ROADMAP TO THE **NEW RULES!**

Federal Civil Rules Handbook

by Steven Baicker-McKee, John Corr, and William Janssen

GAIN IMPORTANT KNOWLEDGE YOU CAN APPLY TO A VARIETY OF SITUATIONS!

The December 1, 2007 restyling effort means that each and every FRCP now reads differently, making this title a "must have" for every litigator in the federal courts. It is also an ideal analytical companion to West's® *Federal Civil Judicial Procedure and Rules* pamphlet.

It provides complete, current text of all procedural rules and all the new federal forms. In addition, you'll find roadmaps that summarize both the stylistic and substantive changes made to each rule – a quick reference tool for rule-by-rule reorientation. Recent topics covered include the effects of the U.S. Supreme Court's decision in *Bell Atlantic Corp. v. Twombly*.

For more information or to order:
Go to **west.thomson.com**
or call **1-800-344-5009**

ON.COM **WEST.®**

THOMSON REUTERS™

© 2008 Thomson Reuters **FD-10**

TAKE YOUR KNOWLEDGE OF FEDERAL RULES TO THE **NEXT LEVEL.**

- **Federal Rules of Civil Procedure, Rules and Commentary**
  by Steven S. Gensler
- **Fundamentals of Federal Litigation**
  by Heidi Kristin Brown
- **Navigating the Federal Trial**
  by Robert E. Larsen
- **Federal Rules of Evidence, 3d**
  by Paul F. Rothstein
- **Federal Testimonial Privileges, 2d**
  by Paul F. Rothstein and Susan W. Crump

Step-by-step guidance you'll appreciate as you take your practice into federal court.

These titles give you what simple federal rules books cannot – the human factor. Judges, practicing attorneys, and scholars have written these books and provided you with not only the text of federal rules, but also valuable practice-tested strategies, tips on avoiding common errors, commentary on the spirit and intent of the rules, and discussion of development of the law since adoption or enactment.

For more information or to order:
Go to **west.thomson.com** or call **1-800-344-5009**

WEST.THOMSON.COM **WEST®**

THOMSON REUTERS™

© 2008 Thomson Reuters **FD-12**

2009 EDITION

FEDERAL CIVIL JUDICIAL PROCEDURE and RULES

Rule amendments received to December 1, 2008

Includes laws through Public Law 110–460, approved December 23, 2008

WEST®

A Thomson Reuters business

Mat#40737934

© 2009 Thomson Reuters

Copyright is not claimed as to any part of the original work prepared by a United States Government officer or employee as part of that person's official duties.

This publication was created to provide you with accurate and authoritative information concerning the subject matter covered; however, this publication was not necessarily prepared by persons licensed to practice law in a particular jurisdiction. The publisher is not engaged in rendering legal or other professional advice and this publication is not a substitute for the advice of an attorney. If you require legal or other expert advice, you should seek the services of a competent attorney or other professional.

ISBN: 978–0–314–99091–4

West's and Westlaw are registered in the U.S. Patent and Trademark Office.

PREFACE

This pamphlet updates the rules and statutes in the 2008 Revised Edition Pamphlet. Rule amendments are current as received to December 1, 2008, and statutes are current through Public Law 110-460, approved December 23, 2008.

Reference should also be made to Westlaw for any interim changes affecting the content in this Pamphlet.

This convenient reference Pamphlet, in form suitable for courtroom and office use, contains the text of the—

Federal Rules of Civil Procedure.

Supplemental Rules—Admiralty or Maritime Claims and Asset Forfeiture Actions.

Rules of Procedure of the Judicial Panel on Multidistrict Litigation.

Rules Governing Habeas Corpus Cases and Motions Attacking Sentence.

Federal Rules of Evidence.

Federal Rules of Appellate Procedure.

Rules of the Supreme Court of the United States.

Title 28, Judiciary and Judicial Procedure.

Miscellaneous provisions from sections 2 to 39 of Act June 25, 1948, c. 646, are set out after the text of Title 28. An Appendix follows these miscellaneous provisions and refers to former provisions relating to judicial personnel financial disclosure requirements in Pub.L. 95–521, title III, sections 301 to 309, and to former provisions relating to the development of mechanisms for resolving minor disputes in Pub.L. 96–190. The Constitution of the United States follows the Appendix. Provisions relating to financial disclosure requirements of federal personnel are set out in Title 5 Appendix 4.

A combined Time Table for Lawyers under Title 28, Judiciary and Judicial Procedure; the Federal Rules of Civil Procedure; the Federal Rules of Appellate Procedure; and the Rules of the Supreme Court are also included. This Table indicates the time for each of the various procedural steps required by the Rules.

A detailed, consolidated Index appears in the back of this pamphlet.

THE PUBLISHER

March, 2009

*

RELATED PRODUCTS IN FEDERAL LAW FROM WEST

FEDERAL PRACTICE

COURTROOM HANDBOOK ON FEDERAL EVIDENCE
Steven Goode and Olin Guy Wellborn III

FEDERAL CIVIL RULES HANDBOOK
Steven Baicker–McKee, William Janssen and John B. Corr

MODERN SCIENTIFIC EVIDENCE
David L. Faigman, David H. Kaye, Michael J. Saks, Joseph Sanders, and Edward K. Cheng

FEDERAL JURY PRACTICE AND INSTRUCTIONS
Kevin F. O'Malley, Jay E. Grenig and William C. Lee
[Also available in CD–ROM]

FEDERAL PRACTICE AND PROCEDURE
Charles Alan Wright, Arthur R. Miller, Mary Kay Kane, Edward H. Cooper, Richard L. Marcus, Kenneth W. Graham, Victor James Gold, Richard D. Freer, Vikram David Amar, Joan E. Steinman, Andrew D. Leipold, Peter J. Henning, Sarah H. Welling, Nancy J. King, Susan R. Klein, Charles H. Koch, Jr., Catherine T. Struve, and Michael H. Graham
[Also available in CD–ROM]

WEST'S FEDERAL ADMINISTRATIVE PRACTICE
Authored by Federal Practice Experts

WEST'S FEDERAL FORMS
Authored by Federal Practice Experts
[Also available in CD–ROM]

FEDERAL COURT OF APPEALS MANUAL
David G. Knibb

FEDERAL PRACTICE AND PROCEDURE—FEDERAL PRACTICE DESKBOOK
Charles Alan Wright and Mary Kay Kane

HANDBOOK OF FEDERAL EVIDENCE
Michael H. Graham

TREATISE ON CONSTITUTIONAL LAW
Ronald D. Rotunda and John E. Nowak

ADMINISTRATIVE LAW AND PRACTICE
Charles H. Koch, Jr.

FEDERAL TRIAL OBJECTIONS
Charles B. Gibbons

BUSINESS AND COMMERCIAL LITIGATION IN FEDERAL COURTS
Robert L. Haig, Editor–In–Chief

RELATED PRODUCTS

NEWBERG ON CLASS ACTIONS, 3rd
Herbert Newberg and Alba Conte

HANDBOOK OF FEDERAL CIVIL DISCOVERY AND DISCLOSURE
Jay E. Grenig and Jeffrey S. Kinsler
[Includes forms on Disk]

ANNOTATED MANUAL FOR COMPLEX LITIGATION
David F. Herr

MULTIDISTRICT LITIGATION MANUAL
David F. Herr

FEDERAL STANDARDS OF REVIEW
Hon. Harry T. Edwards and Linda A. Elliott

United States Code Annotated
West's Federal Practice Digest 4th
United States Code Congressional and Administrative News

CRIMINAL PRACTICE

SEARCH AND SEIZURE
Wayne R. LaFave

SUBSTANTIVE CRIMINAL LAW
Wayne R. LaFave

FEDERAL CRIMINAL RULES HANDBOOK
Laurie L. Levenson

CRIMINAL LAW DEFENSES
Paul H. Robinson

CRIMINAL PROCEDURE
Wayne R. LaFave, Jerold H. Israel, and Nancy J. King

FEDERAL SENTENCING LAW AND PRACTICE
Thomas W. Hutchison, Peter B. Hoffman, Deborah Young, and Sigmund G. Popko

FEDERAL SENTENCING GUIDELINES HANDBOOK
Roger W. Haines, Jr., Frank O. Bowman III, and Jennifer C. Woll

---

Corpus Juris Secundum
West's Federal Case News
Federal Civil Judicial Procedure and Rules
Federal Criminal Code and Rules
Federal Environmental Laws
Federal Immigration Laws and Regulations
Federal Labor Laws

RELATED PRODUCTS

Federal Sentencing Guidelines
Federal Social Security Laws, Selected Statutes and Regulations
Federal Intellectual Property Laws and Regulations
Federal Litigator
Reference Manual on Scientific Evidence, Second
Manual for Complex Litigation, Fourth

TAX PUBLICATIONS

Federal Tax Regulations
Internal Revenue Code
Internal Revenue Acts

Westlaw®

WestCheck.com™

West CD-ROM Libraries™

To order any of these Federal practice tools, call your West Representative or **1-800-328-9352**.

NEED RESEARCH HELP?

You can get quality research results with free help—call the West Reference Attorneys when you have questions concerning Westlaw or West Publications at **1-800-REF-ATTY (1-800-733-2889)**.

INTERNET ACCESS

Contact the West Editorial Department directly with your questions and suggestions by e-mail at west.editor@thomson.com.
Visit West's home page at
west.thomson.com.

*

WESTLAW ELECTRONIC RESEARCH GUIDE

Westlaw—Expanding the Reach of Your Library

Westlaw is West's online legal research service. With Westlaw, you experience the same quality and integrity that you have come to expect from West books, plus quick, easy access to West's vast collection of statutes, case law materials, public records, and other legal resources, in addition to current news articles and business information. For the most current and comprehensive legal research, combine the strengths of West books and Westlaw.

When you research with westlaw.com you get the convenience of the Internet combined with comprehensive and accurate Westlaw content, including exclusive editorial enhancements, plus features found only in westlaw.com such as ResultsPlus™ or StatutesPlus.™

Accessing Databases Using the Westlaw Directory

The Westlaw Directory lists all databases on Westlaw and contains links to detailed information relating to the content of each database. Click **Directory** on the westlaw.com toolbar. There are several ways to access a database even when you don't know the database identifier. Browse a directory view. Scan the directory. Type all or part of a database name in the Search these Databases box. The Find a Database Wizard can help you select relevant databases for your search. You can access up to ten databases at one time for user-defined multibase searching.

Retrieving a Specific Document

To retrieve a specific document by citation or title on westlaw.com click **Find&Print** on the toolbar to display the Find a Document page. If you are unsure of the correct citation format, type the publication abbreviation, e.g., **xx st** (where xx is a state's two-letter postal abbreviation), in the Find this document by citation box and click **Go** to display a fill-in-the-blank template. To retrieve a specific case when you know one or more parties' names, click **Find a Case by Party Name**.

KeyCite®

KeyCite, the citation research service on Westlaw, makes it easy to trace the history of your case, statute, administrative decision or regulation to determine if there are recent updates, and to find other documents that cite your document. KeyCite will also find pending legislation relating to federal or state statutes. Access the powerful features of KeyCite from the westlaw.com toolbar, the **Links** tab, or KeyCite flags in a document display. KeyCite's red and yellow warning flags tell you at a glance whether your document has negative history. Depth-of-treatment stars help you focus on the most important citing references. KeyCite Alert allows you to monitor the status of your case, statute or rule, and automatically sends you updates at the frequency you specify.

ResultsPlus™

ResultsPlus is a Westlaw technology that automatically suggests additional information related to your search. The suggested materials are accessible by a set of links that appear to the right of your westlaw.com search results:

- Go directly to relevant ALR® articles and Am Jur® annotations.
- Find on-point resources by key number.
- See information from related treatises and law reviews.

StatutesPlus™

When you access a statutes database in westlaw.com you are brought to a powerful Search Center which collects, on one toolbar, the tools that are most useful for fast, efficient retrieval of statutes documents:

- Have a few key terms? Click **Statutes Index**.
- Know the common name? Click **Popular Name Table**.
- Familiar with the subject matter? Click **Table of Contents**.
- Have a citation or section number? Click **Find by Citation**.
- Interested in topical surveys providing citations across multiple state statutes? Click **50 State Surveys**.
- Or, simply search with **Natural Language** or **Terms and Connectors.**

When you access a statutes section, click on the **Links** tab for all relevant links for the current document that will also include a KeyCite section with a description of the KeyCite status flag. Depending on your document, links may also include administrative, bill text, and other sources that were previously only available by accessing and searching other databases.

Additional Information

Westlaw is available on the Web at westlaw.com.

For search assistance, call the West Reference Attorneys at 1–800–REF–ATTY (1–800–733–2889).

For technical assistance, call West Customer Technical Support at 1–800–WESTLAW (1–800–937–8529).

TABLE OF CONTENTS

	Page
Federal Rules of Civil Procedure:	
Table of Rules	1
Time Table for Lawyers in Federal Civil Cases	3
Orders of the Supreme Court of the United States Adopting and Amending Rules	28
Text of Rules	41
Appendix of Forms	304
Supplemental Rules for Admiralty or Maritime Claims and Asset Forfeiture Actions	314
Rules of Procedure of the Judicial Panel on Multidistrict Litigation	335
Rules Governing Habeas Corpus Cases	345
Rules Governing Motions Attacking Sentences	370
Federal Rules of Evidence:	
Table of Rules	389
Orders of the Supreme Court of the United States Adopting and Amending Rules	390
Text of Rules	392
Federal Rules of Appellate Procedure:	
Table of Rules	503
Orders of the Supreme Court of the United States Adopting and Amending Rules	504
Text of Rules	508
Appendix of Forms	586
Rules of the Supreme Court of the United States	590
Title 28, U.S. Code, Judiciary and Judicial Procedure	615
Act June 25, 1948, c. 646, §§ 2 to 39, 62 Stat. 985 to 991, as amended, Miscellaneous Provisions	1156
Appendix:	
Judicial Personnel Financial Disclosure Requirements [Repealed]	1161
Development of Mechanisms for Resolving Minor Disputes [Codified]	1161
Constitution of the United States	1162
Title 5, U.S. Code, Government Organization and Employees:	
Appendix 4—Titles I to III, Financial Disclosure Requirements of Federal Personnel	1174
Consolidated Index	I–1

*

PROCEDURES FOR THE CONDUCT OF BUSINESS BY THE JUDICIAL CONFERENCE COMMITTEES ON RULES OF PRACTICE AND PROCEDURE

Scope

These procedures govern the operations of the Judicial Conference Committee on Rules of Practice, Procedure, and Evidence (Standing Committee) and the various Judicial Conference Advisory Committees on Rules of Practice and Procedure in drafting and recommending new rules of practice, procedure, and evidence and amendments to existing rules.

Part I—Advisory Committees

1. Functions

   Each Advisory Committee shall carry on "a continuous study of the operation and effect of the general rules of practice and procedure now or hereafter in use" in its particular field, taking into consideration suggestions and recommendations received from any source, new statutes and court decisions affecting the rules, and legal commentary.

2. Suggestions and Recommendations

   Suggestions and recommendations with respect to the rules should be sent to the Secretary, Committee on Rules of Practice and Procedure, Administrative Office of the United States Courts, Washington, D.C. 20544, who shall, to the extent feasible, acknowledge in writing every written suggestion or recommendation so received and shall refer all suggestions and recommendations to the appropriate Advisory Committee. To the extent feasible, the Secretary, in consultation with the Chairman of the Advisory Committee, shall advise the person making a recommendation or suggestion of the action taken thereon by the Advisory Committee.

3. Drafting Rules Changes

   a. An Advisory Committee shall meet at such times and places as the Chairman may authorize. All Advisory Committee meetings shall be open to the public, except when the committee so meeting, in open session and with a majority present, determines that it is in the public interest that all or part of the remainder of the meeting on that day shall be closed to the public and states the reason for closing the meeting. Each meeting shall be preceded by notice of the time and place of the meeting, including publication in the Federal Register, sufficient to permit interested persons to attend.

   b. The reporter assigned to each Advisory Committee shall, under the direction of the Committee or its Chairman, prepare initial draft rules changes, "Committee Notes" explaining their purpose and intent, copies or summaries of all written recommendations and suggestions received by the Advisory Committee, and shall forward them to the Advisory Committee.

   c. The Advisory Committee shall then meet to consider the draft proposed new rules and rules amendments, together with Committee Notes, make revisions therein, and submit them for approval of publication to the Standing Committee, or its Chairman, with a written report explaining the Committee's action, including any minority or other separate views.

4. Publication and Public Hearings

   a. When publication is approved by the Standing Committee, the Secretary shall arrange for the printing and circulation of the proposed rules changes to the bench and bar, and to the public generally. Publication shall be as wide as practicable. Notice of the proposed rule shall be published in the Federal Register and copies provided to appropriate legal publishing firms with a request that they be timely included in their publications. The Secretary shall also provide copies to the chief justice of the highest court of each state and, insofar as is practicable, to all individuals and organizations that request them.

   b. In order to provide full notice and opportunity for comment on proposed rule changes, a period of at least six months from the time of publication of notice in the Federal Register shall be permitted, unless a shorter period is approved under the provisions of subparagraph d of this paragraph.

   c. An Advisory Committee shall conduct public hearings on all proposed rules changes unless elimination of such hearings is approved under the provisions of subparagraph d of this paragraph. The hearings shall be held at such times and places as determined by the chairman of the Advisory Committee and shall be preceded by adequate notice, including publication in the Federal Register. Proceedings shall be recorded and a transcript prepared. Subject to the provisions of paragraph six, such transcript shall be available for public inspection.

   d. Exceptions to the time period for public comment and the public hearing requirement may be granted by the Standing Committee or its chairman when the Standing Committee or its chairman determines that the administration of justice requires that a proposed rule change should be expedited and that appropriate public notice and comment may be achieved by a shortened comment period, without public hearings, or both. The Standing Committee may eliminate the public notice and comment requirement if, in the case of a technical or conforming amendment, it determines that notice and comment are not appropriate or necessary. Whenever such an exception is made, the Standing Committee shall advise the Judicial Conference of the exception and the reasons for the exception.

5. Subsequent Procedures

   a. At the conclusion of the comment period the reporter shall prepare a summary of the written comments received and the testimony presented at public hearings. The Advisory Committee shall review the proposed rules changes in the light of the comments and testimony. If the Advisory Committee makes any substantial change, an additional period for public notice and comment may be provided.

   b. The Advisory Committee shall submit proposed rules changes and Committee Notes, as finally agreed upon, to the Standing Committee. Each submission shall be accompanied by a separate report of the comments received and shall explain any changes made subsequent to the original publication. The submission shall also include minority views of Advisory Committee members who wish to have separate views recorded.

6. Records

   a. The Chairman of the Advisory Committee shall arrange for the preparation of minutes of all Advisory Committee meetings.

   b. The records of an Advisory Committee shall consist of the written suggestions received from the public; the written comments received on drafts of proposed rules, responses thereto, transcripts of public hearings, and summaries prepared by the reporter; all correspondence relating to proposed rules changes; minutes of Advisory Committee meetings; approved drafts of rules changes; and reports to the Standing Committee. The records shall be maintained at the Administrative Office of the United States Courts for a minimum of two years and shall be available for public inspection during reasonable office hours. Thereafter the records may be transferred to a Government Records Center in accordance with applicable Government retention and disposition schedules.

c. Any portion of minutes, relating to a closed meeting and made available to the public, may contain such deletions as may be necessary to avoid frustrating the purposes of closing the meeting as provided in subparagraph 3a.

d. Copies of records shall be furnished to any person upon payment of a reasonable fee for the cost of reproduction.

Part II—Standing Committee

7. Functions

The Standing Committee shall coordinate the work of the several Advisory Committees, make suggestions of proposals to be studied by them, consider proposals recommended by the Advisory Committees, and transmit such proposals with its recommendation to the Judicial Conference, or recommit them to the appropriate Advisory Committee for further study and consideration.

8. Procedures

a. The Standing Committee shall meet at such times and places as the Chairman may authorize. All Committee meetings shall be open to the public, except when the committee so meeting, in open session and with a majority present, determines that it is in the public interest that all or part of the remainder of the meeting on that day shall be closed to the public and states the reason for closing the meeting. Each meeting shall be preceded by notice of the time and place of the meeting, including publication in the Federal Register, sufficient to permit interested persons to attend.

b. When an Advisory Committee's final recommendations for rules changes have been submitted, the Chairman and Reporter of the Advisory Committee shall attend the Standing Committee meeting to present the proposed rules changes and Committee Notes.

c. The Standing Committee may accept, reject, or modify a proposal. If a modification effects a substantial change, the proposal will be returned to the Advisory Committee with appropriate instructions.

d. The Standing Committee shall transmit to the Judicial Conference the proposed rules changes and Committee Notes approved by it, together with the Advisory Committee report. The Standing Committee's report to the Judicial Conference shall include its recommendations and explain any changes it has made.

9. Records

a. The Secretary shall prepare minutes of all Standing Committee meetings.

b. The records of the Standing Committee shall consist of the minutes of Standing and Advisory Committee meetings, reports to the Judicial Conference, and correspondence concerning rules changes including correspondence with Advisory Committee Chairmen. The records shall be maintained at the Administrative Office of the United States

Courts for a minimum of two years and shall be available for public inspection during reasonable office hours. Thereafter the records may be transferred to a Government Records Center in accordance with applicable Government retention and disposition schedules.

c. Copies of records shall be furnished to any person upon payment of a reasonable fee for the cost of reproduction.

STANDING COMMITTEE ON RULES OF PRACTICE AND PROCEDURE

As Constituted July 1, 2008

Chair:
HONORABLE LEE H. ROSENTHAL

Members:
HONORABLE HARRIS L HARTZ
HONORABLE REENA RAGGI
HONORABLE DIANE P. WOOD
HONORABLE MARILYN L. HUFF
HONORABLE JAMES A. TEILBORG
HONORABLE RONALD M. GEORGE
PROFESSOR DANIEL J. MELTZER
DAVID J. BECK, ESQUIRE
JOHN G. KESTER, ESQUIRE
WILLIAM J. MALEDON, ESQUIRE
DOUGLAS R. COX, ESQUIRE

DEPUTY ATTORNEY GENERAL (EX OFFICIO)
HONORABLE MARK FILIP

Reporter:
PROFESSOR DANIEL R. COQUILLETTE

Advisors and Consultants:
PROFESSOR GEOFFREY C. HAZARD, JR.
PROFESSOR R. JOSEPH KIMBLE
JOSEPH F. SPANIOL, JR., ESQUIRE

Secretary:
PETER G. MCCABE

ADVISORY COMMITTEE ON APPELLATE RULES

As Constituted July 1, 2008

Chair:
HONORABLE CARL E. STEWART

Members:
HONORABLE JEFFREY S. SUTTON
HONORABLE KERMIT EDWARD BYE
HONORABLE T.S. ELLIS III
HONORABLE RANDY J. HOLLAND
DEAN STEPHEN R. MCALLISTER
MARK I. LEVY, ESQUIRE
MAUREEN E. MAHONEY, ESQUIRE
JAMES F. BENNETT, ESQUIRE
ACTING SOLICITOR GENERAL
HONORABLE GREGORY G. GARRE (EX OFFICIO)

APPELLATE LITIGATION COUNSEL
DOUGLAS LETTER

Reporter:
PROFESSOR CATHERINE T. STRUVE

Advisor:
CHARLES R. FULBRUGE, III

Liaison Member:
HONORABLE HARRIS L HARTZ

Secretary:
PETER G. MCCABE

ADVISORY COMMITTEE ON BANKRUPTCY RULES

As Constituted July 1, 2008

Chair:
HONORABLE LAURA TAYLOR SWAIN

Members:
HONORABLE R. GUY COLE, JR.
HONORABLE IRENE M. KEELEY
HONORABLE RICHARD A. SCHELL
HONORABLE WILLIAM H. PAULEY III
HONORABLE EUGENE R. WEDOFF
HONORABLE ELIZABETH L. PERRIS
HONORABLE DAVID H. COAR
HONORABLE JEFFERY P. HOPKINS
DEAN LAWRENCE PONOROFF
J. MICHAEL LAMBERTH, ESQUIRE
G. ERIC BRUNSTAD, JR., ESQUIRE
JOHN RAO, ESQUIRE
DIRECTOR, COMMERCIAL LITIGATION BRANCH, CIVIL DIVISION, U.S. DEPT. OF JUSTICE (EX OFFICIO)
J. CHRISTOPHER KOHN, ESQUIRE

Reporters:
PROFESSOR JEFFREY W. MORRIS
PROFESSOR S. ELIZABETH GIBSON

Advisors and Consultants:
JAMES J. WALDRON
MARK REDMILES, DEPUTY DIRECTOR
PATRICIA S. KETCHUM, ESQUIRE

Liaison Member:
HONORABLE JAMES A. TEILBORG

Liaison from Committee on the Administration of the Bankruptcy System:
HONORABLE JOY FLOWERS CONTI

Secretary:
PETER G. MCCABE

ADVISORY COMMITTEE ON CIVIL RULES

As Constituted July 1, 2008

Chair:
HONORABLE MARK R. KRAVITZ

Members:
HONORABLE STEVEN M. COLLOTON
HONORABLE VAUGHN R. WALKER
HONORABLE MICHAEL M. BAYLSON
HONORABLE DAVID G. CAMPBELL
HONORABLE JOHN G. KOELTL
HONORABLE C. CHRISTOPHER HAGY
PROFESSOR STEVEN S. GENSLER
ROBERT C. HEIM, ESQUIRE
CHILTON DAVIS VARNER, ESQUIRE
DANIEL C. GIRARD, ESQUIRE
ANTON R. VALUKAS, ESQUIRE
PRINCIPAL DEPUTY ASSISTANT ATTORNEY GENERAL
CIVIL DIVISION (EX OFFICIO)
HONORABLE JEFFREY BUCHOLTZ
TED HIRT, ASSISTANT DIRECTOR
FEDERAL PROGRAMS BRANCH
CIVIL DIVISION

Liaison Members:
HONORABLE EUGENE R. WEDOFF
HONORABLE DIANE P. WOOD

Reporter:
PROFESSOR EDWARD H. COOPER

Advisors and Consultants:
PROFESSOR RICHARD L. MARCUS
PROFESSOR THOMAS D. ROWE, JR.

Secretary:
PETER G. MCCABE

ADVISORY COMMITTEE ON CRIMINAL RULES

As Constituted July 1, 2008

Chair:
HONORABLE RICHARD C. TALLMAN

Members:
JUDGE MARK L. WOLF
HONORABLE JAMES P. JONES
HONORABLE JAMES B. ZAGEL
HONORABLE DONALD W. MOLLOY
HONORABLE JOHN F. KEENAN
HONORABLE ANTHONY J. BATTAGLIA
HONORABLE ROBERT H. EDMUNDS, JR.
PROFESSOR ANDREW D. LEIPOLD
LEO P. CUNNINGHAM, ESQUIRE
RACHEL BRILL, ESQUIRE
FEDERAL PUBLIC DEFENDER
THOMAS P. MCNAMARA
ACTING ASSISTANT ATTORNEY GENERAL
CRIMINAL DIVISION (EX OFFICIO)
HONORABLE MATTHEW W. FREIDRICH
DIRECTOR, OFFICE OF POLICY & LEGISLATION
CRIMINAL DIVISION
U.S. DEPT. OF JUSTICE
JONATHAN WROBLEWSKI
DEPUTY CHIEF, APPELLATE SECTION
CRIMINAL DIVISION
U.S. DEPT. OF JUSTICE
KATHLEEN FELTON

Reporters:
PROFESSOR SARA SUN BEALE
PROFESSOR NANCY J. KING

Liaison Member:
HONORABLE REENA RAGGI

Secretary:
PETER G. MCCABE

ADVISORY COMMITTEE ON EVIDENCE RULES

As Constituted July 1, 2008

Chair:
HONORABLE ROBERT L. HINKLE

Members:
HONORABLE JOSEPH F. ANDERSON, JR.
HONORABLE JOAN N. ERICKSEN
HONORABLE ANDREW D. HURWITZ
HONORABLE ANITA B. BRODY
WILLIAM W. TAYLOR, III, ESQUIRE
WILLIAM T. HANGLEY, ESQUIRE
MARJORIE A. MEYERS
FEDERAL PUBLIC DEFENDER
RONALD J. TENPAS
ASSISTANT ATTORNEY GENERAL
ELIZABETH J. SHAPIRO, ASSISTANT DIRECTOR
FEDERAL PROGRAMS BRANCH
CIVIL DIVISION

Liaison Members:
HONORABLE MICHAEL M. BAYLSON
HONORABLE JOHN F. KEENAN
HONORABLE MARILYN L. HUFF

Reporter:
PROFESSOR DANIEL J. CAPRA

Secretary:
PETER G. MCCABE

FEDERAL RULES

CIVIL PROCEDURE

MULTIDISTRICT LITIGATION

HABEAS CORPUS CASES

MOTION ATTACKING SENTENCE

EVIDENCE

APPELLATE PROCEDURE

SUPREME COURT

*

FEDERAL
RULES OF CIVIL PROCEDURE
FOR THE
UNITED STATES DISTRICT COURTS

Amendments received to December 1, 2008

TABLE OF RULES

		Rules
I.	SCOPE OF RULES; FORM OF ACTION	1, 2
II.	COMMENCING AN ACTION; SERVICE OF PROCESS, PLEADINGS, MOTIONS, AND ORDERS	3–6
III.	PLEADINGS AND MOTIONS	7–16
IV.	PARTIES	17–25
V.	DISCLOSURES AND DISCOVERY	26–37
VI.	TRIALS	38–53
VII.	JUDGMENT	54–63
VIII.	PROVISIONAL AND FINAL REMEDIES	64–71
IX.	SPECIAL PROCEEDINGS	71.1–76
X.	DISTRICT COURTS AND CLERKS: CONDUCTING BUSINESS; ISSUING ORDERS	77–80
XI.	GENERAL PROVISIONS	81–86
	APPENDIX OF FORMS (See Rule 84)	
	SUPPLEMENTAL RULES FOR ADMIRALTY OR MARITIME CLAIMS AND ASSET FORFEITURE ACTIONS	

TITLE I. SCOPE OF RULES; FORM OF ACTION

Rule
1. Scope and Purpose.
2. One Form of Action.

TITLE II. COMMENCING AN ACTION; SERVICE OF PROCESS, PLEADINGS, MOTIONS, AND ORDERS

3. Commencing an Action.
4. Summons.
4.1. Serving Other Process.
5. Serving and Filing Pleadings and Other Papers.
5.1. Constitutional Challenge to A Statute—Notice, Certification, and Intervention.
5.2. Privacy Protection For Filings Made with the Court.
6. Computing and Extending Time; Time for Motion Papers.

TITLE III. PLEADINGS AND MOTIONS

7. Pleadings Allowed; Form of Motions and Other Papers.

Rule
TITLE III. PLEADINGS AND MOTIONS—Cont'd

7.1. Disclosure Statement.
8. General Rules of Pleading.
9. Pleading Special Matters.
10. Form of Pleadings.
11. Signing Pleadings, Motions, and Other Papers; Representations to the Court; Sanctions.
12. Defenses and Objections: When and How Presented; Motion for Judgment on the Pleadings; Consolidating Motions; Waiving Defenses; Pretrial Hearing.
13. Counterclaim and Crossclaim.
14. Third-Party Practice.
15. Amended and Supplemental Pleadings.
16. Pretrial Conferences; Scheduling; Management.

TITLE IV. PARTIES

17. Plaintiff and Defendant; Capacity; Public Officers.
18. Joinder of Claims.
19. Required Joinder of Parties.
20. Permissive Joinder of Parties.
21. Misjoinder and Nonjoinder of Parties.
22. Interpleader.
23. Class Actions.
23.1. Derivative Action.
23.2. Actions Relating to Unincorporated Associations.
24. Intervention.
25. Substitution of Parties.

TITLE V. DISCLOSURES AND DISCOVERY

26. Duty to Disclose; General Provisions Governing Discovery.
27. Depositions to Perpetuate Testimony.
28. Persons Before Whom Depositions May Be Taken.
29. Stipulations About Discovery Procedure.
30. Depositions by Oral Examination.
31. Depositions by Written Questions.
32. Using Depositions in Court Proceedings.
33. Interrogatories to Parties.
34. Producing Documents, Electronically Stored Information, and Tangible Things, or Entering onto Land, for Inspection and Other Purposes.
35. Physical and Mental Examinations.
36. Requests for Admission.
37. Failure to Make Disclosures or to Cooperate in Discovery; Sanctions.

Rule

TITLE VI. TRIALS

38. Right to a Jury Trial; Demand.
39. Trial by Jury or by the Court.
40. Scheduling Cases for Trial.
41. Dismissal of Actions.
42. Consolidation; Separate Trials.
43. Taking Testimony.
44. Proving an Official Record.
44.1. Determining Foreign Law.
45. Subpoena.
46. Objecting to a Ruling or Order.
47. Selecting Jurors.
48. Number of Jurors; Verdict.
49. Special Verdict; General Verdict and Questions.
50. Judgment as a Matter of Law in a Jury Trial; Related Motion for a New Trial; Conditional Ruling.
51. Instructions to the Jury; Objections; Preserving a Claim of Error.
52. Findings and Conclusions by the Court; Judgment on Partial Findings.
53. Masters.

TITLE VII. JUDGMENT

54. Judgment; Costs.
55. Default; Default Judgment.
56. Summary Judgment.
57. Declaratory Judgment.
58. Entering Judgment.
59. New Trial; Altering or Amending a Judgment.
60. Relief from a Judgment or Order.
61. Harmless Error.
62. Stay of Proceedings to Enforce a Judgment.
63. Judge's Inability to Proceed.

TITLE VIII. PROVISIONAL AND FINAL REMEDIES

64. Seizing a Person or Property.
65. Injunctions and Restraining Orders.
65.1. Proceedings Against A Surety.
66. Receivers.
67. Deposit into Court.
68. Offer of Judgment.
69. Execution.
70. Enforcing a Judgment for a Specific Act.
71. Enforcing Relief for or Against a Nonparty.

TITLE IX. SPECIAL PROCEEDINGS

71.1. Condemning Real or Personal Property.
72. Magistrate Judges: Pretrial Order.
73. Magistrate Judges: Trial by Consent; Appeal.
74. Method of Appeal From Magistrate Judge to District Judge Under Title 28, U.S.C. § 636(c)(4) and Rule 73(d) [Abrogated].
75. Proceedings On Appeal From Magistrate Judge to District Judge under Rule 73(d) [Abrogated].
76. Judgment of the District Judge On The Appeal under Rule 73(d) and Costs [Abrogated].

Rule

TITLE X. DISTRICT COURTS AND CLERKS: CONDUCTING BUSINESS; ISSUING ORDERS

77. Conducting Business; Clerk's Authority; Notice of an Order or Judgment.
78. Hearing Motions; Submission on Briefs.
79. Records Kept by the Clerk.
80. Stenographic Transcript as Evidence.

TITLE XI. GENERAL PROVISIONS

81. Applicability of the Rules in General; Removed Actions.
82. Jurisdiction and Venue Unaffected.
83. Rules by District Courts; Judge's Directives.
84. Forms.
85. Title.
86. Effective Dates.

APPENDIX OF FORMS

Form

1. Caption.
2. Date, Signature, Address, E–Mail Address, and Telephone Number.
3. Summons.
4. Summons on a Third–Party Complaint.
5. Notice of a Lawsuit and Request to Waive Service of a Summons.
6. Waiver of the Service of Summons.
7. Statement of Jurisdiction.
8. Statement of Reasons for Omitting a Party.
9. Statement Noting a Party's Death.
10. Complaint to Recover a Sum Certain.
11. Complaint for Negligence.
12. Complaint for Negligence when the Plaintiff Does Not Know Who is Responsible.
13. Complaint for Negligence Under the Federal Employers' Liability Act.
14. Complaint for Damages Under the Merchant Marine Act.
15. Complaint for the Conversion of Property.
16. Third–Party Complaint.
17. Complaint for Specific Performance of a Contract to Convey Land.
18. Complaint for Patent Infringement.
19. Complaint for Copyright Infringement and Unfair Competition.
20. Complaint for Interpleader and Declaratory Relief.
21. Complaint on a Claim for a Debt and to Set Aside a Fraudulent Conveyance Under Rule 18(b).
30. Answer Presenting Defenses Under Rule 12(b).
31. Answer to a Complaint for Money Had and Received With a Counterclaim for Interpleader.
40. Motion to Dismiss Under Rule 12(b) for Lack of Jurisdiction, Improper Venue, Insufficient Service of Process, or Failure to State a Claim.
41. Motion to Bring in a Third–Party Defendant.
42. Motion to Intervene as a Defendant Under Rule 24.
50. Request to Produce Documents and Tangible Things, or to Enter onto Land Under Rule 34.
51. Request for Admissions Under Rule 36.
52. Report of the Parties' Planning Meeting.
60. Notice of Condemnation.
61. Complaint for Condemnation.
70. Judgment on a Jury Verdict.

Form
71. Judgment by the Court Without a Jury.
80. Notice of a Magistrate Judge's Availability.
81. Consent to an Assignment to a Magistrate Judge.
82. Order of Assignment to a Magistrate Judge.

SUPPLEMENTAL RULES FOR ADMIRALTY OR MARITIME CLAIMS AND ASSET FORFEITURE ACTIONS

Rule
A. Scope of Rules.

SUPPLEMENTAL RULES FOR ADMIRALTY OR MARITIME CLAIMS AND ASSET FORFEITURE ACTIONS—Cont'd

B. In Personam Actions: Attachment and Garnishment.
C. In Rem Actions: Special Provisions.
D. Possessory, Petitory, and Partition Actions.
E. Actions in Rem and Quasi in Rem: General Provisions.
F. Limitation of Liability.
G. Forfeiture Actions In Rem.

TIME TABLE FOR LAWYERS IN FEDERAL CIVIL CASES

Amended to December 1, 2007

This Time Table, prepared by the Publisher's editorial staff as a guide to the user, indicates the time for each of the steps of a civil action as provided by the Federal Rules of Civil Procedure and the Federal Rules of Appellate Procedure. Certain steps governed by statute and by the Rules of the Supreme Court are also listed. *The user should always consult the actual text of the rule or statute.* Usually the periods permitted for each of these steps may be enlarged by the court in its discretion. In some cases no enlargement is permitted. Citations to supporting authority are in the form "Civ.R. ———" for the Rules of Civil Procedure; "App.R. ———" for the Rules of Appellate Procedure; "28 U.S.C.A. § ———" for statutes; and "Supreme Court Rule ———".

ADMISSIONS

Requests for admissions, service of	On any other party a written request, for purposes of the pending action only. Civ.R. 36(a)(1).
Response to requested admissions	Written answers or objections must be served within 30 days after service of the request, or a shorter or longer time as may be stipulated to under Civ.R. 29 or be ordered by the court. Civ.R. 36(a).
ALTERNATE jurors	The institution of the alternate juror has been abolished. Civ.R. 47, 1991 Advisory Committee note, subd. (b).
ANSWER	**See, also, "Responsive Pleadings", this table.**
To complaint	Service within 20 days after being served with summons and complaint unless another time is specified by Civ.R. 12 or a federal statute. Civ.R. 12(a)(1)(A)(i).
	Service within 60 days after date request is sent for waiver of service of summons or within 90 days after that date if defendant was addressed outside any judicial district of the United States unless another time is specified by Civ.R. 12 or a federal statute. Civ.R. 12(a)(1)(A)(ii).
	Service within 60 days after service on the United States attorney, in action against the United States, a United States agency, or a United States officer or employee sued only in an official capacity. Civ.R. 12(a)(2).
	Service within 60 days after service on the officer or employee or service on the United States attorney, whichever is later, in an action against a United States officer or employee sued in an indi-

ANSWER	**See, also, "Responsive Pleadings", this table.**
	vidual capacity in connection with duties performed on the United States' behalf. Civ.R. 12(a)(3).
	The time for responsive pleading is altered by service of Civ.R. 12 motions. See "Responsive Pleadings", this table.
To counterclaim or cross-claim	
	Service within 20 days after being served with the pleading stating the counterclaim or cross-claim. Civ.R. 12(a)(1)(B).
	60 days for United States, United States agency, or United States officer or employee. Civ.R. 12(a)(2), (3).
	The time for responsive pleading is altered by service of Civ.R. 12(a) motions, see "Responsive Pleadings", this table.
To notice of condemnation	Service within 20 days after service of notice. Civ.R. 71A(e).
Removed actions	20 days after receipt of copy of initial pleading stating the claim for relief, or 20 days after service of summons for an initial pleading on file at time of service, or 5 days after filing of notice of removal, whichever is longest. Civ.R. 81(c).
Proceedings to cancel certificates of citizenship under 8 U.S.C.A. § 1451	60 days after service of petition. Civ.R. 81(a)(3).
ANSWERS (or objections) to interrogatories to party	
	Service within 30 days after service of the interrogatories. A shorter or longer time may be stipulated to under Civ.R. 29 or be ordered by the court. Civ.R. 33(b)(2).
APPEAL	
As of right	30 days from entry of judgment or order. App.R. 4(a)(1)(A).
	60 days in cases in which the United States or its officers, agencies are parties. App.R. 4(a)(1)(B).
	60 days in cases in which the United States or its officers, agencies are parties. App.R. 4(a)(1)(B).
	Entry of a judgment or order in the civil docket under Civ.R. 79(a) is entry for purposes of App.R. 4, unless Civ.R. 58(a)(1) requires a separate document, in which case entry occurs when the judgment or order is entered under Civ.R. 79(a) and either the judgment or order is set forth on a separate document, or 150 days have run from entry of the judgment or order in the civil docket. App.R. 4(a)(7)(A).
	If any party files a timely motion of a type specified below, time for appeal for all parties runs from

APPEAL

entry of order disposing of last such motion outstanding. App.R. 4(a)(4).

(1) motion for judgment under Civ.R. 50(b);
(2) Motion under Civ.R. 52(b) to amend or make additional findings of fact, whether or not granting the motion would alter the judgement;
(3) motion under Civ.R. 59 to alter or amend judgment;
(4) Motion under Civ.R. 54 for attorney's fees if time to appeal extended under Civ.R. 58.
(5) Motion under Civ.R. 59 for new trial.
(6) Motion for relief under Civ.R. 60 if motion filed no later than 10 days after entry of judgement.

App.R. 4(a)(4).

District court may extend for excusable neglect or good cause upon motion filed not later than 30 days after expiration of time prescribed by App.R. 4(a); no extension to exceed 30 days past prescribed time or 10 days from entry of order granting motion, whichever occurs later. App.R. 4(a)(5).

By other parties, within 14 days of filing of first notice of appeal, or within the time otherwise prescribed by App.R. 4(a), whichever last expires. App.R. 4(a)(3).

By permission

Petition filed with circuit clerk with proof of service within time specified by statute or rule authorizing the appeal, or if no such time is specified, within the time provided by App.R. 4(a) for filing a notice of appeal. App.R. 5(a).

Bankruptcy

If a motion for rehearing under Bankruptcy Rule 8015 is filed in a district court or in a bankruptcy appellate panel, time for appeal to court of appeals runs from entry of order disposing of motion. App.R. 6(b)(2)(A).

Class actions

Within 10 days after entry of order of district court granting or denying class action certification. Civ.R. 23(f).

Inmates

A notice of appeal is timely filed if deposited in the institution's internal mail system on or before the last day for filing. App.R. 4(c), 25(a).

Representation statement

Within 10 days after filing notice of appeal unless court of appeals designates another time, attorney who filed notice shall file with the circuit clerk a statement naming each party represented on appeal by that attorney. App.R. 12(b).

Entry of judgment or order, notice of

Lack of notice of entry by clerk does not affect time to appeal or relieve or authorize court to relieve party for failure to appeal within time allowed, except as allowed by App.R. 4(a). Civ.R. 77(d).

Record (Appellant)

Within 10 days after filing notice of appeal or entry of an order disposing of last timely remaining motion specified in App.R. 4(a)(4)(A), whichever is

APPEAL

later: Appellant to place written order for transcript and file copy of order with clerk; if none to be ordered, file a certificate to that effect; unless entire transcript to be included, file a statement of issues and serve appellee a copy of order or certificate and of statement. App.R. 10(b).

Record (Appellee)

Within 10 days after service of appellant's order or certificate and statement, appellee to file and serve on appellant a designation of additional parts of transcript to be included. Unless within 10 days after designation appellant has ordered such parts and so notified appellee, appellee may within following 10 days either order the parts or move in district court for order requiring appellant to do so. App.R. 10(b).

Record (costs)

At time of ordering, party to make satisfactory arrangements with reporter for payment of cost of transcript. App.R. 10(b)(4).

Record (Reporter)

If transcript cannot be completed within 30 days of receipt of order, reporter shall request extension of time from circuit clerk. App.R. 11(b).

Stay of proceedings to enforce judgment

Effective when supersedeas bond is approved by court. Civ.R. 62(d).

Supersedeas bond may be given upon or after filing notice of appeal or after obtaining the order allowing appeal. Civ.R. 62(d).

Briefs

Appellant must serve and file a brief within 40 days after the record is filed. Appellee must serve and file a brief within 30 days after service of the appellant's brief. A reply brief may be filed within 14 days after service of appellee's brief and, except for good cause shown, at least 3 days before argument. A court of appeals may shorten the times allowed for briefs either by local rule for all cases or by order for a particular case. App.R. 31(a).

Transcripts

See "RECORD", ante, this heading.

Tax Court decisions

Review must be obtained by filing a notice of appeal with the Tax Court clerk within 90 days after entry of decision. If a timely notice of appeal is filed by one party, any other party may take an appeal by filing a notice of appeal within 120 days after entry of decision by the Tax Court. If timely motion made to vacate or revise decision, time to file notice of appeal runs from entry of order disposing of motion or entry of new decision, whichever is later. App.R. 13(a).

APPEAL from magistrate judge to district judge under 28 U.S.C.A. § 636(c)(4) and Civ.R. 73(d)

Notice of Appeal

[This Rule provided as follows, prior to its abrogation:] Filed with clerk of district court within 30 days of entry of judgment. Within 60 days if United States or officer or agency thereof is a

APPEAL from magistrate judge to district judge under 28 U.S.C.A. § 636(c)(4) and Civ.R. 73(d)

party. Within 15 days after entry of an interlocutory decision or order. Civ.R. 74(a) [Civ.R. 74 abrogated eff. Dec. 1, 1997].

[This Rule provided as follows, prior to its abrogation:] When timely notice is filed by a party, any other party may file notice within 14 days thereafter or within time otherwise prescribed by Civ.R. 74(a), whichever period last expires. Civ.R. 74(a) [Civ.R. 74 abrogated eff. Dec. 1, 1997].

[This Rule provided as follows, prior to its abrogation:] Upon showing of excusable neglect, time for filing may be extended on motion filed not later than 20 days from expiration of time for filing. Civ.R. 74(a) [Civ.R. 74 abrogated eff. Dec. 1, 1997].

Running of time for filing terminated as to all parties by timely filing of any of the following motions with the magistrate judge by any party, and the full time for appeal from judgment entered commences to run anew from entry of any of the following orders:

(1) granting or denying motion for judgment under Civ.R. 50(b);

(2) granting or denying motion under Civ.R. 52(b) to amend or make additional findings of fact;

(3) granting or denying motion under Civ.R. 59 to alter or amend judgment;

(4) denying motion for new trial under Civ.R. 59. Civ.R. 74(a) [prior to its abrogation] [Civ.R. 74 abrogated eff. Dec. 1, 1997.]

Joint statement of case

Parties could file in lieu of record within 10 days after filing of notice of appeal, under provisions of this rule prior to its abrogation. Civ.R. 75(b)(1) [Civ.R. 75 abrogated eff. Dec. 1, 1997].

Transcript

Within 10 days after filing notice of appeal appellant to make arrangements for production. Unless entire transcript is to be included, description of parts appellant intends to present must be served on the appellee and filed by the appellant within the 10 day period. If appellee deems transcript of other parts to be necessary, designation of additional parts to be included must be served on the appellant and filed within 10 days after service of appellant's statement. Civ.R. 75(b)(2) [Civ.R. 75 abrogated eff. Dec. 1, 1997].

Statement in lieu of transcript

If no record is available for transcription, parties must file a statement of evidence in lieu of transcript within 10 days after filing of notice of appeal. Civ.R. 75(b)(3) [Civ.R. 75 abrogated eff. Dec. 1, 1997].

APPEAL from magistrate judge to district judge under 28 U.S.C.A. § 636(c)(4) and Civ.R. 73(d)	
Briefs	Appellant to serve and file within 20 days after the filing of transcript, statement of case, or statement of evidence. Civ.R. 75(c)(1) [Civ.R. 75 abrogated eff. Dec. 1, 1997].
	Appellee to serve and file within 20 days after service of appellant's brief. Civ.R. 75(c)(2) [Civ.R. 75 abrogated eff. Dec. 1, 1997].
	Appellant may serve and file reply brief within 10 days after service of appellee's brief. Civ.R. 75(c)(3) [Civ.R. 75 abrogated eff. Dec. 1, 1997].
	If appellee files a cross-appeal, appellee may file a reply brief within 10 days after service of the reply brief of the appellant. Civ.R. 75(c)(4) [Civ.R. 75 abrogated eff. Dec. 1, 1997].
Stay of judgments	Decision of district judge stayed for 10 days during which term a party may petition for rehearing. Civ.R. 76(b) [Civ.R. 76 abrogated eff. Dec. 1, 1997].
APPEAL from magistrate judge under 28 U.S.C.A. § 636(c)(3)	Appeal to court of appeals in identical fashion as appeals from other judgments of district courts. App.R. 3.1. [App.R. 3.1 abrogated eff. Dec. 1, 1998].
APPEAL to Supreme Court	
Direct appeals	30 days after entry of interlocutory or final order, decree or judgment holding Act of Congress unconstitutional under circumstances provided by 28 U.S.C.A. §§ 1252, and 1253. 28 U.S.C.A. § 2101(a), as amended by Act May 24, 1949, c. 139, § 106, 63 Stat. 104. [28 U.S.C.A. § 1252 was repealed and 28 U.S.C.A. § 2101(a) was amended by Pub.L. 100–352, §§ 1, 5(b), June 27, 1988, 102 Stat. 662, 663, respectively. For effective date and applicability to cases, see section 7 of Pub.L. 100–352, set out as 28 U.S.C.A. § 1254 note.]
	30 days from interlocutory judgment, order, or decree in any other direct appeal authorized by law from decision of district court. 28 U.S.C.A. § 2101(b).
	60 days from final judgment, order, or decree in any other direct appeal authorized by law from decision of district court. 28 U.S.C.A. § 2101(b).
Other appeals and certiorari	90 days after entry of judgment or decree; justice of Supreme Court for good cause shown may extend time for applying for writ of certiorari for period not exceeding 60 days. 28 U.S.C.A. § 2101(c).
Briefs supporting certiorari	No separate brief supporting petition for certiorari shall be filed; See Supreme Court Rule 14.2.

APPEAL to Supreme Court	
Brief opposing certiorari	30 days after case is placed on the docket unless time is extended by Court or a Justice or by the Clerk; See Supreme Court Rule 15.3.
Brief on merits on appeal or certiorari	By appellant or petitioner, filed within 45 days of the order granting the writ of certiorari or the order noting probable jurisdiction or postponing consideration of jurisdiction; see Supreme Court Rule 25.1.
	By appellee or respondent, filed within 35 days after the brief for the appellant or petitioner is filed; see Supreme Court Rule 25.2.
	Reply brief, if any, filed within 35 days after the brief for appellee or respondent is filed, but any reply brief must actually be received by Clerk not later than one week before the date of oral argument. See Supreme Court Rule 25.3.
Stay of mandate pending petition for certiorari	A stay of mandate pending filing a petition to the Supreme Court for certiorari must not exceed 90 days unless the period is extended for good cause or unless during the period of stay, the party who obtained the stay files a petition for the writ and so notifies the circuit clerk in writing in which case the stay will continue until final disposition by the Supreme Court. The court of appeals must issue the mandate immediately when a copy of the Supreme Court order denying the petition for writ of certiorari is filed. App.R. 41(d)(2).
ATTORNEY'S fees	See "Costs", this table.
BILL of particulars	Abolished. See Civ.R. 12(e), as amended in 1948. See, however, "More definite statement", this table.
CLASS actions	
Certification	At an early practicable time after a person sues or is sued as a class representative, the court must determine by order whether to certify the action as a class action. Civ.R. 23(c)(1)(A).
Settlement, voluntary dismissal, or compromise	Approval by court of settlement, voluntary dismissal, or compromise that would bind class members only after hearing and on finding that it is fair, reasonable, and adequate. Civ.R. 23(e)(2).
Attorney's fees	Claim for award of attorney's fees and nontaxable costs must be made by motion under Civ.R. 54(d)(2) subject to Civ.R. 23(h) at a time the court sets. Notice of motion must be served on all parties and, for motions by class counsel, directed to class members in a reasonable manner. Civ.R. 23(h)(1).
CLERICAL mistakes and mistakes of oversight or omission in judgments, orders, or record	May be corrected whenever found, on motion or on court's own, with or without notice; but after appeal docketed and while pending, may be corrected only with appellate court's leave. Civ.R. 60(a).
COMPLAINT	Filing commences action—must be served with summons. Civ.R. 3, 4(c)(1).

Service of summons and complaint within 120 days after filing. Civ.R. 4(m).

COMPUTATION of time

Exclude day of the act, event, or default that begins the time period. Exclude intermediate Saturdays, Sundays, and legal holidays when the period is less than 11 days. Include last day of the period unless it is a Saturday, Sunday, legal holiday, or, if act to be done is filing a paper in court, a day on which weather or other conditions make the clerk's office inaccessible. When the last day is excluded, the period runs until the end of the next day that is not a Saturday, Sunday, legal holiday, or day when the clerk's office is inaccessible. Civ.R. 6(a).

Intermediate Saturdays, Sundays, and legal holidays are excluded when the period is less than 11 days. Civ.R. 6(a).

Exclude day of the act, event, or default that begins the period. Exclude intermediate Saturdays, Sundays, and legal holidays when the period is less than 11 days, unless stated in calendar days. Include last day of the period unless it is a Saturday, Sunday, legal holiday, or, if the act to be done is filing a paper in court, a day on which weather or other conditions make the clerk's office inaccessible. App.R. 26(a).

Intermediate Saturdays, Sundays, and legal holidays are excluded when the period is less than 11 days, unless stated in calendar days. App.R. 26(a).

Service by mail is complete upon mailing. Civ.R. 5(b).

Service by mail or by commercial carrier is complete upon mailing or delivery to the carrier. App.R. 25(c).

Service under Civ.R. 5(b)(2)(C), (D), (E), or (F) adds three days after the period would otherwise expire under Civ.R. 6(a). Civ.R. 6(d).

When a party is required or permitted to act within a prescribed period after service of a paper upon that party, three calendar days are added to the period unless the paper is delivered on the date of service stated in the proof of service. A paper served electronically is not treated as delivered on the date of service stated in the proof of service. App.R. 26(c).

Legal holidays are defined by Civ.R. 6(a)(4) and App.R. 26(a)(4).

Supreme Court matters—See Supreme Court Rule 30.

CONDEMNATION of property

Answer to notice of condemnation — 20 days after service of notice. Civ.R. 71A(e).

CORPORATE DISCLOSURE	Nongovernmental corporate parties must file, with first appearance, pleading, motion, response, or other request addressed to the court, statement identifying any parent corporation and any publicly held corporation owning 10% or more of its stock or stating that there is no such corporation. Party must promptly file supplemental statement if any required information changes. Civ.R. 7.1.
COSTS	
	Taxation on 1 day's notice. Review taxation of costs on motion served within the next 5 days. Civ.R. 54(d)(1).
	Failure, without good cause, to sign and return requested waiver of service of summons and to return waiver within a reasonable time which must be at least 30 days after request is sent or at least 60 days if sent to a defendant outside any judicial district of the United States. Civ.R. 4(d).
Attorney's fees and related nontaxable expenses	Motion filed no later than 14 days after entry of judgement. Civ.R. 54(d)(2)(B).
CROSS APPEAL	
Optional appeal from magistrate judge to district judge	Appellee may file reply brief within 10 days after service of reply brief of appellant. Civ.R. 75(c)(4) [Civ.R. 75 abrogated eff. Dec. 1, 1997].
Appellate rules	Within 14 days of filing of first notice of appeal or within the time otherwise prescribed by App.R. 4(a), whichever period ends later. App.R. 4(a)(3).
Inmates	Within 14 days after date when first notice of appeal was filed, or within the time otherwise prescribed by App.R. 4(a), whichever period ends later. The 14 day period runs from date district court dockets first notice of appeal. App.R. 4(a)(3), (c).
DEFAULT	
Entry by clerk	No time stated. Civ.R. 55(b).
Entry by court	If party against whom default judgment is sought has appeared personally or by representative, that party or its representative must be served with written notice of application for default judgment at least 3 days before the hearing on such application. Civ.R. 55(b).
DEFENSES and objections, presentation of	
By pleading	See "Answer", this table.
By motion	Motion must be made before pleading if responsive pleading is allowed. Civ.R. 12(b).
At trial	Opposing party may assert at trial any defense to claim for relief to which such party is not required to serve responsive pleading. Civ.R. 12(b).
Motion affects time for responsive pleading	Service of motion under Civ.R. 12 alters times for responsive pleading. See "Responsive Pleadings", this table.

DEMURRERS	Abolished. Civ.R. 7, 20007 Advisory Committee note, relating to Civ.R. 7(c).
DEPOSITIONS	See, also, "Interrogatories to parties", "Depositions on written questions", this table.
Notice of filing	Promptly. Civ.R. 30(f)(4) and Civ.R. 31(c)(2).
Notice of taking	
	Reasonable written notice to every other party. Civ.R. 30(b)(1).
Objections	As to admissibility, objection may be made at hearing or trial, but subject to Civ.R. 28(b) and 32(d)(3). Civ.R. 32(b).
	As to errors or irregularities in the notice, service promptly. Civ.R. 32(d)(1).
	As to disqualification of officer, objection made before deposition begins or promptly after the basis for disqualification becomes known or could have been known with reasonable diligence. Civ.R. 32(d)(2).
	As to competence of deponent or competence, relevance, or materiality of testimony—not waived by failure to make the objection before or during deposition, unless the ground might have been corrected at that time. Civ.R. 32(d)(3)(A).
	As to errors and irregularities at oral examination in manner of taking deposition, in the form of questions or answers, in the oath or affirmation, or in conduct of parties, and other errors that might have been corrected at that time, objection timely made during deposition. Civ.R. 32(d)(3)(B).
	As to form of written questions under Civ.R. 31—service within time allowed for serving responsive questions or, if recross-question, within 5 days after being served with it. Civ.R. 32(d)(3)(C).
	As to completion and return (transcription, signing, certification, sealing, endorsing, sending, or otherwise)—motion to suppress made promptly after error or irregularity becomes known or, with reasonable diligence, could have been known. Civ.R. 32(d)(4).
Protective orders	
	Subsequent to certification that movant has in good faith conferred or attempted to confer with other affected parties to resolve dispute without court action. Civ.R. 26(c)(1).
Motion to terminate or limit examination	
	Any time during a deposition. Civ.R. 30(d)(3).

Perpetuate testimony pending appeal	Motion in court where judgment was rendered on same notice and service as if action was pending in district court. Civ.R. 27(b).
Perpetuate testimony before action	Service of notice and petition at least 20 days before date of hearing. Civ.R. 27(a)(2).
Taking	
	Time specified in the notice of taking. Civ. R. 30(b)(1). Prior notice by a party to deponent and other parties to designate another method for recording deponent's testimony in addition to method specified in original notice. Civ.R. 30(b)(3).
Review of transcript or recording	Request by a party or deponent before completion of deposition. Deponent has 30 days after notice of availability of transcript or recording to review and to sign statement listing changes and reasons for making them. Civ.R. 30(e).
When taken	
	After parties have conferred as required by Civ.R. 26(f), except in proceeding exempted from initial disclosure under Civ.R. 26(a)(1)(B), or when authorized by rules, stipulation, or court order. Civ.R. 26(d).
DEPOSITIONS on written questions	
	See, also, "Depositions", "Interrogatories to parties", this table.
When taken	
	After parties have conferred as required by Civ.R. 26(f), except in proceeding exempted from initial disclosure under Civ.R. 26(a)(1)(B), or when authorized by rules, stipulation, or court order. Civ.R. 26(d).
Cross questions	Service within 14 days after service of the notice and direct questions. Court may extend or shorten time. Civ.R. 31(a)(5).
Redirect questions	Service within 7 days after being served with cross questions. Court may extend or shorten time. Civ.R. 31(a)(5).
Recross questions	
	Service within 7 days after service with redirect questions. Court may extend or shorten time. Civ.R. 31(a)(5).
Notice of filing of deposition	Promptly. Civ.R. 31(c).
Objections to form	Service within the time for serving responsive questions or, if question is a recross-question, within 5 days after being served with it. Civ.R. 32(d)(3)(C).
DISCOVERY	
	See, also, "Admissions", "Depositions", "Depositions on written questions", "Interrogatories to parties", "Production of documents", this Table.

DISCOVERY

Discovery Conference

Except in exempted proceedings or when otherwise ordered, as soon as practicable and at least 21 days before a scheduling conference is to be held or a scheduling order is due under Civ.R. 16(b), the parties must confer to consider the nature and basis of their claims, defenses, and possibility of settling or resolving the case, to make or arrange for disclosures required by Civ.R. 26(a)(1), to discuss any issues about preserving discoverable information, and to develop a proposed discovery plan. A written report outlining the plan is to be submitted to the court within 14 days after the conference. Civ.R. 26(f); See, also, Civ.R. 26(d).

Without awaiting a discovery request and at or within 14 days after the parties' Civ.R. 26(f) conference, a party must provide information specified in Civ.R. 26(a)(1)(A). Disclosure of expert testimony under Civ.R. 26(a)(2), in absence of court order or stipulation, is to be made at least 90 days before trial date or date case is to be ready for trial or if evidence intended solely to contradict or rebut evidence on same subject matter identified by another party under Civ.R. 26(a)(2)(B), within 30 days after the other party's disclosure. Civ.R. 26(a)(2)(C). Disclosures under Civ.R. 26(a)(1) or (2), depositions, interrogatories, requests for documents or tangible things or to permit entry onto land, and requests for admission must not be filed until used in the proceeding or court orders filing. Civ.R. 5(d).

Identification of witnesses, documents, exhibits, including summaries of other evidence, and designation of witnesses whose testimony is expected to be presented by deposition with a transcript of pertinent testimony if deposition is not taken stenographically to be provided to other parties at least 30 days before trial unless otherwise directed by court. Within 14 days thereafter, unless court sets different time, a party may serve and promptly file objections. Civ.R. 26(a)(3).

DISMISSAL for lack of subject-matter jurisdiction

Any time. Civ.R. 12(h)(3).

DISMISSAL by plaintiff voluntarily without court order

By filing notice of dismissal before service of answer or motion for summary judgment. Civ.R. 41(a)(1).

DISMISSAL of counterclaim, crossclaim or third-party claim, voluntary

Before service of responsive pleading, or if none, before introduction of evidence at trial or hearing. Civ.R. 41(c).

DISMISSAL without prejudice

Service of summons and complaint not made within 120 days after filing of complaint. Civ.R. 4(m).

DOCUMENTS, Production of

See "Production of documents", this Table.

ENLARGEMENT of time generally

Act may or must be done within specified time	Court for good cause may extend time (1) with or without motion or notice if court acts, or if request is made, before the original time or its extension expires, or (2) on motion made after the time has expired if party failed to act because of excusable neglect; but court may not extend time for taking any action under Civ.R. 50(b) and (d), 52(b), 59(b), (d) and (e), and 60(b), except as those rules allow. Civ.R. 6(b).
Affidavits in opposition, service	At least 1 day before the hearing, unless court permits service at another time, except as Civ.R. 59(c) provides otherwise. Civ.R. 6(c)(2).
Hearing of motions and defenses	Heard and decided before trial unless court orders deferral until trial. Civ.R. 12(i).
Service under Rule 5(b)(2)(C), (D), (E), or (F)	Adds three days after which the prescribed period after service would otherwise expire under Civ.R. 6(a). Civ.R. 6(d). When a party is required or permitted to act within a prescribed period after service of a paper upon that party, three calendar days are added to the period unless the paper is delivered on the date of service stated in the proof of service. A paper served electronically is not treated as delivered on the day of service stated in the proof of service. App.R. 26(c).
Injunction—temporary restraining order	May be extended 10 days by order of court or for a longer period by consent of party against whom order is directed. Civ.R. 65(b).
Response to request for admissions	Time may be lengthened or shortened by court or as the parties may stipulate to under Civ.R. 29. Civ.R. 36(a).
Optional appeal from magistrate judge to district judge	Upon showing of excusable neglect, time to file notice of appeal may be extended upon motion filed not later than 20 days from expiration of time for filing. Civ.R. 74(a) [Civ.R. 74 abrogated eff. Dec. 1, 1997].
Motion for judgment as a matter of law	No enlargement of the 10 day period except to the extent and under conditions stated in Civ.R. 50(b). Civ.R. 6(b).
Findings by the court, amendment of or make additional findings	No enlargement of the 10 day period except to the extent and under conditions stated in Civ.R. 52(b). Civ.R. 6(b).
Motion for new trial	No enlargement of the 10 day period except to the extent and under conditions stated in Civ.R. 50(d), 59(b), (d), and (e). Civ.R. 6(b).
Motion for relief from judgment or order	No enlargement of the 1 year period except to the extent and under conditions stated in Civ.R. 60(b). Civ.R. 6(b).

ENLARGEMENT of time
generally
Appellate rules — Court for good cause may extend time prescribed by App.Rules or by its order to perform any act or may permit act to be done after expiration of such time; but court may not extend time for filing notice of appeal, or petition for permission to appeal a notice of appeal from or a petition to enjoin, set aside, suspend, modify, enforce or otherwise review an order of an administrative agency, board, commission or officer of the United States, unless specifically authorized by law. App.R. 26(b).

Supreme Court matters, depositions — See Supreme Court Rule 30.

EXCEPTIONS for insufficiency of pleadings — Abolished. Civ.R. 7, 2007 Advisory Committee note, relating to Civ.R. 7(c).

EXECUTION
Stay — Automatically: No execution may issue, nor may proceedings be taken to enforce, until expiration of 10 days after entry of judgment; exceptions—injunctions, receiverships, and patent accountings. Civ.R. 62(a).

Stay according to state law. Civ.R. 62(f).

Motion for new trial or for judgment. Civ.R. 62(b).

Stay in favor of government. Civ.R. 62(e).

Supersedeas on appeal. Civ.R. 62(d).

Stay of judgment as to multiple claims or multiple parties. Civ.R. 62(h).

Stay of judgment pending appeal from magistrate judge to district judge. Civ.R. 74(c). Stay of decision of district judge for 10 days during which time a party may petition for rehearing. Civ.R. 76(b) [Civ.R. 74 and 76 abrogated eff. Dec. 1, 1997].

FILING papers — Filing complaint commences civil action. Civ.R. 3.

Constitutional challenge to a statute. Civ.R. 5.1.

Service of summons and complaint within 120 days after filing of complaint. Civ.R. 4(m).

Any paper after complaint that is required to be served, together with certificate of service, must be filed within reasonable time after service. Civ.R. 5(d).
Any paper after complaint that is required to be served, together with certificate of service, must be filed with clerk unless judge agrees to accept it for filing. Civ.R. 5(d).

Local court rules may allow papers to be filed, signed, or verified by electronic means if consistent with technical standards of Judicial Conference of the United States. A local rule requirement of electronic filing must allow reasonable exceptions.

FILING papers

The clerk must not refuse for filing any paper solely because it is not in the form prescribed by Rules of Civil Procedure or a local rule or practice. Civ.R. 5(d).

Any paper after the complaint required to be served, together with a certificate of service, must be filed with the court within a reasonable time after service. Civ.R. 5(d).

FINDINGS

Motion to amend

10 days after entry of judgment. Civ.R. 52(b). Exception from general rule relating to enlargement. Civ.R. 6(b).

FOREIGN law

Notice by pleading or other writing required of party intending to raise an issue concerning the law of a foreign country. Civ.R. 44.1.

HEARING of motions

A court may establish regular times and places for oral hearings on motions; by rule or order court may provide for submitting and determining motions on briefs, without oral hearings. Civ.R. 78.

Service of notice at least 5 days before time specified for hearing unless motion may be heard ex parte, or otherwise these rules or a court order set a different time. Civ.R. 6(c).

Hearing of certain motions and defenses before trial on application of any party unless court orders deferral until trial. Civ.R. 12(i).

HOLIDAYS

New Year's Day, Birthday of Martin Luther King, Jr., Washington's Birthday, Memorial Day, Independence Day, Labor Day, Columbus Day, Veterans' Day, Thanksgiving Day, Christmas Day, and any other day declared a holiday by the President, Congress or the state in which is located either the district court that rendered the challenged judgment or order, or the circuit clerk's principal office. Civ.R. 6(a); App.R. 26(a).

Exclusion in computation of time. Civ.R. 6(a); App.R. 26(a).

INJUNCTION (Temporary restraining order granted without notice)

Order must state date and hour of issuance, promptly filed in clerk's office, and entered in the record. Civ.R. 65(b).

Expiration within the time after entry, not to exceed 10 days, that court sets, unless before that time the court for good cause extends the order for like period or, with consent of party against whom order is directed, for longer period. Civ.R. 65(b).

Motion for preliminary injunction must be set for hearing at earliest possible time—takes precedence

INJUNCTION (Temporary restraining order granted without notice)	
	over all matters except older ones of same character. Civ.R. 65(b).
	Motion for dissolution or modification on 2 days' notice or shorter notice set by the court; court must then hear and decide motion as promptly as justice requires. Civ.R. 65(b).
INSTRUCTIONS	
Requests	At close of evidence or at an earlier reasonable time that the court orders. After close of evidence for issues that could not reasonably have been anticipated at an earlier time for requests, and untimely requests for instructions on any issue with the court's permission. Civ.R. 51(a).
Proposed	Court must inform parties before instructing jury and before final argument, and give parties opportunity to object before instructions and arguments are delivered. Civ.R. 51(b)(1), (2).
Time of	Court may instruct jury at any time before jury is discharged. Civ.R. 51(b)(3).
Objections	For parties informed of instructions or actions on requests before the jury is instructed and before final jury arguments, at opportunity for objection provided under Civ.R. 51(b)(2). For parties not informed of instructions or actions on requests before time for objection under Civ.R. 51(b)(2), promptly after learning that instruction or request will be, or has been, given or refused. Civ.R. 51(c).
INTERROGATORIES to parties	
	See, also, "Depositions", "Depositions on written questions", this table.
	Service after parties have conferred pursuant to Civ.R. 26(f). Civ.R. 26(d), 33(a).
Answers or objections	Service within 30 days after service of the interrogatories. A shorter or longer time may be stipulated to or ordered by the court. Civ.R. 33(b)(3).
INTERVENTION	
	Upon timely motion. Civ.R. 24(a), (b).
	Person desiring to intervene shall serve a motion to intervene upon the parties as provided in Civ.R. 5. Civ.R. 24(c).
JUDGMENT or order	
Alter or amend judgment, motion to	Shall be filed not later than 10 days after entry of judgment. Civ.R. 59(e). Exception to general rule, relating to enlargement. Civ.R. 6(b).
Clerical mistakes, or from oversight or omission	May be corrected any time; but after an appeal has been docketed in appellate court and while appeal pending may be corrected only with leave of appellate court. Civ.R. 60(a).

JUDGMENT or order

Default	See "Default", this table.
Renewal of motion for judgment after trial	Not later than 10 days after entry of judgment. Exception from general rule relating to enlargement. Civ.R. 6(b).
Entry of judgment	Subject to Civ.R. 54(b), promptly by clerk without awaiting the court's direction, unless court orders otherwise, upon general verdict of jury or upon court decision that a party shall recover only a sum certain or costs or that all relief shall be denied. Promptly approved form of judgment by court, promptly entered by clerk, upon special verdict or general verdict with answers to written questions, or upon court decision granting other relief. Entry may not be delayed in order to tax costs or award fees. Civ.R. 58(b), (e). Time of entry—Entry of a judgment if separate document is not required when judgment is entered in the civil docket under Civ.R. 79(a). If separate document is required, when the judgment is entered in the civil docket under Civ.R. 79(a) and either the judgment is set forth in a separate document, or 150 days have run from entry of the judgment in the civil docket, whichever is earlier. Civ.R. 58(c).
Entry, notice of	Immediately after entry, clerk must serve notice thereof as provided in Civ.R. 5(b) and record service on the docket. Any party may in addition serve a notice of such entry in manner provided in Civ.R. 5(b) for service of papers. Civ.R. 77(d). Lack of notice of entry by clerk does not affect time for appeal or relieve or authorize court to relieve party for failure to appeal within time allowed, except as allowed by App.R. 4(a). Civ.R. 77(d).
Offer of judgment	Service more than 10 days before trial begins. Civ.R. 68. Acceptance, written notice of—service within 10 days after service of offer. Civ.R. 68.
On pleadings, motion for judgment	After pleadings are closed but early enough not to delay the trial. Civ.R. 12(c).
Relief from, on grounds stated in Rule 60(b)	Motion within a reasonable time and not more than 1 year after entry of judgment or order or the date of the proceeding, for following grounds: (1) mistake, inadvertence, surprise, or excusable neglect; (2) newly discovered evidence; (3) fraud, misrepresentation, or other misconduct. Civ.R. 60(b), (c). Exception from general rule relating to enlargement. Civ.R. 6(b). Motion within a reasonable time, for following grounds: (1) judgment void, (2) judgment satisfied, released, or discharged, (3) prior underlying judgment reversed or otherwise vacated, (4) no longer

JUDGMENT or order	
	equitable that judgment have prospective application, (5) any other reason justifying relief. Civ.R. 60(b). Exception from general rule relating to enlargement. Civ.R. 6(b).
Stay	See "Execution", this table.
Summary judgment	See "Summary Judgment", this table.
JURORS	The institution of the alternate juror has been abolished. Civ.R. 47, 1991 Advisory Committee note, subd. (b).
JURY trial	
Demand	Service any time after commencement of action and not later than 10 days after service of last pleading directed to the triable issue. Civ.R. 38(b).
	Adverse party may serve demand for jury trial within 10 days after service of first demand or within a shorter time ordered by the court. Civ.R. 38(c).
Removed actions	If at the time of removal all necessary pleadings have been served, demand for jury trial may be served:
	By petitioner, 10 days after the notice of removal is filed;
	By another party, within 10 days after service on party of the notice of filing the petition. Civ.R. 81(c).
	Demand after removal not necessary in either of two instances: (1) before removal, party has made express demand in accordance with state law; (2) state law does not require express demands and court does not order otherwise. Civ.R. 81(c).
LEGAL HOLIDAY	See "Holidays", this table.
MAGISTRATE JUDGES	
Trial by consent	Consent of parties to magistrate judge's authority to be exercised by filing statement consenting to the referral. Civ.R. 73(b).
Pretrial matters	Objections of parties to order disposing of matter not dispositive of claim or defense to be served and filed within 10 days after being served with copy of order. Civ.R. 72(a).
	Clerk to promptly mail copies to all parties of recommendation of magistrate judge for disposition of matter dispositive of claim or defense of a party or prisoner petition. Specific written objections to recommended disposition may be served and filed within 10 days after service. Response to objections may be made within 10 days after being served with copy. Civ.R. 72(b).

MAIL

Service under Rule 5(b)(2)(C), (D), (E), or (F) adds 3 days after a prescribed period after service would otherwise expire under Civ.R. 6(a). Civ.R. 6(d). When a party is required or permitted to act within a prescribed period after service of a paper upon that party, three calendar days are added to the period unless the paper is delivered on the date of service stated in the proof of service. A paper served electronically is not treated as delivered on the day of service stated in the proof of service. App.R. 26(c).

A brief or appendix is timely filed if on or before the last day for filing it is mailed First-Class or other class at least as expeditious, postage prepaid, or dispatched for delivery within three calendar days by a third-party commercial carrier. App.R. 25(a)(2)(B).

MASTERS

Order appointing master

Court may issue only after master has filed affidavit disclosing whether there is any ground for disqualification under 28 U.S.C. § 455 and, if ground is disclosed, after parties with court's approval waive the disqualification. Civ.R. 53(b)(3).

Amendment of order appointing

Order appointing master may be amended at any time after notice to parties, and opportunity to be heard. Civ.R. 53(b)(4).

Order of master

A master who issues an order must file the order and promptly serve a copy on each party. The clerk must enter the order on the docket. Civ.R. 53(d).

Report of master

Master must report to court as required by appointing order. The master must file the report and promptly serve a copy on each party unless the court orders otherwise. Civ.R. 53(e).

In acting on, the court must give parties notice and an opportunity to be heard. Civ.R. 53(f)(1).

A party may file objections or motion to adopt or modify no later than 20 days from the time the master's order, report, or recommendations are served, unless the court sets a different time. Civ.R. 53(f)(2).

Compensation of master

The court must fix the master's compensation before or after judgment on the basis and terms stated in the appointing order but the court may set a new basis and terms after notice and opportunity to be heard. Civ.R. 53(g)(1)

MORE DEFINITE STATEMENT

Furnished

Must be furnished within 10 days after notice of order or other time fixed by court or court may strike pleading or issue any other appropriate order. Civ.R. 12(e).

Motion for

Must be made before responsive pleading is filed. Civ.R. 12(e).

MOTIONS, notices, and affidavits

See, also, specific headings, this table.

In general

A written motion, supporting affidavits, and notice of hearing thereof—service at least 5 days before time specified for hearing unless motion may be heard ex parte, or a different time is fixed by rule or by order of court. Civ.R. 6(c).

Opposing affidavits must be served at least one day before hearing, unless court permits otherwise. Civ.R. 6(c).

Pleading, written motion, or other paper not signed by attorney or party shall be stricken unless omission of signature is corrected promptly after being called to attention of attorney or party. Civ.R. 11(a).

NEW TRIAL

Motion and affidavits

Motion shall be filed not later than 10 days after entry of judgment. Civ.R. 59(b). Exception from general rule relating to enlargement. Civ.R. 6(b). If motion based on affidavits, they must be filed with motion. Civ.R. 59(c).

Opposing affidavits

Shall be filed within 10 days of service of motion for new trial; period may be extended up to 20 days either by court for good cause shown or by parties by stipulation. Civ.R. 59(c).

Initiative of court

Not later than 10 days after entry of judgment, court may order new trial for any reason that would justify granting one on a party's motion. Civ.R. 59(d). Exception to general rule relating to enlargement. Civ.R. 6(b).

After giving parties notice and opportunity to be heard, court may grant a timely motion for new trial, for reason not stated in the motion. Civ.R. 59(d). Exception to general rule relating to enlargement. Civ.R. 6(b).

Judgment as a matter of law

Party against whom judgment as a matter of law is rendered shall file a motion for a new trial under Civ.R. 59 no later than 10 days after entry of the judgment. Civ.R. 50(d).

OBJECTIONS to orders or rulings of court

At time ruling or order of court is requested or made; if party has no opportunity to object to ruling or order at time it is made, absence of objection does not prejudice the party. Civ.R. 46.

Pretrial matters referred to magistrate judge

Objections of parties to order disposing of matter not dispositive of claim or defense to be served and filed within 10 days after being served with copy of order. Civ.R. 72(a).

Specific written objections to recommended disposition of matter dispositive of claim or defense of a party may be served or filed within 10 days after

OBJECTIONS to orders or rulings of court	
	service. Response to objections may be made within 10 days after being served with copy. Civ.R. 72(b).
OFFER of judgment	
	Must be served more than 10 days before trial. Civ.R. 68(a).
	Acceptance must be served within 10 days after service of offer. Civ.R. 68(a).
ORDERS	See Judgment or order.
PARTICULARS, Bill of	Abolished. Civ.R. 12(e), as amended in 1948. See, however, "More definite statement", this table.
PLEADINGS	
Amendment of	Once as matter of course before responsive pleading served or within 20 days after serving the pleading if no response is allowed and action is not yet on trial calendar. Civ.R. 15(a).
	By leave of court or written consent of opposing parties, at any time. Civ.R. 15(a).
	During trial or after judgment to conform to evidence or to raise an unpleaded issue, but tried by express or implied consent of parties. Civ.R. 15(b).
Supplemental	Upon motion of party—court may upon reasonable notice permit service of supplemental pleading setting out transactions, etc., that happened after the date of pleading sought to be supplemented. Civ.R. 15(d).
	Opposing party plead to supplemental pleading—court may so order, within a specified time. Civ.R. 15(d).
Allegations of time	Such allegations are material when testing the sufficiency of a pleading. Civ.R. 9(f).
Judgment on, motion for	After pleadings are closed but early enough not to delay the trial. Civ.R. 12(c).
Striking of matter from	Motion made before responding to a pleading or, if no responsive pleading allowed, within 20 days after service of pleading. Civ.R. 12(f).
	On court's own initiative at any time. Civ.R. 12(f).
Signing of	Pleading, written motion, or other paper not signed by attorney or party must be stricken unless omission of signature is corrected promptly after being called to attention of attorney or party. Civ.R. 11(a).
PLEAS	Abolished. Civ.R. 7, 2007 Advisory Committee note, relating to Civ.R. 7(c).

PRETRIAL conferences	
	Scheduling order to issue as soon as practicable but in any event within the earlier of 120 days after complaint served on defendant or 90 days after appearance of any defendant. Civ.R. 16(b).
PROCESS	See "Summons", this Table.
PRODUCTION of documents	
Request for, service of	
	Within the scope of Civ.R. 26(b). Civ.R. 34(a).
Response to request	
	Within 30 days after service of the request. A shorter or longer time may be ordered by court or stipulated to under Civ.R. 29. Civ.R. 34(b).
Time of inspection	The request must specify a reasonable time. Civ.R. 34(b).
Subpoena	See "Subpoena", this table.
REHEARING	
Petition for panel rehearing	Petitions for panel rehearings may be filed within 14 days after entry of judgement unless the time is shortened or extended by order or local rule. In all civil cases in which the United States or its agency or officer thereof is a party, the time within which any party may seek a rehearing shall be 45 days after entry of judgement unless the time is shortened or extended by order. App.R. 40(a).
Issuance of mandate	The mandate of the court must issue 7 calendar days after the time to file a petition for rehearing expires, or 7 calendar days after entry of an order denying a timely petition for panel rehearing, petition for rehearing en banc, or motion for stay of mandate, whichever is later. The court may shorten or extend the time. The timely filing of a petition for panel rehearing, petition for rehearing en banc, or motion for stay of mandate, stays the mandate until disposition of the petition or motion, unless the court orders otherwise. App.R. 41(b), (d)(1).
REMOVED actions	
Answers and defenses	Within 20 days after the receipt through service or otherwise of a copy of the initial pleading setting forth the claim for relief upon which the action or proceeding is based, or within 20 days after the service of summons for an initial pleading on file at the time of service, or within 5 days after filing of the notice for removal, whichever period is longest. Civ.R. 81(c).
Demand for jury trial	Demand after removal not necessary in either of two instances: (1) before removal, party has made express demand in accordance with state law; (2) state law does not require express demands and court does not direct otherwise. Civ.R. 81(c).
Notice of removal	Within 30 days after receipt through service or otherwise of a copy of the initial pleading setting forth the claim for relief upon which the action or proceeding is based, or within 30 days after service of summons if such initial pleading has then been filed in court and is not required to be served on

REMOVED actions	
	defendant, whichever period is shorter. 28 U.S.C.A. § 1446(b).
	If the case stated by the initial pleading is not removable, a notice of removal may be filed within 30 days after receipt by the defendant, through service or otherwise, of a copy of an amended pleading, motion, order or other paper from which it may first be ascertained that the case is one which is or has become removable. 28 U.S.C.A. § 1446(b).
	A case may not be removed on the basis of jurisdiction conferred by 28 U.S.C.A. § 1332 more than one year after action's commencement. 28 U.S.C.A. § 1446(b).
REPLY	
	See, also, "Responsive pleadings", this table.
To answer	If ordered by court. Civ.R. 7(a). Service within 20 days after service of order, unless order specifies a different time. Civ.R. 12(a).
To counterclaim or crossclaim	Service within 20 days after service of pleading that states the counterclaim or crossclaim. Civ.R. 12(a).
	United States or agency or officer or employee thereof sued only in an official capacity shall serve reply within 60 days after service on U.S. attorney. Civ.R. 12(a).
	United States officer or employee sued in an individual capacity in connection with duties performed on the United States' behalf shall serve reply within 60 days after service on officer or employee or service on the United States attorney, whichever is later. Civ.R. 12(a).
Alteration of time by service of Civ.R. 12 motion	See "Responsive pleadings", this table.
RESPONSIVE PLEADINGS	
	See, also, "Answer", "Reply", this table.
To amend pleading	Within 10 days after service of amended pleading or within time remaining for response to original pleading, whichever is later, unless court otherwise orders. Civ.R. 15(a).
To supplemental pleading	As ordered by court. Civ.R. 15(d).
Alteration of time by service of Civ.R. 12 motion	Service of motion permitted under Civ.R. 12 alters times for responsive pleadings as follows unless different time fixed by court: (1) if court denies motion or postpones its disposition until trial, service of responsive pleading within 10 days after notice of the court's action; (2) if court grants motion for more definite statement, service of responsive pleading within 10 days after service of the more definite statement. Civ.R. 12(a)(4).

RESTRAINING order, temporary, without notice	See "Injunction", this table.
RETURN	
	The court may allow a summons or proof of service to be amended. Civ.R. 4(a) & (*l*).
	Proof of service must be made to the court by server's affidavit, except for service by United States marshal or deputy marshal. Civ.R. 4(*l*).
SANCTIONS	Presentation to court of a pleading, written motion, or other paper is a certification under Civ.R. 11(b). If after notice and reasonable opportunity to respond, court determines that Civ.R. 11(b) was violated, sanctions may be imposed by a motion for sanctions which must not be filed or presented to court unless, within 21 days after service of the motion or another time period set by the court, the challenged matter is not withdrawn or corrected. Civ.R. 11(c). Sanctions are inapplicable to disclosures and discovery. Civ.R. 11(d).
SATURDAYS AND SUNDAYS, LEGAL HOLIDAYS	Exclusion in computation of time when period is less than 11 days. Civ.R. 6(a); App.R. 26(a).
STAY or supersedeas	See "Appeal", "Execution", this table.
SUBPOENA	
Objection	Before the earlier of 14 days after service of the subpoena or the time specified for compliance, service on the party or attorney designated in the subpoena written objection to production of any or all of the designated materials or of the premises. Civ.R. 45(c)(2)(B).
Motion to compel production	If objection has been made, the party serving the subpoena may, on notice to the person commanded to produce, move at any time for an order to compel the production or inspection. Civ.R. 45(c)(2)(B).
Motion to quash	The court by which a subpoena was issued must quash or modify the subpoena on timely motion under certain circumstances. Civ.R. 45(c)(3)(A).
Witnesses, documentary evidence, etc.	Subpoena specifies time for attendance and giving of testimony or to produce and permit inspection, copying, testing, or sampling of designated documents, electronically stored information, or tangible things in the possession, custody or control of that person, or to permit inspection of premises. Civ.R. 45(a)(1)(A), (C).
SUBSTITUTION of parties	
	In cases of death, incompetency, or transfer of interest—motion to substitute, together with notice of hearing, served on parties as provided in Civ.R. 5 and on nonparties in manner provided in Civ.R. 4 for service of a summons. Civ.R. 25(a), (b), (c).

SUBSTITUTION of parties	
	Dismissal as to deceased party unless motion for substitution is made within 90 days after service of a statement noting the death. Civ.R. 25(a).
	Successor of public officer substituted automatically. Court may order substitution at any time, but absence of order does not affect substitution. Civ.R. 25(d).
SUMMARY JUDGMENT, motion for	
Claimant	May move at any time after 20 days have passed from commencement of action or after service of motion for summary judgment by opposing party. Civ.R. 56(a).
Defending party	May move at any time. Civ.R. 56(b).
Service	Service of motion at least 10 days before the day set for hearing. Civ.R. 56(c).
	Service of opposing affidavits before the hearing day. Civ.R. 56(c).
SUMMONS	
	Served with a copy of complaint. Civ.R. 4(c)(1). If not served within 120 days after filing complaint, court must dismiss action without prejudice, order service be made within a specified time, or extend time for service. Civ.R. 4(m).
	Proof of service must be made to the court by server's affidavit, except for service by United States marshal or deputy marshal. Civ.R. 4(*l*).
	Service by any nonparty at least 18, a United States marshal, deputy marshal, or other person specially appointed by the court. Civ.R. 4(c)(2), (3).
SUPPLEMENTAL pleadings	See "Pleadings", this table.
SUPERSEDEAS or stay	See "Appeal", "Execution", this table.
TERM	Every district court considered always open. Civ.R. 77(a).
	Terms of court have been abolished. 28 U.S.C.A. §§ 138–141, as amended by Pub.L. 88–139, Oct. 16, 1963, 77 Stat. 248.
THIRD-PARTY practice	Third-party plaintiff need not obtain leave if third-party plaintiff files third-party complaint not later than 10 days after serving the original answer. Civ.R. 14(a).
VERDICT	
Renewal of motion for judgment after trial	Movant may renew motion for judgment as a matter of law by filing a motion no later than 10 days after the entry of judgment or — if the motion addresses a jury issue not decided by a verdict — no later than 10 days after the jury was discharged. Civ.R. 50(b).

VERDICT

Exception from general rule relating to enlargement. Civ.R. 6(b).

New trial where judgment as a matter of law rendered

Party against whom judgment as a matter of law is rendered must file a motion for a new trial under Civ.R. 59 no later than 10 days after entry of the judgment. Civ.R. 50(d).

EQUITY RULES REFERENCE TABLE

The Federal Rules of Civil Procedure supplant the Equity Rules since in general they cover the field now covered by the Equity Rules and the Conformity Act (former section 724 of this title).

This table shows the Equity Rules to which references are made in the notes to the Federal Rules of Civil Procedure.

Equity Rules	Federal Rules of Civil Procedure
1	77
2	77
3	79
4	77
5	77
6	78
7	4, 70
8	6, 70
9	70
10	18, 54
11	71
12	3, 4, 5, 12, 55
13	4
14	4
15	4, 45
16	6, 55
17	55
18	7, 8
19	1, 15, 61
20	12
21	11, 12
22	1
23	1, 39
24	11
25	8, 9, 10, 19
26	18, 20, 82
27	23
28	15
29	7, 12, 42, 55
30	8, 13, 82
31	7, 8, 12, 55
32	15
33	7, 12
34	15
35	15
36	11
37	17, 19, 20, 24
38	23
39	19
40	20
41	17
42	19, 20
43	12, 21
44	12, 21
45	25
46	43, 61
47	26
48	43
49	53
50	30, 80
51	30, 53
52	45, 53
53	53
54	26
55	30
56	40
57	40
58	26, 33, 34, 36
59	53
60	53
61	53
61½	53
62	53
63	53
64	26
65	53
66	53
67	53
68	53
69	59
70	17
70½	52
71	54
72	60, 61
73	65
74	62
75	75
76	75
77	76
78	43
79	83
80	6
81	86

ORDERS OF THE SUPREME COURT OF THE UNITED STATES ADOPTING AND AMENDING RULES

ORDER OF DECEMBER 20, 1937

It is ordered that Rules of Procedure for the District Courts of the United States be adopted pursuant to Section 2 of the Act of June 19, 1934, Chapter 651 (48 Stat. 1064), and the Chief Justice is authorized and directed to transmit the Rules as adopted to the Attorney General and to request him, as provided in that section, to report these Rules to the Congress at the beginning of the regular session in January next. MR. JUSTICE BRANDEIS states that he does not approve of the adoption of the Rules.

ORDER OF DECEMBER 28, 1939

1. That the first sentence of Rule 81(a)(6) of the Rules of Civil Procedure be amended so as to read as follows:

"(6) These rules do not apply to proceedings under the Act of September 13, 1888, c. 1015, § 13 (25 Stat. 479) as amended, U.S.C., Title 8, § 282, 8 U.S.C.A. § 282, relating to deportation of Chinese; they apply to proceedings for enforcement or review of compensation orders under the Longshoremen's and Harbor Workers' Compensation Act, Act of March 4, 1927, c. 509, §§ 18, 21 (44 Stat. 1434, 1436), U.S.C., Title 33, §§ 918, 921, 33 U.S.C.A. §§ 918, 921, except to the extent that matters of procedure are provided for in that Act".

2. **Effective Date.** That the foregoing amendment take effect on the day which is three months subsequent to the adjournment of the second regular session of the 76th Congress, but if that day is prior to September 1, 1940, then this amendment shall take effect on September 1, 1940. This amendment governs all proceedings in actions brought after it takes effect and also all further proceedings in actions then pending, except to the extent that in the opinion of the Court its application in a particular action pending when the amendment takes effect would not be feasible or would work injustice, in which event the former procedure applies.

3. That THE CHIEF JUSTICE be authorized to transmit this amendment to the Attorney General with the request that he report it to the Congress at the beginning of the regular session in January, 1940.

MR. JUSTICE BLACK does not approve of the adoption of this amendment.

ORDER OF DECEMBER 27, 1946

1. That subdivisions (a) and (b) of Rule 80 of the Rules of Civil Procedure be, and they hereby are, abrogated.

2. That Rules 6, 7, 12, 13, 14, 17, 24, 26, 27, 28, 33, 34, 36, 41, 45, 52, 54, 56, 58, 59, 60, 62, 65, 66, 68, 73, 75, 77, 79, 81, 84, and 86 of the Rules of Civil Procedure and Forms Nos. 17, 20, 22, and 25, be, and they hereby are, amended as hereinafter set forth.

[See the amendments made thereby under the respective rules and forms, post.]

3. That THE CHIEF JUSTICE be authorized to transmit these amendments to the Attorney General with the request that he report them to the Congress at the beginning of the regular session in January, 1947.

MR. JUSTICE FRANKFURTER joins in approval of the proposed amendments essentially because of his confidence in the informed judgment of the Advisory Committee on Rules of Civil Procedure.

ORDER OF DECEMBER 29, 1948

1. That the title "Rules of Civil Procedure for the District Courts of the United States" be amended to read "Rules of Civil Procedure for the United States District Courts".

2. That Rules 1, 17, 22, 24, 25, 27, 37, 45, 57, 60, 62, 65, 66, 67, 69, 72, 73, 74, 75, 76, 79, 81, 82, and 86 of the Rules of Civil Procedure and Forms Nos. 1, 19, 22, 23, and 27, be, and they hereby are, amended as hereinafter set forth.

[See the amendments made thereby under the respective rules and forms, post.]

3. That THE CHIEF JUSTICE be authorized to transmit these amendments to the Attorney General with the request that he report them to the Congress at the beginning of the regular session in January, 1949.

ORDER OF APRIL 30, 1951

1. That paragraph (7) of Rule 81(a) of the Rules of Civil Procedure, be, and it hereby is, abrogated.

2. That the Rules of Civil Procedure be, and they hereby are, amended by including therein a rule to govern condemnation cases in the United States District Courts, numbered 71A, as follows:

[See text of Rule 71A, post.]

3. Effective Date. That this Rule 71A and the amendment to Rule 81(a) will take effect on August 1, 1951. Rule 71A governs all proceedings in actions brought after it takes effect and also all further proceedings in actions then pending, except to the extent that in the opinion of the court its application in a particular action pending when the rule takes effect would not be feasible or would work injustice, in which event the former procedure applies.

4. That Forms Nos. 28 and 29 be, and they hereby are, approved and added to the Appendix of Forms to the Rules of Civil Procedure. The forms read respectively as follows:

[See text of Forms 28 and 29, post.]

5. That THE CHIEF JUSTICE be authorized to transmit these amendments to the Congress on or before May 1, 1951.

ORDER OF APRIL 17, 1961

1. That Rules 25, 54, 62 and 86 of the Rules of Civil Procedure and Forms Nos. 2 and 19, be, and they hereby are, amended as hereinafter set forth:

[See the amendments made thereby under the respective rules and forms, post.]

2. That THE CHIEF JUSTICE be authorized to transmit these amendments to Congress in accordance with the provisions of Title 28, U.S.C., Sec. 2072.

3. MR. JUSTICE BLACK does not join in approval of the Rules because he believes that it would be better for Congress to act directly by legislation on the matters treated by the Rules.

4. MR. JUSTICE DOUGLAS filed the following statement:

"Most of the proposed changes in the Rules of Civil Procedure are picayune and harmless, yet hardly worth making apart from any overall revision of the Rules. The change in Rule 25 of the Rules of Civil Procedure is, however, a major one; and it seems to me unwise. The policy that a cabinet officer under one administration pursues is often not the policy of the next administration. I would not make the contrary assumption, as does the proposed change. I think the ends served by *Snyder v. Buck*, 340 U.S. 15, 71 S.Ct. 93, 95 L.Ed. 15, are proper ones. The Rule in its present form leaves the burden on the claimant who challenges a particular government policy to re-establish that the controversy he had with a predecessor is a live one as respects the successor. The burden should rest there, not with the newcomer to office.

"The critical language in Rule 25(d) that is changed by the proposed amendment derived from 28 U.S.C. § 780 which the Revised Code dropped in 1949 because it had been incorporated in Rule 25(d). See 28 U.S.C., p. XXIX. The history of § 780 is reviewed in *Snyder v. Buck,* supra, pp. 18–19.

"Congress dealt with the matter beginning with the Act of February 8, 1899, 30 Stat. 822. The care with which it approached the problem is shown in H.R.Rep. No. 960, 55th Cong., 2d Sess., p. 2, where it is said:

" 'A mandamus proceeding against an officer is based upon the claim that he is personally refusing to perform some duty which the law requires of him in his official character, and if decided against him he is properly liable, personally, for all cost of the proceeding, but if he vacates the office before a decision, it might seem harsh to compel his successor to become a party to the suit and to the costs already accrued without having been guilty of any personal neglect of the official duty involved in the proceeding; but to provide against this seeming harshness your committee propose to amend the bill so as to give the succeeding official an opportunity to perform the official act involved in the proceeding and thereby prevent the survival of the action against himself, and if he fails to do so, he can not then complain of being mulct in costs accruing against his predecessor.'

"The provision of § 780 that the action might be continued against the successor in office on the requisite showing within the stated period was added by § 11 of the Judiciary Act of 1925. 43 Stat. 936, 941. The last word Congress spoke on the matter reflected the views in a Report submitted by Chief Justice Taft dated March 11, 1922, which explained § 11 in the following words:

" 'It will be noted ..... that the provision is not mandatory, but leaves it to the sound discretion of the court to determine whether there is a substantial need for continuing the cause and obtaining an adjudication of the questions involved. This will tend to restrict the exercise of the right to cases which have a sound basis.' This language was repeated in the Senate Committee Print, 68th Cong., 1st Sess., of A General Review of H.R. 10479, 67th Cong., p. 16. The language so carefully tailored by Congress is now rejected by the professional group who constitute our advisors in these matters. I do not think we should allow a known and established congressional policy to be so readily abrogated.

"We said in *Snyder v. Buck,* supra, p. 20, that if Rule 25(d) is to be amended in the manner then urged and now adopted 'the amending process is available.' Where we have a matter so heavily encrusted with legislative policy, I think any change should be left to Congress.

"I, therefore, dissent from the submission to Congress of the proposed amendments to Rule 25 of the Rules of Civil Procedure under 28 U.S.C. § 2072. For under that Act the Rules submitted become effective at the expiration of a 90–day period, unless Congress takes contrary action. This machinery seems therefore, inappropriate to me for effecting such a basic change in congressional policy as the proposed Rule 25(d) achieves."

ORDER OF JANUARY 21, 1963

1. That the Rules of Civil Procedure be, and they hereby are, amended by including therein Forms Number 30, 31 and 32, and the amendments to Rules 4, 5, 6, 7, 12, 13, 14, 15, 24, 25, 26, 28, 30, 41, 49, 50, 52, 56, 58, 71A, 77, 79, 81, and 86 and to Forms Number 3, 4, 5, 6, 7, 8, 9, 10, 11, 12, 13, 16, 18, 21, 22–A and 22–B, as hereinafter set forth:

[See additions and amendments made thereby under the respective rules and forms, post.]

2. That THE CHIEF JUSTICE be authorized to transmit these amendments to Congress in accordance with the provisions of Title 28, U.S.C., Sec. 2072.

MR. JUSTICE BLACK and MR. JUSTICE DOUGLAS are opposed to the submission of these rules [1] to the Congress under a statute which permits them to "take effect" and to repeal "all laws in conflict with such rules" without requiring any affirmative consideration, action, or approval of the rules by Congress or by the President.[2] We believe that while some of the Rules of Civil Procedure are simply housekeeping details,[3] many determine matters so substantially affecting the rights of litigants in law suits that in practical effect they are the equivalent of new legislation which, in our judgment, the Constitution requires to be initiated in and enacted by the Congress [4] and approved by the President.[5] The Constitution, as we read it, provides that all laws shall be enacted by the House, the Senate, and the President, not by the mere failure of Congress to reject proposals of an outside agency. Even were there not this constitutional limitation, the authorizing statute itself qualifies this Court's power by imposing upon it a solemn responsibility not to submit rules that "abridge, enlarge or modify any substantive right" and by specifically charging the Court with the duty to "preserve the right to trial by jury as at common law and as declared by the Seventh Amendment to the Constitution." [6] Our chief objections to the rules relate essentially to the fact that many of their provisions do "abridge, enlarge or modify" substantive rights and do not "preserve the right to trial by jury" but actually encroach upon it.

(1)(a) Rule 50(a) is amended by making the order of a judge granting a motion for a directed verdict effective without submitting the question to the jury at all. It was pointed out in *Galloway v. United States,* 319 U.S. 372, 396, 401–407, 63 S.Ct. 1077, 87 L.Ed. 1458 (dissenting opinion), how judges have whittled away or denied the right of trial by jury through the devices of directed verdicts and judgments notwithstanding verdicts. Although the amendment here is not itself a momentous one, it gives formal sanction to the process by which the courts have been wresting from juries the power to render verdicts. Since we do not approve of this sapping of the Seventh Amendment's guarantee of a jury trial, we cannot join even this technical *coup de grace.*

(b) The proposed amendment to 50(c) in practical effect vests appellate courts with more power than they have had to grant or deny new trials. The Court in *Cone v. West Virginia Pulp & Paper Co.,* 330 U.S. 212, 217–218, 67 S.Ct. 752, 91 L.Ed. 849, and *Globe Liquor Co. v. San Roman,* 332 U.S. 571, 68 S.Ct. 246, 92 L.Ed. 177, refused to construe the federal rules then existing to allow Courts of Appeals to interfere with trial judges' discretion to grant new trials. To the extent that jury verdicts are to be set aside and new trials granted, we believe that those who hear the evidence, the trial judges, are the ones who should primarily exercise such discretion.

(c) The proposed amendment to Rule 56(e) imposes additional burdens upon litigants to protect against summary judgments rendered without hearing evidence on the part of witnesses who are confronted by the persons against whom they testify so that these persons can subject the witnesses to cross-examination. The summary judgment procedure, while justified in some cases, is made a handy instrument to let judges rather than juries try law suits and to let those judges try cases not on evidence of witnesses subjected to cross-examination but on ex parte affidavits obtained by parties. Most trial lawyers would agree, we think, that a litigant can frequently obtain in an actual trial favorable testimony which could not have been secured by affidavits or even by depositions.

(d) If there are to be amendments, Rule 49 should be repealed. That rule authorizes judges to require juries to return "only a special verdict in the form of a special written finding upon each issue of fact" or to answer "written interrogatories upon one or more issues of fact the decision of which is necessary to a verdict" in addition to rendering the general verdict. Such devices are used to impair or wholly take away the power of a jury to render a general verdict. One of the ancient, fundamental reasons for having general jury verdicts was to preserve the right of trial by jury as an indispensable part of a free government. Many of the most famous constitutional controversies in England revolved around litigants' insistence, particularly in seditious libel cases, that a jury had the right to render a general verdict without being compelled to return a number of subsidiary findings to support its general verdict. Some English jurors had to go to jail because they insisted upon their right to render general verdicts over the repeated commands of tyrannical judges not to do so. Rule 49 is but another means utilized by courts to weaken the constitutional power of juries and to vest judges with more power to decide cases according to their own judgments. A scrutiny of the special verdict and written interrogatory cases in appellate courts will show the confusion that necessarily results from the employment of these devices and the ease with which judges can use them to take away the right to trial by jury. We believe that Rule 49 be repealed, not amplified.

(2) There is a proposal to amend Rule 41, which provides for dismissal of actions. We believe that, if the Rules are to be changed, a major amendment to this rule is required in the interest of justice. Before dismissing a plaintiff's action for failure of his lawyer to prosecute, the trial judge should be required to have notice served on the plaintiff himself. The hardship that can result from the absence of such requirement is shown by *Link v. Wabash R. Co.,* 370 U.S. 626, 82 S.Ct. 1386, 8 L.Ed.2d 734. Link's lawyer failed to appear in response to a judge's order for a pre-trial conference, and the judge dismissed the case. As pointed out in the dissent, plaintiff had been severely injured, and a fair system of justice should not have penalized him because his lawyer, through neglect or any other reason, failed to appear when ordered. It would do a defendant no injury for the court to refuse to dismiss any apparently bona fide case until the plaintiff has actually had notice that some failure of his lawyer has irked the judge.

(3) MR. JUSTICE BLACK and MR. JUSTICE DOUGLAS object to the changes in Rule 4, which for the first time permit a Federal District Court to obtain jurisdiction over a defendant by service of process outside the state or over his property by garnishment or attachment, under the circumstances and in the manner prescribed by state law. Those changes will apparently have little effect insofar as "federal question" litigation is concerned, since 28 U.S.C. § 1391(b) requires such suits to be brought "only in the judicial district where all defendants reside. . . ." Diversity actions, however, may be greatly increased, for the effect of proposed 4(e) is not limited to suits authorized by such statutes as the Federal Interpleader Act, 28 U.S.C. § 1335. See Advisory Committee Rept., 5–8; 28 U.S.C. § 1391(a); Fed.Rules Civ. Proc. 1. We see no justification for an increase in the number of diversity cases. We also see no reason why the extent of a Federal District Court's personal jurisdiction should depend upon the existence or nonexistence of a state "long-arm" statute. Moreover, at present a state court action commenced by attachment or garnishment can get into a District Court only if a nonresident defendant chooses to appear and remove the case, see 28 U.S.C. § 1441, and there is no good reason, absent a congressional finding, why this should be changed.

Instead of recommending changes to the present Rules, we recommend that the statute authorizing this Court to prescribe Rules of Civil Procedure, if it is to remain a law, be amended to place the responsibility upon the Judicial Conference rather than upon this Court. Since the statute was first enacted in 1934, 48 Stat. 1064, the Judicial Conference has been enlarged and improved and is now very active in its surveillance of the work of the federal courts and in recommending appropriate legislation to Congress. The present Rules produced under 28 U.S.C. § 2072 are not prepared by us but by Committees of the Judicial Conference designated by the Chief Justice, and before coming to us they are approved by the Judicial Conference pursuant to 28 U.S.C. § 331.[7] The Committees and the Conference are composed of able and distinguished members and they render a high public service. It is they, however, who do the work, not we, and the rules have only our imprimatur. The only contribution that we actually make is an occasional exercise of a veto power. If the rule-making for Federal District Courts is to continue under the present plan, we believe that the Supreme Court should not have any part in the task; rather, the statute should be amended to substitute the Judicial Conference. The Judicial Conference can participate more actively in fashioning the rules and affirmatively contribute to their content and design better than we can. Transfer of the function to the Judicial Conference would relieve us of the embarrassment of having to sit in judgment on the constitutionality of rules which we have approved and which as applied in given situations might have to be declared invalid.

[1] See our earlier statements in 368 U.S. 1012–1014 and 346 U.S. 946–947.

[2] 28 U.S.C. § 2072 gives this Court the power to prescribe rules of practice and procedure for Federal District Courts and further provides that such rules

> "shall not take effect until they have been reported to Congress by THE CHIEF JUSTICE at or after the beginning of a regular session thereof but not later than the first day of May, and until the expiration of ninety days after they have been thus reported.
>
> "All laws in conflict with such rules shall be of no further force or effect after such rules have taken effect."

[3] See 368 U.S. 1012.

[4] "All legislative Powers herein granted shall be vested in a Congress of the United States, which shall consist of a Senate and House of Representatives." U.S. Const., Art. I, § 1.

5 Every Bill which shall have passed the House of Representatives and the Senate, shall, before it becomes a Law, be presented to the President of the United States; ...." U.S. Const., Art. I, § 7.

6 28 U.S.C. § 2072.

7 "The Conference shall also carry on a continuous study of the operation and effect of the general rules of practice and procedure now or hereafter in use as prescribed by the Supreme Court for the other courts of the United States pursuant to law. Such changes in and additions to those rules as the Conference may deem desirable to promote simplicity in procedure, fairness in administration, the just determination of litigation, and the elimination of unjustifiable expense and delay shall be recommended by the Conference from time to time to the Supreme Court for its consideration and adoption, modification or rejection, in accordance with law."

ORDER OF FEBRUARY 28, 1966

1. That the Rules of Civil Procedure for the United States District Courts be, and they hereby are, amended by including therein Rules 23.1, 23.2, 44.1 and 65.1, Supplemental Rules A, B, C, D, E and F for Certain Admiralty and Maritime Claims, and amendments to Rules 1, 4, 8, 9, 12, 13, 14, 15, 17, 18, 19, 20, 23, 24, 26, 38, 41, 42, 43, 44, 47, 53, 59, 65, 68, 73, 74, 75, 81 and 82, and to Forms 2 and 15, as hereinafter set forth:

[See added, amended and supplemental Rules and Forms, post.]

2. That the foregoing amendments and additions to the Rules of Civil Procedure shall take effect on July 1, 1966, and shall govern all proceedings in actions brought thereafter and also in all further proceedings in actions then pending, except to the extent that in the opinion of the court their application in a particular action then pending would not be feasible or would work injustice, in which event the former procedure applies.

3. That THE CHIEF JUSTICE be, and he hereby is, authorized to transmit to the Congress the foregoing amendments and additions to the Rules of Civil Procedure in accordance with the provisions of Title 28, U.S.C., §§ 2072 and 2073.

4. That: (a) subdivision (c) of Rule 6 of the Rules of Civil Procedure for the United States District Courts promulgated by this court on December 20, 1937, effective September 16, 1938; (b) Rule 2 of the Rules for Practice and Procedure under section 25 of An Act to amend and consolidate the Acts respecting copyright, approved March 4, 1909, promulgated by this court on June 1, 1909, effective July 1, 1909; and (c) the Rules of Practice in Admiralty and Maritime Cases, promulgated by this court on December 6, 1920, effective March 7, 1921, as revised, amended and supplemented, be, and they hereby are, rescinded, effective July 1, 1966.

MR. JUSTICE BLACK, dissenting.

The Amendments to the Federal Rules of Civil and Criminal Procedure today transmitted to the Congress are the work of very capable advisory committees. Those committees, not the Court, wrote the rules. Whether by this transmittal the individual members of the Court who voted to transmit the rules intended to express approval of the varied policy decisions the rules embody I am not sure. I am reasonably certain, however, that the Court's transmittal does not carry with it a decision that the amended rules are all constitutional. For such a decision would be the equivalent of an advisory opinion which, I assume the Court would unanimously agree, we are without constitutional power to give. And I agree with my Brother DOUGLAS that some of the proposed criminal rules go to the very border line if they do not actually transgress the constitutional right of a defendant not to be compelled to be a witness against himself. This phase of the criminal rules in itself so infects the whole collection of proposals that, without mentioning other objections, I am opposed to transmittal of the proposed amendments to the criminal rules.

I am likewise opposed to transmittal of the proposed revision of the civil rules. In the first place I think the provisions of 28 U.S.C. § 2072 (1964 ed.), under which these rules are transmitted and the corresponding section, 18 U.S.C. § 3771 (1964 ed.), relating to the criminal rules, both of which provide for giving transmitted rules the effect of law as though they had been properly enacted by Congress are unconstitutional for reasons I have previously stated.[1] And in prior dissents I have stated some of the basic reasons for my objections to repeated rules revisions [2] that tend to upset established meanings and need not repeat those grounds of objection here. The confusion created by the adoption of the present rules, over my objection, has been partially dispelled by judicial interpretations of them by this Court and others. New rules and extensive amendments to present rules will mean renewed confusion resulting in new challenges and new reversals and prejudicial "pretrial" dismissals of cases before a trial on the merits for failure of lawyers to understand and comply with new rules of uncertain meaning. Despite my continuing objection to the old rules, it seems to me that since they have at least gained some degree of certainty it would be wiser to "bear those ills we have than fly to others we know not of," unless, of course, we are reasonably sure that the proposed reforms of the old rules are badly needed. But I am not. The new proposals, at least some of them, have, as I view them, objectionable possibilities that cause me to believe our judicial system could get along much better without them.

The momentum given the proposed revision of the old rules by this Court's transmittal makes it practically certain that Congress, just as has this Court, will permit the rules to take effect exactly as they were written by the Advisory Committee on Rules. Nevertheless, I am including here a memorandum I submitted to the Court expressing objections to the Committee's proposals and suggesting changes should they be transmitted. These suggestions chiefly center around rules that grant broad discretion to trial judges with reference to class suits, pretrial procedures, and dismissal of cases with prejudice. Cases coming before the federal courts over the years now filling nearly 40 volumes of Federal Rules Decisions show an accumulation of grievances by lawyers and litigants about the way many trial judges exercise their almost unlimited discretionary powers to use pretrial procedures to dismiss cases without trials. In fact, many of these cases indicate a belief of many judges and legal commentators that the cause of justice is best served in the long run not by trials on the merits but by summary dismissals based on out of court affidavits, pretrial depositions, and other pretrial techniques. My belief is that open court trials on the merits where litigants have the right to prove their case or defense best comports with due process of law.

The proposed rules revisions, instead of introducing changes designed to prevent the continued abuse of pretrial power to dismiss cases summarily without trials, move in the opposite direction. Of course, each such dismissal results in removal of one more case from our congested court dockets, but that factor should not weigh more heavily in our system of justice than assuring a full-fledged due process trial of every bona fide lawsuit brought to vindicate an honest, substantial claim. It is to protect this ancient right of a person to have his case tried rather than summarily thrown out of court that I suggested to the Court that it recommend changes in the Committee's proposals of the nature set out in the following memorandum.

"Dear Brethren:

"I have gone over all the proposed amendments carefully and while there are probably some good suggestions, it is my belief that the bad results that can come from the adoption of these amendments predominate over any good they can bring about. I particularly think that every member of the Court should examine with great care the amendments relating to class suits. It seems to me that they place too much power in the hands of the trial judges and that the rules might almost as well simply provide that 'class suits can be maintained either for or against particular groups whenever in the discretion of a judge he thinks it is wise.' The power given to the judge to dismiss such suits or to divide them up into groups at will subjects members of classes to dangers that could not follow from carefully prescribed legal standards enacted to control class suits.

"In addition, the rules as amended, in my judgment, greatly aggravate the evil of vesting judges with practically uncontrolled power to dismiss with prejudice cases brought by plaintiffs or defenses interposed by defendants. The power to dismiss a plaintiff's case or to render judgments by default against defendants can work great harm to both parties. There are many inherent urges in existence which may subconsciously incline a judge towards disposing of the cases before him without having to go through the burden of a trial. Mr. Chief Justice White, before he became Chief Justice, wrote an opinion in the case of *Hovey v. Elliott*, 167 U.S. 409 [17 S.Ct. 841, 42 L.Ed. 215], which pointed out grave constitutional questions raised by attempting to punish the parties by depriving them of the right to try their law suits or to defend against law suits brought against them by others.

"Rule 41 entitled 'Dismissal of Actions' points up the great power of judges to dismiss actions and provides an automatic method under which a dismissal must be construed as a dismissal 'with prejudice' unless the judge specifically states otherwise. For that reason I suggest to the Conference that if the Rules are accepted, including that one, the last sentence of Rule 41(b) be amended so as to provide that a simple order of dismissal by a judge instead of operating 'as an adjudication upon the merits,' as the amended rule reads, shall provide that such a dismissal 'does not operate as an adjudication upon the merits.'

"As a further guarantee against oppressive dismissals I suggest the addition of the following as subdivision (c) of Rule 41.

" 'No plaintiff's case shall be dismissed or defendant's right to defend be cut off because of the neglect, misfeasance, malfeasance, or failure of their counsel to obey any order of the court, until and unless such plaintiff or defendant shall have been personally served with notice of their counsel's delinquency, and not then unless the parties themselves do or fail to do something on their own part that can legally justify dismissal of the plaintiff's case or of the defendant's defense.'

"This proposed amendment is suggested in order to protect litigants, both plaintiffs and defendants, against being thrown out of court as a penalty for their lawyer's neglect or misconduct. The necessity for such a rule is shown, I think, by the dismissal in the plaintiff's case in *Link v. Wabash R. Co.*, 370 U.S. 626 [82 S.Ct. 1386, 8 L.Ed.2d 734]. The usual argument against this suggestion is that a party to a law suit hires his lawyer and should therefore be responsible for everything his lawyer does in the conduct of his case. This may be a good argument with reference to affluent litigants who not only know the best lawyers but are able to hire them. It is a wholly unrealistic argument, however, to make with reference to individual persons who do not know the ability of various lawyers or who are not financially able to hire those at the top of the bar and who are compelled to rely on the assumption that a lawyer licensed by the State is competent. It seems to me to be an uncivilized practice to punish clients by throwing their cases out of court because of their lawyers' conduct. It may be supportable by good, sound, formal logic but I think has no support whatever in a procedural system supposed to work as far as humanly possible to the end of obtaining equal and exact justice.

"For all the reasons stated above and in my previous objections to the transmittals of rules I dissent from the transmittals here."

[1] In a statement accompanying a previous transmittal of the civil rules, MR. JUSTICE DOUGLAS and I said:

"MR. JUSTICE BLACK and MR. JUSTICE DOUGLAS are opposed to the submission of these rules to the Congress under a statute which permits them to 'take effect' and to repeal 'all laws in conflict with such rules' without requiring any affirmative consideration, action, or approval of the rules by Congress or by the President. We believe that while some of the Rules of Civil Procedure are simply housekeeping details, many determine matters so substantially affecting the rights of litigants in lawsuits that in practical effect they are the equivalent of new legislation which, in our judgment, the Constitution requires to be initiated in and enacted by the Congress and approved by the President. The Constitution, as we read it, provides that all laws shall be enacted by the House, the Senate, and the President, not by the mere failure of Congress to reject proposals of an outside agency. * * *" (Footnotes omitted.) 374 U.S. 865–866.

[2] 346 U.S. 946, 374 U.S. 865. And see 368 U.S. 1011 and 1012.

MR. JUSTICE DOUGLAS, dissenting in part.

I reiterate today what I stated on an earlier occasion (374 U.S. 865, 869–870) (statement of Black and Douglas, JJ.), that the responsibility for promulgating Rules of the kind we send to Congress today should rest with the Judicial Conference and not the Court. It is the Judicial Conference, not the Court, which appoints the Advisory Committee on Criminal Rules which makes the actual recommendations.[1] Members of the Judicial Conference, being in large part judges of the lower courts and attorneys who are using the Rules day in and day out, are in a far better position to make a practical judgment upon their utility or inutility than we.

But since under the statute[2] the Rules go to Congress only on the initiative of the Court, I cannot be only a conduit. I think that placing our imprimatur on the amendments to the Rules entails a large degree of responsibility of judgment concerning them. Some of the criminal Rules which we forward to Congress today are very bothersome—not in the sense that they may be unwieldy or unworkable—but in the sense that they may entrench on important constitutional rights of defendants.

In my judgment, the amendments to Rule 16 dealing with discovery require further reflection. To the extent that they expand the defendant's opportunities for discovery, they accord with the views of a great many commentators who have concluded that a civilized society ought not to tolerate the conduct of a criminal prosecution as a "game." [3] But the proposed changes in the Rule go further. Rule 16(c) would permit a trial judge to condition granting the defendant discovery on the defendant's willingness to permit the prosecution to discover "scientific or medical reports, books, papers, documents, tangible objects, or copies or portions thereof" which (1) are in the defendant's possession; (2) he intends to produce at trial; and (3) are shown to be material to the preparation of the prosecution's case.[4]

The extent to which a court may compel the defendant to disclose information or evidence pertaining to his case without infringing the privilege against self-incrimination is a source of current controversy among judges, prosecutors, defense lawyers, and other legal commentators. A distinguished state court has concluded—although not without a strong dissent—that the privilege is not violated by discovery of the names of expert medical witnesses whose appearance at trial is contemplated by the defense.[5] I mean to imply no views on the point, except to note that a serious constitutional question lurks here.

The prosecution's opportunity to discover evidence in the possession of the defense is somewhat limited in the proposal with which we deal in that it is tied to the exercise by the defense of the right to discover from the prosecution. But *if* discovery, by itself, of information in the possession of the defendant would violate the privilege against self-incrimination, is it any less a violation if conditioned on the defendant's exercise of the opportunity to discover evidence? May benefits be conditioned on the abandonment of constitutional rights? See, e.g., *Sherbert v. Verner,* 374 U.S. 398, 403–406, 83 S.Ct. 1790, 1793–1795, 10 L.Ed.2d 965. To deny a defendant the opportunity to discovery—an opportunity not withheld from defendants who agree to prosecutorial discovery or from whom discovery is not sought—merely because the defendant chooses to exercise the constitutional right to refrain from self-incrimination arguably imposes a penalty upon the exercise of that fundamental privilege. It is said, however, that fairness may require disclosure by a defendant who obtains information from the prosecution.

Perhaps—but the proposed rule establishes no such standards. Its application is mechanical: if the defendant is allowed discovery, so, too, is the prosecution. No requirement is imposed, for example, that the subject matter of the material sought to be discovered by the prosecution be limited to that relating to the subject of the defendant's discovery.

The proposed addition of Rule 17.1 also suggests difficulties, perhaps of constitutional dimension. This rule would establish a pretrial conference procedure. The language of the rule and the Advisory Committee's comments suggest that under some circumstances, the conference might even take place in the absence of the defendant! Cf. *Lewis v. United States,* 146 U.S. 370, 13 S.Ct. 136, 36 L.Ed. 1011; Fed.Rules Crim.Proc. Rule 43.

The proposed amendment to Rule 32(c)(2) states that the trial judge "may" disclose to the defendant or his counsel the contents of a presentence report on which he is relying in fixing sentence. The imposition of sentence is of critical importance to a man convicted of crime. Trial judges need presentence reports so that they may have at their disposal the fullest possible information. See *Williams v. People of State of New York,* 337 U.S. 241, 69 S.Ct. 1079, 93 L.Ed. 1337. But while the formal rules of evidence do not apply to restrict the factors which the sentencing judge may consider, fairness would, in my opinion, require that the defendant be advised of the facts—perhaps very damaging to him—on which the judge intends to rely. The presentence report may be inaccurate, a flaw which may be of constitutional dimension. Cf. *Townsend v. Burke,* 334 U.S. 736, 68 S.Ct. 1252, 92 L.Ed. 1690. It may exaggerate the gravity of the defendant's prior offenses. The investigator may have made an incomplete investigation. See Tappan, Crime, Justice and Correction 556 (1960). There may be countervailing factors not disclosed by the probation report. In many areas we can rely on the sound exercise of discretion by the trial judge; but how can a judge know whether or not the presentence report calls for a reply by the defendant? Its faults may not appear on the face of the document.

Some States require full disclosure of the report to the defense.[6] The proposed Model Penal Code takes the middleground and requires the sentencing judge to disclose to the defense the factual contents of the report so that there is an opportunity to reply.[7] Whatever should be the rule for the federal courts, it ought not to be one which permits a judge to impose sentence on the basis of information of which the defendant may be unaware and to which he has not been afforded an opportunity to reply.

I do not think we should approve Rule 16, 17.1, and 32(c)(2). Instead, we should refer them back to the Judicial Conference and the Advisory Committee for further consideration and reflection, where I believe they were approved only by the narrowest majority.

WILLIAM O. DOUGLAS.

1 28 U.S.C. § 331 (1964 ed.) which establishes the Judicial Conference of the United States, provides that the Conference shall "carry on a continuous study of the operation and effect of the general rules of practice and procedure * * * prescribed by the Supreme Court * * *." The Conference has resolved that a standing Committee on Rules of Practice and Procedure be appointed by the Chief Justice and that, in addition, five advisory committees be established to recommend to the Judicial Conference changes in the rules of practice and procedure for the federal courts. See Annual Report of the Proceedings of the Judicial Conference of the United States 6–7 (1958).

2 18 U.S.C. § 3771 (1964 ed.).

3 See, e.g., Brennan, The Criminal Prosecution: Sporting Event or Quest for Truth?, 1963 Wash.U.L.Q. 279; Louisell, Criminal Discovery: Dilemma Real or Apparent?, 49 Calif.L.Rev. 56 (1961); Traynor, Ground Lost and Found in Criminal Discovery, 39 N.Y.U.L.Rev. 228 (1964).

4 The proposed rule explicitly provides that the prosecution may not discover nonmedical documents or reports "made by the defendant, or his attorneys or agents in connection with the investigation or defense of the case, or of statements made by the defendant, or by government or defense witnesses, or by prospective government or defense witnesses, to the defendant, his agents or attorneys."

5 *Jones v. Superior Court of Nevada County,* 58 Cal.2d 56, 22 Cal. Rptr. 879, 372 P.2d 919, 96 A.L.R.2d 1213. See Comment, 51 Calif.L.Rev. 135; Note, 76 Harv.L.Rev. 838 (1963). The case is more extensively treated in Louisell, Criminal Discovery and Self-Incrimination, 53 Calif.L.Rev. 89 (1965).

6 E.g., Calif.Penal Code § 1203.

[7] Model Penal Code § 7.07(5) (Proposed Official Draft, 1962). The Code provides that the sources of confidential information need not be disclosed. "Less disclosure than this hardly comports with elementary fairness." Comment to § 7.07 (Tent.Draft No. 2, 1954), at 55. A discarded draft of the amendment to Fed.Rules Crim.Proc.Rule 32 would have allowed disclosure to defense counsel of the report, from which the confidential sources would be removed. A defendant not represented by counsel would be told of the "essential facts" in the report. See 8 Moore's Federal Practice ¶¶ 32.03[4], 32.09 (1965).

ORDER OF DECEMBER 4, 1967

1. That the following rules, to be known as the Federal Rules of Appellate Procedure, be, and they hereby are, prescribed, pursuant to sections 3771 and 3772 of Title 18, United States Code, and sections 2072 and 2075 of Title 28, United States Code, to govern the procedure in appeals to United States courts of appeals from the United States district courts, in the review by United States courts of appeals of decisions of the Tax Court of the United States, in proceedings in the United States courts of appeals for the review or enforcement of orders of administrative agencies, boards, commissions and officers, and in applications for writs or other relief which a United States court of appeals or judge thereof is competent to give:

[See text of Rules of Appellate Procedure, post.]

2. That the foregoing rules shall take effect on July 1, 1968, and shall govern all proceedings in appeals and petitions for review or enforcement of orders thereafter brought and in all such proceedings then pending, except to the extent that in the opinion of the court of appeals their application in a particular proceeding then pending would not be feasible or would work injustice, in which case the former procedure may be followed.

3. That Rules 6, 9, 41, 77 and 81 of the Rules of Civil Procedure for the United States District Courts be, and they hereby are, amended, effective July 1, 1968, as hereinafter set forth:

[See the amendments made thereby under the respective rules, post.]

4. That the chapter heading "IX. APPEALS", all of Rules 72, 73, 74, 75 and 76 of the Rules of Civil Procedure for the United States District Courts, and Form 27 annexed to the said rules, be, and they hereby are, abrogated, effective July 1, 1968.

[Paragraphs 5 and 6 of the order pertain to certain Rules of Criminal Procedure for the United States District Courts and to certain Forms annexed to the said rules. For text, see Pamphlet containing Federal Rules of Criminal Procedure.]

7. That THE CHIEF JUSTICE be, and he hereby is, authorized to transmit to the Congress the foregoing new rules and amendments to and abrogation of existing rules, in accordance with the provisions of Title 18, U.S.C., § 3771, and Title 28, U.S.C., §§ 2072 and 2075.

ORDER OF MARCH 30, 1970

1. That subdivision (a) of Rule 5, subdivision (h) of Rule 9 and Rules 26, 29, 30, 31, 32, 33, 34, 35, 36 and 37, and subdivision (d) of Rule 45, subdivision (a) of Rule 69, and Form 24 of the Rules of Civil Procedure for the United States District Courts be, and they hereby are, amended to read as follows:

[See the amendments made thereby under the respective rules and forms, post.]

2. That the foregoing amendments to the Rules of Civil Procedure shall take effect on July 1, 1970, and shall govern all proceedings in actions brought thereafter and also in all further proceedings in actions then pending, except to the extent that in the opinion of the court their application in a particular action then pending would not be feasible or would work injustice, in which event the former procedure applies.

3. That THE CHIEF JUSTICE be, and he hereby is, authorized to transmit to the Congress the foregoing amendments to the Rules of Civil Procedure in accordance with the provisions of Title 28, U.S.C. § 2072.

MR. JUSTICE BLACK and MR. JUSTICE DOUGLAS disapprove of the Amendments to the Federal Rules of Civil Procedure relating to Discovery, and dissent from the action of the Court in transmitting them to the Congress.

ORDER OF MARCH 1, 1971

1. That subdivision (a) of Rule 6, paragraph (4) of subdivision (a) of Rule 27, paragraph (6) of subdivision (b) of Rule 30, subdivision (c) of Rule 77, and paragraph (2) of subdivision (a) of Rule 81 of the Federal Rules of Civil Procedure be, and they hereby are, amended, effective July 1, 1971, to read as follows:

[See amendments made thereby under the respective rules, post.]

2. [*Certain Rules of Criminal Procedure for the United States District Courts amended*].

3. That subdivision (a) of Rule 26 and subdivision (a) of Rule 45 of the Federal Rules of Appellate Procedure be, and they hereby are, amended, effective July 1, 1971, to read as follows:

[See amendments made thereby under the respective Rules of Appellate Procedure, post.]

4. That THE CHIEF JUSTICE be, and he hereby is, authorized to transmit to the Congress the foregoing amendments to the Rules of Civil, Criminal and Appellate Procedure, in accordance with the provisions of Title 18 U.S.C. § 3771, and Title 28 U.S.C. §§ 2072 and 2075.

MR. JUSTICE BLACK and MR. JUSTICE DOUGLAS dissent.

ORDER OF NOVEMBER 20, 1972

1. That the rules hereinafter set forth, to be known as the Federal Rules of Evidence, be, and they hereby are, prescribed pursuant to Sections 3402, 3771, and 3772, Title 18, United States Code, and Sections 2072 and 2075, Title 28, United States Code, to govern procedure, in the proceedings and to the extent set forth therein, in the United States courts of appeals, the United States district courts, the District Court for the District of the Canal Zone and the district courts of Guam and the Virgin Islands, and before United States magistrates.

2. That the aforementioned Federal Rules of Evidence shall take effect on July 1, 1973, and shall be applicable to actions and proceedings brought thereafter and also to fur-

ther procedure in actions and proceedings then pending, except to the extent that in the opinion of the court their application in a particular action or proceeding then pending would not be feasible or would work injustice in which event the former procedure applies.

3. That subdivision (c) of Rule 30 and Rules 43 and 44.1 of the Federal Rules of Civil Procedure be, and they hereby are, amended, effective July 1, 1973, to read as hereinafter set forth:

[See amendments made thereby under the respective rules, post.]

4. That subdivision (c) of Rule 32 of the Federal Rules of Civil Procedure be, and it hereby is, abrogated, effective July 1, 1973.

5. *[Certain Rules of Criminal Procedure for the United States District Courts amended].*

6. That THE CHIEF JUSTICE be, and he hereby is, authorized to transmit the foregoing new rules and amendments to and abrogation of existing rules to the Congress at the beginning of its next regular session, in accordance with the provisions of Title 18 U.S.C. § 3771 and Title 28 U.S.C. §§ 2072 and 2075.

ORDER OF DECEMBER 18, 1972

1. That Rule 43 of the Federal Rules of Civil Procedure, as amended by Order of this Court entered November 20, 1972, be, and it hereby is, further amended, effective July 1, 1973, to read as follows:

[See amendment made thereby under Rule 43 post.]

2. That THE CHIEF JUSTICE be, and he hereby is, authorized to transmit the foregoing amendment of Rule 43 of the Federal Rules of Civil Procedure to the Congress at the beginning of its next regular session in accordance with the provisions of Title 28, U.S.C. § 2072.

CONGRESSIONAL ACTION ON PROPOSED RULES OF EVIDENCE AND 1972 AMENDMENTS TO FEDERAL RULES OF CIVIL PROCEDURE AND FEDERAL RULES OF CRIMINAL PROCEDURE

Pub.L. 93–12, Mar. 30, 1973, 87 Stat. 9, provided: "That notwithstanding any other provisions of law, the Rules of Evidence for United States Courts and Magistrates, the Amendments to the Federal Rules of Civil Procedure, and the Amendments to the Federal Rules of Criminal Procedure, which are embraced by the orders entered by the Supreme Court of the United States on Monday, November 20, 1972, and Monday, December 18, 1972, shall have no force or effect except to the extent, and with such amendments, as they may be expressly approved by Act of Congress."

Pub.L. 93–595, § 3, Jan. 2, 1975, 88 Stat. 1959, provided that: "The Congress expressly approves the amendments to the Federal Rules of Civil Procedure, and the amendments to the Federal Rules of Criminal Procedure, which are embraced by the orders entered by the Supreme Court of the United States on November 20, 1972, and December 18, 1972, and such amendments shall take effect on the one hundred and eightieth day beginning after the date of the enactment of this Act [Jan. 2, 1975]."

ORDER OF APRIL 26, 1976

1. That the rules and forms governing proceedings in the United States District Courts under Section 2254 and Section 2255 of Title 28, United States Code, as approved by the Judicial Conference of the United States be, and they hereby are, prescribed pursuant to Section 2072 of Title 28, United States Code and Sections 3771 and 3772 of Title 18, United States Code.

2. That the aforementioned rules and forms shall take effect August 1, 1976, and shall be applicable to all proceedings then pending except to the extent that in the opinion of the court their application in a particular proceeding would not be feasible or would work injustice.

3. That THE CHIEF JUSTICE be, and he hereby is, authorized to transmit the aforementioned rules and forms governing Section 2254 and Section 2255 proceedings to the Congress in accordance with the provisions of Section 2072 of Title 28 and Sections 3771 and 3772 of Title 18, United States Code.

CONGRESSIONAL ACTION ON PROPOSED RULES AND FORMS GOVERNING PROCEEDINGS UNDER 28 U.S.C. §§ 2254 AND 2255

Pub.L. 94–349, § 2, July 8, 1976, 90 Stat. 822, provided: "That, notwithstanding the provisions of section 2072 of title 28 of the United States Code, the rules and forms governing section 2254 cases in the United States district courts and the rules and forms governing section 2255 proceedings in the United States district courts which are embraced by the order entered by the United States Supreme Court on April 26, 1976, and which were transmitted to the Congress on or about April 26, 1976, shall not take effect until thirty days after the adjournment sine die of the 94th Congress, or until and to the extent approved by Act of Congress, whichever is earlier."

Pub.L. 94–426, § 1, Sept. 28, 1976, 90 Stat. 1334, provided: "That the rules governing section 2254 cases in the United States district courts and the rules governing section 2255 proceedings for the United States district courts, as proposed by the United States Supreme Court, which were delayed by the Act entitled 'An Act to delay the effective date of certain proposed amendments to the Federal Rules of Criminal Procedure and certain other rules promulgated by the United States Supreme Court' (Public Law 94–349), are approved with the amendments set forth in section 2 of this Act and shall take effect as so amended, with respect to petitions under section 2254 and motions under section 2255 of title 28 of the United States Code filed on or after February 1, 1977."

ORDER OF APRIL 29, 1980

1. That the Federal Rules of Civil Procedure be, and they hereby are, amended by including therein amendments to Rules 4, 5, 26, 28, 30, 32, 33, 34, 37 and 45 as hereinafter set forth:

[See amendments made thereby under respective rules, post.]

2. That the foregoing amendments to the Federal Rules of Civil Procedure shall take effect on August 1, 1980, and shall govern all civil proceedings thereafter commenced and, insofar as just and practicable, all proceedings then pending.

3. That subsection (e) of Rule 37 of the Federal Rules of Civil Procedure is hereby abrogated, effective August 1, 1980.

4. That THE CHIEF JUSTICE be, and he hereby is, authorized to transmit to the Congress the foregoing amendments to the Federal Rules of Civil Procedure in accordance with the provisions of Section 2072 of Title 28, United States Code.

MR. JUSTICE POWELL, with whom MR. JUSTICE STEWART and MR. JUSTICE REHNQUIST join, filed a dissenting statement.

I dissent from the Court's adoption of the amendments to Federal Rules of Civil Procedure 26, 33, 34, and 37—the cluster of Rules authorizing and regulating discovery generally, interrogatories, production of documents, and sanctions for failure to make discovery. These amendments are not inherently objectionable. Indeed, they represent the culmination of several years' work by the Judicial Conference's distinguished and conscientious Standing Committee on Rules of Practice and Procedure and Advisory Committee on Civil Rules.[1] But the changes embodied in the amendments fall short of those needed to accomplish reforms in civil litigation that are long overdue.

The American Bar Association proposed significant and substantial reforms.[2] Although the Standing Committee initially favored most of these proposals, it ultimately rejected them in large part. The ABA now accedes to the Standing Committee's amendments because they make some improvements, but the most recent report of the ABA Section of Litigation makes clear that the "serious and widespread abuse of discovery" will remain largely uncontrolled.[3] There are wide differences of opinion within the profession as to the need for reform. The bench and the bar are familiar with the existing Rules, and it often is said that the bar has a vested interest in maintaining the status quo. I imply no criticism of the bar or the Standing Committee when I suggest that the present recommendations reflect a compromise as well as the difficulty of framing satisfactory discovery Rules. But whatever considerations may have prompted the Committee's final decision, I doubt that many judges or lawyers familiar with the proposed amendments believe they will have an appreciable effect on the acute problems associated with discovery. The Court's adoption of these inadequate changes could postpone effective reform for another decade.

When the Federal Rules first appeared in 1938, the discovery provisions properly were viewed as a constructive improvement. But experience under the discovery Rules demonstrates that "not infrequently [they have been] exploited to the disadvantage of justice." *Herbert v. Lando,* 441 U.S. 153, 179 (1979) (POWELL, J., concurring). Properly limited and controlled discovery is necessary in most civil litigation. The present Rules, however, invite discovery of such scope and duration that district judges often cannot keep the practice within reasonable bounds.[4] Even in a relatively simple case, discovery through depositions, interrogatories, and demands for documents may take weeks. In complex litigation, discovery can continue for years. One must doubt whether empirical evidence would demonstrate that untrammeled discovery actually contributes to the just resolution of disputes. If there is disagreement about that, there is none whatever about the effect of discovery practices upon the average citizen's ability to afford legal remedies.

Delay and excessive expense now characterize a large percentage of all civil litigation. The problems arise in significant part, as every judge and litigator knows, from abuse of the discovery procedures available under the Rules.[5] Indeed, the National Conference on the Causes of Popular Dissatisfaction with the Administration of Justice, led by THE CHIEF JUSTICE,[6] identified "Abuse in the use of discovery [as] a major concern" within our legal system.[7] Lawyers devote an enormous number of "chargeable hours" to the practice of discovery. We may assume that discovery usually is conducted in good faith. Yet all too often discovery practices enable the party with greater financial resources to prevail by exhausting the resources of a weaker opponent. The mere threat of delay or unbearable expense denies justice to many actual or prospective litigants. Persons or businesses of comparatively limited means settle unjust claims and relinquish just claims simply because they cannot afford to litigate.[8] Litigation costs have become intolerable, and they cast a lengthening shadow over the basic fairness of our legal system.

I reiterate that I do not dissent because the modest amendments recommended by the Judicial Conference are undesirable. I simply believe that Congress' acceptance of these tinkering changes will delay for years the adoption of genuinely effective reforms. The process of change, as experience teaches, is tortuous and contentious. Favorable congressional action on these amendments will create complacency and encourage inertia. Meanwhile, the discovery Rules will continue to deny justice to those least able to bear the burdens of delay, escalating legal fees, and rising court costs.

The amendments to Rules 26, 33, 34, and 37 recommended by the Judicial Conference should be rejected, and the Conference should be directed to initiate a thorough reexamination of the discovery Rules that have become so central to the conduct of modern civil litigation.

1 This Court's role in the rulemaking process is largely formalistic. Standing and advisory committees of the Judicial Conference make the initial studies, invite comments on their drafts, and prepare the Rules. Both the Judicial Conference and this Court necessarily rely upon the careful work of these committees. Congress should bear in mind that our approval of proposed Rules is more a certification that they are the products of proper procedures than a considered judgment on the merits of the proposals themselves. See generally 409 U.S. 1132, 1133 (1973) (DOUGLAS, J., dissenting from adoption of Federal Rules of Evidence); 383 U.S. 1032 (1966) (BLACK, J., dissenting from adoption of amendment to civil rules); 374 U.S. 865, 869–870 (1963) (statement of BLACK and DOUGLAS, JJ., upon adoption of amendments to Federal Rules of Civil Procedure).

2 American Bar Association, Report of the Section of Litigation Special Committee for the Study of Discovery Abuse (App.Draft 1977).

3 ABA Section of Litigation, Second Report of the Special Committee for the Study of Discovery Abuse, 5 (1980).

4 MR. JUSTICE WHITE, writing for the Court, recently reminded the federal courts that "the discovery provisions . . . are subject to the injunction of Rule 1 that they be 'construed to secure the just, *speedy,* and *inexpensive* determination of every action.' " *Herbert v. Lando,* 441 U.S. 153, 177 (1979).

In his most recent Annual Report on the State of the Judiciary, THE CHIEF JUSTICE declared that "[t]he responsibility for control [of pretrial process] rests on both judges and lawyers. Where existing rules and statutes permit abuse, they must be changed. Where the power lies with judges to prevent or correct abuse and misuse of the system, judges must act." Address to American Bar Association Mid-Year Meeting, 6 (Feb. 3, 1980).

5 Writing from his wide experience as a judge, practicing lawyer, and Attorney General, Griffin B. Bell advised the Standing Committee that "the scope of discovery is far too broad and that excessive discovery has significantly contributed to the delays, complexity and high cost of civil litigation in the federal courts." Letter to The Honorable Roszel C. Thomsen, Chairman of the Committee on Rules of Practice and Procedure of the Judicial Conference, 1 (June 27, 1978).

6 THE CHIEF JUSTICE'S keynote address to this distinguished assembly, popularly known as the Pound Conference, recognized that discovery processes "are being misused and abused." See Burger, Agenda for 2000 A.D.—A Need for Systematic Anticipation, 70 F.R.D. 83, 95–96 (1976).

7 See Erickson, The Pound Conference Recommendations: A Blueprint for the Justice System in the Twenty-first Century, 76 F.R.D. 277, 288 (1978); ABA, Report of Pound Conference Follow-up Task Force, 74 F.R.D. 159, 171–192 (1976).

8 "The principal function of procedural rules," as MR. JUSTICE BLACK observed in another context, "should be to serve as useful guides to help, not hinder, persons who have a legal right to bring their problems before the courts." 346 U.S. 946 (1954) (separate statement upon adoption of revised Supreme Court Rules).

ORDER OF APRIL 28, 1983

1. That the Federal Rules of Civil Procedure be, and they hereby are, amended by including therein new Rules 26(g), 53(f), 72 through 76 and new Official Forms 33 and 34, and amendments to Rules 6(b), 7(b), 11, 16, 26(a) and (b), 52(a), 53(a), (b) and (c) and 67, as hereinafter set forth:

[See additions and amendments made thereby under respective rules and forms, post.]

2. That the foregoing additions and amendments to the Federal Rules of Civil Procedure shall take effect on August 1, 1983 and shall govern all civil proceedings thereafter commenced and, insofar as just and practicable, in proceedings then pending.

3. That THE CHIEF JUSTICE be, and he hereby is, authorized to transmit to the Congress the foregoing additions to and changes in the Federal Rules of Civil Procedure in accordance with the provisions of Section 2072 of Title 28, United States Code.

ORDER OF APRIL 29, 1985

1. That the Federal Rules of Civil Procedure for the United States District Courts be, and they hereby are, amended by including therein a new Rule E(4)(f) to the Supplemental Rules for Certain Admiralty and Maritime Claims; amendments to Rules 6(a), 45(d)(2), 52(a), 71A(h) and 83; amendments to Supplemental Admiralty Rules B(1) and C(3); and amendments to Official Form 18–A, as hereinafter set forth:

[See additions and amendments made thereby under respective rules and forms, post.]

2. That the foregoing addition to and changes in the Federal Rules of Civil Procedure, the Supplemental Rules for Certain Admiralty and Maritime Claims, and the Official Form shall take effect on August 1, 1985 and shall govern all proceedings in civil actions thereafter commenced and, insofar as just and practicable, all proceedings in civil actions then pending.

3. That THE CHIEF JUSTICE be, and he hereby is, authorized to transmit to the Congress the foregoing addition to and changes in the rules of civil procedure in accordance with the provisions of Section 2072 of Title 28, United States Code.

ORDER OF MARCH 2, 1987

1. That the Federal Rules of Civil Procedure and the Supplemental Rules for Certain Admiralty and Maritime Claims be, and they hereby are, amended by including therein amendments to Civil Rules 4, 5, 6, 8, 9, 11, 12, 13, 14, 15, 16, 17, 18, 19, 20, 22, 23, 23.1, 24, 25, 26, 27, 28, 30, 31, 32, 34, 35, 36, 37 38, 41, 43, 44, 44.1, 45, 46, 49, 50, 51, 53, 54, 55, 56, 60, 62, 63, 65, 65.1, 68, 69, 71, 71A, 73, 75, 77, 78, 81, and to the Supplemental Rules for Certain Admiralty and Maritime Claims, Rules B, C, E, and F, as hereinafter set forth:

[See amendments made thereby under respective rules, post.]

2. That the foregoing amendments to the Federal Rules of Civil Procedure and the Supplemental Rules for Certain Admiralty and Maritime Claims shall take effect on August 1, 1987.

3. That THE CHIEF JUSTICE be, and he hereby is, authorized to transmit to the Congress the foregoing amendments in accordance with the provisions of Section 2072 of Title 28, United States Code.

ORDER OF APRIL 25, 1988

1. That the Federal Rules of Civil Procedure be, and they hereby are, amended by including therein amendments to Civil Rules 17 and 71, as hereinafter set forth:

[See amendments made thereby under respective rules, post.]

2. That the foregoing amendments to the Federal Rules of Civil Procedure shall take effect on August 1, 1988.

3. That THE CHIEF JUSTICE be, and he hereby is, authorized to transmit to the Congress the foregoing amendments in accordance with the provisions of Section 2072 of Title 28, United States Code.

ORDER OF APRIL 30, 1991

1. That the Federal Rules of Civil Procedure for the United States District Courts be, and they hereby are, amended by including therein new chapter headings VIII and IX, amendments to Rules C and E of the Supplemental Rules for Certain Admiralty and Maritime Claims, new Forms 1A and 1B to the Appendix of Forms, the abrogation of Form 18A, and amendments to Civil Rules 5, 15, 24, 34, 35, 41, 44, 45, 47, 48, 50, 52, 53, 63, 72, and 77, as hereinafter set forth.

[See additions and amendments made thereby under respective rules and forms, post.]

2. That the foregoing additions to and changes in the Federal Rules of Civil Procedure, the Supplemental Rules for Certain Admiralty and Maritime Claims, and the Civil Forms shall take effect on December 1, 1991, and shall govern all proceedings in civil actions thereafter commenced and, insofar as just and practicable, all proceedings in civil actions then pending.

3. That THE CHIEF JUSTICE be, and hereby is, authorized to transmit to the Congress the foregoing addition to and changes in the Rules of Civil Procedure in accordance

with the provisions of Section 2072 of Title 28, United States Code.

[Congress may postpone the proposed rule and form additions and amendments effective December 1, 1991, may decline to approve such additions and amendments, or may make changes to the additions and amendments.]

ORDER OF APRIL 22, 1993

1. That the Federal Rules of Civil Procedure for the United States District Courts be, and they hereby are, amended by including therein amendments to Civil Rules 1, 4, 5, 11, 12, 15, 16, 26, 28, 29, 30, 31, 32, 33, 34, 36, 37, 38, 50, 52, 53, 54, 58, 71A, 72, 73, 74, 75, and 76, and new Rule 4.1, and abrogation of Form 18–A, and amendments to Forms 2, 33, 34, and 34A, and new Forms 1A, 1B, and 35.

[See amendments made thereby under respective rules and forms, post.]

2. That the foregoing amendments to the Federal Rules of Civil Procedure shall take effect on December 1, 1993, and shall govern all proceedings in civil cases thereafter commenced and, insofar as just and practicable, all proceedings in civil cases then pending.

3. That THE CHIEF JUSTICE be, and he hereby is, authorized to transmit to the Congress the foregoing amendments to the Federal Rules of Civil Procedure in accordance with the provisions of Section 2072 of Title 23, United States Code.

ORDER OF APRIL 27, 1995

1. That the Federal Rules of Civil Procedure for the United States District Courts be, and they hereby are, amended by including therein amendments to Civil Rules 50, 52, 59, and 83.

[See amendments made thereby under respective rules, post.]

2. That the foregoing amendments to the Federal Rules of Civil Procedure shall take effect on December 1, 1995, and shall govern all proceedings in civil cases thereafter commenced and, insofar as just and practicable, all proceedings in civil cases then pending.

3. That THE CHIEF JUSTICE be, and hereby is, authorized to transmit to the Congress the foregoing amendments to the Federal Rules of Civil Procedure in accordance with the provisions of Section 2072 of Title 28, United States Code.

ORDER OF APRIL 23, 1996

1. That the Federal Rules of Civil Procedure for the United States District Courts be, and they hereby are, amended by including therein amendments to Civil Rules 5 and 43.

[See amendments made thereby under respective rules, post]

2. That the foregoing amendments to the Federal Rules of Civil Procedure shall take effect on December 1, 1996, and shall govern all proceedings in civil cases thereafter commenced and, insofar as just and practicable, all proceedings in civil cases then pending.

3. That THE CHIEF JUSTICE be, and hereby is, authorized to transmit to the Congress the foregoing amendments to the Federal Rules of Civil Procedure in accordance with the provisions of Section 2072 of Title 28, United States Code.

ORDER OF APRIL 11, 1997

1. That the Federal Rules of Civil Procedure for the United States District Courts be, and they hereby are, amended by including therein amendments to Civil Rules 9 and 73, and abrogation of Rules 74, 75, and 76, and amendments to Forms 33 and 34.

[See amendments made thereby under respective rules, post]

2. That the foregoing amendments to the Federal Rules of Civil Procedure shall take effect on December 1, 1997, and shall govern all proceedings in civil cases thereafter commenced and, insofar as just and practicable, all proceedings in civil cases then pending.

3. That THE CHIEF JUSTICE be, and hereby is, authorized to transmit to the Congress the foregoing amendments to the Federal Rules of Civil Procedure in accordance with the provisions of Section 2072 of Title 28, United States Code.

ORDER OF APRIL 24, 1998

1. That the Federal Rules of Civil Procedure for the United States District Courts be, and they hereby are, amended by including therein a new Civil Rule 23(f).

[See amendments made thereby under respective rules, post]

2. That the foregoing amendments to the Federal Rules of Civil Procedure shall take effect on December 1, 1998, and shall govern all proceedings in civil cases thereafter commenced and, insofar as just and practicable, all proceedings in civil cases then pending.

3. That THE CHIEF JUSTICE be, and hereby is, authorized to transmit to the Congress the foregoing amendments to the Federal Rules of Civil Procedure in accordance with the provisions of Section 2072 of Title 28, United States Code.

ORDER OF APRIL 26, 1999

1. That the Federal Rules of Civil Procedure for the United States District Courts be, and they hereby are, amended by including therein amendments to Civil Rule 6(b) and Form 2.

[See amendments made thereby under respective rules, post.]

2. That the foregoing amendments to the Federal Rules of Civil Procedure shall take effect on December 1, 1999, and shall govern all proceedings in civil cases thereafter commenced and, insofar as just and practicable, all proceedings in civil cases then pending.

3. That THE CHIEF JUSTICE be, and hereby is, authorized to transmit to the Congress the foregoing amendments to the Federal Rules of Civil Procedure in accordance with the provisions of Section 2072 of Title 28, United States Code.

ORDER OF APRIL 17, 2000

1. That the Federal Rules of Civil Procedure for the United States District Courts be, and they hereby are, amended by including therein amendments to Civil Rules 4, 5, 12, 14, 26, 30, and 37 and to Rules B, C, and E of the Supplemental Rules for Certain Admiralty and Maritime Claims.

[See amendments made thereby under respective rules, post.]

2. That the foregoing amendments to the Federal Rules of Civil Procedure and the Supplemental Rules for Certain Admiralty and Maritime Claims shall take effect on December 1, 2000, and shall govern all proceedings in civil cases thereafter commenced and, insofar as just and practicable, all proceedings in civil cases then pending.

3. That THE CHIEF JUSTICE be, and hereby is, authorized to transmit to the Congress the foregoing amendments to the Federal Rules of Civil Procedure in accordance with the provisions of Section 2072 of Title 28, United States Code.

ORDER OF APRIL 23, 2001

1. That the Federal Rules of Civil Procedure be, and they hereby are, amended by including therein amendments to Civil Rules 5, 6, 65, 77, 81, and 82.

[See amendments made thereby under respective rules, post.]

2. That the foregoing amendments to the Federal Rules of Civil Procedure shall take effect on December 1, 2001, and shall govern in all proceedings in civil cases thereafter commenced and, insofar as just and practicable, all proceedings then pending.

3. That THE CHIEF JUSTICE be, and hereby is, authorized to transmit to the Congress the foregoing amendments to the Federal Rules of Civil Procedure in accordance with the provisions of Section 2072 of Title 28, United States Code.

4. That the Rules for Practice and Procedure under section 25 of An Act To Amend and Consolidate the Acts Respecting Copyright, approved March 4, 1909, promulgated by this Court on June 1, 1909, effective July 1, 1909, as revised, be, and they hereby are, abrogated, effective December 1, 2001.

ORDER OF APRIL 29, 2002

1. That the Federal Rules of Civil Procedure be, and they hereby are, amended by including therein amendments to Civil Rules 54, 58, and 81, and a new Rule 7.1, and Rule C of Supplemental Rules for Certain Admiralty and Maritime Claims.

[See amendments made thereby under respective rules, post.]

2. That the foregoing amendments to the Federal Rules of Civil Procedure shall take effect on December 1, 2002, and shall govern in all proceedings in civil cases thereafter commenced and, insofar as just and practicable, all proceedings then pending.

3. That the CHIEF JUSTICE be, and hereby is, authorized to transmit to the Congress the foregoing amendments to the Federal Rules of Civil Procedure in accordance with the provisions of Section 2072 of Title 28, United States Code.

ORDER OF MARCH 27, 2003

1. That the Federal Rules of Civil Procedure be, and they hereby are, amended by including therein amendments to Civil Rules 23, 51, 53, 54, and 71A.

[See amendments made thereby under respective rules and forms, post.]

2. That Forms 19, 31, and 32 in the Appendix to the Federal Rules of Civil Procedure be, and they hereby are, amended by replacing all references to "19__" with references to "20__."

3. That the foregoing amendments to the Federal Rules of Civil Procedure shall take effect on December 1, 2003, and shall govern in all proceedings in civil cases thereafter commenced and, insofar as just and practicable, all proceedings then pending.

4. That the CHIEF JUSTICE be, and hereby is, authorized to transmit to the Congress the foregoing amendments to the Federal Rules of Civil Procedure in accordance with the provisions of Section 2072 of Title 28, United States Code.

ORDER OF APRIL 25, 2005

1. That the Federal Rules of Civil Procedure be, and they hereby are, amended by including therein the amendments to Civil Rules 6, 27, and 45, and to Rules B and C of the Supplemental Rules for Certain Admiralty and Maritime Claims.

[See amendments made thereby under respective rules and forms, post.]

2. That the foregoing amendments to the Federal Rules of Civil Procedure and the Supplemental Rules for Certain Admiralty and Maritime Claims shall take effect on December 1, 2005, and shall govern in all proceedings thereafter commenced and, insofar as just and practicable, all proceedings then pending.

3. That the CHIEF JUSTICE be, and hereby is, authorized to transmit to the Congress the foregoing amendments to the Federal Rules of Civil Procedure in accordance with the provisions of Section 2072 of Title 28, United States Code.

ORDER OF APRIL 12, 2006

1. That the Federal Rules of Civil Procedure be, and they hereby are, amended by including therein the amendments to Civil Rules 5, 9, 14, 16, 24, 26, 33, 34, 37, 45, 50, and 65.1; Form 35; and new Rule 5.1.

2. That the Supplemental Rules for Admiralty or Maritime Claims and Asset Forfeiture Actions be, and they hereby are, amended by including therein the amendments to Rules A, C, and E, and new Rule G.

[See amendments made thereby under respective rules and forms, post.]

3. That the foregoing amendments to the Federal Rules of Civil Procedure and the Supplemental Rules for Admiralty or Maritime Claims and Asset Forfeiture Actions shall take

effect on December 1, 2006, and shall govern in all proceedings thereafter commenced and, insofar as just and practicable, all proceedings then pending.

4. That THE CHIEF JUSTICE be, and hereby is, authorized to transmit to the Congress the foregoing amendments to the Federal Rules of Civil Procedure in accordance with the provisions of Section 2072 of Title 28, United States Code.

ORDER OF APRIL 30, 2007

1. That the Federal Rules of Civil Procedure be, and they hereby are, amended by including therein the amendments to Civil Rules 1 through 86 and new Rule 5.2.

2. That Forms 1 through 35 in the Appendix to the Federal Rules of Civil Procedure be, and they hereby are, amended to become restyled Forms 1 through 82.

[See amendments made thereby under respective rules and forms, post.]

3. That the foregoing amendments to the Federal Rules of Civil Procedure shall take effect on December 1, 2007, and shall govern in all proceedings thereafter commenced and, insofar as just and practicable, all proceedings then pending.

4. That THE CHIEF JUSTICE be, and hereby is, authorized to transmit to the Congress the foregoing amendments to the Federal Rules of Civil Procedure in accordance with the provisions of Section 2072 of Title 28, United States Code.

ORDER OF APRIL 23, 2008

1. That the Supplemental Rules for Admiralty or Maritime Claims and Asset Forfeiture Actions be, and they hereby are, amended by including therein the amendment to Rule C.

[See amendment made thereby under Rule C post.]

2. That the foregoing amendment to the Supplemental Rules for Admiralty or Maritime Claims and Asset Forfeiture Actions shall take effect on December 1, 2008, and shall govern in all proceedings thereafter commenced and, insofar as just and practicable, all proceedings then pending.

3. That THE CHIEF JUSTICE be, and hereby is, authorized to transmit to the Congress the foregoing amendment to the Supplemental Rules for Admiralty or Maritime Claims and Asset Forfeiture Actions in accordance with the provisions of Section 2072 of Title 28, United States Code.

HISTORICAL NOTES

The original Rules of Civil Procedure for the District Courts were adopted by order of the Supreme Court on Dec. 20, 1937, transmitted to Congress by the Attorney General on Jan. 3, 1938, and became effective on Sept. 16, 1938.

The Rules have been amended Dec. 28, 1939, eff. Apr. 3, 1941; Dec. 27, 1946, eff. Mar. 19, 1948; Dec. 29, 1948, eff. Oct. 20, 1949; Apr. 30, 1951, eff. Aug. 1, 1951; Apr. 17, 1961, eff. July 19, 1961; Jan. 21, 1963, eff. July 1, 1963; Feb. 28, 1966, eff. July 1, 1966; Dec. 4, 1967, eff. July 1, 1968; Mar. 30, 1970, eff. July 1, 1970; Mar. 1, 1971, eff. July 1, 1971; Nov. 20, 1972, and Dec. 18, 1972, eff. July 1, 1975; Apr. 29, 1980, eff. Aug. 1, 1980; Oct. 21, 1980, Pub.L. 96–481, Title II, § 205(a), (b), 94 Stat. 2330; Jan. 12, 1983, Pub.L. 97–462, §§ 2–4, 96 Stat. 2527–2530, eff. Feb. 26, 1983; Apr. 28, 1983, eff. Aug. 1, 1983; Apr. 29, 1985, eff. Aug. 1, 1985; Mar. 2, 1987, eff. Aug. 1, 1987; Apr. 25, 1988, eff. Aug. 1, 1988; Nov. 18, 1988, Pub.L. 100–690, Title VII, §§ 7047(b), 7049, 7050, 102 Stat. 4401; Apr. 30, 1991, eff. Dec. 1, 1991; Apr. 22, 1993, eff. Dec. 1, 1993; Apr. 27, 1995, eff. Dec. 1, 1995; Apr. 23, 1996, eff. Dec. 1, 1996; Apr. 11, 1997, eff. Dec. 1, 1997 Apr. 24, 1998, eff. Dec. 1, 1998; Apr. 26, 1999, eff. Dec. 1, 1999; Apr. 17, 2000, eff. Dec. 1, 2000; Apr. 23, 2001, eff. Dec. 1, 2001; Apr. 29, 2002, eff. Dec. 1, 2002; Mar. 27, 2003, eff. Dec. 1, 2003; Apr. 25, 2005, eff. Dec. 1, 2005; Apr. 12, 2006, eff. Dec. 1, 2006; Apr. 30, 2007, eff. Dec. 1, 2007; April 23, 2008, eff. Dec. 1, 2008, absent contrary Congressional action.

TITLE I. SCOPE OF RULES; FORM OF ACTION

Rule 1. Scope and Purpose

These rules govern the procedure in all civil actions and proceedings in the United States district courts, except as stated in Rule 81. They should be construed and administered to secure the just, speedy, and inexpensive determination of every action and proceeding.

(Amended December 29, 1948, effective October 20, 1949; February 28, 1966, effective July 1, 1966; April 22, 1993, effective December 1, 1993; April 30, 2007, effective December 1, 2007.)

ADVISORY COMMITTEE NOTES

1937 Adoption

1. Rule 81 states certain limitations in the application of these rules to enumerated special proceedings.

2. The expression "district courts of the United States" appearing in the statute authorizing the Supreme Court of the United States to promulgate rules of civil procedure does not include the district courts held in the territories and insular possessions. See *Mookini et al. v. United States*, 1938, 58 S.Ct. 543, 303 U.S. 201, 82 L.Ed. 748.

3. These rules are drawn under the authority of the Act of June 19, 1934, U.S.C., Title 28, § 723b [see 2072] (Rules in actions at law; Supreme Court authorized to make), and § 723c [see 2072] (Union of equity and action at law rules; power of Supreme Court) and also other grants of rule making power to the Court. See Clark and Moore, *A New Federal Civil Procedure—I. The Background*, 44 Yale L.J. 387, 391 (1935). Under § 723b after the rules have taken effect all laws in conflict therewith are of no further force or effect. In accordance with § 723c the Court has united the general rules prescribed for cases in equity with those in actions at law so as to secure one form of civil action and procedure for both. See Rule 2 (One Form of Action). For the former practice in equity and at law see U.S.C.A., Title 28, §§ 723 and 730 [see 2071 et seq.] (conferring power on the Supreme Court to make rules of practice in equity) and the [former] Equity Rules promulgated thereunder; U.S.C., Title 28, [former] § 724 (Conformity act); [former] Equity

Rule 22 (Action at Law Erroneously Begun as Suit in Equity—Transfer); [former] Equity Rule 23 (Matters Ordinarily Determinable at Law When Arising in Suit in Equity to be Disposed of Therein); U.S.C., Title 28, [former] §§ 397 (Amendments to pleadings when case brought to wrong side of court), and 398 (Equitable defenses and equitable relief in actions at law).

4. With the second sentence compare U.S.C., Title 28, [former] §§ 777 (Defects of form; amendments), [former] 767 (Amendment of process); [former] Equity Rule 19 (Amendments Generally).

1948 Amendment

The amendment effective Oct. 20, 1949, substituted the words "United States district courts" for the words "district courts of the United States."

1966 Amendment

This is the fundamental change necessary to effect unification of the civil and admiralty procedure. Just as the 1938 rules abolished the distinction between actions at law and suits in equity, this change would abolish the distinction between civil actions and suits in admiralty. See also Rule 81.

1993 Amendments

The purpose of this revision, adding the words "and administered" to the second sentence, is to recognize the affirmative duty of the court to exercise the authority conferred by these rules to ensure that civil litigation is resolved not only fairly, but also without undue cost or delay. As officers of the court, attorneys share this responsibility with the judge to whom the case is assigned.

2007 Amendment

The language of Rule 1 has been amended as part of the general restyling of the Civil Rules to make them more easily understood and to make style and terminology consistent throughout the rules. These changes are intended to be stylistic only.

The merger of law, equity, and admiralty practice is complete. There is no need to carry forward the phrases that initially accomplished the merger.

The former reference to "suits of a civil nature" is changed to the more modern "civil actions and proceedings." This change does not affect such questions as whether the Civil Rules apply to summary proceedings created by statute. *See SEC v. McCarthy*, 322 F.3d 650 (9th Cir. 2003); *see also New Hampshire Fire Ins. Co. v. Scanlon*, 362 U.S. 404 (1960).

The Style Project

The Civil Rules are the third set of the rules to be restyled. The restyled Rules of Appellate Procedure took effect in 1998. The restyled Rules of Criminal Procedure took effect in 2002. The restyled Rules of Civil Procedure apply the same general drafting guidelines and principles used in restyling the Appellate and Criminal Rules.

1. General Guidelines

Guidance in drafting, usage, and style was provided by Bryan Garner, *Guidelines for Drafting and Editing Court Rules*, Administrative Office of the United States Courts (1996) and Bryan Garner, *Dictionary of Modern Legal Usage* (2d ed. 1995). *See also* Joseph Kimble, *Guiding Principles for Restyling the Civil Rules*, in *Preliminary Draft of Proposed Style Revision of the Federal Rules of Civil Procedure*, at x (Feb. 2005) (available at http://www.uscourts.gov/rules/Prelim_draft_proposed_pt1.pdf).

2. Formatting Changes

Many of the changes in the restyled Civil Rules result from using format to achieve clearer presentation. The rules are broken down into constituent parts, using progressively indented subparagraphs with headings and substituting vertical for horizontal lists. "Hanging indents" are used throughout. These formatting changes make the structure of the rules graphic and make the restyled rules easier to read and understand even when the words are not changed. Rule 14(a) illustrates the benefits of formatting changes.

3. Changes to Reduce Inconsistent, Ambiguous, Redundant, Repetitive, or Archaic Words

The restyled rules reduce the use of inconsistent terms that say the same thing in different ways. Because different words are presumed to have different meanings, such inconsistencies can result in confusion. The restyled rules reduce inconsistencies by using the same words to express the same meaning. For example, consistent expression is achieved without affecting meaning by the changes from "infant" in many rules to "minor" in all rules; from "upon motion or on its own initiative" in Rule 4(m) and variations in many other rules to "on motion or on its own"; and from "deemed" to "considered" in Rules 5(c), 12(e), and elsewhere. Some variations of expression have been carried forward when the context made that appropriate. As an example, "stipulate," "agree," and "consent" appear throughout the rules, and "written" qualifies these words in some places but not others. The number of variations has been reduced, but at times the former words were carried forward. None of the changes, when made, alters the rule's meaning.

The restyled rules minimize the use of inherently ambiguous words. For example, the word "shall" can mean "must," "may," or something else, depending on context. The potential for confusion is exacerbated by the fact that "shall" is no longer generally used in spoken or clearly written English. The restyled rules replace "shall" with "must," "may," or "should," depending on which one the context and established interpretation make correct in each rule.

The restyled rules minimize the use of redundant "intensifiers." These are expressions that attempt to add emphasis, but instead state the obvious and create negative implications for other rules. "The court in its discretion may" becomes "the court may"; "unless the order expressly directs otherwise" becomes "unless the court orders otherwise." The absence of intensifiers in the restyled rules does not change their substantive meaning. For example, the absence of the word "reasonable" to describe the written notice of foreign law required in Rule 44.1 does not mean that "unreasonable" notice is permitted.

The restyled rules also remove words and concepts that are outdated or redundant. The reference to "at law or in equity" in Rule 1 has become redundant with the merger of law and equity. Outdated words and concepts include the reference to "demurrers, pleas, and exceptions" in Rule 7(c);

the reference to "mesne" process in Rule 77(c); and the reference in Rule 81(f) to a now-abolished official position.

The restyled rules remove a number of redundant cross-references. For example, Rule 8(b) states that a general denial is subject to the obligations of Rule 11, but all pleadings are subject to Rule 11. Removing such cross-references does not defeat application of the formerly cross-referenced rule.

4. Rule Numbers

The restyled rules keep the same rule numbers to minimize the effect on research. Subdivisions have been rearranged within some rules to achieve greater clarity and simplicity. The only change that moves one part of a rule to another is the transfer of former Rule 25(d)(2) to Rule 17(d). The restyled rules include a comparison chart to make it easy to identify transfers of provisions between subdivisions and redesignations of some subdivisions.

5. Other Changes

The style changes to the rules are intended to make no changes in substantive meaning. A very small number of minor technical amendments that arguably do change meaning were approved separately from the restyled rules, but become effective at the same time. An example is adding "e-mail address" to the information that must be included in pleadings. These minor changes occur in Rules 4(k), 9(h), 11(a), 14(b), 16(c)(1), 26(g)(1), 30(b), 31, 40, 71.1, and 78.

Rule 2. One Form of Action

There is one form of action—the civil action.

(Amended April 30, 2007, effective December 1, 2007.)

ADVISORY COMMITTEE NOTES

1937 Adoption

1. This rule modifies U.S.C., Title 28, [former] § 384 (Suits in equity, when not sustainable). U.S.C., Title 28, §§ 723 and 730 [sec. 2071, et seq.] (conferring power on the Supreme Court to make rules of practice in equity), are unaffected in so far as they relate to the rule making power in admiralty. These sections, together with § 723b [sec. 2072] (Rules in actions at law; Supreme Court authorized to make) are continued in so far as they are not inconsistent with § 2072, formerly § 723c (Union of equity and action at law rules; power of Supreme Court). See Note 3 to Rule 1. U.S.C., Title 28, [former] §§ 724 (Conformity act), 397 (Amendments to pleadings when case brought to wrong side of court) and 398 (Equitable defenses and equitable relief in actions at law) are superseded.

2. Reference to actions at law or suits in equity in all statutes should now be treated as referring to the civil action prescribed in these rules.

3. This rule follows in substance the usual introductory statements to code practices which provide for a single action and mode of procedure, with abolition of forms of action and procedural distinctions. Representative statutes are N.Y. Code 1848 (Laws 1848, ch. 379) § 62; N.Y.C.P.A. (1937) § 8; Calif.Code Civ.Proc. (Deering, 1937) § 307; 2 Minn.Stat.Ann. 1945 § 540.01; 2 Wash.Rev.Stat.Ann. (Remington, 1932) §§ 153, 255.

2007 Amendment

The language of Rule 2 has been amended as part of the general restyling of the Civil Rules to make them more easily understood and to make style and terminology consistent throughout the rules. These changes are intended to be stylistic only.

TITLE II. COMMENCING AN ACTION; SERVICE OF PROCESS, PLEADINGS, MOTIONS, AND ORDERS

Rule 3. Commencing an Action

A civil action is commenced by filing a complaint with the court.

(Amended April 30, 2007, effective December 1, 2007.)

ADVISORY COMMITTEE NOTES

1937 Adoption

1. Rule 5(e) defines what constitutes filing with the court.

2. This rule governs the commencement of all actions, including those brought by or against the United States or an officer or agency thereof, regardless of whether service is to be made personally pursuant to Rule 4(d), or otherwise pursuant to Rule 4(e).

3. With this rule compare [former] Equity Rule 12 (Issue of Subpoena—Time for Answer) and the following statutes (and other similar statutes) which provide a similar method for commencing an action:

U.S.C., Title 28:

§ 45 [former] (District courts; practice and procedure in certain cases under interstate commerce laws).

§ 762 [see 1402] (Petition in suit against United States).

§ 766 [see 2409] (Partition suits where United States is tenant in common or joint tenant).

4. This rule provides that the first step in an action is the filing of the complaint. Under Rule 4(a) this is to be followed forthwith by issuance of a summons and its delivery to an officer for service. Other rules providing for dismissal for failure to prosecute suggest a method available to attack unreasonable delay in prosecuting an action after it has been commenced. When a Federal or State statute of limitations is pleaded as a defense, a question may arise under this rule whether the mere filing of the complaint stops the running of the statute, or whether any further step is required, such as, service of the summons and complaint or their delivery to the marshal for service. The answer to this question may depend on whether it is competent for the Supreme Court, exercising the power to make rules of procedure without affecting substantive rights, to vary the operation of statutes of limitations. The requirement of rule 4(a) that the clerk shall forthwith issue the summons and deliver it to the marshal for service will reduce the chances of such a question arising.

2007 Amendments

The caption of Rule 3 has been amended as part of the general restyling of the Civil Rules to make them more easily understood and to make style and terminology consistent throughout the rules. These changes are intended to be stylistic only.

Rule 4. Summons

(a) Contents; Amendments.

(1) ***Contents.*** A summons must:

(A) name the court and the parties;

(B) be directed to the defendant;

(C) state the name and address of the plaintiff's attorney or—if unrepresented—of the plaintiff;

(D) state the time within which the defendant must appear and defend;

(E) notify the defendant that a failure to appear and defend will result in a default judgment against the defendant for the relief demanded in the complaint;

(F) be signed by the clerk; and

(G) bear the court's seal.

(2) ***Amendments.*** The court may permit a summons to be amended.

(b) Issuance. On or after filing the complaint, the plaintiff may present a summons to the clerk for signature and seal. If the summons is properly completed, the clerk must sign, seal, and issue it to the plaintiff for service on the defendant. A summons—or a copy of a summons that is addressed to multiple defendants—must be issued for each defendant to be served.

(c) Service.

(1) ***In General.*** A summons must be served with a copy of the complaint. The plaintiff is responsible for having the summons and complaint served within the time allowed by Rule 4(m) and must furnish the necessary copies to the person who makes service.

(2) ***By Whom.*** Any person who is at least 18 years old and not a party may serve a summons and complaint.

(3) ***By a Marshal or Someone Specially Appointed.*** At the plaintiff's request, the court may order that service be made by a United States marshal or deputy marshal or by a person specially appointed by the court. The court must so order if the plaintiff is authorized to proceed in forma pauperis under 28 U.S.C. § 1915 or as a seaman under 28 U.S.C. § 1916.

(d) Waiving Service.

(1) ***Requesting a Waiver.*** An individual, corporation, or association that is subject to service under Rule 4(e), (f), or (h) has a duty to avoid unnecessary expenses of serving the summons. The plaintiff may notify such a defendant that an action has been commenced and request that the defendant waive service of a summons. The notice and request must:

(A) be in writing and be addressed:

(i) to the individual defendant; or

(ii) for a defendant subject to service under Rule 4(h), to an officer, a managing or general agent, or any other agent authorized by appointment or by law to receive service of process;

(B) name the court where the complaint was filed;

(C) be accompanied by a copy of the complaint, two copies of a waiver form, and a prepaid means for returning the form;

(D) inform the defendant, using text prescribed in Form 5, of the consequences of waiving and not waiving service;

(E) state the date when the request is sent;

(F) give the defendant a reasonable time of at least 30 days after the request was sent—or at least 60 days if sent to the defendant outside any judicial district of the United States—to return the waiver; and

(G) be sent by first-class mail or other reliable means.

(2) ***Failure to Waive.*** If a defendant located within the United States fails, without good cause, to sign and return a waiver requested by a plaintiff located within the United States, the court must impose on the defendant:

(A) the expenses later incurred in making service; and

(B) the reasonable expenses, including attorney's fees, of any motion required to collect those service expenses.

(3) ***Time to Answer After a Waiver.*** A defendant who, before being served with process, timely returns a waiver need not serve an answer to the complaint until 60 days after the request was sent—or until 90 days after it was sent to the defendant outside any judicial district of the United States.

(4) ***Results of Filing a Waiver.*** When the plaintiff files a waiver, proof of service is not required and these rules apply as if a summons and complaint had been served at the time of filing the waiver.

(5) ***Jurisdiction and Venue Not Waived.*** Waiving service of a summons does not waive any objection to personal jurisdiction or to venue.

(e) Serving an Individual Within a Judicial District of the United States. Unless federal law provides otherwise, an individual—other than a minor, an incompetent person, or a person whose waiver has been filed—may be served in a judicial district of the United States by:

(1) following state law for serving a summons in an action brought in courts of general jurisdiction in the state where the district court is located or where service is made; or

(2) doing any of the following:

(A) delivering a copy of the summons and of the complaint to the individual personally;

(B) leaving a copy of each at the individual's dwelling or usual place of abode with someone of suitable age and discretion who resides there; or

(C) delivering a copy of each to an agent authorized by appointment or by law to receive service of process.

(f) Serving an Individual in a Foreign Country. Unless federal law provides otherwise, an individual—other than a minor, an incompetent person, or a person whose waiver has been filed—may be served at a place not within any judicial district of the United States:

(1) by any internationally agreed means of service that is reasonably calculated to give notice, such as those authorized by the Hague Convention on the Service Abroad of Judicial and Extrajudicial Documents;

(2) if there is no internationally agreed means, or if an international agreement allows but does not specify other means, by a method that is reasonably calculated to give notice:

(A) as prescribed by the foreign country's law for service in that country in an action in its courts of general jurisdiction;

(B) as the foreign authority directs in response to a letter rogatory or letter of request; or

(C) unless prohibited by the foreign country's law, by:

(i) delivering a copy of the summons and of the complaint to the individual personally; or

(ii) using any form of mail that the clerk addresses and sends to the individual and that requires a signed receipt; or

(3) by other means not prohibited by international agreement, as the court orders.

(g) Serving a Minor or an Incompetent Person. A minor or an incompetent person in a judicial district of the United States must be served by following state law for serving a summons or like process on such a defendant in an action brought in the courts of general jurisdiction of the state where service is made. A minor or an incompetent person who is not within any judicial district of the United States must be served in the manner prescribed by Rule 4(f)(2)(A), (f)(2)(B), or (f)(3).

(h) Serving a Corporation, Partnership, or Association. Unless federal law provides otherwise or the defendant's waiver has been filed, a domestic or foreign corporation, or a partnership or other unincorporated association that is subject to suit under a common name, must be served:

(1) in a judicial district of the United States:

(A) in the manner prescribed by Rule 4(e)(1) for serving an individual; or

(B) by delivering a copy of the summons and of the complaint to an officer, a managing or general agent, or any other agent authorized by appointment or by law to receive service of process and—if the agent is one authorized by statute and the statute so requires—by also mailing a copy of each to the defendant; or

(2) at a place not within any judicial district of the United States, in any manner prescribed by Rule 4(f) for serving an individual, except personal delivery under (f)(2)(C)(i).

(i) Serving the United States and Its Agencies, Corporations, Officers, or Employees.

(1) ***United States.*** To serve the United States, a party must:

(A)(i) deliver a copy of the summons and of the complaint to the United States attorney for the district where the action is brought—or to an assistant United States attorney or clerical employee whom the United States attorney designates in a writing filed with the court clerk—or

(ii) send a copy of each by registered or certified mail to the civil-process clerk at the United States attorney's office;

(B) send a copy of each by registered or certified mail to the Attorney General of the United States at Washington, D.C.; and

(C) if the action challenges an order of a nonparty agency or officer of the United States, send a copy of each by registered or certified mail to the agency or officer.

(2) ***Agency; Corporation; Officer or Employee Sued in an Official Capacity.*** To serve a United States agency or corporation, or a United States officer or employee sued only in an official capacity, a party must serve the United States and also send a copy of the summons and of the complaint by registered or certified mail to the agency, corporation, officer, or employee.

(3) ***Officer or Employee Sued Individually.*** To serve a United States officer or employee sued in an individual capacity for an act or omission occurring in connection with duties performed on the United States' behalf (whether or not the officer or employee is also sued in an official capacity), a party must serve the United States and also serve the officer or employee under Rule 4(e), (f), or (g).

(4) ***Extending Time.*** The court must allow a party a reasonable time to cure its failure to:

(A) serve a person required to be served under Rule 4(i)(2), if the party has served either the United States attorney or the Attorney General of the United States; or

(B) serve the United States under Rule 4(i)(3), if the party has served the United States officer or employee.

(j) Serving a Foreign, State, or Local Government.

(1) ***Foreign State.*** A foreign state or its political subdivision, agency, or instrumentality must be served in accordance with 28 U.S.C. § 1608.

(2) ***State or Local Government.*** A state, a municipal corporation, or any other state-created governmental organization that is subject to suit must be served by:

(A) delivering a copy of the summons and of the complaint to its chief executive officer; or

(B) serving a copy of each in the manner prescribed by that state's law for serving a summons or like process on such a defendant.

(k) Territorial Limits of Effective Service.

(1) ***In General.*** Serving a summons or filing a waiver of service establishes personal jurisdiction over a defendant:

(A) who is subject to the jurisdiction of a court of general jurisdiction in the state where the district court is located;

(B) who is a party joined under Rule 14 or 19 and is served within a judicial district of the United States and not more than 100 miles from where the summons was issued; or

(C) when authorized by a federal statute.

(2) ***Federal Claim Outside State-Court Jurisdiction.*** For a claim that arises under federal law, serving a summons or filing a waiver of service establishes personal jurisdiction over a defendant if:

(A) the defendant is not subject to jurisdiction in any state's courts of general jurisdiction; and

(B) exercising jurisdiction is consistent with the United States Constitution and laws.

(*l*) Proving Service.

(1) ***Affidavit Required.*** Unless service is waived, proof of service must be made to the court. Except for service by a United States marshal or deputy marshal, proof must be by the server's affidavit.

(2) ***Service Outside the United States.*** Service not within any judicial district of the United States must be proved as follows:

(A) if made under Rule 4(f)(1), as provided in the applicable treaty or convention; or

(B) if made under Rule 4(f)(2) or (f)(3), by a receipt signed by the addressee, or by other evidence satisfying the court that the summons and complaint were delivered to the addressee.

(3) ***Validity of Service; Amending Proof.*** Failure to prove service does not affect the validity of service. The court may permit proof of service to be amended.

(m) Time Limit for Service. If a defendant is not served within 120 days after the complaint is filed, the court—on motion or on its own after notice to the plaintiff—must dismiss the action without prejudice against that defendant or order that service be made within a specified time. But if the plaintiff shows good cause for the failure, the court must extend the time for service for an appropriate period. This subdivision (m) does not apply to service in a foreign country under Rule 4(f) or 4(j)(1).

(n) Asserting Jurisdiction over Property or Assets.

(1) ***Federal Law.*** The court may assert jurisdiction over property if authorized by a federal statute. Notice to claimants of the property must be given as provided in the statute or by serving a summons under this rule.

(2) ***State Law.*** On a showing that personal jurisdiction over a defendant cannot be obtained in the district where the action is brought by

reasonable efforts to serve a summons under this rule, the court may assert jurisdiction over the defendant's assets found in the district. Jurisdiction is acquired by seizing the assets under the circumstances and in the manner provided by state law in that district.

(Amended January 21, 1963, effective July 1, 1963; February 28, 1966, effective July 1, 1966; April 29, 1980, effective August 1, 1980; amended by Pub.L. 97-462, § 2, January 12, 1983, 96 Stat. 2527, effective 45 days after January 12, 1983; amended March 2, 1987, effective August 1, 1987; April 22, 1993, effective December 1, 1993; April 17, 2000, effective December 1, 2000; April 30, 2007, effective December 1, 2007.)

ADVISORY COMMITTEE NOTES

1937 Adoption

Note to Subdivision (a). With the provision permitting additional summons upon request of the plaintiff, compare former Equity Rule 14 (Alias Subpoena) and the last sentence of former Equity Rule 12 (Issue of Subpoena—Time for Answer).

Note to Subdivision (b). This rule prescribes a form of summons which follows substantially the requirements stated in former Equity Rules 12 (Issue of Subpoena—Time for Answer) and 7 (Process, Mesne and Final).

U.S.C., Title 28, § 721 [now 1691] (Sealing and testing of writs) is substantially continued insofar as it applies to a summons, but its requirements as to teste of process are superseded. U.S.C., Title 28, [former] § 722 (Teste of process, day of) is superseded.

See Rule 12(a) for a statement of the time within which the defendant is required to appear and defend.

Note to Subdivision (c). This rule does not affect U.S.C., Title 28, § 503 [see 566], as amended June 15, 1935 (Marshals; duties) and such statutes as the following insofar as they provide for service of process by a marshal, but modifies them in so far as they may imply service by a marshal only:

U.S.C., Title 15:

§ 5 (Bringing in additional parties) (Sherman Act)

§ 10 (Bringing in additional parties)

§ 25 (Restraining violations; procedure)

U.S.C., Title 28:

§ 45 [former] (Practice and procedure in certain cases under the interstate commerce laws)

Compare [former] Equity Rule 15 (Process, by Whom Served).

Note to Subdivision (d). Under this rule the complaint must always be served with the summons.

Paragraph (1). For an example of a statute providing for service upon an agent of an individual see U.S.C., Title 28, § 109 [now 1400, 1694] (Patent cases).

Paragraph (3). This enumerates the officers and agents of a corporation or of a partnership or other unincorporated association upon whom service of process may be made, and permits service of process only upon the officers, managing or general agents, or agents authorized by appointment or by law, of the corporation, partnership or unincorporated association against which the action is brought. See *Christian v. International Ass'n of Machinists,* 7 F.(2d) 481 (D.C.Ky. 1925) and *Singleton v. Order of Railway Conductors of America,* 9 F.Supp. 417 (D.C.Ill.1935). Compare *Operative Plasterers' and Cement Finishers' International Ass'n of the United States and Canada v. Case,* 93 F.(2d) 56 (App.D.C. 1937).

For a statute authorizing service upon a specified agent and requiring mailing to the defendant, see U.S.C., Title 6, § 7 (Surety companies as sureties; appointment of agents; service of process).

Paragraphs (4) and (5) provide a uniform and comprehensive method of service for all actions against the United States or an officer or agency thereof. For statutes providing for such service, see U.S.C., Title 7, §§ 217 (Proceedings for suspension of orders) 499k (Injunctions; application of injunction laws governing orders of Interstate Commerce Commission), 608c(15)(B) (Court review of ruling of Secretary of Agriculture), and 855 (making § 608c(15)(B) applicable to orders of the Secretary of Agriculture as to handlers of anti-hog-cholera serum and hog-cholera virus); U.S.C., Title 26, § 3679, (Bill in chancery to clear title to realty on which the United States has a lien for taxes); U.S.C., Title 28, former §§ 45, (District Courts; practice and procedure in certain cases under the interstate commerce laws), [former] 763 (Petition in suit against the United States; service; appearance by district attorney), 766 [now 2409] (Partition suits where United States is tenant in common or joint tenant), 902 [now 2410] (Foreclosure of mortgages or other liens on property in which the United States has an interest). These and similar statutes are modified in so far as they prescribe a different method of service or dispense with the service of a summons.

For the [former] Equity Rule on service, see [former] Equity Rule 13, Manner of Serving Subpoena.

Note to Subdivision (e). The provisions for the service of a summons or of notice or of an order in lieu of summons contained in U.S.C., Title 8, § 405 (Cancellation of certificates of citizenship fraudulently or illegally procured) (service by publication in accordance with State law); U.S.C., Title 28, § 118 [now 1655] (Absent defendants in suits to enforce liens); U.S.C., Title 35, § 72a [now 146, 291] (Jurisdiction of District Court of United States for the District of Columbia in certain equity suits where adverse parties reside elsewhere) (service by publication against parties residing in foreign countries); U.S.C., Title 38, § 445 [now 784] (Action against the United States on a veteran's contract of insurance) (parties not inhabitants of or not found within the district may be served with an order of the court, personally or by publication) and similar statutes are continued by this rule. Title 24, § 378 [now title 13, § 336] of the Code of the District of Columbia (Publication against non-resident; those absent for six months; unknown heirs or devisees; for divorce or in rem; actual service beyond District) is continued by this rule.

Note to Subdivision (f). This rule enlarges to some extent the present rule as to where service may be made. It does not, however, enlarge the jurisdiction of the district courts.

U.S.C., Title 28, §§ 113 [now 1392] (Suits in States containing more than one district) (where there are two or more defendants residing in different districts), [former] 115 (Suits of a local nature), 116 [now 1392] (Property in different districts in same state), [former] 838 (Executions run in all districts of state); U.S.C., Title 47, § 13 (Action for damages against a railroad or telegraph company whose officer or agent in control of a telegraph line refuses or fails to operate such line in a certain manner—"upon any agent of the company found in such state"); U.S.C., Title 49, § 321(c) [now 10330(b)] (Requiring designation of a process agent by interstate motor carriers and in case of failure so to do, service may be made upon any agent in the state) and similar statutes, allowing the running of process throughout a state, are substantially continued.

U.S.C., Title 15, §§ 5 (Bringing in additional parties) (Sherman Act), 25 (Restraining violations; procedure); U.S.C., Title 28, §§ 44 [now 2321] (Procedure in certain cases under interstate commerce laws; service of processes of court), 117 [now 754, 1692] (Property in different states in same circuit; jurisdiction of receiver), 839 [now 2413] (Executions; run in every State and Territory) and similar statutes, providing for the running of process beyond the territorial limits of a State, are expressly continued.

Note to Subdivision (g). With the second sentence compare [former] Equity Rule 15, (Process, by Whom Served).

Note to Subdivision (h). This rule substantially continues U.S.C., Title 28, [former] § 767 (Amendment of process).

1963 Amendment

Subdivision (b). Under amended subdivision (e) of this rule, an action may be commenced against a nonresident of the State in which the district court is held by complying with State procedures. Frequently the form of the summons or notice required in these cases by State law differs from the Federal form of summons described in present subdivision (b) and exemplified in Form 1. To avoid confusion, the amendment of subdivision (b) states that a form of summons or notice, corresponding "as nearly as may be" to the State form, shall be employed. See also a corresponding amendment of Rule 12(a) with regard to the time to answer.

Subdivision (d)(4). This paragraph, governing service upon the United States, is amended to allow the use of certified mail as an alternative to registered mail for sending copies of the papers to the Attorney General or to a United States officer or agency. Cf. N.J. Rule 4:5–2. See also the amendment of Rule 30(f)(1).

Subdivision (d)(7). Formerly a question was raised whether this paragraph, in the context of the rule as a whole, authorized service in original Federal actions pursuant to State statutes permitting service on a State official as a means of bringing a nonresident motorist defendant into court. It was argued in *McCoy v. Siler,* 205 F.2d 498, 501–2 (3d Cir.) (concurring opinion), cert. denied, 346 U.S. 872, 74 S.Ct. 120, 98 L.Ed. 380 (1953), that the effective service in those cases occurred not when the State official was served but when notice was given to the defendant outside the State, and that subdivision (f) (Territorial limits of effective service), as then worded, did not authorize out-of-State service. This contention found little support. A considerable number of cases held the service to be good, either by fixing upon the service on the official within the State as the effective service, thus satisfying the wording of subdivision (f) as it then stood, see *Holbrook v. Cafiero,* 18 F.R.D. 218 (D.Md. 1955); *Pasternack v. Dalo,* 17 F.R.D. 420 (W.D.Pa.1955); *Super Prods. Corp. v. Parkin,* 20 F.R.D. 377 (S.D.N.Y.1957), or by reading paragraph (7) as not limited by subdivision (f). See *Giffin v. Ensign,* 234 F.2d 307 (3d Cir. 1956); 2 Moore's *Federal Practice,* ¶4.19 (2d ed. 1948); 1 Barron & Holtzoff, *Federal Practice & Procedure* § 182.1 (Wright ed. 1960); Comment, 27 U. of Chi.L.Rev. 751 (1960). See also *Olberding v. Illinois Central R.R.,* 201 F.2d 582 (6th Cir.), rev'd on other grounds, 346 U.S. 338, 74 S.Ct. 83, 98 L.Ed. 39 (1953); *Feinsinger v. Bard,* 195 F.2d 45 (7th Cir. 1952).

An important and growing class of State statutes base personal jurisdiction over nonresidents on the doing of acts or on other contacts within the State, and permit notice to be given the defendant outside the State without any requirement of service on a local State official. See, e.g., Ill.Ann. Stat., c. 110, §§ 16, 17 (Smith–Hurd 1956); Wis.Stat. § 262.06 (1959). This service, employed in original Federal actions pursuant to paragraph (7), has also been held proper. See *Farr & Co. v. Cia. Intercontinental de Nav. de Cuba,* 243 F.2d 342 (2d Cir. 1957); *Kappus v. Western Hills Oil, Inc.,* 24 F.R.D. 123 (E.D.Wis.1959); *Star v. Rogalny,* 162 F.Supp. 181 (E.D.Ill.1957). It has also been held that the clause of paragraph (7) which permits service "in the manner prescribed by the law of the state," etc., is not limited by subdivision (c) requiring that service of all process be made by certain designated persons. See *Farr & Co. v. Cia. Intercontinental de Nav. de Cuba, supra.* But *cf. Sappia v. Lauro Lines,* 130 F.Supp. 810 (S.D.N.Y.1955).

The salutary results of these cases are intended to be preserved. See paragraph (7), with a clarified reference to State law, and amended subdivisions (e) and (f).

Subdivision (e). For the general relation between subdivisions (d) and (e), see 2 Moore, supra, ¶4.32.

The amendment of the first sentence inserting the word "thereunder" supports the original intention that the "order of court" must be authorized by a specific United States statute. See 1 Barron & Holtzoff, supra, at 731. The clause added at the end of the first sentence expressly adopts the view taken by commentators that, if no manner of service is prescribed in the statute or order, the service may be made in a manner stated in Rule 4. See 2 Moore, supra, ¶4.32, at 1004; Smit, *International Aspects of Federal Civil Procedure,* 61 Colum.L.Rev. 1031, 1036–39 (1961). But see Commentary, 5 Fed. Rules Serv. 791 (1942).

Examples of the statutes to which the first sentence relates are 28 U.S.C. § 2361 (Interpleader; process and procedure); 28 U.S.C. § 1655 (Lien enforcement; absent defendants).

The second sentence, added by amendment, expressly allows resort in original Federal actions to the procedures provided by State law for effecting service on nonresident parties (as well as on domiciliaries not found within the State). See, as illustrative, the discussion under amended subdivision (d)(7) of service pursuant to State nonresident motorist statutes and other comparable State statutes. Of particular interest is the change brought about by the reference in this sentence to State procedures for commencing actions against nonresidents by attachment and the like, accompanied by notice. Although an action commenced in a State court by attachment may be removed to the Federal court if ordinary conditions for removal are satisfied, see 28 U.S.C. § 1450; *Rorick v. Devon Syndicate, Ltd.,* 307 U.S. 299, 59 S.Ct. 877, 83 L.Ed. 1303 (1939); *Clark v. Wells,* 203 U.S. 164, 27 S.Ct. 43, 51 L.Ed. 138 (1906), there has heretofore been no provision recognized by the courts for commencing an original Federal civil action by attachment. See

Currie, *Attachment and Garnishment in the Federal Courts,* 59 Mich.L.Rev. 337 (1961), arguing that this result came about through historical anomaly. Rule 64, which refers to attachment, garnishment, and similar procedures under State law, furnishes only provisional remedies in actions otherwise validly commenced. See *Big Vein Coal Co. v. Read,* 229 U.S. 31, 33 S.Ct. 694, 57 L.Ed. 1053 (1913); *Davis v. Ensign–Bickford Co.,* 139 F.2d 624 (8th Cir. 1944); 7 Moore's *Federal Practice* ¶64.05 (2d ed. 1954); 3 Barron & Holtzoff, *Federal Practice & Procedure* § 1423 (Wright ed. 1958); but cf. Note, 13 So.Calif.L.Rev. 361 (1940). The amendment will now permit the institution of original Federal actions against nonresidents through the use of familiar State procedures by which property of these defendants is brought within the custody of the court and some appropriate service is made upon them.

The necessity of satisfying subject-matter jurisdictional requirements and requirements of venue will limit the practical utilization of these methods of effecting service. Within those limits, however, there appears to be no reason for denying plaintiffs means of commencing actions in Federal courts which are generally available in the State courts. See 1 Barron & Holtzoff, supra, at 374–80; Nordbye, *Comments on Proposed Amendments to Rules of Civil Procedure for the United States District Courts,* 18 F.R.D. 105, 106 (1956); Note, 34 Corn.L.Q. 103 (1948); Note, 13 So.Calif.L.Rev. 361 (1940).

If the circumstances of a particular case satisfy the applicable Federal law (first sentence of Rule 4(e), as amended) and the applicable State law (second sentence), the party seeking to make the service may proceed under the Federal or the State law, at his option.

See also amended Rule 13(a), and the Advisory Committee's Note thereto.

Subdivision (f). The first sentence is amended to assure the effectiveness of service outside the territorial limits of the State in all the cases in which any of the rules authorize service beyond those boundaries. Besides the preceding provisions of Rule 4, see Rule 71A(d)(3). In addition, the new second sentence of the subdivision permits effective service within a limited area outside the State in certain special situations, namely, to bring in additional parties to a counterclaim or cross-claim (Rule 13 (h)), impleaded parties (Rule 14), and indispensable or conditionally necessary parties to a pending action (Rule 19); and to secure compliance with an order of commitment for civil contempt. In those situations effective service can be made at points not more than 100 miles distant from the courthouse in which the action is commenced, or to which it is assigned or transferred for trial.

The bringing in of parties under the 100-mile provision in the limited situations enumerated is designed to promote the objective of enabling the court to determine entire controversies. In the light of present-day facilities for communication and travel, the territorial range of the service allowed, analogous to that which applies to the service of a subpoena under Rule 45(e)(1), can hardly work hardship on the parties summoned. The provision will be especially useful in metropolitan areas spanning more than one State. Any requirements of subject-matter jurisdiction and venue will still have to be satisfied as to the parties brought in, although these requirements will be eased in some instances when the parties can be regarded as "ancillary." See *Pennsylvania R.R. v. Erie Avenue Warehouse Co.,* 5 F.R.Serv.2d 14a.62, Case 2 (3d Cir.1962); *Dery v. Wyer,* 265 F.2d 804 (2d Cir.1959); *United Artists Corp. v. Masterpiece Productions, Inc.,* 221 F.2d 213 (2d Cir.1955); *Lesnik v. Public Industrials Corp.,* 144 F.2d 968 (2d Cir.1944); *Vaughn v. Terminal Transp. Co.,* 162 F.Supp. 647 (E.D.Tenn.1957); and compare the fifth paragraph of the Advisory Committee's Note to Rule 4(e), as amended. The amendment is but a moderate extension of the territorial reach of Federal process and has ample practical justification. See 2 Moore, supra, § 4.01[13] (Supp. 1960); 1 Barron & Holtzoff, supra, § 184; Note, 51 Nw. U.L.Rev. 354 (1956). But cf. Nordbye, *Comments on Proposed Amendments to Rules of Civil Procedure for the United States District Courts,* 18 F.R.D. 105, 106 (1956).

As to the need for enlarging the territorial area in which orders of commitment for civil contempt may be served, see *Graber v. Graber,* 93 F.Supp. 281 (D.D.C.1950); *Teele Soap Mfg. Co. v. Pine Tree Products Co., Inc.,* 8 F.Supp. 546 (D.N.H.1934); *Mitchell v. Dexter,* 244 Fed. 926 (1st Cir. 1917); *In re Graves,* 29 Fed. 60 (N.D.Iowa 1886).

As to the Court's power to amend subdivisions (e) and (f) as here set forth, see *Mississippi Pub. Corp. v. Murphree,* 326 U.S. 438, 66 S.Ct. 242, 90 L.Ed. 185 (1946).

Subdivision (i). The continual increase of civil litigation having international elements makes it advisable to consolidate, amplify, and clarify the provisions governing service upon parties in foreign countries. See generally Jones, *International Judicial Assistance: Procedural Chaos and a Program for Reform,* 62 Yale L.J. 515 (1953); Longley, *Serving Process, Subpoenas and Other Documents in Foreign Territory,* Proc.A.B.A., Sec.Int'l & Comp.L. 34 (1959); Smit, *International Aspects of Federal Civil Procedure,* 61 Colum.L.Rev. 1031 (1961).

As indicated in the opening lines of new subdivision (i), referring to the provisions of subdivision (e), the authority for effecting foreign service must be found in a statute of the United States or a statute or rule of court of the State in which the district court is held providing in terms or upon proper interpretation for service abroad upon persons not inhabitants of or found within the State. See the Advisory Committee's Note to amended Rule 4(d)(7) and Rule 4(e). For examples of Federal and State statutes expressly authorizing such service, see 8 U.S.C. § 1451(b); 35 U.S.C. §§ 146, 293; Me.Rev.Stat., ch. 22, § 70 (Supp.1961); Minn.Stat.Ann. § 303.13 (1947); N.Y.Veh. & Tfc.Law § 253. Several decisions have construed statutes to permit service in foreign countries, although the matter is not expressly mentioned in the statutes. See, e.g., *Chapman v. Superior Court,* 162 Cal.App.2d 421, 328 P.2d 23 (Dist.Ct.App.1958); *Sperry v. Fliegers,* 194 Misc. 438, 86 N.Y.S.2d 830 (Sup.Ct.1949); *Ewing v. Thompson,* 233 N.C. 564, 65 S.E.2d 17 (1951); *Rushing v. Bush,* 260 S.W.2d 900 (Tex.Ct.Civ.App.1953). Federal and State statutes authorizing service on nonresidents in such terms as to warrant the interpretation that service abroad is permissible include 15 U.S.C. §§ 77v(a), 78aa, 79y; 28 U.S.C. § 1655; 38 U.S.C. § 784(a); Ill.Ann.Stat., c. 110, §§ 16, 17 (Smith–Hurd 1956); Wis.Stat. § 262.06 (1959).

Under subdivisions (e) and (i), when authority to make foreign service is found in a Federal statute or statute or rule of court of a State, it is always sufficient to carry out the service in the manner indicated therein. Subdivision (i) introduces considerable further flexibility by permitting the foreign service and return thereof to be carried out in any of a number of other alternative ways that are also declared to be sufficient. Other aspects of foreign service continue to be governed by the other provisions of Rule 4. Thus, for example, subdivision (i) effects no change in the form of the summons, or the issuance of separate or additional summons, or the amendment of service.

Service of process beyond the territorial limits of the United States may involve difficulties not encountered in the case of domestic service. Service abroad may be considered by a foreign country to require the performance of judicial, and therefore, "sovereign," acts within its territory, which that country may conceive to be offensive to its policy or contrary to its law. See Jones, supra, at 537. For example, a person not qualified to serve process according to the law of the foreign country may find himself subject to sanctions if he attempts service therein. See Inter-American Juridical Committee, *Report on Uniformity of Legislation on International Cooperation in Judicial Procedures* 20 (1952). The enforcement of a judgment in the foreign country in which the service was made may be embarrassed or prevented if the service did not comport with the law of that country. See ibid.

One of the purposes of subdivision (i) is to allow accommodation to the policies and procedures of the foreign country. It is emphasized, however, that the attitudes of foreign countries vary considerably and that the question of recognition of United States judgments abroad is complex. Accordingly, if enforcement is to be sought in the country of service, the foreign law should be examined before a choice is made among the methods of service allowed by subdivision (i).

Subdivision (i)(1). Subparagraph (a) of paragraph (1), permitting service by the method prescribed by the law of the foreign country for service on a person in that country in a civil action in any of its courts of general jurisdiction, provides an alternative that is likely to create least objection in the place of service and also is likely to enhance the possibilities of securing ultimate enforcement of the judgment abroad. See *Report on Uniformity of Legislation on International Cooperation in Judicial Procedures,* supra.

In certain foreign countries service in aid of litigation pending in other countries can lawfully be accomplished only upon request to the foreign courts, which in turn directs the service to be made. In many countries this has long been a customary way of accomplishing the service. See *In re Letters Rogatory out of First Civil Court of City of Mexico,* 261 Fed. 652 (S.D.N.Y.1919); Jones, supra, at 543; Comment, 44 Colum.L.Rev. 72 (1944); Note 58 Yale L.J. 1193 (1949). Subparagraph (B) of paragraph (1), referring to a letter rogatory, validates this method. A proviso, applicable to this subparagraph and the preceding one, requires, as a safeguard, that the service made shall be reasonably calculated to give actual notice of the proceedings to the party. See *Milliken v. Meyer,* 311 U.S. 457, 61 S.Ct. 339, 85 L.Ed. 278 (1940).

Subparagraph (C) of paragraph (1), permitting foreign service by personal delivery on individuals and corporations, partnerships, and associations, provides for a manner of service that is not only traditionally preferred, but also is most likely to lead to actual notice. Explicit provision for this manner of service was thought desirable because a number of Federal and State statutes permitting foreign service do not specifically provide for service by personal delivery abroad, see e.g., 35 U.S.C. §§ 146, 293; 46 U.S.C. § 1292; Calif.Ins.Code § 1612; N.Y.Veh. & Tfc. Law § 253, and it also may be unavailable under the law of the country in which the service is made.

Subparagraph (D) of paragraph (1), permitting service by certain types of mail, affords a manner of service that is inexpensive and expeditious, and requires a minimum of activity within the foreign country. Several statutes specifically provide for service in a foreign country by mail, e.g., Hawaii Rev.Laws §§ 230–31, 230–32 (1955); Minn.Stat.Ann. § 303.13 (1947); N.Y.Civ.Prac.Act, § 229–b; N.Y.Veh. & Tfc. Law § 253, and it has been sanctioned by the courts even in the absence of statutory provision specifying that form of service. *Zurini v. United States,* 189 F.2d 722 (8th Cir. 1951); *United States v. Cardillo,* 135 F.Supp. 798 (W.D.Pa. 1955); *Autogiro Co. v. Kay Gyroplanes, Ltd.,* 55 F.Supp. 919 (D.D.C.1944). Since the reliability of postal service may vary from country to country, service by mail is proper only when it is addressed to the party to be served and a form of mail requiring a signed receipt is used. An additional safeguard is provided by the requirement that the mailing be attended to by the clerk of the court. See also the provisions of paragraph (2) of this subdivision (i) regarding proof of service by mail.

Under the applicable law it may be necessary, when the defendant is an infant or incompetent person, to deliver the summons and complaint to a guardian, committee, or similar fiduciary. In such a case it would be advisable to make service under subparagraph (A), (B), or (E).

Subparagraph (E) of paragraph (1) adds flexibility by permitting the court by order to tailor the manner of service to fit the necessities of a particular case or the peculiar requirements of the law of the country in which the service is to be made. A similar provision appears in a number of statutes, e.g., 35 U.S.C. §§ 146, 293; 38 U.S.C. § 784(a); 46 U.S.C. § 1292.

The next-to-last sentence of paragraph (1) permits service under (C) and (E) to be made by any person who is not a party and is not less than 18 years of age or who is designated by court order or by the foreign court. Cf. Rule 45(c); N.Y.Civ.Prac.Act §§ 233, 235. This alternative increases the possibility that the plaintiff will be able to find a process server who can proceed unimpeded in the foreign country; it also may improve the changes of enforcing the judgment in the country of service. Especially is this alternative valuable when authority for the foreign service is found in a statute or rule of court that limits the group of eligible process servers to designated officials or special appointees who, because directly connected with another "sovereign," may be particularly offensive to the foreign country. See generally Smit, supra, at 1040–41. When recourse is had to subparagraph (A) or (B) the identity of the process server always will be determined by the law of the foreign country in which the service is made.

The last sentence of paragraph (1) sets forth an alternative manner for the issuance and transmission of the summons for service. After obtaining the summons from the clerk, the plaintiff must ascertain the best manner of delivering the summons and complaint to the person, court, or officer who will make the service. Thus the clerk is not burdened with the task of determining who is permitted to serve process under the law of a particular country or the appropriate governmental or nongovernmental channel for forwarding a letter rogatory. Under (D), however, the papers must always be posted by the clerk.

Subdivision (i)(2). When service is made in a foreign country, paragraph (2) permits methods for proof of service in addition to those prescribed by subdivision (g). Proof of service in accordance with the law of the foreign country is permitted because foreign process servers, unaccustomed to the form or the requirement of return of service prevalent in the United States, have on occasion been unwilling to execute the affidavit required by Rule 4(g). See Jones, supra, at 537; Longley, supra, at 35. As a corollary of the alternate manner of service in subdivision (i)(1)(E), proof of service as directed by order of the court is permitted. The special provision for proof of service by mail is intended as an additional safeguard when that method is used. On the type of evidence of delivery that may be satisfactory to a court in lieu of a signed receipt, see *Aero Associates, Inc. v. La Metropolitana,* 183 F.Supp. 357 (S.D.N.Y.1960).

1966 Amendment

The wording of Rule 4(f) is changed to accord with the amendment of Rule 13(h) referring to Rule 19 as amended.

1980 Amendment

Subdivision (a). This is a technical amendment to conform this subdivision with the amendment of subdivision (c).

Subdivision (c). The purpose of this amendment is to authorize service of process to be made by any person who is authorized to make service in actions in the courts of general jurisdiction of the state in which the district court is held or in which service is made.

There is a troublesome ambiguity in Rule 4. Rule 4(c) directs that all process is to be served by the marshal, by his deputy, or by a person specially appointed by the court. But Rule 4(d)(7) authorizes service in certain cases "in the manner prescribed by the law of the state in which the district court is held. . . ." And Rule 4(e), which authorizes service beyond the state and service in quasi in rem cases when state law permits such service, directs that "service may be made . . . under the circumstances and in the manner prescribed in the [state] statute or rule." State statutes and rules of the kind referred to in Rule 4(d)(7) and Rule 4(e) commonly designate the persons who are to make the service provided for, e.g., a sheriff or a plaintiff. When that is so, may the persons so designated by state law make service, or is service in all cases to be made by a marshal or by one specially appointed under present Rule 4(c)? The commentators have noted the ambiguity and have suggested the desirability of an amendment. See 2 Moore's *Federal Practice* ¶4.08 (1974); Wright & Miller, *Federal Practice and Procedure:* Civil § 1092 (1969). And the ambiguity has given rise to unfortunate results. See *United States for the use of Tanos v. St. Paul Mercury Ins. Co.,* 361 F.2d 838 (5th Cir. 1966); *Veeck v. Commodity Enterprises, Inc.,* 487 F.2d 423 (9th Cir.1973).

The ambiguity can be resolved by specific amendments to Rules 4(d)(7) and 4(e), but the Committee is of the view that there is no reason why Rule 4(c) should not generally authorize service of process in all cases by anyone authorized to make service in the courts of general jurisdiction of the state in which the district court is held or in which service is made. The marshal continues to be the obvious, always effective officer for service of process.

1987 Amendment

The amendments are technical. No substantive change is intended.

1993 Amendments

SPECIAL NOTE: Mindful of the constraints of the Rules Enabling Act, the Committee calls the attention of the Supreme Court and Congress to new subdivision (k)(2). Should this limited extension of service be disapproved, the Committee nevertheless recommends adoption of the balance of the rule, with subdivision (k)(1) becoming simply subdivision (k). The Committee Notes would be revised to eliminate references to subdivision (k)(2).

Purposes of Revision. The general purpose of this revision is to facilitate the service of the summons and complaint. The revised rule explicitly authorizes a means for service of the summons and complaint on any defendant. While the methods of service so authorized always provide appropriate notice to persons against whom claims are made, effective service under this rule does not assure that personal jurisdiction has been established over the defendant served.

First, the revised rule authorizes the use of any means of service provided by the law not only of the forum state, but also of the state in which a defendant is served, unless the defendant is a minor or incompetent.

Second, the revised rule clarifies and enhances the cost-saving practice of securing the assent of the defendant to dispense with actual service of the summons and complaint. This practice was introduced to the rule in 1983 by an act of Congress authorizing "service-by-mail," a procedure that effects economic service with cooperation of the defendant. Defendants that magnify costs of service by requiring expensive service not necessary to achieve full notice of an action brought against them are required to bear the wasteful costs. This provision is made available in actions against defendants who cannot be served in the districts in which the actions are brought.

Third, the revision reduces the hazard of commencing an action against the United States or its officers, agencies, and corporations. A party failing to effect service on all the offices of the United States as required by the rule is assured adequate time to cure defects in service.

Fourth, the revision calls attention to the important effect of the Hague Convention and other treaties bearing on service of documents in foreign countries and favors the use of internationally agreed means of service. In some respects, these treaties have facilitated service in foreign countries but are not fully known to the bar.

Finally, the revised rule extends the reach of federal courts to impose jurisdiction over the person of all defendant against whom federal law claims are made and who can be constitutionally subjected to the jurisdiction of the courts of the United States. The present territorial limits on the effectiveness of service to subject a defendant to the jurisdiction of the court over the defendant's person are retained for all actions in which there is a state in which personal jurisdiction can be asserted consistently with state law and the Fourteenth Amendment. A new provision enables district courts to exercise jurisdiction, if permissible under the

Constitution and not precluded by statute, when a federal claim is made against a defendant not subject to the jurisdiction of any single state.

The revised rule is reorganized to make its provisions more accessible to those not familiar with all of them. Additional subdivisions in this rule allow for more captions; several overlaps among subdivisions are eliminated; and several disconnected provisions are removed, to be relocated in a new Rule 4.1.

The Caption of the Rule. Prior to this revision, Rule 4 was entitled "Process" and applied to the service of not only the summons but also other process as well, although these are not covered by the revised rule. Service of process in eminent domain proceedings is governed by Rule 71A. Service of a subpoena is governed by Rule 45, and service of papers such as orders, motions, notices, pleadings, and other documents is governed by Rule 5.

The revised rule is entitled "Summons" and applies only to that form of legal process. Unless service of the summons is waived, a summons must be served whenever a person is joined as a party against whom a claim is made. Those few provisions of the former rule which relate specifically to service of process other than a summons are relocated in Rule 4.1 in order to simplify the text of this rule.

Subdivision (a). Revised subdivision (a) contains most of the language of the former subdivision (b). The second sentence of the former subdivision (b) has been stricken, so that the federal court summons will be the same in all cases. Few states now employ, distinctive requirements of form for a summons and the applicability of such a requirement in federal court can only serve as a trap for an unwary party or attorney. A sentence is added to this subdivision authorizing an amendment of a summons. This sentence replaces the rarely used former subdivision 4(h). See 4A Wright & Miller, Federal Practice and Procedure § 1131 (2d ed. 1987).

Subdivision (b). Revised subdivision (b) replaces the former subdivision (a). The revised text makes clear that the responsibility for filling in the summons falls on the plaintiff, not the clerk of the court. If there are multiple defendants, the plaintiff may secure issuance of a summons for each defendant, or may serve copies of a single original bearing the names of multiple defendants if the addressee of the summons is effectively identified.

Subdivision (c). Paragraph (1) of revised subdivision (c) retains language from the former subdivision (d)(1). Paragraph (2) retains language from the former subdivision (a), and adds an appropriate caution regarding the time limit for service set forth in subdivision (m).

The 1983 revision of Rule 4 relieved the marshals' offices of much of the burden of serving the summons. Subdivision (c) eliminates the requirement for service by the marshal's office in actions in which the party seeking service is the United States. The United States, like other civil litigants, is now permitted to designate any person who is 18 years of age and not a party to serve its summons.

The court remains obligated to appoint a marshal, a deputy, or some other person to effect service of a summons in two classes of cases specified by statute: actions brought in forma pauperis or by a seaman. 28 U.S.C. §§ 1915, 1916. The court also retains discretion to appoint a process server on motion of a party. If a law enforcement presence appears to be necessary or advisable to keep the peace, the court should appoint a marshal or deputy or other official person to make the service. The Department of Justice may also call upon the Marshals Service to perform services in actions brought by the United States. 28 U.S.C. § 651.

Subdivision (d). This text is new, but is substantially derived from the former subdivisions (c)(2)(C) and (D), added to the rule by Congress in 1983. The aims of the provision are to eliminate the costs of service of a summons on many parties and to foster cooperation among adversaries and counsel. The rule operates to impose upon the defendant those costs that could have been avoided if the defendant had cooperated reasonably in the manner prescribed. This device is useful in dealing with defendants who are furtive, who reside in places not easily reached by process servers, or who are outside the United States and can be served only at substantial and unnecessary expense. Illustratively, there is no useful purpose achieved by requiring a plaintiff to comply with all the formalities of service in a foreign country, including costs of translation, when suing a defendant manufacturer, fluent in English, whose products are widely distributed in the United States. See Bankston v. Toyota Motor Corp., 889 F.2d 172 (8th Cir.1989).

The former text described this process as service-by-mail. This language misled some plaintiffs into thinking that service could be effected by mail without the affirmative cooperation of the defendant. E.g., Gulley v. Mayo Foundation, 886 F.2d 161 (8th Cir.1989). It is more accurate to describe the communication sent to the defendant as a request for a waiver of formal service.

The request for waiver of service may be sent only to defendants subject to service under subdivision (e), (f), or (h). The United States is not expected to waive service for the reason that its mail receiving facilities are inadequate to assure that the notice is actually received by the correct person in the Department of Justice. The same principle is applied to agencies, corporations, and officers of the United States and to other governments and entities subject to service under subdivision (j). Moreover, there are policy reasons why governmental entities should not be confronted with the potential for bearing costs of service in cases in which they ultimately prevail. Infants or incompetent persons likewise are not called upon to waive service because, due to their presumed inability to understand the request and its consequences, they must generally be served through fiduciaries.

It was unclear whether the former rule authorized, mailing of a request for "acknowledgement of service" to defendants outside the forum state. See 1 R. Casad, Jurisdiction in Civil Actions (2d Ed.) 5–29, 30 (1991) and cases cited. But, as Professor Casad observed, there was no reason not to employ this device in an effort to obtain service outside the state, and there are many instances in which it was in fact so used, with respect both to defendants within the United States and to defendants in other countries.

The opportunity for waiver has distinct advantages to a foreign defendant. By waiving service, the defendant can reduce the costs that may ultimately be taxed against it if unsuccessful in the lawsuit, including the sometimes substantial expense of translation that may be wholly unnecessary for defendants fluent in English. Moreover, a foreign defendant that waives service is afforded substantially more time to defend against the action than if it had been formally served: under Rule 12, a defendant ordinarily has only 20 days after service in which to file its answer or raise objections by motion, but by signing a waiver it is allowed 90 days after the date the request for waiver was mailed in which to submit its defenses. Because of the additional time needed for mailing and the unreliability of some foreign mail services, a period of 60 days (rather than the 30 days required for domestic transmissions) is provided for a return of a waiver sent to a foreign country.

It is hoped that, since transmission of the notice and waiver forms is a private nonjudicial act, does not purport to effect service, and is not accompanied by any summons or directive from a court, use of the procedure will not offend foreign sovereignties, even those that have withheld their assent to formal service by mail or have objected to the "service-by-mail" provisions of the former rule. Unless the addressee consents, receipt of the request under the revised rule does not give rise to any obligation to answer the lawsuit, does not provide a basis for default judgment, and does not suspend the statute of limitations in those states where the period continues to run until service. Nor are there any adverse consequences to a foreign defendant, since the provisions for shifting the expense of service to a defendant that declines to waive service apply only if the plaintiff and defendant are both located in the United States.

With respect to a defendant located in a foreign country like the United Kingdom, which accepts documents in English, whose Central Authority acts promptly in effecting service, and whose policies discourage its residents from waiving formal service, there will be little reason for a plaintiff to send the notice and request under subdivision (d) rather than use convention methods. On the other hand, the procedure offers significant potential benefits to a plaintiff when suing a defendant that, though fluent in English, is located in a country where, as a condition to formal service under a convention, documents must be translated into another language or where formal service will be otherwise costly or time-consuming.

Paragraph (1) is explicit that a timely waiver of service of a summons does not prejudice the right of a defendant to object by means of a motion authorized by Rule 12(b)(2) to the absence of jurisdiction over the defendant's person, or to assert other defenses that may be available. The only issues eliminated are those involving the sufficiency of the summons or the sufficiency of the method by which it is served.

Paragraph (2) states what the present rule implies: the defendant has a duty to avoid costs associated with the service of a summons not needed to inform the defendant regarding the commencement of an action. The text of the rule also sets forth the requirements for a Notice and Request for Waiver sufficient to put the cost-shifting provision in place. These requirements are illustrated in Forms 1A and 1B, which replace the former Form 18–A.

Paragraph (2)(A) is explicit that a request for waiver of service by a corporate defendant must be addressed to a person qualified to receive service. The general mail rooms of large organizations cannot be required to identify the appropriate individual recipient for an institutional summons.

Paragraph (2)(B) permits the use of alternatives to the United States mails in sending the Notice and Request. While private messenger services or electronic communications may be more expensive than the mail, they may be equally reliable and on occasion more convenient to the parties. Especially with respect to transmissions to foreign countries, alternative means may be desirable, for in some countries facsimile transmission is the most efficient and economical means of communication. If electronic means such as facsimile transmission are employed, the sender should maintain a record of the transmission to assure proof of transmission if receipt is denied, but a party receiving such a transmission has a duty to cooperate and cannot avoid liability for the resulting cost of formal service if the transmission is prevented at the point of receipt.

A defendant failing to comply with a request for waiver shall be given an opportunity to show good cause for the failure, but sufficient cause should be rare. It is not a good cause for failure to waive service that the claim is unjust or that the court lacks jurisdiction. Sufficient cause not to shift the cost of service would exist, however, if the defendant did not receive the request or was insufficiently literate in English to understand it. It should be noted that the provisions for shifting the cost of service apply only if the plaintiff and the defendant are both located in the United States, and accordingly a foreign defendant need not show "good cause" for its failure to waive service.

Paragraph (3) extends the time for answer if, before being served with process, the defendant waives formal service. The extension is intended to serve as an inducement to waive service and to assure that a defendant will not gain any delay be declining to waive service and thereby causing the additional time needed to effect service. By waiving service, a defendant is not called upon to respond to the complaint until 60 days from the date the notice was sent to it—90 days if the notice was sent to a foreign country—rather than within the 20 day period from date of service specified in Rule 12.

Paragraph (4) clarifies the effective date of service when service is waived; the provision is needed to resolve an issue arising when applicable law requires service of process to toll the statute of limitations. E.g., Morse v. Elmira Country Club, 752 F.2d 35 (2d Cir.1984). Cf. Walker v. Armco Steel Corp., 446 U.S. 740 (1980).

The provisions in former subdivision (c)(2)(C)(ii) of this rule may have been misleading to some parties. Some plaintiffs, not reading the rule carefully, supposed that receipt by the defendant of the mailed complaint had the effect both of establishing the jurisdiction of the court over the defendant's person and of tolling the statute of limitations in actions in which service of the summons is required to toll the limitations period. The revised rule is clear that, if the waiver is not returned and filed, the limitations period under such a law is not tolled and the action will not otherwise proceed until formal service of process is effected.

Some state limitations laws may toll an otherwise applicable statute at the time when the defendant receives notice of the action. Nevertheless, the device of requested waiver of service is not suitable if a limitations period which is about to expire is not tolled by filing the action. Unless there is ample time, the plaintiff should proceed directly to the formal methods for service identified in subdivisions (e), (f), or (h).

The procedure of requesting waiver of service should also not be used if the time for service under subdivision (m) will expire before the date on which the waiver must be returned. While a plaintiff has been allowed additional time for service in that situation, e.g., Prather v. Raymond Constr. Co., 570 F.Supp. 278 (N.D.Ga.1983), the court could refuse a request for additional time unless the defendant appears to have evaded service pursuant to subdivision (e) or (h). It may be noted that the presumptive time limit for service under subdivision (m) does not apply to service in a foreign country.

Paragraph (5) is a cost-shifting provision retained from the former rule. The costs that may be imposed on the defendant could include, for example, the cost of the time of a process server required to make contact with a defendant residing in a guarded apartment house or residential development. The paragraph is explicit that the costs of enforcing the cost-shifting provision are themselves recoverable from a defendant who fails to return the waiver. In the absence of such a provision, the purpose of the rule would be frustrated by the cost of its enforcement, which is likely to be high in relation to the small benefit secured by the plaintiff.

Some plaintiffs may send a notice and request for waiver and, without waiting for return of the waiver, also proceed with efforts to effect formal service on the defendant. To discourage this practice, the cost-shifting provisions in paragraphs (2) and (5) are limited to costs of effecting service incurred after the time expires for the defendant to return the waiver. Moreover, by returning the waiver within the time allowed and before being served with process, a defendant receives the benefit of the longer period for responding to the complaint afforded for waivers under paragraph (3).

Subdivision (e). This subdivision replaces former subdivisions (c)(2)(C)(i) and (d)(1). It provides a means for service of summons on individuals within a judicial district of the United States. Together with subdivision (f), it provides for service on persons anywhere, subject to constitutional and statutory constraints.

Service of the summons under this subdivision does not conclusively establish the jurisdiction of the court over the person of the defendant. A defendant may assert the territorial limits of the court's reach set forth in subdivision (k), including the constitutional limitations that may be imposed by the Due Process Clause of the Fifth Amendment.

Paragraph (1) authorizes service in any judicial district in conformity with state law. This paragraph sets forth the language of former subdivision (c)(2)(C)(i), which authorized the use of the law of the state in which the district court sits, but adds as an alternative the use of the law of the state in which the service is effected.

Paragraph (2) retains the text of the former subdivision (d)(1) and authorizes the use of the familiar methods of personal or abode service or service on an authorized agent in any judicial district.

To conform to these provisions, the former subdivision (e) bearing on proceedings against parties not found within the state is stricken. Likewise stricken is the first sentence of the former subdivision (f), which had restricted the authority of the federal process server to the state in which the district court sits.

Subdivision (f). This subdivision provides for service on individuals who are in a foreign country, replacing the former subdivision (i) that was added to Rule 4 in 1963. Reflecting the pattern of Rule 4 in incorporating state law limitations on the exercise of jurisdiction over persons, the former subdivision (i) limited service outside the United States to cases in which extraterritorial service was authorized by state or federal law. The new rule eliminates the requirement of explicit authorization. On occasion, service in a foreign country was held to be improper for lack of statutory authority. E.g., Martens v. Winder, 341 F.2d 197 (9th Cir.), cert. denied, 382 U.S. 937 (1965). This authority, however, was found to exist by implication. E.g., SEC v. VTR, Inc., 39 F.R.D. 19 (S.D.N.Y.1966). Given the substantial increase in the number of international transactions and events that are the subject of litigation in federal courts, it is appropriate to infer a general legislative authority to effect service on defendants in a foreign country.

A secondary effect of this provision for foreign service of a federal summons is to facilitate the use of federal long-arm law in actions brought to enforce the federal law against defendants who cannot be served under any state law but who can be constitutionally subjected to the jurisdiction of the federal court. Such a provision is set forth in paragraph (2) of subdivision (k) of this rule, applicable only to persons not subject to the territorial jurisdiction of any particular state.

Paragraph (1) gives effect to the Hague Convention on the Service Abroad of Judicial and Extrajudicial Documents, which entered into force for the United States on February 10, 1969. See 28 U.S.C.A., Fed.R.Civ.P. 4 (Supp.1986). This Convention is an important means of dealing with problems of service in a foreign country. See generally 1 B. Ristau, International Judicial Assistance §§ 4–1–1 to 4–5–2 (1990). Use of the Convention procedures, when available, is mandatory if documents must be transmitted abroad to effect service. See Volkswagenwerk Aktiengesellschaft v. Schlunk, 486 U.S. 694 (1988) (noting that voluntary use of these procedures may be desirable even when service could constitutionally be effected in another manner); J. Weis, The Federal Rules and the Hague Conventions: Concerns of Conformity and Comity, 50 U.Pitt.L.Rev. 903 (1989). Therefore, this paragraph provides that, when service is to be effected outside a judicial district of the United States, the methods of service appropriate under an applicable treaty shall be employed if available and if the treaty so requires.

The Hague Convention furnishes safeguards against the abridgment of rights of parties through inadequate notice. Article 15 provides for verification of actual notice or a demonstration that process was served by a method prescribed by the internal laws of the foreign state before a default judgment may be entered. Article 16 of the Convention also enables the judge to extend the time for appeal after judgment if the defendant shows a lack of adequate notice either to defend or to appeal the judgment, or has disclosed a prima facie case on the merits.

The Hague Convention does not specify a time within which a foreign country's Central Authority must effect service, but Article 15 does provide that alternate methods may be used if a Central Authority does not respond within six months. Generally, a Central Authority can be expected to respond much more quickly than that limit might permit, but there have been occasions when the signatory state was dilatory or refused to cooperate for substantive reasons. In such cases, resort may be had to the provision set forth in subdivision (f)(3).

Two minor changes in the text reflect the Hague Convention. First, the term "letter of request" has been added. Although these words are synonymous with "letter rogatory," "letter of request" is preferred in modern usage. The provision should not be interpreted to authorize use of a letter of request when there is in fact no treaty obligation on the receiving country to honor such a request from this country or when the United States does not extend diplomatic recognition to the foreign nation. Second, the passage formerly found in subdivision (i)(1)(B), "when service in either case is reasonably calculated to give actual notice," has been relocated.

Paragraph (2) provides alternative methods for use when internationally agreed methods are not intended to be exclusive, or where there is no international agreement applicable. It contains most of the language formerly set forth in subdivision (i) of the rule. Service by methods that would violate foreign law is not generally authorized. Subparagraphs (A) and (B) prescribe the more appropriate methods for conforming to local practice or using a local authority. Subparagraph (C) prescribes other methods authorized by the former rule.

Paragraph (3) authorizes the court to approve other methods of service not prohibited by international agreements. The Hague Convention, for example, authorizes special forms of service in cases of urgency if convention methods will not permit service within the time required by the circumstances. Other circumstances that might justify the use of additional methods include the failure of the foreign country's Central Authority to effect service within the six-month period provided by the Convention, or the refusal of the Central Authority to serve a complaint seeking punitive damages or to enforce the antitrust laws of the United States. In such cases, the court may direct a special method of service not explicitly authorized by international agreement if not prohibited by the agreement. Inasmuch as our Constitution requires that reasonable notice be given, an earnest effort should be made to devise a method of communication that is consistent with due process and minimizes offense to foreign law. A court may in some instances specially authorize use of ordinary mail. Cf. Levin v. Ruby Trading Corp., 248 F.Supp. 537 (S.D.N.Y.1965).

Subdivision (g). This subdivision retains the text of former subdivision (d)(2). Provision is made for service upon an infant or incompetent person in a foreign country.

Subdivision (h). This subdivision retains the text of former subdivision (d)(3), with changes reflecting those made in subdivision (e). It also contains the provisions for service on a corporation or association in a foreign country, as formerly found in subdivision (i).

Frequent use should be made of the Notice and Request procedure set forth in subdivision (d) in actions against corporations. Care must be taken, however, to address the request to an individual officer or authorized agent of the corporation. It is not effective use of the Notice and Request procedure if the mail is sent undirected to the mail room of the organization.

Subdivision (i). This subdivision retains much of the text of former subdivisions (d)(4) and (d)(5). Paragraph (1) provides for service of a summons on the United States; it amends former subdivision (d)(4) to permit the United States attorney to be served by registered or certified mail. The rule does not authorize the use of the Notice and Request procedure of revised subdivision (d) when the United States is the defendant. To assure proper handling of mail in the United States attorney's office, the authorized mail service must be specifically addressed to the civil process clerk of the office of the United States attorney.

Paragraph (2) replaces former subdivision (d)(5). Paragraph (3) saves the plaintiff from the hazard of losing a substantive right because of failure to comply with the complex requirements of multiple service under this subdivision. That risk has proved to be more than nominal. E.g., Whale v. United States, 792 F.2d 951 (9th Cir.1986). This provision should be read in connection with the provisions of subdivision (c) of Rule 15 to preclude the loss of substantive rights against the United States or its agencies, corporations, or officers resulting from a plaintiff's failure to correctly identify and serve all the persons who should be named or served.

Subdivision (j). This subdivision retains the text of former subdivision (d)(6) without material change. The waiver-of-service provision is also inapplicable to actions against governments subject to service pursuant to this subdivision.

The revision adds a new paragraph (1) referring to the statute governing service of a summons on a foreign state and its political subdivisions, agencies, and instrumentalities, the Foreign Sovereign Immunities Act of 1976, 28 U.S.C. § 1608. The caption of the subdivision reflects that change.

Subdivision (k). This subdivision replaces the former subdivision (f), with no change in the title. Paragraph (1) retains the substance of the former rule in explicitly authorizing the exercise of personal jurisdiction over persons who can be reached under state long-arm law, the "100–mile bulge" provision added in 1963, or the federal interpleader act. Paragraph (1)(D) is new, but merely calls attention to federal legislation that may provide for nationwide or even world-wide service of process in cases arising under particular federal laws. Congress has provided for nationwide service of process and full exercise of territorial jurisdiction by all district courts with respect to specified federal actions. See 1 R. Casad, Jurisdiction in Civil Actions (2d Ed.) chap. 5 (1991).

Paragraph (2) is new. It authorizes the exercise of territorial jurisdiction over the person of any defendant against whom is made a claim arising under any federal law if that person is subject to personal jurisdiction in no state. This addition is a companion to the amendments made in revised subdivisions (e) and (f).

This paragraph corrects a gap in the enforcement of federal law. Under the former rule, a problem was presented when the defendant was a non-resident of the United States having contacts with the United States sufficient to justify the application of United States law and to satisfy federal standards of forum selection, but having insufficient contact with any single state to support jurisdiction under state long-arm legislation or meet the requirements of the Fourteenth Amendment limitation on state court territorial jurisdiction. In such cases, the defendant was shielded from the enforcement of federal law by the fortuity of a favorable limitation on the power of state courts, which was incorporated into the federal practice by the former rule. In this respect, the revision responds to the suggestion of the Supreme Court made in Omni Capital Int'l. v. Rudolf Wolff & Co., Ltd., 484 U.S. 97, 111 (1987).

There remain constitutional limitations on the exercise of territorial jurisdiction by federal courts over persons outside the United States. These restrictions arise from the Fifth Amendment rather than from the Fourteenth Amendment, which limits state-court reach and which was incorporated into federal practice by the reference to state law in the text of the former subdivision (e) that is deleted by this revision. The Fifth Amendment requires that any defendant have affiliating contacts with the United States sufficient to justify the exercise of personal jurisdiction over that party. Cf. Wells Fargo & Co. v. Wells Fargo Express Co., 556 F.2d 406, 418 (9th Cir.1977). There also may be a further Fifth Amendment constraint in that a plaintiff's forum selection might be so inconvenient to a defendant that it would be a denial of "fair play and substantial justice" required by the due process clause, even though the defendant had significant affiliating contacts with the United States. See DeJames v. Magnificent Carriers, 654 F.2d 280, 286 n. 3 (3rd Cir.), cert. denied, 454 U.S. 1085 (1981). Compare World-Wide Volkswagen Corp. v. Woodson, 444 U.S. 286, 293–294 (1980); Insurance Corp. of Ireland v. Compagnie des Bauxites de Guinee, 456 U.S. 694, 702–03 (1982); Burger King Corp. v. Rudzewicz, 471 U.S. 462, 476–78 (1985); Asahi Metal Indus. v. Superior Court of Cal., Solano County, 480 U.S. 102, 108–13 (1987). See generally R. Lusardi, Nationwide Service of Process: Due Process Limitations on the Power of the Sovereign, 33 Vill.L.Rev. 1 (1988).

This provision does not affect the operation of federal venue legislation. See generally 28 U.S.C. § 1391. Nor does it affect the operation of federal law providing for the change of venue. 28 U.S.C. §§ 1404, 1406. The availability of transfer for fairness and convenience under § 1404 should preclude most conflicts between the full exercise of territorial jurisdiction permitted by this rule and the Fifth Amendment requirement of "fair play and substantial justice."

The district court should be especially scrupulous to protect aliens who reside in a foreign country from forum selections so onerous that injustice could result. "[G]reat care and reserve should be exercised when extending our notions of personal jurisdiction into the international field." Asahi Metal Indus. v. Superior Court of Cal., Solano County, 480 U.S. 102, 115 (1987), quoting United States v. First Nat'l City Bank, 379 U.S. 378, 404 (1965) (Harlan, J., dissenting).

This narrow extension of the federal reach applies only if a claim is made against the defendant under federal law. It does not establish personal jurisdiction if the only claims are those arising under state law or the law of another country, even though there might be diversity or alienage subject matter jurisdiction as to such claims. If, however, personal jurisdiction is established under this paragraph with respect to a federal claim, then 28 U.S.C. § 1367(a) provides supplemental jurisdiction over related claims against that defendant, subject to the court's discretion to decline exercise of that jurisdiction under 28 U.S.C. § 1367(c).

Subdivision (*l*). This subdivision assembles in one place all the provisions of the present rule bearing on proof of service. No material change in the rule is effected. The provision that proof of service can be amended by leave of court is retained from the former subdivision (h). See generally 4A Wright & Miller, Federal Practice and Procedure § 1132 (2d ed. 1987).

Subdivision (m). This subdivision retains much of the language of the present subdivision (j).

The new subdivision explicitly provides that the court shall allow additional time if there is good cause for the plaintiff's failure to effect service in the prescribed 120 days, and authorizes the court to relieve a plaintiff of the consequences of an application of this subdivision even if there is no good cause shown. Such relief formerly was afforded in some cases, partly in reliance on Rule 6(b). Relief may be justified, for example, if the applicable statute of limitations would bar the refiled action, or if the defendant is evading service or conceals a defect in attempted service. E.g., Ditkof v. Owens–Illinois, Inc., 114 F.R.D. 104 (E.D.Mich. 1987). A specific instance of good cause is set forth in paragraph (3) of this rule, which provides for extensions if necessary to correct oversights in compliance with the requirements of multiple service in actions against the United States or its officers, agencies, and corporations. The district court should also take care to protect pro se plaintiffs from consequences of confusion or delay attending the resolution of an in forma pauperis petition. Robinson v. America's Best Contacts & Eyeglasses, 876 F.2d 596 (7th Cir. 1989).

The 1983 revision of this subdivision referred to the "party on whose behalf such service was required," rather than to the "plaintiff," a term used generically elsewhere in this rule to refer to any party initiating a claim against a person who is not a party to the action. To simplify the text, the revision returns to the usual practice in the rule of referring simply to the plaintiff even though its principles apply with equal force to defendants who may assert claims against nonparties under Rules 13(h), 14, 19, 20, or 21.

Subdivision (n). This subdivision provides for in rem and quasi-in-rem jurisdiction. Paragraph (1) incorporates any requirements of 28 U.S.C. § 1655 or similar provisions bearing on seizures or liens.

Paragraph (2) provides for other uses of quasi-in-rem jurisdiction but limits its use to exigent circumstances. Provisional remedies may be employed as a means to secure jurisdiction over the property of a defendant whose person is not within reach of the court, but occasions for the use of this provision should be rare, as where the defendant is a fugitive or assets are in imminent danger of disappearing. Until 1963, it was not possible under Rule 4 to assert jurisdiction in a federal court over the property of a defendant not personally served. The 1963 amendment to subdivision (e) authorized the use of state law procedures authorizing seizures of assets as a basis for jurisdiction. Given the liberal availability of long-arm jurisdiction, the exercise of power quasi-in-rem has become almost an anachronism. Circumstances too spare to affiliate the defendant to the forum state sufficiently to support long-arm jurisdiction over the defendant's person are also inadequate to support seizure of the defendant's assets fortuitously found within the state. Shaffer v. Heitner, 433 U.S. 186 (1977).

2000 Amendment

Paragraph (2)(B) is added to Rule 4(i) to require service on the United States when a United States officer or employee is sued in an individual capacity for acts or omissions occurring in connection with duties performed on behalf of the United States. Decided cases provide uncertain guidance on the question whether the United States must be served in such actions. *See Vaccaro v. Dobre*, 81 F.3d 854, 856–857 (9th Cir.1996); *Armstrong v. Sears*, 33 F.3d 182, 185–187 (2d Cir.1994); *Ecclesiastical Order of the Ism of Am v. Chasin*, 845 F.2d 113, 116 (6th Cir.1988); *Light v. Wolf*, 816 F.2d 746 (D.C.Cir.1987); *see also Simpkins v. District of Columbia*, 108 F.3d 366, 368–369 (D.C.Cir.1997). Service on the United States will help to protect the interest of the individual defendant in securing representation by the United States, and will expedite the process of determining whether the United States will provide representation. It has been understood that the individual defendant must be served as an individual defendant, a requirement that is made explicit. Invocation of the individual service provisions of subdivisions (e), (f), and (g) invokes also the waiver-of-service provisions of subdivision (d).

Paragraph 2(B) reaches service when an officer or employee of the United States is sued in an individual capacity "for acts or omissions occurring in connection with the performance of duties on behalf of the United States." This phrase has been chosen as a functional phrase that can be applied without the occasionally distracting associations of such phrases as "scope of employment," "color of office," or "arising out of the employment." Many actions are brought against individual federal officers or employees of the United States for acts or omissions that have no connection whatever to their governmental roles. There is no reason to require service on the United States in these actions. The connection to federal employment that requires service on the United States must be determined as a practical matter, considering whether the individual defendant has reasonable grounds to look to the United States for assistance and whether the United States has reasonable grounds for demanding formal notice of the action.

An action against a former officer or employee of the United States is covered by paragraph (2)(B) in the same way as an action against a present officer or employee. Termination of the relationship between the individual defendant and the United States does not reduce the need to serve the United States.

Paragraph (3) is amended to ensure that failure to serve the United States in an action governed by paragraph 2(B) does not defeat an action. This protection is adopted because there will be cases in which the plaintiff reasonably fails to appreciate the need to serve the United States . There is no requirement, however, that the plaintiff show that the failure to serve the United States was reasonable. A reasonable time to effect service on the United States must be allowed after the failure is pointed out. An additional change ensures that if the United States or United States attorney is served in an action governed by paragraph 2(A), additional time is to be allowed even though no officer, employee, agency, or corporation of the United States was served.

GAP Report

The most important changes were made to ensure that no one would read the seemingly independent provisions of paragraphs 2(A) and 2(B) to mean that service must be made twice both on the United States and on the United States employee when the employee is sued in both official and individual capacities. The word "only" was added in subparagraph (A) and the new phrase "whether or not the officer or employee is sued also in an individual capacity" was inserted in subparagraph (B).

Minor changes were made to include "Employees" in the catch-line for subdivision (i), and to add "or employee" in paragraph 2(A). Although it may seem awkward to think of suit against an employee in an official capacity, there is no clear definition that separates "officers" from "employees" for this purpose. The published proposal to amend Rule 12(a)(3) referred to actions against an employee sued in an official capacity, and it seemed better to make the rules parallel by adding "employee" to Rule 4(i)(2)(A) than by deleting it from Rule 12(a)(3)(A).

2007 Amendment

The language of Rule 4 has been amended as part of the general restyling of the Civil Rules to make them more easily understood and to make style and terminology consistent throughout the rules. These changes are intended to be stylistic only.

Rule 4(d)(1)(C) corrects an inadvertent error in former Rule 4(d)(2)(G). The defendant needs two copies of the waiver form, not an extra copy of the notice and request.

Rule 4(g) changes "infant" to "minor." "Infant" in the present rule means "minor." Modern word usage suggests that "minor" will better maintain the intended meaning. The same change from "infant" to "minor" is made throughout the rules. In addition, subdivision (f)(3) is added to the description of methods of service that the court may order; the addition ensures the evident intent that the court not order service by means prohibited by international agreement.

Rule 4(i)(4) corrects a misleading reference to "the plaintiff" in former Rule 4(i)(3). A party other than a plaintiff may need a reasonable time to effect service. Rule 4(i)(4) properly covers any party.

Former Rule 4(j)(2) refers to service upon an "other governmental organization subject to suit." This is changed to "any other state-created governmental organization that is subject to suit." The change entrenches the meaning indicated by the caption ("Serving a Foreign, State, or Local Government"), and the invocation of state law. It excludes any risk that this rule might be read to govern service on a federal agency, or other entities not created by state law.

The former provision describing service on interpleader claimants [former (k)(1)(C)] is deleted as redundant in light of the general provision in (k)(1)(C) recognizing personal jurisdiction authorized by a federal statute.

HISTORICAL NOTES

Effective and Applicability Provisions

1983 Acts. Amendment by Pub.L. 97–462 effective 45 days after Jan. 12, 1983, see section 4 of Pub.L. 97–462, set out as a note under section 2071 of this title.

LEGISLATIVE STATEMENT

1983 Amendment

128 Congressional Record H 9848, Dec. 15, 1982. Mr. EDWARDS of California. Mr. Speaker, in July Mr. McClory and I brought before the House a bill to delay the effective date of proposed changes in rule 4 of the Federal Rules of Civil Procedure dealing with service of process. The Congress enacted that legislation and delayed the effective date so that we could cure certain problems in the proposed amendments to rule 4.

Since that time, Mr. McClory and I introduced a bill, H.R. 7154, that cures those problems. It was drafted in consultation with representatives of the Department of Justice, the Judicial Conference of the United States, and others.

The Department of Justice and the Judicial Conference have endorsed the bill and have urged its prompt enactment. Indeed, the Department of Justice has indicated that the changes occasioned by the bill will facilitate its collection of debts owed to the Government.

I have a letter from the Office of Legislative Affairs of the Department of Justice supporting the bill that I will submit for the Record. Also, I am submitting for the Record a section-by-section analysis of the bill.

H.R. 7154 makes much needed changes in rule 4 of the Federal Rules of Civil Procedure and is supported by all interested parties. I urge my colleagues to support it.

U.S. DEPARTMENT OF JUSTICE,
OFFICE OF LEGISLATIVE AFFAIRS,
Washington, D.C., December 10, 1982.

Hon. Peter W. Rodino, Jr.
Chairman, Committee on the Judiciary House of Representatives, Washington, D.C.

Dear Mr. Chairman: This is to proffer the views of the Department of Justice on H.R. 7154, the proposed Federal Rules of Civil Procedure Amendments Act of 1982. While the agenda is extremely tight and we appreciate that fact, we do reiterate that this Department strongly endorses the enactment of H.R. 7154. We would greatly appreciate your watching for any possible way to enact this legislation expeditiously.

H.R. 7154 would amend Rule 4 of the Federal Rules of Civil Procedure to relieve effectively the United States Marshals Service of the duty of routinely serving summonses and complaints for private parties in civil actions and would thus achieve a goal this Department has long sought. Experience has shown that the Marshals Service's increasing workload and limited budget require such major relief from the burdens imposed by its role as process-server in all civil actions.

The bill would also amend Rule 4 to permit certain classes of defendants to be served by first class mail with a notice and acknowledgment of receipt form enclosed. We have previously expressed a preference for the service-by-mail provisions of the proposed amendments to Rule 4 which the Supreme Court transmitted to Congress on April 28, 1982.

The amendments proposed by the Supreme Court would permit service by registered or certified mail, return receipt requested. We had regarded the Supreme Court proposal as the more efficient because it would not require an affirmative act of signing and mailing on the part of a defendant. Moreover, the Supreme Court proposal would permit the entry of a default judgment if the record contained a returned receipt showing acceptance by the defendant or a returned envelope showing refusal of the process by the defendant and subsequent service and notice by first class mail. However, critics of that system of mail service have argued that certified mail is not an effective method of providing actual notice to defendants of claims against them because signatures may be illegible or may not match the name of the defendant, or because it may be difficult to determine whether mail has been "unclaimed" or "refused," the latter providing the sole basis for a default judgment.

As you know, in light of these criticisms the Congress enacted Public Law 97–227 (H.R. 6663) postponing the effective date of the proposed amendments to Rule 4 until October 1, 1983, so as to facilitate further review of the problem. This Department opposed the delay in the effective date, primarily because the Supreme Court's proposed amendments also contained urgently needed provisions designed to relieve the United States Marshals of the burden of serving summonses and complaints in private civil actions. In our view, these necessary relief provisions are readily separable from the issues of service by certified mail and the propriety of default judgment after service by certified mail which the Congress felt warranted additional review.

During the floor consideration of H.R. 6663 Congressman Edwards and other proponents of the delayed effective date pledged to expedite the review of the proposed amendments to Rule 4, given the need to provide prompt relief for the Marshals Service in the service of process area. In this spirit Judiciary Committee staff consulted with representatives of this Department, the Judicial Conference, and others who had voiced concern about the proposed amendments.

H.R. 7154 is the product of those consultations and accommodated the concerns of the Department in a very workable and acceptable manner.

Accordingly, we are satisfied that the provisions of H.R. 7154 merit the support of all three branches of the Federal Government and everyone else who has a stake in the fair and efficient service of process in civil actions. We urge prompt consideration of H.R. 7154 by the Committee.[1]

The Office of Management and Budget has advised that there is no objection to the submission of this report from the standpoint of the Administration's program.

Sincerely,
ROBERT A. MCCONNELL,
Assistant Attorney General

[1] In addition to amending Rule 4, we have previously recommended: (a) amendments to 28 U.S.C. § 569(b) redefining the Marshals traditional role by eliminating the statutory requirement that they serve subpoenas, as well as summonses and complaints, and; (b) amendments to 28 U.S.C. § 1921 changing the manner and level in which marshal fees are charged for serving private civil process. These legislative changes are embodied in Section 10 of S. 2567 and the Department's proposed fiscal year 1983 Appropriations Authorization bill. If, in the Committee's judgment, efforts to incorporate these suggested amendments in H.R. 7154 would in any way impede consideration of the bill during the few remaining legislative days in the 97th Congress, we would urge that they be separately considered early in the 98th Congress.

H.R. 7154—Federal Rules of Civil Procedure Amendments Act of 1982

BACKGROUND

The Federal Rules of Civil Procedure set forth the procedures to be followed in civil actions and proceedings in United States district courts. These rules are usually amended by a process established by 28 U.S.C. 2072, often referred to as the "Rules Enabling Act". The Rules Enabling Act provides that the Supreme Court can propose new rules of "practice and procedure" and amendments to existing rules by transmitting them to Congress after the start of a regular session but not later than May 1. The rules and amendments so proposed take effect 90 days after transmittal unless legislation to the contrary is enacted.[1]

On April 28, 1982, the Supreme Court transmitted to Congress several proposed amendments to the Federal Rules of Civil Procedure, the Federal Rules of Criminal Procedure (which govern criminal cases and proceedings in Federal courts), and the Rules and Forms Governing Proceedings in the United States District Courts under sections 2254 and 2255 of Title 28, United States Code (which govern habeas corpus proceedings). These amendments were to have taken effect on August 1, 1982.

The amendments to Rule 4 of the Federal Rules of Civil Procedure were intended primarily to relieve United States marshals of the burden of serving summonses and complaints in private civil actions. Appendix II, at 7 (Report of the Committee on Rules of Practice and Procedure), 16 (Advisory Committee Note). The Committee received numerous complaints that the changes not only failed to achieve that goal, but that in the process the changes saddled litigators with flawed mail service, deprived litigants of the use of effective local procedures for service, and created a time limit for service replete with ambiguities that could only be resolved by costly litigation. See House Report No. 97–662, at 2–4 (1982).

In order to consider these criticisms, Congress enacted Public Law 97–227, postponing the effective date of the proposed amendments to Rule 4 until October 1, 1983.[2] Accordingly, in order to help shape the policy behind, and the form of, the proposed amendments, Congress must enact legislation before October 1, 1983.[3]

With that deadline and purpose in mind, consultations were held with representatives of the Judicial Conference, the Department of Justice, and others who had voiced concern about the proposed amendments. H.R. 7154 is the product of those consultations. The bill seeks to effectuate the policy of relieving the Marshals Service of the duty of routinely serving summonses and complaints. It provides a system of service by mail modeled upon a system found to be effective in California, and finally, it makes appropriate stylistic, grammatical, and other changes in Rule 4.

Need for the Legislation

1. *Current Rule 4*

Rule 4 of the Federal Rules of Civil Procedure relates to the issuance and service of process. Subsection (c) authorizes service of process by personnel of the Marshals Service, by a person specially appointed by the Court, or "by a person authorized to serve process in an action brought in the courts of general jurisdiction of the state in which the district court is held or in which service is made." Subsection (d) describes how a summons and complaint must be served and designates those persons who must be served in cases involving specified categories of defendants. Mail service is not directly authorized. Subsection (d)(7), however, authorizes service under the law of the state in which the district court sits upon defendants described in subsections (d)(1) (certain individuals) and (d)(3) (organizations). Thus, if state law authorizes service by mail of a summons and complaint upon an individual or organization described in subsections (d)(1) or (3), then subsection (d)(7) authorizes service by mail for United States district courts in that state.[4]

2. *Reducing the role of marshals*

The Supreme Court's proposed modifications of Rule 4 were designed to alleviate the burden on the Marshals Service of serving summonses and complaints in private civil actions. Appendix II, at 7 (Report of the Committee on Rules of Practice and Procedure), 16 (Advisory Committee Note). While the Committee received no complaints about the goal of reducing the role of the Marshals Service, the Court's proposals simply failed to achieve that goal. See House Report No. 97–662, at 2–3 (1982).

The Court's proposed Rule 4(c)(2)(B) required the Marshals Service to serve summonses and complaints "pursuant to any statutory provision expressly providing for service by a United States Marshal or his deputy."[5] One such statutory provision is 28 U.S.C. 569(b), which compels marshals to "execute *all* lawful writs, process and orders issued under authority of the United States, *including those of the courts* * * *." (emphasis added). Thus, any party could have invoked 28 U.S.C. 569(b) to utilize a marshal for service of a summons and complaint, thereby thwarting the intent of the new subsection to limit the use of marshals. The Justice Department acknowledges that the proposed subsection did not accomplish its objectives.[6]

Had 28 U.S.C. 569(b) been inconsistent with proposed Rule 4(c)(2)(B), the latter would have nullified the former under 28 U.S.C. 2072, which provides that "All laws in conflict with such rules shall be of no further force or effect after such rules have taken effect." Since proposed Rule 4(c)(2)(B) specifically referred to statutes such as 28 U.S.C. 569(b), however, the new subsection did not conflict with 28 U.S.C. 569(b) and did not, therefore, supersede it.

H.R. 7154 cures this problem and achieves the desired reduction in the role of the Marshals Service by authorizing marshals to serve summonses and complaints "on behalf of the United States". By so doing, H.R. 7154 eliminates the loophole in the Court's proposed language and still provides for service by marshals on behalf of the Government.[7]

3. *Mail service*

The Supreme Court's proposed subsection (d)(7) and (8) authorized, as an alternative to personal service, mail service of summonses and complaints on individuals and organizations described in subsection (d)(1) and (3), but only through registered or certified mail, restricted delivery. Critics of that system of mail service argued that registered and certified mail were not necessarily effective methods of providing actual notice to defendants of claims against them. This was so, they argued, because signatures may be illegible or may not match the name of the defendant, or because it may be difficult to determine whether mail has been "unclaimed" or "refused", the latter apparently providing the sole basis for a default judgment.[8]

H.R. 7154 provides for a system of service by mail similar to the system now used in California. See Cal.Civ.Pro. § 415.30 (West 1973). Service would be by ordinary mail with a notice and acknowledgment of receipt form enclosed. If the defendant returns the acknowledgment form to the sender within 20 days of mailing, the sender files the return and service is complete. If the acknowledgment is not returned within 20 days of mailing, then service must be effected through some other means provided for in the Rules.

This system of mail service avoids the notice problems created by the registered and certified mail procedures proposed by the Supreme Court. If the proper person receives the notice and returns the acknowledgment, service is complete. If the proper person does not receive the mailed form, or if the proper person receives the notice but fails to return the acknowledgment form, another method of service authorized by law is required.[9] In either instance, however, the defendant will receive actual notice of the claim. In order to encourage defendants to return the acknowledgment form, the court can order a defendant who does not return it to pay the costs of service unless the defendant can show good cause for the failure to return it.

4. *The local option*

The Court's proposed amendments to Rule 4 deleted the provision in current subsection (d)(7) that authorizes service of a summons and complaint upon individuals and organizations "in the manner prescribed by the law of the state in which the district court is held for the service of summons or other like process upon any such defendant in an action brought in the courts of general jurisdiction of that state." The Committee received a variety of complaints about the deletion of this provision. Those in favor of preserving the local option saw no reason to forego systems of service that had been successful in achieving effective notice.[10]

H.R. 7154 carries forward the policy of the current rule and permits a party to serve a summons and complaint upon individuals and organizations described in Rule 4(d)(1) and (3) in accordance with the law of the state in which the district court sits. Thus, the bill authorizes four methods of serving a summons and complaint on such defendants: (1) service by a nonparty adult (Rule 4(c)(2)(A)); (2) service by personnel of the Marshals Service, if the party qualifies, such as because the party is proceeding in forma pauperis (Rule 4(c)(2)(B)); (3) service in any manner authorized by the law of the state in which the district court is held (Rule 4(c)(2)(C)(i)); or (4) service by regular mail with a notice and acknowledgment of receipt form enclosed (Rule 4(c)(2)(C)(ii)).[11]

5. *Time limits*

Rule 4 does not currently provide a time limit within which service must be completed. Primarily because United States marshals currently effect service of process, no time restriction has been deemed necessary, Appendix II, at 18 (Advisory Committee Note). Along with the proposed changes to subdivisions (c) and (d) to reduce the role of the Marshals Service, however, came new subdivision (j), requiring that service of a summons and complaint be made within 120 days of the filing of the complaint. If service were not accomplished within that time, proposed subdivision (j) required that the action "be dismissed as to that defendant without prejudice upon motion or upon the court's own initiative". Service by mail was deemed made for purposes of subdivision (j) "as of the date on which the process was accepted, refused, or returned as unclaimed".[12]

H.R. 7154 adopts a policy of limiting the time to effect service. It provides that if a summons and complaint have not been served within 120 days of the filing of the complaint and the plaintiff fails to show "good cause" for not completing service within that time, then the court must dismiss the action as to the unserved defendant. H.R. 7154 ensures that a plaintiff will be notified of an attempt to dismiss the action. If dismissal for failure to serve is raised by the court upon its own motion, the legislation requires that the court provide notice to the plaintiff. If dismissal is sought by someone else, Rule 5(a) of the Federal Rules of Civil Procedure requires that the motion be served upon the plaintiff.

Like proposed subsection (j), H.R. 7154 provides that a dismissal for failure to serve within 120 days shall be "without prejudice". Proposed subsection (j) was criticized by some for ambiguity because, it was argued, neither the text of subsection (j) nor the Advisory Committee Note indicated whether a dismissal without prejudice would toll a statute of limitation. *See* House Report 97–662, at 3–4 (1982). The problem would arise when a plaintiff files the complaint within the applicable statute of limitation period but does not effect service within 120 days. If the statute of limitation period expires during that period, and if the plaintiff's action is dismissed "without prejudice", can the plaintiff refile the complaint and maintain the action? The answer depends upon how the statute of limitation is tolled.[13]

If the law provides that the statute of limitation is tolled by filing and service of the complaint, then a dismissal under H.R. 7154 for failure to serve within the 120 days would, by the terms of the law controlling the tolling bar the plaintiff from later maintaining the cause of action.[14] If the law provides that the statute of limitation is tolled by filing alone, then the status of the plaintiff's cause of action turns upon the plaintiff's diligence. If the plaintiff has not been diligent, the court will dismiss the complaint for failure to serve within 120 days, and the plaintiff will be barred from later maintaining the cause of action because the statute of limitation has run. A dismissal without prejudice does not confer upon the plaintiff any rights that the plaintiff does otherwise possess and leaves a plaintiff whose action has been dismissed in the same position as if the action had never been filed.[15] If, on the other hand, the plaintiff has made reasonable efforts to effect service, then the plaintiff can move under Rule 6(b) to enlarge the time within which to serve or can oppose dismissal for failure to serve. A court would undoubtedly permit such a plaintiff additional time within which to effect service. Thus, a diligent plaintiff can preserve the cause of action. This result is consistent with the policy behind the time limit for service and with statutes of limitation, both of which are designed to encourage prompt movement of civil actions in the federal courts.

6. *Conforming and clarifying subsections (d)(4) and (5)*

Current subsections (d)(4) and (5) prescribe which persons must be served in cases where an action is brought against the United States or an officer or agency of the United States. Under subsection (d)(4), where the United States is the named defendant, service must be made as follows: (1) personal service upon the United States attorney, an assistant United States attorney, or a designated clerical employee of the United States attorney in the district in which the action is brought; (2) registered or certified mail service to the Attorney General of the United States in Washington, D.C.; and (3) registered or certified mail service to the appropriate officer or agency if the action attacks an order of that officer or agency but does not name the officer or agency as a defendant. Under subsection (d)(5), where an officer or agency of the United States is named as a defendant, service must be made as in subsection (d)(4), except that personal service upon the officer or agency involved is required.[16]

The time limit for effecting service in H.R. 7154 would present significant difficulty to a plaintiff who has to arrange for personal service upon an officer or agency that may be thousands of miles away. There is little reason to require different types of service when the officer or agency is named as a party, and H.R. 7154 therefore conforms the manner of service under subsection (d)(5) to the manner of service under subsection (d)(4).

Section-By-Section Analysis

Section 1

Section 1 provides that the short title of the bill is the "Federal Rules of Civil Procedure Amendments Act of 1982".

Section 2

Section 2 of the bill consists of 7 numbered paragraphs, each amending a different part of Rule 4 of the Federal Rules of Civil Procedure.

Paragraph (1) deletes the requirement in present Rule 4(a) that a summons be delivered for service to the marshal or other person authorized to serve it. As amended by the legislation, Rule 4(a) provides that the summons be delivered to "the plaintiff or the plaintiff's attorney, who shall be responsible for prompt service of the summons and complaint". This change effectuates the policy proposed by the Supreme Court. See Appendix II, at — (Advisory Committee Note).

Paragraph (2) amends current Rule 4(c), which deals with the service of process. New Rule 4(c)(1) requires that all process, other than a subpoena or a summons and complaint, be served by the Marshals Service or by a person especially appointed for that purpose. Thus, the Marshals Service or persons specially appointed will continue to serve all process other than subpoenas and summonses and complaints, a policy identical to that proposed by the Supreme Court. See Appendix II, at 8 (Report of the Judicial Conference Committee on Rules of Practice and Procedure). The service of subpoenas is governed by Rule 45,[17] and the service of summonses and complaints is governed by new Rule 4(c)(2).

New Rule 4(c)(2)(A) sets forth the general rule that summonses and complaints shall be served by someone who is at least 18 years old and not a party to the action or proceeding. This is consistent with the Court's proposal. Appendix II, at 16 (Advisory Committee Note). Subparagraphs (B) and (C) of new Rule 4(c)(2) set forth exceptions to this general rule.

Subparagraph (B) sets forth 3 exceptions to the general rule. First, subparagraph (B)(i) requires the Marshals Service (or someone specially appointed by the court) to serve summonses and complaints on behalf of a party proceeding in forma pauperis or a seaman authorized to proceed under 28 U.S.C. 1916. This is identical to the Supreme Court's proposal. *See* Appendix II, at 3 (text of proposed rule), 16 (Advisory Committee Note). Second, subparagraph (B)(ii) requires the Marshals Service (or someone specially appointed by the court) to serve a summons and complaint when the court orders the marshals to do so in order properly to effect service in that particular action.[18] This, except for nonsubstantive changes in phrasing, is identical to the Supreme Court's proposal. See Appendix II, at 3 (text of proposed rule), 16 (Advisory Committee Note).

Subparagraph (C) of new Rule 4(c)(2) provides 2 exceptions to the general rule of service by a nonparty adult. These exceptions apply only when the summons and complaint is to be served upon persons described in Rule 4(d)(1) (certain individuals) or Rule 4(d)(3) (organizations).[19] First, subparagraph (C)(i) permits service of a summons and complaint in a manner authorized by the law of the state in which the court sits. This restates the option to follow local law currently found in Rule 4(d)(7) and would authorize service by mail if the state law so allowed. The method of mail service in that instance would, of course, be the method permitted by state law.

Second, subparagraph (C)(ii) permits service of a summons and complaint by regular mail. The sender must send to the defendant, by first-class mail, postage prepaid, a copy of the summons and complaint, together with 2 copies of a notice and acknowledgment of receipt of summons and complaint form and a postage prepaid return envelope addressed to the sender. If a copy of the notice and acknowledgment form is not received by the sender within 20 days after the date of mailing, then service must be made under Rule 4(c)(2)(A) or (B) (i.e., by a nonparty adult or, if the person qualifies,[20] by personnel of the Marshals Service or a person specially appointed by the court) in the manner prescribed by Rule 4(d)(1) or (3) (i.e., personal or substituted service).

New Rule 4(c)(2)(D) permits a court to penalize a person who avoids service by mail. It authorizes the court to order a person who does not return the notice and acknowledgment form within 20 days after mailing to pay the costs of service, unless that person can show good cause for failing to return the form. The purpose of this provision is to encourage the prompt return of the form so that the action can move forward without unnecessary delay. Fairness requires that a person who causes another additional and unnecessary expense in effecting service ought to reimburse the party who was forced to bear the additional expense.

Subparagraph (E) of Rule 4(c)(2) requires that the notice and acknowledgment form described in new Rule 4(c)(2)(C)(ii) be executed under oath or affirmation. This provision tracks the language of 28 U.S.C. 1746, which permits the use of unsworn declarations under penalty of perjury whenever an oath or affirmation is required. Statements made under penalty of perjury are subject to 18 U.S.C. 1621(2), which provides felony penalties for someone who "willfully subscribes as true any material matter which he does not believe to be true". The requirement that the form be executed under oath or affirmation is intended to encourage truthful submissions to the court, as the information contained in the form is important to the parties.[21]

New Rule 4(c)(3) authorizes the court freely to make special appointments to serve summonses and complaints under Rule 4(c)(2)(B) and all other process under Rule 4(c)(1). This carries forward the policy of present Rule 4(c).

Paragraph (3) of section 2 of the bill makes a non-substantive change in the caption of Rule 4(d) in order to reflect more accurately the provisions of Rule 4(d). Paragraph (3) also deletes a provision on service of a summons and complaint pursuant to state law. This provision is redundant in view of new Rule 4(c)(2)(C)(i).

Paragraph (4) of section 2 of the bill conforms Rule 4(d)(5) to present Rule 4(d)(4). Rule 4(d)(5) is amended to provide that service upon a named defendant agency or officer of the United States shall be made by "sending" a copy of the summons and complaint "by registered or certified mail" to the defendant.[22] Rule 4(d)(5) currently provides for service by "delivering" the copies to the defendant, but 28 U.S.C.

1391(e) authorizes delivery upon a defendant agency or officer outside of the district in which the action is brought by means of certified mail. Hence, the change is not a marked departure from current practice.

Paragraph (5) of section 2 of the bill amends the caption of Rule 4(e) in order to describe subdivision (e) more accurately.

Paragraph (6) of section 2 of the bill amends Rule 4(g), which deals with return of service. Present rule 4(g) is not changed except to provide that, if service is made pursuant to the new system of mail service (Rule 4(c)(2)(C)(ii)), the plaintiff or the plaintiff's attorney must file the court the signed acknowledgment form returned by the person served.

Paragraph (7) of section 2 of the bill adds new subsection (j) to provide a time limitation for the service of a summons and complaint. New Rule 4(j) retains the Supreme Court's requirement that a summons and complaint be served within 120 days of the filing of the complaint. See Appendix II, at 18 (Advisory Committee Note).[23] The plaintiff must be notified of an effort or intention to dismiss the action. This notification is mandated by subsection (j) if the dismissal is being raised on the court's own initiative and will be provided pursuant to Rule 5 (which requires service of motions upon the adverse party) if the dismissal is sought by someone else.[24] The plaintiff may move under Rule 6(b) to enlarge the time period. See Appendix II, at Id. (Advisory Committee Note). If service is not made within the time period or enlarged time period, however, and if the plaintiff fails to show "good cause" for not completing service, then the court must dismiss the action as to the unserved defendant. The dismissal is "without prejudice". The term "without prejudice" means that the dismissal does not constitute an adjudication of the merits of the complaint. A dismissal "without prejudice" leaves a plaintiff whose action has been dismissed in the position in which that person would have been if the action had never been filed.

Section 3

Section 3 of the bill amends the Appendix of Forms at the end of the Federal Rules of Civil Procedure by adding a new form 18A, "Notice and Acknowledgment for Service by Mail". This new form is required by new Rule 4(c)(2)(C)(ii), which requires that the notice and acknowledgment form used with service by regular mail conform substantially to Form 18A.

Form 18A as set forth in section 3 of the bill is modeled upon a form used in California.[25] It contains 2 parts. The first part is a notice to the person being served that tells that person that the enclosed summons and complaint is being served pursuant to Rule 4(c)(2)(C)(ii); advises that person to sign and date the acknowledgment form and indicate the authority to receive service if the person served is not the party to the action (e.g., the person served is an officer of the organization being served); and warns that failure to return the form to the sender within 20 days may result in the court ordering the party being served to pay the expenses involved in effecting service. The notice also warns that if the complaint is not responded to within 20 days, a default judgment can be entered against the party being served. The notice is dated under penalty of perjury by the plaintiff or the plaintiff's attorney.[26]

The second part of the form contains the acknowledgment of receipt of the summons and complaint. The person served must declare on this part of the form, under penalty of perjury, the date and place of service and the person's authority to receive service.

Section 4

Section 4 of the bill provides that the changes in Rule 4 made by H.R. 7154 will take effect 45 days after enactment, thereby giving the bench and bar, as well as other interested persons and organizations (such as the Marshals Service), an opportunity to prepare to implement the changes made by the legislation. The delayed effective date means that service of process issued before the effective date will be made in accordance with current Rule 4. Accordingly, all process in the hands of the Marshals Service prior to the effective date will be served by the Marshals Service under the present rule.

Section 5

Section 5 of the bill provides that the amendments to Rule 4 proposed by the Supreme Court (whose effective date was postponed by Public Law 97–227) shall not take effect. This is necessary because under Public Law 97–227 the proposed amendments will take effect on October 1, 1983.

1 The drafting of the rules and amendments is actually done by a committee of the Judicial Conference of the United States. In the case of the Federal Rules of Civil Procedure, the initial draft is prepared by the Advisory Committee on Civil Rules. The Advisory Committee's draft is then reviewed by the Committee on Rules of Practice and Procedure, which must give its approval to the draft. Any draft approved by that committee is forwarded to the Judicial Conference. If the Judicial Conference approves the draft, it forwards the draft to the Supreme Court. The Judicial Conference's role in the rule-making process is defined by 28 U.S.C. 331.

For background information about how the Judicial Conference committees operate, see Wright, "Procedural Reform: Its Limitation and Its Future," 1 Ga.L.Rev. 563, 565–66 (1967) (civil rules); statement of United States District Judge Roszel C. Thomsen, Hearings on Proposed Amendments to the Federal Rules of Criminal Procedure Before the Subcommittee on Criminal Justice of the House Committee on the Judiciary, 93d Cong., 2d Sess. at 25 (1974) (criminal rules); statement of United States Circuit Judge J. Edward Lumbard, id. at 203 (criminal rules); J. Weinstein, Reform of Federal Court Rulemaking Procedure (1977); Weinstein, "Reform of Federal Rulemaking Procedures," 76 Colum.L.Rev. 905 (1976).

2 All of the other amendments, including all of the proposed amendments to the Federal Rules of Criminal Procedure and the Rules and Forms Governing Proceedings in the United States District Courts under sections 2254 and 2255 of Title 28, United States Code, took effect on August 1, 1982, as scheduled.

3 The President has urged Congress to act promptly. See President's Statement on Signing H.R. 6663 into Law, 18 Weekly Comp. of Pres. Doc. 982 (August 2, 1982).

4 Where service of a summons is to be made upon a party who is neither an inhabitant of, nor found within, the state where the district court sits, subsection (e) authorizes service under a state statute or rule of court that provides for service upon such a party. This would authorize mail service if the state statute or rule of court provided for service by mail.

5 The Court's proposal authorized service by the Marshals Service in other situations. This authority, however, was not seen as thwarting the underlying policy of limiting the use of marshals. *See* Appendix II, at 16, 17 (Advisory Committee Note).

6 Appendix I, at 2 (letter of Assistant Attorney General Robert A. McConnell).

7 The provisions of H.R. 7154 conflict with 28 U.S.C. 569(b) because the latter is a broader command to marshals to serve all federal court

process. As a later statutory enactment, however, H.R. 7154 supersedes 28 U.S.C. 569(b), thereby achieving the goal of reducing the role of marshals.

8 Proposed Rule 4(d)(8) provided that "Service ... shall not be the basis for the entry of a default or a judgment by default unless the record contains a return receipt showing acceptance by the defendant or a returned envelope showing refusal of the process by the defendant." This provision reflects a desire to preclude default judgments on unclaimed mail. See Appendix II, at 7 (Report of the Committee on Rules of Practice and Procedure).

The interpretation of Rule 4(d)(8) to require a refusal of delivery in order to have a basis for a default judgment, while undoubtedly the interpretation intended and the interpretation that reaches the fairest result, may not be the only possible interpretation. Since a default judgment can be entered for defendant's failure to respond to the complaint once defendant has been served and the time to answer the complaint has run, it can be argued that a default judgment can be obtained where the mail was unclaimed because proposed subsection (j), which authorized dismissal of a complaint not served within 120 days, provided that mail service would be deemed made "on the date on which the process was accepted, refused, or *returned as unclaimed*" (emphasis added).

9 *See* p. 15 infra.

10 Proponents of the California system of mail service, in particular, saw no reason to supplant California's proven method of mail service with a certified mail service that they believed likely to result in default judgments without actual notice to defendants. See House Report No. 97–662, at 3 (1982).

11 The parties may, of course, stipulate to service, as is frequently done now.

12 While return of the letter as unclaimed was deemed service for the purpose of determining whether the plaintiff's action could be dismissed, return of the letter as unclaimed was not service for the purpose of entry of a default judgment against the defendant. See note 8 supra.

13 The law governing the tolling of a statute of limitation depends upon the type of civil action involved. In a diversity action, state law governs tolling. *Walker v. Armco Steel Corp.,* 446 U.S. 740 (1980). In *Walker,* plaintiff had filed his complaint and thereby commenced the action under Rule 3 of the Federal Rules of Civil Procedure within the statutory period. He did not, however, serve the summons and complaint until after the statutory period had run. The Court held that state law (which required both filing and service within the statutory period) governed, barring plaintiff's action.

In the federal question action, the courts of appeals have generally held that Rule 3 governs, so that the filing of the complaint tolls a statute of limitation. *United States v. Wahl,* 538 F.2d 285 (6th Cir. 1978); *Windbrooke Dev. Co. v. Environmental Enterprises Inc. of Fla.,* 524 F.2d 461 (5th Cir. 1975); *Metropolitan Paving Co. v. International Union of Operating Engineers,* 439 F.2d 300 (10th Cir. 1971); *Moore Co. v. Sid Richardson Carbon & Gasoline Co.,* 347 F.2d 921 (8th Cir.), cert. denied, 383 U.S. 925, reh. denied, 384 U.S. 914 (1965); *Hoffman v. Halden,* 268 F.2d 280 (9th Cir. 1959). The continued validity of this line of cases, however, must be questioned in light of the *Walker* case, even though the Court in that case expressly reserved judgment about federal question actions, *see Walker v. Armco Steel Corp.,* 446 U.S. 741, 751 n.11 (1980).

14 The same result obtains even if service occurs within the 120 day period, if the service occurs after the statute of limitation has run.

15 See p. 19 infra.

16 See p. 17 infra.

17 Rule 45(c) provides that "A subpoena may be served by the marshal, by his deputy, or by any other person who is not a party and is not less than 18 years of age."

18 Some litigators have voiced concern that there may be situations in which personal service by someone other than a member of the Marshals Service may present a risk of injury to the person attempting to make the service. For example, a hostile defendant may have a history of injuring persons attempting to serve process. Federal judges undoubtedly will consider the risk of harm to private persons who would be making personal service when deciding whether to order the Marshals Service to make service under Rule 4(c)(2)(B)(iii).

19 The methods of service authorized by Rule 4(c)(2)(C) may be invoked by any person seeking to effect service. Thus, a nonparty adult who receives the summons and complaint for service under Rule 4(c)(1) may serve them personally or by mail in the manner authorized by Rule 4(c)(2)(C)(ii). Similarly, the Marshals Service may utilize the mail service authorized by Rule 4(c)(2)(C)(ii) when serving a summons and complaint under Rule 4(c)(2)(B)(i)(iii). When serving a summons and complaint under Rule 4(c)(2)(B)(ii), however, the Marshals Service must serve in the manner set forth in the court's order. If no particular manner of service is specified, then the Marshals Service may utilize Rule 4(c)(2)(C)(ii). It would not seem to be appropriate, however, for the Marshals Service to utilize Rule 4(c)(2)(C)(ii) in a situation where a previous attempt to serve by mail failed. Thus, it would not seem to be appropriate for the Marshals Service to attempt service by regular mail when serving a summons and complaint on behalf of a plaintiff who is proceeding in forma pauperis if that plaintiff previously attempted unsuccessfully to serve the defendant by mail.

20 To obtain service by personnel of the Marshals Service or someone specially appointed by the court, a plaintiff who has unsuccessfully attempted mail service under Rule 4(c)(2)(C)(ii) must meet the conditions of Rule 4(c)(2)(B)—for example, the plaintiff must be proceeding *in forma pauperis.*

21 For example, the sender must state the date of mailing on the form. If the form is not returned to the sender within 20 days of that date, then the plaintiff must serve the defendant in another manner and the defendant may be liable for the costs of such service. Thus, a defendant would suffer the consequences of a misstatement about the date of mailing.

22 See p. 12 supra.

23 The 120 day period begins to run upon the filing of each complaint. Thus, where a defendant files a cross-claim against the plaintiff, the 120 day period begins to run upon the filing of the cross-complaint, not upon the filing of the plaintiff's complaint initiating the action.

24 The person who may move to dismiss can be the putative defendant (i.e., the person named as defendant in the complaint filed with the court) or, in multi-party actions, another party to the action. (If the putative defendant moves to dismiss and the failure to effect service is due to that person's evasion of service, a court should not dismiss because the plaintiff has "good cause" for not completing service.)

25 See Cal.Civ.Pro. § 415.30 (West 1973).

26 See p. 16 supra.

TREATIES AND CONVENTIONS

Convention On The Service Abroad Of Judicial And Extrajudicial Documents In Civil Or Commercial Matters

The States signatory to the present Convention,

Desiring to create appropriate means to ensure that judicial and extrajudicial documents to be served abroad shall be brought to the notice of the addressee in sufficient time,

Desiring to improve the organisation of mutual judicial assistance for that purpose by simplifying and expediting the procedure,

Have resolved to conclude a Convention to this effect and have agreed upon the following provisions:

Article 1

The present Convention shall apply in all cases, in civil or commercial matters, where there is occasion to transmit a judicial or extrajudicial document for service abroad.

This Convention shall not apply where the address of the person to be served with the document is not known.

CHAPTER I—JUDICIAL DOCUMENTS

Article 2

Each contracting State shall designate a Central Authority which will undertake to receive requests for service coming from other contracting States and to proceed in conformity with the provisions of articles 3 to 6.

Each State shall organise the Central Authority in conformity with its own law.

Article 3

The authority or judicial officer competent under the law of the State in which the documents originate shall forward to the Central Authority of the State addressed a request conforming to the model annexed to the present Convention, without any requirement of legalisation or other equivalent formality.

The document to be served or a copy thereof shall be annexed to the request. The request and the document shall both be furnished in duplicate.

Article 4

If the Central Authority considers that the request does not comply with the provisions of the present Convention it shall promptly inform the applicant and specify its objections to the request.

Article 5

The Central Authority of the State addressed shall itself serve the document or shall arrange to have it served by an appropriate agency, either—

(a) by a method prescribed by its internal law for the service of documents in domestic actions upon persons who are within its territory, or

(b) by a particular method requested by the applicant, unless such a method is incompatible with the law of the State addressed.

Subject to sub-paragraph (b) of the first paragraph of this article, the document may always be served by delivery to an addressee who accepts it voluntarily.

If the document is to be served under the first paragraph above, the Central Authority may require the document to be written in, or translated into, the official language or one of the official languages of the State addressed.

That part of the request, in the form attached to the present Convention, which contains a summary of the document to be served, shall be served with the document.

Article 6

The Central Authority of the State addressed or any authority which it may have designated for that purpose, shall complete a certificate in the form of the model annexed to the present Convention.

The certificate shall state that the document has been served and shall include the method, the place and the date of service and the person to whom the document was delivered. If the document has not been served, the certificate shall set out the reasons which have prevented service.

The applicant may require that a certificate not completed by a Central Authority or by a judicial authority shall be countersigned by one of these authorities.

The certificate shall be forwarded directly to the applicant.

Article 7

The standard terms in the model annexed to the present Convention shall in all cases be written either in French or in English. They may also be written in the official language, or in one of the official languages, of the State in which the documents originate.

The corresponding blanks shall be completed either in the language of the State addressed or in French or in English.

Article 8

Each contracting State shall be free to effect service of judicial documents upon persons abroad, without application of any compulsion, directly through its diplomatic or consular agents.

Any State may declare that it is opposed to such service within its territory, unless the document is to be served upon a national of the State in which the documents originate.

Article 9

Each contracting State shall be free, in addition, to use consular channels to forward documents, for the purpose of service, to those authorities of another contracting State which are designated by the latter for this purpose.

Each contracting State may, if exceptional circumstances so require, use diplomatic channels for the same purpose.

Article 10

Provided the State of destination does not object, the present Convention shall not interfere with—

(a) the freedom to send judicial documents, by postal channels, directly to persons abroad,

(b) the freedom of judicial officers, officials or other competent persons of the State of origin to effect service of judicial documents directly through the judicial officers, officials or other competent persons of the State of destination,

(c) the freedom of any person interested in a judicial proceeding to effect service of judicial documents directly through the judicial officers, officials or other competent persons of the State of destination.

Article 11

The present Convention shall not prevent two or more contracting States from agreeing to permit, for the purpose of service of judicial documents, channels of transmission other than those provided for in the preceding articles and, in particular, direct communication between their respective authorities.

Article 12

The service of judicial documents coming from a contracting State shall not give rise to any payment or reimbursement of taxes or costs for the services rendered by the State addressed.

The applicant shall pay or reimburse the costs occasioned by—

(a) the employment of a judicial officer or of a person competent under the law of the State of destination,

(b) the use of a particular method of service.

Article 13

Where a request for service complies with the terms of the present Convention, the State addressed may refuse to comply therewith only if it deems that compliance would infringe its sovereignty or security.

It may not refuse to comply solely on the ground that, under its internal law, it claims exclusive jurisdiction over the subject-matter of the action or that its internal law would not permit the action upon which the application is based.

The Central Authority shall, in case of refusal, promptly inform the applicant and state the reasons for the refusal.

Article 14

Difficulties which may arise in connection with the transmission of judicial documents for service shall be settled through diplomatic channels.

Article 15

Where a writ of summons or an equivalent document had to be transmitted abroad for the purpose of service, under the provisions of the present Convention, and the defendant has not appeared, judgment shall not be given until it is established that—

(a) the document was served by a method prescribed by the internal law of the State addressed for the service of documents in domestic actions upon persons who are within its territory, or

(b) the document was actually delivered to the defendant or to his residence by another method provided for by this Convention,

and that in either of these cases the service or the delivery was effected in sufficient time to enable the defendant to defend.

Each contracting State shall be free to declare that the judge, notwithstanding the provisions of the first paragraph of this article, may give judgment even if no certificate of service or delivery has been received, if all the following conditions are fulfilled—

(a) the document was transmitted by one of the methods provided for in this Convention,

(b) a period of time of not less than six months, considered adequate by the judge in the particular case, has elapsed since the date of the transmission of the document,

(c) no certificate of any kind has been received, even though every reasonable effort has been made to obtain it through the competent authorities of the State addressed.

Notwithstanding the provisions of the preceding paragraphs the judge may order, in case of urgency, any provisional or protective measures.

Article 16

When a writ of summons or an equivalent document had to be transmitted abroad for the purpose of service, under the provisions of the present Convention, and a judgment has been entered against a defendant who has not appeared, the judge shall have the power to relieve the defendant from the effects of the expiration of the time for appeal from the judgment if the following conditions are fulfilled—

(a) the defendant, without any fault on his part, did not have knowledge of the document in sufficient time to defend, or knowledge of the judgment in sufficient time to appeal, and

(b) the defendant has disclosed a *prima facie* defense to the action on the merits.

An application for relief may be filed only within a reasonable time after the defendant has knowledge of the judgment.

Each contracting State may declare that the application will not be entertained if it is filed after the expiration of a time to be stated in the declaration, but which shall in no case be less than one year following the date of the judgment.

This article shall not apply to judgments concerning status or capacity of persons.

CHAPTER II—EXTRAJUDICIAL DOCUMENTS

Article 17

Extrajudicial documents emanating from authorities and judicial officers of a contracting State may be transmitted for the purpose of service in another contracting State by the methods and under the provisions of the present Convention.

CHAPTER III—GENERAL CLAUSES

Article 18

Each contracting State may designate other authorities in addition to the Central Authority and shall determine the extent of their competence.

The applicant shall, however, in all cases, have the right to address a request directly to the Central Authority.

Federal States shall be free to designate more than one Central Authority.

Article 19

To the extent that the internal law of a contracting State permits methods of transmission, other than those provided for in the preceding articles, of documents coming from abroad, for service within its territory, the present Convention shall not affect such provisions.

Article 20

The present Convention shall not prevent an agreement between any two or more contracting States to dispense with—

(a) the necessity for duplicate copies of transmitted documents as required by the second paragraph of article 3,

(b) the language requirements of the third paragraph of article 5 and article 7,

(c) the provisions of the fourth paragraph of article 5,

(d) the provisions of the second paragraph of article 12.

Article 21

Each contracting State shall, at the time of the deposit of its instrument of ratification or accession, or at a later date, inform the Ministry of Foreign Affairs of the Netherlands of the following—

(a) the designation of authorities, pursuant to articles 2 and 18,

(b) the designation of the authority competent to complete the certificate pursuant to article 6,

(c) the designation of the authority competent to receive documents transmitted by consular channels, pursuant to article 9.

Each contracting State shall similarly inform the Ministry, where appropriate, of—

(a) opposition to the use of methods of transmission pursuant to articles 8 and 10,

(b) declarations pursuant to the second paragraph of article 15 and the third paragraph of article 16,

(c) all modifications of the above designations, oppositions and declarations.

Article 22

Where Parties to the present Convention are also Parties to one or both of the Conventions on civil procedure signed at The Hague on 17th July 1905 [99 BFSP 990], and on 1st March 1954 [286 UNTS 265], this Convention shall replace as between them articles 1 to 7 of the earlier Conventions.

Article 23

The present Convention shall not affect the application of article 23 of the Convention on civil procedure signed at The Hague on 17th July 1905, or of article 24 of the Convention on civil procedure signed at The Hague on 1st March 1954.

These articles shall, however, apply only if methods of communication, identical to those provided for in these Conventions, are used.

Article 24

Supplementary agreements between parties to the Conventions of 1905 and 1954 shall be considered as equally applicable to the present Convention, unless the Parties have otherwise agreed.

Article 25

Without prejudice to the provisions of articles 22 and 24, the present Convention shall not derogate from Conventions containing provisions on the matters governed by this Convention to which the contracting States are, or shall become, Parties.

Article 26

The present Convention shall be open for signature by the States represented at the Tenth Session of the Hague Conference on Private International Law.

It shall be ratified, and the instruments of ratification shall be deposited with the Ministry of Foreign Affairs of the Netherlands.

Article 27

The present Convention shall enter into force on the sixtieth day after the deposit of the third instrument of ratification referred to in the second paragraph of article 26.

The Convention shall enter into force for each signatory State which ratifies subsequently on the sixtieth day after the deposit of its instrument of ratification.

Article 28

Any State not represented at the Tenth Session of the Hague Conference on Private International Law may accede to the present Convention after it has entered into force in accordance with the first paragraph of article 27. The instrument of accession shall be deposited with the Ministry of Foreign Affairs of the Netherlands.

The Convention shall enter into force for such a State in the absence of any objection from a State, which has ratified the Convention before such deposit, notified to the Ministry of Foreign Affairs of the Netherlands within a period of six months after the date on which the said Ministry has notified it of such accession.

In the absence of any such objection, the Convention shall enter into force for the acceding State on the first day of the month following the expiration of the last of the periods referred to in the preceding paragraph.

Article 29

Any State may, at the time of signature, ratification or accession, declare that the present Convention shall extend to all the territories for the international relations of which it is responsible, or to one or more of them. Such a declaration shall take effect on the date of entry into force of the Convention for the State concerned.

At any time thereafter, such extensions shall be notified to the Ministry of Foreign Affairs of the Netherlands.

The Convention shall enter into force for the territories mentioned in such an extension on the sixtieth day after the notification referred to in the preceding paragraph.

Article 30

The present Convention shall remain in force for five years from the date of its entry into force in accordance with the first paragraph of article 27, even for States which have ratified it or acceded to it subsequently.

If there has been no denunciation, it shall be renewed tacitly every five years.

Any denunciation shall be notified to the Ministry of Foreign Affairs of the Netherlands at least six months before the end of the five year period.

It may be limited to certain of the territories to which the Convention applies.

The denunciation shall have effect only as regards the State which has notified it. The Convention shall remain in force for the other contracting States.

Article 31

The Ministry of Foreign Affairs of the Netherlands shall give notice to the States referred to in article 26, and to the States which have acceded in accordance with article 28, of the following—

(a) the signatures and ratifications referred to in article 26;

(b) the date on which the present Convention enters into force in accordance with the first paragraph of article 27;

(c) the accessions referred to in article 28 and the dates on which they take effect;

(d) the extensions referred to in article 29 and the dates on which they take effect;

(e) the designations, oppositions and declarations referred to in article 21;

(f) the denunciations referred to in the third paragraph of article 30.

IN WITNESS WHEREOF the undersigned, being duly authorised thereto, have signed the present Convention.

DONE at The Hague, on the 15th day of November, 1965, in the English and French languages, both texts being equally authentic, in a single copy which shall be deposited in the archives of the Government of the Netherlands, and of which a certified copy shall be sent, through the diplomatic channel, to each of The States represented at the Tenth Session of the Hague Conference on Private International Law.

[Signatures omitted.]

Service of Documents Convention
ANNEX TO THE CONVENTION

Forms *

* These forms may be obtained from the Offices of United States Marshals.

REQUEST
FOR SERVICE ABROAD OF JUDICIAL OR EXTRAJUDICIAL DOCUMENTS

Convention on the service abroad of judicial and extrajudicial documents in civil or commercial matters, signed at The Hague, November 15, 1965.

Identity and address of the applicant

Address of receiving authority

The undersigned applicant has the honour to transmit—in duplicate—the documents listed below and, in conformity with article 5 of the above-mentioned Convention, requests prompt service of one copy thereof on the addressee, i.e., (identity and address) .....
.....

(*a*) in accordance with the provisions of sub-paragraph (*a*) of the first paragraph of article 5 of the Convention*.

(*b*) in accordance with the following particular method (sub-paragraph (*b*) of the first paragraph of article 5)*:
.....
.....
.....

(*c*) by delivery to the addressee, if he accepts it voluntarily (second paragraph of article 5)*.

The authority is requested to return or to have returned to the applicant a copy of the documents—and of the annexes*—with a certificate as provided on the reverse side.

List of documents
.....
.....
.....
.....
.....
.....
.....

Done at .....,
the .....
.....
.....

Signature and/or stamp.

* Delete if inappropriate.

Reverse of the request

CERTIFICATE

The undersigned authority has the honour to certify, in conformity with article 6 of the Convention,

1) that the document has been served *
— the (date) .....
— at (place, street, number) .....
.....
— in one of the following methods authorised by article 5—

(*a*) in accordance with the provisions of sub-paragraph (*a*) of the first paragraph of article 5 of the Convention*.

(*b*) in accordance with the following particular method *: .....
.....

(*c*) by delivery to the addressee, who accepted it voluntarily*.

The documents referred to in the request have been delivered to:
—(identity and description of person) .....
.....
—relationship to the addressee (family, business or other) .
.....

2) that the document has not been served, by reason of the following facts*:
.....
.....
.....

In conformity with the second paragraph of article 12 of the Convention, the applicant is requested to pay or reimburse the expenses detailed in the attached statement *.

Annexes

Documents returned: .....
.....
.....
.....
..... Done at ....., the .....

In appropriate cases, documents establishing the service:
.....
.....
..... Signature and/or stamp.

*Delete if inappropriate.

SUMMARY OF THE DOCUMENT TO BE SERVED

Convention on the service abroad of judicial and extrajudicial documents in civil or commercial matters, signed at The Hague, the 15th of November 1965.

(article 5, fourth paragraph)

Name and address of the requesting authority: .....

.....

.....

Particulars of the parties*:

.....

.....

.....

JUDICIAL DOCUMENT **

Nature and purpose of the document:

.....

.....

.....

Nature and purpose of the proceedings and, where appropriate, the amount in dispute: .....

Date and place for entering appearance**:

.....

.....

Court which has given judgment **:

.....

.....

Date of judgment **: .....

Time limits stated in the document **:

.....

.....

EXTRAJUDICIAL DOCUMENT **

Nature and purpose of the document:

.....

.....

.....

Time limits stated in the document **:

.....

.....

.....

* If appropriate, identity and address of the person interested in the transmission of the document.

** Delete if inappropriate.

Convention on the service abroad of judicial and extrajudicial documents in civil or commercial matters. Done at The Hague November 15, 1965; entered into force for the United States February 10, 1969. 20 UST 361; TIAS 6638; 658 UNTS 163.

Notes and Annotations to the Convention

Litigants wishing to serve a person in one of the Convention countries should request copies in duplicate of the three forms prescribed by the Convention: the "Request", the "Certificate" and the "Summary." These forms may be obtained from the offices of the United States Marshals. Upon completion of these forms, the litigants must then transmit them, together with the documents to be served—all in duplicate—to the local process server.

The local process server thereupon mails all these documents to the "Central Authority" abroad. After service has been effected, one copy of the documents served and an executed "Certificate" all be returned to the local process server, who will transmit these documents to the litigant who initiated the request.

—— Annotations

"The Effect of the Hague Convention on Service Abroad of Judicial and Extrajudicial Documents in Civil or Commercial Matters", 2 Cornell Int'l L.J. 125 (1969).

Julen v. Larson, 25 Cal.App.3d 325, 101 Cal. 796 (1972).

Shoei Kako Co., Ltd. v. Superior Court, 33 Cal.App.3d 808, 109 Cal. 402 (1973).

Rule 4.1. Serving Other Process

(a) In General. Process—other than a summons under Rule 4 or a subpoena under Rule 45—must be served by a United States marshal or deputy marshal or by a person specially appointed for that purpose. It may be served anywhere within the territorial limits of the state where the district court is located and, if authorized by a federal statute, beyond those limits. Proof of service must be made under Rule 4(*l*).

(b) Enforcing Orders: Committing for Civil Contempt. An order committing a person for civil contempt of a decree or injunction issued to enforce federal law may be served and enforced in any district. Any other order in a civil-contempt proceeding may be served only in the state where the issuing court is located or elsewhere in the United States within 100 miles from where the order was issued.

(Adopted April 22, 1993, effective December 1, 1993; amended April 30, 2007, effective December 1, 2007.)

ADVISORY COMMITTEE NOTES

1993 Adoption

This is a new rule. Its purpose is to separate those few provisions of the former Rule 4 bearing on matters other than service of a summons to allow greater textual clarity in Rule 4. Subdivision (a) contains no new language.

Subdivision (b) replaces the final clause of the penultimate sentence of the former subdivision 4(f), a clause added to the rule in 1963. The new rule provides for nationwide service of orders of civil commitment enforcing decrees of injunctions issued to compel compliance with federal law. The rule makes no change in the practice with respect to the enforcement of injunctions or decrees not involving the enforcement of federally-created rights.

Service of process is not required to notify a party of a decree or injunction, or of an order that the party show cause why that party should not be held in contempt of such an order. With respect to a party who has once been served with a summons, the service of the decree or injunction itself or of an order to show cause can be made pursuant to Rule 5.

Thus, for example, an injunction may be served on a party through that person's attorney. *Chagas v. United States,* 369 F.2d 643 (5th Cir.1966). The same is true for service of an order to show cause. *Waffenschmidt v. Mackay,* 763 F.2d 711 (5th Cir.1985).

The new rule does not affect the reach of the court to impose criminal contempt sanctions. Nationwide enforcement of federal decrees and injunctions is already available with respect to criminal contempt: a federal court may effect the arrest of a criminal contemnor anywhere in the United States, 28 U.S.C. § 3041, and a contemnor when arrested may be subject to removal to the district in which punishment may be imposed. Fed.R.Crim.P. 40. Thus, the present law permits criminal contempt enforcement against a contemnor wherever that person may be found.

The effect of the revision is to provide a choice of civil or criminal contempt sanctions in those situations to which it applies. Contempt proceedings, whether civil or criminal, must be brought in the court that was allegedly defied by a contumacious act. *Ex parte Bradley,* 74 U.S. 366 (1869). This is so even if the offensive conduct or inaction occurred outside the district of the court in which the enforcement proceeding must be conducted. *E.g., McCourtney v. United States,* 291 Fed. 497 (8th Cir.), *cert. denied,* 263 U.S. 714 (1923). For this purpose, the rule as before does not distinguish between parties and other persons subject to contempt sanctions by reason of their relation or connection to parties.

2007 Amendment

The language of Rule 4.1 has been amended as part of the general restyling of the Civil Rules to make them more easily understood and to make style and terminology consistent throughout the rules. These changes are intended to be stylistic only.

Rule 5. Serving and Filing Pleadings and Other Papers

(a) Service: When Required.

(1) ***In General.*** Unless these rules provide otherwise, each of the following papers must be served on every party:

(A) an order stating that service is required;

(B) a pleading filed after the original complaint, unless the court orders otherwise under Rule 5(c) because there are numerous defendants;

(C) a discovery paper required to be served on a party, unless the court orders otherwise;

(D) a written motion, except one that may be heard ex parte; and

(E) a written notice, appearance, demand, or offer of judgment, or any similar paper.

(2) ***If a Party Fails to Appear.*** No service is required on a party who is in default for failing to appear. But a pleading that asserts a new claim for relief against such a party must be served on that party under Rule 4.

(3) ***Seizing Property.*** If an action is begun by seizing property and no person is or need be named as a defendant, any service required before the filing of an appearance, answer, or claim must be made on the person who had custody or possession of the property when it was seized.

(b) Service: How Made.

(1) ***Serving an Attorney.*** If a party is represented by an attorney, service under this rule must be made on the attorney unless the court orders service on the party.

(2) ***Service in General.*** A paper is served under this rule by:

(A) handing it to the person;

(B) leaving it:

(i) at the person's office with a clerk or other person in charge or, if no one is in charge, in a conspicuous place in the office; or

(ii) if the person has no office or the office is closed, at the person's dwelling or usual place of abode with someone of suitable age and discretion who resides there;

(C) mailing it to the person's last known address—in which event service is complete upon mailing;

(D) leaving it with the court clerk if the person has no known address;

(E) sending it by electronic means if the person consented in writing—in which event service is complete upon transmission, but is not effective if the serving party learns that it did not reach the person to be served; or

(F) delivering it by any other means that the person consented to in writing—in which event service is complete when the person making service delivers it to the agency designated to make delivery.

(3) ***Using Court Facilities.*** If a local rule so authorizes, a party may use the court's transmission facilities to make service under Rule 5(b)(2)(E).

(c) Serving Numerous Defendants.

(1) ***In General.*** If an action involves an unusually large number of defendants, the court may, on motion or on its own, order that:

(A) defendants' pleadings and replies to them need not be served on other defendants;

(B) any crossclaim, counterclaim, avoidance, or affirmative defense in those pleadings and replies to them will be treated as denied or avoided by all other parties; and

(C) filing any such pleading and serving it on the plaintiff constitutes notice of the pleading to all parties.

(2) ***Notifying Parties.*** A copy of every such order must be served on the parties as the court directs.

(d) Filing.

(1) ***Required Filings; Certificate of Service.*** Any paper after the complaint that is required to be served—together with a certificate of service—must be filed within a reasonable time after service. But disclosures under Rule 26(a)(1) or (2) and the following discovery requests and responses must not be filed until they are used in the proceeding or the court orders filing: depositions, interrogatories, requests for documents or tangible things or to permit entry onto land, and requests for admission.

(2) ***How Filing Is Made—In General.*** A paper is filed by delivering it:

(A) to the clerk; or

(B) to a judge who agrees to accept it for filing, and who must then note the filing date on the paper and promptly send it to the clerk.

(3) ***Electronic Filing, Signing, or Verification.*** A court may, by local rule, allow papers to be filed, signed, or verified by electronic means that are consistent with any technical standards established by the Judicial Conference of the United States. A local rule may require electronic filing only if reasonable exceptions are allowed. A paper filed electronically in compliance with a local rule is a written paper for purposes of these rules.

(4) ***Acceptance by the Clerk.*** The clerk must not refuse to file a paper solely because it is not in the form prescribed by these rules or by a local rule or practice.

(Amended January 21, 1963, effective July 1, 1963; March 30, 1970, effective July 1, 1970; April 29, 1980, effective August 1, 1980; March 2, 1987, effective August 1, 1987; April 30, 1991, effective December 1, 1991; April 22, 1993, effective December 1, 1993; April 23, 1996, effective December 1, 1996; April 17, 2000, effective December 1, 2000; April 23, 2001, effective December 1, 2001; April 12, 2006, effective December 1, 2006; April 30, 2007, effective December 1, 2007.)

ADVISORY COMMITTEE NOTES

1937 Adoption

Note to Subdivisions (a) and (b). Compare 2 Minn.Stat. (1927) §§ 9240, 9241, 9242; N.Y.C.P.A. (1937) §§ 163, 164 and N.Y.R.C.P. (1937) Rules 20, 21; 2 Wash.Rev.Stat.Ann. (Remington, 1932) §§ 244 to 249.

Note to Subdivision (d). Compare the present practice under former Equity Rule 12 (Issue of Subpoena—Time for Answer).

1963 Amendment

The words "affected thereby," stricken out by the amendment, introduced a problem of interpretation. See 1 Barron & Holtzoff, *Federal Practice & Procedure* 760–61 (Wright ed. 1960). The amendment eliminates this difficulty and promotes full exchange of information among the parties by requiring service of papers on all the parties to the action, except as otherwise provided in the rules. See also subdivision (c) of Rule 5. So, for example, a third-party defendant is required to serve his answer to the third-party complaint not only upon the defendant but also upon the plaintiff. See amended Form 22–A and the Advisory Committee's Note thereto.

As to the method of serving papers upon a party whose address is unknown, see Rule 5(b).

1970 Amendment

The amendment makes clear that all papers relating to discovery which are required to be served on any party must be served on all parties, unless the court orders otherwise. The present language expressly includes notices and demands, but it is not explicit as to answers or responses as provided in Rules 33, 34, and 36. Discovery papers may be voluminous or the parties numerous, and the court is empowered to vary the requirement if in a given case it proves needlessly onerous.

In actions begun by seizure of property, service will at times have to be made before the absent owner of the property has filed an appearance. For example, a prompt deposition may be needed in a maritime action in rem. See Rules 30(a) and 30(b)(2) and the related notes. A provision is added authorizing service on the person having custody or possession of the property at the time of its seizure.

1980 Amendment

Subdivision (d). By the terms of this rule and Rule 30(f)(1) discovery materials must be promptly filed, although it often happens that no use is made of the materials after they are filed. Because the copies required for filing are an added expense and the large volume of discovery filings presents serious problems of storage in some districts, the Committee in 1978 first proposed that discovery materials not be filed unless on order of the court or for use in the proceedings. But such materials are sometimes of interest to those who may have no access to them except by a requirement of filing, such as members of a class, litigants similarly situated, or the public generally. Accordingly, this amendment and a change in Rule 30(f)(1) continue the requirement of filing but make it subject to an order of the court that discovery materials not be filed unless filing is requested by the court or is effected by parties who wish to use the materials in the proceeding.

1987 Amendment

The amendments are technical. No substantive change is intended.

1991 Amendment

Subdivision (d). This subdivision is amended to require that the person making service under the rule certify that service has been effected. Such a requirement has generally been imposed by local rule.

Having such information on file may be useful for many purposes, including proof of service if an issue arises concerning the effectiveness of the service. The certificate will generally specify the date as well as the manner of service, but parties employing private delivery services may sometimes be unable to specify the date of delivery. In the latter circumstance, a specification of the date of transmission of the paper to the delivery service may be sufficient for the purposes of this rule.

Subdivision (e). The words *"pleading and other"* are stricken as unnecessary. Pleadings are papers within the meaning of the rule. The revision also accommodates the development of the use of facsimile transmission for filing.

Several local district rules have directed the office of the clerk to refuse to accept for filing papers not conforming to certain requirements of form imposed by local rules or practice. This is not a suitable role for the office of the clerk, and the practice exposes litigants to the hazards of time bars; for these reasons, such rules are proscribed by this revision. The enforcement of these rules and of the local rules is a role for a judicial officer. A clerk may of course advise a party or counsel that a particular instrument is not in proper form, and may be directed to so inform the court.

1993 Amendments

This is a technical amendment, using the broader language of Rule 25 of the Federal Rules of Appellate Procedure. The district court—and the bankruptcy court by virtue of a cross-reference in Bankruptcy Rule 7005—can, by local rule, permit filing not only by facsimile transmissions but also by other electronic means, subject to standards approved by the Judicial Conference.

1996 Amendments

The present Rule 5(e) has authorized filing by facsimile or other electronic means on two conditions. The filing must be authorized by local rule. Use of this means of filing must be authorized by the Judicial Conference of the United States and must be consistent with standards established by the Judicial Conference. Attempts to develop Judicial Conference standards have demonstrated the value of several adjustments in the rule.

The most significant change discards the requirement that the Judicial Conference authorize local electronic filing rules. As before, each district may decide for itself whether it has the equipment and personnel required to establish electronic filing, but a district that wishes to establish electronic filing need no longer await Judicial Conference action.

The role of Judicial Conference standards is clarified by specifying that the standards are to govern technical matters. Technical standards can provide nationwide uniformity, enabling ready use of electronic filing without pausing to adjust for the otherwise inevitable variations among local rules. Judicial Conference adoption of technical standards should prove superior to specification in these rules. Electronic technology has advanced with great speed. The process of adopting Judicial Conference standards should prove speedier and more flexible in determining the time for the first uniform standards, in adjusting standards at appropriate intervals, and in sparing the Supreme Court and Congress the need to consider technological details. Until Judicial Conference standards are adopted, however, uniformity will occur only to the extent that local rules deliberately seek to copy other local rules.

It is anticipated that Judicial Conference standards will govern such technical specifications as data formatting, speed of transmission, means to transmit copies of supporting documents, and security of communication. Perhaps more important, standards must be established to assure proper maintenance and integrity of the record and to provide appropriate access and retrieval mechanisms. Local rules must address these issues until Judicial Conference standards are adopted.

The amended rule also makes clear the equality of filing by electronic means with written filings. An electronic filing that complies with the local rule satisfies all requirements for filing on paper, signature, or verification. An electronic filing that otherwise satisfies the requirements of 28 U.S.C. § 1746 need not be separately made in writing. Public access to electronic filings is governed by the same rules as govern written filings.

The separate reference to filing by facsimile transmission is deleted. Facsimile transmission continues to be included as an electronic means.

2000 Amendment

Subdivision (d). Rule 5(d) is amended to provide that disclosures under Rule 26(a)(1) and (2), and discovery requests and responses under Rules 30, 31, 33, 34, and 36 must not be filed until they are used in the action. "Discovery requests" includes deposition notices and "discovery responses" includes objections. The rule supersedes and invalidates local rules that forbid, permit, or require filing of these materials before they are used in the action. The former Rule 26(a)(4) requirement that disclosures under Rule 26(a)(1) and (2) be filed has been removed. Disclosures under Rule 26(a)(3), however, must be promptly filed as provided in Rule 26(a)(3). Filings in connection with Rule 35 examinations, which involve a motion proceeding when the parties do not agree, are unaffected by these amendments.

Recognizing the costs imposed on parties and courts by required filing of discovery materials that are never used in an action, Rule 5(d) was amended in 1980 to authorize court orders that excuse filing. Since then, many districts have adopted local rules that excuse or forbid filing. In 1989 the Judicial Conference Local Rules Project concluded that these local rules were inconsistent with Rule 5(d), but urged the Advisory Committee to consider amending the rule. *Local Rules Project* at 92 (1989). The Judicial Conference of the Ninth Circuit gave the Committee similar advice in 1997. The reality of nonfiling reflected in these local rules has even been assumed in drafting the national rules. In 1993, Rule 30(f)(1) was amended to direct that the officer presiding at a deposition file it with the court or send it to the attorney who arranged for the transcript or recording. The Committee

Note explained that this alternative to filing was designed for "courts which direct that depositions not be automatically filed." Rule 30(f)(1) has been amended to conform to this change in Rule 5(d).

Although this amendment is based on widespread experience with local rules, and confirms the results directed by these local rules, it is designed to supersede and invalidate local rules. There is no apparent reason to have different filing rules in different districts. Even if districts vary in present capacities to store filed materials that are not used in an action, there is little reason to continue expending court resources for this purpose. These costs and burdens would likely change as parties make increased use of audio- and videotaped depositions. Equipment to facilitate review and reproduction of such discovery materials may prove costly to acquire, maintain, and operate.

The amended rule provides that discovery materials and disclosures under Rule 26(a)(1) and (a)(2) must not be filed until they are "used in the proceeding." This phrase is meant to refer to proceedings in court. This filing requirement is not triggered by "use" of discovery materials in other discovery activities, such as depositions. In connection with proceedings in court, however, the rule is to be interpreted broadly; any use of discovery materials in court in connection with a motion, a pretrial conference under Rule 16, or otherwise, should be interpreted as use in the proceeding.

Once discovery or disclosure materials are used in the proceeding, the filing requirements of Rule 5(d) should apply to them. But because the filing requirement applies only with regard to materials that are used, only those parts of voluminous materials that are actually used need be filed. Any party would be free to file other pertinent portions of materials that are so used. *See* Fed. R. Evid. 106; *cf.* Rule 32(a)(4). If the parties are unduly sparing in their submissions, the court may order further filings. By local rule, a court could provide appropriate direction regarding the filing of discovery materials, such as depositions, that are used in proceedings.

"Shall" is replaced by "must" under the program to conform amended rules to current style conventions when there is no ambiguity.

GAP Report

The Advisory Committee recommends no changes to either the amendments to Rule 5(d) or the Committee Note as published.

2001 Amendments

Rule 5(b) is restyled.

Rule 5(b)(1) makes it clear that the provision for service on a party's attorney applies only to service made under Rules 5(a) and 77(d). Service under Rules 4, 4.1, 45(b), and 71A(d)(3)—as well as rules that invoke those rules—must be made as provided in those rules.

Subparagraphs (A), (B), and (C) of Rule 5(b)(2) carry forward the method-of-service provisions of former Rule 5(b).

Subparagraph (D) of Rule 5(b)(2) is new. It authorizes service by electronic means or any other means, but only if consent is obtained from the person served. The consent must be express, and cannot be implied from conduct. Early experience with electronic filing as authorized by Rule 5(d) is positive, supporting service by electronic means as well. Consent is required, however, because it is not yet possible to assume universal entry into the world of electronic communication. Subparagraph (D) also authorizes service by nonelectronic means. The Rule 5(b)(2)(B) provision making mail service complete on mailing is extended in subparagraph (D) to make service by electronic means complete on transmission; transmission is effected when the sender does the last act that must be performed by the sender. Service by other agencies is complete on delivery to the designated agency.

Finally, subparagraph (D) authorizes adoption of local rules providing for service through the court. Electronic case filing systems will come to include the capacity to make service by using the court's facilities to transmit all documents filed in the case. It may prove most efficient to establish an environment in which a party can file with the court, making use of the court's transmission facilities to serve the filed paper on all other parties. Transmission might be by such means as direct transmission of the paper, or by transmission of a notice of filing that includes an electronic link for direct access to the paper. Because service is under subparagraph (D), consent must be obtained from the persons served.

Consent to service under Rule 5(b)(2)(D) must be in writing, which can be provided by electronic means. Parties are encouraged to specify the scope and duration of the consent. The specification should include at least the persons to whom service should be made, the appropriate address or location for such service—such as the e-mail address or facsimile machine number, and the format to be used for attachments. A district court may establish a registry or other facility that allows advance consent to service by specified means for future actions.

Rule 6(e) is amended to allow additional time to respond when service is made under Rule 5(b)(2)(D). The additional time does not relieve a party who consents to service under Rule 5(b)(2)(D) of the responsibilities to monitor the facility designated for receiving service and to provide prompt notice of any address change.

Paragraph (3) addresses a question that may arise from a literal reading of the provision that service by electronic means is complete on transmission. Electronic communication is rapidly improving, but lawyers report continuing failures of transmission, particularly with respect to attachments. Ordinarily the risk of non-receipt falls on the person being served, who has consented to this form of service. But the risk should not extend to situations in which the person attempting service learns that the attempted service in fact did not reach the person to be served. Given actual knowledge that the attempt failed, service is not effected. The person attempting service must either try again or show circumstances that justify dispensing with service.

Paragraph (3) does not address the similar questions that may arise when a person attempting service learns that service by means other than electronic means in fact did not reach the person to be served. Case law provides few illustrations of circumstances in which a person attempting service actually knows that the attempt failed but seeks to act as if service had been made. This negative history suggests there is no need to address these problems in Rule 5(b)(3). This silence does not imply any view on these issues, nor on the circumstances that justify various forms of judicial action even though service has not been made.

Changes Made After Publication and Comments

Rule 5(b)(2)(D) was changed to require that consent be "in writing."

Rule 5(b)(3) is new. The published proposal did not address the question of failed service in the text of the rule. Instead, the Committee Note included this statement: "As with other modes of service, however, actual notice that the transmission was not received defeats the presumption of receipt that arises from the provision that service is complete on transmission. The sender must take additional steps to effect service. Service by other agencies is complete on delivery to the designated agency." The addition of paragraph (3) was prompted by consideration of the draft Appellate Rule 25(c) that was prepared for the meeting of the Appellate Rules Advisory Committee. This draft provided: "Service by electronic means is complete on transmission, unless the party making service is notified that the paper was not received." Although Appellate Rule 25(c) is being prepared for publication and comment, while Civil Rule 5(b) has been published and otherwise is ready to recommend for adoption, it seemed desirable to achieve some parallel between the two rules.

The draft Rule 5(b)(3) submitted for consideration by the Advisory Committee covered all means of service except for leaving a copy with the clerk of the court when the person to be served has no known address. It was not limited to electronic service for fear that a provision limited to electronic service might generate unintended negative implications as to service by other means, particularly mail. This concern was strengthened by a small number of opinions that say that service by mail is effective, because complete on mailing, even when the person making service has prompt actual notice that the mail was not delivered. The Advisory Committee voted to limit Rule 5(b)(3) to service by electronic means because this means of service is relatively new, and seems likely to miscarry more frequently than service by post. It was suggested during the Advisory Committee meeting that the question of negative implication could be addressed in the Committee Note. There was little discussion of this possibility. The Committee Note submitted above includes a "no negative implications" paragraph prepared by the Reporter for consideration by the Standing Committee.

The Advisory Committee did not consider at all a question that was framed during the later meeting of the Appellate Rules Advisory Committee. As approved by the Advisory Committee, Rule 5(b)(3) defeats service by electronic means "if the party making service learns that the attempted service did not reach the person to be served." It says nothing about the time relevant to learning of the failure. The omission may seem glaring. Curing the omission, however, requires selection of a time. As revised, proposed Appellate Rule 25(c) requires that the party making service learn of the failure within three calendar days. The Appellate Rules Advisory Committee will have the luxury of public comment and another year to consider the desirability of this short period. If Civil Rule 5(b) is to be recommended for adoption now, no such luxury is available. This issue deserves careful consideration by the Standing Committee.

Several changes are made in the Committee Note. (1) It requires that consent "be express, and cannot be implied from conduct." This addition reflects a more general concern stimulated by a reported ruling that an e-mail address on a firm's letterhead implied consent to e-mail service. (2) The paragraph discussing service through the court's facilities is expanded by describing alternative methods, including an "electronic link." (3) There is a new paragraph that states that the requirement of written consent can be satisfied by electronic means, and that suggests matters that should be addressed by the consent. (4) A paragraph is added to note the additional response time provided by amended Rule 6(e). (5) The final two paragraphs address newly added Rule 5(b)(3). The first explains the rule that electronic service is not effective if the person making service learns that it did not reach the person to be served. The second paragraph seeks to defeat any negative implications that might arise from limiting Rule 5(b)(3) to electronic service, not mail, not other means consented to such as commercial express service, and not service on another person on behalf of the person to be served.

Rule 6(e)

The Advisory Committee recommended that no change be made in Civil Rule 6(e) to reflect the provisions of Civil Rule 5(b)(2)(D) that, with the consent of the person to be served, would allow service by electronic or other means. Absent change, service by these means would not affect the time for acting in response to the paper served. Comment was requested, however, on the alternative that would allow an additional 3 days to respond. The alternative Rule 6(e) amendments are cast in a form that permits ready incorporation in the Bankruptcy Rules. Several of the comments suggest that the added three days should be provided. Electronic transmission is not always instantaneous, and may fail for any of a number of reasons. It may take three days to arrange for transmission in readable form. Providing added time to respond will not discourage people from asking for consent to electronic transmission, and may encourage people to give consent. The more who consent, the quicker will come the improvements that will make electronic service ever more attractive. Consistency with the Bankruptcy Rules will be a good thing, and the Bankruptcy Rules Advisory Committee believes the additional three days should be allowed.

2006 Amendment

Amended Rule 5(e) acknowledges that many courts have required electronic filing by means of a standing order, procedures manual, or local rule. These local practices reflect the advantages that courts and most litigants realize from electronic filing. Courts that mandate electronic filing recognize the need to make exceptions when requiring electronic filing imposes a hardship on a party. Under amended Rule 5(e), a local rule that requires electronic filing must include reasonable exceptions, but Rule 5(e) does not define the scope of those exceptions. Experience with the local rules that have been adopted and that will emerge will aid in drafting new local rules and will facilitate gradual convergence on uniform exceptions, whether in local rules or in an amended Rule 5(e).

2007 Amendment

The language of Rule 5 has been amended as part of the general restyling of the Civil Rules to make them more easily understood and to make style and terminology consistent throughout the rules. These changes are intended to be stylistic only.

Rule 5(a)(1)(E) omits the former reference to a designation of record on appeal. Appellate Rule 10 is a self-contained provision for the record on appeal, and provides for service.

Former Rule 5(b)(2)(D) literally provided that a local rule may authorize use of the court's transmission facilities to make service by non-electronic means agreed to by the parties. That was not intended. Rule 5(b)(3) restores the intended meaning—court transmission facilities can be used only for service by electronic means.

Rule 5(d)(2)(B) provides that "a" judge may accept a paper for filing, replacing the reference in former Rule 5(e) to "the" judge. Some courts do not assign a designated judge to each case, and it may be important to have another judge accept a paper for filing even when a case is on the individual docket of a particular judge. The ministerial acts of accepting the paper, noting the time, and transmitting the paper to the court clerk do not interfere with the assigned judge's authority over the action.

Rule 5.1. Constitutional Challenge to A Statute—Notice, Certification, and Intervention

(a) Notice by a Party. A party that files a pleading, written motion, or other paper drawing into question the constitutionality of a federal or state statute must promptly:

(1) file a notice of constitutional question stating the question and identifying the paper that raises it, if:

(A) a federal statute is questioned and the parties do not include the United States, one of its agencies, or one of its officers or employees in an official capacity; or

(B) a state statute is questioned and the parties do not include the state, one of its agencies, or one of its officers or employees in an official capacity; and

(2) serve the notice and paper on the Attorney General of the United States if a federal statute is questioned—or on the state attorney general if a state statute is questioned—either by certified or registered mail or by sending it to an electronic address designated by the attorney general for this purpose.

(b) Certification by the Court. The court must, under 28 U.S.C. § 2403, certify to the appropriate attorney general that a statute has been questioned.

(c) Intervention; Final Decision on the Merits. Unless the court sets a later time, the attorney general may intervene within 60 days after the notice is filed or after the court certifies the challenge, whichever is earlier. Before the time to intervene expires, the court may reject the constitutional challenge, but may not enter a final judgment holding the statute unconstitutional.

(d) No Forfeiture. A party's failure to file and serve the notice, or the court's failure to certify, does not forfeit a constitutional claim or defense that is otherwise timely asserted.

(Effective December 1, 2006; amended April 30, 2007, effective December 1, 2007.)

ADVISORY COMMITTEE NOTES

2006 Adoption

Rule 5.1 implements 28 U.S.C. § 2403, replacing the final three sentences of Rule 24(c). New Rule 5.1 requires a party that files a pleading, written motion, or other paper drawing in question the constitutionality of a federal or state statute to file a notice of constitutional question and serve it on the United States Attorney General or state attorney general. The party must promptly file and serve the notice of constitutional question. This notice requirement supplements the court's duty to certify a constitutional challenge to the United States Attorney General or state attorney general. The notice of constitutional question will ensure that the attorney general is notified of constitutional challenges and has an opportunity to exercise the statutory right to intervene at the earliest possible point in the litigation. The court's certification obligation remains, and is the only notice when the constitutionality of a federal or state statute is drawn in question by means other than a party's pleading, written motion, or other paper.

Moving the notice and certification provisions from Rule 24(c) to a new rule is designed to attract the parties' attention to these provisions by locating them in the vicinity of the rules that require notice by service and pleading.

Rule 5.1 goes beyond the requirements of § 2403 and the former Rule 24(c) provisions by requiring notice and certification of a constitutional challenge to any federal or state statute, not only those "affecting the public interest." It is better to assure, through notice, that the attorney general is able to determine whether to seek intervention on the ground that the act or statute affects a public interest. Rule 5.1 refers to a "federal statute," rather than the § 2403 reference to an "Act of Congress," to maintain consistency in the Civil Rules vocabulary. In Rule 5.1 "statute" means any congressional enactment that would qualify as an "Act of Congress."

Unless the court sets a later time, the 60–day period for intervention runs from the time a party files a notice of constitutional question or from the time the court certifies a constitutional challenge, whichever is earlier. Rule 5.1(a) directs that a party promptly serve the notice of constitutional question. The court may extend the 60–period [So in original. Probably should read "60-day period".] on its own or on motion. One occasion for extension may arise if the court certifies a challenge under § 2403 after a party files a notice of constitutional question. Pretrial activities may continue without interruption during the intervention period, and the court retains authority to grant interlocutory relief. The court may reject a constitutional challenge to a statute at any time. But the court may not enter a final judgment holding a statute unconstitutional before the attorney general has responded or the intervention period has expired without response. This rule does not displace any of the statutory or rule procedures that permit dismissal of all or part of an action — including a constitutional challenge — at any time, even before service of process.

2007 Amendment

The language of Rule 5.1 has been amended as part of the general restyling of the Civil Rules to make them more easily understood and to make style and terminology consistent throughout the rules. These changes are intended to be stylistic only.

Rule 5.2. Privacy Protection For Filings Made with the Court

(a) **Redacted Filings.** Unless the court orders otherwise, in an electronic or paper filing with the court that contains an individual's social-security number, taxpayer-identification number, or birth date, the name of an individual known to be a minor, or a financial-account number, a party or nonparty making the filing may include only:

(1) the last four digits of the social-security number and taxpayer-identification number;

(2) the year of the individual's birth;

(3) the minor's initials; and

(4) the last four digits of the financial-account number.

(b) **Exemptions from the Redaction Requirement.** The redaction requirement does not apply to the following:

(1) a financial-account number that identifies the property allegedly subject to forfeiture in a forfeiture proceeding;

(2) the record of an administrative or agency proceeding;

(3) the official record of a state-court proceeding;

(4) the record of a court or tribunal, if that record was not subject to the redaction requirement when originally filed;

(5) a filing covered by Rule 5.2(c) or (d); and

(6) a pro se filing in an action brought under 28 U.S.C. §§ 2241, 2254, or 2255.

(c) **Limitations on Remote Access to Electronic Files; Social–Security Appeals and Immigration Cases.** Unless the court orders otherwise, in an action for benefits under the Social Security Act, and in an action or proceeding relating to an order of removal, to relief from removal, or to immigration benefits or detention, access to an electronic file is authorized as follows:

(1) the parties and their attorneys may have remote electronic access to any part of the case file, including the administrative record;

(2) any other person may have electronic access to the full record at the courthouse, but may have remote electronic access only to:

(A) the docket maintained by the court; and

(B) an opinion, order, judgment, or other disposition of the court, but not any other part of the case file or the administrative record.

(d) **Filings Made Under Seal.** The court may order that a filing be made under seal without redaction. The court may later unseal the filing or order the person who made the filing to file a redacted version for the public record.

(e) **Protective Orders.** For good cause, the court may by order in a case:

(1) require redaction of additional information; or

(2) limit or prohibit a nonparty's remote electronic access to a document filed with the court.

(f) **Option for Additional Unredacted Filing Under Seal.** A person making a redacted filing may also file an unredacted copy under seal. The court must retain the unredacted copy as part of the record.

(g) **Option for Filing a Reference List.** A filing that contains redacted information may be filed together with a reference list that identifies each item of redacted information and specifies an appropriate identifier that uniquely corresponds to each item listed. The list must be filed under seal and may be amended as of right. Any reference in the case to a listed identifier will be construed to refer to the corresponding item of information.

(h) **Waiver of Protection of Identifiers.** A person waives the protection of Rule 5.2(a) as to the person's own information by filing it without redaction and not under seal.

(Adopted April 30, 2007, effective December 1, 2007.)

ADVISORY COMMITTEE NOTES

2007 Adoption

The rule is adopted in compliance with section 205(c)(3) of the E–Government Act of 2002, Public Law 107–347. Section 205(c)(3) requires the Supreme Court to prescribe rules "to protect privacy and security concerns relating to electronic filing of documents and the public availability . . . of documents filed electronically." The rule goes further than the E–Government Act in regulating paper filings even when they are not converted to electronic form. But the number of filings that remain in paper form is certain to diminish over time. Most districts scan paper filings into the electronic case file, where they become available to the public in the same way as documents initially filed in electronic form. It is electronic availability, not the form of the initial filing, that raises the privacy and security concerns addressed in the E–Government Act.

The rule is derived from and implements the policy adopted by the Judicial Conference in September 2001 to address the privacy concerns resulting from public access to electronic case files. See http://www.privacy.uscourts.gov/Policy.htm. The Judicial Conference policy is that documents in case files generally should be made available electronically to the same extent they are available at the courthouse, provided that certain "personal data identifiers" are not included in the public file.

While providing for the public filing of some information, such as the last four digits of an account number, the rule does not intend to establish a presumption that this information never could or should be protected. For example, it may well be necessary in individual cases to prevent remote access by nonparties to any part of an account number or social security number. It may also be necessary to protect information not covered by the redaction requirement—such as driver's license numbers and alien registration numbers—in a particular case. In such cases, protection may be sought under subdivision (d) or (e). Moreover, the Rule does not affect the protection available under other rules, such as Civil Rules 16 and 26(c), or under other sources of protective authority.

Parties must remember that any personal information not otherwise protected by sealing or redaction will be made available over the internet. Counsel should notify clients of this fact so that an informed decision may be made on what information is to be included in a document filed with the court.

The clerk is not required to review documents filed with the court for compliance with this rule. The responsibility to redact filings rests with counsel and the party or non-party making the filing.

Subdivision (c) provides for limited public access in Social Security cases and immigration cases. Those actions are entitled to special treatment due to the prevalence of sensitive information and the volume of filings. Remote electronic access by nonparties is limited to the docket and the written dispositions of the court unless the court orders otherwise. The rule contemplates, however, that nonparties can obtain full access to the case file at the courthouse, including access through the court's public computer terminal.

Subdivision (d) reflects the interplay between redaction and filing under seal. It does not limit or expand the judicially developed rules that govern sealing. But it does reflect the possibility that redaction may provide an alternative to sealing.

Subdivision (e) provides that the court can by order in a particular case for good cause require more extensive redaction than otherwise required by the Rule. Nothing in this subdivision is intended to affect the limitations on sealing that are otherwise applicable to the court.

Subdivision (f) allows a person who makes a redacted filing to file an unredacted document under seal. This provision is derived from section 205(c)(3)(iv) of the E–Government Act.

Subdivision (g) allows the option to file a register of redacted information. This provision is derived from section 205(c)(3)(v) of the E–Government Act, as amended in 2004. In accordance with the E–Government Act, subdivision (g) refers to "redacted" information. The term "redacted" is intended to govern a filing that is prepared with abbreviated identifiers in the first instance, as well as a filing in which a personal identifier is edited after its preparation.

Subdivision (h) allows a person to waive the protections of the rule as to that person's own personal information by filing it unsealed and in unredacted form. One may wish to waive the protection if it is determined that the costs of redaction outweigh the benefits to privacy. If a person files an unredacted identifier by mistake, that person may seek relief from the court.

Trial exhibits are subject to the redaction requirements of Rule 5.2 to the extent they are filed with the court. Trial exhibits that are not initially filed with the court must be redacted in accordance with the rule if and when they are filed as part of an appeal or for other reasons.

Rule 6. Computing and Extending Time; Time for Motion Papers

(a) Computing Time. The following rules apply in computing any time period specified in these rules or in any local rule, court order, or statute:

(1) ***Day of the Event Excluded.*** Exclude the day of the act, event, or default that begins the period.

(2) ***Exclusions from Brief Periods.*** Exclude intermediate Saturdays, Sundays, and legal holidays when the period is less than 11 days.

(3) ***Last Day.*** Include the last day of the period unless it is a Saturday, Sunday, legal holiday, or—if the act to be done is filing a paper in court—a day on which weather or other conditions make the clerk's office inaccessible. When the last day is excluded, the period runs until the end of the next day that is not a Saturday, Sunday, legal holiday, or day when the clerk's office is inaccessible.

(4) ***"Legal Holiday" Defined.*** As used in these rules, "legal holiday" means:

(A) the day set aside by statute for observing New Year's Day, Martin Luther King Jr.'s Birthday, Washington's Birthday, Memorial Day, Independence Day, Labor Day, Columbus Day, Veterans' Day, Thanksgiving Day, or Christmas Day; and

(B) any other day declared a holiday by the President, Congress, or the state where the district court is located.

(b) Extending Time.

(1) ***In General.*** When an act may or must be done within a specified time, the court may, for good cause, extend the time:

(A) with or without motion or notice if the court acts, or if a request is made, before the original time or its extension expires; or

(B) on motion made after the time has expired if the party failed to act because of excusable neglect.

(2) ***Exceptions.*** A court must not extend the time to act under Rules 50(b) and (d), 52(b), 59(b), (d), and (e), and 60(b), except as those rules allow.

(c) Motions, Notices of Hearing, and Affidavits.

(1) ***In General.*** A written motion and notice of the hearing must be served at least 5 days before the time specified for the hearing, with the following exceptions:

(A) when the motion may be heard ex parte;

(B) when these rules set a different time; or

(C) when a court order—which a party may, for good cause, apply for ex parte—sets a different time.

(2) ***Supporting Affidavit.*** Any affidavit supporting a motion must be served with the motion. Except as Rule 59(c) provides otherwise, any opposing affidavit must be served at least 1 day before the hearing, unless the court permits service at another time.

(d) Additional Time After Certain Kinds of Service. When a party may or must act within a specified time after service and service is made under Rule 5(b)(2)(C), (D), (E), or (F), 3 days are added after the period would otherwise expire under Rule 6(a).

(Amended December 27, 1946, effective March 19, 1948; January 21, 1963, effective July 1, 1963; February 28, 1966, effective July 1, 1966; December 4, 1967, effective July 1, 1968; March 1, 1971, effective July 1, 1971; April 28, 1983, effective August 1, 1983; April 29, 1985, effective August 1, 1985; March 2, 1987, effective August 1, 1987; April 29, 1999, effective December 1, 1999; April 23, 2001, effective December 1, 2001; April 25, 2005, effective December 1, 2005; April 30, 2007, effective December 1, 2007.)

ADVISORY COMMITTEE NOTES

1937 Adoption

Note to Subdivisions (a) and (b). These are amplifications along lines common in state practices, of [former] Equity Rule 80 (Computation of Time—Sundays and Holidays) and of the provisions for enlargement of time found in [former] Equity Rules 8 (Enforcement of Final Decrees) and 16 (Defendant to Answer—Default—Decree Pro Confesso). See also Rule XIII, Rules and Forms in Criminal Cases, 1934, 292 U.S. 661, 666. Compare Ala.Code Ann. (Michie, 1928) § 13 and former Law Rule 8 of the Rules of the Supreme Court of the District of Columbia (1924), superseded in 1929 by Law Rule 8, Rules of the District Court of the United States for the District of Columbia (1937).

Note to Subdivision (c). This eliminates the difficulties caused by the expiration of terms of court. Such statutes as U.S.C., Title 28, [former] § 12 (Trials not discontinued by new term) are not affected. Compare Rules of the United States District Court of Minnesota, Rule 25 (Minn.Stat. (Mason, Supp.1936), p. 1089).

Note to Subdivision (d). Compare 2 Minn.Stat. (Mason, 1927) § 9246; N.Y.R.C.P. (1937) Rules 60 and 64.

1946 Amendment

Note to Subdivision (b). The purpose of the amendment is to clarify the finality of judgments. Prior to the advent of the Federal Rules of Civil Procedure, the general rule that a court loses jurisdiction to disturb its judgments, upon the expiration of the term at which they were entered, had long been the classic device which (together with the statutory limits on the time for appeal) gave finality to judgments. See note to rule 73(a). Rule 6(c) abrogates that limit on judicial power. That limit was open to many objections, one of them being inequality of operation because, under it, the time for vacating a judgment rendered early in a term was much longer than for a judgment rendered near the end of the term.

The question to be met under rule 6(b) is: how far should the desire to allow correction of judgments be allowed to postpone their finality? The rules contain a number of provisions permitting the vacation or modification of judgments on various grounds. Each of these rules contains express time limits on the motions for granting of relief. Rule 6(b) is a rule of general application giving wide discretion to the court to enlarge these time limits or revive them after they have expired, the only exceptions stated in the original rule being a prohibition against enlarging the time specified in Rule 59(b) and (d) for making motions for or granting new trials, and a prohibition against enlarging the time fixed by law for taking an appeal. It should also be noted that Rule 6(b) itself contains no limitation of time within which the court may exercise its discretion, and since the expiration of the term does not end its power, there is now no time limit on the exercise of its discretion under Rule 6(b).

Decisions of lower federal courts suggest that some of the rules containing time limits which may be set aside under Rule 6(b) are Rules 25, 50(b), 52(b), 60(b), and 73(g).

In a number of cases the effect of Rule 6(b) on the time limitations of these rules has been considered. Certainly the rule is susceptible of the interpretation that the court is given the power in its discretion to relieve a party from failure to act within the times specified in any of these other rules, with only the exceptions stated in Rule 6(b), and in some cases the rule has been so construed.

With regard to Rule 25(a) for substitution, it was held in *Anderson v. Brady,* Ky.1941, 1 F.R.D. 589, 4 Fed.Rules Service 25a.1, Case 1, and in *Anderson v. Yungkau,* C.C.A.6, 1946, 153 F.2d 685, certiorari granted 66 S.Ct. 1025, 328 U.S. 829, 90 L.Ed. 1606, that under Rule 6(b) the court had no authority to allow substitution of parties after the expiration of the limit fixed in Rule 25(a).

As to Rules 50(b) for judgments notwithstanding the verdict and 52(b) for amendment of findings and vacation of judgment, it was recognized in *Leishman v. Associated Wholesale Electric Co.,* 1943, 63 S.Ct. 543, 318 U.S. 203, 87 L.Ed. 714, that Rule 6(b) allowed the district court to enlarge the time to make a motion for amended findings and judgment beyond the limit expressly fixed in Rule 52(b). See *Coca-Cola v. Busch,* E.D.Pa.1943, 7 Fed.Rules Service, 59b.2,

Case 4. Obviously, if the time limit in Rule 52(b) could be set aside under Rule 6(b), the time limit in Rule 50(b) for granting judgment notwithstanding the verdict (and thus vacating the judgment entered "forthwith" on the verdict) likewise could be set aside.

As to Rule 59 on motions for a new trial, it has been settled that the time limits in Rule 59(b) and (d) for making motions for or granting new trial could not be set aside under Rule 6(b), because Rule 6(b) expressly refers to Rule 59, and forbids it. See *Safeway Stores, Inc. v. Coe,* App.D.C. 1943, 136 F.2d 771, 78 U.S.App.D.C. 19; *Jusino v. Morales & Tio,* C.C.A.1, 1944, 139 F.2d 946; *Coca-Cola Co. v. Busch,* E.D.Pa.1943, 7 Fed.Rules Service 59b.2, Case 4; *Peterson v. Chicago Great Western Ry. Co.,* D.Neb.1943, 3 F.R.D. 346, 7 Fed.Rules Service 59b.2, Case 1; *Leishman v. Associated Wholesale Electric Co.,* 1943, 63 S.Ct. 543, 318 U.S. 203, 87 L.Ed. 714.

As to Rule 60(b) for relief from a judgment, it was held in *Schram v. O'Connor,* Mich.1941, 5 Fed.Rules Serv. 6b.31, Case 1, 2 F.R.D. 192, s.c. 5 Fed.Rules Serv. 6b.31, Case 2, 2 F.R.D. 192, that the six-months time limit in original rule 60(b) for making a motion for relief from a judgment for surprise, mistake, or excusable neglect could be set aside under Rule 6(b). The contrary result was reached in *Wallace v. United States,* C.C.A.2, 1944, 142 F.2d 240, certiorari denied 65 S.Ct. 37, 323 U.S. 712, 89 L.Ed. 573; *Reed v. South Atlantic Steamship Co. of Del.,* Del.1942, 2 F.R.D. 475, 6 Fed.Rules Serv. 60b.31, Case 1.

As to Rule 73(g), fixing the time for docketing an appeal, it was held in *Ainsworth v. Gill Glass & Fixture Co.,* C.C.A.3, 1939, 104 F.2d 83, that under Rule 6(b) the district court, upon motion made after the expiration of the forty-day period, stated in Rule 73(g), but before the expiration of the ninety-day period therein specified, could permit the docketing of the appeal on a showing of excusable neglect. The contrary was held in *Mutual Benefit Health & Accident Ass'n v. Snyder,* C.C.A.6, 1940, 109 F.2d 469 and in *Burke v. Canfield,* 1940, 111 F.2d 526, 72 App.D.C. 127.

The amendment of Rule 6(b) now proposed is based on the view that there should be a definite point where it can be said a judgment is final; that the right method of dealing with the problem is to list in Rule 6(b) the various other rules whose time limits may not be set aside, and then, if the time limit in any of those other rules is too short, to amend that other rule to give a longer time. The further argument is that Rule 6(c) abolished the long standing device to produce finality in judgments through expiration of the term, and since that limitation on the jurisdiction of courts to set aside their own judgments has been removed by Rule 6(c), some other limitation must be substituted or judgments never can be said to be final.

In this connection reference is made to the established rule that if a motion for new trial is seasonably made, the mere making or pendency of the motion destroys the finality of the judgment, and even though the motion is ultimately denied, the full time for appeal starts anew from the date of denial. Also, a motion to amend the findings under Rule 52(b) has the same effect on the time for appeal. *Leishman v. Associated Wholesale Electric Co.,* 1943, 63 S.Ct. 543, 318 U.S. 203, 87 L.Ed. 714. By the same reasoning a motion for judgment under Rule 50(b), involving as it does the vacation of a judgment entered "forthwith" on the verdict (Rule 58), operates to postpone, until an order is made, the running of the time for appeal. The Committee believes that the abolition by Rule 6(c) of the old rule that a court's power over its judgments ends with the term, requires a substitute limitation, and that unless Rule 6(b) is amended to prevent enlargement of the times specified in Rules 50(b), 52(b) and 60(b), and the limitation as to Rule 59(b) and (d) is retained, no one can say when a judgment is final. This is also true with regard to proposed Rule 59(e), which authorizes a motion to alter or amend a judgment, hence that rule is also included in the enumeration in amended Rule 6(b). In consideration of the amendment, however, it should be noted that Rule 60(b) is also to be amended so as to lengthen the six-months period originally prescribed in that rule to one year.

As to Rule 25 on substitution, while finality is not involved, the limit there fixed should be controlling. That rule, as amended, gives the court power, upon showing of a reasonable excuse, to permit substitution after the expiration of the two-year period.

As to Rule 73(g), it is believed that the conflict in decisions should be resolved and not left to further litigation, and that the rule should be listed as one whose limitation may not be set aside under Rule 6(b).

As to Rule 59(c), fixing the time for serving affidavits on motion for new trial, it is believed that the court should have authority under Rule 6(b) to enlarge the time, because, once the motion for new trial is made, the judgment no longer has finality, and the extension of time for affidavits thus does not of itself disturb finality.

Other changes proposed in Rule 6(b) are merely clarifying and conforming. Thus "request" is substituted for "application" in clause (1) because an application is defined as a motion under Rule 7(b). The phrase "extend the time" is substituted for "enlarge the period" because the former is a more suitable expression and relates more clearly to both clauses (1) and (2). The final phrase in Rule 6(b), "or the period for taking an appeal as provided by law", is deleted and a reference to Rule 73(a) inserted, since it is proposed to state in that rule the time for appeal to a circuit court of appeals, which is the only appeal governed by the Federal Rules, and allows an extension of time. See Rule 72.

Subdivision (c). The purpose of this amendment is to prevent reliance upon the continued existence of a term as a source of power to disturb the finality of a judgment upon grounds other than those stated in these rules. See *Hill v. Hawes,* 1944, 64 S.Ct. 334, 320 U.S. 520, 88 L.Ed. 283; *Boaz v. Mutual Life Ins. Co. of New York,* C.C.A.8, 1944, 146 F.2d 321; *Bucy v. Nevada Construction Co.,* C.C.A.9, 1942, 125 F.2d 213.

1963 Amendment

Subdivision (a). This amendment is related to the amendment of Rule 77(c) changing the regulation of the days on which the clerk's office shall be open.

The wording of the first sentence of Rule 6(a) is clarified and the subdivision is made expressly applicable to computing periods of time set forth in local rules.

Saturday is to be treated in the same way as Sunday or a "legal holiday" in that it is not to be included when it falls on the last day of a computed period, nor counted as an intermediate day when the period is less than 7 days. "Legal holiday" is defined for purposes of this subdivision and amended Rule 77(c). Compare the definition of "holiday" in 11 U.S.C. § 1(18); also 5 U.S.C. § 86a; Executive Order No. 10358, *"Observance of Holidays,"* June 9, 1952, 17 Fed.Reg. 5269. In the light of these changes the last sentence of the present subdivision, dealing with half holidays, is eliminated.

With Saturdays and State holidays made "dies non" in certain cases by the amended subdivision, computation of the usual 5-day notice of motion or the 2-day notice to dissolve or modify a temporary restraining order may work out so as to cause embarrassing delay in urgent cases. The delay can be obviated by applying to the court to shorten the time, see Rules 6(d) and 65(b).

Subdivision (b). The prohibition against extending the time for taking action under Rule 25 (Substitution of parties) is eliminated. The only limitation of time provided for in amended Rule 25 is the 90-day period following a suggestion upon the record of the death of a party within which to make a motion to substitute the proper parties for the deceased party. See Rule 25(a)(1), as amended, and the Advisory Committee's Note thereto. It is intended that the court shall have discretion to enlarge that period.

1966 Amendment

P.L. 88–139, § 1, 77 Stat. 248, approved on October 16, 1963, amended 28 U.S.C. § 138 to read as follows: "The district court shall not hold formal terms." Thus Rule 6(c) is rendered unnecessary, and it is rescinded.

1967 Amendment

The amendment eliminates the references to Rule 73, which is to be abrogated.

1971 Amendment

The amendment adds Columbus Day to the list of legal holidays to conform the subdivision to the Act of June 28, 1968, 82 Stat. 250, which constituted Columbus Day a legal holiday effective after January 1, 1971.

The Act, which amended Title 5, U.S.C. § 6103(a), changes the day on which certain holidays are to be observed. Washington's Birthday, Memorial Day and Veterans Day are to be observed on the third Monday in February, the last Monday in May and the fourth Monday in October, respectively, rather than, as heretofore, on February 22, May 30, and November 11, respectively, Columbus Day is to be observed on the second Monday in October. New Year's Day, Independence Day, Thanksgiving Day and Christmas continue to be observed on the traditional days.

1983 Amendment

Subdivision (b). The amendment confers finality upon the judgments of magistrates by foreclosing enlargement of the time for appeal except as provided in new Rule 74(a) (20 day period for demonstration of excusable neglect).

1985 Amendment

Rule 6(a) is amended to acknowledge that weather conditions or other events may render the clerk's office inaccessible one or more days. Parties who are obliged to file something with the court during that period should not be penalized if they cannot do so. The amendment conforms to changes made in Federal Rule of Criminal Procedure 45(a), effective August 1, 1982.

The Rule also is amended to extend the exclusion of intermediate Saturdays, Sundays, and legal holidays to the computation of time periods less than 11 days. Under the current version of the Rule, parties bringing motions under rules with 10-day periods could have as few as 5 working days to prepare their motions. This hardship would be especially acute in the case of Rules 50(b) and (c)(2), 52(b), and 59(b), (d), and (e), which may not be enlarged at the discretion of the court. See Rule 6(b). If the exclusion of Saturdays, Sundays, and legal holidays will operate to cause excessive delay in urgent cases, the delay can be obviated by applying to the court to shorten the time. See Rule 6(b).

The Birthday of Martin Luther King, Jr., which becomes a legal holiday effective in 1986, has been added to the list of legal holidays enumerated in the Rule.

1987 Amendment

The amendments are technical. No substantive change is intended.

1999 Amendment

The reference to Rule 74(a) is stricken from the catalogue of time periods that cannot be extended by the district court. The change reflects the 1997 abrogation of Rule 74(a).

2001 Amendments

The additional three days provided by Rule 6(e) is extended to the means of service authorized by the new paragraph (D) added to Rule 5(b), including—with the consent of the person served—service by electronic or other means. The three-day addition is provided as well for service on a person with no known address by leaving a copy with the clerk of the court.

Changes Made After Publication and Comments

Proposed Rule 6(e) is the same as the "alternative proposal" that was published in August 1999.

2005 Amendments

Rule 6(e) is amended to remove any doubt as to the method for extending the time to respond after service by mail, leaving with the clerk of court, electronic means, or other means consented to by the party served. Three days are added after the prescribed period otherwise expires under Rule 6(a). Intermediate Saturdays, Sundays, and legal holidays are included in counting these added three days. If the third day is a Saturday, Sunday, or legal holiday, the last day to act is the next day that is not a Saturday, Sunday, or legal holiday. The effect of invoking the day when the prescribed period would otherwise expire under Rule 6(a) can be illustrated by assuming that the thirtieth day of a thirty-day period is a Saturday. Under Rule 6(a) the period expires on the next day that is not a Sunday or legal holiday. If the following Monday is a legal holiday, under Rule 6(a) the period expires on Tuesday. Three days are then added—Wednesday, Thursday, and Friday as the third and final day to act. If the period prescribed expires on a Friday, the three added days are Saturday, Sunday, and Monday, which is the third and final day to act unless it is a legal holiday. If

Monday is a legal holiday, the next day that is not a legal holiday is the third and final day to act.

Application of Rule 6(e) to a period that is less than eleven days can be illustrated by a paper that is served by mailing on a Friday. If ten days are allowed to respond, intermediate Saturdays, Sundays, and legal holidays are excluded in determining when the period expires under Rule 6(a). If there is no legal holiday, the period expires on the Friday two weeks after the paper was mailed. The three added Rule 6(e) days are Saturday, Sunday, and Monday, which is the third and final day to act unless it is a legal holiday. If Monday is a legal holiday, the next day that is not a legal holiday is the final day to act.

2007 Amendment

The language of Rule 6 has been amended as part of the general restyling of the Civil Rules to make them more easily understood and to make style and terminology consistent throughout the rules. These changes are intended to be stylistic only.

HISTORICAL NOTES

Effective and Applicability Provisions

1946 Amendments. Effective date of amendment to this rule, see rule 86(b).

TITLE III. PLEADINGS AND MOTIONS

Rule 7. Pleadings Allowed; Form of Motions and Other Papers

(a) Pleadings. Only these pleadings are allowed:

(1) a complaint;

(2) an answer to a complaint;

(3) an answer to a counterclaim designated as a counterclaim;

(4) an answer to a crossclaim;

(5) a third-party complaint;

(6) an answer to a third-party complaint; and

(7) if the court orders one, a reply to an answer.

(b) Motions and Other Papers.

(1) ***In General.*** A request for a court order must be made by motion. The motion must:

(A) be in writing unless made during a hearing or trial;

(B) state with particularity the grounds for seeking the order; and

(C) state the relief sought.

(2) ***Form.*** The rules governing captions and other matters of form in pleadings apply to motions and other papers.

(Amended December 27, 1946, effective March 19, 1948; January 21, 1963, effective July 1, 1963; April 28, 1983, effective August 1, 1983; April 30, 2007, effective December 1, 2007.)

ADVISORY COMMITTEE NOTES

1937 Adoption

1. A provision designating pleadings and defining a motion is common in the state practice acts. See Smith-Hurd Ill.Stats. ch. 110, § 156 (Designation and order of pleadings); 2 Minn.Stat. (Mason, 1927) § 9246 (Definition of motion); and N.Y.C.P.A. (1937) § 113 (Definition of motion). Former Equity Rules 18 (Pleadings—Technical Forms Abrogated), 29 (Defenses—How Presented), and 33 (Testing Sufficiency of Defense) abolished technical forms of pleading, demurrers and pleas, and exceptions for insufficiency of an answer.

2. Note to Subdivision (a). This preserves the substance of [former] Equity Rule 31 (Reply—When Required—When Cause at Issue). Compare the English practice, *English Rules under the Judicature Act* (The Annual Practice, 1937) O. 23, r.r. 1, 2 (Reply to counterclaim; amended, 1933, to be subject to the rules applicable to defenses, O. 21). See O. 21, r.r. 1–14; O. 27, r. 13 (When pleadings deemed denied and put in issue). Under the codes the pleadings are generally limited. A reply is sometimes required to an affirmative defense in the answer. 1 Colo.Stat.Ann. (1935) § 66; Ore. Code Ann. (1930) §§ 1–614, 1–616. In other jurisdictions no reply is necessary to an affirmative defense in the answer, but a reply may be ordered by the court. N.C.Code Ann. (1935) § 525; 1 S.D.Comp.Laws (1929) § 2357. A reply to a counterclaim is usually required. Ark.Civ.Code (Crawford, 1934) §§ 123 to 125; Wis.Stat. (1935) §§ 263.20, 263.21. U.S.C. Title 28, [former] § 45 (District courts; practice and procedure in certain cases) is modified insofar as it may dispense with a reply to a counterclaim.

For amendment of pleadings, see Rule 15 dealing with amended and supplemental pleadings.

3. All statutes which use the words "petition", "bill of complaint", "plea", "demurrer", and other such terminology are modified in form by this rule.

1946 Amendment

Note. This amendment eliminates any question as to whether the compulsory reply, where a counterclaim is pleaded, is a reply only to the counterclaim or is a general reply to the answer containing the counterclaim. The Commentary, *Scope of Reply where Defendant Has Pleaded Counterclaim,* 1939, 1 Fed.Rules Serv. 672; *Fort Chartres and Ivy Landing Drainage and Levee District No. Five v. Thompson,* Ill.1945, 8 Fed.Rules Serv. 13.32, Case 1.

1963 Amendment

Certain redundant words are eliminated and the subdivision is modified to reflect the amendment of Rule 14(a) which in certain cases eliminates the requirement of obtaining leave to bring in a third-party defendant.

1983 Amendment

One of the reasons sanctions against improper motion practice have been employed infrequently is the lack of clarity of Rule 7. That rule has stated only generally that the pleading requirements relating to captions, signing, and other matters of form also apply to motions and other papers. The addition of Rule 7(b)(3) makes explicit the applicability of the signing requirement and the sanctions of Rule 11, which have been amplified.

2007 Amendment

The language of Rule 7 has been amended as part of the general restyling of the Civil Rules to make them more easily understood and to make style and terminology consistent throughout the rules. These changes are intended to be stylistic only.

Former Rule 7(a) stated that "there shall be * * * an answer to a cross-claim, if the answer contains a cross-claim * * *." Former Rule 12(a)(2) provided more generally that "[a] party served with a pleading stating a cross-claim against that party shall serve an answer thereto * * *." New Rule 7(a) corrects this inconsistency by providing for an answer to a crossclaim.

For the first time, Rule 7(a)(7) expressly authorizes the court to order a reply to a counterclaim answer. A reply may be as useful in this setting as a reply to an answer, a third-party answer, or a crossclaim answer.

Former Rule 7(b)(1) stated that the writing requirement is fulfilled if the motion is stated in a written notice of hearing. This statement was deleted as redundant because a single written document can satisfy the writing requirements both for a motion and for a Rule 6(c)(1) notice.

The cross-reference to Rule 11 in former Rule 7(b)(3) is deleted as redundant. Rule 11 applies by its own terms. The force and application of Rule 11 are not diminished by the deletion.

Former Rule 7(c) is deleted because it has done its work. If a motion or pleading is described as a demurrer, plea, or exception for insufficiency, the court will treat the paper as if properly captioned.

HISTORICAL NOTES

Effective and Applicability Provisions

1946 Amendments. Effective date of amendment to this rule, see rule 86(b).

Rule 7.1. Disclosure Statement

(a) Who Must File; Contents. A nongovernmental corporate party must file two copies of a disclosure statement that:

(1) identifies any parent corporation and any publicly held corporation owning 10% or more of its stock; or

(2) states that there is no such corporation.

(b) Time to File; Supplemental Filing. A party must:

(1) file the disclosure statement with its first appearance, pleading, petition, motion, response, or other request addressed to the court; and

(2) promptly file a supplemental statement if any required information changes.

(Adopted April 29, 2002, effective December 1, 2002; April 30, 2007, effective December 1, 2007.)

ADVISORY COMMITTEE NOTES

2002 Adoption

Rule 7.1 is drawn from Rule 26.1 of the Federal Rules of Appellate Procedure, with changes to adapt to the circumstances of district courts that dictate different provisions for the time of filing, number of copies, and the like. The information required by Rule 7.1(a) reflects the "financial interest" standard of Canon 3C(1)(c) of the Code of Conduct for United States Judges. This information will support properly informed disqualification decisions in situations that call for automatic disqualification under Canon 3C(1)(c). It does not cover all of the circumstances that may call for disqualification under the financial interest standard, and does not deal at all with other circumstances that may call for disqualification.

Although the disclosures required by Rule 7.1(a) may seem limited, they are calculated to reach a majority of the circumstances that are likely to call for disqualification on the basis of financial information that a judge may not know or recollect. Framing a rule that calls for more detailed disclosure will be difficult. Unnecessary disclosure requirements place a burden on the parties and on courts. Unnecessary disclosure of volumes of information may create a risk that a judge will overlook the one bit of information that might require disqualification, and also may create a risk that unnecessary disqualifications will be made rather than attempt to unravel a potentially difficult question. It has not been feasible to dictate more detailed disclosure requirements in Rule 7.1(a).

Rule 7.1 does not prohibit local rules that require disclosures in addition to those required by Rule 7.1. Developing experience with local disclosure practices and advances in electronic technology may provide a foundation for adopting more detailed disclosure requirements by future amendments of Rule 7.1.

Changes Made After Publication and Comment. The provisions that would require disclosure of additional information that may be required by the Judicial Conference have been deleted.

2007 Amendment

The language of Rule 7.1 has been amended as part of the general restyling of the Civil Rules to make them more easily understood and to make style and terminology consistent throughout the rules. These changes are intended to be stylistic only.

Rule 8. General Rules of Pleading

(a) Claim for Relief. A pleading that states a claim for relief must contain:

(1) a short and plain statement of the grounds for the court's jurisdiction, unless the court already has jurisdiction and the claim needs no new jurisdictional support;

(2) a short and plain statement of the claim showing that the pleader is entitled to relief; and

(3) a demand for the relief sought, which may include relief in the alternative or different types of relief.

(b) Defenses; Admissions and Denials.

(1) ***In General.*** In responding to a pleading, a party must:

(A) state in short and plain terms its defenses to each claim asserted against it; and

(B) admit or deny the allegations asserted against it by an opposing party.

(2) ***Denials—Responding to the Substance.*** A denial must fairly respond to the substance of the allegation.

(3) ***General and Specific Denials.*** A party that intends in good faith to deny all the allegations of a pleading—including the jurisdictional grounds—may do so by a general denial. A party that does not intend to deny all the allegations must either specifically deny designated allegations or generally deny all except those specifically admitted.

(4) ***Denying Part of an Allegation.*** A party that intends in good faith to deny only part of an allegation must admit the part that is true and deny the rest.

(5) ***Lacking Knowledge or Information.*** A party that lacks knowledge or information sufficient to form a belief about the truth of an allegation must so state, and the statement has the effect of a denial.

(6) ***Effect of Failing to Deny.*** An allegation—other than one relating to the amount of damages—is admitted if a responsive pleading is required and the allegation is not denied. If a responsive pleading is not required, an allegation is considered denied or avoided.

(c) Affirmative Defenses.

(1) ***In General.*** In responding to a pleading, a party must affirmatively state any avoidance or affirmative defense, including:

- accord and satisfaction;
- arbitration and award;
- assumption of risk;
- contributory negligence;
- discharge in bankruptcy;
- duress;
- estoppel;
- failure of consideration;
- fraud;
- illegality;
- injury by fellow servant;
- laches;
- license;
- payment;
- release;
- res judicata;
- statute of frauds;
- statute of limitations; and
- waiver.

(2) ***Mistaken Designation.*** If a party mistakenly designates a defense as a counterclaim, or a counterclaim as a defense, the court must, if justice requires, treat the pleading as though it were correctly designated, and may impose terms for doing so.

(d) Pleading to Be Concise and Direct; Alternative Statements; Inconsistency.

(1) ***In General.*** Each allegation must be simple, concise, and direct. No technical form is required.

(2) ***Alternative Statements of a Claim or Defense.*** A party may set out 2 or more statements of a claim or defense alternatively or hypothetically, either in a single count or defense or in separate ones. If a party makes alternative statements, the pleading is sufficient if any one of them is sufficient.

(3) ***Inconsistent Claims or Defenses.*** A party may state as many separate claims or defenses as it has, regardless of consistency.

(e) Construing Pleadings. Pleadings must be construed so as to do justice.

(Amended February 28, 1966, effective July 1, 1966; March 2, 1987, effective August 1, 1987; April 30, 2007, effective December 1, 2007.)

ADVISORY COMMITTEE NOTES

1937 Adoption

Note to Subdivision (a). See [former] Equity Rules 25 (Bill of Complaint—Contents), and 30 (Answer—Contents—Counterclaim). Compare 2 Ind.Stat.Ann. (Burns, 1933) §§ 2–1004, 2–1015; 2 Ohio Gen.Code Ann. (Page, 1926) §§ 11305, 11314; Utah Rev.Stat.Ann. (1933) §§ 104–7–2, 104–9–1.

See Rule 19(c) for the requirement of a statement in a claim for relief of the names of persons who ought to be parties and the reason for their omission.

See Rule 23(b) for particular requirements as to the complaint in a secondary action by shareholders.

Note to Subdivision (b). 1. This rule supersedes the methods of pleading prescribed in U.S.C., Title 19, § 508 (Persons making seizures pleading general issue and proving special matter); U.S.C. Title 35, [former] §§ 40d (Proving under general issue, upon notice, that a statement in application for an extended patent is not true), 69 [now 282] (Pleading and proof in actions for infringement) and similar statutes.

2. This rule is, in part, [former] Equity Rule 30 (Answer—Contents—Counterclaim), with the matter on denials

largely from the Connecticut practice. See Conn. Practice Book (1934) §§ 107, 108, and 122; Conn.Gen.Stat. (1930) §§ 5508 to 5514. Compare the English practice, *English Rules Under the Judicature Act* (The Annual Practice, 1937) O. 19, r.r. 17–20.

Note to Subdivision (c). This follows substantially *English Rules Under the Judicature Act* (The Annual Practice, 1937) O. 19, r. 15 and N.Y.C.P.A. (1937) § 242, with "surprise" omitted in this rule.

Note to Subdivision (d). The first sentence is similar to former Equity Rule 30 (Answer—Contents—Counterclaim). For the second sentence see former Equity Rule 31 (Reply—When Required—When Cause at Issue). This is similar to *English Rules Under the Judicature Act* (The Annual Practice, 1937) O. 19, r.r. 13, 18; and to the practice of the States.

Note to Subdivision (e). This rule is an elaboration upon [former] Equity Rule 30 (Answer—Contents—Counterclaim), plus a statement of the actual practice under some codes. Compare also [former] Equity Rule 18 (Pleadings—Technical Forms Abrogated). See Clark, *Code Pleading* (1928), pp. 171–4, 432–5; Hankin, *Alternative and Hypothetical Pleading* (1924), 33 Yale L.J. 365.

Note to Subdivision (f). A provision of like import is of frequent occurrence in the codes. Smith-Hurd Ill.Stats. ch. 110, § 157(3); 2 Minn.Stat. (Mason, 1927) § 9266; N.Y.C.P.A. (1937) § 275; 2 N.D.Comp.Laws Ann. (1913) § 7458.

1966 Amendment

The change here is consistent with the broad purposes of unification.

1987 Amendment

The amendments are technical. No substantive change is intended.

2007 Amendment

The language of Rule 8 has been amended as part of the general restyling of the Civil Rules to make them more easily understood and to make style and terminology consistent throughout the rules. These changes are intended to be stylistic only.

The former Rule 8(b) and 8(e) cross-references to Rule 11 are deleted as redundant. Rule 11 applies by its own terms. The force and application of Rule 11 are not diminished by the deletion.

Former Rule 8(b) required a pleader denying part of an averment to "specify so much of it as is true and material and * * * deny only the remainder." "[A]nd material" is deleted to avoid the implication that it is proper to deny something that the pleader believes to be true but not material.

Deletion of former Rule 8(e)(2)'s "whether based on legal, equitable, or maritime grounds" reflects the parallel deletions in Rule 1 and elsewhere. Merger is now successfully accomplished.

Rule 9. Pleading Special Matters

(a) Capacity or Authority to Sue; Legal Existence.

(1) ***In General.*** Except when required to show that the court has jurisdiction, a pleading need not allege:

(A) a party's capacity to sue or be sued;

(B) a party's authority to sue or be sued in a representative capacity; or

(C) the legal existence of an organized association of persons that is made a party.

(2) ***Raising Those Issues.*** To raise any of those issues, a party must do so by a specific denial, which must state any supporting facts that are peculiarly within the party's knowledge.

(b) Fraud or Mistake; Conditions of Mind. In alleging fraud or mistake, a party must state with particularity the circumstances constituting fraud or mistake. Malice, intent, knowledge, and other conditions of a person's mind may be alleged generally.

(c) Conditions Precedent. In pleading conditions precedent, it suffices to allege generally that all conditions precedent have occurred or been performed. But when denying that a condition precedent has occurred or been performed, a party must do so with particularity.

(d) Official Document or Act. In pleading an official document or official act, it suffices to allege that the document was legally issued or the act legally done.

(e) Judgment. In pleading a judgment or decision of a domestic or foreign court, a judicial or quasi-judicial tribunal, or a board or officer, it suffices to plead the judgment or decision without showing jurisdiction to render it.

(f) Time and Place. An allegation of time or place is material when testing the sufficiency of a pleading.

(g) Special Damages. If an item of special damage is claimed, it must be specifically stated.

(h) Admiralty or Maritime Claim.

(1) ***How Designated.*** If a claim for relief is within the admiralty or maritime jurisdiction and also within the court's subject-matter jurisdiction on some other ground, the pleading may designate the claim as an admiralty or maritime claim for purposes of Rules 14(c), 38(e), and 82 and the Supplemental Rules for Admiralty or Maritime Claims and Asset Forfeiture Actions. A claim cognizable only in the admiralty or maritime jurisdiction is an admiralty or maritime claim for those purposes, whether or not so designated.

(2) ***Designation for Appeal.*** A case that includes an admiralty or maritime claim within this

subdivision (h) is an admiralty case within 28 U.S.C. § 1292(a)(3).

(Amended February 28, 1966, effective July 1, 1966; December 4, 1967, effective July 1, 1968; March 30, 1970, effective July 1, 1970; March 2, 1987, effective August 1, 1987; April 11, 1997, effective December 1, 1997; April 12, 2006, effective December 1, 2006; April 30, 2007, effective December 1, 2007.)

ADVISORY COMMITTEE NOTES

1937 Adoption

Note to Subdivision (a). Compare [former] Equity Rule 25 (Bill of Complaint—Contents) requiring disability to be stated; Utah Rev.Stat.Ann. (1933) § 104–13–15, enumerating a number of situations where a general averment of capacity is sufficient. For provisions governing averment of incorporation, see 2 Minn.Stat. (Mason, 1927) § 9271; N.Y.R.C.P. (1937) Rule 93; 2 N.D.Comp.Laws Ann. (1913) § 7981 et seq.

Note to Subdivision (b). See *English Rules Under the Judicature Act* (The Annual Practice, 1937) O. 19, r. 22.

Note to Subdivision (c). The codes generally have this or a similar provision. See *English Rules Under the Judicature Act* (The Annual Practice, 1937) O. 19, r. 14; 2 Minn. Stat. (Mason, 1927) § 9273; N.Y.R.C.P. (1937) Rule 92; 2 N.D.Comp.Laws Ann. (1913) § 7461; 2 Wash.Rev.Stat.Ann. (Remington, 1932) § 288.

Note to Subdivision (e). The rule expands the usual code provisions on pleading a judgment by including judgments or decisions of administrative tribunals and foreign courts. Compare Ark.Civ.Code (Crawford, 1934) § 141; 2 Minn.Stat. (Mason, 1927) § 9269; N.Y.R.C.P. (1937) Rule 95; 2 Wash. Rev.Stat.Ann. (Remington, 1932) § 287.

1966 Amendment

Certain distinctive features of the admiralty practice must be preserved for what are now suits in admiralty. This raises the question: After unification, when a single form of action is established, how will the counterpart of the present suit in admiralty be identifiable? In part the question is easily answered. Some claims for relief can only be suits in admiralty, either because the admiralty jurisdiction is exclusive or because no nonmaritime ground of federal jurisdiction exists. Many claims, however, are cognizable by the district courts whether asserted in admiralty or in a civil action, assuming the existence of a nonmaritime ground of jurisdiction. Thus at present the pleader has power to determine procedural consequences by the way in which he exercises the classic privilege given by the saving-to-suitors clause (28 U.S.C. § 1333) or by equivalent statutory provisions. For example, a longshoreman's claim for personal injuries suffered by reason of the unseaworthiness of a vessel may be asserted in a suit in admiralty or, if diversity of citizenship exists, in a civil action. One of the important procedural consequences is that in the civil action either party may demand a jury trial, while in the suit in admiralty there is no right to jury trial except as provided by statute.

It is no part of the purpose of unification to inject a right to jury trial into those admiralty cases in which that right is not provided by statute. Similarly as will be more specifically noted below, there is no disposition to change the present law as to interlocutory appeals in admiralty, or as to the venue of suits in admiralty; and, of course, there is no disposition to inject into the civil practice as it now is the distinctively maritime remedies (maritime attachment and garnishment, actions in rem, possessory, petitory and partition actions and limitation of liability). The unified rules must therefore provide some device for preserving the present power of the pleader to determine whether these historically maritime procedures shall be applicable to his claim or not; the pleader must be afforded some means of designating his claim as the counterpart of the present suit in admiralty, where its character as such is not clear.

The problem is different from the similar one concerning the identification of claims that were formerly suits in equity. While that problem is not free from complexities, it is broadly true that the modern counterpart of the suit in equity is distinguishable from the former action at law by the character of the relief sought. This mode of identification is possible in only a limited category of admiralty cases. In large numbers of cases the relief sought in admiralty is simple money damages, indistinguishable from the remedy afforded by the common law. This is true, for example, in the case of the longshoreman's action for personal injuries stated above. After unification has abolished the distinction between civil actions and suits in admiralty, the complaint in such an action would be almost completely ambiguous as to the pleader's intentions regarding the procedure invoked. The allegation of diversity of citizenship might be regarded as a clue indicating an intention to proceed as at present under the saving-to-suitors clause; but this, too, would be ambiguous if there were also reference to the admiralty jurisdiction, and the pleader ought not be required to forego mention of all available jurisdictional grounds.

Other methods of solving the problem were carefully explored, but the Advisory Committee concluded that the preferable solution is to allow the pleader who now has power to determine procedural consequences by filing a suit in admiralty to exercise that power under unification, for the limited instances in which procedural differences will remain, by a simple statement in his pleading to the effect that the claim is an admiralty or maritime claim.

The choice made by the pleader in identifying or in failing to identify his claim as an admiralty or maritime claim is not an irrevocable election. The rule provides that the amendment of a pleading to add or withdraw an identifying statement is subject to the principles of Rule 15.

1968 Amendment

The amendment eliminates the reference to Rule 73 which is to be abrogated and transfers to Rule 9(h) the substance of Subsection (h) of Rule 73 which preserved the right to an interlocutory appeal in admiralty cases which is provided by 28 U.S.C. § 1292(a)(3).

1970 Amendment

The reference to Rule 26(a) is deleted, in light of the transfer of that subdivision to Rule 30(a) and the elimination of the de bene esse procedure therefrom. See the Advisory Committee's note to Rule 30(a).

1987 Amendment

The amendment is technical. No substantive change is intended.

1997 Amendment

Section 1292(a)(3) of the Judicial Code provides for appeal from "[i]nterlocutory decrees of * * * district courts * * * determining the rights and liabilities of the parties to admiralty cases in which appeals from final decrees are allowed."

Rule 9(h) was added in 1966 with the unification of civil and admiralty procedure. Civil Rule 73(h) was amended at the same time to provide that the § 1292(a)(3) reference "to admiralty cases shall be construed to mean admiralty and maritime claims within the meaning of Rule 9(h)." This provision was transferred to Rule 9(h) when the Appellate Rules were adopted.

A single case can include both admiralty or maritime claims and nonadmiralty claims or parties. This combination reveals an ambiguity in the statement in present Rule 9(h) that an admiralty "claim" is an admiralty "case." An order "determining the rights and liabilities of the parties" within the meaning of § 1292(a)(3) may resolve only a nonadmiralty claim, or may simultaneously resolve interdependent admiralty and non-admiralty claims. Can appeal be taken as to the nonadmiralty matter, because it is part of a case that includes an admiralty claim, or is appeal limited to the admiralty claim?

The courts of appeals have not achieved full uniformity in applying the § 1292(a)(3) requirement that an order "determin[e] the rights and liabilities of the parties." It is common to assert that the statute should be construed narrowly, under the general policy that exceptions to the final judgment rule should be construed narrowly. This policy would suggest that the ambiguity should be resolved by limiting the interlocutory appeal right to orders that determine the rights and liabilities of the parties to an admiralty claim.

A broader view is chosen by this amendment for two reasons. The statute applies to admiralty "cases," and may itself provide for appeal from an order that disposes of a nonadmiralty claim that is joined in a single case with an admiralty claim. Although a rule of court may help to clarify and implement a statutory grant of jurisdiction, the line is not always clear between permissible implementation and impermissible withdrawal of jurisdiction. In addition, so long as an order truly disposes of the rights and liabilities of the parties within the meaning of § 1292(a)(3), it may prove important to permit appeal as to the non-admiralty claim. Disposition of the non-admiralty claim, for example, may make it unnecessary to consider the admiralty claim and have the same effect on the case and parties as disposition of the admiralty claim. Or the admiralty and non-admiralty claims may be interdependent. An illustration is provided by Roco Carriers, Ltd. v. M/V Nurnberg Express, 899 F.2d 1292 (2d Cir.1990). Claims for losses of ocean shipments were made against two defendants, one subject to admiralty jurisdiction and the other not. Summary judgment was granted in favor of the admiralty defendant and against the nonadmiralty defendant. The nonadmiralty defendant's appeal was accepted, with the explanation that the determination of its liability was "integrally linked with the determination of non-liability" of the admiralty defendant, and that "section 1292(a)(3) is not limited to admiralty claims; instead, it refers to admiralty cases." 899 F.2d at 1297. The advantages of permitting appeal by the nonadmiralty defendant would be particularly clear if the plaintiff had appealed the summary judgment in favor of the admiralty defendant.

It must be emphasized that this amendment does not rest on any particular assumptions as to the meaning of the § 1292(a)(3) provision that limits interlocutory appeal to orders that determine the rights and liabilities of the parties. It simply reflects the conclusion that so long as the case involves an admiralty claim and an order otherwise meets statutory requirements, the opportunity to appeal should not turn on the circumstance that the order does—or does not—dispose of an admiralty claim. No attempt is made to invoke the authority conferred by 28 U.S.C. § 1292(e) to provide by rule for appeal of an interlocutory decision that is not otherwise provided for by other subsections of § 1292.

GAP Report on Rule 9(h). No changes have been made in the published proposal.

2006 Amendment

Rule 9(h) is amended to conform to the changed title of the Supplemental Rules.

2007 Amendment

The language of Rule 9 has been amended as part of the general restyling of the Civil Rules to make them more easily understood and to make style and terminology consistent throughout the rules. These changes are intended to be stylistic only.

Rule 15 governs pleading amendments of its own force. The former redundant statement that Rule 15 governs an amendment that adds or withdraws a Rule 9(h) designation as an admiralty or maritime claim is deleted. The elimination of paragraph (2) means that "(3)" will be redesignated as "(2)" in Style Rule 9(h).

Rule 10. Form of Pleadings

(a) Caption; Names of Parties. Every pleading must have a caption with the court's name, a title, a file number, and a Rule 7(a) designation. The title of the complaint must name all the parties; the title of other pleadings, after naming the first party on each side, may refer generally to other parties.

(b) Paragraphs; Separate Statements. A party must state its claims or defenses in numbered paragraphs, each limited as far as practicable to a single set of circumstances. A later pleading may refer by number to a paragraph in an earlier pleading. If doing so would promote clarity, each claim founded on a separate transaction or occurrence—and each defense other than a denial—must be stated in a separate count or defense.

(c) Adoption by Reference; Exhibits. A statement in a pleading may be adopted by reference elsewhere in the same pleading or in any other pleading or motion. A copy of a written instrument that is an exhibit to a pleading is a part of the pleading for all purposes.

(Amended April 30, 2007, effective December 1, 2007.)

ADVISORY COMMITTEE NOTES

1937 Adoption

The first sentence is derived in part from the opening statement of former Equity Rule 25 (Bill of Complaint—Contents). The remainder of the rule is an expansion in conformity with usual state provisions. For numbered paragraphs and separate statements, see Conn.Gen.Stat., 1930, § 5513; Smith-Hurd Ill.Stats. ch. 110, § 157(2); N.Y.R.C.P., (1937) Rule 90. For incorporation by reference, see N.Y.R.C.P., (1937) Rule 90. For written instruments as exhibits, see Smith-Hurd Ill.Stats. ch. 110, § 160.

2007 Amendment

The language of Rule 10 has been amended as part of the general restyling of the Civil Rules to make them more easily understood and to make style and terminology consistent throughout the rules. These changes are intended to be stylistic only.

Rule 11. Signing Pleadings, Motions, and Other Papers; Representations to the Court; Sanctions

(a) Signature. Every pleading, written motion, and other paper must be signed by at least one attorney of record in the attorney's name—or by a party personally if the party is unrepresented. The paper must state the signer's address, e-mail address, and telephone number. Unless a rule or statute specifically states otherwise, a pleading need not be verified or accompanied by an affidavit. The court must strike an unsigned paper unless the omission is promptly corrected after being called to the attorney's or party's attention.

(b) Representations to the Court. By presenting to the court a pleading, written motion, or other paper—whether by signing, filing, submitting, or later advocating it—an attorney or unrepresented party certifies that to the best of the person's knowledge, information, and belief, formed after an inquiry reasonable under the circumstances:

(1) it is not being presented for any improper purpose, such as to harass, cause unnecessary delay, or needlessly increase the cost of litigation;

(2) the claims, defenses, and other legal contentions are warranted by existing law or by a nonfrivolous argument for extending, modifying, or reversing existing law or for establishing new law;

(3) the factual contentions have evidentiary support or, if specifically so identified, will likely have evidentiary support after a reasonable opportunity for further investigation or discovery; and

(4) the denials of factual contentions are warranted on the evidence or, if specifically so identified, are reasonably based on belief or a lack of information.

(c) Sanctions.

(1) ***In General.*** If, after notice and a reasonable opportunity to respond, the court determines that Rule 11(b) has been violated, the court may impose an appropriate sanction on any attorney, law firm, or party that violated the rule or is responsible for the violation. Absent exceptional circumstances, a law firm must be held jointly responsible for a violation committed by its partner, associate, or employee.

(2) ***Motion for Sanctions.*** A motion for sanctions must be made separately from any other motion and must describe the specific conduct that allegedly violates Rule 11(b). The motion must be served under Rule 5, but it must not be filed or be presented to the court if the challenged paper, claim, defense, contention, or denial is withdrawn or appropriately corrected within 21 days after service or within another time the court sets. If warranted, the court may award to the prevailing party the reasonable expenses, including attorney's fees, incurred for the motion.

(3) ***On the Court's Initiative.*** On its own, the court may order an attorney, law firm, or party to show cause why conduct specifically described in the order has not violated Rule 11(b).

(4) ***Nature of a Sanction.*** A sanction imposed under this rule must be limited to what suffices to deter repetition of the conduct or comparable conduct by others similarly situated. The sanction may include nonmonetary directives; an order to pay a penalty into court; or, if imposed on motion and warranted for effective deterrence, an order directing payment to the movant of part or all of the reasonable attorney's fees and other expenses directly resulting from the violation.

(5) ***Limitations on Monetary Sanctions.*** The court must not impose a monetary sanction:

(A) against a represented party for violating Rule 11(b)(2); or

(B) on its own, unless it issued the show-cause order under Rule 11(c)(3) before voluntary dismissal or settlement of the claims made by or against the party that is, or whose attorneys are, to be sanctioned.

(6) ***Requirements for an Order.*** An order imposing a sanction must describe the sanctioned conduct and explain the basis for the sanction.

(d) Inapplicability to Discovery. This rule does not apply to disclosures and discovery requests, responses, objections, and motions under Rules 26 through 37.

(Amended April 28, 1983, effective August 1, 1983; March 2, 1987, effective August 1, 1987; April 22, 1993, effective December 1, 1993; April 30, 2007, effective December 1, 2007.)

ADVISORY COMMITTEE NOTES

1937 Adoption

This is substantially the content of [former] Equity Rules 24 (Signature of Counsel) and 21 (Scandal and Impertinence) consolidated and unified. Compare former Equity Rule 36 (Officers Before Whom Pleadings Verified). Compare to similar purposes, *English Rules Under the Judicature Act* (The Annual Practice, 1937) O. 19, r. 4, and *Great Australian Gold Mining Co. v. Martin*, L.R. 5 Ch.Div. 1, 10 (1877). Subscription of pleadings is required in many codes. 2 Minn.Stat. (Mason, 1927) § 9265; N.Y.R.C.P. (1937) Rule 91; 2 N.D.Comp.Laws Ann. (1913) § 7455.

This rule expressly continues any statute which requires a pleading to be verified or accompanied by an affidavit, such as: U.S.C., Title 28:

§ 381 [former] (Preliminary injunctions and temporary restraining orders)

§ 762 [now 1402] (Suit against the United States)

U.S.C., Title 28, § 829 [now 1927] (Costs; attorney liable for, when) is unaffected by this rule.

For complaints which must be verified under these rules, see Rules 23(b) (Secondary Action by Shareholders) and 65 (Injunctions).

For abolition of former rule in equity that the averments of an answer under oath must be overcome by the testimony of two witnesses or of one witness sustained by corroborating circumstances, see 12 P.S.Pa. § 1222; for the rule in equity itself, see *Greenfield v. Blumenthal*, C.C.A.3, 1934, 69 F.2d 294.

1983 Amendment

Since its original promulgation, Rule 11 has provided for the striking of pleadings and the imposition of disciplinary sanctions to check abuses in the signing of pleadings. Its provisions have always applied to motions and other papers by virtue of incorporation by reference in Rule 7(b)(2). The amendment and the addition of Rule 7(b)(3) expressly confirms this applicability.

Experience shows that in practice Rule 11 has not been effective in deterring abuses. See 6 Wright & Miller, *Federal Practice and Procedure: Civil* § 1334 (1971). There has been considerable confusion as to (1) the circumstances that should trigger striking a pleading or motion or taking disciplinary action, (2) the standard of conduct expected of attorneys who sign pleadings and motions, and (3) the range of available and appropriate sanctions. See Rodes, Ripple & Mooney, *Sanctions Imposable for Violations of the Federal Rules of Civil Procedure* 64–65, Federal Judicial Center (1981). The new language is intended to reduce the reluctance of courts to impose sanctions, see Moore, *Federal Practice* ¶ 7.05, at 1547, by emphasizing the responsibilities of the attorney and reenforcing those obligations by the imposition of sanctions.

The amended rule attempts to deal with the problem by building upon and expanding the equitable doctrine permitting the court to award expenses, including attorney's fees, to a litigant whose opponent acts in bad faith in instituting or conducting litigation. See, e.g., *Roadway Express, Inc. v. Piper*, 447 U.S. 752 (1980); *Hall v. Cole*, 412 U.S. 1, 5 (1973). Greater attention by the district courts to pleading and motion abuses and the imposition of sanctions when appropriate, should discourage dilatory or abusive tactics and help to streamline the litigation process by lessening frivolous claims or defenses.

The expanded nature of the lawyer's certification in the fifth sentence of amended Rule 11 recognizes that the litigation process may be abused for purposes other than delay. See, e.g., *Browning Debenture Holders' Committee v. DASA Corp.*, 560 F.2d 1078 (2d Cir.1977).

The words "good ground to support" the pleading in the original rule were interpreted to have both factual and legal elements. See, e.g., *Heart Disease Research Foundation v. General Motors Corp.*, 15 Fed.R.Serv.2d 1517, 1519 (S.D.N.Y.1972). They have been replaced by a standard of conduct that is more focused.

The new language stresses the need for some prefiling inquiry into both the facts and the law to satisfy the affirmative duty imposed by the rule. The standard is one of reasonableness under the circumstances. See *Kinee v. Abraham Lincoln Fed. Sav. & Loan Ass'n*, 365 F.Supp. 975 (E.D.Pa.1973). This standard is more stringent than the original good-faith formula and thus it is expected that a greater range of circumstances will trigger its violation. See *Nemeroff v. Abelson*, 620 F.2d 339 (2d Cir.1980).

The rule is not intended to chill an attorney's enthusiasm or creativity in pursuing factual or legal theories. The court is expected to avoid using the wisdom of hindsight and should test the signer's conduct by inquiring what was reasonable to believe at the time the pleading, motion, or other paper was submitted. Thus, what constitutes a reasonable inquiry may depend on such factors as how much time for investigation was available to the signer; whether he had to rely on a client for information as to the facts underlying the pleading, motion, or other paper; whether the pleading, motion, or other paper was based on a plausible view of the law; or whether he depended on forwarding counsel or another member of the bar.

The rule does not require a party or an attorney to disclose privileged communications or work product in order to show that the signing of the pleading, motion, or other paper is substantially justified. The provisions of Rule 26(c), including appropriate orders after *in camera* inspection by the court, remain available to protect a party claiming privilege or work product protection.

Amended Rule 11 continues to apply to anyone who signs a pleading, motion, or other paper. Although the standard is the same for unrepresented parties, who are obliged themselves to sign the pleadings, the court has sufficient discretion to take account of the special circumstances that often arise in *pro se* situations. See *Haines v. Kerner*, 404 U.S. 519 (1972).

The provision in the original rule for striking pleadings and motions as sham and false has been deleted. The passage has rarely been utilized, and decisions thereunder have tended to confuse the issue of attorney honesty with the merits of the action. See generally Risinger, *Honesty in Pleading and its Enforcement: Some "Striking" Problems with Fed.R.Civ.P. 11,* 61 Minn.L.Rev. 1 (1976). Motions under this provision generally present issues better dealt with under Rules 8, 12, or 56. See *Murchison v. Kirby,* 27 F.R.D. 14 (S.D.N.Y.1961); 5 Wright & Miller, *Federal Practice and Procedure: Civil* § 1334 (1969).

The former reference to the inclusion of scandalous or indecent matter, which is itself strong indication that an improper purpose underlies the pleading, motion, or other paper, also has been deleted as unnecessary. Such matter may be stricken under Rule 12(f) as well as dealt with under the more general language of amended Rule 11.

The text of the amended rule seeks to dispel apprehensions that efforts to obtain enforcement will be fruitless by insuring that the rule will be applied when properly invoked. The word "sanctions" in the caption, for example, stresses a deterrent orientation in dealing with improper pleadings, motions or other papers. This corresponds to the approach in imposing sanctions for discovery abuses. See *National Hockey League v. Metropolitan Hockey Club,* 427 U.S. 639 (1976) (per curiam). And the words "shall impose" in the last sentence focus the court's attention on the need to impose sanctions for pleading and motion abuses. The court, however, retains the necessary flexibility to deal appropriately with violations of the rule. It has discretion to tailor sanctions to the particular facts of the case, with which it should be well acquainted.

The references in the former text to wilfulness as a prerequisite to disciplinary action has been deleted. However, in considering the nature and severity of the sanctions to be imposed, the court should take account of the state of the attorney's or party's actual or presumed knowledge when the pleading or other paper was signed. Thus, for example, when a party is not represented by counsel, the absence of legal advice is an appropriate factor to be considered.

Courts currently appear to believe they may impose sanctions on their own motion. See *North American Trading Corp. v. Zale Corp.,* 73 F.R.D. 293 (S.D.N.Y.1979). Authority to do so has been made explicit in order to overcome the traditional reluctance of courts to intervene unless requested by one of the parties. The detection and punishment of a violation of the signing requirement, encouraged by the amended rule, is part of the court's responsibility for securing the system's effective operation.

If the duty imposed by the rule is violated, the court should have the discretion to impose sanctions on either the attorney, the party the signing attorney represents, or both, or on an unrepresented party who signed the pleading, and the new rule so provides. Although Rule 11 has been silent on the point, courts have claimed the power to impose sanctions on an attorney personally, either by imposing costs or employing the contempt technique. See 5 Wright & Miller, *Federal Practice and Procedure: Civil* § 1334 (1969); 2A Moore, *Federal Practice* ¶ 11.02, at 2104 n. 8. This power has been used infrequently. The amended rule should eliminate any doubt as to the propriety of assessing sanctions against the attorney.

Even though it is the attorney whose signature violates the rule, it may be appropriate under the circumstances of the case to impose a sanction on the client. See *Browning Debenture Holders' Committee v. DASA Corp.,* supra. This modification brings Rule 11 in line with practice under Rule 37, which allows sanctions for abuses during discovery to be imposed upon the party, the attorney, or both.

A party seeking sanctions should give notice to the court and the offending party promptly upon discovering a basis for doing so. The time when sanctions are to be imposed rests in the discretion of the trial judge. However, it is anticipated that in the case of pleadings the sanctions issue under Rule 11 normally will be determined at the end of the litigation, and in the case of motions at the time when the motion is decided or shortly thereafter. The procedure obviously must comport with due process requirements. The particular format to be followed should depend on the circumstances of the situation and the severity of the sanction under consideration. In many situations the judge's participation in the proceedings provides him with full knowledge of the relevant facts and little further inquiry will be necessary.

To assure that the efficiencies achieved through more effective operation of the pleading regimen will not be offset by the cost of satellite litigation over the imposition of sanctions, the court must to the extent possible limit the scope of sanction proceedings to the record. Thus, discovery should be conducted only by leave of the court, and then only in extraordinary circumstances.

Although the encompassing reference to "other papers" in new Rule 11 literally includes discovery papers, the certification requirement in that context is governed by proposed new Rule 26(g). Discovery motions, however, fall within the ambit of Rule 11.

1987 Amendment

The amendments are technical. No substantive change is intended.

1993 Amendments

Purpose of revision. This revision is intended to remedy problems that have arisen in the interpretation and application of the 1983 revision of the rule. For empirical examination of experience under the 1983 rule, see, *e.g.,* New York State Bar Committee on Federal Courts, *Sanctions and Attorneys' Fees* (1987); T. Willging, *The Rule 11 Sanctioning Process* (1989); American Judicature Society, *Report of the Third Circuit Task Force on Federal Rule of Civil Procedure 11* (S. Burbank ed., 1989); E. Wiggins, T. Willging, and D. Stienstra, *Report on Rule 11* (Federal Judicial Center 1991). For book-length analyses of the case law, see G. Joseph, *Sanctions: The Federal Law of Litigation Abuse* (1989); J. Solovy, *The Federal Law of Sanctions* (1991); G. Vairo, *Rule 11 Sanctions: Case Law Perspectives and Preventive Measures* (1991).

The rule retains the principle that attorneys and pro se litigants have an obligation to the court to refrain from conduct that frustrates the aims of Rule 1. The revision broadens the scope of this obligation, but places greater constraints on the imposition of sanctions and should reduce the number of motions for sanctions presented to the court. New subdivision (d) removes from the ambit of this rule all discovery requests, responses, objections, and motions subject to the provisions of Rule 26 through 37.

Subdivision (a). Retained in this subdivision are the provisions requiring signatures on pleadings, written motions, and other papers. Unsigned papers are to be received by the Clerk, but then are to be stricken if the omission of the signature is not corrected promptly after being called to the attention of the attorney or pro se litigant. Correction can be made by signing the paper on file or by submitting a duplicate that contains the signature. A court may require by local rule that papers contain additional identifying information regarding the parties or attorneys, such as telephone numbers to facilitate facsimile transmissions, though, as for omission of a signature, the paper should not be rejected for failure to provide such information.

The sentence in the former rule relating to the effect of answers under oath is no longer needed and has been eliminated. The provision in the former rule that signing a paper constitutes a certificate that it has been read by the signer also has been eliminated as unnecessary. The obligations imposed under subdivision (b) obviously require that a pleading, written motion, or other paper be read before it is filed or submitted to the court.

Subdivisions (b) and (c). These subdivisions restate the provisions requiring attorneys and pro se litigants to conduct a reasonable inquiry into the law and facts before signing pleadings, written motions, and other documents, and prescribing sanctions for violation of these obligations. The revision in part expands the responsibilities of litigants to the court, while providing greater constraints and flexibility in dealing with infractions of the rule. The rule continues to require litigants to "stop-and-think" before initially making legal or factual contentions. It also, however, emphasizes the duty of candor by subjecting litigants to potential sanctions for insisting upon a position after it is no longer tenable and by generally providing protection against sanctions if they withdraw or correct contentions after a potential violation is called to their attention.

The rule applies only to assertions contained in papers filed with or submitted to the court. It does not cover matters arising for the first time during oral presentations to the court, when counsel may make statements that would not have been made if there had been more time for study and reflection. However, a litigant's obligations with respect to the contents of these papers are not measured solely as of the time they are filed with or submitted to the court, but include reaffirming to the court and advocating positions contained in those pleadings and motions after learning that they cease to have any merit. For example, an attorney who during a pretrial conference insists on a claim or defense should be viewed as "presenting to the court" that contention and would be subject to the obligations of subdivision (b) measured as of that time. Similarly, if after a notice of removal is filed, a party urges in federal court the allegations of a pleading filed in state court (whether as claims, defenses, or in disputes regarding removal or remand), it would be viewed as "presenting"—and hence certifying to the district court under Rule 11—those allegations.

The certification with respect to allegations and other factual contentions is revised in recognition that sometimes a litigant may have good reason to believe that a fact is true or false but may need discovery, formal or informal, from opposing parties or third persons to gather and confirm the evidentiary basis for the allegation. Tolerance of factual contentions in initial pleadings by plaintiffs or defendants when specifically identified as made on information and belief does not relieve litigants from the obligation to conduct an appropriate investigation into the facts that is reasonable under the circumstances; it is not a license to join parties, make claims, or present defenses without any factual basis or justification. Moreover, if evidentiary support is not obtained after a reasonable opportunity for further investigation or discovery, the party has a duty under the rule not to persist with that contention. Subdivision (b) does not require a formal amendment to pleadings for which evidentiary support is not obtained, but rather calls upon a litigant not thereafter to advocate such claims or defenses.

The certification is that there is (or likely will be) "evidentiary support" for the allegation, not that the party will prevail with respect to its contention regarding the fact. That summary judgment is rendered against a party does not necessarily mean, for purposes of this certification, that it had no evidentiary support for its position. On the other hand, if a party has evidence with respect to a contention that would suffice to defeat a motion for summary judgment based thereon, it would have sufficient "evidentiary support" for purposes of Rule 11.

Denials of factual contentions involve somewhat different considerations. Often, of course, a denial is premised upon the existence of evidence contradicting the alleged fact. At other times a denial is permissible because, after an appropriate investigation, a party has no information concerning the matter or, indeed, has a reasonable basis for doubting the credibility of the only evidence relevant to the matter. A party should not deny an allegation it knows to be true; but it is not required, simply because it lacks contradictory evidence, to admit an allegation that it believes is not true.

The changes in subdivisions (b)(3) and (b)(4) will serve to equalize the burden of the rule upon plaintiffs and defendants, who under Rule 8(b) are in effect allowed to deny allegations by stating that from their initial investigation they lack sufficient information to form a belief as to the truth of the allegation. If, after further investigation or discovery, a denial is no longer warranted, the defendant should not continue to insist on that denial. While sometimes helpful, formal amendment of the pleadings to withdraw an allegation or denial is not required by subdivision (b).

Arguments for extensions, modifications, or reversals of existing law or for creation of new law do not violate subdivision (b)(2) provided they are "nonfrivolous." This establishes an objective standard, intended to eliminate any "empty-head pure-heart" justification for patently frivolous arguments. However, the extent to which a litigant has researched the issues and found some support for its theories even in minority opinions, in law review articles, or through consultation with other attorneys should certainly be taken into account in determining whether paragraph (2) has been violated. Although arguments for a change of law are not required to be specifically so identified, a contention that is so identified should be viewed with greater tolerance under the rule.

The court has available a variety of possible sanctions to impose for violations, such as striking the offending paper; issuing an admonition, reprimand, or censure; requiring participation in seminars or other educational programs; ordering a fine payable to the court; referring the matter to disciplinary authorities (or, in the case of government attorneys, to the Attorney General, Inspector General, or agency head), etc. *See Manual for Complex Litigation, Second,* § 42.3. The rule does not attempt to enumerate the factors a court should consider in deciding whether to impose a sanction or what sanctions would be appropriate in the circumstances; but, for emphasis, it does specifically note that a sanction may be nonmonetary as well as monetary. Whether the improper conduct was willful, or negligent; whether it was part of a pattern of activity, or an isolated event; whether it infected the entire pleading, or only one particular count or defense; whether the person has engaged in similar conduct in other litigation; whether it was intended to injure; what effect it had on the litigation process in time or expense; whether the responsible person is trained in the law; what amount, given the financial resources of the responsible person, is needed to deter that person from repetition in the same case; what amount is needed to deter similar activity by other litigants: all of these may in a particular case be proper considerations. The court has significant discretion in determining what sanctions, if any, should be imposed for a violation, subject to the principle that the sanctions should not be more severe than reasonably necessary to deter repetition of the conduct by the offending person or comparable conduct by similarly situated persons.

Since the purpose of Rule 11 sanctions is to deter rather than to compensate, the rule provides that, if a monetary sanction is imposed, it should ordinarily be paid into court as a penalty. However, under unusual circumstances, particularly for (b)(1) violations, deterrence may be ineffective unless the sanction not only requires the person violating the rule to make a monetary payment, but also directs that some or all of this payment be made to those injured by the violation. Accordingly, the rule authorizes the court, if requested in a motion and if so warranted, to award attorney's fees to another party. Any such award to another party, however, should not exceed the expenses and attorneys' fees for the services directly and unavoidably caused by the violation of the certification requirement. If, for example, a wholly unsupportable count were included in a multi-count complaint or counterclaim for the purpose of needlessly increasing the cost of litigation to an impecunious adversary, any award of expenses should be limited to those directly caused by inclusion of the improper count, and not those resulting from the filing of the complaint or answer itself. The award should not provide compensation for services that could have been avoided by an earlier disclosure of evidence or an earlier challenge to the groundless claims or defenses. Moreover, partial reimbursement of fees may constitute a sufficient deterrent with respect to violations by persons having modest financial resources. In cases brought under statutes providing for fees to be awarded to prevailing parties, the court should not employ cost-shifting under this rule in a manner that would be inconsistent with the standards that govern the statutory award of fees, such as stated in *Christiansburg Garment Co. v. EEOC,* 434 U.S. 412 (1978).

The sanction should be imposed on the persons—whether attorneys, law firms, or parties—who have violated the rule or who may be determined to be responsible for the violation. The person signing, filing, submitting, or advocating a document has a nondelegable responsibility to the court, and in most situations is the person to be sanctioned for a violation. Absent exceptional circumstances, a law firm is to be held also responsible when, as a result of a motion under subdivision (c)(1)(A), one of its partners, associates, or employees is determined to have violated the rule. Since such a motion may be filed only if the offending paper is not withdrawn or corrected within 21 days after service of the motion, it is appropriate that the law firm ordinarily be viewed as jointly responsible under established principles of agency. This provision is designed to remove the restrictions of the former rule. *Cf. Pavelic & LeFlore v. Marvel Entertainment Group,* 493 U.S. 120 (1989) (1983 version of Rule 11 does not permit sanctions against law firm of attorney signing groundless complaint).

The revision permits the court to consider whether other attorneys in the firm, co-counsel, other law firms, or the party itself should be held accountable for their part in causing a violation. When appropriate, the court can make an additional inquiry in order to determine whether the sanction should be imposed on such persons, firms, or parties either in addition to or, in unusual circumstances, instead of the person actually making the presentation to the court. For example, such an inquiry may be appropriate in cases involving governmental agencies or other institutional parties that frequently impose substantial restrictions on the discretion of individual attorneys employed by it.

Sanctions that involve monetary awards (such as a fine or an award of attorney's fees) may not be imposed on a represented party for causing a violation of subdivision (b)(2), involving frivolous contentions of law. Monetary responsibility for such violations is more properly placed solely on the party's attorneys. With this limitation, the rule should not be subject to attack under the Rules Enabling Act. See *Willy v. Coastal Corp.,* 503 U.S. 131 (1992); *Business Guides, Inc. v. Chromatic Communications Enter. Inc.,* 498 U.S. 533 (1991). This restriction does not limit the court's power to impose sanctions or remedial orders that may have collateral financial consequences upon a party, such as dismissal of a claim, preclusion of a defense, or preparation of amended pleadings.

Explicit provision is made for litigants to be provided notice of the alleged violation and an opportunity to respond before sanctions are imposed. Whether the matter should be decided solely on the basis of written submissions or should be scheduled for oral argument (or, indeed, for evidentiary presentation) will depend on the circumstances. If the court imposes a sanction, it must, unless waived, indicate its reasons in a written order or on the record; the court should not ordinarily have to explain its denial of a motion for sanctions. Whether a violation has occurred and what sanctions, if any, to impose for a violation are matters committed to the discretion of the trial court; accordingly, as under current law, the standard for appellate review of these decisions will be for abuse of discretion. *See Cooter & Gell v. Hartmarx Corp.,* 496 U.S. 384 (1990) (noting, however, that an abuse would be established if the court based its ruling on an erroneous view of the law or on a clearly erroneous assessment of the evidence).

The revision leaves for resolution on a case-by-case basis, considering the particular circumstances involved, the question as to when a motion for violation of Rule 11 should be served and when, if filed, it should be decided. Ordinarily the motion should be served promptly after the inappropriate paper is filed, and, if delayed too long, may be viewed as untimely. In other circumstances, it should not be served until the other party has had a reasonable opportunity for discovery. Given the "safe harbor" provisions discussed below, a party cannot delay serving its Rule 11 motion until conclusion of the case (or judicial rejection of the offending contention).

Rule 11 motions should not be made or threatened for minor, inconsequential violations of the standards prescribed by subdivision (b). They should not be employed as a discovery device or to test the legal sufficiency or efficacy of allegations in the pleadings; other motions are available for those purposes. Nor should Rule 11 motions be prepared to emphasize the merits of a party's position, to exact an unjust settlement, to intimidate an adversary into withdrawing contentions that are fairly debatable, to increase the costs of litigation, to create a conflict of interest between attorney and client, or to seek disclosure of matters otherwise protected by the attorney-client privilege or the work-product doctrine. As under the prior rule, the court may defer its ruling (or its decision as to the identity of the persons to be sanctioned) until final resolution of the case in order to avoid immediate conflicts of interest and to reduce the disruption created if a disclosure of attorney-client communications is needed to determine whether a violation occurred or to identify the person responsible for the violation.

The rule provides that requests for sanctions must be made as a separate motion, *i.e.*, not simply included as an additional prayer for relief contained in another motion. The motion for sanctions is not, however, to be filed until at least 21 days (or such other period as the court may set) after being served. If, during this period, the alleged violation is corrected, as by withdrawing (whether formally or informally) some allegation or contention, the motion should not be filed with the court. These provisions are intended to provide a type of "safe harbor" against motions under Rule 11 in that a party will not be subject to sanctions on the basis of another party's motion unless, after receiving the motion, it refuses to withdraw that position or to acknowledge candidly that it does not currently have evidence to support a specified allegation. Under the former rule, parties were sometimes reluctant to abandon a questionable contention lest that be viewed as evidence of a violation of Rule 11; under the revision, the timely withdrawal of a contention will protect a party against a motion for sanctions.

To stress the seriousness of a motion for sanctions and to define precisely the conduct claimed to violate the rule, the revision provides that the "safe harbor" period begins to run only upon service of the motion. In most cases, however, counsel should be expected to give informal notice to the other party, whether in person or by a telephone call or letter, of a potential violation before proceeding to prepare and serve a Rule 11 motion.

As under former Rule 11, the filing of a motion for sanctions is itself subject to the requirements of the rule and can lead to sanctions. However, service of a cross motion under Rule 11 should rarely be needed since under the revision the court may award to the person who prevails on a motion under Rule 11—whether the movant or the target of the motion—reasonable expenses, including attorney's fees, incurred in presenting or opposing the motion.

The power of the court to act on its own initiative is retained, but with the condition that this be done through a show cause order. This procedure provides the person with notice and an opportunity to respond. The revision provides that a monetary sanction imposed after a court-initiated show cause order be limited to a penalty payable to the court and that it be imposed only if the show cause order is issued before any voluntary dismissal or an agreement of the parties to settle the claims made by or against the litigant. Parties settling a case should not be subsequently faced with an unexpected order from the court leading to monetary sanctions that might have affected their willingness to settle or voluntarily dismiss a case. Since show cause orders will ordinarily be issued only in situations that are akin to a contempt of court, the rule does not provide a "safe harbor" to a litigant for withdrawing a claim, defense, etc., after a show cause order has been issued on the court's own initiative. Such corrective action, however, should be taken into account in deciding what—if any—sanction to impose if, after consideration of the litigant's response, the court concludes that a violation has occurred.

Subdivision (d). Rules 26(g) and 37 establish certification standards and sanctions that apply to discovery disclosures, requests, responses, objections, and motions. It is appropriate that Rules 26 through 37, which are specially designed for the discovery process, govern such documents and conduct rather than the more general provisions of Rule 11. Subdivision (d) has been added to accomplish this result.

Rule 11 is not the exclusive source for control of improper presentations of claims, defenses, or contentions. It does not supplant statutes permitting awards of attorney's fees to prevailing parties or alter the principles governing such awards. It does not inhibit the court in punishing for contempt, in exercising its inherent powers, or in imposing sanctions, awarding expenses, or directing remedial action authorized under other rules or under 28 U.S.C. § 1927. *See Chambers v. NASCO,* 501 U.S. 32 (1991). Chambers cautions, however, against reliance upon inherent powers if appropriate sanctions can be imposed under provisions such as Rule 11, and the procedures specified in Rule 11—notice, opportunity to respond, and findings—should ordinarily be employed when imposing a sanction under the court's inherent powers. Finally, it should be noted that Rule 11 does not preclude a party from initiating an independent action for malicious prosecution or abuse of process.

2007 Amendment

The language of Rule 11 has been amended as part of the general restyling of the Civil Rules to make them more easily understood and to make style and terminology consistent throughout the rules. These changes are intended to be stylistic only.

Providing an e-mail address is useful, but does not of itself signify consent to filing or service by e-mail.

Rule 12. Defenses and Objections: When and How Presented; Motion for Judgment on the Pleadings; Consolidating Motions; Waiving Defenses; Pretrial Hearing

(a) Time to Serve a Responsive Pleading.

(1) ***In General.*** Unless another time is specified by this rule or a federal statute, the time for serving a responsive pleading is as follows:

(A) A defendant must serve an answer:

(i) within 20 days after being served with the summons and complaint; or

(ii) if it has timely waived service under Rule 4(d), within 60 days after the request for a waiver was sent, or within 90 days after it was sent to the defendant outside any judicial district of the United States.

(B) A party must serve an answer to a counterclaim or crossclaim within 20 days after being served with the pleading that states the counterclaim or crossclaim.

(C) A party must serve a reply to an answer within 20 days after being served with an order to reply, unless the order specifies a different time.

(2) ***United States and Its Agencies, Officers, or Employees Sued in an Official Capacity.*** The United States, a United States agency, or a United States officer or employee sued only in an official capacity must serve an answer to a complaint, counterclaim, or crossclaim within 60 days after service on the United States attorney.

(3) ***United States Officers or Employees Sued in an Individual Capacity.*** A United States officer or employee sued in an individual capacity for an act or omission occurring in connection with duties performed on the United States' behalf must serve an answer to a complaint, counterclaim, or crossclaim within 60 days after service on the officer or employee or service on the United States attorney, whichever is later.

(4) ***Effect of a Motion.*** Unless the court sets a different time, serving a motion under this rule alters these periods as follows:

(A) if the court denies the motion or postpones its disposition until trial, the responsive pleading must be served within 10 days after notice of the court's action; or

(B) if the court grants a motion for a more definite statement, the responsive pleading must be served within 10 days after the more definite statement is served.

(b) How to Present Defenses. Every defense to a claim for relief in any pleading must be asserted in the responsive pleading if one is required. But a party may assert the following defenses by motion:

(1) lack of subject-matter jurisdiction;

(2) lack of personal jurisdiction;

(3) improper venue;

(4) insufficient process;

(5) insufficient service of process;

(6) failure to state a claim upon which relief can be granted; and

(7) failure to join a party under Rule 19.

A motion asserting any of these defenses must be made before pleading if a responsive pleading is allowed. If a pleading sets out a claim for relief that does not require a responsive pleading, an opposing party may assert at trial any defense to that claim. No defense or objection is waived by joining it with one or more other defenses or objections in a responsive pleading or in a motion.

(c) Motion for Judgment on the Pleadings. After the pleadings are closed—but early enough not to delay trial—a party may move for judgment on the pleadings.

(d) Result of Presenting Matters Outside the Pleadings. If, on a motion under Rule 12(b)(6) or 12(c), matters outside the pleadings are presented to and not excluded by the court, the motion must be treated as one for summary judgment under Rule 56. All parties must be given a reasonable opportunity to present all the material that is pertinent to the motion.

(e) Motion for a More Definite Statement. A party may move for a more definite statement of a pleading to which a responsive pleading is allowed but which is so vague or ambiguous that the party cannot reasonably prepare a response. The motion must be made before filing a responsive pleading and must point out the defects complained of and the details desired. If the court orders a more definite statement and the order is not obeyed within 10 days after notice of the order or within the time the court sets, the court may strike the pleading or issue any other appropriate order.

(f) Motion to Strike. The court may strike from a pleading an insufficient defense or any redundant, immaterial, impertinent, or scandalous matter. The court may act:

(1) on its own; or

(2) on motion made by a party either before responding to the pleading or, if a response is not allowed, within 20 days after being served with the pleading.

(g) Joining Motions.

(1) ***Right to Join.*** A motion under this rule may be joined with any other motion allowed by this rule.

(2) ***Limitation on Further Motions.*** Except as provided in Rule 12(h)(2) or (3), a party that makes a motion under this rule must not

make another motion under this rule raising a defense or objection that was available to the party but omitted from its earlier motion.

(h) Waiving and Preserving Certain Defenses.

(1) ***When Some Are Waived.*** A party waives any defense listed in Rule 12(b)(2)-(5) by:

(A) omitting it from a motion in the circumstances described in Rule 12(g)(2); or

(B) failing to either:

(i) make it by motion under this rule; or

(ii) include it in a responsive pleading or in an amendment allowed by Rule 15(a)(1) as a matter of course.

(2) ***When to Raise Others.*** Failure to state a claim upon which relief can be granted, to join a person required by Rule 19(b), or to state a legal defense to a claim may be raised:

(A) in any pleading allowed or ordered under Rule 7(a);

(B) by a motion under Rule 12(c); or

(C) at trial.

(3) ***Lack of Subject-Matter Jurisdiction.*** If the court determines at any time that it lacks subject-matter jurisdiction, the court must dismiss the action.

(i) Hearing Before Trial. If a party so moves, any defense listed in Rule 12(b)(1)-(7)—whether made in a pleading or by motion—and a motion under Rule 12(c) must be heard and decided before trial unless the court orders a deferral until trial.

(Amended December 27, 1946, effective March 19, 1948; January 21, 1963, effective July 1, 1963; February 28, 1966, effective July 1, 1966; March 2, 1987, effective August 1, 1987; April 22, 1993, effective December 1, 1993; April 17, 2000, effective December 1, 2000; April 30, 2007, effective December 1, 2007.)

ADVISORY COMMITTEE NOTES

1937 Adoption

Note to Subdivision (a). 1. Compare [former] Equity Rules 12 (Issue of Subpoena—Time for Answer) and 31 (Reply—When Required—When Cause at Issue); 4 Mont. Rev.Codes Ann. (1935) §§ 9107, 9158; N.Y.C. P.A. (1937) § 263; N.Y.R.C.P. (1937) Rules 109–111.

2. U.S.C., Title 28, § 763 (now § 547) (Petition in action against United States; service; appearance by district attorney) provides that the United States as a defendant shall have 60 days within which to answer or otherwise defend. This and other statutes which provide 60 days for the United States or an officer or agency thereof to answer or otherwise defend are continued by this rule. In so far as any statutes not excepted in rule 81 provide a different time for a defendant to defend, such statutes are modified. See U.S.C., Title 28, [former] § 45 (District courts; practice and procedure in certain cases under the interstate commerce laws) (30 days).

3. Compare the last sentence of [former] Equity Rule 29 (Defenses—How Presented) and N.Y.C.P.A. (1937) § 283. See Rule 15(a) for time within which to plead to an amended pleading.

Note to Subdivisions (b) and (d). 1. See generally [former] Equity Rules 29 (Defenses—How Presented), 33 (Testing Sufficiency of Defense), 43 (Defect of Parties—Resisting Objection), and 44 (Defect of Parties—Tardy Objection); N.Y.C.P.A. (1937) §§ 277–280; N.Y.R.C.P. (1937) Rules 106–112; *English Rules Under the Judicature Act* (The Annual Practice, 1937) O. 25, r.r. 1–4; Clark, *Code Pleading,* 1928, pp. 371–381.

2. For provisions authorizing defenses to be made in the answer or reply see *English Rules Under the Judicature Act,* (The Annual Practice, 1937) O. 25, r.r. 1–4; 1 Miss.Code Ann. (1930) §§ 378, 379. Compare Equity Rule 29 (Defenses—How Presented); U.S.C.A., Title 28, [former] § 45 (District Courts; practice and procedure in certain cases under the interstate commerce laws). U.S.C., Title 28, [former] § 45, substantially continued by this rule, provides: "No replication need be filed to the answer, and objections to the sufficiency of the petition or answer as not setting forth a cause of action or defense must be taken at the final hearing or by motion to dismiss the petition based on said grounds, which motion may be made at any time before answer is filed." Compare Calif.Code Civ.Proc., (Deering, 1937) § 433; 4 Nev.Comp.Laws (Hillyer, 1929) § 8600. For provisions that the defendant may demur and answer at the same time, see Calif.Code Civ.Proc. (Deering, 1937) § 431; 4 Nev.Comp. Laws (Hillyer, 1929) § 8598.

3. [Former] Equity Rule 29 (Defenses—How Presented) abolished demurrers and provided that defenses in point of law arising on the face of the bill should be made by motion to dismiss or in the answer, with further provision that every such point of law going to the whole or material part of the cause or causes stated might be called up and disposed of before final hearing "at the discretion of the court." Likewise many state practices have abolished the demurrer, or retain it only to attack substantial and not formal defects. See 6 Tenn.Code Ann. (Williams, 1934) § 8784; Ala.Code Ann. (Michie, 1928) § 9479; 2 Mass.Gen.Laws (Ter.Ed., 1932) ch. 231, §§ 15–18; Kansas Gen.Stat.Ann. (1935) §§ 60–705, 60–706.

Note to Subdivision (c). Compare [former] Equity Rule 33 (Testing Sufficiency of Defense); N.Y.R.C.P. (1937) Rules 111 and 112.

Note to Subdivisions (e) and (f). Compare [former] Equity Rules 20 (Further and Particular Statement in Pleading May be Required) and 21 (Scandal and Impertinence); *English Rules Under the Judicature Act* (The Annual Practice, 1937) O. 19, r.r. 7, 7a, 7b, 8; 4 Mont.Rev.Codes Ann. (1935) §§ 9166, 9167; N.Y.C.P.A. (1937) § 247; N.Y.C.P.A. (1937) Rules 103, 115, 116, 117; Wyo.Rev.Stat.Ann. (Courtright, 1931) §§ 89–1033, 89–1034.

Note to Subdivision (g). Compare Rules of the District Court of the United States for the District of Columbia (1937) Equity Rule 11; N.M. Rules of Pleading, Practice and Procedure, 38 N.M.Rep. vii. [105–408] (1934); Wash.Gen. Rules of the Superior Courts, 1 Wash.Rev.Stat.Ann. (Remington, 1932) p. 160, Rule VI(e) and (f).

Note to Subdivision (h). Compare Calif.Code Civ.Proc. (Deering, 1937) § 434; 2 Minn.Stat. (Mason, 1927) § 9252;

N.Y.C.P.A. (1937) §§ 278 and 279; Wash.Gen.Rules of the Superior Courts, 1 Wash.Rev.Stat.Ann. (Remington, 1932) p. 160, Rule VI(e). This rule continues U.S.C.A., Title 28, former § 80 [now 1359, 1447, 1919] (Dismissal or remand) (of action over which district court lacks jurisdiction), while U.S.C.A., Title 28, § 399 (Amendments to show diverse citizenship) is continued by Rule 15.

1946 Amendment

Note. Subdivision (a). Various minor alterations in language have been made to improve the statement of the rule. All references to bills of particulars have been stricken in accordance with changes made in subdivision (e).

Subdivision (b). The addition of defense (7), "failure to join an indispensable party", cures an omission in the rules which are silent as to the mode of raising such failure. See Commentary, *Manner of Raising Objection of Non-Joinder of Indispensable Party,* 1940, 2 Fed.Rules Serv. 658, and, 1942, 5 Fed.Rules Serv. 820. In one case, *United States v. Metropolitan Life Ins. Co.*, E.D.Pa.1941, 36 F.Supp. 399, the failure to join an indispensable party was raised under Rule 12(c).

Rule 12(b)(6), permitting a motion to dismiss for failure of the complaint to state a claim on which relief can be granted, is substantially the same as the old demurrer for failure of a pleading to state a cause of action. Some courts have held that as the rule by its terms refers to statements in the complaint, extraneous matter on affidavits, depositions or otherwise, may not be introduced in support of the motion, or to resist it. On the other hand, in many cases the district courts have permitted the introduction of such material. When these cases have reached circuit courts of appeals in situations where the extraneous material so received shows that there is no genuine issue as to any material question of fact and that on the undisputed facts as disclosed by the affidavits or depositions, one party or the other is entitled to judgment as a matter of law, the circuit courts, properly enough, have been reluctant to dispose of the case merely on the face of the pleading, and in the interest of prompt disposition of the action have made a final disposition of it. In dealing with such situations the Second Circuit has made the sound suggestion that whatever its label or original basis, the motion may be treated as a motion for summary judgment and disposed of as such. *Samara v. United States*, C.C.A.2, 1942, 129 F.2d 594, certiorari denied 63 S.Ct. 258, 317 U.S. 686, 87 L.Ed. 549; *Boro Hall Corp. v. General Motors Corp.,* C.C.A.2, 1942, 124 F.2d 822, certiorari denied 63 S.Ct. 436, 317 U.S. 695, 87 L.Ed. 556. See, also, *Kithcart v. Metropolitan Life Ins. Co.,* C.C.A.8, 1945, 150 F.2d 997.

It has also been suggested that this practice could be justified on the ground that the federal rules permit "speaking" motions. The Committee entertains the view that on motion under Rule 12(b)(6) to dismiss for failure of the complaint to state a good claim, the trial court should have authority to permit the introduction of extraneous matter, such as may be offered on a motion for summary judgment, and if it does not exclude such matter the motion should then be treated as a motion for summary judgment and disposed of in the manner and on the conditions stated in Rule 56 relating to summary judgments, and, of course, in such a situation, when the case reaches the circuit court of appeals, that court should treat the motion in the same way. The Committee believes that such practice, however, should be tied to the summary judgment rule. The term "speaking motion" is not mentioned in the rules, and if there is such a thing its limitations are undefined. Where extraneous matter is received, by tying further proceedings to the summary judgment rule the courts have a definite basis in the rules for disposing of the motion.

The Committee emphasizes particularly the fact that the summary judgment rule does not permit a case to be disposed of by judgment on the merits on affidavits, which disclose a conflict on a material issue of fact, and unless this practice is tied to the summary judgment, rule, the extent to which a court, on the introduction of such extraneous matter, may resolve questions of fact on conflicting proof would be left uncertain.

The decisions dealing with this general situation may be generally grouped as follows: (1) cases dealing with the use of affidavits and other extraneous material on motions; (2) cases reversing judgments to prevent final determination on mere pleading allegations alone.

Under group (1) are: *Boro Hall Corp. v. General Motors Corp.*, C.C.A.2, 1942, 124 F.2d 822, certiorari denied 1943, 63 S.Ct. 436, 317 U.S. 695, 87 L.Ed. 556; *Gallup v. Caldwell,* C.C.A.3, 1941, 120 F.2d 90; *Central Mexico Light & Power Co. v. Munch,* C.C.A.2, 1940, 116 F.2d 85; *National Labor Relations Board v. Montgomery Ward & Co.*, 1944, 144 F.2d 528, 79 U.S.App.D.C. 200, certiorari denied 1944, 65 S.Ct. 134, 323 U.S. 774, 89 L.Ed. 619; *Urquhart v. American-La France Foamite Corp.*, 1944, 144 F.2d 542, 79 U.S.App.D.C. 219; *Samara v. United States*, C.C.A.2, 1942, 129 F.2d 594; *Cohen v. American Window Glass Co.*, C.C.A.2, 1942, 126 F.2d 111; *Sperry Products Inc. v. Association of American Railroads,* C.C.A.2, 1942, 132 F.2d 408; *Joint Council Dining Car Employees Local 370 v. Delaware, Lackawanna and Western R. Co.*, C.C.A.2, 1946, 157 F.2d 417; *Weeks v. Bareco Oil Co.,* C.C.A.7, 1941, 125 F.2d 84; *Carroll v. Morrison Hotel Corp.*, C.C.A.7, 1945, 149 F.2d 404; *Victory v. Manning,* C.C.A.3, 1942, 128 F.2d 415; *Locals No. 1470, No. 1469, and No. 1512 of International Longshoremen's Association v. Southern Pacific Co.*, C.C.A.5, 1942, 131 F.2d 605; *Lucking v. Delano,* C.C.A.6, 1942, 129 F.2d 283; *San Francisco Lodge No. 68 of International Association of Machinists v. Forrestal,* Cal.1944, 58 F.Supp. 466; *Benson v. Export Equipment Corp.,* 1945, 164 P.2d 380, 49 N.M. 356, construing New Mexico rule identical with Rule 12(b)(6); *F. E. Myers & Bros. Co. v. Gould Pumps, Inc.*, W.D.N.Y.1946, 9 Fed.Rules Serv. 12b.33, Case 2, 5 F.R.D. 132. Cf. *Kohler v. Jacobs,* C.C.A.5, 1943, 138 F.2d 440; *Cohen v. United States*, C.C.A.8, 1942, 129 F.2d 733.

Under group (2) are: *Sparks v. England,* C.C.A.8, 1940, 113 F.2d 579; *Continental Collieries, Inc. v. Shober,* C.C.A.3, 1942, 130 F.2d 631; *Downey v. Palmer,* C.C.A.2, 1940, 114 F.2d 116; *DeLoach v. Crowley's Inc.*, C.C.A.5, 1942, 128 F.2d 378; *Leimer v. State Mutual Life Assurance Co. of Worcester, Mass.,* C.C.A.8, 1940, 108 F.2d 302; *Rossiter v. Vogel,* C.C.A.2, 1943, 134 F.2d 908, compare s.c., C.C.A.2, 1945, 148 F.2d 292; *Karl Kiefer Machine Co. v. United States Bottlers Machinery Co.*, C.C.A.7, 1940, 113 F.2d 356; *Chicago Metallic Mfg. Co. v. Edward Katzinger Co.*, C.C.A.7, 1941, 123 F.2d 518; *Louisiana Farmers' Protective Union, Inc. v. Great Atlantic & Pacific Tea Co. of America, Inc.*, C.C.A.8, 1942, 131 F.2d 419; *Publicity Bldg. Realty Corp. v. Hannegan,* C.C.A.8, 1943, 139 F.2d 583; *Dioguardi v. Durning,* C.C.A.2, 1944, 139 F.2d 774; *Package Closure Corp. v.*

Sealright Co., Inc., C.C.A.2, 1944, 141 F.2d 972; *Tahir Erk v. Glenn L. Martin Co.*, C.C.A.4, 1941, 116 F.2d 865; *Bell v. Preferred Life Assurance Society of Montgomery, Ala.*, 1943, 64 S.Ct. 5, 320 U.S. 238, 88 L.Ed. 15.

The addition at the end of subdivision (b) makes it clear that on a motion under Rule 12(b)(6) extraneous material may not be considered if the court excludes it, but that if the court does not exclude such material the motion shall be treated as a motion for summary judgment and disposed of as provided in Rule 56. It will also be observed that if a motion under Rule 12(b)(6) is thus converted into a summary judgment motion, the amendment insures that both parties shall be given a reasonable opportunity to submit affidavits and extraneous proofs to avoid taking a party by surprise through the conversion of the motion into a motion for summary judgment. In this manner and to this extent the amendment regularizes the practice above described. As the courts are already dealing with cases in this way, the effect of this amendment is really only to define the practice carefully and apply the requirements of the summary judgment rule in the disposition of the motion.

Subdivision (c). The sentence appended to subdivision (c) performs the same function and is grounded on the same reasons as the corresponding sentence added in subdivision (b).

Subdivision (d). The change here was made necessary because of the addition of defense (7) in subdivision (b).

Subdivision (e). References in this subdivision to a bill of particulars have been deleted, and the motion provided for is confined to one for more definite statement to be obtained only in cases where the movant cannot reasonably be required to frame an answer or other responsive pleading to the pleading in question. With respect to preparations for trial, the party is properly relegated to the various methods of examination and discovery provided in the rules for that purpose. *Slusher v. Jones*, E.D.Ky.1943, 7 Fed.Rules Serv. 12e.231, Case 5, 3 F.R.D. 168; *Best Foods, Inc. v. General Mills, Inc.*, D.Del.1943, 7 Fed.Rules Serv. 12e.231, Case 7, 3 F.R.D. 275; *Braden v. Callaway*, E.D.Tenn.1943, 8 Fed. Rules Serv. 12e.231, Case 1 (". . . most courts . . . conclude that the definiteness required is only such as will be sufficient for the party to prepare responsive pleadings"). Accordingly, the reference to the 20 day time limit has also been eliminated, since the purpose of this present provision is to state a time period where the motion for a bill is made for the purpose of preparing for trial.

Rule 12(e) as originally drawn has been the subject of more judicial rulings than any other part of the rules, and has been much criticized by commentators, judges and members of the bar. See general discussion and cases cited in 1 Moore's *Federal Practice*, 1938, Cum.Supplement, § 12.07, under "Page 657"; also, Holtzoff, *New Federal Procedure and the Courts*, 1940, 35–41. And compare vote of Second Circuit Conference of Circuit and District Judges, June 1940, recommending the abolition of the bill of particulars; *Sun Valley Mfg. Co. v. Mylish*, E.D.Pa.1944, 8 Fed.Rules Serv. 12e.231, Case 6 ("Our experience . . . has demonstrated not only that 'the office of the bill of particulars is fast becoming obsolete' . . . but that in view of the adequate discovery procedure available under the Rules, motions for bills of particulars should be abolished altogether."); *Walling v. American Steamship Co.*, W.D.N.Y.1945, 4 F.R.D. 355, 8 Fed.Rules Serv. 12e.244, Case 8 (". . . the adoption of the rule was ill advised. It has led to confusion, duplication and delay.") The tendency of some courts freely to grant extended bills of particulars has served to neutralize any helpful benefits derived from rule 8, and has overlooked the intended use of the rules on depositions and discovery. The words "or to prepare for trial"—eliminated by the proposed amendment—have sometimes been seized upon as grounds for compulsory statement in the opposing pleading of all the details which the movant would have to meet at the trial. On the other hand, many courts have in effect read these words out of the rule. See *Walling v. Alabama Pipe Co.*, W.D.Mo. 1942, 3 F.R.D. 159, 6 Fed.Rules Serv. 12e.244, Case 7; *Fleming v. Mason & Dixon Lines, Inc.*, E.D.Tenn.1941, 42 F.Supp. 230; *Kellogg Co. v. National Biscuit Co.*, D.N.J. 1941, 38 F.Supp. 643; *Brown v. H. L. Green Co.*, S.D.N.Y. 1943, 7 Fed.Rules Serv. 12e.231, Case 6; *Pedersen v. Standard Accident Ins. Co.*, W.D.Mo.1945, 8 Fed.Rules Serv. 12e.231, Case 8; *Bowles v. Ohse*, D.Neb.1945, 4 F.R.D. 403, 9 Fed.Rules Serv. 12e.231, Case 1; *Klages v. Cohen*, E.D.N.Y. 1945, 9 Fed.Rules Serv. 8a.25, Case 4; *Bowles v. Lawrence*, D.Mass.1945, 8 Fed.Rules Serv. 12e.231, Case 19; *McKinney Tool & Mfg. Co. v. Hoyt*, N.D.Ohio 1945, 9 Fed.Rules Serv. 12e.235, Case 1; *Bowles v. Jack*, D.Minn.1945, 5 F.R.D. 1, 9 Fed.Rules Serv. 12e.244, Case 9. And it has been urged from the bench that the phrase be stricken, *Poole v. White*, N.D.W.Va.1941, 5 Fed.Rules Serv. 12e.231, Case 4, 2 F.R.D. 40. See also *Bowles v. Gabel*, W.D.Mo.1946, 9 Fed.Rules Serv. 12e.244, Case 10. ("The courts have never favored that portion of the rules which undertook to justify a motion of this kind for the purpose of aiding counsel in preparing his case for trial.").

Subdivision (f). This amendment affords a specific method of raising the insufficiency of a defense, a matter which has troubled some courts, although attack has been permitted in one way or another. See *Dysart v. Remington-Rand, Inc.*, D.Conn.1939, 31 F.Supp. 296; *Eastman Kodak Co. v. McAuley*, S.D.N.Y.1941, 4 Fed.Rules Serv., 12f.21, Case 8, 2 F.R.D. 21; *Schenley Distillers Corp. v. Renken*, E.D.S.C. 1940, 34 F.Supp. 678; *Yale Transport Corp. v. Yellow Truck & Coach Mfg. Co.*, S.D.N.Y.1944, 3 F.R.D. 440; *United States v. Turner Milk Co.*, N.D.Ill.1941, 4 Fed.Rules Serv. 12b.51, Case 3, 1 F.R.D. 643; *Teiger v. Stephan Oderwald, Inc.*, S.D.N.Y.1940, 31 F.Supp. 626; *Teplitsky v. Pennsylvania R. Co.*, N.D.Ill.1941, 38 F.Supp. 535; *Callagher v. Carroll*, E.D.N.Y.1939, 27 F.Supp. 568; *United States v. Palmer*, S.D.N.Y.1939, 28 F.Supp. 936. And see *Indemnity Ins. Co. of North America v. Pan American Airways, Inc.*, S.D.N.Y. 1944, 58 F.Supp. 338; Commentary, *Modes of Attacking Insufficient Defenses in the Answer*, 901, 1939, 1 Fed.Rules Serv. 669, 1940, 2 Fed.Rules Serv. 640.

Subdivision (g). The change in title conforms with the companion provision in subdivision (h).

The alteration of the "except" clause requires that other than provided in subdivision (h) a party who resorts to a motion to raise defenses specified in the rule, must include in one motion all that are then available to him. Under the original rule defenses which could be raised by motion were divided into two groups which could be the subjects of two successive motions.

Subdivision (h). The addition of the phrase relating to indispensable parties is one of necessity.

1963 Amendment

This amendment conforms to the amendment of Rule 4(e). See also the Advisory Committee's Note to amended Rule 4(b).

1966 Amendment

Subdivision (b)(7). The terminology of this subdivision is changed to accord with the amendment of Rule 19. See the Advisory Committee's Note to Rule 19, as amended, especially the third paragraph therein before the caption "Subdivision (c)."

Subdivision (g). Subdivision (g) has forbidden a defendant who makes a preanswer motion under this rule from making a further motion presenting any defense or objection which was available to him at the time he made the first motion and which he could have included, but did not in fact include therein. Thus if the defendant moves before answer to dismiss the complaint for failure to state a claim, he is barred from making a further motion presenting the defense of improper venue, if that defense was available to him when he made his original motion. Amended subdivision (g) is to the same effect. This required consolidation of defenses and objections in a Rule 12 motion is salutary in that it works against piecemeal consideration of a case. For exceptions to the requirement of consolidation, see the last clause of subdivision (g), referring to new subdivision (h)(2).

Subdivision (h). The question has arisen whether an omitted defense which cannot be made the basis of a second motion may nevertheless be pleaded in the answer. Subdivision (h) called for waiver of "* * * defenses and objections which he [defendant] does not present * * * by motion * * * or, if he has made no motion, in his answer * * *." If the clause "if he has made no motion," was read literally, it seemed that the omitted defense was waived and could not be pleaded in the answer. On the other hand, the clause might be read as adding nothing of substance to the preceding words; in that event it appeared that a defense was not waived by reason of being omitted from the motion and might be set up in the answer. The decisions were divided. Favoring waiver, see *Keef v. Derounian*, 6 F.R.D. 11 (N.D.Ill.1946); *Elbinger v. Precision Metal Workers Corp.*, 18 F.R.D. 467 (E.D.Wis.1956); see also *Rensing v. Turner Aviation Corp.*, 166 F.Supp. 790 (N.D.Ill.1958); *P. Beiersdorf & Co. v. Duke Laboratories, Inc.*, 10 F.R.D. 282 (S.D.N.Y. 1950); *Neset v. Christensen*, 92 F.Supp. 78 (E.D.N.Y.1950). Opposing waiver, see *Phillips v. Baker*, 121 F.2d 752 (9th Cir.1941); *Crum v. Graham*, 32 F.R.D. 173 (D.Mont.1963) (regretfully following the Phillips case); see also *Birnbaum v. Birrell*, 9 F.R.D. 72 (S.D.N.Y.1948); *Johnson v. Joseph Schlitz Brewing Co.*, 33 F.Supp. 176 (E.D.Tenn.1940); cf. *Carter v. American Bus Lines, Inc.*, 22 F.R.D. 323 (D.Neb. 1958).

Amended subdivision (h)(1)(A) eliminates the ambiguity and states that certain specified defenses which were available to a party when he made a preanswer motion, but which he omitted from the motion, are waived. The specified defenses are lack of jurisdiction over the person, improper venue, insufficiency of process, and insufficiency of service of process (see Rule 12(b)(2)–(5)). A party who by motion invites the court to pass upon a threshold defense should bring forward all the specified defenses he then has and thus allow the court to do a reasonably complete job. The waiver reinforces the policy of subdivision (g) forbidding successive motions.

By amended subdivision (h)(1)(B), the specified defenses, even if not waived by the operation of (A), are waived by the failure to raise them by a motion under Rule 12 or in the responsive pleading or any amendment thereof to which the party is entitled as a matter of course. The specified defenses are of such a character that they should not be delayed and brought up for the first time by means of an application to the court to amend the responsive pleading.

Since the language of the subdivisions is made clear, the party is put on fair notice of the effect of his actions and omissions and can guard himself against unintended waiver. It is to be noted that while the defenses specified in subdivision (h)(1) are subject to waiver as there provided, the more substantial defenses of failure to state a claim upon which relief can be granted, failure to join a party indispensable under Rule 19, and failure to state a legal defense to a claim (see Rule 12(b)(6), (7), (f)), as well as the defense of lack of jurisdiction over the subject matter (see Rule 12(b)(1)), are expressly preserved against waiver by amended subdivision (h)(2) and (3).

1987 Amendment

The amendments are technical. No substantive change is intended.

1993 Amendment

Subdivision (a) is divided into paragraphs for greater clarity, and paragraph (1)(B) is added to reflect amendments to Rule 4. Consistent with Rule 4(d)(3), a defendant that timely waives service is allowed 60 days from the date the request was mailed in which to respond to the complaint, with an additional 30 days afforded if the request was sent out of the country. Service is timely waived if the waiver is returned within the time specified in the request (30 days after the request was mailed, or 60 days if mailed out of the country) and before being formally served with process. Sometimes a plaintiff may attempt to serve a defendant with process while also sending the defendant a request for waiver of service; if the defendant executes the waiver of service within the time specified and before being served with process, it should have the longer time to respond afforded by waiving service.

The date of sending the request is to be inserted by the plaintiff on the face of the request for waiver and on the waiver itself. This date is used to measure the return day for the waiver form, so that the plaintiff can know on a day certain whether formal service of process will be necessary; it is also a useful date to measure the time for answer when service is waived. The defendant who returns the waiver is given additional time for answer in order to assure that it loses nothing by waiving service of process.

2000 Amendment

Rule 12(a)(3)(B) is added to complement the addition of Rule 4(i)(2)(B). The purposes that underlie the requirement that service be made on the United States in an action that asserts individual liability of a United States officer or employee for acts occurring in connection with the performance of duties on behalf of the United States also require that the time to answer be extended to 60 days. Time is needed for the United States to determine whether to provide representation to the defendant officer or employee. If the United States provides representation, the need for an extended answer period is the same as in actions against the United States, a United States agency, or a United States officer sued in an official capacity.

An action against a former officer or employee of the United States is covered by subparagraph (3)(B) in the same way as an action against a present officer or employee. Termination of the relationship between the individual defendant and the United States does not reduce the need for additional time to answer.

GAP Report

No changes are recommended for Rule 12 as published.

2007 Amendment

The language of Rule 12 has been amended as part of the general restyling of the Civil Rules to make them more easily understood and to make style and terminology consistent throughout the rules. These changes are intended to be stylistic only.

Former Rule 12(a)(4)(A) referred to an order that postpones disposition of a motion "until the trial on the merits." Rule 12(a)(4) now refers to postponing disposition "until trial." The new expression avoids the ambiguity that inheres in "trial on the merits," which may become confusing when there is a separate trial of a single issue or another event different from a single all-encompassing trial.

Rule 13. Counterclaim and Crossclaim

(a) Compulsory Counterclaim.

(1) ***In General.*** A pleading must state as a counterclaim any claim that—at the time of its service—the pleader has against an opposing party if the claim:

(A) arises out of the transaction or occurrence that is the subject matter of the opposing party's claim; and

(B) does not require adding another party over whom the court cannot acquire jurisdiction.

(2) ***Exceptions.*** The pleader need not state the claim if:

(A) when the action was commenced, the claim was the subject of another pending action; or

(B) the opposing party sued on its claim by attachment or other process that did not establish personal jurisdiction over the pleader on that claim, and the pleader does not assert any counterclaim under this rule.

(b) Permissive Counterclaim. A pleading may state as a counterclaim against an opposing party any claim that is not compulsory.

(c) Relief Sought in a Counterclaim. A counterclaim need not diminish or defeat the recovery sought by the opposing party. It may request relief that exceeds in amount or differs in kind from the relief sought by the opposing party.

(d) Counterclaim Against the United States. These rules do not expand the right to assert a counterclaim—or to claim a credit—against the United States or a United States officer or agency.

(e) Counterclaim Maturing or Acquired After Pleading. The court may permit a party to file a supplemental pleading asserting a counterclaim that matured or was acquired by the party after serving an earlier pleading.

(f) Omitted Counterclaim. The court may permit a party to amend a pleading to add a counterclaim if it was omitted through oversight, inadvertence, or excusable neglect or if justice so requires.

(g) Crossclaim Against a Coparty. A pleading may state as a crossclaim any claim by one party against a coparty if the claim arises out of the transaction or occurrence that is the subject matter of the original action or of a counterclaim, or if the claim relates to any property that is the subject matter of the original action. The crossclaim may include a claim that the coparty is or may be liable to the cross-claimant for all or part of a claim asserted in the action against the cross-claimant.

(h) Joining Additional Parties. Rules 19 and 20 govern the addition of a person as a party to a counterclaim or crossclaim.

(i) Separate Trials; Separate Judgments. If the court orders separate trials under Rule 42(b), it may enter judgment on a counterclaim or crossclaim under Rule 54(b) when it has jurisdiction to do so, even if the opposing party's claims have been dismissed or otherwise resolved.

(Amended December 27, 1946, effective March 19, 1948; January 21, 1963, effective July 1, 1963; February 28, 1966, effective July 1, 1966; March 2, 1987, effective August 1, 1987; April 30, 2007, effective December 1, 2007.)

ADVISORY COMMITTEE NOTES

1937 Adoption

1. This is substantially [former] Equity Rule 30 (Answer—Contents—Counterclaim), broadened to include legal as well as equitable counterclaims.

2. Compare the English practice, *English Rules Under the Judicature Act* (The Annual Practice, 1937) O. 19, r.r. 2 and 3, and O. 21, r.r. 10–17; *Beddall v. Maitland*, L.R. 17 Ch.Div. 174, 181, 182 (1881).

3. Certain States have also adopted almost unrestricted provisions concerning both the subject matter of and the parties to a counterclaim. This seems to be the modern tendency. Ark.Civ.Code (Crawford, 1934) §§ 117 (as amended) and 118; N.J.Comp.Stat. (2 Cum.Supp. 1911–1924); N.Y.C.P.A. (1937) §§ 262, 266, 267 (all as amended, Laws of 1936, ch. 324), 268, 269, and 271; Wis.Stat. (1935) § 263.14(1)(c).

4. Most codes do not expressly provide for a counterclaim in the reply. Clark, *Code Pleading* (1928), p. 486. Ky.Codes (Carroll, 1932) Civ.Pract. § 98 does provide, however, for such counterclaim.

5. The provisions of this rule respecting counterclaims are subject to Rule 82 (Jurisdiction and Venue Unaffected). For a discussion of Federal jurisdiction and venue in regard to counterclaims and cross-claims, see Shulman and Jaegerman, *Some Jurisdictional Limitations in Federal Procedure* (1936), 45 Yale L.J. 393, 410 et seq.

6. This rule does not affect such statutes of the United States as U.S.C., Title 28, § 41(1) (now §§ 1332, 1345, 1359) (United States as plaintiff; civil suits at common law and in equity), relating to assigned claims in actions based on diversity of citizenship.

7. If the action proceeds to judgment without the interposition of a counterclaim as required by subdivision (a) of this rule, the counterclaim is barred. See *American Mills Co. v. American Surety Co.*, 260 U.S. 360, 43 S.Ct. 149, 67 L.Ed. 306 (1922); *Marconi Wireless Telegraph Co. v. National Electric Signalling Co.*, 206 Fed. 295 (E.D.N.Y., 1913); Hopkins, *Federal Equity Rules* (8th ed., 1933), p. 213; Simkins, *Federal Practice* (1934), p. 663.

8. For allowance of credits against the United States see U.S.C., Title 26, §§ 1672–1673 [sec. 7442] (Suits for refunds of internal revenue taxes—limitations); U.S.C., Title 28, § 774 (now § 2406) (Suits by United States against individuals; credits), [former] § 775 (Suits under postal laws; credits); U.S.C., Title 31, § 227 [now 3728] (Offsets against judgments and claims against United States).

1946 Amendment

Note. Subdivision (a). The use of the word "filing" was inadvertent. The word "serving" conforms with subdivision (e) and with usage generally throughout the rules.

The removal of the phrase "not the subject of a pending action" and the addition of the new clause at the end of the subdivision is designed to eliminate the ambiguity noted in *Prudential Insurance Co. of America v. Saxe,* App.D.C.1943, 77 U.S.App.D.C. 144, 134 F.2d 16, 33–34, cert. den., 1943, 319 U.S. 745, 63 S.Ct. 1033. The rewording of the subdivision in this respect insures against an undesirable possibility presented under the original rule whereby a party having a claim which would be the subject of a compulsory counterclaim could avoid stating it as such by bringing an independent action in another court after the commencement of the federal action but before serving his pleading in the federal action.

Subdivision (g). The amendment is to care for a situation such as where a second mortgagee is made defendant in a foreclosure proceeding and wishes to file a cross-complaint against the mortgagor in order to secure a personal judgment for the indebtedness and foreclose his lien. A claim of this sort by the second mortgagee may not necessarily arise out of the transaction or occurrence that is the subject matter of the original action under the terms of Rule 13(g).

Subdivision (h). The change clarifies the interdependence of Rules 13(i) and 54(b).

1963 Amendment

When a defendant, if he desires to defend his interest in property, is obliged to come in and litigate in a court to whose jurisdiction he could not ordinarily be subjected, fairness suggests that he should not be required to assert counterclaims, but should rather be permitted to do so at his election. If, however, he does elect to assert a counterclaim, it seems fair to require him to assert any other which is compulsory within the meaning of Rule 13(a). Clause (2), added by amendment to Rule 13(a), carries out this idea. It will apply to various cases described in Rule 4(e), as amended, where service is effected through attachment or other process by which the court does not acquire jurisdiction to render a personal judgment against the defendant. Clause (2) will also apply to actions commenced in State courts jurisdictionally grounded on attachment or the like, and removed to the Federal courts.

1966 Amendment

Rule 13(h), dealing with the joinder of additional parties to a counterclaim or cross-claim, has partaken of some of the textual difficulties of Rule 19 on necessary joinder of parties. See Advisory Committee's Note to Rule 19, as amended; cf. 3 *Moore's Federal Practice,* par. 13.39 (2d ed. 1963), and Supp. thereto; 1A Barron & Holtzoff, *Federal Practice and Procedure* § 399 (Wright ed. 1960). Rule 13(h) has also been inadequate in failing to call attention to the fact that a party pleading a counterclaim or cross-claim may join additional persons when the conditions for permissive joinder of parties under Rule 20 are satisfied.

The amendment of Rule 13(h) supplies the latter omission by expressly referring to Rule 20, as amended, and also incorporates by direct reference the revised criteria and procedures of Rule 19, as amended. Hereafter, for the purpose of determining who must or may be joined as additional parties to a counterclaim or cross-claim, the party pleading the claim is to be regarded as a plaintiff and the additional parties as plaintiffs or defendants as the case may be, and amended Rules 19 and 20 are to be applied in the usual fashion. See also Rules 13(a) (compulsory counterclaims) and 22 (interpleader).

The amendment of Rule 13(h), like the amendment of Rule 19, does not attempt to regulate Federal jurisdiction or venue. See Rule 82. It should be noted, however, that in some situations the decisional law has recognized "ancillary" Federal jurisdiction over counterclaims and cross-claims and "ancillary" venue as to parties to these claims.

1987 Amendment

The amendments are technical. No substantive change is intended.

2007 Amendment

The language of Rule 13 has been amended as part of the general restyling of the Civil Rules to make them more easily understood and to make style and terminology consistent throughout the rules. These changes are intended to be stylistic only.

The meaning of former Rule 13(b) is better expressed by deleting "not arising out of the transaction or occurrence that is the subject matter of the opposing party's claim." Both as a matter of intended meaning and current practice, a party may state as a permissive counterclaim a claim that does grow out of the same transaction or occurrence as an opposing party's claim even though one of the exceptions in Rule 13(a) means the claim is not a compulsory counterclaim.

Rule 14. Third-Party Practice

(a) When a Defending Party May Bring in a Third Party.

(1) ***Timing of the Summons and Complaint.*** A defending party may, as third-party plaintiff, serve a summons and complaint on a nonparty who is or may be liable to it for all or part of the claim against it. But the third-party plaintiff must, by motion, obtain the court's leave if it files the third-party complaint more than 10 days after serving its original answer.

(2) ***Third-Party Defendant's Claims and Defenses.*** The person served with the summons and third-party complaint—the "third-party defendant":

(A) must assert any defense against the third-party plaintiff's claim under Rule 12;

(B) must assert any counterclaim against the third-party plaintiff under Rule 13(a), and may assert any counterclaim against the third-party plaintiff under Rule 13(b) or any crossclaim against another third-party defendant under Rule 13(g);

(C) may assert against the plaintiff any defense that the third-party plaintiff has to the plaintiff's claim; and

(D) may also assert against the plaintiff any claim arising out of the transaction or occurrence that is the subject matter of the plaintiff's claim against the third-party plaintiff.

(3) ***Plaintiff's Claims Against a Third-Party Defendant.*** The plaintiff may assert against the third-party defendant any claim arising out of the transaction or occurrence that is the subject matter of the plaintiff's claim against the third-party plaintiff. The third-party defendant must then assert any defense under Rule 12 and any counterclaim under Rule 13(a), and may assert any counterclaim under Rule 13(b) or any crossclaim under Rule 13(g).

(4) ***Motion to Strike, Sever, or Try Separately.*** Any party may move to strike the third-party claim, to sever it, or to try it separately.

(5) ***Third-Party Defendant's Claim Against a Nonparty.*** A third-party defendant may proceed under this rule against a nonparty who is or may be liable to the third-party defendant for all or part of any claim against it.

(6) ***Third-Party Complaint In Rem.*** If it is within the admiralty or maritime jurisdiction, a third-party complaint may be in rem. In that event, a reference in this rule to the "summons" includes the warrant of arrest, and a reference to the defendant or third-party plaintiff includes, when appropriate, a person who asserts a right under Supplemental Rule C(6)(a)(i) in the property arrested.

(b) When a Plaintiff May Bring in a Third Party. When a claim is asserted against a plaintiff, the plaintiff may bring in a third party if this rule would allow a defendant to do so.

(c) Admiralty or Maritime Claim.

(1) ***Scope of Impleader.*** If a plaintiff asserts an admiralty or maritime claim under Rule 9(h), the defendant or a person who asserts a right under Supplemental Rule C(6)(a)(i) may, as a third-party plaintiff, bring in a third-party defendant who may be wholly or partly liable—either to the plaintiff or to the third-party plaintiff—for remedy over, contribution, or otherwise on account of the same transaction, occurrence, or series of transactions or occurrences.

(2) ***Defending Against a Demand for Judgment for the Plaintiff.*** The third-party plaintiff may demand judgment in the plaintiff's favor against the third-party defendant. In that event, the third-party defendant must defend under Rule 12 against the plaintiff's claim as well as the third-party plaintiff's claim; and the action proceeds as if the plaintiff had sued both the third-party defendant and the third-party plaintiff.

(Amended December 27, 1946, effective March 19, 1948; January 21, 1963, effective July 1, 1963; February 28, 1966, effective July 1, 1966; March 2, 1987, effective August 1, 1987; April 17, 2000, effective December 1, 2000; April 12, 2006, effective December 1, 2006; April 30, 2007, effective December 1, 2007.)

ADVISORY COMMITTEE NOTES

1937 Adoption

Third-party impleader is in some aspects a modern innovation in law and equity although well known in admiralty. Because of its many advantages a liberal procedure with respect to it has developed in England, in the federal admiralty courts, and in some American state jurisdictions. See *English Rules Under the Judicature Act* (The Annual Practice, 1937) O. 16A, r.r. 1–13; United States Supreme Court Admiralty Rules (1920), Rule 56 (Right to Bring in Party Jointly Liable); 12 P.S.Pa. § 141; Wis.Stat. (1935) §§ 260.19, 260.20; N.Y.C.P.A. (1937) §§ 193(2), 211(a). Compare La.

Code Pract. (Dart, 1932) §§ 378–388. For the practice in Texas as developed by judicial decision, see *Lottman v. Cuilla*, Tex.1926, 288 S.W. 123, 126. For a treatment of this subject see Gregory, *Legislative Loss Distribution in Negligence Actions* (1936); *Shulman and Jaegerman, Some Jurisdictional Limitations on Federal Procedure (1936)*, 45 Yale L.J. 393, 417 et seq.

Third-party impleader under the conformity act has been applied in actions at law in the Federal courts. *Lowry and Co., Inc. v. National City Bank of New York*, N.Y.1928, 28 F.2d 895; *Yellow Cab Co. of Philadelphia v. Rodgers*, C.C.A.3, 1932, 61 F.2d 729.

1946 Amendment

Note. The provisions in Rule 14(a) which relate to the impleading of a third party who is or may be liable to the plaintiff have been deleted by the proposed amendment. It has been held that under Rule 14(a) the plaintiff need not amend his complaint to state a claim against such third party if he does not wish to do so. *Satink v. Holland Township*, D.N.J.1940, 31 F.Supp. 229, noted, 1940, 88 U.Pa.L.Rev. 751; *Connelly v. Bender*, E.D.Mich.1941, 36 F.Supp. 368; *Whitmire v. Partin (Milton)*, E.D.Tenn.1941, 2 F.R.D. 83, 5 Fed.Rules Serv. 14a.513, Case 2; *Crim v. Lumbermen's Mutual Casualty Co.*, D.D.C.1939, 26 F.Supp. 715; *Carbola Chemical Co., Inc. v. Trundle*, S.D.N.Y.1943, 3 F.R.D. 502, 7 Fed.Rules Serv. 14a.224, Case 1; *Roadway Express, Inc. v. Automobile Ins. Co. of Hartford, Conn., (Providence Washington Ins. Co.)* N.D.Ohio 1945, 8 Fed.Rules Serv. 14a.513, Case 3. In *Delano v. Ives*, E.D.Pa.1941, 40 F.Supp. 672, the court said: ". . . the weight of authority is to the effect that a defendant cannot compel the plaintiff, who has sued him, to sue also a third party whom he does not wish to sue, by tendering in a third party complaint the third party as an additional defendant directly liable to the plaintiff." Thus impleader here amounts to no more than a mere offer of a party to the plaintiff, and if he rejects it, the attempt is a time-consuming futility. See *Satink v. Holland Township, supra; Malkin v. Arundel Corp.*, D.Md.1941, 36 F.Supp. 948; also Koenigsberger, *Suggestions for Changes in the Federal Rules of Civil Procedure*, 1941, 4 Fed.Rules Serv. 1010. But cf. *Atlantic Coast Line R. Co. v. United States Fidelity & Guaranty Co.*, Ga.1943, 52 F.Supp. 177. Moreover, in any case where the plaintiff could not have joined the third party originally because of jurisdictional limitations such as lack of diversity of citizenship, the majority view is that any attempt by the plaintiff to amend his complaint and assert a claim against the impleaded third party would be unavailing. *Hoskie v. Prudential Ins. Co. of America, (Lorrac Real Estate Corp.)*, E.D.N.Y.1941, 39 F.Supp. 305; *Johnson v. G. J. Sherrard Co., (New England Telephone & Telegraph Co.)*, D.Mass.1941, 5 Fed.Rules Serv. 14a.511, Case 1, 2 F.R.D. 164; *Thompson v. Cranston*, W.D.N.Y.1942, 6 Fed.Rules Serv. 14a.511, Case 1, 2 F.R.D. 270, affirmed CCA2d, 1942, 132 F.2d 631, certiorari denied 1945, 63 S.Ct. 1028, 319 U.S. 741, 87 L.Ed. 1698; *Friend v. Middle Atlantic Transportation Co.*, C.C.A.2, 1946, 153 F.2d 778, certiorari denied 1946, 66 S.Ct. 1370, 328 U.S. 865, 90 L.Ed. 1635; *Herrington v. Jones*, E.D.La.1941, 5 Fed.Rules Serv. 14a.511, Case 2, 2 F.R.D. 108; *Banks v. Employers' Liability Assurance Corp., (Central Surety & Ins. Corp.)* W.D.Mo.1943, 7 Fed.Rules Serv. 14a.11, Case 2; *Saunders v. Baltimore & Ohio R. Co.*, S.D.W.Va.1945, 9 Fed.Rules Serv. 14a.62, Case 2; *Hull v. United States Rubber Co. (Johnson Larsen and Co.)*, E.D.Mich.1945, 9 Fed.Rules Serv. 14a.62, Case 3. See also concurring opinion of Circuit Judge Minton in *People of State of Illinois for Use of Trust Co. of Chicago v. Maryland Casualty Co.*, C.C.A.7, 1942, 132 F.2d 850, 853. Contra: *Sklar v. Hayes (Singer)*, E.D.Pa.1941, 4 Fed.Rules Serv. 14a.511, Case 2, 1 F.R.D. 594. Discussion of the problem will be found in Commentary, *Amendment of Plaintiff's Pleading to Assert Claim Against Third-Party Defendant*, 1942, 5 Fed.Rules Serv. 811; Commentary, *Federal Jurisdiction in Third-Party Practice*, 1943, 6 Fed.Rules Serv. 766; Holtzoff, *Some Problems Under Federal Third-Party Practice*, 1941, 3 La.L.Rev. 408, 419–420; 1 Moore's *Federal Practice*, 1938, Cum.Supplement § 14.08. For these reasons therefore, the words "or to the plaintiff" in the first sentence of subdivision (a) have been removed by the amendment; and in conformance therewith the words "the plaintiff" in the second sentence of the subdivision, and the words "or to the third-party plaintiff" in the concluding sentence thereof have likewise been eliminated.

The third sentence of rule 14(a) has been expanded to clarify the right of the third-party defendant to assert any defenses which the third-party plaintiff may have to the plaintiff's claim. This protects the impleaded third-party defendant where the third-party plaintiff fails or neglects to assert a proper defense to the plaintiff's action. A new sentence has also been inserted giving the third-party defendant the right to assert directly against the original plaintiff any claim arising out of the transaction or occurrence that is the subject matter of the plaintiff's claim against the third-party plaintiff. This permits all claims arising out of the same transaction or occurrence to be heard and determined in the same action. See *Atlantic Coast Line R. Co. v. United States Fidelity & Guaranty Co.*, Ga.1943, 52 F.Supp. 177. Accordingly, the next to the last sentence of subdivision (a) has also been revised to make clear that the plaintiff may, if he desires, assert directly against the third-party defendant either by amendment or by a new pleading any claim he may have against him arising out of the transaction or occurrence that is the subject matter of the plaintiff's claim against the third-party plaintiff. In such a case, the third-party defendant then is entitled to assert the defenses, counter-claims and cross-claims provided in Rules 12 and 13.

The sentence reading "The third-party defendant is bound by the adjudication of the third-party plaintiff's liability to the plaintiff, as well as of his own to the plaintiff, or to the third-party plaintiff" has been stricken from Rule 14(a), not to change the law, but because the sentence states a rule of substantive law which is not within the scope of a procedural rule. It is not the purpose of the rules to state the effect of a judgment.

The elimination of the words "the third-party plaintiff, or any other party" from the second sentence of rule 14(a), together with the insertion of the new phrases therein, are not changes of substance but are merely for the purpose of clarification.

1963 Amendment

Under the amendment of the initial sentences of the subdivision, a defendant as a third-party plaintiff may freely and without leave of court bring in a third-party defendant if he files the third-party complaint not later than 10 days after he serves his original answer. When the impleader comes so early in the case, there is little value in requiring a preliminary ruling by the court on the propriety of the impleader.

After the third-party defendant is brought in, the court has discretion to strike the third-party claim if it is obviously unmeritorious and can only delay or prejudice the disposition of the plaintiff's claim, or to sever the third-party claim or accord it separate trial if confusion or prejudice would otherwise result. This discretion, applicable not merely to the cases covered by the amendment where the third-party defendant is brought in without leave, but to all impleaders under the rule, is emphasized in the next-to-last sentence of the subdivision, added by amendment.

In dispensing with leave of court for an impleader filed not later than 10 days after serving the answer, but retaining the leave requirement for impleaders sought to be effected thereafter, the amended subdivision takes a moderate position on the lines urged by some commentators, see Note, 43 Minn.L.Rev. 115 (1958); cf. Pa.R.Civ.P. 2252–53 (60 days after service on the defendant; Minn.R.Civ.P. 14.01 (45 days). Other commentators would dispense with the requirement of leave regardless of the time when impleader is effected, and would rely on subsequent action by the court to dismiss the impleader if it would unduly delay or complicate the litigation or would be otherwise objectionable. See 1A Barron & Holtzoff, *Federal Practice & Procedure* 649–50 (Wright ed. 1960); Comment, 58 Colum.L.Rev. 532, 546 (1958); cf. N.Y.Civ.Prac.Act § 193–a; Me.R.Civ.P. 14. The amended subdivision preserves the value of a preliminary screening, through the leave procedure, of impleaders attempted after the 10-day period.

The amendment applies also when an impleader is initiated by a third-party defendant against a person who may be liable to him, as provided in the last sentence of the subdivision.

1966 Amendment

Rule 14 was modeled on Admiralty Rule 56. An important feature of Admiralty Rule 56 was that it allowed impleader not only of a person who might be liable to the defendant by way of remedy over, but also of any person who might be liable to the plaintiff. The importance of this provision was that the defendant was entitled to insist that the plaintiff proceed to judgment against the third-party defendant. In certain cases this was a valuable implementation of a substantive right. For example, in a case of ship collision where a finding of mutual fault is possible, one shipowner, if sued alone, faces the prospect of an absolute judgment for the full amount of the damage suffered by an innocent third party; but if he can implead the owner of the other vessel, and if mutual fault is found, the judgment against the original defendant will be in the first instance only for a moiety of the damages; liability for the remainder will be conditioned on the plaintiff's inability to collect from the third-party defendant.

This feature was originally incorporated in Rule 14, but was eliminated by the amendment of 1946, so that under the amended rule a third party could not be impleaded on the basis that he might be liable to the plaintiff. One of the reasons for the amendment was that the Civil Rule, unlike the Admiralty Rule, did not require the plaintiff to go to judgment against the third-party defendant. Another reason was that where jurisdiction depended on diversity of citizenship the impleader of an adversary having the same citizenship as the plaintiff was not considered possible.

Retention of the admiralty practice in those cases that will be counterparts of a suit in admiralty is clearly desirable.

1987 Amendment

The amendments are technical. No substantive change is intended.

2000 Amendment

Subdivisions (a) and (c) are amended to reflect revisions in Supplemental Rule C(6).

GAP Report

Rule B(1)(a) was modified by moving "in an in personam action" out of paragraph (a) and into the first line of subdivision (1). This change makes it clear that all paragraphs of subdivision (1) apply when attachment is sought in an in personam action. Rule B(1)(d) was modified by changing the requirement that the clerk deliver the summons and process to the person or organization authorized to serve it. The new form requires only that the summons and process be delivered, not that the clerk effect the delivery. This change conforms to present practice in some districts and will facilitate rapid service. It matches the spirit of Civil Rule 4(b), which directs the clerk to issue the summons "to the plaintiff for service on the defendant." A parallel change is made in Rule C(3)(b).

2006 Amendment

Rule 14 is amended to conform to changes in designating the paragraphs of Supplemental Rule C(6).

2007 Amendment

The language of Rule 14 has been amended as part of the general restyling of the Civil Rules to make them more easily understood and to make style and terminology consistent throughout the rules. These changes are intended to be stylistic only.

Former Rule 14 twice refers to counterclaims under Rule 13. In each case, the operation of Rule 13(a) depends on the state of the action at the time the pleading is filed. If plaintiff and third-party defendant have become opposing parties because one has made a claim for relief against the other, Rule 13(a) requires assertion of any counterclaim that grows out of the transaction or occurrence that is the subject matter of that claim. Rules 14(a)(2)(B) and (a)(3) reflect the distinction between compulsory and permissive counterclaims.

A plaintiff should be on equal footing with the defendant in making third-party claims, whether the claim against the plaintiff is asserted as a counterclaim or as another form of claim. The limit imposed by the former reference to "counterclaim" is deleted.

Rule 15. Amended and Supplemental Pleadings

(a) Amendments Before Trial.

(1) ***Amending as a Matter of Course.*** A party may amend its pleading once as a matter of course:

(A) before being served with a responsive pleading; or

(B) within 20 days after serving the pleading if a responsive pleading is not allowed and the action is not yet on the trial calendar.

(2) ***Other Amendments.*** In all other cases, a party may amend its pleading only with the opposing party's written consent or the court's leave. The court should freely give leave when justice so requires.

(3) ***Time to Respond.*** Unless the court orders otherwise, any required response to an amended pleading must be made within the time remaining to respond to the original pleading or within 10 days after service of the amended pleading, whichever is later.

(b) Amendments During and After Trial.

(1) ***Based on an Objection at Trial.*** If, at trial, a party objects that evidence is not within the issues raised in the pleadings, the court may permit the pleadings to be amended. The court should freely permit an amendment when doing so will aid in presenting the merits and the objecting party fails to satisfy the court that the evidence would prejudice that party's action or defense on the merits. The court may grant a continuance to enable the objecting party to meet the evidence.

(2) ***For Issues Tried by Consent.*** When an issue not raised by the pleadings is tried by the parties' express or implied consent, it must be treated in all respects as if raised in the pleadings. A party may move—at any time, even after judgment—to amend the pleadings to conform them to the evidence and to raise an unpleaded issue. But failure to amend does not affect the result of the trial of that issue.

(c) Relation Back of Amendments.

(1) ***When an Amendment Relates Back.*** An amendment to a pleading relates back to the date of the original pleading when:

(A) the law that provides the applicable statute of limitations allows relation back;

(B) the amendment asserts a claim or defense that arose out of the conduct, transaction, or occurrence set out—or attempted to be set out—in the original pleading; or

(C) the amendment changes the party or the naming of the party against whom a claim is asserted, if Rule 15(c)(1)(B) is satisfied and if, within the period provided by Rule 4(m) for serving the summons and complaint, the party to be brought in by amendment:

(i) received such notice of the action that it will not be prejudiced in defending on the merits; and

(ii) knew or should have known that the action would have been brought against it, but for a mistake concerning the proper party's identity.

(2) ***Notice to the United States.*** When the United States or a United States officer or agency is added as a defendant by amendment, the notice requirements of Rule 15(c)(1)(C)(i) and (ii) are satisfied if, during the stated period, process was delivered or mailed to the United States attorney or the United States attorney's designee, to the Attorney General of the United States, or to the officer or agency.

(d) Supplemental Pleadings. On motion and reasonable notice, the court may, on just terms, permit a party to serve a supplemental pleading setting out any transaction, occurrence, or event that happened after the date of the pleading to be supplemented. The court may permit supplementation even though the original pleading is defective in stating a claim or defense. The court may order that the opposing party plead to the supplemental pleading within a specified time.

(Amended January 21, 1963, effective July 1, 1963; February 28, 1966, effective July 1, 1966; March 2, 1987, effective August 1, 1987; April 30, 1991, effective December 1, 1991; amended by Pub.L. 102–198, § 11, December 9, 1991, 105 Stat. 1626; amended April 22, 1993, effective December 1, 1993; April 30, 2007, effective December 1, 2007.)

ADVISORY COMMITTEE NOTES

1937 Adoption

See generally for the present federal practice, [former] Equity Rules 19 (Amendments Generally), 28 (Amendment of Bill as of Course), 32 (Answer to Amended Bill), 34 (Supplemental Pleading), and 35 (Bills of Revivor and Supplemental Bills—Form); U.S.C. Title 28, § 399 [now 1653] (Amendments to show diverse citizenship) and [former] 777 (Defects of form; amendments). See *English Rules Under the Judicature Act* (The Annual Practice, 1937) O. 28, r. r. 1–13; O. 20, r. 4; O. 24, r. r. 1–3.

Note to Subdivision (a). The right to serve an amended pleading once as of course is common. 4 Mont.Rev.Codes Ann. (1935) § 9186; 1 Ore.Code Ann. (1930) § 1–904; 1 S.C.Code (Michie, 1932) § 493; *English Rules Under the Judicature Act* (The Annual Practice, 1937) O. 28, r. 2. Provision for amendment of pleading before trial, by leave of court, is in almost every code. If there is no statute the power of the court to grant leave is said to be inherent. Clark, *Code Pleading* (1928), pp. 498, 509.

Note to Subdivision (b). Compare [former] Equity Rule 19 (Amendments Generally) and code provisions which allow an amendment "at any time in furtherance of justice," (e.g., Ark.Civ.Code (Crawford, 1934) § 155) and which allow an amendment of pleadings to conform to the evidence, where the adverse party has not been misled and prejudiced (e.g., N.M.Stat.Ann. (Courtright, 1929) §§ 105–601, 105–602).

Note to Subdivision (c). "Relation back" is a well recognized doctrine of recent and now more frequent application. Compare Ala.Code Ann. (Michie, 1928) § 9513; Smith-Hurd Ill.Stats. ch. 110, § 170(2); 2 Wash.Rev.Stat.Ann. (Remington, 1932) § 308–3(4). See U.S.C., Title 28, § 399 [now 1653] (Amendments to show diverse citizenship) for a provision for "relation back".

Note to Subdivision (d). This is an adaptation of former Equity Rule 34 (Supplemental Pleading).

1963 Amendment

Rule 15(d) is intended to give the court broad discretion in allowing a supplemental pleading. However, some cases, opposed by other cases and criticized by the commentators, have taken the rigid and formalistic view that where the original complaint fails to state a claim upon which relief can be granted, leave to serve a supplemental complaint must be denied. See *Bonner v. Elizabeth Arden, Inc.,* 177 F.2d 703 (2d Cir. 1949); *Bowles v. Senderowitz,* 65 F.Supp. 548 (E.D.Pa.), rev'd on other grounds, 158 F.2d 435 (3d Cir. 1946), cert. denied, *Senderowitz v. Fleming,* 330 U.S. 848, 67 S.Ct. 1091, 91 L.Ed. 1292 (1947); cf. *LaSalle Nat. Bank v. 222 East Chestnut St. Corp.,* 267 F.2d 247 (7th Cir.), cert. denied, 361 U.S. 836, 80 S.Ct. 88, 4 L.Ed.2d 77 (1959). But see *Camilla Cotton Oil Co. v. Spencer Kellogg & Sons,* 257 F.2d 162 (5th Cir. 1958); *Genuth v. National Biscuit Co.,* 81 F.Supp. 213 (S.D.N.Y.1948), app. dism., 177 F.2d 962 (2d Cir. 1949); 3 Moore's *Federal Practice* ¶15.01[5] (Supp.1960); 1A Barron & Holtzoff, *Federal Practice & Procedure* 820–21 (Wright ed. 1960). Thus plaintiffs have sometimes been needlessly remitted to the difficulties of commencing a new action even though events occurring after the commencement of the original action have made clear the right to relief.

Under the amendment the court has discretion to permit a supplemental pleading despite the fact that the original pleading is defective. As in other situations where a supplemental pleading is offered, the court is to determine in the light of the particular circumstances whether filing should be permitted, and if so, upon what terms. The amendment does not attempt to deal with such questions as the relation of the statute of limitations to supplemental pleadings, the operation of the doctrine of laches, or the availability of other defenses. All these questions are for decision in accordance with the principles applicable to supplemental pleadings generally. Cf. *Blau v. Lamb,* 191 F.Supp. 906 (S.D.N.Y.1961); *Lendonsol Amusement Corp. v. B. & Q. Assoc., Inc.,* 23 F.R.Serv. 15d.3, Case 1 (D.Mass.1957).

1966 Amendment

Rule 15(c) is amplified to state more clearly when an amendment of a pleading changing the party against whom a claim is asserted (including an amendment to correct a misnomer or misdescription of a defendant) shall "relate back" to the date of the original pleading.

The problem has arisen most acutely in certain actions by private parties against officers or agencies of the United States. Thus an individual denied social security benefits by the Secretary of Health, Education, and Welfare may secure review of the decision by bringing a civil action against that officer within sixty days. 42 U.S.C. § 405(g) (Supp. III, 1962). In several recent cases the claimants instituted timely action but mistakenly named as defendant the United States, the Department of HEW, the "Federal Security Administration" (a nonexistent agency), and a Secretary who had retired from the office nineteen days before. Discovering their mistakes, the claimants moved to amend their complaints to name the proper defendant; by this time the statutory sixty-day period had expired. The motions were denied on the ground that the amendment "would amount to the commencement of a new proceeding and would not relate back in time so as to avoid the statutory provision * * * that suit be brought within sixty days * * *" *Cohn v. Federal Security Adm.,* 199 F.Supp. 884, 885 (W.D.N.Y.1961); see also *Cunningham v. United States,* 199 F.Supp. 541 (W.D.Mo.1958); *Hall v. Department of HEW,* 199 F.Supp. 833 (S.D.Tex.1960); *Sandridge v. Folsom, Secretary of HEW,* 200 F.Supp. 25 (M.D.Tenn.1959). [The Secretary of Health, Education, and Welfare has approved certain ameliorative regulations under 42 U.S.C. § 405(g). See 29 Fed. Reg. 8209 (June 30, 1964); Jacoby, *The Effect of Recent Changes in the Law of "Nonstatutory" Judicial Review,* 53 Geo.L.J. 19, 42–43 (1964); see also *Simmons v. United States Dept. HEW,* 328 F.2d 86 (3d Cir. 1964).]

Analysis in terms of "new proceeding" is traceable to *Davis v. L. L. Cohen & Co.,* 268 U.S. 638 (1925), and *Mellon v. Arkansas Land & Lumber Co.,* 275 U.S. 460 (1928), but those cases antedate the adoption of the Rules which import different criteria for determining when an amendment is to "relate back". As lower courts have continued to rely on the *Davis* and *Mellon* cases despite the contrary intent of the Rules, clarification of Rule 15(c) is considered advisable.

Relation back is intimately connected with the policy of the statute of limitations. The policy of the statute limiting the time for suit against the Secretary of HEW would not have been offended by allowing relation back in the situations described above. For the government was put on notice of the claim within the stated period—in the particular instances, by means of the initial delivery of process to a responsible government official (see Rule 4(d)(4) and (5)). In these circumstances, characterization of the amendment as a new proceeding is not responsive to the realty [sic], but is merely question-begging; and to deny relation back is to defeat unjustly the claimant's opportunity to prove his case. See the full discussion by Byse, *Suing the "Wrong" Defendant in Judicial Review of Federal Administrative Action: Proposals for Reform,* 77 Harv.L.Rev. 40 (1963); see also Ill.Civ.P. Act § 46(4).

Much the same question arises in other types of actions against the government (see *Byse,* supra, at 45 n. 15). In actions between private parties, the problem of relation back of amendments changing defendants has generally been better handled by the courts, but incorrect criteria have sometimes been applied, leading sporadically to doubtful results. See 1A Barron & Holtzoff, *Federal Practice & Procedure* § 451 (Wright ed. 1960); 1 id. § 186 (1960); 2 id. § 543 (1961); 3 *Moore's Federal Practice,* par. 15.15 (Cum.Supp. 1962); Annot., *Change in Party After Statute of Limitations Has Run,* 8 A.L.R.2d 6 (1949). Rule 15(c) has been amplified to provide a general solution. An amendment changing the party against whom a claim is asserted relates back if the amendment satisfies the usual condition of Rule 15(c) of "arising out of the conduct * * * set forth * * * in the original pleading," and if, within the applicable limitations period, the party brought in by amendment, first, received such notice of the institution of the action—the notice need not be formal—that he would not be prejudiced in defending the action, and, second, knew or should have known that the action would have been brought against him initially had there not been a mistake concerning the identity of the proper party. Revised Rule 15(c) goes on to provide specifically in the government cases that the first and second requirements are satisfied when the government has been notified in the manner there described (see Rule 4(d)(4) and (5)). As applied to the government cases, revised Rule 15(c) further advances the objectives of the 1961 amendment of Rule 25(d) (substitution of public officers).

The relation back of amendments changing plaintiffs is not expressly treated in revised Rule 15(c) since the problem is generally easier. Again the chief consideration of policy is that of the statute of limitations, and the attitude taken in revised Rule 15(c) toward change of defendants extends by analogy to amendments changing plaintiffs. Also relevant is the amendment of Rule 17(a) (real party in interest). To avoid forfeitures of just claims, revised Rule 17(a) would provide that no action shall be dismissed on the ground that it is not prosecuted in the name of the real party in interest until a reasonable time has been allowed for correction of the defect in the manner there stated.

1987 Amendment

The amendments are technical. No substantive change is intended.

1991 Amendment

The rule has been revised to prevent parties against whom claims are made from taking unjust advantage of otherwise inconsequential pleading errors to sustain a limitations defense.

Paragraph (c)(1). This provision is new. It is intended to make it clear that the rule does not apply to preclude any relation back that may be permitted under the applicable limitations law. Generally, the applicable limitations law will be state law. If federal jurisdiction is based on the citizenship of the parties, the primary reference is the law of the state in which the district court sits. *Walker v. Armco Steel Corp.,* 446 U.S. 740 (1980). If federal jurisdiction is based on a federal question, the reference may be to the law of the state governing relations between the parties. *E.g., Board of Regents v. Tomanio,* 446 U.S. 478 (1980). In some circumstances, the controlling limitations law may be federal law. *E.g., West v. Conrail, Inc.,* 107 S.Ct. 1538 (1987). Cf. *Burlington Northern R. Co. v. Woods,* 480 U.S. 1 (1987); *Stewart Organization v. Ricoh,* 108 S.Ct. 2239 (1988). Whatever may be the controlling body of limitations law, if that law affords a more forgiving principle of relation back than the one provided in this rule, it should be available to save the claim. Accord, *Marshall v. Mulrenin,* 508 F.2d 39 (1st cir.1974). If *Schiavone v. Fortune,* 106 S.Ct. 2379 (1986) implies the contrary, this paragraph is intended to make a material change in the rule.

Paragraph (c)(3). This paragraph has been revised to change the result in *Schiavone v. Fortune, supra,* with respect to the problem of a misnamed defendant. An intended defendant who is notified of an action within the period allowed by Rule 4(m) [subdivision (m) in Rule 4 was a proposed subdivision which was withdrawn by the Supreme Court] for service of a summons and complaint may not under the revised rule defeat the action on account of a defect in the pleading with respect to the defendant's name, provided that the requirements of clauses (A) and (B) have been met. If the notice requirement is met within the Rule 4(m) [subdivision (m) in Rule 4 was a proposed subdivision which was withdrawn by the Supreme Court] period, a complaint may be amended at any time to correct a formal defect such as a misnomer or misidentification. On the basis of the text of the former rule, the Court reached a result in *Schiavone v. Fortune* that was inconsistent with the liberal pleading practices secured by Rule 8. See Bauer, Schiavone: *An Un-Fortune-ate Illustration of the Supreme Court's Role as Interpreter of the Federal Rules of Civil Procedure,* 63 Notre Dame L.Rev. 720 (1988); Brussack, *Outrageous Fortune: The Case for Amending Rule 15(c) Again,* 61 S.Cal. L.Rev. 671 (1988); Lewis, *The Excessive History of Federal Rule 15(c) and Its Lessons for Civil Rules Revision,* 86 Mich.L.Rev. 1507 (1987).

In allowing a name-correcting amendment within the time allowed by Rule 4(m), this rule allows not only the 120 days specified in that rule, but also any additional time resulting from any extension ordered by the court pursuant to that rule, as may be granted, for example, if the defendant is a fugitive from service of the summons.

This revision, together with the revision of Rule 4(i) with respect to the failure of a plaintiff in an action against the United States to effect timely service on all the appropriate officials, is intended to produce results contrary to those reached in *Gardner v. Gartman,* 880 F.2d 797 (4th Cir. 1989), *Rys v. U.S. Postal Service,* 886 F.2d 443 (1st Cir. 1989), *Martin's Food & Liquor, Inc. v. U.S. Dept. of Agriculture,* 14 F.R.D.3d 86 (N.D.Ill.1988). *But cf. Montgomery v. United States Postal Service,* 867 F.2d 900 (5th Cir. 1989), *Warren v. Department of the Army,* 867 F.2d 1156 (8th Cir. 1989); *Miles v. Department of the Army,* 881 F.2d 777 (9th Cir. 1989), *Barsten v. Department of the Interior,* 896 F.2d 422 (9th Cir. 1990); *Brown v. Georgia Dept. of Revenue,* 881 F.2d 1018 (11th Cir. 1989).

1993 Amendments

The amendment conforms the cross reference to Rule 4 to the revision of that rule.

2007 Amendment

The language of Rule 15 has been amended as part of the general restyling of the Civil Rules to make them more easily understood and to make style and terminology consistent throughout the rules. These changes are intended to be stylistic only.

Former Rule 15(c)(3)(A) called for notice of the "institution" of the action. Rule 15(c)(1)(C)(i) omits the reference to "institution" as potentially confusing. What counts is that the party to be brought in have notice of the existence of the action, whether or not the notice includes details as to its "institution."

HISTORICAL NOTES

Effective and Applicability Provisions

1991 Acts. Section 11(a) of Pub.L. 102–198 amended subd. (c)(3) of this rule, as transmitted to the Congress by the Supreme Court pursuant to section 2074 of title 28, United States Code, to become effective on December 1, 1991.

Rule 16. Pretrial Conferences; Scheduling; Management

(a) Purposes of a Pretrial Conference. In any action, the court may order the attorneys and any unrepresented parties to appear for one or more pretrial conferences for such purposes as:

(1) expediting disposition of the action;

(2) establishing early and continuing control so that the case will not be protracted because of lack of management;

(3) discouraging wasteful pretrial activities;

(4) improving the quality of the trial through more thorough preparation; and

(5) facilitating settlement.

(b) Scheduling.

(1) ***Scheduling Order.*** Except in categories of actions exempted by local rule, the district judge—or a magistrate judge when authorized by local rule—must issue a scheduling order:

(A) after receiving the parties' report under Rule 26(f); or

(B) after consulting with the parties' attorneys and any unrepresented parties at a scheduling conference or by telephone, mail, or other means.

(2) ***Time to Issue.*** The judge must issue the scheduling order as soon as practicable, but in any event within the earlier of 120 days after any defendant has been served with the complaint or 90 days after any defendant has appeared.

(3) ***Contents of the Order.***

(A) *Required Contents.* The scheduling order must limit the time to join other parties, amend the pleadings, complete discovery, and file motions.

(B) *Permitted Contents.* The scheduling order may:

(i) modify the timing of disclosures under Rules 26(a) and 26(e)(1);

(ii) modify the extent of discovery;

(iii) provide for disclosure or discovery of electronically stored information;

(iv) include any agreements the parties reach for asserting claims of privilege or of protection as trial-preparation material after information is produced;

(v) set dates for pretrial conferences and for trial; and

(vi) include other appropriate matters.

(4) ***Modifying a Schedule.*** A schedule may be modified only for good cause and with the judge's consent.

(c) Attendance and Matters for Consideration at a Pretrial Conference.

(1) ***Attendance.*** A represented party must authorize at least one of its attorneys to make stipulations and admissions about all matters that can reasonably be anticipated for discussion at a pretrial conference. If appropriate, the court may require that a party or its representative be present or reasonably available by other means to consider possible settlement.

(2) ***Matters for Consideration.*** At any pretrial conference, the court may consider and take appropriate action on the following matters:

(A) formulating and simplifying the issues, and eliminating frivolous claims or defenses;

(B) amending the pleadings if necessary or desirable;

(C) obtaining admissions and stipulations about facts and documents to avoid unnecessary proof, and ruling in advance on the admissibility of evidence;

(D) avoiding unnecessary proof and cumulative evidence, and limiting the use of testimony under Federal Rule of Evidence 702;

(E) determining the appropriateness and timing of summary adjudication under Rule 56;

(F) controlling and scheduling discovery, including orders affecting disclosures and discovery under Rule 26 and Rules 29 through 37;

(G) identifying witnesses and documents, scheduling the filing and exchange of any pretrial briefs, and setting dates for further conferences and for trial;

(H) referring matters to a magistrate judge or a master;

(I) settling the case and using special procedures to assist in resolving the dispute when authorized by statute or local rule;

(J) determining the form and content of the pretrial order;

(K) disposing of pending motions;

(L) adopting special procedures for managing potentially difficult or protracted actions that may involve complex issues, multiple parties, difficult legal questions, or unusual proof problems;

(M) ordering a separate trial under Rule 42(b) of a claim, counterclaim, crossclaim, third-party claim, or particular issue;

(N) ordering the presentation of evidence early in the trial on a manageable issue that might, on the evidence, be the basis for a judgment as a matter of law under Rule 50(a) or a judgment on partial findings under Rule 52(c);

(O) establishing a reasonable limit on the time allowed to present evidence; and

(P) facilitating in other ways the just, speedy, and inexpensive disposition of the action.

(d) **Pretrial Orders.** After any conference under this rule, the court should issue an order reciting the action taken. This order controls the course of the action unless the court modifies it.

(e) **Final Pretrial Conference and Orders.** The court may hold a final pretrial conference to formulate a trial plan, including a plan to facilitate the admission of evidence. The conference must be held as close to the start of trial as is reasonable, and must be attended by at least one attorney who will conduct the trial for each party and by any unrepresented party. The court may modify the order issued after a final pretrial conference only to prevent manifest injustice.

(f) **Sanctions.**

(1) ***In General.*** On motion or on its own, the court may issue any just orders, including those authorized by Rule 37(b)(2)(A)(ii)-(vii), if a party or its attorney:

(A) fails to appear at a scheduling or other pretrial conference;

(B) is substantially unprepared to participate—or does not participate in good faith—in the conference; or

(C) fails to obey a scheduling or other pretrial order.

(2) ***Imposing Fees and Costs.*** Instead of or in addition to any other sanction, the court must order the party, its attorney, or both to pay the reasonable expenses—including attorney's fees—incurred because of any noncompliance with this rule, unless the noncompliance was substantially justified or other circumstances make an award of expenses unjust.

(Amended April 28, 1983, effective August 1, 1983; March 2, 1987, effective August 1, 1987; April 22, 1993, effective December 1, 1993; April 12, 2006, effective December 1, 2006; April 30, 2007, effective December 1, 2007.)

ADVISORY COMMITTEE NOTES

1937 Adoption

1. Similar rules of pre-trial procedure are now in force in Boston, Cleveland, Detroit, and Los Angeles, and a rule substantially like this one has been proposed for the urban centers of New York state. For a discussion of the successful operation of pre-trial procedure in relieving the congested condition of trial calendars of the courts in such cities and for the proposed New York plan, see *A Proposal for Minimizing Calendar Delay in Jury Cases* (Dec. 1936—published by the New York Law Society); *Pre-Trial Procedure and Administration,* Third Annual Report of the Judicial Council of the State of New York (1937), pages 207–243; *Report of the Commission on the Administration of Justice in New York State* (1934), pp. (288) to (290). See also *Pre-Trial Procedure in the Wayne Circuit Court,* Detroit, Michigan, Sixth Annual Report of the Judicial Council of Michigan (1936), pp. 63 to 75; and Sunderland, *The Theory and Practice of Pre-trial Procedure* (Dec. 1937) 36 Mich.L.Rev. 215–226, 21 J.Am.Jud. Soc. 125. Compare the English procedure known as the "summons for directions", *English Rules Under the Judicature Act* (The Annual Practice, 1937) O. 38a; and a similar procedure in New Jersey, N.J.S.A. 2:27–135, 2:27–136, 2:27–160; N.J. Supreme Court Rules, 2 N.J.Misc.Rep. (1924) 1230, Rules 94, 92, 93, 95 (the last three as amended 1933, 11 N.J.Misc.Rep. (1933) 955).

2. Compare the similar procedure under Rule 56(d) (Summary Judgment—Case Not Fully Adjudicated on Motion). Rule 12(g) (Consolidation of Motions), by requiring to some extent the consolidation of motions dealing with matters preliminary to trial, is a step in the same direction. In connection with clause (5) of this rule, see Rules 53(b) (Masters; Reference) and 53(e)(3) (Master's Report; In Jury Actions).

1983 Amendment

Introduction

Rule 16 has not been amended since the Federal Rules were promulgated in 1938. In many respects, the rule has been a success. For example, there is evidence that pretrial conferences may improve the quality of justice rendered in the federal courts by sharpening the preparation and presentation of cases, tending to eliminate trial surprise, and improving, as well as facilitating, the settlement process. See 6 Wright & Miller, *Federal Practice and Procedure:* Civil § 1522 (1971). However, in other respects particularly with regard to case management, the rule has not always been as helpful as it might have been. Thus there has been a widespread feeling that amendment is necessary to encourage pretrial management that meets the needs of modern litigation. See *Report of the National Commission for the Review of Antitrust Laws and Procedures* (1979).

Major criticism of Rule 16 has centered on the fact that its application can result in over-regulation of some cases and under-regulation of others. In simple, run-of-the-mill cases, attorneys have found pretrial requirements burdensome. It is claimed that over-administration leads to a series of mini-trials that result in a waste of an attorney's time and needless expense to a client. Pollack, *Pretrial Procedures More Effectively Handled,* 65 F.R.D. 475 (1974). This is especially likely to be true when pretrial proceedings occur long before trial. At the other end of the spectrum, the discretionary character of Rule 16 and its orientation toward a single conference late in the pretrial process has led to under-administration of complex or protracted cases. Without judicial guidance beginning shortly after institution, these cases often become mired in discovery.

Four sources of criticism of pretrial have been identified. First, conferences often are seen as a mere exchange of legalistic contentions without any real analysis of the particular case. Second, the result frequently is nothing but a formal agreement on minutiae. Third, the conferences are seen as unnecessary and time-consuming in cases that will be settled before trial. Fourth, the meetings can be ceremonial and ritualistic, having little effect on the trial and being of minimal value, particularly when the attorneys attending the sessions are not the ones who will try the case or lack authority to enter into binding stipulations. See generally *McCargo v. Hedrick,* 545 F.2d 393 (4th Cir.1976); Pollack, *Pretrial Procedures More Effectively Handled,* 65 F.R.D. 475 (1974); Rosenberg, *The Pretrial Conference and Effective Justice* 45 (1964).

There also have been difficulties with the pretrial orders that issue following Rule 16 conferences. When an order is entered far in advance of trial, some issues may not be properly formulated. Counsel naturally are cautious and often try to preserve as many options as possible. If the judge who tries the case did not conduct the conference, he could find it difficult to determine exactly what was agreed to at the conference. But any insistence on a detailed order may be too burdensome, depending on the nature or posture of the case.

Given the significant changes in federal civil litigation since 1938 that are not reflected in Rule 16, it has been extensively rewritten and expanded to meet the challenges of modern litigation. Empirical studies reveal that when a trial judge intervenes personally at an early stage to assume judicial control over a case and to schedule dates for completion by the parties of the principal pretrial steps, the case is disposed of by settlement or trial more efficiently and with less cost and delay than when the parties are left to their own devices. Flanders, *Case Management and Court Management in United States District Courts* 17, Federal Judicial Center (1977). Thus, the rule mandates a pretrial scheduling order. However, although scheduling and pretrial conferences are encouraged in appropriate cases, they are not mandated.

Discussion

Subdivision (a); Pretrial Conferences; Objectives. The amended rule makes scheduling and case management an express goal of pretrial procedure. This is done in Rule 16(a) by shifting the emphasis away from a conference focused solely on the trial and toward a process of judicial management that embraces the entire pretrial phase, especially motions and discovery. In addition, the amendment explicitly recognizes some of the objectives of pretrial conferences and the powers that many courts already have assumed. Rule 16 thus will be a more accurate reflection of actual practice.

Subdivision (b); Scheduling and Planning. The most significant change in Rule 16 is the mandatory scheduling order described in Rule 16(b), which is based in part on Wisconsin Civil Procedure Rule 802.10. The idea of scheduling orders is not new. It has been used by many federal courts. See, *e.g.,* Southern District of Indiana, Local Rule 19.

Although a mandatory scheduling order encourages the court to become involved in case management early in the litigation, it represents a degree of judicial involvement that is not warranted in many cases. Thus, subdivision (b) permits each district court to promulgate a local rule under Rule 83 exempting certain categories of cases in which the burdens of scheduling orders exceed the administrative efficiencies that would be gained. See Eastern District of Virginia, Local Rule 12(1). Logical candidates for this treatment include social security disability matters, habeas corpus petitions, forfeitures, and reviews of certain administrative actions.

A scheduling conference may be requested either by the judge, a magistrate when authorized by district court rule, or a party within 120 days after the summons and complaint are filed. If a scheduling conference is not arranged within that time and the case is not exempted by local rule, a scheduling order must be issued under Rule 16(b), after some communication with the parties, which may be by telephone or mail rather than in person. The use of the term "judge" in subdivision (b) reflects the Advisory Committee's judgment that it is preferable that this task should be handled by a district judge rather than a magistrate, except when the magistrate is acting under 28 U.S.C. § 636(c). While personal supervision by the trial judge is preferred, the rule, in recognition of the impracticality or difficulty of complying with such a requirement in some districts, authorizes a district by local rule to delegate the duties to a magistrate. In order to formulate a practicable scheduling order, the judge, or a magistrate when authorized by district court rule, and attorneys are required to develop a timetable for the matters listed in Rule 16(b)(1)–(3). As indicated in Rule 16(b)(4)–(5), the order may also deal with a wide range of other matters. The rule is phrased permissively as to clauses (4) and (5), however, because scheduling these items at an early point may not be feasible or appropriate. Even though subdivision (b) relates only to scheduling, there is no reason why some of the procedural matters listed in Rule 16(c) cannot be addressed at the same time, at least when a scheduling conference is held.

Item (1) assures that at some point both the parties and the pleadings will be fixed, by setting a time within which joinder of parties shall be completed and the pleadings amended.

Item (2) requires setting time limits for interposing various motions that otherwise might be used as stalling techniques.

Item (3) deals with the problem of procrastination and delay by attorneys in a context in which scheduling is especially important-discovery. Scheduling the completion of discovery can serve some of the same functions as the conference described in Rule 26(f).

Item (4) refers to setting dates for conferences and for trial. Scheduling multiple pretrial conferences may well be desirable if the case is complex and the court believes that a more elaborate pretrial structure, such as that described in the *Manual for Complex Litigation,* should be employed.

On the other hand, only one pretrial conference may be necessary in an uncomplicated case.

As long as the case is not exempted by local rule, the court must issue a written scheduling order even if no scheduling conference is called. The order, like pretrial orders under the former rule and those under new Rule 16(c), normally will "control the subsequent course of the action." See Rule 16(e). After consultation with the attorneys for the parties and any unrepresented parties-a formal motion is not necessary-the court may modify the schedule on a showing of good cause if it cannot reasonably be met despite the diligence of the party seeking the extension. Since the scheduling order is entered early in the litigation, this standard seems more appropriate than a "manifest injustice" or "substantial hardship" test. Otherwise, a fear that extensions will not be granted may encourage counsel to request the longest possible periods for completing pleading, joinder, and discovery. Moreover, changes in the court's calendar sometimes will oblige the judge or magistrate when authorized by district court rule to modify the scheduling order.

The district courts undoubtedly will develop several prototype scheduling orders for different types of cases. In addition, when no formal conference is held, the court may obtain scheduling information by telephone, mail, or otherwise. In many instances this will result in a scheduling order better suited to the individual case than a standard order, without taking the time that would be required by a formal conference.

Rule 16(b) assures that the judge will take some early control over the litigation, even when its character does not warrant holding a scheduling conference. Despite the fact that the process of preparing a scheduling order does not always bring the attorneys and judge together, the fixing of time limits serves

> to stimulate litigants to narrow the areas of inquiry and advocacy to those they believe are truly relevant and material. Time limits not only compress the amount of time for litigation, they should also reduce the amount of resources invested in litigation. Litigants are forced to establish discovery priorities and thus to do the most important work first.

Report of the National Commission for the Review of Antitrust Laws and Procedures 28 (1979).

Thus, except in exempted cases, the judge or a magistrate when authorized by district court rule will have taken some action in every case within 120 days after the complaint is filed that notifies the attorneys that the case will be moving toward trial. Subdivision (b) is reenforced by subdivision (f), which makes it clear that the sanctions for violating a scheduling order are the same as those for violating a pretrial order.

Subdivision (c); Subjects to be Discussed at Pretrial Conferences. This subdivision expands upon the list of things that may be discussed at a pretrial conference that appeared in original Rule 16. The intention is to encourage better planning and management of litigation. Increased judicial control during the pretrial process accelerates the processing and termination of cases. Flanders, *Case Management and Court Management in United States District Courts,* 39 Federal Judicial Center (1977). See also *Report of the National Commission for the Review of Antitrust Laws and Procedures* (1979).

The reference in Rule 16(c)(1) to "formulation" is intended to clarify and confirm the court's power to identify the litigable issues. It has been added in the hope of promoting efficiency and conserving judicial resources by identifying the real issues prior to trial, thereby saving time and expense for everyone. See generally *Meadow Gold Prods. Co. v. Wright,* 278 F.2d 867 (D.C.Cir.1960). The notion is emphasized by expressly authorizing the elimination of frivolous claims or defenses at a pretrial conference. There is no reason to require that this await a formal motion for summary judgment. Nor is there any reason for the court to wait for the parties to initiate the process called for in Rule 16(c)(1).

The timing of any attempt at issue formulation is a matter of judicial discretion. In relatively simple cases it may not be necessary or may take the form of a stipulation between counsel or a request by the court that counsel work together to draft a proposed order.

Counsel bear a substantial responsibility for assisting the court in identifying the factual issues worthy of trial. If counsel fail to identify an issue for the court, the right to have the issue tried is waived. Although an order specifying the issues is intended to be binding, it may be amended at trial to avoid manifest injustice. See Rule 16(e). However, the rule's effectiveness depends on the court employing its discretion sparingly.

Clause (6) acknowledges the widespread availability and use of magistrates. The corresponding provision in the original rule referred only to masters and limited the function of the reference to the making of "findings to be used as evidence" in a case to be tried to a jury. The new text is not limited and broadens the potential use of a magistrate to that permitted by the Magistrate's Act.

Clause (7) explicitly recognizes that it has become commonplace to discuss settlement at pretrial conferences. Since it obviously eases crowded court dockets and results in savings to the litigants and the judicial system, settlement should be facilitated at as early a stage of the litigation as possible. Although it is not the purpose of Rule 16(b)(7) to impose settlement negotiations on unwilling litigants, it is believed that providing a neutral forum for discussing the subject might foster it. See Moore's *Federal Practice* ¶ 16.17; 6 Wright & Miller, *Federal Practice and Procedure: Civil* § 1522 (1971). For instance, a judge to whom a case has been assigned may arrange, on his own motion or at a party's request, to have settlement conferences handled by another member of the court or by a magistrate. The rule does not make settlement conferences mandatory because they would be a waste of time in many cases. See Flanders, *Case Management and Court Management in the United States District Courts,* 39 Federal Judicial Center (1977). Requests for a conference from a party indicating a willingness to talk settlement normally should be honored, unless thought to be frivolous or dilatory.

A settlement conference is appropriate at any time. It may be held in conjunction with a pretrial or discovery conference, although various objectives of pretrial management, such as moving the case toward trial, may not always be compatible with settlement negotiations, and thus a separate settlement conference may be desirable. See 6 Wright & Miller, *Federal Practice and Procedure: Civil* § 1522, at p. 571 (1971).

In addition to settlement, Rule 16(c)(7) refers to exploring the use of procedures other than litigation to resolve the dispute. This includes urging the litigants to employ adjudicatory techniques outside the courthouse. See, for example, the experiment described in *Green, Marks & Olson, Settling Large Case Litigation: An Alternative Approach,* 11 Loyola of L.A.L.Rev. 493 (1978).

Rule 16(c)(10) authorizes the use of special pretrial procedures to expedite the adjudication of potentially difficult or protracted cases. Some district courts obviously have done so for many years. See Rubin, *The Managed Calendar: Some Pragmatic Suggestions About Achieving the Just, Speedy and Inexpensive Determination of Civil Cases in Federal Courts,* 4 Just.Sys.J. 135 (1976). Clause 10 provides an explicit authorization for such procedures and encourages their use. No particular techniques have been described; the Committee felt that flexibility and experience are the keys to efficient management of complex cases. Extensive guidance is offered in such documents as the *Manual for Complex Litigation.*

The rule simply identifies characteristics that make a case a strong candidate for special treatment. The four mentioned are illustrative, not exhaustive, and overlap to some degree. But experience has shown that one or more of them will be present in every protracted or difficult case and it seems desirable to set them out. See Kendig, *Procedures for Management of Non-Routine Cases,* 3 Hofstra L.Rev. 701 (1975).

The last sentence of subdivision (c) is new. See Wisconsin Civil Procedure Rule 802.11(2). It has been added to meet one of the criticisms of the present practice described earlier and insure proper preconference preparation so that the meeting is more than a ceremonial or ritualistic event. The reference to "authority" is not intended to insist upon the ability to settle the litigation. Nor should the rule be read to encourage the judge conducting the conference to compel attorneys to enter into stipulations or to make admissions that they consider to be unreasonable, that touch on matters that could not normally have been anticipated to arise at the conference, or on subjects of a dimension that normally require prior consultation with and approval from the client.

Subdivision (d); Final Pretrial Conference. This provision has been added to make it clear that the time between any final pretrial conference (which in a simple case may be the **only** pretrial conference) and trial should be as short as possible to be certain that the litigants make substantial progress with the case and avoid the inefficiency of having that preparation repeated when there is a delay between the last pretrial conference and trial. An optimum time of 10 days to two weeks has been suggested by one federal judge. Rubin, *The Managed Calendar: Some Pragmatic Suggestions About Achieving the Just, Speedy and Inexpensive Determination of Civil Cases in Federal Courts,* 4 Just. Sys.J. 135, 141 (1976). The Committee, however, concluded that it would be inappropriate to fix a precise time in the rule, given the numerous variables that could bear on the matter. Thus the timing has been left to the court's discretion.

At least one of the attorneys who will conduct the trial for each party must be present at the final pretrial conference. At this late date there should be no doubt as to which attorney or attorneys this will be. Since the agreements and stipulations made at this final conference will control the trial, the presence of lawyers who will be involved in it is especially useful to assist the judge in structuring the case, and to lead to a more effective trial.

Subdivision (e); Pretrial Orders. Rule 16(e) does not substantially change the portion of the original rule dealing with pretrial orders. The purpose of an order is to guide the course of the litigation and the language of the original rule making that clear has been retained. No compelling reason has been found for major revision, especially since this portion of the rule has been interpreted and clarified by over forty years of judicial decisions with comparatively little difficulty. See 6 Wright & Miller, *Federal Practice and Procedure: Civil* §§ 1521–30 (1971). Changes in language therefore have been kept to a minimum to avoid confusion.

Since the amended rule encourages more extensive pretrial management than did the original, two or more conferences may be held in many cases. The language of Rule 16(e) recognizes this possibility and the corresponding need to issue more than one pretrial order in a single case.

Once formulated, pretrial orders should not be changed lightly; but total inflexibility is undesirable. See, *e.g., Clark v. Pennsylvania R.R. Co.,* 328 F.2d 591 (2d Cir.1964). The exact words used to describe the standard for amending the pretrial order probably are less important than the meaning given them in practice. By not imposing any limitation on the ability to modify a pretrial order, the rule reflects the reality that in any process of continuous management, what is done at one conference may have to be altered at the next. In the case of the final pretrial order, however, a more stringent standard is called for and the words "to prevent manifest injustice," which appeared in the original rule, have been retained. They have the virtue of familiarity and adequately describe the restraint the trial judge should exercise.

Many local rules make the plaintiff's attorney responsible for drafting a proposed pretrial order, either before or after the conference. Others allow the court to appoint any of the attorneys to perform the task, and others leave it to the court. See Note, *Pretrial Conference: A Critical Examination of Local Rules Adopted by Federal District Courts,* 64 Va.L.Rev. 467 (1978). Rule 16 has never addressed this matter. Since there is no consensus about which method of drafting the order works best and there is no reason to believe that nationwide uniformity is needed, the rule has been left silent on the point. See *Handbook for Effective Pretrial Procedure,* 37 F.R.D. 225 (1964).

Subdivision (f); Sanctions. Original Rule 16 did not mention the sanctions that might be imposed for failing to comply with the rule. However, courts have not hesitated to enforce it by appropriate measures. See, e.g., *Link v. Wabash R. Co.,* 370 U.S. 628 (1962) (district court's dismissal under Rule 41(b) after plaintiff's attorney failed to appear at a pretrial conference upheld); *Admiral Theatre Corp. v. Douglas Theatre,* 585 F.2d 877 (8th Cir.1978) (district court has discretion to exclude exhibits or refuse to permit the testimony of a witness not listed prior to trial in contravention of its pretrial order).

To reflect that existing practice, and to obviate dependence upon Rule 41(b) or the court's inherent power to regulate litigation, *cf. Societe Internationale Pour Participations Industrielles et Commerciales, S.A. v. Rogers,* 357 U.S. 197 (1958), Rule 16(f) expressly provides for imposing sanctions on disobedient or recalcitrant parties, their attorneys, or both in four types of situations. Rodes, Ripple & Mooney,

Sanctions Imposable for Violations of the Federal Rules of Civil Procedure 65–67, 80–84, Federal Judicial Center (1981). Furthermore, explicit reference to sanctions reenforces the rule's intention to encourage forceful judicial management.

Rule 16(f) incorporates portions of Rule 37(b)(2), which prescribes sanctions for failing to make discovery. This should facilitate application of Rule 16(f), since courts and lawyers already are familiar with the Rule 37 standards. Among the sanctions authorized by the new subdivision are: preclusion order, striking a pleading, staying the proceeding, default judgment, contempt, and charging a party, his attorney, or both with the expenses, including attorney's fees, caused by noncompliance. The contempt sanction, however, is only available for a violation of a court order. The references in Rule 16(f) are not exhaustive.

As is true under Rule 37(b)(2), the imposition of sanctions may be sought by either the court or a party. In addition, the court has discretion to impose whichever sanction it feels is appropriate under the circumstances. Its action is reviewable under the abuse-of-discretion standard. See *National Hockey League v. Metropolitan Hockey Club, Inc.*, 427 U.S. 639 (1976).

1987 Amendment

The amendments are technical. No substantive change is intended.

1993 Amendments

Subdivision (b). One purpose of this amendment is to provide a more appropriate deadline for the initial scheduling order required by the rule. The former rule directed that the order be entered within 120 days from the filing of the complaint. This requirement has created problems because Rule 4(m) allows 120 days for service and ordinarily at least one defendant should be available to participate in the process of formulating the scheduling order. The revision provides that the order is to be entered within 90 days after the date a defendant first appears (whether by answer or by a motion under Rule 12) or, if earlier (as may occur in some actions against the United States or if service is waived under Rule 4), within 120 days after service of the complaint on a defendant. The longer time provided by the revision is not intended to encourage unnecessary delays in entering the scheduling order. Indeed, in most cases the order can and should be entered at a much earlier date. Rather, the additional time is intended to alleviate problems in multidefendant cases and should ordinarily be adequate to enable participation by all defendants initially named in the action.

In many cases the scheduling order can and should be entered before this deadline. However, when setting a scheduling conference, the court should take into account the effect this setting will have in establishing deadlines for the parties to meet under revised Rule 26(f) and to exchange information under revised Rule 26(a)(1). While the parties are expected to stipulate to additional time for making their disclosures when warranted by the circumstances, a scheduling conference held before defendants have had time to learn much about the case may result in diminishing the value of the Rule 26(f) meeting, the parties' proposed discovery plan, and indeed the conference itself.

New paragraph (4) has been added to highlight that it will frequently be desirable for the scheduling order to include provisions relating to the timing of disclosures under Rule 26(a). While the initial disclosures required by Rule 26(a)(1) will ordinarily have been made before entry of the scheduling order, the timing and sequence for disclosure of expert testimony and of the witnesses and exhibits to be used at trial should be tailored to the circumstances of the case and is a matter that should be considered at the initial scheduling conference. Similarly, the scheduling order might contain provisions modifying the extent of discovery (*e.g.*, number and length of depositions) otherwise permitted under these rules or by a local rule.

The report from the attorneys concerning their meeting and proposed discovery plan, as required by revised Rule 26(f), should be submitted to the court before the scheduling order is entered. Their proposals, particularly regarding matters on which they agree, should be of substantial value to the court in setting the timing and limitations on discovery and should reduce the time of the court needed to conduct a meaningful conference under Rule 16(b). As under the prior rule, while a scheduling order is mandated, a scheduling conference is not. However, in view of the benefits to be derived from the litigants and a judicial officer meeting in person, a Rule 16(b) conference should, to the extent practicable, be held in all cases that will involve discovery.

This subdivision, as well as subdivision (c)(8), also is revised to reflect the new title of United States Magistrate Judges pursuant to the Judicial Improvements Act of 1990.

Subdivision (c). The primary purposes of the changes in subdivision (c) are to call attention to the opportunities for structuring of trial under Rules 42, 50, and 52 and to eliminate questions that have occasionally been raised regarding the authority of the court to make appropriate orders designed either to facilitate settlement or to provide for an efficient and economical trial. The prefatory language of this subdivision is revised to clarify the court's power to enter appropriate orders at a conference notwithstanding the objection of a party. Of course settlement is dependent upon agreement by the parties and, indeed, a conference is most effective and productive when the parties participate in a spirit of cooperation and mindful of their responsibilities under Rule 1.

Paragraph (4) is revised to clarify that in advance of trial the court may address the need for, and possible limitations on, the use of expert testimony under Rule 702 of the Federal Rules of Evidence. Even when proposed expert testimony might be admissible under the standards of Rules 403 and 702 of the evidence rules, the court may preclude or limit such testimony if the cost to the litigants—which may include the cost to adversaries of securing testimony on the same subjects by other experts—would be unduly expensive given the needs of the case and the other evidence available at trial.

Paragraph (5) is added (and the remaining paragraphs renumbered) in recognition that use of Rule 56 to avoid or reduce the scope of trial is a topic that can, and often should, be considered at a pretrial conference. Renumbered paragraph (11) enables the court to rule on pending motions for summary adjudication that are ripe for decision at the time of the conference. Often, however, the potential use of Rule 56 is a matter that arises from discussions during a conference. The court may then call for motions to be filed.

Paragraph (6) is added to emphasize that a major objective of pretrial conferences should be to consider appropriate controls on the extent and timing of discovery. In many cases the court should also specify the times and sequence for disclosure of written reports from experts under revised Rule 26(a)(2)(B) and perhaps direct changes in the types of experts from whom written reports are required. Consideration should also be given to possible changes in the timing or form of the disclosure of trial witnesses and documents under Rule 26(a)(3).

Paragraph (9) is revised to describe more accurately the various procedures that, in addition to traditional settlement conferences, may be helpful in settling litigation. Even if a case cannot immediately be settled, the judge and attorneys can explore possible use of alternative procedures such as mini-trials, summary jury trials, mediation, neutral evaluation, and nonbinding arbitration that can lead to consensual resolution of the dispute without a full trial on the merits. The rule acknowledges the presence of statutes and local rules or plans that may authorize use of some of these procedures even when not agreed to by the parties. See 28 U.S.C. §§ 473(a)(6), 473(b)(4), 651–58; Section 104(b)(2), Pub.L. 101–650. The rule does not attempt to resolve questions as to the extent a court would be authorized to require such proceedings as an exercise of its inherent powers.

The amendment of paragraph (9) should be read in conjunction with the sentence added to the end of subdivision (c), authorizing the court to direct that, in appropriate cases, a responsible representative of the parties be present or available by telephone during a conference in order to discuss possible settlement of the case. The sentence refers to participation by a party or its representative. Whether this would be the individual party, an officer of a corporate party, a representative from an insurance carrier, or someone else would depend on the circumstances. Particularly in litigation in which governmental agencies or large amounts of money are involved, there may be no one with on-the-spot settlement authority, and the most that should be expected is access to a person who would have a major role in submitting a recommendation to the body or board with ultimate decision-making responsibility. The selection of the appropriate representative should ordinarily be left to the party and its counsel. Finally, it should be noted that the unwillingness of a party to be available, even by telephone, for a settlement conference may be a clear signal that the time and expense involved in pursuing settlement is likely to be unproductive and that personal participation by the parties should not be required.

The explicit authorization in the rule to require personal participation in the manner stated is not intended to limit the reasonable exercise of the court's inherent powers, *e.g., G. Heileman Brewing Co. v. Joseph Oat Corp.*, 871 F.2d 648 (7th Cir.1989), or its power to require party participation under the Civil Justice Reform Act of 1990. See 28 U.S.C. § 473(b)(5) (civil justice expense and delay reduction plans adopted by district courts may include requirement that representatives "with authority to bind [parties] in settlement discussions" be available during settlement conferences).

New paragraphs (13) and (14) are added to call attention to the opportunities for structuring of trial under Rule 42 and under revised Rules 50 and 52.

Paragraph (15) is also new. It supplements the power of the court to limit the extent of evidence under Rules 403 and 611(a) of the Federal Rules of Evidence, which typically would be invoked as a result of developments during trial. Limits on the length of trial established at a conference in advance of trial can provide the parties with a better opportunity to determine priorities and exercise selectivity in presenting evidence than when limits are imposed during trial. Any such limits must be reasonable under the circumstances, and ordinarily the court should impose them only after receiving appropriate submissions from the parties outlining the nature of the testimony expected to be presented through various witnesses, and the expected duration of direct and cross-examination.

2006 Amendment

The amendment to Rule 16(b) is designed to alert the court to the possible need to address the handling of discovery of electronically stored information early in the litigation if such discovery is expected to occur. Rule 26(f) is amended to direct the parties to discuss discovery of electronically stored information if such discovery is contemplated in the action. Form 35 is amended to call for a report to the court about the results of this discussion. In many instances, the court's involvement early in the litigation will help avoid difficulties that might otherwise arise.

Rule 16(b) is also amended to include among the topics that may be addressed in the scheduling order any agreements that the parties reach to facilitate discovery by minimizing the risk of waiver of privilege or work-product protection. Rule 26(f) is amended to add to the discovery plan the parties' proposal for the court to enter a case-management or other order adopting such an agreement. The parties may agree to various arrangements. For example, they may agree to initial provision of requested materials without waiver of privilege or protection to enable the party seeking production to designate the materials desired or protection for actual production, with the privilege review of only those materials to follow. Alternatively, they may agree that if privileged or protected information is inadvertently produced, the producing party may by timely notice assert the privilege or protection and obtain return of the materials without waiver. Other arrangements are possible. In most circumstances, a party who receives information under such an arrangement cannot assert that production of the information waived a claim of privilege or of protection as trial-preparation material.

An order that includes the parties' agreement may be helpful in avoiding delay and excessive cost in discovery. *See Manual for Complex Litigation* (4th) § 11.446. Rule 16(b)(6) recognizes the propriety of including such agreements in the court's order. The rule does not provide the court with authority to enter such a case-management or other order without party agreement, or limit the court's authority to act on motion.

2007 Amendment

The language of Rule 16 has been amended as part of the general restyling of the Civil Rules to make them more easily understood and to make style and terminology consistent throughout the rules. These changes are intended to be stylistic only.

When a party or its representative is not present, it is enough to be reasonably available by any suitable means, whether telephone or other communication device.

HISTORICAL NOTES

Change of Name

Reference to United States magistrate or to magistrate deemed to refer to United States magistrate judge pursuant to section 321 of Pub.L. 101–650, set out as a note under section 631 of this title.

TITLE IV. PARTIES

Rule 17. Plaintiff and Defendant; Capacity; Public Officers

(a) Real Party in Interest.

(1) ***Designation in General.*** An action must be prosecuted in the name of the real party in interest. The following may sue in their own names without joining the person for whose benefit the action is brought:

(A) an executor;

(B) an administrator;

(C) a guardian;

(D) a bailee;

(E) a trustee of an express trust;

(F) a party with whom or in whose name a contract has been made for another's benefit; and

(G) a party authorized by statute.

(2) ***Action in the Name of the United States for Another's Use or Benefit.*** When a federal statute so provides, an action for another's use or benefit must be brought in the name of the United States.

(3) ***Joinder of the Real Party in Interest.*** The court may not dismiss an action for failure to prosecute in the name of the real party in interest until, after an objection, a reasonable time has been allowed for the real party in interest to ratify, join, or be substituted into the action. After ratification, joinder, or substitution, the action proceeds as if it had been originally commenced by the real party in interest.

(b) Capacity to Sue or Be Sued. Capacity to sue or be sued is determined as follows:

(1) for an individual who is not acting in a representative capacity, by the law of the individual's domicile;

(2) for a corporation, by the law under which it was organized; and

(3) for all other parties, by the law of the state where the court is located, except that:

(A) a partnership or other unincorporated association with no such capacity under that state's law may sue or be sued in its common name to enforce a substantive right existing under the United States Constitution or laws; and

(B) *28 U.S.C.* §§ 754 and 959(a) govern the capacity of a receiver appointed by a United States court to sue or be sued in a United States court.

(c) Minor or Incompetent Person.

(1) ***With a Representative.*** The following representatives may sue or defend on behalf of a minor or an incompetent person:

(A) a general guardian;

(B) a committee;

(C) a conservator; or

(D) a like fiduciary.

(2) ***Without a Representative.*** A minor or an incompetent person who does not have a duly appointed representative may sue by a next friend or by a guardian ad litem. The court must appoint a guardian ad litem—or issue another appropriate order—to protect a minor or incompetent person who is unrepresented in an action.

(d) Public Officer's Title and Name. A public officer who sues or is sued in an official capacity may be designated by official title rather than by name, but the court may order that the officer's name be added.

(Amended December 27, 1946, effective March 19, 1948; December 29, 1948, effective October 20, 1949; February 28, 1966, effective July 1, 1966; March 2, 1987, effective August 1, 1987; April 25, 1988, effective August 1, 1988; amended by Pub.L. 100–690, Title VII, § 7049, November 18, 1988, 102 Stat. 4401 (although amendment by Pub.L. 100–690 could not be executed due to prior amendment by Court order which made the same change effective August 1, 1988); April 30, 2007, effective December 1, 2007.)

ADVISORY COMMITTEE NOTES

1937 Adoption

Note to Subdivision (a). The real party in interest provision, except for the last clause which is new, is taken verbatim from [former] Equity Rule 37 (Parties Generally—Intervention), except that the word "expressly" has been omitted. For similar provisions see N.Y.C.P.A., (1937) § 210; Wyo.Rev.Stat.Ann. (1931) §§ 89–501, 89–502, 89–503; *English Rules Under the Judicature Act* (The Annual Practice, 1937) O. 16, r. 8. See, also Equity Rule 41 (Suit to Execute Trusts of Will—Heir as Party). For examples of statutes of the United States providing particularly for an action for the use or benefit of another in the name of the United States, see U.S.C., Title 40, § 270b [see now 40 U.S.C.A. § 3133(b)] (Suit by persons furnishing labor and material for work on public building contracts * * * may sue on a payment bond, "in the name of the United States for the use of the person suing"); and U.S.C., Title 25, § 201 (Penalties under laws relating to Indians—how recovered). Compare U.S.C., Title 26, Int.Rev.Code [1939], § 3745(c) [former § 1645(c)] (Suits for penalties, fines, and forfeitures, under this title, where not otherwise provided for, to be in name of United States).

Note to Subdivision (b). For capacity see generally Clark and Moore, *New Federal Civil Procedure*—II. Pleadings and Parties, 44 Yale L.J. 1291, 1312–1317 (1935) and specifically *Coppedge v. Clinton*, 72 F.2d 531 (C.C.A.10th, 1934) (natural person); *David Lupton's Sons Co. v. Automobile Club of America*, 225 U.S. 489, 32 S.Ct. 711, 56 L.Ed. 1177, Ann.Cas.1914A, 699 (1912) (corporation); *Puerto Rico v. Russell & Co.*, 288 U.S. 476, 53 S.Ct. 447, 77 L.Ed. 903 (1933) (unincorporated assn.); *United Mine Workers of America v. Coronado Coal Co.*, 259 U.S. 344, 42 S.Ct. 570, 66 L.Ed. 975, 27 A.L.R. 762 (1922) (federal substantive right enforced against unincorporated association by suit against the association in its common name without naming all its members as parties). This rule follows the existing law as to such associations, as declared in the case last cited above. Compare *Moffat Tunnel League v. United States*, 289 U.S. 113, 53 S.Ct. 543, 77 L.Ed. 1069 (1933). See note to Rule 23, clause (1).

Note to Subdivision (c). The provision for infants and incompetent persons is substantially former Equity Rule 70 (Suits by or Against Incompetents) with slight additions. Compare the more detailed English provisions, *English Rules Under the Judicature Act* (The Annual Practice, 1937) O. 16, r.r. 16–21.

1946 Amendment

Note. The new matter [in subdivision (b)] makes clear the controlling character of Rule 66 regarding suits by or against a federal receiver in a federal court.

1948 Amendment

The amendment effective October 20, 1949, deleted the words "Rule 66" at the end of subdivision (b) and substituted the words "Title 28, U.S.C., §§ 754 and 959(a)".

1966 Amendment

The minor change in the text of the rule is designed to make it clear that the specific instances enumerated are not exceptions to, but illustrations of, the rule. These illustrations, of course, carry no negative implication to the effect that there are not other instances of recognition as the real party in interest of one whose standing as such may be in doubt. The enumeration is simply of cases in which there might be substantial doubt as to the issue but for the specific enumeration. There are other potentially arguable cases that are not excluded by the enumeration. For example, the enumeration states that the promisee in a contract for the benefit of a third party may sue as real party in interest; it does not say, because it is obvious, that the third-party beneficiary may sue (when the applicable law gives him that right.)

The rule adds to the illustrative list of real parties in interest a bailee—meaning, of course, a bailee suing on behalf of the bailor with respect to the property bailed. (When the possessor of property other than the owner sues for an invasion of the possessory interest he is the real party in interest.) The word "bailee" is added primarily to preserve the admiralty practice whereby the owner of a vessel as bailee of the cargo, or the master of the vessel as bailee of both vessel and cargo, sues for damage to either property interest or both. But there is no reason to limit such a provision to maritime situations. The owner of a warehouse in which household furniture is stored is equally entitled to sue on behalf of the numerous owners of the furniture stored. Cf. *Gulf Oil Corp. v. Gilbert*, 330 U.S. 501 (1947).

The provision that no action shall be dismissed on the ground that it is not prosecuted in the name of the real party in interest until a reasonable time has been allowed, after the objection has been raised, for ratification, substitution, etc., is added simply in the interests of justice. In its origin the rule concerning the real party in interest was permissive in purpose: it was designed to allow an assignee to sue in his own name. That having been accomplished, the modern function of the rule in its negative aspect is simply to protect the defendant against a subsequent action by the party actually entitled to recover, and to insure generally that the judgment will have its proper effect as res judicata.

This provision keeps pace with the law as it is actually developing. Modern decisions are inclined to be lenient when an honest mistake has been made in choosing the party in whose name the action is to be filed—in both maritime and nonmaritime cases. See *Levinson v. Deupree*, 345 U.S. 648 (1953); *Link Aviation, Inc. v. Downs*, 325 F.2d 613 (D.C.Cir. 1963). The provision should not be misunderstood or distorted. It is intended to prevent forfeiture when determination of the proper party to sue is difficult or when an understandable mistake has been made. It does not mean, for example, that, following an airplane crash in which all aboard were killed, an action may be filed in the name of John Doe (a fictitious person), as personal representative of Richard Roe (another fictitious person), in the hope that at a later time the attorney filing the action may substitute the real name of the real personal representative of a real victim, and have the benefit of suspension of the limitation period. It does not even mean, when an action is filed by the personal representative of John Smith, of Buffalo, in the good faith belief that he was aboard the flight, that upon discovery that Smith is alive and well, having missed the fatal flight, the representative of James Brown, of San Francisco, an actual victim, can be substituted to take advantage of the suspension of the limitation period. It is, in cases of this sort, intended to insure against forfeiture and injustice—in short, to codify in broad terms the salutary principle of *Levinson v. Deupree*, 345 U.S. 648 (1953), and *Link Aviation, Inc. v. Downs*, 325 F.2d 613 (D.C.Cir. 1963).

1987 Amendment

The amendments are technical. No substantive change is intended.

1988 Amendment

The amendment is technical. No substantive change is intended.

2007 Amendment

The language of Rule 17 has been amended as part of the general restyling of the Civil Rules to make them more easily understood and to make style and terminology consistent throughout the rules. These changes are intended to be stylistic only.

Rule 17(d) incorporates the provisions of former Rule 25(d)(2), which fit better with Rule 17.

Rule 18. Joinder of Claims

(a) In General. A party asserting a claim, counterclaim, crossclaim, or third-party claim may join, as independent or alternative claims, as many claims as it has against an opposing party.

(b) Joinder of Contingent Claims. A party may join two claims even though one of them is contingent on the disposition of the other; but the court may grant relief only in accordance with the parties' relative substantive rights. In particular, a plaintiff may state a claim for money and a claim to set aside a conveyance that is fraudulent as to that plaintiff, without first obtaining a judgment for the money.

(Amended February 28, 1966, effective July 1, 1966; March 2, 1987, effective August 1, 1987; April 30, 2007, effective December 1, 2007.)

ADVISORY COMMITTEE NOTES

1937 Adoption

Note to Subdivision (a). 1. Recent development, both in code and common law states, has been toward unlimited joinder of actions. See Ill.Rev.Stat. (1937) ch. 110, § 168; N.J.S.A. 2:27–37, as modified by N.J.Sup.Ct.Rules, Rule 21, 2 N.J.Misc. 1208 (1924); N.Y.C.P.A. (1937) § 258 as amended by Laws of 1935, ch. 339.

2. This provision for joinder of actions has been patterned upon [former] Equity Rule 26 (Joinder of Causes of Action) and broadened to include multiple parties. Compare the English practice, *English Rules Under the Judicature Act* (The Annual Practice, 1937) O. 18, r.r. 1–9 (noting rules 1 and 6). The earlier American codes set forth classes of joinder, following the now abandoned New York rule. See N.Y.C.P.A. § 258 before amended in 1935; Compare Kan. Gen.Stat.Ann. (1935) § 60–601; Wis.Stat.(1935) § 263.04 for the more liberal practice.

3. The provisions of this rule for the joinder of claims are subject to Rule 82 (Jurisdiction and Venue Unaffected). For the jurisdictional aspects of joinder of claims, see Shulman and Jaegerman, *Some Jurisdictional Limitations on Federal Procedure* (1936), 45 Yale L.J. 393, 397–410. For separate trials of joined claims, see Rule 42(b).

Note to Subdivision (b). This rule is inserted to make it clear that in a single action a party should be accorded all the relief to which he is entitled regardless of whether it is legal or equitable or both. This necessarily includes a deficiency judgment in foreclosure actions formerly provided for in [former] Equity Rule 10 (Decree for Deficiency in Foreclosures, Etc.). In respect to fraudulent conveyances the rule changes the former rule requiring a prior judgment against the owner (*Braun v. American Laundry Mach. Co.*, 56 F.2d 197 (S.D.N.Y. 1932)) to conform to the provisions of the Uniform Fraudulent Conveyance Act, §§ 9 and 10. See McLaughlin, *Application of the Uniform Fraudulent Conveyance Act*, 46 Harv.L.Rev. 404, 444 (1933).

1966 Amendment

The Rules "proceed upon the theory that no inconvenience can result from the joinder of any two or more matters in the pleadings, but only from trying two or more matters together which have little or nothing in common." Sunderland, *The New Federal Rules*, 45 W.Va.L.Q. 5, 13 (1938); see Clark, Code Pleading 58 (2d ed. 1947). Accordingly, Rule 18(a) has permitted a party to plead multiple claims of all types against an opposing party, subject to the court's power to direct an appropriate procedure for trying the claims. See Rules 42(b), 20(b), 21.

The liberal policy regarding joinder of claims in the pleadings extends to cases with multiple parties. However, the language used in the second sentence of Rule 18(a)—"if the requirements of Rules 19 [necessary joinder of parties], 20 [permissive joinder of parties], and 22 [interpleader] are satisfied"—has led some courts to infer that the rules regulating joinder of parties are intended to carry back to Rule 18(a) and to impose some special limits on joinder of claims in multiparty cases. In particular, Rule 20(a) has been read as restricting the operation of Rule 18(a) in certain situations in which a number of parties have been permissively joined in an action. In *Federal Housing Admr. v. Christianson*, 26 F.Supp. 419 (D.Conn.1939), the indorsee of two notes sued the three comakers of one note, and sought to join in the action a count on a second note which had been made by two of the three defendants. There was no doubt about the propriety of the joinder of the three parties defendant, for a right to relief was being asserted against all three defendants which arose out of a single "transaction" (the first note) and a question of fact or law "common" to all three defendants would arise in the action. See the text of Rule 20(a). The court, however, refused to allow the joinder of the count on the second note, on the ground that this right to relief, assumed to arise from a distinct transaction, did not involve a question common to all the defendants but only two of them. For analysis of the *Christianson* case and other authorities, see 2 Barron & Holtzoff, *Federal Practice & Procedure*, § 533.1 (Wright ed. 1961); 3 Moore's *Federal Practice*, par. 18.04[3] (2d ed. 1963).

If the court's view is followed, it becomes necessary to enter at the pleading stage into speculations about the exact relation between the claim sought to be joined against fewer than all the defendants properly joined in the action, and the claims asserted against all the defendants. Cf. Wright, *Joinder of Claims and Parties Under Modern Pleading Rules*, 36 Minn.L.Rev. 580, 605–06 (1952). Thus if it could be found in the Christianson situation that the claim on the second note arose out of the same transaction as the claim on the first or out of a transaction forming part of a "series," and that any question of fact or law with respect to the second note also arose with regard to the first, it would be held that the claim on the second note could be joined in the complaint. See 2 Barron & Holtzoff, supra, at 109; see also id. at 198 n. 60.4; cf. 3 Moore's *Federal Practice,* supra, at 1811. Such pleading niceties provide a basis for delaying and wasteful maneuver. It is more compatible with the design of the Rules to allow the claim to be joined in the pleading, leaving the question of possible separate trial of that claim to be later decided. See 2 Barron & Holtzoff, supra, § 533.1; Wright, supra, 36 Minn.L.Rev. at 604–11; *Developments in the Law—Multiparty Litigation in the Federal Courts,* 71 Harv. 874, 970–71 (1958); Commentary, *Relation Between Joinder of Parties and Joinder of Claims,* 5 F.R.Serv. 822 (1942). It is instructive to note that the court in the *Christianson* case, while holding that the claim on the second note could not be joined as a matter of pleading, held open the possibility that both claims would later be consolidated for trial under Rule 42(a). See 26 F.Supp. 419.

Rule 18(a) is now amended not only to overcome the *Christianson* decision and similar authority, but also to state clearly as a comprehensive proposition, that a party asserting a claim (an original claim, counterclaim, cross-claim, or third-party claim) may join as many claims as he has against an opposing party. See *Noland Co., Inc. v. Graver Tank & Mfg. Co.,* 301 F.2d 43, 49–51 (4th Cir.1962); but cf. *C. W. Humphrey Co. v. Security Alum. Co.,* 31 F.R.D. 41 (E.D.Mich.1962). This permitted joinder of claims is not affected by the fact that there are multiple parties in the action. The joinder of parties is governed by other rules operating independently.

It is emphasized that amended Rule 18(a) deals only with pleading. As already indicated, a claim properly joined as a matter of pleading need not be proceeded with together with the other claims if fairness or convenience justifies separate treatment.

Amended Rule 18(a), like the rule prior to amendment, does not purport to deal with questions of jurisdiction or venue which may arise with respect to claims properly joined as a matter of pleading. See Rule 82.

See also the amendment of Rule 20(a) and the Advisory Committee's Note thereto.

Free joinder of claims and remedies is one of the basic purposes of unification of the admiralty and civil procedure. The amendment accordingly provides for the inclusion in the rule of maritime claims as well as those which are legal and equitable in character.

1987 Amendment

The amendments are technical. No substantive change is intended.

2007 Amendment

The language of Rule 18 has been amended as part of the general restyling of the Civil Rules to make them more easily understood and to make style and terminology consistent throughout the rules. These changes are intended to be stylistic only.

Modification of the obscure former reference to a claim "heretofore cognizable only after another claim has been prosecuted to a conclusion" avoids any uncertainty whether Rule 18(b)'s meaning is fixed by retrospective inquiry from some particular date.

Rule 19. Required Joinder of Parties

(a) Persons Required to Be Joined if Feasible.

(1) ***Required Party.*** A person who is subject to service of process and whose joinder will not deprive the court of subject-matter jurisdiction must be joined as a party if:

(A) in that person's absence, the court cannot accord complete relief among existing parties; or

(B) that person claims an interest relating to the subject of the action and is so situated that disposing of the action in the person's absence may:

(i) as a practical matter impair or impede the person's ability to protect the interest; or

(ii) leave an existing party subject to a substantial risk of incurring double, multiple, or otherwise inconsistent obligations because of the interest.

(2) ***Joinder by Court Order.*** If a person has not been joined as required, the court must order that the person be made a party. A person who refuses to join as a plaintiff may be made either a defendant or, in a proper case, an involuntary plaintiff.

(3) ***Venue.*** If a joined party objects to venue and the joinder would make venue improper, the court must dismiss that party.

(b) When Joinder Is Not Feasible. If a person who is required to be joined if feasible cannot be joined, the court must determine whether, in equity and good conscience, the action should proceed among the existing parties or should be dismissed. The factors for the court to consider include:

(1) the extent to which a judgment rendered in the person's absence might prejudice that person or the existing parties;

(2) the extent to which any prejudice could be lessened or avoided by:

(A) protective provisions in the judgment;

(B) shaping the relief; or

(C) other measures;

(3) whether a judgment rendered in the person's absence would be adequate; and

(4) whether the plaintiff would have an adequate remedy if the action were dismissed for nonjoinder.

(c) Pleading the Reasons for Nonjoinder. When asserting a claim for relief, a party must state:

(1) the name, if known, of any person who is required to be joined if feasible but is not joined; and

(2) the reasons for not joining that person.

(d) Exception for Class Actions. This rule is subject to Rule 23.

(Amended February 28, 1966, effective July 1, 1966; March 2, 1987, effective August 1, 1987; April 30, 2007, effective December 1, 2007.)

ADVISORY COMMITTEE NOTES

1937 Adoption

Note to Subdivision (a). The first sentence with verbal differences (e.g., "united" interest for "joint" interest) is to be found in [former] Equity Rule 37 (Parties Generally—Intervention). Such compulsory joinder provisions are common. Compare Alaska Comp.Laws (1933) § 3392 (containing in same sentence a "class suit" provision); Wyo.Rev.Stat. Ann. (Courtright, 1931) § 89–515 (immediately followed by "class suit" provisions, § 89–516). See also former Equity Rule 42 (Joint and Several Demands). For example of a proper case for involuntary plaintiff, see *Independent Wireless Telegraph Co. v. Radio Corp. of America,* 269 U.S. 459, 46 S.Ct. 166, 70 L.Ed. 357 (1926).

The joinder provisions of this rule are subject to Rule 82 (Jurisdiction and Venue Unaffected).

Note to Subdivision (b). For the substance of this rule see [former] Equity Rule 39 (Absence of Persons Who Would be Proper Parties) and U.S.C., Title 28, § 111 [now § 1391] (When part of several defendants cannot be served); *Camp v. Gress,* 250 U.S. 308, 39 S.Ct. 478, 63 L.Ed. 997 (1919). See also the second and third sentences of [former] Equity Rule 37 (Parties Generally—Intervention).

Note to Subdivision (c). For the substance of this rule see the fourth subdivision of [former] Equity Rule 25 (Bill of Complaint—Contents).

1966 Amendment

General Considerations

Whenever feasible, the persons materially interested in the subject of an action—see the more detailed description of these persons in the discussion of new subdivision (a) below—should be joined as parties so that they may be heard and a complete disposition made. When this comprehensive joinder cannot be accomplished—a situation which may be encountered in Federal courts because of limitations on service of process, subject matter jurisdiction, and venue—the case should be examined pragmatically and a choice made between the alternatives of proceeding with the action in the absence of particular interested persons, and dismissing the action.

Even if the court is mistaken in its decision to proceed in the absence of an interested person, it does not by that token deprive itself of the power to adjudicate as between the parties already before it through proper service of process. But the court can make a legally binding adjudication only between the parties actually joined in the action. It is true that an adjudication between the parties before the court may on occasion adversely affect the absent person as a practical matter, or leave a party exposed to a later inconsistent recovery by the absent person. These are factors which should be considered in deciding whether the action should proceed, or should rather be dismissed; but they do not themselves negate the court's power to adjudicate as between the parties who have been joined.

Defects in the Original Rule

The foregoing propositions were well understood in the older equity practice, see Hazard, *Indispensable Party: The Historical Origin of a Procedural Phantom,* 61 Colum.L.Rev. 1254 (1961), and Rule 19 could be and often was applied in consonance with them. But experience showed that the rule was defective in its phrasing and did not point clearly to the proper basis of decision.

Textual defects.—(1) The expression "persons * * * who ought to be parties if complete relief is to be accorded between those already parties," appearing in original subdivision (b), was apparently intended as a description of the persons whom it would be desirable to join in the action, all questions of feasibility of joinder being put to one side; but it was not adequately descriptive of those persons.

(2) The word "indispensable," appearing in original subdivision (b), was apparently intended as an inclusive reference to the interested persons in whose absence it would be advisable, all factors having been considered, to dismiss the action. Yet the sentence implied that there might be interested persons, not "indispensable," in whose absence the action ought also to be dismissed. Further, it seemed at least superficially plausible to equate the word "indispensable" with the expression "having a joint interest," appearing in subdivision (a). See *United States v. Washington Inst. of Tech., Inc.,* 138 F.2d 25, 26 (3d Cir. 1943); cf. *Chidester v. City of Newark,* 162 F.2d 598 (3d Cir. 1947). But persons holding an interest technically "joint" are not always so related to an action that it would be unwise to proceed without joining all of them, whereas persons holding an interest not technically "joint" may have this relation to an action. See Reed, *Compulsory Joinder of Parties in Civil Actions,* 55 Mich.L.Rev. 327, 356 ff., 483 (1957).

(3) The use of "indispensable" and "joint interest" in the context of original Rule 19 directed attention to the technical or abstract character of the rights or obligations of the persons whose joinder was in question, and correspondingly distracted attention from the pragmatic considerations which should be controlling.

(4) The original rule, in dealing with the feasibility of joining a person as a party to the action, besides referring to whether the person was "subject to the jurisdiction of the court as to both service of process and venue," spoke of whether the person could be made a party "without depriving the court of jurisdiction of the parties before it." The second quoted expression used "jurisdiction" in the sense of the competence of the court over the subject matter of the action, and in this sense the expression was apt. However, by a familiar confusion, the expression seems to have suggested to some that the absence from the lawsuit of a person who was "indispensable" or "who ought to be [a] part[y]" itself deprived the court of the power to adjudicate as between the parties already joined. See *Samuel Goldwyn, Inc. v. United Artists Corp.,* 113 F.2d 703, 707 (3d Cir. 1940); *McArthur v. Rosenbaum Co. of Pittsburgh,* 180 F.2d 617, 621 (3d Cir. 1949); cf. *Calcote v. Texas Pac. Coal & Oil Co.,* 157 F.2d 216 (5th Cir. 1946), cert. denied, 329 U.S. 782 (1946),

noted in 56 Yale L.J. 1088 (1947); Reed, supra, 55 Mich. L.Rev. at 332–34.

Failure to point to correct basis of decision. The original rule did not state affirmatively what factors were relevant in deciding whether the action should proceed or be dismissed when joinder of interested persons was infeasible. In some instances courts did not undertake the relevant inquiry or were misled by the "jurisdiction" fallacy. In other instances there was undue preoccupation with abstract classifications of rights or obligations, as against consideration of the particular consequences of proceeding with the action and the ways by which these consequences might be ameliorated by the shaping of final relief or other precautions.

Although these difficulties cannot be said to have been general analysis of the cases showed that there was good reason for attempting to strengthen the rule. The literature also indicated how the rule should be reformed. See Reed, supra (discussion of the important case of *Shields v. Barrow,* 17 How. (58 U.S.) 130 (1854), appears at 55 Mich.L.Rev., p. 340 ff.); Hazard, supra; N.Y. Temporary Comm. on Courts, First Preliminary Report, Legis.Doc.1957, No. 6(b), pp. 28, 233; N.Y. Judicial Council, Twelfth Ann.Rep., Legis.Doc.1946, No. 17, p. 163; Joint Comm. on Michigan Procedural Revision, Final Report, Pt. III, p. 69 (1960); Note, *Indispensable Parties in the Federal Courts,* 65 Harv.L.Rev. 1050 (1952); *Developments in the Law—Multiparty Litigation in the Federal Courts,* 71 Harv.L.Rev. 874, 879 (1958); Mich.Gen.Court Rules, R. 205 (effective Jan. 1, 1963); N.Y.Civ.Prac.Law & Rules, § 1001 (effective Sept. 1, 1963).

The Amended Rule

New subdivision (a) defines the persons whose joinder in the action is desirable. Clause (1) stresses the desirability of joining those persons in whose absence the court would be obliged to grant partial or "hollow" rather than complete relief to the parties before the court. The interests that are being furthered here are not only those of the parties, but also that of the public in avoiding repeated lawsuits on the same essential subject matter. Clause (2)(i) recognizes the importance of protecting the person whose joinder is in question against the practical prejudice to him which may arise through a disposition of the action in his absence. Clause (2)(ii) recognizes the need for considering whether a party may be left, after the adjudication, in a position where a person not joined can subject him to a double or otherwise inconsistent liability. See Reed, supra, 55 Mich.L.Rev. at 330, 338; Note, supra, 65 Harv.L.Rev. at 1052–57; *Developments in the Law,* supra, 71 Harv.L.Rev. at 881–85.

The subdivision (a) definition of persons to be joined is not couched in terms of the abstract nature of their interests—"joint," "united," "separable," or the like. See N.Y. Temporary Comm. on Courts, First Preliminary Report, supra; Developments in the Law, supra, at 880. It should be noted particularly, however, that the description is not at variance with the settled authorities holding that a tortfeasor with the usual "joint-and-several" liability is merely a permissive party to an action against another with like liability. See 3 Moore's *Federal Practice* 2153 (2d ed. 1963); 2 Barron & Holtzoff, *Federal Practice & Procedure* § 513.8 (Wright ed. 1961). Joinder of these tortfeasors continues to be regulated by Rule 20; compare Rule 14 on third-party practice.

If a person as described in subdivision (a)(1)(2) is amenable to service of process and his joinder would not deprive the court of jurisdiction in the sense of competence over the action, he should be joined as a party; and if he has not been joined, the court should order him to be brought into the action. If a party joined has a valid objection to the venue and chooses to assert it, he will be dismissed from the action.

Subdivision (b).—When a person as described in subdivision (a)(1)–(2) cannot be made a party, the court is to determine whether in equity and good conscience the action should proceed among the parties already before it, or should be dismissed. That this decision is to be made in the light of pragmatic considerations has often been acknowledged by the courts. See *Roos v. Texas Co.,* 23 F.2d 171 (2d Cir. 1927), cert. denied 277 U.S. 587 (1928); *Niles-Bement-Pond Co. v. Iron Moulders' Union,* 254 U.S. 77, 80 (1920). The subdivision sets out four relevant considerations drawn from the experience revealed in the decided cases. The factors are to a certain extent overlapping, and they are not intended to exclude other considerations which may be applicable in particular situations.

The first factor brings in a consideration of what a judgment in the action would mean to the absentee. Would the absentee be adversely affected in a practical sense, and if so, would the prejudice be immediate and serious, or remote and minor? The possible collateral consequences of the judgment upon the parties already joined are also to be appraised. Would any party be exposed to a fresh action by the absentee, and if so, how serious is the threat? See the elaborate discussion in Reed, supra; cf. *A. L. Smith Iron Co. v. Dickson,* 141 F.2d 3 (2d Cir. 1944); *Caldwell Mfg. Co. v. Unique Balance Co.,* 18 F.R.D. 258 (S.D.N.Y.1955).

The second factor calls attention to the measures by which prejudice may be averted or lessened. The "shaping of relief" is a familiar expedient to this end. See, e.g., the award of money damages in lieu of specific relief where the latter might affect an absentee adversely. *Ward v. Deavers,* 203 F.2d 72 (D.C.Cir.1953); *Miller & Lux, Inc. v. Nickel,* 141 F.Supp. 41 (N.D.Calif.1956). On the use of "protective provisions," see *Roos v. Texas Co.,* supra; *Atwood v. Rhode Island Hosp. Trust Co.,* 275 Fed. 513, 519 (1st Cir. 1921), cert. denied, 257 U.S. 661 (1922); cf. *Stumpf v. Fidelity Gas Co.,* 294 F.2d 886 (9th Cir. 1961); and the general statement in *National Licorice Co. v. Labor Board,* 309 U.S. 350, 363 (1940).

Sometimes the party is himself able to take measures to avoid prejudice. Thus a defendant faced with a prospect of a second suit by an absentee may be in a position to bring the latter into the action by defensive interpleader. See *Hudson v. Newell,* 172 F.2d 848, 852 mod., 176 F.2d 546 (5th Cir. 1949); *Gauss v. Kirk,* 198 F.2d 83, 86 (D.C.Cir. 1952); *Abel v. Brayton Flying Service, Inc.,* 248 F.2d 713, 716 (5th Cir. 1957) (suggestion of possibility of counter-claim under Rule 13(h)); cf. *Parker Rust-Proof Co. v. Western Union Tel. Co.,* 105 F.2d 976 (2d Cir. 1939), cert. denied, 308 U.S. 597 (1939). So also the absentee may sometimes be able to avert prejudice to himself by voluntarily appearing in the action or intervening on an ancillary basis. See *Developments in the Law,* supra, 71 Harv.L.Rev. at 882; Annot., *Intervention or Subsequent Joinder of Parties as Affecting Jurisdiction of Federal Court Based on Diversity of Citizenship,* 134 A.L.R. 335 (1941); *Johnson v. Middleton,* 175 F.2d 535 (7th Cir. 1949); *Kentucky Nat. Gas Corp. v. Duggins,* 165 F.2d 1011 (6th Cir. 1948); *McComb v. McCormack,* 159 F.2d 219 (5th Cir. 1947). The court should consider whether this, in turn, would impose undue hardship on the absentee. (For the possibility of the court's informing an absentee of the pendency of the action, see comment under subdivision (c) below.)

The third factor—whether an "adequate" judgment can be rendered in the absence of a given person—calls attention to the extent of the relief that can be accorded among the parties joined. It meshes with the other factors, especially the "shaping of relief" mentioned under the second factor. Cf. *Kroese v. General Steel Castings Corp.*, 179 F.2d 760 (3d Cir. 1949), cert. denied, 339 U.S. 983 (1950).

The fourth factor, looking to the practical effects of a dismissal, indicates that the court should consider whether there is any assurance that the plaintiff, if dismissed, could sue effectively in another forum where better joinder would be possible. See *Fitzgerald v. Haynes*, 241 F.2d 417, 420 (3d Cir. 1957); *Fouke v. Schenewerk*, 197 F.2d 234, 236 (5th Cir. 1952); cf. *Warfield v. Marks*, 190 F.2d 178 (5th Cir. 1951).

The subdivision uses the word "indispensable" only in a conclusory sense, that is, a person is "regarded as indispensable" when he cannot be made a party and, upon consideration of the factors above mentioned, it is determined that in his absence it would be preferable to dismiss the action, rather than to retain it.

A person may be added as a party at any stage of the action on motion or on the court's initiative (see Rule 21); and a motion to dismiss, on the ground that a person has not been joined and justice requires that the action should not proceed in his absence, may be made as late as the trial on the merits (see Rule 12(h)(2), as amended; cf. Rule 12(b)(7), as amended). However, when the moving party is seeking dismissal in order to protect himself against a later suit by the absent person (subdivision (a)(2)(ii)), and is not seeking vicariously to protect the absent person against a prejudicial judgment (subdivision (a)(2)(i)), his undue delay in making the motion can properly be counted against him as a reason for denying the motion. A joinder question should be decided with reasonable promptness, but decision may properly be deferred if adequate information is not available at the time. Thus the relationship of an absent person to the action, and the practical effects of an adjudication upon him and others, may not be sufficiently revealed at the pleading stage; in such a case it would be appropriate to defer decision until the action was further advanced. Cf. Rule 12(d).

The amended rule makes no special provision for the problem arising in suits against subordinate Federal officials where it has often been set up as a defense that some superior officer must be joined. Frequently this defense has been accompanied by or intermingled with defenses of sovereign community or lack of consent of the United States to suit. So far as the issue of joinder can be isolated from the rest, the new subdivision seems better adapted to handle it than the predecessor provision. See the discussion in *Johnson v. Kirkland*, 290 F.2d 440, 446–47 (5th Cir. 1961) (stressing the practical orientation of the decisions); *Shaughnessy v. Pedreiro*, 349 U.S. 48, 54 (1955). Recent legislation, P.L. 87–748, 76 Stat. 744, approved October 5, 1962, adding §§ 1361, 1391(e) to Title 28, U.S.C., vests original jurisdiction in the District Courts over actions in the nature of mandamus to compel officials of the United States to perform their legal duties, and extends the range of service of process and liberalizes venue in these actions. If, then, it is found that a particular official should be joined in the action, the legislation will make it easy to bring him in.

Subdivision (c) parallels the predecessor subdivision (c) of Rule 19. In some situations it may be desirable to advise a person who has not been joined of the fact that the action is pending, and in particular cases the court in its discretion may itself convey this information by directing a letter or other informal notice to the absentee.

Subdivision (d) repeats the exception contained in the first clause of the predecessor subdivision (a).

1987 Amendment

The amendments are technical. No substantive change is intended.

2007 Amendment

The language of Rule 19 has been amended as part of the general restyling of the Civil Rules to make them more easily understood and to make style and terminology consistent throughout the rules. These changes are intended to be stylistic only.

Former Rule 19(b) described the conclusion that an action should be dismissed for inability to join a Rule 19(a) party by carrying forward traditional terminology: "the absent person being thus regarded as indispensable." "Indispensable" was used only to express a conclusion reached by applying the tests of Rule 19(b). It has been discarded as redundant.

Rule 20. Permissive Joinder of Parties

(a) Persons Who May Join or Be Joined.

(1) ***Plaintiffs.*** Persons may join in one action as plaintiffs if:

(A) they assert any right to relief jointly, severally, or in the alternative with respect to or arising out of the same transaction, occurrence, or series of transactions or occurrences; and

(B) any question of law or fact common to all plaintiffs will arise in the action.

(2) ***Defendants.*** Persons—as well as a vessel, cargo, or other property subject to admiralty process in rem—may be joined in one action as defendants if:

(A) any right to relief is asserted against them jointly, severally, or in the alternative with respect to or arising out of the same transaction, occurrence, or series of transactions or occurrences; and

(B) any question of law or fact common to all defendants will arise in the action.

(3) ***Extent of Relief.*** Neither a plaintiff nor a defendant need be interested in obtaining or defending against all the relief demanded. The court may grant judgment to one or more plaintiffs according to their rights, and against one or more defendants according to their liabilities.

(b) Protective Measures. The court may issue orders—including an order for separate trials—to protect a party against embarrassment, delay, expense, or other prejudice that arises from including a person against whom the party asserts no claim and who asserts no claim against the party.

(Amended February 28, 1966, effective July 1, 1966; March 2, 1987, effective August 1, 1987; April 30, 2007, effective December 1, 2007.)

ADVISORY COMMITTEE NOTES

1937 Adoption

The provisions for joinder here stated are in substance the provisions found in England, California, Illinois, New Jersey, and New York. They represent only a moderate expansion of the present federal equity practice to cover both law and equity actions.

With this rule compare also [former] Equity Rules 26 (Joinder of Causes of Action), 37 (Parties Generally—Intervention), 40 (Nominal Parties), and 42 (Joint and Several Demands).

The provisions of this rule for the joinder of parties are subject to Rule 82 (Jurisdiction and Venue Unaffected).

Note to Subdivision (a). The first sentence is derived from *English Rules Under the Judicature Act* (The Annual Practice, 1937) O. 16, r. 1. Compare Calif.Code Civ.Proc. (Deering, 1937) §§ 378, 379a; Ill.Rev.Stat. (1937) ch. 110, § 147–148; N.J.Comp.Stat. (2 Cum.Supp., 1911–1924), N.Y.C.P.A. (1937) §§ 209, 211. The second sentence is derived from *English Rules Under the Judicature Act* (The Annual Practice, 1937) O. 16, r. 4. The third sentence is derived from O. 16, r. 5, and the fourth from O. 16, r.r. 1 and 4.

Note to Subdivision (b). This is derived from *English Rules Under the Judicature Act* (The Annual Practice, 1937) O. 16, r.r. 1 and 5.

1966 Amendment

See the amendment of Rule 18(a) and the Advisory Committee's Note thereto. It has been thought that a lack of clarity in the antecedent of the word "them," as it appeared in two places in Rule 20(a), contributed to the view, taken by some courts, that this rule limited the joinder of claims in certain situations of permissive party joinder. Although the amendment of Rule 18(a) should make clear that this view is untenable, it has been considered advisable to amend Rule 20(a) to eliminate any ambiguity. See 2 Barron & Holtzoff, *Federal Practice & Procedure* 202 (Wright Ed. 1961).

A basic purpose of unification of admiralty and civil procedure is to reduce barriers to joinder; hence the reference to "any vessel," etc.

1987 Amendment

The amendments are technical. No substantive change is intended.

2007 Amendment

The language of Rule 20 has been amended as part of the general restyling of the Civil Rules to make them more easily understood and to make style and terminology consistent throughout the rules. These changes are intended to be stylistic only.

Rule 21. Misjoinder and Nonjoinder of Parties

Misjoinder of parties is not a ground for dismissing an action. On motion or on its own, the court may at any time, on just terms, add or drop a party. The court may also sever any claim against a party.

(Amended April 30, 2007, effective December 1, 2007.)

ADVISORY COMMITTEE NOTES

1937 Adoption

See *English Rules Under the Judicature Act* (The Annual Practice, 1937) O. 16, r. 11. See also [former] Equity Rules 43 (Defect of Parties—Resisting Objection) and 44 (Defect of Parties—Tardy Objection).

For separate trials see Rules 13(i) (Counterclaims and Cross-Claims: Separate Trials; Separate Judgments), 20(b) (Permissive Joinder of Parties: Separate Trials), and 42(b) (Separate Trials, generally) and the note to the latter rule.

2007 Amendment

The language of Rule 21 has been amended as part of the general restyling of the Civil Rules to make them more easily understood and to make style and terminology consistent throughout the rules. These changes are intended to be stylistic only.

Rule 22. Interpleader

(a) Grounds.

(1) ***By a Plaintiff.*** Persons with claims that may expose a plaintiff to double or multiple liability may be joined as defendants and required to interplead. Joinder for interpleader is proper even though:

(A) the claims of the several claimants, or the titles on which their claims depend, lack a common origin or are adverse and independent rather than identical; or

(B) the plaintiff denies liability in whole or in part to any or all of the claimants.

(2) ***By a Defendant.*** A defendant exposed to similar liability may seek interpleader through a crossclaim or counterclaim.

(b) Relation to Other Rules and Statutes. This rule supplements—and does not limit—the joinder of parties allowed by Rule 20. The remedy this rule provides is in addition to—and does not supersede or limit—the remedy provided by 28 U.S.C. §§ 1335, 1397, and 2361. An action under those statutes must be conducted under these rules.

(Amended December 29, 1948, effective October 20, 1949; March 2, 1987, effective August 1, 1987; April 30, 2007, effective December 1, 2007.)

ADVISORY COMMITTEE NOTES

1937 Adoption

The first paragraph provides for interpleader relief along the newer and more liberal lines of joinder in the alternative. It avoids the confusion and restrictions that developed around actions of strict interpleader and actions in the nature of interpleader. Compare *John Hancock Mutual Life Insurance Co. v. Kegan et al.*, 22 F.Supp. 326 (D.C.Md.1938). It does not change the rules on service of process, jurisdiction, and venue, as established by judicial decision.

The second paragraph allows an action to be brought under the recent interpleader statute when applicable. By this paragraph all remedies under the statute are continued, but the manner of obtaining them is in accordance with these rules. For temporary restraining orders and preliminary injunctions under this statute, see Rule 65(e).

This rule substantially continues such statutory provisions as U.S.C., Title 38, § 445 [now 784] (Actions on claims; jurisdiction; parties; procedure; limitation; witnesses; definitions) (actions upon veterans' contracts of insurance with the United States), providing for interpleader by the United States where it acknowledges indebtedness under a contract of insurance with the United States; U.S.C., Title 49, § 97 (Interpleader of conflicting claimants) (by carrier which has issued bill of lading). See Chaffee, *The Federal Interpleader Act of 1936: I and II* (1936), 45 Yale L.J. 963, 1161.

1948 Amendment

The amendment effective October 20, 1949, substituted the reference to "Title 28, U.S.C., §§ 1335, 1397, and 2361," at the end of the first sentence of paragraph (2), for the reference to "Section 24(26) of the Judicial Code, as amended, U.S.C., Title 28, § 41(26)." The amendment also substituted the words "those provisions" in the second sentence of paragraph (2) for the words "that section."

1987 Amendment

The amendment is technical. No substantive change is intended.

2007 Amendment

The language of Rule 22 has been amended as part of the general restyling of the Civil Rules to make them more easily understood and to make style and terminology consistent throughout the rules. These changes are intended to be stylistic only.

Rule 23. Class Actions

(a) Prerequisites. One or more members of a class may sue or be sued as representative parties on behalf of all members only if:

(1) the class is so numerous that joinder of all members is impracticable;

(2) there are questions of law or fact common to the class;

(3) the claims or defenses of the representative parties are typical of the claims or defenses of the class; and

(4) the representative parties will fairly and adequately protect the interests of the class.

(b) Types of Class Actions. A class action may be maintained if Rule 23(a) is satisfied and if:

(1) prosecuting separate actions by or against individual class members would create a risk of:

(A) inconsistent or varying adjudications with respect to individual class members that would establish incompatible standards of conduct for the party opposing the class; or

(B) adjudications with respect to individual class members that, as a practical matter, would be dispositive of the interests of the other members not parties to the individual adjudications or would substantially impair or impede their ability to protect their interests;

(2) the party opposing the class has acted or refused to act on grounds that apply generally to the class, so that final injunctive relief or corresponding declaratory relief is appropriate respecting the class as a whole; or

(3) the court finds that the questions of law or fact common to class members predominate over any questions affecting only individual members, and that a class action is superior to other available methods for fairly and efficiently adjudicating the controversy. The matters pertinent to these findings include:

(A) the class members' interests in individually controlling the prosecution or defense of separate actions;

(B) the extent and nature of any litigation concerning the controversy already begun by or against class members;

(C) the desirability or undesirability of concentrating the litigation of the claims in the particular forum; and

(D) the likely difficulties in managing a class action.

(c) Certification Order; Notice to Class Members; Judgment; Issues Classes; Subclasses.

(1) ***Certification Order.***

(A) *Time to Issue.* At an early practicable time after a person sues or is sued as a class representative, the court must determine by order whether to certify the action as a class action.

(B) *Defining the Class; Appointing Class Counsel.* An order that certifies a class action must define the class and the class claims, issues, or defenses, and must appoint class counsel under Rule 23(g).

(C) *Altering or Amending the Order.* An order that grants or denies class certification may be altered or amended before final judgment.

(2) ***Notice.***

(A) *For (b)(1) or (b)(2) Classes.* For any class certified under Rule 23(b)(1) or (b)(2), the court may direct appropriate notice to the class.

(B) *For (b)(3) Classes.* For any class certified under Rule 23(b)(3), the court must direct to class members the best notice that is practicable under the circumstances, including individual notice to all members who can be identified through reasonable effort. The notice must clearly and concisely state in plain, easily understood language:

(i) the nature of the action;

(ii) the definition of the class certified;

(iii) the class claims, issues, or defenses;

(iv) that a class member may enter an appearance through an attorney if the member so desires;

(v) that the court will exclude from the class any member who requests exclusion;

(vi) the time and manner for requesting exclusion; and

(vii) the binding effect of a class judgment on members under Rule 23(c)(3).

(3) ***Judgment.*** Whether or not favorable to the class, the judgment in a class action must:

(A) for any class certified under Rule 23(b)(1) or (b)(2), include and describe those whom the court finds to be class members; and

(B) for any class certified under Rule 23(b)(3), include and specify or describe those to whom the Rule 23(c)(2) notice was directed, who have not requested exclusion, and whom the court finds to be class members.

(4) ***Particular Issues.*** When appropriate, an action may be brought or maintained as a class action with respect to particular issues.

(5) ***Subclasses.*** When appropriate, a class may be divided into subclasses that are each treated as a class under this rule.

(d) Conducting the Action.

(1) ***In General.*** In conducting an action under this rule, the court may issue orders that:

(A) determine the course of proceedings or prescribe measures to prevent undue repetition or complication in presenting evidence or argument;

(B) require—to protect class members and fairly conduct the action—giving appropriate notice to some or all class members of:

(i) any step in the action;

(ii) the proposed extent of the judgment; or

(iii) the members' opportunity to signify whether they consider the representation fair and adequate, to intervene and present claims or defenses, or to otherwise come into the action;

(C) impose conditions on the representative parties or on intervenors;

(D) require that the pleadings be amended to eliminate allegations about representation of absent persons and that the action proceed accordingly; or

(E) deal with similar procedural matters.

(2) ***Combining and Amending Orders.*** An order under Rule 23(d)(1) may be altered or amended from time to time and may be combined with an order under Rule 16.

(e) Settlement, Voluntary Dismissal, or Compromise. The claims, issues, or defenses of a certified class may be settled, voluntarily dismissed, or compromised only with the court's approval. The following procedures apply to a proposed settlement, voluntary dismissal, or compromise:

(1) The court must direct notice in a reasonable manner to all class members who would be bound by the proposal.

(2) If the proposal would bind class members, the court may approve it only after a hearing and on finding that it is fair, reasonable, and adequate.

(3) The parties seeking approval must file a statement identifying any agreement made in connection with the proposal.

(4) If the class action was previously certified under Rule 23(b)(3), the court may refuse to approve a settlement unless it affords a new opportunity to request exclusion to individual class members who had an earlier opportunity to request exclusion but did not do so.

(5) Any class member may object to the proposal if it requires court approval under this subdivision (e); the objection may be withdrawn only with the court's approval.

(f) Appeals. A court of appeals may permit an appeal from an order granting or denying class-action certification under this rule if a petition for permission to appeal is filed with the circuit clerk within 10 days after the order is entered. An appeal does not stay proceedings in the district court unless the district judge or the court of appeals so orders.

(g) Class Counsel.

(1) ***Appointing Class Counsel.*** Unless a statute provides otherwise, a court that certifies a class must appoint class counsel. In appointing class counsel, the court:

(A) must consider:

(i) the work counsel has done in identifying or investigating potential claims in the action;

(ii) counsel's experience in handling class actions, other complex litigation, and the types of claims asserted in the action;

(iii) counsel's knowledge of the applicable law; and

(iv) the resources that counsel will commit to representing the class;

(B) may consider any other matter pertinent to counsel's ability to fairly and adequately represent the interests of the class;

(C) may order potential class counsel to provide information on any subject pertinent to the appointment and to propose terms for attorney's fees and nontaxable costs;

(D) may include in the appointing order provisions about the award of attorney's fees or nontaxable costs under Rule 23(h); and

(E) may make further orders in connection with the appointment.

(2) ***Standard for Appointing Class Counsel.*** When one applicant seeks appointment as class counsel, the court may appoint that applicant only if the applicant is adequate under Rule 23(g)(1) and (4). If more than one adequate applicant seeks appointment, the court must appoint the applicant best able to represent the interests of the class.

(3) ***Interim Counsel.*** The court may designate interim counsel to act on behalf of a putative class before determining whether to certify the action as a class action.

(4) ***Duty of Class Counsel.*** Class counsel must fairly and adequately represent the interests of the class.

(h) Attorney's Fees and Nontaxable Costs. In a certified class action, the court may award reasonable attorney's fees and nontaxable costs that are authorized by law or by the parties' agreement. The following procedures apply:

(1) A claim for an award must be made by motion under Rule 54(d)(2), subject to the provisions of this subdivision (h), at a time the court sets. Notice of the motion must be served on all parties and, for motions by class counsel, directed to class members in a reasonable manner.

(2) A class member, or a party from whom payment is sought, may object to the motion.

(3) The court may hold a hearing and must find the facts and state its legal conclusions under Rule 52(a).

(4) The court may refer issues related to the amount of the award to a special master or a magistrate judge, as provided in Rule 54(d)(2)(D).

(Amended February 28, 1966, effective July 1, 1966; March 2, 1987, effective August 1, 1987; April 24, 1998, effective December 1, 1998; March 27, 2003, effective December 1, 2003; April 30, 2007, effective December 1, 2007.)

ADVISORY COMMITTEE NOTES

1937 Adoption

Note to Subdivision (a). This is a substantial restatement of [former] Equity Rule 38 (Representatives of Class) as that rule has been construed. It applies to all actions, whether formerly denominated legal or equitable. For a general analysis of class actions, effect of judgment, and requisites of jurisdiction see Moore, *Federal Rules of Civil Procedure: Some Problems Raised by the Preliminary Draft,* 25 Georgetown L.J. 551, 570 et seq. (1937); Moore and Cohn, *Federal Class Actions,* 32 Ill.L.Rev. 307 (1937); Moore and Cohn, *Federal Class Actions—Jurisdiction and Effect of Judgment,* 32 Ill.L.Rev. 555–567 (1938); Lesar, *Class Suits and the Federal Rules,* 22 Minn.L.Rev. 34 (1937); cf. Arnold and James, *Cases on Trials, Judgments and Appeals* (1936) 175; and see Blume, *Jurisdictional Amount in Representative Suits,* 15 Minn.L.Rev. 501 (1931).

The general test of [former] Equity Rule 38 (Representatives of Class) that the question should be "one of common or general interest to many persons constituting a class so numerous as to make it impracticable to bring them all before the court," is a common test. For states which require the two elements of a common or general interest and numerous persons, as provided for in [former] Equity Rule 38, see Del.Ch. Rule 113; Fla.Comp.Gen.Laws Ann. (Supp., 1936) § 4918(7); Georgia Code (1933) § 37–1002, and see *English Rules Under the Judicature Act* (The Annual Practice, 1937) O. 16, r. 9. For statutory provisions providing for class actions when the question is one of common or general interest or when the parties are numerous, see Ala.Code Ann. (Michie, 1928) § 5701; 2 Ind.Stat.Ann. (Burns, 1933) § 2–220; N.Y.C.P.A. (1937) 195; Wis.Stat. (1935) § 260.12. These statutes have, however, been uniformly construed as though phrased in the conjunctive. See *Garfein v. Stiglitz,* 260 Ky. 430, 86 S.W.2d 155 (1935). The rule adopts the test of [former] Equity Rule 38, but defines what constitutes a "common or general interest". Compare with code provisions which make the action dependent upon the propriety of joinder of the parties. See Blume, *The "Common Questions" Principle in the Code Provision for Representative Suits,* 30 Mich.L.Rev. 878 (1932). For discussion of what constitutes "numerous persons" see Wheaton, *Representative Suits Involving Numerous Litigants,* 19 Corn.L.Q. 399 (1934); Note, 36 Harv.L.Rev. 89 (1922).

Clause (1), Joint, Common, or Secondary Right. This clause is illustrated in actions brought by or against representatives of an unincorporated association. See *Oster v. Brotherhood of Locomotive Firemen and Enginemen,* 271 Pa. 419, 114 Atl. 377 (1921); *Pickett v. Walsh,* 192 Mass. 572, 78 N.E. 753, 6 L.R.A., N.S., 1067 (1906); *Colt v. Hicks,* 97 Ind.App. 177, 179 N.E. 335 (1932). Compare Rule 17(b) as to when an unincorporated association has capacity to sue or be sued in its common name; *United Mine Workers of America v. Coronado Coal Co.,* 42 S.Ct. 570, 259 U.S. 344, 66 L.Ed. 975, 27 A.L.R. 762 (1922) (an unincorporated association was sued as an entity for the purpose of enforcing against it a federal substantive right); Moore, *Federal Rules of Civil Procedure: Some Problems Raised by the Preliminary Draft,* 25 Georgetown L.J. 551, 566 (for discussion of jurisdictional requisites when an unincorporated association sues or is sued in its common name and jurisdiction is founded upon diversity of citizenship). For an action brought by representatives of one group against representatives of another group for distribution of a fund held by an unincorporated association, see *Smith v. Swormstedt,* 16 How. 288, 14 L.Ed. 942 (U.S. 1853). Compare *Christopher, et al. v. Brusselback,* 1938, 58 S.Ct. 350, 302 U.S. 500, 82 L.Ed. 388.

For an action to enforce rights held in common by policyholders against the corporate issuer of the policies, see *Supreme Tribe of Ben Hur v. Cauble,* 255 U.S. 356, 41 S.Ct. 338, 65 L.Ed. 673 (1921). See also *Terry v. Little,* 101 U.S. 216, 25 L.Ed. 864 (1880); *John A. Roebling's Sons Co. v. Kinnicutt,* 248 Fed. 596 (D.C.N.Y., 1917) dealing with the right held in common by creditors to enforce the statutory liability of stockholders.

Typical of a secondary action is a suit by stockholders to enforce a corporate right. For discussion of the general nature of these actions see *Ashwander v. Tennessee Valley Authority,* 297 U.S. 288, 56 S.Ct. 466, 80 L.Ed. 688 (1936); Glenn, *The Stockholder's Suit—Corporate and Individual Grievances,* 33 Yale L.J. 580 (1924); McLaughlin, *Capacity of Plaintiff-Stockholder to Terminate a Stockholder's Suit,* 46 Yale L.J. 421 (1937). See also Subdivision (b) of this rule which deals with Shareholder's Action; Note, 15 Minn.L.Rev. 453 (1931).

Clause (2). A creditor's action for liquidation or reorganization of a corporation is illustrative of this clause. An action by a stockholder against certain named defendants as representatives of numerous claimants presents a situation converse to the creditor's action.

Clause (3). See *Everglades Drainage League v. Napoleon Broward Drainage Dist.,* 253 Fed. 246 (D.C.Fla., 1918); *Gramling v. Maxwell,* 52 F.2d 256 (D.C.N.C., 1931), approved in 30 Mich.L.Rev. 624 (1932); *Skinner v. Mitchell,* 108 Kan. 861, 197 Pac. 569 (1921); *Duke of Bedford v. Ellis* (1901) A.C. 1, for class actions when there were numerous persons and there was only a question of law or fact common to them; and see Blume, *The "Common Questions" Principle in the Code Provision for Representative Suits,* 30 Mich. L.Rev. 878 (1932).

Note to Subdivision (b). This is [former] Equity Rule 27 (Stockholder's Bill) with verbal changes. See also *Hawes v. Oakland,* 104 U.S. 450, 26 L.Ed. 827 (1882) and former Equity Rule 94, promulgated January 23, 1882, 104 U.S. IX.

Note to Subdivision (c). See McLaughlin, Capacity of Plaintiff-Stockholder to Terminate a Stockholder's Suit, 46 Yale L.J. 421 (1937).

Supplementary Note

Note. Subdivision (b), relating to secondary actions by shareholders, provides among other things, that in such an action the complainant "shall aver (1) that the plaintiff was a shareholder at the time of the transaction of which he complains or that his share thereafter devolved on him by operation of law * * *".

As a result of the decision in *Erie R. Co. v. Tompkins,* 1938, 304 U.S. 64, 58 S.Ct. 817 (decided April 25, 1938, after this rule was promulgated by the Supreme Court, though before it took effect) a question has arisen as to whether the provision above quoted deals with a matter of substantive right or is a matter of procedure. If it is a matter of substantive law or right, then under *Erie R. Co. v. Tompkins* clause (1) may not be validly applied in cases pending in states whose local law permits a shareholder to maintain such actions, although not a shareholder at the time of the transactions complained of. The Advisory Committee, believing the question should be settled in the courts, proposes no change in Rule 23 but thinks rather that the situation should be explained in an appropriate note.

The rule has a long history. In *Hawes v. Oakland,* 1882, 104 U.S. 450, the Court held that a shareholder could not maintain such an action unless he owned shares at the time of the transactions complained of, or unless they devolved on him by operation of law. At that time the decision in *Swift v. Tyson,* 1842, 16 Peters 1, was the law, and the federal courts considered themselves free to establish their own principles of equity jurisprudence, so the Court was not in 1882 and has not been, until *Erie R. Co. v. Tompkins* in 1938, concerned with the question whether *Hawes v. Oakland* dealt with substantive right or procedure.

Following the decision in *Hawes v. Oakland,* and at the same term, the Court, to implement its decision, adopted [former] Equity Rule 94, which contained the same provision above quoted from Rule 23 F.R.C.P. The provision in [former] Equity Rule 94 was later embodied in [former] Equity Rule 27, of which the present Rule 23 is substantially a copy.

In *City of Quincy v. Steel,* 1887, 120 U.S. 241, 245, 7 S.Ct. 520, the Court referring to *Hawes v. Oakland* said: "In order to give effect to the principles there laid down, this Court at that term adopted Rule 94 of the rules of practice for courts of equity of the United States."

Some other cases dealing with [former] Equity Rules 94 or 27 prior to the decision in *Erie R. Co. v. Tompkins* are *Dimpfel v. Ohio & Miss. R.R.,* 1884, 3 S.Ct. 573, 110 U.S. 209, 28 L.Ed. 121; *Illinois Central R. Co. v. Adams,* 1901, 21 S.Ct. 251, 180 U.S. 28, 34, 45L.Ed. 410; *Venner v. Great Northern Ry.,* 1908, 28 S.Ct. 328, 209 U.S. 24, 30, 52 L.Ed. 666; *Jacobson v. General Motors Corp.,* S.D.N.Y.1938, 22 F.Supp. 255, 257. These cases generally treat *Hawes v. Oakland* as establishing a "principle" of equity, or as dealing not with jurisdiction but with the "right" to maintain an action, or have said that the defense under the equity rule is analogous to the defense that the plaintiff has no "title" and results in a dismissal "for want of equity."

Those state decisions which held that a shareholder acquiring stock after the event may maintain a derivative action are founded on the view that it is a right belonging to the shareholder at the time of the transaction and which passes as a right to the subsequent purchaser. See *Pollitz v. Gould*, 1911, 202 N.Y. 11, 94 N.E. 1088.

The first case arising after the decision in *Erie R. Co. v. Tompkins*, in which this problem was involved, was *Summers v. Hearst*, S.D.N.Y.1938, 23 F.Supp. 986. It concerned [former] Equity Rule 27, as Federal Rule 23 was not then in effect. In a well considered opinion Judge Leibell reviewed the decisions and said: "The federal cases that discuss this section of [former] Rule 27 support the view that it states a principle of substantive law." He quoted *Pollitz v. Gould*, 1911, 202 N.Y. 11, 94 N.E. 1088, as saying that the United States Supreme Court "seems to have been more concerned with establishing this rule as one of practice than of substantive law" but that "whether it be regarded as establishing a principle of law or a rule of practice, this authority has been subsequently followed in the United States courts."

He then concluded that, although the federal decisions treat the equity rule as "stating a principle of substantive law", if "[former] Equity Rule 27 is to be modified or revoked in view of *Erie R. Co. v. Tompkins*, it is not the province of this Court to suggest it, much less impliedly to follow that course by disregarding the mandatory provisions of the Rule."

In *Piccard v. Sperry Corporation*, S.D.N.Y.1941, 36 F.Supp. 1006, 1009–10, affirmed without opinion, C.C.A.2d 1941, 120 F.2d 328, a shareholder, not such at the time of the transactions complained of, sought to intervene. The court held an intervenor was as much subject to Rule 23 as an original plaintiff; and that the requirement of Rule 23(b) was "a matter of practice," not substance, and applied in New York where the state law was otherwise, despite *Erie R. Co. v. Tompkins*. In *New York v. Guaranty Trust Co. of New York*, C.C.A.2, 1944, 143 F.2d 503, rev'd on other grounds, 1945, 65 S.Ct. 1464, the court said: "Restrictions on the bringing of stockholders' actions, such as those imposed by F.R.C.P. 23(b) or other state statutes are procedural," citing the *Piccard* and other cases.

Some other federal decisions since 1938 touch the question.

In *Gallup v. Caldwell*, C.C.A.3, 1941, 120 F.2d 90, 95 arising in New Jersey, the point was raised but not decided, the court saying that it was not satisfied that the then New Jersey rule differed from Rule 23(b), and that "under the circumstances the proper course was to follow Rule 23(b)."

In *Mullins v. DeSoto Securities Co.*, W.D.La.1942, 45 F.Supp. 871, 878, the point was not decided, because the court found the Louisiana rule to be the same as that stated in Rule 23(b).

In *Toebelman v. Missouri-Kansas Pipe Line Co.*, D.Del. 1941, 41 F.Supp. 334, 340, the court dealt only with another part of Rule 23(b), relating to prior demands on the stockholders and did not discuss *Erie R. Co. v. Tompkins*, or its effect on the rule.

In *Perrott v. United States Banking Corp.*, D.Del.1944, 53 F.Supp. 953, it appeared that the Delaware law does not require the plaintiff to have owned shares at the time of the transaction complained of. The court sustained Rule 23(b), after discussion of the authorities, saying:

"It seems to me the rule does not go beyond procedure. * * * Simply because a particular plaintiff cannot qualify as a proper party to maintain such an action does not destroy or even whittle at the cause of action. The cause of action exists until a qualified plaintiff can get it started in a federal court."

In *Bankers Nat. Corp. v. Barr*, S.D.N.Y.1945, 9 Fed.Rules Serv. 23b.11, Case 1, the court held Rule 23(b) to be one of procedure, but that whether the plaintiff was a stockholder was a substantive question to be settled by state law.

The New York rule, as stated in *Pollitz v. Gould*, supra, has been altered by an act of the New York Legislature, Chapter 667, Laws of 1944, effective April 9, 1944, General Corporation Law, § 61, which provides that "in any action brought by a shareholder in the right of a * * * corporation, it must appear that the plaintiff was a stockholder at the time of the transaction of which he complains, or that his stock thereafter devolved upon him by operation of law." At the same time a further and separate provision was enacted, requiring under certain circumstances the giving of security for reasonable expenses and attorney's fees, to which security the corporation in whose right the action is brought and the defendants therein may have recourse. (Chapter 668, Laws of 1944, effective April 9, 1944, General Corporation Law, § 61–b.) These provisions are aimed at so-called "strike" stockholders' suits and their attendant abuses. *Shielcrawt v. Moffett*, Ct.App.1945, 294 N.Y. 180, 61 N.E.2d 435, rev'g 51 N.Y.S.2d 188, aff'g 49 N.Y.S.2d 64; *Noel Associates, Inc. v. Merrill*, Sup.Ct.1944, 184 Misc. 646, 63 N.Y.S.2d 143.

Insofar as § 61 is concerned, it has been held that the section is procedural in nature. *Klum v. Clinton Trust Co.*, Sup.Ct.1944, 183 Misc. 340, 48 N.Y.S.2d 267; *Noel Associates, Inc. v. Merrill*, supra. In the latter case the court pointed out that "The 1944 amendment to Section 61 rejected the rule laid down in the Pollitz case and substituted, in place thereof, in its precise language, the rule which has long prevailed in the Federal Courts and which is now Rule 23(b) * * *". There is, nevertheless, a difference of opinion regarding the application of the statute to pending actions. See *Klum v. Clinton Trust Co.*, supra (applicable); *Noel Associates, Inc. v. Merrill*, supra (inapplicable).

With respect to § 61–b, which may be regarded as a separate problem, *Noel Associates, Inc. v. Merrill*, supra, it has been held that even though the statute is procedural in nature—a matter not definitely decided—the Legislature evinced no intent that the provisions should apply to actions pending when it became effective. *Shielcrawt v. Moffett*, supra. As to actions instituted after the effective date of the legislation, the constitutionality of § 61–b is in dispute. See *Wolf v. Atkinson*, Sup.Ct.1944, 182 Misc. 675, 49 N.Y.S.2d 703 (constitutional); *Citron v. Mangel Stores Corp.*, Sup.Ct. 1944, 50 N.Y.S.2d 416 (unconstitutional); Zlinkoff, *The American Investor and the Constitutionality of § 61–b of the New York General Corporation Law*, 1945, 54 Yale L.J. 352.

New Jersey also enacted a statute, similar to Chapters 667 and 668 of the New York law. See P.L.1945, Ch. 131, R.S.Cum.Supp. 14:3–15. The New Jersey provision similar to Chapter 668, § 61–b, differs, however, in that it specifically applies retroactively. It has been held that this provision is procedural and hence will not govern a pending action brought against a New Jersey corporation in the New York courts. *Shielcrawt v. Moffett*, Sup.Ct.N.Y.1945, 184 Misc. 1074, 56 N.Y.S.2d 134.

See, also generally, 2 Moore's *Federal Practice*, 1938, 2250–2253, and Cum.Supplement § 23.05.

The decisions here discussed show that the question is a debatable one, and that there is respectable authority for either view, with a recent trend towards the view that Rule 23(b)(1) is procedural. There is reason to say that the question is one which should not be decided by the Supreme Court ex parte, but left to await a judicial decision in a litigated case, and that in the light of the material in this note, the only inference to be drawn from a failure to amend Rule 23(b) would be that the question is postponed to await a litigated case.

The Advisory Committee is unanimously of the opinion that this course should be followed.

If, however, the final conclusion is that the rule deals with a matter of substantive right, then the rule should be amended by adding a provision that Rule 23(b)(1) does not apply in jurisdictions where state law permits a shareholder to maintain a secondary action, although he was not a shareholder at the time of the transactions of which he complains.

1966 Amendment

Difficulties with the original rule. The categories of class actions in the original rule were defined in terms of the abstract nature of the rights involved: the so-called "true" category was defined as involving "joint, common, or secondary rights"; the "hybrid" category, as involving "several" rights related to "specific property"; the "spurious" category, as involving "several" rights affected by a common question and related to common relief. It was thought that the definitions accurately described the situations amenable to the class-suit device, and also would indicate the proper extent of the judgment in each category, which would in turn help to determine the res judicata effect of the judgment if questioned in a later action. Thus the judgments in "true" and "hybrid" class actions would extend to the class (although in somewhat different ways); the judgment in a "spurious" class action would extend only to the parties including intervenors. See Moore, *Federal Rules of Civil Procedure: Some Problems Raised by the Preliminary Draft*, 25 Geo.L.J. 551, 570–76 (1937).

In practice the terms "joint," "common," etc., which were used as the basis of the Rule 23 classification proved obscure and uncertain. See Chafee, *Some Problems of Equity* 245–46, 256–57 (1950); Kalven & Rosenfield, *The Contemporary Function of the Class Suit*, 8 U. of Chi.L.Rev. 684, 707 & n. 73 (1941); Keeffe, Levy & Donovan, *Lee Defeats Ben Hur*, 33 Corn.L.Q. 327, 329–36 (1948); *Developments in the Law: Multiparty Litigation in the Federal Courts*, 71 Harv. L.Rev. 874, 931 (1958); Advisory Committee's Note to Rule 19, as amended. The courts had considerable difficulty with these terms. See, e.g., *Gullo v. Veterans' Coop. H. Assn.*, 13 F.R.D. 11 (D.D.C.1952); *Shipley v. Pittsburgh & L.E.R. Co.*, 70 F.Supp. 870 (W.D.Pa.1947); *Deckert v. Independence Shares Corp.*, 27 F.Supp. 763 (E.D.Pa.1939), rev'd 108 F.2d 51 (3d Cir. 1939), rev'd, 311 U.S. 282 (1940), on remand, 39 F.Supp. 592 (E.D.Pa.1941), rev'd sub nom. *Pennsylvania Co. for Ins. on Lives v. Deckert*, 123 F.2d 979 (3d Cir.1941) (see Chafee, supra, at 264–65).

Nor did the rule provide an adequate guide to the proper extent of the judgments in class actions. First, we find instances of the courts classifying actions as "true" or intimating that the judgments would be decisive for the class where these results seemed appropriate but were reached by dint of depriving the word "several" of coherent meaning. See, e.g., *System Federation No. 91 v. Reed*, 180 F.2d 991 (6th Cir.1950); *Wilson v. City of Paducah*, 100 F.Supp. 116 (W.D.Ky.1951); *Citizens Banking Co. v. Monticello State Bank*, 143 F.2d 261 (8th Cir.1944); *Redmond v. Commerce Trust Co.*, 144 F.2d 140 (8th Cir.1944), cert. denied, 323 U.S. 776 (1944); *United States v. American Optical Co.*, 97 F.Supp. 66 (N.D.Ill.1951); *National Hairdressers' & C. Assn. v. Philad Co.*, 34 F.Supp. 264 (D.Del.1940); 41 F.Supp. 701 (D.Del.1940), aff'd mem., 129 F.2d 1020 (3d Cir.1942). Second, we find cases classified by the courts as "spurious" in which, on a realistic view, it would seem fitting for the judgments to extend to the class. See, e.g., *Knapp v. Bankers Sec. Corp.*, 17 F.R.D. 245 (E.D.Pa.1954), aff'd 230 F.2d 717 (3d Cir.1956); *Giesecke v. Denver Tramway Corp.*, 81 F.Supp. 957 (D.Del.1949); *York v. Guaranty Trust Co.*, 143 F.2d 503 (2d Cir.1944), rev'd on grounds not here relevant, 326 U.S. 99 (1945) (see Chafee, supra, at 208); cf. *Webster Eisenlohr, Inc. v. Kalodner*, 145 F.2d 316, 320 (3d Cir.1944), cert. denied, 325 U.S. 867 (1945). But cf. the early decisions, *Duke of Bedford v. Ellis*, [1901] A.C. 1; *Sheffield Waterworks v. Yeomans*, L.R. 2 Ch.App. 8 (1866); *Brown v. Vermuden*, 1 Ch.Cas. 272, 22 Eng.Rep. 796 (1676).

The "spurious" action envisaged by original Rule 23 was in any event an anomaly because, although denominated a "class" action and pleaded as such, it was supposed not to adjudicate the rights or liabilities of any person not a party. It was believed to be an advantage of the "spurious" category that it would invite decisions that a member of the "class" could, like a member of the class in a "true" or "hybrid" action, intervene on an ancillary basis without being required to show an independent basis of Federal jurisdiction, and have the benefit of the date of the commencement of the action for purposes of the statute of limitations. See 3 Moore's *Federal Practice*, pars. 23.10[1], 23.12 (2d ed.1963). These results were attained in some instances but not in others. On the statute of limitations, see *Union Carbide & Carbon Corp. v. Nisley*, 300 F.2d 561 (10th Cir.1961), pet. cert. dism., 371 U.S. 801 (1963); but cf. *P. W. Husserl, Inc. v. Newman*, 25 F.R.D. 264 (S.D.N.Y.1960); *Athas v. Day*, 161 F.Supp. 916 (D.Colo.1958). On ancillary intervention, see *Amen v. Black*, 234 F.2d 12 (10th Cir.1956), cert. granted, 352 U.S. 888 (1956), dism. on stip., 355 U.S. 600 (1958); but cf. *Wagner v. Kemper*, 13 F.R.D. 128 (W.D.Mo.1952). The results, however, can hardly depend upon the mere appearance of a "spurious" category in the rule; they should turn on more basic considerations. See discussion of subdivision (c)(1) below.

Finally, the original rule did not squarely address itself to the question of the measures that might be taken during the course of the action to assure procedural fairness, particularly giving notice to members of the class, which may in turn be related in some instances to the extension of the judgment to the class. See Chafee, supra, at 230–31; Keeffe, Levy & Donovan, supra; *Developments in the law*, supra, 71 Harv. L.Rev. at 937–38; Note, *Binding Effect of Class Actions*, 67 Harv.L.Rev. 1059, 1062–65 (1954); Note, *Federal Class Actions: A Suggested Revision of Rule 23*, 46 Colum.L.Rev. 818, 833–36 (1946); Mich.Gen.Court R. 208.4 (effective Jan. 1,

1963); Idaho R.Civ.P. 23(d); Minn.R.Civ.P. 23.04; N.Dak.R.Civ.P. 23(d).

The amended rule describes in more practical terms the occasions for maintaining class actions; provides that all class actions maintained to the end as such will result in judgments including those whom the court finds to be members of the class, whether or not the judgment is favorable to the class; and refers to the measures which can be taken to assure the fair conduct of these actions.

Subdivision (a) states the prerequisites for maintaining any class action in terms of the numerousness of the class making joinder of the members impracticable, the existence of questions common to the class, and the desired qualifications of the representative parties. See Weinstein, *Revision of Procedure: Some Problems in Class Actions,* 9 Buffalo L.Rev. 433, 458–59 (1960); 2 Barron & Holtzoff, *Federal Practice & Procedure* § 562, at 265, § 572, at 351–52 (Wright ed. 1961). These are necessary but not sufficient conditions for a class action. See, e.g., *Giordano v. Radio Corp. of Am.,* 183 F.2d 558, 560 (3d Cir.1950); *Zachman v. Erwin,* 186 F.Supp. 681 (S.D.Tex.1959); *Baim & Blank, Inc. v. Warren-Connelly Co., Inc.,* 19 F.R.D. 108 (S.D.N.Y.1956). Subdivision (b) describes the additional elements which in varying situations justify the use of a class action.

Subdivision (b)(1). The difficulties which would be likely to arise if resort were had to separate actions by or against the individual members of the class here furnish the reasons for, and the principal key to, the propriety and value of utilizing the class-action device. The considerations stated under clauses (A) and (B) are comparable to certain of the elements which define the persons whose joinder in an action is desirable as stated in Rule 19(a), as amended. See amended Rule 19(a)(2)(i) and (ii), and the Advisory Committee's Note thereto; Hazard, *Indispensable Party: The Historical Origin of a Procedural Phantom,* 61 Colum.L.Rev. 1254, 1259–60 (1961); cf. 3 Moore, supra, par. 23.08, at 3435.

Clause (A): One person may have rights against, or be under duties toward, numerous persons constituting a class, and be so positioned that conflicting or varying adjudications in lawsuits with individual members of the class might establish incompatible standards to govern his conduct. The class action device can be used effectively to obviate the actual or virtual dilemma which would thus confront the party opposing the class. The matter has been stated thus: "The felt necessity for a class action is greatest when the courts are called upon to order or sanction the alteration of the status quo in circumstances such that a large number of persons are in a position to call on a single person to alter the status quo, or to complain if it is altered, and the possibility exists that [the] actor might be called upon to act in inconsistent ways." Louisell & Hazard, *Pleading and Procedure: State and Federal* 719 (1962); see *Supreme Tribe of Ben-Hur v. Cauble,* 255 U.S. 356, 366–67 (1921). To illustrate: Separate actions by individuals against a municipality to declare a bond issue invalid or condition or limit it, to prevent or limit the making of a particular appropriation or to compel or invalidate an assessment, might create a risk of inconsistent or varying determinations. In the same way, individual litigations of the rights and duties of riparian owners, or of landowners' rights and duties respecting a claimed nuisance, could create a possibility of incompatible adjudications. Actions by or against a class provide a ready and fair means of achieving unitary adjudication. See *Maricopa County Mun. Water Con. Dist. v. Looney,* 219 F.2d 529 (9th Cir.1955); *Rank v. Krug,* 142 F.Supp. 1, 154–59 (S.D.Calif.1956), on app., *State of California v. Rank,* 293 F.2d 340, 348 (9th Cir.1961); *Gart v. Cole,* 263 F.2d 244 (2d Cir.1959), cert. denied 359 U.S. 978 (1959); cf. *Martinez v. Maverick Cty. Water Con. & Imp. Dist.,* 219 F.2d 666 (5th Cir.1955); 3 Moore, supra, par. 23.11[2], at 3458–59.

Clause (B): This clause takes in situations where the judgment in a nonclass action by or against an individual member of the class, while not technically concluding the other members, might do so as a practical matter. The vice of an individual action would lie in the fact that the other members of the class, thus practically concluded, would have had no representation in the lawsuit. In an action by policy holders against a fraternal benefit association attacking a financial reorganization of the society, it would hardly have been practical, if indeed it would have been possible, to confine the effects of a validation of the reorganization to the individual plaintiffs. Consequently a class action was called for with adequate representation of all members of the class. See *Supreme Tribe of Ben-Hur v. Cauble,* 255 U.S. 356 (1921); *Waybright v. Columbian Mut. Life Ins. Co.,* 30 F.Supp. 885 (W.D.Tenn.1939); cf. *Smith v. Swormstedt,* 16 How. (57 U.S.) 288 (1853). For much the same reason actions by shareholders to compel the declaration of a dividend[,] the proper recognition and handling of redemption or pre-emption rights, or the like (or actions by the corporation for corresponding declarations of rights), should ordinarily be conducted as class actions, although the matter has been much obscured by the insistence that each shareholder has an individual claim. See *Knapp v. Bankers Securities Corp.,* 17 F.R.D. 245 (E.D.Pa.1954), aff'd, 230 F.2d 717 (3d Cir. 1956); *Giesecke v. Denver Tramway Corp.,* 81 F.Supp. 957 (D.Del.1949); *Zahn v. Transamerica Corp.,* 162 F.2d 36 (3d Cir.1947); *Speed v. Transamerica Corp.,* 100 F.Supp. 461 (D.Del.1951); *Sobel v. Whittier Corp.,* 95 F.Supp. 643 (E.D.Mich.1951), app. dism., 195 F.2d 361 (6th Cir.1952); *Goldberg v. Whittier Corp.,* 111 F.Supp. 382 (E.D.Mich.1953); *Dann v. Studebaker-Packard Corp.,* 288 F.2d 201 (6th Cir. 1961); *Edgerton v. Armour & Co.,* 94 F.Supp. 549 (S.D.Calif.1950); *Ames v. Mengel Co.,* 190 F.2d 344 (2d Cir.1951). (These shareholders' actions are to be distinguished from derivative actions by shareholders dealt with in new Rule 23.1). The same reasoning applies to an action which charges a breach of trust by an indenture trustee or other fiduciary similarly affecting the members of a large class of security holders or other beneficiaries, and which requires an accounting or like measures to restore the subject of the trust. See *Boesenberg v. Chicago T. & T. Co.,* 128 F.2d 245 (7th Cir.1942); *Citizens Banking Co. v. Monticello State Bank,* 143 F.2d 261 (8th Cir.1944); *Redmond v. Commerce Trust Co.,* 144 F.2d 140 (8th Cir.1944), cert. denied, 323 U.S. 776 (1944); cf. *York v. Guaranty Trust Co.,* 143 F.2d 503 (2d Cir.1944), rev'd on grounds not here relevant, 326 U.S. 99 (1945).

In various situations an adjudication as to one or more members of the class will necessarily or probably have an adverse practical effect on the interests of other members who should therefore be represented in the lawsuit. This is plainly the case when claims are made by numerous persons against a fund insufficient to satisfy all claims. A class action by or against representative members to settle the validity of the claims as a whole, or in groups, followed by separate proof of the amount of each valid claim and proportionate distribution of the fund, meets the problem. Cf. *Dickinson v. Burnham*, 197 F.2d 973 (2d Cir.1952), cert. denied, 344 U.S. 875 (1952); 3 Moore, supra, at par. 23.09. The same reasoning applies to an action by a creditor to set aside a fraudulent conveyance by the debtor and to appropriate the property to his claim, when the debtor's assets are insufficient to pay all creditors' claims. See *Heffernan v. Bennett & Armour*, 110 Cal.App.2d 564, 243 P.2d 846 (1952); cf. *City & County of San Francisco v. Market Street Ry.*, 95 Cal.App.2d 648, 213 P.2d 780 (1950). Similar problems, however, can arise in the absence of a fund either present or potential. A negative or mandatory injunction secured by one of a numerous class may disable the opposing party from performing claimed duties toward the other members of the class or materially affect his ability to do so. An adjudication as to movie "clearances and runs" nominally affecting only one exhibitor would often have practical effects on all the exhibitors in the same territorial area. Cf. *United States v. Paramount Pictures, Inc.*, 66 F.Supp. 323, 341–46 (S.D.N.Y. 1946); 334 U.S. 131, 144–48 (1948). Assuming a sufficiently numerous class of exhibitors, a class action would be advisable. (Here representation of subclasses of exhibitors could become necessary; see subdivision (c)(3)(B).)

Subdivision (b)(2). This subdivision is intended to reach situations where a party has taken action or refused to take action with respect to a class, and final relief of an injunctive nature or of a corresponding declaratory nature, settling the legality of the behavior with respect to the class as a whole, is appropriate. Declaratory relief "corresponds" to injunctive relief when as a practical matter it affords injunctive relief or serves as a basis for later injunctive relief. The subdivision does not extend to cases in which the appropriate final relief relates exclusively or predominantly to money damages. Action or inaction is directed to a class within the meaning of this subdivision even if it has taken effect or is threatened only as to one or a few members of the class, provided it is based on grounds which have general application to the class.

Illustrative are various actions in the civil-rights field where a party is charged with discriminating unlawfully against a class, usually one whose members are incapable of specific enumeration. See *Potts v. Flax*, 313 F.2d 284 (5th Cir. 1963); *Bailey v. Patterson*, 323 F.2d 201 (5th Cir. 1963), cert. denied, 376 U.S. 910, (1964); *Brunson v. Board of Trustees of School District No. 1, Clarendon Cty., S.C.*, 311 F.2d 107 (4th Cir. 1962), cert. denied, 373 U.S. 933 (1963); *Green v. School Bd. of Roanoke, Va.*, 304 F.2d 118 (4th Cir. 1962); *Orleans Parish School Bd. v. Bush*, 242 F.2d 156 (5th Cir. 1957), cert. denied, 354 U.S. 921 (1957); *Mannings v. Board of Public Inst. of Hillsborough County, Fla.*, 277 F.2d 370 (5th Cir. 1960); *Northcross v. Board of Ed. of City of Memphis*, 302 F.2d 818 (6th Cir. 1962), cert. denied, 370 U.S. 944 (1962); *Frasier v. Board of Trustees of Univ. of N.C.*, 134 F.Supp. 589 (M.D.N.C.1955, 3-judge court), aff'd 350 U.S. 979 (1956). Subdivision (b)(2) is not limited to civil-rights cases. Thus an action looking to specific or declaratory relief could be brought by a numerous class of purchasers, say retailers of a given description, against a seller alleged to have undertaken to sell to that class at prices higher than those set for other purchasers, say retailers of another description, when the applicable law forbids such a pricing differential. So also a patentee of a machine, charged with selling or licensing the machine on condition that purchasers or licensees also purchase or obtain licenses to use an ancillary unpatented machine, could be sued on a class basis by a numerous group of purchasers or licensees, or by a numerous group of competing sellers or licensors of the unpatented machine, to test the legality of the "tying" condition.

Subdivision (b)(3). In the situations to which this subdivision relates, class-action treatment is not as clearly called for as in those described above, but it may nevertheless be convenient and desirable depending upon the particular facts. Subdivision (b)(3) encompasses those cases in which a class action would achieve economies of time, effort, and expense, and promote uniformity of decision as to persons similarly situated, without sacrificing procedural fairness or bringing about other undesirable results. Cf. Chafee, supra, at 201.

The court is required to find, as a condition of holding that a class action may be maintained under this subdivision, that the questions common to the class predominate over the questions affecting individual members. It is only where this predominance exists that economies can be achieved by means of the class-action device. In this view, a fraud perpetrated on numerous persons by the use of similar misrepresentations may be an appealing situation for a class action, and it may remain so despite the need, if liability is found, for separate determination of the damages suffered by individuals within the class. On the other hand, although having some common core, a fraud case may be unsuited for treatment as a class action if there was material variation in the representations made or in the kinds or degrees of reliance by the persons to whom they were addressed. See *Oppenheimer v. F. J. Young & Co., Inc.*, 144 F.2d 387 (2d Cir. 1944); *Miller v. National City Bank of N.Y.*, 166 F.2d 723 (2d Cir. 1948); and for like problems in other contexts, see *Hughes v. Encyclopaedia Britannica*, 199 F.2d 295 (7th Cir. 1952); *Sturgeon v. Great Lakes Steel Corp.*, 143 F.2d 819 (6th Cir. 1944). A "mass accident" resulting in injuries to numerous persons is ordinarily not appropriate for a class action because of the likelihood that significant questions, not only of damages but of liability and defenses of liability, would be present, affecting the individuals in different ways. In these circumstances an action conducted nominally as a class action would degenerate in practice into multiple lawsuits separately tried. See *Pennsylvania R.R. v. United States*, 111 F.Supp. 80 (D.N.J.1953); cf. Weinstein, supra, 9 Buffalo L.Rev. at 469. Private damage claims by numerous individuals arising out of concerted antitrust violations may or may not involve predominating common questions. See *Union Carbide & Carbon Corp. v. Nisley*, 300 F.2d 561 (10th Cir. 1961), pet. cert. dism., 371 U.S. 801 (1963); cf. *Weeks v. Bareco Oil Co.*, 125 F.2d 84 (7th Cir. 1941); *Kainz v. Anheuser-Busch, Inc.*, 194 F.2d 737 (7th Cir. 1952); *Hess v. Anderson, Clayton & Co.*, 20 F.R.D. 466 (S.D.Calif.1957).

That common questions predominate is not itself sufficient to justify a class action under subdivision (b)(3), for another method of handling the litigious situation may be available which has greater practical advantages. Thus one or more actions agreed to by the parties as test or model actions may be preferable to a class action; or it may prove feasible and preferable to consolidate actions. Cf. Weinstein, supra, 9 Buffalo L.Rev. at 438–54. Even when a number of separate actions are proceeding simultaneously, experience shows that the burdens on the parties and the courts can sometimes be reduced by arrangements for avoiding repetitious discovery or the like. Currently the Coordinating Committee on Multiple Litigation in the United States District Courts (a subcommittee of the Committee on Trial Practice and Technique of the Judicial Conference of the United States) is charged with developing methods for expediting such massive litigation. To reinforce the point that the court with the aid of the parties ought to assess the relative advantages of alternative procedures for handling the total controversy, subdivision (b)(3) requires, as a further condition of maintaining the class action, that the court shall find that that procedure is "superior" to the others in the particular circumstances.

Factors (A)–(D) are listed, non-exhaustively, as pertinent to the findings. The court is to consider the interests of individual members of the class in controlling their own litigations and carrying them on as they see fit. See *Weeks v. Bareco Oil Co.*, 125 F.2d 84, 88–90, 93–94 (7th Cir. 1941) (anti-trust action); see also *Pentland v. Dravo Corp.*, 152 F.2d 851 (3d Cir. 1945), and Chafee, supra, at 273–75, regarding policy of Fair Labor Standards Act of 1938, § 16(b), 29 U.S.C. § 216(b), prior to amendment by Portal-to-Portal Act of 1947, § 5(a). [The present provisions of 29 U.S.C. § 216(b) are not intended to be affected by Rule 23, as amended.]

In this connection the court should inform itself of any litigation actually pending by or against the individuals. The interests of individuals in conducting separate lawsuits may be so strong as to call for denial of a class action. On the other hand, these interests may be theoretic rather than practical; the class may have a high degree of cohesion and prosecution of the action through representatives would be quite unobjectionable, or the amounts at stake for individuals may be so small that separate suits would be impracticable. The burden that separate suits would impose on the party opposing the class, or upon the court calendars, may also fairly be considered. (See the discussion, under subdivision (c)(2) below, of the right of members to be excluded from the class upon their request.)

Also pertinent is the question of the desirability of concentrating the trial of the claims in the particular forum by means of a class action, in contrast to allowing the claims to be litigated separately in forums to which they would ordinarily be brought. Finally, the court should consider the problems of management which are likely to arise in the conduct of a class action.

Subdivision (c)(1). In order to give clear definition to the action, this provision requires the court to determine, as early in the proceedings as may be practicable, whether an action brought as a class action is to be so maintained. The determination depends in each case on satisfaction of the terms of subdivision (a) and the relevant provisions of subdivision (b).

An order embodying a determination can be conditional; the court may rule, for example, that a class action may be maintained only if the representation is improved through intervention of additional parties of a stated type. A determination once made can be altered or amended before the decision on the merits if, upon fuller development of the facts, the original determination appears unsound. A negative determination means that the action should be stripped of its character as a class action. See subdivision (d)(4). Although an action thus becomes a nonclass action, the court may still be receptive to interventions before the decision on the merits so that the litigation may cover as many interests as can be conveniently handled; the questions whether the intervenors in the nonclass action shall be permitted to claim "ancillary" jurisdiction or the benefit of the date of the commencement of the action for purposes of the statute of limitations are to be decided by reference to the laws governing jurisdiction and limitations as they apply in particular contexts.

Whether the court should require notice to be given to members of the class of its intention to make a determination, or of the order embodying it, is left to the court's discretion under subdivision (d)(2).

Subdivision (c)(2) makes special provision for class actions maintained under subdivision (b)(3). As noted in the discussion of the latter subdivision, the interests of the individuals in pursing their own litigations may be so strong here as to warrant denial of a class action altogether. Even when a class action is maintained under subdivision (b)(3), this individual interest is respected. Thus the court is required to direct notice to the members of the class of the right of each member to be excluded from the class upon his request. A member who does not request exclusion may, if he wishes, enter an appearance in the action through his counsel; whether or not he does so, the judgment in the action will embrace him.

The notice[,] setting forth the alternatives open to the members of the class, is to be the best practicable under the circumstances, and shall include individual notice to the members who can be identified through reasonable effort. (For further discussion of this notice, see the statement under subdivision (d)(2) below.)

Subdivision (c)(3). The judgment in a class action maintained as such to the end will embrace the class, that is, in a class action under subdivision (b)(1) or (b)(2), those found by the court to be class members; in a class action under subdivision (b)(3), those to whom the notice prescribed by subdivision (c)(2) was directed, excepting those who requested exclusion or who are ultimately found by the court not to be members of the class. The judgment has this scope whether it is favorable or unfavorable to the class. In a (b)(1) or (b)(2) action the judgment "describes" the members of the class, but need not specify the individual members; in a (b)(3) action the judgment "specifies" the individual members who have been identified and described the others.

Compare subdivision (c)(4) as to actions conducted as class actions only with respect to particular issues. Where the class-action character of the lawsuit is based solely on the existence of a "limited fund," the judgment, while extending to all claims of class members against the fund, has ordinarily left unaffected the personal claims of nonappearing members against the debtor. See 3 Moore, supra, par. 23.11[4].

Hitherto, in a few actions conducted as "spurious" class actions and thus nominally designed to extend only to parties and others intervening before the determination of liability, courts have held or intimated that class members might be permitted to intervene after a decision on the merits favorable to their interests, in order to secure the benefits of the decision for themselves, although they would presumably be unaffected by an unfavorable decision. See, as to the propriety of this so-called "one-way" intervention in "spurious" actions, the conflicting views expressed in *Union Carbide & Carbon Corp. v. Nisley*, 300 F.2d 561 (10th Cir. 1961), pet. cert. dism., 371 U.S. 801 (1963); *York v. Guaranty Trust Co.*, 143 F.2d 503, 529 (2d Cir. 1944), rev'd on grounds not here relevant, 326 U.S. 99 (1945); *Pentland v. Dravo Corp.*, 152

F.2d 851, 856 (3d Cir. 1945); *Speed v. Transamerica Corp.*, 100 F.Supp. 461, 463 (D.Del.1951); *State Wholesale Grocers v. Great Atl. & Pac. Tea Co.*, 24 F.R.D. 510 (N.D.Ill.1959); *Alabama Ind. Serv. Stat. Assn. v. Shell Pet. Corp.*, 28 F.Supp. 386, 390 (N.D.Ala.1939); *Tolliver v. Cudahy Packing Co.*, 39 F.Supp. 337, 339 (E.D.Tenn.1941); Kalven & Rosenfield, supra, 8 U. of Chi.L.Rev. 684 (1941); Comment, 53 Nw.U.L.Rev. 627, 632–33 (1958); *Developments in the Law*, supra, 71 Harv.L.Rev. at 935; 2 Barron & Holtzoff, supra, § 568; but cf. *Lockwood v. Hercules Powder Co.*, 7 F.R.D. 24, 28–29 (W.D.Mo.1947); *Abram v. San Joaquin Cotton Oil Co.*, 46 F.Supp. 969, 976–77 (S.D.Calif.1942); Chafee, supra, at 280, 285; 3 Moore, supra, par. 23.12, at 3476. Under proposed subdivision (c)(3), one-way intervention is excluded; the action will have been early determined to be a class or nonclass action, and in the former case the judgment, whether or not favorable, will include the class, as above stated.

Although thus declaring that the judgment in a class action includes the class, as defined, subdivision (c)(3) does not disturb the recognized principle that the court conducting the action cannot predetermine the *res judicata* effect of the judgment; this can be tested only in a subsequent action. See Restatement, Judgments § 86, comment (h), § 116 (1942). The court, however, in framing the judgment in any suit brought as a class action, must decide what its extent or coverage shall be, and if the matter is carefully considered, questions of *res judicata* are less likely to be raised at a later time and if raised will be more satisfactorily answered. See Chafee, supra, at 294; Weinstein, supra, 9 Buffalo L.Rev. at 460.

Subdivision (c)(4). This provision recognizes that an action may be maintained as a class action as to particular issues only. For example, in a fraud or similar case the action may retain its "class" character only through the adjudication of liability to the class; the members of the class may thereafter be required to come in individually and prove the amounts of their respective claims.

Two or more classes may be represented in a single action. Where a class is found to include subclasses divergent in interest, the class may be divided correspondingly, and each subclass treated as a class.

Subdivision (d) is concerned with the fair and efficient conduct of the action and lists some types of orders which may be appropriate.

The court should consider how the proceedings are to be arranged in sequence, and what measures should be taken to simplify the proof and argument. See subdivision (d)(1). The orders resulting from this consideration, like the others referred to in subdivision (d), may be combined with a pretrial order under Rule 16, and are subject to modification as the case proceeds.

Subdivision (d)(2) sets out a non-exhaustive list of possible occasions for orders requiring notice to the class. Such notice is not a novel conception. For example, in "limited fund" cases, members of the class have been notified to present individual claims after the basic class decision. Notice has gone to members of a class so that they might express any opposition to the representation, see *United States v. American Optical Co.*, 97 F.Supp. 66 (N.D.Ill.1951), and 1950–51 CCH Trade Cases 64573–74 (par. 62869); cf. *Weeks v. Bareco Oil Co.*, 125 F.2d 84, 94 (7th Cir. 1941), and notice may encourage interventions to improve the representation of the class. Cf. *Oppenheimer v. F. J. Young & Co.*, 144 F.2d 387 (2d Cir. 1944). Notice has been used to poll members on a proposed modification of a consent decree. See record in *Sam Fox Publishing Co. v. United States*, 366 U.S. 683 (1961).

Subdivision (d)(2) does not require notice at any stage, but rather calls attention to its availability and invokes the court's discretion. In the degree that there is cohesiveness or unity in the class and the representation is effective, the need for notice to the class will tend toward a minimum. These indicators suggest that notice under subdivision (d)(2) may be particularly useful and advisable in certain class actions maintained under subdivision (b)(3), for example, to permit members of the class to object to the representation. Indeed, under subdivision (c)(2), notice must be ordered, and is not merely discretionary, to give the members in a subdivision (b)(3) class action an opportunity to secure exclusion from the class. This mandatory notice pursuant to subdivision (c)(2), together with any discretionary notice which the court may find it advisable to give under subdivision (d)(2), is designed to fulfill requirements of due process to which the class action procedure is of course subject. See *Hansberry v. Lee*, 311 U.S. 32 (1940); *Mullane v. Central Hanover Bank & Trust Co.*, 339 U.S. 306 (1950); cf. *Dickinson v. Burnham*, 197 F.2d 973, 979 (2d Cir. 1952), and studies cited at 979 in 4; see also *All American Airways, Inc. v. Elderd*, 209 F.2d 247, 249 (2d Cir. 1954); *Gart v. Cole*, 263 F.2d 244, 248–49 (2d Cir. 1959), cert. denied, 359 U.S. 978 (1959).

Notice to members of the class, whenever employed under amended Rule 23, should be accommodated to the particular purpose but need not comply with the formalities for service of process. See Chafee, supra, at 230–31; *Brendle v. Smith*, 7 F.R.D. 119 (S.D.N.Y.1946). The fact that notice is given at one stage of the action does not mean that it must be given at subsequent stages. Notice is available fundamentally "for the protection of the members of the class or otherwise for the fair conduct of the action" and should not be used merely as a device for the undesirable solicitation of claims. See the discussion in *Cherner v. Transitron Electronic Corp.*, 201 F.Supp. 934 (D.Mass.1962); *Hormel v. United States*, 17 F.R.D. 303 (S.D.N.Y.1955).

In appropriate cases the court should notify interested government agencies of the pendency of the action or of particular steps therein.

Subdivision (d)(3) reflects the possibility of conditioning the maintenance of a class action, e.g., on the strengthening of the representation, see subdivision (c)(1) above; and recognizes that the imposition of conditions on intervenors may be required for the proper and efficient conduct of the action.

As to orders under subdivision (d)(4), see subdivision (c)(1) above.

Subdivision (e) requires approval of the court, after notice, for the dismissal or compromise of any class action.

1987 Amendment

The amendments are technical. No substantive change is intended.

1998 Amendments

Subdivision (f). This permissive interlocutory appeal provision is adopted under the power conferred by 28 U.S.C. § 1292(e). Appeal from an order granting or denying class certification is permitted in the sole discretion of the court of appeals. No other type of Rule 23 order is covered by this provision. The court of appeals is given unfettered discretion whether to permit the appeal, akin to the discretion exercised by the Supreme Court in acting on a petition for certiorari. This discretion suggests an analogy to the provision in 28 U.S.C. § 1292(b) for permissive appeal on certification by a district court. Subdivision (f), however, departs from the § 1291(b) model in two significant ways. It does not require that the district court certify the certification ruling for appeal, although the district court often can assist the parties and court of appeals by offering advice on the desirability of appeal. And it does not include the potentially limiting requirements of § 1292(b) that the district court order "involve[] a controlling question of law as to which there is substantial ground for difference of opinion and that an immediate appeal from the order may materially advance the ultimate termination of the litigation.

The courts of appeals will develop standards for granting review that reflect the changing areas of uncertainty in class litigation. The Federal Judicial Center study supports the view that many suits with class-action allegations present familiar and almost routine issues that are no more worthy of immediate appeal than many other interlocutory rulings. Yet several concerns justify expansion of present opportunities to appeal. An order denying certification may confront the plaintiff with a situation in which the only sure path to appellate review is by proceeding to final judgment on the merits of an individual claim that, standing alone, is far smaller than the costs of litigation. An order granting certification, on the other hand, may force a defendant to settle rather than incur the costs of defending a class action and run the risk of potentially ruinous liability. These concerns can be met at low cost by establishing in the court of appeals a discretionary power to grant interlocutory review in cases that show appeal-worthy certification issues.

Permission to appeal may be granted or denied on the basis of any consideration that the court of appeals finds persuasive. Permission is most likely to be granted when the certification decision turns on a novel or unsettled question of law, or when, as a practical matter, the decision on certification is likely dispositive of the litigation.

The district court, having worked through the certification decision, often will be able to provide cogent advice on the factors that bear on the decision whether to permit appeal. This advice can be particularly valuable if the certification decision is tentative. Even as to a firm certification decision, a statement of reasons bearing on the probably benefits and costs of immediate appeal can help focus the court of appeals decision, and may persuade the disappointed party that an attempt to appeal would be fruitless.

The 10-day period for seeking permission to appeal is designed to reduce the risk that attempted appeals will disrupt continuing proceedings. It is expected that the courts of appeals will act quickly in making the preliminary determination whether to permit appeal. Permission to appeal does not stay trial court proceedings. A stay should be sought first from the trial court. If the trial court refuses a stay, its action and any explanation of its views should weigh heavily with the court of appeals.

Appellate Rule 5 has been modified to establish the procedure for petitioning for leave to appeal under subdivision (f).

2003 Amendments

Subdivision (c). Subdivision (c) is amended in several respects. The requirement that the court determine whether to certify a class "as soon as practicable after commencement of an action" is replaced by requiring determination "at an early practicable time." The notice provisions are substantially revised.

Paragraph (1). Subdivision (c)(1)(A) is changed to require that the determination whether to certify a class be made "at an early practicable time." The "as soon as practicable" exaction neither reflects prevailing practice nor captures the many valid reasons that may justify deferring the initial certification decision. See Willging, Hooper & Niemic, *Empirical Study of Class Actions in Four Federal District Courts: Final Report to the Advisory Committee on Civil Rules 26–36* (Federal Judicial Center 1996).

Time may be needed to gather information necessary to make the certification decision. Although an evaluation of the probable outcome on the merits is not properly part of the certification decision, discovery in aid of the certification decision often includes information required to identify the nature of the issues that actually will be presented at trial. In this sense it is appropriate to conduct controlled discovery into the "merits," limited to those aspects relevant to making the certification decision on an informed basis. Active judicial supervision may be required to achieve the most effective balance that expedites an informed certification determination without forcing an artificial and ultimately wasteful division between "certification discovery" and "merits discovery." A critical need is to determine how the case will be tried. An increasing number of courts require a party requesting class certification to present a "trial plan" that describes the issues likely to be presented at trial and tests whether they are susceptible of class-wide proof. See Manual For Complex Litigation Third, § 21.213, p. 44; § 30.11, p. 214; § 30.12, p. 215.

Other considerations may affect the timing of the certification decision. The party opposing the class may prefer to win dismissal or summary judgment as to the individual plaintiffs without certification and without binding the class that might have been certified. Time may be needed to explore designation of class counsel under Rule 23(g), recognizing that in many cases the need to progress toward the certification determination may require designation of interim counsel under Rule 23(g)(2)(A).

Although many circumstances may justify deferring the certification decision, active management may be necessary to ensure that the certification decision is not unjustifiably delayed.

Subdivision (c)(1)(C) reflects two amendments. The provision that a class certification "may be conditional" is deleted. A court that is not satisfied that the requirements of Rule 23 have been met should refuse certification until they have been met. The provision that permits alteration or amendment of an order granting or denying class certification is amended to set the cut-off point at final judgment rather than "the decision on the merits." This change avoids the possible ambiguity in referring to "the decision on the merits." Following a determination of liability, for example, proceedings to define the remedy may demonstrate the need to amend the class definition or subdivide the class. In this setting the final judgment concept is pragmatic. It is not the same as the concept used for appeal purposes, but it should be flexible, particularly in protracted litigation.

The authority to amend an order under Rule 23(c)(1) before final judgment does not restore the practice of "one-way intervention" that was rejected by the 1966 revision of Rule 23. A determination of liability after certification, however, may show a need to amend the class definition. Decertification may be warranted after further proceedings.

If the definition of a class certified under Rule 23(b)(3) is altered to include members who have not been afforded notice and an opportunity to request exclusion, notice—including an opportunity to request exclusion—must be directed to the new class members under Rule 23(c)(2)(B).

Paragraph (2). The first change made in Rule 23(c)(2) is to call attention to the court's authority—already established in part by Rule 23(d)(2)—to direct notice of certification to a Rule 23(b)(1) or (b)(2) class. The present rule expressly requires notice only in actions certified under Rule 23(b)(3). Members of classes certified under Rules 23(b)(1) or (b)(2) have interests that may deserve protection by notice.

The authority to direct notice to class members in a (b)(1) or (b)(2) class action should be exercised with care. For several reasons, there may be less need for notice than in a (b)(3) class action. There is no right to request exclusion from a (b)(1) or (b)(2) class. The characteristics of the class may reduce the need for formal notice. The cost of providing notice, moreover, could easily cripple actions that do not seek damages. The court may decide not to direct notice after balancing the risk that notice costs may deter the pursuit of class relief against the benefits of notice.

When the court does direct certification notice in a (b)(1) or (b)(2) class action, the discretion and flexibility established by subdivision (c)(2)(A) extend to the method of giving notice. Notice facilitates the opportunity to participate. Notice calculated to reach a significant number of class members often will protect the interests of all. Informal methods may prove effective. A simple posting in a place visited by many class members, directing attention to a source of more detailed information, may suffice. The court should consider the costs of notice in relation to the probable reach of inexpensive methods.

If a Rule 23(b)(3) class is certified in conjunction with a (b)(2) class, the (c)(2)(B) notice requirements must be satisfied as to the (b)(3) class.

The direction that class-certification notice be couched in plain, easily understood language is a reminder of the need to work unremittingly at the difficult task of communicating with class members. It is difficult to provide information about most class actions that is both accurate and easily understood by class members who are not themselves lawyers. Factual uncertainty, legal complexity, and the complication of class-action procedure raise the barriers high. The Federal Judicial Center has created illustrative clear-notice forms that provide a helpful starting point for actions similar to those described in the forms.

Subdivision (e). Subdivision (e) is amended to strengthen the process of reviewing proposed class-action settlements. Settlement may be a desirable means of resolving a class action. But court review and approval are essential to assure adequate representation of class members who have not participated in shaping the settlement.

Paragraph (1). Subdivision (e)(1)(A) expressly recognizes the power of a class representative to settle class claims, issues, or defenses.

Rule 23(e)(1)(A) resolves the ambiguity in former Rule 23(e)'s reference to dismissal or compromise of "a class action." That language could be—and at times was—read to require court approval of settlements with putative class representatives that resolved only individual claims. See Manual for Complex Litigation Third, § 30.41. The new rule requires approval only if the claims, issues, or defenses of a certified class are resolved by a settlement, voluntary dismissal, or compromise.

Subdivision (e)(1)(B) carries forward the notice requirement of present Rule 23(e) when the settlement binds the class through claim or issue preclusion; notice is not required when the settlement binds only the individual class representatives. Notice of a settlement binding on the class is required either when the settlement follows class certification or when the decisions on certification and settlement proceed simultaneously.

Reasonable settlement notice may require individual notice in the manner required by Rule 23(c)(2)(B) for certification notice to a Rule 23(b)(3) class. Individual notice is appropriate, for example, if class members are required to take action—such as filing claims—to participate in the judgment, or if the court orders a settlement opt-out opportunity under Rule 23(e)(3).

Subdivision (e)(1)(C) confirms and mandates the already common practice of holding hearings as part of the process of approving settlement, voluntary dismissal, or compromise that would bind members of a class.

Subdivision (e)(1)(C) states the standard for approving a proposed settlement that would bind class members. The settlement must be fair, reasonable, and adequate. A helpful review of many factors that may deserve consideration is provided by *In re: Prudential Ins. Co. America Sales Practice Litigation Agent Actions,* 148 F.3d 283, 316–324 (3d Cir. 1998). Further guidance can be found in the Manual for Complex Litigation.

The court must make findings that support the conclusion that the settlement is fair, reasonable, and adequate. The findings must be set out in sufficient detail to explain to class members and the appellate court the factors that bear on applying the standard.

Settlement review also may provide an occasion to review the cogency of the initial class definition. The terms of the settlement themselves, or objections, may reveal divergent interests of class members and demonstrate the need to redefine the class or to designate subclasses. Redefinition of a class certified under Rule 23(b)(3) may require notice to new class members under Rule 23(c)(2)(B). See Rule 23(c)(1)(C).

Paragraph (2). Subdivision (e)(2) requires parties seeking approval of a settlement, voluntary dismissal, or compromise under Rule 23(e)(1) to file a statement identifying any agreement made in connection with the settlement. This provision does not change the basic requirement that the parties disclose all terms of the settlement or compromise that the court must approve under Rule 23(e)(1). It aims instead at related undertakings that, although seemingly separate, may have influenced the terms of the settlement by trading away possible advantages for the class in return for advantages for others. Doubts should be resolved in favor of identification.

Further inquiry into the agreements identified by the parties should not become the occasion for discovery by the parties or objectors. The court may direct the parties to provide to the court or other parties a summary or copy of the full terms of any agreement identified by the parties. The court also may direct the parties to provide a summary or copy of any agreement not identified by the parties that the court considers relevant to its review of a proposed settlement. In exercising discretion under this rule, the court may act in steps, calling first for a summary of any agreement that may have affected the settlement and then for a complete version if the summary does not provide an adequate basis for review. A direction to disclose a summary or copy of an agreement may raise concerns of confidentiality. Some agreements may include information that merits protection against general disclosure. And the court must provide an opportunity to claim work-product or other protections.

Paragraph (3). Subdivision (e)(3) authorizes the court to refuse to approve a settlement unless the settlement affords class members a new opportunity to request exclusion from a class certified under Rule 23(b)(3) after settlement terms are known. An agreement by the parties themselves to permit class members to elect exclusion at this point by the settlement agreement may be one factor supporting approval of the settlement. Often there is an opportunity to opt out at this point because the class is certified and settlement is reached in circumstances that lead to simultaneous notice of certification and notice of settlement. In these cases, the basic opportunity to elect exclusion applies without further complication. In some cases, particularly if settlement appears imminent at the time of certification, it may be possible to achieve equivalent protection by deferring notice and the opportunity to elect exclusion until actual settlement terms are known. This approach avoids the cost and potential confusion of providing two notices and makes the single notice more meaningful. But notice should not be delayed unduly after certification in the hope of settlement.

Rule 23(e)(3) authorizes the court to refuse to approve a settlement unless the settlement affords a new opportunity to elect exclusion in a case that settles after a certification decision if the earlier opportunity to elect exclusion provided with the certification notice has expired by the time of the settlement notice. A decision to remain in the class is likely to be more carefully considered and is better informed when settlement terms are known.

The opportunity to request exclusion from a proposed settlement is limited to members of a (b)(3) class. Exclusion may be requested only by individual class members; no class member may purport to opt out other class members by way of another class action.

The decision whether to approve a settlement that does not allow a new opportunity to elect exclusion is confided to the court's discretion. The court may make this decision before directing notice to the class under Rule 23(e)(1)(B) or after the Rule 23(e)(1)(C) hearing. Many factors may influence the court's decision. Among these are changes in the information available to class members since expiration of the first opportunity to request exclusion, and the nature of the individual class members' claims.

The terms set for permitting a new opportunity to elect exclusion from the proposed settlement of a Rule 23(b)(3) class action may address concerns of potential misuse. The court might direct, for example, that class members who elect exclusion are bound by rulings on the merits made before the settlement was proposed for approval. Still other terms or conditions may be appropriate.

Paragraph (4). Subdivision (e)(4) confirms the right of class members to object to a proposed settlement, voluntary dismissal, or compromise. The right is defined in relation to a disposition that, because it would bind the class, requires court approval under subdivision (e)(1)(C).

Subdivision (e)(4)(B) requires court approval for withdrawal of objections made under subdivision (e)(4)(A). Review follows automatically if the objections are withdrawn on terms that lead to modification of the settlement with the class. Review also is required if the objector formally withdraws the objections. If the objector simply abandons pursuit of the objection, the court may inquire into the circumstances.

Approval under paragraph (4)(B) may be given or denied with little need for further inquiry if the objection and the disposition go only to a protest that the individual treatment afforded the objector under the proposed settlement is unfair because of factors that distinguish the objector from other class members. Different considerations may apply if the objector has protested that the proposed settlement is not fair, reasonable, or adequate on grounds that apply generally to a class or subclass. Such objections, which purport to represent class-wide interests, may augment the opportunity for obstruction or delay. If such objections are surrendered on terms that do not affect the class settlement or the objector's participation in the class settlement, the court often can approve withdrawal of the objections without elaborate inquiry.

Once an objector appeals, control of the proceeding lies in the court of appeals. The court of appeals may undertake review and approval of a settlement with the objector, perhaps as part of appeal settlement procedures, or may remand to the district court to take advantage of the district court's familiarity with the action and settlement.

Subdivision (g). Subdivision (g) is new. It responds to the reality that the selection and activity of class counsel are often critically important to the successful handling of a class action. Until now, courts have scrutinized proposed class counsel as well as the class representative under Rule 23(a)(4). This experience has recognized the importance of judicial evaluation of the proposed lawyer for the class, and this new subdivision builds on that experience rather than introducing an entirely new element into the class certification process. Rule 23(a)(4) will continue to call for scrutiny of the proposed class representative, while this subdivision will guide the court in assessing proposed class counsel as part of the certification decision. This subdivision recognizes the importance of class counsel, states the obligation to represent the interests of the class, and provides a framework for selection of class counsel. The procedure and standards for appointment vary depending on whether there are multiple applicants to be class counsel. The new subdivision also provides a method by which the court may make directions from the outset about the potential fee award to class counsel in the event the action is successful.

Paragraph (1) sets out the basic requirement that class counsel be appointed if a class is certified and articulates the obligation of class counsel to represent the interests of the class, as opposed to the potentially conflicting interests of individual class members. It also sets out the factors the court should consider in assessing proposed class counsel.

Paragraph (1)(A) requires that the court appoint class counsel to represent the class. Class counsel must be appointed for all classes, including each subclass that the court certifies to represent divergent interests.

Paragraph (1)(A) does not apply if "a statute provides otherwise." This recognizes that provisions of the Private Securities Litigation Reform Act of 1995, Pub. L. No. 104–67, 109 Stat. 737 (1995) (codified in various sections of 15 U.S.C.), contain directives that bear on selection of a lead plaintiff and the retention of counsel. This subdivision does not purport to supersede or to affect the interpretation of those provisions, or any similar provisions of other legislation.

Paragraph 1(B) recognizes that the primary responsibility of class counsel, resulting from appointment as class counsel, is to represent the best interests of the class. The rule thus establishes the obligation of class counsel, an obligation that may be different from the customary obligations of counsel to individual clients. Appointment as class counsel means that the primary obligation of counsel is to the class rather than to any individual members of it. The class representatives do not have an unfettered right to "fire" class counsel. In the same vein, the class representatives cannot command class counsel to accept or reject a settlement proposal. To the contrary, class counsel must determine whether seeking the court's approval of a settlement would be in the best interests of the class as a whole.

Paragraph (1)(C) articulates the basic responsibility of the court to appoint class counsel who will provide the adequate representation called for by paragraph (1)(B). It identifies criteria that must be considered and invites the court to consider any other pertinent matters. Although couched in terms of the court's duty, the listing also informs counsel seeking appointment about the topics that should be addressed in an application for appointment or in the motion for class certification.

The court may direct potential class counsel to provide additional information about the topics mentioned in paragraph (1)(C) or about any other relevant topic. For example, the court may direct applicants to inform the court concerning any agreements about a prospective award of attorney fees or nontaxable costs, as such agreements may sometimes be significant in the selection of class counsel. The court might also direct that potential class counsel indicate how parallel litigation might be coordinated or consolidated with the action before the court.

The court may also direct counsel to propose terms for a potential award of attorney fees and nontaxable costs. Attorney fee awards are an important feature of class action practice, and attention to this subject from the outset may often be a productive technique. Paragraph (2)(C) therefore authorizes the court to provide directions about attorney fees and costs when appointing class counsel. Because there will be numerous class actions in which this information is not likely to be useful, the court need not consider it in all class actions.

Some information relevant to class counsel appointment may involve matters that include adversary preparation in a way that should be shielded from disclosure to other parties. An appropriate protective order may be necessary to preserve confidentiality.

In evaluating prospective class counsel, the court should weigh all pertinent factors. No single factor should necessarily be determinative in a given case. For example, the resources counsel will commit to the case must be appropriate to its needs, but the court should be careful not to limit consideration to lawyers with the greatest resources.

If, after review of all applicants, the court concludes that none would be satisfactory class counsel, it may deny class certification, reject all applications, recommend that an application be modified, invite new applications, or make any other appropriate order regarding selection and appointment of class counsel.

Paragraph (2). This paragraph sets out the procedure that should be followed in appointing class counsel. Although it affords substantial flexibility, it provides the framework for appointment of class counsel in all class actions. For counsel who filed the action, the materials submitted in support of the motion for class certification may suffice to justify appointment so long as the information described in paragraph (g)(1)(C) is included. If there are other applicants, they ordinarily would file a formal application detailing their suitability for the position.

In a plaintiff class action the court usually would appoint as class counsel only an attorney or attorneys who have sought appointment. Different considerations may apply in defendant class actions.

The rule states that the court should appoint "class counsel." In many instances, the applicant will be an individual attorney. In other cases, however, an entire firm, or perhaps numerous attorneys who are not otherwise affiliated but are collaborating on the action will apply. No rule of thumb exists to determine when such arrangements are appropriate; the court should be alert to the need for adequate staffing of the case, but also to the risk of overstaffing or an ungainly counsel structure.

Paragraph (2)(A) authorizes the court to designate interim counsel during the pre-certification period if necessary to protect the interests of the putative class. Rule 23(c)(1)(B) directs that the order certifying the class include appointment of class counsel. Before class certification, however, it will usually be important for an attorney to take action to prepare for the certification decision. The amendment to Rule 23(c)(1) recognizes that some discovery is often necessary for that determination. It also may be important to make or respond to motions before certification. Settlement may be discussed before certification. Ordinarily, such work is handled by the lawyer who filed the action. In some cases, however, there may be rivalry or uncertainty that makes formal designation of interim counsel appropriate. Rule 23(g)(2)(A) authorizes the court to designate interim counsel to act on behalf of the putative class before the certification decision is made. Failure to make the formal designation does not prevent the attorney who filed the action from proceeding in it. Whether or not formally designated interim counsel, an attorney who acts on behalf of the class before certification must act in the best interests of the class as a whole. For example, an attorney who negotiates a pre-certification settlement must seek a settlement that is fair, reasonable, and adequate for the class.

Rule 23(c)(1) provides that the court should decide whether to certify the class "at an early practicable time," and directs that class counsel should be appointed in the order certifying the class. In some cases, it may be appropriate for the court to allow a reasonable period after commencement of the action for filing applications to serve as class counsel. The primary ground for deferring appointment would be that there is reason to anticipate competing applications to serve as class counsel. Examples might include instances in which more than one class action has been filed, or in which other attorneys have filed individual actions on behalf of putative class members. The purpose of facilitating competing applications in such a case is to afford the best possible representation for the class. Another possible reason for deferring appointment would be that the initial applicant was found inadequate, but it seems appropriate to permit additional applications rather than deny class certification.

Paragraph (2)(B) states the basic standard the court should use in deciding whether to certify the class and appoint class counsel in the single applicant situation—that the applicant be able to provide the representation called for by paragraph (1)(B) in light of the factors identified in paragraph (1)(C).

If there are multiple adequate applicants, paragraph (2)(B) directs the court to select the class counsel best able to represent the interests of the class. This decision should also be made using the factors outlined in paragraph (1)(C), but in the multiple applicant situation the court is to go beyond scrutinizing the adequacy of counsel and make a comparison of the strengths of the various applicants. As with the decision whether to appoint the sole applicant for the posit ion, no single factor should be dispositive in selecting class counsel in cases in which there are multiple applicants. The fact that a given attorney filed the instant action, for example, might not weigh heavily in the decision if that lawyer had not done significant work identifying or investigating claims. Depending on the nature of the case, one important consideration might be the applicant's existing attorney-client relationship with the proposed class representative.

Paragraph (2)(C) builds on the appointment process by authorizing the court to include provisions regarding attorney fees in the order appointing class counsel. Courts may find it desirable to adopt guidelines for fees or nontaxable costs, or to direct class counsel to report to the court at regular intervals on the efforts undertaken in the action, to facilitate the court's later determination of a reasonable attorney fee.

Subdivision (h). Subdivision (h) is new. Fee awards are a powerful influence on the way attorneys initiate, develop, and conclude class actions. Class action attorney fee awards have heretofore been handled, along with all other attorney fee awards, under Rule 54(d)(2), but that rule is not addressed to the particular concerns of class actions. This subdivision is designed to work in tandem with new subdivision (g) on appointment of class counsel, which may afford an opportunity for the court to provide an early framework for an eventual fee award, or for monitoring the work of class counsel during the pendency of the action.

Subdivision (h) applies to "an action certified as a class action." This includes cases in which there is a simultaneous proposal for class certification and settlement even though technically the class may not be certified unless the court approves the settlement pursuant to review under Rule 23(e). When a settlement is proposed for Rule 23(e) approval, either after certification or with a request for certification, notice to class members about class counsel's fee motion would ordinarily accompany the notice to the class about the settlement proposal itself.

This subdivision does not undertake to create new grounds for an award of attorney fees or nontaxable costs. Instead, it applies when such awards are authorized by law or by agreement of the parties. Against that background, it provides a format for all awards of attorney fees and nontaxable costs in connection with a class action, not only the award to class counsel. In some situations, there may be a basis for making an award to other counsel whose work produced a beneficial result for the class, such as attorneys who acted for the class before certification but were not appointed class counsel, or attorneys who represented objectors to a proposed settlement under Rule 23(e) or to the fee motion of class counsel. Other situations in which fee awards are authorized by law or by agreement of the parties may exist.

This subdivision authorizes an award of "reasonable" attorney fees and nontaxable costs. This is the customary term for measurement of fee awards in cases in which counsel may obtain an award of fees under the "common fund" theory that applies in many class actions, and is used in many fee-shifting statutes. Depending on the circumstances, courts have approached the determination of what is reasonable in different ways. In particular, there is some variation among courts about whether in "common fund" cases the court should use the lodestar or a percentage method of determining what fee is reasonable. The rule does not attempt to resolve the question whether the lodestar or percentage approach should be viewed as preferable.

Active judicial involvement in measuring fee awards is singularly important to the proper operation of the class-action process. Continued reliance on caselaw development of fee-award measures does not diminish the court's responsibility. In a class action, the district court must ensure that the amount and mode of payment of attorney fees are fair and proper whether the fees come from a common fund or are otherwise paid. Even in the absence of objections, the court bears this responsibility.

Courts discharging this responsibility have looked to a variety of factors. One fundamental focus is the result actually achieved for class members, a basic consideration in any case in which fees are sought on the basis of a benefit achieved for class members. The Private Securities Litigation Reform Act of 1995 explicitly makes this factor a cap for a fee award in actions to which it applies. See 15 U.S.C. §§ 77z–1(a)(6); 78u–4(a)(6) (fee award should not exceed a "reasonable percentage of the amount of any damages and prejudgment interest actually paid to the class"). For a percentage approach to fee measurement, results achieved is the basic starting point.

In many instances, the court may need to proceed with care in assessing the value conferred on class members. Settlement regimes that provide for future payments, for example, may not result in significant actual payments to class members. In this connection, the court may need to scrutinize the manner and operation of any applicable claims procedure. In some cases, it may be appropriate to defer some portion of the fee award until actual payouts to class members are known. Settlements involving nonmonetary provisions for class members also deserve careful scrutiny to ensure that these provisions have actual value to the class. On occasion the court's Rule 23(e) review will provide a solid basis for this sort of evaluation, but in any event it is also important to assessing the fee award for the class.

At the same time, it is important to recognize that in some class actions the monetary relief obtained is not the sole determinant of an appropriate attorney fees award. Cf. *Blanchard v. Bergeron,* 489 U.S. 87, 95 (1989) (cautioning in an individual case against an "undesirable emphasis" on "the importance of the recovery of damages in civil rights litigation" that might "shortchange efforts to seek effective injunctive or declaratory relief").

Any directions or orders made by the court in connection with appointing class counsel under Rule 23(g) should weigh heavily in making a fee award under this subdivision.

Courts have also given weight to agreements among the parties regarding the fee motion, and to agreements between class counsel and others about the fees claimed by the motion. Rule 54(d)(2)(B) provides: "If directed by the court, the motion shall also disclose the terms of any agreement with respect to fees to be paid for the services for which claim is made." The agreement by a settling party not to oppose a fee application up to a certain amount, for example, is worthy of consideration, but the court remains responsible to determine a reasonable fee. "Side agreements" regarding fees provide at least perspective pertinent to an appropriate fee award.

In addition, courts may take account of the fees charged by class counsel or other attorneys for representing individual claimants or objectors in the case. In determining a fee for class counsel, the court's objective is to ensure an overall fee that is fair for counsel and equitable within the class. In some circumstances individual fee agreements between class counsel and class members might have provisions inconsistent with those goals, and the court might determine that adjustments in the class fee award were necessary as a result.

Finally, it is important to scrutinize separately the application for an award covering nontaxable costs. If costs were addressed in the order appointing class counsel, those directives should be a presumptive starting point in determining what is an appropriate award.

Paragraph (1). Any claim for an award of attorney fees must be sought by motion under Rule 54(d)(2), which invokes the provisions for timing of appeal in Rule 58 and Appellate Rule 4. Owing to the distinctive features of class action fee motions, however, the provisions of this subdivision control disposition of fee motions in class actions, while Rule 54(d)(2) applies to matters not addressed in this subdivision.

The court should direct when the fee motion must be filed. For motions by class counsel in cases subject to court review of a proposed settlement under Rule 23(e), it would be important to require the filing of at least the initial motion in time for inclusion of information about the motion in the notice to the class about the proposed settlement that is required by Rule 23(e). In cases litigated to judgment, the court might also order class counsel's motion to be filed promptly so that notice to the class under this subdivision (h) can be given.

Besides service of the motion on all parties, notice of class counsel's motion for attorney fees must be "directed to the class in a reasonable manner." Because members of the class have an interest in the arrangements for payment of class counsel whether that payment comes from the class fund or is made directly by another party, notice is required in all instances. In cases in which settlement approval is contemplated under Rule 23(e), notice of class counsel's fee motion should be combined with notice of the proposed settlement, and the provision regarding notice to the class is parallel to the requirements for notice under Rule 23(e). In adjudicated class actions, the court may calibrate the notice to avoid undue expense.

Paragraph (2). A class member and any party from whom payment is sought may object to the fee motion. Other parties—for example, nonsettling defendants—may not object because they lack a sufficient interest in the amount the court awards. The rule does not specify a time limit for making an objection. In setting the date objections are due, the court should provide sufficient time after the full fee motion is on file to enable potential objectors to examine the motion.

The court may allow an objector discovery relevant to the objections. In determining whether to allow discovery, the court should weigh the need for the information against the cost and delay that would attend discovery. See Rule 26(b)(2). One factor in determining whether to authorize discovery is the completeness of the material submitted in support of the fee motion, which depends in part on the fee measurement standard applicable to the case. If the motion provides thorough information, the burden should be on the objector to justify discovery to obtain further information.

Paragraph (3). Whether or not there are formal objections, the court must determine whether a fee award is justified and, if so, set a reasonable fee. The rule does not require a formal hearing in all cases. The form and extent of a hearing depend on the circumstances of the case. The rule does require findings and conclusions under Rule 52(a).

Paragraph (4). By incorporating Rule 54(d)(2), this provision gives the court broad authority to obtain assistance in determining the appropriate amount to award. In deciding whether to direct submission of such questions to a special master or magistrate judge, the court should give appropriate consideration to the cost and delay that such a process might entail.

2007 Amendment

The language of Rule 23 has been amended as part of the general restyling of the Civil Rules to make them more easily understood and to make style and terminology consistent throughout the rules. These changes are intended to be stylistic only.

Amended Rule 23(d)(2) carries forward the provisions of former Rule 23(d) that recognize two separate propositions. First, a Rule 23(d) order may be combined with a pretrial order under Rule 16. Second, the standard for amending the Rule 23(d) order continues to be the more open-ended standard for amending Rule 23(d) orders, not the more exacting standard for amending Rule 16 orders.

As part of the general restyling, intensifiers that provide emphasis but add no meaning are consistently deleted. Amended Rule 23(f) omits as redundant the explicit reference to court of appeals discretion in deciding whether to permit an interlocutory appeal. The omission does not in any way limit the unfettered discretion established by the original rule.

HISTORICAL NOTES

Amendments to Civil Rules Proposed March 27, 2003

Pub.L. 109–2, § 7, Feb. 18, 2005, 119 Stat. 13, provided that amendments to rule 23 of the Federal Rules of Civil Procedure, which are set forth in the order entered by the Supreme Court of the United States on March 27, 2003, shall take effect on the date of enactment of that Act [Feb. 18, 2005] or on December 1, 2003 (as specified in that order), whichever occurred first, see Pub.L. 109–2, § 7, set out as a note under 28 U.S.C.A. § 2074.

Rule 23.1. Derivative Actions

(a) **Prerequisites.** This rule applies when one or more shareholders or members of a corporation or an unincorporated association bring a derivative action to enforce a right that the corporation or association may properly assert but has failed to enforce. The derivative action may not be maintained if it appears that the plaintiff does not fairly and adequately represent the interests of shareholders or members who are similarly situated in enforcing the right of the corporation or association.

(b) **Pleading Requirements.** The complaint must be verified and must:

(1) allege that the plaintiff was a shareholder or member at the time of the transaction complained of, or that the plaintiff's share or membership later devolved on it by operation of law;

(2) allege that the action is not a collusive one to confer jurisdiction that the court would otherwise lack; and

(3) state with particularity:

(A) any effort by the plaintiff to obtain the desired action from the directors or comparable authority and, if necessary, from the shareholders or members; and

(B) the reasons for not obtaining the action or not making the effort.

(c) **Settlement, Dismissal, and Compromise.** A derivative action may be settled, voluntarily dismissed, or compromised only with the court's approval. Notice of a proposed settlement, voluntary dismissal, or compromise must be given to shareholders or members in the manner that the court orders.

(Adopted February 28, 1966, effective July 1, 1966; amended March 2, 1987, effective August 1, 1987; April 30, 2007, effective December 1, 2007.)

ADVISORY COMMITTEE NOTES

1966 Addition

A derivative action by a shareholder of a corporation or by a member of an unincorporated association has distinctive aspects which require the special provisions set forth in the new rule. The next-to-the-last sentence recognizes that the question of adequacy of representation may arise when the plaintiff is one of a group of shareholders or members. Cf. 3 Moore's *Federal Practice*, par. 23.08 (2d ed. 1963).

The court has inherent power to provide for the conduct of the proceedings in a derivative action, including the power to determine the course of the proceedings and require that any appropriate notice be given to shareholders or members.

1987 Amendment

The amendments are technical. No substantive change is intended.

2007 Amendment

The language of Rule 23.1 has been amended as part of the general restyling of the Civil Rules to make them more easily understood and to make style and terminology consistent throughout the rules. These changes are intended to be stylistic only.

Rule 23.2. Actions Relating to Unincorporated Associations

This rule applies to an action brought by or against the members of an unincorporated association as a class by naming certain members as representative parties. The action may be maintained only if it appears that those parties will fairly and adequately protect the interests of the association and its members. In conducting the action, the court may issue any appropriate orders corresponding with those in Rule 23(d), and the procedure for settlement, voluntary dismissal, or compromise must correspond with the procedure in Rule 23(e).

(Adopted February 28, 1966, effective July 1, 1966; amended April 30, 2007, effective December 1, 2007.)

ADVISORY COMMITTEE NOTES

1966 Addition

Although an action by or against representatives of the membership of an unincorporated association has often been viewed as a class action, the real or main purpose of this characterization has been to give "entity treatment" to the association when for formal reasons it cannot sue or be sued as a jural person under Rule 17(b). See Louisell & Hazard, *Pleading and Procedure: State and Federal* 718 (1962); 3 Moore's *Federal Practice*, par. 23.08 (2d ed. 1963); Story, J. in *West v. Randall*, 29 Fed.Cas. 718, 722–23, No. 17,424 (C.C.D.R.I.1820); and, for examples, *Gibbs v. Buck*, 307 U.S. 66 (1939); *Tunstall v. Brotherhood of Locomotive F. & E.*, 148 F.2d 403 (4th Cir. 1945); *Oskoian v. Canuel*, 269 F.2d 311 (1st Cir. 1959). Rule 23.2 deals separately with these actions, referring where appropriate to Rule 23.

2007 Amendment

The language of Rule 23.2 has been amended as part of the general restyling of the Civil Rules to make them more easily understood and to make style and terminology consistent throughout the rules. These changes are intended to be stylistic only.

Rule 24. Intervention

(a) Intervention of Right. On timely motion, the court must permit anyone to intervene who:

(1) is given an unconditional right to intervene by a federal statute; or

(2) claims an interest relating to the property or transaction that is the subject of the action, and is so situated that disposing of the action may as a practical matter impair or impede the movant's ability to protect its interest, unless existing parties adequately represent that interest.

(b) Permissive Intervention.

(1) ***In General.*** On timely motion, the court may permit anyone to intervene who:

(A) is given a conditional right to intervene by a federal statute; or

(B) has a claim or defense that shares with the main action a common question of law or fact.

(2) ***By a Government Officer or Agency.*** On timely motion, the court may permit a federal or state governmental officer or agency to intervene if a party's claim or defense is based on:

(A) a statute or executive order administered by the officer or agency; or

(B) any regulation, order, requirement, or agreement issued or made under the statute or executive order.

(3) ***Delay or Prejudice.*** In exercising its discretion, the court must consider whether the intervention will unduly delay or prejudice the adjudication of the original parties' rights.

(c) Notice and Pleading Required. A motion to intervene must be served on the parties as provided in Rule 5. The motion must state the grounds for intervention and be accompanied by a pleading that sets out the claim or defense for which intervention is sought.

(Amended December 27, 1946, effective March 19, 1948; December 29, 1948, effective October 20, 1949; January 21, 1963, effective July 1, 1963; February 28, 1966, effective July 1, 1966; March 2, 1987, effective August 1, 1987; April 30, 1991, effective December 1, 1991; April 12, 2006, effective December 1, 2006; April 30, 2007, effective December 1, 2007.)

ADVISORY COMMITTEE NOTES

1937 Adoption

The right to intervene given by the following and similar statutes is preserved, but the procedure for its assertion is governed by this rule:

U.S.C., Title 28 former sections:

45a [now 2323] (Special attorneys; participation by Interstate Commerce Commission; intervention) (in certain cases under interstate commerce laws)

48 [now 2322] (Suits to be against United States; intervention by United States)

401 [now 2403] (Intervention by United States; constitutionality of Federal statute)

U.S.C., Title 40:

276a–2(b) [now 3162(a)(2)] (Bonds of contractors for public buildings or works; rights of persons furnishing labor and materials).

Compare with the last sentence of [former] Equity Rule 37 (Parties Generally—Intervention). This rule amplifies and restates the present federal practice at law and in equity. For the practice in admiralty see Admiralty Rules 34 (How Third Party May Intervene) and 42 (Claims Against Proceeds in Registry). See generally Moore and Levi, *Federal Intervention: I The Right to Intervene and Reorganization* (1936), 45 Yale L.J. 565. Under the codes two types of intervention are provided, one for the recovery of specific real or personal property (2 Ohio Gen.Code Ann. (Page, 1926) § 11263; Wyo.Rev.Stat.Ann. (Courtright, 1931) § 89–522), and the other allowing intervention generally when the applicant has an interest in the matter in litigation (1 Colo.Stat.Ann. (1935) Code Civ.Proc. § 22; La.Code Pract. (Dart, 1932) Arts. 389–394; Utah Rev.Stat.Ann. (1933) § 104–3–24). The English intervention practice is based upon various rules and decisions and falls into the two categories of absolute right and discretionary right. For the absolute right see *English Rules Under the Judicature Act* (The Annual Practice, 1937) O. 12, r. 24 (admiralty), r. 25 (land), r. 23 (probate); O. 57, r. 12 (execution); J.A. (1925) §§ 181, 182, 183(2) (divorce); *In re Metropolitan Amalgamated Estates, Ltd.,* (1912) 2 Ch. 497 (receivership); *Wilson v. Church,* 9 Ch.D. 552 (1878) (representative action). For the discretionary right see O. 16, r. 11 (non-joinder) and *Re Fowler,* 142 L.T.Jo. 94 (Ch.1916), *Vavasseur v. Krupp,* 9 Ch.D. 351 (1878) (persons out of the jurisdiction).

1946 Amendment

Note. Subdivision (a). The addition to subdivision (a)(3) covers the situation where property may be in the actual custody of some other officer or agency—such as the Secretary of the Treasury—but the control and disposition of the property is lodged in the court wherein the action is pending.

Subdivision (b). The addition in subdivision (b) permits the intervention of governmental officers or agencies in proper cases and thus avoids exclusionary constructions of the rule. For an example of the latter, see *Matter of Bender Body Co.,* Ref. Ohio 1941, 47 F.Supp. 224, holding that the Administrator of the Office of Price Administration, then acting under the authority of an Executive Order of the President, could not intervene in a bankruptcy proceeding to protest the sale of assets above ceiling prices. Compare, however, *Securities and Exchange Commission v. United States Realty & Improvement Co.,* 1940, 310 U.S. 434, 60 S.Ct. 1044, where permissive intervention of the Commission to protect the public interest in an arrangement proceeding under Chapter XI of the Bankruptcy Act was upheld. See also dissenting opinion in *Securities and Exchange Commission v. Long Island Lighting Co.,* C.C.A.2d 1945, 148 F.2d

252, judgment vacated as moot and case remanded with direction to dismiss complaint, 1945, 325 U.S. 833, 65 S.Ct. 1085. For discussion see Commentary, *Nature of Permissive Intervention Under Rule 24b,* 1940, 3 Fed.Rules Serv. 704; Berger, *Intervention by Public Agencies in Private Litigation in the Federal Courts,* 1940, 50 Yale L.J. 65.

Regarding the construction of subdivision (b)(2), see *Allen Calculators, Inc. v. National Cash Register Co.,* 1944, 64 S.Ct. 905, 322 U.S. 137, 88 L.Ed. 1188.

1948 Amendment

The amendment effective Oct. 20, 1949, substituted the reference to "Title 28, U.S.C.A. § 2403" at the end of subdivision (c) for the reference to "the Act of August 24, 1937, c. 754, § 1."

1963 Amendment

This amendment conforms to the amendment of Rule 5(a). See the Advisory Committee's Note to that amendment.

1966 Amendment

In attempting to overcome certain difficulties which have arisen in the application of present Rule 24(a)(2) and (3), this amendment draws upon the revision of the related Rules 19 (joinder of persons needed for just adjudication) and 23 (class actions), and the reasoning underlying that revision.

Rule 24(a)(3) as amended in 1948 provided for intervention of right where the applicant established that he would be adversely affected by the distribution or disposition of property involved in an action to which he had not been made a party. Significantly, some decided cases virtually disregarded the language of this provision. Thus Professor Moore states: "The concept of a fund has been applied so loosely that it is possible for a court to find a fund in almost any in personam action." 4 Moore's *Federal Practice,* par. 24.09[3], at 55 (2d ed. 1962), and see, e.g., *Formulabs, Inc. v. Hartley Pen Co.,* 275 F.2d 52 (9th Cir.1960). This development was quite natural, for Rule 24(a)(3) was unduly restricted. If an absentee would be substantially affected in a practical sense by the determination made in an action, he should, as a general rule, be entitled to intervene, and his right to do so should not depend on whether there is a fund to be distributed or otherwise disposed of. Intervention of right is here seen to be a kind of counterpart to Rule 19(a)(2)(i) on joinder of persons needed for a just adjudication: where, upon motion of a party in an action, an absentee should be joined so that he may protect his interest which as a practical matter may be substantially impaired by the disposition of the action, he ought to have a right to intervene in the action on his own motion. See Louisell & Hazard, *Pleading and Procedure: State and Federal* 749–50 (1962).

The general purpose of original Rule 24(a)(2) was to entitle an absentee, purportedly represented by a party, to intervene in the action if he could establish with fair probability that the representation was inadequate. Thus, where an action is being prosecuted or defended by a trustee, a beneficiary of the trust should have a right to intervene if he can show that the trustee's representation of his interest probably is inadequate; similarly a member of a class should have the right to intervene in a class action if he can show the inadequacy of the representation of his interest by the representative parties before the court.

Original Rule 24(a)(2), however, made it a condition of intervention that "the applicant is or may be bound by a judgment in the action," and this created difficulties with intervention in class actions. If the "bound" language was read literally in the sense of res judicata, it could defeat intervention in some meritorious cases. A member of a class to whom a judgment in a class action extended by its terms (see Rule 23(c)(3), as amended) might be entitled to show in a later action, when the judgment in the class action was claimed to operate as res judicata against him, that the "representative" in the class action had not in fact adequately represented him. If he could make this showing, the class-action judgment might be held not to bind him. See *Hansberry v. Lee,* 311 U.S. 32 (1940). If a class member sought to intervene in the class action proper, while it was still pending, on grounds of inadequacy of representation, he could be met with the argument: if the representation was in fact inadequate, he would not be "bound" by the judgment when it was subsequently asserted against him as res judicata, hence he was not entitled to intervene; if the representation was in fact adequate, there was no occasion or ground for intervention. See *Sam Fox Publishing Co. v. United States,* 366 U.S. 683 (1961); cf. *Sutphen Estates, Inc. v. United States,* 342 U.S. 19 (1951). This reasoning might be linguistically justified by original Rule 24(a)(2); but it could lead to poor results. Compare the discussion in *International M. & I. Corp. v. Von Clemm,* 301 F.2d 857 (2d Cir.1962); *Atlantic Refining Co. v. Standard Oil Co.,* 304 F.2d 387 (D.C.Cir. 1962). A class member who claims that his "representative" does not adequately represent him, and is able to establish that proposition with sufficient probability, should not be put to the risk of having a judgment entered in the action which by its terms extends to him, and be obliged to test the validity of the judgment as applied to his interest by a later collateral attack. Rather he should, as a general rule, be entitled to intervene in the action.

The amendment provides that an applicant is entitled to intervene in an action when his position is comparable to that of a person under Rule 19(a)(2)(i), as amended, unless his interest is already adequately represented in the action by existing parties. The Rule 19(a)(2)(i) criterion imports practical considerations, and the deletion of the "bound" language similarly frees the rule from undue preoccupation with strict considerations of res judicata.

The representation whose adequacy comes into question under the amended rule is not confined to formal representation like that provided by a trustee for his beneficiary or a representative party in a class action for a member of the class. A party to an action may provide practical representation to the absentee seeking intervention although no such formal relationship exists between them, and the adequacy of this practical representation will then have to be weighed. See *International M. & I. Crop. v. Von Clemm,* and *Atlantic Refining Co. v. Standard Oil Co.,* both supra; *Wolpe v. Poretsky,* 144 F.2d 505 (D.C.Cir.1944), cert. denied, 323 U.S. 777 (1944); cf. *Ford Motor Co. v. Bisanz Bros.,* 249 F.2d 22 (8th Cir.1957); and generally, Annot., 84 A.L.R.2d 1412 (1961).

An intervention of right under the amended rule may be subject to appropriate conditions or restrictions responsive among other things to the requirements of efficient conduct of the proceedings.

1987 Amendment

The amendments are technical. No substantive change is intended.

1991 Amendment

Language is added to bring Rule 24(c) into conformity with the statute cited, resolving some confusion reflected in district court rules. As the text provides, counsel challenging the constitutionality of legislation in an action in which the appropriate government is not a party should call the attention of the court to its duty to notify the appropriate governmental officers. The statute imposes the burden of notification on the court, not the party making the constitutional challenge, partly in order to protect against any possible waiver of constitutional rights by parties inattentive to the need for notice. For this reason, the failure of a party to call the court's attention to the matter cannot be treated as a waiver.

2006 Amendment

New Rule 5.1 replaces the final three sentences of Rule 24(c), implementing the provisions of 28 U.S.C. § 2403. Section 2403 requires notification to the Attorney General of the United States when the constitutionality of an Act of Congress is called in question, and to the state attorney general when the constitutionality of a state statute is drawn into question.

2007 Amendment

The language of Rule 24 has been amended as part of the general restyling of the Civil Rules to make them more easily understood and to make style and terminology consistent throughout the rules. These changes are intended to be stylistic only.

The former rule stated that the same procedure is followed when a United States statute gives a right to intervene. This statement is deleted because it added nothing.

Rule 25. Substitution of Parties

(a) Death.

(1) ***Substitution if the Claim Is Not Extinguished.*** If a party dies and the claim is not extinguished, the court may order substitution of the proper party. A motion for substitution may be made by any party or by the decedent's successor or representative. If the motion is not made within 90 days after service of a statement noting the death, the action by or against the decedent must be dismissed.

(2) ***Continuation Among the Remaining Parties.*** After a party's death, if the right sought to be enforced survives only to or against the remaining parties, the action does not abate, but proceeds in favor of or against the remaining parties. The death should be noted on the record.

(3) ***Service.*** A motion to substitute, together with a notice of hearing, must be served on the parties as provided in Rule 5 and on nonparties as provided in Rule 4. A statement noting death must be served in the same manner. Service may be made in any judicial district.

(b) Incompetency. If a party becomes incompetent, the court may, on motion, permit the action to be continued by or against the party's representative. The motion must be served as provided in Rule 25(a)(3).

(c) Transfer of Interest. If an interest is transferred, the action may be continued by or against the original party unless the court, on motion, orders the transferee to be substituted in the action or joined with the original party. The motion must be served as provided in Rule 25(a)(3).

(d) Public Officers; Death or Separation from Office. An action does not abate when a public officer who is a party in an official capacity dies, resigns, or otherwise ceases to hold office while the action is pending. The officer's successor is automatically substituted as a party. Later proceedings should be in the substituted party's name, but any misnomer not affecting the parties' substantial rights must be disregarded. The court may order substitution at any time, but the absence of such an order does not affect the substitution.

(Amended December 29, 1948, effective October 20, 1949; April 17, 1961, effective July 19, 1961; January 21, 1963, effective July 1, 1963; March 2, 1987, effective August 1, 1987; April 30, 2007, effective December 1, 2007.)

ADVISORY COMMITTEE NOTES

1937 Adoption

Note to Subdivision (a). 1. The first paragraph of this rule is based upon [former] Equity Rule 45 (Death of Party—Revivor) and U.S.C., Title 28, former § 778 (Death of parties; substitution of executor or administrator). The *scire facias* procedure provided for in the statute cited is superseded and the writ is abolished by Rule 81(b). Paragraph two states the content of U.S.C., Title 28, former § 779 (Death of one of several plaintiffs or defendants). With these two paragraphs compare generally *English Rules Under the Judicature Act* (The Annual Practice, 1937) O. 17, r.r. 1–10.

2. This rule modifies U.S.C., Title 28, [former] §§ 778 (Death of parties; substitution of executor or administrator), 779 (Death of one of several plaintiffs or defendants), and 780 (Survival of actions, suits, or proceedings, etc.), in so far as they differ from it.

Note to Subdivisions (b) and (c). These are a combination and adaptation of N.Y.C.P.A. (1937) § 83 and Calif.Code Civ.Proc. (1937) § 385; see also 4 Nev.Comp.Laws (Hillyer, 1929) § 8561.

Note to Subdivision (d). With the first and last sentences compare U.S.C.A., Title 28, former § 780 (Survival of actions, suits, or proceedings, etc.). With the second sentence of this subdivision compare *Ex parte La Prade,* 1933, 53 S.Ct. 682, 289 U.S. 444, 77 L.Ed. 1311.

1948 Amendment

The amendment effective October 19, 1949, inserted the words, "the Canal Zone, a territory, an insular possession," in the first sentence of subdivision (d), and, in the same sentence, after the phrase "or other governmental agency," deleted the words, "or any other officer specified in the Act of February 13, 1925, c. 229, § 11 (43 Stat. 941), formerly section 780 of this title."

1961 Amendment

Subdivision (d)(1). Present Rule 25(d) is generally considered to be unsatisfactory. 4 Moore's *Federal Practice* ¶25.01[7] (2d ed. 1950); Wright, *Amendments to the Federal Rules: The Function of a Continuing Rules Committee,* 7 Vand.L.Rev. 521, 529 (1954); *Developments in the Law—Remedies Against the United States and Its Officials,* 70 Harv.L.Rev. 827, 931–34 (1957). To require, as a condition of substituting a successor public officer as a party to a pending action, that an application be made with a showing that there is substantial need for continuing the litigation, can rarely serve any useful purpose and fosters a burdensome formality. And to prescribe a short, fixed time period for substitution which cannot be extended even by agreement, see *Snyder v. Buck,* 340 U.S. 15, 19 (1950), with the penalty of dismissal of the action, "makes a trap for unsuspecting litigants which seems unworthy of a great government." *Vibra Brush Corp. v. Schaffer,* 256 F.2d 681, 684 (2d Cir. 1958). Although courts have on occasion found means of undercutting the rule, e.g. *Acheson v. Furusho,* 212 F.2d 284 (9th Cir.1954) (substitution of defendant officer unnecessary on theory that only a declaration of status was sought), it has operated harshly in many instances, e.g. *Snyder v. Buck,* supra; *Poindexter v. Folsom,* 242 F.2d 516 (3d Cir.1957).

Under the amendment, the successor is automatically substituted as a party without an application or showing of need to continue the action. An order of substitution is not required, but may be entered at any time if a party desires or the court thinks fit.

The general term "public officer" is used in preference to the enumeration which appears in the present rule. It comprises Federal, State, and local officers.

The expression "in his official capacity" is to be interpreted in its context as part of a simple procedural rule for substitution; care should be taken not to distort its meaning by mistaken analogies to the doctrine of sovereign immunity from suit or the Eleventh Amendment. The amended rule will apply to all actions brought by public officers for the government, and to any action brought in form against a named officer, but intrinsically against the government or the office or the incumbent thereof whoever he may be from time to time during the action. Thus the amended rule will apply to actions against officers to compel performance of official duties or to obtain judicial review of their orders. It will also apply to actions to prevent officers from acting in excess of their authority or under authority not validly conferred, cf. *Philadelphia Co. v. Stimson,* 223 U.S. 605 (1912), or from enforcing unconstitutional enactments, cf. *Ex parte Young,* 209 U.S. 123 (1908); *Ex parte La Prade,* 289 U.S. 444 (1933). In general it will apply whenever effective relief would call for corrective behavior by the one then having official status and power, rather than one who has lost that status and power through ceasing to hold office. Cf. *Land v. Dollar,* 330 U.S. 731 (1947); *Larson v. Domestic & Foreign Commerce Corp.,* 337 U.S. 682 (1949). Excluded from the operation of the amended rule will be the relatively infrequent actions which are directed to securing money judgments against the named officers enforceable against their personal assets; in these cases Rule 25(a)(1), not Rule 25(d), applies to the question of substitution. Examples are actions against officers seeking to make them pay damages out of their own pockets for defamatory utterances or other misconduct in some way related to the office, see *Barr v. Matteo,* 360 U.S. 564 (1959); *Howard v. Lyons,* 360 U.S. 593 (1959); *Gregoire v. Biddle,* 177 F.2d 579 (2d Cir.1949), cert. denied, 339 U.S. 949 (1950). Another example is the anomalous action for a tax refund against a collector of internal revenue, see *Ignelzi v. Granger,* 16 F.R.D. 517 (W.D.Pa.1955), 28 U.S.C. § 2006, 4 Moore, supra, ¶25.05, p. 531; but see 28 U.S.C. § 1346(a)(1), authorizing the bringing of such suits against the United States rather than the officer.

Automatic substitution under the amended rule, being merely a procedural device for substituting a successor for a past officeholder as a party, is distinct from and does not affect any substantive issues which may be involved in the action. Thus a defense of immunity from suit will remain in the case despite a substitution.

Where the successor does not intend to pursue the policy of his predecessor which gave rise to the lawsuit, it will be open to him, after substitution, as plaintiff to seek voluntary dismissal of the action, or as defendant to seek to have the action dismissed as moot or to take other appropriate steps to avert a judgment or decree. Contrast *Ex parte La Prade,* supra; *Allen v. Regents of the University System,* 304 U.S. 439 (1938); *McGrath v. National Assn. of Mfgrs.,* 344 U.S. 804 (1952); *Danenberg v. Cohen,* 213 F.2d 944 (7th Cir.1954).

As the present amendment of Rule 25(d)(1) eliminates a specified time period to secure substitution of public officers, the reference in Rule 6(b) (regarding enlargement of time) to Rule 25 will no longer apply to these public-officer substitutions.

As to substitution on appeal, the rules of the appellate courts should be consulted.

Subdivision (d)(2). This provision, applicable in "official capacity" cases as described above, will encourage the use of the official title without any mention of the officer individually, thereby recognizing the intrinsic character of the action and helping to eliminate concern with the problem of substitution. If for any reason it seems desirable to add the individual's name, this may be done upon motion or on the court's initiative; thereafter the procedure of amended Rule 25(d)(1) will apply if the individual named ceases to hold office.

For examples of naming the officer or title rather than the officeholder, see *Annot.,* 102 A.L.R. 943, 948–52; *Comment,* 50 Mich.L.Rev. 443, 450 (1952); cf. 26 U.S.C. § 7484. Where an action is brought by or against a board or agency with continuity of existence, it has been often decided that there is no need to name the individual members and substitution is unnecessary when the personnel changes. 4 Moore, supra,

¶25.09, p. 536. The practice encouraged by amended Rule 25(d)(2) is similar.

1963 Amendment

Present Rule 25(a)(1), together with present Rule 6(b), results in an inflexible requirement that an action be dismissed as to a deceased party if substitution is not carried out within a fixed period measured from the time of the death. The hardships and inequities of this unyielding requirement plainly appear from the cases. See, e.g., *Anderson v. Yungkau,* 329 U.S. 482, 67 S.Ct. 428, 91 L.Ed. 436 (1947); *Iovino v. Waterson,* 274 F.2d 41 (1959), cert. denied, *Carlin v. Sovino,* 362 U.S. 949, 80 S.Ct. 860, 4 L.Ed.2d 867 (1960); *Perry v. Allen,* 239 F.2d 107 (5th Cir.1956); *Starnes v. Pennsylvania R.R.,* 26 F.R.D. 625 (E.D.N.Y.), aff'd per curiam, 295 F.2d 704 (2d Cir.1961), cert. denied, 369 U.S. 813, 82 S.Ct. 688, 7 L.Ed.2d 612 (1962); *Zdanok v. Glidden Co.,* 28 F.R.D. 346 (S.D.N.Y.1961). See also 4 Moore's *Federal Practice* ¶25.01[9] (Supp.1960); 2 Barron & Holtzoff, *Federal Practice & Procedure* § 621, at 420–21 (Wright ed.1961).

The amended rule establishes a time limit for the motion to substitute based not upon the time of the death, but rather upon the time information of the death is provided by means of a suggestion of death upon the record, i.e. service of a statement of the fact of the death. Cf. Ill.Ann.Stat., c. 110, § 54(2) (Smith-Hurd 1956). The motion may not be made later than 90 days after the service of the statement unless the period is extended pursuant to Rule 6(b), as amended. See the Advisory Committee's Note to amended Rule 6(b). See also the new Official Form 30.

A motion to substitute may be made by any party or by the representative of the deceased party without awaiting the suggestion of death. Indeed, the motion will usually be so made. If a party or the representative of the deceased party desires to limit the time within which another may make the motion, he may do so by suggesting the death upon the record.

A motion to substitute made within the prescribed time will ordinarily be granted, but under the permissive language of the first sentence of the amended rule ("the court may order") it may be denied by the court in the exercise of a sound discretion if made long after the death—as can occur if the suggestion of death is not made or is delayed—and circumstances have arisen rendering it unfair to allow substitution. Cf. *Anderson v. Yungkau,* supra, 329 U.S. at 485, 486, 67 S.Ct. at 430, 431, 91 L.Ed. 436, where it was noted under the present rule that settlement and distribution of the estate of a deceased defendant might be so far advanced as to warrant denial of a motion for substitution even though made within the time limit prescribed by that rule. Accordingly, a party interested in securing substitution under the amended rule should not assume that he can rest indefinitely awaiting the suggestion of death before he makes his motion to substitute.

1987 Amendment

The amendments are technical. No substantive change is intended.

2007 Amendment

The language of Rule 25 has been amended as part of the general restyling of the Civil Rules to make them more easily understood and to make style and terminology consistent throughout the rules. These changes are intended to be stylistic only.

Former Rule 25(d)(2) is transferred to become Rule 17(d) because it deals with designation of a public officer, not substitution.

HISTORICAL NOTES

Effective and Applicability Provisions

1961 Amendments. Amendment adopted on Apr. 17, 1961, effective July 19, 1961, see rule 86(d).

TITLE V. DISCLOSURES AND DISCOVERY

ADVISORY COMMITTEE'S EXPLANATORY STATEMENT CONCERNING 1970 AMENDMENTS TO DISCOVERY RULES

This statement is intended to serve as a general introduction to the amendments of Rules 26–37, concerning discovery, as well as related amendments of other rules. A separate note of customary scope is appended to amendments proposed for each rule. This statement provides a framework for the consideration of individual rule changes.

Changes in the Discovery Rules

The discovery rules, as adopted in 1938, were a striking and imaginative departure from tradition. It was expected from the outset that they would be important, but experience has shown them to play an even larger role than was initially foreseen. Although the discovery rules have been amended since 1938, the changes were relatively few and narrowly focused, made in order to remedy specific defects. The amendments now proposed reflect the first comprehensive review of the discovery rules undertaken since 1938. These amendments make substantial changes in the discovery rules. Those summarized here are among the more important changes.

Scope of Discovery. New provisions are made and existing provisions changed affecting the scope of discovery: (1) The contents of insurance policies are made discoverable (Rule 26(b)(2)). (2) A showing of good cause is no longer required for discovery of documents and things and entry upon land (Rule 34). However, a showing of need is required for discovery of "trial preparation" materials other than a party's discovery of his own statement and a witness' discovery of his own statement; and protection is afforded against disclosure in such documents of mental impressions, conclusions, opinions, or legal theories concerning the litigation. (Rule 26(b)(3)). (3) Provision is made for discovery with respect to experts retained for trial preparation, and particularly those experts who will be called to testify at trial (Rule 26(b)(4)). (4) It is provided that interrogatories and requests for admission are not objectionable simply because they relate to matters of opinion or contention, subject of course to the supervisory power of the court (Rules 33(b), 36(a)). (5) Medical examination is made available as to certain nonparties. (Rule 35(a)).

Mechanics of Discovery. A variety of changes are made in the mechanics of the discovery process, affecting the sequence and timing of discovery, the respective obligations of the parties with respect to requests, responses, and motions for court orders, and the related powers of the court to enforce discovery requests and to protect against their abusive use. A new provision eliminates the automatic grant of priority in discovery to one side (Rule 26(d)). Another provides that a party is not under a duty to supplement his responses to requests for discovery, except as specified (Rule 26(e)).

Other changes in the mechanics of discovery are designed to encourage extrajudicial discovery with a minimum of court intervention. Among these are the following: (1) The requirement that a plaintiff seek leave of court for early discovery requests is eliminated or reduced, and motions for a court order under Rule 34 are made unnecessary. Motions under Rule 35 are continued. (2) Answers and objections are to be served together and an enlargement of the time for response is provided. (3) The party seeking discovery, rather than the objecting party, is made responsible for invoking judicial determination of discovery disputes not resolved by the parties. (4) Judicial sanctions are tightened with respect to unjustified insistence upon or objection to discovery. These changes bring Rules 33, 34, and 36 substantially into line with the procedure now provided for depositions.

Failure to amend Rule 35 in the same way is based upon two considerations. First, the Columbia Survey (described below) finds that only about 5 percent of medical examinations require court motions, of which about half result in court orders. Second and of greater importance, the interest of the person to be examined in the privacy of his person was recently stressed by the Supreme Court in *Schlagenhauf v. Holder*, 379 U.S. 104 (1964). The court emphasized the trial judge's responsibility to assure that the medical examination was justified, particularly as to its scope.

Rearrangement of Rules. A limited rearrangement of the discovery rules has been made, whereby certain provisions are transferred from one rule to another. The reasons for this rearrangement are discussed below in a separate section of this statement and the details are set out in a table at the end of this statement.

Optional Procedures. In two instances, new optional procedures have been made available. A new procedure is provided to a party seeking to take the deposition of a corporation or other organization (Rule 30(b)(6)). A party on whom interrogatories have been served requesting information derivable from his business records may under specified circumstances produce the records rather than give answers (Rule 33(c)).

Other Changes. This summary of changes is by no means exhaustive. Various changes have been made in order to improve, tighten, or clarify particular provisions, to resolve conflicts in the case law, and to improve language. All changes, whether mentioned here or not, are discussed in the appropriate note for each rule.

A Field Survey of Discovery Practice

Despite widespread acceptance of discovery as an essential part of litigation, disputes have inevitably arisen concerning the values claimed for discovery and abuses alleged to exist. Many disputes about discovery relate to particular rule provisions or court decisions and can be studied in traditional fashion with a view to specific amendment. Since discovery is in large measure extra-judicial, however, even these disputes may be enlightened by a study of discovery "in the field." And some of the larger questions concerning discovery can be pursued only by a study of its operation at the law office level and in unreported cases.

The Committee, therefore, invited the Project for Effective Justice of Columbia Law School to conduct a field survey of discovery. Funds were obtained from the Ford Foundation and the Walter E. Meyer Research Institute of Law, Inc. The survey was carried on under the direction of Prof. Maurice Rosenberg of Columbia Law School. The Project for Effective Justice has submitted a report to the Committee entitled "Field Survey of Federal Pretrial Discovery" (hereafter referred to as the Columbia Survey). The Committee is deeply grateful for the benefit of this extensive undertaking and is most appreciative of the cooperation of the Project and the funding organizations. The Committee is particularly grateful to Professor Rosenberg who not only directed the survey but has given much time in order to assist the Committee in assessing the results.

The Columbia Survey concludes, in general, that there is no empirical evidence to warrant a fundamental change in the philosophy of the discovery rules. No widespread or profound failings are disclosed in the scope or availability of discovery. The costs of discovery do not appear to be oppressive, as a general matter, either in relation to ability to pay or to the stakes of the litigation. Discovery frequently provides evidence that would not otherwise be available to the parties and thereby makes for a fairer trial or settlement. On the other hand, no positive evidence is found that discovery promotes settlement.

More specific findings of the Columbia Survey are described in other Committee notes, in relation to particular rule provisions and amendments. Those interested in more detailed information may obtain it from the Project for Effective Justice.

Rearrangement of the Discovery Rules

The present discovery rules are structured entirely in terms of individual discovery devices, except for Rule 27 which deals with perpetuation of testimony, and Rule 37 which provides sanctions to enforce discovery. Thus, Rules 26 and 28 to 32 are in terms addressed only to the taking of a deposition of a party or third person. Rules 33 to 36 then deal in succession with four additional discovery devices: Written interrogatories to parties, production for inspection of documents and things, physical or mental examination and requests for admission.

Under the rules as promulgated in 1938, therefore, each of the discovery devices was separate and self-contained. A defect of this arrangement is that there is no natural location in the discovery rules for provisions generally applicable to all discovery or to several discovery devices. From 1938 until the present, a few amendments have applied a discovery provision to several rules. For example, in 1948, the scope of deposition discovery in Rule 26(b) and the provision for protective orders in Rule 30(b) were incorporated by reference in Rules 33 and 34. The arrangement was adequate so long as there were few provisions governing discovery generally and these provisions were relatively simple.

As will be seen, however, a series of amendments are now proposed which govern most or all of the discovery devices. Proposals of a similar nature will probably be made in the future. Under these circumstances, it is very desirable, even necessary, that the discovery rules contain one rule addressing itself to discovery generally.

Rule 26 is obviously the most appropriate rule for this purpose. One of its subdivisions, Rule 26(b), in terms governs only scope of deposition discovery, but it has been expressly incorporated by reference in Rules 33 and 34 and is treated by courts as setting a general standard. By means of a transfer to Rule 26 of the provisions for protective orders now contained in Rule 30(b), and a transfer from Rule 26 of provisions addressed exclusively to depositions, Rule 26 is converted into a rule concerned with discovery generally. It becomes a convenient vehicle for the inclusion of new provisions dealing with the scope, timing, and regulation of discovery. Few additional transfers are needed. See table showing rearrangement of rules, set out following this statement.

There are, to be sure, disadvantages in transferring any provision from one rule to another. Familiarity with the present pattern, reinforced by the references made by prior court decisions and the various secondary writings about the rules, is not lightly to be sacrificed. Revision of treatises and other reference works is burdensome and costly. Moreover, many States have adopted the existing pattern as a model for their rules.

On the other hand, the amendments now proposed will in any event require revision of texts and reference works as well as reconsideration by States following the Federal model. If these amendments are to be incorporated in an understandable way, a rule with general discovery provisions is needed. As will be seen, the proposed rearrangement produces a more coherent and intelligible pattern for the discovery rules taken as a whole. The difficulties described are those encountered whenever statutes are reexamined and revised. Failure to rearrange the discovery rules now would freeze the present scheme, making future change even more difficult.

Table Showing Rearrangement of Rules

Existing Rule No.	New Rule No.
26(a)	30(a), 31(a)
26(c)	30(c)
26(d)	32(a)
26(e)	32(b)
26(f)	32(c)
30(a)	30(b)
30(b)	26(c)
32	32(d)

Rule 26. Duty to Disclose; General Provisions Governing Discovery

(a) Required Disclosures.

(1) ***Initial Disclosure.***

(A) *In General.* Except as exempted by Rule 26(a)(1)(B) or as otherwise stipulated or ordered by the court, a party must, without awaiting a discovery request, provide to the other parties:

(i) the name and, if known, the address and telephone number of each individual likely to have discoverable information—along with the subjects of that information—that the disclosing party may use to support its claims or defenses, unless the use would be solely for impeachment;

(ii) a copy—or a description by category and location—of all documents, electronically stored information, and tangible things that the disclosing party has in its possession, custody, or control and may use to support its claims or defenses, unless the use would be solely for impeachment;

(iii) a computation of each category of damages claimed by the disclosing party—who must also make available for inspection and copying as under Rule 34 the documents or other evidentiary material, unless privileged or protected from disclosure, on which each computation is based, including materials bearing on the nature and extent of injuries suffered; and

(iv) for inspection and copying as under Rule 34, any insurance agreement under which an insurance business may be liable to satisfy all or part of a possible judgment in the action or to indemnify or reimburse for payments made to satisfy the judgment.

(B) *Proceedings Exempt from Initial Disclosure.* The following proceedings are exempt from initial disclosure:

(i) an action for review on an administrative record;

(ii) a forfeiture action in rem arising from a federal statute;

(iii) a petition for habeas corpus or any other proceeding to challenge a criminal conviction or sentence;

(iv) an action brought without an attorney by a person in the custody of the United States, a state, or a state subdivision;

(v) an action to enforce or quash an administrative summons or subpoena;

(vi) an action by the United States to recover benefit payments;

(vii) an action by the United States to collect on a student loan guaranteed by the United States;

(viii) a proceeding ancillary to a proceeding in another court; and

(ix) an action to enforce an arbitration award.

(C) *Time for Initial Disclosures—In General.* A party must make the initial disclosures at or within 14 days after the parties' Rule 26(f) conference unless a different time is set by stipulation or court order, or unless a party objects during the conference that initial disclosures are not appropriate in this action and states the objection in the proposed discovery plan. In ruling on the objection, the court must determine what disclosures, if any, are to be made and must set the time for disclosure.

(D) *Time for Initial Disclosures—For Parties Served or Joined Later.* A party that is first served or otherwise joined after the Rule 26(f) conference must make the initial disclosures within 30 days after being served or joined, unless a different time is set by stipulation or court order.

(E) *Basis for Initial Disclosure; Unacceptable Excuses.* A party must make its initial disclosures based on the information then reasonably available to it. A party is not excused from making its disclosures because it has not fully investigated the case or because it challenges the sufficiency of another party's disclosures or because another party has not made its disclosures.

(2) ***Disclosure of Expert Testimony.***

(A) *In General.* In addition to the disclosures required by Rule 26(a)(1), a party must disclose to the other parties the identity of any witness it may use at trial to present evidence under Federal Rule of Evidence 702, 703, or 705.

(B) *Written Report.* Unless otherwise stipulated or ordered by the court, this disclosure must be accompanied by a written report—prepared and signed by the witness—if the witness is one retained or specially employed to provide expert testimony in the case or one whose duties as the party's employee regularly involve giving expert testimony. The report must contain:

(i) a complete statement of all opinions the witness will express and the basis and reasons for them;

(ii) the data or other information considered by the witness in forming them;

(iii) any exhibits that will be used to summarize or support them;

(iv) the witness's qualifications, including a list of all publications authored in the previous 10 years;

(v) a list of all other cases in which, during the previous four years, the witness testified as an expert at trial or by deposition; and

(vi) a statement of the compensation to be paid for the study and testimony in the case.

(C) *Time to Disclose Expert Testimony.* A party must make these disclosures at the times and in the sequence that the court orders. Absent a stipulation or a court order, the disclosures must be made:

(i) at least 90 days before the date set for trial or for the case to be ready for trial; or

(ii) if the evidence is intended solely to contradict or rebut evidence on the same subject matter identified by another party under Rule 26(a)(2)(B), within 30 days after the other party's disclosure.

(D) *Supplementing the Disclosure.* The parties must supplement these disclosures when required under Rule 26(e).

(3) ***Pretrial Disclosures.***

(A) *In General.* In addition to the disclosures required by Rule 26(a)(1) and (2), a party must provide to the other parties and promptly file the following information about the evidence that it may present at trial other than solely for impeachment:

(i) the name and, if not previously provided, the address and telephone number of each witness—separately identifying those the party expects to present and those it may call if the need arises;

(ii) the designation of those witnesses whose testimony the party expects to present by deposition and, if not taken stenographically, a transcript of the pertinent parts of the deposition; and

(iii) an identification of each document or other exhibit, including summaries of other evidence—separately identifying those items the party expects to offer and those it may offer if the need arises.

(B) *Time for Pretrial Disclosures; Objections.* Unless the court orders otherwise, these disclosures must be made at least 30 days before trial. Within 14 days after they are made, unless the court sets a different time, a party may serve and promptly file a list of the following objections: any objections to the use under Rule 32(a) of a deposition designated by another party under Rule 26(a)(3)(A)(ii); and any objection, together with the grounds for it, that may be made to the admissibility of materials identified under Rule 26(a)(3)(A)(iii). An objection not so made—except for one under Federal Rule of Evidence 402 or 403—is waived unless excused by the court for good cause.

(4) ***Form of Disclosures.*** Unless the court orders otherwise, all disclosures under Rule 26(a) must be in writing, signed, and served.

(b) Discovery Scope and Limits.

(1) ***Scope in General.*** Unless otherwise limited by court order, the scope of discovery is as follows: Parties may obtain discovery regarding any nonprivileged matter that is relevant to any party's claim or defense—including the existence, description, nature, custody, condition, and location of any documents or other tangible things and the identity and location of persons who know of any discoverable matter. For good cause, the court may order discovery of any matter relevant to the subject matter involved in the action. Relevant information need not be admissible at the trial if the discovery appears reasonably calculated to lead to the discovery of admissible evidence. All discovery is subject to the limitations imposed by Rule 26(b)(2)(C).

(2) ***Limitations on Frequency and Extent.***

(A) *When Permitted.* By order, the court may alter the limits in these rules on the number of depositions and interrogatories or on the length of depositions under Rule 30. By order or local rule, the court may also limit the number of requests under Rule 36.

(B) *Specific Limitations on Electronically Stored Information.* A party need not provide discovery of electronically stored information from sources that the party identifies as not reasonably accessible because of undue burden or cost. On motion to compel discovery or for a protective order, the party from whom discovery is sought must show that the information is not reasonably accessible because of undue burden or cost. If that showing is made, the court may nonetheless order discovery from such sources if the requesting party shows good cause, considering the limitations of Rule 26(b)(2)(C). The court may specify conditions for the discovery.

(C) *When Required.* On motion or on its own, the court must limit the frequency or extent of discovery otherwise allowed by these rules or by local rule if it determines that:

(i) the discovery sought is unreasonably cumulative or duplicative, or can be obtained from some other source that is more convenient, less burdensome, or less expensive;

(ii) the party seeking discovery has had ample opportunity to obtain the information by discovery in the action; or

(iii) the burden or expense of the proposed discovery outweighs its likely benefit, considering the needs of the case, the amount in controversy, the parties' resources, the importance of the issues at stake in the action, and the importance of the discovery in resolving the issues.

(3) ***Trial Preparation: Materials.***

(A) *Documents and Tangible Things.* Ordinarily, a party may not discover documents and tangible things that are prepared in anticipation of litigation or for trial by or for another party or its representative (including the other party's attorney, consultant, surety, indemnitor, insurer, or agent). But, subject to Rule 26(b)(4), those materials may be discovered if:

(i) they are otherwise discoverable under Rule 26(b)(1); and

(ii) the party shows that it has substantial need for the materials to prepare its case and cannot, without undue hardship, obtain their substantial equivalent by other means.

(B) *Protection Against Disclosure.* If the court orders discovery of those materials, it must protect against disclosure of the mental impressions, conclusions, opinions, or legal theories of a party's attorney or other representative concerning the litigation.

(C) *Previous Statement.* Any party or other person may, on request and without the required showing, obtain the person's own previous statement about the action or its subject matter. If the request is refused, the person may move for a court order, and Rule 37(a)(5) applies to the award of expenses. A previous statement is either:

(i) a written statement that the person has signed or otherwise adopted or approved; or

(ii) a contemporaneous stenographic, mechanical, electrical, or other recording—or a transcription of it—that recites substantially verbatim the person's oral statement.

(4) ***Trial Preparation: Experts.***

(A) *Expert Who May Testify.* A party may depose any person who has been identified as an expert whose opinions may be presented at trial. If Rule 26(a)(2)(B) requires a report from the expert, the deposition may be conducted only after the report is provided.

(B) *Expert Employed Only for Trial Preparation.* Ordinarily, a party may not, by interrogatories or deposition, discover facts known or opinions held by an expert who has been retained or specially employed by another party in anticipation of litigation or to prepare for trial and who is not expected to be called as a witness at trial. But a party may do so only:

(i) as provided in Rule 35(b); or

(ii) on showing exceptional circumstances under which it is impracticable for the party to obtain facts or opinions on the same subject by other means.

(C) *Payment.* Unless manifest injustice would result, the court must require that the party seeking discovery:

(i) pay the expert a reasonable fee for time spent in responding to discovery under Rule 26(b)(4)(A) or (B); and

(ii) for discovery under (B), also pay the other party a fair portion of the fees and expenses it reasonably incurred in obtaining the expert's facts and opinions.

(5) ***Claiming Privilege or Protecting Trial-Preparation Materials.***

(A) *Information Withheld.* When a party withholds information otherwise discoverable by claiming that the information is privileged or subject to protection as trial-preparation material, the party must:

(i) expressly make the claim; and

(ii) describe the nature of the documents, communications, or tangible things not produced or disclosed—and do so in a manner that, without revealing information itself privileged or protected, will enable other parties to assess the claim.

(B) *Information Produced.* If information produced in discovery is subject to a claim of privilege or of protection as trial-preparation material, the party making the claim may notify any party that received the information of the claim and the basis for it. After being notified, a party must promptly return, sequester, or destroy the specified information and any copies it has; must not use or disclose the information until the claim is resolved; must take reasonable steps to retrieve the information if the party disclosed it before being notified; and may promptly present the information to the court under seal for a determination of the claim. The producing party must preserve the information until the claim is resolved.

(c) Protective Orders.

(1) ***In General.*** A party or any person from whom discovery is sought may move for a protective order in the court where the action is pending—or as an alternative on matters relating to a deposition, in the court for the district where the deposition will be taken. The motion must include a certification that the movant has in good faith conferred or attempted to confer with other affected parties in an effort to resolve the dispute without court action. The court may, for good cause, issue an order to protect a party or person from annoyance, embarrassment, oppression, or undue burden or expense, including one or more of the following:

(A) forbidding the disclosure or discovery;

(B) specifying terms, including time and place, for the disclosure or discovery;

(C) prescribing a discovery method other than the one selected by the party seeking discovery;

(D) forbidding inquiry into certain matters, or limiting the scope of disclosure or discovery to certain matters;

(E) designating the persons who may be present while the discovery is conducted;

(F) requiring that a deposition be sealed and opened only on court order;

(G) requiring that a trade secret or other confidential research, development, or commercial information not be revealed or be revealed only in a specified way; and

(H) requiring that the parties simultaneously file specified documents or information in sealed envelopes, to be opened as the court directs.

(2) ***Ordering Discovery.*** If a motion for a protective order is wholly or partly denied, the court may, on just terms, order that any party or person provide or permit discovery.

(3) ***Awarding Expenses.*** Rule 37(a)(5) applies to the award of expenses.

(d) Timing and Sequence of Discovery.

(1) ***Timing.*** A party may not seek discovery from any source before the parties have conferred as required by Rule 26(f), except in a proceeding exempted from initial disclosure under Rule 26(a)(1)(B), or when authorized by these rules, by stipulation, or by court order.

(2) ***Sequence.*** Unless, on motion, the court orders otherwise for the parties' and witnesses' convenience and in the interests of justice:

(A) methods of discovery may be used in any sequence; and

(B) discovery by one party does not require any other party to delay its discovery.

(e) Supplementing Disclosures and Responses.

(1) ***In General.*** A party who has made a disclosure under Rule 26(a)—or who has responded to an interrogatory, request for production, or request for admission—must supplement or correct its disclosure or response:

(A) in a timely manner if the party learns that in some material respect the disclosure or response is incomplete or incorrect, and if the additional or corrective information has not otherwise been made known to the other parties during the discovery process or in writing; or

(B) as ordered by the court.

(2) ***Expert Witness.*** For an expert whose report must be disclosed under Rule 26(a)(2)(B), the party's duty to supplement extends both to information included in the report and to information given during the expert's deposition. Any additions or changes to this information must be disclosed by the time the party's pretrial disclosures under Rule 26(a)(3) are due.

(f) Conference of the Parties; Planning for Discovery.

(1) ***Conference Timing.*** Except in a proceeding exempted from initial disclosure under Rule 26(a)(1)(B) or when the court orders otherwise, the parties must confer as soon as practicable—and in any event at least 21 days before a scheduling conference is to be held or a scheduling order is due under Rule 16(b).

(2) ***Conference Content; Parties' Responsibilities.*** In conferring, the parties must consider the nature and basis of their claims and defenses and the possibilities for promptly settling or resolving the case; make or arrange for the disclosures required by Rule 26(a)(1); discuss any issues about preserving discoverable information; and develop a proposed discovery plan. The attorneys of record and all unrepresented parties that have appeared in the case are jointly responsible for arranging the conference, for attempting in good faith to agree on the proposed discovery plan, and for submitting to the court within 14 days after the conference a written report outlining the plan. The court may order the parties or attorneys to attend the conference in person.

(3) ***Discovery Plan.*** A discovery plan must state the parties' views and proposals on:

(A) what changes should be made in the timing, form, or requirement for disclosures under Rule 26(a), including a statement of when initial disclosures were made or will be made;

(B) the subjects on which discovery may be needed, when discovery should be completed, and whether discovery should be conducted in phases or be limited to or focused on particular issues;

(C) any issues about disclosure or discovery of electronically stored information, including the form or forms in which it should be produced;

(D) any issues about claims of privilege or of protection as trial-preparation materials, including—if the parties agree on a procedure to assert these claims after production—whether to ask the court to include their agreement in an order;

(E) what changes should be made in the limitations on discovery imposed under these rules or by local rule, and what other limitations should be imposed; and

(F) any other orders that the court should issue under Rule 26(c) or under Rule 16(b) and (c).

(4) ***Expedited Schedule.*** If necessary to comply with its expedited schedule for Rule 16(b) conferences, a court may by local rule:

(A) require the parties' conference to occur less than 21 days before the scheduling conference is held or a scheduling order is due under Rule 16(b); and

(B) require the written report outlining the discovery plan to be filed less than 14 days after the parties' conference, or excuse the parties from submitting a written report and permit them to report orally on their discovery plan at the Rule 16(b) conference.

(g) Signing Disclosures and Discovery Requests, Responses, and Objections.

(1) ***Signature Required; Effect of Signature.*** Every disclosure under Rule 26(a)(1) or (a)(3) and every discovery request, response, or objection must be signed by at least one attorney of record in the attorney's own name—or by the party personally, if unrepresented—and must state the signer's address, e-mail address, and telephone number. By signing, an attorney or party certifies that to the best of the person's knowledge, information, and belief formed after a reasonable inquiry:

(A) with respect to a disclosure, it is complete and correct as of the time it is made; and

(B) with respect to a discovery request, response, or objection, it is:

(i) consistent with these rules and warranted by existing law or by a nonfrivolous argument for extending, modifying, or reversing existing law, or for establishing new law;

(ii) not interposed for any improper purpose, such as to harass, cause unnecessary delay, or needlessly increase the cost of litigation; and

(iii) neither unreasonable nor unduly burdensome or expensive, considering the needs of the case, prior discovery in the case, the amount in controversy, and the importance of the issues at stake in the action.

(2) ***Failure to Sign.*** Other parties have no duty to act on an unsigned disclosure, request, response, or objection until it is signed, and the court must strike it unless a signature is promptly supplied after the omission is called to the attorney's or party's attention.

(3) ***Sanction for Improper Certification.*** If a certification violates this rule without substantial justification, the court, on motion or on its own, must impose an appropriate sanction on the signer, the party on whose behalf the signer was acting, or both. The sanction may include an order to pay the reasonable expenses, including attorney's fees, caused by the violation.

(Amended December 27, 1946, effective March 19, 1948; January 21, 1963, effective July 1, 1963; February 28, 1966, effective July 1, 1966; March 30, 1970, effective July 1, 1970; April 29, 1980, effective August 1, 1980; April 28, 1983, effective August 1, 1983; March 2, 1987, effective August 1, 1987; April 22, 1993, effective December 1, 1993; April 17, 2000, effective December 1, 2000; April 12, 2006, effective December 1, 2006; April 30, 2007, effective December 1, 2007.)

ADVISORY COMMITTEE NOTES

1937 Adoption

Note to Subdivision (a). This rule freely authorizes the taking of depositions under the same circumstances and by the same methods whether for the purpose of discovery or for the purpose of obtaining evidence. Many states have adopted this practice on account of its simplicity and effectiveness, safeguarding it by imposing such restrictions upon the subsequent use of the deposition at the trial or hearing as are deemed advisable. See Ark.Civ.Code (Crawford, 1934) §§ 606 to 607; Calif.Code Civ.Proc. (Deering, 1937) § 2021; 1 Colo.Stat.Ann. (1935) Code Civ.Proc. § 376; Idaho Code Ann. (1932) § 16–906; Ill.Rules of Pract.Rule 19 (Smith-Hurd Ill.Stats. c. 110, § 259.19); Smith-Hurd Ill.Stats. c. 51, § 24; 2 Ind.Stat.Ann. (Burns, 1933) §§ 2–1501, 2–1506; Ky. Codes (Carroll, 1932) Civ.Pract. § 557; 1 Mo.Rev.Stat. (1929) § 1753; 4 Mont.Rev.Codes Ann. (1935) § 10645; Neb.Comp. Stat. (1929) ch. 20, §§ 1246–7; 4 Nev.Comp.Laws (Hillyer, 1929) § 9001; 2 N.H.Pub.Laws (1926) ch. 337, § 1; N.C.Code Ann. (1935) § 1809; 2 N.D.Comp.Laws Ann. (1913) §§ 7889 to 7897; 2 Ohio Gen.Code Ann. (Page, 1926) §§ 11525–6; 1 Ore.Code Ann. (1930) Tit. 9, § 1503; 1 S.D.Comp.Laws (1929) §§ 2713–16; Vernon's Ann.Civ.Stats. Tex. arts. 3738, 3752, 3769; Utah Rev.Stat.Ann. (1933) § 104–51–7; Wash.Rules of Practice adopted by the Supreme Ct., Rule 8, 2 Wash.Rev.Stat.Ann. (Remington, 1932) § 308–8; W.Va.Code (1931) ch. 57, art. 4, § 1. Compare [former] Equity Rules 47 (Depositions—To be Taken in Exceptional Instances); 54 (Depositions Under Revised Statutes, §§ 863, 865, 866, 867—Cross Examination); 58 (Discovery—Interrogatories—Inspection and Production of Documents—Admission of Execution or Genuineness).

This and subsequent rules incorporate, modify, and broaden the provisions for depositions under U.S.C., Title 28, [former] §§ 639 (Depositions *de bene esse;* when and where taken; notice), 640 (Same; mode of taking), 641 (Same; transmission to court), 644 (Depositions under *dedimus potestatem* and *in perpetuam*), 646 (Deposition under *dedimus potestatem*; how taken). These statutes are superseded in so far as they differ from this and subsequent rules. U.S.C. Title 28, [former] § 643 (Depositions; taken in mode prescribed by State laws) is superseded by the third sentence of Subdivision (a).

While a number of states permit discovery only from parties or their agents, others either make no distinction between parties or agents of parties and ordinary witnesses, or authorize the taking of ordinary depositions, without restriction, from any persons who have knowledge of relevant facts. See Ark.Civ.Code (Crawford, 1934) §§ 606 to

607; 1 Idaho Code Ann. (1932) § 16–906; Ill.Rules of Pract., Rule 19 (Smith-Hurd Ill.Stats. c. 110, § 259.19); Smith-Hurd Ill.Stats. c. 51, § 24; 2 Ind.Stat.Ann. (Burns, 1933) § 2–1501; Ky.Codes (Carroll, 1932) Civ.Pract. §§ 554 to 558; 2 Md. Ann.Code (Bagby, 1924) Art. 35, § 21; 2 Minn.Stat. (Mason, 1927) § 9820; Mo.St.Ann. §§ 1753, 1759, pp. 4023, 4026; Neb.Comp.Stat. (1929) ch. 20, §§ 1246–7; 2 N.H.Pub.Laws (1926) ch. 337, § 1; 2 N.D.Comp.Laws Ann. (1913) § 7897; 2 Ohio Gen.Code Ann. (Page, 1926) §§ 11525–6; 1 S.D.Comp. Laws (1929) §§ 2713–16; Vernon's Ann.Civil Stats.Tex. arts. 3738, 3752, 3769; Utah Rev.Stat.Ann. (1933) § 104–51–7; Wash.Rules of Practice adopted by Supreme Ct., Rule 8, 2 Wash.Rev.Stat.Ann. (Remington, 1932) § 308–8; W.Va.Code (1931) ch. 57, art. 4, § 1.

The more common practice in the United States is to take depositions on notice by the party desiring them, without any order from the court, and this has been followed in these rules. See Calif.Code Civ.Proc. (Deering, 1937) § 2031; 2 Fla.Comp.Gen.Laws Ann. (1927) §§ 4405–7; 1 Idaho Code Ann. (1932) § 16–902; Ill.Rules of Pract., Rule 19 (Smith-Hurd Ill.Stats. c. 110, § 259.19); Smith-Hurd Ill.Stats. c. 51, § 24; 2 Ind.Stat.Ann. (Burns, 1933) § 2–1502; Kan.Gen.Stat. Ann. (1935) § 60–2827; Ky.Codes (Carroll, 1932) Civ.Pract. § 565; 2 Minn.Stat. (Mason, 1927) § 9820; Mo.St.Ann. § 1761, p. 4029; 4 Mont.Rev.Codes Ann. (1935) § 10651; Nev.Comp.Laws (Hillyer, 1929) § 9002; N.C.Code Ann. (1935) § 1809; 2 N.D.Comp.Laws Ann. (1913) § 7895; Utah Rev.Stat.Ann. (1933) § 104–51–8.

Note to Subdivision (b). While the old chancery practice limited discovery to facts supporting the case of the party seeking it, this limitation has been largely abandoned by modern legislation. See Ala.Code Ann. (Michie, 1928) §§ 7764 to 7773; 2 Ind.Stat.Ann. (Burns, 1933) §§ 2–1028, 2–1506, 2–1728–2–1732; Iowa Code (1935) § 11185; Ky. Codes (Carroll, 1932) Civ.Pract. §§ 557, 606(8); La.Code Pract. (Dart, 1932) arts. 347–356; 2 Mass.Gen.Laws (Ter.Ed., 1932) ch. 231, §§ 61 to 67; Mo.St.Ann. §§ 1753, 1759, pp. 4023, 4026; Neb.Comp.Stat. (1929) §§ 20–1246, 20–1247; 2 N.H.Pub.Laws (1926) ch. 337, § 1; 2 Ohio Gen.Code Ann. (Page, 1926) §§ 11497, 11526; Vernon's Ann.Civ.Stats.Tex. arts. 3738, 3753, 3769; Wis.Stat. (1935) § 326.12; Ontario Consol.Rules of Pract. (1928) Rules 237–347; Quebec Code of Civ.Proc. (Curran, 1922) §§ 286 to 290.

Note to Subdivisions (d), (e), and (f). The restrictions here placed upon the use of depositions at the trial or hearing are substantially the same as those provided in U.S.C., Title 28, [former] § 641, for depositions taken, *de bene esse,* with the additional provision that any deposition may be used when the court finds the existence of exceptional circumstances. Compare English Rules Under the Judicature Act (The Annual Practice, 1937) O. 37, r. 18 (with additional provision permitting use of deposition by consent of the parties). See also [former] Equity Rule 64 (Former Depositions, Etc. May be Used Before Master); and 2 Minn. Stat. (Mason, 1927) § 9835 (Use in a subsequent action of a deposition filed in a previously dismissed action between the same parties and involving the same subject matter).

1946 Amendment

Note. Subdivision (a). The amendment eliminates the requirement of leave of court for the taking of a deposition except where a plaintiff seeks to take a deposition within 20 days after the commencement of the action. The retention of the requirement where a deposition is sought by a plaintiff within 20 days of the commencement of the action protects a defendant who has not had an opportunity to retain counsel and inform himself as to the nature of the suit; the plaintiff, of course, needs no such protection. The present rule forbids the plaintiff to take a deposition, without leave of court, before the answer is served. Sometimes the defendant delays the serving of an answer for more than 20 days, but as 20 days are sufficient time for him to obtain a lawyer, there is no reason to forbid the plaintiff to take a deposition without leave merely because the answer has not been served. In all cases, Rule 30(a) empowers the court, for cause shown, to alter the time of the taking of a deposition, and Rule 30(b) contains provisions giving ample protection to persons who are unreasonably pressed. The modified practice here adopted is along the line of that followed in various states. See e.g., 8 Mo.Rev.Stat.Ann.1939, § 1917; 2 Burns' Ind.Stat.Ann.1933, § 2–1506.

Subdivision (b). The amendments to subdivision (b) make clear the broad scope of examination and that it may cover not only evidence for use at the trial but also inquiry into matters in themselves inadmissible as evidence but which will lead to the discovery of such evidence. The purpose of discovery is to allow a broad search for facts, the names of witnesses, or any other matters which may aid a party in the preparation or presentation of his case. *Engl v. Aetna Life Ins. Co.*, C.C.A.2, 1943, 139 F.2d 469; *Mahler v. Pennsylvania R. Co.*, E.D.N.Y.1945, 8 Fed.Rules Serv. 33.351, Case 1. In such a preliminary inquiry admissibility at trial should not be the test as to whether the information sought is within the scope of proper examination. Such a standard unnecessarily curtails the utility of discovery practice. Of course, matters entirely without bearing either as direct evidence or as leads to evidence are not within the scope of inquiry, but to the extent that the examination develops useful information, it functions successfully as an instrument of discovery, even if it produces no testimony directly admissible. *Lewis v. United Air Lines Transportation Corp.*, D.Conn.1939, 27 F.Supp. 946; *Engl v. Aetna Life Ins. Co.*, supra; *Mahler v. Pennsylvania R. Co.*, supra; *Bloomer v. Sirian Lamp Co.*, D.Del.1944, 8 Fed.Rules Serv. 26b.31, Case 3; *Rosseau v. Langley*, N.Y.1945, 9 Fed.Rules Serv. 34.41, Case 1 (Rule 26 contemplates "examinations not merely for the narrow purpose of adducing testimony which may be offered in evidence but also for the broad discovery of information which may be useful in preparation for trial."); *Olson Transportation Co. v. Socony-Vacuum Co.*, E.D.Wis. 1944, 8 Fed.Rules Serv. 34.41, Case 2 (". . . the Rules . . . permit 'fishing' for evidence as they should."); Note, 1945, 45 Col.L.Rev. 482. Thus hearsay, while inadmissible itself, may suggest testimony which properly may be proved. Under Rule 26(b) several cases, however, have erroneously limited discovery on the basis of admissibility, holding that the word "relevant" in effect meant "material and competent under the rules of evidence". *Poppino v. Jones Store Co.*, W.D.Mo.1940, 1 F.R.D. 215, 3 Fed.Rules Serv. 26b.5, Case 1; *Benevento v. A. & P. Food Stores, Inc.*, E.D.N.Y.1939, 26 F.Supp. 424. Thus it has been said that inquiry might not be made into statements or other matters which, when disclosed, amounted only to hearsay. *See Maryland for use of Montvila v. Pan-American Bus Lines, Inc.*, D.Md.1940, 1 F.R.D. 213, 3 Fed.Rules Serv. 26b.211, Case 3; *Gitto v. "Italia," Societa Anonima Di Navigazione*, E.D.N.Y.1940, 31 F.Supp. 567; *Rose Silk Mills, Inc. v. Insurance Co. of North*

America, S.D.N.Y.1939, 29 F.Supp. 504; *Colpak v. Hetterick,* E.D.N.Y.1941, 40 F.Supp. 350; *Matthies v. Peter F. Connolly Co.,* E.D.N.Y.1941, 6 Fed.Rules Serv. 30a.22, Case 1, 2 F.R.D. 277; *Matter of Examination of Citizens Casualty Co. of New York,* S.D.N.Y.1942, 3 F.R.D. 171, 7 Fed.Rules Serv. 26b.211, Case 1; *United States v. Silliman,* D.C.N.J.1944, 8 Fed.Rules Serv. 26b.52, Case 1. The contrary and better view, however, has often been stated. See, e.g., *Engl v. Aetna Life Ins. Co.,* supra; *Stevenson v. Melady,* S.D.N.Y. 1940, 3 Fed.Rules Serv. 26b.31, Case 1, 1 F.R.D. 329; *Lewis v. United Air Lines Transport Corp.,* supra; *Application of Zenith Radio Corp.,* E.D.Pa.1941, 4 Fed.Rules Serv. 30b.21, Case 1, 1 F.R.D. 627; *Steingut v. Guaranty Trust Co. of New York,* S.D.N.Y.1941, 1 F.R.D. 723, 4 Fed.Rules Serv. 26b.5, Case 2; *DeSeversky v. Republic Aviation Corp.,* E.D.N.Y.1941, 2 F.R.D. 183, 5 Fed.Rules Serv. 26b.31, Case 5; *Moore v. George A. Hormel & Co.,* S.D.N.Y.1942, 6 Fed.Rules Serv. 30b.41, Case 1, 2 F.R.D. 340; *Hercules Powder Co. v. Rohm & Haas Co.,* D.Del.1943, 7 Fed.Rules Serv. 45b.311, Case 2, 3 F.R.D. 302; *Bloomer v. Sirian Lamp Co.,* supra; *Crosby Steam Gage & Valve Co. v. Manning, Maxwell & Moore, Inc.,* D.Mass.1944, 8 Fed.Rules Serv. 26b.31, Case 1; *Patterson Oil Terminals, Inc. v. Charles Kurz & Co., Inc.,* E.D.Pa.1945, 9 Fed.Rules Serv. 33.321, Case 2; *Pueblo Trading Co. v. Reclamation Dist. No. 1500,* N.D.Cal.1945, 9 Fed.Rules Serv. 33.321, Case 4, 4 F.R.D. 471. See also discussion as to the broad scope of discovery in *Hoffman v. Palmer,* C.C.A.2, 1942, 129 F.2d 976, 995–997, affirmed 63 S.Ct. 477, 318 U.S. 109, 87 L.Ed. 645; Note, 1945, 45 Col.L.Rev. 482.

1963 Amendment

This amendment conforms to the amendment of Rule 28(b). See the next-to-last paragraph of the Advisory Committee's Note to that amendment.

1966 Amendment

The requirement that the plaintiff obtain leave of court in order to serve notice of taking of a deposition within 20 days after commencement of the action gives rise to difficulties when the prospective deponent is about to become unavailable for examination. The problem is not confined to admiralty, but has been of special concern in that context because of the mobility of vessels and their personnel. When Rule 26 was adopted as Admiralty Rule 30A in 1961, the problem was alleviated by permitting depositions *de bene esse,* for which leave of court is not required. See Advisory Committee's Note to Admiralty Rule 30A (1961).

A continuing study is being made in the effort to devise a modification of the 20-day rule appropriate to both the civil and admiralty practice to the end that Rule 26(a) shall state a uniform rule applicable alike to what are now civil actions and suits in admiralty. Meanwhile, the exigencies of maritime litigation require preservation, for the time being at least, of the traditional *de bene esse* procedure for the post-unification counterpart of the present suit in admiralty. Accordingly, the amendment provides for continued availability of that procedure in admiralty and maritime claims within the meaning of Rule 9(h).

1970 Amendment

A limited rearrangement of the discovery rules is made, whereby certain rule provisions are transferred, as follows: Existing Rule 26(a) is transferred to Rules 30(a) and 31(a). Existing Rule 26(c) is transferred to Rule 30(c). Existing Rules 26(d), (e), and (f) are transferred to Rule 32. Revisions of the transferred provisions, if any, are discussed in the notes appended to Rules 30, 31, and 32. In addition, Rule 30(b) is transferred to Rule 26(c). The purpose of this rearrangement is to establish Rule 26 as a rule governing discovery in general. (The reasons are set out in the Advisory Committee's explanatory statement.)

Subdivision (a)—Discovery Devices. This is a new subdivision listing all of the discovery devices provided in the discovery rules and establishing the relationship between the general provisions of Rule 26 and the specific rules for particular discovery devices. The provision that the frequency of use of these methods is not limited confirms existing law. It incorporates in general form a provision now found in Rule 33.

Subdivision (b)—Scope of Discovery. This subdivision is recast to cover the scope of discovery generally. It regulates the discovery obtainable through any of the discovery devices listed in Rule 26(a).

All provisions as to scope of discovery are subject to the initial qualification that the court may limit discovery in accordance with these rules. Rule 26(c) (transferred from 30(b)) confers broad powers on the courts to regulate or prevent discovery even though the materials sought are within the scope of 26(b), and these powers have always been freely exercised. For example, a party's income tax return is generally held not privileged, 2A Barron & Holtzoff, *Federal Practice and Procedure,* § 651.2 (Wright ed. 1961), and yet courts have recognized that interests in privacy may call for a measure of extra protection. E.g., *Wiesenberger v. W. E. Hutton & Co.,* 35 F.R.D. 556 (S.D.N.Y.1964). Similarly, the courts have in appropriate circumstances protected materials that are primarily of an impeaching character. These two types of materials merely illustrate the many situations, not capable of governance by precise rule, in which courts must exercise judgment. The new subsections in Rule 26(b) do not change existing law with respect to such situations.

Subdivision (b)(1)—In General. The language is changed to provide for the scope of discovery in general terms. The existing subdivision, although in terms applicable only to depositions, is incorporated by reference in existing Rules 33 and 34. Since decisions as to relevance to the subject matter of the action are made for discovery purposes well in advance of trial, a flexible treatment of relevance is required and the making of discovery, whether voluntary or under court order, is not a concession or determination of relevance for purposes of trial. *Cf.* 4 *Moore's Federal Practice* ¶26–16[1] (2d ed. 1966).

Subdivision (b)(2)—Insurance Policies. Both the cases and commentators are sharply in conflict on the question whether defendant's liability insurance coverage is subject to discovery in the usual situation when the insurance coverage is not itself admissible and does not bear on another issue in the case. Examples of Federal cases requiring disclosure and supporting comments: *Cook v. Welty,* 253 F.Supp. 875 (D.D.C.1966) (cases cited); *Johanek v. Aberle,* 27 F.R.D. 272

(D.Mont.1961); Williams, *Discovery of Dollar Limits in Liability Policies in Automobile Tort Cases,* 10 Ala.L.Rev. 355 (1958); Thode, *Some Reflections on the 1957 Amendments to the Texas Rules,* 37 Tex.L.Rev. 33, 40–42 (1958). Examples of Federal cases refusing disclosure and supporting comments: *Bisserier v. Manning,* 207 F.Supp. 476 (D.N.J.1962); *Cooper v. Stender,* 30 F.R.D. 389 (E.D.Tenn.1962); Frank, *Discovery and Insurance, Coverage,* 1959 Ins.L.J. 281; Fournier, *Pre-trial Discovery of Insurance Coverage and Limits,* 28 Ford.L.Rev. 215 (1959).

The division in reported cases is close. State decisions based on provisions similar to the federal rules are similarly divided. See cases collected in 2A Barron & Holtzoff, *Federal Practice and Procedure* § 647.1, nn. 45.5, 45.6 (Wright ed. 1961). It appears to be difficult if not impossible to obtain appellate review of the issue. Resolution by rule amendment is indicated. The question is essentially procedural in that it bears upon preparation for trial and settlement before trial, and courts confronting the question, however they have decided it, have generally treated it as procedural and governed by the rules.

The amendment resolves this issue in favor of disclosure. Most of the decisions denying discovery, some explicitly, reason from the text of Rule 26(b) that it permits discovery only of matters which will be admissible in evidence or appear reasonably calculated to lead to such evidence; they avoid considerations of policy, regarding them as foreclosed. See *Bisserier v. Manning, supra.* Some note also that facts about a defendant's financial status are not discoverable as such, prior to judgment with execution unsatisfied, and fear that, if courts hold insurance coverage discoverable, they must extend the principle to other aspects of the defendant's financial status. The cases favoring disclosure rely heavily on the practical significance of insurance in the decisions lawyers make about settlement and trial preparation. In *Clauss v. Danker,* 264 F.Supp. 246 (S.D.N.Y.1967), the court held that the rules forbid disclosure but called for an amendment to permit it.

Disclosure of insurance coverage will enable counsel for both sides to make the same realistic appraisal of the case, so that settlement and litigation strategy are based on knowledge and not speculation. It will conduce to settlement and avoid protracted litigation in some cases, though in others it may have an opposite effect. The amendment is limited to insurance coverage, which should be distinguished from any other facts concerning defendant's financial status (1) because insurance is an asset created specifically to satisfy the claim; (2) because the insurance company ordinarily controls the litigation; (3) because information about coverage is available only from defendant or his insurer; and (4) because disclosure does not involve a significant invasion of privacy.

Disclosure is required when the insurer "may be liable" on part or all of the judgment. Thus, an insurance company must disclose even when it contests liability under the policy, and such disclosure does not constitute a waiver of its claim. It is immaterial whether the liability is to satisfy the judgment directly or merely to indemnify or reimburse another after he pays the judgment.

The provision applies only to persons "carrying on an insurance business" and thus covers insurance companies and not the ordinary business concern that enters into a contract of indemnification. *Cf.* N.Y.Ins.Law § 41. Thus, the provision makes no change in existing law on discovery of indemnity agreements other than insurance agreements by persons carrying on an insurance business. Similarly, the provision does not cover the business concern that creates a reserve fund for purposes of self-insurance.

For some purposes other than discovery, an application for insurance is treated as a part of the insurance agreement. The provision makes clear that, for discovery purposes, the application is not to be so treated. The insurance application may contain personal and financial information concerning the insured, discovery of which is beyond the purpose of this provision.

In no instance does disclosure make the facts concerning insurance coverage admissible in evidence.

Subdivision (b)(3)—Trial Preparation: Materials. Some of the most controversial and vexing problems to emerge from the discovery rules have arisen out of requests for the production of documents or things prepared in anticipation of litigation or for trial. The existing rules make no explicit provision for such materials. Yet, two verbally distinct doctrines have developed, each conferring a qualified immunity on these materials—the "good cause" requirement in Rule 34 (now generally held applicable to discovery of documents via deposition under Rule 45 and interrogatories under Rule 33) and the work-product doctrine of *Hickman v. Taylor,* 329 U.S. 495 (1947). Both demand a showing of justification before production can be had, the one of "good cause" and the other variously described in the *Hickman* case: "necessity or justification," "denial * * * would unduly prejudice the preparation of petitioner's case," or "cause hardship or injustice" 329 U.S. at 509–510.

In deciding the *Hickman* case, the Supreme Court appears to have expressed a preference in 1947 for an approach to the problem of trial preparation materials by judicial decision rather than by rule. Sufficient experience has accumulated, however, with lower court applications of the *Hickman* decision to warrant a reappraisal.

The major difficulties visible in the existing case law are (1) confusion and disagreement as to whether "good cause" is made out by a showing of relevance and lack of privilege, or requires an additional showing of necessity, (2) confusion and disagreement as to the scope of the *Hickman* work-product doctrine, particularly whether it extends beyond work actually performed by lawyers, and (3) the resulting difficulty of relating the "good cause" required by Rule 34 and the "necessity or justification" of the work-product doctrine, so that their respective roles and the distinctions between them are understood.

Basic Standard.—Since Rule 34 in terms requires a showing of "good cause" for the production of all documents and things, whether or not trial preparation is involved, courts have felt that a single formula is called for and have differed over whether a showing of relevance and lack of privilege is enough or whether more must be shown. When the facts of the cases are studied, however, a distinction emerges based upon the type of materials. With respect to documents not obtained or prepared with an eye to litigation, the decisions, while not uniform, reflect a strong and increasing tendency to relate "good cause" to a showing that the documents are relevant to the subject matter of the action. *E.g., Connecticut Mutual Life Ins. Co. v. Shields,* 17 F.R.D. 273 (S.D.N.Y. 1959), with cases cited; *Houdry Process Corp. v. Commonwealth Oil Refining Co.,* 24 F.R.D. 58 (S.D.N.Y.1955); see *Bell v. Commercial Ins. Co.,* 280 F.2d 514, 517 (3d Cir. 1960).

When the party whose documents are sought shows that the request for production is unduly burdensome or oppressive, courts have denied discovery for lack of "good cause", although they might just as easily have based their decision on the protective provisions of existing Rule 30(b) (new Rule 26(c)). *E.g., Lauer v. Tankrederi,* 39 F.R.D. 334 (E.D.Pa. 1966).

As to trial-preparation materials, however, the courts are increasingly interpreting "good cause" as requiring more than relevance. When lawyers have prepared or obtained the materials for trial, all courts require more than relevance; so much is clearly commanded by *Hickman.* But even as to the preparatory work of nonlawyers, while some courts ignore work-product and equate "good cause" with relevance, *e.g., Brown v. New York, N.H. & H.R.R.,* 17 F.R.D. 324 (S.D.N.Y.1955), the more recent trend is to read "good cause" as requiring inquiry into the importance of and need for the materials as well as into alternative sources for securing the same information. In *Guilford Nat'l Bank v. Southern Ry.,* 297 F.2d 921 (4th Cir. 1962), statements of witnesses obtained by claim agents were held not discoverable because both parties had had equal access to the witnesses at about the same time, shortly after the collision in question. The decision was based solely on Rule 34 and "good cause"; the court declined to rule on whether the statements were work-products. The court's treatment of "good cause" is quoted at length and with approval in *Schlagenhauf v. Holder,* 379 U.S. 104, 117–118 (1964). See also *Mitchell v. Bass,* 252 F.2d 513 (8th Cir. 1958); *Hauger v. Chicago, R.I. & Pac. R.R.,* 216 F.2d 501 (7th Cir. 1954); *Burke v. United States,* 32 F.R.D. 213 (E.D.N.Y.1963). While the opinions dealing with "good cause" do not often draw an explicit distinction between trial preparation materials and other materials, in fact an overwhelming proportion of the cases in which a special showing is required are cases involving trial preparation materials.

The rules are amended by eliminating the general requirement of "good cause" from Rule 34 but retaining a requirement of a special showing for trial preparation materials in this subdivision. The required showing is expressed, not in terms of "good cause" whose generality has tended to encourage confusion and controversy, but in terms of the elements of the special showing to be made: substantial need of the materials in the preparation of the case and inability without undue hardship to obtain the substantial equivalent of the materials by other means.

These changes conform to the holdings of the cases, when viewed in light of their facts. Apart from trial preparation, the fact that the materials sought are documentary does not in and of itself require a special showing beyond relevance and absence of privilege. The protective provisions are of course available, and if the party from whom production is sought raises a special issue of privacy (as with respect to income tax returns or grand jury minutes) or points to evidence primarily impeaching, or can show serious burden or expense, the court will exercise its traditional power to decide whether to issue a protective order. On the other hand, the requirement of a special showing for discovery of trial preparation materials reflects the view that each side's informal evaluation of its case should be protected, that each side should be encouraged to prepare independently, and that one side should not automatically have the benefit of the detailed preparatory work of the other side. See Field and McKusick, *Maine Civil Practice* 264 (1959).

Elimination of a "good cause" requirement from Rule 34 and the establishment of a requirement of a special showing in this subdivision will eliminate the confusion caused by having two verbally distinct requirements of justification that the courts have been unable to distinguish clearly. Moreover, the language of the subdivision suggests the factors which the courts should consider in determining whether the requisite showing has been made. The importance of the materials sought to the party seeking them in preparation of his case and the difficulty he will have obtaining them by other means are factors noted in the *Hickman* case. The courts should also consider the likelihood that the party, even if he obtains the information by independent means, will not have the substantial equivalent of the documents the production of which he seeks.

Consideration of these factors may well lead the court to distinguish between witness statements taken by an investigator, on the one hand, and other parts of the investigative file, on the other. The court in *Southern Ry. v. Lanham,* 403 F.2d 119 (5th Cir. 1968), while it naturally addressed itself to the "good cause" requirements of Rule 34, set forth as controlling considerations the factors contained in the language of this subdivision. The analysis of the court suggests circumstances under which witness statements will be discoverable. The witness may have given a fresh and contemporaneous account in a written statement while he is available to the party seeking discovery only a substantial time thereafter. *Lanham, supra* at 127–128; *Guilford, supra* at 926. Or he may be reluctant or hostile. *Lanham, supra* at 128–129; *Brookshire v. Pennsylvania RR,* 14 F.R.D. 154 (N.D.Ohio 1953); *Diamond v. Mohawk Rubber Co.,* 33 F.R.D. 264 (D.Colo.1963). Or he may have a lapse of memory. *Tannenbaum v. Walker,* 16 F.R.D. 570 (E.D.Pa. 1954). Or he may probably be deviating from his prior statement. *Cf. Hauger v. Chicago, R.I. & Pac. RR,* 216 F.2d 501 (7th Cir. 1954). On the other hand, a much stronger showing is needed to obtain evaluative materials in an investigator's reports. *Lanham, supra* at 131–133; *Pickett v. L. R. Ryan, Inc.,* 237 F.Supp. 198 (E.D.S.C.1965).

Materials assembled in the ordinary course of business, or pursuant to public requirements unrelated to litigation, or for other nonlitigation purposes are not under the qualified immunity provided by this subdivision. *Goosman v. A. Duie Pyle, Inc.,* 320 F.2d 45 (4th Cir. 1963); cf. *United States v. New York Foreign Trade Zone Operators, Inc.,* 304 F.2d 792 (2d Cir. 1962). No change is made in the existing doctrine, noted in the *Hickman* case, that one party may discover relevant facts known or available to the other party, even though such facts are contained in a document which is not itself discoverable.

Treatment of Lawyers; Special Protection of Mental Impressions, Conclusions, Opinions, and Legal Theories Concerning the Litigation.—The courts are divided as to whether the work-product doctrine extends to the preparatory work only of lawyers. The *Hickman* case left this issue open since the statements in that case were taken by a lawyer. As to courts of appeals compare *Alltmont v. United States,* 177 F.2d 971, 976 (3d Cir. 1949), cert. denied, 339 U.S. 967 (1950) (*Hickman* applied to statements obtained by FBI agents on theory it should apply to "all statements of prospective witnesses which a party has obtained for his trial counsel's use"), with *Southern Ry. v. Campbell,* 309 F.2d 569 (5th Cir. 1962) (Statements taken by claim agents not work-product), and *Guilford Nat'l Bank v. Southern Ry.,* 297 F.2d 921 (4th Cir. 1962) (avoiding issue of work-product as to claim agents, deciding case instead under Rule 34 "good cause"). Similarly, the district courts are divided on statements obtained by claim agents, compare, e.g., *Brown v. New York, N.H. & H.R.R.,* 17 F.R.D. 324 (S.D.N.Y.1955) with *Hanke v. Milwaukee Electric Ry. & Transp. Co.,* 7 F.R.D. 540 (E.D.Wis.1947); investigators, compare *Burke v. United States,* 32 F.R.D. 213 (E.D.N.Y.1963) with *Snyder v. United States,* 20 F.R.D. 7 (E.D.N.Y.1956); and insurers, compare *Gottlieb v. Bresler,* 24 F.R.D. 371 (D.D.C.1959) with *Burns v. Mulder,* 20 F.R.D. 605 (E.D.Pa.1957). See 4 Moore's *Federal Practice* ¶26.23[8.1] (2d ed. 1966); 2A Barron & Holtzoff, *Federal Practice and Procedure* § 652.2 (Wright ed. 1961).

A complication is introduced by the use made by courts of the "good cause" requirement of Rule 34, as described above. A court may conclude that trial preparation materials are not work-product because not the result of lawyer's work and yet hold that they are not producible because "good cause" has not been shown. *Cf. Guilford Nat'l Bank v. Southern Ry.,* 297 F.2d 921 (4th Cir. 1962), cited and described above. When the decisions on "good cause" are taken into account, the weight of authority affords protection of the preparatory work of both lawyers and nonlawyers (though not necessarily to the same extent) by requiring more than a showing of relevance to secure production.

Subdivision (b)(3) reflects the trend of the cases by requiring a special showing, not merely as to materials prepared by an attorney, but also as to materials prepared in anticipation of litigation or preparation for trial by or for a party or any representative acting on his behalf. The subdivision then goes on to protect against disclosure the mental impressions, conclusions, opinions, or legal theories concerning the litigation of an attorney or other representative of a party. The *Hickman* opinion drew special attention to the need for protecting an attorney against discovery of memoranda prepared from recollection of oral interviews. The courts have steadfastly safeguarded against disclosure of lawyers' mental impressions and legal theories, as well as mental impressions and subjective evaluations of investigators and claim-agents. In enforcing this provision of the subdivision, the courts will sometimes find it necessary to order disclosure of a document but with portions deleted.

Rules 33 and 36 have been revised in order to permit discovery calling for opinions, contentions, and admissions relating not only to fact but also to the application of law to fact. Under those rules, a party and his attorney or other representative may be required to disclose, to some extent, mental impressions, opinions, or conclusions. But documents or parts of documents containing these matters are protected against discovery by this subdivision. Even though a party may ultimately have to disclose in response to interrogatories or requests to admit, he is entitled to keep confidential documents containing such matters prepared for internal use.

Party's Right to Own Statement—An exception to the requirement of this subdivision enables a party to secure production of his own statement without any special showing. The cases are divided. Compare, *e.g., Safeway Stores, Inc. v. Reynolds,* 176 F.2d 476 (D.C. Cir.1949); *Shupe v. Pennsylvania R.R.,* 19 F.R.D. 144 (W.D.Pa.1956); with *e.g., New York Central R.R. v. Carr,* 251 F.2d 433 (4th Cir. 1957); *Belback v. Wilson Freight Forwarding Co.,* 40 F.R.D. 16 (W.D.Pa.1966).

Courts which treat a party's statement as though it were that of any witness overlook the fact that the party's statement is, without more, admissible in evidence. Ordinarily, a party gives a statement without insisting on a copy because he does not yet have a lawyer and does not understand the legal consequences of his actions. Thus, the statement is given at a time when he functions at a disadvantage. Discrepancies between his trial testimony and earlier statement may result from lapse of memory or ordinary inaccuracy; a written statement produced for the first time at trial may give such discrepancies a prominence which they do not deserve. In appropriate cases the court may order a party to be deposed before his statement is produced. *E.g., Smith v. Central Linen Service Co.,* 39 F.R.D. 15 (D.Md.1966); *McCoy v. General Motors Corp.,* 33 F.R.D. 354 (W.D.Pa. 1963).

Commentators strongly support the view that a party be able to secure his statement without a showing. 4 *Moore's Federal Practice* ¶26.23[8.4] (2d ed. 1966); 2A Barron & Holtzoff, *Federal Practice and Procedure* § 652.3 (Wright ed. 1961); see also Note, *Developments in the Law—Discovery,* 74 Harv.L.Rev. 940, 1039 (1961). The following states have by statute or rule taken the same position: *Statutes:* Fla.Stat.Ann. § 92.33; Ga.Code Ann. § 38–2109(b); La.Stat. Ann.R.S. 13:3732; Mass.Gen.Laws Ann. c. 271, § 44; Minn. Stat.Ann. § 602.01; N.Y.C.P.L.R. § 3101(e); *Rules:* Mo. R.C.P. 56.01(a); N.Dak.R.C.P. 34(b); Wyo.R.C.P. 34(b); *cf.* Mich.G.C.R. 306.2.

In order to clarify and tighten the provision on statements by a party, the term "statement" is defined. The definition is adapted from 18 U.S.C. § 3500(e) (Jencks Act). The statement of a party may of course be that of plaintiff or defendant, and it may be that of an individual or of a corporation or other organization.

Witness' Right to Own Statement.—A second exception to the requirement of this subdivision permits a non-party witness to obtain a copy of his own statement without any special showing. Many, though not all, of the considerations supporting a party's right to obtain his statement apply also to the non-party witness. Insurance companies are increasingly recognizing that a witness is entitled to a copy of his statement and are modifying their regular practice accordingly.

Subdivision (b)(4)—Trial Preparation: Experts. This is a new provision dealing with discovery of information (including facts and opinions) obtained by a party from an expert retained by that party in relation to litigation or obtained by the expert and not yet transmitted to the party. The subdivision deals separately with those experts whom the party expects to call as trial witnesses and with those experts who have been retained or specially employed by the party but who are not expected to be witnesses. It should be noted that the subdivision does not address itself to the expert whose information was not acquired in preparation for trial but rather because he was an actor or viewer with respect to transactions or occurrences that are part of the subject matter of the lawsuit. Such an expert should be treated as an ordinary witness.

Subsection (b)(4)(A) deals with discovery of information obtained by or through experts who will be called as witnesses at trial. The provision is responsive to problems suggested by a relatively recent line of authorities. Many of these cases present intricate and difficult issues as to which expert testimony is likely to be determinative. Prominent among them are food and drug, patent, and condemnation cases. See, *e.g., United States v. Nysco Laboratories, Inc.,* 26 F.R.D. 159, 162 (E.D.N.Y.1960) (food and drug); *E. I. du Pont de Nemours & Co. v. Phillips Petroleum Co.,* 24 F.R.D. 416, 421 (D.Del.1959) (patent); *Cold Metal Process Co. v. Aluminum Co. of America,* 7 F.R.D. 425 (N.D.Ohio 1947), aff'd, *Sachs v. Aluminum Co. of America,* 167 F.2d 570 (6th Cir. 1948) (same); *United States v. 50.34 Acres of Land,* 13 F.R.D. 19 (E.D.N.Y.1952) (condemnation).

In cases of this character, a prohibition against discovery of information held by expert witnesses produces in acute form the very evils that discovery has been created to prevent. Effective cross-examination of an expert witness requires advance preparation. The lawyer even with the help of his own experts frequently cannot anticipate the particular approach his adversary's expert will take or the data on which he will base his judgment on the stand. McGlothlin, *Some Practical Problems in Proof of Economic, Scientific, and Technical Facts,* 23 F.R.D. 467, 478 (1958). A California study of discovery and pretrial in condemnation cases notes that the only substitute for discovery of experts' valuation materials is "lengthy—and often fruitless—cross-examination during trial," and recommends pretrial exchange of such material. Calif.Law Rev.Comm'n, Discovery in Eminent Domain Proceedings 707–710 (Jan. 1963). Similarly, effective rebuttal requires advance knowledge of the line of testimony of the other side. If the latter is foreclosed by a rule against discovery, then the narrowing of issues and elimination of surprise which discovery normally produces are frustrated.

These considerations appear to account for the broadening of discovery against experts in the cases cited where expert testimony was central to the case. In some instances, the opinions are explicit in relating expanded discovery to improved cross-examination and rebuttal at trial. *Franks v. National Dairy Products Corp.,* 41 F.R.D. 234 (W.D.Tex. 1966); *United States v. 23.76 Acres,* 32 F.R.D. 593 (D.Md. 1963); see also an unpublished opinion of Judge Hincks, quoted in *United States v. 48 Jars, etc.,* 23 F.R.D. 192, 198 (D.D.C.1958). On the other hand, the need for a new provision is shown by the many cases in which discovery of expert trial witnesses is needed for effective cross-examination and rebuttal, and yet courts apply the traditional doctrine and refuse disclosure. *E.g., United States v. Certain Parcels of Land,* 25 F.R.D. 192 (N.D.Cal.1959); *United States v. Certain Acres,* 18 F.R.D. 98 (M.D.Ga.1955).

Although the trial problems flowing from lack of discovery of expert witnesses are most acute and noteworthy when the case turns largely on experts, the same problems are encountered when a single expert testifies. Thus, subdivision (b)(4)(A) draws no line between complex and simple cases, or between cases with many experts and those with but one. It establishes by rule substantially the procedure adopted by decision of the court in *Knighton v. Villian & Fassio,* 39 F.R.D. 11 (D.Md.1965). For a full analysis of the problem and strong recommendations to the same effect, see Friedenthal, *Discovery and Use of an Adverse Party's Expert Information,* 14 Stan.L.Rev. 455, 485–488 (1962); Long, *Discovery and Experts under the Federal Rules of Civil Procedure,* 38 F.R.D. 111 (1965).

Past judicial restrictions on discovery of an adversary's expert, particularly as to his opinions, reflect the fear that one side will benefit unduly from the other's better preparation. The procedure established in subsection (b)(4)(A) holds the risk to a minimum. Discovery is limited to trial witnesses, and may be obtained only at a time when the parties know who their expert witnesses will be. A party must as a practical matter prepare his own case in advance of that time, for he can hardly hope to build his case out of his opponent's experts.

Subdivision (b)(4)(A) provides for discovery of an expert who is to testify at the trial. A party can require one who intends to use the expert to state the substance of the testimony that the expert is expected to give. The court may order further discovery, and it has ample power to regulate its timing and scope and to prevent abuse. Ordinarily, the order for further discovery shall compensate the expert for his time, and may compensate the party who intends to use the expert for past expenses reasonably incurred in obtaining facts or opinions from the expert. Those provisions are likely to discourage abusive practices.

Subdivision (b)(4)(B) deals with an expert who has been retained or specially employed by the party in anticipation of litigation or preparation for trial (thus excluding an expert who is simply a general employee of the party not specially employed on the case), but who is not expected to be called as a witness. Under its provisions, a party may discover facts known or opinions held by such an expert only on a showing of exceptional circumstances under which it is impracticable for the party seeking discovery to obtain facts or opinions on the same subject by other means.

Subdivision (b)(4)(B) is concerned only with experts retained or specially consulted in relation to trial preparation. Thus the subdivision precludes discovery against experts who were informally consulted in preparation for trial, but not retained or specially employed. As an ancillary procedure, a party may on a proper showing require the other party to name experts retained or specially employed, but not those informally consulted.

These new provisions of subdivision (b)(4) repudiate the few decisions that have held an expert's information privileged simply because of his status as an expert, *e.g., American Oil Co. v. Pennsylvania Petroleum Products Co.,* 23 F.R.D. 680, 685–686 (D.R.I.1959). See *Louisell, Modern California Discovery* 315–316 (1963). They also reject as ill-considered the decisions which have sought to bring expert information within the work-product doctrine. See *United States v. McKay,* 372 F.2d 174, 176–177 (5th Cir. 1967). The provisions adopt a form of the more recently developed doctrine of "unfairness". See *e.g., United States v. 23.76 Acres of Land,* 32 F.R.D. 593, 597 (D.Md.1963); Louisell, *supra,* at 317–318; 4 *Moore's Federal Practice* 26.24 (2d ed. 1966).

Under subdivision (b)(4)(C), the court is directed or authorized to issue protective orders, including an order that the expert be paid a reasonable fee for time spent in responding to discovery, and that the party whose expert is made subject to discovery be paid a fair portion of the fees and expenses that the party incurred in obtaining information from the expert. The court may issue the latter order as a condition of discovery, or it may delay the order until after discovery is completed. These provisions for fees and expenses meet the objection that it is unfair to permit one side to obtain without cost the benefit of an expert's work for which the other side has paid, often a substantial sum. E.g., *Lewis v. United Air Lines Transp. Corp.*, 32 F.Supp. 21 (W.D.Pa.1940); *Walsh v. Reynolds Metal Co.*, 15 F.R.D. 376 (D.N.J.1954). On the other hand, a party may not obtain discovery simply by offering to pay fees and expenses. Cf. *Boynton v. R. J. Reynolds Tobacco Co.*, 36 F.Supp. 593 (D.Mass.1941).

In instances of discovery under subdivision (b)(4)(B), the court is directed to award fees and expenses to the other party, since the information is of direct value to the discovering party's preparation of his case. In ordering discovery under (b)(4)(A)(ii), the court has discretion whether to award fees and expenses to the other party; its decision should depend upon whether the discovering party is simply learning about the other party's case or is going beyond this to develop his own case. Even in cases where the court is directed to issue a protective order, it may decline to do so if it finds that manifest injustice would result. Thus, the court can protect, when necessary and appropriate, the interests of an indigent party.

Subdivision (c)—Protective Orders. The provisions of existing Rule 30(b) are transferred to this subdivision (c), as part of the rearrangement of Rule 26. The language has been changed to give it application to discovery generally. The subdivision recognizes the power of the court in the district where a deposition is being taken to make protective orders. Such power is needed when the deposition is being taken far from the court where the action is pending. The court in the district where the deposition is being taken may, and frequently will, remit the deponent or party to the court where the action is pending.

In addition, drafting changes are made to carry out and clarify the sense of the rule. Insertions are made to avoid any possible implication that a protective order does not extend to "time" as well as to "place" or may not safeguard against "undue burden or expense."

The new reference to trade secrets and other confidential commercial information reflects existing law. The courts have not given trade secrets automatic and complete immunity against disclosure, but have in each case weighed their claim to privacy against the need for disclosure. Frequently, they have been afforded a limited protection. See, *e.g.*, *Covey Oil Co. v. Continental Oil Co.*, 340 F.2d 993 (10th Cir. 1965); *Julius M. Ames Co. v. Bostitch, Inc.*, 235 F.Supp. 856 (S.D.N.Y.1964).

The subdivision contains new matter relating to sanctions. When a motion for a protective order is made and the court is disposed to deny it, the court may go a step further and issue an order to provide or permit discovery. This will bring the sanctions of Rule 37(b) directly into play. Since the court has heard the contentions of all interested persons, an affirmative order is justified. See *Rosenberg, Sanctions to Effectuate Pretrial Discovery*, 58 Col.L.Rev. 480, 492–493 (1958). In addition, the court may require the payment of expenses incurred in relation to the motion.

Subdivision (d)—Sequence and Priority. This new provision is concerned with the sequence in which parties may proceed with discovery and with related problems of timing. The principal effects of the new provision are first, to eliminate any fixed priority in the sequence of discovery, and second, to make clear and explicit the court's power to establish priority by an order issued in a particular case.

A priority rule developed by some courts, which confers priority on the party who first serves notice of taking a deposition, is unsatisfactory in several important respects:

First, this priority rule permits a party to establish a priority running to all depositions as to which he has given earlier notice. Since he can on a given day serve notice of taking many depositions he is in a position to delay his adversary's taking of depositions for an inordinate time. Some courts have ruled that deposition priority also permits a party to delay his answers to interrogatories and production of documents. *E.g., E. I. du Pont de Nemours & Co. v. Phillips Petroleum Co.*, 23 F.R.D. 237 (D.Del.1959); *but cf. Sturdevant v. Sears, Roebuck & Co.*, 32 F.R.D. 426 (W.D.Mo. 1963).

Second, since notice is the key to priority, if both parties wish to take depositions first a race results. See *Caldwell-Clements, Inc. v. McGraw-Hill Pub. Co.*, 11 F.R.D. 156 (S.D.N.Y.1951) (description of tactics used by parties). But the existing rules on notice of deposition create a race with runners starting from different positions. The plaintiff may not give notice without leave of court until 20 days after commencement of the action, whereas the defendant may serve notice at any time after commencement. Thus, a careful and prompt defendant can almost always secure priority. This advantage of defendants is fortuitous, because the purpose of requiring plaintiff to wait 20 days is to afford defendant an opportunity to obtain counsel, not to confer priority.

Third, although courts have ordered a change in the normal sequence of discovery on a number of occasions, *e.g.*, *Kaeppler v. James H. Matthews & Co.*, 200 F.Supp. 229 (E.D.Pa.1961); *Park & Tilford Distillers Corp. v. Distillers Co.*, 19 F.R.D. 169 (S.D.N.Y.1956), and have at all times avowed discretion to vary the usual priority, most commentators are agreed that courts in fact grant relief only for "the most obviously compelling reasons." 2A Barron & Holtzoff, *Federal Practice and Procedure* 44–47 (Wright ed. 1961); see also Younger, *Priority of Pretrial Examination in the Federal Courts—A Comment*, 34 N.Y.U.L.Rev. 1271 (1959); Freund, *The Pleading and Pretrial of an Antitrust Claim*, 46 Corn.L.Q. 555, 564 (1964). Discontent with the fairness of actual practice has been evinced by other observers. Comments, 59 Yale L.J. 117, 134–136 (1949); Yudkin, *Some Refinements in Federal Discovery Procedure*, 11 Fed.B.J. 289, 296–297 (1951); *Developments in the Law-Discovery*, 74 Harv.L.Rev. 940, 954–958 (1961).

Despite these difficulties, some courts have adhered to the priority rule, presumably because it provides a test which is easily understood and applied by the parties without much court intervention. It thus permits deposition discovery to function extrajudicially, which the rules provide for and the courts desire. For these same reasons, courts are reluctant to make numerous exceptions to the rule.

The Columbia Survey makes clear that the problem of priority does not affect litigants generally. It found that most litigants do not move quickly to obtain discovery. In over half of the cases, both parties waited at least 50 days. During the first 20 days after commencement of the action—the period when defendant might assure his priority by noticing depositions—16 percent of the defendants acted to obtain discovery. A race could not have occurred in more than 16 percent of the cases and it undoubtedly occurred in fewer. On the other hand, five times as many defendants as plaintiffs served notice of deposition during the first 19 days. To the same effect, see Comment, *Tactical Use and Abuse of Depositions Under the Federal Rules,* 59 Yale L.J. 117, 134 (1949).

These findings do not mean, however, that the priority rule is satisfactory or that a problem of priority does not exist. The court decisions show that parties do battle on this issue and carry their disputes to court. The statistics show that these court cases are not typical. By the same token, they reveal that more extensive exercise of judicial discretion to vary the priority will not bring a flood of litigation, and that a change in the priority rule will in fact affect only a small fraction of the cases.

It is contended by some that there is no need to alter the existing priority practice. In support, it is urged that there is no evidence that injustices in fact result from present practice and that, in any event, the courts can and do promulgate local rules, as in New York, to deal with local situations and issue orders to avoid possible injustice in particular cases.

Subdivision (d) is based on the contrary view that the rule of priority based on notice is unsatisfactory and unfair in its operation. Subdivision (d) follows an approach adapted from Civil Rule 4 of the District Court for the Southern District of New York. That rule provides that starting 40 days after commencement of the action, unless otherwise ordered by the court, the fact that one party is taking a deposition shall not prevent another party from doing so "concurrently." In practice, the depositions are not usually taken simultaneously; rather, the parties work out arrangements for alternation in the taking of depositions. One party may take a complete deposition and then the other, or, if the depositions are extensive, one party deposes for a set time, and then the other. See *Caldwell-Clements, Inc. v. McCraw-Hill Pub. Co.,* 11 F.R.D. 156 (S.D.N.Y.1951).

In principle, one party's initiation of discovery should not wait upon the other's completion, unless delay is dictated by special considerations. Clearly the principle is feasible with respect to all methods of discovery other than depositions. And the experience of the Southern District of New York shows that the principle can be applied to depositions as well. The courts have not had an increase in motion business on this matter. Once it is clear to lawyers that they bargain on an equal footing, they are usually able to arrange for an orderly succession of depositions without judicial intervention. Professor Moore has called attention to Civil Rule 4 and suggested that it may usefully be extended to other areas. 4 *Moore's Federal Practice* 1154 (2d ed. 1966).

The court may upon motion and by order grant priority in a particular case. But a local court rule purporting to confer priority in certain classes of cases would be inconsistent with this subdivision and thus void.

Subdivision (e)—Supplementation of Responses. The rules do not now state whether interrogatories (and questions at deposition as well as requests for inspection and admissions) impose a "continuing burden" on the responding party to supplement his answers if he obtains new information. The issue is acute when new information renders substantially incomplete or inaccurate an answer which was complete and accurate when made. It is essential that the rules provide an answer to this question. The parties can adjust to a rule either way, once they know what it is. See 4 *Moore's Federal Practice* ¶33.25[4] (2d ed. 1966).

Arguments can be made both ways. Imposition of a continuing burden reduces the proliferation of additional sets of interrogatories. Some courts have adopted local rules establishing such a burden. *E.g.,* E.D.Pa.R. 20(f), quoted in *Taggart v. Vermont Transp. Co.,* 32 F.R.D. 587 (E.D.Pa. 1963); D.Me.R. 15(c). Others have imposed the burden by decision. *E.g., Chenault v. Nebraska Farm Products, Inc.,* 9 F.R.D. 529, 533 (D.Nebr.1949). On the other hand, there are serious objections to the burden, especially in protracted cases. Although the party signs the answers, it is his lawyer who understands their significance and bears the responsibility to bring answers up to date. In a complex case all sorts of information reaches the party, who little understands its bearing on answers previously given to interrogatories. In practice, therefore, the lawyer under a continuing burden must periodically recheck all interrogatories and canvass all new information. But a full set of new answers may no longer be needed by the interrogating party. Some issues will have been dropped from the case, some questions are now seen as unimportant, and other questions must in any event be reformulated. See *Novick v. Pennsylvania R.R.,* 18 F.R.D. 296, 298 (W.D.Pa.1955).

Subdivision (e) provides that a party is not under a continuing burden except as expressly provided. Cf. Note, 68 Harv.L.Rev. 673, 677 (1955). An exception is made as to the identity of persons having knowledge of discoverable matters, because of the obvious importance to each side of knowing all witnesses and because information about witnesses routinely comes to each lawyer's attention. Many of the decisions on the issue of a continuing burden have in fact concerned the identity of witnesses. An exception is also made as to expert trial witnesses in order to carry out the provisions of Rule 26(b)(4). See *Diversified Products Corp. v. Sports Center Co.,* 42 F.R.D. 3 (D.Md.1967).

Another exception is made for the situation in which a party, or more frequently his lawyer, obtains actual knowledge that a prior response is incorrect. This exception does not impose a duty to check the accuracy of prior responses, but it prevents knowing concealment by a party or attorney. Finally, a duty to supplement may be imposed by order of the court in a particular case (including an order resulting from a pretrial conference) or by agreement of the parties. A party may of course make a new discovery request which requires supplementation of prior responses.

The duty will normally be enforced, in those limited instances where it is imposed, through sanctions imposed by the trial court, including exclusion of evidence, continuance, or other action, as the court may deem appropriate.

1980 Amendment

Subdivision (f). This subdivision is new. There has been widespread criticism of abuse of discovery. The Committee has considered a number of proposals to eliminate abuse, including a change in Rule 26(b)(1) with respect to the scope of discovery and a change in Rule 33(a) to limit the number of questions that can be asked by interrogatories to parties.

The Committee believes that abuse of discovery, while very serious in certain cases, is not so general as to require such basic changes in the rules that govern discovery in all cases. A very recent study of discovery in selected metropolitan districts tends to support its belief. P. Connolly, E. Holleman, & M. Kuhlman, *Judicial Controls and the Civil Litigative Process: Discovery* (Federal Judicial Center, 1978). In the judgment of the Committee abuse can best be prevented by intervention by the court as soon as abuse is threatened.

To this end this subdivision provides that counsel who has attempted without success to effect with opposing counsel a reasonable program or plan for discovery is entitled to the assistance of the court.

It is not contemplated that requests for discovery conferences will be made routinely. A relatively narrow discovery dispute should be resolved by resort to Rules 26(c) or 37(a), and if it appears that a request for a conference is in fact grounded in such a dispute, the court may refer counsel to those rules. If the court is persuaded that a request is frivolous or vexatious, it can strike it. See Rules 11 and 7(b)(2).

A number of courts routinely consider discovery matters in preliminary pretrial conferences held shortly after the pleadings are closed. This subdivision does not interfere with such a practice. It authorizes the court to combine a discovery conference with a pretrial conference under Rule 16 if a pretrial conference is held sufficiently early to prevent or curb abuse.

1983 Amendment

Excessive discovery and evasion or resistance to reasonable discovery requests pose significant problems. Recent studies have made some attempt to determine the sources and extent of the difficulties. See Brazil, *Civil Discovery: Lawyers' Views of its Effectiveness, Principal Problems and Abuses,* American Bar Foundation (1980); Connolly, Holleman & Kuhlman, *Judicial Controls and the Civil Litigative Process: Discovery,* Federal Judicial Center (1978); Ellington, *A Study of Sanctions for Discovery Abuse,* Department of Justice (1979); Schroeder & Frank, *The Proposed Changes in the Discovery Rules,* 1978 Ariz.St.L.J. 475.

The purpose of discovery is to provide a mechanism for making relevant information available to the litigants. "Mutual knowledge of all the relevant facts gathered by both parties is essential to proper litigation." *Hickman v. Taylor,* 329 U.S. 495, 507 (1947). Thus the spirit of the rules is violated when advocates attempt to use discovery tools as tactical weapons rather than to expose the facts and illuminate the issues by overuse of discovery or unnecessary use of defensive weapons or evasive responses. All of this results in excessively costly and time-consuming activities that are disproportionate to the nature of the case, the amount involved, or the issues or values at stake.

Given our adversary tradition and the current discovery rules, it is not surprising that there are many opportunities, if not incentives, for attorneys to engage in discovery that, although authorized by the broad, permissive terms of the rules, nevertheless results in delay. See Brazil, *The Adversary Character of Civil Discovery: A Critique and Proposals for Change,* 31 Vand.L.Rev. 1259 (1978). As a result, it has been said that the rules have "not infrequently [been] exploited to the disadvantage of justice." *Herbert v. Lando,* 441 U.S. 153, 179 (1979) (Powell, J., concurring). These practices impose costs on an already overburdened system and impede the fundamental goal of the "just, speedy, and inexpensive determination of every action." Fed.R.Civ.P. 1.

Subdivision (a); Discovery Methods. The deletion of the last sentence of Rule 26(a)(1), which provided that unless the court ordered otherwise under Rule 26(c) "the frequency of use" of the various discovery methods was not to be limited, is an attempt to address the problem of duplicative, redundant, and excessive discovery and to reduce it. The amendment, in conjunction with the changes in Rule 26(b)(1), is designed to encourage district judges to identify instances of needless discovery and to limit the use of the various discovery devices accordingly. The question may be raised by one of the parties, typically on a motion for a protective order, or by the court on its own initiative. It is entirely appropriate to consider a limitation on the frequency of use of discovery at a discovery conference under Rule 26(f) or at any other pretrial conference authorized by these rules. In considering the discovery needs of a particular case, the court should consider the factors described in Rule 26(b)(1).

Subdivision (b); Discovery Scope and Limits. Rule 26(b)(1) has been amended to add a sentence to deal with the problem of over-discovery. The objective is to guard against redundant or disproportionate discovery by giving the court authority to reduce the amount of discovery that may be directed to matters that are otherwise proper subjects of inquiry. The new sentence is intended to encourage judges to be more aggressive in identifying and discouraging discovery overuse. The grounds mentioned in the amended rule for limiting discovery reflect the existing practice of many courts in issuing protective orders under Rule 26(c). See, e.g., *Carlson Cos. v. Sperry & Hutchinson Co.,* 374 F.Supp. 1080 (D.Minn.1974); *Dolgow v. Anderson,* 53 F.R.D. 661 (E.D.N.Y.1971); *Mitchell v. American Tobacco Co.,* 33 F.R.D. 262 (M.D.Pa.1963); *Welty v. Clute,* 1 F.R.D. 446 (W.D.N.Y.1941). On the whole, however, district judges have been reluctant to limit the use of the discovery devices. See, *e.g., Apco Oil Co. v. Certified Transp., Inc.,* 46 F.R.D. 428 (W.D.Mo.1969). See generally 8 Wright & Miller, *Federal Practice and Procedure: Civil* §§ 2036, 2037, 2039, 2040 (1970).

The first element of the standard, Rule 26(b)(1)(i), is designed to minimize redundancy in discovery and encourage attorneys to be sensitive to the comparative costs of different methods of securing information. Subdivision (b)(1)(ii) also seeks to reduce repetitiveness and to oblige lawyers to think through their discovery activities in advance so that full utilization is made of each deposition, document request, or set of interrogatories. The elements of Rule 26(b)(1)(iii) address the problem of discovery that is disproportionate to the individual lawsuit as measured by such matters as its nature and complexity, the importance of the issues at stake in a case seeking damages, the limitations on a financially weak litigant to withstand extensive opposition to a discovery program or to respond to discovery requests, and the significance of the substantive issues, as measured in philosophic, social, or institutional terms. Thus the rule recognizes that many cases in public policy spheres, such as employment practices, free speech, and other matters, may have importance far beyond the monetary amount involved. The court must apply the standards in an even-handed manner that will prevent use of discovery to wage a war of attrition or as a device to coerce a party, whether financially weak or affluent.

The rule contemplates greater judicial involvement in the discovery process and thus acknowledges the reality that it cannot always operate on a self-regulating basis. See Connolly, Holleman & Kuhlman, *Judicial Controls and the Civil Litigative Process: Discovery* 77, Federal Judicial Center (1978). In an appropriate case the court could restrict the number of depositions, interrogatories, or the scope of a production request. But the court must be careful not to deprive a party of discovery that is reasonably necessary to afford a fair opportunity to develop and prepare the case.

The court may act on motion, or its own initiative. It is entirely appropriate to resort to the amended rule in conjunction with a discovery conference under Rule 26(f) or one of the other pretrial conferences authorized by the rules.

Subdivision (g); Signing of Discovery Requests, Responses, and Objections. Rule 26(g) imposes an affirmative duty to engage in pretrial discovery in a responsible manner that is consistent with the spirit and purposes of Rules 26 through 37. In addition, Rule 26(g) is designed to curb discovery abuse by explicitly encouraging the imposition of sanctions. The subdivision provides a deterrent to both excessive discovery and evasion by imposing a certification requirement that obliges each attorney to stop and think about the legitimacy of a discovery request, a response thereto, or an objection. The term "response" includes answers to interrogatories and to requests to admit as well as responses to production requests.

If primary responsibility for conducting discovery is to continue to rest with the litigants, they must be obliged to act responsibly and avoid abuse. With this in mind, Rule 26(g), which parallels the amendments to Rule 11, requires an attorney or unrepresented party to sign each discovery request, response, or objection. Motions relating to discovery are governed by Rule 11. However, since a discovery request, response, or objection usually deals with more specific subject matter than motions or papers, the elements that must be certified in connection with the former are spelled out more completely. The signature is a certification of the elements set forth in Rule 26(g).

Although the certification duty requires the lawyer to pause and consider the reasonableness of his request, response, or objection, it is not meant to discourage or restrict necessary and legitimate discovery. The rule simply requires that the attorney make a reasonable inquiry into the factual basis of his response, request, or objection.

The duty to make a "reasonable inquiry" is satisfied if the investigation undertaken by the attorney and the conclusions drawn therefrom are reasonable under the circumstances. It is an objective standard similar to the one imposed by Rule 11. See the Advisory Committee Note to Rule 11. See also *Kinee v. Abraham Lincoln Fed. Sav. & Loan Ass'n,* 365 F.Supp. 975 (E.D.Pa.1973). In making the inquiry, the attorney may rely on assertions by the client and on communications with other counsel in the case as long as that reliance is appropriate under the circumstances. Ultimately, what is reasonable is a matter for the court to decide on the totality of the circumstances.

Rule 26(g) does not require the signing attorney to certify the truthfulness of the client's factual responses to a discovery request. Rather, the signature certifies that the lawyer has made a reasonable effort to assure that the client has provided all the information and documents available to him that are responsive to the discovery demand. Thus, the lawyer's certification under Rule 26(g) should be distinguished from other signature requirements in the rules, such as those in Rules 30(e) and 33.

Nor does the rule require a party or an attorney to disclose privileged communications or work product in order to show that a discovery request, response, or objection is substantially justified. The provisions of Rule 26(c), including appropriate orders after *in camera* inspection by the court, remain available to protect a party claiming privilege or work product protection.

The signing requirement means that every discovery request, response, or objection should be grounded on a theory that is reasonable under the precedents or a good faith belief as to what should be the law. This standard is heavily dependent on the circumstances of each case. The certification speaks as of the time it is made. The duty to supplement discovery responses continues to be governed by Rule 26(e).

Concern about discovery abuse has led to widespread recognition that there is a need for more aggressive judicial control and supervision. *ACF Industries, Inc. v. EEOC,* 439 U.S. 1081 (1979) (certiorari denied) (Powell, J., dissenting). Sanctions to deter discovery abuse would be more effective if they were diligently applied "not merely to penalize those whose conduct may be deemed to warrant such a sanction, but to deter those who might be tempted to such conduct in the absence of such a deterrent." *National Hockey League v. Metropolitan Hockey Club,* 427 U.S. 639, 643 (1976). See also Note, *The Emerging Deterrence Orientation in the Imposition of Discovery Sanctions,* 91 Harv.L.Rev. 1033 (1978). Thus the premise of Rule 26(g) is that imposing sanctions on attorneys who fail to meet the rule's standards will significantly reduce abuse by imposing disadvantages therefor.

Because of the asserted reluctance to impose sanctions on attorneys who abuse the discovery rules, see Brazil, *Civil Discovery: Lawyers' Views of its Effectiveness, Principal Problems and Abuses,* American Bar Foundation (1980); Ellington, *A Study of Sanctions for Discovery Abuse,* Department of Justice (1979), Rule 26(g) makes explicit the authority judges now have to impose appropriate sanctions and requires them to use it. This authority derives from Rule 37, 28 U.S.C. § 1927, and the court's inherent power. See *Roadway Express, Inc. v. Piper,* 447 U.S. 752 (1980); *Martin v. Bell Helicopter Co.,* 85 F.R.D. 654, 661–62 (D.Col. 1980); Note, *Sanctions Imposed by Courts on Attorneys Who Abuse the Judicial Process,* 44 U.Chi.L.Rev. 619 (1977). The new rule mandates that sanctions be imposed on attorneys who fail to meet the standards established in the first portion of Rule 26(g). The nature of the sanction is a matter of judicial discretion to be exercised in light of the particular circumstances. The court may take into account any failure by the party seeking sanctions to invoke protection under Rule 26(c) at an early stage in the litigation.

The sanctioning process must comport with due process requirements. The kind of notice and hearing required will depend on the facts of the case and the severity of the sanction being considered. To prevent the proliferation of the sanction procedure and to avoid multiple hearings, discovery in any sanction proceeding normally should be permitted only when it is clearly required by the interests of justice. In most cases the court will be aware of the circumstances and only a brief hearing should be necessary.

1987 Amendment

The amendments are technical. No substantive change is intended.

1993 Amendments

Subdivision (a). Through the addition of paragraphs (1)–(4), this subdivision imposes on parties a duty to disclose, without awaiting formal discovery requests, certain basic information that is needed in most cases to prepare for trial or make an informed decision about settlement. The rule requires all parties (1) early in the case to exchange information regarding potential witnesses, documentary evidence, damages, and insurance, (2) at an appropriate time during the discovery period to identify expert witnesses and provide a detailed written statement of the testimony that may be offered at trial through specially retained experts, and (3) as the trial date approaches to identify the particular evidence that may be offered at trial. The enumeration in Rule 26(a) of items to be disclosed does not prevent a court from requiring by order or local rule that the parties disclose additional information without a discovery request. Nor are parties precluded from using traditional discovery methods to obtain further information regarding these matters, as for example asking an expert during a deposition about testimony given in other litigation beyond the four-year period specified in Rule 26(a)(2)(B).

A major purpose of the revision is to accelerate the exchange of basic information about the case and to eliminate the paper work involved in requesting such information, and the rule should be applied in a manner to achieve those objectives. The concepts of imposing a duty of disclosure were set forth in Brazil, *The Adversary Character of Civil Discovery: A Critique and Proposals for Change,* 31 *Vand. L.Rev.* 1348 (1978), and Schwarzer, *The Federal Rules, the Adversary Process, and Discovery Reform,* 50 *U.Pitt.L.Rev. 703, 721–23 (1989).*

The rule is based upon the experience of district courts that have required disclosure of some of this information through local rules, court-approved standard interrogatories, and standing orders. Most have required pretrial disclosure of the kind of information described in Rule 26(a)(3). Many have required written reports from experts containing information like that specified in Rule 26(a)(2)(B). While far more limited, the experience of the few state and federal courts that have required pre-discovery exchange of core information such as is contemplated in Rule 26(a)(1) indicates that savings in time and expense can be achieved, particularly if the litigants meet and discuss the issues in the case as a predicate for this exchange and if a judge supports the process, as by using the results to guide further proceedings in the case. Courts in Canada and the United Kingdom have for many years required disclosure of certain information without awaiting a request from an adversary.

Paragraph (1). As the functional equivalent of court-ordered interrogatories, this paragraph requires early disclosure, without need for any request, of four types of information that have been customarily secured early in litigation through formal discovery. The introductory clause permits the court, by local rule, to exempt all or particular types of cases from these disclosure requirement *[sic]* or to modify the nature of the information to be disclosed. It is expected that courts would, for example, exempt cases like Social Security reviews and government collection cases in which discovery would not be appropriate or would be unlikely. By order the court may eliminate or modify the disclosure requirements in a particular case, and similarly the parties, unless precluded by order or local rule, can stipulate to elimination or modification of the requirements for that case. The disclosure obligations specified in paragraph (1) will not be appropriate for all cases, and it is expected that changes in these obligations will be made by the court or parties when the circumstances warrant.

Authorization of these local variations is, in large measure, included in order to accommodate the Civil Justice Reform Act of 1990, which implicitly directs districts to experiment during the study period with differing procedures to reduce the time and expense of civil litigation. The civil justice delay and expense reduction plans adopted by the courts under the Act differ as to the type, form, and timing of disclosures required. Section 105(c)(1) of the Act calls for a report by the Judicial Conference to Congress by December 31, 1995, comparing experience in twenty of these courts; and section 105(c)(2)(B) contemplates that some changes in the Rules may then be needed. While these studies may indicate the desirability of further changes in Rule 26(a)(1), these changes probably could not become effective before December 1998 at the earliest. In the meantime, the present revision puts in place a series of disclosure obligations that, unless a court acts affirmatively to impose other requirements or indeed to reject all such requirements for the present, are designed to eliminate certain discovery, help focus the discovery that is needed, and facilitate preparation for trial or settlement.

Subparagraph (A) requires identification of all persons who, based on the investigation conducted thus far, are likely to have discoverable information relevant to the factual disputes between the parties. All persons with such information should be disclosed, whether or not their testimony will be supportive of the position of the disclosing party. As officers of the court, counsel are expected to disclose the identity of those persons who may be used by them as witnesses or who, if their potential testimony were known, might reasonably be expected to be deposed or called as a witness by any of the other parties. Indicating briefly the general topics on which such persons have information should not be burdensome, and will assist other parties in deciding which depositions will actually be needed.

Subparagraph (B) is included as a substitute for the inquiries routinely made about the existence and location of documents and other tangible things in the possession, custody, or control of the disclosing party. Although, unlike subdivision (a)(3)(C), an itemized listing of each exhibit is not required, the disclosure should describe and categorize, to the extent identified during the initial investigation, the nature and location of potentially relevant documents and records, including computerized data and other electronically-recorded information, sufficiently to enable opposing parties (1) to make an informed decision concerning which documents might need to be examined, at least initially, and (2) to frame their document requests in a manner likely to avoid squabbles resulting from the wording of the requests. As with potential witnesses, the requirement for disclosure of documents applies to all potentially relevant items then known to the party, whether or not supportive of its contentions in the case.

Unlike subparagraphs (C) and (D), subparagraph (B) does not require production of any documents. Of course, in cases involving few documents a disclosing party may prefer to provide copies of the documents rather than describe them, and the rule is written to afford this option to the disclosing party. If, as will be more typical, only the description is provided, the other parties are expected to obtain the documents desired by proceeding under Rule 34 or through informal requests. The disclosing party does not, by describing documents under subparagraph (B), waive its right to object to production on the basis of privilege or work product protection, or to assert that the documents are not sufficiently relevant to justify the burden or expense of production.

The initial disclosure requirements of subparagraphs (A) and (B) are limited to identification of potential evidence "relevant to disputed facts alleged with particularity in the pleadings." There is no need for a party to identify potential evidence with respect to allegations that are admitted. Broad, vague, and conclusory allegations sometimes tolerated in notice pleading—for example, the assertion that a product with many component parts is defective in some unspecified manner—should not impose upon responding parties the obligation at that point to search for and identify all persons possibly involved in, or all documents affecting, the design, manufacture, and assembly of the product. The greater the specificity and clarity of the allegations in the pleadings, the more complete should be the listing of potential witnesses and types of documentary evidence. Although paragraphs (1)(A) and (1)(B) by their terms refer to the factual disputes defined in the pleadings, the rule contemplates that these issues would be informally refined and clarified during the meeting of the parties under subdivision (f) and that the disclosure obligations would be adjusted in the light of these discussions. The disclosure requirements should, in short, be applied with common sense in light of the principles of Rule 1, keeping in mind the salutary purposes that the rule is intended to accomplish. The litigants should not indulge in gamesmanship with respect to the disclosure obligations.

Subparagraph (C) imposes a burden of disclosure that includes the functional equivalent of a standing Request for Production under Rule 34. A party claiming damages or other monetary relief must, in addition to disclosing the calculation of such damages, make available the supporting documents for inspection and copying as if a request for such materials had been made under Rule 34. This obligation applies only with respect to documents then reasonably available to it and not privileged or protected as work product. Likewise, a party would not be expected to provide a calculation of damages which, as in many patent infringement actions, depends on information in the possession of another party or person.

Subparagraph (D) replaces subdivision (b)(2) of Rule 26, and provides that liability insurance policies be made available for inspection and copying. The last two sentences of that subdivision have been omitted as unnecessary, not to signify any change of law. The disclosure of insurance information does not thereby render such information admissible in evidence. See Rule 411, Federal Rules of Evidence. Nor does subparagraph (D) require disclosure of applications for insurance, though in particular cases such information may be discoverable in accordance with revised subdivision (a)(5).

Unless the court directs a different time, the disclosures required by subdivision (a)(1) are to be made at or within 10 days after the meeting of the parties under subdivision (f). One of the purposes of this meeting is to refine the factual disputes with respect to which disclosures should be made under paragraphs (1)(A) and (1)(B), particularly if an answer has not been filed by a defendant, or, indeed, to afford the parties an opportunity to modify by stipulation the timing or scope of these obligations. The time of this meeting is generally left to the parties provided it is held at least 14 days before a scheduling conference is held or before a scheduling order is due under Rule 16(b). In cases in which no scheduling conference is held, this will mean that the meeting must ordinarily be held within 75 days after a defendant has first appeared in the case and hence that the initial disclosures would be due no later than 85 days after the first appearance of a defendant.

Before making its disclosures, a party has the obligation under subdivision (g)(1) to make a reasonable inquiry into the facts of the case. The rule does not demand an exhaustive investigation at this stage of the case, but one that is reasonable under the circumstances, focusing on the facts that are alleged with particularity in the pleadings. The type of investigation that can be expected at this point will vary based upon such factors as the number and complexity of the issues; the location, nature, number, and availability of potentially relevant witnesses and documents; the extent of past working relationships between the attorney and the client, particularly in handling related or similar litigation; and of course how long the party has to conduct an investigation, either before or after filing of the case. As provided in the last sentence of subdivision (a)(1), a party is not excused from the duty of disclosure merely because its investigation is incomplete. The party should make its initial disclosures based on the pleadings and the information then reasonably available to it. As its investigation continues and as the issues in the pleadings are clarified, it should supplement its disclosures as required by subdivision (e)(1). A party is not relieved from its obligation of disclosure merely because another party has not made its disclosures or has made an inadequate disclosure.

It will often be desirable, particularly if the claims made in the complaint are broadly stated, for the parties to have their Rule 26(f) meeting early in the case, perhaps before a defendant has answered the complaint or had time to conduct other than a cursory investigation. In such circumstances, in order to facilitate more meaningful and useful initial disclosures, they can and should stipulate to a period of more than 10 days after the meeting in which to make these disclosures, at least for defendants who had no advance notice of the potential litigation. A stipulation at an early meeting affording such a defendant at least 60 days after receiving the complaint in which to make its disclosures under subdivision (a)(1)—a period that is two weeks longer than the time formerly specified for responding to interrogatories served with a complaint—should be adequate and appropriate in most cases.

Paragraph (2). This paragraph imposes an additional duty to disclose information regarding expert testimony sufficiently in advance of trial that opposing parties have a reasonable opportunity to prepare for effective cross examination and perhaps arrange for expert testimony from other witnesses. Normally the court should prescribe a time for these disclosures in a scheduling order under Rule 16(b), and in most cases the party with the burden of proof on an issue should disclose its expert testimony on that issue before other parties are required to make their disclosures with respect to that issue. In the absence of such a direction, the disclosures are to be made by all parties at least 90 days before the trial date or the date by which the case is to be ready for trial, except that an additional 30 days is allowed (unless the court specifies another time) for disclosure of expert testimony to be used solely to contradict or rebut the testimony that may be presented by another party's expert. For a discussion of procedures that have been used to enhance the reliability of expert testimony, see M. Graham, *Expert Witness Testimony and the Federal Rules of Evidence: Insuring Adequate Assurance of Trustworthiness,* 1986 U.Ill.L.Rev. 90.

Paragraph (2)(B) requires that persons retained or specially employed to provide expert testimony, or whose duties as an employee of the party regularly involve the giving of expert testimony, must prepare a detailed and complete written report, stating the testimony the witness is expected to present during direct examination, together with the reasons therefor. The information disclosed under the former rule in answering interrogatories about the "substance" of expert testimony was frequently so sketchy and vague that it rarely dispensed with the need to depose the expert and often was even of little help in preparing for a deposition of the witness. Revised Rule 37(c)(1) provides an incentive for full disclosure; namely, that a party will not ordinarily be permitted to use on direct examination any expert testimony not so disclosed. Rule 26(a)(2)(B) does not preclude counsel from providing assistance to experts in preparing the reports, and indeed, with experts such as automobile mechanics, this assistance may be needed. Nevertheless, the report, which is intended to set forth the substance of the direct examination, should be written in a manner that reflects the testimony to be given by the witness and it must be signed by the witness.

The report is to disclose the data and other information considered by the expert and any exhibits or charts that summarize or support the expert's opinions. Given this obligation of disclosure, litigants should no longer be able to argue that materials furnished to their experts to be used in forming their opinions—whether or not ultimately relied upon by the expert—are privileged or otherwise protected from disclosure when such persons are testifying or being deposed.

Revised subdivision (b)(4)(A) authorizes the deposition of expert witnesses. Since depositions of experts required to prepare a written report may be taken only after the report has been served, the length of the deposition of such experts should be reduced, and in many cases the report may eliminate the need for a deposition. Revised subdivision (e)(1) requires disclosure of any material changes made in the opinions of an expert from whom a report is required, whether the changes are in the written report or in testimony given at a deposition.

For convenience, this rule and revised Rule 30 continue to use the term "expert" to refer to those persons who will testify under Rule 702 of the Federal Rules of Evidence with respect to scientific, technical, and other specialized matters. The requirement of a written report in paragraph (2)(B), however, applies only to those experts who are retained or specially employed to provide such testimony in the case or whose duties as an employee of a party regularly involve the giving of such testimony. A treating physician, for example, can be deposed or called to testify at trial without any requirement for a written report. By local rule, order, or written stipulation, the requirement of a written report may be waived for particular experts or imposed upon additional persons who will provide opinions under Rule 702.

Paragraph (3). This paragraph imposes an additional duty to disclose, without any request, information customarily needed in final preparation for trial. These disclosures are to be made in accordance with schedules adopted by the court under Rule 16(b) or by special order. If no such schedule is directed by the court, the disclosures are to be made at least 30 days before commencement of the trial. By its terms, rule 26(a)(3) does not require disclosure of evidence to be used solely for impeachment purposes; however, disclosure of such evidence—as well as other items relating to conduct of trial—may be required by local rule or a pretrial order.

Subparagraph (A) requires the parties to designate the persons whose testimony they may present as substantive evidence at trial, whether in person or by deposition. Those who will probably be called as witnesses should be listed separately from those who are not likely to be called but who are being listed in order to preserve the right to do so if needed because of developments during trial. Revised Rule 37(c)(1) provides that only persons so listed may be used at trial to present substantive evidence. This restriction does not apply unless the omission was "without substantial justification" and hence would not bar an unlisted witness if the need for such testimony is based upon developments during trial that could not reasonably have been anticipated—*e.g.,* a change of testimony.

Listing a witness does not obligate the party to secure the attendance of the person at trial, but should preclude the party from objecting if the person is called to testify by another party who did not list the person as a witness.

Subparagraph (B) requires the party to indicate which of these potential witnesses will be presented by deposition at trial. A party expecting to use at trial a deposition not recorded by stenographic means is required by revised Rule 32 to provide the court with a transcript of the pertinent portions of such depositions. This rule requires that copies of the transcript of a nonstenographic deposition be provided to other parties in advance of trial for verification, an obvious concern since counsel often utilize their own personnel to prepare transcripts from audio or video tapes. By order or local rule, the court may require that parties designate the particular portions of stenographic depositions to be used at trial.

Subparagraph (C) requires disclosure of exhibits, including summaries (whether to be offered in lieu of other documentary evidence or to be used as an aid in understanding such evidence), that may be offered as substantive evidence. The rule requires a separate listing of each such exhibit, though it should permit voluminous items of a similar or standardized character to be described by meaningful categories. For example, unless the court has otherwise directed, a series of vouchers might be shown collectively as a single exhibit with their starting and ending dates. As with witnesses, the exhibits that will probably be offered are to be listed separately from those which are unlikely to be offered but which are listed in order to preserve the right to do so if needed because of developments during trial. Under revised Rule 37(c)(1) the court can permit use of unlisted documents the need for which could not reasonably have been anticipated in advance of trial.

Upon receipt of these final pretrial disclosures, other parties have 14 days (unless a different time is specified by the court) to disclose any objections they wish to preserve to the usability of the deposition testimony or to the admissibility of the documentary evidence (other than under Rules 402 and 403 of the Federal Rules of Evidence). Similar provisions have become commonplace either in pretrial orders or by local rules, and significantly expedite the presentation of evidence at trial, as well as eliminate the need to have available witnesses to provide "foundation" testimony for most items of documentary evidence. The listing of a potential objection does not constitute the making of that objection or require the court to rule on the objection; rather, it preserves the right of the party to make the objection when and as appropriate during trial. The court may, however, elect to treat the listing as a motion "in limine" and rule upon the objections in advance of trial to the extent appropriate.

The time specified in the rule for the final pretrial disclosures is relatively close to the trial date. The objective is to eliminate the time and expense in making these disclosures of evidence and objections in those cases that settle shortly before trial, while affording a reasonable time for final preparation for trial in those cases that do not settle. In many cases, it will be desirable for the court in a scheduling or pretrial order to set an earlier time for disclosures of evidence and provide more time for disclosing potential objections.

Paragraph (4). This paragraph prescribes the form of disclosures. A signed written statement is required, reminding the parties and counsel of the solemnity of the obligations imposed; and the signature on the initial or pretrial disclosure is a certification under subdivision (g)(1) that it is complete and correct as of the time when made. Consistent with Rule 5(d), these disclosures are to be filed with the court unless otherwise directed. It is anticipated that many courts will direct that expert reports required under paragraph (2)(B) not be filed until needed in connection with a motion or for trial.

Paragraph (5). This paragraph is revised to take note of the availability of revised Rule 45 for inspection from nonparties of documents and premises without the need for a deposition.

Subdivision (b). This subdivision is revised in several respects. First, former paragraph (1) is subdivided into two paragraphs for ease of reference and to avoid renumbering of paragraphs (3) and (4). Textual changes are then made in new paragraph (2) to enable the court to keep tighter rein on the extent of discovery. The information explosion of recent decades has greatly increased both the potential cost of wide-ranging discovery and the potential for discovery to be used as an instrument for delay or oppression. Amendments to Rules 30, 31, and 33 place presumptive limits on the number of depositions and interrogatories, subject to leave of court to pursue additional discovery. The revisions in Rule 26(b)(2) are intended to provide the court with broader discretion to impose additional restrictions on the scope and extent of discovery and to authorize courts that develop case tracking systems based on the complexity of cases to increase or decrease by local rule the presumptive number of depositions and interrogatories allowed in particular types or classifications of cases. The revision also dispels any doubt as to the power of the court to impose limitations on the length of depositions under Rule 30 or on the number of requests for admission under Rule 36.

Second, former paragraph (2), relating to insurance, has been relocated as part of the required initial disclosures under subdivision (a)(1)(D), and revised to provide for disclosure of the policy itself.

Third, paragraph (4)(A) is revised to provide that experts who are expected to be witnesses will be subject to deposition prior to trial, conforming the norm stated in the rule to the actual practice followed in most courts, in which depositions of experts have become standard. Concerns regarding the expense of such depositions should be mitigated by the fact that the expert's fees for the deposition will ordinarily be borne by the party taking the deposition. The requirement under subdivision (a)(2)(B) of a complete and detailed report of the expected testimony of certain forensic experts may, moreover, eliminate the need for some such depositions or at least reduce the length of the depositions. Accordingly, the deposition of an expert required by subdivision (a)(2)(B) to provide a written report may be taken only after the report has been served.

Paragraph (4)(C), bearing on compensation of experts, is revised to take account of the changes in paragraph (4)(A).

Paragraph (5) is a new provision. A party must notify other parties if it is withholding materials otherwise subject to disclosure under the rule or pursuant to a discovery request because it is asserting a claim of privilege or work product protection. To withhold materials without such notice is contrary to the rule, subjects the party to sanctions under Rule 37(b)(2), and may be viewed as a waiver of the privilege or protection.

The party must also provide sufficient information to enable other parties to evaluate the applicability of the claimed privilege or protection. Although the person from whom the discovery is sought decides whether to claim a privilege or protection, the court ultimately decides whether, if this claim is challenged, the privilege or protection applies. Providing information pertinent to the applicability of the privilege or protection should reduce the need for in camera examination of the documents.

The rule does not attempt to define for each case what information must be provided when a party asserts a claim of privilege or work product protection. Details concerning time, persons, general subject matter, etc., may be appropriate if only a few items are withheld, but may be unduly burdensome when voluminous documents are claimed to be privileged or protected, particularly if the items can be described by categories. A party can seek relief through a protective order under subdivision (c) if compliance with the requirement for providing this information would be an unreasonable burden. In rare circumstances some of the pertinent information affecting applicability of the claim, such as the identity of the client, may itself be privileged; the rule provides that such information need not be disclosed.

The obligation to provide pertinent information concerning withheld privileged materials applies only to items "otherwise discoverable." If a broad discovery request is made—for example, for all documents of a particular type during a twenty year period—and the responding party believes in good faith that production of documents for more than the past three years would be unduly burdensome, it should make its objection to the breadth of the request and, with respect to the documents generated in that three year period, produce the unprivileged documents and describe those withheld under the claim of privilege. If the court later rules that documents for a seven year period are properly discoverable, the documents for the additional four years should then be either produced (if not privileged) or described (if claimed to be privileged).

Subdivision (c). The revision requires that before filing a motion for a protective order the movant must confer—either in person or by telephone—with the other affected parties in a good faith effort to resolve the discovery dispute without the need for court intervention. If the movant is unable to get opposing parties even to discuss the matter, the efforts in attempting to arrange such a conference should be indicated in the certificate.

Subdivision (d). This subdivision is revised to provide that formal discovery—as distinguished from interviews of potential witnesses and other informal discovery—not commence until the parties have met and conferred as required by subdivision (f). Discovery can begin earlier if authorized under Rule 30(a)(2)(C) (deposition of person about to leave the country) or by local rule, order, or stipulation. This will be appropriate in some cases, such as those involving requests for a preliminary injunction or motions challenging personal jurisdiction. If a local rule exempts any types of cases in which discovery may be needed from the requirement of a meeting under Rule 26(f), it should specify when discovery may commence in those cases.

The meeting of counsel is to take place as soon as practicable and in any event at least 14 days before the date of the scheduling conference under Rule 16(b) or the date a scheduling order is due under Rule 16(b). The court can assure that discovery is not unduly delayed either by entering a special order or by setting the case for a scheduling conference.

Subdivision (e). This subdivision is revised to provide that the requirement for supplementation applies to all disclosures required by subdivisions (a)(1)–(3). Like the former rule, the duty, while imposed on a "party," applies whether the corrective information is learned by the client or by the attorney. Supplementations need not be made as each new item of information is learned but should be made at appropriate intervals during the discovery period, and with special promptness as the trial date approaches. It may be useful for the scheduling order to specify the time or times when supplementations should be made.

The revision also clarifies that the obligation to supplement responses to formal discovery requests applies to interrogatories, requests for production, and requests for admissions, but not ordinarily to deposition testimony. However, with respect to experts from whom a written report is required under subdivision (a)(2)(B), changes in the opinions expressed by the expert whether in the report or at a subsequent deposition are subject to a duty of supplemental disclosure under subdivision (e)(1).

The obligation to supplement disclosures and discovery responses applies whenever a party learns that its prior disclosures or responses are in some material respect incomplete or incorrect. There is, however, no obligation to provide supplemental or corrective information that has been otherwise made known to the parties in writing or during the discovery process, as when a witness not previously disclosed is identified during the taking of a deposition or when an expert during a deposition corrects information contained in an earlier report.

Subdivision (f). This subdivision was added in 1980 to provide a party threatened with abusive discovery with a special means for obtaining judicial intervention other than through discrete motions under Rules 26(c) and 37(a). The amendment envisioned a two-step process: first, the parties would attempt to frame a mutually agreeable plan; second, the court would hold a "discovery conference" and then enter an order establishing a schedule and limitations for the conduct of discovery. It was contemplated that the procedure, an elective one triggered on request of a party, would be used in special cases rather than as a routine matter. As expected, the device has been used only sparingly in most courts, and judicial controls over the discovery process have ordinarily been imposed through scheduling orders under Rule 16(b) or through rulings on discovery motions.

The provisions relating to a conference with the court are removed from subdivision (f). This change does not signal any lessening of the importance of judicial supervision. Indeed, there is a greater need for early judicial involvement to consider the scope and timing of the disclosure requirements of Rule 26(a) and the presumptive limits on discovery imposed under these rules or by local rules. Rather, the change is made because the provisions addressing the use of conferences with the court to control discovery are more properly included in Rule 16, which is being revised to highlight the court's powers regarding the discovery process.

The desirability of some judicial control of discovery can hardly be doubted. Rule 16, as revised, requires that the court set a time for completion of discovery and authorizes various other orders affecting the scope, timing, and extent of discovery and disclosures. Before entering such orders, the court should consider the views of the parties, preferably by means of a conference, but at the least through written submissions. Moreover, it is desirable that the parties' proposals regarding discovery be developed through a process where they meet in person, informally explore the nature and basis of the issues, and discuss how discovery can be conducted most efficiently and economically.

As noted above, former subdivision (f) envisioned the development of proposed discovery plans as an optional procedure to be used in relatively few cases. The revised rule directs that in all cases not exempted by local rule or special order the litigants must meet in person and plan for discovery. Following this meeting, the parties submit to the court their proposals for a discovery plan and can begin formal discovery. Their report will assist the court in seeing that the timing and scope of disclosures under revised Rule 26(a) and the limitations on the extent of discovery under these rules and local rules are tailored to the circumstances of the particular case.

To assure that the court has the litigants' proposals before deciding on a scheduling order and that the commencement of discovery is not delayed unduly, the rule provides that the meeting of the parties take place as soon as practicable and in any event at least 14 days before a scheduling conference is held or before a scheduling order is due under Rule 16(b). (Rule 16(b) requires that a scheduling order be entered within 90 days after the first appearance of a defendant or, if earlier, within 120 days after the complaint has been served on any defendant.) The obligation to participate in the planning process is imposed on all parties that have appeared in the case, including defendants who, because of a pending Rule 12 motion, may not have yet filed an answer in the case. Each such party should attend the meeting, either through one of its attorneys or in person if unrepresented. If more parties are joined or appear after the initial meeting, an additional meeting may be desirable.

Subdivision (f) describes certain matters that should be accomplished at the meeting and included in the proposed discovery plan. This listing does not exclude consideration of other subjects, such as the time when any dispositive motions should be filed and when the case should be ready for trial.

The parties are directed under subdivision (a)(1) to make the disclosures required by that subdivision at or within 10 days after this meeting. In many cases the parties should use the meeting to exchange, discuss, and clarify their respective disclosures. In other cases, it may be more useful if the disclosures are delayed until after the parties have discussed at the meeting the claims and defenses in order to define the issues with respect to which the initial disclosures should be made. As discussed in the Notes to subdivision (a)(1), the parties may also need to consider whether a stipulation extending this 10–day period would be appropriate, as when a defendant would otherwise have less than 60 days after being served in which to make its initial disclosure. The parties should also discuss at the meeting what additional information, although not subject to the disclosure requirements, can be made available informally without the necessity for formal discovery requests.

The report is to be submitted to the court within 10 days after the meeting and should not be difficult to prepare. In most cases counsel should be able to agree that one of them will be responsible for its preparation and submission to the court. Form 35 has been added in the Appendix to the Rules, both to illustrate the type of report that is contemplated and to serve as a checklist for the meeting.

The litigants are expected to attempt in good faith to agree on the contents of the proposed discovery plan. If they cannot agree on all aspects of the plan, their report to the court should indicate the competing proposals of the parties on those items, as well as the matters on which they agree. Unfortunately, there may be cases in which, because of disagreements about time or place or for other reasons, the meeting is not attended by all parties or, indeed, no meeting takes place. In such situations, the report—or reports—should describe the circumstances and the court may need to consider sanctions under Rule 37(g).

By local rule or special order, the court can exempt particular cases or types of cases from the meet-and-confer requirement of subdivision (f). In general this should include any types of cases which are exempted by local rule from the requirement for a scheduling order under Rule 16(b), such as cases in which there will be no discovery (*e.g.*, bankruptcy appeals and reviews of social security determinations). In addition, the court may want to exempt cases in which discovery is rarely needed (*e.g.*, government collection cases and proceedings to enforce administrative summonses) or in which a meeting of the parties might be impracticable (*e.g.*, actions by unrepresented prisoners). Note that if a court exempts from the requirements for a meeting any types of cases in which discovery may be needed, it should indicate when discovery may commence in those cases.

Subdivision (g). Paragraph (1) is added to require signatures on disclosures, a requirement that parallels the provisions of paragraph (2) with respect to discovery requests, responses, and objections. The provisions of paragraph (3) have been modified to be consistent with Rules 37(a)(4) and 37(c)(1); in combination, these rules establish sanctions for violation of the rules regarding disclosures and discovery matters. Amended Rule 11 no longer applies to such violations.

2000 Amendment

Purposes of amendments. The Rule 26(a)(1) initial disclosure provisions are amended to establish a nationally uniform practice. The scope of the disclosure obligation is narrowed to cover only information that the disclosing party may use to support its position. In addition, the rule exempts specified categories of proceedings from initial disclosure, and permits a party who contends that disclosure is not appropriate in the circumstances of the case to present its objections to the court, which must then determine whether disclosure should be made. Related changes are made in Rules 26(d) and (f).

The initial disclosure requirements added by the 1993 amendments permitted local rules directing that disclosure would not be required or altering its operation. The inclusion of the "opt out" provision reflected the strong opposition to initial disclosure felt in some districts, and permitted experimentation with differing disclosure rules in those districts that were favorable to disclosure. The local option also recognized that—partly in response to the first publication in 1991 of a proposed disclosure rule—many districts had adopted a variety of disclosure programs under the aegis of the Civil Justice Reform Act. It was hoped that developing experience under a variety of disclosure systems would support eventual refinement of a uniform national disclosure practice. In addition, there was hope that local experience could identify categories of actions in which disclosure is not useful.

A striking array of local regimes in fact emerged for disclosure and related features introduced in 1993. *See* D. Stienstra, *Implementation of Disclosure in United States District Courts, With Specific Attention to Courts' Responses to Selected Amendments to Federal Rule of Civil Procedure 26* (Federal Judicial Center, March 30, 1998) (describing and categorizing local regimes). In its final report to Congress on the CJRA experience, the Judicial Conference recommended reexamination of the need for national uniformity, particularly in regard to initial disclosure. Judicial Conference, *Alternative Proposals for Reduction of Cost and Delay: Assessment of Principles, Guidelines and Techniques,* 175 F.R.D. 62, 98 (1997).

At the Committee's request, the Federal Judicial Center undertook a survey in 1997 to develop information on current disclosure and discovery practices. *See* T. Willging, J. Shapard, D. Stienstra & D. Miletich, *Discovery and Disclosure Practice, Problems, and Proposals for Change* (Federal Judicial Center, 1997). In addition, the Committee convened two conferences on discovery involving lawyers from around the country and received reports and recommendations on possible discovery amendments from a number of bar groups. Papers and other proceedings from the second conference are published in 39 Boston Col. L. Rev. 517–840 (1998).

The Committee has discerned widespread support for national uniformity. Many lawyers have experienced difficulty in coping with divergent disclosure and other practices as they move from one district to another. Lawyers surveyed by the Federal Judicial Center ranked adoption of a uniform national disclosure rule second among proposed rule changes (behind increased availability of judges to resolve discovery disputes) as a means to reduce litigation expenses without interfering with fair outcomes. *Discovery and Disclosure Practice, supra,* at 44–45. National uniformity is also a central purpose of the Rules Enabling Act of 1934, as amended, 28 U.S.C. §§ 2072–2077.

These amendments restore national uniformity to disclosure practice. Uniformity is also restored to other aspects of discovery by deleting most of the provisions authorizing local rules that vary the number of permitted discovery events or the length of depositions. Local rule options are also deleted from Rules 26(d) and (f).

Subdivision (a)(1). The amendments remove the authority to alter or opt out of the national disclosure requirements by local rule, invalidating not only formal local rules but also informal "standing" orders of an individual judge or court that purport to create exemptions from—or limit or expand—the disclosure provided under the national rule. *See* Rule 83. Case-specific orders remain proper, however, and are expressly required if a party objects that initial disclosure is not appropriate in the circumstances of the action. Specified categories of proceedings are excluded from initial disclosure under subdivision (a)(1)(E). In addition, the parties can stipulate to forgo disclosure, as was true before. But even in a case excluded by subdivision (a)(1)(E) or in which the parties stipulate to bypass disclosure, the court can order exchange of similar information in managing the action under Rule 16.

The initial disclosure obligation of subdivisions (a)(1)(A) and (B) has been narrowed to identification of witnesses and documents that the disclosing party may use to support its claims or defenses. "Use" includes any use at a pretrial conference, to support a motion, or at trial. The disclosure obligation is also triggered by intended use in discovery, apart from use to respond to a discovery request; use of a document to question a witness during a deposition is a common example. The disclosure obligation attaches both to witnesses and documents a party intends to use and also to witnesses and to documents the party intends to use if—in the language of Rule 26(a)(3)—"the need arises."

A party is no longer obligated to disclose witnesses or documents, whether favorable or unfavorable, that it does not intend to use. The obligation to disclose information the party may use connects directly to the exclusion sanction of Rule 37(c)(1). Because the disclosure obligation is limited to material that the party may use, it is no longer tied to particularized allegations in the pleadings. Subdivision (e)(1), which is unchanged, requires supplementation if information later acquired would have been subject to the disclosure requirement. As case preparation continues, a party must supplement its disclosures when it determines that it may use a witness or document that it did not previously intend to use.

The disclosure obligation applies to "claims and defenses," and therefore requires a party to disclose information it may use to support its denial or rebuttal of the allegations, claim, or defense of another party. It thereby bolsters the requirements of Rule 11(b)(4), which authorizes denials "warranted on the evidence," and disclosure should include the identity of any witness or document that the disclosing party may use to support such denials.

Subdivision (a)(3) presently excuses pretrial disclosure of information solely for impeachment. Impeachment information is similarly excluded from the initial disclosure requirement.

Subdivisions (a)(1)(C) and (D) are not changed. Should a case be exempted from initial disclosure by Rule 26(a)(1)(E) or by agreement or order, the insurance information described by subparagraph (D) should be subject to discovery, as it would have been under the principles of former Rule 26(b)(2), which was added in 1970 and deleted in 1993 as redundant in light of the new initial disclosure obligation.

New subdivision (a)(1)(E) excludes eight specified categories of proceedings from initial disclosure. The objective of this listing is to identify cases in which there is likely to be little or no discovery, or in which initial disclosure appears unlikely to contribute to the effective development of the case. The list was developed after a review of the categories excluded by local rules in various districts from the operation of Rule 16(b) and the conference requirements of subdivision (f). Subdivision (a)(1)(E) refers to categories of "proceedings" rather than categories of "actions" because some might not properly be labeled " actions." Case designations made by the parties or the clerk's office at the time of filing do not control application of the exemptions. The descriptions in the rule are generic and are intended to be administered by the parties—and, when needed, the courts—with the flexibility needed to adapt to gradual evolution in the types of proceedings that fall within these general categories. The exclusion of an action for review on an administrative record, for example, is intended to reach a proceeding that is framed as an " appeal" based solely on an administrative record. The exclusion should not apply to a proceeding in a form that commonly permits admission of new evidence to supplement the record. Item (vii), excluding a proceeding ancillary to proceedings in other courts, does not refer to bankruptcy proceedings; application of the Civil Rules to bankruptcy proceedings is determined by the Bankruptcy Rules.

Subdivision (a)(1)(E) is likely to exempt a substantial proportion of the cases in most districts from the initial disclosure requirement. Based on 1996 and 1997 case filing statistics, Federal Judicial Center staff estimate that, nationwide, these categories total approximately one-third of all civil filings.

The categories of proceedings listed in subdivision (a)(1)(E) are also exempted from the subdivision (f) conference requirement and from the subdivision (d) moratorium on discovery. Although there is no restriction on commencement of discovery in these cases, it is not expected that this opportunity will often lead to abuse since there is likely to be little or no discovery in most such cases. Should a defendant need more time to respond to discovery requests filed at the beginning of an exempted action, it can seek relief by motion under Rule 26(c) if the plaintiff is unwilling to defer the due date by agreement.

Subdivision (a)(1)(E)'s enumeration of exempt categories is exclusive. Although a case-specific order can alter or excuse initial disclosure, local rules or "standing" orders that purport to create general exemptions are invalid. *See* Rule 83.

The time for initial disclosure is extended to 14 days after the subdivision (f) conference unless the court orders otherwise. This change is integrated with corresponding changes requiring that the subdivision (f) conference be held 21 days before the Rule 16(b) scheduling conference or scheduling order, and that the report on the subdivision (f) conference be submitted to the court 14 days after the meeting. These changes provide a more orderly opportunity for the parties to review the disclosures, and for the court to consider the report. In many instances, the subdivision (f) conference and the effective preparation of the case would benefit from disclosure before the conference, and earlier disclosure is encouraged.

The presumptive disclosure date does not apply if a party objects to initial disclosure during the subdivision (f) conference and states its objection in the subdivision (f) discovery plan. The right to object to initial disclosure is not intended to afford parties an opportunity to "opt out" of disclosure unilaterally. It does provide an opportunity for an objecting party to present to the court its position that disclosure would be "inappropriate in the circumstances of the action." Making the objection permits the objecting party to present the question to the judge before any party is required to make disclosure. The court must then rule on the objection and determine what disclosures—if any—should be made. Ordinarily, this determination would be included in the Rule 16(b) scheduling order, but the court could handle the matter in a different fashion. Even when circumstances warrant suspending some disclosure obligations, others—such as the damages and insurance information called for by subdivisions (a)(1)(C) and (D)—may continue to be appropriate.

The presumptive disclosure date is also inapplicable to a party who is "first served or otherwise joined" after the subdivision (f) conference. This phrase refers to the date of service of a claim on a party in a defensive posture (such as a defendant or third-party defendant), and the date of joinder of a party added as a claimant or an intervenor. Absent court order or stipulation, a new party has 30 days in which to make its initial disclosures. But it is expected that later-added parties will ordinarily be treated the same as the original parties when the original parties have stipulated to forgo initial disclosure, or the court has ordered disclosure in a modified form.

Subdivision (a)(3). The amendment to Rule 5(d) forbids filing disclosures under subdivisions (a)(1) and (a)(2) until they are used in the proceeding, and this change is reflected in an amendment to subdivision (a)(4) . Disclosures under subdivision (a)(3), however, may be important to the court in connection with the final pretrial conference or otherwise in preparing for trial. The requirement that objections to certain matters be filed points up the court's need to be provided with these materials. Accordingly, the requirement that subdivision (a)(3) materials be filed has been moved from subdivision (a)(4) to subdivision (a)(3), and it has also been made clear that they—and any objections—should be filed "promptly."

Subdivision (a)(4). The filing requirement has been removed from this subdivision. Rule 5(d) has been amended to provide that disclosures under subdivisions (a)(1) and (a)(2) must not be filed until used in the proceeding. Subdivision (a)(3) has been amended to require that the disclosures it directs, and objections to them, be filed promptly. Subdivision (a)(4) continues to require that all disclosures under subdivisions (a)(1), (a)(2), and (a)(3) be in writing, signed, and served.

"Shall" is replaced by "must" under the program to conform amended rules to current style conventions when there is no ambiguity.

GAP Report

The Advisory Committee recommends that the amendments to Rules 26(a)(1)(A) and (B) be changed so that initial disclosure applies to information the disclosing party "may use to support" its claims or defenses. It also recommends changes in the Committee Note to explain that disclosure requirement. In addition, it recommends inclusion in the Note of further explanatory matter regarding the exclusion from initial disclosure provided in new Rule 26(a)(1)(E) for actions for review on an administrative record and the impact of these exclusions on bankruptcy proceedings. Minor wording improvements in the Note are also proposed.

Subdivision (b)(1). In 1978, the Committee published for comment a proposed amendment, suggested by the Section of Litigation of the American Bar Association, to refine the scope of discovery by deleting the "subject matter" language. This proposal was withdrawn, and the Committee has since then made other changes in the discovery rules to address concerns about overbroad discovery. Concerns about costs and delay of discovery have persisted nonetheless, and other bar groups have repeatedly renewed similar proposals for amendment to this subdivision to delete the "subject matter" language. Nearly one-third of the lawyers surveyed in 1997 by the Federal Judicial Center endorsed narrowing the scope of discovery as a means of reducing litigation expense without interfering with fair case resolutions. *Discovery and Disclosure Practice, supra*, at 44–45 (1997). The Committee has heard that in some instances, particularly cases involving large quantities of discovery, parties seek to justify discovery requests that sweep far beyond the claims and defenses of the parties on the ground that they nevertheless have a bearing on the "subject matter" involved in the action.

The amendments proposed for subdivision (b)(1) include one element of these earlier proposals but also differ from these proposals in significant ways. The similarity is that the amendments describe the scope of party-controlled discovery in terms of matter relevant to the claim or defense of any party. The court, however, retains authority to order discovery of any matter relevant to the subject matter involved in the action for good cause. The amendment is designed to involve the court more actively in regulating the breadth of sweeping or contentious discovery. The Committee has been informed repeatedly by lawyers that involvement of the court in managing discovery is an important method of controlling problems of inappropriately broad discovery. Increasing the availability of judicial officers to resolve discovery disputes and increasing court management of discovery were both strongly endorsed by the attorneys surveyed by the Federal Judicial Center. *See Discovery and Disclosure Practice, supra*, at 44. Under the amended provisions, if there is an objection that discovery goes beyond material relevant to the parties' claims or defenses, the court would become involved to determine whether the discovery is relevant to the claims or defenses and, if not, whether good cause exists for authorizing it so long as it is relevant to the subject matter of the action. The good-cause standard warranting broader discovery is meant to be flexible.

The Committee intends that the parties and the court focus on the actual claims and defenses involved in the action. The dividing line between information relevant to the claims and defenses and that relevant only to the subject matter of the action cannot be defined with precision. A variety of types of information not directly pertinent to the incident in suit could be relevant to the claims or defenses raised in a given action. For example, other incidents of the same type, or involving the same product, could be properly discoverable under the revised standard. Information about organizational arrangements or filing systems of a party could be discoverable if likely to yield or lead to the discovery of admissible information. Similarly, information that could be used to impeach a likely witness, although not otherwise relevant to the claims or defenses, might be properly discoverable. In each instance, the determination whether such information is discoverable because it is relevant to the claims or defenses depends on the circumstances of the pending action.

The rule change signals to the court that it has the authority to confine discovery to the claims and defenses asserted in the pleadings, and signals to the parties that they have no entitlement to discovery to develop new claims or defenses that are not already identified in the pleadings. In general, it is hoped that reasonable lawyers can cooperate to manage discovery without the need for judicial intervention. When judicial intervention is invoked, the actual scope of discovery should be determined according to the reasonable needs of the action. The court may permit broader discovery in a particular case depending on the circumstances of the case, the nature of the claims and defenses, and the scope of the discovery requested.

The amendments also modify the provision regarding discovery of information not admissible in evidence. As added in 1946, this sentence was designed to make clear that otherwise relevant material could not be withheld because it was hearsay or otherwise inadmissible. The Committee was concerned that the "reasonably calculated to lead to the discovery of admissible evidence" standard set forth in this sentence might swallow any other limitation on the scope of discovery. Accordingly, this sentence has been amended to clarify that information must be relevant to be discoverable, even though inadmissible, and that discovery of such material is permitted if reasonably calculated to lead to the discovery of admissible evidence. As used here, "relevant" means within the scope of discovery as defined in this subdivision, and it would include information relevant to the subject matter involved in the action if the court has ordered discovery to that limit based on a showing of good cause.

Finally, a sentence has been added calling attention to the limitations of subdivision (b)(2)(i), (ii), and (iii). These limitations apply to discovery that is otherwise within the scope of subdivision (b)(1). The Committee has been told repeatedly that courts have not implemented these limitations with the vigor that was contemplated. *See 8 Federal Practice & Procedure* § 2008.1 at 121. This otherwise redundant cross-reference has been added to emphasize the need for active judicial use of subdivision (b)(2) to control excessive discovery. *Cf. Crawford-El v. Britton*, 118 S. Ct. 1584, 1597 (1998) (quoting Rule 26(b)(2)(iii) and stating that "Rule 26 vests the trial judge with broad discretion to tailor discovery narrowly").

GAP Report

The Advisory Committee recommends changing the rule to authorize the court to expand discovery to any "matter"—not "information"—relevant to the subject matter involved in the action. In addition, it recommends additional clarifying material in the Committee Note about the impact of the change on some commonly disputed discovery topics, the relationship between cost-bearing under Rule 26(b)(2) and expansion of the scope of discovery on a showing of good cause, and the meaning of "relevant" in the revision to the last sentence of current subdivision (b)(1). In addition, some minor clarifications of language changes have been proposed for the Committee Note .

Subdivision (b)(2). Rules 30, 31, and 33 establish presumptive national limits on the numbers of depositions and interrogatories. New Rule 30(d)(2) establishes a presumptive limit on the length of depositions. Subdivision (b)(2) is amended to remove the previous permission for local rules that establish different presumptive limits on these discovery activities. There is no reason to believe that unique circumstances justify varying these nationally-applicable presumptive limits in certain districts. The limits can be modified by court order or agreement in an individual action, but "standing" orders imposing different presumptive limits are not authorized. Because there is no national rule limiting the number of Rule 36 requests for admissions, the rule continues to authorize local rules that impose numerical limits on them. This change is not intended to interfere with differentiated case management in districts that use this technique by case-specific order as part of their Rule 16 process.

Subdivision (d). The amendments remove the prior authority to exempt cases by local rule from the moratorium on discovery before the subdivision (f) conference, but the categories of proceedings exempted from initial disclosure under subdivision (a)(1)(E) are excluded from subdivision (d). The parties may agree to disregard the moratorium where it applies, and the court may so order in a case, but "standing" orders altering the moratorium are not authorized.

Subdivision (f). As in subdivision (d), the amendments remove the prior authority to exempt cases by local rule from the conference requirement. The Committee has been informed that the addition of the conference was one of the most successful changes made in the 1993 amendments, and it therefore has determined to apply the conference requirement nationwide. The categories of proceedings exempted from initial disclosure under subdivision (a)(1)(E) are exempted from the conference requirement for the reasons that warrant exclusion from initial disclosure. The court may order that the conference need not occur in a case where otherwise required, or that it occur in a case otherwise exempted by subdivision (a)(1)(E). "Standing" orders altering the conference requirement for categories of cases are not authorized.

The rule is amended to require only a "conference" of the parties, rather than a "meeting." There are important benefits to face-to-face discussion of the topics to be covered in the conference, and those benefits may be lost if other means of conferring were routinely used when face-to-face meetings would not impose burdens. Nevertheless, geographic conditions in some districts may exact costs far out of proportion to these benefits. The amendment allows the court by case-specific order to require a face-to-face meeting, but "standing" orders so requiring are not authorized.

As noted concerning the amendments to subdivision (a)(1), the time for the conference has been changed to at least 21 days before the Rule 16 scheduling conference, and the time for the report is changed to no more than 14 days after the Rule 26(f) conference. This should ensure that the court will have the report well in advance of the scheduling conference or the entry of the scheduling order.

Since Rule 16 was amended in 1983 to mandate some case management activities in all courts, it has included deadlines for Completing these tasks to ensure that all courts do so within a reasonable time. Rule 26(f) was fit into this scheme when it was adopted in 1993. It was never intended, however, that the national requirements that certain activities be completed by a certain time should delay case management in districts that move much faster than the national rules direct, and the rule is therefore amended to permit such a court to adopt a local rule that shortens the period specified for the completion of these tasks.

"Shall" is replaced by "must," "does," or an active verb under the program to conform amended rules to current style conventions when there is no ambiguity.

GAP Report

The Advisory Committee recommends adding a sentence to the published amendments to Rule 26(f) authorizing local rules shortening the time between the attorney conference and the court's action under Rule 16(b), and addition to the Committee Note of explanatory material about this change to the rule. This addition can be made without republication in response to public comments.

2006 Amendment

Subdivision (a). Rule 26(a)(1)(B) is amended to parallel Rule 34(a) by recognizing that a party must disclose electronically stored information as well as documents that it may use to support its claims or defenses. The term "electronically stored information" has the same broad meaning in Rule 26(a)(1) as in Rule 34(a). This amendment is consistent with the 1993 addition of Rule 26(a)(1)(B). The term "data compilations" is deleted as unnecessary because it is a subset of both documents and electronically stored information.

[Subdivision (a)(1)(E).] Civil forfeiture actions are added to the list of exemptions from Rule 26(a)(1) disclosure requirements. These actions are governed by new Supplemental Rule G. Disclosure is not likely to be useful.

Subdivision (b)(2). The amendment to Rule 26(b)(2) is designed to address issues raised by difficulties in locating, retrieving, and providing discovery of some electronically stored information. Electronic storage systems often make it easier to locate and retrieve information. These advantages are properly taken into account in determining the reasonable scope of discovery in a particular case. But some sources of electronically stored information can be accessed only with substantial burden and cost. In a particular case, these burdens and costs may make the information on such sources not reasonably accessible.

It is not possible to define in a rule the different types of technological features that may affect the burdens and costs of accessing electronically stored information. Information systems are designed to provide ready access to information used in regular ongoing activities. They also may be designed so as to provide ready access to information that is not regularly used. But a system may retain information on sources that are accessible only by incurring substantial burdens or costs. Subparagraph (B) is added to regulate discovery from such sources.

Under this rule, a responding party should produce electronically stored information that is relevant, not privileged, and reasonably accessible, subject to the (b)(2)(C) limitations that apply to all discovery. The responding party must also identify, by category or type, the sources containing potentially responsive information that it is neither searching nor producing. The identification should, to the extent possible, provide enough detail to enable the requesting party to evaluate the burdens and costs of providing the discovery and the likelihood of finding responsive information on the identified sources.

A party's identification of sources of electronically stored information as not reasonably accessible does not relieve the party of its common-law or statutory duties to preserve evidence. Whether a responding party is required to preserve unsearched sources of potentially responsive information that it believes are not reasonably accessible depends on the circumstances of each case. It is often useful for the parties to discuss this issue early in discovery.

The volume of — and the ability to search — much electronically stored information means that in many cases the responding party will be able to produce information from reasonably accessible sources that will fully satisfy the parties' discovery needs. In many circumstances the requesting party should obtain and evaluate the information from such sources before insisting that the responding party search and produce information contained on sources that are not reasonably accessible. If the requesting party continues to seek discovery of information from sources identified as not reasonably accessible, the parties should discuss the burdens and costs of accessing and retrieving the information, the needs that may establish good cause for requiring all or part of the requested discovery even if the information sought is not reasonably accessible, and conditions on obtaining and producing the information that may be appropriate.

If the parties cannot agree whether, or on what terms, sources identified as not reasonably accessible should be searched and discoverable information produced, the issue may be raised either by a motion to compel discovery or by a motion for a protective order. The parties must confer before bringing either motion. If the parties do not resolve the issue and the court must decide, the responding party must show that the identified sources of information are not reasonably accessible because of undue burden or cost. The requesting party may need discovery to test this assertion. Such discovery might take the form of requiring the responding party to conduct a sampling of information contained on the sources identified as not reasonably accessible; allowing some form of inspection of such sources; or taking depositions of witnesses knowledgeable about the responding party's information systems.

Once it is shown that a source of electronically stored information is not reasonably accessible, the requesting party may still obtain discovery by showing good cause, considering the limitations of Rule 26(b)(2)(C) that balance the costs and potential benefits of discovery. The decision whether to require a responding party to search for and produce information that is not reasonably accessible depends not only on the burdens and costs of doing so, but also on whether those burdens and costs can be justified in the circumstances of the case. Appropriate considerations may include: (1) the specificity of the discovery request; (2) the quantity of information available from other and more easily accessed sources; (3) the failure to produce relevant information that seems likely to have existed but is no longer available on more easily accessed sources; (4) the likelihood of finding relevant, responsive information that cannot be obtained from other, more easily accessed sources; (5) predictions as to the importance and usefulness of the further information; (6) the importance of the issues at stake in the litigation; and (7) the parties' resources.

The responding party has the burden as to one aspect of the inquiry — whether the identified sources are not reasonably accessible in light of the burdens and costs required to search for, retrieve, and produce whatever responsive information may be found. The requesting party has the burden of showing that its need for the discovery outweighs the burdens and costs of locating, retrieving, and producing the information. In some cases, the court will be able to determine whether the identified sources are not reasonably accessible and whether the requesting party has shown good cause for some or all of the discovery, consistent with the limitations of Rule 26(b)(2)(C), through a single proceeding or presentation. The good-cause determination, however, may be complicated because the court and parties may know little about what information the sources identified as not reasonably accessible might contain, whether it is relevant, or how valuable it may be to the litigation. In such cases, the parties may need some focused discovery, which may include sampling of the sources, to learn more about what burdens and costs are involved in accessing the information, what the information consists of, and how valuable it is for the litigation in light of information that can be obtained by exhausting other opportunities for discovery.

The good-cause inquiry and consideration of the Rule 26(b)(2)(C) limitations are coupled with the authority to set conditions for discovery. The conditions may take the form of limits on the amount, type, or sources of information required to be accessed and produced. The conditions may also include payment by the requesting party of part or all of the reasonable costs of obtaining information from sources that are not reasonably accessible. A requesting party's willingness to share or bear the access costs may be weighed by the court in determining whether there is good cause. But the producing party's burdens in reviewing the information for relevance and privilege may weigh against permitting the requested discovery.

The limitations of Rule 26(b)(2)(C) continue to apply to all discovery of electronically stored information, including that stored on reasonably accessible electronic sources.

Subdivision (b)(5). The Committee has repeatedly been advised that the risk of privilege waiver, and the work necessary to avoid it, add to the costs and delay of discovery. When the review is of electronically stored information, the risk of waiver, and the time and effort required to avoid it, can increase substantially because of the volume of electronically stored information and the difficulty in ensuring that all information to be produced has in fact been reviewed. Rule 26(b)(5)(A) provides a procedure for a party that has withheld information on the basis of privilege or protection as trial-preparation material to make the claim so that the requesting party can decide whether to contest the claim and the court can resolve the dispute. Rule 26(b)(5)(B) is added to provide a procedure for a party to assert a claim of privilege or trial-preparation material protection after information is produced in discovery in the action and, if the claim is contested, permit any party that received the information to present the matter to the court for resolution.

Rule 26(b)(5)(B) does not address whether the privilege or protection that is asserted after production was waived by the production. The courts have developed principles to determine whether, and under what circumstances, waiver results from inadvertent production of privileged or protected information. Rule 26(b)(5)(B) provides a procedure for presenting and addressing these issues. Rule 26(b)(5)(B) works in tandem with Rule 26(f), which is amended to direct the parties to discuss privilege issues in preparing their discovery plan, and which, with amended Rule 16(b), allows the parties to ask the court to include in an order any agreements the parties reach regarding issues of privilege or trial-preparation material protection. Agreements reached under Rule 26(f)(4) and orders including such agreements entered under Rule 16(b)(6) may be considered when a court determines whether a waiver has occurred. Such agreements and orders ordinarily control if they adopt procedures different from those in Rule 26(b)(5)(B).

A party asserting a claim of privilege or protection after production must give notice to the receiving party. That notice should be in writing unless the circumstances preclude it. Such circumstances could include the assertion of the claim during a deposition. The notice should be as specific as possible in identifying the information and stating the basis for the claim. Because the receiving party must decide whether to challenge the claim and may sequester the information and submit it to the court for a ruling on whether the claimed privilege or protection applies and whether it has been waived, the notice should be sufficiently detailed so as to enable the receiving party and the court to understand the basis for the claim and to determine whether waiver has occurred. Courts will continue to examine whether a claim of privilege or protection was made at a reasonable time when delay is part of the waiver determination under the governing law.

After receiving notice, each party that received the information must promptly return, sequester, or destroy the information and any copies it has. The option of sequestering or destroying the information is included in part because the receiving party may have incorporated the information in protected trial-preparation materials. No receiving party may use or disclose the information pending resolution of the privilege claim. The receiving party may present to the court the questions whether the information is privileged or protected as trial-preparation material, and whether the privilege or protection has been waived. If it does so, it must provide the court with the grounds for the privilege or protection specified in the producing party's notice, and serve all parties. In presenting the question, the party may use the content of the information only to the extent permitted by the applicable law of privilege, protection for trial-preparation material, and professional responsibility.

If a party disclosed the information to nonparties before receiving notice of a claim of privilege or protection as trial-preparation material, it must take reasonable steps to retrieve the information and to return it, sequester it until the claim is resolved, or destroy it.

Whether the information is returned or not, the producing party must preserve the information pending the court's ruling on whether the claim of privilege or of protection is properly asserted and whether it was waived. As with claims made under Rule 26(b)(5)(A), there may be no ruling if the other parties do not contest the claim.

Subdivision (f). Rule 26(f) is amended to direct the parties to discuss discovery of electronically stored information during their discovery-planning conference. The rule focuses on "issues relating to disclosure or discovery of electronically stored information"; the discussion is not required in cases not involving electronic discovery, and the amendment imposes no additional requirements in those cases. When the parties do anticipate disclosure or discovery of electronically stored information, discussion at the outset may avoid later difficulties or ease their resolution.

When a case involves discovery of electronically stored information, the issues to be addressed during the Rule 26(f) conference depend on the nature and extent of the contemplated discovery and of the parties' information systems. It may be important for the parties to discuss those systems, and accordingly important for counsel to become familiar with those systems before the conference. With that information, the parties can develop a discovery plan that takes into account the capabilities of their computer systems. In appropriate cases identification of, and early discovery from, individuals with special knowledge of a party's computer systems may be helpful.

The particular issues regarding electronically stored information that deserve attention during the discovery planning stage depend on the specifics of the given case. *See Manual for Complex Litigation* (4th) § 40.25(2) (listing topics for discussion in a proposed order regarding meet-and-confer sessions). For example, the parties may specify the topics for such discovery and the time period for which discovery will be sought. They may identify the various sources of such information within a party's control that should be searched for electronically stored information. They may discuss whether the information is reasonably accessible to the party that has it, including the burden or cost of retrieving and reviewing the information. *See* Rule 26(b)(2)(B). Rule 26(f)(3) explicitly directs the parties to discuss the form or forms in which electronically stored information might be produced. The parties may be able to reach agreement on the forms of production, making discovery more efficient. Rule 34(b) is amended to permit a requesting party to specify the form or forms in which it wants electronically stored information produced. If the requesting party does not specify a form, Rule 34(b) directs the responding party to state the forms it intends to use in the production. Early discussion of the forms of production may facilitate the application of Rule 34(b) by allowing the parties to determine what forms of production will meet both parties' needs. Early identification of disputes over the forms of production may help avoid the expense and delay of searches or productions using inappropriate forms.

Rule 26(f) is also amended to direct the parties to discuss any issues regarding preservation of discoverable information during their conference as they develop a discovery plan. This provision applies to all sorts of discoverable information, but can be particularly important with regard to electronically stored information. The volume and dynamic nature of electronically stored information may complicate preservation obligations. The ordinary operation of computers involves both the automatic creation and the automatic deletion or overwriting of certain information. Failure to address preservation issues early in the litigation increases uncertainty and raises a risk of disputes.

The parties' discussion should pay particular attention to the balance between the competing needs to preserve relevant evidence and to continue routine operations critical to ongoing activities. Complete or broad cessation of a party's routine computer operations could paralyze the party's activities. *Cf. Manual for Complex Litigation* (4th) § 11.422 ("A blanket preservation order may be prohibitively expensive and unduly burdensome for parties dependent on computer systems for their day-to-day operations.") The parties should take account of these considerations in their discussions, with the goal of agreeing on reasonable preservation steps.

The requirement that the parties discuss preservation does not imply that courts should routinely enter preservation orders. A preservation order entered over objections should be narrowly tailored. Ex parte preservation orders should issue only in exceptional circumstances.

Rule 26(f) is also amended to provide that the parties should discuss any issues relating to assertions of privilege or of protection as trial-preparation materials, including whether the parties can facilitate discovery by agreeing on procedures for asserting claims of privilege or protection after production and whether to ask the court to enter an order that includes any agreement the parties reach. The Committee has repeatedly been advised about the discovery difficulties that can result from efforts to guard against waiver of privilege and work-product protection. Frequently parties find it necessary to spend large amounts of time reviewing materials requested through discovery to avoid waiving privilege. These efforts are necessary because materials subject to a claim of privilege or protection are often difficult to identify. A failure to withhold even one such item may result in an argument that there has been a waiver of privilege as to all other privileged materials on that subject matter. Efforts to avoid the risk of waiver can impose substantial costs on the party producing the material and the time required for the privilege review can substantially delay access for the party seeking discovery.

These problems often become more acute when discovery of electronically stored information is sought. The volume of such data, and the informality that attends use of e-mail and some other types of electronically stored information, may make privilege determinations more difficult, and privilege review correspondingly more expensive and time consuming. Other aspects of electronically stored information pose particular difficulties for privilege review. For example, production may be sought of information automatically included in electronic files but not apparent to the creator or to readers. Computer programs may retain draft language, editorial comments, and other deleted matter (sometimes referred to as "embedded data" or "embedded edits") in an electronic file but not make them apparent to the reader. Information describing the history, tracking, or management of an electronic file (sometimes called "metadata") is usually not apparent to the reader viewing a hard copy or a screen image. Whether this information should be produced may be among the topics discussed in the Rule 26(f) conference. If it is, it may need to be reviewed to ensure that no privileged information is included, further complicating the task of privilege review.

Parties may attempt to minimize these costs and delays by agreeing to protocols that minimize the risk of waiver. They may agree that the responding party will provide certain requested materials for initial examination without waiving any privilege or protection — sometimes known as a "quick peek." The requesting party then designates the documents it wishes to have actually produced. This designation is the Rule 34 request. The responding party then responds in the usual course, screening only those documents actually requested for formal production and asserting privilege claims as provided in Rule 26(b)(5)(A). On other occasions, parties enter agreements — sometimes called "clawback agreements"— that production without intent to waive privilege or protection should not be a waiver so long as the responding party identifies the documents mistakenly produced, and that the documents should be returned under those circumstances. Other voluntary arrangements may be appropriate depending on the circumstances of each litigation. In most circumstances, a party who receives information under such an arrangement cannot assert that production of the information waived a claim of privilege or of protection as trial-preparation material.

Although these agreements may not be appropriate for all cases, in certain cases they can facilitate prompt and economical discovery by reducing delay before the discovering party obtains access to documents, and by reducing the cost and burden of review by the producing party. A case-management or other order including such agreements may further facilitate the discovery process. Form 35 is amended to include a report to the court about any agreement regarding protections against inadvertent forfeiture or waiver of privilege or protection that the parties have reached, and Rule 16(b) is amended to recognize that the court may include such an agreement in a case-management or other order. If the parties agree to entry of such an order, their proposal should be included in the report to the court.

Rule 26(b)(5)(B) is added to establish a parallel procedure to assert privilege or protection as trial-preparation material after production, leaving the question of waiver to later determination by the court.

2007 Amendment

The language of Rule 26 has been amended as part of the general restyling of the Civil Rules to make them more easily understood and to make style and terminology consistent throughout the rules. These changes are intended to be stylistic only.

Former Rule 26(a)(5) served as an index of the discovery methods provided by later rules. It was deleted as redundant. Deletion does not affect the right to pursue discovery in addition to disclosure.

Former Rule 26(b)(1) began with a general statement of the scope of discovery that appeared to function as a preface to each of the five numbered paragraphs that followed. This preface has been shifted to the text of paragraph (1) because it does not accurately reflect the limits embodied in paragraphs (2), (3), or (4), and because paragraph (5) does not address the scope of discovery.

The reference to discovery of "books" in former Rule 26(b)(1) was deleted to achieve consistent expression throughout the discovery rules. Books remain a proper subject of discovery.

Amended Rule 26(b)(3) states that a party may obtain a copy of the party's own previous statement "on request." Former Rule 26(b)(3) expressly made the request procedure available to a nonparty witness, but did not describe the procedure to be used by a party. This apparent gap is closed by adopting the request procedure, which ensures that a party need not invoke Rule 34 to obtain a copy of the party's own statement.

Rule 26(e) stated the duty to supplement or correct a disclosure or discovery response "to include information thereafter acquired." This apparent limit is not reflected in practice; parties recognize the duty to supplement or correct by providing information that was not originally provided although it was available at the time of the initial disclosure or response. These words are deleted to reflect the actual meaning of the present rule.

Former Rule 26(e) used different phrases to describe the time to supplement or correct a disclosure or discovery response. Disclosures were to be supplemented "at appropriate intervals." A prior discovery response must be "seasonably * * * amend[ed]." The fine distinction between these phrases has not been observed in practice. Amended Rule 26(e)(1)(A) uses the same phrase for disclosures and discovery responses. The party must supplement or correct "in a timely manner."

Former Rule 26(g)(1) did not call for striking an unsigned disclosure. The omission was an obvious drafting oversight. Amended Rule 26(g)(2) includes disclosures in the list of matters that the court must strike unless a signature is provided "promptly * * * after being called to the attorney's or party's attention."

Former Rule 26(b)(2)(A) referred to a "good faith" argument to extend existing law. Amended Rule 26(b)(1)(B)(i) changes this reference to a "nonfrivolous" argument to achieve consistency with Rule 11(b)(2).

As with the Rule 11 signature on a pleading, written motion, or other paper, disclosure and discovery signatures should include not only a postal address but also a telephone number and electronic-mail address. A signer who lacks one or more of those addresses need not supply a nonexistent item.

Rule 11(b)(2) recognizes that it is legitimate to argue for establishing new law. An argument to establish new law is equally legitimate in conducting discovery.

Rule 27. Depositions to Perpetuate Testimony

(a) Before an Action Is Filed.

(1) ***Petition.*** A person who wants to perpetuate testimony about any matter cognizable in a United States court may file a verified petition in the district court for the district where any expected adverse party resides. The petition must ask for an order authorizing the petitioner to depose the named persons in order to perpetuate their testimony. The petition must be titled in the petitioner's name and must show:

(A) that the petitioner expects to be a party to an action cognizable in a United States court but cannot presently bring it or cause it to be brought;

(B) the subject matter of the expected action and the petitioner's interest;

(C) the facts that the petitioner wants to establish by the proposed testimony and the reasons to perpetuate it;

(D) the names or a description of the persons whom the petitioner expects to be adverse parties and their addresses, so far as known; and

(E) the name, address, and expected substance of the testimony of each deponent.

(2) ***Notice and Service.*** At least 20 days before the hearing date, the petitioner must serve each expected adverse party with a copy of the petition and a notice stating the time and place of the hearing. The notice may be served either inside or outside the district or state in the manner provided in Rule 4. If that service cannot be made with reasonable diligence on an expected adverse party, the court may order service by publication or otherwise. The court must appoint an attorney to represent persons not served in the manner provided in Rule 4 and to cross-examine the deponent if an unserved person is not otherwise represented. If any expected adverse party is a minor or is incompetent, Rule 17(c) applies.

(3) ***Order and Examination.*** If satisfied that perpetuating the testimony may prevent a failure or delay of justice, the court must issue an order that designates or describes the persons whose depositions may be taken, specifies the subject matter of the examinations, and states whether the depositions will be taken orally or by written interrogatories. The depositions may then be taken under these rules, and the court may issue orders like those authorized by Rules 34 and 35. A reference in these rules to the court where an action is pending means, for purposes of this rule, the court where the petition for the deposition was filed.

(4) ***Using the Deposition.*** A deposition to perpetuate testimony may be used under Rule 32(a) in any later-filed district-court action involving the same subject matter if the deposition either was taken under these rules or, although not so taken, would be admissible in evidence in the courts of the state where it was taken.

(b) Pending Appeal.

(1) ***In General.*** The court where a judgment has been rendered may, if an appeal has been taken or may still be taken, permit a party to depose witnesses to perpetuate their testimony for use in the event of further proceedings in that court.

(2) ***Motion.*** The party who wants to perpetuate testimony may move for leave to take the depositions, on the same notice and service as if the action were pending in the district court. The motion must show:

(A) the name, address, and expected substance of the testimony of each deponent; and

(B) the reasons for perpetuating the testimony.

(3) ***Court Order.*** If the court finds that perpetuating the testimony may prevent a failure or delay of justice, the court may permit the depositions to be taken and may issue orders like those authorized by Rules 34 and 35. The depositions may be taken and used as any other deposition taken in a pending district-court action.

(c) Perpetuation by an Action. This rule does not limit a court's power to entertain an action to perpetuate testimony.

(Amended December 27, 1946, effective March 19, 1948; December 29, 1948, effective October 20, 1949; March 1, 1971, effective July 1, 1971; March 2, 1987, effective August 1, 1987; April 25, 2005, effective December 1, 2005; April 30, 2007, effective December 1, 2007.)

ADVISORY COMMITTEE NOTES

1937 Adoption

Note to Subdivision (a). This rule offers a simple method of perpetuating testimony in cases where it is usually allowed under equity practice or under modern statutes. See *Arizona v. California,* 1934, 54 S.Ct. 735, 292 U.S. 341, 78 L.Ed. 1298; *Todd Engineering Dry Dock and Repair Co. v. United States,* C.C.A.5, 1929, 32 F.2d 734; *Hall v. Stout,* 4 Del.Ch. 269 (1871). For comparable state statutes see Ark.Civ.Code (Crawford, 1934) §§ 666 to 670; Calif.Code Civ.Proc. (Deering, 1937) 2083–2089; Smith-Hurd Ill.Stats. c. 51, §§ 39 to 46; Iowa Code (1935) §§ 11400 to 11407; 2 Mass.Gen.Laws (Ter.Ed., 1932) ch. 233, §§ 46 to 63; N.Y.C.P.A. (1937) § 295; Ohio Gen.Code Ann. (Throckmorton, 1936) §§ 12216 to 12222; Va.Code Ann. (Michie, 1936) § 6235; Wis.Stat. (1935) §§ 326.27 to 326.29. The appointment of an attorney to represent absent parties or parties not personally notified, or a guardian ad litem to represent minors and incompetents, is provided for in several of the above statutes.

Note to Subdivision (b). This follows the practice approved in *Richter v. Union Trust Co.,* 1885, 5 S.Ct. 1162, 115 U.S. 55, 29 L.Ed. 345, by extending the right to perpetuate testimony to cases pending an appeal.

Note to Subdivision (c). This preserves the right to employ a separate action to perpetuate testimony under

U.S.C., Title 28, [former] § 644 (Depositions under *dedimus potestatem* and *in perpetuam*) as an alternate method.

1946 Amendment

Note. Since the second sentence in subdivision (a)(3) refers only to depositions, it is arguable that Rules 34 and 35 are inapplicable in proceedings to perpetuate testimony. The new matter [in subdivisions (a)(3) and (b)] clarifies. A conforming change is also made in subdivision (b).

1948 Amendment

The amendment effective October 1949, substituted the words "United States district court" in subdivision (a)(1) and (4) for "district court of the United States."

1971 Amendment

The reference intended in this subdivision is to the rule governing the use of depositions in court proceedings. Formerly Rule 26(d), that rule is now Rule 32(a). The subdivision is amended accordingly.

1987 Amendment

The amendments are technical. No substantive change is intended.

2005 Amendment

The outdated cross-reference to former Rule 4(d) is corrected to incorporate all Rule 4 methods of service. Former Rule 4(d) has been allocated to many different subdivisions of Rule 4. Former Rule 4(d) did not cover all categories of defendants or modes of service, and present Rule 4 reaches further than all of former Rule 4. But there is no reason to distinguish between the different categories of defendants and modes of service encompassed by Rule 4. Rule 4 service provides effective notice. Notice by such means should be provided to any expected adverse party that comes within Rule 4.

Other changes are made to conform Rule 27(a)(2) to current style conventions.

2007 Amendment

The language of Rule 27 has been amended as part of the general restyling of the Civil Rules to make them more easily understood and to make style and terminology consistent throughout the rules. These changes are intended to be stylistic only.

Rule 28. Persons Before Whom Depositions May Be Taken

(a) Within the United States.

(1) ***In General.*** Within the United States or a territory or insular possession subject to United States jurisdiction, a deposition must be taken before:

(A) an officer authorized to administer oaths either by federal law or by the law in the place of examination; or

(B) a person appointed by the court where the action is pending to administer oaths and take testimony.

(2) ***Definition of "Officer".*** The term "officer" in Rules 30, 31, and 32 includes a person appointed by the court under this rule or designated by the parties under Rule 29(a).

(b) In a Foreign Country.

(1) ***In General.*** A deposition may be taken in a foreign country:

(A) under an applicable treaty or convention;

(B) under a letter of request, whether or not captioned a "letter rogatory";

(C) on notice, before a person authorized to administer oaths either by federal law or by the law in the place of examination; or

(D) before a person commissioned by the court to administer any necessary oath and take testimony.

(2) ***Issuing a Letter of Request or a Commission.*** A letter of request, a commission, or both may be issued:

(A) on appropriate terms after an application and notice of it; and

(B) without a showing that taking the deposition in another manner is impracticable or inconvenient.

(3) ***Form of a Request, Notice, or Commission.*** When a letter of request or any other device is used according to a treaty or convention, it must be captioned in the form prescribed by that treaty or convention. A letter of request may be addressed "To the Appropriate Authority in [name of country]." A deposition notice or a commission must designate by name or descriptive title the person before whom the deposition is to be taken.

(4) ***Letter of Request—Admitting Evidence.*** Evidence obtained in response to a letter of request need not be excluded merely because it is not a verbatim transcript, because the testimony was not taken under oath, or because of any similar departure from the requirements for depositions taken within the United States.

(c) Disqualification. A deposition must not be taken before a person who is any party's relative, employee, or attorney; who is related to or employed by any party's attorney; or who is financially interested in the action.

(Amended December 27, 1946, effective March 19, 1948; January 21, 1963, effective July 1, 1963; April 29, 1980, effective August 1, 1980; March 2, 1987, effective August 1, 1987; April 22, 1993, effective December 1, 1993; April 30, 2007, effective December 1, 2007.)

ADVISORY COMMITTEE NOTES

1937 Adoption

In effect this rule is substantially the same as U.S.C., Title 28, [former] § 639 (Depositions *de bene esse*; when and where taken; notice). U.S.C., Title 28, [former] § 642 (Depositions, acknowledgments, and affidavits taken by notaries public) does not conflict with subdivision (a).

1946 Amendments

Note. The added language [in subdivision (a)] provides for the situation, occasionally arising, when depositions must be taken in an isolated place where there is no one readily available who has the power to administer oaths and take testimony according to the terms of the rule as originally stated. In addition, the amendment affords a more convenient method of securing depositions in the case where state lines intervene between the location of various witnesses otherwise rather closely grouped. The amendment insures that the person appointed shall have adequate power to perform his duties. It has been held that a person authorized to act in the premises, as, for example, a master, may take testimony outside the district of his appointment. *Consolidated Fastener Co. v. Columbian Button & Fastener Co.,* C.C.N.D.N.Y.1898, 85 Fed. 54; *Mathieson Alkali Works v. Arnold, Hoffman & Co.,* C.C.A.1, 1929, 31 F.2d 1.

1963 Amendments

The amendment of clause (1) is designed to facilitate depositions in foreign countries by enlarging the class of persons before whom the depositions may be taken on notice. The class is no longer confined, as at present, to a secretary of embassy or legation, consul general, consul, vice consul, or consular agent of the United States. In a country that regards the taking of testimony by a foreign official in aid of litigation pending in a court of another country as an infringement upon its sovereignty, it will be expedient to notice depositions before officers of the country in which the examination is taken. See generally *Symposium, Letters Rogatory* (Grossman ed. 1956); Doyle, *Taking Evidence by Deposition and Letters Rogatory and Obtaining Documents in Foreign Territory,* Proc.A.B.A., Sec.Int'l & Comp.L. 37 (1959); Heilpern, *Procuring Evidence Abroad,* 14 Tul.L.Rev. 29 (1939); Jones, *International Judicial Assistance: Procedural Chaos and a Program for Reform,* 62 Yale L.J. 515, 526–29 (1953); Smit, *International Aspects of Federal Civil Procedure,* 61 Colum.L.Rev. 1031, 1056–58 (1961).

Clause (2) of amended subdivision (b), like the corresponding provision of subdivision (a) dealing with depositions taken in the United States, makes it clear that the appointment of a person by commission in itself confers power upon him to administer any necessary oath.

It has been held that a letter rogatory will not be issued unless the use of a notice or commission is shown to be impossible or impractical. See, e.g., *United States v. Matles,* 154 F.Supp. 574 (E.D.N.Y.1957); *The Edmund Fanning,* 89 F.Supp. 282 (E.D.N.Y.1950); *Branyan v. Koninklijke Luchtvaart Maatschappij,* 13 F.R.D. 425 (S.D.N.Y.1953). See also *Ali Akber Kiachif v. Philco International Corp.,* 10 F.R.D. 277 (S.D.N.Y.1950). The intent of the fourth sentence of the amended subdivision is to overcome this judicial antipathy and to permit a sound choice between depositions under a letter rogatory and on notice or by commission in the light of all the circumstances. In a case in which the foreign country will compel a witness to attend or testify in aid of a letter rogatory but not in aid of a commission, a letter rogatory may be preferred on the ground that it is less expensive to execute, even if there is plainly no need for compulsive process. A letter rogatory may also be preferred when it cannot be demonstrated that a witness will be recalcitrant or when the witness states that he is willing to testify voluntarily, but the contingency exists that he will change his mind at the last moment. In the latter case, it may be advisable to issue both a commission and a letter rogatory, the latter to be executed if the former fails. The choice between a letter rogatory and a commission may be conditioned by other factors, including the nature and extent of the assistance that the foreign country will give to the execution of either.

In executing a letter rogatory the courts of other countries may be expected to follow their customary procedure for taking testimony. See *United States v. Paraffin Wax,* 2255 Bags, 23 F.R.D. 289 (E.D.N.Y.1959). In many noncommon-law countries the judge questions the witness, sometimes without first administering an oath, the attorneys put any supplemental questions either to the witness or through the judge, and the judge dictates a summary of the testimony, which the witness acknowledges as correct. See *Jones, supra,* at 530–32; *Doyle, supra,* at 39–41. The last sentence of the amended subdivision provides, contrary to the implications of some authority, that evidence recorded in such a fashion need not be excluded on that account. See *The Mandu,* 11 F.Supp. 845 (E.D.N.Y.1935). But *cf. Nelson v. United States,* 17 Fed.Cas. 1340 (No. 10,116) (C.C.D.Pa. 1816); *Winthrop v. Union Ins. Co.,* 30 Fed.Cas. 376 (No. 17901) (C.C.D.Pa.1807). The specific reference to the lack of an oath or a verbatim transcript is intended to be illustrative. Whether or to what degree the value or weight of the evidence may be affected by the method of taking or recording the testimony is left for determination according to the circumstances of the particular case, *cf. Uebersee Finanz-Korporation, A.G. v. Brownell,* 121 F.Supp. 420 (D.D.C. 1954); *Danisch v. Guardian Life Ins. Co.,* 19 F.R.D. 235 (S.D.N.Y.1956); the testimony may indeed be so devoid of substance or probative value as to warrant its exclusion altogether.

Some foreign countries are hostile to allowing a deposition to be taken in their country, especially by notice or commission, or to lending assistance in the taking of a deposition. Thus compliance with the terms of amended subdivision (b) may not in all cases ensure completion of a deposition abroad. Examination of the law and policy of the particular foreign country in advance of attempting a deposition is therefore advisable. See 4 *Moore's Federal Practice* ¶¶28.05–28.08 (2d ed. 1950).

1980 Amendments

The amendments are clarifying.

1987 Amendments

The amendment is technical. No substantive change is intended.

1993 Amendments

This revision is intended to make effective use of the Hague Convention on the Taking of Evidence Abroad in Civil or Commercial Matters, and of any similar treaties that the United States may enter into in the future which provide procedures for taking depositions abroad. The party taking the deposition is ordinarily obliged to conform to an applicable treaty or convention if an effective deposition can be taken by such internationally approved means, even though a verbatim transcript is not available or testimony cannot be taken under oath. For a discussion of the impact of such treaties upon the discovery process, and of the application of principles of comity upon discovery in countries not signatories to a convention, see *Société Nationale Industrielle Aérospatiale v. United States District Court*, 482 U.S. 522 (1987).

The term "letter of request" has been substituted in the rule for the term "letter rogatory" because it is the primary method provided by the Hague Convention. A letter rogatory is essentially a form of letter of request. There are several other minor changes that are designed merely to carry out the intent of the other alterations.

2007 Amendment

The language of Rule 28 has been amended as part of the general restyling of the Civil Rules to make them more easily understood and to make style and terminology consistent throughout the rules. These changes are intended to be stylistic only.

Rule 29. Stipulations About Discovery Procedure

Unless the court orders otherwise, the parties may stipulate that:

(a) a deposition may be taken before any person, at any time or place, on any notice, and in the manner specified—in which event it may be used in the same way as any other deposition; and

(b) other procedures governing or limiting discovery be modified—but a stipulation extending the time for any form of discovery must have court approval if it would interfere with the time set for completing discovery, for hearing a motion, or for trial.

(Amended March 30, 1970, effective July 1, 1970; April 22, 1993, effective December 1, 1993; April 30, 2007, effective December 1, 2007.)

ADVISORY COMMITTEE NOTES

1970 Amendment

There is no provision for stipulations varying the procedures by which methods of discovery other than depositions are governed. It is common practice for parties to agree on such variations, and the amendment recognizes such agreements and provides a formal mechanism in the rules for giving them effect. Any stipulation varying the procedures may be superseded by court order, and stipulations extending the time for response to discovery under Rules 33, 34, and 36 require court approval.

1993 Amendments

This rule is revised to give greater opportunity for litigants to agree upon modifications to the procedures governing discovery or to limitations upon discovery. Counsel are encouraged to agree on less expensive and time-consuming methods to obtain information, as through voluntary exchange of documents, use of interviews in lieu of depositions, etc. Likewise, when more depositions or interrogatories are needed than allowed under these rules or when more time is needed to complete a deposition than allowed under a local rule, they can, by agreeing to the additional discovery, eliminate the need for a special motion addressed to the court.

Under the revised rule, the litigants ordinarily are not required to obtain the court's approval of these stipulations. By order or local rule, the court can, however, direct that its approval be obtained for particular types of stipulations; and, in any event, approval must be obtained if a stipulation to extend the 30–day period for responding to interrogatories, requests for production, or requests for admissions would interfere with dates set by the court for completing discovery, for hearing of a motion, or for trial.

2007 Amendment

The language of Rule 29 has been amended as part of the general restyling of the Civil Rules to make them more easily understood and to make style and terminology consistent throughout the rules. These changes are intended to be stylistic only.

Rule 30. Depositions by Oral Examination

(a) When a Deposition May Be Taken.

(1) ***Without Leave.*** A party may, by oral questions, depose any person, including a party, without leave of court except as provided in Rule 30(a)(2). The deponent's attendance may be compelled by subpoena under Rule 45.

(2) ***With Leave.*** A party must obtain leave of court, and the court must grant leave to the extent consistent with Rule 26(b)(2):

(A) if the parties have not stipulated to the deposition and:

(i) the deposition would result in more than 10 depositions being taken under this rule or Rule 31 by the plaintiffs, or by the defendants, or by the third-party defendants;

(ii) the deponent has already been deposed in the case; or

(iii) the party seeks to take the deposition before the time specified in Rule 26(d), unless the party certifies in the notice, with supporting facts, that the deponent is expected to leave the United States and be unavailable for examination in this country after that time; or

(B) if the deponent is confined in prison.

(b) Notice of the Deposition; Other Formal Requirements.

(1) ***Notice in General.*** A party who wants to depose a person by oral questions must give reasonable written notice to every other party. The notice must state the time and place of the deposition and, if known, the deponent's name and address. If the name is unknown, the notice must provide a general description sufficient to identify the person or the particular class or group to which the person belongs.

(2) ***Producing Documents.*** If a subpoena duces tecum is to be served on the deponent, the materials designated for production, as set out in the subpoena, must be listed in the notice or in an attachment. The notice to a party deponent may be accompanied by a request under Rule 34 to produce documents and tangible things at the deposition.

(3) ***Method of Recording.***

(A) *Method Stated in the Notice.* The party who notices the deposition must state in the notice the method for recording the testimony. Unless the court orders otherwise, testimony may be recorded by audio, audiovisual, or stenographic means. The noticing party bears the recording costs. Any party may arrange to transcribe a deposition.

(B) *Additional Method.* With prior notice to the deponent and other parties, any party may designate another method for recording the testimony in addition to that specified in the original notice. That party bears the expense of the additional record or transcript unless the court orders otherwise.

(4) ***By Remote Means.*** The parties may stipulate—or the court may on motion order—that a deposition be taken by telephone or other remote means. For the purpose of this rule and Rules 28(a), 37(a)(2), and 37(b)(1), the deposition takes place where the deponent answers the questions.

(5) ***Officer's Duties.***

(A) *Before the Deposition.* Unless the parties stipulate otherwise, a deposition must be conducted before an officer appointed or designated under Rule 28. The officer must begin the deposition with an on-the-record statement that includes:

(i) the officer's name and business address;

(ii) the date, time, and place of the deposition;

(iii) the deponent's name;

(iv) the officer's administration of the oath or affirmation to the deponent; and

(v) the identity of all persons present.

(B) *Conducting the Deposition; Avoiding Distortion.* If the deposition is recorded nonstenographically, the officer must repeat the items in Rule 30(b)(5)(A)(i)-(iii) at the beginning of each unit of the recording medium. The deponent's and attorneys' appearance or demeanor must not be distorted through recording techniques.

(C) *After the Deposition.* At the end of a deposition, the officer must state on the record that the deposition is complete and must set out any stipulations made by the attorneys about custody of the transcript or recording and of the exhibits, or about any other pertinent matters.

(6) ***Notice or Subpoena Directed to an Organization.*** In its notice or subpoena, a party may name as the deponent a public or private corporation, a partnership, an association, a governmental agency, or other entity and must describe with reasonable particularity the matters for examination. The named organization must then designate one or more officers, directors, or managing agents, or designate other persons who consent to testify on its behalf; and it may set out the matters on which each person designated will testify. A subpoena must advise a nonparty organization of its duty to make this designation. The persons designated must testify about information known or reasonably available to the organization. This paragraph (6) does not preclude a deposition by any other procedure allowed by these rules.

(c) Examination and Cross-Examination; Record of the Examination; Objections; Written Questions.

(1) ***Examination and Cross-Examination.*** The examination and cross-examination of a deponent proceed as they would at trial under the Federal Rules of Evidence, except Rules 103 and 615. After putting the deponent under oath or affirmation, the officer must record the testimony by the method designated under Rule 30(b)(3)(A). The testimony must be recorded by the officer personally or by a person acting in the presence and under the direction of the officer.

(2) ***Objections.*** An objection at the time of the examination—whether to evidence, to a par-

ty's conduct, to the officer's qualifications, to the manner of taking the deposition, or to any other aspect of the deposition—must be noted on the record, but the examination still proceeds; the testimony is taken subject to any objection. An objection must be stated concisely in a nonargumentative and nonsuggestive manner. A person may instruct a deponent not to answer only when necessary to preserve a privilege, to enforce a limitation ordered by the court, or to present a motion under Rule 30(d)(3).

(3) ***Participating Through Written Questions.*** Instead of participating in the oral examination, a party may serve written questions in a sealed envelope on the party noticing the deposition, who must deliver them to the officer. The officer must ask the deponent those questions and record the answers verbatim.

(d) Duration; Sanction; Motion to Terminate or Limit.

(1) ***Duration.*** Unless otherwise stipulated or ordered by the court, a deposition is limited to 1 day of 7 hours. The court must allow additional time consistent with Rule 26(b)(2) if needed to fairly examine the deponent or if the deponent, another person, or any other circumstance impedes or delays the examination.

(2) ***Sanction.*** The court may impose an appropriate sanction—including the reasonable expenses and attorney's fees incurred by any party—on a person who impedes, delays, or frustrates the fair examination of the deponent.

(3) ***Motion to Terminate or Limit.***

(A) *Grounds.* At any time during a deposition, the deponent or a party may move to terminate or limit it on the ground that it is being conducted in bad faith or in a manner that unreasonably annoys, embarrasses, or oppresses the deponent or party. The motion may be filed in the court where the action is pending or the deposition is being taken. If the objecting deponent or party so demands, the deposition must be suspended for the time necessary to obtain an order.

(B) *Order.* The court may order that the deposition be terminated or may limit its scope and manner as provided in Rule 26(c). If terminated, the deposition may be resumed only by order of the court where the action is pending.

(C) *Award of Expenses.* Rule 37(a)(5) applies to the award of expenses.

(e) Review by the Witness; Changes.

(1) ***Review; Statement of Changes.*** On request by the deponent or a party before the deposition is completed, the deponent must be allowed 30 days after being notified by the officer that the transcript or recording is available in which:

(A) to review the transcript or recording; and

(B) if there are changes in form or substance, to sign a statement listing the changes and the reasons for making them.

(2) ***Changes Indicated in the Officer's Certificate.*** The officer must note in the certificate prescribed by Rule 30(f)(1) whether a review was requested and, if so, must attach any changes the deponent makes during the 30-day period.

(f) Certification and Delivery; Exhibits; Copies of the Transcript or Recording; Filing.

(1) ***Certification and Delivery.*** The officer must certify in writing that the witness was duly sworn and that the deposition accurately records the witness's testimony. The certificate must accompany the record of the deposition. Unless the court orders otherwise, the officer must seal the deposition in an envelope or package bearing the title of the action and marked "Deposition of [witness's name]" and must promptly send it to the attorney who arranged for the transcript or recording. The attorney must store it under conditions that will protect it against loss, destruction, tampering, or deterioration.

(2) ***Documents and Tangible Things.***

(A) *Originals and Copies.* Documents and tangible things produced for inspection during a deposition must, on a party's request, be marked for identification and attached to the deposition. Any party may inspect and copy them. But if the person who produced them wants to keep the originals, the person may:

(i) offer copies to be marked, attached to the deposition, and then used as originals—after giving all parties a fair opportunity to verify the copies by comparing them with the originals; or

(ii) give all parties a fair opportunity to inspect and copy the originals after they are marked—in which event the originals may be used as if attached to the deposition.

(B) *Order Regarding the Originals.* Any party may move for an order that the originals be attached to the deposition pending final disposition of the case.

(3) ***Copies of the Transcript or Recording.*** Unless otherwise stipulated or ordered by the court, the officer must retain the stenographic notes of a deposition taken stenographically or a copy of the recording of a deposition taken by another method. When paid reasonable charges, the officer must furnish a copy of the transcript or recording to any party or the deponent.

(4) ***Notice of Filing.*** A party who files the deposition must promptly notify all other parties of the filing.

(g) Failure to Attend a Deposition or Serve a Subpoena; Expenses. A party who, expecting a deposition to be taken, attends in person or by an attorney may recover reasonable expenses for attending, including attorney's fees, if the noticing party failed to:

(1) attend and proceed with the deposition; or

(2) serve a subpoena on a nonparty deponent, who consequently did not attend.

(Amended January 21, 1963, effective July 1, 1963; March 30, 1970, effective July 1, 1970; March 1, 1971, effective July 1, 1971; November 20, 1972, effective July 1, 1975; April 29, 1980, effective August 1, 1980; March 2, 1987, effective August 1, 1987; April 22, 1993, effective December 1, 1993; April 17, 2000, effective December 1, 2000; April 30, 2007, effective December 1, 2007.)

ADVISORY COMMITTEE NOTES

1937 Adoption

Note to Subdivision (a). This is in accordance with common practice. See U.S.C., Title 28, [former] § 639 (Depositions *de bene esse*; when and where taken; notice), the relevant provisions of which are incorporated in this rule; West's Ann.Code Civ.Proc. § 2031; and statutes cited in respect to notice in the Note to Rule 26(a). The provision for enlarging or shortening the time of notice has been added to give flexibility to the rule.

Note to Subdivisions (b) and (d). These are introduced as a safeguard for the protection of parties and deponents on account of the unlimited right of discovery given by Rule 26.

Note to Subdivisions (c) and (e). These follow the general plan of [former] Equity Rule 51 (Evidence Taken Before Examiners, Etc.) and U.S.C., Title 28, [former] §§ 640 (Depositions *de bene esse*; mode of taking), and [former] 641 (Same; transmission to court), but are more specific. They also permit the deponent to require the officer to make changes in the deposition if the deponent is not satisfied with it. See also [former] Equity Rule 50 (Stenographer—Appointment—Fees.)

Note to Subdivision (f). Compare [former] Equity Rule 55 (Depositions Deemed Published When Filed.)

Note to Subdivision (g). This is similar to 2 Minn.Stat. (Mason, 1927) § 9833, but is more extensive.

1963 Amendments

This amendment corresponds to the change in Rule 4(d)(4). See Advisory Committee's Note to that amendment.

1970 Amendments

Subdivision (a). This subdivision contains the provisions of existing Rule 26(a), transferred here as part of the rearrangement relating to Rule 26. Existing Rule 30(a) is transferred to 30(b). Changes in language have been made to conform to the new arrangement.

This subdivision is further revised in regard to the requirement of leave of court for taking a deposition. The present procedure, requiring a plaintiff to obtain leave of court if he serves notice of taking a deposition within 20 days after commencement of the action, is changed in several respects. First, leave is required by reference to the time the deposition is to be taken rather than the date of serving notice of taking. Second, the 20-day period is extended to 30 days and runs from the service of summons and complaint on any defendant, rather than the commencement of the action. *Cf.* Ill.S.Ct.R. 19–1 S-H Ill.Ann.Stat. § 101.19–1. Third, leave is not required beyond the time that defendant initiates discovery, thus showing that he has retained counsel. As under the present practice, a party not afforded a reasonable opportunity to appear at a deposition, because he has not yet been served with process, is protected against use of the deposition at trial against him. See Rule 32(a), transferred from 26(d). Moreover, he can later redepose the witness if he so desires.

The purpose of requiring the plaintiff to obtain leave of court is, as stated by the Advisory Committee that proposed the present language of Rule 26(a), to protect "a defendant who has not had an opportunity to retain counsel and inform himself as to the nature of the suit." Note to 1948 amendment of Rule 26(a), quoted in 3A Barron & Holtzoff, *Federal Practice and Procedure* 455–456 (Wright ed. 1958). In order to assure defendant of this opportunity, the period is lengthened to 30 days. This protection, however, is relevant to the time of taking the deposition, not to the time that notice is served. Similarly, the protective period should run from the service of process rather than the filing of the complaint with the court. As stated in the note to Rule 26(d), the courts have used the service of notice as a convenient reference point for assigning priority in taking depositions, but with the elimination of priority in new Rule 26(d) the reference point is no longer needed. The new procedure is consistent in principle with the provisions of Rules 33, 34, and 36 as revised.

Plaintiff is excused from obtaining leave even during the initial 30-day period if he gives the special notice provided in subdivision (b)(2). The required notice must state that the person to be examined is about to go out of the district where the action is pending and more than 100 miles from the place of trial, or out of the United States, or on a voyage to sea, and will be unavailable for examination unless deposed within the 30-day period. These events occur most often in maritime litigation, when seamen are transferred from one port to another or are about to go to sea. Yet, there are analogous situations in nonmaritime litigation, and although the maritime problems are more common, a rule limited to claims in the admiralty and maritime jurisdiction is not justified.

In the recent unification of the civil and admiralty rules, this problem was temporarily met through addition in Rule 26(a) of a provision that depositions *de bene esse* may continue to be taken as to admiralty and maritime claims within the meaning of Rule 9(h). It was recognized at the time that "a uniform rule applicable alike to what are now civil actions and suits in admiralty" was clearly preferable, but the de bene esse procedure was adopted "for the time being at least." See Advisory Committee's Note in Report of the Judicial Conference: Proposed Amendments to Rules of Civil Procedure 43–44 (1966).

The changes in Rule 30(a) and the new Rule 30(b)(2) provide a formula applicable to ordinary civil as well as maritime claims. They replace the provision for depositions *de bene esse*. They authorize an early deposition without leave of court where the witness is about to depart and, unless his deposition is promptly taken, (1) it will be impossible or very difficult to depose him before trial or (2) his deposition can later be taken but only with substantially increased effort and expense. *Cf. S.S. Hai Chang,* 1966 A.M.C. 2239 (S.D.N.Y.1966), in which the deposing party is required to prepay expenses and counsel fees of the other party's lawyer when the action is pending in New York and depositions are to be taken on the West Coast. Defendant is protected by a provision that the deposition cannot be used against him if he was unable through exercise of diligence to obtain counsel to represent him.

The distance of 100 miles from place of trial is derived from the *de bene esse* provision and also conforms to the reach of a subpoena of the trial court, as provided in Rule 45(e). See also S.D.N.Y. Civ.R. 5(a). Some parts of the *de bene esse* provision are omitted from Rule 30(b)(2). Modern deposition practice adequately covers the witness who lives more than 100 miles away from place of trial. If a witness is aged or infirm, leave of court can be obtained.

Subdivision (b). Existing Rule 30(b) on protective orders has been transferred to Rule 26(c), and existing Rule 30(a) relating to the notice of taking deposition has been transferred to this subdivision. Because new material has been added, subsection numbers have been inserted.

Subdivision (b)(1). If a subpoena duces tecum is to be served, a copy thereof or a designation of the materials to be produced must accompany the notice. Each party is thereby enabled to prepare for the deposition more effectively.

Subdivision (b)(2). This subdivision is discussed in the note to subdivision (a), to which it relates.

Subdivision (b)(3). This provision is derived from existing Rule 30(a), with a minor change of language.

Subdivision (b)(4). In order to facilitate less expensive procedures, provision is made for the recording of testimony by other than stenographic means—*e.g.*, by mechanical, electronic, or photographic means. Because these methods give rise to problems of accuracy and trustworthiness, the party taking the deposition is required to apply for a court order. The order is to specify how the testimony is to be recorded, preserved, and filed, and it may contain whatever additional safeguards the court deems necessary.

Subdivision (b)(5). A provision is added to enable a party, through service of notice, to require another party to produce documents or things at the taking of his deposition. This may now be done as to a nonparty deponent through use of a subpoena duces tecum as authorized by Rule 45, but some courts have held that documents may be secured from a party only under Rule 34. See 2A Barron & Holtzoff, *Federal Practice and Procedure* § 644.1 n. 83.2, § 792 n. 16 (Wright ed. 1961). With the elimination of "good cause" from Rule 34, the reason for this restrictive doctrine has disappeared. *Cf.* N.Y.C.P.L.R. § 3111.

Whether production of documents or things should be obtained directly under Rule 34 or at the deposition under this rule will depend on the nature and volume of the documents or things. Both methods are made available. When the documents are few and simple, and closely related to the oral examination, ability to proceed via this rule will facilitate discovery. If the discovering party insists on examining many and complex documents at the taking of the deposition, thereby causing undue burdens on others, the latter may, under Rules 26(c) or 30(d), apply for a court order that the examining party proceed via Rule 34 alone.

Subdivision (b)(6). A new provision is added, whereby a party may name a corporation, partnership, association, or governmental agency as the deponent and designate the matters on which he requests examination, and the organization shall then name one or more of its officers, directors, or managing agents, or other persons consenting to appear and testify on its behalf with respect to matters known or reasonably available to the organization. *Cf.* Alberta Sup.Ct.R. 255. The organization may designate persons other than officers, directors, and managing agents, but only with their consent. Thus, an employee or agent who has an independent or conflicting interest in the litigation—for example, in a personal injury case—can refuse to testify on behalf of the organization.

This procedure supplements the existing practice whereby the examining party designates the corporate official to be deposed. Thus, if the examining party believes that certain officials who have not testified pursuant to this subdivision have added information, he may depose them. On the other hand, a court's decision whether to issue a protective order may take account of the availability and use made of the procedures provided in this subdivision.

The new procedure should be viewed as an added facility for discovery, one which may be advantageous to both sides as well as an improvement in the deposition process. It will reduce the difficulties now encountered in determining, prior to the taking of a deposition, whether a particular employee or agent is a "managing agent." See Note, *Discovery Against Corporations Under the Federal Rules*, 47 Iowa L.Rev. 1006–1016 (1962). It will curb the "bandying" by which officers or managing agents of a corporation are deposed in turn but each disclaims knowledge of facts that are clearly known to persons in the organization and thereby to it. *Cf. Haney v. Woodward & Lothrop, Inc.*, 330 F.2d 940, 944 (4th Cir. 1964). The provision should also assist organizations which find that an unnecessarily large number of their officers and agents are being deposed by a party uncertain of who in the organization has knowledge. Some courts have held that under the existing rules a corporation should not be burdened with choosing which person is to appear for it. E.g., *United States v. Gahagan Dredging Corp.*, 24 F.R.D. 328, 329 (S.D.N.Y.1958). This burden is not essentially different from that of answering interrogatories under Rule 33, and is in any case lighter than that of an examining party ignorant of who in the corporation has knowledge.

Subdivision (c). A new sentence is inserted at the beginning, representing the transfer of existing Rule 26(c) to this subdivision. Another addition conforms to the new provision in subdivision (b)(4).

The present rule provides that transcription shall be carried out unless all parties waive it. In view of the many depositions taken from which nothing useful is discovered, the revised language provides that transcription is to be performed if any party requests it. The fact of the request is relevant to the exercise of the court's discretion in determining who shall pay for transcription.

Parties choosing to serve written questions rather than participate personally in an oral deposition are directed to serve their questions on the party taking the deposition, since the officer is often not identified in advance. Confidentiality is preserved, since the questions may be served in a sealed envelope.

Subdivision (d). The assessment of expenses incurred in relation to motions made under this subdivision (d) is made subject to the provisions of Rule 37(a). The standards for assessment of expenses are more fully set out in Rule 37(a), and these standards should apply to the essentially similar motions of this subdivision.

Subdivision (e). The provision relating to the refusal of a witness to sign his deposition is tightened through insertion of a 30-day time period.

Subdivision (f)(1). A provision is added which codifies in a flexible way the procedure for handling exhibits related to the deposition and at the same time assures each party that he may inspect and copy documents and things produced by a nonparty witness in response to a subpoena duces tecum. As a general rule and in the absence of agreement to the contrary or order of the court, exhibits produced without objection are to be annexed to and returned with the deposition, but a witness may substitute copies for purposes of marking and he may obtain return of the exhibits. The right of the parties to inspect exhibits for identification and to make copies is assured. *Cf.* N.Y.C.P.L.R. § 3116(c).

1971 Amendments

The subdivision permits a party to name a corporation or other form of organization as a deponent in the notice of examination and to describe in the notice the matters about which discovery is desired. The organization is then obliged to designate natural persons to testify on its behalf. The amendment clarifies the procedure to be followed if a party desires to examine a non-party organization through persons designated by the organization. Under the rules, a subpoena rather than a notice of examination is served on a non-party to compel attendance at the taking of a deposition. The amendment provides that a subpoena may name a non-party organization as the deponent and may indicate the matters about which discovery is desired. In that event, the non-party organization must respond by designating natural persons, who are then obliged to testify as to matters known or reasonably available to the organization. To insure that a non-party organization that is not represented by counsel has knowledge of its duty to designate, the amendment directs the party seeking discovery to advise of the duty in the body of the subpoena.

1972 Amendments

Subdivision (c). Existing Rule 43(b), which is to be abrogated, deals with the use of leading questions, the calling, interrogation, impeachment, and scope of cross-examination of adverse parties, officers, etc. These topics are dealt with in many places in the Rules of Evidence. Moreover, many pertinent topics included in the Rules of Evidence are not mentioned in Rule 43(b), e.g. privilege. A reference to the Rules of Evidence generally is therefore made in subdivision (c) of Rule 30.

1980 Amendments

Subdivision (b)(4). It has been proposed that electronic recording of depositions be authorized as a matter of course, subject to the right of a party to seek an order that a deposition be recorded by stenographic means. The Committee is not satisfied that a case has been made for a reversal of present practice. The amendment is made to encourage parties to agree to the use of electronic recording of depositions so that conflicting claims with respect to the potential of electronic recording for reducing costs of depositions can be appraised in the light of greater experience. The provision that the parties may stipulate that depositions may be recorded by other than stenographic means seems implicit in Rule 29. The amendment makes it explicit. The provision that the stipulation or order shall designate the person before whom the deposition is to be taken is added to encourage the naming of the recording technician as that person, eliminating the necessity of the presence of one whose only function is to administer the oath. See Rules 28(a) and 29.

Subdivision (b)(7). Depositions by telephone are now authorized by Rule 29 upon stipulation of the parties. The amendment authorizes that method by order of the court. The final sentence is added to make it clear that when a deposition is taken by telephone it is taken in the district and at the place where the witness is to answer the questions rather than that where the questions are propounded.

Subdivision (f)(1). For the reasons set out in the Note following the amendment of Rule 5(d), the court may wish to permit the parties to retain depositions unless they are to be used in the action. The amendment of the first paragraph permits the court to so order.

The amendment of the second paragraph is clarifying. The purpose of the paragraph is to permit a person who produces materials at a deposition to offer copies for marking and annexation to the deposition. Such copies are a "substitute" for the originals, which are not to be marked and which can thereafter be used or even disposed of by the person who produces them. In the light of that purpose, the former language of the paragraph had been justly termed "opaque." Wright & Miller, *Federal Practice and Procedure: Civil* § 2114.

1987 Amendments

The amendments are technical. No substantive change is intended.

1993 Amendments

Subdivision (a). Paragraph (1) retains the first and third sentences from the former subdivision (a) without significant modification. The second and fourth sentences are relocated.

Paragraph (2) collects all provisions bearing on requirements of leave of court to take a deposition.

Paragraph (2)(A) is new. It provides a limit on the number of depositions the parties may take, absent leave of court or stipulation with the other parties. One aim of this revision is to assure judicial review under the standards stated in Rule 26(b)(2) before any side will be allowed to take more than ten depositions in a case without agreement of the other parties. A second objective is to emphasize that counsel have a professional obligation to develop a mutual cost-effective plan for discovery in the case. Leave to take additional depositions should be granted when consistent with the principles of Rule 26(b)(2), and in some cases the ten-per-side limit should be reduced in accordance with those same principles. Consideration should ordinarily be given at the planning meeting of the parties under Rule 26(f) and at the time of a scheduling conference under Rule 16(b) as to enlargements or reductions in the number of depositions, eliminating the need for special motions.

A deposition under Rule 30(b)(6) should, for purposes of this limit, be treated as a single deposition even though more than one person may be designated to testify.

In multi-party cases, the parties on any side are expected to confer and agree as to which depositions are most needed, given the presumptive limit on the number of depositions they can take without leave of court. If these disputes cannot be amicably resolved, the court can be requested to resolve the dispute or permit additional depositions.

Paragraph (2)(B) is new. It requires leave of court if any witness is to be deposed in the action more than once. This requirement does not apply when a deposition is temporarily recessed for convenience of counsel or the deponent or to enable additional materials to be gathered before resuming the deposition. If significant travel costs would be incurred to resume the deposition, the parties should consider the feasibility of conducting the balance of the examination by telephonic means.

Paragraph (2)(C) revises the second sentence of the former subdivision (a) as to when depositions may be taken. Consistent with the changes made in Rule 26(d), providing that formal discovery ordinarily not commence until after the litigants have met and conferred as directed in revised Rule 26(f), the rule requires leave of court or agreement of the parties if a deposition is to be taken before that time (except when a witness is about to leave the country).

Subdivision (b). The primary change in subdivision (b) is that parties will be authorized to record deposition testimony by nonstenographic means without first having to obtain permission of the court or agreement from other counsel.

Former subdivision (b)(2) is partly relocated in subdivision (a)(2)(C) of this rule. The latter two sentences of the first paragraph are deleted, in part because they are redundant to Rule 26(g) and in part because Rule 11 no longer applies to discovery requests. The second paragraph of the former subdivision (b)(2), relating to use of depositions at trial where a party was unable to obtain counsel in time for an accelerated deposition, is relocated in Rule 32.

New paragraph (2) confers on the party taking the deposition the choice of the method of recording, without the need to obtain prior court approval for one taken other than stenographically. A party choosing to record a deposition only by videotape or audiotape should understand that a transcript will be required by Rule 26(a)(3)(B) and Rule 32(c) if the deposition is later to be offered as evidence at trial or on a dispositive motion under Rule 56. Objections to the nonstenographic recording of a deposition, when warranted by the circumstances, can be presented to the court under Rule 26(c).

Paragraph (3) provides that other parties may arrange, at their own expense, for the recording of a deposition by a means (stenographic, visual, or sound) in addition to the method designated by the person noticing the deposition. The former provisions of this paragraph, relating to the court's power to change the date of a deposition, have been eliminated as redundant in view of Rule 26(c)(2).

Revised paragraph (4) requires that all depositions be recorded by an officer designated or appointed under Rule 28 and contains special provisions designed to provide basic safeguards to assure the utility and integrity of recordings taken other than stenographically.

Paragraph (7) is revised to authorize the taking of a deposition not only by telephone but also by other remote electronic means, such as satellite television, when agreed to by the parties or authorized by the court.

Subdivision (c). Minor changes are made in this subdivision to reflect those made in subdivision (b) and to complement the new provisions of subdivision (d)(1), aimed at reducing the number of interruptions during depositions.

In addition, the revision addresses a recurring problem as to whether other potential deponents can attend a deposition. Courts have disagreed, some holding that witnesses should be excluded through invocation of Rule 615 of the evidence rules, and others holding that witnesses may attend unless excluded by an order under Rule 26(c)(5). The revision provides that other witnesses are not automatically excluded from a deposition simply by the request of a party. Exclusion, however, can be ordered under Rule 26(c)(5) when appropriate; and, if exclusion is ordered, consideration should be given as to whether the excluded witnesses likewise should be precluded from reading, or being otherwise informed about, the testimony given in the earlier depositions. The revision addresses only the matter of attendance by potential deponents, and does not attempt to resolve issues concerning attendance by others, such as members of the public or press.

Subdivision (d). The first sentence of new paragraph (1) provides that any objections during a deposition must be made concisely and in a non-argumentative and non-suggestive manner. Depositions frequently have been unduly prolonged, if not unfairly frustrated, by lengthy objections and colloquy, often suggesting how the deponent should respond. While objections may, under the revised rule, be made during a deposition, they ordinarily should be limited to those that under Rule 32(d)(3) might be waived if not made at that time, *i.e.,* objections on grounds that might be immediately obviated, removed, or cured, such as to the form of a question or the responsiveness of an answer. Under Rule 32(b), other objections can, even without the so-called "usual stipulation" preserving objections, be raised for the first time at trial and therefore should be kept to a minimum during a deposition.

Directions to a deponent not to answer a question can be even more disruptive than objections. The second sentence of new paragraph (1) prohibits such directions except in the three circumstances indicated: to claim a privilege or protection against disclosure (*e.g.*, as work product), to enforce a court directive limiting the scope or length of permissible discovery, or to suspend a deposition to enable presentation of a motion under paragraph (3).

Paragraph (2) is added to this subdivision to dispel any doubts regarding the power of the court by order or local rule to establish limits on the length of depositions. The rule also explicitly authorizes the court to impose the cost resulting from obstructive tactics that unreasonably prolong a deposition on the person engaged in such obstruction. This sanction may be imposed on a non-party witness as well as a party or attorney, but is otherwise congruent with Rule 26(g).

It is anticipated that limits on the length of depositions prescribed by local rules would be presumptive only, subject to modification by the court or by agreement of the parties. Such modifications typically should be discussed by the parties in their meeting under Rule 26(f) and included in the scheduling order required by Rule 16(b). Additional time, moreover, should be allowed under the revised rule when justified under the principles stated in Rule 26(b)(2). To reduce the number of special motions, local rules should ordinarily permit—and indeed encourage—the parties to agree to additional time, as when, during the taking of a deposition, it becomes clear that some additional examination is needed.

Paragraph (3) authorizes appropriate sanctions not only when a deposition is unreasonably prolonged, but also when an attorney engages in other practices that improperly frustrate the fair examination of the deponent, such as making improper objections or giving directions not to answer prohibited by paragraph (1). In general, counsel should not engage in any conduct during a deposition that would not be allowed in the presence of a judicial officer. The making of an excessive number of unnecessary objections may itself constitute sanctionable conduct, as may the refusal of an attorney to agree with other counsel on a fair apportionment of the time allowed for examination of a deponent or a refusal to agree to a reasonable request for some additional time to complete a deposition, when that is permitted by the local rule or order.

Subdivision (e). Various changes are made in this subdivision to reduce problems sometimes encountered when depositions are taken stenographically. Reporters frequently have difficulties obtaining signatures—and the return of depositions—from deponents. Under the revision pre-filing review by the deponent is required only if requested before the deposition is completed. If review is requested, the deponent will be allowed 30 days to review the transcript or recording and to indicate any changes in form or substance. Signature of the deponent will be required only if review is requested and changes are made.

Subdivision (f). Minor changes are made in this subdivision to reflect those made in subdivision (b). In courts which direct that depositions not be automatically filed, the reporter can transmit the transcript or recording to the attorney taking the deposition (or ordering the transcript or record), who then becomes custodian for the court of the original record of the deposition. Pursuant to subdivision (f)(2), as under the prior rule, any other party is entitled to secure a copy of the deposition from the officer designated to take the deposition; accordingly, unless ordered or agreed, the officer must retain a copy of the recording or the stenographic notes.

2000 Amendment

Subdivision (d). Paragraph (1) has been amended to clarify the terms regarding behavior during depositions. The references to objections " to evidence" and limitations "on evidence" have been removed to avoid disputes about what is "evidence" and whether an objection is to, or a limitation is on, discovery instead. It is intended that the rule apply to any objection to a question or other issue arising during a deposition, and to any limitation imposed by the court in connection with a deposition, which might relate to duration or other matters.

The current rule places limitations on instructions that a witness not answer only when the instruction is made by a "party." Similar limitations should apply with regard to anyone who might purport to instruct a witness not to answer a question. Accordingly, the rule is amended to apply the limitation to instructions by any person. The amendment is not intended to confer new authority on nonparties to instruct witnesses to refuse to answer deposition questions. The amendment makes it clear that, whatever the legitimacy of giving such instructions, the nonparty is subject to the same limitations as parties.

Paragraph (2) imposes a presumptive durational limitation of one day of seven hours for any deposition. The Committee has been informed that overlong depositions can result in undue costs and delays in some circumstances. This limitation contemplates that there will be reasonable breaks during the day for lunch and other reasons, and that the only time to be counted is the time occupied by the actual deposition. For purposes of this durational limit, the deposition of each person designated under Rule 30(b)(6) should be considered a separate deposition. The presumptive duration may be extended, or otherwise altered, by agreement. Absent agreement, a court order is needed. The party seeking a court order to extend the examination, or otherwise alter the limitations, is expected to show good cause to justify such an order.

Parties considering extending the time for a deposition—and courts asked to order an extension—might consider a variety of factors. For example, if the witness needs an interpreter, that may prolong the examination. If the examination will cover events occurring over a long period of time, that may justify allowing additional time. In cases in which the witness will be questioned about numerous or lengthy documents, it is often desirable for the interrogating party to send copies of the documents to the witness sufficiently in advance of the deposition so that the witness can become familiar with them. Should the witness nevertheless not read the documents in advance, thereby prolonging the deposition, a court could consider that a reason for extending the time limit. If the examination reveals that documents have been requested but not produced, that may justify further examination once production has occurred. In multi-party cases, the need for each party to examine the witness may warrant additional time, although duplicative questioning should be avoided and parties with similar interests should strive to designate one lawyer to question about areas of common interest. Similarly, should the lawyer for the witness want to examine the witness, that may require additional time. Finally, with regard to expert witnesses, there may more often be a need for additional time—even after the submission of the report required by Rule 26(a)(2)—for full exploration of the theories upon which the witness relies.

It is expected that in most instances the parties and the witness will make reasonable accommodations to avoid the need for resort to the court. The limitation is phrased in terms of a single day on the assumption that ordinarily a single day would be preferable to a deposition extending over multiple days; if alternative arrangements would better suit the parties, they may agree to them. It is also assumed that there will be reasonable breaks during the day. Preoccupation with timing is to be avoided.

The rule directs the court to allow additional time where consistent with Rule 26(b)(2) if needed for a fair examination of the deponent. In addition, if the deponent or another person impedes or delays the examination, the court must authorize extra time. The amendment makes clear that additional time should also be allowed where the examination is impeded by an "other circumstance," which might include a power outage, a health emergency, or other event.

In keeping with the amendment to Rule 26(b)(2), the provision added in 1993 granting authority to adopt a local rule limiting the time permitted for depositions has been removed. The court may enter a case-specific order directing shorter depositions for all depositions in a case or with regard to a specific witness. The court may also order that a deposition be taken for limited periods on several days.

Paragraph (3) includes sanctions provisions formerly included in paragraph (2). It authorizes the court to impose an appropriate sanction on any person responsible for an impediment that frustrated the fair examination of the deponent. This could include the deponent, any party, or any other person involved in the deposition. If the impediment or delay results from an "other circumstance" under paragraph (2), ordinarily no sanction would be appropriate.

Former paragraph (3) has been renumbered (4) but is otherwise unchanged .

Subdivision (f)(1): This subdivision is amended because Rule 5(d) has been amended to direct that discovery materials, including depositions, ordinarily should not be filed. The rule already has provisions directing that the lawyer who arranged for the transcript or recording preserve the deposition. Rule 5(d) provides that, once the deposition is used in the proceeding, the attorney must file it with the court.

"Shall" is replaced by "must" or "may" under the program to conform amended rules to current style conventions when there is no ambiguity.

GAP Report

The Advisory Committee recommends deleting the requirement in the published proposed amendments that the deponent consent to extending a deposition beyond one day, and adding an amendment to Rule 30(f)(1) to conform to the published amendment to Rule 5(d) regarding filing of depositions. It also recommends conforming the Committee Note with regard to the deponent veto, and adding material to the Note to provide direction on computation of the durational limitation on depositions, to provide examples of situations in which the parties might agree—or the court order—that a deposition be extended, and to make clear that no new authority to instruct a witness is conferred by the amendment. One minor wording improvement in the Note is also suggested.

2007 Amendment

The language of Rule 30 has been amended as part of the general restyling of the Civil Rules to make them more easily understood and to make style and terminology consistent throughout the rules. These changes are intended to be stylistic only.

The right to arrange a deposition transcription should be open to any party, regardless of the means of recording and regardless of who noticed the deposition.

"[O]ther entity" is added to the list of organizations that may be named as deponent. The purpose is to ensure that the deposition process can be used to reach information known or reasonably available to an organization no matter what abstract fictive concept is used to describe the organization. Nothing is gained by wrangling over the place to fit into current rule language such entities as limited liability companies, limited partnerships, business trusts, more exotic common-law creations, or forms developed in other countries.

HISTORICAL NOTES

Effective Date of Amendment Proposed November 20, 1972

Amendment of this rule embraced by the order entered by the Supreme Court of the United States on November 20, 1972, effective on the 180th day beginning after January 2, 1975, see section 3 of Pub.L. 93-595, Jan. 2, 1975, 88 Stat. 1959, set out as a note under section 2071 of Title 28.

Rule 31. Depositions by Written Questions

(a) When a Deposition May Be Taken.

(1) ***Without Leave.*** A party may, by written questions, depose any person, including a party, without leave of court except as provided in Rule 31(a)(2). The deponent's attendance may be compelled by subpoena under Rule 45.

(2) ***With Leave.*** A party must obtain leave of court, and the court must grant leave to the extent consistent with Rule 26(b)(2):

(A) if the parties have not stipulated to the deposition and:

(i) the deposition would result in more than 10 depositions being taken under this rule or Rule 30 by the plaintiffs, or by the defendants, or by the third-party defendants;

(ii) the deponent has already been deposed in the case; or

(iii) the party seeks to take a deposition before the time specified in Rule 26(d); or

(B) if the deponent is confined in prison.

(3) ***Service; Required Notice.*** A party who wants to depose a person by written questions must serve them on every other party, with a notice stating, if known, the deponent's name and address. If the name is unknown, the notice must provide a general description sufficient to identify the person or the particular class or group to which the person belongs. The notice must also state the name or descriptive title and the address of the officer before whom the deposition will be taken.

(4) ***Questions Directed to an Organization.*** A public or private corporation, a partnership, an association, or a governmental agency may be deposed by written questions in accordance with Rule 30(b)(6).

(5) ***Questions from Other Parties.*** Any questions to the deponent from other parties must be served on all parties as follows: cross-questions, within 14 days after being served with the notice and direct questions; redirect questions, within 7 days after being served with cross-questions; and recross-questions, within 7 days after being served with redirect questions. The court may, for good cause, extend or shorten these times.

(b) Delivery to the Officer; Officer's Duties. The party who noticed the deposition must deliver to the officer a copy of all the questions served and of the notice. The officer must promptly proceed in the manner provided in Rule 30(c), (e), and (f) to:

(1) take the deponent's testimony in response to the questions;

(2) prepare and certify the deposition; and

(3) send it to the party, attaching a copy of the questions and of the notice.

(c) Notice of Completion or Filing.

(1) ***Completion.*** The party who noticed the deposition must notify all other parties when it is completed.

(2) ***Filing.*** A party who files the deposition must promptly notify all other parties of the filing.

(Amended March 30, 1970, effective July 1, 1970; March 2, 1987, effective August 1, 1987; April 22, 1993, effective December 1, 1993; April 30, 2007, effective December 1, 2007.)

ADVISORY COMMITTEE NOTES

1937 Adoption

This rule is in accordance with common practice. In most of the states listed in the Note to Rule 26(a), provisions similar to this rule will be found in the statutes which in their respective statutory compilations follow those cited in the Note to Rule 26(a).

1970 Amendment

Confusion is created by the use of the same terminology to describe both the taking of a deposition upon "written interrogatories" pursuant to this rule and the serving of "written interrogatories" upon parties pursuant to Rule 33. The distinction between these two modes of discovery will be more readily and clearly grasped through substitution of the word "questions" for "interrogatories" throughout this rule.

Subdivision (a). A new paragraph is inserted at the beginning of this subdivision to conform to the rearrangement of provisions in Rules 26(a), 30(a), and 30(b).

The revised subdivision permits designation of the deponent by general description or by class or group. This conforms to the practice for depositions on oral examination.

The new procedure provided in Rule 30(b)(6) for taking the deposition of a corporation or other organization through persons designated by the organization is incorporated by reference.

The service of all questions, including cross, redirect, and recross, is to be made on all parties. This will inform the parties and enable them to participate fully in the procedure.

The time allowed for service of cross, redirect, and recross questions has been extended. Experience with the existing time limits shows them to be unrealistically short. No special restriction is placed on the time for serving the notice of taking the deposition and the first set of questions. Since no party is required to serve cross questions less than 30 days after the notice and questions are served, the defendant has sufficient time to obtain counsel. The court may for cause shown enlarge or shorten the time.

Subdivision (d). Since new Rule 26(c) provides for protective orders with respect to all discovery, and expressly provides that the court may order that one discovery device be used in place of another, subdivision (d) is eliminated as unnecessary.

1987 Amendment

The amendments are technical. No substantive change is intended.

1993 Amendments

Subdivision (a). The first paragraph of subdivision (a) is divided into two subparagraphs, with provisions comparable to those made in the revision of Rule 30. Changes are made in the former third paragraph, numbered in the revision as paragraph (4), to reduce the total time for developing cross-examination, redirect, and recross questions from 50 days to 28 days.

2007 Amendment

The language of Rule 31 has been amended as part of the general restyling of the Civil Rules to make them more easily understood and to make style and terminology consistent throughout the rules. These changes are intended to be stylistic only.

The party who noticed a deposition on written questions must notify all other parties when the deposition is completed, so that they may make use of the deposition. A deposition is completed when it is recorded and the deponent has either waived or exercised the right of review under Rule 30(e)(1).

Rule 32. Using Depositions in Court Proceedings

(a) Using Depositions.

(1) ***In General.*** At a hearing or trial, all or part of a deposition may be used against a party on these conditions:

(A) the party was present or represented at the taking of the deposition or had reasonable notice of it;

(B) it is used to the extent it would be admissible under the Federal Rules of Evidence if the deponent were present and testifying; and

(C) the use is allowed by Rule 32(a)(2) through (8).

(2) ***Impeachment and Other Uses.*** Any party may use a deposition to contradict or impeach the testimony given by the deponent as a witness, or for any other purpose allowed by the Federal Rules of Evidence.

(3) ***Deposition of Party, Agent, or Designee.*** An adverse party may use for any purpose the deposition of a party or anyone who, when deposed, was the party's officer, director, managing agent, or designee under Rule 30(b)(6) or 31(a)(4).

(4) ***Unavailable Witness.*** A party may use for any purpose the deposition of a witness, whether or not a party, if the court finds:

(A) that the witness is dead;

(B) that the witness is more than 100 miles from the place of hearing or trial or is outside the United States, unless it appears that the witness's absence was procured by the party offering the deposition;

(C) that the witness cannot attend or testify because of age, illness, infirmity, or imprisonment;

(D) that the party offering the deposition could not procure the witness's attendance by subpoena; or

(E) on motion and notice, that exceptional circumstances make it desirable—in the interest of justice and with due regard to the importance of live testimony in open court—to permit the deposition to be used.

(5) ***Limitations on Use.***

(A) *Deposition Taken on Short Notice.* A deposition must not be used against a party who, having received less than 11 days' notice of the deposition, promptly moved for a protective order under Rule 26(c)(1)(B) requesting that it not be taken or be taken at a different time or place—and this motion was still pending when the deposition was taken.

(B) *Unavailable Deponent; Party Could Not Obtain an Attorney.* A deposition taken without leave of court under the unavailability provision of Rule 30(a)(2)(A)(iii) must not be used against a party who shows that, when served with the notice, it could not, despite diligent efforts, obtain an attorney to represent it at the deposition.

(6) ***Using Part of a Deposition.*** If a party offers in evidence only part of a deposition, an adverse party may require the offeror to introduce other parts that in fairness should be considered with the part introduced, and any party may itself introduce any other parts.

(7) ***Substituting a Party.*** Substituting a party under Rule 25 does not affect the right to use a deposition previously taken.

(8) ***Deposition Taken in an Earlier Action.*** A deposition lawfully taken and, if required, filed in any federal- or state-court action may be used in a later action involving the same subject matter between the same parties, or their representatives or successors in interest, to the same extent as if taken in the later action. A deposition previously taken may also be used as allowed by the Federal Rules of Evidence.

(b) Objections to Admissibility. Subject to Rules 28(b) and 32(d)(3), an objection may be made at a hearing or trial to the admission of any deposition testimony that would be inadmissible if the witness were present and testifying.

(c) Form of Presentation. Unless the court orders otherwise, a party must provide a transcript of any deposition testimony the party offers, but may provide the court with the testimony in nontranscript form as well. On any party's request, deposition testimony offered in a jury trial for any purpose other than impeachment must be presented in nontranscript form, if available, unless the court for good cause orders otherwise.

(d) Waiver of Objections.

(1) ***To the Notice.*** An objection to an error or irregularity in a deposition notice is waived unless promptly served in writing on the party giving the notice.

(2) ***To the Officer's Qualification.*** An objection based on disqualification of the officer before whom a deposition is to be taken is waived if not made:

(A) before the deposition begins; or

(B) promptly after the basis for disqualification becomes known or, with reasonable diligence, could have been known.

(3) ***To the Taking of the Deposition.***

(A) *Objection to Competence, Relevance, or Materiality.* An objection to a deponent's competence—or to the competence, relevance, or materiality of testimony—is not waived by a failure to make the objection before or during the deposition, unless the ground for it might have been corrected at that time.

(B) *Objection to an Error or Irregularity.* An objection to an error or irregularity at an oral examination is waived if:

(i) it relates to the manner of taking the deposition, the form of a question or answer, the oath or affirmation, a party's conduct, or other matters that might have been corrected at that time; and

(ii) it is not timely made during the deposition.

(C) *Objection to a Written Question.* An objection to the form of a written question under Rule 31 is waived if not served in writing on the party submitting the question within the time for serving responsive questions or, if the question is a recross-question, within 5 days after being served with it.

(4) ***To Completing and Returning the Deposition.*** An objection to how the officer transcribed the testimony—or prepared, signed, certified, sealed, endorsed, sent, or otherwise dealt with the deposition—is waived unless a motion to suppress is made promptly after the error or irregularity becomes known or, with reasonable diligence, could have been known.

(Amended March 30, 1970, effective July 1, 1970; November 20, 1972, effective July 1, 1975; April 29, 1980, effective August 1, 1980; March 2, 1987, effective August 1, 1987; April 22, 1993, effective December 1, 1993; April 30, 2007, effective December 1, 2007.)

ADVISORY COMMITTEE NOTES

1937 Adoption

This rule is in accordance with common practice. In most of the states listed in the note to rule 26, provisions similar to this rule will be found in the statutes which in their respective statutory compilations follow those cited in the Note to Rule 26.

1970 Amendment

As part of the rearrangement of the discovery rules, existing subdivisions (d), (e), and (f) of Rule 26 are transferred to Rule 32 as new subdivisions (a), (b), and (c). The provisions of Rule 32 are retained as subdivision (d) of Rule 32 with appropriate changes in the lettering and numbering of subheadings. The new rule is given a suitable new title. A beneficial byproduct of the rearrangement is that provisions which are naturally related to one another are placed in one rule.

A change is made in new Rule 32(a), whereby it is made clear that the rules of evidence are to be applied to depositions offered at trial as though the deponent were then present and testifying at trial. This eliminates the possibility of certain technical hearsay objections which are based, not on the contents of deponent's testimony, but on his absence from court. The language of present Rule 26(d) does not appear to authorize these technical objections, but it is not entirely clear. Note present Rule 26(e), transferred to Rule 32(b); see 2A Barron & Holtzoff, *Federal Practice and Procedure* 164–166 (Wright ed. 1961).

An addition in Rule 32(a)(2) provides for use of a deposition of a person designated by a corporation or other organization, which is a party, to testify on its behalf. This complements the new procedure for taking the deposition of a corporation or other organization provided in Rules 30(b)(6) and 31(a). The addition is appropriate, since the deposition is in substance and effect that of the corporation or other organization which is a party.

A change is made in the standard under which a party offering part of a deposition in evidence may be required to introduce additional parts of the deposition. The new standard is contained in a proposal made by the Advisory Committee on Rules of Evidence. See Rule 1–07 and accompanying Note, *Preliminary Draft of Proposed Rules of Evidence for the United States District Courts and Magistrates* 21–22 (March, 1969).

References to other rules are changed to conform to the rearrangement, and minor verbal changes have been made for clarification. The time for objecting to written questions served under Rule 31 is slightly extended.

1972 Amendment

Subdivision (c). The concept of "making a person one's own witness" appears to have had significance principally in two respects: impeachment and waiver of incompetency. Neither retains any vitality under the Rules of Evidence. The old prohibition against impeaching one's own witness is eliminated by Evidence Rule 607. The lack of recognition in the Rules of Evidence of state rules of incompetency in the Dead Man's area renders it unnecessary to consider aspects of waiver arising from calling the incompetent party-witness. Subdivision (c) is deleted because it appears to be no longer necessary in the light of the Rules of Evidence.

1980 Amendment

Subdivision (a)(1). Rule 801(d) of the Federal Rules of Evidence permits a prior inconsistent statement of a witness in a deposition to be used as substantive evidence. And Rule 801(d)(2) makes the statement of an agent or servant admissible against the principal under the circumstances described in the Rule. The language of the present subdivision is, therefore, too narrow.

Subdivision (a)(4). The requirement that a prior action must have been dismissed before depositions taken for use in it can be used in a subsequent action was doubtless an oversight, and the courts have ignored it. See Wright & Miller, *Federal Practice and Procedure: Civil* § 2150. The final sentence is added to reflect the fact that the Federal Rules of Evidence permit a broader use of depositions previously taken under certain circumstances. For example, Rule 804(b)(1) of the Federal Rules of Evidence provides that if a witness is unavailable, as that term is defined by the rule, his deposition in any earlier proceeding can be used against a party to the prior proceeding who had an opportunity and similar motive to develop the testimony of the witness.

1987 Amendment

The amendment is technical. No substantive change is intended.

1993 Amendments

Subdivision (a). The last sentence of revised subdivision (a) not only includes the substance of the provisions formerly contained in the second paragraph of Rule 30(b)(2), but adds a provision to deal with the situation when a party, receiving minimal notice of a proposed deposition, is unable to obtain a court ruling on its motion for a protective order seeking to delay or change the place of the deposition. Ordinarily a party does not obtain protection merely by the filing of a motion for a protective order under Rule 26(c); any protection is dependent upon the court's ruling. Under the revision, a party receiving less than 11 days notice of a deposition can, provided its motion for a protective order is filed promptly, be spared the risks resulting from nonattendance at the deposition held before its motion is ruled upon. Although the revision of Rule 32(a) covers only the risk that the deposition could be used against the non-appearing movant, it should also follow that, when the proposed deponent is the movant, the deponent would have "just cause" for failing to appear for purposes of Rule 37(d)(1). Inclusion of this provision is not intended to signify that 11 days' notice is the minimum advance notice for all depositions or that greater than 10 days should necessarily be deemed sufficient in all situations.

Subdivision (c). This new subdivision, inserted at the location of a subdivision previously abrogated, is included in view of the increased opportunities for video-recording and audio-recording of depositions under revised Rule 30(b). Under this rule a party may offer deposition testimony in any of the forms authorized under Rule 30(b) but, if offering it in a nonstenographic form, must provide the court with a transcript of the portions so offered. On request of any party in a jury trial, deposition testimony offered other than for impeachment purposes is to be presented in a nonstenographic form if available, unless the court directs otherwise. Note that under Rule 26(a)(3)(B) a party expecting to use nonstenographic deposition testimony as substantive evidence is required to provide other parties with a transcript in advance of trial.

2007 Amendment

The language of Rule 32 has been amended as part of the general restyling of the Civil Rules to make them more easily understood and to make style and terminology consistent throughout the rules. These changes are intended to be stylistic only.

Former Rule 32(a) applied "[a]t the trial or upon the hearing of a motion or an interlocutory proceeding." The amended rule describes the same events as "a hearing or trial."

The final paragraph of former Rule 32(a) allowed use in a later action of a deposition "lawfully taken and duly filed in the former action." Because of the 2000 amendment of Rule 5(d), many depositions are not filed. Amended Rule 32(a)(8) reflects this change by excluding use of an unfiled deposition only if filing was required in the former action.

HISTORICAL NOTES

Effective Date of Amendment Proposed November 20, 1972

Amendment of this rule embraced by the order entered by the Supreme Court of the United States on November 20, 1972, effective on the 180th day beginning after January 2, 1975, see section 3 of Pub.L. 93–595, Jan. 2, 1975, 88 Stat. 1959, set out as a note under section 2071 of Title 28.

Rule 33. Interrogatories to Parties

(a) In General.

(1) ***Number.*** Unless otherwise stipulated or ordered by the court, a party may serve on any other party no more than 25 written interrogatories, including all discrete subparts. Leave to serve additional interrogatories may be granted to the extent consistent with Rule 26(b)(2).

(2) ***Scope.*** An interrogatory may relate to any matter that may be inquired into under Rule 26(b). An interrogatory is not objectionable merely because it asks for an opinion or contention that relates to fact or the application of law to fact, but the court may order that the interrogatory need not be answered until designated discovery is complete, or until a pretrial conference or some other time.

(b) Answers and Objections.

(1) ***Responding Party.*** **The interrogatories must be answered:**

(A) by the party to whom they are directed; or

(B) if that party is a public or private corporation, a partnership, an association, or a governmental agency, by any officer or agent, who must furnish the information available to the party.

(2) ***Time to Respond.*** The responding party must serve its answers and any objections within 30 days after being served with the interrogatories. A shorter or longer time may

be stipulated to under Rule 29 or be ordered by the court.

(3) ***Answering Each Interrogatory.*** Each interrogatory must, to the extent it is not objected to, be answered separately and fully in writing under oath.

(4) ***Objections.*** The grounds for objecting to an interrogatory must be stated with specificity. Any ground not stated in a timely objection is waived unless the court, for good cause, excuses the failure.

(5) ***Signature.*** The person who makes the answers must sign them, and the attorney who objects must sign any objections.

(c) Use. An answer to an interrogatory may be used to the extent allowed by the Federal Rules of Evidence.

(d) Option to Produce Business Records. If the answer to an interrogatory may be determined by examining, auditing, compiling, abstracting, or summarizing a party's business records (including electronically stored information), and if the burden of deriving or ascertaining the answer will be substantially the same for either party, the responding party may answer by:

(1) specifying the records that must be reviewed, in sufficient detail to enable the interrogating party to locate and identify them as readily as the responding party could; and

(2) giving the interrogating party a reasonable opportunity to examine and audit the records and to make copies, compilations, abstracts, or summaries.

(Amended December 27, 1946, effective March 19, 1948; March 30, 1970, effective July 1, 1970; April 29, 1980, effective August 1, 1980; April 22, 1993, effective December 1, 1993; April 12, 2006, effective December 1, 2006; April 30, 2007, effective December 1, 2007.)

ADVISORY COMMITTEE NOTES

1937 Adoption

This rule restates the substance of [former] Equity Rule 58 (Discovery—Interrogatories—Inspection and Production of Documents—Admission of Execution or Genuineness), with modifications to conform to these rules.

1946 Amendment

Note. The added second sentence in the first paragraph of Rule 33 conforms with a similar change in Rule 26(a) and will avoid litigation as to when the interrogatories may be served. Original Rule 33 does not state the times at which parties may serve written interrogatories upon each other. It has been the accepted view, however, that the times were the same in Rule 33 as those stated in Rule 26(a). *United States v. American Solvents & Chemical Corp. of California,* D.Del.1939, 30 F.Supp. 107; *Sheldon v. Great Lakes Transit Corp.,* W.D.N.Y.1942, 2 F.R.D. 272, 5 Fed.Rules Serv. 33.11, Case 3; *Musher Foundation, Inc., v. Alba Trading Co.,* S.D.N.Y.1941, 42 F.Supp. 281; 2 *Moore's Federal Practice,* 1938, 2621. The time within which leave of court must be secured by a plaintiff has been fixed at 10 days, in view of the fact that a defendant has 10 days within which to make objections in any case, which should give him ample time to engage counsel and prepare.

Further in the first paragraph of Rule 33, the word "service" is substituted for "delivery" in conformance with the use of the word "serve" elsewhere in the rule and generally throughout the rules. See also Note to Rule 13(a) herein. The portion of the rule dealing with practice on objections has been revised so as to afford a clearer statement of the procedure. The addition of the words "to interrogatories to which objection is made" insures that only the answers to the objectionable interrogatories may be deferred, and that the answers to interrogatories not objectionable shall be forthcoming within the time prescribed in the rule. Under the original wording, answers to all interrogatories may be withheld until objections, sometimes to but a few interrogatories, are determined. The amendment expedites the procedure of the rule and serves to eliminate the strike value of objections to minor interrogatories. The elimination of the last sentence of the original rule is in line with the policy stated subsequently in this note.

The added second paragraph in Rule 33 contributes clarity and specificity as to the use and scope of interrogatories to the parties. The field of inquiry will be as broad as the scope of examination under Rule 26(b). There is no reason why interrogatories should be more limited than depositions, particularly when the former represent an inexpensive means of securing useful information. See *Hoffman v. Wilson Line, Inc.,* E.D.Pa.1946, 9 Fed.Rules Serv. 33.514, Case 2; *Brewster v. Technicolor, Inc.,* N.Y.1941, 2 F.R.D. 186, 5 Fed.Rules Serv. 33.319, Case 3; *Kingsway Press, Inc. v. Farrell Publishing Corp.,* S.D.N.Y.1939, 30 F.Supp. 775. Under present Rule 33 some courts have unnecessarily restricted the breadth of inquiry on various grounds. See *Auer v. Hershey Creamery Co.,* D.N.J.1939, 2 Fed.Rules Serv. 33.31, Case 2, 1 F.R.D. 14; *Tudor v. Leslie,* D.Mass.1940, 1 F.R.D. 448, 4 Fed.Rules Serv. 33.324, Case 1. Other courts have read into the rule the requirement that interrogation should be directed only towards "important facts", and have tended to fix a more or less arbitrary limit as to the number of interrogatories which could be asked in any case. See *Knox v. Alter,* W.D.Pa.1942, 2 F.R.D. 337, 6 Fed.Rules Serv. 33.352, Case 1; *Byers Theaters, Inc. v. Murphy,* W.D.Va.1940, 3 Fed.Rules Serv. 33.31, Case 3, 1 F.R.D. 286; *Coca-Cola Co. v. Dixi-Cola Laboratories, Inc.,* D.Md.1939, 30 F.Supp. 275. See also comment on these restrictions in Holtzoff, *Instruments of Discovery under Federal Rules of Civil Procedure,* 1942, 41 Mich.L.Rev. 205, 216–217. Under amended Rule 33, the party interrogated is given the right to invoke such protective orders under Rule 30(b) as are appropriate to the situation. At the same time, it is provided that the number of or number of sets of interrogatories to be served may not be limited arbitrarily or as a general policy to any particular number, but that a limit may be fixed only as justice requires to avoid annoyance, expense, embarrassment or oppression in individual cases. The party interrogated, therefore, must show the necessity for limitation on that basis. It will be noted that in accord with this change the last sentence of the present rule, restricting the sets of interrogatories to be served, has been stricken. In *J. Schoeneman, Inc. v. Brauer,* W.D.Mo.1940, 1 F.R.D. 292, 3 Fed.Rules Serv. 33.31, Case 2, the court said: "Rule 33 * * * has been interpreted * * * as being just as broad in its implications as in the case of depositions * * * It makes no difference therefore, how many interrogatories are propounded. If the inquiries are pertinent the opposing party cannot complain." To the same effect, see *Canuso v. City of Niagara Falls,* W.D.N.Y.1945, 8 Fed.Rules Serv. 33.352, Case 1; *Hoffman v. Wilson Line, Inc.,* supra.

By virtue of express language in the added second paragraph of Rule 33, as amended, any uncertainty as to the use of the answers to interrogatories is removed. The omission of a provision on this score in the original rule has caused some difficulty. See, e.g., *Bailey v. New England Mutual Life Ins. Co.,* S.D.Cal.1940, 1 F.R.D. 494, 4 Fed.Rules Serv. 33.46, Case 1.

The second sentence of the second paragraph in Rule 33, as amended, concerns the situation where a party wishes to serve interrogatories on a party after having taken his deposition, or vice versa. It has been held that an oral examination of a party, after the submission to him and answer of interrogatories, would be permitted. *Howard v. State Marine Corp.,* S.D.N.Y.1940, 4 Fed.Rules Serv. 33.62, Case 1, 1 F.R.D. 499; *Stevens v. Minder Construction Co.,* S.D.N.Y.1943, 3 F.R.D. 498, 7 Fed.Rules Serv. 30b.31, Case 2. But objections have been sustained to interrogatories served after the oral deposition of a party had been taken. *McNally v. Simons,* S.D.N.Y.1940, 3 Fed.Rules Serv. 33.61, Case 1, 1 F.R.D. 254; *Currier v. Currier,* S.D.N.Y.1942, 3 F.R.D. 21, 6 Fed.Rules Serv. 33.61, Case 1. Rule 33, as amended, permits either interrogatories after a deposition or a deposition after interrogatories. It may be quite desirable or necessary to elicit additional information by the inexpensive method of interrogatories where a deposition has already been taken. The party to be interrogated, however, may seek a protective order from the court under Rule 30(b) where the additional deposition or interrogation works a hardship or injustice on the party from whom it is sought.

1970 Amendment

Subdivision (a). The mechanics of the operation of Rule 33 are substantially revised by the proposed amendment, with a view to reducing court intervention. There is general agreement that interrogatories spawn a greater percentage of objections and motions than any other discovery device. The Columbia Survey shows that, although half of the litigants resorted to depositions and about one-third used interrogatories, about 65 percent of the objections were made with respect to interrogatories and 26 percent related to depositions. See also Speck, *The Use of Discovery in United States District Courts,* 60 Yale L.J. 1132, 1144, 1151 (1951); Note, 36 Minn.L.Rev. 364, 379 (1952).

The procedures now provided in Rule 33 seem calculated to encourage objections and court motions. The time periods now allowed for responding to interrogatories—15 days for answers and 10 days for objections—are too short. The Columbia Survey shows that tardy response to interrogatories is common, virtually expected. The same was reported in Speck, *supra,* 60 Yale L.J. 1132, 1144. The time pressures tend to encourage objections as a means of gaining time to answer.

The time for objections is even shorter than for answers, and the party runs the risk that if he fails to object in time he may have waived his objections. *E.g., Cleminshaw v. Beech Aircraft Corp.,* 21 F.R.D. 300 (D.Del.1957); See 4 *Moore's Federal Practice,* ¶33.27 (2d ed. 1966); 2A Barron & Holtzoff, *Federal Practice and Procedure* 372–373 (Wright ed. 1961). It often seems easier to object than to seek an extension of time. Unlike Rules 30(d) and 37(a), Rule 33 imposes no sanction of expenses on a party whose objections are clearly unjustified.

Rule 33 assures that the objections will lead directly to court, through its requirement that they be served with a notice of hearing. Although this procedure does not preclude an out-of-court resolution of the dispute, the procedure tends to discourage informal negotiations. If answers are served and they are thought inadequate, the interrogating party may move under Rule 37(a) for an order compelling adequate answers. There is no assurance that the hearing on objections and that on inadequate answers will be heard together.

The amendment improves the procedure of Rule 33 in the following respects:

(1) The time allowed for response is increased to 30 days and this time period applies to both answers and objections, but a defendant need not respond in less than 45 days after service of the summons and complaint upon him. As is true under existing law, the responding party who believes that some parts or all of the interrogatories are objectionable may choose to seek a protective order under new Rule 26(c) or may serve objections under this rule. Unless he applies for a protective order, he is required to serve answers or objections in response to the interrogatories, subject to the sanctions provided in Rule 37(d). Answers and objections are served together, so that a response to each interrogatory is encouraged, and any failure to respond is easily noted.

(2) In view of the enlarged time permitted for response, it is no longer necessary to require leave of court for service of interrogatories. The purpose of this requirement—that defendant have time to obtain counsel before a response must be made—is adequately fulfilled by the requirement that interrogatories be served upon a party with or after service of the summons and complaint upon him.

Some would urge that the plaintiff nevertheless not be permitted to serve interrogatories with the complaint. They fear that a routine practice might be invited, whereby form interrogatories would accompany most complaints. More fundamentally, they feel that, since very general complaints are permitted in present-day pleading, it is fair that the defendant have a right to take the lead in serving interrogatories. (These views apply also to Rule 36.) The amendment of Rule 33 rejects these views, in favor of allowing both parties to go forward with discovery, each free to obtain the information he needs respecting the case.

(3) If objections are made, the burden is on the interrogating party to move under Rule 37(a) for a court order compelling answers, in the course of which the court will pass on the objections. The change in the burden of going forward does not alter the existing obligation of an objecting party to justify his objections. *E.g., Pressley v. Bochlke,* 33 F.R.D. 316 (W.D.N.C. 1963). If the discovering party asserts that an answer is incomplete or evasive, again he may look to Rule 37(a) for relief, and he should add this assertion to his motion to overrule objections. There is no require-

ment that the parties consult informally concerning their differences, but the new procedure should encourage consultation, and the court may by local rule require it.

The proposed changes are similar in approach to those adopted by California in 1961. See Calif.Code Civ.Proc. § 2030(a). The experience of the Los Angeles Superior Court is informally reported as showing that the California amendment resulted in a significant reduction in court motions concerning interrogatories. Rhode Island takes a similar approach. See R. 33, *R.I.R. Civ.Proc. Official Draft,* p. 74 (Boston Law Book Co.).

A change is made in subdivision (a) which is not related to the sequence of procedures. The restriction to "adverse" parties is eliminated. The courts have generally construed this restriction as precluding interrogatories unless an issue between the parties is disclosed by the pleadings—even though the parties may have conflicting interests. E.g., *Mozeika v. Kaufman Construction Co.,* 25 F.R.D. 233 (E.D.Pa.1960) (plaintiff and third-party defendant); *Biddle v. Hutchinson,* 24 F.R.D. 256 (M.D.Pa.1959) (codefendants). The resulting distinctions have often been highly technical. In *Schlagenhauf v. Holder,* 379 U.S. 104 (1964), the Supreme Court rejected a contention that examination under Rule 35 could be had only against an "opposing" party, as not in keeping "with the aims of a liberal, nontechnical application of the Federal Rules." 379 U.S. at 116. Eliminating the requirement of "adverse" parties from Rule 33 brings it into line with all other discovery rules.

A second change in subdivision (a) is the addition of the term "governmental agency" to the listing of organizations whose answers are to be made by any officer or agent of the organization. This does not involve any change in existing law. Compare the similar listing in Rule 30(b)(6).

The duty of a party to supplement his answers to interrogatories is governed by a new provision in Rule 26(e).

Subdivision (b). There are numerous and conflicting decisions on the question whether and to what extent interrogatories are limited to matters "of fact," or may elicit opinions, contentions, and legal conclusions. Compare, e.g., *Payer, Hewitt & Co. v. Bellanca Corp.,* 26 F.R.D. 219 (D.Del.1960) (opinions bad); *Zinsky v. New York Central R.R.,* 36 F.R.D. 680 (N.D.Ohio 1964) (factual opinion or contention good, but legal theory bad); *United States v. Carter Products, Inc.,* 28 F.R.D. 373 (S.D.N.Y.1961) (factual contentions and legal theories bad) with *Taylor v. Sound Steamship Lines, Inc.,* 100 F.Supp. 388 (D.Conn.1951) (opinions good); *Bynum v. United States,* 36 F.R.D. 14 (E.D.La.1964) (contentions as to facts constituting negligence good). For lists of the many conflicting authorities, see 4 *Moore's Federal Practice* ¶33.17 (2d ed. 1966); 2A Barron & Holtzoff, *Federal Practice and Procedure* § 768 (Wright ed. 1961).

Rule 33 is amended to provide that an interrogatory is not objectionable merely because it calls for an opinion or contention that relates to fact or the application of law to fact. Efforts to draw sharp lines between facts and opinions have invariably been unsuccessful, and the clear trend of the cases is to permit "factual" opinions. As to requests for opinions or contentions that call for the application of law to fact, they can be most useful in narrowing and sharpening the issues, which is a major purpose of discovery. See *Diversified Products Corp. v. Sports Center Co.,* 42 F.R.D. 3 (D.Md. 1967); Moore, *supra;* Field & McKusick, *Maine Civil Practice* § 26.18 (1959). On the other hand, under the new language interrogatories may not extend to issues of "pure law," *i.e.,* legal issues unrelated to the facts of the case. *Cf. United States v. Maryland & Va. Milk Producers Assn., Inc.,* 22 F.R.D. 300 (D.D.C.1958).

Since interrogatories involving mixed questions of law and fact may create disputes between the parties which are best resolved after much or all of the other discovery has been completed, the court is expressly authorized to defer an answer. Likewise, the court may delay determination until pretrial conference, if it believes that the dispute is best resolved in the presence of the judge.

The principal question raised with respect to the cases permitting such interrogatories is whether they reintroduce undesirable aspects of the prior pleading practice, whereby parties were chained to misconceived contentions or theories, and ultimate determination on the merits was frustrated. See James, *The Revival of Bills of Particulars under the Federal Rules,* 71 Harv.L.Rev. 1473 (1958). But there are few if any instances in the recorded cases demonstrating that such frustration has occurred. The general rule governing the use of answers to interrogatories is that under ordinary circumstances they do not limit proof. See, *e.g., McElroy v. United Air Lines, Inc.,* 21 F.R.D. 100 (W.D.Mo.1967); *Pressley v. Boehlke,* 33 F.R.D. 316, 317 (W.D.N.C.1963). Although in exceptional circumstances reliance on an answer may cause such prejudice that the court will hold the answering party bound to his answer, *e.g., Zielinski v. Philadelphia Piers, Inc.,* 139 F.Supp. 408 (E.D.Pa.1956), the interrogating party will ordinarily not be entitled to rely on the unchanging character of the answers he receives and cannot base prejudice on such reliance. The rule does not affect the power of a court to permit withdrawal or amendment of answers to interrogatories.

The use of answers to interrogatories at trial is made subject to the rules of evidence. The provisions governing use of depositions, to which Rule 33 presently refers, are not entirely apposite to answers to interrogatories, since deposition practice contemplates that all parties will ordinarily participate through cross-examination. See 4 *Moore's Federal Practice* ¶33.29[1] (2d ed. 1966).

Certain provisions are deleted from subdivision (b) because they are fully covered by new Rule 26(c) providing for protective orders and Rules 26(a) and 26(d). The language of the subdivision is thus simplified without any change of substance.

Subdivision (c). This is a new subdivision, adapted from Calif.Code Civ.Proc. § 2030(c), relating especially to interrogatories which require a party to engage in burdensome or expensive research into his own business records in order to give an answer. The subdivision gives the party an option to make the records available and place the burden of research of the party who seeks the information. "This provision, without undermining the liberal scope of interrogatory discovery, places the burden of discovery upon its potential benefittee," Louisell, *Modern California Discovery,* 124–125 (1963), and alleviates a problem which in the past has troubled Federal courts. See Speck, *The Use of Discovery in United States District Courts,* 60 Yale L.J. 1132, 1142–1144 (1951). The interrogating party is protected against abusive use of this provision through the requirement that the burden of ascertaining the answer be substantially the same for both sides. A respondent may not impose on an interrogating party a mass of records as to which research is feasible only for one familiar with the records. At the same time, the respondent unable to invoke this subdivision does not on that account lose the protection available to him under new Rule 26(c) against oppressive or unduly burdensome or expensive interrogatories. And even when the respondent successfully invokes the subdivision, the court is not deprived of its usual power, in appropriate cases, to require that the interrogating party reimburse the respondent for the expense of assembling his records and making them intelligible.

1980 Amendment

Subdivision (c). The Committee is advised that parties upon whom interrogatories are served have occasionally responded by directing the interrogating party to a mass of business records or by offering to make all of their records available, justifying the response by the option provided by this subdivision. Such practices are an abuse of the option. A party who is permitted by the terms of this subdivision to offer records for inspection in lieu of answering an interrogatory should offer them in a manner than permits the same direct and economical access that is available to the party. If the information sought exists in the form of compilations, abstracts or summaries then available to the responding party, those should be made available to the interrogating party. The final sentence is added to make it clear that a responding party has the duty to specify, by category and location, the records from which answers to interrogatories can be derived.

1993 Amendments

Purpose of Revision. The purpose of this revision is to reduce the frequency and increase the efficiency of interrogatory practice. The revision is based on experience with local rules. For ease of reference, subdivision (a) is divided into two subdivisions and the remaining subdivisions renumbered.

Subdivision (a). Revision of this subdivision limits interrogatory practice. Because Rule 26(a)(1)–(3) requires disclosure of much of the information previously obtained by this form of discovery, there should be less occasion to use it. Experience in over half of the district courts has confirmed that limitations on the number of interrogatories are useful and manageable. Moreover, because the device can be costly and may be used as a means of harassment, it is desirable to subject its use to the control of the court consistent with the principles stated in Rule 26(b)(2), particularly in multi-party cases where it has not been unusual for the same interrogatory to be propounded to a party by more than one of its adversaries.

Each party is allowed to serve 25 interrogatories upon any other party, but must secure leave of court (or a stipulation from the opposing party) to serve a larger number. Parties cannot evade this presumptive limitation through the device of joining as "subparts" questions that seek information about discrete separate subjects. However, a question asking about communications of a particular type should be treated as a single interrogatory even though it requests that the time, place, persons present, and contents be stated separately for each such communication.

As with the number of depositions authorized by Rule 30, leave to serve additional interrogatories is to be allowed when consistent with Rule 26(b)(2). The aim is not to prevent needed discovery, but to provide judicial scrutiny before parties make potentially excessive use of this discovery device. In many cases it will be appropriate for the court to permit a larger number of interrogatories in the scheduling order entered under Rule 16(b).

Unless leave of court is obtained, interrogatories may not be served prior to the meeting of the parties under Rule 26(f).

When a case with outstanding interrogatories exceeding the number permitted by this rule is removed to federal court, the interrogating party must seek leave allowing the additional interrogatories, specify which twenty-five are to be answered, or resubmit interrogatories that comply with the rule. Moreover, under Rule 26(d), the time for response would be measured from the date of the parties' meeting under Rule 26(f). See Rule 81(c), providing that these rules govern procedures after removal.

Subdivision (b). A separate subdivision is made of the former second paragraph of subdivision (a). Language is added to paragraph (1) of this subdivision to emphasize the duty of the responding party to provide full answers to the extent not objectionable. If, for example, an interrogatory seeking information about numerous facilities or products is deemed objectionable, but an interrogatory seeking information about a lesser number of facilities or products would not have been objectionable, the interrogatory should be answered with respect to the latter even though an objection is raised as to the balance of the facilities or products. Similarly, the fact that additional time may be needed to respond to some questions (or to some aspects of questions) should not justify a delay in responding to those questions (or other aspects of questions) that can be answered within the prescribed time.

Paragraph (4) is added to make clear that objections must be specifically justified, and that unstated or untimely grounds for objection ordinarily are waived. Note also the provisions of revised Rule 26(b)(5), which require a responding party to indicate when it is withholding information under a claim of privilege or as trial preparation materials.

These provisions should be read in light of Rule 26(g), authorizing the court to impose sanctions on a party and attorney making an unfounded objection to an interrogatory.

Subdivisions (c) and (d). The provisions of former subdivisions (b) and (c) are renumbered.

2006 Amendment

Rule 33(d) is amended to parallel Rule 34(a) by recognizing the importance of electronically stored information. The term "electronically stored information" has the same broad meaning in Rule 33(d) as in Rule 34(a). Much business information is stored only in electronic form; the Rule 33(d) option should be available with respect to such records as well.

Special difficulties may arise in using electronically stored information, either due to its form or because it is dependent on a particular computer system. Rule 33(d) allows a responding party to substitute access to documents or electronically stored information for an answer only if the burden of deriving the answer will be substantially the same for either party. Rule 33(d) states that a party electing to respond to an interrogatory by providing electronically stored information must ensure that the interrogating party can locate and identify it "as readily as can the party served," and that the responding party must give the interrogating party a "reasonable opportunity to examine, audit, or inspect" the information. Depending on the circumstances, satisfying these provisions with regard to electronically stored information may require the responding party to provide some combination of technical support, information on application software, or other assistance. The key question is whether such support enables the interrogating party to derive or ascertain the answer from the electronically stored information as readily as the responding party. A party that wishes to invoke Rule 33(d) by specifying electronically stored information may be required to provide direct access to its electronic information system, but only if that is necessary to afford the requesting party an adequate opportunity to derive or ascertain the answer to the interrogatory. In that situation, the responding party's need to protect sensitive interests of confidentiality or privacy may mean that it must derive or ascertain and provide the answer itself rather than invoke Rule 33(d).

2007 Amendment

The language of Rule 33 has been amended as part of the general restyling of the Civil Rules to make them more easily understood and to make style and terminology consistent throughout the rules. These changes are intended to be stylistic only.

The final sentence of former Rule 33(a) was a redundant cross-reference to the discovery moratorium provisions of Rule 26(d). Rule 26(d) is now familiar, obviating any need to carry forward the redundant cross-reference.

Former Rule 33(b)(5) was a redundant reminder of Rule 37(a) procedure and is omitted as no longer useful.

Former Rule 33(c) stated that an interrogatory "is not necessarily objectionable merely because an answer * * * involves an opinion or contention * * *." "[I]s not necessarily" seemed to imply that the interrogatory might be objectionable merely for this reason. This implication has been ignored in practice. Opinion and contention interrogatories are used routinely. Amended Rule 33(a)(2) embodies the current meaning of Rule 33 by omitting "necessarily."

Rule 34. Producing Documents, Electronically Stored Information, and Tangible Things, or Entering onto Land, for Inspection and Other Purposes

(a) In General. A party may serve on any other party a request within the scope of Rule 26(b):

(1) to produce and permit the requesting party or its representative to inspect, copy, test, or sample the following items in the responding party's possession, custody, or control:

(A) any designated documents or electronically stored information—including writings, drawings, graphs, charts, photographs, sound recordings, images, and other data or data compilations—stored in any medium from which information can be obtained either directly or, if necessary, after translation by the responding party into a reasonably usable form; or

(B) any designated tangible things; or

(2) to permit entry onto designated land or other property possessed or controlled by the responding party, so that the requesting party may inspect, measure, survey, photograph, test, or sample the property or any designated object or operation on it.

(b) Procedure.

(1) ***Contents of the Request.*** The request:

(A) must describe with reasonable particularity each item or category of items to be inspected;

(B) must specify a reasonable time, place, and manner for the inspection and for performing the related acts; and

(C) may specify the form or forms in which electronically stored information is to be produced.

(2) ***Responses and Objections.***

(A) *Time to Respond.* The party to whom the request is directed must respond in writing within 30 days after being served. A shorter or longer time may be stipulated to under Rule 29 or be ordered by the court.

(B) *Responding to Each Item.* For each item or category, the response must either state that inspection and related activities will be permitted as requested or state an objection to the request, including the reasons.

(C) *Objections.* An objection to part of a request must specify the part and permit inspection of the rest.

(D) *Responding to a Request for Production of Electronically Stored Information.* The response may state an objection to a requested form for producing electronically stored information. If the responding party objects to a requested form—or if no form was specified in the request—the party must state the form or forms it intends to use.

(E) *Producing the Documents or Electronically Stored Information.* Unless otherwise stipulated or ordered by the court, these procedures apply to producing documents or electronically stored information:

(i) A party must produce documents as they are kept in the usual course of business or must organize and label them to correspond to the categories in the request;

(ii) If a request does not specify a form for producing electronically stored information, a party must produce it in a form or forms in which it is ordinarily maintained or in a reasonably usable form or forms; and

(iii) A party need not produce the same electronically stored information in more than one form.

(c) Nonparties. As provided in Rule 45, a nonparty may be compelled to produce documents and tangible things or to permit an inspection.

(Amended December 27, 1946, effective March 19, 1948; March 30, 1970, effective July 1, 1970; April 29, 1980, effective August 1, 1980; March 2, 1987, effective August 1, 1987; April 30, 1991, effective December 1, 1991; April 22, 1993, effective December 1, 1993; April 12, 2006, effective December 1, 2006; April 30, 2007, effective December 1, 2007.)

ADVISORY COMMITTEE NOTES

1937 Adoption

In England orders are made for the inspection of documents, *English Rules Under the Judicature Act (The Annual Practice,* 1937) O. 31, r.r. 14, et seq., or for the inspection of tangible property or for entry upon land, O. 50, r. 3. Michigan provides for inspection of damaged property when such damage is the ground of the action. Mich.Court Rules Ann. (Searl, 1933) Rule 41, § 2.

Practically all states have statutes authorizing the court to order parties in possession or control of documents to permit other parties to inspect and copy them before trial. See Ragland, *Discovery Before Trial* (1932) Appendix, p. 267, setting out the statutes.

Compare [former] Equity Rule 58 (Discovery—Interrogatories—Inspection and Production of Documents—Admission of Execution or Genuineness) (fifth paragraph).

1946 Amendment

Note. The changes in clauses (1) and (2) correlate the scope of inquiry permitted under Rule 34 with that provided in Rule 26(b), and thus remove any ambiguity created by the former differences in language. As stated in *Olson Transportation Co. v. Socony-Vacuum Oil Co.,* E.D.Wis.1944, 8 Fed.Rules Serv. 34.41, Case 2, "* * * Rule 34 is a direct and simple method of discovery." At the same time the addition of the words following the term "parties" makes certain that the person in whose custody, possession, or control the evidence reposes may have the benefit of the applicable protective orders stated in Rule 30(b). This change should be considered in the light of the proposed expansion of Rule 30(b).

An objection has been made that the word "designated" in Rule 34 has been construed with undue strictness in some district court cases so as to require great and impracticable specificity in the description of documents, papers, books, etc., sought to be inspected. The Committee, however, believes that no amendment is needed, and that the proper meaning of "designated" as requiring specificity has already been delineated by the Supreme Court. *See Brown v. United States,* 1928, 48 S.Ct. 288, 276 U.S. 134, 143, 72 L.Ed. 500 ("The subpoena * * * specifies * * * with reasonable particularity the subjects to which the documents called for related."); *Consolidated Rendering Co. v. Vermont,* 1908, 28 S.Ct. 178, 207 U.S. 541, 543–544, 52 L.Ed. 327 ("We see no reason why all such books, papers and correspondence which related to the subject of inquiry, and were described with reasonable detail, should not be called for and the company directed to produce them. Otherwise, the State would be compelled to designate each particular paper which it desired, which presupposes an accurate knowledge of such papers, which the tribunal desiring the papers would probably rarely, if ever, have.").

1970 Amendment

Rule 34 is revised to accomplish the following major changes in the existing rule: (1) to eliminate the requirement of good cause; (2) to have the rule operate extrajudicially; (3) to include testing and sampling as well as inspecting or photographing tangible things; and (4) to make clear that the rule does not preclude an independent action for analogous discovery against persons not parties.

Subdivision (a). Good cause is eliminated because it has furnished an uncertain and erratic protection to the parties from whom production is sought and is now rendered unnecessary by virtue of the more specific provisions added to Rule 26(b) relating to materials assembled in preparation for trial and to experts retained or consulted by parties.

The good cause requirement was originally inserted in Rule 34 as a general protective provision in the absence of experience with the specific problems that would arise thereunder. As the note to Rule 26(b)(3) on trial preparation materials makes clear, good cause has been applied differently to varying classes of documents, though not without confusion. It has often been said in court opinions that good cause requires a consideration of need for the materials and of alternative means of obtaining them, i.e., something more than relevance and lack of privilege. But the overwhelming proportion of the cases in which the formula of good cause has been applied to require a special showing are those involving trial preparation. In practice, the courts have not treated documents as having a special immunity to discovery simply because of their being documents. Protection may be afforded to claims of privacy or secrecy or of undue burden or expense under what is now Rule 26(c) (previously Rule 30(b)). To be sure, an appraisal of "undue" burden inevitably entails consideration of the needs of the party seeking discovery. With special provisions added to govern trial preparation materials and experts, there is no longer any occasion to retain the requirement of good cause.

The revision of Rule 34 to have it operate extrajudicially, rather than by court order, is to a large extent a reflection of existing law office practice. The Columbia Survey shows that of the litigants seeking inspection of documents or things, only about 25 percent filed motions for court orders. This minor fraction nevertheless accounted for a significant number of motions. About half of these motions were uncontested and in almost all instances the party seeking production ultimately prevailed. Although an extrajudicial procedure will not drastically alter existing practice under Rule 34—it will conform to it in most cases—it has the potential of saving court time in a substantial though proportionately small number of cases tried annually.

The inclusion of testing and sampling of tangible things and objects or operations on land reflects a need frequently encountered by parties in preparation for trial. If the operation of a particular machine is the basis of a claim for negligent injury, it will often be necessary to test its operating parts or to sample and test the products it is producing. *Cf.* Mich.Gen.Ct.R. 310.1(1) (1963) (testing authorized).

The inclusive description of "documents" is revised to accord with changing technology. It makes clear that Rule 34 applies to electronics data compilations from which information can be obtained only with the use of detection devices, and that when the data can as a practical matter be made usable by the discovering party only through respondent's devices, respondent may be required to use his devices to translate the data into usable form. In many instances, this means that respondent will have to supply a print-out of computer data. The burden thus placed on respondent will vary from case to case, and the courts have ample power under Rule 26(c) to protect respondent against undue burden or expense, either by restricting discovery or requiring that the discovering party pay costs. Similarly, if the discovering party needs to check the electronic source itself, the court may protect respondent with respect to preservation of his records, confidentiality of nondiscoverable matters, and costs.

Subdivision (b). The procedure provided in Rule 34 is essentially the same as that in Rule 33, as amended, and the discussion in the note appended to that rule is relevant to Rule 34 as well. Problems peculiar to Rule 34 relate to the specific arrangements that must be worked out for inspection and related acts of copying, photographing, testing, or sampling. The rule provides that a request for inspection shall set forth the items to be inspected either by item or category, describing each with reasonable particularity, and shall specify a reasonable time, place, and manner of making the inspection.

Subdivision (c). Rule 34 as revised continues to apply only to parties. Comments from the bar make clear that in the preparation of cases for trial it is occasionally necessary to enter land or inspect large tangible things in the possession of a person not a party, and that some courts have dismissed independent actions in the nature of bills in equity for such discovery on the ground that Rule 34 is preemptive. While an ideal solution to this problem is to provide for discovery against persons not parties in Rule 34, both the jurisdictional and procedural problems are very complex. For the present, this subdivision makes clear that Rule 34 does not preclude independent actions for discovery against persons not parties.

1980 Amendment

Subdivision (b). The Committee is advised that, "It is apparently not rare for parties deliberately to mix critical documents with others in the hope of obscuring significance." *Report of the Special Committee for the Study of Discovery Abuse, Section of Litigation of the American Bar Association* (1977) 22. The sentence added by this subdivision follows the recommendation of the *Report.*

1987 Amendment

The amendment is technical. No substantive change is intended.

1991 Amendment

This amendment reflects the change effected by revision of Rule 45 to provide for subpoenas to compel non-parties to produce documents and things and to submit to inspections of premises. The deletion of the text of the former paragraph is not intended to preclude an independent action for production of documents or things or for permission to enter upon land, but such actions may no longer be necessary in light of this revision.

1993 Amendments

The rule is revised to reflect the change made by Rule 26(d), preventing a party from seeking formal discovery prior to the meeting of the parties required by Rule 26(f). Also, like a change made in Rule 33, the rule is modified to make clear that, if a request for production is objectionable only in part, production should be afforded with respect to the unobjectionable portions.

When a case with outstanding requests for production is removed to federal court, the time for response would be measured from the date of the parties' meeting. See Rule 81(c), providing that these rules govern procedures after removal.

2006 Amendment

Subdivision (a). As originally adopted, Rule 34 focused on discovery of "documents" and "things." In 1970, Rule 34(a) was amended to include discovery of data compilations, anticipating that the use of computerized information would increase. Since then, the growth in electronically stored information and in the variety of systems for creating and storing such information has been dramatic. Lawyers and judges interpreted the term "documents" to include electronically stored information because it was obviously improper to allow a party to evade discovery obligations on the basis that the label had not kept pace with changes in information technology. But it has become increasingly difficult to say that all forms of electronically stored information, many dynamic in nature, fit within the traditional concept of a "document." Electronically stored information may exist in dynamic databases and other forms far different from fixed expression on paper. Rule 34(a) is amended to confirm that discovery of electronically stored information stands on equal footing with discovery of paper documents. The change clarifies that Rule 34 applies to information that is fixed in a tangible form and to information that is stored in a medium from which it can be retrieved and examined. At the same time, a Rule 34 request for production of "documents" should be understood to encompass, and the response should include, electronically stored information unless discovery in the action has clearly distinguished between electronically stored information and "documents."

Discoverable information often exists in both paper and electronic form, and the same or similar information might exist in both. The items listed in Rule 34(a) show different ways in which information may be recorded or stored. Images, for example, might be hard-copy documents or electronically stored information. The wide variety of computer systems currently in use, and the rapidity of technological change, counsel against a limiting or precise definition of electronically stored information. Rule 34(a)(1) is expansive and includes any type of information that is stored electronically. A common example often sought in discovery is electronic communications, such as e-mail. The rule covers — either as documents or as electronically stored information — information "stored in any medium," to encompass future developments in computer technology. Rule 34(a)(1) is intended to be broad enough to cover all current types of computer-based information, and flexible enough to encompass future changes and developments.

References elsewhere in the rules to "electronically stored information" should be understood to invoke this expansive approach. A companion change is made to Rule 33(d), making it explicit that parties choosing to respond to an interrogatory by permitting access to responsive records may do so by providing access to electronically stored information. More generally, the term used in Rule 34(a)(1) appears in a number of other amendments, such as those to Rules 26(a)(1), 26(b)(2), 26(b)(5)(B), 26(f), 34(b), 37(f), and 45. In each of these rules, electronically stored information has the same broad meaning it has under Rule 34(a)(1). References to "documents" appear in discovery rules that are not amended, including Rules 30(f), 36(a), and 37(c)(2). These references should be interpreted to include electronically stored information as circumstances warrant.

The term "electronically stored information" is broad, but whether material that falls within this term should be produced, and in what form, are separate questions that must be addressed under Rules 26(b), 26(c), and 34(b).

The Rule 34(a) requirement that, if necessary, a party producing electronically stored information translate it into reasonably usable form does not address the issue of translating from one human language to another. *See In re Puerto Rico Elect. Power Auth.*, 687 F.2d 501, 504–510 (1st Cir. 1989).

Rule 34(a)(1) is also amended to make clear that parties may request an opportunity to test or sample materials sought under the rule in addition to inspecting and copying them. That opportunity may be important for both electronically stored information and hard-copy materials. The current rule is not clear that such testing or sampling is authorized; the amendment expressly permits it. As with any other form of discovery, issues of burden and intrusiveness raised by requests to test or sample can be addressed under Rules 26(b)(2) and 26(c). Inspection or testing of certain types of electronically stored information or of a responding party's electronic information system may raise issues of confidentiality or privacy. The addition of testing and sampling to Rule 34(a) with regard to documents and electronically stored information is not meant to create a routine right of direct access to a party's electronic information system, although such access might be justified in some circumstances. Courts should guard against undue intrusiveness resulting from inspecting or testing such systems.

Rule 34(a)(1) is further amended to make clear that tangible things must — like documents and land sought to be examined — be designated in the request.

Subdivision (b). Rule 34(b) provides that a party must produce documents as they are kept in the usual course of business or must organize and label them to correspond with the categories in the discovery request. The production of electronically stored information should be subject to comparable requirements to protect against deliberate or inadvertent production in ways that raise unnecessary obstacles for the requesting party. Rule 34(b) is amended to ensure similar protection for electronically stored information.

The amendment to Rule 34(b) permits the requesting party to designate the form or forms in which it wants electronically stored information produced. The form of production is more important to the exchange of electronically stored information than of hard-copy materials, although a party might specify hard copy as the requested form. Specification of the desired form or forms may facilitate the orderly, efficient, and cost-effective discovery of electronically stored information. The rule recognizes that different forms of production may be appropriate for different types of electronically stored information. Using current technology, for example, a party might be called upon to produce word processing documents, e-mail messages, electronic spreadsheets, different image or sound files, and material from databases. Requiring that such diverse types of electronically stored information all be produced in the same form could prove impossible, and even if possible could increase the cost and burdens of producing and using the information. The rule therefore provides that the requesting party may ask for different forms of production for different types of electronically stored information.

The rule does not require that the requesting party choose a form or forms of production. The requesting party may not have a preference. In some cases, the requesting party may not know what form the producing party uses to maintain its electronically stored information, although Rule 26(f)(3) is amended to call for discussion of the form of production in the parties' prediscovery conference.

The responding party also is involved in determining the form of production. In the written response to the production request that Rule 34 requires, the responding party must state the form it intends to use for producing electronically stored information if the requesting party does not specify a form or if the responding party objects to a form that the requesting party specifies. Stating the intended form before the production occurs may permit the parties to identify and seek to resolve disputes before the expense and work of the production occurs. A party that responds to a discovery request by simply producing electronically stored information in a form of its choice, without identifying that form in advance of the production in the response required by Rule 34(b), runs a risk that the requesting party can show that the produced form is not reasonably usable and that it is entitled to production of some or all of the information in an additional form. Additional time might be required to permit a responding party to assess the appropriate form or forms of production.

If the requesting party is not satisfied with the form stated by the responding party, or if the responding party has objected to the form specified by the requesting party, the parties must meet and confer under Rule 37(a)(2)(B) in an effort to resolve the matter before the requesting party can file a motion to compel. If they cannot agree and the court resolves the dispute, the court is not limited to the forms initially chosen by the requesting party, stated by the responding party, or specified in this rule for situations in which there is no court order or party agreement.

If the form of production is not specified by party agreement or court order, the responding party must produce electronically stored information either in a form or forms in which it is ordinarily maintained or in a form or forms that are reasonably usable. Rule 34(a) requires that, if necessary, a responding party "translate" information it produces into a "reasonably usable" form. Under some circumstances, the responding party may need to provide some reasonable amount of technical support, information on application software, or other reasonable assistance to enable the requesting party to use the information. The rule does not require a party to produce electronically stored information in the form it which it is ordinarily maintained, as long as it is produced in a reasonably usable form. But the option to produce in a reasonably usable form does not mean that a responding party is free to convert electronically stored information from the form in which it is ordinarily maintained to a different form that makes it more difficult or burdensome for the requesting party to use the information efficiently in the litigation. If the responding party ordinarily maintains the information it is producing in a way that makes it searchable by electronic means, the information should not be produced in a form that removes or significantly degrades this feature.

Some electronically stored information may be ordinarily maintained in a form that is not reasonably usable by any party. One example is "legacy" data that can be used only by superseded systems. The questions whether a producing party should be required to convert such information to a more usable form, or should be required to produce it at all, should be addressed under Rule 26(b)(2)(B).

Whether or not the requesting party specified the form of production, Rule 34(b) provides that the same electronically stored information ordinarily need be produced in only one form.

2007 Amendment

The language of Rule 34 has been amended as part of the general restyling of the Civil Rules to make them more easily understood and to make style and terminology consistent throughout the rules. These changes are intended to be stylistic only.

The final sentence in the first paragraph of former Rule 34(b) was a redundant cross-reference to the discovery moratorium provisions of Rule 26(d). Rule 26(d) is now familiar, obviating any need to carry forward the redundant cross-reference.

The redundant reminder of Rule 37(a) procedure in the second paragraph of former Rule 34(b) is omitted as no longer useful.

Rule 35. Physical and Mental Examinations

(a) Order for an Examination.

(1) ***In General.*** The court where the action is pending may order a party whose mental or physical condition—including blood group—is in controversy to submit to a physical or mental examination by a suitably licensed or certified examiner. The court has the same authority to order a party to produce for examination a person who is in its custody or under its legal control.

(2) ***Motion and Notice; Contents of the Order.*** The order:

(A) may be made only on motion for good cause and on notice to all parties and the person to be examined; and

(B) must specify the time, place, manner, conditions, and scope of the examination, as well as the person or persons who will perform it.

(b) Examiner's Report.

(1) ***Request by the Party or Person Examined.*** The party who moved for the examination must, on request, deliver to the requester a copy of the examiner's report, together with like reports of all earlier examinations of the same condition. The request may be made by the party against whom the examination order was issued or by the person examined.

(2) ***Contents.*** The examiner's report must be in writing and must set out in detail the examiner's findings, including diagnoses, conclusions, and the results of any tests.

(3) ***Request by the Moving Party.*** After delivering the reports, the party who moved for the examination may request—and is entitled to receive—from the party against whom the examination order was issued like reports of all earlier or later examinations of the same condition. But those reports need not be delivered by the party with custody or control of the person examined if the party shows that it could not obtain them.

(4) ***Waiver of Privilege.*** By requesting and obtaining the examiner's report, or by deposing the examiner, the party examined waives any privilege it may have—in that action or any other action involving the same controversy—concerning testimony about all examinations of the same condition.

(5) ***Failure to Deliver a Report.*** The court on motion may order—on just terms—that a party deliver the report of an examination. If the report is not provided, the court may exclude the examiner's testimony at trial.

(6) ***Scope.*** This subdivision (b) applies also to an examination made by the parties' agreement, unless the agreement states otherwise. This subdivision does not preclude obtaining an examiner's report or deposing an examiner under other rules.

(Amended March 30, 1970, effective July 1, 1970; March 2, 1987, effective August 1, 1987; amended by Pub.L. 100-690, Title VII, § 7047(b), November 18, 1988, 102 Stat. 4401; amended April 30, 1991, effective December 1, 1991; April 30, 2007, effective December 1, 2007.)

ADVISORY COMMITTEE NOTES

1937 Adoption

Physical examination of parties before trial is authorized by statute or rule in a number of states. See Ariz.Rev. Code Ann. (Struckmeyer, 1928) § 4468; Mich. Court Rules Ann.

(Searl, 1933) Rule 41, § 2; 2 N.J.Comp.Stat. (1910); N.Y.C.P.A. (1937) § 306; 1 S.D.Comp.Laws (1929) § 2716A; 3 Wash.Rev.Stat.Ann. (Remington, 1932) § 1230–1.

Mental examination of parties is authorized in Iowa. Iowa Code (1935) ch. 491–F1. See McCash, *The Evolution of the Doctrine of Discovery and Its Present Status in Iowa*, 20 Ia.L.Rev. 68 (1934).

The constitutionality of legislation providing for physical examination of parties was sustained in *Lyon v. Manhattan Railway Co.*, 1894, 37 N.E. 113, 142 N.Y. 298, and *McGovern v. Hope*, 1899, 42 A. 830, 63 N.J.L. 76. In *Union Pacific Ry. Co. v. Botsford*, 1891, 11 S.Ct. 1000, 141 U.S. 250, 35 L.Ed. 734, it was held that the court could not order the physical examination of a party in the absence of statutory authority. But in *Camden and Suburban Ry. Co. v. Stetson*, 1900, 20 S.Ct. 617, 177 U.S. 172, 44 L.Ed. 721 where there was statutory authority for such examination, derived from a state statute made operative by the conformity act, the practice was sustained. Such authority is now found in the present rule made operative by the Act of June 19, 1934, c. 651, U.S.C., Title 28, § 2072, formerly §§ 723b (Rules in actions at law; Supreme Court authorized to make) and 723c (Union of equity and action at law rules; power of Supreme Court).

1970 Amendment

Subdivision (a). Rule 35(a) has hitherto provided only for an order requiring a party to submit to an examination. It is desirable to extend the rule to provide for an order against the party for examination of a person in his custody or under his legal control. As appears from the provisions of amended Rule 37(b)(2) and the comment under that rule, an order to "produce" the third person imposes only an obligation to use good faith efforts to produce the person.

The amendment will settle beyond doubt that a parent or guardian suing to recover for injuries to a minor may be ordered to produce the minor for examination. Further, the amendment expressly includes blood examination within the kinds of examinations that can be ordered under the rule. See *Beach v. Beach*, 114 F.2d 479 (D.C. Cir. 1940). Provisions similar to the amendment have been adopted in at least 10 States: Calif. Code Civ.Proc. § 2032; Ida.R.Civ.P. 35; Ill. S–H Ann. c. 110A, § 215; Md.R.P. 420; Mich.Gen.Ct.R. 311; Minn.R.Civ.P. 35; Mo.Vern.Ann.R.Civ.p. 60.01; N.Dak.R.Civ.P. 35; N.Y.C.P.L. § 3121; Wyo.R.Civ.P. 35.

The amendment makes no change in the requirements of Rule 35 that, before a court order may issue, the relevant physical or mental condition must be shown to be "in controversy" and "good cause" must be shown for the examination. Thus, the amendment has no effect on the recent decision of the Supreme Court in *Schlagenhauf v. Holder*, 379 U.S. 104 (1964), stressing the importance of these requirements and applying them to the facts of the case. The amendment makes no reference to employees of a party. Provisions relating to employees in the State statutes and rules cited above appear to have been virtually unused.

Subdivision (b)(1). This subdivision is amended to correct an imbalance in Rule 35(b)(1) as heretofore written. Under that text, a party causing a Rule 35(a) examination to be made is required to furnish to the party examined, on request, a copy of the examining physician's report. If he delivers this copy, he is in turn entitled to receive from the party examined reports of all examinations of the same condition previously or later made. But the rule has not in terms entitled the examined party to receive from the party causing the Rule 35(a) examination any reports of earlier examinations of the same condition to which the latter may have access. The amendment cures this defect. See La. Stat.Ann., Civ.Proc. art 1495 (1960); Utah R.Civ.P. 35(c).

The amendment specifies that the written report of the examining physician includes results of all tests made, such as results of X-rays and cardiograms. It also embodies changes required by the broadening of Rule 35(a) to take in persons who are not parties.

Subdivision (b)(3). This new subdivision removes any possible doubt that reports of examination may be obtained although no order for examination has been made under Rule 35(a). Examinations are very frequently made by agreement, and sometimes before the party examined has an attorney. The courts have uniformly ordered that reports be supplied, see 4 *Moore's Federal Practice* ¶35.06, n. 1 (2d ed. 1966); 2A Barron & Holtzoff, *Federal Practice and Procedure* § 823, n. 22 (Wright ed. 1961), and it appears best to fill the technical gap in the present rule.

The subdivision also makes clear that reports of examining physicians are discoverable not only under Rule 35(b), but under other rules as well. To be sure, if the report is privileged, then discovery is not permissible under any rule other than Rule 35(b) and it is permissible under Rule 35(b) only if the party requests a copy of the report of examination made by the other party's doctor. *Sher v. De Haven*, 199 F.2d 777 (D.C. Cir. 1952), *cert. denied* 345 U.S. 936 (1953). But if the report is unprivileged and is subject to discovery under the provisions of rules other than Rule 35(b)—such as Rules 34 or 26(b)(3) or (4)—discovery should not depend upon whether the person examined demands a copy of the report. Although a few cases have suggested the contrary, *e.g., Galloway v. National Dairy Products Corp.*, 24 F.R.D. 362 (E.D.Pa.1959), the better considered district court decisions hold that Rule 35(b) is not preemptive. *E.g., Leszynski v. Russ*, 29 F.R.D. 10, 12 (D.Md.1961) and cases cited. The question was recently given full consideration in *Buffington v. Wood*, 351 F.2d 292 (3d Cir. 1965), holding that Rule 35(b) is not preemptive.

1987 Amendment

The amendments are technical. No substantive change is intended.

1991 Amendment

The revision authorizes the court to require physical or mental examinations conducted by any person who is suitably licensed or certified.

The rule was revised in 1988 by Congressional enactment to authorize mental examinations by licensed clinical psychologists. This revision extends that amendment to include other certified or licensed professionals, such as dentists or occupational therapists, who are not physicians or clinical psychologists, but who may be well-qualified to give valuable testimony about the physical or mental condition that is the subject of dispute.

The requirement that the examiner be *suitably* licensed or certified is a new requirement. The court is thus expressly authorized to assess the credentials of the examiner to assure that no person is subjected to a court-ordered examination by an examiner whose testimony would be of such limited value that it would be unjust to require the person to undergo the invasion of privacy associated with the examination. This authority is not wholly new, for under the former rule, the court retained discretion to refuse to order an examination, or to restrict an examination. 8 WRIGHT & MILLER, FEDERAL PRACTICE & PROCEDURE § 2234 (1986 Supp.). The revision is intended to encourage the exercise of this discretion, especially with respect to examinations by persons having narrow qualifications.

The court's responsibility to determine the suitability of the examiner's qualifications applies even to a proposed examination by a physician. If the proposed examination and testimony calls for an expertise that the proposed examiner does not have, it should not be ordered, even if the proposed examiner is a physician. The rule does not, however, require that the license or certificate be conferred by the jurisdiction in which the examination is conducted.

2007 Amendment

The language of Rule 35 has been amended as part of the general restyling of the Civil Rules to make them more easily understood and to make style and terminology consistent throughout the rules. These changes are intended to be stylistic only.

Rule 36. Requests for Admission

(a) Scope and Procedure.

(1) ***Scope.*** A party may serve on any other party a written request to admit, for purposes of the pending action only, the truth of any matters within the scope of Rule 26(b)(1) relating to:

(A) facts, the application of law to fact, or opinions about either; and

(B) the genuineness of any described documents.

(2) ***Form; Copy of a Document.*** Each matter must be separately stated. A request to admit the genuineness of a document must be accompanied by a copy of the document unless it is, or has been, otherwise furnished or made available for inspection and copying.

(3) ***Time to Respond; Effect of Not Responding.*** A matter is admitted unless, within 30 days after being served, the party to whom the request is directed serves on the requesting party a written answer or objection addressed to the matter and signed by the party or its attorney. A shorter or longer time for responding may be stipulated to under Rule 29 or be ordered by the court.

(4) ***Answer.*** If a matter is not admitted, the answer must specifically deny it or state in detail why the answering party cannot truthfully admit or deny it. A denial must fairly respond to the substance of the matter; and when good faith requires that a party qualify an answer or deny only a part of a matter, the answer must specify the part admitted and qualify or deny the rest. The answering party may assert lack of knowledge or information as a reason for failing to admit or deny only if the party states that it has made reasonable inquiry and that the information it knows or can readily obtain is insufficient to enable it to admit or deny.

(5) ***Objections.*** The grounds for objecting to a request must be stated. A party must not object solely on the ground that the request presents a genuine issue for trial.

(6) ***Motion Regarding the Sufficiency of an Answer or Objection.*** The requesting party may move to determine the sufficiency of an answer or objection. Unless the court finds an objection justified, it must order that an answer be served. On finding that an answer does not comply with this rule, the court may order either that the matter is admitted or that an amended answer be served. The court may defer its final decision until a pretrial conference or a specified time before trial. Rule 37(a)(5) applies to an award of expenses.

(b) Effect of an Admission; Withdrawing or Amending It. A matter admitted under this rule is conclusively established unless the court, on motion, permits the admission to be withdrawn or amended. Subject to Rule 16(e), the court may permit withdrawal or amendment if it would promote the presentation of the merits of the action and if the court is not persuaded that it would prejudice the requesting party in maintaining or defending the action on the merits. An admission under this rule is not an admission for any other purpose and cannot be used against the party in any other proceeding.

(Amended December 27, 1946, effective March 19, 1948; March 30, 1970, effective July 1, 1970; March 2, 1987, effective August 1, 1987; April 22, 1993, effective December 1, 1993; April 30, 2007, effective December 1, 2007.)

ADVISORY COMMITTEE NOTES

1937 Adoption

Compare similar rules: [Former] Equity Rule 58 (last paragraph, which provides for the admission of the execution and genuineness of documents); *English Rules Under the Judicature Act* (The Annual Practice, 1937) O. 32; Ill.Rev. Stat. (1937) ch. 110, § 182 and Rule 18 (Ill.Rev.Stat. (1937) ch. 110, § 259.18); 2 Mass.Gen.Laws (Ter.Ed., 1932) ch. 231, § 69; Mich. Court Rules Ann. (Searl, 1933) Rule 42; N.J. Comp.Stat. (2 Cum.Supp. 1911–1924); N.Y.C.P.A. (1937) §§ 322, 323; Wis.Stat. (1935) § 327.22.

1946 Amendment

Note. The first change in the first sentence of Rule 36(a) and the addition of the new second sentence, specifying when requests for admissions may be served, bring Rule 36 in line with amended Rules 26(a) and 33. There is no reason why these rules should not be treated alike. Other provisions of Rule 36(a) give the party whose admissions are requested adequate protection.

The second change in the first sentence of the rule [subdivision (a)] removes any uncertainty as to whether a party can be called upon to admit matters of fact other than those set forth in relevant documents described in and exhibited with the request. In *Smyth v. Kaufman*, C.C.A.2, 1940, 114 F.2d 40, it was held that the word "therein", now stricken from the rule [said subdivision] referred to the request and that a matter of fact not related to any document could be presented to the other party for admission or denial. The rule of this case is now clearly stated.

The substitution of the word "served" for "delivered" in the third sentence of the amended rule [said subdivision] is in conformance with the use of the word "serve" elsewhere in the rule and generally throughout the rules. See also Notes to Rules 13(a) and 33 herein. The substitution [in said subdivision] of "shorter or longer" for "further" will enable a court to designate a lesser period than 10 days for answer. This conforms with a similar provision already contained in Rule 33.

The addition of clause (1) [in said subdivision] specifies the method by which a party may challenge the propriety of a request to admit. There has been considerable difference of judicial opinion as to the correct method, if any, available to secure relief from an allegedly improper request. See Commentary, *Methods of Objecting to Notice to Admit*, 1942, 5 Fed.Rules Serv. 835; *International Carbonic Engineering Co. v. Natural Carbonic Products, Inc.*, S.D.Cal.1944, 57 F.Supp. 248. The changes in clause (1) are merely of a clarifying and conforming nature.

The first of the added last two sentences [in said subdivision] prevents an objection to a part of a request from holding up the answer, if any, to the remainder. See similar proposed change in Rule 33. The last sentence strengthens the rule by making the denial accurately reflect the party's position. It is taken, with necessary changes, from Rule 8(b).

1970 Amendment

Rule 36 serves two vital purposes, both of which are designed to reduce trial time. Admissions are sought, first to facilitate proof with respect to issues that cannot be eliminated from the case, and secondly, to narrow the issues by eliminating those that can be. The changes made in the rule are designed to serve these purposes more effectively. Certain disagreements in the courts about the proper scope of the rule are resolved. In addition, the procedural operation of the rule is brought into line with other discovery procedures, and the binding effect of an admission is clarified. See generally Finman, *The Request for Admissions in Federal Civil Procedure*, 71 Yale L.J. 371 (1962).

Subdivision (a). As revised, the subdivision provides that a request may be made to admit any matters within the scope of Rule 26(b) that relate to statements or opinions of fact or of the application of law to fact. It thereby eliminates the requirement that the matters be "of fact." This change resolves conflicts in the court decisions as to whether a request to admit matters of "opinion" and matters involving "mixed law and fact" is proper under the rule. As to "opinion," compare, *e.g., Jackson Buff Corp. v. Marcelle*, 20 F.R.D. 139 (E.D.N.Y.1957); *California v. The S. S. Jules Fribourg*, 19 F.R.D. 432 (N.D.Calif.1955), with *e.g., Photon, Inc. v. Harris Intertype, Inc.*, 28 F.R.D. 327 (D.Mass.1961); *Hise v. Lockwood Grader Corp.*, 153 F.Supp. 276 (D.Nebr.1957). As to "mixed law and fact" the majority of courts sustain objections, *e.g., Minnesota Mining and Mfg. Co. v. Norton Co.*, 36 F.R.D. 1 (N.D.Ohio 1964), but *McSparran v. Hanigan*, 225 F.Supp. 628 (E.D.Pa.1963) is to the contrary.

Not only is it difficult as a practical matter to separate "fact" from "opinion," see 4 *Moore's Federal Practice* ¶36.04 (2d ed. 1966); cf. 2A Barron & Holtzoff, *Federal Practice and Procedure* 317 (Wright ed. 1961), but an admission on a matter of opinion may facilitate proof or narrow the issues or both. An admission of a matter involving the application of law to fact may, in a given case, even more clearly narrow the issues. For example, an admission that an employee acted in the scope of his employment may remove a major issue from the trial. In *McSparran v. Hanigan, supra*, plaintiff admitted that "the premises on which said accident occurred, were occupied or under the control" of one of the defendants, 225 F.Supp. at 636. This admission, involving law as well as fact, removed one of the issues from the lawsuit and thereby reduced the proof required at trial. The amended provision does not authorize requests for admissions of law unrelated to the facts of the case.

Requests for admission involving the application of law to fact may create disputes between the parties which are best resolved in the presence of the judge after much or all of the other discovery has been completed. Power is therefore expressly conferred upon the court to defer decision until a pretrial conference is held or until a designated time prior to trial. On the other hand, the court should not automatically defer decision; in many instances, the importance of the admission lies in enabling the requesting party to avoid the burdensome accumulation of proof prior to the pretrial conference.

Courts have also divided on whether an answering party may properly object to request for admission as to matters which that party regards as "in dispute." Compare, *e.g., Syracuse Broadcasting Corp. v. Newhouse*, 271 F.2d 910, 917 (2d Cir. 1959); *Driver v. Gindy Mfg. Corp.*, 24 F.R.D. 473 (E.D.Pa.1959); with, *e.g., McGonigle v. Baxter*, 27 F.R.D. 504 (E.D.Pa.1961); *United States v. Ehbauer*, 13 F.R.D. 462 (W.D.Mo.1952). The proper response in such cases is an answer. The very purpose of the request is to ascertain whether the answering party is prepared to admit or regards the matter as presenting a genuine issue for trial. In his answer, the party may deny, or he may give as his reason for inability to admit or deny the existence of a genuine issue. The party runs no risk of sanctions if the matter is genuinely in issue, since Rule 37(c) provides a sanction of costs only when there are no good reasons for a failure to admit.

On the other hand, requests to admit may be so voluminous and so framed that the answering party finds the task of identifying what is in dispute and what is not unduly burdensome. If so, the responding party may obtain a protective order under Rule 26(c). Some of the decisions sustaining objections on "disputability" grounds could have been justified by the burdensome character of the requests. See, *e.g., Syracuse Broadcasting Corp. v. Newhouse, supra.*

Another sharp split of authority exists on the question whether a party may base his answer on lack of information or knowledge without seeking out additional information. One line of cases has held that a party may answer on the basis of such knowledge as he has at the time he answers. *E.g., Jackson Buff Corp. v. Marcelle,* 20 F.R.D. 139 (E.D.N.Y.1957); *Sladek v. General Motors Corp.,* 16 F.R.D. 104 (S.D.Iowa 1954). A larger group of cases, supported by commentators, has taken the view that if the responding party lacks knowledge, he must inform himself in reasonable fashion. *E.g., Hise v. Lockwood Grader Corp.,* 153 F.Supp. 276 (D.Nebr. 1957); *E. H. Tate Co. v. Jiffy Enterprises, Inc.,* 16 F.R.D. 571 (E.D.Pa.1954); Finman, *supra,* 71 Yale L.J. 371, 404–409; 4 *Moore's Federal Practice* ¶36.04 (2d ed. 1966); 2A Barron & Holtzoff, *Federal Practice and Procedure* 509 (Wright ed. 1961).

The rule as revised adopts the majority view, as in keeping with a basic principle of the discovery rules that a reasonable burden may be imposed on the parties when its discharge will facilitate preparation for trial and ease the trial process. It has been argued against this view that one side should not have the burden of "proving" the other side's case. The revised rule requires only that the answering party make reasonable inquiry and secure such knowledge and information as are readily obtainable by him. In most instances, the investigation will be necessary either to his own case or to preparation for rebuttal. Even when it is not, the information may be close enough at hand to be "readily obtainable." Rule 36 requires only that the party state that he has taken these steps. The sanction for failure of a party to inform himself before he answers lies in the award of costs after trial, as provided in Rule 37(c).

The requirement that the answer to a request for admission be sworn is deleted, in favor of a provision that the answer be signed by the party or by his attorney. The provisions of Rule 36 make it clear that admissions function very much as pleadings do. Thus, when a party admits in part and denies in part, his admission is for purposes of the pending action only and may not be used against him in any other proceeding. The broadening of the rule to encompass mixed questions of law and fact reinforces this feature. Rule 36 does not lack a sanction for false answers; Rule 37(c) furnishes an appropriate deterrent.

The existing language describing the available grounds for objection to a request for admission is eliminated as neither necessary nor helpful. The statement that objection may be made to any request which is "improper" adds nothing to the provisions that the party serve an answer or objection addressed to each matter and that he state his reasons for any objection. None of the other discovery rules sets forth grounds for objection, except so far as all are subject to the general provisions of Rule 26.

Changes are made in the sequence of procedures in Rule 36 so that they conform to the new procedures in Rules 33 and 34. The major changes are as follows:

(1) The normal time for response to a request for admissions is lengthened from 10 to 30 days, conforming more closely to prevailing practice. A defendant need not respond, however, in less than 45 days after service of the summons and complaint upon him. The court may lengthen or shorten the time when special situations require it.

(2) The present requirement that the plaintiff wait 10 days to serve requests without leave of court is eliminated. The revised provision accords with those in Rules 33 and 34.

(3) The requirement that the objecting party move automatically for a hearing on his objection is eliminated, and the burden is on the requesting party to move for an order. The change in the burden of going forward does not modify present law on burden of persuasion. The award of expenses incurred in relation to the motion is made subject to the comprehensive provisions of Rule 37(a)(4).

(4) A problem peculiar to Rule 36 arises if the responding party serves answers that are not in conformity with the requirements of the rule—for example, a denial is not "specific," or the explanation of inability to admit or deny is not "in detail." Rule 36 now makes no provision for court scrutiny of such answers before trial, and it seems to contemplate that defective answers bring about admissions just as effectively as if no answer had been served. Some cases have so held. *E.g., Southern Ry. Co. v. Crosby,* 201 F.2d 878 (4th Cir. 1953); *United States v. Laney,* 96 F.Supp. 482 (E.D.S.C.1951).

Giving a defective answer the automatic effect of an admission may cause unfair surprise. A responding party who purported to deny or to be unable to admit or deny will for the first time at trial confront the contention that he has made a binding admission. Since it is not always easy to know whether a denial is "specific" or an explanation is "in detail," neither party can know how the court will rule at trial and whether proof must be prepared. Some courts, therefore, have entertained motions to rule on defective answers. They have at times ordered that amended answers be served, when the defects were technical, and at other times have declared that the matter was admitted. *E.g., Woods v. Stewart,* 171 F.2d 544 (5th Cir. 1948); *SEC v. Kaye, Real & Co.,* 122 F.Supp. 639 (S.D.N.Y.1954); *Sieb's Hatcheries, Inc. v. Lindley,* 13 F.R.D. 113 (W.D.Ark.1952). The rule as revised conforms to the latter practice.

Subdivision (b). The rule does not how indicate the extent to which a party is bound by his admission. Some courts view admissions as the equivalent of sworn testimony. *E.g., Ark–Tenn Distributing Corp. v. Breidt,* 209 F.2d 359 (3d Cir. 1954); *United States v. Lemons,* 125 F.Supp. 686 (W.D.Ark.1954); 4 *Moore's Federal Practice* ¶36.08 (2d ed. 1966 Supp.). At least in some jurisdictions a party may rebut his own testimony, *e.g., Alamo v. Del Rosario,* 98 F.2d 328 (D.C.Cir.1938), and by analogy an admission made pursuant to Rule 36 may likewise be thought rebuttable. The courts in *Ark–Tenn* and *Lemons, supra,* reasoned in this way, although the results reached may be supported on different grounds. In *McSparran v. Hanigan,* 225 F.Supp. 628, 636–637 (E.D.Pa.1963), the court held that an admission is conclusively binding, though noting the confusion created by prior decisions.

The new provisions give an admission a conclusively binding effect, for purposes only of the pending action, unless the admission is withdrawn or amended. In form and substance a Rule 36 admission is comparable to an admission in pleadings or a stipulation drafted by counsel for use at trial, rather than to an evidentiary admission of a party. Louisell, *Modern California Discovery* § 8.07 (1963); 2A Barron & Holtzoff, *Federal Practice and Procedure* § 838 (Wright ed.

1961). Unless the party securing an admission can depend on its binding effect, he cannot safely avoid the expense of preparing to prove the very matters on which he has secured the admission, and the purpose of the rule is defeated. Field v. McKusick, *Maine Civil Practice* § 36.4 (1959); Finman, *supra*, 71 Yale L.J. 371, 418–426; Comment, 56 Nw.U.L.Rev. 679, 682–683 (1961).

Provision is made for withdrawal or amendment of an admission. This provision emphasizes the importance of having the action resolved on the merits, while at the same time assuring each party that justified reliance on an admission in preparation for trial will not operate to his prejudice. *Cf. Moosman v. Joseph P. Blitz, Inc.*, 358 F.2d 686 (2d Cir. 1966).

1987 Amendment

The amendments are technical. No substantive change is intended.

1993 Amendments

The rule is revised to reflect the change made by Rule 26(d), preventing a party from seeking formal discovery until after the meeting of the parties required by Rule 26(f).

2007 Amendment

The language of Rule 36 has been amended as part of the general restyling of the Civil Rules to make them more easily understood and to make style and terminology consistent throughout the rules. These changes are intended to be stylistic only.

The final sentence of the first paragraph of former Rule 36(a) was a redundant cross-reference to the discovery moratorium provisions of Rule 26(d). Rule 26(d) is now familiar, obviating any need to carry forward the redundant cross-reference. The redundant reminder of Rule 37(c) in the second paragraph was likewise omitted.

Rule 37. Failure to Make Disclosures or to Cooperate in Discovery; Sanctions

(a) Motion for an Order Compelling Disclosure or Discovery.

(1) ***In General.*** On notice to other parties and all affected persons, a party may move for an order compelling disclosure or discovery. The motion must include a certification that the movant has in good faith conferred or attempted to confer with the person or party failing to make disclosure or discovery in an effort to obtain it without court action.

(2) ***Appropriate Court.*** A motion for an order to a party must be made in the court where the action is pending. A motion for an order to a nonparty must be made in the court where the discovery is or will be taken.

(3) ***Specific Motions.***

(A) *To Compel Disclosure.* If a party fails to make a disclosure required by Rule 26(a), any other party may move to compel disclosure and for appropriate sanctions.

(B) *To Compel a Discovery Response.* A party seeking discovery may move for an order compelling an answer, designation, production, or inspection. This motion may be made if:

(i) a deponent fails to answer a question asked under Rule 30 or 31;

(ii) a corporation or other entity fails to make a designation under Rule 30(b)(6) or 31(a)(4);

(iii) a party fails to answer an interrogatory submitted under Rule 33; or

(iv) a party fails to respond that inspection will be permitted—or fails to permit inspection—as requested under Rule 34.

(C) *Related to a Deposition.* When taking an oral deposition, the party asking a question may complete or adjourn the examination before moving for an order.

(4) ***Evasive or Incomplete Disclosure, Answer, or Response.*** For purposes of this subdivision (a), an evasive or incomplete disclosure, answer, or response must be treated as a failure to disclose, answer, or respond.

(5) ***Payment of Expenses; Protective Orders.***

(A) *If the Motion Is Granted (or Disclosure or Discovery Is Provided After Filing).* If the motion is granted—or if the disclosure or requested discovery is provided after the motion was filed—the court must, after giving an opportunity to be heard, require the party or deponent whose conduct necessitated the motion, the party or attorney advising that conduct, or both to pay the movant's reasonable expenses incurred in making the motion, including attorney's fees. But the court must not order this payment if:

(i) the movant filed the motion before attempting in good faith to obtain the disclosure or discovery without court action;

(ii) the opposing party's nondisclosure, response, or objection was substantially justified; or

(iii) other circumstances make an award of expenses unjust.

(B) *If the Motion Is Denied.* If the motion is denied, the court may issue any protective order authorized under Rule 26(c) and must, after giving an opportunity to be heard, require the movant, the attorney filing the motion, or both to pay the party or deponent who opposed the motion its reasonable expenses incurred in opposing the motion, including attorney's fees. But the court must not order this payment if the motion was substantially justified or other circumstances make an award of expenses unjust.

(C) *If the Motion Is Granted in Part and Denied in Part.* If the motion is granted in part and denied in part, the court may issue any protective order authorized under Rule 26(c) and may, after giving an opportunity to be heard, apportion the reasonable expenses for the motion.

(b) Failure to Comply with a Court Order.

(1) ***Sanctions in the District Where the Deposition Is Taken.*** If the court where the discovery is taken orders a deponent to be sworn or to answer a question and the deponent fails to obey, the failure may be treated as contempt of court.

(2) ***Sanctions in the District Where the Action Is Pending.***

(A) *For Not Obeying a Discovery Order.* If a party or a party's officer, director, or managing agent—or a witness designated under Rule 30(b)(6) or 31(a)(4)—fails to obey an order to provide or permit discovery, including an order under Rule 26(f), 35, or 37(a), the court where the action is pending may issue further just orders. They may include the following:

(i) directing that the matters embraced in the order or other designated facts be taken as established for purposes of the action, as the prevailing party claims;

(ii) prohibiting the disobedient party from supporting or opposing designated claims or defenses, or from introducing designated matters in evidence;

(iii) striking pleadings in whole or in part;

(iv) staying further proceedings until the order is obeyed;

(v) dismissing the action or proceeding in whole or in part;

(vi) rendering a default judgment against the disobedient party; or

(vii) treating as contempt of court the failure to obey any order except an order to submit to a physical or mental examination.

(B) *For Not Producing a Person for Examination.* If a party fails to comply with an order under Rule 35(a) requiring it to produce another person for examination, the court may issue any of the orders listed in Rule 37(b)(2)(A)(i)-(vi), unless the disobedient party shows that it cannot produce the other person.

(C) *Payment of Expenses.* Instead of or in addition to the orders above, the court must order the disobedient party, the attorney advising that party, or both to pay the reasonable expenses, including attorney's fees, caused by the failure, unless the failure was substantially justified or other circumstances make an award of expenses unjust.

(c) Failure to Disclose, to Supplement an Earlier Response, or to Admit.

(1) ***Failure to Disclose or Supplement.*** If a party fails to provide information or identify a witness as required by Rule 26(a) or (e), the party is not allowed to use that information or witness to supply evidence on a motion, at a hearing, or at a trial, unless the failure was substantially justified or is harmless. In addition to or instead of this sanction, the court, on motion and after giving an opportunity to be heard:

(A) may order payment of the reasonable expenses, including attorney's fees, caused by the failure;

(B) may inform the jury of the party's failure; and

(C) may impose other appropriate sanctions, including any of the orders listed in Rule 37(b)(2)(A)(i)-(vi).

(2) ***Failure to Admit.*** If a party fails to admit what is requested under Rule 36 and if the requesting party later proves a document to be genuine or the matter true, the requesting party may move that the party who failed to admit pay the reasonable expenses, including attorney's fees, incurred in making that proof. The court must so order unless:

(A) the request was held objectionable under Rule 36(a);

(B) the admission sought was of no substantial importance;

(C) the party failing to admit had a reasonable ground to believe that it might prevail on the matter; or

(D) there was other good reason for the failure to admit.

(d) Party's Failure to Attend Its Own Deposition, Serve Answers to Interrogatories, or Respond to a Request for Inspection.

(1) ***In General.***

(A) *Motion; Grounds for Sanctions.* The court where the action is pending may, on motion, order sanctions if:

(i) a party or a party's officer, director, or managing agent—or a person designated under Rule 30(b)(6) or 31(a)(4)—fails, after being served with proper notice, to appear for that person's deposition; or

(ii) a party, after being properly served with interrogatories under Rule 33 or a request for inspection under Rule 34, fails to serve its answers, objections, or written response.

(B) *Certification.* A motion for sanctions for failing to answer or respond must include a certification that the movant has in good faith conferred or attempted to confer with the party failing to act in an effort to obtain the answer or response without court action.

(2) ***Unacceptable Excuse for Failing to Act.*** A failure described in Rule 37(d)(1)(A) is not excused on the ground that the discovery sought was objectionable, unless the party failing to act has a pending motion for a protective order under Rule 26(c).

(3) ***Types of Sanctions.*** Sanctions may include any of the orders listed in Rule 37(b)(2)(A)(i)-(vi). Instead of or in addition to these sanctions, the court must require the party failing to act, the attorney advising that party, or both to pay the reasonable expenses, including attorney's fees, caused by the failure, unless the failure was substantially justified or other circumstances make an award of expenses unjust.

(e) Failure to Provide Electronically Stored Information. Absent exceptional circumstances, a court may not impose sanctions under these rules on a party for failing to provide electronically stored information lost as a result of the routine, good-faith operation of an electronic information system.

(f) Failure to Participate in Framing a Discovery Plan. If a party or its attorney fails to participate in good faith in developing and submitting a proposed discovery plan as required by Rule 26(f), the court may, after giving an opportunity to be heard, require that party or attorney to pay to any other party the reasonable expenses, including attorney's fees, caused by the failure.

(Amended December 29, 1948, effective October 20, 1949; March 30, 1970, effective July 1, 1970; April 29, 1980, effective August 1, 1980; amended by Pub.L. 96–481, Title II, § 205(a), October 21, 1980, 94 Stat. 2330, effective October 1, 1981; amended March 2, 1987, effective August 1, 1987; April 22, 1993, effective December 1, 1993; April 17, 2000, effective December 1, 2000; April 12, 2006, effective December 1, 2006; April 30, 2007, effective December 1, 2007.)

ADVISORY COMMITTEE NOTES

1937 Adoption

The provisions of this rule authorizing orders establishing facts or excluding evidence or striking pleadings, or authorizing judgments of dismissal or default, for refusal to answer questions or permit inspection or otherwise make discovery, are in accord with *Hammond Packing Co. v. Arkansas,* 1909, 29 S.Ct. 370, 212 U.S. 322, 53 L.Ed. 530, 15 Ann.Cas. 645, which distinguishes between the justifiable use of such measures as a means of compelling the production of evidence, and their unjustifiable use, as in *Hovey v. Elliott,* 1897, 17 S.Ct. 841, 167 U.S. 409, 42 L.Ed. 215, for the mere purpose of punishing for contempt.

1948 Amendment

The amendment effective October 1949, substituted the reference to "Title 28, U.S.C., § 1783" in subdivision (e) for the reference to "the Act of July 3, 1926, c. 762, § 1 (44 Stat. 835), U.S.C., Title 28, § 711."

1970 Amendment

Rule 37 provides generally for sanctions against parties or persons unjustifiably resisting discovery. Experience has brought to light a number of defects in the language of the rule as well as instances in which it is not serving the purposes for which it was designed. See Rosenberg, *Sanctions to Effectuate Pretrial Discovery,* 58 Col.L.Rev. 480 (1958). In addition, changes being made in other discovery rules require conforming amendments to Rule 37.

Rule 37 sometimes refers to a "failure" to afford discovery and at other times to a "refusal" to do so. Taking note of this dual terminology, courts have imported into "refusal" a requirement of "wilfullness." See *Roth v. Paramount Pictures Corp.,* 8 F.R.D. 31 (W.D.Pa.1948); *Campbell v. Johnson,* 101 F.Supp. 705, 707 (S.D.N.Y.1951). In *Societe Internationale v. Rogers,* 357 U.S. 197 (1958), the Supreme Court concluded that the rather random use of these two terms in Rule 37 showed no design to use them with consistently distinctive meanings, that "refused" in Rule 37(b)(2) meant simply a failure to comply, and that wilfullness was relevant only to the selection of sanctions, if any, to be imposed. Nevertheless, after the decision in *Societe,* the court in *Hinson v. Michigan Mutual Liability Co.,* 275 F.2d 537 (5th Cir. 1960) once again ruled that "refusal" required wilfullness. Substitution of "failure" for "refusal" throughout Rule 37 should eliminate this confusion and bring the rule into harmony with the *Societe Internationale* decision. See Rosenberg, *supra,* 58 Col.L.Rev. 480, 489–490 (1958).

Subdivision (a). Rule 37(a) provides relief to a party seeking discovery against one who, with or without stated objections, fails to afford the discovery sought. It has always fully served this function in relation to depositions, but the amendments being made to Rules 33 and 34 give Rule 37(a) added scope and importance. Under existing Rule 33, a party objecting to interrogatories must make a motion for court hearing on his objections. The changes now made in Rules 33 and 37(a) make it clear that the interrogating party must move to compel answers, and the motion is provided for in Rule 37(a). Existing Rule 34, since it requires a court order prior to production of documents or things or permission to enter on land, has no relation to Rule 37(a). Amendments of Rules 34 and 37(a) create a procedure similar to that provided for Rule 33.

Subdivision (a)(1). This is a new provision making clear to which court a party may apply for an order compelling discovery. Existing Rule 37(a) refers only to the court in which the deposition is being taken; nevertheless, it has been held that the court where the action is pending has "inherent power" to compel a party deponent to answer. *Lincoln Laboratories, Inc. v. Savage Laboratories, Inc.*, 27 F.R.D. 476 (D.Del.1961). In relation to Rule 33 interrogatories and Rule 34 requests for inspection, the court where the action is pending is the appropriate enforcing tribunal. The new provision eliminates the need to resort to inherent power by spelling out the respective roles of the court where the action is pending and the court where the deposition is taken. In some instances, two courts are available to a party seeking to compel answers from a party deponent. The party seeking discovery may choose the court to which he will apply, but the court has power to remit the party to the other court as a more appropriate forum.

Subdivision (a)(2). This subdivision contains the substance of existing provisions of Rule 37(a) authorizing motions to compel answers to questions put at depositions and to interrogatories. New provisions authorize motions for orders compelling designation under Rules 30(b)(6) and 31(a) and compelling inspection in accordance with a request made under Rule 34. If the court denies a motion, in whole or part, it may accompany the denial with issuance of a protective order. Compare the converse provision in Rule 26(c).

Subdivision (a)(3). This new provision makes clear that an evasive or incomplete answer is to be considered, for purposes of subdivision (a), a failure to answer. The courts have consistently held that they have the power to compel adequate answers. *E.g., Cone Mills Corp. v. Joseph Bancroft & Sons Co.*, 33 F.R.D. 318 (D.Del.1963). This power is recognized and incorporated into the rule.

Subdivision (a)(4). This subdivision amends the provisions for award of expenses, including reasonable attorney's fees, to the prevailing party or person when a motion is made for an order compelling discovery. At present, an award of expenses is made only if the losing party or person is found to have acted without substantial justification. The change requires that expenses be awarded unless the conduct of the losing party or person is found to have been substantially justified. The test of "substantial justification" remains, but the change in language is intended to encourage judges to be more alert to abuses occurring in the discovery process.

On many occasions, to be sure, the dispute over discovery between the parties is genuine, though ultimately resolved one way or the other by the court. In such cases, the losing party is substantially justified in carrying the matter to court. But the rules should deter the abuse implicit in carrying or forcing a discovery dispute to court when no genuine dispute exists. And the potential or actual imposition of expenses is virtually the sole formal sanction in the rules to deter a party from pressing to a court hearing frivolous requests for or objections to discovery.

The present provision of Rule 37(a) that the court shall require payment if it finds that the defeated party acted without "substantial justification" may appear adequate, but in fact it has been little used. Only a handful of reported cases include an award of expenses, and the Columbia Survey found that in only one instance out of about 50 motions decided under Rule 37(a) did the court award expenses. It appears that the courts do not utilize the most important available sanction to deter abusive resort to the judiciary.

The proposed change provides in effect that expenses should ordinarily be awarded unless a court finds that the losing party acted justifiably in carrying his point to court. At the same time, a necessary flexibility is maintained, since the court retains the power to find that other circumstances make an award of expenses unjust—as where the prevailing party also acted unjustifiably. The amendment does not significantly narrow the discretion of the court, but rather presses the court to address itself to abusive practices. The present provision that expenses may be imposed upon either the party or his attorney or both is unchanged. But it is not contemplated that expenses will be imposed upon the attorney merely because the party is indigent.

Subdivision (b). This subdivision deals with sanctions for failure to comply with a court order. The present captions for subsections (1) and (2) entitled, "Contempt" and "Other Consequences," respectively, are confusing. One of the consequences listed in (2) is the arrest of the party, representing the exercise of the contempt power. The contents of the subsections show that the first authorizes the sanction of contempt (and no other) by the court in which the deposition is taken, whereas the second subsection authorizes a variety of sanctions, including contempt, which may be imposed by the court in which the action is pending. The captions of the subsections are changed to reflect their contents.

The scope of Rule 37(b)(2) is broadened by extending it to include any order "to provide or permit discovery," including orders issued under Rules 37(a) and 35. Various rules authorize orders for discovery—*e.g.*, Rule 35(b)(1), Rule 26(c) as revised, Rule 37(d). See Rosenberg, *supra*, 58 Col.L.Rev. 480, 484–486. Rule 37(b)(2) should provide comprehensively for enforcement of all these orders. *Cf. Societe Internationale v. Rogers*, 357 U.S. 197, 207 (1958). On the other hand, the reference to Rule 34 is deleted to conform to the changed procedure in that rule.

A new subsection (E) provides that sanctions which have been available against a party for failure to comply with an order under Rule 35(a) to submit to examination will now be available against him for his failure to comply with a Rule 35(a) order to produce a third person for examination, unless he shows that he is unable to produce the person. In this context, "unable" means in effect "unable in good faith." See *Societe Internationale v. Rogers*, 357 U.S. 197 (1958).

Subdivision (b)(2) is amplified to provide for payment of reasonable expenses caused by the failure to obey the order. Although Rules 37(b)(2) and 37(d) have been silent as to award of expenses, courts have nevertheless ordered them on occasion. *E.g., United Sheeplined Clothing Co. v. Arctic Fur Cap Corp.*, 165 F.Supp. 193 (S.D.N.Y.1958); *Austin Theatre, Inc. v. Warner Bros. Pictures, Inc.*, 22 F.R.D. 302 (S.D.N.Y.

1958). The provision places the burden on the disobedient party to avoid expenses by showing that his failure is justified or that special circumstances make an award of expenses unjust. Allocating the burden in this way conforms to the changed provisions as to expenses in Rule 37(a), and is particularly appropriate when a court order is disobeyed.

An added reference to directors of a party is similar to a change made in subdivision (d) and is explained in the note to that subdivision. The added reference to persons designated by a party under Rules 30(b)(6) or 31(a) to testify on behalf of the party carries out the new procedure in those rules for taking a deposition of a corporation or other organization.

Subdivision (c). Rule 37(c) provides a sanction for the enforcement of Rule 36 dealing with requests for admission. Rule 36 provides the mechanism whereby a party may obtain from another party in appropriate instances either (1) an admission, or (2) a sworn and specific denial or (3) a sworn statement "setting forth in detail the reasons why he cannot truthfully admit or deny." If the party obtains the second or third of these responses, in proper form, Rule 36 does not provide for a pretrial hearing on whether the response is warranted by the evidence thus far accumulated. Instead, Rule 37(c) is intended to provide posttrial relief in the form of a requirement that the party improperly refusing the admission pay the expenses of the other side in making the necessary proof at trial.

Rule 37(c), as now written, addresses itself in terms only to the sworn denial and is silent with respect to the statement of reasons for an inability to admit or deny. There is no apparent basis for this distinction, since the sanction provided in Rule 37(c) should deter all unjustified failures to admit. This omission in the rule has caused confused and diverse treatment in the courts. One court has held that if a party give inadequate reasons, he should be treated before trial as having denied the request, so that Rule 37(c) may apply. *Bertha Bldg. Corp. v. National Theatres Corp.*, 15 F.R.D. 339 (E.D.N.Y.1954). Another has held that the party should be treated as having admitted the request. *Heng Hsin Co. v. Stern, Morgenthau & Co.*, 20 Fed.Rules Serv. 36a.52, Case 1 (S.D.N.Y. Dec. 10, 1954). Still another has ordered a new response, without indicating what the outcome should be if the new response were inadequate. *United States Plywood Corp. v. Hudson Lumber Co.*, 127 F.Supp. 489, 497–498 (S.D.N.Y.1954). See generally Finman, *The Request for Admissions in Federal Civil Procedure*, 71 Yale L.J. 371, 426–430 (1962). The amendment eliminates this defect in Rule 37(c) by bringing within its scope all failures to admit.

Additional provisions in Rule 37(c) protect a party from having to pay expenses if the request for admission was held objectionable under Rule 36(a) or if the party failing to admit had reasonable ground to believe that he might prevail on the matter. The latter provision emphasizes that the true test under Rule 37(c) is not whether a party prevailed at trial but whether he acted reasonably in believing that he might prevail.

Subdivision (d). The scope of subdivision (d) is broadened to include responses to requests for inspection under Rule 34, thereby conforming to the new procedures of Rule 34.

Two related changes are made in subdivision (d): the permissible sanctions are broadened to include such orders "as are just"; and the requirement that the failure to appear or respond be "wilful" is eliminated. Although Rule 37(d) in terms provides for only three sanctions, all rather severe, the courts have interpreted it as permitting softer sanctions than those which it sets forth. E.g., *Gill v. Stolow*, 240 F.2d 669 (2d Cir.1957); *Saltzman v. Birrell*, 156 F.Supp. 538 (S.D.N.Y.1957); 2A Barron & Holtzoff, *Federal Practice and Procedure* 554–557 (Wright ed. 1961). The rule is changed to provide the greater flexibility as to sanctions which the cases show is needed.

The resulting flexibility as to sanctions eliminates any need to retain the requirement that the failure to appear or respond be "wilful." The concept of "wilful failure" is at best subtle and difficult, and the cases do not supply a bright line. Many courts have imposed sanctions without referring to wilfullness. E.g., *Milewski v. Schneider Transportation Co.*, 238 F.2d 397 (6th Cir.1956); *Dictograph Products, Inc. v. Kentworth Corp.*, 7 F.R.D. 543 (W.D.Ky.1947). In addition, in view of the possibility of light sanctions, even a negligent failure should come within Rule 37(d). If default is caused by counsel's ignorance of Federal practice, cf. *Dunn v. Pa. R.R.*, 96 F.Supp. 597 (N.D.Ohio 1951), or by his preoccupation with another aspect of the case, *cf. Maurer–Neuer, Inc. v. United Packinghouse Workers*, 26 F.R.D. 139 (D.Kans.1960), dismissal of the action and default judgment are not justified, but the imposition of expenses and fees may well be. "Wilfullness" continues to play a role, along with various other factors, in the choice of sanctions. Thus, the scheme conforms to Rule 37(b) as construed by the Supreme Court in *Societe Internationale v. Rogers*, 357 U.S. 197, 208 (1958).

A provision is added to make clear that a party may not properly remain completely silent even when he regards a notice to take his deposition or a set of interrogatories or requests to inspect as improper and objectionable. If he desires not to appear or not to respond, he must apply for a protective order. The cases are divided on whether a protective order must be sought. Compare *Collins v. Wayland*, 139 F.2d 677 (9th Cir. 1944), *cert. den.* 322 U.S. 744; *Bourgeois v. El Paso Natural Gas Co.*, 20 F.R.D. 358 (S.D.N.Y. 1957); *Loosley v. Stone*, 15 F.R.D. 373 (S.D.Ill.1954), with *Scarlatos v. Kulukundis*, 21 F.R.D. 185 (S.D.N.Y.1957); *Ross v. True Temper Corp.*, 11 F.R.D. 307 (N.D.Ohio 1951). Compare also Rosenberg, *supra*, 58 Col.L.Rev. 480, 496 (1958) with 2A Barron & Holtzoff, *Federal Practice and Procedure* 530–531 (Wright ed. 1961). The party from whom discovery is sought is afforded, through Rule 26(c), a fair and effective procedure whereby he can challenge the request made. At the same time, the total noncompliance with which Rule 37(d) is concerned may impose severe inconvenience or hardship on the discovering party and substantially delay the discovery process. Cf. 2B Barron & Holtzoff, *Federal Practice and Procedure* 306–307 (Wright ed. 1961) (response to a subpoena).

The failure of an officer or managing agent of a party to make discovery as required by present Rule 37(d) is treated as the failure of the party. The rule as revised provides similar treatment for a director of a party. There is slight warrant for the present distinction between officers and managing agents on the one hand and directors on the other. Although the legal power over a director to compel his making discovery may not be as great as over officers or managing agents, *Campbell v. General Motors Corp.*, 13 F.R.D. 331 (S.D.N.Y.1952), the practical differences are negligible. That a director's interests are normally aligned with those of his corporation is shown by the provisions of old Rule 26(d)(2), transferred to 32(a)(2) (deposition of director of party may be used at trial by an adverse party for any purpose) and of Rule 43(b) (director of party may be treated at trial as a hostile witness on direct examination by any adverse party). Moreover, in those rare instances when a corporation is unable through good faith efforts to compel a director to make discovery, it is unlikely that the court will impose sanctions. Cf. *Societe Internationale v. Rogers*, 357 U.S. 197 (1958).

Subdivision (e). The change in the caption conforms to the language of 28 U.S.C. § 1783, as amended in 1964.

Subdivision (f). Until recently, costs of a civil action could be awarded against the United States only when expressly provided by Act of Congress, and such provision was rarely made. See H.R.Rep.No. 1535, 89th Cong., 2d Sess., 2–3 (1966). To avoid any conflict with this doctrine, Rule 37(f) has provided that expenses and attorney's fees may not be imposed upon the United States under Rule 37. See 2A Barron & Holtzoff, *Federal Practice and Procedure* 857 (Wright ed. 1961).

A major change in the law was made in 1966, 80 Stat. 308, 28 U.S.C. § 2412 (1966), whereby a judgment for costs may ordinarily be awarded to the prevailing party in any civil action brought by or against the United States. Costs are not to include the fees and expenses of attorneys. In light of this legislative development, Rule 37(f) is amended to permit the award of expenses and fees against the United States under Rule 37, but only to the extent permitted by statute. The amendment brings Rule 37(f) into line with present and future statutory provisions.

1980 Amendment

Subdivision (b)(2). New Rule 26(f) provides that if a discovery conference is held, at its close the court shall enter an order respecting the subsequent conduct of discovery. The amendment provides that the sanctions available for violation of other court orders respecting discovery are available for violation of the discovery conference order.

Subdivision (e). Subdivision (e) is stricken. Title 28, U.S.C. § 1783 no longer refers to sanctions. The subdivision otherwise duplicates Rule 45(e)(2).

Subdivision (g). New Rule 26(f) imposes a duty on parties to participate in good faith in the framing of a discovery plan by agreement upon the request of any party. This subdivision authorizes the court to award to parties who participate in good faith in an attempt to frame a discovery plan the expenses incurred in the attempt if any party or his attorney fails to participate in good faith and thereby causes additional expense.

Failure of United States to Participate in Good Faith in Discovery. Rule 37 authorizes the court to direct that parties or attorneys who fail to participate in good faith in the discovery process pay the expenses, including attorneys' fees, incurred by other parties as a result of that failure. Since attorneys' fees cannot ordinarily be awarded against the United States (28 U.S.C. § 2412), there is often no practical remedy for the misconduct of its officers and attorneys. However, in the case of a government attorney who fails to participate in good faith in discovery, nothing prevents a court in an appropriate case from giving written notification of that fact to the Attorney General of the United States and other appropriate heads of offices or agencies thereof.

1987 Amendment

The amendments are technical. No substantive change is intended.

1993 Amendments

Subdivision (a). This subdivision is revised to reflect the revision of Rule 26(a), requiring disclosure of matters without a discovery request.

Pursuant to new subdivision (a)(2)(A), a party dissatisfied with the disclosure made by an opposing party may under this rule move for an order to compel disclosure. In providing for such a motion, the revised rule parallels the provisions of the former rule dealing with failures to answer particular interrogatories. Such a motion may be needed when the information to be disclosed might be helpful to the party seeking the disclosure but not to the party required to make the disclosure. If the party required to make the disclosure would need the material to support its own contentions, the more effective enforcement of the disclosure requirement will be to exclude the evidence not disclosed, as provided in subdivision (c)(1) of this revised rule.

Language is included in the new paragraph and added to the subparagraph (B) that requires litigants to seek to resolve discovery disputes by informal means before filing a motion with the court. This requirement is based on successful experience with similar local rules of court promulgated pursuant to Rule 83.

The last sentence of paragraph (2) is moved into paragraph (4).

Under revised paragraph (3), evasive or incomplete disclosures and responses to interrogatories and production requests are treated as failures to disclose or respond. Interrogatories and requests for production should not be read or interpreted in an artificially restrictive or hypertechnical manner to avoid disclosure of information fairly covered by the discovery request, and to do so is subject to appropriate sanctions under subdivision (a).

Revised paragraph (4) is divided into three subparagraphs for ease of reference, and in each the phrase "after opportunity for hearing" is changed to "after affording an opportunity to be heard" to make clear that the court can consider such questions on written submissions as well as on oral hearings.

Subparagraph (A) is revised to cover the situation where information that should have been produced without a motion to compel is produced after the motion is filed but before it is brought on for hearing. The rule also is revised to provide that a party should not be awarded its expenses for filing a motion that could have been avoided by conferring with opposing counsel.

Subparagraph (C) is revised to include the provision that formerly was contained in subdivision (a)(2) and to include the same requirement of an opportunity to be heard that is specified in subparagraphs (A) and (B).

Subdivision (c). The revision provides a self-executing sanction for failure to make a disclosure required by Rule 26(a), without need for a motion under subdivision (a)(2)(A).

Paragraph (1) prevents a party from using as evidence any witnesses or information that, without substantial justification, has not been disclosed as required by Rules 26(a) and 26(e)(1). This automatic sanction provides a strong inducement for disclosure of material that the disclosing party would expect to use as evidence, whether at a trial, at a hearing, or on a motion, such as one under Rule 56. As disclosure of evidence offered solely for impeachment purposes is not required under those rules, this preclusion sanction likewise does not apply to that evidence.

Limiting the automatic sanction to violations "without substantial justification," coupled with the exception for violations that are "harmless," is needed to avoid unduly harsh penalties in a variety of situations: *e.g.*, the inadvertent omission from a Rule 26(a)(1)(A) disclosure of the name of a potential witness known to all parties; the failure to list as a trial witness a person so listed by another party; or the lack of knowledge of a pro se litigant of the requirement to make disclosures. In the latter situation, however, exclusion would be proper if the requirement for disclosure had been called to the litigant's attention by either the court or another party.

Preclusion of evidence is not an effective incentive to compel disclosure of information that, being supportive of the position of the opposing party, might advantageously be concealed by the disclosing party. However, the rule provides the court with a wide range of other sanctions—such as declaring specified facts to be established, preventing contradictory evidence, or, like spoliation of evidence, allowing the jury to be informed of the fact of nondisclosure—that, though not self-executing, can be imposed when found to be warranted after a hearing. The failure to identify a witness or document in a disclosure statement would be admissible under the Federal Rules of Evidence under the same principles that allow a party's interrogatory answers to be offered against it.

Subdivision (d). This subdivision is revised to require that, where a party fails to file any response to interrogatories or a Rule 34 request, the discovering party should informally seek to obtain such responses before filing a motion for sanctions.

The last sentence of this subdivision is revised to clarify that it is the pendency of a motion for protective order that may be urged as an excuse for a violation of subdivision (d). If a party's motion has been denied, the party cannot argue that its subsequent failure to comply would be justified. In this connection, it should be noted that the filing of a motion under Rule 26(c) is not self-executing—the relief authorized under that rule depends on obtaining the court's order to that effect.

Subdivision (g). This subdivision is modified to conform to the revision of Rule 26(f).

2000 Amendment

Subdivision (c)(1). When this subdivision was added in 1993 to direct exclusion of materials not disclosed as required, the duty to supplement discovery responses pursuant to Rule 26(e)(2) was omitted. In the face of this omission, courts may rely on inherent power to sanction for failure to supplement as required by Rule 26(e)(2), *see 8 Federal Practice & Procedure* § 2050 at 607–09, but that is an uncertain and unregulated ground for imposing sanctions. There is no obvious occasion for a Rule 37(a) motion in connection with failure to supplement, and ordinarily only Rule 37(c)(1) exists as rule-based authority for sanctions if this supplementation obligation is violated.

The amendment explicitly adds failure to comply with Rule 26(e)(2) as a ground for sanctions under Rule 37(c)(1), including exclusion of withheld materials. The rule provides that this sanction power only applies when the failure to supplement was "without substantial justification." Even if the failure was not substantially justified, a party should be allowed to use the material that was not disclosed if the lack of earlier notice was harmless.

"Shall" is replaced by "is" under the program to conform amended rules to current style conventions when there is no ambiguity.

GAP Report

The Advisory Committee recommends that the published amendment proposal be modified to state that the exclusion sanction can apply to failure "to amend a prior response to discovery as required by Rule 26(e)(2)." In addition, one minor phrasing change is recommended for the Committee Note.

2006 Amendment

Subdivision (f). Subdivision (f) is new. It focuses on a distinctive feature of computer operations, the routine alteration and deletion of information that attends ordinary use. Many steps essential to computer operation may alter or destroy information, for reasons that have nothing to do with how that information might relate to litigation. As a result, the ordinary operation of computer systems creates a risk that a party may lose potentially discoverable information without culpable conduct on its part. Under Rule 37(f), absent exceptional circumstances, sanctions cannot be imposed for loss of electronically stored information resulting from the routine, good-faith operation of an electronic information system.

Rule 37(f) applies only to information lost due to the "routine operation of an electronic information system" — the ways in which such systems are generally designed, programmed, and implemented to meet the party's technical and business needs. The "routine operation" of computer systems includes the alteration and overwriting of information, often without the operator's specific direction or awareness, a feature with no direct counterpart in hard-copy documents. Such features are essential to the operation of electronic information systems.

Rule 37(f) applies to information lost due to the routine operation of an information system only if the operation was in good faith. Good faith in the routine operation of an information system may involve a party's intervention to modify or suspend certain features of that routine operation to prevent the loss of information, if that information is subject to a preservation obligation. A preservation obligation may arise from many sources, including common law, statutes, regulations, or a court order in the case. The good faith requirement of Rule 37(f) means that a party is not permitted to exploit the routine operation of an information system to thwart discovery obligations by allowing that operation to continue in order to destroy specific stored information that it is required to preserve. When a party is under a duty to preserve information because of pending or reasonably anticipated litigation, intervention in the routine operation of an information system is one aspect of what is often called a "litigation hold." Among the factors that bear on a party's good faith in the routine operation of an information system are the steps the party took to comply with a court order in the case or party agreement requiring preservation of specific electronically stored information.

Whether good faith would call for steps to prevent the loss of information on sources that the party believes are not reasonably accessible under Rule 26(b)(2) depends on the circumstances of each case. One factor is whether the party reasonably believes that the information on such sources is likely to be discoverable and not available from reasonably accessible sources.

The protection provided by Rule 37(f) applies only to sanctions "under these rules." It does not affect other sources of authority to impose sanctions or rules of professional responsibility.

This rule restricts the imposition of "sanctions." It does not prevent a court from making the kinds of adjustments frequently used in managing discovery if a party is unable to provide relevant responsive information. For example, a court could order the responding party to produce an additional witness for deposition, respond to additional interrogatories, or make similar attempts to provide substitutes or alternatives for some or all of the lost information.

2007 Amendment

The language of Rule 37 has been amended as part of the general restyling of the Civil Rules to make them more easily understood and to make style and terminology consistent throughout the rules. These changes are intended to be stylistic only.

HISTORICAL NOTES

Effective and Applicability Provisions

1980 Acts. Amendment by Pub.L. 96–481 effective Oct. 1, 1981, and applicable to adversary adjudication defined in section 504(b)(1)(C) of Title 5, and to civil actions and adversary adjudications described in section 2412 of Title 28, Judiciary and Judicial Procedure, which are pending on, or commenced on or after Oct. 1, 1981, see section 208 of Pub.L. 96–481, set out as an Effective Date note under section 504 of Title 5, Government Organization and Employees.

TITLE VI. TRIALS

Rule 38. Right to a Jury Trial; Demand

(a) **Right Preserved.** The right of trial by jury as declared by the Seventh Amendment to the Constitution—or as provided by a federal statute—is preserved to the parties inviolate.

(b) **Demand.** On any issue triable of right by a jury, a party may demand a jury trial by:

(1) serving the other parties with a written demand—which may be included in a pleading—no later than 10 days after the last pleading directed to the issue is served; and

(2) filing the demand in accordance with Rule 5(d).

(c) **Specifying Issues.** In its demand, a party may specify the issues that it wishes to have tried by a jury; otherwise, it is considered to have demanded a jury trial on all the issues so triable. If the party has demanded a jury trial on only some issues, any other party may—within 10 days after being served with the demand or within a shorter time ordered by the court—serve a demand for a jury trial on any other or all factual issues triable by jury.

(d) **Waiver; Withdrawal.** A party waives a jury trial unless its demand is properly served and filed. A proper demand may be withdrawn only if the parties consent.

(e) **Admiralty and Maritime Claims.** These rules do not create a right to a jury trial on issues in a claim that is an admiralty or maritime claim under Rule 9(h).

(Amended February 28, 1966, effective July 1, 1966; March 2, 1987, effective August 1, 1987; April 22, 1993, effective December 1, 1993; April 30, 2007, effective December 1, 2007.)

ADVISORY COMMITTEE NOTES

1937 Adoption

This rule provides for the preservation of the constitutional right of trial by jury as directed in the enabling act (act of June 19, 1934, 48 Stat. 1064, U.S.C., Title 28, § 723c [sec. 2072]), and it and the next rule make definite provision for claim and waiver of jury trial, following the method used in many American states and in England and the British Dominions. Thus the claim must be made at once on initial pleading or appearance under Ill.Rev.Stat. (1937) ch. 110, § 188; 6 Tenn.Code Ann. (Williams, 1934) § 8734; compare Wyo.Rev.Stat.Ann. (1931) § 89–1320 (with answer or reply); within 10 days after the pleadings are completed or the case is at issue under 2 Conn.Gen.Stat. (1930) § 5624; Hawaii Rev.Laws (1935) § 4101; 2 Mass.Gen.Laws (Ter.Ed.1932) ch. 231, § 60; 3 Mich.Comp.Laws (1929) § 14263; Mich. Court Rules Ann. (Searl, 1933) Rule 33 (15 days); England (until 1933) O. 36, r.r. 2 and 6; and Ontario Jud. Act (1927) § 57(1) (4 days, or, where prior notice of trial, 2 days from such notice); or at a definite time varying under different codes, from 10 days before notice of trial to 10 days after notice, or, as in many, when the case is called for assignment, Ariz.Rev. Code Ann. (Struckmeyer, 1928) § 3802; Calif. Code Civ.Proc. (Deering, 1937) § 631, par. 4; Iowa Code (1935) § 10724; 4 Nev.Comp.Laws (Hillyer, 1929) § 8782; N.M. Stat.Ann. (Courtright, 1929) § 105–814; N.Y.C.P.A. (1937) § 426, subdivision 5 (applying to New York, Bronx, Richmond, Kings, and Queens Counties); R.I. Pub. Laws (1929), ch. 1327, amending R.I. Gen.Laws (1923) ch. 337, § 6; Utah Rev.Stat. Ann. (1933) § 104–23–6; 2 Wash.Rev.Stat.Ann. (Remington, 1932) § 316; England (4 days after notice of trial), Administration of Justice Act (1933) § 6 and amended rule under the Judicature Act (The Annual Practice, 1937), O. 36, r. 1; Australia High Court Procedure Act (1921) § 12, Rules, O. 33, r. 2; Alberta Rules of Ct. (1914) 172, 183, 184; British Columbia Sup.Ct.Rules (1925) O. 36, r.r. 2, 6, 11, and 16; New Brunswick Jud. Act (1927) O. 36, r.r. 2 and 5. See James, Trial by Jury and the New Federal Rules of Procedure (1936), 45 Yale L.J. 1022.

Rule 81(c) provides for claim for jury trial in removed actions.

The right to trial by jury as declared in U.S.C., Title 28, § 770 (Trial of issues of fact; by jury; exceptions), and similar statutes, is unaffected by this rule. This rule modifies U.S.C., Title 28, [former] § 773 (Trial of issues of fact; by court).

1966 Amendments

See Note to Rule 9(h), supra.

1987 Amendments

The amendments are technical. No substantive change is intended.

1993 Amendments

Language requiring the filing of a jury demand as provided in subdivision (d) is added to subdivision (b) to eliminate an apparent ambiguity between the two subdivisions. For proper scheduling of cases, it is important that jury demands not only be served on other parties, but also be filed with the court.

2007 Amendment

The language of Rule 38 has been amended as part of the general restyling of the Civil Rules to make them more easily understood and to make style and terminology consistent throughout the rules. These changes are intended to be stylistic only.

Rule 39. Trial by Jury or by the Court

(a) When a Demand Is Made. When a jury trial has been demanded under Rule 38, the action must be designated on the docket as a jury action. The trial on all issues so demanded must be by jury unless:

(1) the parties or their attorneys file a stipulation to a nonjury trial or so stipulate on the record; or

(2) the court, on motion or on its own, finds that on some or all of those issues there is no federal right to a jury trial.

(b) When No Demand Is Made. Issues on which a jury trial is not properly demanded are to be tried by the court. But the court may, on motion, order a jury trial on any issue for which a jury might have been demanded.

(c) Advisory Jury; Jury Trial by Consent. In an action not triable of right by a jury, the court, on motion or on its own:

(1) may try any issue with an advisory jury; or

(2) may, with the parties' consent, try any issue by a jury whose verdict has the same effect as if a jury trial had been a matter of right, unless the action is against the United States and a federal statute provides for a nonjury trial.

(Amended April 30, 2007, effective December 1, 2007.)

ADVISORY COMMITTEE NOTES

1937 Adoption

The provisions for express waiver of jury trial found in U.S.C., Title 28, [former] § 773 (Trial of issues of fact; by court) are incorporated in this rule. See Rule 38, however, which extends the provisions for waiver of jury. U.S.C., Title 28, [former] § 772 (Trial of issues of fact; in equity in patent causes) is unaffected by this rule. When certain of the issues are to be tried by jury and others by the court, the court may determine the sequence in which such issues shall be tried. *See Liberty Oil Co. v. Condon Nat. Bank,* 260 U.S. 235, 43 S.Ct. 118, 67 L.Ed. 232 (1922).

A discretionary power in the courts to send issues of fact to the jury is common in state procedure. Compare Calif. Code Civ.Proc. (Deering, 1937) § 592; 1 Colo.Stat.Ann. (1935) Code Civ.Proc., ch. 12, § 191; Conn.Gen.Stat. (1930) § 5625; 2 Minn.Stat. (Mason, 1927) § 9288; 4 Mont.Rev. Codes Ann. (1935) § 9327; N.Y.C.P.A. (1937) § 430; 2 Ohio Gen.Code Ann. (Page, 1926) § 11380; 1 Okla.Stat.Ann. (Harlow, 1931) § 351 [12 Okl.St.Ann. § 557]; Utah Rev.Stat.Ann. (1933) § 104–23–5; 2 Wash.Rev.Stat.Ann. (Remington, 1932) § 315; Wis.Stat. (1935) § 270.07. See [former] Equity Rule 23 (Matters Ordinarily Determinable at Law When Arising in Suit in Equity to be Disposed of Therein) and U.S.C., Title 28 [former] § 772 (Trial of issues of fact; in equity in patent causes); *Colleton Merc. Mfg. Co. v. Savannah River Lumber Co.,* C.C.A.4, 1922, 280 F. 358; *Fed. Res. Bk. of San Francisco v. Idaho Grimm Alfalfa Seed Growers' Ass'n,* C.C.A.9, 1925, 8 F.2d 922, certiorari denied 46 S.Ct. 347, 270 U.S. 646, 70 L.Ed. 778 (1926); *Watt v. Starke,* 1879, 101 U.S. 247, 25 L.Ed. 826.

2007 Amendment

The language of Rule 39 has been amended as part of the general restyling of the Civil Rules to make them more easily understood and to make style and terminology consistent throughout the rules. These changes are intended to be stylistic only.

Rule 40. Scheduling Cases for Trial

Each court must provide by rule for scheduling trials. The court must give priority to actions entitled to priority by a federal statute.

(Amended April 30, 2007, effective December 1, 2007.)

ADVISORY COMMITTEE NOTES

1937 Adoption

U.S.C., Title 28, [former] § 769 (Notice of case for trial) is modified. See former Equity Rule 56 (On Expiration of Time for Depositions, Case Goes on Trial Calendar). See also [former] Equity Rule 57 (Continuances).

For examples of statutes giving precedence, see U.S.C., Title 28, § 47 (now §§ 1253, 2101, 2325) (Injunctions as to orders of Interstate Commerce Commission); § 380 (now §§ 1253, 2101, 2284) (Injunctions; alleged unconstitutionality of state statutes); § 380a (now §§ 1253, 2101, 2284) (Same; Constitutionality of federal statute); [former] § 768 (Priority of cases where a state is party); Title 15, § 28 (Antitrust laws; suits against monopolies expedited); Title 22, § 240 (Petition for restoration of property seized as munitions of war, etc.); and Title 49, [former] § 44 (Proceedings in equity under interstate commerce laws; expedition of suits).

2007 Amendment

The language of Rule 40 has been amended as part of the general restyling of the Civil Rules to make them more easily understood and to make style and terminology consistent throughout the rules. These changes are intended to be stylistic only.

The best methods for scheduling trials depend on local conditions. It is useful to ensure that each district adopts an explicit rule for scheduling trials. It is not useful to limit or dictate the provisions of local rules.

Rule 41. Dismissal of Actions

(a) Voluntary Dismissal.

(1) *By the Plaintiff.*

(A) *Without a Court Order.* Subject to Rules 23(e), 23.1(c), 23.2, and 66 and any applicable federal statute, the plaintiff may dismiss an action without a court order by filing:

(i) a notice of dismissal before the opposing party serves either an answer or a motion for summary judgment; or

(ii) a stipulation of dismissal signed by all parties who have appeared.

(B) *Effect.* Unless the notice or stipulation states otherwise, the dismissal is without prejudice. But if the plaintiff previously dismissed any federal-or state-court action based on or including the same claim, a notice of dismissal operates as an adjudication on the merits.

(2) *By Court Order; Effect.* Except as provided in Rule 41(a)(1), an action may be dismissed at the plaintiff's request only by court order, on terms that the court considers proper. If a defendant has pleaded a counterclaim before being served with the plaintiff's motion to dismiss, the action may be dismissed over the defendant's objection only if the counterclaim can remain pending for independent adjudication. Unless the order states otherwise, a dismissal under this paragraph (2) is without prejudice.

(b) Involuntary Dismissal; Effect. If the plaintiff fails to prosecute or to comply with these rules or a court order, a defendant may move to dismiss the action or any claim against it. Unless the dismissal order states otherwise, a dismissal under this subdivision (b) and any dismissal not under this rule—except one for lack of jurisdiction, improper venue, or failure to join a party under Rule 19—operates as an adjudication on the merits.

(c) Dismissing a Counterclaim, Crossclaim, or Third–Party Claim. This rule applies to a dismissal of any counterclaim, crossclaim, or third-party claim. A claimant's voluntary dismissal under Rule 41(a)(1)(A)(i) must be made:

(1) before a responsive pleading is served; or

(2) if there is no responsive pleading, before evidence is introduced at a hearing or trial.

(d) Costs of a Previously Dismissed Action. If a plaintiff who previously dismissed an action in any court files an action based on or including the same claim against the same defendant, the court:

(1) may order the plaintiff to pay all or part of the costs of that previous action; and

(2) may stay the proceedings until the plaintiff has complied.

(Amended December 27, 1946, effective March 19, 1948; January 21, 1963, effective July 1, 1963; February 28, 1966, effective July 1, 1966; December 4, 1967, effective July 1, 1968; March 2, 1987, effective August 1, 1987; April 30, 1991, effective December 1, 1991; April 30, 2007, effective December 1, 2007.)

ADVISORY COMMITTEE NOTES

1937 Adoption

Note to Subdivision (a). Compare Ill.Rev.Stat. (1937) c. 110, § 176, and *English Rules Under the Judicature Act* (The Annual Practice, 1937) O. 26.

Provisions regarding dismissal in such statutes as U.S.C., Title 8, § 164 [see 1329] (Jurisdiction of district courts in immigration cases) and U.S.C., Title 31, § 232 [now 3730] (Liability of persons making false claims against United States; suits) are preserved by paragraph (1).

Note to Subdivision (b). This provides for the equivalent of a nonsuit on motion by the defendant after the completion of the presentation of evidence by the plaintiff. Also, for actions tried without a jury, it provides the equivalent of the directed verdict practice for jury actions which is regulated by Rule 50.

1946 Amendment

Note. Subdivision (a). The insertion of the reference to Rule 66 correlates Rule 41(a)(1) with the express provisions concerning dismissal set forth in amended Rule 66 on receivers.

The change in Rule 41(a)(1)(i) gives the service of a motion for summary judgment by the adverse party the same effect in preventing unlimited dismissal as was originally given only to the service of an answer. The omission of reference to a motion for summary judgment in the original rule was subject to criticism. 3 *Moore's Federal Practice,* 1938, 3037–3038, n. 12. A motion for summary judgment may be forthcoming prior to answer, and if well taken will eliminate the necessity for an answer. Since such a motion may require even more research and preparation than the answer itself, there is good reason why the service of the motion, like that of the answer, should prevent a voluntary dismissal by the adversary without court approval.

The word "generally" has been stricken from Rule 41(a)(1)(ii) in order to avoid confusion and to conform with the elimination of the necessity for special appearance by original Rule 12(b).

Subdivision (b). In some cases tried without a jury, where at the close of plaintiff's evidence the defendant moves for dismissal under Rule 41(b) on the ground that plaintiff's evidence is insufficient for recovery, the plaintiff's own evidence may be conflicting or present questions of credibility. In ruling on the defendant's motion, questions arise as to the function of the judge in evaluating the testimony and whether findings should be made if the motion is sustained. Three circuits hold that as the judge is the trier of the facts in such a situation his function is not the same as on a motion to direct a verdict, where the jury is the trier of the facts, and that the judge in deciding such a motion in a non-jury case may pass on conflicts of evidence and credibility, and if he performs that function of evaluating the testimony and grants the motion on the merits, findings are required. *Young v. United States,* C.C.A.9, 1940, 111 F.2d 823; *Gary Theatre Co. v. Columbia Pictures Corporation,* C.C.A.7, 1941, 120 F.2d 891; *Bach v. Friden Calculating Machine Co., Inc.,* C.C.A.6, 1945, 148 F.2d 407. Cf. *Mateas v. Fred Harvey, a Corporation,* C.C.A.9, 1945, 146 F.2d 989. The Third Circuit has held that on such a motion the function of the court is the same as on a motion to direct in a jury case, and that the court should only decide whether there is evidence which would support a judgment for the plaintiff, and therefore, findings are not required by Rule 52. *Federal Deposit Insurance Corp. v. Mason,* C.C.A.3, 1940, 115 F.2d 548; *Schad v. Twentieth Century-Fox Film Corp.,* C.C.A.3, 1943, 136 F.2d 991. The added sentence in Rule 41(b) incorporates the view of the Sixth, Seventh and Ninth Circuits. See also 3 *Moore's Federal Practice,* 1938, Cum.Supplement § 41.03, under "Page 3045"; Commentary, *The Motion to Dismiss in Non-Jury Cases,* 1946, 9 Fed.Rules Serv., Comm.Pg. 41b.14.

1963 Amendment

Under the present text of the second sentence of this subdivision, the motion for dismissal at the close of the plaintiff's evidence may be made in a case tried to a jury as well as in a case tried without a jury. But, when made in a jury-tried case, this motion overlaps the motion for a directed verdict under Rule 50(a), which is also available in the same situation. It has been held that the standard to be applied in deciding the Rule 41(b) motion at the close of the plaintiff's evidence in a jury-tried case is the same as that used upon a motion for a directed verdict made at the same stage; and, just as the court need not make findings pursuant to Rule 52(a) when it directs a verdict, so in a jury-tried case it may omit these findings in granting the Rule 41(b) motion. See generally *O'Brien v. Westinghouse Electric Corp.,* 293 F.2d 1, 5–10 (3d Cir. 1961).

As indicated by the discussion in the *O'Brien* case, the overlap has caused confusion. Accordingly, the second and third sentences of Rule 41(b) are amended to provide that the motion for dismissal at the close of the plaintiff's evidence shall apply only to nonjury cases (including cases tried with an advisory jury). Hereafter the correct motion in jury-tried cases will be the motion for a directed verdict. This involves no change of substance. It should be noted that the court upon a motion for a directed verdict may in appropriate circumstances deny that motion and grant instead a new trial, or a voluntary dismissal without prejudice under Rule 41(a)(2). See 6 *Moore's Federal Practice* ¶59.08[5] (2d ed. 1954); *cf. Cone v. West Virginia Pulp & Paper Co.,* 330 U.S. 212, 217, 67 S.Ct. 752, 91 L.Ed. 849 (1947).

The first sentence of Rule 41(b), providing for dismissal for failure to prosecute or to comply with the Rules or any order of court, and the general provisions of the last sentence remain applicable in jury as well as nonjury cases.

The amendment of the last sentence of Rule 41(b) indicates that a dismissal for lack of an indispensable party does not operate as an adjudication on the merits. Such a dismissal does not bar a new action, for it is based merely "on a plaintiff's failure to comply with a precondition requisite to the Court's going forward to determine the merits of his substantive claim." See *Costello v. United States,* 365 U.S. 265, 284–288, 81 S.Ct. 534, 5 L.Ed.2d 551 & n. 5 (1961); *Mallow v. Hinde,* 12 Wheat. (25 U.S.) 193, 6 L.Ed. 599 (1827); Clark, *Code Pleading* 602 (2d ed. 1947); *Restatement of Judgments* § 49, comm. a, b (1942). This amendment corrects an omission from the rule and is consistent with an earlier amendment, effective in 1948, adding "the defense of failure to join an indispensable party" to clause (1) of Rule 12(h).

1966 Amendment

The terminology is changed to accord with the amendment of Rule 19. See that amended rule and the Advisory Committee's Note thereto.

1968 Amendment

The amendment corrects an inadvertent error in the reference to amended Rule 23.

1987 Amendment

The amendment is technical. No substantive change is intended.

1991 Amendment

Language is deleted that authorized the use of this rule as a means of terminating a non-jury action on the merits when the plaintiff has failed to carry a burden of proof in presenting the plaintiff's case. The device is replaced by the new provisions of Rule 52(c), which authorize entry of judgment against the defendant as well as the plaintiff, and earlier than the close of the case of the party against whom judgment is rendered. A motion to dismiss under Rule 41 on the ground that a plaintiff's evidence is legally insufficient should now be treated as a motion for judgment on partial findings as provided in Rule 52(c).

2007 Amendment

The language of Rule 41 has been amended as part of the general restyling of the Civil Rules to make them more easily understood and to make style and terminology consistent throughout the rules. These changes are intended to be stylistic only.

When Rule 23 was amended in 1966, Rules 23.1 and 23.2 were separated from Rule 23. Rule 41(a)(1) was not then amended to reflect the Rule 23 changes. In 1968 Rule 41(a)(1) was amended to correct the cross-reference to what had become Rule 23(e), but Rules 23.1 and 23.2 were inadvertently overlooked. Rules 23.1 and 23.2 are now added to the list of exceptions in Rule 41(a)(1)(A). This change does not affect established meaning. Rule 23.2 explicitly incorporates Rule 23(e), and thus was already absorbed directly into the exceptions in Rule 41(a)(1). Rule 23.1 requires court approval of a compromise or dismissal in language parallel to Rule 23(e) and thus supersedes the apparent right to dismiss by notice of dismissal.

Rule 42. Consolidation; Separate Trials

(a) Consolidation. If actions before the court involve a common question of law or fact, the court may:

(1) join for hearing or trial any or all matters at issue in the actions;

(2) consolidate the actions; or

(3) issue any other orders to avoid unnecessary cost or delay.

(b) Separate Trials. For convenience, to avoid prejudice, or to expedite and economize, the court may order a separate trial of one or more separate issues, claims, crossclaims, counterclaims, or third-party claims. When ordering a separate trial, the court must preserve any federal right to a jury trial.

(Amended February 28, 1966, effective July 1, 1966; April 30, 2007, effective December 1, 2007.)

ADVISORY COMMITTEE NOTES

1937 Adoption

Subdivision (a) is based upon U.S.C., Title 28, [former] § 734 (Orders to save costs; consolidation of causes of like nature) but in so far as the statute differs from this rule, it is modified.

For comparable statutes dealing with consolidation see Ark.Dig.Stat. (Crawford & Moses, 1921) § 1081; Calif.Code Civ.Proc. (Deering, 1937) § 1048; N.M.Stat.Ann. (Courtright, 1929) § 105–828; N.Y.C.P.A. (1937) §§ 96, 96a, and 97; American Judicature Society, Bulletin XIV, (1919) Art. 26.

For severance or separate trials see Calif.Code Civ.Proc. (Deering, 1937) § 1048; N.Y.C.P.A. (1937) § 96; American Judicature Society, Bulletin XIV (1919) Art. 3, § 2 and Art. 10, § 10. See also the third sentence of Equity Rule 29 (Defenses—How Presented) providing for discretionary separate hearing and disposition before trial of pleas in bar or abatement, and see also Rule 12(d) of these rules for preliminary hearings of defenses and objections.

For the entry of separate judgments, see Rule 54(b) (Judgment at Various Stages).

1966 Amendment

In certain suits in admiralty separation for trial of the issues of liability and damages (or of the extent of liability other than damages, such as salvage and general average) has been conducive to expedition and economy, especially because of the statutory right to interlocutory appeal in admiralty cases (which is of course preserved by these Rules). While separation of issues for trial is not to be routinely ordered, it is important that it be encouraged where experience has demonstrated its worth. Cf. Weinstein, *Routine Bifurcation of Negligence Trials,* 14 Vand. L.Rev. 831 (1961).

In cases (including some cases within the admiralty and maritime jurisdiction) in which the parties have a constitutional or statutory right of trial by jury, separation of issues may give rise to problems. See *e.g., United Air Lines, Inc. v. Wiener,* 286 F.2d 302 (9th Cir.1961). Accordingly, the proposed change in Rule 42 reiterates the mandate of Rule 38 respecting preservation of the right to jury trial.

2007 Amendment

The language of Rule 42 has been amended as part of the general restyling of the Civil Rules to make them more easily understood and to make style and terminology consistent throughout the rules. These changes are intended to be stylistic only.

Rule 43. Taking Testimony

(a) In Open Court. At trial, the witnesses' testimony must be taken in open court unless a federal statute, the Federal Rules of Evidence, these rules, or other rules adopted by the Supreme Court provide otherwise. For good cause in compelling circumstances and with appropriate safeguards, the court may permit testimony in open court by contemporaneous transmission from a different location.

(b) Affirmation Instead of an Oath. When these rules require an oath, a solemn affirmation suffices.

(c) Evidence on a Motion. When a motion relies on facts outside the record, the court may hear the matter on affidavits or may hear it wholly or partly on oral testimony or on depositions.

(d) Interpreter. The court may appoint an interpreter of its choosing; fix reasonable compensation to be paid from funds provided by law or by one or more parties; and tax the compensation as costs.

(Amended February 28, 1966, effective July 1, 1966; November 20, 1972, and December 18, 1972, effective July 1, 1975; March 2, 1987, effective August 1, 1987; April 23, 1996, effective December 1, 1996; April 30, 2007, effective December 1, 2007.)

ADVISORY COMMITTEE NOTES

1937 Adoption

Note to Subdivision (a). The first sentence is a restatement of the substance of U.S.C., Title 28, § 635 (Proof in common-law actions), [former] § 637 (see §§ 2072, 2073) (Proof in equity and admiralty), and [former] Equity Rule 46 (Trial—Testimony Usually Taken in Open Court—Rulings on Objections to Evidence). This rule abolishes in patent and trademark actions, the practice under [former] Equity Rule 48 of setting forth in affidavits the testimony in chief of expert witnesses whose testimony is directed to matters of opinion. The second and third sentences on admissibility of evidence and Subdivision (b) on contradiction and cross-examination modify U.S.C., Title 28, § 725 (now 1652) (Laws of states as rules of decision) insofar as that statute has been construed to prescribe conformity to state rules of evidence. Compare Callahan and Ferguson, *Evidence and the New Federal Rules of Civil Procedure,* 45 Yale L.J. 622 (1936), and *Same: 2,* 47 Yale L.J. 195 (1937). The last sentence modifies to the extent indicated U.S.C., Title 28, [former] § 631 (Competency of witnesses governed by State laws).

Note to Subdivision (b). See 4 *Wigmore on Evidence* (2d ed., 1923) § 1885 et seq.

Note to Subdivision (c). See [former] Equity Rule 46 (Trial—Testimony Usually Taken in Open Court-Rulings on Objections to Evidence). With the last sentence compare *Dowagiac v. Lochren,* 143 Fed. 211 (C.C.A. 8th, 1906). See also *Blease v. Garlington,* 92 U.S. 1, 23 L.Ed. 521 (1876); *Nelson v. United States,* 201 U.S. 92, 114, 26 S.Ct. 358, 50 L.Ed. 673 (1906); *Unkle v. Wills,* 281 Fed. 29 (C.C.A. 8th, 1922).

See Rule 61 for harmless error in either the admission or exclusion of evidence.

Note to Subdivision (d). See [former] Equity Rule 78 (Affirmation in Lieu of Oath) and U.S.C., Title 1, § 1 (Words importing singular number, masculine gender, etc.; extended application), providing for affirmation in lieu of oath.

Supplementary Note on Advisory Committee Regarding Rules 43 and 44

Note. These rules have been criticized and suggested improvements offered by commentators. 1 *Wigmore on Evidence,* 3d ed. 1940, 200–204; Green, *The Admissibility of Evidence Under the Federal Rules,* 1941, 55 Harv.L.Rev. 197. Cases indicate, however, that the rule is working better than these commentators had expected. *Boerner v. United States,* C.C.A.2d, 1941, 117 F.2d 387, cert. den., 1941, 313 U.S. 587, 61 S.Ct. 1120; *Mosson v. Liberty Fast Freight Co.,* C.C.A.2d, 1942, 124 F.2d, 448; *Hartford Accident & Indemnity Co. v. Olivier,* C.C.A. 5th, 1941, 123 F.2d 709; *Anzano v. Metropolitan Life Ins. Co. of New York,* C.C.A.3d, 1941, 118 F.2d 430; *Franzen v. E. I. DuPont De Nemours & Co.,* C.C.A.3d, 1944, 146 F.2d 837; *Fakouri v. Cadais,* C.C.A. 5th, 1945, 147 F.2d 667; *In re C. & P. Co.,* S.D.Cal.1945, 63 F.Supp. 400, 408. But cf. *United States v. Aluminum Co. of America,* S.D.N.Y.1938, 1 Fed.Rules Serv. 43a.3, Case 1; Note, 1946, 46 Col.L.Rev. 267. While consideration of a comprehensive and detailed set of rules of evidence seems very desirable, it has not been feasible for the Committee so far to undertake this important task. Such consideration should include the adaptability to federal practice of all or parts of the proposed Code of Evidence of the American Law Institute. See Armstrong, *Proposed Amendments to Federal Rules of Civil Procedure,* 4 F.R.D. 124, 137–138.

1966 Amendment

Note to Subdivision (f). This new subdivision [subdivision (f)] authorizes the court to appoint interpreters (including interpreters for the deaf), to provide for their compensation, and to tax the compensation as costs. Compare proposed subdivision (b) of Rule 28 of the Federal Rules of Criminal Procedure.

1972 Amendment

Rule 43, entitled Evidence, has heretofore served as the basic rule of evidence for civil cases in federal courts. Its very general provisions are superseded by the detailed provisions of the new Rules of Evidence. The original title and many of the provisions of the rule are, therefore, no longer appropriate.

Subdivision (a). The provision for taking testimony in open court is not duplicated in the Rules of Evidence and is retained. Those dealing with admissibility of evidence and competency of witnesses, however, are no longer needed or appropriate since those topics are covered at large in the Rules of Evidence. They are accordingly deleted. The language is broadened, however, to take account of acts of Congress dealing with the taking of testimony, as well as of the Rules of Evidence and any other rules adopted by the Supreme Court.

Subdivision (b). The subdivision is no longer needed or appropriate since the matters with which it deals are treated in the Rules of Evidence. The use of leading questions, both generally and in the interrogation of an adverse party or witness identified with him, is the subject of Evidence Rule 611(c). Who may impeach is treated in Evidence Rule 601 [sic; probably means 607], and scope of cross-examination is covered in Evidence Rule 611(b). The subdivision is accordingly deleted.

Subdivision (c). Offers of proof and making a record of excluded evidence are treated in Evidence Rule 103. The subdivision is no longer needed or appropriate and is deleted.

1987 Amendment

The amendment is technical. No substantive change is intended.

1996 Amendment

Rule 43(a) is revised to conform to the style conventions adopted for simplifying the present Civil Rules. The only intended changes of meaning are described below.

The requirement that testimony be taken "orally" is deleted. The deletion makes it clear that testimony of a witness may be given in open court by other means if the witness is not able to communicate orally. Writing or sign language are common examples. The development of advanced technology may enable testimony to be given by other means. A witness unable to sign or write by hand may be able to communicate through a computer or similar device.

Contemporaneous transmission of testimony from a different location is permitted only on showing good cause in compelling circumstances. The importance of presenting live testimony in court cannot be forgotten. The very ceremony of trial and the presence of the factfinder may exert a powerful force for truthtelling. The opportunity to judge the demeanor of a witness face-to-face is accorded great value in our tradition. Transmission cannot be justified merely by showing that it is inconvenient for the witness to attend the trial.

The most persuasive showings of good cause and compelling circumstances are likely to arise when a witness is unable to attend trial for unexpected reasons, such as accident or illness, but remains able to testify from a different place. Contemporaneous transmission may be better than an attempt to reschedule the trial, particularly if there is a risk that other—and perhaps more important—witnesses might not be available at a later time.

Other possible justifications for remote transmission must be approached cautiously. Ordinarily depositions, including video depositions, provide a superior means of securing the testimony of a witness who is beyond the reach of a trial subpoena, or of resolving difficulties in scheduling a trial that can be attended by all witnesses. Deposition procedures ensure the opportunity of all parties to be represented while the witness is testifying. An unforeseen need for the testimony of a remote witness that arises during trial, however, may establish good cause and compelling circumstances. Justification is particularly likely if the need arises from the interjection of new issues during trial or from the unexpected inability to present testimony as planned from a different witness.

Good cause and compelling circumstances may be established with relative ease if all parties agree that testimony should be presented by transmission. The court is not bound by a stipulation, however, and can insist on live testimony. Rejection of the parties' agreement will be influenced, among other factors, by the apparent importance of the testimony in the full context of the trial.

A party who could reasonably foresee the circumstances offered to justify transmission of testimony will have special difficulty in showing good cause and the compelling nature of the circumstances. Notice of a desire to transmit testimony from a different location should be given as soon as the reasons are known, to enable other parties to arrange a deposition, or to secure an advance ruling on transmission so as to know whether to prepare to be present with the witness while testifying.

No attempt is made to specify the means of transmission that may be used. Audio transmission without video images may be sufficient in some circumstances, particularly as to less important testimony. Video transmission ordinarily should be preferred when the cost is reasonable in relation to the matters in dispute, the means of the parties, and the circumstances that justify transmission. Transmission that merely produces the equivalent of a written statement ordinarily should not be used.

Safeguards must be adopted that ensure accurate identification of the witness and that protect against influence by persons present with the witness. Accurate transmission likewise must be assured.

Other safeguards should be employed to ensure that advance notice is given to all parties of foreseeable circumstances that may lead the proponent to offer testimony by transmission. Advance notice is important to protect the opportunity to argue for attendance of the witness at trial. Advance notice also ensures an opportunity to depose the witness, perhaps by video record, as a means of supplementing transmitted testimony.

2007 Amendment

The language of Rule 43 has been amended as part of the general restyling of the Civil Rules to make them more easily understood and to make style and terminology consistent throughout the rules. These changes are intended to be stylistic only.

HISTORICAL NOTES

Effective Date of Amendments Proposed November 20, 1972, and December 18, 1972

Amendments of this rule embraced by orders entered by the Supreme Court of the United States on November 20, 1972, and December 18, 1972, effective on the 180th day beginning after January 2, 1975, see section 3 of Pub.L. 93–595, Jan. 2, 1975, 88 Stat. 1959, set out as a note under section 2071 of Title 28.

Rule 44. Proving an Official Record

(a) Means of Proving.

(1) ***Domestic Record.*** Each of the following evidences an official record—or an entry in it—that is otherwise admissible and is kept within the United States, any state, district, or commonwealth, or any territory subject to the administrative or judicial jurisdiction of the United States:

(A) an official publication of the record; or

(B) a copy attested by the officer with legal custody of the record—or by the officer's deputy—and accompanied by a certificate that the officer has custody. The certificate must be made under seal:

(i) by a judge of a court of record in the district or political subdivision where the record is kept; or

(ii) by any public officer with a seal of office and with official duties in the district or political subdivision where the record is kept.

(2) ***Foreign Record.***

(A) *In General.* Each of the following evidences a foreign official record—or an entry in it—that is otherwise admissible:

(i) an official publication of the record; or

(ii) the record—or a copy—that is attested by an authorized person and is accompanied either by a final certification of genuineness or by a certification under a treaty or convention to which the United States and the country where the record is located are parties.

(B) *Final Certification of Genuineness.* A final certification must certify the genuineness of the signature and official position of the attester or of any foreign official whose certificate of genuineness relates to the attestation or is in a chain of certificates of genuineness relating to the attestation. A final certification may be made by a secretary of a United States embassy or legation; by a consul general, vice consul, or consular agent of the United States; or by a diplomatic or consular official of the foreign country assigned or accredited to the United States.

(C) *Other Means of Proof.* If all parties have had a reasonable opportunity to investigate a foreign record's authenticity and accuracy, the court may, for good cause, either:

(i) admit an attested copy without final certification; or

(ii) permit the record to be evidenced by an attested summary with or without a final certification.

(b) Lack of a Record. A written statement that a diligent search of designated records revealed no record or entry of a specified tenor is admissible as evidence that the records contain no such record or entry. For domestic records, the statement must be authenticated under Rule 44(a)(1). For foreign records, the statement must comply with (a)(2)(C)(ii).

(c) Other Proof. A party may prove an official record—or an entry or lack of an entry in it—by any other method authorized by law.

(Amended February 28, 1966, effective July 1, 1966; March 2, 1987, effective August 1, 1987; April 30, 1991, effective December 1, 1991; April 30, 2007, effective December 1, 2007.)

ADVISORY COMMITTEE NOTES

1937 Adoption

This rule provides a simple and uniform method of proving public records, and entry or lack of entry therein, in all cases including those specifically provided for by statutes of the United States. Such statutes are not superseded, however, and proof may also be made according to their provisions whenever they differ from this rule. Some of those statutes are:

U.S.C., Title 28 [former sections]:

§ 661[now 1733] (Copies of department or corporation records and papers; admissibility; seal)

§ 662[now 1733] (Same; in office of General Counsel of the Treasury)

§ 663[now 1733] (Instruments and papers of Comptroller of Currency; admissibility)

§ 664[now 1733] (Organization certificates of national banks; admissibility)

§ 665[now 1733] (Transcripts from books of Treasury in suits against delinquents; admissibility)

§ 666[now 1733] (Same; certificate by Secretary or Assistant Secretary)

§ 670[now 1743] (Admissibility of copies of statements of demands by Post Office Department)

§ 671[now 1733] (Admissibility of copies of post office records and statement of accounts)

§ 672[former] (Admissibility of copies of records in General Land Office)

§ 673[now 1744] (Admissibility of copies of records, and so forth, of Patent Office)

§ 674[now 1745] (Copies of foreign letters patent as prima facie evidence)

§ 675[former] (Copies of specifications and drawings of patents admissible)

§ 676[now 1736] (Extracts from Journals of Congress admissible when injunction of secrecy removed)

§ 677[now 1740] (Copies of records in offices of United States consuls admissible)

§ 678[former] (Books and papers in certain district courts)

§ 679[former] (Records in clerks' offices, Western District of North Carolina)

§ 680[former] (Records in clerks' offices of former district of California)

§ 681[now 1734] (Original records lost or destroyed; certified copy admissible)

§ 682[now 1734] (Same; when certified copy not obtainable)

§ 685[now 1735] (Same; certified copy of official papers)

§ 687[now 1738] (Authentication of legislative acts; proof of judicial proceedings of State)

§ 688[now 1739] (Proofs of records in offices not pertaining to courts)

§ 689[now 1742] (Copies of foreign records relating to land titles)

§ 695[now 1732] (Writings and records made in regular course of business; admissibility)

§ 695e[now 1741] (Foreign documents on record in public offices; certification)

U.S.C., Title 1:

§ 30[now 112] (Statutes at large; contents; admissibility in evidence)

§ 30a[now 113] ("Little and Brown's" edition of laws and treaties competent evidence of Acts of Congress)

§ 54[now 204] (Codes and supplements as establishing prima facie the laws of United States and District of Columbia, etc.)

§ 55[now 208] (Copies of supplements to Code of Laws of United States and of District of Columbia Code and supplements; conclusive evidence of original)

U.S.C., Title 5:

§ 490[former] (Records of Department of Interior; authenticated copies as evidence)

U.S.C., Title 6:

§ 7[now Title 31, § 9306] (Surety Companies as sureties; appointment of agents; service of process)

U.S.C., Title 8:

§ 9a[see 1435(c)] (Citizenship of children of persons naturalized under certain laws; repatriation of native-born women married to aliens prior to September 22, 1922; copies of proceedings)

§ 356[see 1443] (Regulations for execution of naturalization laws; certified copies of papers as evidence)

§ 399b(d)[see 1443] (Certifications of naturalization records; authorization; admissibility as evidence)

U.S.C., Title 11:

§ 44(d), (e), (f), (g)[former] (Bankruptcy court proceedings and orders as evidence)

§ 204[former] (Extensions extended, etc.; evidence of confirmation)

§ 207(j)[former] (Corporate reorganizations; certified copy of decree as evidence)

U.S.C., Title 15:

§ 127 (Trade-mark records in Patent Office; copies as evidence)

U.S.C., Title 20:

§ 52 (Smithsonian Institution; evidence of title to site and buildings)

U.S.C., Title 25:

§ 6 (Bureau of Indian Affairs; seal; authenticated and certified documents; evidence)

U.S.C., Title 31:

§ 46[now 704] (Laws governing General Accounting Office; copies of books, records, etc., thereof as evidence)

U.S.C., Title 38:

§ 11g[see 202] (Seal of Veterans' Administration; authentication of copies of records)

U.S.C., Title 40:

§ 238 [former 44 U.S.C.A. § 300h] (National Archives; seal; reproduction of archives; fee; admissibility in evidence of reproductions)

§ 270c [see now 40 U.S.C.A. § 3133(a)] (Bonds of contractors for public works; right of person furnishing labor or material to copy of bond)

U.S.C., Title 43:

§§ 57–59 (Copies of land surveys, etc., in certain states and districts admissible as evidence)

§ 83 (General Land Office registers and receivers; transcripts of records as evidence)

U.S.C., Title 46:

§ 823 (Records of Maritime Commission; copies; publication of reports; evidence)

U.S.C., Title 47:

§ 154(m) (Federal Communications Commission; copies of reports and decisions as evidence)

§ 412 (Documents filed with Federal Communications Commission as public records; prima facie evidence; confidential records)

U.S.C., Title 49:

§ 14(3)[now 10310] (Interstate Commerce Commission reports and decisions; printing and distribution of copies)

§ 16(13)[now 10303(b)] (Copies of schedules, tariffs, etc. filed with Interstate Commerce Commission as evidence)

§ 19a(i)[now 10785(c)] (Valuation of property of carriers by Interstate Commerce Commission; final published valuations as evidence)

Supplementary Note of Advisory Committee Regarding Rules 43 and 44.

For supplementary note of Advisory Committee on this rule, see note under Rule 43.

1966 Amendment

Note to Subdivision (a)(1). These provisions on proof of official records kept within the United States are similar in substance to those heretofore appearing in Rule 44. There is a more exact description of the geographical areas covered. An official record kept in one of the areas enumerated qualifies for proof under subdivision (a)(1) even though it is not a United States official record. For example, an official record kept in one of these areas by a government in exile falls within subdivision (a)(1). It also falls within subdivision (a)(2) which may be availed of alternatively. Cf. *Banco de Espana v. Federal Reserve Bank,* 114 F.2d 438 (2d Cir. 1940).

Note to Subdivision (a)(2). Foreign official records may be proved, as heretofore, by means of official publications thereof. See *United States v. Aluminum Co. of America,* 1 F.R.D. 71 (S.D.N.Y.1939). Under this rule, a document that, on its face, appears to be an official publication, is admissible, unless a party opposing its admission into evidence shows that it lacks that character.

The rest of subdivision (a)(2) aims to provide greater clarity, efficiency, and flexibility in the procedure for authenticating copies of foreign official records.

The reference to attestation by "the officer having the legal custody of the record," hitherto appearing in Rule 44, has been found inappropriate for official records kept in foreign countries where the assumed relation between custody and the authority to attest does not obtain. See 2B Barron & Holtzoff, Federal Practice & Procedure § 992 (Wright ed. 1961). Accordingly it is provided that an attested copy may be obtained from any person authorized by the law of the foreign country to make the attestation without regard to whether he is charged with responsibility for maintaining the record or keeping it in his custody.

Under Rule 44 a United States foreign service officer has been called on to certify to the authority of the foreign official attesting the copy as well as the genuineness of his signature and his official position. See Schlesinger, *Comparative Law 57* (2d ed. 1959); Smit, *International Aspects of Federal Civil Procedure,* 61 Colum.L.Rev. 1031, 1063 (1961); 22 C.F.R. § 92.41(a), (e) (1958). This has created practical difficulties. For example, the question of the authority of the foreign officer might raise issues of foreign law which were beyond the knowledge of the United States officer. The difficulties are met under the amended rule by eliminating the element of the authority of the attesting foreign official from the scope of the certifying process, and by specifically permitting use of the chain-certificate method. Under this method, it is sufficient if the original attestation purports to have been issued by an authorized person and is accompanied by a certificate of another foreign official whose certificate may in turn be followed by that of a foreign official of higher rank. The process continues until a foreign official is reached as to whom the United States foreign service official (or a diplomatic or consular officer of the foreign country assigned or accredited to the United States) has adequate information upon which to base a "final certification." See *New York Life Ins. Co. v. Aronson,* 38 F.Supp. 687 (W.D.Pa.1941); 22 C.F.R. § 92.37 (1958).

The final certification (a term used in contradistinction to the certificates prepared by the foreign officials in a chain) relates to the incumbency and genuineness of signature of the foreign official who attested the copy of the record or, where the chain-certificate method is used, of a foreign official whose certificate appears in the chain, whether that certificate is the last in the chain or not. A final certification may be prepared on the basis of material on file in the consulate or any other satisfactory information.

Although the amended rule will generally facilitate proof of foreign official records, it is recognized that in some situations it may be difficult or even impossible to satisfy the basic requirements of the rule. There may be no United States consul in a particular foreign country; the foreign officials may not cooperate, peculiarities may exist or arise hereafter in the law or practice of a foreign country. See *United States v. Grabina,* 119 F.2d 863 (2d Cir. 1941); and, generally, Jones, *International Judicial Assistance: Procedural Chaos and a Program for Reform,* 62 Yale L.J. 515, 548–49 (1953). Therefore the final sentence of subdivision (a)(2) provides the court with discretion to admit an attested copy of a record without a final certification, or an attested summary of a record with or without a final certification. See Rep. of Comm. on Comparative Civ.Proc. & Prac., Proc. A.B.A., Sec. Int'l & Comp.L. 123, 130–31 (1952); Model Code of Evidence §§ 517, 519 (1942). This relaxation should be permitted only when it is shown that the party has been unable to satisfy the basic requirements of the amended rule despite his reasonable efforts. Moreover it is specially provided that the parties must be given a reasonable opportunity in these cases to examine into the authenticity and accuracy of the copy or summary.

Note to Subdivision (b). This provision relating to proof of lack of record is accommodated to the changes made in subdivision (a).

Note to Subdivision (c). The amendment insures that international agreements of the United States are unaffected by the rule. Several consular conventions contain provisions for reception of copies or summaries of foreign official records. See, e.g., Consular Conv. with Italy, May 8, 1878, art. X, 20 Stat. 725, T.S. No. 178 (Dept. State 1878). See also 28 U.S.C. §§ 1740–42, 1745; *Fakouri v. Cadais,* 149 F.2d 321 (5th Cir.1945), cert. denied 326 U.S. 742 (1945); 5 *Moore's Federal Practice,* par. 44.05 (2d ed. 1951).

1987 Amendment

The amendments are technical. No substantive change is intended.

1991 Amendment

The amendment to paragraph (a)(1) strikes the references to specific territories, two of which are no longer subject to the jurisdiction of the United States, and adds a generic term to describe governments having a relationship with the United States such that their official records should be treated as domestic records.

The amendment to paragraph (a)(2) adds a sentence to dispense with the final certification by diplomatic officers when the United States and the foreign country where the record is located are parties to a treaty or convention that abolishes or displaces the requirement. In that event the treaty or convention is to be followed. This changes the former procedure for authenticating foreign official records only with respect to records from countries that are parties to the Hague Convention Abolishing the Requirement of Legalization for Foreign Public Documents. Moreover, it does not affect the former practice of attesting the records, but only changes the method of certifying the attestation.

The Hague Public Documents Convention provides that the requirement of a final certification is abolished and replaced with a model *apostille,* which is to be issued by officials of the country where the records are located. See Hague Public Documents Convention, Arts. 2–4. The *apostille* certifies the signature, official position, and seal of the attesting officer. The authority who issues the *apostille* must maintain a register or card index showing the serial number of the *apostille* and other relevant information recorded on it. A foreign court can then check the serial number and information on the *apostille* with the issuing authority in order to guard against the use of fraudulent *apostilles.* This system provides a reliable method for maintaining the integrity of the authentication process, and the *apostille* can be accorded greater weight than the normal authentication procedure because foreign officials are more likely to know the precise capacity under their law of the attesting officer than would an American official. See generally Comment, *The United States and the Hague Convention Abolishing the Requirement of Legalization for Foreign Public Documents,* 11 HARV. INT'L L.J. 476, 482, 488 (1970).

2007 Amendment

The language of Rule 44 has been amended as part of the general restyling of the Civil Rules to make them more easily understood and to make style and terminology consistent throughout the rules. These changes are intended to be stylistic only.

TREATIES AND CONVENTIONS

Convention Abolishing the Requirement of Legalisation for Foreign Public Documents

The States signatory to the present Convention,

Desiring to abolish the requirement of diplomatic or consular legalisation for foreign public documents,

Have resolved to conclude a Convention to this effect and have agreed upon the following provisions:

ARTICLE 1

The present Convention shall apply to public documents which have been executed in the territory of one contracting State and which have to be produced in the territory of another contracting State.

For the purposes of the present Convention, the following are deemed to be public documents:

(a) Documents emanating from an authority or an official connected with the courts or tribunals of the State, including those emanating from a public prosecutor, a clerk of a court or a process server ("huissier de justice");

(b) Administrative documents;

(c) Notarial acts;

(d) Official certificates which are placed on documents signed by persons in their private capacity, such as official certificates recording the registration of a document or the fact that it was in existence on a certain date and official and notarial authentications of signatures.

However, the present Convention shall not apply:

(a) To documents executed by diplomatic or consular agents;

(b) To administrative documents dealing directly with commercial or customs operations.

ARTICLE 2

Each contracting State shall exempt from legalisation documents to which the present Convention applies and which have to be produced in its territory. For the purposes of the present Convention, legalisation means only the formality by which the diplomatic or consular agents of the country in which the document has to be produced certify the authenticity of the signature, the capacity in which the person signing the document has acted and, where appropriate, the identity of the seal or stamp which it bears.

ARTICLE 3

The only formality that may be required in order to certify the authenticity of the signature, the capacity in which the person signing the document has acted and, where appropriate, the identity of the seal or stamp which it bears, is the addition of the certificate described in Article 4, issued by the competent authority of the State from which the document emanates.

However, the formality mentioned in the preceding paragraph cannot be required when either the laws, regulations, or practice in force in the State where the document is produced or an agreement between two or more contracting States have abolished or simplified it, or exempt the document itself from legalisation.

ARTICLE 4

The certificate referred to in the first paragraph of Article 3 shall be placed on the document itself or on an "allonge"; it shall be in the form of the model annexed to the present Convention.

It may, however, be drawn up in the official language of the authority which issues it. The standard terms appearing therein may be in a second language also. The title "Apostille (Convention de La Haye du 5 octobre 1961)" shall be in the French language.

ARTICLE 5

The certificate shall be issued at the request of the person who has signed the document or of any bearer.

When properly filled in, it will certify the authenticity of the signature, the capacity in which the person signing the document has acted and, where appropriate, the identity of the seal or stamp which the document bears.

The signature, seal and stamp on the certificate are exempt from all certification.

ARTICLE 6

Each contracting State shall designate by reference to their official function, the authorities who are competent to issue the certificate referred to in the first paragraph of Article 3.

It shall give notice of such designation to the Ministry of Foreign Affairs of the Netherlands at the time it deposits its instrument of ratification or of accession or its declaration of extension. It shall also give notice of any change in the designated authorities.

ARTICLE 7

Each of the authorities designated in accordance with Article 6 shall keep a register or card index in which it shall record the certificates issued, specifying:

(a) The number and date of the certificate,

(b) The name of the person signing the public document and the capacity in which he has acted, or in the case of unsigned documents, the name of the authority which has affixed the seal or stamp.

At the request of any interested person, the authority which has issued the certificate shall verify whether the particulars in the certificate correspond with those in the register or card index.

ARTICLE 8

When a treaty, convention or agreement between two or more contracting States contains provisions which subject the certification of a signature, seal or stamp to certain formalities, the present Convention will only override such provisions if those formalities are more rigorous than the formality referred to in Articles 3 and 4.

ARTICLE 9

Each contracting State shall take the necessary steps to prevent the performance of legalisations by its diplomatic or consular agents in cases where the present Convention provides for exemption.

ARTICLE 10

The present Convention shall be open for signature by the States represented at the Ninth session of the Hague Conference on Private International Law and Iceland, Ireland, Liechtenstein and Turkey.

It shall be ratified, and the instruments of ratification shall be deposited with the Ministry of Foreign Affairs of the Netherlands.

ARTICLE 11

The present Convention shall enter into force on the sixtieth day after the deposit of the third instrument of ratification referred to in the second paragraph of Article 10.

The Convention shall enter into force for each signatory State which ratifies subsequently on the sixtieth day after the deposit of its instrument of ratification.

ARTICLE 12

Any State not referred to in Article 10 may accede to the present Convention after it has entered into force in accordance with the first paragraph of Article 11. The instrument of accession shall be deposited with the Ministry of Foreign Affairs of the Netherlands.

Such accession shall have effect only as regards the relations between the acceding State and those contracting States which have not raised an objection to its accession in the six months after the receipt of the notification referred to in sub-paragraph (d) of Article 15. Any such objection shall be notified to the Ministry of Foreign Affairs of the Netherlands.

The Convention shall enter into force as between the acceding State and the States which have raised no objection to its accession on the sixtieth day after the expiry of the period of six months mentioned in the preceding paragraph.

ARTICLE 13

Any State may, at the time of signature, ratification or accession, declare that the present Convention shall extend to all the territories for the international relations of which it is responsible, or to one or more of them. Such a declaration shall take effect on the date of entry into force of the Convention for the State concerned.

At any time thereafter, such extension shall be notified to the Ministry of Foreign Affairs of the Netherlands.

When the declaration of extension is made by a State which has signed and ratified, the Convention shall enter into force for the territories concerned in accordance with Article 11. When the declaration of extension is made by a State which has acceded, the Convention shall enter into force for the territories concerned in accordance with Article 12.

ARTICLE 14

The present Convention shall remain in force for five years from the date of its entry into force in accordance with the first paragraph of Article 11, even for States which have ratified it or acceded to it subsequently.

If there has been no denunciation, the Convention shall be renewed tacitly every five years.

Any denunciation shall be notified to the Ministry of Foreign Affairs of the Netherlands at least six months before the end of the five year period.

It may be limited to certain of the territories to which the Convention applies.

The denunciation will only have effect as regards the State which has notified it. The Convention shall remain in force for the other contracting States.

ARTICLE 15

The Ministry of Foreign Affairs of the Netherlands shall give notice to the States referred to in Article 10, and to the States which have acceded in accordance with Article 12, of the following:

(a) The notifications referred to in the second paragraph of Article 6;

(b) The signatures and ratifications referred to in Article 10;

(c) The date on which the present Convention enters into force in accordance with the first paragraph of Article 11;

(d) The accessions and objections referred to in Article 12 and the date on which such accessions take effect;

(e) The extensions referred to in Article 13 and the date on which they take effect;

(f) The denunciations referred to in the third paragraph of Article 14.

In witness whereof the undersigned, being duly authorised thereto, have signed the present Convention.

Done at The Hague the 5th October 1961, in French and in English, the French text prevailing in case of divergence between the two texts, in a single copy which shall be deposited in the archives of the Government of the Netherlands, and of which a certified copy shall be sent, through the diplomatic channel, to each of the States represented at the Ninth session of the Hague Conference on Private International Law and also to Iceland, Ireland, Liechtenstein and Turkey.

[Signatures omitted.]

ANNEX TO THE CONVENTION

Model of certificate

The certificate will be in the form of a square with sides at least 9 centimetres long

APOSTILLE

(Convention de La Haye du 5 octobre 1961)

1. Country: .....
   This public document
2. has been signed by .....
3. acting in the capacity of .....
4. bears the seal/stamp of .....
   .....

Certified

5. at ..... 6. the .....
7. by .....
8. N° .....
9. Seal/stamp: 10. Signature:
   .....

Convention abolishing the requirement of legalization for foreign public documents, with annex. Done at The Hague October 5, 1961; entered into force for the United States October 15, 1981. (TIAS 10072; 527 UNTS 189).

Rule 44.1. Determining Foreign Law

A party who intends to raise an issue about a foreign country's law must give notice by a pleading or other writing. In determining foreign law, the court may consider any relevant material or source, including testimony, whether or not submitted by a party or admissible under the Federal Rules of Evidence. The court's determination must be treated as a ruling on a question of law.

(Adopted February 28, 1966, effective July 1, 1966; amended November 20, 1972, effective July 1, 1975; March 2, 1987, effective August 1, 1987; April 30, 2007, effective December 1, 2007.)

ADVISORY COMMITTEE NOTES

1966 Adoption

Rule 44.1 is added by amendment to furnish Federal courts with a uniform and effective procedure for raising and determining an issue concerning the law of a foreign country.

To avoid unfair surprise, the *first sentence* of the new rule requires that a party who intends to raise an issue of foreign law shall give notice thereof. The uncertainty under Rule 8(a) about whether foreign law must be pleaded—compare *Siegelman v. Cunard White Star, Ltd.,* 221 F.2d 189 (2d Cir.1955), and *Pedersen v. United States,* 191 F.Supp. 95 (D. Guam 1961), with *Harrison v. United Fruit Co.,* 143 F.Supp. 598 (S.D.N.Y.1956)—is eliminated by the provision that the notice shall be "written" and "reasonable." It may, but need not be, incorporated in the pleadings. In some situations the pertinence of foreign law is apparent from the outset; accordingly the necessary investigation of that law will have been accomplished by the party at the pleading stage, and the notice can be given conveniently in the pleadings. In other situations the pertinence of foreign law may remain doubtful until the case is further developed. A requirement that notice of foreign law be given only through the medium of the pleadings would tend in the latter instances to force the party to engage in a peculiarly burdensome type of investigation which might turn out to be unnecessary; and correspondingly the adversary would be forced into a possible wasteful investigation. The liberal provisions for amendment of the pleadings afford help if the pleadings are used as the medium of giving notice of the foreign law; but it seems best to permit a written notice to be given outside of and later than the pleadings, provided the notice is reasonable.

The new rule does not attempt to set any definite limit on the party's time for giving the notice of an issue of foreign law; in some cases the issue may not become apparent until the trial and notice then given may still be reasonable. The stage which the case had reached at the time of the notice, the reason proffered by the party for his failure to give earlier notice, and the importance to the case as a whole of the issue of foreign law sought to be raised, are among the factors which the court should consider in deciding a question of the reasonableness of a notice. If notice is given by one party it need not be repeated by any other and serves as a basis for presentation of material on the foreign law by all parties.

The *second sentence* of the new rule describes the materials to which the court may resort in determining an issue of foreign law. Heretofore the district courts, applying Rule 43(a), have looked in certain cases to State law to find the rules of evidence by which the content of foreign-country law is to be established. The State laws vary; some embody procedures which are inefficient, time consuming and expensive. See, generally, Nussbaum, *Proving the Law of Foreign Countries,* 3 Am. J. Comp. L. 60 (1954). In all events the ordinary rules of evidence are often inapposite to the problem of determining foreign law and have in the past prevented examination of material which could have provided a proper basis for the determination. The new rule permits consideration by the court of any relevant material, including testimony, without regard to its admissibility under Rule 43. Cf. N.Y. Civ. Prac. Law & Rules, R. 4511 (effective Sept. 1, 1963); 2 Va. Code Ann. tit. 8, § 8-273; 2 W. Va. Code Ann. § 5711.

In further recognition of the peculiar nature of the issue of foreign law, the new rule provides that in determining this law the court is not limited by material presented by the parties; it may engage in its own research and consider any relevant material thus found. The court may have at its disposal better foreign law materials than counsel have presented, or may wish to reexamine and amplify material that has been presented by counsel in partisan fashion or in insufficient detail. On the other hand, the court is free to insist on a complete presentation by counsel.

There is no requirement that the court give formal notice to the parties of its intention to engage in its own research on an issue of foreign law which has been raised by them, or of its intention to raise and determine independently an issue not raised by them. Ordinarily the court should inform the parties of material it has found diverging substantially from the material which they have presented; and in general the court should give the parties an opportunity to analyze and counter new points upon which it proposes to rely. See Schlesinger, *Comparative Law* 142 (2d ed. 1959); Wyzanski, *A Trial Judge's Freedom and Responsibility,* 65 Harv. L.Rev. 1281, 1296 (1952); cf. *Siegelman v. Cunard White Star, Ltd.,* supra, 221 F.2d at 197. To require, however, that the court give formal notice from time to time as it proceeds with its study of the foreign law would add an element of undesirable rigidity to the procedure for determining issues of foreign law.

The new rule refrains from imposing an obligation on the court to take "judicial notice" of foreign law because this would put an extreme burden on the court in many cases; and it avoids use of the concept of "judicial notice" in any form because of the uncertain meaning of that concept as applied to foreign law. See, e.g., Stern, *Foreign Law in the Courts: Judicial Notice and Proof,* 45 Calif.L.Rev. 23, 43 (1957). Rather the rule provides flexible procedures for presenting and utilizing material on issues of foreign law by which a sound result can be achieved with fairness to the parties.

Under the *third sentence,* the court's determination of an issue of foreign law is to be treated as a ruling on a question of "law," not "fact," so that appellate review will not be narrowly confined by the "clearly erroneous" standard of Rule 52(a). *Cf. Uniform Judicial Notice of Foreign Law Act* § 3; Note, 72 Harv.L.Rev. 318 (1958).

The new rule parallels Article IV of the Uniform Interstate and International Procedure Act, approved by the Commissioners on Uniform State Laws in 1962, except that § 4.03 of Article IV states that "[t]he court, not the jury" shall determine foreign law. The new rule does not address itself to this problem, since the Rules refrain from allocating functions as between the court and the jury. See Rule 38(a). It has long been thought, however, that the jury is not the appropriate body to determine issues of foreign law. See, e.g., Story, *Conflict of Laws,* § 638 (1st ed. 1834, 8th ed. 1883); 1 Greenleaf, *Evidence,* § 486 (1st ed. 1842, 16th ed. 1899); 4 Wigmore, *Evidence* § 2558 (1st ed. 1905); 9 id. § 2558 (3d ed. 1940). The majority of the States have committed such issues to determination by the court. See Article 5 of the Uniform Judicial Notice of Foreign Law Act, adopted by twenty-six states, 9A U.L.A. 318 (1957) (Suppl.1961, at 134); N.Y.Civ.Prac.Law & Rules, R. 4511 (effective Sept. 1, 1963); Wigmore, loc. cit. And Federal courts that have considered the problem in recent years have reached the same conclusion without reliance on statute. See *Jansson v. Swedish American Line*, 185 F.2d 212, 216 (1st Cir.1950); *Bank of Nova Scotia v. San Miguel*, 196 F.2d 950, 957, n. 6 (1st Cir.1952); *Liechti v. Roche*, 198 F.2d 174 (5th Cir.1952); *Daniel Lumber Co. v. Empresas Hondurenas, S.A.*, 215 F.2d 465 (5th Cir.1954).

1972 Amendment

Since the purpose of the provision is to free the judge, in determining foreign law, from any restrictions imposed by evidence rules, a general reference to the Rules of Evidence is appropriate and is made.

1987 Amendment

The amendment is technical. No substantive change is intended.

2007 Amendment

The language of Rule 44.1 has been amended as part of the general restyling of the Civil Rules to make them more easily understood and to make style and terminology consistent throughout the rules. These changes are intended to be stylistic only.

HISTORICAL NOTES

Effective Date of Amendment Proposed November 20, 1972

Amendment of this rule embraced by the order entered by the Supreme Court of the United States on November 20, 1972, effective on the 180th day beginning after January 2, 1975, see section 3 of Pub.L. 93–595, Jan. 2, 1975, 88 Stat. 1959, set out as a note under section 2071 of Title 28.

Rule 45. Subpoena

(a) In General.

(1) ***Form and Contents.***

(A) *Requirements—In General.* Every subpoena must:

(i) state the court from which it issued;

(ii) state the title of the action, the court in which it is pending, and its civil-action number;

(iii) command each person to whom it is directed to do the following at a specified time and place: attend and testify; produce designated documents, electronically stored information, or tangible things in that person's possession, custody, or control; or permit the inspection of premises; and

(iv) set out the text of Rule 45(c) and (d).

(B) *Command to Attend a Deposition—Notice of the Recording Method.* A subpoena commanding attendance at a deposition must state the method for recording the testimony.

(C) *Combining or Separating a Command to Produce or to Permit Inspection; Specifying the Form for Electronically Stored Information.* A command to produce documents, electronically stored information, or tangible things or to permit the inspection of premises may be included in a subpoena commanding attendance at a deposition, hearing, or trial, or may be set out in a separate subpoena. A subpoena may specify the form or forms in which electronically stored information is to be produced.

(D) *Command to Produce; Included Obligations.* A command in a subpoena to produce documents, electronically stored information, or tangible things requires the responding party to permit inspection, copying, testing, or sampling of the materials.

(2) ***Issued from Which Court.*** **A subpoena must issue as follows:**

(A) for attendance at a hearing or trial, from the court for the district where the hearing or trial is to be held;

(B) for attendance at a deposition, from the court for the district where the deposition is to be taken; and

(C) for production or inspection, if separate from a subpoena commanding a person's attendance, from the court for the district where the production or inspection is to be made.

(3) ***Issued by Whom.*** The clerk must issue a subpoena, signed but otherwise in blank, to a party who requests it. That party must complete it before service. An attorney also may issue and sign a subpoena as an officer of:

(A) a court in which the attorney is authorized to practice; or

(B) a court for a district where a deposition is to be taken or production is to be made, if the attorney is authorized to practice in the court where the action is pending.

(b) Service.

(1) ***By Whom; Tendering Fees; Serving a Copy of Certain Subpoenas.*** Any person who is at least 18 years old and not a party may serve a subpoena. Serving a subpoena requires delivering a copy to the named person and, if the subpoena requires that person's attendance, tendering the fees for 1 day's attendance and the mileage allowed by law. Fees and mileage need not be tendered when the subpoena issues on behalf of the United States or any of its officers or agencies. If the subpoena commands the production of documents, electronically stored information, or tangible things or the inspection of premises before trial, then before it is served, a notice must be served on each party.

(2) ***Service in the United States.*** Subject to Rule 45(c)(3)(A)(ii), a subpoena may be served at any place:

(A) within the district of the issuing court;

(B) outside that district but within 100 miles of the place specified for the deposition, hearing, trial, production, or inspection;

(C) within the state of the issuing court if a state statute or court rule allows service at that place of a subpoena issued by a state court of general jurisdiction sitting in the place specified for the deposition, hearing, trial, production, or inspection; or

(D) that the court authorizes on motion and for good cause, if a federal statute so provides.

(3) ***Service in a Foreign Country.*** 28 U.S.C. § 1783 governs issuing and serving a subpoena directed to a United States national or resident who is in a foreign country.

(4) ***Proof of Service.*** Proving service, when necessary, requires filing with the issuing court a statement showing the date and manner of service and the names of the persons served. The statement must be certified by the server.

(c) Protecting a Person Subject to a Subpoena.

(1) ***Avoiding Undue Burden or Expense; Sanctions.*** A party or attorney responsible for issuing and serving a subpoena must take reasonable steps to avoid imposing undue burden or expense on a person subject to the subpoena. The issuing court must enforce this duty and impose an appropriate sanction—which may include lost earnings and reasonable attorney's fees—on a party or attorney who fails to comply.

(2) ***Command to Produce Materials or Permit Inspection.***

(A) *Appearance Not Required.* A person commanded to produce documents, electronically stored information, or tangible things, or to permit the inspection of premises, need not appear in person at the place of production or inspection unless also commanded to appear for a deposition, hearing, or trial.

(B) *Objections.* A person commanded to produce documents or tangible things or to permit inspection may serve on the party or attorney designated in the subpoena a written objection to inspecting, copying, testing or sampling any or all of the materials or to inspecting the premises—or to producing electronically stored information in the form or forms requested. The objection must be served before the earlier of the time specified for compliance or 14 days after the subpoena is served. If an objection is made, the following rules apply:

(i) At any time, on notice to the commanded person, the serving party may move the issuing court for an order compelling production or inspection.

(ii) These acts may be required only as directed in the order, and the order must protect a person who is neither a party nor a party's officer from significant expense resulting from compliance.

(3) ***Quashing or Modifying a Subpoena.***

(A) *When Required.* On timely motion, the issuing court must quash or modify a subpoena that:

(i) fails to allow a reasonable time to comply;

(ii) requires a person who is neither a party nor a party's officer to travel more than 100 miles from where that person resides, is employed, or regularly transacts business in person—except that, subject to Rule 45(c)(3)(B)(iii), the person may be commanded to attend a trial by traveling from any such place within the state where the trial is held;

(iii) requires disclosure of privileged or other protected matter, if no exception or waiver applies; or

(iv) subjects a person to undue burden.

(B) *When Permitted.* To protect a person subject to or affected by a subpoena, the issuing court may, on motion, quash or modify the subpoena if it requires:

(i) disclosing a trade secret or other confidential research, development, or commercial information;

(ii) disclosing an unretained expert's opinion or information that does not describe specific occurrences in dispute and results from the expert's study that was not requested by a party; or

(iii) a person who is neither a party nor a party's officer to incur substantial expense to travel more than 100 miles to attend trial.

(C) *Specifying Conditions as an Alternative.* In the circumstances described in Rule 45(c)(3)(B), the court may, instead of quashing or modifying a subpoena, order appearance or production under specified conditions if the serving party:

(i) shows a substantial need for the testimony or material that cannot be otherwise met without undue hardship; and

(ii) ensures that the subpoenaed person will be reasonably compensated.

(d) Duties in Responding to a Subpoena.

(1) ***Producing Documents or Electronically Stored Information.*** These procedures apply to producing documents or electronically stored information:

(A) *Documents.* A person responding to a subpoena to produce documents must produce them as they are kept in the ordinary course of business or must organize and label them to correspond to the categories in the demand.

(B) *Form for Producing Electronically Stored Information Not Specified.* If a subpoena does not specify a form for producing electronically stored information, the person responding must produce it in a form or forms in which it is ordinarily maintained or in a reasonably usable form or forms.

(C) *Electronically Stored Information Produced in Only One Form.* The person responding need not produce the same electronically stored information in more than one form.

(D) *Inaccessible Electronically Stored Information.* The person responding need not provide discovery of electronically stored information from sources that the person identifies as not reasonably accessible because of undue burden or cost. On motion to compel discovery or for a protective order, the person responding must show that the information is not reasonably accessible because of undue burden or cost. If that showing is made, the court may nonetheless order discovery from such sources if the requesting party shows good cause, considering the limitations of Rule 26(b)(2)(C). The court may specify conditions for the discovery.

(2) ***Claiming Privilege or Protection.***

(A) *Information Withheld.* A person withholding subpoenaed information under a claim that it is privileged or subject to protection as trial-preparation material must:

(i) expressly make the claim; and

(ii) describe the nature of the withheld documents, communications, or tangible things in a manner that, without revealing information itself privileged or protected, will enable the parties to assess the claim.

(B) *Information Produced.* If information produced in response to a subpoena is subject to a claim of privilege or of protection as trial-preparation material, the person making the claim may notify any party that received the information of the claim and the basis for it. After being notified, a party must promptly return, sequester, or destroy the specified information and any copies it has; must not use or disclose the information until the claim is resolved; must take reasonable steps to retrieve the information if the party disclosed it before being notified; and may promptly present the information to the court under seal for a determination of the claim. The person who produced the information must preserve the information until the claim is resolved.

(e) Contempt. The issuing court may hold in contempt a person who, having been served, fails without adequate excuse to obey the subpoena. A nonparty's failure to obey must be excused if the subpoena purports to require the nonparty to attend or produce at a place outside the limits of Rule 45(c)(3)(A)(ii).

(Amended December 27, 1946, effective March 19, 1948; December 29, 1948, effective October 20, 1949; March 30, 1970, effective July 1, 1970; April 29, 1980, effective August 1, 1980; April 29, 1985, effective August 1, 1985; March 2, 1987, effective August 1, 1987; April 30, 1991, effective December 1, 1991; April 25, 2005, effective December 1, 2005; April 12, 2006, effective December 1, 2006; April 30, 2007, effective December 1, 2007.)

ADVISORY COMMITTEE NOTES

1937 Adoption

This rule applies to subpoenas ad testificandum and duces tecum issued by the district courts for attendance at a hearing or a trial, or to take depositions. It does not apply to the enforcement of subpoenas issued by administrative officers and commissions pursuant to statutory authority. The enforcement of such subpoenas by the district courts is regulated by appropriate statutes. Many of these statutes do not place any territorial limits on the validity of subpoenas so issued, but provide that they may be served anywhere within the United States. Among such statutes are the following:

U.S.C., Title 7, §§ 222 and 511n (Secretary of Agriculture)

U.S.C., Title 15, § 49 (Federal Trade Commission)

U.S.C., Title 15, §§ 77v(b), 78u(c), 79r(d) (Securities and Exchange Commission)

U.S.C., Title 16, §§ 797(g) and 825f (Federal Power Commission)

U.S.C., Title 19, § 1333(b) (Tariff Commission)

U.S.C., Title 22, §§ 268, 270d and 270e (International Commissions, etc.)

U.S.C., Title 26, §§ 614, 619(b) [see 7456] (Board of Tax Appeals)

U.S.C., Title 26, § 1523(a) [see 7608] (Internal Revenue Officers)

U.S.C., Title 29, § 161 (Labor Relations Board)

U.S.C., Title 33, § 506 (Secretary of Army)

U.S.C., Title 35, §§ 54 to 56 [now 24] (Patent Office proceedings)

U.S.C., Title 38, [former] § 133 (Veterans' Administration)

U.S.C., Title 41, § 39 (Secretary of Labor)

U.S.C., Title 45, § 157 Third. (h) (Board of Arbitration under Railway Labor Act)

U.S.C., Title 45, § 222(b) (Investigation Commission under Railroad Retirement Act of 1935)

U.S.C., Title 46, § 1124(b) (Maritime Commission)

U.S.C., Title 47, § 409(c) and (d) (Federal Communications Commission)

U.S.C., Title 49, § 12(2) and (3) [now 10321] (Interstate Commerce Commission)

U.S.C., Title 49, § 173a [see 1484] (Secretary of Commerce)

Note to Subdivisions (a) and (b). These simplify the form of subpoena as provided in U.S.C., Title 28, [former] § 655 (Witnesses; subpoena; form; attendance under); and broaden U.S.C, Title 28, [former] § 636 (Production for books and writings) to include all actions, and to extend to any person. With the provision for relief from an oppressive or unreasonable subpoena duces tecum, compare N.Y.C.P.A. (1937) § 411.

Note to Subdivision (c). This provides for the simple and convenient method of service permitted under many state codes; e.g., N.Y.C.P.A. (1937) §§ 220, 404, J.Ct.Act, § 191; 3 Wash.Rev.Stat.Ann. (Remington, 1932) § 1218. Compare former Equity Rule 15 (Process, by Whom Served).

For statutes governing fees and mileage of witnesses see:

U.S.C., Title 28 former sections:

600a[now 1871] (Per diem; mileage)

600c[now 1821, 1823] (Amount per diem and mileage for witnesses; subsistence)

600d[former] (Fees and mileage in certain states)

601[former] (Witnesses' fees; enumeration)

602[now 1824] (Fees and mileage of jurors and witnesses)

603[see Title 5, §§ 5515, 5537] (No officer of court to have witness fees)

Note to Subdivision (d). The method provided in paragraph (1) for the authorization of the issuance of subpoenas has been employed in some districts. See *Henning v. Boyle*, S.D.N.Y.1901, 112 F. 397. The requirement of an order for the issuance of a subpoena duces tecum is in accordance with U.S.C., Title 28, [former] § 647 (Deposition under dedimus potestatem; subpoena duces tecum). The provisions of paragraph (2) are in accordance with common practice. See U.S.C., Title 28, former § 648 (Deposition under dedimus potestatem; witnesses, when required to attend); N.Y.C.P.A. (1937) § 300; 1 N.J.Rev.Stat. (1937) 2:27–174.

Note to Subdivision (e). The first paragraph continues the substance of U.S.C., Title 28, [former] § 654 (Witnesses; subpoenas; may run into another district). Compare U.S.C., Title 11, [former] § 69 (Referees in bankruptcy; contempts before) (production of books and writings) which is not affected by this rule. For examples of statutes which allow the court, upon proper application and cause shown, to authorize the clerk of the court to issue a subpoena for a witness who lives in another district and at a greater distance than 100 miles from the place of the hearing or trial, see:

U.S.C., Title 15:

§ 23 (Suits by United States; subpoenas for witnesses) (under antitrust laws).

U.S.C., Title 38:

§ 445[now 784] (Actions on claims; jurisdiction; parties; procedure; limitation; witnesses; definitions) (Veterans' insurance contracts).

The second paragraph continues the present procedure applicable to certain witnesses who are in foreign countries. See U.S.C., Title 28, §§ 711 [now 1783] (Letters rogatory to take testimony of witness, addressed to court of foreign country; failure of witness to appear; subpoena) and 713 [now 1783] (Service of Subpoena on witness in foreign country).

Note to Subdivision (f). Compare [former] Equity Rule 52 (Attendance of Witnesses Before Commissioner, Master, or Examiner).

1946 Amendment

Note to Subdivision (b). The added words, "or tangible things" in subdivision (b) merely make the rule for the subpoena duces tecum at the trial conform to that of subdivision (d) for the subpoena at the taking of depositions. The insertion of the words "or modify" in clause (1) affords desirable flexibility.

Subdivision (d). The added last sentence of amended subdivision (d)(1) properly gives the subpoena for documents or tangible things the same scope as provided in Rule 26(b), thus promoting uniformity. The requirement in the last sentence of original Rule 45(d)(1)—to the effect that leave of court should be obtained for the issuance of such a subpoena—has been omitted. This requirement is unnecessary and oppressive on both counsel and court, and it had been criticized by district judges. There is no satisfactory reason for a differentiation between a subpoena for the production of documentary evidence by a witness at a trial (Rule 45(a)) and for the production of the same evidence at the taking of a deposition. Under this amendment, the person subpoenaed may obtain the protection afforded by any of the orders permitted under Rule 30(b) or Rule 45(b). See *Application* *of Zenith Radio Corp.*, E.D.Pa.1941, 4 F.Rules Serv. 30b.21. Case 1, 1 F.R.D. 627; *Fox v. House*, Okla.1939, 29 F.Supp. 673; *United States of America for the Use of Tilo Roofing Co., Inc. v. J. Slotnik Co.*, Conn.1944, 3 F.R.D. 408.

The changes in subdivisions (d)(2) give the court the same power in the case of residents of the district as is conferred in the case of non-residents, and permit the court to fix a place for attendance which may be more convenient and accessible for the parties than that specified in the rule.

1948 Amendment

The amendment effective October 1949, substituted the reference to "Title 28, U.S.C., § 1783" at the end of subdivision (e)(2) for the reference to "the Act of July 3, 1926, c. 762, §§ 1, 3 (44 Stat. 835), U.S.C., Title 28, § 713."

1970 Amendment

At present, when a subpoena duces tecum is issued to a deponent, he is required to produce the listed materials at the deposition, but is under no clear compulsion to permit their inspection and copying. This results in confusion and uncertainty before the time the deposition is taken, with no mechanism provided whereby the court can resolve the matter. Rule 45(d)(1), as revised, makes clear that the subpoena authorizes inspection and copying of the materials produced. The deponent is afforded full protection since he can object, thereby forcing the party serving the subpoena to obtain a court order if he wishes to inspect and copy. The procedure is thus analogous to that provided in Rule 34.

The changed references to other rules conform to changes made in those rules. The deletion of words in the clause describing the proper scope of the subpoena conforms to a change made in the language of Rule 34. The reference to Rule 26(b) is unchanged but encompasses new matter in that subdivision. The changes make it clear that the scope of discovery through a subpoena is the same as that applicable to Rule 34 and the other discovery rules.

1980 Amendment

Subdivision (d)(1). The amendment defines the term "proof of service" as used in the first sentence of the present subdivision. For want of a definition, the district court clerks have been obliged to fashion their own, with results that vary from district to district. All that seems required is a simple certification on a copy of the notice to take a deposition that the notice has been served on every other party to the action. That is the proof of service required by Rule 25(d) of both the Federal Rules of Appellate Procedure and the Supreme Court Rules.

Subdivision (e)(1). The amendment makes the reach of a subpoena of a district court at least as extensive as that of the state courts of general jurisdiction in the state in which the district court is held. Under the present rule the reach of a district court subpoena is often greater, since it extends throughout the district. No reason appears why it should be less, as it sometimes is because of the accident of district lines. Restrictions upon the reach of subpoenas are imposed to prevent undue inconvenience to witnesses. State statutes and rules of court are quite likely to reflect the varying degrees of difficulty and expense attendant upon local travel.

1985 Amendment

Present Rule 45(d)(2) has two sentences setting forth the territorial scope of deposition subpoenas. The first sentence is directed to depositions taken in the judicial district in which the deponent resides; the second sentence addresses situations in which the deponent is not a resident of the district in which the deposition is to take place. The Rule, as currently constituted, creates anomalous situations that often cause logistical problems in conducting litigation.

The first sentence of the present Rule states that a deponent may be required to attend only in the *county* wherein that person resides or is employed or transacts business in person, that is, where the person lives or works. Under this provision a deponent can be compelled, without court order, to travel from one end of that person's home county to the other, no matter how far that may be. The second sentence of the Rule is somewhat more flexible, stating that someone who does not reside in the district in which the deposition is to be taken can be required to attend in the county where the person is served with the subpoena, *or* within 40 miles from the place of service.

Under today's conditions there is no sound reason for distinguishing between residents of the district or county in which a deposition is to be taken and nonresidents, and the Rule is amended to provide that any person may be subpoenaed to attend a deposition within a specified radius from that person's residence, place of business, or where the person was served. The 40-mile radius has been increased to 100 miles.

1987 Amendment

The amendments are technical. No substantive change is intended.

1991 Amendment

Purposes of Revision. The purposes of this revision are (1) to clarify and enlarge the protections afforded persons who are required to assist the court by giving information or evidence; (2) to facilitate access outside the deposition procedure provided by Rule 30 to documents and other information in the possession of persons who are not parties; (3) to facilitate service of subpoenas for depositions or productions of evidence at places distant from the district in which an action is proceeding; (4) to enable the court to compel a witness found within the state in which the court sits to attend trial; (5) to clarify the organization of the text of the rule.

Subdivision (a). This subdivision is amended in seven significant respects.

First, Paragraph (a)(3) modifies the requirement that a subpoena be issued by the clerk of court. Provision is made for the issuance of subpoenas by attorneys as officers of the court. This revision perhaps culminates an evolution. Subpoenas were long issued by specific order of the court. As this became a burden to the court, general orders were made authorizing clerks to issue subpoenas on request. Since 1948, they have been issued in blank by the clerk of any federal court to any lawyer, the clerk serving as stationer to the bar. In allowing counsel to issue the subpoena, the rule is merely a recognition of present reality.

Although the subpoena is in a sense the command of the attorney who completes the form, defiance of a subpoena is nevertheless an act in defiance of a court order and exposes the defiant witness to contempt sanctions. In *ICC v. Brimson*, 154 U.S. 447 (1894), the Court upheld a statute directing federal courts to issue subpoenas to compel testimony before the ICC. In *CAB v. Hermann*, 353 U.S. 322 (1957), the Court approved as established practice the issuance of administrative subpoenas as a matter of absolute agency right. And in *NLRB v. Warren Co.*, 350 U.S. 107 (1955), the Court held that the lower court had no discretion to withhold sanctions against a contemnor who violated such subpoenas. The 1948 revision of Rule 45 put the attorney in a position similar to that of the administrative agency, as a public officer entitled to use the court's contempt power to investigate facts in dispute. Two courts of appeals have touched on the issue and have described lawyer-issued subpoenas as mandates of the court. *Waste Conversion, Inc. v. Rollins Environmental Services (NJ), Inc.*, 893 F.2d 605 (3d cir., 1990); *Fisher v. Marubent Cotton Corp.*, 526 F.2d 1338, 1340 (8th cir., 1975). Cf. *Young v. United States ex rel Vuitton et Fils S.A.*, 481 U.S. 787, 821 (1987) (Scalia, J., concurring). This revision makes the rule explicit that the attorney acts as an officer of the court in issuing and signing subpoenas.

Necessarily accompanying the evolution of this power of the lawyer as officer of the court is the development of increased responsibility and liability for the misuse of this power. The latter development is reflected in the provisions of subdivision (c) of this rule, and also in the requirement imposed by paragraph (3) of this subdivision that the attorney issuing a subpoena must sign it.

Second, Paragraph (a)(3) authorizes attorneys in distant districts to serve as officers authorized to issue commands in the name of the court. Any attorney permitted to represent a client in a federal court, even one admitted pro haec vice, has the same authority as a clerk to issue a subpoena from any federal court for the district in which the subpoena is served and enforced. In authorizing attorneys to issue subpoenas from distant courts, the amended rule effectively authorizes service of a subpoena anywhere in the United States by an attorney representing any party. This change is intended to ease the administrative burdens of interdistrict law practice. The former rule resulted in delay and expense caused by the need to secure forms from clerks' offices some distance from the place at which the action proceeds. This change does not enlarge the burden on the witness.

Pursuant to Paragraph (a)(2), a subpoena for a deposition must still issue from the court in which the deposition or production would be compelled. Accordingly, a motion to quash such a subpoena if it overbears the limits of the subpoena power must, as under the previous rule, be presented to the court for the district in which the deposition would occur. Likewise, the court in whose name the subpoena is issued is responsible for its enforcement.

Third, in order to relieve attorneys of the need to secure an appropriate seal to affix to a subpoena issued as an officer of a distant court, the requirement that a subpoena be under seal is abolished by the provisions of Paragraph (a)(1).

Fourth, Paragraph (a)(1) authorizes the issuance of a subpoena to compel a non-party to produce evidence independent of any deposition. This revision spares the necessity of a deposition of the custodian of evidentiary material required to be produced. A party seeking additional production from a person subject to such a subpoena may serve an additional subpoena requiring additional production at the same time and place.

Fifth, Paragraph (a)(2) makes clear that the person subject to the subpoena is required to produce materials in that person's control whether or not the materials are located within the district or within the territory within which the subpoena can be served. The non-party witness is subject to the same scope of discovery under this rule as that person would be as a party to whom a request is addressed pursuant to Rule 34.

Sixth, Paragraph (a)(1) requires that the subpoena include a statement of the rights and duties of witnesses by setting forth in full the text of the new subdivisions (c) and (d).

Seventh, the revised rule authorizes the issuance of a subpoena to compel the inspection of premises in the possession of a non-party. Rule 34 has authorized such inspections of premises in the possession of a party as discovery compelled under Rule 37, but prior practice required an independent proceeding to secure such relief ancillary to the federal proceeding when the premises were not in the possession of a party. Practice in some states has long authorized such use of a subpoena for this purpose without apparent adverse consequence.

Subdivision (b). Paragraph (b)(1) retains the text of the former subdivision (c) with minor changes.

The reference to the United States marshal and deputy marshal is deleted because of the infrequency of the use of these officers for this purpose. Inasmuch as these officers meet the age requirement, they may still be used if available.

A provision requiring service of prior notice pursuant to Rule 5 of compulsory pretrial production or inspection has been added to paragraph (b)(1). The purpose of such notice is to afford other parties an opportunity to object to the production or inspection, or to serve a demand for additional documents or things. Such additional notice is not needed with respect to a deposition because of the requirement of notice imposed by Rule 30 or 31. But when production or inspection is sought independently of a deposition, other parties may need notice in order to monitor the discovery and in order to pursue access to any information that may or should be produced.

Paragraph (b)(2) retains language formerly set forth in subdivision (e) and extends its application to subpoenas for depositions or production.

Paragraph (b)(3) retains language formerly set forth in paragraph (d)(1) and extends its applications to subpoenas for trial or hearing or production.

Subdivision (c). This provision is new and states the rights of witnesses. It is not intended to diminish rights conferred by Rules 26–37 or any other authority.

Paragraph (c)(1) gives specific application to the principle stated in Rule 26(g) and specifies liability for earnings lost by a non-party witness as a result of a misuse of the subpoena. No change in existing law is thereby effected. Abuse of a subpoena is an actionable tort, *Board of Ed. v. Farmingdale Classroom Teach. Ass'n*, 38 N.Y.2d 397, 380 N.Y.S.2d 635, 343 N.E.2d 278 (1975), and the duty of the attorney to the non-party is also embodied in Model Rule of Professional Conduct 4.4. The liability of the attorney is correlative to the expanded power of the attorney to issue subpoenas. The liability may include the cost of fees to collect attorneys' fees owed as a result of a breach of this duty.

Paragraph (c)(2) retains language from the former subdivision (b) and paragraph (d)(1). The 10-day period for response to a subpoena is extended to 14 days to avoid the complex calculations associated with short time periods under Rule 6 and to allow a bit more time for such objections to be made.

A non-party required to produce documents or materials is protected against significant expense resulting from involuntary assistance to the court. This provision applies, for example, to a non-party required to provide a list of class members. The court is not required to fix the costs in advance of production, although this will often be the most satisfactory accommodation to protect the party seeking discovery from excessive costs. In some instances, it may be preferable to leave uncertain costs to be determined after the materials have been produced, provided that the risk of uncertainty is fully disclosed to the discovering party. See, *e.g., United States v. Columbia Broadcasting Systems, Inc.*, 666 F.2d 364 (9th Cir.1982).

Paragraph (c)(3) explicitly authorizes the quashing of a subpoena as a means of protecting a witness from misuse of the subpoena power. It replaces and enlarges on the former subdivision (b) of this rule and tracks the provisions of Rule 26(c). While largely repetitious, this rule is addressed to the witness who may read it on the subpoena, where it is required to be printed by the revised paragraph (a)(1) of this rule.

Subparagraph (c)(3)(A) identifies those circumstances in which a subpoena must be quashed or modified. It restates the former provisions with respect to the limits of mandatory travel that are set forth in the former paragraphs (d)(2) and (e)(1), with one important change. Under the revised rule, a federal court can compel a witness to come from any place in the state to attend trial, whether or not the local state law so provides. This extension is subject to the qualification provided in the next paragraph, which authorizes the court to condition enforcement of a subpoena compelling a non-party witness to bear substantial expense to attend trial. The traveling non-party witness may be entitled to reasonable compensation for the time and effort entailed.

Clause (c)(3)(A)(iv) requires the court to protect all persons from undue burden imposed by the use of the subpoena power. Illustratively, it might be unduly burdensome to compel an adversary to attend trial as a witness if the adversary is known to have no personal knowledge of matters in dispute, especially so if the adversary would be required to incur substantial travel burdens.

Subparagraph (c)(3)(B) identifies circumstances in which a subpoena should be quashed unless the party serving the subpoena shows a substantial need and the court can devise an appropriate accommodation to protect the interests of the witness. An additional circumstance in which such action is required is a request for costly production of documents; that situation is expressly governed by subparagraph (b)(2)(B)[1].

Clause (c)(3)(B)(i) authorizes the court to quash, modify, or condition a subpoena to protect the person subject to or affected by the subpoena from unnecessary or unduly harmful disclosures of confidential information. It corresponds to Rule 26(c)(7).

Clause (c)(3)(B)(ii) provides appropriate protection for the intellectual property of the non-party witness; it does not apply to the expert retained by a party, whose information is subject to the provisions of Rule 26(b)(4). A growing problem has been the use of subpoenas to compel the giving of evidence and information by unretained experts. Experts are not exempt from the duty to give evidence, even if they cannot be compelled to prepare themselves to give effective testimony, *e.g., Carter-Wallace, Inc. v. Otte*, 474 F.2d 529 (2d Cir.1972), but compulsion to give evidence may threaten the intellectual property of experts denied the opportunity to bargain for the value of their services. See generally Maurer, *Compelling the Expert Witness: Fairness and Utility Under the Federal Rules of Civil Procedure*, 19 GA.L.REV. 71 (1984); Note, *Discovery and Testimony of Unretained Experts*, 1987 DUKE L.J. 140. Arguably the compulsion to testify can be regarded as a "taking" of intellectual property. The rule establishes the right of such persons to withhold their expertise, at least unless the party seeking it makes the kind of showing required for a conditional denial of a motion to quash as provided in the final sentence of subparagraph (c)(3)(B); that requirement is the same as that necessary to secure work product under Rule 26(b)(3) and gives assurance of reasonable compensation. The Rule thus approves the accommodation of competing interests exemplified in *United States v. Columbia Broadcasting Systems Inc.*, 666 F.2d 364 (9th Cir.1982). See also *Wright v. Jeep Corporation*, 547 F.Supp. 871 (E.D.Mich.1982).

As stated in *Kaufman v. Edelstein*, 539 F.2d 811, 822 (2d Cir.1976), the district court's discretion in these matters should be informed by "the degree to which the expert is being called because of his knowledge of facts relevant to the case rather than in order to give opinion testimony; the difference between testifying to a previously formed or expressed opinion and forming a new one; the possibility that, for other reasons, the witness is a unique expert; the extent to which the calling party is able to show the unlikelihood that any comparable witness will willingly testify; and the degree to which the witness is able to show that he has been oppressed by having continually to testify. . . ."

Clause (c)(3)(B)(iii) protects non-party witnesses who may be burdened to perform the duty to travel in order to provide testimony at trial. The provision requires the court to condition a subpoena requiring travel of more than 100 miles on reasonable compensation.

Subdivision (d). This provision is new. Paragraph (d)(1) extends to non-parties the duty imposed on parties by the last paragraph of Rule 34(b), which was added in 1980.

Paragraph (d)(2) is new and corresponds to the new Rule 26(b)(5) [paragraph (5) in Rule 26(b) was a proposed paragraph which was withdrawn by the Supreme Court]. Its purpose is to provide a party whose discovery is constrained by a claim of privilege or work product protection with information sufficient to evaluate such a claim and to resist if it seems unjustified. The person claiming a privilege or protection cannot decide the limits of that party's own entitlement.

A party receiving a discovery request who asserts a privilege or protection but fails to disclose that claim is at risk of waiving the privilege or protection. A person claiming a privilege or protection who fails to provide adequate information about the privilege or protection claim to the party seeking the information is subject to an order to show cause why the person should not be held in contempt under subdivision (e). Motions for such orders and responses to motions are subject to the sanctions provisions of Rules 7 and 11.

A person served a subpoena that is too broad may be faced with a burdensome task to provide full information regarding all that person's claims to privilege or work product protection. Such a person is entitled to protection that may be secured through an objection made pursuant to paragraph (c)(2).

Subdivision (e). This provision retains most of the language of the former subdivision (f).

"Adequate cause" for a failure to obey a subpoena remains undefined. In at least some circumstances, a non-party might be guilty of contempt for refusing to obey a subpoena even though the subpoena manifestly overreaches the appropriate limits of the subpoena power. *E.g., Walker v. City of Birmingham*, 388 U.S. 307 (1967). But, because the command of the subpoena is not in fact one uttered by a judicial officer, contempt should be very sparingly applied when the non-party witness has been overborne by a party or attorney. The language added to subdivision (f) is intended to assure that result where a non-party has been commanded, on the signature of an attorney, to travel greater distances than can be compelled pursuant to this rule.

[1] So in original. Probably should be "subparagraph (c)(2)(B)".

2005 Amendments

This amendment closes a small gap in regard to notifying witnesses of the manner for recording a deposition. A deposition subpoena must state the method for recording the testimony.

Rule 30(b)(2) directs that the party noticing a deposition state in the notice the manner for recording the testimony, but the notice need not be served on the deponent. The deponent learns of the recording method only if the deponent is a party or is informed by a party. Rule 30(b)(3) permits another party to designate an additional method of recording with prior notice to the deponent and the other parties. The deponent thus has notice of the recording method when an additional method is designated. This amendment completes the notice provisions to ensure that a nonparty deponent has notice of the recording method when the recording method is described only in the deposition notice.

A subpoenaed witness does not have a right to refuse to proceed with a deposition due to objections to the manner of recording. But under rare circumstances, a nonparty witness might have a ground for seeking a protective order under Rule 26(c) with regard to the manner of recording or the use of the deposition if recorded in a certain manner. Should such a witness not learn of the manner of recording until the deposition begins, undesirable delay or complication might result. Advance notice of the recording method affords an opportunity to raise such protective issues.

Other changes are made to conform Rule 45(a)(2) to current style conventions.

2006 Amendments

Rule 45 is amended to conform the provisions for subpoenas to changes in other discovery rules, largely related to discovery of electronically stored information. Rule 34 is amended to provide in greater detail for the production of electronically stored information. Rule 45(a)(1)(C) is amended to recognize that electronically stored information, as defined in Rule 34(a), can also be sought by subpoena. Like Rule 34(b), Rule 45(a)(1) is amended to provide that the subpoena can designate a form or forms for production of electronic data. Rule 45(c)(2) is amended, like Rule 34(b), to authorize the person served with a subpoena to object to the requested form or forms. In addition, as under Rule 34(b), Rule 45(d)(1)(B) is amended to provide that if the subpoena does not specify the form or forms for electronically stored information, the person served with the subpoena must produce electronically stored information in a form or forms in which it is usually maintained or in a form or forms that are reasonably usable. Rule 45(d)(1)(C) is added to provide that the person producing electronically stored information should not have to produce the same information in more than one form unless so ordered by the court for good cause.

As with discovery of electronically stored information from parties, complying with a subpoena for such information may impose burdens on the responding person. Rule 45(c) provides protection against undue impositions on nonparties. For example, Rule 45(c)(1) directs that a party serving a subpoena "shall take reasonable steps to avoid imposing undue burden or expense on a person subject to the subpoena," and Rule 45(c)(2)(B) permits the person served with the subpoena to object to it and directs that an order requiring compliance "shall protect a person who is neither a party nor a party's officer from significant expense resulting from" compliance. Rule 45(d)(1)(D) is added to provide that the responding person need not provide discovery of electronically stored information from sources the party identifies as not reasonably accessible, unless the court orders such discovery for good cause, considering the limitations of Rule 26(b)(2)(C), on terms that protect a nonparty against significant expense. A parallel provision is added to Rule 26(b)(2).

Rule 45(a)(1)(B) is also amended, as is Rule 34(a), to provide that a subpoena is available to permit testing and sampling as well as inspection and copying. As in Rule 34, this change recognizes that on occasion the opportunity to perform testing or sampling may be important, both for documents and for electronically stored information. Because testing or sampling may present particular issues of burden or intrusion for the person served with the subpoena, however, the protective provisions of Rule 45(c) should be enforced with vigilance when such demands are made. Inspection or testing of certain types of electronically stored information or of a person's electronic information system may raise issues of confidentiality or privacy. The addition of sampling and testing to Rule 45(a) with regard to documents and electronically stored information is not meant to create a routine right of direct access to a person's electronic information system, although such access might be justified in some circumstances. Courts should guard against undue intrusiveness resulting from inspecting or testing such systems.

Rule 45(d)(2) is amended, as is Rule 26(b)(5), to add a procedure for assertion of privilege or of protection as trial-preparation materials after production. The receiving party may submit the information to the court for resolution of the privilege claim, as under Rule 26(b)(5)(B).

Other minor amendments are made to conform the rule to the changes described above.

2007 Amendment

The language of Rule 45 has been amended as part of the general restyling of the Civil Rules to make them more easily understood and to make style and terminology consistent throughout the rules. These changes are intended to be stylistic only.

The reference to discovery of "books" in former Rule 45(a)(1)(C) was deleted to achieve consistent expression throughout the discovery rules. Books remain a proper subject of discovery.

Former Rule 45(b)(1) required "prior notice" to each party of any commanded production of documents and things or inspection of premises. Courts have agreed that notice must be given "prior" to the return date, and have tended to converge on an interpretation that requires notice to the parties before the subpoena is served on the person commanded to produce or permit inspection. That interpretation is adopted in amended Rule 45(b)(1) to give clear notice of general present practice.

The language of former Rule 45(d)(2) addressing the manner of asserting privilege is replaced by adopting the wording of Rule 26(b)(5). The same meaning is better expressed in the same words.

Rule 46. Objecting to a Ruling or Order

A formal exception to a ruling or order is unnecessary. When the ruling or order is requested or made, a party need only state the action that it wants the court to take or objects to, along with the grounds for the request or objection. Failing to object does not prejudice a party who had no opportunity to do so when the ruling or order was made.

(Amended March 2, 1987, effective August 1, 1987; April 30, 2007, effective December 1, 2007.)

ADVISORY COMMITTEE NOTES

1937 Adoption

Abolition of formal exceptions is often provided by statute. See Ill.Rev.Stat. (1937), ch. 110, § 204; Neb.Comp.Stat. (1929) § 20–1139; N.M.Stat.Ann. (Courtright, 1929) § 105–830; 2 N.D.Comp.Laws Ann. (1913) § 7653; Ohio Code Ann. (Throckmorton, 1936) § 11560; 1 S.D.Comp.Laws (1929) § 2542; Utah Rev.Stat.Ann. (1933) §§ 104–39–2, 104–24–18; Va.Rules of Court, Rule 22, 163 Va. v. xii (1935); Wis.Stat. (1935) § 270.39. Compare N.Y.C.P.A. (1937) §§ 583, 445, and 446, all as amended by L.1936, ch. 915. Rule 51 deals with objections to the court's instructions to the jury.

U.S.C., Title 28, [former] § 776 (Bill of exceptions; authentication; signing of by judge) and [former] § 875 (Review of findings in cases tried without a jury) are superseded insofar as they provide for formal exceptions, and a bill of exceptions.

1987 Amendment

The amendments are technical. No substantive change is intended.

2007 Amendments

The language of Rule 46 has been amended as part of the general restyling of the Civil Rules to make them more easily understood and to make style and terminology consistent throughout the rules. These changes are intended to be stylistic only.

Rule 47. Selecting Jurors

(a) **Examining Jurors.** The court may permit the parties or their attorneys to examine prospective jurors or may itself do so. If the court examines the jurors, it must permit the parties or their attorneys to make any further inquiry it considers proper, or must itself ask any of their additional questions it considers proper.

(b) **Peremptory Challenges.** The court must allow the number of peremptory challenges provided by 28 U.S.C. § 1870.

(c) **Excusing a Juror.** During trial or deliberation, the court may excuse a juror for good cause.

(Amended February 28, 1966, effective July 1, 1966; April 30, 1991, effective December 1, 1991; April 30, 2007, effective December 1, 2007.)

ADVISORY COMMITTEE NOTES

1937 Adoption

Note to Subdivision (a). This permits a practice found very useful by Federal trial judges. For an example of a state practice in which the examination by the court is supplemented by further inquiry by counsel, see Rule 27 of the Code of Rules for the District Courts of Minnesota, 186 Minn. xxxiii (1932), 3 Minn.Stat. (Mason, Supp.1936) Appendix 4, p. 1062.

Note to Subdivision (b). The provision for an alternate juror is one often found in modern state codes. See N.C.Code (1935) § 2330(a); Ohio Gen.Code Ann. (Page, Supp.1926–1935) § 11419–47; Pa.Stat.Ann. (Purdon, Supp. 1936) Title 17, § 1153; compare U.S.C., Title 28, [former] § 417a (Alternate jurors in criminal trials); 1 N.J.Rev.Stat. (1937) 2:91A–1, 2:91A–2, 2:91A–3.

Provisions for qualifying, drawing, and challenging of jurors are found in U.S.C., Title 28:

§ 411 [now 1861] (Qualifications and exemptions)

§ 412 [now 1864] (Manner of drawing)

§ 413 [now 1865] (Apportioned in district)

§ 415 [see 1862] (Not disqualified because of race or color)

§ 416 [now 1867] (Venire; service and return)

§ 417 [now 1866] (Talesmen for petit jurors)

§ 418 [now 1866] (Special juries)

§ 423 [now 1869] (Jurors not to serve more than once a year)

§ 424 [now 1870] (Challenges)

and D.C.Code (1930) Title 18, §§ 341 to 360 (Juries and Jury Commission) and Title 6, § 366 (Peremptory challenges).

1966 Amendment

The revision of this subdivision brings it into line with the amendment of Rule 24(c) of this Federal Rules of Criminal Procedure. That rule previously allowed four alternate jurors, as contrasted with the two allowed in civil cases, and the amendments increase the number to a maximum of six in all cases. The Advisory Committee's Note to amended Criminal Rule 24(c) points to experience demonstrating that four alternates may not be enough in some lengthy criminal trials; and the same may be said of civil trials. The Note adds:

"The words 'or are found to be' are added to the second sentence to make clear that an alternate juror may be called in the situation where it is first discovered during the trial that a juror was unable or disqualified to perform his duties at the time he was sworn."

1991 Amendment

Subdivision (b). The former provision for alternate jurors is stricken and the institution of the alternate juror abolished.

The former rule reflected the long-standing assumption that a jury would consist of exactly twelve members. It provided for additional jurors to be used as substitutes for jurors who are for any reason excused or disqualified from service after the commencement of the trial. Additional jurors were traditionally designated at the outset of the trial, and excused at the close of the evidence if they had not been promoted to full service on account of the elimination of one of the original jurors.

The use of alternate jurors has been a source of dissatisfaction with the jury system because of the burden it places on alternates who are required to listen to the evidence but denied the satisfaction of participating in its evaluation.

Subdivision (c). This provision makes it clear that the court may in appropriate circumstances excuse a juror during the jury deliberations without causing a mistrial. Sickness, family emergency or juror misconduct that might occasion a mistrial are examples of appropriate grounds for excusing a juror. It is not grounds for the dismissal of a juror that the juror refuses to join with fellow jurors in reaching a unanimous verdict.

2007 Amendments

The language of Rule 47 has been amended as part of the general restyling of the Civil Rules to make them more easily understood and to make style and terminology consistent throughout the rules. These changes are intended to be stylistic only.

Rule 48. Number of Jurors; Verdict

A jury must initially have at least 6 and no more than 12 members, and each juror must participate in the verdict unless excused under Rule 47(c). Unless the parties stipulate otherwise, the verdict must be unanimous and be returned by a jury of at least 6 members.

(Amended April 30, 1991, effective December 1, 1991; April 30, 2007, effective December 1, 2007.)

ADVISORY COMMITTEE NOTES

1937 Adoption

For provisions in state codes, compare Utah Rev.Stat.Ann. (1933) § 48–0–5 (In civil cases parties may agree in open court on lesser number of jurors); 2 Wash.Rev.Stat.Ann. (Remington, 1932) § 323 (Parties may consent to any number of jurors not less than three).

1991 Amendment

The former rule was rendered obsolete by the adoption in many districts of local rules establishing six as the standard size for a civil jury.

It appears that the minimum size of a jury consistent with the Seventh Amendment is six. *Cf. Ballew v. Georgia*, 435 U.S. 223 (1978) (holding that a conviction based on a jury of less than six is a denial of due process of law). If the parties agree to trial before a smaller jury, a verdict can be taken, but the parties should not other than in exceptional circumstances be encouraged to waive the right to a jury of six, not only because of the constitutional stature of the right, but also because smaller juries are more erratic and less effective in serving to distribute responsibility for the exercise of judicial power.

Because the institution of the alternate juror has been abolished by the proposed revision of Rule 47, it will ordinarily be prudent and necessary, in order to provide for sickness or disability among jurors, to seat more than six jurors. The use of jurors in excess of six increases the representativeness of the jury and harms no interest of a party. *Ray v. Parkside Surgery Center*, 13 F.R.Serv. 585 (6th Cir.1989).

If the court takes the precaution of seating a jury larger than six, an illness occurring during the deliberation period will not result in a mistrial, as it did formerly, because all seated jurors will participate in the verdict and a sufficient number will remain to render a unanimous verdict of six or more.

In exceptional circumstances, as where a jury suffers depletions during trial and deliberation that are greater than can reasonably be expected, the parties may agree to be bound by a verdict rendered by fewer than six jurors. The court should not, however, rely upon the availability of such an agreement, for the use of juries smaller than six is problematic for reasons fully explained in *Ballew v. Georgia*, supra.

2007 Amendments

The language of Rule 48 has been amended as part of the general restyling of the Civil Rules to make them more easily understood and to make style and terminology consistent throughout the rules. These changes are intended to be stylistic only.

Rule 49. Special Verdict; General Verdict and Questions

(a) Special Verdict.

(1) ***In General.*** The court may require a jury to return only a special verdict in the form of a special written finding on each issue of fact. The court may do so by:

(A) submitting written questions susceptible of a categorical or other brief answer;

(B) submitting written forms of the special findings that might properly be made under the pleadings and evidence; or

(C) using any other method that the court considers appropriate.

(2) ***Instructions.*** The court must give the instructions and explanations necessary to enable the jury to make its findings on each submitted issue.

(3) ***Issues Not Submitted.*** A party waives the right to a jury trial on any issue of fact raised by the pleadings or evidence but not submitted to the jury unless, before the jury retires, the party demands its submission to the jury. If the party does not demand submission, the court may make a finding on the issue. If the court makes no finding, it is considered to have made a finding consistent with its judgment on the special verdict.

(b) General Verdict with Answers to Written Questions.

(1) ***In General.*** The court may submit to the jury forms for a general verdict, together with written questions on one or more issues of fact that the jury must decide. The court must give the instructions and explanations necessary to enable the jury to render a general verdict and answer the questions in writing, and must direct the jury to do both.

(2) ***Verdict and Answers Consistent.*** When the general verdict and the answers are consistent, the court must approve, for entry under Rule 58, an appropriate judgment on the verdict and answers.

(3) ***Answers Inconsistent with the Verdict.*** When the answers are consistent with each other but one or more is inconsistent with the general verdict, the court may:

(A) approve, for entry under Rule 58, an appropriate judgment according to the answers, notwithstanding the general verdict;

(B) direct the jury to further consider its answers and verdict; or

(C) order a new trial.

(4) ***Answers Inconsistent with Each Other and the Verdict.*** When the answers are inconsistent with each other and one or more is also inconsistent with the general verdict, judgment must not be entered; instead, the court must direct the jury to further consider its answers and verdict, or must order a new trial.

(Amended January 21, 1963, effective July 1, 1963; March 2, 1987, effective August 1, 1987; April 30, 2007, effective December 1, 2007.)

ADVISORY COMMITTEE NOTES

1937 Adoption

The Federal courts are not bound to follow state statutes authorizing or requiring the court to ask a jury to find a special verdict or to answer interrogatories. *Victor American Fuel Co. v. Peccarich*, 209 Fed. 568 (C.C.A.8th, 1913), cert. den. 232 U.S. 727, 34 S.Ct. 603, 58 L.Ed. 817 (1914); *Spokane and I.E.R. Co. v. Campbell*, 217 Fed. 518 (C.C.A.9th, 1914), affd. 241 U.S. 497, 36 S.Ct. 683, 60 L.Ed. 1125 (1916); Simkins, *Federal Practice* (1934) § 186. The power of a territory to adopt by statute the practice under Subdivision (b) has been sustained. *Walker v. New Mexico and Southern Pacific R.R.*, 165 U.S. 593, 17 S.Ct. 421, 41 L.Ed. 837 (1897); *Southwestern Brewery and Ice Co. v. Schmidt*, 226 U.S. 162, 33 S.Ct. 68, 57 L.Ed. 170 (1912).

Compare Wis.Stat. (1935) §§ 270.27, 270.28 and 270.30; Green, *A New Development in Jury Trial* (1927), 13 A.B.A.J. 715; *Morgan, A Brief History of Special Verdicts and Special Interrogatories*, 1923, 32 Yale L.J. 575.

The provisions of U.S.C., Title 28, [former] § 400(3) (now §§ 2201, 2202) (Declaratory judgments authorized; procedure) permitting the submission of issues of fact to a jury are covered by this rule.

1963 Amendment

This amendment conforms to the amendment of Rule 58. See the Advisory Committee's Note to Rule 58, as amended.

1987 Amendment

The amendments are technical. No substantive change is intended.

2007 Amendments

The language of Rule 49 has been amended as part of the general restyling of the Civil Rules to make them more easily understood and to make style and terminology consistent throughout the rules. These changes are intended to be stylistic only.

Rule 50. Judgment as a Matter of Law in a Jury Trial; Related Motion for a New Trial; Conditional Ruling

(a) Judgment as a Matter of Law.

(1) ***In General.*** If a party has been fully heard on an issue during a jury trial and the court finds that a reasonable jury would not have a legally sufficient evidentiary basis to find for the party on that issue, the court may:

(A) resolve the issue against the party; and

(B) grant a motion for judgment as a matter of law against the party on a claim or defense that, under the controlling law, can be maintained or defeated only with a favorable finding on that issue.

(2) ***Motion.*** A motion for judgment as a matter of law may be made at any time before the case is submitted to the jury. The motion must specify the judgment sought and the law and facts that entitle the movant to the judgment.

(b) Renewing the Motion After Trial; Alternative Motion for a New Trial. If the court does not grant a motion for judgment as a matter of law made under Rule 50(a), the court is considered to have submitted the action to the jury subject to the court's later deciding the legal questions raised by the motion. No later than 10 days after the entry of judgment—or if the motion addresses a jury issue not decided by a verdict, no later than 10 days after the jury was discharged—the movant may file a renewed motion for judgment as a matter of law and may include an alternative or joint request for a new trial under Rule 59. In ruling on the renewed motion, the court may:

(1) allow judgment on the verdict, if the jury returned a verdict;

(2) order a new trial; or

(3) direct the entry of judgment as a matter of law.

(c) Granting the Renewed Motion; Conditional Ruling on a Motion for a New Trial.

(1) ***In General.*** If the court grants a renewed motion for judgment as a matter of law, it must also conditionally rule on any motion for a new trial by determining whether a new trial should be granted if the judgment is later vacated or reversed. The court must state the grounds for conditionally granting or denying the motion for a new trial.

(2) ***Effect of a Conditional Ruling.*** Conditionally granting the motion for a new trial does not affect the judgment's finality; if the judgment is reversed, the new trial must proceed unless the appellate court orders otherwise. If the motion for a new trial is conditionally denied, the appellee may assert error in that denial; if the judgment is reversed, the case must proceed as the appellate court orders.

(d) Time for a Losing Party's New-Trial Motion. Any motion for a new trial under Rule 59 by a party against whom judgment as a matter of law is rendered must be filed no later than 10 days after the entry of the judgment.

(e) Denying the Motion for Judgment as a Matter of Law; Reversal on Appeal. If the court denies the motion for judgment as a matter of law, the prevailing party may, as appellee, assert grounds entitling it to a new trial should the appellate court conclude that the trial court erred in denying the motion. If the appellate court reverses the judgment, it may order a new trial, direct the trial court to determine whether a new trial should be granted, or direct the entry of judgment.

(Amended January 21, 1963, effective July 1, 1963; March 2, 1987, effective August 1, 1987; April 30, 1991, effective December 1, 1991; April 22, 1993, effective December 1, 1993; April 27, 1995, effective December 1, 1995; April 12, 2006, effective December 1, 2006; April 30, 2007, effective December 1, 2007.)

ADVISORY COMMITTEE NOTES

1937 Adoption

Note to Subdivision (a). The present federal rule is changed to the extent that the formality of an express reservation of rights against waiver is no longer necessary. See *Sampliner v. Motion Picture Patents Co.,* 41 S.Ct. 79, 254 U.S. 233, 65 L.Ed. 240 (1920); *Union Indemnity Co. v. United States,* 74 F.2d 645 (C.C.A. 6th, 1935). The requirement that specific grounds for the motion for a directed verdict must be stated settles a conflict in the federal cases. See Simkins, *Federal Practice* (1934) § 189.

Note to Subdivision (b). For comparable state practice upheld under the conformity act, see *Baltimore and Carolina Line v. Redman,* 55 S.Ct. 890, 295 U.S. 654, 79 L.Ed. 1636 (1935); compare *Slocum v. New York Life Ins. Co.,* 33 S.Ct. 523, 228 U.S. 364, 57 L.Ed. 879, Ann.Cas.1914D, 1029 (1913).

See *Northern Ry. Co. v. Page,* 47 S.Ct. 491, 274 U.S. 65, 71 L.Ed. 929 (1927), following the Massachusetts practice of alternative verdicts, explained in Thorndike, *Trial by Jury in United States Courts,* 26 Harv.L.Rev. 732 (1913). See also Thayer, *Judicial Administration,* 63 U. of Pa.L.Rev. 585, 600–601, and note 32 (1915); Scott, *Trial by Jury and the Reform of Civil Procedure,* 31 Harv.L.Rev. 669, 685 (1918); Comment, 34 Mich.L.Rev. 93, 98 (1935).

1963 Amendment

Subdivision (a). The practice, after the court has granted a motion for a directed verdict, of requiring the jury to express assent to a verdict they did not reach by their own deliberations serves no useful purpose and may give offense to the members of the jury. See 2B Barron & Holtzoff, *Federal Practice & Procedure* § 1072, at 367 (Wright ed. 1961); Blume, *Origin and Development of the Directed Verdict,* 48 Mich.L.Rev. 555, 582–85, 589–90 (1950). The final sentence of the subdivision, added by amendment, provides that the court's order granting a motion for a directed verdict is effective in itself, and that no action need be taken by the foreman or other members of the jury. See Ariz. R.Civ.P. 50(c); cf. Fed.R.Crim.P. 29(a). No change is intended in the standard to be applied in deciding the motion. To assure this interpretation, and in the interest of simplicity, the traditional term, "directed verdict," is retained.

Subdivision (b). A motion for judgment notwithstanding the verdict will not lie unless it was preceded by a motion for a directed verdict made at the close of all the evidence.

The amendment of the second sentence of this subdivision sets the time limit for making the motion for judgment n.o.v.

at 10 days after the entry of judgment, rather than 10 days after the reception of the verdict. Thus the time provision is made consistent with that contained in Rule 59(b) (time for motion for new trial) and Rule 52(b) (time for motion to amend findings by the court).

Subdivision (c) deals with the situation where a party joins a motion for a new trial with his motion for judgment n.o.v., or prays for a new trial in the alternative, and the motion for judgment n.o.v. is granted. The procedure to be followed in making rulings on the motion for the new trial, and the consequences of the rulings thereon, were partly set out in *Montgomery Ward & Co. v. Duncan,* 311 U.S. 243, 253, 61 S.Ct. 189, 85 L.Ed. 147 (1940), and have been further elaborated in later cases. See *Cone v. West Virginia Pulp & Paper Co.,* 330 U.S. 212, 67 S.Ct. 752, 91 L.Ed. 849 (1947); *Globe Liquor Co., Inc. v. San Roman,* 332 U.S. 571, 68 S.Ct. 246, 92 L.Ed. 177 (1948); *Fountain v. Filson,* 336 U.S. 681, 69 S.Ct. 754, 93 L.Ed. 971 (1949); *Johnson v. New York, N.H. & H.R.R. Co.,* 344 U.S. 48, 73 S.Ct. 125, 97 L.Ed. 77 (1952). However, courts as well as counsel have often misunderstood the procedure, and it will be helpful to summarize the proper practice in the text of the rule. The amendments do not alter the effects of a jury verdict or the scope of appellate review.

In the situation mentioned, subdivision (c)(1) requires that the court make a "conditional" ruling on the new-trial motion, i.e., a ruling which goes on the assumption that the motion for judgment n.o.v. was erroneously granted and will be reversed or vacated; and the court is required to state its grounds for the conditional ruling. Subdivision (c)(1) then spells out the consequences of a reversal of the judgment in the light of the conditional ruling on the new-trial motion.

If the motion for new trial has been conditionally granted, and the judgment is reversed, "the new trial shall proceed unless the appellate court has otherwise ordered." The party against whom the judgment n.o.v. was entered below may, as appellant, besides seeking to overthrow that judgment, also attack the conditional grant of the new trial. And the appellate court, if it reverses the judgment n.o.v., may in an appropriate case also reverse the conditional grant of the new trial and direct that judgment be entered on the verdict. See *Bailey v. Slentz,* 189 F.2d 406 (10th Cir. 1951); *Moist Cold Refrigerator Co. v. Lou Johnson Co.,* 249 F.2d 246 (9th Cir. 1957), cert. denied, 356 U.S. 968, 78 S.Ct. 1008, 2 L.Ed.2d 1074 (1958); *Peters v. Smith,* 221 F.2d 721 (3d Cir. 1955); *Dailey v. Timmer,* 292 F.2d 824 (3d Cir. 1961), explaining *Lind v. Schenley Industries, Inc.,* 278 F.2d 79 (3d Cir.), cert. denied, 364 U.S. 835, 81 S.Ct. 58, 5 L.Ed.2d 60 (1960); *Cox v. Pennsylvania R.R.,* 120 A.2d 214 (D.C.Mun. Ct.App.1956); 3 Barron & Holtzoff, *Federal Practice & Procedure* § 1302.1 at 346–47 (Wright ed. 1958); 6 *Moore's Federal Practice* ¶59.16 at 3915 n. 8a (2d ed. 1954).

If the motion for a new trial has been conditionally denied, and the judgment is reversed, "subsequent proceedings shall be in accordance with the order of the appellate court." The party in whose favor judgment n.o.v. was entered below may, as appellee, besides seeking to uphold that judgment, also urge on the appellate court that the trial court committed error in conditionally denying the new trial. The appellee may assert this error in his brief, without taking a cross-appeal. *Cf. Patterson v. Pennsylvania R.R.,* 238 F.2d 645, 650 (6th Cir. 1956); *Hughes v. St. Louis Nat. L. Baseball Club, Inc.,* 359 Mo. 993, 997, 224 S.W.2d 989, 992 (1949). If the appellate court concludes that the judgment cannot stand, but accepts the appellee's contention that there was error in the conditional denial of the new trial, it may order a new trial in lieu of directing the entry of judgment upon the verdict.

Subdivision (c)(2), which also deals with the situation where the trial court has granted the motion for judgment n.o.v., states that the verdict-winner may apply to the trial court for a new trial pursuant to Rule 59 after the judgment n.o.v. has been entered against him. In arguing to the trial court in opposition to the motion for judgment n.o.v., the verdict-winner may, and often will, contend that he is entitled, at the least, to a new trial, and the court has a range of discretion to grant a new trial or (where plaintiff won the verdict) to order a dismissal of the action without prejudice instead of granting judgment n.o.v. See *Cone v. West Virginia Pulp & Paper Co.,* supra, 330 U.S. at 217, 218, 67 S.Ct. at 755, 756, 91 L.Ed. 849. Subdivision (c)(2) is a reminder that the verdict-winner is entitled, even after entry of judgment n.o.v. against him, to move for a new trial in the usual course. If in these circumstances the motion is granted, the judgment is superseded.

In some unusual circumstances, however, the grant of the new-trial motion may be only conditional, and the judgment will not be superseded. See the situation in *Tribble v. Bruin,* 279 F.2d 424 (4th Cir. 1960) (upon a verdict for plaintiff, defendant moves for and obtains judgment n.o.v.; plaintiff moves for a new trial on the ground of inadequate damages; trial court might properly have granted plaintiff's motion, conditional upon reversal of the judgment n.o.v.).

Even if the verdict-winner makes no motion for a new trial, he is entitled upon his appeal from the judgment n.o.v. not only to urge that that judgment should be reversed and judgment entered upon the verdict, but that errors were committed during the trial which at the least entitle him to a new trial.

Subdivision (d) deals with the situation where judgment has been entered on the jury verdict, the motion for judgment n.o.v. and any motion for a new trial having been denied by the trial court. The verdict-winner, as appellee, besides seeking to uphold the judgment may urge upon the appellate court that in case the trial court is found to have erred in entering judgment on the verdict, there are grounds for granting him a new trial instead of directing the entry of judgment for his opponent. In appropriate cases the appellate court is not precluded from itself directing that a new trial be had. See *Weade v. Dichmann, Wright & Pugh, Inc.,* 337 U.S. 801, 69 S.Ct. 1326, 93 L.Ed. 1704 (1949). Nor is it precluded in proper cases from remanding the case for a determination by the trial court as to whether a new trial should be granted. The latter course is advisable where the grounds urged are suitable for the exercise of trial court discretion.

Subdivision (d) does not attempt a regulation of all aspects of the procedure where the motion for judgment n.o.v. and any accompanying motion for a new trial are denied, since the problems have not been fully canvassed in the decisions and the procedure is in some respects still in a formative stage. It is, however, designed to give guidance on certain important features of the practice.

1987 Amendment

The amendments are technical. No substantive change is intended.

1991 Amendment

Subdivision (a). The revision of this subdivision aims to facilitate the exercise by the court of its responsibility to assure the fidelity of its judgment to the controlling law, a responsibility imposed by the Due Process Clause of the Fifth Amendment. *Cf. Galloway v. United States,* 319 U.S. 372 (1943).

The revision abandons the familiar terminology of *direction of verdict* for several reasons. The term is misleading as a description of the relationship between judge and jury. It is also freighted with anachronisms some of which are the subject of the text of former subdivision (a) of this rule that is deleted in this revision. Thus, it should not be necessary to state in the text of this rule that a motion made pursuant to it is not a waiver of the right to jury trial, and only the antiquities of directed verdict practice suggest that it might have been. The term "judgment as a matter of law" is an almost equally familiar term and appears in the text of Rule 56; its use in Rule 50 calls attention to the relationship between the two rules. Finally, the change enables the rule to refer to preverdict and post-verdict motions with a terminology that does not conceal the common identity of two motions made at different times in the proceeding.

If a motion is denominated a motion for directed verdict or for judgment notwithstanding the verdict, the party's error is merely formal. Such a motion should be treated as a motion for judgment as a matter of law in accordance with this rule.

Paragraph (a)(1) articulates the standard for the granting of a motion for judgment as a matter of law. It effects no change in the existing standard. That existing standard was not expressed in the former rule, but was articulated in longstanding case law. *See generally* Cooper, *Directions for Directed Verdicts: A Compass for Federal Courts,* 55 MINN.L.REV. 903 (1971). The expressed standard makes clear that action taken under the rule is a performance of the court's duty to assure enforcement of the controlling law and is not an intrusion on any responsibility for factual determinations conferred on the jury by the Seventh Amendment or any other provision of federal law. Because this standard is also used as a reference point for entry of summary judgment under 56(a), it serves to link the two related provisions.

The revision authorizes the court to perform its duty to enter judgment as a matter of law at any time during the trial, as soon as it is apparent that either party is unable to carry a burden of proof that is essential to that party's case. Thus, the second sentence of paragraph (a)(1) authorizes the court to consider a motion for judgment as a matter of law as soon as a party has completed a presentation on a fact essential to that party's case. Such early action is appropriate when economy and expedition will be served. In no event, however, should the court enter judgment against a party who has not been apprised of the materiality of the dispositive fact and been afforded an opportunity to present any available evidence bearing on that fact. In order further to facilitate the exercise of the authority provided by this rule, Rule 16 is also revised to encourage the court to schedule an order of trial that proceeds first with a presentation on an issue that is likely to be dispositive, if such an issue is identified in the course of pretrial. Such scheduling can be appropriate where the court is uncertain whether favorable action should be taken under Rule 56. Thus, the revision affords the court the alternative of denying a motion for summary judgment while scheduling a separate trial of the issue under Rule 42(b) or scheduling the trial to begin with a presentation on that essential fact which the opposing party seems unlikely to be able to maintain.

Paragraph (a)(2) retains the requirement that a motion for judgment be made prior to the close of the trial, subject to renewal after a jury verdict has been rendered. The purpose of this requirement is to assure the responding party an opportunity to cure any deficiency in that party's proof that may have been overlooked until called to the party's attention by a late motion for judgment. Cf. *Farley Transp. Co. v. Santa Fe Trail Transp. Co.,* 786 F.2d 1342 (9th Cir.1986) ("If the moving party is then permitted to make a later attack on the evidence through a motion for judgment notwithstanding the verdict or an appeal, the opposing party may be prejudiced by having lost the opportunity to present additional evidence before the case was submitted to the jury"); *Benson v. Allphin,* 786 F.2d 268 (7th Cir.1986) ("the motion for directed verdict at the close of all the evidence provides the nonmovant an opportunity to do what he can to remedy the deficiencies in his case . . .); *McLaughlin v. The Fellows Gear Shaper Co.,* 4 F.R.Serv.3d 607 (3d Cir.1986) (per Adams, J., dissenting: "This Rule serves important practical purposes in ensuring that neither party is precluded from presenting the most persuasive case possible and in preventing unfair surprise after a matter has been submitted to the jury"). At one time, this requirement was held to be of constitutional stature, being compelled by the Seventh Amendment. Cf. *Slocum v. New York Insurance Co.,* 228 U.S. 364 (1913). But cf. *Baltimore & Carolina Line v. Redman,* 295 U.S. 654 (1935).

The second sentence of paragraph (a)(2) does impose a requirement that the moving party articulate the basis on which a judgment as a matter of law might be rendered. The articulation is necessary to achieve the purpose of the requirement that the motion be made before the case is submitted to the jury, so that the responding party may seek to correct any overlooked deficiencies in the proof. The revision thus alters the result in cases in which courts have used various techniques to avoid the requirement that a motion for a directed verdict be made as a predicate to a motion for judgment notwithstanding the verdict. E.g., *Benson v. Allphin,* 788 F.2d 268 (7th Cir.1986) ("this circuit has allowed something less than a formal motion for directed verdict to preserve a party's right to move for judgment notwithstanding the verdict"). *See generally* 9 WRIGHT & MILLER, FEDERAL PRACTICE AND PROCEDURE § 2537 (1971 and Supp.). The information required with the motion may be supplied by explicit reference to materials and argument previously supplied to the court.

This subdivision deals only with the entry of judgment and not with the resolution of particular factual issues as a matter of law. The court may, as before, properly refuse to instruct a jury to decide an issue if a reasonable jury could on the evidence presented decide that issue in only one way.

Subdivision (b). This provision retains the concept of the former rule that the post-verdict motion is a renewal of an earlier motion made at the close of the evidence. One purpose of this concept was to avoid any question arising under the Seventh Amendment. *Montgomery Ward & Co. v. Duncan*, 311 U.S. 243 (1940). It remains useful as a means of defining the appropriate issue posed by the post-verdict motion. A post-trial motion for judgment can be granted only on grounds advanced in the pre-verdict motion. *E.g., Kutner Buick, Inc. v. American Motors Corp.*, 848 F.2d 614 (3d Cir.1989).

Often it appears to the court or to the moving party that a motion for judgment as a matter of law made at the close of the evidence should be reserved for a post-verdict decision. This is so because a jury verdict for the moving party moots the issue and because a preverdict ruling gambles that a reversal may result in a new trial that might have been avoided. For these reasons, the court may often wisely decline to rule on a motion for judgment as a matter of law made at the close of the evidence, and it is not inappropriate for the moving party to suggest such a postponement of the ruling until after the verdict has been rendered.

In ruling on such a motion, the court should disregard any jury determination for which there is no legally sufficient evidentiary basis enabling a reasonable jury to make it. The court may then decide such issues as a matter of law and enter judgment if all other material issues have been decided by the jury on the basis of legally sufficient evidence, or by the court as a matter of law.

The revised rule is intended for use in this manner with Rule 49. Thus, the court may combine facts established as a matter of law either before trial under Rule 56 or at trial on the basis of the evidence presented with other facts determined by the jury under instructions provided under Rule 49 to support a proper judgment under this rule.

This provision also retains the former requirement that a post-trial motion under the rule must be made within 10 days after entry of a contrary judgment. The renewed motion must be served and filed as provided by Rule 5. A purpose of this requirement is to meet the requirements of F.R.App.P. 4(a)(4).

Subdivision (c). Revision of this subdivision conforms the language to the change in diction set forth in subdivision (a) of this revised rule.

Subdivision (d). Revision of this subdivision conforms the language to that of the previous subdivisions.

1993 Amendments

This technical amendment corrects an ambiguity in the text of the 1991 revision of the rule, which, as indicated in the Notes, was not intended to change the existing standards under which "directed verdicts" could be granted. This amendment makes clear that judgments as a matter of law in jury trials may be entered against both plaintiffs and defendants and with respect to issues or defenses that may not be wholly dispositive of a claim or defense.

1995 Amendments

The only change, other than stylistic, intended by this revision is to prescribe a uniform explicit time for filing of post-judgment motions under this rule—no later than 10 days after entry of the judgment. Previously, there was an inconsistency in the wording of Rules 50, 52, and 59 with respect to whether certain post-judgment motions had to be filed, or merely served, during that period. This inconsistency caused special problems when motions for a new trial were joined with other post-judgment motions. These motions affect the finality of the judgment, a matter often of importance to third persons as well as the parties and the court. The Committee believes that each of these rules should be revised to require filing before end of the 10–day period. Filing is an event that can be determined with certainty from court records. The phrase "no later than" is used—rather than "within"—to include post-judgment motions that sometimes are filed before actual entry of the judgment by the clerk. It should be noted that under Rule 6(a) Saturdays, Sundays, and legal holidays are excluded in measuring the 10–day period, and that under Rule 5 the motions when filed are to contain a certificate of service on other parties.

2006 Amendment

The language of Rule 50(a) has been amended as part of the general restyling of the Civil Rules to make them more easily understood and to make style and terminology consistent throughout the rules. These changes are intended to be stylistic only.

Rule 50(b) is amended to permit renewal of any Rule 50(a) motion for judgment as a matter of law, deleting the requirement that a motion be made at the close of all the evidence. Because the Rule 50(b) motion is only a renewal of the preverdict motion, it can be granted only on grounds advanced in the preverdict motion. The earlier motion informs the opposing party of the challenge to the sufficiency of the evidence and affords a clear opportunity to provide additional evidence that may be available. The earlier motion also alerts the court to the opportunity to simplify the trial by resolving some issues, or even all issues, without submission to the jury. This fulfillment of the functional needs that underlie present Rule 50(b) also satisfies the Seventh Amendment. Automatic reservation of the legal questions raised by the motion conforms to the decision in *Baltimore & Carolina Line v. Redman*, 297 U.S. 654 (1935).

This change responds to many decisions that have begun to move away from requiring a motion for judgment as a matter of law at the literal close of all the evidence. Although the requirement has been clearly established for several decades, lawyers continue to overlook it. The courts are slowly working away from the formal requirement. The amendment establishes the functional approach that courts have been unable to reach under the present rule and makes practice more consistent and predictable.

Many judges expressly invite motions at the close of all the evidence. The amendment is not intended to discourage this useful practice.

Finally, an explicit time limit is added for making a posttrial motion when the trial ends without a verdict or with a verdict that does not dispose of all issues suitable for resolution by verdict. The motion must be made no later than 10 days after the jury was discharged.

2007 Amendments

The language of Rule 50 has been amended as part of the general restyling of the Civil Rules to make them more easily understood and to make style and terminology consistent throughout the rules. These changes are intended to be stylistic only.

Former Rule 50(b) stated that the court reserves ruling on a motion for judgment as a matter of law made at the close of all the evidence "[i]f, for any reason, the court does not grant" the motion. The words "for any reason" reflected the proposition that the reservation is automatic and inescapable. The ruling is reserved even if the court explicitly denies the motion. The same result follows under the amended rule. If the motion is not granted, the ruling is reserved.

Amended Rule 50(e) identifies the appellate court's authority to direct the entry of judgment. This authority was not described in former Rule 50(d), but was recognized in *Weisgram v. Marley Co.*, 528 U.S. 440 (2000), and in *Neely v. Martin K. Eby Construction Company*, 386 U.S. 317 (1967). When Rule 50(d) was drafted in 1963, the Committee Note stated that "[s]ubdivision (d) does not attempt a regulation of all aspects of the procedure where the motion for judgment n.o.v. and any accompanying motion for a new trial are denied * * *." Express recognition of the authority to direct entry of judgment does not otherwise supersede this caution.

Rule 51. Instructions to the Jury; Objections; Preserving a Claim of Error

(a) Requests.

(1) ***Before or at the Close of the Evidence.*** At the close of the evidence or at any earlier reasonable time that the court orders, a party may file and furnish to every other party written requests for the jury instructions it wants the court to give.

(2) ***After the Close of the Evidence.*** After the close of the evidence, a party may:

(A) file requests for instructions on issues that could not reasonably have been anticipated by an earlier time that the court set for requests; and

(B) with the court's permission, file untimely requests for instructions on any issue.

(b) Instructions. The court:

(1) must inform the parties of its proposed instructions and proposed action on the requests before instructing the jury and before final jury arguments;

(2) must give the parties an opportunity to object on the record and out of the jury's hearing before the instructions and arguments are delivered; and

(3) may instruct the jury at any time before the jury is discharged.

(c) Objections.

(1) ***How to Make.*** A party who objects to an instruction or the failure to give an instruction must do so on the record, stating distinctly the matter objected to and the grounds for the objection.

(2) ***When to Make.*** An objection is timely if:

(A) a party objects at the opportunity provided under Rule 51(b)(2); or

(B) a party was not informed of an instruction or action on a request before that opportunity to object, and the party objects promptly after learning that the instruction or request will be, or has been, given or refused.

(d) Assigning Error; Plain Error.

(1) ***Assigning Error.*** A party may assign as error:

(A) an error in an instruction actually given, if that party properly objected; or

(B) a failure to give an instruction, if that party properly requested it and—unless the court rejected the request in a definitive ruling on the record—also properly objected.

(2) ***Plain Error.*** A court may consider a plain error in the instructions that has not been preserved as required by Rule 51(d)(1) if the error affects substantial rights.

(Amended March 2, 1987, effective August 1, 1987; March 27, 2003, effective December 1, 2003; April 30, 2007, effective December 1, 2007.)

ADVISORY COMMITTEE NOTES

1937 Adoption

Supreme Court Rule 8 requires exceptions to the charge of the court to the jury which shall distinctly state the several matters of law in the charge to which exception is taken. Similar provisions appear in the rules of the various Circuit Courts of Appeals.

1987 Amendment

Although Rule 51 in its present form specifies that the court shall instruct the jury only after the arguments of the parties are completed, in some districts (typically those in states where the practice is otherwise) it is common for the parties to stipulate to instruction before the arguments. The purpose of the amendment is to give the court discretion to instruct the jury either before or after argument. Thus, the rule as revised will permit resort to the long-standing federal practice or to an alternative procedure, which has been praised because it gives counsel the opportunity to explain the instructions, argue their application to the facts and thereby give the jury the maximum assistance in determining the issues and arriving at a good verdict on the law and the evidence. As an ancillary benefit, this approach aids counsel by supplying a natural outline so that arguments may be directed to the essential fact issues which the jury must decide. See generally Raymond, *Merits and Demerits of the Missouri System of Instructing Juries*, 5 St. Louis U.L.J. 317 (1959). Moreover, if the court instructs before an argument, counsel then know the precise words the court has chosen and need not speculate as to the words the court will later use in its instructions. Finally, by instructing ahead of argument the court has the attention of the jurors when they are fresh and can give their full attention to the court's instructions. It is more difficult to hold the attention of jurors after lengthy arguments.

2003 Amendments

Rule 51 is revised to capture many of the interpretations that have emerged in practice. The revisions in text will make uniform the conclusions reached by a majority of decisions on each point. Additions also are made to cover some practices that cannot now be anchored in the text of Rule 51.

Scope. Rule 51 governs instructions to the trial jury on the law that governs the verdict. A variety of other instructions cannot practicably be brought within Rule 51. Among these instructions are preliminary instructions to a venire, and cautionary or limiting instructions delivered in immediate response to events at trial.

Requests. Subdivision (a) governs requests. Apart from the plain error doctrine recognized in subdivision (d)(2), a court is not obliged to instruct the jury on issues raised by the evidence unless a party requests an instruction. The revised rule recognizes the court's authority to direct that requests be submitted before trial.

The close-of-the-evidence deadline may come before trial is completed on all potential issues. Trial may be formally bifurcated or may be sequenced in some less formal manner. The close of the evidence is measured by the occurrence of two events: completion of all intended evidence on an identified phase of the trial and impending submission to the jury with instructions.

The risk in directing a pretrial request deadline is that trial evidence may raise new issues or reshape issues the parties thought they had understood. Courts need not insist on pretrial requests in all cases. Even if the request time is set before trial or early in the trial, subdivision (a)(2)(A) permits requests after the close of the evidence to address issues that could not reasonably have been anticipated at the earlier time for requests set by the court.

Subdivision (a)(2)(B) expressly recognizes the court's discretion to act on an untimely request. The most important consideration in exercising the discretion confirmed by subdivision (a)(2)(B) is the importance of the issue to the case—the closer the issue lies to the "plain error" that would be recognized under subdivision (d)(2), the better the reason to give an instruction. The cogency of the reason for failing to make a timely request also should be considered. To be considered under subdivision (a)(2)(B) a request should be made before final instructions and before final jury arguments. What is a "final" instruction and argument depends on the sequence of submitting the case to the jury. If separate portions of the case are submitted to the jury in sequence, the final arguments and final instructions are those made on submitting to the jury the portion of the case addressed by the arguments and instructions.

Instructions. Subdivision (b)(1) requires the court to inform the parties, before instructing the jury and before final jury arguments related to the instruction, of the proposed instructions as well as the proposed action on instruction requests. The time limit is addressed to final jury arguments to reflect the practice that allows interim argument s during trial in complex cases; it may not be feasible to develop final instructions before such interim arguments. It is enough that counsel know of the intended instructions before making final arguments addressed to the issue. If the trial is sequenced or bifurcated, the final arguments addressed to an issue may occur before the close of the entire trial.

Subdivision (b)(2) complements subdivision (b)(1) by carrying forward the opportunity to object established by present Rule 51. It makes explicit the opportunity to object on the record, ensuring a clear memorial of the objection.

Subdivision (b)(3) reflects common practice by authorizing instructions at any time after trial begins and before the jury is discharged.

Objections. Subdivision (c) states the right to object to an instruction or the failure to give an instruction. It carries forward the formula of present Rule 51 requiring that the objection state distinctly the matter objected to and the grounds of the objection, and makes explicit the requirement that the objection be made on the record. The provisions on the time to object make clear that it is timely to object promptly after learning of an instruction or action on a request when the court has not provided advance information as required by subdivision (b)(1). The need to repeat a request by way of objection is continued by new subdivision (d)(1)(B) except where the court made a definitive ruling on the record.

Preserving a claim of error and plain error. Many cases hold that a proper request for a jury instruction is not alone enough to preserve the right to appeal failure to give the instruction. The request must be renewed by objection. This doctrine is appropriate when the court may not have sufficiently focused on the request, or may believe that the request has been granted in substance although in different words. But this doctrine may also prove a trap for the unwary who fail to add an objection after the court has made it clear that the request has been considered and rejected on the merits. Subdivision (d)(1)(B) establishes authority to review the failure to grant a timely request, despite a failure to add an objection, when the court has made a definitive ruling on the record rejecting the request.

Many circuits have recognized that an error not preserved under Rule 51 may be reviewed in exceptional circumstances. The language adopted to capture these decisions in subdivision (d)(2) is borrowed from Criminal Rule 52. Although the language is the same, the context of civil litigation often differs from the context of criminal prosecution; actual application of the plain-error standard takes account of the differences. The Supreme Court has summarized application of Criminal Rule 52 as involving four elements: (1) there must be an error; (2) the error must be plain; (3) the error must affect substantial rights; and (4) the error must seriously affect the fairness, integrity, or public reputation of judicial proceedings. Johnson v. U.S., 520 U.S. 461, 466–467, 469–470 (1997). (The Johnson case quoted the fourth element from its decision in a civil action, U.S. v. Atkinson, 297 U.S. 157, 160 (1936): "In exceptional circumstances, especially in criminal cases, appellate courts, in the public interest, may, of their own motion, notice errors to which no exception has been taken, if the errors are obvious, or if they otherwise substantially affect the fairness, integrity, or public reputation of judicial proceedings.")

The court's duty to give correct jury instructions in a civil action is shaped by at least four factors.

The factor most directly implied by a "plain" error rule is the obviousness of the mistake. The importance of the error is a second major factor. The costs of correcting an error reflect a third factor that is affected by a variety of circumstances. In a case that seems close to the fundamental error line, account also may be taken of the impact a verdict may have on nonparties.

2007 Amendments

The language of Rule 51 has been amended as part of the general restyling of the Civil Rules to make them more easily understood and to make style and terminology consistent throughout the rules. These changes are intended to be stylistic only.

Rule 52. Findings and Conclusions by the Court; Judgment on Partial Findings

(a) Findings and Conclusions.

(1) ***In General.*** In an action tried on the facts without a jury or with an advisory jury, the court must find the facts specially and state its conclusions of law separately. The findings and conclusions may be stated on the record after the close of the evidence or may appear in an opinion or a memorandum of decision filed by the court. Judgment must be entered under Rule 58.

(2) ***For an Interlocutory Injunction.*** In granting or refusing an interlocutory injunction, the court must similarly state the findings and conclusions that support its action.

(3) ***For a Motion.*** The court is not required to state findings or conclusions when ruling on a motion under Rule 12 or 56 or, unless these rules provide otherwise, on any other motion.

(4) ***Effect of a Master's Findings.*** A master's findings, to the extent adopted by the court, must be considered the court's findings.

(5) ***Questioning the Evidentiary Support.*** A party may later question the sufficiency of the evidence supporting the findings, whether or not the party requested findings, objected to them, moved to amend them, or moved for partial findings.

(6) ***Setting Aside the Findings.*** Findings of fact, whether based on oral or other evidence, must not be set aside unless clearly erroneous, and the reviewing court must give due regard to the trial court's opportunity to judge the witnesses' credibility.

(b) Amended or Additional Findings. On a party's motion filed no later than 10 days after the entry of judgment, the court may amend its findings—or make additional findings—and may amend the judgment accordingly. The motion may accompany a motion for a new trial under Rule 59.

(c) Judgment on Partial Findings. If a party has been fully heard on an issue during a nonjury trial and the court finds against the party on that issue, the court may enter judgment against the party on a claim or defense that, under the controlling law, can be maintained or defeated only with a favorable finding on that issue. The court may, however, decline to render any judgment until the close of the evidence. A judgment on partial findings must be supported by findings of fact and conclusions of law as required by Rule 52(a).

(Amended December 27, 1946, effective March 19, 1948; January 21, 1963, effective July 1, 1963; April 28, 1983, effective August 1, 1983; April 29, 1985, effective August 1, 1985; April 30, 1991, effective December 1, 1991; April 22, 1993, effective December 1, 1993; April 27, 1995, effective December 1, 1995; April 30, 2007, effective December 1, 2007.)

ADVISORY COMMITTEE NOTES

1937 Adoption

See [former] Equity Rule 70½, as amended Nov. 25, 1935, (Findings of Fact and Conclusions of Law) and U.S.C., Title 28, [former] § 764 (Opinion, findings, and conclusions in action against United States) which are substantially continued in this rule. The provisions of U.S.C., Title 28, [former] §§ 773 (Trial of issues of fact; by court) and [former] 875 (Review in cases tried without a jury) are superseded in so far as they provide a different method of finding facts and a different method of appellate review. The rule stated in the third sentence of Subdivision (a) accords with the decisions on the scope of the review in modern federal equity practice. It is applicable to all classes of findings in cases tried without a jury whether the finding is of a fact concerning which there was conflict of testimony, or of a fact deduced or inferred from uncontradicted testimony. See *Silver King Coalition Mines Co. v. Silver King Consolidated Mining Co.*, C.C.A.8, 1913, 204 F. 166, certiorari denied 33 S.Ct. 1051, 229 U.S. 624, 57 L.Ed. 1356; *Warren v. Keep*, 1894, 15 S.Ct. 83, 155 U.S. 265, 39 L.Ed. 144; *Furrer v. Ferris*, 1892, 12 S.Ct. 821, 145 U.S. 132, 36 L.Ed. 649; *Tilghman v. Proctor*, 1888, 8 S.Ct. 894, 125 U.S. 136, 149, 31 L.Ed. 664; *Kimberly v. Arms*, 1889, 9 S.Ct. 355, 129 U.S. 512, 524, 32 L.Ed. 764. Compare *Kaeser & Blair Inc. v. Merchants' Ass'n*, C.C.A.6, 1933, 64 F.2d 575, 576; *Dunn v. Trefry*, C.C.A.1, 1919, 260 F. 147.

In the following states findings of fact are required in all cases tried without a jury (waiver by the parties being permitted as indicated at the end of the listing): Arkansas, Civ.Code (Crawford, 1934) § 364; California, Code Civ.Proc. (Deering, 1937) §§ 632, 634; Colorado, 1 Stat.Ann. (1935) Code Civ.Proc. §§ 232, 291 (in actions before referees or for possession of and damages to land); Connecticut, Gen.Stats. §§ 5660, 5664; Idaho, 1 Code Ann. (1932) §§ 7–302 through 7–305; Massachusetts (equity cases), 2 Gen.Laws (Ter.Ed., 1932) ch. 214, § 23; Minnesota, 2 Stat. (Mason, 1927) § 9311; Nevada, 4 Comp.Laws (Hillyer, 1929) §§ 8783–8784; New Jersey, Sup.Ct.Rule 113, 2 N.J.Misc. 1197, 1239 (1924); New

Mexico, Stat.Ann. (Courtright, 1929) §§ 105–813; North Carolina, Code (1935) § 569; North Dakota, 2 Comp.Laws Ann. (1913) § 7641; Oregon, 2 Code Ann. (1930) §§ 2–502; South Carolina, Code (Michie, 1932) § 649; South Dakota, 1 Comp. Laws (1929) §§ 2525–2526; Utah, Rev.Stat.Ann. (1933) §§ 104–26–2, 104–26–3; Vermont (where jury trial waived), Pub.Laws (1933) § 2069; Washington, 2 Rev.Stat.Ann. (Remington, 1932) § 367; Wisconsin, Stat. (1935) § 270.33. The parties may waive this requirement for findings in California, Idaho, North Dakota, Nevada, New Mexico, Utah, and South Dakota.

In the following states the review of findings of fact in all non-jury cases, including jury waived cases, is assimilated to the equity review: Alabama, Code Ann. (Michie, 1928) §§ 9498, 8599; California, Code Civ.Proc. (Derring, 1937) § 956a; but see 20 Calif.Law Rev. 171 (1932); Colorado, *Johnson v. Kountze,* 1895, 43 P. 445, 21 Colo. 486, semble; Illinois, *Baker v. Hinricks,* 1934, 194 N.E. 284, 359 Ill. 138; *Weininger v. Metropolitan Fire Ins. Co.,* 1935, 195 N.E. 420, 359 Ill. 584, 98 A.L.R. 169; Minnesota, *State Bank of Gibbon v. Walter,* 1926, 208 N.W. 423, 167 Minn. 37; *Waldron v. Page,* 1934, 253 N.W. 894, 191 Minn. 302; New Jersey N.J.S.A. 2:27–241, 2:27–363, as interpreted in *Bussy v. Hatch,* 1920, 111 A. 546, 95 N.J.L. 56; New York, *York Mortgage Corporation v. Clotar Const. Corp.,* 1930, 172 N.E. 265, 254 N.Y. 128; North Dakota, Comp.Laws Ann. (1913) § 7846, as amended by N.D.Laws 1933, c. 208; *Milnor Holding Co. v. Holt,* 1933, 248 N.W. 315, 63 N.D. 362, 370; Oklahoma, *Wichita Mining and Improvement Co. v. Hale,* 1908, 94 P. 530, 20 Okl. 159; South Dakota, *Randall v. Burk Township,* 4 S.D. 337, 57 N.W. 4 (1893); Texas, *Custard v. Flowers,* 1929, 14 S.W.2d 109; Utah, Rev.Stat.Ann. (1933) § 104–41–5; Vermont, *Roberge v. Troy,* 1933, 163 A. 770, 105 Vt. 134; Washington, 2 Rev.Stat.Ann. (Remington, 1932) §§ 309–316; *McCullough v. Puget Sound Realty Associates,* 1913, 136 Pac. 1146, 76 Wash. 700, but see *Cornwall v. Anderson,* 1915, 148 P. 1, 85 Wash. 369; West Virginia, *Kinsey v. Carr,* 1906, 55 S.E. 1004, 60 W.Va. 449, semble; Wisconsin, Stat. (1935) § 251.09; *Campbell v. Sutliff,* 1927, 214 N.W. 374, 193 Wis. 370; *Gessler v. Erwin Co.,* 1924, 193 N.W. 303, 182 Wis. 315.

For examples of an assimilation of the review of findings of fact in cases tried without a jury to the review at law as made in several states, see Clark and Stone, *Review of Findings of Fact,* 4 U. of Chi.L.Rev. 190, 215 (1937).

1946 Amendment

Note to Subdivision (a). The amended rule makes clear that the requirement for findings of fact and conclusions of law thereon applies in a case with an advisory jury. This removes an ambiguity in the rule as originally stated, but carries into effect what has been considered its intent. 3 *Moore's Federal Practice,* 1938, 3119. *Hurwitz v. Hurwitz,* 1943, 136 F.2d 796, 78 U.S.App.D.C. 66.

The two sentences added at the end of Rule 52(a) eliminate certain difficulties which have arisen concerning findings and conclusions. The first of the two sentences permits findings of fact and conclusions of law to appear in an opinion or memorandum of decision. See, e.g., *United States v. One 1941 Ford Sedan,* S.D.Tex.1946, 65 F.Supp. 84. Under original Rule 52(a) some courts have expressed the view that findings and conclusions could not be incorporated in an opinion. *Detective Comics, Inc. v. Bruns Publications,* S.D.N.Y.1939, 28 F.Supp. 399; *Pennsylvania Co. for Insurance on Lives & Granting Annuities v. Cincinnati & L.E.R. Co.,* S.D.Ohio 1941, 43 F.Supp. 5; *United States v. Aluminum Co. of America,* S.D.N.Y.1941, 2 F.R.D. 224, 5 Fed. Rules Serv. 52a.11, Case 3; see also s.c., 44 F.Supp. 97. But, to the contrary, see *Wellman v. United States,* D.Mass.1938, 25 F.Supp. 868; *Cook v. United States,* D.Mass.1939, 26 F.Supp. 253; *Proctor v. White,* D.Mass.1939, 28 F.Supp. 161; *Green Valley Creamery, Inc. v. United States,* C.C.A.1, 1939, 108 F.2d 342. See also *Matton Oil Transfer Corp. v. The Dynamic,* C.C.A.2, 1941, 123 F.2d 999; *Carter Coal Co. v. Litz,* C.C.A.4, 1944, 140 F.2d 934; *Woodruff v. Heiser,* C.C.A.10, 1945, 150 F.2d 869; *Coca Cola Co. v. Busch,* Pa.1943, 7 Fed. Rules Serv. 59b.2, Case 4; Oglebay, *Some Developments in Bankruptcy Law,* 1944, 18 J. of Nat'l Ass'n of Ref. 68, 69. Findings of fact aid in the process of judgment and in defining for future cases the precise limitations of the issues and the determination thereon. Thus they not only aid the appellate court on review, *Hurwitz v. Hurwitz,* App.D.C.1943, 136 F.2d 796, 78 U.S.App.D.C. 66, but they are an important factor in the proper application of the doctrines of res judicata and estoppel by judgment. Nordbye, *Improvements in Statement of Findings of Fact and Conclusions of Law,* 1 F.R.D. 25, 26–27; *United States v. Forness,* C.C.A.2, 1942, 125 F.2d 928, certiorari denied 1942, 62 S.Ct. 1293, 316 U.S. 694, 86 L.Ed. 1764. These findings should represent the judge's own determination and not the long, often argumentative statements of successful counsel. *United States v. Forness,* supra; *United States v. Crescent Amusement Co.,* 1944, 1945, 65 S.Ct. 254, 323 U.S. 173, 89 L.Ed. 160. Consequently, they should be a part of the judge's opinion and decision, either stated therein or stated separately. *Matton Oil Transfer Corp. v. The Dynamic,* supra. But the judge need only make brief, definite, pertinent findings and conclusions upon the contested matters; there is no necessity for over-elaboration of detail or particularization of facts. *United States v. Forness,* supra; *United States v. Crescent Amusement Co.,* supra. See also *Petterson Lighterage & Towing Corp. v. New York Central R. Co.,* C.C.A.2, 1942, 126 F.2d 992; *Brown Paper Mill Co., Inc. v. Irwin,* C.C.A.8, 1943, 134 F.2d 337; *Allen Bradley Co. v. Local Union No. 3, I.B.E.W.,* C.C.A.2, 1944, 145 F.2d 215, reversed on other grounds 65 S.Ct. 1533, 325 U.S. 797; *Young v. Murphy, Ohio* 1946, 9 Fed.Rules Serv. 52a.11, Case 2.

The last sentence of Rule 52(a) as amended will remove any doubt that findings and conclusions are unnecessary upon decision of a motion, particularly one under Rule 12 or Rule 56, except as provided in amended Rule 41(b). As so holding, see *Thomas v. Peyser,* App.D.C.1941, 118 F.2d 369; *Schad v. Twentieth Century-Fox Corp.,* C.C.A.3, 1943, 136 F.2d 991; *Prudential Ins. Co. of America v. Goldstein,* N.Y.1942, 43 F.Supp. 767; *Somers Coal Co. v. United States,* N.D.Ohio 1942, 2 F.R.D. 532, 6 Fed.Rules Serv. 52a.1, Case 1; *Pen-Ken Oil & Gas Corp. v. Warfield Natural Gas Co.,* E.D.Ky.1942, 2 F.R.D. 355, 5 Fed. Rules Serv. 52a.1, Case 3; also Commentary, *Necessity of Findings of Fact,* 1941, 4 Fed. Rules Serv. 936.

1963 Amendment

This amendment conforms to the amendment of Rule 58. See the Advisory Committee's Note to Rule 58, as amended.

1983 Amendment

Rule 52(a) has been amended to revise its penultimate sentence to provide explicitly that the district judge may make the findings of fact and conclusions of law required in nonjury cases orally. Nothing in the prior text of the rule forbids this practice, which is widely utilized by district judges. See Christensen, *A Modest Proposal for Immeasurable Improvement,* 64 A.B.A.J. 693 (1978). The objective is to lighten the burden on the trial court in preparing findings in nonjury cases. In addition, the amendment should reduce the number of published district court opinions that embrace written findings.

1985 Amendment

Rule 52(a) has been amended (1) to avoid continued confusion and conflicts among the circuits as to the standard of appellate review of findings of fact by the court, (2) to eliminate the disparity between the standard of review as literally stated in Rule 52(a) and the practice of some courts of appeals, and (3) to promote nationwide uniformity. See Note, *Rule 52(a): Appellate Review of Findings of Fact Based on Documentary or Undisputed Evidence,* 49 Va. L.Rev. 506, 536 (1963).

Some courts of appeal have stated that when a trial court's findings do not rest on demeanor evidence and evaluation of a witness' credibility, there is no reason to defer to the trial court's findings and the appellate court more readily can find them to be clearly erroneous. See, e.g., *Marcum v. United States,* 621 F.2d 142, 144–45 (5th Cir.1980). Others go further, holding that appellate review may be had without application of the "clearly erroneous" test since the appellate court is in as good a position as the trial court to review a purely documentary record. See, *e.g., Atari, Inc. v. North American Philips Consumer Electronics Corp.,* 672 F.2d 607, 614 (7th Cir.), cert. denied, 459 U.S. 880 (1982); *Lydle v. United States,* 635 F.2d 763, 765 n. 1 (6th Cir.1981); *Swanson v. Baker Indus., Inc.,* 615 F.2d 479, 483 (8th Cir.1980); *Taylor v. Lombard,* 606 F.2d 371, 372 (2d Cir.1979), cert. denied, 445 U.S. 946 (1980); *Jack Kahn Music Co. v. Baldwin Piano & Organ Co.,* 604 F.2d 755, 758 (2d Cir.1979); *John R. Thompson Co. v. United States,* 477 F.2d 164, 167 (7th Cir.1973).

A third group has adopted the view that the "clearly erroneous" rule applies in all nonjury cases even when findings are based solely on documentary evidence or on inferences from undisputed facts. See, *e.g., Maxwell v. Sumner,* 673 F.2d 1031, 1036 (9th Cir.), *cert. denied,* 459 U.S. 976 (1982); *United States v. Texas Education Agency,* 647 F.2d 504, 506–07 (5th Cir.1981), *cert. denied,* 454 U.S. 1143 (1982); *Constructora Maza, Inc. v. Banco de Ponce,* 616 F.2d 573, 576 (1st Cir.1980); *In re Sierra Trading Corp.,* 482 F.2d 333, 337 (10th Cir.1973); *Case v. Morrisette,* 475 F.2d 1300, 1306–07 (D.C.Cir.1973).

The commentators also disagree as to the proper interpretation of the Rule. *Compare* Wright, *The Doubtful Omniscience of Appellate Courts,* 41 Minn.L.Rev. 751, 769–70 (1957) (language and intent of Rule support view that "clearly erroneous" test should apply to all forms of evidence), *and* 9 C. Wright & A. Miller, *Federal Practice and Procedure: Civil § 2587,* at 740 (1971) (language of the Rule is clear), *with* 5A J. Moore, *Federal Practice* ¶ 52.04, 2687–88 (2d ed. 1982) (Rule as written supports broader review of findings based on non-demeanor testimony).

The Supreme Court has not clearly resolved the issue. See, *Bose Corp. v. Consumers Union of United States, Inc.,* 466 U.S. 485, 104 S.Ct. 1949, 1958 (1984); *Pullman Standard v. Swint,* 456 U.S. 273, 293 (1982); *United States v. General Motors Corp.,* 384 U.S. 127, 141 n. 16 (1966); *United States v. United States Gypsum Co.,* 333 U.S. 364, 394–96 (1948).

The principal argument advanced in favor of a more searching appellate review of findings by the district court based solely on documentary evidence is that the rationale of Rule 52(a) does not apply when the findings do not rest on the trial court's assessment of credibility of the witnesses but on an evaluation of documentary proof and the drawing of inferences from it, thus eliminating the need for any special deference to the trial court's findings. These considerations are outweighed by the public interest in the stability and judicial economy that would be promoted by recognizing that the trial court, not the appellate tribunal, should be the finder of the facts. To permit courts of appeals to share more actively in the fact-finding function would tend to undermine the legitimacy of the district courts in the eyes of litigants, multiply appeals by encouraging appellate retrial of some factual issues, and needlessly reallocate judicial authority.

1991 Amendment

Subdivision (c) is added. It parallels the revised Rule 50(a), but is applicable to non-jury trials. It authorizes the court to enter judgment at any time that it can appropriately make a dispositive finding of fact on the evidence.

The new subdivision replaces part of Rule 41(b), which formerly authorized a dismissal at the close of the plaintiff's case if the plaintiff had failed to carry an essential burden of proof. Accordingly, the reference to Rule 41 formerly made in subdivision (a) of this rule is deleted.

As under the former Rule 41(b), the court retains discretion to enter no judgment prior to the close of the evidence.

Judgment entered under this rule differs from a summary judgment under Rule 56 in the nature of the evaluation made by the court. A judgment on partial findings is made after the court has heard all the evidence bearing on the crucial issue of fact, and the finding is reversible only if the appellate court finds it to be "clearly erroneous." A summary judgment, in contrast, is made on the basis of facts established on account of the absence of contrary evidence or presumptions; such establishments of fact are rulings on questions of law as provided in Rule 56(a) and are not shielded by the "clear error" standard of review.

1993 Amendments

This technical amendment corrects an ambiguity in the text of the 1991 revision of the rule, similar to the revision being made to Rule 50. This amendment makes clear that judgments as a matter of law in nonjury trials may be entered against both plaintiffs and defendants and with respect to issues or defenses that may not be wholly dispositive of a claim or defense.

1995 Amendments

The only change, other than stylistic, intended by this revision is to require that any motion to amend or add findings after a nonjury trial must be filed no later than 10 days after entry of the judgment. Previously, there was an inconsistency in the wording of Rules 50, 52, and 59 with respect to whether certain post-judgment motions had to be filed, or merely served, during that period. This inconsistency caused special problems when motions for a new trial were joined with other post-judgment motions. These motions affect the finality of the judgment, a matter often of importance to third persons as well as the parties and the court. The Committee believes that each of these rules should be revised to require filing before end of the 10–day period. Filing is an event that can be determined with certainty from court records. The phrase "no later than" is used—rather than "within"—to include post-judgment motions that sometimes are filed before actual entry of the judgment by the clerk. It should be noted that under Rule 6(a) Saturdays, Sundays, and legal holidays are excluded in measuring the 10–day period, and that under Rule 5 the motions when filed are to contain a certificate of service on other parties.

2007 Amendments

The language of Rule 52 has been amended as part of the general restyling of the Civil Rules to make them more easily understood and to make style and terminology consistent throughout the rules. These changes are intended to be stylistic only.

Former Rule 52(a) said that findings are unnecessary on decisions of motions "except as provided in subdivision (c) of this rule." Amended Rule 52(a)(3) says that findings are unnecessary "unless these rules provide otherwise." This change reflects provisions in other rules that require Rule 52 findings on deciding motions. Rules 23(e), 23(h), and 54(d)(2)(C) are examples.

Amended Rule 52(a)(5) includes provisions that appeared in former Rule 52(a) and 52(b). Rule 52(a) provided that requests for findings are not necessary for purposes of review. It applied both in an action tried on the facts without a jury and also in granting or refusing an interlocutory injunction. Rule 52(b), applicable to findings "made in actions tried without a jury," provided that the sufficiency of the evidence might be "later questioned whether or not in the district court the party raising the question objected to the findings, moved to amend them, or moved for partial findings." Former Rule 52(b) did not explicitly apply to decisions granting or refusing an interlocutory injunction. Amended Rule 52(a)(5) makes explicit the application of this part of former Rule 52(b) to interlocutory injunction decisions.

Former Rule 52(c) provided for judgment on partial findings, and referred to it as "judgment as a matter of law." Amended Rule 52(c) refers only to "judgment," to avoid any confusion with a Rule 50 judgment as a matter of law in a jury case. The standards that govern judgment as a matter of law in a jury case have no bearing on a decision under Rule 52(c).

Rule 53. Masters

(a) Appointment.

(1) ***Scope.*** Unless a statute provides otherwise, a court may appoint a master only to:

(A) perform duties consented to by the parties;

(B) hold trial proceedings and make or recommend findings of fact on issues to be decided without a jury if appointment is warranted by:

(i) some exceptional condition; or

(ii) the need to perform an accounting or resolve a difficult computation of damages; or

(C) address pretrial and posttrial matters that cannot be effectively and timely addressed by an available district judge or magistrate judge of the district.

(2) ***Disqualification.*** A master must not have a relationship to the parties, attorneys, action, or court that would require disqualification of a judge under 28 U.S.C. § 455, unless the parties, with the court's approval, consent to the appointment after the master discloses any potential grounds for disqualification.

(3) ***Possible Expense or Delay.*** In appointing a master, the court must consider the fairness of imposing the likely expenses on the parties and must protect against unreasonable expense or delay.

(b) Order Appointing a Master.

(1) ***Notice.*** Before appointing a master, the court must give the parties notice and an opportunity to be heard. Any party may suggest candidates for appointment.

(2) ***Contents.*** The appointing order must direct the master to proceed with all reasonable diligence and must state:

(A) the master's duties, including any investigation or enforcement duties, and any limits on the master's authority under Rule 53(c);

(B) the circumstances, if any, in which the master may communicate ex parte with the court or a party;

(C) the nature of the materials to be preserved and filed as the record of the master's activities;

(D) the time limits, method of filing the record, other procedures, and standards for reviewing the master's orders, findings, and recommendations; and

(E) the basis, terms, and procedure for fixing the master's compensation under Rule 53(g).

(3) ***Issuing.*** The court may issue the order only after:

(A) the master files an affidavit disclosing whether there is any ground for disqualification under 28 U.S.C. § 455; and

(B) if a ground is disclosed, the parties, with the court's approval, waive the disqualification.

(4) ***Amending.*** The order may be amended at any time after notice to the parties and an opportunity to be heard.

(c) Master's Authority.

(1) ***In General.*** Unless the appointing order directs otherwise, a master may:

(A) regulate all proceedings;

(B) take all appropriate measures to perform the assigned duties fairly and efficiently; and

(C) if conducting an evidentiary hearing, exercise the appointing court's power to compel, take, and record evidence.

(2) ***Sanctions.*** The master may by order impose on a party any noncontempt sanction provided by Rule 37 or 45, and may recommend a contempt sanction against a party and sanctions against a nonparty.

(d) Master's Orders. A master who issues an order must file it and promptly serve a copy on each party. The clerk must enter the order on the docket.

(e) Master's Reports. A master must report to the court as required by the appointing order. The master must file the report and promptly serve a copy on each party, unless the court orders otherwise.

(f) Action on the Master's Order, Report, or Recommendations.

(1) ***Opportunity for a Hearing; Action in General.*** In acting on a master's order, report, or recommendations, the court must give the parties notice and an opportunity to be heard; may receive evidence; and may adopt or affirm, modify, wholly or partly reject or reverse, or resubmit to the master with instructions.

(2) ***Time to Object or Move to Adopt or Modify.*** A party may file objections to—or a motion to adopt or modify—the master's order, report, or recommendations no later than 20 days after a copy is served, unless the court sets a different time.

(3) ***Reviewing Factual Findings.*** The court must decide de novo all objections to findings of fact made or recommended by a master, unless the parties, with the court's approval, stipulate that:

(A) the findings will be reviewed for clear error; or

(B) the findings of a master appointed under Rule 53(a)(1)(A) or (C) will be final.

(4) ***Reviewing Legal Conclusions.*** The court must decide de novo all objections to conclusions of law made or recommended by a master.

(5) ***Reviewing Procedural Matters.*** Unless the appointing order establishes a different standard of review, the court may set aside a master's ruling on a procedural matter only for an abuse of discretion.

(g) Compensation.

(1) ***Fixing Compensation.*** Before or after judgment, the court must fix the master's compensation on the basis and terms stated in the appointing order, but the court may set a new basis and terms after giving notice and an opportunity to be heard.

(2) ***Payment.*** The compensation must be paid either:

(A) by a party or parties; or

(B) from a fund or subject matter of the action within the court's control.

(3) ***Allocating Payment.*** The court must allocate payment among the parties after considering the nature and amount of the controversy, the parties' means, and the extent to which any party is more responsible than other parties for the reference to a master. An interim allocation may be amended to reflect a decision on the merits.

(h) Appointing a Magistrate Judge. A magistrate judge is subject to this rule only when the order referring a matter to the magistrate judge states that the reference is made under this rule.

(Amended February 28, 1966, effective July 1, 1966; April 28, 1983, effective August 1, 1983; March 2, 1987, effective August 1, 1987; April 30, 1991, effective December 1, 1991; April 22, 1993, effective December 1, 1993; March 27, 2003, effective December 1, 2003; April 30, 2007, effective December 1, 2007.)

ADVISORY COMMITTEE NOTES

1937 Adoption

Note to Subdivision (a). This is a modification of former Equity Rule 68 (Appointment and Compensation of Masters).

Note to Subdivision (b). This is substantially the first sentence of [former] Equity Rule 59 (Reference to Master—Exceptional, Not Usual) extended to actions formerly legal. See *Ex parte Peterson,* 1920, 40 S.Ct. 543, 253 U.S. 300, 64 L.Ed. 919.

Note to Subdivision (c). This is [former] Equity Rules 62 (Powers of Master) and 65 (Claimants Before Master Examinable by Him) with slight modifications. Compare [former] Equity Rules 49 (Evidence Taken Before Examiners, Etc.) and 51 (Evidence Taken Before Examiners, Etc.).

Note to Subdivision (d). (1) This is substantially a combination of the second sentence of [former] Equity Rule 59 (Reference to Master—Exceptional, Not Usual) and [former] Equity Rule 60 (Proceedings Before Master). Compare [former] Equity Rule 53 (Notice of Taking Testimony Before Examiner, Etc.).

(2) This is substantially [former] Equity Rule 52 (Attendance of Witnesses Before Commissioner, Master, or Examiner).

(3) This is substantially [former] Equity Rule 63 (Form of Accounts Before Master).

Note to Subdivision (e). This contains the substance of [former] Equity Rules 61 (Master's Report—Documents Identified but not Set Forth), 61½ (Master's Report—Presumption as to Correctness—Review), and 66 (Return of Master's Report—Exceptions—Hearing), with modifications as to the form and effect of the report and for inclusion of reports by auditors, referees, and examiners, and references in actions formerly legal. Compare [former] Equity Rules 49 (Evidence Taken Before Examiners, Etc.) and 67 (Costs on Exceptions to Master's Report). See *Camden v. Stuart,* 144 U.S. 104, 12 S.Ct. 585, 36 L.Ed. 363 (1892); *Ex parte Peterson,* 253 U.S. 300, 40 S.Ct. 543, 64 L.Ed. 919 (1920).

1966 Amendment

These changes are designed to preserve the admiralty practice whereby difficult computations are referred to a commissioner or assessor, especially after an interlocutory judgment determining liability. As to separation of issues for trial see Rule 42(b).

1983 Amendment

Subdivision (a). The creation of full-time magistrates, who serve at government expense and have no nonjudicial duties competing for their time, eliminates the need to appoint standing masters. Thus the prior provision in Rule 53(a) authorizing the appointment of standing masters is deleted. Additionally, the definition of "master" in subdivision (a) now eliminates the superseded office of commissioner.

The term "special master" is retained in Rule 53 in order to maintain conformity with 28 U.S.C. § 636(b)(2), authorizing a judge to designate a magistrate "to serve as a special master pursuant to the applicable provisions of this title and the Federal Rules of Civil Procedure for the United States District Courts." Obviously, when a magistrate serves as a special master, the provisions for compensation of masters are inapplicable, and the amendment to subdivision (a) so provides.

Although the existence of magistrates may make the appointment of outside masters unnecessary in many instances, see, e.g., *Gautreaux v. Chicago Housing Authority,* 384 F.Supp. 37 (N.D.Ill.1974), mandamus denied *sub nom., Chicago Housing Authority v. Austin,* 511 F.2d 82 (7th Cir. 1975); *Avco Corp. v. American Tel. & Tel. Co.,* 68 F.R.D. 532 (S.D.Ohio 1975), such masters may prove useful when some special expertise is desired or when a magistrate is unavailable for lengthy and detailed supervision of a case.

Subdivision (b). The provisions of 28 U.S.C. § 636(b)(2) not only permit magistrates to serve as masters under Rule 53(b) but also eliminate the exceptional condition requirement of Rule 53(b) when the reference is made with the consent of the parties. The amendment to subdivision (b) brings Rule 53 into harmony with the statute by exempting magistrates, appointed with the consent of the parties, from the general requirement that some exceptional condition requires the reference. It should be noted that subdivision (b) does not address the question, raised in recent decisional law and commentary, as to whether the exceptional condition requirement is applicable when *private masters* who are not magistrates are appointed with the consent of the parties. See Silberman, *Masters and Magistrates Part II: The American Analogue,* 50 N.Y.U.L.Rev. 1297, 1354 (1975).

Subdivision (c). The amendment recognizes the abrogation of Federal Rule 43(c) by the Federal Rules of Evidence.

Subdivision (f). The new subdivision responds to confusion flowing from the dual authority for references of pretrial matters to magistrates. Such references can be made, with or without the consent of the parties, pursuant to Rule 53 or under 28 U.S.C. § 636(b)(1)(A) and (b)(1)(B). There are a number of distinctions between references made under the statute and under the rule. For example, under the statute nondispositive pretrial matters may be referred to a magistrate, without consent, for final determination with reconsideration by the district judge if the magistrate's order is clearly erroneous or contrary to law. Under the rule, however, the appointment of a master, without consent of the parties, to supervise discovery would require some exceptional condition (Rule 53(b)) and would subject the proceedings to the report procedures of Rule 53(e). If an order of reference does not clearly articulate the source of the court's authority the resulting proceedings could be subject to attack on grounds of the magistrate's noncompliance with the provisions of Rule 53. This subdivision therefore establishes a presumption that the limitations of Rule 53 are not applicable unless the reference is specifically made subject to Rule 53.

A magistrate serving as a special master under 28 U.S.C. § 636(b)(2) is governed by the provisions of Rule 53, with the exceptional condition requirement lifted in the case of a consensual reference.

1987 Amendment

The amendments are technical. No substantive change is intended.

1991 Amendment

The purpose of the revision is to expedite proceedings before a master. The former rule required only a filing of the master's report, with the clerk then notifying the parties of the filing. To receive a copy, a party would then be required to secure it from the clerk. By transmitting directly to the parties, the master can save some efforts of counsel. Some local rules have previously required such action by the master.

1993 Amendments

This revision is made to conform the rule to changes made by the Judicial Improvements Act of 1990.

2003 Amendments

Rule 53 is revised extensively to reflect changing practices in using masters. From the beginning in 1938, Rule 53 focused primarily on special masters who perform trial functions. Since then, however, courts have gained experience with masters appointed to perform a variety of pretrial and post-trial functions. See Willging, Hooper, Leary, Miletich, Reagan, & Shapard, *Special Masters' Incidence and Activity* (Federal Judicial Center 2000). This revised Rule 53 recognizes that in appropriate circumstances masters may properly be appointed to perform these functions and regulates such appointments. Rule 53 continues to address trial masters as well, but permits appointment of a trial master in an action to be tried to a jury only if the parties consent. The new rule clarifies the provisions that govern the appointment and function of masters for all purposes. Rule 53(g) also changes the standard of review for findings of fact made or recommended by a master. The core of the original Rule 53 remains, including its prescription that appointment of a master must be the exception and not the rule.

Special masters are appointed in many circumstances outside the Civil Rules. Rule 53 applies only to proceedings that Rule 1 brings within its reach.

Subdivision (a)(1)

District judges bear primary responsibility for the work of their courts. A master should be appointed only in limited circumstances. Subdivision (a)(1) describes three different standards, relating to appointments by consent of the parties, appointments for trial duties, and appointments for pretrial or post-trial duties.

Consent Masters. Subparagraph (a)(1)(A) authorizes appointment of a master with the parties' consent. Party consent does not require that the court make the appointment; the court retains unfettered discretion to refuse appointment.

Trial Masters. Use of masters for the core functions of trial has been progressively limited. These limits are reflected in the provisions of subparagraph (a)(1)(B) that restrict appointments to exercise trial functions. The Supreme Court gave clear direction to this trend in *La Buy v. Howes Leather Co.*, 352 U.S. 249 (1957); earlier roots are sketched in *Los Angeles Brush Mfg. Corp. v. James*, 272 U.S. 701 (1927). As to nonjury trials, this trend has developed through elaboration of the "exceptional condition" requirement in present Rule 53(b). This phrase is retained, and will continue to have the same force as it has developed. Although the provision that a reference "shall be the exception and not the rule" is deleted, its meaning is embraced for this setting by the exceptional condition requirement.

Subparagraph (a)(1)(B)(ii) carries forward the approach of present Rule 53(b), which exempts from the "exceptional condition" requirement "matters of account and of difficult computation of damages." This approach is justified only as to essentially ministerial determinations that require mastery of much detailed information but that do not require extensive determinations of credibility. Evaluations of witness credibility should only be assigned to a trial master when justified by an exceptional condition.

The use of a trial master without party consent is abolished as to matters to be decided by a jury unless a statute provides for this practice.

Abolition of the direct power to appoint a trial master as to issues to be decided by a jury leaves the way free to appoint a trial master with the consent of all parties. A trial master should be appointed in a jury case, with consent of the parties and concurrence of the court, only if the parties waive jury trial with respect to the issues submitted to the master or if the master's findings are to be submitted to the jury as evidence in the manner provided by former Rule 53(e)(3). In no circumstance may a master be appointed to preside at a jury trial.

The central function of a trial master is to preside over an evidentiary hearing on the merits of the claims or defenses in the action. This function distinguishes the trial master from most functions of pretrial and post-trial masters. If any master is to be used for such matters as a preliminary injunction hearing or a determination of complex damages issues, for example, the master should be a trial master. The line, however, is not distinct. A pretrial master might well conduct an evidentiary hearing on a discovery dispute, and a post-trial master might conduct evidentiary hearings on questions of compliance.

Rule 53 has long provided authority to report the evidence without recommendations in nonjury trials. This authority is omitted from Rule 53(a)(1)(B). In some circumstances a master may be appointed under Rule 53(a)(1)(A) or (C) to take evidence and report without recommendations.

For nonjury cases, a master also may be appointed to assist the court in discharging trial duties other than conducting an evidentiary hearing.

Pretrial and Post–Trial Masters. Subparagraph (a)(1)(C) authorizes appointment of a master to address pretrial or post-trial matters. Appointment is limited to matters that cannot be addressed effectively and in a timely fashion by an available district judge or magistrate judge of the district. A master's pretrial or post-trial duties may include matters that could be addressed by a judge, such as reviewing discovery documents for privilege, or duties that might not be suitable for a judge. Some forms of settlement negotiations, investigations, or administration of an organization are familiar examples of duties that a judge might not feel free to undertake.

Magistrate Judges. Particular attention should be paid to the prospect that a magistrate judge may be available for special assignments. United States magistrate judges are authorized by statute to perform many pretrial functions in civil actions. 28 U.S.C. § 636(b)(1). Ordinarily a district judge who delegates these functions should refer them to a magistrate judge acting as magistrate judge.

There is statutory authority to appoint a magistrate judge as special master. 28 U.S.C. § 636(b)(2). In special circumstances, or when expressly authorized by a statute other than § 636(b)(2), it may be appropriate to appoint a magistrate judge as a master when needed to perform functions outside those listed in § 636(b)(1). There is no apparent reason to appoint a magistrate judge to perform as master duties that could be performed in the role of magistrate judge. Party consent is required for trial before a magistrate judge, moreover, and this requirement should not be undercut by resort to Rule 53 unless specifically authorized by statute; see 42 U.S.C. § 2000e–5(f)(5).

Pretrial Masters. The appointment of masters to participate in pretrial proceedings has developed extensively over the last two decades as some district courts have felt the need for additional help in managing complex litigation. This practice is not well regulated by present Rule 53, which focuses on masters as trial participants. Rule 53 is amended to confirm the authority to appoint—and to regulate the use of—pretrial masters.

A pretrial master should be appointed only when the need is clear. Direct judicial performance of judicial functions may be particularly important in cases that involve important public issues or many parties. At the extreme, a broad delegation of pretrial responsibility as well as a delegation of trial responsibilities can run afoul of Article III.

A master also may be appointed to address matters that blur the divide between pretrial and trial functions. The court's responsibility to interpret patent claims as a matter of law, for example, may be greatly assisted by appointing a master who has expert knowledge of the field in which the patent operates. Review of the master's findings will be de novo under Rule 53(g)(4), but the advantages of initial determination by a master may make the process more effective and timely than disposition by the judge acting alone. Determination of foreign law may present comparable difficulties. The decision whether to appoint a master to address such matters is governed by subdivision (a)(1)(C), not the trial-master provisions of subdivision (a)(1)(B).

Post–Trial Masters. Courts have come to rely on masters to assist in framing and enforcing complex decrees. Present Rule 53 does not directly address this practice. Amended Rule 53 authorizes appointment of post-trial masters for these and similar purposes. The constraint of subdivision (a)(1)(C) limits this practice to cases in which the master's duties cannot be performed effectively and in a timely fashion by an available district judge or magistrate judge of the district.

Reliance on a master is appropriate when a complex decree requires complex policing, particularly when a party has proved resistant or intransigent. This practice has been recognized by the Supreme Court, see *Local 28, Sheet Metal Workers' Internat. Assn. v. EEOC*, 478 U.S. 421, 481–482 (1986). The master's role in enforcement may extend to investigation in ways that are quite unlike the traditional role of judicial officers in an adversary system.

Expert Witness Overlap. This rule does not address the difficulties that arise when a single person is appointed to perform overlapping roles as master and as court-appointed expert witness under Evidence Rule 706. Whatever combination of functions is involved, the Rule 53(a)(1)(B) limit that confines trial masters to issues to be decided by the court does not apply to a person who also is appointed as an expert witness under Evidence Rule 706.

Subdivision (a)(2) and (3)

Masters are subject to the Code of Conduct for United States Judges, with exceptions spelled out in the Code. Special care must be taken to ensure that there is no actual or apparent conflict of interest involving a master. The standard of disqualification is established by 28 U.S.C. § 455. The affidavit required by Rule 53(b)(3) provides an important source of information about possible grounds for disqualification, but careful inquiry should be made at the time of making the initial appointment. The disqualification standards established by § 455 are strict. Because a master is not a public judicial officer, it may be appropriate to permit the parties to consent to appointment of a particular person as master in circumstances that would require disqualification of a judge. The judge must be careful to ensure that no party feels any pressure to consent, but with such assurances—and with the judge's own determination that there is no troubling conflict of interests or disquieting appearance of impropriety—consent may justify an otherwise barred appointment.

One potential disqualification issue is peculiar to the master's role. It may happen that a master who is an attorney represents a client whose litigation is assigned to the judge who appointed the attorney as master. Other parties to the litigation may fear that the attorney-master will gain special respect from the judge. A flat prohibition on appearance before the appointing judge during the time of service as master, however, might in some circumstances unduly limit the opportunity to make a desirable appointment. These matters may be regulated to some extent by state rules of professional responsibility. The question of present conflicts, and the possibility of future conflicts, can be considered at the time of appointment. Depending on the circumstances, the judge may consider it appropriate to impose a non-appearance condition on the lawyer-master, and perhaps on the master's firm as well.

Subdivision (b)

The order appointing a pretrial master is vitally important in informing the master and the parties about the nature and extent of the master's duties and authority. Care must be taken to make the order as precise as possible. The parties must be given notice and opportunity to be heard on the question whether a master should be appointed and on the terms of the appointment. To the extent possible, the notice should describe the master's proposed duties, time to complete the duties, standards of review, and compensation. Often it will be useful to engage the parties in the process of identifying the master, inviting nominations, and reviewing potential candidates. Party involvement may be particularly useful if a pretrial master is expected to promote settlement.

The hearing requirement of Rule 53(b)(1) can be satisfied by an opportunity to make written submissions unless the circumstances require live testimony.

Rule 53(b)(2) requires precise designation of the master's duties and authority. Clear identification of any investigating or enforcement duties is particularly important. Clear delineation of topics for any reports or recommendations is also an important part of this process. And it is important to protect against delay by establishing a time schedule for performing the assigned duties. Early designation of the procedure for fixing the master's compensation also may provide useful guidance to the parties.

Ex parte communications between a master and the court present troubling questions. Ordinarily the order should prohibit such communications, assuring that the parties know where authority is lodged at each step of the proceedings. Prohibiting ex parte communications between master and court also can enhance the role of a settlement master by assuring the parties that settlement can be fostered by confidential revelations that will not be shared with the court. Yet there may be circumstances in which the master's role is enhanced by the opportunity for ex parte communications with the court. A master assigned to help coordinate multiple proceedings, for example, may benefit from off-the-record exchanges with the court about logistical matters. The rule does not directly regulate these matters. It requires only that the court exercise its discretion and address the topic in the order of appointment.

Similarly difficult questions surround ex part e communications between a master and the parties. Ex parte communications may be essential in seeking to advance settlement. Ex parte communications also may prove useful in other settings, as with in camera review of documents to resolve privilege questions. In most settings, however, ex parte communications with the parties should be discouraged or prohibited. The rule requires that the court address the topic in the order of appointment.

Subdivision (b)(2)(C) provides that the appointment order must state the nature of the materials to be preserved and filed as the record of the master's activities, and (b)(2)(D) requires that the order state the method of filing the record. It is not feasible to prescribe the nature of the record without regard to the nature of the master's duties. The records appropriate to discovery duties may be different from those appropriate to encouraging settlement, investigating possible violations of a complex decree, or making recommendations for trial findings. A basic requirement, however, is that the master must make and file a complete record of the evidence considered in making or recommending findings of fact on the basis of evidence. The order of appointment should routinely include this requirement unless the nature of the appointment precludes any prospect that the master will make or recommend evidence-based findings of fact. In some circumstances it may be appropriate for a party to file materials directly with the court as provided by Rule 5(e), but in many circumstances filing with the court may be inappropriate. Confidentiality is important with respect to many materials that may properly be considered by a master. Materials in the record can be transmitted to the court, and filed, in connection with review of a master's order, report, or recommendations under subdivisions (f) and (g). Independently of review proceedings, the court may direct filing of any materials that it wishes to make part of the public record.

The provision in subdivision (b)(2)(D) that the order must state the standards for reviewing the master's orders, findings, or recommendations is a reminder of the provisions of subdivision (g)(3) that recognize stipulations for review less searching than the presumptive requirement of de novo decision by the court. Subdivision (b)(2)(D) does not authorize the court to supersede the limits of subdivision (g)(3).

In setting the procedure for fixing the master's compensation, it is useful at the outset to establish specific guidelines to control total expense. The court has power under subdivision (h) to change the basis and terms for determining compensation after notice to the parties.

Subdivision (b)(3) permits entry of the order appointing a master only after the master has filed an affidavit disclosing whether there is any ground for disqualification under 28 U.S.C. § 455. If the affidavit discloses a possible ground for disqualification, the order can enter only if the court determines that there is no ground for disqualification or if the parties, knowing of the ground for disqualification, consent with the court's approval to waive the disqualification.

The provision in Rule 53(b)(4) for amending the order of appointment is as import ant as the provisions for the initial order. Anything that could be done in the initial order can be done by amendment. The hearing requirement can be satisfied by an opportunity to make written submissions unless the circumstances require live testimony.

Subdivision (c)

Subdivision (c) is a simplification of the provisions scattered throughout present Rule 53. It is intended to provide the broad and flexible authority necessary to discharge the master's responsibilities. The most important delineation of a master's authority and duties is provided by the Rule 53(b) appointing order.

Subdivision (d)

The subdivision (d) provisions for evidentiary hearings are reduced from the extensive provisions in current Rule 53. This simplification of the rule is not intended to diminish the authority that may be delegated to a master. Reliance is placed on the broad and general terms of subdivision (c).

Subdivision (e)

Subdivision (e) provides that a master's order must be filed and entered on the docket. It must be promptly served on the parties, a task ordinarily accomplished by mailing or other means as permitted by Rule 5(b). In some circumstances it may be appropriate to have the clerk's office assist the master in mailing the order to the parties.

Subdivision (f)

Subdivision (f) restates some of the provisions of present Rule 53(e)(1). The report is the master's primary means of communication with the court. The materials to be provided to support review of the report will depend on the nature of the report. The master should provide all portions of the record preserved under Rule 53(b)(2)(C) that the master deems relevant to the report. The parties may designate additional materials from the record, and may seek permission to supplement the record with evidence. The court may direct that additional materials from the record be provided and filed. Given the wide array of tasks that may be assigned to a pretrial master, there may be circumstances that justify sealing a report or review record against public access—a report on continuing or failed settlement efforts is the most likely example. A post-trial master may be assigned duties in formulating a decree that deserve similar protection. Such circumstances may even justify denying access to the report or review materials by the parties, although this step should be taken only for the most compelling reasons. Sealing is much less likely to be appropriate with respect to a trial master's report.

Before formally making an order, report, or recommendations, a master may find it helpful to circulate a draft to the parties for review and comment. The usefulness of this practice depends on the nature of the master's proposed action.

Subdivision (g)

The provisions of subdivision (g)(1), describing the court's powers to afford a hearing, take evidence, and act on a master's order, report, or recommendations are drawn from present Rule 53(e)(2), but are not limited, as present Rule 53(e)(2) is limited, to the report of a trial master in a nonjury action. The requirement that the court must afford an opportunity to be heard can be satisfied by taking written submissions when the court acts on the report without taking live testimony.

The subdivision (g)(2) time limits for objecting to—or seeking adoption or modification of—a master's order, report, or recommendations, are important. They are not jurisdictional. Although a court may properly refuse to entertain untimely review proceedings, the court may excuse the failure to seek timely review. The basic time period is lengthened to 20 days because the present 10–day period may be too short to permit thorough study and response to a complex report dealing with complex litigation. If no party asks the court to act on a master's report, the court is free to adopt the master's action or to disregard it at any relevant point in the proceedings.

Subdivision (g)(3) establishes the standards of review for a master's findings of fact or recommended findings of fact. The court must decide de novo all objections to findings of fact made or recommended by the master unless the parties stipulate, with the court's consent, that the findings will be reviewed for clear error or—with respect to a master appointed on the parties' consent or appointed to address pretrial or post-trial matters—that the findings will be final. Clear-error review is more likely to be appropriate with respect to findings that do not go to the merits of the underlying claims or defenses, such as findings of fact bearing on a privilege objection to a discovery request. Even if no objection is made, the court is free to decide the facts de novo; to review for clear error if an earlier approved stipulation provided clear-error review; or to withdraw its consent to a stipulation for clear-error review or finality, and then to decide de novo. If the court withdraws its consent to a stipulation for finality or clear-error review, it may reopen the opportunity to object.

Under Rule 53(g)(4), the court must decide de novo all objections to conclusions of law made or recommended by a master. As with findings of fact, the court also may decide conclusions of law de novo when no objection is made.

Apart from factual and legal questions, masters often make determinations that, when made by a trial court, would be treated as matters of procedural discretion. The court may set a standard for review of such matters in the order of appointment, and may amend the order to establish the standard. If no standard is set by the original or amended order appointing the master, review of procedural matters is for abuse of discretion. The subordinate role of the master means that the trial court's review for abuse of discretion may be more searching than the review that an appellate court makes of a trial court.

If a master makes a recommendation on any matter that does not fall within Rule 53(g)(3), (4), or (5), the court may act on the recommendation under Rule 53(g)(1).

Subdivision (h)

The need to pay compensation is a substantial reason for care in appointing private persons as masters.

Payment of the master's fees must be allocated among the parties and any property or subject-matter within the court's control. The amount in controversy and the means of the parties may provide some guidance in making the allocation. The nature of the dispute also may be important—parties pursuing matters of public interest, for example, may deserve special protection. A party whose unreasonable behavior has occasioned the need to appoint a master, on the other hand, may properly be charged all or a major portion of the master's fees. It may be proper to revise an interim allocation after decision on the merits. The revision need not await a decision that is final for purposes of appeal, but may be made to reflect disposition of a substantial portion of the case.

The basis and terms for fixing compensation should be stated in the order of appointment. The court retains power to alter the initial basis and terms, after notice and an opportunity to be heard, but should protect the parties against unfair surprise.

The provision of former Rule 53(a) that the "provision for compensation shall not apply when a United States Magistrate Judge is designated to serve as a master" is deleted as unnecessary. Other provisions of law preclude compensation.

Subdivision (i)

Rule 53(i) carries forward unchanged former Rule 53(f).

2007 Amendments

The language of Rule 53 has been amended as part of the general restyling of the Civil Rules to make them more easily understood and to make style and terminology consistent throughout the rules. These changes are intended to be stylistic only.

HISTORICAL NOTES

Change of Name

United States magistrate appointed under section 631 of Title 28, Judiciary and Judicial Procedure, to be known as United States magistrate judge after Dec. 1, 1990, with any reference to United States magistrate or magistrate in Title 28, in any other Federal statute, etc., deemed a reference to United States magistrate judge appointed under section 631 of Title 28, see section 321 of Pub.L. 101–650, set out as a note under section 631 of Title 28.

TITLE VII. JUDGMENT

Rule 54. Judgment; Costs

(a) Definition; Form. "Judgment" as used in these rules includes a decree and any order from which an appeal lies. A judgment should not include recitals of pleadings, a master's report, or a record of prior proceedings.

(b) Judgment on Multiple Claims or Involving Multiple Parties. When an action presents more than one claim for relief—whether as a claim, counterclaim, crossclaim, or third-party claim—or when multiple parties are involved, the court may direct entry of a final judgment as to one or more, but fewer than all, claims or parties only if the court expressly determines that there is no just reason for delay. Otherwise, any order or other decision, however designated, that adjudicates fewer than all the claims or the rights and liabilities of fewer than all the parties does not end the action as to any of the claims or parties and may be revised at any time before the entry of a judgment adjudicating all the claims and all the parties' rights and liabilities.

(c) Demand for Judgment; Relief to Be Granted. A default judgment must not differ in kind from, or exceed in amount, what is demanded in the pleadings. Every other final judgment should grant the relief to which each party is entitled, even if the party has not demanded that relief in its pleadings.

(d) Costs; Attorney's Fees.

(1) ***Costs Other Than Attorney's Fees.*** Unless a federal statute, these rules, or a court order provides otherwise, costs—other than attorney's fees—should be allowed to the prevailing party. But costs against the United States, its officers, and its agencies may be imposed only to the extent allowed by law. The clerk may tax costs on 1 day's notice. On motion served within the next 5 days, the court may review the clerk's action.

(2) ***Attorney's Fees.***

(A) *Claim to Be by Motion.* A claim for attorney's fees and related nontaxable expenses must be made by motion unless the substantive law requires those fees to be proved at trial as an element of damages.

(B) *Timing and Contents of the Motion.* Unless a statute or a court order provides otherwise, the motion must:

(i) be filed no later than 14 days after the entry of judgment;

(ii) specify the judgment and the statute, rule, or other grounds entitling the movant to the award;

(iii) state the amount sought or provide a fair estimate of it; and

(iv) disclose, if the court so orders, the terms of any agreement about fees for the services for which the claim is made.

(C) *Proceedings.* Subject to Rule 23(h), the court must, on a party's request, give an opportunity for adversary submissions on the motion in accordance with Rule 43(c) or 78. The court may decide issues of liability for fees before receiving submissions on the value of services. The court must find the facts and state its conclusions of law as provided in Rule 52(a).

(D) *Special Procedures by Local Rule; Reference to a Master or a Magistrate Judge.* By local rule, the court may establish special procedures to resolve fee-related issues without extensive evidentiary hearings. Also, the court may refer issues concerning the value of services to a special master under Rule 53 without regard to the limitations of Rule 53(a)(1), and may refer a motion for attorney's fees to a magistrate judge under Rule 72(b) as if it were a dispositive pretrial matter.

(E) *Exceptions.* Subparagraphs (A)-(D) do not apply to claims for fees and expenses as sanctions for violating these rules or as sanctions under 28 U.S.C. § 1927.

(Amended December 27, 1946, effective March 19, 1948; April 17, 1961, effective July 19, 1961; March 2, 1987, effective August 1, 1987; April 22, 1993, effective December 1, 1993; April 29, 2002, effective December 1, 2002; March 27, 2003, effective December 1, 2003; April 30, 2007, effective December 1, 2007.)

ADVISORY COMMITTEE NOTES

1937 Adoption

Note to Subdivision (a). The second sentence is derived substantially from [former] Equity Rule 71 (Form of Decree).

Note to Subdivision (b). This provides for the separate judgment of equity and code practice. See Wis.Stat. (1935) § 270.54; Compare N.Y.C.P.A. (1937) § 476.

Note to Subdivision (c). For the limitation on default contained in the first sentence, see 2 N.D.Comp.Laws Ann. (1913) § 7680; N.Y.C.P.A. (1937) § 479. Compare *English Rules Under the Judicature Act* (The Annual Practice, 1937) O. 13, r.r. 3–12. The remainder is a usual code provision. It makes clear that a judgment should give the relief to which a party is entitled, regardless of whether it is legal or equitable or both. This necessarily includes the deficiency judgment in foreclosure cases formerly provided for by Equity Rule 10 (Decree for Deficiency in Foreclosures, Etc.).

Note to Subdivision (d). For the present rule in common law actions, see *Ex parte Peterson,* 253 U.S. 300, 40 S.Ct. 543, 64 L.Ed. 919 (1920); Payne, *Costs in Common Law Actions in the Federal Courts* (1935), 21 Va.L.Rev. 397.

The provisions as to costs in actions in forma pauperis contained in U.S.C., Title 28, former §§ 832–836 [now 1915] are unaffected by this rule. Other sections of U.S.C., Title 28, which are unaffected by this rule are: [former] §§ 815 (Costs; plaintiff not entitled to, when), 821 [now 1928] (Costs; infringement of patent; disclaimer), 825 (Costs; several actions), 829 [now 1927] (Costs; attorney liable for, when), and 830 [now 1920] (Costs; bill of; taxation).

The provisions of the following and similar statutes as to costs against the United States and its officers and agencies are specifically continued:

U.S.C., Title 15, §§ 77v(a), 78aa, 79y (Securities and Exchange Commission)

U.S.C., Title 16, § 825p (Federal Power Commission)

U.S.C., Title 26, [former] §§ 3679(d) and 3745(d) (Internal revenue actions)

U.S.C., Title 26, [former] § 3770(b)(2) (Reimbursement of costs of recovery against revenue officers)

U.S.C., Title 28, [former] § 817 (Internal revenue actions)

U.S.C., Title 28, § 836 [now 1915] (United States—actions in *forma pauperis*)

U.S.C., Title 28, § 842 [now 2006] (Actions against revenue officers)

U.S.C., Title 28, § 870 [now 2408] (United States—in certain cases)

U.S.C., Title 28, [former] § 906 (United States—foreclosure actions)

U.S.C., Title 47, § 401 (Communications Commission)

The provisions of the following and similar statutes as to costs are unaffected:

U.S.C., Title 7, § 210(f) (Actions for damages based on an order of the Secretary of Agriculture under Stockyards Act)

U.S.C., Title 7, § 499g(c) (Appeals from reparations orders of Secretary of Agriculture under Perishable Commodities Act)

U.S.C., Title 8, [former] § 45 (Action against district attorneys in certain cases)

U.S.C., Title 15, § 15 (Actions for injuries due to violation of antitrust laws)

U.S.C., Title 15, § 72 (Actions for violation of law forbidding importation or sale of articles at less than market value or wholesale prices)

U.S.C., Title 15, § 77k (Actions by persons acquiring securities registered with untrue statements under Securities Act of 1933)

U.S.C., Title 15, § 78i(e) (Certain actions under the Securities Exchange Act of 1934)

U.S.C., Title 15, § 78r (Similar to 78i(e))

U.S.C., Title 15, § 96 (Infringement of trade-mark—damages)

U.S.C., Title 15, § 99 (Infringement of trade-mark—injunctions)

U.S.C., Title 15, § 124 (Infringement of trade-mark—damages)

U.S.C., Title 19, § 274 (Certain actions under customs law)

U.S.C., Title 30, § 32 (Action to determine right to possession of mineral lands in certain cases)

U.S.C., Title 31, §§ 232 [now 3730] and 234 [former] (Action for making false claims upon United States)

U.S.C., Title 33, § 926 (Actions under Harbor Workers' Compensation Act)

U.S.C., Title 35, § 67 [now 281, 284] (Infringement of patent—damages)

U.S.C., Title 35, § 69 [now 282] (Infringement of patent—pleading and proof)

U.S.C., Title 35, § 71 [now 288] (Infringement of patent—when specification too broad)

U.S.C., Title 45, § 153p (Actions for non-compliance with an order of National R.R. Adjustment Board for payment of money)

U.S.C., Title 46, [former] § 38 (Action for penalty for failure to register vessel)

U.S.C., Title 46, § 829 (Action based on non-compliance with an order of Maritime Commission for payment of money)

U.S.C., Title 46, § 941 (Certain actions under Ship Mortgage Act)

U.S.C., Title 46, § 1227 (Actions for damages for violation of certain provisions of the Merchant Marine Act, 1936)

U.S.C., Title 47, § 206 (Actions for certain violations of Communications Act of 1934)

U.S.C., Title 49, § 16(2) [now 11705] (Action based on non-compliance with an order of I.C.C. for payment of money)

1946 Amendment

Note. The historic rule in the federal courts has always prohibited piecemeal disposal of litigation and permitted appeals only from final judgments except in those special instances covered by statute. *Hohorst v. Hamburg—American Packet Co.,* 1893, 13 S.Ct. 590, 148 U.S. 262, 37 L.Ed. 443; *Rexford v. Brunswick-Balke-Collender Co.,* 1913, 33 S.Ct. 515, 228 U.S. 339, 57 L.Ed. 864; *Collins v. Miller,* 1920, 40 S.Ct. 347, 252 U.S. 364, 64 L.Ed. 616. Rule 54(b) was originally adopted in view of the wide scope and possible content of the newly created "civil action" in order to avoid the possible injustice of a delay in judgment of a distinctly separate claim to await adjudication of the entire case. It was not designed to overturn the settled federal rule stated above, which, indeed, has more recently been reiterated in *Catlin v. United States,* 1945, 65 S.Ct. 631, 324 U.S. 229, 89 L.Ed. 911. See also *United States v. Florian,* 1941, 61 S.Ct. 713, 312 U.S. 656, 85 L.Ed. 1105; *Reeves v. Beardall,* 1942, 62 S.Ct. 1085, 316 U.S. 283, 86 L.Ed. 1478.

Unfortunately, this was not always understood, and some confusion ensued. Hence situations arose where district courts made a piecemeal disposition of an action and entered what the parties thought amounted to a judgment, although a trial remained to be had on other claims similar or identical with those disposed of. In the interim the parties did not know their ultimate rights, and accordingly took an appeal, thus putting the finality of the partial judgment in question. While most appellate courts have reached a result generally in accord with the intent of the rule, yet there have been divergent precedents and division of views which have served to render the issues more clouded to the parties appellant. It hardly seems a case where multiplicity of precedents will tend to remove the problem from debate. The problem is presented and discussed in the following cases: *Atwater v. North American Coal Corp.,* C.C.A.2, 1940, 111 F.2d 125; *Rosenblum v. Dingfelder,* C.C.A.2, 1940, 111 F.2d 406; *Audi-Vision, Inc. v. RCA Mfg. Co., Inc.,* C.C.A.2, 1943, 136 F.2d 621; *Zalkind v. Scheinman,* C.C.A.2, 1943, 139 F.2d 895; *Oppenheimer v. F. J. Young & Co., Inc.,* C.C.A.2, 1944, 144 F.2d 387; *Libbey-Owens-Ford Glass Co. v. Sylvania Industrial Corp.,* C.C.A.2, 1946, 154 F.2d 814, certiorari denied 1946, 66 S.Ct. 1353, 328 U.S. 859, 90 L.Ed. 1630; *Zarati Steamship Co. v. Park Bridge Corp.,* C.C.A.2, 1946, 154 F.2d 377; *Baltimore and Ohio R. Co. v. United Fuel Gas Co.,* C.C.A.4, 1946, 154 F.2d 545; *Jefferson Electric Co. v. Sola Electric Co.,* C.C.A.7, 1941, 122 F.2d 124; *Leonard v. Socony-Vacuum Oil Co.,* C.C.A.7, 1942, 130 F.2d 535; *Markham v. Kasper,* C.C.A.7, 1945, 152 F.2d 270; *Hanney v. Franklin*

Fire Ins. Co. of Philadelphia, C.C.A.9, 1944, 142 F.2d 864; *Toomey v. Toomey,* App.D.C.1945, 149 F.2d 19, 80 U.S.App. D.C. 77.

In view of the difficulty thus disclosed, the Advisory Committee in its two preliminary drafts of proposed amendments attempted to redefine the original rule with particular stress upon the interlocutory nature of partial judgments which did not adjudicate all claims arising out of a single transaction or occurrence. This attempt appeared to meet with almost universal approval from those of the profession commenting upon it, although there were, of course, helpful suggestions for additional changes in language or clarification of detail. But cf. Circuit Judge Frank's dissenting opinion in *Libbey-Owens-Ford Glass Co. v. Sylvania Industrial Corp.,* supra, n. 21 of the dissenting opinion. The Committee, however, became convinced on careful study of its own proposals that the seeds of ambiguity still remained, and that it had not completely solved the problem of piecemeal appeals. After extended consideration, it concluded that a retention of the older federal rule was desirable, and that this rule needed only the exercise of a discretionary power to afford a remedy in the infrequent harsh case to provide a simple, definite, workable rule. This is afforded by amended Rule 54(b). It re-establishes an ancient policy with clarity and precision. For the possibility of staying execution where not all claims are disposed of under Rule 54(b), see amended Rule 62(h).

1961 Amendment

This rule permitting appeal, upon the trial court's determination of "no just reason for delay," from a judgment upon one or more but less than all the claims in an action, has generally been given a sympathetic construction by the courts and its validity is settled. *Reeves v. Beardall,* 316 U.S. 283 (1942); *Sears, Roebuck & Co. v. Mackey,* 351 U.S. 427 (1956); *Cold Metal Process Co. v. United Engineering & Foundry Co.,* 351 U.S. 445 (1956).

A serious difficulty has, however, arisen because the rule speaks of claims but nowhere mentions parties. A line of cases has developed in the circuits consistently holding the rule to be inapplicable to the dismissal, even with the requisite trial court determination, of one or more but less than all defendants jointly charged in an action, i.e. charged with various forms of concerted or related wrongdoing or related liability. See *Mull v. Ackerman,* 279 F.2d 25 (2d Cir. 1960); *Richards v. Smith,* 276 F.2d 652 (5th Cir. 1960); *Hardy v. Bankers Life & Cas. Co.,* 222 F.2d 827 (7th Cir. 1955); *Steiner v. 20th Century-Fox Film Corp.,* 220 F.2d 105 (9th Cir. 1955). For purposes of Rule 54(b) it was arguable that there were as many "claims" as there were parties defendant and that the rule in its present text applied where less than all of the parties were dismissed, cf. *United Artists Corp. v. Masterpiece Productions, Inc.,* 221 F.2d 213, 215 (2d Cir. 1955); *Bowling Machines, Inc. v. First Nat. Bank,* 283 F.2d 39 (1st Cir. 1960); but the Courts of Appeals are now committed to an opposite view.

The danger of hardship through delay of appeal until the whole action is concluded may be at least as serious in the multiple-parties situations as in multiple-claims cases, see *Pabellon v. Grace Line, Inc.,* 191 F.2d 169, 179 (2d Cir. 1951), cert. denied, 342 U.S. 893 (1951), and courts and commentators have urged that Rule 54(b) be changed to take in the former. See *Reagan v. Traders & General Ins. Co.,* 255 F.2d 845 (5th Cir. 1958); *Meadows v. Greyhound Corp.,* 235 F.2d 233 (5th Cir. 1956); *Steiner v. 20th Century-Fox Film Corp.,* supra; 6 Moore's Federal Practice ¶54.34[2] (2d ed. 1953); 3 Barron & Holtzoff, *Federal Practice & Procedure* § 1193.2 (Wright ed. 1958); *Developments in the Law—Multiparty Litigation,* 71 Harv.L.Rev. 874, 981 (1958); Note, 62 Yale L.J. 263, 271 (1953); Ill.Ann.Stat. ch. 110, § 50(2) (Smith-Hurd 1956). The amendment accomplishes this purpose by referring explicitly to parties.

There has been some recent indication that interlocutory appeal under the provisions of 28 U.S.C. § 1292(b), added in 1958, may now be available for the multiple-parties cases here considered. See *Jaftex Corp. v. Randolph Mills, Inc.,* 282 F.2d 508 (2d Cir. 1960). The Rule 54(b) procedure seems preferable for those cases, and § 1292(b) should be held inapplicable to them when the rule is enlarged as here proposed. See *Luckenbach Steamship Co., Inc., v. H. Muehlstein & Co., Inc.,* 280 F.2d 755, 757 (2d Cir. 1960); 1 Barron & Holtzoff, supra, § 58.1, p. 321 (Wright ed. 1960).

1987 Amendment

The amendment is technical. No substantive change is intended.

1993 Amendments

Subdivision (d). This revision adds paragraph (2) to this subdivision to provide for a frequently recurring form of litigation not initially contemplated by the rules—disputes over the amount of attorneys' fees to be awarded in the large number of actions in which prevailing parties may be entitled to such awards or in which the court must determine the fees to be paid from a common fund. This revision seeks to harmonize and clarify procedures that have been developed through case law and local rules.

Paragraph (1). Former subdivision (d), providing for taxation of costs by the clerk, is renumbered as paragraph (1) and revised to exclude applications for attorneys' fees.

Paragraph (2). This new paragraph establishes a procedure for presenting claims for attorneys' fees, whether or not denominated as "costs." It applies also to requests for reimbursement of expenses, not taxable as costs, when recoverable under governing law incident to the award of fees. *Cf. West Virginia Univ. Hosp. v. Casey,* 499 U.S. 83 (1991), holding, prior to the Civil Rights Act of 1991, that expert witness fees were not recoverable under 42 U.S.C. § 1988. As noted in subparagraph (A), it does not, however, apply to fees recoverable as an element of damages, as when sought under the terms of a contract; such damages typically are to be claimed in a pleading and may involve issues to be resolved by a jury. Nor, as provided in subparagraph (E), does it apply to awards of fees as sanctions authorized or mandated under these rules or under 28 U.S.C. § 1927.

Subparagraph (B) provides a deadline for motions for attorneys' fees—14 days after final judgment unless the court or a statute specifies some other time. One purpose of this provision is to assure that the opposing party is informed of the claim before the time for appeal has elapsed. Prior law did not prescribe any specific time limit on claims for attorneys' fees. White v. New Hampshire Dep't of Employment Sec., 455 U.S. 445 (1982). In many nonjury cases the court will want to consider attorneys' fee issues immediately after rendering its judgment on the merits of the case. Note that the time for making claims is specifically stated in some legislation, such as the Equal Access to Justice Act, 28 U.S.C. § 2412(d)(1)(B) (30–day filing period).

Prompt filing affords an opportunity for the court to resolve fee disputes shortly after trial, while the services performed are freshly in mind. It also enables the court in appropriate circumstances to make its ruling on a fee request in time for any appellate review of a dispute over fees to proceed at the same time as review on the merits of the case.

Filing a motion for fees under this subdivision does not affect the finality or the appealability of a judgment, though revised Rule 58 provides a mechanism by which prior to appeal the court can suspend the finality to resolve a motion for fees. If an appeal on the merits of the case is taken, the court may rule on the claim for fees, may defer its ruling on the motion, or may deny the motion without prejudice, directing under subdivision (d)(2)(B) a new period for filing after the appeal has been resolved. A notice of appeal does not extend the time for filing a fee claim based on the initial judgment, but the court under subdivision (d)(2)(B) may effectively extend the period by permitting claims to be filed after resolution of the appeal. A new period for filing will automatically begin if a new judgment is entered following a reversal or remand by the appellate court or the granting of a motion under Rule 59.

The rule does not require that the motion be supported at the time of filing with the evidentiary material bearing on the fees. This material must of course be submitted in due course, according to such schedule as the court may direct in light of the circumstances of the case. What is required is the filing of a motion sufficient to alert the adversary and the court that there is a claim for fees, and the amount of such fees (or a fair estimate).

If directed by the court, the moving party is also required to disclose any fee agreement, including those between attorney and client, between attorneys sharing a fee to be awarded, and between adversaries made in partial settlement of a dispute where the settlement must be implemented by court action as may be required by Rules 23(e) and 23.1 or other like provisions. With respect to the fee arrangements requiring court approval, the court may also by local rule require disclosure immediately after such arrangements are agreed to. *E.g.*, Rule 5 of United States District Court for the Eastern District of New York; *cf. In re "Agent Orange" Product Liability Litigation (MDL 381)*, 611 F.Supp. 1452, 1464 (E.D.N.Y.1985).

In the settlement of class actions resulting in a common fund from which fees will be sought, courts frequently have required that claims for fees be presented in advance of hearings to consider approval of the proposed settlement. The rule does not affect this practice, as it permits the court to require submissions of fee claims in advance of entry of judgment.

Subparagraph (C) assures the parties of an opportunity to make an appropriate presentation with respect to issues involving the evaluation of legal services. In some cases, an evidentiary hearing may be needed, but this is not required in every case. The amount of time to be allowed for the preparation of submissions both in support of and in opposition to awards should be tailored to the particular case.

The court is explicitly authorized to make a determination of the liability for fees before receiving submissions by the parties bearing on the amount of an award. This option may be appropriate in actions in which the liability issue is doubtful and the evaluation issues are numerous and complex.

The court may order disclosure of additional information, such as that bearing on prevailing local rates or on the appropriateness of particular services for which compensation is sought.

On rare occasion, the court may determine that discovery under Rules 26–37 would be useful to the parties. *Compare* Rules Governing Section 2254 Cases in the U.S. District Courts, Rule 6. *See* Note, *Determining the Reasonableness of Attorneys' Fees—the Discoverability of Billing Records*, 64 *B.U.L.Rev.* 241 (1984). In complex fee disputes, the court may use case management techniques to limit the scope of the dispute or to facilitate the settlement of fee award disputes.

Fee awards should be made in the form of a separate judgment under Rule 58 since such awards are subject to review in the court of appeals. To facilitate review, the paragraph provides that the court set forth its findings and conclusions as under Rule 52(a), though in most cases this explanation could be quite brief.

Subparagraph (D) explicitly authorizes the court to establish procedures facilitating the efficient and fair resolution of fee claims. A local rule, for example, might call for matters to be presented through affidavits, or might provide for issuance of proposed findings by the court, which would be treated as accepted by the parties unless objected to within a specified time. A court might also consider establishing a schedule reflecting customary fees or factors affecting fees within the community, as implicitly suggested by Justice O'Connor in *Pennsylvania v. Delaware Valley Citizens' Council*, 483 U.S. 711, 733 (1987) (O'Connor, J., concurring) (how particular markets compensate for contingency). *Cf. Thompson v. Kennickell*, 710 F.Supp. 1 (D.D.C.1989) (use of findings in other cases to promote consistency). The parties, of course, should be permitted to show that in the circumstances of the case such a schedule should not be applied or that different hourly rates would be appropriate.

The rule also explicitly permits, without need for a local rule, the court to refer issues regarding the amount of a fee award in a particular case to a master under Rule 53. The district judge may designate a magistrate judge to act as a master for this purpose or may refer a motion for attorneys' fees to a magistrate judge for proposed findings and recommendations under Rule 72(b). This authorization eliminates any controversy as to whether such references are permitted under Rule 53(b) as "matters of account and of difficult computation of damages" and whether motions for attorneys' fees can be treated as the equivalent of a dispositive pretrial matter that can be referred to a magistrate judge. For consistency and efficiency, all such matters might be referred to the same magistrate judge.

Subparagraph (E) excludes from this rule the award of fees as sanctions under these rules or under 28 U.S.C. § 1927.

2002 Amendments

Subdivision (d)(2)(C) is amended to delete the requirement that judgment on a motion for attorney fees be set forth in a separate document. This change complements the amendment of Rule 58(a)(1), which deletes the separate document requirement for an order disposing of a motion for attorney fees under Rule 54. These changes are made to support amendment of Rule 4 of the Federal Rules of Appellate Procedure. It continues to be important that a district court make clear its meaning when it intends an order to be the final disposition of a motion for attorney fees.

The requirement in subdivision (d)(2)(B) that a motion for attorney fees be not only filed but also served no later than 14 days after entry of judgment is changed to require filing only, to establish a parallel with Rules 50, 52, and 59. Service continues to be required under Rule 5(a).

2003 Amendments

Rule 54(d)(2)(D) is revised to reflect amendments to Rule 53.

2007 Amendments

The language of Rule 54 has been amended as part of the general restyling of the Civil Rules to make them more easily understood and to make style and terminology consistent throughout the rules. These changes are intended to be stylistic only.

The words "or class member" have been removed from Rule 54(d)(2)(C) because Rule 23(h)(2) now addresses objections by class members to attorney-fee motions. Rule 54(d)(2)(C) is amended to recognize that Rule 23(h) now controls those aspects of attorney-fee motions in class actions to which it is addressed.

HISTORICAL NOTES

Effective and Applicability Provisions

1961 Amendments. Amendment adopted on Apr. 17, 1961, effective July 19, 1961, see Rule 86(d).

Rule 55. Default; Default Judgment

(a) Entering a Default. When a party against whom a judgment for affirmative relief is sought has failed to plead or otherwise defend, and that failure is shown by affidavit or otherwise, the clerk must enter the party's default.

(b) Entering a Default Judgment.

(1) ***By the Clerk.*** If the plaintiff's claim is for a sum certain or a sum that can be made certain by computation, the clerk—on the plaintiff's request, with an affidavit showing the amount due—must enter judgment for that amount and costs against a defendant who has been defaulted for not appearing and who is neither a minor nor an incompetent person.

(2) ***By the Court.*** In all other cases, the party must apply to the court for a default judgment. A default judgment may be entered against a minor or incompetent person only if represented by a general guardian, conservator, or other like fiduciary who has appeared. If the party against whom a default judgment is sought has appeared personally or by a representative, that party or its representative must be served with written notice of the application at least 3 days before the hearing. The court may conduct hearings or make referrals—preserving any federal statutory right to a jury trial—when, to enter or effectuate judgment, it needs to:

(A) conduct an accounting;

(B) determine the amount of damages;

(C) establish the truth of any allegation by evidence; or

(D) investigate any other matter.

(c) Setting Aside a Default or a Default Judgment. The court may set aside an entry of default for good cause, and it may set aside a default judgment under Rule 60(b).

(d) Judgment Against the United States. A default judgment may be entered against the United States, its officers, or its agencies only if the claimant establishes a claim or right to relief by evidence that satisfies the court.

(Amended March 2, 1987, effective August 1, 1987; April 30, 2007, effective December 1, 2007.)

ADVISORY COMMITTEE NOTES

1937 Adoption

This represents the joining of the equity decree *pro confesso* (former Equity Rules 12 (Issue of Subpoena—Time for Answer), 16 (Defendant to Answer—Default—Decree *Pro Confesso*), 17 (Decree *Pro Confesso* to be Followed by Final Decree—Setting Aside Default), 29 (Defenses—How Presented), 31 (Reply—When Required—When Cause at Issue)) and the judgment by default now governed by U.S.C., Title 28, [former] § 724 (Conformity act). For dismissal of an action for failure to comply with these rules or any order of the court, see Rule 41(b).

Note to Subdivision (a). The provision for the entry of default comes from the Massachusetts practice, 2 Mass.Gen. Laws (Ter.Ed., 1932) ch. 231, § 57. For affidavit of default, see 2 Minn.Stat. (Mason, 1927) § 9256.

Note to Subdivision (b). The provision in paragraph (1) for the entry of judgment by the clerk when plaintiff claims a sum certain is found in the N.Y.C.P.A. (1937) § 485, in Calif.Code Civ.Proc. (Deering, 1937) § 585(1), and in Conn.Practice Book (1934) § 47. For provisions similar to paragraph (2), compare Calif.Code, *supra*, § 585(2); N.Y.C.P.A. (1937) § 490; 2 Minn.Stat. (Mason, 1927) § 9256(3); 2 Wash.Rev.Stat.Ann. (Remington, 1932) § 411(2). U.S.C., Title 28, § 1874, formerly § 785 (Action to recover forfeiture in bond) and similar statutes are preserved by the last clause of paragraph (2).

Note to Subdivision (e). This restates substantially the last clause of U.S.C., Title 28, [former] § 763 (Action against the United States under the Tucker Act). As this rule governs in all actions against the United States, U.S.C., Title 28, [former] § 45 (Practice and procedure in certain cases under the interstate commerce laws) and similar statutes are modified insofar as they contain anything inconsistent therewith.

Supplementary Note

Note. The operation of Rule 55(b) (Judgment) is directly affected by the Soldiers' and Sailors' Civil Relief Act of 1940, 50 U.S.C. Appendix, § 501 et seq. Section 200 of the Act [50 U.S.C. Appendix, § 520] imposes specific requirements which must be fulfilled before a default judgment can be entered, e.g., *Ledwith v. Storkan,* D.Neb.1942, 6 Fed.Rules Serv. 60b.24, Case 2, 2 F.R.D. 539, and also provides for the vacation of a judgment in certain circumstances. See discussion in Commentary, Effect of Conscription Legislation on the Federal Rules, 1940, 3 Fed.Rules Serv. 725; 3 *Moore's Federal Practice,* 1938, Cum.Supplement § 55.02.

1987 Amendment

The amendments are technical. No substantive change is intended.

2007 Amendments

The language of Rule 55 has been amended as part of the general restyling of the Civil Rules to make them more easily understood and to make style and terminology consistent throughout the rules. These changes are intended to be stylistic only.

Former Rule 55(a) directed the clerk to enter a default when a party failed to plead or otherwise defend "as provided by these rules." The implication from the reference to defending "as provided by these rules" seemed to be that the clerk should enter a default even if a party did something showing an intent to defend, but that act was not specifically described by the rules. Courts in fact have rejected that implication. Acts that show an intent to defend have frequently prevented a default even though not connected to any particular rule. "[A]s provided by these rules" is deleted to reflect Rule 55(a)'s actual meaning.

Amended Rule 55 omits former Rule 55(d), which included two provisions. The first recognized that Rule 55 applies to described claimants. The list was incomplete and unnecessary. Rule 55(a) applies Rule 55 to any party against whom a judgment for affirmative relief is requested. The second provision was a redundant reminder that Rule 54(c) limits the relief available by default judgment.

Rule 56. Summary Judgment

(a) By a Claiming Party. A party claiming relief may move, with or without supporting affidavits, for summary judgment on all or part of the claim. The motion may be filed at any time after:

(1) 20 days have passed from commencement of the action; or

(2) the opposing party serves a motion for summary judgment.

(b) By a Defending Party. A party against whom relief is sought may move at any time, with or without supporting affidavits, for summary judgment on all or part of the claim.

(c) Serving the Motion; Proceedings. The motion must be served at least 10 days before the day set for the hearing. An opposing party may serve opposing affidavits before the hearing day. The judgment sought should be rendered if the pleadings, the discovery and disclosure materials on file, and any affidavits show that there is no genuine issue as to any material fact and that the movant is entitled to judgment as a matter of law.

(d) Case Not Fully Adjudicated on the Motion.

(1) ***Establishing Facts.*** If summary judgment is not rendered on the whole action, the court should, to the extent practicable, determine what material facts are not genuinely at issue. The court should so determine by examining the pleadings and evidence before it and by interrogating the attorneys. It should then issue an order specifying what facts—including items of damages or other relief—are not genuinely at issue. The facts so specified must be treated as established in the action.

(2) ***Establishing Liability.*** An interlocutory summary judgment may be rendered on liability alone, even if there is a genuine issue on the amount of damages.

(e) Affidavits; Further Testimony.

(1) ***In General.*** A supporting or opposing affidavit must be made on personal knowledge, set out facts that would be admissible in evidence, and show that the affiant is competent to testify on the matters stated. If a paper or part of a paper is referred to in an affidavit, a sworn or certified copy must be attached to or served with the affidavit. The court may permit an affidavit to be supplemented or opposed by depositions, answers to interrogatories, or additional affidavits.

(2) ***Opposing Party's Obligation to Respond.*** When a motion for summary judgment is properly made and supported, an opposing party may not rely merely on allegations or denials in its own pleading; rather, its response must—by affidavits or as otherwise provided in this rule—set out specific facts showing a genuine issue for trial. If the opposing party does not so respond, summary judgment should, if appropriate, be entered against that party.

escape notes

(f) When Affidavits Are Unavailable. If a party opposing the motion shows by affidavit that, for specified reasons, it cannot present facts essential to justify its opposition, the court may:

(1) deny the motion;

(2) order a continuance to enable affidavits to be obtained, depositions to be taken, or other discovery to be undertaken; or

(3) issue any other just order.

(g) **Affidavit Submitted in Bad Faith.** If satisfied that an affidavit under this rule is submitted in bad faith or solely for delay, the court must order the submitting party to pay the other party the reasonable expenses, including attorney's fees, it incurred as a result. An offending party or attorney may also be held in contempt.

(Amended December 27, 1946, effective March 19, 1948; January 21, 1963, effective July 1, 1963; March 2, 1987, effective August 1, 1987; April 30, 2007, effective December 1, 2007.)

ADVISORY COMMITTEE NOTES

1937 Adoption

This rule is applicable to all actions, including those against the United States or an officer or agency thereof.

Summary judgment procedure is a method for promptly disposing of actions in which there is no genuine issue as to any material fact. It has been extensively used in England for more than 50 years and has been adopted in a number of American states. New York, for example, has made great use of it. During the first nine years after its adoption there, the records of New York county alone show 5,600 applications for summary judgments. Report of the Commission on the Administration of Justice in New York State (1934), p. 383. See also *Third Annual Report of the Judicial Council of the State of New York* (1937), p. 30.

In England it was first employed only in cases of liquidated claims, but there has been a steady enlargement of the scope of the remedy until it is now used in actions to recover land or chattels and in all other actions at law, for liquidated or unliquidated claims, except for a few designated torts and breach of promise of marriage. *English Rules Under the Judicature Act* (The Annual Practice, 1937) O. 3, r. 6; Orders 14, 14A, and 15; see also O. 32, r. 6, authorizing an application for judgment at any time upon admissions. In Michigan (3 Comp.Laws (1929) § 14260) and Illinois (Smith-Hurd Ill.Stats. c. 110, §§ 181, 259.15, 259.16), it is not limited to liquidated demands. New York (N.Y.R.C.P. (1937) Rule 113; see also Rule 107) has brought so many classes of actions under the operation of the rule that the Commission on Administration of Justice in New York State (1934) recommend that all restrictions be removed and that the remedy be available "in any action" (p. 287). For the history and nature of the summary judgment procedure and citations of state statutes, see Clark and Samenow, *The Summary Judgment* (1929), 38 Yale L.J. 423.

Note to Subdivision (d). See Rule 16 (Pre-Trial Procedure; Formulating Issues) and the Note thereto.

Note to Subdivisions (e) and (f). These are similar to rules in Michigan. Mich.Court Rules Ann. (Searl, 1933) Rule 30.

1946 Amendment

Note to Subdivision (a). The amendment allows a claimant to move for a summary judgment at any time after the expiration of 20 days from the commencement of the action or after service of a motion for summary judgment by the adverse party. This will normally operate to permit an earlier motion by the claimant than under the original rule, where the phrase "at any time after the pleading in answer thereto has been served" operates to prevent a claimant from moving for summary judgment, even in a case clearly proper for its exercise, until a formal answer has been filed. Thus in *Peoples Bank v. Federal Reserve Bank of San Francisco,* N.D.Cal.1944, 58 F.Supp. 25, the plaintiff's countermotion for a summary judgment was stricken as premature, because the defendant had not filed an answer. Since Rule 12(a) allows at least 20 days for an answer, that time plus the 10 days required in Rule 56(c) means that under original Rule 56(a) a minimum period of 30 days necessarily has to elapse in every case before the claimant can be heard on his right to a summary judgment. An extension of time by the court or the service of preliminary motions of any kind will prolong that period even further. In many cases this merely represents unnecessary delay. See *United States v. Adler's Creamery, Inc.,* C.C.A.2, 1939, 107 F.2d 987. The changes are in the interest of more expeditious litigation. The 20-day period, as provided, gives the defendant an opportunity to secure counsel and determine a course of action. But in a case where the defendant himself makes a motion for summary judgment within that time, there is no reason to restrict the plaintiff and the amended rule so provides.

Subdivision (c). The amendment of Rule 56(c), by the addition of the final sentence, resolves a doubt expressed in *Sartor v. Arkansas Natural Gas Corp.,* 1944, 64 S.Ct. 724, 321 U.S. 620, 88 L.Ed. 967. See also Commentary, Summary Judgment as to Damages, 1944, 7 Fed.Rules Serv. 974; *Madeirense Do Brasil S/A v. Stulman-Emrick Lumber Co.,* C.C.A.2d, 1945, 147 F.2d 399, certiorari denied 1945, 65 S.Ct. 1201, 325 U.S. 861, 89 L.Ed. 1982. It makes clear that although the question of recovery depends on the amount of damages, the summary judgment rule is applicable and summary judgment may be granted in a proper case. If the case is not fully adjudicated it may be dealt with as provided in subdivision (d) of Rule 56, and the right to summary recovery determined by a preliminary order, interlocutory in character, and the precise amount of recovery left for trial.

Subdivision (d). Rule 54(a) defines "judgment" as including a decree and "any order from which an appeal lies." Subdivision (d) of Rule 56 indicates clearly, however, that a partial summary "judgment" is not a final judgment, and, therefore, that it is not appealable, unless in the particular case some statute allows an appeal from the interlocutory order involved. The partial summary judgment is merely a pretrial adjudication that certain issues shall be deemed established for the trial of the case. This adjudication is more nearly akin to the preliminary order under Rule 16, and likewise serves the purpose of speeding up litigation by eliminating before trial matters wherein there is no genuine issue of fact. See *Leonard v. Socony-Vacuum Oil Co.,* C.C.A.7, 1942, 130 F.2d 535; *Biggins v. Oltmer Iron Works,* C.C.A.7, 1946, 154 F.2d 214; 3 *Moore's Federal Practice,* 1938, 3190–3192. Since interlocutory appeals are not allowed, except where specifically provided by statute, see 3 Moore, op. cit. supra, 3155–3156, this interpretation is in line with that policy, *Leonard v. Socony-Vacuum Oil Co.*, supra. See also *Audi Vision Inc. v. RCA Mfg. Co.*, C.C.A.2, 1943, 136 F.2d 621; *Toomey v. Toomey*, 1945, 149 F.2d 19, 80 U.S.App.D.C. 77; *Biggins v. Oltmer Iron Works*, supra; *Catlin v. United States*, 1945, 65 S.Ct. 631, 324 U.S. 229, 89 L.Ed. 911.

1963 Amendment

Subdivision (c). By the amendment "answers to interrogatories" are included among the materials which may be considered on motion for summary judgment. The phrase was inadvertently omitted from the rule, see 3 Barron & Holtzoff, *Federal Practice & Procedure* 159–60 (Wright ed. 1958), and the courts have generally reached by interpretation the result which will hereafter be required by the text of the amended rule. See Annot., 74 A.L.R.2d 984 (1960).

Subdivision (e). The words "answers to interrogatories" are added in the third sentence of this subdivision to conform to the amendment of subdivision (c).

The last two sentences are added to overcome a line of cases, chiefly in the Third Circuit, which has impaired the utility of the summary judgment device. A typical case is as follows: A party supports his motion for summary judgment by affidavits or other evidentiary matter sufficient to show that there is no genuine issue as to a material fact. The adverse party, in opposing the motion, does not produce any evidentiary matter, or produces some but not enough to establish that there is a genuine issue for trial. Instead, the adverse party rests on averments of his pleadings which on their face present an issue. In this situation Third Circuit cases have taken the view that summary judgment must be denied, at least if the averments are "well-pleaded," and not suppositious, conclusory, or ultimate. See *Frederick Hart & Co., Inc. v. Recordgraph Corp.*, 169 F.2d 580 (3d Cir. 1948); *United States ex rel. Kolton v. Halpern*, 260 F.2d 590 (3d Cir. 1958); *United States ex rel. Nobles v. Ivey Bros. Constr. Co., Inc.*, 191 F.Supp. 383 (D.Del.1961); *Jamison v. Pennsylvania Salt Mfg. Co.*, 22 F.R.D. 238 (W.D.Pa.1958); *Bunny Bear, Inc. v. Dennis Mitchell Industries*, 139 F.Supp. 542 (E.D.Pa.1956); *Levy v. Equitable Life Assur. Society*, 18 F.R.D. 164 (E.D.Pa.1955).

The very mission of the summary judgment procedure is to pierce the pleadings and to assess the proof in order to see whether there is a genuine need for trial. The Third Circuit doctrine, which permits the pleadings themselves to stand in the way of granting an otherwise justified summary judgment, is incompatible with the basic purpose of the rule. See 6 *Moore's Federal Practice* 2069 (2d ed. 1953); 3 Barron & Holtzoff, supra, § 1235.1.

It is hoped that the amendment will contribute to the more effective utilization of the salutary device of summary judgment.

The amendment is not intended to derogate from the solemnity of the pleadings. Rather it recognizes that, despite the best efforts of counsel to make his pleadings accurate, they may be overwhelmingly contradicted by the proof available to his adversary.

Nor is the amendment designed to affect the ordinary standards applicable to the summary judgment motion. So, for example: Where an issue as to a material fact cannot be resolved without observation of the demeanor of witnesses in order to evaluate their credibility, summary judgment is not appropriate. Where the evidentiary matter in support of the motion does not establish the absence of a genuine issue, summary judgment must be denied even if no opposing evidentiary matter is presented. And summary judgment may be inappropriate where the party opposing it shows under subdivision (f) that he cannot at the time present facts essential to justify his opposition.

1987 Amendment

The amendments are technical. No substantive change is intended.

2007 Amendments

The language of Rule 56 has been amended as part of the general restyling of the Civil Rules to make them more easily understood and to make style and terminology consistent throughout the rules. These changes are intended to be stylistic only.

Former Rule 56(a) and (b) referred to summary-judgment motions on or against a claim, counterclaim, or crossclaim, or to obtain a declaratory judgment. The list was incomplete. Rule 56 applies to third-party claimants, intervenors, claimants in interpleader, and others. Amended Rule 56(a) and (b) carry forward the present meaning by referring to a party claiming relief and a party against whom relief is sought.

Former Rule 56(c), (d), and (e) stated circumstances in which summary judgment "shall be rendered," the court "shall if practicable" ascertain facts existing without substantial controversy, and "if appropriate, shall" enter summary judgment. In each place "shall" is changed to "should." It is established that although there is no discretion to enter summary judgment when there is a genuine issue as to any material fact, there is discretion to deny summary judgment when it appears that there is no genuine issue as to any material fact. *Kennedy v. Silas Mason Co.*, 334 U.S. 249, 256–257 (1948). Many lower court decisions are gathered in 10A Wright, Miller & Kane, Federal Practice & Procedure: Civil 3d, § 2728. "Should" in amended Rule 56(c) recognizes that courts will seldom exercise the discretion to deny summary judgment when there is no genuine issue as to any material fact. Similarly sparing exercise of this discretion is appropriate under Rule 56(e)(2). Rule 56(d)(1), on the other hand, reflects the more open-ended discretion to decide whether it is practicable to determine what material facts are not genuinely at issue.

Former Rule 56(d) used a variety of different phrases to express the Rule 56(c) standard for summary judgment—that there is no genuine issue as to any material fact. Amended Rule 56(d) adopts terms directly parallel to Rule 56(c).

Rule 57. Declaratory Judgment

These rules govern the procedure for obtaining a declaratory judgment under 28 U.S.C. § 2201. Rules 38 and 39 govern a demand for a jury trial. The existence of another adequate remedy does not preclude a declaratory judgment that is otherwise appropriate. The court may order a speedy hearing of a declaratory-judgment action.

(Amended December 29, 1948, effective October 20, 1949; April 30, 2007, effective December 1, 2007.)

ADVISORY COMMITTEE NOTES

1937 Adoption

The fact that a declaratory judgment may be granted "whether or not further relief is or could be prayed" indicates that declaratory relief is alternative or cumulative and not exclusive or extraordinary. A declaratory judgment is appropriate when it will "terminate the controversy" giving rise on undisputed or relatively undisputed facts, it operates frequently as a summary proceeding, justifying docketing the case for early hearing as on a motion, as provided for in California (Code Civ.Proc. (Deering, 1937) § 1062a), Michigan (3 Comp.Laws (1929) § 13904), and Kentucky (Codes (Carroll, 1932) Civ.Pract. § 639a–3).

The "controversy" must necessarily be "of a justiciable nature, thus excluding an advisory decree upon a hypothetical state of facts." *Ashwander v. Tennessee Valley Authority,* 1936, 56 S.Ct. 466, 473, 297 U.S. 288, 80 L.Ed. 688. The existence or non-existence of any right, duty, power, liability, privilege, disability, or immunity or of any fact upon which such legal relations depend, or of a status, may be declared. The petitioner must have a practical interest in the declaration sought and all parties having an interest therein or adversely affected must be made parties or be cited. A declaration may not be rendered if a special statutory proceeding has been provided for the adjudication of some special type of case, but general ordinary or extraordinary legal remedies, whether regulated by statute or not, are not deemed special statutory proceedings.

When declaratory relief will not be effective in settling the controversy, the court may decline to grant it. But the fact that another remedy would be equally effective affords no ground for declining declaratory relief. The demand for relief shall state with precision the declaratory judgment relief, cumulatively or in the alternative; but when coercive relief only is sought but is deemed ungrantable, or inappropriate, the court may *sua sponte,* if it serves a useful purpose, grant instead a declaration of rights. *Hasselbring v. Koepke,* 1933, 248 N.W. 869, 263 Mich. 466, 93 A.L.R. 1170. Written instruments, including ordinances and statutes, may be construed before or after breach at the petition of a properly interested party, process being served on the private parties or public officials interested. In other respects the Uniform Declaratory Judgment Act affords a guide to the scope and function of the Federal act. Compare *Aetna Life Insurance Co. v. Haworth,* 1937, 57 S.Ct. 461, 300 U.S. 227, 81 L.Ed. 617, 108 A.L.R. 1000; *Nashville, Chattanooga & St. Louis Ry. v. Wallace,* 1933, 53 S.Ct. 345, 288 U.S. 249, 77 L.Ed. 730, 87 A.L.R. 1191; *Gully, Tax Collector v. Interstate Natural Gas Co.,* 82 F.2d 145 (C.C.A.5, 1936); *Ohio Casualty Ins. Co. v. Plummer,* Tex.1935, 13 F.Supp. 169; Borchard, Declaratory Judgments (1934), *passim.*

1948 Amendment

The amendment effective October 1949, substituted the reference to "Title 28, U.S.C., § 2201" in the first sentence for the reference to "Section 274(d) of the Judicial Code, as amended, U.S.C., Title 28, § 400".

2007 Amendments

The language of Rule 57 has been amended as part of the general restyling of the Civil Rules to make them more easily understood and to make style and terminology consistent throughout the rules. These changes are intended to be stylistic only.

Rule 58. Entering Judgment

(a) **Separate Document.** Every judgment and amended judgment must be set out in a separate document, but a separate document is not required for an order disposing of a motion:

(1) for judgment under Rule 50(b);

(2) to amend or make additional findings under Rule 52(b);

(3) for attorney's fees under Rule 54;

(4) for a new trial, or to alter or amend the judgment, under Rule 59; or

(5) for relief under Rule 60.

(b) **Entering Judgment.**

(1) ***Without the Court's Direction.*** Subject to Rule 54(b) and unless the court orders otherwise, the clerk must, without awaiting the court's direction, promptly prepare, sign, and enter the judgment when:

(A) the jury returns a general verdict;

(B) the court awards only costs or a sum certain; or

(C) the court denies all relief.

(2) ***Court's Approval Required.*** Subject to Rule 54(b), the court must promptly approve the form of the judgment, which the clerk must promptly enter, when:

(A) the jury returns a special verdict or a general verdict with answers to written questions; or

(B) the court grants other relief not described in this subdivision (b).

(c) **Time of Entry.** For purposes of these rules, judgment is entered at the following times:

(1) if a separate document is not required, when the judgment is entered in the civil docket under Rule 79(a); or

(2) if a separate document is required, when the judgment is entered in the civil docket under Rule 79(a) and the earlier of these events occurs:

(A) it is set out in a separate document; or

(B) 150 days have run from the entry in the civil docket.

(d) **Request for Entry.** A party may request that judgment be set out in a separate document as required by Rule 58(a).

(e) **Cost or Fee Awards.** Ordinarily, the entry of judgment may not be delayed, nor the time for appeal extended, in order to tax costs or award fees. But if a timely motion for attorney's fees is made under Rule 54(d)(2), the court may act before a notice of appeal has been filed and become effective to order that the motion have the same effect under Federal Rule of Appellate Procedure 4(a)(4) as a timely motion under Rule 59.

(Amended December 27, 1946, effective March 19, 1948; January 21, 1963, effective July 1, 1963; April 22, 1993, effective December 1, 1993; April 29, 2002, effective December 1, 2002; April 30, 2007, effective December 1, 2007.)

ADVISORY COMMITTEE NOTES

1937 Adoption

See Wis.Stat. (1935) § 270.31 (judgment entered forthwith on verdict of jury unless otherwise ordered), § 270.65 (where trial is by the court, entered by direction of the court), § 270.63 (entered by clerk on judgment on admitted claim for money). Compare 1 Idaho Code Ann. (1932) § 7–1101, and 4 Mont.Rev.Codes Ann. (1935) § 9403, which provide that judgment in jury cases be entered by clerk within 24 hours after verdict unless court otherwise directs. Conn.Practice Book (1934), § 200, provides that all judgments shall be entered within one week after rendition. In some States such as Washington, 2 Rev.Stat.Ann. (Remington, 1932), § 431, in jury cases the judgment is entered two days after the return of verdict to give time for making motion for new trial; § 435 (*ibid.*), provides that all judgments shall be entered by the clerk, subject to the court's direction.

1946 Amendment

Note. The reference to Rule 54(b) is made necessary by the amendment of that rule.

Two changes have been made in Rule 58 in order to clarify the practice. The substitution of the more inclusive phrase "all relief be denied" for the words "there be no recovery", makes it clear that the clerk shall enter the judgment forthwith in the situations specified without awaiting the filing of a formal judgment approved by the court. The phrase "all relief be denied" covers cases such as the denial of a bankrupt's discharge and similar situations where the relief sought is refused but there is literally no denial of a "recovery".

The addition of the last sentence in the rule emphasizes that judgments are to be entered promptly by the clerk without waiting for the taxing of costs. Certain district court rules, for example, Civil Rule 22 of the Southern District of New York—until its annulment Oct. 1, 1945, for conflict with this rule—and the like rule of the Eastern District of New York, are expressly in conflict with this provision, although the federal law is of long standing and well settled. *Fowler v. Hamill,* 1891, 11 S.Ct. 663, 139 U.S. 549, 35 L.Ed. 266; *Craig v. The Hartford,* C.C.Cal.1856, Fed.Cas. No. 3,333; *Tuttle v. Claflin,* C.C.A.2, 1895, 60 F. 7, certiorari denied 1897; 17 S.Ct. 992, 166 U.S. 721, 41 L.Ed. 1188; *Prescott & A.C. Ry. Co. v. Atchison, T. & S.F.R. Co.,* C.C.A.2, 1897, 84 F. 213; *Stallo v. Wagner,* C.C.A.2, 1917, 245 F. 636, 639–40; *Brown v. Parker,* C.C.A.8, 1899, 97 F. 446; *Allis-Chalmers v. United States,* C.C.A.7, 1908, 162 F. 679. And this applies even though state law is to the contrary. *United States v. Nordbye,* C.C.A.8, 1935, 75 F.2d 744, certiorari denied 56 S.Ct. 103, 296 U.S. 572, 80 L.Ed. 404. Inasmuch as it has been held that failure of the clerk thus to enter judgment is a "misprision" "not to be excused", *The Washington,* C.C.A.2, 1926, 16 F.2d 206, such a district court rule may have serious consequences for a district court clerk. Rules of this sort also provide for delay in entry of the judgment contrary to Rule 58. See *Commissioner of Internal Revenue v. Bedford's Estate,* 1945, 65 S.Ct. 1157, 325 U.S. 283, 91 L.Ed. 1611.

1963 Amendment

Under the present rule a distinction has sometimes been made between judgments on general jury verdicts, on the one hand, and, on the other, judgments upon decisions of the court that a party shall recover only money or costs or that all relief shall be denied. In the first situation, it is clear that the clerk should enter the judgment without awaiting a direction by the court unless the court otherwise orders. In the second situation it was intended that the clerk should similarly enter the judgment forthwith upon the court's decision; but because of the separate listing in the rule, and the use of the phrase "upon receipt . . . of the direction," the rule has sometimes been interpreted as requiring the clerk to await a separate direction of the court. All these judgments are usually uncomplicated, and should be handled in the same way. The amended rule accordingly deals with them as a single group in clause (1) (substituting the expression "only a sum certain" for the present expression "only money"), and requires the clerk to prepare, sign and enter them forthwith, without awaiting court direction, unless the court makes a contrary order. (The clerk's duty is ministerial and may be performed by a deputy clerk in the name of the clerk. See 28 U.S.C. § 956; cf. *Gilbertson v. United States,* 168 Fed. 672 (7th Cir. 1909).) The more complicated judgments described in clause (2) must be approved by the court before they are entered.

Rule 58 is designed to encourage all reasonable speed in formulating and entering the judgment when the case has been decided. Participation by the attorneys through the submission of forms of judgment involves needless expenditure of time and effort and promotes delay, except in special cases where counsel's assistance can be of real value. See *Matteson v. United States,* 240 F.2d 517, 518–19 (2d Cir. 1956). Accordingly, the amended rule provides that attorneys shall not submit forms of judgment unless directed to do so by the court. This applies to the judgments mentioned in clause (2) as well as clause (1).

Hitherto some difficulty has arisen, chiefly where the court has written an opinion or memorandum containing some apparently directive or dispositive words, e.g., "the plaintiff's motion [for summary judgment] is granted," see *United States v. F. & M. Schaefer Brewing Co.,* 356 U.S. 227, 229, 78 S.Ct. 674, 2 L.Ed.2d 721 (1958). Clerks on occasion have viewed these opinions or memoranda as being in themselves a sufficient basis for entering judgment in the civil docket as provided by Rule 79(a). However, where the opinion or memorandum has not contained all the elements of a judgment, or where the judge has later signed a formal judgment, it has become a matter of doubt whether the purported entry of judgment was effective, starting the time running for post-verdict motions and for the purpose of appeal. See id.; and compare *Blanchard v. Commonwealth Oil Co.,* 294 F.2d 834 (5th Cir. 1961); *United States v. Higginson,* 238

F.2d 439 (1st Cir. 1956); *Danzig v. Virgin Isle Hotel, Inc.*, 278 F.2d 580 (3d Cir. 1960); *Sears v. Austin*, 282 F.2d 340 (9th Cir. 1960), with *Matteson v. United States*, supra; *Erstling v. Southern Bell Tel. & Tel. Co.*, 255 F.2d 93 (5th Cir. 1958); *Barta v. Oglala Sioux Tribe*, 259 F.2d 553 (8th Cir. 1958) cert. denied, 358 U.S. 932, 79 S.Ct. 320, 3 L.Ed.2d 304 (1959); *Beacon Fed. S. & L. Assn. v. Federal Home L. Bank Bd.*, 266 F.2d 246 (7th Cir.), cert. denied, 361 U.S. 823, 80 S.Ct. 70, 4 L.Ed.2d 67 (1959); *Ram v. Paramount Film D. Corp.*, 278 F.2d 191 (4th Cir. 1960).

The amended rule eliminates these uncertainties by requiring that there be a judgment set out on a separate document—distinct from any opinion or memorandum—which provides the basis for the entry of judgment. That judgment shall be on separate documents is also indicated in Rule 79(b); and see General Rule 10 of the U.S. District Courts for the Eastern and Southern Districts of New York; *Ram v. Paramount Film D. Corp.*, supra, at 194.

See the amendment of Rule 79(a) and the new specimen forms of judgment, Forms 31 and 32.

See also Rule 55(b)(1) and (2) covering the subject of judgments by default.

1993 Amendments

Ordinarily the pendency or post-judgment filing of a claim for attorney's fees will not affect the time for appeal from the underlying judgment. See Budinich v. Becton Dickinson & Co., 486 U.S. 196 (1988). Particularly if the claim for fees involves substantial issues or is likely to be affected by the appellate decision, the district court may prefer to defer consideration of the claim for fees until after the appeal is resolved. However, in many cases it may be more efficient to decide fee questions before an appeal is taken so that appeals relating to the fee award can be heard at the same time as appeals relating to the merits of the case. This revision permits, but does not require, the court to delay the finality of the judgment for appellate purposes under revised Fed.R.App.P. 4(a) until the fee dispute is decided. To accomplish this result requires entry of an order by the district court before the time a notice of appeal becomes effective for appellate purposes. If the order is entered, the motion for attorney's fees is treated in the same manner as a timely motion under Rule 59.

2002 Amendments

Rule 58 has provided that a judgment is effective only when set forth on a separate document and entered as provided in Rule 79(a). This simple separate document requirement has been ignored in many cases. The result of failure to enter judgment on a separate document is that the time for making motions under Rules 50, 52, 54(d)(2)(B), 59, and some motions under Rule 60, never begins to run. The time to appeal under Appellate Rule 4(a) also does not begin to run. There have been few visible problems with respect to Rule 50, 52, 54(d)(2)(B), 59, or 60 motions, but there have been many and horridly confused problems under Appellate Rule 4(a). These amendments are designed to work in conjunction with Appellate Rule 4(a) to ensure that appeal time does not linger on indefinitely, and to maintain the integration of the time periods set for Rules 50, 52, 54(d)(2)(B), 59, and 60 with Appellate Rule 4(a).

Rule 58(a) preserves the core of the present separate document requirement, both for the initial judgment and for any amended judgment. No attempt is made to sort through the confusion that some courts have found in addressing the elements of a separate document. It is easy to prepare a separate document that recites the terms of the judgment without offering additional explanation or citation of authority. Forms 31 and 32 provide examples.

Rule 58 is amended, however, to address a problem that arises under Appellate Rule 4(a). Some courts treat such orders as those that deny a motion for new trial as a "judgment," so that appeal time does not start to run until the order is entered on a separate document. Without attempting to address the question whether such orders are appealable, and thus judgments as defined by Rule 54(a), the amendment provides that entry on a separate document is not required for an order disposing of the motions listed in Appellate Rule 4(a). The enumeration of motions drawn from the Appellate Rule 4(a) list is generalized by omitting details that are important for appeal time purposes but that would unnecessarily complicate the separate document requirement. As one example, it is not required that any of the enumerated motions be timely. Many of the enumerated motions are frequently made before judgment is entered. The exemption of the order disposing of the motion does not excuse the obligation to set forth the judgment itself on a separate document. And if disposition of the motion results in an amended judgment, the amended judgment must be set forth on a separate document.

Rule 58(b) discards the attempt to define the time when a judgment becomes "effective." Taken in conjunction with the Rule 54(a) definition of a judgment to include "any order from which an appeal lies," the former Rule 58 definition of effectiveness could cause strange difficulties in implementing pretrial orders that are appealable under interlocutory appeal provisions or under expansive theories of finality. Rule 58(b) replaces the definition of effectiveness with a new provision that defines the time when judgment is entered. If judgment is promptly set forth on a separate document, as should be done when required by Rule 58(a)(1), the new provision will not change the effect of Rule 58. But in the cases in which court and clerk fail to comply with this simple requirement, the motion time periods set by Rules 50, 52, 54, 59, and 60 begin to run after expiration of 150 days from entry of the judgment in the civil docket as required by Rule 79(a).

A companion amendment of Appellate Rule 4(a)(7) integrates these changes with the time to appeal.

The new all-purpose definition of the entry of judgment must be applied with common sense to other questions that may turn on the time when judgment is entered. If the 150–day provision in Rule 58(b)(2)(B)—designed to integrate the time for post-judgment motions with appeal time—serves no purpose, or would defeat the purpose of another rule, it should be disregarded. In theory, for example, the separate document requirement continues to apply to an interlocutory order that is appealable as a final decision under collateral-order doctrine. Appealability under collateral-order doctrine should not be complicated by failure to enter the order as a judgment on a separate document—there is little reason to force trial judges to speculate about the potential appealability of every order, and there is no means to ensure that the trial judge will always reach the same conclusion as the court of appeals. Appeal time should start to run when the collateral order is entered without regard to creation of a separate document and without awaiting expiration of the 150 days provided by Rule 58(b)(2). Drastic surgery on Rules 54(a) and 58 would be required to address this and related issues, however, and it is better to leave this conundrum to the pragmatic disregard that seems its present fate. The present amendments do not seem to make matters worse, apart from one false appearance. If a pretrial order is set forth on a separate document that meets the requirements of Rule 58(b), the time to move for reconsideration seems to begin to run, perhaps years before final judgment. And even if there is no separate document, the time to move for reconsideration seems to begin 150 days after entry in the civil docket. This apparent problem is resolved by Rule 54(b), which expressly permits revision of all orders not made final under Rule 54(b) "at any time before the entry of judgment adjudicating all the claims and the rights and liabilities of all the parties."

New Rule 58(d) replaces the provision that attorneys shall not submit forms of judgment except on direction of the court. This provision was added to Rule 58 to avoid the delays that were frequently encountered by the former practice of directing the attorneys for the prevailing party to prepare a form of judgment, and also to avoid the occasionally inept drafting that resulted from attorney-prepared judgments. See *11 Wright, Miller & Kane, Federal Practice & Procedure: Civil 2d, § 2786*. The express direction in Rule 58(a)(2) for prompt action by the clerk, and by the court if court action is required, addresses this concern. The new provision allowing any party to move for entry of judgment on a separate document will protect all needs for prompt commencement of the periods for motions, appeals, and execution or other enforcement.

Changes Made After Publication and Comment Minor style changes were made. The definition of the time of entering judgment in Rule 58(b) was extended to reach all Civil Rules, not only the Rules described in the published version—Rules 50, 52, 54(d)(2)(B), 59, 60, and 62. And the time of entry was extended from 60 days to 150 days after entry in the civil docket without a required separate document.

2007 Amendments

The language of Rule 58 has been amended as part of the general restyling of the Civil Rules to make them more easily understood and to make style and terminology consistent throughout the rules. These changes are intended to be stylistic only.

Rule 59. New Trial; Altering or Amending a Judgment

(a) In General.

(1) ***Grounds for New Trial.*** The court may, on motion, grant a new trial on all or some of the issues—and to any party—as follows:

(A) after a jury trial, for any reason for which a new trial has heretofore been granted in an action at law in federal court; or

(B) after a nonjury trial, for any reason for which a rehearing has heretofore been granted in a suit in equity in federal court.

(2) ***Further Action After a Nonjury Trial.*** After a nonjury trial, the court may, on motion for a new trial, open the judgment if one has been entered, take additional testimony, amend findings of fact and conclusions of law or make new ones, and direct the entry of a new judgment.

(b) Time to File a Motion for a New Trial. A motion for a new trial must be filed no later than 10 days after the entry of judgment.

(c) Time to Serve Affidavits. When a motion for a new trial is based on affidavits, they must be filed with the motion. The opposing party has 10 days after being served to file opposing affidavits; but that period may be extended for up to 20 days, either by the court for good cause or by the parties' stipulation. The court may permit reply affidavits.

(d) New Trial on the Court's Initiative or for Reasons Not in the Motion. No later than 10 days after the entry of judgment, the court, on its own, may order a new trial for any reason that would justify granting one on a party's motion. After giving the parties notice and an opportunity to be heard, the court may grant a timely motion for a new trial for a reason not stated in the motion. In either event, the court must specify the reasons in its order.

(e) Motion to Alter or Amend a Judgment. A motion to alter or amend a judgment must be filed no later than 10 days after the entry of the judgment.

(Amended December 27, 1946, effective March 19, 1948; February 28, 1966, effective July 1, 1966; April 27, 1995, effective December 1, 1995; April 30, 2007, effective December 1, 2007.)

ADVISORY COMMITTEE NOTES

1937 Adoption

This rule represents an amalgamation of the petition for rehearing of [former] Equity Rule 69 (Petition for Rehearing) and the motion for new trial of 28 U.S.C., § 2111, formerly § 391 (New trials; harmless error), made in the light of the experience and provision of the code States. Compare Calif.Code Civ.Proc., Deering, 1937, §§ 656 to 663a, 28 U.S.C., § 2111, formerly § 391 (New trials; harmless error) is thus substantially continued in this rule. U.S.C., Title 28, [former] § 840 (Executions; stay on conditions) is modified insofar as it contains time provisions inconsistent with Subdivision (b). For the effect of the motion for new trial upon the time for taking an appeal see *Morse v. United States*, 1926, 46 S.Ct. 241, 270 U.S. 151, 70 L.Ed. 518; *Aspen*

Mining and Smelting Co. v. Billings, 1893, 14 S.Ct. 4, 150 U.S. 31, 37 L.Ed. 986.

For partial new trials which are permissible under Subdivision (a), see *Gasoline Products Co., Inc. v. Champlin Refining Co.,* 1931, 51 S.Ct. 513, 283 U.S. 494, 75 L.Ed. 1188; *Schuerholz v. Roach,* C.C.A.4, 1932, 58 F.2d 32; *Simmons v. Fish,* 1912, 97 N.E. 102, 210 Mass. 563, Ann.Cas.1912D, 588 (sustaining and recommending the practice and citing federal cases and cases in accord from about sixteen States and contra from three States). The procedure in several States provides specifically for partial new trials. Ariz.Rev.Code Ann., Struckmeyer, 1928, § 3852; Calif.Code Civ.Proc., Deering, 1937, §§ 657, 662; Smith-Hurd Ill.Stats., 1937, c. 110, § 216 (Par. (f)); Md.Ann.Code, Bagby, 1924, Art. 5, §§ 25, 26; Mich.Court Rules Ann., Searl, 1933, Rule 47, § 2; Miss.Sup.Ct.Rule 12, 161 Miss. 903, 905, 1931; N.J.Sup.Ct. Rules 131, 132, 147, 2 N.J.Misc. 1197, 1246–1251, 1255, 1924; 2 N.D.Comp.Laws Ann., 1913, § 7844, as amended by N.D.Laws 1927, ch. 214.

1946 Amendment

Note. Subdivision (b). With the time for appeal to a circuit court of appeals reduced in general to 30 days by the proposed amendment of Rule 73(a), the utility of the original "except" clause, which permits a motion for a new trial on the ground of newly discovered evidence to be made before the expiration of the time for appeal, would have been seriously restricted. It was thought advisable, therefore, to take care of this matter in another way. By amendment of Rule 60(b), newly discovered evidence is made the basis for relief from a judgment, and the maximum time limit has been extended to one year. Accordingly the amendment of Rule 59(b) eliminates the "except" clause and its specific treatment of newly discovered evidence as a ground for a motion for new trial. This ground remains, however, as a basis for a motion for new trial served not later than 10 days after the entry of judgment. See also Rule 60(b).

As to the effect of a motion under subdivision (b) upon the running of appeal time, see amended Rule 73(a) and Note.

Note to Subdivision (e). This subdivision has been added to care for a situation such as that arising in *Boaz v. Mutual Life Ins. Co. of New York,* C.C.A.8, 1944, 146 F.2d 321, and makes clear that the district court possesses the power asserted in that case to alter or amend a judgment after its entry. The subdivision deals only with alteration or amendment of the original judgment in a case and does not relate to a judgment upon motion as provided in Rule 50(b). As to the effect of a motion under subdivision (e) upon the running of appeal time, see amended Rule 73(a) and Note.

The title of Rule 59 has been expanded to indicate the inclusion of this subdivision.

1966 Amendment

By narrow interpretation of Rule 59(b) and (d), it has been held that the trial court is without power to grant a motion for a new trial, timely served, by an order made more than 10 days after the entry of judgment, based upon a ground not stated in the motion but perceived and relied on by the trial court sua sponte. *Freid v. McGrath,* 133 F.2d 350 (D.C.Cir. 1942); *National Farmers Union Auto. & Cas. Co. v. Wood,* 207 F.2d 659 (10th Cir. 1953); *Bailey v. Slentz,* 189 F.2d 406 (10th Cir. 1951); *Marshall's U.S. Auto Supply, Inc. v. Cashman,* 111 F.2d 140 (10th Cir. 1940), cert. denied, 311 U.S. 667 (1940); but see *Steinberg v. Indemnity Ins. Co.,* 36 F.R.D. 253 (E.D.La.1964).

The result is undesirable. Just as the court has power under Rule 59(d) to grant a new trial of its own initiative within the 10 days, so it should have power, when an effective new trial motion has been made and is pending, to decide it on grounds thought meritorious by the court although not advanced in the motion. The second sentence added by amendment to Rule 59(d) confirms the court's power in the latter situation, with provision that the parties be afforded a hearing before the power is exercised. See 6 *Moore's Federal Practice,* par. 59.09[2] (2d ed. 1953).

In considering whether a given ground has or has not been advanced in the motion made by the party, it should be borne in mind that the particularity called for in stating the grounds for a new trial motion is the same as that required for all motions by Rule 7(b)(1). The latter rule does not require ritualistic detail but rather a fair indication to court and counsel of the substance of the grounds relied on. See *Lebeck v. William A. Jarvis Co.,* 250 F.2d 285 (3d Cir. 1957); *Tsai v. Rosenthal,* 297 F.2d 614 (8th Cir. 1961); *General Motors Corp. v. Perry,* 303 F.2d 544 (7th Cir. 1962); cf. *Grimm v. California Spray-Chemical Corp.,* 264 F.2d 145 (9th Cir. 1959); *Cooper v. Midwest Feed Products Co.,* 271 F.2d 177 (8th Cir. 1959).

1995 Amendments

The only change, other than stylistic, intended by this revision is to add explicit time limits for filing motions for a new trial, motions to alter or amend a judgment, and affidavits opposing a new trial motion. Previously, there was an inconsistency in the wording of Rules 50, 52, and 59 with respect to whether certain post-judgment motions had to be filed, or merely served, during the prescribed period. This inconsistency caused special problems when motions for a new trial were joined with other post-judgment motions. These motions affect the finality of the judgment, a matter often of importance to third persons as well as the parties and the court. The Committee believes that each of these rules should be revised to require filing before end of the 10–day period. Filing is an event that can be determined with certainty from court records. The phrase "no later than" is used—rather than "within"—to include post-judgment motions that sometimes are filed before actual entry of the judgment by the clerk. It should be noted that under Rule 5 the motions when filed are to contain a certificate of service on other parties. It also should be noted that under Rule 6(a) Saturdays, Sundays, and legal holidays are excluded in measuring the 10–day period, but that Bankruptcy Rule 9006(a) excludes intermediate Saturdays, Sundays, and legal holidays only in computing periods less than 8 days.

2007 Amendments

The language of Rule 59 has been amended as part of the general restyling of the Civil Rules to make them more easily understood and to make style and terminology consistent throughout the rules. These changes are intended to be stylistic only.

Rule 60. Relief from a Judgment or Order

(a) Corrections Based on Clerical Mistakes; Oversights and Omissions. The court may correct a clerical mistake or a mistake arising from oversight or omission whenever one is found in a judgment, order, or other part of the record. The court may do so on motion or on its own, with or without notice. But after an appeal has been docketed in the appellate court and while it is pending, such a mistake may be corrected only with the appellate court's leave.

(b) Grounds for Relief from a Final Judgment, Order, or Proceeding. On motion and just terms, the court may relieve a party or its legal representative from a final judgment, order, or proceeding for the following reasons:

(1) mistake, inadvertence, surprise, or excusable neglect;

(2) newly discovered evidence that, with reasonable diligence, could not have been discovered in time to move for a new trial under Rule 59(b);

(3) fraud (whether previously called intrinsic or extrinsic), misrepresentation, or misconduct by an opposing party;

(4) the judgment is void;

(5) the judgment has been satisfied, released or discharged; it is based on an earlier judgment that has been reversed or vacated; or applying it prospectively is no longer equitable; or

(6) any other reason that justifies relief.

(c) Timing and Effect of the Motion.

(1) ***Timing.*** A motion under Rule 60(b) must be made within a reasonable time—and for reasons (1), (2), and (3) no more than a year after the entry of the judgment or order or the date of the proceeding.

(2) ***Effect on Finality.*** The motion does not affect the judgment's finality or suspend its operation.

(d) Other Powers to Grant Relief. This rule does not limit a court's power to:

(1) entertain an independent action to relieve a party from a judgment, order, or proceeding;

(2) grant relief under 28 U.S.C. § 1655 to a defendant who was not personally notified of the action; or

(3) set aside a judgment for fraud on the court.

(e) Bills and Writs Abolished. The following are abolished: bills of review, bills in the nature of bills of review, and writs of coram nobis, coram vobis, and audita querela.

(Amended December 27, 1946, effective March 19, 1948; December 29, 1948, effective October 20, 1949; March 2, 1987, effective August 1, 1987; April 30, 2007, effective December 1, 2007.)

ADVISORY COMMITTEE NOTES

1937 Adoption

Note to Subdivision (a). See [former] Equity Rule 72 (Correction of Clerical Mistakes in Orders and Decrees); Mich.Court Rules Ann. (Searl, 1933) Rule 48, § 3; 2 Wash. Rev.Stat.Ann. (Remington, 1932) § 464(3); Wyo.Rev.Stat. Ann. (Courtright, 1931) § 89–2301(3). For an example of a very liberal provision for the correction of clerical errors and for amendment after judgment, see Va.Code Ann. (Michie, 1936) §§ 6329, 6333.

Note to Subdivision (b). Application to the court under this subdivision does not extend the time for taking an appeal, as distinguished from the motion for new trial. This section is based upon Calif.Code Civ.Proc. (Deering, 1937) § 473. See also N.Y.C.P.A. (1937) § 108; 2 Minn.Stat. (Mason, 1927) § 9283.

For the independent action to relieve against mistake, etc., see Dobie, *Federal Procedure,* pages 760 to 765, compare 639; and Simkins, *Federal Practice,* ch. CXXI (pp. 820 to 830) and ch. CXXII (pp. 831 to 834), compare § 214.

1946 Amendment

Note. Subdivision (a). The amendment incorporates the view expressed in *Perlman v. 322 West Seventy-Second Street, Co., Inc.,* C.C.A.2d, 1942, 127 F.2d 716; 3 *Moore's Federal Practice,* 1938, 3276, and further permits correction after docketing, with leave of the appellate court. Some courts have thought that upon the taking of an appeal the district court lost its power to act. See *Schram v. Safety Investment Co.,* E.D.Mich.1942, 45 F.Supp. 636; also *Miller v. United States,* C.C.A.7th, 1940, 114 F.2d 267.

Subdivision (b). When promulgated, the rules contained a number of provisions, including those found in Rule 60(b), describing the practice by a motion to obtain relief from judgments, and these rules, coupled with the reservation in Rule 60(b) of the right to entertain a new action to relieve a party from a judgment, were generally supposed to cover the field. Since the rules have been in force, decisions have been rendered that the use of bills of review, coram nobis, or audita querela, to obtain relief from final judgments is still proper, and that various remedies of this kind still exist although they are not mentioned in the rules and the practice is not prescribed in the rules. It is obvious that the rules should be complete in this respect and define the practice with respect to any existing rights or remedies to obtain relief from final judgments. For extended discussion of the old common law writs and equitable remedies, the interpretation of Rule 60, and proposals for change, see Moore and Rogers, *Federal Relief from Civil Judgments,* 1946, 55 Yale L.J. 623. See also 3 *Moore's Federal Practice,* 1938, 3254 et seq.; Commentary, *Effect of Rule 60b on Other Methods of Relief From Judgment,* 1941, 4 Fed.Rules Serv. 942, 945; *Wallace v. United States,* C.C.A.2d, 1944, 142 F.2d 240, certiorari denied 65 S.Ct. 37, 323 U.S. 712, 89 L.Ed. 573.

The reconstruction of Rule 60(b) has for one of its purposes a clarification of this situation. Two types of procedure to obtain relief from judgments are specified in the rules as it is proposed to amend them. One procedure is by motion in the court and in the action in which the judgment was rendered. The other procedure is by a new or independent action to obtain relief from a judgment, which action may or may not be begun in the court which rendered the judgment. Various rules, such as the one dealing with a motion for new trial and for amendment of judgments, Rule 59, one for amended findings, Rule 52, and one for judgment notwithstanding the verdict, Rule 50(b), and including the provisions of Rule 60(b) as amended, prescribe the various types of cases in which the practice by motion is permitted. In each case there is a limit upon the time within which resort to a motion is permitted, and this time limit may not be enlarged under Rule 6(b). If the right to make a motion is lost by the expiration of the time limits fixed in these rules, the only other procedural remedy is by a new or independent action to set aside a judgment upon those principles which have heretofore been applied in such an action. Where the independent action is resorted to, the limitations of time are those of laches or statutes of limitations. The Committee has endeavored to ascertain all the remedies and types of relief heretofore available by coram nobis, coram vobis, audita querela, bill of review, or bill in the nature of a bill of review. See Moore and Rogers, *Federal Relief from Civil Judgments,* 1946, 55 Yale L.J. 623, 659 to 682. It endeavored then to amend the rules to permit, either by motion or by independent action, the granting of various kinds of relief from judgments which were permitted in the federal courts prior to the adoption of these rules, and the amendment concludes with a provision abolishing the use of bills of review and the other common law writs referred to, and requiring the practice to be by motion or by independent action.

To illustrate the operation of the amendment, it will be noted that under Rule 59(b) as it now stands, without amendment, a motion for new trial on the ground of newly discovered evidence is permitted within ten days after the entry of the judgment, or after that time upon leave of the court. It is proposed to amend Rule 59(b) by providing that under that rule a motion for new trial shall be served not later than ten days after the entry of the judgment, whatever the ground be for the motion, whether error by the court or newly discovered evidence. On the other hand, one of the purposes of the bill of review in equity was to afford relief on the ground of newly discovered evidence long after the entry of the judgment. Therefore, to permit relief by a motion similar to that heretofore obtained on bill of review, Rule 60(b) as amended permits an application for relief to be made by motion, on the ground of newly discovered evidence, within one year after judgment. Such a motion under Rule 60(b) does not affect the finality of the judgment, but a motion under Rule 59, made within 10 days, does affect finality and the running of the time for appeal.

If these various amendments, including principally those to Rule 60(b), accomplish the purpose for which they are intended, the federal rules will deal with the practice in every sort of case in which relief from final judgments is asked, and prescribe the practice. With reference to the question whether, as the rules now exist, relief by coram nobis, bills of review, and so forth, is permissible, the generally accepted view is that the remedies are still available, although the precise relief obtained in a particular case by use of these ancillary remedies is shrouded in ancient lore and mystery. See *Wallace v. United States,* C.C.A.2d, 1944, 142 F.2d 240, certiorari denied 65 S.Ct. 37, 323 U.S. 712, 89 L.Ed. 573; *Fraser v. Doing,* App.D.C.1942, 130 F.2d 617; *Jones v. Watts,* C.C.A.5th, 1944, 142 F.2d 575; *Preveden v. Hahn,* S.D.N.Y.1941, 36 F.Supp. 952; *Cavallo v. Agwilines, Inc.,* S.D.N.Y.1942, 6 Fed.Rules Serv. 60b.31, Case 2, 2 F.R.D. 526; *McGinn v. United States,* D.C.Mass.1942, 6 Fed.Rules Serv. 60b.51, Case 3, 2 F.R.D. 562; *City of Shattuck, Oklahoma ex rel. Versluis v. Oliver,* W.D.Okl.1945, 8 Fed.Rules Serv. 60b.31, Case 3; Moore and Rogers, *Federal Relief from Civil Judgments,* 1946, 55 Yale L.J. 623, 631 to 653; 3 *Moore's Federal Practice,* 1938, 3254 et seq.; Commentary, *Effect of Rule 60b on Other Methods of Relief From Judgment,* op. cit. supra. Cf. *Norris v. Camp,* C.C.A.10th, 1944, 144 F.2d 1; *Reed v. South Atlantic Steamship Co. of Delaware,* D.Del.1942, 2 F.R.D. 475, 6 Fed.Rules Serv. 60b.31, Case 1; *Laughlin v. Berens,* D.D.C.1945, 8 Fed.Rules Serv. 60b.51, Case 1, 73 W.L.R. 209.

The transposition of the words "the court" and the addition of the word "and" at the beginning of the first sentence are merely verbal changes. The addition of the qualifying word "final" emphasizes the character of the judgments, orders or proceedings from which Rule 60(b) affords relief; and hence interlocutory judgments are not brought within the restrictions of the rule, but rather they are left subject to the complete power of the court rendering them to afford such relief from them as justice requires.

The qualifying pronoun "his" has been eliminated on the basis that it is too restrictive, and that the subdivision should include the mistake or neglect of others which may be just as material and call just as much for supervisory jurisdiction as where the judgment is taken against the party through *his* mistake, inadvertence, etc.

Fraud, whether intrinsic or extrinsic, misrepresentation, or other misconduct of an adverse party are express grounds for relief by motion under amended subdivision (b). There is no sound reason for their exclusion. The incorporation of fraud and the like within the scope of the rule also removes confusion as to the proper procedure. It has been held that relief from a judgment obtained by extrinsic fraud could be secured by motion within a "reasonable time," which might be after the time stated in the rule had run. *Fiske v. Buder,* C.C.A.8th, 1942, 125 F.2d 841; see also inferentially *Bucy v. Nevada Construction Co.,* C.C.A.9th, 1942, 125 F.2d 213. On the other hand, it has been suggested that in view of the fact that fraud was omitted from original Rule 60(b) as a ground for relief, an independent action was the only proper remedy. Commentary, *Effect of Rule 60b on Other Methods of Relief From Judgment,* 1941, 4 Fed.Rules Serv. 942, 945. The amendment settles this problem by making fraud an express ground for relief by motion; and under the saving clause, fraud may be urged as a basis for relief by independent action insofar as established doctrine permits. See Moore and Rogers, *Federal Relief from Civil Judgments,* 1946, 55 Yale L.J. 623, 653 to 659; 3 Moore's Federal Practice, 1938, 3267 et seq. And the rule expressly does not limit the power of the court, when fraud has been perpetrated upon it, to give relief under the saving clause. As an illustration of this situation, see *Hazel-Atlas Glass Co. v. Hartford Empire Co.,* 1944, 64 S.Ct. 997, 322 U.S. 238, 88 L.Ed. 1250.

The time limit for relief by motion in the court and in the action in which the judgment was rendered has been enlarged from six months to one year.

It should be noted that Rule 60(b) does not assume to define the substantive law as to the grounds for vacating judgments, but merely prescribes the practice in proceedings to obtain relief. It should also be noted that under § 200(4) of the Soldiers' and Sailors' Civil Relief Act of 1940, § 501 et seq. [§ 520(4)] of the Appendix to Title 50, a judgment rendered in any action or proceeding governed by the section may be vacated under certain specified circumstances upon proper application to the court.

1948 Amendment

The amendment effective October, 1949 substituted the reference to "Title 28, U.S.C. § 1655," in the next to the last sentence of subdivision (b), for the reference to "Section 57 of the Judicial Code, U.S.C., Title 28, § 118".

1987 Amendment

The amendment is technical. No substantive change is intended.

2007 Amendments

The language of Rule 60 has been amended as part of the general restyling of the Civil Rules to make them more easily understood and to make style and terminology consistent throughout the rules. These changes are intended to be stylistic only.

The final sentence of former Rule 60(b) said that the procedure for obtaining any relief from a judgment was by motion as prescribed in the Civil Rules or by an independent action. That provision is deleted as unnecessary. Relief continues to be available only as provided in the Civil Rules or by independent action.

Rule 61. Harmless Error

Unless justice requires otherwise, no error in admitting or excluding evidence—or any other error by the court or a party—is ground for granting a new trial, for setting aside a verdict, or for vacating, modifying, or otherwise disturbing a judgment or order. At every stage of the proceeding, the court must disregard all errors and defects that do not affect any party's substantial rights.

(Amended April 30, 2007, effective December 1, 2007.)

ADVISORY COMMITTEE NOTES

1937 Adoption

A combination of U.S.C., Title 28, § 2111, [former] § 391 (New trials; harmless error) and [former] § 777 (Defects of form; amendments) with modifications. See *McCandless v. United States,* 1936, 56 S.Ct. 764, 298 U.S. 342, 80 L.Ed. 1205. Compare [former] Equity Rule 72 (Correction of Clerical Mistakes in Orders and Decrees); and last sentence of [former] Equity Rule 46 (Trial—Testimony Usually Taken in Open Court—Rulings on Objections to Evidence). For the last sentence see the last sentence of [former] Equity Rule 19 (Amendments Generally).

2007 Amendments

The language of Rule 61 has been amended as part of the general restyling of the Civil Rules to make them more easily understood and to make style and terminology consistent throughout the rules. These changes are intended to be stylistic only.

Rule 62. Stay of Proceedings to Enforce a Judgment

(a) Automatic Stay; Exceptions for Injunctions, Receiverships, and Patent Accountings. Except as stated in this rule, no execution may issue on a judgment, nor may proceedings be taken to enforce it, until 10 days have passed after its entry. But unless the court orders otherwise, the following are not stayed after being entered, even if an appeal is taken:

(1) an interlocutory or final judgment in an action for an injunction or a receivership; or

(2) a judgment or order that directs an accounting in an action for patent infringement.

(b) Stay Pending the Disposition of a Motion. On appropriate terms for the opposing party's security, the court may stay the execution of a judgment—or any proceedings to enforce it—pending disposition of any of the following motions:

(1) under Rule 50, for judgment as a matter of law;

(2) under Rule 52(b), to amend the findings or for additional findings;

(3) under Rule 59, for a new trial or to alter or amend a judgment; or

(4) under Rule 60, for relief from a judgment or order.

(c) Injunction Pending an Appeal. While an appeal is pending from an interlocutory order or final judgment that grants, dissolves, or denies an injunction, the court may suspend, modify, restore, or grant an injunction on terms for bond or other terms that secure the opposing party's rights. If the judgment appealed from is rendered by a statutory three-judge district court, the order must be made either:

(1) by that court sitting in open session; or

(2) by the assent of all its judges, as evidenced by their signatures.

(d) Stay with Bond on Appeal. If an appeal is taken, the appellant may obtain a stay by supersedeas bond, except in an action described in Rule 62(a)(1) or (2). The bond may be given upon or after filing the notice of appeal or after obtaining the order allowing the appeal. The stay takes effect when the court approves the bond.

(e) Stay Without Bond on an Appeal by the United States, Its Officers, or Its Agencies. The court must not require a bond, obligation, or other security from the appellant when granting a stay on an appeal by the United States, its officers, or its agencies or on an appeal directed by a department of the federal government.

(f) Stay in Favor of a Judgment Debtor Under State Law. If a judgment is a lien on the judgment debtor's property under the law of the state where the court is located, the judgment debtor is entitled to the same stay of execution the state court would give.

(g) Appellate Court's Power Not Limited. This rule does not limit the power of the appellate court or one of its judges or justices:

(1) to stay proceedings—or suspend, modify, restore, or grant an injunction—while an appeal is pending; or

(2) to issue an order to preserve the status quo or the effectiveness of the judgment to be entered.

(h) Stay with Multiple Claims or Parties. A court may stay the enforcement of a final judgment entered under Rule 54(b) until it enters a later judgment or judgments, and may prescribe terms necessary to secure the benefit of the stayed judgment for the party in whose favor it was entered.

(Amended December 27, 1946, effective March 19, 1948; December 29, 1948, effective October 20, 1949; April 17, 1961, effective July 19, 1961; March 2, 1987, effective August 1, 1987; April 30, 2007, effective December 1, 2007.)

ADVISORY COMMITTEE NOTES

1937 Adoption

Note to Subdivision (a). The first sentence states the substance of the last sentence of U.S.C., Title 28, [former] § 874 (Supersedeas). The remainder of the subdivision states the substance of the last clause of U.S.C., Title 28, § 1292, [formerly] § 227 (Appeals in proceedings for injunctions; receivers; and admiralty), and of §§ 1292, 2107, [formerly] § 227a (Appeals in suits in equity for infringement of letters patent for inventions; stay of proceedings for accounting), but extended to include final as well as interlocutory judgments.

Note to Subdivision (b). This modifies U.S.C., Title 28, [former] § 840 (Executions; stay on conditions).

Note to Subdivision (c). Compare [former] Equity Rule 74 (Injunction Pending Appeal); and *Cumberland Telephone and Telegraph Co. v. Louisiana Public Service Commission*, 1922, 43 S.Ct. 75, 260 U.S. 212, 67 L.Ed. 217. See Simkins, Federal Practice (1934), § 916, in regard to the effect of appeal on injunctions and the giving of bonds. See U.S.C., [former] Title 6 (Official and Penal Bonds) for bonds by surety companies. For statutes providing for a specially constituted district court of three judges, see:

U.S.C., Title 7:

§ 217 (Proceedings for suspension of orders of Secretary of Agriculture under Stockyards Act)—by reference.

§ 499k (Injunctions; application of injunction laws governing orders of Interstate Commerce Commission to orders of Secretary of Agriculture under Perishable Commodities Act)—by reference.

U.S.C., Title 15:

§ 28 (Antitrust laws; suits against monopolies expedited)

U.S.C., Title 28, former:

§ 47 [now 2325 (repealed)] (Injunctions as to orders of Interstate Commerce Commission, etc.)

§ 380 [now 2284] (Injunctions; alleged unconstitutionality of State statutes)

§ 380a [now 2284] (Same; constitutionality of federal statute)

U.S.C., Title 49:

§ 44 [former] (Suits in equity under interstate commerce laws; expedition of suits)

Note to Subdivision (d). This modifies U.S.C., Title 28, [former] § 874 (Supersedeas). See Rule 36(2), Rules of the Supreme Court of the United States, which governs supersedeas bonds on direct appeals to the Supreme Court, and Rule 73(d), of these rules, which governs supersedeas bonds on appeals to a circuit court of appeals. The provisions governing supersedeas bonds in both kinds of appeals are substantially the same.

Note to Subdivision (e). This states the substance of U.S.C., Title 28, § 2408, formerly § 870 (Bond; not required of the United States).

Note to Subdivision (f). This states the substance of U.S.C., Title 28, [former] § 841 (Executions; stay of one term) with appropriate modification to conform to the provisions of Rule 6(c) as to terms of court.

1946 Amendment

Note. Subdivision (a). [This subdivision not amended]. Sections 203 and 204 of the Soldiers' and Sailors' Civil Relief Act of 1940, 50 U.S.C., Appendix, § 501 et seq. [§§ 523, 524], provide under certain circumstances for the issuance and continuance of a stay of execution of any judgment or order entered against a person in military service. See *Bowsman v. Peterson*, D.Neb.1942, 45 F.Supp. 741. Section 201 of the Act [50 U.S.C. App. § 521] permits under certain circumstances the issuance of a stay of any action or proceeding at any stage thereof, where either the plaintiff or defendant is a person in military service. See also note to Rule 64 herein.

Subdivision (b). This change was necessary because of the proposed addition to Rule 59 of subdivision (e).

Subdivision (h). In proposing to revise Rule 54(b), the Committee thought it advisable to include a separate provision in Rule 62 for stay of enforcement of a final judgment in cases involving multiple claims.

1948 Amendment

The amendment effective October 1949 deleted at the end of subdivision (g) the following language which originally appeared after the word "entered": "and these rules do not supersede the provisions of Section 210 of the Judicial Code, as amended, U.S.C., Title 28, [former] § 47a, or of other statutes of the United States to the effect that stays pending appeals to the Supreme Court may be granted only by that court or a justice thereof."

1961 Amendment

The amendment adopted Apr. 17, 1961, effective July 19, 1961, eliminated words "on some but not all of the claims presented in the action" which followed "final judgment".

1987 Amendment

The amendment is technical. No substantive change is intended.

2007 Amendments

The language of Rule 62 has been amended as part of the general restyling of the Civil Rules to make them more easily understood and to make style and terminology consistent throughout the rules. These changes are intended to be stylistic only.

The final sentence of former Rule 62(a) referred to Rule 62(c). It is deleted as an unnecessary. Rule 62(c) governs of its own force.

Rule 63. Judge's Inability to Proceed

If a judge conducting a hearing or trial is unable to proceed, any other judge may proceed upon certifying familiarity with the record and determining that the case may be completed without prejudice to the parties. In a hearing or a nonjury trial, the successor judge must, at a party's request, recall any witness whose testimony is material and disputed and who is available to testify again without undue burden. The successor judge may also recall any other witness. (Amended March 2, 1987, effective August 1, 1987; April 30, 1991, effective December 1, 1991; April 30, 2007, effective December 1, 2007.)

ADVISORY COMMITTEE NOTES

1937 Adoption

This rule adapts and extends the provisions of U.S.C., Title 28, [former] § 776 (Bill of exceptions; authentication; signing of by judge) to include all duties to be performed by the judge after verdict or judgment. The statute is therefore superseded.

1987 Amendment

The amendments are technical. No substantive change is intended.

1991 Amendment

The revision substantially displaces the former rule. The former rule was limited to the disability of the judge, and made no provision for disqualification or possible other reasons for the withdrawal of the judge during proceedings. In making provision for other circumstances, the revision is not intended to encourage judges to discontinue participation in a trial for any but compelling reasons. Cf. *United States v. Lane*, 708 F.2d 1394, 1395–1397 (9th Cir.1983). Manifestly, a substitution should not be made for the personal convenience of the court, and the reasons for a substitution should be stated on the record.

The former rule made no provision for the withdrawal of the judge during the trial, but was limited to disqualification after trial. Several courts concluded that the text of the former rule prohibited substitution of a new judge prior to the points described in the rule, thus requiring a new trial, whether or not a fair disposition was within reach of a substitute judge. *E.g., Whalen v. Ford Motor Credit Co.*, 684 F.2d 272 (4th Cir.1982, en banc) *cert. denied*, 459 U.S. 910 (1982) (jury trial); *Arrow–Hart, Inc. v. Philip Carey Co.*, 552 F.2d 711 (6th Cir.1977) (non-jury trial). *See generally* Comment, *The Case of the Dead Judge: Fed.R.Civ.P. 63: Whalen v. Ford Motor Credit Co.*, 67 MINN.L.REV. 827 (1983).

The increasing length of federal trials has made it likely that the number of trials interrupted by the disability of the judge will increase. An efficient mechanism for completing these cases without unfairness is needed to prevent unnecessary expense and delay. To avoid the injustice that may result if the substitute judge proceeds despite unfamiliarity with the action, the new Rule provides, in language similar to Federal Rule of Criminal Procedure 25(a), that the successor judge must certify familiarity with the record and determine that the case may be completed before that judge without prejudice to the parties. This will necessarily require that there be available a transcript or a videotape of the proceedings prior to substitution. If there has been a long but incomplete jury trial, the prompt availability of the transcript or videotape is crucial to the effective use of this rule, for the jury cannot long be held while an extensive transcript is prepared without prejudice to one or all parties.

The revised text authorizes the substitute judge to make a finding of fact at a bench trial based on evidence heard by a different judge. This may be appropriate in limited circumstances. First, if a witness has become unavailable, the testimony recorded at trial can be considered by the successor judge pursuant to F.R.Ev. 804, being equivalent to a recorded deposition available for use at trial pursuant to Rule 32. For this purpose, a witness who is no longer subject to a subpoena to compel testimony at trial is unavailable. Secondly, the successor judge may determine that particular testimony is not material or is not disputed, and so need not be reheard. The propriety of proceeding in this manner may be marginally affected by the availability of a videotape record; a judge who has reviewed a trial on videotape may be entitled to greater confidence in his or her ability to proceed.

The court would, however, risk error to determine the credibility of a witness not seen or heard who is available to be recalled. Cf. *Anderson v. City of Bessemer City NC*, 470 U.S. 564, 575 (1985); *Marshall v. Jerrico Inc.*, 446 U.S. 238, 242 (1980). See also *United States v. Radatz*, 447 U.S. 667 (1980).

2007 Amendments

The language of Rule 63 has been amended as part of the general restyling of the Civil Rules to make them more easily understood and to make style and terminology consistent throughout the rules. These changes are intended to be stylistic only.

TITLE VIII. PROVISIONAL AND FINAL REMEDIES

ADVISORY COMMITTEE NOTES

1991 Amendment

The purpose of the revision is to divide this chapter of the Rules into two. No substantive change is effected.

Rule 64. Seizing a Person or Property

(a) Remedies Under State Law—In General. At the commencement of and throughout an action, every remedy is available that, under the law of the state where the court is located, provides for seizing a person or property to secure satisfaction of the potential judgment. But a federal statute governs to the extent it applies.

(b) Specific Kinds of Remedies. The remedies available under this rule include the following—however designated and regardless of whether state procedure requires an independent action:

- arrest;
- attachment;
- garnishment;
- replevin;
- sequestration; and
- other corresponding or equivalent remedies.

(Amended April 30, 2007, effective December 1, 2007.)

ADVISORY COMMITTEE NOTES

1937 Adoption

This rule adopts the existing Federal law, except that it specifies the applicable State law to be that of the time when the remedy is sought. Under U.S.C., Title 28, [former] § 726 (Attachments as provided by State laws) the plaintiff was entitled to remedies by attachment or other process which were on June 1, 1872, provided by the applicable State law, and the district courts might, from time to time, by general rules, adopt such State laws as might be in force. This statute is superseded as are district court rules which are rendered unnecessary by the rule.

Lis pendens. No rule concerning lis pendens is stated, for this would appear to be a matter of substantive law affecting State laws of property. It has been held that in the absence of a State statute expressly providing for the recordation of notice of the pendency of Federal actions, the commencement of a Federal action is notice to all persons affected. *King v. Davis,* 137 F. 198 (W.D.Va., 1903). It has been held, however, that when a state statute does so provide expressly, its provisions are binding. *United States v. Calcasieu Timber Co.,* 236 F. 196 (C.C.A.5th, 1916).

For statutes of the United States on attachment, see, e.g.:

U.S.C., Title 28 former:

§ 737 [now 2710] (Attachment in postal suits)

§ 738 [now 2711] (Attachment; application for warrant)

§ 739 [now 2712] (Attachment; issue of warrant)

§ 740 [now 2713] (Attachment; trial of ownership of property)

§ 741 [now 2714] (Attachment; investment of proceeds of attached property)

§ 742 [now 2715] (Attachment; publication of attachment)

§ 743 [now 2716] (Attachment; personal notice of attachment)

§ 744 [now 2717] (Attachment; discharge; bond)

§ 745 [former] (Attachment; accrued rights not affected)

§ 746 (Attachments dissolved in conformity with State laws)

For statutes of the United States on garnishment, see, e.g.:

U.S.C., Title 28, former:

§ 748 [now 2405] (Garnishees in suits by United States against a corporation)

§ 749 [now 2405] (Same; issue tendered on denial of indebtedness)

§ 750 [now 2405] (Same; garnishee failing to appear)

For statutes of the United States on arrest, see, e.g.:

U.S.C., Title 28 former:

§ 376 [now 1651] (Writs of ne exeat)

§ 755 [former] (Special bail in suits for duties and penalties)

§ 756 [former] (Defendant giving bail in one district and committed in another)

§ 757 [former] (Defendant giving bail in one district and committed in another; defendant held until judgment in first suit)

§ 758 [former] (Bail and affidavits; taking by commissioners)

§ 759 [former] (Calling of bail in Kentucky)

§ 760 [former] (Clerks may take bail de bene esse)

§ 843 [now 2007] (Imprisonment for debt)

§ 844 [now 2007] (Imprisonment for debt; discharge according to State laws)

§ 845 [now 2007] (Imprisonment for debt; jail limits)

For statutes of the United States on replevin, see, e.g.:

U.S.C., Title 28:

§ 2463, formerly § 747 (Replevy of property taken under revenue laws).

Supplementary Note

Note. Sections 203 and 204 of the Soldiers' and Sailors' Civil Relief Act of 1940, 50 U.S.C.Appendix, § 501 et seq. [§§ 523 and 524], provide under certain circumstances for the issuance and continuance of a stay of the execution of any judgment entered against a person in military service, or the vacation or stay of any attachment or garnishment directed against such person's property, money, or debts in the hands of another. See also Note to Rule 62 herein.

2007 Amendments

The language of Rule 64 has been amended as part of the general restyling of the Civil Rules to make them more easily understood and to make style and terminology consistent throughout the rules. These changes are intended to be stylistic only.

Former Rule 64 stated that the Civil Rules govern an action in which any remedy available under Rule 64(a) is used. The Rules were said to govern from the time the action is commenced if filed in federal court, and from the time of removal if removed from state court. These provisions are deleted as redundant. Rule 1 establishes that the Civil Rules apply to all actions in a district court, and Rule 81(c)(1) adds reassurance that the Civil Rules apply to a removed action "after it is removed."

Rule 65. Injunctions and Restraining Orders

(a) Preliminary Injunction.

(1) ***Notice.*** The court may issue a preliminary injunction only on notice to the adverse party.

(2) ***Consolidating the Hearing with the Trial on the Merits.*** Before or after beginning the hearing on a motion for a preliminary injunction, the court may advance the trial on the merits and consolidate it with the hearing. Even when consolidation is not ordered, evidence that is received on the motion and that would be admissible at trial becomes part of the trial record and need not be repeated at trial. But the court must preserve any party's right to a jury trial.

(b) Temporary Restraining Order.

(1) ***Issuing Without Notice.*** The court may issue a temporary restraining order without written or oral notice to the adverse party or its attorney only if:

(A) specific facts in an affidavit or a verified complaint clearly show that immediate and irreparable injury, loss, or damage will result to the movant before the adverse party can be heard in opposition; and

(B) the movant's attorney certifies in writing any efforts made to give notice and the reasons why it should not be required.

(2) ***Contents; Expiration.*** Every temporary restraining order issued without notice must state the date and hour it was issued; describe the injury and state why it is irreparable; state why the order was issued without notice; and be promptly filed in the clerk's office and entered in the record. The order expires at the time after entry—not to exceed 10 days—that the court sets, unless before that time the court, for good cause, extends it for a like period or the adverse party consents to a longer extension. The reasons for an extension must be entered in the record.

(3) ***Expediting the Preliminary-Injunction Hearing.*** If the order is issued without notice, the motion for a preliminary injunction must be set for hearing at the earliest possible time, taking precedence over all other matters except hearings on older matters of the same character. At the hearing, the party who obtained the order must proceed with the motion; if the party does not, the court must dissolve the order.

(4) ***Motion to Dissolve.*** On 2 days' notice to the party who obtained the order without notice—or on shorter notice set by the court—the adverse party may appear and move to dissolve or modify the order. The court must then hear and decide the motion as promptly as justice requires.

(c) Security. The court may issue a preliminary injunction or a temporary restraining order only if the movant gives security in an amount that the court considers proper to pay the costs and damages sustained by any party found to have been wrongfully enjoined or restrained. The United States, its officers, and its agencies are not required to give security.

(d) Contents and Scope of Every Injunction and Restraining Order.

(1) ***Contents.*** Every order granting an injunction and every restraining order must:

(A) state the reasons why it issued;

(B) state its terms specifically; and

(C) describe in reasonable detail—and not by referring to the complaint or other document—the act or acts restrained or required.

(2) ***Persons Bound.*** The order binds only the following who receive actual notice of it by personal service or otherwise:

(A) the parties;

(B) the parties' officers, agents, servants, employees, and attorneys; and

(C) other persons who are in active concert or participation with anyone described in Rule 65(d)(2)(A) or (B).

(e) Other Laws Not Modified. These rules do not modify the following:

(1) any federal statute relating to temporary restraining orders or preliminary injunctions in actions affecting employer and employee;

(2) 28 U.S.C. § 2361, which relates to preliminary injunctions in actions of interpleader or in the nature of interpleader; or

(3) 28 U.S.C. § 2284, which relates to actions that must be heard and decided by a three-judge district court.

(f) Copyright Impoundment. This rule applies to copyright-impoundment proceedings.

(Amended December 27, 1946, effective March 19, 1948; December 29, 1948, effective October 20, 1949; February 28, 1966, effective July 1, 1966; March 2, 1987, effective August 1, 1987; April 23, 2001, effective December 1, 2001; April 30, 2007, effective December 1, 2007.)

ADVISORY COMMITTEE NOTES

1937 Adoption

Note to Subdivisions (a) and (b). These are taken from U.S.C., Title 28, [former] § 381 (Injunctions; preliminary injunctions and temporary restraining orders).

Note to Subdivision (c). Except for the last sentence, this is substantially U.S.C., Title 28, [former] § 382 (Injunctions; security on issuance of). The last sentence continues the following and similar statutes which expressly except the United States or an officer or agency thereof from such security requirements: U.S.C. Title 15, §§ 77t(b), 78u(e), and 79r(f) (Securities and Exchange Commission). It also excepts the United States or an officer or agency thereof from such security requirements in any action in which a restraining order or interlocutory judgment of injunction issues in its favor whether there is an express statutory exception from such security requirements or not.

See U.S.C., [former] Title 6 (Official and Penal Bonds) for bonds by surety companies.

Note to Subdivision (d). This is substantially U.S.C., Title 28, [former] § 383 (Injunctions; requisites of order; binding effect).

Note to Subdivision (e). The words "relating to temporary restraining orders and preliminary injunctions in actions affecting employer and employee" are words of description and not of limitation.

Compare [former] Equity Rule 73 (Preliminary Injunctions and Temporary Restraining Orders) which is substantially equivalent to the statutes.

For other statutes dealing with injunctions which are continued, see e.g.:

U.S.C., Title 28 former:

§ 46 [now 2324] (Suits to enjoin orders of Interstate Commerce Commission to be against United States)

§ 47 [now 2325] (Injunctions as to orders of Interstate Commerce Commission; appeal to Supreme Court; time for taking)

§ 378 [former] (Injunctions; when granted)

§ 379 [now 2283] (Injunctions; stay in State courts)

§ 380 [now 1253, 2101, 2281, 2284] (Injunctions; alleged unconstitutionality of State statutes; appeal to Supreme Court)

§ 380a [now 1253, 2101, 2281, 2284] (Injunctions; constitutionality of Federal statute; application for hearing; appeal to Supreme Court)

U.S.C., Title 7:

§ 216 (Court proceedings to enforce orders; injunction)

§ 217 (Proceedings for suspension of orders)

U.S.C., Title 15:

§ 4 (Jurisdiction of courts; duty of district attorney; procedure)

§ 25 (Restraining violations; procedure)

§ 26 (Injunctive relief for private parties; exceptions)

§ 77t(b) (Injunctions and prosecution of offenses)

1946 Amendment

Note. It has been held that in actions on preliminary injunction bonds the district court has discretion to grant relief in the same proceeding or to require the institution of a new action on the bond. *Russell v. Farley,* 1881, 105 U.S. 433, 466. It is believed, however, that in all cases the litigant should have a right to proceed on the bond in the same proceeding, in the manner provided in Rule 73(f) for a similar situation. The paragraph added to Rule 65(c) insures this result and is in the interest of efficiency. There is no reason why Rules 65(c) and 73(f) should operate differently. Compare § 50, sub. n of the Bankruptcy Act, 11 U.S.C. § 78, sub. n, under which actions on all bonds furnished pursuant to the Act may be proceeded upon summarily in the bankruptcy court. See 2 *Collier on Bankruptcy,* 14th ed. by Moore and Oglebay, 1853–1854.

1948 Amendment

The amendment effective October 1949, changed subdivision (e) in the following respects: in the first clause the amendment substituted the words "any statute of the United States" for the words "the Act of October 15, 1914, c. 323, §§ 1 and 20 (38 Stat. 730), U.S.C., Title 29, §§ 52 and 53, or the Act of March 23, 1932, c. 90 (47 Stat. 70), U.S.C., Title 29, c. 6"; in the second clause of subdivision (e) the amendment substituted the reference to "Title 28, U.S.C., § 2361" for the reference to "Section 24(26) of the Judicial Code as amended, U.S.C., Title 28, § 41(26)"; and the third clause was amended to read "Title 28, U.S.C., § 2284," etc., as at present, instead of "the Act of August 24, 1937, c. 754, § 3, relating to actions to enjoin the enforcement of acts of Congress."

1966 Amendment

Subdivision (a)(2). This new subdivision provides express authority for consolidating the hearing of an application for a preliminary injunction with the trial on the merits. The authority can be exercised with particular profit when it appears that a substantial part of the evidence offered on the application will be relevant to the merits and will be presented in such form as to qualify for admission on the trial proper. Repetition of evidence is thereby avoided. The fact that the proceedings have been consolidated should cause no delay in the disposition of the application for the preliminary injunction, for the evidence will be directed in the first instance to that relief, and the preliminary injunction, if justified by the proof, may be issued in the course of the consolidated proceedings. Furthermore, to consolidate the proceedings will tend to expedite the final disposition of the action. It is believed that consolidation can be usefully availed of in many cases.

The subdivision further provides that even when consolidation is not ordered, evidence received in connection with an application for a preliminary injunction which would be admissible on the trial on the merits forms part of the trial record. This evidence need not be repeated on the trial. On the other hand, repetition is not altogether prohibited. That would be impractical and unwise. For example, a witness testifying comprehensively on the trial who has previously testified upon the application for a preliminary injunction might sometimes be hamstrung in telling his story if he could not go over some part of his prior testimony to connect it with his present testimony. So also, some repetition of testimony may be called for where the trial is conducted by a judge who did not hear the application for the preliminary injunction. In general, however, repetition can be avoided with an increase of efficiency in the conduct of the case and without any distortion of the presentation of evidence by the parties.

Since an application for a preliminary injunction may be made in an action in which, with respect to all or part of the merits, there is a right to trial by jury, it is appropriate to add the caution appearing in the last sentence of the subdivision. In such a case the jury will have to hear all the evidence bearing on its verdict, even if some part of the evidence has already been heard by the judge alone on the application for the preliminary injunction.

The subdivision is believed to reflect the substance of the best current practice and introduces no novel conception.

Subdivision (b). In view of the possibly drastic consequences of a temporary restraining order, the opposition should be heard, if feasible, before the order is granted. Many judges have properly insisted that, when time does not permit of formal notice of the application to the adverse party, some expedient, such as telephonic notice to the attorney for the adverse party, be resorted to if this can reasonably be done. On occasion, however, temporary restraining orders have been issued without any notice when it was feasible for some fair, although informal, notice to be given. See the emphatic criticisms in *Pennsylvania Rd. Co. v. Transport Workers Union,* 278 F.2d 693, 694 (3d Cir. 1960); *Arvida Corp. v. Sugarman,* 259 F.2d 428, 429 (2d Cir. 1958); *Lummus Co. v. Commonwealth Oil Ref. Co., Inc.,* 297 F.2d 80, 83 (2d Cir. 1961), cert. denied, 368 U.S. 986 (1962).

Heretofore the first sentence of subdivision (b), in referring to a notice "served" on the "adverse party" on which a "hearing" could be held, perhaps invited the interpretation that the order might be granted without notice if the circumstances did not permit of a formal hearing on the basis of a formal notice. The subdivision is amended to make it plain that informal notice, which may be communicated to the attorney rather than the adverse party, is to be preferred to no notice at all.

Before notice can be dispensed with, the applicant's counsel must give his certificate as to any efforts made to give notice and the reasons why notice should not be required. This certificate is in addition to the requirement of an affidavit or verified complaint setting forth the facts as to the irreparable injury which would result before the opposition could be heard.

The amended subdivision continues to recognize that a temporary restraining order may be issued without any notice when the circumstances warrant.

Subdivision (c). Original Rules 65 and 73 contained substantially identical provisions for summary proceedings against sureties on bonds required or permitted by the rules. There was fragmentary coverage of the same subject in the Admiralty Rules. Clearly, a single comprehensive rule is required, and is incorporated as Rule 65.1.

1987 Amendment

The amendments are technical. No substantive change is intended.

2001 Amendments

New subdivision (f) is added in conjunction with abrogation of the antiquated Copyright Rules of Practice adopted for proceedings under the 1909 Copyright Act. Courts have naturally turned to Rule 65 in response to the apparent inconsistency of the former Copyright Rules with the discretionary impoundment procedure adopted in 1976, 17 U.S.C. § 503(a). Rule 65 procedures also have assuaged well-founded doubts whether the Copyright Rules satisfy more contemporary requirements of due process. See, e.g., *Religious Technology Center v. Netcom On-Line Communications Servs., Inc.*, 923 F.Supp. 1231, 1260–1265 (N.D.Cal.1995); *Paramount Pictures Corp. v. Doe*, 821 F.Supp. 82 (E.D.N.Y. 1993); *WPOW, Inc. v. MRLJ Enterprises*, 584 F.Supp. 132 (D.D.C.1984).

A common question has arisen from the experience that notice of a proposed impoundment may enable an infringer to defeat the court's capacity to grant effective relief. Impoundment may be ordered on an ex parte basis under subdivision (b) if the applicant makes a strong showing of the reasons why notice is likely to defeat effective relief. Such no-notice procedures are authorized in trademark infringement proceedings, see 15 U.S.C. § 1116(d), and courts have provided clear illustrations of the kinds of showings that support ex parte relief. See *Matter of Vuitton et Fils S.A.*, 606 F.2d 1 (2d Cir.1979); *Vuitton v. White*, 945 F.2d 569 (3d Cir.1991). In applying the tests for no-notice relief, the court should ask whether impoundment is necessary, or whether adequate protection can be had by a less intrusive form of no-notice relief shaped as a temporary restraining order.

This new subdivision (f) does not limit use of trademark procedures in cases that combine trademark and copyright claims. Some observers believe that trademark procedures should be adopted for all copyright cases, a proposal better considered by Congressional processes than by rulemaking processes.

2007 Amendments

The language of Rule 65 has been amended as part of the general restyling of the Civil Rules to make them more easily understood and to make style and terminology consistent throughout the rules. These changes are intended to be stylistic only.

The final sentence of former Rule 65(c) referred to Rule 65.1. It is deleted as unnecessary. Rule 65.1 governs of its own force.

Rule 65(d)(2) clarifies two ambiguities in former Rule 65(d). The former rule was adapted from former 28 U.S.C. § 363, but omitted a comma that made clear the common doctrine that a party must have actual notice of an injunction in order to be bound by it. Amended Rule 65(d) restores the meaning of the earlier statute, and also makes clear the proposition that an injunction can be enforced against a person who acts in concert with a party's officer, agent, servant, employee, or attorney.

Rule 65.1. Proceedings Against A Surety

Whenever these rules (including the Supplemental Rules for Admiralty or Maritime Claims and Asset Forfeiture Actions) require or allow a party to give security, and security is given through a bond or other undertaking with one or more sureties, each surety submits to the court's jurisdiction and irrevocably appoints the court clerk as its agent for receiving service of any papers that affect its liability on the bond or undertaking. The surety's liability may be enforced on motion without an independent action. The motion and any notice that the court orders may be served on the court clerk, who must promptly mail a copy of each to every surety whose address is known.

(Adopted February 28, 1966, effective July 1, 1966; amended March 2, 1987, effective August 1, 1987; April 12, 2006, effective December 1, 2006; April 30, 2007, effective December 1, 2007.)

ADVISORY COMMITTEE NOTES

1966 Addition

See Note to Rule 65.

1987 Amendment

The amendments are technical. No substantive change is intended.

2006 Amendment

Rule 65.1 is amended to conform to the changed title of the Supplemental Rules.

2007 Amendments

The language of Rule 65.1 has been amended as part of the general restyling of the Civil Rules to make them more easily understood and to make style and terminology consistent throughout the rules. These changes are intended to be stylistic only.

Rule 66. Receivers

These rules govern an action in which the appointment of a receiver is sought or a receiver sues or is sued. But the practice in administering an estate by a receiver or a similar court-appointed officer must accord with the historical practice in federal courts or with a local rule. An action in which a receiver has been appointed may be dismissed only by court order.

(Amended December 27, 1946, effective March 19, 1948; December 29, 1948, effective October 20, 1949; April 30, 2007, effective December 1, 2007.)

ADVISORY COMMITTEE NOTES

1946 Amendment

Note. The title of Rule 66 has been expanded to make clear the subject of the rule, i.e., federal equity receivers.

The first sentence added to Rule 66 prevents a dismissal by any party, after a federal equity receiver has been appointed, except upon leave of court. A party should not be permitted to oust the court and its officer without the consent of that court. See Civil Rule 31(e), Eastern District of Washington.

The second sentence added at the beginning of the rule deals with suits by or against a federal equity receiver. The first clause thereof eliminates the formal ceremony of an ancillary appointment before suit can be brought by a receiver, and is in accord with the more modern state practice, and with more expeditious and less expensive judicial administration. 2 *Moore's Federal Practice,* 1938, 2088–2091. For the rule necessitating ancillary appointment, see *Sterrett v. Second Nat. Bank,* 1918, 39 S.Ct. 27, 248 U.S. 73, 63 L.Ed. 135; *Kelley v. Queeney,* W.D.N.Y.1941, 41 F.Supp. 1015; see also *McCandless v. Furlaud,* 1934, 55 S.Ct. 42, 293 U.S. 67, 79 L.Ed. 202. This rule has been extensively criticized. First, *Extraterritorial Powers of Receivers,* 1932, 27 Ill.L.Rev. 271; Rose, *Extraterritorial Actions by Receivers,* 1933, 17 Minn. L.Rev. 704; Laughlin, *The Extraterritorial Powers of Receivers,* 1932, 45 Harv.L.Rev. 429; Clark and Moore, *A New Federal Civil Procedure—II, Pleadings and Parties,* 1935, 44 Yale L.J. 1291, 1312–1315; Note, 1932, 30 Mich.L.Rev. 1322. See also comment in *Bicknell v. Lloyd-Smith,* C.C.A.2d, 1940, 109 F.2d 527, certiorari denied 61 S.Ct. 15, 311 U.S. 650, 85 L.Ed. 416. The second clause of the sentence merely incorporates the well-known and general rule that, absent statutory authorization, a federal receiver cannot be sued without leave of the court which appointed him, applied in the federal courts since *Barton v. Barbour,* 1881, 104 U.S. 126. See also 1 *Clark on Receivers,* 2d ed., § 549. Under [§ 959 of this title, formerly] 28 U.S.C. § 125 leave of court is unnecessary when a receiver is sued "in respect of any act or transaction of his in carrying on the business" connected with the receivership property, but such suit is subject to the general equity jurisdiction of the court in which the receiver was appointed, so far as justice necessitates.

Capacity of a state court receiver to sue or be sued in Federal court is governed by Rule 17(b).

The last sentence added to Rule 66 assures the application of the rules in all matters except actual administration of the receivership estate itself. Since this implicitly carries with it the applicability of those rules relating to appellate procedure, the express reference thereto contained in Rule 66 has been stricken as superfluous. Under Rule 81(a)(1) the rules do not apply to bankruptcy proceedings except as they may be made applicable by order of the Supreme Court. Rule 66 is applicable to what is commonly known as a federal "chancery" or "equity" receiver, or similar type of court officer. It is not designed to regulate or affect receivers in bankruptcy, which are governed by the Bankruptcy Act and the General Orders. Since the Federal Rules are applicable in bankruptcy by virtue of General Orders in Bankruptcy 36 and 37 [see Appendix II following Rules of Bankruptcy Procedure, Title 11] only to the extent that they are not inconsistent with the Bankruptcy Act or the General Orders, Rule 66 is not applicable to bankruptcy receivers. See 1 *Collier on Bankruptcy*, 14th ed. by Moore and Oglebay, ¶¶2.23–2.36.

1948 Amendment

The amendment effective October 1949 deleted a sentence which formerly appeared immediately following the first sentence and which read as follows: "A receiver shall have the capacity to sue in any district court without ancillary appointment; but actions against a receiver may not be commenced without leave of the court appointing him except when authorized by a statute of the United States."

2007 Amendments

The language of Rule 66 has been amended as part of the general restyling of the Civil Rules to make them more easily understood and to make style and terminology consistent throughout the rules. These changes are intended to be stylistic only.

Rule 67. Deposit into Court

(a) Depositing Property. If any part of the relief sought is a money judgment or the disposition of a sum of money or some other deliverable thing, a party—on notice to every other party and by leave of court—may deposit with the court all or part of the money or thing, whether or not that party claims any of it. The depositing party must deliver to the clerk a copy of the order permitting deposit.

(b) Investing and Withdrawing Funds. Money paid into court under this rule must be deposited and withdrawn in accordance with 28 U.S.C. §§ 2041 and 2042 and any like statute. The money must be deposited in an interest-bearing account or invested in a court-approved, interest-bearing instrument.

(Amended December 29, 1948, effective October 20, 1949; April 28, 1983, effective August 1, 1983; April 30, 2007, effective December 1, 2007.)

ADVISORY COMMITTEE NOTES

1937 Adoption

This rule provides for deposit in court generally, continuing similar special provisions contained in such statutes as U.S.C., Title 28, [§§ 1335, 1397, 2361, formerly] § 41(26) (Original jurisdiction of bills of interpleader, and of bills in the nature of interpleader). See generally *Howard v. United States*, 1902, 22 S.Ct. 543, 184 U.S. 676, 46 L.Ed. 754; United States Supreme Court Admiralty Rules (1920), Rules 37 (Bringing Funds into Court), 41 (Funds in Court Registry), and 42 (Claims Against Proceeds in Registry). With the first sentence, compare *English Rules Under the Judicature Act* (The Annual Practice, 1937) O. 22, r. 1(1).

1948 Amendment

The amendment effective October 1949 substituted the reference to "Title 28, U.S.C.A., §§ 2041, and 2042" for the reference to "Sections 995 and 996, Revised Statutes, as amended, U.S.C.A., Title 28, §§ 851, 852." The amendment also added the words "as amended" following the citation of the Act of June 26, 1934, c. 756, § 23, and, in the parenthetical citation immediately following, added the reference to "58 Stat. 845".

1983 Amendment

Rule 67 has been amended in three ways. The first change is the addition of the clause in the first sentence. Some courts have construed the present rule to permit deposit only when the party making it claims no interest in the fund or thing deposited. E.g., *Blasin-Stern v. Beech-Nut Life Savers Corp.*, 429 F.Supp. 533 (D. Puerto Rico 1975); *Dinkins v. General Aniline & Film Corp.*, 214 F.Supp. 281 (S.D.N.Y.1963). However, there are situations in which a litigant may wish to be relieved of responsibility for a sum or thing, but continue to claim an interest in all or part of it. In these cases the deposit-in-court procedure should be available; in addition to the advantages to the party making the deposit, the procedure gives other litigants assurance that any judgment will be collectable. The amendment is intended to accomplish that.

The second change is the addition of a requirement that the order of deposit be served on the clerk of the court in which the sum or thing is to be deposited. This is simply to assure that the clerk knows what is being deposited and what his responsibilities are with respect to the deposit. The latter point is particularly important since the rule as amended contemplates that deposits will be placed in interest-bearing accounts; the clerk must know what treatment has been ordered for the particular deposit.

The third change is to require that any money be deposited in an interest-bearing account or instrument approved by the court.

2007 Amendments

The language of Rule 67 has been amended as part of the general restyling of the Civil Rules to make them more easily understood and to make style and terminology consistent throughout the rules. These changes are intended to be stylistic only.

Rule 68. Offer of Judgment

(a) Making an Offer; Judgment on an Accepted Offer. More than 10 days before the trial begins, a party defending against a claim may serve on an opposing party an offer to allow judgment on specified terms, with the costs then accrued. If, within 10 days after being served, the opposing party serves written notice accepting the offer, either party may then file the offer and notice of acceptance, plus proof of service. The clerk must then enter judgment.

(b) Unaccepted Offer. An unaccepted offer is considered withdrawn, but it does not preclude a later offer. Evidence of an unaccepted offer is not admissible except in a proceeding to determine costs.

(c) **Offer After Liability Is Determined.** When one party's liability to another has been determined but the extent of liability remains to be determined by further proceedings, the party held liable may make an offer of judgment. It must be served within a reasonable time—but at least 10 days—before a hearing to determine the extent of liability.

(d) **Paying Costs After an Unaccepted Offer.** If the judgment that the offeree finally obtains is not more favorable than the unaccepted offer, the offeree must pay the costs incurred after the offer was made.

(Amended December 27, 1946, effective March 19, 1948; February 28, 1966, effective July 1, 1966; March 2, 1987, effective August 1, 1987; April 30, 2007, effective December 1, 2007.)

ADVISORY COMMITTEE NOTES

1937 Adoption

See 2 Minn.Stat. (Mason, 1927) § 9323; 4 Mont.Rev.Codes Ann. (1935) § 9770; N.Y.C.P.A. (1937) § 177.

For the recovery of costs against the United States, see Rule 54(d).

1946 Amendment

Note. The third sentence of Rule 68 has been altered to make clear that evidence of an unaccepted offer is admissible in a proceeding to determine the costs of the action but is not otherwise admissible.

The two sentences substituted for the deleted last sentence of the rule assure a party the right to make a second offer where the situation permits—as, for example, where a prior offer was not accepted but the plaintiff's judgment is nullified and a new trial ordered, whereupon the defendant desires to make a second offer. It is implicit, however, that as long as the case continues—whether there be a first, second or third trial—and the defendant makes no further offer, his first and only offer will operate to save him the costs from the time of that offer if the plaintiff ultimately obtains a judgment less than the sum offered. In the case of successive offers not accepted, the offeror is saved the costs incurred after the making of the offer which was equal to or greater than the judgment ultimately obtained. These provisions should serve to encourage settlements and avoid protracted litigation.

The phrase "before the trial begins", in the first sentence of the rule, has been construed in *Cover v. Chicago Eye Shield Co.,* C.C.A.7th, 1943, 136 F.2d 374, certiorari denied 64 S.Ct. 53, 320 U.S. 749, 88 L.Ed. 445.

1966 Amendment

This logical extension of the concept of offer of judgment is suggested by the common admiralty practice of determining liability before the amount of liability is determined.

1987 Amendment

The amendments are technical. No substantive change is intended.

2007 Amendments

The language of Rule 68 has been amended as part of the general restyling of the Civil Rules to make them more easily understood and to make style and terminology consistent throughout the rules. These changes are intended to be stylistic only.

Rule 69. Execution

(a) **In General.**

(1) ***Money Judgment; Applicable Procedure.*** A money judgment is enforced by a writ of execution, unless the court directs otherwise. The procedure on execution—and in proceedings supplementary to and in aid of judgment or execution—must accord with the procedure of the state where the court is located, but a federal statute governs to the extent it applies.

(2) ***Obtaining Discovery.*** In aid of the judgment or execution, the judgment creditor or a successor in interest whose interest appears of record may obtain discovery from any person—including the judgment debtor—as provided in these rules or by the procedure of the state where the court is located.

(b) **Against Certain Public Officers.** When a judgment has been entered against a revenue officer in the circumstances stated in 28 U.S.C. § 2006, or against an officer of Congress in the circumstances stated in 2 U.S.C. § 118, the judgment must be satisfied as those statutes provide.

(Amended December 29, 1948, effective October 20, 1949; March 30, 1970, effective July 1, 1970; March 2, 1987 effective August 1, 1987; April 30, 2007, effective December 1, 2007.)

ADVISORY COMMITTEE NOTES

1937 Adoption

Note to Subdivision (a). This follows in substance U.S.C. Title 28, [former] §§ 727 (Executions as provided by State laws) and [former 729] [now Title 42, § 1988] (Proceedings in vindication of civil rights), except that, as in the similar case of attachments (see note to Rule 64), the rule specifies the applicable state law to be that of the time when the remedy is sought, and thus renders unnecessary, as well as supersedeas, local district court rules.

Statutes of the United States on execution, when applicable, govern under this rule. Among these are:

U.S.C., Title 12:

§ 91 (Transfers by bank and other acts in contemplation of insolvency)

§ 632 (Jurisdiction of United States district courts in cases arising out of foreign banking jurisdiction where Federal reserve bank a party)

U.S.C., Title 19:

§ 199 (Judgments for customs duties, how payable)

U.S.C., Title 26 [I.R.C.1939]:

§ 1610(a) [former] (Surrender of property subject to distraint)

U.S.C., Title 28 former:

§ 122 [now 1656] (Creation of new district or transfer of territory; lien)

§ 350 [now 2101] (Time for making application for appeal or certiorari; stay pending application for certiorari)

§ 489 [now 547] (District Attorneys; reports to Department of Justice)

§ 574 [now 1921] (Marshals, fees enumerated)

§ 786 [former] (Judgments for duties; collected in coin)

§ 811 [now 1961] (Interest on judgments)

§ 838 [former] (Executions; run in all districts of State)

§ 839 [now 2413] (Executions; run in every State and Territory)

§ 840 [former] (Executions; stay on conditions), as modified by Rule 62(b)

§ 841 [former] (Executions; stay of one term), as modified by Rule 62(f)

§ 842 [now 2006] (Executions; against officers of revenue in cases of probable cause), as incorporated in Subdivision (b) of this rule

§ 843 [now 2007] (Imprisonment for debt)

§ 844 [now 2007] (Imprisonment for debt; discharge according to State laws)

§ 845 [now 2007] (Imprisonment for debt; jail limits)

§ 846 [now 2005] (Fieri Facias; appraisal of goods; appraisers)

§ 847 [now 2001] (Sales; real property under order or decree)

§ 848 [now 2004] (Sales; personal property under order or decree)

§ 849 [now 2002] (Sales; necessity of notice)

§ 850 [now 2003] (Sales; death of marshall after levy or after sale)

§ 869 [former] (Bond in former error and on appeal), as incorporated in Rule 73(c)

§ 874 [former] (Supersedeas), as modified by Rules 62(d) and 73(d)

U.S.C., Title 31:

§ 195 [now 3715] (Purchase on execution)

U.S.C., Title 33:

§ 918 (Collection of defaulted payments)

U.S.C., Title 49:

§ 74(g) [former] (Causes of action arising out of Federal control of railroads; execution and other process)

Special statutes of the United States on exemption from execution are also continued. Among these are:

U.S.C., Title 2:

§ 118 (Actions against officers of Congress for official acts)

U.S.C., Title 5 former:

§ 729 [see 8346, 8470] (Federal employees retirement annuities not subject to assignment, execution, levy or other legal process)

U.S.C., Title 10 former:

§ 610 [now 3690, 8690] (Exemption of enlisted men from arrest on civil process)

U.S.C., Title 22 former:

§ 21(h) [see 4060] (Foreign service retirement and disability system; establishment; rules and regulations; annuities; nonassignable; exemption from legal process)

U.S.C., Title 33:

§ 916 (Assignment and exemption from claims of creditors) (Longshoremen's and Harborworkers' Compensation Act)

U.S.C., Title 38 former:

§ 54 [see 3101] (Attachment, levy or seizure of moneys due pensioners prohibited)

§ 393 [former] (Army and Navy Medal of Honor Roll; pensions additional to other pensions; liability to attachment, etc.) Compare [former] Title 34, § 365(c) (Medal of Honor Roll; special pension to persons enrolled)

§ 618 [see 3101] (Benefits exempt from seizure under process and taxation; no deductions for indebtedness to United States)

U.S.C., Title 43:

§ 175 (Exemption from execution of homestead land)

U.S.C., Title 48 former:

§ 1371*o* (Panama canal and railroad retirement annuities, exemption from execution and so forth.)

Supplementary Note

Note. With respect to the provisions of the Soldiers' and Sailors' Civil Relief Act of 1940, 50 U.S.C. Appendix, § 501 et seq., see notes to Rules 62 and 64 herein.

1948 Amendment

The amendment effective October 1949, substituted the citation of "Title 28, U.S.C., § 2006" in subdivision (b) in place of the citation to "Section 989, Revised Statutes, U.S.C., Title 28, § 842".

1970 Amendment

The amendment assures that, in aid of execution on a judgment, all discovery procedures provided in the rules are available and not just discovery via the taking of a deposition. Under the present language, one court had held that Rule 34 discovery is unavailable to the judgment creditor. *M. Lowenstein & Sons, Inc. v. American Underwear Mfg. Co.*, 11 F.R.D. 172 (E.D.Pa.1951). Notwithstanding the language, and relying heavily on legislative history referring to Rule 33, the Fifth Circuit has held that a judgment creditor may invoke Rule 33 interrogatories. *United States v. McWhirter*, 376 F.2d 102 (5th Cir. 1967). But the court's reasoning does not extend to discovery except as provided in Rules 26–33. One commentator suggests that the existing language might properly be stretched to all discovery, 7 *Moore's Federal*

Practice ¶69.05[1] (2d ed. 1966), but another believes that a rules amendment is needed. 3 Barron & Holtzoff, *Federal Practice and Procedure* 1484 (Wright ed. 1958). Both commentators and the court in *McWhirter* are clear that, as a matter of policy, Rule 69 should authorize the use of all discovery devices provided in the rules.

1987 Amendment

The amendments are technical. No substantive change is intended.

2007 Amendments

The language of Rule 69 has been amended as part of the general restyling of the Civil Rules to make them more easily understood and to make style and terminology consistent throughout the rules. These changes are intended to be stylistic only.

Amended Rule 69(b) incorporates directly the provisions of 2 U.S.C. § 118 and 28 U.S.C. § 2006, deleting the incomplete statement in former Rule 69(b) of the circumstances in which execution does not issue against an officer.

Rule 70. Enforcing a Judgment for a Specific Act

(a) Party's Failure to Act; Ordering Another to Act. If a judgment requires a party to convey land, to deliver a deed or other document, or to perform any other specific act and the party fails to comply within the time specified, the court may order the act to be done—at the disobedient party's expense—by another person appointed by the court. When done, the act has the same effect as if done by the party.

(b) Vesting Title. If the real or personal property is within the district, the court—instead of ordering a conveyance—may enter a judgment divesting any party's title and vesting it in others. That judgment has the effect of a legally executed conveyance.

(c) Obtaining a Writ of Attachment or Sequestration. On application by a party entitled to performance of an act, the clerk must issue a writ of attachment or sequestration against the disobedient party's property to compel obedience.

(d) Obtaining a Writ of Execution or Assistance. On application by a party who obtains a judgment or order for possession, the clerk must issue a writ of execution or assistance.

(e) Holding in Contempt. The court may also hold the disobedient party in contempt.

(Amended April 30, 2007, effective December 1, 2007.)

ADVISORY COMMITTEE NOTES

1937 Adoption

Compare [former] Equity Rules 7 (Process, Mesne and Final), 8 (Enforcement of Final Decrees), and 9 (Writ of Assistance). To avoid possible confusion, both old and new denominations for attachment (sequestration) and execution (assistance) are used in this rule. Compare with the provision in this rule that the judgment may itself vest title, 6 Tenn.Ann.Code (Williams, 1934), § 10594; 2 Conn.Gen.Stat. (1930), § 5455; N.M.Stat.Ann. (Courtright, 1929), § 117–117; 2 Ohio Gen.Code Ann. (Page, 1926), § 11590; and England, Supreme Court of Judicature Act (1925), § 47.

2007 Amendments

The language of Rule 70 has been amended as part of the general restyling of the Civil Rules to make them more easily understood and to make style and terminology consistent throughout the rules. These changes are intended to be stylistic only.

Rule 71. Enforcing Relief for or Against a Nonparty

When an order grants relief for a nonparty or may be enforced against a nonparty, the procedure for enforcing the order is the same as for a party.

(Amended March 2, 1987, effective August 1, 1987; April 30, 2007, effective December 1, 2007.)

ADVISORY COMMITTEE NOTES

1937 Adoption

Compare [former] Equity Rule 11 (Process in Behalf of and Against Persons Not Parties). Compare also *Terrell v. Allison*, 1875, 21 Wall. 289, 22 L.Ed. 634; *Farmers' Loan and Trust Co. v. Chicago and A. Ry. Co.*, C.C.Ind.1890, 44 F. 653; *Robert Findlay Mfg. Co. v. Hygrade Lighting Fixture Corp.*, E.D.N.Y.1923, 288 F. 80; *Thompson v. Smith*, C.C.Minn.1870, Fed.Cas. No. 13,977.

1987 Amendment

The amendments are technical. No substantive change is intended.

2007 Amendments

The language of Rule 71 has been amended as part of the general restyling of the Civil Rules to make them more easily understood and to make style and terminology consistent throughout the rules. These changes are intended to be stylistic only.

TITLE IX. SPECIAL PROCEEDINGS

Rule 71.1. Condemning Real or Personal Property

(a) **Applicability of Other Rules.** These rules govern proceedings to condemn real and personal property by eminent domain, except as this rule provides otherwise.

(b) **Joinder of Properties.** The plaintiff may join separate pieces of property in a single action, no matter whether they are owned by the same persons or sought for the same use.

(c) **Complaint.**

(1) ***Caption.*** The complaint must contain a caption as provided in Rule 10(a). The plaintiff must, however, name as defendants both the property—designated generally by kind, quantity, and location—and at least one owner of some part of or interest in the property.

(2) ***Contents.*** The complaint must contain a short and plain statement of the following:

(A) the authority for the taking;

(B) the uses for which the property is to be taken;

(C) a description sufficient to identify the property;

(D) the interests to be acquired; and

(E) for each piece of property, a designation of each defendant who has been joined as an owner or owner of an interest in it.

(3) ***Parties.*** When the action commences, the plaintiff need join as defendants only those persons who have or claim an interest in the property and whose names are then known. But before any hearing on compensation, the plaintiff must add as defendants all those persons who have or claim an interest and whose names have become known or can be found by a reasonably diligent search of the records, considering both the property's character and value and the interests to be acquired. All others may be made defendants under the designation "Unknown Owners."

(4) ***Procedure.*** Notice must be served on all defendants as provided in Rule 71.1(d), whether they were named as defendants when the action commenced or were added later. A defendant may answer as provided in Rule 71.1(e). The court, meanwhile, may order any distribution of a deposit that the facts warrant.

(5) ***Filing; Additional Copies.*** In addition to filing the complaint, the plaintiff must give the clerk at least one copy for the defendants' use and additional copies at the request of the clerk or a defendant.

(d) **Process.**

(1) ***Delivering Notice to the Clerk.*** On filing a complaint, the plaintiff must promptly deliver to the clerk joint or several notices directed to the named defendants. When adding defendants, the plaintiff must deliver to the clerk additional notices directed to the new defendants.

(2) ***Contents of the Notice.***

(A) *Main Contents.* Each notice must name the court, the title of the action, and the defendant to whom it is directed. It must describe the property sufficiently to identify it, but need not describe any property other than that to be taken from the named defendant. The notice must also state:

(i) that the action is to condemn property;

(ii) the interest to be taken;

(iii) the authority for the taking;

(iv) the uses for which the property is to be taken;

(v) that the defendant may serve an answer on the plaintiff's attorney within 20 days after being served with the notice;

(vi) that the failure to so serve an answer constitutes consent to the taking and to the court's authority to proceed with the action and fix the compensation; and

(vii) that a defendant who does not serve an answer may file a notice of appearance.

(B) *Conclusion.* The notice must conclude with the name, telephone number, and e-mail address of the plaintiff's attorney and an address within the district in which the action is brought where the attorney may be served.

(3) ***Serving the Notice.***

(A) *Personal Service.* When a defendant whose address is known resides within the United States or a territory subject to the administrative or judicial jurisdiction of the United States, personal service of the notice (without a copy of the complaint) must be made in accordance with Rule 4.

(B) Service by Publication.

(i) A defendant may be served by publication only when the plaintiff's attorney files a certificate stating that the attorney believes the defendant cannot be personally served, because after diligent inquiry within the state where the complaint is filed, the defendant's place of residence is still unknown or, if known, that it is beyond the territorial limits of personal service. Service is then made by publishing the notice—once a week for at least 3 successive weeks—in a newspaper published in the county where the property is located or, if there is no such newspaper, in a newspaper with general circulation where the property is located. Before the last publication, a copy of the notice must also be mailed to every defendant who cannot be personally served but whose place of residence is then known. Unknown owners may be served by publication in the same manner by a notice addressed to "Unknown Owners."

(ii) Service by publication is complete on the date of the last publication. The plaintiff's attorney must prove publication and mailing by a certificate, attach a printed copy of the published notice, and mark on the copy the newspaper's name and the dates of publication.

(4) ***Effect of Delivery and Service.*** Delivering the notice to the clerk and serving it have the same effect as serving a summons under Rule 4.

(5) ***Amending the Notice; Proof of Service and Amending the Proof.*** Rule 4(a)(2) governs amending the notice. Rule 4(*l*) governs proof of service and amending it.

(e) Appearance or Answer.

(1) ***Notice of Appearance.*** A defendant that has no objection or defense to the taking of its property may serve a notice of appearance designating the property in which it claims an interest. The defendant must then be given notice of all later proceedings affecting the defendant.

(2) ***Answer.*** A defendant that has an objection or defense to the taking must serve an answer within 20 days after being served with the notice. The answer must:

(A) identify the property in which the defendant claims an interest;

(B) state the nature and extent of the interest; and

(C) state all the defendant's objections and defenses to the taking.

(3) ***Waiver of Other Objections and Defenses; Evidence on Compensation.*** A defendant waives all objections and defenses not stated in its answer. No other pleading or motion asserting an additional objection or defense is allowed. But at the trial on compensation, a defendant—whether or not it has previously appeared or answered—may present evidence on the amount of compensation to be paid and may share in the award.

(f) Amending Pleadings. Without leave of court, the plaintiff may—as often as it wants—amend the complaint at any time before the trial on compensation. But no amendment may be made if it would result in a dismissal inconsistent with Rule 71.1(i)(1) or (2). The plaintiff need not serve a copy of an amendment, but must serve notice of the filing, as provided in Rule 5(b), on every affected party who has appeared and, as provided in Rule 71.1(d), on every affected party who has not appeared. In addition, the plaintiff must give the clerk at least one copy of each amendment for the defendants' use, and additional copies at the request of the clerk or a defendant. A defendant may appear or answer in the time and manner and with the same effect as provided in Rule 71.1(e).

(g) Substituting Parties. If a defendant dies, becomes incompetent, or transfers an interest after being joined, the court may, on motion and notice of hearing, order that the proper party be substituted. Service of the motion and notice on a nonparty must be made as provided in Rule 71.1(d)(3).

(h) Trial of the Issues.

(1) ***Issues Other Than Compensation; Compensation.*** In an action involving eminent domain under federal law, the court tries all issues, including compensation, except when compensation must be determined:

(A) by any tribunal specially constituted by a federal statute to determine compensation; or

(B) if there is no such tribunal, by a jury when a party demands one within the time to answer or within any additional time the court sets, unless the court appoints a commission.

(2) ***Appointing a Commission; Commission's Powers and Report.***

(A) *Reasons for Appointing.* If a party has demanded a jury, the court may instead appoint a three-person commission to determine compensation because of the character, location, or quantity of the property to be condemned or for other just reasons.

(B) *Alternate Commissioners.* The court may appoint up to two additional persons to serve as alternate commissioners to hear the case and replace commissioners who, before a decision is filed, the court finds unable or disqualified to perform their duties. Once the commission renders its final decision, the court must discharge any alternate who has not replaced a commissioner.

(C) *Examining the Prospective Commissioners.* Before making its appointments, the court must advise the parties of the identity and qualifications of each prospective commissioner and alternate, and may permit the parties to examine them. The parties may not suggest appointees, but for good cause may object to a prospective commissioner or alternate.

(D) *Commission's Powers and Report.* A commission has the powers of a master under Rule 53(c). Its action and report are determined by a majority. Rule 53(d), (e), and (f) apply to its action and report.

(i) Dismissal of the Action or a Defendant.

(1) *Dismissing the Action.*

(A) *By the Plaintiff.* If no compensation hearing on a piece of property has begun, and if the plaintiff has not acquired title or a lesser interest or taken possession, the plaintiff may, without a court order, dismiss the action as to that property by filing a notice of dismissal briefly describing the property.

(B) *By Stipulation.* Before a judgment is entered vesting the plaintiff with title or a lesser interest in or possession of property, the plaintiff and affected defendants may, without a court order, dismiss the action in whole or in part by filing a stipulation of dismissal. And if the parties so stipulate, the court may vacate a judgment already entered.

(C) *By Court Order.* At any time before compensation has been determined and paid, the court may, after a motion and hearing, dismiss the action as to a piece of property. But if the plaintiff has already taken title, a lesser interest, or possession as to any part of it, the court must award compensation for the title, lesser interest, or possession taken.

(2) *Dismissing a Defendant.* The court may at any time dismiss a defendant who was unnecessarily or improperly joined.

(3) *Effect.* A dismissal is without prejudice unless otherwise stated in the notice, stipulation, or court order.

(j) Deposit and Its Distribution.

(1) *Deposit.* The plaintiff must deposit with the court any money required by law as a condition to the exercise of eminent domain and may make a deposit when allowed by statute.

(2) *Distribution; Adjusting Distribution.* After a deposit, the court and attorneys must expedite the proceedings so as to distribute the deposit and to determine and pay compensation. If the compensation finally awarded to a defendant exceeds the amount distributed to that defendant, the court must enter judgment against the plaintiff for the deficiency. If the compensation awarded to a defendant is less than the amount distributed to that defendant, the court must enter judgment against that defendant for the overpayment.

(k) Condemnation Under a State's Power of Eminent Domain. This rule governs an action involving eminent domain under state law. But if state law provides for trying an issue by jury—or for trying the issue of compensation by jury or commission or both—that law governs.

(*l*) Costs. Costs are not subject to Rule 54(d).

(Adopted April 30, 1951, effective August 1, 1951; amended January 21, 1963, effective July 1, 1963; April 29, 1985, effective August 1, 1985; March 2, 1987, effective August 1, 1987; April 25, 1988, effective August 1, 1988; amended by Pub.L. 100–690, Title VII, § 7050, November 18, 1988, 102 Stat. 4401 (although amendment by Pub.L. 100–690 could not be executed due to prior amendment by Court order which made the same change effective August 1, 1988); amended April 22, 1993, effective December 1, 1993; March 27, 2003, effective December 1, 2003; April 30, 2007, effective December 1, 2007.)

ADVISORY COMMITTEE NOTES

1951 Addition

Supplementary Report

The Court will remember that at its conference on December 2, 1948, the discussion was confined to subdivision (h) of the rule (* * *), the particular question being whether the tribunal to award compensation should be a commission or a jury in cases where the Congress has not made specific provision on the subject. The Advisory Committee was agreed from the outset that a rule should not be promulgated which would overturn the decision of the Congress as to the kind of tribunal to fix compensation, provided that the system established by Congress was found to be working well. We found two instances where the Congress had specified the kind of tribunal to fix compensation. One case was the District of Columbia ([former] §§ 361 to 386 of Title 40 [now D.C. Code, Title 16, § 1301 et seq.]) where a rather unique system exists under which the court is required in all cases to order the selection of a "jury" of five from among not less than twenty names drawn from "the special box provided by law." They must have the usual qualifications of jurors and in addition must be freeholders of the District and not in the service of the United States or the District. That system has been in effect for many years, and our inquiry revealed that it works well under the conditions prevailing in the District, and is satisfactory to the courts of the District, the legal profession and to property owners.

The other instance is that of the Tennessee Valley Authority, where the act of Congress (section 831x of Title 16) provides that compensation is fixed by three disinterested commissioners appointed by the court, whose award goes before the District Court for confirmation or modification. The Advisory Committee made a thorough inquiry into the practical operation of the TVA commission system. We obtained from counsel for the TVA the results of their experience, which afforded convincing proof that the commission system is preferable under the conditions affecting TVA and that the jury system would not work satisfactorily. We then, under date of February 6, 1947, wrote every Federal judge who had ever sat in a TVA condemnation case, asking his views as to whether the commission system is satisfactory and whether a jury system should be preferred. Of 21 responses from the judges 17 approved the commission system and opposed the substitution of a jury system for the TVA. Many of the judges went further and opposed the use of juries in any condemnation cases. Three of the judges preferred the jury system, and one dealt only with the TVA provision for a three judge district court. The Advisory Committee has not considered abolition of the three judge requirement of the TVA Act, because it seemed to raise a question of jurisdiction, which cannot be altered by rule. Nevertheless the Department of Justice continued its advocacy of the jury system for its asserted expedition and economy; and others favored a uniform procedure. In consequence of these divided counsels the Advisory Committee was itself divided, but in its May 1948 Report to the Court recommended the following rule as approved by a majority (* * *):

(h) Trial. If the action involves the exercise of the power of eminent domain under the law of the United States, any tribunal especially constituted by an Act of Congress governing the case for the trial of the issue of just compensation shall be the tribunal for the determination of that issue; but if there is no such specially constituted tribunal any party may have a trial by jury of the issue of just compensation by filing a demand therefor within the time allowed for answer or within such further time as the court may fix. Trial of all issues shall otherwise be by the court.

The effect of this was to preserve the existing systems in the District of Columbia and in TVA cases, but to provide for a jury to fix compensation in all other cases.

Before the Court's conference of December 2, 1948, the Chief Justice informed the Committee that the Court was particularly interested in the views expressed by Judge John Paul, Judge of the United States District Court for the Western District of Virginia, in a letter from him to the chairman of the Advisory Committee, dated February 13, 1947. Copies of all the letters from judges who had sat in TVA cases had been made available to the Court, and this letter from Judge Paul is one of them. Judge Paul strongly opposed jury trials and recommended the commission system in large projects like the TVA, and his views seemed to have impressed the Court and to have been the occasion for the conference.

The reasons which convinced the Advisory Committee that the use of commissioners instead of juries is desirable in TVA cases were these:

1. The TVA condemns large areas of land of similar kind, involving many owners. Uniformity in awards is essential. The commission system tends to prevent discrimination and provide for uniformity in compensation. The jury system tends to lack of uniformity. Once a reasonable and uniform standard of values for the area has been settled by a commission, litigation ends and settlements result.

2. Where large areas are involved many small landowners reside at great distances from the place where a court sits. It is a great hardship on humble people to have to travel long distances to attend a jury trial. A commission may travel around and receive the evidence of the owner near his home.

3. It is impracticable to take juries long distances to view the premises.

4. If the cases are tried by juries the burden on the time of the courts is excessive.

These considerations are the very ones Judge Paul stressed in his letter. He pointed out that they applied not only to the TVA but to other large governmental projects, such as flood control, hydroelectric power, reclamation, national forests, and others. So when the representatives of the Advisory Committee appeared at the Court's conference December 2, 1948, they found it difficult to justify the proposed provision in subdivision (h) of the rule that a jury should be used to fix compensation in all cases where Congress had not specified the tribunal. If our reasons for preserving the TVA system were sound, provision for a jury in similar projects of like magnitude seemed unsound.

Aware of the apparent inconsistency between the acceptance of the TVA system and the provision for a jury in all other cases, the members of the Committee attending the conference of December 2, 1948, then suggested that in the other cases the choice of jury or commission be left to the discretion of the District Court, going back to a suggestion previously made by Committee members and reported at page 15 of the Preliminary Draft of June 1947. They called the attention of the Court to the fact that the entire Advisory Committee had not been consulted about this suggestion and proposed that the draft be returned to the Committee for further consideration, and that was done.

The proposal we now make for subdivision (h) is as follows:

(h) Trial. If the action involves the exercise of the power of eminent domain under the law of the United States, any tribunal specially constituted by an Act of Congress governing the case for the trial of the issue of just compensation shall be the tribunal for the determination of that issue; but if there is no such specially constituted tribunal any party may have a trial by jury of the issue of just compensation by filing a demand therefor within the time allowed for answer or within such further time as the court may fix, unless the court in its discretion orders that, because of the character, location, or quantity of the property to be condemned, or for other reasons in the interest of justice, the issue of compensation shall be determined by a commission of three persons appointed by it. If a commission is appointed it shall have the powers of a master provided in subdivision (c) of Rule 53 and proceedings before it shall be governed by the provisions of paragraphs (1) and (2) of subdivision (d) of Rule 53. Its action and report shall be determined by a majority and its findings and report shall have the effect, and be dealt with by the court in accordance with the practice, prescribed in paragraph (2) of subdivision (e) of Rule 53. Trial of all issues shall otherwise be by the court.

In the 1948 draft the Committee had been almost evenly divided as between jury or commission and that made it easy for us to agree on the present draft. It would be difficult to state in a rule the various conditions to control the District Court in its choice and we have merely stated generally the matters which should be considered by the District Court.

The rule as now drafted seems to meet Judge Paul's objection. In large projects like the TVA the court may decide to use a commission. In a great number of cases involving only sites for buildings or other small areas, where use of a jury is appropriate, a jury may be chosen. The District Court's discretion may also be influenced by local preference or habit, and the preference of the Department of Justice and the reasons for its preference will doubtless be given weight. The Committee is convinced that there are some types of cases in which use of a commission is preferable and others in which a jury may be appropriately used, and that it would be a mistake to provide that the same kind of tribunal should be used in all cases. We think the available evidence clearly leads to that conclusion.

When this suggestion was made at the conference of December 2, 1948, representatives of the Department of Justice opposed it, expressing opposition to the use of a commission in any case. Their principal ground for opposition to commissions was then based on the assertion that the commission system is too expensive because courts allow commissioners too large compensation. The obvious answer to that is that the compensation of commissioners ought to be fixed or limited by law, as was done in the TVA Act, and the agency dealing with appropriations—either the Administrative Office or some other interested department of the government—should correct that evil, if evil there be, by obtaining such legislation. Authority to promulgate rules of procedure does not include power to fix compensation of government employees. The Advisory Committee is not convinced that even without such legislation the commission system is more expensive than the jury system. The expense of jury trials includes not only the per diem and mileage of the jurors impaneled for a case but like items for the entire venire. In computing cost of jury trials, the salaries of court officials, judges, clerks, marshals and deputies must be considered. No figures have been given to the Committee to establish that the cost of the commission system is the greater.

We earnestly recommend the rule as now drafted for promulgation by the Court, in the public interest.

The Advisory Committee have given more time to this rule, including time required for conferences with the Department of Justice to hear statements of its representatives, than has been required by any other rule. The rule may not be perfect but if faults develop in practice they may be promptly cured. Certainly the present conformity system is atrocious.

Under state practices, just compensation is normally determined by one of three methods: by commissioners; by commissioners with a right of appeal to and trial de novo before a jury; and by a jury, without a commission. A trial to the court or to the court including a master are, however, other methods that are occasionally used. Approximately 5 states use only commissioners; 23 states use commissioners with a trial de novo before a jury; and 18 states use only the jury. This classification is advisedly stated in approximate terms, since the same state may utilize diverse methods, depending upon different types of condemnations or upon the locality of the property, and since the methods used in a few states do not permit of a categorical classification. To reject the proposed rule and leave the situation as it is would not satisfy the views of the Department of Justice. The Department and the Advisory Committee agree that the use of a commission, with appeal to a jury, is a wasteful system.

The Department of Justice has a voluminous "Manual on Federal Eminent Domain," the 1940 edition of which has 948 pages with an appendix of 73 more pages. The title page informs us the preparation of the manual was begun during the incumbency of Attorney General Cummings, was continued under Attorney General Murphy, and completed during the incumbency of Attorney General Jackson. The preface contains the following statement:

It should also be mentioned that the research incorporated in the manual would be of invaluable assistance in the drafting of a new uniform code, or rules of court, for federal condemnation proceedings, which are now greatly confused, not only by the existence of over seventy federal statutes governing condemnations for different purposes—statutes which sometimes conflict with one another—but also by the countless problems occasioned by the requirements of conformity to state law. Progress of the work has already demonstrated that the need for such reform exists.

It is not surprising that more than once Attorneys General have asked the Advisory Committee to prepare a federal rule and rescue the government from this morass.

The Department of Justice has twice tried and failed to persuade the Congress to provide that juries shall be used in all condemnation cases. The debates in Congress show that part of the opposition to the Department of Justice's bills came from representatives opposed to jury trials in all cases, and in part from a preference for the conformity system. Our present proposal opens the door for district judges to yield to local preferences on the subject. It does much for the Department's points of view. It is a great improvement over the present so-called conformity system. It does away with the wasteful "double" system prevailing in 23 states where awards by commissions are followed by jury trials.

Aside from the question as to the choice of a tribunal to award compensation, the proposed rule would afford a simple and improved procedure.

We turn now to an itemized explanation of the other changes we have made in the 1948 draft. Some of these result from recent amendments to the Judicial Code. Others result from a reconsideration by the Advisory Committee of provisions which we thought could be improved.

1. In the amended Judicial Code, the district courts are designated as "United States District Courts" instead of "District Courts of the United States," and a corresponding change has been made in the rule.

2. After the 1948 draft was referred back to the committee, the provision in subdivision (c)(2), relating to naming defendants, * * * which provided that the plaintiff shall add as defendants all persons having or claiming an interest in that property whose names can be ascertained by a search of the records to the extent commonly made by competent searchers of title in the vicinity "in light of the type and value of the property involved," the phrase in quotation marks was changed to read "in the light of the character and value of the property involved and the interests to be acquired."

The Department of Justice made a counter proposal * * * that there be substituted the words "reasonably diligent search of the records, considering the type." When the American Bar Association thereafter considered the draft, it approved the Advisory Committee's draft of this subdivision, but said that it had no objection to the Department's suggestion. Thereafter, in an effort to eliminate controversy, the Advisory Committee accepted the Department's suggestion as to (c)(2), using the word "character" instead of the word "type."

The Department of Justice also suggested that in subdivision (d)(3)(ii) relating to service by publication, the search for a defendant's residence as a preliminary to publication be limited to the state in which the complaint is filed. Here again the American Bar Association's report expressed the view that the Department's suggestion was unobjectionable and the Advisory Committee thereupon adopted it.

3. Subdivision (k) of the 1948 draft is as follows:

(k) Condemnation Under a State's Power of Eminent Domain. If the action involves the exercise of the power of eminent domain under the law of a state, the practice herein prescribed may be altered to the extent necessary to observe and enforce any condition affecting the substantial rights of a litigant attached by the state law to the exercise of the state's power of eminent domain.

Occasionally condemnation cases under a state's power of eminent domain reach a United States District Court because of diversity of citizenship. Such cases are rare, but provision should be made for them.

The 1948 draft of (k) required a district court to decide whether a provision of state law specifying the tribunal to award compensation is or is not a "condition" attached to the exercise of the state's power. On reconsideration we concluded that it would be wise to redraft (k) so as to avoid that troublesome question. As to conditions in state laws which affect the substantial rights of a litigant, the district courts would be bound to give them effect without any rule on the subject. Accordingly we present two alternative revisions. One suggestion supported by a majority of the Advisory Committee is as follows:

(k) Condemnation Under a State's Power of Eminent Domain. The practice herein prescribed governs in actions involving the exercise of the power of eminent domain under the law of a state, provided that if the state law makes provision for trial of any issue by jury, or for trial of the issue of compensation by jury or commission or both, that provision shall be followed.

The other is as follows:

(k) Condemnation Under a State's Power of Eminent Domain. The practice herein prescribed governs in actions involving the exercise of the power of eminent domain under the law of a state, provided that if the state law gives a right to a trial by jury such a trial shall in any case be allowed to the party demanding it within the time permitted by these rules, and in that event no hearing before a commission shall be had.

The first proposal accepts the state law as to the tribunals to fix compensation, and in that respect leaves the parties in precisely the same situation as if the case were pending in a state court, including the use of a commission with appeal to a jury, if the state law so provides. It has the effect of avoiding any question as to whether the decisions in *Erie R. Co. v. Tompkins* and later cases have application to a situation of this kind.

The second proposal gives the parties a right to a jury trial if that is provided for by state law, but prevents the use of both commission and jury. Those members of the Committee who favor the second proposal do so because of the obvious objections to the double trial, with a commission and appeal to a jury. As the decisions in *Erie R. Co. v. Tompkins* and later cases may have a bearing on this point, and the Committee is divided, we think both proposals should be placed before the Court.

4. The provision * * * of the 1948 draft * * * prescribing the effective date of the rule was drafted before the recent amendment of the Judicial Code on that subject. On May 10, 1950, the President approved an act which amended section 2072 of Title 28, United States Code, to read as follows:

> Such rules shall not take effect until they have been reported to Congress by the Chief Justice at or after the beginning of a regular session thereof but not later than the first day of May, and until the expiration of ninety days after they have been thus reported.

To conform to the statute now in force, we suggest a provision as follows:

Effective Date. This Rule 71A and the amendment to Rule 81(a) will take effect on August 1, 1951. Rule 71A governs all proceedings in actions brought after it takes effect and also all further proceedings in actions then pending, except to the extent that in the opinion of the court its application in a particular action pending when the rule takes effect would not be feasible or would work injustice, in which event the former procedure applies.

If the rule is not reported to Congress by May 1, 1951, this provision must be altered.

[Par. 3 of Supreme Court Order adopted Apr. 30, 1951, setting out this rule and providing for the abrogation of par. (7) of Rule 81(a), and providing for the Effective Date, as stated herein, was transmitted to Congress on May 1, 1951 by the Chief Justice of the United States (House Document No. 121, May 1, 1951, 82nd Cong., 1st Sess.), in conformity with § 2072 of this title. As no action was taken by Congress within the 90-day period required by that section, this rule and the abrogation of par. (7) of Rule 81(a) took effect on Aug. 1, 1951, as provided in said order.]

5. We call attention to the fact that the proposed rule does not contain a provision for the procedure to be followed in order to exercise the right of the United States to take immediate possession or title, when the condemnation proceeding is begun. There are several statutes conferring such a right which are cited in the original notes to the May 1948 draft * * *. The existence of this right is taken into account in the rule. In subdivision (c)(2), * * * it is stated: "Upon the commencement of the action, the plaintiff need join as defendants only the persons having or claiming an interest in the property whose names are then known." That is to enable the United States to exercise the right to immediate title or possession without the delay involved in ascertaining the names of all interested parties. The right is also taken into account in the provision relating to dismissal (paragraph (i), subdivisions (1), (2), and (3), * * *); also in paragraph (j) relating to deposits and their distribution.

The Advisory Committee considered whether the procedure for exercising the right should be specified in the rule and decided against it, as the procedure now being followed seems to be giving no trouble, and to draft a rule to fit all the statutes on the subject might create confusion.

The American Bar Association has taken an active interest in a rule for condemnation cases. In 1944 its House of Delegates adopted a resolution which among other things resolved:

That before adoption by the Supreme Court of the United States of any redraft of the proposed rule, time and opportunity should be afforded to the bar to consider and make recommendations concerning any such redraft.

Accordingly, in 1950 the revised draft was submitted to the American Bar Association and its section of real property, probate and trust law appointed a committee to consider it. That committee was supplied with copies of the written statement from the Department of Justice giving the reasons relied on by the Department for preferring a rule to use juries in all cases. The Advisory Committee's report was approved at a meeting of the section of real property law, and by the House of Delegates at the annual meeting of September 1950. The American Bar Association report gave particular attention to the question whether juries or commissions should be used to fix compensation, approved the Advisory Committee's solution appearing in their latest draft designed to allow use of commissions in projects comparable to the TVA, and rejected the proposal for use of juries in all cases.

In November 1950 a committee of the Federal Bar Association, the chairman of which was a Special Assistant to the Attorney General, made a report which reflected the attitude of the Department of Justice on the condemnation rule.

Aside from subdivision (h) about the tribunal to award compensation the final draft of the condemnation rule here presented has the approval of the American Bar Association and, we understand, the Department of Justice, and we do not know of any opposition to it. Subdivision (h) has the unanimous approval of the Advisory Committee and has been approved by the American Bar Association. The use of commissions in TVA cases, and, by fair inference, in cases comparable to the TVA, is supported by 17 out of 20 judges who up to 1947 had sat in TVA cases. The legal staff of the TVA has vigorously objected to the substitution of juries for commissions in TVA cases. We regret to report that the Department of Justice still asks that subdivision (h) be altered to provide for jury trials in an cases where Congress has not specified the tribunal. We understand that the Department approves the proposal that the system prevailing in 23 states for the "double" trial, by commission with appeal to and trial de novo before a jury, should be abolished, and also asks that on demand a jury should be substituted for a commission, in those states where use of a commission alone is now required. The Advisory Committee has no evidence that commissions do not operate satisfactorily in the case of projects comparable to the TVA.

Original Report

General Statement. 1. Background. When the Advisory Committee was formulating its recommendations to the Court concerning rules of procedure, which subsequently became the Federal Rules of 1938, the Committee concluded at an early stage not to fix the procedure in condemnation cases. This is a matter principally involving the exercise of the federal power of eminent domain, as very few condemnation cases involving the state's power reach the United States District Courts. The Committee's reasons at that time were that inasmuch as condemnation proceedings by the United States are governed by statutes of the United States, prescribing different procedure for various agencies and departments of the government, or, in the absence of such statutes, by local state practice under the Conformity Act (former § 258 of Title 40), it would be extremely difficult to draft a uniform rule satisfactory to the various agencies and departments of the government and to private parties; and that there was no general demand for a uniform rule. The Committee continued in that belief until shortly before the preparation of the April 1937 Draft of the Rules, when the officials of the Department of Justice having to do with condemnation cases urgently requested the Committee to propose rules on this subject. The Committee undertook the task and drafted a Condemnation Rule which appeared for the first time as Rule 74 of the April 1937 Draft. After the publication and distribution of this initial draft many objections were urged against it by counsel for various governmental agencies, whose procedure in condemnation cases was prescribed by federal statutes. Some of these agencies wanted to be excepted in whole or in part from the operation of the uniform rule proposed in April 1937. And the Department of Justice changed its position and stated that it preferred to have government condemnations conducted by local attorneys familiar with the state practice, which was applied under the Conformity Act where the Acts of Congress do not prescribe the practice; that it preferred to work under the Conformity Act without a uniform rule of procedure. The profession generally showed little interest in the proposed uniform rule. For these reasons the Advisory Committee in its Final Report to the Court in November 1937 proposed that all of Rule 74 be stricken and that the Federal Rules be made applicable only to appeals in condemnation cases. See note to Rule 74 of the Final Report.

Some of six or seven years later when the Advisory Committee was considering the subject of amendments to the Federal Rules both government officials and the profession generally urged the adoption of some uniform procedure. This demand grew out of the volume of condemnation proceedings instituted during the war, and the general feeling of dissatisfaction with the diverse condemnation procedures that were applicable in the federal courts. A strongly held belief was that both the sovereign's power to condemn and the property owner's right to compensation could be promoted by a simplified rule. As a consequence the Committee proposed a Rule 71A on the subject of condemnation in its Preliminary Draft of May 1944. In the Second Preliminary Draft of May 1945 this earlier proposed Rule 71A was, however, omitted. The Committee did not then feel that it had sufficient time to prepare a revised draft satisfactorily to it which would meet legitimate objections made to the draft of May 1944. To avoid unduly delaying the proposed amendments to existing rules the Committee concluded to proceed in the regular way with the preparation of the amendments to these rules and deal with the question of a condemnation rule as an independent matter. As a consequence it made no recommendations to the Court on condemnation in its Final Report of Proposed Amendments of June 1946; and the amendments which the Court adopted in December 1946 did not deal with condemnation. After concluding its task relative to amendments, the Committee returned to a consideration of eminent domain, its proposed Rule 71A of May 1944, the suggestions and criticisms that had been presented in the interim, and in June 1947 prepared and distributed to the profession another draft of a proposed condemnation rule. This draft contained several alternative provisions, specifically called attention to and asked for opinion relative to these matters, and in particular as to the constitution of the tribunal to award compensation. The present draft was based on the June 1947 formulation, in light of the advice of the profession on both matters of substance and form.

2. Statutory Provisions. The need for a uniform condemnation rule in the federal courts arises from the fact that by various statutes Congress has prescribed diverse procedures for certain condemnation proceedings, and, in the absence of such statutes, has prescribed conformity to local state practice under former § 258 of Title 40. This general conformity adds to the diversity of procedure since in the United States there are multifarious methods of procedure in existence. Thus in 1931 it was said that there were 269 different methods of judicial procedure in different classes of condemnation cases and 56 methods of nonjudicial or administrative procedure. First Report of Judicial Council of Michigan, 1931, § 46, pp. 55 to 56. These numbers have not decreased. Consequently, the general requirement of conformity to state practice and procedure, particularly where the condemnor is the United States, leads to expense, delay and uncertainty. In advocacy of a uniform federal rule, see Armstrong, *Proposed Amendments to Federal Rules for Civil Procedure,* 1944, 4 F.R.D. 124, 134; id., *Report of the Advisory Committee on Federal Rules of Civil Procedure Recommending Amendments,* 1946, 5 F.R.D. 339, 357.

There are a great variety of Acts of Congress authorizing the exercise of the power of eminent domain by the United States and its officers and agencies. These statutes for the most part do not specify the exact procedure to be followed, but where procedure is prescribed, it is by no means uniform.

The following are instances of Acts which merely authorize the exercise of the power without specific declaration as to the procedure:

U.S.C., Title 16:

§ 404c–11 (Mammoth Cave National Park; acquisition of lands, interests in lands or other property for park by the Secretary of the Interior).

§ 426d (Stones River National Park; acquisition of land for parks by the Secretary of the Army).

§ 450aa (George Washington Carver National Monument; acquisition of land by the Secretary of the Interior).

§ 517 (National forest reservation; title to lands to be acquired by the Secretary of Agriculture).

U.S.C., Title 42:

§§ 1805(b)(5), 1813(b) [now §§ 2061 and 2112, and §§ 2221 to 2224, respectively, of Title 42] (Atomic Energy Act).

The following are instances of Acts which authorized condemnation and declare that the procedure is to conform what that of similar actions in state courts:

U.S.C., Title 16:

§ 423k (Richmond National Battlefield Park; acquisition of lands by the Secretary of the Interior).

§ 814 (Exercise by water power licensee of power of eminent domain).

U.S.C., Title 24:

§ 78 [Repealed] (Condemnation of land for the former National Home for Disabled Volunteer Soldiers).

U.S.C., Title 33:

§ 591 (Condemnation of lands and materials for river and harbor improvement by the Secretary of the Army).

U.S.C., Title 40:

§ 257 [now § 3113] (Condemnation of realty for sites for public building and for other public uses by the Secretary of the Treasury authorized).

§ 258 [Omitted as superseded by this rule] (Same procedure).

U.S.C., Title 50:

§ 171 [Repealed and is now covered by § 2663 of Title 10] (Acquisition of land by the Secretary of the Army for national defense).

§ 172 [Repealed and is now covered by §§ 2664 and 2665 of Title 10] (Acquisition of property by the Secretary of the Army, etc., for production of lumber).

§ 632 App. [Omitted as terminated by § 645 of the Appendix to Title 50] (Second War Powers Act, 1942; acquisition of real property for war purposes by the Secretary of Army, the Secretary of the Navy and others).

The following are Acts in which a more or less complete code of procedure is set forth in connection with the taking:

U.S.C., Title 16:

§ 831x (Condemnation by Tennessee Valley Authority).

U.S.C., Title 40:

§ 361–386 [Repealed] [now D.C.Code, Title 16, § 1301 et seq.] (Acquisition of lands in District of Columbia for use of United States; condemnation).

3. Adjustment of Rule to Statutory Provisions. While it was apparent that the principle of uniformity should be the basis for a rule to replace the multiple diverse procedures set out above, there remained a serious question as to whether an exception could properly be made relative to the method of determining compensation. Where Congress had provided for conformity to state law the following were the general methods in use: an initial determination by commissioners, with appeal to a judge; an initial award, likewise made by commissioners, but with the appeal to a jury; and determination by a jury without a previous award by commissioners. In two situations Congress had specified the tribunal to determine the issue of compensation: condemnation by the Tennessee Valley Authority; and condemnation in the District of Columbia. Under the TVA procedure the initial determination of value is by three disinterested commissioners, appointed by the court, from a locality other than the one in which the land lies. Either party may except to the award of the commission; in that case the exceptions are to be heard by three district judges (unless the parties stipulate for a lesser number), with a right of appeal to the circuit court of appeals. The TVA is a regional agency. It is faced with the necessity of acquiring a very substantial acreage within a relatively small area, and charged with the task of carrying on within the Tennessee Valley and in cooperation with the local people a permanent program involving navigation and flood control, electric power, soil conservation, and general regional development. The success of this program is partially dependent upon the good will and cooperation of the people of the Tennessee Valley, and this in turn partially depends upon the land acquisition program. Disproportionate awards among landowners would create dissatisfaction and ill will. To secure uniformity in treatment Congress provided the rather unique procedure of the three-judge court to review de novo the initial award of the commissioners. This procedure has worked to the satisfaction of the property owners and the TVA. A full statement of the TVA position and experience is set forth in Preliminary Draft of Proposed Rule to Govern Condemnation Cases (June, 1947) 15–19. A large majority of the district judges with experience under this procedure approve it, subject to some objection to the requirement for a three-judge district court to review commissioners' awards. A statutory three-judge requirement is, however, jurisdictional and must be strictly followed. *Stratton v. St. Louis, Southwestern Ry. Co.*, 1930, 51 S.Ct. 8, 282 U.S. 10, 75 L.Ed. 135; *Ayrshire Collieries Corp. v. United States*, 1947, 67 S.Ct. 1168, 331 U.S. 132, 91 L.Ed. 1391. Hence except insofar as the TVA statute itself authorizes the parties to stipulate for a court of less than three judges, the requirement must be followed, and would seem to be beyond alteration by court rule even if change were thought desirable. Accordingly the TVA procedure is retained for the determination of compensation in TVA condemnation cases. It was also thought desirable to retain the specific method Congress had prescribed for the District of Columbia, which is a so-called jury of five appointed by the court. This is a local matter and the specific treatment accorded by Congress has given local satisfaction.

Aside from the foregoing limited exceptions dealing with the TVA and the District of Columbia, the question was whether a uniform method for determining compensation should be a commission with appeal to a district judge, or a commission with appeal to a jury, or a jury without a commission. Experience with the commission on a nationwide basis, and in particular with the utilization of a commission followed by an appeal to a jury, has been that the commission is time consuming and expensive. Furthermore, it is largely a futile procedure where it is preparatory to jury trial. Since in the bulk of states a land owner is entitled eventually to a jury trial, since the jury is a traditional tribunal for the determination of questions of value, and since experience with juries has proved satisfactory to both government and land owner, the right to jury trial is adopted as the general rule. Condemnation involving the TVA and the District of Columbia are the two exceptions. See Note to Subdivision (h), infra.

Note to Subdivision (a). As originally promulgated the Federal Rules governed appeals in condemnation proceedings but were not otherwise applicable. Rule 81(a)(7). Pre-appeal procedure, in the main, conformed to state procedure. See statutes and discussion, supra. The purpose of Rule 71A is to provide a uniform procedure for condemnation in the federal district courts, including the District of Columbia. To achieve this purpose Rule 71A prescribes such specialized procedure as is required by condemnation proceedings, otherwise it utilizes the general framework of the Federal Rules where specific detail is unnecessary. The adoption of Rule 71A, of course, renders paragraph (7) of Rule 81(a) unnecessary.

The promulgation of a rule for condemnation procedure is within the rulemaking power. The Enabling Act [Act of June 19, 1934, c. 651, §§ 1, 2 (48 Stat. 1064), former §§ 723b, 723c, now § 2072, of this title] gives the Supreme Court "the power to prescribe, by general rules * * * the forms of process, writs, pleadings, and motions, and the practice and procedure in civil actions at law." Such rules, however, must not abridge, enlarge, or modify substantive rights. In *Kohl v. United States*, 1875, 91 U.S. 367, 23 L.Ed. 449, a proceeding instituted by the United States to appropriate land for a postoffice site under a statute enacted for such purpose, the Supreme Court held that "a proceeding to take land in virtue of the government's eminent domain, and determining the compensation to be made for it, is * * * a suit at common law, when initiated in a court." See, also, *Madisonville Traction Co. v. Saint Bernard Mining Co.*, 1905, 25 S.Ct. 251, 196 U.S. 239, 49 L.Ed. 462, infra, under subdivision (k). And the Conformity Act [former § 258 of Title 40], which is superseded by Rule 71A, deals only with "practice, pleadings, forms and proceedings and not with matters of substantive laws." *United States v. 243.22 Acres of Land in Village of Farmingdale, Town of Babylon, Suffolk County, N.Y.*, D.C.N.Y.1942, 43 F.Supp. 561, affirmed 129 F.2d 678, certiorari denied 63 S.Ct. 441, 317 U.S. 698, 87 L.Ed. 558.

Rule 71A affords a uniform procedure for all cases of condemnation invoking the national power of eminent domain, and, to the extent stated in subdivision (k), for cases invoking a state's power of eminent domain; and supplants all statutes prescribing a different procedure. While the almost exclusive utility of the rule is for the condemnation of real property, it also applies to the condemnation of personal property, either as an incident to real property or as the sole object of the proceeding, when permitted or required by statute. See former § 438j [now § 5001] of Title 38 (World War Veterans' Relief Act); former §§ 1805, 1811, and 1813 of Title 42 (Atomic Energy Act); former § 79 [now § 100] of Title 50 (Nitrates Act); former §§ 161 to 165 and § 166, of Title 50 (Helium Gas Act). Requisitioning of personal property with the right in the owner to sue the United States, where the compensation cannot be agreed upon (see former § 1813 [now §§ 2221 to 2224] of Title 42, for example) will continue to be the normal method of acquiring personal property and Rule 71A in no way interferes with or restricts any such right. Only where the law requires or permits the formal procedure of condemnation to be utilized will the rule have any applicability to the acquisition of personal property.

Rule 71A is not intended to and does not supersede the Act of February 26, 1931, c. 307, §§ 1 to 5 (46 Stat. 1421), §§ 258a to 258e of Title 40, which is a supplementary condemnation statute, permissive in its nature and designed to permit the prompt acquisition of title by the United States, pending the condemnation proceeding, upon a deposit in court. See *United States v. 76,800 Acres, More or Less, of Land, in Bryan and Liberty Counties, Ga.*, D.C.Ga.1942, 44 F.Supp. 653; *United States v. 17,280 Acres of Land, More or Less, Situated in Saunders County, Neb.*, D.C.Neb.1942, 47 F.Supp. 267. The same is true insofar as the following or any other statutes authorize the acquisition of title or the taking of immediate possession:

U.S.C., Title 33:

§ 594 (When immediate possession of land may be taken; for a work of river and harbor improvements.)

U.S.C., Title 42:

§ 1813(b) [now §§ 2221 to 2224 of Title 42] (When immediate possession may be taken under Atomic Energy Act).

U.S.C., Title 50:

§ 171 [Repealed and is now covered by § 2663 of Title 10] (Acquisition of land by the Secretary of the Army for national defense).

§ 632 App. [Omitted as terminated by § 645 of the Appendix to Title 50] (Second War Powers Act, 1942; acquisition of real property for war purposes by the Secretary of the Army, the Secretary of the Navy, and others).

Note to Subdivision (b). This subdivision provides for broad joinder in accordance with the tenor of other rules such as Rule 18. To require separate condemnation proceedings for each piece of property separately owned would be unduly burdensome and would serve no useful purpose. And a restriction that only properties may be joined which are to be acquired for the same public use would also cause difficulty. For example, a unified project to widen a street, construct a bridge across a navigable river, and for the construction of approaches to the level of the bridge on both sides of the river might involve acquiring property for different public uses. Yet it is eminently desirable that the plaintiff may in one proceeding condemn all the property interests and rights necessary to carry out this project. Rule 21 which allows the court to sever and proceed separately with any claim against a party, and Rule 42(b) giving the court broad discretion to order separate trials give adequate protection to all defendants in condemnation proceedings.

Note to Subdivision (c). Since a condemnation proceeding is in rem and since a great many property owners are often involved, paragraph (1) requires the property to be named and only one of the owners. In other respects and caption will contain the name of the court, the title of the action, file number, and a designation of the pleading as a complaint in accordance with Rule 10(a).

Since the general standards of pleading are stated in other rules, paragraph (2) prescribes only the necessary detail for condemnation proceedings. Certain statutes allow the United States to acquire title or possession immediately upon commencement of an action. See the Act of February 26, 1931, c. 307, §§ 1 to 5 (46 Stat. 1421), §§ 258a to 258e of Title 40; and § 594 of Title 33, former § 1813(b) of Title 42, former § 171 of Title 50, former § 632 of the Appendix to Title 50, supra. To carry out the purpose of such statutes and to aid the condemnor in instituting the action even where title is not acquired at the outset, the plaintiff is initially required to join as defendants only the persons having or claiming an interest in the property whose names are then known. This is no way prejudices the property owner, who must eventually be joined as a defendant, served with process, and allowed to answer before there can be any hearing involving the compensation to be paid for his piece of property. The rule requires the plaintiff to name all persons having or claiming an interest in the property of whom the plaintiff has learned and, more importantly, those appearing of record. By charging the plaintiff with the necessity to make "a search of the records of the extent commonly made by competent searches of title in the vicinity in light of the type and value of the property involved" both the plaintiff and property owner are protected. Where a short term interest in property of little value is involved, as a two or three year easement over a vacant land for purposes of ingress and egress to other property, a search of the records covering a long period of time is not required. Where on the other hand fee simple title in valuable property is being condemned the search must necessarily cover a much longer period of time and be commensurate with the interests involved. But even here the search is related to the type made by competent title searchers in the vicinity. A search that extends back to the original patent may be feasible in some midwestern and western states and be proper under certain circumstances. In the Atlantic seaboard states such a search is normally not feasible nor desirable. There is a common sense business accommodation of what title searchers can and should do. For state statutes requiring persons appearing as owners or otherwise interested in the property to be named as defendants, see 3 Colo.Stat.Ann., 1935, c. 61, § 2; Ill.Ann.Stat. (Smith-Hurd) c. 47, § 2; 1 Iowa Code, 1946, § 472.3; Kans.Stat.Ann., 1935, § 26–101; 2 Mass.Laws Ann., 1932, c. 80A, § 4; 7 Mich.Stat.Ann., 1936, § 8.2; 2 Minn.Stat., Mason 1927, § 6541; 20 N.J.Stat.Ann., 1939, § 1–2; 3 Wash.Revised Stat., Remington, 1932, Title 6, § 891. For state provisions allowing persons whose names are not known to be designated under the descriptive term of "unknown owner", see Hawaii Revised Laws, 1945, c. 8, § 310 ("such [unknown] defendant may be joined in the petition under a fictitious name."); Ill.Ann.Stat. (Smith-Hurd) c. 47, § 2 ("Persons interested, whose names are unknown, may be made parties defendant by the description of the unknown owners; * * *"); Maryland Code Ann., 1939, Art. 33A, § 1 ("In case any owner or owners is or are not known, he or they may be described in such petition as the unknown owner or owners, or the unknown heir or heirs of a deceased owner."); 2 Mass.Laws Ann., 1932, c. 80A, § 4 ("Persons not in being, unascertained or unknown who may have an interest in any of such land shall be made parties respondent by such description as seems appropriate, * * *"); New Mex.Stat.Ann., 1941, § 25–901 ("the owners * * * shall be parties defendant, by name, if the names are known, and by description of the unknown owners of the land therein described, if their names are unknown."); Utah Code Ann., 1943, § 104–61–7 ("The names of all owners and claimants of the property, if known, or a statement that they are unknown, who must be styled defendants").

The last sentence of paragraph (2) enables the court to expedite the distribution of a deposit, in whole or in part, as soon as pertinent facts of ownership, value and the like are established. See also subdivision (j).

The signing of the complaint is governed by Rule 11.

Note to Subdivision (d). In lieu of a summons, which is the initial process in other civil actions under Rule 4(a), subdivision (d) provides for a notice which is to contain sufficient information so that the defendant in effect obtains the plaintiff's statement of his claim against the defendant to whom the notice is directed. Since the plaintiff's attorney is an officer of the court and to prevent unduly burdening the clerk of the court, paragraph (1) of subdivision (d) provides that plaintiff's attorney shall prepare and deliver a notice or notices to the clerk. Flexibility is provided by the provision for joint or several notices, and for additional notices. Where there are only a few defendants it may be convenient to prepare but one notice directed to all the defendants. In other cases where there are many defendants it will be more convenient to prepare two or more notices; but in any event a notice must be directed to each named defendant. Paragraph (2) provides that the notice is to be signed by the plaintiff's attorney. Since the notice is to be delivered to the clerk, the issuance of the notice will appear of record in the court. The clerk should forthwith deliver the notice or notices for service to the marshal or to a person specially appointed to serve the notice. Rule 4(a). The form of the notice is such that, in addition to informing the defendant of the plaintiff's statement of claim, it tells the defendant precisely what his rights are. Failure on the part of the defendant to serve an answer constitutes a consent to the taking and to the authority of the court to proceed to fix compensation therefor, but it does not preclude the defendant from presenting evidence as to the amount of compensation due him or in sharing the award of distribution. See subdivision (e); Form 28.

While under Rule 4(f) the territorial limits of a summons are normally the territorial limits of the state in which the district court is held, the territorial limits for personal service of a notice under Rule 71A(d)(3) are those of the nation. This extension of process is here proper since the aim of the condemnation proceeding is not to enforce any personal liability and the property owner is helped, not imposed upon, by the best type of service possible. If personal service cannot be made either because the defendant's whereabouts cannot be ascertained, or, if ascertained, the defendant cannot be personally served, as where he resides in a foreign country such as Canada or Mexico, then service by publication is proper. The provisions for this type of service are set forth in the rule and are in no way governed by § 118 [now § 1655] of this title.

Note to Subdivision (e). Departing from the scheme of Rule 12, subdivision (e) requires all defenses and objections to be presented in an answer and does not authorize a preliminary motion. There is little need for the latter in condemnation proceedings. The general standard of pleading is governed by other rules, particularly Rule 8, and this subdivision (e) merely prescribes what matters the answer should set forth. Merely by appearing in the action a defendant can receive notice of all proceedings affecting him. And without the necessity of answering a defendant may present evidence as to the amount of compensation due him, and he may share in the distribution of the award. See also subdivision (d)(2); Form 28.

Note to Subdivision (f). Due to the number of persons who may be interested in the property to be condemned, there is a likelihood that the plaintiff will need to amend his complaint, perhaps many times, to add new parties or state new issues. This subdivision recognizes that fact and does not burden the court with applications by the plaintiff for leave to amend. At the same time all defendants are adequately protected; and their need to amend the answer is adequately protected by Rule 15, which is applicable by virtue of subdivision (a) of this Rule 71A.

Note to Subdivision (g). A condemnation action is a proceeding in rem. Commencement of the action as against a defendant by virtue of his joinder pursuant to subdivision (c)(2) is the point of cut-off and there is no mandatory requirement for substitution because of a subsequent change of interest, although the court is given ample power to require substitution. Rule 25 is inconsistent with subdivision (g) and hence inapplicable. Accordingly, the time periods of Rule 25 do not govern to require dismissal nor to prevent substitution.

Note to Subdivision (h). This subdivision prescribes the method for determining the issue of just compensation in cases involving the federal power of eminent domain. The method of jury trial provided by subdivision (h) will normally apply in cases involving the state power by virtue of subdivision (k).

Congress has specially constituted a tribunal for the trial of the issue of just compensation in two instances: condemnation under the Tennessee Valley Authority Act; and condemnation in the District of Columbia. These tribunals are retained for reasons set forth in the General Statement: 3. Adjustment of Rule to Statutory Provisions, supra. Subdivision (h) also has prospective application so that if Congress should create another special tribunal, that tribunal will determine the issue of just compensation. Subject to these exceptions the general method of trial of that issue is to be by jury if any party demands it, otherwise that issue, as well as all other issues, are to be tried by the court.

As to the TVA procedure that is continued, § 831x of Title 16 requires that three commissioners be appointed to fix the compensation; that exceptions to their award are to be heard by three district judges (unless the parties stipulate for a lesser number) and that the district judges try the question de novo; that an appeal to the circuit court of appeals may be taken within 30 days from the filing of the decision of the district judges; and that the circuit court of appeals shall on the record fix compensation "without regard to the awards of findings theretofore made by the commissioners or the district judges." The mode of fixing compensation in the District of Columbia, which is also continued, is prescribed in former §§ 361 to 386 of Title 40. Under former § 371 the court is required in all cases to order the selection of a jury of five from among not less than 20 names, drawn "from the special box provided by law." They must have the usual qualifications of jurors and in addition must be freeholders of the District, and not in the service of the United States or the District. A special oath is administered to the chosen jurors. The trial proceeds in the ordinary way, except that the jury is allowed to separate after they have begun to consider their verdict.

There is no constitutional right to jury trial in a condemnation proceeding. *Bauman v. Ross*, 1897, 17 S.Ct. 966, 167 U.S. 548, 42 L.Ed. 270. See, also, Hines, *Does the Seventh Amendment to the Constitution of the United States Require Jury Trials in all Condemnation Proceedings?*, 1925, 11 Va.L.Rev. 505; Blair, *Federal Condemnation Proceedings and the Seventh Amendment,* 1927, 41 Harv.L.Rev. 29; 3 *Moore's Federal Practice,* 1938, 3007. Prior to Rule 71A, jury trial in federal condemnation proceedings was, however, enjoyed under the general conformity statute, former § 258 of Title 40, in states which provided for jury trial. See generally, 2 Lewis, *Eminent Domain,* 3d ed. 1909, §§ 509, 510; 3 Moore, op. cit. supra. Since the general conformity statute is superseded by Rule 71A, see supra under subdivision (a), and since it was believed that the rule to be substituted should likewise give a right to jury trial, subdivision (h) establishes that method as the general one for determining the issue of just compensation.

Note to Subdivision (i). Both the right of the plaintiff to dismiss by filing a notice of dismissal and the right of the court to permit a dismissal are circumscribed to the extent that where the plaintiff has acquired the title or a lesser interest or possession, viz., any property interest for which just compensation should be paid, the action may not be dismissed, without the defendant's consent, and the property owner remitted to another court, such as the Court of Claims, to recover just compensation for the property right taken. Circuity of action is thus prevented without increasing the liability of the plaintiff to pay just compensation for any interest that is taken. Freedom of dismissal is accorded, where both the condemnor and condemnee agree, up to the time of the entry of judgment vesting plaintiff with title. And power is given to the court, where the parties agree, to vacate the judgment and thus revest title in the property owner. In line with Rule 21, the court may at any time drop a defendant who has been unnecessarily or improperly joined as where it develops that he has no interest.

Note to Subdivision (j). Whatever the substantive law is concerning the necessity of making a deposit will continue to govern. For statutory provisions concerning deposit in court in condemnation proceedings by the United States, see § 258a of [former] Title 40; § 594 of Title 33; acquisition of title and possession statutes referred to in note to subdivision (a), supra. If the plaintiff is invoking the state's power of eminent domain the necessity of deposit will be governed by the state law. For discussion of such law, see 1 Nichols, Eminent Domain, 2d ed. 1917, §§ 209 to 216. For discussion of the function of deposit and the power of the court to enter judgment in cases both of deficiency and overpayment, see *United States v. Miller,* 1943, 63 S.Ct. 276, 317 U.S. 369, 87 L.Ed. 336, 147 A.L.R. 55, rehearing denied 63 S.Ct. 557, 318 U.S. 798, 87 L.Ed. 1162 (judgment in favor of plaintiff for overpayment ordered).

The court is to make distribution of the deposit as promptly as the facts of the case warrant. See also subdivision (c)(2).

Note to Subdivision (k). While the overwhelming number of cases that will be brought in the federal courts under this rule will be actions involving the federal power of eminent domain, a small percentage of cases may be instituted in the federal court or removed thereto on the basis of diversity or alienage which will involve the power of eminent domain under the law of a state. See *Boom Co. v. Patterson,* 1878, 98 U.S. 403, 25 L.Ed. 206; *Searl v. School District No. 2,* 1888, 8 S.Ct. 460, 124 U.S. 197, 31 L.Ed. 415; *Madisonville Traction Co. v. Saint Bernard Mining Co.,* 1905, 25 S.Ct. 251, 196 U.S. 239, 49 L.Ed. 462. In the Madisonville case, and in cases cited therein, it has been held that condemnation actions brought by state corporations in the exercise of a power delegated by the state might be governed by procedure prescribed by the laws of the United States, whether the cases were begun in or removed to the federal court. See, also, *Franzen v. Chicago, M. & St. P. Ry. Co.,* C.C.A.7th, 1921, 278 F. 370, 372.

Any condition affecting the substantial right of a litigant attached by state law is to be observed and enforced, such as making a deposit in court where the power of eminent domain is conditioned upon so doing. (See also subdivision (j). Subject to this qualification, subdivision (k) provides that in cases involving the state power of eminent domain, the practice prescribed by other subdivisions of Rule 71A shall govern.

Note to Subdivision (*l*). Since the condemnor will normally be the prevailing party and since he should not recover his costs against the property owner, Rule 54(d), which provides generally that costs shall go to the prevailing party, is made inapplicable. Without attempting to state what the rule on costs is, the effect of subdivision (*l*) is that costs shall be awarded in accordance with the law that has developed in condemnation cases. This has been summarized as follows: "Costs of condemnation proceedings are not assessable against the condemnee, unless by stipulation he agrees to assume some or all of them. Such normal expenses of the proceeding as bills for publication of notice, commissioners' fees, the cost of transporting commissioners and jurors to take a view, fees for attorneys to represent defendants who have failed to answer, and witness' fees, are properly charged to the government, though not taxed as costs. Similarly, if it is necessary that a conveyance be executed by a commissioner, the United States pay his fees and those for recording the deed. However, the distribution of the award is a matter in which the United States has no legal interest. Expenses incurred in ascertaining the identity of distributees and deciding between conflicting claimants are properly chargeable against the award, not against the United States, although United States attorneys are expected to aid the court in such matters as amici curiae." Lands Division Manual 861. For other discussion and citation, see *Grand River Dam Authority v. Jarvis,* C.C.A.10th, 1942, 124 F.2d 914. Costs may not be taxed against the United States except to the extent permitted by law. *United States v. 125.71 Acres of Land in Loyalhanna Tp., Westmoreland County, Pa.,* D.C.Pa.1944, 54 F.Supp. 193; Lands Division Manual 859. Even if it were thought desirable to allow the property owner's costs to be taxed against the United States, this is a matter for legislation and not court rule.

1963 Amendment

This amendment conforms to the amendment of Rule 4(f).

1985 Amendment

Rule 71A(h) provides that except when Congress has provided otherwise, the issue of just compensation in a condemnation case may be tried by a jury if one of the parties so demands, unless the court in its discretion orders the issue determined by a commission of three persons. In 1980, the Comptroller General of the United States in a Report to Congress recommended that use of the commission procedure should be encouraged in order to improve and expedite the trial of condemnation cases. The Report noted that long delays were being caused in many districts by such factors as crowded dockets, the precedence given criminal cases, the low priority accorded condemnation matters, and the high turnover of Assistant United States Attorneys. The Report concluded that revising Rule 71A to make the use of the commission procedure more attractive might alleviate the situation.

Accordingly, Rule 71A(h) is being amended in a number of respects designed to assure the quality and utility of a Rule 71A commission. First, the amended Rule will give the court discretion to appoint, in addition to the three members of a commission, up to two additional persons as alternate commissioners who would hear the case and be available, at any time up to the filing of the decision by the three-member commission, to replace any commissioner who becomes unable or disqualified to continue. The discretion to appoint alternate commissioners can be particularly useful in protracted cases, avoiding expensive retrials that have been required in some cases because of the death or disability of a commissioner. Prior to replacing a commissioner an alternate would not be present at, or participate in, the commission's deliberations.

Second, the amended Rule requires the court, before appointment, to advise the parties of the identity and qualifications of each prospective commissioner and alternate. The court then may authorize the examination of prospective appointees by the parties and each party has the right to challenge for cause. The objective is to insure that unbiased and competent commissioners are appointed.

The amended Rule does not prescribe a qualification standard for appointment to a commission, although it is understood that only persons possessing background and ability to appraise real estate valuation testimony and to award fair and just compensation on the basis thereof would be appointed. In most situations the chairperson should be a lawyer and all members should have some background qualifying them to weigh proof of value in the real estate field and, when possible, in the particular real estate market embracing the land in question.

The amended Rule should give litigants greater confidence in the commission procedure by affording them certain rights to participate in the appointment of commission members that are roughly comparable to the practice with regard to jury selection. This is accomplished by giving the court permission to allow the parties to examine prospective commissioners and by recognizing the right of each party to object to the appointment of any person for cause.

1987 Amendment

The amendments are technical. No substantive change is intended.

1988 Amendment

The amendment is technical. No substantive change is intended.

1993 Amendments

The references to the subdivisions of Rule 4 are deleted in light of the revision of that rule.

2003 Amendments

The references to specific subdivisions of Rule 53 are deleted or revised to reflect amendments of Rule 53.

2007 Amendments

The language of Rule 71A has been amended as part of the general restyling of the Civil Rules to make them more easily understood and to make style and terminology consistent throughout the rules. These changes are intended to be stylistic only.

Former Rule 71A has been redesignated as Rule 71.1 to conform to the designations used for all other rules added with the original numbering system.

Rule 71.1(e) allows a defendant to appear without answering. Former form 28 (now form 60) includes information about this right in the Rule 71.1(d)(2) notice. It is useful to confirm this practice in the rule.

The information that identifies the attorney is changed to include telephone number and electronic-mail address, in line with similar amendments to Rules 11(a) and 26(g)(1).

Rule 72. Magistrate Judges: Pretrial Order

(a) Nondispositive Matters. When a pretrial matter not dispositive of a party's claim or defense is referred to a magistrate judge to hear and decide, the magistrate judge must promptly conduct the required proceedings and, when appropriate, issue a written order stating the decision. A party may serve and file objections to the order within 10 days after being served with a copy. A party may not assign as error a defect in the order not timely objected to. The district judge in the case must consider timely objections and modify or set aside any part of the order that is clearly erroneous or is contrary to law.

(b) Dispositive Motions and Prisoner Petitions.

(1) ***Findings and Recommendations.*** A magistrate judge must promptly conduct the required proceedings when assigned, without the parties' consent, to hear a pretrial matter dispositive of a claim or defense or a prisoner petition challenging the conditions of confinement. A record must be made of all evidentiary proceedings and may, at the magistrate judge's discretion, be made of any other proceedings. The magistrate judge must enter a recommended disposition, including, if appropriate, proposed findings of fact. The clerk must promptly mail a copy to each party.

(2) ***Objections.*** Within 10 days after being served with a copy of the recommended disposition, a party may serve and file specific written objections to the proposed findings and recommendations. A party may respond to another party's objections within 10 days after being served with a copy. Unless the district judge

orders otherwise, the objecting party must promptly arrange for transcribing the record, or whatever portions of it the parties agree to or the magistrate judge considers sufficient.

(3) ***Resolving Objections.*** The district judge must determine de novo any part of the magistrate judge's disposition that has been properly objected to. The district judge may accept, reject, or modify the recommended disposition; receive further evidence; or return the matter to the magistrate judge with instructions.

(Former Rule 72 abrogated December 4, 1967, effective July 1, 1968; new Rule 72 adopted April 28, 1983, effective August 1, 1983; amended April 30, 1991, effective December 1, 1991; April 22, 1993, effective December 1, 1993; April 30, 2007, effective December 1, 2007.)

ADVISORY COMMITTEE NOTES

1983 Addition

Subdivision (a). This subdivision addresses court-ordered referrals of nondispositive matters under 28 U.S.C. § 636(b)(1)(A). The rule calls for a written order of the magistrate's disposition to preserve the record and facilitate review. An oral order read into the record by the magistrate will satisfy this requirement.

No specific procedures or timetables for raising objections to the magistrate's rulings on nondispositive matters are set forth in the Magistrates Act. The rule fixes a 10-day period in order to avoid uncertainty and provide uniformity that will eliminate the confusion that might arise if different periods were prescribed by local rule in different districts. It also is contemplated that a party who is successful before the magistrate will be afforded an opportunity to respond to objections raised to the magistrate's ruling.

The last sentence of subdivision (a) specifies that reconsideration of a magistrate's order, as provided for in the Magistrates Act, shall be by the district judge to whom the case is assigned. This rule does not restrict experimentation by the district courts under 28 U.S.C. § 636(b)(3) involving references of matters other than pretrial matters, such as appointment of counsel, taking of default judgments, and acceptance of jury verdicts when the judge is unavailable.

Subdivision (b). This subdivision governs court-ordered referrals of dispositive pretrial matters and prisoner petitions challenging conditions of confinement, pursuant to statutory authorization in 28 U.S.C. § 636(b)(1)(B). This rule does not extend to habeas corpus petitions, which are covered by the specific rules relating to proceedings under Sections 2254 and 2255 of Title 28.

This rule implements the statutory procedures for making objections to the magistrate's proposed findings and recommendations. The 10–day period, as specified in the statute, is subject to Rule 6(e) which provides for an additional 3–day period when service is made by mail. Although no specific provision appears in the Magistrates Act, the rule specifies a 10–day period for a party to respond to objections to the magistrate's recommendation.

Implementing the statutory requirements, the rule requires the district judge to whom the case is assigned to make a de novo determination of those portions of the report, findings, or recommendations to which timely objection is made. The term "de novo" signifies that the magistrate's findings are not protected by the clearly erroneous doctrine, but does not indicate that a second evidentiary hearing is required. See *United States v. Raddatz,* 417 [447] U.S. 667 (1980). See also Silberman, *Masters and Magistrates Part II: The American Analogue,* 50 N.Y.U. L.Rev. 1297, 1367 (1975). When no timely objection is filed, the court need only satisfy itself that there is no clear error on the face of the record in order to accept the recommendation. See *Campbell v. United States Dist. Court,* 501 F.2d 196, 206 (9th Cir.1974), cert. denied, 419 U.S. 879, quoted in House Report No. 94–1609, 94th Cong.2d Sess. (1976) at 3. Compare *Park Motor Mart, Inc. v. Ford Motor Co.,* 616 F.2d 603 (1st Cir.1980). Failure to make timely objection to the magistrate's report prior to its adoption by the district judge may constitute a waiver of appellate review of the district judge's order. *See United States v. Walters,* 638 F.2d 947 (6th Cir.1981).

1991 Amendment

This amendment is intended to eliminate a discrepancy in measuring the 10 days for serving and filing objections to a magistrate's action under subdivisions (a) and (b) of this Rule. The rule as promulgated in 1983 required objections to the magistrate's handling of nondispositive matters to be served and filed within 10 days of entry of the order, but required objections to dispositive motions to be made within 10 days of being served with a copy of the recommended disposition. Subdivision (a) is here amended to conform to subdivision (b) to avoid any confusion or technical defaults, particularly in connection with magistrate orders that rule on both dispositive and nondispositive matters.

The amendment is also intended to assure that objections to magistrate's orders that are not timely made shall not be considered. *Compare* Rule 51.

1993 Amendments

This revision is made to conform the rule to changes made by the Judicial Improvements Act of 1990.

2007 Amendments

The language of Rule 72 has been amended as part of the general restyling of the Civil Rules to make them more easily understood and to make style and terminology consistent throughout the rules. These changes are intended to be stylistic only.

Rule 73. Magistrate Judges: Trial by Consent; Appeal

(a) Trial by Consent. When authorized under 28 U.S.C. § 636(c), a magistrate judge may, if all parties consent, conduct a civil action or proceeding, including a jury or nonjury trial. A record must be made in accordance with 28 U.S.C. § 636(c)(5).

(b) Consent Procedure.

(1) ***In General.*** When a magistrate judge has been designated to conduct civil actions or proceedings, the clerk must give the parties written notice of their opportunity to consent under 28 U.S.C. § 636(c). To signify their consent, the parties must jointly or separately file a statement consenting to the referral. A district judge or magistrate judge may be informed of a party's response to the clerk's notice only if all parties have consented to the referral.

(2) ***Reminding the Parties About Consenting.*** A district judge, magistrate judge, or other court official may remind the parties of the magistrate judge's availability, but must also advise them that they are free to withhold consent without adverse substantive consequences.

(3) ***Vacating a Referral.*** On its own for good cause—or when a party shows extraordinary circumstances—the district judge may vacate a referral to a magistrate judge under this rule.

(c) Appealing a Judgment. In accordance with 28 U.S.C. § 636(c)(3), an appeal from a judgment entered at a magistrate judge's direction may be taken to the court of appeals as would any other appeal from a district-court judgment.

(Former Rule 73 abrogated December 4, 1967, effective July 1, 1968; new Rule 73 adopted April 28, 1983, effective August 1, 1983; amended March 2, 1987, effective August 1, 1987; April 22, 1993, effective December 1, 1993; April 11, 1997, effective December 1, 1997; April 30, 2007, effective December 1, 2007.)

ADVISORY COMMITTEE NOTES

1983 Addition

Subdivision (a). This subdivision implements the broad authority of the 1979 amendments to the Magistrates Act, 28 U.S.C. § 636(c), which permit a magistrate to sit in lieu of a district judge and exercise civil jurisdiction over a case, when the parties consent. See McCabe, *The Federal Magistrate Act of 1979,* 16 Harv.J.Legis. 343, 364–79 (1979). In order to exercise this jurisdiction, a magistrate must be specially designated under 28 U.S.C. § 636(c)(1) by the district court or courts he serves. The only exception to a magistrate's exercise of civil jurisdiction, which includes the power to conduct jury and nonjury trials and decide dispositive motions, is the contempt power. A hearing on contempt is to be conducted by the district judge upon certification of the facts and an order to show cause by the magistrate. See 28 U.S.C. § 639(e). In view of 28 U.S.C. § 636(c)(1) and this rule, it is unnecessary to amend Rule 58 to provide that the decision of a magistrate is a "decision by the court" for the purposes of that rule and a "final decision of the district court" for purposes of 28 U.S.C. § 1291 governing appeals.

Subdivision (b). This subdivision implements the blind consent provision of 28 U.S.C. § 636(c)(2) and is designed to ensure that neither the judge nor the magistrate attempts to induce a party to consent to reference of a civil matter under this rule to a magistrate. See House Rep. No. 96–444, 96th Cong. 1st Sess. 8 (1979).

The rule opts for a uniform approach in implementing the consent provision by directing the clerk to notify the parties of their opportunity to elect to proceed before a magistrate and by requiring the execution and filing of a consent form or forms setting forth the election. However, flexibility at the local level is preserved in that local rules will determine how notice shall be communicated to the parties, and local rules will specify the time period within which an election must be made.

The last paragraph of subdivision (b) reiterates the provision in 28 U.S.C. § 636(c)(6) for vacating a reference to the magistrate.

Subdivision (c). Under 28 U.S.C. § 636(c)(3), the normal route of appeal from the judgment of a magistrate—the only route that will be available unless the parties otherwise agree in advance—is an appeal by the aggrieved party "directly to the appropriate United States court of appeals from the judgment of the magistrate in the same manner as an appeal from any other judgment of a district court." The quoted statutory language indicates Congress' intent that the same procedures and standards of appealability that govern appeals from district court judgments govern appeals from magistrates' judgments.

Subdivision (d). 28 U.S.C. § 636(c)(4) offers parties who consent to the exercise of civil jurisdiction by a magistrate an alternative appeal route to that provided in subdivision (c) of this rule. This optional appellate route was provided by Congress in recognition of the fact that not all civil cases warrant the same appellate treatment. In cases where the amount in controversy is not great and there are no difficult questions of law to be resolved, the parties may desire to avoid the expense and delay of appeal to the court of appeals by electing an appeal to the district judge. See McCabe, *The Federal Magistrate Act of 1979,* 16 Harv.J.Legis, 343, 388 (1979). This subdivision provides that the parties may elect the optional appeal route at the time of reference to a magistrate. To this end, the notice by the clerk under subdivision (b) of this rule shall explain the appeal option and the corollary restriction on review by the court of appeals. This approach will avoid later claims of lack of consent to the avenue of appeal. The choice of the alternative appeal route to the judge of the district court should be made by the parties in their forms of consent. Special appellate rules to govern appeals from a magistrate to a district judge appear in new Rules 74 through 76.

1987 Amendment

The amendment is technical. No substantive change is intended.

1993 Amendments

This revision is made to conform the rule to changes made by the Judicial Improvements Act of 1990. The Act requires that, when being reminded of the availability of a magistrate judge, the parties be advised that withholding of consent will have no "adverse substantive consequences." They may, however, be advised if the withholding of consent will have the adverse procedural consequence of a potential delay in trial.

1997 Amendments

The Federal Courts Improvement Act of 1996 repealed the former provisions of 28 U.S.C. § 636(c)(4) and (5) that enabled parties that had agreed to trial before a magistrate judge to agree also that appeal should be taken to the district court. Rule 73 is amended to conform to this change. Rules 74, 75, and 76 are abrogated for the same reason. The portions of Form 33 and Form 34 that referred to appeals to the district court also are deleted.

2007 Amendments

The language of Rule 73 has been amended as part of the general restyling of the Civil Rules to make them more easily understood and to make style and terminology consistent throughout the rules. These changes are intended to be stylistic only.

HISTORICAL NOTES

Change of Name

Reference to United States magistrate or to magistrate deemed to refer to United States magistrate judge pursuant to section 321 of Pub.L. 101–650, set out as a note under section 631 of this title.

Rule 74. Method of Appeal From Magistrate Judge to District Judge Under Title 28, U.S.C. § 636(c)(4) and Rule 73(d) [Abrogated]

(Former Rule 74 abrogated December 4, 1967, effective July 1, 1968; new Rule 74 adopted April 28, 1983, effective August 1, 1983; amended April 22, 1993, effective December 1, 1993; abrogated April 11, 1997, effective December 1, 1997; April 30, 2007, effective December 1, 2007.)

ADVISORY COMMITTEE NOTES

1997 Amendment

Rule 74 is abrogated for the reasons described in the Note to Rule 73.

2007 Amendment

Rule 74 was abrogated in 1997 to reflect repeal of the statute providing for appeal from a magistrate judge's judgment to the district court. The rule number is reserved for possible future use.

Rule 75. Proceedings On Appeal From Magistrate Judge to District Judge under Rule 73(d) [Abrogated]

(Former Rule 75 abrogated December 4, 1967, effective July 1, 1968; new Rule 75 adopted April 28, 1983, effective August 1, 1983; amended March 2, 1987, effective August 1, 1987; April 22, 1993, effective December 1, 1993; abrogated April 11, 1997, effective December 1, 1997; April 30, 2007, effective December 1, 2007.)

ADVISORY COMMITTEE NOTES

1997 Amendment

Rule 75 is abrogated for the reasons described in the Note to Rule 73.

2007 Amendment

Rule 75 was abrogated in 1997 to reflect repeal of the statute providing for appeal from a magistrate judge's judgment to the district court. The rule number is reserved for possible future use.

Rule 76. Judgment of the District Judge On The Appeal under Rule 73(d) and Costs [Abrogated]

(Former Rule 76 abrogated December 4, 1967, effective July 1, 1968; new Rule 76 adopted April 28, 1983, effective August 1, 1983; amended April 22, 1993, effective December 1, 1993; abrogated April 11, 1997, effective December 1, 1997; April 30, 2007, effective December 1, 2007.)

ADVISORY COMMITTEE NOTES

1997 Amendment

Rule 76 is abrogated for the reasons described in the Note to Rule 73.

2007 Amendment

Rule 76 was abrogated in 1997 to reflect repeal of the statute providing for appeal from a magistrate judge's judgment to the district court. The rule number is reserved for possible future use.

TITLE X. DISTRICT COURTS AND CLERKS: CONDUCTING BUSINESS; ISSUING ORDERS

Rule 77. Conducting Business; Clerk's Authority; Notice of an Order or Judgment

(a) **When Court Is Open.** Every district court is considered always open for filing any paper, issuing and returning process, making a motion, or entering an order.

(b) **Place for Trial and Other Proceedings.** Every trial on the merits must be conducted in open court and, so far as convenient, in a regular courtroom. Any other act or proceeding may be done or conducted by a judge in chambers, without the attendance of the clerk or other court official, and anywhere inside or outside the district. But no hearing—other than one ex parte—may be conducted outside the district unless all the affected parties consent.

(c) Clerk's Office Hours; Clerk's Orders.

(1) ***Hours.*** The clerk's office—with a clerk or deputy on duty—must be open during business hours every day except Saturdays, Sundays, and legal holidays. But a court may, by local rule or order, require that the office be open for specified hours on Saturday or a particular legal holiday other than one listed in Rule 6(a)(4)(A).

(2) ***Orders.*** Subject to the court's power to suspend, alter, or rescind the clerk's action for good cause, the clerk may:

(A) issue process;

(B) enter a default;

(C) enter a default judgment under Rule 55(b)(1); and

(D) act on any other matter that does not require the court's action.

(d) Serving Notice of an Order or Judgment.

(1) ***Service.*** Immediately after entering an order or judgment, the clerk must serve notice of the entry, as provided in Rule 5(b), on each party who is not in default for failing to appear. The clerk must record the service on the docket. A party also may serve notice of the entry as provided in Rule 5(b).

(2) ***Time to Appeal Not Affected by Lack of Notice.*** Lack of notice of the entry does not affect the time for appeal or relieve—or authorize the court to relieve—a party for failing to appeal within the time allowed, except as allowed by Federal Rule of Appellate Procedure (4)(a).

(Amended December 27, 1946, effective March 19, 1948; January 21, 1963, effective July 1, 1963; December 4, 1967, effective July 1, 1968; March 1, 1971, effective July 1, 1971; March 2, 1987, effective August 1, 1987; April 30, 1991, effective December 1, 1991; April 23, 2001, effective December 1, 2001; April 30, 2007, effective December 1, 2007.)

ADVISORY COMMITTEE NOTES

1937 Adoption

This rule states the substance of U.S.C., Title 28, § 452, formerly § 13 (Courts open as courts of admiralty and equity). Compare [former] Equity Rules 1 (District Court Always Open For Certain Purposes—Orders at Chambers), 2 (Clerk's Office Always Open, Except, Etc.), 4 (Notice of Orders), and 5 (Motions Grantable of Course by Clerk).

1946 Amendment

Note. Rule 77(d) has been amended to avoid such situations as the one arising in *Hill v. Hawes,* 1944, 64 S.Ct. 334, 320 U.S. 520, 88 L.Ed. 283. In that case, an action instituted in the District Court for the District of Columbia, the clerk failed to give notice of the entry of a judgment for defendant as required by Rule 77(d). The time for taking an appeal then was 20 days under Rule 10 of the Court of Appeals (later enlarged by amendment to thirty days), and due to lack of notice of the entry of judgment the plaintiff failed to file his notice of appeal within the prescribed time. On this basis the trial court vacated the original judgment and then re-entered it, whereupon notice of appeal was filed. The Court of Appeals dismissed the appeal as taken too late. The Supreme Court, however, held that although rule 77(d) did not purport to attach any consequence to the clerk's failure to give notice as specified, the terms of the rule were such that the appellant was entitled to rely on it, and the trial court in such a case, in the exercise of a sound discretion, could vacate the former judgment and enter a new one, so that the appeal would be within the allowed time.

Because of Rule 6(c), which abolished the old rule that the expiration of the term ends a court's power over its judgment, the effect of the decision in *Hill v. Hawes* is to give the district court power, in its discretion and without time limit, and long after the term may have expired, to vacate a judgment and reenter it for the purpose of reviving the right of appeal. This seriously affects the finality of judgments. See also proposed Rule 6(c) and Note; proposed Rule 60(b) and Note; and proposed Rule 73(a) and Note.

Rule 77(d) as amended makes it clear that notification by the clerk of the entry of a judgment has nothing to do with the starting of the time for appeal; that time starts to run from the date of entry of judgment and not from the date of notice of the entry. Notification by the clerk is merely for the convenience of litigants. And lack of such notification in itself has no effect upon the time for appeal; but in considering an application for extension of time for appeal as provided in Rule 73(a), the court may take into account, as one of the factors affecting its decision, whether the clerk failed to give notice as provided in Rule 77(d) or the party failed to receive the clerk's notice. It need not, however, extend the time for appeal merely because the clerk's notice was not sent or received. It would, therefore, be entirely unsafe for a party to rely on absence of notice from the clerk of the entry of a judgment, or to rely on the adverse party's failure to serve notice of the entry of a judgment. Any party may, of course, serve timely notice of the entry of a judgment upon the adverse party and thus preclude a successful application, under Rule 73(a), for the extension of the time for appeal.

1963 Amendment

Subdivision (c). The amendment authorizes closing of the clerk's office on Saturday as far as civil business is concerned. However, a district court may require its clerk's office to remain open for specified hours on Saturdays or "legal holidays" other than those enumerated ("Legal holiday" is defined in Rule 6(a), as amended.) The clerk's offices of many district courts have customarily remained open on some of the days appointed as holidays by State law. This practice could be continued by local rule or order.

Subdivision (d). This amendment conforms to the amendment of Rule 5(a). See the Advisory Committee's Note to that amendment.

1968 Amendment

The provisions of Rule 73(a) are incorporated in Rule 4(a) of the Federal Rules of Appellate Procedure.

1971 Amendment

The amendment adds Columbus Day to the list of legal holidays. See the Note accompanying the amendment of Rule 6(a).

1987 Amendment

The amendments are technical. No substantive change is intended. The Birthday of Martin Luther King, Jr. is added to the list of national holidays in Rule 77.

1991 Amendment

This revision is a companion to the concurrent amendment to Rule 4 of the Federal Rules of Appellate Procedure. The purpose of the revisions is to permit district courts to ease strict sanctions now imposed on appellants whose notices of appeal are filed late because of their failure to receive notice of entry of a judgment. See, e.g. *Tucker v. Commonwealth Land Title Ins. Co.*, 800 F.2d 1054 (11th Cir.1986); *Ashby Enterprises, Ltd. v. Weitzman, Dym & Associates*, 780 F.2d 1043 (D.C.Cir.1986); *In re OPM Leasing Services, Inc.*, 769 F.2d 911 (2d Cir.1985); *Spika v. Village of Lombard, Ill.*, 763 F.2d 282 (7th Cir.1985); *Hall v. Community Mental Health Center of Beaver County*, 772 F.2d 42 (3d Cir.1985); *Wilson v. Atwood v. Stark*, 725 F.2d 255 (5th Cir. en banc), cert. dismissed, 105 S.Ct. 17 (1984); *Case v. BASF Wyandotte*, 727 F.2d 1034 (Fed.Cir.1984), cert. denied, 105 S.Ct. 386 (1984); *Hensley v. Chesapeake & Ohio R.R. Co.*, 651 F.2d 226 (4th Cir.1981); *Buckeye Cellulose Corp. v. Electric Construction Co.*, 569 F.2d 1036 (8th Cir.1978).

Failure to receive notice may have increased in frequency with the growth in the caseload in the clerks' offices. The present strict rule imposes a duty on counsel to maintain contact with the court while a case is under submission. Such contact is more difficult to maintain if counsel is outside the district, as is increasingly common, and can be a burden to the court as well as counsel.

The effect of the revisions is to place a burden on prevailing parties who desire certainty that the time for appeal is running. Such parties can take the initiative to assure that their adversaries receive effective notice. An appropriate procedure for such notice is provided in Rule 5.

The revised rule lightens the responsibility but not the workload of the clerk's offices, for the duty of that office to give notice of entry of judgment must be maintained.

2001 Amendments

Rule 77(d) is amended to reflect changes in Rule 5(b). A few courts have experimented with serving Rule 77(d) notices by electronic means on parties who consent to this procedure. The success of these experiments warrants express authorization. Because service is made in the manner provided in Rule 5(b), party consent is required for service by electronic or other means described in Rule 5(b)(2)(D). The same provision is made for a party who wishes to ensure actual communication of the Rule 77(d) notice by also serving notice.

Changes Made After Publication and Comments

Rule 77(d) was amended to correct an oversight in the published version. The clerk is to note "service," not "mailing," on the docket.

2007 Amendments

The language of Rule 77 has been amended as part of the general restyling of the Civil Rules to make them more easily understood and to make style and terminology consistent throughout the rules. These changes are intended to be stylistic only.

Rule 78. Hearing Motions; Submission on Briefs

(a) Providing a Regular Schedule for Oral Hearings. A court may establish regular times and places for oral hearings on motions.

(b) Providing for Submission on Briefs. By rule or order, the court may provide for submitting and determining motions on briefs, without oral hearings.

(Amended March 2, 1987, effective August 1, 1987; April 30, 2007, effective December 1, 2007.)

ADVISORY COMMITTEE NOTES

1937 Adoption

Compare [former] Equity Rule 6 (Motion Day) with the first paragraph of this rule. The second paragraph authorizes a procedure found helpful for the expedition of business in some of the Federal and State courts. See Rule 43(e) of these rules dealing with evidence on motions. Compare *Civil Practice Rules of the Municipal Court of Chicago* (1935), Rules 269, 270, 271.

1987 Amendment

The amendment is technical. No substantive change is intended.

2007 Amendments

The language of Rule 78 has been amended as part of the general restyling of the Civil Rules to make them more easily understood and to make style and terminology consistent throughout the rules. These changes are intended to be stylistic only.

Rule 16 has superseded any need for the provision in former Rule 78 for orders for the advancement, conduct, and hearing of actions.

Rule 79. Records Kept by the Clerk

(a) Civil Docket.

(1) ***In General.*** The clerk must keep a record known as the "civil docket" in the form and manner prescribed by the Director of the Administrative Office of the United States Courts with the approval of the Judicial Conference of the United States. The clerk must enter each civil action in the docket. Actions must be assigned consecutive file numbers, which must be noted in the docket where the first entry of the action is made.

(2) ***Items to be Entered.*** The following items must be marked with the file number and entered chronologically in the docket:

(A) papers filed with the clerk;

(B) process issued, and proofs of service or other returns showing execution; and

(C) appearances, orders, verdicts, and judgments.

(3) ***Contents of Entries; Jury Trial Demanded.*** Each entry must briefly show the nature of the paper filed or writ issued, the substance of each proof of service or other return, and the substance and date of entry of each order and judgment. When a jury trial has been properly demanded or ordered, the clerk must enter the word "jury" in the docket.

(b) **Civil Judgments and Orders.** The clerk must keep a copy of every final judgment and appealable order; of every order affecting title to or a lien on real or personal property; and of any other order that the court directs to be kept. The clerk must keep these in the form and manner prescribed by the Director of the Administrative Office of the United States Courts with the approval of the Judicial Conference of the United States.

(c) **Indexes; Calendars.** Under the court's direction, the clerk must:

(1) keep indexes of the docket and of the judgments and orders described in Rule 79(b); and

(2) prepare calendars of all actions ready for trial, distinguishing jury trials from nonjury trials.

(d) **Other Records.** The clerk must keep any other records required by the Director of the Administrative Office of the United States Courts with the approval of the Judicial Conference of the United States.

(Amended December 27, 1946, effective March 19, 1948; December 29, 1948, effective October 20, 1949; January 21, 1963, effective July 1, 1963; April 30, 2007, effective December 1, 2007.)

ADVISORY COMMITTEE NOTES

1937 Adoption

Compare [former] Equity Rule 3 (Books Kept by Clerk and Entries Therein). In connection with this rule, see also the following statutes of the United States:

U.S.C., Title 5 former:

§ 301 [See Title 28, § 526] (Officials for investigation of official acts, records and accounts of marshals, attorneys, clerks of courts, United States commissioners, referees and trustees)

§ 318 [former] (Accounts of district attorneys)

U.S.C., Title 28 former:

§ 556 [former] (Clerks of district courts; books open to inspection)

§ 567 [now 751] (Same; accounts)

§ 568 [now 751] (Same; reports and accounts of moneys received; dockets)

§ 813 [former] (Indices of judgment debtors to be kept by clerks)

And see "Instructions to United States Attorneys, Marshals, Clerks and Commissioners" issued by the Attorney General of the United States.

1946 Amendment

Note. Subdivision (a). The amendment substitutes the Director of the Administrative Office of the United States Courts, acting subject to the approval of the Judicial Conference of Senior Circuit Judges, in the place of the Attorney General as a consequence of and in accordance with the provisions of the act establishing the Administrative Office and transferring functions thereto. Act of August 7, 1939, c. 501, §§ 1 to 7, 53 Stat. 1223, 28 U.S.C.A. §§ 601 to 610, formerly §§ 444 to 450.

Subdivision (b). The change in this subdivision does not alter the nature of the judgments and orders to be recorded in permanent form but it does away with the express requirement that they be recorded in a book. This merely gives latitude for the preservation of court records in other than book form, if that shall seem advisable, and permits with the approval of the Judicial Conference the adoption of such modern, space-saving methods as microphotography. See *Proposed Improvements in the Administration of the Offices of Clerks of United States District Courts,* prepared by the Bureau of the Budget, 1941, 38–42. See also Rule 55, Federal Rules of Criminal Procedure.

Subdivision (c). The words "Separate and" have been deleted as unduly rigid. There is no sufficient reason for requiring that the indices in all cases be separate; on the contrary, the requirement frequently increases the labor of persons searching the records as well as the labor of the clerk's force preparing them. The matter should be left to administrative discretion.

The other changes in the subdivision merely conform with those made in subdivision (b) of the rule.

Subdivision (d). Subdivision (d) is a new provision enabling the Administrative Office, with the approval of the Judicial Conference, to carry out any improvements in clerical procedure with respect to books and records which may be deemed advisable. See report cited in Note to subdivision (b), supra.

1948 Amendment

The amendment effective October 1949, substituted the name, "Judicial Conference of the United States," for "Judicial Conference of Senior Circuit Judges," in the first sentence of subdivision (a), and in subdivisions (b) and (d).

1963 Amendment

The terminology is clarified without any change of the prescribed practice. See amended Rule 58, and the Advisory Committee's Note thereto.

2007 Amendments

The language of Rule 79 has been amended as part of the general restyling of the Civil Rules to make them more easily understood and to make style and terminology consistent throughout the rules. These changes are intended to be stylistic only.

Rule 80. Stenographic Transcript as Evidence

If stenographically reported testimony at a hearing or trial is admissible in evidence at a later trial, the testimony may be proved by a transcript certified by the person who reported it.

(Amended December 27, 1946, effective March 19, 1948; April 30, 2007, effective December 1, 2007.)

ADVISORY COMMITTEE NOTES

1937 Adoption

Note to Subdivision (a). This follows substantially [former] Equity Rule 50 (Stenographer— Appointment— Fees). [This subdivision was abrogated. See amendment note of Advisory Committee below.]

Note to Subdivision (b). See *Reports of Conferences of Senior Circuit Judges with the Chief Justice of the United States* (1936), 22 A.B.A.J. 818, 819; (1937), 24 A.B.A.J. 75, 77. [This subdivision was abrogated. See amendment note of Advisory Committee below.]

Note to Subdivision (c). Compare Iowa Code (1935) § 11353.

1946 Amendment

Note. Subdivisions (a) and (b) of Rule 80 have been abrogated because of Public Law 222, 78th Cong., c. 3, 2d Sess., approved Jan. 20, 1944, 28 U.S.C. §§ 550, 604, 753, 1915, 1920, formerly § 9a, providing for the appointment of official stenographers for each district court, prescribing their duties, providing for the furnishing of transcripts, the taxation of the fees therefor as costs, and other related matters. This statute has now been implemented by Congressional appropriation available for the fiscal year beginning July 1, 1945.

Subdivision (c) of Rule 80 (Stenographic Report or Transcript as Evidence) has been retained unchanged.

2007 Amendments

The language of Rule 80 has been amended as part of the general restyling of the Civil Rules to make them more easily understood and to make style and terminology consistent throughout the rules. These changes are intended to be stylistic only.

TITLE XI. GENERAL PROVISIONS

Rule 81. Applicability of the Rules in General; Removed Actions

(a) Applicability to Particular Proceedings.

(1) ***Prize Proceedings.*** These rules do not apply to prize proceedings in admiralty governed by 10 U.S.C. §§ 7651–7681.

(2) ***Bankruptcy.*** These rules apply to bankruptcy proceedings to the extent provided by the Federal Rules of Bankruptcy Procedure.

(3) ***Citizenship.*** These rules apply to proceedings for admission to citizenship to the extent that the practice in those proceedings is not specified in federal statutes and has previously conformed to the practice in civil actions. The provisions of 8 U.S.C. § 1451 for service by publication and for answer apply in proceedings to cancel citizenship certificates.

(4) ***Special Writs.*** These rules apply to proceedings for habeas corpus and for quo warranto to the extent that the practice in those proceedings:

(A) is not specified in a federal statute, the Rules Governing Section 2254 Cases, or the Rules Governing Section 2255 Cases; and

(B) has previously conformed to the practice in civil actions.

(5) ***Proceedings Involving a Subpoena.*** These rules apply to proceedings to compel testimony or the production of documents through a subpoena issued by a United States officer or agency under a federal statute, except as otherwise provided by statute, by local rule, or by court order in the proceedings.

(6) ***Other Proceedings.*** These rules, to the extent applicable, govern proceedings under the following laws, except as these laws provide other procedures:

(A) 7 U.S.C. §§ 292, 499g(c), for reviewing an order of the Secretary of Agriculture;

(B) 9 U.S.C., relating to arbitration;

(C) 15 U.S.C. § 522, for reviewing an order of the Secretary of the Interior;

(D) 15 U.S.C. § 715d(c), for reviewing an order denying a certificate of clearance;

(E) 29 U.S.C. §§ 159, 160, for enforcing an order of the National Labor Relations Board;

(F) 33 U.S.C. §§ 918, 921, for enforcing or reviewing a compensation order under the Longshore and Harbor Workers' Compensation Act; and

(G) 45 U.S.C. § 159, for reviewing an arbitration award in a railway-labor dispute.

(b) Scire Facias and Mandamus. The writs of scire facias and mandamus are abolished. Relief previously available through them may be obtained by appropriate action or motion under these rules.

(c) Removed Actions.

(1) ***Applicability.*** These rules apply to a civil action after it is removed from a state court.

(2) ***Further Pleading.*** After removal, repleading is unnecessary unless the court orders it. A defendant who did not answer before removal must answer or present other defenses or objections under these rules within the longest of these periods:

(A) 20 days after receiving—through service or otherwise—a copy of the initial pleading stating the claim for relief;

(B) 20 days after being served with the summons for an initial pleading on file at the time of service; or

(C) 5 days after the notice of removal is filed.

(3) ***Demand for a Jury Trial.***

(A) *As Affected by State Law.* A party who, before removal, expressly demanded a jury trial in accordance with state law need not renew the demand after removal. If the state law did not require an express demand for a jury trial, a party need not make one after removal unless the court orders the parties to do so within a specified time. The court must so order at a party's request and may so order on its own. A party who fails to make a demand when so ordered waives a jury trial.

(B) *Under Rule 38.* If all necessary pleadings have been served at the time of removal, a party entitled to a jury trial under Rule 38 must be given one if the party serves a demand within 10 days after:

(i) it files a notice of removal; or

(ii) it is served with a notice of removal filed by another party.

(d) Law Applicable.

(1) ***State Law.*** When these rules refer to state law, the term "law" includes the state's statutes and the state's judicial decisions.

(2) ***District of Columbia.*** The term "state" includes, where appropriate, the District of Columbia. When these rules provide for state law to apply, in the District Court for the District of Columbia:

(A) the law applied in the District governs; and

(B) the term "federal statute" includes any Act of Congress that applies locally to the District.

(Amended December 28, 1939, effective April 3, 1941; December 27, 1946, effective March 19, 1948; December 29, 1948, effective October 20, 1949; April 30, 1951, effective August 1, 1951; January 21, 1963, effective July 1, 1963; February 28, 1966, effective July 1, 1966; December 4, 1967, effective July 1, 1968; March 1, 1971, effective July 1, 1971; March 2, 1987, effective August 1, 1987; April 23, 2001, effective December 1, 2001; April 29, 2002, effective December 1, 2002; April 30, 2007, effective December 1, 2007.)

ADVISORY COMMITTEE NOTES

1937 Adoption

Note to Subdivision (a). Paragraph (1): Compare the enabling act, Act of June 19, 1934, U.S.C., Title 28, § 2072, formerly § 723b (Rules in actions at law; Supreme Court authorized to make) and § 2072, formerly § 723c (Union of equity and action at law rules; power of Supreme Court). For the application of these rules in bankruptcy and copyright proceedings, see Orders xxxvi and xxxvii in Bankruptcy and Rule 1 of Rules of Practice and Procedure under § 25 of the copyright act, Act of March 4, 1909, U.S.C., Title 17, former § 25 [see 412, 501 et seq.] (Infringement and rules of procedure).

For examples of statutes which are preserved by paragraph (2) see: U.S.C., Title 8, [former] ch. 9 (Naturalization); Title 28, former ch. 14 [now 153] (Habeas corpus); Title 28, former §§ 377a to 377c [now D.C.Code, Title 16 § 3501 et seq.] (Quo warranto); and such forfeiture statutes as U.S.C., Title 7, former § 116 (Misbranded seeds, confiscation), and Title 21, § 334(b), formerly § 14 (Pure Food and Drug Act—condemnation of adulterated or misbranded Food; procedure). See also *443 Cans of Frozen Eggs Product v. U.S.*, 1912, 33 S.Ct. 50, 226 U.S. 172, 57 L.Ed. 174.

For examples of statutes which under paragraph (7) will continue to govern procedure in condemnation cases, see U.S.C. [former] Title 40, [former] § 258 (Condemnation of realty for sites for public building, etc., procedure); U.S.C., Title 16, § 831x (Condemnation by Tennessee Valley Authority); U.S.C., [former] Title 40, § 120 (Acquisition of lands for public use in District of Columbia); [former] Title 40, ch. 7 [now D.C.Code, Title 16, § 1301 et seq.] (Acquisition of lands in District of Columbia for use of United States; condemnation).

Note to Subdivision (b). Some statutes which will be affected by this subdivision are;

U.S.C., Title 7:

§ 222 (Federal Trade Commission powers adopted for enforcement of Stockyards Act) (By reference to Title 15, § 49)

U.S.C., Title 15:

§ 49 (Enforcement of Federal Trade Commission orders and antitrust laws)

§ 77t(c) (Enforcement of Securities and Exchange Commission orders and Securities Act of 1933)

§ 78u(f) (Same; Securities Exchange Act of 1934)

§ 79r(g) (Same; Public Utility Holding Company Act of 1935)

U.S.C., Title 16:

§ 820 (Proceedings in equity for revocation or to prevent violations of license of Federal Power Commission licensee)

§ 825m(b) (Mandamus to compel compliance with Federal Water Power Act, etc.)

U.S.C., Title 19:

§ 1333(c) (Mandamus to compel compliance with orders of Tariff Commission, etc.)

U.S.C., Title 28, former:

§ 377 [now 1651] (Power to issue writs)

§ 572 [now 1923] (Fees, attorneys, solicitors and proctors)

§ 778 [former] (Death of parties; substitution of executor or administrator). Compare Rule 25(a) (Substitution of parties; death), and the note thereto.

U.S.C., Title 33:

§ 495 (Removal of bridges over navigable waters)

U.S.C., Title 45:

§ 88 (Mandamus against Union Pacific Railroad Company)

§ 153(p) (Mandamus to enforce orders of Adjustment Board under Railway Labor Act)

§ 185 (Same; National Air Transport Adjustment Board) (By reference to § 153)

U.S.C., Title 47:

§ 11 (Powers of Federal Communications Commission)

§ 401(a) (Enforcement of Federal Communications Act and orders of Commission)

§ 406 (Same; Compelling furnishing of facilities; mandamus)

U.S.C., Title 49:

§ 19a(*l*) [now 11703] (Mandamus to compel compliance with Interstate Commerce Act)

§ 20(9) [now 11703] (Jurisdiction to compel compliance with interstate commerce laws by mandamus)

For comparable provisions in state practice see Smith-Hurd Ill.Stats.c. 110, § 179 (1937); Calif.Code Civ.Proc. (Deering, 1937) § 802.

Note to Subdivision (c). Such statutes as the following dealing with the removal of actions are substantially continued and made subject to these rules:

U.S.C., Title 28 former:

§ 71 [now 1441, 1445, 1447] (Removal of suits from state courts)

§ 72 [now 1446, 1447] (Same; procedure)

§ 73 [former] (Same; suits under grants of land from different states)

§ 74 [now 1443, 1446, 1447] (Same; causes against persons denied civil rights)

§ 75 [now 1446] (Same; petitioner in actual custody of state court)

§ 76 [now 1442, 1446, 1447] (Same; suits and prosecutions against revenue officers)

§ 77 [now 1442] (Same; suits by aliens)

§ 78 [now 1449] (Same; copies of records refused by clerk of state court)

§ 79 [now 1450] (Same; previous attachment bonds or orders)

§ 80 [now 1359, 1447, 1919] (Same; dismissal or remand)

§ 81 [now 1447] (Same; proceedings in suits removed)

§ 82 [former] (Same; record; filing and return)

§ 83 [now 1447, 1448] (Service of process after removal)

U.S.C., Title 28, §§ 1446, 1447, formerly § 72, supra, however, is modified by shortening the time for pleading in removed actions.

Note to Subdivision (e). The last sentence of this subdivision modifies U.S.C., Title 28, § 1652, formerly § 725 (Laws of States as rules of decision) in so far as that statute has been construed to govern matters of procedure and to exclude state judicial decisions relative thereto.

1946 Amendment

Note to Subdivision (a). Despite certain dicta to the contrary, *Lynn v. United States,* C.C.A.5th, 1940, 110 F.2d 586; *Mount Tivy Winery, Inc. v. Lewis,* N.D.Cal.1942, 42 F.Supp. 636, it is manifest that the rules apply to actions against the United States under the Tucker Act [28 U.S.C., §§ 41(20), 250, 251, 254, 257, 258, 287, 289, 292, 761–765 [now 791, 1346, 1401, 1402, 1491, 1493, 1496, 1501, 1503, 2071, 2072, 2411, 2412, 2501, 2506, 2509, 2510]]. See United States to use of *Foster Wheeler Corp. v. American Surety Co. of New York,* E.D.N.Y.1939, 25 F.Supp. 700; *Boerner v. United States,* E.D.N.Y.1939, 26 F.Supp. 769; *United States v. Gallagher,* C.C.A.9th, 1945, 151 F.2d 556. Rules 1 and 81 provide that the rules shall apply to all suits of a civil nature, whether cognizable as cases at law or in equity except those specifically excepted; and the character of the various proceedings excepted by express statement in Rule 81, as well as the language of the rules generally, shows that the term "civil action" [Rule 2] includes actions against the United States. Moreover, the rules in many places expressly make provision for the situation wherein the United States is a party as either plaintiff or defendant. See Rules 4(d)(4), 12(a), 13(d), 25(d), 37(f), 39(c), 45(c), 54(d), 55(e), 62(e), and 65(c). In *United States v. Sherwood,* 1941, 61 S.Ct. 767, 312 U.S. 584, 85 L.Ed. 1058, the Solicitor General expressly conceded in his brief for the United States that the rules apply to Tucker Act cases. The Solicitor General stated: "The Government, of course, recognizes that the Federal Rules of Civil Procedure apply to cases brought under the Tucker Act." (Brief for the United States, p. 31). Regarding *Lynn v. United States,* supra, the Solicitor General said: "In *Lynn v. United States* . . . the Circuit Court of Appeals for the Fifth Circuit went beyond the Government's contention there, and held that an action under the Tucker Act is neither an action at law nor a suit in equity and, seemingly, that the Federal Rules of Civil Procedure are, therefore, inapplicable. We think the suggestion is erroneous. Rules 4(d), 12(a), 39(c), and 55(e) expressly contemplate suits against the United States, and nothing in the enabling Act (48 Stat. 1064, 28 U.S.C. §§ 723b, 723c [see 2072]) suggests that the Rules are inapplicable to Tucker Act proceedings, which in terms are to accord with court rules and their subsequent modifications (Sec. 4, Act of March 3, 1887, 24 Stat. 505, 28 U.S.C. § 761 [see 2071, 2072]).." (Brief for the United States, p. 31, n. 17.)

United States v. Sherwood, supra, emphasizes, however, that the application of the rules in Tucker Act cases affects only matters of procedure and does not operate to extend jurisdiction. See also Rule 82. In the Sherwood case, the New York Supreme Court, acting under § 795 of the New York Civil Practice Act, made an order, authorizing Sherwood, as a judgment creditor, to maintain a suit under the Tucker Act to recover damages from the United States for breach of its contract with the judgment debtor, Kaiser, for construction of a post office building. Sherwood brought suit against the United States and Kaiser in the District Court for the Eastern District of New York. The question before the United States Supreme Court was whether a United States District Court had jurisdiction to entertain a suit against the United States wherein private parties were joined as parties defendant. It was contended that either the Federal Rules of Civil Procedure or the Tucker Act, or both, embodied the consent of the United States to be sued in litigations in which issues between the plaintiff and third persons were to be adjudicated. Regarding the effect of the Federal Rules, the Court declared that nothing in the rules, so far as they may be applicable in Tucker Act cases, authorized the maintenance of any suit against the United States to which it had not otherwise consented. The matter involved was not one of procedure but of jurisdiction, the limits of which were marked by the consent of the United States to be sued. The jurisdiction thus limited is unaffected by the Federal Rules of Civil Procedure.

Subdivision (a)(2). The added sentence makes it clear that the rules have not superseded the requirements of U.S.C., Title 28, § 2253, formerly § 466. *Schenk v. Plummer,* C.C.A.9, 1940, 113 F.2d 726.

For correct application of the rules in proceedings for forfeiture of property for violation of a statute of the United States, such as under U.S.C., Title 22, § 405 (seizure of war materials intended for unlawful export) or U.S.C., Title 21, § 334(b) (Federal Food, Drug, and Cosmetic Act; formerly Title 21, U.S.C. § 14, Pure Food and Drug Act), see *Reynal v. United States,* C.C.A.5, 1945, 153 F.2d 929; *United States v. 108 Boxes of Cheddar Cheese,* S.D.Iowa 1943, 3 F.R.D. 40.

Subdivision (a)(3). The added sentence makes it clear that the rules apply to appeals from proceedings to enforce administrative subpoenas. See *Perkins v. Endicott Johnson Corp.,* C.C.A.2d 1942, 128 F.2d 208, affirmed on other grounds 63 S.Ct. 339, 317 U.S. 501, 87 L.Ed. 424; *Walling v. News Printing Inc.,* C.C.A.3, 1945, 148 F.2d 57; *McCrone v. United States,* 1939, 59 S.Ct. 685, 307 U.S. 61, 83 L.Ed. 1108. And, although the provision allows full recognition of the fact that the rigid application of the rules in the proceedings themselves may conflict with the summary determination desired, *Goodyear Tire & Rubber Co. v. National Relations Board,* C.C.A.6, 1941, 122 F.2d 450; *Cudahy Packing Co. v. National Labor Relations Board,* C.C.A.10, 1941, 117 F.2d 692, it is drawn so as to permit application of any of the rules in the proceedings whenever the district court deems them helpful. See, e.g., *Peoples Natural Gas Co. v. Federal Power Commission,* App.D.C.1942, 127 F.2d 153, certiorari denied 62 S.Ct. 1298, 316 U.S. 700, 86 L.Ed. 1769; *Martin v. Chandis Securities Co.,* C.C.A.9th, 1942, 128 F.2d 731. Compare the application of the rules in summary proceedings in bankruptcy under General Order 37. See 1 *Collier on Bankruptcy,* 14th ed. by Moore and Oglebay, 326–327; 2 Collier, op.cit.supra, 1401–1402; 3 Collier, op.cit.supra, 228–231; 4 Collier, op.cit.supra, 1199–1202.

Subdivision (a)(6). Section 405 of U.S.C., Title 8 originally referred to in the last sentence of paragraph (6), has been repealed and § 738 [now 1451], U.S.C., Title 8, has been enacted in its stead. The last sentence of paragraph (6) has, therefore, been amended in accordance with this change. The sentence has also been amended so as to refer directly to the statute regarding the provision of time for answer, thus avoiding any confusion attendant upon a change in the statute.

That portion of subdivision (a)(6) making the rules applicable to proceedings for enforcement or review of compensation orders under the Longshoremen's and Harbor Workers' Compensation Act [33 U.S.C. § 901 et seq.] was added by an amendment made pursuant to order of the Court, December 28, 1939, effective three months subsequent to the adjournment of the 76th Congress, January 3, 1941.

Subdivision (c). The change in subdivision (c) effects more speedy trials in removed actions. In some states many of the courts have only two terms a year. A case, if filed 20 days before a term, is returnable to that term, but if filed less than 20 days before a term, is returnable to the following term, which convenes six months later. Hence, under the original wording of Rule 81(c), where a case is filed less than 20 days before the term and is removed within a few days but before answer, it is possible for the defendant to delay interposing his answer or presenting his defenses by motion for six months or more. The rule as amended prevents this result.

Subdivision (f). The use of the phrase "the United States or an officer or agency thereof" in the rules (as e.g., in Rule 12(a) and amended Rule 73(a)) could raise the question of whether "officer" includes a collector of internal revenue, a former collector, or the personal representative of a deceased collector, against whom suits for tax refunds are frequently instituted. Difficulty might ensue for the reason that a suit against a collector or his representative has been held to be a personal action. *Sage v. United States,* 1919, 39 S.Ct. 415, 250 U.S. 33, 63 L.Ed. 828; *Smietanka v. Indiana Steel Co.,* 1921, 42 S.Ct. 1, 257 U.S. 1, 66 L.Ed. 99; *United States v. Nunnally Investment Co.,* 1942, 62 S.Ct. 1064, 316 U.S. 258, 86 L.Ed. 1455. The addition of subdivision (f) to Rule 81 dispels any doubts on the matter and avoids further litigation.

1948 Amendment

The amendment effective October 1949, substituted the words "United States District Court" for the words "District Court of the United States" in the last sentence of subdivision (a)(1) and in the first and third sentences of subdivision (e). The amendment substituted the words "United States district courts" in lieu of "district courts of the United States" in subdivision (a)(4) and (5) and in the first sentence of subdivision (c).

The amendment effective October 20, 1949, also made the following changes:

In subdivision (a)(1), the reference to "Title 17, U.S.C." was substituted for the reference to "the Act of March 4, 1909, c. 320, § 25 (35 Stat. 1081), as amended, U.S.C., Title 17, § 25."

In subdivision (a)(2), the reference to "Title 28, U.S.C., § 2253" was substituted for "U.S.C., Title 28, § 466."

In subdivision (a)(3), the reference in the first sentence to "Title 9, U.S.C.," was substituted for "the Act of February 12, 1925, c. 213 (43 Stat. 883), U.S.C., Title 9".

In subdivision (a)(5), the words "as amended" were inserted after the parenthetical citation of "(49 Stat. 453)," and after the citations of "Title 29, §§ 159 and 160," former references to subdivisions "(e), (g), and (i)" were deleted.

In subdivision (a)(6), after the words "These rules" at the beginning of the first sentence, the following words were deleted: "do not apply to proceedings under the Act of September 13, 1888, c. 1015, § 13 (25 Stat. 479), as amended, U.S.C., Title 8, [former] § 282, relating to deportation of Chinese; they". Also in the first sentence, after the parenthetical citation of "(44 Stat. 1434, 1436)," the words "as amended" were added. In the last sentence, the words "October 14, 1940, c. 876, § 338 (54 Stat. 1158)" were inserted in lieu of the words "June 29, 1906, c. 3592, § 15 (34 Stat. 601), as amended."

In subdivision (c), the word "all" originally appearing in the first sentence between the words "govern" and "procedure" was deleted. In the third sentence, the portion beginning with the words "20 days after the receipt" and including all the remainder of that sentence was substituted for the following language: "the time allowed for answer by the law of the state or within 5 days after the filing of the transcript of the record in the district court of the United States, whichever period is longer, but in any event within 20 days after the filing of the transcript". In the fourth or last sentence, after the words at the beginning of the sentence, "If at the time of removal all necessary pleadings have been," the word "served" was inserted in lieu of the word "filed," and the concluding words of the sentence, "petition for removal is filed if he is the petitioner," together with the final clause immediately following, were substituted for the words "record of the action is filed in the district court of the United States."

1963 Amendment

Subdivision (a)(4). This change reflects the transfer of functions from the Secretary of Commerce to the Secretary of the Interior made by 1939 Reorganization Plan No. II, § 4(e), 53 Stat. 1433.

Subdivision (a)(6). The proper current reference is to the 1952 statute superseding the 1940 statute.

Subdivision (c). Most of the cases have held that a party who has made a proper express demand for jury trial in the State court is not required to renew the demand after removal of the action. *Zakoscielny v. Waterman Steamship Corp.,* 16 F.R.D. 314 (D.Md.1954); *Talley v. American Bakeries Co.,* 15 F.R.D. 391 (E.D.Tenn.1954); *Rehrer v. Service Trucking Co.,* 15 F.R.D. 113 (D.Del.1953); 5 *Moore's Federal Practice* ¶38.39[3] (2d ed. 1951); 1 Barron & Holtzoff, *Federal Practice & Procedure* § 132 (Wright ed. 1960). But there is some authority to the contrary. *Petsel v. Chicago, B. & Q.R. Co.,* 101 F.Supp. 1006 (S.D.Iowa 1951); *Nelson v. American Nat. Bank & Trust Co.,* 9 F.R.D. 680 (E.D.Tenn. 1950). The amendment adopts the preponderant view.

In order still further to avoid unintended waivers of jury trial, the amendment provides that where by State law applicable in the court from which the case is removed a party is entitled to jury trial without making an express demand, he need not make a demand after removal. However, the district court for calendar or other purposes may on its own motion direct the parties to state whether they demand a jury, and the court must make such a direction upon the request of any party. Under the amendment a district court may find it convenient to establish a routine practice of giving these directions to the parties in appropriate cases.

Subdivision (f). The amendment recognizes the change of nomenclature made by Treasury Dept. Order 150–26(2), 18 Fed.Reg. 3499 (1953).

As to a special problem arising under Rule 25 (Substitution of parties) in actions for refund of taxes, see the Advisory Committee's Note to the amendment of Rule 25(d), effective July 19, 1961; and 4 *Moore's Federal Practice* ¶25.09 at 531 (2d ed. 1950).

1966 Amendment

See Note to Rule 1, supra.

Statutory proceedings to forfeit property for violation of the laws of the United States, formerly governed by the admiralty rules, will be governed by the unified and supplemental rules. See Supplemental Rule A.

Upon the recommendation of the judges of the United States District Court for the District of Columbia, the Federal Rules of Civil Procedure are made applicable to probate proceedings in that court. The exception with regard to adoption proceedings is removed because the court no longer has jurisdiction of those matters; and the words "mental health" are substituted for "lunacy" to conform to the current characterization in the District.

The purpose of the amendment to paragraph (3) is to permit the deletion from Rule 73(a) of the clause "unless a shorter time is provided by law." The 10 day period fixed for an appeal under 45 U.S.C. § 159 is the only instance of a shorter time provided for appeals in civil cases. Apart from the unsettling effect of the clause, it is eliminated because its retention would preserve the 15 day period heretofore allowed by 28 U.S.C. § 2107 for appeals from interlocutory decrees in admiralty, it being one of the purposes of the amendment to make the time for appeals in civil and admiralty cases uniform under the unified rules. See Advisory Committee's Note to subdivision (a) of Rule 73.

1968 Amendment

The amendments eliminate inappropriate references to appellate procedure.

1971 Amendment

Title 28, U.S.C., § 2243 now requires that the custodian of a person detained must respond to an application for a writ of habeas corpus "within three days unless for good cause additional time, not exceeding twenty days, is allowed." The amendment increases to forty days the additional time that the district court may allow in habeas corpus proceedings involving persons in custody pursuant to a judgment of a state court. The substantial increase in the number of such proceedings in recent years has placed a considerable burden on state authorities. Twenty days has proved in practice too short a time in which to prepare and file the return in many such cases. Allowance of additional time should, of course, be granted only for good cause.

While the time allowed in such a case for the return of the writ may not exceed forty days, this does not mean that the state must necessarily be limited to that period of time to provide for the federal court the transcript of the proceedings of a state trial or plenary hearing if the transcript must be prepared after the habeas corpus proceeding has begun in the federal court.

1987 Amendment

The amendments are technical. No substantive change is intended.

2001 Amendments

Former Copyright Rule 1 made the Civil Rules applicable to copyright proceedings except to the extent the Civil Rules were inconsistent with Copyright Rules. Abrogation of the Copyright Rules leaves the Civil Rules fully applicable to copyright proceedings. Rule 81(a)(1) is amended to reflect this change.

The District of Columbia Court Reform and Criminal Procedure Act of 1970, Pub.L. 91–358, 84 Stat. 473, transferred mental health proceedings formerly held in the United States District Court for the District of Columbia to local District of Columbia courts. The provision that the Civil Rules do not apply to these proceedings is deleted as superfluous.

The reference to incorporation of the Civil Rules in the Federal Rules of Bankruptcy Procedure has been restyled.

Changes Made After Publication and Comments

The Committee Note was amended to correct the inadvertent omission of a negative. As revised, it correctly reflects the language that is stricken from the rule.

2002 Amendments

This amendment brings Rule 81(a)(2) into accord with the Rules Governing § 2254 and § 2255 proceedings. In its present form, Rule 81(a)(2) includes return-time provisions that are inconsistent with the provisions in the Rules Governing §§ 2254 and 2255. The inconsistency should be eliminated, and it is better that the time provisions continue to be set out in the other rules without duplication in Rule 81. Rule 81 also directs that the writ be directed to the person having custody of the person detained. Similar directions exist in the § 2254 and § 2255 rules, providing additional detail for applicants subject to future custody. There is no need for partial duplication in Rule 81.

The provision that the civil rules apply to the extent that practice is not set forth in the § 2254 and § 2255 rules dovetails with the provisions in Rule 11 of the § 2254 rules and Rule 12 of the § 2255 rules.

Changes Made After Publication and Comment The only change since publication is deletion of an inadvertent reference to § 2241 proceedings.

2007 Amendments

The language of Rule 81 has been amended as part of the general restyling of the Civil Rules to make them more easily understood and to make style and terminology consistent throughout the rules. These changes are intended to be stylistic only.

Rule 81(c) has been revised to reflect the amendment of 28 U.S.C. § 1446(a) that changed the procedure for removal from a petition for removal to a notice of removal.

Former Rule 81(e), drafted before the decision in *Erie R.R. v. Tompkins*, 304 U.S. 64 (1938), defined state law to include "the statutes of that state and the state judicial decisions construing them." The *Erie* decision reinterpreted the Rules of Decision Act, now 28 U.S.C. § 1652, recognizing that the "laws" of the states include the common law established by judicial decisions. Long-established practice reflects this understanding, looking to state common law as well as statutes and court rules when a Civil Rule directs use of state law. Amended Rule 81(d)(1) adheres to this practice, including all state judicial decisions, not only those that construe state statutes.

Former Rule 81(f) is deleted. The office of district director of internal revenue was abolished by restructuring under the Internal Revenue Service Restructuring and Reform Act of 1998, Pub.L. 105–206, July 22, 1998, 26 U.S.C. § 1 Note.

HISTORICAL NOTES

Pending Actions

For applicability of Supreme Court amendments to pending cases, see Orders of the Supreme Court of the United States Adopting and Amending Rules set out preceding Rule 1 of these rules.

Rule 82. Jurisdiction and Venue Unaffected

These rules do not extend or limit the jurisdiction of the district courts or the venue of actions in those courts. An admiralty or maritime claim under Rule 9(h) is not a civil action for purposes of 28 U.S.C. §§ 1391–1392.

(Amended December 29, 1948, effective October 20, 1949; February 28, 1966, effective July 1, 1966; April 23, 2001, effective December 1, 2001; April 30, 2007, effective December 1, 2007.)

ADVISORY COMMITTEE NOTES

1937 Adoption

These rules grant extensive power of joining claims and counterclaims in one action, but, as this rule states, such grant does not extend federal jurisdiction. The rule is declaratory of existing practice under the [former] Federal Equity Rules with regard to such provisions as [former] Equity Rule 26 on Joinder of Causes of Action and [former] Equity Rule 30 on Counterclaims. Compare Shulman and Jaegerman, *Some Jurisdictional Limitations on Federal Procedure*, 45 Yale L.J. 393 (1936).

1948 Amendment

The amendment effective October 1949, substituted the words "United States district courts" for "district courts of the United States."

1966 Amendment

Title 28, U.S.C., § 1391(b) provides: "A civil action wherein jurisdiction is not founded solely on diversity of citizenship may be brought only in the judicial district where all defendants reside, except as otherwise provided by law." This provision cannot appropriately be applied to what were formerly suits in admiralty. The rationale of decisions holding it inapplicable rests largely on the use of the term "civil action": i.e., a suit in admiralty is not a "civil action" within the statute. By virtue of the amendment to Rule 1, the provisions of Rule 2 convert suits in admiralty into civil actions. The added sentence is necessary to avoid an undesirable change in existing law with respect to venue.

2001 Amendments

The final sentence of Rule 82 is amended to delete the reference to 28 U.S.C. § 1393, which has been repealed.

Style Comment

The recommendation that the change be made without publication carries with it a recommendation that style changes not be made. Styling would carry considerable risks. The first sentence of Rule 82, for example, states that the Civil Rules do not "extend or limit the jurisdiction of the United States district courts." That sentence is a flat lie if "jurisdiction" includes personal or quasi-in rem jurisdiction. The styling project on this rule requires publication and comment.

2007 Amendments

The language of Rule 82 has been amended as part of the general restyling of the Civil Rules to make them more easily understood and to make style and terminology consistent throughout the rules. These changes are intended to be stylistic only.

Rule 83. Rules by District Courts; Judge's Directives

(a) Local Rules.

(1) ***In General.*** After giving public notice and an opportunity for comment, a district court, acting by a majority of its district judges, may adopt and amend rules governing its practice. A local rule must be consistent with—but not duplicate—federal statutes and rules adopted under 28 U.S.C. §§ 2072 and 2075, and must conform to any uniform numbering system prescribed by the Judicial Conference of the United States. A local rule takes effect on the date specified by the district court and remains in effect unless amended by the court or abrogated by the judicial council of the circuit. Copies of rules and amendments must, on their adoption, be furnished to the judicial council and the Administrative Office of the United States Courts and be made available to the public.

(2) ***Requirement of Form.*** A local rule imposing a requirement of form must not be enforced in a way that causes a party to lose any right because of a nonwillful failure to comply.

(b) Procedure When There Is No Controlling Law. A judge may regulate practice in any manner consistent with federal law, rules adopted under 28 U.S.C. §§ 2072 and 2075, and the district's local rules. No sanction or other disadvantage may be imposed for noncompliance with any requirement not in federal law, federal rules, or the local rules unless the alleged violator has been furnished in the particular case with actual notice of the requirement.

(Amended April 29, 1985, effective August 1, 1985; April 27, 1995, effective December 1, 1995; April 30, 2007, effective December 1, 2007.)

ADVISORY COMMITTEE NOTES

1937 Adoption

This rule substantially continues U.S.C., Title 28, § 2071, formerly § 731 (Rules of practice in district courts) with the additional requirement that copies of such rules and amendments be furnished to the Supreme Court of the United States. See [former] Equity Rule 79 (Additional Rules by District Court). With the last sentence compare United States Supreme Court Admiralty Rules, 1920, Rule 44 (Right of Trial Courts to Make Rules of Practice) (originally promulgated in 1842).

1985 Amendment

Rule 83, which has not been amended since the Federal Rules were promulgated in 1938, permits each district to adopt local rules not inconsistent with the Federal Rules by a majority of the judges. The only other requirement is that copies be furnished to the Supreme Court.

The widespread adoption of local rules and the modest procedural prerequisites for their promulgation have led many commentators to question the soundness of the process as well as the validity of some rules. See 12 C. Wright & A. Miller, *Federal Practice and Procedure: Civil* § 3152, at 217 (1973); Caballero, *Is There an Over-Exercise of Local Rule-Making Powers by the United States District Courts?,* 24 Fed.Bar News 325 (1977). Although the desirability of local rules for promoting uniform practice within a district is widely accepted, several commentators also have suggested reforms to increase the quality, simplicity, and uniformity of the local rules. See Note, *Rule 83 and the Local Federal Rules,* 67 Colum.L.Rev. 1251 (1967), and Comment, *The Local Rules of Civil Procedure in the Federal District Courts—A Survey,* 1966 Duke L.J. 1011.

The amended Rule attempts, without impairing the procedural validity of existing local rules, to enhance the local rulemaking process by requiring appropriate public notice of proposed rules and an opportunity to comment on them. Although some district courts apparently consult the local bar before promulgating rules, many do not, which has led to criticism of a process that has district judges consulting only with each other. See 12 C. Wright & A. Miller, *supra,* § 3152, at 217; Blair, *The New Local Rules for Federal Practice in Iowa,* 23 Drake L.Rev. 517 (1974). The new language subjects local rulemaking to scrutiny similar to that accompanying the Federal Rules, administrative rulemaking, and legislation. It attempts to assure that the expert advice of practitioners and scholars is made available to the district court before local rules are promulgated. See Weinstein, *Reform of Court Rule-Making Procedures* 84–87, 127–37, 151 (1977).

The amended Rule does not detail the procedure for giving notice and an opportunity to be heard since conditions vary from district to district. Thus, there is no explicit requirement for a public hearing, although a district may consider that procedure appropriate in all or some rulemaking situations. See generally, Weinstein, *supra,* at 117–37, 151. The new Rule does not foreclose any other form of consultation. For example, it can be accomplished through the mechanism of an "Advisory Committee" similar to that employed by the Supreme Court in connection with the Federal Rules themselves.

The amended Rule provides that a local rule will take effect upon the date specified by the district court and will remain in effect unless amended by the district court or abrogated by the judicial council. The effectiveness of a local rule should not be deferred until approved by the judicial council because that might unduly delay promulgation of a local rule that should become effective immediately, especially since some councils do not meet frequently. Similarly, it was thought that to delay a local rule's effectiveness for a fixed period of time would be arbitrary and that to require the judicial council to abrogate a local rule within a specified time would be inconsistent with its power under 28 U.S.C. § 332 (1976) to nullify a local rule at any time. The expectation is that the judicial council will examine all local rules, including those currently in effect, with an eye toward determining whether they are valid and consistent with the Federal Rules, promote inter-district uniformity and efficiency, and do not undermine the basic objectives of the Federal Rules.

The amended Rule requires copies of local rules to be sent upon their promulgation to the judicial council and the Administrative Office of the United States Courts rather than to the Supreme Court. The Supreme Court was the appropriate filing place in 1938, when Rule 83 originally was promulgated, but the establishment of the Administrative Office makes it a more logical place to develop a centralized file of local rules. This procedure is consistent with both the Criminal and the Appellate Rules. See Fed.R.Crim.P. 57(a); Fed.R.App.P. 47. The Administrative Office also will be able to provide improved utilization of the file because of its recent development of a Local Rules Index.

The practice pursued by some judges of issuing standing orders has been controversial, particularly among members of the practicing bar. The last sentence in Rule 83 has been amended to make certain that standing orders are not inconsistent with the Federal Rules or any local district court rules. Beyond that, it is hoped that each district will adopt procedures, perhaps by local rule, for promulgating and reviewing single-judge standing orders.

1995 Amendments

Subdivision (a). This rule is amended to reflect the requirement that local rules be consistent not only with the national rules but also with Acts of Congress. The amendment also states that local rules should not repeat Acts of Congress or national rules.

The amendment also requires that the numbering of local rules conform with any uniform numbering system that may be prescribed by the Judicial Conference. Lack of uniform numbering might create unnecessary traps for counsel and litigants. A uniform numbering system would make it easier for an increasingly national bar and for litigants to locate a local rule that applies to a particular procedural issue.

Paragraph (2) is new. Its aim is to protect against loss of rights in the enforcement of local rules relating to matters of form. For example, a party should not be deprived of a right to a jury trial because its attorney, unaware of—or forgetting—a local rule directing that jury demands be noted in the caption of the case, includes a jury demand only in the body of the pleading. The proscription of paragraph (2) is narrowly drawn—covering only violations attributable to nonwillful failure to comply and only those involving local rules directed to matters of form. It does not limit the court's power to impose substantive penalties upon a party if it or its attorney contumaciously or willfully violates a local rule, even one involving merely a matter of form. Nor does it affect the court's power to enforce local rules that involve more than mere matters of form—for example, a local rule requiring parties to identify evidentiary matters relied upon to support or oppose motions for summary judgment.

Subdivision (b). This rule provides flexibility to the court in regulating practice when there is no controlling law. Specifically, it permits the court to regulate practice in any manner consistent with Acts of Congress, with rules adopted under 28 U.S.C. §§ 2072 and 2075, and with the district local rules.

This rule recognizes that courts rely on multiple directives to control practice. Some courts regulate practice through the published Federal Rules and the local rules of the court. Some courts also have used internal operating procedures, standing orders, and other internal directives. Although such directives continue to be authorized, they can lead to problems. Counsel or litigants may be unaware of various directives. In addition, the sheer volume of directives may impose an unreasonable barrier. For example, it may be difficult to obtain copies of the directives. Finally, counsel or litigants may be unfairly sanctioned for failing to comply with a directive. For these reasons, the amendment to this rule disapproves imposing any sanction or other disadvantage on a person for noncompliance with such an internal directive, unless the alleged violator has been furnished actual notice of the requirement in a particular case.

There should be no adverse consequence to a party or attorney for violating special requirements relating to practice before a particular court unless the party or attorney has actual notice of those requirements. Furnishing litigants with a copy outlining the judge's practices—or attaching instructions to a notice setting a case for conference or trial—would suffice to give actual notice, as would an order in a case specifically adopting by reference a judge's standing order and indicating how copies can be obtained.

2007 Amendments

The language of Rule 83 has been amended as part of the general restyling of the Civil Rules to make them more easily understood and to make style and terminology consistent throughout the rules. These changes are intended to be stylistic only.

Rule 84. Forms

The forms in the Appendix suffice under these rules and illustrate the simplicity and brevity that these rules contemplate.

(Amended December 27, 1946, effective March 19, 1948; April 30, 2007, effective December 1, 2007.)

ADVISORY COMMITTEE NOTES

1937 Adoption

In accordance with the practice found useful in many codes, provision is here made for a limited number of official forms which may serve as guides in pleading. Compare 2 Mass.Gen.Laws (Ter.Ed., 1932) ch. 231, § 147, Forms 1–47; *English Annual Practice* (1937) Appendix A to M, inclusive; *Conn.Practice Book* (1934) Rules, 47–68, pp. 123 to 427.

1946 Amendment

Note. The amendment serves to emphasize that the forms contained in the Appendix of Forms are sufficient to withstand attack under the rules under which they are drawn, and that the practitioner using them may rely on them to that extent. The circuit courts of appeals generally have upheld the use of the forms as promoting desirable simplicity and brevity of statement. *Sierocinski v. E. I. DuPont DeNemours & Co.,* C.C.A.3, 1939, 103 F.2d 843; *Swift & Co. v. Young,* C.C.A.4, 1939, 107 F.2d 170; *Sparks v. England,* C.C.A.8, 1940, 113 F.2d 579; *Ramsouer v. Midland Valley R. Co.,* C.C.A.8, 1943, 135 F.2d 101. And the forms as a whole have met with widespread approval in the courts. See cases cited in 1 Moore's Federal Practice, 1938, Cum. Supplement § 8.07, under "Page 554"; see also Commentary, The Official Forms, 1941, 4 Fed.Rules Serv. 954. In Cook, "Facts" and "Statements of Fact", 1937, 4 U.Chi.L.Rev. 233, 245–246, it is said with reference to what is now Rule 84: ". . . pleaders in the federal courts are not to be left to guess as to the meaning of [the] language" in Rule 8(a) regarding the form of the complaint. "All of which is as it should be. In no other way can useless litigation be avoided." Ibid. The amended rule will operate to discourage isolated results such as those found in *Washburn v. Moorman Mfg. Co.,* S.D.Cal. 1938, 25 F.Supp. 546; *Employers Mutual Liability Ins. Co. of Wisconsin v. Blue Line Transfer Co.,* W.D.Mo.1941, 2 F.R.D. 121, 5 Fed.Rules Serv. 12e.235, Case 2.

2007 Amendments

The language of Rule 84 has been amended as part of the general restyling of the Civil Rules to make them more easily understood and to make style and terminology consistent throughout the rules. These changes are intended to be stylistic only.

Rule 85. Title

These rules may be cited as the Federal Rules of Civil Procedure.

(Amended April 30, 2007, effective December 1, 2007.)

ADVISORY COMMITTEE NOTES

2007 Amendments

The language of Rule 85 has been amended as part of the general restyling of the Civil Rules to make them more easily understood and to make style and terminology consistent throughout the rules. These changes are intended to be stylistic only.

Rule 86. Effective Dates

(a) In General. These rules and any amendments take effect at the time specified by the Supreme Court, subject to 28 U.S.C. § 2074. They govern:

(1) proceedings in an action commenced after their effective date; and

(2) proceedings after that date in an action then pending unless:

(A) the Supreme Court specifies otherwise; or

(B) the court determines that applying them in a particular action would be infeasible or work an injustice.

(b) December 1, 2007 Amendments. If any provision in Rules 1–5.1, 6–73, or 77–86 conflicts with another law, priority in time for the purpose of 28 U.S.C. § 2072(b) is not affected by the amendments taking effect on December 1, 2007.

(Amended December 27, 1946, effective March 19, 1948; December 29, 1948, effective October 20, 1949; April 17, 1961, effective July 19, 1961; January 21, 1963, and March 18, 1963, effective July 1, 1963; April 30, 2007, effective December 1, 2007.)

ADVISORY COMMITTEE NOTES

1937 Adoption

See former Equity Rule 81 (These Rules Effective February 1, 1913—Old Rules Abrogated).

2007 Amendments

The language of Rule 86 has been amended as part of the general restyling of the Civil Rules to make them more easily understood and to make style and terminology consistent throughout the rules. These changes are intended to be stylistic only.

The subdivisions that provided a list of the effective dates of the original Civil Rules and amendments made up to 1963 are deleted as no longer useful.

Rule 86(b) is added to clarify the relationship of amendments taking effect on December 1, 2007, to other laws for the purpose of applying the "supersession" clause in 28 U.S.C. § 2072(b). Section 2072(b) provides that a law in conflict with an Enabling Act Rule "shall be of no further force or effect after such rule[] ha[s] taken effect." The amendments that take effect on December 1, 2007, result from the general restyling of the Civil Rules and from a small number of technical revisions adopted on a parallel track. None of these amendments is intended to affect resolution of any conflict that might arise between a rule and another law. Rule 86(b) makes this intent explicit. Any conflict that arises should be resolved by looking to the date the specific conflicting rule provision first became effective.

HISTORICAL NOTES

Effective and Applicability Provisions

1948 Amendments. The first regular session of the 81st Congress adjourned sine die on Oct. 19, 1949, therefore the amendments to Rules 1, 17, 22, 24, 25, 27, 37, 45, 57, 60, 65, 66, 67, 69, 72–76, 79, 81, 82, and 86 and to forms 1, 19, 22, 23, and 27 became effective on Oct. 20, 1949, following the adjournment as provided for in subsection (c) of this rule.

1946 Amendments. The first regular session of the 80th Congress adjourned sine die on Friday, Dec. 19, 1947, therefore the amendments to Rules 6, 7, 12, 13, 14, 17, 24, 26, 27, 28, 33, 34, 36, 41, 45, 52, 54, 56, 58, 59, 60, 62, 65, 66, 68, 73,

75, 77, 79, 80, 81, 84, and 86, became effective Mar. 19, 1948 as provided for in subsection (b) of this rule.

Effective Date of 1970 Amendments; Transmission to Congress

Sections 2 and 3 of the Order of the Supreme Court, dated Mar. 30, 1970, provided:

"2. That the foregoing amendments to the Rules of Civil Procedure shall take effect on July 1, 1970, and shall govern all proceedings in actions brought thereafter and also in all further proceedings in actions then pending, except to the extent that in the opinion of the court their application in a particular action then pending would not be feasible or would work injustice, in which event the former procedure applies.

"3. That the Chief Justice be, and he hereby is, authorized to transmit to the Congress the foregoing amendments to the Rules of Civil Procedure in accordance with the provisions of Title 28, U.S.C. § 2072."

Effective Date of 1966 Amendment; Transmission to Congress; Rescission

Sections 2 to 4 of the Order of the Supreme Court, dated Feb. 28, 1966, 383 U.S. 1031, provided:

"2. That the foregoing amendments and additions to the Rules of Civil Procedure shall take effect on July 1, 1966, and shall govern all proceedings in actions brought thereafter and also in all further proceedings in actions then pending, except to the extent that in the opinion of the court their application in a particular action then pending would not be feasible or would work injustice, in which event the former procedure applies.

"3. That the Chief Justice be, and he hereby is, authorized to transmit to the Congress the foregoing amendments and additions to the Rules of Civil Procedure in accordance with the provisions of Title 28, U.S.C., §§ 2072 and 2073.

"4. That: (a) subdivision (c) of Rule 6 of the Rules of Civil Procedure for the United States District Courts promulgated by this court on December 20, 1937, effective September 16, 1938; (b) Rule 2 of the Rules for Practice and Procedure under section 25 of An Act To amend and consolidate the Acts respecting copyright, approved March 4, 1909, promulgated by this court on June 1, 1909, effective July 1, 1909; and (c) the Rules of Practice in Admiralty and Maritime Cases, promulgated by this court on December 6, 1920, effective March 7, 1921, as revised, amended and supplemented, be, and they hereby are, rescinded, effective July 1, 1966."

APPENDIX OF FORMS

(See Rule 84)

Form 1. Caption

(Use on every summons, complaint, answer, motion, or other document.)

United States District Court
for the
_____ District of _____

A B, Plaintiff v. C D, Defendant v. E F, Third-Party Defendant *(Use if needed.)*	))))))))))

Civil Action No. _____

(Name of Document)

(Added Apr. 30, 2007, eff. Dec. 1, 2007.)

Form 2. Date, Signature, Address, E-Mail Address, and Telephone Number

(Use at the conclusion of pleadings and other papers that require a signature.)

Date _____

_____
(Signature of the attorney or unrepresented party)

_____
(Printed name)

_____
(Address)

_____
(E-mail address)

_____
(Telephone number)

(Added Apr. 30, 2007, eff. Dec. 1, 2007.)

Form 3. Summons

(Caption—See Form 1.)

To *name the defendant*:

A lawsuit has been filed against you.

Within 20 days after service of this summons on you (not counting the day you received it), you must serve on the plaintiff an answer to the attached complaint or a motion under Rule 12 of the Federal Rules of Civil Procedure. The answer or motion must be served on the plaintiff's attorney, _____, whose address is _____. If you fail to do so, judgment by default will be entered against you for the relief demanded in the complaint. You also must file your answer or motion with the court.

Date _____

_____
Clerk of Court

(Court Seal)

(Use 60 days if the defendant is the United States or a United States agency, or is an officer or employee of the United States allowed 60 days by Rule 12(a)(3).)

(Added Apr. 30, 2007, eff. Dec. 1, 2007.)

Form 4. Summons on a Third-Party Complaint

(Caption—See Form 1.)

To *name the third-party defendant*:

A lawsuit has been filed against defendant _____, who as third-party plaintiff is making this claim against you to pay part or all of what [he] may owe to the plaintiff _____.

Within 20 days after service of this summons on you (not counting the day you received it), you must serve on the plaintiff and on the defendant an answer to the attached third-party complaint or a motion under Rule 12 of the Federal Rules of Civil Procedure. The answer or motion must be served on the defendant's attorney, _____, whose address is, _____, and also on the plaintiff's attorney, _____, whose address is, _____. If you fail to do so, judgment by default will be entered against you for the relief demanded in the third-party complaint. You also must file the answer or motion with the court and serve it on any other parties.

A copy of the plaintiff's complaint is also attached. You may—but are not required to—respond to it.

Date _____

_____

Clerk of Court

(Court Seal)

(Added Apr. 30, 2007, eff. Dec. 1, 2007.)

Form 5. Notice of a Lawsuit and Request to Waive Service of a Summons

(Caption—See Form 1.)

To *(name the defendant—or if the defendant is a corporation, partnership, or association name an officer or agent authorized to receive service)*:

Why are you getting this?

A lawsuit has been filed against you, or the entity you represent, in this court under the number shown above. A copy of the complaint is attached.

This is not a summons, or an official notice from the court. It is a request that, to avoid expenses, you waive formal service of a summons by signing and returning the enclosed waiver. To avoid these expenses, you must return the signed waiver within *(give at least 30 days or at least 60 days if the defendant is outside any judicial district of the United States)* from the date shown below, which is the date this notice was sent. Two copies of the waiver form are enclosed, along with a stamped, self-addressed envelope or other prepaid means for returning one copy. You may keep the other copy.

What happens next?

If you return the signed waiver, I will file it with the court. The action will then proceed as if you had been served on the date the waiver is filed, but no summons will be served on you and you will have 60 days from the date this notice is sent (see the date below) to answer the complaint (or 90 days if this notice is sent to you outside any judicial district of the United States).

If you do not return the signed waiver within the time indicated, I will arrange to have the summons and complaint served on you. And I will ask the court to require you, or the entity you represent, to pay the expenses of making service.

Please read the enclosed statement about the duty to avoid unnecessary expenses.

I certify that this request is being sent to you on the date below.

(Date and sign—See Form 2.)

(Added Apr. 30, 2007, eff. Dec. 1, 2007.)

Form 6. Waiver of the Service of Summons

(Caption—See Form 1.)

To *name the plaintiff's attorney or the unrepresented plaintiff*:

I have received your request to waive service of a summons in this action along with a copy of the complaint, two copies of this waiver form, and a prepaid means of returning one signed copy of the form to you.

I, or the entity I represent, agree to save the expense of serving a summons and complaint in this case.

I understand that I, or the entity I represent, will keep all defenses or objections to the lawsuit, the court's jurisdiction, and the venue of the action, but that I waive any objections to the absence of a summons or of service.

I also understand that I, or the entity I represent, must file and serve an answer or a motion under Rule 12 within 60 days from _____, the date when this request was sent (or 90 days if it was sent outside the United States). If I fail to do so, a default judgment will be entered against me or the entity I represent.

(Date and sign—See Form 2.)

(Attach the following to Form 6.)

Duty to Avoid Unnecessary Expenses of Serving a Summons

Rule 4 of the Federal Rules of Civil Procedure requires certain defendants to cooperate in saving unnecessary expenses of serving a summons and complaint. A defendant who is located in the United States and who fails to return a signed waiver of service requested by a plaintiff located in the United States will be required to pay the expenses of service, unless the defendant shows good cause for the failure.

"Good cause" does *not* include a belief that the lawsuit is groundless, or that it has been brought in an improper venue, or that the court has no jurisdiction over this matter or over the defendant or the defendant's property.

If the waiver is signed and returned, you can still make these and all other defenses and objections, but you cannot object to the absence of a summons or of service.

If you waive service, then you must, within the time specified on the waiver form, serve an answer or a motion under Rule 12 on the plaintiff and file a copy with the court. By signing and returning the waiver form, you are allowed more time to respond than if a summons had been served.

(Added Apr. 30, 2007, eff. Dec. 1, 2007.)

Form 7. Statement of Jurisdiction

a. (*For diversity-of-citizenship jurisdiction.*) The plaintiff is [a citizen of *Michigan*] [a corporation incorporated under the laws of *Michigan* with its principal place of business in *Michigan*]. The defendant is [a citizen of *New York*] [a corporation incorporated under the laws of *New York* with its principal place of business in *New York*]. The amount in controversy, without interest and costs, exceeds the sum or value specified by 28 U.S.C. § 1332.

b. (*For federal-question jurisdiction.*) This action arises under [the United States Constitution, *specify the article or amendment and the section*] [a United States treaty *specify*] [a federal statute, ___ U.S.C. § ___].

c. (*For a claim in the admiralty or maritime jurisdiction.*) This is a case of admiralty or maritime jurisdiction. (*To invoke admiralty status under Rule 9(h) use the following:* This is an admiralty or maritime claim within the meaning of Rule 9(h).)

(Added Apr. 30, 2007, eff. Dec. 1, 2007.)

Form 8. Statement of Reasons for Omitting a Party

(*If a person who ought to be made a party under Rule 19(a) is not named, include this statement in accordance with Rule 19(c).*)

This complaint does not join as a party *name* who [is not subject to this court's personal jurisdiction] [cannot be made a party without depriving this court of subject-matter jurisdiction] because *state the reason.*

(Added Apr. 30, 2007, eff. Dec. 1, 2007.)

Form 9. Statement Noting a Party's Death

(Caption—See Form 1.)

In accordance with Rule 25(a) *name the person,* who is [a party to this action] [a representative of or successor to the deceased party] notes the death during the pendency of this action of *name*, [*describe as party* in this action].

(Date and sign—See Form 2.)

(Added Apr. 30, 2007, eff. Dec. 1, 2007.)

Form 10. Complaint to Recover a Sum Certain

(Caption—See Form 1.)

1. (Statement of Jurisdiction—See Form 7.)

(*Use one or more of the following as appropriate and include a demand for judgment.*)

(a) On a Promissory Note

2. On *date,* the defendant executed and delivered a note promising to pay the plaintiff on *date* the sum of $_____ with interest at the rate of ___ percent. A copy of the note [is attached as Exhibit A] [is summarized as follows: _____.]

3. The defendant has not paid the amount owed.

(b) On an Account

2. The defendant owes the plaintiff $_____ according to the account set out in Exhibit A.

(c) For Goods Sold and Delivered

2. The defendant owes the plaintiff $_____ for goods sold and delivered by the plaintiff to the defendant from *date* to *date*.

(d) For Money Lent

2. The defendant owes the plaintiff $_____ for money lent by the plaintiff to the defendant on *date*.

(e) For Money Paid by Mistake

2. The defendant owes the plaintiff $_____ for money paid by mistake to the defendant on *date* under these circumstances: *describe with particularity in accordance with Rule 9(b).*

(f) For Money Had and Received

2. The defendant owes the plaintiff $_____ for money that was received from *name* on *date* to be paid by the defendant to the plaintiff.

Demand for Judgment

Therefore, the plaintiff demands judgment against the defendant for $_____, plus interest and costs.

(Date and sign—See Form 2.)

(Added Apr. 30, 2007, eff. Dec. 1, 2007.)

Form 11. Complaint for Negligence

(Caption—See Form 1.)

1. (Statement of Jurisdiction—See Form 7.)

2. On *date*, at *place*, the defendant negligently drove a motor vehicle against the plaintiff.

3. As a result, the plaintiff was physically injured, lost wages or income, suffered physical and mental pain, and incurred medical expenses of $_____.

Therefore, the plaintiff demands judgment against the defendant for $_____, plus costs.

(Date and sign—See Form 2).

(Added Apr. 30, 2007, eff. Dec. 1, 2007.)

Form 12. Complaint for Negligence when the Plaintiff Does Not Know Who is Responsible

(Caption—See Form 1.)

1. (Statement of Jurisdiction—See Form 7.)
2. On *date*, at *place*, defendant *name* or defendant *name* or both of them willfully or recklessly or negligently drove, or caused to be driven, a motor vehicle against the plaintiff.
3. As a result, the plaintiff was physically injured, lost wages or income, suffered mental and physical pain, and incurred medical expenses of $_____.

Therefore, the plaintiff demands judgment against one or both defendants for $_____, plus costs.

(Date and sign—See Form 2.)

(Added Apr. 30, 2007, eff. Dec. 1, 2007.)

Form 13. Complaint for Negligence Under the Federal Employers' Liability Act

(Caption—See Form 1.)

1. (Statement of Jurisdiction—See Form 7.)
2. At the times below, the defendant owned and operated in interstate commerce a railroad line that passed through a tunnel located at _____.
3. On *date*, the plaintiff was working to repair and enlarge the tunnel to make it convenient and safe for use in interstate commerce.
4. During this work, the defendant, as the employer, negligently put the plaintiff to work in a section of the tunnel that the defendant had left unprotected and unsupported.
5. The defendant's negligence caused the plaintiff to be injured by a rock that fell from an unsupported portion of the tunnel.
6. As a result, the plaintiff was physically injured, lost wages or income, suffered mental and physical pain, and incurred medical expenses of $_____.

Therefore, the plaintiff demands judgment against the defendant for $_____, and costs.

(Date and sign—See Form 2.)

(Added Apr. 30, 2007, eff. Dec. 1, 2007.)

Form 14. Complaint for Damages Under the Merchant Marine Act

(Caption—See Form 1.)

1. (Statement of Jurisdiction—See Form 7.)
2. At the times below, the defendant owned and operated the vessel *name* and used it to transport cargo for hire by water in interstate and foreign commerce.
3. On *date*, at *place*, the defendant hired the plaintiff under seamen's articles of customary form for a voyage from _____ to _____ and return at a wage of $_____ a month and found, which is equal to a shore worker's wage of $_____ a month.
4. On *date*, the vessel was at sea on the return voyage. (*Describe the weather and the condition of the vessel.*)
5. (*Describe as in Form 11 the defendant's negligent conduct.*)
6. As a result of the defendant's negligent conduct and the unseaworthiness of the vessel, the plaintiff was physically injured, has been incapable of any gainful activity, suffered mental and physical pain, and has incurred medical expenses of $_____.

Therefore, the plaintiff demands judgment against the defendant for $_____, plus costs.

(Date and sign—See Form 2.)

(Added Apr. 30, 2007, eff. Dec. 1, 2007.)

Form 15. Complaint for the Conversion of Property

(Caption—See Form 1.)

1. (Statement of Jurisdiction—See Form 7.)
2. On *date*, at *place*, the defendant converted to the defendant's own use property owned by the plaintiff. The property converted consists of *describe*.
3. The property is worth $_____.

Therefore, the plaintiff demands judgment against the defendant for $_____, plus costs.

(Date and sign—See Form 2.)

(Added Apr. 30, 2007, eff. Dec. 1, 2007.)

Form 16. Third-Party Complaint

(Caption—See Form 1.)

1. Plaintiff *name* has filed against defendant *name* a complaint, a copy of which is attached.
2. (*State grounds entitling defendant's name to recover from third-party defendant's name for (all or an identified share) of any judgment for plaintiff's name against defendant's name.*)

Therefore, the defendant demands judgment against *third-party defendant's name* for *all or an identified share* of sums that may be adjudged against the defendant in the plaintiff's favor.

(Date and sign—See Form 2.)

(Added Apr. 30, 2007, eff. Dec. 1, 2007.)

Form 17. Complaint for Specific Performance of a Contract to Convey Land

(Caption—See Form 1.)

1. (Statement of Jurisdiction—See Form 7.)
2. On *date*, the parties agreed to the contract [attached as Exhibit A][summarize the contract].
3. As agreed, the plaintiff tendered the purchase price and requested a conveyance of the land, but the defendant refused to accept the money or make a conveyance.
4. The plaintiff now offers to pay the purchase price.

Therefore, the plaintiff demands that:

(a) the defendant be required to specifically perform the agreement and pay damages of $_____, plus interest and costs, or

(b) if specific performance is not ordered, the defendant be required to pay damages of $_____, plus interest and costs.

(Date and sign—See Form 2.)

(Added Apr. 30, 2007, eff. Dec. 1, 2007.)

Form 18. Complaint for Patent Infringement

(Caption—See Form 1.)

1. (Statement of Jurisdiction—See Form 7.)
2. On *date*, United States Letters Patent No. _____ were issued to the plaintiff for an invention in an *electric motor*. The plaintiff owned the patent throughout the period of the defendant's infringing acts and still owns the patent.
3. The defendant has infringed and is still infringing the Letters Patent by making, selling, and using *electric motors* that embody the patented invention, and the defendant will continue to do so unless enjoined by this court.
4. The plaintiff has complied with the statutory requirement of placing a notice of the Letters Patent on all *electric motors* it manufactures and sells and has given the defendant written notice of the infringement.

Therefore, the plaintiff demands:

(a) a preliminary and final injunction against the continuing infringement;

(b) an accounting for damages; and

(c) interest and costs.

(Date and sign—See Form 2.)

(Added Apr. 30, 2007, eff. Dec. 1, 2007.)

Form 19. Complaint for Copyright Infringement and Unfair Competition

(Caption—See Form 1.)

1. (Statement of Jurisdiction—See Form 7.)
2. Before *date*, the plaintiff, a United States citizen, wrote a book entitled _____.
3. The book is an original work that may be copyrighted under United States law. A copy of the book is attached as Exhibit A.
4. Between *date* and *date*, the plaintiff applied to the copyright office and received a certificate of registration dated _____ and identified as *date, class, number*.
5. Since *date*, the plaintiff has either published or licensed for publication all copies of the book in compliance with the copyright laws and has remained the sole owner of the copyright.
6. After the copyright was issued, the defendant infringed the copyright by publishing and selling a book entitled _____, which was copied largely from the plaintiff's book. A copy of the defendant's book is attached as Exhibit B.
7. The plaintiff has notified the defendant in writing of the infringement.
8. The defendant continues to infringe the copyright by continuing to publish and sell the infringing book in violation of the copyright, and further has engaged in unfair trade practices and unfair competition in connection with its publication and sale of the infringing book, thus causing irreparable damage.

Therefore, the plaintiff demands that:

(a) until this case is decided the defendant and the defendant's agents be enjoined from disposing of any copies of the defendant's book by sale or otherwise;

(b) the defendant account for and pay as damages to the plaintiff all profits and advantages gained from unfair trade practices and unfair competition in selling the defendant's book, and all profits and advantages gained from infringing the plaintiff's copyright (but no less than the statutory minimum);

(c) the defendant deliver for impoundment all copies of the book in the defendant's possession or control and deliver for destruction all infringing copies and all plates, molds, and other materials for making infringing copies;

(d) the defendant pay the plaintiff interest, costs, and reasonable attorney's fees; and

(e) the plaintiff be awarded any other just relief.

(Date and sign—See Form 2.)

(Added Apr. 30, 2007, eff. Dec. 1, 2007.)

Form 20. Complaint for Interpleader and Declaratory Relief

(Caption—See Form 1.)

1. (Statement of Jurisdiction—See Form 7.)
2. On *date*, the plaintiff issued a life insurance policy on the life of *name* with *name* as the named beneficiary.
3. As a condition for keeping the policy in force, the policy required payment of a premium during the first year and then annually.
4. The premium due on *date* was never paid, and the policy lapsed after that date.
5. On *date* , after the policy had lapsed, both the insured and the named beneficiary died in an automobile collision.
6. Defendant *name* claims to be the beneficiary in place of *name* and has filed a claim to be paid the policy's full amount.
7. The other two defendants are representatives of the deceased persons' estates. Each defendant has filed a claim on behalf of each estate to receive payment of the policy's full amount.
8. If the policy was in force at the time of death, the plaintiff is in doubt about who should be paid.

Therefore, the plaintiff demands that:

(a) each defendant be restrained from commencing any action against the plaintiff on the policy;

(b) a judgment be entered that no defendant is entitled to the proceeds of the policy or any part of it, but if the court determines that the policy was in effect at the time of the insured's death, that the defendants be required to interplead and settle among themselves their rights to the proceeds, and that the plaintiff be discharged from all liability except to the defendant determined to be entitled to the proceeds; and

(c) the plaintiff recover its costs.

(Date and sign—See Form 2.)

(Added Apr. 30, 2007, eff. Dec. 1, 2007.)

Form 21. Complaint on a Claim for a Debt and to Set Aside a Fraudulent Conveyance Under Rule 18(b)

(Caption—See Form 1.)

1. (Statement of Jurisdiction—See Form 7.)
2. On *date*, defendant *name* signed a note promising to pay to the plaintiff on *date* the sum of $_____ with interest at the rate of ___ percent. [The pleader may, but need not, attach a copy or plead the note verbatim.]
3. Defendant *name* owes the plaintiff the amount of the note and interest.
4. On *date*, defendant *name* conveyed all defendant's real and personal property *if less than all, describe it fully* to defendant *name* for the purpose of defrauding the plaintiff and hindering or delaying the collection of the debt.

Therefore, the plaintiff demands that:

(a) judgment for $_____, plus costs, be entered against defendant(s) *name(s)*; and

(b) the conveyance to defendant *name* be declared void and any judgment granted be made a lien on the property.

(Date and sign—See Form 2.)

(Added Apr. 30, 2007, eff. Dec. 1, 2007.)

Form 30. Answer Presenting Defenses Under Rule 12(b)

(Caption—See Form 1.)

Responding to Allegations in the Complaint

1. Defendant admits the allegations in paragraphs _____.
2. Defendant lacks knowledge or information sufficient to form a belief about the truth of the allegations in paragraphs _____.
3. Defendant admits *identify part of the allegation* in paragraph _____ and denies or lacks knowledge or information sufficient to form a belief about the truth of the rest of the paragraph.

Failure to State a Claim

4. The complaint fails to state a claim upon which relief can be granted.

Failure to Join a Required Party

5. If there is a debt, it is owed jointly by the defendant and *name* who is a citizen of _____. This person can be made a party

without depriving this court of jurisdiction over the existing parties.

Affirmative Defense–Statute of Limitations

6. The plaintiff's claim is barred by the statute of limitations because it arose more than _____ years before this action was commenced.

Counterclaim

7. (*Set forth any counterclaim in the same way a claim is pleaded in a complaint. Include a further statement of jurisdiction if needed.*)

Crossclaim

8. (*Set forth a crossclaim against a coparty in the same way a claim is pleaded in a complaint. Include a further statement of jurisdiction if needed.*)

(Date and sign—See Form 2.)

(Added Apr. 30, 2007, eff. Dec. 1, 2007.)

Form 31. Answer to a Complaint for Money Had and Received With a Counterclaim for Interpleader

(Caption—See Form 1.)

Response to the Allegations in the Complaint

(See Form 30.)

Counterclaim for Interpleader

1. The defendant received from *name* a deposit of $_____.
2. The plaintiff demands payment of the deposit because of a purported assignment from *name*, who has notified the defendant that the assignment is not valid and who continues to hold the defendant responsible for the deposit.

Therefore, the defendant demands that:

(a) *name* be made a party to this action;

(b) the plaintiff and *name* be required to interplead their respective claims;

(c) the court decide whether the plaintiff or *name* or either of them is entitled to the deposit and discharge the defendant of any liability except to the person entitled to the deposit; and

(d) the defendant recover costs and attorney's fees.

(Date and sign—See Form 2.)

(Added Apr. 30, 2007, eff. Dec. 1, 2007.)

Form 40. Motion to Dismiss Under Rule 12(b) for Lack of Jurisdiction, Improper Venue, Insufficient Service of Process, or Failure to State a Claim

(Caption—See Form 1.)

The defendant moves to dismiss the action because:

1. the amount in controversy is less than the sum or value specified by 28 U.S.C. § 1332;
2. the defendant is not subject to the personal jurisdiction of this court;
3. venue is improper (this defendant does not reside in this district and no part of the events or omissions giving rise to the claim occurred in the district);
4. the defendant has not been properly served, as shown by the attached affidavits of _____; or
5. the complaint fails to state a claim upon which relief can be granted.

(Date and sign—See Form 2.)

(Added Apr. 30, 2007, eff. Dec. 1, 2007.)

Form 41. Motion to Bring in a Third-Party Defendant

(Caption—See Form 1.)

The defendant, as third-party plaintiff, moves for leave to serve on *name* a summons and third-party complaint, copies of which are attached.

(Date and sign—See Form 2.)

(Added Apr. 30, 2007, eff. Dec. 1, 2007.)

Form 42. Motion to Intervene as a Defendant Under Rule 24

(Caption—See Form 1.)

1. *name* moves for leave to intervene as a defendant in this action and to file the attached answer.

(State grounds under Rule 24(a) or (b).)

2. The plaintiff alleges patent infringement. We manufacture and sell to the defendant the articles involved, and we have a defense to the plaintiff's claim.
3. Our defense presents questions of law and fact that are common to this action.

(Date and sign—See Form 2.)

[An Intervener's Answer must be attached. See Form 30.]

(Added Apr. 30, 2007, eff. Dec. 1, 2007.)

Form 50. Request to Produce Documents and Tangible Things, or to Enter onto Land Under Rule 34

(Caption—See Form 1.)

The plaintiff *name* requests that the defendant *name* respond within ____ days to the following requests:

1. To produce and permit the plaintiff to inspect and copy and to test or sample the following documents, including electronically stored information:

(*Describe each document and the electronically stored information, either individually or by category.*)

(*State the time, place, and manner of the inspection and any related acts.*)

2. To produce and permit the plaintiff to inspect and copy—and to test or sample—the following tangible things:

(*Describe each thing, either individually or by category.*)

(*State the time, place, and manner of the inspection and any related acts.*)

3. To permit the plaintiff to enter onto the following land to inspect, photograph, test, or sample the property or an object or operation on the property.

(*Describe the property and each object or operation.*)

(*State the time and manner of the inspection and any related acts.*)

(Date and sign—See Form 2.)

(Added Apr. 30, 2007, eff. Dec. 1, 2007.)

Form 51. Request for Admissions Under Rule 36

(Caption—See Form 1.)

The plaintiff *name* asks the defendant *name* to respond within 30 days to these requests by admitting, for purposes of this action only and subject to objections to admissibility at trial:

1. The genuineness of the following documents, copies of which [are attached] [are or have been furnished or made available for inspection and copying].

(*List each document.*)

2. The truth of each of the following statements:

(*List each statement.*)

(Date and sign—See Form 2.)

(Added Apr. 30, 2007, eff. Dec. 1, 2007.)

Form 52. Report of the Parties' Planning Meeting

(Caption—See Form 1.)

1. The following persons participated in a Rule 26(f) conference on *date* by *state the method of conferring*:

(*e.g., name* representing the plaintiff.)

2. Initial Disclosures. The parties [have completed] [will complete by *date*] the initial disclosures required by Rule 26(a)(1).
3. Discovery Plan. The parties propose this discovery plan:

(*Use separate paragraphs or subparagraphs if the parties disagree.*)

(a) Discovery will be needed on these subjects: (*describe.*)

(b) (Dates for commencing and completing discovery, including discovery to be commenced or completed before other discovery.)

(c) (Maximum number of interrogatories by each party to another party, along with the dates the answers are due.)

(d) (Maximum number of requests for admission, along with the dates responses are due.)

(e) (Maximum number of depositions by each party.)

(f) (Limits on the length of depositions, in hours.)

(g) (Dates for exchanging reports of expert witnesses.)

(h) (Dates for supplementations under Rule 26(e).)

4. Other Items:

(a) (A date if the parties ask to meet with the court before a scheduling order.)

(b) (Requested dates for pretrial conferences.)

(c) (Final dates for the plaintiff to amend pleadings or to join parties.)

(d) (Final dates for the defendant to amend pleadings or to join parties.)

(e) (Final dates to file dispositive motions.)

(f) (State the prospects for settlement.)

(g) (Identify any alternative dispute resolution procedure that may enhance settlement prospects.)

(h) (Final dates for submitting Rule 26(a)(3) witness lists, designations of witnesses whose testimony will be presented by deposition, and exhibit lists.)

(i) (Final dates to file objections under Rule 26(a)(3).)

(j) (Suggested trial date and estimate of trial length.)

(k) (Other matters.)

(Date and sign—see Form 2.)

(Added Apr. 30, 2007, eff. Dec. 1, 2007.)

Form 60. Notice of Condemnation

(Caption—See Form 1.)

To *name the defendant*.

1. A complaint in condemnation has been filed in the United States District Court for the _____District of _____, to take property to use for *purpose*. The interest to be taken is *describe*. *The court is located in the United States courthouse at this address:* _____.
2. The property to be taken is described below. You have or claim an interest in it.

(*Describe the property.*)

3. The authority for taking this property is *cite*.
4. If you want to object or present any defense to the taking you must serve an answer on the plaintiff's attorney within 20 days [after being served with this notice][from *(insert the date of the last publication of notice)*]. Send your answer to this address: _____.
5. Your answer must identify the property in which you claim an interest, state the nature and extent of that interest, and state all your objections and defenses to the taking. Objections and defenses not presented are waived.
6. If you fail to answer you consent to the taking and the court will enter a judgment that takes your described property interest.
7. Instead of answering, you may serve on the plaintiff's attorney a notice of appearance that designates the property in which you claim an interest. After you do that, you will receive a notice of any proceedings that affect you. Whether or not you have previously appeared or answered, you may present evidence at a trial to determine compensation for the property and share in the overall award.

(Date and sign—See Form 2.)

(Added Apr. 30, 2007, eff. Dec. 1, 2007.)

Form 61. Complaint for Condemnation

(Caption—See Form 1; name as defendants the property and at least one owner.)

1. (Statement of Jurisdiction—See Form 7.)
2. This is an action to take property under the power of eminent domain and to determine just compensation to be paid to the owners and parties in interest.
3. The authority for the taking is _____.
4. The property is to be used for _____.
5. The property to be taken is (*describe in enough detail for identification—or attach the description and state "is described in Exhibit A, attached."*)
6. The interest to be acquired is _____.
7. The persons known to the plaintiff to have or claim an interest in the property are: _____. (*For each person include the interest claimed.*)
8. There may be other persons who have or claim an interest in the property and whose names could not be found after a reasonably diligent search. They are made parties under the designation "Unknown Owners."

Therefore, the plaintiff demands judgment:

(a) condemning the property;

(b) determining and awarding just compensation; and

(c) granting any other lawful and proper relief.

(Date and sign—See Form 2.)

(Added Apr. 30, 2007, eff. Dec. 1, 2007.)

Form 70. Judgment on a Jury Verdict

(Caption—See Form 1.)

This action was tried by a jury with Judge _____ presiding, and the jury has rendered a verdict.

It is ordered that:

[the plaintiff *name* recover from the defendant *name* the amount of $_____ with interest at the rate of ___%, along with costs.]

[the plaintiff recover nothing, the action be dismissed on the merits, and the defendant *name* recover costs from the plaintiff *name*.]

Date _____

_____

Clerk of Court

(Added Apr. 30, 2007, eff. Dec. 1, 2007.)

Form 71. Judgment by the Court Without a Jury

(Caption—See Form 1.)

This action was tried by Judge _____ without a jury and the following decision was reached:

It is ordered that [the plaintiff *name* recover from the defendant *name* the amount of $_____, with prejudgment interest at the rate of ___%, post-judgment interest at the rate of ___%, along with costs.] [the plaintiff recover nothing, the action be dismissed on the merits, and the defendant *name* recover costs from the plaintiff *name*.]

Date_____

_____

Clerk of Court

(Added Apr. 30, 2007, eff. Dec. 1, 2007.)

Form 80. Notice of a Magistrate Judge's Availability

1. A magistrate judge is available under title 28 U.S.C. § 636(c) to conduct the proceedings in this case, including a jury or nonjury trial and the entry of final judgment. But a magistrate judge can be assigned only if all parties voluntarily consent.
2. You may withhold your consent without adverse substantive consequences. The identity of any party consenting or withholding consent will not be disclosed to the judge to whom the case is assigned or to any magistrate judge.
3. If a magistrate judge does hear your case, you may appeal directly to a United States court of appeals as you would if a district judge heard it.

A form called *Consent to an Assignment to a United States Magistrate Judge* is available from the court clerk's office.

(Added Apr. 30, 2007, eff. Dec. 1, 2007.)

Form 81. Consent to an Assignment to a Magistrate Judge

(Caption—See Form 1.)

I voluntarily consent to have a United States magistrate judge conduct all further proceedings in this case, including a trial, and order the entry of final judgment. (Return this form to the court clerk—not to a judge or magistrate judge.)

Date_____

_____

Signature of the Party

(Added Apr. 30, 2007, eff. Dec. 1, 2007.)

Form 82. Order of Assignment to a Magistrate Judge

(Caption—See Form 1.)

With the parties' consent it is ordered that this case be assigned to United States Magistrate Judge _____ of this district to conduct all proceedings and enter final judgment in accordance with 28 U.S.C. § 636(c).

Date _____

_____

United States District Judge

(Added Apr. 30, 2007, eff. Dec. 1, 2007.)

SUPPLEMENTAL RULES FOR ADMIRALTY OR MARITIME CLAIMS AND ASSET FORFEITURE ACTIONS

Adopted February 28, 1966, effective July 1, 1966
Amendments received to December 1, 2008

The former Rules of Practice in Admiralty and Maritime Cases, promulgated by the Supreme Court on December 6, 1920, effective March 7, 1921, as revised, amended and supplemented, were rescinded, effective July 1, 1966.

Rule A. Scope of Rules

(1) These Supplemental Rules apply to:

(A) the procedure in admiralty and maritime claims within the meaning of Rule 9(h) with respect to the following remedies:

(i) maritime attachment and garnishment,

(ii) actions in rem,

(iii) possessory, petitory, and partition actions, and

(iv) actions for exoneration from or limitation of liability;

(B) forfeiture actions in rem arising from a federal statute; and

(C) the procedure in statutory condemnation proceedings analogous to maritime actions in rem, whether within the admiralty and maritime jurisdiction or not. Except as otherwise provided, references in these Supplemental Rules to actions in rem include such analogous statutory condemnation proceedings.

(2) The Federal Rules of Civil Procedure also apply to the foregoing proceedings except to the extent that they are inconsistent with these Supplemental Rules. (Added Feb. 28, 1966, eff. July 1, 1966, and amended Apr. 12, 2006, eff. Dec. 1, 2006)

ADVISORY COMMITTEE NOTES

1966 Adoption

Certain distinctively maritime remedies must be preserved in unified rules. The commencement of an action by attachment or garnishment has heretofore been practically unknown in federal jurisprudence except in admiralty, although the amendment of Rule 4(e) effective July 1, 1963, makes available that procedure in accordance with state law. The maritime proceeding in rem is unique, except as it has been emulated by statute, and is closely related to the substantive maritime law relating to liens. Arrest of the vessel or other maritime property is an historic remedy in controversies over title or right to possession, and in disputes among co-owners over the vessel's employment. The statutory right to limit liability is limited to owners of vessels, and has its own complexities. While the unified federal rules are generally applicable to these distinctive proceedings, certain special rules dealing with them are needed.

Arrest of the person and imprisonment for debt are not included because there remedies are not peculiarly maritime. The practice is not uniform but conforms to state law. See 2 Benedict § 286 [Note: reference is to the 6th Edition of Benedict on Admiralty and not to the current 7th Edition]; 28 U.S.C., § 2007; FRCP 64, 69. The relevant provisions of Admiralty Rules 2, 3, and 4 are unnecessary or obsolete.

No attempt is here made to compile a complete and self-contained code governing these distinctively maritime remedies. The more limited objective is to carry forward the relevant provisions of the former Rules of Practice for Admiralty and Maritime Cases, modernized and revised to some extent but still in the context of history and precedent. Accordingly, these Rules are not to be construed as limiting or impairing the traditional power of a district court, exercising the admiralty and maritime jurisdiction, to adapt its procedures and its remedies in the individual case, consistently with these rules, to secure the just, speedy, and inexpensive determination of every action. (See *Swift & Co., Packers v. Compania Columbiana Del Caribe, S/A,* 339 U.S. 684, (1950); Rule 1). In addition, of course, the district courts retain the power to make local rules not inconsistent with these rules. See Rule 83; cf. Admiralty Rule 44.

2006 Amendment

Rule A is amended to reflect the adoption of Rule G to govern procedure in civil forfeiture actions. Rule G(1) contemplates application of other Supplemental Rules to the extent that Rule G does not address an issue. One example is the Rule E(4)(c) provision for arresting intangible property.

Rule B. In Personam Actions: Attachment and Garnishment

(1) When Available; Complaint, Affidavit, Judicial Authorization, and Process. In an in personam action:

(a) If a defendant is not found within the district when a verified complaint praying for attachment and the affidavit required by Rule B(1)(b) are filed, a verified complaint may contain a prayer for process to attach the defendant's tangible or intangible personal property—up to the amount sued for—in the hands of garnishees named in the process.

(b) The plaintiff or the plaintiff's attorney must sign and file with the complaint an affidavit stating that, to the affiant's knowledge, or on information and belief, the defendant cannot be found within the district. The court must review the complaint and affidavit and, if the conditions of this Rule B appear to exist, enter an order so stating and authorizing process of attachment and garnishment. The clerk may issue supplemental process enforcing the court's order upon application without further court order.

(c) If the plaintiff or the plaintiff's attorney certifies that exigent circumstances make court review impracticable, the clerk must issue the summons and process of attachment and garnishment. The plaintiff has the burden in any post-attachment hearing under Rule E(4)(f) to show that exigent circumstances existed.

(d)(i) If the property is a vessel or tangible property on board a vessel, the summons, process, and any supplemental process must be delivered to the marshal for service.

(ii) If the property is other tangible or intangible property, the summons, process, and any supplemental process must be delivered to a person or organization authorized to serve it, who may be (A) a marshal; (B) someone under contract with the United States; (C) someone specially appointed by the court for that purpose; or, (D) in an action brought by the United States, any officer or employee of the United States.

(e) The plaintiff may invoke state-law remedies under Rule 64 for seizure of person or property for the purpose of securing satisfaction of the judgment.

(2) Notice to Defendant. No default judgment may be entered except upon proof—which may be by affidavit—that:

(a) the complaint, summons, and process of attachment or garnishment have been served on the defendant in a manner authorized by Rule 4;

(b) the plaintiff or the garnishee has mailed to the defendant the complaint, summons, and process of attachment or garnishment, using any form of mail requiring a return receipt; or

(c) the plaintiff or the garnishee has tried diligently to give notice of the action to the defendant but could not do so.

(3) Answer.

(a) By Garnishee. The garnishee shall serve an answer, together with answers to any interrogatories served with the complaint, within 20 days after service of process upon the garnishee. Interrogatories to the garnishee may be served with the complaint without leave of court. If the garnishee refuses or neglects to answer on oath as to the debts, credits, or effects of the defendant in the garnishee's hands, or any interrogatories concerning such debts, credits, and effects that may be propounded by the plaintiff, the court may award compulsory process against the garnishee. If the garnishee admits any debts, credits, or effects, they shall be held in the garnishee's hands or paid into the registry of the court, and shall be held in either case subject to the further order of the court.

(b) By Defendant. The defendant shall serve an answer within 30 days after process has been executed, whether by attachment of property or service on the garnishee.

(Added Feb. 28, 1966, eff. July 1, 1966, and amended Apr. 29, 1985, eff. Aug. 1, 1985; Mar. 2, 1987, eff. Aug. 1, 1987; Apr. 17, 2000, eff. Dec. 1, 2000; Apr. 25, 2005, eff. Dec. 1, 2005.)

ADVISORY COMMITTEE NOTES

1966 Adoption

Subdivision (1)

This preserves the traditional maritime remedy of attachment and garnishment, and carries forward the relevant substance of Admiralty Rule 2. In addition, or in the alternative, provision is made for the use of similar state remedies made available by the amendment of Rule 4(e) effective July 1, 1963. On the effect of appearance to defend against attachment see Rule E(8).

The rule follows closely the language of Admiralty Rule 2. No change is made with respect to the property subject to attachment. No change is made in the condition that makes the remedy available. The rules have never defined the clause, "if the defendant shall not be found within the district," and no definition is attempted here. The subject seems one best left for the time being to development on a case-by-case basis. The proposal does shift from the marshal (on whom it now rests in theory) to the plaintiff the burden of establishing that the defendant cannot be found in the district.

A change in the context of the practice is brought about by Rule 4(f), which will enable summons to be served throughout the state instead of, as heretofore, only within the district. The Advisory Committee considered whether the rule on attachment and garnishment should be correspondingly changed to permit those remedies only when the defendant cannot be found within the state and concluded that the remedy should not be so limited.

The effect is to enlarge the class of cases in which the plaintiff may proceed by attachment or garnishment although jurisdiction of the person of the defendant may be independently obtained. This is possible at the present time where, for example, a corporate defendant has appointed an agent within the district to accept service of process but is not carrying on activities there sufficient to subject it to jurisdiction. (*Seawind Compania, S.A. v. Crescent Line, Inc.*, 320 F.2d 580 (2d Cir.1963)), or where, though the foreign corporation's activities in the district are sufficient to subject it personally to the jurisdiction, there is in the district no officer on whom process can be served (*United States v. Cia. Naviera Continental, S.A.*, 178 F.Supp. 561, (S.D.N.Y.1959)).

Process of attachment or garnishment will be limited to the district. See Rule E(3)(a).

Subdivision (2)

The former Admiralty Rules did not provide for notice to the defendant in attachment and garnishment proceedings. None is required by the principles of due process, since it is assumed that the garnishee or custodian of the property attached will either notify the defendant or be deprived of the right to plead the judgment as a defense in an action against him by the defendant. *Harris v. Balk*, 198 U.S. 215 (1905); *Pennoyer v. Neff*, 95 U.S. 714 (1878). Modern conceptions of fairness, however, dictate that actual notice be given to persons known to claim an interest in the property that is the subject of the action where that is reasonably practicable. In attachment and garnishment proceedings the persons whose interests will be affected by the judgment are identified by the complaint. No substantial burden is imposed on the plaintiff by a simple requirement that he notify the defendant of the action by mail.

In the usual case the defendant is notified of the pendency of the proceedings by the garnishee or otherwise, and appears to claim the property and to make his answer. Hence notice by mail is not routinely required in all cases, but only in those in which the defendant has not appeared prior to the time when a default judgment is demanded. The rule therefore provides only that no default judgment shall be entered except upon proof of notice, or of inability to give notice despite diligent efforts to do so. Thus the burden of giving notice is further minimized.

In some cases the plaintiff may prefer to give notice by serving process in the usual way instead of simply by mail. (Rule 4(d).) In particular, if the defendant is in a foreign country the plaintiff may wish to utilize the modes of notice recently provided to facilitate compliance with foreign laws and procedures (Rule 4(i)). The rule provides for these alternatives.

The rule does not provide for notice by publication because there is no problem concerning unknown claimants, and publication has little utility in proportion to its expense where the identity of the defendant is known.

Subdivision (3)

Subdivision (a) incorporates the substance of Admiralty Rule 36.

The Admiralty Rules were silent as to when the garnishee and the defendant were to answer. See also 2 Benedict ch. XXIV [Reference is to the 6th Edition of Benedict on Admiralty and not to the current 7th Edition].

The rule proceeds on the assumption that uniform and definite periods of time for responsive pleadings should be substituted for return days (see the discussion under Rule C(6), below). Twenty days seems sufficient time for the garnishee to answer (cf. FRCP 12(a)), and an additional 10 days should suffice for the defendant. When allowance is made for the time required for notice to reach the defendant this gives the defendant in attachment and garnishment approximately the same time that defendants have to answer when personally served.

1985 Amendment

Rule B(1) has been amended to provide for judicial scrutiny before the issuance of any attachment or garnishment process. Its purpose is to eliminate doubts as to whether the Rule is consistent with the principles of procedural due process enunciated by the Supreme Court in *Sniadach v. Family Finance Corp.*, 395 U.S. 337 (1969); and later developed in *Fuentes v. Shevin*, 407 U.S. 67 (1972); *Mitchell v. W.T. Grant Co.*, 416 U.S. 600 (1974); and *North Georgia Finishing, Inc. v. Di-Chem, Inc.*, 419 U.S. 601 (1975). Such doubts were raised in *Grand Bahama Petroleum Co. v. Canadian Transportation Agencies, Ltd.*, 450 F.Supp. 447 (W.D.Wash.1978); and *Schiffahartsgesellschaft Leonhardt & Co. v. A. Bottacchi S.A. de Navegacion*, 552 F.Supp. 771 (S.D.Ga.1982), which was reversed, 732 F.2d 1543 (11th Cir. 1984). But compare *Polar Shipping Ltd. v. Oriental Shipping Corp.*, 680 F.2d 627 (9th Cir.1982), in which a majority of the panel upheld the constitutionality of Rule B because of the unique commercial context in which it is invoked. The practice described in Rule B(1) has been adopted in some districts by local rule. E.g., N.D. Calif. Local Rule 603.3; W.D.Wash. Local Admiralty Rule 15(d).

The rule envisions that the order will issue when the plaintiff makes a prima facie showing that he has a maritime claim against the defendant in the amount sued for and the defendant is not present in the district. A simple order with conclusory findings is contemplated. The reference to review by the "court" is broad enough to embrace review by a magistrate as well as by a district judge.

The new provision recognizes that in some situations, such as when the judge is unavailable and the ship is about to depart from the jurisdiction, it will be impracticable, if not impossible, to secure the judicial review contemplated by Rule B(1). When "exigent circumstances" exist, the rule enables the plaintiff to secure the issuance of the summons and process of attachment and garnishment, subject to a later showing that the necessary circumstances actually existed. This provision is intended to provide a safety valve without undermining the requirement of preattachment scrutiny. Thus, every effort to secure judicial review, including conducting a hearing by telephone, should be pursued before resorting to the exigent-circumstances procedure.

Rule B(1) also has been amended so that the garnishee shall be named in the "process" rather than in the "complaint." This should solve the problem presented in *Filia Compania Naviera, S.A. v. Petroship, S.A.*, 1983 A.M.C. 1 (S.D.N.Y.1982), and eliminate any need for an additional judicial review of the complaint and affidavit when a garnishee is added.

1987 Amendment

The amendments are technical. No substantive change is intended.

2000 Amendment

Rule B(1) is amended in two ways, and style changes have been made.

The service provisions of Rule C(3) are adopted in paragraph (d), providing alternatives to service by a marshal if the property to be seized is not a vessel or tangible property on board a vessel.

The provision that allows the plaintiff to invoke state attachment and garnishment remedies is amended to reflect the 1993 amendments of Civil Rule 4. Former Civil Rule 4(e), incorporated in Rule B(1), allowed general use of state quasi-in-rem jurisdiction if the defendant was not an inhabitant of, or found within, the state. Rule 4(e) was replaced in 1993 by Rule 4(n)(2), which permits use of state law to seize a defendant's assets only if personal jurisdiction over the defendant cannot be obtained in the district where the action is brought. Little purpose would be served by incorporating Rule 4(n)(2) in Rule B, since maritime attachment and garnishment are available whenever the defendant is not found within the district, a concept that allows attachment or garnishment even in some circumstances in which personal jurisdiction also can be asserted. In order to protect against any possibility that elimination of the reference to state quasi-in-rem jurisdiction remedies might seem to defeat continued use of state security devices, paragraph (e) expressly incorporates Civil Rule 64. Because Rule 64 looks only to security, not jurisdiction, the former reference to Rule E(8) is deleted as no longer relevant.

Rule B(2)(a) is amended to reflect the 1993 redistribution of the service provisions once found in Civil Rule 4(d) and (i). These provisions are now found in many different subdivisions of Rule 4. The new reference simply incorporates Rule 4, without designating the new subdivisions, because the function of Rule B(2) is simply to describe the methods of notice that suffice to support a default judgment. Style changes also have been made.

2005 Amendments

Rule B(1) is amended to incorporate the decisions in *Heidmar, Inc. v. Anomina Ravennate Di Armamento Sp.A. of Ravenna*, 132 F.3d 264, 267–268 (5th Cir. 1998), and *Navieros InterAmericanos, S.A. v. M/V Vasilia Express*, 120 F.3d 304, 314–315 (1st Cir. 1997). The time for determining whether a defendant is "found" in the district is set at the time of filing the verified complaint that prays for attachment and the affidavit required by Rule B(1)(b). As provided by Rule B(1)(b), the affidavit must be filed with the complaint. A defendant cannot defeat the security purpose of attachment by appointing an agent for service of process after the complaint and affidavit are filed. The complaint praying for attachment need not be the initial complaint. So long as the defendant is not found in the district, the prayer for attachment may be made in an amended complaint; the affidavit that the defendant cannot be found must be filed with the amended complaint.

Rule C. In Rem Actions: Special Provisions

(1) When Available. An action in rem may be brought:

(a) To enforce any maritime lien;

(b) Whenever a statute of the United States provides for a maritime action in rem or a proceeding analogous thereto.

Except as otherwise provided by law a party who may proceed in rem may also, or in the alternative, proceed in personam against any person who may be liable.

Statutory provisions exempting vessels or other property owned or possessed by or operated by or for the United States from arrest or seizure are not affected by this rule. When a statute so provides, an action against the United States or an instrumentality thereof may proceed on in rem principles.

(2) Complaint. In an action in rem the complaint must:

(a) be verified;

(b) describe with reasonable particularity the property that is the subject of the action; and

(c) state that the property is within the district or will be within the district while the action is pending.

(3) Judicial Authorization and Process.

(a) Arrest Warrant.

(i) The court must review the complaint and any supporting papers. If the conditions for an in rem action appear to exist, the court must issue an order directing the clerk to issue a warrant for the arrest of the vessel or other property that is the subject of the action.

(ii) If the plaintiff or the plaintiff's attorney certifies that exigent circumstances make court review impracticable, the clerk must promptly issue a summons and a warrant for the arrest of the vessel or other property that is the subject of the action. The plaintiff has the burden in any post-arrest hearing under Rule E(4)(f) to show that exigent circumstances existed.

(b) Service.

(i) If the property that is the subject of the action is a vessel or tangible property on board a vessel, the warrant and any supplemental process must be delivered to the marshal for service.

(ii) If the property that is the subject of the action is other property, tangible or intangible, the warrant and any supplemental process must be delivered to a person or organization authorized to enforce it, who may be: (A) a marshal; (B) someone under contract with the United States; (C) someone specially appointed by the court for that purpose; or, (D) in an action brought by the United States, any officer or employee of the United States.

(c) Deposit in Court. If the property that is the subject of the action consists in whole or in part of freight, the proceeds of property sold, or other intangible property, the clerk must issue—in addition to the warrant—a summons directing any person controlling the property to show cause why it should not be deposited in court to abide the judgment.

(d) Supplemental Process. The clerk may upon application issue supplemental process to enforce the court's order without further court order.

(4) Notice. No notice other than execution of process is required when the property that is the subject of the action has been released under Rule E(5). If the property is not released within 10 days after execution, the plaintiff must promptly—or within the time that the court allows—give public notice of the action and arrest in a newspaper designated by court order and having general circulation in the district, but publication may be terminated if the property is released before publication is completed. The notice must specify the time under Rule C(6) to file a statement of interest in or right against the seized property and to answer. This rule does not affect the notice requirements in an action to foreclose a preferred ship mortgage under 46 U.S.C. §§ 31301 et seq., as amended.

(5) Ancillary Process. In any action in rem in which process has been served as provided by this rule, if any part of the property that is the subject of the action has not been brought within the control of the court because it has been removed or sold, or because it is intangible property in the hands of a person who has not been served with process, the court may, on motion, order any person having possession or control of such property or its proceeds to show cause why it should not be delivered into the custody of the marshal or other person or organization having a warrant for the arrest of the property, or paid into court to abide the judgment; and, after hearing, the court may enter such judgment as law and justice may require.

(6) Responsive Pleading; Interrogatories.

(a) Statement of Interest; Answer. In an action in rem:

(i) a[1] person who asserts a right of possession or any ownership interest in the property that is the subject of the action must file a verified statement of right or interest:

(A) within 10 days after the execution of process, or

(B) within the time that the court allows;

(ii) the statement of right or interest must describe the interest in the property that supports the person's demand for its restitution or right to defend the action;

(iii) an agent, bailee, or attorney must state the authority to file a statement of right or interest on behalf of another; and

(iv) a person who asserts a right of possession or any ownership interest must serve an answer within 20 days after filing the statement of interest or right.

(b) Interrogatories. Interrogatories may be served with the complaint in an in rem action without leave of court. Answers to the interrogatories must be served with the answer to the complaint.

(Added Feb. 28, 1966, eff. July 1, 1966, and amended Apr. 29, 1985, eff. Aug. 1, 1985; Mar. 2, 1987, eff. Aug. 1, 1987; Apr. 30, 1991, eff. Dec. 1, 1991; Apr. 17, 2000, eff. Dec. 1, 2000; Apr. 29, 2002, eff. Dec. 1, 2002; Apr. 25, 2005, eff. Dec. 1, 2005; Apr. 12, 2006, eff. Dec. 1, 2006; Apr. 23, 2008, eff. Dec. 1, 2008.)

[1] Text begins so in original.

ADVISORY COMMITTEE NOTES

1966 Adoption

Subdivision (1).

This rule is designed not only to preserve the proceeding in rem as it now exists in admiralty cases, but to preserve the substance of Admiralty Rules 13–18. The general reference to enforcement of any maritime lien is believed to state the existing law, and is an improvement over the enumeration in the former Admiralty Rules, which is repetitious and incomplete (e.g., there was no reference to general average). The reference to any maritime lien is intended to include liens created by state law which are enforceable in admiralty.

The main concern of Admiralty Rules 13–18 was with the question whether certain actions might be brought in rem or also, or in the alternative, in personam. Essentially, therefore, these rules deal with questions of substantive law, for in general an action in rem may be brought to enforce any maritime lien, and no action in personam may be brought when the substantive law imposes no personal liability.

These rules may be summarized as follows:

1. Cases in which the plaintiff may proceed in rem and/or in personam:

a. Suits for seamen's wages;

b. Suits by materialmen for supplies, repairs, etc.;

c. Suits for pilotage;

d. Suits for collision damages;

e. Suits founded on mere maritime hypothecation;

f. Suits for salvage.

2. Cases in which the plaintiff may proceed only in personam:

a. Suits for assault and beating.

3. Cases in which the plaintiff may proceed only in rem:

a. Suits on bottomry bonds.

The coverage is incomplete, since the rules omit mention of many cases in which the plaintiff may proceed in rem or in personam. This revision proceeds on the principle that it is preferable to make a general statement as to the availability of the remedies, leaving out conclusions on matters of substantive law. Clearly it is not necessary to enumerate the cases listed under Item 1, above, nor to try to complete the list.

The rule eliminates the provision of Admiralty Rule 15 that actions for assault and beating may be brought only in personam. A preliminary study fails to disclose any reason for the rule. It is subject to so many exceptions that it is calculated to deceive rather than to inform. A seaman may sue in rem when he has been beaten by a fellow member of the crew so vicious as to render the vessel unseaworthy, *The Rolph,* 293 Fed. 269, aff'd 299 Fed. 52 (9th Cir. 1923), or where the theory of the action is that a beating by the master is a breach of the obligation under the shipping articles to treat the seaman with proper kindness, *The David Evans,* 187 Fed. 775 (D.Hawaii 1911); and a passenger may sue in rem on the theory that the assault is a breach of the contract of passage, *The Western States,* 159 Fed. 354 (2d Cir. 1908). To say that an action for money damages may be brought only in personam seems equivalent to saying that a maritime lien shall not exist; and that, in turn, seems equivalent to announcing a rule of substantive law rather than a rule of procedure. Dropping the rule will leave it to the courts to determine whether a lien exists as a matter of substantive law.

The specific reference to bottomry bonds is omitted because, as a matter of hornbook substantive law, there is no personal liability on such bonds.

Subdivision (2).

This incorporates the substance of Admiralty Rules 21 and 22.

Subdivision (3).

Derived from Admiralty Rules 10 and 37. The provision that the warrant is to be issued by the clerk is new, but is assumed to state existing law.

There is remarkably little authority bearing on Rule 37, although the subject would seem to be an important one. The rule appears on its face to have provided for a sort of ancillary process, and this may well be the case when tangible property, such as a vessel, is arrested, and intangible property such as freight is incidentally involved. It can easily happen, however, that the only property against which the action may be brought is intangible, as where the owner of a vessel under charter has a lien on subfreights. See 2 Benedict § 299 and cases cited. [Reference is to the 6th Edition of Benedict on Admiralty and not to the current 7th Edition]. In such cases it would seem that the order to the person holding the fund is equivalent to original process, taking the place of the warrant for arrest. That being so, it would also seem that (1) there should be some provision for notice, comparable to that given when tangible property is arrested, and (2) it should not be necessary, as Rule 37 provided, to petition the court for issuance of the process, but that it should issue as of course. Accordingly the substance of Rule 37 is included in the rule covering ordinary process, and notice will be required by Rule C(4). Presumably the rules omit any requirement of notice in these cases because the holder of the funds (e.g., the cargo owner) would be required on general principles (cf. *Harris v. Balk*, 198 U.S. 215 (1905)) to notify his obligee (e.g., the charterer); but in actions in rem such notice seems plainly inadequate because there may be adverse claims to the fund (e.g., there may be liens against the subfreights for seamen's wages, etc.). Compare Admiralty Rule 9.

Subdivision (4).

This carries forward the notice provision of Admiralty Rule 10, with one modification. Notice by publication is too expensive and ineffective a formality to be routinely required. When, as usually happens, the vessel or other property is released on bond or otherwise there is no point in publishing notice; the vessel is freed from the claim of the plaintiff and no other interest in the vessel can be affected by the proceedings. If, however, the vessel is not released, general notice is required in order that all persons, including unknown claimants, may appear and be heard, and in order that the judgment in rem shall be binding on all the world.

Subdivision (5).

This incorporates the substance of Admiralty Rule 9.

There are remarkably few cases dealing directly with the rule. In The *George Prescott*, 10 Fed.Cas. 222 (No. 5,339) (E.D.N.Y.1865), the master and crew of a vessel libeled her for wages, and other lienors also filed libels. One of the lienors suggested to the court that prior to the arrest of the vessel the master had removed the sails, and asked that he be ordered to produce them. He admitted removing the sails and selling them, justifying on the ground that he held a mortgage on the vessel. He was ordered to pay the proceeds into court. Cf. *United States v. The Zarko*, 187 F.Supp. 371 (S.D.Cal.1960), where an armature belonging to a vessel subject to a preferred ship mortgage was in possession of a repairman claiming a lien.

It is evident that, though the rule has had a limited career in the reported cases, it is a potentially important one. It is also evident that the rule is framed in terms narrower than the principle that supports it. There is no apparent reason for limiting it to ships and their appurtenances (2 Benedict § 299) [Reference is to the 6th Edition of Benedict on Admiralty and not to the current 7th Edition]. Also, the reference to "third parties" in the existing rule seems unfortunate. In *The George Prescott*, the person who removed and sold the sails was a plaintiff in the action, and relief against him was just as necessary as if he had been a stranger.

Another situation in which process of this kind would seem to be useful is that in which the principal property that is the subject of the action is a vessel, but her pending freight is incidentally involved. The warrant of arrest, and notice of its service, should be all that is required by way of original process and notice; ancillary process without notice should suffice as to the incidental intangibles.

The distinction between Admiralty Rules 9 and 37 is not at once apparent, but seems to be this: Where the action was against property that could not be seized by the marshal because it was intangible, the original process was required to be similar to that issued against a garnishee, and general notice was required (though not provided for by the present rule; cf. Advisory Committee's Note to Rule C(3)). Under Admiralty Rule 9 property had been arrested and general notice had been given, but some of the property had been removed or for some other reason could not be arrested. Here no further notice was necessary.

The rule also makes provision for this kind of situation: The proceeding is against a vessel's pending freight only; summons has been served on the person supposedly holding the funds, and general notice has been given; it develops that another person holds all or part of the funds. Ancillary process should be available here without further notice.

Subdivision (6).

Adherence to the practice of return days seems unsatisfactory. The practice varies significantly from district to district. A uniform rule should be provided so that any claimant or defendant can readily determine when he is required to file or serve a claim or answer.

A virtue of the return-day practice is that it requires claimants to come forward and identify themselves at an early stage of the proceedings—before they could fairly be required to answer. The draft is designed to preserve this feature of the present practice by requiring early filing of the claim. The time schedule contemplated in the draft is closely comparable to the present practice in the Southern District of New York, where the claimant has a minimum of 8 days to claim and three weeks thereafter to answer.

This rule also incorporates the substance of Admiralty Rule 25. The present rule's emphasis on "the true and bona fide owner" is omitted, since anyone having the right to possession can claim (2 Benedict § 324) [Reference is to the 6th Edition of Benedict on Admiralty and not to the current 7th Edition].

1985 Amendment

Rule C(3) has been amended to provide for judicial scrutiny before the issuance of any warrant of arrest. Its purpose is to eliminate any doubt as to the rule's constitutionality under the *Sniadach* line of cases. *Sniadach v. Family Finance Corp.*, 395 U.S. 337 (1969); *Fuentes v. Shevin*, 407 U.S. 67 (1972); *Mitchell v. W.T. Grant Co.*, 416 U.S. 600 (1974); and *North Georgia Finishing, Inc. v. Di-Chem, Inc.*, 419 U.S. 601 (1975). This was thought desirable even though both the Fourth and the Fifth Circuits have upheld the existing rule. *Amstar Corp. v. S/S Alexandros T.*, 664 F.2d 904 (4th Cir.1981); *Merchants National Bank of Mobile v. The Dredge General G.L. Gillespie*, 663 F.2d 1338 (5th Cir.1981), *cert. dismissed*, 456 U.S. 966 (1982). A contrary view was taken by Judge Tate in the *Merchants National Bank* case and by the district court in *Alyeska Pipeline Service Co. v. The Vessel Bay Ridge*, 509 F.Supp. 1115 (D.Alaska 1981), *appeal dismissed*, 703 F.2d 381 (9th Cir. 1983).

The rule envisions that the order will issue upon a prima facie showing that the plaintiff has an action in rem against the defendant in the amount sued for and that the property is within the district. A simple order with conclusory findings is contemplated. The reference to review by the "court" is broad enough to embrace a magistrate as well as a district judge.

The new provision recognizes that in some situations, such as when a judge is unavailable and the vessel is about to depart from the jurisdiction, it will be impracticable, if not impossible, to secure the judicial review contemplated by Rule C(3). When "exigent circumstances" exist, the rule enables the plaintiff to secure the issuance of the summons and warrant of arrest, subject to a later showing that the necessary circumstances actually existed. This provision is intended to provide a safety valve without undermining the requirement of pre-arrest scrutiny. Thus, every effort to secure judicial review, including conducting a hearing by telephone, should be pursued before invoking the exigent-circumstances procedure.

The foregoing requirements for prior court review or proof of exigent circumstances do not apply to actions by the United States for forfeitures for federal statutory violations. In such actions a prompt hearing is not constitutionally required, *United States v. Eight Thousand Eight Hundred and Fifty Dollars*, 103 S.Ct. 2005 (1983); *Calero-Toledo v. Pearson Yacht Leasing Co.*, 416 U.S. 663 (1974), and could prejudice the government in its prosecution of the claimants as defendants in parallel criminal proceedings since the forfeiture hearing could be misused by the defendants to obtain by way of civil discovery information to which they would not otherwise be entitled and subject the government and the courts to the unnecessary burden and expense of two hearings rather than one.

1987 Amendment

The amendments are technical. No substantive change is intended.

1991 Amendment

These amendments are designed to conform the rule to Fed.R.Civ.P. 4, as amended. As with recent amendments to Rule 4, it is intended to relieve the Marshals Service of the burden of using its limited personnel and facilities for execution of process in routine circumstances. Doing so may involve a contractual arrangement with a person or organization retained by the government to perform these services, or the use of other government officers and employees, or the special appointment by the court of persons available to perform suitably.

The seizure of a vessel, with or without cargo, remains a task assigned to the Marshal. Successful arrest of a vessel frequently requires the enforcement presence of an armed government official and the cooperation of the United States Coast Guard and other governmental authorities. If the marshal is called upon to seize the vessel, it is expected that the same officer will also be responsible for the seizure of any property on board the vessel at the time of seizure that is to be the object of arrest or attachment.

2000 Amendment

Style changes have been made throughout the revised portions of Rule C. Several changes of meaning have been made as well.

Subdivision 2. In rem jurisdiction originally extended only to property within the judicial district. Since 1986, Congress has enacted a number of jurisdictional and venue statutes for forfeiture and criminal matters that in some circumstances permit a court to exercise authority over property outside the district. 28 U.S.C. § 1355(b)(1) allows a forfeiture action in the district where an act or omission giving rise to forfeiture occurred, or in any other district where venue is established by § 1395 or by any other statute. Section 1355(b)(2) allows an action to be brought as provided in (b)(1) or in the United States District Court for the District of Columbia when the forfeiture property is located in a foreign country or has been seized by authority of a foreign government. Section 1355(d) allows a court with jurisdiction under § 1355(b) to cause service in any other district of process required to bring the forfeiture property before the court. Section 1395 establishes venue of a civil proceeding for forfeiture in the district where the forfeiture accrues or the defendant is found; in any district where the property is found; in any district into which the property is brought, if the property initially is outside any judicial district; or in any district where the vessel is arrested if the proceeding is an admiralty proceeding to forfeit a vessel. Section 1395(e) deals with a vessel or cargo entering a port of entry closed by the President, and transportation to or from a state or section declared to be in insurrection. 18 U.S.C. § 981(h) creates expanded jurisdiction and venue over property located elsewhere that is related to a criminal prosecution pending in the district. These amendments, and related amendments of Rule E(3), bring these Rules into step with the new statutes. No change is made as to admiralty and maritime proceedings that do not involve a forfeiture governed by one of the new statutes.

Subdivision (2) has been separated into lettered paragraphs to facilitate understanding.

Subdivision (3). Subdivision (3) has been rearranged and divided into lettered paragraphs to facilitate understanding.

Paragraph (b)(i) is amended to make it clear that any supplemental process addressed to a vessel or tangible property on board a vessel, as well as the original warrant, is to be served by the marshal.

Subdivision (4). Subdivision (4) has required that public notice state the time for filing an answer, but has not required that the notice set out the earlier time for filing a statement of interest or claim. The amendment requires that both times be stated.

A new provision is added, allowing termination of publication if the property is released more than 10 days after execution but before publication is completed. Termination will save money, and also will reduce the risk of confusion as to the status of the property.

Subdivision (6). Subdivision (6) has applied a single set of undifferentiated provisions to civil forfeiture proceedings and to in rem admiralty proceedings. Because some differences in procedure are desirable, these proceedings are separated by adopting a new paragraph (a) for civil forfeiture proceedings and recasting the present rule as paragraph (b) for in rem admiralty proceedings. The provision for interrogatories and answers is carried forward as paragraph (c). Although this established procedure for serving interrogatories with the complaint departs from the general provisions of Civil Rule 26(d), the special needs of expedition that often arise in admiralty justify continuing the practice.

Both paragraphs (a) and (b) require a statement of interest or right rather than the "claim" formerly required. The new wording permits parallel drafting, and facilitates cross-references in other rules. The substantive nature of the statement remains the same as the former claim. The requirements of (a) and (b) are, however, different in some respects.

In a forfeiture proceeding governed by paragraph (a), a statement must be filed by a person who asserts an interest in or a right against the property involved. This category includes every right against the property, such as a lien, whether or not it establishes ownership or a right to possession. In determining who has an interest in or a right against property, courts may continue to rely on precedents that have developed the meaning of "claims" or "claimants" for the purpose of civil forfeiture proceedings.

In an admiralty and maritime proceeding governed by paragraph (b), a statement is filed only by a person claiming a right of possession or ownership. Other claims against the property are advanced by intervention under Civil Rule 24, as it may be supplemented by local admiralty rules. The reference to ownership includes every interest that qualifies as ownership under domestic or foreign law. If an ownership interest is asserted, it makes no difference whether its character is legal, equitable, or something else.

Paragraph (a) provides more time than paragraph (b) for filing a statement. Admiralty and maritime in rem proceedings often present special needs for prompt action that do not commonly arise in forfeiture proceedings .

Paragraphs (a) and (b) do not limit the right to make a restricted appearance under Rule E(8).

2002 Amendments

Rule C(3) is amended to reflect the provisions of 18 U.S.C. § 985, enacted by the Civil Asset Forfeiture Reform Act of 2000, 114 Stat. 202, 214–215. Section 985 provides, subject to enumerated exceptions, that real property that is the subject of a civil forfeiture action is not to be seized until an order of forfeiture is entered. A civil forfeiture action is initiated by filing a complaint, posting notice, and serving notice on the property owner. The summons and arrest procedure is no longer appropriate.

Rule C(6)(a)(i)(A) is amended to adopt the provision enacted by 18 U.S.C. § 983(a)(4)(A), shortly before Rule C(6)(a)(i)(A) took effect, that sets the time for filing a verified statement as 30 days rather than 20 days, and that sets the first alternative event for measuring the 30 days as the date of service of the Government's complaint.

Rule C(6)(a)(iii) is amended to give notice of the provision enacted by 18 U.S.C. § 983(a)(4)(B) that requires that the answer in a forfeiture proceeding be filed within 20 days. Without this notice, unwary litigants might rely on the provision of Rule 5(d) that allows a reasonable time for filing after service.

Rule C(6)(b)(iv) is amended to change the requirement that an answer be filed within 20 days to a requirement that it be served within 20 days. Service is the ordinary requirement, as in Rule 12(a). Rule 5(d) requires filing within a reasonable time after service.

Changes Made After Publication and Comment No changes have been made since publication.

2005 Amendments

Rule C(6)(b)(i)(A) is amended to delete the reference to a time 10 days after completed publication under Rule C(4). This change corrects an oversight in the amendments made in 2000. Rule C(4) requires publication of notice only if the property that is the subject of the action is not released within 10 days after execution of process. Execution of process will always be earlier than publication.

2006 Amendment

Rule C is amended to reflect the adoption of Rule G to govern procedure in civil forfeiture actions.

2008 Amendments

Supplemental Rule C(6)(a)(i) is amended to correct an inadvertent omission in the 2006 amendment to Rule C. The amendment is technical and stylistic in nature. No substantive change is intended.

Rule D. Possessory, Petitory, and Partition Actions

In all actions for possession, partition, and to try title maintainable according to the course of the admiralty practice with respect to a vessel, in all actions so maintainable with respect to the possession of cargo or other maritime property, and in all actions by one or more part owners against the others to obtain security for the return of the vessel from any voyage undertaken without their consent, or by one or more part owners against the others to obtain possession of the vessel for any voyage on giving security for its safe return, the process shall be by a warrant of arrest of the vessel, cargo, or other property, and by

notice in the manner provided by Rule B(2) to the adverse party or parties.
(Added Feb. 28, 1966, eff. July 1, 1966.)

ADVISORY COMMITTEE NOTES

1966 Adoption

This carries forward the substance of Admiralty Rule 19.

Rule 19 provided the remedy of arrest in controversies involving title and possession in general. See *The Tilton*, 23 Fed.Cas.1277 (No. 14,054) (C.C.D.Mass.1830). In addition it provided that remedy in controversies between co-owners respecting the employment of a vessel. It did not deal comprehensively with controversies between co-owners, omitting the remedy of partition. Presumably the omission is traceable to the fact that, when the rules were originally promulgated, concepts of substantive law (sometimes stated as concepts of jurisdiction) denied the remedy of partition except where the parties in disagreement were the owners of equal shares. See *The Steamboat Orleans*, 36 U.S. (11 Pet.) 175 (1837). The Supreme Court has now removed any doubt as to the jurisdiction of the district courts to partition a vessel, and has held in addition that no fixed principle of federal admiralty law limits the remedy to the case of equal shares. *Madruga v. Superior Court*, 346 U.S. 556 (1954). It is therefore appropriate to include a reference to partition in the rule.

Rule E. Actions in Rem and Quasi in Rem: General Provisions

(1) Applicability. Except as otherwise provided, this rule applies to actions in personam with process of maritime attachment and garnishment, actions in rem, and petitory, possessory, and partition actions, supplementing Rules B, C, and D.

(2) Complaint; Security.

(a) *Complaint.* In actions to which this rule is applicable the complaint shall state the circumstances from which the claim arises with such particularity that the defendant or claimant will be able, without moving for a more definite statement, to commence an investigation of the facts and to frame a responsive pleading.

(b) *Security for Costs.* Subject to the provisions of Rule 54(d) and of relevant statutes, the court may, on the filing of the complaint or on the appearance of any defendant, claimant, or any other party, or at any later time, require the plaintiff, defendant, claimant, or other party to give security, or additional security, in such sum as the court shall direct to pay all costs and expenses that shall be awarded against the party by any interlocutory order or by the final judgment, or on appeal by any appellate court.

(3) Process.

(a) In admiralty and maritime proceedings process in rem or of maritime attachment and garnishment may be served only within the district.

(b) Issuance and Delivery. Issuance and delivery of process in rem, or of maritime attachment and garnishment, shall be held in abeyance if the plaintiff so requests.

(4) Execution of Process; Marshal's Return; Custody of Property; Procedures for Release.

(a) *In General.* Upon issuance and delivery of the process, or, in the case of summons with process of attachment and garnishment, when it appears that the defendant cannot be found within the district, the marshal or other person or organization having a warrant shall forthwith execute the process in accordance with this subdivision (4), making due and prompt return.

(b) *Tangible Property.* If tangible property is to be attached or arrested, the marshal or other person or organization having the warrant shall take it into the marshal's possession for safe custody. If the character or situation of the property is such that the taking of actual possession is impracticable, the marshal or other person executing the process shall affix a copy thereof to the property in a conspicuous place and leave a copy of the complaint and process with the person having possession or the person's agent. In furtherance of the marshal's custody of any vessel the marshal is authorized to make a written request to the collector of customs not to grant clearance to such vessel until notified by the marshal or deputy marshal or by the clerk that the vessel has been released in accordance with these rules.

(c) *Intangible Property.* If intangible property is to be attached or arrested the marshal or other person or organization having the warrant shall execute the process by leaving with the garnishee or other obligor a copy of the complaint and process requiring the garnishee or other obligor to answer as provided in Rules B(3)(a) and C(6); or the marshal may accept for payment into the registry of the court the amount owed to the extent of the amount claimed by the plaintiff with interest and costs, in which event the garnishee or other obligor shall not be required to answer unless alias process shall be served.

(d) *Directions With Respect to Property in Custody.* The marshal or other person or organization having the warrant may at any time apply to the court for directions with respect to property that has been attached or arrested, and shall give notice of such application to any or all of the parties as the court may direct.

(e) *Expenses of Seizing and Keeping Property; Deposit.* These rules do not alter the provisions of Title 28, U.S.C., § 1921, as amended, relative to the expenses of seizing and keeping property attached or arrested and to the requirement of deposits to cover such expenses.

(f) *Procedure for Release From Arrest or Attachment.* Whenever property is arrested or attached, any person claiming an interest in it shall be entitled to a prompt hearing at which the plaintiff shall be required to show why the arrest or attachment should not be vacated or other relief granted consistent with these rules. This subdivision shall have no application to suits for seamen's wages when process is issued upon a certification of sufficient cause filed pursuant to Title 46, U.S.C. §§ 603 and 604 or to actions by the United States for forfeitures for violation of any statute of the United States.

(5) Release of Property.

(a) *Special Bond.* Whenever process of maritime attachment and garnishment or process in rem is issued the execution of such process shall be stayed, or the property released, on the giving of security, to be approved by the court or clerk, or by stipulation of the parties, conditioned to answer the judgment of the court or of any appellate court. The parties may stipulate the amount and nature of such security. In the event of the inability or refusal of the parties so to stipulate the court shall fix the principal sum of the bond or stipulation at an amount sufficient to cover the amount of the plaintiff's claim fairly stated with accrued interest and costs; but the principal sum shall in no event exceed (i) twice the amount of the plaintiff's claim or (ii) the value of the property on due appraisement, whichever is smaller. The bond or stipulation shall be conditioned for the payment of the principal sum and interest thereon at 6 per cent per annum.

(b) *General Bond.* The owner of any vessel may file a general bond or stipulation, with sufficient surety, to be approved by the court, conditioned to answer the judgment of such court in all or any actions that may be brought thereafter in such court in which the vessel is attached or arrested. Thereupon the execution of all such process against such vessel shall be stayed so long as the amount secured by such bond or stipulation is at least double the aggregate amount claimed by plaintiffs in all actions begun and pending in which such vessel has been attached or arrested. Judgments and remedies may be had on such bond or stipulation as if a special bond or stipulation had been filed in each of such actions. The district court may make necessary orders to carry this rule into effect, particularly as to the giving of proper notice of any action against or attachment of a vessel for which a general bond has been filed. Such bond or stipulation shall be indorsed by the clerk with a minute of the actions wherein process is so stayed. Further security may be required by the court at any time.

If a special bond or stipulation is given in a particular case, the liability on the general bond or stipulation shall cease as to that case.

(c) *Release by Consent or Stipulation; Order of Court or Clerk; Costs.* Any vessel, cargo, or other property in the custody of the marshal or other person or organization having the warrant may be released forthwith upon the marshal's acceptance and approval of a stipulation, bond, or other security, signed by the party on whose behalf the property is detained or the party's attorney and expressly authorizing such release, if all costs and charges of the court and its officers shall have first been paid. Otherwise no property in the custody of the marshal, other person or organization having the warrant, or other officer of the court shall be released without an order of the court; but such order may be entered as of course by the clerk, upon the giving of approved security as provided by law and these rules, or upon the dismissal or discontinuance of the action; but the marshal or other person or organization having the warrant shall not deliver any property so released until the costs and charges of the officers of the court shall first have been paid.

(d) *Possessory, Petitory, and Partition Actions.* The foregoing provisions of this subdivision (5) do not apply to petitory, possessory, and partition actions. In such cases the property arrested shall be released only by order of the court, on such terms and conditions and on the giving of such security as the court may require.

(6) Reduction or Impairment of Security. Whenever security is taken the court may, on motion and hearing, for good cause shown, reduce the amount of security given; and if the surety shall be or become insufficient, new or additional sureties may be required on motion and hearing.

(7) Security on Counterclaim.

(a) When a person who has given security for damages in the original action asserts a counterclaim that arises from the transaction or occurrence that is the subject of the original action, a plaintiff for whose benefit the security has been given must give security for damages demanded in the counterclaim unless the court for cause shown, directs otherwise. Proceedings on the original claim must be stayed until this security is given unless the court directs otherwise.

(b) The plaintiff is required to give security under Rule E(7)(a) when the United States or its corporate instrumentality counterclaims and would have been required to give security to respond in damages if a private party but is relieved by law from giving security.

(8) Restricted Appearance. An appearance to defend against an admiralty and maritime claim with respect to which there has issued process in rem, or process of attachment and garnishment, may be expressly restricted to the defense of such claim, and in that event is not an appearance for the purposes of any other claim with respect to which such process is not available or has not been served.

(9) Disposition of Property; Sales.

(a) Interlocutory Sales; Delivery.

(i) On application of a party, the marshal, or other person having custody of the property, the court may order all or part of the property sold—with the sales proceeds, or as much of them as will satisfy the judgment, paid into court to await further orders of the court—if:

(A) the attached or arrested property is perishable, or liable to deterioration, decay, or injury by being detained in custody pending the action;

(B) the expense of keeping the property is excessive or disproportionate; or

(C) there is an unreasonable delay in securing release of the property.

(ii) In the circumstances described in Rule E(9)(a)(i), the court, on motion by a defendant or a person filing a statement of interest or right under Rule C(6), may order that the property, rather than being sold, be delivered to the movant upon giving security under these rules.

(b) Sales; Proceeds. All sales of property shall be made by the marshal or a deputy marshal, or by other person or organization having the warrant, or by any other person assigned by the court where the marshal or other person or organization having the warrant is a party in interest; and the proceeds of sale shall be forthwith paid into the registry of the court to be disposed of according to law.

(10) Preservation of Property. When the owner or another person remains in possession of property attached or arrested under the provisions of Rule E(4)(b) that permit execution of process without taking actual possession, the court, on a party's motion or on its own, may enter any order necessary to preserve the property and to prevent its removal.

(Added Feb. 28, 1966, eff. July 1, 1966, and amended Apr. 29, 1985, eff. Aug. 1, 1985; Mar. 2, 1987, eff. Aug. 1, 1987; Apr. 30, 1991, eff. Dec. 1, 1991; Apr. 17, 2000, eff. Dec. 1, 2000; Apr. 12, 2006, eff. Dec. 1, 2006.)

ADVISORY COMMITTEE NOTES

1966 Adoption

Subdivisions (1), (2).

Adapted from Admiralty Rule 24. The rule is based on the assumption that there is no more need for security for costs in maritime personal actions than in civil cases generally, but that there is reason to retain the requirement for actions in which property is seized. As to proceedings for limitation of liability see Rule F(1).

Subdivision (3).

The Advisory Committee has concluded for practical reasons that process requiring seizure of property should continue to be served only within the geographical limits of the district. Compare Rule B(1), continuing the condition that process of attachment and garnishment may be served only if the defendant is not found within the district.

The provisions of Admiralty Rule 1 concerning the persons by whom process is to be served will be superseded by FRCP 4(c).

Subdivision (4).

This rule is intended to preserve the provisions of Admiralty Rules 10 and 36 relating to execution of process, custody of property seized by the marshal, and the marshal's return. It is also designed to make express provision for matters not heretofore covered.

The provision relating to clearance in subdivision (b) is suggested by Admiralty Rule 44 of the District of Maryland.

Subdivision (d) is suggested by English Rule 12, Order 75.

28 U.S.C., § 1921 as amended in 1962 contains detailed provisions relating to the expenses of seizing and preserving property attached or arrested.

Subdivision (5).

In addition to Admiralty Rule 11 (see Rule E(9)), the release of property seized on process of attachment or in rem was dealt with by Admiralty Rules 5, 6, 12, and 57, and 28 U.S.C., § 2464 (formerly Rev.Stat. § 941). The rule consolidates these provisions and makes them uniformly applicable to attachment and garnishment and actions in rem.

The rule restates the substance of Admiralty Rule 5. Admiralty Rule 12 dealt only with ships arrested on in rem process. Since the same ground appears to be covered more generally by 28 U.S.C., § 2464, the subject matter of Rule 12 is omitted. The substance of Admiralty Rule 57 is retained. 28 U.S.C., § 2464 is incorporated with changes of terminology, and with a substantial change as to the amount of the bond. See 2 Benedict 395 n. 1a [Reference is to the 6th Edition of Benedict on Admiralty and not to the current 7th Edition.] *The Lotosland*, 2 F.Supp. 42 (S.D.N.Y.1933). The provision for general bond is enlarged to include the contingency of attachment as well as arrest of the vessel.

Subdivision (6).

Adapted from Admiralty Rule 8.

Subdivision (7).

Derived from Admiralty Rule 50.

Title 46, U.S.C., § 783 extends the principle of Rule 50 to the Government when sued under the Public Vessels Act, presumably on the theory that the credit of the Government is the equivalent of the best security. The rule adopts this principle and extends it to all cases in which the Government is defendant although the Suits in Admiralty Act contains no parallel provisions.

Subdivision (8).

Under the liberal joinder provisions of unified rules the plaintiff will be enabled to join with maritime actions in rem, or maritime actions in personam with process of attachment and garnishment, claims with respect to which such process is not available, including nonmaritime claims. Unification should not, however, have the result that, in order to defend against an admiralty and maritime claim with respect to which process in rem or quasi in rem has been served, the claimant or defendant must subject himself personally to the jurisdiction of the court with reference to other claims with respect to which such process is not available or has not been served, especially when such other claims are nonmaritime. So far as attachment and garnishment are concerned this principle holds true whether process is issued according to admiralty tradition and the Supplemental Rules or according to Rule 4(e) as incorporated by Rule B(1).

A similar problem may arise with respect to civil actions other than admiralty and maritime claims within the meaning of Rule 9(h). That is to say, in an ordinary civil action, whether maritime or not, there may be joined in one action claims with respect to which process of attachment and garnishment is available under state law and Rule 4(e) and claims with respect to which such process is not available or has not been served. The general Rules of Civil Procedure do not specify whether an appearance in such cases to defend the claim with respect to which process of attachment and garnishment has issued is an appearance for the purposes of the other claims. In that context the question has been considered best left to case-by-case development. Where admiralty and maritime claims within the meaning of Rule 9(h) are concerned, however, it seems important to include a specific provision to avoid an unfortunate and unintended effect of unification. No inferences whatever as to the effect of such an appearance in an ordinary civil action should be drawn from the specific provision here and the absence of such a provision in the general Rules.

Subdivision (9).

Adapted from Admiralty Rules 11, 12, and 40. Subdivision (a) is necessary because of various provisions as to disposition of property in forfeiture proceedings. In addition to particular statutes, note the provisions of 28 U.S.C., §§ 2461–65.

The provision of Admiralty Rule 12 relating to unreasonable delay was limited to ships but should have broader application. See 2 Benedict 404 [Reference is to the 6th Edition of Benedict on Admiralty and not to the current 7th Edition]. Similarly, both Rules 11 and 12 were limited to actions in rem, but should equally apply to attached property.

1985 Amendment

Rule E(4)(f) makes available the type of prompt post-seizure hearing in proceedings under Supplemental Rules B and C that the Supreme Court has called for in a number of cases arising in other contexts. See *North Georgia Finishing, Inc. v. Di-Chem, Inc.*, 419 U.S. 601 (1975); *Mitchell v. W.T. Grant Co.*, 416 U.S. 600 (1974). Although post-attachment and post-arrest hearings always have been available on motion, an explicit statement emphasizing promptness and elaborating the procedure has been lacking in the Supplemental Rules. Rule E(4)(f) is designed to satisfy the constitutional requirement of due process by guaranteeing to the shipowner a prompt post-seizure hearing at which he can attack the complaint, the arrest, the security demanded, or any other alleged deficiency in the proceedings. The amendment also is intended to eliminate the previously disparate treatment under local rules of defendants whose property has been seized pursuant to Supplemental Rules B and C.

The new Rule E(4)(f) is based on a proposal by the Maritime Law Association of the United States and on local admiralty rules in the Eastern, Northern, and Southern Districts of New York. E.D.N.Y. Local Rule 13; N.D.N.Y. Local Rule 13; S.D.N.Y. Local Rule 12. Similar provisions have been adopted by other maritime districts. E.g., N.D.Calif. Local Rule 603.4; W.D.La. Local Admiralty Rule 21. Rule E(4)(f) will provide uniformity in practice and reduce constitutional uncertainties.

Rule E(4)(f) is triggered by the defendant or any other person with an interest in the property seized. Upon an oral or written application similar to that used in seeking a temporary restraining order, see Rule 65(b), the court is required to hold a hearing as promptly as possible to determine whether to allow the arrest or attachment to stand. The plaintiff has the burden of showing why the seizure should not be vacated. The hearing also may determine the amount of security to be granted or the propriety of imposing counter-security to protect the defendant from an improper seizure.

The foregoing requirements for prior court review or proof of exigent circumstances do not apply to actions by the United States for forfeitures for federal statutory violations. In such actions a prompt hearing is not constitutionally required, *United States v. Eight Thousand Eight Hundred and Fifty Dollars*, 103 S.Ct. 2005 (1983); *Calero-Toledo v. Pearson Yacht Leasing Co.*, 416 U.S. 663 (1974), and could prejudice the government in its prosecution of the claimants as defendants in parallel criminal proceedings since the forfeiture hearing could be misused by the defendants to obtain by way of civil discovery information to which they would not otherwise be entitled and subject the government and the courts to the unnecessary burden and expense of two hearings rather than one.

1987 Amendment

The amendments are technical. No substantive change is intended.

1991 Amendment

These amendments are designed to conform this rule to Fed.R.Civ.P. 4, as amended. They are intended to relieve the Marshals Service of the burden of using its limited personnel and facilities for execution of process in routine circumstances. Doing so may involve a contractual arrangement with a person or organization retained by the government to perform these services, or the use of other government officers and employees, or the special appointment by the court of persons available to perform suitably.

2000 Amendment

Style changes have been made throughout the revised portions of Rule E. Several changes of meaning have been made as well.

Subdivision (3). Subdivision (3) is amended to reflect the distinction drawn in Rule C(2)(c) and (d). Service in an admiralty or maritime proceeding still must be made within the district, as reflected in Rule C(2)(c), while service in forfeiture proceedings may be made outside the district when authorized by statute, as reflected in Rule C(2)(d).

Subdivision (7). Subdivision (7)(a) is amended to make it clear that a plaintiff need give security to meet a counterclaim only when the counterclaim is asserted by a person who has given security to respond in damages in the original action.

Subdivision (8). Subdivision (8) is amended to reflect the change in Rule B(1)(e) that deletes the former provision incorporating state quasi-in-rem jurisdiction. A restricted appearance is not appropriate when state law is invoked only for security under Civil Rule 64, not as a basis of quasi-in-rem jurisdiction. But if state law allows a special, limited, or restricted appearance as an incident of the remedy adopted from state law, the state practice applies through Rule 64 "in the manner provided by" state law.

Subdivision (9). Subdivision 9(b)(ii) is amended to reflect the change in Rule C(6) that substitutes a statement of interest or right for a claim.

Subdivision (10). Subdivision 10 is new. It makes clear the authority of the court to preserve and to prevent removal of attached or arrested property that remains in the possession of the owner or other person under Rule E(4)(b).

2006 Amendment

Rule E is amended to reflect the adoption of Rule G to govern procedure in civil forfeiture actions.

HISTORICAL NOTES

References in Text

Sections 603 and 604 of Title 46, referred to in subd. (4)(f), were repealed by Pub.L. 98–89, § 4(b), Aug. 26, 1983, 97 Stat. 600, section 1 of which enacted Title 46, Shipping.

Rule F. Limitation of Liability

(1) Time for Filing Complaint; Security. Not later than six months after receipt of a claim in writing, any vessel owner may file a complaint in the appropriate district court, as provided in subdivision (9) of this rule, for limitation of liability pursuant to statute. The owner (a) shall deposit with the court, for the benefit of claimants, a sum equal to the amount or value of the owner's interest in the vessel and pending freight, or approved security therefor, and in addition such sums, or approved security therefor, as the court may from time to time fix as necessary to carry out the provisions of the statutes as amended; or (b) at the owner's option shall transfer to a trustee to be appointed by the court, for the benefit of claimants, the owner's interest in the vessel and pending freight, together with such sums, or approved security therefor, as the court may from time to time fix as necessary to carry out the provisions of the statutes as amended. The plaintiff shall also give security for costs and, if the plaintiff elects to give security, for interest at the rate of 6 percent per annum from the date of the security.

(2) Complaint. The complaint shall set forth the facts on the basis of which the right to limit liability is asserted and all facts necessary to enable the court to determine the amount to which the owner's liability shall be limited. The complaint may demand exoneration from as well as limitation of liability. It shall state the voyage if any, on which the demands sought to be limited arose, with the date and place of its termination; the amount of all demands including all unsatisfied liens or claims of lien, in contract or in tort or otherwise, arising on that voyage, so far as known to the plaintiff, and what actions and proceedings, if any, are pending thereon; whether the vessel was damaged, lost, or abandoned, and, if so, when and where; the value of the vessel at the close of the voyage or, in case of wreck, the value of her wreckage, strippings, or proceeds, if any, and where and in whose possession they are; and the amount of any pending freight recovered or recoverable. If the plaintiff elects to transfer the plaintiff's interest in the vessel to a trustee, the complaint must further show any prior paramount liens thereon, and what voyages or trips, if any, she has made since the voyage or trip on which the claims sought to be limited arose, and any existing liens arising upon any such subsequent voyage or trip, with the amounts and causes thereof, and the names and addresses of the lienors, so far as known; and whether the vessel sustained any injury upon or by reason of such subsequent voyage or trip.

(3) Claims Against Owner; Injunction. Upon compliance by the owner with the requirements of subdivision (1) of this rule all claims and proceedings against the owner or the owner's property with respect to the matter in question shall cease. On application of the plaintiff the court shall enjoin the further prosecution of any action or proceeding against the plaintiff or the plaintiff's property with respect to any claim subject to limitation in the action.

(4) Notice to Claimants. Upon the owner's compliance with subdivision (1) of this rule the court shall issue a notice to all persons asserting claims with respect to which the complaint seeks limitation, admonishing them to file their respective claims with the clerk of the court and to serve on the attorneys for the plaintiff a copy thereof on or before a date to be named in the notice. The date so fixed shall not be less than 30 days after issuance of the notice. For cause shown, the court may enlarge the time within which claims may be filed. The notice shall be published in such newspaper or newspapers as the court may direct once a week for four successive weeks prior to the date fixed for the filing of claims. The plaintiff not later than the day of second publication shall also mail a copy of the notice to every person known to have made any claim against the vessel or the plaintiff arising out of the voyage or trip on which the claims sought to be limited arose. In cases involving death a copy of such notice shall be mailed to the decedent at the decedent's last known address, and also to any person who shall be known to have made any claim on account of such death.

(5) Claims and Answer. Claims shall be filed and served on or before the date specified in the notice provided for in subdivision (4) of this rule. Each claim shall specify the facts upon which the claimant relies in support of the claim, the items thereof, and the dates on which the same accrued. If a claimant desires to contest either the right to exoneration from or the right to limitation of liability the claimant shall file and serve an answer to the complaint unless the claim has included an answer.

(6) Information to be Given Claimants. Within 30 days after the date specified in the notice for filing claims, or within such time as the court thereafter may allow, the plaintiff shall mail to the attorney for each claimant (or if the claimant has no attorney to the claimant) a list setting forth (a) the name of each claimant, (b) the name and address of the claimant's attorney (if the claimant is known to have one), (c) the nature of the claim, i.e., whether property loss, property damage, death, personal injury etc., and (d) the amount thereof.

(7) Insufficiency of Fund or Security. Any claimant may by motion demand that the funds deposited in court or the security given by the plaintiff be increased on the ground that they are less than the value of the plaintiff's interest in the vessel and pending freight. Thereupon the court shall cause due appraisement to be made of the value of the plaintiff's interest in the vessel and pending freight; and if the court finds that the deposit or security is either insufficient or excessive it shall order its increase or reduction. In like manner any claimant may demand that the deposit or security be increased on the ground that it is insufficient to carry out the provisions of the statutes relating to claims in respect of loss of life or bodily injury; and, after notice and hearing, the court may similarly order that the deposit or security be increased or reduced.

(8) Objections to Claims: Distribution of Fund. Any interested party may question or controvert any claim without filing an objection thereto. Upon determination of liability the fund deposited or secured, or the proceeds of the vessel and pending freight, shall be divided pro rata, subject to all relevant provisions of law, among the several claimants in proportion to the amounts of their respective claims, duly proved, saving, however, to all parties any priority to which they may be legally entitled.

(9) Venue; Transfer. The complaint shall be filed in any district in which the vessel has been attached or arrested to answer for any claim with respect to which the plaintiff seeks to limit liability; or, if the vessel has not been attached or arrested, then in any district in which the owner has been sued with respect to any such claim. When the vessel has not been attached or arrested to answer the matters aforesaid, and suit has not been commenced against the owner, the proceedings may be had in the district in which the vessel may be, but if the vessel is not within any district and no suit has been commenced in any district, then the complaint may be filed in any district. For the convenience of parties and witnesses, in the interest of justice, the court may transfer the action to any district; if venue is wrongly laid the court shall dismiss or, if it be in the interest of justice, transfer the action to any district in which it could have been brought. If the vessel shall have been sold, the proceeds shall represent the vessel for the purposes of these rules.

(Added Feb. 28, 1966, eff. July 1, 1966, and amended Mar. 2, 1987, eff. Aug. 1, 1987.)

ADVISORY COMMITTEE NOTES

1966 Adoption

Subdivision (1).

The amendments of 1936 to the Limitation Act superseded to some extent the provisions of Admiralty Rule 51, especially with respect to the time of filing the complaint and with respect to security. The rule here incorporates in substance the 1936 amendment of the Act (46 U.S.C., § 185) with a slight modification to make it clear that the complaint may be filed at any time not later than six months after a claim has been lodged with the owner.

Subdivision (2).

Derived from Admiralty Rules 51 and 53.

Subdivision (3).

This is derived from the last sentence of 46 U.S.C. § 185 and the last paragraph of Admiralty Rule 51.

Subdivision (4).

Derived from Admiralty Rule 51.

Subdivision (5).

Derived from Admiralty Rules 52 and 53.

Subdivision (6).

Derived from Admiralty Rule 52.

Subdivision (7).

Derived from Admiralty Rule 52 and 46 U.S.C., § 185.

Subdivision (8).

Derived from Admiralty Rule 52.

Subdivision (9).

Derived from Admiralty Rule 54. The provision for transfer is revised to conform closely to the language of 28 U.S.C. §§ 1404(a) and 1406(a), though it retains the existing rule's provision for transfer to any district for convenience. The revision also makes clear what has been doubted: that the court may transfer if venue is wrongly laid.

1987 Amendment

The amendments are technical. No substantive change is intended.

Rule G. Forfeiture Actions In Rem

(1) Scope. This rule governs a forfeiture action in rem arising from a federal statute. To the extent that this rule does not address an issue, Supplemental

Rules C and E and the Federal Rules of Civil Procedure also apply.

(2) **Complaint.** The complaint must:

(a) be verified;

(b) state the grounds for subject-matter jurisdiction, in rem jurisdiction over the defendant property, and venue;

(c) describe the property with reasonable particularity;

(d) if the property is tangible, state its location when any seizure occurred and — if different — its location when the action is filed;

(e) identify the statute under which the forfeiture action is brought; and

(f) state sufficiently detailed facts to support a reasonable belief that the government will be able to meet its burden of proof at trial.

(3) **Judicial Authorization and Process.**

(a) **Real Property.** If the defendant is real property, the government must proceed under 18 U.S.C. § 985.

(b) **Other Property; Arrest Warrant.** If the defendant is not real property:

(i) the clerk must issue a warrant to arrest the property if it is in the government's possession, custody, or control;

(ii) the court—on finding probable cause—must issue a warrant to arrest the property if it is not in the government's possession, custody, or control and is not subject to a judicial restraining order; and

(iii) a warrant is not necessary if the property is subject to a judicial restraining order.

(c) **Execution of Process.**

(i) The warrant and any supplemental process must be delivered to a person or organization authorized to execute it, who may be: (A) a marshal or any other United States officer or employee; (B) someone under contract with the United States; or (C) someone specially appointed by the court for that purpose.

(ii) The authorized person or organization must execute the warrant and any supplemental process on property in the United States as soon as practicable unless:

(A) the property is in the government's possession, custody, or control; or

(B) the court orders a different time when the complaint is under seal, the action is stayed before the warrant and supplemental process are executed, or the court finds other good cause.

(iii) The warrant and any supplemental process may be executed within the district or, when authorized by statute, outside the district.

(iv) If executing a warrant on property outside the United States is required, the warrant may be transmitted to an appropriate authority for serving process where the property is located.

(4) **Notice.**

(a) **Notice by Publication.**

(i) **When Publication Is Required.** A judgment of forfeiture may be entered only if the government has published notice of the action within a reasonable time after filing the complaint or at a time the court orders. But notice need not be published if:

(A) the defendant property is worth less than $1,000 and direct notice is sent under Rule G(4)(b) to every person the government can reasonably identify as a potential claimant; or

(B) the court finds that the cost of publication exceeds the property's value and that other means of notice would satisfy due process.

(ii) **Content of the Notice.** Unless the court orders otherwise, the notice must:

(A) describe the property with reasonable particularity;

(B) state the times under Rule G(5) to file a claim and to answer; and

(C) name the government attorney to be served with the claim and answer.

(iii) **Frequency of Publication.** Published notice must appear:

(A) once a week for three consecutive weeks; or

(B) only once if, before the action was filed, notice of nonjudicial forfeiture of the same property was published on an official internet government forfeiture site for at least 30 consecutive days, or in a newspaper of general circulation for three consecutive weeks in a district where publication is authorized under Rule G(4)(a)(iv).

(iv) **Means of Publication.** The government should select from the following options a means of publication reasonably calculated to notify potential claimants of the action:

(A) if the property is in the United States, publication in a newspaper generally circulated in the district where the action is filed, where the property was seized, or where property that was not seized is located;

(B) if the property is outside the United States, publication in a newspaper generally circulated in a district where the action is filed, in a newspaper generally circulated in the country where the property is located, or in legal notices published and generally circulated in the country where the property is located; or

(C) instead of (A) or (B), posting a notice on an official internet government forfeiture site for at least 30 consecutive days.

(b) Notice to Known Potential Claimants.

(i) Direct Notice Required. The government must send notice of the action and a copy of the complaint to any person who reasonably appears to be a potential claimant on the facts known to the government before the end of the time for filing a claim under Rule G(5)(a)(ii)(B).

(ii) Content of the Notice. The notice must state:

(A) the date when the notice is sent;

(B) a deadline for filing a claim, at least 35 days after the notice is sent;

(C) that an answer or a motion under Rule 12 must be filed no later than 20 days after filing the claim; and

(D) the name of the government attorney to be served with the claim and answer.

(iii) Sending Notice.

(A) The notice must be sent by means reasonably calculated to reach the potential claimant.

(B) Notice may be sent to the potential claimant or to the attorney representing the potential claimant with respect to the seizure of the property or in a related investigation, administrative forfeiture proceeding, or criminal case.

(C) Notice sent to a potential claimant who is incarcerated must be sent to the place of incarceration.

(D) Notice to a person arrested in connection with an offense giving rise to the forfeiture who is not incarcerated when notice is sent may be sent to the address that person last gave to the agency that arrested or released the person.

(E) Notice to a person from whom the property was seized who is not incarcerated when notice is sent may be sent to the last address that person gave to the agency that seized the property.

(iv) When Notice Is Sent. Notice by the following means is sent on the date when it is placed in the mail, delivered to a commercial carrier, or sent by electronic mail.

(v) Actual Notice. A potential claimant who had actual notice of a forfeiture action may not oppose or seek relief from forfeiture because of the government's failure to send the required notice.

(5) Responsive Pleadings.

(a) Filing a Claim.

(i) A person who asserts an interest in the defendant property may contest the forfeiture by filing a claim in the court where the action is pending. The claim must:

(A) identify the specific property claimed;

(B) identify the claimant and state the claimant's interest in the property;

(C) be signed by the claimant under penalty of perjury; and

(D) be served on the government attorney designated under Rule G(4)(a)(ii)(C) or (b)(ii)(D).

(ii) Unless the court for good cause sets a different time, the claim must be filed:

(A) by the time stated in a direct notice sent under Rule G(4)(b);

(B) if notice was published but direct notice was not sent to the claimant or the claimant's attorney, no later than 30 days after final publication of newspaper notice or legal notice under Rule G(4)(a) or no later than 60 days after the first day of publication on an official internet government forfeiture site; or

(C) if notice was not published and direct notice was not sent to the claimant or the claimant's attorney:

(1) if the property was in the government's possession, custody, or control when the complaint was filed, no later than 60 days after the filing, not counting any time when the complaint was under seal or when the action was stayed before execution of a warrant issued under Rule G(3)(b); or

(2) if the property was not in the government's possession, custody, or control when the complaint was filed, no later than 60 days after the government complied with 18 U.S.C. § 985(c) as to real property, or 60 days after process was executed on the property under Rule G(3).

(iii) A claim filed by a person asserting an interest as a bailee must identify the bailor, and if filed on the bailor's behalf must state the authority to do so.

(b) Answer. A claimant must serve and file an answer to the complaint or a motion under Rule 12 within 20 days after filing the claim. A claimant waives an objection to in rem jurisdiction or to venue if the objection is not made by motion or stated in the answer.

(6) Special Interrogatories.

(a) Time and Scope. The government may serve special interrogatories limited to the claimant's identity and relationship to the defendant property without the court's leave at any time after the claim is filed and before discovery is closed.

But if the claimant serves a motion to dismiss the action, the government must serve the interrogatories within 20 days after the motion is served.

(b) Answers or Objections. Answers or objections to these interrogatories must be served within 20 days after the interrogatories are served.

(c) Government's Response Deferred. The government need not respond to a claimant's motion to dismiss the action under Rule G(8)(b) until 20 days after the claimant has answered these interrogatories.

(7) Preserving, Preventing Criminal Use, and Disposing of Property; Sales.

(a) Preserving and Preventing Criminal Use of Property. When the government does not have actual possession of the defendant property the court, on motion or on its own, may enter any order necessary to preserve the property, to prevent its removal or encumbrance, or to prevent its use in a criminal offense.

(b) Interlocutory Sale or Delivery.

(i) Order to Sell. On motion by a party or a person having custody of the property, the court may order all or part of the property sold if:

(A) the property is perishable or at risk of deterioration, decay, or injury by being detained in custody pending the action;

(B) the expense of keeping the property is excessive or is disproportionate to its fair market value;

(C) the property is subject to a mortgage or to taxes on which the owner is in default; or

(D) the court finds other good cause.

(ii) Who Makes the Sale. A sale must be made by a United States agency that has authority to sell the property, by the agency's contractor, or by any person the court designates.

(iii) Sale Procedures. The sale is governed by 28 U.S.C. §§ 2001, 2002, and 2004, unless all parties, with the court's approval, agree to the sale, aspects of the sale, or different procedures.

(iv) Sale Proceeds. Sale proceeds are a substitute res subject to forfeiture in place of the property that was sold. The proceeds must be held in an interest-bearing account maintained by the United States pending the conclusion of the forfeiture action.

(v) Delivery on a Claimant's Motion. The court may order that the property be delivered to the claimant pending the conclusion of the action if the claimant shows circumstances that would permit sale under Rule G(7)(b)(i) and gives security under these rules.

(c) Disposing of Forfeited Property. Upon entry of a forfeiture judgment, the property or proceeds from selling the property must be disposed of as provided by law.

(8) Motions.

(a) Motion To Suppress Use of the Property as Evidence. If the defendant property was seized, a party with standing to contest the lawfulness of the seizure may move to suppress use of the property as evidence. Suppression does not affect forfeiture of the property based on independently derived evidence.

(b) Motion To Dismiss the Action.

(i) A claimant who establishes standing to contest forfeiture may move to dismiss the action under Rule 12(b).

(ii) In an action governed by 18 U.S.C. § 983(a)(3)(D) the complaint may not be dismissed on the ground that the government did not have adequate evidence at the time the complaint was filed to establish the forfeitability of the property. The sufficiency of the complaint is governed by Rule G(2).

(c) Motion To Strike a Claim or Answer.

(i) At any time before trial, the government may move to strike a claim or answer:

(A) for failing to comply with Rule G(5) or (6), or

(B) because the claimant lacks standing.

(ii) The motion:

(A) must be decided before any motion by the claimant to dismiss the action; and

(B) may be presented as a motion for judgment on the pleadings or as a motion to determine after a hearing or by summary judgment whether the claimant can carry the burden of establishing standing by a preponderance of the evidence.

(d) Petition To Release Property.

(i) If a United States agency or an agency's contractor holds property for judicial or nonjudicial forfeiture under a statute governed by 18 U.S.C. § 983(f), a person who has filed a claim to the property may petition for its release under § 983(f).

(ii) If a petition for release is filed before a judicial forfeiture action is filed against the property, the petition may be filed either in the district where the property was seized or in the district where a warrant to seize the property issued. If a judicial forfeiture action against the property is later filed in another district — or if the government shows that the action will be filed in another district — the petition may be transferred to that district under 28 U.S.C. § 1404.

(e) Excessive Fines. A claimant may seek to mitigate a forfeiture under the Excessive Fines Clause of the Eighth Amendment by motion for summary judgment or by motion made after entry of a forfeiture judgment if:

(i) the claimant has pleaded the defense under Rule 8; and

(ii) the parties have had the opportunity to conduct civil discovery on the defense.

(9) Trial. Trial is to the court unless any party demands trial by jury under Rule 38.

(Added Apr. 12, 2006, eff. Dec. 1, 2006.)

ADVISORY COMMITTEE NOTES

2006 Adoption

Rule G is added to bring together the central procedures that govern civil forfeiture actions. Civil forfeiture actions are in rem proceedings, as are many admiralty proceedings. As the number of civil forfeiture actions has increased, however, reasons have appeared to create sharper distinctions within the framework of the Supplemental Rules. Civil forfeiture practice will benefit from distinctive provisions that express and focus developments in statutory, constitutional, and decisional law. Admiralty practice will be freed from the pressures that arise when the needs of civil forfeiture proceedings counsel interpretations of common rules that may not be suitable for admiralty proceedings.

Rule G generally applies to actions governed by the Civil Asset Forfeiture Reform Act of 2000 (CAFRA) and also to actions excluded from it. The rule refers to some specific CAFRA provisions; if these statutes are amended, the rule should be adapted to the new provisions during the period required to amend the rule.

Rule G is not completely self-contained. Subdivision (1) recognizes the need to rely at times on other Supplemental Rules and the place of the Supplemental Rules within the basic framework of the Civil Rules.

Supplemental Rules A, C, and E are amended to reflect the adoption of Rule G.

Subdivision (1).

Rule G is designed to include the distinctive procedures that govern a civil forfeiture action. Some details, however, are better supplied by relying on Rules C and E. Subdivision (1) incorporates those rules for issues not addressed by Rule G. This general incorporation is at times made explicit — subdivision (7)(b)(v), for example, invokes the security provisions of Rule E. But Rules C and E are not to be invoked to create conflicts with Rule G. They are to be used only when Rule G, fairly construed, does not address the issue.

The Civil Rules continue to provide the procedural framework within which Rule G and the other Supplemental Rules operate. Both Rule G(1) and Rule A state this basic proposition. Rule G, for example, does not address pleadings amendments. Civil Rule 15 applies, in light of the circumstances of a forfeiture action.

Subdivision (2).

Rule E(2)(a) requires that the complaint in an admiralty action "state the circumstances from which the claim arises with such particularity that the defendant or claimant will be able, without moving for a more definite statement, to commence an investigation of the facts and to frame a responsive pleading." Application of this standard to civil forfeiture actions has evolved to the standard stated in subdivision (2)(f). The complaint must state sufficiently detailed facts to support a reasonable belief that the government will be able to meet its burden of proof at trial. *See U. S. v. Mondragon*, 313 F.3d 862 (4th Cir. 2002). Subdivision (2)(f) carries this forfeiture case law forward without change.

Subdivision (3).

Subdivision (3) governs in rem process in a civil forfeiture action.

Paragraph (a). Paragraph (a) reflects the provisions of 18 U.S.C. § 985.

Paragraph (b). Paragraph (b) addresses arrest warrants when the defendant is not real property. Subparagraph (i) directs the clerk to issue a warrant if the property is in the government's possession, custody, or control. If the property is not in the government's possession, custody, or control and is not subject to a restraining order, subparagraph (ii) provides that a warrant issues only if the court finds probable cause to arrest the property. This provision departs from former Rule C(3)(a)(i), which authorized issuance of summons and warrant by the clerk without a probable-cause finding. The probable-cause finding better protects the interests of persons interested in the property. Subparagraph (iii) recognizes that a warrant is not necessary if the property is subject to a judicial restraining order. The government remains free, however, to seek a warrant if it anticipates that the restraining order may be modified or vacated.

Paragraph (c). Subparagraph (ii) requires that the warrant and any supplemental process be served as soon as practicable unless the property is already in the government's possession, custody, or control. But it authorizes the court to order a different time. The authority to order a different time recognizes that the government may have secured orders sealing the complaint in a civil forfeiture action or have won a stay after filing. The seal or stay may be ordered for reasons, such as protection of an ongoing criminal investigation, that would be defeated by prompt service of the warrant. Subparagraph (ii) does not reflect any independent ground for ordering a seal or stay, but merely reflects the consequences for execution when sealing or a stay is ordered. A court also may order a different time for service if good cause is shown for reasons unrelated to a seal or stay. Subparagraph (iv) reflects the uncertainty surrounding service of an arrest warrant on property not in the United States. It is not possible to identify in the rule the appropriate authority for serving process in all other countries. Transmission of the warrant to an appropriate authority, moreover, does not ensure that the warrant will be executed. The rule requires only that the warrant be transmitted to an appropriate authority.

Subdivision (4).

Paragraph (a). Paragraph (a) reflects the traditional practice of publishing notice of an in rem action.

Subparagraph (i) recognizes two exceptions to the general publication requirement. Publication is not required if the defendant property is worth less than $1,000 and direct notice is sent to all reasonably identifiable potential claimants as required by subdivision (4)(b). Publication also is not required if the cost would exceed the property's value and the court finds that other means of notice would satisfy due process. Publication on a government-established internet forfeiture site, as contemplated by subparagraph (iv), would be at a low marginal publication cost, which would likely be the cost to compare to the property value.

Subparagraph (iv) states the basic criterion for selecting the means and method of publication. The purpose is to adopt a means reasonably calculated to reach potential claimants. The government should choose from among these means a method that is reasonably likely to reach potential claimants at a cost reasonable in the circumstances.

If the property is in the United States and newspaper notice is chosen, publication may be where the action is filed, where the property was seized, or — if the property was not seized — where the property is located. Choice among these places is influenced by the probable location of potential claimants.

If the property is not in the United States, account must be taken of the sensitivities that surround publication of legal notices in other countries. A foreign country may forbid local publication. If potential claimants are likely to be in the United States, publication in the district where the action is filed may be the best choice. If potential claimants are likely to be located abroad, the better choice may be publication by means generally circulated in the country where the property is located.

Newspaper publication is not a particularly effective means of notice for most potential claimants. Its traditional use is best defended by want of affordable alternatives. Paragraph (iv)(C) contemplates a government-created internet forfeiture site that would provide a single easily identified means of notice. Such a site could allow much more direct access to notice as to any specific property than publication provides.

Paragraph (b). Paragraph (b) is entirely new. For the first time, Rule G expressly recognizes the due process obligation to send notice to any person who reasonably appears to be a potential claimant.

Subparagraph (i) states the obligation to send notice. Many potential claimants will be known to the government because they have filed claims during the administrative forfeiture stage. Notice must be sent, however, no matter what source of information makes it reasonably appear that a person is a potential claimant. The duty to send notice terminates when the time for filing a claim expires.

Notice of the action does not require formal service of summons in the manner required by Rule 4 to initiate a personal action. The process that begins an in rem forfeiture action is addressed by subdivision (3). This process commonly gives notice to potential claimants. Publication of notice is required in addition to this process. Due process requirements have moved beyond these traditional means of notice, but are satisfied by practical means that are reasonably calculated to accomplish actual notice.

Subparagraph (ii)(B) directs that the notice state a deadline for filing a claim that is at least 35 days after the notice is sent. This provision applies both in actions that fall within 18 U.S.C. § 983(a)(4)(A) and in other actions. Section 983(a)(4)(A) states that a claim should be filed no later than 30 days after service of the complaint. The variation introduced by subparagraph (ii)(B) reflects the procedure of § 983(a)(2)(B) for nonjudicial forfeiture proceedings. The nonjudicial procedure requires that a claim be filed "not later than the deadline set forth in a personal notice letter (which may be not earlier than 35 days after the date the letter is sent) * * *." This procedure is as suitable in a civil forfeiture action as in a nonjudicial forfeiture proceeding. Thirty-five days after notice is sent ordinarily will extend the claim time by no more than a brief period; a claimant anxious to expedite proceedings can file the claim before the deadline; and the government has flexibility to set a still longer period when circumstances make that desirable.

Subparagraph (iii) begins by stating the basic requirement that notice must be sent by means reasonably calculated to reach the potential claimant. No attempt is made to list the various means that may be reasonable in different circumstances. It may be reasonable, for example, to rely on means that have already been established for communication with a particular potential claimant. The government's interest in choosing a means likely to accomplish actual notice is bolstered by its desire to avoid post-forfeiture challenges based on arguments that a different method would have been more likely to accomplish actual notice. Flexible rule language accommodates the rapid evolution of communications technology.

Notice may be directed to a potential claimant through counsel, but only to counsel already representing the claimant with respect to the seizure of the property, or in a related investigation, administrative forfeiture proceeding, or criminal case.

Subparagraph (iii)(C) reflects the basic proposition that notice to a potential claimant who is incarcerated must be sent to the place of incarceration. Notice directed to some other place, such as a pre-incarceration residence, is less likely to reach the potential claimant. This provision does not address due process questions that may arise if a particular prison has deficient procedures for delivering notice to prisoners. *See Dusenbery v. U.S.*, 534 U.S. 161 (2002).

Items (D) and (E) of subparagraph (iii) authorize the government to rely on an address given by a person who is not incarcerated. The address may have been given to the agency that arrested or released the person, or to the agency that seized the property. The government is not obliged to undertake an independent investigation to verify the address.

Subparagraph (iv) identifies the date on which notice is considered to be sent for some common means, without addressing the circumstances for choosing among the identified means or other means. The date of sending should be determined by analogy for means not listed. Facsimile transmission, for example, is sent upon transmission. Notice by personal delivery is sent on delivery.

Subparagraph (v), finally, reflects the purpose to effect actual notice by providing that a potential claimant who had actual notice of a forfeiture proceeding cannot oppose or seek relief from forfeiture because the government failed to comply with subdivision (4)(b).

Subdivision (5).

Paragraph (a). Paragraph (a) establishes that the first step of contesting a civil forfeiture action is to file a claim. A claim is required by 18 U.S.C. § 983(a)(4)(A) for actions covered by § 983. Paragraph (a) applies this procedure as well to actions not covered by § 983. "Claim" is used to describe this first pleading because of the statutory references to claim and claimant. It functions in the same way as the statement of interest prescribed for an admiralty proceeding by Rule C(6), and is not related to the distinctive meaning of "claim" in admiralty practice.

If the claimant states its interest in the property to be as bailee, the bailor must be identified. A bailee who files a claim on behalf of a bailor must state the bailee's authority to do so.

The claim must be signed under penalty of perjury by the person making it. An artificial body that can act only through an agent may authorize an agent to sign for it. Excusable inability of counsel to obtain an appropriate signature may be grounds for an extension of time to file the claim.

Paragraph (a)(ii) sets the time for filing a claim. Item (C) applies in the relatively rare circumstance in which notice is not published and the government did not send direct notice to the claimant because it did not know of the claimant or did not have an address for the claimant.

Paragraph (b). Under 18 U.S.C. § 983(a)(4)(B), which governs many forfeiture proceedings, a person who asserts an interest by filing a claim "shall file an answer to the Government's complaint for forfeiture not later than 20 days after the date of the filing of the claim." Paragraph (b) recognizes that this statute works within the general procedures established by Civil Rule 12. Rule 12(a)(4) suspends the time to answer when a Rule 12 motion is served within the time allowed to answer. Continued application of this rule to proceedings governed by § 983(a)(4)(B) serves all of the purposes advanced by Rule 12(a)(4), *see U. S. v. $8,221,877.16*, 330 F.3d 141 (3d Cir. 2003); permits a uniform procedure for all civil forfeiture actions; and recognizes that a motion under Rule 12 can be made only after a claim is filed that provides background for the motion.

Failure to present an objection to in rem jurisdiction or to venue by timely motion or answer waives the objection. Waiver of such objections is familiar. An answer may be amended to assert an objection initially omitted. But Civil Rule 15 should be applied to an amendment that for the first time raises an objection to in rem jurisdiction by analogy to the personal jurisdiction objection provision in Civil Rule 12(h)(1)(B). The amendment should be permitted only if it is permitted as a matter of course under Rule 15(a).

A claimant's motion to dismiss the action is further governed by subdivisions (6)(c), (8)(b), and (8)(c).

Subdivision (6).

Subdivision (6) illustrates the adaptation of an admiralty procedure to the different needs of civil forfeiture. Rule C(6) permits interrogatories to be served with the complaint in an in rem action without limiting the subjects of inquiry. Civil forfeiture practice does not require such an extensive departure from ordinary civil practice. It remains useful, however, to permit the government to file limited interrogatories at any time after a claim is filed to gather information that bears on the claimant's standing. Subdivisions (8)(b) and (c) allow a claimant to move to dismiss only if the claimant has standing, and recognize the government's right to move to dismiss a claim for lack of standing. Subdivision (6) interrogatories are integrated with these provisions in that the interrogatories are limited to the claimant's identity and relationship to the defendant property. If the claimant asserts a relationship to the property as bailee, the interrogatories can inquire into the bailor's interest in the property and the bailee's relationship to the bailor. The claimant can accelerate the time to serve subdivision (6) interrogatories by serving a motion to dismiss — the interrogatories must be served within 20 days after the motion is served. Integration is further accomplished by deferring the government's obligation to respond to a motion to dismiss until 20 days after the claimant moving to dismiss has answered the interrogatories.

Special interrogatories served under Rule G(6) do not count against the presumptive 25–interrogatory limit established by Rule 33(a). Rule 33 procedure otherwise applies to these interrogatories.

Subdivision (6) supersedes the discovery "moratorium" of Rule 26(d) and the broader interrogatories permitted for admiralty proceedings by Rule C(6).

Subdivision (7).

Paragraph (a). Paragraph (a) is adapted from Rule E(9)(b). It provides for preservation orders when the government does not have actual possession of the defendant property. It also goes beyond Rule E(9) by recognizing the need to prevent use of the defendant property in ongoing criminal offenses.

Paragraph (b). Paragraph (b)(i)(C) recognizes the authority, already exercised in some cases, to order sale of property subject to a defaulted mortgage or to defaulted taxes. The authority is narrowly confined to mortgages and tax liens; other lien interests may be addressed, if at all, only through the general good-cause provision. The court must carefully weigh the competing interests in each case.

Paragraph (b)(i)(D) establishes authority to order sale for good cause. Good cause may be shown when the property is subject to diminution in value. Care should be taken before ordering sale to avoid diminished value.

Paragraph (b)(iii) recognizes that if the court approves, the interests of all parties may be served by their agreement to sale, aspects of the sale, or sale procedures that depart from governing statutory procedures.

Paragraph (c) draws from Rule E(9)(a), (b), and (c). Disposition of the proceeds as provided by law may require resolution of disputed issues. A mortgagee's claim to the property or sale proceeds, for example, may be disputed on the ground that the mortgage is not genuine. An undisputed lien claim, on the other hand, may be recognized by payment after an interlocutory sale.

Subdivision (8).

Subdivision (8) addresses a number of issues that are unique to civil forfeiture actions.

Paragraph (a). Standing to suppress use of seized property as evidence is governed by principles distinct from the principles that govern claim standing. A claimant with standing to contest forfeiture may not have standing to seek suppression. Rule G does not of itself create a basis of suppression standing that does not otherwise exist.

Paragraph (b). Paragraph (b)(i) is one element of the system that integrates the procedures for determining a claimant's standing to claim and for deciding a claimant's motion to dismiss the action. Under paragraph (c)(ii), a motion to dismiss the action cannot be addressed until the court has decided any government motion to strike the claim or answer. This procedure is reflected in the (b)(i) reminder that a motion to dismiss the forfeiture action may be made only by a claimant who establishes claim standing. The government, moreover, need not respond to a claimant's motion to dismiss until 20 days after the claimant has answered any subdivision (6) interrogatories.

Paragraph (b)(ii) mirrors 18 U.S.C. § 983(a)(3)(D). It applies only to an action independently governed by § 983(a)(3)(D), implying nothing as to actions outside § 983(a)(3)(D). The adequacy of the complaint is measured against the pleading requirements of subdivision (2), not against the quality of the evidence available to the government when the complaint was filed.

Paragraph (c). As noted with paragraph (b), paragraph (c) governs the procedure for determining whether a claimant has standing. It does not address the principles that govern claim standing.

Paragraph (c)(i)(A) provides that the government may move to strike a claim or answer for failure to comply with the pleading requirements of subdivision (5) or to answer subdivision (6) interrogatories. As with other pleadings, the court should strike a claim or answer only if satisfied that an opportunity should not be afforded to cure the defects under Rule 15. Not every failure to respond to subdivision (6) interrogatories warrants an order striking the claim. But the special role that subdivision (6) plays in the scheme for determining claim standing may justify a somewhat more demanding approach than the general approach to discovery sanctions under Rule 37.

Paragraph (c)(ii) directs that a motion to strike a claim or answer be decided before any motion by the claimant to dismiss the action. A claimant who lacks standing is not entitled to challenge the forfeiture on the merits.

Paragraph (c)(ii) further identifies three procedures for addressing claim standing. If a claim fails on its face to show facts that support claim standing, the claim can be dismissed by judgment on the pleadings. If the claim shows facts that would support claim standing, those facts can be tested by a motion for summary judgment. If material facts are disputed, precluding a grant of summary judgment, the court may hold an evidentiary hearing. The evidentiary hearing is held by the court without a jury. The claimant has the burden to establish claim standing at a hearing; procedure on a government summary judgment motion reflects this allocation of the burden.

Paragraph (d). The hardship release provisions of 18 U.S.C. § 983(f) do not apply to a civil forfeiture action exempted from § 983 by § 983(i).

Paragraph (d)(ii) reflects the venue provisions of 18 U.S.C. § 983(f)(3)(A) as a guide to practitioners. In addition, it makes clear the status of a civil forfeiture action as a "civil action" eligible for transfer under 28 U.S.C. § 1404. A transfer decision must be made on the circumstances of the particular proceeding. The district where the forfeiture action is filed has the advantage of bringing all related proceedings together, avoiding the waste that flows from consideration of different parts of the same forfeiture proceeding in the court where the warrant issued or the court where the property was seized. Transfer to that court would serve consolidation, the purpose that underlies nationwide enforcement of a seizure warrant. But there may be offsetting advantages in retaining the petition where it was filed. The claimant may not be able to litigate, effectively or at all, in a distant court. Issues relevant to the petition may be better litigated where the property was seized or where the warrant issued. One element, for example, is whether the claimant has sufficient ties to the community to provide assurance that the property will be available at the time of trial. Another is whether continued government possession would prevent the claimant from working. Determining whether seizure of the claimant's automobile prevents work may turn on assessing the realities of local public transit facilities.

Paragraph (e). The Excessive Fines Clause of the Eighth Amendment forbids an excessive forfeiture. *U.S. v. Bajakajian*, 524 U.S. 321 (1998). 18 U.S.C. § 983(g) provides a "petition" "to determine whether the forfeiture was constitutionally excessive" based on finding "that the forfeiture is grossly disproportional to the offense." Paragraph (e) describes the procedure for § 983(g) mitigation petitions and adopts the same procedure for forfeiture actions that fall outside § 983(g). The procedure is by motion, either for summary judgment or for mitigation after a forfeiture judgment is entered. The claimant must give notice of this defense by pleading, but failure to raise the defense in the initial answer may be cured by amendment under Rule 15. The issues that bear on mitigation often are separate from the issues that determine forfeiture. For that reason it may be convenient to resolve the issue by summary judgment before trial on the forfeiture issues. Often, however, it will be more convenient to determine first whether the property is to be forfeited. Whichever time is chosen to address mitigation, the parties must have had the opportunity to conduct civil discovery on the defense. The extent and timing of discovery are governed by the ordinary rules.

Subdivision (9).

Subdivision (9) serves as a reminder of the need to demand jury trial under Rule 38. It does not expand the right to jury trial. *See U.S. v. One Parcel of Property Located at 32 Medley Lane*, 2005 WL 465421 (D.Conn.2005), ruling that the court, not the jury, determines whether a forfeiture is constitutionally excessive.

RULES OF PROCEDURE OF THE JUDICIAL PANEL ON MULTIDISTRICT LITIGATION

Amendments received to December 1, 2008

I. GENERAL RULES/RULES FOR MULTIDISTRICT LITIGATION UNDER 28 U.S.C. § 1407

Rule

1.1. Definitions.
1.2. Practice.
1.3. Failure to Comply with Rules.
1.4. Admission to Practice Before the Panel and Representation in Transferred Actions.
1.5. Effect of the Pendency of an Action Before the Panel.
1.6. Transfer of Files.
5.1. Keeping Records and Files.
5.11. Place of Filing of Papers.
5.12. Manner of Filing of Papers.
5.13. Filing of Papers: Computer Generated Disk Required.
5.2. Service of Papers Filed.
5.3. Corporate Disclosure Statement.
6.2. Applications for Extensions of Time.

Rule

7.1. Form of Papers Filed.
7.2. Motion Practice.
7.3. Show Cause Orders.
7.4. Conditional Transfer Orders for "Tag–Along Actions".
7.5. Miscellaneous Provisions Concerning "Tag–Along Actions".
7.6. Termination and Remand.
16.1. Hearing Sessions and Oral Argument.

II. RULES FOR MULTICIRCUIT PETITIONS FOR REVIEW UNDER 28 U.S.C. § 2112(a)(3)

17.1. Random Selection.
25.1. Filing of Notices.
25.2. Accompaniments to Notices.
25.3. Service of Notices.
25.4. Form of Notices.
25.5. Service of Panel Consolidation Order.

I. GENERAL RULES/RULES FOR MULTIDISTRICT LITIGATION UNDER 28 U.S.C. § 1407

Rule 1.1. Definitions

As used in these Rules "Panel" means the members of the Judicial Panel on Multidistrict Litigation appointed by the Chief Justice of the United States pursuant to Section 1407, Title 28, United States Code.

"Clerk of the Panel" means the official appointed by the Panel to act as Clerk of the Panel and shall include those deputized by the Clerk of the Panel to perform or assist in the performance of the duties of the Clerk of the Panel.

"Chairman" means the Chairman of the Judicial Panel on Multidistrict Litigation appointed by the Chief Justice of the United States pursuant to Section 1407, or the member of the Panel designated by the Panel to act as Chairman in the absence or inability of the appointed Chairman.

A "tag-along action" refers to a civil action pending in a district court and involving common questions of fact with actions previously transferred under Section 1407.

(Added May 3, 1993, eff. July 1, 1993, and amended Sept. 1, 1998, eff. Nov. 2, 1998; Apr. 2, 2001, eff. Apr. 2, 2001.)

Rule 1.2. Practice

Where not fixed by statute or rule, the practice shall be that heretofore customarily followed by the Panel.

(Added May 3, 1993, eff. July 1, 1993, and amended Sept. 1, 1998, eff. Nov. 2, 1998; Apr. 2, 2001, eff. Apr. 2, 2001.)

Rule 1.3. Failure to Comply with Rules

The Clerk of the Panel may, when a paper submitted for filing is not in compliance with the provisions of these Rules, advise counsel of the deficiencies and a date for full compliance. If full compliance is not accomplished within the established time, the non-complying paper shall nonetheless be filed by the Clerk of the Panel but it may be stricken by order of the Chairman of the Panel.

(Added May 3, 1993, eff. July 1, 1993, and amended Sept. 1, 1998, eff. Nov. 2, 1998; Apr. 2, 2001, eff. Apr. 2, 2001.)

Rule 1.4. Admission to Practice Before the Panel and Representation in Transferred Actions

Every member in good standing of the Bar of any district court of the United States is entitled without condition to practice before the Judicial Panel on Multidistrict Litigation. Any attorney of record in any action transferred under Section 1407 may continue to represent his or her client in any district court of the United States to which such action is transferred. Parties to any action transferred under Section 1407 are not required to obtain local counsel in the district to which such action is transferred.

(Added May 3, 1993, eff. July 1, 1993, and amended Sept. 1, 1998, eff. Nov. 2, 1998; Apr. 2, 2001, eff. Apr. 2, 2001.)

Rule 1.5. Effect of the Pendency of an Action Before the Panel

The pendency of a motion, order to show cause, conditional transfer order or conditional remand order before the Panel concerning transfer or remand of an action pursuant to 28 U.S.C. § 1407 does not affect or suspend orders and pretrial proceedings in the district court in which the action is pending and does not in any way limit the pretrial jurisdiction of that court. A transfer or remand pursuant to 28 U.S.C. § 1407 shall be effective when the transfer or remand order is filed in the office of the clerk of the district court of the transferee district.

(Added May 3, 1993, eff. July 1, 1993, and amended Sept. 1, 1998, eff. Nov. 2, 1998; Apr. 2, 2001, eff. Apr. 2, 2001.)

Rule 1.6. Transfer of Files

(a) Upon receipt of a certified copy of a transfer order from the clerk of the transferee district court, the clerk of the transferor district court shall forward to the clerk of the transferee district court the complete original file and a certified copy of the docket sheet for each transferred action.

(b) If an appeal is pending, or a notice of appeal has been filed, or leave to appeal has been sought under 28 U.S.C. § 1292(b) or a petition for an extraordinary writ is pending, in any action included in an order of transfer under 28 U.S.C. § 1407, and the original file or parts thereof have been forwarded to the court of appeals, the clerk of the transferor district court shall notify the clerk of the court of appeals of the order of transfer and secure the original file long enough to prepare and transmit to the clerk of the transferee district court a certified copy of all papers contained in the original file and a certified copy of the docket sheet.

(c) If the transfer order provides for the separation and simultaneous remand of any claim, cross-claim, counterclaim, or third-party claim, the clerk of the transferor district court shall retain the original file and shall prepare and transmit to the clerk of the transferee district court a certified copy of the docket sheet and copies of all papers except those relating exclusively to separated and remanded claims.

(d) Upon receipt of an order to remand from the Clerk of the Panel, the transferee district court shall prepare and send to the clerk of the transferor district court the following:

(i) a certified copy of the individual docket sheet for each action being remanded;

(ii) a certified copy of the master docket sheet, if applicable;

(iii) the entire file for each action being remanded, as originally received from the transferor district court and augmented as set out in this rule;

(iv) a certified copy of the final pretrial order, if applicable; and

(v) a "record on remand" to be composed of those parts of the files and records produced during coordinated or consolidated pretrial proceedings which have been stipulated to or designated by counsel as being necessary for any or all proceedings to be conducted following remand. It shall be the responsibility of counsel originally preparing or filing any document to be included in the "record on remand" to furnish on request sufficient copies to the clerk of the transferee district court.

(e) The Clerk of the Panel shall be notified when any files have been transmitted pursuant to this Rule.

(Added May 3, 1993, eff. July 1, 1993, and amended Sept. 1, 1998, eff. Nov. 2, 1998; Apr. 2, 2001, eff. Apr. 2, 2001.)

Rule 5.1. Keeping Records and Files

(a) The records and files of the Panel shall be kept by the Clerk of the Panel at the offices of the Panel. Records and files may be temporarily or permanently removed to such places at such times as the Panel or the Chairman of the Panel shall direct. The Clerk of the Panel may charge fees, as prescribed by the Judicial Conference of the United States, for duplicating records and files. Records and files may be transferred whenever appropriate to the Federal Records Center.

(b) In order to assist the Panel in carrying out its functions, the Clerk of the Panel shall obtain the complaints and docket sheets in all actions under consideration for transfer under 28 U.S.C. § 1407 from the clerk of each district court wherein such actions are pending. The Clerk of the Panel shall similarly obtain any other pleadings and orders that could affect the Panel's decision under 28 U.S.C. § 1407.

(Added May 3, 1993, eff. July 1, 1993, and amended Sept. 1, 1998, eff. Nov. 2, 1998; Apr. 2, 2001, eff. Apr. 2, 2001.)

Rule 5.11. Place of Filing of Papers

All papers for consideration by the Panel shall be submitted for filing to the Clerk of the Panel by mailing or delivering to:

Clerk of the Panel
Judicial Panel on Multidistrict Litigation
Thurgood Marshall Federal Judiciary Building
One Columbus Circle, N.E., Room G–255, North Lobby
Washington, D.C. 20002–8004

No papers shall be left with or mailed to a Judge of the Panel.

(Added May 3, 1993, eff. July 1, 1993, and amended Sept. 1, 1998, eff. Nov. 2, 1998; Apr. 2, 2001, eff. Apr. 2, 2001.)

Rule 5.12. Manner of Filing of Papers

(a) An original of the following papers shall be submitted for filing to the Clerk of the Panel: a proof of service pursuant to Rule 5.2(a) and (b) of these Rules, a notice of appearance pursuant to Rule 5.2(c) and (d) of these Rules, a corporate disclosure statement pursuant to Rule 5.3 of these Rules, a status notice pursuant to Rules 7.2(f), 7.3(e) and 7.4(b) of these Rules, a notice of opposition pursuant to Rules 7.4(c) and 7.6(f)(ii) of these Rules, a notice of related action pursuant to Rules 7.2(i), 7.3(a) and 7.5(e) of these Rules, an application for extension of time pursuant to Rule 6.2 of these Rules, or a notice of presentation or waiver of oral argument pursuant to Rule 16.1(d) of these Rules. An original and ~~eleven~~four copies [1] of all other papers shall be submitted for filing to the Clerk of the Panel. The Clerk of the Panel may require that additional copies also be submitted for filing.

(b) When papers are submitted for filing, the Clerk of the Panel shall endorse thereon the date for filing.

(c) Copies of motions for transfer of an action or actions pursuant to 28 U.S.C. § 1407 shall be filed in each district court in which an action is pending that will be affected by the motion. Copies of a motion for remand pursuant to 28 U.S.C. § 1407 shall be filed in the Section 1407 transferee district court in which any action affected by the motion is pending.

(d) Papers requiring only an original may be faxed to the Panel office with prior approval of the Clerk of the Panel. No papers requiring multiple copies shall be accepted via fax.

(Added May 3, 1993, eff. July 1, 1993, and amended Sept. 1, 1998, eff. Nov. 2, 1998; Apr. 2, 2001, eff. Apr. 2, 2001.)

[1] An order issued by the Judicial Panel on Multidistrict Litigation filed April 19, 2005, entitled "Order Partially Suspending Panel Rule 5.12(a), Manner of Filing Papers" provided that, "IT IS HEREBY ORDERED that, because the Panel is utilizing filed papers and electronic distribution of those papers, Panel Rule 5.12(a), Manner of Filing Papers, R.P.J.P.M.L., 199 F.R.D. 425, 429 (2001), is partially suspended insofar as papers submitted for filing requiring an original and eleven copies shall be reduced to four copies along with an original."

Rule 5.13. Filing of Papers: Computer Generated Disk Required

(a) Whenever an original paper and eleven copies is required to be submitted for filing to the Clerk of the Panel pursuant to Rule 5.12(a) of these Rules, and where a party is represented by counsel, one copy of that paper must also be submitted on a computer readable disk and shall be filed at the time the party's paper is filed. The disk shall contain the entire paper exclusive of computer non-generated exhibits. The label of the disk shall include i) "MDL #___," ii) an abbreviated version of the MDL descriptive title, or other appropriate descriptive title, if not yet designated by the Panel, iii) the identity of the type of paper being filed (i.e. motion, response, reply, etc.), iv) the name of the counsel who signed the paper, and v) the first named represented party on the paper.

(b) The paper must be on a disk in Adobe Acrobat (PDF) format.

(c) One copy of the disk may be served on each party separately represented by counsel. If a party chooses to serve a copy of the disk, the proof of service, as required by Rule 5.2 of these Rules, must indicate service of the paper in both paper and electronic format.

(d) A party may be relieved from the requirements of this Rule by submitting a written application for a waiver, in a timely manner in advance of submission of the paper, certifying that compliance with the Rule would impose undue hardship, that the text of the paper is not available on disk, or that other unusual circumstances preclude compliance with this Rule. The requirements of this Rule shall not apply to parties appearing pro se. Papers embraced by this Rule and submitted by counsel after June 1, 2000 without a computer disk copy or Panel-approved waiver of the requirements of this Rule shall be governed by Rule 1.3 of these Rules.

(Added May 22, 2000, eff. June 1, 2000; amended Apr. 2, 2001, eff. Apr. 2, 2001; July 30, 2007, eff. July 30, 2007.)

Rule 5.2. Service of Papers Filed

(a) All papers filed with the Clerk of the Panel shall be accompanied by proof of previous or simultaneous service on all other parties in all actions involved in the litigation. Service and proof of service shall be made as provided in Rules 5 and 6 of the Federal Rules of Civil Procedure. The proof of service shall indicate the name and complete address of each person served and shall indicate the party represented by each. If a party is not represented by counsel, the proof of service shall indicate the name of the party and the party's last known address. The proof of service shall indicate why any person named as a party in a constituent complaint was not served with the Section 1407 pleading. The original proof of service shall be filed with the Clerk of the Panel and copies thereof shall be sent to each person included within the proof of service. After the "Panel Service List" described in subsection (d) of this Rule has been received from the Clerk of the Panel, the "Panel Service List" shall be utilized for service of responses to motions and all other filings. In such instances, the "Panel Service List" shall be attached to the proof of service and shall be supplemented in the proof of service in the event of the presence of additional parties or subsequent corrections relating to any party, counsel or address already on the "Panel Service List."

(b) The proof of service pertaining to motions for transfer of actions pursuant to 28 U.S.C. § 1407 shall certify that copies of the motions have been mailed or otherwise delivered for filing to the clerk of each district court in which an action is pending that will be affected by the motion. The proof of service pertaining to a motion for remand pursuant to 28 U.S.C. § 1407 shall certify that a copy of the motion has been mailed or otherwise delivered for filing to the clerk of the Section 1407 transferee district court in which any action affected by the motion is pending.

(c) Within eleven days of filing of a motion to transfer, an order to show cause or a conditional transfer order, each party or designated attorney shall notify the Clerk of the Panel, in writing, of the name and address of the attorney designated to receive service of all pleadings, notices, orders and other papers relating to practice before the Judicial Panel on Multidistrict Litigation. Only one attorney shall be designated for each party. Any party not represented by counsel shall be served by mailing such pleadings to the party's last known address. Requests for an extension of time to file the designation of attorney shall not be granted except in extraordinary circumstances.

(d) In order to facilitate compliance with subsection (a) of this Rule, the Clerk of the Panel shall prepare and serve on all counsel and parties not represented by counsel, a "Panel Service List" containing the names and addresses of the designated attorneys and the party or parties they represent in the actions under consideration by the Panel and the names and addresses of the parties not represented by counsel in the actions under consideration by the Panel. After the "Panel Service List" has been received from the Clerk of the Panel, notice of subsequent corrections relating to any party, counsel or address on the "Panel Service List" shall be served on all other parties in all actions involved in the litigation.

(e) If following transfer of any group of multidistrict litigation, the transferee district court appoints liaison counsel, this Rule shall be satisfied by serving each party in each affected action and all liaison counsel. Liaison counsel designated by the transferee district court shall receive copies of all Panel orders concerning their particular litigation and shall be responsible for distribution to the parties for whom he or she serves as liaison counsel.

(Added May 3, 1993, eff. July 1, 1993, and amended Sept. 1, 1998, eff. Nov. 2, 1998; Apr. 2, 2001, eff. Apr. 2, 2001.)

Rule 5.3. Corporate Disclosure Statement

(a) Any nongovernmental corporate party to a matter before the Panel shall file a statement identifying all its parent corporations and listing any publicly held company that owns 10% or more of the party's stock.

(b) A party shall file the corporate disclosure statement within eleven days of the filing of a motion to transfer or remand, an order to show cause, or a motion to vacate a conditional transfer order or a conditional remand order.

(c) Once a corporate disclosure statement by a party has been filed in an MDL docket pursuant to subsection (b) of this Rule, such a party is required to update the statement to reflect any change in the information therein i) until the matter before the Panel is decided, and ii) within eleven days of the filing of any subsequent motion to transfer or remand, order to show cause, or motion to vacate a conditional transfer order or a conditional remand order in that docket.

(Added Apr. 2, 2001, eff. Apr. 2, 2001.)

Rule 6.2. Applications for Extensions of Time

Any application for an extension of time to file a pleading or perform an act required by these Rules must be in writing, must request a specific number of additional days and may be acted upon by the Clerk of the Panel. Such an application will be evaluated in relation to the impact on the Panel's calendar as well as on the basis of the reasons set forth in support of the application. Any party aggrieved by the Clerk of the Panel's action on such application may submit its objections to the Panel for consideration. Absent exceptional circumstances, no extensions of time shall be granted to file a notice of opposition to either a conditional transfer order or a conditional remand order. All applications for extensions of time shall be filed and served in conformity with Rules 5.12, 5.2 and 7.1 of these Rules.

(Added May 3, 1993, eff. July 1, 1993, and amended Sept. 1, 1998, eff. Nov. 2, 1998; Apr. 2, 2001, eff. Apr. 2, 2001.)

Rule 7.1. Form of Papers Filed

(a) Averments in any motion seeking action by the Panel shall be made in numbered paragraphs, each of which shall be limited, as far as practicable, to a statement of a single factual averment.

(b) Responses to averments in motions shall be made in numbered paragraphs, each of which shall correspond to the number of the paragraph of the motion to which the responsive paragraph is directed. Each responsive paragraph shall admit or deny wholly or in part the averment of the motion, and shall contain the respondent's version of the subject matter when the averment or the motion is not wholly admitted.

(c) Each pleading filed shall be:

(i) flat and unfolded;

(ii) plainly written, typed in double space, printed or prepared by means of a duplicating process, without erasures or interlineations which materially deface it;

(iii) on opaque, unglazed, white paper (not onionskin);

(iv) approximately 8–1/2 x 11 inches in size; and

(v) fastened at the top-left corner without side binding or front or back covers.

(d) The heading on the first page of each pleading shall commence not less than three inches from the top of the page. Each pleading shall bear the heading "Before the Judicial Panel on Multidistrict Litigation," the identification "MDL Docket No.___" and the descriptive title designated by the Panel for the litigation involved. If the Panel has not yet designated a title, an appropriate descriptive title shall be used.

(e) The final page of each pleading shall contain the name, address and telephone number of the attorney or party in active charge of the case. Each attorney shall also include the name of each party represented.

(f) Except with the approval of the Panel, each brief submitted for filing with the Panel shall be limited to twenty pages, exclusive of exhibits. Absent exceptional circumstances, motions to exceed page limits shall not be granted.

(g) Exhibits exceeding a cumulative total of 50 pages shall be fastened separately from the accompanying pleading.

(h) Proposed Panel orders shall not be submitted with papers for filing.

(Added May 3, 1993, eff. July 1, 1993, and amended Sept. 1, 1998, eff. Nov. 2, 1998; Apr. 2, 2001, eff. Apr. 2, 2001.)

Rule 7.2. Motion Practice

(a) All requests for action by the Panel under 28 U.S.C. § 1407 shall be made by written motion. Every motion shall be accompanied by:

(i) a brief in support thereof in which the background of the litigation and factual and legal contentions of the movant shall be concisely stated in separate portions of the brief with citation of applicable authorities; and

(ii) a schedule giving

(A) the complete name of each action involved, listing the full name of each party included as such on the district court's docket sheet, not shortened by the use of references such as "et al." or "etc.";

(B) the district court and division in which each action is pending;

(C) the civil action number of each action; and

(D) the name of the judge assigned each action, if known.

(b) The Clerk of the Panel shall notify recipients of a motion of the filing date, caption, MDL docket number, briefing schedule and pertinent Panel policies.

(c) Within twenty days after filing of a motion, all other parties shall file a response thereto. Failure of a party to respond to a motion shall be treated as that party's acquiescence to the action requested in the motion.

(d) The movant may, within five days after the lapse of the time period for filing responsive briefs, file a single brief in reply to any opposition.

(e) Motions, their accompaniments, responses, and replies shall also be governed by Rules 5.12, 5.2 and 7.1 of these Rules.

(f) With respect to any action that is the subject of Panel consideration, counsel shall promptly notify the Clerk of the Panel of any development that would partially or completely moot the matter before the Panel.

(g) A joinder in a motion shall not add any action to the previous motion.

(h) Once a motion is filed, any other pleading that purports to be a "motion" in the docket shall be filed by the Clerk of the Panel as a response unless the "motion" adds an action. The Clerk of the Panel, upon designating such a pleading as a motion, shall acknowledge that designation by the distribution of a briefing schedule to all parties in the docket. Response time resulting from an additional motion shall ordinarily be extended only to those parties directly affected by the additional motion. An accelerated briefing schedule for the additional motion may be set by the Clerk of the Panel to conform with the hearing session schedule established by the Chairman.

(i) Any party or counsel in a new group of actions under consideration by the Panel for transfer under Section 1407 shall promptly notify the Clerk of the Panel of any potential tag-along action in which that party is also named or in which that counsel appears.

(Added May 3, 1993, eff. July 1, 1993, and amended Sept. 1, 1998, eff. Nov. 2, 1998; Apr. 2, 2001, eff. Apr. 2, 2001.)

Rule 7.3. Show Cause Orders

(a) When transfer of multidistrict litigation is being considered on the initiative of the Panel pursuant to 28 U.S.C. § 1407(c)(i), an order shall be filed by the Clerk of the Panel directing the parties to show cause why the action or actions should not be transferred for coordinated or consolidated pretrial proceedings. Any party or counsel in such actions shall promptly notify the Clerk of the Panel of any other federal district court actions related to the litigation encompassed by the show cause order. Such notification shall be made for additional actions pending at the time of the issuance of the show cause order and whenever new actions are filed.

(b) Any party may file a response to the show cause order within twenty days of the filing of said order unless otherwise provided for in the order. Failure of a party to respond to a show cause order shall be treated as that party's acquiescence to the Panel action contemplated in the order.

(c) Within five days after the lapse of the time period for filing a response, any party may file a reply limited to new matters.

(d) Responses and replies shall be filed and served in conformity with Rules 5.12, 5.2 and 7.1 of these Rules.

(e) With respect to any action that is the subject of Panel consideration, counsel shall promptly notify the Clerk of the Panel of any development that would partially or completely moot the matter before the Panel.

(Added May 3, 1993, eff. July 1, 1993, and amended Sept. 1, 1998, eff. Nov. 2, 1998; Apr. 2, 2001, eff. Apr. 2, 2001.)

Rule 7.4. Conditional Transfer Orders for "Tag-Along Actions"

(a) Upon learning of the pendency of a potential "tag-along action," as defined in Rule 1.1 of these Rules, an order may be entered by the Clerk of the Panel transferring that action to the previously designated transferee district court on the basis of the prior hearing session(s) and for the reasons expressed in previous opinions and orders of the Panel in the litigation. The Clerk of the Panel shall serve this order on each party to the litigation but, in order to afford all parties the opportunity to oppose transfer, shall not send the order to the clerk of the transferee district court for fifteen days from the entry thereof.

(b) Parties to an action subject to a conditional transfer order shall notify the Clerk of the Panel within the fifteen-day period if that action is no longer pending in its transferor district court.

(c) Any party opposing the transfer shall file a notice of opposition with the Clerk of the Panel within the fifteen-day period. If a notice of opposition is received by the Clerk of the Panel within this fifteen-day period, the Clerk of the Panel shall not transmit said order to the clerk of the transferee district court until further order of the Panel. The Clerk of the Panel shall notify the parties of the briefing schedule.

(d) Within fifteen days of the filing of its notice of opposition, the party opposing transfer shall file a motion to vacate the conditional transfer order and brief in support thereof. The Chairman of the Panel shall set the motion for the next appropriate hearing session of the Panel. Failure to file and serve a motion and brief shall be treated as withdrawal of the opposition and the Clerk of the Panel shall forthwith transmit the order to the clerk of the transferee district court.

(e) Conditional transfer orders do not become effective unless and until they are filed with the clerk of the transferee district court.

(f) Notices of opposition and motions to vacate such orders of the Panel and responses thereto shall be governed by Rules 5.12, 5.2, 7.1 and 7.2 of these Rules.

(Added May 3, 1993, eff. July 1, 1993, and amended Sept. 1, 1998, eff. Nov. 2, 1998; Apr. 2, 2001, eff. Apr. 2, 2001.)

Rule 7.5. Miscellaneous Provisions Concerning "Tag-Along Actions"

(a) Potential "tag-along actions" filed in the transferee district require no action on the part of the Panel and requests for assignment of such actions to the Section 1407 transferee judge should be made in accordance with local rules for the assignment of related actions.

(b) Upon learning of the pendency of a potential "tag-along action" and having reasonable anticipation of opposition to transfer of that action, the Panel may direct the Clerk of the Panel to file a show cause order, in accordance with Rule 7.3 of these Rules, instead of a conditional transfer order.

(c) Failure to serve one or more of the defendants in a potential "tag-along action" with the complaint and summons as required by Rule 4 of the Federal Rules of Civil Procedure does not preclude transfer of such action under Section 1407. Such failure, however, may be submitted by such a defendant as a basis for opposing the proposed transfer if prejudice can be shown. The inability of the Clerk of the Panel to serve a conditional transfer order on all plaintiffs or defendants or their counsel shall not render the transfer of the action void but can be submitted by such a party as a basis for moving to remand as to such party if prejudice can be shown.

(d) A civil action apparently involving common questions of fact with actions under consideration by the Panel for transfer under Section 1407, which was either not included in a motion under Rule 7.2 of these Rules, or was included in such a motion that was filed too late to be included in the initial hearing session, will ordinarily be treated by the Panel as a potential "tag-along action."

(e) Any party or counsel in actions previously transferred under Section 1407 or under consideration by the Panel for transfer under Section 1407 shall promptly notify the Clerk of the Panel of any potential "tag-along actions" in which that party is also named or in which that counsel appears.

(Added May 3, 1993, eff. July 1, 1993, and amended Sept. 1, 1998, eff. Nov. 2, 1998; Apr. 2, 2001, eff. Apr. 2, 2001.)

Rule 7.6. Termination and Remand

In the absence of unusual circumstances—

(a) Actions terminated in the transferee district court by valid judgment, including but not limited to summary judgment, judgment of dismissal and judgment upon stipulation, shall not be remanded by the Panel and shall be dismissed by the transferee district court. The clerk of the transferee district court shall send a copy of the order terminating the action to the Clerk of the Panel but shall retain the original files and records unless otherwise directed by the transferee judge or by the Panel.

(b) Each action transferred only for coordinated or consolidated pretrial proceedings that has not been terminated in the transferee district court shall be remanded by the Panel to the transferor district for trial. Actions that were originally filed in the transferee district require no action by the Panel to be reassigned to another judge in the transferee district at the conclusion of the coordinated or consolidated pretrial proceedings affecting those actions.

(c) The Panel shall consider remand of each transferred action or any separable claim, cross-claim, counterclaim or third-party claim at or before the conclusion of coordinated or consolidated pretrial proceedings on

(i) motion of any party,

(ii) suggestion of the transferee district court, or

(iii) the Panel's own initiative, by entry of an order to show cause, a conditional remand order or other appropriate order.

(d) The Panel is reluctant to order remand absent a suggestion of remand from the transferee district court. If remand is sought by motion of a party, the motion shall be accompanied by:

(i) an affidavit reciting

(A) whether the movant has requested a suggestion of remand from the transferee district court, how the court responded to any request, and, if no such request was made, why;

(B) whether all common discovery and other pretrial proceedings have been completed in the action sought to be remanded, and if not, what remains to be done; and

(C) whether all orders of the transferee district court have been satisfactorily complied with, and if not, what remains to be done; and

(ii) a copy of the transferee district court's final pretrial order, where such order has been entered.

Motions to remand and responses thereto shall be governed by Rules 5.12, 5.2, 7.1 and 7.2 of these Rules.

(e) When an order to show cause why an action or actions should not be remanded is entered pursuant to subsection (c), paragraph (iii) of this Rule, any party may file a response within twenty days of the filing of said order unless otherwise provided for in the order. Within five days of filing of a party's response, any party may file a reply brief limited to new matters. Failure of a party to respond to a show cause order regarding remand shall be treated as that party's acquiescence to the remand. Responses and replies shall be filed and served in conformity with Rules 5.12, 5.2 and 7.1 of these Rules.

(f) Conditional Remand Orders.

(i) When the Panel has been advised by the transferee district judge, or otherwise has reason to believe, that pretrial proceedings in the litigation assigned to the transferee district judge are concluded or that remand of an action or actions is otherwise appropriate, an order may be entered by the Clerk of the Panel remanding the action or actions to the transferor district court. The Clerk of the Panel shall serve this order on each party to the litigation but, in order to afford all parties the opportunity to oppose remand, shall not send the order to the clerk of the transferee district court for fifteen days from the entry thereof.

(ii) Any party opposing the remand shall file a notice of opposition with the Clerk of the Panel within the fifteen-day period. If a notice of opposition is received by the Clerk of the Panel within this fifteen-day period, the Clerk of the Panel shall not transmit said order to the clerk of the transferee district court until further order of the Panel. The Clerk of the Panel shall notify the parties of the briefing schedule.

(iii) Within fifteen days of the filing of its notice of opposition, the party opposing remand shall file a motion to vacate the conditional remand order and brief in support thereof. The Chairman of the Panel shall set the motion for the next appropriate hearing session of the Panel. Failure to file and serve a motion and brief shall be treated as a withdrawal of the opposition and the Clerk of the Panel shall forthwith transmit the order to the clerk of the transferee district court.

(iv) Conditional remand orders do not become effective unless and until they are filed with the clerk of the transferee district court.

(v) Notices of opposition and motions to vacate such orders of the Panel and responses thereto shall be governed by Rules 5.12, 5.2, 7.1 and 7.2 of these Rules.

(g) Upon receipt of an order to remand from the Clerk of the Panel, the parties shall furnish forthwith to the transferee district clerk a stipulation or designation of the contents of the record or part thereof to be remanded and furnish the transferee district clerk all necessary copies of any pleading or other matter filed so as to enable the transferee district clerk to comply with the order of remand.

(Added May 3, 1993, eff. July 1, 1993, and amended Sept. 1, 1998, eff. Nov. 2, 1998; Apr. 2, 2001, eff. Apr. 2, 2001.)

Rule 16.1. Hearing Sessions and Oral Argument

(a) Hearing sessions of the Panel for the presentation of oral argument and consideration of matters taken under submission without oral argument shall be held as ordered by the Panel. The Panel shall convene whenever and wherever desirable or necessary in the judgment of the Chairman. The Chairman shall determine which matters shall be considered at each hearing session and the Clerk of the Panel shall give notice to counsel for all parties involved in the litigation to be so considered of the time, place and subject matter of such hearing session.

(b) Each party filing a motion or a response to a motion or order of the Panel under Rules 7.2, 7.3, 7.4 or 7.6 of these Rules may file simultaneously therewith a separate statement limited to one page setting forth reasons why oral argument should, or need not, be heard. Such statements shall be captioned "Reasons Why Oral Argument Should [Need Not] Be Heard," and shall be filed and served in conformity with Rules 5.12 and 5.2 of these Rules.

(c) No transfer or remand determination regarding any action pending in the district court shall be made by the Panel when any party timely opposes such transfer or remand unless a hearing session has been held for the presentation of oral argument except that the Panel may dispense with oral argument if it determines that:

(i) the dispositive issue(s) have been authoritatively decided; or

(ii) the facts and legal arguments are adequately presented in the briefs and record, and the decisional process would not be significantly aided by oral argument.

Unless otherwise ordered by the Panel, all other matters before the Panel, such as a motion for reconsideration, shall be considered and determined upon the basis of the papers filed.

(d) In those matters in which oral argument is not scheduled by the Panel, counsel shall be promptly advised. If oral argument is scheduled in a matter the Clerk of the Panel may require counsel for all parties who wish to make or to waive oral argument to file and serve notice to that effect within a stated time in conformity with Rules 5.12 and 5.2 of these Rules. Failure to do so shall be deemed a waiver of oral argument by that party. If oral argument is scheduled but not attended by a party, the matter shall not be rescheduled and that party's position shall be treated as submitted for decision by the Panel on the basis of the papers filed.

(e) Except for leave of the Panel on a showing of good cause, only those parties to actions scheduled for oral argument who have filed a motion or written response to a motion or order shall be permitted to appear before the Panel and present oral argument.

(f) Counsel for those supporting transfer or remand under Section 1407 and counsel for those opposing such transfer or remand are to confer separately prior to the oral argument for the purpose of organizing their arguments and selecting representatives to present all views without duplication.

(g) Unless otherwise ordered by the Panel, a maximum of twenty minutes shall be allotted for oral argument in each matter. The time shall be divided equally among those with varying viewpoints. Counsel for the moving party or parties shall generally be heard first.

(h) So far as practicable and consistent with the purposes of Section 1407, the offering of oral testimony before the Panel shall be avoided. Accordingly, oral testimony shall not be received except upon notice, motion and order of the Panel expressly providing for it.

(i) After an action or group of actions has been set for a hearing session, consideration of such action(s) may be continued only by order of the Panel on good cause shown.

(Added May 3, 1998, eff. July 1, 1993, and amended Sept. 1, 1998, eff. Nov. 2, 1998; Apr. 2, 2001, eff. Apr. 2, 2001.)

II. RULES FOR MULTICIRCUIT PETITIONS FOR REVIEW UNDER 28 U.S.C. § 2112(a)(3)

Rule 17.1. Random Selection

(a) Upon filing a notice of multicircuit petitions for review, the Clerk of the Panel or designated deputy shall randomly select a circuit court of appeals from a drum containing an entry for each circuit wherein a constituent petition for review is pending. Multiple petitions for review pending in a single circuit shall be allotted only a single entry in the drum. This random selection shall be witnessed by the Clerk of the Panel or a designated deputy other than the random selector. Thereafter, an order on behalf of the Panel shall be issued, signed by the random selector and the witness,

(i) consolidating the petitions for review in the court of appeals for the circuit that was randomly selected; and

(ii) designating that circuit as the one in which the record is to be filed pursuant to Rules 16 and 17 of the Federal Rules of Appellate Procedure.

(b) A consolidation of petitions for review shall be effective when the Panel's consolidation order is filed at the offices of the Panel by the Clerk of the Panel.

(Added May 3, 1993, eff. July 1, 1993, and amended Sept. 1, 1998, eff. Nov. 2, 1998; Apr. 2, 2001, eff. Apr. 2, 2001.)

Rule 25.1. Filing of Notices

(a) An original of a notice of multicircuit petitions for review pursuant to 28 U.S.C. § 2112(a)(3) shall be submitted for filing to the Clerk of the Panel by the affected agency, board, commission or officer. The term "agency" as used in Section II of these Rules shall include agency, board, commission or officer.

(b) All notices of multicircuit petitions for review submitted by the affected agency for filing with the Clerk of the Panel shall embrace exclusively petitions for review filed in the courts of appeals within ten days after issuance of an agency order and received by the affected agency from the petitioners within that ten-day period.

(c) When a notice of multicircuit petitions for review is submitted for filing to the Clerk of the Panel, the Clerk of the Panel shall file the notice and endorse thereon the date of filing.

(d) Copies of notices of multicircuit petitions for review shall be filed by the affected agency with the clerk of each circuit court of appeals in which a petition for review is pending that is included in the notice.

(Added May 3, 1993, eff. July 1, 1993, and amended Sept. 1, 1998, eff. Nov. 2, 1998; Apr. 2, 2001, eff. Apr. 2, 2001.)

Rule 25.2. Accompaniments to Notices

(a) All notices of multicircuit petitions for review shall be accompanied by:

(i) a copy of each involved petition for review as the petition for review is defined in 28 U.S.C. § 2112(a)(2); and

(ii) a schedule giving

(A) the date of the relevant agency order;

(B) the case name of each petition for review involved;

(C) the circuit court of appeals in which each petition for review is pending;

(D) the appellate docket number of each petition for review;

(E) the date of filing by the court of appeals of each petition for review; and

(F) the date of receipt by the agency of each petition for review.

(b) The schedule in Subsection (a)(ii) of this Rule shall also be governed by Rules 25.1, 25.3 and 25.4(a) of these Rules.

(Added May 3, 1993, eff. July 1, 1993, and amended Sept. 1, 1998, eff. Nov. 2, 1998; Apr. 2, 2001, eff. Apr. 2, 2001.)

Rule 25.3. Service of Notices

(a) All notices of multicircuit petitions for review shall be accompanied by proof of service by the affected agency on all other parties in all petitions for review included in the notice. Service and proof of service shall be made as provided in Rule 25 of the Federal Rules of Appellate Procedure. The proof of service shall state the name and address of each person served and shall indicate the party represented by each. If a party is not represented by counsel, the proof of service shall indicate the name of the party and his or her last known address. The original proof of service shall be submitted by the affected agency for filing with the Clerk of the Panel and copies thereof shall be sent by the affected agency to each person included within the proof of service.

(b) The proof of service pertaining to notices of multicircuit petitions for review shall certify that copies of the notices have been mailed or otherwise delivered by the affected agency for filing to the clerk of each circuit court of appeals in which a petition for review is pending that is included in the notice.

(Added May 3, 1993, eff. July 1, 1993, and amended Sept. 1, 1998, eff. Nov. 2, 1998; Apr. 2, 2001, eff. Apr. 2, 2001.)

Rule 25.4. Form of Notices

(a) Each notice of multicircuit petitions for review shall be

(i) flat and unfolded;

(ii) plainly written, typed in double space, printed or prepared by means of a duplicating process, without erasures or interlineations which materially deface it;

(iii) on opaque, unglazed white paper (not onionskin);

(iv) approximately 8–1/2 x 11 inches in size; and

(v) fastened at the top-left corner without side binding or front or back covers.

(b) The heading on the first page of each notice of multicircuit petitions for review shall commence not less that three inches from the top of the page. Each notice shall bear the heading "Notice to the Judicial Panel on Multidistrict Litigation of Multicircuit Petitions for Review," followed by a brief caption identifying the involved agency, the relevant agency order, and the date of the order.

(c) The final page of each notice of multicircuit petitions for review shall contain the name, address and telephone number of the individual or individuals who submitted the notice on behalf of the agency.

(Added May 3, 1993, eff. July 1, 1993, and amended Sept. 1, 1998, eff. Nov. 2, 1998; Apr. 2, 2001, eff. Apr. 2, 2001.)

Rule 25.5. Service of Panel Consolidation Order

(a) The Clerk of the Panel shall serve the Panel's consolidation order on the affected agency through the individual or individuals, as identified in Rule 25.4(c) of these Rules, who submitted the notice of multicircuit petitions for review on behalf of the agency.

(b) That individual or individuals, or anyone else designated by the agency, shall promptly serve the Panel's consolidation order on all other parties in all petitions for review included in the Panel's consolidation order, and shall promptly submit a proof of that service to the Clerk of the Panel. Service and proof of that service shall also be governed by Rule 25.3 of these Rules.

(c) The Clerk of the Panel shall serve the Panel's consolidation order on the clerks of all circuit courts of appeals that were among the candidates for the Panel's random selection.

(Added May 3, 1993, eff. July 1, 1993, and amended Sept. 1, 1998, eff. Nov. 2, 1998; Apr. 2, 2001, eff. Apr. 2, 2001.)

RULES GOVERNING SECTION 2254 CASES IN THE UNITED STATES DISTRICT COURTS

Effective February 1, 1977
Amendments received to December 1, 2008

Rule

1. Scope.
2. The Petition.
3. Filing the Petition; Inmate Filing.
4. Preliminary Review; Serving the Petition and Order.
5. The Answer and the Reply.
6. Discovery.
7. Expanding the Record.
8. Evidentiary Hearing.
9. Second or Successive Petitions.
10. Powers of a Magistrate Judge.
11. Applicability of the Federal Rules of Civil Procedure.

APPENDIX OF FORMS

Petition for Relief From a Conviction or Sentence By a Person in State Custody.
(Petition Under 28 U.S.C. § 2254 for a Writ of Habeas Corpus).

ORDERS OF THE SUPREME COURT OF THE UNITED STATES ADOPTING AND AMENDING RULES GOVERNING SECTION 2254 PROCEEDINGS IN THE UNITED STATES DISTRICT COURTS

ORDER OF APRIL 26, 1976

1. That the rules and forms governing proceedings in the United States District Courts under Section 2254 and Section 2255 of Title 28, United States Code, as approved by the Judicial Conference of the United States be, and they hereby are, prescribed pursuant to Section 2072 of Title 28, United States Code and Sections 3771 and 3772 of Title 18, United States Code.

2. That the aforementioned rules and forms shall take effect August 1, 1976, and shall be applicable to all proceedings then pending except to the extent that in the opinion of the court their application in a particular proceeding would not be feasible or would work injustice.

3. That THE CHIEF JUSTICE be, and he hereby is, authorized to transmit the aforementioned rules and forms governing Section 2254 and Section 2255 proceedings to the Congress in accordance with the provisions of Section 2072 of Title 28 and Sections 3771 and 3772 of Title 18, United States Code.

CONGRESSIONAL ACTION ON PROPOSED RULES AND FORMS GOVERNING PROCEEDING UNDER 28 U.S.C. §§ 2254 AND 2255

Pub.L. 94–349, § 2, July 8, 1976, 90 Stat. 822, provided: "That, notwithstanding the provisions of section 2072 of title 28 of the United States Code, the rules and forms governing section 2254 cases in the United States district courts and the rules and forms governing section 2255 proceedings in the United States district courts which are embraced by the order entered by the United States Supreme Court on April 26, 1976, and which were transmitted to the Congress on or about April 26, 1976, shall not take effect until thirty days after the adjournment sine die of the 94th Congress, or until and to the extent approved by Act of Congress, whichever is earlier."

Pub.L. 94–426, § 1, Sept. 28, 1976, 90 Stat. 1334, provided: "That the rules governing section 2254 cases in the United States district courts and the rules governing section 2255 proceedings for the United States Supreme Court, which were delayed by the Act entitled 'An Act to delay the effective date of certain proposed amendments to the Federal Rules of Criminal Procedure and certain other rules promulgated by the United States Supreme Court' (Public Law 94–349), are approved with the amendments set forth in section 2 of this Act and shall take effect as so amended, with respect to petitions under section 2254 and motions under section 2255 of title 28 of the United States Code filed on or after February 1, 1977."

ORDER OF APRIL 30, 1979

1. That Rule 10 of the Rules Governing Proceedings in the United States District Courts on application under Section 2254 of Title 28, United States Code, be, and hereby is, amended to read as follows:

[See amendment made thereby under Rule 10, post.]

2. That Rules 10 and 11 of the Rules Governing Proceedings in the United States District Courts on a motion under Section 2255 of Title 28, United States Code, be, and they hereby are, amended to read as follows:

[See amendments made hereby under Rules 10 and 11 set out following section 2255.]

3. That the foregoing amendments to the Rules Governing Proceedings in the United States District Courts under Section 2254 and Section 2255 of Title 28, United States Code, shall take effect on August 1, 1979, and shall be applicable to all proceedings then pending except to the extent that in the opinion of the court their application in a particular proceeding would not be feasible or would work injustice.

4. That THE CHIEF JUSTICE be, and he hereby is, authorized to transmit the aforementioned amendments to the Rules Governing Section 2254 and Section 2255 Proceedings to the Congress in accordance with the provisions of

Section 2072 of Title 28, United States Code, and Sections 3771 and 3772 of Title 18, United States Code.

ORDER OF APRIL 28, 1982

1. That the rules and forms governing proceedings in the United States district courts under Section 2254 and Section 2255 of Title 28, United States Code, be, and they hereby are, amended by including therein an amendment to Rule 2(c) of the rules for Section 2254 cases, an amendment to Rule 2(b) of the rules for Section 2255 proceedings, and amendments to the model forms for use in applications under Section 2254 and motions under Section 2255, as hereinafter set forth:

[See amendments made thereby under respective rules and forms post and following section 2255.]

2. That the aforementioned amendments shall take effect August 1, 1982, and shall be applicable to all proceedings thereafter commenced and, insofar as just and practicable, all proceedings then pending.

3. That THE CHIEF JUSTICE be, and he hereby is, authorized to transmit the aforementioned amendments to the Congress in accordance with Section 2072 of Title 28 and Sections 3771 and 3772 of Title 18, United States Code.

ORDER OF APRIL 26, 2004

1. That the Federal Rules of Criminal Procedure be, and they hereby are, amended by including therein an amendment to Criminal Rule 35.

2. That the rules and forms governing cases in the United States District Courts under Section 2254 and Section 2255 of Title 28, United States Code, be, and they hereby are, amended by including therein amendments to Rules 1 through 11 of the Rules Governing Section 2254 Cases in the United States District Courts, Rules 1 through 12 of the Rules Governing Section 2255 Cases in the United States District Courts, and forms for use in applications under Section 2254 and motions under Section 2255.

[See amendments made thereby under respective rules, post.]

3. That the foregoing amendments to the Federal Rules of Criminal Procedure, the Rules Governing Section 2254 Cases in the United States District Courts, and the Rules Governing Section 2255 Cases in the United States District Courts shall take effect on December 1, 2004, and shall govern in all proceedings thereafter commenced and, insofar as just and practicable, all proceedings then pending.

4. That the CHIEF JUSTICE be, and hereby is, authorized to transmit to the Congress the foregoing amendments to the Federal Rules of Criminal Procedure, the Rules Governing Section 2254 Cases in the United States District Courts, and the Rules Governing Section 2255 Cases in the United States District Courts in accordance with the provisions of Section 2072 of Title 28, United States Code.

HISTORICAL NOTES

Effective Date of Rules; 1976 Act

Rules governing section 2254 cases, and the amendments thereto by Pub.L. 94–426, Sept. 28, 1976, 90 Stat. 1334, effective with respect to petitions under section 2254 of this title and motions under section 2255 of this title filed on or after Feb. 1, 1977, see section 1 of Pub.L. 94–426, set out as a note under section 2074 and 2254 of this title.

Rule 1. Scope

(a) Cases Involving a Petition under 28 U.S.C. § 2254. These rules govern a petition for a writ of habeas corpus filed in a United States district court under 28 U.S.C. § 2254 by:

(1) a person in custody under a state-court judgment who seeks a determination that the custody violates the Constitution, laws, or treaties of the United States; and

(2) a person in custody under a state-court or federal-court judgment who seeks a determination that future custody under a state-court judgment would violate the Constitution, laws, or treaties of the United States.

(b) Other Cases. The district court may apply any or all of these rules to a habeas corpus petition not covered by Rule 1(a).

(As amended Apr. 26, 2004, eff. Dec. 1, 2004.)

ADVISORY COMMITTEE NOTES

1976 Adoption

Rule 1 provides that the habeas corpus rules are applicable to petitions by persons in custody pursuant to a judgment of a state court. See *Preiser v. Rodriguez,* 411 U.S. 475, 484 (1973). Whether the rules ought to apply to other situations (*e.g.*, person in active military service, *Glazier v. Hackel,* 440 F.2d 592 (9th Cir. 1971); or a reservist called to active duty but not reported, *Hammond v. Lenfest,* 398 F.2d 705 (2d Cir. 1968)) is left to the discretion of the court.

The basic scope of habeas corpus is prescribed by statute. 28 U.S.C. § 2241(c) provides that the "writ of habeas corpus shall not extend to a prisoner unless * * * (h)e is *in custody* in violation of the Constitution." 28 U.S.C. § 2254 deals specifically with state custody, providing that habeas corpus shall apply only "in behalf of a person in custody pursuant to a judgment of a state court * * *."

In *Preiser v. Rodriguez, supra*, the court said: "It is clear . . . that the essence of habeas corpus is an attack by a person in custody upon the legality of that custody, and that the traditional function of the writ is to secure release from illegal custody." 411 U.S. at 484.

Initially the Supreme Court held that habeas corpus was appropriate only in those situations in which petitioner's claim would, if upheld, result in an immediate release from a present custody. *McNally v. Hill,* 293 U.S. 131 (1934). This was changed in *Peyton v. Rowe,* 391 U.S. 54 (1968), in which the court held that habeas corpus was a proper way to attack a consecutive sentence to be served in the future, expressing the view that consecutive sentences resulted in present custody under both judgments, not merely the one imposing the first sentence. This view was expanded in *Carafas v. LaVallee,* 391 U.S. 234 (1968), to recognize the propriety of habeas corpus in a case in which petitioner was in custody when the petition had been originally filed but had since been unconditionally released from custody.

See also *Preiser v. Rodriguez,* 411 U.S. at 486 et seq.

Since *Carafas,* custody has been construed more liberally by the courts so as to make a § 2255 motion or habeas corpus petition proper in more situations. "In custody" now includes a person who is: on parole, *Jones v. Cunningham,* 371 U.S. 236 (1963); at large on his own recognizance but subject to several conditions pending execution of his sentence, *Hensley v. Municipal Court,* 411 U.S. 345 (1973); or released on bail after conviction pending final disposition of his case, *Lefkowitz v. Newsome,* 95 S.Ct. 886 (1975). See also *United States v. Re,* 372 F.2d 641 (2d Cir.), cert. denied, 388 U.S. 912 (1967) (on probation); *Walker v. North Carolina,* 262 F.Supp. 102 (W.D.N.C.1966), aff'd per curiam, 372 F.2d 129 (4th Cir.), cert. denied, 388 U.S. 917 (1967) (recipient of a conditionally suspended sentence); *Burris v. Ryan,* 397 F.2d 553 (7th Cir. 1968); *Marden v. Purdy,* 409 F.2d 784 (5th Cir. 1969) (free on bail); *United States ex rel. Smith v. Dibella,* 314 F.Supp. 446 (D.Conn.1970) (release on own recognizance); *Choung v. California,* 320 F.Supp. 625 (E.D.Cal.1970) (federal stay of state court sentence); *United States ex rel. Meadows v. New York,* 426 F.2d 1176 (2d Cir. 1970), cert. denied, 401 U.S. 941 (1971) (subject to parole detainer warrant); *Capler v. City of Greenville,* 422 F.2d 299 (5th Cir. 1970) (released on appeal bond); *Glover v. North Carolina,* 301 F.Supp. 364 (E.D.N.C.1969) (sentence served, but as convicted felon disqualified from engaging in several activities).

The courts are not unanimous in dealing with the above situations, and the boundaries of custody remain somewhat unclear. In *Morgan v. Thomas,* 321 F.Supp. 565 (S.D.Miss. 1970), the court noted:

> It is axiomatic that actual physical custody or restraint is not required to confer habeas jurisdiction. Rather, the term is synonymous with restraint of liberty. The real question is how much restraint of one's liberty is necessary before the right to apply for the writ comes into play. * * *
>
> It is clear however, that something more than moral restraint is necessary to make a case for habeas corpus.

321 F.Supp. at 573

Hammond v. Lenfest, 398 F.2d 705 (2d Cir. 1968), reviewed prior "custody" doctrine and reaffirmed a generalized flexible approach to the issue. In speaking about 28 U.S.C. § 2241, the first section in the habeas corpus statutes, the court said:

> While the language of the Act indicates that a writ of habeas corpus is appropriate only when a petitioner is "in custody" * * * the Act "does not attempt to mark the boundaries of 'custody' nor in any way other than by use of that word attempt to limit the situations in which the writ can be used." * * * And, recent Supreme Court decisions have made clear that "[i]t [habeas corpus] is not now and never has been a static, narrow, formalistic remedy; its scope has grown to achieve its grand purpose—the protection of individuals against erosion of their right to be free from wrongful restraints upon their liberty." * * * "[B]esides physical imprisonment, there are other restraints on a man's liberty, restraints not shared by the public generally, which have been thought sufficient in the English-speaking world to support the issuance of habeas corpus."

398 F.2d at 710–711

There is, as of now, no final list of the situations which are appropriate for habeas corpus relief. It is not the intent of these rules or notes to define or limit "custody."

It is, however, the view of the Advisory Committee that claims of improper conditions of custody or confinement (not related to the propriety of the custody itself), can better be handled by other means such as 42 U.S.C. § 1983 and other related statutes. In *Wilwording v. Swanson,* 404 U.S. 249 (1971), the court treated a habeas corpus petition by a state prisoner challenging the conditions of confinement as a claim for relief under 42 U.S.C. § 1983, the Civil Rights Act. Compare *Johnson v. Avery,* 393 U.S. 483 (1969).

The distinction between duration of confinement and conditions of confinement may be difficult to draw. Compare *Preiser v. Rodriguez,* 411 U.S. 475 (1973), with *Clutchette v. Procunier,* 497 F.2d 809 (9th Cir. 1974), modified, 510 F.2d 613 (1975).

2004 Amendments

The language of Rule 1 has been amended as part of general restyling of the rules to make them more easily understood and to make style and terminology consistent throughout the rules. These changes are intended to be stylistic and no substantive change is intended.

Rule 2. The Petition

(a) Current Custody; Naming the Respondent. If the petitioner is currently in custody under a state-court judgment, the petition must name as respondent the state officer who has custody.

(b) Future Custody; Naming the Respondents and Specifying the Judgment. If the petitioner is not yet in custody—but may be subject to future custody—under the state-court judgment being contested, the petition must name as respondents both the officer who has current custody and the attorney general of the state where the judgment was entered. The petition must ask for relief from the state-court judgment being contested.

(c) Form. The petition must:

(1) specify all the grounds for relief available to the petitioner;

(2) state the facts supporting each ground;

(3) state the relief requested;

(4) be printed, typewritten, or legibly handwritten; and

(5) be signed under penalty of perjury by the petitioner or by a person authorized to sign it for the petitioner under 28 U.S.C. § 2242.

(d) Standard Form. The petition must substantially follow either the form appended to these rules or a form prescribed by a local district-court rule. The clerk must make forms available to petitioners without charge.

(e) Separate Petitions for Judgments of Separate Courts. A petitioner who seeks relief from judgments of more than one state court must file a separate petition covering the judgment or judgments of each court.

(As amended Pub.L. 94–426, § 2(1), (2), Sept. 28, 1976, 90 Stat. 1334; Apr. 28, 1982, eff. Aug. 1, 1982; Apr. 26, 2004, eff. Dec. 1, 2004.)

ADVISORY COMMITTEE NOTES

1976 Adoption

Rule 2 describes the requirements of the actual petition, including matters relating to its form, contents, scope, and sufficiency. The rule provides more specific guidance for a petitioner and the court than 28 U.S.C. § 2242, after which it is patterned.

Subdivision (a) provides that an applicant challenging a state judgment, pursuant to which he is presently in custody, must make his application in the form of a petition for a writ of habeas corpus. It also requires that the state officer having custody of the applicant be named as respondent. This is consistent with 28 U.S.C. § 2242, which says in part, [Application for a writ of habeas corpus] shall allege * * * the name of the person who has custody over [the applicant] * * *." The proper person to be served in the usual case is either the warden of the institution in which the petitioner is incarcerated (*Sanders v. Bennett*, 148 F.2d 19 (D.C.Cir. 1945)) or the chief officer in charge of state penal institutions.

Subdivision (b) prescribes the procedure to be used for a petition challenging a judgment under which the petitioner will be subject to custody in the future. In this event the relief sought will usually not be released from present custody, but rather for a declaration that the judgment being attacked is invalid. Subdivision (b) thus provides for a prayer for "appropriate relief." It is also provided that the attorney general of the state of the judgment as well as the state officer having actual custody of the petitioner shall be named as respondents. This is appropriate because no one will have custody of the petitioner in the state of the judgment being attacked, and the habeas corpus action will usually be defended by the attorney general. The attorney general is in the best position to inform the court as to who the proper party respondent is. If it is not the attorney general, he can move for a substitution of party.

Since the concept of "custody" requisite to the consideration of a petition for habeas corpus has been enlarged significantly in recent years, it may be worthwhile to spell out the various situations which might arise and who should be named as respondent(s) for each situation.

(1) The applicant is in jail, prison, or other actual physical restraint due to the state action he is attacking. The named respondent shall be the state officer who has official custody of the petitioner (for example, the warden of the prison).

(2) The applicant is on probation or parole due to the state judgment he is attacking. The named respondents shall be the particular probation or parole officer responsible for supervising the applicant, and the official in charge of the parole or probation agency, or the state correctional agency, as appropriate.

(3) The applicant is in custody in any other manner differing from (1) and (2) above due to the effects of the state action he seeks relief from. The named respondent should be the attorney general of the state wherein such action was taken.

(4) The applicant is in jail, prison, or other actual physical restraint but is attacking a state action which will cause him to be kept in custody in the future rather than the government action under which he is presently confined. The named respondents shall be the state or federal officer who has official custody of him at the time the petition is filed and the attorney general of the state whose action subjects the petitioner to future custody.

(5) The applicant is in custody, although not physically restrained, and is attacking a state action which will result in his future custody rather than the government action out of which his present custody arises. The named respondent(s) shall be the attorney general of the state whose action subjects the petitioner to future custody, as well as the government officer who has present official custody of the petitioner if there is such an officer and his identity is ascertainable.

In any of the above situations the judge may require or allow the petitioner to join an additional or different party as a respondent if to do so would serve the ends of justice.

As seen in rule 1 and paragraphs (4) and (5) above, these rules contemplate that a petitioner currently in federal custody will be permitted to apply for habeas relief from a state restraint which is to go into effect in the future. There has been disagreement in the courts as to whether they have jurisdiction of the habeas application under these circumstances (compare *Piper v. United States*, 306 F.Supp. 1259 (D.Conn.1969), with *United States ex rel. Meadows v. New York*, 426 F.2d 1176 (2d Cir. 1970), cert. denied, 401 U.S. 941 (1971)). This rule seeks to make clear that they do have such jurisdiction.

Subdivision (c) provides that unless a district court requires otherwise by local rule, the petition must be in the form annexed to these rules. Having a standard prescribed form has several advantages. In the past, petitions have frequently contained mere conclusions of law, unsupported by any facts. Since it is the relationship of the facts to the claim asserted that is important, these petitions were obviously deficient. In addition, lengthy and often illegible petitions, arranged in no logical order, were submitted to judges who have had to spend hours deciphering them. For example, in *Passic v. Michigan*, 98 F.Supp. 1015, 1016 (E.D.Mich. 1951), the court dismissed a petition for habeas corpus, describing it as "two thousand pages of irrational, prolix and redundant pleadings * * *."

Administrative convenience, of benefit to both the court and the petitioner, results from the use of a prescribed form. Judge Hubert L. Will briefly described the experience with the use of a standard form in the Northern District of Illinois:

> Our own experience, though somewhat limited, has been quite satisfactory. * * *
>
> In addition, [petitions] almost always contain the necessary basic information * * *. Very rarely do we get the kind of hybrid federal-state habeas corpus petition with civil rights allegations thrown in which were not uncom-

mon in the past. * * * [W]hen a real constitutional issue is raised it is quickly apparent * * *.

33 F.R.D. 363, 384

Approximately 65 to 70% of all districts have adopted forms or local rules which require answers to essentially the same questions as contained in the standard form annexed to these rules. All courts using forms have indicated the petitions are time-saving and more legible. The form is particularly helpful in getting information about whether there has been an exhaustion of state remedies or, at least, where that information can be obtained.

The requirement of a standard form benefits the petitioner as well. His assertions are more readily apparent, and a meritorious claim is more likely to be properly raised and supported. The inclusion in the form of the ten most frequently raised grounds in habeas corpus petitions is intended to encourage the applicant to raise all his asserted grounds in one petition. It may better enable him to recognize if an issue he seeks to raise is cognizable under habeas corpus and hopefully inform him of those issues as to which he must first exhaust his state remedies.

Some commentators have suggested that the use of forms is of little help because the questions usually are too general, amounting to little more than a restatement of the statute. They contend the blanks permit a prisoner to fill in the same ambiguous answers he would have offered without the aid of a form. See Comment, Developments in the Law—Federal Habeas Corpus, 83 Harv.L.Rev. 1038, 1177–1178 (1970). Certainly, as long as the statute requires factual pleading, the adequacy of a petition will continue to be affected largely by the petitioner's intelligence and the legal advice available to him. On balance, however, the use of forms has contributed enough to warrant mandating their use.

Giving the petitioner a list of often—raised grounds may, it is said, encourage perjury. See Comment, Developments in the Law—Federal Habeas Corpus, 83 Harv.L.Rev. 1038, 1178 (1970). Most inmates are aware of, or have access to, some common constitutional grounds for relief. Thus, the risk of perjury is not likely to be substantially increased and the benefit of the list for some inmates seems sufficient to outweigh any slight risk that perjury will increase. There is a penalty for perjury, and this would seem the most appropriate way to try to discourage it.

Legal assistance is increasingly available to inmates either through paraprofessional programs involving law students or special programs staffed by members of the bar. See Jacob and Sharma, Justice After Trial: Prisoners' Need for Legal Services in the Criminal-Correctional Process, 18 Kan.L.Rev. 493 (1970). In these situations, the prescribed form can be filled out more competently, and it does serve to ensure a degree of uniformity in the manner in which habeas corpus claims are presented.

Subdivision (c) directs the clerk of the district court to make available to applicants upon request, without charge, blank petitions in the prescribed form.

Subdivision (c) also requires that all available grounds for relief be presented in the petition, including those grounds of which, by the exercise of reasonable diligence, the petitioner should be aware. This is reinforced by rule 9(b), which allows dismissal of a second petition which fails to allege new grounds or, if new grounds are alleged, the judge finds an inexcusable failure to assert the ground in the prior petition.

Both subdivision (c) and the annexed form require a legibly handwritten or typewritten petition. As required by 28 U.S.C. § 2242, the petition must be signed and sworn to by the petitioner (or someone acting in his behalf).

Subdivision (d) provides that a single petition may assert a claim only against the judgment or judgments of a single state court (*i.e.*, a court of the same county or judicial district or circuit). This permits, but does not require, an attack in a single petition on judgments based upon separate indictments or on separate counts even though sentences were imposed on separate days by the same court. A claim against a judgment of a court of a different political subdivision must be raised by means of a separate petition.

Subdivision (e) allows the clerk to return an insufficient petition to the petitioner, and it must be returned if the clerk is so directed by a judge of the court. Any failure to comply with the requirements of rule 2 or 3 is grounds for insufficiency. In situations where there may be arguable noncompliance with another rule, such as rule 9, the judge, not the clerk, must make the decision. If the petition is returned it must be accompanied by a statement of the reason for its return. No petitioner should be left to speculate as to why or in what manner his petition failed to conform to these rules.

Subdivision (e) also provides that the clerk shall retain one copy of the insufficient petition. If the prisoner files another petition, the clerk will be in a better position to determine the sufficiency of the new petition. If the new petition is insufficient, comparison with the prior petition may indicate whether the prisoner has failed to understand the clerk's prior explanation for its insufficiency, so that the clerk can make another, hopefully successful, attempt at transmitting this information to the petitioner. If the petitioner insists that the original petition was in compliance with the rules, a copy of the original petition is available for the consideration of the judge. It is probably better practice to make a photocopy of a petition which can be corrected by the petitioner, thus saving the petitioner the task of completing an additional copy.

1982 Amendment

Subdivision (c). The amendment takes into account 28 U.S.C. § 1746, enacted after adoption of the § 2254 rules. Section 1746 provides that in lieu of an affidavit an unsworn statement may be given under penalty of perjury in substantially the following form if executed within the United States, its territories, possessions or commonwealths: "I declare (or certify, verify, or state) under penalty of perjury that the foregoing is true and correct. Executed on (date). (Signature)." The statute is "intended to encompass prisoner litigation," and the statutory alternative is especially appropriate in such cases because a notary might not be readily available. *Carter v. Clark*, 616 F.2d 228 (5th Cir. 1980). The § 2254 forms have been revised accordingly.

2004 Amendments

The language of Rule 2 has been amended as part of general restyling of the rules to make them more easily understood and to make style and terminology consistent throughout the rules. These changes are intended to be stylistic and no substantive change is intended, except as described below.

Revised Rule 2(c)(5) has been amended by removing the requirement that the petition be signed personally by the petitioner. As reflected in 28 U.S.C. § 2242, an application for habeas corpus relief may be filed by the person who is seeking relief, or by someone acting on behalf of that person. *See, e.g., Whitmore v. Arkansas,* 495 U.S. 149 (1990) (discussion of requisites for "next friend" standing in petition for habeas corpus). Thus, under the, amended rule the petition may be signed by petitioner personally or by someone acting on behalf of the petitioner, assuming that the person is authorized to do so, for example, an attorney for the petitioner. The Committee envisions that the courts will apply third-party, or "next-friend," standing analysis in deciding whether the signer was actually authorized to sign the petition on behalf of the petitioner.

The language in new Rule 2(d) has been changed to reflect that a petitioner must substantially follow the standard form, which is appended to the rules, or a form provided by the court. The current rule, Rule 2(c), seems to indicate a preference for the standard "national" form. Under the amended rule, there is no stated preference. The Committee understood that current practice in some courts is that if the petitioner first files a petition using the national form, the courts may then ask the petitioner to supplement it with the local form.

Current Rule 2(e), which provided for returning an insufficient petition, has been deleted. The Committee believed that the approach in Federal Rule of Civil Procedure 5(e) was more appropriate for dealing with petitions that do not conform to the form requirements of the rule. That Rule provides that the clerk may not refuse to accept a filing solely for the reason that it fails to comply with these rules or local rules. Before the adoption of a one-year statute of limitations in the Antiterrorism and Effective Death Penalty Act of 1996, 110 Stat. 1214, the petitioner suffered no penalty, other than delay, if the petition was deemed insufficient. Now that a one-year statute of limitations applies to petitions filed under § 2254, *see* 28 U.S.C. § 2244(d)(1), the court's dismissal of a petition because it is not in proper form may pose a significant penalty for a petitioner, who may not be able to file another petition within the one-year limitations period. Now, under revised Rule 3(b), the clerk is required to file a petition, even though it may otherwise fail to comply with the provisions in revised Rule 2(c). The Committee believed that the better procedure was to accept the defective petition and require the petitioner to submit a corrected petition that conforms to Rule 2(c).

Rule 3. Filing the Petition; Inmate Filing

(a) Where to File; Copies; Filing Fee. An original and two copies of the petition must be filed with the clerk and must be accompanied by:

(1) the applicable filing fee, or

(2) a motion for leave to proceed in forma pauperis, the affidavit required by 28 U.S.C. § 1915, and a certificate from the warden or other appropriate officer of the place of confinement showing the amount of money or securities that the petitioner has in any account in the institution.

(b) Filing. The clerk must file the petition and enter it on the docket.

(c) Time to File. The time for filing a petition is governed by 28 U.S.C. § 2244(d).

(d) Inmate Filing. A paper filed by an inmate confined in an institution is timely if deposited in the institution's internal mailing system on or before the last day for filing. If an institution has a system designed for legal mail, the inmate must use that system to receive the benefit of this rule. Timely filing may be shown by a declaration in compliance with 28 U.S.C. § 1746 or by a notarized statement, either of which must set forth the date of deposit and state that first-class postage has been prepaid.

(As amended Apr. 26, 2004, eff. Dec. 1, 2004.)

ADVISORY COMMITTEE NOTES

1976 Adoption

Rule 3 sets out the procedures to be followed by the petitioner and the court in filing the petition. Some of its provisions are currently dealt with by local rule or practice, while others are innovations. Subdivision (a) specifies the petitioner's responsibilities. It requires that the petition, which must be accompanied by two conformed copies thereof, be filed in the office of the clerk of the district court. The petition must be accompanied by the filing fee prescribed by law (presently $5; see 28 U.S.C. § 1914(a)), unless leave to prosecute the petition in forma pauperis is applied for and granted. In the event the petitioner desires to prosecute the petition in forma pauperis, he must file the affidavit required by 28 U.S.C. § 1915, together with a certificate showing the amount of funds in his institutional account.

Requiring that the petition be filed in the office of the clerk of the district court provides an efficient and uniform system of filing habeas corpus petitions.

Subdivision (b) requires the clerk to file the petition. If the filing fee accompanies the petition, it may be filed immediately, and, if not, it is contemplated that prompt attention will be given to the request to proceed in forma pauperis. The court may delegate the issuance of the order to the clerk in those cases in which it is clear from the petition that there is full compliance with the requirements to proceed in forma pauperis.

Requiring the copies of the petition to be filed with the clerk will have an impact not only upon administrative matters, but upon more basic problems as well. In districts with more than one judge, a petitioner under present circumstances may send a petition to more than one judge. If no central filing system exists for each district, two judges may independently take different action on the same petition. Even if the action taken is consistent, there may be needless duplication of effort.

The requirement of an additional two copies of the form of the petition is a current practice in many courts. An efficient filing system requires one copy for use by the court (central file), one for the respondent (under 3(b), the respondent receives a copy of the petition whether an answer is required or not), and one for petitioner's counsel, if appointed. Since rule 2 provides that blank copies of the petition in the prescribed form are to be furnished to the applicant free of charge, there should be no undue burden created by this requirement.

Attached to copies of the petition supplied in accordance with rule 2 is an affidavit form for the use of petitioners desiring to proceed in forma pauperis. The form requires information concerning the petitioner's financial resources.

In forma pauperis cases, the petition must also be accompanied by a certificate indicating the amount of funds in the petitioner's institution account. Usually the certificate will be from the warden. If the petitioner is on probation or parole, the court might want to require a certificate from the supervising officer. Petitions by persons on probation or parole are not numerous enough, however, to justify making special provision for this situation in the text of the rule.

The certificate will verify the amount of funds credited to the petitioner in an institution account. The district court may by local rule require that any amount credited to the petitioner, in excess of a stated maximum, must be used for the payment of the filing fee. Since prosecuting an action in forma pauperis is a privilege (see *Smart v. Heinze,* 347 F.2d 114, 116 (9th Cir. 1965), it is not to be granted when the petitioner has sufficient resources.

Subdivision (b) details the clerk's duties with regard to filing the petition. If the petition does not appear on its face to comply with the requirements of rules 2 and 3, it may be returned in accordance with rule 2(e). If it appears to comply, it must be filed and entered on the docket in the clerk's office. However, under this subdivision the respondent is not required to answer or otherwise move with respect to the petition unless so ordered by the court.

2004 Amendments

The language of Rule 3 has been amended as part of general restyling of the rules to make them more easily understood and to make style and terminology consistent throughout the rules. These changes are intended to be stylistic and no substantive change is intended except as described below.

The last sentence of current Rule 3(b), dealing with an answer being filed by the respondent, has been moved to revised Rule 5(a).

Revised Rule 3(b) is new and is intended to parallel Federal Rule of Civil Procedure 5(e), which provides that the clerk may not refuse to accept a filing solely for the reason that it fails to comply with these rules or local rules. Before the adoption of a one-year statute of limitations in the Antiterrorism and Effective Death Penalty Act of 1996, 110 Stat. 1214, the petitioner suffered no penalty, other than delay, if the petition was deemed insufficient. That Act, however, added a one-year statute of limitations to petitions filed under § 2254, *see* 28 U.S.C. § 2244(d)(1). Thus, a court's dismissal of a defective petition may pose a significant penalty for a petitioner who may not be able to file a corrected petition within the one-year limitations period. The Committee believed that the better procedure was to accept the defective petition and require the petitioner to submit a corrected petition that conforms to Rule 2. Thus, revised Rule 3(b) requires the clerk to file a petition, even though it may otherwise fail to comply with Rule 2. The rule, however, is not limited to those instances where the petition is defective only in form; the clerk would also be required, for example, to file the petition even though it lacked the requisite filing fee or an *in forma pauperis* form.

Revised Rule 3(c), which sets out a specific reference to 28 U.S.C. § 2244(d), is new and has been added to put petitioners on notice that a one-year statute of limitations applies to petitions filed under these Rules. Although the rule does not address the issue, every circuit that has addressed the issue has taken the position that equitable tolling of the statute of limitations is available in appropriate circumstances. *See, e.g., Smith v. McGinnis,* 208 F.3d 13, 17–18 (2d Cir. 2000); *Miller v. New Jersey State Department of Corrections,* 145 F.3d 616, 618–19 (3d Cir. 1998); *Harris v. Hutchinson,* 209 F.3d 325, 330 (4th Cir. 2000). The Supreme Court has not addressed the question directly. *See Duncan v. Walker,* 533 U.S. 167, 181 (2001) ("We . . . have no occasion to address the question that Justice Stevens raises concerning the availability of equitable tolling.").

Rule 3(d) is new and provides guidance on determining whether a petition from an inmate is considered to have been filed in a timely fashion. The new provision parallels Federal Rule of Appellate Procedure 25(a)(2)(C).

Rule 4. Preliminary Review; Serving the Petition and Order

The clerk must promptly forward the petition to a judge under the court's assignment procedure, and the judge must promptly examine it. If it plainly appears from the petition and any attached exhibits that the petitioner is not entitled to relief in the district court, the judge must dismiss the petition and direct the clerk to notify the petitioner. If the petition is not dismissed, the judge must order the respondent to file an answer, motion, or other response within a fixed time, or to take other action the judge may order. In every case, the clerk must serve a copy of the petition and any order on the respondent and on the attorney general or other appropriate officer of the state involved.

(As amended Apr. 26, 2004, eff. Dec. 1, 2004.)

ADVISORY COMMITTEE NOTES

1976 Adoption

Rule 4 outlines the options available to the court after the petition is properly filed. The petition must be promptly presented to and examined by the judge to whom it is assigned. If it plainly appears from the face of the petition and any exhibits attached thereto that the petitioner is not entitled to relief in the district court, the judge must enter an order summarily dismissing the petition and cause the petitioner to be notified. If summary dismissal is not ordered, the judge must order the respondent to file an answer or to otherwise plead to the petition within a time period to be fixed in the order.

28 U.S.C. § 2243 requires that the writ shall be awarded, or an order to show cause issued, "unless it appears from the application that the applicant or person detained is not entitled thereto." Such consideration may properly encompass any exhibits attached to the petition, including, but not limited to, transcripts, sentencing records, and copies of state court opinions. The judge may order any of these items for

his consideration if they are not yet included with the petition. See 28 U.S.C. § 753(f) which authorizes payment for transcripts in habeas corpus cases.

It has been suggested that an answer should be required in every habeas proceeding, taking into account the usual petitioner's lack of legal expertise and the important functions served by the return. See Developments in the Law—Federal Habeas Corpus, 83 Harv.L.Rev. 1038, 1178 (1970). However, under § 2243 it is the duty of the court to screen out frivolous applications and eliminate the burden that would be placed on the respondent by ordering an unnecessary answer. *Allen v. Perini*, 424 F.2d 134, 141 (6th Cir. 1970). In addition, "notice" pleading is not sufficient, for the petition is expected to state facts that point to a "real possibility of constitutional error." See *Aubut v. State of Maine*, 431 F.2d 688, 689 (1st Cir. 1970).

In the event an answer is ordered under rule 4, the court is accorded greater flexibility than under § 2243 in determining within what time period an answer must be made. Under § 2243, the respondent must make a return within three days after being so ordered, with additional time of up to forty days allowed under the Federal Rules of Civil Procedure, Rule 81(a)(2), for good cause. In view of the widespread state of work overload in prosecutors' offices (see, *e.g.*, *Allen*, 424 F.2d at 141), additional time is granted in some jurisdictions as a matter of course. Rule 4, which contains no fixed time requirement, gives the court the discretion to take into account various factors such as the respondent's workload and the availability of transcripts before determining a time within which an answer must be made.

Rule 4 authorizes the judge to "take such other action as the judge deems appropriate." This is designed to afford the judge flexibility in a case where either dismissal or an order to answer may be inappropriate. For example, the judge may want to authorize the respondent to make a motion to dismiss based upon information furnished by respondent, which may show that petitioner's claims have already been decided on the merits in a federal court; that petitioner has failed to exhaust state remedies; that the petitioner is not in custody within the meaning of 28 U.S.C. § 2254; or that a decision in the matter is pending in state court. In these situations, a dismissal may be called for on procedural grounds, which may avoid burdening the respondent with the necessity of filing an answer on the substantive merits of the petition. In other situations, the judge may want to consider a motion from respondent to make the petition more certain. Or the judge may want to dismiss some allegations in the petition, requiring the respondent to answer only those claims which appear to have some arguable merit.

Rule 4 requires that a copy of the petition and any order be served by certified mail on the respondent and the attorney general of the state involved. See 28 U.S.C. § 2252. Presently, the respondent often does not receive a copy of the petition unless the court directs an answer under 28 U.S.C. § 2243. Although the attorney general is served, he is not required to answer if it is more appropriate for some other agency to do so. Although the rule does not specifically so provide, it is assumed that copies of the court orders to respondent will be mailed to petitioner by the court.

2004 Amendments

The language of Rule 4 has been amended as part of general restyling of the rules to make them more easily understood and to make style and terminology consistent throughout the rules. These changes are intended to be stylistic and no substantive change is intended, except as described below.

The amended rule reflects that the response to a habeas petition may be a motion.

The requirement that in every case the clerk must serve a copy of the petition on the respondent by certified mail has been deleted. In addition, the current requirement that the petition be sent to the Attorney General of the state has been modified to reflect practice in some jurisdictions that the appropriate state official may be someone other than the Attorney General, for example, the officer in charge of a local confinement facility. This comports with a similar provision in 28 U.S.C. § 2252, which addresses notice of habeas corpus proceedings to the state's attorney general or other appropriate officer of the state.

Rule 5. The Answer and the Reply

(a) When Required. The respondent is not required to answer the petition unless a judge so orders.

(b) Contents: Addressing the Allegations; Stating a Bar. The answer must address the allegations in the petition. In addition, it must state whether any claim in the petition is barred by a failure to exhaust state remedies, a procedural bar, non-retroactivity, or a statute of limitations.

(c) Contents: Transcripts. The answer must also indicate what transcripts (of pretrial, trial, sentencing, or post-conviction proceedings) are available, when they can be furnished, and what proceedings have been recorded but not transcribed. The respondent must attach to the answer parts of the transcript that the respondent considers relevant. The judge may order that the respondent furnish other parts of existing transcripts or that parts of untranscribed recordings be transcribed and furnished. If a transcript cannot be obtained, the respondent may submit a narrative summary of the evidence.

(d) Contents: Briefs on Appeal and Opinions. The respondent must also file with the answer a copy of:

(1) any brief that the petitioner submitted in an appellate court contesting the conviction or sentence, or contesting an adverse judgment or order in a post-conviction proceeding;

(2) any brief that the prosecution submitted in an appellate court relating to the conviction or sentence; and

(3) the opinions and dispositive orders of the appellate court relating to the conviction or the sentence.

(e) Reply. The petitioner may submit a reply to the respondent's answer or other pleading within a time fixed by the judge.

(As amended Apr. 26, 2004, eff. Dec. 1, 2004.)

ADVISORY COMMITTEE NOTES

1976 Adoption

Rule 5 details the contents of the "answer". (This is a change in terminology from "return," which is still used below when referring to prior practice.) The answer plays an obviously important role in a habeas proceeding:

> The return serves several important functions: it permits the court and the parties to uncover quickly the disputed issues; it may reveal to the petitioner's attorney grounds for release that the petitioner did not know; and it may demonstrate that the petitioner's claim is wholly without merit.
>
> Developments in the Law—Federal Habeas Corpus, 83 Harv.L.Rev. 1083, 1178 (1970).

The answer must respond to the allegations of the petition. While some districts require this by local rule (see, *e.g.*, E.D.N.C.R. 17(B)), under 28 U.S.C. § 2243 little specificity is demanded. As a result, courts occasionally receive answers which contain only a statement certifying the true cause of detention, or a series of delaying motions such as motions to dismiss. The requirement of the proposed rule that the "answer shall respond to the allegations of the petition" is intended to ensure that a responsive pleading will be filed and thus the functions of the answer fully served.

The answer must also state whether the petitioner has exhausted his state remedies. This is a prerequisite to eligibility for the writ under 28 U.S.C. § 2254(b) and applies to every ground the petitioner raises. Most form petitions now in use contain questions requiring information relevant to whether the petitioner has exhausted his remedies. However, the exhaustion requirement is often not understood by the unrepresented petitioner. The attorney general has both the legal expertise and access to the record and thus is in a much better position to inform the court on the matter of exhaustion of state remedies. An alleged failure to exhaust state remedies as to any ground in the petition may be raised by a motion by the attorney general, thus avoiding the necessity of a formal answer as to that ground.

The rule requires the answer to indicate what transcripts are available, when they can be furnished, and also what proceedings have been recorded and not transcribed. This will serve to inform the court and petitioner as to what factual allegations can be checked against the actual transcripts. The transcripts include pretrial transcripts relating, for example, to pretrial motions to suppress; transcripts of the trial or guilty plea proceeding; and transcripts of any post-conviction proceedings which may have taken place. The respondent is required to furnish those portions of the transcripts which he believes relevant. The court may order the furnishing of additional portions of the transcripts upon the request of petitioner or upon the court's own motion.

Where transcripts are unavailable, the rule provides that a narrative summary of the evidence may be submitted.

Rule 5 (and the general procedure set up by this entire set of rules) does not contemplate a traverse to the answer, except under special circumstances. See advisory committee note to rule 9. Therefore, the old common law assumption of verity of the allegations of a return until impeached, as codified in 28 U.S.C. § 2248, is no longer applicable. The meaning of the section, with its exception to the assumption "to the extent that the judge finds from the evidence that they (the allegations) are not true," has given attorneys and courts a great deal of difficulty. It seems that when the petition and return pose an issue of fact, no traverse is required; *Stewart v. Overholser*, 186 F.2d 339 (D.C.Cir. 1950).

> We read § 2248 of the Judicial Code as not requiring a traverse when a factual issue has been clearly framed by the petition and the return or answer. This section provides that the allegations of a return or answer to an order to show cause shall be accepted as true if not traversed, except to the extent the judge finds from the evidence that they are not true. This contemplates that where the petition and return or answer do present an issue of fact material to the legality of detention, evidence is required to resolve that issue despite the absence of a traverse. This reference to evidence assumes a hearing on issues raised by the allegations of the petition and the return or answer to the order to show cause.
>
> **186 F.2d at 342, n. 5**

In actual practice, the traverse tends to be a mere pro forma refutation of the return, serving little if any expository function. In the interests of a more streamlined and manageable habeas corpus procedure, it is not required except in those instances where it will serve a truly useful purpose. Also, under rule 11 the court is given the discretion to incorporate Federal Rules of Civil Procedure when appropriate, so civil rule 15(a) may be used to allow the petitioner to amend his petition when the court feels this is called for by the contents of the answer.

Rule 5 does not indicate who the answer is to be served upon, but it necessarily implies that it will be mailed to the petitioner (or to his attorney if he has one). The number of copies of the answer required is left to the court's discretion. Although the rule requires only a copy of petitioner's brief on appeal, respondent is free also to file a copy of respondent's brief. In practice, courts have found it helpful to have a copy of respondent's brief.

2004 Amendments

The language of Rule 5 has been amended as part of general restyling of the rules to make them more easily understood and to make style and terminology consistent throughout the rules. These changes are intended to be stylistic and no substantive change is intended, except as described below.

Revised Rule 5(a), which provides that the respondent is not required to file an answer to the petition, unless a judge so orders, is taken from current Rule 3(b). The revised rule does not address the practice in some districts, where the respondent files a pre-answer motion to dismiss the petition. But revised Rule 4 permits that practice and reflects the view that if the court does not dismiss the petition, it may require (or permit) the respondent to file a motion.

Rule 5(b) has been amended to require that the answer address not only failure to exhaust state remedies, but also procedural bars, non-retroactivity, and any statute of limitations. Although the latter three matters are not addressed in the current rule, the Committee intends no substantive change with the additional new language. *See, e.g.,* 28 U.S.C. § 2254(b)(3). Instead, the Committee believes that the explicit mention of those issues in the rule conforms to current case law and statutory provisions. *See, e.g.,* 28 U.S.C. § 2244(d)(1).

Revised Rule 5(d) includes new material. First, Rule 5(d)(2), requires a respondent—assuming an answer is filed—to provide the court with a copy of any brief submitted by the prosecution to the appellate court. And Rule 5(d)(3) now provides that the respondent also file copies of any opinions and dispositive orders of the appellate court concerning the conviction or sentence. These provisions are intended to ensure that the court is provided with additional information that may assist it in resolving the issues raised, or not raised, in the petition.

Finally, revised Rule 5(e) adopts the practice in some jurisdictions of giving the petitioner an opportunity to file a reply to the respondent's answer. Rather than using terms such as "traverse," *see* 28 U.S.C. § 2248, to identify the petitioner's response to the answer, the rule uses the more general term "reply." The Rule prescribes that the court set the time for such responses and in lieu of setting specific time limits in each case, the court may decide to include such time limits in its local rules.

Rule 6. Discovery

(a) Leave of Court Required. A judge may, for good cause, authorize a party to conduct discovery under the Federal Rules of Civil Procedure and may limit the extent of discovery. If necessary for effective discovery, the judge must appoint an attorney for a petitioner who qualifies to have counsel appointed under 18 U.S.C. § 3006A.

(b) Requesting Discovery. A party requesting discovery must provide reasons for the request. The request must also include any proposed interrogatories and requests for admission, and must specify any requested documents.

(c) Deposition Expenses. If the respondent is granted leave to take a deposition, the judge may require the respondent to pay the travel expenses, subsistence expenses, and fees of the petitioner's attorney to attend the deposition.

(As amended Apr. 26, 2004, eff. Dec. 1, 2004.)

ADVISORY COMMITTEE NOTES

1976 Adoption

This rule prescribes the procedures governing discovery in habeas corpus cases. Subdivision (a) provides that any party may utilize the processes of discovery available under the Federal Rules of Civil Procedure (rules 26–37) if, and to the extent that, the judge allows. It also provides for the appointment of counsel for a petitioner who qualifies for this when counsel is necessary for effective utilization of discovery procedures permitted by the judge.

Subdivision (a) is consistent with *Harris v. Nelson,* 394 U.S. 286 (1969). In that case the court noted,

> [I]t is clear that there was no intention to extend to habeas corpus, as a matter of right, the broad discovery provisions * * * of the new [Federal Rules of Civil Procedure].

394 U.S. at 295

However, citing the lack of methods for securing information in habeas proceedings, the court pointed to an alternative.

> Clearly, in these circumstances * * * the courts may fashion appropriate modes of procedure, by analogy to existing rules or otherwise in conformity with judicial usage. * * * Their authority is expressly confirmed in the All Writs Act, 28 U.S.C. § 1651.

394 U.S. at 299

The court concluded that the issue of discovery in habeas corpus cases could best be dealt with as part of an effort to provide general rules of practice for habeas corpus cases:

> In fact, it is our view that the rulemaking machinery should be invoked to formulate rules of practice with respect to federal habeas corpus and § 2255 proceedings, on a comprehensive basis and not merely one confined to discovery. The problems presented by these proceedings are materially different from those dealt with in the Federal Rules of Civil Procedure and the Federal Rules of Criminal Procedure, and reliance upon usage and the opaque language of Civil Rule 81(a)(2) is transparently inadequate. In our view the results of a meticulous formulation and adoption of special rules for federal habeas corpus and § 2255 proceedings would promise much benefit.

394 U.S. at 301 n. 7

Discovery may, in appropriate cases, aid in developing facts necessary to decide whether to order an evidentiary hearing or to grant the writ following an evidentiary hearing:

> We are aware that confinement sometimes induces fantasy which has its basis in the paranoia of prison rather than in fact. But where specific allegations before the court show reason to believe that the petitioner may, if the facts are fully developed, be able to demonstrate that he is confined illegally and is therefore entitled to relief, it is the duty of the court to provide the necessary facilities and procedures for an adequate inquiry. Obviously, in exercising this power, the court may utilize familiar procedures, as appropriate, whether these are found in the civil or criminal rules or elsewhere in the "usages and principles."

Granting discovery is left to the discretion of the court, discretion to be exercised where there is a showing of good cause why discovery should be allowed. Several commentators have suggested that at least some discovery should be permitted without leave of court. It is argued that the courts will be burdened with weighing the propriety of requests to which the discovered party has no objection. Additionally, the availability of protective orders under Fed. R.Civ.R., Rules 30(b) and 31(d) will provide the necessary safeguards. See Developments in the Law—Federal Habeas Corpus, 83 Harv.L.Rev. 1038, 1186–87 (1970); Civil Discovery in Habeas Corpus, 67 Colum.L.Rev. 1296, 1310 (1967).

Nonetheless, it is felt the requirement of prior court approval of all discovery is necessary to prevent abuse, so this requirement is specifically mandated in the rule.

While requests for discovery in habeas proceedings normally follow the granting of an evidentiary hearing, there may be instances in which discovery would be appropriate beforehand. Such an approach was advocated in *Wagner v. United States*, 418 F.2d 618, 621 (9th Cir.1969), where the opinion stated the trial court could permit interrogatories, provide for deposing witnesses, "and take such other pre-hearing steps as may be appropriate." While this was an action under § 2255, the reasoning would apply equally well to petitions by state prisoners. Such pre-hearing discovery may show an evidentiary hearing to be unnecessary, as when there are "no disputed issues of law or fact." 83 Harv.L.Rev. 1038, 1181 (1970). The court in Harris alluded to such a possibility when it said "the court may * * * authorize such proceedings with respect to development, *before or in conjunction with the hearing* of the facts * * *." [emphasis added] 394 U.S. at 300. Such pre-hearing discovery, like all discovery under rule 6, requires leave of court. In addition, the provisions in rule 7 for the use of an expanded record may eliminate much of the need for this type of discovery. While probably not as frequently sought or granted as discovery in conjunction with a hearing, it may nonetheless serve a valuable function.

In order to make pre-hearing discovery meaningful, subdivision (a) provides that the judge should appoint counsel for a petitioner who is without counsel and qualifies for appointment when this is necessary for the proper utilization of discovery procedures. Rule 8 provides for the appointment of counsel at the evidentiary hearing stage (see rule 8(b) and advisory committee note), but this would not assist the petitioner who seeks to utilize discovery to stave off dismissal of his petition (see rule 9 and advisory committee note) or to demonstrate that an evidentiary hearing is necessary. Thus, if the judge grants a petitioner's request for discovery prior to making a decision as to the necessity for an evidentiary hearing, he should determine whether counsel is necessary for the effective utilization of such discovery and, if so, appoint counsel for the petitioner if the petitioner qualifies for such appointment.

This rule contains very little specificity as to what types and methods of discovery should be made available to the parties in a habeas proceeding, or how, once made available, these discovery procedures should be administered. The purpose of this rule is to get some experience in how discovery would work in actual practice by letting district court judges fashion their own rules in the context of individual cases. When the results of such experience are available it would be desirable to consider whether further, more specific codification should take place.

Subdivision (b) provides for judicial consideration of all matters subject to discovery. A statement of the interrogatories, or requests for admission sought to be answered, and a list of any documents sought to be produced, must accompany a request for discovery. This is to advise the judge of the necessity for discovery and enable him to make certain that the inquiry is relevant and appropriately narrow.

Subdivision (c) refers to the situation where the respondent is granted leave to take the deposition of the petitioner or any other person. In such a case the judge may direct the respondent to pay the expenses and fees of counsel for the petitioner to attend the taking of the deposition, as a condition granting the respondent such leave. While the judge is not required to impose this condition subdivision (c) will give the court the means to do so. Such a provision affords some protection to the indigent petitioner who may be prejudiced by his inability to have counsel, often court-appointed, present at the taking of a deposition. It is recognized that under 18 U.S.C. § 3006A(g), court-appointed counsel in a § 2254 proceeding is entitled to receive up to $250 and reimbursement for expenses reasonably incurred. (Compare Fed.R.Crim.P. 15(c).) Typically, however, this does not adequately reimburse counsel if he must attend the taking of depositions or be involved in other pre-hearing proceedings. Subdivision (c) is intended to provide additional funds, if necessary, to be paid by the state government (respondent) to petitioner's counsel.

Although the rule does not specifically so provide, it is assumed that a petitioner who qualifies for the appointment of counsel under 18 U.S.C. § 3006A(g) and is granted leave to take a deposition will be allowed witness costs. This will include recording and transcription of the witness's statement. Such costs are payable pursuant to 28 U.S.C. § 1825. See Opinion of Comptroller General, February 28, 1974.

Subdivision (c) specifically recognizes the right of the respondent to take the deposition of the petitioner. Although the petitioner could not be called to testify against his will in a criminal trial, it is felt the nature of the habeas proceeding, along with the safeguards accorded by the Fifth Amendment and the presence of counsel, justify this provision. See 83 Harv.L.Rev. 1038, 1183–84 (1970).

2004 Amendments

The language of Rule 6 has been amended as part of general restyling of the rules to make them more easily understood and to make style and terminology consistent throughout the rules. These changes are intended to be stylistic and no substantive change is intended.

Although current Rule 6(b) contains no requirement that the parties provide reasons for the requested discovery, the revised rule does so and also includes a requirement that the request be accompanied by any proposed interrogatories and requests for admission, and must specify any requested documents. The Committee believes that the revised rule makes explicit what has been implicit in current practice.

Rule 7. Expanding the Record

(a) In General. If the petition is not dismissed, the judge may direct the parties to expand the record by submitting additional materials relating to the petition. The judge may require that these materials be authenticated.

(b) Types of Materials. The materials that may be required include letters predating the filing of the petition, documents, exhibits, and answers under oath to written interrogatories propounded by the judge. Affidavits may also be submitted and considered as part of the record.

(c) Review by the Opposing Party. The judge must give the party against whom the additional materials are offered an opportunity to admit or deny their correctness.

(As amended Apr. 26, 2004, eff. Dec. 1, 2004.)

ADVISORY COMMITTEE NOTES

1976 Adoption

This rule provides that the judge may direct that the record be expanded. The purpose is to enable the judge to dispose of some habeas petitions not dismissed on the pleadings, without the time and expense required for an evidentiary hearing. An expanded record may also be helpful when an evidentiary hearing is ordered.

The record may be expanded to include additional material relevant to the merits of the petition. While most petitions are dismissed either summarily or after a response has been made, of those that remain, by far the majority require an evidentiary hearing. In the fiscal year ending June 30, 1970, for example, of 8,423 § 2254 cases terminated, 8,231 required court action. Of these, 7,812 were dismissed before a prehearing conference and 469 merited further court action (*e.g.*, expansion of the record, prehearing conference, or an evidentiary hearing). Of the remaining 469 cases, 403 required an evidentiary hearing, often time-consuming, costly, and, at least occasionally, unnecessary. See Director of the Administrative Office of the United States Courts, Annual Report, 245a–245c (table C4) (1970). In some instances these hearings were necessitated by slight omissions in the state record which might have been cured by the use of an expanded record.

Authorizing expansion of the record will, hopefully, eliminate some unnecessary hearings. The value of this approach was articulated in *Raines v. United States*, 423 F.2d 526, 529–530 (4th Cir. 1970):

> Unless it is clear from the pleadings and the files and records that the prisoner is entitled to no relief, the statute makes a hearing mandatory. We think there is a permissible intermediate step that may avoid the necessity for an expensive and time consuming evidentiary hearing in every Section 2255 case. It may instead be perfectly appropriate, depending upon the nature of the allegations, for the district court to proceed by requiring that the record be expanded to include letters, documentary evidence, and, in an appropriate case, even affidavits. *United States v. Carlino*, 400 F.2d 56 (2nd Cir. 1968); *Mirra v. United States*, 379 F.2d 782 (2nd Cir. 1967); *Accardi v. United States*, 379 F.2d 312 (2nd Cir. 1967). When the issue is one of credibility, resolution on the basis of affidavits can rarely be conclusive, but that is not to say they may not be helpful.

In *Harris v. Nelson*, 394 U.S. 286, 300 (1969), the court said:

> At any time in the proceedings * * * *either on [the court's] own motion* or upon cause shown by the petitioner, it may issue such writs and take or authorize such proceedings * * * *before* or in conjunction with the hearing of the facts * * *. [emphasis added]

Subdivision (b) specifies the materials which may be added to the record. These include, without limitation, letters predating the filing of the petition in the district court, documents, exhibits, and answers under oath directed to written interrogatories propounded by the judge. Under this subdivision affidavits may be submitted and considered part of the record. Subdivision (b) is consistent with 28 U.S.C. §§ 2246 and 2247 and the decision in *Raines* with regard to types of material that may be considered upon application for a writ of habeas corpus. See *United States v. Carlino*, 400 F.2d 56, 58 (2d Cir. 1968), and *Machibroda v. United States*, 368 U.S. 487 (1962).

Under subdivision (c) all materials proposed to be included in the record must be submitted to the party against whom they are to be offered.

Under subdivision (d) the judge can require authentication if he believes it desirable to do so.

2004 Amendments

The language of Rule 7 has been amended as part of general restyling of the rules to make them more easily understood and to make style and terminology consistent throughout the rules. These changes are intended to be stylistic and no substantive change is intended, except as noted below.

Revised Rule 7(a) is not intended to restrict the court's authority to expand the record through means other than requiring the parties themselves to provide the information. Further, the rule has been changed to remove the reference to the "merits" of the petition in the recognition that a court may wish to expand the record in order to assist it in deciding an issue other than the merits of the petition.

The language in current Rule 7(d), which deals with authentication of materials in the expanded record, has been moved to revised Rule 7(a).

Rule 8. Evidentiary Hearing

(a) Determining Whether to Hold a Hearing. If the petition is not dismissed, the judge must review the answer, any transcripts and records of state-court proceedings, and any materials submitted under Rule 7 to determine whether an evidentiary hearing is warranted.

(b) Reference to a Magistrate Judge. A judge may, under 28 U.S.C. § 636(b), refer the petition to a magistrate judge to conduct hearings and to file proposed findings of fact and recommendations for disposition. When they are filed, the clerk must promptly serve copies of the proposed findings and recommendations on all parties. Within 10 days after being served, a party may file objections as provided by local court rule. The judge must determine *de novo* any proposed finding or recommendation to which objection is made. The judge may accept, reject, or modify any proposed finding or recommendation.

(c) Appointing Counsel; Time of Hearing. If an evidentiary hearing is warranted, the judge must appoint an attorney to represent a petitioner who qualifies to have counsel appointed under 18 U.S.C. § 3006A. The judge must conduct the hearing as soon as practicable after giving the attorneys adequate time to investigate and prepare. These rules do not limit the appointment of counsel under § 3006A at any stage of the proceeding.

(As amended Pub.L. 94–426, § 2(5), Sept. 28, 1976, 90 Stat. 1334; Pub.L. 94–577, § 2(a)(1), (b)(1), Oct. 21, 1976, 90 Stat. 2730, 2731; Apr. 26, 2004, eff. Dec. 1, 2004.)

ADVISORY COMMITTEE NOTES

1976 Adoption

This rule outlines the procedure to be followed by the court immediately prior to and after the determination of whether to hold an evidentiary hearing.

The provisions are applicable if the petition has not been dismissed at a previous stage in the proceeding [including a summary dismissal under Rule 4; a dismissal pursuant to a motion by the respondent; a dismissal after the answer and petition are considered; or a dismissal after consideration of the pleadings and an expanded record].

If dismissal has not been ordered, the court must determine whether an evidentiary hearing is required. This determination is to be made upon a review of the answer, the transcript and record of state court proceedings, and if there is one, the expanded record. As the United States Supreme Court noted in *Townsend v. Sam,* 372 U.S. 293, 319 (1963):

> Ordinarily [the complete state-court] record—including the transcript of testimony (or if unavailable some adequate substitute, such as a narrative record), the pleadings, court opinions, and other pertinent documents—is indispensable to determining whether the habeas applicant received a full and fair state-court evidentiary hearing resulting in reliable findings.

Subdivision (a) contemplates that all of these materials, if available, will be taken into account. This is especially important in view of the standard set down in *Townsend* for determining *when* a hearing in the federal habeas proceeding is mandatory.

> The appropriate standard * * * is this: Where the facts are in dispute, the federal court in habeas corpus must hold an evidentiary hearing if the habeas applicant did not receive a full and fair evidentiary hearing in a state court, either at the time of the trial or in a collateral proceeding.

372 U.S. at 312

The circumstances under which a federal hearing is mandatory are now specified in 28 U.S.C. § 2254(d). The 1966 amendment clearly places the burden on the petitioner, when there has already been a state hearing, to show that it was not a fair or adequate hearing for one or more of the specifically enumerated reasons, in order to force a federal evidentiary hearing. Since the function of an evidentiary hearing is to try issues of fact (372 U.S. at 309), such a hearing is unnecessary when only issues of law are raised. See, *e.g., Yeaman v. United States,* 326 F.2d 293 (9th Cir. 1963).

In situations in which an evidentiary hearing is not mandatory, the judge may nonetheless decide that an evidentiary hearing is desirable:

> The purpose of the test is to indicate the situations in which the holding of an evidentiary hearing is mandatory. In all other cases where the material facts are in dispute, the holding of such a hearing is in the discretion of the district judge.

372 U.S. at 318

If the judge decides that an evidentiary hearing is neither required nor desirable, he shall make such a disposition of the petition "as justice shall require." Most habeas petitions are dismissed before the prehearing conference stage (see Director of the Administrative Office of the United States Courts, Annual Report 245–245c (table C4) (1970)) and of those not dismissed, the majority raise factual issues that necessitate an evidentiary hearing. If no hearing is required, most petitions are dismissed, but in unusual cases the court may grant the relief sought without a hearing. This includes immediate release from custody or nullification of a judgment under which the sentence is to be served in the future.

Subdivision (b) provides that a magistrate, when so empowered by rule of the district court, may recommend to the district judge that an evidentiary hearing be held or that the petition be dismissed, provided he gives the district judge a sufficiently detailed description of the facts so that the judge may decide whether or not to hold an evidentiary hearing. This provision is not inconsistent with the holding in *Wingo v. Wedding,* 418 U.S. 461 (1974), that the Federal Magistrates Act did not change the requirement of the habeas corpus statute that federal judges personally conduct habeas evidentiary hearings, and that consequently a local district court rule was invalid insofar as it authorized a magistrate to hold such hearings. 28 U.S.C. § 636(b) provides that a district court may by rule authorize any magistrate to perform certain additional duties, including preliminary review of applications for posttrial relief made by individuals convicted of criminal offenses, and submission of a report and recommendations to facilitate the decision of the district judge having jurisdiction over the case as to whether there should be a hearing.

As noted in *Wingo,* review "by Magistrates of applications for post-trial relief is thus limited to review for the purpose of proposing, not holding, evidentiary hearings."

Utilization of the magistrate as specified in subdivision (b) will aid in the expeditious and fair handling of habeas petitions.

> A qualified, experienced magistrate will, it is hoped, acquire an expertise in examining these [postconviction review] applications and summarizing their important contents for the district judge, thereby facilitating his decisions. Law clerks are presently charged with this responsibility by many judges, but judges have noted that the normal 1-year clerkship does not afford law clerks the time or experience necessary to attain real efficiency in handling such applications.

S.Rep. No. 371, 90th Cong., 1st Sess., 26 (1967).

Under subdivision (c) there are two provisions that differ from the procedure set forth in 28 U.S.C. § 2243. These are the appointment of counsel and standard for determining how soon the hearing will be held.

If an evidentiary hearing is required the judge must appoint counsel for a petitioner who qualified [sic] for appointment under the Criminal Justice Act. Currently, the appointment of counsel is not recognized as a right at any stage of a habeas proceeding. See, *e.g., United States ex rel. Marshall v. Wilkins,* 338 F.2d 404 (2d Cir. 1964). Some district courts have, however, by local rule, required that counsel must be provided for indigent petitioners in cases requiring a hearing. See, *e.g., D.N.M.R. 21(f), E.D.N.Y.R. 26(d).* Appointment of counsel at this stage is mandatory under subdivision (c). This requirement will not limit the authority of the court to provide counsel at an earlier stage if it is thought desirable to do so as is done in some courts under current practice. At the evidentiary hearing stage, however, an indigent petitioner's access to counsel should not depend on local practice and, for this reason, the furnishing of counsel is made mandatory.

Counsel can perform a valuable function benefiting both the court and the petitioner. The issues raised can be more clearly identified if both sides have the benefit of trained legal personnel. The presence of counsel at the prehearing conference may help to expedite the evidentiary hearing or make it unnecessary, and counsel will be able to make better use of available prehearing discovery procedures. Compare ABA Project on Standards for Criminal Justice, Standards Relating to Post-Conviction Remedies § 4.4, p. 66 (Approved Draft 1968). At a hearing, the petitioner's claims are more likely to be effectively and properly presented by counsel.

Under 18 U.S.C. § 3006A(g), payment is allowed counsel up to $250, plus reimbursement for expenses reasonably incurred. The standards of indigency under this section are less strict than those regarding eligibility to prosecute a petition in forma pauperis, and thus many who cannot qualify to proceed under 28 U.S.C. § 1915 will be entitled to the benefits of counsel under 18 U.S.C. § 3006A(g). Under Rule 6(c), the court may order the respondent to reimburse counsel from state funds for fees and expenses incurred as the result of the utilization of discovery procedures by the respondent.

Subdivision (c) provides that the hearing shall be conducted as promptly as possible, taking into account "the need of counsel for both parties for adequate time for investigation and preparation." This differs from the language of 28 U.S.C. § 2243, which requires that the day for the hearing be set "not more than five days after the return unless for good cause additional time is allowed." This time limit fails to take into account the function that may be served by a prehearing conference and the time required to prepare adequately for an evidentiary hearing. Although "additional time" is often allowed under § 2243, subdivision (c) provides more flexibility to take account of the complexity of the case, the availability of important materials, the workload of the attorney general, and the time required by appointed counsel to prepare.

While the rule does not make specific provision for a prehearing conference, the omission is not intended to cast doubt upon the value of such a conference:

> The conference may limit the questions to be resolved, identify areas of agreement and dispute, and explore evidentiary problems that may be expected to arise. * * * [S]uch conferences may also disclose that a hearing is unnecessary * * *.
>
> ABA Project on Standards for Criminal Justice, Standards Relating to Post-Conviction Remedies § 4.6, commentary pp. 74–75. (Approved Draft, 1968.)

See also Developments in the Law—Federal Habeas Corpus, 83 Harv.L.Rev. 1038, 1188 (1970).

The rule does not contain a specific provision on the subpoenaing of witnesses. It is left to local practice to determine the method for doing this. The implementation of 28 U.S.C. § 1825 on the payment of witness fees is dealt with in an opinion of the Comptroller General, February 28, 1974.

2004 Amendments

The language of Rule 8 has been amended as part of general restyling of the rules to make them more easily understood and to make style and terminology consistent throughout the rules. These changes are intended to be stylistic and no substantive change is intended.

Rule 8(a) is not intended to supersede the restrictions on evidentiary hearings contained in 28 U.S.C. § 2254(e)(2).

The requirement in current Rule 8(b)(2) that a copy of the magistrate judge's findings must be promptly mailed to all parties has been changed in revised Rule 8(b) to require that copies of those findings be served on all parties. As used in this rule, "service" means service consistent with Federal Rule of Civil Procedure 5(b), which allows mailing the copies.

HISTORICAL NOTES

Effective and Applicability Provisions

1976 Acts. Section 2(c) of Pub.L. 94–577 provided that: "The amendments made by this section [amending subdivs. (b) and (c) of this rule and Rule 8(b), (c) of the Rules Governing Proceedings Under Section 2255 of this title] shall take effect with respect to petitions under section 2254 and motions under section 2255 of title 28 of the United States Code filed on or after February 1, 1977."

Rule 9. Second or Successive Petitions

Before presenting a second or successive petition, the petitioner must obtain an order from the appropriate court of appeals authorizing the district court to consider the petition as required by 28 U.S.C. § 2244(b)(3) and (4).

(As amended Pub.L. 94–426, § 2(7), (8), Sept. 28, 1976, 90 Stat. 1335; Apr. 26, 2004, eff. Dec. 1, 2004.)

ADVISORY COMMITTEE NOTES

1976 Adoption

This rule is intended to minimize abuse of the writ of habeas corpus by limiting the right to assert stale claims and to file multiple petitions. Subdivision (a) deals with the delayed petition. Subdivision (b) deals with the second or successive petition.

Subdivision (a) provides that a petition attacking the judgment of a state court may be dismissed on the grounds of delay if the petitioner knew or should have known of the existence of the grounds he is presently asserting in the petition and the delay has resulted in the state being prejudiced in its ability to respond to the petition. If the delay is more than five years after the judgment of conviction, prejudice is presumed, although this presumption is rebuttable by the petitioner. Otherwise, the state has the burden of showing such prejudice.

The assertion of stale claims is a problem which is not likely to decrease in frequency. Following the decisions in *Jones v. Cunningham*, 371 U.S. 236 (1963), and *Benson v. California*, 328 F.2d 159 (9th Cir. 1964), the concept of custody expanded greatly, lengthening the time period during which a habeas corpus petition may be filed. The petitioner who is not unconditionally discharged may be on parole or probation for many years. He may at some date, perhaps ten or fifteen years after conviction, decide to challenge the state court judgment. The grounds most often troublesome to the courts are ineffective counsel, denial of right of appeal, plea of guilty unlawfully induced, use of a coerced confession, and illegally constituted jury. The latter four grounds are often interlocked with the allegation of ineffective counsel. When they are asserted after the passage of many years, both the attorney for the defendant and the state have difficulty in ascertaining what the facts are. It often develops that the defense attorney has little or no recollection as to what took place and that many of the participants in the trial are dead or their whereabouts unknown. The court reporter's notes may have been lost or destroyed, thus eliminating any exact record of what transpired. If the case was decided on a guilty plea, even if the record is intact, it may not satisfactorily reveal the extent of the defense attorney's efforts in behalf of the petitioner. As a consequence, there is obvious difficulty in investigating petitioner's allegations.

The interest of both the petitioner and the government can best be served if claims are raised while the evidence is still fresh. The American Bar Association has recognized the interest of the state in protecting itself against stale claims by limiting the right to raise such claims after completion of service of a sentence imposed pursuant to a challenged judgment. See ABA Standards Relating to Post-Conviction Remedies § 2.4(c), p. 45 (Approved Draft, 1968). Subdivision (a) is not limited to those who have completed their sentence. Its reach is broader, extending to all instances where delay by the petitioner has prejudiced the state, subject to the qualifications and conditions contained in the subdivision.

In *McMann v. Richardson*, 397 U.S. 759 (1970), the court made reference to the issue of the stale claim:

> What is at stake in this phase of the case is not the integrity of the state convictions obtained on guilty pleas, *but whether, years later*, defendants must be permitted to withdraw their pleas, which were perfectly valid when made, and be given another choice between admitting their guilt and putting the State to its proof. [Emphasis added.]

397 U.S. at 773

The court refused to allow this, intimating its dislike of collateral attacks on sentences long since imposed which disrupt the state's interest in finality of convictions which were constitutionally valid when obtained.

Subdivision (a) is not a statute of limitations. Rather, the limitation is based on the equitable doctrine of laches. "Laches is such delay in enforcing one's rights as works disadvantage to another." 30A C.J.S. Equity § 112, p. 19. Also, the language of the subdivision, "a petition *may* be dismissed" [emphasis added], is permissive rather than mandatory. This clearly allows the court which is considering the petition to use discretion in assessing the equities of the particular situation.

The use of a flexible rule analogous to laches to bar the assertion of stale claims is suggested in ABA Standards Relating to Post-Conviction Remedies § 2.4, commentary at 48 (Approved Draft, 1968). Additionally, in *Fay v. Noia*, 372 U.S. 391 (1963), the Supreme Court noted:

> Furthermore, habeas corpus has traditionally been regarded as governed by equitable principles. *United States ex rel. Smith v. Baldi*, 344 U.S. 561, 573 (dissenting opinion). Among them is the principle that a suitor's conduct in relation to the matter at hand may disentitle him to the relief he seeks.

372 U.S. at 438

Finally, the doctrine of laches has been applied with reference to another postconviction remedy, the writ of coram nobis. See 24 C.J.S. Criminal Law § 1606(25), p. 779.

The standard used for determining if the petitioner shall be barred from asserting his claim is consistent with that used in laches provisions generally. The petitioner is held to a standard of reasonable diligence. Any inference or presumption arising by reason of the failure to attack collaterally a conviction may be disregarded where (1) there has been a change of law or fact (new evidence) or (2) where the court, in the interest of justice, feels that the collateral attack should be entertained and the prisoner makes a proper showing as to why he has not asserted a particular ground for relief.

Subdivision (a) establishes the presumption that the passage of more than five years from the time of the judgment of conviction to the time of filing a habeas petition is prejudicial to the state. "Presumption" has the meaning given it by Fed.R.Evid. 301. The prisoner has "the burden of going forward with evidence to rebut or meet the presumption" that the state has not been prejudiced by the passage of a substantial period of time. This does not impose too heavy a burden on the petitioner. He usually knows what persons are important to the issue of whether the state has been prejudiced. Rule 6 can be used by the court to allow petitioner liberal discovery to learn whether witnesses have died or whether other circumstances prejudicial to the state have occurred. Even if the petitioner should fail to overcome the presumption of prejudice to the state, he is not automatically barred from asserting his claim. As discussed previously, he may proceed if he neither knew nor, by the exercise of reasonable diligence, could have known of the grounds for relief.

The presumption of prejudice does not come into play if the time lag is not more than five years.

The time limitation should have a positive effect in encouraging petitioners who have knowledge of it to assert all their claims as soon after conviction as possible. The implementation of this rule can be substantially furthered by the development of greater legal resources for prisoners. See ABA Standards Relating to Post-Conviction Remedies § 3.1, pp. 49–50 (Approved Draft, 1968).

Subdivision (a) does not constitute an abridgement or modification of a substantive right under 28 U.S.C. § 2072. There are safeguards for the hardship case. The rule provides a flexible standard for determining when a petition will be barred.

Subdivision (b) deals with the problem of successive habeas petitions. It provides that the judge may dismiss a second or successive petition (1) if it fails to allege new or different grounds for relief or (2) if new or different grounds for relief are alleged and the judge finds the failure of the petitioner to assert those grounds in a prior petition is inexcusable.

In *Sanders v. United States*, 373 U.S. 1 (1963), the court, in dealing with the problem of successive applications, stated:

> Controlling weight *may* be given to denial of a prior application for federal habeas corpus or § 2255 relief only

if (1) the same ground presented in the subsequent application was determined adversely to the applicant on the prior application, (2) the prior determination was on the merits, and (3) the ends of justice would not be served by reaching the merits of the subsequent application. [Emphasis added.]

373 U.S. at 15

The requirement is that the prior determination of the same ground has been on the merits. This requirement is in 28 U.S.C. § 2244(b) and has been reiterated in many cases since *Sanders.* See *Gains v. Allgood,* 391 F.2d 692 (5th Cir. 1968); *Hutchinson v. Craven,* 415 F.2d 278 (9th Cir. 1969); *Brown v. Peyton,* 435 F.2d 1352 (4th Cir. 1970).

With reference to a successive application asserting a new ground or one not previously decided on the merits, the court in *Sanders* noted:

> In either case, full consideration of the merits of the new application can be avoided only if there has been an abuse of the writ * * * and this the Government has the burden of pleading. * * *
>
> Thus, for example, if a prisoner deliberately withholds one of two grounds for federal collateral relief at the time of filing his first application, * * * he may be deemed to have waived his right to a hearing on a second application presenting the withheld ground.

373 U.S. at 17–18

Subdivision (b) has incorporated this principle and requires that the judge find petitioner's failure to have asserted the new grounds in the prior petition to be inexcusable.

Sanders, 18 [sic] U.S.C. § 2244, and subdivision (b) make it clear that the court has discretion to entertain a successive application.

The burden is on the government to plead abuse of the writ. See *Sanders v. United States,* 373 U.S. 1, 10 (1963); *Dixon v. Jacobs,* 427 F.2d 589, 596 (D.C.Cir.1970); cf. *Johnson v. Copinger,* 420 F.2d 395 (4th Cir. 1969). Once the government has done this, the petitioner has the burden of proving that he has not abused the writ. In *Price v. Johnston,* 334 U.S. 266, 292 (1948), the court said:

> [I]f the Government chooses * * * to claim that the prisoner has abused the writ of *habeas corpus,* it rests with the Government to make that claim with clarity and particularity in its return to the order to show cause. That is not an intolerable burden. The Government is usually well acquainted with the facts that are necessary to make such a claim. Once a particular abuse has been alleged, the prisoner has the burden of answering that allegation and of proving that he has not abused the writ.

Subdivision (b) is consistent with the important and well established purpose of habeas corpus. It does not eliminate a remedy to which the petitioner is rightfully entitled. However, in *Sanders,* the court pointed out:

> Nothing in the traditions of habeas corpus requires the federal courts to tolerate needless piecemeal litigation, or to entertain collateral proceedings whose only purpose is to vex, harass, or delay.

373 U.S. at 18

There are instances in which petitioner's failure to assert a ground in a prior petition is excusable. A retroactive change in the law and newly discovered evidence are examples. In rare instances, the court may feel a need to entertain a petition alleging grounds that have already been decided on the merits. *Sanders,* 373 U.S. at 1, 16. However, abusive use of the writ should be discouraged, and instances of abuse are frequent enough to require a means of dealing with them. For example, a successive application, already decided on the merits, may be submitted in the hope of getting before a different judge in multijudge courts. A known ground may be deliberately withheld in the hope of getting two or more hearings or in the hope that delay will result in witnesses and records being lost. There are instances in which a petitioner will have three or four petitions pending at the same time in the same court. There are many hundreds of cases where the application is at least the second one by the petitioner. This subdivision is aimed at screening out the abusive petitions from this large volume, so that the more meritorious petitions can get quicker and fuller consideration.

The form petition, supplied in accordance with Rule 2(c), encourages the petitioner to raise all of his available grounds in one petition. It sets out the most common grounds asserted so that these may be brought to his attention.

Some commentators contend that the problem of abuse of the writ of habeas corpus is greatly overstated:

> Most prisoners, of course, are interested in being released as soon as possible; only rarely will one inexcusably neglect to raise all available issues in his first federal application. The purpose of the "abuse" bar is apparently to deter repetitious applications from those few bored or vindictive prisoners * * *.

83 Harv.L.Rev. at 1153–1154

See also ABA Standards Relating to Post-Conviction Remedies § 6.2, commentary at 92 (Approved Draft, 1968), which states: "The occasional, highly litigious prisoner stands out as the rarest exception." While no recent systematic study of repetitious applications exists, there is no reason to believe that the problem has decreased in significance in relation to the total number of § 2254 petitions filed. That number has increased from 584 in 1949 to 12,088 in 1971. See Director of the Administrative Office of the United States Courts, Annual Report, table 16 (1971). It is appropriate that action be taken by rule to allow the courts to deal with this problem, whatever its specific magnitude. The bar set up by subdivision (b) is not one of rigid application, but rather is within the discretion of the courts on a case-by-case basis.

If it appears to the court after examining the petition and answer (where appropriate) that there is a high probability that the petition will be barred under either subdivision of Rule 9, the court ought to afford petitioner an opportunity to explain his apparent abuse. One way of doing this is by the use of the form annexed hereto. The use of a form will ensure a full airing of the issue so that the court is in a better position to decide whether the petition should be barred. This conforms with *Johnson v. Copinger,* 420 F.2d 395 (4th Cir. 1969), where the court stated:

> [T]he petitioner is obligated to present facts demonstrating that his earlier failure to raise his claims is excusable and does not amount to an abuse of the writ. However, it is

inherent in this obligation placed upon the petitioner that he must be given an opportunity to make his explanation, if he has one. If he is not afforded such an opportunity, the requirement that he satisfy the court that he has not abused the writ is meaningless. Nor do we think that a procedure which allows the imposition of a forfeiture for abuse of the writ, without allowing the petitioner an opportunity to be heard on the issue, comports with the minimum requirements of fairness.

420 F.2d at 399

Use of the recommended form will contribute to an orderly handling of habeas petitions and will contribute to the ability of the court to distinguish the excusable from the inexcusable delay or failure to assert a ground for relief in a prior petition.

2004 Amendments

The language of Rule 9 has been amended as part of general restyling of the rules to make them more easily understood and to make style and terminology consistent throughout the rules. These changes are intended to be stylistic and no substantive change is intended, except as noted below.

First, current Rule 9(a) has been deleted as unnecessary in light of the applicable one-year statute of limitations for § 2254 petitions, added as part of the Antiterrorism and Effective Death Penalty Act of 1996, 28 U.S.C. § 2244(d).

Second, current Rule 9(b), now Rule 9, has been changed to also reflect provisions in the Antiterrorism and Effective Death Penalty Act of 1996, 28 U.S.C. § 2244(b)(3) and (4), which now require a petitioner to obtain approval from the appropriate court of appeals before filing a second or successive petition.

Finally, the title of Rule 9 has been changed to reflect the fact that the only topic now addressed in the rules is that of second or successive petitions.

Rule 10. Powers of a Magistrate Judge

A magistrate judge may perform the duties of a district judge under these rules, as authorized under 28 U.S.C. § 636.

(As amended Pub.L. 94–426, § 2(11), Sept. 28, 1976, 90 Stat. 1335; Apr. 30, 1979, eff. Aug. 1, 1979; Apr. 26, 2004, eff. Dec. 1, 2004.)

ADVISORY COMMITTEE NOTES

1976 Adoption

Under this rule the duties imposed upon the judge of the district court by rules 2, 3, 4, 6, and 7 may be performed by a magistrate if and to the extent he is empowered to do so by a rule of the district court. However, when such duties involve the making of an order under rule 4 disposing of the petition, that order must be made by the court. The magistrate in such instances must submit to the court his report as to the facts and his recommendation with respect to the order.

The Federal Magistrates Act allows magistrates, when empowered by local rule, to perform certain functions in proceedings for post-trial relief. See 28 U.S.C. § 636(b)(3). The performance of such functions, when authorized, is intended to "afford some degree of relief to district judges and their law clerks, who are presently burdened with burgeoning numbers of habeas corpus petitions and applications under 28 U.S.C. § 2255." Committee on the Judiciary, The Federal Magistrates Act, S.Rep. No. 371, 90th Cong., 1st sess., 26 (1967).

Under 28 U.S.C. § 636(b), any district court,

> by the concurrence of a majority of all the judges of such district court, may establish rules pursuant to which any full-time United States magistrate * * * may be assigned within the territorial jurisdiction of such court such additional duties as are not inconsistent with the Constitution and laws of the United States.

The proposed rule recognizes the limitations imposed by 28 U.S.C. § 636(b) upon the powers of magistrates to act in federal postconviction proceedings. These limitations are: (1) that the magistrate may act only pursuant to a rule passed by the majority of the judges in the district court in which the magistrate serves, and (2) that the duties performed by the magistrate pursuant to such rule be consistent with the Constitution and laws of the United States.

It has been suggested magistrates be empowered by law to hold hearings and make final decisions in habeas proceedings. See Proposed Reformation of Federal Habeas Corpus Procedure: Use of Federal Magistrates, 54 Iowa L.Rev. 1147, 1158 (1969). However, the Federal Magistrates Act does not authorize such use of magistrates. *Wingo v. Wedding*, 418 U.S. 461 (1974). See advisory committee note to Rule 8. While the use of magistrates can help alleviate the strain imposed on the district courts by the large number of unmeritorious habeas petitions, neither 28 U.S.C. § 636(b) nor this rule contemplate the abdication by the court of its decision-making responsibility. See also Developments in the Law—Federal Habeas Corpus, 83 Harv.L.Rev. 1038, 1188 (1970).

Where a full-time magistrate is not available, the duties contemplated by this rule may be assigned to a part-time magistrate.

2004 Amendments

The language of Rule 10 has been amended as part of general restyling of the rules to make them more easily understood and to make style and terminology consistent throughout the rules. These changes are intended to be stylistic and no substantive change is intended.

HISTORICAL NOTES

Change of Name

United States magistrate appointed under section 631 of Title 28, Judiciary and Judicial Procedure, to be known as United States magistrate judge after Dec. 1, 1990, with any reference to United States magistrate or magistrate in Title 28, in any other Federal statute, etc., deemed a reference to United States magistrate judge appointed under section 631 of Title 28, see section 321 of Pub.L. 101–650, set out as a note under section 631 of Title 28.

Rule 11. Applicability of the Federal Rules of Civil Procedure

The Federal Rules of Civil Procedure, to the extent that they are not inconsistent with any statutory provisions or these rules, may be applied to a proceeding under these rules.

(As amended Apr. 26, 2004, eff. Dec. 1, 2004.)

ADVISORY COMMITTEE NOTES

1976 Adoption

Habeas corpus proceedings are characterized as civil in nature. See, *e.g.*, *Fisher v. Baker*, 203 U.S. 174, 181 (1906). However, under Fed.R.Civ.P. 81(a)(2), the applicability of the civil rules to habeas corpus actions has been limited, although the various courts which have considered this problem have had difficulty in setting out the boundaries of this limitation. See *Harris v. Nelson*, 394 U.S. 286 (1969) at 289, footnote 1. Rule 11 is intended to conform with the Supreme Court's approach in the *Harris* case. There the court was dealing with the petitioner's contention that Civil Rule 33 granting the right to discovery via written interrogatories is wholly applicable to habeas corpus proceedings. The court held:

> We agree with the Ninth Circuit that Rule 33 of the Federal Rules of Civil Procedure is not applicable to habeas corpus proceedings and that 28 U.S.C. § 2246 does not authorize interrogatories except in limited circumstances not applicable to this case; but we conclude that, in appropriate circumstances, a district court, confronted by a petition for habeas corpus which establishes a prima facie case for relief, may use or authorize the use of suitable discovery procedures, including interrogatories, reasonably fashioned to elicit facts necessary to help the court to "dispose of the matter as law and justice require" 28 U.S.C. § 2243.

394 U.S. at 290

The court then went on to consider the contention that the "conformity" provision of Rule 81(a)(2) should be rigidly applied so that the civil rules would be applicable only to the extent that habeas corpus practice had conformed to the practice in civil actions at the time of the adoption of the Federal Rules of Civil Procedure on September 16, 1938. The court said:

> Although there is little direct evidence, relevant to the present problem, of the purpose of the "conformity" provision of Rule 81(a)(2), the concern of the draftsmen, as a general matter, seems to have been to provide for the continuing applicability of the "civil" rules in their new form to those areas of practice in habeas corpus and other enumerated proceedings in which the "specified" proceedings had theretofore utilized the modes of civil practice. Otherwise, those proceedings were to be considered outside of the scope of the rules without prejudice, of course, to the use of particular rules by analogy or otherwise, where appropriate.

394 U.S. at 294

The court then reiterated its commitment to judicial discretion in formulating rules and procedures for habeas corpus proceedings by stating:

> [T]he habeas corpus jurisdiction and the duty to exercise it being present, the courts may fashion appropriate modes of procedure, by analogy to existing rules or otherwise in conformity with judicial usage.

Where their duties require it, this is the inescapable obligation of the courts. Their authority is expressly confirmed in the All Writs Act, 28 U.S.C. § 1651.

394 U.S. at 299

Rule 6 of these proposed rules deals specifically with the issue of discovery in habeas actions in a manner consistent with *Harris*. Rule 11 extends this approach to allow the court considering the petition to use any of the rules of civil procedure (unless inconsistent with these rules of habeas corpus) when in its discretion the court decides they are appropriate under the circumstances of the particular case. The court does not have to rigidly apply rules which would be inconsistent or inequitable in the overall framework of habeas corpus. Rule 11 merely recognizes and affirms their discretionary power to use their judgment in promoting the ends of justice.

Rule 11 permits application of the civil rules only when it would be appropriate to do so. Illustrative of an inappropriate application is that rejected by the Supreme Court in *Pitchess v. Davis*, 95 S.Ct. 1748 (1975), holding that Fed. R.Civ.P. 60(b) should not be applied in a habeas case when it would have the effect of altering the statutory exhaustion requirement of 28 U.S.C. § 2254.

2004 Amendments

The language of Rule 11 has been amended as part of general restyling of the rules to make them more easily understood and to make style and terminology consistent throughout the rules. These changes are intended to be stylistic and no substantive change is intended.

APPENDIX OF FORMS

Petition for Relief From a Conviction or Sentence By a Person in State Custody (Petition Under 28 U.S.C. § 2254 for a Writ of Habeas Corpus)

Instructions

1. To use this form, you must be a person who is currently serving a sentence under a judgment against you in a state court. You are asking for relief from the conviction or the sentence. This form is your petition for relief.

2. You may also use this form to challenge a state judgment that imposed a sentence to be served in the future, but you must fill in the name of the state where the judgment was entered. If you want to challenge a federal judgment that imposed a sentence to be served in the future, you should file a motion under 28 U.S.C. § 2255 in the federal court that entered the judgment.

3. Make sure the form is typed or neatly written.

4. You must tell the truth and sign the form. If you make a false statement of a material fact, you may be prosecuted for perjury.

5. Answer all the questions. You do not need to cite law. You may submit additional pages if necessary. If you do not fill out the form properly, you will be asked to submit additional or correct information. If you want to submit a brief or arguments, you must submit them in a separate memorandum.

6. You must pay a fee of $5. If the fee is paid, your petition will be filed. If you cannot pay the fee, you may ask to proceed *in forma pauperis* (as a poor person). To do that, you must fill out the last page of this form. Also, you must submit a certificate signed by an officer at the institution where you are confined showing the amount of money that the institution is holding for you. If your account exceeds $___, you must pay the filing fee.

7. In this petition, you may challenge the judgment entered by only one court. If you want to challenge a judgment entered by a different court (either in the same state or in different states), you must file a separate petition.

8. When you have completed the form, send the original and two copies to the Clerk of the United States District Court at this address:

   Clerk, United States District Court for _____
   Address
   City, State Zip Code

9. **CAUTION: You must include in this petition all the grounds for relief from the conviction or sentence that you challenge. And you must state the facts that support each ground. If you fail to set forth all the grounds in this petition, you may be barred from presenting additional grounds at a later date.**

10. **CAPITAL CASES: If you are under a sentence of death, you are entitled to the assistance of counsel and should request the appointment of counsel.**

PETITION UNDER 28 U.S.C. § 2254 FOR WRIT OF HABEAS CORPUS BY A PERSON IN STATE CUSTODY

Name (under which you were convicted): Docket or Case No.:

Place of Confinement: Prisoner No.:

Petitioner (include the name under which you were convicted) Respondent (authorized person having custody of petitioner)

v.

The Attorney General of the State of

PETITION

1. (a) Name and location of court that entered the judgment of conviction you are challenging: _____

(b) Criminal docket or case number (if you know): ___

2. (a) Date of the judgment of conviction (if you know): _____

(b) Date of sentencing: _____

3. Length of sentence: _____

4. In this case, were you convicted on more than one count or of more than one crime? Yes ☐ No ☐

5. Identify all crimes of which you were convicted and sentenced in this case: _____

6. (a) What was your plea? (Check one)

(1) Not guilty ☐ (3) Nolo contendere (no contest) ☐

(2) Guilty ☐ (4) Insanity plea ☐

(b) If you entered a guilty plea to one count or charge and a not guilty plea to another count or charge, what did you plead guilty to and what did you plead not guilty to? _____

(c) If you went to trial, what kind of trial did you have? (Check one)

Jury ☐ Judge only ☐

7. Did you testify at a pretrial hearing, trial, or a post-trial hearing?

Yes ☐ No ☐

8. Did you appeal from the judgment of conviction?

Yes ☐ No ☐

9. If you did appeal, answer the following:

(a) Name of court: _____

(b) Docket or case number (if you know): _____

(c) Result: _____

(d) Date of result (if you know): _____

(e) Citation to the case (if you know): _____

(f) Grounds raised: _____

(g) Did you seek further review by a higher state court? Yes ☐ No ☐

If yes, answer the following:

(1) Name of court: _____

(2) Docket or case number (if you know): _____

(3) Result: _____

(4) Date of result (if you know): _____

(5) Citation to the case (if you know): _____

(6) Grounds raised: _____

(h) Did you file a petition for certiorari in the United States Supreme Court?

Yes ☐ No ☐

If yes, answer the following:

(1) Docket or case number (if you know): _____

(2) Result: _____

(3) Date of result (if you know): _____

(4) Citation to the case (if you know): _____

10. Other than the direct appeals listed above, have you previously filed any other petitions, applications, or motions concerning this judgment of conviction in any state court?

Yes ☐ No ☐

11. If your answer to Question 10 was "Yes," give the following information:

(a) (1) Name of court: _____

(2) Docket or case number (if you know): _____

(3) Date of filing (if you know): _____

(4) Nature of the proceeding: _____

(5) Grounds raised: _____

(6) Did you receive a hearing where evidence was given on your petition, application, or motion?

Yes ☐ No ☐

(7) Result: _____

(8) Date of result (if you know): _____

(b) If you filed any second petition, application, or motion, give the same information:

(1) Name of court: _____

(2) Docket or case number (if you know): _____

(3) Date of filing (if you know): _____

(4) Nature of the proceeding: _____

(5) Grounds raised: _____

(6) Did you receive a hearing where evidence was given on your petition, application, or motion?
Yes ☐ No ☐
(7) Result:
(8) Date of result (if you know):

(c) If you filed any third petition, application, or motion, give the same information:
(1) Name of court:
(2) Docket or case number (if you know):
(3) Date of filing (if you know):
(4) Nature of the proceeding:
(5) Grounds raised:

(6) Did you receive a hearing where evidence was given on your petition, application, or motion?
Yes ☐ No ☐
(7) Result:
(8) Date of result (if you know):

(d) Did you appeal to the highest state court having jurisdiction over the action taken on your petition, application, or motion?
(1) First petition: Yes ☐ No ☐
(2) Second petition: Yes ☐ No ☐
(3) Third petition: Yes ☐ No ☐

(e) If you did not appeal to the highest state court having jurisdiction, explain why you did not:

12. For this petition, state every ground on which you claim that you are being held in violation of the Constitution, laws, or treaties of the United States. Attach additional pages if you have more than four grounds. State the facts supporting each ground.

CAUTION: To proceed in the federal court, you must ordinarily first exhaust (use up) your available state-court remedies on each ground on which you request action by the federal court. Also, if you fail to set forth all the grounds in this petition, you may be barred from presenting additional grounds at a later date.

GROUND ONE:

(a) Supporting facts (Do not argue or cite law. Just state the specific facts that support your claim.):

(b) If you did not exhaust your state remedies on Ground One, explain why:

(c) **Direct Appeal of Ground One:**
(1) If you appealed from the judgment of conviction, did you raise this issue?
Yes ☐ No ☐
(2) If you did not raise this issue in your direct appeal, explain why:

(d) **Post-Conviction Proceedings:**
(1) Did you raise this issue through a post-conviction motion or petition for habeas corpus in a state trial court?
Yes ☐ No ☐
(2) If your answer to Question (d)(1) is "Yes," state:
Type of motion or petition:
Name and location of the court where the motion or petition was filed:
Docket or case number (if you know):
Date of the court's decision:
Result (attach a copy of the court's opinion or order, if available):

(3) Did you receive a hearing on your motion or petition?
Yes ☐ No ☐
(4) Did you appeal from the denial of your motion or petition?
Yes ☐ No ☐
(5) If your answer to Question (d)(4) is "Yes," did you raise this issue in the appeal?
Yes ☐ No ☐
(6) If your answer to Question (d)(4) is "Yes," state:
Name and location of the court where the appeal was filed:
Docket or case number (if you know):
Date of the court's decision:
Result (attach a copy of the court's opinion or order, if available):

(7) If your answer to Question (d)(4) or Question (d)(5) is "No," explain why you did not raise this issue:

(e) **Other Remedies:** Describe any other procedures (such as habeas corpus, administrative remedies, etc.) that you have used to exhaust your state remedies on Ground One:

GROUND TWO:

(a) Supporting facts (Do not argue or cite law. Just state the specific facts that support your claim.): _____

(b) If you did not exhaust your state remedies on Ground Two, explain why: _____

(c) **Direct Appeal of Ground Two:**

(1) If you appealed from the judgment of conviction, did you raise this issue?

Yes ☐ No ☐

(2) If you did not raise this issue in your direct appeal, explain why: _____

(d) **Post-Conviction Proceedings:**

(1) Did you raise this issue through a post-conviction motion or petition for habeas corpus in a state trial court?

Yes ☐ No ☐

(2) If your answer to Question (d)(1) is "Yes," state:

Type of motion or petition: _____

Name and location of the court where the motion or petition was filed: _____

Docket or case number (if you know): _____

Date of the court's decision: _____

Result (attach a copy of the court's opinion or order, if available): _____

(3) Did you receive a hearing on your motion or petition?

Yes ☐ No ☐

(4) Did you appeal from the denial of your motion or petition?

Yes ☐ No ☐

(5) If your answer to Question (d)(4) is "Yes," did you raise this issue in the appeal?

Yes ☐ No ☐

(6) If your answer to Question (d)(4) is "Yes," state:

Name and location of the court where the appeal was filed: _____

Docket or case number (if you know): _____

Date of the court's decision: _____

Result (attach a copy of the court's opinion or order, if available): _____

(7) If your answer to Question (d)(4) or Question (d)(5) is "No," explain why you did not raise this issue: _____

(e) **Other Remedies:** Describe any other procedures (such as habeas corpus, administrative remedies, etc.) that you have used to exhaust your state remedies on Ground Two: _____

GROUND THREE: _____

(a) Supporting facts (Do not argue or cite law. Just state the specific facts that support your claim.): _____

(b) If you did not exhaust your state remedies on Ground Three, explain why: _____

(c) **Direct Appeal of Ground Three:**

(1) If you appealed from the judgment of conviction, did you raise this issue?

Yes ☐ No ☐

(2) If you did not raise this issue in your direct appeal, explain why: _____

(d) **Post-Conviction Proceedings:**

(1) Did you raise this issue through a post-conviction motion or petition for habeas corpus in a state trial court?

Yes ☐ No ☐

(2) If your answer to Question (d)(1) is "Yes," state:

Type of motion or petition: _____

Name and location of the court where the motion or petition was filed: _____

Docket or case number (if you know): _____

Date of the court's decision: _____

Result (attach a copy of the court's opinion or order, if available): _____

(3) Did you receive a hearing on your motion or petition?

Yes ☐ No ☐

(4) Did you appeal from the denial of your motion or petition?

Yes ☐ No ☐

(5) If your answer to Question (d)(4) is "Yes," did you raise this issue in the appeal?

Yes ☐ No ☐

(6) If your answer to Question (d)(4) is "Yes," state:

Name and location of the court where the appeal was filed: _____

Docket or case number (if you know): _____

Date of the court's decision: _____

Result (attach a copy of the court's opinion or order, if available): _____

(7) If your answer to Question (d)(4) or Question (d)(5) is "No," explain why you did not raise this issue: ____

(e) **Other Remedies:** Describe any other procedures (such as habeas corpus, administrative remedies, etc.) that you have used to exhaust your state remedies on Ground Three: ____

GROUND FOUR: ____

(a) Supporting facts (Do not argue or cite law. Just state the specific facts that support your claim.): ____

(b) If you did not exhaust your state remedies on Ground Four, explain why: ____

(c) **Direct Appeal of Ground Four:**

(1) If you appealed from the judgment of conviction, did you raise this issue?

Yes ☐ No ☐

(2) If you did not raise this issue in your direct appeal, explain why:

(d) **Post-Conviction Proceedings:**

(1) Did you raise this issue through a post-conviction motion or petition for habeas corpus in a state trial court?

Yes ☐ No ☐

(2) If your answer to Question (d)(1) is "Yes," state:

Type of motion or petition: ____

Name and location of the court where the motion or petition was filed: ____

Docket or case number (if you know): ____

Date of the court's decision: ____

Result (attach a copy of the court's opinion or order, if available): ____

(3) Did you receive a hearing on your motion or petition?

Yes ☐ No ☐

(4) Did you appeal from the denial of your motion or petition?

Yes ☐ No ☐

(5) If your answer to Question (d)(4) is "Yes," did you raise this issue in the appeal?

Yes ☐ No ☐

(6) If your answer to Question (d)(4) is "Yes," state:

Name and location of the court where the appeal was filed: ____

Docket or case number (if you know): ____

Date of the court's decision: ____

Result (attach a copy of the court's opinion or order, if available): ____

(7) If your answer to Question (d)(4) or Question (d)(5) is "No," explain why you did not raise this issue: ____

(e) **Other Remedies:** Describe any other procedures (such as habeas corpus, administrative remedies, etc.) that you have used to exhaust your state remedies on Ground Four:

13. Please answer these additional questions about the petition you are filing:

(a) Have all grounds for relief that you have raised in this petition been presented to the highest state court having jurisdiction? Yes ☐ No ☐

If your answer is "No," state which grounds have not been so presented and give your reason(s) for not presenting them: ____

(b) Is there any ground in this petition that has not been presented in some state or federal court? If so, which ground or grounds have not been presented, and state your reasons for not presenting them: ____

14. Have you previously filed any type of petition, application, or motion in a federal court regarding the conviction that you challenge in this petition? Yes ☐ No ☐

If "Yes," state the name and location of the court, the docket or case number, the type of proceeding, the issues raised, the date of the court's decision, and the result for each petition, application, or motion filed. Attach a copy of any court opinion or order, if available. ____

15. Do you have any petition or appeal now pending (filed and not decided yet) in any court, either state or federal, for the judgment you are challenging? Yes ☐ No ☐

If "Yes," state the name and location of the court, the docket or case number, the type of proceeding, and the issues raised. ____

16. Give the name and address, if you know, of each attorney who represented you in the following stages of the judgment you are challenging:

(a) At preliminary hearing: ____

(b) At arraignment and plea: ____

(c) At trial: _____

(d) At sentencing: _____

(e) On appeal: _____

(f) In any post-conviction proceeding: _____

(g) On appeal from any ruling against you in a post-conviction proceeding: _____

17. Do you have any future sentence to serve after you complete the sentence for the judgment that you are challenging? Yes ☐ No ☐
(a) If so, give name and location of court that imposed the other sentence you will serve in the future: _____

(b) Give the date the other sentence was imposed: _____

(c) Give the length of the other sentence: _____

(d) Have you filed, or do you plan to file, any petition that challenges the judgment or sentence to be served in the future? Yes ☐ No ☐

18. TIMELINESS OF PETITION: If your judgment of conviction became final over one year ago, you must explain why the one-year statute of limitations as contained in 28 U.S.C. § 2244(d) does not bar your petition.*

_____

* The Antiterrorism and Effective Death Penalty Act of 1996 ("AEDPA") as contained in 28 U.S.C. § 2244(d) provides in part that:

(1) A one-year period of limitation shall apply to an application for a writ of habeas corpus by a person in custody pursuant to the judgment of a State court. The limitation period shall run from the latest of—

(A) the date on which the judgment became final by the conclusion of direct review or the expiration of the time for seeking such review;

(B) the date on which the impediment to filing an application created by State action in violation of the Constitution or laws of the United States is removed, if the applicant was prevented from filing by such state action;

(C) the date on which the constitutional right asserted was initially recognized by the Supreme Court, if the right has been newly recognized by the Supreme Court and made retroactively applicable to cases on collateral review; or

(D) the date on which the factual predicate of the claim or claims presented could have been discovered through the exercise of due diligence.

(2) The time during which a properly filed application for State post-conviction or other collateral review with respect to the pertinent judgment or claim is pending shall not be counted toward any period of limitation under this subsection.

Therefore, petitioner asks that the Court grant the following relief: _____

or any other relief to which petitioner may be entitled.

_____
Signature of Attorney (if any)

I declare (or certify, verify, or state) under penalty of perjury that the foregoing is true and correct and that this Petition for Writ of Habeas Corpus was placed in the prison mailing system on _____ (month, date, year).

_____
Executed (signed) on (date).

_____
Signature of Petitioner

If the person signing is not petitioner, state relationship to petitioner and explain why petitioner is not signing this petition. _____

IN FORMA PAUPERIS DECLARATION

[Insert appropriate court]

_____ (Petitioner)	DECLARATION IN SUPPORT OF REQUEST TO PROCEED *IN FORMA PAUPERIS*
v.	
_____ (Respondent(s))	

I, _____, declare that I am the petitioner in the above entitled case; that in support of my motion to proceed without being required to prepay fees, costs or give security therefor, I state that because of my poverty I am unable to pay the costs of said proceeding or to give security therefor; that I believe I am entitled to relief.

1. Are you presently employed? Yes ☐ No ☐
   a. If the answer is "yes," state the amount of your salary or wages per month, and give the name and address of your employer.

   _____

   _____

   b. If the answer is "no," state the date of last employment and the amount of the salary and wages per month which you received.

   _____

   _____

2. Have you received within the past twelve months any money from any of the following sources?
   a. Business, profession or form of self-employment? Yes ☐ No ☐
   b. Rent payments, interest or dividends? Yes ☐ No ☐
   c. Pensions, annuities or life insurance payments? Yes ☐ No ☐
   d. Gifts or inheritances? Yes ☐ No ☐
   e. Any other sources? Yes ☐ No ☐

   If the answer to any of the above is "yes," describe each source of money and state the amount received from each during the past twelve months.

   _____

   _____

   _____

   _____

3. Do you own cash, or do you have money in a checking or savings account?

   Yes ☐ No ☐ (Include any funds in prison accounts.)

   If the answer is "yes," state the total value of the items owned.

   _____

   _____

   _____

4. Do you own any real estate, stocks, bonds, notes, automobiles, or other valuable property (excluding ordinary household furnishings and clothing)?

   Yes ☐ No ☐

   If the answer is "yes," describe the property and state its approximate value.

   _____

   _____

   _____

5. List the persons who are dependent upon you for support, state your relationship to those persons, and indicate how much you contribute toward their support.

   _____

   _____

   _____

I declare (or certify, verify, or state) under penalty of perjury that the foregoing is true and correct. Executed on _____.

(date)

_____

Signature of Petitioner

CERTIFICATE

I hereby certify that the petitioner herein has the sum of $_____ on account to his credit at the _____ institution where he is confined. I further certify that petitioner likewise has the following securities to his credit according to the records of said _____ institution:

_____

_____

_____

_____

_____

Authorized Officer of Institution

(As amended Apr. 28, 1982, eff. Aug. 1, 1982; Apr. 26, 2004, eff. Dec. 1, 2004.)

RULES GOVERNING SECTION 2255 PROCEEDINGS FOR THE UNITED STATES DISTRICT COURTS

Effective February 1, 1977
Amendments received to December 1, 2008

Rule

1. Scope.
2. The Motion.
3. Filing the Motion; Inmate Filing.
4. Preliminary Review.
5. The Answer and the Reply.
6. Discovery.
7. Expanding the Record.
8. Evidentiary Hearing.
9. Second or Successive Motions.
10. Powers of a Magistrate Judge.
11. Time to Appeal.
12. Applicability of the Federal Rules of Civil Procedure and the Federal Rules of Criminal Procedure.

APPENDIX OF FORMS

Motion to Vacate, Set Aside, or Correct a Sentence By a Person in Federal Custody
(Motion Under 28 U.S.C. § 2255)

ORDERS OF THE SUPREME COURT OF THE UNITED STATES ADOPTING AND AMENDING RULES GOVERNING SECTION 2255 PROCEEDINGS

ORDER OF APRIL 26, 1976

1. That the rules and forms governing proceedings in the United States District Courts under Section 2254 and Section 2255 of Title 28, United States Code, as approved by the Judicial Conference of the United States be, and they hereby are, prescribed pursuant to Section 2072 of Title 28, United States Code and Sections 3771 and 3772 of Title 18, United States Code.

2. That the aforementioned rules and forms shall take effect August 1, 1976, and shall be applicable to all proceedings then pending except to the extent that in the opinion of the court their application in a particular proceeding would not be feasible or would work injustice.

3. That THE CHIEF JUSTICE be, and he hereby is, authorized to transmit the aforementioned rules and forms governing Section 2254 and Section 2255 proceedings to the Congress in accordance with the provisions of Section 2072 of Title 28 and Sections 3771 and 3772 of Title 18, United States Code.

CONGRESSIONAL ACTION ON PROPOSED RULES AND FORMS GOVERNING PROCEEDING UNDER 28 U.S.C. §§ 2254 AND 2255

Pub.L. 94–349, § 2, July 8, 1976, 90 Stat. 822, provided: "That, notwithstanding the provisions of section 2072 of title 28 of the United States Code, the rules and forms governing section 2254 cases in the United States district courts and the rules and forms governing section 2255 proceedings in the United States district courts which are embraced by the order entered by the United States Supreme Court on April 26, 1976, and which were transmitted to the Congress on or about April 26, 1976, shall not take effect until thirty days after the adjournment sine die of the 94th Congress, or until and to the extent approved by Act of Congress, whichever is earlier."

Pub.L. 94–426, § 1, Sept. 28, 1976, 90 Stat. 1334, provided: "That the rules governing section 2254 cases in the United States district courts and the rules governing section 2255 proceedings for the United States district courts, as proposed by the United States Supreme Court, which were delayed by the Act entitled 'An Act to delay the effective date of certain proposed amendments to the Federal Rules of Criminal Procedure and certain other rules promulgated by the United States Supreme Court' (Public Law 94–349), are approved with the amendments set forth in section 2 of this Act and shall take effect as so amended, with respect to petitions under section 2254 and motions under section 2255 of title 28 of the United States Code filed on or after February 1, 1977."

ORDER OF APRIL 30, 1979

1. That Rule 10 of the Rules Governing Proceedings in the United States District Courts on application under Section 2254 of Title 28, United States Code, be, and hereby is, amended to read as follows:

[See amendment made thereby under Rule 10 set out following section 2254.]

2. That Rules 10 and 11 of the Rules Governing Proceedings in the United States District Courts on a motion under Section 2255 of Title 28, United States Code, be, and they hereby are, amended to read as follows:

[See amendments made thereby under the respective rules, post.]

3. That the foregoing amendments to the Rules Governing Proceedings in the United States District Courts under Section 2254 and Section 2255 of Title 28, United States Code, shall take effect on August 1, 1979, and shall be applicable to all proceedings then pending except to the extent that in the opinion of the court their application in a particular proceeding would not be feasible or would work injustice.

4. That THE CHIEF JUSTICE be, and he hereby is, authorized to transmit the aforementioned amendments to the Rules Governing Section 2254 and Section 2255 Proceedings to the Congress in accordance with the provisions of Section 2072 of Title 28, United States Code, and Sections 3771 and 3772 of Title 18, United States Code.

ORDER OF APRIL 28, 1982

1. That the rules and forms governing proceedings in the United States district courts under Section 2254 and Section 2255 of Title 28, United States Code, be, and they hereby are, amended by including therein an amendment to Rule 2(c) of the rules for Section 2254 cases, an amendment to Rule 2(b) of the rules for Section 2255 proceedings, and amendments to the model forms for use in applications under Section 2254 and motions under Section 2255, as hereinafter set forth:

[See amendments made thereby under respective rules and forms post and following section 2254.]

2. That the aforementioned amendments shall take effect August 1, 1982, and shall be applicable to all proceedings thereafter commenced and, insofar as just and practicable, all proceedings then pending.

3. That THE CHIEF JUSTICE be, and he hereby is, authorized to transmit the aforementioned amendments to the Congress in accordance with Section 2072 of Title 28 and Sections 3771 and 3772 of Title 18, United States Code.

ORDER OF APRIL 22, 1993

1. That the Federal Rules of Criminal Procedure for the United States District Courts be, and they hereby are, amended by including therein amendments to Criminal Rules 1, 3, 4, 5, 5.1, 6, 9, 12, 16, 17, 26.2, 32, 32.1, 40, 41, 44, 46, 49, 50, 54, 55, 57, and 58, and new Rule 26.3, and an amendment to Rule 8 of the Rules Governing Section 2255 Proceedings.

[See amendments made thereby under the respective rules set out in the Federal Criminal Code and Rules and under Rule 8, post.]

2. That the foregoing amendments to the Federal Rules of Criminal Procedure shall take effect on December 1, 1993, and shall govern all proceedings in criminal cases thereafter commenced and, insofar as just and practicable, all proceedings in criminal cases then pending.

3. That THE CHIEF JUSTICE be, and he hereby is, authorized to transmit to the Congress the foregoing amendments to the Federal Rules of Criminal Procedure in accordance with the provisions of Section 2072 of Title 28, United States Code.

ORDER OF APRIL 26, 2004

1. That the Federal Rules of Criminal Procedure be, and they hereby are, amended by including therein an amendment to Criminal Rule 35.

2. That the rules and forms governing cases in the United States District Courts under Section 2254 and Section 2255 of Title 28, United States Code, be, and they hereby are, amended by including therein amendments to Rules 1 through 11 of the Rules Governing Section 2254 Cases in the United States District Courts, Rules 1 through 12 of the Rules Governing Section 2255 Cases in the United States District Courts, and forms for use in applications under Section 2254 and motions under Section 2255.

[See amendments made thereby under respective rules, post.]

3. That the foregoing amendments to the Federal Rules of Criminal Procedure, the Rules Governing Section 2254 Cases in the United States District Courts, and the Rules Governing Section 2255 Cases in the United States District Courts shall take effect on December 1, 2004, and shall govern in all proceedings thereafter commenced and, insofar as just and practicable, all proceedings then pending.

4. That the CHIEF JUSTICE be, and hereby is, authorized to transmit to the Congress the foregoing amendments to the Federal Rules of Criminal Procedure, the Rules Governing Section 2254 Cases in the United States District Courts, and the Rules Governing Section 2255 Cases in the United States District Courts in accordance with the provisions of Section 2072 of Title 28, United States Code.

HISTORICAL NOTES

Effective Date of Rules; 1976 Act

Rules, and the amendments thereto by Pub.L. 94–426, Sept. 28, 1976, 90 Stat. 1334, effective with respect to petitions under section 2254 of this title and motions under section 2255 of this title filed on or after Feb. 1, 1977, see section 1 of Pub.L. 94–426, set out as a note under section 2074 and 2255 of this title.

Rule 1. Scope

These rules govern a motion filed in a United States district court under 28 U.S.C. § 2255 by:

(a) a person in custody under a judgment of that court who seeks a determination that:

(1) the judgment violates the Constitution or laws of the United States;

(2) the court lacked jurisdiction to enter the judgment;

(3) the sentence exceeded the maximum allowed by law; or

(4) the judgment or sentence is otherwise subject to collateral review; and

(b) a person in custody under a judgment of a state court or another federal court, and subject to future custody under a judgment of the district court, who seeks a determination that:

(1) future custody under a judgment of the district court would violate the Constitution or laws of the United States;

(2) the district court lacked jurisdiction to enter the judgment;

(3) the district court's sentence exceeded the maximum allowed by law; or

(4) the district court's judgment or sentence is otherwise subject to collateral review.

(As amended Apr. 26, 2004, eff. Dec. 1, 2004.)

ADVISORY COMMITTEE NOTES

1976 Adoption

The basic scope of this postconviction remedy is prescribed by 28 U.S.C. § 2255. Under these rules the person seeking relief from federal custody files a motion to vacate, set aside, or correct sentence, rather than a petition for habeas corpus. This is consistent with the terminology used in section 2255 and indicates the difference between this remedy and federal habeas for a state prisoner. Also, habeas corpus is available to the person in federal custody if his "remedy by motion is inadequate or ineffective to test the legality of his detention."

Whereas sections 2241–2254 (dealing with federal habeas corpus for those in state custody) speak of the district court judge "issuing the writ" as the operative remedy, section 2255 provides that, if the judge finds the movant's assertions to be meritorious, he "shall discharge the prisoner or resentence him or grant a new trial or correct the sentence as may appear appropriate." This is possible because a motion under § 2255 is a further step in the movant's criminal case and not a separate civil action, as appears from the legislative history of section 2 of S. 20, 80th Congress, the provisions of which were incorporated by the same Congress in title 28 U.S.C. as § 2255. In reporting S. 20 favorably the Senate Judiciary Committee said (Sen.Rep. 1526, 80th Cong.2d Sess., p. 2):

The two main advantages of such motion remedy over the present habeas corpus are as follows:

First, habeas corpus is a separate civil action and not a further step in the criminal case in which petitioner is sentenced (Ex parte *Tom Tong,* 108 U.S. 556, 559 (1883)). It is not a determination of guilt or innocence of the charge upon which petitioner was sentenced. Where a prisoner sustains his right to discharge in habeas corpus, it is usually because some right—such as lack of counsel—has been denied which reflects no determination of his guilt or innocence but affects solely the fairness of his earlier criminal trial. Even under the broad power in the statute "to dispose of the party as law and justice require" (28 U.S.C.A., sec. 461), the court or judge is by no means in the same advantageous position in habeas corpus to do justice as would be so if the matter were determined in the criminal proceeding (see *Medley,* petitioner, 134 U.S. 160, 174 (1890)). For instance, the judge (by habeas corpus) cannot grant a new trial in the criminal case. Since the motion remedy is in the criminal proceeding, this section 2 affords the opportunity and expressly gives the broad powers to set aside the judgment and to "discharge the prisoner or resentence him or grant a new trial or correct the sentence as may appear appropriate."

The fact that a motion under § 2255 is a further step in the movant's criminal case rather than a separate civil action has significance at several points in these rules. See, *e.g.,* advisory committee note to Rule 3 (re no filing fee), advisory committee note to Rule 4 (re availability of files, etc., relating to the judgment), advisory committee note to Rule 6 (re availability of discovery under criminal procedure rules), advisory committee note to Rule 11 (re no extension of time for appeal), and advisory committee note to Rule 12 (re applicability of federal criminal rules). However, the fact that Congress has characterized the motion as a further step in the criminal proceedings does *not* mean that proceedings upon such a motion are of necessity governed by the legal principles which are applicable at a criminal trial regarding such matters as counsel, presence, confrontation, self-incrimination, and burden of proof.

The challenge of decisions such as the revocation of probation or parole are not appropriately dealt with under 28 U.S.C. § 2255, which is a continuation of the original criminal action. Other remedies, such as habeas corpus, are available in such situations.

Although Rule 1 indicates that these rules apply to a motion for a determination that the judgment was imposed "in violation of the . . . laws of the United States," the language of 28 U.S.C. § 2255, it is not the intent of these rules to define or limit what is encompassed within that phrase. See *Davis v. United States,* 417 U.S. 333 (1974), holding that it is not true "that every asserted error of law can be raised on a § 2255 motion," and that the appropriate inquiry is "whether the claimed error of law was 'a fundamental defect which inherently results in a complete miscarriage of justice,' and whether '[i]t . . . present[s] exceptional circumstances where the need for the remedy afforded by the writ of habeas corpus is apparent.' "

For a discussion of the "custody" requirement and the intended limited scope of this remedy, see advisory committee note to § 2254 Rule 1.

2004 Amendments

The language of Rule 1 has been amended as part of general restyling of the rules to make them more easily understood and to make style and terminology consistent throughout the rules. These changes are intended to be stylistic and no substantive change is intended.

Rule 2. The Motion

(a) Applying for Relief. The application must be in the form of a motion to vacate, set aside, or correct the sentence.

(b) Form. The motion must:

(1) specify all the grounds for relief available to the moving party;

(2) state the facts supporting each ground;

(3) state the relief requested;

(4) be printed, typewritten, or legibly handwritten; and

(5) be signed under penalty of perjury by the movant or by a person authorized to sign it for the movant.

(c) Standard Form. The motion must substantially follow either the form appended to these rules or a form prescribed by a local district-court rule. The clerk must make forms available to moving parties without charge.

(d) Separate Motions for Separate Judgments. A moving party who seeks relief from more than one judgment must file a separate motion covering each judgment.

(As amended Pub.L. 94–426, § 2(3), (4), Sept. 28, 1976, 90 Stat. 1334; Apr. 28, 1982, eff. Aug. 1, 1982; Apr. 26, 2004, eff. Dec. 1, 2004.)

ADVISORY COMMITTEE NOTES

1976 Adoption

Under these rules the application for relief is in the form of a motion rather than a petition (see Rule 1 and advisory committee note). Therefore, there is no requirement that the movant name a respondent. This is consistent with 28 U.S.C. § 2255. The United States Attorney for the district in which the judgment under attack was entered is the proper party to oppose the motion since the federal government is the movant's adversary of record.

If the movant is attacking a federal judgment which will subject him to future custody, he must be in present custody (see Rule 1 and advisory committee note) as the result of a state or federal governmental action. He need not alter the nature of the motion by trying to include the government officer who presently has official custody of him as a pseudo-respondent, or third-party plaintiff, or other fabrication. The court hearing his motion attacking the future custody can exercise jurisdiction over those having him in present custody without the use of artificial pleading devices.

There is presently a split among the courts as to whether a person currently in state custody may use a § 2255 motion to obtain relief from a federal judgment under which he will be subjected to custody in the future. Negative, see *Newton v. United States,* 329 F.Supp. 90 (S.D. Texas 1971); affirmative, see *Desmond v. The United States Board of Parole,* 397 F.2d 386 (1st Cir.1968), *cert. denied,* 393 U.S. 919 (1968); and *Paalino v. United States,* 314 F.Supp. 875 (C.D.Cal.1970). It is intended that these rules settle the matter in favor of the prisoner's being able to file a § 2255 motion for relief under those circumstances. The proper district in which to file such a motion is the one in which is situated the court which rendered the sentence under attack.

Under Rule 35, Federal Rules of Criminal Procedure, the court may correct an illegal sentence or a sentence imposed in an illegal manner, or may reduce the sentence. This remedy should be used, rather than a motion under these § 2255 rules, whenever applicable, but there is some overlap between the two proceedings which has caused the courts difficulty.

The movant should not be barred from an appropriate remedy because he has misstyled his motion. See *United States v. Morgan,* 346 U.S. 502, 505 (1954). The court should construe it as whichever one is proper under the circumstances and decide it on its merits. For a § 2255 motion construed as a Rule 35 motion, see *Heflin v. United States,* 358 U.S. 415 (1959); and *United States v. Coke,* 404 F.2d 836 (2d Cir.1968). For writ of error coram nobis treated as a Rule 35 motion, see *Hawkins v. United States,* 324 F.Supp. 223 (E.D. Texas, Tyler Division 1971). For a Rule 35 motion treated as a § 2255 motion, see *Moss v. United States,* 263 F.2d 615 (5th Cir.1959); *Jones v. United States,* 400 F.2d 892 (8th Cir.1968), cert. denied 394 U.S. 991 (1969); and *United States v. Brown,* 413 F.2d 878 (9th Cir.1969), cert. denied, 397 U.S. 947 (1970).

One area of difference between § 2255 and Rule 35 motions is that for the latter there is no requirement that the movant be "in custody." *Heflin v. United States,* 358 U.S. 415, 418, 422 (1959); *Duggins v. United States,* 240 F.2d 479, 483 (6th Cir.1957). Compare with Rule 1 and advisory committee note for § 2255 motions. The importance of this distinction has decreased since *Peyton v. Rowe,* 391 U.S. 54 (1968), but it might still make a difference in particular situations.

A Rule 35 motion is used to attack the sentence imposed, not the basis for the sentence. The court in *Gilinsky v. United States,* 335 F.2d 914, 916 (9th Cir.1964), stated, "a Rule 35 motion presupposes a valid conviction. * * * [C]ollateral attack on errors allegedly committed at trial is not permissible under Rule 35." By illustration the court noted at page 917: "a Rule 35 proceeding contemplates the correction of a sentence of a court having jurisdiction. * * * [J]urisdictional defects * * * involve a collateral attack, they must ordinarily be presented under 28 U.S.C. § 2255." In *United States v. Semet,* 295 F.Supp. 1084 (E.D.Okla.1968), the prisoner moved under Rule 35 and § 2255 to invalidate the sentence he was serving on the grounds of his failure to understand the charge to which he pleaded guilty. The court said:

> As regards Defendant's Motion under Rule 35, said Motion must be denied as its [sic] presupposes a valid conviction of the offense with which he was charged and may be used only to attack the sentence. It may not be used to examine errors occurring prior to the imposition of sentence.

295 F.Supp. at 1085

See also: *Moss v. United States,* 263 F.2d at 616; *Duggins v. United States,* 240 F.2d at 484; *Migdal v. United States,* 298 F.2d 513, 514 (9th Cir.1961); *Jones v. United States,* 400 F.2d at 894; *United States v. Coke,* 404 F.2d at 847; and *United States v. Brown,* 413 F.2d at 879.

A major difficulty in deciding whether Rule 35 or § 2255 is the proper remedy is the uncertainty as to what is meant by an "illegal sentence." The Supreme Court dealt with this issue in *Hill v. United States,* 368 U.S. 424 (1962). The prisoner brought a § 2255 motion to vacate sentence on the ground that he had not been given a Fed.R.Crim.P. 32(a) opportunity to make a statement in his own behalf at the time of sentencing. The majority held this was not an error subject to collateral attack under § 2255. The five-member majority considered the motion as one brought pursuant to Rule 35, but denied relief, stating:

> [T]he narrow function of Rule 35 is to permit correction at any time of an illegal *sentence,* not to re-examine errors occurring at the trial or other proceedings prior to the imposition of sentence. The sentence in this case was not illegal. The punishment meted out was not in excess of that prescribed by the relevant statutes, multiple terms were not imposed for the same offense, nor were the terms of the sentence itself legally or constitutionally invalid in any other respect.

368 U.S. at 430

The four dissenters felt the majority definition of "illegal" was too narrow.

> [Rule 35] provides for the correction of an "illegal sentence" without regard to the reasons why that sentence is illegal and contains not a single word to support the Court's conclusion that only a sentence illegal by reason of the punishment it imposes is "illegal" within the meaning of the Rule. I would have thought that a sentence imposed in an illegal manner—whether the amount or form of the punishment meted out constitutes an additional

violation of law or not—would be recognized as an "illegal sentence" under any normal reading of the English language.

368 U.S. at 431–432

The 1966 amendment of Rule 35 added language permitting correction of a sentence imposed in an "illegal manner." However, there is a 120-day time limit on a motion to do this, and the added language does not clarify the intent of the rule or its relation to § 2255.

The courts have been flexible in considering motions under circumstances in which relief might appear to be precluded by *Hill v. United States.* In *Peterson v. United States,* 432 F.2d 545 (8th Cir.1970), the court was confronted with a motion for reduction of sentence by a prisoner claiming to have received a harsher sentence than his codefendants because he stood trial rather than plead guilty. He alleged that this violated his constitutional right to a jury trial. The court ruled that, even though it was past the 120-day time period for a motion to reduce sentence, the claim was still cognizable under Rule 35 as a motion to correct an illegal sentence.

The courts have made even greater use of § 2255 in these types of situations. In *United States v. Lewis,* 392 F.2d 440 (4th Cir.1968), the prisoner moved under § 2255 and Rule 35 for relief from a sentence he claimed was the result of the judge's misunderstanding of the relevant sentencing law. The court held that he could not get relief under Rule 35 because it was past the 120 days for correction of a sentence imposed in an illegal manner and under *Hill v. United States* it was not an illegal sentence. However, § 2255 was applicable because of its "otherwise subject to collateral attack" language. The flaw was not a mere trial error relating to the finding of guilt, but a rare and unusual error which amounted to "exceptional circumstances" embraced in § 2255's words "collateral attack." See 368 U.S. at 444 for discussion of other cases allowing use of § 2255 to attack the sentence itself in similar circumstances, especially where the judge has sentenced out of a misapprehension of the law.

In *United States v. McCarthy,* 433 F.2d 591, 592 (1st Cir.1970), the court allowed a prisoner who was past the time limit for a proper Rule 35 motion to use § 2255 to attack the sentence which he received upon a plea of guilty on the ground that it was induced by an unfulfilled promise of the prosecutor to recommend leniency. The court specifically noted that under § 2255 this was a proper collateral attack on the sentence and there was no need to attack the conviction as well.

The court in *United States v. Malcolm,* 432 F.2d 809, 814, 818 (2d Cir.1970), allowed a prisoner to challenge his sentence under § 2255 without attacking the conviction. It held Rule 35 inapplicable because the sentence was not illegal on its face, but the manner in which the sentence was imposed raised a question of the denial of due process in the sentencing itself which was cognizable under § 2255.

The flexible approach taken by the courts in the above cases seems to be the reasonable way to handle these situations in which Rule 35 and § 2255 appear to overlap. For a further discussion of this problem, see C. Wright, Federal Practice and Procedure: Criminal §§ 581–587 (1969, Supp. 1975).

See the advisory committee note to Rule 2 of the § 2254 rules for further discussion of the purposes and intent of Rule 2 of these § 2255 rules.

1982 Amendment

Subdivision (b). The amendment takes into account 28 U.S.C. § 1746, enacted after adoption of the § 2255 rules. Section 1746 provides that in lieu of an affidavit an unsworn statement may be given under penalty of perjury in substantially the following form if executed within the United States, its territories, possessions or commonwealths: "I declare (or certify, verify, or state) under penalty of perjury that the foregoing is true and correct. Executed on (date). (Signature)." The statute is "intended to encompass prisoner litigation," and the statutory alternative is especially appropriate in such cases because a notary might not be readily available. *Carter v. Clark,* 616 F.2d 228 (5th Cir.1980). The § 2255 forms have been revised accordingly.

2004 Amendments

The language of Rule 2 has been amended as part of general restyling of the rules to make them more easily understood and to make style and terminology consistent throughout the rules. These changes are intended to be stylistic and no substantive change is intended, except as described below.

Revised Rule 2(b)(5) has been amended by removing the requirement that the motion be signed personally by the moving party. Thus, under the amended rule the motion may be signed by movant personally or by someone acting on behalf of the movant, assuming that the person is authorized to do so, for example, an attorney for the movant. The Committee envisions that the courts would apply third-party, or "next-friend," standing analysis in deciding whether the signer was actually authorized to sign the motion on behalf of the movant. *See generally Whitmore v. Arkansas,* 495 U.S. 149 (1990) (discussion of requisites for "next friend" standing in habeas petitions). *See also* 28 U.S.C. § 2242 (application for state habeas corpus relief may be filed by the person who is seeking relief, or by someone acting on behalf of that person).

The language in new Rule 2(c) has been changed to reflect that a moving party must substantially follow the standard form, which is appended to the rules, or a form provided by the court. The current rule, Rule 2(c), seems to indicate a preference for the standard "national" form. Under the amended rule, there is no stated preference. The Committee understood that the current practice in some courts is that if the moving party first files a motion using the national form, that courts may ask the moving party to supplement it with the local form.

Current Rule 2(d), which provided for returning an insufficient motion has been deleted. The Committee believed that the approach in Federal Rule of Civil Procedure 5(e) was more appropriate for dealing with motions that do not conform to the form requirements of the rule. That Rule provides that the clerk may not refuse to accept a filing solely for the reason that it fails to comply with these rules or local rules. Before the adoption of a one-year statute of limitations in the Antiterrorism and Effective Death Penalty Act of 1996, 110 Stat. 1214, the moving party suffered no penalty, other than delay, if the motion was deemed insufficient. Now that a one-year statute of limitations applies to motions filed under § 2255, *see* 28 U.S.C. § 2244(d) (1), the court's dismissal of a motion because it is not in proper form may pose a significant penalty for a moving party, who may not be able to file another motion within the one-year limitations period. Now, under revised Rule 3(b), the clerk is required to file a motion, even though it may otherwise fail to comply with the provisions in revised Rule 2(b). The Committee believed that the better procedure was to accept the defective motion and require the moving party to submit a corrected motion that conforms to Rule 2(b).

Rule 3. Filing the Motion; Inmate Filing

(a) Where to File; Copies. An original and two copies of the motion must be filed with the clerk.

(b) Filing and Service. The clerk must file the motion and enter it on the criminal docket of the case in which the challenged judgment was entered. The clerk must then deliver or serve a copy of the motion on the United States attorney in that district, together with a notice of its filing.

(c) Time to File. The time for filing a motion is governed by 28 U.S.C. § 2255 para. 6.

(d) Inmate Filing. A paper filed by an inmate confined in an institution is timely if deposited in the institution's internal mailing system on or before the last day for filing. If an institution has a system designed for legal mail, the inmate must use that system to receive the benefit of this rule. Timely filing may be shown by a declaration in compliance with 28 U.S.C. § 1746 or by a notarized statement, either of which must set forth the date of deposit and state that first-class postage has been prepaid.

(As amended Apr. 26, 2004, eff. Dec. 1, 2004.)

ADVISORY COMMITTEE NOTES

1976 Adoption

There is no filing fee required of a movant under these rules. This is a change from the practice of charging $15 and is done to recognize specifically the nature of a § 2255 motion as being a continuation of the criminal case whose judgment is under attack.

The long-standing practice of requiring a $15 filing fee has followed from 28 U.S.C. § 1914(a) whereby "parties instituting any civil action * * * pay a filing fee of $15, except that on an application for a writ of habeas corpus the filing fee shall be $5." This has been held to apply to a proceeding under § 2255 despite the rationale that such a proceeding is a motion and thus a continuation of the criminal action. (See note to Rule 1.)

> A motion under Section 2255 is a civil action and the clerk has no choice but to charge a $15.00 filing fee unless by leave of court it is filed in forma pauperis.

McCune v. United States, 406 F.2d 417, 419 (6th Cir.1969).

Although the motion has been considered to be a new civil action in the nature of habeas corpus for filing purposes, the reduced fee for habeas has been held not applicable. The Tenth Circuit considered the specific issue in *Martin v. United States,* 273 F.2d 775 (10th Cir.1960), cert. denied, 365 U.S. 853 (1961), holding that the reduced fee was exclusive to habeas petitions.

> Counsel for Martin insists that, if a docket fee must be paid, the amount is $5 rather than $15 and bases his contention on the exception contained in 28 U.S.C. § 1914 that in habeas corpus the fee is $5. This reads into § 1914 language which is not there. While an application under § 2255 may afford the same relief as that previously obtainable by habeas corpus, it is not a petition for a writ of habeas corpus. A change in § 1914 must come from Congress.

273 F.2d at 778

Although for most situations § 2255 is intended to provide to the federal prisoner a remedy equivalent to habeas corpus as used by state prisoners, there is a major distinction between the two. Calling a § 2255 request for relief a motion rather than a petition militates toward charging no new filing fee, not an increased one. In the absence of convincing evidence to the contrary, there is no reason to suppose that Congress did not mean what it said in making a § 2255 action a motion. Therefore, as in other motions filed in a criminal action, there is no requirement of a filing fee. It is appropriate that the present situation of docketing a § 2255 motion as a new action and charging a $15 filing fee be remedied by the rule when the whole question of § 2255 motions is thoroughly thought through and organized.

Even though there is no need to have a forma pauperis affidavit to proceed with the action since there is no requirement of a fee for filing the motion the affidavit remains attached to the form to be supplied potential movants. Most such movants are indigent, and this is a convenient way of getting this into the official record so that the judge may appoint counsel, order the government to pay witness fees, allow docketing of an appeal, and grant any other rights to which an indigent is entitled in the course of a § 2255 motion, when appropriate to the particular situation, without the need for an indigency petition and adjudication at such later point in the proceeding. This should result in a streamlining of the process to allow quicker disposition of these motions.

For further discussion of this rule, see the advisory committee note to Rule 3 of the § 2254 rules.

2004 Amendments

The language of Rule 3 has been amended as part of general restyling of the rules to make them more easily understood and to make style and terminology consistent throughout the rules. These changes are intended to be stylistic and no substantive change is intended, except as indicated below.

Revised Rule 3(b) is new and is intended to parallel Federal Rule of Civil Procedure 5(e), which provides that the clerk may not refuse to accept a filing solely for the reason that it fails to comply with these rules or local rules. Before the adoption of a one-year statute of limitations in the Antiterrorism and Effective Death Penalty Act of 1996, 110 Stat. 1214, the moving party suffered no penalty, other than delay, if the petition was deemed insufficient. That Act, however, added a one-year statute of limitations to motions filed under § 2255, *see* 28 U.S.C. § 2244(d)(1). Thus, a court's dismissal of a defective motion may pose a significant penalty for a moving party who may not be able to file a corrected motion within the one-year limitation period. The Committee believed that the better procedure was to accept the defective motion and require the moving party to submit a corrected motion that conforms to Rule 2. Thus, revised Rule 3(b) requires the clerk to file a motion, even though it may otherwise fail to comply with Rule 2.

Revised Rule 3(c), which sets out a specific reference to 28 U.S.C. § 2255, paragraph 6, is new and has been added to put moving parties on notice that a one-year statute of limitations applies to motions filed under these Rules. Although the rule does not address the issue, every circuit that has addressed the issue has taken the position that equitable tolling of the statute of limitations is available in appropriate circumstances. *See, e.g., Dunlap v. United States,* 250 F.3d 1001, 1004–07 (6th Cir. 2001); *Moore v. United States,* 173 F.3d 1131, 1133–35 (8th Cir. 1999); *Sandvik v. United States,* 177 F.3d 1269, 1270–72 (11th Cir. 1999). The Supreme Court has not addressed the question directly. *See Duncan v. Walker,* 533 U.S. 167, 181 (2001) ("We . . . have no occasion to address the question that Justice Stevens raises concerning the availability of equitable tolling.").

Rule 3(d) is new and provides guidance on determining whether a motion from an inmate is considered to have been filed in a timely fashion. The new provision parallels Federal Rule of Appellate Procedure 25(a)(2)(C).

Rule 4. Preliminary Review

(a) Referral to a Judge. The clerk must promptly forward the motion to the judge who conducted the trial and imposed sentence or, if the judge who imposed sentence was not the trial judge, to the judge who conducted the proceedings being challenged. If the appropriate judge is not available, the clerk must forward the motion to a judge under the court's assignment procedure.

(b) Initial Consideration by the Judge. The judge who receives the motion must promptly examine it. If it plainly appears from the motion, any attached exhibits, and the record of prior proceedings that the moving party is not entitled to relief, the judge must dismiss the motion and direct the clerk to notify the moving party. If the motion is not dismissed, the judge must order the United States attorney to file an answer, motion, or other response within a fixed time, or to take other action the judge may order.

(As amended Apr. 26, 2004, eff. Dec. 1, 2004.)

ADVISORY COMMITTEE NOTES

1976 Adoption

Rule 4 outlines the procedure for assigning the motion to a specific judge of the district court and the options available to the judge and the government after the motion is properly filed.

The long-standing majority practice in assigning motions made pursuant to § 2255 has been for the trial judge to determine the merits of the motion. In cases where the § 2255 motion is directed against the sentence, the merits have traditionally been decided by the judge who imposed sentence. The reasoning for this was first noted in *Carvell v. United States,* 173 F.2d 348–349 (4th Cir.1949):

> Complaint is made that the judge who tried the case passed upon the motion. Not only was there no impropriety in this, but it is highly desirable in such cases that the motions be passed on by the judge who is familiar with the facts and circumstances surrounding the trial, and is consequently not likely to be misled by false allegations as to what occurred.

This case, and its reasoning, has been almost unanimously endorsed by other courts dealing with the issue.

Commentators have been critical of having the motion decided by the trial judge. See Developments in the Law—Federal Habeas Corpus, 83 Harv.L.Rev. 1038, 1206–1208 (1970).

> [T]he trial judge may have become so involved with the decision that it will be difficult for him to review it objectively. Nothing in the legislative history suggests that "court" refers to a specific judge, and the procedural advantages of section 2255 are available whether or not the trial judge presides at the hearing.
>
> The theory that Congress intended the trial judge to preside at a section 2255 hearing apparently originated in *Carvell v. United States,* 173 F.2d 348 (4th Cir.1949) (per curiam), where the panel of judges included Chief Judge Parker of the Fourth Circuit, chairman of the Judicial Conference committee which drafted section 2255. But the legislative history does not indicate that Congress wanted the trial judge to preside. Indeed the advantages of section 2255 can all be achieved if the case is heard in the sentencing district, regardless of which judge hears it. According to the Senate committee report the purpose of the bill was to make the proceeding a part of the criminal action so the court could resentence the applicant, or grant him a new trial. (A judge presiding over a habeas corpus action does not have these powers.) In addition, Congress did not want the cases heard in the district of confinement because that tended to concentrate the burden on a few districts, and made it difficult for witnesses and records to be produced.

83 Harv.L.Rev. at 1207–1208

The Court of Appeals for the First Circuit has held that a judge other than the trial judge should rule on the 2255 motion. See *Halliday v. United States,* 380 F.2d 270 (1st Cir.1967).

There is a procedure by which the movant can have a judge other than the trial judge decide his motion in courts adhering to the majority rule. He can file an affidavit alleging bias in order to disqualify the trial judge. And there are circumstances in which the trial judge will, on his own, disqualify himself. See, *e.g., Webster v. United States,* 330 F.Supp. 1080 (1972). However, there has been some questioning of the effectiveness of this procedure. See Developments in the Law—Federal Habeas Corpus, 83 Harv.L.Rev. 1038, 1200–1207 (1970).

Subdivision (a) adopts the majority rule and provides that the trial judge, or sentencing judge if different and appropriate for the particular motion, will decide the motion made pursuant to these rules, recognizing that, under some circumstances, he may want to disqualify himself. A movant is not without remedy if he feels this is unfair to him. He can file an affidavit of bias. And there is the right to appellate review if the trial judge refuses to grant his motion. Because the trial judge is thoroughly familiar with the case, there is obvious administrative advantage in giving him the first opportunity to decide whether there are grounds for granting the motion.

Since the motion is part of the criminal action in which was entered the judgment to which it is directed, the files, records, transcripts, and correspondence relating to that judgment are automatically available to the judge in his consideration of the motion. He no longer need order them incorporated for that purpose.

Rule 4 has its basis in § 2255 (rather than 28 U.S.C. § 2243 in the corresponding habeas corpus rule) which does not have a specific time limitation as to when the answer must be made. Also, under § 2255, the United States Attorney for the district is the party served with the notice and a copy of the motion and required to answer (when appropriate). Subdivision (b) continues this practice since there is no respondent involved in the motion (unlike habeas) and the United States Attorney, as prosecutor in the case in question, is the most appropriate one to defend the judgment and oppose the motion.

The judge has discretion to require an answer or other appropriate response from the United States Attorney. See advisory committee note to Rule 4 of the § 2254 rules.

2004 Amendments

The language of Rule 4 has been amended as part of general restyling of the rules to make them more easily understood and to make style and terminology consistent throughout the rules. These changes are intended to be stylistic and no substantive change is intended.

The amended rule reflects that the response to a Section 2255 motion may be a motion to dismiss or some other response.

Rule 5. The Answer and the Reply

(a) When Required. The respondent is not required to answer the motion unless a judge so orders.

(b) Contents. The answer must address the allegations in the motion. In addition, it must state whether the moving party has used any other federal remedies, including any prior post-conviction motions under these rules or any previous rules, and whether the moving party received an evidentiary hearing.

(c) Records of Prior Proceedings. If the answer refers to briefs or transcripts of the prior proceedings that are not available in the court's records, the judge must order the government to furnish them within a reasonable time that will not unduly delay the proceedings.

(d) Reply. The moving party may submit a reply to the respondent's answer or other pleading within a time fixed by the judge.

(As amended Apr. 26, 2004, eff. Dec. 1, 2004.)

ADVISORY COMMITTEE NOTES

1976 Adoption

Unlike the habeas corpus statutes (see 28 U.S.C. §§ 2243, 2248) § 2255 does not specifically call for a return or answer by the United States Attorney or set any time limits as to when one must be submitted. The general practice, however, if the motion is not summarily dismissed, is for the government to file an answer to the motion as well as counter-affidavits, when appropriate. Rule 4 provides for an answer to the motion by the United States Attorney, and Rule 5 indicates what its contents should be.

There is no requirement that the movant exhaust his remedies prior to seeking relief under § 2255. However, the courts have held that such a motion is inappropriate if the movant is simultaneously appealing the decision.

> We are of the view that there is no jurisdictional bar to the District Court's entertaining a Section 2255 motion during the pendency of a direct appeal but that the orderly administration of criminal law precludes considering such a motion absent extraordinary circumstances.
>
> ***Womack v. United States*, 395 F.2d 630, 631 (D.C.Cir.1968)**

Also see *Masters v. Eide*, 353 F.2d 517 (8th Cir.1965). The answer may thus cut short consideration of the motion if it discloses the taking of an appeal which was omitted from the form motion filed by the movant.

There is nothing in § 2255 which corresponds to the § 2248 requirement of a traverse to the answer. Numerous cases have held that the government's answer and affidavits are not conclusive against the movant, and if they raise disputed issues of fact a hearing must be held. *Machibroda v. United States*, 368 U.S. 487, 494, 495 (1962); *United States v. Salerno*, 290 F.2d 105, 106 (2d Cir.1961); *Romero v. United States*, 327 F.2d 711, 712 (5th Cir.1964); *Scott v. United States*, 349 F.2d 641, 642, 643 (6th Cir.1965); *Schiebelhut v. United States*, 357 F.2d 743, 745 (6th Cir.1966); and *Del Piano v. United States*, 362 F.2d 931, 932, 933 (3d Cir.1966). None of these cases make any mention of a traverse by the movant to the government's answer. As under Rule 5 of the § 2254 rules, there is no intention here that such a traverse be required, except under special circumstances. See advisory committee note to Rule 9.

Subdivision (b) provides for the government to supplement its answers with appropriate copies of transcripts or briefs if for some reason the judge does not already have them under his control. This is because the government will in all probability have easier access to such papers than the movant, and it will conserve the court's time to have the government produce them rather than the movant, who would in most instances have to apply in forma pauperis for the government to supply them for him anyway.

For further discussion, see the advisory committee note to Rule 5 of the § 2254 rules.

2004 Amendments

The language of Rule 5 has been amended as part of general restyling of the rules to make them more easily understood and to make style and terminology consistent throughout the rules. These changes are intended to be stylistic and no substantive change is intended.

Revised Rule 5(a), which provides that the respondent is not required to file an answer to the motion, unless a judge so orders, is taken from current Rule 3(b). The revised rule does not address the practice in some districts, where the respondent files a pre-answer motion to dismiss the motion. But revised Rule 4(b) contemplates that practice and has been changed to reflect the view that if the court does not dismiss the motion, it may require (or permit) the respondent to file a motion.

Finally, revised Rule 5(d) adopts the practice in some jurisdictions giving the movant an opportunity to file a reply to the respondent's answer. Rather than using terms such as "traverse," *see* 28 U.S.C. § 2248, to identify the movant's response to the answer, the rule uses the more general term " reply." The Rule prescribes that the court set the time for such responses, and in lieu of setting specific time limits in each case, the court may decide to include such time limits in its local rules.

Rule 6. Discovery

(a) Leave of Court Required. A judge may, for good cause, authorize a party to conduct discovery under the Federal Rules of Criminal Procedure or Civil Procedure, or in accordance with the practices and principles of law. If necessary for effective discovery, the judge must appoint an attorney for a moving party who qualifies to have counsel appointed under 18 U.S.C. § 3006A.

(b) Requesting Discovery. A party requesting discovery must provide reasons for the request. The request must also include any proposed interrogatories and requests for admission, and must specify any requested documents.

(c) Deposition Expenses. If the government is granted leave to take a deposition, the judge may require the government to pay the travel expenses, subsistence expenses, and fees of the moving party's attorney to attend the deposition.

(As amended Apr. 26, 2004, eff. Dec. 1, 2004.)

ADVISORY COMMITTEE NOTES

1976 Adoption

This rule differs from the corresponding discovery rule under the § 2254 rules in that it includes the processes of discovery available under the Federal Rules of Criminal Procedure as well as the civil. This is because of the nature of a § 2255 motion as a continuing part of the criminal proceeding (see advisory committee note to Rule 1) as well as a remedy analogous to habeas corpus by state prisoners.

See the advisory committee note to rule 6 of the § 2254 rules. The discussion there is fully applicable to discovery under these rules for § 2255 motions.

2004 Amendments

The language of Rule 6 has been amended as part of general restyling of the rules to make them more easily understood and to make style and terminology consistent throughout the rules. These changes are intended to be stylistic and no substantive change is intended, except as indicated below.

Although current Rule 6(b) contains no requirement that the parties provide reasons for the requested discovery, the revised rule does so and also includes a requirement that the request be accompanied by any proposed interrogatories and requests for admission, and must specify any requested documents. The Committee believes that the revised rule makes explicit what has been implicit in current practice.

Rule 7. Expanding the Record

(a) In General. If the motion is not dismissed, the judge may direct the parties to expand the record by submitting additional materials relating to the motion. The judge may require that these materials be authenticated.

(b) Types of Materials. The materials that may be required include letters predating the filing of the motion, documents, exhibits, and answers under oath to written interrogatories propounded by the judge. Affidavits also may be submitted and considered as part of the record.

(c) Review by the Opposing Party. The judge must give the party against whom the additional materials are offered an opportunity to admit or deny their correctness.

(As amended Apr. 26, 2004, eff. Dec. 1, 2004.)

ADVISORY COMMITTEE NOTES

1976 Adoption

It is less likely that the court will feel the need to expand the record in a § 2255 proceeding than in a habeas corpus proceeding, because the trial (or sentencing) judge is the one hearing the motion (see Rule 4) and should already have a complete file on the case in his possession. However, Rule 7 provides a convenient method for supplementing his file if the case warrants it.

See the advisory committee note to Rule 7 of the § 2254 rules for a full discussion of reasons and procedures for expanding the record.

2004 Amendments

The language of Rule 7 has been amended as part of general restyling of the rules to make them more easily understood and to make style and terminology consistent throughout the rules. These changes are intended to be stylistic and no substantive change is intended.

Revised Rule 7(a) is not intended to restrict the court's authority to expand the record through means other than requiring the parties themselves to provide the information.

The language in current Rule 7(d), which deals with authentication of materials in the expanded record, has been moved to revised Rule 7(a).

Rule 8. Evidentiary Hearing

(a) Determining Whether to Hold a Hearing. If the motion is not dismissed, the judge must review the answer, any transcripts and records of prior proceedings, and any materials submitted under Rule 7 to determine whether an evidentiary hearing is warranted.

(b) Reference to a Magistrate Judge. A judge may, under 28 U.S.C. § 636(b), refer the motion to a magistrate judge to conduct hearings and to file proposed findings of fact and recommendations for disposition. When they are filed, the clerk must promptly serve copies of the proposed findings and recommendations on all parties. Within 10 days after being served, a party may file objections as provided by local court rule. The judge must determine *de novo* any proposed finding or recommendation to which objection is made. The judge may accept, reject, or modify any proposed finding or recommendation.

(c) Appointing Counsel; Time of Hearing. If an evidentiary hearing is warranted, the judge must appoint an attorney to represent a moving party who qualifies to have counsel appointed under 18 U.S.C. § 3006A. The judge must conduct the hearing as soon as practicable after giving the attorneys adequate time to investigate and prepare. These rules do not limit the appointment of counsel under § 3006A at any stage of the proceeding.

(d) Producing a Statement. Federal Rule of Criminal Procedure 26.2(a)–(d) and (f) applies at a hearing under this rule. If a party does not comply with a Rule 26.2(a) order to produce a witness's statement, the court must not consider that witness's testimony.

(As amended Pub.L. 94–426, § 2(6), Sept. 28, 1976, 90 Stat. 1335; Pub.L. 94–577, § 2(a)(2), (b)(2), Oct. 21, 1976, 90 Stat. 2730, 2731; Apr. 22, 1993, eff. Dec. 1, 1993; Apr. 26, 2004, eff. Dec. 1, 2004.)

ADVISORY COMMITTEE NOTES

1976 Adoption

The standards for § 2255 hearings are essentially the same as for evidentiary hearings under a habeas petition, except that the previous federal fact-finding proceeding is in issue rather than the state's. Also § 2255 does not set specific time limits for holding the hearing, as does § 2243 for a habeas action. With these minor differences in mind, see the advisory committee note to Rule 8 of § 2254 rules, which is applicable to Rule 8 of these § 2255 rules.

1993 Amendment

The amendment to Rule 8 is one of a series of parallel amendments to Federal Rules of Criminal Procedure 32, 32.1, and 46 which extend the scope of Rule 26.2 (Production of Witness Statements) to proceedings other than the trial itself. The amendments are grounded on the compelling need for accurate and credible information in making decisions concerning the defendant's liberty. *See* the Advisory Committee Note to Rule 26.2(g). A few courts have recognized the authority of a judicial officer to order production of prior statements by a witness at a Section 2255 hearing, see, e.g., *United States v. White*, 342 F.2d 379, 382, n. 4 (4th Cir.1959). The amendment to Rule 8 grants explicit authority to do so. The amendment is not intended to require production of a witness's statement before the witness actually presents oral testimony.

2004 Amendments

The language of Rule 8 has been amended as part of general restyling of the rules to make them more easily understood and to make style and terminology consistent throughout the rules. These changes are intended to be stylistic and no substantive change is intended, except as described below.

The requirement in current Rule 8(b)(2) that a copy of the magistrate judge's findings must be promptly mailed to all parties has been changed in revised Rule 8(b) to require that copies of those findings be served on all parties. As used in this rule, "service" means service consistent with Federal Rule of Civil Procedure 5(b), which allows mailing the copies.

HISTORICAL NOTES

Effective and Applicability Provisions

1976 Acts. Amendments made by Pub.L. 94–577 effective with respect to motions under section 2255 of this title filed on or after Feb. 1, 1977, see section 2(c) of Pub.L. 94–577, set out as a note under Rule 8 of the Rules Governing Cases Under Section 2254 of this title.

Rule 9. Second or Successive Motions

Before presenting a second or successive motion, the moving party must obtain an order from the appropriate court of appeals authorizing the district court to consider the motion, as required by 28 U.S.C. § 2255, para. 8.

(As amended Pub.L. 94–426, § 2(9), (10), Sept. 28, 1976, 90 Stat. 1335; Apr. 26, 2004, eff. Dec. 1, 2004.)

ADVISORY COMMITTEE NOTES

1976 Adoption

Unlike the statutory provisions on habeas corpus (28 U.S.C. §§ 2241–2254), § 2255 specifically provides that "a motion for such relief may be made *at any time*." [Emphasis added.] Subdivision (a) provides that delayed motions may be barred from consideration if the government has been prejudiced in its ability to respond to the motion by the delay and the movant's failure to seek relief earlier is not excusable within the terms of the rule. Case law, dealing with this issue, is in conflict.

Some courts have held that the literal language of § 2255 precludes any possible time bar to a motion brought under it. In *Heflin v. United States*, 358 U.S. 415 (1959), the concurring opinion noted:

> The statute [28 U.S.C. § 2255] further provides: "A motion * * * may be made at any time." This * * * simply means that, as in habeas corpus, there is no statute of limitations, no *res judicata*, and that the doctrine of laches is inapplicable.

358 U.S. at 420

McKinney v. United States, 208 F.2d 844 (D.C.Cir.1953) reversed the district court's dismissal of a § 2255 motion for being too late, the court stating:

McKinney's present application for relief comes late in the day: he has served some fifteen years in prison. But tardiness is irrelevant where a constitutional issue is raised and where the prisoner is still confined.

208 F.2d at 846, 847

In accord, see; *Juelich v. United States,* 300 F.2d 381, 383 (5th Cir.1962); *Conners v. United States,* 431 F.2d 1207, 1208 (9th Cir.1970); *Sturrup v. United States,* 218 F.Supp. 279, 281 (E.D.N.Car.1963); and *Banks v. United States,* 319 F.Supp. 649, 652 (S.D.N.Y.1970).

It has also been held that delay in filing a § 2255 motion does not bar the movant because of lack of reasonable diligence in pressing the claim.

> The statute [28 U.S.C. § 2255], when it states that the motion may be made at any time, excludes the addition of a showing of diligence in delayed filings. A number of courts have considered contentions similar to those made here and have concluded that there are no time limitations. This result excludes the requirement of diligence which is in reality a time limitation.

***Haier v. United States,* 334 F.2d 441, 442 (10th Cir.1964)**

Other courts have recognized that delay may have a negative effect on the movant. In *Raines v. United States,* 423 F.2d 526 (4th Cir.1970), the court stated:

> [B]oth petitioners' silence for extended periods, one for 28 months and the other for nine years, serves to render their allegations less believable. "Although a delay in filing a section 2255 motion is not a controlling element * * * it may merit some consideration * * *."

423 F.2d at 531

In *Aiken v. United States,* 191 F.Supp. 43, 50 (M.D.N.Car. 1961), aff'd 296 F.2d 604 (4th Cir.1961), the court said: "While motions under 28 U.S.C. § 2255 may be made at any time, the lapse of time affects the good faith and credibility of the moving party." For similar conclusions, see: *Parker v. United States,* 358 F.2d 50, 54 n. 4 (7th Cir.1965), cert. denied, 386 U.S. 916 (1967); *Le Clair v. United States,* 241 F.Supp. 819, 824 (N.D.Ind.1965); *Malone v. United States,* 299 F.2d 254, 256 (6th Cir.1962), cert. denied, 371 U.S. 863 (1962); *Howell v. United States,* 442 F.2d 265, 274 (7th Cir.1971); and *United States v. Wiggins,* 184 F.Supp. 673, 676 (D.C.Cir.1960).

There have been holdings by some courts that a delay in filing a § 2255 motion operates to increase the burden of proof which the movant must meet to obtain relief. The reasons for this, as expressed in *United States v. Bostic,* 206 F.Supp. 855 (D.C.Cir.1962), are equitable in nature.

> Obviously, the burden of proof on a motion to vacate a sentence under 28 U.S.C. § 2255 is on the moving party. . . . The burden is particularly heavy if the issue is one of fact and a long time has elapsed since the trial of the case. While neither the statute of limitations nor laches can bar the assertion of a constitutional right, nevertheless, the passage of time may make it impracticable to retry a case if the motion is granted and a new trial is ordered. No doubt, at times such a motion is a product of an afterthought. Long delay may raise a question of good faith.

206 F.Supp. at 856–857

See also *United States v. Wiggins,* 184 F.Supp. at 676.

A requirement that the movant display reasonable diligence in filing a § 2255 motion has been adopted by some courts dealing with delayed motions. The court in *United States v. Moore,* 166 F.2d 102 (7th Cir.1948), cert. denied, 334 U.S. 849 (1948), did this, again for equitable reasons.

> [W]e agree with the District Court that the petitioner has too long slept upon his rights. * * * [A]pparently there is no limitation of time within which * * * a motion to vacate may be filed, except that an applicant must show reasonable diligence in presenting his claim. * * *
>
> The reasons which support the rule requiring diligence seem obvious. * * * Law enforcement officials change, witnesses die, memories grow dim. The prosecuting tribunal is put to a disadvantage if an unexpected retrial should be necessary after long passage of time.

166 F.2d at 105

In accord see *Desmond v. United States,* 333 F.2d 378, 381 (1st Cir.1964), on remand, 345 F.2d 225 (1st Cir.1965).

One of the major arguments advanced by the courts which would penalize a movant who waits an unduly long time before filing a § 2255 motion is that such delay is highly prejudicial to the prosecution. In *Desmond v. United States,* writing of a § 2255 motion alleging denial of effective appeal because of deception by movant's own counsel, the court said:

> [A]pplications for relief such as this must be made promptly. It will not do for a prisoner to wait until government witnesses have become unavailable as by death, serious illness or absence from the country, or until the memory of available government witnesses has faded. It will not even do for a prisoner to wait any longer than is reasonably necessary to prepare appropriate moving papers, however inartistic, after discovery of the deception practiced upon him by his attorney.

333 F.2d at 381

In a similar vein are *United States v. Moore* and *United States v. Bostic,* supra, and *United States v. Wiggins,* 184 F.Supp. at 676.

Subdivision (a) provides a flexible, equitable time limitation based on laches to prevent movants from withholding their claims so as to prejudice the government both in meeting the allegations of the motion and in any possible retrial. It includes a reasonable diligence requirement for ascertaining possible grounds for relief. If the delay is found to be excusable, or nonprejudicial to the government, the time bar is inoperative.

Subdivision (b) is consistent with the language of § 2255 and relevant case law.

The annexed form is intended to serve the same purpose as the comparable one included in the § 2254 rules.

For further discussion applicable to this rule, see the advisory committee note to Rule 9 of the § 2254 rules.

2004 Amendments

The language of Rule 9 has been amended as part of general restyling of the rules to make them more easily understood and to make style and terminology consistent throughout the rules. These changes are intended to be stylistic and no substantive change is intended, except as indicated below.

First, current Rule 9(a) has been deleted as unnecessary in light of the applicable one-year statute of limitations for § 2255 motions, added as part of the Antiterrorism and Effective Death Penalty Act of 1996, 28 U.S.C. § 2255, para. 6.

Second, the remainder of revised Rule 9 reflects provisions in the Antiterrorism and Effective Death Penalty Act of 1996, 28 U.S.C. § 2255, para. 8, which now require a moving party to obtain approval from the appropriate court of appeals before filing a second or successive motion.

Finally, the title of the rule has been changed to reflect the fact that the revised version addresses only the topic of second or successive motions.

Rule 10. Powers of a Magistrate Judge

A magistrate judge may perform the duties of a district judge under these rules, as authorized by 28 U.S.C. § 636.

(As amended Pub.L. 94–426, § 2(12), Sept. 28, 1976, 90 Stat. 1335; Apr. 30, 1979, eff. Aug. 1, 1979; Apr. 26, 2004, eff. Dec. 1, 2004.)

ADVISORY COMMITTEE NOTES

1976 Adoption

See the advisory committee note to Rule 10 of the § 2254 rules for a discussion fully applicable here as well.

1979 Amendment

This amendment conforms the rule to 18 U.S.C. § 636. See Advisory Committee Note to Rule 10 of the Rules Governing Section 2254 Cases in the United States District Courts.

2004 Amendments

The language of Rule 10 has been amended as part of general restyling of the rules to make them more easily understood and to make style and terminology consistent throughout the rules. These changes are intended to be stylistic and no substantive change is intended.

HISTORICAL NOTES

Change of Name

United States magistrate appointed under section 631 of Title 28, Judiciary and Judicial Procedure, to be known as United States magistrate judge after Dec. 1, 1990, with any reference to United States magistrate or magistrate in Title 28, in any other Federal statute, etc., deemed a reference to United States magistrate judge appointed under section 631 of Title 28, see section 321 of Pub.L. 101–650, set out as a note under section 631 of Title 28.

Rule 11. Time to Appeal

Federal Rule of Appellate Procedure 4(a) governs the time to appeal an order entered under these rules. These rules do not extend the time to appeal the original judgment of conviction.

(As amended Apr. 30, 1979, eff. Aug. 1, 1979; Apr. 26, 2004, eff. Dec. 1, 2004.)

ADVISORY COMMITTEE NOTES

1976 Adoption

Rule 11 is intended to make clear that, although a § 2255 action is a continuation of the criminal case, the bringing of a § 2255 action does not extend the time.

1979 Amendment

Prior to the promulgation of the Rules Governing Section 2255 Proceedings, the courts consistently held that the time for appeal in a section 2255 case is as provided in Fed. R.App.P. 4(a), that is, 60 days when the government is a party, rather than as provided in appellate rule 4(b), which says that the time is 10 days in criminal cases. This result has often been explained on the ground that rule 4(a) has to do with civil cases and that "proceedings under section 2255 are civil in nature." E.g., *Rothman v. United States*, 508 F.2d 648 (3d Cir.1975). Because the new section 2255 rules are based upon the premise "that a motion under § 2255 is a further step in the movant's criminal case rather than a separate civil action," see Advisory Committee Note to Rule 1, the question has arisen whether the new rules have the effect of shortening the time for appeal to that provided in appellate rule 4(b). A sentence has been added to Rule 11 in order to make it clear that this is not the case.

Even though section 2255 proceedings are a further step in the criminal case, the added sentence correctly states current law. In *United States v. Hayman*, 342 U.S. 205 (1952), the Supreme Court noted that such appeals "are governed by the civil rules applicable to appeals from final judgments in habeas corpus actions." In support, the Court cited *Mercado v. United States*, 183 F.2d 486 (1st Cir.1950), a case rejecting the argument that because § 2255 proceedings are criminal in nature the time for appeal is only 10 days. The *Mercado* court concluded that the situation was governed by that part of 28 U.S.C. § 2255 which reads: "An appeal may be taken to the court of appeals from the order entered on the motion as from a final judgment on application for a writ of habeas corpus." Thus, because appellate rule 4(a) is applicable in habeas cases, it likewise governs in § 2255 cases even though they are criminal in nature.

2004 Amendments

The language of Rule 11 has been amended as part of general restyling of the rules to make them more easily understood and to make style and terminology consistent throughout the rules. These changes are intended to be stylistic and no substantive change is intended.

Rule 12. Applicability of the Federal Rules of Civil Procedure and the Federal Rules of Criminal Procedure

The Federal Rules of Civil Procedure and the Federal Rules of Criminal Procedure, to the extent that they are not inconsistent with any statutory provisions or these rules, may be applied to a proceeding under these rules.

(As amended Apr. 26, 2004, eff. Dec. 1, 2004.)

ADVISORY COMMITTEE NOTES

1976 Adoption

This rule differs from rule 11 of the § 2254 rules in that it includes the Federal Rules of Criminal Procedure as well as the civil. This is because of the nature of a § 2255 motion as a continuing part of the criminal proceeding (see advisory committee note to Rule 1) as well as a remedy analogous to habeas corpus by state prisoners.

Since § 2255 has been considered analogous to habeas as respects the restrictions in Fed.R.Civ.P. 81(a) (2) (see *Sullivan v. United States,* 198 F.Supp. 624 (S.D.N.Y.1961)), Rule 12 is needed. For discussion, see the advisory committee note to Rule 11 of the § 2254 rules.

2004 Amendments

The language of Rule 12 has been amended as part of general restyling of the rules to make them more easily understood and to make style and terminology consistent throughout the rules. These changes are intended to be stylistic and no substantive change is intended.

APPENDIX OF FORMS

Motion to Vacate, Set Aside, or Correct a Sentence By a Person in Federal Custody
(Motion Under 28 U.S.C. § 2255)

Instructions

1. To use this form, you must be a person who is serving a sentence under a judgment against you in a federal court. You are asking for relief from the conviction or the sentence. This form is your motion for relief.

2. You must file the form in the United States district court that entered the judgment that you are challenging. If you want to challenge a federal judgment that imposed a sentence to be served in the future, you should file the motion in the federal court that entered that judgment.

3. Make sure the form is typed or neatly written.

4. You must tell the truth and sign the form. If you make a false statement of a material fact, you may be prosecuted for perjury.

5. Answer all the questions. You do not need to cite law. You may submit additional pages if necessary. If you do not fill out the form properly, you will be asked to submit additional or correct information. If you want to submit a brief or arguments, you must submit them in a separate memorandum.

6. If you cannot pay for the costs of this motion (such as costs for an attorney or transcripts), you may ask to proceed *in forma pauperis* (as a poor person). To do that, you must fill out the last page of this form. Also, you must submit a certificate signed by an officer at the institution where you are confined showing the amount of money that the institution is holding for you.

7. In this motion, you may challenge the judgment entered by only one court. If you want to challenge a judgment entered by a different judge or division (either in the same district or in a different district), you must file a separate motion.

8. When you have completed the form, send the original and two copies to the Clerk of the United States District Court at this address:

   Clerk, United States District Court for
   _____
   Address
   City, State Zip Code

9. **CAUTION: You must include in this motion all the grounds for relief from the conviction or sentence that you challenge. And you must state the facts that support each ground. If you fail to set forth all the grounds in this motion, you may be barred from presenting additional grounds at a later date.**

10. **CAPITAL CASES: If you are under a sentence of death, you are entitled to the assistance of counsel and should request the appointment of counsel.**

MOTION UNDER 28 U.S.C. § 2255 TO VACATE, SET ASIDE, OR CORRECT SENTENCE BY A PERSON IN FEDERAL CUSTODY

Name (under which you were convicted): Docket or Case No.:

Place of Confinement: Prisoner No.:

UNITED STATES OF AMERICA Movant (include name under which convicted)

v.

MOTION

1. (a) Name and location of court that entered the judgment of conviction you are challenging: _____

(b) Criminal docket or case number (if you know): _____

2. (a) Date of the judgment of conviction (if you know): _____

(b) Date of sentencing: _____

3. Length of sentence: _____

4. Nature of crime (all counts): _____

5. (a) What was your plea? (Check one)
(1) Not guilty ☐ (2) Guilty ☐ (3) Nolo contendere (no contest) ☐

(b) If you entered a guilty plea to one count or indictment, and a not guilty plea to another count or indictment, what did you plead guilty to and what did you plead not guilty to? _____

6. If you went to trial, what kind of trial did you have? (Check one) Jury ☐ Judge only ☐

7. Did you testify at a pretrial hearing, trial, or post-trial hearing? Yes ☐ No ☐

8. Did you appeal from the judgment of conviction? Yes ☐ No ☐

9. If you did appeal, answer the following:
(a) Name of court: _____
(b) Docket or case number (if you know): _____
(c) Result: _____
(d) Date of result (if you know): _____
(e) Citation to the case (if you know): _____
(f) Grounds raised: _____

(g) Did you file a petition for certiorari in the United States Supreme Court?
Yes ☐ No ☐

If "Yes," answer the following:
(1) Docket or case number (if you know): _____
(2) Result: _____
(3) Date of result (if you know): _____
(4) Citation to the case (if you know): _____
(5) Grounds raised: _____

10. Other than the direct appeals listed above, have you previously filed any other motions, petitions, or applications concerning this judgment of conviction in any court?
Yes ☐ No ☐

11. If your answer to Question 10 was "Yes," give the following information:

(a) (1) Name of court: _____
(2) Docket or case number (if you know): _____
(3) Date of filing (if you know): _____
(4) Nature of the proceeding: _____
(5) Grounds raised: _____

(6) Did you receive a hearing where evidence was given on your motion, petition, or application?
Yes ☐ No ☐
(7) Result: _____
(8) Date of result (if you know): _____

(b) If you filed any second motion, petition, or application, give the same information:
(1) Name of court: _____
(2) Docket or case number (if you know): _____
(3) Date of filing (if you know): _____
(4) Nature of the proceeding: _____
(5) Grounds raised: _____

(6) Did you receive a hearing where evidence was given on your motion, petition, or application?
Yes ☐ No ☐
(7) Result: _____
(8) Date of result (if you know): _____

(c) Did you appeal to a federal appellate court having jurisdiction over the action taken on your motion, petition, or application?
(1) First petition: Yes ☐ No ☐
(2) Second petition: Yes ☐ No ☐

(d) If you did not appeal from the action on any motion, petition, or application, explain briefly why you did not: _____

12. For this motion, state every ground on which you claim that you are being held in violation of the Constitution, laws, or treaties of the United States. Attach additional pages if you have more than four grounds. State the facts supporting each ground.

GROUND ONE:

(a) Supporting facts (Do not argue or cite law. Just state the specific facts that support your claim.):

(b) **Direct Appeal of Ground One:**
(1) If you appealed from the judgment of conviction, did you raise this issue?
Yes ☐ No ☐
(2) If you did not raise this issue in your direct appeal, explain why:

(c) **Post-Conviction Proceedings:**
(1) Did you raise this issue in any post-conviction motion, petition, or application?
Yes ☐ No ☐
(2) If your answer to Question (c)(1) is "Yes," state:
Type of motion or petition:
Name and location of the court where the motion or petition was filed:
Docket or case number (if you know):
Date of the court's decision:
Result (attach a copy of the court's opinion or order, if available):
(3) Did you receive a hearing on your motion, petition, or application?
Yes ☐ No ☐
(4) Did you appeal from the denial of your motion, petition, or application?
Yes ☐ No ☐
(5) If your answer to Question (c)(4) is "Yes," did you raise this issue in the appeal?
Yes ☐ No ☐
(6) If your answer to Question (c)(4) is "Yes," state:
Name and location of the court where the appeal was filed:
Docket or case number (if you know):
Date of the court's decision:
Result (attach a copy of the court's opinion or order, if available):
(7) If your answer to Question (c)(4) or Question (c)(5) is "No," explain why you did not appeal or raise this issue:

GROUND TWO:

(a) Supporting facts (Do not argue or cite law. Just state the specific facts that support your claim.):

(b) **Direct Appeal of Ground Two:**
(1) If you appealed from the judgment of conviction, did you raise this issue?
Yes ☐ No ☐
(2) If you did not raise this issue in your direct appeal, explain why:

(c) **Post-Conviction Proceedings:**
(1) Did you raise this issue in any post-conviction motion, petition, or application?
Yes ☐ No ☐
(2) If your answer to Question (c)(1) is "Yes," state:
Type of motion or petition:
Name and location of the court where the motion or petition was filed:
Docket or case number (if you know):
Date of the court's decision:
Result (attach a copy of the court's opinion or order, if available):
(3) Did you receive a hearing on your motion, petition, or application?
Yes ☐ No ☐
(4) Did you appeal from the denial of your motion, petition, or application?
Yes ☐ No ☐
(5) If your answer to Question (c)(4) is "Yes," did you raise this issue in the appeal?
Yes ☐ No ☐
(6) If your answer to Question (c)(4) is "Yes," state:
Name and location of the court where the appeal was filed:
Docket or case number (if you know):
Date of the court's decision:
Result (attach a copy of the court's opinion or order, if available):
(7) If your answer to Question (c)(4) or Question (c)(5) is "No," explain why you did not appeal or raise this issue:

GROUND THREE:

(a) Supporting facts (Do not argue or cite law. Just state the specific facts that support your claim.):

(b) **Direct Appeal of Ground Three:**
(1) If you appealed from the judgment of conviction, did you raise this issue?
Yes ☐ No ☐
(2) If you did not raise this issue in your direct appeal, explain why:

(c) **Post-Conviction Proceedings:**
(1) Did you raise this issue in any post-conviction motion, petition, or application?
Yes ☐ No ☐
(2) If your answer to Question (c)(1) is "Yes," state:
Type of motion or petition:
Name and location of the court where the motion or petition was filed:
Docket or case number (if you know):
Date of the court's decision:
Result (attach a copy of the court's opinion or order, if available):
(3) Did you receive a hearing on your motion, petition, or application?
Yes ☐ No ☐
(4) Did you appeal from the denial of your motion, petition, or application?
Yes ☐ No ☐
(5) If your answer to Question (c)(4) is "Yes," did you raise this issue in the appeal?
Yes ☐ No ☐
(6) If your answer to Question (c)(4) is "Yes," state:
Name and location of the court where the appeal was filed:
Docket or case number (if you know):
Date of the court's decision:
Result (attach a copy of the court's opinion or order, if available):
(7) If your answer to Question (c)(4) or Question (c)(5) is "No," explain why you did not appeal or raise this issue:

GROUND FOUR:

(a) Supporting facts (Do not argue or cite law. Just state the specific facts that support your claim.):

(b) **Direct Appeal of Ground Four:**
(1) If you appealed from the judgment of conviction, did you raise this issue?
Yes ☐ No ☐
(2) If you did not raise this issue in your direct appeal, explain why:

(c) **Post-Conviction Proceedings:**
(1) Did you raise this issue in any post-conviction motion, petition, or application?
Yes ☐ No ☐
(2) If your answer to Question (c)(1) is "Yes," state:
Type of motion or petition:
Name and location of the court where the motion or petition was filed:
Docket or case number (if you know):
Date of the court's decision:
Result (attach a copy of the court's opinion or order, if available):
(3) Did you receive a hearing on your motion, petition, or application?
Yes ☐ No ☐
(4) Did you appeal from the denial of your motion, petition, or application?
Yes ☐ No ☐
(5) If your answer to Question (c)(4) is "Yes," did you raise this issue in the appeal?
Yes ☐ No ☐
(6) If your answer to Question (c)(4) is "Yes," state:
Name and location of the court where the appeal was filed:
Docket or case number (if you know):
Date of the court's decision:
Result (attach a copy of the court's opinion or order, if available):
(7) If your answer to Question (c)(4) or Question (c)(5) is "No," explain why you did not appeal or raise this issue:

13. Is there any ground in this motion that you have not previously presented in some federal court? If so, which ground or grounds have not been presented, and state your reasons for not presenting them:

14. Do you have any motion, petition, or appeal now pending (filed and not decided yet) in any court for the judgment you are challenging? Yes ☐ No ☐
If "Yes," state the name and location of the court, the docket or case number, the type of proceeding, and the issues raised. _____

15. Give the name and address, if known, of each attorney who represented you in the following stages of the judgment you are challenging:
(a) At preliminary hearing: _____
(b) At arraignment and plea: _____
(c) At trial: _____
(d) At sentencing: _____
(e) On appeal: _____
(f) In any post-conviction proceeding: _____
(g) On appeal from any ruling against you in a post-conviction proceeding: _____

16. Were you sentenced on more than one count of an indictment, or on more than one indictment, in the same court and at the same time? Yes ☐ No ☐

17. Do you have any future sentence to serve after you complete the sentence for the judgment that you are challenging? Yes ☐ No ☐
(a) If so, give name and location of court that imposed the other sentence you will serve in the future: _____
(b) Give the date the other sentence was imposed: _____
(c) Give the length of the other sentence: _____
(d) Have you filed, or do you plan to file, any motion, petition, or application that challenges the judgment or sentence to be served in the future? Yes ☐ No ☐

18. TIMELINESS OF MOTION: If your judgment of conviction became final over one year ago, you must explain why the one-year statute of limitations as contained in 28 U.S.C. § 2255 does not bar your motion.* _____

* The Antiterrorism and Effective Death Penalty Act of 1996 ("AEDPA") as contained in 28 U.S.C. § 2255, paragraph 6, provides in part that:

> A one-year period of limitation shall apply to a motion under this section. The limitation period shall run from the latest of—
>
> (1) the date on which the judgment of conviction became final;
>
> (2) the date on which the impediment to making a motion created by governmental action in violation of the Constitution or laws of the United States is removed, if the movant was prevented from making such a motion by such governmental action;
>
> (3) the date on which the right asserted was initially recognized by the Supreme Court, if that right has been newly recognized by the Supreme Court and made retroactively applicable to cases on collateral review; or
>
> (4) the date on which the facts supporting the claim or claims presented could have been discovered through the exercise of due diligence.

Therefore, movant asks that the Court grant the following relief: _____

or any other relief to which movant may be entitled.

_____
Signature of Attorney (if any)

I declare (or certify, verify, or state) under penalty of perjury that the foregoing is true and correct and that this Motion Under 28 U.S.C. § 2255 was placed in the prison mailing system on _____ (month, date, year).

Executed (signed) on _____ (date).

_____
Signature of Movant

If the person signing is not movant, state relationship to movant and explain why movant is not signing this motion. _____

IN FORMA PAUPERIS DECLARATION

[INSERT APPROPRIATE COURT]

United States v. _____ (Movant)	DECLARATION IN SUPPORT OF REQUEST TO PROCEED *IN FORMA PAUPERIS*

I, _____, declare that I am the movant in the above entitled case; that in support of my motion to proceed without being required to prepay fees, costs or give security therefor, I state that because of my poverty, I am unable to pay the costs of said proceeding or to give security therefor; that I believe I am entitled to relief.

1. Are you presently employed? Yes ☐ No ☐
   a. If the answer is "yes," state the amount of your salary or wages per month, and give the name and address of your employer.
   b. If the answer is "no," state the date of last employment and the amount of the salary and wages per month which you received.
2. Have you received within the past twelve months any money from any of the following sources?
   a. Business, profession or form of self-employment? Yes ☐ No ☐
   b. Rent payments, interest or dividends? Yes ☐ No ☐
   c. Pensions, annuities or life insurance payments? Yes ☐ No ☐
   d. Gifts or inheritances? Yes ☐ No ☐
   e. Any other sources? Yes ☐ No ☐

   If the answer to any of the above is "yes," describe each source of money and state the amount received from each during the past twelve months.
3. Do you own any cash, or do you have money in a checking or savings account?
   Yes ☐ No ☐ (Include any funds in prison accounts)

   If the answer is "yes," state the total value of the items owned.
4. Do you own real estate, stocks, bonds, notes, automobiles, or other valuable property (excluding ordinary household furnishings and clothing)?
   Yes ☐ No ☐

   If the answer is "yes," describe the property and state its approximate value.
5. List the persons who are dependent upon you for support, state your relationship to those persons, and indicate how much you contribute toward their support.

I declare (or certify, verify, or state) under penalty of perjury that the foregoing is true and correct. Executed on _____.
(date)

_____
Signature of Movant

CERTIFICATE

I hereby certify that the movant herein has the sum of $_____ on account to his credit at the _____ institution where he is confined. I further certify that movant likewise has the following securities to his credit according to the records of said _____ institution:

_____
Authorized Officer of Institution

(As amended Apr. 28, 1982, eff. Aug. 1, 1982; Apr. 26, 2004, eff. Dec. 1, 2004.)

RULES OF EVIDENCE FOR UNITED STATES COURTS AND MAGISTRATES

Pub.L. 93–595, § 1, January 2, 1975, 88 Stat. 1926
Amendments received to December 1, 2008

ARTICLE I. GENERAL PROVISIONS

Rule
101. Scope.
102. Purpose and Construction.
103. Rulings on Evidence.
104. Preliminary Questions.
105. Limited Admissibility.
106. Remainder of or Related Writings or Recorded Statements.

ARTICLE II. JUDICIAL NOTICE

201. Judicial Notice of Adjudicative Facts.

ARTICLE III. PRESUMPTIONS IN CIVIL ACTIONS AND PROCEEDINGS

301. Presumptions in General in Civil Actions and Proceedings.
302. Applicability of State Law in Civil Actions and Proceedings.

ARTICLE IV. RELEVANCY AND ITS LIMITS

401. Definition of "Relevant Evidence".
402. Relevant Evidence Generally Admissible; Irrelevant Evidence Inadmissible.
403. Exclusion of Relevant Evidence on Grounds of Prejudice, Confusion, or Waste of Time.
404. Character Evidence Not Admissible To Prove Conduct; Exceptions; Other Crimes.
405. Methods of Proving Character.
406. Habit; Routine Practice.
407. Subsequent Remedial Measures.
408. Compromise and Offers to Compromise.
409. Payment of Medical and Similar Expenses.
410. Inadmissibility of Pleas, Plea Discussions, and Related Statements.
411. Liability Insurance.
412. Sex Offense Cases; Relevance of Alleged Victim's Past Sexual Behavior or Alleged Sexual Predisposition.
413. Evidence of Similar Crimes in Sexual Assault Cases.
414. Evidence of Similar Crimes in Child Molestation Cases.
415. Evidence of Similar Acts in Civil Cases Concerning Sexual Assault or Child Molestation.

ARTICLE V. PRIVILEGES

501. General Rule.
502. Attorney–Client Privilege and Work Product; Limitations on Waiver.

Rule

ARTICLE VI. WITNESSES

601. General Rule of Competency.
602. Lack of Personal Knowledge.
603. Oath or Affirmation.
604. Interpreters.
605. Competency of Judge as Witness.
606. Competency of Juror as Witness.
607. Who May Impeach.
608. Evidence of Character and Conduct of Witness.
609. Impeachment by Evidence of Conviction of Crime.
610. Religious Beliefs or Opinions.
611. Mode and Order of Interrogation and Presentation.
612. Writing Used to Refresh Memory.
613. Prior Statements of Witnesses.
614. Calling and Interrogation of Witnesses by Court.
615. Exclusion of Witnesses.
616 to 700. Reserved.

ARTICLE VII. OPINIONS AND EXPERT TESTIMONY

701. Opinion Testimony by Lay Witnesses.
702. Testimony by Experts.
703. Bases of Opinion Testimony by Experts.
704. Opinion on Ultimate Issue.
705. Disclosure of Facts or Data Underlying Expert Opinion.
706. Court Appointed Experts.

ARTICLE VIII. HEARSAY

801. Definitions.
802. Hearsay Rule.
803. Hearsay Exceptions; Availability of Declarant Immaterial.
804. Hearsay Exceptions; Declarant Unavailable.
805. Hearsay Within Hearsay.
806. Attacking and Supporting Credibility of Declarant.
807. Residual Exception.

ARTICLE IX. AUTHENTICATION AND IDENTIFICATION

901. Requirement of Authentication or Identification.
902. Self-authentication.
903. Subscribing Witness' Testimony Unnecessary.

ARTICLE X. CONTENTS OF WRITINGS, RECORDINGS AND PHOTOGRAPHS

1001. Definitions.
1002. Requirement of Original.

Rule

ARTICLE X. CONTENTS OF WRITINGS, RECORDINGS AND PHOTOGRAPHS —Cont'd

1003. Admissibility of Duplicates.
1004. Admissibility of Other Evidence of Contents.
1005. Public Records.
1006. Summaries.
1007. Testimony or Written Admission of Party.
1008. Functions of Court and Jury.

ARTICLE XI. MISCELLANEOUS RULES

1101. Applicability of Rules.
1102. Amendments.
1103. Title.

ORDERS OF THE SUPREME COURT OF THE UNITED STATES ADOPTING AND AMENDING RULES

ORDER OF NOVEMBER 20, 1972

1. That the rules hereinafter set forth, to be known as the Federal Rules of Evidence, be, and they hereby are, prescribed pursuant to Sections 3402, 3771, and 3772, Title 18, United States Code, and Sections 2072 and 2075, Title 28, United States Code, to govern procedure, in the proceedings and to the extent set forth therein, in the United States courts of appeals, the United States district courts, the District Court for the District of the Canal Zone and the district courts of Guam and the Virgin Islands, and before United States magistrates.

2. That the aforementioned Federal Rules of Evidence shall take effect on July 1, 1973, and shall be applicable to actions and proceedings brought thereafter and also to further procedure in actions and proceedings then pending, except to the extent that in the opinion of the court their application in a particular action or proceeding then pending would not be feasible or would work injustice in which event the former procedure applies.

3. That subdivision (c) of Rule 30 and Rules 43 and 44.1 of the Federal Rules of Civil Procedure be, and they hereby are, amended, effective July 1, 1973, to read as hereinafter set forth:

[See amendments made thereby under the respective Rules of Civil Procedure.]

4. That subdivision (c) of Rule 32 of the Federal Rules of Civil Procedure be, and it hereby is, abrogated, effective July 1, 1973.

5. That Rules 26, 26.1 and 28 of the Federal Rules of Criminal Procedure be, and they hereby are, amended effective July 1, 1973, to read as hereinafter set forth.

[See amendments made thereby under the respective Rules of Criminal Procedure.]

6. That the Chief Justice be, and he hereby is, authorized to transmit the foregoing new rules and amendments to and abrogation of existing rules to the Congress at the beginning of its next regular session, in accordance with the provisions of Title 18 U.S.C. § 3771 and Title 28 U.S.C. §§ 2072 and 2075.

CONGRESSIONAL ACTION ON PROPOSED RULES OF EVIDENCE AND 1972 AMENDMENTS TO FEDERAL RULES OF CIVIL PROCEDURE AND FEDERAL RULES OF CRIMINAL PROCEDURE

Pub.L. 93–12, Mar. 30, 1973, 87 Stat. 9, provided: "That notwithstanding any other provisions of law, the Rules of Evidence for United States Courts and Magistrates, the Amendments to the Federal Rules of Civil Procedure, and the Amendments to the Federal Rules of Criminal Procedure, which are embraced by the orders entered by the Supreme Court of the United States on Monday, November 20, 1972, and Monday, December 18, 1972, shall have no force or effect except to the extent, and with such amendments, as they may be expressly approved by Act of Congress."

Pub.L. 93–595, § 3, Jan. 2, 1975, 88 Stat. 1959, provided that: "The Congress expressly approves the amendments to the Federal Rules of Civil Procedure, and the amendments to the Federal Rules of Criminal Procedure, which are embraced by the orders entered by the Supreme Court of the United States on November 20, 1972, and December 18, 1972, and such amendments shall take effect on the one hundred and eightieth day beginning after the date of the enactment of this Act [Jan. 2, 1975]."

ORDER OF APRIL 30, 1979

1. That Rule 410 of the Federal Rules of Evidence be, and it hereby is, amended to read as follows:

[See amendment made thereby following Rule 410, post.]

2. That the foregoing amendment to the Federal Rules of Evidence shall take effect on November 1, 1979, and shall be applicable to all proceedings then pending except to the extent that in the opinion of the court the application of the amended rule in a particular proceeding would not be feasible or would work injustice.

3. That THE CHIEF JUSTICE be, and he hereby is, authorized to transmit to the Congress the foregoing amendment to the Federal Rules of Evidence in accordance with the provisions of 28 U.S.C. § 2076.

CONGRESSIONAL ACTION ON AMENDMENT PROPOSED APRIL 30, 1979

Pub.L. 96–42, July 31, 1979, 93 Stat. 326, provided that the amendment proposed and transmitted to the Federal Rules of Evidence affecting rule 410, shall not take effect until Dec. 1, 1980, or until and then only to the extent approved by Act of Congress, whichever is earlier.

ORDER OF MARCH 2, 1987

1. That the Federal Rules of Evidence be, and they hereby are, amended by including therein amendments to Rules 101, 104, 106, 404, 405, 411, 602, 603, 604, 606, 607, 608, 609, 610, 611, 612, 613, 615, 701, 703, 705, 706, 801, 803, 804, 806, 902, 1004, 1007 and 1101, as hereinafter set forth:

[See amendments made thereby under respective rules, post.]

2. That the foregoing changes in the Federal Rules of Evidence shall take effect on October 1, 1987.

3. That THE CHIEF JUSTICE be, and he hereby is, authorized to transmit to the Congress the foregoing changes

in the rules of evidence in accordance with the provisions of Section 2076 of Title 28, United States Code.

ORDER OF APRIL 25, 1988

1. That the Federal Rules of Evidence be, and they hereby are, amended by including therein amendments to Rules 101, 602, 608, 613, 615, 902, and 1101, as hereinafter set forth:

[See amendments made thereby under respective rules, post.]

2. That the foregoing changes in the Federal Rules of Evidence shall take effect on November 1, 1988.

3. That THE CHIEF JUSTICE be, and he hereby is, authorized to transmit to the Congress the foregoing changes in the rules of evidence in accordance with the provisions of Section 2076 of Title 28, United States Code.

ORDER OF JANUARY 26, 1990

1. That the Federal Rules of Evidence be, and they hereby are, amended by including therein amendments to Rule 609(a)(1) and (2), as hereinafter set forth:

[See amendment made thereby, post].

2. That the foregoing changes in the Federal Rules of Evidence shall take effect on December 1, 1990.

3. That THE CHIEF JUSTICE be, and he hereby is, authorized to transmit to the Congress the foregoing changes in the rules of evidence in accordance with the provisions of Section 2074 of Title 28, United States Code.

ORDER OF APRIL 30, 1991

1. That the Federal Rules of Evidence for the United States District Courts be, and they hereby are, amended by including therein amendments to Evidence Rules 404(b) and 1102.

[See amendments made thereby under respective rules, post.]

2. That the foregoing amendments to the Federal Rules of Evidence shall take effect on December 1, 1991, and shall govern in all proceedings thereafter commenced and, insofar as just and practicable, all proceedings then pending.

3. That THE CHIEF JUSTICE be, and he hereby is, authorized to transmit to the Congress the foregoing amendments to the Federal Rules of Evidence in accordance with the provisions of Section 2072 of Title 28, United States Code.

ORDER OF APRIL 22, 1993

1. That the Federal Rules of Evidence for the United States District Courts be, and they hereby are, amended by including therein amendments to Evidence Rules 101, 705, and 1101.

[See amendments made thereby under respective rules, post.]

2. That the foregoing amendments to the Federal Rules of Evidence shall take effect on December 1, 1993, and shall govern in all proceedings thereafter commenced and, insofar as just and practicable, all proceedings then pending.

3. That THE CHIEF JUSTICE be, and he hereby is, authorized to transmit to the Congress the foregoing amendments to the Federal Rules of Evidence in accordance with the provisions of Section 2072 of Title 28, United States Code.

ORDER OF APRIL 29, 1994

ORDERED:

1. That the Federal Rules of Evidence for the United States District Courts be, and they hereby are, amended by including therein an amendment to Evidence Rule 412.

[See amendment made hereby under Rule 412, post.]

2. That the foregoing amendment to the Federal Rules of Evidence shall take effect on December 1, 1994, and shall govern in all proceedings thereafter commenced and, insofar as just and practicable, all proceedings then pending.

3. That THE CHIEF JUSTICE be, and he hereby is, authorized to transmit to the Congress the foregoing amendment to the Federal Rules of Evidence in accordance with the provisions of Section 2072 of Title 28, United States Code.

ORDER OF APRIL 11, 1997

ORDERED:

1. That the Federal Rules of Evidence be, and they hereby are, amended by including therein amendments to Evidence Rules 407, 801, 803(24), 804(b)(5), and 806, and new Rules 804(b)(6) and 807.

[See amendments made thereby under respective rules, post.]

2. That the foregoing amendments to the Federal Rules of Evidence shall take effect on December 1, 1997, and shall govern in all proceedings thereafter commenced and, insofar as just and practicable, all proceedings then pending.

3. That THE CHIEF JUSTICE be, and hereby is, authorized to transmit to the Congress the foregoing amendments to the Federal Rules of Evidence in accordance with the provisions of Section 2072 of Title 28, United States Code.

ORDER OF APRIL 24, 1998

ORDERED:

1. That the Federal Rules of Evidence be, and they hereby are, amended by including therein amendments to Evidence Rule 615.

[See amendments made thereby under respective rules, post.]

2. That the foregoing amendments to the Federal Rules of Evidence shall take effect on December 1, 1998, and shall govern in all proceedings thereafter commenced and, insofar as just and practicable, all proceedings then pending.

3. That THE CHIEF JUSTICE be, and hereby is, authorized to transmit to the Congress the foregoing amendments to the Federal Rules of Evidence in accordance with the provisions of Section 2072 of Title 28, United States Code.

ORDER OF APRIL 17, 2000

ORDERED:

1. That the Federal Rules of Evidence for the United States District Courts be, and they hereby are, amended by including therein amendments to Evidence Rules 103, 404, 701, 702, 703, 803(6), and 902.

[See amendments made thereby under respective rules, post.]

2. That the foregoing amendments to the Federal Rules of Evidence shall take effect on December 1, 2000, and shall govern all proceedings thereafter commenced and, insofar as just and practicable, all proceedings then pending .

3. That THE CHIEF JUSTICE be, and hereby is, authorized to transmit to the Congress the foregoing amendments to the Federal Rules of Evidence in accordance with the provisions of Section 2072 of Title 28, United States Code.

ORDER OF MARCH 27, 2003

ORDERED:

1. That the Federal Rules of Evidence be, and they hereby are, amended by including therein the amendments to Evidence Rule 608(b).

[See amendments made thereby under respective rules, post.]

2. That the foregoing amendments to the Federal Rules of Evidence shall take effect on December 1, 2003, and shall govern in all proceedings thereafter commenced and, insofar as just and practicable, all proceedings then pending.

3. That THE CHIEF JUSTICE be, and hereby is, authorized to transmit to the Congress the foregoing amendments to the Federal Rules of Evidence in accordance with the provisions of Section 2072 of Title 28, United States Code.

ORDER OF APRIL 12, 2006

1. That the Federal Rules of Evidence be, and they hereby are, amended by including therein the amendments to Evidence Rules 404, 408, 606, and 609.

[See amendments made thereby under respective rules, post.]

2. That the foregoing amendments to the Federal Rules of Evidence shall take effect on December 1, 2006, and shall govern in all proceedings thereafter commenced and, insofar as just and practicable, all proceedings then pending.

3. That THE CHIEF JUSTICE be, and hereby is, authorized to transmit to the Congress the foregoing amendments to the Federal Rules of Evidence in accordance with the provisions of Section 2072 of Title 28, United States Code.

HISTORICAL NOTES

Effective Date and Application of Rules

The Federal Rules of Evidence were adopted by order of the Supreme Court on Nov. 20, 1972, transmitted to Congress by the Chief Justice on Feb. 5, 1973, and to have become effective on July 1, 1973. Pub.L. 93–12, Mar. 30, 1973, 87 Stat. 9, provided that the proposed rules "shall have no force or effect except to the extent, and with such amendments, as they may be expressly approved by Act of Congress". Pub.L. 93–595, Jan. 2, 1975, 88 Stat. 1926, enacted the Federal Rules of Evidence proposed by the Supreme Court, with amendments made by Congress, to take effect on July 1, 1975.

The Rules have been amended Oct. 16, 1975, Pub.L. 94–113, § 1, 89 Stat. 576, eff. Oct. 31, 1975; Dec. 12, 1975, Pub.L. 94–149, § 1, 89 Stat. 805; Oct. 28, 1978, Pub.L. 95–540, § 2, 92 Stat. 2046; Nov. 6, 1978, Pub.L. 95–598, Title II, § 251, 92 Stat. 2673, eff. Oct. 1, 1979; Apr. 30, 1979, eff. Dec. 1, 1980; Apr. 2, 1982, Pub.L. 97–164, Title I, § 142, Title IV, § 402, 96 Stat. 45, 57, eff. Oct. 1, 1982; Oct. 12, 1984, Pub.L. 98–473, Title IV, § 406, 98 Stat. 2067; Mar. 2, 1987, eff. Oct. 1, 1987; Apr. 25, 1988, eff. Nov. 1, 1988; Nov. 18, 1988, Pub.L. 100–690, Title VII, §§ 7046, 7075, 102 Stat. 4400, 4405; Jan. 26, 1990, eff. Dec. 1, 1990; Apr. 30, 1991, eff. Dec. 1, 1991; Apr. 22, 1993, eff. Dec. 1, 1993; Apr. 29, 1994, eff. Dec. 1, 1994; Apr. 11, 1997, eff. Dec. 1, 1997; Apr. 24, 1998, eff. Dec. 1, 1998; Apr. 17, 2000, eff. Dec. 1, 2000; Mar. 27, 2003, eff. Dec. 1, 2003; Apr. 12, 2006, eff. Dec. 1, 2006.

ARTICLE I. GENERAL PROVISIONS

HISTORICAL NOTES

Change of Name

United States magistrate appointed under section 631 of Title 28, Judiciary and Judicial Procedure, to be known as United States magistrate judge after Dec. 1, 1990, with any reference to United States magistrate or magistrate in Title 28, in any other Federal statute, etc., deemed a reference to United States magistrate judge appointed under section 631 of Title 28, see section 321 of Pub.L. 101–650, set out as a note under section 631 of Title 28.

Rule 101. Scope

These rules govern proceedings in the courts of the United States and before the United States bankruptcy judges and United States magistrate judges, to the extent and with the exceptions stated in rule 1101. (Pub.L. 93–595, § 1, Jan. 2, 1975, 88 Stat. 1929; Mar. 2, 1987, eff. Oct. 1, 1987; Apr. 25, 1988, eff. Nov. 1, 1988; Apr. 22, 1993, eff. Dec. 1, 1993.)

1972 Proposed Rules

Rule 1101 specifies in detail the courts, proceedings, questions, and stages of proceedings to which the rules apply in whole or in part.

1987 Amendments

United States bankruptcy judges are added to conform this rule with Rule 1101(b) and Bankruptcy Rule 9017.

1988 Amendments

The amendment is technical. No substantive change is intended.

1993 Amendments

This revision is made to conform the rule to changes made by the Judicial Improvements Act of 1990.

HISTORICAL NOTES

Change of Name

United States magistrate appointed under section 631 of Title 28, Judiciary and Judicial Procedure, to be known as United States magistrate judge after Dec. 1, 1990, with any reference to United States magistrate or magistrate in Title 28, in any other Federal statute, etc., deemed a reference to United States magistrate judge appointed under section 631 of Title 28, see section 321 of Pub.L. 101–650, set out as a note under section 631 of Title 28.

Rule 102. Purpose and Construction

These rules shall be construed to secure fairness in administration, elimination of unjustifiable expense and delay, and promotion of growth and development of the law of evidence to the end that the truth may be ascertained and proceedings justly determined.

(Pub.L. 93–595, § 1, Jan. 2, 1975, 88 Stat.1929.)

1972 Proposed Rules

For similar provisions see Rule 2 of the Federal Rules of Criminal Procedure, Rule 1 of the Federal Rules of Civil Procedure, California Evidence Code § 2, and New Jersey Evidence Rule 5.

Rule 103. Rulings on Evidence

(a) Effect of Erroneous Ruling.—Error may not be predicated upon a ruling which admits or excludes evidence unless a substantial right of the party is affected, and

(1) Objection.—In case the ruling is one admitting evidence, a timely objection or motion to strike appears of record, stating the specific ground of objection, if the specific ground was not apparent from the context; or

(2) Offer of Proof.—In case the ruling is one excluding evidence, the substance of the evidence was made known to the court by offer or was apparent from the context within which questions were asked.

Once the court makes a definitive ruling on the record admitting or excluding evidence, either at or before trial, a party need not renew an objection or offer of proof to preserve a claim of error for appeal.

(b) Record of Offer and Ruling.—The court may add any other or further statement which shows the character of the evidence, the form in which it was offered, the objection made, and the ruling thereon. It may direct the making of an offer in question and answer form.

(c) Hearing of Jury.—In jury cases, proceedings shall be conducted, to the extent practicable, so as to prevent inadmissible evidence from being suggested to the jury by any means, such as making statements or offers of proof or asking questions in the hearing of the jury.

(d) Plain Error.—Nothing in this rule precludes taking notice of plain errors affecting substantial rights although they were not brought to the attention of the court.

(Pub.L. 93–595, § 1, Jan. 2, 1975, 88 Stat. 1929; Apr. 17, 2000, eff. Dec. 1, 2000.)

1972 Proposed Rules

Note to Subdivision (a). Subdivision (a) states the law as generally accepted today. Rulings on evidence cannot be assigned as error unless (1) a substantial right is affected, and (2) the nature of the error was called to the attention of the judge, so as to alert him to the proper course of action and enable opposing counsel to take proper corrective measures. The objection and the offer of proof are the techniques for accomplishing these objectives. For similar provisions see Uniform Rules 4 and 5; California Evidence Code §§ 353 and 354; Kansas Code of Civil Procedure §§ 60–404 and 60–405. The rule does not purport to change the law with respect to harmless error. See 28 USC § 2111, F.R.Civ.P. 61, F.R.Crim.P. 52, and decisions construing them. The status of constitutional error as harmless or not is treated in Chapman v. California, 386 U.S. 18, 87 S.Ct. 824, 17 L.Ed.2d 705 (1967), reh. denied id. 987, 87 S.Ct. 1283, 18 L.Ed.2d 241.

Note to Subdivision (b). The first sentence is the third sentence of Rule 43(c) of the Federal Rules of Civil Procedure virtually verbatim. Its purpose is to reproduce for an appellate court, insofar as possible, a true reflection of what occurred in the trial court. The second sentence is in part derived from the final sentence of Rule 43(c). It is designed to resolve doubts as to what testimony the witness would have in fact given, and, in nonjury cases, to provide the appellate court with material for a possible final disposition of the case in the event of reversal of a ruling which excluded evidence. See 5 Moore's Federal Practice § 43.11 (2d ed. 1968). Application is made discretionary in view of the practical impossibility of formulating a satisfactory rule in mandatory terms.

Note to Subdivision (c). This subdivision proceeds on the supposition that a ruling which excludes evidence in a jury case is likely to be a pointless procedure if the excluded evidence nevertheless comes to the attention of the jury. *Bruton v. United States,* 389 U.S. 818, 88 S.Ct. 126, 19 L.Ed.2d 70 (1968). Rule 43(c) of the Federal Rules of Civil Procedure provides: "The court may require the offer to be made out of the hearing of the jury." *In re McConnell,* 370 U.S. 230, 82 S.Ct. 1288, 8 L.Ed.2d 434 (1962), left some doubt whether questions on which an offer is based must first be asked in the presence of the jury. The subdivision answers in the negative. The judge can foreclose a particular line of testimony and counsel can protect his record without a series of questions before the jury, designed at best to waste time and at worst "to waft into the jury box" the very matter sought to be excluded.

Note to Subdivision (d). This wording of the plain error principle is from Rule 52(b) of the Federal Rules of Criminal Procedure. While judicial unwillingness to be constructed by mechanical breakdowns of the adversary system has been more pronounced in criminal cases, there is no scarcity of decisions to the same effect in civil cases. In general, see Campbell, Extent to Which Courts of Review Will Consider Questions Not Properly Raised and Preserved, 7 Wis.L.Rev. 91, 160 (1932); Vestal, Sua Sponte Consideration in Appellate Review, 27 Fordham L.Rev. 477 (1958–59); 64 Harv.L.Rev. 652 (1951). In the nature of things the application of the plain error rule will be more likely with respect to the admission of evidence than to exclusion, since failure to comply with normal requirements of offers of proof is likely to produce a record which simply does not disclose the error.

2000 Amendment

The amendment applies to all rulings on evidence whether they occur at or before trial, including so-called "*in limine*" rulings. One of the most difficult questions arising from *in limine* and other evidentiary rulings is whether a losing party must renew an objection or offer of proof when the evidence is or would be offered at trial, in order to preserve a claim of error on appeal. Courts have taken differing approaches to this question. Some courts have held that a renewal at the time the evidence is to be offered at trial is always required. *See, e.g., Collins v. Wayne Corp.*, 621 F.2d 777 (5th Cir. 1980). Some courts have taken a more flexible approach, holding that renewal is not required if the issue decided is one that (1) was fairly presented to the trial court for an initial ruling, (2) may be decided as a final matter before the evidence is actually offered, and (3) was ruled on definitively by the trial judge, *See, e.g., Rosenfeld v. Basquiat*, 78 F.3d 84 (2d Cir. 1996) (admissibility of former testimony under the Dead Man's Statute; renewal not required). Other courts have distinguished between objections to evidence, which must be renewed when evidence is offered, and offers of proof, which need not be renewed after a definitive determination is made that the evidence is inadmissible. *See, e.g., Fusco v. General Motors Corp.*, 11 F.3d 259 (1st Cir. 1993). Another court, aware of this Committee's proposed amendment, has adopted its approach. *Wilson v. Williams*, 182 F. 3d 562 (7th Cir.1999) (en banc). Differing views on this question create uncertainty for litigants and unnecessary work for the appellate courts.

The amendment provides that a claim of error with respect to a definitive ruling is preserved for review when the party has otherwise satisfied the objection or offer of proof requirements of Rule 103(a). When the ruling is definitive, a renewed objection or offer of proof at the time the evidence is to be offered is more a formalism than a necessity. *See* Fed.R.Civ.P. 46 (formal exceptions unnecessary); Fed. R.Cr.P. 51 (same); *United States v. Mejia–Alarcon*, 995 F.2d 982, 986 (10th Cir. 1993) ("Requiring a party to renew an objection when the district court has issued a definitive ruling on a matter that can be fairly decided before trial would be in the nature of a formal exception and therefore unnecessary."). On the other hand, when the trial court appears to have reserved its ruling or to have indicated that the ruling is provisional, it makes sense to require the party to bring the issue to the court's attention subsequently. *See, e.g., United States v. Vest*, 116 F.3d 1179, 1188 (7th Cir. 1997) (where the trial court ruled *n limine* that testimony from defense witnesses could not be admitted, but allowed the defendant to seek leave at trial to call the witnesses should their testimony turn out to be relevant, the defendant's failure to seek such leave at trial meant that it was "too late to reopen the issue now on appeal"); *United States v. Valenti*, 60 F.3d 941 (2d Cir. 1995) (failure to proffer evidence at trial waives any claim of error where the trial judge had stated that he would reserve judgment on the *in limine* motion until he had heard the trial evidence).

The amendment imposes the obligation on counsel to clarify whether an *in limine* or other evidentiary ruling is definitive when there is doubt on that point. *See, e.g., Walden v. Georgia–Pacific Corp.*, 126 F.3d 506, 520 (3d Cir. 1997) (although "the district court told plaintiffs' counsel not to reargue every ruling, it did not countermand its clear opening statement that all of its rulings were tentative, and counsel never requested clarification, as he might have done.").

Even where the court's ruling is definitive, nothing in the amendment prohibits the court from revisiting its decision when the evidence is to be offered. If the court changes its initial ruling, or if the opposing party violates the terms of the initial ruling, objection must be made when the evidence is offered to preserve the claim of error for appeal. The error, if any, in such a situation occurs only when the evidence is offered and admitted. *United States Aviation Underwriters, Inc. v. Olympia Wings, Inc.*, 896 F.2d 949, 956 (5th Cir. 1990) ("objection is required to preserve error when an opponent, or the court itself, violates a motion *in limine* that was granted"); *United States v. Roenigk*, 810 F.2d 809 (8th Cir. 1987) (claim of error was not preserved where the defendant failed to object at trial to secure the benefit of a favorable advance ruling).

A definitive advance ruling is reviewed in light of the facts and circumstances before the trial court at the time of the ruling. If the relevant facts and circumstances change materially after the advance ruling has been made, those facts and circumstances cannot be relied upon on appeal unless they have been brought to the attention of the trial court by way of a renewed, and timely, objection, offer of proof, or motion to strike. *See Old Chief v. United States*, 519 U.S. 172, 182, n.6 (1997) ("It is important that a reviewing court evaluate the trial court's decision from its perspective when it had to rule and not indulge in review by hindsight."). Similarly, if the court decides in an advance ruling that proffered evidence is admissible subject to the eventual introduction by the proponent of a foundation for the evidence, and that foundation is never provided, the opponent cannot claim error based on the failure to establish the foundation unless the opponent calls that failure to the court's attention by a timely motion to strike or other suitable motion. *See Huddleston v. United States*, 485 U.S. 681, 690, n.7 (1988) ("It is, of course, not the responsibility of the judge *sua sponte* to ensure that the foundation evidence is offered; the objector must move to strike the evidence if at the close of the trial the offeror has failed to satisfy the condition.").

Nothing in the amendment is intended to affect the provisions of Fed.R.Civ.P. 72(a) or 28 U.S.C. § 636(b)(1) pertaining to nondispositive pretrial rulings by magistrate judges in proceedings that are not before a magistrate judge by consent of the parties. Fed.R.Civ.P. 72(a) provides that a party who fails to file a written objection to a magistrate judge's nondispositive order within ten days of receiving a copy "may not thereafter assign as error a defect" in the order. 28 U.S.C. § 636(b)(1) provides that any party "may serve and file written objections to such proposed findings and recommendations as provided by rules of court" within ten days of receiving a copy of the order. Several courts have held that a party must comply with this statutory provision in order to preserve a claim of error. *See, e.g., Wells v. Shriners Hospital*, 109 F.3d 198, 200 (4th Cir. 1997)("[i]n this circuit, as in others, a party 'may' file objections within ten days or he may not, as he chooses, but he 'shall' do so if he wishes further consideration."). When Fed.R.Civ.P. 72(a) or 28 U.S.C. § 636(b)(1) is operative, its requirement must be satisfied in order for a party to preserve a claim of error on appeal, even where Evidence Rule 103(a) would not require a subsequent objection or offer of proof.

Nothing in the amendment is intended to affect the rule set forth in *Luce v. United States*, 469 U.S. 38 (1984), and its progeny. The amendment provides that an objection or offer of proof need not be renewed to preserve a claim of error with respect to a definitive pretrial ruling. *Luce* answers affirmatively a separate question: whether a criminal defendant must testify at trial in order to preserve a claim of error predicated upon a trial court's decision to admit the defendant's prior convictions for impeachment. The *Luce* principle has been extended by many lower courts to other situations. *See United States v. DiMatteo*, 759 F.2d 831 (11th Cir. 1985) (applying *Luce* where the defendant's witness would be impeached with evidence offered under Rule 608). *See also United States v. Goldman*, 41 F.3d 785, 788 (1st Cir. 1994) ("Although *Luce* involved impeachment by conviction under Rule 609, the reasons given by the Supreme Court for requiring the defendant to testify apply with full force to the kind of Rule 403 and 404 objections that are advanced by Goldman in this case."); *Palmieri v. DeFaria*, 88 F.3d 136 (2d Cir. 1996) (where the plaintiff decided to take an adverse judgment rather than challenge an advance ruling by putting on evidence at trial, the *in limine* ruling would not be reviewed on appeal); *United States v. Ortiz*, 857 F.2d 900 (2d Cir. 1988) (where uncharged misconduct is ruled admissible if the defendant pursues a certain defense, the defendant must actually pursue that defense at trial in order to preserve a claim of error on appeal); *United States v. Bond*, 87 F.3d 695 (5th Cir. 1996) (where the trial court rules *in limine* that the defendant would waive his fifth amendment privilege were he to testify, the defendant must take the stand and testify in order to challenge that ruling on appeal).

The amendment does not purport to answer whether a party who objects to evidence that the court finds admissible in a definitive ruling, and who then offers the evidence to "remove the sting" of its anticipated prejudicial effect, thereby waives the right to appeal the trial court's ruling. *See, e.g., United States v. Fisher*, 106 F.3d 622 (5th Cir. 1997) (where the trial judge ruled *in limine* that the government could use a prior conviction to impeach the defendant if he testified, the defendant did not waive his right to appeal by introducing the conviction on direct examination); *Judd v. Rodman*, 105 F.3d 1339 (11th Cir. 1997) (an objection made *in limine* is sufficient to preserve a claim of error when the movant, as a matter of trial strategy, presents the objectionable evidence herself on direct examination to minimize its prejudicial effect); *Gill v. Thomas*, 83 F.3d 537, 540 (1st Cir. 1996) ("by offering the misdemeanor evidence himself, Gill waived his opportunity to object and thus did not preserve the issue for appeal"); *United States v. Williams*, 939 F.2d 721 (9th Cir. 1991) (objection to impeachment evidence was waived where the defendant was impeached on direct examination).

GAP Report—Proposed Amendment to Rule 103(a)

The Committee made the following changes to the published draft of the proposed amendment to Evidence Rule 103(a):

1. A minor stylistic change was made in the text, in accordance with the suggestion of the Style Subcommittee of the Standing Committee on Rules of Practice and Procedure.

2. The second sentence of the amended portion of the published draft was deleted, and the Committee Note was amended to reflect the fact that nothing in the amendment is intended to affect the rule of *Luce v. United States*.

3. The Committee Note was updated to include cases decided after the proposed amendment was issued for public comment.

4. The Committee Note was amended to include a reference to a Civil Rule and a statute requiring objections to certain Magistrate Judge rulings to be made to the District Court.

5. The Committee Note was revised to clarify that an advance ruling does not encompass subsequent developments at trial that might be the subject of an appeal.

HISTORICAL NOTES

Conference Committee Notes, House Report No. 93–1597

The House bill contains the word "judge". The Senate amendment substitutes the word "court" in order to conform with usage elsewhere in the House bill.

The Conference adopts the Senate amendment.

Rule 104. Preliminary Questions

(a) Questions of admissibility generally. Preliminary questions concerning the qualification of a person to be a witness, the existence of a privilege, or the admissibility of evidence shall be determined by the court, subject to the provisions of subdivision (b). In making its determination it is not bound by the rules of evidence except those with respect to privileges.

(b) Relevancy conditioned on fact. When the relevancy of evidence depends upon the fulfillment of a condition of fact, the court shall admit it upon, or subject to, the introduction of evidence sufficient to support a finding of the fulfillment of the condition.

(c) Hearing of jury. Hearings on the admissibility of confessions shall in all cases be conducted out of the hearing of the jury. Hearings on other preliminary matters shall be so conducted when the interests of justice require, or when an accused is a witness and so requests.

(d) Testimony by accused. The accused does not, by testifying upon a preliminary matter, become subject to cross-examination as to other issues in the case.

(e) Weight and credibility. This rule does not limit the right of a party to introduce before the jury evidence relevant to weight or credibility.

(Pub.L. 93–595, § 1, Jan. 2, 1975, 88 Stat.1930; Mar. 2, 1987, eff. Oct. 1, 1987.)

1972 Proposed Rule

Note to Subdivision (a). The applicability of a particular rule of evidence often depends upon the existence of a condition. Is the alleged expert a qualified physician? Is a witness whose former testimony is offered unavailable? Was a stranger present during a conversation between attorney and client? In each instance the admissibility of evidence will turn upon the answer to the question of the existence of the condition. Accepted practice, incorporated in the rule, places on the judge the responsibility for these determinations. McCormick § 53; Morgan, Basic Problems of Evidence 45–50 (1962).

To the extent that these inquiries are factual, the judge acts as a trier of fact. Often, however, rulings on evidence call for an evaluation in terms of a legally set standard. Thus when a hearsay statement is offered as a declaration against interest, a decision must be made whether it possesses the required against-interest characteristics. These decisions, too, are made by the judge.

In view of these considerations, this subdivision refers to preliminary requirements generally by the broad term "questions," without attempt at specification.

This subdivision is of general application. It must, however, be read as subject to the special provisions for "conditional relevancy" in subdivision (b) and those for confessions in subdivision (d).

If the question is factual in nature, the judge will of necessity receive evidence pro and con on the issue. The rule provides that the rules of evidence in general do not apply to this process. McCormick § 53, p. 123, n. 8, points out that the authorities are "scattered and inconclusive," and observes:

"Should the exclusionary law of evidence, 'the child of the jury system' in Thayer's phrase, be applied to this hearing before the judge? Sound sense backs the view that it should not, and that the judge should be empowered to hear any relevant evidence, such as affidavits or other reliable hearsay."

This view is reinforced by practical necessity in certain situations. An item, offered and objected to, may itself be considered in ruling on admissibility, though not yet admitted in evidence. Thus, the content of an asserted declaration against interest must be considered in ruling whether it is against interest. Again, common practice calls for considering the testimony of a witness, particularly a child, in determining competency. Another example is the requirement of Rule 602 dealing with personal knowledge. In the case of hearsay, it is enough, if the declarant "so far as appears [has] had an opportunity to observe the fact declared." McCormick, § 10, p. 19.

If concern is felt over the use of affidavits by the judge in preliminary hearings on admissibility, attention is directed to the many important judicial determinations made on the basis of affidavits. Rule 47 of the Federal Rules of Criminal Procedure provides:

"An application to the court for an order shall be by motion. * * * It may be supported by affidavit."

The Rules of Civil Procedure are more detailed. Rule 43(e), dealing with motions generally, provides:

"When a motion is based on facts not appearing of record the court may hear the matter on affidavits presented by the respective parties, but the court may direct that the matter be heard wholly or partly on oral testimony or depositions." Rule 4(g) provides for proof of service by affidavit. Rule 56 provides in detail for the entry of summary judgment based on affidavits. Affidavits may supply the foundation for temporary restraining orders under Rule 65(b).

The study made for the California Law Revision Commission recommended an amendment to Uniform Rule 2 as follows:

"In the determination of the issue aforesaid [preliminary determination], exclusionary rules shall not apply, subject, however, to Rule 45 and any valid claim of privilege." Tentative Recommendation and a Study Relating to the Uniform Rules of Evidence (Article VIII, Hearsay), Cal.Law Revision Comm'n, Rep., Rec. & Studies, 470 (1962). The proposal was not adopted in the California Evidence Code. The Uniform Rules are likewise silent on the subject. However, New Jersey Evidence Rule 8(1), dealing with preliminary inquiry by the judge, provides:

"In his determination the rules of evidence shall not apply except for Rule 4 [exclusion on grounds of confusion, etc.] or a valid claim of privilege."

Note to Subdivision (b). In some situations, the relevancy of an item of evidence, in the large sense, depends upon the existence of a particular preliminary fact. Thus when a spoken statement is relied upon to prove notice to X, it is without probative value unless X heard it. Or if a letter purporting to be from Y is relied upon to establish an admission by him, it has no probative value unless Y wrote or authorized it. Relevance in this sense has been labelled "conditional relevancy." Morgan, Basic Problems of Evidence 45–46 (1962). Problems arising in connection with it are to be distinguished from problems of logical relevancy, e.g., evidence in a murder case that accused on the day before purchased a weapon of the kind used in the killing, treated in Rule 401.

If preliminary questions of conditional relevancy were determined solely by the judge, as provided in subdivision (a), the functioning of the jury as a trier of fact would be greatly restricted and in some cases virtually destroyed. These are appropriate questions for juries. Accepted treatment, as provided in the rule, is consistent with that given fact questions generally. The judge makes a preliminary determination whether the foundation evidence is sufficient to support a finding of fulfillment of the condition. If so, the item is admitted. If after all the evidence on the issue is in, pro and con, the jury could reasonably conclude that fulfillment of the condition is not established, the issue is for them. If the evidence is not such as to allow a finding, the judge withdraws the matter from their consideration. Morgan, *supra;* California Evidence Code § 403; New Jersey Rule 8(2). See also Uniform Rules 19 and 67.

The order of proof here, as generally, is subject to the control of the judge.

Note to Subdivision (c). Preliminary hearings on the admissibility of confessions must be conducted outside the hearing of the jury. See *Jackson v. Denno,* 378 U.S. 368, 84 S.Ct. 1774, 12 L.Ed.2d 908 (1964). Otherwise, detailed treatment of when preliminary matters should be heard outside the hearing of the jury is not feasible. The procedure is time consuming. Not infrequently the same evidence which is relevant to the issue of establishment of fulfillment of a condition precedent to admissibility is also relevant to weight or credibility, and time is saved by taking foundation proof in the presence of the jury. Much evidence on preliminary questions, though not relevant to jury issues, may be heard by the jury with no adverse effect. A great deal must be left to the discretion of the judge who will act as the interests of justice require.

Note to Subdivision (d). The limitation upon cross-examination is designed to encourage participation by the accused in the determination of preliminary matters. He may testify concerning them without exposing himself to cross-examination generally. The provision is necessary because of the breadth of cross-examination under Rule 611(b).

The rule does not address itself to questions of the subsequent use of testimony given by an accused at a hearing on a preliminary matter. See *Walder v. United States,* 347 U.S. 62 (1954); *Simmons v. United States,* 390 U.S. 377 (1968); *Harris v. New York,* 401 U.S. 222 (1971).

Note to Subdivision (e). For similar provisions see Uniform Rule 8; California Evidence Code § 406; Kansas Code of Civil Procedure § 60–408; New Jersey Evidence Rule 8(1).

1974 Enactment

Rule 104(c) as submitted to the Congress provided that hearings on the admissibility of confessions shall be conducted outside the presence of the jury and hearings on all other preliminary matters should be so conducted when the interests of justice require. The Committee amended the Rule to provide that where an accused is a witness as to a preliminary matter, he has the right, upon his request, to be heard outside the jury's presence. Although recognizing that in some cases duplication of evidence would occur and that the procedure could be subject to abuse, the Committee believed that a proper regard for the right of an accused not to testify generally in the case dictates that he be given an option to testify out of the presence of the jury on preliminary matters.

The Committee construes the second sentence of subdivision (c) as applying to civil actions and proceedings as well as to criminal cases, and on this assumption has left the sentence unamended. House Report No. 93–650.

Under rule 104(c) the hearing on a preliminary matter may at times be conducted in front of the jury. Should an accused testify in such a hearing, waiving his privilege against self-incrimination as to the preliminary issue, rule 104(d) provides that he will not generally be subject to cross-examination as to any other issue. This rule is not, however, intended to immunize the accused from cross-examination where, in testifying about a preliminary issue, he injects other issues into the hearing. If he could not be cross-examined about any issues gratuitiously raised by him beyond the scope of the preliminary matters, injustice might result. Accordingly, in order to prevent any such unjust result, the committee intends the rule to be construed to provide that the accused may subject himself to cross-examination as to issues raised by his own testimony upon a preliminary matter before a jury. Senate Report No. 93–1277.

1987 Amendments

The amendments are technical. No substantive change is intended.

Rule 105. Limited Admissibility

When evidence which is admissible as to one party or for one purpose but not admissible as to another party or for another purpose is admitted, the court, upon request, shall restrict the evidence to its proper scope and instruct the jury accordingly.

(Pub.L. 93–595, § 1, Jan. 2, 1975, 88 Stat. 1930.)

1972 Proposed Rules

A close relationship exists between this rule and Rule 403 which requires exclusion when "probative value is substantially outweighed by the danger of unfair prejudice, confusion of the issues, or misleading the jury." The present rule recognizes the practice of admitting evidence for a limited purpose and instructing the jury accordingly. The availability and effectiveness of this practice must be taken into consideration in reaching a decision whether to exclude for unfair prejudice under Rule 403. In *Bruton v. United States,* 389 U.S. 818, 88 S.Ct. 126, 19 L.Ed.2d 70 (1968), the Court ruled that a limiting instruction did not effectively protect the accused against the prejudicial effect of admitting in evidence the confession of a codefendant which implicated him. The decision does not, however, bar the use of limited admissibility with an instruction where the risk of prejudice is less serious.

Similar provisions are found in Uniform Rule 6; California Evidence Code § 355; Kansas Code of Civil Procedure § 60–406; New Jersey Evidence Rule 6. The wording of the present rule differs, however, in repelling any implication that limiting or curative instructions are sufficient in all situations.

1974 Enactment

Rule 106 as submitted by the Supreme Court (now Rule 105 in the bill) dealt with the subject of evidence which is admissible as to one party or for one purpose but is not admissible against another party or for another purpose. The Committee adopted this Rule without change on the understanding that it does not affect the authority of a court to order a severance in a multi-defendant case. House Report No. 93–650.

Rule 106. Remainder of or Related Writings or Recorded Statements

When a writing or recorded statement or part thereof is introduced by a party, an adverse party may require the introduction at that time of any other part or any other writing or recorded statement which ought in fairness to be considered contemporaneously with it.

(Pub.L. 93–595, § 1, Jan. 2, 1975, 88 Stat. 1930; Mar. 2, 1987, eff. Oct. 1, 1987.)

1972 Proposed Rules

The rule is an expression of the rule of completeness. McCormick § 56. It is manifested as to depositions in Rule 32(a)(4) of the Federal Rules of Civil Procedure, of which the proposed rule is substantially a restatement.

The rule is based on two considerations. The first is the misleading impression created by taking matters out of context. The second is the inadequacy of repair work when delayed to a point later in the trial. See McCormick § 56; California Evidence Code § 356. The rule does not in any way circumscribe the right of the adversary to develop the matter on cross-examination or as part of his own case.

For practical reasons, the rule is limited to writings and recorded statements and does not apply to conversations.

1987 Amendments

The amendments are technical. No substantive change is intended.

ARTICLE II. JUDICIAL NOTICE

Rule 201. Judicial Notice of Adjudicative Facts

(a) Scope of rule. This rule governs only judicial notice of adjudicative facts.

(b) Kinds of facts. A judicially noticed fact must be one not subject to reasonable dispute in that it is either (1) generally known within the territorial jurisdiction of the trial court or (2) capable of accurate and ready determination by resort to sources whose accuracy cannot reasonably be questioned.

(c) When discretionary. A court may take judicial notice, whether requested or not.

(d) When mandatory. A court shall take judicial notice if requested by a party and supplied with the necessary information.

(e) Opportunity to be heard. A party is entitled upon timely request to an opportunity to be heard as to the propriety of taking judicial notice and the tenor of the matter noticed. In the absence of prior notification, the request may be made after judicial notice has been taken.

(f) Time of taking notice. Judicial notice may be taken at any stage of the proceeding.

(g) Instructing jury. In a civil action or proceeding, the court shall instruct the jury to accept as conclusive any fact judicially noticed. In a criminal case, the court shall instruct the jury that it may, but is not required to, accept as conclusive any fact judicially noticed.

(Pub.L. 93–595, § 1, Jan. 2, 1975, 88 Stat. 1930.)

1972 Proposed Rules

Note to Subdivision (a). This is the only evidence rule on the subject of judicial notice. It deals only with judicial notice of "adjudicative" facts. No rule deals with judicial notice of "legislative" facts. Judicial notice of matters of foreign law is treated in Rule 44.1 of the Federal Rules of Civil Procedure and Rule 26.1 of the Federal Rules of Criminal Procedure.

The omission of any treatment of legislative facts results from fundamental differences between adjudicative facts and legislative facts. Adjudicative facts are simply the facts of the particular case. Legislative facts, on the other hand, are those which have relevance to legal reasoning and the lawmaking process, whether in the formulation of a legal principle or ruling by a judge or court or in the enactment of a legislative body. The terminology was coined by Professor Kenneth Davis in his article An Approach to Problems of Evidence in the Administrative Process, 55 Harv.L.Rev. 364, 404–407 (1942). The following discussion draws extensively upon his writings. In addition, see the same author's Judicial Notice, 55 Colum.L.Rev. 945 (1955); Administrative Law Treatise, ch. 15 (1958); A System of Judicial Notice Based on Fairness and Convenience, in Perspectives of Law 69 (1964).

The usual method of establishing adjudicative facts is through the introduction of evidence, ordinarily consisting of the testimony of witnesses. If particular facts are outside the area of reasonable controversy, this process is dispensed with as unnecessary. A high degree of indisputability is the essential prerequisite.

Legislative facts are quite different. As Professor Davis says:

"My opinion is that judge-made law would stop growing if judges, in thinking about questions of law and policy, were forbidden to take into account the facts they believe, as distinguished from facts which are 'clearly * * * within the domain of the indisputable.' Facts most needed in thinking about difficult problems of law and policy have a way of being outside the domain of the clearly indisputable." A System of Judicial Notice Based on Fairness and Convenience, *supra*, at 82.

An illustration is *Hawkins v. United States*, 358 U.S. 74, 79 S.Ct. 136, 3 L.Ed.2d 125 (1958), in which the Court refused to discard the common law rule that one spouse could not testify against the other, saying, "Adverse testimony given in criminal proceedings would, we think, be likely to destroy almost any marriage." This conclusion has a large intermixture of fact, but the factual aspect is scarcely "indisputable." See Hutchins and Slesinger, Some Observations on the Law of Evidence—Family Relations, 13 Minn.L.Rev. 675 (1929). If the destructive effect of the giving of adverse testimony by a spouse is not indisputable, should the Court have refrained from considering it in the absence of supporting evidence?

"If the Model Code or the Uniform Rules had been applicable, the Court would have been barred from thinking about the essential factual ingredient of the problems before it, and such a result would be obviously intolerable. What the law needs at its growing points is more, not less, judicial thinking about the factual ingredients of problems of what the law ought to be, and the needed facts are seldom 'clearly' indisputable." Davis, *supra*, at 83.

Professor Morgan gave the following description of the methodology of determining domestic law:

"In determining the content or applicability of a rule of domestic law, the judge is unrestricted in his investigation and conclusion. He may reject the propositions of either party or of both parties. He may consult the sources of pertinent data to which they refer, or he may refuse to do so. He may make an independent search for persuasive data or rest content with what he has or what the parties present. * * * [T]he parties do no more than to assist; they control no part of the process." Morgan, Judicial Notice, 57 Harv. L.Rev. 269, 270–271 (1944).

This is the view which should govern judicial access to legislative facts. It renders inappropriate any limitation in the form of indisputability, any formal requirements of notice other than those already inherent in affording opportunity to hear and be heard and exchanging briefs, and any requirement of formal findings at any level. It should, however leave open the possibility of introducing evidence through regular channels in appropriate situations. See *Borden's Farm Products Co. v. Baldwin*, 293 U.S. 194, 55 S.Ct. 187, 79 L.Ed. 281 (1934), where the cause was remanded for the taking of evidence as to the economic conditions and trade practices underlying the New York Milk Control Law.

Similar considerations govern the judicial use of non-adjudicative facts in ways other than formulating laws and rules. Thayer described them as a part of the judicial reasoning process.

"In conducting a process of judicial reasoning, as of other reasoning, not a step can be taken without assuming something which has not been proved; and the capacity to do this with competent judgment and efficiency, is imputed to judges and juries as part of their necessary mental outfit." Thayer, Preliminary Treatise on Evidence 279–280 (1898).

As Professor Davis points out, A System of Judicial Notice Based on Fairness and Convenience, in Perspectives of Law 69, 73 (1964), every case involves the use of hundreds or thousands of non-evidence facts. When a witness in an automobile accident case says "car," everyone, judge and jury included, furnishes, from non-evidence sources within himself, the supplementing information that the "car" is an automobile, not a railroad car, that it is self-propelled, probably by an internal combustion engine, that it may be assumed to have four wheels with pneumatic rubber tires, and so on. The judicial process cannot construct every case from scratch, like Descartes creating a world based on the postulate *Cogito, ergo sum.* These items could not possibly be introduced into evidence, and no one suggests that they be. Nor are they appropriate subjects for any formalized treatment of judicial notice of facts. See Levin and Levy, Persuading the Jury with Facts Not in Evidence: The Fiction–Science Spectrum, 105 U.Pa.L.Rev. 139 (1956).

Another aspect of what Thayer had in mind is the use of non-evidence facts to appraise or assess the adjudicative facts of the case. Pairs of cases from two jurisdictions illustrate this use and also the difference between non-evidence facts thus used and adjudicative facts. In People v. Strook, 347 Ill. 460, 179 N.E. 821 (1932), venue in Cook County had been held not established by testimony that the crime was committed at 7956 South Chicago Avenue, since judicial notice would not be taken that the address was in Chicago. However, the same court subsequently ruled that venue in Cook County was established by testimony that a crime occurred at 8900 South Anthony Avenue, since notice would be taken of the common practice of omitting the name of the city when speaking of local addresses, and the witness was testifying in Chicago. *People v. Pride*, 16 Ill.2d 82, 156 N.E.2d 551 (1951). And in *Hughes v. Vestal*, 264 N.C. 500, 142 S.E.2d 361 (1965), the Supreme Court of North Carolina disapproved the trial judge's admission in evidence of a state-published table of automobile stopping distances on the basis of judicial notice, though the court itself had referred to the same table in an earlier case in a "rhetorical and illustrative" way in determining that the defendant could not have stopped her car in time to avoid striking a child who suddenly appeared in the highway and that a nonsuit was properly granted. *Ennis v. Dupree*, 262 N.C. 224, 136 S.E.2d 702 (1964). See also *Brown v. Hale*, 263 N.C. 176, 139 S.E.2d 210 (1964); *Clayton v. Rimmer*, 262 N.C. 302, 136 S.E.2d 562 (1964). It is apparent that this use of non-evidence facts in evaluating the adjudicative facts of the case is not an appropriate subject for a formalized judicial notice treatment.

In view of these considerations, the regulation of judicial notice of facts by the present rule extends only to adjudicative facts.

What, then, are "adjudicative" facts? Davis refers to them as those "which relate to the parties," or more fully:

"When a court or an agency finds facts concerning the immediate parties—who did what, where, when, how, and with what motive or intent—the court or agency is performing an adjudicative function, and the facts are conveniently called adjudicative facts. * * *

"Stated in other terms, the adjudicative facts are those to which the law is applied in the process of adjudication. They are the facts that normally go to the jury in a jury case. They relate to the parties, their activities, their properties, their businesses." 2 Administrative Law Treatise 353.

Note to Subdivision (b). With respect to judicial notice of adjudicative facts, the tradition has been one of caution in requiring that the matter be beyond reasonable controversy. This tradition of circumspection appears to be soundly based, and no reason to depart from it is apparent. As Professor Davis says:

"The reason we use trial-type procedure, I think, is that we make the practical judgment, on the basis of experience, that taking evidence, subject to cross-examination and rebuttal, is the best way to resolve controversies involving disputes of adjudicative facts, that is, facts pertaining to the parties. The reason we require a determination on the record is that we think fair procedure in resolving disputes of adjudicative facts calls for giving each party a chance to meet in the appropriate fashion the facts that come to the tribunal's attention, and the appropriate fashion for meeting disputed adjudicative facts includes rebuttal evidence, cross-examination, usually confrontation, and argument (either written or oral or both). The key to a fair trial is opportunity to use the appropriate weapons (rebuttal evidence, cross-examination, and argument) to meet adverse materials that come to the tribunal's attention." A System of Judicial Notice Based on Fairness and Convenience, in Perspectives of Law 69, 93 (1964).

The rule proceeds upon the theory that these considerations call for dispensing with traditional methods of proof only in clear cases. Compare Professor Davis' conclusion that judicial notice should be a matter of convenience, subject to requirements of procedural fairness. *Id.*, 94.

This rule is consistent with Uniform Rule 9(1) and (2) which limit judicial notice of facts to those "so universally known that they cannot reasonably be the subject of dispute," those "so generally known or of such common notoriety within the territorial jurisdiction of the court that they cannot reasonably be the subject of dispute," and those "capable of immediate and accurate determination by resort to easily accessible sources of indisputable accuracy." The traditional textbook treatment has included these general categories (matters of common knowledge, facts capable of verification), McCormick §§ 324, 325, and then has passed on into detailed treatment of such specific topics as facts relating to the personnel and records of the court, *Id.* § 327, and other governmental facts, *Id.* § 328. The California draftsmen, with a background of detailed statutory regulation of judicial notice, followed a somewhat similar pattern. California Evidence Code §§ 451, 452. The Uniform Rules, however, were drafted on the theory that these particular matters are included within the general categories and need no specific mention. This approach is followed in the present rule.

The phrase "propositions of generalized knowledge," found in Uniform Rule 9(1) and (2) is not included in the present rule. It was, it is believed, originally included in Model Code Rules 801 and 802 primarily in order to afford some minimum recognition to the right of the judge in his "legislative" capacity (not acting as the trier of fact) to take judicial notice of very limited categories of generalized knowledge. The limitations thus imposed have been discarded herein as undesirable, unworkable, and contrary to existing practice. What is left, then, to be considered, is the status of a "proposition of generalized knowledge" as an "adjudicative" fact to be noticed judicially and communicated by the judge to the jury. Thus viewed, it is considered to be lacking practical significance. While judges use judicial notice of "propositions of generalized knowledge" in a variety of situations: determining the validity and meaning of statutes, formulating common law rules, deciding whether evidence should be admitted, assessing the sufficiency and effect of evidence, all are essentially nonadjudicative in nature. When judicial notice is seen as a significant vehicle for progress in the law, these are the areas involved, particularly in developing fields of scientific knowledge. See McCormick 712. It is not believed that judges now instruct juries as to "propositions of generalized knowledge" derived from encyclopedias or other sources, or that they are likely to do so, or, indeed, that it is desirable that they do so. There is a vast difference between ruling on the basis of judicial notice that radar evidence of speed is admissible and explaining to the jury its principles and degree of accuracy, or between using a table of stopping distances of automobiles at various speeds in a judicial evaluation of testimony and telling the jury its precise application in the case. For cases raising doubt as to the propriety of the use of medical texts by lay triers of fact in passing on disability claims in administrative proceedings, see *Sayers v. Gardner*, 380 F.2d 940 (6th Cir.1967); *Ross v. Gardner*, 365 F.2d 554 (6th Cir.1966); *Sosna v. Celebrezze*, 234 F.Supp. 289 (E.D.Pa.1964); *Glendenning v. Ribicoff*, 213 F.Supp. 301 (W.D.Mo.1962).

Notes to Subdivisions (c) and (d). Under subdivision (c) the judge has a discretionary authority to take judicial notice, regardless of whether he is so requested by a party. The taking of judicial notice is mandatory, under subdivision (d), only when a party requests it and the necessary information is supplied. This scheme is believed to reflect existing practice. It is simple and workable. It avoids troublesome distinctions in the many situations in which the process of taking judicial notice is not recognized as such.

Compare Uniform Rule 9 making judicial notice of facts universally known mandatory without request, and making judicial notice of facts generally known in the jurisdiction or capable of determination by resort to accurate sources discretionary in the absence of request but mandatory if request is made and the information furnished. But see Uniform Rule 10(3), which directs the judge to decline to take judicial notice if available information fails to convince him that the matter falls clearly within Uniform Rule 9 or is insufficient to enable him to notice it judicially. Substantially the same approach is found in California Evidence Code §§ 451–453 and in New Jersey Evidence Rule 9. In contrast, the present rule treats alike all adjudicative facts which are subject to judicial notice.

Note to Subdivision (e). Basic considerations of procedural fairness demand an opportunity to be heard on the propriety of taking judicial notice and the tenor of the matter noticed. The rule requires the granting of that opportunity upon request. No formal scheme of giving notice is provided. An adversely affected party may learn in advance that judicial notice is in contemplation, either by virtue of being served with a copy of a request by another party under subdivision (d) that judicial notice be taken, or through an advance indication by the judge. Or he may have no advance notice at all. The likelihood of the latter is enhanced by the frequent failure to recognize judicial notice as such. And in the absence of advance notice, a request made after the fact could not in fairness be considered untimely. See the provision for hearing on timely request in the Administrative Procedure Act, 5 U.S.C. § 556(e). See also Revised Model State Administrative Procedure Act (1961), 9C U.L.A. § 10(4) (Supp.1967).

Note to Subdivision (f). In accord with the usual view, judicial notice may be taken at any stage of the proceedings, whether in the trial court or on appeal. Uniform Rule 12; California Evidence Code § 459; Kansas Rules of Evidence § 60–412; New Jersey Evidence Rule 12; McCormick § 330, p. 712.

Note to Subdivision (g). Much of the controversy about judicial notice has centered upon the question whether evidence should be admitted in disproof of facts of which judicial notice is taken.

The writers have been divided. Favoring admissibility are Thayer, Preliminary Treatise on Evidence 308 (1898); 9 Wigmore § 2567; Davis, A System of Judicial Notice Based on Fairness and Convenience, in Perspectives of Law, 69, 76–77 (1964). Opposing admissibility are Keeffe, Landis and Shaad, Sense and Nonsense about Judicial Notice, 2 Stan. L.Rev. 664, 668 (1950); McNaughton, Judicial Notice—Excerpts Relating to the Morgan–Whitmore Controversy, 14 Vand.L.Rev. 779 (1961); Morgan, Judicial Notice, 57 Harv.

L.Rev. 269, 279 (1944); McCormick 710–711. The Model Code and the Uniform Rules are predicated upon indisputability of judicially noticed facts.

The proponents of admitting evidence in disproof have concentrated largely upon legislative facts. Since the present rule deals only with judicial notice of adjudicative facts, arguments directed to legislative facts lose their relevancy.

Within its relatively narrow area of adjudicative facts, the rule contemplates there is to be no evidence before the jury in disproof. The judge instructs the jury to take judicially noticed facts as established. This position is justified by the undesirable effects of the opposite rule in limiting the rebutting party, though not his opponent, to admissible evidence, in defeating the reasons for judicial notice, and in affecting the substantive law to an extent and in ways largely unforeseeable. Ample protection and flexibility are afforded by the broad provision for opportunity to be heard on request, set forth in subdivision (e).

Authority upon the propriety of taking judicial notice against an accused in a criminal case with respect to matters other than venue is relatively meager. Proceeding upon the theory that the right of jury trial does not extend to matters which are beyond reasonable dispute, the rule does not distinguish between criminal and civil cases. *People v. Mayes*, 113 Cal. 618, 45 P. 860 (1896); *Ross v. United States*, 374 F.2d 97 (8th Cir.1967). Cf. *State v. Main*, 94 R.I. 338, 180 A.2d 814 (1962); *State v. Lawrence*, 120 Utah 323, 234 P.2d 600 (1951).

Note on Judicial Notice of Law. By rules effective July 1, 1966, the method of invoking the law of a foreign country is covered elsewhere. Rule 44.1 of the Federal Rules of Civil Procedure; Rule 26.1 of the Federal Rules of Criminal Procedure. These two new admirably designed rules are founded upon the assumption that the manner in which law is fed into the judicial process is never a proper concern of the rules of evidence but rather of the rules of procedure. The Advisory Committee on Evidence, believing that this assumption is entirely correct, proposes no evidence rule with respect to judicial notice of law, and suggests that those matters of law which, in addition to foreign-country law, have traditionally been treated as requiring pleading and proof and more recently as the subject of judicial notice be left to the Rules of Civil and Criminal Procedure.

1974 Enactment

Rule 201(g) as received from the Supreme Court provided that when judicial notice of a fact is taken, the court shall instruct the jury to accept that fact as established. Being of the view that mandatory instruction to a jury in a criminal case to accept as conclusive any fact judicially noticed is inappropriate because contrary to the spirit of the Sixth Amendment right to a jury trial, the Committee adopted the 1969 Advisory Committee draft of this subsection, allowing a mandatory instruction in civil actions and proceedings and a discretionary instruction in criminal cases. House Report No. 93–650.

ARTICLE III. PRESUMPTIONS IN CIVIL ACTIONS AND PROCEEDINGS

Rule 301. Presumptions in General in Civil Actions and Proceedings

In all civil actions and proceedings not otherwise provided for by Act of Congress or by these rules, a presumption imposes on the party against whom it is directed the burden of going forward with evidence to rebut or meet the presumption, but does not shift to such party the burden of proof in the sense of the risk of nonpersuasion, which remains throughout the trial upon the party on whom it was originally cast.

(Pub.L. 93–595, § 1, Jan. 2, 1975, 88 Stat. 1931.)

1972 Proposed Rules

This rule governs presumptions generally. See Rule 302 for presumptions controlled by state law and Rule 303 [deleted] for those against an accused in a criminal case.

Presumptions governed by this rule are given the effect of placing upon the opposing party the burden of establishing the nonexistence of the presumed fact, once the party invoking the presumption establishes the basic facts giving rise to it. The same considerations of fairness, policy, and probability which dictate the allocation of the burden of the various elements of a case as between the prima facie case of a plaintiff and affirmative defenses also underlie the creation of presumptions. These considerations are not satisfied by giving a lesser effect to presumptions. Morgan and Maguire, Looking Backward and Forward at Evidence, 50 Harv. L.Rev. 909, 913 (1937); Morgan, Instructing the Jury upon Presumptions and Burden of Proof, 47 Harv.L.Rev. 59, 82 (1933); Cleary, Presuming and Pleading: An Essay on Juristic Immaturity, 12 Stan.L.Rev. 5 (1959).

The so-called "bursting bubble" theory, under which a presumption vanishes upon the introduction of evidence which would support a finding of the nonexistence of the presumed fact, even though not believed, is rejected as according presumptions too "slight and evanescent" an effect. Morgan and Maguire, *supra*, at p. 913.

In the opinion of the Advisory Committee, no constitutional infirmity attends this view of presumptions. In *Mobile, J. & K. C. R. Co. v. Turnipseed*, 219 U.S. 35, 31 S.Ct. 136, 55 L.Ed. 78 (1910), the Court upheld a Mississippi statute which provided that in actions against railroads proof of injury inflicted by the running of trains should be prima facie evidence of negligence by the railroad. The injury in the case had resulted from a derailment. The opinion made the points (1) that the only effect of the statute was to impose on the railroad the duty of producing some evidence to the contrary, (2) that an inference may be supplied by law if there is a rational connection between the fact proved and the fact presumed, as long as the opposite party is not precluded from presenting his evidence to the contrary, and (3) that considerations of public policy arising from the character of the business justified the application in question. Nineteen years later, in *Western & Atlantic R. Co. v. Henderson*, 279 U.S. 639, 49 S.Ct. 445, 73 L.Ed. 884 (1929), the Court overturned a Georgia statute making railroads liable for damages done by trains, unless the railroad made it appear that reasonable care had been used, the presumption being against the railroad. The declaration alleged the death of plaintiff's husband from a grade crossing collision, due to specified acts of negligence by defendant. The jury were instructed that proof of the injury raised a presumption of negligence; the burden shifted to the railroad to prove ordinary care; and unless it did so, they should find for plaintiff. The instruction was held erroneous in an opinion stating (1) that there was no rational connection between the mere fact of collision and negligence on the part of anyone, and (2) that the statute was different from that in *Turnipseed* in imposing a burden upon the railroad. The reader is left in a state of some confusion. Is the difference between a derailment and a grade crossing collision of no significance? Would the *Turnipseed* presumption have been bad if it had imposed a burden of persuasion on defendant, although that would in nowise have impaired its "rational connection"? If *Henderson* forbids imposing a burden of persuasion on defendants, what happens to affirmative defenses?

Two factors serve to explain *Henderson.* The first was that it was common ground that negligence was indispensable to liability. Plaintiff thought so, drafted her complaint accordingly, and relied upon the presumption. But how in logic could the same presumption establish her alternative grounds of negligence that the engineer was so blind he could not see decedent's truck and that he failed to stop after he saw it? Second, take away the basic assumption of no liability without fault, as *Turnipseed* intimated might be done ("considerations of public policy arising out of the character of the business"), and the structure of the decision in *Henderson* fails. No question of logic would have arisen if the statute had simply said: a prima facie case of liability is made by proof of injury by a train; lack of negligence is an affirmative defense, to be pleaded and proved as other affirmative defenses. The problem would be one of economic due process only. While it seems likely that the Supreme Court of 1929 would have voted that due process was denied, that result today would be unlikely. See, for example, the shift in the direction of absolute liability in the consumer cases. Prosser, The Assault upon the Citadel (Strict Liability to the Consumer), 69 Yale L.J. 1099 (1960).

Any doubt as to the constitutional permissibility of a presumption imposing a burden of persuasion of the nonexistence of the presumed fact in civil cases is laid at rest by *Dick v. New York Life Ins. Co.,* 359 U.S. 437, 79 S.Ct. 921, 3 L.Ed.2d 935 (1959). The Court unhesitatingly applied the North Dakota rule that the presumption against suicide imposed on defendant the burden of proving that the death of insured, under an accidental death clause, was due to suicide.

"Proof of coverage and of death by gunshot wound shifts the burden to the insurer to establish that the death of the insured was due to his suicide." 359 U.S. at 443, 79 S.Ct. at 925.

"In a case like this one, North Dakota presumes that death was accidental and places on the insurer the burden of proving that death resulted from suicide." *Id.* at 446, 79 S.Ct. at 927.

The rational connection requirement survives in criminal cases, *Tot v. United States,* 319 U.S. 463, 63 S.Ct. 1241, 87 L.Ed. 1519 (1943), because the Court has been unwilling to extend into that area the greater-includes-the-lesser theory of *Ferry v. Ramsey,* 277 U.S. 88, 48 S.Ct. 443, 72 L.Ed. 796 (1928). In that case the Court sustained a Kansas statute under which bank directors were personally liable for deposits made with their assent and with knowledge of insolvency, and the fact of insolvency was prima facie evidence of assent and knowledge of insolvency. Mr. Justice Holmes pointed out that the state legislature could have made the directors personally liable to depositors in every case. Since the statute imposed a less stringent liability, "the thing to be considered is the result reached, not the possibly inartificial or clumsy way of reaching it." *Id.* at 94, 48 S.Ct. at 444. Mr. Justice Sutherland dissented: though the state could have created an absolute liability, it did not purport to do so; a rational connection was necessary, but lacking, between the liability created and the prima facie evidence of it; the result might be different if the basis of the presumption were being open for business.

The Sutherland view has prevailed in criminal cases by virtue of the higher standard of notice there required. The fiction that everyone is presumed to know the law is applied to the substantive law of crimes as an alternative to complete unenforceability. But the need does not extend to criminal evidence and procedure, and the fiction does not encompass them. "Rational connection" is not fictional or artificial, and so it is reasonable to suppose that Gainey should have known that his presence at the site of an illicit still could convict him of being connected with (carrying on) the business, *United States v. Gainey,* 380 U.S. 63, 85 S.Ct. 754, 13 L.Ed.2d 658 (1965), but not that Romano should have known that his presence at a still could convict him of possessing it, *United States v. Romano,* 382 U.S. 136, 86 S.Ct. 279, 15 L.Ed.2d 210 (1965).

In his dissent in Gainey, Mr. Justice Black put it more artistically:

"It might be argued, although the Court does not so argue or hold, that Congress if it wished could make presence at a still a crime in itself, and so Congress should be free to create crimes which are called 'possession' and 'carrying on an illegal distillery business' but which are defined in such a way that unexplained presence is sufficient and indisputable evidence in all cases to support conviction for those offenses. See *Ferry v. Ramsey,* 277 U.S. 88, 48 S.Ct. 443, 72 L.Ed. 796. Assuming for the sake of argument that Congress could make unexplained presence a criminal act, and ignoring also the refusal of this Court in other cases to uphold a statutory presumption on such a theory, see *Heiner v. Donnan,* 285 U.S. 312, 52 S.Ct. 358, 76 L.Ed. 772, there is no indication here that Congress intended to adopt such a misleading method of draftsmanship, nor in my judgment could the statutory provisions if so construed escape condemnation for vagueness, under the principles applied in *Lanzetta v. New Jersey,* 306 U.S. 451, 59 S.Ct. 618, 83 L.Ed. 888, and many other cases." 380 U.S. at 84, n. 12, 85 S.Ct. at 766.

And the majority opinion in *Romano* agreed with him:

"It may be, of course, that Congress has the power to make presence at an illegal still a punishable crime, but we find no clear indication that it intended to so exercise this power. The crime remains possession, not presence, and with all due deference to the judgment of Congress, the former may not constitutionally be inferred from the latter." 382 U.S. at 144, 86 S.Ct. at 284.

The rule does not spell out the procedural aspects of its application. Questions as to when the evidence warrants submission of a presumption and what instructions are proper under varying states of fact are believed to present no particular difficulties.

1974 Enactment

Rule 301 as submitted by the Supreme Court provided that in all cases a presumption imposes on the party against whom it is directed the burden of proving that the nonexistence of the presumed fact is more probable than its existence. The Committee limited the scope of Rule 301 to "civil actions and proceedings" to effectuate its decision not to deal with the question of presumptions in criminal cases. (See note on [proposed] Rule 303 in discussion of Rules deleted). With respect to the weight to be given a presumption in a civil case, the Committee agreed with the judgment implicit in the Court's version that the so-called "bursting bubble" theory of presumptions, whereby a presumption vanishes upon the appearance of any contradicting evidence by the other party, gives to presumptions too slight an effect. On the other hand, the Committee believed that the Rule proposed by the Court, whereby a presumption permanently alters the burden of persuasion, no matter how much contradicting evidence is introduced—a view shared by only a few courts—lends too great a force to presumptions. Accordingly, the Committee amended the Rule to adopt an intermediate position under which a presumption does not vanish upon the introduction of contradicting evidence, and does not change the burden of persuasion; instead it is merely deemed sufficient evidence of the fact presumed, to be considered by the jury or other finder of fact. House Report No. 93–650.

The rule governs presumptions in civil cases generally. Rule 302 provides for presumptions in cases controlled by State law.

As submitted by the Supreme Court, presumptions governed by this rule were given the effect of placing upon the opposing party the burden of establishing the nonexistence of the presumed fact, once the party invoking the presumption established the basic facts giving rise to it.

Instead of imposing a burden of persuasion on the party against whom the presumption is directed, the House adopted a provision which shifted the burden of going forward with the evidence. They further provided that "even though met with contradicting evidence, a presumption is sufficient evidence of the fact presumed, to be considered by the trier of fact." The effect of the amendment is that presumptions are to be treated as evidence.

The committee feels the House amendment is ill-advised. As the joint committees (the Standing Committee on Practice and Procedure of the Judicial Conference and the Advisory Committee on the Rules of Evidence) stated: "Presumptions are not evidence, but ways of dealing with evidence." This treatment requires juries to perform the task of considering "as evidence" facts upon which they have no direct evidence and which may confuse them in performance of their duties. California had a rule much like that contained in the House amendment. It was sharply criticized by Justice Traynor in *Speck v. Sarver* [20 Cal.2d 585, 128 P.2d 16, 21 (1942)] and was repealed after 93 troublesome years [Cal.Ev.Code 1965 § 600].

Professor McCormick gives a concise and compelling critique of the presumption as evidence rule:

"Another solution, formerly more popular than now, is to instruct the jury that the presumption is 'evidence', to be weighed and considered with the testimony in the case. This avoids the danger that the jury may infer that the presumption is conclusive, but it probably means little to the jury, and certainly runs counter to accepted theories of the nature of evidence." [McCormick, Evidence, 669 (1954); *Id.* 825 (2d ed. 1972)].

For these reasons the committee has deleted that provision of the House-passed rule that treats presumptions as evidence. The effect of the rule as adopted by the committee is to make clear that while evidence of facts giving rise to a presumption shifts the burden of coming forward with evidence to rebut or meet the presumption, it does not shift the burden of persuasion on the existence of the presumed facts. The burden of persuasion remains on the party to whom it is allocated under the rules governing the allocation in the first instance.

The court may instruct the jury that they may infer the existence of the presumed fact from proof of the basic facts giving rise to the presumption. However, it would be inappropriate under this rule to instruct the jury that the inference they are to draw is conclusive. Senate Report 93–1277.

The House bill provides that a presumption in civil actions and proceedings shifts to the party against whom it is directed the burden of going forward with evidence to meet or rebut it. Even though evidence contradicting the presumption is offered, a presumption is considered sufficient evidence of the presumed fact to be considered by the jury. The Senate amendment provides that a presumption shifts to the party against whom it is directed the burden of going forward with evidence to meet or rebut the presumption, but it does not shift to that party the burden of persuasion on the existence of the presumed fact.

Under the Senate amendment, a presumption is sufficient to get a party past an adverse party's motion to dismiss made at the end of his case-in-chief. If the adverse party offers no evidence contradicting the presumed fact, the court will instruct the jury that if it finds the basic facts, it may presume the existence of the presumed fact. If the adverse party does offer evidence contradicting the presumed fact, the court cannot instruct the jury that it may *presume* the existence of the presumed fact from proof of the basic facts. The court may, however, instruct the jury that it may infer the existence of the presumed fact from proof of the basic facts.

The conference adopts the Senate amendment. House Conference Report No. 93–1597.

Rule 302. Applicability of State Law in Civil Actions and Proceedings

In civil actions and proceedings, the effect of a presumption respecting a fact which is an element of a claim or defense as to which State law supplies the rule of decision is determined in accordance with State law.

(Pub.L. 93–595, § 1, Jan. 2, 1975, 88 Stat. 1931.)

1972 Proposed Rules

A series of Supreme Court decisions in diversity cases leaves no doubt of the relevance of *Erie Railroad Co. v. Tompkins,* 304 U.S. 64, 58 S.Ct. 817, 82 L.Ed. 1188 (1938), to questions of burden of proof. These decisions are *Cities Service Oil Co. v. Dunlap,* 308 U.S. 208, 60 S.Ct. 201, 84 L.Ed. 196 (1939), *Palmer v. Hoffman,* 318 U.S. 109, 63 S.Ct. 477, 87 L.Ed. 645 (1943), and *Dick v. New York Life Ins. Co.,* 359 U.S. 437, 79 S.Ct. 921, 3 L.Ed.2d 935 (1959). They involved burden of proof, respectively, as to status as bona fide purchaser, contributory negligence, and nonaccidental death (suicide) of an insured. In each instance the state rule was held to be applicable. It does not follow, however, that all presumptions in diversity cases are governed by state law. In each case cited, the burden of proof question had to do with a substantive element of the claim or defense. Application of the state law is called for only when the presumption operates upon such an element. Accordingly the rule does not apply state law when the presumption operates upon a lesser aspect of the case, i.e. "tactical" presumptions.

The situations in which the state law is applied have been tagged for convenience in the preceding discussion as "diversity cases." The designation is not a completely accurate one since *Erie* applies to any claim or issue having its source in state law, regardless of the basis of federal jurisdiction, and does not apply to a federal claim or issue, even though jurisdiction is based on diversity. *Vestal, Erie R.R. v. Tompkins:* A Projection, 48 Iowa L.Rev. 248, 257 (1963); Hart and Wechsler, The Federal Courts and the Federal System, 697 (1953); 1A Moore, Federal Practice ¶ 0.305[3] (2d ed. 1965); Wright, Federal Courts, 217–218 (1963). Hence the rule employs, as appropriately descriptive, the phrase "as to which state law supplies the rule of decision." See A.L.I. Study of the Division of Jurisdiction Between State and Federal Courts, § 2344(c), p. 40, P.F.D. No. 1 (1965).

ARTICLE IV. RELEVANCY AND ITS LIMITS

Rule 401. Definition of "Relevant Evidence"

"Relevant evidence" means evidence having any tendency to make the existence of any fact that is of consequence to the determination of the action more probable or less probable than it would be without the evidence.

(Pub.L. 93–595, § 1, Jan. 2, 1975, 88 Stat.1931.)

1972 Proposed Rules

Problems of relevancy call for an answer to the question whether an item of evidence, when tested by the processes of legal reasoning, possesses sufficient probative value to justify receiving it in evidence. Thus, assessment of the probative value of evidence that a person purchased a revolver shortly prior to a fatal shooting with which he is charged is a matter of analysis and reasoning.

The variety of relevancy problems is coextensive with the ingenuity of counsel in using circumstantial evidence as a means of proof. An enormous number of cases fall in no set pattern, and this rule is designed as a guide for handling them. On the other hand, some situations recur with sufficient frequency to create patterns susceptible of treatment by specific rules. Rule 404 and those following it are of that variety; they also serve as illustrations of the application of the present rule as limited by the exclusionary principles of Rule 403.

Passing mention should be made of so-called "conditional" relevancy. Morgan, Basic Problems of Evidence 45–46 (1962). In this situation, probative value depends not only upon satisfying the basic requirement of relevancy as described above but also upon the existence of some matter of fact. For example, if evidence of a spoken statement is relied upon to prove notice, probative value is lacking unless the person sought to be charged heard the statement. The problem is one of fact, and the only rules needed are for the purpose of determining the respective functions of judge and jury. See Rules 104(b) and 901. The discussion which follows in the present note is concerned with relevancy generally, not with any particular problem of conditional relevancy.

Relevancy is not an inherent characteristic of any item of evidence but exists only as a relation between an item of evidence and a matter properly provable in the case. Does the item of evidence tend to prove the matter sought to be proved? Whether the relationship exists depends upon principles evolved by experience or science, applied logically to the situation at hand. James, Relevancy, Probability and the Law, 29 Calif.L.Rev. 689, 696, n. 15 (1941), in Selected Writings on Evidence and Trial 610, 615, n. 15 (Fryer ed. 1957). The rule summarizes this relationship as a "tendency to make the existence" of the fact to be proved "more probable or less probable." Compare Uniform Rule 1(2) which states the crux of relevancy as "a tendency in reason," thus perhaps emphasizing unduly the logical process and ignoring the need to draw upon experience or science to validate the general principle upon which relevancy in a particular situation depends.

The standard of probability under the rule is "more * * * probable than it would be without the evidence." Any more stringent requirement is unworkable and unrealistic. As McCormick § 152, p. 317, says, "A brick is not a wall," or, as Falknor, Extrinsic Policies Affecting Admissibility, 10 Rutgers L.Rev. 574, 576 (1956), quotes Professor McBaine, "* * * [I]t is not to be supposed that every witness can make a home run." Dealing with probability in the language of the rule has the added virtue of avoiding confusion between questions of admissibility and questions of the sufficiency of the evidence.

The rule uses the phrase "fact that is of consequence to the determination of the action" to describe the kind of fact to which proof may properly be directed. The language is that of California Evidence Code § 210; it has the advantage of avoiding the loosely used and ambiguous word "material." Tentative Recommendation and a Study Relating to the Uniform Rules of Evidence (Art. I. General Provisions), Cal.Law Revision Comm'n, Rep., Rec. & Studies, 10–11 (1964). The fact to be proved may be ultimate, intermediate, or evidentiary; it matters not, so long as it is of consequence in the determination of the action. Cf. Uniform Rule 1(2) which requires that the evidence relate to a "material" fact.

The fact to which the evidence is directed need not be in dispute. While situations will arise which call for the exclusion of evidence offered to prove a point conceded by the opponent, the ruling should be made on the basis of such considerations as waste of time and undue prejudice (see Rule 403), rather than under any general requirement that evidence is admissible only if directed to matters in dispute. Evidence which is essentially background in nature can scarcely be said to involve disputed matter, yet it is universally offered and admitted as an aid to understanding. Charts, photographs, views of real estate, murder weapons, and many other items of evidence fall in this category. A rule limiting admissibility to evidence directed to a controversial point would invite the exclusion of this helpful evidence, or at least the raising of endless questions over its admission. Cf. California Evidence Code § 210, defining relevant evidence in terms of tendency to prove a disputed fact.

Rule 402. Relevant Evidence Generally Admissible; Irrelevant Evidence Inadmissible

All relevant evidence is admissible, except as otherwise provided by the Constitution of the United States, by Act of Congress, by these rules, or by other rules prescribed by the Supreme Court pursuant to statutory authority. Evidence which is not relevant is not admissible.

(Pub.L. 93–595, § 1, Jan. 2, 1975, 88 Stat. 1931.)

1972 Proposed Rules

The provisions that all relevant evidence is admissible, with certain exceptions, and that evidence which is not relevant is not admissible are "a presupposition involved in the very conception of a rational system of evidence." Thayer, Preliminary Treatise on Evidence 264 (1898). They constitute the foundation upon which the structure of admission and exclusion rests. For similar provisions see California Evidence Code §§ 350, 351. Provisions that all relevant evidence is admissible are found in Uniform Rule 7(f); Kansas Code of Civil Procedure § 60–407(f); and New Jersey Evidence Rule 7(f); but the exclusion of evidence which is not relevant is left to implication.

Not all relevant evidence is admissible. The exclusion of relevant evidence occurs in a variety of situations and may be called for by these rules, by the Rules of Civil and Criminal Procedure, by Bankruptcy Rules, by Act of Congress, or by constitutional considerations.

Succeeding rules in the present article, in response to the demands of particular policies, require the exclusion of evidence despite its relevancy. In addition, Article V recognizes a number of privileges; Article VI imposes limitations upon witnesses and the manner of dealing with them; Article VII specifies requirements with respect to opinions and expert testimony; Article VIII excludes hearsay not falling within an exception; Article IX spells out the handling of authentication and identification; and Article X restricts the manner of proving the contents of writings and recordings.

The Rules of Civil and Criminal Procedure in some instances require the exclusion of relevant evidence. For example, Rules 30(b) and 32(a)(3) of the Rules of Civil Procedure, by imposing requirements of notice and unavailability of the deponent, place limits on the use of relevant depositions. Similarly, Rule 15 of the Rules of Criminal Procedure restricts the use of depositions in criminal cases, even though relevant. And the effective enforcement of the command, originally statutory and now found in Rule 5(a) of the Rules of Criminal Procedure, that an arrested person be taken without unnecessary delay before a commissioner or other similar officer is held to require the exclusion of statements elicited during detention in violation thereof. *Mallory v. United States,* 354 U.S. 449, 77 S.Ct. 1356, 1 L.Ed.2d 1479 (1957); 18 U.S.C. § 3501(c).

While congressional enactments in the field of evidence have generally tended to expand admissibility beyond the scope of the common law rules, in some particular situations they have restricted the admissibility of relevant evidence. Most of this legislation has consisted of the formulation of a privilege or of a prohibition against disclosure. 8 U.S.C. § 1202(f), records of refusal of visas or permits to enter United States confidential, subject to discretion of Secretary of State to make available to court upon certification of need; 10 U.S.C. § 3693, replacement certificate of honorable discharge from Army not admissible in evidence; 10 U.S.C. § 8693, same as to Air Force; 11 U.S.C. § 25(a)(10), testimony given by bankrupt on his examination not admissible in criminal proceedings against him, except that given in hearing upon objection to discharge; 11 U.S.C. § 205(a), railroad reorganization petition, if dismissed, not admissible in evidence; 11 U.S.C. § 403(a), list of creditors filed with municipal composition plan not an admission; 13 U.S.C. § 9(a), census information confidential, retained copies of reports privileged; 47 U.S.C. § 605, interception and divulgence of wire or radio communications prohibited unless authorized by sender. These statutory provisions would remain undisturbed by the rules.

The rule recognizes but makes no attempt to spell out the constitutional considerations which impose basic limitations upon the admissibility of relevant evidence. Examples are evidence obtained by unlawful search and seizure. *Weeks v. United States,* 232 U.S. 383, 34 S.Ct. 341, 58 L.Ed. 652 (1914); *Katz v. United States,* 389 U.S. 347, 88 S.Ct. 507, 19 L.Ed.2d 576 (1967); incriminating statement elicited from an accused in violation of right to counsel. *Massiah v. United States,* 377 U.S. 201, 84 S.Ct. 1199, 12 L.Ed.2d 246 (1964).

1974 Enactment

Rule 402 as submitted to the Congress contained the phrase "or by other rules adopted by the Supreme Court". To accommodate the view that the Congress should not appear to acquiesce in the Court's judgment that it has authority under the existing Rules Enabling Acts to promulgate Rules of Evidence, the Committee amended the above phrase to read "or by other rules prescribed by the Supreme Court pursuant to statutory authority" in this and other Rules where the reference appears. House Report No. 93–650.

Rule 403. Exclusion of Relevant Evidence on Grounds of Prejudice, Confusion, or Waste of Time

Although relevant, evidence may be excluded if its probative value is substantially outweighed by the danger of unfair prejudice, confusion of the issues, or misleading the jury, or by considerations of undue delay, waste of time, or needless presentation of cumulative evidence.

(Pub.L. 93–595, § 1, Jan. 2, 1975, 88 Stat. 1932.)

1972 Proposed Rules

The case law recognizes that certain circumstances call for the exclusion of evidence which is of unquestioned relevance. These circumstances entail risks which range all the way from inducing decision on a purely emotional basis, at one extreme, to nothing more harmful than merely wasting time, at the other extreme. Situations in this area call for balancing the probative value of and need for the evidence against the harm likely to result from its admission. Slough, Relevancy Unraveled, 5 Kan.L.Rev. 1, 12–15 (1956); Trautman, Logical or Legal Relevancy—A Conflict in Theory, 5 Van. L.Rev. 385, 392 (1952); McCormick § 152, pp. 319–321. The rules which follow in this Article are concrete applications evolved for particular situations. However, they reflect the policies underlying the present rule, which is designed as a guide for the handling of situations for which no specific rules have been formulated.

Exclusion for risk of unfair prejudice, confusion of issues, misleading the jury, or waste of time, all find ample support in the authorities. "Unfair prejudice" within its context means an undue tendency to suggest decision on an improper basis, commonly, though not necessarily, an emotional one.

The rule does not enumerate surprise as a ground for exclusion, in this respect following Wigmore's view of the common law. 6 Wigmore § 1849. Cf. McCormick § 152, p. 320, n. 29, listing unfair surprise as a ground for exclusion but stating that it is usually "coupled with the danger of prejudice and confusion of issues." While Uniform Rule 45 incorporates surprise as a ground and is followed in Kansas Code of Civil Procedure § 60–445, surprise is not included in California Evidence Code § 352 or New Jersey Rule 4, though both the latter otherwise substantially embody Uniform Rule 45. While it can scarcely be doubted that claims of unfair surprise may still be justified despite procedural requirements of notice and instrumentalities of discovery, the granting of a continuance is a more appropriate remedy than exclusion of the evidence. Tentative Recommendation and a Study Relating to the Uniform Rules of Evidence (Art. VI. Extrinsic Policies Affecting Admissibility), Cal.Law Revision Comm'n, Rep., Rec. & Studies, 612 (1964). Moreover, the impact of a rule excluding evidence on the ground of surprise would be difficult to estimate.

In reaching a decision whether to exclude on grounds of unfair prejudice, consideration should be given to the probable effectiveness or lack of effectiveness of a limiting instruction. See Rule 106 [now 105] and Advisory Committee's Note thereunder. The availability of other means of proof may also be an appropriate factor.

Rule 404. Character Evidence Not Admissible To Prove Conduct; Exceptions; Other Crimes

(a) Character evidence generally.—Evidence of a person's character or a trait of character is not admissible for the purpose of proving action in conformity therewith on a particular occasion, except:

(1) Character of accused.—In a criminal case, evidence of a pertinent trait of character offered by an accused, or by the prosecution to rebut the same, or if evidence of a trait of character of the alleged victim of the crime is offered by an accused and admitted under Rule 404(a)(2), evidence of the same trait of character of the accused offered by the prosecution;

(2) Character of alleged victim.—In a criminal case, and subject to the limitations imposed by Rule 412, evidence of a pertinent trait of character of the alleged victim of the crime offered by an accused, or by the prosecution to rebut the same, or evidence of a character trait of peacefulness of the alleged victim offered by the prosecution in a homicide case to rebut evidence that the alleged victim was the first aggressor;

(3) Character of witness.—Evidence of the character of a witness, as provided in Rules 607, 608, and 609.

(b) Other Crimes, Wrongs, or Acts.—Evidence of other crimes, wrongs, or acts is not admissible to prove the character of a person in order to show action in conformity therewith. It may, however, be admissible for other purposes, such as proof of motive, opportunity, intent, preparation, plan, knowledge, identity, or absence of mistake or accident, provided that upon request by the accused, the prosecution in a criminal case shall provide reasonable notice in advance of trial, or during trial if the court excuses pretrial notice on good cause shown, of the general nature of any such evidence it intends to introduce at trial.

(Pub.L. 93–595, § 1, Jan. 2, 1975, 88 Stat.1932; Mar. 2, 1987, eff. Oct. 1, 1987; Apr. 30, 1991, eff. Dec. 1, 1991; Apr. 17, 2000, eff. Dec. 1, 2000; Apr. 12, 2006, eff. Dec. 1, 2006.)

1972 Proposed Rules

Note to Subdivision (a). This subdivision deals with the basic question whether character evidence should be admitted. Once the admissibility of character evidence in some form is established under this rule, reference must then be made to Rule 405, which follows, in order to determine the appropriate method of proof. If the character is that of a witness, see Rules 608 and 610 for methods of proof.

Character questions arise in two fundamentally different ways. (1) Character may itself be an element of a crime, claim, or defense. A situation of this kind is commonly referred to as "character in issue." Illustrations are: the chastity of the victim under a statute specifying her chastity as an element of the crime of seduction, or the competency of the driver in an action for negligently entrusting a motor vehicle to an incompetent driver. No problem of the general relevancy of character evidence is involved, and the present rule therefore has no provision on the subject. The only question relates to allowable methods of proof, as to which see Rule 405, immediately following. (2) Character evidence is susceptible of being used for the purpose of suggesting an inference that the person acted on the occasion in question consistently with his character. This use of character is often described as "circumstantial." Illustrations are: evidence of a violent disposition to prove that the person was the aggressor in an affray, or evidence of honesty in disproof of a charge of theft. This circumstantial use of character evidence raises questions of relevancy as well as questions of allowable methods of proof.

In most jurisdictions today, the circumstantial use of character is rejected but with important exceptions: (1) an accused may introduce pertinent evidence of good character (often misleadingly described as "putting his character in issue"), in which event the prosecution may rebut with evidence of bad character; (2) an accused may introduce pertinent evidence of the character of the victim, as in support of a claim of self-defense to a charge of homicide or consent in a case of rape, and the prosecution may introduce similar evidence in rebuttal of the character evidence, or, in a homicide case, to rebut a claim that deceased was the first aggressor, however proved; and (3) the character of a witness may be gone into as bearing on his credibility. McCormick §§ 155–161. This pattern is incorporated in the rule. While its basis lies more in history and experience than in logic an underlying justification can fairly be found in terms of the relative presence and absence of prejudice in the various situations. Falknor, Extrinsic Policies Affecting Admissibility, 10 Rutgers L.Rev. 574, 584 (1956); McCormick § 157. In any event, the criminal rule is so deeply imbedded in our jurisprudence as to assume almost constitutional proportions and to override doubts of the basic relevancy of the evidence.

The limitation to pertinent traits of character, rather than character generally, in paragraphs (1) and (2) is in accordance with the prevailing view. McCormick § 158, p. 334. A similar provision in Rule 608, to which reference is made in paragraph (3), limits character evidence respecting witnesses to the trait of truthfulness or untruthfulness.

The argument is made that circumstantial use of character ought to be allowed in civil cases to the same extent as in criminal cases, i.e. evidence of good (nonprejudicial) character would be admissible in the first instance, subject to rebuttal by evidence of bad character. Falknor, Extrinsic Policies Affecting Admissibility, 10 Rutgers L.Rev. 574, 581–583 (1956); Tentative Recommendation and a Study Relating to the Uniform Rules of Evidence (Art. VI. Extrinsic Policies Affecting Admissibility), Cal.Law Revision Comm'n, Rep., Rec. & Studies, 657–658 (1964). Uniform Rule 47 goes farther, in that it assumes that character evidence in general satisfies the conditions of relevancy, except as provided in Uniform Rule 48. The difficulty with expanding the use of character evidence in civil cases is set forth by the California Law Revision Commission in its ultimate rejection of Uniform Rule 47, *id.*, 615:

"Character evidence is of slight probative value and may be very prejudicial. It tends to distract the trier of fact from the main question of what actually happened on the particular occasion. It subtly permits the trier of fact to reward the good man and to punish the bad man because of their respective characters despite what the evidence in the case shows actually happened."

Much of the force of the position of those favoring greater use of character evidence in civil cases is dissipated by their support of Uniform Rule 48 which excludes the evidence in negligence cases, where it could be expected to achieve its maximum usefulness. Moreover, expanding concepts of "character," which seem of necessity to extend into such areas as psychiatric evaluation and psychological testing, coupled with expanded admissibility, would open up such vistas of mental examinations as caused the Court concern in *Schlagenhauf v. Holder*, 379 U.S. 104, 85 S.Ct. 234, 13 L.Ed.2d 152 (1964). It is believed that those espousing change have not met the burden of persuasion.

Note to Subdivision (b). Subdivision (b) deals with a specialized but important application of the general rule excluding circumstantial use of character evidence. Consistently with that rule, evidence of other crimes, wrongs, or acts is not admissible to prove character as a basis for suggesting the inference that conduct on a particular occasion was in conformity with it. However, the evidence may be offered for another purpose, such as proof of motive, opportunity, and so on, which does not fall within the prohibition. In this situation the rule does not require that the evidence be excluded. No mechanical solution is offered. The determination must be made whether the danger of undue prejudice outweighs the probative value of the evidence in view of the availability of other means of proof and other facts appropriate for making decision of this kind under Rule 403. Slough and Knightly, Other Vices, Other Crimes, 41 Iowa L.Rev. 325 (1956).

1974 Enactment

Note to Subdivision (b). The second sentence of Rule 404(b) as submitted to the Congress began with the words "This subdivision does not exclude the evidence when offered". The Committee amended this language to read "It may, however, be admissible", the words used in the 1971 Advisory Committee draft, on the ground that this formulation properly placed greater emphasis on admissibility than did the final Court version. House Report No. 93–650.

Note to Subdivision (b). This rule provides that evidence of other crimes, wrongs, or acts is not admissible to prove character but may be admissible for other specified purposes such as proof of motive.

Although your committee sees no necessity in amending the rule itself, it anticipates that the use of the discretionary word "may" with respect to the admissibility of evidence of crimes, wrongs, or acts is not intended to confer any arbitrary discretion on the trial judge. Rather, it is anticipated that with respect to permissible uses for such evidence, the trial judge may exclude it only on the basis of those considerations set forth in Rule 403, i.e., prejudice, confusion or waste of time. Senate Report No. 93–1277.

1987 Amendments

The amendments are technical. No substantive change is intended.

1991 Amendments

Rule 404(b) has emerged as one of the most cited Rules in the Rules of Evidence. And in many criminal cases evidence of an accused's extrinsic acts is viewed as an important asset in the prosecution's case against an accused. Although there are a few reported decisions on use of such evidence by the defense, *see, e.g., United States v. McClure,* 546 F.2d 670 (5th Cir.1990) (acts of informant offered in entrapment defense), the overwhelming number of cases involve introduction of that evidence by the prosecution.

The amendment to Rule 404(b) adds a pretrial notice requirement in criminal cases and is intended to reduce surprise and promote early resolution on the issue of admissibility. The notice requirement thus places Rule 404(b) in the mainstream with notice and disclosure provisions in other rules of evidence. *See, e.g.,* Rule 412 (written motion of intent to offer evidence under rule), Rule 609 (written notice of intent to offer conviction older than 10 years), Rule 803(24) and 804(b)(5) (notice of intent to use residual hearsay exceptions).

The Rule expects that counsel for both the defense and the prosecution will submit the necessary request and information in a reasonable and timely fashion. Other than requiring pretrial notice, no specific time limits are stated in recognition that what constitutes a reasonable request or disclosure will depend largely on the circumstances of each case. *Compare* Fla.Stat.Ann. § 90.404(2)(b) (notice must be given at least 10 days before trial) *with* Tex.R.Evid. 404(b) (no time limit).

Likewise, no specific form of notice is required. The Committee considered and rejected a requirement that the notice satisfy the particularity requirements normally required of language used in a charging instrument. *Cf.* Fla.Stat.Ann. § 90.404(2)(b) (written disclosure must describe uncharged misconduct with particularity required of an indictment or information). Instead, the Committee opted for a generalized notice provision which requires the prosecution to apprise the defense of the general nature of the evidence of extrinsic acts. The Committee does not intend that the amendment will supercede other rules of admissibility or disclosure, such as the Jencks Act, 18 U.S.C. § 3500, et. seq. nor require the prosecution to disclose directly or indirectly the names and addresses of its witnesses, something it is currently not required to do under Federal Rule of Criminal Procedure 16.

The amendment requires the prosecution to provide notice, regardless of how it intends to use the extrinsic act evidence at trial, i.e., during its case-in-chief, for impeachment, or for possible rebuttal. The court in its discretion may, under the facts, decide that the particular request or notice was not reasonable, either because of the lack of timeliness or completeness. Because the notice requirement serves as condition precedent to admissibility of 404(b) evidence, the offered evidence is inadmissible if the court decides that the notice requirement has not been met.

Nothing in the amendment precludes the court from requiring the government to provide it with an opportunity to rule *in limine* on 404(b) evidence before it is offered or even mentioned during trial. When ruling *in limine,* the court may require the government to disclose to it the specifics of such evidence which the court must consider in determining admissibility.

The amendment does not extend to evidence of acts which are "intrinsic" to the charged offense, *see United States v. Williams,* 900 F.2d 823 (5th Cir.1990) (noting distinction between 404(b) evidence and intrinsic offense evidence). Nor is the amendment intended to redefine what evidence would otherwise be admissible under Rule 404(b). Finally, the Committee does not intend through the amendment to affect the role of the court and the jury in considering such evidence. *See United States v. Huddleston,* 485 U.S. 681, 108 S.Ct. 1496 (1988).

2000 Amendments

Rule 404(a)(1) has been amended to provide that when the accused attacks the character of an alleged victim under subdivision (a)(2) of this Rule, the door is opened to an attack on the same character trait of the accused. Current law does not allow the government to introduce negative character evidence as to the accused unless the accused introduces evidence of good character. *See, e.g., United States v. Fountain,* 768 F.2d 790 (7th Cir. 1985) (when the accused offers proof of self-defense, this permits proof of the alleged victim's character trait for peacefulness, but it does not permit proof of the accused's character trait for violence).

The amendment makes clear that the accused cannot attack the alleged victim's character and yet remain shielded from the disclosure of equally relevant evidence concerning the same character trait of the accused. For example, in a murder case with a claim of self-defense, the accused, to bolster this defense, might offer evidence of the alleged victim's violent disposition. If the government has evidence that the accused has a violent character, but is not allowed to offer this evidence as part of its rebuttal, the jury has only part of the information it needs for an informed assessment of the probabilities as to who was the initial aggressor. This may be the case even if evidence of the accused's prior violent acts is admitted under Rule 404(b), because such evidence can be admitted only for limited purposes and not to show action in conformity with the accused's character on a specific occasion. Thus, the amendment is designed to permit a more balanced presentation of character evidence when an accused chooses to attack the character of the alleged victim.

The amendment does not affect the admissibility of evidence of specific acts of uncharged misconduct offered for a purpose other than proving character under Rule 404(b). Nor does it affect the standards for proof of character by evidence of other sexual behavior or sexual offenses under Rules 412–415. By its placement in Rule 404(a)(1), the amendment covers only proof of character by way of reputation or opinion.

The amendment does not permit proof of the accused's character if the accused merely uses character evidence for a purpose other than to prove the alleged victim's propensity to act in a certain way. *See United States v. Burks,* 470 F.2d 432, 434–5 (D.C.Cir. 1972) (evidence of the alleged victim's violent character, when known by the accused, was admissible "on the issue of whether or not the defendant reasonably feared he was in danger of imminent great bodily harm"). Finally, the amendment does not permit proof of the accused's character when the accused attacks the alleged victim's character as a witness under Rule 608 or 609.

The term "alleged" is inserted before each reference to "victim" in the Rule, in order to provide consistency with Evidence Rule 412.

GAP Report—Proposed Amendment to Rule 404(a)

The Committee made the following changes to the published draft of the proposed amendment to Evidence Rule 404(a):

1. The term "a pertinent trait of character" was changed to "the same trait of character," in order to limit the scope of the government's rebuttal. The Committee Note was revised to accord with this change in the text.

2. The word "alleged" was added before each reference in the Rule to a "victim" in order to provide consistency with Evidence Rule 412. The Committee Note was amended to accord with this change in the text.

3. The Committee Note was amended to clarify that rebuttal is not permitted under this Rule if the accused proffers evidence of the alleged victim's character for a purpose other than to prove the alleged victim's propensity to act in a certain manner.

2006 Amendments

The Rule has been amended to clarify that in a civil case evidence of a person's character is never admissible to prove that the person acted in conformity with the character trait. The amendment resolves the dispute in the case law over whether the exceptions in subdivisions (a)(1) and (2) permit the circumstantial use of character evidence in civil cases. *Compare Carson v. Polley*, 689 F.2d 562, 576 (5th Cir. 1982) ("when a central issue in a case is close to one of a criminal nature, the exceptions to the Rule 404(a) ban on character evidence may be invoked"), *with SEC v. Towers Financial Corp.*, 966 F.Supp. 203 (S.D.N.Y. 1997) (relying on the terms "accused" and "prosecution" in Rule 404(a) to conclude that the exceptions in subdivisions (a)(1) and (2) are inapplicable in civil cases). The amendment is consistent with the original intent of the Rule, which was to prohibit the circumstantial use of character evidence in civil cases, even where closely related to criminal charges. *See Ginter v. Northwestern Mut. Life Ins. Co.*, 576 F.Supp. 627, 629–30 (D. Ky.1984) ("It seems beyond peradventure of doubt that the drafters of F.R.Evi. 404(a) explicitly intended that all character evidence, except where 'character is at issue' was to be excluded" in civil cases).

The circumstantial use of character evidence is generally discouraged because it carries serious risks of prejudice, confusion and delay. *See Michelson v. United States*, 335 U.S. 469, 476 (1948) ("The overriding policy of excluding such evidence, despite its admitted probative value, is the practical experience that its disallowance tends to prevent confusion of issues, unfair surprise and undue prejudice."). In criminal cases, the so-called "mercy rule" permits a criminal defendant to introduce evidence of pertinent character traits of the defendant and the victim. But that is because the accused, whose liberty is at stake, may need "a counterweight against the strong investigative and prosecutorial resources of the government." C. Mueller & L. Kirkpatrick, *Evidence: Practice Under the Rules*, pp. 264–5 (2d ed. 1999). See also Richard Uviller, *Evidence of Character to Prove Conduct: Illusion, Illogic, and Injustice in the Courtroom*, 130 U.Pa. L.Rev. 845, 855 (1982) (the rule prohibiting circumstantial use of character evidence "was relaxed to allow the criminal defendant with so much at stake and so little available in the way of conventional proof to have special dispensation to tell the factfinder just what sort of person he really is"). Those concerns do not apply to parties in civil cases.

The amendment also clarifies that evidence otherwise admissible under Rule 404(a)(2) may nonetheless be excluded in a criminal case involving sexual misconduct. In such a case, the admissibility of evidence of the victim's sexual behavior and predisposition is governed by the more stringent provisions of Rule 412.

Nothing in the amendment is intended to affect the scope of Rule 404(b). While Rule 404(b) refers to the "accused," the "prosecution," and a "criminal case," it does so only in the context of a notice requirement. The admissibility standards of Rule 404(b) remain fully applicable to both civil and criminal cases.

Rule 405. Methods of Proving Character

(a) Reputation or opinion. In all cases in which evidence of character or a trait of character of a person is admissible, proof may be made by testimony as to reputation or by testimony in the form of an opinion. On cross-examination, inquiry is allowable into relevant specific instances of conduct.

(b) Specific instances of conduct. In cases in which character or a trait of character of a person is an essential element of a charge, claim, or defense, proof may also be made of specific instances of that person's conduct.

(Pub.L. 93–595, § 1, Jan. 2, 1975, 88 Stat. 1932; Mar. 2, 1987, eff. Oct. 1, 1987.)

1972 Proposed Rules

The rule deals only with allowable methods of proving character, not with the admissibility of character evidence, which is covered in Rule 404.

Of the three methods of proving character provided by the rule, evidence of specific instances of conduct is the most convincing. At the same time it possesses the greatest capacity to arouse prejudice, to confuse, to surprise, and to consume time. Consequently the rule confines the use of evidence of this kind to cases in which character is, in the strict sense, in issue and hence deserving of a searching inquiry. When character is used circumstantially and hence occupies a lesser status in the case, proof may be only by reputation and opinion. These latter methods are also available when character is in issue. This treatment is, with respect to specific instances of conduct and reputation, conventional contemporary common law doctrine. McCormick § 153.

In recognizing opinion as a means of proving character, the rule departs from usual contemporary practice in favor of that of an earlier day. See 7 Wigmore § 1986, pointing out that the earlier practice permitted opinion and arguing strongly for evidence based on personal knowledge and belief as contrasted with "the secondhand, irresponsible product of multiplied guesses and gossip which we term 'reputation'."

It seems likely that the persistence of reputation evidence is due to its largely being opinion in disguise. Traditionally character has been regarded primarily in moral overtones of good and bad: chaste, peaceable, truthful, honest. Nevertheless, on occasion nonmoral considerations crop up, as in the case of the incompetent driver, and this seems bound to happen increasingly. If character is defined as the kind of person one is, then account must be taken of varying ways of arriving at the estimate. These may range from the opinion of the employer who has found the man honest to the opinion of the psychiatrist based upon examination and testing. No effective dividing line exists between character and mental capacity, and the latter traditionally has been provable by opinion.

According to the great majority of cases, on cross-examination inquiry is allowable as to whether the reputation witness has heard of particular instances of conduct pertinent to the trait in question. *Michelson v. United States,* 335 U.S. 469, 69 S.Ct. 213, 93 L.Ed. 168 (1948); Annot., 47 A.L.R.2d 1258. The theory is that, since the reputation witness relates what he has heard, the inquiry tends to shed light on the accuracy of his hearing and reporting. Accordingly, the opinion witness would be asked whether he knew, as well as whether he had heard. The fact is, of course, that these distinctions are of slight if any practical significance, and the second sentence of subdivision (a) eliminates them as a factor in formulating questions. This recognition of the propriety of inquiring into specific instances of conduct does not circumscribe inquiry otherwise into the bases of opinion and reputation testimony.

The express allowance of inquiry into specific instances of conduct on cross-examination in subdivision (a) and the express allowance of it as part of a case in chief when character is actually in issue in subdivision (b) contemplate that testimony of specific instances is not generally permissible on the direct examination of an ordinary opinion witness to character. Similarly as to witnesses to the character of witnesses under Rule 608(b). Opinion testimony on direct in these situations ought in general to correspond to reputation testimony as now given, *i.e.,* be confined to the nature and extent of observation and acquaintance upon which the opinion is based. See Rule 701.

1974 Enactment

Note to Subdivision (a). Rule 405(a) as submitted proposed to change existing law by allowing evidence of character in the form of opinion as well as reputation testimony. Fearing, among other reasons, that wholesale allowance of opinion testimony might tend to turn a trial into a swearing contest between conflicting character witnesses, the Committee decided to delete from this Rule, as well as from Rule 608(a) which involves a related problem, reference to opinion testimony. House Report No. 93–650.

The Senate makes two language changes in the nature of conforming amendments. The Conference adopts the Senate amendments. House Report No. 93–1597.

1987 Amendments

The amendment is technical. No substantive change is intended.

Rule 406. Habit; Routine Practice

Evidence of the habit of a person or of the routine practice of an organization, whether corroborated or not and regardless of the presence of eyewitnesses, is relevant to prove that the conduct of the person or organization on a particular occasion was in conformity with the habit or routine practice.

(Pub.L. 93–595, § 1, Jan. 2, 1975, 88 Stat. 1932.)

1972 Proposed Rules

An oft-quoted paragraph, McCormick, § 162, p. 340, describes habit in terms effectively contrasting it with character:

"Character and habit are close akin. Character is a generalized description of one's disposition, or of one's disposition in respect to a general trait, such as honesty, temperance, or peacefulness. 'Habit,' in modern usage, both lay and psychological, is more specific. It describes one's regular response to a repeated specific situation. If we speak of character for care, we think of the person's tendency to act prudently in all the varying situations of life, in business, family life, in handling automobiles and in walking across the street. A habit, on the other hand, is the person's regular practice of meeting a particular kind of situation with a specific type of conduct, such as the habit of going down a particular stairway two stairs at a time, or of giving the hand-signal for a left turn, or of alighting from railway cars while they are moving. The doing of the habitual acts may become semi-automatic."

Equivalent behavior on the part of a group is designated "routine practice of an organization" in the rule.

Agreement is general that habit evidence is highly persuasive as proof of conduct on a particular occasion. Again quoting McCormick § 162, p. 341:

"Character may be thought of as the sum of one's habits though doubtless it is more than this. But unquestionably the uniformity of one's response to habit is far greater than the consistency with which one's conduct conforms to character or disposition. Even though character comes in only exceptionally as evidence of an act, surely any sensible man in investigating whether X did a particular act would be greatly helped in his inquiry by evidence as to whether he was in the habit of doing it."

When disagreement has appeared, its focus has been upon the question what constitutes habit, and the reason for this is readily apparent. The extent to which instances must be multiplied and consistency of behavior maintained in order to rise to the status of habit inevitably gives rise to differences of opinion. Lewan, Rationale of Habit Evidence, 16 Syracuse L.Rev. 39, 49 (1964). While adequacy of sampling and uniformity of response are key factors, precise standards for measuring their sufficiency for evidence purposes cannot be formulated.

The rule is consistent with prevailing views. Much evidence is excluded simply because of failure to achieve the status of habit. Thus, evidence of intemperate "habits" is generally excluded when offered as proof of drunkenness in accident cases, Annot., 46 A.L.R.2d 103, and evidence of other assaults is inadmissible to prove the instant one in a civil assault action, Annot., 66 A.L.R.2d 806. In *Levin v.*

United States, 119 U.S.App.D.C. 156, 338 F.2d 265 (1964), testimony as to the religious "habits" of the accused, offered as tending to prove that he was at home observing the Sabbath rather than out obtaining money through larceny by trick, was held properly excluded:

"It seems apparent to us that an individual's religious practices would not be the type of activities which would lend themselves to the characterization of 'invariable regularity.' [1 Wigmore 520.] Certainly the very volitional basis of the activity raises serious questions as to its invariable nature, and hence its probative value." *Id.* at 272.

These rulings are not inconsistent with the trend towards admitting evidence of business transactions between one of the parties and a third person as tending to prove that he made the same bargain or proposal in the litigated situation. Slough, Relevancy Unraveled, 6 Kan.L.Rev. 38–41 (1957). Nor are they inconsistent with such cases as *Whittemore v. Lockheed Aircraft Corp.,* 65 Cal.App.2d 737, 151 P.2d 670 (1944), upholding the admission of evidence that plaintiff's intestate had on four other occasions flown planes from defendant's factory for delivery to his employer airline, offered to prove that he was piloting rather than a guest on a plane which crashed and killed all on board while en route for delivery.

A considerable body of authority has required that evidence of the routine practice of an organization be corroborated as a condition precedent to its admission in evidence. Slough, Relevancy Unraveled, 5 Kan.L.Rev. 404, 449 (1957). This requirement is specifically rejected by the rule on the ground that it relates to the sufficiency of the evidence rather than admissibility. A similar position is taken in New Jersey Rule 49. The rule also rejects the requirement of the absence of eyewitnesses, sometimes encountered with respect to admitting habit evidence to prove freedom from contributory negligence in wrongful death cases. For comment critical of the requirements see Frank, J., in *Cereste v. New York,* N.H. & H.R. Co., 231 F.2d 50 (2d Cir.1956), cert. denied 351 U.S. 951, 76 S.Ct. 848, 100 L.Ed. 1475, 10 Vand.L.Rev. 447 (1957); McCormick § 162, p. 342. The omission of the requirement from the California Evidence Code is said to have effected its elimination. Comment, Cal.Ev.Code § 1105.

Rule 407. Subsequent Remedial Measures

When, after an injury or harm allegedly caused by an event, measures are taken that, if taken previously, would have made the injury or harm less likely to occur, evidence of the subsequent measures is not admissible to prove negligence, culpable conduct, a defect in a product, a defect in a product's design, or a need for a warning or instruction. This rule does not require the exclusion of evidence of subsequent measures when offered for another purpose, such as proving ownership, control, or feasibility of precautionary measures, if controverted, or impeachment.

(Pub.L. 93–595, § 1, Jan. 2, 1975, 88 Stat. 1932; Apr. 11, 1997, eff. Dec. 1, 1997.)

1972 Proposed Rules

The rule incorporates conventional doctrine which excludes evidence of subsequent remedial measures as proof of an admission of fault. The rule rests on two grounds. (1) The conduct is not in fact an admission, since the conduct is equally consistent with injury by mere accident or through contributory negligence. Or, as Baron Bramwell put it, the rule rejects the notion that "because the world gets wiser as it gets older, therefore it was foolish before." *Hart v. Lancashire & Yorkshire Ry. Co.,* 21 L.T.R. N.S. 261, 263 (1869). Under a liberal theory of relevancy this ground alone would not support exclusion as the inference is still a possible one. (2) The other, and more impressive, ground for exclusion rests on a social policy of encouraging people to take, or at least not discouraging them from taking, steps in furtherance of added safety. The courts have applied this principle to exclude evidence of subsequent repairs, installation of safety devices, changes in company rules, and discharge of employees, and the language of the present rule is broad enough to encompass all of them. See Falknor, Extrinsic Policies Affecting Admissibility, 10 Rutgers L.Rev. 574, 590 (1956).

The second sentence of the rule directs attention to the limitations of the rule. Exclusion is called for only when the evidence of subsequent remedial measures is offered as proof of negligence or culpable conduct. In effect it rejects the suggested inference that fault is admitted. Other purposes are, however, allowable, including ownership or control, existence of duty, and feasibility of precautionary measures, if controverted, and impeachment. 2 Wigmore § 283; Annot., 64 A.L.R.2d 1296. Two recent federal cases are illustrative. *Boeing Airplane Co. v. Brown,* 291 F.2d 310 (9th Cir.1961), an action against an airplane manufacturer for using an allegedly defectively designed alternator shaft which caused a plane crash, upheld the admission of evidence of subsequent design modification for the purpose of showing that design changes and safeguards were feasible. And *Powers v. J.B. Michael & Co.,* 329 F.2d 674 (6th Cir.1964), an action against a road contractor for negligent failure to put out warning signs, sustained the admission of evidence that defendant subsequently put out signs to show that the portion of the road in question was under defendant's control. The requirement that the other purpose be controverted calls for automatic exclusion unless a genuine issue be present and allows the opposing party to lay the groundwork for exclusion by making an admission. Otherwise the factors of undue prejudice, confusion of issues, misleading the jury, and waste of time remain for consideration under Rule 403.

For comparable rules, see Uniform Rule 51; California Evidence Code § 1151; Kansas Code of Civil Procedure § 60–451; New Jersey Evidence Rule 51.

1997 Amendments

The amendment to Rule 407 makes two changes in the rule. First, the words "an injury or harm allegedly caused by" were added to clarify that the rule applies only to changes made after the occurrence that produced the damages giving rise to the action. Evidence of measures taken by the defendant prior to the "event" causing "injury or harm" do not fall within the exclusionary scope of Rule 407 even if they occurred after the manufacture or design of the product. See *Chase v. General Motors Corp.,* 856 F.2d 17, 21–22 (4th Cir. 1988).

Second, Rule 407 has been amended to provide that evidence of subsequent remedial measures may not be used to prove "a defect in a product or its design, or that a warning or instruction should have accompanied a product." This amendment adopts the view of a majority of the circuits that have interpreted Rule 407 to apply to products liability actions. See *Raymond v. Raymond Corp., 938 F.2d 1518, 1522 (1st Cir. 1991); In re Joint Eastern District and Southern District Asbestos Litigation v. Armstrong World industries, Inc.*, 995 F.2d 343 (2d Cir. 1993); *Cann v. Ford Motor Co.*, 658 F.2d 54, 60 (2d Cir. 1981), *cert. denied*, 456 U.S. 960 (1982); *Kelly v. Crown Equipment Co.*, 970 F.2d 1273, 1275 (3d Cir. 1992); *Werner v. Upjohn, Inc.*, 628 F.2d 848 (4th Cir. 1980); *cert. denied*, 449 U.S. 1080 (1981); *Grenada Steel Industries, Inc. v. Alabama Oxygen Co., Inc.*, 695 F.2d 883 (5th Cir. 1983); *Bauman v. Volkswagenwerk Aktiengesellschaft*, 621 F.2d 230, 232 (6th Cir. 1980); *Flaminio v. Honda Motor Company, Ltd.*, 733 F.2d 463, 469 (7th Cir. 1984); *Gauthier v. AMF, Inc.*, 788 F.2d 634, 636–37 (9th Cir. 1986).

Although this amendment adopts a uniform federal rule, it should be noted that evidence of subsequent remedial measures may be admissible pursuant to the second sentence of Rule 407. Evidence of subsequent measures that is not barred by Rule 407 may still be subject to exclusion on Rule 403 grounds when the dangers of prejudice or confusion substantially outweigh the probative value of the evidence.

Rule 408. Compromise and Offers to Compromise

(a) Prohibited uses.—Evidence of the following is not admissible on behalf of any party, when offered to prove liability for, invalidity of, or amount of a claim that was disputed as to validity or amount, or to impeach through a prior inconsistent statement or contradiction:

(1) furnishing or offering or promising to furnish—or accepting or offering or promising to accept—a valuable consideration in compromising or attempting to compromise the claim; and

(2) conduct or statements made in compromise negotiations regarding the claim, except when offered in a criminal case and the negotiations related to a claim by a public office or agency in the exercise of regulatory, investigative, or enforcement authority.

(b) Permitted uses.—This rule does not require exclusion if the evidence is offered for purposes not prohibited by subdivision (a). Examples of permissible purposes include proving a witness's bias or prejudice; negating a contention of undue delay; and proving an effort to obstruct a criminal investigation or prosecution.

(Pub.L. 93–595, § 1, Jan. 2, 1975, 88 Stat. 1933; Apr. 12, 2006, eff. Dec. 1, 2006.)

1972 Proposed Rules

As a matter of general agreement, evidence of an offer to compromise a claim is not receivable in evidence as an admission of, as the case may be, the validity or invalidity of the claim. As with evidence of subsequent remedial measures, dealt with in Rule 407, exclusion may be based on two grounds. (1) The evidence is irrelevant, since the offer may be motivated by a desire for peace rather than from any concession of weakness of position. The validity of this position will vary as the amount of the offer varies in relation to the size of the claim and may also be influenced by other circumstances. (2) A more consistently impressive ground is promotion of the public policy favoring the compromise and settlement of disputes. McCormick §§ 76, 251. While the rule is ordinarily phrased in terms of offers of compromise, it is apparent that a similar attitude must be taken with respect to completed compromises when offered against a party thereto. This latter situation will not, of course, ordinarily occur except when a party to the present litigation has compromised with a third person.

The same policy underlies the provision of Rule 68 of the Federal Rules of Civil Procedure that evidence of an unaccepted offer of judgment is not admissible except in a proceeding to determine costs.

The practical value of the common law rule has been greatly diminished by its inapplicability to admissions of fact, even though made in the course of compromise negotiations, unless hypothetical, stated to be "without prejudice," or so connected with the offer as to be inseparable from it. McCormick § 251, pp. 540–541. An inevitable effect is to inhibit freedom of communication with respect to compromise, even among lawyers. Another effect is the generation of controversy over whether a given statement falls within or without the protected area. These considerations account for the expansion of the rule herewith to include evidence of conduct or statements made in compromise negotiations, as well as the offer or completed compromise itself. For similar provisions see California Evidence Code §§ 1152, 1154.

The policy considerations which underlie the rule do not come into play when the effort is to induce a creditor to settle an admittedly due amount for a lesser sum. McCormick § 251, p. 540. Hence the rule requires that the claim be disputed as to either validity or amount.

The final sentence of the rule serves to point out some limitations upon its applicability. Since the rule excludes only when the purpose is proving the validity or invalidity of the claim or its amount, an offer for another purpose is not within the rule. The illustrative situations mentioned in the rule are supported by the authorities. As to proving bias or prejudice of a witness, see Annot., 161 A.L.R. 395, *contra, Fenberg v. Rosenthal*, 348 Ill.App. 510, 109 N.E.2d 402 (1952), and negativing a contention of lack of due diligence in presenting a claim, 4 Wigmore § 1061. An effort to "buy off" the prosecution or a prosecuting witness in a criminal case is not within the policy of the rule of exclusion. McCormick § 251, p. 542.

For other rules of similar import, see Uniform Rules 52 and 53; California Evidence Code §§ 1152, 1154; Kansas Code of Civil Procedure §§ 60–452, 60–453; New Jersey Evidence Rules 52 and 53.

1974 Enactment

Under existing federal law evidence of conduct and statements made in compromise negotiations is admissible in subsequent litigation between the parties. The second sentence of Rule 408 as submitted by the Supreme Court proposed to reverse that doctrine in the interest of further promoting non-judicial settlement of disputes. Some agencies of government expressed the view that the Court formulation was likely to impede rather than assist efforts to achieve settlement of disputes. For one thing, it is not always easy to tell when compromise negotiations begin, and informal dealings end. Also, parties dealing with government agencies would be reluctant to furnish factual information at preliminary meetings; they would wait until "compromise negotiations" began and thus hopefully effect an immunity for themselves with respect to the evidence supplied. In light of these considerations, the Committee recast the Rule so that admissions of liability or opinions given during compromise negotiations continue inadmissible, but evidence of unqualified factual assertions is admissible. The latter aspect of the Rule is drafted, however, so as to preserve other possible objections to the introduction of such evidence. The Committee intends no modification of current law whereby a party may protect himself from future use of his statements by couching them in hypothetical conditional form. House Report No. 93–650.

This rule as reported makes evidence of settlement or attempted settlement of a disputed claim inadmissible when offered as an admission of liability or the amount of liability. The purpose of this rule is to encourage settlements which would be discouraged if such evidence were admissible.

Under present law, in most jurisdictions, statements of fact made during settlement negotiations, however, are excepted from this ban and are admissible. The only escape from admissibility of statements of fact made in a settlement negotiation is if the declarant or his representative expressly states that the statement is hypothetical in nature or is made without prejudice. Rule 408 as submitted by the Court reversed the traditional rule. It would have brought statements of fact within the ban and made them, as well as an offer of settlement, inadmissible.

The House amended the rule and would continue to make evidence of facts disclosed during compromise negotiations admissible. It thus reverted to the traditional rule. The House committee report states that the committee intends to preserve current law under which a party may protect himself by couching his statements in hypothetical form [See House Report No. 93–650 above]. The real impact of this amendment, however, is to deprive the rule of much of its salutary effect. The exception for factual admissions was believed by the Advisory Committee to hamper free communication between parties and thus to constitute an unjustifiable restraint upon efforts to negotiate settlements—the encouragement of which is the purpose of the rule. Further, by protecting hypothetically phrased statements, it constituted a preference for the sophisticated, and a trap for the unwary.

Three States which had adopted rules of evidence patterned after the proposed rules prescribed by the Supreme Court opted for versions of rule 408 identical with the Supreme Court draft with respect to the inadmissibility of conduct or statements made in compromise negotiations [Nev.Rev.Stats. § 48.105; N.Mex.Stats.Anno. (1973 Supp.) § 20–4–408; West's Wis.Stats.Anno. (1973 Supp.) § 904.08].

For these reasons, the committee has deleted the House amendment and restored the rule to the version submitted by the Supreme Court with one additional amendment. This amendment adds a sentence to insure that evidence, such as documents, is not rendered inadmissible merely because it is presented in the course of compromise negotiations if the evidence is otherwise discoverable. A party should not be able to immunize from admissibility documents otherwise discoverable merely by offering them in a compromise negotiation. Senate Report No. 93–1277.

The House bill provides that evidence of admissions of liability or opinions given during compromise negotiations is not admissible, but that evidence of facts disclosed during compromise negotiations is not inadmissible by virtue of having been first disclosed in the compromise negotiations. The Senate amendment provides that evidence of conduct or statements made in compromise negotiations is not admissible. The Senate amendment also provides that the rule does not require the exclusion of any evidence otherwise discoverable merely because it is presented in the course of compromise negotiations.

The House bill was drafted to meet the objection of executive agencies that under the rule as proposed by the Supreme Court, a party could present a fact during compromise negotiations and thereby prevent an opposing party from offering evidence of that fact at trial even though such evidence was obtained from independent sources. The Senate amendment expressly precludes this result.

The Conference adopts the Senate amendment. House Report No. 93–1597.

2006 Amendment

Rule 408 has been amended to settle some questions in the courts about the scope of the Rule, and to make it easier to read. First, the amendment provides that Rule 408 does not prohibit the introduction in a criminal case of statements or conduct during compromise negotiations regarding a civil dispute by a government regulatory, investigative, or enforcement agency. *See, e.g., United States v. Prewitt*, 34 F.3d 436, 439 (7th Cir. 1994) (admissions of fault made in compromise of a civil securities enforcement action were admissible against the accused in a subsequent criminal action for mail fraud). Where an individual makes a statement in the presence of government agents, its subsequent admission in a criminal case should not be unexpected. The individual can seek to protect against subsequent disclosure through negotiation and agreement with the civil regulator or an attorney for the government.

Statements made in compromise negotiations of a claim by a government agency may be excluded in criminal cases where the circumstances so warrant under Rule 403. For example, if an individual was unrepresented at the time the statement was made in a civil enforcement proceeding, its probative value in a subsequent criminal case may be minimal. But there is no absolute exclusion imposed by Rule 408.

In contrast, statements made during compromise negotiations of other disputed claims are not admissible in subsequent criminal litigation, when offered to prove liability for, invalidity of, or amount of those claims. When private parties enter into compromise negotiations they cannot protect against the subsequent use of statements in criminal cases by way of private ordering. The inability to guarantee protection against subsequent use could lead to parties refusing to admit fault, even if by doing so they could favorably settle the private matter. Such a chill on settlement negotiations would be contrary to the policy of Rule 408.

The amendment distinguishes statements and conduct (such as a direct admission of fault) made in compromise negotiations of a civil claim by a government agency from an offer or acceptance of a compromise of such a claim. An offer or acceptance of a compromise of any civil claim is excluded under the Rule if offered against the defendant as an admission of fault. In that case, the predicate for the evidence would be that the defendant, by compromising with the government agency, has admitted the validity and amount of the civil claim, and that this admission has sufficient probative value to be considered as evidence of guilt. But unlike a direct statement of fault, an offer or acceptance of a compromise is not very probative of the defendant's guilt. Moreover, admitting such an offer or acceptance could deter a defendant from settling a civil regulatory action, for fear of evidentiary use in a subsequent criminal action. *See, e.g.*, Fishman, *Jones on Evidence, Civil and Criminal*, § 22:16 at 199, n.83 (7th ed. 2000) ("A target of a potential criminal investigation may be unwilling to settle civil claims against him if by doing so he increases the risk of prosecution and conviction.").

The amendment retains the language of the original rule that bars compromise evidence only when offered as evidence of the "validity," "invalidity," or "amount" of the disputed claim. The intent is to retain the extensive case law finding Rule 408 inapplicable when compromise evidence is offered for a purpose other than to prove the validity, invalidity, or amount of a disputed claim. *See, e.g., Athey v. Farmers Ins. Exchange*, 234 F.3d 357 (8th Cir. 2000) (evidence of settlement offer by insurer was properly admitted to prove insurer's bad faith); *Coakley & Williams v. Structural Concrete Equip.*, 973 F.2d 349 (4th Cir. 1992) (evidence of settlement is not precluded by Rule 408 where offered to prove a party's intent with respect to the scope of a release); *Cates v. Morgan Portable Bldg. Corp.*, 708 F.2d 683 (7th Cir. 1985) (Rule 408 does not bar evidence of a settlement when offered to prove a breach of the settlement agreement, as the purpose of the evidence is to prove the fact of settlement as opposed to the validity or amount of the underlying claim); *Uforma/Shelby Bus. Forms, Inc. v. NLRB*, 111 F.3d 1284 (6th Cir. 1997) (threats made in settlement negotiations were admissible; Rule 408 is inapplicable when the claim is based upon a wrong that is committed during the course of settlement negotiations). So for example, Rule 408 is inapplicable if offered to show that a party made fraudulent statements in order to settle a litigation.

The amendment does not affect the case law providing that Rule 408 is inapplicable when evidence of the compromise is offered to prove notice. *See, e.g., United States v. Austin*, 54 F.3d 394 (7th Cir. 1995) (no error to admit evidence of the defendant's settlement with the FTC, because it was offered to prove that the defendant was on notice that subsequent similar conduct was wrongful); *Spell v. McDaniel*, 824 F.2d 1380 (4th Cir. 1987) (in a civil rights action alleging that an officer used excessive force, a prior settlement by the City of another brutality claim was properly admitted to prove that the City was on notice of aggressive behavior by police officers).

The amendment prohibits the use of statements made in settlement negotiations when offered to impeach by prior inconsistent statement or through contradiction. Such broad impeachment would tend to swallow the exclusionary rule and would impair the public policy of promoting settlements. *See McCormick on Evidence* at 186 (5th ed. 1999) ("Use of statements made in compromise negotiations to impeach the testimony of a party, which is not specifically treated in Rule 408, is fraught with danger of misuse of the statements to prove liability, threatens frank interchange of information during negotiations, and generally should not be permitted."). *See also EEOC v. Gear Petroleum, Inc.*, 948 F.2d 1542 (10th Cir.1991) (letter sent as part of settlement negotiation cannot be used to impeach defense witnesses by way of contradiction or prior inconsistent statement; such broad impeachment would undermine the policy of encouraging uninhibited settlement negotiations).

The amendment makes clear that Rule 408 excludes compromise evidence even when a party seeks to admit its own settlement offer or statements made in settlement negotiations. If a party were to reveal its own statement or offer, this could itself reveal the fact that the adversary entered into settlement negotiations. The protections of Rule 408 cannot be waived unilaterally because the Rule, by definition, protects both parties from having the fact of negotiation disclosed to the jury. Moreover, proof of statements and offers made in settlement would often have to be made through the testimony of attorneys, leading to the risks and costs of disqualification. *See generally Pierce v. F.R. Tripler & Co.*, 955 F.2d 820, 828 (2d Cir. 1992) (settlement offers are excluded under Rule 408 even if it is the offeror who seeks to admit them; noting that the "widespread admissibility of the substance of settlement offers could bring with it a rash of motions for disqualification of a party's chosen counsel who would likely become a witness at trial").

The sentence of the Rule referring to evidence "otherwise discoverable" has been deleted as superfluous. *See, e.g.*, Advisory Committee Note to Maine Rule of Evidence 408 (refusing to include the sentence in the Maine version of Rule 408 and noting that the sentence "seems to state what the law would be if it were omitted"); Advisory Committee Note to Wyoming Rule of Evidence 408 (refusing to include the sentence in Wyoming Rule 408 on the ground that it was "superfluous"). The intent of the sentence was to prevent a party from trying to immunize admissible information, such as a pre-existing document, through the pretense of disclosing it during compromise negotiations. *See Ramada Development Co. v. Rauch*, 644 F.2d 1097 (5th Cir. 1981). But even without the sentence, the Rule cannot be read to protect pre-existing information simply because it was presented to the adversary in compromise negotiations.

Rule 409. Payment of Medical and Similar Expenses

Evidence of furnishing or offering or promising to pay medical, hospital, or similar expenses occasioned by an injury is not admissible to prove liability for the injury.

(Pub.L. 93–595, § 1, Jan. 2, 1975, 88 Stat.1933.)

1972 Proposed Rules

The considerations underlying this rule parallel those underlying Rules 407 and 408, which deal respectively with subsequent remedial measures and offers of compromise. As stated in Annot., 20 A.L.R.2d 291, 293:

"[G]enerally, evidence of payment of medical, hospital, or similar expenses of an injured party by the opposing party, is not admissible, the reason often given being that such payment or offer is usually made from humane impulses and not from an admission of liability, and that to hold otherwise would tend to discourage assistance to the injured person."

Contrary to Rule 408, dealing with offers of compromise, the present rule does not extend to conduct or statements not a part of the act of furnishing or offering or promising to pay. This difference in treatment arises from fundamental differences in nature. Communication is essential if compromises are to be effected, and consequently broad protection of statements is needed. This is not so in cases of payments or offers or promises to pay medical expenses, where factual statements may be expected to be incidental in nature.

For rules on the same subject, but phrased in terms of "humanitarian motives," see Uniform Rule 52; California Evidence Code § 1152; Kansas Code of Civil Procedure § 60–452; New Jersey Evidence Rule 52.

Rule 410. Inadmissibility of Pleas, Plea Discussions, and Related Statements

Except as otherwise provided in this rule, evidence of the following is not, in any civil or criminal proceeding, admissible against the defendant who made the plea or was a participant in the plea discussions:

(1) a plea of guilty which was later withdrawn;

(2) a plea of nolo contendere;

(3) any statement made in the course of any proceedings under Rule 11 of the Federal Rules of Criminal Procedure or comparable state procedure regarding either of the foregoing pleas; or

(4) any statement made in the course of plea discussions with an attorney for the prosecuting authority which do not result in a plea of guilty or which result in a plea of guilty later withdrawn.

However, such a statement is admissible (i) in any proceeding wherein another statement made in the course of the same plea or plea discussions has been introduced and the statement ought in fairness be considered contemporaneously with it, or (ii) in a criminal proceeding for perjury or false statement if the statement was made by the defendant under oath, on the record and in the presence of counsel.

(Pub.L. 93–595, § 1, Jan. 2, 1975, 88 Stat. 1933; Pub.L. 94–149, § 1(9), Dec. 12, 1975, 89 Stat. 805; Apr. 30, 1979, eff. Dec. 1, 1980.)

1972 Proposed Rules

Withdrawn pleas of guilty were held inadmissible in federal prosecutions in *Kercheval v. United States,* 274 U.S. 220, 47 S.Ct. 582, 71 L.Ed. 1009 (1927). The Court pointed out that to admit the withdrawn plea would effectively set at naught the allowance of withdrawal and place the accused in a dilemma utterly inconsistent with the decision to award him a trial. The New York Court of Appeals, in *People v. Spitaleri,* 9 N.Y.2d 168, 212 N.Y.S.2d 53, 173 N.E.2d 35 (1961), reexamined and overturned its earlier decisions which had allowed admission. In addition to the reasons set forth in Kercheval, which was quoted at length, the court pointed out that the effect of admitting the plea was to compel defendant to take the stand by way of explanation and to open the way for the prosecution to call the lawyer who had represented him at the time of entering the plea. State court decisions for and against admissibility are collected in Annot., 86 A.L.R.2d 326.

Pleas of *nolo contendere* are recognized by Rule 11 of the Rules of Criminal Procedure, although the law of numerous States is to the contrary. The present rule gives effect to the principal traditional characteristic of the *nolo* plea, i.e. avoiding the admission of guilt which is inherent in pleas of guilty. This position is consistent with the construction of Section 5 of the Clayton Act, 15 U.S.C. § 16(a), recognizing the inconclusive and compromise nature of judgments based on *nolo* pleas. *General Electric Co. v. City of San Antonio,* 334 F.2d 480 (5th Cir.1964); *Commonwealth Edison Co. v. Allis–Chalmers Mfg. Co.,* 323 F.2d 412 (7th Cir.1963), cert. denied 376 U.S. 939, 84 S.Ct. 794, 11 L.Ed.2d 659; *Armco Steel Corp. v. North Dakota,* 376 F.2d 206 (8th Cir.1967); *City of Burbank v. General Electric Co.,* 329 F.2d 825 (9th Cir.1964). See also state court decisions in Annot., 18 A.L.R.2d 1287, 1314.

Exclusion of offers to plead guilty or *nolo* has as its purpose the promotion of disposition of criminal cases by compromise. As pointed out in McCormick § 251, p. 543.

"Effective criminal law administration in many localities would hardly be possible if a large proportion of the charges were not disposed of by such compromises."

See also *People v. Hamilton,* 60 Cal.2d 105, 32 Cal.Rptr. 4, 383 P.2d 412 (1963), discussing legislation designed to achieve this result. As with compromise offers generally, Rule 408, free communication is needed, and security against having an offer of compromise or related statement admitted in evidence effectively encourages it.

Limiting the exclusionary rule to use against the accused is consistent with the purpose of the rule, since the possibility of use for or against other persons will not impair the effectiveness of withdrawing pleas or the freedom of discussion which the rule is designed to foster. See A.B.A. Standards Relating to Pleas of Guilty § 2.2 (1968). See also the narrower provisions of New Jersey Evidence Rule 52(2) and the unlimited exclusion provided in California Evidence Code § 1153.

1974 Enactment

The Committee added the phrase "Except as otherwise provided by Act of Congress" to Rule 410 as submitted by the Court in order to preserve particular congressional policy judgments as to the effect of a plea of guilty or of nolo contendere. See 15 U.S.C. 16(a). The Committee intends that its amendment refers to both present statutes and statutes subsequently enacted. House Report No. 93–650.

As adopted by the House, rule 410 would make inadmissible pleas of guilty or nolo contendere subsequently withdrawn as well as offers to make such pleas. Such a rule is clearly justified as a means of encouraging pleading. However, the House rule would then go on to render inadmissible for any purpose statements made in connection with these pleas or offers as well.

The committee finds this aspect of the House rule unjustified. Of course, in certain circumstances such statements should be excluded. If, for example, a plea is vitiated because of coercion, statements made in connection with the plea may also have been coerced and should be inadmissible on that basis. In other cases, however, voluntary statements of an accused made in court on the record, in connection with a plea, and determined by a court to be reliable should be admissible even though the plea is subsequently withdrawn. This is particularly true in those cases where, if the House rule were in effect, a defendant would be able to contradict his previous statements and thereby lie with impunity [See *Harris v. New York,* 401 U.S. 222 (1971)]. To prevent such an injustice, the rule has been modified to permit the use of such statements for the limited purposes of impeachment and in subsequent perjury or false statement prosecutions. Senate Report No. 93–1277.

The House bill provides that evidence of a guilty or nolo contendere plea, of an offer of either plea, or of statements made in connection with such pleas or offers of such pleas, is inadmissible in any civil or criminal action, case or proceeding against the person making such plea or offer. The Senate amendment makes the rule inapplicable to a voluntary and reliable statement made in court on the record where the statement is offered in a subsequent prosecution of the declarant for perjury or false statement.

The issues raised by Rule 410 are also raised by proposed Rule 11(e)(6) of the Federal Rules of Criminal Procedure presently pending before Congress. This proposed rule, which deals with the admissibility of pleas of guilty or nolo contendere, offers to make such pleas, and statements made in connection with such pleas, was promulgated by the Supreme Court on April 22, 1974, and in the absence of congressional action will become effective on August 1, 1975. The conferees intend to make no change in the presently-existing case law until that date, leaving the courts free to develop rules in this area on a case-by-case basis.

The Conferees further determined that the issues presented by the use of guilty and nolo contendere pleas, offers of such pleas, and statements made in connection with such pleas or offers, can be explored in greater detail during Congressional consideration of Rule 11(e)(6) of the Federal Rules of Criminal Procedure. The Conferees believe, therefore, that it is best to defer its effective date until August 1, 1975. The Conferees intend that Rule 410 would be superseded by any subsequent Federal Rule of Criminal Procedure or act of Congress with which it is inconsistent, if the Federal Rule of Criminal Procedure or Act of Congress takes effect or becomes law after the date of the enactment of the act establishing the rules of evidence.

The conference adopts the Senate amendment with an amendment that expresses the above intentions. House Report No. 93–1597.

1979 Amendments

Present rule 410 conforms to rule 11(e)(6) of the Federal Rules of Criminal Procedure. A proposed amendment to rule 11(e)(6) would clarify the circumstances in which pleas, plea discussions and related statements are inadmissible in evidence: see Advisory Committee Note thereto. The amendment proposed above would make comparable changes in rule 410.

HISTORICAL NOTES

References in Text

Rule 11 of the Federal Rules of Criminal Procedure, referred to in par. (3), is classified to Title 18, Federal Rules of Criminal Procedure.

Rule 411. Liability Insurance

Evidence that a person was or was not insured against liability is not admissible upon the issue whether the person acted negligently or otherwise wrongfully. This rule does not require the exclusion of evidence of insurance against liability when offered for another purpose, such as proof of agency, ownership, or control, or bias or prejudice of a witness. (Pub.L. 93–595, § 1, Jan. 2, 1975, 88 Stat.1933; Mar. 2, 1987, eff. Oct. 1, 1987.)

1972 Proposed Rules

The courts have with substantial unanimity rejected evidence of liability insurance for the purpose of proving fault, and absence of liability insurance as proof of lack of fault. At best the inference of fault from the fact of insurance coverage is a tenuous one, as is its converse. More important, no doubt, has been the feeling that knowledge of the presence or absence of liability insurance would induce juries to decide cases on improper grounds. McCormick § 168; Annot., 4 A.L.R.2d 761. The rule is drafted in broad terms so as to include contributory negligence or other fault of a plaintiff as well as fault of a defendant.

The second sentence points out the limits of the rule, using well established illustrations. *Id.*

For similar rules see Uniform Rule 54; California Evidence Code § 1155; Kansas Code of Civil Procedure § 60–454; New Jersey Evidence Rule 54.

1987 Amendments

The amendment is technical. No substantive change is intended.

Rule 412. Sex Offense Cases; Relevance of Alleged Victim's Past Sexual Behavior or Alleged Sexual Predisposition

(a) Evidence generally inadmissible.—**The following evidence is not admissible in any civil or criminal proceeding involving alleged sexual misconduct except as provided in subdivisions (b) and (c):**

(1) Evidence offered to prove that any alleged victim engaged in other sexual behavior.

(2) Evidence offered to prove any alleged victim's sexual predisposition.

(b) Exceptions.—

(1) In a criminal case, the following evidence is admissible, if otherwise admissible under these rules:

(A) evidence of specific instances of sexual behavior by the alleged victim offered to prove that a person other than the accused was the source of semen, injury or other physical evidence;

(B) evidence of specific instances of sexual behavior by the alleged victim with respect to the person accused of the sexual misconduct offered by the accused to prove consent or by the prosecution; and

(C) evidence the exclusion of which would violate the constitutional rights of the defendant.

(2) In a civil case, evidence offered to prove the sexual behavior or sexual predisposition of any alleged victim is admissible if it is otherwise admissible under these rules and its probative value substantially outweighs the danger of harm to any victim and of unfair prejudice to any party. Evidence of an alleged victim's reputation is admissible only if it has been placed in controversy by the alleged victim.

(c) Procedure to determine admissibility.—

(1) A party intending to offer evidence under subdivision (b) must—

(A) file a written motion at least 14 days before trial specifically describing the evidence and stating the purpose for which it is offered unless the court, for good cause requires a different time for filing or permits filing during trial; and

(B) serve the motion on all parties and notify the alleged victim or, when appropriate, the alleged victim's guardian or representative.

(2) Before admitting evidence under this rule the court must conduct a hearing in camera and afford the victim and parties a right to attend and be heard. The motion, related papers, and the record of the hearing must be sealed and remain under seal unless the court orders otherwise.

(Added Pub.L. 95–540, § 2(a), Oct. 28, 1978, 92 Stat. 2046, and amended Pub.L. 100–690, Title VII, § 7046(a), Nov. 18, 1988, 102 Stat. 4400; Apr. 29, 1994, eff. Dec. 1, 1994; Pub.L. 103–322, Title IV, § 40141(b), Sept. 13, 1994, 108 Stat. 1919.)

1994 Amendments

Rule 412 has been revised to diminish some of the confusion engendered by the original rule and to expand the protection afforded alleged victims of sexual misconduct. Rule 412 applies to both civil and criminal proceedings. The rule aims to safeguard the alleged victim against the invasion of privacy, potential embarrassment and sexual stereotyping that is associated with public disclosure of intimate sexual details and the infusion of sexual innuendo into the factfinding process. By affording victims protection in most instances, the rule also encourages victims of sexual misconduct to institute and to participate in legal proceedings against alleged offenders

Rule 412 seeks to achieve these objectives by barring evidence relating to the alleged victim's sexual behavior or alleged sexual predisposition, whether offered as substantive evidence of for impeachment, except in designated circumstances in which the probative value of the evidence significantly outweighs possible harm to the victim.

The revised rule applies in all cases involving sexual misconduct without regard to whether the alleged victim or person accused is a party to the litigation. Rule 412 extends to "pattern" witnesses in both criminal and civil cases whose testimony about other instances of sexual misconduct by the person accused is otherwise admissible. When the case does not involve alleged sexual misconduct, evidence relating to a third-party witness' alleged sexual activities is not within the ambit of Rule 412. The witness will, however, be protected by other rules such as Rules 404 and 608, as well as Rule 403.

The terminology "alleged victim" is used because there will frequently be a factual dispute as to whether sexual misconduct occurred. It does not connote any requirement that the misconduct be alleged in the pleadings. Rule 412 does not, however, apply unless the person against whom the evidence is offered can reasonably be characterized as a "victim of alleged sexual misconduct." When this is not the case, as for instance in a defamation action involving statements concerning sexual misconduct in which the evidence is offered to show that the alleged defamatory statements were true or did not damage the plaintiff's reputation, neither Rule 404 nor this rule will operate to bar the evidence; Rule 401 and 403 will continue to control. Rule 412 will, however, apply in a Title VII action in which the plaintiff has alleged sexual harassment.

The reference to a person "accused" is also used in a nontechnical sense. There is no requirement that there be a criminal charge pending against the person or even that the misconduct would constitute a criminal offense. Evidence offered to prove allegedly false prior claims by the victim is not barred by Rule 412. However, the evidence is subject to the requirements of Rule 404.

Subdivision (a). As amended, Rule 412 bars evidence offered to prove the victim's sexual behavior and alleged sexual predisposition. Evidence, which might otherwise be admissible under Rules 402, 404(b), 405, 607, 608, 609 of some other evidence rule, must be excluded if Rule 412 so requires. The word "other" is used to suggest some flexibility in admitting evidence "intrinsic" to the alleged sexual misconduct. *Cf.* Committee Note to 1991 amendment to Rule 404(b)

Past sexual behavior connotes all activities that involve actual physical conduct, i.e. sexual intercourse or sexual contact. *See, e.g., United States v. Galloway*, 937 F.2d 542 (10th Cir. 1991), *cert. denied*, 113 S.Ct. 418 (1992) (use of contraceptives inadmissible since use implies sexual activity); *United States v. One Feather*, 702 F.2d 736 (8th Cir. 1983) (birth of an illegitimate child inadmissible); *State v. Carmichael*, 727 P.2d 918, 925 (Kan. 1986) (evidence of venereal disease inadmissible). In addition, the word "behavior" should be construed to include activities of the mind, such as fantasies of dreams. *See* 23 C. Wright and K. Graham, Jr., *Federal Practice and Procedure*, § 5384 at p. 548 (1980) ("While there may be some doubt under statutes that require 'conduct,' it would seem that the language of Rule 412 is broad enough to encompass the behavior of the mind.").

The rule has been amended to also exclude all other evidence relating to an alleged victim of sexual misconduct that is offered to prove a sexual predisposition. This amendment is designed to exclude evidence that does not directly refer to sexual activities or thoughts but that the proponent believes may have a sexual connotation for the factfinder. Admission of such evidence would contravene Rule 412's objectives of shielding the alleged victim from potential embarrassment and safeguarding the victim against stereotypical thinking. Consequently, unless the (b)(2) exception is satisfied, evidence such as that relating to the alleged victim's mode of dress, speech, or life-style will not be admissible.

The introductory phrase in subdivision (a) was deleted because it lacked clarity and contained no explicit reference to the other provisions of the law that were intended to be overridden. The conditional clause, "except as provided in subdivisions (b) and (c)" is intended to make clear that evidence of the types described in subdivision (a) is admissible only under the strictures of those sections.

The reason for extending the rule to all criminal cases is obvious. The strong social policy of protecting a victim's privacy and encouraging victims to come forward to report criminal acts is not confined to cases that involve a charge of sexual assault. The need to protect the victim is equally great when a defendant is charged with kidnapping, and evidence is offered, either to prove motive or as background, that the defendant sexually assaulted the victim.

The reason for extending Rule 412 to civil cases is equally obvious. The need to protect alleged victims against invasions of privacy, potential embarrassment, and unwarranted sexual stereotyping, and the wish to encourage victims to come forward when they have been sexually molested do not disappear because the context has shifted from a criminal prosecution to a claim for damages or injunctive relief. There is a strong social policy in not only punishing those who engage in sexual misconduct, but in also providing relief to the victim. Thus, Rule 412 applies in any civil case in which a person claims to be the victim of sexual misconduct, such as actions for sexual battery or sexual harassment.

Subdivision (b). Subdivision (b) spells out the specific circumstances in which some evidence may be admissible that would otherwise be barred by the general rule expressed in subdivision (a). As amended, Rule 412 will be virtually unchanged in criminal cases, but will provide protection to any person alleged to be a victim of sexual misconduct regardless of the charge actually brought against an accused. A new exception has been added for civil cases.

In a criminal case, evidence may be admitted under subdivision (b)(1) pursuant to three possible exceptions, provided the evidence also satisfies other requirements for admissibility specified in the Federal Rules of Evidence, including Rule 403. Subdivisions (b)(1)(A) and (b)(1)(B) require proof in the form of specific instances of sexual behavior in recognition of the limited probative value and dubious reliability of evidence of reputation or evidence in the form of an opinion.

Under subdivision (b)(1)(A), evidence of specific instances of sexual behavior with persons other than the person whose sexual misconduct is alleged may be admissible if it is offered to prove that another person was the source of semen, injury or other physical evidence. Where the prosecution has directly or indirectly asserted that the physical evidence originated with the accused, the defendant must be afforded an opportunity to prove that another person was responsible. See *United States v. Begay*, 937 F.2d 515, 523 n. 10 (10th Cir. 1991). Evidence offered for the specific purpose identified in this subdivision may still be excluded if it does not satisfy Rules 401 or 403. *See, e.g., United States v. Azure*, 845 F.2d 1503, 1505-06 (8th Cir. 1988) (10 year old victim's injuries indicated recent use of force; court excluded evidence of consensual sexual activities with witness who testified at in camera hearing that he had never hurt victim and failed to establish recent activities).

Under the exception in subdivision (b)(1)(B), evidence of specific instances of sexual behavior with respect to the person whose sexual misconduct is alleged is admissible if offered to prove consent, or offered by the prosecution. Admissible pursuant to this exception might be evidence of prior instances of sexual activities between the alleged victim and the accused, as well as statements in which the alleged victim expresses an intent to engage in sexual intercourse with the accused, or voiced sexual fantasies involving that specific accused. In a prosecution for child sexual abuse, for example, evidence of uncharged sexual activity between the accused and the alleged victim offered by the prosecution may be admissible pursuant to Rule 404(b) to show a pattern of behavior. Evidence relating to the victim's alleged sexual predisposition is not admissible pursuant to this exception.

Under subdivision (b)(1)(C), evidence of specific instances of conduct may not be excluded if the result would be to deny a criminal defendant the protections afforded by the Constitution. For example, statements in which the victim has expressed an intent to have sex with the first person encountered on a particular occasion might not be excluded without violating the due process right of a rape defendant seeking to prove consent. Recognition of this basic principle was expressed on subdivision (b)(1) of the original rule. The United States Supreme Court has recognized that in various circumstances a defendant may have a right to introduce evidence otherwise precluded by an evidence rule under the Confrontation Clause. *See, e.g., Olden v. Kentucky*, 488 U.S. 227 (1988) (defendant in rape cases had right to inquire into alleged victim's cohabitation with another man to show bias).

Subdivision (b)(2) governs the admissibility of otherwise proscribed evidence in civil cases. It employs a balancing test rather than the specific exceptions stated in subdivision (b)(1) in recognition of the difficulty of foreseeing future developments in the law. Greater flexibility is needed to accommodate evolving causes of action such as claims for sexual harassment.

The balancing test requires the proponent of the evidence, whether plaintiff or defendant, to convince the court that the probative value of the proffered evidence "substantially outweighs the danger of harm to any victim and of unfair prejudice of any party." This test for admitting evidence offered to prove sexual behavior or sexual propensity in civil cases differs in three respects from the general rule governing admissibility set forth in Rule 403. First, it Reverses that usual procedure spelled out in Rule 403 by shifting the burden to the proponent to demonstrate admissibility rather than making the opponent justify exclusion of the evidence. Second, the standard expressed in subdivision (b)(2) is more stringent than in the original rule; it raises the threshold for admission by requiring that the probative value of the evidence *substantially* outweigh the specified dangers. Finally, the Rule 412 test puts "harm to the victim" on the scale in addition to prejudice to the parties.

Evidence of reputation may be received in a civil case only if the alleged victim has put his or her reputation into controversy. The victim may do so without making a specific allegation in a pleading. *Cf.* Fed.R.Civ.P. 35(a).

Subdivision (c). Amended subdivision (c) is more concise and understandable than the subdivision it replaces. The requirement of a motion before trial is continued in the amended rule, as is the provision that a late motion may be permitted for good cause shown. In deciding whether to permit late filing, the court may take into account the conditions previously included in the rule: namely whether the evidence is newly discovered and could not have been obtained earlier through the existence of due diligence, and whether the issue to which such evidence relates has newly arisen in the case. The rule recognizes that in some instances the circumstances that justify an application to introduce evidence otherwise barred by Rule 412 will not become apparent until trial.

The amended rule provides that before admitting evidence that falls within that prohibition of Rule 412(a), the court must hold a hearing in camera at which the alleged victim and any party must be afforded the right to be present and an opportunity to be heard. All papers connected with the motion must be kept and remain under seal during the course of trial and appellate proceedings unless otherwise ordered. This is to assure that the privacy of the alleged victim is preserved in all cases in which the court rules that proffered evidence is not admissible, and in which the hearing refers to matters that are not received, or are received in another form.

The procedures set forth in subdivision (c) do not apply to discovery of a victim's past sexual conduct or predisposition in civil cases, which will be continued to be governed by Fed. R. Civ. P. 26. In order not to undermine the rationale of Rule 412, however, courts should enter appropriate orders pursuant to Fed. R. Civ. P. 26 (c) to protect the victim against unwarranted inquiries and to ensure confidentiality. Courts should presumptively issue protective orders barring discovery unless the party seeking discovery makes a showing that the evidence sought to be discovered would be relevant under the facts and theories of the particular case, and cannot be obtained except through discovery. In an action for sexual harassment, for instance, while some evidence of the alleged victim's sexual behavior and/or predisposition in the workplace may perhaps be relevant, non-work place conduct will usually be irrelevant. *Cf. Burns v. McGregor Electronic Industries, Inc.*, 989 F.2d 959, 962-63 (8th Cir. 1993) (posing for a nude magazine outside work hours is irrelevant to issue of unwelcomeness of sexual advances at work). Confidentiality orders should be presumptively granted as well.

One substantive change made in subdivision (c) is the elimination of the following sentence: "Notwithstanding subdivision (b) of Rule 104, if the relevancy of the evidence which the accused seeks to offer in trial depends upon the fulfillment of a condition of fact, the court, at the hearing in chambers or at a subsequent hearing in chambers scheduled for such purpose, shall accept evidence on the issue of whether such condition of fact is fulfilled and shall determine such issue." On its face, this language would appear to authorize a trial judge to exclude evidence of past sexual conduct between alleged victim and an accused or a defendant in a civil case based upon the judge's belief that such past acts did not occur. Such an authorization raises questions of invasion of the right to a jury trial under the Sixth and Seventh Amendments. *See* 1 S. Saltzburg & M. Martin, *Federal Rules of Evidence Manual*, 396-97 (5th ed. 1990).

The Advisory Committee concluded that the amended rule provided adequate protection for all persons claiming to be the victims of sexual misconduct, and that it was inadvisable to continue to include a provision in the rule that has been confusing and that raises substantial constitutional issues. [Advisory Committee Note adopted by Congressional Conference Report accompanying Pub.L. 103–322. See H.R. Conf. Rep. No. 103–711, 103rd Cong., 2nd Sess., 383 (1994).]

Congressional Discussion

The following discussion in the House of Representatives of October 10, 1978, preceded passage of H.R. 4727, which enacted Rule 412. The discussion appears in 124 Cong.Record, at page H. 11944.

Mr. MANN. Mr. Speaker, I yield myself such time as I may consume.

Mr. Speaker, for many years in this country, evidentiary rules have permitted the introduction of evidence about a rape victim's prior sexual conduct. Defense lawyers were permitted great latitude in bringing out intimate details about a rape victim's life. Such evidence quite often serves no real purpose and only results in embarrassment to the rape victim and unwarranted public intrusion into her private life.

The evidentiary rules that permit such inquiry have in recent years come under question; and the States have taken the lead to change and modernize their evidentiary rules about evidence of a rape victim's prior sexual behavior. The bill before us similarly seeks to modernize the Federal Evidentiary rules.

The present Federal Rules of Evidence reflect the traditional approach. If a defendant in a rape case raises the defense of consent, that defendant may then offer evidence about the victim's prior sexual behavior. Such evidence may be in the form of opinion evidence, evidence of reputation, or evidence of specific instances of behavior. Rule 404(a)(2) of the Federal Rules of Evidence permits the introduction of evidence of a "pertinent character trait." The advisory committee note to that rule cites, as an example of what the rule covers, the character of a rape victim when the issue is consent. Rule 405 of the Federal Rules of Evidence permits the use of opinion or reputation evidence or the use of evidence of specific behavior to show a character trait.

Thus, Federal evidentiary rules permit a wide ranging inquiry into the private conduct of a rape victim, even though that conduct may have at best a tenuous connection to the offense for which the defendant is being tried.

H.R. 4727 amends the Federal Rules of Evidence to add a new rule, applicable only in criminal cases, to spell out when, and under what conditions, evidence of a rape victim's prior sexual behavior can be admitted. The new rule provides that reputation or opinion evidence about a rape victim's prior sexual behavior is not admissible. The new rule also provides that a court cannot admit evidence of specific instances of a rape victim's prior sexual conduct except in three circumstances.

The first circumstance is where the Constitution requires that the evidence be admitted. This exception is intended to cover those infrequent instances where, because of an unusual chain of circumstances, the general rule of inadmissibility, if followed, would result in denying the defendant a constitutional right.

The second circumstance in which the defendant can offer evidence of specific instances of a rape victim's prior sexual behavior is where the defendant raises the issue of consent and the evidence is of sexual behavior with the defendant. To admit such evidence, however, the court must find that the evidence is relevant and that its probative value outweighs the danger of unfair prejudice.

The third circumstance in which a court can admit evidence of specific instances of a rape victim's prior sexual behavior is where the evidence is of behavior with someone other than the defendant and is offered by the defendant on the issue of whether or not he was the source of semen or injury. Again, such evidence will be admitted only if the court finds that the evidence is relevant and that its probative value outweighs the danger of unfair prejudice.

The new rule further provides that before evidence is admitted under any of these exceptions, there must be an in camera hearing—that is, a proceeding that takes place in the judge's chambers out of the presence of the jury and the general public. At this hearing, the defendant will present the evidence he intends to offer and be able to argue why it should be admitted. The prosecution, of course, will be able to argue against that evidence being admitted.

The purpose of the in camera hearing is twofold. It gives the defendant an opportunity to demonstrate to the court why certain evidence is admissible and ought to be presented to the jury. At the same time, it protects the privacy of the rape victim in those instances when the court finds that evidence is inadmissible. Of course, if the court finds the evidence to be admissible, the evidence will be presented to the jury in open court.

The effect of this legislation, therefore, is to preclude the routine use of evidence of specific instances of a rape victim's prior sexual behavior. Such evidence will be admitted only in clearly and narrowly defined circumstances and only after an in camera hearing. In determining the admissibility of such evidence, the court will consider all of the facts and circumstances surrounding the evidence, such as the amount of time that lapsed between the alleged prior act and the rape charged in the prosecution. The greater the lapse of time, of course, the less likely it is that such evidence will be admitted.

Mr. Speaker, the principal purpose of this legislation is to protect rape victims from the degrading and embarrassing disclosure of intimate details about their private lives. It does so by narrowly circumscribing when such evidence may be admitted. It does not do so, however, by sacrificing any constitutional right possessed by the defendant. The bill before us fairly balances the interests involved—the rape victim's interest in protecting her private life from unwarranted public exposure; the defendant's interest in being able adequately to present a defense by offering relevant and probative evidence; and society's interest in a fair trial, one where unduly prejudicial evidence is not permitted to becloud the issues before the jury.

I urge support of the bill.

Mr. WIGGINS. Mr. Speaker, I yield myself such time as I may consume.

(Mr. WIGGINS asked and was given permission to revise and extend his remarks.)

Mr. WIGGINS. Mr. Speaker, this legislation addresses itself to a subject that is certainly a proper one for our consideration. Many of us have been troubled for years about the indiscriminate and prejudicial use of testimony with respect to a victim's prior sexual behavior in rape and similar cases. This bill deals with that problem. It is not, in my opinion, Mr. Speaker, a perfect bill in the manner in which it deals with the problem, but my objections are not so fundamental as would lead me to oppose the bill.

I think, Mr. Speaker, that it is unwise to adopt a per se rule absolutely excluding evidence of reputation and opinion with respect to the victim—and this bill does that—but it is difficult for me to foresee the specific case in which such evidence might be admissible. The trouble is this, Mr. Speaker: None of us can foresee perfectly all of the various circumstances under which the propriety of evidence might be before the court. If this bill has a defect, in my view it is because it adopts a per se rule with respect to opinion and reputation evidence.

Alternatively we might have permitted that evidence to be considered in camera as we do other evidence under the bill.

I should note, however, in fairness, having expressed minor reservations, that the bill before the House at this time does improve significantly upon the bill which was presented to our committee.

I will not detail all of those improvements but simply observe that the bill upon which we shall soon vote is a superior product to that which was initially considered by our subcommittee.

Mr. Speaker, I ask my colleagues to vote for this legislation as being, on balance, worthy of their support, and urge its adoption.

I reserve the balance of my time.

Mr. MANN. Mr. Speaker, this legislation has more than 100 cosponsors, but its principal sponsor, as well as its architect is the gentlewoman from New York (Ms. Holtzman). As the drafter of the legislation she will be able to provide additional information about the probable scope and effect of the legislation.

I yield such time as she may consume to the gentlewoman from New York (Ms. Holtzman).

(Ms. HOLTZMAN asked and was given permission to revise and extend her remarks.)

Ms. HOLTZMAN. Mr. Speaker, I would like to begin first by complimenting the distinguished gentleman from South Carolina (Mr. Mann), the chairman of the subcommittee, for his understanding of the need for corrective legislation in this area and for the fairness with which he has conducted the subcommittee hearings. I would like also to compliment the other members of the subcommittee, including the gentleman from California (Mr. Wiggins).

Too often in this country victims of rape are humiliated and harassed when they report and prosecute the rape. Bullied and cross-examined about their prior sexual experiences, many find the trial almost as degrading as the rape itself. Since rape trials become inquisitions into the victim's morality, not trials of the defendant's innocence or guilt, it is not surprising that it is the least reported crime. It is estimated that as few as one in ten rapes is ever reported.

Mr. Speaker, over 30 States have taken some action to limit the vulnerability of rape victims to such humiliating cross-examination of their past sexual experiences and intimate personal histories. In federal courts, however, it is permissible still to subject rape victims to brutal cross-examination about their past sexual histories. H.R. 4727 would rectify this problem in Federal courts and I hope, also serve as a model to suggest to the remaining states that reform of existing rape laws is important to the equity of our criminal justice system.

H.R. 4727 applies only to criminal rape cases in Federal courts. The bill provides that neither the prosecution nor the defense can introduce any reputation or opinion evidence about the victim's past sexual conduct. It does permit, however, the introduction of specific evidence about the victim's past sexual conduct in three very limited circumstances.

First, this evidence can be introduced if it deals with the victim's past sexual relations with the defendant and is relevant to the issue of whether she consented. Second, when the defendant claims he had no relations with the victim, he can use evidence of the victim's past sexual relations with others if the evidence rebuts the victim's claim that the rape caused certain physical consequences, such as semen or injury. Finally, the evidence can be introduced if it is constitutionally required. This last exception, added in subcommittee, will insure that the defendant's constitutional rights are protected.

Before any such evidence can be introduced, however, the court must determine at a hearing in chambers that the evidence falls within one of the exceptions.

Furthermore, unless constitutionally required, the evidence of specific instances of prior sexual conduct cannot be introduced at all it if would be more prejudicial and inflammatory that probative.

Mr. Speaker, I urge adoption of this bill. It will protect women from both injustice and indignity.

Mr. MANN. Mr. Speaker, I have no further requests for time, and I yield back the balance of my time.

Mr. WIGGINS. Mr. Speaker, I have no further requests for time, and yield back the balance of my time.

The SPEAKER pro tempore. The question is on the motion offered by the gentleman from South Carolina (Mr. Mann) that the House suspend the rules and pass the bill H.R. 4727, as amended.

The question was taken; and (two-thirds having voted in favor thereof) the rules were suspended and the bill, as amended, was passed.

A motion to reconsider was laid on the table.

HISTORICAL NOTES

Effective and Applicability Provisions

1978 Acts. Section 3 of Pub.L. 95–540 provided that: "The amendments made by this Act [enacting this rule] shall apply to trials which begin more than thirty days after the date of the enactment of this Act [Oct. 28, 1978]."

Rule 413. Evidence of Similar Crimes in Sexual Assault Cases

(a) In a criminal case in which the defendant is accused of an offense of sexual assault, evidence of the defendant's commission of another offense or offenses of sexual assault is admissible, and may be considered for its bearing on any matter to which it is relevant.

(b) In a case in which the Government intends to offer evidence under this rule, the attorney for the Government shall disclose the evidence to the defendant, including statements of witnesses or a summary of the substance of any testimony that is expected to be offered, at least fifteen days before the scheduled date of trial or at such later time as the court may allow for good cause.

(c) This rule shall not be construed to limit the admission or consideration of evidence under any other rule.

(d) For purposes of this rule and Rule 415, "offense of sexual assault" means a crime under Federal law or the law of a State (as defined in section 513 of title 18, United States Code) that involved—

(1) any conduct proscribed by chapter 109A of title 18, United States Code;

(2) contact, without consent, between any part of the defendant's body or an object and the genitals or anus of another person;

(3) contact, without consent, between the genitals or anus of the defendant and any part of another person's body;

(4) deriving sexual pleasure or gratification from the infliction of death, bodily injury, or physical pain on another person; or

(5) an attempt or conspiracy to engage in conduct described in paragraphs (1)–(4).

(Added Pub.L. 103–322, Title XXXII, § 320935(a), Sept. 13, 1994, 108 Stat. 2136.)

HISTORICAL NOTES

Effective and Applicability Provisions

Section 320935(b) to (e) of Pub.L. 103–322, as amended Pub.L. 104–208, Div. A, Title I, § 101(a), [Title I, § 120], Sept. 30, 1996, 110 Stat. 3009–25, provided that:

"**(b) Implementation.**—The amendments made by subsection (a) [enacting Federal Rules of Evidence 413, 414, and 415] shall become effective pursuant to subsection (d).

"**(c) Recommendations by Judicial Conference.**—Not later than 150 days after the date of enactment of this Act [Sept. 13, 1994], the Judicial Conference of the United States shall transmit to Congress a report containing recommendations for amending the Federal Rules of Evidence as they affect the admission of evidence of a defendant's prior sexual assault or child molestation crimes in cases involving sexual assault and child molestation. The Rules Enabling Act [28 U.S.C.A. § 2072] shall not apply to the recommendations made by the Judicial Conference pursuant to this section.

"**(d)** Congressional action.—

"**(1)** If the recommendations described in subsection (c) are the same as the amendment made by subsection (a) [enacting Federal Rules of Evidence 413, 414, and 415], then the amendments made by subsection (a) shall become effective 30 days after the transmittal of the recommendations.

"(2) If the recommendations described in subsection (c) are different than the amendments made by subsection (a) [enacting Federal Rules of Evidence 413, 414, and 415], the amendments made by subsection (a) shall become effective 150 days after the transmittal of the recommendations unless otherwise provided by law.

"(3) If the Judicial Conference fails to comply with subsection (c), the amendments made by subsection (a) [enacting Federal of Evidence 413, 414, and 415] shall become effective 150 days after the date the recommendations were due under subsection (c) unless otherwise provided by law.

"**(e) Application.**—The amendments made by subsection (a) [enacting Federal Rules of Evidence 413, 414, and 415] shall apply to proceedings commenced on or after the effective date of such amendments, including all trials commenced on or after the effective date of such amendments."

[The Judicial Conference transmitted a report to Congress on Feb. 9, 1995, containing recommendations described in subsec. (c) different than the amendments made by section 320935(a) of Pub.L. 103–322. Congress did not follow the recommendations submitted or provide otherwise by law. Accordingly, Rules 413, 414, and 415, as added by section 320935(a) of Pub.L. 103–322, became effective on July 9, 1995.]

Submitted to the Congress in accordance with section 320935 of the Violent Crime Control and Law Enforcement Act of 1994 (Pub.L. No. 103–322)

I. INTRODUCTION

This report is transmitted to Congress in accordance with the Violent Crime Control and Law Enforcement Act of 1994, Pub.L. No. 103–322 (September 13, 1994). Section 320935 of the Act invited the Judicial Conference of the United States within 150 days (February 10, 1995) to submit "a report containing recommendations for amending the Federal Rules of Evidence as they affect the admission of evidence of a defendant's prior sexual assault or child molestation crimes in cases involving sexual assault or child molestation."

Under the Act, new Rules 413, 414, and 415 would be added to the Federal Rules of Evidence. These Rules would admit evidence of a defendant's past similar acts in criminal and civil cases involving a sexual assault or child molestation offense for its bearing on any matter to which it is relevant. The effective date of new Rules 413–415 is contingent in part upon the nature of the recommendations submitted by the Judicial Conference.

After careful study, the Judicial Conference urges Congress to reconsider its decision on the policy questions underlying the new rules for reasons set out in Part III below.

If Congress does not reconsider its decision on the underlying policy questions, the Judicial Conference recommends incorporation of the provisions of new Rules 413–415 as amendments to Rules 404 and 405 of the Federal Rules of Evidence. The amendments would not change the substance of the congressional enactment but would clarify drafting ambiguities and eliminate possible constitutional infirmities.

II. BACKGROUND

Under the Act, the Judicial Conference was provided 150 days within which to make and submit to Congress alternative recommendations to new Evidence Rules 413–415. Consideration of Rules 413–415 by the Judicial Conference was specifically excepted from the exacting review procedures set forth in the Rules Enabling Act (codified at 28 U.S.C. §§ 2071–2077). Although the Conference acted on these new rules on an expedited basis to meet the Act's deadlines, the review process was thorough.

The new rules would apply to both civil and criminal cases. Accordingly, the Judicial Conference's Advisory Committee on Criminal Rules and the Advisory Committee on Civil Rules reviewed the rules at separate meetings in October 1994. At the same time and in preparation for its consideration of the new rules, the Advisory Committee on Evidence Rules sent out a notice soliciting comment on new Evidence Rules 413, 414, and 415. The notice was sent to the courts, including all federal judges, about 900 evidence law professors, 40 women's rights organizations, and 1,000 other individuals and interested organizations.

III. DISCUSSION

On October 17–18, 1994, the Advisory Committee on Evidence Rules met in Washington, D.C. It considered the public responses, which included 84 written comments, representing 112 individuals, 8 local and 8 national legal organizations. The overwhelming majority of judges, lawyers, law professors, and legal organizations who responded opposed new Evidence Rules 413, 414, and 415. The principal objections expressed were that the rules would permit the admission of unfairly prejudicial evidence and contained numerous drafting problems not intended by their authors.

The Advisory Committee on Evidence Rules submitted its report to the Judicial Conference Committee on Rules of Practice and Procedure (Standing Committee) for review at its January 11–13, 1995 meeting. The committee's report was unanimous except for a dissenting vote by the representative of the Department of Justice. The advisory committee believed that the concerns expressed by Congress and embodied in new Evidence Rules 413, 414, and 415 are already adequately addressed in the existing Federal Rules of Evidence. In particular, Evidence Rule 404(b) now allows the admission of evidence against a criminal defendant of the commission of prior crimes, wrongs, or acts for specified purposes, including to show intent, plan, motive, preparation, identity, knowledge, or absence of mistake or accident.

Furthermore, the new rules, which are not supported by empirical evidence, could diminish significantly the protections that have safeguarded persons accused in criminal cases and parties in civil cases against undue prejudice. These protections form a fundamental part of American jurisprudence and have evolved under long-standing rules and case law. A significant concern identified by the committee was the danger of convicting a criminal defendant for past, as opposed to charged, behavior or for being a bad person.

In addition, the advisory committee concluded that, because prior bad acts would be admissible even though not the subject of a conviction, mini-trials within trials concerning those acts would result when a defendant seeks to rebut such evidence. The committee also noticed that many of the comments received had concluded that the Rules, as drafted, were mandatory—that is, such evidence had to be admitted regardless of other rules of evidence such as the hearsay rule or the Rule 403 balancing test. The committee believed that this position was arguable because Rules 413–415 declare without qualification that such evidence "is admissible." In contrast, the new Rule 412, passed as part of the same legislation, provided that certain evidence "is admissible if it is otherwise admissible under these Rules." Fed.R.Evid. 412(b)(2). If the critics are right, Rules 413–415 free the prosecution from rules that apply to the defendant—including the hearsay rule and Rule 403. If so, serious constitutional questions would arise.

The Advisory Committees on Criminal and Civil Rules unanimously, except for representatives of the Department of Justice, also opposed the new rules. Those committees also concluded that the new rules would permit the introduction of unreliable but highly prejudicial evidence and would complicate trials by causing mini-trials of other alleged wrongs. After the advisory committees reported, the Standing Committee unanimously, again except for the representative of the Department of Justice, agreed with the view of the advisory committees.

It is important to note the highly unusual unanimity of the members of the Standing and Advisory Committees, composed of over 40 judges, practicing lawyers, and academicians, in taking the view that Rules 413–415 are undesirable. Indeed, the only supporters of the Rules were representatives of the Department of Justice.

For these reasons, the Standing Committee recommended that Congress reconsider its decision on the policy questions embodied in new Evidence Rules 413, 414, and 415.

However, if Congress will not reconsider its decision on the policy questions, the Standing Committee recommended that Congress consider an alternative draft recommended by the Advisory Committee on Evidence Rules. That Committee drafted proposed amendments to existing Evidence Rules 404 and 405 that would both correct ambiguities and possible constitutional infirmities identified in new Evidence Rules 413, 414, and 415 yet still effectuate Congressional intent. In particular, the proposed amendments:

(1) expressly apply the other rules of evidence to evidence offered under the new rules;

(2) expressly allow the party against whom such evidence is offered to use similar evidence in rebuttal;

(3) expressly enumerate the factors to be weighed by a court in making its Rule 403 determination;

(4) render the notice provisions consistent with the provisions in existing Rule 404 regarding criminal cases;

(5) eliminate the special notice provisions of Rules 413–415 in civil cases so that notice will be required as provided in the Federal Rules of Civil Procedure; and

(6) permit reputation or opinion evidence after such evidence is offered by the accused or defendant.

The Standing Committee reviewed the new rules and the alternative recommendations. It concurred with the views of the Evidence Rules Committee and recommended that the Judicial Conference adopt them.

IV. RECOMMENDATIONS

The Judicial Conference concurs with the views of the Standing Committee and urges that Congress reconsider its policy determinations underlying Evidence Rules 413–415. In the alternative, the attached amendments to Evidence Rules 404 and 405 are recommended, in lieu of new Evidence Rules 413, 414, and 415. The alternative amendments to Evidence Rules 404 and 405 are accompanied by the Advisory Committee Notes, which explain them in detail.

RULE 404. CHARACTER EVIDENCE NOT ADMISSIBLE TO PROVE CONDUCT; EXCEPTIONS; OTHER CRIMES

* * * * * * *

(4) **Character in sexual misconduct cases.** Evidence of another act of sexual assault or child molestation, or evidence to rebut such proof or an inference therefrom, if that evidence is otherwise admissible under these rules, in a criminal case in which the accused is charged with sexual assault or child molestation, or in a civil case in which a claim is predicated on a party's alleged commission of sexual assault or child molestation.

(A) In weighing the probative value of such evidence, the court may, as part of its rule 403 determination, consider:

(i) proximity in time to the charged or predicate misconduct;

(ii) similarity to the charged or predicate misconduct;

(iii) frequency of the other acts;

(iv) surrounding circumstances;

(v) relevant intervening events; and

(vi) other relevant similarities or differences.

(B) In a criminal case in which the prosecution intends to offer evidence under this subdivision, it must disclose the evidence, including statements of witnesses or a summary of the substance of any testimony, at a reasonable time in advance of trial, or during trial if the court excuses pretrial notice on good cause shown.

(C) For purposes of this subdivision.

(i) "sexual assault" means conduct—or an attempt or conspiracy to engage in conduct—of the type proscribed by chapter 109A of title 18, United States Code, or conduct that involved deriving sexual pleasure or gratification from inflicting death, bodily injury, or physical pain on another person irrespective of the age of the victim—regardless of whether that conduct would have subjected the actor to federal jurisdiction.

(ii) "child molestation" means conduct—or an attempt or conspiracy to engage in conduct—of the type proscribed by chapter 110 of title 18, United States Code, or conduct, committed in relation to a child below the age of 14 years, either of the type proscribed by chapter 109A of title 18, United States Code, or that involved deriving sexual pleasure or gratification from inflicting death, bodily injury, or physical pain on another person—regardless of whether that conduct would have subjected the actor to federal jurisdiction.

(b) **Other crimes, wrongs, or acts.** Evidence of other crimes, wrongs, or acts is not admissible to prove the character of a person in order to show action in conformity therewith except as provided in subdivision (a). . . .

Note to Rule 404(a)(4)

The Committee has redrafted Rules 413, 414 and 415 which the Violent Crime Control and Law Enforcement Act of 1994 conditionally added to the Federal Rules of Evidence.[1] These modifications do not change the substance of the congressional enactment. The changes were made in order to integrate the provisions both substantively and stylistically with the existing Rules of Evidence; to illuminate the intent expressed by the principal drafters of the measure; to clarify drafting ambiguities that might necessitate considerable judicial attention if they remained unresolved; and to eliminate possible constitutional infirmities.

The Committee placed the new provisions in Rule 404 because this rule governs the admissibility of character evidence. The congressional enactment constitutes a new exception to the general rule stated in subdivision (a). The Committee also combined the three separate rules proposed by Congress into one subdivision (a)(4) in accordance with the rules' customary practice of treating criminal and civil issues jointly. An amendment to Rule 405 has been added because the authorization of a new form of character evidence in this rule has an impact on methods of proving character that were not explicitly addressed by Congress. The stylistic changes are self-evident. They are particularly noticeable in the definition section in subdivision (a)(4)(C) in which the Committee eliminated, without any change in meaning, graphic details of sexual acts.

The Committee added language that explicitly provides that evidence under this subdivision must satisfy other rules of evidence such as the hearsay rules in Article VIII and the expert testimony rules in Article VII. Although principal sponsors of the legislation had stated that they intended other evidentiary rules to apply, the Committee believes that the opening phrase of the new subdivision 'if otherwise admissible under these rules' is needed to clarify the relationship between subdivision (a)(4) and other evidentiary provisions.

The Committee also expressly made subdivision (a)(4) subject to Rule 403 balancing in accordance with the repeatedly stated objectives of the legislation's sponsors with which representatives of the Justice Department expressed agreement. Many commentators on Rules 413–415 had objected that Rule 403's applicability was obscured by the actual language employed.

In addition to clarifying the drafters' intent, an explicit reference to Rule 403 may be essential to insulate the rule against constitutional challenge. Constitutional concerns also led the Committee to acknowledge specifically the opposing party's right to offer in rebuttal character evidence that the rules would otherwise bar, including evidence of a third person's prior acts of sexual misconduct offered to prove that the third person rather than the party committed the acts in issue.

In order to minimize the need for extensive and time-consuming judicial interpretation, the Committee listed factors that a court may consider in discharging Rule 403 balancing. Proximity in time is taken into account in a related rule. See Rule 609(b). Similarity, frequency and surrounding circumstances have long been considered by courts in handling other crimes evidence pursuant to Rule 404(b). Relevant intervening events, such as extensive medical treatment of the accused between the time of the prior proffered act and the charged act, may affect the strength of the propensity inference for which the evidence is offered. The final factor—'other relevant similarities or differences'—is added in recognition of the endless variety of circumstances that confront a trial court in rulings on admissibility. Although subdivision (4)(A) explicitly refers to factors that bear on probative value, this enumeration does not eliminate a judge's responsibility to take into account the other factors mentioned in Rule 403 itself—'the danger of unfair prejudice, confusion of the issues, . . . misleading the jury, . . . undue delay, waste of time, or needless presentation of cumulative evidence.' In addition, the Advisory Committee Note to Rule 403 reminds judges that 'The availability of other means of proof may also be an appropriate factor.'

The Committee altered slightly the notice provision in criminal cases. Providing the trial court with some discretion to excuse pretrial notice was thought preferable to the inflexible 15–day rule provided in Rules 414 and 415. Furthermore, the formulation is identical to that contained in the 1991 amendment to Rule 404(b) so that no confusion will result from having two somewhat different notice provisions in the same rule. The Committee eliminated the notice provision for civil cases stated in Rule 415 because it did not believe that Congress intended to alter the usual time table for disclosure and discovery provided by the Federal Rules of Civil Procedure.

The definition section was simplified with no change in meaning. The reference to 'the law of a State' was eliminated as unnecessarily confusing and restrictive. Conduct committed outside the United States ought equally to be eligible for admission. Evidence offered pursuant to subdivision (a)(4) must relate to a form of conduct proscribed by either chapter 109A or 110 of title 18, United States Code, regardless of whether the actor was subject to federal jurisdiction.

RULE 405. METHODS OF PROVING CHARACTER

(a) Reputation or opinion. In all cases in which evidence of character or a trait of character of a person is admissible, proof may be made by testimony as to reputation or by testimony in the form of an opinion except as provided in subdivision (c) of this rule. On cross-examination, inquiry is allowable into relevant specific instances of conduct.

* * * * * * *

(c) Proof in sexual misconduct cases. In a case in which evidence is offered under rule 404(a)(4), proof may be made by specific instances of conduct, testimony as to reputation, or testimony in the form of an opinion, except that the prosecution or claimant may offer reputation or opinion testimony only after the opposing party has offered such testimony.

Note to Rule 405(c)

The addition of a new subdivision (a)(4) to Rule 404 necessitates adding a new subdivision (c) to Rule 405 to govern methods of proof. Congress clearly intended no change in the preexisting law that precludes the prosecution or a claimant from offering reputation or opinion testimony in its case in chief to prove that the opposing party acted in conformity with character. When evidence is admissible pursuant to Rule 404(a)(4), the proponents proof must consist of specific instances of conduct. The opposing party, however, is free to respond with reputation or opinion testimony (including expert testimony if otherwise admissible) as well as evidence of specific instances. In a criminal case, the admissibility of reputation or opinion testimony would, in any event, be authorized by Rule 404(a)(1). The extension to civil cases is essential in order to provide the opponent with an adequate opportunity to refute allegations about a character for sexual misconduct. Once the opposing party offers reputation or opinion testimony, however, the prosecution or claimant may counter using such methods of proof.

[1] Congress provided that the rules would take effect unless within a specified time period the Judicial Conference made recommendations to amend the rules that Congress enacted.

Congressional Discussion

Floor Statement of the Principal House Sponsor, Representative Susan Molinari, Concerning the Prior Crimes Evidence Rules for Sexual Assault and Child Molestation Cases (Cong.Rec. H8991-92, Aug. 21, 1994):

Mr. Speaker, the revised conference bill contains a critical reform that I have long sought to protect the public from crimes of sexual violence—general rules of admissibility in sexual assault and child molestation cases for evidence that the defendant has committed offenses of the same type on other occasions. The enactment of this reform is first and foremost a triumph for the public—for the women who will not be raped and the children who will not be molested because we have strengthened the legal system's tools for bringing the perpetrators of these atrocious crimes to justice.

Senator Dole and I initially proposed this reform in February of 1991 in the Women's Equal Opportunity Act bill, and we later re-introduced it in the Sexual Assault Prevention Act bills of the 102d and 103d Congresses. The proposal also enjoyed the strong support of the Administration in the 102d Congress, and was included in President Bush's violent crime bill of that Congress, S. 635. The Senate passed the proposed rules on Nov. 5, 1993, by a vote of 75 to 19, in a crime bill amendment offered by Senate Dole. This Chamber endorsed the same rules on June 29, 1994, by a vote of 348 to 62, through a motion to instruct conferees that I offered.

The rules in the revised conference bill are substantially identical to our earlier proposals. We have agreed to a temporary deferral of the effective date of the new rules, pending a report by the Judicial Conference, in order to accommodate procedural objections raised by opponents of the reform. However, regardless of what the Judicial Conference may recommend, the new rules will take effect within at most 300 days of the enactment of this legislation, unless repealed or modified by subsequent legislation.

The need for these rules, their precedential support, their interpretation, and the issues and policy questions they raise have been analyzed at length in the legislative history of this proposal. I would direct the Members' attention particularly to two earlier statements:

The first is the portion of the section-by-section analysis accompanying these rules in section 801 of S. 635, which President Bush transmitted to Congress in 1991. That statement appears on pages S 3238 [to] S 3242 of the daily edition of the Congressional Record for March 13, 1991.

The second is the prepared text of an address—entitled "Evidence of Propensity and Probability in Sex Offense Cases and Other Cases"—by Senior Counsel David J. Karp of the Office of Policy Development of the U.S. Department of Justice. Mr. Karp, who is the author of the new evidence rules, presented this statement on behalf of the Justice Department to the Evidence Section of the Association of American Law Schools on January 9, 1993. The statement provided a detailed account of the views of the legislative sponsors and the Administration concerning the proposed reform, and should also be considered an authoritative part of its legislative history.

These earlier statements address the issues raised by this reform in considerable detail. In my present remarks, I will simply emphasize the following essential points:

The new rules will supersede in sex offense cases the restrictive aspects of Federal Rule of Evidence 404(b). In contrast to Rule 404(b)'s general prohibition of evidence of character or propensity, the new rules for sex offense cases authorize admission and consideration of evidence of an uncharged offense for its bearing "on any matter to which it is relevant." This includes the defendant's propensity to commit sexual assault or child molestation offenses, and assessment of the probability or improbability that the defendant has been falsely or mistakenly accused of such an offense.

In other respects, the general standards of the rules of evidence will continue to apply, including the restrictions on hearsay evidence and the court's authority under Evidence Rule 403 to exclude evidence whose probative value is substantially outweighed by its prejudicial effect. Also, the government (or the plaintiff in a civil case) will generally have to disclose to the defendant any evidence that is to be offered under the new rules at least 15 days before trial.

The proposed reform is critical to the protection of the public from rapists and child molesters, and is justified by the distinctive characteristics of the cases it will affect. In child molestation cases, for example, a history of similar acts tends to be exceptionally probative because it shows an unusual disposition of the defendant—a sexual or sadosexual interest in children—that simply does not exist in ordinary people. Moreover, such cases require reliance on child victims whose credibility can readily be attacked in the absence of substantial corroboration. In such cases, there is a compelling public interest in admitting all significant evidence that will illumine the credibility of the charge and any denial by the defense.

Similarly, adult-victim sexual assault cases are distinctive, and often turn on difficult credibility determinations. Alleged consent by the victim is rarely an issue in prosecutions for other violent crimes—the accused mugger does not claim that the victim freely handed over [his] wallet as a gift—but the defendant in a rape case often contends that the victim engaged in consensual sex and then falsely accused him. Knowledge that the defendant has committed rapes on other occasions is frequently critical in assessing the relative plausibility of these claims and accurately deciding cases that would otherwise become unresolvable swearing matches.

The practical effect of the new rules is to put evidence of uncharged offenses in sexual assault and child molestation cases on the same footing as other types of relevant evidence that are not subject to a special exclusionary rule. The presumption is in favor of admission. The underlying legislative judgment is that the evidence admissible pursuant to the proposed rules is typically relevant and probative, and that its probative value is normally not outweighed by any risk of prejudice or other adverse effects.

In line with this judgment, the rules do not impose arbitrary or artificial restrictions on the admissibility of evidence. Evidence of offenses for which the defendant has not previously been prosecuted or convicted will be admissible, as well as evidence of prior convictions. No time limit is imposed on the uncharged offenses for which evidence may be admitted; as a practical matter, evidence of other sex offenses by the defendant is often probative and properly admitted, notwithstanding very substantial lapses of time in relation to the charged offense or offenses. *See, e.g., United States v. Hadley*, 918 F.2d 848, 850–51 (9th Cir. 1990), *cert. dismissed*, 113 S.Ct. 486 (1992) (evidence of offenses occurring up to 15 years earlier admitted); *State v. Plymate*, 345 N.W.2d 327 (Neb.1984) (evidence of defendant's commission of other child molestations more than 20 years earlier admitted).

Finally, the practical efficacy of these rules will depend on faithful execution by judges of the will of Congress in adopting this critical reform. To implement the legislative intent, the courts must liberally construe these rules to provide the basis for a fully informed decision of sexual assault and child molestation cases, including assessment of the defendant's propensities and questions of probability in light of the defendant's past conduct.

Rule 414. Evidence of Similar Crimes in Child Molestation Cases

(a) In a criminal case in which the defendant is accused of an offense of child molestation, evidence of the defendant's commission of another offense or offenses of child molestation is admissible, and may be considered for its bearing on any matter to which it is relevant.

(b) In a case in which the Government intends to offer evidence under this rule, the attorney for the Government shall disclose the evidence to the defendant, including statements of witnesses or a summary of the substance of any testimony that is expected to be offered, at least fifteen days before the scheduled date of trial or at such later time as the court may allow for good cause.

(c) This rule shall not be construed to limit the admission or consideration of evidence under any other rule.

(d) For purposes of this rule and Rule 415, "child" means a person below the age of fourteen, and "offense of child molestation" means a crime under Federal law or the law of a State (as defined in section 513 of title 18, United States Code) that involved—

(1) any conduct proscribed by chapter 109A of title 18, United States Code, that was committed in relation to a child;

(2) any conduct proscribed by chapter 110 of title 18, United States Code;

(3) contact between any part of the defendant's body or an object and the genitals or anus of a child;

(4) contact between the genitals or anus of the defendant and any part of the body of a child;

(5) deriving sexual pleasure or gratification from the infliction of death, bodily injury, or physical pain on a child; or

(6) an attempt or conspiracy to engage in conduct described in paragraphs (1)–(5).

(Added Pub.L. 103–322, Title XXXII, § 320935(a), Sept. 13, 1994, 108 Stat. 2135.)

HISTORICAL NOTES

Effective and Applicability Provisions

1995 Acts. Rule effective July 9, 1995, see section 320935(b) to (e) of Pub.L. 103–322, set out as a note under rule 413 of these rules.

Congressional Discussion

See Floor Statement following Rule 413.

Rule 415. Evidence of Similar Acts in Civil Cases Concerning Sexual Assault or Child Molestation

(a) In a civil case in which a claim for damages or other relief is predicated on a party's alleged commission of conduct constituting an offense of sexual assault or child molestation, evidence of that party's commission of another offense or offenses of sexual assault or child molestation is admissible and may be considered as provided in Rule 413 and Rule 414 of these rules.

(b) A party who intends to offer evidence under this Rule shall disclose the evidence to the party against whom it will be offered, including statements of witnesses or a summary of the substance of any testimony that is expected to be offered, at least fifteen days before the scheduled date of trial or at such later time as the court may allow for good cause.

(c) This rule shall not be construed to limit the admission or consideration of evidence under any other rule.

(Added Pub.L. 103–322, Title XXXII, § 320935(a), Sept. 13, 1994, 108 Stat. 2137.)

HISTORICAL NOTES

Effective and Applicability Provisions

1995 Acts. Rule effective July 9, 1995, see section 320935(b) to (e) of Pub.L. 103–322, set out as a note under rule 413 of these rules.

Congressional Discussion

See Floor Statement following Rule 413.

ARTICLE V. PRIVILEGES

Rule 501. General Rule

Except as otherwise required by the Constitution of the United States or provided by Act of Congress or in rules prescribed by the Supreme Court pursuant to statutory authority, the privilege of a witness, person, government, State, or political subdivision thereof shall be governed by the principles of the common law as they may be interpreted by the courts of the United States in the light of reason and experience. However, in civil actions and proceedings, with respect to an element of a claim or defense as to which State law supplies the rule of decision, the privilege of a witness, person, government, State, or political subdivision thereof shall be determined in accordance with State law.

(Pub.L. 93–595, § 1, Jan. 2, 1975, 88 Stat. 1933.)

1974 Enactment

Article V as submitted to Congress contained thirteen Rules. Nine of those Rules defined specific non-constitutional privileges which the federal courts must recognize (i.e. required reports, lawyer-client, psychotherapist-patient, husband-wife, communications to clergymen, political vote, trade secrets, secrets of state and other official information, and identity of informer.) Another Rule provided that only those privileges set forth in Article V or in some other Act of Congress could be recognized by the federal courts. The three remaining Rules addressed collateral problems as to waiver of privilege by voluntary disclosure, privileged matter disclosed under compulsion or without opportunity to claim privilege, comment upon or inference from a claim of privilege, and jury instruction with regard thereto.

The Committee amended Article V to eliminate all of the Court's specific Rules on privileges. Instead, the Committee, through a single Rule, 501, left the law of privileges in its present state and further provided that privileges shall continue to be developed by the courts of the United States under a uniform standard applicable both in civil and criminal cases. That standard, derived from Rule 26 of the Federal Rules of Criminal Procedure, mandates the application of the principles of the common law as interpreted by the courts of the United States in the light of reason and experience. The words "person, government, State, or political subdivision thereof" were added by the Committee to the lone term "witnesses" used in Rule 26 to make clear that, as under present law, not only witnesses may have privileges. The Committee also included in its amendment a proviso modeled after Rule 302 and similar to language added by the Committee to Rule 601 relating to the competency of witnesses. The proviso is designed to require the application of State privilege law in civil actions and proceedings governed by *Erie R. Co. v. Tompkins,* 304 U.S. 64 (1938), a result in accord with current federal court decisions. See *Republic Gear Co. v. Borg–Warner Corp.,* 381 F.2d 551, 555–556 n. 2 (2nd Cir.1967). The Committee deemed the proviso to be necessary in the light of the Advisory Committee's view (see its note to Court [proposed] Rule 501) that this result is not mandated under *Erie.*

The rationale underlying the proviso is that federal law should not supersede that of the States in substantive areas such as privilege absent a compelling reason. The Committee believes that in civil cases in the federal courts where an element of a claim or defense is not grounded upon a federal question, there is no federal interest strong enough to justify departure from State policy. In addition, the Committee considered that the Court's proposed Article V would have promoted forum shopping in some civil actions, depending upon differences in the privilege law applied as among the State and federal courts. The Committee's proviso, on the other hand, under which the federal courts are bound to apply the State's privilege law in actions founded upon a State-created right or defense, removes the incentive to "shop". House Report No. 93–650.

Article V as submitted to Congress contained 13 rules. Nine of those rules defined specific nonconstitutional privileges which the Federal courts must recognize (i.e., required reports, lawyer-client, psychotherapist-patient, husband-wife, communications to clergymen, political vote, trade secrets, secrets of state and other official information, and identity of informer). Many of these rules contained controversial modifications or restrictions upon common law privileges. As noted supra, the House amended article V to eliminate all of the Court's specific rules on privileges. Through a single rule, 501, the House provided that privileges shall be governed by the principles of the common law as interpreted by the courts of the United States in the light of reason and experience (a standard derived from rule 26 of the Federal Rules of Criminal Procedure) except in the case of an element of a civil claim or defense as to which State law supplies the rule of decision, in which event state privilege law was to govern.

The committee agrees with the main thrust of the House amendment: that a federally developed common law based on modern reason and experience shall apply except where the State nature of the issues renders deference to State privilege law the wiser course, as in the usual diversity case. The committee understands that thrust of the House amendment to require that State privilege law be applied in "diversity" cases (actions on questions of State law between citizens of different States arising under 28 U.S.C. § 1332). The language of the House amendment, however, goes beyond this in some respects, and falls short of it in others: State privilege law applies even in nondiversity, Federal question civil cases, where an issue governed by State substantive law is the object of the evidence (such issues do sometimes arise in such cases); and, in all instances where State privilege law is to be applied, e.g., on proof of a State issue in a diversity case, a close reading reveals that State privilege law is not to be applied unless the matter to be proved is an element of that state claim or defense, as distinguished from a step along the way in the proof of it.

The committee is concerned that the language used in the House amendment could be difficult to apply. It provides that "in civil actions * * * with respect to an element of a claim or defense as to which State law supplies the rule of decision," State law on privilege applies. The question of what is an element of a claim or defense is likely to engender considerable litigation. If the matter in question constitutes an element of a claim, State law supplies the privilege rule; whereas if it is a mere item of proof with respect to a claim, then, even though State law might supply the rule of decision, Federal law on the privilege would apply. Further, disputes will arise as to how the rule should be applied in an antitrust action or in a tax case where the Federal statute is silent as to a particular aspect of the substantive law in question, but Federal cases had incorporated State law by reference to State law. [For a discussion of reference to State substantive law, see note on Federal Incorporation by Reference of State Law, Hart & Wechsler, The Federal Courts and the Federal System, pp. 491–494 (2d ed. 1973).] Is a claim (or defense) based on such a reference a claim or defense as to which federal or State law supplies the rule of decision?

Another problem not entirely avoidable is the complexity or difficulty the rule introduces into the trial of a Federal case containing a combination of Federal and State claims and defenses, e.g. an action involving Federal antitrust and State unfair competition claims. Two different bodies of privilege law would need to be consulted. It may even develop that the same witness-testimony might be relevant on both counts and privileged as to one but not the other. [The problems with the House formulation are discussed in Rothstein, The Proposed Amendments to the Federal Rules of Evidence, 62 Georgetown University Law Journal 125 (1973) at notes 25, 26 and 70–74 and accompanying text.]

The formulation adopted by the House is pregnant with litigious mischief. The committee has, therefore, adopted what we believe will be a clearer and more practical guideline for determining when courts should respect State rules of privilege. Basically, it provides that in criminal and Federal question civil cases, federally evolved rules on privilege should apply since it is Federal policy which is being enforced. [It is also intended that the Federal law of privileges should be applied with respect to pendent State law claims when they arise in a Federal question case.] Conversely, in diversity cases where the litigation in question turns on a substantive question of State law, and is brought in the Federal courts because the parties reside in different States, the committee believes it is clear that State rules of privilege should apply unless the proof is directed at a claim or defense for which Federal law supplies the rule of decision (a situation which would not commonly arise.) [While such a situation might require use of two bodies of privilege law, federal and state, in the same case, nevertheless the occasions on which this would be required are considerably reduced as compared with the House version, and confined to situations where the Federal and State interests are such as to justify application of neither privilege law to the case as a whole. If the rule proposed here results in two conflicting bodies of privilege law applying to the same piece of evidence in the same case, it is contemplated that the rule favoring reception of the evidence should be applied. This policy is based on the present rule 43(a) of the Federal Rules of Civil Procedure which provides: In any case, the statute or rule which favors the reception of the evidence governs and the evidence shall be presented according to the most convenient method prescribed in any of the statutes or rules to which reference is herein made.] It is intended that the State rules of privilege should apply equally in original diversity actions and diversity actions removed under 28 U.S.C. § 1441(b).

Two other comments on the privilege rule should be made. The committee has received a considerable volume of correspondence from psychiatric organizations and psychiatrists concerning the deletion of rule 504 of the rule submitted by the Supreme Court. It should be clearly understood that, in approving this general rule as to privileges, the action of Congress should not be understood as disapproving any recognition of a psychiatrist-patient, or husband-wife, or any other of the enumerated privileges contained in the Supreme Court rules. Rather, our action should be understood as reflecting the view that the recognition of a privilege based on a confidential relationship and other privileges should be determined on a case-by-case basis.

Further, we would understand that the prohibition against spouses testifying against each other is considered a rule of privilege and covered by this rule and not by rule 601 of the competency of witnesses. Senate Report No. 93–1277.

Rule 501 deals with the privilege of a witness not to testify. Both the House and Senate bills provide that federal privilege law applies in criminal cases. In civil actions and proceedings, the House bill provides that state privilege law applies "to an element of a claim or defense as to which State law supplies the rule of decision." The Senate bill provides that "in civil actions and proceedings arising under 28 U.S.C. § 1332 or 28 U.S.C. § 1335, or between citizens of different States and removed under 28 U.S.C. § 1441(b) the privilege of a witness, person, government, State or political subdivision thereof is determined in accordance with State law, unless with respect to the particular claim or defense, Federal law supplies the rule of decision."

The wording of the House and Senate bills differs in the treatment of civil actions and proceedings. The rule in the House bill applies to evidence that relates to "an element of a claim or defense." If an item of proof tends to support or defeat a claim or defense, or an element of a claim or defense, and if state law supplies the rule of decision for that claim or defense, then state privilege law applies to that item of proof.

Under the provision in the House bill, therefore, state privilege law will usually apply in diversity cases. There may be diversity cases, however, where a claim or defense is based upon federal law. In such instances, federal privilege law will apply to evidence relevant to the federal claim or defense. See *Sola Electric Co. v. Jefferson Electric Co.*, 317 U.S. 173 (1942).

In nondiversity jurisdiction civil cases, federal privilege law will generally apply. In those situations where a federal court adopts or incorporates state law to fill interstices or gaps in federal statutory phrases, the court generally will apply federal privilege law. As Justice Jackson has said:

> A federal court sitting in a non-diversity case such as this does not sit as a local tribunal. In some cases it may see fit for special reasons to give the law of a particular state highly persuasive or even controlling effect, but in the last analysis its decision turns upon the law of the United States, not that of any state.

D'Oench, Duhme & Co. v. Federal Deposit Insurance Corp., 315 U.S. 447, 471 (1942) (Jackson, J., concurring). When a federal court chooses to absorb state law, it is applying the state law as a matter of federal common law. Thus, state law does not supply the rule of decision (even though the federal court may apply a rule derived from state decisions), and state privilege law would not apply. See C.A. Wright,

Federal Courts 251–252 (2d ed. 1970); *Holmberg v. Armbrecht*, 327 U.S. 392 (1946); *DeSylva v. Ballentine*, 351 U.S. 570, 581 (1956); 9 Wright & Miller, Federal Rules and Procedure § 2408.

In civil actions and proceedings, where the rule of decision as to a claim or defense or as to an element of a claim or defense is supplied by state law, the House provision requires that state privilege law apply.

The Conference adopts the House provision. House Report No. 93–1597.

Rule 502. Attorney-Client Privilege and Work Product; Limitations on Waiver

The following provisions apply, in the circumstances set out, to disclosure of a communication or information covered by the attorney-client privilege or work-product protection.

(a) Disclosure made in a Federal proceeding or to a Federal office or agency; scope of a waiver.—When the disclosure is made in a Federal proceeding or to a Federal office or agency and waives the attorney-client privilege or work-product protection, the waiver extends to an undisclosed communication or information in a Federal or State proceeding only if:

(1) the waiver is intentional;

(2) the disclosed and undisclosed communications or information concern the same subject matter; and

(3) they ought in fairness to be considered together.

(b) Inadvertent disclosure.—When made in a Federal proceeding or to a Federal office or agency, the disclosure does not operate as a waiver in a Federal or State proceeding if:

(1) the disclosure is inadvertent;

(2) the holder of the privilege or protection took reasonable steps to prevent disclosure; and

(3) the holder promptly took reasonable steps to rectify the error, including (if applicable) following Federal Rule of Civil Procedure 26(b)(5)(B).

(c) Disclosure made in a State proceeding.—When the disclosure is made in a State proceeding and is not the subject of a State-court order concerning waiver, the disclosure does not operate as a waiver in a Federal proceeding if the disclosure:

(1) would not be a waiver under this rule if it had been made in a Federal proceeding; or

(2) is not a waiver under the law of the State where the disclosure occurred.

(d) Controlling effect of a court order.—A Federal court may order that the privilege or protection is not waived by disclosure connected with the litigation pending before the court—in which event the disclosure is also not a waiver in any other Federal or State proceeding.

(e) Controlling effect of a party agreement.—An agreement on the effect of disclosure in a Federal proceeding is binding only on the parties to the agreement, unless it is incorporated into a court order.

(f) Controlling effect of this rule.—Notwithstanding Rules 101 and 1101, this rule applies to State proceedings and to Federal court-annexed and Federal court-mandated arbitration proceedings, in the circumstances set out in the rule. And notwithstanding Rule 501, this rule applies even if State law provides the rule of decision.

(g) Definitions.—In this rule:

(1) "attorney-client privilege" means the protection that applicable law provides for confidential attorney-client communications; and

(2) "work-product protection" means the protection that applicable law provides for tangible material (or its intangible equivalent) prepared in anticipation of litigation or for trial.

(Pub.L. 110–322, § 1(a), Sept. 19, 2008, 122 Stat. 3537.)

Explanatory Note (Revised 11/28/2007)

This new rule has two major purposes:

1) It resolves some longstanding disputes in the courts about the effect of certain disclosures of communications or information protected by the attorney-client privilege or as work product—specifically those disputes involving inadvertent disclosure and subject matter waiver.

2) It responds to the widespread complaint that litigation costs necessary to protect against waiver of attorney-client privilege or work product have become prohibitive due to the concern that any disclosure (however innocent or minimal) will operate as a subject matter waiver of all protected communications or information. This concern is especially troubling in cases involving electronic discovery. *See, e.g., Hopson v. City of Baltimore*, 232 F.R.D. 228, 244 (D.Md. 2005) (electronic discovery may encompass "millions of documents" and to insist upon "record-by-record pre-production privilege review, on pain of subject matter waiver, would impose upon parties costs of production that bear no proportionality to what is at stake in the litigation").

The rule seeks to provide a predictable, uniform set of standards under which parties can determine the consequences of a disclosure of a communication or information covered by the attorney-client privilege or work-product protection. Parties to litigation need to know, for example, that if they exchange privileged information pursuant to a confidentiality order, the court's order will be enforceable. Moreover, if a federal court's confidentiality order is not enforceable in a state court then the burdensome costs of privilege review and retention are unlikely to be reduced.

The rule makes no attempt to alter federal or state law on whether a communication or information is protected under the attorney-client privilege or work-product immunity as an initial matter. Moreover, while establishing some exceptions to waiver, the rule does not purport to supplant applicable waiver doctrine generally.

The rule governs only certain waivers by disclosure. Other common-law waiver doctrines may result in a finding of waiver even where there is no disclosure of privileged information or work product. *See, e.g., Nguyen v. Excel Corp.*, 197 F.3d 200 (5th Cir. 1999) (reliance on an advice of counsel defense waives the privilege with respect to attorney-client communications pertinent to that defense); *Ryers v. Burleson*, 100 F.R.D. 436 (D.D.C. 1983) (allegation of lawyer malpractice constituted a waiver of confidential communications under the circumstances). The rule is not intended to displace or modify federal common law concerning waiver of privilege or work product where no disclosure has been made.

Subdivision (a). The rule provides that a voluntary disclosure in a federal proceeding or to a federal office or agency, if a waiver, generally results in a waiver only of the communication or information disclosed; a subject matter waiver (of either privilege or work product) is reserved for those unusual situations in which fairness requires a further disclosure of related, protected information, in order to prevent a selective and misleading presentation of evidence to the disadvantage of the adversary. *See, e.g., In re United Mine Workers of America Employee Benefit Plans Litig.*, 159 F.R.D. 307, 312 (D.D.C. 1994) (waiver of work product limited to materials actually disclosed, because the party did not deliberately disclose documents in an attempt to gain a tactical advantage). Thus, subject matter waiver is limited to situations in which a party intentionally puts protected information into the litigation in a selective, misleading and unfair manner. It follows that an inadvertent disclosure of protected information can never result in a subject matter waiver. *See* Rule 502(b). The rule rejects the result in *In re Sealed Case*, 877 F.2d 976 (D.C.Cir. 1989), which held that inadvertent disclosure of documents during discovery automatically constituted a subject matter waiver.

The language concerning subject matter waiver—"ought in fairness"—is taken from Rule 106, because the animating principle is the same. Under both Rules, a party that makes a selective, misleading presentation that is unfair to the adversary opens itself to a more complete and accurate presentation.

To assure protection and predictability, the rule provides that if a disclosure is made at the federal level, the federal rule on subject matter waiver governs subsequent state court determinations on the scope of the waiver by that disclosure.

Subdivision (b). Courts are in conflict over whether an inadvertent disclosure of a communication or information protected as privileged or work product constitutes a waiver. A few courts find that a disclosure must be intentional to be a waiver. Most courts find a waiver only if the disclosing party acted carelessly in disclosing the communication or information and failed to request its return in a timely manner. And a few courts hold that any inadvertent disclosure of a communication or information protected under the attorney-client privilege or as work product constitutes a waiver without regard to the protections taken to avoid such a disclosure. *See generally Hopson v. City of Baltimore*, 232 F.R.D. 228 (D.Md. 2005), for a discussion of this case law.

The rule opts for the middle ground: inadvertent disclosure of protected communications or information in connection with a federal proceeding or to a federal office or agency does not constitute a waiver if the holder took reasonable steps to prevent disclosure and also promptly took reasonable steps to rectify the error. This position is in accord with the majority view on whether inadvertent disclosure is a waiver.

Cases such as *Lois Sportswear, U.S.A., Inc. v. Levi Strauss & Co.*, 104 F.R.D. 103, 105 (S.D.N.Y. 1985) and *Hartford Fire Ins. Co. v. Garvey*, 109 F.R.D. 323, 332 (N.D.Cal. 1985), set out a multi-factor test for determining whether inadvertent disclosure is a waiver. The stated factors (none of which is dispositive) are the reasonableness of precautions taken, the time taken to rectify the error, the scope of discovery, the extent of disclosure and the overriding issue of fairness. The rule does not explicitly codify that test, because it is really a set of non-determinative guidelines that vary from case to case. The rule is flexible enough to accommodate any of those listed factors. Other considerations bearing on the reasonableness of a producing party's efforts include the number of documents to be reviewed and the time constraints for production. Depending on the circumstances, a party that uses advanced analytical software applications and linguistic tools in screening for privilege and work product may be found to have taken "reasonable steps" to prevent inadvertent disclosure. The implementation of an efficient system of records management before litigation may also be relevant.

The rule does not require the producing party to engage in a post-production review to determine whether any protected communication or information has been produced by mistake. But the rule does require the producing party to follow up on any obvious indications that a protected communication or information has been produced inadvertently.

The rule applies to inadvertent disclosures made to a federal office or agency, including but not limited to an office or agency that is acting in the course of its regulatory, investigative or enforcement authority. The consequences of waiver, and the concomitant costs of pre-production privilege review, can be as great with respect to disclosures to offices and agencies as they are in litigation.

Subdivision (c). Difficult questions can arise when 1) a disclosure of a communication or information protected by the attorney-client privilege or as work product is made in a state proceeding, 2) the communication or information is offered in a subsequent federal proceeding on the ground that the disclosure waived the privilege or protection, and 3) the state and federal laws are in conflict on the question of waiver. The Committee determined that the proper solution for the federal court is to apply the law that is most protective of privilege and work product. If the state law is more protective (such as where the state law is that an inadvertent disclosure can never be a waiver), the holder of the privilege or protection may well have relied on that law when making the disclosure in the state proceeding. Moreover, applying a more restrictive federal law of waiver could impair the state objective of preserving the privilege or work-product protection for disclosures made in state proceedings. On the other hand, if the federal law is more protective, applying the state law of waiver to determine admissibility in federal court is likely to undermine the federal objective of limiting the costs of production.

The rule does not address the enforceability of a state court confidentiality order in a federal proceeding, as that question is covered both by statutory law and principles of federalism and comity. *See* 28 U.S.C. § 1738 (providing that state judicial proceedings "shall have the same full faith and credit in every court within the United States . . . as they have by law or usage in the courts of such State . . . from which they are taken"). *See also Tucker v. Ohtsu Tire & Rubber Co.*, 191 F.R.D. 495, 499 (D.Md. 2000) (noting that a federal court considering the enforceability of a state confidentiality order is "constrained by principles of comity, courtesy, and . . . federalism"). Thus, a state court order finding no waiver in connection with a disclosure made in a state court proceeding is enforceable under existing law in subsequent federal proceedings.

Subdivision (d). Confidentiality orders are becoming increasingly important in limiting the costs of privilege review and retention, especially in cases involving electronic discovery. But the utility of a confidentiality order in reducing discovery costs is substantially diminished if it provides no protection outside the particular litigation in which the order is entered. Parties are unlikely to be able to reduce the costs of pre-production review for privilege and work product if the consequence of disclosure is that the communications or information could be used by non-parties to the litigation.

There is some dispute on whether a confidentiality order entered in one case is enforceable in other proceedings. *See generally Hopson v. City of Baltimore*, 232 F.R.D. 228 (D.Md. 2005), for a discussion of this case law. The rule provides that when a confidentiality order governing the consequences of disclosure in that case is entered in a federal proceeding, its terms are enforceable against non-parties in any federal or state proceeding. For example, the court order may provide for return of documents without waiver irrespective of the care taken by the disclosing party; the rule contemplates enforcement of "claw-back" and "quick peek" arrangements as a way to avoid the excessive costs of pre-production review for privilege and work product. *See Zubulake v. UBS Warburg LLC*, 216 F.R.D. 280, 290 (S.D.N.Y. 2003) (noting that parties may enter into "so-called 'claw-back' agreements that allow the parties to forego privilege review altogether in favor of an agreement to return inadvertently produced privilege documents"). The rule provides a party with a predictable protection from a court order—predictability that is needed to allow the party to plan in advance to limit the prohibitive costs of privilege and work product review and retention.

Under the rule, a confidentiality order is enforceable whether or not it memorializes an agreement among the parties to the litigation. Party agreement should not be a condition of enforceability of a federal court's order.

Under subdivision (d), a federal court may order that disclosure of privileged or protected information "in connection with" a federal proceeding does not result in waiver. But subdivision (d) does not allow the federal court to enter an order determining the waiver effects of a separate disclosure of the same information in other proceedings, state or federal. If a disclosure has been made in a state proceeding (and is not the subject of a state-court order on waiver), then subdivision (d) is inapplicable. Subdivision (c) would govern the federal court's determination whether the state-court disclosure waived the privilege or protection in the federal proceeding.

Subdivision (e). Subdivision (e) codifies the well-established proposition that parties can enter an agreement to limit the effect of waiver by disclosure between or among them. Of course such an agreement can bind only the parties to the agreement. The rule makes clear that if parties want protection against non-parties from a finding of waiver by disclosure, the agreement must be made part of a court order.

Subdivision (f). The protections against waiver provided by Rule 502 must be applicable when protected communications or information disclosed in federal proceedings are subsequently offered in state proceedings. Otherwise the holders of protected communications and information, and their lawyers, could not rely on the protections provided by the Rule, and the goal of limiting costs in discovery would be substantially undermined. Rule 502(f) is intended to resolve any potential tension between the provisions of Rule 502 that apply to state proceedings and the possible limitations on the applicability of the Federal Rules of Evidence otherwise provided by Rules 101 and 1101.

The rule is intended to apply in all federal court proceedings, including court-annexed and court-ordered arbitrations, without regard to any possible limitations of Rules 101 and 1101. This provision is not intended to raise an inference about the applicability of any other rule of evidence in arbitration proceedings more generally.

The costs of discovery can be equally high for state and federal causes of action, and the rule seeks to limit those costs in all federal proceedings, regardless of whether the claim arises under state or federal law. Accordingly, the rule applies to state law causes of action brought in federal court.

Subdivision (g). The rule's coverage is limited to attorney-client privilege and work product. The operation of waiver by disclosure, as applied to other evidentiary privileges, remains a question of federal common law. Nor does the rule purport to apply to the Fifth Amendment privilege against compelled self-incrimination.

The definition of work product "materials" is intended to include both tangible and intangible information. *See In re Cendant Corp. Sec. Litig.*, 343 F.3d 658, 662 (3d Cir. 2003) ("work product protection extends to both tangible and intangible work product").

Committee Letter

The letter from the Committee on Rules of Practice and Procedure of the Judicial Conference of the United States to the Committee on the Judiciary of the U.S. Senate and House of Representatives, dated September 26, 2007, provided:

On behalf of the Judicial Conference of the United States, I respectfully submit a proposed addition to the Federal Rules of Evidence. The Conference recommends that Congress adopt this proposed rule as Federal Rule of Evidence 502.

The Rule provides for protections against waiver of the attorney-client privilege or work product immunity. The Conference submits this proposal directly to Congress because of the limitations on the rulemaking function of the federal courts in matters dealing with evidentiary privilege. Unlike all other federal rules of procedure prescribed under the Rules Enabling Act, those rules governing evidentiary privilege must by approved by an Act of Congress, 28 U.S.C. § 2074(b).

Description of the Process Leading to the Proposed Rule

The Judicial Conference Rules Committees have long been concerned about the rising costs of litigation, much of which has been caused by the review, required under current law, of every document produced in discovery, in order to determine whether the document contains privileged information. In 2006, the House Judiciary Committee Chair suggested that the Judicial Conference consider proposing a rule dealing with waiver of attorney-client privilege and work product, in order to limit these rising costs. The Judicial Conference was urged to proceed with rulemaking that would:

- protect against the forfeiture of privilege when a disclosure in discovery is the result of an innocent mistake; and
- permit parties, and courts, to protect against the consequences of waiver by permitting disclosures of privileged information between the parties to litigation.

The task of drafting a proposed rule was referred to the Advisory Committee on Evidence Rules (the "Advisory Committee"). The Advisory Committee prepared a draft Rule 502 and invited a select group of judges, lawyers, and academics to testify before the Advisory Committee about the need for the rule, and to suggest any improvements. The Advisory Committee considered all the testimony presented by these experts and redrafted the rule accordingly. At its Spring 2006 meeting, the Advisory Committee approved for release for public comment a proposed Rule 502 that would provide certain exceptions to the federal common law on waiver of privileges and work product. That rule was approved for release for public comment by the Committee on Rules of Practice and Procedure ("the Standing Committee"). The public comment period began in August 2006 and ended February 15, 2007. The Advisory Committee received more that [sic] 70 public comments, and also heard the testimony of more than 20 witnesses at two public hearings. The rule released for public comment was also carefully reviewed by the Standing Committee's Subcommittee on Style. In April 2007, the Advisory Committee issued a revised proposed Rule 502 taking into account the public comment, the views of the Subcommittee on Style, and its own judgment. The revised rule was approved by the Standing Committee and the Judicial Conference. It is enclosed with this letter.

In order to inform Congress of the legal issues involved in this rule, the proposed Rule 502 also includes a proposed Committee Note of the kind that accompanies all rules adopted through the Rules Enabling Act. This Committee Note may be incorporated as all or part of the legislative history of the rule if it is adopted by Congress. *See, e.g.*, House Conference Report 103–711 (stating that the "Conferees intend that the Advisory Committee Note on [Evidence] Rule 412, as transmitted by the Judicial Conference of the United States to the Supreme Court on October 25, 1993, applies to Rule 412 as enacted by this section" of the Violent Crime Control and Law Enforcement Act of 1994).

Problems Addressed by the Proposed Rule

In drafting the proposed Rule, the Advisory Committee concluded that the current law on waiver of privilege and work product is responsible in large part for the rising costs of discovery, especially discovery of electronic information. In complex litigation the lawyers spend significant amounts of time and effort to preserve the privilege and work product. The reason is that if a protected document is produced, there is a risk that a court will find a subject matter waiver that will apply not only to the instant case and document but to other cases and documents as well. Moreover, an enormous amount of expense is put into document production in order to protect against inadvertent disclosure of privileged information, because the producing party risks a ruling that even a mistaken disclosure can result in a subject matter waiver. Advisory Committee members also expressed the view that the fear of waiver leads to extravagant claims of privilege. Members concluded that if there were a way to produce documents in discovery without risking subject matter waiver, the discovery process could be made much less expensive. The Advisory Committee noted that the existing law on the effect of inadvertent disclosures and on the scope of waiver is far from consistent or certain. It also noted that agreements between parties with regard to the effect of disclosure on privilege are common, but are unlikely to decrease the costs of discovery due to the ineffectiveness of such agreements as to persons not party to them.

Proposed Rule 502 does not attempt to deal comprehensively with either attorney-client privilege or work-product protection. It also does not purport to cover all issues concerning waiver or forfeiture of either the attorney-client privilege or work-product protection. Rather, it deals primarily with issues involved in the disclosure of protected information in federal court proceedings or to a federal public office or agency. The rule binds state courts only with regard to disclosures made in federal proceedings. It deals with disclosures made in state proceedings only to the extent that the effect of those disclosures becomes an issue in federal litigation. The Rule covers issues of scope of waiver, inadvertent disclosure, and the controlling effect of court orders and agreements.

Rule 502 provides the following protections against waiver of privilege or work product:

- *Limitations on Scope of Waiver.* Subdivision (a) provides that if a waiver is found, it applies only to the information disclosed, unless a broader waiver is made necessary by the holder's intentional and misleading use of privileged or protected communications or information.
- *Protections Against Inadvertent Disclosure.* Subdivision (b) provides that an inadvertent disclosure of privileged or protected communications or information, when made at the federal level, does not operate as a waiver if the holder took reasonable steps to prevent such a disclosure and employed reasonably prompt measures to retrieve the mistakenly disclosed communications or information.
- *Effect on State Proceedings and Disclosures Made in State Courts.* Subdivision (c) provides that 1) if there is a disclosure of privileged or protected communications or information at the federal level, then state courts must honor Rule 502 in subsequent state proceedings; and 2) if there is a disclosure of privileged or protected communications or information in a state proceeding, then admissibility in a subsequent federal proceeding is determined by the law that is most protective against waiver.
- *Orders Protecting Privileged Communications Binding on Non-Parties.* Subdivision (d) provides that if a federal court enters an order providing that a disclosure of privileged or protected communications or information does not constitute a waiver, that order is enforceable against all

persons and entities in any federal or state proceeding. This provision allows parties in an action in which such an order is entered to limit their costs of pre-production privilege review.

•*Agreements Protecting Privileged Communications Binding on Parties.* Subdivision (e) provides that parties in a federal proceeding can enter into a confidentiality agreement providing for mutual protection against waiver in that proceeding. While those agreements bind the signatory parties, they are not binding on non-parties unless incorporated into a court order.

Drafting Choices Made by the Advisory Committee

The Advisory Committee made a number of important drafting choices in Rule 502. This section explains those choices.

1) The effect in state proceedings of disclosures initially made in state proceedings. Rule 502 does not apply to a disclosure made in a state proceeding when the disclosed communication or information is subsequently offered in another state proceeding. The first draft of Rule 502 provided for uniform waiver rules in federal and state proceedings, regardless of where the initial disclosure was made. This draft raised the objections of the Conference of State Chief Justices. State judges argued that the Rule as drafted offended principles of federalism and comity, by superseding state law of privilege waiver, even for disclosures that are made initially in state proceedings—and even when the disclosed material is then offered in a state proceeding (the so-called "state-to-state" problem). In response to these objections, the Advisory Committee voted unanimously to scale back the Rule, so that it would not cover the "state-to-state" problem. Under the current proposal state courts are bound by the Federal Rule only when a disclosure is made at the federal level and the disclosed communication or information is later offered in a state proceeding (the so-called "federal-to-state" problem).

During the public comment period on the scaled-back rule, the Advisory Committee received many requests from lawyers and lawyer groups to return to the original draft and provide a uniform rule of privilege waiver that would bind both state and federal courts, for disclosures made in either state or federal proceedings. These comments expressed the concern that if states were not bound by a uniform federal rule on privilege waiver, the protections afforded by Rule 502 would be undermined; parties and their lawyers might not be able to rely on the protections of the Rule, for fear that a state law would find a waiver even though the Federal Rule would not.

The Advisory Committee determined that these comments raised a legitimate concern, but decided not to extend Rule 502 to govern a state court's determination of waiver with respect to disclosures made in state proceedings. The Committee relied on the following considerations:

- Rule 502 is located in the Federal Rules of Evidence, a body of rules determining the admissibility of evidence in federal proceedings. Parties in a state proceeding determining the effect of a disclosure made in that proceeding or in other state courts would be unlikely to look to the Federal Rules of Evidence for the answer.
- In the Advisory Committee's view, Rule 502, as proposed herein, does fulfill its primary goal of reducing the costs of discovery in *federal* proceedings. Rule 502 by its terms governs state courts with regard to the effect of disclosures initially made in federal proceedings or to federal offices or agencies. Parties and their lawyers in federal proceedings can therefore predict the consequences of disclosure by referring to Rule 502; there is no possibility that a state court could find a waiver when Rule 502 would not, when the disclosure is initially made at the federal level.

The Judicial Conference has no position on the merits of separate legislation to cover the problem of waiver of privilege and work product when the disclosure is made at the state level and the consequence is to be determined in a state court.

2) Other applications of Rule 502 to state court proceedings. Although disclosures made in state court proceedings and later offered in state proceedings would not be covered, Rule 502 would have an effect on state court proceedings where the disclosure is initially made in a federal proceeding or to a federal office or agency. Most importantly, state courts in such circumstances would be bound by federal protection orders. The other protections against waiver in Rule 502—against mistaken disclosure and subject matter waiver—would also bind state courts as to disclosures initially made at the federal level. The Rule, as submitted, specifically provides that it applies to state proceedings under the circumstances set out in the Rule. This protection is needed, otherwise parties could not rely on Rule 502 even as to federal disclosures, for fear that a state court would find waiver even when a federal court would not.

3) Disclosures made in state proceedings and offered in a subsequent federal proceeding. Earlier drafts of proposed Rule 502 did not determine the question of what rule would apply when a disclosure is made in state court and the waiver determination is to be made in a subsequent federal proceeding. Proposed Rule 502 as submitted herein provides that all of the provisions of Rule 502 apply unless the state law of privilege is more protective (less likely to find waiver) than the federal law. The Advisory Committee determined that this solution best preserved federal interests in protecting against waiver, and also provided appropriate respect for state attempts to give greater protection to communications and information covered by the attorney-client privilege or work-product doctrine.

4) Selective waiver. At the suggestion of the House Judiciary Committee Chair, the Advisory Committee considered a rule that would allow persons and entities to cooperate with government agencies without waiving all privileges as to other parties in subsequent litigation. Such a rule is known as a "selective waiver" rule, meaning that disclosure of protected communications or information to the government waives the protection only selectively—to the government—and not to any other person or entity.

The selective waiver provision proved to be very controversial. The Advisory Committee determined that it would not propose adoption of a selective waiver provision; but in light of the request from the House Judiciary Committee, the Advisory Committee did prepare language for a selective waiver provision should Congress decide to proceed. The draft language for a selective waiver provision is available on request.

Conclusion

Proposed Rule 502 is respectfully submitted for consideration by Congress as a rule that will effectively limit the skyrocketing costs of discovery. Members of the Standing Committee, the Advisory Committee, as well as their reporters and consultants, are ready to assist Congress in any way it sees fit.

Sincerely,

Lee H. Rosenthal
Chair, Committee on Rules of Practice and Procedure

HISTORICAL NOTES

Effective and Applicability Provisions

2008 Acts. Pub.L. 110–322, § 1(c), Sept. 19, 2008, 122 Stat. 3538, provided that: "The amendments made by this Act [enacting this rule] shall apply in all proceedings commenced after the date of enactment of this Act [Sept. 19, 2008] and, insofar as is just and practicable, in all proceedings pending on such date of enactment [Sept. 19, 2008]."

ARTICLE VI. WITNESSES

Rule 601. General Rule of Competency

Every person is competent to be a witness except as otherwise provided in these rules. However, in civil actions and proceedings, with respect to an element of a claim or defense as to which State law supplies the rule of decision, the competency of a witness shall be determined in accordance with State law.

(Pub.L. 93–595, § 1, Jan. 2, 1975, 88 Stat.1934.)

1972 Proposed Rules

This general ground-clearing eliminates all grounds of incompetency not specifically recognized in the succeeding rules of this Article. Included among the grounds thus abolished are religious belief, conviction of crime, and connection with the litigation as a party or interested person or spouse of a party or interested person. With the exception of the so-called Dead Man's Acts, American jurisdictions generally have ceased to recognize these grounds.

The Dead Man's Acts are surviving traces of the common law disqualification of parties and interested persons. They exist in variety too great to convey conviction of their wisdom and effectiveness. These rules contain no provision of this kind. For the reasoning underlying the decision not to give effect to state statutes in diversity cases, see the Advisory Committee's Note to Rule 501.

No mental or moral qualifications for testifying as a witness are specified. Standards of mental capacity have proved elusive in actual application. A leading commentator observes that few witnesses are disqualified on that ground. Weihofen, Testimonial Competence and Credibility, 34 Geo. Wash.L.Rev. 53 (1965). Discretion is regularly exercised in favor of allowing the testimony. A witness wholly without capacity is difficult to imagine. The question is one particularly suited to the jury as one of weight and credibility, subject to judicial authority to review the sufficiency of the evidence. 2 Wigmore §§ 501, 509. Standards of moral qualification in practice consist essentially of evaluating a person's truthfulness in terms of his own answers about it. Their principal utility is in affording an opportunity on voir dire examination to impress upon the witness his moral duty. This result may, however, be accomplished more directly, and without haggling in terms of legal standards, by the manner of administering the oath or affirmation under Rule 603.

Admissibility of religious belief as a ground of impeachment is treated in Rule 610. Conviction of crime as a ground of impeachment is the subject of Rule 609. Marital relationship is the basis for privilege under Rule 505. Interest in the outcome of litigation and mental capacity are, of course, highly relevant to credibility and require no special treatment to render them admissible along with other matters bearing upon the perception, memory, and narration of witnesses.

1974 Enactment

Rule 601 as submitted to the Congress provided that "Every person is competent to be a witness except as otherwise provided in these rules." One effect of the Rule as proposed would have been to abolish age, mental capacity, and other grounds recognized in some State jurisdictions as making a person incompetent as a witness. The greatest controversy centered around the Rule's rendering inapplicable in the federal courts the so-called Dead Man's Statutes which exist in some States. Acknowledging that there is substantial disagreement as to the merit of Dead Man's Statutes, the Committee nevertheless believed that where such statutes have been enacted they represent State policy which should not be overturned in the absence of a compelling federal interest. The Committee therefore amended the Rule to make competency in civil actions determinable in accordance with State law with respect to elements of claims or defenses as to which State law supplies the rule of decision. Cf. *Courtland v. Walston & Co., Inc.,* 340 F.Supp. 1076, 1087–1092 (S.D.N.Y.1972). House Report No. 93–650.

The amendment to rule 601 parallels the treatment accorded Rule 501 discussed immediately above. Senate Report No. 93–1277.

Rule 601 deals with competency of witnesses. Both the House and Senate bills provide that federal competency law applies in criminal cases. In civil actions and proceedings, the House bill provides that state competency law applies "to an element of a claim or defense as to which State law supplies the rule of decision." The Senate bill provides that "in civil actions and proceedings arising under 28 U.S.C. § 1332 or 28 U.S.C. § 1335, or between citizens of different States and removed under 28 U.S.C. § 1441(b) the competency of a witness, person, government, State or political subdivision thereof is determined in accordance with State law, unless with respect to the particular claim or defense, Federal law supplies the rule of decision."

The wording of the House and Senate bills differs in the treatment of civil actions and proceedings. The rule in the House bill applies to evidence that relates to "an element of a claim or defense." If an item of proof tends to support or defeat a claim or defense, or an element of a claim or defense, and if state law supplies the rule of decision for that claim or defense, then state competency law applies to that item of proof.

For reasons similar to those underlying its action on Rule 501, the Conference adopts the House provision. House Report No. 93–1597.

Rule 602. Lack of Personal Knowledge

A witness may not testify to a matter unless evidence is introduced sufficient to support a finding that the witness has personal knowledge of the matter. Evidence to prove personal knowledge may, but need not, consist of the witness' own testimony. This rule is subject to the provisions of rule 703, relating to opinion testimony by expert witnesses.

(Pub.L. 93–595, § 1, Jan. 2, 1975, 88 Stat. 1934; Mar. 2, 1987, eff. Oct. 1, 1987; Apr. 25, 1988, eff. Nov. 1, 1988.)

1972 Proposed Rules

" * * * [T]he rule requiring that a witness who testifies to a fact which can be perceived by the senses must have had an opportunity to observe, and must have actually observed the fact" is a "most pervasive manifestation" of the common law insistence upon "the most reliable sources of information." McCormick § 10, p. 19. These foundation requirements may, of course, be furnished by the testimony of the witness himself; hence personal knowledge is not an absolute but may consist of what the witness thinks he knows from personal perception. 2 Wigmore § 650. It will be observed that the rule is in fact a specialized application of the provisions of Rule 104(b) on conditional relevancy.

This rule does not govern the situation of a witness who testifies to a hearsay statement as such, if he has personal knowledge of the making of the statement. Rules 801 and 805 would be applicable. This rule would, however, prevent him from testifying to the subject matter of the hearsay statement, as he has no personal knowledge of it.

The reference to Rule 703 is designed to avoid any question of conflict between the present rule and the provisions of that rule allowing an expert to express opinions based on facts of which he does not have personal knowledge.

1987 Amendments

The amendments are technical. No substantive change is intended.

1988 Amendments

The amendment is technical. No substantive change is intended.

Rule 603. Oath or Affirmation

Before testifying, every witness shall be required to declare that the witness will testify truthfully, by oath or affirmation administered in a form calculated to awaken the witness' conscience and impress the witness' mind with the duty to do so.

(Pub.L. 93–595, § 1, Jan. 2, 1975, 88 Stat. 1934; Mar. 2, 1987, eff. Oct. 1, 1987.)

1972 Proposed Rules

The rule is designed to afford the flexibility required in dealing with religious adults, atheists, conscientious objectors, mental defectives, and children. Affirmation is simply a solemn undertaking to tell the truth; no special verbal formula is required. As is true generally, affirmation is recognized by federal law. "Oath" includes affirmation, 1 U.S.C. § 1; judges and clerks may administer oaths and affirmations, 28 U.S.C. §§ 459, 953; and affirmations are acceptable in lieu of oaths under Rule 43(d) of the Federal Rules of Civil Procedure. Perjury by a witness is a crime, 18 U.S.C. § 1621.

1987 Amendments

The amendments are technical. No substantive change is intended.

Rule 604. Interpreters

An interpreter is subject to the provisions of these rules relating to qualification as an expert and the administration of an oath or affirmation to make a true translation.

(Pub.L. 93–595, § 1, Jan. 2, 1975, 88 Stat. 1934; Mar. 2, 1987, eff. Oct. 1, 1987.)

1972 Proposed Rules

The rule implements Rule 43(f) of the Federal Rules of Civil Procedure and Rule 28(b) of the Federal Rules of Criminal Procedure, both of which contain provisions for the appointment and compensation of interpreters.

1987 Amendments

The amendment is technical. No substantive change is intended.

Rule 605. Competency of Judge as Witness

The judge presiding at the trial may not testify in that trial as a witness. No objection need be made in order to preserve the point.

(Pub.L. 93–595, § 1, Jan. 2, 1975, 88 Stat. 1934.)

1972 Proposed Rules

In view of the mandate of 28 U.S.C. § 455 that a judge disqualify himself in "any case in which he * * * is or has been a material witness," the likelihood that the presiding judge in a federal court might be called to testify in the trial over which he is presiding is slight. Nevertheless the possibility is not totally eliminated.

The solution here presented is a broad rule of incompetency, rather than such alternatives as incompetency only as to material matters, leaving the matter to the discretion of the judge, or recognizing no incompetency. The choice is the result of inability to evolve satisfactory answers to questions which arise when the judge abandons the bench for the witness stand. Who rules on objections? Who compels him to answer? Can he rule impartially on the weight and admissibility of his own testimony? Can he be impeached or cross-examined effectively? Can he, in a jury trial, avoid conferring his seal of approval on one side in the eyes of the jury? Can he, in a bench trial, avoid an involvement destructive of impartiality? The rule of general incompetency has substantial support. See Report of the Special Committee on the Propriety of Judges Appearing as Witnesses, 36 A.B.A.J. 630 (1950); cases collected in Annot. 157 A.L.R. 311; McCormick § 68, p. 147; Uniform Rule 42; California Evidence Code § 703; Kansas Code of Civil Procedure § 60–442; New Jersey Evidence Rule 42. Cf. 6 Wigmore § 1909, which advocates leaving the matter to the discretion of the judge, and statutes to that effect collected in Annot. 157 A.L.R. 311.

The rule provides an "automatic" objection. To require an actual objection would confront the opponent with a choice between not objecting, with the result of allowing the testimony, and objecting, with the probable result of excluding the testimony but at the price of continuing the trial before a judge likely to feel that his integrity had been attacked by the objector.

Rule 606. Competency of Juror as Witness

(a) At the trial. A member of the jury may not testify as a witness before that jury in the trial of the case in which the juror is sitting. If the juror is called so to testify, the opposing party shall be afforded an opportunity to object out of the presence of the jury.

(b) Inquiry into validity of verdict or indictment. Upon an inquiry into the validity of a verdict or indictment, a juror may not testify as to any matter or statement occurring during the course of the jury's deliberations or to the effect of anything upon that or any other juror's mind or emotions as influencing the juror to assent to or dissent from the verdict or indictment or concerning the juror's mental processes in connection therewith. But a juror may testify about (1) whether extraneous prejudicial information was improperly brought to the jury's attention, (2) whether any outside influence was improperly brought to bear upon any juror, or (3) whether there was a mistake in entering the verdict onto the verdict form. A juror's affidavit or evidence of any statement by the juror may not be received on a matter about which the juror would be precluded from testifying.

(Pub.L. 93–595, § 1, Jan. 2, 1975, 88 Stat. 1934; Pub.L. 94–149, § 1(10), Dec. 12, 1975, 89 Stat. 805; Mar. 2, 1987, eff. Oct. 1, 1987; Apr. 12, 2006, eff. Dec. 1, 2006.)

1972 Proposed Rules

Note to Subdivision (a). The considerations which bear upon the permissibility of testimony by a juror in the trial in which he is sitting as juror bear an obvious similarity to those evoked when the judge is called as a witness. See Advisory Committee's Note to Rule 605. The judge is not, however in this instance so involved as to call for departure from usual principles requiring objection to be made; hence the only provision on objection is that opportunity be afforded for its making out of the presence of the jury. Compare Rule 605.

Note to Subdivision (b). Whether testimony, affidavits, or statements of jurors should be received for the purpose of invalidating or supporting a verdict or indictment, and if so, under what circumstances, has given rise to substantial differences of opinion. The familiar rubric that a juror may not impeach his own verdict, dating from Lord Mansfield's time, is a gross oversimplification. The values sought to be promoted by excluding the evidence include freedom of deliberation, stability and finality of verdicts, and protection of jurors against annoyance and embarrassment. *McDonald v. Pless,* 238 U.S. 264, 35 S.Ct. 783, 59 L.Ed. 1300 (1915). On the other hand, simply putting verdicts beyond effective reach can only promote irregularity and injustice. The rule offers an accommodation between these competing considerations.

The mental operations and emotional reactions of jurors in arriving at a given result would, if allowed as a subject of inquiry, place every verdict at the mercy of jurors and invite tampering and harassment. See *Grenz v. Werre,* 129 N.W.2d 681 (N.D.1964). The authorities are in virtually complete accord in excluding the evidence. Fryer, Note on Disqualification of Witnesses, Selected Writings on Evidence and Trial 345, 347 (Fryer ed. 1957); Maguire, Weinstein, et al., Cases on Evidence 887 (5th ed. 1965); 8 Wigmore § 2349 (McNaughton Rev.1961). As to matters other than mental operations and emotional reactions of jurors, substantial authority refuses to allow a juror to disclose irregularities which occur in the jury room, but allows his testimony as to irregularities occurring outside and allows outsiders to testify as to occurrences both inside and out. 8 Wigmore § 2354 (McNaughton Rev.1961). However, the door of the jury room is not necessarily a satisfactory dividing point, and the Supreme Court has refused to accept it for every situation. *Mattox v. United States,* 146 U.S. 140, 13 S.Ct. 50, 36 L.Ed. 917 (1892).

Under the federal decisions the central focus has been upon insulation of the manner in which the jury reached its verdict, and this protection extends to each of the components of deliberation, including arguments, statements, discussions, mental and emotional reactions, votes, and any other feature of the process. Thus testimony or affidavits of jurors have been held incompetent to show a compromise verdict. *Hyde v. United States,* 225 U.S. 347, 382 (1912); a quotient verdict, *McDonald v. Pless,* 238 U.S. 264 (1915); speculation as to insurance coverage. *Holden v. Porter,* 405 F.2d 878 (10th Cir.1969); *Farmers Coop. Elev. Ass'n v. Strand,* 382 F.2d 224, 230 (8th Cir.1967), cert. denied 389 U.S. 1014; misinterpretation of instructions, *Farmers Coop. Elev. Ass'n v. Strand,* supra; mistake in returning verdict, *United States v. Chereton,* 309 F.2d 197 (6th Cir.1962); interpretation of guilty plea by one defendant as implicating others, *United States v. Crosby,* 294 F.2d 928, 949 (2d Cir.1961). The policy does not, however, foreclose testimony by jurors as to prejudicial extraneous information or influences injected into or brought to bear upon the deliberative process. Thus a juror is recognized as competent to testify to statements by the bailiff or the introduction of a prejudicial newspaper account into the jury room, *Mattox v. United States,* 146 U.S. 140 (1892). See also *Parker v. Gladden,* 385 U.S. 363 (1966).

This rule does not purport to specify the substantive grounds for setting aside verdicts for irregularity; it deals only with the competency of jurors to testify concerning those grounds. Allowing them to testify as to matters other than their own inner reactions involves no particular hazard to the values sought to be protected. The rule is based upon this conclusion. It makes no attempt to specify the substantive grounds for setting aside verdicts for irregularity.

See also Rule 6(e) of the Federal Rules of Criminal Procedure and 18 U.S.C. § 3500, governing the secrecy of grand jury proceedings. The present rule does not relate to secrecy and disclosure but to the competency of certain witnesses and evidence.

1974 Enactment

Note to Subdivision (b). As proposed by the Court, Rule 606(b) limited testimony by a juror in the course of an inquiry into the validity of a verdict or indictment. He could testify as to the influence of extraneous prejudicial information brought to the jury's attention (e.g. a radio newscast or a newspaper account) or an outside influence which improperly had been brought to bear upon a juror (e.g. a threat to the safety of a member of his family), but he could not testify as to other irregularities which occurred in the jury room. Under this formulation a quotient verdict could not be attacked through the testimony of a juror, nor could a juror testify to the drunken condition of a fellow juror which so disabled him that he could not participate in the jury's deliberations.

The 1969 and 1971 Advisory Committee drafts would have permitted a member of the jury to testify concerning these kinds of irregularities in the jury room. The Advisory Committee note in the 1971 draft stated that "* * * the door of the jury room is not a satisfactory dividing point, and the Supreme Court has refused to accept it." The Advisory Committee further commented that—

> The trend has been to draw the dividing line between testimony as to mental processes, on the one hand, and as to the existence of conditions or occurrences of events calculated improperly to influence the verdict on the other hand, without regard to whether the happening is within or without the jury room. * * * The jurors are the persons who know what really happened. Allowing them to testify as to matters other than their own reactions involves no particular hazard to the values sought to be protected. The rule is based upon this conclusion. It makes no attempt to specify the substantive grounds for setting aside verdicts for irregularity.

Objective jury misconduct may be testified to in California, Florida, Iowa, Kansas, Nebraska, New Jersey, North Dakota, Ohio, Oregon, Tennessee, Texas, and Washington.

Persuaded that the better practice is that provided for in the earlier drafts, the Committee amended subdivision (b) to read in the text of those drafts. House Report No. 93–650.

Note to Subdivision (b). As adopted by the House, this rule would permit the impeachment of verdicts by inquiry into, not the mental processes of the jurors, but what happened in terms of conduct in the jury room. This extension of the ability to impeach a verdict is felt to be unwarranted and ill-advised.

The rule passed by the House embodies a suggestion by the Advisory Committee of the Judicial Conference that is considerably broader than the final version adopted by the Supreme Court, which embodied long-accepted Federal law. Although forbidding the impeachment of verdicts by inquiry into the jurors' mental processes, it deletes from the Supreme Court version the proscription against testimony "as to any matter or statement occurring during the course of the jury's deliberations." This deletion would have the effect of opening verdicts up to challenge on the basis of what happened during the jury's internal deliberations, for example, where a juror alleged that the jury refused to follow the trial judge's instructions or that some of the jurors did not take part in deliberations.

Permitting an individual to attack a jury verdict based upon the jury's internal deliberations has long been recognized as unwise by the Supreme Court. In *McDonald v. Pless,* the Court stated:

* * * * * * *

> [L]et it once be established that verdicts solemnly made and publicly returned into court can be attacked and set aside on the testimony of those who took part in their publication and all verdicts could be, and many would be, followed by an inquiry in the hope of discovering something which might invalidate the finding. Jurors would be harassed and beset by the defeated party in an effort to secure from them evidence of facts which might establish misconduct sufficient to set aside a verdict. If evidence thus secured could be thus used, the result would be to make what was intended to be a private deliberation, the constant subject of public investigation—to the destruction of all frankness and freedom of discussion and conference [238 U.S. 264, at 267 (1914)].

* * * * * * *

As it stands then, the rule would permit the harassment of former jurors by losing parties as well as the possible exploitation of disgruntled or otherwise badly-motivated ex-jurors.

Public policy requires a finality to litigation. And common fairness requires that absolute privacy be preserved for jurors to engage in the full and free debate necessary to the attainment of just verdicts. Jurors will not be able to function effectively if their deliberations are to be scrutinized in post-trial litigation. In the interest of protecting the jury system and the citizens who make it work, rule 606 should not permit any inquiry into the internal deliberations of the jurors. Senate Report No. 93–1277.

Note to Subdivision (b). Rule 606(b) deals with juror testimony in an inquiry into the validity of a verdict or indictment. The House bill provides that a juror cannot testify about his mental processes or about the effect of anything upon his or another juror's mind as influencing him to assent to or dissent from a verdict or indictment. Thus, the House bill allows a juror to testify about objective matters occurring during the jury's deliberation, such as the misconduct of another juror or the reaching of a quotient verdict. The Senate bill does not permit juror testimony about any matter or statement occurring during the course of the jury's deliberations. The Senate bill does provide, however, that a juror may testify on the question whether extraneous prejudicial information was improperly brought to the jury's attention and on the question whether any outside influence was improperly brought to bear on any juror.

The Conference adopts the Senate amendment. The Conferees believe that jurors should be encouraged to be conscientious in promptly reporting to the court misconduct that occurs during jury deliberations. House Report No. 93–1597.

1987 Amendments

The amendments are technical. No substantive change is intended.

2006 Amendments

Rule 606(b) has been amended to provide that juror testimony may be used to prove that the verdict reported was the result of a mistake in entering the verdict on the verdict form. The amendment responds to a divergence between the text of the Rule and the case law that has established an exception for proof of clerical errors. *See, e.g., Plummer v. Springfield Term. Ry.*, 5 F.3d 1, 3 (1st Cir. 1993) ("A number of circuits hold, and we agree, that juror testimony regarding an alleged clerical error, such as announcing a verdict different than that agreed upon, does not challenge the validity of the verdict or the deliberation of mental processes, and therefore is not subject to Rule 606(b)."); *Teevee Toons, Inc., v. MP3.Com, Inc.*, 148 F.Supp.2d 276, 278 (S.D.N.Y. 2001) (noting that Rule 606(b) has been silent regarding inquiries designed to confirm the accuracy of a verdict).

In adopting the exception for proof of mistakes in entering the verdict on the verdict form, the amendment specifically rejects the broader exception, adopted by some courts, permitting the use of juror testimony to prove that the jurors were operating under a misunderstanding about the consequences of the result that they agreed upon. *See, e.g., Attridge v. Cencorp Div. of Dover Techs. Int'l, Inc.*, 836 F.2d 113, 116 (2d Cir. 1987); *Eastridge Development Co., v. Halpert Associates, Inc.*, 853 F.2d 772 (10th Cir. 1988). The broader exception is rejected because an inquiry into whether the jury misunderstood or misapplied an instruction goes to the jurors' mental processes underlying the verdict, rather than the verdict's accuracy in capturing what the jurors had agreed upon. *See, e.g. , Karl v. Burlington Northern R.R.*, 880 F.2d 68, 74 (8th Cir. 1989) (error to receive juror testimony on whether verdict was the result of jurors' misunderstanding of instructions: "The jurors did not state that the figure written by the foreman was different from that which they agreed upon, but indicated that the figure the foreman wrote down was intended to be a net figure, not a gross figure. Receiving such statements violates Rule 606(b) because the testimony relates to how the jury interpreted the court's instructions, and concerns the jurors' 'mental processes,' which is forbidden by the rule."); *Robles v. Exxon Corp.*, 862 F.2d 1201, 1208 (5th Cir. 1989) ("the alleged error here goes to the substance of what the jury was asked to decide, necessarily implicating the jury's mental processes insofar as it questions the jury's understanding of the court's instructions and application of those instructions to the facts of the case"). Thus, the exception established by the amendment is limited to cases such as "where the jury foreperson wrote down, in response to an interrogatory, a number different from that agreed upon by the jury, or mistakenly stated that the defendant was 'guilty' when the jury had actually agreed that the defendant was not guilty." *Id.*

It should be noted that the possibility of errors in the verdict form will be reduced substantially by polling the jury. Rule 606(b) does not, of course, prevent this precaution. *See* 8 C. Wigmore, *Evidence*, § 2350 at 691 (McNaughten ed. 1961) (noting that the reasons for the rule barring juror testimony, "namely, the dangers of uncertainty and of tampering with the jurors to procure testimony, disappear in large part if such investigation as may be desired is *made by the judge* and takes place *before the jurors' discharge* and separation") (emphasis in original). Errors that come to light after polling the jury "may be corrected on the spot, or the jury may be sent out to continue deliberations, or, if necessary, a new trial may be ordered." C. Mueller & L. Kirkpatrick, *Evidence Under the Rules* at 671 (2d ed. 1999) (citing *Sincox v. United States*, 571 F.2d 876, 878–79 (5th Cir. 1978)).

Rule 607. Who May Impeach

The credibility of a witness may be attacked by any party, including the party calling the witness.

(Pub.L. 93–595, § 1, Jan. 2, 1975, 88 Stat.1934; Mar. 2, 1987, eff. Oct. 1, 1987.)

1972 Proposed Rules

The traditional rule against impeaching one's own witness is abandoned as based on false premises. A party does not hold out his witnesses as worthy of belief, since he rarely has a free choice in selecting them. Denial of the right leaves the party at the mercy of the witness and the adversary. If the impeachment is by a prior statement, it is free from hearsay dangers and is excluded from the category of hearsay under Rule 801(d)(1). Ladd, Impeachment of One's Own Witness—New Developments, 4 U.Chi.L.Rev. 69 (1936); McCormick § 38; 3 Wigmore §§ 896–918. The substantial inroads into the old rule made over the years by decisions, rules, and statutes are evidence of doubts as to its basic soundness and workability. Cases are collected in 3 Wigmore § 905. Revised Rule 32(a)(1) of the Federal Rules of Civil Procedure allows any party to impeach a witness by means of his deposition, and Rule 43(b) has allowed the calling and impeachment of an adverse party or person identified with him. Illustrative statutes allowing a party to impeach his own witness under varying circumstances are Ill.Rev.Stats.1967, c. 110, § 60; Mass.Laws Annot. 1959, c. 233, § 23; 20 N.M.Stats.Annot. 1953, § 20–2–4; N.Y. CPLR § 4514 (McKinney 1963); 12 Vt.Stats.Annot.1959, §§ 1641a, 1642. Complete judicial rejection of the old rule is found in *United States v. Freeman*, 302 F.2d 347 (2d Cir.1962). The same result is reached in Uniform Rule 20; California Evidence Code § 785; Kansas Code of Civil Procedure § 60–420. See also New Jersey Evidence Rule 20.

1987 Amendments

The amendment is technical. No substantive change is intended.

Rule 608. Evidence of Character and Conduct of Witness

(a) Opinion and reputation evidence of character. The credibility of a witness may be attacked or supported by evidence in the form of opinion or reputation, but subject to these limitations: (1) the evidence may refer only to character for truthfulness or untruthfulness, and (2) evidence of truthful character is admissible only after the character of the witness for truthfulness has been attacked by opinion or reputation evidence or otherwise.

(b) Specific instances of conduct. Specific instances of the conduct of a witness, for the purpose of attacking or supporting the witness' character for truthfulness, other than conviction of crime as provided in rule 609, may not be proved by extrinsic evidence. They may, however, in the discretion of the court, if probative of truthfulness or untruthfulness, be inquired into on cross-examination of the witness (1) concerning the witness' character for truthfulness or untruthfulness, or (2) concerning the character for truthfulness or untruthfulness of another witness as to which character the witness being cross-examined has testified.

The giving of testimony, whether by an accused or by any other witness, does not operate as a waiver of the accused's or the witness' privilege against self-incrimination when examined with respect to matters that relate only to character for truthfulness.

(Pub.L. 93–595, § 1, Jan. 2, 1975, 88 Stat.1935; Mar. 2, 1987, eff. Oct. 1, 1987; Apr. 25, 1988, eff. Nov. 1, 1988; Mar. 27, 2003, eff. Dec. 1, 2003.)

1972 Proposed Rules

Note to Subdivision (a). In Rule 404(a) the general position is taken that character evidence is not admissible for the purpose of proving that the person acted in conformity therewith, subject, however, to several exceptions, one of which is character evidence of a witness as bearing upon his credibility. The present rule develops that exception.

In accordance with the bulk of judicial authority, the inquiry is strictly limited to character for veracity, rather than allowing evidence as to character generally. The result is to sharpen relevancy, to reduce surprise, waste of time, and confusion, and to make the lot of the witness somewhat less unattractive. McCormick § 44.

The use of opinion and reputation evidence as means of proving the character of witnesses is consistent with Rule 405(a). While the modern practice has purported to exclude opinion, witnesses who testify to reputation seem in fact often to be giving their opinions, disguised somewhat misleadingly as reputation. See McCormick § 44. And even under the modern practice, a common relaxation has allowed inquiry as to whether the witnesses would believe the principal witness under oath. *United States v. Walker*, 313 F.2d 236 (6th Cir.1963), and cases cited therein; McCormick § 44, pp. 94–95, n. 3.

Character evidence in support of credibility is admissible under the rule only after the witness' character has first been attacked, as has been the case at common law. Maguire, Weinstein, et al., Cases on Evidence 295 (5th ed. 1965); McCormick § 49, p. 105; 4 Wigmore § 1104. The enormous needless consumption of time which a contrary practice would entail justifies the limitation. Opinion or reputation that the witness is untruthful specifically qualifies as an attack under the rule, and evidence of misconduct, including conviction of crime, and of corruption also fall within this category. Evidence of bias or interest does not. McCormick § 49; 4 Wigmore §§ 1106, 1107. Whether evidence in the form of contradiction is an attack upon the character of the witness must depend upon the circumstances. McCormick § 49. Cf. 4 Wigmore §§ 1108, 1109.

As to the use of specific instances on direct by an opinion witness, see the Advisory Committee's Note to Rule 405, *supra*.

Note to Subdivision (b). In conformity with Rule 405, which forecloses use of evidence of specific incidents as proof in chief of character unless character is an issue in the case, the present rule generally bars evidence of specific instances of conduct of a witness for the purpose of attacking or supporting his credibility. There are, however, two exceptions: (1) specific instances are provable when they have been the subject of criminal conviction, and (2) specific instances may be inquired into on cross-examination of the principal witness or of a witness giving an opinion of his character for truthfulness.

(1) Conviction of crime as a technique of impeachment is treated in detail in Rule 609, and here is merely recognized as an exception to the general rule excluding evidence of specific incidents for impeachment purposes.

(2) Particular instances of conduct, though not the subject of criminal conviction, may be inquired into on cross-examination of the principal witness himself or of a witness who testifies concerning his character for truthfulness. Effective cross-examination demands that some allowance be made for going into matters of this kind, but the possibilities of abuse are substantial. Consequently safeguards are erected in the form of specific requirements that the instances inquired into be probative of truthfulness or its opposite and not remote in time. Also, the overriding protection of Rule 403 requires that probative value not be outweighed by danger of unfair prejudice, confusion of issues, or misleading the jury, and that of Rule 611 bars harassment and undue embarrassment.

The final sentence constitutes a rejection of the doctrine of such cases as *People v. Sorge*, 301 N.Y. 198, 93 N.E.2d 637 (1950), that any past criminal act relevant to credibility may be inquired into on cross-examination, in apparent disregard of the privilege against self-incrimination. While it is clear that an ordinary witness cannot make a partial disclosure of incriminating matter and then invoke the privilege on cross-examination, no tenable contention can be made that merely by testifying he waives his right to foreclose inquiry on cross-examination into criminal activities for the purpose of attacking his credibility. So to hold would reduce the privilege to a nullity. While it is true that an accused, unlike an ordinary witness, has an option whether to testify, if the option can be exercised only at the price of opening up inquiry as to any and all criminal acts committed during his lifetime, the right to testify could scarcely be said to possess much vitality. In *Griffin v. California*, 380 U.S. 609, 85 S.Ct. 1229, 14 L.Ed.2d 106 (1965), the Court held that allowing comment on the election of an accused not to testify exacted a constitutionally impermissible price, and so here. While no specific provision in terms confers constitutional status on the right of an accused to take the stand in his own defense, the existence of the right is so completely recognized that a denial of it or substantial infringement upon it would surely be of due process dimensions. See *Ferguson v. Georgia*, 365 U.S. 570, 81 S.Ct. 756, 5 L.Ed.2d 783 (1961); McCormick § 131; 8 Wigmore § 2276 (McNaughton Rev.1961). In any event, wholly aside from constitutional considerations, the provision represents a sound policy.

1974 Enactment

Note to Subdivision (a). Rule 608(a) as submitted by the Court permitted attack to be made upon the character for truthfulness or untruthfulness of a witness either by reputation or opinion testimony. For the same reason underlying its decision to eliminate the admissibility of opinion testimony in Rule 405(a), the Committee amended Rule 608(a) to delete the reference to opinion testimony.

Note to Subdivision (b). The second sentence of Rule 608(b) as submitted by the Court permitted specific instances of misconduct of a witness to be inquired into on cross-examination for the purpose of attacking his credibility, if probative of truthfulness or untruthfulness, "and not remote in time". Such cross-examination could be of the witness himself or of another witness who testifies as to "his" character for truthfulness or untruthfulness.

The Committee amended the Rule to emphasize the discretionary power of the court in permitting such testimony and deleted the reference to remoteness in time as being unnecessary and confusing (remoteness from time of trial or remoteness from the incident involved?). As recast, the Committee amendment also makes clear the antecedent of "his" in the original Court proposal. House Report No. 93–650.

The Senate amendment adds the words "opinion or" to conform the first sentence of the rule with the remainder of the rule.

The Conference adopts the Senate amendment. House Report No. 93–1597.

1987 Amendments

The amendments are technical. No substantive change is intended.

1988 Amendments

The amendment is technical. No substantive change is intended.

2003 Amendments

The Rule has been amended to clarify that the absolute prohibition on extrinsic evidence applies only when the sole reason for proffering that evidence is to attack or support the witness' character for truthfulness. *See United States v. Abel*, 469 U.S. 45 (1984); *United States v. Fusco*, 748 F.2d 996 (5th Cir. 1984) (Rule 608(b) limits the use of evidence "designed to show that the witness has done things, unrelated to the suit being tried, that make him more or less believable per se"); Ohio R.Evid. 608(b). On occasion the Rule's use of the overbroad term "credibility" has been read "to bar extrinsic evidence for bias, competency and contradiction impeachment since they too deal with credibility." American Bar Association Section of Litigation, *Emerging Problems Under the Federal Rules of Evidence* at 161 (3d ed. 1998). The amendment conforms the language of the Rule to its original intent, which was to impose an absolute bar on extrinsic evidence only if the sole purpose for offering the evidence was to prove the witness' character for veracity. *See* Advisory Committee Note to Rule 608(b) (stating that the Rule is "[i]n conformity with Rule 405, which forecloses use of evidence of specific incidents as proof in chief of character unless character is in issue in the case . . . ").

By limiting the application of the Rule to proof of a witness' character for truthfulness, the amendment leaves the admissibility of extrinsic evidence offered for other grounds of impeachment (such as contradiction, prior inconsistent statement, bias and mental capacity) to Rules 402 and 403. *See, e.g., United States v. Winchenbach*, 197 F.3d 548 (1st Cir. 1999) (admissibility of a prior inconsistent statement offered for impeachment is governed by Rules 402 and 403, not Rule 608(b)); *United States v. Tarantino*, 846 F.2d 1384 (D.C. Cir. 1988) (admissibility of extrinsic evidence offered to contradict a witness is governed by Rules 402 and 403); *United States v. Lindemann*, 85 F.3d 1232 (7th Cir. 1996) (admissibility of extrinsic evidence of bias is governed by Rules 402 and 403).

It should be noted that the extrinsic evidence prohibition of Rule 608(b) bars any reference to the consequences that a witness might have suffered as a result of an alleged bad act. For example, Rule 608(b) prohibits counsel from mentioning that a witness was suspended or disciplined for the conduct that is the subject of impeachment, when that conduct is offered only to prove the character of the witness. *See United States v. Davis*, 183 F.3d 231, 257 n.12 (3d Cir. 1999) (emphasizing that in attacking the defendant's character for truthfulness "the government cannot make reference to Davis's forty-four day suspension or that Internal Affairs found that he lied about" an incident because "[s]uch evidence would not only be hearsay to the extent it contains assertion of fact, it would be inadmissible extrinsic evidence under Rule 608(b)"). *See also* Stephen A. Saltzburg, *Impeaching the Witness: Prior Bad Acts and Extrinsic Evidence*, 7 Crim. Just. 28, 31 (Winter 1993) ("counsel should not be permitted to circumvent the no-extrinsic-evidence provision by tucking a third person's opinion about prior acts into a question asked of the witness who has denied the act").

For purposes of consistency the term "credibility" has been replaced by the term "character for truthfulness" in the last sentence of subdivision (b). The term "credibility" is also used in subdivision (a). But the Committee found it unnecessary to substitute "character for truthfulness" for "credibility" in Rule 608(a), because subdivision (a)(1) already serves to limit impeachment to proof of such character.

Rules 609(a) and 610 also use the term "credibility" when the intent of those Rules is to regulate impeachment of a witness' character for truthfulness. No inference should be derived from the fact that the Committee proposed an amendment to Rule 608(b) but not to Rules 609 and 610.

Rule 609. Impeachment by Evidence of Conviction of Crime

(a) General rule.—For the purpose of attacking the character for truthfulness of a witness,

(1) evidence that a witness other than an accused has been convicted of a crime shall be admitted, subject to Rule 403, if the crime was punishable by death or imprisonment in excess of one year under the law under which the witness was convicted, and evidence that an accused has been convicted of such a crime shall be admitted if the court determines that the probative value of admitting this evidence outweighs its prejudicial effect to the accused; and

(2) evidence that any witness has been convicted of a crime shall be admitted regardless of the punishment, if it readily can be determined that establishing the elements of the crime required proof or admission of an act of dishonesty or false statement by the witness.

(b) Time limit. Evidence of a conviction under this rule is not admissible if a period of more than ten years has elapsed since the date of the conviction or of the release of the witness from the confinement imposed for that conviction, whichever is the later date, unless the court determines, in the interests of justice, that the probative value of the conviction supported by specific facts and circumstances substantially outweighs its prejudicial effect. However, evidence of a conviction more than 10 years old as calculated herein, is not admissible unless the proponent gives to the adverse party sufficient advance written notice of intent to use such evidence to provide the adverse party with a fair opportunity to contest the use of such evidence.

(c) Effect of pardon, annulment, or certificate of rehabilitation.—Evidence of a conviction is not admissible under this rule if (1) the conviction has been the subject of a pardon, annulment, certificate of rehabilitation, or other equivalent procedure based on a finding of the rehabilitation of the person convicted, and that person has not been convicted of a subsequent crime that was punishable by death or imprisonment in excess of one year, or (2) the conviction has been the subject of a pardon, annulment, or other equivalent procedure based on a finding of innocence.

(d) Juvenile adjudications. Evidence of juvenile adjudications is generally not admissible under this rule. The court may, however, in a criminal case allow evidence of a juvenile adjudication of a witness other than the accused if conviction of the offense would be admissible to attack the credibility of an adult and the court is satisfied that admission in evidence is necessary for a fair determination of the issue of guilt or innocence.

(e) Pendency of appeal. The pendency of an appeal therefrom does not render evidence of a conviction inadmissible. Evidence of the pendency of an appeal is admissible.

(Pub.L. 93–595, § 1, Jan. 2, 1975, 88 Stat.1935; Mar. 2, 1987, eff. Oct. 1, 1987; Jan. 26, 1990, eff. Dec. 1, 1990; Apr. 12, 2006, eff. Dec. 1, 2006.)

1972 Proposed Rules

As a means of impeachment, evidence of conviction of crime is significant only because it stands as proof of the commission of the underlying criminal act. There is little dissent from the general proposition that at least some crimes are relevant to credibility but much disagreement among the cases and commentators about which crimes are usable for this purpose. See McCormick § 43; 2 Wright, Federal Practice and Procedure: Criminal § 416 (1969). The weight of traditional authority has been to allow use of felonies generally, without regard to the nature of the particular offense, and of *crimen falsi* without regard to the grade of the offense. This is the view accepted by Congress in the 1970 amendment of § 14–305 of the District of Columbia Code, P.L. 91–358, 84 Stat. 473. Uniform Rule 21 and Model Code Rule 106 permit only crimes involving "dishonesty or false statement." Others have thought that the trial judge should have discretion to exclude convictions if the probative value of the evidence of the crime is substantially outweighed by the danger of unfair prejudice. *Luck v. United States*, 121 U.S.App.D.C. 151, 348 F.2d 763 (1965); McGowan, Impeachment of Criminal Defendants by Prior Convictions, 1970 Law & Soc.Order 1. Whatever may be the merits of those views, this rule is drafted to accord with the Congressional policy manifested in the 1970 legislation.

The proposed rule incorporates certain basic safeguards, in terms applicable to all witnesses but of particular significance to an accused who elects to testify. These protections include the imposition of definite time limitations, giving effect to demonstrated rehabilitation, and generally excluding juvenile adjudications.

Note to Subdivision (a). For purposes of impeachment, crimes are divided into two categories by the rule: (1) those of what is generally regarded as felony grade, without particular regard to the nature of the offense, and (2) those involving dishonesty or false statement, without regard to the grade of the offense. Probable convictions are not limited to violations of federal law. By reason of our constitutional structure, the federal catalog of crimes is far from being a complete one, and resort must be had to the laws of the states for the specification of many crimes. For example, simple theft as compared with theft from interstate commerce. Other instances of borrowing are the Assimilative Crimes Act, making the state law of crimes applicable to the special territorial and maritime jurisdiction of the United States, 18 U.S.C. § 13, and the provision of the Judicial Code disqualifying persons as jurors on the grounds of state as well as federal convictions, 28 U.S.C. § 1865. For evaluation of the crime in terms of seriousness, reference is made to the congressional measurement of felony (subject to imprisonment in excess of one year) rather than adopting state definitions which vary considerably. See 28 U.S.C. § 1865, *supra*, disqualifying jurors for conviction in state or federal court of crime punishable by imprisonment for more than one year.

Note to Subdivision (b). Few statutes recognize a time limit on impeachment by evidence of conviction. However, practical considerations of fairness and relevancy demand that some boundary be recognized. See Ladd, Credibility Tests—Current Trends, 89 U.Pa.L.Rev. 166, 176–177 (1940). This portion of the rule is derived from the proposal advanced in Recommendation Proposing in Evidence Code, § 788(5), p. 142, Cal.Law Rev.Comm'n (1965), though not adopted. See California Evidence Code § 788.

Note to Subdivision (c). A pardon or its equivalent granted solely for the purpose of restoring civil rights lost by virtue of a conviction has no relevance to an inquiry into character. If, however, the pardon or other proceeding is hinged upon a showing of rehabilitation the situation is otherwise. The result under the rule is to render the conviction inadmissible. The alternative of allowing in evidence both the conviction and the rehabilitation has not been adopted for reasons of policy, economy of time, and difficulties of evaluation.

A similar provision is contained in California Evidence Code § 788. Cf. A.L.I. Model Penal Code, Proposed Official Draft § 306.6(3)(e) (1962), and discussion in A.L.I. Proceedings 310 (1961).

Pardons based on innocence have the effect, of course, of nullifying the conviction *ab initio*.

Note to Subdivision (d). The prevailing view has been that a juvenile adjudication is not usable for impeachment. *Thomas v. United States*, 74 App.D.C. 167, 121 F.2d 905 (1941); *Cotton v. United States*, 355 F.2d 480 (10th Cir.1966). This conclusion was based upon a variety of circumstances. By virtue of its informality, frequently diminished quantum of required proof, and other departures from accepted standards for criminal trials under the theory of *parens patriae*, the juvenile adjudication was considered to lack the precision and general probative value of the criminal conviction. While *In re Gault*, 387 U.S. 1, 87 S.Ct. 1428, 18 L.Ed.2d 527 (1967), no doubt eliminates these characteristics insofar as objectionable, other obstacles remain. Practical problems of administration are raised by the common provisions in juvenile legislation that records be kept confidential and that they be destroyed after a short time. While *Gault* was skeptical as to the realities of confidentiality of juvenile records, it also saw no constitutional obstacles to improvement. 387 U.S. at 25, 87 S.Ct. 1428. See also Note, Rights and Rehabilitation in the Juvenile Courts, 67 Colum.L.Rev. 281, 289 (1967). In addition, policy considerations much akin to those which dictate exclusion of adult convictions after rehabilitation has been established strongly suggest a rule of excluding juvenile adjudications. Admittedly, however, the rehabilitative process may in a given case be a demonstrated failure, or the strategic importance of a given witness may be so great as to require the overriding of general policy in the interests of particular justice. See *Giles v. Maryland*, 386 U.S. 66, 87 S.Ct. 793, 17 L.Ed.2d 737 (1967). Wigmore was outspoken in his condemnation of the disallowance of juvenile adjudications to impeach, especially when the witness is the complainant in a case of molesting a minor. 1 Wigmore § 196; 3 *Id.* §§ 924a, 980. The rule recognizes discretion in the judge to effect an accommodation among these various factors by departing from the general principle of exclusion. In deference to the general pattern and policy of juvenile statutes, however, no discretion is accorded when the witness is the accused in a criminal case.

Note to Subdivision (e). The presumption of correctness which ought to attend judicial proceedings supports the position that pendency of an appeal does not preclude use of a conviction for impeachment. *United States v. Empire Packing Co.*, 174 F.2d 16 (7th Cir.1949), cert. denied 337 U.S. 959, 69 S.Ct. 1534, 93 L.Ed. 1758; *Bloch v. United States*, 226 F.2d 185 (9th Cir.1955), cert. denied 350 U.S. 948, 76 S.Ct. 323, 100 L.Ed. 826 and 353 U.S. 959, 77 S.Ct. 868, 1 L.Ed.2d 910; and see *Newman v. United States*, 331 F.2d 968 (8th Cir.1964). *Contra, Campbell v. United States*, 85 U.S.App.D.C. 133, 176 F.2d 45 (1949). The pendency of an appeal is, however, a qualifying circumstance properly considerable.

1974 Enactment

Note to Subdivision (a). Rule 609(a) as submitted by the Court was modeled after Section 133(a) of Public Law 91–358, 14 D.C.Code 305(b)(1), enacted in 1970. The Rule provided that:

> For the purpose of attacking the credibility of a witness, evidence that he has been convicted of a crime is admissible but only if the crime (1) was punishable by death or imprisonment in excess of one year under the law under which he was convicted or (2) involved dishonesty or false statement regardless of the punishment.

As reported to the Committee by the Subcommittee, Rule 609(a) was amended to read as follows:

> For the purpose of attacking the credibility of a witness, evidence that he has been convicted of a crime is admissible only if the crime (1) was punishable by death or imprisonment in excess of one year, unless the court determines that the danger of unfair prejudice outweighs the probative value of the evidence of the conviction, or (2) involved dishonesty or false statement.

In full committee, the provision was amended to permit attack upon the credibility of a witness by prior conviction only if the prior crime involved dishonesty or false statement. While recognizing that the prevailing doctrine in the federal courts and in most States allows a witness to be impeached by evidence of prior felony convictions without restriction as to type, the Committee was of the view that, because of the danger of unfair prejudice in such practice and the deterrent effect upon an accused who might wish to testify, and even upon a witness who was not the accused, cross-examination by evidence of prior conviction should be limited to those kinds of convictions bearing directly on credibility, *i.e.*, crimes involving dishonesty or false statement.

Note to Subdivision (b). Rule 609(b) as submitted by the Court was modeled after Section 133(a) of Public Law 91–358, 14 D.C.Code 305(b)(2)(B), enacted in 1970. The Rule provided:

> Evidence of a conviction under this rule is not admissible if a period of more than ten years has elapsed since the date of the release of the witness from confinement imposed for his most recent conviction, or the expiration of the period of his parole, probation, or sentence granted or imposed with respect to his most recent conviction, whichever is the later date.

Under this formulation, a witness' entire past record of criminal convictions could be used for impeachment (provided the conviction met the standard of subdivision (a)), if the witness had been most recently released from confinement, or the period of his parole or probation had expired, within ten years of the conviction.

The Committee amended the Rule to read in the text of the 1971 Advisory Committee version to provide that upon the expiration of ten years from the date of a conviction of a witness, or of his release from confinement for that offense, that conviction may no longer be used for impeachment. The Committee was of the view that after ten years following a person's release from confinement (or from the date of his conviction) the probative value of the conviction with respect to that person's credibility diminished to a point where it should no longer be admissible.

Note to Subdivision (c). Rule 609(c) as submitted by the Court provided in part that evidence of a witness' prior conviction is not admissible to attack his credibility if the conviction was the subject of a pardon, annulment, or other equivalent procedure, based on a showing of rehabilitation, and the witness has not been convicted of a subsequent crime. The Committee amended the Rule to provide that the "subsequent crime" must have been "punishable by death or imprisonment in excess of one year", on the ground that a subsequent conviction of an offense not a felony is insufficient to rebut the finding that the witness has been rehabilitated. The Committee also intends that the words "based on a finding of the rehabilitation of the person convicted" apply not only to "certificate of rehabilitation, or other equivalent procedure", but also to "pardon" and "annulment.". House Report No. 93–650.

Note to Subdivision (a). As proposed by the Supreme Court, the rule would allow the use of prior convictions to impeach if the crime was a felony or a misdemeanor if the misdemeanor involved dishonesty or false statement. As modified by the House, the rule would admit prior convictions for impeachment purposes only if the offense, whether felony or misdemeanor, involved dishonesty or false statement.

The committee has adopted a modified version of the House-passed rule. In your committee's view, the danger of unfair prejudice is far greater when the accused, as opposed to other witnesses, testifies, because the jury may be prejudiced not merely on the question of credibility but also on the ultimate question of guilt or innocence. Therefore, with respect to defendants, the committee agreed with the House limitation that only offenses involved false statement or dishonesty may be used. By that phrase, the committee means crimes such as perjury or subornation of perjury, false statement, criminal fraud, embezzlement or false pretense, or any other offense, in the nature of *crimen falsi* the commission of which involves some element of untruthfulness, deceit or falsification bearing on the accused's propensity to testify truthfully.

With respect to other witnesses, in addition to any prior conviction involving false statement or dishonesty, any other felony may be used to impeach if, and only if, the court finds that the probative value of such evidence outweighs its prejudicial effect against the party offering that witness.

Notwithstanding this provision, proof of any prior offense otherwise admissible under Rule 404 could still be offered for the purposes sanctioned by that rule. Furthermore, the committee intends that notwithstanding this rule, a defendant's misrepresentation regarding the existence or nature of prior convictions may be met by rebuttal evidence, including the record of such prior convictions. Similarly, such records may be offered to rebut representations made by the defendant regarding his attitude toward or willingness to commit a general category of offense, although denials or other representations by the defendant regarding the specific conduct which forms the basis of the charge against him shall not make prior convictions admissible to rebut such statement.

In regard to either type of representation, of course, prior convictions may be offered in rebuttal only if the defendant's statement is made in response to defense counsel's questions or is made gratuitously in the course of cross-examination. Prior convictions may not be offered as rebuttal evidence if the prosecution has sought to circumvent the purpose of this rule by asking questions which elicit such representations from the defendant.

One other clarifying amendment has been added to this subsection, that is, to provide that the admissibility of evidence of a prior conviction is permitted only upon cross-examination of a witness. It is not admissible if a person does not testify. It is to be understood, however, that a court record of a prior conviction is admissible to prove that conviction if the witness has forgotten or denies its existence.

Note to Subdivision (b). Although convictions over ten years old generally do not have much probative value, there may be exceptional circumstances under which the conviction substantially bears on the credibility of the witness. Rather than exclude all convictions over 10 years old, the committee adopted an amendment in the form of a final clause to the section granting the court discretion to admit convictions over 10 years old, but only upon a determination by the court that the probative value of the conviction supported by specific facts and circumstances, substantially outweighs its prejudicial effect.

It is intended that convictions over 10 years old will be admitted very rarely and only in exceptional circumstances. The rules provide that the decision be supported by specific facts and circumstances thus requiring the court to make specific findings on the record as to the particular facts and circumstances it has considered in determining that the probative value of the conviction substantially outweighs its prejudicial impact. It is expected that, in fairness, the court will give the party against whom the conviction is introduced a full and adequate opportunity to contest its admission. Senate Report No. 93–1277.

Rule 609 defines when a party may use evidence of a prior conviction in order to impeach a witness. The Senate amendments make changes in two subsections of Rule 609.

Note to Subdivision (a). The House bill provides that the credibility of a witness can be attacked by proof of prior conviction of a crime only if the crime involves dishonesty or false statement. The Senate amendment provides that a witness' credibility may be attacked if the crime (1) was punishable by death or imprisonment in excess of one year under the law under which he was convicted or (2) involves dishonesty or false statement, regardless of the punishment.

The Conference adopts the Senate amendment with an amendment. The Conference amendment provides that the credibility of a witness, whether a defendant or someone else, may be attacked by proof of a prior conviction but only if the crime: (1) was punishable by death or imprisonment in excess of one year under the law under which he was convicted and the court determines that the probative value of the conviction outweighs its prejudicial effect to the defendant; or (2) involved dishonesty or false statement regardless of the punishment.

By the phrase "dishonesty and false statement" the Conference means crimes such as perjury or subornation of perjury, false statement, criminal fraud, embezzlement, or false pretense, or any other offense in the nature of *crimen falsi,* the commission of which involves some element of deceit, untruthfulness, or falsification bearing on the accused's propensity to testify truthfully.

The admission of prior convictions involving dishonesty and false statement is not within the discretion of the Court. Such convictions are peculiarly probative of credibility and, under this rule, are always to be admitted. Thus, judicial discretion granted with respect to the admissibility of other prior convictions is not applicable to those involving dishonesty or false statement.

With regard to the discretionary standard established by paragraph (1) of Rule 609(a), the Conference determined that the prejudicial effect to be weighed against the probative value of the conviction is specifically the prejudicial effect *to the defendant.* The danger of prejudice to a witness other than the defendant (such as injury to the witness' reputation in his community) was considered and rejected by the Conference as an element to be weighed in determining admissibility. It was the judgment of the Conference that the danger of prejudice to a nondefendant witness is outweighed by the need for the trier of fact to have as much relevant evidence on the issue of credibility as possible. Such evidence should only be excluded where it presents a danger of improperly influencing the outcome of the trial by persuading the trier of fact to convict the defendant on the basis of his prior criminal record.

Note to Subdivision (b). The House bill provides in subsection (b) that evidence of conviction of a crime may not be used for impeachment purposes under subsection (a) if more than ten years have elapsed since the date of the conviction or the date the witness was released from confinement imposed for the conviction, whichever is later. The Senate amendment permits the use of convictions older than ten years, if the court determines, in the interests of justice, that the probative value of the conviction, supported by specific facts and circumstances, substantially outweighs its prejudicial effect.

The Conference adopts the Senate amendment with an amendment requiring notice by a party that he intends to request that the court allow him to use a conviction older than ten years. The Conferees anticipate that a written notice, in order to give the adversary a fair opportunity to contest the use of the evidence, will ordinarily include such information as the date of the conviction, the jurisdiction, and the offense or statute involved. In order to eliminate the possibility that the flexibility of this provision may impair the ability of a party-opponent to prepare for trial, the Conferees intend that the notice provision operate to avoid surprise. House Report No. 93–1597.

1987 Amendments

The amendments are technical. No substantive change is intended.

1990 Amendments

The amendment to Rule 609(a) makes two changes in the rule. The first change removes from the rule the limitation that the conviction may only be elicited during cross-examination, a limitation that virtually every circuit has found to be inapplicable. It is common for witnesses to reveal on direct examination their convictions to "remove the sting" of the impeachment. *See e.g., United States v. Bad Cob,* 560 F.2d 877 (8th Cir.1977). The amendment does not contemplate that a court will necessarily permit proof of prior convictions through testimony, which might be time-consuming and more prejudicial than proof through a written record. Rules 403 and 611(a) provide sufficient authority for the court to protect against unfair or disruptive methods of proof.

The second change effected by the amendment resolves an ambiguity as to the relationship of Rules 609 and 403 with respect to impeachment of witnesses other than the criminal defendant. *See, Green v. Bock Laundry Machine Co.,* 109 S.Ct. 1981, 490 U.S. 504 (1989). The amendment does not disturb the special balancing test for the criminal defendant who chooses to testify. Thus, the rule recognizes that, in virtually every case in which prior convictions are used to impeach the testifying defendant, the defendant faces a unique risk of prejudice—*i.e.,* the danger that convictions that would be excluded under Fed.R.Evid. 404 will be misused by a jury as propensity evidence despite their introduction solely for impeachment purposes. Although the rule does not forbid all use of convictions to impeach a defendant, it requires that the government show that the probative value of convictions as impeachment evidence outweighs their prejudicial effect.

Prior to the amendment, the rule appeared to give the defendant the benefit of the special balancing test when defense witnesses other than the defendant were called to testify. In practice, however, the concern about unfairness to the defendant is most acute when the defendant's own convictions are offered as evidence. Almost all of the decided cases concern this type of impeachment, and the amendment does not deprive the defendant of any meaningful protection, since Rule 403 now clearly protects against unfair impeachment of any defense witness other than the defendant. There are cases in which a defendant might be prejudiced when a defense witness is impeached. Such cases may arise, for example, when the witness bears a special relationship to the defendant such that the defendant is likely to suffer some spill-over effect from impeachment of the witness.

The amendment also protects other litigants from unfair impeachment of their witnesses. The danger of prejudice from the use of prior convictions is not confined to criminal defendants. Although the danger that prior convictions will be misused as character evidence is particularly acute when the defendant is impeached, the danger exists in other situations as well. The amendment reflects the view that it is desirable to protect all litigants from the unfair use of prior convictions, and that the ordinary balancing test of Rule 403, which provides that evidence shall not be excluded unless its prejudicial effect substantially outweighs its probative value, is appropriate for assessing the admissibility of prior convictions for impeachment of any witness other than a criminal defendant.

The amendment reflects a judgment that decisions interpreting Rule 609(a) as requiring a trial court to admit convictions in civil cases that have little, if anything, to do with credibility reach undesirable results. *See, e.g., Diggs v. Lyons,* 741 F.2d 577 (3d Cir.1984), *cert. denied,* 105 S.Ct. 2157 (1985). The amendment provides the same protection against unfair prejudice arising from prior convictions used for impeachment purposes as the rules provide for other evidence. The amendment finds support in decided cases. *See, e.g., Petty v. Ideco,* 761 F.2d 1146 (5th Cir.1985); *Czaka v. Hickman,* 703 F.2d 317 (8th Cir.1983).

Fewer decided cases address the question whether Rule 609(a) provides any protection against unduly prejudicial prior convictions used to impeach government witnesses. Some courts have read Rule 609(a) as giving the government no protection for its witnesses. *See, e.g., United States v. Thorne,* 547 F.2d 56 (8th Cir.1976); *United States v. Nevitt,* 563 F.2d 406 (9th Cir.1977), *cert. denied,* 444 U.S. 847 (1979). This approach also is rejected by the amendment. There are cases in which impeachment of government witnesses with prior convictions that have little, if anything, to do with credibility may result in unfair prejudice to the government's interest in a fair trial and unnecessary embarrassment to a witness. Fed.R.Evid. 412 already recognizes this and excluded certain evidence of past sexual behavior in the context of prosecutions for sexual assaults.

The amendment applies the general balancing test of Rule 403 to protect all litigants against unfair impeachment of witnesses. The balancing test protects civil litigants, the government in criminal cases, and the defendant in a criminal case who calls other witnesses. The amendment addresses prior convictions offered under Rule 609, not for other purposes, and does not run afoul, therefore, of *Davis v. Alaska,* 415 U.S. 308 (1974). *Davis* involved the use of a prior juvenile adjudication not to prove a past law violation, but to prove bias. The defendant in a criminal case has the right to demonstrate the bias of a witness and to be assured a fair trial, but not to unduly prejudice a trier of fact. *See generally* Rule 412. In any case in which the trial court believes that confrontation rights require admission of impeachment evidence, obviously the Constitution would take precedence over the rule.

The probability that prior convictions of an ordinary government witness will be unduly prejudicial is low in most criminal cases. Since the behavior of the witness is not the issue in dispute in most cases, there is little chance that the trier of fact will misuse the convictions offered as impeachment evidence as propensity evidence. Thus, trial courts will be skeptical when the government objects to impeachment of its witnesses with prior convictions. Only when the government is able to point to a real danger of prejudice that is sufficient to outweigh substantially the probative value of the conviction for impeachment purposes will the conviction be excluded.

The amendment continues to divide subdivision (a) into subsections (1) and (2) thus facilitating retrieval under current computerized research programs which distinguish the two provisions. The Committee recommended no substantive change in subdivision (a)(2), even though some cases raise a concern about the proper interpretation of the words "dishonesty or false statement." These words were used but not explained in the original Advisory Committee Note accompanying Rule 609. Congress extensively debated the rule, and the Report of the House and Senate Conference Committee states that "[b]y the phrase 'dishonesty and false statement,' the Conference means crimes such as perjury, subornation of perjury, false statement, criminal fraud, embezzlement, or false pretense, or any other offense in the nature of *crimen falsi,* commission of which involves some element of deceit, untruthfulness, or falsification bearing on the accused's propensity to testify truthfully." The Advisory Committee concluded that the Conference Report provides sufficient guidance to trial courts and that no amendment is necessary, notwithstanding some decisions that take an unduly broad view of "dishonesty," admitting convictions such as for bank robbery or bank larceny. Subsection (a)(2) continues to apply to any witness, including a criminal defendant.

Finally, the Committee determined that it was unnecessary to add to the rule language stating that, when a prior conviction is offered under Rule 609, the trial court is to consider the probative value of the prior conviction *for impeachment,* not for other purposes. The Committee concluded that the title of the rule, its first sentence, and its placement among the impeachment rules clearly establish that evidence offered under Rule 609 is offered only for purposes of impeachment.

2006 Amendments

The amendment provides that Rule 609(a)(2) mandates the admission of evidence of a conviction only when the conviction required the proof of (or in the case of a guilty plea, the admission of) an act of dishonesty or false statement. Evidence of all other convictions is inadmissible under this subsection, irrespective of whether the witness exhibited dishonesty or made a false statement in the process of the commission of the crime of conviction. Thus, evidence that a witness was convicted for a crime of violence, such as murder, is not admissible under Rule 609(a)(2), even if the witness acted deceitfully in the course of committing the crime.

The amendment is meant to give effect to the legislative intent to limit the convictions that are to be automatically admitted under subdivision (a)(2). The Conference Committee provided that by "dishonesty and false statement" it meant "crimes such as perjury, subornation of perjury, false statement, criminal fraud, embezzlement, or false pretense, or any other offense in the nature of *crimen falsi,* the commission of which involves some element of deceit, untruthfulness, or falsification bearing on the [witness's] propensity to testify truthfully." Historically, offenses classified as *crimina falsi* have included only those crimes in which the ultimate criminal act was itself an act of deceit. *See* Green, *Deceit and the Classification of Crimes: Federal Rule of Evidence 609(a)(2) and the Origins of* Crimen Falsi, 90 J. Crim. L. & Criminology 1087 (2000).

Evidence of crimes in the nature of *crimina falsi* must be admitted under Rule 609(a)(2), regardless of how such crimes are specifically charged. For example, evidence that a witness was convicted of making a false claim to a federal agent is admissible under this subdivision regardless of whether the crime was charged under a section that expressly references deceit (e.g., 18 U.S.C. § 1001, Material Misrepresentation to the Federal Government) or a section that does not (*e.g.*, 18 U.S.C. § 1503, Obstruction of Justice).

The amendment requires that the proponent have ready proof that the conviction required the factfinder to find, or the defendant to admit, an act of dishonesty or false statement. Ordinarily, the statutory elements of the crime will indicate whether it is one of dishonesty or false statement. Where the deceitful nature of the crime is not apparent from the statute and the face of the judgment — as, for example, where the conviction simply records a finding of guilt for a statutory offense that does not reference deceit expressly — a proponent may offer information such as an indictment, a statement of admitted facts, or jury instructions to show that the factfinder had to find, or the defendant had to admit, an act of dishonesty or false statement in order for the witness to have been convicted. *Cf. Taylor v. United States*, 495 U.S. 575, 602 (1990) (providing that a trial court may look to a charging instrument or jury instructions to ascertain the nature of a prior offense where the statute is insufficiently clear on its face); *Shepard v. United States*, 125 S.Ct. 1254 (2005) (the inquiry to determine whether a guilty plea to a crime defined by a nongeneric statute necessarily admitted elements of the generic offense was limited to the charging document's terms, the terms of a plea agreement or transcript of colloquy between judge and defendant in which the factual basis for the plea was confirmed by the defendant, or a comparable judicial record). But the amendment does not contemplate a "mini-trial" in which the court plumbs the record of the previous proceeding to determine whether the crime was in the nature of *crimen falsi*.

The amendment also substitutes the term "character for truthfulness" for the term "credibility" in the first sentence of the Rule. The limitations of Rule 609 are not applicable if a conviction is admitted for a purpose other than to prove the witness's character for untruthfulness. *See, e.g., United States v. Lopez*, 979 F.2d 1024 (5th Cir. 1992) (Rule 609 was not applicable where the conviction was offered for purposes of contradiction). The use of the term "credibility" in subdivision (d) is retained, however, as that subdivision is intended to govern the use of a juvenile adjudication for any type of impeachment.

Rule 610. Religious Beliefs or Opinions

Evidence of the beliefs or opinions of a witness on matters of religion is not admissible for the purpose of showing that by reason of their nature the witness' credibility is impaired or enhanced.

(Pub.L. 93–595, § 1, Jan. 2, 1975, 88 Stat.1936; Mar. 2, 1987, eff. Oct. 1, 1987.)

1972 Proposed Rules

While the rule forecloses inquiry into the religious beliefs or opinions of a witness for the purpose of showing that his character for truthfulness is affected by their nature, an inquiry for the purpose of showing interest or bias because of them is not within the prohibition. Thus disclosure of affiliation with a church which is a party to the litigation would be allowable under the rule. Cf. Tucker v. Reil, 51 Ariz. 357, 77 P.2d 203 (1938). To the same effect, though less specifically worded, is California Evidence Code § 789. See 3 Wigmore § 936.

1987 Amendments

The amendment is technical. No substantive change is intended.

Rule 611. Mode and Order of Interrogation and Presentation

(a) Control by court. The court shall exercise reasonable control over the mode and order of interrogating witnesses and presenting evidence so as to (1) make the interrogation and presentation effective for the ascertainment of the truth, (2) avoid needless consumption of time, and (3) protect witnesses from harassment or undue embarrassment.

(b) Scope of cross-examination. Cross-examination should be limited to the subject matter of the direct examination and matters affecting the credibility of the witness. The court may, in the exercise of discretion, permit inquiry into additional matters as if on direct examination.

(c) Leading questions. Leading questions should not be used on the direct examination of a witness except as may be necessary to develop the witness' testimony. Ordinarily leading questions should be permitted on cross-examination. When a party calls a hostile witness, an adverse party, or a witness identified with an adverse party, interrogation may be by leading questions.

(Pub.L. 93–595, § 1, Jan. 2, 1975, 88 Stat. 1936; Mar. 2, 1987, eff. Oct. 1, 1987.)

1972 Proposed Rules

Note to Subdivision (a). Spelling out detailed rules to govern the mode and order of interrogating witnesses and presenting evidence is neither desirable nor feasible. The ultimate responsibility for the effective working of the adversary system rests with the judge. The rule sets forth the objectives which he should seek to attain.

Item (1) restates in broad terms the power and obligation of the judge as developed under common law principles. It covers such concerns as whether testimony shall be in the form of a free narrative or responses to specific questions, McCormick § 5, the order of calling witnesses and presenting evidence, 6 Wigmore § 1867, the use of demonstrative evidence, McCormick § 179, and the many other questions arising during the course of a trial which can be solved only by the judge's common sense and fairness in view of the particular circumstances.

Item (2) is addressed to avoidance of needless consumption of time, a matter of daily concern in the disposition of cases. A companion piece is found in the discretion vested in the judge to exclude evidence as a waste of time in Rule 403(b).

Item (3) calls for a judgment under the particular circumstances whether interrogation tactics entail harassment or undue embarrassment. Pertinent circumstances include the importance of the testimony, the nature of the inquiry, its relevance to credibility, waste of time, and confusion. McCormick § 42. In *Alford v. United States*, 282 U.S. 687,

694, 51 S.Ct. 218, 75 L.Ed. 624 (1931), the Court pointed out that, while the trial judge should protect the witness from questions which "go beyond the bounds of proper cross-examination merely to harass, annoy or humiliate," this protection by no means forecloses efforts to discredit the witness. Reference to the transcript of the prosecutor's cross-examination in *Berger v. United States,* 295 U.S. 78, 55 S.Ct. 629, 79 L.Ed. 1314 (1935), serves to lay at rest any doubts as to the need for judicial control in this area.

The inquiry into specific instances of conduct of a witness allowed under Rule 608(b) is, of course, subject to this rule.

Note to Subdivision (b). The tradition in the federal courts and in numerous state courts has been to limit the scope of cross-examination to matters testified to on direct, plus matters bearing upon the credibility of the witness. Various reasons have been advanced to justify the rule of limited cross-examination. (1) A party vouches for his own witness but only to the extent of matters elicited on direct. *Resurrection Gold Mining Co. v. Fortune Gold Mining Co.,* 129 F. 668, 675 (8th Cir.1904), quoted in Maguire, Weinstein, et al., Cases on Evidence 277, n. 38 (5th ed. 1965). But the concept of vouching is discredited, and Rule 607 rejects it. (2) A party cannot ask his own witness leading questions. This is a problem properly solved in terms of what is necessary for a proper development of the testimony rather than by a mechanistic formula similar to the vouching concept. See discussion under subdivision (c). (3) A practice of limited cross-examination promotes orderly presentation of the case. *Finch v. Weiner,* 109 Conn. 616, 145 A. 31 (1929). While this latter reason has merit, the matter is essentially one of the order of presentation and not one in which involvement at the appellate level is likely to prove fruitful. See, for example, *Moyer v. Aetna Life Ins. Co.,* 126 F.2d 141 (3rd Cir.1942); *Butler v. New York Central R. Co.,* 253 F.2d 281 (7th Cir.1958); *United States v. Johnson,* 285 F.2d 35 (9th Cir.1960); *Union Automobile Indemnity Ass'n v. Capitol Indemnity Ins. Co.,* 310 F.2d 318 (7th Cir.1962). In evaluating these considerations, McCormick says:

"The foregoing considerations favoring the wide-open or restrictive rules may well be thought to be fairly evenly balanced. There is another factor, however, which seems to swing the balance overwhelmingly in favor of the wide-open rule. This is the consideration of economy of time and energy. Obviously, the wide-open rule presents little or no opportunity for dispute in its application. The restrictive practice in all its forms, on the other hand, is productive in many court rooms, of continual bickering over the choice of the numerous variations of the 'scope of the direct' criterion, and of their application to particular cross-questions. These controversies are often reventilated on appeal, and reversals for error in their determination are frequent. Observance of these vague and ambiguous restrictions is a matter of constant and hampering concern to the cross-examiner. If these efforts, delays and misprisions were the necessary incidents to the guarding of substantive rights or the fundamentals of fair trial, they might be worth the cost. As the price of the choice of an obviously debatable regulation of the order of evidence, the sacrifice seems misguided. The American Bar Association's Committee for the Improvement of the Law of Evidence for the year 1937–38 said this:

'The rule limiting cross-examination to the precise subject of the direct examination is probably the most frequent rule (except the Opinion rule) leading in the trial practice today to refined and technical quibbles which obstruct the progress of the trial, confuse the jury, and give rise to appeal on technical grounds only. Some of the instances in which Supreme Courts have ordered new trials for the mere transgression of this rule about the order of evidence have been astounding.

'We recommend that the rule allowing questions upon any part of the issue known to the witness * * * be adopted. * * *'" McCormick, § 27, p. 51. See also 5 Moore's Federal Practice ¶ 43.10 (2nd ed. 1964).

The provision of the second sentence, that the judge may in the interests of justice limit inquiry into new matters on cross-examination, is designed for those situations in which the result otherwise would be confusion, complication, or protraction of the case, not as a matter of rule but as demonstrable in the actual development of the particular case.

The rule does not purport to determine the extent to which an accused who elects to testify thereby waives his privilege against self-incrimination. The question is a constitutional one, rather than a mere matter of administering the trial. Under *Simmons v. United States,* 390 U.S. 377, 88 S.Ct. 967, 19 L.Ed.2d 1247 (1968), no general waiver occurs when the accused testifies on such preliminary matters as the validity of a search and seizure or the admissibility of a confession. Rule 104(d), *supra.* When he testifies on the merits, however, can he foreclose inquiry into an aspect or element of the crime by avoiding it on direct? The affirmative answer given in *Tucker v. United States,* 5 F.2d 818 (8th Cir.1925), is inconsistent with the description of the waiver as extending to "all other relevant facts" in *Johnson v. United States,* 318 U.S. 189, 195, 63 S.Ct. 549, 87 L.Ed. 704 (1943). See also *Brown v. United States,* 356 U.S. 148, 78 S.Ct. 622, 2 L.Ed.2d 589 (1958). The situation of an accused who desires to testify on some but not all counts of a multiple-count indictment is one to be approached, in the first instance at least, as a problem of severance under Rule 14 of the Federal Rules of Criminal Procedure. *Cross v. United States,* 118 U.S.App. D.C. 324, 335 F.2d 987 (1964). Cf. *United States v. Baker,* 262 F.Supp. 657, 686 (D.D.C.1966). In all events, the extent of the waiver of the privilege against self-incrimination ought not to be determined as a by-product of a rule on scope of cross-examination.

Note to Subdivision (c). The rule continues the traditional view that the suggestive powers of the leading question are as a general proposition undesirable. Within this tradition, however, numerous exceptions have achieved recognition: The witness who is hostile, unwilling, or biased; the child witness or the adult with communication problems; the witness whose recollection is exhausted; and undisputed preliminary matters. 3 Wigmore §§ 774–778. An almost total unwillingness to reverse for infractions has been manifested by appellate courts. See cases cited in 3 Wigmore § 770. The matter clearly falls within the area of control by the judge over the mode and order of interrogation and presentation and accordingly is phrased in words of suggestion rather than command.

The rule also conforms to tradition in making the use of leading questions on cross-examination a matter of right. The purpose of the qualification "ordinarily" is to furnish a basis for denying the use of leading questions when the cross-examination is cross-examination in form only and not in fact, as for example the "cross-examination" of a party by his own counsel after being called by the opponent (savoring more of re-direct) or of an insured defendant who proves to be friendly to the plaintiff.

The final sentence deals with categories of witnesses automatically regarded and treated as hostile. Rule 43(b) of the Federal Rules of Civil Procedure has included only "an adverse party or an officer, director, or managing agent of a public or private corporation or of a partnership or association which is an adverse party." This limitation virtually to persons whose statements would stand as admissions is believed to be an unduly narrow concept of those who may safely be regarded as hostile without further demonstration. See, for example, *Maryland Casualty Co. v. Kador,* 225 F.2d 120 (5th Cir.1955), and *Degelos v. Fidelity and Casualty Co.,* 313 F.2d 809 (5th Cir.1963), holding despite the language of Rule 43(b) that an insured fell within it, though not a party in an action under the Louisiana direct action statute. The phrase of the rule, "witness identified with" an adverse party, is designed to enlarge the category of persons thus callable.

1974 Enactment

Note to Subdivision (b). As submitted by the Court, Rule 611(b) provided:

> A witness may be cross-examined on any matter relevant to any issue in the case, including credibility. In the interests of justice, the judge may limit cross-examination with respect to matters not testified to on direct examination.

The Committee amended this provision to return to the rule which prevails in the federal courts and thirty-nine State jurisdictions. As amended, the Rule is in the text of the 1969 Advisory Committee draft. It limits cross-examination to credibility and to matters testified to on direct examination, unless the judge permits more, in which event the cross-examiner must proceed as if on direct examination. This traditional rule facilitates orderly presentation by each party at trial. Further, in light of existing discovery procedures, there appears to be no need to abandon the traditional rule.

Note to Subdivision (c). The third sentence of Rule 611(c) as submitted by the Court provided that:

> In civil cases, a party is entitled to call an adverse party or witness identified with him and interrogate by leading questions.

The Committee amended this Rule to permit leading questions to be used with respect to any hostile witness, not only an adverse party or person identified with such adverse party. The Committee also substituted the word "When" for the phrase "In civil cases" to reflect the possibility that in criminal cases a defendant may be entitled to call witnesses identified with the government, in which event the Committee believed the defendant should be permitted to inquire with leading questions. House Report No. 93–650.

Note to Subdivision (b). Rule 611(b) as submitted by the Supreme Court permitted a broad scope of cross-examination: "cross-examination on any matter relevant to any issue in the case" unless the judge, in the interests of justice, limited the scope of cross-examination.

The House narrowed the Rule to the more traditional practice of limiting cross-examination to the subject matter of direct examination (and credibility), but with discretion in the judge to permit inquiry into additional matters in situations where that would aid in the development of the evidence or otherwise facilitate the conduct of the trial.

The committee agrees with the House amendment. Although there are good arguments in support of broad cross-examination from perspectives of developing all relevant evidence, we believe the factors of insuring an orderly and predictable development of the evidence weigh in favor of the narrower rule, especially when discretion is given to the trial judge to permit inquiry into additional matters. The committee expressly approves this discretion and believes it will permit sufficient flexibility allowing a broader scope of cross-examination whenever appropriate.

The House amendment providing broader discretionary cross-examination permitted inquiry into additional matters only as if on direct examination. As a general rule, we concur with this limitation, however, we would understand that this limitation would not preclude the utilization of leading questions if the conditions of subsection (c) of this rule were met, bearing in mind the judge's discretion in any case to limit the scope of cross-examination [see McCormick on Evidence, §§ 24–26 (especially 24) (2d ed. 1972)].

Further, the committee has received correspondence from Federal judges commenting on the applicability of this rule to section 1407 of title 28. It is the committee's judgment that this rule as reported by the House is flexible enough to provide sufficiently broad cross-examination in appropriate situations in multidistrict litigation.

Note to Subdivision (c). As submitted by the Supreme Court, the rule provided: "In civil cases, a party is entitled to call an adverse party or witness identified with him and interrogate by leading questions."

The final sentence of subsection (c) was amended by the House for the purpose of clarifying the fact that a "hostile witness"—that is a witness who is hostile in fact—could be subject to interrogation by leading questions. The rule as submitted by the Supreme Court declared certain witnesses hostile as a matter of law and thus subject to interrogation by leading questions without any showing of hostility in fact. These were adverse parties or witnesses identified with adverse parties. However, the wording of the first sentence of subsection (c) while generally prohibiting the use of leading questions on direct examination, also provides "except as may be necessary to develop his testimony." Further, the first paragraph of the Advisory Committee note explaining the subsection makes clear that they intended that leading questions could be asked of a hostile witness or a witness who was unwilling or biased and even though that witness was not associated with an adverse party. Thus, we question whether the House amendment was necessary.

However, concluding that it was not intended to affect the meaning of the first sentence of the subsection and was intended solely to clarify the fact that leading questions are permissible in the interrogation of a witness, who is hostile in fact, the committee accepts that House amendment.

The final sentence of this subsection was also amended by the House to cover criminal as well as civil cases. The committee accepts this amendment, but notes that it may be difficult in criminal cases to determine when a witness is "identified with an adverse party," and thus the rule should be applied with caution. Senate Report No. 93–1277.

1987 Amendments

The amendment is technical. No substantive change is intended.

Rule 612. Writing Used to Refresh Memory

Except as otherwise provided in criminal proceedings by section 3500 of title 18, United States Code, if a witness uses a writing to refresh memory for the purpose of testifying, either—

(1) while testifying, or

(2) before testifying, if the court in its discretion determines it is necessary in the interests of justice,

an adverse party is entitled to have the writing produced at the hearing, to inspect it, to cross-examine the witness thereon, and to introduce in evidence those portions which relate to the testimony of the witness. If it is claimed that the writing contains matters not related to the subject matter of the testimony the court shall examine the writing in camera, excise any portions not so related, and order delivery of the remainder to the party entitled thereto. Any portion withheld over objections shall be preserved and made available to the appellate court in the event of an appeal. If a writing is not produced or delivered pursuant to order under this rule, the court shall make any order justice requires, except that in criminal cases when the prosecution elects not to comply, the order shall be one striking the testimony or, if the court in its discretion determines that the interests of justice so require, declaring a mistrial.

(Pub.L. 93–595, § 1, Jan. 2, 1975, 88 Stat. 1936; Mar. 2, 1987, eff. Oct. 1, 1987.)

1972 Proposed Rules

The treatment of writings used to refresh recollection while on the stand is in accord with settled doctrine. McCormick § 9, p. 15. The bulk of the case law has, however, denied the existence of any right to access by the opponent when the writing is used prior to taking the stand, though the judge may have discretion in the matter. *Goldman v. United States,* 316 U.S. 129, 62 S.Ct. 993, 86 L.Ed. 1322 (1942); *Needelman v. United States,* 261 F.2d 802 (5th Cir.1958), cert. dismissed 362 U.S. 600, 80 S.Ct. 960, 4 L.Ed.2d 980, rehearing denied 363 U.S. 858, 80 S.Ct. 1606, 4 L.Ed.2d 1739, Annot., 82 A.L.R.2d 473, 562 and 7 A.L.R.3d 181, 247. An increasing group of cases has repudiated the distinction. *People v. Scott,* 29 Ill.2d 97, 193 N.E.2d 814 (1963); *State v. Mucci,* 25 N.J. 423, 136 A.2d 761 (1957); *State v. Hunt,* 25 N.J. 514, 138 A.2d 1 (1958); *State v. Deslovers,* 40 R.I. 89, 100 A. 64 (1917), and this position is believed to be correct. As Wigmore put it, "the risk of imposition and the need of safeguard is just as great" in both situations. 3 Wigmore § 762, p. 111. To the same effect is McCormick, § 9, p. 17.

The purpose of the phrase "for the purpose of testifying" is to safeguard against using the rule as a pretext for wholesale exploration of an opposing party's files and to insure that access is limited only to those writings which may fairly be said in fact to have an impact upon the testimony of the witness.

The purpose of the rule is the same as that of the *Jencks* statute, 18 U.S.C. § 3500: to promote the search of credibility and memory. The same sensitivity to disclosure of government files may be involved; hence the rule is expressly made subject to the statute, subdivision (a) of which provides: "In any criminal prosecution brought by the United States, no statement or report in the possession of the United States which was made by a Government witness or prospective Government witness (other than the defendant) shall be the subject of subpena, discovery, or inspection until said witness has testified on direct examination in the trial of the case." Items falling within the purview of the statute are producible only as provided by its terms, *Palermo v. United States,* 360 U.S. 343, 351 (1959), and disclosure under the rule is limited similarly by the statutory conditions. With this limitation in mind, some differences of application may be noted. The *Jencks* statute applies only to statements of witnesses; the rule is not so limited. The statute applies only to criminal cases; the rule applies to all cases. The statute applies only to government witnesses; the rule applies to all witnesses. The statute contains no requirement that the statement be consulted for purposes of refreshment before or while testifying; the rule so requires. Since many writings would qualify under either statute or rule, a substantial overlap exists, but the identity of procedures makes this of no importance.

The consequences of nonproduction by the government in a criminal case are those of the *Jencks* statute, striking the testimony or in exceptional cases a mistrial. 18 U.S.C. § 3500(d). In other cases these alternatives are unduly limited, and such possibilities as contempt, dismissal, finding issues against the offender, and the like are available. See Rule 16(g) of the Federal Rules of Criminal Procedure and Rule 37(b) of the Federal Rules of Civil Procedure for appropriate sanctions.

1974 Enactment

As submitted to Congress, Rule 612 provided that except as set forth in 18 U.S.C. 3500, if a witness uses a writing to refresh his memory for the purpose of testifying, "either before or while testifying," an adverse party is entitled to have the writing produced at the hearing, to inspect it, to cross-examine the witness on it, and to introduce in evidence those portions relating to the witness' testimony. The Committee amended the Rule so as still to require the production of writings used by a witness while testifying, but to render the production of writings used by a witness to refresh his memory before testifying discretionary with the court in the interests of justice, as is the case under existing federal law. See Goldman v. United States, 316 U.S. 129 (1942). The Committee considered that permitting an adverse party to require the production of writings used before testifying could result in fishing expeditions among a multitude of papers which a witness may have used in preparing for trial.

The Committee intends that nothing in the Rule be construed as barring the assertion of a privilege with respect to writings used by a witness to refresh his memory. House Report No. 93–650.

1987 Amendments

The amendment is technical. No substantive change is intended.

Rule 613. Prior Statements of Witnesses

(a) Examining witness concerning prior statement. In examining a witness concerning a prior statement made by the witness, whether written or not, the statement need not be shown nor its contents disclosed to the witness at that time, but on request the same shall be shown or disclosed to opposing counsel.

(b) Extrinsic evidence of prior inconsistent statement of witness. Extrinsic evidence of a prior inconsistent statement by a witness is not admissible unless the witness is afforded an opportunity to explain or deny the same and the opposite party is afforded an opportunity to interrogate the witness thereon, or the interests of justice otherwise require. This provision does not apply to admissions of a party-opponent as defined in rule 801(d)(2).

(Pub.L. 93–595, § 1, Jan. 2, 1975, 88 Stat.1936; Mar. 2, 1987, eff. Oct. 1, 1987; Apr. 25, 1988, eff. Nov. 1, 1988.)

1972 Proposed Rules

Note to Subdivision (a). The Queen's Case, 2 Br. & B. 284, 129 Eng.Rep. 976 (1820), laid down the requirement that a cross-examiner, prior to questioning the witness about his own prior statement in writing, must first show it to the witness. Abolished by statute in the country of its origin, the requirement nevertheless gained currency in the United States. The rule abolishes this useless impediment, to cross-examination. Ladd, Some Observations on Credibility: Impeachment of Witnesses, 52 Cornell L.Q. 239, 246–247 (1967); McCormick § 28; 4 Wigmore §§ 1259–1260. Both oral and written statements are included.

The provision for disclosure to counsel is designed to protect against unwarranted insinuations that a statement has been made when the fact is to the contrary.

The rule does not defeat the application of Rule 1002 relating to production of the original when the contents of a writing are sought to be proved. Nor does it defeat the application of Rule 26(b)(3) of the Rules of Civil Procedure, as revised, entitling a person on request to a copy of his own statement, though the operation of the latter may be suspended temporarily.

Note to Subdivision (b). The familiar foundation requirement that an impeaching statement first be shown to the witness before it can be proved by extrinsic evidence is preserved but with some modifications. See Ladd, Some Observations on Credibility: Impeachment of Witnesses, 52 Cornell L.Q. 239, 247 (1967). The traditional insistence that the attendance of the witness be directed to the statement on cross-examination is relaxed in favor of simply providing the witness an opportunity to explain and the opposite party an opportunity to examine on the statement, with no specification of any particular time or sequence. Under this procedure, several collusive witnesses can be examined before disclosure of a joint prior inconsistent statement. See Comment to California Evidence Code § 770. Also, dangers of oversight are reduced. See McCormick § 37, p. 68.

In order to allow for such eventualities as the witness becoming unavailable by the time the statement is discovered, a measure of discretion is conferred upon the judge. Similar provisions are found in California Evidence Code § 770 and New Jersey Evidence Rule 22(b).

Under principles of *expression unius* the rule does not apply to impeachment by evidence of prior inconsistent conduct. The use of inconsistent statements to impeach a hearsay declaration is treated in Rule 806.

1987 Amendments

The amendments are technical. No substantive change is intended.

1988 Amendments

The amendment is technical. No substantive change is intended.

Rule 614. Calling and Interrogation of Witnesses by Court

(a) Calling by court. The court may, on its own motion or at the suggestion of a party, call witnesses, and all parties are entitled to cross-examine witnesses thus called.

(b) Interrogation by court. The court may interrogate witnesses, whether called by itself or by a party.

(c) Objections. Objections to the calling of witnesses by the court or to interrogation by it may be made at the time or at the next available opportunity when the jury is not present.

(Pub.L. 93–595, § 1, Jan. 2, 1975, 88 Stat.1937.)

1972 Proposed Rules

Note to Subdivision (a). While exercised more frequently in criminal than in civil cases, the authority of the judge to call witnesses is well established. McCormick § 8, p. 14; Maguire, Weinstein, et al., Cases on Evidence 303–304 (5th ed. 1965); 9 Wigmore § 2484. One reason for the practice, the old rule against impeaching one's own witness, no longer exists by virtue of Rule 607, *supra*. Other reasons remain, however, to justify the continuation of the practice of calling court's witnesses. The right to cross-examine, with all it implies, is assured. The tendency of juries to associate a witness with the party calling him, regardless of technical aspects of vouching, is avoided. And the judge is not imprisoned within the case as made by the parties.

Note to Subdivision (b). The authority of the judge to question witnesses is also well established. McCormick § 8, pp. 12–13; Maguire, Weinstein, et al., Cases on Evidence 737–739 (5th ed. 1965); 3 Wigmore § 784. The authority is, of course, abused when the judge abandons his proper role and assumes that of advocate, but the manner in which interrogation should be conducted and the proper extent of its exercise are not susceptible of formulation in a rule. The omission in no sense precludes courts of review from continuing to reverse for abuse.

Note to Subdivision (c). The provision relating to objections is designed to relieve counsel of the embarrassment attendant upon objecting to questions by the judge in the presence of the jury, while at the same time assuring that objections are made in apt time to afford the opportunity to take possible corrective measures. Compare the "automatic" objection feature of Rule 605 when the judge is called as a witness.

Rule 615. Exclusion of Witnesses

At the request of a party the court shall order witnesses excluded so that they cannot hear the testimony of other witnesses, and it may make the order of its own motion. This rule does not authorize exclusion of (1) a party who is a natural person, or (2) an officer or employee of a party which is not a natural person designated as its representative by its attorney, or (3) a person whose presence is shown by a party to be essential to the presentation of the party's cause, or (4) a person authorized by statute to be present. (Pub.L. 93–595, § 1, Jan. 2, 1975, 88 Stat.1937; Mar. 2, 1987, eff. Oct. 1, 1987; Apr. 25, 1988, eff. Nov. 1, 1988; Pub.L. 100–690, Nov. 18, 1988, Title VII, § 7075(a), 102 Stat. 4405; Apr. 24, 1998, eff. Dec. 1, 1998.)

1972 Proposed Rules

The efficacy of excluding or sequestering witnesses has long been recognized as a means of discouraging and exposing fabrication, inaccuracy, and collusion. 6 Wigmore §§ 1837–1838. The authority of the judge is admitted, the only question being whether the matter is committed to his discretion or one of right. The rule takes the latter position. No time is specified for making the request.

Several categories of persons are excepted. (1) Exclusion of persons who are parties would raise serious problems of confrontation and due process. Under accepted practice they are not subject to exclusion. 6 Wigmore § 1841. (2) As the equivalent of the right of a natural-person party to be present, a party which is not a natural person is entitled to have a representative present. Most of the cases have involved allowing a police officer who has been in charge of an investigation to remain in court despite the fact that he will be a witness. United States v. Infanzon, 235 F.2d 318, (2d Cir.1956); *Portomene v. United States,* 221 F.2d 582 (5th Cir.1955); *Powell v. United States,* 208 F.2d 618 (6th Cir. 1953); *Jones v. United States,* 252 F.Supp. 781 (W.D.Okl. 1966). Designation of the representative by the attorney rather than by the client may at first glance appear to be an inversion of the attorney-client relationship, but it may be assumed that the attorney will follow the wishes of the client, and the solution is simple and workable. See California Evidence Code § 777. (3) The category contemplates such persons as an agent who handled the transaction being litigated or an expert needed to advise counsel in the management of the litigation. See 6 Wigmore § 1841, n. 4.

1974 Enactment

Many district courts permit government counsel to have an investigative agent at counsel table throughout the trial although the agent is or may be a witness. The practice is permitted as an exception to the rule of exclusion and compares with the situation defense counsel finds himself in—he always has the client with him to consult during the trial. The investigative agent's presence may be extremely important to government counsel, especially when the case is complex or involves some specialized subject matter. The agent, too, having lived with the case for a long time, may be able to assist in meeting trial surprises where the best-prepared counsel would otherwise have difficulty. Yet, it would not seem the Government could often meet the burden under rule 615 of showing that the agent's presence is essential. Furthermore, it could be dangerous to use the agent as a witness as early in the case as possible, so that he might then help counsel as a nonwitness, since the agent's testimony could be needed in rebuttal. Using another, nonwitness agent from the same investigative agency would not generally meet government counsel's needs.

This problem is solved if it is clear that investigative agents are within the group specified under the second exception made in the rule, for "an officer or employee of a party which is not a natural person designated as its representative by its attorney." It is our understanding that this was the intention of the House committee. It is certainly this committee's construction of the rule. Senate Report No. 93–1277.

1987 Amendments

The amendment is technical. No substantive change is intended.

1988 Amendments

The amendment is technical. No substantive change is intended.

1998 Amendments

The amendment is in response to: (1) the Victim's Rights and Restitution Act of 1990, 42 U.S.C. § 10606, which guarantees, within certain limits, the right of a crime victim to attend the trial; and (2) the Victim Rights Clarification Act of 1997 (18 U.S.C. § 3510).

Rules 616 to 700. Reserved for future legislation

ARTICLE VII. OPINIONS AND EXPERT TESTIMONY

Rule 701. Opinion Testimony by Lay Witnesses

If the witness is not testifying as an expert, the witness' testimony in the form of opinions or inferences is limited to those opinions or inferences which are (a) rationally based on the perception of the witness, (b) helpful to a clear understanding of the witness' testimony or the determination of a fact in issue, and (c) not based on scientific, technical, or other specialized knowledge within the scope of Rule 702.

(Pub.L. 93–595, § 1, Jan. 2, 1975, 88 Stat.1937; Mar. 2, 1987, eff. Oct. 1, 1987; Apr. 17, 2000, eff. Dec. 1, 2000.)

1972 Proposed Rules

The rule retains the traditional objective of putting the trier of fact in possession of an accurate reproduction of the event.

Limitation (a) is the familiar requirement of first-hand knowledge or observation.

Limitation (b) is phrased in terms of requiring testimony to be helpful in resolving issues. Witnesses often find difficulty in expressing themselves in language which is not that of an opinion or conclusion. While the courts have made concessions in certain recurring situations, necessity as a standard for permitting opinions and conclusions has proved too elusive and too unadaptable to particular situations for purposes of satisfactory judicial administration. McCormick § 11. Moreover, the practical impossibility of determining by rule what is a "fact," demonstrated by a century of litigation of the question of what is a fact for purposes of pleading under the Field Code, extends into evidence also. 7 Wigmore § 1919. The rule assumes that the natural characteristics of the adversary system will generally lead to an acceptable result, since the detailed account carries more conviction than the broad assertion, and a lawyer can be expected to display his witness to the best advantage. If he fails to do so, cross-examination and argument will point up the weakness. See Ladd, Expert Testimony, 5 Vand.L.Rev. 414, 415–417 (1952). If, despite these considerations, attempts are made to introduce meaningless assertions which amount to little more than choosing up sides, exclusion for lack of helpfulness is called for by the rule.

The language of the rule is substantially that of Uniform Rule 56(1). Similar provisions are California Evidence Code § 800; Kansas Code of Civil Procedure § 60–456(a); New Jersey Evidence Rule 56(1).

1987 Amendments

The amendments are technical. No substantive change is intended.

2000 Amendments

Rule 701 has been amended to eliminate the risk that the reliability requirements set forth in Rule 702 will be evaded through the simple expedient of proffering an expert in lay witness clothing. Under the amendment, a witness' testimony must be scrutinized under the rules regulating expert opinion to the extent that the witness is providing testimony based on scientific, technical, or other specialized knowledge within the scope of Rule 702. *See generally Asplundh Mfg. Div. v. Benton Harbor Eng'g*, 57 F.3d 1190 (3d Cir. 1995). By channeling testimony that is actually expert testimony to Rule 702, the amendment also ensures that a party will not evade the expert witness disclosure requirements set forth in Fed.R.Civ.P. 26 and Fed.R.Crim.P. 16 by simply calling an expert witness in the guise of a layperson. *See* Joseph, *Emerging Expert Issues Under the 1993 Disclosure Amendments to the Federal Rules of Civil Procedure*, 164 F.R.D. 97, 108 (1996) (noting that "there is no good reason to allow what is essentially surprise expert testimony." and that "the Court should be vigilant to preclude manipulative conduct designed to thwart the expert disclosure and discovery process") *See also United States v. Figueroa–Lopez*, 125 F.3d 1241, 1246 (9th Cir. 1997) (law enforcement agents testifying that the defendant's conduct was consistent with that of a drug trafficker could not testify as lay witnesses; to permit such testimony under Rule 701 "subverts the requirements of Federal Rule of Criminal Procedure 16(a)(1)(E)").

The amendment does not distinguish between expert and lay *witnesses*, but rather between expert and lay *testimony*. Certainly it is possible for the same witness to provide both lay and expert testimony in a single case. *See, e.g, United States v. Figueroa–Lopez*, 125 F.3d 1241, 1246 (9th Cir. 1997) (law enforcement agents could testify that the defendant was acting suspiciously, without being qualified as experts; however, the rules on experts were applicable where the agents testified on the basis of extensive experience that the defendant was using code words to refer to drug quantities and prices). The amendment makes clear that any part of a witness' testimony that is based upon scientific, technical, or other specialized knowledge within the scope of Rule 702 is governed by the standards of Rule 702 and the corresponding disclosure requirements of the Civil and Criminal Rules.

The amendment is not intended to affect the "prototypical example[s] of the type of evidence contemplated by the adoption of Rule 701 relat[ing] to the appearance of persons or things, identity, the manner of conduct, competency of a person, degrees of light or darkness, sound, size, weight, distance, and an endless number of items that cannot be described factually in words apart from inferences." *Asplundh Mfg. Div. v. Benton Harbor Eng' g*, 57 F.3d 1190, 1196 (3d Cir. 1995).

For example, most courts have permitted the owner or officer of a business to testify to the value or projected profits of the business, without the necessity of qualifying the witness as an accountant, appraiser, or similar expert. *See, e.g., Lightning Lube, Inc. v. Witco Corp.* 4 F.3d 1153 (3d Cir. 1993) (no abuse of discretion in permitting the plaintiff's owner to give lay opinion testimony as to damages, as it was based on his knowledge and participation in the day-to-day affairs of the business). Such opinion testimony is admitted not because of experience, training or specialized knowledge within the realm of an expert, but because of the particularized knowledge that the witness has by virtue of his or her position in the business. The amendment does not purport to change this analysis. Similarly, courts have permitted lay witnesses to testify that a substance appeared to be a narcotic, so long as a foundation of familiarity with the substance is established. *See, e.g., United States v. Westbrook*, 896 F.2d 330 (8th Cir. 1990) (two lay witnesses who were heavy amphetamine users were properly permitted to testify that a substance was amphetamine; but it was error to permit another witness to make such an identification where she had no experience with amphetamines). Such testimony is not based on specialized knowledge within the scope of Rule 702, but rather is based upon a layperson's personal knowledge. If, however, that witness were to describe how a narcotic was manufactured, or to describe the intricate workings of a narcotic distribution network, then the witness would have to qualify as an expert under Rule 702. *United States v . Figueroa–Lopez, supra.*

The amendment incorporates the distinctions set forth in *State v. Brown*, 836 S.W.2d 530, 549 (1992), a case involving former Tennessee Rule of Evidence 701, a rule that precluded lay witness testimony based on "special knowledge." In *Brown*, the court declared that the distinction between lay and expert witness testimony is that lay testimony "results from a process of reasoning familiar in everyday life," while expert testimony "results from a process of reasoning which can be mastered only by specialists in the field." The court in *Brown* noted that a lay witness with experience could testify that a substance appeared to be blood, but that a witness would have to qualify as an expert before he could testify that bruising around the eyes is indicative of skull trauma. That is the kind of distinction made by the amendment to this Rule.

GAP Report—Proposed Amendment to Rule 701

The Committee made the following changes to the published draft of the proposed amendment to Evidence Rule 701:

1. The words "within the scope of Rule 702" were added at the end of the proposed amendment, to emphasize that the Rule does not require witnesses to qualify as experts unless their testimony is of the type traditionally considered within the purview of Rule 702. The Committee Note was amended to accord with this textual change.

2. The Committee Note was revised to provide further examples of the kind of testimony that could and could not be proffered under the limitation imposed by the proposed amendment.

Rule 702. Testimony by Experts

If scientific, technical, or other specialized knowledge will assist the trier of fact to understand the evidence or to determine a fact in issue, a witness qualified as an expert by knowledge, skill, experience, training, or education, may testify thereto in the form of an opinion or otherwise, if (1) the testimony is based upon sufficient facts or data, (2) the testimony is the product of reliable principles and methods, and (3) the witness has applied the principles and methods reliably to the facts of the case.

(Pub.L. 93–595, § 1, Jan. 2, 1975, 88 Stat. 1937; Apr. 17, 2000, eff. Dec. 1, 2000.)

1972 Proposed Rules

An intelligent evaluation of facts is often difficult or impossible without the application of some scientific, technical, or other specialized knowledge. The most common source of this knowledge is the expert witness, although there are other techniques for supplying it.

Most of the literature assumes that experts testify only in the form of opinions. The assumption is logically unfounded. The rule accordingly recognizes that an expert on the stand may give a dissertation or exposition of scientific or other principles relevant to the case, leaving the trier of fact to apply them to the facts. Since much of the criticism of expert testimony has centered upon the hypothetical question, it seems wise to recognize that opinions are not indispensable and to encourage the use of expert testimony in non-opinion form when counsel believes the trier can itself draw the requisite inference. The use of opinions is not abolished by the rule, however. It will continue to be permissible for the experts to take the further step of suggesting the inference which should be drawn from applying the specialized knowledge to the facts. See Rules 703 to 705.

Whether the situation is a proper one for the use of expert testimony is to be determined on the basis of assisting the trier. "There is no more certain test for determining when experts may be used than the common sense inquiry whether the untrained layman would be qualified to determine intelligently and to the best possible degree the particular issue without enlightenment from those having a specialized understanding of the subject involved in the dispute." Ladd, Expert Testimony, 5 Vand.L.Rev. 414, 418 (1952). When opinions are excluded, it is because they are unhelpful and therefore superfluous and a waste of time. 7 Wigmore § 1918.

The rule is broadly phrased. The fields of knowledge which may be drawn upon are not limited merely to the "scientific" and "technical" but extend to all "specialized" knowledge. Similarly, the expert is viewed, not in a narrow sense, but as a person qualified by "knowledge, skill, experience, training or education." Thus within the scope of the rule are not only experts in the strictest sense of the word, e.g., physicians, physicists, and architects, but also the large group sometimes called "skilled" witnesses, such as bankers or landowners testifying to land values.

2000 Amendments

Rule 702 has been amended in response to *Daubert v. Merrell Dow Pharmaceuticals, Inc.*, 509 U.S. 579 (1993), and to the many cases applying *Daubert*, including *Kumho Tire Co. v. Carmichael*, 119 S.Ct. 1167 (1999). In *Daubert* the Court charged trial judges with the responsibility of acting as gatekeepers to exclude unreliable expert testimony, and the Court in *Kumho* clarified that this gatekeeper function applies to all expert testimony, not just testimony based in science. *See also Kumho*, 119 S.Ct. at 1178 (citing the Committee Note to the proposed amendment to Rule 702, which had been released for public comment before the date of the *Kumho* decision). The amendment affirms the trial court's role as gatekeeper and provides some general standards that the trial court must use to assess the reliability and helpfulness of proffered expert testimony. Consistently with *Kumho*, the Rule as amended provides that all types of expert testimony present questions of admissibility for the trial court in deciding whether the evidence is reliable and helpful. Consequently, the admissibility of all expert testimony is governed by the principles of Rule 104(a). Under that Rule, the proponent has the burden of establishing that the pertinent admissibility requirements are met by a preponderance of the evidence. *See Bourjaily v. United States*, 483 U.S. 171 (1987).

Daubert set forth a non-exclusive checklist for trial courts to use in assessing the reliability of scientific expert testimony. The specific factors explicated by the *Daubert* Court are (1) whether the expert's technique or theory can be or has been tested—that is, whether the expert's theory can be challenged in some objective sense, or whether it is instead simply a subjective, conclusory approach that cannot reasonably be assessed for reliability; (2) whether the technique or theory has been subject to peer review and publication; (3) the known or potential rate of error of the technique or theory when applied; (4) the existence and maintenance of standards and controls; and (5) whether the technique or theory has been generally accepted in the scientific community. The Court in *Kumho* held that these factors might also be applicable in assessing the reliability of non-scientific expert testimony, depending upon "the particular circumstances of the particular case at issue." 119 S.Ct. at 1175.

No attempt has been made to "codify" these specific factors. *Daubert* itself emphasized that the factors were neither exclusive nor dispositive. Other cases have recognized that not all of the specific *Daubert* factors can apply to every type of expert testimony. In addition to *Kumho*, 119 S.Ct. at 1175, *see Tyus v. Urban Search Management*, 102 F.3d 256 (7th Cir. 1996) (noting that the factors mentioned by the Court in *Daubert* do not neatly apply to expert testimony from a sociologist). *See also Kannankeril v. Terminix Int'l, Inc.*, 128 F.3d 802, 809 (3d Cir. 1997) (holding that lack of peer review or publication was not dispositive where the expert's opinion was supported by "widely accepted scientific knowledge"). The standards set forth in the amendment are broad enough to require consideration of any or all of the specific *Daubert* factors where appropriate.

Courts both before and after *Daubert* have found other factors relevant in determining whether expert testimony is sufficiently reliable to be considered by the trier of fact. These factors include:

(1) Whether experts are "proposing to testify about matters growing naturally and directly out of research they have conducted independent of the litigation, or whether they have developed their opinions expressly for purposes of testifying." *Daubert v. Merrell Dow Pharmaceuticals, Inc.*, 43 F.3d 1311, 1317 (9th Cir. 1995).

(2) Whether the expert has unjustifiably extrapolated from an accepted premise to an unfounded conclusion. *See General Elec. Co. v. Joiner*, 522 U.S. 136, 146 (1997) (noting that in some cases a trial court "may conclude that there is simply too great an analytical gap between the data and the opinion proffered").

(3) Whether the expert has adequately accounted for obvious alternative explanations. *See Claar v. Burlington N.R.R.*, 29 F.3d 499 (9th Cir. 1994) (testimony excluded where the expert failed to consider other obvious causes for the plaintiff's condition). *Compare Ambrosini v. Labarraque*, 101 F.3d 129 (D.C. Cir. 1996) (the possibility of some uneliminated causes presents a question of weight, so long as the most obvious causes have been considered and reasonably ruled out by the expert).

(4) Whether the expert "is being as careful as he would be in his regular professional work outside his paid litigation consulting." *Sheehan v. Daily Racing Form, Inc.*, 104 F.3d 940, 942 (7th Cir. 1997). *See Kumho Tire Co. v. Carmichael*, 119 S.Ct. 1167, 1176 (1999) (*Daubert* requires the trial court to assure itself that the expert "employs in the courtroom the same level of intellectual rigor that characterizes the practice of an expert in the relevant field").

(5) Whether the field of expertise claimed by the expert is known to reach reliable results for the type of opinion the expert would give. *See Kumho Tire Co. v. Carmichael*, 119 S.Ct.1167, 1175 (1999) (*Daubert's* general acceptance factor does not "help show that an expert's testimony is reliable where the discipline itself lacks reliability, as for example, do theories grounded in any so-called generally accepted principles of astrology or necromancy."), *Moore v. Ashland Chemical, Inc.*, 151 F.3d 269 (5th Cir. 1998) (en banc) (clinical doctor was properly precluded from testifying to the toxicological cause of the plaintiff's respiratory problem, where the opinion was not sufficiently grounded in scientific methodology); *Sterling v. Velsicol Chem. Corp.*, 855 F.2d 1188 (6th Cir. 1988) (rejecting testimony based on "clinical ecology" as unfounded and unreliable).

All of these factors remain relevant to the determination of the reliability of expert testimony under the Rule as amended. Other factors may also be relevant. *See Kumho*, 119 S.Ct. 1167, 1176 ("[W]e conclude that the trial judge must have considerable leeway in deciding in a particular case how to go about determining whether particular expert testimony is reliable."). Yet no single factor is necessarily dispositive of the reliability of a particular expert's testimony. *See, e.g., Heller v. Shaw Industries, Inc.*, 167 F.3d 146, 155 (3d Cir. 1999) ("not only must each stage of the expert's testimony be reliable, but each stage must be evaluated practically and flexibly without bright-line exclusionary (or inclusionary) rules."); *Daubert v. Merrell Dow Pharmaceuticals, Inc.*, 43 F.3d 1311, 1317, n.5 (9th Cir. 1995) (noting that some expert disciplines "have the courtroom as a principal theatre of operations" and as to these disciplines "the fact that the expert has developed an expertise principally for purposes of litigation will obviously not be a substantial consideration.").

A review of the caselaw after *Daubert* shows that the rejection of expert testimony is the exception rather than the rule. *Daubert* did not work a "seachange over federal evidence law," and "the trial court's role as gatekeeper is not intended to serve as a replacement for the adversary system." *United States v. 14.38 Acres of Land Situated in Leflore County, Mississippi*, 80 F.3d 1074, 1078 (5th Cir. 1996). As the Court in *Daubert* stated: "Vigorous cross-examination, presentation of contrary evidence, and careful instruction on the burden of proof are the traditional and appropriate means of attacking shaky but admissible evidence." 509 U.S. at 595. Likewise, this amendment is not intended to provide an excuse for an automatic challenge to the testimony of every expert. *See Kumho Tire Co. v . Carmichael*, 119 S.Ct.1167, 1176 (1999) (noting that the trial judge has the discretion "both to avoid unnecessary 'reliability' proceedings in ordinary cases where the reliability of an expert's methods is properly taken for granted, and to require appropriate proceedings in the less usual or more complex cases where cause for questioning the expert's reliability arises.").

When a trial court, applying this amendment, rules that an expert's testimony is reliable, this does not necessarily mean that contradictory expert testimony is unreliable. The amendment is broad enough to permit testimony that is the product of competing principles or methods in the same field of expertise. *See, e.g., Heller v. Shaw Industries, Inc.*, 167 F.3d 146, 160 (3d Cir. 1999) (expert testimony cannot be excluded simply because the expert uses one test rather than another, when both tests are accepted in the field and both reach reliable results). As the court stated in *In re Paoli R.R. Yard PCB Litigation*, 35 F.3d 717, 744 (3d Cir. 1994), proponents "do not have to demonstrate to the judge by a preponderance of the evidence that the assessments of their experts are correct, they only have to demonstrate by a preponderance of evidence that their opinions are reliable.... The evidentiary requirement of reliability is lower than the merits standard of correctness." *See also Daubert v. Merrell Dow Pharmaceuticals, Inc.*, 43 F.3d 1311, 1318 (9th Cir. 1995) (scientific experts might be permitted to testify if they could show that the methods they used were also employed by "a recognized minority of scientists in their field."); *Ruiz-Troche v. Pepsi Cola*, 161 F.3d 77, 85 (1st Cir. 1998) ("*Daubert* neither requires nor empowers trial courts to determine which of several competing scientific theories has the best provenance.").

The Court in *Daubert* declared that the "focus, of course, must be solely on principles and methodology, not on the conclusions they generate." 509 U.S. at 595. Yet as the Court later recognized, "conclusions and methodology are not entirely distinct from one another." *General Elec. Co. v. Joiner*, 522 U.S. 136, 146 (1997). Under the amendment, as under *Daubert*, when an expert purports to apply principles and methods in accordance with professional standards, and yet reaches a conclusion that other experts in the field would not reach, the trial court may fairly suspect that the principles and methods have not been faithfully applied. *See Lust v. Merrell Dow Pharmaceuticals, Inc.*, 89 F.3d 594, 598 (9th Cir. 1996). The amendment specifically provides that the trial court must scrutinize not only the principles and methods used by the expert, but also whether those principles and methods have been properly applied to the facts of the case. As the court noted in *In re Paoli R.R. Yard PCB Litig.*, 35 F.3d 717, 745 (3d Cir. 1994), "*any* step that renders the analysis unreliable . . . renders the expert's testimony inadmissible. *This is true whether the step completely changes a reliable methodology or merely misapplies that methodology.*"

If the expert purports to apply principles and methods to the facts of the case, it is important that this application be conducted reliably. Yet it might also be important in some cases for an expert to educate the factfinder about general principles, without ever attempting to apply these principles to the specific facts of the case. For example, experts might instruct the factfinder on the principles of thermodynamics, or bloodclotting, or on how financial markets respond to corporate reports, without ever knowing about or trying to tie their testimony into the facts of the case. The amendment does not alter the venerable practice of using expert testimony to educate the factfinder on general principles. For this kind of generalized testimony, Rule 702 simply requires that: (1) the expert be qualified; (2) the testimony address a subject matter on which the factfinder can be assisted by an expert; (3) the testimony be reliable; and (4) the testimony "fit" the facts of the case.

As stated earlier, the amendment does not distinguish between scientific and other forms of expert testimony. The trial court's gatekeeping function applies to testimony by any expert. *See Kumho Tire Co. v. Carmichael*, 119 S.Ct. 1167, 1171 (1999) ("We conclude that *Daubert's* general holding—setting forth the trial judge's general 'gatekeeping' obligation—applies not only to testimony based on 'scientific' knowledge, but also to testimony based on 'technical' and 'other specialized' knowledge."). While the relevant factors for determining reliability will vary from expertise to expertise, the amendment rejects the premise that an expert's testimony should be treated more permissively simply because it is outside the realm of science. An opinion from an expert who is not a scientist should receive the same degree of scrutiny for reliability as an opinion from an expert who purports to be a scientist. *See Watkins v. Telsmith, Inc.*, 121 F.3d 984, 991 (5th Cir. 1997) ("[I]t seems exactly backwards that experts who purport to rely on general engineering principles and practical experience might escape screening by the district court simply by stating that their conclusions were not reached by any particular method or technique."). Some types of expert testimony will be more objectively verifiable, and subject to the expectations of falsifiability, peer review, and publication, than others. Some types of expert testimony will not rely on anything like a scientific method, and so will have to be evaluated by reference to other standard principles attendant to the particular area of expertise. The trial judge in all cases of proffered expert testimony must find that it is properly grounded, well-reasoned, and not speculative before it can be admitted. The expert's testimony must be grounded in an accepted body of learning or experience in the expert's field, and the expert must explain how the conclusion is so grounded. *See, e.g.*, American College of Trial Lawyers, *Standards and Procedures for Determining the Admissibility of Expert Testimony* after *Daubert*, 157 F.R.D. 571, 579 (1994) ("[W] hether the testimony concerns economic principles, accounting standards, property valuation or other non-scientific subjects, it should be evaluated by reference to the 'knowledge and experience' of that particular field.").

The amendment requires that the testimony must be the product of reliable principles and methods that are reliably applied to the facts of the case. While the terms "principles" and "methods" may convey a certain impression when applied to scientific knowledge, they remain relevant when applied to testimony based on technical or other specialized knowledge. For example, when a law enforcement agent testifies regarding the use of code words in a drug transaction, the principle used by the agent is that participants in such transactions regularly use code words to conceal the nature of their activities. The method used by the agent is the application of extensive experience to analyze the meaning of the conversations. So long as the principles and methods are reliable and applied reliably to the facts of the case, this type of testimony should be admitted.

Nothing in this amendment is intended to suggest that experience alone—or experience in conjunction with other knowledge, skill, training or education—may not provide a sufficient foundation for expert testimony. To the contrary, the text of Rule 702 expressly contemplates that an expert may be qualified on the basis of experience. In certain fields, experience is the predominant, if not sole, basis for a great deal of reliable expert testimony. *See, e.g., United States v. Jones*, 107 F.3d 1147 (6th Cir. 1997) (no abuse of discretion in admitting the testimony of a handwriting examiner who had years of practical experience and extensive training, and who explained his methodology in detail); *Tassin v. Sears Roebuck*, 946 F.Supp. 1241, 1248 (M.D.La. 1996) (design engineer's testimony can be admissible when the expert's opinions "are based on facts, a reasonable investigation, and traditional technical/mechanical expertise, and he provides a reasonable link between the information and procedures he uses and the conclusions he reaches"). *See also Kumho Tire Co. v. Carmichael*, 119 S.Ct. 1167, 1178 (1999) (stating that "no one denies that an expert might draw a conclusion from a set of observations based on extensive and specialized experience.").

If the witness is relying solely or primarily on experience, then the witness must explain how that experience leads to the conclusion reached, why that experience is a sufficient basis for the opinion, and how that experience is reliably applied to the facts. The trial court's gatekeeping function requires more than simply "taking the expert's word for it." *See Daubert v. Merrell Dow Pharmaceuticals, Inc.*, 43 F.3d 1311, 1319 (9th Cir. 1995) ("We've been presented with only the experts' qualifications, their conclusions and their assurances of reliability. Under *Daubert*, that's not enough."). The more subjective and controversial the expert's inquiry, the more likely the testimony should be excluded as unreliable. *See O'Conner v. Commonwealth Edison Co.*, 13 F.3d 1090 (7th Cir. 1994) (expert testimony based on a completely subjective methodology held properly excluded). *See also Kumho Tire Co. v. Carmichael*, 119 S.Ct . 1167, 1176 (1999) ("[I]t will at times be useful to ask even of a witness whose expertise is based purely on experience, say, a perfume tester able to distinguish among 140 odors at a sniff, whether his preparation is of a kind that others in the field would recognize as acceptable.").

Subpart (1) of Rule 702 calls for a quantitative rather than qualitative analysis. The amendment requires that expert testimony be based on sufficient underlying "facts or data." The term "data" is intended to encompass the reliable opinions of other experts. See the original Advisory Committee Note to Rule 703. The language "facts or data" is broad enough to allow an expert to rely on hypothetical facts that are supported by the evidence. *Id.*

When facts are in dispute, experts sometimes reach different conclusions based on competing versions of the facts. The emphasis in the amendment on " sufficient facts or data" is not intended to authorize a trial court to exclude an expert's testimony on the ground that the court believes one version of the facts and not the other.

There has been some confusion over the relationship between Rules 702 and 703. The amendment makes clear that the sufficiency of the basis of an expert' s testimony is to be decided under Rule 702. Rule 702 sets forth the overarching requirement of reliability, and an analysis of the sufficiency of the expert's basis cannot be divorced from the ultimate reliability of the expert's opinion. In contrast, the "reasonable reliance" requirement of Rule 703 is a relatively narrow inquiry. When an expert relies on inadmissible information, Rule 703 requires the trial court to determine whether that information is of a type reasonably relied on by other experts in the field. If so, the expert can rely on the information in reaching an opinion. However, the question whether the expert is relying on a *sufficient* basis of information—whether admissible information or not—is governed by the requirements of Rule 702.

The amendment makes no attempt to set forth procedural requirements for exercising the trial court's gatekeeping function over expert testimony. *See* Daniel J. Capra, *The Daubert Puzzle*, 38 Ga.L.Rev. 699, 766 (1998) ("Trial courts should be allowed substantial discretion in dealing with *Daubert* questions; any attempt to codify procedures will likely give rise to unnecessary changes in practice and create difficult questions for appellate review."). Courts have shown considerable ingenuity and flexibility in considering challenges to expert testimony under *Daubert*, and it is contemplated that this will continue under the amended Rule. *See, e.g., Cortes-Irizarry v. Corporacion Insular*, 111 F.3d 184 (1st Cir. 1997) (discussing the application of *Daubert* in ruling on a motion for summary judgment); *In re Paoli R.R. Yard PCB Litig.*, 35 F.3d 717, 736, 739 (3d Cir. 1994) (discussing the use of *in limine* hearings); *Claar v. Burlington N.R.R.*, 29 F.3d 499, 502–05 (9th Cir. 1994) (discussing the trial court's technique of ordering experts to submit serial affidavits explaining the reasoning and methods underlying their conclusions).

The amendment continues the practice of the original Rule in referring to a qualified witness as an "expert." This was done to provide continuity and to minimize change. The use of the term "expert" in the Rule does not, however, mean that a jury should actually be informed that a qualified witness is testifying as an "expert." Indeed, there is much to be said for a practice that prohibits the use of the term "expert" by both the parties and the court at trial. Such a practice "ensures that trial courts do not inadvertently put their stamp of authority" on a witness's opinion, and protects against the jury's being "overwhelmed by the so-called 'experts'." Hon. Charles Richey, *Proposals to Eliminate the Prejudicial Effect of the Use of the Word "Expert" Under the Federal Rules of Evidence in Criminal and Civil Jury Trials*, 154 F.R.D. 537, 559 (1994) (setting forth limiting instructions and a standing order employed to prohibit the use of the term " expert" injury trials).

GAP Report—Proposed Amendment to Rule 702

The Committee made the following changes to the published draft of the proposed amendment to Evidence Rule 702:

1. The word "reliable" was deleted from Subpart (1) of the proposed amendment, in order to avoid an overlap with Evidence Rule 703, and to clarify that an expert opinion need not be excluded simply because it is based on hypothetical facts. The Committee Note was amended to accord with this textual change.

2. The Committee Note was amended throughout to include pertinent references to the Supreme Court's decision in *Kumho Tire Co. v. Carmichael*, which was rendered after the proposed amendment was released for public comment. Other citations were updated as well.

3. The Committee Note was revised to emphasize that the amendment is not intended to limit the right to jury trial, nor to permit a challenge to the testimony of every expert, nor to preclude the testimony of experience-based experts, nor to prohibit testimony based on competing methodologies within a field of expertise.

4. Language was added to the Committee Note to clarify that no single factor is necessarily dispositive of the reliability inquiry mandated by Evidence Rule 702.

Rule 703. Bases of Opinion Testimony by Experts

The facts or data in the particular case upon which an expert bases an opinion or inference may be those perceived by or made known to the expert at or before the hearing. If of a type reasonably relied upon by experts in the particular field in forming opinions or inferences upon the subject, the facts or data need not be admissible in evidence in order for the opinion or inference to be admitted. Facts or data that are otherwise inadmissible shall not be disclosed to the jury by the proponent of the opinion or inference unless the court determines that their probative value in assisting the jury to evaluate the expert's opinion substantially outweighs their prejudicial effect.

(Pub.L. 93–595, § 1, Jan. 2, 1975, 88 Stat.1937; Mar. 2, 1987, eff. Oct. 1, 1987; Apr. 17, 2000, eff. Dec. 1, 2000.)

1972 Proposed Rules

Facts or data upon which expert opinions are based may, under the rule, be derived from three possible sources. The first is the firsthand observation of the witness with opinions based thereon traditionally allowed. A treating physician affords an example. Rheingold, The Basis of Medical Testimony, 15 Vand.L.Rev. 473, 489 (1962). Whether he must first relate his observations is treated in Rule 705. The second source, presentation at the trial, also reflects existing practice. The technique may be the familiar hypothetical question or having the expert attend the trial and hear the testimony establishing the facts. Problems of determining what testimony the expert relied upon, when the latter technique is employed and the testimony is in conflict, may be resolved by resort to Rule 705. The third source contemplated by the rule consists of presentation of data to the expert outside of court and other than by his own perception. In this respect the rule is designed to broaden the basis for expert opinions beyond that current in many jurisdictions and to bring the judicial practice into line with the practice of the experts themselves when not in court. Thus a physician in his own practice bases his diagnosis on information from numerous sources and of considerable variety, including statements by patients and relatives, reports and opinions from nurses, technicians and other doctors, hospital records, and X rays. Most of them are admissible in evidence, but only with the expenditure of substantial time in producing and examining various authenticating witnesses. The physician makes life-and-death decisions in reliance upon them. His validation, expertly performed and subject to cross-examination, ought to suffice for judicial purposes. Rheingold, *supra*, at 531; McCormick § 15. A similar provision is California Evidence Code § 801(b).

The rule also offers a more satisfactory basis for ruling upon the admissibility of public opinion poll evidence. Attention is directed to the validity of the techniques employed rather than to relatively fruitless inquiries whether hearsay is involved. See Judge Feinberg's careful analysis in Zippo Mfg. Co. v. Rogers Imports, Inc., 216 F.Supp. 670 (S.D.N.Y. 1963). See also Blum et al., The Art of Opinion Research: A Lawyer's Appraisal of an Emerging Service, 24 U.Chi.L.Rev. 1 (1956); Bonynge Trademark Surveys and Techniques and Their Use in Litigation, 48 A.B.A.J. 329 (1962); Zeisel, The Uniqueness of Survey Evidence, 45 Cornell L.Q. 322 (1960); Annot., 76 A.L.R.2d 919.

If it be feared that enlargement of permissible data may tend to break down the rules of exclusion unduly, notice should be taken that the rule requires that the facts or data "be of a type reasonably relied upon by experts in the particular field." The language would not warrant admitting in evidence the opinion of an "accidentologist" as to the point of impact in an automobile collision based on statements of bystanders since this requirement is not satisfied. See Comment, Cal.Law Rev.Comm'n, Recommendation Proposing an Evidence Code 148–150 (1965).

1987 Amendments

The amendment is technical. No substantive change is intended.

2000 Amendments

Rule 703 has been amended to emphasize that when an expert reasonably relies on inadmissible information to form an opinion or inference, the underlying information is not admissible simply because the opinion or inference is admitted. Courts have reached different results on how to treat inadmissible information when it is reasonably relied upon by an expert in forming an opinion or drawing an inference. *Compare United States v. Rollins*, 862 F.2d 1282 (7th Cir. 1988) (admitting, as part of the basis of an FBI agent's expert opinion on the meaning of code language, the hearsay statements of an informant), *with United States v. 0.59 Acres of Land*, 109 F.3d 1493 (9th Cir. 1997) (error to admit hearsay offered as the basis of an expert opinion, without a limiting instruction). Commentators have also taken differing views. *See e.g.*, Ronald Carlson, *Policing the Bases of Modern Expert Testimony*, 39 Vand.L.Rev. 577 (1986) (advocating limits on the jury's consideration of otherwise inadmissible evidence used as the basis for an expert opinion); Paul Rice, *Inadmissible Evidence as a Basis for Expert Testimony: A Response to Professor Carlson*, 40 Vand.L.Rev. 583 (1987) (advocating unrestricted use of information reasonably relied upon by an expert).

When information is reasonably relied upon by an expert and yet is admissible only for the purpose of assisting the jury in evaluating an expert's opinion, a trial court applying this Rule must consider the information's probative value in assisting the jury to weigh the expert's opinion on the one hand, and the risk of prejudice resulting from the jury's potential misuse of the information for substantive purposes on the other. The information may be disclosed to the jury, upon objection, only if the trial court finds that the probative value of the information in assisting the jury to evaluate the expert's opinion substantially outweighs its prejudicial effect. If the otherwise inadmissible information is admitted under this balancing test, the trial judge must give a limiting instruction upon request, informing the jury that the underlying information must not be used for substantive purposes. *See* Rule 105. In determining the appropriate course, the trial court should consider the probable effectiveness or lack of effectiveness of a limiting instruction under the particular circumstances.

The amendment governs only the disclosure to the jury of information that is reasonably relied on by an expert, when that information is not admissible for substantive purposes. It is not intended to affect the admissibility of an expert's testimony. Nor does the amendment prevent an expert from relying on information that is inadmissible for substantive purposes.

Nothing in this Rule restricts the presentation of underlying expert facts or data when offered by an adverse party. *See* Rule 705. Of course, an adversary's attack on an expert's basis will often open the door to a proponent's rebuttal with information that was reasonably relied upon by the expert, even if that information would not have been discloseable initially under the balancing test provided by this amendment. Moreover, in some circumstances the proponent might wish to disclose information that is relied upon by the expert in order to "remove the sting" from the opponent's anticipated attack, and thereby prevent the jury from drawing an unfair negative inference. The trial court should take this consideration into account in applying the balancing test provided by this amendment.

This amendment covers facts or data that cannot be admitted for any purpose other than to assist the jury to evaluate the expert's opinion. The balancing test provided in this amendment is not applicable to facts or data that are admissible for any other purpose but have not yet been offered for such a purpose at the time the expert testifies.

The amendment provides a presumption against disclosure to the jury of information used as the basis of an expert's opinion and not admissible for any substantive purpose, when that information is offered by the proponent of the expert. In a multi-party case, where one party proffers an expert whose testimony is also beneficial to other parties, each such party should be deemed a "proponent" within the meaning of the amendment.

GAP Report—Proposed Amendment to Rule 703

The Committee made the following changes to the published draft of the proposed amendment to Evidence Rule 703:

1. A minor stylistic change was made in the text, in accordance with the suggestion of the Style Subcommittee of the Standing Committee on Rules of Practice and Procedure.

2. The words "in assisting the jury to evaluate the expert's opinion" were added to the text, to specify the proper purpose for offering the otherwise inadmissible information relied on by an expert. The Committee Note was revised to accord with this change in the text.

3. Stylistic changes were made to the Committee Note.

4. The Committee Note was revised to emphasize that the balancing test set forth in the proposal should be used to determine whether an expert's basis may be disclosed to the jury either (1) in rebuttal or (2) on direct examination to "remove the sting" of an opponent's anticipated attack on an expert's basis.

Rule 704. Opinion on Ultimate Issue

(a) Except as provided in subdivision (b), testimony in the form of an opinion or inference otherwise admissible is not objectionable because it embraces an ultimate issue to be decided by the trier of fact.

(b) No expert witness testifying with respect to the mental state or condition of a defendant in a criminal case may state an opinion or inference as to whether the defendant did or did not have the mental state or condition constituting an element of the crime charged or of a defense thereto. Such ultimate issues are matters for the trier of fact alone.

(Pub.L. 93–595, § 1, Jan. 2, 1975, 88 Stat. 1937; Pub.L. 98–473, Title IV, § 406, Oct. 12, 1984, 98 Stat. 2067.)

1972 Proposed Rules

The basic approach to opinions, lay and expert, in these rules is to admit them when helpful to the trier of fact. In order to render this approach fully effective and to allay any doubt on the subject, the so-called "ultimate issue" rule is specifically abolished by the instant rule.

The older cases often contained strictures against allowing witnesses to express opinions upon ultimate issues, as a particular aspect of the rule against opinions. The rule was unduly restrictive, difficult of application, and generally served only to deprive the trier of fact of useful information. 7 Wigmore §§ 1920, 1921; McCormick § 12. The basis usually assigned for the rule, to prevent the witness from "usurping the province of the jury," is aptly characterized as "empty rhetoric." 7 Wigmore § 1920, p. 17. Efforts to meet the felt needs of particular situations led to odd verbal circumlocutions which were said not to violate the rule. Thus a witness could express his estimate of the criminal responsibility of an accused in terms of sanity or insanity, but not in terms of ability to tell right from wrong or other more modern standard. And in cases of medical causation, witnesses were sometimes required to couch their opinions in cautious phrases of "might or could," rather than "did," though the result was to deprive many opinions of the positiveness to which they were entitled, accompanied by the hazard of a ruling of insufficiency to support a verdict. In other instances the rule was simply disregarded, and, as concessions to need, opinions were allowed upon such matters as intoxication, speed, handwriting, and value, although more precise coincidence with an ultimate issue would scarcely be possible.

Many modern decisions illustrate the trend to abandon the rule completely. People v. Wilson, 25 Cal.2d 341, 153 P.2d 720 (1944), whether abortion necessary to save life of patient; *Clifford–Jacobs Forging Co. v. Industrial Comm.*, 19 Ill.2d 236, 166 N.E.2d 582 (1960), medical causation; *Dowling v. L. H. Shattuck*, Inc., 91 N.H. 234, 17 A.2d 529 (1941), proper method of shoring ditch; *Schweiger v. Solbeck*, 191 Or. 454, 230 P.2d 195 (1951), cause of landslide. In each instance the opinion was allowed.

The abolition of the ultimate issue rule does not lower the bars so as to admit all opinions. Under Rules 701 and 702, opinions must be helpful to the trier of fact, and Rule 403 provides for exclusion of evidence which wastes time. These provisions afford ample assurances against the admission of opinions which would merely tell the jury what result to reach, somewhat in the manner of the oath-helpers of an earlier day. They also stand ready to exclude opinions phrased in terms of inadequately explored legal criteria. Thus the question, "Did T have capacity to make a will?" would be excluded, while the question, "Did T have sufficient mental capacity to know the nature and extent of his property and the natural objects of his bounty and to formulate a rational scheme of distribution?" would be allowed. McCormick § 12.

For similar provisions see Uniform Rule 56(4); California Evidence Code § 805; Kansas Code of Civil Procedure § 60–456(d); New Jersey Evidence Rule 56(3).

Rule 705. Disclosure of Facts or Data Underlying Expert Opinion

The expert may testify in terms of opinion or inference and give reasons therefor without first testifying to the underlying facts or data, unless the court requires otherwise. The expert may in any event be required to disclose the underlying facts or data on cross-examination.

(Pub.L. 93–595, § 1, Jan. 2, 1975, 88 Stat. 1938; Mar. 2, 1987, eff. Oct. 1, 1987; Apr. 22, 1993, eff. Dec. 1, 1993.)

1972 Proposed Rules

The hypothetical question has been the target of a great deal of criticism as encouraging partisan bias, affording an opportunity for summing up in the middle of the case, and as complex and time consuming. Ladd, Expert Testimony, 5 Vand.L.Rev. 414, 426–427 (1952). While the rule allows counsel to make disclosure of the underlying facts or data as a preliminary to the giving of an expert opinion, if he chooses, the instances in which he is required to do so are reduced. This is true whether the expert bases his opinion on data furnished him at secondhand or observed by him at firsthand.

The elimination of the requirement of preliminary disclosure at the trial of underlying facts or data has a long background of support. In 1937 the Commissioners on Uniform State Laws incorporated a provision to this effect in their Model Expert Testimony Act, which furnished the basis for Uniform Rules 57 and 58. Rule 4515, N.Y. CPLR (McKinney 1963), provides:

"Unless the court orders otherwise, questions calling for the opinion of an expert witness need not be hypothetical in form, and the witness may state his opinion and reasons without first specifying the data upon which it is based. Upon cross-examination, he may be required to specify the data * * *."

See also California Evidence Code § 802; Kansas Code of Civil Procedure §§ 60–456, 60–457; New Jersey Evidence Rules 57, 58.

If the objection is made that leaving it to the cross-examiner to bring out the supporting data is essentially unfair, the answer is that he is under no compulsion to bring out any facts or data except those unfavorable to the opinion. The answer assumes that the cross-examiner has the advance knowledge which is essential for effective cross-examination. This advance knowledge has been afforded, though imperfectly, by the traditional foundation requirement. Rule 26(b)(4) of the Rules of Civil Procedure, as revised, provides for substantial discovery in this area, obviating in large measure the obstacles which have been raised in some instances to discovery of findings, underlying data, and even the identity of the experts. Friedenthal Discovery and Use of an Adverse Party's Expert Information, 14 Stan.L.Rev. 455 (1962).

These safeguards are reinforced by the discretionary power of the judge to require preliminary disclosure in any event.

1987 Amendment

The amendment is technical. No substantive change is intended.

1993 Amendment

This rule, which relates to the manner of presenting testimony at trial, is revised to avoid an arguable conflict with revised Rules 26(a)(2)(B) and 26(e)(1) of the Federal Rules of Civil Procedure or with revised Rule 16 of the Federal Rules of Criminal Procedure, which require disclosure in advance of trial of the basis and reasons for an expert's opinions.

If a serious question is raised under Rule 702 or 703 as to the admissibility of expert testimony, disclosure of the underlying facts or data on which opinions are based may, of course, be needed by the court before deciding whether, and to what extent, the person should be allowed to testify. This rule does not preclude such an inquiry.

Rule 706. Court Appointed Experts

(a) Appointment. The court may on its own motion or on the motion of any party enter an order to show cause why expert witnesses should not be appointed, and may request the parties to submit nominations. The court may appoint any expert witnesses agreed upon by the parties, and may appoint expert witnesses of its own selection. An expert witness shall not be appointed by the court unless the witness consents to act. A witness so appointed shall be informed of the witness' duties by the court in writing, a copy of which shall be filed with the clerk, or at a conference in which the parties shall have opportunity to participate. A witness so appointed shall advise the parties of the witness' findings, if any; the witness' deposition may be taken by any party; and the witness may be called to testify by the court or any party. The witness shall be subject to cross-examination by each party, including a party calling the witness.

(b) Compensation. Expert witnesses so appointed are entitled to reasonable compensation in whatever sum the court may allow. The compensation thus fixed is payable from funds which may be provided by law in criminal cases and civil actions and proceedings involving just compensation under the fifth amendment. In other civil actions and proceedings the compensation shall be paid by the parties in such proportion and at such time as the court directs, and thereafter charged in like manner as other costs.

(c) Disclosure of appointment. In the exercise of its discretion, the court may authorize disclosure to the jury of the fact that the court appointed the expert witness.

(d) Parties' experts of own selection. Nothing in this rule limits the parties in calling expert witnesses of their own selection.

(Pub.L. 93–595, § 1, Jan. 2, 1975, 88 Stat.1938; Mar. 2, 1987, eff. Oct. 1, 1987.)

1972 Proposed Rules

The practice of shopping for experts, the venality of some experts, and the reluctance of many reputable experts to involve themselves in litigation, have been matters of deep concern. Though the contention is made that court appointed experts acquire an aura of infallibility to which they are not entitled, Levy, Impartial Medical Testimony—Revisited, 34 Temple L.Q. 416 (1961), the trend is increasingly to provide for their use. While experience indicates that actual appointment is a relatively infrequent occurrence, the assumption may be made that the availability of the procedure in itself decreases the need for resorting to it. The ever-present possibility that the judge may appoint an expert in a given case must inevitably exert a sobering effect on the expert witness of a party and upon the person utilizing his services.

The inherent power of a trial judge to appoint an expert of his own choosing is virtually unquestioned. *Scott v. Spanjer Bros., Inc.*, 298 F.2d 928 (2d Cir.1962); *Danville Tobacco Assn. v. Bryant-Buckner Associates*, Inc., 333 F.2d 202 (4th Cir.1964); Sink, The Unused Power of a Federal Judge to Call His Own Expert Witnesses, 29 S.Cal.L.Rev. 195 (1956); 2 Wigmore § 563, 9 *id.* § 2484; Annot., 95 A.L.R.2d 383. Hence the problem becomes largely one of detail.

The New York plan is well known and is described in Report by Special Committee of the Association of the Bar of the City of New York: Impartial Medical Testimony (1956). On recommendation of the Section of Judicial Administration, local adoption of an impartial medical plan was endorsed by the American Bar Association. 82 A.B.A.Rep. 184–185 (1957). Descriptions and analyses of plans in effect in various parts of the country are found in Van Dusen, A United States District Judge's View of the Impartial Medical Expert System, 32 F.R.D. 498 (1963); Wick and Kightlinger, Impartial Medical Testimony Under the Federal Civil Rules: A Tale of Three Doctors, 34 Ins. Counsel J. 115 (1967); and numerous articles collected in Klein, Judicial Administration and the Legal Profession 393 (1963). Statutes and rules include California Evidence Code §§ 730–733; Illinois Supreme Court Rule 215(d), Ill.Rev.Stat.1969, c. 110A, § 215(d); Burns Indiana Stats.1956, § 9–1702; Wisconsin Stats.Annot.1958, § 957.27.

In the federal practice, a comprehensive scheme for court appointed experts was initiated with the adoption of Rule 28 of the Federal Rules of Criminal Procedure in 1946. The Judicial Conference of the United States in 1953 considered court appointed experts in civil cases, but only with respect to whether they should be compensated from public funds, a proposal which was rejected. Report of the Judicial Conference of the United States 23 (1953). The present rule expands the practice to include civil cases.

Note to Subdivision (a). Subdivision (a) is based on Rule 28 of the Federal Rules of Criminal Procedure, with a few changes, mainly in the interest of clarity. Language has been added to provide specifically for the appointment either on motion of a party or on the judge's own motion. A provision subjecting the court appointed expert to deposition procedures has been incorporated. The rule has been revised to make definite the right of any party, including the party calling him, to cross-examine.

Note to Subdivision (b). Subdivision (b) combines the present provision for compensation in criminal cases with what seems to be a fair and feasible handling of civil cases, originally found in the Model Act and carried from there into Uniform Rule 60. See also California Evidence Code §§ 730–731. The special provision for Fifth Amendment compensation cases is designed to guard against reducing constitutionally guaranteed just compensation by requiring the recipient to pay costs. See Rule 71A(*l*) of the Rules of Civil Procedure.

Note to Subdivision (c). Subdivision (c) seems to be essential if the use of court appointed experts is to be fully effective. Uniform Rule 61 so provides.

Note to Subdivision (d). Subdivision (d) is in essence the last sentence of Rule 28(a) of the Federal Rules of Criminal Procedure.

1987 Amendment

The amendments are technical. No substantive change is intended.

ARTICLE VIII. HEARSAY

1972 Proposed Rules

Introductory Note; The Hearsay Problem. The factors to be considered in evaluating the testimony of a witness are perception, memory, and narration. Morgan, Hearsay Dangers and the Application of the Hearsay Concept, 62 Harv. L.Rev. 177 (1948), Selected Writings on Evidence and Trial 764, 765 (Fryer ed. 1957); Shientag, Cross-Examination—A Judge's Viewpoint, 3 Record 12 (1948); Strahorn, A Reconsideration of the Hearsay Rule and Admissions, 85 U.Pa. L.Rev. 484, 485 (1937), Selected Writings, *supra*, 756, 757; Weinstein, Probative Force of Hearsay, 46 Iowa L.Rev. 331 (1961). Sometimes a fourth is added, sincerity, but in fact it seems merely to be an aspect of the three already mentioned.

In order to encourage the witness to do his best with respect to each of these factors, and to expose any inaccuracies which may enter in, the Anglo-American tradition has evolved three conditions under which witnesses will ideally be required to testify: (1) under oath, (2) in the personal presence of the trier of fact, (3) subject to cross-examination.

(1) Standard procedure calls for the swearing of witnesses. While the practice is perhaps less effective than in an earlier time, no disposition to relax the requirement is apparent, other than to allow affirmation by persons with scruples against taking oaths.

(2) The demeanor of the witness traditionally has been believed to furnish trier and opponent with valuable clues. *Universal Camera Corp. v. N.L.R.B.*, 340 U.S. 474, 495–496, 71 S.Ct. 456, 95 L.Ed. 456 (1951); Sahm, Demeanor Evidence: Elusive and Intangible Imponderables, 47 A.B.A.J. 580 (1961), quoting numerous authorities. The witness himself will probably be impressed with the solemnity of the occasion and the possibility of public disgrace. Willingness to falsify may reasonably become more difficult in the presence of the person against whom directed. Rules 26 and 43(a) of the Federal Rules of Criminal and Civil Procedure, respectively, include the general requirement that testimony be taken orally in open court. The Sixth Amendment right of confrontation is a manifestation of these beliefs and attitudes.

(3) Emphasis on the basis of the hearsay rule today tends to center upon the condition of cross-examination. All may not agree with Wigmore that cross-examination is "beyond doubt the greatest legal engine ever invented for the discovery of truth," but all will agree with his statement that it has become a "vital feature" of the Anglo–American system. 5 Wigmore § 1367, p. 29. The belief, or perhaps hope, that cross-examination is effective in exposing imperfections of perception, memory, and narration is fundamental. Morgan, Foreword to Model Code of Evidence 37 (1942).

The logic of the preceding discussion might suggest that no testimony be received unless in full compliance with the three ideal conditions. No one advocates this position. Common sense tells that much evidence which is not given under the three conditions may be inherently superior to much that is. Moreover, when the choice is between evidence which is less than best and no evidence at all, only clear folly would dictate an across-the-board policy of doing without. The problem thus resolves itself into effecting a sensible accommodation between these considerations and the desirability of giving testimony under the ideal conditions.

The solution evolved by the common law has been a general rule excluding hearsay but subject to numerous exceptions under circumstances supposed to furnish guarantees of trustworthiness. Criticisms of this scheme are that it is bulky and complex, fails to screen good from bad hearsay realistically, and inhibits the growth of the law of evidence.

Since no one advocates excluding all hearsay, three possible solutions may be considered: (1) abolish the rule against hearsay and admit all hearsay; (2) admit hearsay possessing sufficient probative force, but with procedural safeguards; (3) revise the present system of class exceptions.

(1) Abolition of the hearsay rule would be the simplest solution. The effect would not be automatically to abolish the giving of testimony under ideal conditions. If the declarant were available, compliance with the ideal conditions would be optional with either party. Thus the proponent could call the declarant as a witness as a form of presentation more impressive than his hearsay statement. Or the opponent could call the declarant to be cross-examined upon his statement. This is the tenor of Uniform Rule 63(1), admitting the hearsay declaration of a person "who is present at the hearing and available for cross-examination." Compare the treatment of declarations of available declarants in Rule 801(d)(1) of the instant rules. If the declarant were unavailable, a rule of free admissibility would make no distinctions in terms of degrees of noncompliance with the ideal conditions and would exact no quid pro quo in the form of assurances of trustworthiness. Rule 503 of the Model Code did exactly that, providing for the admissibility of any hearsay declaration by an unavailable declarant, finding support in the Massachusetts act of 1898, enacted at the instance of Thayer, Mass.Gen.L.1932, c. 233, § 65, and in the English act of 1938, St.1938, c. 28, Evidence. Both are limited to civil cases. The draftsmen of the Uniform Rules chose a less advanced and more conventional position. Comment, Uniform Rule 63. The present Advisory Committee has been unconvinced of the wisdom of abandoning the traditional requirement of some particular assurance of credibility as a condition precedent to admitting the hearsay declaration of an unavailable declarant.

In criminal cases, the Sixth Amendment requirement of confrontation would no doubt move into a large part of the area presently occupied by the hearsay rule in the event of the abolition of the latter. The resultant split between civil and criminal evidence is regarded as an undesirable development.

(2) Abandonment of the system of class exceptions in favor of individual treatment in the setting of the particular case, accompanied by procedural safeguards, has been impressively advocated. Weinstein, The Probative Force of Hearsay, 46 Iowa L.Rev. 331 (1961). Admissibility would be determined by weighing the probative force of the evidence against the possibility of prejudice, waste of time, and the availability of more satisfactory evidence. The bases of the traditional hearsay exceptions would be helpful in assessing probative force. Ladd, The Relationship of the Principles of Exclusionary Rules of Evidence to the Problem of Proof, 18 Minn.L.Rev. 506 (1934). Procedural safeguards would consist of notice of intention to use hearsay, free comment by the judge on the weight of the evidence, and a greater measure of authority in both trial and appellate judges to deal with evidence on the basis of weight. The Advisory Committee has rejected this approach to hearsay as involving too great a measure of judicial discretion, minimizing the predictability of rulings, enhancing the difficulties of preparation for trial, adding a further element to the already overcomplicated congeries of pretrial procedures, and requiring substantially different rules for civil and criminal cases. The only way in which the probative force of hearsay differs from the probative force of other testimony is in the absence of oath, demeanor, and cross-examination as aids in determining credibility. For a judge to exclude evidence because he does not believe it has been described as "altogether atypical, extraordinary. * * *" Chadbourn, Bentham and the Hearsay Rule—A Benthamic View of Rule 63(4)(c) of the Uniform Rules of Evidence, 75 Harv.L.Rev. 932, 947 (1962).

(3) The approach to hearsay in these rules is that of the common law, i.e., a general rule excluding hearsay, with exceptions under which evidence is not required to be excluded even though hearsay. The traditional hearsay exceptions are drawn upon for the exceptions, collected under two rules, one dealing with situations where availability of the declarant is regarded as immaterial and the other with those where unavailability is made a condition to the admission of the hearsay statement. Each of the two rules concludes with a provision for hearsay statements not within one of the specified exceptions "but having comparable circumstantial guarantees of trustworthiness." Rules 803(24) and 804(b)(6). This plan is submitted as calculated to encourage growth and development in this area of the law, while conserving the values and experience of the past as a guide to the future.

Confrontation and Due Process. Until very recently, decisions invoking the confrontation clause of the Sixth Amendment were surprisingly few, a fact probably explainable by the former inapplicability of the clause to the states and by the hearsay rule's occupancy of much the same ground. The pattern which emerges from the earlier cases invoking the clause is substantially that of the hearsay rule, applied to criminal cases: an accused is entitled to have the witnesses against him testify under oath, in the presence of himself and trier, subject to cross-examination; yet considerations of public policy and necessity require the recognition of such exceptions as dying declarations and former testimony of unavailable witnesses. *Mattox v. United States,* 156 U.S. 237, 15 S.Ct. 337, 39 L.Ed. 409 (1895); *Motes v. United States,* 178 U.S. 458, 20 S.Ct. 993, 44 L.Ed. 1150 (1900); *Delaney v. United States,* 263 U.S. 586, 44 S.Ct. 206, 68 L.Ed. 462 (1924). Beginning with *Snyder v. Massachusetts,* 291 U.S. 97, 54 S.Ct. 330, 78 L.Ed. 674 (1934), the Court began to speak of confrontation as an aspect of procedural due process, thus extending its applicability to state cases and to federal cases other than criminal. The language of *Snyder* was that of an elastic concept of hearsay. The deportation case of *Bridges v. Wixon,* 326 U.S. 135, 65 S.Ct. 1443, 89 L.Ed. 2103 (1945), may be read broadly as imposing a strictly construed right of confrontation in all kinds of cases or narrowly as the product of a failure of the Immigration and Naturalization Service to follow its own rules. *In re Oliver,* 333 U.S. 257, 68 S.Ct. 499, 92 L.Ed. 682 (1948), ruled that cross-examination was essential to due process in a state contempt proceeding, but in *United States v. Nugent,* 346 U.S. 1, 73 S.Ct. 991, 97 L.Ed. 1417 (1953), the court held that it was not an essential aspect of a "hearing" for a conscientious objector under the Selective Service Act. *Stein v. New York,* 346 U.S. 156, 196, 73 S.Ct. 1077, 97 L.Ed. 1522 (1953), disclaimed any purpose to read the hearsay rule into the Fourteenth Amendment, but in *Greene v. McElroy,* 360 U.S. 474, 79 S.Ct. 1400, 3 L.Ed.2d 1377 (1959), revocation of security clearance without confrontation and cross-examination was held unauthorized, and a similar result was reached in *Willner v. Committee on Character,* 373 U.S. 96, 83 S.Ct. 1175, 10 L.Ed.2d 224 (1963). Ascertaining the constitutional dimensions of the confrontation-hearsay aggregate against the background of these cases is a matter of some difficulty, yet the general pattern is at least not inconsistent with that of the hearsay rule.

In 1965 the confrontation clause was held applicable to the states. *Pointer v. Texas,* 380 U.S. 400, 85 S.Ct. 1065, 13 L.Ed.2d 923 (1965). Prosecution use of former testimony given at a preliminary hearing where petitioner was not represented by counsel was a violation of the clause. The same result would have followed under conventional hearsay doctrine read in the light of a constitutional right to counsel, and nothing in the opinion suggests any difference in essential outline between the hearsay rule and the right of confrontation. In the companion case of *Douglas v. Alabama,* 380 U.S. 415, 85 S.Ct. 1074, 13 L.Ed.2d 934 (1965), however, the result reached by applying the confrontation clause is one reached less readily via the hearsay rule. A confession implicating petitioner was put before the jury by reading it to the witness in portions and asking if he made that statement. The witness refused to answer on grounds of self-incrimination. The result, said the Court, was to deny cross-examination, and hence confrontation. True, it could broadly be said that the confession was a hearsay statement which for all practical purposes was put in evidence. Yet a more easily accepted explanation of the opinion is that its real thrust was in the direction of curbing undesirable prosecutorial behavior, rather than merely applying rules of exclusion, and that the confrontation clause was the means selected to achieve this end. Comparable facts and a like result appeared in *Brookhart v. Janis,* 384 U.S. 1, 86 S.Ct. 1245, 16 L.Ed.2d 314 (1966).

The pattern suggested in *Douglas* was developed further and more distinctly in a pair of cases at the end of the 1966 term. *United States v. Wade,* 388 U.S. 218, 87 S.Ct. 1926, 18 L.Ed.2d 1149 (1967), and *Gilbert v. California,* 388 U.S. 263, 87 S.Ct. 1951, 18 L.Ed.2d 1178 (1967), hinged upon practices followed in identifying accused persons before trial. This pretrial identification was said to be so decisive an aspect of the case that accused was entitled to have counsel present; a pretrial identification made in the absence of counsel was not itself receivable in evidence and, in addition, might fatally infect a courtroom identification. The presence of counsel at the earlier identification was described as a necessary prerequisite for "a meaningful confrontation at trial." *United States v. Wade, supra,* 388 U.S. at p. 236, 87 S.Ct. at p. 1937. *Wade* involved no evidence of the fact of a prior identification and hence was not susceptible of being decided on hearsay grounds. In *Gilbert,* witnesses did testify to an earlier identification, readily classifiable as hearsay under a fairly strict view of what constitutes hearsay. The Court, however, carefully avoided basing the decision on the hearsay ground, choosing confrontation instead. 388 U.S. 263, 272, n. 3, 87 S.Ct. 1951. See also *Parker v. Gladden,* 385 U.S. 363, 87 S.Ct. 468, 17 L.Ed.2d 420 (1966), holding that the right of confrontation was violated when the bailiff made prejudicial statements to jurors, and Note, 75 Yale L.J. 1434 (1966).

Under the earlier cases, the confrontation clause may have been little more than a constitutional embodiment of the hearsay rule, even including traditional exceptions but with some room for expanding them along similar lines. But under the recent cases the impact of the clause clearly extends beyond the confines of the hearsay rule. These considerations have led the Advisory Committee to conclude that a hearsay rule can function usefully as an adjunct to the confrontation right in constitutional areas and independently in nonconstitutional areas. In recognition of the separateness of the confrontation clause and the hearsay rule, and to avoid inviting collisions between them or between the hearsay rule and other exclusionary principles, the exceptions set forth in Rules 803 and 804 are stated in terms of exemption from the general exclusionary mandate of the hearsay rule, rather than in positive terms of admissibility. See Uniform Rule 63(1) to (31) and California Evidence Code §§ 1200–1340.

Rule 801. Definitions

The following definitions apply under this article:

(a) Statement. A "statement" is (1) an oral or written assertion or (2) nonverbal conduct of a person, if it is intended by the person as an assertion.

(b) Declarant. A "declarant" is a person who makes a statement.

(c) Hearsay. "Hearsay" is a statement, other than one made by the declarant while testifying at the trial or hearing, offered in evidence to prove the truth of the matter asserted.

(d) Statements which are not hearsay. A statement is not hearsay if—

(1) Prior statement by witness. The declarant testifies at the trial or hearing and is subject to cross-examination concerning the statement, and the statement is (A) inconsistent with the declarant's testimony, and was given under oath subject to the penalty of perjury at a trial, hearing, or other proceeding, or in a deposition, or (B) consistent with the declarant's testimony and is offered to rebut an express or implied charge against the declarant of recent fabrication or improper influence or motive, or (C) one of identification of a person made after perceiving the person; or

(2) Admission by party-opponent. The statement is offered against a party and is (A) the party's own statement, in either an individual or a representative capacity or (B) a statement of which the party has manifested an adoption or belief in its truth, or (C) a statement by a person authorized by the party to make a statement concerning the subject, or (D) a statement by the party's agent or servant concerning a matter within the scope of the agency or employment, made during the existence of the relationship, or (E) a statement by a coconspirator of a party during the course and in furtherance of the conspiracy. The contents of the statement shall be considered but are not alone sufficient to establish the declarant's authority under subdivision (C), the agency or employment relationship and scope thereof under subdivision (D), or the existence of the conspiracy and the participation therein of the declarant and the party against whom the statement is offered under subdivision (E).

(Pub.L. 93–595, § 1, Jan. 2, 1975, 88 Stat.1938; Pub.L. 94–113, § 1, Oct. 16, 1975, 89 Stat. 576; Mar. 2, 1987, eff. Oct. 1, 1987; Apr. 11, 1997, eff. Dec. 1, 1997.)

1972 Proposed Rules

Note to Subdivision (a). The definition of "statement" assumes importance because the term is used in the definition of hearsay in subdivision (c). The effect of the definition of "statement" is to exclude from the operation of the hearsay rule all evidence of conduct, verbal or nonverbal, not intended as an assertion. The key to the definition is that nothing is an assertion unless intended to be one.

It can scarcely be doubted that an assertion made in words is intended by the declarant to be an assertion. Hence verbal assertions readily fall into the category of "statement." Whether nonverbal conduct should be regarded as a statement for purposes of defining hearsay requires further consideration. Some nonverbal conduct, such as the act of pointing to identify a suspect in a lineup, is clearly the equivalent of words, assertive in nature, and to be regarded as a statement. Other nonverbal conduct, however, may be offered as evidence that the person acted as he did because of his belief in the existence of the condition sought to be proved, from which belief the existence of the condition may be inferred. This sequence is, arguably, in effect an assertion of the existence of the condition and hence properly includable within the hearsay concept. See Morgan, Hearsay Dangers and the Application of the Hearsay Concept, 62 Harv.L.Rev. 177, 214, 217 (1948), and the elaboration in Finman, Implied Assertions as Hearsay: Some Criticisms of the Uniform Rules of Evidence, 14 Stan.L.Rev. 682 (1962). Admittedly evidence of this character is untested with respect to the perception, memory, and narration (or their equivalents) of the actor, but the Advisory Committee is of the view that these dangers are minimal in the absence of an intent to assert and do not justify the loss of the evidence on hearsay grounds. No class of evidence is free of the possibility of fabrication, but the likelihood is less with nonverbal than with assertive verbal conduct. The situations giving rise to the nonverbal conduct are such as virtually to eliminate questions of sincerity. Motivation, the nature of the conduct, and the presence or absence of reliance will bear heavily upon the weight to be given the evidence. Falknor, The "Hear–Say" Rule as a "See–Do" Rule: Evidence of Conduct, 33 Rocky Mt.L.Rev. 133 (1961). Similar considerations govern nonassertive verbal conduct and verbal conduct which is assertive but offered as a basis for inferring something other than the matter asserted, also excluded from the definition of hearsay by the language of subdivision (c).

When evidence of conduct is offered on the theory that it is not a statement, and hence not hearsay, a preliminary determination will be required to determine whether an assertion is intended. The rule is so worded as to place the burden upon the party claiming that the intention existed; ambiguous and doubtful cases will be resolved against him and in favor of admissibility. The determination involves no greater difficulty than many other preliminary questions of fact. Maguire, The Hearsay System: Around and Through the Thicket, 14 Vand.L.Rev. 741, 765–767 (1961).

For similar approaches, see Uniform Rule 62(1); California Evidence Code §§ 225, 1200; Kansas Code of Civil Procedure § 60–459(a); New Jersey Evidence Rule 62(1).

Note to Subdivision (c). The definition follows along familiar lines in including only statements offered to prove the truth of the matter asserted. McCormick § 225; 5 Wigmore § 1361, 6 *id.* § 1766. If the significance of an offered statement lies solely in the fact that it was made, no issue is raised as to the truth of anything asserted, and the statement is not hearsay. *Emich Motors Corp. v. General Motors Corp.,* 181 F.2d 70 (7th Cir.1950), rev'd on other grounds 340 U.S. 558, 71 S.Ct. 408, 95 L.Ed. 534, letters of complaint from customers offered as a reason for cancellation of dealer's franchise, to rebut contention that franchise was revoked for refusal to finance sales through affiliated finance company. The effect is to exclude from hearsay the entire category of "verbal acts" and "verbal parts of an act," in which the statement itself affects the legal rights of the parties or is a circumstance bearing on conduct affecting their rights.

The definition of hearsay must, of course, be read with reference to the definition of statement set forth in subdivision (a).

Testimony given by a witness in the course of court proceedings is excluded since there is compliance with all the ideal conditions for testifying.

Note to Subdivision (d). Several types of statements which would otherwise literally fall within the definition are expressly excluded from it:

(1) *Prior statement by witness.* Considerable controversy has attended the question whether a prior out-of-court statement by a person now available for cross-examination concerning it, under oath and in the presence of the trier of fact, should be classed as hearsay. If the witness admits on the stand that he made the statement and that it was true, he adopts the statement and there is no hearsay problem. The hearsay problem arises when the witness on the stand denies having made the statement or admits having made it but denies its truth. The argument in favor of treating these latter statements as hearsay is based upon the ground that the conditions of oath, cross-examination, and demeanor observation did not prevail at the time the statement was made and cannot adequately be supplied by the later examination. The logic of the situation is troublesome. So far as concerns the oath, its mere presence has never been regarded as sufficient to remove a statement from the hearsay category, and it receives much less emphasis than cross-examination as a truth-compelling device. While strong expressions are found to the effect that no conviction can be had or important right taken away on the basis of statements not made under fear of prosecution for perjury, *Bridges v. Wixon*, 326 U.S. 135, 65 S.Ct. 1443, 89 L.Ed. 2103 (1945), the fact is that, of the many common law exceptions to the hearsay rule, only that for reported testimony has required the statement to have been made under oath. Nor is it satisfactorily explained why cross-examination cannot be conducted subsequently with success. The decisions contending most vigorously for its inadequacy in fact demonstrate quite thorough exploration of the weaknesses and doubts attending the earlier statement. *State v. Saporen*, 205 Minn. 358, 285 N.W. 898 (1939); *Ruhala v. Roby*, 379 Mich. 102, 150 N.W.2d 146 (1967); *People v. Johnson*, 68 Cal.2d 646, 68 Cal.Rptr. 599, 441 P.2d 111 (1968). In respect to demeanor, as Judge Learned Hand observed in *Di Carlo v. United States*, 6 F.2d 364 (2d Cir.1925), when the jury decides that the truth is not what the witness says now, but what he said before, they are still deciding from what they see and hear in court. The bulk of the case law nevertheless has been against allowing prior statements of witnesses to be used generally as substantive evidence. Most of the writers and Uniform Rule 63(1) have taken the opposite position.

The position taken by the Advisory Committee in formulating this part of the rule is funded upon an unwillingness to countenance the general use of prior prepared statements as substantive evidence, but with a recognition that particular circumstances call for a contrary result. The judgment is one more of experience than of logic. The rule requires in each instance, as a general safeguard, that the declarant actually testify as a witness, and it then enumerates three situations in which the statement is excepted from the category of hearsay. Compare Uniform Rule 63(1) which allows any out-of-court statement of a declarant who is present at the trial and available for cross-examination.

(A) Prior inconsistent statements traditionally have been admissible to impeach but not as substantive evidence. Under the rule they are substantive evidence. As has been said by the California Law Revision Commission with respect to a similar provision:

"Section 1235 admits inconsistent statements of witnesses because the dangers against which the hearsay rule is designed to protect are largely nonexistent. The declarant is in court and may be examined and cross-examined in regard to his statements and their subject matter. In many cases, the inconsistent statement is more likely to be true than the testimony of the witness at the trial because it was made nearer in time to the matter to which it relates and is less likely to be influenced by the controversy that gave rise to the litigation. The trier of fact has the declarant before it and can observe his demeanor and the nature of his testimony as he denies or tries to explain away the inconsistency. Hence, it is in as good a position to determine the truth or falsity of the prior statement as it is to determine the truth or falsity of the inconsistent testimony given in court. Moreover, Section 1235 will provide a party with desirable protection against the 'turncoat' witness who changes his story on the stand and deprives the party calling him of evidence essential to his case." Comment, California Evidence Code § 1235. See also McCormick § 39. The Advisory Committee finds these views more convincing than those expressed in *People v. Johnson*, 68 Cal.2d 646, 68 Cal.Rptr. 599, 441 P.2d 111 (1968). The constitutionality of the Advisory Committee's view was upheld in *California v. Green*, 399 U.S. 149, 90 S.Ct. 1930, 26 L.Ed.2d 489 (1970). Moreover, the requirement that the statement be inconsistent with the testimony given assures a thorough exploration of both versions while the witness is on the stand and bars any general and indiscriminate use of previously prepared statements.

(B) Prior consistent statements traditionally have been admissible to rebut charges of recent fabrication or improper influence or motive but not as substantive evidence. Under the rule they are substantive evidence. The prior statement is consistent with the testimony given on the stand, and, if the opposite party wishes to open the door for its admission in evidence, no sound reason is apparent why it should not be received generally.

(C) The admission of evidence of identification finds substantial support, although it falls beyond a doubt in the category of prior out-of-court statements. Illustrative are *People v. Gould*, 54 Cal.2d 621, 7 Cal.Rptr. 273, 354 P.2d 865 (1960); *Judy v. State*, 218 Md. 168, 146 A.2d 29 (1958); *State v. Simmons*, 63 Wash.2d 17, 385 P.2d 389 (1963); California Evidence Code § 1238; New Jersey Evidence Rule 63(1)(c); N.Y.Code of Criminal Procedure § 393–b. Further cases are found in 4 Wigmore § 1130. The basis is the generally unsatisfactory and inconclusive nature of courtroom identifications as compared with those made at an earlier time under less suggestive conditions. The Supreme Court considered the admissibility of evidence of prior identification in *Gilbert v. California*, 388 U.S. 263, 87 S.Ct. 1951, 18 L.Ed.2d 1178 (1967). Exclusion of lineup identification was held to be required because the accused did not then have the assistance of counsel. Significantly, the Court carefully refrained from placing its decision on the ground that testimony as to the making of a prior out-of-court identification ("That's the man") violated either the hearsay rule or the right of confrontation because not made under oath, subject to immediate cross-examination, in the presence of the trier. Instead the Court observed:

"There is a split among the States concerning the admissibility of prior extra-judicial identifications, as independent evidence of identity, both by the witness and third parties present at the prior identification. See 71 ALR2d 449. It has been held that the prior identification is hearsay, and, when admitted through the testimony of the identifier, is merely a prior consistent statement. The recent trend, however, is to admit the prior identification under the exception that admits as substantive evidence a prior communication by a witness who is available for cross-examination at the trial. See 5 ALR2d Later Case Service 1225–1228. * * * " 388 U.S. at 272, n. 3, 87 S.Ct. at 1956.

(2) *Admissions.* Admissions by a party-opponent are excluded from the category of hearsay on the theory that their admissibility in evidence is the result of the adversary system rather than satisfaction of the conditions of the hearsay rule. Strahorn, A Reconsideration of the Hearsay Rule and Admissions, 85 U.Pa.L.Rev. 484, 564 (1937); Morgan, Basic Problems of Evidence 265 (1962); 4 Wigmore § 1048. No guarantee of trustworthiness is required in the case of an admission. The freedom which admissions have enjoyed from technical demands of searching for an assurance of truthworthiness in some against-interest circumstance, and from the restrictive influences of the opinion rule and the rule requiring firsthand knowledge, when taken with the apparently prevalent satisfaction with the results, calls for generous treatment of this avenue to admissibility.

The rule specifies five categories of statements for which the responsibility of a party is considered sufficient to justify reception in evidence against him:

(A) A party's own statement is the classic example of an admission. If he has a representative capacity and the statement is offered against him in that capacity, no inquiry whether he was acting in the representative capacity in making the statement is required; the statement need only be relevant to represent affairs. To the same effect in California Evidence Code § 1220. Compare Uniform Rule 63(7), requiring a statement to be made in a representative capacity to be admissible against a party in a representative capacity.

(B) Under established principles an admission may be made by adopting or acquiescing in the statement of another. While knowledge of contents would ordinarily be essential, this is not inevitably so: "X is a reliable person and knows what he is talking about." See McCormick § 246, p. 527, n. 15. Adoption or acquiescence may be manifested in any appropriate manner. When silence is relied upon, the theory is that the person would, under the circumstances, protest the statement made in his presence, if untrue. The decision in each case calls for an evaluation in terms of probable human behavior. In civil cases, the results have generally been satisfactory. In criminal cases, however, troublesome questions have been raised by decisions holding that failure to deny is an admission: the inference is a fairly weak one, to begin with; silence may be motivated by advice of counsel or realization that "anything you say may be used against you"; unusual opportunity is afforded to manufacture evidence; and encroachment upon the privilege against self-incrimination seems inescapably to be involved. However, recent decisions of the Supreme Court relating to custodial interrogation and the right to counsel appear to resolve these difficulties. Hence the rule contains no special provisions concerning failure to deny in criminal cases.

(C) No authority is required for the general proposition that a statement authorized by a party to be made should have the status of an admission by the party. However, the question arises whether only statements to third persons should be so regarded, to the exclusion of statements by the agent to the principal. The rule is phrased broadly so as to encompass both. While it may be argued that the agent authorized to make statements to his principal does not speak for him, Morgan, Basic Problems of Evidence 273 (1962), communication to an outsider has not generally been thought to be an essential characteristic of an admission. Thus a party's books or records are usable against him, without regard to any intent to disclose to third persons. 5 Wigmore § 1557. See also McCormick § 78, pp. 159–161. In accord is New Jersey Evidence Rule 63(8)(a). Cf. Uniform Rule 63(8)(a) and California Evidence Code § 1222 which limit status as an admission in this regard to statements authorized by the party to be made "for" him, which is perhaps an ambiguous limitation to statements to third persons. Falknor, Vicarious Admissions and the Uniform Rules, 14 Vand.L.Rev. 855, 860–861 (1961).

(D) The tradition has been to test the admissibility of statements by agents, as admissions, by applying the usual test of agency. Was the admission made by the agent acting in the scope of his employment? Since few principals employ agents for the purpose of making damaging statements, the usual result was exclusion of the statement. Dissatisfaction with this loss of valuable and helpful evidence has been increasing. A substantial trend favors admitting statements related to a matter within the scope of the agency or employment. *Grayson v. Williams,* 256 F.2d 61 (10th Cir. 1958); *Koninklijke Luchtvaart Maatschappij N.V. KLM Royal Dutch Airlines v. Tuller,* 110 U.S.App.D.C. 282, 292 F.2d 775, 784 (1961); *Martin v. Savage Truck Lines,* Inc., 121 F.Supp. 417 (D.D.C.1954), and numerous state court decisions collected in 4 Wigmore, 1964 Supp. pp. 66–73, with comments by the editor that the statements should have been excluded as not within scope of agency. For the traditional view see *Northern Oil Co. v. Socony Mobil Oil Co.,* 347 F.2d 81, 85 (2d Cir.1965) and cases cited therein. Similar provisions are found in Uniform Rule 63(9)(a), Kansas Code of Civil Procedure § 60–460(i)(1), and New Jersey Evidence Rule 63(9)(a).

(E) The limitation upon the admissibility of statements of co-conspirators to those made "during the course and in furtherance of the conspiracy" is in the accepted pattern. While the broadened view of agency taken in item (iv) might suggest wider admissibility of statements of co-conspirators, the agency theory of conspiracy is at best a fiction and ought not to serve as a basis for admissibility beyond that already established. See Levie, Hearsay and Conspiracy, 52 Mich. L.Rev. 1159 (1954); Comment, 25 U.Chi.L.Rev. 530 (1958). The rule is consistent with the position of the Supreme Court in denying admissibility to statements made after the objectives of the conspiracy have either failed or been achieved. *Krulewitch v. United States,* 336 U.S. 440, 69 S.Ct. 716, 93 L.Ed. 790 (1949); *Wong Sun v. United States,* 371 U.S. 471, 490, 83 S.Ct. 407, 9 L.Ed.2d 441 (1963). For similarly limited provisions see California Evidence Code § 1223 and New Jersey Rule 63(9)(b). Cf. Uniform Rule 63(9)(b).

1974 Enactment

Note to Subdivision (d)(1). Present federal law, except in the Second Circuit, permits the use of prior inconsistent statements of a witness for impeachment only. Rule 801(d)(1) as proposed by the Court would have permitted all such statements to be admissible as substantive evidence, an approach followed by a small but growing number of State jurisdictions and recently held constitutional in California v. Green, 399 U.S. 149 (1970). Although there was some support expressed for the Court Rule, based largely on the need to counteract the effect of witness intimidation in criminal cases, the Committee decided to adopt a compromise version of the Rule similar to the position of the Second Circuit. The Rule as amended draws a distinction between types of prior inconsistent statements (other than statements of identification of a person made after perceiving him which are currently admissible, see United States v. Anderson, 406 F.2d 719, 720 (4th Cir.), cert. denied, 395 U.S. 967 (1969)) and allows only those made while the declarant was subject to cross-examination at a trial or hearing or in a deposition, to be admissible for their truth. Compare United States v. DeSisto, 329 F.2d 929 (2nd Cir.), cert. denied, 377 U.S. 979 (1964); United States v. Cunningham, 446 F.2d 194 (2nd Cir.1971) (restricting the admissibility of prior inconsistent statements as substantive evidence to those made under oath in a formal proceeding, but not requiring that there have been an opportunity for cross-examination). The rationale for the Committee's decision is that (1) unlike in most other situations involving unsworn or oral statements, there can be no dispute as to whether the prior statement was made; and (2) the context of a formal proceeding, an oath, and the opportunity for cross-examination provide firm additional assurances of the reliability of the prior statement. House Report No. 93–650.

Note to Subdivision (d)(1)(A). Rule 801 defines what is and what is not hearsay for the purpose of admitting a prior statement as substantive evidence. A prior statement of a witness at a trial or hearing which is inconsistent with his testimony is, of course, always admissible for the purpose of impeaching the witness' credibility.

As submitted by the Supreme Court, subdivision (d)(1)(A) made admissible as substantive evidence the prior statement of a witness inconsistent with his present testimony.

The House severely limited the admissibility of prior inconsistent statements by adding a requirement that the prior statement must have been subject to cross-examination, thus precluding even the use of grand jury statements. The requirement that the prior statement must have been subject to cross-examination appears unnecessary since this rule comes into play only when the witness testifies in the present trial. At that time, he is on the stand and can explain an earlier position and be cross-examined as to both.

The requirement that the statement be under oath also appears unnecessary. Notwithstanding the absence of an oath contemporaneous with the statement, the witness, when on the stand, qualifying or denying the prior statement, is under oath. In any event, of all the many recognized exceptions to the hearsay rule, only one (former testimony) requires that the out-of-court statement have been made under oath. With respect to the lack of evidence of the demeanor of the witness at the time of the prior statement, it would be difficult to improve upon Judge Learned Hand's observation that when the jury decides that the truth is not what the witness says now but what he said before, they are still deciding from what they see and hear in court. [*Di Carlo v. U.S.*, 6 F.2d 364 (2d Cir.1925)].

The rule as submitted by the Court has positive advantages. The prior statement was made nearer in time to the events, when memory was fresher and intervening influences had not been brought into play. A realistic method is provided for dealing with the turncoat witness who changes his story on the stand [see Comment, California Evidence Code § 1235; McCormick, Evidence, § 38 (2nd ed. 1972)].

New Jersey, California, and Utah have adopted a rule similar to this one; and Nevada, New Mexico, and Wisconsin have adopted the identical Federal rule.

For all of these reasons, we think the House amendment should be rejected and the rule as submitted by the Supreme Court reinstated. [It would appear that some of the opposition to this Rule is based on a concern that a person could be convicted solely upon evidence admissible under this Rule. The Rule, however, is not addressed to the question of the sufficiency of evidence to send a case to the jury, but merely as to its admissibility. Factual circumstances could well arise where, if this were the sole evidence, dismissal would be appropriate.]

Note to Subdivision (d)(1)(C). As submitted by the Supreme Court and as passed by the House, subdivision (d)(1)(C) of rule 801 made admissible the prior statement identifying a person made after perceiving him. The committee decided to delete this provision because of the concern that a person could be convicted solely upon evidence admissible under this subdivision.

Note to Subdivision 801(d)(2)(E). The House approved the long-accepted rule that "a statement by a coconspirator of a party during the course and in furtherance of the conspiracy" is not hearsay as it was submitted by the Supreme Court. While the rule refers to a coconspirator, it is this committee's understanding that the rule is meant to carry forward the universally accepted doctrine that a joint venturer is considered as a coconspirator for the purposes of this rule even though no conspiracy has been charged. *United States v. Rinaldi,* 393 F.2d 97, 99 (2d Cir.), cert. denied 393 U.S. 913 (1968); *United States v. Spencer,* 415 F.2d 1301, 1304 (7th Cir., 1969). Senate Report No. 93–1277.

Rule 801 supplies some basic definitions for the rules of evidence that deal with hearsay. Rule 801(d)(1) defines certain statements as not hearsay. The Senate amendments make two changes in it.

Note to Subdivision (d)(1)(A). The House bill provides that a statement is not hearsay if the declarant testifies and is subject to cross-examination concerning the statement and if the statement is inconsistent with his testimony and was given under oath subject to cross-examination and subject to the penalty of perjury at a trial or hearing or in a deposition. The Senate amendment drops the requirement that the prior statement be given under oath subject to cross-examination and subject to the penalty of perjury at a trial or hearing or in a deposition.

The Conference adopts the Senate amendment with an amendment, so that the rule now requires that the prior inconsistent statement be given under oath subject to the penalty of perjury at a trial, hearing, or other proceeding, or in a deposition. The rule as adopted covers statements before a grand jury. Prior inconsistent statements may, of course, be used for impeaching the credibility of a witness. When the prior inconsistent statement is one made by a defendant in a criminal case, it is covered by Rule 801(d)(2).

Note to Subdivision (d)(1)(C). The House bill provides that a statement is not hearsay if the declarant testifies and is subject to cross-examination concerning the statement and the statement is one of identification of a person made after perceiving him. The Senate amendment eliminated this provision.

The Conference adopts the Senate amendment. House Report No. 93–1597.

1987 Amendment

The amendments are technical. No substantive change is intended.

1997 Amendment

Rule 801(d)(2) has been amended in order to respond to three issues raised by *Bourjaily v. United States*, 483 U.S. 171 (1987). First, the amendment codifies the holding in *Bourjaily* by stating expressly that a court shall consider the contents of a coconspirator's statement in determining "the existence of the conspiracy and the participation therein of the declarant and the party against whom the statement is offered." According to *Bourjaily*, Rule 104(a) requires these preliminary questions to be established by a preponderance of the evidence.

Second, the amendment resolves an issue on which the Court had reserved decision. It provides that the contents of the declarant's statement do not alone suffice to establish a conspiracy in which the declarant and the defendant participated. The court must consider in addition the circumstances surrounding the statement, such as the identity of the speaker, the context in which the statement was made, or evidence corroborating the contents of the statement in making its determination as to each preliminary question. This amendment is in accordance with existing practice. Every court of appeals that has resolved this issue requires some evidence in addition to the contents of the statement. *See, e.g.*, *United States v. Beckham*, 968 F.2d 47, 51 (D.C.Cir. 1992); *United States v. Sepulveda*, 15 F.3d 1161, 1181–82 (1st Cir.1993), *cert. denied*, 114 S.Ct. 2714 (1994); *United States v. Daly*, 842 F.2d 1380, 1386 (2d Cir.), *cert. denied*, 488 U.S. 821 (1988); *United States v. Clark*, 18 F.3d 1337, 1341–42 (6th Cir.), *cert. denied*, 115 S.Ct. 152 (1994); *United States v. Zambrana*, 841 F.2d 1320, 1344–45 (7th Cir.1988); *United States v. Silverman*, 861 F.2d 571, 577 (9th Cir.1988); *United States v. Gordon*, 844 F.2d 1397, 1402 (9th Cir.1988); *United States v. Hernandez*, 829 F.2d 988, 993 (10th Cir. 1987), *cert. denied*, 485 U.S. 1013 (1988); *United States v. Byrom*, 910 F.2d 725, 736 (11th Cir.1990).

Third, the amendment extends the reasoning of Bourjaily to statements offered under subdivisions (C) and (D) of Rule 801(d)(2). In Bourjaily, the Court rejected treating foundational facts pursuant to the law of agency in favor of an evidentiary approach governed by Rule 104(a). The Advisory Committee believes it appropriate to treat analogously preliminary questions relating to the declarant's authority under subdivision (C), and the agency or employment relationship and scope thereof under subdivision (D).

GAP Report on Rule 801. The word "shall" was substituted for the word "may" in line 19. The second sentence of the committee note was changed accordingly.

HISTORICAL NOTES

For legislative history and purpose of Pub.L. 94–113, see 1975 U.S.Code Cong. and Adm.News, p. 1092.

Effective and Applicability Provisions

1975 Acts. Section 2 of Pub.L. 94–113 provided that: "This Act [enacting cl. (c) of subd. (d)] shall become effective on the fifteenth day after the date of the enactment of this Act [Oct. 16, 1975]."

Rule 802. Hearsay Rule

Hearsay is not admissible except as provided by these rules or by other rules prescribed by the Supreme Court pursuant to statutory authority or by Act of Congress.

(Pub.L. 93–595, § 1, Jan. 2, 1975, 88 Stat. 1939.)

1972 Proposed Rules

The provision excepting from the operation of the rule hearsay which is made admissible by other rules adopted by the Supreme Court or by Act of Congress continues the admissibility thereunder of hearsay which would not qualify under these Evidence Rules. The following examples illustrate the working of the exception:

Federal Rules of Civil Procedure

Rule 4(g): proof of service by affidavit.

Rule 32: admissibility of depositions.

Rule 43(e): affidavits when motion based on facts not appearing of record.

Rule 56: affidavits in summary judgment proceedings.

Rule 65(b): showing by affidavit for temporary restraining order.

Federal Rules of Criminal Procedure

Rule 4(a): affidavits to show grounds for issuing warrants.

Rule 12(b)(4): affidavits to determine issues of fact in connection with motions.

Acts of Congress

10 U.S.C. § 7730: affidavits of unavailable witnesses in actions for damages caused by vessel in naval service, or towage or salvage of same, when taking of testimony or bringing of action delayed or stayed on security grounds.

29 U.S.C. § 161(4): affidavit as proof of service in NLRB proceedings.

38 U.S.C. § 5206: affidavit as proof of posting notice of sale of unclaimed property by Veterans Administration.

Rule 803. Hearsay Exceptions; Availability of Declarant Immaterial

The following are not excluded by the hearsay rule, even though the declarant is available as a witness:

(1) Present sense impression. A statement describing or explaining an event or condition made while the declarant was perceiving the event or condition, or immediately thereafter.

(2) Excited utterance. A statement relating to a startling event or condition made while the declarant was under the stress of excitement caused by the event or condition.

(3) Then existing mental, emotional, or physical condition. A statement of the declarant's then existing state of mind, emotion, sensation, or physical condition (such as intent, plan, motive, design, mental feeling, pain, and bodily health), but not including a statement of memory or belief to prove the fact remembered or believed unless it relates to the execution, revocation, identification, or terms of declarant's will.

(4) Statements for purposes of medical diagnosis or treatment. Statements made for purposes of medical diagnosis or treatment and describing medical history, or past or present symptoms, pain, or sensations, or the inception or general character of the cause or external source thereof insofar as reasonably pertinent to diagnosis or treatment.

(5) Recorded recollection. A memorandum or record concerning a matter about which a witness once had knowledge but now has insufficient recollection to enable the witness to testify fully and accurately, shown to have been made or adopted by the witness when the matter was fresh in the witness' memory and to reflect that knowledge correctly. If admitted, the memorandum or record may be read into evidence but may not itself be received as an exhibit unless offered by an adverse party.

(6) Records of Regularly Conducted Activity.—A memorandum, report, record, or data compilation, in any form, of acts, events, conditions, opinions, or diagnoses, made at or near the time by, or from information transmitted by, a person with knowledge, if kept in the course of a regularly conducted business activity, and if it was the regular practice of that business activity to make the memorandum, report, record or data compilation, all as shown by the testimony of the custodian or other qualified witness, or by certification that complies with Rule 902(11), Rule 902(12), or a statute permitting certification, unless the source of information or the method or circumstances of preparation indicate lack of trustworthiness. The term "business" as used in this paragraph includes business, institution, association, profession, occupation, and calling of every kind, whether or not conducted for profit.

(7) Absence of entry in records kept in accordance with the provisions of paragraph (6). Evidence that a matter is not included in the memoranda reports, records, or data compilations, in any form, kept in accordance with the provisions of paragraph (6), to prove the nonoccurrence or nonexistence of the matter, if the matter was of a kind of which a memorandum, report, record, or data compilation was regularly made and preserved, unless the sources of information or other circumstances indicate lack of trustworthiness.

(8) Public records and reports. Records, reports, statements, or data compilations, in any form, of public offices or agencies, setting forth (A) the activities of the office or agency, or (B) matters observed pursuant to duty imposed by law as to which matters there was a duty to report, excluding, however, in criminal cases matters observed by police officers and other law enforcement personnel, or (C) in civil actions and proceedings and against the Government in criminal cases, factual findings resulting from an investigation made pursuant to authority granted by law, unless the sources of information or other circumstances indicate lack of trustworthiness.

(9) Records of vital statistics. Records or data compilations, in any form, of births, fetal deaths, deaths, or marriages, if the report thereof was made to a public office pursuant to requirements of law.

(10) Absence of public record or entry. To prove the absence of a record, report, statement, or data compilation, in any form, or the nonoccurrence or nonexistence of a matter of which a record, report, statement, or data compilation, in any form, was regularly made and preserved by a public office or agency, evidence in the form of a certification in accordance with rule 902, or testimony, that diligent search failed to disclose the record, report, statement, or data compilation, or entry.

(11) Records of religious organizations. Statements of births, marriages, divorces, deaths, legitimacy, ancestry, relationship by blood or marriage, or other similar facts of personal or family history, contained in a regularly kept record of a religious organization.

(12) Marriage, baptismal, and similar certificates. Statements of fact contained in a certificate that the maker performed a marriage or other ceremony or administered a sacrament, made by a clergyman, public official, or other person authorized by the rules or practices of a religious organization or by law to perform the act certified, and purporting to have been issued at the time of the act or within a reasonable time thereafter.

(13) Family records. Statements of fact concerning personal or family history contained in family Bibles, genealogies, charts, engravings on rings, inscriptions on family portraits, engravings on urns, crypts, or tombstones, or the like.

(14) Records of documents affecting an interest in property. The record of a document purporting to establish or affect an interest in property, as proof of the content of the original recorded document and its execution and delivery by each person by whom it purports to have been executed, if the record is a record of a public office and an applicable statute authorizes the recording of documents of that kind in that office.

(15) Statements in documents affecting an interest in property. A statement contained in a document purporting to establish or affect an interest in property if the matter stated was relevant to the purpose of the document, unless dealings with the property since the document was made have been inconsistent with the truth of the statement or the purport of the document.

(16) Statements in ancient documents. Statements in a document in existence twenty years or more the authenticity of which is established.

(17) Market reports, commercial publications. Market quotations, tabulations, lists, directories, or other published compilations, generally used and relied upon by the public or by persons in particular occupations.

(18) Learned treatises. To the extent called to the attention of an expert witness upon cross-examination or relied upon by the expert witness in direct examination, statements contained in published treatises, periodicals, or pamphlets on a subject of history, medicine, or other science or art, established as a reliable authority by the testimony or admission of the witness or by other expert testimony or by judicial notice. If admitted, the statements may be read into evidence but may not be received as exhibits.

(19) Reputation concerning personal or family history. Reputation among members of a person's family by blood, adoption, or marriage, or among a person's associates, or in the community, concerning a person's birth, adoption, marriage, divorce, death, legitimacy, relationship by blood, adoption, or marriage, ancestry, or other similar fact of personal or family history.

(20) Reputation concerning boundaries or general history. Reputation in a community, arising before the controversy, as to boundaries of or customs affecting lands in the community, and reputation as to events of general history important to the community or State or nation in which located.

(21) Reputation as to character. Reputation of a person's character among associates or in the community.

(22) Judgment of previous conviction. Evidence of a final judgment, entered after a trial or upon a plea of guilty (but not upon a plea of nolo contendere), adjudging a person guilty of a crime punishable by death or imprisonment in excess of one year, to prove any fact essential to sustain the judgment, but not including, when offered by the Government in a criminal prosecution for purposes other than impeachment, judgments against persons other than the accused. The pendency of an appeal may be shown but does not affect admissibility.

(23) Judgment as to personal, family, or general history, or boundaries. Judgments as proof of matters of personal, family or general history, or boundaries, essential to the judgment, if the same would be provable by evidence of reputation.

(24) [Transferred to Rule 807]

(Pub.L. 93–595, § 1, Jan. 2, 1975, 88 Stat. 1939; Pub.L. 94–149, § 1(11), Dec. 12, 1975, 89 Stat. 805; Mar. 2, 1987, eff. Oct. 1, 1987; Apr. 11, 1997, eff. Dec. 1, 1997; Apr. 17, 2000, eff. Dec. 1, 2000.)

1972 Proposed Rules

The exceptions are phrased in terms of nonapplication of the hearsay rule, rather than in positive terms of admissibility, in order to repel any implication that other possible grounds for exclusion are eliminated from consideration.

The present rule proceeds upon the theory that under appropriate circumstances a hearsay statement may possess circumstantial guarantees of trustworthiness sufficient to justify nonproduction of the declarant in person at the trial even though he may be available. The theory finds vast support in the many exceptions to the hearsay rule developed by the common law in which unavailability of the declarant is not a relevant factor. The present rule is a synthesis of them, with revision where modern developments and conditions are believed to make that course appropriate.

In a hearsay situation, the declarant is, of course, a witness, and neither this rule nor Rule 804 dispenses with the requirement of firsthand knowledge. It may appear from his statement or be inferable from circumstances. See Rule 602.

Note to Paragraphs (1) and (2). In considerable measure these two examples overlap, though based on somewhat different theories. The most significant practical difference will lie in the time lapse allowable between event and statement.

The underlying theory of Exception [paragraph] (1) is that substantial contemporaneity of event and statement negate the likelihood of deliberate or conscious misrepresentation. Moreover, if the witness is the declarant, he may be examined on the statement. If the witness is not the declarant, he may be examined as to the circumstances as an aid in evaluating the statement. Morgan, Basic Problems of Evidence 340–341 (1962).

The theory of Exception [paragraph] (2) is simply that circumstances may produce a condition of excitement which temporarily stills the capacity of reflection and produces utterances free of conscious fabrication. 6 Wigmore § 1747, p. 135. Spontaneity is the key factor in each instance, though arrived at by somewhat different routes. Both are needed in order to avoid needless niggling.

While the theory of Exception [paragraph] (2) has been criticized on the ground that excitement impairs accuracy of observation as well as eliminating conscious fabrication, Hutchins and Slesinger, Some Observations on the Law of Evidence: Spontaneous Exclamations, 28 Colum.L.Rev. 432 (1928), it finds support in cases without number. See cases in 6 Wigmore § 1750; Annot. 53 A.L.R.2d 1245 (statements as to cause of or responsibility for motor vehicle accident); Annot., 4 A.L.R.3d 149 (accusatory statements by homicide victims). Since unexciting events are less likely to evoke comment, decisions involving Exception [paragraph] (1) are far less numerous. Illustrative are *Tampa Elec. Co. v. Getrost*, 151 Fla. 558, 10 So.2d 83 (1942); *Houston Oxygen Co. v. Davis*, 139 Tex. 1, 161 S.W.2d 474 (1942); and cases cited in McCormick § 273, p. 585, n. 4.

With respect to the *time element*, Exception [paragraph] (1) recognizes that in many, if not most, instances precise contemporaneity is not possible and hence a slight lapse is allowable. Under Exception [paragraph] (2) the standard of measurement is the duration of the state of excitement. "How long can excitement prevail? Obviously there are no pat answers and the character of the transaction or event will largely determine the significance of the time factor." Slough, Spontaneous Statements and State of Mind, 46 Iowa L.Rev. 224, 243 (1961); McCormick § 272, p. 580.

Participation by the declarant is not required: a non-participant may be moved to describe what he perceives, and one may be startled by an event in which he is not an actor. Slough, *supra;* McCormick, *supra;* 6 Wigmore § 1755; Annot. 78 A.L.R.2d 300.

Whether *proof of the startling event* may be made by the statement itself is largely an academic question, since in most cases there is present at least circumstantial evidence that something of a startling nature must have occurred. For cases in which the evidence consists of the condition of the declarant (injuries, state of shock), see *Insurance Co. v. Mosely,* 75 U.S. (8 Wall.) 397, 19 L.Ed. 437 (1869); *Wheeler v. United States,* 93 U.S. App.D.C. 159, 211 F.2d 19 (1953), cert. denied 347 U.S. 1019, 74 S.Ct. 876, 98 L.Ed. 1140; *Wetherbee v. Safety Casualty Co.,* 219 F.2d 274 (5th Cir. 1955); *Lampe v. United States,* 97 U.S.App.D.C. 160, 229 F.2d 43 (1956). Nevertheless, on occasion the only evidence may be the content of the statement itself, and rulings that it may be sufficient are described as "increasing," Slough, *supra* at 246, and as the "prevailing practice," McCormick § 272, p. 579. Illustrative are *Armour & Co. v. Industrial Commission,* 78 Colo. 569, 243 P. 546 (1926); *Young v. Stewart,* 191 N.C. 297, 131 S.E. 735 (1926). Moreover, under Rule 104(a) the judge is not limited by the hearsay rule in passing upon preliminary questions of fact.

Proof of declarant's perception by his statement presents similar considerations when declarant is identified. *People v. Poland,* 22 Ill.2d 175, 174 N.E.2d 804 (1961). However, when declarant is an unidentified bystander, the cases indicate hesitancy in upholding the statement alone as sufficient, *Garrett v. Howden,* 73 N.M. 307, 387 P.2d 874 (1963); *Beck v. Dye,* 200 Wash. 1, 92 P.2d 1113 (1939), a result which would under appropriate circumstances be consistent with the rule.

Permissible *subject matter* of the statement is limited under Exception [paragraph] (1) to description or explanation of the event or condition, the assumption being that spontaneity, in the absence of a startling event, may extend no farther. In Exception [paragraph] (2), however, the statement need only "relate" to the startling event or condition, thus affording a broader scope of subject matter coverage. 6 Wigmore §§ 1750, 1754. See *Sanitary Grocery Co. v. Snead,* 67 App.D.C. 129, 90 F.2d 374 (1937), slip-and-fall case sustaining admissibility of clerk's statement. "That has been on the floor for a couple of hours," and *Murphy Auto Parts Co., Inc. v. Ball,* 101 U.S.App.D.C. 416, 249 F.2d 508 (1957), upholding admission, on issue of driver's agency, of his statement that he had to call on a customer and was in a hurry to get home. Quick, Hearsay, Excitement, Necessity and the Uniform Rules: A Reappraisal of Rule 63(4), 6 Wayne L.Rev. 204, 206–209 (1960).

Similar provisions are found in Uniform Rule 63(4)(a) and (b); California Evidence Code § 1240 (as to Exception (2) only); Kansas Code of Civil Procedure § 60–460(d)(1) and (2); New Jersey Evidence Rule 63(4).

Note to Paragraph (3). Exception [paragraph] (3) is essentially a specialized application of Exception [paragraph] (1), presented separately to enhance its usefulness and accessibility. See McCormick §§ 265, 268.

The exclusion of "statements of memory or belief to prove the fact remembered or believed" is necessary to avoid the virtual destruction of the hearsay rule which would otherwise result from allowing state of mind, provable by a hearsay statement, to serve as the basis for an inference of the happening of the event which produced the state of mind. *Shepard v. United States,* 290 U.S. 96, 54 S.Ct. 22, 78 L.Ed. 196 (1933); Maguire, The Hillmon Case—Thirty-three Years After, 38 Harv.L.Rev. 709, 719–731 (1925); Hinton, States of Mind and the Hearsay Rule, 1 U.Chi.L.Rev. 394, 421–423 (1934). The rule of *Mutual Life Ins. Co. v. Hillmon,* 145 U.S. 285, 12 S.Ct. 909, 36 L.Ed. 706 (1892), allowing evidence of intention as tending to prove the doing of the act intended, is, of course, left undisturbed.

The carving out, from the exclusion mentioned in the preceding paragraph, of declarations relating to the execution, revocation, identification, or terms of declarant's will represents and *ad hoc* judgment which finds ample reinforcement in the decisions, resting on practical grounds of necessity and expediency rather than logic. McCormick § 271, pp. 577–578; Annot. 34 A.L.R.2d 588, 62 A.L.R.2d 855. A similar recognition of the need for and practical value of this kind of evidence is found in California Evidence Code § 1260.

Note to Paragraph (4). Even those few jurisdictions which have shied away from generally admitting statements of present condition have allowed them if made to a physician for purposes of diagnosis and treatment in view of the patient's strong motivation to be truthful. McCormick § 266, p. 563. The same guarantee of trustworthiness extends to statements of past conditions and medical history, made for purposes of diagnosis or treatment. It also extends to statements as to causation, reasonably pertinent to the same purposes, in accord with the current trend. *Shell Oil Co. v. Industrial Commission,* 2 Ill.2d 590, 119 N.E.2d 224 (1954); McCormick § 266, p. 564; New Jersey Evidence Rule 63(12)(c). Statements as to fault would not ordinarily qualify under this latter language. Thus a patient's statement that he was struck by an automobile would qualify but not his statement that the car was driven through a red light. Under the exception the statement need not have been made to a physician. Statements to hospital attendants, ambulance drivers, or even members of the family might be included.

Conventional doctrine has excluded from the hearsay exception, as not within its guarantee of truthfulness, statements to a physician consulted only for the purpose of enabling him to testify. While these statements were not admissible as substantive evidence, the expert was allowed to state the basis of his opinion, including statements of this kind. The distinction thus called for was one most unlikely to be made by juries. The rule accordingly rejects the limitation. This position is consistent with the provision of Rule 703 that the facts on which expert testimony is based need not be admissible in evidence if of a kind ordinarily relied upon by experts in the field.

Note to Paragraph (5). A hearsay exception for recorded recollection is generally recognized and has been described as having "long been favored by the federal and practically all the state courts that have had occasion to decide the question." *United States v. Kelly,* 349 F.2d 720, 770 (2d Cir.1965), citing numerous cases and sustaining the exception against a claimed denial of the right of confrontation. Many additional cases are cited in Annot., 82 A.L.R.2d 473, 520. The guarantee of trustworthiness is found in the reliability inherent in a record made while events were still fresh in mind and accurately reflecting them. *Owens v. State,* 67 Md. 307, 316, 10 A. 210, 212 (1887).

The principal controversy attending the exception has centered, not upon the propriety of the exception itself, but upon the question whether a preliminary requirement of impaired memory on the part of the witness should be imposed. The authorities are divided. If regard be had only to the accuracy of the evidence, admittedly impairment of the memory of the witness adds nothing to it and should not be required. McCormick § 277, p. 593; 3 Wigmore § 738, p. 76; *Jordan v. People,* 151 Colo. 133, 376 P.2d 699 (1962), cert. denied 373 U.S. 944, 83 S.Ct. 1553, 10 L.Ed.2d 699; *Hall v. State,* 223 Md. 158, 162 A.2d 751 (1960); *State v. Bindhammer,* 44 N.J. 372, 209 A.2d 124 (1965). Nevertheless, the absence of the requirement, it is believed, would encourage the use of statements carefully prepared for purposes of litigation under the supervision of attorneys, investigators, or claim adjusters. Hence the example includes a requirement that the witness not have "sufficient recollection to enable him to testify fully and accurately." To the same effect are California Evidence Code § 1237 and New Jersey Rule 63(1)(b), and this has been the position of the federal courts. *Vicksburg & Meridian R.R. v. O'Brien,* 119 U.S. 99, 7 S.Ct. 118, 30 L.Ed. 299 (1886); Ahern v. Webb, 268 F.2d 45 (10th Cir.1959); and see *N.L.R.B. v. Hudson Pulp and Paper Corp.,* 273 F.2d 660, 665 (5th Cir.1960); *N.L.R.B. v. Federal Dairy Co.,* 297 F.2d 487 (1st Cir.1962). But cf. *United States v. Adams,* 385 F.2d 548 (2d Cir.1967).

No attempt is made in the exception to spell out the method of establishing the initial knowledge or the contemporaneity and accuracy of the record, leaving them to be dealt with as the circumstances of the particular case might indicate. Multiple person involvement in the process of observing and recording, as in *Rathbun v. Brancatella,* 93 N.J.L. 222, 107 A. 279 (1919), is entirely consistent with the exception.

Locating the exception at this place in the scheme of the rules is a matter of choice. There were two other possibilities. The first was to regard the statement as one of the group of prior statements of a testifying witness which are excluded entirely from the category of hearsay by Rule 801(d)(1). That category, however, requires that declarant be "subject to cross-examination," as to which the impaired memory aspect of the exception raises doubts. The other possibility was to include the exception among those covered by Rule 804. Since unavailability is required by that rule and lack of memory is listed as a species of unavailability by the definition of the term in Rule 804(a)(3), that treatment at first impression would seem appropriate. The fact is, however, that the unavailability requirement of the exception is of a limited and peculiar nature. Accordingly, the exception is located at this point rather than in the context of a rule where unavailability is conceived of more broadly.

Note to Paragraph (6). Exception [paragraph] (6) represents an area which has received much attention from those seeking to improve the law of evidence. The Commonwealth Fund Act was the result of a study completed in 1927 by a distinguished committee under the chairmanship of Professor Morgan. Morgan et al., The Law of Evidence: Some Proposals for its Reform 63 (1927). With changes too minor to mention, it was adopted by Congress in 1936 as the rule for federal courts. 28 U.S.C. § 1732. A number of states took similar action. The Commissioners on Uniform State Laws in 1936 promulgated the Uniform Business Records as Evidence Act, 9A U.L.A. 506, which has acquired a substantial following in the states. Model Code Rule 514 and Uniform Rule 63(13) also deal with the subject. Difference of varying degrees of importance exist among these various treatments.

These reform efforts were largely within the context of business and commercial records, as the kind usually encountered, and concentrated considerable attention upon relaxing the requirement of producing as witnesses, or accounting for the nonproduction of, all participants in the process of gathering, transmitting, and recording information which the common law had evolved as a burdensome and crippling aspect of using records of this type. In their areas of primary emphasis on witnesses to be called and the general admissibility of ordinary business and commercial records, the Commonwealth Fund Act and the Uniform Act appear to have worked well. The exception seeks to preserve their advantages.

On the subject of what witnesses must be called, the Commonwealth Fund Act eliminated the common law requirement of calling or accounting for all participants by failing to mention it. *United States v. Mortimer,* 118 F.2d 266 (2d Cir.1941); *La Porte v. United States,* 300 F.2d 878 (9th Cir.1962); McCormick § 290, p. 608. Model Code Rule 514 and Uniform Rule 63(13) did likewise. The Uniform Act, however, abolished the common law requirement in express terms, providing that the requisite foundation testimony might be furnished by "the custodian or other qualified witness." Uniform Business Records as Evidence Act, § 2; 9A U.L.A. 506. The exception follows the Uniform Act in this respect.

The element of unusual reliability of business records is said variously to be supplied by systematic checking, by regularity and continuity which produce habits of precision, by actual experience of business in relying upon them, or by a duty to make an accurate record as part of a continuing job or occupation. McCormick §§ 281, 286, 287; Laughlin, Business Entries and the Like, 46 Iowa L.Rev. 276 (1961). The model statutes and rules have sought to capture these factors and to extend their impact by employing the phrase "regular course of business," in conjunction with a definition of "business" far broader than its ordinarily accepted meaning. The result is a tendency unduly to emphasize a requirement of routineness and repetitiveness and an insistence that other types of records be squeezed into the fact patterns which give rise to traditional business records. The rule therefore adopts the phrase "the course of a regularly conducted activity" as capturing the essential basis of the hearsay exception as it has evolved and the essential element which can be abstracted from the various specifications of what is a "business."

Amplification of the kinds of activities producing admissible records has given rise to problems which conventional business records by their nature avoid. They are problems of the source of the recorded information, of entries in opinion form, of motivation, and of involvement as participant in the matters recorded.

Sources of information presented no substantial problem with ordinary business records. All participants, including the observer or participant furnishing the information to be recorded, were acting routinely, under a duty of accuracy, with employer reliance on the result, or in short "in the regular course of business." If, however, the supplier of the information does not act in the regular course, an essential link is broken; the assurance of accuracy does not extend to the information itself, and the fact that it may be recorded with scrupulous accuracy is of no avail. An illustration is the police report incorporating information obtained from a bystander: the officer qualifies as acting in the regular course but the informant does not. The leading case, *Johnson v. Lutz*, 253 N.Y. 124, 170 N.E. 517 (1930), held that a report thus prepared was inadmissible. Most of the authorities have agreed with the decision. Gencarella v. Fyfe, 171 F.2d 419 (1st Cir.1948); *Gordon v. Robinson*, 210 F.2d 192 (3d Cir.1954); *Standard Oil Co. of California v. Moore*, 251 F.2d 188, 214 (9th Cir.1957), cert. denied 356 U.S. 975, 78 S.Ct. 1139, 2 L.Ed.2d 1148; *Yates v. Bair Transport*, Inc., 249 F.Supp. 681 (S.D.N.Y.1965); Annot., 69 A.L.R.2d 1148. Cf. *Hawkins v. Gorea Motor Express, Inc.*, 360 F.2d 933 (2d Cir.1966); *Contra*, 5 Wigmore § 1530a, n. 1, pp. 391–392. The point is not dealt with specifically in the Commonwealth Fund Act, the Uniform Act, or Uniform Rule 63(13). However, Model Code Rule 514 contains the requirement "that it was the regular course of that business for one with personal knowledge * * * to make such a memorandum or record or to transmit information thereof to be included in such a memorandum or record * * *." The rule follows this lead in requiring an informant with knowledge acting in the course of the regularly conducted activity.

Entries in the form of opinions were not encountered in traditional business records in view of the purely factual nature of the items recorded, but they are now commonly encountered with respect to medical diagnoses, prognoses, and test results, as well as occasionally in other areas. The Commonwealth Fund Act provided only for records of an "act, transaction, occurrence, or event," while the Uniform Act, Model Code Rule 514, and Uniform Rule 63(13) merely added the ambiguous term "condition." The limited phrasing of the Commonwealth Fund Act, 28 U.S.C. § 1732, may account for the reluctance of some federal decisions to admit diagnostic entries. *New York Life Ins. Co. v. Taylor*, 79 U.S.App.D.C. 66, 147 F.2d 297 (1945); *Lyles v. United States*, 103 U.S.App.D.C. 22, 254 F.2d 725 (1957), cert. denied 356 U.S. 961, 78 S.Ct. 997, 2 L.Ed.2d 1067; *England v. United States*, 174 F.2d 466 (5th Cir.1949); *Skogen v. Dow Chemical Co.*, 375 F.2d 692 (8th Cir.1967). Other federal decisions, however, experienced no difficulty in freely admitting diagnostic entries. *Reed v. Order of United Commercial Travelers*, 123 F.2d 252 (2d Cir.1941); *Buckminster's Estate v. Commissioner of Internal Revenue*, 147 F.2d 331 (2d Cir.1944); *Medina v. Erickson*, 226 F.2d 475 (9th Cir. 1955); *Thomas v. Hogan*, 308 F.2d 355 (4th Cir.1962); *Glawe v. Rulon*, 284 F.2d 495 (8th Cir.1960). In the state courts, the trend favors admissibility. Borucki v. MacKenzie Bros. Co., 125 Conn. 92, 3 A.2d 224 (1938); *Allen v. St. Louis Public Service Co.*, 365 Mo. 677, 285 S.W.2d 663, 55 A.L.R.2d 1022 (1956); *People v. Kohlmeyer*, 284 N.Y. 366, 31 N.E.2d 490 (1940); *Weis v. Weis*, 147 Ohio St. 416, 72 N.E.2d 245 (1947). In order to make clear its adherence to the latter position, the rule specifically includes both diagnoses and opinions, in addition to acts, events, and conditions, as proper subjects of admissible entries.

Problems of the motivation of the informant have been a source of difficulty and disagreement. In *Palmer v. Hoffman*, 318 U.S. 109, 63 S.Ct. 477, 87 L.Ed. 645 (1943), exclusion of an accident report made by the since deceased engineer, offered by defendant railroad trustees in a grade crossing collision case, was upheld. The report was not "in the regular course of business," not a record of the systematic conduct of the business as a business, said the Court. The report was prepared for use in litigating, not railroading. While the opinion mentions the motivation of the engineer only obliquely, the emphasis on records of routine operations is significant only by virtue of impact on motivation to be accurate. Absence of routineness raises lack of motivation to be accurate. The opinion of the Court of Appeals had gone beyond mere lack of motive to be accurate: the engineer's statement was "dripping with motivations to misrepresent." *Hoffman v. Palmer*, 129 F.2d 976, 991 (2d Cir.1942). The direct introduction of motivation is a disturbing factor, since absence of motive to misrepresent has not traditionally been a requirement of the rule; that records might be self-serving has not been a ground for exclusion. Laughlin, Business Records and the Like, 46 Iowa L.Rev. 276, 285 (1961). As Judge Clark said in his dissent, "I submit that there is hardly a grocer's account book which could not be excluded on that basis." 129 F.2d at 1002. A physician's evaluation report of a personal injury litigant would appear to be in the routine of his business. If the report is offered by the party at whose instance it was made, however, it has been held inadmissible, *Yates v. Bair Transport, Inc.*, 249 F.Supp. 681 (S.D.N.Y.1965), otherwise if offered by the opposite party, *Korte v. New York, N.H. & H.R. Co.*, 191 F.2d 86 (2d Cir.1951), cert. denied 342 U.S. 868, 72 S.Ct. 108, 96 L.Ed. 652.

The decisions hinge on motivation and which party is entitled to be concerned about it. Professor McCormick believed that the doctor's report or the accident report were sufficiently routine to justify admissibility. McCormick § 287, p. 604. Yet hesitation must be experienced in admitting everything which is observed and recorded in the course of a regularly conducted activity. Efforts to set a limit are illustrated by *Hartzog v. United States*, 217 F.2d 706 (4th Cir.1954), error to admit worksheets made by since deceased deputy collector in preparation for the instant income tax evasion prosecution, and *United States v. Ware*, 247 F.2d 698 (7th Cir.1957), error to admit narcotics agents' records of purchases. See also Exception [paragraph] (8), *infra*, as to the public record aspects of records of this nature. Some decisions have been satisfied as to motivation of an accident report if made pursuant to statutory duty, United States v. New York Foreign Trade Zone Operators, 304 F.2d 792 (2d Cir.1962); Taylor v. Baltimore & O.R. Co., 344 F.2d 281 (2d Cir.1965), since the report was oriented in a direction other than the litigation which ensued. Cf. Matthews v. United States, 217 F.2d 409 (5th Cir.1954). The formulation of specific terms which would assure satisfactory results in all cases is not possible. Consequently the rule proceeds from the base that records made in the course of a regularly conducted activity will be taken as admissible but subject to authority to exclude if "the sources of information or other circumstances indicate lack of trustworthiness."

Occasional decisions have reached for enhanced accuracy by requiring involvement as a participant in matters reported. *Clainos v. United States*, 82 U.S.App.D.C. 278, 163 F.2d 593 (1947), error to admit police records of convictions;

Standard Oil Co. of California v. Moore, 251 F.2d 188 (9th Cir.1957), cert. denied 356 U.S. 975, 78 S.Ct. 1139, 2 L.Ed.2d 1148, error to admit employees' records of observed business practices of others. The rule includes no requirement of this nature. Wholly acceptable records may involve matters merely observed, e.g. the weather.

The form which the "record" may assume under the rule is described broadly as a "memorandum, report, record, or data compilation, in any form." The expression "data compilation" is used as broadly descriptive of any means of storing information other than the conventional words and figures in written or documentary form. It includes, but is by no means limited to, electronic computer storage. The term is borrowed from revised Rule 34(a) of the Rules of Civil Procedure.

Note to Paragraph (7). Failure of a record to mention a matter which would ordinarily be mentioned is satisfactory evidence of its nonexistence. Uniform Rule 63(14), Comment. While probably not hearsay as defined in Rule 801, *supra,* decisions may be found which class the evidence not only as hearsay but also as not within any exception. In order to set the question at rest in favor of admissibility, it is specifically treated here. McCormick § 289, p. 609; Morgan, Basic Problems of Evidence 314 (1962); 5 Wigmore § 1531; Uniform Rule 63(14); California Evidence Code § 1272; Kansas Code of Civil Procedure § 60–460(n); New Jersey Evidence Rule 63(14).

Note to Paragraph (8). Public records are a recognized hearsay exception at common law and have been the subject of statutes without number. McCormick § 291. See, for example, 28 U.S.C. § 1733, the relative narrowness of which is illustrated by its nonapplicability to nonfederal public agencies, thus necessitating resort to the less appropriate business record exception to the hearsay rule. *Kay v. United States,* 255 F.2d 476 (4th Cir.1958). The rule makes no distinction between federal and nonfederal offices and agencies.

Justification for the exception is the assumption that a public official will perform his duty properly and the unlikelihood that he will remember details independently of the record. *Wong Wing Foo v. McGrath,* 196 F.2d 120 (9th Cir.1952), and see *Chesapeake & Delaware Canal Co. v. United States,* 250 U.S. 123, 39 S.Ct. 407, 63 L.Ed. 889 (1919). As to items (a) and (b), further support is found in the reliability factors underlying records of regularly conducted activities generally. See Exception [paragraph] (6), supra.

(a) Cases illustrating the admissibility of records of the office's or agency's own activities are numerous. *Chesapeake & Delaware Canal Co. v. United States,* 250 U.S. 123, 39 S.Ct. 407, 63 L.Ed. 889 (1919), Treasury records of miscellaneous receipts and disbursements; *Howard v. Perrin,* 200 U.S. 71, 26 S.Ct. 195, 50 L.Ed. 374 (1906), General Land Office records; *Ballew v. United States,* 160 U.S. 187, 16 S.Ct. 263, 40 L.Ed. 388 (1895). Pension Office records.

(b) Cases sustaining admissibility of records of matters observed are also numerous. *United States v. Van Hook,* 284 F.2d 489 (7th Cir.1960), remanded for resentencing 365 U.S. 609, 81 S.Ct. 823, 5 L.Ed.2d 821, letter from induction officer to District Attorney, pursuant to army regulations, stating fact and circumstances of refusal to be inducted; *T'Kach v. United States,* 242 F.2d 937 (5th Cir.1957), affidavit of White House personnel officer that search of records showed no employment of accused, charged with fraudulently representing himself as an envoy of the President; *Minnehaha County v. Kelley,* 150 F.2d 356 (8th Cir.1945); Weather Bureau records of rainfall; *United States v. Meyer,* 113 F.2d 387 (7th Cir.1940), cert. denied 311 U.S. 706, 61 S.Ct. 174, 85 L.Ed. 459, map prepared by government engineer from information furnished by men working under his supervision.

(c) The more controversial area of public records is that of the so-called "evaluative" report. The disagreement among the decisions has been due in part, no doubt, to the variety of situations encountered, as well as to differences in principle. Sustaining admissibility are such cases as *United States v. Dumas,* 149 U.S. 278, 13 S.Ct. 872, 37 L.Ed. 734 (1893), statement of account certified by Postmaster General in action against postmaster; *McCarty v. United States,* 185 F.2d 520 (5th Cir.1950), reh. denied 187 F.2d 234, Certificate of Settlement of General Accounting Office showing indebtedness and letter from Army official stating Government had performed, in action on contract to purchase and remove waste food from Army camp; *Moran v. Pittsburgh–Des Moines Steel Co.,* 183 F.2d 467 (3d Cir.1950), report of Bureau of Mines as to cause of gas tank explosion; Petition of W___, 164 F.Supp. 659 (E.D.Pa.1958), report by Immigration and Naturalization Service investigator that petitioner was known in community as wife of man to whom she was not married. To the opposite effect and denying admissibility are *Franklin v. Skelly Oil Co.,* 141 F.2d 568 (10th Cir. 1944), State Fire Marshal's report of cause of gas explosion; *Lomax Transp. Co. v. United States,* 183 F.2d 331 (9th Cir.1950), Certificate of Settlement from General Accounting Office in action for naval supplies lost in warehouse fire; *Yung Jin Teung v. Dulles,* 229 F.2d 244 (2d Cir.1956), "Status Reports" offered to justify delay in processing passport applications. Police reports have generally been excluded except to the extent to which they incorporate firsthand observations of the officer. Annot., 69 A.L.R.2d 1148. Various kinds of evaluative reports are admissible under federal statutes: 7 U.S.C. § 78, findings of Secretary of Agriculture prima facie evidence of true grade of grain; 7 U.S.C. § 210(f), findings of Secretary of Agriculture prima facie evidence in action for damages against stockyard owner; 7 U.S.C. § 292, order by Secretary of Agriculture prima facie evidence in judicial enforcement proceedings against producers association monopoly; 7 U.S.C. § 1622(h), Department of Agriculture inspection certificates of products shipped in interstate commerce prima facie evidence; 8 U.S.C. § 1440(c), separation of alien from military service on conditions other than honorable provable by certificate from department in proceedings to revoke citizenship; 18 U.S.C. § 4245, certificate of Director of Prisons that convicted person has been examined and found probably incompetent at time of trial prima facie evidence in court hearing on competency; 42 U.S.C. § 269(b), bill of health by appropriate official prima facie evidence of vessel's sanitary history and condition and compliance with regulations; 46 U.S.C. § 679, certificate of consul presumptive evidence of refusal of master to transport destitute seamen to United States. While these statutory exceptions to the hearsay rule are left undisturbed, Rule 802, the willingness of Congress to recognize a substantial measure of admissibility for evaluative reports is a helpful guide.

Factors which may be of assistance in passing upon the admissibility of evaluative reports include: (1) the timeliness of the investigation, McCormick, Can the Courts Make Wider

Use of Reports of Official Investigations? 42 Iowa L.Rev. 363 (1957); (2) the special skill or experience of the official, *id.*, (3) whether a hearing was held and the level at which conducted, Franklin v. Skelly Oil Co., 141 F.2d 568 (10th Cir.1944); (4) possible motivation problems suggested by Palmer v. Hoffman, 318 U.S. 109, 63 S.Ct. 477, 87 L.Ed. 645 (1943). Others no doubt could be added.

The formulation of an approach which would give appropriate weight to all possible factors in every situation is an obvious impossibility. Hence the rule, as in Exception [paragraph] (6), assumes admissibility in the first instance but with ample provision for escape if sufficient negative factors are present. In one respect, however, the rule with respect to evaluative reports under item (c) is very specific: they are admissible only in civil cases and against the government in criminal cases in view of the almost certain collision with confrontation rights which would result from their use against the accused in a criminal case.

Note to Paragraph (9). Records of vital statistics are commonly the subject of particular statutes making them admissible in evidence, Uniform Vital Statistics Act, 9C U.L.A. 350 (1957). The rule is in principle narrower than Uniform Rule 63(16) which includes reports required of persons performing functions authorized by statute, yet in practical effect the two are substantially the same. Comment Uniform Rule 63(16). The exception as drafted is in the pattern of California Evidence Code § 1281.

Note to Paragraph (10). The principle of proving nonoccurrence of an event by evidence of the absence of a record which would regularly be made of its occurrence, developed in Exception [paragraph] (7) with respect to regularly conducted activities, is here extended to public records of the kind mentioned in Exceptions [paragraphs] (8) and (9). 5 Wigmore § 1633(6), p. 519. Some harmless duplication no doubt exists with Exception [paragraph] (7). For instances of federal statutes recognizing this method of proof, see 8 U.S.C. § 1284(b), proof of absence of alien crewman's name from outgoing manifest prima facie evidence of failure to detain or deport, and 42 U.S.C. § 405(c)(3), (4)(B), (4)(C), absence of HEW [Department of Health, Education, and Welfare] record prima facie evidence of no wages or self-employment income.

The rule includes situations in which absence of a record may itself be the ultimate focal point of inquiry, e.g. People v. Love, 310 Ill. 558, 142 N.E. 204 (1923), certificate of Secretary of State admitted to show failure to file documents required by Securities Law, as well as cases where the absence of a record is offered as proof of the nonoccurrence of an event ordinarily recorded.

The refusal of the common law to allow proof by certificate of the lack of a record or entry has no apparent justification, 5 Wigmore § 1678(7), p. 752. The rule takes the opposite position, as to Uniform Rule 63(17); California Evidence Code § 1284; Kansas Code of Civil Procedure § 60–460(c); New Jersey Evidence Rule 63(17). Congress has recognized certification as evidence of the lack of a record. 8 U.S.C. § 1360(d), certificate of Attorney General or other designated officer that no record of Immigration and Naturalization Service of specified nature or entry therein is found, admissible in alien cases.

Note to Paragraph (11). Records of activities of religious organizations are currently recognized as admissible at least to the extent of the business records exception to the hearsay rule, 5 Wigmore § 1523, p. 371, and Exception [paragraph] (6) would be applicable. However, both the business record doctrine and Exception [paragraph] (6) require that the person furnishing the information be one in the business or activity. The result is such decisions as Daily v. Grand Lodge, 311 Ill. 184, 142 N.E. 478 (1924), holding a church record admissible to prove fact, date, and place of baptism, but not age of child except that he had at least been born at the time. In view of the unlikelihood that false information would be furnished on occasions of this kind, the rule contains no requirement that the informant be in the course of the activity. See California Evidence Code § 1315 and Comment.

Note to Paragraph (12). The principle of proof by certification is recognized as to public officials in Exceptions [paragraphs] (8) and (10), and with respect to authentication in Rule 902. The present exception is a duplication to the extent that it deals with a certificate by a public official, as in the case of a judge who performs a marriage ceremony. The area covered by the rule is, however, substantially larger and extends the certification procedure to clergymen and the like who perform marriages and other ceremonies or administer sacraments. Thus certificates of such matters as baptism or confirmation, as well as marriage, are included. In principle they are as acceptable evidence as certificates of public officers. See 5 Wigmore § 1645, as to marriage certificates. When the person executing the certificate is not a public official, the self-authenticating character of documents purporting to emanate from public officials, see Rule 902, is lacking and proof is required that the person was authorized and did make the certificate. The time element, however, may safely be taken as supplied by the certificate, once authority and authenticity are established, particularly in view of the presumption that a document was executed on the date it bears.

For similar rules, some limited to certificates of marriage, with variations in foundation requirements, see Uniform Rule 63(18); California Evidence Code § 1316; Kansas Code of Civil Procedure § 60–460(p); New Jersey Evidence Rule 63(18).

Note to Paragraph (13). Records of family history kept in family Bibles have by long tradition been received in evidence. 5 Wigmore §§ 1495, 1496, citing numerous statutes and decisions. See also Regulations, Social Security Administration, 20 C.F.R. § 404.703(c), recognizing family Bible entries as proof of age in the absence of public or church records. Opinions in the area also include inscriptions on tombstones, publicly displayed pedigrees, and engravings on rings. Wigmore, *supra.* The rule is substantially identical in coverage with California Evidence Code § 1312.

Note to Paragraph (14). The recording of title documents is a purely statutory development. Under any theory of the admissibility of public records, the records would be receivable as evidence of the contents of the recorded document, else the recording process would be reduced to a nullity. When, however, the record is offered for the further purpose of proving execution and delivery, a problem of lack of firsthand knowledge by the recorder, not present as to contents, is presented. This problem is solved, seemingly in all jurisdictions, by qualifying for recording only those documents shown by a specified procedure, either acknowledgement or a form of probate, to have been executed and delivered. 5 Wigmore §§ 1647–1651. Thus what may appear in the rule, at first glance, as endowing the record with an effect independently of local law and inviting difficulties of an *Erie* nature under *Cities Service Oil Co. v. Dunlap,* 308 U.S. 208, 60 S.Ct. 201, 84 L.Ed. 196 (1939), is not present, since the local law in fact governs under the example.

Note to Paragraph (15). Dispositive documents often contain recitals of fact. Thus a deed purporting to have been executed by an attorney in fact may recite the existence of the power of attorney, or a deed may recite that the grantors are all the heirs of the last record owner. Under the rule, these recitals are exempted from the hearsay rule. The circumstances under which dispositive documents are executed and the requirement that the recital be germane to the purpose of the document are believed to be adequate guarantees of trustworthiness, particularly in view of the nonapplicability of the rule if dealings with the property have been inconsistent with the document. The age of the document is of no significance, though in practical application the document will most often be an ancient one. See Uniform Rule 63(29), Comment.

Similar provisions are contained in Uniform Rule 63(29); California Evidence Code § 1330; Kansas Code of Civil Procedure § 60–460(aa); New Jersey Evidence Rule 63(29).

Note to Paragraph (16). Authenticating a document as ancient, essentially in the pattern of the common law, as provided in Rule 901(b)(8), leaves open as a separate question the admissibility of assertive statements contained therein as against a hearsay objection. 7 Wigmore § 2145a. Wigmore further states that the ancient document technique of authentication is universally conceded to apply to all sorts of documents, including letters, records, contracts, maps, and certificates, in addition to title documents, citing numerous decisions. *Id.* § 2145. Since most of these items are significant evidentially only insofar as they are assertive, their admission in evidence must be as a hearsay exception. But see 5 *id.* § 1573, p. 429, referring to recitals in ancient deeds as a "limited" hearsay exception. The former position is believed to be the correct one in reason and authority. As pointed out in McCormick § 298, danger of mistake is minimized by authentication requirements, and age affords assurance that the writing antedates the present controversy. See *Dallas County v. Commercial Union Assurance Co.,* 286 F.2d 388 (5th Cir.1961), upholding admissibility of 58–year–old newspaper story. Cf. Morgan, Basic Problems of Evidence 364 (1962), but see *id.* 254.

For a similar provision, but with the added requirement that "the statement has since generally been acted upon as true by persons having an interest in the matter," see California Evidence Code § 1331.

Note to Paragraph (17). Ample authority at common law supported the admission in evidence of items falling in this category. While Wigmore's text is narrowly oriented to lists, etc., prepared for the use of a trade or profession, 6 Wigmore § 1702, authorities are cited which include other kinds of publications, for example, newspaper market reports, telephone directories, and city directories. *Id.* §§ 1702–1706. The basis of trustworthiness is general reliance by the public or by a particular segment of it, and the motivation of the compiler to foster reliance by being accurate.

For similar provisions, see Uniform Rule 63(30); California Evidence Code § 1340; Kansas Code of Civil Procedure § 60–460(bb); New Jersey Evidence Rule 63(30). Uniform Commercial Code § 2–724 provides for admissibility in evidence of "reports in official publications or trade journals or in newspapers or periodicals of general circulation published as the reports of such [established commodity] market."

Note to Paragraph (18). The writers have generally favored the admissibility of learned treatises, McCormick § 296, p. 621; Morgan, Basic Problems of Evidence 366 (1962); 6 Wigmore § 1692, with the support of occasional decisions and rules, *City of Dothan v. Hardy,* 237 Ala. 603, 188 So. 264 (1939); *Lewandowski v. Preferred Risk Mut. Ins. Co.,* 33 Wis.2d 69, 146 N.W.2d 505 (1966), 66 Mich.L.Rev. 183 (1967); Uniform Rule 63(31); Kansas Code of Civil Procedure § 60–460(cc), but the great weight of authority has been that learned treatises are not admissible as substantive evidence though usable in the cross-examination of experts. The foundation of the minority view is that the hearsay objection must be regarded as unimpressive when directed against treatises since a high standard of accuracy is engendered by various factors: the treatise is written primarily and impartially for professionals, subject to scrutiny and exposure for inaccuracy, with the reputation of the writer at stake. 6 Wigmore § 1692. Sound as this position may be with respect to trustworthiness, there is, nevertheless, an additional difficulty in the likelihood that the treatise will be misunderstood and misapplied without expert assistance and supervision. This difficulty is recognized in the cases demonstrating unwillingness to sustain findings relative to disability on the basis of judicially noticed medical texts. *Ross v. Gardner,* 365 F.2d 554 (6th Cir.1966); *Sayers v. Gardner,* 380 F.2d 940 (6th Cir.1967); *Colwell v. Gardner,* 386 F.2d 56 (6th Cir.1967); *Glendenning v. Ribicoff,* 213 F.Supp. 301 (W.D.Mo.1962); *Cook v. Celebrezze,* 217 F.Supp. 366 (W.D.Mo.1963); *Sosna v. Celebrezze,* 234 F.Supp. 289 (E.D.Pa.1964); and see *McDaniel v. Celebrezze,* 331 F.2d 426 (4th Cir.1964). The rule avoids the danger of misunderstanding and misapplication by limiting the use of treatises as substantive evidence to situations in which an expert is on the stand and available to explain and assist in the application of the treatise if desired. The limitation upon receiving the publication itself physically in evidence, contained in the last sentence, is designed, to further this policy.

The relevance of the use of treatises on cross-examination is evident. This use of treatises has been the subject of varied views. The most restrictive position is that the witness must have stated expressly on direct his reliance upon the treatise. A slightly more liberal approach still insists upon reliance but allows it to be developed on cross-examination. Further relaxation dispenses with reliance but requires recognition as an authority by the witness, developable on cross-examination. The greatest liberality is found in decisions allowing use of the treatise on cross-examination when its status as an authority is established by any means. Annot., 60 A.L.R.2d 77. The exception is hinged upon this last position, which is that of the Supreme Court, *Reilly v. Pinkus,* 338 U.S. 269, 70 S.Ct. 110, 94 L.Ed. 63 (1949), and of recent well considered state court decisions, *City of St. Petersburg v. Ferguson,* 193 So.2d 648 (Fla.App.1967), cert. denied Fla., 201 So.2d 556; *Darling v. Charleston Memorial Community Hospital,* 33 Ill.2d 326, 211 N.E.2d 253 (1965); *Dabroe v. Rhodes Co.,* 64 Wash.2d 431, 392 P.2d 317 (1964).

In Reilly v. Pinkus, *supra,* the Court pointed out that testing of professional knowledge was incomplete without exploration of the witness' knowledge of and attitude toward established treatises in the field. The process works equally well in reverse and furnishes the basis of the rule.

The rule does not require that the witness rely upon or recognize the treatise as authoritative, thus avoiding the possibility that the expert may at the outset block cross-examination by refusing to concede reliance or authoritativeness. Dabroe v. Rhodes Co., *supra.* Moreover, the rule avoids the unreality of admitting evidence for the purpose of impeachment only, with an instruction to the jury not to consider it otherwise. The parallel to the treatment of prior inconsistent statements will be apparent. See Rules 613(b) and 801(d)(1).

Note to Paragraphs (19), (20) and (21). Trustworthiness in reputation evidence is found "when the topic is such that the facts are likely to have been inquired about and that persons having personal knowledge have disclosed facts which have thus been discussed in the community; and thus the community's conclusion, if any has been formed, is likely to be a trustworthy one." 5 Wigmore § 1580, p. 444, and see also § 1583. On this common foundation, reputation as to land boundaries, customs, general history, character, and marriage have come to be regarded as admissible. The breadth of the underlying principle suggests the formulation of an equally broad exception, but tradition has in fact been much narrower and more particularized, and this is the pattern of these exceptions in the rule.

Exception [paragraph] (19) is concerned with matters of personal and family history. Marriage is universally conceded to be a proper subject of proof by evidence of reputation in the community. 5 Wigmore § 1602. As to such items as legitimacy, relationship, adoption, birth, and death, the decisions are divided. *Id.* § 1605. All seem to be susceptible to being the subject of well founded repute. The "world" in which the reputation may exist may be family, associates, or community. This world has proved capable of expanding with changing times from the single uncomplicated neighborhood, in which all activities take place, to the multiple and unrelated worlds of work, religious affiliation, and social activity, in each of which a reputation may be generated. *People v. Reeves,* 360 Ill. 55, 195 N.E. 443 (1935); *State v. Axilrod,* 248 Minn. 204, 79 N.W.2d 677 (1956); Mass.Stat. 1947, c. 410, M.G.L.A. c. 233 § 21A; 5 Wigmore § 1616. The family has often served as the point of beginning for allowing community reputation. 5 Wigmore § 1488. For comparable provisions see Uniform Rule 63(26), (27)(c); California Evidence Code §§ 1313, 1314; Kansas Code of Civil Procedure § 60–460(x), (y)(3); New Jersey Evidence Rule 63(26), (27)(c).

The first portion of Exception [paragraph] (20) is based upon the general admissibility of evidence of reputation as to land boundaries and land customs, expanded in this country to include private as well as public boundaries. McCormick § 299, p. 625. The reputation is required to antedate the controversy, though not to be ancient. The second portion is likewise supported by authority, *id.,* and is designed to facilitate proof of events when judicial notice is not available. The historical character of the subject matter dispenses with any need that the reputation antedate the controversy with respect to which it is offered. For similar provisions see Uniform Rule 63(27)(a), (b); California Evidence Code §§ 1320–1322; Kansas Code of Civil Procedure § 60–460(y), (1), (2); New Jersey Evidence Rule 63(27)(a), (b).

Exception [paragraph] (21) recognizes the traditional acceptance of reputation evidence as a means of proving human character. McCormick §§ 44, 158. The exception deals only with the hearsay aspect of this kind of evidence. Limitations upon admissibility based on other grounds will be found in Rules 404, relevancy of character evidence generally, and 608, character of witness. The exception is in effect a reiteration, in the context of hearsay, of Rule 405(a). Similar provisions are contained in Uniform Rule 63(28); California Evidence Code § 1324; Kansas Code of Civil Procedure § 60–460(z); New Jersey Evidence Rule 63(28).

Note to Paragraph (22). When the status of a former judgment is under consideration in subsequent litigation, three possibilities must be noted: (1) the former judgment is conclusive under the doctrine of res judicata, either as a bar or a collateral estoppel; or (2) it is admissible in evidence for what it is worth; or (3) it may be of no effect at all. The first situation does not involve any problem of evidence except in the way that principles of substantive law generally bear upon the relevancy and materiality of evidence. The rule does not deal with the substantive effect of the judgment as a bar or collateral estoppel. When, however, the doctrine of res judicata does not apply to make the judgment either a bar or a collateral estoppel, a choice is presented between the second and third alternatives. The rule adopts the second for judgments of criminal conviction of felony grade. This is the direction of the decisions, Annot., 18 A.L.R.2d 1287, 1299, which manifest an increasing reluctance to reject *in toto* the validity of the law's factfinding processes outside the confines of res judicata and collateral estoppel. While this may leave a jury with the evidence of conviction but without means to evaluate it, as suggested by Judge Hinton, Note 27 Ill.L.Rev. 195 (1932), it seems safe to assume that the jury will give it substantial effect unless defendant offers a satisfactory explanation, a possibility not foreclosed by the provision. But see *North River Ins. Co. v. Militello,* 104 Colo. 28, 88 P.2d 567 (1939), in which the jury found for plaintiff on a fire policy despite the introduction of his conviction for arson. For supporting federal decisions see Clark, J., in *New York & Cuba Mail S.S. Co. v. Continental Cas. Co.,* 117 F.2d 404, 411 (2d Cir.1941); *Connecticut Fire Ins. Co. v. Farrara,* 277 F.2d 388 (8th Cir.1960).

Practical considerations require exclusion of convictions of minor offenses, not because the administration of justice in its lower echelons must be inferior, but because motivation to defend at this level is often minimal or nonexistent. *Cope v. Goble,* 39 Cal.App.2d 448, 103 P.2d 598 (1940); *Jones v. Talbot,* 87 Idaho 498, 394 P.2d 316 (1964); *Warren v. Marsh,* 215 Minn. 615, 11 N.W.2d 528 (1943); Annot., 18 A.L.R.2d 1287, 1295–1297; 16 Brooklyn L.Rev. 286 (1950); 50 Colum.L.Rev. 529 (1950); 35 Cornell L.Q. 872 (1950). Hence the rule includes only convictions of felony grade, measured by federal standards.

Judgments of conviction based upon pleas of *nolo contendere* are not included. This position is consistent with the treatment of *nolo* pleas in Rule 410 and the authorities cited in the Advisory Committee's Note in support thereof.

While these rules do not in general purport to resolve constitutional issues, they have in general been drafted with a view to avoiding collision with constitutional principles. Consequently the exception does not include evidence of the conviction of a third person, offered against the accused in a criminal prosecution to prove any fact essential to sustain the judgment of conviction. A contrary position would seem clearly to violate the right of confrontation. *Kirby v. United States,* 174 U.S. 47, 19 S.Ct. 574, 43 L.Ed. 890 (1899), error to convict of possessing stolen postage stamps with the only evidence of theft being the record of conviction of the thieves. The situation is to be distinguished from cases in which conviction of another person is an element of the crime, e.g. 15 U.S.C. § 902(d), interstate shipment of firearms to a known convicted felon, and, as specifically provided, from impeachment.

For comparable provisions see Uniform Rule 63(20); California Evidence Code § 1300; Kansas Code of Civil Procedure § 60–460(r); New Jersey Evidence Rule 63(20).

Note to Paragraph (23). A hearsay exception in this area was originally justified on the ground that verdicts were evidence of reputation. As trial by jury graduated from the category of neighborhood inquests, this theory lost its validity. It was never valid as to chancery decrees. Nevertheless the rule persisted, though the judges and writers shifted ground and began saying that the judgment or decree was as good evidence as reputation. See *City of London v. Clerke,* Carth. 181, 90 Eng.Rep. 710 (K.B. 1691); *Neill v. Duke of Devonshire,* 8 App.Cas. 135 (1882). The shift appears to be correct, since the process of inquiry, sifting, and scrutiny which is relied upon to render reputation reliable is present in perhaps greater measure in the process of litigation. While this might suggest a broader area of application, the affinity to reputation is strong, and paragraph [paragraph] (23) goes no further, not even including character.

The leading case in the *United States, Patterson v. Gaines,* 47 U.S. (6 How.) 550, 599, 12 L.Ed. 553 (1847), follows in the pattern of the English decisions, mentioning as illustrative matters thus provable: manorial rights, public rights of way, immemorial custom, disputed boundary, and pedigree. More recent recognition of the principle is found in *Grant Bros. Construction Co. v. United States,* 232 U.S. 647, 34 S.Ct. 452, 58 L.Ed. 776 (1914), in action for penalties under Alien Contract Labor Law, decision of board of inquiry of Immigration Service admissible to prove alienage of laborers, as a matter of pedigree; *United States v. Mid-Continent Petroleum Corp.,* 67 F.2d 37 (10th Cir.1933), records of commission enrolling Indians admissible on pedigree; *Jung Yen Loy v. Cahill,* 81 F.2d 809 (9th Cir.1936), board decisions as to citizenship of plaintiff's father admissible in proceeding for declaration of citizenship. *Contra,* In re Estate of Cunha, 49 Haw. 273, 414 P.2d 925 (1966).

1974 Enactment

Note to Paragraph (3). Rule 803(3) was approved in the form submitted by the Court to Congress. However, the Committee intends that the Rule be construed to limit the doctrine of *Mutual Life Insurance Co. v. Hillmon,* 145 U.S. 285, 295–300 (1892), so as to render statements of intent by a declarant admissible only to prove his future conduct, not the future conduct of another person.

Note to Paragraph (4). After giving particular attention to the question of physical examination made solely to enable a physician to testify, the Committee approved Rule 803(4) as submitted to Congress, with the understanding that it is not intended in any way to adversely affect present privilege rules or those subsequently adopted.

Note to Paragraph (5). Rule 803(5) as submitted by the Court permitted the reading into evidence of a memorandum or record concerning a matter about which a witness once had knowledge but now has insufficient recollection to enable him to testify accurately and fully, "shown to have been made when the matter was fresh in his memory and to reflect that knowledge correctly." The Committee amended this Rule to add the words "or adopted by the witness" after the phrase "shown to have been made", a treatment consistent with the definition of "statement" in the Jencks Act, 18 U.S.C. 3500. Moreover, it is the Committee's understanding that a memorandum or report, although barred under this Rule, would nonetheless be admissible if it came within another hearsay exception. This last stated principle is deemed applicable to all the hearsay rules.

Note to Paragraph (6). Rule 803(6) as submitted by the Court permitted a record made "in the course of a regularly conducted activity" to be admissible in certain circumstances. The Committee believed there were insufficient guarantees of reliability in records made in the course of activities falling outside the scope of "business" activities as that term is broadly defined in 28 U.S.C. 1732. Moreover, the Committee concluded that the additional requirement of Section 1732 that it must have been the regular practice of a business to make the record is a necessary further assurance of its trustworthiness. The Committee accordingly amended the Rule to incorporate these limitations.

Note to Paragraph (7). Rule 803(7) as submitted by the Court concerned the *absence* of entry in the records of a "regularly conducted activity." The Committee amended this Rule to conform with its action with respect to Rule 803(6).

Note to Paragraph (8). The Committee approved Rule 803(8) without substantive change from the form in which it was submitted by the Court. The Committee intends that the phrase "factual findings" be strictly construed and that evaluations or opinions contained in public reports shall not be admissible under this Rule.

Note to Paragraph (13). The Committee approved this Rule in the form submitted by the Court, intending that the phrase "Statements of fact concerning personal or family history" be read to include the specific types of such statements enumerated in Rule 803(11). House Report No. 93–650.

Note to Paragraph (4). The House approved this rule as it was submitted by the Supreme Court "with the understanding that it is not intended in any way to adversely affect present privilege rules." We also approve this rule, and we would point out with respect to the question of its relation to privileges, it must be read in conjunction with rule 35 of the Federal Rules of Civil Procedure which provides that whenever the physical or mental condition of a party (plaintiff or defendant) is in controversy, the court may require him to submit to an examination by a physician. It is these examinations which will normally be admitted under this exception.

Note to Paragraph (5). Rule 803(5) as submitted by the Court permitted the reading into evidence of a memorandum or record concerning a matter about which a witness once had knowledge but now has insufficient recollection to enable him to testify accurately and fully, "shown to have been made when the matter was fresh in his memory and to reflect that knowledge correctly." The House amended the rule to add the words "or adopted by the witness" after the phrase "shown to have been made," language parallel to the Jencks Act [18 U.S.C. § 3500].

The committee accepts the House amendment with the understanding and belief that it was not intended to narrow the scope of applicability of the rule. In fact, we understand it to clarify the rule's applicability to a memorandum adopted by the witness as well as one made by him. While the rule as submitted by the Court was silent on the question of who made the memorandum, we view the House amendment as a helpful clarification, noting, however, that the Advisory Committee's note to this rule suggests that the important thing is the accuracy of the memorandum rather than who made it.

The committee does not view the House amendment as precluding admissibility in situations in which multiple participants were involved.

When the verifying witness has not prepared the report, but merely examined it and found it accurate, he has adopted the report, and it is therefore admissible. The rule should also be interpreted to cover other situations involving multiple participants, e.g., employer dictating to secretary, secretary making memorandum at direction of employer, or information being passed along a chain of persons, as in *Curtis v. Bradley* [65 Conn. 99, 31 Atl. 591 (1894); see, also, *Rathbun v. Brancatella*, 93 N.J.L. 222, 107 Atl. 279 (1919); see, also, McCormick on Evidence, § 303 (2d ed. 1972)].

The committee also accepts the understanding of the House that a memorandum or report, although barred under this rule, would nonetheless be admissible if it came within another hearsay exception. We consider this principle to be applicable to all the hearsay rules.

Note to Paragraph (6). Rule 803(6) as submitted by the Supreme Court permitted a record made in the course of a regularly conducted activity to be admissible in certain circumstances. This rule constituted a broadening of the traditional business records hearsay exception which has been long advocated by scholars and judges active in the law of evidence.

The House felt there were insufficient guarantees of reliability of records not within a broadly defined business records exception. We disagree. Even under the House definition of "business" including profession, occupation, and "calling of every kind," the records of many regularly conducted activities will, or may be, excluded from evidence. Under the principle of ejusdem generis, the intent of "calling of every kind" would seem to be related to work-related endeavors—e.g., butcher, baker, artist, etc.

Thus, it appears that the records of many institutions or groups might not be admissible under the House amendments. For example, schools, churches, and hospitals will not normally be considered businesses within the definition. Yet, these are groups which keep financial and other records on a regular basis in a manner similar to business enterprises. We believe these records are of equivalent trustworthiness and should be admitted into evidence.

Three states, which have recently codified their evidence rules, have adopted the Supreme Court version of rule 803(6), providing for admission of memoranda of a "regularly conducted activity." None adopted the words "business activity" used in the House amendment. [See Nev.Rev.Stats. § 15.135; N.Mex.Stats. (1973 Supp.) § 20–4–803(6); West's Wis.Stats.Anno. (1973 Supp.) § 908.03(6).]

Therefore, the committee deleted the word "business" as it appears before the word "activity". The last sentence then is unnecessary and was also deleted.

It is the understanding of the committee that the use of the phrase "person with knowledge" is not intended to imply that the party seeking to introduce the memorandum, report, record, or data compilation must be able to produce, or even identify, the specific individual upon whose first-hand knowledge the memorandum, report, record or data compilation was based. A sufficient foundation for the introduction of such evidence will be laid if the party seeking to introduce the evidence is able to show that it was the regular practice of the activity to base such memorandums, reports, records, or data compilations upon a transmission from a person with knowledge, e.g., in the case of the content of a shipment of goods, upon a report from the company's receiving agent or in the case of a computer printout, upon a report from the company's computer programmer or one who has knowledge of the particular record system. In short, the scope of the phrase "person with knowledge" is meant to be coterminous with the custodian of the evidence or other qualified witness. The committee believes this represents the desired rule in light of the complex nature of modern business organizations.

Note to Paragraph (8). The House approved rule 803(8), as submitted by the Supreme Court, with one substantive change. It excluded from the hearsay exception reports containing matters observed by police officers and other law enforcement personnel in criminal cases. Ostensibly, the reason for this exclusion is that observations by police officers at the scene of the crime or the apprehension of the defendant are not as reliable as observations by public officials in other cases because of the adversarial nature of the confrontation between the police and the defendant in criminal cases.

The committee accepts the House's decision to exclude such recorded observations where the police officer is available to testify in court about his observation. However, where he is unavailable as unavailability is defined in rule 804(a)(4) and (a)(5), the report should be admitted as the best available evidence. Accordingly, the committee has amended rule 803(8) to refer to the provision of [proposed] rule 804(b)(5) [deleted], which allows the admission of such reports, records or other statements where the police officer or other law enforcement officer is unavailable because of death, then existing physical or mental illness or infirmity, or not being successfully subject to legal process.

The House Judiciary Committee report contained a statement of intent that "the phrase 'factual findings' in subdivision (c) be strictly construed and that evaluations or opinions contained in public reports shall not be admissible under this rule." The committee takes strong exception to this limiting understanding of the application of the rule. We do not think it reflects an understanding of the intended operation of the rule as explained in the Advisory Committee notes to this subsection. The Advisory Committee notes on subsection (c) of this subdivision point out that various kinds of evaluative reports are now admissible under Federal statutes. 7 U.S.C. § 78, findings of Secretary of Agriculture prima facie evidence of true grade of grain; 42 U.S.C. § 269(b), bill of health by appropriate official prima facie evidence of vessel's sanitary history and condition and compliance with regulations. These statutory exceptions to the hearsay rule are preserved. Rule 802. The willingness of

Congress to recognize these and other such evaluative reports provides a helpful guide in determining the kind of reports which are intended to be admissible under this rule. We think the restrictive interpretation of the House overlooks the fact that while the Advisory Committee assumes admissibility in the first instance of evaluative reports, they are not admissible if, as the rule states, "the sources of information or other circumstances indicate lack of trustworthiness."

The Advisory Committee explains the factors to be considered:

* * * * * * *

Factors which may be assistance in passing upon the admissibility of evaluative reports include: (1) the timeliness of the investigation, McCormick, Can the Courts Make Wider Use of Reports of Official Investigations? 42 Iowa L.Rev. 363 (1957); (2) the special skill or experience of the official, id.; (3) whether a hearing was held and the level at which conducted, *Franklin v. Skelly Oil Co.,* 141 F.2d 568 (19th Cir.1944); (4) possible motivation problems suggested by *Palmer v. Hoffman,* 318 U.S. 109, 63 S.Ct. 477, 87 L.Ed. 645 (1943). Others no doubt could be added.

* * * * * * *

The committee concludes that the language of the rule together with the explanation provided by the Advisory Committee furnish sufficient guidance on the admissibility of evaluative reports.

Note to Paragraph (24). The proposed Rules of Evidence submitted to Congress contained identical provisions in rules 803 and 804 (which set forth the various hearsay exceptions), admitting any hearsay statement not specifically covered by any of the stated exceptions, if the hearsay statement was found to have "comparable circumstantial guarantees of trustworthiness." The House deleted these provisions (proposed rules 803(24) and 804(b)(6)[(5)]) as injecting "too much uncertainty" into the law of evidence and impairing the ability of practitioners to prepare for trial. The House felt that rule 102, which directs the courts to construe the Rules of Evidence so as to promote growth and development, would permit sufficient flexibility to admit hearsay evidence in appropriate cases under various factual situations that might arise.

We disagree with the total rejection of a residual hearsay exception. While we view rule 102 as being intended to provide for a broader construction and interpretation of these rules, we feel that, without a separate residual provision, the specifically enumerated exceptions could become tortured beyond any reasonable circumstances which they were intended to include (even if broadly construed). Moreover, these exceptions, while they reflect the most typical and well recognized exceptions to the hearsay rule, may not encompass every situation in which the reliability and appropriateness of a particular piece of hearsay evidence make clear that it should be heard and considered by the trier of fact.

The committee believes that there are certain exceptional circumstances where evidence which is found by a court to have guarantees of trustworthiness equivalent to or exceeding the guarantees reflected by the presently listed exceptions, and to have a high degree of prolativeness [sic] and necessity could properly be admissible.

The case of *Dallas County v. Commercial Union Assoc. Co., Ltd.,* 286 F.2d 388 (5th Cir.1961) illustrates the point. The issue in that case was whether the tower of the county courthouse collapsed because it was struck by lightning (covered by insurance) or because of structural weakness and deterioration of the structure (not covered). Investigation of the structure revealed the presence of charcoal and charred timbers. In order to show that lightning may not have been the cause of the charring, the insurer offered a copy of a local newspaper published over 50 years earlier containing an unsigned article describing a fire in the courthouse while it was under construction. The court found that the newspaper did not qualify for admission as a business record or an ancient document and did not fit within any other recognized hearsay exception. The court concluded, however, that the article was trustworthy because it was inconceivable that a newspaper reporter in a small town would report a fire in the courthouse if none had occurred. See also *United States v. Barbati,* 284 F.Supp. 409 (E.D.N.Y.1968).

Because exceptional cases like the *Dallas County* case may arise in the future, the committee has decided to reinstate a residual exception for rules 803 and 804(b).

The committee, however, also agrees with those supporters of the House version who felt that an overly broad residual hearsay exception could emasculate the hearsay rule and the recognized exceptions or vitiate the rationale behind codification of the rules.

Therefore, the committee has adopted a residual exception for rules 803 and 804(b) of much narrower scope and applicability than the Supreme Court version. In order to qualify for admission, a hearsay statement not falling within one of the recognized exceptions would have to satisfy at least four conditions. First, it must have "equivalent circumstantial guarantees of trustworthiness." Second, it must be offered as evidence of a material fact. Third, the court must determine that the statement "is more probative on the point for which it is offered than any other evidence which the proponent can procure through reasonable efforts." This requirement is intended to insure that only statements which have high probative value and necessity may qualify for admission under the residual exceptions. Fourth, the court must determine that "the general purposes of these rules and the interests of justice will best be served by admission of the statement into evidence."

It is intended that the residual hearsay exceptions will be used very rarely, and only in exceptional circumstances. The committee does not intend to establish a broad license for trial judges to admit hearsay statements that do not fall within one of the other exceptions contained in rules 803 and 804(b). The residual exceptions are not meant to authorize major judicial revisions of the hearsay rule, including its present exceptions. Such major revisions are best accomplished by legislative action. It is intended that in any case in which evidence is sought to be admitted under these subsections, the trial judge will exercise no less care, reflection and caution than the courts did under the common law in establishing the now-recognized exceptions to the hearsay rule.

In order to establish a well-defined jurisprudence, the special facts and circumstances which, in the court's judgment, indicates that the statement has a sufficiently high degree of trustworthiness and necessity to justify its admission should be stated on the record. It is expected that the court will give the opposing party a full and adequate opportunity to contest the admission of any statement sought to be introduced under these subsections. Senate Report No. 93–1277.

Rule 803 defines when hearsay statements are admissible in evidence even though the declarant is available as a witness. The Senate amendments make three changes in this rule.

Note to Paragraph (6). The House bill provides in subsection (6) that records of a regularly conducted "business" activity qualify for admission into evidence as an exception to the hearsay rule. "Business" is defined as including "business, profession, occupation and calling of every kind." The Senate amendment drops the requirement that the records be those of a "business" activity and eliminates the definition of "business." The Senate amendment provides that records are admissible if they are records of a regularly conducted "activity."

The Conference adopts the House provision that the records must be those of a regularly conducted "business" activity. The Conferees changed the definition of "business" contained in the House provision in order to make it clear that the records of institutions and associations like schools, churches and hospitals are admissible under this provision. The records of public schools and hospitals are also covered by Rule 803(8), which deals with public records and reports.

Note to Paragraph (8). The Senate amendment adds language, not contained in the House bill, that refers to another rule that was added by the Senate in another amendment ([proposed] Rule 804(b)(5)—Criminal law enforcement records and reports [deleted]).

In view of its action on [proposed] Rule 804(b)(5) (Criminal law enforcement records and reports) [deleted], the Conference does not adopt the Senate amendment and restores the bill to the House version.

Note to Paragraph (24). The Senate amendment adds a new subsection, (24), which makes admissible a hearsay statement not specifically covered by any of the previous twenty-three subsections, if the statement has equivalent circumstantial guarantees of trustworthiness and if the court determines that (A) the statement is offered as evidence of a material fact; (B) the statement is more probative on the point for which it is offered than any other evidence the proponent can procure through reasonable efforts; and (C) the general purposes of these rules and the interests of justice will best be served by admission of the statement into evidence.

The House bill eliminated a similar, but broader, provision because of the conviction that such a provision injected too much uncertainty into the law of evidence regarding hearsay and impaired the ability of a litigant to prepare adequately for trial.

The Conference adopts the Senate amendment with an amendment that provides that a party intending to request the court to use a statement under this provision must notify any adverse party of this intention as well as of the particulars of the statement, including the name and address of the declarant. This notice must be given sufficiently in advance of the trial or hearing to provide any adverse party with a fair opportunity to prepare to contest the use of the statement. House Report No. 93–1597.

1987 Amendment

The amendments are technical. No substantive change is intended.

1997 Amendment

The contents of Rule 803(24) and Rule 804(b)(5) have been combined and transferred to a new Rule 807. This was done to facilitate additions to Rules 803 and 804. No change in meaning is intended.

GAP Report on Rule 803. The words "Transferred to Rule 807" were substituted for "Abrogated."

2000 Amendment

The amendment provides that the foundation requirements of Rule 803(6) can be satisfied under certain circumstances without the expense and inconvenience of producing time-consuming foundation witnesses. Under current law, courts have generally required foundation witnesses to testify. *See, e.g., Tongil Co., Ltd. v. Hyundai Merchant Marine Corp.*, 968 F.2d 999 (9th Cir. 1992) (reversing a judgment based on business records where a qualified person filed an affidavit but did not testify). Protections are provided by the authentication requirements of Rule 902(11) for domestic records, Rule 902(12) for foreign records in civil cases, and 18 U.S.C. § 3505 for foreign records in criminal cases.

GAP Report—Proposed Amendment to Rule 803(6)

The Committee made no changes to the published draft of the proposed amendment to Evidence Rule 803(6).

Rule 804. Hearsay Exceptions; Declarant Unavailable

(a) Definition of unavailability. "Unavailability as a witness" includes situations in which the declarant—

(1) is exempted by ruling of the court on the ground of privilege from testifying concerning the subject matter of the declarant's statement; or

(2) persists in refusing to testify concerning the subject matter of the declarant's statement despite an order of the court to do so; or

(3) testifies to a lack of memory of the subject matter of the declarant's statement; or

(4) is unable to be present or to testify at the hearing because of death or then existing physical or mental illness or infirmity; or

(5) is absent from the hearing and the proponent of a statement has been unable to procure the declarant's attendance (or in the case of a hearsay exception under subdivision (b)(2), (3), or (4), the declarant's attendance or testimony) by process or other reasonable means.

A declarant is not unavailable as a witness if exemption, refusal, claim of lack of memory, inability, or absence is due to the procurement or wrongdoing of the proponent of a statement for the purpose of preventing the witness from attending or testifying.

(b) Hearsay exceptions. The following are not excluded by the hearsay rule if the declarant is unavailable as a witness:

(1) Former testimony. Testimony given as a witness at another hearing of the same or a different proceeding, or in a deposition taken in compliance with law in the course of the same or another proceeding, if the party against whom the testimony is now offered, or, in a civil action or proceeding, a predecessor in interest, had an opportunity and similar motive to develop the testimony by direct, cross, or redirect examination.

(2) Statement under belief of impending death. In a prosecution for homicide or in a civil action or proceeding, a statement made by a declarant while believing that the declarant's death was imminent, concerning the cause or circumstances of what the declarant believed to be impending death.

(3) Statement against interest. A statement which was at the time of its making so far contrary to the declarant's pecuniary or proprietary interest, or so far tended to subject the declarant to civil or criminal liability, or to render invalid a claim by the declarant against another, that a reasonable person in the declarant's position would not have made the statement unless believing it to be true. A statement tending to expose the declarant to criminal liability and offered to exculpate the accused is not admissible unless corroborating circumstances clearly indicate the trustworthiness of the statement.

(4) Statement of personal or family history. (A) A statement concerning the declarant's own birth, adoption, marriage, divorce, legitimacy, relationship by blood, adoption, or marriage, ancestry, or other similar fact of personal or family history, even though declarant had no means of acquiring personal knowledge of the matter stated; or (B) a statement concerning the foregoing matters, and death also, of another person, if the declarant was related to the other by blood, adoption, or marriage or was so intimately associated with the other's family as to be likely to have accurate information concerning the matter declared.

(5) [Transferred to Rule 807]

(6) Forfeiture by wrongdoing. A statement offered against a party that has engaged or acquiesced in wrongdoing that was intended to, and did, procure the unavailability of the declarant as a witness.

(Pub.L. 93–595, § 1, Jan. 2, 1975, 88 Stat. 1942; Pub.L. 94–149, § 1(12), (13), Dec. 12, 1975, 89 Stat. 806; Mar. 2, 1987, eff. Oct. 1, 1987; Pub.L. 100–690, Title VII, § 7075(b), Nov. 18, 1988, 102 Stat. 4405; Apr. 11, 1997, eff. Dec. 1, 1997.)

1972 Proposed Rules

As to firsthand knowledge on the part of hearsay declarants, see the introductory portion of the Advisory Committee's Note to Rule 803.

Note to Subdivision (a). The definition of unavailability implements the division of hearsay exceptions into two categories by Rules 803 and 804(b).

At common law the unavailability requirement was evolved in connection with particular hearsay exceptions rather than along general lines. For example, see the separate explications of unavailability in relation to former testimony, declarations against interest, and statements of pedigree, separately developed in McCormick §§ 234, 257, and 297. However, no reason is apparent for making distinctions as to what satisfies unavailability for the different exceptions. The treatment in the rule is therefore uniform although differences in the range of process for witnesses between civil and criminal cases will lead to a less exacting requirement under item (5). See Rule 45(e) of the Federal Rules of Civil Procedure and Rule 17(e) of the Federal Rules of Criminal Procedure.

Five instances of unavailability are specified:

(1) Substantial authority supports the position that exercise of a claim of privilege by the declarant satisfies the requirement of unavailability (usually in connection with former testimony). *Wyatt v. State*, 35 Ala.App. 147, 46 So.2d 837 (1950); *State v. Stewart*, 85 Kan. 404, 116 P. 489 (1911); Annot., 45 A.L.R.2d 1354; Uniform Rule 62(7)(a); California Evidence Code § 240(a)(1); Kansas Code of Civil Procedure § 60–459(g)(1). A ruling by the judge is required, which clearly implies that an actual claim of privilege must be made.

(2) A witness is rendered unavailable if he simply refuses to testify concerning the subject matter of his statement despite judicial pressures to do so, a position supported by similar considerations of practicality. *Johnson v. People*, 152 Colo. 586, 384 P.2d 454 (1963); *People v. Pickett*, 339 Mich. 294, 63 N.W.2d 681, 45 A.L.R.2d 1341 (1954). *Contra, Pleau v. State*, 255 Wis. 362, 38 N.W.2d 496 (1949).

(3) The position that a claimed lack of memory by the witness of the subject matter of his statement constitutes unavailability likewise finds support in the cases, though not without dissent. McCormick § 234, p. 494. If the claim is successful, the practical effect is to put the testimony beyond reach, as in the other instances. In this instance, however, it will be noted that the lack of memory must be established by the testimony of the witness himself, which clearly contemplates his production and subjection to cross-examination.

(4) Death and infirmity find general recognition as grounds. McCormick §§ 234, 257, 297; Uniform Rule 62(7)(c); California Evidence Code § 240(a)(3); Kansas Code of Civil Procedure § 60–459(g)(3); New Jersey Evidence Rule 62(6)(c). See also the provisions on use of depositions in Rule 32(a)(3) of the Federal Rules of Civil Procedure and Rule 15(e) of the Federal Rules of Criminal Procedure.

(5) Absence from the hearing coupled with inability to compel attendance by process or other reasonable means also

satisfies the requirement. McCormick § 234; Uniform Rule 62(7)(d) and (e); California Evidence Code § 240(a)(4) and (5); Kansas Code of Civil Procedure § 60–459(g)(4) and (5); New Jersey Rule 62(6)(b) and (d). See the discussion of procuring attendance of witnesses who are nonresidents or in custody in *Barber v. Page*, 390 U.S. 719, 88 S.Ct. 1318, 20 L.Ed.2d 255 (1968).

If the conditions otherwise constituting unavailability result from the procurement or wrongdoing of the proponent of the statement, the requirement is not satisfied. The rule contains no requirement that an attempt be made to take the deposition of a declarant.

Note to Subdivision (b). Rule 803, *supra*, is based upon the assumption that a hearsay statement falling within one of its exceptions possesses qualities which justify the conclusion that whether the declarant is available or unavailable is not a relevant factor in determining admissibility. The instant rule proceeds upon a different theory: hearsay which admittedly is not equal in quality to testimony of the declarant on the stand may nevertheless be admitted if the declarant is unavailable and if his statement meets a specified standard. The rule expresses preferences: testimony given on the stand in person is preferred over hearsay, and hearsay, if of the specified quality, is preferred over complete loss of the evidence of the declarant. The exceptions evolved at common law with respect to declarations of unavailable declarants furnish the basis for the exceptions enumerated in the proposal. The term "unavailable" is defined in subdivision (a).

Exception (1). Former testimony does not rely upon some set of circumstances to substitute for oath and cross-examination, since both oath and opportunity to cross-examine were present in fact. The only missing one of the ideal conditions for the giving of testimony is the presence of trier and opponent ("demeanor evidence"). This is lacking with all hearsay exceptions. Hence it may be argued that former testimony is the strongest hearsay and should be included under Rule 803, supra. However, opportunity to observe demeanor is what in a large measure confers depth and meaning upon oath and cross-examination. Thus in cases under Rule 803 demeanor lacks the significance which it possesses with respect to testimony. In any event, the tradition, founded in experience, uniformly favors production of the witness if he is available. The exception indicates continuation of the policy. This preference for the presence of the witness is apparent also in rules and statutes on the use of depositions, which deal with substantially the same problem.

Under the exception, the testimony may be offered (1) against the party *against* whom it was previously offered or (2) against the party *by* whom it was previously offered. In each instance the question resolves itself into whether fairness allows imposing, upon the party against whom now offered, the handling of the witness of the earlier occasion. (1) If the party against whom now offered is the one against whom the testimony was offered previously, no unfairness is apparent in requiring him to accept his own prior conduct of cross-examination or decision not to cross-examine. Only demeanor has been lost, and that is inherent in the situation. (2) If the party against whom now offered is the one *by* whom the testimony was offered previously, a satisfactory answer becomes somewhat more difficult. One possibility is to proceed somewhat along the line of an adoptive admission, i.e. by offering the testimony proponent in effect adopts it. However, this theory savors of discarded concepts of witnesses' belonging to a party, of litigants' ability to pick and choose witnesses, and of vouching for one's own witnesses. Cf. McCormick § 246, pp. 526–527; 4 Wigmore § 1075. A more direct and acceptable approach is simply to recognize direct and redirect examination of one's own witness as the equivalent of cross-examining an opponent's witness. Falknor, Former Testimony and the Uniform Rules: A Comment, 38 N.Y.U.L.Rev. 651, n. 1 (1963); McCormick § 231, p. 483. See also 5 Wigmore § 1389. Allowable techniques for dealing with hostile, double-crossing, forgetful, and mentally deficient witnesses leave no substance to a claim that one could not adequately develop his own witness at the former hearing. An even less appealing argument is presented when failure to develop fully was the result of a deliberate choice.

The common law did not limit the admissibility of former testimony to that given in an earlier trial of the same case, although it did require identity of issues as a means of insuring that the former handling of the witness was the equivalent of what would now be done if the opportunity were presented. Modern decisions reduce the requirement to "substantial" identity. McCormick § 233. Since identity of issues is significant only in that it bears on motive and interest in developing fully the testimony of the witness, expressing the matter in the latter terms is preferable. *Id.* Testimony given at a preliminary hearing was held in *California v. Green*, 399 U.S. 149, 90 S.Ct. 1930, 26 L.Ed.2d 489 (1970), to satisfy confrontation requirements in this respect.

As a further assurance of fairness in thrusting upon a party the prior handling of the witness, the common law also insisted upon identity of parties, deviating only to the extent of allowing substitution of successors in a narrowly construed privity. Mutuality as an aspect of identity is now generally discredited, and the requirement of identity of the offering party disappears except as it might affect motive to develop the testimony. Falknor, *supra*, at 652; McCormick § 232, pp. 487–488. The question remains whether strict identity, or privity, should continue as a requirement with respect to the party against whom offered. The rule departs to the extent of allowing substitution of one with the right and opportunity to develop the testimony with similar motive and interest. This position is supported by modern decisions. McCormick § 232, pp. 489–490; 5 Wigmore § 1388.

Provisions of the same tenor will be found in Uniform Rule 63(3)(b); California Evidence Code §§ 1290–1292; Kansas Code of Civil Procedure § 60–460(c)(2); New Jersey Evidence Rule 63(3). Unlike the rule, the latter three provide either that former testimony is not admissible if the right of confrontation is denied or that it is not admissible if the accused was not a party to the prior hearing. The genesis of these limitations is a caveat in Uniform Rule 63(3) Comment that use of former testimony against an accused may violate his right of confrontation. *Mattox v. United States*, 156 U.S. 237, 15 S.Ct. 337, 39 L.Ed. 409 (1895), held that the right was not violated by the Government's use, on a retrial of the same case, of testimony given at the first trial by two witnesses since deceased. The decision leaves open the questions (1) whether direct and redirect are equivalent to cross-examination for purposes of confrontation, (2) whether testimony given in a different proceeding is acceptable, and (3) whether the accused must himself have been a party to the earlier proceeding or whether a similarly situated person will serve the purpose. Professor Falknor concluded that, if a dying declaration untested by cross-examination is constitutionally admissible, former testimony tested by the cross-examination of one similarly situated does not offend against confrontation. Falknor, *supra*, at 659–660. The constitutional acceptability of dying declarations has often been conceded. *Mattox v. United States*, 156 U.S. 237, 243, 15 S.Ct. 337, 39 L.Ed. 409 (1895); *Kirby v. United States*, 174 U.S. 47, 61, 19 S.Ct. 574, 43 L.Ed. 890 (1899); *Pointer v. Texas*, 380 U.S. 400, 407, 85 S.Ct. 1065, 13 L.Ed.2d 923 (1965).

Exception (2). The exception is the familiar dying declaration of the common law, expanded somewhat beyond its traditionally narrow limits. While the original religious justification for the exception may have lost its conviction for some persons over the years, it can scarcely be doubted that powerful psychological pressures are present. See 5 Wigmore § 1443 and the classic statement of Chief Baron Eyre in Rex v. Woodcock, 1 Leach 500, 502, 168 Eng.Rep. 352, 353 (K.B.1789).

The common law required that the statement be that of the victim, offered in a prosecution for criminal homicide. Thus declarations by victims in prosecutions for other crimes, e.g. a declaration by a rape victim who dies in childbirth, and all declarations in civil cases were outside the scope of the exception. An occasional statute has removed these restrictions, as in Colo.R.S. § 52–1–20, or has expanded the area of offenses to include abortions, 5 Wigmore § 1432, p. 224, n. 4. Kansas by decision extended the exception to civil cases. *Thurston v. Fritz*, 91 Kan. 468, 138 P. 625 (1914). While the common law exception no doubt originated as a result of the exceptional need for the evidence in homicide cases, the theory of admissibility applies equally in civil cases and in prosecutions for crimes other than homicide. The same considerations suggest abandonment of the limitation to circumstances attending the event in question, yet when the statement deals with matters other than the supposed death, its influence is believed to be sufficiently attenuated to justify the limitation. Unavailability is not limited to death. See subdivision (a) of this rule. Any problem as to declarations phrased in terms of opinion is laid at rest by Rule 701, and continuation of a requirement of firsthand knowledge is assured by Rule 602.

Comparable provisions are found in Uniform Rule 63(5); California Evidence Code § 1242; Kansas Code of Civil Procedure § 60–460(e); New Jersey Evidence Rule 63(5).

Exception (3). The circumstantial guaranty of reliability for declarations against interest is the assumption that persons do not make statements which are damaging to themselves unless satisfied for good reason that they are true. *Hileman v. Northwest Engineering Co.*, 346 F.2d 668 (6th Cir.1965). If the statement is that of a party, offered by his opponent, it comes in as an admission, Rule 803(d)(2) [sic; probably should be "Rule 801(d)(2)"], and there is no occasion to inquire whether it is against interest, this not being a condition precedent to admissibility of admissions by opponents.

The common law required that the interest declared against be pecuniary or proprietary but within this limitation demonstrated striking ingenuity in discovering an against-interest aspect. Higham v. Ridgway, 10 East 109, 103 Eng.Rep. 717 (K.B.1808); Reg. v. Overseers of Birmingham, 1 B. & S. 763, 121 Eng.Rep. 897 (Q.B.1861); McCormick, § 256, p. 551, nn. 2 and 3.

The exception discards the common law limitation and expands to the full logical limit. One result is to remove doubt as to the admissibility of declarations tending to establish a tort liability against the declarant or to extinguish one which might be asserted by him, in accordance with the trend of the decisions in this country. McCormick § 254, pp. 548–549. Another is to allow statements tending to expose declarant to hatred, ridicule, or disgrace, the motivation here being considered to be as strong as when financial interests are at stake. McCormick § 255, p. 551. And finally, exposure to criminal liability satisfies the against-interest requirement. The refusal of the common law to concede the adequacy of a penal interest was no doubt indefensible in logic, see the dissent of Mr. Justice Holmes in *Donnelly v. United States*, 228 U.S. 243, 33 S.Ct. 449, 57 L.Ed. 820 (1913), but one senses in the decisions a distrust of evidence of confessions by third persons offered to exculpate the accused arising from suspicions of fabrication either of the fact of the making of the confession or in its contents, enhanced in either instance by the required unavailability of the declarant. Nevertheless, an increasing amount of decisional law recognizes exposure to punishment for crime as a sufficient stake. *People v. Spriggs*, 60 Cal.2d 868, 36 Cal.Rptr. 841, 389 P.2d 377 (1964); *Sutter v. Easterly*, 354 Mo. 282, 189 S.W.2d 284 (1945); Band's Refuse Removal, Inc. v. Fairlawn Borough, 62 N.J.Super. 522, 163 A.2d 465 (1960); *Newberry v. Commonwealth*, 191 Va. 445, 61 S.E.2d 318 (1950); Annot., 162 A.L.R. 446. The requirement of corroboration is included in the rule in order to effect an accommodation between these competing considerations. When the statement is offered by the accused by way of exculpation, the resulting situation is not adapted to control by rulings as to the weight of the evidence, and hence the provision is cast in terms of a requirement preliminary to admissibility. Cf. Rule 406(a). The requirement of corroboration should be construed in such a manner as to effectuate its purpose of circumventing fabrication.

Ordinarily the third-party confession is thought of in terms of exculpating the accused, but this is by no means always or necessarily the case: it may include statements implicating him, and under the general theory of declarations against interest they would be admissible as related statements. Douglas v. Alabama, 380 U.S. 415, 85 S.Ct. 1074, 13 L.Ed.2d 934 (1965), and Bruton v. United States, 389 U.S. 818, 88 S.Ct. 126, 19 L.Ed.2d 70 (1968), both involved confessions by codefendants which implicated the accused. While the confession was not actually offered in evidence in *Douglas*, the procedure followed effectively put it before the jury, which the Court ruled to be error. Whether the confession might have been admissible as a declaration against penal interest was not considered or discussed. *Bruton* assumed the inadmissibility, as against the accused, of the implicating confession of his codefendant, and centered upon the question of the effectiveness of a limiting instruction. These decisions, however, by no means require that all statements implicating another person be excluded from the category of declarations against interest. Whether a statement is in fact against interest must be determined from the circumstances of each case. Thus a statement admitting guilt and implicating another person, made while in custody, may well be motivated by a desire to curry favor with the authorities and hence fail to qualify as against interest. See the dissenting opinion of Mr. Justice White in *Bruton.* On the other hand, the same words spoken under different circumstances, e.g., to an acquaintance, would have no difficulty in qualifying. The rule does not purport to deal with questions of the right of confrontation.

The balancing of self-serving against dissenting aspects of a declaration is discussed in McCormick § 256.

For comparable provisions, see Uniform Rule 63(10); California Evidence Code § 1230; Kansas Code of Civil Procedure § 60–460(j); New Jersey Evidence Rule 63(10).

Exception (4). The general common law requirement that a declaration in this area must have been made *ante litem motam* has been dropped, as bearing more appropriately on weight than admissibility. See 5 Wigmore § 1483. Item (i)[(A)] specifically disclaims any need of firsthand knowledge respecting declarant's own personal history. In some instances it is self-evident (marriage) and in others impossible and traditionally not required (date of birth). Item (ii)[(B)] deals with declarations concerning the history of another person. As at common law, declarant is qualified if related by blood or marriage. 5 Wigmore § 1489. In addition, and contrary to the common law, declarant qualifies by virtue of intimate association with the family. *Id.,* § 1487. The requirement sometimes encountered that when the subject of the statement is the relationship between two other persons the declarant must qualify as to both is omitted. Relationship is reciprocal. *Id.,* § 1491.

For comparable provisions, see Uniform Rule 63(23), (24), (25); California Evidence Code §§ 1310, 1311; Kansas Code of Civil Procedure § 60–460(u), (v), (w); New Jersey Evidence Rules 63–23), 63(24), 63(25).

1974 Enactment

Note to Subdivision (a)(3). Rule 804(a)(3) was approved in the form submitted by the Court. However, the Committee intends no change in existing federal law under which the court may choose to disbelieve the declarant's testimony as to his lack of memory. See *United States v. Insana,* 423 F.2d 1165, 1169–1170 (2nd Cir.), cert. denied, 400 U.S. 841 (1970).

Note to Subdivision (a)(5). Rule 804(a)(5) as submitted to the Congress provided, as one type of situation in which a declarant would be deemed "unavailable", that he be "absent from the hearing and the proponent of his statement has been unable to procure his attendance by process or other reasonable means." The Committee amended the Rule to insert after the word "attendance" the parenthetical expression "(or, in the case of a hearsay exception under subdivision (b)(2), (3), or (4), his attendance or testimony)". The amendment is designed primarily to require that an attempt be made to depose a witness (as well as to seek his attendance) as a precondition to the witness being deemed unavailable. The Committee, however, recognized the propriety of an exception to this additional requirement when it is the declarant's former testimony that is sought to be admitted under subdivision (b)(1).

Note to Subdivision (b)(1). Rule 804(b)(1) as submitted by the Court allowed prior testimony of an unavailable witness to be admissible if the party against whom it is offered or a person "with motive and interest similar" to his had an opportunity to examine the witness. The Committee considered that it is generally unfair to impose upon the party against whom the hearsay evidence is being offered responsibility for the manner in which the witness was previously handled by another party. The sole exception to this, in the Committee's view, is when a party's predecessor in interest in a civil action or proceeding had an opportunity and similar motive to examine the witness. The Committee amended the Rule to reflect these policy determinations.

Note to Subdivision (b)(2). Rule 804(b)(3) as submitted by the Court (now Rule 804(b)(2) in the bill) proposed to expand the traditional scope of the dying declaration exception (i.e. a statement of the victim in a homicide case as to the cause or circumstances of his believed imminent death) to allow such statements in all criminal and civil cases. The Committee did not consider dying declarations as among the most reliable forms of hearsay. Consequently, it amended the provision to limit their admissibility in criminal cases to homicide prosecutions, where exceptional need for the evidence is present. This is existing law. At the same time, the Committee approved the expansion to civil actions and proceedings where the stakes do not involve possible imprisonment, although noting that this could lead to forum shopping in some instances.

Note to Subdivision (b)(3). Rule 804(b)(4) as submitted by the Court (now Rule 804(b)(3) in the bill) provided as follows:

Statement against interest.—A statement which was at the time of its making so far contrary to the declarant's pecuniary or proprietary interest or so far tended to subject him to civil or criminal liability or to render invalid a claim by him against another or to make him an object of hatred, ridicule, or disgrace, that a reasonable man in his position would not have made the statement unless he believed it to be true. A statement tending to exculpate the accused is not admissible unless corroborated.

The Committee determined to retain the traditional hearsay exception for statements against pecuniary or proprietary interest. However, it deemed the Court's additional references to statements tending to subject a declarant to civil liability or to render invalid a claim by him against another to be redundant as included within the scope of the reference to statements against pecuniary or proprietary interest. See *Gichner v. Antonio Triano Tile and Marble Co.,* 410 F.2d 238 (D.C.Cir.1968). Those additional references were accordingly deleted.

The Court's Rule also proposed to expand the hearsay limitation from its present federal limitation to include statements subjecting the declarant to criminal liability and statements tending to make him an object of hatred, ridicule, or disgrace. The Committee eliminated the latter category from the subdivision as lacking sufficient guarantees of reliability. See *United States v. Dovico,* 380 F.2d 325, 327 nn. 2, 4 (2nd Cir.), cert. denied, 389 U.S. 944 (1967). As for statements against penal interest, the Committee shared the view of the Court that some such statements do possess adequate assurances of reliability and should be admissible. It believed, however, as did the Court, that statements of this type tending to exculpate the accused are more suspect and so should have their admissibility conditioned upon some further provision insuring trustworthiness. The proposal in the Court Rule to add a requirement of simple corroboration was, however, deemed ineffective to accomplish this purpose since the accused's own testimony might suffice while not necessarily increasing the reliability of the hearsay statement. The Committee settled upon the language "unless corroborating circumstances clearly indicate the trustworthiness of the statement" as affording a proper standard and degree of discretion. It was contemplated that the result in such cases as *Donnelly v. United States*, 228 U.S. 243 (1912), where the circumstances plainly indicated reliability, would be changed. The Committee also added to the Rule the final sentence from the 1971 Advisory Committee draft, designed to codify the doctrine of *Bruton v. United States*, 391 U.S. 123 (1968). The Committee does not intend to affect the existing exception to the *Bruton* principle where the codefendant takes the stand and is subject to cross-examination, but believed there was no need to make specific provision for this situation in the Rule, since in that event the declarant would not be "unavailable". House Report No. 93–650.

Note to Subdivision (a)(5). Subdivision (a) of rule 804 as submitted by the Supreme Court defined the conditions under which a witness was considered to be unavailable. It was amended in the House.

The purpose of the amendment, according to the report of the House Committee on the Judiciary, is "primarily to require that an attempt be made to depose a witness (as well as to seek his attendance) as a precondition to the witness being unavailable."

Under the House amendment, before a witness is declared unavailable, a party must try to depose a witness (declarant) with respect to dying declarations, declarations against interest, and declarations of pedigree. None of these situations would seem to warrant this needless, impractical and highly restrictive complication. A good case can be made for eliminating the unavailability requirement entirely for declarations against interest cases. [Uniform rule 63(10); Kan. Stat.Anno. 60–460(j); 2A N.J.Stats.Anno. 84–63(10).]

In dying declaration cases, the declarant will usually, though not necessarily, be deceased at the time of trial. Pedigree statements which are admittedly and necessarily based largely on word of mouth are not greatly fortified by a deposition requirement.

Depositions are expensive and time-consuming. In any event, deposition procedures are available to those who wish to resort to them. Moreover, the deposition procedures of the Civil Rules and Criminal Rules are only imperfectly adapted to implementing the amendment. No purpose is served unless the deposition, if taken, may be used in evidence. Under Civil Rule (a)(3) the Criminal Rule 15(e), a deposition, though taken, may not be admissible, and under Criminal Rule 15(a) substantial obstacles exist in the way of even taking a deposition.

For these reasons, the committee deleted the House amendment.

The committee understands that the rule as to unavailability, as explained by the Advisory Committee "contains no requirement that an attempt be made to take the deposition of a declarant." In reflecting the committee's judgment, the statement is accurate insofar as it goes. Where, however, the proponent of the statement, with knowledge of the existence of the statement, fails to confront the declarant with the statement at the taking of the deposition, then the proponent should not, in fairness, be permitted to treat the declarant as "unavailable" simply because the declarant was not amenable to process compelling his attendance at trial. The committee does not consider it necessary to amend the rule to this effect because such a situation abuses, not conforms to, the rule. Fairness would preclude a person from introducing a hearsay statement on a particular issue if the person taking the deposition was aware of the issue at the time of the deposition but failed to depose the unavailable witness on that issue.

Note to Subdivision (b)(1). Former testimony.—Rule 804(b)(1) as submitted by the Court allowed prior testimony of an unavailable witness to be admissible if the party against whom it is offered or a person "with motive and interest similar" to his had an opportunity to examine the witness.

The House amended the rule to apply only to a party's predecessor in interest. Although the committee recognizes considerable merit to the rule submitted by the Supreme Court, a position which has been advocated by many scholars and judges, we have concluded that the difference between the two versions is not great and we accept the House amendment.

Note to Subdivision (b)(3). The rule defines those statements which are considered to be against interest and thus of sufficient trustworthiness to be admissible even though hearsay. With regard to the type of interest declared against, the version submitted by the Supreme Court included inter alia, statements tending to subject a declarant to civil liability or to invalidate a claim by him against another. The House struck these provisions as redundant. In view of the conflicting case law construing pecuniary or proprietary interests narrowly so as to exclude, e.g., tort cases, this deletion could be misconstrued.

Three States which have recently codified their rules of evidence have followed the Supreme Court's version of this rule, i.e., that a statement is against interest if it tends to subject a declarant to civil liability. [Nev.Rev.Stats. § 51.345; N.Mex.Stats. (1973 Supp.) § 20–4–804(4); West's Wis.Stats.Anno. (1973 Supp.) § 908.045(4).]

The committee believes that the reference to statements tending to subject a person to civil liability constitutes a desirable clarification of the scope of the rule. Therefore, we have reinstated the Supreme Court language on this matter.

The Court rule also proposed to expand the hearsay limitation from its present federal limitation to include statements subjecting the declarant to statements tending to make him an object of hatred, ridicule, or disgrace. The House eliminated the latter category from the subdivision as lacking sufficient guarantees of reliability. Although there is considerable support for the admissibility of such statements (all three of the State rules referred to supra, would admit such statements), we accept the deletion by the House.

The House amended this exception to add a sentence making inadmissible a statement or confession offered against the accused in a criminal case, made by a codefendant or other person implicating both himself and the accused. The sentence was added to codify the constitutional principle announced in *Bruton v. United States*, 391 U.S. 123 (1968). Bruton held that the admission of the extrajudicial hearsay statement of one codefendant inculpating a second codefendant violated the confrontation clause of the sixth amendment.

The committee decided to delete this provision because the basic approach of the rules is to avoid codifying, or attempting to codify, constitutional evidentiary principles, such as the fifth amendment's right against self-incrimination and, here, the sixth amendment's right of confrontation. Codification of a constitutional principle is unnecessary and, where the principle is under development, often unwise. Furthermore, the House provision does not appear to recognize the exceptions to the *Bruton* rule, e.g. where the codefendant takes the stand and is subject to cross examination; where the accused confessed, see *United States v. Mancusi*, 404 F.2d 296 (2d Cir.1968), cert. denied 397 U.S. 942 (1907); where the accused was placed at the scene of the crime, see *United States v. Zelker*, 452 F.2d 1009 (2d Cir.1971). For these reasons, the committee decided to delete this provision.

Note to Subdivision (b)(5). See Note to Paragraph (24), Notes of Committee on the Judiciary, Senate Report No. 93–1277, set out as a note under rule 803 of these rules. Senate Report No. 93–1277.

Rule 804 defines what hearsay statements are admissible in evidence if the declarant is unavailable as a witness. The Senate amendments make four changes in the rule.

Note to Subdivision (a)(5). Subsection (a) defines the term "unavailability as a witness". The House bill provides in subsection (a)(5) that the party who desires to use the statement must be unable to procure the declarant's attendance by process or other reasonable means. In the case of dying declarations, statements against interest and statements of personal or family history, the House bill requires that the proponent must also be unable to procure the declarant's *testimony* (such as by deposition or interrogatories) by process or other reasonable means. The Senate amendment eliminates this latter provision.

The Conference adopts the provision contained in the House bill.

Note to Subdivision (b)(3). The Senate amendment to subsection (b)(3) provides that a statement is against interest and not excluded by the hearsay rule when the declarant is unavailable as a witness, if the statement tends to subject a person to civil or criminal liability or renders invalid a claim by him against another. The House bill did not refer specifically to civil liability and to rendering invalid a claim against another. The Senate amendment also deletes from the House bill the provision that subsection (b)(3) does not apply to a statement or confession, made by a codefendant or another, which implicates the accused and the person who made the statement, when that statement or confession is offered against the accused in a criminal case.

The Conference adopts the Senate amendment. The Conferees intend to include within the purview of this rule, statements subjecting a person to civil liability and statements rendering claims invalid. The Conferees agree to delete the provision regarding statements by a codefendant, thereby reflecting the general approach in the Rules of Evidence to avoid attempting to codify constitutional evidentiary principles.

Note to Subdivision (b)(5). The Senate amendment adds a new subsection, (b)(6) [now (b)(5)], which makes admissible a hearsay statement not specifically covered by any of the five previous subsections, if the statement has equivalent circumstantial guarantees of trustworthiness and if the court determines that (A) the statement is offered as evidence of a material fact; (B) the statement is more probative on the point for which it is offered than any other evidence the proponent can procure through reasonable efforts; and (C) the general purposes of these rules and the interests of justice will best be served by admission of the statement into evidence.

The House bill eliminated a similar, but broader, provision because of the conviction that such a provision injected too much uncertainty into the law of evidence regarding hearsay and impaired the ability of a litigant to prepare adequately for trial.

The Conference adopts the Senate amendment with an amendment that renumbers this subsection and provides that a party intending to request the court to use a statement under this provision must notify any adverse party of this intention as well as of the particulars of the statement, including the name and address of the declarant. This notice must be given sufficiently in advance of the trial or hearing to provide any adverse party with a fair opportunity to prepare to contest the use of the statement. House Report No. 93–1597.

1987 Amendments

The amendments are technical. No substantive change is intended.

1997 Amendments

Subdivision (b)(5). The contents of Rule 803(24) and Rule 804(b)(5) have been combined and transferred to a new Rule 807. This was done to facilitate additions to Rules 803 and 804. No change in meaning is intended.

Subdivision (b)(6). Rule 804(b)(6) has been added to provide that a party forfeits the right to object on hearsay grounds to the admission of a declarant's prior statement when the party's deliberate wrongdoing or acquiescence therein procured the unavailability of the declarant as a witness. This recognizes the need for a prophylactic rule to deal with abhorrent behavior "which strikes at the heart of the system of justice itself." *United States v. Mastrangelo*, 693 F.2d 269, 273 (2d Cir.1982), *cert. denied*, 467 U.S. 1204 (1984). The wrongdoing need not consist of a criminal act. The rule applies to all parties, including the government.

Every circuit that has resolved the question has recognized the principle of forfeiture by misconduct, although the tests for determining whether there is a forfeiture have varied. *See, e.g., United States v. Aguiar*, 975 F.2d 45, 47 (2d Cir.1992); *United States v. Potamitis*, 739 F.2d 784, 789 (2d Cir.), *cert. denied*, 469 U.S. 918 (1984); *Steele v. Taylor*, 684 F.2d 1193, 1199 (6th Cir.1982), *cert. denied*, 460 U.S. 1053 (1983); United States v. Balano, 618 F.2d 624, 629 (10th Cir.1979), *cert. denied*, 449 U.S. 840 (1980); *United States v. Carlson*, 547 F.2d 1346, 1358–59 (8th Cir.), *cert. denied*, 431 U.S. 914 (1977). The foregoing cases apply a preponderance of the evidence standard. *Contra United States v. Thevis*, 665 F.2d 616, 631 (5th Cir.) (clear and convincing standard), *cert. denied*, 459 U.S. 825 (1982). The usual Rule 104(a) preponderance of the evidence standard has been adopted in light of the behavior the new Rule 804(b)(6) seeks to discourage.

GAP Report on Rule 804(b)(5). The words "Transferred to Rule 807" were substituted for "Abrogated".

GAP Report on Rule 804(b)(6). The title of the rule was changed to "Forfeiture by wrongdoing." The word "who" in line 24 was changed to "that" to indicate that the rule is potentially applicable against the government. Two sentences were added to the first paragraph of the committee note to clarify that the wrongdoing need not be criminal in nature, and to indicate the rule's potential applicability to the government. The word "forfeiture" was substituted for "waiver" in the note.

Rule 805. Hearsay Within Hearsay

Hearsay included within hearsay is not excluded under the hearsay rule if each part of the combined statements conforms with an exception to the hearsay rule provided in these rules.

(Pub.L. 93–595, § 1, Jan. 2, 1975, 88 Stat. 1943.)

1972 Proposed Rules

On principle it scarcely seems open to doubt that the hearsay rule should not call for exclusion of a hearsay statement which includes a further hearsay statement when both conform to the requirements of a hearsay exception. Thus a hospital record might contain an entry of the patient's age based on information furnished by his wife. The hospital record would qualify as a regular entry except that the person who furnished the information was not acting in the routine of the business. However, her statement independently qualifies as a statement of pedigree (if she is unavailable) or as a statement made for purposes of diagnosis or treatment, and hence each link in the chain falls under sufficient assurances. Or, further to illustrate, a dying declaration may incorporate a declaration against interest by another declarant. See McCormick § 290, p. 611.

Rule 806. Attacking and Supporting Credibility of Declarant

When a hearsay statement, or a statement defined in Rule 801(d)(2)(C), (D), or (E), has been admitted in evidence, the credibility of the declarant may be attacked, and if attacked may be supported, by any evidence which would be admissible for those purposes if declarant had testified as a witness. Evidence of a statement or conduct by the declarant at any time, inconsistent with the declarant's hearsay statement, is not subject to any requirement that the declarant may have been afforded an opportunity to deny or explain. If the party against whom a hearsay statement has been admitted calls the declarant as a witness, the party is entitled to examine the declarant on the statement as if under cross-examination.

(Pub.L. 93–595, § 1, Jan. 2, 1975, 88 Stat. 1943; Mar. 2, 1987, eff. Oct. 1, 1987; Apr. 11, 1997, eff. Dec. 1, 1997.)

1972 Proposed Rules

The declarant of a hearsay statement which is admitted in evidence is in effect a witness. His credibility should in fairness be subject to impeachment and support as though he had in fact testified. See Rules 608 and 609. There are however, some special aspects of the impeaching of a hearsay declarant which require consideration. These special aspects center upon impeachment by inconsistent statement, arise from factual differences which exist between the use of hearsay and an actual witness and also between various kinds of hearsay, and involve the question of applying to declarants the general rule disallowing evidence of an inconsistent statement to impeach a witness unless he is afforded an opportunity to deny or explain. See Rule 613(b).

The principal difference between using hearsay and an actual witness is that the inconsistent statement will in the case of the witness almost inevitably of necessity in the nature of things be a *prior* statement, which it is entirely possible and feasible to call to his attention, while in the case of hearsay the inconsistent statement may well be a *subsequent* one, which practically precludes calling it to the attention of the declarant. The result of insisting upon observation of this impossible requirement in the hearsay situation is to deny the opponent, already barred from cross-examination, any benefit of this important technique of impeachment. The writers favor allowing the subsequent statement. McCormick § 37, p. 69; 3 Wigmore § 1033. The cases, however, are divided. Cases allowing the impeachment include *People v. Collup,* 27 Cal.2d 829, 167 P.2d 714 (1946); *People v. Rosoto,* 58 Cal.2d 304, 23 Cal.Rptr. 779, 373 P.2d 867 (1962); *Carver v. United States,* 164 U.S. 694, 17 S.Ct. 228, 41 L.Ed. 602 (1897). *Contra, Mattox v. United States,* 156 U.S. 237, 15 S.Ct. 337, 39 L.Ed. 409 (1895); *People v. Hines,* 284 N.Y. 93, 29 N.E.2d 483 (1940). The force of *Mattox,* where the hearsay was the former testimony of a deceased witness and the denial of use of a subsequent inconsistent statement was upheld, is much diminished by *Carver,* where the hearsay was a dying declaration and denial of use of a subsequent inconsistent statement resulted in reversal. The difference in the particular brand of hearsay seems unimportant when the inconsistent statement is a *subsequent* one. True, the opponent is not totally deprived of cross-examination when the hearsay is former testimony or a deposition but he is deprived of cross-examining on the statement or along lines suggested by it. Mr. Justice Shiras, with two justices joining him, dissented vigorously in *Mattox.*

When the impeaching statement was made prior to the hearsay statement, differences in the kinds of hearsay appear which arguably may justify differences in treatment. If the hearsay consisted of a simple statement by the witness, e.g. a dying declaration or a declaration against interest, the feasibility of affording him an opportunity to deny or explain encounters the same practical impossibility as where the statement is a subsequent one, just discussed, although here the impossibility arises from the total absence of anything resembling a hearing at which the matter could be put to him. The courts by a large majority have ruled in favor of allowing the statement to be used under these circumstances. McCormick § 37, p. 69; 3 Wigmore § 1033. If, however, the hearsay consists of former testimony or a deposition, the possibility of calling the prior statement to the attention of the witness or deponent is not ruled out, since the opportunity to cross-examine was available. It might thus be concluded that with former testimony or depositions the conventional foundation should be insisted upon. Most of the cases involve depositions, and Wigmore describes them as divided. 3 Wigmore § 1031. Deposition procedures at best are cumbersome and expensive, and to require the laying of the foundation may impose an undue burden. Under the federal practice, there is no way of knowing with certainty at the time of taking a deposition whether it is merely for discovery or will ultimately end up in evidence. With respect to both former testimony and depositions the possibility exists that knowledge of the statement might not be acquired until after the time of the cross-examination. Moreover, the expanded admissibility of former testimony and depositions under Rule 804(b)(1) calls for a correspondingly expanded approach to impeachment. The rule dispenses with the requirement in all hearsay situations, which is readily administered and best calculated to lead to fair results.

Notice should be taken that Rule 26(f) of the Federal Rules of Civil Procedure, as originally submitted by the Advisory Committee, ended with the following:

" * * * and, without having first called them to the deponent's attention, may show statements contradictory thereto made at any time by the deponent."

This language did not appear in the rule as promulgated in December, 1937. See 4 Moore's Federal Practice ¶¶ 26.01[9], 26.35 (2d ed.1967). In 1951, Nebraska adopted a provision strongly resembling the one stricken from the federal rule:

"Any party may impeach any adverse deponent by self-contradiction without having laid foundation for such impeachment at the time such deposition was taken." R.S.Neb. § 25–1267.07.

For similar provisions, see Uniform Rule 65; California Evidence Code § 1202; Kansas Code of Civil Procedure § 60–462; New Jersey Evidence Rule 65.

The provision for cross-examination of a declarant upon his hearsay statement is a corollary of general principles of cross-examination. A similar provision is found in California Evidence Code § 1203.

1974 Enactment

Rule 906, as passed by the House and as proposed by the Supreme Court provides that whenever a hearsay statement is admitted, the credibility of the declarant of the statement may be attacked, and if attacked may be supported, by any evidence which would be admissible for those purposes if the declarant had testified as a witness. Rule 801 defines what is a hearsay statement. While statements by a person authorized by a party-opponent to make a statement concerning the subject, by the party-opponent's agent or by a coconspirator of a party—see rule 801(d)(2)(c), (d) and (e)—are traditionally defined as exceptions to the hearsay rule, rule 801 defines such admission by a party-opponent as statements which are not hearsay. Consequently, rule 806 by referring exclusively to the admission of hearsay statements, does not appear to allow the credibility of the declarant to be attacked when the declarant is a coconspirator, agent or authorized spokesman. The committee is of the view that such statements should open the declarant to attacks on his credibility. Indeed, the reason such statements are excluded from the operation of rule 806 is likely attributable to the drafting technique used to codify the hearsay rule, viz. some statements, instead of being referred to as exceptions to the hearsay rule, are defined as statements which are not hearsay. The phrase "or a statement defined in rule 801(d)(2)(c), (d) and (e)" is added to the rule in order to subject the declarant of such statements, like the declarant of hearsay statements, to attacks on his credibility. [The committee considered it unnecessary to include statements contained in rule 801(d)(2)(A) and (B)—the statement by the party-opponent himself or the statement of which he has manifested his adoption—because the credibility of the party-opponent is always subject to an attack on his credibility]. Senate Report No. 93–1277.

The Senate amendment permits an attack upon the credibility of the declarant of a statement if the statement is one by a person authorized by a party-opponent to make a statement concerning the subject, one by an agent of a party-opponent, or one by a coconspirator of the party-opponent, as these statements are defined in Rules 801(d)(2)(C), (D) and (E). The House bill has no such provision.

The Conference adopts the Senate amendment. The Senate amendment conforms the rule to present practice. House Report No. 93–1597.

1987 Amendments

The amendments are technical. No substantive change is intended.

1997 Amendments

The amendment is technical. No substantive change is intended.

GAP Report. Restylization changes in the rule were eliminated.

Rule 807. Residual Exception

A statement not specifically covered by Rule 803 or 804 but having equivalent circumstantial guarantees of trustworthiness, is not excluded by the hearsay rule, if the court determines that (A) the statement is offered as evidence of a material fact; (B) the statement is more probative on the point for which it is offered than any other evidence which the proponent can procure through reasonable efforts; and (C) the general purposes of these rules and the interests of justice will best be served by admission of the statement into evidence. However, a statement may not be admitted under this exception unless the proponent of it makes known to the adverse party sufficiently in advance of the trial or hearing to provide the adverse party with a fair opportunity to prepare to meet it, the proponent's intention to offer the statement and the particulars of it, including the name and address of the declarant.

(Added Apr. 11, 1997, eff. Dec. 1, 1997.)

1997 Amendments

The contents of Rule 803(24) and Rule 804(b)(5) have been combined and transferred to a new Rule 807. This was done to facilitate additions to Rules 803 and 804. No change in meaning is intended.

GAP Report on Rule 807. Restylization changes in the rule were eliminated.

ARTICLE IX. AUTHENTICATION AND IDENTIFICATION

Rule 901. Requirement of Authentication or Identification

(a) General provision. The requirement of authentication or identification as a condition precedent to admissibility is satisfied by evidence sufficient to support a finding that the matter in question is what its proponent claims.

(b) Illustrations. By way of illustration only, and not by way of limitation, the following are examples of authentication or identification conforming with the requirements of this rule:

(1) Testimony of witness with knowledge. Testimony that a matter is what it is claimed to be.

(2) Nonexpert opinion on handwriting. Nonexpert opinion as to the genuineness of handwriting, based upon familiarity not acquired for purposes of the litigation.

(3) Comparison by trier or expert witness. Comparison by the trier of fact or by expert witnesses with specimens which have been authenticated.

(4) Distinctive characteristics and the like. Appearance, contents, substance, internal patterns, or other distinctive characteristics, taken in conjunction with circumstances.

(5) Voice identification. Identification of a voice, whether heard firsthand or through mechanical or electronic transmission or recording, by opinion based upon hearing the voice at any time under circumstances connecting it with the alleged speaker.

(6) Telephone conversations. Telephone conversations, by evidence that a call was made to the number assigned at the time by the telephone company to a particular person or business, if (A) in the case of a person, circumstances, including self-identification, show the person answering to be the one called, or (B) in the case of a business, the call was made to a place of business and the conversation related to business reasonably transacted over the telephone.

(7) Public records or reports. Evidence that a writing authorized by law to be recorded or filed and in fact recorded or filed in a public office, or a purported public record, report, statement, or data compilation, in any form, is from the public office where items of this nature are kept.

(8) Ancient documents or data compilation. Evidence that a document or data compilation, in any form, (A) is in such condition as to create no suspicion concerning its authenticity, (B) was in a place where it, if authentic, would likely be, and (C) has been in existence 20 years or more at the time it is offered.

(9) Process or system. Evidence describing a process or system used to produce a result and showing that the process or system produces an accurate result.

(10) Methods provided by statute or rule. Any method of authentication or identification provided by Act of Congress or by other rules prescribed by the Supreme Court pursuant to statutory authority.

(Pub.L. 93–595, § 1, Jan. 2, 1975, 88 Stat.1943.)

1972 Proposed Rules

Note to Subdivision (a). Authentication and identification represent a special aspect of relevancy. Michael and Adler, Real Proof, 5 Vand.L.Rev. 344, 362 (1952); McCormick §§ 179, 185; Morgan, Basic Problems of Evidence 378 (1962). Thus a telephone conversation may be irrelevant because on an unrelated topic or because the speaker is not identified. The latter aspect is the one here involved. Wigmore describes the need for authentication as "an inherent logical necessity." 7 Wigmore § 2129, p. 564.

This requirement of showing authenticity or identity falls in the category of relevancy dependent upon fulfillment of a condition of fact and is governed by the procedure set forth in Rule 104(b).

The common law approach to authentication of documents has been criticized as an "attitude of agnosticism," McCormick, Cases on Evidence 388, n. 4 (3rd ed. 1956), as one which "departs sharply from men's customs in ordinary affairs," and as presenting only a slight obstacle to the introduction of forgeries in comparison to the time and expense devoted to proving genuine writings which correctly show their origin on their face, McCormick § 185, pp. 395, 396. Today, such available procedures as requests to admit and pretrial conference afford the means of eliminating much of the need for authentication or identification. Also, significant inroads upon the traditional insistence on authentication and identification have been made by accepting as at least prima facie genuine items of the kind treated in Rule 902, *infra*. However, the need for suitable methods of proof still remains, since criminal cases pose their own obstacles to the use of preliminary procedures, unforeseen contingencies may arise, and cases of genuine controversy will still occur.

Note to Subdivision (b). The treatment of authentication and identification draws largely upon the experience embodied in the common law and in statutes to furnish illustrative applications of the general principle set forth in subdivision (a). The examples are not intended as an exclusive enumeration of allowable methods but are meant to guide and suggest, leaving room for growth and development in this area of the law.

The examples relate for the most part to documents, with some attention given to voice communications and computer printouts. As Wigmore noted, no special rules have been developed for authenticating chattels. Wigmore, Code of Evidence § 2086 (3rd ed. 1942).

It should be observed that compliance with requirements of authentication or identification by no means assures admission of an item into evidence, as other bars, hearsay for example, may remain.

Example (1). Example (1) contemplates a broad spectrum ranging from testimony of a witness who was present at the signing of a document to testimony establishing narcotics as taken from an accused and accounting for custody through the period until trial, including laboratory analysis. See California Evidence Code § 1413, eyewitness to signing.

Example (2). Example (2) states conventional doctrine as to lay identification of handwriting, which recognizes that a sufficient familiarity with the handwriting of another person may be acquired by seeing him write, by exchanging correspondence, or by other means, to afford a basis for identifying it on subsequent occasions. McCormick § 189. See also California Evidence Code § 1416. Testimony based upon familiarity acquired for purposes of the litigation is reserved to the expert under the example which follows.

Example (3). The history of common law restrictions upon the technique of proving or disproving the genuineness of a disputed specimen of handwriting through comparison with a genuine specimen, by either the testimony of expert witnesses or direct viewing by the triers themselves, is detailed in 7 Wigmore §§ 1991–1994. In breaking away, the English Common Law Procedure Act of 1854, 17 and 18 Vict., c. 125, § 27, cautiously allowed expert or trier to use exemplars "proved to the satisfaction of the judge to be genuine" for purposes of comparison. The language found its way into numerous statutes in this country, e.g., California Evidence Code §§ 1417, 1418. While explainable as a measure of prudence in the process of breaking with precedent in the handwriting situation, the reservation to the judge of the question of the genuineness of exemplars and the imposition of an unusually high standard of persuasion are at variance with the general treatment of relevancy which depends upon fulfillment of a condition of fact. Rule 104(b). No similar attitude is found in other comparison situations, e.g., ballistics comparison by jury, as in *Evans v. Commonwealth,* 230 Ky. 411, 19 S.W.2d 1091 (1929), or by experts, Annot., 26 A.L.R.2d 892, and no reason appears for its continued existence in handwriting cases. Consequently Example (3) sets no higher standard for handwriting specimens and treats all comparison situations alike, to be governed by Rule 104(b). This approach is consistent with 28 U.S.C. § 1731: "The admitted or proved handwriting of any person shall be admissible, for purposes of comparison, to determine genuineness of other handwriting attributed to such person."

Precedent supports the acceptance of visual comparison as sufficiently satisfying preliminary authentication requirements for admission in evidence. *Brandon v. Collins,* 267 F.2d 731 (2d Cir.1959); *Wausau Sulphate Fibre Co. v. Commissioner of Internal Revenue,* 61 F.2d 879 (7th Cir. 1932); *Desimone v. United States,* 227 F.2d 864 (9th Cir. 1955).

Example (4). The characteristics of the offered item itself, considered in the light of circumstances, afford authentication techniques in great variety. Thus a document or telephone conversation may be shown to have emanated from a particular person by virtue of its disclosing knowledge of facts known peculiarly to him; *Globe Automatic Sprinkler Co. v. Braniff,* 89 Okl. 105, 214 P. 127 (1923); California Evidence Code § 1421; similarly, a letter may be authenticated by content and circumstances indicating it was in reply to a duly authenticated one. McCormick § 192; California Evidence Code § 1420. Language patterns may indicate authenticity or its opposite. *Magnuson v. State,* 187 Wis. 122, 203 N.W. 749 (1925); Arens and Meadow, Psycholinguistics and the Confession Dilemma, 56 Colum.L.Rev. 19 (1956).

Example (5). Since aural voice identification is not a subject of expert testimony, the requisite familiarity may be acquired either before or after the particular speaking which is the subject of the identification, in this respect resembling visual identification of a person rather than identification of handwriting. Cf. Example (2), *supra, People v. Nichols,* 378 Ill. 487, 38 N.E.2d 766 (1942); *McGuire v. State,* 200 Md. 601, 92 A.2d 582 (1952); *State v. McGee,* 336 Mo. 1082, 83 S.W.2d 98 (1935).

Example (6). The cases are in agreement that a mere assertion of his identity by a person talking on the telephone is not sufficient evidence of the authenticity of the conversation and that additional evidence of his identity is required. The additional evidence need not fall in any set pattern. Thus the content of his statements or the reply technique, under Example (4), *supra,* or voice identification under Example (5), may furnish the necessary foundation. Outgoing calls made by the witness involve additional factors bearing upon authenticity. The calling of a number assigned by the telephone company reasonably supports the assumption that the listing is correct and that the number is the one reached. If the number is that of a place of business, the mass of authority allows an ensuing conversation if it relates to business reasonably transacted over the telephone, on the theory that the maintenance of the telephone connection is an invitation to do business without further identification. *Matton v. Hoover Co.,* 350 Mo. 506, 166 S.W.2d 557 (1942); *City of Pawhuska v. Crutchfield,* 147 Okl. 4, 293 P. 1095 (1930); *Zurich General Acc. & Liability Ins. Co. v. Baum,* 159 Va. 404, 165 S.E. 518 (1932). Otherwise, some additional circumstance of identification of the speaker is required. The authorities divide on the question whether the self-identifying statement of the person answering suffices. Example (6) answers in the affirmative on the assumption that usual conduct respecting telephone calls furnish adequate assurances of regularity, bearing in mind that the entire matter is open to exploration before the trier of fact. In general, see McCormick § 193; 7 Wigmore § 2155; Annot., 71 A.L.R. 5, 105 id. 326.

Example (7). Public records are regularly authenticated by proof of custody, without more. McCormick § 191; 7 Wigmore §§ 2158, 2159. The example extends the principle to include data stored in computers and similar methods, of which increasing use in the public records area may be expected. See California Evidence Code §§ 1532, 1600.

Example (8). The familiar ancient document rule of the common law is extended to include data stored electronically or by other similar means. Since the importance of appearance diminishes in this situation, the importance of custody or place where found increases correspondingly. This expansion is necessary in view of the widespread use of methods of storing data in forms other than conventional written records.

Any time period selected is bound to be arbitrary. The common law period of 30 years is here reduced to 20 years, with some shift of emphasis from the probable unavailability of witnesses to the unlikeliness of a still viable fraud after the lapse of time. The shorter period is specified in the English Evidence Act of 1938, 1 & 2 Geo. 6, c. 28, and in Oregon R.S.1963, § 41.360(34). See also the numerous statutes prescribing periods of less than 30 years in the case of recorded documents. 7 Wigmore § 2143.

The application of Example (8) is not subject to any limitation to title documents or to any requirement that possession, in the case of a title document, has been consistent with the document. See McCormick § 190.

Example (9). Example (9) is designed for situations in which the accuracy of a result is dependent upon a process or system which produces it. X rays afford a familiar instance. Among more recent developments is the computer, as to which see Transport Indemnity Co. v. Seib, 178 Neb. 253, 132 N.W.2d 871 (1965); *State v. Veres,* 7 Ariz.App. 117, 436 P.2d 629 (1968); *Merrick v. United States Rubber Co.,* 7 Ariz.App. 433, 440 P.2d 314 (1968); Freed, Computer Print-Outs as Evidence, 16 Am.Jur.Proof of Facts 273; Symposium, Law and Computers in the Mid-Sixties, ALI-ABA (1966); 37 Albany L.Rev. 61 (1967). Example (9) does not, of course, foreclose taking judicial notice of the accuracy of the process or system.

Example (10). The example makes clear that methods of authentication provided by Act of Congress and by the Rules of Civil and Criminal Procedure or by Bankruptcy Rules are not intended to be superseded. Illustrative are the provisions for authentication of official records in Civil Procedure Rule 44 and Criminal Procedure Rule 27, for authentication of records of proceedings by court reporters in 28 U.S.C. § 753(b) and Civil Procedure Rule 80(c), and for authentication of depositions in Civil Procedure Rule 30(f).

Rule 902. Self-authentication

Extrinsic evidence of authenticity as a condition precedent to admissibility is not required with respect to the following:

(1) Domestic public documents under seal. A document bearing a seal purporting to be that of the United States, or of any State, district, Commonwealth, territory, or insular possession thereof, or the Panama Canal Zone, or the Trust Territory of the Pacific Islands, or of a political subdivision, department, officer, or agency thereof, and a signature purporting to be an attestation or execution.

(2) Domestic public documents not under seal. A document purporting to bear the signature in the official capacity of an officer or employee of any entity included in paragraph (1) hereof, having no seal, if a public officer having a seal and having official duties in the district or political subdivision of the officer or employee certifies under seal that the signer has the official capacity and that the signature is genuine.

(3) Foreign public documents. A document purporting to be executed or attested in an official capacity by a person authorized by the laws of a foreign country to make the execution or attestation, and accompanied by a final certification as to the genuineness of the signature and official position (A) of the executing or attesting person, or (B) of any foreign official whose certificate of genuineness of signature and official position relates to the execution or attestation or is in a chain of certificates of genuineness of signature and official position relating to the execution or attestation. A final certification may be made by a secretary of an embassy or legation, consul general, consul, vice consul, or consular agent of the United States, or a diplomatic or consular official of the foreign country assigned or accredited to the United States. If reasonable opportunity has been given to all parties to investigate the authenticity and accuracy of official documents, the court may, for good cause shown, order that they be treated as presumptively authentic without final certification or permit them to be evidenced by an attested summary with or without final certification.

(4) Certified copies of public records. A copy of an official record or report or entry therein, or of a document authorized by law to be recorded or filed and actually recorded or filed in a public office, including data compilations in any form, certified as correct by the custodian or other person authorized to make the certification, by certificate complying with paragraph (1), (2), or (3) of this rule or complying with any Act of Congress or rule prescribed by the Supreme Court pursuant to statutory authority.

(5) Official publications. Books, pamphlets, or other publications purporting to be issued by public authority.

(6) Newspapers and periodicals. Printed materials purporting to be newspapers or periodicals.

(7) Trade inscriptions and the like. Inscriptions, signs, tags, or labels purporting to have been affixed in the course of business and indicating ownership, control, or origin.

(8) Acknowledged documents. Documents accompanied by a certificate of acknowledgment executed in the manner provided by law by a notary public or other officer authorized by law to take acknowledgments.

(9) Commercial paper and related documents. Commercial paper, signatures thereon, and documents relating thereto to the extent provided by general commercial law.

(10) Presumptions under Acts of Congress. Any signature, document, or other matter declared by Act of Congress to be presumptively or prima facie genuine or authentic.

(11) Certified Domestic Records of Regularly Conducted Activity.—The original or a duplicate of a domestic record of regularly conducted activity that would be admissible under Rule 803(6) if accompanied by a written declaration of its custodian or other qualified person, in a manner complying with any Act of Congress or rule prescribed by the Supreme Court pursuant to statutory authority, certifying that the record—

(A) was made at or near the time of the occurrence of the matters set forth by, or from information transmitted by, a person with knowledge of those matters;

(B) was kept in the course of the regularly conducted activity; and

(C) was made by the regularly conducted activity as a regular practice.

A party intending to offer a record into evidence under this paragraph must provide written notice of that intention to all adverse parties, and must make the record and declaration available for inspection sufficiently in advance of their offer into evidence to provide an adverse party with a fair opportunity to challenge them.

(12) Certified Foreign Records of Regularly Conducted Activity.—In a civil case, the original or a duplicate of a foreign record of regularly conducted activity that would be admissible under Rule 803(6) if accompanied by a written declaration by its custodian or other qualified person certifying that the record—

(A) was made at or near the time of the occurrence of the matters set forth by, or from information transmitted by, a person with knowledge of those matters;

(B) was kept in the course of the regularly conducted activity; and

(C) was made by the regularly conducted activity as a regular practice.

The declaration must be signed in a manner that, if falsely made, would subject the maker to criminal penalty under the laws of the country where the declaration is signed. A party intending to offer a record into evidence under this paragraph must provide written notice of that intention to all adverse parties, and must make the record and declaration available for inspection sufficiently in advance of their offer into evidence to provide an adverse party with a fair opportunity to challenge them.

(Pub.L. 93–595, § 1, Jan. 2, 1975, 88 Stat. 1944; Mar. 2, 1987, eff. Oct. 1, 1987; Apr. 25, 1988, eff. Nov. 1, 1988; Apr. 17, 2000, eff. Dec. 1, 2000.)

1972 Proposed Rules

Case law and statutes have, over the years, developed a substantial body of instances in which authenticity is taken as sufficiently established for purposes of admissibility without extrinsic evidence to that effect, sometimes for reasons of policy but perhaps more often because practical considerations reduce the possibility of unauthenticity to a very small dimension. The present rule collects and incorporates these situations, in some instances expanding them to occupy a larger area which their underlying considerations justify. In no instance is the opposite party foreclosed from disputing authenticity.

Note to Paragraph (1). The acceptance of documents bearing a public seal and signature, most often encountered in practice in the form of acknowledgments or certificates authenticating copies of public records, is actually of broad application. Whether theoretically based in whole or in part upon judicial notice, the practical underlying considerations are that forgery is a crime and detection is fairly easy and certain. 7 Wigmore § 2161, p. 638; California Evidence Code § 1452. More than 50 provisions for judicial notice of official seals are contained in the United States Code.

Note to Paragraph (2). While statutes are found which raise a presumption of genuineness of purported official signatures in the absence of an official seal, 7 Wigmore § 2167; California Evidence Code § 1453, the greater ease of effecting a forgery under these circumstances is apparent. Hence this paragraph of the rule calls for authentication by an officer who has a seal. Notarial acts by members of the armed forces and other special situations are covered in paragraph (10).

Note to Paragraph (3). Paragraph (3) provides a method for extending the presumption of authenticity to foreign official documents by a procedure of certification. It is derived from Rule 44(a)(2) of the Rules of Civil Procedure but is broader in applying to public documents rather than being limited to public records.

Note to Paragraph (4). The common law and innumerable statutes have recognized the procedure of authenticating copies of public records by certificate. The certificate qualifies as a public document, receivable as authentic when in conformity with paragraph (1), (2), or (3). Rule 44(a) of the Rules of Civil Procedure and Rule 27 of the Rules of Criminal Procedure have provided authentication procedures of this nature for both domestic and foreign public records. It will be observed that the certification procedure here provided extends only to public records, reports, and recorded documents, all including data compilations, and does not apply to public documents generally. Hence documents provable when presented in original form under paragraphs (1), (2), or (3) may not be provable by certified copy under paragraph (4).

Note to Paragraph (5). Dispensing with preliminary proof of the genuineness of purportedly official publications, most commonly encountered in connection with statutes, court reports, rules, and regulations, has been greatly enlarged by statutes and decisions. 5 Wigmore § 1684. Paragraph (5), it will be noted, does not confer admissibility upon all official publications; it merely provides a means whereby their authenticity may be taken as established for purposes of admissibility. Rule 44(a) of the Rules of Civil Procedure has been to the same effect.

Note to Paragraph (6). The likelihood of forgery of newspapers or periodicals is slight indeed. Hence no danger is apparent in receiving them. Establishing the authenticity of the publication may, of course, leave still open questions of authority and responsibility for items therein contained. See 7 Wigmore § 2150. Cf. 39 U.S.C. § 4005(b), public advertisement prima facie evidence of agency of person named, in postal fraud order proceeding; Canadian Uniform Evidence Act, Draft of 1936, printed copy of newspaper prima facie evidence that notices or advertisements were authorized.

Note to Paragraph (7). Several factors justify dispensing with preliminary proof of genuineness of commercial and mercantile labels and the like. The risk of forgery is minimal. Trademark infringement involves serious penalties. Great efforts are devoted to inducing the public to buy in reliance on brand names, and substantial protection is given them. Hence the fairness of this treatment finds recognition in the cases. *Curtiss Candy Co. v. Johnson,* 163 Miss. 426, 141 So. 762 (1932), Baby Ruth candy bar; *Doyle v. Continental Baking Co.,* 262 Mass. 516, 160 N.E. 325 (1928), loaf of bread; *Weiner v. Mager & Throne, Inc.,* 167 Misc. 338, 3 N.Y.S.2d 918 (1938), same. And see W.Va.Code 1966, § 47–3–5, trademark on bottle prima facie evidence of ownership. *Contra, Keegan v. Green Giant Co.,* 150 Me. 283, 110 A.2d 599 (1954); *Murphy v. Campbell Soup Co.,* 62 F.2d 564 (1st Cir.1933). Cattle brands have received similar acceptance in the western states. Rev.Code Mont.1947, § 46–606, *State v. Wolfley,* 75 Kan. 406, 89 P. 1046 (1907); Annot., 11 L.R.A.(N.S.) 87. Inscriptions on trains and vehicles are held to be prima facie evidence of ownership or control. *Pittsburgh, Ft. W. & C. Ry. v. Callaghan,* 157 Ill. 406, 41 N.E. 909 (1895); 9 Wigmore § 2510a. See also the provision of 19 U.S.C. § 1615(2) that marks, labels, brands, or stamps indicating foreign origin are prima facie evidence of foreign origin of merchandise.

Note to Paragraph (8). In virtually every state, acknowledged title documents are receivable in evidence without further proof. Statutes are collected in 5 Wigmore § 1676. If this authentication suffices for documents of the importance of those affecting titles, logic scarcely permits denying this method when other kinds of documents are involved. Instances of broadly inclusive statutes are California Evidence Code § 1451 and N.Y.CPLR 4538, McKinney's Consol.Laws 1963.

Note to Paragraph (9). Issues of the authenticity of commercial paper in federal courts will usually arise in diversity cases, will involve an element of a cause of action or defense, and with respect to presumptions and burden of proof will be controlled by *Erie Railroad Co. v. Tompkins,* 304 U.S. 64, 58 S.Ct. 817, 82 L.Ed. 1188 (1938). Rule 302, *supra.* There may, however, be questions of authenticity involving lesser segments of a case or the case may be one governed by federal common law. *Clearfield Trust Co. v. United States,* 318 U.S. 363, 63 S.Ct. 573, 87 L.Ed. 838 (1943). Cf. *United States v. Yazell,* 382 U.S. 341, 86 S.Ct. 500, 15 L.Ed.2d 404 (1966). In these situations, resort to the useful authentication provisions of the Uniform Commercial Code is provided for. While the phrasing is in terms of "general commercial law," in order to avoid the potential complications inherent in borrowing local statutes, today one would have difficulty in determining the general commercial law without referring to the Code. See *Williams v. Walker–Thomas Furniture Co.,* 121 U.S.App.D.C. 315, 350 F.2d 445 (1965). Pertinent Code provisions are sections 1–202, 3–307, and 3–510, dealing with third-party documents, signatures on negotiable instruments, protests, and statements of dishonor.

Note to Paragraph (10). The paragraph continues in effect dispensations with preliminary proof of genuineness provided in various Acts of Congress. See, for example, 10 U.S.C. § 936, signature, without seal, together with title, prima facie evidence of authenticity of acts of certain military personnel who are given notarial powers; 15 U.S.C. § 77f(a), signature on SEC registration presumed genuine; 26 U.S.C. § 6064, signature to tax return prima facie genuine.

1974 Enactment

Note to Paragraph (8). Rule 902(8) as submitted by the Court referred to certificates of acknowledgment "under the hand and seal of" a notary public or other officer authorized by law to take acknowledgments. The Committee amended the Rule to eliminate the requirement, believed to be inconsistent with the law in some States, that a notary public must affix a seal to a document acknowledged before him. As amended the Rule merely requires that the document be executed in the manner prescribed by State law.

Note to Paragraph (9). The Committee approved Rule 902(9) as submitted by the Court. With respect to the meaning of the phrase "general commercial law", the Committee intends that the Uniform Commercial Code, which has been adopted in virtually every State, will be followed generally, but that federal commercial law will apply where federal commercial paper is involved. See Clearfield Trust Co. v. United States, 318 U.S. 363 (1943). Further, in those instances in which the issues are governed by Erie R. Co. v. Tompkins, 304 U.S. 64 (1938), State law will apply irrespective of whether it is the Uniform Commercial Code. House Report No. 93–650.

1987 Amendments

The amendments are technical. No substantive change is intended.

1988 Amendments

These two sentences were inadvertently eliminated from the 1987 amendments. The amendment is technical. No substantive change is intended.

2000 Amendments

The amendment adds two new paragraphs to the rule on self-authentication. It sets forth a procedure by which parties can authenticate certain records of regularly conducted activity, other than through the testimony of a foundation witness. See the amendment to Rule 803(6). 18 U.S.C. § 3505 currently provides a means for certifying foreign records of regularly conducted activity in criminal cases, and this amendment is intended to establish a similar procedure for domestic records, and for foreign records offered in civil cases.

A declaration that satisfies 28 U.S.C. § 1746 would satisfy the declaration requirement of Rule 902(11), as would any comparable certification under oath.

The notice requirement in Rules 902(11) and (12) is intended to give the opponent of the evidence a full opportunity to test the adequacy of the foundation set forth in the declaration.

GAP Report—Proposed Amendment to Rule 902

The Committee made the following changes to the published draft of the proposed amendment to Evidence Rule 902:

1. Minor stylistic changes were made in the text, in accordance with suggestions of the Style Subcommittee of the Standing Committee on Rules of Practice and Procedure.

2. The phrase "in a manner complying with any Act of Congress or rule prescribed by the Supreme Court pursuant to statutory authority" was added to proposed Rule 902(11), to provide consistency with Evidence Rule 902(4). The Committee Note was amended to accord with this textual change.

3. Minor stylistic changes were made in the text to provide a uniform construction of the terms "declaration" and "certifying."

4. The notice provisions in the text were revised to clarify that the proponent must make both the declaration and the underlying record available for inspection.

Rule 903. Subscribing Witness' Testimony Unnecessary

The testimony of a subscribing witness is not necessary to authenticate a writing unless required by the laws of the jurisdiction whose laws govern the validity of the writing.

(Pub.L. 93–595, § 1, Jan. 2, 1975, 88 Stat.1945.)

1972 Proposed Rules

The common law required that attesting witnesses be produced or accounted for. Today the requirement has generally been abolished except with respect to documents which must be attested to be valid, e.g. wills in some states. McCormick § 188. Uniform Rule 71; California Evidence Code § 1411; Kansas Code of Civil Procedure § 60–468; New Jersey Evidence Rule 71; New York CPLR Rule 4537.

ARTICLE X. CONTENTS OF WRITINGS, RECORDINGS AND PHOTOGRAPHS

Rule 1001. Definitions

For purposes of this article the following definitions are applicable:

(1) Writings and recordings. "Writings" and "recordings" consist of letters, words, or numbers, or their equivalent, set down by handwriting, typewriting, printing, photostating, photographing, magnetic impulse, mechanical or electronic recording, or other form of data compilation.

(2) Photographs. "Photographs" include still photographs, X-ray films, video tapes, and motion pictures.

(3) Original. An "original" of a writing or recording is the writing or recording itself or any counterpart intended to have the same effect by a person executing or issuing it. An "original" of a photograph includes the negative or any print therefrom. If data are stored in a computer or similar device, any printout or other output readable by sight, shown to reflect the data accurately, is an "original".

(4) Duplicate. A "duplicate" is a counterpart produced by the same impression as the original, or from the same matrix, or by means of photography, including enlargements and miniatures, or by mechanical or electronic re-recording, or by chemical reproduction, or by other equivalent techniques which accurately reproduces the original.

(Pub.L. 93–595, § 1, Jan. 2, 1975, 88 Stat. 1945.)

1972 Proposed Rules

In an earlier day, when discovery and other related procedures were strictly limited, the misleading named "best evidence rule" afforded substantial guarantees against inaccuracies and fraud by its insistence upon production or original documents. The great enlargement of the scope of discovery and related procedures in recent times has measurably reduced the need for the rule. Nevertheless important areas of usefulness persist: discovery of documents outside the jurisdiction may require substantial outlay of time and money; the unanticipated document may not practically be discoverable; criminal cases have built-in limitations on discovery. Cleary and Strong, The Best Evidence Rule: An Evaluation in Context, 51 Iowa L.Rev. 825 (1966).

Note to Paragraph (1). Traditionally the rule requiring the original centered upon accumulations of data and expressions affecting legal relations set forth in words and figures. this meant that the rule was one essentially related to writings. Present day techniques have expanded methods of storing data, yet the essential form which the information ultimately assumes for usable purposes is words and figures. Hence the considerations underlying the rule dictate its expansion to include computers, photographic systems, and other modern developments.

Note to Paragraph (3). In most instances, what is an original will be self-evident and further refinement will be unnecessary. However, in some instances particularized definition is required. A carbon copy of a contract executed in duplicate becomes an original, as does a sales ticket carbon copy given to a customer. While strictly speaking the original of a photograph might be thought to be only the negative, practicality and common usage require that any print from the negative be regarded as an original. Similarly, practicality and usage confer the status of original upon any computer printout. *Transport Indemnity Co. v. Seib,* 178 Neb. 253, 132 N.W.2d 871 (1965).

Note to Paragraph (4). The definition describes "copies" produced by methods possessing an accuracy which virtually eliminates the possibility of error. Copies thus produced are given the status of originals in large measure by Rule 1003, *infra.* Copies subsequently produced manually, whether handwritten or typed, are not within the definition. It should be noted that what is an original for some purposes may be a duplicate for others. Thus a bank's microfilm record of checks cleared is the original as a record. However, a print offered as a copy of a check whose contents are in controversy is a duplicate. This result is substantially consistent with 28 U.S.C. § 1732(b). Compare 26 U.S.C. § 7513(c), giving full status as originals to photographic reproductions of tax returns and other documents, made by authority of the Secretary of the Treasury, and 44 U.S.C. § 399(a), giving original status to photographic copies in the National Archives.

1974 Enactment

Note to Paragraph (2). The Committee amended this Rule expressly to include "video tapes" in the definition of "photographs." House Report No. 93–650.

Rule 1002. Requirement of Original

To prove the content of a writing, recording, or photograph, the original writing, recording, or photograph is required, except as otherwise provided in these rules or by Act of Congress.

(Pub.L. 93–595, § 1, Jan. 2, 1975, 88 Stat. 1946.)

1972 Proposed Rules

The rule is the familiar one requiring production of the original of a document to prove its contents, expanded to include writings, recordings, and photographs, as defined in Rule 1001(1) and (2), *supra*.

Application of the rule requires a resolution of the question whether contents are sought to be proved. Thus an event may be proved by nondocumentary evidence, even though a written record of it was made. If, however, the event is sought to be proved by the written record, the rule applies. For example, payment may be proved without producing the written receipt which was given. Earnings may be proved without producing books of account in which they are entered. McCormick § 198; 4 Wigmore § 1245. Nor does the rule apply to testimony that books or records have been examined and found not to contain any reference to a designated matter.

The assumption should not be made that the rule will come into operation on every occasion when use is made of a photograph in evidence. On the contrary, the rule will seldom apply to ordinary photographs. In most instances a party *wishes* to introduce the item and the question raised is the propriety of receiving it in evidence. Cases in which an offer is made of the testimony of a witness as to what he saw in a photograph or motion picture, without producing the same, are most unusual. The usual course is for a witness on the stand to identify the photograph or motion picture as a correct representation of events which he saw or of a scene with which he is familiar. In fact he adopts the picture as his testimony, or, in common parlance, uses the picture to illustrate his testimony. Under these circumstances, no effort is made to prove the contents of the picture, and the rule is inapplicable. Paradis, The Celluloid Witness, 37 U.Colo. L.Rev. 235, 249–251 (1965).

On occasion, however, situations arise in which contents are sought to be proved. Copyright, defamation, and invasion of privacy by photograph or motion picture falls in this category. Similarly as to situations in which the picture is offered as having independent probative value, e.g. automatic photograph of bank robber. See *People v. Doggett*, 83 Cal.App.2d 405, 188 P.2d 792 (1948), photograph of defendants engaged in indecent act; Mouser and Philbin, Photographic Evidence—Is There a Recognized Basis for Admissibility? 8 Hastings L.J. 310 (1957). the most commonly encountered of this latter group is of course, the X ray, with substantial authority calling for production of the original. *Daniels v. Iowa City*, 191 Iowa 811, 183 N.W. 415 (1921); *Cellamare v. Third Acc. Transit Corp.*, 273 App.Div. 260, 77 N.Y.S.2d 91 (1948); *Patrick & Tilman v. Matkin*, 154 Okl. 232, 7 P.2d 414 (1932); *Mendoza v. Rivera*, 78 P.R.R. 569 (1955).

It should be noted, however, that Rule 703, *supra*, allows an expert to give an opinion based on matters not in evidence, and the present rule must be read as being limited accordingly in its application. Hospital records which may be admitted as business records under Rule 803(6) commonly contain reports interpreting X-rays by the staff radiologist, who qualifies as an expert, and these reports need not be excluded from the records by the instant rule.

The reference to Acts of Congress is made in view of such statutory provisions as 26 U.S.C. § 7513, photographic reproductions of tax returns and documents, made by authority of the Secretary of the Treasury, treated as originals, and 44 U.S.C. § 399(a), photographic copies in National Archives treated as originals.

Rule 1003. Admissibility of Duplicates

A duplicate is admissible to the same extent as an original unless (1) a genuine question is raised as to the authenticity of the original or (2) in the circumstances it would be unfair to admit the duplicate in lieu of the original.

(Pub.L. 93–595, § 1, Jan. 2, 1975, 88 Stat. 1946.)

1972 Proposed Rules

When the only concern is with getting the words or other contents before the court with accuracy and precision, then a counterpart serves equally as well as the original, if the counterpart is the product of a method which insures accuracy and genuineness. By definition in Rule 1001(4), *supra*, a "duplicate" possesses this character.

Therefore, if no genuine issue exists as to authenticity and no other reason exists for requiring the original, a duplicate is admissible under the rule. This position finds support in the decisions, *Myrick v. United States*, 332 F.2d 279 (5th Cir.1964), no error in admitting photostatic copies of checks instead of original microfilm in absence of suggestion to trial judge that photostats were incorrect; *Johns v. United States*, 323 F.2d 421 (5th Cir.1963), not error to admit concededly accurate tape recording made from original wire recording; *Sauget v. Johnston*, 315 F.2d 816 (9th Cir.1963), not error to admit copy of agreement when opponent had original and did not on appeal claim any discrepancy. Other reasons for acquiring the original may be present when only a part of the original is reproduced and the remainder is needed for cross-examination or may disclose matters qualifying the part offered or otherwise useful to the opposing party. *United States v. Alexander*, 326 F.2d 736 (4th Cir. 1964). And see *Toho Bussan Kaisha, Ltd. v. American President Lines, Ltd.*, 265 F.2d 418, 76 A.L.R.2d 1344 (2d Cir.1959).

1974 Enactment

The Committee approved this Rule in the form submitted by the Court, with the expectation that the courts would be liberal in deciding that a "genuine question is raised as to the authenticity of the original." House Report No. 93–650.

Rule 1004. Admissibility of Other Evidence of Contents

The original is not required, and other evidence of the contents of a writing, recording, or photograph is admissible if—

(1) Originals lost or destroyed. All originals are lost or have been destroyed, unless the proponent lost or destroyed them in bad faith; or

(2) Original not obtainable. No original can be obtained by any available judicial process or procedure; or

(3) Original in possession of opponent. At a time when an original was under the control of the party against whom offered, that party was put on notice, by the pleadings or otherwise, that the contents would be a subject of proof at the hearing, and that party does not produce the original at the hearing; or

(4) Collateral matters. The writing, recording, or photograph is not closely related to a controlling issue.

(Pub.L. 93–595, § 1, Jan. 2, 1975, 88 Stat. 1946; Mar. 2, 1987, eff. Oct. 1, 1987.)

1972 Proposed Rules

Basically the rule requiring the production of the original as proof of contents has developed as a rule of preference: if failure to produce the original is satisfactorily explained, secondary evidence is admissible. The instant rule specifies the circumstances under which production of the original is excused.

The rule recognizes no "degrees" of secondary evidence. While strict logic might call for extending the principle of preference beyond simply preferring the original, the formulation of a hierarchy of preferences and a procedure for making it effective is believed to involve unwarranted complexities. Most, if not all, that would be accomplished by an extended scheme of preferences will, in any event, be achieved through the normal motivation of a party to present the most convincing evidence possible and the arguments and procedures available to his opponent if he does not. Compare McCormick § 207.

Note to Paragraph (1). Loss or destruction of the original, unless due to bad faith of the proponent, is a satisfactory explanation of nonproduction. McCormick § 201.

Note to Paragraph (2). When the original is in the possession of a third person, inability to procure it from him by resort to process or other judicial procedure is a sufficient explanation of nonproduction. Judicial procedure includes subpoena duces tecum as an incident to the taking of a deposition in another jurisdiction. No further showing is required. See McCormick § 202.

Note to Paragraph (3). A party who has an original in his control has no need for the protection of the rule if put on notice that proof of contents will be made. He can ward off secondary evidence by offering the original. The notice procedure here provided is not to be confused with orders to produce or other discovery procedures, as the purpose of the procedure under this rule is to afford the opposite party an opportunity to produce the original, not to compel him to do so. McCormick § 203.

Note to Paragraph (4). While difficult to define with precision, situations arise in which no good purpose is served by production of the original. Examples are the newspaper in an action for the price of publishing defendant's advertisement, *Foster–Holcomb Investment Co. v. Little Rock Publishing Co.*, 151 Ark. 449, 236 S.W. 597 (1922), and the streetcar transfer of plaintiff claiming status as a passenger, *Chicago City Ry. Co. v. Carroll*, 206 Ill. 318, 68 N.E. 1087 (1903). Numerous cases are collected in McCormick § 200, p. 412, n. 1.

1974 Enactment

Note to Paragraph (1). The Committee approved Rule 1004(1) in the form submitted to Congress. However, the Committee intends that loss or destruction of an original by another person at the instigation of the proponent should be considered as tantamount to loss or destruction in bad faith by the proponent himself. House Report No. 93–650.

1987 Amendments

The amendments are technical. No substantive change is intended.

Rule 1005. Public Records

The contents of an official record, or of a document authorized to be recorded or filed and actually recorded or filed, including data compilations in any form, if otherwise admissible, may be proved by copy, certified as correct in accordance with rule 902 or testified to be correct by a witness who has compared it with the original. If a copy which complies with the foregoing cannot be obtained by the exercise of reasonable diligence, then other evidence of the contents may be given.

(Pub.L. 93–595, § 1, Jan. 2, 1975, 88 Stat. 1946.)

1972 Proposed Rules

Public records call for somewhat different treatment. Removing them from their usual place of keeping would be attended by serious inconvenience to the public and to the custodian. As a consequence judicial decisions and statutes commonly hold that no explanation need be given for failure to produce the original of a public record. McCormick § 204; 4 Wigmore §§ 1215–1228. This blanket dispensation from producing or accounting for the original would open the door to the introduction of every kind of secondary evidence of contents of public records were it not for the preference given certified or compared copies. Recognition of degrees of secondary evidence in this situation is an appropriate *quid pro quo* for not applying the requirement of producing the original.

The provisions of 28 U.S.C. § 1733(b) apply only to departments or agencies of the United States. The rule, however, applies to public records generally and is comparable in scope in this respect to Rule 44(a) of the Rules of Civil Procedure.

Rule 1006. Summaries

The contents of voluminous writings, recordings, or photographs which cannot conveniently be examined in court may be presented in the form of a chart, summary, or calculation. The originals, or duplicates, shall be made available for examination or copying, or both, by other parties at reasonable time and place. The court may order that they be produced in court.

(Pub.L. 93–595, § 1, Jan. 2, 1975, 88 Stat. 1946.)

1972 Proposed Rules

The admission of summaries of voluminous books, records, or documents offers the only practicable means of making their contents available to judge and jury. The rule recognizes this practice, with appropriate safeguards. 4 Wigmore § 1230.

Rule 1007. Testimony or Written Admission of Party

Contents of writings, recordings, or photographs may be proved by the testimony or deposition of the party against whom offered or by that party's written admission, without accounting for the nonproduction of the original.

(Pub.L. 93–595, § 1, Jan. 2, 1975, 88 Stat. 1947; Mar. 2, 1987, eff. Oct. 1, 1987.)

1972 Proposed Rules

While the parent case, *Slatterie v. Pooley,* 6 M. & W. 664, 151 Eng.Rep. 579 (Exch.1840), allows proof of contents by evidence of an oral admission by the party against whom offered, without accounting for nonproduction of the original, the risk of inaccuracy is substantial and the decision is at odds with the purpose of the rule giving preference to the original. See 4 Wigmore § 1255. The instant rule follows Professor McCormick's suggestion of limiting this use of admissions to those made in the course of giving testimony or in writing. McCormick § 208, p. 424. The limitation, of course, does not call for excluding evidence of an oral admission when nonproduction of the original has been accounted for and secondary evidence generally has become admissible. Rule 1004, supra.

A similar provision is contained in New Jersey Evidence Rule 70(1)(h).

1987 Amendments

The amendment is technical. No substantive change is intended.

Rule 1008. Functions of Court and Jury

When the admissibility of other evidence of contents of writings, recordings, or photographs under these rules depends upon the fulfillment of a condition of fact, the question whether the condition has been fulfilled is ordinarily for the court to determine in accordance with the provisions of rule 104. However, when an issue is raised (a) whether the asserted writing ever existed, or (b) whether another writing, recording, or photograph produced at the trial is the original, or (c) whether other evidence of contents correctly reflects the contents, the issue is for the trier of fact to determine as in the case of other issues of fact.

(Pub.L. 93–595, § 1, Jan. 2, 1975, 88 Stat. 1947.)

1972 Proposed Rules

Most preliminary questions of fact in connection with applying the rule preferring the original as evidence of contents are for the judge, under the general principles announced in Rule 104, *supra.* Thus, the question whether the loss of the originals has been established, or of the fulfillment of other conditions specified in Rule 1004, supra, is for the judge. However, questions may arise which go beyond the mere administration of the rule preferring the original and into the merits of the controversy. For example, plaintiff offers secondary evidence of the contents of an alleged contract, after first introducing evidence of loss of the original, and defendant counters with evidence that no such contract was ever executed. If the judge decides that the contract was never executed and excludes the secondary evidence, the case is at an end without ever going to the jury on a central issue. Levin, Authentication and Content of Writings, 10 Rutgers L.Rev. 632, 644 (1956). The latter portion of the instant rule is designed to insure treatment of these situations as raising jury questions. The decision is not one for uncontrolled discretion of the jury but is subject to the control exercised generally by the judge over jury determinations. See Rule 104(b), *supra.*

For similar provisions, see Uniform Rule 70(2); Kansas Code of Civil Procedure § 60–467(b); New Jersey Evidence Rule 70(2), (3).

ARTICLE XI. MISCELLANEOUS RULES

Rule 1101. Applicability of Rules

(a) Courts and judges. These rules apply to the United States district courts, the District Court of Guam, the District Court of the Virgin Islands, the District Court for the Northern Mariana Islands, the United States courts of appeals, the United States Claims Court, and to United States bankruptcy judges and United States magistrate judges, in the actions, cases, and proceedings and to the extent hereinafter set forth. The terms "judge" and "court" in these rules include United States bankruptcy judges and United States magistrate judges.

(b) Proceedings generally. These rules apply generally to civil actions and proceedings, including admiralty and maritime cases, to criminal cases and proceedings, to contempt proceedings except those in which the court may act summarily, and to proceedings and cases under title 11, United States Code.

(c) Rule of privilege. The rule with respect to privileges applies at all stages of all actions, cases, and proceedings.

(d) Rules inapplicable. The rules (other than with respect to privileges) do not apply in the following situations:

(1) Preliminary questions of fact. The determination of questions of fact preliminary to admissibility of evidence when the issue is to be determined by the court under rule 104.

(2) Grand jury. Proceedings before grand juries.

(3) Miscellaneous proceedings. Proceedings for extradition or rendition; preliminary examinations in criminal cases; sentencing, or granting or revoking probation; issuance of warrants for arrest, criminal summonses, and search warrants; and proceedings with respect to release on bail or otherwise.

(e) Rules applicable in part. In the following proceedings these rules apply to the extent that matters of evidence are not provided for in the statutes which govern procedure therein or in other rules prescribed by the Supreme Court pursuant to statutory authority: the trial of misdemeanors and other petty offenses before United States magistrate judges; review of agency actions when the facts are subject to trial de novo under section 706(2)(F) of title 5, United States Code; review of orders of the Secretary of Agriculture under section 2 of the Act entitled "An Act to authorize association of producers of agricultural products" approved February 18, 1922 (7 U.S.C. 292), and under sections 6 and 7(c) of the Perishable Agricultural Commodities Act, 1930 (7 U.S.C. 499f, 499g(c)); naturalization and revocation of naturalization under sections 310–318 of the Immigration and Nationality Act (8 U.S.C. 1421–1429); prize proceedings in admiralty under sections 7651–7681 of title 10, United States Code; review of orders of the Secretary of the Interior under section 2 of the Act entitled "An Act authorizing associations of producers of aquatic products" approved June 25, 1934 (15 U.S.C. 522); review of orders of petroleum control boards under section 5 of the Act entitled "An Act to regulate interstate and foreign commerce in petroleum and its products by prohibiting the shipment in such commerce of petroleum and its products produced in violation of State law, and for other purposes", approved February 22, 1935 (15 U.S.C. 715d); actions for fines, penalties, or forfeitures under part V of title IV of the Tariff Act of 1930 (19 U.S.C. 1581–1624), or under the Anti-Smuggling Act (19 U.S.C. 1701–1711); criminal libel for condemnation, exclusion of imports, or other proceedings under the Federal Food, Drug, and Cosmetic Act (21 U.S.C. 301–392); disputes between seamen under sections 4079, 4080, and 4081 of the Revised Statutes (22 U.S.C. 256–258); habeas corpus under sections 2241–2254 of title 28, United States Code; motions to vacate, set aside or correct sentence under section 2255 of title 28, United States Code; actions for penalties for refusal to transport destitute seamen under section 4578 of the Revised Statutes (46 U.S.C. 679); actions against the United States under the Act entitled "An Act authorizing suits against the United States in admiralty for damage caused by and salvage service rendered to public vessels belonging to the United States, and for other purposes", approved March 3, 1925 (46 U.S.C. 781–790), as implemented by section 7730 of title 10, United States Code.

(Pub.L. 93–595, § 1, Jan. 2, 1975, 88 Stat. 1947; Pub.L. 94–149, § 1(14), Dec. 12, 1975, 89 Stat. 806; Pub.L. 95–598, Title II, § 251, Nov. 6, 1978, 92 Stat. 2673; Pub.L. 97–164, Title I, § 142, Apr. 2, 1982, 96 Stat. 45; Mar. 2, 1987, eff. Oct. 1, 1987; Apr. 25, 1988, eff. Nov. 1, 1988; Pub.L. 100–690, Title VII, § 7075(c), Nov. 18, 1988, 102 Stat. 4405; Apr. 22, 1993, eff. Dec. 1, 1993.)

1972 Proposed Rules

Note to Subdivision (a). The various enabling acts contain differences in phraseology in their descriptions of the courts over which the Supreme Court's power to make rules of practice and procedure extends. The act concerning civil actions, as amended in 1966, refers to "the district courts * * * of the United States in civil actions, including admiralty and maritime cases. * * *" 28 U.S.C. § 2072, Pub.L. 89–773, § 1, 80 Stat. 1323. The bankruptcy authorization is for rules of practice and procedure "under the Bankruptcy Act." 28 U.S.C. § 2075, Pub.L. 88–623, § 1, 78 Stat. 1001. The Bankruptcy Act in turn creates bankruptcy courts of "the United States district courts and the district courts of the Territories and possessions to which this title is or may hereafter be applicable." 11 U.S.C. §§ 1(10), 11(a). The provision as to criminal rules up to and including verdicts applies to "criminal cases and proceedings to punish for criminal contempt of court in the United States district courts, in the district courts for the districts of the Canal Zone and Virgin Islands, in the Supreme Court of Puerto Rico, and in proceedings before United States magistrates." 18 U.S.C. § 3771.

These various provisions do not in terms describe the same courts. In congressional usage the phrase "district courts of the United States," without further qualification, traditionally has included the district courts established by Congress in the states under Article III of the Constitution, which are "constitutional" courts, and has not included the territorial courts created under Article IV, Section 3, clause 2, which are "legislative" courts. *Hornbuckle v. Toombs*, 85 U.S. 648, 21 L.Ed. 966 (1873). However, any doubt as to the inclusion of the District Court for the District of Columbia in the phrase is laid at rest by the provisions of the Judicial Code constituting the judicial districts, 28 U.S.C. § 81 et seq., creating district courts therein, id. § 132, and specifically providing that the term "district court of the United States" means the court so constituted. *Id.* § 451. The District of Columbia is included. *Id.* § 88. Moreover, when these provisions were enacted, reference to the District of Columbia was deleted from the original civil rules enabling act. 28 U.S.C. § 2072. Likewise Puerto Rico is made a district, with a district court, and included in the term. *Id.* § 119. The question is simply one of the extent of the authority conferred by Congress. With respect to civil rules it seems clearly to include the district courts in the states, the District Court for the District of Columbia, and the District Court for the District of Puerto Rico.

The bankruptcy coverage is broader. The bankruptcy courts include "the United States district courts," which includes those enumerated above. Bankruptcy courts also include "the district courts of the Territories and possessions to which this title is or may hereafter be applicable." 11 U.S.C. §§ 1(10), 11(a). These courts include the district courts of Guam and the Virgin Islands. 48 U.S.C. §§ 1424(b), 1615. Professor Moore points out that whether the District Court for the District of the Canal Zone is a court of bankruptcy "is not free from doubt in view of the fact that no other statute expressly or inferentially provides for the applicability of the Bankruptcy Act in the Zone." He further observes that while there seems to be little doubt that the Zone is a territory or possession within the meaning of the Bankruptcy Act, 11 U.S.C. § 1(10), it must be noted that the appendix to the Canal Zone Code of 1934 did not list the Act among the laws of the United States applicable to the Zone. 1 Moore's Collier on Bankruptcy ¶ 1.10, pp. 67, 72, n. 25 (14th ed. 1967). The Code of 1962 confers on the district court jurisdiction of:

"(4) actions and proceedings involving laws of the United States applicable to the Canal Zone; and

"(5) other matters and proceedings wherein jurisdiction is conferred by this Code or any other law." Canal Zone Code, 1962, Title 3, § 141.

Admiralty jurisdiction is expressly conferred. *Id.* § 142. General powers are conferred on the district court, "if the course of proceeding is not specifically prescribed by this Code, by the statute, or by applicable rule of the Supreme Court of the United States * * *" *Id.* § 279. Neither these provisions nor § 1(10) of the Bankruptcy Act ("district courts of the Territories and possessions to which this title is or may hereafter be applicable") furnishes a satisfactory answer as to the status of the District Court for the District of the Canal Zone as a court of bankruptcy. However, the fact is that this court exercises no bankruptcy jurisdiction in practice.

The criminal rules enabling act specified United States district courts, district courts for the districts of the Canal Zone and the Virgin Islands, the Supreme Court of the Commonwealth of Puerto Rico, and proceedings before United States commissioners. Aside from the addition of commissioners, now magistrates, this scheme differs from the bankruptcy pattern in that it makes no mention of the District Court of Guam but by specific mention removes the Canal Zone from the doubtful list.

The further difference in including the Supreme Court of the Commonwealth of Puerto Rico seems not to be significant for present purposes, since the Supreme Court of the Commonwealth of Puerto Rico is an appellate court. The Rules of Criminal Procedure have not been made applicable to it, as being unneeded and inappropriate, Rule 54(a) of the Federal Rules of Criminal Procedure, and the same approach is indicated with respect to rules of evidence.

If one were to stop at this point and frame a rule governing the applicability of the proposed rules of evidence in terms of the authority conferred by the three enabling acts, an irregular pattern would emerge as follows:

Civil actions, including admiralty and maritime cases—district courts in the states, District of Columbia, and Puerto Rico.

Bankruptcy—same as civil actions, plus Guam and Virgin Islands.

Criminal cases—same as civil actions, plus Canal Zone and Virgin Islands (but not Guam).

This irregular pattern need not, however, be accepted. Originally the Advisory Committee on the Rules of Civil Procedure took the position that, although the phrase "district courts of the United States" did not include territorial courts, provisions in the organic laws of Puerto Rico and Hawaii would make the rules applicable to the district courts thereof, though this would not be so as to Alaska, the Virgin Islands, or the Canal Zone, whose organic acts contained no corresponding provisions. At the suggestion of the Court, however, the Advisory Committee struck from its notes a statement to the above effect. 2 Moore's Federal Practice ¶ 1.07 (2nd ed. 1967); 1 Barron and Holtzoff, Federal Practice and Procedure § 121 (Wright ed. 1960). Congress thereafter by various enactments provided that the rules and future amendments thereto should apply to the district courts of Hawaii, 53 Stat. 841 (1939), Puerto Rico, 54 Stat. 22 (1940), Alaska, 63 Stat. 445 (1949), Guam, 64 Stat. 384–390 (1950), and the Virgin Islands, 68 Stat. 497, 507 (1954). The original enabling act for rules of criminal procedure specifically mentioned the district courts of the Canal Zone and the Virgin Islands. The Commonwealth of Puerto Rico was blanketed in by creating its court a "district court of the United States" as previously described. Although Guam is not mentioned in either the enabling act or in the expanded definition of "district court of the United States," the Supreme Court in 1956 amended Rule 54(a) to state that the

Rules of Criminal Procedure are applicable in Guam. The Court took this step following the enactment of legislation by Congress in 1950 that rules theretofore or thereafter promulgated by the Court in civil cases, admiralty, criminal cases and bankruptcy should apply to the District Court of Guam, 48 U.S.C. § 1424(b), and two Ninth Circuit decisions upholding the applicability of the Rules of Criminal Procedure to Guam. *Pugh v. United States,* 212 F.2d 761 (9th Cir.1954); *Hatchett v. Guam,* 212 F.2d 767 (9th Cir.1954); Orfield, The Scope of the Federal Rules of Criminal Procedure, 38 U. of Det.L.J. 173, 187 (1960).

From this history, the reasonable conclusion is that Congressional enactment of a provision that rules and future amendments shall apply in the courts of a territory or possession is the equivalent of mention in an enabling act and that a rule on scope and applicability may properly be drafted accordingly. Therefore the pattern set by Rule 54 of the Federal Rules of Criminal Procedure is here followed.

The substitution of magistrates in lieu of commissioners is made in pursuance of the Federal Magistrates Act, P.L. 90–578, approved October 17, 1968, 82 Stat. 1107.

Note to Subdivision (b). Subdivision (b) is a combination of the language of the enabling acts, supra, with respect to the kinds of proceedings in which the making of rules is authorized. It is subject to the qualifications expressed in the subdivisions which follow.

Note to Subdivision (c). Subdivision (c) singling out the rules of privilege for special treatment, is made necessary by the limited applicability of the remaining rules.

Note to Subdivision (d). The rule is not intended as an expression as to when due process or other constitutional provisions may require an evidentiary hearing. Paragraph (1) restates, for convenience, the provisions of the second sentence of Rule 104(a), *supra.* See Advisory Committee's Note to that rule.

(2) While some states have statutory requirements that indictments be based on "legal evidence," and there is some case law to the effect that the rules of evidence apply to grand jury proceedings, 1 Wigmore § 4(5), the Supreme Court has not accepted this view. In *Costello v. United States,* 350 U.S. 359, 76 S.Ct. 406, 100 L.Ed. 397 (1965), the Court refused to allow an indictment to be attacked, for either constitutional or policy reasons, on the ground that only hearsay evidence was presented.

"It would run counter to the whole history of the grand jury institution, in which laymen conduct their inquiries unfettered by technical rules. Neither justice nor the concept of a fair trial requires such a change." *Id.* at 364. The rule as drafted does not deal with the evidence required to support an indictment.

(3) The rule exempts preliminary examinations in criminal cases. Authority as to the applicability of the rules of evidence to preliminary examinations has been meagre and conflicting. Goldstein, The State and the Accused: Balance of Advantage in Criminal Procedure, 69 Yale L.J. 1149, 1168, n. 53 (1960); Comment, Preliminary Hearings on Indictable Offenses in Philadelphia, 106 U. of Pa.L.Rev. 589, 592–593 (1958). Hearsay testimony is, however, customarily received in such examinations. Thus in a Dyer Act case, for example, an affidavit may properly be used in a preliminary examination to prove ownership of the stolen vehicle, thus saving the victim of the crime the hardship of having to travel twice to a distant district for the sole purpose of testifying as to ownership. It is believed that the extent of the applicability of the Rules of Evidence to preliminary examinations should be appropriately dealt with by the Federal Rules of Criminal Procedure which regulate those proceedings.

Extradition and rendition proceedings are governed in detail by statute. 18 U.S.C. §§ 3181–3195. They are essentially administrative in character. Traditionally the rules of evidence have not applied. 1 Wigmore § 4(6). Extradition proceedings are accepted from the operation of the Rules of Criminal Procedure. Rule 54(b)(5) of Federal Rules of Criminal Procedure.

The rules of evidence have not been regarded as applicable to sentencing or probation proceedings, where great reliance is placed upon the presentence investigation and report. Rule 32(c) of the Federal Rules of Criminal Procedure requires a presentence investigation and report in every case unless the court otherwise directs. In *Williams v. New York,* 337 U.S. 241, 69 S.Ct. 1079, 93 L.Ed. 1337 (1949), in which the judge overruled a jury recommendation of life imprisonment and imposed a death sentence, the Court said that due process does not require confrontation or cross-examination in sentencing or passing on probation, and that the judge has broad discretion as to the sources and types of information relied upon. Compare the recommendation that the substance of all derogatory information be disclosed to the defendant, in A.B.A. Project on Minimum Standards for Criminal Justice, Sentencing Alternatives and Procedures § 4.4, Tentative Draft (1967, Sobeloff, Chm.). Williams was adhered to in *Specht v. Patterson,* 386 U.S. 605, 87 S.Ct. 1209, 18 L.Ed.2d 326 (1967), but not extended to a proceeding under the Colorado Sex Offenders Act, which was said to be a new charge leading in effect to punishment, more like the recidivist statutes where opportunity must be given to be heard on the habitual criminal issue.

Warrants for arrest, criminal summonses, and search warrants are issued upon complaint or affidavit showing probable cause. Rules 4(a) and 41(c) of the Federal Rules of Criminal Procedure. The nature of the proceedings makes application of the formal rules of evidence inappropriate and impracticable.

Criminal contempts are punishable summarily if the judge certifies that he saw or heard the contempt and that it was committed in the presence of the court. Rule 42(a) of the Federal Rules of Criminal Procedure. The circumstances which preclude application of the rules of evidence in this situation are not present, however, in other cases of criminal contempt.

Proceedings with respect to release on bail or otherwise do not call for application of the rules of evidence. The governing statute specifically provides:

"Information stated in, or offered in connection with, any order entered pursuant to this section need not conform to the rules pertaining to the admissibility of evidence in a court of law." 18 U.S.C.A. § 3146(f). This provision is consistent with the type of inquiry contemplated in A.B.A. Project on Minimum Standards for Criminal Justice, Standards Relating to Pretrial Release, § 4.5(b), (c), p. 16 (1968). The references to the weight of the evidence against the accused, in Rule 46(a)(1), (c) of the Federal Rules of Criminal Procedure and in 18 U.S.C.A. § 3146(b), as a factor to be considered, clearly do not have in view evidence introduced at a hearing under the rules of evidence.

The rule does not exempt habeas corpus proceedings. The Supreme Court held in *Walker v. Johnston*, 312 U.S. 275, 61 S.Ct. 574, 85 L.Ed. 830 (1941), that the practice of disposing of matters of fact on affidavit, which prevailed in some circuits, did not "satisfy the command of the statute that the judge shall proceed 'to determine the facts of the case, by hearing the testimony and arguments.'" This view accords with the emphasis in *Townsend v. Sain*, 372 U.S. 293, 83 S.Ct. 745, 9 L.Ed.2d 770 (1963), upon trial-type proceedings, *id.* 311, 83 S.Ct. 745, with demeanor evidence as a significant factor, *id.* 322, 83 S.Ct. 745, in applications by state prisoners aggrieved by unconstitutional detentions. Hence subdivision (3) applies the rules to habeas corpus proceedings to the extent not inconsistent with the statute.

Note to Subdivision (e). In a substantial number of special proceedings, *ad hoc* evaluation has resulted in the promulgation of particularized evidentiary provisions, by Act of Congress or by rule adopted by the Supreme Court. Well adapted to the particular proceedings, though not apt candidates for inclusion in a set of general rules, they are left undisturbed. Otherwise, however, the rules of evidence are applicable to the proceedings enumerated in the subdivision.

1974 Enactment

Note to Subdivision (a). Subdivision (a) as submitted to the Congress, in stating the courts and judges to which the Rules of Evidence apply, omitted the Court of Claims and commissioners of that Court. At the request of the Court of Claims, the Committee amended the Rule to include the Court and its commissioners within the purview of the Rules.

Note to Subdivision (b). Subdivision (b) was amended merely to substitute positive law citations for those which were not. House Report No. 93–650.

1987 Amendments

Subdivision (a) is amended to delete the reference to the District Court for the District of the Canal Zone, which no longer exists, and to add the District Court for the Northern Mariana Islands. The United States bankruptcy judges are added to conform the subdivision with Rule 1101(b) and Bankruptcy Rule 9017.

1988 Amendments

The amendments are technical. No substantive change is intended.

1993 Amendments

This revision is made to conform the rule to changes in terminology made by Rule 58 of the Federal Rules of Criminal Procedure and to the changes in the title of United States magistrates made by the Judicial Improvements Act of 1990.

HISTORICAL NOTES

References in Text

The Tariff Act of 1930, referred to in subsec. (e), is Act June 17, 1930, c. 497, 46 Stat. 590, as amended, which is classified principally to chapter 4 (section 1202 et seq.) of Title 19, Customs Duties. Part V of Title IV of the Tariff Act of 1930 enacted part V (section 1581 et seq.) of subtitle III of chapter 4 of Title 19. For complete classification of this Act to the Code, see section 1654 of Title 19 and Tables.

The Anti–Smuggling Act (19 U.S.C. 1701–1711), referred to in subsec. (e), is Act Aug. 5, 1935, c. 438, 49 Stat. 517, as amended, which is classified principally to chapter 5 (section 1701 et seq.) of Title 19, Customs Duties. For complete classification of this Act to the Code, see section 1711 of Title 19 and Tables.

The Federal Food, Drug, and Cosmetic Act (21 U.S.C. 301–392), referred to in subsec. (e), is Act June 25, 1938, c. 675, 52 Stat. 1040, as amended, which is classified generally to chapter 9 (section 301 et seq.) of Title 21, Food and Drugs. For complete classification of this Act to the Code, see section 301 of Title 21 and Tables.

"An Act authorizing suits against the United States in admiralty for damage caused by and salvage service rendered to public vessels belonging to the United States, and for other purposes," approved Mar. 3, 1925 (46 U.S.C. 781–790), referred to in subsec. (e), is Act Mar. 3, 1925, c. 428, 43 Stat. 1112, as amended, known as the "Public Vessels Act", which is classified generally to chapter 22 (section 781 et seq.) of Title 46, Shipping. For complete classification of this Act to the Code, see Short Title note set out under section 781 of Title 46 and Tables.

1988 Amendments

Subd. (a). Pub.L. 100–690, § 7075(c)(1), (2), substituted "rules" and "courts of appeals" for "Rules" and "Courts of Appeals".

1982 Amendments

Subd. (a). Pub.L. 97–164 substituted "United States Claims Court" for "Court of Claims" and struck out "and commissioners of the Court of Claims" following "these rules include United States magistrates".

1978 Amendments

Subd. (a). Pub.L. 95–598, § 251(a), struck out ", referees in bankruptcy," following "United States magistrates".

1978 Amendments

Subd. (a). Pub.L. 95–598, § 252, directed the amendment of this subd. by adding "the United States bankruptcy courts," after "the United States district courts,", which amendment did not become effective pursuant to section 402(b) of Pub.L. 95–598, as amended, set out as an Effective Date note preceding section 101 of Title 11, Bankruptcy.

Subd. (b). Pub.L. 95–598, § 251(b), substituted "title 11, United States Code" for "the Bankruptcy Act".

1975 Amendments

Subd. (e). Pub.L. 94–149 substituted "admiralty" for "admirality".

Effective and Applicability Provisions

1982 Acts. Amendment by Pub.L. 97–164 effective Oct. 1, 1982, see section 402 of Pub.L. 97–164, set out as a note under section 171 of this title.

1978 Acts. Amendment of subds. (a) and (b) of this rule by section 251 of Pub.L. 95–598 effective Oct. 1, 1979, see section 402(c) of Pub.L. 95–598, set out as a note preceding section 101 of Title 11, Bankruptcy.

Change of Name

United States magistrate appointed under section 631 of Title 28, Judiciary and Judicial Procedure, to be known as

United States magistrate judge after Dec. 1, 1990, with any reference to United States magistrate or magistrate in Title 28, in any other Federal statute, etc., deemed a reference to United States magistrate judge appointed under section 631 of Title 28, see section 321 of Pub.L. 101–650, set out as a note under section 631 of Title 28.

Pending Actions

Amendments of Supreme Court to the Federal Rules of Evidence effective December 1, 1993, applicable, insofar as just and practicable, in all proceedings then pending, pursuant to the Order of April 22, 1993.

Rule 1102. Amendments

Amendments to the Federal Rules of Evidence may be made as provided in section 2072 of title 28 of the United States Code.

(Pub.L. 93–595, § 1, Jan. 2, 1975, 88 Stat.1948); Apr. 30, 1991, eff. Dec. 1, 1991.)

1991 Amendments

The amendment is technical. No substantive change is intended.

Rule 1103. Title

These rules may be known and cited as the Federal Rules of Evidence.

(Pub.L. 93–595, § 1, Jan. 2, 1975, 88 Stat.1948.)

HISTORICAL NOTES

Short Title

1978 Amendments. Pub.L. 95–540, § 1, Oct. 28, 1978, 92 Stat. 2046, provided: "That this Act [enacting rule 412 of these rules and a provision set out as a note under rule 412 of these rules] may be cited as the 'Privacy Protection for Rape Victims Act of 1978'."

FEDERAL RULES OF APPELLATE PROCEDURE

Amendments received to December 1, 2008

TITLE I. APPLICABILITY OF RULES

Rule

1. Scope of Rules; Title.
2. Suspension of Rules.

TITLE II. APPEAL FROM A JUDGMENT OR ORDER OF A DISTRICT COURT

3. Appeal as of Right—How Taken.
3.1. Abrogated Apr. 24, 1998, eff. Dec. 1, 1998].
4. Appeal as of Right—When Taken.
5. Appeal by Permission.
5.1. Appeal by Leave Under 28 U.S.C. § 636(c)(5)] (Abrogated Apr. 24, 1998, eff. Dec. 1, 1998).
6. Appeal in a Bankruptcy Case From a Final Judgment, Order, or Decree of a District Court or Bankruptcy Appellate Panel.
7. Bond for Costs on Appeal in a Civil Case.
8. Stay or Injunction Pending Appeal.
9. Release in a Criminal Case.
10. The Record on Appeal.
11. Forwarding the Record.
12. Docketing the Appeal; Filing a Representation Statement; Filing the Record.

TITLE III. REVIEW OF A DECISION OF THE UNITED STATES TAX COURT

13. Review of a Decision of the Tax Court.
14. Applicability of Other Rules to the Review of a Tax Court Decision.

TITLE IV. REVIEW OR ENFORCEMENT OF AN ORDER OF AN ADMINISTRATIVE AGENCY, BOARD, COMMISSION, OR OFFICER

15. Review or Enforcement of an Agency Order—How Obtained; Intervention.
15.1. Briefs and Oral Argument in a National Labor Relations Board Proceeding.
16. The Record on Review or Enforcement.
17. Filing the Record.
18. Stay Pending Review.
19. Settlement of a Judgment Enforcing an Agency Order in Part.
20. Applicability of Rules to the Review or Enforcement of an Agency Order.

TITLE V. EXTRAORDINARY WRITS

21. Writs of Mandamus and Prohibition, and Other Extraordinary Writs.

Rule

TITLE VI. HABEAS CORPUS; PROCEEDINGS IN FORMA PAUPERIS

22. Habeas Corpus and Section 2255 Proceedings.
23. Custody or Release of a Prisoner in a Habeas Corpus Proceeding.
24. Proceeding in Forma Pauperis.

TITLE VII. GENERAL PROVISIONS

25. Filing and Service.
26. Computing and Extending Time.
26.1. Corporate Disclosure Statement.
27. Motions.
28. Briefs.
28.1. Cross-Appeals.
29. Brief of an Amicus Curiae.
30. Appendix to the Briefs.
31. Serving and Filing Briefs.
32. Form of Briefs, Appendices, and Other Papers.
32.1. Citing Judicial Dispositions.
33. Appeal Conferences.
34. Oral Argument.
35. En Banc Determination.
36. Entry of Judgment; Notice.
37. Interest on Judgment.
38. Frivolous Appeal—Damages and Costs.
39. Costs.
40. Petition for Panel Rehearing.
41. Mandate: Contents; Issuance and Effective Date; Stay.
42. Voluntary Dismissal.
43. Substitution of Parties.
44. Case Involving a Constitutional Question When the United States or the Relevant State is Not a Party.
45. Clerk's Duties.
46. Attorneys.
47. Local Rules by Courts of Appeals.
48. Masters.

APPENDIX OF FORMS

Form

1. Notice of Appeal to a Court of Appeals From a Judgment or Order of a District Court.
2. Notice of Appeal to a Court of Appeals From a Decision of the United States Tax Court.
3. Petition for Review of Order of an Agency, Board, Commission or Officer.
4. Affidavit Accompanying Motion for Permission to Appeal In Forma Pauperis.
5. Notice of Appeal to a Court of Appeals from a Judgment or Order of a District Court or a Bankruptcy Appellate Panel.
6. Certificate of Compliance with Rule 32(a).

ORDERS OF THE SUPREME COURT OF THE UNITED STATES ADOPTING AND AMENDING RULES

ORDER OF DECEMBER 4, 1967

ORDERED:

1. That the following rules, to be known as the Federal Rules of Appellate Procedure, be, and they hereby are, prescribed, pursuant to sections 3771 and 3772 of Title 18, United States Code, and sections 2072 and 2075 of Title 28, United States Code, to govern the procedure in appeals to United States courts of appeals from the United States district courts, in the review by United States courts of appeals of decisions of the Tax Court of the United States, in proceedings in the United States courts of appeals for the review or enforcement of orders of administrative agencies, boards, commissions and officers, and in applications for writs or other relief which a United States court of appeals or judge thereof is competent to give:

[See text of Rules of Appellate Procedure, post]

2. That the foregoing rules shall take effect on July 1, 1968, and shall govern all proceedings in appeals and petitions for review or enforcement of orders thereafter brought and in all such proceedings then pending, except to the extent that in the opinion of the court of appeals their application in a particular proceeding then pending would not be feasible or would work injustice, in which case the former procedure may be followed.

3. That Rules 6, 9, 41, 77 and 81 of the Rules of Civil Procedure for the United States District Courts be, and they hereby are, amended, effective July 1, 1968, as hereinafter set forth:

[See amendments made thereby under the Rules of Civil Procedure, ante]

4. That the chapter heading "IX. APPEALS", all of Rules 72, 73, 74, 75 and 76 of the Rules of Civil Procedure for the United States District Courts, and Form 27 annexed to the said rules, be, and they hereby are, abrogated, effective July 1, 1968.

5. That Rules 45, 49, 56 and 57 of the Rules of Criminal Procedure for the United States District Courts be, and they hereby are, amended, effective July 1, 1968, as hereinafter set forth:

[For text of amendments, see pamphlet containing Federal Rules of Criminal Procedure]

6. That the chapter heading "VIII. APPEAL", all of Rules 37 and 39, and subdivisions (b) and (c) of Rule 38, of the Rules of Criminal Procedure for the United States District Courts, and Forms 26 and 27 annexed to the said rules, be, and they hereby are, abrogated, effective July 1, 1968.

7. That the Chief Justice be, and he hereby is, authorized to transmit to the Congress the foregoing new rules and amendments to and abrogation of existing rules, in accordance with the provisions of Title 18, U.S.C., § 3771, and Title 28, U.S.C., §§ 2072 and 2075.

ORDER OF MARCH 30, 1970

1. That subdivisions (a) and (c) of Rule 30 and subdivision (a) of Rule 31 of the Federal Rules of Appellate Procedure be, and they hereby are, amended as follows:

[See the amendments made thereby under the respective rules, post]

2. That the foregoing amendments to the Federal Rules of Appellate Procedure shall take effect on July 1, 1970, and shall govern all proceedings in actions brought thereafter and also in all further proceedings in actions then pending, except to the extent that in the opinion of the court their application in a particular action then pending would not be feasible or would work injustice, in which event the former procedure applies.

3. That the Chief Justice be, and he hereby is, authorized to transmit to the Congress the foregoing amendments to existing rules, in accordance with the provisions of Title 18, U.S.C., § 3772, and Title 28, U.S.C., §§ 2072 and 2075.

ORDER OF MARCH 1, 1971

1. That subdivision (a) of Rule 6, paragraph (4) of subdivision (a) of Rule 27, paragraph (6) of subdivision (b) of Rule 30, subdivision (c) of Rule 77, and paragraph (2) of subdivision (a) of Rule 81 of the Federal Rules of Civil Procedure be, and hereby are, amended, effective July 1, 1971, to read as follows:

[See amendments made thereby under the Rules of Civil Procedure, ante]

2. That subdivision (a) of Rule 45 and all of Rule 56 of the Federal Rules of Criminal Procedure be, and they hereby are, amended, effective July 1, 1971, to read as follows:

[For text of amendments, see pamphlet containing Federal Rules of Criminal Procedure]

3. That subdivision (a) of Rule 26 and subdivision (a) of Rule 45 of the Federal Rules of Appellate Procedure be, and they hereby are, amended, effective July 1, 1971, to read as follows:

[See amendments made thereby under the respective rules, post]

4. That THE CHIEF JUSTICE be, and he hereby is, authorized to transmit to the Congress the foregoing amendments to the Rules of Civil, Criminal and Appellate Procedure, in accordance with the provisions of Title 18, U.S.C., § 3771, and Title 28, U.S.C., §§ 2072 and 2075.

MR. JUSTICE BLACK and MR. JUSTICE DOUGLAS dissent.

ORDER OF APRIL 24, 1972

1. That Rules 1, 3, 4(b) & (c), 5, 5.1, 6(b), 7(c), 9(b), (c) & (d), 17(a) & (g), 31(e), 32(b), 38(a), 40, 41, 44, 46, 50, 54 and 55 of the Federal Rules of Criminal Procedure be, and they hereby are, amended effective October 1, 1972, to read as follows:

[For text of amendments, see pamphlet containing Federal Rules of Criminal Procedure]

2. That Rule 9(c) of the Federal Rules of Appellate Procedure be, and hereby is amended, effective October 1, 1972, to read as follows:

[See amendments made thereby under the respective rules, post]

3. That THE CHIEF JUSTICE be, and he hereby is, authorized to transmit to the Congress the foregoing amendments to Rules of Criminal and Appellate Procedure, in accordance with the provisions of Title 18, U.S.Code, §§ 3771 and 3772.

MR. JUSTICE DOUGLAS dissented to adoption of Rule 50(b) of the Federal Rules of Criminal Procedure.

ORDER OF APRIL 30, 1979

1. That the Federal Rules of Appellate Procedure be, and they hereby are, amended by including therein amendments to Rules 1(a), 3(c), (d) and (e), 4(a), 5(d), 6(d), 7, 10(b), 11(a), (b), (c) and (d), 12, 13(a), 24(b), 27(b), 28(g) and (j), 34(a) and (b), 35(b) and (c), 39(c) and (d), and 40 as hereinafter set forth:

[See amendments made thereby under the respective rules, post]

2. That the foregoing amendments to the Federal Rules of Appellate Procedure shall take effect on August 1, 1979, and shall govern all appellate proceedings thereafter commenced and, insofar as just and practicable, all proceedings then pending.

3. That THE CHIEF JUSTICE be, and he hereby is, authorized to transmit to the Congress the foregoing amendments to the Federal Rules of Appellate Procedure in accordance with the provisions of Section 3772 of Title 18, United States Code, and Sections 2072 and 2075 of Title 28, United States Code.

ORDER OF MARCH 10, 1986

1. That the Federal Rules of Appellate Procedure be, and they hereby are, amended by including therein new Appellate Rules 3.1, 5.1 and 15.1 and amendments to Appellate Rules 3(d), 8(b), 10(b) and (c), 11(b), 12(a), 19, 23(b) and (c), 24(a), 25(a) and (b), 26(a) and (c), 28(c) and (j), 30(a), (b) and (c), 31(a) and (c), 34(a) and (e), 39(c) and (d), 43(a) and (c), 45(a), (b), and (d), and 46(a) and (b), as hereinafter set forth:

[See amendments made thereby under the respective rules, post]

2. That the foregoing additions to and changes in the Federal Rules of Appellate Procedure, shall take effect on July 1, 1986 and shall govern all proceedings in appellate actions thereafter commenced and, insofar as just and practicable, all proceedings in appellate actions then pending.

3. That THE CHIEF JUSTICE be, and he hereby is, authorized to transmit to the Congress the foregoing additions to and changes in the rules of appellate procedure in accordance with the provisions of Section 3772 of Title 18 and Section 2072 of Title 28, United States Code.

ORDER OF APRIL 25, 1989

1. That the Federal Rules of Appellate Procedure be, and they hereby are, amended by including therein amendments to Appellate Rules 1(a), 3(a), 26(a), 27(a), 28(g) and new Rules 6 and 26.1, and a new Form 5 as hereinafter set forth:

[See amendments made thereby under the respective rules, post]

2. That the foregoing additions to and changes in the Federal Rules of Appellate Procedure, shall take effect on December 1, 1989 and shall govern all proceedings in appellate actions thereafter commenced and, insofar as just and practicable, all proceedings in appellate actions then pending.

3. That THE CHIEF JUSTICE be, and he hereby is, authorized to transmit to the Congress the foregoing additions to and changes in the rules of appellate procedure in accordance with the provisions of Section 2072 of Title 28, United States Code.

ORDER OF APRIL 30, 1991

1. That the Federal Rules of Appellate Procedure be, and they hereby are, amended by including therein amendments to Appellate Rules 4(a), 6, 10(c), 25(a), 26(a), 26.1, 28(a), (b), and (h), 30(b), and 34(d).

[See amendments made thereby under the respective rules, post]

2. That the foregoing amendments to the Federal Rules of Appellate Procedure shall take effect on December 1, 1991, and shall govern all proceedings in appellate cases thereafter commenced and, insofar as just and practicable, all proceedings in appellate cases then pending.

3. That THE CHIEF JUSTICE be, and he hereby is, authorized to transmit to the Congress the foregoing amendments to the Federal Rules of Appellate Procedure in accordance with the provisions of Section 2072 of Title 28, United States Code.

ORDER OF APRIL 22, 1993

1. That the Federal Rules of Appellate Procedure be, and they hereby are, amended by including therein amendments to Appellate Rules 3, 3.1, 4, 5.1, 6, 10, 12, 15, 25, 28, and 34, and to Forms 1, 2, and 3.

[See amendments made thereby under the respective rules and forms, post.]

2. That the foregoing amendments to the Federal Rules of Appellate Procedure shall take effect on December 1, 1993, and shall govern all proceedings in appellate cases thereafter commenced and, insofar as just and practicable, all proceedings in appellate cases then pending.

3. That THE CHIEF JUSTICE be, and he hereby is, authorized to transmit to the Congress the foregoing amendments to the Federal Rules of Appellate Procedure in accordance with the provisions of Section 2072 of Title 28, United States Code.

ORDER OF APRIL 29, 1994

1. That the Federal Rules of Appellate Procedure be, and they hereby are, amended by including therein amendments to Appellate Rules 1, 3, 5, 5.1, 9, 13, 21, 25, 26.1, 27, 28, 30, 31, 33, 35, 38, 40, 41, and 48.

[See amendments made hereby under respective rules, post]

2. That the foregoing amendments to the Federal Rules of Appellate Procedure shall take effect on December 1, 1994, and shall govern all proceedings in appellate cases

thereafter commenced and, insofar as just and practicable, all proceedings in appellate cases then pending.

3. That THE CHIEF JUSTICE be, and he hereby is, authorized to transmit to the Congress the foregoing amendments to the Federal Rules of Appellate Procedure in accordance with the provisions of Section 2072 of Title 28, United States Code.

ORDER OF APRIL 27, 1995

1. That the Federal Rules of Appellate Procedure be, and they hereby are, amended by including therein amendments to Appellate Rules 4, 8, 10, and 47.

[See amendments made thereby under the respective rules, post.]

2. That the foregoing amendments to the Federal Rules of Appellate Procedure shall take effect on December 1, 1995, and shall govern all proceedings in appellate cases thereafter commenced and, insofar as just and practicable, all proceedings in appellate cases then pending.

3. That THE CHIEF JUSTICE be, and he hereby is, authorized to transmit to the Congress the foregoing amendments to the Federal Rules of Appellate Procedure in accordance with the provisions of Section 2072 of Title 28, United States Code.

ORDER OF APRIL 23, 1996

1. That the Federal Rules of Appellate Procedure be, and they hereby are, amended by including therein amendments to Appellate Rules 21, 25, and 26.

[See amendments made thereby under respective rules, post]

2. That the foregoing amendments to the Federal Rules of Appellate Procedure shall take effect on December 1, 1996, and shall govern all proceedings in appellate cases thereafter commenced and, insofar as just and practicable, all proceedings in appellate cases then pending.

3. That THE CHIEF JUSTICE be, and hereby is, authorized to transmit to the Congress the foregoing amendments to the Federal Rules of Appellate Procedure in accordance with the provisions of Section 2072 of Title 28, United States Code.

ORDER OF APRIL 24, 1998

1. That the Federal Rules of Appellate Procedure be, and they hereby are, amended by including therein amendments to Appellate Rules 1–48 and to Form 4.

[See amendments made thereby under respective rules, post]

2. That the foregoing amendments to the Federal Rules of Appellate Procedure shall take effect on December 1, 1998, and shall govern in all proceedings thereafter commenced and, insofar as just and practicable, all proceedings then pending.

3. That THE CHIEF JUSTICE be, and hereby is, authorized to transmit to the Congress the foregoing amendments to the Federal Rules of Appellate Procedure in accordance with the provisions of Section 2072 of Title 28, United States Code.

ORDER OF APRIL 29, 2002

1. That the Federal Rules of Appellate Procedure be, and they hereby are, amended by including therein amendments to Appellate Rules 1, 4, 5, 21, 24, 25, 26, 26.l, 27, 28, 31, 32, 36, 41, 44, and 45 and new Form 6.

[See amendments made thereby under respective rules and forms, post]

2. That the foregoing amendments to the Federal Rules of Appellate Procedure shall take effect on December 1, 2002, and shall govern in all proceedings in appellate cases thereafter commenced and, insofar as just and practicable, all proceedings then pending.

3. That THE CHIEF JUSTICE be, and hereby is, authorized to transmit to the Congress the foregoing amendments to the Federal Rules of Appellate Procedure in accordance with the provisions of Section 2072 of Title 28, United States Code.

ORDER OF MARCH 27, 2003

1. That Forms 1, 2, 3, and 5 in the Appendix to the Federal Rules of Appellate Procedure be, and they hereby are, amended by replacing all references to "19___" with references to "20___"

[See amendments made thereby under respective forms, post]

2. That the foregoing amendments to the forms in the Appendix to the Federal Rules of Appellate Procedure shall take effect on December 1, 2003, and shall govern in all proceedings in appellate cases thereafter commenced and, insofar as just and practicable, all proceedings then pending.

3. That THE CHIEF JUSTICE be, and hereby is, authorized to transmit to the Congress the foregoing amendments to the Federal Rules of Appellate Procedure in accordance with the provisions of Section 2072 of Title 28, United States Code.

ORDER OF APRIL 25, 2005

1. That the Federal Rules of Appellate Procedure be, and they hereby are, amended by including therein amendments to Appellate Rules 4, 26, 27, 28, 32, 34, 35, 45, and new Rule 28.1.

[See amendments made thereby under respective rules, post]

2. That the foregoing amendments to the Federal Rules of Appellate Procedure shall take effect on December 1, 2005, and shall govern in all proceedings thereafter commenced and, insofar as just and practicable, all proceedings then pending.

3. That THE CHIEF JUSTICE be, and hereby is, authorized to transmit to the Congress the foregoing amendments to the Federal Rules of Appellate Procedure in accordance with the provisions of Section 2072 of Title 28, United States Code.

ORDER OF APRIL 12, 2006

1. That the Federal Rules of Appellate Procedure be, and they hereby are, amended by including therein an amendment to Appellate Rule 25 and a new Rule 32.1.

[See amendments made thereby under respective rules, post]

2. That the foregoing amendment and new rule shall take effect on December 1, 2006, and shall govern in all proceedings thereafter commenced and, insofar as just and practicable, all proceedings then pending.

3. That the CHIEF JUSTICE be, and hereby is, authorized to transmit to the Congress the foregoing amendments to the Federal Rules of Appellate Procedure in accordance with the provisions of Section 2072 of Title 28, United States Code.

ORDER OF APRIL 30, 2007

1. That the Federal Rules of Appellate Procedure be, and they hereby are, amended by including therein an amendment to Appellate Rule 25.

[See amendments made thereby under respective rules, post]

2. That the foregoing amendment to the Federal Rules of Appellate Procedure shall take effect on December 1, 2007, and shall govern in all proceedings thereafter commenced and, insofar as just and practicable, all proceedings then pending.

3. That the CHIEF JUSTICE be, and hereby is, authorized to transmit to the Congress the foregoing amendment to the Federal Rules of Appellate Procedure in accordance with the provisions of Section 2072 of Title 28, United States Code.

HISTORICAL NOTES

Effective and Applicability Provisions; Application; Transmission to Congress

The Federal Rules of Appellate Procedure were adopted by order of the Supreme Court on Dec. 4, 1967, transmitted to Congress by the Chief Justice on Jan. 15, 1968, and became effective on July 1, 1968.

The Rules have been amended Mar. 30, 1970, eff. July 1, 1970; Mar. 1, 1971, eff. July 1, 1971; Apr. 24, 1972, eff. Oct. 1, 1972; Apr. 30, 1979, eff. Aug. 1, 1979; Oct. 12, 1984, Pub.L. 98–473, Title II, § 210, 98 Stat. 1987; Mar. 10, 1986, eff. July 1, 1986; Nov. 18, 1988, Pub.L. 100–690, Title VII, § 7111, 102 Stat. 4419; Apr. 25, 1989, eff. Dec. 1, 1989; Apr. 30, 1991, eff. Dec. 1, 1991; Apr. 22, 1993, eff. Dec. 1, 1993; Apr. 29, 1994, eff. Dec. 1, 1994; Apr. 27, 1995, eff. Dec. 1, 1995; Apr. 23, 1996, eff. Dec. 1, 1996; Apr. 24, 1998, eff. Dec. 1, 1998; Apr. 29, 2002, eff. Dec. 1, 2002; Mar. 27, 2003, eff. Dec. 1, 2003; Apr. 25, 2005, eff. Dec. 1, 2005; Apr. 12, 2006, eff. Dec. 1, 2006; Apr. 30, 2007, eff. Dec. 1, 2007.

TITLE I. APPLICABILITY OF RULES

Rule 1. Scope of Rules; Title

(a) Scope of Rules.

(1) These rules govern procedure in the United States courts of appeals.

(2) When these rules provide for filing a motion or other document in the district court, the procedure must comply with the practice of the district court.

(b) [Abrogated]

(c) Title. These rules are to be known as the Federal Rules of Appellate Procedure.

(As amended Apr. 30, 1979, eff. Aug. 1, 1979; Apr. 25, 1989, eff. Dec. 1, 1989; Apr. 29, 1994, eff. Dec. 1, 1994; Apr. 24, 1998, eff. Dec. 1, 1998; Apr. 29, 2002, eff. Dec. 1, 2002.)

1967 Adoption

These rules are drawn under the authority of 28 U.S.C. § 2072 as amended by the Act of November 6, 1966, 80 Stat. 1323 (1 U.S.Code Cong. & Ad.News, p. 1546 (1966)) (Rules of Civil Procedure); 28 U.S.C. § 2075 (Bankruptcy Rules); and 18 U.S.C. §§ 3771 [§ 3771 of Title 18, Crimes and Criminal Procedure] (Procedure to and including verdict) and 3772 [§ 3772 of Title 18] (Procedure after verdict). Those statutes combine to give to the Supreme Court power to make rules of practice and procedure for all cases within the jurisdiction of the courts of appeals. By the terms of the statutes, after the rules have taken effect all laws in conflict with them are of no further force or effect. Practice and procedure in the eleven courts of appeals are now regulated by rules promulgated by each court under the authority of 28 U.S.C. § 2071. Rule 47 expressly authorizes the courts of appeals to make rules of practice not inconsistent with these rules.

As indicated by the titles under which they are found, the following rules are of special application: Rules 3 through 12 apply to appeals from judgments and orders of the district courts; Rules 13 and 14 apply to appeals from decisions of the Tax Court (Rule 13 establishes an appeal as the mode of review of decisions of the Tax Court in place of the present petition for review); Rules 15 through 20 apply to proceedings for review or enforcement of orders of administrative agencies, boards, commissions and officers. Rules 22 through 24 regulate habeas corpus proceedings and appeals in forma pauperis. All other rules apply to all proceedings in the courts of appeals.

1979 Amendment

The Federal Rules of Appellate Procedure were designed as an integrated set of rules to be followed in appeals to the courts of appeals, covering all steps in the appellate process, whether they take place in the district court or in the court of appeals, and with their adoption Rules 72 to 76 of the F.R.C.P. [rules 72 to 76, Federal Rules of Civil Procedure] were abrogated. In some instances, however, the F.R.A.P. provide that a motion or application for relief may, or must, be made in the district court. See Rules 4(a), 10(b) and 24. The proposed amendment would make it clear that when this is so the motion or application is to be made in the form and manner prescribed by the F.R.C.P. or F.R.Cr.P. [Federal Rules Criminal Procedure] and local rules relating to the form and presentation of motions and is not governed by Rule 27 of the F.R.A.P. See Rule 7(b) of the F.R.C.P. [rule 7(b), Federal Rules of Civil Procedure] and Rule 47 of the F.R.Cr.P. [rule 47, Federal Rules of Criminal Procedure].

1989 Amendment

The amendment is technical. No substantive change is intended.

1994 Amendment

Subdivision (c). A new subdivision is added to the rule. The text of new subdivision (c) has been moved from Rule 48 to Rule 1 to allow the addition of new rules at the end of the existing set of appellate rules without burying the title provision among other rules. In a similar fashion the Bankruptcy Rules combine the provisions governing the scope of the rules and the title in the first rule.

1998 Amendments

The language and organization of the rule are amended to make the rule more easily understood. In addition to changes made to improve the understanding, the Advisory Committee has changed language to make style and terminology consistent throughout the appellate rules. These changes are intended to be stylistic only. The Advisory Committee recommends deleting the language in subdivision (a) that describes the different types of proceedings that may be brought in a court of appeals. The Advisory Committee believes that the language is unnecessary and that it s omission does not work any substantive change.

2002 Amendments

Subdivision (b). Two recent enactments make it likely that, in the future, one or more of the Federal Rules of Appellate Procedure ("FRAP") will extend or limit the jurisdiction of the courts of appeals. In 1990, Congress amended the Rules Enabling Act to give the Supreme Court authority to use the federal rules of practice and procedure to define when a ruling of a district court is final for purposes of 28 U.S.C. § 1291. *See* 28 U.S.C. § 2072(c). In 1992, Congress amended 28 U.S.C. § 1292 to give the Supreme Court authority to use the federal rules of practice and procedure to provide for appeals of interlocutory decisions that are not already authorized by 28 U.S.C. § 1292. *See* 28 U.S.C. § 1292(e). Both § 1291 and § 1292 are unquestionably jurisdictional statutes, and thus, as soon as FRAP is amended to define finality for purposes of the former or to authorize interlocutory appeals not provided for by the latter, FRAP will "extend or limit the jurisdiction of the courts of appeals," and subdivision (b) will become obsolete. For that reason, subdivision (b) has been abrogated.

Changes Made After Publication and Comments No changes were made to the text of the proposed amendment or to the Committee Note.

HISTORICAL NOTES

Pending Actions

Amendments of Supreme Court to Federal Rules of Appellate Procedure effective December 1, 1993, applicable, insofar as just and practicable, in all proceedings then pending, pursuant to the Order of April 22, 1993.

Rule 2. Suspension of Rules

On its own or a party's motion, a court of appeals may—to expedite its decision or for other good cause—suspend any provision of these rules in a particular case and order proceedings as it directs, except as otherwise provided in Rule 26(b).

(As amended Apr. 24, 1998, eff. Dec. 1, 1998.)

1967 Adoption

The primary purpose of this rule is to make clear the power of the courts of appeals to expedite the determination of cases of pressing concern to the public or to the litigants by prescribing a time schedule other than that provided by the rules. The rule also contains a general authorization to the courts to relieve litigants of the consequences of default where manifest injustice would otherwise result. Rule 26(b) prohibits a court of appeals from extending the time for taking appeal or seeking review.

1998 Amendments

The language of the rule is amended to make the rule more easily understood. In addition to changes made to improve the understanding, the Advisory Committee has changed the language to make style and terminology consistent throughout the appellate rules. These changes are intended to by stylistic only.

TITLE II. APPEAL FROM A JUDGMENT OR ORDER OF A DISTRICT COURT

Rule 3. Appeal as of Right—How Taken

(a) Filing the Notice of Appeal.

(1) An appeal permitted by law as of right from a district court to a court of appeals may be taken only by filing a notice of appeal with the district clerk within the time allowed by Rule 4. At the time of filing, the appellant must furnish the clerk with enough copies of the notice to enable the clerk to comply with Rule 3(d).

(2) An appellant's failure to take any step other than the timely filing of a notice of appeal does not affect the validity of the appeal, but is ground only for the court of appeals to act as it considers appropriate, including dismissing the appeal.

(3) An appeal from a judgment by a magistrate judge in a civil case is taken in the same way as an appeal from any other district court judgment.

(4) An appeal by permission under 28 U.S.C. § 1292(b) or an appeal in a bankruptcy case may be taken only in the manner prescribed by Rules 5 and 6, respectively.

(b) Joint or Consolidated Appeals.

(1) When two or more parties are entitled to appeal from a district-court judgment or order, and their interests make joinder practicable, they may file a joint notice of appeal. They may then proceed on appeal as a single appellant.

(2) When the parties have filed separate timely notices of appeal, the appeals may be joined or consolidated by the court of appeals.

(c) Contents of the Notice of Appeal.

(1) The notice of appeal must:

(A) specify the party or parties taking the appeal by naming each one in the caption or body of the notice, but an attorney representing more than one party may describe those parties with such terms as "all plaintiffs," "the defendants," "the plaintiffs A, B, et al.," or "all defendants except X";

(B) designate the judgment, order, or part thereof being appealed; and

(C) name the court to which the appeal is taken.

(2) A pro se notice of appeal is considered filed on behalf of the signer and the signer's spouse and minor children (if they are parties), unless the notice clearly indicates otherwise.

(3) In a class action, whether or not the class has been certified, the notice of appeal is sufficient if it names one person qualified to bring the appeal as representative of the class.

(4) An appeal must not be dismissed for informality of form or title of the notice of appeal, or for failure to name a party whose intent to appeal is otherwise clear from the notice.

(5) Form 1 in the Appendix of Forms is a suggested form of a notice of appeal.

(d) Serving the Notice of Appeal.

(1) The district clerk must serve notice of the filing of a notice of appeal by mailing a copy to each party's counsel of record—excluding the appellant's—or, if a party is proceeding pro se, to the party's last known address. When a defendant in a criminal case appeals, the clerk must also serve a copy of the notice of appeal on the defendant, either by personal service or by mail addressed to the

defendant. The clerk must promptly send a copy of the notice of appeal and of the docket entries—and any later docket entries—to the clerk of the court of appeals named in the notice. The district clerk must note, on each copy, the date when the notice of appeal was filed.

(2) If an inmate confined in an institution files a notice of appeal in the manner provided by Rule 4(c), the district clerk must also note the date when the clerk docketed the notice.

(3) The district clerk's failure to serve notice does not affect the validity of the appeal. The clerk must note on the docket the names of the parties to whom the clerk mails copies, with the date of mailing. Service is sufficient despite the death of a party or the party's counsel.

(e) Payment of Fees. Upon filing a notice of appeal, the appellant must pay the district clerk all required fees. The district clerk receives the appellate docket fee on behalf of the court of appeals.

(As amended Apr. 30, 1979, eff. Aug. 1, 1979; Mar. 10, 1986, eff. July 1, 1986; Apr. 25, 1989, eff. Dec. 1, 1989; Apr. 22, 1993, eff. Dec. 1, 1993; Apr. 29, 1994, eff. Dec. 1, 1994; Apr. 24, 1998, eff. Dec. 1, 1998.)

1967 Adoption

General Note. Rule 3 and Rule 4 combine to require that a notice of appeal be filed with the clerk of the district court within the time prescribed for taking an appeal. Because the timely filing of a notice of appeal is "mandatory and jurisdictional," *United States v. Robinson*, 361 U.S. 220, 224, 80 S.Ct. 282, 4 L.Ed.2d 259 (1960), compliance with the provisions of those rules is of the utmost importance. But the proposed rules merely restate, in modified form, provisions now found in the civil and criminal rules (FRCP 5(e), 73 [Rules 5(e) and 73, Federal Rules of Civil Procedure]; FRCrP 37 [rule 37, Federal Rules of Criminal Procedure], and decisions under the present rules which dispense with literal compliance in cases in which it cannot fairly be exacted should control interpretation of these rules. Illustrative decisions are: *Fallen v. United States*, 378 U.S. 139, 84 S.Ct. 1689, 12 L.Ed.2d 760 (1964) (notice of appeal by a prisoner, in the form of a letter delivered, well within the time fixed for appeal, to prison authorities for mailing to the clerk of the district court held timely filed notwithstanding that it was received by the clerk after expiration of the time for appeal; the appellant "did all he could" to effect timely filing); *Richey v. Wilkins*, 335 F.2d 1 (2d Cir. 1964) (notice filed in the court of appeals by a prisoner without assistance of counsel held sufficient); *Halfen v. United States*, 324 F.2d 52 (10th Cir. 1963) (notice mailed to district judge in time to have been received by him in normal course held sufficient); *Riffle v. United States*, 299 F.2d 802 (5th Cir. 1962) (letter of prisoner to judge of court of appeals held sufficient). Earlier cases evidencing "a liberal view of papers filed by indigent and incarcerated defendants" are listed in *Coppedge v. United States*, 369 U.S. 438, 442, n. 5, 82 S.Ct. 917, 8 L.Ed.2d 21 (1962).

Subdivision (a). The substance of this subdivision is derived from FRCP 73(a) [rule 73(a), Federal Rules of Civil Procedure] and FRCrP 37(a)(1) [rule 37(a)(1), Federal Rules of Criminal Procedure]. The proposed rule follows those rules in requiring nothing other than the filing of a notice of appeal in the district court for the perfection of the appeal. The petition for allowance (except for appeals governed by Rules 5 and 6), citations, assignments of error, summons and severance—all specifically abolished by earlier modern rules—are assumed to be sufficiently obsolete as no longer to require pointed abolition.

Subdivision (b). The first sentence is derived from FRCP 74 [rule 74, Federal Rules of Civil Procedure]. The second sentence is added to encourage consolidation of appeals whenever feasible.

Subdivision (c). This subdivision is identical with corresponding provisions in FRCP 73(b) [rule 73(b), Federal Rules of Civil Procedure] and FRCrP 37(a)(1) [rule 37(a)(1), Federal Rules of Criminal Procedure].

Subdivision (d). This subdivision is derived from FRCP 73(b) [rule 73(b), Federal Rules of Civil Procedure] and FRCrP 37(a)(1) [rule 37(a)(1), Federal Rules of Criminal Procedure]. The duty of the clerk to forward a copy of the notice of appeal and of the docket entries to the court of appeals in a criminal case is extended to habeas corpus and 28 U.S.C. § 2255 proceedings.

1979 Amendments

Subdivision (c). The proposed amendment would add the last sentence. Because of the fact that the timely filing of the notice of appeal has been characterized as jurisdictional (see, e.g., Brainerd v. Real (C.A. 7th, 1974) 498 F.2d 901, in which the filing of a notice of appeal one day late was fatal), it is important that the right to appeal not be lost by mistakes of mere form. In a number of decided cases it has been held that so long as the function of notice is met by the filing of a paper indicating an intention to appeal, the substance of the rule has been complied with. See, e.g., Cobb v. Lewis (C.A. 5th, 1974), 488 F.2d 41; *Holley v. Capps* (C.A. 5th, 1972) 468 F.2d 1366. The proposed amendment would give recognition to this practice.

When a notice of appeal is filed, the clerk should ascertain whether any judgment designated therein has been entered in compliance with Rules 58 and 79(a) of the F.R.C.P. [rules 58 and 79(a), Federal Rules of Civil Procedure]. See Note to Rule 4(a)(6), *infra*.

Subdivision (d). The proposed amendment would extend to civil cases the present provision applicable to criminal cases, habeas corpus cases, and proceedings under 28 U.S.C. § 2255, requiring the clerk of the district court to transmit to the clerk of the court of appeals a copy of the notice of appeal and of the docket entries, which should include reference to compliance with the requirements for payment of fees. See Note to (e), *infra*.

This requirement is the initial step in proposed changes in the rules to place in the court of appeals an increased practical control over the early steps in the appeal.

Subdivision (e). Proposed new Rule 3(e) represents the second step in shifting to the court of appeals the control of the early stages of an appeal. See Note to Rule 3(d) above. Under the present rules the payment of the fee prescribed by 28 U.S.C. 1917 is not covered. Under the statute, however, this fee is paid to the clerk of the district court at the time the notice of appeal is filed. Under present Rule 12, the "docket fee" fixed by the Judicial Conference of the United States under 28 U.S.C. § 1913 must be paid to the clerk of the court of appeals within the time fixed for transmission of the record, ". . . and the clerk shall thereupon enter the appeal upon the docket."

Under the proposed new Rule 3(e) both fees would be paid to the clerk of the district court at the time the notice of appeal is filed, the clerk of the district court receiving the docket fee on behalf of the court of appeals.

In view of the provision in Rule 3(a) that "[f]ailure of an appellant to take any step other than the timely filing of a notice of appeal does not affect the validity of the appeal, but is ground only for such action as the court of appeals deems appropriate, which may include dismissal of the appeal," the case law indicates that the failure to prepay the statutory filing fee does not constitute a jurisdictional defect. See *Parissi v. Telechron*, 349 U.S. 46 (1955); *Gould v. Members of N.J. Division of Water Policy & Supply*, 555 F.2d 340 (3d Cir. 1977). Similarly, under present Rule 12, failure to pay the docket fee within the time prescribed may be excused by the court of appeals. See, e.g., *Walker v. Mathews*, 546 F.2d 814 (9th Cir. 1976). Proposed new Rule 3(e) adopts the view of these cases, requiring that both fees be paid at the time the notice of appeal is filed, but subject to the provisions of Rule 26(b) preserving the authority of the court of appeals to permit late payment.

1986 Amendments

The amendments to Rule 3(d) are technical. No substantive change is intended.

1989 Amendments

The amendment is technical. No substantive change is intended.

1993 Amendments

Note to subdivision (c). The amendment is intended to reduce the amount of satellite litigation spawned by the Supreme Court's decision in Torres v. Oakland Scavenger Co., 487 U.S. 312 (1988). In Torres the Supreme Court held that the language in Rule 3(c) requiring a notice of appeal to "specify the party or parties taking the appeal" is a jurisdictional requirement and that naming the first named party and adding "et al.," without any further specificity is insufficient to identify the appellants. Since the Torres decision, there has been a great deal of litigation regarding whether a notice of appeal that contains some indication of the appellants' identities but does not name the appellants is sufficiently specific.

The amendment states a general rule that specifying the parties should be done by naming them. Naming an appellant in an otherwise timely and proper notice of appeal ensures that the appellant has perfected an appeal. However, in order to prevent the loss of a right to appeal through inadvertent omission of a party's name or continued use of such terms as "et al.," which are sufficient in all district court filings after the complaint, the amendment allows an attorney representing more than one party the flexibility to indicate which parties are appealing without naming them individually. The test established by the rule for determining whether such designations are sufficient is whether it is objectively clear that a party intended to appeal. A notice of appeal filed by a party proceeding pro se is filed on behalf of the party signing the notice and the signer's spouse and minor children, if they are parties, unless the notice clearly indicates a contrary intent.

In class actions, naming each member of a class as an appellant may be extraordinarily burdensome or even impossible. In class actions if class certification has been denied, named plaintiffs may appeal the order denying the class certification on their own behalf and on behalf of putative class members, *United States Parole Comm'n v. Geraghty*, 445 U.S. 388 (1980); or if the named plaintiffs choose not to appeal the order denying the class certification, putative class members may appeal, *United Airlines, Inc. v. McDonald*, 432 U.S. 385 (1977). If no class has been certified, naming each of the putative class members as an appellant would often be impossible. Therefore the amendment provides that in class actions, whether or not the class has been certified, it is sufficient for the notice to name one person qualified to bring the appeal as a representative of the class.

Finally, the rule makes it clear that dismissal of an appeal should not occur when it is otherwise clear from the notice that the party intended to appeal. If a court determines it is objectively clear that a party intended to appeal, there are neither administrative concerns nor fairness concerns that should prevent the appeal from going forward.

Note to subdivision (d). The amendment requires the district court clerk to send to the clerk of the court of appeals a copy of every docket entry in a case after the filing of a notice of appeal. This amendment accompanies the amendment to Rule 4(a)(4), which provides that when one of the posttrial motions enumerated in Rule 4(a)(4) is filed, a notice of appeal filed before the disposition of the motion becomes effective upon disposition of the motion. The court of appeals needs to be advised that the filing of a posttrial motion has suspended a notice of appeal. The court of appeals also needs to know when the district court has ruled on the motion. Sending copies of all docket entries after the filing of a notice of appeal should provide the courts of appeals with the necessary information.

1994 Amendments

Subdivision (a). The amendment requires a party filing a notice of appeal to provide the court with sufficient copies of the notice for service on all other parties.

1998 Amendments

The language and organization of the rule are amended to make the rule more easily understood. In addition to changes made to improve the understanding, the Advisory Committee has changed language to make style and terminology consistent throughout the appellate rules. These changes are generally intended to by stylistic only; in this rule, however, substantive changes are made in subdivisions (a), (b), and (d).

Subdivision (a). The provision in paragraph (a)(3) is transferred from former Rule 3.1(b). The Federal Courts Improvement Act of 1996, Pub.L. No. 104–317, repealed paragraphs (4) and (5) of 28 U.S.C. § 636(c). That statutory change made the continued separate existence of Rule 3.1 unnecessary. New paragraph (a)(3) of this rule simply makes it clear that an appeal from a judgment by a magistrate judge is taken in identical fashion to any other appeal from a district-court judgment.

Subdivision (b). A joint appeal is authorized only when two or more persons may appeal from a single judgment or order. A joint appeal is treated as a single appeal and the joint appellants file a single brief. Under existing Rule 3(b) parties decide whether to join their appeals. They may do so by filing a joint notice of appeal or by joining their appeals after filing separate notices of appeal.

In consolidated appeals the separate appeals do not merge into one. The parties do not proceed as a single appellant. Under existing Rule 3(b) it is unclear whether appeals may be consolidated without court order if the parties stipulate to consolidation. The language resolves that ambiguity by requiring court action.

The language also requires court action to join appeals after separate notices of appeal have been filed.

Subdivision (d). Paragraph (d)(2) has been amended to require that when an inmate files a notice of appeal by depositing the notice in the institution's internal mail system, the clerk must note the docketing date—rather than the receipt date—on the notice of appeal before serving copies of it. This change conforms to a change in Rule 4(c). Rule 4(c) is amended to provide that when an inmate files the first notice of appeal in a civil case by depositing the notice in an institution's internal mail system, the time for filing a cross-appeal runs from the date the district court dockets the inmate's notice of appeal. Existing Rule 4(c) says that in such a case the time for filing a cross-appeal runs from the date the district court receives the inmate's notice of appeal. A court may "receive" a paper when its mail is delivered to it even if the mail is not processed for a day or two, making the date of receipt uncertain. "Docketing" is an easily identified event. The change is made to eliminate the uncertainty.

[Rule 3.1. Abrogated Apr. 24, 1998, eff. Dec. 1, 1998]

1998 Amendments

The Federal Courts Improvement Act of 1996, Pub.L. No. 104-317, repealed paragraphs (4) and (5) of 28 U.S.C. § 636(c). That statutory change means that when parties consent to trial before a magistrate judge, appeal lies directly, and as a matter of right, to the court of appeals under § 636(c)(3). The parties may not choose to appeal first to a district judge and thereafter seek discretionary review in the court of appeals.

As a result of the statutory amendments, subdivision (a) of Rule 3.1 is no longer necessary. Since Rule 3.1 existed primarily because of the provisions in subdivision (a), subdivision (b) has been moved to Rule 3(a)(3) and Rule 3.1 has been abrogated.

HISTORICAL NOTES

The abrogated rule provided that: "When the parties consent to a trial before a magistrate judge under 28 U.S.C. § 636(c)(1), any appeal from the judgment must be heard by the court of appeals in accordance with 28 U.S.C. § 636(c)(3), unless the parties consent to an appeal on the record to a district judge and thereafter, by petition only, to the court of appeals, in accordance with 28 U.S.C. § 636(c)(4). An appeal under 28 U.S.C. § 636(c)(3) must be taken in identical fashion as an appeal from any other judgment of the district court."

Rule 4. Appeal as of Right—When Taken

(a) Appeal in a Civil Case.

(1) Time for Filing a Notice of Appeal.

(A) In a civil case, except as provided in Rules 4(a)(1)(B), 4(a)(4), and 4(c), the notice of appeal required by Rule 3 must be filed with the district clerk within 30 days after the judgment or order appealed from is entered.

(B) When the United States or its officer or agency is a party, the notice of appeal may be filed by any party within 60 days after the judgment or order appealed from is entered.

(C) An appeal from an order granting or denying an application for a writ of error coram nobis is an appeal in a civil case for purposes of Rule 4(a).

(2) Filing Before Entry of Judgment. A notice of appeal filed after the court announces a decision or order—but before the entry of the judgment or order—is treated as filed on the date of and after the entry.

(3) Multiple Appeals. If one party timely files a notice of appeal, any other party may file a notice of appeal within 14 days after the date when the first notice was filed, or within the time otherwise prescribed by this Rule 4(a), whichever period ends later.

(4) Effect of a Motion on a Notice of Appeal.

(A) If a party timely files in the district court any of the following motions under the Federal Rules of Civil Procedure, the time to file an appeal runs for all parties from the entry of the order disposing of the last such remaining motion:

(i) for judgment under Rule 50(b);

(ii) to amend or make additional factual findings under Rule 52(b), whether or not granting the motion would alter the judgment;

(iii) for attorney's fees under Rule 54 if the district court extends the time to appeal under Rule 58;

(iv) to alter or amend the judgment under Rule 59;

(v) for a new trial under Rule 59; or

(vi) for relief under Rule 60 if the motion is filed no later than 10 days after the judgment is entered.

(B)(i) If a party files a notice of appeal after the court announces or enters a judgment—but before it disposes of any motion listed in Rule 4(a)(4)(A)—the notice becomes effective to appeal a judgment or order, in whole or in part, when the order disposing of the last such remaining motion is entered.

(ii) A party intending to challenge an order disposing of any motion listed in Rule 4(a)(4)(A), or a judgment altered or amended upon such a motion, must file a notice of appeal, or an amended notice of appeal—in compliance with Rule 3(c)—within the time prescribed by this Rule measured from the entry of the order disposing of the last such remaining motion.

(iii) No additional fee is required to file an amended notice.

(5) Motion for Extension of Time.

(A) The district court may extend the time to file a notice of appeal if:

(i) a party so moves no later than 30 days after the time prescribed by this Rule 4(a) expires; and

(ii) regardless of whether its motion is filed before or during the 30 days after the time prescribed by this Rule 4(a) expires, that party shows excusable neglect or good cause.

(B) A motion filed before the expiration of the time prescribed in Rule 4(a)(1) or (3) may be ex parte unless the court requires otherwise. If the motion is filed after the expiration of the prescribed time, notice must be given to the other parties in accordance with local rules.

(C) No extension under this Rule 4(a)(5) may exceed 30 days after the prescribed time or 10 days after the date when the order granting the motion is entered, whichever is later.

(6) Reopening the Time to File an Appeal. The district court may reopen the time to file an appeal for a period of 14 days after the date when its order to reopen is entered, but only if all the following conditions are satisfied:

(A) the court finds that the moving party did not receive notice under Federal Rule of Civil Procedure 77(d) of the entry of the judgment or order sought to be appealed within 21 days after entry;

(B) the motion is filed within 180 days after the judgment or order is entered or within 7 days after the moving party receives notice under Federal Rule of Civil Procedure 77(d) of the entry, whichever is earlier; and

(C) the court finds that no party would be prejudiced.

(7) Entry Defined.

(A) A judgment or order is entered for purposes of this Rule 4(a):

(i) if Federal Rule of Civil Procedure 58(a)(1) does not require a separate document, when the judgment or order is entered in the civil docket under Federal Rule of Civil Procedure 79(a); or

(ii) if Federal Rule of Civil Procedure 58(a)(1) requires a separate document, when the judgment or order is entered in the civil docket under Federal Rule of Civil Procedure 79(a) and when the earlier of these events occurs:

- the judgment or order is set forth on a separate document, or
- 150 days have run from entry of the judgment or order in the civil docket under Federal Rule of Civil Procedure 79(a).

(B) A failure to set forth a judgment or order on a separate document when required by Federal Rule of Civil Procedure 58(a)(1) does not affect the validity of an appeal from that judgment or order.

(b) Appeal in a Criminal Case.

(1) Time for Filing a Notice of Appeal.

(A) In a criminal case, a defendant's notice of appeal must be filed in the district court within 10 days after the later of:

(i) the entry of either the judgment or the order being appealed; or

(ii) the filing of the government's notice of appeal.

(B) When the government is entitled to appeal, its notice of appeal must be filed in the district court within 30 days after the later of:

(i) the entry of the judgment or order being appealed; or

(ii) the filing of a notice of appeal by any defendant.

(2) Filing Before Entry of Judgment. A notice of appeal filed after the court announces a decision, sentence, or order—but before the entry of the judgment or order—is treated as filed on the date of and after the entry.

(3) Effect of a Motion on a Notice of Appeal.

(A) If a defendant timely makes any of the following motions under the Federal Rules of Criminal Procedure, the notice of appeal from a judgment of conviction must be filed within 10 days after the entry of the order disposing of the last such remaining motion, or within 10 days after the entry of the judgment of conviction, whichever period ends later. This provision applies to a timely motion:

(i) for judgment of acquittal under Rule 29;

(ii) for a new trial under Rule 33, but if based on newly discovered evidence, only if the motion is made no later than 10 days after the entry of the judgment; or

(iii) for arrest of judgment under Rule 34.

(B) A notice of appeal filed after the court announces a decision, sentence, or order—but before it disposes of any of the motions referred to in Rule 4(b)(3)(A)—becomes effective upon the later of the following:

(i) the entry of the order disposing of the last such remaining motion; or

(ii) the entry of the judgment of conviction.

(C) A valid notice of appeal is effective—without amendment—to appeal from an order disposing of any of the motions referred to in Rule 4(b)(3)(A).

(4) Motion for Extension of Time. Upon a finding of excusable neglect or good cause, the district court may—before or after the time has expired, with or without motion and notice—extend the time to file a notice of appeal for a period not to exceed 30 days from the expiration of the time otherwise prescribed by this Rule 4(b).

(5) Jurisdiction. The filing of a notice of appeal under this Rule 4(b) does not divest a district court of jurisdiction to correct a sentence under Federal Rule of Criminal Procedure 35(a), nor does the filing of a motion under 35(a) affect the validity of a notice of appeal filed before entry of the order disposing of the motion. The filing of a motion under Federal Rule of Criminal Procedure 35(a) does not suspend the time for filing a notice of appeal from a judgment of conviction.

(6) Entry Defined. A judgment or order is entered for purposes of this Rule 4(b) when it is entered on the criminal docket.

(c) Appeal by an Inmate Confined in an Institution.

(1) If an inmate confined in an institution files a notice of appeal in either a civil or a criminal case, the notice is timely if it is deposited in the institution's internal mail system on or before the last day for filing. If an institution has a system designed for legal mail, the inmate must use that system to receive the benefit of this rule. Timely filing may be shown by a declaration in compliance with 28 U.S.C. § 1746 or by a notarized statement, either of which must set forth the date of deposit and state that first-class postage has been prepaid.

(2) If an inmate files the first notice of appeal in a civil case under this Rule 4(c), the 14-day period provided in Rule 4(a)(3) for another party to file a notice of appeal runs from the date when the district court dockets the first notice.

(3) When a defendant in a criminal case files a notice of appeal under this Rule 4(c), the 30-day period for the government to file its notice of appeal runs from the entry of the judgment or order appealed from or from the district court's docketing of the defendant's notice of appeal, whichever is later.

(d) Mistaken Filing in the Court of Appeals. If a notice of appeal in either a civil or a criminal case is mistakenly filed in the court of appeals, the clerk of that court must note on the notice the date when it was received and send it to the district clerk. The notice is then considered filed in the district court on the date so noted.

(As amended Apr. 30, 1979, eff. Aug. 1, 1979; Nov. 18, 1988, Pub.L. 100-690, Title VII, § 7111, 102 Stat. 4419; Apr. 30, 1991, eff. Dec. 1, 1991; Apr. 22, 1993, eff. Dec. 1, 1993; Apr. 27, 1995, eff. Dec. 1, 1995; Apr. 24, 1998, eff. Dec. 1, 1998; Apr. 29, 2002, eff. Dec. 1, 2002; Apr. 25, 2005, eff. Dec. 1, 2005.)

1967 Adoption

Subdivision (a). This subdivision is derived from FRCP 73(a) [rule 73(a), Federal Rules of Civil Procedure, this title] without any change of substance. The requirement that a request for an extension of time for filing the notice of appeal made after expiration of the time be made by motion and on notice codifies the result reached under the present provisions of FRCP 73(a) and 6(b) [rules 73(a) and 6(b), Federal Rules of Civil Procedure]. *North Umberland Mining Co. v. Standard Accident Ins. Co.*, 193 F.2d 951 (9th Cir., 1952); *Cohen v. Plateau Natural Gas Co.*, 303 F.2d 273 (10th Cir., 1962); *Plant Economy, Inc. v. Mirror Insulation Co.*, 308 F.2d 275 (3d Cir., 1962).

Since this subdivision governs appeals in all civil cases, it supersedes the provisions of § 25 of the Bankruptcy Act (11 U.S.C. § 48). Except in cases to which the United States or an officer or agency thereof is a party, the change is a minor one, since a successful litigant in a bankruptcy proceeding may, under § 25, oblige an aggrieved party to appeal within 30 days after entry of judgment—the time fixed by this subdivision in cases involving private parties only—by serving him with notice of entry on the day thereof, and by the terms of § 25 and aggrieved party must in any event appeal within 40 days after entry of judgment. No reason appears why the time for appeal in bankruptcy should not be the same as that in civil cases generally. Furthermore, § 25 is a potential trap for the uninitiated. The time for appeal which it provides is not applicable to all appeals which may fairly be termed appeals in bankruptcy. Section 25 governs only those cause referred to in § 24 as "proceedings in bankruptcy" and "controversies arising in proceedings in bankruptcy." *Lowenstein v. Reikes*, 54 F.2d 481 (2d Cir., 1931), cert. den., 285 U.S. 539, 52 S.Ct. 311, 76 L.Ed. 932 (1932). The distinction between such cases and other cases which arise out of bankruptcy is often difficult to determine. See 2 Moore's Collier on Bankruptcy ¶24.12 through ¶24.36 (1962). As a result it is not always clear whether an appeal is governed by § 25 or by FRCP 73(a) [rule 73(a), Federal Rules of Civil Procedure, this title], which is applicable to such appeals in bankruptcy as are not governed by § 25.

In view of the unification of the civil and admiralty procedure accomplished by the amendments of the Federal Rules of Civil Procedure effective July 1, 1966, this subdivision governs appeals in those civil actions which involve admiralty or maritime claims and which prior to that date were known as suits in admiralty.

The only other change possibly effected by this subdivision is in the time for appeal from a decision of a district court on a petition for impeachment of an award of a board of arbitration under the Act of May 20, 1926, c. 347, § 9 (44 Stat. 585), 45 U.S.C. § 159. The act provides that a notice of appeal from such a decision shall be filed within 10 days of the decision. This singular provision was apparently repealed by the enactment in 1948 of 28 U.S.C. § 2107, which fixed 30 days from the date of entry of judgment as the time for appeal in all actions a civil nature except actions in admiralty or bankruptcy matters or those in which the United States is a party. But it was not expressly repealed, and its status is in doubt. See 7 Moore's Federal Practice ¶73.09[2] (1966). The doubt should be resolved, and no reason appears why appeals in such cases should not be taken within the time provided for civil cases generally.

Subdivision (b). This subdivision is derived from FRCrP 37(a)(2) [rule 37(a)(2), Federal Rules of Criminal Procedure] without change of substance.

1979 Amendment

Subdivision (a)(1). The words "(including a civil action which involves an admiralty or maritime claim and a proceeding in bankruptcy or a controversy arising therein)," which appear in the present rule are struck out as unnecessary and perhaps misleading in suggesting that there may be other categories that are not either civil or criminal within the meaning of Rule 4(a) and (b).

The phrases "within 30 days of such entry" and "within 60 days of such entry" have been changed to read "after" instead of "or." The change is for clarity only, since the word "of" in the present rule appears to be used to mean "after." Since the proposed amended rule deals directly with the premature filing of a notice of appeal, it was thought useful to emphasize the fact that except as provided, the period during which a notice of appeal may be filed is the 30 days, or 60 days as the case may be, following the entry of the judgment or order appealed from. See Notes to Rule 4(a)(2) and (4), below.

Subdivision (a)(2). The proposed amendment to Rule 4(a)(2) would extend to civil cases the provisions of Rule 4(b), dealing with criminal cases, designed to avoid the loss of the right to appeal by filing the notice of appeal prematurely. Despite the absence of such a provision in Rule 4(a) the courts of appeals quite generally have held premature appeals effective. See, e.g., *Matter of Grand Jury Empanelled Jan. 21, 1975*, 541 F.2d 373 (3d Cir. 1976); *Hodge v. Hodge*, 507 F.2d 87 (3d Cir. 1976); *Song Jook Suh v. Rosenberg*, 437 F.2d 1098 (9th Cir. 1971); *Ruby v. Secretary of the Navy*, 365 F.2d 385 (9th Cir. 1966); *Firchau v. Diamond Nat'l Corp.*, 345 F.2d 269 (9th Cir. 1965).

The proposed amended rule would recognize this practice but make an exception in cases in which a post trial motion has destroyed the finality of the judgment. See Note to Rule 4(a)(4) below.

Subdivision (a)(4). The proposed amendment would make it clear that after the filing of the specified post trial motions, a notice of appeal should await disposition of the motion. Since the proposed amendments to Rules 3, 10, and 12 contemplate that immediately upon the filing of the notice of appeal the fees will be paid and the case docketed in the court of appeals, and the steps toward its disposition set in motion, it would be undesirable to proceed with the appeal while the district court has before it a motion the granting of which would vacate or alter the judgment appealed from. See, e.g., *Keith v. Newcourt*, 530 F.2d 826 (8th Cir. 1976). Under the present rule, since docketing may not take place until the record is transmitted, premature filing is much less likely to involve waste effort. See, e.g. *Stockes v. Peyton's Inc.*, 508 F.2d 1287 (5th Cir. 1975). Further, since a notice of appeal filed before the disposition of a post trial motion, even if it were treated as valid for purposes of jurisdiction, would not embrace objections to the denial of the motion, it is obviously preferable to postpone the notice of appeal until after the motion is disposed of.

The present rule, since it provides for the "termination" of the "running" of the appeal time, is ambiguous in its application to a notice of appeal filed prior to a post trial motion filed within the 10 day limit. The amendment would make it clear that in such circumstances the appellant should not proceed with the appeal during pendency of the motion but should file a new notice of appeal after the motion is disposed of.

Subdivision (a)(5). Under the present rule it is provided that upon a showing of excusable neglect the district court at any time may extend the time for the filing of a notice of appeal for a period not to exceed 30 days from the expiration of the time otherwise prescribed by the rule, but that if the application is made after the original time has run, the order may be made only on motion with such notice as the court deems appropriate.

A literal reading of this provision would require that the extension be ordered and the notice of appeal filed within the 30 day period, but despite the surface clarity of the rule, it has produced considerable confusion. See the discussion by Judge Friendly in In re Orbitek, 520 F.2d 358 (2d Cir. 1975). The proposed amendment would make it clear that a motion to extend the time must be filed no later than 30 days after the expiration of the original appeal time, and that if the motion is timely filed the district court may act upon the motion at a later date, and may extend the time not in excess of 10 days measured from the date on which the order granting the motion is entered.

Under the present rule there is a possible implication that prior to the time the initial appeal time has run, the district court may extend the time on the basis of an informal application. The amendment would require that the application must be made by motion, though the motion may be made *ex parte*. After the expiration of the initial time a motion for the extension of the time must be made in compliance with the F.R.C.P. [Federal Rules of Civil Procedure] and local rules of the district court. See Note to proposed amended Rule 1, *supra*. And see Rules 6(d), 7(b) of the F.R.C.P. [rules 6(d) and 7(b), Federal Rules of Civil Procedure].

The proposed amended rule expands to some extent the standard for the grant of an extension of time. The present rule requires a "showing of excusable neglect." While this was an appropriate standard in cases in which the motion is made after the time for filing the notice of appeal has run, and remains so, it has never fit exactly the situation in which the appellant seeks an extension before the expiration of the initial time. In such a case "good cause," which is the standard that is applied in the granting of other extensions of time under Rule 26(b) seems to be more appropriate.

Subdivision (a)(6). The proposed amendment would call attention to the requirement of Rule 58 of the F.R.C.P. [Federal Rules of Civil Procedure] that the judgment constitute a separate document. See *United States v. Indrelunas*, 411 U.S. 216 (1973). When a notice of appeal is filed, the clerk should ascertain whether any judgment designated therein has been entered in compliance with Rules 58 and 79(a) and if not, so advise all parties and the district judge. While the requirement of Rule 58 is not jurisdictional, (see *Bankers Trust Co. v. Mallis*, 431 U.S. 928 (1977)), compliance is important since the time for the filing of a notice of appeal by other parties is measured by the time at which the judgment is properly entered.

1991 Amendment

The amendment provides a limited opportunity for relief in circumstances where the notice of entry of a judgment or order, required to be mailed by the clerk of the district court pursuant to Rule 77(d) of the Federal Rules of Civil Procedure, is either not received by a party or is received so late as to impair the opportunity to file a timely notice of appeal. The amendment adds a new subdivision (6) allowing a district court to reopen for a brief period the time for appeal upon a finding that notice of entry of a judgment or order was not received from the clerk or a party within 21 days of its entry and that no party would be prejudiced. By "prejudice" the Committee means some adverse consequence other than the cost of having to oppose the appeal and encounter the risk of reversal, consequences that are present in every appeal. Prejudice might arise, for example, if the appellee had taken some action in reliance on the expiration of the normal time period for filing a notice of appeal.

Reopening may be ordered only upon a motion filed within 180 days of the entry of a judgment or order or within 7 days of receipt of notice of such entry, whichever is earlier. This provision establishes an outer time limit of 180 days for a party who fails to receive timely notice of entry of a judgment to seek additional time to appeal and enables any winning party to shorten the 180–day period by sending (and establishing proof of receipt of) its own notice of entry of a judgment, as authorized by Fed.R.Civ.P. 77(d). Winning parties are encouraged to send their own notice in order to lessen the chance that a judge will accept a claim of nonreceipt in the face of evidence that notices were sent by both the clerk and the winning party. Receipt of a winning party's notice will shorten only the time for reopening the time for appeal under this subdivision, leaving the normal time periods for appeal unaffected.

If the motion is granted, the district court may reopen the time for filing a notice of appeal only for a period of 14 days from the date of entry of the order reopening the time for appeal.

Transmittal Note: Upon transmittal of this rule to Congress, the Advisory Committee recommends that the attention of Congress be called to the fact that language in the fourth paragraph of 28 U.S.C. § 2107 might appropriately be revised in light of this proposed rule.

1993 Amendment

Note to Paragraph (a)(1). The amendment is intended to alert readers to the fact that paragraph (a)(4) extends the time for filing an appeal when certain posttrial motions are filed. The Committee hopes that awareness of the provisions of paragraph (a)(4) will prevent the filing of a notice of appeal when a posttrial tolling motion is pending.

Note to Paragraph (a)(2). The amendment treats a notice of appeal filed after the announcement of a decision or order, but before its formal entry, as if the notice had been filed after entry. The amendment deletes the language that made paragraph (a)(2) inapplicable to a notice of appeal filed after announcement of the disposition of a posttrial motion enumerated in paragraph (a)(4) but before the entry of the order, see *Acosta v. Louisiana Dep't of Health & Human Resources*, 478 U.S. 251 (1986) (per curiam); *Alerte v. McGinnis*, 898 F.2d 69 (7th Cir.1990). Because the amendment of paragraph (a)(4) recognizes all notices of appeal filed after announcement or entry of judgment—even those that are filed while the posttrial motions enumerated in paragraph (a)(4) are pending—the amendment of this paragraph is consistent with the amendment of paragraph (a)(4).

Note to Paragraph (a)(3). The amendment is technical in nature; no substantive change is intended.

Note to Paragraph (a)(4). The 1979 amendment of this paragraph created a trap for an unsuspecting litigant who files a notice of appeal before a posttrial motion, or while a posttrial motion is pending. The 1979 amendment requires a party to file a new notice of appeal after the motion's disposition. Unless a new notice is filed, the court of appeals lacks jurisdiction to hear the appeal. *Griggs v. Provident Consumer Discount Co.*, 459 U.S. 56 (1982). Many litigants, especially pro se litigants, fail to file the second notice of appeal, and several courts have expressed dissatisfaction with the rule. See, e.g., *Averhart v. Arrendondo*, 773 F.2d 919 (7th Cir.1985); *Harcon Barge Co. v. D & G Boat Rentals, Inc.*, 746 F.2d 278 (5th Cir.1984), cert. denied, 479 U.S. 930 (1986).

The amendment provides that a notice of appeal filed before the disposition of a specified posttrial motion will become effective upon disposition of the motion. A notice filed before the filing of one of the specified motions or after the filing of a motion but before disposition of the motion is, in effect, suspended until the motion is disposed of, whereupon, the previously filed notice effectively places jurisdiction in the court of appeals.

Because a notice of appeal will ripen into an effective appeal upon disposition of a posttrial motion, in some instances there will be an appeal from a judgment that has been altered substantially because the motion was granted in whole or in part. Many such appeals will be dismissed for want of prosecution when the appellant fails to meet the briefing schedule. But, the appellee may also move to strike the appeal. When responding to such a motion, the appellant would have an opportunity to state that, even though some relief sought in a posttrial motion was granted, the appellant still plans to pursue the appeal. Because the appellant's response would provide the appellee with sufficient notice of the appellant's intentions, the Committee does not believe that an additional notice of appeal is needed.

The amendment provides that a notice of appeal filed before the disposition of a posttrial tolling motion is sufficient to bring the underlying case, as well as any orders specified in the original notice, to the court of appeals. If the judgment is altered upon disposition of a posttrial motion, however, and if a party wishes to appeal from the disposition of the motion, the party must amend the notice to so indicate. When a party files an amended notice, no additional fees are required because the notice is an amendment of the original and not a new notice of appeal.

Paragraph (a)(4) is also amended to include, among motions that extend the time for filing a notice of appeal, a Rule 60 motion that is served within 10 days after entry of judgment. This eliminates the difficulty of determining whether a posttrial motion made within 10 days after entry of a judgment is a Rule 59(e) motion, which tolls the time for filing an appeal, or a Rule 60 motion, which historically has not tolled the time. The amendment comports with the practice in several circuits of treating all motions to alter or amend judgments that are made within 10 days after entry of judgment as Rule 59(e) motions for purposes of Rule 4(a)(4). See, e.g., *Finch v. City of Vernon*, 845 F.2d 256 (11th Cir.1988); *Rados v. Celotex Corp.*, 809 F.2d 170 (2d Cir.1986); *Skagerberg v. Oklahoma*, 797 F.2d 881 (10th Cir. 1986). To conform to a recent Supreme Court decision, however—*Budinich v. Becton Dickinson and Co.*, 486 U.S. 196 (1988)—the amendment excludes motions for attorney's fees from the class of motions that extend the filing time unless a district court, acting under Rule 58, enters an order extending the time for appeal. This amendment is to be read in conjunction with the amendment of Fed.R.Civ.P. 58.

Note to subdivision (b). The amendment grammatically restructures the portion of this subdivision that lists the types of motions that toll the time for filing an appeal. This restructuring is intended to make the rule easier to read. No substantive change is intended other than to add a motion for judgment of acquittal under Criminal Rule 29 to the list of tolling motions. Such a motion is the equivalent of a Fed.R.Civ.P. 50(b) motion for judgment notwithstanding the verdict, which tolls the running of time for an appeal in a civil case.

The proposed amendment also eliminates an ambiguity from the third sentence of this subdivision. Prior to this amendment, the third sentence provided that if one of the specified motions was filed, the time for filing an appeal would run from the entry of an order denying the motion. That sentence, like the parallel provision in Rule 4(a)(4), was intended to toll the running of time for appeal if one of the posttrial motions is timely filed. In a criminal case, however, the time for filing the motions runs not from entry of judgment (as it does in civil cases), but from the verdict or finding of guilt. Thus, in a criminal case, a posttrial motion may be disposed of more than 10 days before sentence is imposed, i.e. before the entry of judgment. *United States v. Hashagen*, 816 F.2d 899, 902 n. 5 (3d Cir.1987). To make it clear that a notice of appeal need not be filed before entry of judgment, the amendment states that an appeal may be taken within 10 days after the entry of an order disposing of the motion, or within 10 days after the entry of judgment, whichever is later. The amendment also changes the language in the third sentence providing that an appeal may be taken within 10 days after the entry of an order *denying* the motion; the amendment says instead that an appeal may be taken within 10 days after the entry of an order *disposing* of the last such motion outstanding. (Emphasis added) The change recognizes that there may be multiple posttrial motions filed and that, although one or more motions may be granted in whole or in part, a defendant may still wish to pursue an appeal.

The amendment also states that a notice of appeal filed before the disposition of any of the posttrial tolling motions becomes effective upon disposition of the motions. In most circuits this language simply restates the current practice. See *United States v. Cortes*, 895 F.2d 1245 (9th Cir.), cert. denied, 495 U.S. 939 (1990). Two circuits, however, have questioned that practice in light of the language of the rule, see *United States v. Gargano*, 826 F.2d 610 (7th Cir.1987), and *United States v. Jones*, 669 F.2d 559 (8th Cir.1982), and the Committee wishes to clarify the rule. The amendment is consistent with the proposed amendment of Rule 4(a)(4).

Subdivision (b) is further amended in light of new Fed. R.Crim.P. 35(c), which authorizes a sentencing court to correct any arithmetical, technical, or other clear errors in sentencing within 7 days after imposing the sentence. The Committee believes that a sentencing court should be able to act under Criminal Rule 35(c) even if a notice of appeal has already been filed; and that a notice of appeal should not be affected by the filing of a Rule 35(c) motion or by correction of a sentence under Rule 35(c).

Note to subdivision (c). In *Houston v. Lack*, 487 U.S. 266 (1988), the Supreme Court held that a *pro se* prisoner's notice of appeal is "filed" at the moment of delivery to prison authorities for forwarding to the district court. The amendment reflects that decision. The language of the amendment is similar to that in Supreme Court Rule 29.2.

Permitting an inmate to file a notice of appeal by depositing it in an institutional mail system requires adjustment of the rules governing the filing of cross-appeals. In a civil case, the time for filing a cross-appeal ordinarily runs from the date when the first notice of appeal is filed. If an inmate's notice of appeal is filed by depositing it in an institution's mail system, it is possible that the notice of appeal will not arrive in the district court until several days after the "filing" date and perhaps even after the time for filing a cross-appeal has expired. To avoid that problem, subdivision (c) provides that in a civil case when an institutionalized person files a notice of appeal by depositing it in the institution's mail system, the time for filing a cross-appeal runs from the district court's receipt of the notice. The amendment makes a parallel change regarding the time for the government to appeal in a criminal case.

1995 Amendment

Subdivision (a). Fed.R.Civ.P. 50, 52, and 59 were previously inconsistent with respect to whether certain postjudgment motions had to be filed or merely served no later than 10 days after entry of judgment. As a consequence Rule 4(a)(4) spoke of making or serving such motions rather than filing them. Civil Rules 50, 52, and 59, are being revised to require filing before the end of the 10–day period. As a consequence, this rule is being amended to provide that 'filing' must occur within the 10 day period in order to affect the finality of the judgment and extend the period for filing a notice of appeal.

The Civil Rules require the filing of postjudgment motions 'no later than 10 days after entry of judgment'—rather than 'within' 10 days—to include postjudgment motions that are filed before actual entry of the judgment by the clerk. This rule is amended, therefore, to use the same terminology.

The rule is further amended to clarify the fact that a party who wants to obtain review of an alteration or amendment of a judgment must file a notice of appeal or amend a previously filed notice to indicate intent to appeal from the altered judgment.

1998 Amendments

The language and organization of the rule are amended to make the rule more easily understood. In addition to changes made to improve the understanding the Advisory Committee has changed language to make style and terminology consistent throughout the appellate rules. These changes are intended to be stylistic only; in this rule, however, substantive changes are made in paragraphs (a)(6) and (b)(4), and in subdivision (c).

Subdivision (a), paragraph (1). Although the Advisory Committee does not intend to make any substantive changes in this paragraph, cross-references to Rules 4(a)(1)(B) and (4)(c) have been added to subparagraph (a)(1)(A).

Subdivision (a), paragraph (4). Item (iv) in subparagraph (A) of Rule 4(a)(4) provides that filing a motion for relief under Fed.R.Civ.P. 60 will extend the time for filing a notice of appeal if the Rule 60 motion is filed no later than 10 days after judgment is entered. Again, the Advisory Committee does not intend to make any substantive change in this paragraph. But because Fed.R.Civ.P. 6(a) and Fed.R.App.P. 26(a) have different methods for computing time, one might be uncertain whether the 10–day period referred to in Rule 4(a)(4) is computed using Civil Rule 6(a) or Appellate Rule 26(a). Because the Rule 60 motion is filed in the district court, and because Fed.R.App.P. 1(a)(2) says that when the appellate rules provide for filing a motion in the district court, "the procedure must comply with the practice of the district court," the rule provides that the 10–day period is computed using Fed.R.Civ.P. 6(a)

Subdivision (a), paragraph (6). Paragraph (6) permits a district court to reopen the time for appeal if a party has not received notice of the entry of judgment and no party would be prejudiced by the reopening. Before reopening the time for appeal, the existing rule requires the district court to find that the moving party was entitled to notice of the entry of judgment and did not receive it "from the clerk or any party within 21 days of its entry." The Advisory Committee makes a substantive change. The finding must be that the movant did not receive notice "from the district court or any party within 21 days after entry." This change broadens the type of notice that can preclude reopening the time for appeal. The existing rule provides that only notice from a party or from the clerk bars reopening. The new language precludes reopening if the movant has received notice from "the court."

Subdivision (b). Two substantive changes are made in what will be paragraph (b)(4). The current rule permits an extension of time to file a notice of appeal if there is a "showing of excusable neglect." First, the rule is amended to permit a court to extend the time for "good cause" as well as for excusable neglect. Rule 4(a) permits extensions for both reasons in civil cases and the Advisory Committee believes that "good cause" should be sufficient in criminal cases as well. The amendment does not limit extensions for good cause to instances in which the motion for extension of time is filed before the original time has expired. The rule gives the district court discretion to grant extensions for good cause whenever the court believes it appropriate to do so provided that the extended period does not exceed 30 days after the expiration of the time otherwise prescribed by Rule 4(b). Second, paragraph (b)(4) is amended to require only a "finding" of excusable neglect or good cause and not a "showing" of them. Because the rule authorizes the court to provide an extension without a motion, a "showing" is obviously not required; a "finding" is sufficient.

Subdivision (c). Substantive amendments are made in this subdivision. The current rule provides that if an inmate confined in an institution files a notice of appeal by depositing it in the institution's internal mail system, the notice is timely filed if deposited on or before the last day for filing. Some institutions have special internal mail systems for handling legal mail; such systems often record the date of deposit of mail by an inmate, the date of delivery of mail to an inmate, etc. The Advisory Committee amends the rule to require an inmate to use the system designed for legal mail, if there is one, in order to receive the benefit of this subdivision.

When an inmate uses the filing method authorized by subdivision (c), the current rule provides that the time for other parties to appeal begins to run from the date the district court "receives" the inmate's notice of appeal. The rule is amended so that the time for other parties begins to run when the district court "dockets" the inmates appeal. A court may "receive" a paper when its mail is delivered to it even if the mail is not processed for a day or two, making the date of receipt uncertain. "Docketing" is an easily identified event. The change eliminates uncertainty. Paragraph (c)(3) is further amended to make it clear that the time for the government to file its appeal runs from the later of the entry of the judgment or order appealed from or the district court's docketing of a defendant's notice filed under this paragraph (c).

2002 Amendments

Subdivision (a)(1)(C). The federal courts of appeals have reached conflicting conclusions about whether an appeal from an order granting or denying an application for a writ of error *coram nobis* is governed by the time limitations of Rule 4(a) (which apply in civil cases) or by the time limitations of Rule 4(b) (which apply in criminal cases). *Compare United States v. Craig*, 907 F.2d 653, 655–57, *amended* 919 F.2d 57 (7th Cir. 1990); *United States v. Cooper*, 876 F.2d 1192, 1193–94 (5th Cir. 1989); and *United States v. Keogh*, 391 F.2d 138, 140 (2d Cir. 1968) (applying the time limitations of Rule 4(a)); *with Yasui v. United States*, 772 F.2d 1496, 1498–99 (9th Cir. 1985); and *United States v. Mills*, 430 F.2d 526, 527–28 (8th Cir. 1970) (applying the time limitations of Rule 4(b)). A new part (C) has been added to Rule 4(a)(1) to resolve this conflict by providing that the time limitations of Rule 4(a) will apply.

Subsequent to the enactment of Fed. R. Civ. P. 60(b) and 28 U.S.C. § 2255, the Supreme Court has recognized the continued availability of a writ of error *coram nobis* in at least one narrow circumstance. In 1954, the Court permitted a litigant who had been convicted of a crime, served his full sentence, and been released from prison, but who was continuing to suffer a legal disability on account of the conviction, to seek a writ of error *coram nobis* to set aside the conviction. *United States v. Morgan*, 346 U.S. 502 (1954). As the Court recognized, in the *Morgan* situation an application for a writ of error *coram nobis* "is of the same general character as [a motion] under 28 U.S.C. § 2255." *Id.* at 506 n.4. Thus, it seems appropriate that the time limitations of

Rule 4(a), which apply when a district court grants or denies relief under 28 U.S.C. § 2255, should also apply when a district court grants or denies a writ of error *coram nobis*. In addition, the strong public interest in the speedy resolution of criminal appeals that is reflected in the shortened deadlines of Rule 4(b) is not present in the *Morgan* situation, as the party seeking the writ of error *coram nobis* has already served his or her full sentence.

Notwithstanding *Morgan*, it is not clear whether the Supreme Court continues to believe that the writ of error *coram nobis* is available in federal court. In civil cases, the writ has been expressly abolished by Fed. R. Civ. P. 60(b). In criminal cases, the Supreme Court has recently stated that it has become " 'difficult to conceive of a situation' " in which the writ " 'would be necessary or appropriate.' " *Carlisle v. United States*, 517 U.S. 416, 429 (1996) (quoting *United States v. Smith*, 331 U.S. 469, 475 n.4 (1947)). The amendment to Rule 4(a)(1) is not intended to express any view on this issue; rather, it is merely meant to specify time limitations for appeals.

Rule 4(a)(1)(C) applies only to motions that are in substance, and not merely in form, applications for writs of error *coram nobis*. Litigants may bring and label as applications for a writ of error *coram nobis* what are in reality motions for a new trial under Fed. R. Crim. P. 33 or motions for correction or reduction of a sentence under Fed. R. Crim. P. 35. In such cases, the time limitations of Rule 4(b), and not those of Rule 4(a), should be enforced.

Changes Made After Publication and Comments No changes were made to the text of the proposed amendment or to the Committee Note.

Subdivision (a)(4)(A)(vi). Rule 4(a)(4)(A)(vi) has been amended to remove a parenthetical that directed that the 10–day deadline be "computed using Federal Rule of Civil Procedure 6(a)." That parenthetical has become superfluous because Rule 26(a)(2) has been amended to require that all deadlines under 11 days be calculated as they are under Fed. R. Civ. P. 6(a).

Changes Made After Publication and Comments No changes were made to the text of the proposed amendment or to the Committee Note.

Subdivision (a)(5)(A)(ii). Rule 4(a)(5)(A) permits the district court to extend the time to file a notice of appeal if two conditions are met. First, the party seeking the extension must file its motion no later than 30 days after the expiration of the time originally prescribed by Rule 4(a). Second, the party seeking the extension must show either excusable neglect or good cause. The text of Rule 4(a)(5)(A) does not distinguish between motions filed prior to the expiration of the original deadline and those filed after the expiration of the original deadline. Regardless of whether the motion is filed before or during the 30 days after the original deadline expires, the district court may grant an extension if a party shows either excusable neglect or good cause.

Despite the text of Rule 4(a)(5)(A), most of the courts of appeals have held that the good cause standard applies only to motions brought prior to the expiration of the original deadline and that the excusable neglect standard applies only to motions brought during the 30 days following the expiration of the original deadline. *See Pontarelli v. Stone*, 930 F.2d 104, 109–10 (1st Cir. 1991) (collecting cases from the Second, Fifth, Sixth, Seventh, Eighth, Ninth, and Eleventh Circuits). These courts have relied heavily upon the Advisory Committee Note to the 1979 amendment to Rule 4(a)(5). But the Advisory Committee Note refers to a draft of the 1979 amendment that was ultimately rejected. The rejected draft directed that the good cause standard apply only to motions filed prior to the expiration of the original deadline. Rule 4(a)(5), as actually amended, did not. *See* 16A CHARLES ALAN WRIGHT, ET AL., FEDERAL PRACTICE AND PROCEDURE § 3950.3, at 148–49 (2d ed. 1996).

The failure of the courts of appeals to apply Rule 4(a)(5)(A) as written has also created tension between that rule and Rule 4(b)(4). As amended in 1998, Rule 4(b)(4) permits the district court to extend the time for filing a notice of appeal in a *criminal* case for an additional 30 days upon a finding of excusable neglect or good cause. Both Rule 4(b)(4) and the Advisory Committee Note to the 1998 amendment make it clear that an extension can be granted for either excusable neglect or good cause, regardless of whether a motion for an extension is filed before or during the 30 days following the expiration of the original deadline.

Rule 4(a)(5)(A)(ii) has been amended to correct this misunderstanding and to bring the rule in harmony in this respect with Rule 4(b)(4). A motion for an extension filed prior to the expiration of the original deadline may be granted if the movant shows either excusable neglect or good cause. Likewise, a motion for an extension filed during the 30 days following the expiration of the original deadline may be granted if the movant shows either excusable neglect or good cause.

The good cause and excusable neglect standards have "different domains." *Lorenzen v. Employees Retirement Plan*, 896 F.2d 228, 232 (7th Cir. 1990). They are not interchangeable, and one is not inclusive of the other. The excusable neglect standard applies in situations in which there is fault; in such situations, the need for an extension is usually occasioned by something within the control of the movant. The good cause standard applies in situations in which there is no fault—excusable or otherwise. In such situations, the need for an extension is usually occasioned by something that is not within the control of the movant.

Thus, the good cause standard can apply to motions brought during the 30 days following the expiration of the original deadline. If, for example, the Postal Service fails to deliver a notice of appeal, a movant might have good cause to seek a post-expiration extension. It may be unfair to make such a movant prove that its "neglect" was excusable, given that the movant may not have been neglectful at all. Similarly, the excusable neglect standard can apply to motions brought prior to the expiration of the original deadline. For example, a movant may bring a pre-expiration motion for an extension of time when an error committed by the movant makes it unlikely that the movant will be able to meet the original deadline.

Changes Made After Publication and Comments No changes were made to the text of the proposed amendment. The stylistic changes to the Committee Note suggested by Judge Newman were adopted. In addition, two paragraphs were added at the end of the Committee Note to clarify the difference between the good cause and excusable neglect standards.

Subdivision (a)(7). Several circuit splits have arisen out of uncertainties about how Rule 4(a)(7)'s definition of when a judgment or order is "entered" interacts with the requirement in Fed. R. Civ. P. 58 that, to be "effective," a judgment must be set forth on a separate document. Rule 4(a)(7) and Fed. R. Civ. P. 58 have been amended to resolve those splits.

1. The first circuit split addressed by the amendments to Rule 4(a)(7) and Fed. R. Civ. P. 58 concerns the extent to which orders that dispose of post-judgment motions must be set forth on separate documents. Under Rule 4(a)(4)(A), the filing of certain post-judgment motions tolls the time to appeal the underlying judgment until the "entry" of the order disposing of the last such remaining motion. Courts have disagreed about whether such an order must be set forth on a separate document before it is treated as "entered." This disagreement reflects a broader dispute among courts about whether Rule 4(a)(7) independently imposes a separate document requirement (a requirement that is distinct from the separate document requirement that is imposed by the Federal Rules of Civil Procedure ("FRCP")) or whether Rule 4(a)(7) instead incorporates the separate document requirement as it exists in the FRCP. Further complicating the matter, courts in the former "camp" disagree among themselves about the scope of the separate document requirement that they interpret Rule 4(a)(7) as imposing, and courts in the latter "camp" disagree among themselves about the scope of the separate document requirement imposed by the FRCP.

Rule 4(a)(7) has been amended to make clear that it simply incorporates the separate document requirement as it exists in Fed. R. Civ. P. 58. If Fed. R. Civ. P. 58 does not require that a judgment or order be set forth on a separate document, then neither does Rule 4(a)(7); the judgment or order will be deemed entered for purposes of Rule 4(a) when it is entered in the civil docket. If Fed. R. Civ. P. 58 requires that a judgment or order be set forth on a separate document, then so does Rule 4(a)(7); the judgment or order will not be deemed entered for purposes of Rule 4(a) until it is so set forth and entered in the civil docket (with one important exception, described below).

In conjunction with the amendment to Rule 4(a)(7), Fed. R. Civ. P. 58 has been amended to provide that orders disposing of the postjudgment motions listed in new Fed. R. Civ. P. 58(a)(1) (which postjudgment motions include, but are not limited to, the post-judgment motions that can toll the time to appeal under Rule 4(a)(4)(A)) do not have to be set forth on separate documents. *See* Fed. R. Civ. P. 58(a)(1). Thus, such orders are entered for purposes of Rule 4(a) when they are entered in the civil docket pursuant to Fed. R. Civ. P. 79(a). *See* Rule 4(a)(7)(A)(1).

2. The second circuit split addressed by the amendments to Rule 4(a)(7) and Fed. R. Civ. P. 58 concerns the following question: When a judgment or order is required to be set forth on a separate document under Fed. R. Civ. P. 58 but is not, does the time to appeal the judgment or order—or the time to bring post-judgment motions, such as a motion for a new trial under Fed. R. Civ. P. 59—ever begin to run? According to every circuit except the First Circuit, the answer is "no." The First Circuit alone holds that parties will be deemed to have waived their right to have a judgment or order entered on a separate document three months after the judgment or order is entered in the civil docket. *See Fiore v. Washington County Community Mental Health Ctr.*, 960 F.2d 229, 236 (1st Cir. 1992) (en banc). Other circuits have rejected this cap as contrary to the relevant rules. *See, e.g., United States v. Haynes*, 158 F.3d 1327, 1331 (D.C. Cir. 1998); *Hammack v. Baroid Corp.*, 142 F.3d 266, 269–70 (5th Cir. 1998); *Rubin v. Schottenstein, Zox & Dunn*, 110 F.3d 1247, 1253 n.4 (6th Cir. 1997), *vacated on other grounds*, 143 F.3d 263 (6th Cir. 1998) (en banc). However, no court has questioned the wisdom of imposing such a cap as a matter of policy.

Both Rule 4(a)(7)(A) and Fed. R. Civ. P. 58 have been amended to impose such a cap. Under the amendments, a judgment or order is generally treated as entered when it is entered in the civil docket pursuant to Fed. R. Civ. P. 79(a). There is one exception: When Fed. R. Civ. P. 58(a)(1) requires the judgment or order to be set forth on a separate document, that judgment or order is not treated as entered until it is set forth on a separate document (in addition to being entered in the civil docket) or until the expiration of 150 days after its entry in the civil docket, whichever occurs first. This cap will ensure that parties will not be given forever to appeal (or to bring a postjudgment motion) when a court fails to set forth a judgment or order on a separate document in violation of Fed. R. Civ. P. 58(a)(1).

3. The third circuit split—this split addressed only by the amendment to Rule 4(a)(7)—concerns whether the appellant may waive the separate document requirement over the objection of the appellee. In *Bankers Trust Co. v. Mallis*, 435 U.S. 381, 387 (1978) (per curiam), the Supreme Court held that the "parties to an appeal may waive the separate-judgment requirement of Rule 58." Specifically, the Supreme Court held that when a district court enters an order and "clearly evidence[s] its intent that the . . . order . . . represent[s] the final decision in the case," the order is a "final decision" for purposes of 28 U.S.C. § 1291, even if the order has not been set forth on a separate document for purposes of Fed. R. Civ. P. 58. *Id.* Thus, the parties can choose to appeal without waiting for the order to be set forth on a separate document.

Courts have disagreed about whether the consent of all parties is necessary to waive the separate document requirement. Some circuits permit appellees to object to attempted *Mallis* waivers and to force appellants to return to the trial court, request that judgment be set forth on a separate document, and appeal a second time. *See, e.g., Selletti v. Carey*, 173 F.3d 104, 109–10 (2d Cir. 1999); *Williams v. Borg*, 139 F.3d 737, 739–40 (9th Cir. 1998); *Silver Star Enters., Inc. v. M/V Saramacca*, 19 F.3d 1008, 1013 (5th Cir. 1994). Other courts disagree and permit *Mallis* waivers even if the appellee objects. *See, e.g., Haynes*, 158 F.3d at 1331; *Miller v. Artistic Cleaners*, 153 F.3d 781, 783–84 (7th Cir. 1998); *Alvord-Polk, Inc. v. F. Schumacher & Co.*, 37 F.3d 996, 1006 n.8 (3d Cir. 1994).

New Rule 4(a)(7)(B) is intended both to codify the Supreme Court's holding in *Mallis* and to make clear that the decision whether to waive the requirement that the judgment or order be set forth on a separate document is the appellant's alone. It is, after all, the appellant who needs a clear signal as to when the time to file a notice of appeal has begun to run. If the appellant chooses to bring an appeal without waiting for the judgment or order to be set forth on a separate document, then there is no reason why the appellee should be able to object. All that would result from honoring the appellee's objection would be delay.

4. The final circuit split addressed by the amendment to Rule 4(a)(7) concerns the question whether an appellant who chooses to waive the separate document requirement must

appeal within 30 days (60 days if the government is a party) from the entry in the civil docket of the judgment or order that should have been set forth on a separate document but was not. In *Townsend v. Lucas*, 745 F.2d 933 (5th Cir. 1984), the district court dismissed a 28 U.S.C. § 2254 action on May 6, 1983, but failed to set forth the judgment on a separate document. The plaintiff appealed on January 10, 1984. The Fifth Circuit dismissed the appeal, reasoning that, if the plaintiff waived the separate document requirement, then his appeal would be from the May 6 order, and if his appeal was from the May 6 order, then it was untimely under Rule 4(a)(1). The Fifth Circuit stressed that the plaintiff could return to the district court, move that the judgment be set forth on a separate document, and appeal from that judgment within 30 days. *Id.* at 934. Several other cases have embraced the *Townsend* approach. *See, e.g.*, *Armstrong v. Ahitow*, 36 F.3d 574, 575 (7th Cir. 1994) (per curiam); *Hughes v. Halifax County Sch. Bd.*, 823 F.2d 832, 835–36 (4th Cir. 1987); *Harris v. McCarthy*, 790 F.2d 753, 756 n.1 (9th Cir. 1986).

Those cases are in the distinct minority. There are numerous cases in which courts have heard appeals that were not filed within 30 days (60 days if the government was a party) from the judgment or order that should have been set forth on a separate document but was not. *See, e.g.*, *Haynes*, 158 F.3d at 1330–31; *Clough v. Rush*, 959 F.2d 182, 186 (10th Cir. 1992); *McCalden v. California Library Ass'n*, 955 F.2d 1214, 1218–19 (9th Cir. 1990). In the view of these courts, the remand in *Townsend* was "precisely the purposeless spinning of wheels abjured by the Court in the [*Mallis*] case." 15B CHARLES ALAN WRIGHT ET AL., FEDERAL PRACTICE AND PROCEDURE § 3915, at 259 n.8 (3d ed. 1992).

The Committee agrees with the majority of courts that have rejected the *Townsend* approach. In drafting new Rule 4(a)(7)(B), the Committee has been careful to avoid phrases such as "otherwise timely appeal" that might imply an endorsement of *Townsend*.

Changes Made After Publication and Comments No changes were made to the text of proposed Rule 4(a)(7)(B) or to the third or fourth numbered sections of the Committee Note, except that, in several places, references to a judgment being "entered" on a separate document were changed to references to a judgment being "set forth" on a separate document. This was to maintain stylistic consistency. The appellate rules and the civil rules consistently refer to "entering" judgments on the civil docket and to "setting forth" judgments on separate documents.

Two major changes were made to the text of proposed Rule 4(a)(7)(A)—one substantive and one stylistic. The substantive change was to increase the "cap" from 60 days to 150 days. The Appellate Rules Committee and the Civil Rules Committee had to balance two concerns that are implicated whenever a court fails to enter its final decision on a separate document. On the one hand, potential appellants need a clear signal that the time to appeal has begun to run, so that they do not unknowingly forfeit their rights. On the other hand, the time to appeal cannot be allowed to run forever. A party who receives no notice whatsoever of a judgment has only 180 days to move to reopen the time to appeal from that judgment. *See* Rule 4(a)(6)(A). It hardly seems fair to give a party who *does* receive notice of a judgment an unlimited amount of time to appeal, merely because that judgment was not set forth on a separate piece of paper. Potential appellees and the judicial system need *some* limit on the time within which appeals can be brought.

The 150–day cap properly balances these two concerns. When an order is not set forth on a separate document, what signals litigants that the order is final and appealable is a lack of further activity from the court. A 60–day period of inactivity is not sufficiently rare to signal to litigants that the court has entered its last order. By contrast, 150 days of inactivity is much less common and thus more clearly signals to litigants that the court is done with their case.

The major stylistic change to Rule 4(a)(7) requires some explanation. In the published draft, proposed Rule 4(a)(7)(A) provided that "[a] judgment or order is entered for purposes of this Rule 4(a) when it is entered for purposes of Rule 58(b) of the Federal Rules of Civil Procedure." In other words, Rule 4(a)(7)(A) told readers to look to FRCP 58(b) to ascertain when a judgment is entered for purposes of starting the running of the time to appeal. Sending appellate lawyers to the civil rules to discover when time began to run for purposes of the appellate rules was itself somewhat awkward, but it was made more confusing by the fact that, when readers went to proposed FRCP 58(b), they found this introductory clause: "Judgment is entered for purposes of Rules 50, 52, 54(d)(2)(B), 59, 60, and 62 when. . . . "

This introductory clause was confusing for both appellate lawyers and trial lawyers. It was confusing for appellate lawyers because Rule 4(a)(7) informed them that FRCP 58(b) would tell them when the time begins to run for purposes of the *appellate* rules, but when they got to FRCP 58(b) they found a rule that, by its terms, dictated only when the time begins to run for purposes of certain *civil* rules. The introductory clause was confusing for trial lawyers because FRCP 58(b) described when judgment is entered for some purposes under the civil rules, but then was completely silent about when judgment is entered for other purposes.

To avoid this confusion, the Civil Rules Committee, on the recommendation of the Appellate Rules Committee, changed the introductory clause in FRCP 58(b) to read simply: "Judgment is entered for purposes of *these Rules* when. . . . " In addition, Rule 4(a)(7)(A) was redrafted [1] so that the triggering events for the running of the time to appeal (entry in the civil docket, and being set forth on a separate document or passage of 150 days) were incorporated directly into Rule 4(a)(7), rather than indirectly through a reference to FRCP 58(b). This eliminates the need for appellate lawyers to examine Rule 58(b) and any chance that Rule 58(b)'s introductory clause (even as modified) might confuse them.

We do not believe that republication of Rule 4(a)(7) or FRCP 58 is necessary. In *substance*, rewritten Rule 4(a)(7)(A) and FRCP 58(b) operate identically to the published versions, except that the 60–day cap has been replaced with a 150–day cap—a change that was suggested by some of the commentators and that makes the cap more forgiving.

1. A redraft of Rule 4(a)(7) was faxed to members of the Appellate Rules Committee two weeks after our meeting in New Orleans. The Committee consented to the redraft without objection.

Subdivision (b)(5). Federal Rule of Criminal Procedure 35(a) permits a district court, acting within 7 days after the imposition of sentence, to correct an erroneous sentence in a criminal case. Some courts have held that the filing of a motion for correction of a sentence suspends the time for filing a notice of appeal from the judgment of conviction. *See, e.g.*, *United States v. Carmouche*, 138 F.3d 1014, 1016 (5th

Cir. 1998) (per curiam); *United States v. Morillo*, 8 F.3d 864, 869 (1st Cir. 1993). Those courts establish conflicting timetables for appealing a judgment of conviction after the filing of a motion to correct a sentence. In the First Circuit, the time to appeal is suspended only for the period provided by Fed. R. Crim. P. 35(a) for the district court to correct a sentence; the time to appeal begins to run again once 7 days have passed after sentencing, even if the motion is still pending. By contrast, in the Fifth Circuit, the time to appeal does not begin to run again until the district court actually issues an order disposing of the motion.

Rule 4(b)(5) has been amended to eliminate the inconsistency concerning the effect of a motion to correct a sentence on the time for filing a notice of appeal. The amended rule makes clear that the time to appeal continues to run, even if a motion to correct a sentence is filed. The amendment is consistent with Rule 4(b)(3)(A), which lists the motions that toll the time to appeal, and notably omits any mention of a Fed. R. Crim. P. 35(a) motion. The amendment also should promote certainty and minimize the likelihood of confusion concerning the time to appeal a judgment of conviction.

If a district court corrects a sentence pursuant to Fed. R. Crim. P. 35(a), the time for filing a notice of appeal of the corrected sentence under Rule 4(b)(1) would begin to run when the court enters a new judgment reflecting the corrected sentence.

Changes Made After Publication and Comments The reference to Federal Rule of Criminal Procedure 35(c) was changed to Rule 35(a) to reflect the pending amendment of Rule 35. The proposed amendment to Criminal Rule 35, if approved, will take effect at the same time that the proposed amendment to Appellate Rule 4 will take effect, if approved.

2005 Amendments

Rule 4(a)(6) has permitted a district court to reopen the time to appeal a judgment or order upon finding that four conditions were satisfied. First, the district court had to find that the appellant did not receive notice of the entry of the judgment or order from the district court or any party within 21 days after the judgment or order was entered. Second, the district court had to find that the appellant moved to reopen the time to appeal within 7 days after the appellant received notice of the entry of the judgment or order. Third, the district court had to find that the appellant moved to reopen the time to appeal within 180 days after the judgment or order was entered. Finally, the district court had to find that no party would be prejudiced by the reopening of the time to appeal.

Rule 4(a)(6) has been amended to specify more clearly what type of "notice" of the entry of a judgment or order precludes a party from later moving to reopen the time to appeal. In addition, Rule 4(a)(6) has been amended to address confusion about what type of "notice" triggers the 7-day period to bring a motion to reopen. Finally, Rule 4(a)(6) has been reorganized to set forth more logically the conditions that must be met before a district court may reopen the time to appeal.

Subdivision (a)(6)(A). Former subdivision (a)(6)(B) has been redesignated as subdivision (a)(6)(A), and one substantive change has been made. As amended, the subdivision will preclude a party from moving to reopen the time to appeal a judgment or order only if the party receives (within 21 days) formal notice of the entry of that judgment or order under Civil Rule 77(d). No other type of notice will preclude a party.

The reasons for this change take some explanation. Prior to 1998, former subdivision (a)(6)(B) permitted a district court to reopen the time to appeal if it found "that a party entitled to notice of the entry of a judgment or order did not receive such notice from the clerk or any party within 21 days of its entry." The rule was clear that the "notice" to which it referred was the notice required under Civil Rule 77(d), which must be served by the clerk pursuant to Civil Rule 5(b) and may also be served by a party pursuant to that same rule. In other words, prior to 1998, former subdivision (a)(6)(B) was clear that, if a party did not receive formal notice of the entry of a judgment or order under Civil Rule 77(d), that party could later move to reopen the time to appeal (assuming that the other requirements of subdivision (a)(6) were met).

In 1998, former subdivision (a)(6)(B) was amended to change the description of the type of notice that would preclude a party from moving to reopen. As a result of the amendment, former subdivision (a)(6)(B) no longer referred to the failure of the moving party to receive "*such* notice"—that is, the notice required by Civil Rule 77(d)—but instead referred to the failure of the moving party to receive "*the* notice." And former subdivision (a)(6)(B) no longer referred to the failure of the moving party to receive notice from "the *clerk* or any party," both of whom are explicitly mentioned in Civil Rule 77(d). Rather, former subdivision (a)(6)(B) referred to the failure of the moving party to receive notice from "the *district court* or any party."

The 1998 amendment meant, then, that the type of notice that precluded a party from moving to reopen the time to appeal was no longer limited to Civil Rule 77(d) notice. Under the 1998 amendment, *some* type of notice, in addition to Civil Rule 77(d) notice, precluded a party. But the text of the amended rule did not make clear what type of notice qualified. This was an invitation for litigation, confusion, and possible circuit splits.

To avoid such problems, former subdivision (a)(6)(B)—new subdivision (a)(6)(A)—has been amended to restore its pre-1998 simplicity. Under new subdivision (a)(6)(A), if the court finds that the moving party was not notified under Civil Rule 77(d) of the entry of the judgment or order that the party seeks to appeal within 21 days after that judgment or order was entered, then the court is authorized to reopen the time to appeal (if all of the other requirements of subdivision (a)(6) are met). Because Civil Rule 77(d) requires that notice of the entry of a judgment or order be formally served under Civil Rule 5(b), any notice that is not so served will not operate to preclude the reopening of the time to appeal under new subdivision (a)(6)(A).

Subdivision (a)(6)(B). Former subdivision (a)(6)(A) required a party to move to reopen the time to appeal "within 7 days after the moving party receives notice of the entry [of the judgment or order sought to be appealed]." Former subdivision (a)(6)(A) has been redesignated as subdivision (a)(6)(B), and one important substantive change has been made: The subdivision now makes clear that only formal notice of the entry of a judgment or order under Civil Rule 77(d) will trigger the 7-day period to move to reopen the time to appeal.

The circuits have been split over what type of "notice" is sufficient to trigger the 7-day period. The majority of circuits that addressed the question held that only *written* notice was sufficient, although nothing in the text of the rule suggested such a limitation. *See, e.g., Bass v. United States Dep't of Agric.*, 211 F.3d 959, 963 (5th Cir. 2000). By contrast, the Ninth Circuit held that while former subdivision (a)(6)(A) did not require written notice, "the quality of the communication [had to] rise to the functional equivalent of written notice." *Nguyen v. Southwest Leasing & Rental, Inc.*, 282 F.3d 1061, 1066 (9th Cir. 2002). Other circuits suggested in dicta that former subdivision (a)(6)(A) required only "actual notice," which, presumably, could have included oral notice that was not "the functional equivalent of written notice." *See, e.g., Lowry v. McDonnell Douglas Corp.*, 211 F.3d 457, 464 (8th Cir. 2000). And still other circuits read into former subdivision (a)(6)(A) restrictions that appeared only in former subdivision (a)(6)(B) (such as the requirement that notice be received "from the district court or any party," *see Benavides v. Bureau of Prisons*, 79 F.3d 1211, 1214 (D.C. Cir. 1996)) or that appeared in neither former subdivision (a)(6)(A) nor former subdivision (a)(6)(B) (such as the requirement that notice be served in the manner prescribed by Civil Rule 5, *see Ryan v. First Unum Life Ins. Co.*, 174 F.3d 302, 304–05 (2d Cir. 1999)).

Former subdivision (a)(6)(A)—new subdivision (a)(6)(B)—has been amended to resolve this circuit split by providing that only formal notice of the entry of a judgment or order under Civil Rule 77(d) will trigger the 7-day period. Using Civil Rule 77(d) notice as the trigger has two advantages: First, because Civil Rule 77(d) is clear and familiar, circuit splits are unlikely to develop over its meaning. Second, because Civil Rule 77(d) notice must be served under Civil Rule 5(b), establishing whether and when such notice was provided should generally not be difficult.

Using Civil Rule 77(d) notice to trigger the 7-day period will not unduly delay appellate proceedings. Rule 4(a)(6) applies to only a small number of cases—cases in which a party was not notified of a judgment or order by either the clerk or another party within 21 days after entry. Even with respect to those cases, an appeal cannot be brought more than 180 days after entry, no matter what the circumstances. In addition, Civil Rule 77(d) permits parties to serve notice of the entry of a judgment or order. The winning party can prevent Rule 4(a)(6) from even coming into play simply by serving notice of entry within 21 days. Failing that, the winning party can always trigger the 7-day deadline to move to reopen by serving belated notice.

Rule 5. Appeal by Permission

(a) Petition for Permission to Appeal.

(1) To request permission to appeal when an appeal is within the court of appeals' discretion, a party must file a petition for permission to appeal. The petition must be filed with the circuit clerk with proof of service on all other parties to the district-court action.

(2) The petition must be filed within the time specified by the statute or rule authorizing the appeal or, if no such time is specified, within the time provided by Rule 4(a) for filing a notice of appeal.

(3) If a party cannot petition for appeal unless the district court first enters an order granting permission to do so or stating that the necessary conditions are met, the district court may amend its order, either on its own or in response to a party's motion, to include the required permission or statement. In that event, the time to petition runs from entry of the amended order.

(b) Contents of the Petition; Answer or Cross-Petition; Oral Argument.

(1) The petition must include the following:

(A) the facts necessary to understand the question presented;

(B) the question itself;

(C) the relief sought;

(D) the reasons why the appeal should be allowed and is authorized by a statute or rule; and

(E) an attached copy of:

(i) the order, decree, or judgment complained of and any related opinion or memorandum, and

(ii) any order stating the district court's permission to appeal or finding that the necessary conditions are met.

(2) A party may file an answer in opposition or a cross-petition within 7 days after the petition is served.

(3) The petition and answer will be submitted without oral argument unless the court of appeals orders otherwise.

(c) Form of Papers; Number of Copies. All papers must conform to Rule 32(c)(2). Except by the court's permission, a paper must not exceed 20 pages, exclusive of the disclosure statement, the proof of service, and the accompanying documents required by Rule 5(b)(1)(E). An original and 3 copies must be filed unless the court requires a different number by local rule or by order in a particular case.

(d) Grant of Permission; Fees; Cost Bond; Filing the Record.

(1) Within 10 days after the entry of the order granting permission to appeal, the appellant must:

(A) pay the district clerk all required fees; and

(B) file a cost bond if required under Rule 7.

(2) A notice of appeal need not be filed. The date when the order granting permission to appeal is entered serves as the date of the notice of appeal for calculating time under these rules.

(3) The district clerk must notify the circuit clerk once the petitioner has paid the fees. Upon receiving this notice, the circuit clerk must enter the appeal on the docket. The record must be forwarded and filed in accordance with Rules 11 and 12(c).

(As amended Apr. 30, 1979, eff. Aug. 1, 1979; Apr. 29, 1994, eff. Dec. 1, 1994; Apr. 24, 1998, eff. Dec. 1, 1998; Apr. 29, 2002, eff. Dec. 1, 2002.)

1967 Adoption

This rule is derived in the main from Third Circuit Rule 11(2), which is similar to the rule governing appeals under 28 U.S.C. § 1292(b) in a majority of the circuits. The second sentence of subdivision (a) resolves a conflict over the question of whether the district court can amend an order by supplying the statement required by § 1292(b) at any time after entry of the order, with the result that the time fixed by the statute commences to run on the date of entry of the order as amended. Compare *Milbert v. Bison Laboratories*, 260 F.2d 431 (3d Cir., 1958) with *Sperry Rand Corporation v. Bell Telephone Laboratories*, 272 F.2d 29 (2d Cir., 1959), *Hadjipateras v. Pacifica, S.A.*, 290 F.2d 697 (5th Cir., 1961) and *Houston Fearless Corporation v. Teter*, 313 F.2d 91 (10th Cir., 1962). The view taken by the Second, Fifth and Tenth Circuits seems theoretically and practically sound, and the rule adopts it. Although a majority of the circuits now require the filing of a notice of appeal following the grant of permission to appeal, filing of the notice serves no function other than to provide a time from which the time for transmitting the record and docketing the appeal begins to run.

1979 Amendment

The proposed amendment [to subdivision (d)] adapts to the practice in appeals from interlocutory orders under 28 U.S.C. § 1292(b) the provisions of proposed Rule 3(e) above, requiring payment of all fees in the district court upon the filing of the notice of appeal. See Note to proposed amended Rule 3(e), *supra*.

1994 Amendments

Subdivision (c). The amendment makes it clear that a court may require a different number of copies either by rule or by order in an individual case. The number of copies of any document that a court of appeals needs varies depending upon the way in which the court conducts business. The internal operation of the courts of appeals necessarily varies from circuit to circuit because of differences in the number of judges, the geographic area included within the circuit, and other such factors. Uniformity could be achieved only by setting the number of copies artificially high so that parties in all circuits file enough copies to satisfy the needs of the court requiring the greatest number. Rather than do that, the Committee decided to make it clear that local rules may require a greater or lesser number of copies and that, if the circumstances of a particular case indicate the need for a different number of copies in that case, the court may so order.

1998 Amendments

In 1992 Congress added subsection (e) to 28 U.S.C. § 1292. Subsection (e) says that the Supreme Court has power to prescribe rules that "provide for an appeal of an interlocutory decision to the courts of appeals that is not otherwise provided for" in section 1292. The amendment of Rule 5 was prompted by the possibility of new rules authorizing additional interlocutory appeals. Rather than add a separate rule governing each such appeal, the Committee believes it is preferable to amend Rule 5 so that it will govern all such appeals.

In addition the Federal Courts Improvement Act of 12996, Pub.L. 104–317, abolished appeals by permission under 28 U.S.C. § 636(c)(5), making Rule 5.1 obsolete.

This new Rule 5 is intended to govern all discretionary appeals from district-court orders, judgments, or decrees. At this time that includes interlocutory appeals under 28 U.S.C. § 1292(b), (c)(1), (d)(1) & (2). If additional interlocutory appeals are authorized under § 1292(e), the new Rule is intended to govern them if the appeals are discretionary.

Subdivision (a). Paragraph (a)(1) says that when granting an appeal is within a court of appeals' discretion, a party may file a petition for permission to appeal. The time for filing provision states only that the petition must be filed within the time provided in the statute or rule authorizing the appeal or, if no such time is specified, within the time provided by Rule 4(a) for filing a notice of appeal.

Section 1292(b), (c), and (d) provide that the petition must be filed within 10 days after entry of the order containing the statement prescribed in the statute. Existing Rule 5(a) provides that if a district court amends an order to contain the prescribed statement, the petition must be filed within 10 days after entry of the amended order. The new rule similarly says that if a party cannot petition without the district court's permission or statement that necessary circumstances are present, the district court may amend its order to include such a statement and the time to petition runs from entry of the amended order.

The provision that the Rule 4(a) time for filing a notice of appeal should apply if the statute or rule is silent about the filing time was drawn from existing Rule 5.1

Subdivision (b). The changes made in the provisions in paragraph (b)(1) are intended only to broaden them sufficiently to make them appropriate for all discretionary appeals.

In paragraph (b)(2) a uniform time—7 days—is established for filing an answer in opposition or cross-petition. Seven days is the time for responding under existing Rule 5 and is an appropriate length of time when dealing with an interlocutory appeal. Although existing Rule 5.1 provides 14 days for responding, the Committee does not believe that the longer response time is necessary.

Subdivision (c). Subdivision (c) is substantively unchanged.

Subdivision (d). Paragraph (d)(2) is amended to state that "the date when the order granting permission to appeal is entered serves as the date of the notice of appeal" for purposes of calculating time under the rules. That language simply clarifies existing practice.

2002 Amendments

Subdivision (c). A petition for permission to appeal, a cross-petition for permission to appeal, and an answer to a petition or cross-petition for permission to appeal are all "other papers" for purposes of Rule 32(c)(2), and all of the requirements of Rule 32(a) apply to those papers, except as provided in Rule 32(c)(2). During the 1998 restyling of the Federal Rules of Appellate Procedure, Rule 5(c) was inadvertently changed to suggest that only the requirements of Rule 32(a)(1) apply to such papers. Rule 5(c) has been amended to correct that error.

Rule 5(c) has been further amended to limit the length of papers filed under Rule 5.

Changes Made After Publication and Comments No changes were made to the text of the proposed amendment or to the Committee Note.

[Rule 5.1. Appeal by Leave Under 28 U.S.C. § 636(c)(5)] (Abrogated Apr. 24, 1998, eff. Dec. 1, 1998)

1998 Amendments

The Federal Courts Improvement Act of 1996, Pub.L. No. 104–317, abolished appeals by permission under 28 U.S.C. § 636(c)(5), making Rule 5.1 obsolete. Rule 5.1 is, therefore, abrogated.

HISTORICAL NOTES

The abrogated rule provided that:

"**(a) Petition for Leave to Appeal; Answer or Cross Petition.** An appeal from a district court judgment, entered after an appeal under 28 U.S.C. § 636(c)(4) to a district judge from a judgment entered upon direction of a magistrate judge in a civil case, may be sought by filing a petition for leave to appeal. An appeal on petition for leave to appeal is not a matter of right, but its allowance is a matter of sound judicial discretion. The petition shall be filed with the clerk of the court of appeals within the time provided by Rule 4(a) for filing a notice of appeal, with proof of service on all parties to the action in the district court. A notice of appeal need not be filed. Within 14 days after service of the petition, a party may file an answer in opposition or a cross petition.

"**(b) Content of Petition; Answer.** The petition for leave to appeal shall contain a statement of the facts necessary to an understanding of the questions to be presented by the appeal; a statement of those questions and of the relief sought; a statement of the reasons why in the opinion of the petitioner the appeal should be allowed; and a copy of the order, decree or judgment complained of and any opinion or memorandum relating thereto. The petition and answer shall be submitted to a panel of judges of the court of appeals without oral argument unless otherwise ordered.

"**(c) Form of Papers; Number of Copies.** All papers may be typewritten. An original and three copies must be filed unless the court requires the filing of a different number by local rule or by order in a particular case.

"**(d) Allowance of the Appeal; Fees; Cost Bond; Filing of Record.** Within 10 days after the entry of an order granting the appeal, the appellant shall (1) pay to the clerk of the district court the fees established by statute and the docket fee prescribed by the Judicial Conference of the United States and (2) file a bond for costs if required pursuant to Rule 7. The clerk of the district court shall notify the clerk of the court of appeals of the payment of the fees. Upon receipt of such notice, the clerk of the court of appeals shall enter the appeal upon the docket. The record shall be transmitted and filed in accordance with Rules 11 and 12(b)."

Rule 6. Appeal in a Bankruptcy Case From a Final Judgment, Order, or Decree of a District Court or Bankruptcy Appellate Panel

(a) Appeal From a Judgment, Order, or Decree of a District Court Exercising Original Jurisdiction in a Bankruptcy Case. An appeal to a court of appeals from a final judgment, order, or decree of a district court exercising jurisdiction under 28 U.S.C. § 1334 is taken as any other civil appeal under these rules.

(b) Appeal From a Judgment, Order, or Decree of a District Court or Bankruptcy Appellate Panel Exercising Appellate Jurisdiction in a Bankruptcy Case.

(1) Applicability of Other Rules. These rules apply to an appeal to a court of appeals under 28 U.S.C. § 158(d) from a final judgment, order, or decree of a district court or bankruptcy appellate panel exercising appellate jurisdiction under 28 U.S.C. § 158(a) or (b). But there are 3 exceptions:

(A) Rules 4(a)(4), 4(b), 9, 10, 11, 12(b), 13–20, 22–23, and 24(b) do not apply;

(B) the reference in Rule 3(c) to 'Form 1 in the Appendix of Forms' must be read as a reference to Form 5; and

(C) when the appeal is from a bankruptcy appellate panel, the term 'district court,' as used in any applicable rule, means 'appellate panel.'

(2) Additional Rules. In addition to the rules made applicable by Rule 6(b)(1), the following rules apply:

(A) Motion for rehearing.

(i) If a timely motion for rehearing under Bankruptcy Rule 8015 is filed, the time to appeal for all parties runs from the entry of the order disposing of the motion. A notice of appeal filed after the district court or bankruptcy appellate panel announces or enters a judgment, order, or decree—but before disposition of the motion for rehearing—becomes effective when the order disposing of the motion for rehearing is entered.

(ii) Appellate review of the order disposing of the motion requires the party, in compliance with Rules 3(c) and 6(b)(1)(B), to amend a previously filed notice of appeal. A party intending to challenge an altered or amended judgment, order, or decree must file a notice of appeal or amended notice of appeal within the time prescribed by Rule 4—excluding Rules 4(a)(4) and 4(b)—measured from the entry of the order disposing of the motion.

(iii) No additional fee is required to file an amended notice.

(B) The record on appeal.

(i) Within 10 days after filing the notice of appeal, the appellant must file with the clerk possessing the record assembled in accordance with Bankruptcy Rule 8006—and serve on the appellee—a statement of the issues to be presented on appeal and a designation of the record to be certified and sent to the circuit clerk.

(ii) An appellee who believes that other parts of the record are necessary must, within 10 days after being served with the appellant's designation, file with the clerk and serve on the appellant a designation of additional parts to be included.

(iii) The record on appeal consists of:

- the redesignated record as provided above;
- the proceedings in the district court or bankruptcy appellate panel; and
- a certified copy of the docket entries prepared by the clerk under Rule 3(d).

(C) Forwarding the record.

(i) When the record is complete, the district clerk or bankruptcy appellate panel clerk must number the documents constituting the record and send them promptly to the circuit clerk together with a list of the documents correspondingly numbered and reasonably identified. Unless directed to do so by a party or the circuit clerk, the clerk will not send to the court of appeals documents of unusual bulk or weight, physical exhibits other than documents, or other parts of the record designated for omission by local rule of the court of appeals. If the exhibits are unusually bulky or heavy, a party must arrange with the clerks in advance for their transportation and receipt.

(ii) All parties must do whatever else is necessary to enable the clerk to assemble and forward the record. The court of appeals may provide by rule or order that a certified copy of the docket entries be sent in place of the redesignated record, but any party may request at any time during the pendency of the appeal that the redesignated record be sent.

(D) Filing the record. Upon receiving the record—or a certified copy of the docket entries sent in place of the redesignated record—the circuit clerk must file it and immediately notify all parties of the filing date.

(Added Apr. 25, 1989, eff. Dec. 1, 1989, and amended Apr. 30, 1991, eff. Dec. 1, 1991; Apr. 22, 1993, eff. Dec. 1, 1993; Apr. 24, 1998, eff. Dec. 1, 1998.)

1989 Addition

A new Rule 6 is proposed. The Bankruptcy Reform Act of 1978, Pub.L. No. 95–598, 92 Stat. 2549, the Supreme Court decision in *Northern Pipeline Construction Co. v. Marathon Pipe Line Co.*, 458 U.S. 50 (1982), and the Bankruptcy Amendments and Federal Judgeship Act of 1984, Pub.L. No. 98–353, 98 Stat. 333, have made the existing Rule 6 obsolete.

Subdivision (a). Subdivision (a) provides that when a district court exercises original jurisdiction in a bankruptcy matter, rather than referring it to a bankruptcy judge for a final determination, the appeal should be taken in identical fashion as appeals from district court decisions in other civil actions. A district court exercises original jurisdiction and this subdivision applies when the district court enters a final order or judgment upon consideration of a bankruptcy judge's proposed findings of fact and conclusions of law in a non-core proceeding pursuant to 28 U.S.C. § 157(c)(1) or when a district court withdraws a proceeding pursuant to 28 U.S.C. § 157(d). This subdivision is included to avoid uncertainty arising from the question of whether a bankruptcy case is a civil case. The rules refer at various points to the procedure "in a civil case", *see,* e.g. Rule 4(a)(1). Subdivision (a) makes it clear that such rules apply to an appeal from a district court bankruptcy decision.

Subdivision (b). Subdivision (b) governs appeals that follow intermediate review of a bankruptcy judge's decision by a district court or a bankruptcy appellate panel.

Subdivision (b)(1). Subdivision (b)(1) provides for the general applicability of the Federal Rules of Appellate Procedure, with specified exceptions, to appeals covered by subdivision (b) and makes necessary word adjustments.

Subdivision (b)(2). Paragraph (i) provides that the time for filing a notice of appeal shall begin to run anew from the entry of an order denying a rehearing or from the entry of a subsequent judgment. The Committee deliberately omitted from the rule any provision governing the validity of a notice of appeal filed prior to the entry of an order denying a rehearing; the Committee intended to leave undisturbed the current state of the law on that issue. Paragraph (ii) calls for a redesignation of the appellate record assembled in the bankruptcy court pursuant to Rule 8006 of the Rules of Bankruptcy Procedure. After an intermediate appeal, a party may well narrow the focus of its efforts on the second appeal and a redesignation of the record may eliminate unnecessary material. The proceedings during the first appeal are included to cover the possibility that independent error in the intermediate appeal, for example failure to follow appropriate procedures, may be assigned in the court of appeals. Paragraph (iii) provides for the transmission of the record and tracks the appropriate subsections of Rule 11. Paragraph (iv) provides for the filing of the record and notices to the parties. Paragraph (ii) and Paragraph (iv) both refer to "a certified copy of the docket entries". The "docket entries" referred to are the docket entries in the district court or the bankruptcy appellate panel, not the entire docket in the bankruptcy court.

1993 Amendments

Note to Subparagraph (b)(2)(i). The amendment accompanies concurrent changes to Rule 4(a)(4). Although Rule 6 never included language such as that being changed in Rule 4(a)(4), language that made a notice of appeal void if it was filed before, or during the pendency of, certain posttrial motions, courts have found that a notice of appeal is premature if it is filed before the court disposes of a motion for rehearing. See, e.g., *In re X-Cel, Inc.*, 823 F.2d 192 (7th

Cir.1987); *In re Shah*, 859 F.2d 1463 (10th Cir.1988). The Committee wants to achieve the same result here as in Rule 4, the elimination of a procedural trap.

1998 Amendments

The language and organization of the rule are amended to make the rule more easily understood. In addition to changes made to improve the understanding, the Advisory Committee has changed language to make style and terminology consistent throughout the appellate rules. These changes are intended to be stylistic only.

Subdivision (b). Language is added to Rule 6(b)(2)(A)(ii) to conform with the corresponding provision in Rule 4(a)(4). The new language is clarifying rather than substantive. The existing rule states that a party intending to challenge an alteration or amendment of a judgment must file an amended notice of appeal. Of course, if a party has not previously filed a notice of appeal, the party would simply file a notice of appeal not an amended one. The new language states that the party must file "a notice of appeal or amended notice of appeal."

Rule 7. Bond for Costs on Appeal in a Civil Case

In a civil case, the district court may require an appellant to file a bond or provide other security in any form and amount necessary to ensure payment of costs on appeal. Rule 8(b) applies to a surety on a bond given under this rule.

(As amended Apr. 30, 1979, eff. Aug. 1, 1979; Apr. 24, 1998, eff. Dec. 1, 1998.)

1967 Adoption

This rule is derived from FRCP 73(c) [rule 73(c), Federal Rules of Civil Procedure, this title] without change in substance.

1979 Amendment

The amendment would eliminate the provision of the present rule that requires the appellant to file a $250 bond for costs on appeal at the time of filing his notice of appeal. The $250 provision was carried forward in the F.R.App.P. [these rules] from former Rule 73(c) of the F.R.Civ.P. [rule 73(c), Federal Rules of Civil Procedure], and the $250 figure has remained unchanged since the adoption of that rule in 1937. Today it bears no relationship to actual costs. The amended rule would leave the question of the need for a bond for costs and its amount in the discretion of the court.

1998 Amendments

The language of the rule is amended to make the rule more easily understood. In addition to changes made to improve the understanding, the Advisory Committee has changed language to make style and terminology consistent throughout the appellate rules. These changes are intended to be stylistic only.

Rule 8. Stay or Injunction Pending Appeal

(a) Motion for Stay.

(1) Initial Motion in the District Court. A party must ordinarily move first in the district court for the following relief:

(A) a stay of the judgment or order of a district court pending appeal;

(B) approval of a supersedeas bond; or

(C) an order suspending, modifying, restoring, or granting an injunction while an appeal is pending.

(2) Motion in the Court of Appeals; Conditions on Relief. A motion for the relief mentioned in Rule 8(a)(1) may be made to the court of appeals or to one of its judges.

(A) The motion must:

(i) show that moving first in the district court would be impracticable; or

(ii) state that, a motion having been made, the district court denied the motion or failed to afford the relief requested and state any reasons given by the district court for its action.

(B) The motion must also include:

(i) the reasons for granting the relief requested and the facts relied on;

(ii) originals or copies of affidavits or other sworn statements supporting facts subject to dispute; and

(iii) relevant parts of the record.

(C) The moving party must give reasonable notice of the motion to all parties.

(D) A motion under this Rule 8(a)(2) must be filed with the circuit clerk and normally will be considered by a panel of the court. But in an exceptional case in which time requirements make that procedure impracticable, the motion may be made to and considered by a single judge.

(E) The court may condition relief on a party's filing a bond or other appropriate security in the district court.

(b) Proceeding Against a Surety. If a party gives security in the form of a bond or stipulation or other undertaking with one or more sureties, each surety submits to the jurisdiction of the district court and irrevocably appoints the district clerk as the surety's agent on whom any papers affecting the surety's liability on the bond or undertaking may be served. On motion, a surety's liability may be enforced in the district court without the necessity of an independent action. The motion and any notice that the district court prescribes may be served on the district clerk, who must promptly mail a copy to each surety whose address is known.

(c) Stay in a Criminal Case. Rule 38 of the Federal Rules of Criminal Procedure governs a stay in a criminal case.

(As amended Mar. 10, 1986, eff. July 1, 1986; Apr. 27, 1995, eff. Dec. 1, 1995; Apr. 24, 1998, eff. Dec. 1, 1998.)

1967 Adoption

Subdivision (a). While the power of a court of appeals to stay proceedings in the district court during the pendency of an appeal is not explicitly conferred by statute, it exists by virtue of the all writs statute, 28 U.S.C. § 1651. *Eastern Greyhound Lines v. Fusco*, 310 F.2d 632 (6th Cir., 1962); *United States v. Lynd*, 301 F.2d 818 (5th Cir., 1962); *Public Utilities Commission of Dist. of Col. v. Capital Transit Co.*, 94 U.S.App.D.C. 140, 214 F.2d 242 (1954). And the Supreme Court has termed the power "inherent" (*In re McKenzie*, 180 U.S. 536, 551, 21 S.Ct. 468, 45 L.Ed. 657 (1901)) and "part of its (the court of appeals') traditional equipment for the administration of justice." (*Scripps-Howard Radio v. F.C.C.*, 316 U.S. 4, 9–10, 62 S.Ct. 875, 86 L.Ed. 1229 (1942)). The power of a single judge of the court of appeals to grant a stay pending appeal was recognized in *In re McKenzie, supra. Alexander v. United States*, 173 F.2d 865 (9th Cir., 1949) held that a single judge could not stay the judgment of a district court, but it noted the absence of a rule of court authorizing the practice. FRCP 62(g) [rule 62(g), Federal Rules of Civil Procedure] adverts to the grant of a stay by a single judge of the appellate court. The requirement that application be first made to the district court is the case law rule. *Cumberland Tel. & Tel. Co. v. Louisiana Public Service Commission*, 260 U.S. 212, 219, 43 S.Ct. 75, 67 L.Ed. 217 (1922); *United States v. El-O-Pathic Pharmacy*, 192 F.2d 62 (9th Cir., 1951); *United States v. Hansell*, 109 F.2d 613 (2d Cir., 1940). The requirement is explicitly stated in FRCrP 38(c) [rule 38(c), Federal Rules of Criminal Procedure] and in the rules of the First, Third, Fourth and Tenth Circuits. See also Supreme Court Rules 18 and 27.

The statement of the requirement in the proposed rule would work a minor change in present practice. FRCP 73(e) [rule 73(e), Federal Rules of Civil Procedure] requires that if a bond for costs on appeal or a supersedeas bond is offered after the appeal is docketed, leave to file the bond must be obtained from the court of appeals. There appears to be no reason why matters relating to supersedeas and cost bonds should not be initially presented to the district court whenever they arise prior to the disposition of the appeal. The requirement of FRCP 73(e) appears to be a concession of the view that once an appeal is perfected, the district court loses all power over its judgment. See *In re Federal Facilities Realty Trust*, 227 F.2d 651 (7th Cir., 1955) and cases cited at 654–655. No reason appears why all questions related to supersedeas or the bond for costs on appeal should not be presented in the first instance to the district court in the ordinary case.

Subdivision (b). The provisions respecting a surety upon a bond or other undertaking are based upon FRCP 65.1 [rule 65.1, Federal Rules of Civil Procedure].

1986 Amendment

The amendments to Rule 8(b) are technical. No substantive change is intended.

1995 Amendment

Subdivision (c). The amendment conforms subdivision (c) to previous amendments to Fed.R.Crim.P. 38. This amendment strikes the reference to subdivision (a) of Fed. R.Crim.P. 38 so that Fed.R.App.P. 8(c) refers instead to all of Criminal Rule 38. When Rule 8(c) was adopted Fed. R.Crim.P. 38(a) included the procedures for obtaining a stay of execution when the sentence in question was death, imprisonment, a fine, or probation. Criminal Rule 38 was later amended and now addresses those topics in separate subdivisions. Subdivision 38(a) now addresses only stays of death sentences. The proper cross reference is to all of Criminal Rule 38.

1998 Amendments

The language and organization of the rule are amended to make the rule more easily understood. In addition to changes made to improve the understanding, the Advisory Committee has changed language to make style and terminology consistent throughout the appellate rules. These changes are intended to by stylistic only.

Rule 9. Release in a Criminal Case

(a) Release Before Judgment of Conviction.

(1) The district court must state in writing, or orally on the record, the reasons for an order regarding the release or detention of a defendant in a criminal case. A party appealing from the order must file with the court of appeals a copy of the district court's order and the court's statement of reasons as soon as practicable after filing the notice of appeal. An appellant who questions the factual basis for the district court's order must file a transcript of the release proceedings or an explanation of why a transcript was not obtained.

(2) After reasonable notice to the appellee, the court of appeals must promptly determine the appeal on the basis of the papers, affidavits, and parts of the record that the parties present or the court requires. Unless the court so orders, briefs need not be filed.

(3) The court of appeals or one of its judges may order the defendant's release pending the disposition of the appeal.

(b) Release After Judgment of Conviction. A party entitled to do so may obtain review of a district-court order regarding release after a judgment of conviction by filing a notice of appeal from that order in the district court, or by filing a motion in the court of appeals if the party has already filed a notice of appeal from the judgment of conviction. Both the order and the review are subject to Rule 9(a). The papers filed by the party seeking review must include a copy of the judgment of conviction.

(c) Criteria for Release. The court must make its decision regarding release in accordance with the applicable provisions of 18 U.S.C. §§ 3142, 3143, and 3145(c).

(As amended Apr. 24, 1972, eff. Oct. 1, 1972; Oct. 12, 1984, Pub.L. 98–473, Title II, § 210, 98 Stat. 1987; Apr. 29, 1994, eff. Dec. 1, 1994; Apr. 24, 1998, eff. Dec. 1, 1998.)

1967 Adoption

Subdivision (a). The appealability of release orders entered prior to a judgment of conviction is determined by the provisions of 18 U.S.C. § 3147, as qualified by 18 U.S.C. § 3148, and by the rule announced in *Stack v. Boyle*, 342 U.S. 1, 72 S.Ct. 1, 96 L.Ed. 3 (1951), holding certain orders respecting release appealable as final orders under 28 U.S.C. § 1291. The language of the rule, "(a)n appeal authorized by law from an order refusing or imposing conditions of release," is intentionally broader than that used in 18 U.S.C. § 3147 in describing orders made appealable by that section. The summary procedure ordained by the rule is intended to apply to all appeals from orders respecting release, and it would appear that at least some orders not made appealable by 18 U.S.C. § 3147 are nevertheless appealable under the *Stack v. Boyle* rationale. See, for example, *United States v. Foster*, 278 F.2d 567 (2d Cir., 1960), holding appealable an order refusing to extend bail limits. Note also the provisions of 18 U.S.C. § 3148, which after withdrawing from persons charged with an offense punishable by death and from those who have been convicted of an offense the right of appeal granted by 18 U.S.C. § 3147, expressly preserves "other rights to judicial review of conditions of release or orders of detention."

The purpose of the subdivision is to insure the expeditious determination of appeals respecting release orders, an expedition commanded by 18 U.S.C. § 3147 and by the Court in *Stack v. Boyle*, supra. It permits such appeals to be heard on an informal record without the necessity of briefs and on reasonable notice. Equally important to the just and speedy disposition of these appeals is the requirement that the district court state the reasons for its decision. See *Jones v. United States*, 358 F.2d 543 (D.C.Cir., 1966); *Rhodes v. United States*, 275 F.2d 78 (4th Cir., 1960); *United States v. Williams*, 253 F.2d 144 (7th Cir., 1958).

Subdivision (b). This subdivision regulates procedure for review of an order respecting release at a time when the jurisdiction of the court of appeals has already attached by virtue of an appeal from the judgment of conviction. Notwithstanding the fact that jurisdiction has passed to the court of appeals, both 18 U.S.C. § 3148 and FRCrP 38(c) [rule 38(c), Federal Rules of Criminal Procedure] contemplate that the initial determination of whether a convicted defendant is to be released pending the appeal is to be made by the district court. But at this point there is obviously no need for a separate appeal from the order of the district court respecting release. The court of appeals or a judge thereof has power to effect release on motion as an incident to the pending appeal. See FRCrP 38(c) and 46(a)(2) [rules 38(c) and 46(a)(2), Federal Rules of Criminal Procedure. But the motion is functionally identical with the appeal regulated by subdivision (a) and requires the same speedy determination if relief is to be effective. Hence the similarity of the procedure outlined in the two subdivisions.

1972 Amendment

Subdivision (c) is intended to bring the rule into conformity with 18 U.S.C. § 3148 and to allocate to the defendant the burden of establishing that he will not flee and that he poses no danger to pay other person or to the community. The burden is placed upon the defendant in the view that the fact of his conviction justifies retention in custody in situations where doubt exists as to whether he can be safely released pending disposition of his appeal. Release pending appeal may also be denied if "it appears that an appeal is frivolous or taken for delay." 18 U.S.C. § 3148. The burden of establishing the existence of these criteria remains with the government.

1994 Amendments

Rule 9 has been entirely rewritten. The basic structure of the rule has been retained. Subdivision (a) governs appeals from bail decisions made before the judgment of conviction is entered at the time of sentencing. Subdivision (b) governs review of bail decisions made after sentencing and pending appeal.

Subdivision (a). The subdivision applies to appeals from "an order regarding release or detention" of a criminal defendant before judgment of conviction, *i.e.*, before sentencing. *See* Fed. R. Crim. P. 32. The old rule applied only to a defendant's appeal from an order "refusing or imposing conditions of release." The new broader language is needed because the government is now permitted to appeal bail decisions in certain circumstances. 18 U.S.C. §§ 3145 and 3731. For the same reason, the rule now requires a district court to state reasons for its decision in all instances, not only when it refuses release or imposes conditions on release.

The rule requires a party appealing from a district court's decision to supply the court of appeals with a copy of the district court's order and its statement of reasons. In addition, an appellant who questions the factual basis for the district court's decision must file a transcript of the release proceedings, if possible. The rule also permits a court to require additional papers. A court must act promptly to decide these appeals; lack of pertinent information can cause delays. The old rule left the determination of what should be filed entirely within the party's, discretion; it stated that the court of appeals would hear the appeal "upon such papers, affidavits, and portions of the record as the parties shall present."

Subdivision (b). This subdivision applies to review of a district court's decision regarding release made after judgment of conviction. As in subdivision (a), the language has been changed to accommodate the government's ability to seek review.

The word "review" is used in this subdivision, rather than "appeal" because review may be obtained, in some instances, upon motion. Review may be obtained by motion if the party has already filed a notice of appeal from the judgment of conviction. If the party desiring review of the release decision has not filed such a notice of appeal, review may be obtained only by filing a notice of appeal from the order regarding release.

The requirements of subdivision (a) apply to both the order and the review. That is, the district court must state its reasons for the order. The party seeking review must supply the court of appeals with the same information required by subdivision (a). In addition, the party seeking review must also supply the court with information about the conviction and the sentence.

Subdivision (c). This subdivision has been amended to include references to the correct statutory provisions.

1998 Amendments

The language and organization of the rule are amended to make the rule more easily understood. In addition to changes made to improve the understanding, the Advisory Committee has changed language to make style and terminology consistent throughout the appellate rules. These changes are intended to by stylistic only.

Rule 10. The Record on Appeal

(a) Composition of the Record on Appeal. The following items constitute the record on appeal:

(1) the original papers and exhibits filed in the district court;

(2) the transcript of proceedings, if any; and

(3) a certified copy of the docket entries prepared by the district clerk.

(b) The Transcript of Proceedings.

(1) Appellant's Duty to Order. Within 10 days after filing the notice of appeal or entry of an order disposing of the last timely remaining motion of a type specified in Rule 4(a)(4)(A), whichever is later, the appellant must do either of the following:

(A) order from the reporter a transcript of such parts of the proceedings not already on file as the appellant considers necessary, subject to a local rule of the court of appeals and with the following qualifications:

(i) the order must be in writing;

(ii) if the cost of the transcript is to be paid by the United States under the Criminal Justice Act, the order must so state; and

(iii) the appellant must, within the same period, file a copy of the order with the district clerk; or

(B) file a certificate stating that no transcript will be ordered.

(2) Unsupported Finding or Conclusion. If the appellant intends to urge on appeal that a finding or conclusion is unsupported by the evidence or is contrary to the evidence, the appellant must include in the record a transcript of all evidence relevant to that finding or conclusion.

(3) Partial Transcript. Unless the entire transcript is ordered:

(A) the appellant must—within the 10 days provided in Rule 10(b)(1)—file a statement of the issues that the appellant intends to present on the appeal and must serve on the appellee a copy of both the order or certificate and the statement;

(B) if the appellee considers it necessary to have a transcript of other parts of the proceedings, the appellee must, within 10 days after the service of the order or certificate and the statement of the issues, file and serve on the appellant a designation of additional parts to be ordered; and

(C) unless within 10 days after service of that designation the appellant has ordered all such parts, and has so notified the appellee, the appellee may within the following 10 days either order the parts or move in the district court for an order requiring the appellant to do so.

(4) Payment. At the time of ordering, a party must make satisfactory arrangements with the reporter for paying the cost of the transcript.

(c) Statement of the Evidence When the Proceedings Were Not Recorded or When a Transcript Is Unavailable. If the transcript of a hearing or trial is unavailable, the appellant may prepare a statement of the evidence or proceedings from the best available means, including the appellant's recollection. The statement must be served on the appellee, who may serve objections or proposed amendments within 10 days after being served. The statement and any objections or proposed amendments must then be submitted to the district court for settlement and approval. As settled and approved, the statement must be included by the district clerk in the record on appeal.

(d) Agreed Statement as the Record on Appeal. In place of the record on appeal as defined in Rule 10(a), the parties may prepare, sign, and submit to the district court a statement of the case showing how the issues presented by the appeal arose and were decided in the district court. The statement must set forth only those facts averred and proved or sought to be proved that are essential to the court's resolution of the issues. If the statement is truthful, it—together with any additions that the district court may consider necessary to a full presentation of the issues on appeal—must be approved by the district court and must then be certified to the court of appeals as the record on appeal. The district clerk must then send it to the circuit clerk within the time provided by Rule 11. A copy of the agreed statement may be filed in place of the appendix required by Rule 30.

(e) Correction or Modification of the Record.

(1) If any difference arises about whether the record truly discloses what occurred in the district court, the difference must be submitted to and settled by that court and the record conformed accordingly.

(2) If anything material to either party is omitted from or misstated in the record by error or accident, the omission or misstatement may be correct-

ed and a supplemental record may be certified and forwarded:

(A) on stipulation of the parties;

(B) by the district court before or after the record has been forwarded; or

(C) by the court of appeals.

(3) All other questions as to the form and content of the record must be presented to the court of appeals.

(As amended Apr. 30, 1979, eff. Aug. 1, 1979; Mar. 10, 1986, eff. July 1, 1986; Apr. 30, 1991, eff. Dec. 1, 1991; Apr. 22, 1993, eff. Dec. 1, 1993; Apr. 27, 1995, eff. Dec. 1, 1995; Apr. 24, 1998, eff. Dec. 1, 1998.)

1967 Adoption

This rule is derived from FRCP 75(a), (b), (c) and (d) and FRCP 76 [rule 75(a), (b), (c) and (d) and rule 76, Federal Rules of Civil Procedure], without change in substance.

1979 Amendment

The proposed amendments to Rule 10(b) would require the appellant to place with the reporter a written order for the transcript of proceedings and file a copy with the clerk, and to indicate on the order if the transcript is to be provided under the Criminal Justice Act. If the appellant does not plan to order a transcript of any of the proceedings, he must file a certificate to that effect. These requirements make the appellant's steps in readying the appeal a matter of record and give the district court notice of requests for transcripts at the expense of the United States under the Criminal Justice Act. They are also the third step in giving the court of appeals some control over the production and transmission of the record. See Note to Rules 3(d)(e) above and Rule 11 below.

In the event the appellant orders no transcript, or orders a transcript of less than all the proceedings, the procedure under the proposed amended rule remains substantially as before. The appellant must serve on the appellee a copy of his order or in the event no order is placed, of the certificate to that effect, and a statement of the issues he intends to present on appeal, and the appellee may thereupon designate additional parts of the transcript to be included, and upon appellant's refusal to order the additional parts, may either order them himself or seek an order requiring the appellant to order them. The only change proposed in this procedure is to place a 10 day time limit on motions to require the appellant to order the additional portions.

Rule 10(b) is made subject to local rules of the courts of appeals in recognition of the practice in some circuits in some classes of cases, e.g., appeals by indigents in criminal cases after a short trial, of ordering immediate preparation of a complete transcript, thus making compliance with the rule unnecessary.

1986 Amendment

The amendments to Rules 10(b) and (c) are technical. No substantive change is intended.

1993 Amendment

The amendment is technical and no substantive change is intended.

1995 Amendment

Subdivision (b)(1). The amendment conforms this rule to amendments made in Rule 4(a)(4) in 1993. The amendments to Rule 4(a)(4) provide that certain postjudgment motions have the effect of suspending a filed notice of appeal until the disposition of the last of such motions. The purpose of this amendment is to suspend the 10–day period for ordering a transcript if a timely postjudgment motion is made and a notice of appeal is suspended under Rule 4(a)(4). The 10–day period set forth in the first sentence of this rule begins to run when the order disposing of the last of such postjudgment motions outstanding is entered.

1998 Amendments

The language and organization of the rule are amended to make the rule more easily understood. In addition to changes made to improve the understanding, the Advisory Committee has changed language to make style and terminology consistent throughout the appellate rules. These changes are intended to by stylistic only.

HISTORICAL NOTES

References in Text

The Criminal Justice Act, referred to in subd. (b)(1), probably means the Criminal Justice Act of 1964, Pub.L. 88–455, Aug. 20, 1964, 78 Stat. 552, which is classified to § 3006A of Title 18, Crimes and Criminal Procedure.

Rule 11. Forwarding the Record

(a) Appellant's Duty. An appellant filing a notice of appeal must comply with Rule 10(b) and must do whatever else is necessary to enable the clerk to assemble and forward the record. If there are multiple appeals from a judgment or order, the clerk must forward a single record.

(b) Duties of Reporter and District Clerk.

(1) Reporter's Duty to Prepare and File a Transcript. The reporter must prepare and file a transcript as follows:

(A) Upon receiving an order for a transcript, the reporter must enter at the foot of the order the date of its receipt and the expected completion date and send a copy, so endorsed, to the circuit clerk.

(B) If the transcript cannot be completed within 30 days of the reporter's receipt of the order, the reporter may request the circuit clerk to grant additional time to complete it. The clerk must note on the docket the action taken and notify the parties.

(C) When a transcript is complete, the reporter must file it with the district clerk and notify the circuit clerk of the filing.

(D) If the reporter fails to file the transcript on time, the circuit clerk must notify the district judge and do whatever else the court of appeals directs.

(2) **District Clerk's Duty to Forward.** When the record is complete, the district clerk must number the documents constituting the record and send them promptly to the circuit clerk together with a list of the documents correspondingly numbered and reasonably identified. Unless directed to do so by a party or the circuit clerk, the district clerk will not send to the court of appeals documents of unusual bulk or weight, physical exhibits other than documents, or other parts of the record designated for omission by local rule of the court of appeals. If the exhibits are unusually bulky or heavy, a party must arrange with the clerks in advance for their transportation and receipt.

(c) Retaining the Record Temporarily in the District Court for Use in Preparing the Appeal. The parties may stipulate, or the district court on motion may order, that the district clerk retain the record temporarily for the parties to use in preparing the papers on appeal. In that event the district clerk must certify to the circuit clerk that the record on appeal is complete. Upon receipt of the appellee's brief, or earlier if the court orders or the parties agree, the appellant must request the district clerk to forward the record.

(d) [Abrogated.]

(e) Retaining the Record by Court Order.

(1) The court of appeals may, by order or local rule, provide that a certified copy of the docket entries be forwarded instead of the entire record. But a party may at any time during the appeal request that designated parts of the record be forwarded.

(2) The district court may order the record or some part of it retained if the court needs it while the appeal is pending, subject, however, to call by the court of appeals.

(3) If part or all of the record is ordered retained, the district clerk must send to the court of appeals a copy of the order and the docket entries together with the parts of the original record allowed by the district court and copies of any parts of the record designated by the parties.

(f) Retaining Parts of the Record in the District Court by Stipulation of the Parties. The parties may agree by written stipulation filed in the district court that designated parts of the record be retained in the district court subject to call by the court of appeals or request by a party. The parts of the record so designated remain a part of the record on appeal.

(g) Record for a Preliminary Motion in the Court of Appeals. If, before the record is forwarded, a party makes any of the following motions in the court of appeals:

- for dismissal;
- for release;
- for a stay pending appeal;
- for additional security on the bond on appeal or on a supersedeas bond; or
- for any other intermediate order—

the district clerk must send the court of appeals any parts of the record designated by any party.

(As amended Apr. 30, 1979, eff. Aug. 1, 1979; Mar. 10, 1986, eff. July 1, 1986; Apr. 24, 1998, eff. Dec. 1, 1998.)

1967 Adoption

Subdivisions (a) and (b). These subdivisions are derived from FRCP 73(g) and FRCP 75(e) [rules 73(g) and 75(e), Federal Rules of Civil Procedure]. FRCP 75(e) presently directs the clerk of the district court to transmit the record within the time allowed or fixed for its filing, which, under the provisions of FRCP 73(g) is within 40 days from the date of filing the notice of appeal, unless an extension is obtained from the district court. The precise time at which the record must be transmitted thus depends upon the time required for delivery of the record from the district court to the court of appeals, since, to permit its timely filing, it must reach the court of appeals before expiration of the 40-day period or an extension thereof. Subdivision (a) of this rule provides that the record is to be transmitted within the 40-day period, or any extension thereof; subdivision (b) provides that transmission is effected when the clerk of the district court mails or otherwise forwards the record to the clerk of the court of appeals; Rule 12(b) directs the clerk of the court of appeals to file the record upon its receipt following timely docketing and transmittal. It can thus be determined with certainty precisely when the clerk of the district court must forward the record to the clerk of the court of appeals in order to effect timely filing: the final day of the 40-day period or of any extension thereof.

Subdivision (c). This subdivision is derived from FRCP 75(e) [rule 75(e), Federal Rules of Civil Procedure] without change of substance.

Subdivision (d). This subdivision is derived from FRCP 73(g) [rule 73(g), Federal Rules of Civil Procedure] and FRCrP 39(c) [rule 39(c), Federal Rules of Criminal Procedure]. Under present rules the district court is empowered to extend the time for filing the record and docketing the appeal. Since under the proposed rule timely transmission now insures timely filing (see note to subdivisions (a) and (b) above) the power of the district court is expressed in terms of its power to extend the time for transmitting the record. Restriction of that power to a period of 90 days after the filing of the notice of appeal represents a change in the rule with respect to appeals in criminal cases. FRCrP 39(c) now permits the district court to extend the time for filing and docketing without restriction. No good reason appears for a difference between the civil and criminal rule in this regard, and subdivision (d) limits the power of the district court to extend the time for transmitting the record in all cases to 90 days from the date of filing the notice of appeal, just as its power is now limited with respect to docketing and filing in civil cases. Subdivision (d) makes explicit the power of the court of appeals to permit the record to be filed at any time. See *Pyramid Motor Freight Corporation v. Ispass*, 330 U.S. 695, 67 S.Ct. 954, 91 L.Ed. 1184 (1947).

Subdivisions (e), (f) and (g). These subdivisions are derived from FRCP 75(f) [rule 75(f), Federal Rules of Civil Procedure], (a) and (g), respectively, without change of substance.

1979 Amendment

Under present Rule 11(a) it is provided that the record shall be transmitted to the court of appeals within 40 days after the filing of the notice of appeal. Under present Rule 11(d) the district court, on request made during the initial time or any extension thereof, and cause shown, may extend the time for the transmission of the record to a point not more than 90 days after the filing of the first notice of appeal. If the district court is without authority to grant a request to extend the time, or denies a request for extension, the appellant may make a motion for extension of time in the court of appeals. Thus the duty to see that the record is transmitted is placed on the appellant. Aside from ordering the transcript within the time prescribed the appellant has no control over the time at which the record is transmitted, since all steps beyond this point are in the hands of the reporter and the clerk. The proposed amendments recognize this fact and place the duty directly on the reporter and the clerk. After receiving the written order for the transcript (See Note to Rule 10(b) above), the reporter must acknowledge its receipt, indicate when he expects to have it completed, and mail the order so endorsed to the clerk of the court of appeals. Requests for extensions of time must be made by the reporter to the clerk of the court of appeals and action on such requests is entered on the docket. Thus from the point at which the transcript is ordered the clerk of the court of appeals is made aware of any delays. If the transcript is not filed on time, the clerk of the court of appeals will notify the district judge.

Present Rule 11(b) provides that the record shall be transmitted when it is "complete for the purposes of the appeal." The proposed amended rule continues this requirement. The record is complete for the purposes of the appeal when it contains the original papers on file in the clerk's office, all necessary exhibits, and the transcript, if one is to be included. Cf. present Rule 11(c). The original papers will be in the custody of the clerk of the district court at the time the notice of appeal is filed. See Rule 5(e) of the F.R.C.P. [rule 5(e), Federal Rules of Civil Procedure]. The custody of exhibits is often the subject of local rules. Some of them require that documentary exhibits must be deposited with the clerk. See Local Rule 13 of the Eastern District of Virginia. Others leave exhibits with counsel, subject to order of the court. See Local Rule 33 of the Northern District of Illinois. If under local rules the custody of exhibits is left with counsel, the district court should make adequate provision for their preservation during the time during which an appeal may be taken, the prompt deposit with the clerk of such as under Rule 11(b) are to be transmitted to the court of appeals, and the availability of others in the event that the court of appeals should require their transmission. Cf. Local Rule 11 of the Second Circuit [rule 11, U.S.Ct. of App. 2d Cir.].

Usually the record will be complete with the filing of the transcript. While the proposed amendment requires transmission "forthwith" when the record is complete, it was not designed to preclude a local requirement by the court of appeals that the original papers and exhibits be transmitted when complete without awaiting the filing of the transcript.

The proposed amendments continue the provision in the present rule that documents of unusual bulk or weight and physical exhibits other than documents shall not be transmitted without direction by the parties or by the court of appeals, and the requirement that the parties make special arrangements for transmission and receipt of exhibits of unusual bulk or weight. In addition, they give recognition to local rules that make transmission of other record items subject to order of the court of appeals. See Local Rule 4 of the Seventh Circuit [rule 4, U.S.Ct. of App. 7th Cir., this title].

1986 Amendment

The amendments to Rule 11(b) are technical. No substantive change is intended.

1998 Amendments

The language and organization of the rule are amended to make the rule more easily understood. In addition to changes made to improve the understanding, the Advisory Committee has changed language to make style and terminology consistent throughout the appellate rules. These changes are intended to be stylistic only.

Rule 12. Docketing the Appeal; Filing a Representation Statement; Filing the Record

(a) Docketing the Appeal. Upon receiving the copy of the notice of appeal and the docket entries from the district clerk under Rule 3(d), the circuit clerk must docket the appeal under the title of the district-court action and must identify the appellant, adding the appellant's name if necessary.

(b) Filing a Representation Statement. Unless the court of appeals designates another time, the attorney who filed the notice of appeal must, within 10 days after filing the notice, file a statement with the circuit clerk naming the parties that the attorney represents on appeal.

(c) Filing the Record, Partial Record, or Certificate. Upon receiving the record, partial record, or district clerk's certificate as provided in Rule 11, the circuit clerk must file it and immediately notify all parties of the filing date.

(As amended Apr. 30, 1979, eff. Aug. 1, 1979; Mar. 10, 1986, eff. July 1, 1986; Apr. 22, 1993, eff. Dec. 1, 1993; Apr. 24, 1998, eff. Dec. 1, 1998.)

1967 Adoption

Subdivision (a). All that is involved in the docketing of an appeal is the payment of the docket fee. In practice, after the clerk of the court of appeals receives the record from the clerk of the district court he notifies the appellant of its receipt and requests payment of the fee. Upon receipt of the fee, the clerk enters the appeal upon the docket and files the record. The appellant is allowed to pay the fee at any time within the time allowed or fixed for transmission of the record and thereby to discharge his responsibility for docketing. The final sentence is added in the interest of facilitating future reference and citation and location of cases in indexes. Compare 3d Cir.Rule 10(2) [rule 10(2), U.S.Ct. of App. 3d Cir.]; 4th Cir.Rule 9(8) [rule 9(8), U.S.Ct. of App. 4th Cir.]; 6th Cir.Rule 14(1) [rule 14(1), U.S.Ct. of App. 6th Cir.].

Subdivision (c). The rules of the circuits generally permit the appellee to move for dismissal in the event the appellant fails to effect timely filing of the record. See 1st Cir.Rule 21(3) [rule 21(3), U.S.Ct. of App. 1st Cir.]; 3d Cir.Rule 21(4) [rule 21(4), U.S.Ct. of App. 3d Cir.]; 5th Cir.Rule 16(1) [rule 16(1), U.S.Ct. of App. 5th Cir.]; 8th Cir.Rule 7(d) [rule 7(d), U.S.Ct. of App. 8th Cir.].

1979 Amendments

Subdivision (a). Under present Rule 12(a) the appellant must pay the docket fee within the time fixed for the transmission of the record, and upon timely payment of the fee, the appeal is docketed. The proposed amendment takes the docketing out of the hands of the appellant. The fee is paid at the time the notice of appeal is filed and the appeal is entered on the docket upon receipt of a copy of the notice of appeal and of the docket entries, which are sent to the court of appeals under the provisions of Rule 3(d). This is designed to give the court of appeals control of its docket at the earliest possible time so that within the limits of its facilities and personnel it can screen cases for appropriately different treatment, expedite the proceedings through prehearing conferences or otherwise, and in general plan more effectively for the prompt disposition of cases.

Subdivision (b). The proposed amendment conforms the provision to the changes in Rule 11.

1986 Amendments

The amendment to Rule 12(a) is technical. No substantive change is intended.

1993 Amendments

Note to new subdivision (b). This amendment is a companion to the amendment of Rule 3(c). The Rule 3(c) amendment allows an attorney who represents more than one party on appeal to "specify" the appellants by general description rather than by naming them individually. The requirement added here is that whenever an attorney files a notice of appeal, the attorney must soon thereafter file a statement indicating all parties represented on the appeal by that attorney. Although the notice of appeal is the jurisdictional document and it must clearly indicate who is bringing the appeal, the representation statement will be helpful especially to the court of appeals in identifying the individual appellants.

The rule allows a court of appeals to require the filing of the representation statement at some time other than specified in the rule so that if a court of appeals requires a docketing statement or appearance form the representation statement may be combined with it.

1998 Amendments

The language of the rule are amended to make the rule more easily understood. In addition to changes made to improve the understanding, the Advisory Committee has changed language to make style and terminology consistent throughout the appellate rules. These changes are intended to by stylistic only.

TITLE III. REVIEW OF A DECISION OF THE UNITED STATES TAX COURT

Rule 13. Review of a Decision of the Tax Court

(a) How Obtained; Time for Filing Notice of Appeal.

(1) Review of a decision of the United States Tax Court is commenced by filing a notice of appeal with the Tax Court clerk within 90 days after the entry of the Tax Court's decision. At the time of filing, the appellant must furnish the clerk with enough copies of the notice to enable the clerk to comply with Rule 3(d). If one party files a timely notice of appeal, any other party may file a notice of appeal within 120 days after the Tax Court's decision is entered.

(2) If, under Tax Court rules, a party makes a timely motion to vacate or revise the Tax Court's decision, the time to file a notice of appeal runs from the entry of the order disposing of the motion or from the entry of a new decision, whichever is later.

(b) Notice of Appeal; How Filed. The notice of appeal may be filed either at the Tax Court clerk's office in the District of Columbia or by mail addressed to the clerk. If sent by mail the notice is considered filed on the postmark date, subject to § 7502 of the Internal Revenue Code, as amended, and the applicable regulations.

(c) Contents of the Notice of Appeal; Service; Effect of Filing and Service. Rule 3 prescribes the contents of a notice of appeal, the manner of service, and the effect of its filing and service. Form 2 in the Appendix of Forms is a suggested form of a notice of appeal.

(d) The Record on Appeal; Forwarding; Filing.

(1) An appeal from the Tax Court is governed by the parts of Rules 10, 11, and 12 regarding the record on appeal from a district court, the time and manner of forwarding and filing, and the docketing in the court of appeals. References in those rules and in Rule 3 to the district court and district clerk are to be read as referring to the Tax Court and its clerk.

(2) If an appeal from a Tax Court decision is taken to more than one court of appeals, the original record must be sent to the court named in the first notice of appeal filed. In an appeal to any other court of appeals, the appellant must apply to that other court to make provision for the record.

(As amended Apr. 30, 1979, eff. Aug. 1, 1979; Apr. 29, 1994, eff. Dec. 1, 1994; Apr. 24, 1998, eff. Dec. 1, 1998.)

1967 Adoption

Subdivision (a). This subdivision effects two changes in practice respecting review of Tax Court decisions: (1) § 7483 of the Internal Revenue Code, 68A Stat. 891, 26 U.S.C. § 7483, provides that review of a Tax Court decision may be obtained by filing a petition for review. The subdivision provides for review by the filing of the simple and familiar notice of appeal used to obtain review of district court judgments; (2) § 7483, supra, requires that a petition for review be filed within 3 months after a decision is rendered, and provides that if a petition is so filed by one party, any other party may file a petition for review within 4 months after the decision is rendered. In the interest of fixing the time for review with precision, the proposed rule substitutes "90 days" and "120 days" for the statutory "3 months" and "4 months", respectively. The power of the Court to regulate these details of practice is clear. Title 28 U.S.C. § 2072, as amended by the Act of November 6, 1966, 80 Stat. 1323 (1 U.S.Code Cong. & Ad. News, p. 1546 (1966)), authorizes the Court to regulate ". . . practice and procedure in proceedings for the review by the courts of appeals of decisions of the Tax Court of the United States. . . ."

The second paragraph states the settled teaching of the case law. See *Robert Louis Stevenson Apartments, Inc. v. C.I.R.*, 337 F.2d 681, 10 A.L.R.3d 112 (8th Cir., 1964); *Denholm & McKay Co. v. C.I.R.*, 132 F.2d 243 (1st Cir., 1942); *Helvering v. Continental Oil Co.*, 63 App.D.C. 5, 68 F.2d 750 (1934); *Burnet v. Lexington Ice & Coal Co.*, 62 F.2d 906 (4th Cir.1933); *Griffiths v. C.I.R.*, 50 F.2d 782 (7th Cir., 1931).

Subdivision (b). The subdivision incorporates the statutory provision (Title 26, U.S.C., § 7502) that timely mailing is to be treated as timely filing. The statute contains special provisions respecting other than ordinary mailing. If the notice of appeal is sent by registered mail, registration is deemed prima facie evidence that the notice was delivered to the clerk of the Tax Court, and the date of registration is deemed the postmark date. If the notice of appeal is sent by certified mail, the effect of certification with respect to prima facie evidence of delivery and the postmark date depends upon regulations of the Secretary of the Treasury. The effect of a postmark made other than by the United States Post Office likewise depends upon regulations of the Secretary. Current regulations are found in 26 CFR § 301.7502–1.

1979 Amendments

The proposed amendment reflects the change in the title of the Tax Court to "United States Tax Court." See 26 U.S.C. § 7441.

1994 Amendments

Subdivision (a). The amendment requires a party filing a notice of appeal to provide the court with sufficient copies of the notice for service on all other parties.

1998 Amendments

The language and organization of the rule are amended to make the rule more easily understood. In addition to changes made to improve the understanding, the Advisory Committee has changed language to make style and terminology consistent throughout the appellate rules. These changes are intended to by stylistic only.

Rule 14. Applicability of Other Rules to the Review of a Tax Court Decision

All provisions of these rules, except Rules 4–9, 15–20, and 22–23, apply to the review of a Tax Court decision.

(As amended Apr. 24, 1998, eff. Dec. 1, 1998.)

1967 Adoption

The proposed rule continues the present uniform practice of the circuits of regulating review of decisions of the Tax Court by the general rules applicable to appeals from judgments of the district courts.

1998 Amendments

The language of the rule are amended to make the rule more easily understood. In addition to changes made to improve the understanding, the Advisory Committee has changed language to make style and terminology consistent throughout the appellate rules. These changes are intended to by stylistic only.

TITLE IV. REVIEW OR ENFORCEMENT OF AN ORDER OF AN ADMINISTRATIVE AGENCY, BOARD, COMMISSION, OR OFFICER

Rule 15. Review or Enforcement of an Agency Order—How Obtained; Intervention

(a) Petition for Review; Joint Petition.

(1) Review of an agency order is commenced by filing, within the time prescribed by law, a petition for review with the clerk of a court of appeals authorized to review the agency order. If their interests make joinder practicable, two or more persons may join in a petition to the same court to review the same order.

(2) The petition must:

(A) name each party seeking review either in the caption or the body of the petition—using such terms as 'et al.,' 'petitioners,' or 'respondents' does not effectively name the parties;

(B) name the agency as a respondent (even though not named in the petition, the United States is a respondent if required by statute); and

(C) specify the order or part thereof to be reviewed.

(3) Form 3 in the Appendix of Forms is a suggested form of a petition for review.

(4) In this rule 'agency' includes an agency, board, commission, or officer; 'petition for review' includes a petition to enjoin, suspend, modify, or otherwise review, or a notice of appeal, whichever form is indicated by the applicable statute.

(b) Application or Cross-Application to Enforce an Order; Answer; Default.

(1) An application to enforce an agency order must be filed with the clerk of a court of appeals authorized to enforce the order. If a petition is filed to review an agency order that the court may enforce, a party opposing the petition may file a cross-application for enforcement.

(2) Within 20 days after the application for enforcement is filed, the respondent must serve on the applicant an answer to the application and file it with the clerk. If the respondent fails to answer in time, the court will enter judgment for the relief requested.

(3) The application must contain a concise statement of the proceedings in which the order was entered, the facts upon which venue is based, and the relief requested.

(c) Service of the Petition or Application. The circuit clerk must serve a copy of the petition for review, or an application or cross-application to enforce an agency order, on each respondent as prescribed by Rule 3(d), unless a different manner of service is prescribed by statute. At the time of filing, the petitioner must:

(1) serve, or have served, a copy on each party admitted to participate in the agency proceedings, except for the respondents;

(2) file with the clerk a list of those so served; and

(3) give the clerk enough copies of the petition or application to serve each respondent.

(d) Intervention. Unless a statute provides another method, a person who wants to intervene in a proceeding under this rule must file a motion for leave to intervene with the circuit clerk and serve a copy on all parties. The motion—or other notice of intervention authorized by statute—must be filed within 30 days after the petition for review is filed and must contain a concise statement of the interest of the moving party and the grounds for intervention.

(e) Payment of Fees. When filing any separate or joint petition for review in a court of appeals, the petitioner must pay the circuit clerk all required fees. (As amended Apr. 22, 1993, eff. Dec. 1, 1993; Apr. 24, 1998, eff. Dec. 1, 1998.)

1967 Adoption

General Note. The power of the Supreme Court to prescribe rules of practice and procedure for the judicial review or enforcement of orders of administrative agencies, boards, commissions, and officers is conferred by 28 U.S.C. § 2072, as amended by the Act of November 6, 1966, § 1, 80 Stat. 1323 (1 U.S.Code Cong. & Ad. News, p. 1546 (1966). Section 11 of the Hobbs Administrative Orders Review Act of 1950, 64 Stat. 1132, reenacted as 28 U.S.C. § 2352 (28 U.S.C.A. § 2352 (Supp.1966)), repealed by the Act of November 6, 1966, § 4, supra, directed the courts of appeals to adopt and promulgate, subject to approval by the Judicial Conference rules governing practice and procedure in proceedings to review the orders of boards, commissions and officers whose orders were made reviewable in the courts of appeals by the Act. Thereafter, the Judicial Conference approved a uniform rule, and that rule, with minor variations, is now in effect in all circuits. Third Circuit Rule 18 [rule 18, U.S.Ct. of App. 3rd Cir.] is a typical circuit rule, and for convenience it is referred to as the uniform rule in the notes which accompany rules under this Title.

Subdivision (a). The uniform rule (see General Note above) requires that the petition for review contain "a concise statement, in barest outline, of the nature of the proceedings as to which relief is sought, the facts upon which venue is based, the grounds upon which relief is sought, and the relief prayed." That language is derived from § 4 of the Hobbs Administrative Orders Review Act of 1950, 64 Stat. 1130, reenacted as 28 U.S.C. § 2344 (28 U.S.C.A. § 2344 (Supp.

1966)). A few other statutes also prescribe the content of the petition, but the great majority are silent on the point. The proposed rule supersedes 28 U.S.C. § 2344 and other statutory provisions prescribing the form of the petition for review and permits review to be initiated by the filing of a simple petition similar in form to the notice of appeal used in appeals from judgments of district courts. The more elaborate form of petition for review now required is rarely useful either to the litigants or to the courts. There is no effective, reasonable way of obliging petitioners to come to the real issues before those issues are formulated in the briefs. Other provisions of this subdivision are derived from §§ 1 and 2 of the uniform rule.

Subdivision (b). This subdivision is derived from §§ 3, 4 and 5 of the uniform rule.

Subdivision (c). This subdivision is derived from § 1 of the uniform rule.

Subdivision (d). This subdivision is based upon § 6 of the uniform rule. Statutes occasionally permit intervention by the filing of a notice of intention to intervene. The uniform rule does not fix a time limit for intervention, and the only time limits fixed by statute are the 30-day periods found in the Communications Act Amendments, 1952, § 402(e), 66 Stat. 719, 47 U.S.C. § 402(e), and the Sugar Act of 1948, § 205(d), 61 Stat. 927, 7 U.S.C. § 1115(d).

1993 Amendments

Subdivision (a). The amendment is a companion to the amendment of Rule 3(c). Both Rule 3(c) and Rule 15(a) state that a notice of appeal or petition for review must name the parties seeking appellate review. Rule 3(c), however, provides an attorney who represents more than one party on appeal the flexibility to describe the parties in general terms rather than naming them individually. Rule 15(a) does not allow that flexibility; each petitioner must be named. A petition for review of an agency decision is the first filing in any court and, therefore, is analogous to a complaint in which all parties must be named.

Subdivision (e). The amendment adds subdivision (e). Subdivision (e) parallels Rule 3(e) that requires the payment of fees when filing a notice of appeal. The omission of such a requirement from Rule 15 is an apparent oversight. Five circuits have local rules requiring the payment of such fees, see, e.g., Fifth Cir.Loc.R. 15.1, and Fed.Cir.Loc.R. 15(a)(2).

1998 Amendments

The language and organization of the rule are amended to make the rule more easily understood. In addition to changes made to improve the understanding, the Advisory Committee has changed language to make style and terminology consistent throughout the appellate rules. These changes are intended to by stylistic only.

Rule 15.1. Briefs and Oral Argument in a National Labor Relations Board Proceeding

In either an enforcement or a review proceeding, a party adverse to the National Labor Relations Board proceeds first on briefing and at oral argument, unless the court orders otherwise.

(Added Mar. 10, 1986, eff. July 1, 1986, and amended Apr. 24, 1998, eff. Dec. 1, 1998.)

1986 Addition

This rule simply confirms the existing practice in most circuits.

1998 Amendments

The language of the rule are amended to make the rule more easily understood. In addition to changes made to improve the understanding, the Advisory Committee has changed language to make style and terminology consistent throughout the appellate rules. These changes are intended to by stylistic only.

Rule 16. The Record on Review or Enforcement

(a) Composition of the Record. The record on review or enforcement of an agency order consists of:

(1) the order involved;

(2) any findings or report on which it is based; and

(3) the pleadings, evidence, and other parts of the proceedings before the agency.

(b) Omissions From or Misstatements in the Record. The parties may at any time, by stipulation, supply any omission from the record or correct a misstatement, or the court may so direct. If necessary, the court may direct that a supplemental record be prepared and filed.

(As amended Apr. 24, 1998, eff. Dec. 1, 1998.)

1967 Adoption

Subdivision (a) is based upon 28 U.S.C § 2112(b). There is no distinction between the record compiled in the agency proceeding and the record on review; they are one and the same. The record in agency cases is thus the same as that in appeals from the district court—the original papers, transcripts and exhibits in the proceeding below. Subdivision (b) is based upon § 8 of the uniform rule (see General Note following Rule 15).

1998 Amendments

The language and organization of the rule are amended to make the rule more easily understood. In addition to changes made to improve the understanding, the Advisory Committee has changed language to make style and terminology consistent throughout the appellate rules. These changes are intended to by stylistic only.

Rule 17. Filing the Record

(a) Agency to File; Time for Filing; Notice of Filing. The agency must file the record with the circuit clerk within 40 days after being served with a petition for review, unless the statute authorizing review provides otherwise, or within 40 days after it files an application for enforcement unless the respondent fails to answer or the court orders otherwise. The court may shorten or extend the time to file the record. The clerk must notify all parties of the date when the record is filed.

(b) Filing—What Constitutes.

(1) The agency must file:

(A) the original or a certified copy of the entire record or parts designated by the parties; or

(B) a certified list adequately describing all documents, transcripts of testimony, exhibits, and other material constituting the record, or describing those parts designated by the parties.

(2) The parties may stipulate in writing that no record or certified list be filed. The date when the stipulation is filed with the circuit clerk is treated as the date when the record is filed.

(3) The agency must retain any portion of the record not filed with the clerk. All parts of the record retained by the agency are a part of the record on review for all purposes and, if the court or a party so requests, must be sent to the court regardless of any prior stipulation.

(As amended Apr. 24, 1998, eff. Dec. 1, 1998.)

1967 Adoption

Subdivision (a). This subdivision is based upon § 7 of the uniform rule (see General Note following Rule 15). That rule does not prescribe a time for filing the record in enforcement cases. Forty days are allowed in order to avoid useless preparation of the record or certified list in cases where the application for enforcement is not contested.

Subdivision (b). This subdivision is based upon 28 U.S.C. § 2112 and § 7 of the uniform rule. It permits the agency to file either the record itself or a certified list of its contents. It also permits the parties to stipulate against transmission of designated parts of the record without the fear that an inadvertent stipulation may "diminish" the record. Finally, the parties may, in cases where consultation of the record is unnecessary, stipulate that neither the record nor a certified list of its contents be filed.

1998 Amendments

The language and organization of the rule are amended to make the rule more easily understood. In addition to changes made to improve the understanding, the Advisory Committee has changed language to make style and terminology consistent throughout the appellate rules. These changes are intended to by stylistic only; a substantive change is made, however, in subdivision (b).

Subdivision (b). The current rule provides that when a court of appeals is asked to review or enforce an agency order, the agency must file either "the entire record or such parts thereof as the parties may designate by stipulation filed with the agency" or a certified list describing the documents, transcripts, exhibits, and other material constituting the record. If the agency is not filing a certified list, the current rule requires the agency to file the entire record unless the parties file a "stipulation" designating only parts of the record. Such a "stipulation" presumably requires agreement of the parties as to the parts to be filed. The amended language in subparagraph (b)(1)(A) permits the filing of less than the entire record even when the parties do not agree as to which parts should be filed. Each party can designate the parts that it wants filed; the agency can then forward the parts designated by each party. In contrast, paragraph (b)(2) continues to require stipulation, that is agreement of the parties, that the agency need not file either the record or a certified list.

Rule 18. Stay Pending Review

(a) Motion for a Stay.

(1) Initial Motion Before the Agency. A petitioner must ordinarily move first before the agency for a stay pending review of its decision or order.

(2) Motion in the Court of Appeals. A motion for a stay may be made to the court of appeals or one of its judges.

(A) The motion must:

(i) show that moving first before the agency would be impracticable; or

(ii) state that, a motion having been made, the agency denied the motion or failed to afford the relief requested and state any reasons given by the agency for its action.

(B) The motion must also include:

(i) the reasons for granting the relief requested and the facts relied on;

(ii) originals or copies of affidavits or other sworn statements supporting facts subject to dispute; and

(iii) relevant parts of the record.

(C) The moving party must give reasonable notice of the motion to all parties.

(D) The motion must be filed with the circuit clerk and normally will be considered by a panel of the court. But in an exceptional case in which time requirements make that procedure impracticable, the motion may be made to and considered by a single judge.

(b) Bond. The court may condition relief on the filing of a bond or other appropriate security.

(As amended Apr. 24, 1998, eff. Dec. 1, 1998.)

1967 Adoption

While this rule has no counterpart in present rules regulating review of agency proceedings, it merely assimilates the procedure for obtaining stays in agency proceedings with that for obtaining stays in appeals from the district courts. The same considerations which justify the requirement of an initial application to the district court for a stay pending appeal support the requirement of an initial application to the agency pending review. See Note accompanying Rule 8.

Title 5, U.S.C. § 705 (5 U.S.C.A. § 705 (1966 Pamphlet)), confers general authority on both agencies and reviewing courts to stay agency action pending review. Many of the statutes authorizing review of agency action by the courts of appeals deal with the question of stays, and at least one, the Act of June 15, 1936, 49 Stat. 1499 (7 U.S.C. § 10a), prohibits a stay pending review. The proposed rule in nowise affects such statutory provisions respecting stays. By its terms, it simply indicates the procedure to be followed when a stay is sought.

1998 Amendments

The language and organization of the rule are amended to make the rule more easily understood. In addition to changes made to improve the understanding, the Advisory Committee has changed language to make style and terminology consistent throughout the appellate rules. These changes are intended to by stylistic only.

Rule 19. Settlement of a Judgment Enforcing an Agency Order in Part

When the court files an opinion directing entry of judgment enforcing the agency's order in part, the agency must within 14 days file with the clerk and serve on each other party a proposed judgment conforming to the opinion. A party who disagrees with the agency's proposed judgment must within 7 days file with the clerk and serve the agency with a proposed judgment that the party believes conforms to the opinion. The court will settle the judgment and direct entry without further hearing or argument.
(As amended Mar. 10, 1986, eff. July 1, 1986; Apr. 24, 1998, eff. Dec. 1, 1998.)

1967 Adoption

This is § 12 of the uniform rule (see General Note following Rule 15) with changes in phraseology.

1986 Amendment

The deletion of the words "in whole or" is designed to eliminate delay in the issuance of a judgment when the court of appeals has either enforced completely the order of an agency or denied completely such enforcement. In such a clear-cut situation, it serves no useful purpose to delay the issuance of the judgment until a proposed judgment is submitted by the agency and reviewed by the respondent. This change conforms the Rule to the existing practice in most circuits. Other amendments are technical and no substantive change is intended.

1998 Amendments

The language of the rule are amended to make the rule more easily understood. In addition to changes made to improve the understanding, the Advisory Committee has changed language to make style and terminology consistent throughout the appellate rules. These changes are intended to by stylistic only.

Rule 20. Applicability of Rules to the Review or Enforcement of an Agency Order

All provisions of these rules, except Rules 3–14 and 22–23, apply to the review or enforcement of an agency order. In these rules, 'appellant' includes a petitioner or applicant, and 'appellee' includes a respondent.
(As amended Apr. 24, 1998, eff. Dec. 1, 1998.)

1967 Adoption

The proposed rule continues the present uniform practice of the circuits of regulating agency review or enforcement proceedings by the general rules applicable to appeals from judgments of the district courts.

1998 Amendments

The language of the rule are amended to make the rule more easily understood. In addition to changes made to improve the understanding, the Advisory Committee has changed language to make style and terminology consistent throughout the appellate rules. These changes are intended to by stylistic only.

TITLE V. EXTRAORDINARY WRITS

Rule 21. Writs of Mandamus and Prohibition, and Other Extraordinary Writs

(a) Mandamus or Prohibition to a Court: Petition, Filing, Service, and Docketing.

(1) A party petitioning for a writ of mandamus or prohibition directed to a court must file a petition with the circuit clerk with proof of service on all parties to the proceeding in the trial court. The party must also provide a copy to the trial-court judge. All parties to the proceeding in the trial court other than the petitioner are respondents for all purposes.

(2)(A) The petition must be titled 'In re [name of petitioner].'

(B) The petition must state:

(i) the relief sought;

(ii) the issues presented;

(iii) the facts necessary to understand the issue presented by the petition; and

(iv) the reasons why the writ should issue.

(C) The petition must include a copy of any order or opinion or parts of the record that may be essential to understand the matters set forth in the petition.

(3) Upon receiving the prescribed docket fee, the clerk must docket the petition and submit it to the court.

(b) Denial; Order Directing Answer; Briefs; Precedence.

(1) The court may deny the petition without an answer. Otherwise, it must order the respondent, if any, to answer within a fixed time.

(2) The clerk must serve the order to respond on all persons directed to respond.

(3) Two or more respondents may answer jointly.

(4) The court of appeals may invite or order the trial-court judge to address the petition or may invite an amicus curiae to do so. The trial-court judge may request permission to address the petition but may not do so unless invited or ordered to do so by the court of appeals.

(5) If briefing or oral argument is required, the clerk must advise the parties, and when appropriate, the trial-court judge or amicus curiae.

(6) The proceeding must be given preference over ordinary civil cases.

(7) The circuit clerk must send a copy of the final disposition to the trial-court judge.

(c) Other Extraordinary Writs. An application for an extraordinary writ other than one provided for in Rule 21(a) must be made by filing a petition with the circuit clerk with proof of service on the respondents. Proceedings on the application must conform, so far as is practicable, to the procedures prescribed in Rule 21(a) and (b).

(d) Form of Papers; Number of Copies. All papers must conform to Rule 32(c)(2). Except by the court's permission, a paper must not exceed 30 pages, exclusive of the disclosure statement, the proof of service, and the accompanying documents required by Rule 21(a)(2)(C). An original and 3 copies must be filed unless the court requires the filing of a different number by local rule or by order in a particular case.

(As amended Apr. 29, 1994, eff. Dec. 1, 1994; Apr. 23, 1996, eff. Dec. 1, 1996; Apr. 24, 1998, eff. Dec. 1, 1998; Apr. 29, 2002, eff. Dec. 1, 2002.)

1967 Adoption

The authority of courts of appeals to issue extraordinary writs is derived from 28 U.S.C. § 1651. Subdivisions (a) and (b) regulate in detail the procedure surrounding the writs most commonly sought—mandamus or prohibition directed to a judge or judges. Those subdivisions are based upon Supreme Court Rule 31, with certain changes which reflect the uniform practice among the circuits (Seventh Circuit Rule 19 is a typical circuit rule). Subdivision (c) sets out a very general procedure to be followed in applications for the variety of other writs which may be issued under the authority of 28 U.S.C. § 1651.

1994 Amendments

Subdivision (d). The amendment makes it clear that a court may require a different number of copies either by rule or by order in an individual case. The number of copies of any document that a court of appeals needs varies depending upon the way in which the court conducts business. The internal operation of the courts of appeals necessarily varies from circuit to circuit because of differences in the number of judges, the geographic area included within the circuit, and other such factors. Uniformity could be achieved only by setting the number of copies artificially high so that parties in all circuits file enough copies to satisfy the needs of the courts requiring the greatest number. Rather than do that, the Committee decided to make it clear that local rules may require a greater or lesser number of copies and that, if the circumstances of a particular case indicate the need for a different number of copies in that case, the court may so order.

1996 Amendments

In most instances, a writ of mandamus or prohibition is not actually directed to a judge in any more personal way than is an order reversing a court's judgment. Most often a petition for a writ of mandamus seeks review of the intrinsic merits of a judge's action and is in reality an adversary proceeding between the parties. See, *e.g.*, *Walker v. Columbia Broadcasting System, Inc.*, 443 F.2d 33 (7th Cir.1971). In order to change the tone of the rule and of mandamus proceedings generally, the rule is amended so that the judge is not treated as a respondent. The caption and subdivision (a) are amended by deleting the reference to the writs as being "directed to a judge or judges."

Subdivision (a). Subdivision (a) applies to writs of mandamus or prohibition directed to a court, but it is amended so that a petition for a writ of mandamus or prohibition does not bear the name of the judge. The amendments to subdivision (a) speak, however, about mandamus or prohibition "directed to a court." This language is inserted to distinguish subdivision (a) from subdivision (c). Subdivision (c) governs all other extraordinary writs, including a writ of mandamus or prohibition directed to an administrative agency rather than to a court and a writ of habeas corpus.

The amendments require the petitioner to provide a copy of the petition to the trial court judge. This will alert the judge to the filing of the petition. This is necessary because the trial court judge is not treated as a respondent and, as a result, is not served. A companion amendment is made in subdivision (b). It requires the circuit clerk to send a copy of the disposition of the petition to the trial court judge.

Subdivision (b). The amendment provides that even if relief is requested of a particular judge, although the judge may request permission to respond, the judge may not do so unless the court invites or orders a response.

The court of appeals ordinarily will be adequately informed not only by the opinions or statements made by the trial court judge contemporaneously with the entry of the challenged order but also by the arguments made on behalf of the party opposing the relief. The latter does not create an attorney-client relationship between the party's attorney and the judge whose action is challenged, nor does it give rise to any right to compensation from the judge.

If the court of appeals desires to hear from the trial court judge, however, the court may invite or order the judge to respond. In some instances, especially those involving court administration or the failure of a judge to act, it may be that no one other than the judge can provide a thorough explanation of the matters at issue. Because it is ordinarily undesirable to place the trial court judge, even temporarily, in an adversarial posture with a litigant, the rule permits a court of appeals to invite an *amicus curiae* to provide a response to the petition. In those instances in which the respondent does not oppose issuance of the writ or does not have sufficient perspective on the issue to provide an adequate response, participation of an *amicus* may avoid the need for the trial judge to participate.

Subdivision (c). The changes are stylistic only. No substantive changes are intended.

1998 Amendments

The language and organization of the rule are amended to make the rule more easily understood. In addition to changes made to improve the understanding, the Advisory Committee has changed language to make style and terminology consistent throughout the appellate rules. These changes are intended to by stylistic only.

2002 Amendments

Subdivision (d). A petition for a writ of mandamus or prohibition, an application for another extraordinary writ, and an answer to such a petition or application are all "other papers" for purposes of Rule 32(c)(2), and all of the requirements of Rule 32(a) apply to those papers, except as provided in Rule 32(c)(2). During the 1998 restyling of the Federal Rules of Appellate Procedure, Rule 21(d) was inadvertently changed to suggest that only the requirements of Rule 32(a)(1) apply to such papers. Rule 21(d) has been amended to correct that error.

Rule 21(d) has been further amended to limit the length of papers filed under Rule 21.

Changes Made After Publication and Comments No changes were made to the text of the proposed amendment or to the Committee Note, except that the page limit was increased from 20 pages to 30 pages. The Committee was persuaded by some commentators that petitions for extraordinary writs closely resemble principal briefs on the merits and should be allotted more than 20 pages.

TITLE VI. HABEAS CORPUS; PROCEEDINGS IN FORMA PAUPERIS

Rule 22. Habeas Corpus and Section 2255 Proceedings

(a) Application for the Original Writ. An application for a writ of habeas corpus must be made to the appropriate district court. If made to a circuit judge, the application must be transferred to the appropriate district court. If a district court denies an application made or transferred to it, renewal of the application before a circuit judge is not permitted. The applicant may, under 28 U.S.C. § 2253, appeal to the court of appeals from the district court's order denying the application.

(b) Certificate of Appealability.

(1) In a habeas corpus proceeding in which the detention complained of arises from process issued by a state court, or in a 28 U.S.C. § 2255 proceeding, the applicant cannot take an appeal unless a circuit justice or a circuit or district judge issues a certificate of appealability under 28 U.S.C. § 2253(c). If an applicant files a notice of appeal, the district judge who rendered the judgment must either issue a certificate of appealability or state why a certificate should not issue. The district clerk must send the certificate or statement to the court of appeals with the notice of appeal and the file of the district-court proceedings. If the district judge has denied the certificate, the applicant may request a circuit judge to issue the certificate.

(2) A request addressed to the court of appeals may be considered by a circuit judge or judges, as the court prescribes. If no express request for a certificate is filed, the notice of appeal constitutes a request addressed to the judges of the court of appeals.

(3) A certificate of appealability is not required when a state or its representative or the United States or its representative appeals.

(As amended Pub.L. 104–132, Title I, § 103, Apr. 24, 1996, 110 Stat. 1218; Apr. 24, 1998, eff. Dec. 1, 1998.)

1967 Adoption

Subdivision (a). Title 28 U.S.C. § 2241(a) authorizes circuit judges to issue the writ of habeas corpus. Section 2241(b) [§ 2241(b) of this title], however, authorizes a circuit judge to decline to entertain an application and to transfer it to the appropriate district court, and this is the usual practice. The first two sentences merely make present practice explicit. Title 28 U.S.C. § 2253 seems clearly to contemplate that once an application is presented to a district judge and is denied by him, the remedy is an appeal from the order of denial. But the language of 28 U.S.C. § 2241 seems to authorize a second original application to a circuit judge following a denial by a district judge. *In re Gersing*, 79 U.S.App.D. 245, 145 F.2d 481 (D.C.Cir., 1944) and *Chapman v. Teets*, 241 F.2d 186 (9th Cir., 1957) acknowledge the availability of such a procedure. But the procedure is ordinarily a waste of time for all involved, and the final sentence attempts to discourage it.

A court of appeals has no jurisdiction as a court to grant an original writ of habeas corpus, and courts of appeals have dismissed applications addressed to them. *Loum v. Alvis*,

263 F.2d 836 (6th Cir., 1959); *In re Berry*, 221 F.2d 798 (9th Cir., 1955); *Posey v. Dowd*, 134 F.2d 613 (7th Cir., 1943). The fairer and more expeditious practice is for the court of appeals to regard an application addressed to it as being addressed to one of its members, and to transfer the application to the appropriate district court in accordance with the provisions of this rule. Perhaps such a disposition is required by the rationale of *In re Burwell*, 350 U.S. 521, 76 S.Ct. 539, 100 L.Ed. 666 (1956).

Subdivision (b). Title 28 U.S.C. § 2253 provides that an appeal may not be taken in a habeas corpus proceeding where confinement is under a judgment of a state court unless the judge who rendered the order in the habeas corpus proceeding, or a circuit justice or judge, issues a certificate of probable cause. In the interest of insuring that the matter of the certificate will not be overlooked and that, if the certificate is denied, the reasons for denial in the first instance will be available on any subsequent application, the proposed rule requires the district judge to issue the certificate or to state reasons for its denial.

While 28 U.S.C. § 2253 does not authorize the court of appeals as a court to grant a certificate of probable cause, *In re Burwell*, 350 U.S. 521, 76 S.Ct. 539, 100 L.Ed. 666 (1956) makes it clear that a court of appeals may not decline to consider a request for the certificate addressed to it as a court but must regard the request as made to the judges thereof. The fourth sentence incorporates the Burwell rule.

Although 28 U.S.C. § 2253 appears to require a certificate of probable cause even when an appeal is taken by a state or its representative, the legislative history strongly suggests that the intention of Congress was to require a certificate only in the case in which an appeal is taken by an applicant for the writ. See *United States ex rel. Tillery v. Cavell*, 294 F.2d 12 (3d Cir., 1960). Four of the five circuits which have ruled on the point have so interpreted § 2253. *United States ex rel. Tillery v. Cavell*, supra; *Buder v. Bell*, 306 F.2d 71 (6th Cir., 1962); *United States ex rel. Calhoun v. Pate*, 341 F.2d 885 (7th Cir., 1965); *State of Texas v. Graves*, 352 F.2d 514 (5th Cir., 1965). Cf. *United States ex rel. Carrol v. LaVallee*, 342 F.2d 641 (2d Cir., 1965). The final sentence makes it clear that a certificate of probable cause is not required of a state or its representative.

1998 Amendments

The language and organization of the rule are amended to make the rule more easily understood. In addition to changes made to improve the understanding, the Advisory Committee has changed language to make style and terminology consistent throughout the appellate rules. These changes are intended to by stylistic only; in this rule, however, substantive changes are made in paragraphs (b)(1) and (b)(3).

Subdivision (b), paragraph (1). Two substantive changes are made in this paragraph. First, the paragraph is made applicable to 28 U.S.C. § 2255 proceedings. This brings the rule into conformity with 28 U.S.C. § 2253 as amended by the Anti-Terrorism and Effective Death Penalty Act of 1996, Pub.L. No. 104–132. Second, the rule states that a certificate of appealability may be issued by a "circuit justice or a circuit or district judge." That language adds a reference to the circuit justice which also brings the rule into conformity with section 2253. The language continues to state that in addition to the circuit justice, both a circuit and a district judge may issue a certificate of appealability. The language of section 2253 is ambiguous; it states that a certificate of appealability may be issued by "a circuit justice or judge." Since the enactment of the Anti–Terrorism and Effective Death Penalty Act, three circuits have held that both district and circuit judges, as well as the circuit justice, may issue a certificate of appealability. *Else v. Johnson*, 104 F.3d 82 (5th Cir. 1997); *Lyons v. Ohio Adult Parole Authority*, 105 F.3d 1063 (6th Cir. 1997); and *Hunter v. United States*, 101 F.3d 1565 (11th Cir. 1996). The approach taken by the rule is consistent with those decisions.

Subdivision (b), paragraph (3). The Anti-Terrorism and Effective Death Penalty Act of 1996, Pub.L. No. 104–132, amended 28 U.S.C. § 2253 to make it applicable to § 2255 proceedings. Accordingly, paragraph (3) is amended to provide that when the United States or its representative appeals, a certificate of appealability is not required.

Rule 23. Custody or Release of a Prisoner in a Habeas Corpus Proceeding

(a) Transfer of Custody Pending Review. Pending review of a decision in a habeas corpus proceeding commenced before a court, justice, or judge of the United States for the release of a prisoner, the person having custody of the prisoner must not transfer custody to another unless a transfer is directed in accordance with this rule. When, upon application, a custodian shows the need for a transfer, the court, justice, or judge rendering the decision under review may authorize the transfer and substitute the successor custodian as a party.

(b) Detention or Release Pending Review of Decision Not to Release. While a decision not to release a prisoner is under review, the court or judge rendering the decision, or the court of appeals, or the Supreme Court, or a judge or justice of either court, may order that the prisoner be:

(1) detained in the custody from which release is sought;

(2) detained in other appropriate custody; or

(3) released on personal recognizance, with or without surety.

(c) Release Pending Review of Decision Ordering Release. While a decision ordering the release of a prisoner is under review, the prisoner must—unless the court or judge rendering the decision, or the court of appeals, or the Supreme Court, or a judge or justice of either court orders otherwise—be released on personal recognizance, with or without surety.

(d) Modification of the Initial Order on Custody. An initial order governing the prisoner's custody or release, including any recognizance or surety, continues in effect pending review unless for special reasons shown to the court of appeals or the Supreme Court, or to a judge or justice of either court, the order is modified or an independent order regarding custody, release, or surety is issued.

(As amended Mar. 10, 1986, eff. July 1, 1986; Apr. 24, 1998, eff. Dec. 1, 1998.)

1967 Adoption

The rule is the same as Supreme Court Rule 49 as amended on June 12, 1967, effective October 2, 1967.

1986 Amendment

The amendments to Rules 23(b) and (c) are technical. No substantive change is intended.

1998 Amendments

The language and organization of the rule are amended to make the rule more easily understood. In addition to changes made to improve the understanding, the Advisory Committee has changed language to make style and terminology consistent throughout the appellate rules. These changes are intended to by stylistic only.

Subdivision (d). The current rule states that the initial order governing custody or release "shall govern review" in the court of appeals. The amended language says that the initial order generally "continues in effect" pending review.

When Rule 23 was adopted it used the same language as Supreme Court Rule 49, which then governed custody of prisoners in habeas corpus proceedings. The "shall govern review" language was drawn from the Supreme Court Rule. The Supreme Court has since amended its rule, now Rule 36, to say that the initial order "shall continue in effect" unless for reasons shown it is modified or a new order is entered. Rule 23 is amended to similarly state that the initial order "continues in effect." The new language is clearer. It removes the possible implication that the initial order created law of the case, a strange notion to attach to an order regarding custody or release.

Rule 24. Proceeding in Forma Pauperis

(a) Leave to Proceed in Forma Pauperis.

(1) Motion in the District Court. Except as stated in Rule 24(a)(3), a party to a district-court action who desires to appeal in forma pauperis must file a motion in the district court. The party must attach an affidavit that:

(A) shows in the detail prescribed by Form 4 of the Appendix of Forms the party's inability to pay or to give security for fees and costs;

(B) claims an entitlement to redress; and

(C) states the issues that the party intends to present on appeal.

(2) Action on the Motion. If the district court grants the motion, the party may proceed on appeal without prepaying or giving security for fees and costs, unless a statute provides otherwise. If the district court denies the motion, it must state its reasons in writing.

(3) Prior Approval. A party who was permitted to proceed in forma pauperis in the district-court action, or who was determined to be financially unable to obtain an adequate defense in a criminal case, may proceed on appeal in forma pauperis without further authorization, unless:

(A) the district court—before or after the notice of appeal is filed—certifies that the appeal is not taken in good faith or finds that the party is not otherwise entitled to proceed in forma pauperis and states in writing its reasons for the certification or finding; or

(B) a statute provides otherwise.

(4) Notice of District Court's Denial. The district clerk must immediately notify the parties and the court of appeals when the district court does any of the following:

(A) denies a motion to proceed on appeal in forma pauperis;

(B) certifies that the appeal is not taken in good faith; or

(C) finds that the party is not otherwise entitled to proceed in forma pauperis.

(5) Motion in the Court of Appeals. A party may file a motion to proceed on appeal in forma pauperis in the court of appeals within 30 days after service of the notice prescribed in Rule 24(a)(4). The motion must include a copy of the affidavit filed in the district court and the district court's statement of reasons for its action. If no affidavit was filed in the district court, the party must include the affidavit prescribed by Rule 24(a)(1).

(b) Leave to Proceed in Forma Pauperis on Appeal or Review of an Administrative–Agency Proceeding. When an appeal or review of a proceeding before an administrative agency, board, commission, or officer (including for the purpose of this rule the United States Tax Court) proceeds directly in a court of appeals, a party may file in the court of appeals a motion for leave to proceed on appeal in forma pauperis with an affidavit prescribed by Rule 24(a)(1).

(c) Leave to Use Original Record. A party allowed to proceed on appeal in forma pauperis may request that the appeal be heard on the original record without reproducing any part.

(As amended Apr. 30, 1979, eff. Aug. 1, 1979; Mar. 10, 1986, eff. July 1, 1986; Apr. 24, 1998, eff. Dec. 1, 1998; Apr. 29, 2002, eff. Dec. 1, 2002.)

1967 Adoption

Subdivision (a). Authority to allow prosecution of an appeal in forma pauperis is vested in "[a]ny court of the United States" by 28 U.S.C. § 1915(a). The second paragraph of § 1915(a) seems to contemplate initial application to the district court for permission to proceed in forma pauperis, and although the circuit rules are generally silent on the question, the case law requires initial application to the district court. *Hayes v. United States*, 258 F.2d 400 (5th Cir., 1958), cert. den. 358 U.S. 856, 79 S.Ct. 87, 3 L.Ed.2d 89

(1958); *Elkins v. United States*, 250 F.2d 145 (9th Cir., 1957) see 364 U.S. 206, 80 S.Ct. 1437, 4 L.Ed.2d 1669 (1960); *United States v. Farley*, 238 F.2d 575 (2d Cir., 1956) see 354 U.S. 521, 77 S.Ct. 1371, 1 L.Ed.2d 1529 (1957). D.C.Cir. Rule 41(a) requires initial application to the district court. The content of the affidavit follows the language of the statute; the requirement of a statement of the issues comprehends the statutory requirement of a statement of "the nature of the . . . appeal. . . ." The second sentence is in accord with the decision in *McGann v. United States*, 362 U.S. 309, 80 S.Ct. 725, 4 L.Ed.2d 734 (1960). The requirement contained in the third sentence has no counterpart in present circuit rules, but it has been imposed by decision in at least two circuits. *Ragan v. Cox*, 305 F.2d 58 (10th Cir., 1962); *United States ex rel. Breedlove v. Dowd*, 269 F.2d 693 (7th Cir., 1959).

The second paragraph permits one whose indigency has been previously determined by the district court to proceed on appeal in forma pauperis without the necessity of a redetermination of indigency, while reserving to the district court its statutory authority to certify that the appeal is not taken in good faith, 28 U.S.C. § 1915(a), and permitting an inquiry into whether the circumstances of the party who was originally entitled to proceed in forma pauperis have changed during the course of the litigation. Cf. Sixth Circuit Rule 26 [rule 26, U.S.Ct. of App. 6th Cir.].

The final paragraph establishes a subsequent motion in the court of appeals, rather than an appeal from the order of denial or from the certification of lack of good faith, as the proper procedure for calling in question the correctness of the action of the district court. The simple and expeditious motion procedure seems clearly preferable to an appeal. This paragraph applies only to applications for leave to appeal in forma pauperis. The order of a district court refusing leave to initiate an action in the district court in forma pauperis is reviewable on appeal. See *Roberts v. United States District Court*, 339 U.S. 844, 70 S.Ct. 954, 94 L.Ed. 1326 (1950).

Subdivision (b). Authority to allow prosecution in forma pauperis is vested only in a "court of the United States" (see Note to subdivision (a), above). Thus in proceedings brought directly in a court of appeals to review decisions of agencies or of the Tax Court, authority to proceed in forma pauperis should be sought in the court of appeals. If initial review of agency action is had in a district court, an application to appeal to a court of appeals in forma pauperis from the judgment of the district court is governed by the provisions of subdivision (a).

1979 Amendment

The proposed amendment reflects the change in the title of the Tax Court to "United States Tax Court." See 26 U.S.C. § 7441.

1986 Amendment

The amendments to Rule 24(a) are technical. No substantive change is intended.

1998 Amendments

The language and organization of the rule are amended to make the rule more easily understood. In addition to changes made to improve the understanding, the Advisory Committee has changed language to make style and terminology consistent throughout the appellate rules. These changes are intended to by stylistic only. The Advisory Committee deletes the language in subdivision (c) authorizing a party proceeding in forma pauperis to file papers in typewritten form because the authorization is unnecessary. The rules permit all parties to file typewritten documents.

2002 Amendments

Subdivision (a)(2). Section 804 of the Prison Litigation Reform Act of 1995 ("PLRA") amended 28 U.S.C. § 1915 to require that prisoners who bring civil actions or appeals from civil actions must "pay the full amount of a filing fee." 28 U.S.C. § 1915(b)(1). Prisoners who are unable to pay the full amount of the filing fee at the time that their actions or appeals are filed are generally required to pay part of the fee and then to pay the remainder of the fee in installments. 28 U.S.C. § 1915(b). By contrast, Rule 24(a)(2) has provided that, after the district court grants a litigant's motion to proceed on appeal in forma pauperis, the litigant may proceed "without prepaying or giving security for fees and costs." Thus, the PLRA and Rule 24(a)(2) appear to be in conflict.

Rule 24(a)(2) has been amended to resolve this conflict. Recognizing that future legislation regarding prisoner litigation is likely, the Committee has not attempted to incorporate into Rule 24 all of the requirements of the current version of 28 U.S.C. § 1915. Rather, the Committee has amended Rule 24(a)(2) to clarify that the rule is not meant to conflict with anything required by the PLRA or any other statute.

Subdivision (a)(3). Rule 24(a)(3) has also been amended to eliminate an apparent conflict with the PLRA. Rule 24(a)(3) has provided that a party who was permitted to proceed in forma pauperis in the district court may continue to proceed in forma pauperis in the court of appeals without further authorization, subject to certain conditions. The PLRA, by contrast, provides that a prisoner who was permitted to proceed in forma pauperis in the district court and who wishes to continue to proceed in forma pauperis on appeal may not do so "automatically," but must seek permission. *See, e.g., Morgan v. Haro*, 112 F.3d 788, 789 (5th Cir. 1997) ("A prisoner who seeks to proceed IFP on appeal must obtain leave to so proceed despite proceeding IFP in the district court.").

Rule 24(a)(3) has been amended to resolve this conflict. Again, recognizing that future legislation regarding prisoner litigation is likely, the Committee has not attempted to incorporate into Rule 24 all of the requirements of the current version of 28 U.S.C. § 1915. Rather, the Committee has amended Rule 24(a)(3) to clarify that the rule is not meant to conflict with anything required by the PLRA or any other statute.

Changes Made After Publication and Comments No changes were made to the text of the proposed amendment or to the Committee Note, except that "a statute provides otherwise" was substituted in place of "the law requires otherwise" in the text of the rule and conforming changes (as well as a couple of minor stylistic changes) were made to the Committee Note.

TITLE VII. GENERAL PROVISIONS

Rule 25. Filing and Service

(a) Filing.

(1) Filing with the Clerk. A paper required or permitted to be filed in a court of appeals must be filed with the clerk.

(2) Filing: Method and Timeliness.

(A) In general. Filing may be accomplished by mail addressed to the clerk, but filing is not timely unless the clerk receives the papers within the time fixed for filing.

(B) A brief or appendix. A brief or appendix is timely filed, however, if on or before the last day for filing, it is:

(i) mailed to the clerk by First–Class Mail, or other class of mail that is at least as expeditious, postage prepaid; or

(ii) dispatched to a third-party commercial carrier for delivery to the clerk within 3 calendar days.

(C) Inmate filing. A paper filed by an inmate confined in an institution is timely if deposited in the institution's internal mailing system on or before the last day for filing. If an institution has a system designed for legal mail, the inmate must use that system to receive the benefit of this rule. Timely filing may be shown by a declaration in compliance with 28 U.S.C. § 1746 or by a notarized statement, either of which must set forth the date of deposit and state that first-class postage has been prepaid.

(D) Electronic filing. A court of appeals may by local rule permit or require papers to be filed, signed, or verified by electronic means that are consistent with technical standards, if any, that the Judicial Conference of the United States establishes. A local rule may require filing by electronic means only if reasonable exceptions are allowed. A paper filed by electronic means in compliance with a local rule constitutes a written paper for the purpose of applying these rules.

(3) Filing a Motion with a Judge. If a motion requests relief that may be granted by a single judge, the judge may permit the motion to be filed with the judge; the judge must note the filing date on the motion and give it to the clerk.

(4) Clerk's Refusal of Documents. The clerk must not refuse to accept for filing any paper presented for that purpose solely because it is not presented in proper form as required by these rules or by any local rule or practice.

(5) Privacy Protection. An appeal in a case whose privacy protection was governed by Federal Rule of Bankruptcy Procedure 9037, Federal Rule of Civil Procedure 5.2, or Federal Rule of Criminal Procedure 49.1 is governed by the same rule on appeal. In all other proceedings, privacy protection is governed by Federal Rule of Civil Procedure 5.2, except that Federal Rule of Criminal Procedure 49.1 governs when an extraordinary writ is sought in a criminal case.

(b) Service of All Papers Required. Unless a rule requires service by the clerk, a party must, at or before the time of filing a paper, serve a copy on the other parties to the appeal or review. Service on a party represented by counsel must be made on the party's counsel.

(c) Manner of Service.

(1) Service may be any of the following:

(A) personal, including delivery to a responsible person at the office of counsel;

(B) by mail;

(C) by third-party commercial carrier for delivery within 3 calendar days; or

(D) by electronic means, if the party being served consents in writing.

(2) If authorized by local rule, a party may use the court's transmission equipment to make electronic service under Rule 25(c)(1)(D).

(3) When reasonable considering such factors as the immediacy of the relief sought, distance, and cost, service on a party must be by a manner at least as expeditious as the manner used to file the paper with the court.

(4) Service by mail or by commercial carrier is complete on mailing or delivery to the carrier. Service by electronic means is complete on transmission, unless the party making service is notified that the paper was not received by the party served.

(d) Proof of Service.

(1) A paper presented for filing must contain either of the following:

(A) an acknowledgment of service by the person served; or

(B) proof of service consisting of a statement by the person who made service certifying:

(i) the date and manner of service;

(ii) the names of the persons served; and

(iii) their mail or electronic addresses, facsimile numbers, or the addresses of the places of delivery, as appropriate for the manner of service.

(2) When a brief or appendix is filed by mailing or dispatch in accordance with Rule 25(a)(2)(B), the proof of service must also state the date and manner by which the document was mailed or dispatched to the clerk.

(3) Proof of service may appear on or be affixed to the papers filed.

(e) Number of Copies. When these rules require the filing or furnishing of a number of copies, a court may require a different number by local rule or by order in a particular case.

(As amended Mar. 10, 1986, eff. July 1, 1986; Apr. 30, 1991, eff. Dec. 1, 1991; Apr. 22, 1993, eff. Dec. 1, 1993; Apr. 29, 1994, eff. Dec. 1, 1994; Apr. 23, 1996, eff. Dec. 1, 1996; Apr. 24, 1998, eff. Dec. 1, 1998; Apr. 29, 2002, eff. Dec. 1, 2002; Apr. 12, 2006, eff. Dec. 1, 2006; Apr. 30, 2007, eff. Dec. 1, 2007.)

1967 Adoption

The rule that filing is not timely unless the papers filed are received within the time allowed is the familiar one. *Ward v. Atlantic Coast Line R.R. Co.*, 265 F.2d 75 (5th Cir., 1959), rev'd on other grounds 362 U.S. 396, 80 S.Ct. 789, 4 L.Ed.2d 820 (1960); *Kahler-Ellis Co. v. Ohio Turnpike Commission*, 225 F.2d 922 (6th Cir., 1955). An exception is made in the case of briefs and appendices in order to afford the parties the maximum time for their preparation. By the terms of the exception, air mail delivery must be used whenever it is the most expeditious manner of delivery.

A majority of the circuits now require service of all papers filed with the clerk. The usual provision in present rules is for service on "adverse" parties. In view of the extreme simplicity of service by mail, there seems to be no reason why a party who files a paper should not be required to serve all parties to the proceeding in the court of appeals, whether or not they may be deemed adverse. The common requirement of proof of service is retained, but the rule permits it to be made by simple certification, which may be endorsed on the copy which is filed.

1986 Amendment

The amendments to Rules 25(a) and (b) are technical. No substantive change is intended.

1991 Amendment

Subdivision (a). The amendment permits, but does not require, courts of appeals to adopt local rules that allow filing of papers by electronic means. However, courts of appeals cannot adopt such local rules until the Judicial Conference of the United States authorizes filing by facsimile or other electronic means.

1993 Amendment

The amendment accompanies new subdivision (c) of Rule 4 and extends the holding in *Houston v. Lack*, 487 U.S. 266 (1988), to all papers filed in the courts of appeals by persons confined in institutions.

1994 Amendment

Subdivision (a). Several circuits have local rules that authorize the office of the clerk to refuse to accept for filing papers that are not in the form required by these rules or by local rules. This is not a suitable role for the office of the clerk and the practice exposes litigants to the hazards of time bars; for these reasons, such rules are proscribed by this rule. This provision is similar to Fed.R.Civ.P. 5(e) and Fed.R.Bankr.P. 5005.

The Committee wishes to make it clear that the provision prohibiting a clerk from refusing a document does not mean that a clerk's office may no longer screen documents to determine whether they comply with the rules. A court may delegate to the clerk authority to inform a party about any noncompliance with the rules and, if the party is willing to correct the document, to determine a date by which the corrected document must be resubmitted. If a party refuses to take the steps recommended by the clerk or if in the clerk's judgment the party fails to correct the noncompliance, the clerk must refer the matter to the court for a ruling.

Subdivision (d). Two changes have been made in this subdivision. Subdivision (d) provides that a paper presented for filing must contain proof of service.

The last sentence of subdivision (d) has been deleted as unnecessary. That sentence stated that a clerk could permit papers to be filed without the acknowledgment or proof of service but must require that it be filed promptly thereafter. In light of the change made in subdivision (a) which states that a clerk may not refuse to accept for filing a document because it is not in the proper form, there is no further need for a provision stating that a clerk may accept a paper lacking a proof of service. The clerk must accept such a paper. That portion of the deleted sentence stating that the clerk must require that proof of service be filed promptly after the filing of the document if the proof is not filed concurrently with the document is also unnecessary.

The second amendment requires that the certificate of service must state the addresses to which the papers were mailed or at which they were delivered. The Federal Circuit has a similar local rule, Fed.Cir.R. 25.

Subdivision (e). Subdivision (e) is a new subdivision. It makes it clear that whenever these rules require a party to file or furnish a number of copies a court may require a different number of copies either by rule or by order in an individual case. The number of copies of any document that a court of appeals needs varies depending upon the way in which the court conducts business. The internal operation of the courts of appeals necessarily varies from circuit to circuit because of differences in the number of judges, the geographic area included within the circuit, and other such factors. Uniformity could be achieved only by setting the number of copies artificially high so that parties in all circuits file enough copies to satisfy the needs of the court requiring the greatest number. Rather than do that, the Committee decided to make it clear that local rules may require a greater or lesser number of copies and that, if the circumstances of a particular case indicate the need for a different number of copies in that case, the court may so order.

A party must consult local rules to determine whether the court requires a different number than that specified in these national rules. The Committee believes it would be helpful if each circuit either: 1) included a chart at the beginning of its local rules showing the number of copies of each document required to be filed with the court along with citation to the controlling rule; or 2) made available such a chart to each party upon commencement of an appeal; or both. If a party fails to file the required number of copies, the failure does not create a jurisdictional defect. Rule 3(a) states: "Failure of an appellant to take any step other than the timely filing of a notice of appeal does not affect the validity of the appeal, but is ground only for such action as the court of appeals deems appropriate...."

1996 Amendments

Subdivision (a). The amendment deletes the language requiring a party to use "the most expeditious form of delivery by mail, except special delivery" in order to file a brief using the mailbox rule. That language was adopted before the Postal Service offered Express Mail and other expedited delivery services. The amendment makes it clear that it is sufficient to use First–Class Mail. Other equally or more expeditious classes of mail service, such as Express Mail, also may be used. In addition, the amendment permits the use of commercial carriers. The use of private, overnight courier services has become commonplace in law practice. Expedited services offered by commercial carriers often provide faster delivery than First–Class Mail; therefore, there should be no objection to the use of commercial carriers as long as they are reliable. In order to make use of the mailbox rule when using a commercial carrier, the amendment requires that the filer employ a carrier who undertakes to deliver the document in no more than three calendar days. The three-calendar-day period coordinates with the three-day extension provided by Rule 26(c).

Subdivision (c). The amendment permits service by commercial carrier if the carrier is to deliver the paper to the party being served within three days of the carrier's receipt of the paper. The amendment also expresses a desire that when reasonable, service on a party be accomplished by a manner as expeditious as the manner used to file the paper with the court. When a brief or motion is filed with the court by hand delivering the paper to the clerk's office, or by overnight courier, the copies should be served on the other parties by an equally expeditious manner—meaning either by personal service, if distance permits, or by overnight courier, if mail delivery to the party is not ordinarily accomplished overnight. The reasonableness standard is included so that if a paper is hand delivered to the clerk's office for filing but the other parties must be served in a different city, state, or region, personal service on them ordinarily will not be expected. If use of an equally expeditious manner of service is not reasonable, use of the next most expeditious manner may be. For example, if the paper is filed by hand delivery to the clerk's office but the other parties reside in distant cities, service on them need not be personal but in most instances should be by overnight courier. Even that may not be required, however, if the number of parties that must be served would make the use of overnight service too costly. A factor that bears upon the reasonableness of serving parties expeditiously is the immediacy of the relief requested.

Subdivision (d). The amendment adds a requirement that when a brief or appendix is filed by mail or commercial carrier, the certificate of service state the date and manner by which the document was mailed or dispatched to the clerk. Including that information in the certificate of service avoids the necessity for a separate certificate concerning the date and manner of filing.

1998 Amendments

The language and organization of the rule are amended to make the rule more easily understood. In addition to changes made to improve the understanding, the Advisory Committee has changed language to make style and terminology consistent throughout the appellate rules. These changes are intended to by stylistic only; a substantive amendment is made, however, in subdivision (a).

Subdivision (a). The substantive amendment in this subdivision is in subparagraph (a)(2)(C) and is a companion to an amendment in Rule 4(c). Currently Rule 25(a)(2(C) provides that if an inmate confined in an institution files a document by depositing it in the institution's internal mail system, the document is timely filed if deposited on or before the last day for filing. Some institutions have special internal mail systems for handling legal mail; such systems often record the date of deposit of mail by an inmate, the date of delivery of mail to an inmate, etc. The Advisory Committee amends the rule to require an inmate to use the system designed for legal mail, if there is one, in order to receive the benefit of this subparagraph

2002 Amendments

Rule 25(a)(2)(D) presently authorizes the courts of appeals to permit papers to be *filed* by electronic means. Rule 25 has been amended in several respects to permit papers also to be *served* electronically. In addition, Rule 25(c) has been reorganized and subdivided to make it easier to understand.

Subdivision (c)(1)(D). New subdivision (c)(1)(D) has been added to permit service to be made electronically, such as by e-mail or fax. No party may be served electronically, either by the clerk or by another party, unless the party has consented in writing to such service.

A court of appeals may not, by local rule, forbid the use of electronic service on a party that has consented to its use. At the same time, courts have considerable discretion to use local rules to regulate electronic service. Difficult and presently unforeseeable questions are likely to arise as electronic service becomes more common. Courts have the flexibility to use their local rules to address those questions. For example, courts may use local rules to set forth specific procedures that a party must follow before the party will be deemed to have given written consent to electronic service.

Parties also have the flexibility to define the terms of their consent; a party's consent to electronic service does not have to be "all-or-nothing." For example, a party may consent to service by facsimile transmission, but not by electronic mail; or a party may consent to electronic service only if "courtesy" copies of all transmissions are mailed within 24 hours; or a party may consent to electronic service of only documents that were created with Corel WordPerfect.

Subdivision (c)(2). The courts of appeals are authorized under Rule 25(a)(2)(D) to permit papers to be filed electronically. Technological advances may someday make it possible for a court to forward an electronically filed paper to all parties automatically or semi-automatically. When such court-facilitated service becomes possible, courts may decide to permit parties to use the courts' transmission facilities to serve electronically filed papers on other parties who have consented to such service. Court personnel would use the court's computer system to forward the papers, but the papers would be considered served by the filing parties, just as papers that are carried from one address to another by the United States Postal Service are considered served by the sending parties. New subdivision (c)(2) has been added so that the courts of appeals may use local rules to authorize such use of their transmission facilities, as well as to address the many questions that court-facilitated electronic service is likely to raise.

Subdivision (c)(4). The second sentence of new subdivision (c)(4) has been added to provide that electronic service is complete upon transmission. Transmission occurs when the sender performs the last act that he or she must perform to transmit a paper electronically; typically, it occurs when the sender hits the "send" or "transmit" button on an electronic mail program. There is one exception to the rule that electronic service is complete upon transmission: If the sender is notified—by the sender's e-mail program or otherwise—that the paper was not received, service is not complete, and the sender must take additional steps to effect service. A paper has been "received" by the party on which it has been served as long as the party has the ability to retrieve it. A party cannot defeat service by choosing not to access electronic mail on its server.

Changes Made After Publication and Comments No changes were made to the text of the proposed amendment. A paragraph was added to the Committee Note to clarify that consent to electronic service is not an "all-or-nothing" matter.

Subdivision (d)(1)(B)(iii). Subdivision (d)(1)(B)(iii) has been amended to require that, when a paper is served electronically, the proof of service of that paper must include the electronic address or facsimile number to which the paper was transmitted.

Changes Made After Publication and Comments The text of the proposed amendment was changed to refer to "electronic" addresses (instead of to "e-mail" addresses), to include "facsimile numbers," and to add the concluding phrase "as appropriate for the manner of service." Conforming changes were made to the Committee Note.

2006 Amendment

Subdivision (a)(2)(D). Amended Rule 25(a)(2)(D) acknowledges that many courts have required electronic filing by means of a standing order, procedures manual, or local rule. These local practices reflect the advantages that courts and most litigants realize from electronic filing. Courts that mandate electronic filing recognize the need to make exceptions when requiring electronic filing imposes a hardship on a party. Under Rule 25(a)(2)(D), a local rule that requires electronic filing must include reasonable exceptions, but Rule 25(a)(2)(D) does not define the scope of those exceptions. Experience with the local rules that have been adopted and that will emerge will aid in drafting new local rules and will facilitate gradual convergence on uniform exceptions, whether in local rules or in an amended Rule 25(a)(2)(D).

A local rule may require that both electronic and "hard" copies of a paper be filed. Nothing in the last sentence of Rule 25(a)(2)(D) is meant to imply otherwise.

2007 Amendments

Subdivision (a)(5). Section 205(c)(3)(A)(i) of the E-Government Act of 2002 (Public Law 107-347, as amended by Public Law 108-281) requires that the rules of practice and procedure be amended "to protect privacy and security concerns relating to electronic filing of documents and the public availability ... of documents filed electronically." In response to that directive, the Federal Rules of Bankruptcy, Civil, and Criminal Procedure have been amended, not merely to address the privacy and security concerns raised by documents that are filed electronically, but also to address similar concerns raised by documents that are filed in paper form. *See* Fed. R. Bankr. P. 9037; Fed. R. Civ. P. 5.2; and Fed. R. Crim. P. 49.1.

Appellate Rule 25(a)(5) requires that, in cases that arise on appeal from a district court, bankruptcy appellate panel, or bankruptcy court, the privacy rule that applied to the case below will continue to apply to the case on appeal. With one exception, all other cases—such as cases involving the review or enforcement of an agency order, the review of a decision of the tax court, or the consideration of a petition for an extraordinary writ—will be governed by Civil Rule 5.2. The only exception is when an extraordinary writ is sought in a criminal case—that is, a case in which the related trial-court proceeding is governed by Criminal Rule 49.1. In such a case, Criminal Rule 49.1 will govern in the court of appeals as well.

Rule 26. Computing and Extending Time

(a) Computing Time. The following rules apply in computing any period of time specified in these rules or in any local rule, court order, or applicable statute:

(1) Exclude the day of the act, event, or default that begins the period.

(2) Exclude intermediate Saturdays, Sundays, and legal holidays when the period is less than 11 days, unless stated in calendar days.

(3) Include the last day of the period unless it is a Saturday, Sunday, legal holiday, or—if the act to be done is filing a paper in court—a day on which the weather or other conditions make the clerk's office inaccessible.

(4) As used in this rule, "legal holiday" means New Year's Day, Martin Luther King, Jr.'s Birthday, Washington's Birthday, Memorial Day, Independence Day, Labor Day, Columbus Day, Veterans' Day, Thanksgiving Day, Christmas Day, and any other day declared a holiday by the President, Congress, or the state in which is located either the district court that rendered the challenged judgment or order, or the circuit clerk's principal office.

(b) Extending Time. For good cause, the court may extend the time prescribed by these rules or by its order to perform any act, or may permit an act to be done after that time expires. But the court may not extend the time to file:

(1) a notice of appeal (except as authorized in Rule 4) or a petition for permission to appeal; or

(2) a notice of appeal from or a petition to enjoin, set aside, suspend, modify, enforce, or otherwise review an order of an administrative agency, board,

commission, or officer of the United States, unless specifically authorized by law.

(c) Additional Time after Service. When a party is required or permitted to act within a prescribed period after a paper is served on that party, 3 calendar days are added to the prescribed period unless the paper is delivered on the date of service stated in the proof of service. For purposes of this Rule 26(c), a paper that is served electronically is not treated as delivered on the date of service stated in the proof of service.

(As amended Mar. 1, 1971, eff. July 1, 1971; Mar. 10, 1986, eff. July 1, 1986; Apr. 25, 1989, eff. Dec. 1, 1989; Apr. 30, 1991, eff. Dec. 1, 1991; Apr. 23, 1996, eff. Dec. 1, 1996; Apr. 24, 1998, eff. Dec. 1, 1998; Apr. 29, 2002, eff. Dec. 1, 2002; Apr. 25, 2005, eff. Dec. 1, 2005.)

1967 Adoption

The provisions of this rule are based upon FRCP 6(a), (b) and (e) [rule 6(a), (b) and (e), Federal Rules of Civil Procedure]. See also Supreme Court Rule 34 and FRCrP 45 [rule 45, Federal Rules of Criminal Procedure]. Unlike FRCP 6(b), this rule, read with Rule 27, requires that every request for enlargement of time be made by motion, with proof of service on all parties. This is the simplest, most convenient way of keeping all parties advised of developments. By the terms of Rule 27(b) a motion for enlargement of time under Rule 26(b) may be entertained and acted upon immediately, subject to the right of any party to seek reconsideration. Thus the requirement of motion and notice will not delay the granting of relief of a kind which a court is inclined to grant as of course. Specifically, if a court is of the view that an extension of time sought before expiration of the period originally prescribed or as extended by a previous order ought to be granted in effect ex parte, as FRCP 6(b) permits, it may grant motions seeking such relief without delay.

1971 Amendments

The amendment adds Columbus Day to the list of legal holidays to conform the subdivision to the Act of June 28, 1968, 82 Stat. 250, which constituted Columbus Day a legal holiday effective after January 1, 1971.

The Act, which amended Title 5, U.S.C. § 6103(a), changes the day on which certain holidays are to be observed. Washington's Birthday, Memorial Day and Veterans Day are to be observed on the third Monday in February, the last Monday in May and the fourth Monday in October, respectively, rather than, as heretofore, on February 22, May 30, and November 11, respectively. Columbus Day is to be observed on the second Monday in October. New Year's Day, Independence Day, Thanksgiving Day and Christmas continue to be observed on the traditional days.

1986 Amendments

The Birthday of Martin Luther King, Jr. is added to the list of national holidays in Rule 26(a). The amendment to Rule 26(c) is technical. No substantive change is intended.

1989 Amendments

The proposed amendment brings Rule 26(a) into conformity with the provisions of Rule 6(a) of the Rules of Civil Procedure, Rule 45(a) of the Rules of Criminal Procedure, and Rule 9006(a) of the Rules of Bankruptcy Procedure which allow additional time for filing whenever a clerk's office is inaccessible on the last day for filing due to weather or other conditions.

1996 Amendments

The amendment is a companion to the proposed amendments to Rule 25 that permit service on a party by commercial carrier. The amendments to subdivision (c) of this rule make the three-day extension applicable not only when service is accomplished by mail, but whenever delivery to the party being served occurs later than the date of service stated in the proof of service. When service is by mail or commercial carrier, the proof of service recites the date of mailing or delivery to the commercial carrier. If the party being served receives the paper on a later date, the three-day extension applies. If the party being served receives the paper on the same date as the date of service recited in the proof of service, the three-day extension is not available.

The amendment also states that the three-day extension is three calendar days. Rule 26(a) states that when a period prescribed or allowed by the rules is less than seven days, intermediate Saturdays, Sundays, and legal holidays do not count. Whether the three-day extension in Rule 26(c) is such a period, meaning that three-days could actually be five or even six days, is unclear. The D.C. Circuit recently held that the parallel three-day extension provided in the Civil Rules is not such a period and that weekends and legal holidays do count. *CNPq v. Inter-Trade, 50 F.3d 56 (D.C.Cir.1995).* The Committee believes that is the right result and that the issue should be resolved. Providing that the extension is three calendar days means that if a period would otherwise end on Thursday but the three-day extension applies, the paper must be filed on Monday. Friday, Saturday, and Sunday are the extension days. Because the last day of the period as extended is Sunday, the paper must be filed the next day, Monday.

1998 Amendments

The language and organization of the rule are amended to make the rule more easily understood. In addition to changes made to improve the understanding, the Advisory Committee has changed language to make style and terminology consistent throughout the appellate rules. These changes are intended to by stylistic only; two substantive changes are made, however, in subdivision (a).

Subdivision (a). First, the amendments make the computation method prescribed in this rule applicable to any time period imposed by a local rule. This means that if a local rule establishing a time limit is permitted, the national rule will govern the computation of that period.

Second, paragraph (a)(2) includes language clarifying that whenever the rules establish a time period in "calendar days," weekends and legal holidays are counted.

2002 Amendments

Subdivision (a)(2). The Federal Rules of Civil Procedure and the Federal Rules of Criminal Procedure compute time differently than the Federal Rules of Appellate Procedure. Fed. R. Civ. P. 6(a) and Fed. R. Crim. P. 45(a) provide that, in computing any period of time, "[w]hen the period of time prescribed or allowed is less than 11 days, intermediate Saturdays, Sundays, and legal holidays shall be excluded in the computation." By contrast, Rule 26(a)(2) provides that, in computing any period of time, a litigant should "[e]xclude intermediate Saturdays, Sundays, and legal holidays when the period is less than 7 days, unless stated in calendar days." Thus, deadlines of 7, 8, 9, and 10 days are calculated differently under the rules of civil and criminal procedure than they are under the rules of appellate procedure. This creates a trap for unwary litigants. No good reason for this discrepancy is apparent, and thus Rule 26(a)(2) has been amended so that, under all three sets of rules, intermediate Saturdays, Sundays, and legal holidays will be excluded when computing deadlines under 11 days but will be counted when computing deadlines of 11 days and over.

Changes Made After Publication and Comments No changes were made to the text of the proposed amendment or to the Committee Note.

Subdivision (c). Rule 26(c) has been amended to provide that when a paper is served on a party by electronic means, and that party is required or permitted to respond to that paper within a prescribed period, 3 calendar days are added to the prescribed period. Electronic service is usually instantaneous, but sometimes it is not, because of technical problems. Also, if a paper is electronically transmitted to a party on a Friday evening, the party may not realize that he or she has been served until two or three days later. Finally, extending the "3-day rule" to electronic service will encourage parties to consent to such service under Rule 25(c).

Changes Made After Publication and Comments No changes were made to the text of the proposed amendment or to the Committee Note.

2005 Amendments

Subdivision (a)(4). Rule 26(a)(4) has been amended to refer to the third Monday in February as "Washington's Birthday." A federal statute officially designates the holiday as "Washington's Birthday," reflecting the desire of Congress specially to honor the first president of the United States. *See* 5 U.S.C. § 6103(a). During the 1998 restyling of the Federal Rules of Appellate Procedure, references to "Washington's Birthday" were mistakenly changed to "Presidents' Day." The amendment corrects that error.

Rule 26.1. Corporate Disclosure Statement

(a) Who Must File. Any nongovernmental corporate party to a proceeding in a court of appeals must file a statement that identifies any parent corporation and any publicly held corporation that owns 10% or more of its stock or states that there is no such corporation.

(b) Time for Filing; Supplemental Filing. A party must file the Rule 26.1(a) statement with the principal brief or upon filing a motion, response, petition, or answer in the court of appeals, whichever occurs first, unless a local rule requires earlier filing. Even if the statement has already been filed, the party's principal brief must include the statement before the table of contents. A party must supplement its statement whenever the information that must be disclosed under Rule 26.1(a) changes.

(c) Number of Copies. If the Rule 26.1(a) statement is filed before the principal brief, or if a supplemental statement is filed, the party must file an original and 3 copies unless the court requires a different number by local rule or by order in a particular case.

(Added Apr. 25, 1989, eff. Dec. 1, 1989, and amended Apr. 30, 1991, eff. Dec. 1, 1991; Apr. 29, 1994, eff. Dec. 1, 1994; Apr. 24, 1998, eff. Dec. 1, 1998; Apr. 29, 2002, eff. Dec. 1, 2002.)

1989 Addition

The purpose of this rule is to assist judges in making a determination of whether they have any interests in any of a party's related corporate entities that would disqualify the judges from hearing the appeal. The committee believes that this rule represents minimum disclosure requirements. If a Court of Appeals wishes to require additional information, a court is free to do so by local rule. However, the committee requests the courts to consider the desirability of uniformity and the burden that varying circuit rules creates on attorneys who practice in many circuits.

1994 Amendment

The amendment requires a party to file three copies of the disclosure statement whenever the statement is filed before the party's principle brief. Because the statement is included in each copy of the party's brief, there is no need to require the filing of additional copies at that time. A court of appeals may require the filing of a different number of copies by local rule or by order in a particular case.

1998 Amendments

The language and organization of the rule are amended to make the rule more easily understood. In addition to changes made to improve the understanding, the Advisory Committee has changed language to make style and terminology consistent throughout the appellate rules. These changes are intended to by stylistic only; a substantive change is made, however, in subdivision (a).

Subdivision (a). The amendment deletes the requirement that a corporate party identify subsidiaries and affiliates that have issued shares to the public. Although several circuit rules require identification of such entities, the Committee believes that such disclosure is unnecessary.

A disclosure statement assists a judge in ascertaining whether or not the judge has an interest that should cause the judge to recuse himself or herself from the case. Given that purpose, disclosure of entities that would not be adversely affected by a decision in the case is unnecessary.

Disclosure of a party's parent corporation is necessary because a judgment against a subsidiary can negatively impact the parent. A judge who owns stock in the parent corporation, therefore, has an interest in litigation involving the subsidiary. The rule requires disclosure of all of a party's parent corporations meaning grandparent and great grandparent corporations as well. For example, if a party is a closely held corporation, the majority shareholder of which is a corporation formed by a publicly traded corporation for the purpose of acquiring and holding the shares of the party, the publicly traded grandparent corporation should be disclosed. Conversely, disclosure of a party's subsidiaries or affiliated corporations is ordinarily unnecessary. For example, if a party is a part owner of a corporation in which a judge owns stock, the possibility is quite remote that the judge might be biased by the fact that the judge and the litigant are co-owners of a corporation.

The amendment, however, adds a requirement that the party lists all its stockholders that are publicly held companies owning 10% or more of the stock of the party. A judgment against a corporate party can adversely affect the value of the company's stock and, therefore, persons owning stock in the party have an interest in the outcome of the litigation. A judge owning stock in a corporate party ordinarily recuses himself or herself. The new requirement takes the analysis one step further and assumes that if a judge owns stock in a publicly held corporation which in turn owns 10% or more of the stock in the party, the judge may have sufficient interest in the litigation to require recusal. The 10% threshold ensures that the corporation in which the judge may own stock is itself sufficiently invested in the party that a judgment adverse to the party could have an adverse impact upon the investing corporation in which the judge may own stock. This requirement is modeled on the Seventh Circuit's disclosure requirement.

Subdivision (b). The language requiring inclusion of the disclosure statement in a party's principal brief is moved to this subdivision because it deals with the time for filing the statement.

2002 Amendments

Subdivision (a). Rule 26.1(a) requires nongovernmental corporate parties to file a "corporate disclosure statement." In that statement, a nongovernmental corporate party is required to identify all of its parent corporations and all publicly held corporations that own 10% or more of its stock. The corporate disclosure statement is intended to assist judges in determining whether they must recuse themselves by reason of "a financial interest in the subject matter in controversy." Code of Judicial Conduct, Canon 3C(1)(c) (1972).

Rule 26.1(a) has been amended to require that nongovernmental corporate parties who have not been required to file a corporate disclosure statement—that is, nongovernmental corporate parties who do not have any parent corporations and at least 10% of whose stock is not owned by any publicly held corporation—inform the court of that fact. At present, when a corporate disclosure statement is not filed, courts do not know whether it has not been filed because there was nothing to report or because of ignorance of Rule 26.1.

Subdivision (b). Rule 26.1(b) has been amended to require parties to file supplemental disclosure statements whenever there is a change in the information that Rule 26.1(a) requires the parties to disclose. For example, if a publicly held corporation acquires 10% or more of a party's stock after the party has filed its disclosure statement, the party should file a supplemental statement identifying that publicly held corporation.

Subdivision (c). Rule 26.1(c) has been amended to provide that a party who is required to file a supplemental disclosure statement must file an original and 3 copies, unless a local rule or an order entered in a particular case provides otherwise.

Changes Made After Publication and Comments The Committee is submitting two versions of proposed Rule 26.1 for the consideration of the Standing Committee.

The first version—"Alternative One"—is the same as the version that was published, except that the rule has been amended to refer to "any information that may be *publicly designated* by the Judicial Conference" instead of to "any information that may be *required* by the Judicial Conference." At its April meeting, the Committee gave unconditional approval to all of "Alternative One," except the Judicial Conference provisions. The Committee conditioned its approval of the Judicial Conference provisions on the Standing Committee's assuring itself that lawyers would have ready access to any standards promulgated by the Judicial Conference and that the Judicial Conference provisions were consistent with the Rules Enabling Act.

The second version—"Alternative Two"—is the same as the version that was published, except that the Judicial Conference provisions have been eliminated. The Civil Rules Committee met several days after the Appellate Rules Committee and joined the Bankruptcy Rules Committee in disapproving the Judicial Conference provisions. Given the decreasing likelihood that the Judicial Conference provisions will be approved by the Standing Committee, I asked Prof. Schiltz to draft, and the Appellate Rules Committee to approve, a version of Rule 26.1 that omitted those provisions. "Alternative Two" was circulated to and approved by the Committee in late April.

I should note that, at its April meeting, the Appellate Rules Committee discussed the financial disclosure provision that was approved by the Bankruptcy Rules Committee. That provision defines the scope of the financial disclosure obligation much differently than the provisions approved by the Appellate, Civil, and Criminal Rules Committees, which are based on existing Rule 26.1. For example, the bankruptcy provision requires disclosure when a party "directly or indirectly" owns 10 percent or more of "any class" of a publicly *or* privately held corporation's "equity interests." Members of the Appellate Rules Committee expressed several concerns about the provision approved by the Bankruptcy Rules Committee, objecting both to its substance and to its ambiguity.

Rule 27. Motions

(a) In General.

(1) Application for Relief. An application for an order or other relief is made by motion unless these rules prescribe another form. A motion must be in writing unless the court permits otherwise.

(2) Contents of a Motion.

(A) Grounds and relief sought. A motion must state with particularity the grounds for the motion, the relief sought, and the legal argument necessary to support it.

(B) Accompanying documents.

(i) Any affidavit or other paper necessary to support a motion must be served and filed with the motion.

(ii) An affidavit must contain only factual information, not legal argument.

(iii) A motion seeking substantive relief must include a copy of the trial court's opinion or agency's decision as a separate exhibit.

(C) Documents barred or not required.

(i) A separate brief supporting or responding to a motion must not be filed.

(ii) A notice of motion is not required.

(iii) A proposed order is not required.

(3) Response.

(A) Time to file. Any party may file a response to a motion; Rule 27(a)(2) governs its contents. The response must be filed within 8 days after service of the motion unless the court shortens or extends the time. A motion authorized by Rules 8, 9, 18, or 41 may be granted before the 8–day period runs only if the court gives reasonable notice to the parties that it intends to act sooner.

(B) Request for affirmative relief. A response may include a motion for affirmative relief. The time to respond to the new motion, and to reply to that response, are governed by Rule 27(a)(3)(A) and (a)(4). The title of the response must alert the court to the request for relief.

(4) Reply to Response. Any reply to a response must be filed within 5 days after service of the response. A reply must not present matters that do not relate to the response.

(b) Disposition of a Motion for a Procedural Order. The court may act on a motion for a procedural order—including a motion under Rule 26(b)—at any time without awaiting a response, and may, by rule or by order in a particular case, authorize its clerk to act on specified types of procedural motions. A party adversely affected by the court's, or the clerk's, action may file a motion to reconsider, vacate, or modify that action. Timely opposition filed after the motion is granted in whole or in part does not constitute a request to reconsider, vacate, or modify the disposition; a motion requesting that relief must be filed.

(c) Power of a Single Judge to Entertain a Motion. A circuit judge may act alone on any motion, but may not dismiss or otherwise determine an appeal or other proceeding. A court of appeals may provide by rule or by order in a particular case that only the court may act on any motion or class of motions. The court may review the action of a single judge.

(d) Form of Papers; Page Limits; and Number of Copies.

(1) Format.

(A) Reproduction. A motion, response, or reply may be reproduced by any process that yields a clear black image on light paper. The paper must be opaque and unglazed. Only one side of the paper may be used.

(B) Cover. A cover is not required, but there must be a caption that includes the case number, the name of the court, the title of the case, and a brief descriptive title indicating the purpose of the motion and identifying the party or parties for whom it is filed. If a cover is used, it must be white.

(C) Binding. The document must be bound in any manner that is secure, does not obscure the text, and permits the document to lie reasonably flat when open.

(D) Paper size, line spacing, and margins. The document must be on 8½ by 11 inch paper. The text must be double-spaced, but quotations more than two lines long may be indented and single-spaced. Headings and footnotes may be single-spaced. Margins must be at least one inch on all four sides. Page numbers may be placed in the margins, but no text may appear there.

(E) Typeface and type styles. The document must comply with the typeface requirements of Rule 32(a)(5) and the type-style requirements of Rule 32(a)(6).

(2) Page Limits. A motion or a response to a motion must not exceed 20 pages, exclusive of the corporate disclosure statement and accompanying documents authorized by Rule 27(a)(2)(B), unless the court permits or directs otherwise. A reply to a response must not exceed 10 pages.

(3) Number of Copies. An original and 3 copies must be filed unless the court requires a different number by local rule or by order in a particular case.

(e) Oral Argument. A motion will be decided without oral argument unless the court orders otherwise.

(As amended Apr. 30, 1979, eff. Aug. 1, 1979; Apr. 25, 1989, eff. Dec. 1, 1989; Apr. 29, 1994, eff. Dec. 1, 1994; Apr. 24, 1998, eff. Dec. 1, 1998; Apr. 29, 2002, eff. Dec. 1, 2002; Apr. 25, 2005, eff. Dec. 1, 2005.)

1967 Adoption

Subdivisions (a) and (b). Many motions seek relief of a sort which is ordinarily unopposed or which is granted as of course. The provision of subdivision (a) which permits any party to file a response in opposition to a motion within 7 days after its service upon him assumes that the motion is one of substance which ought not be acted upon without affording affected parties an opportunity to reply. A motion to dismiss or otherwise determine an appeal is clearly such a motion. Motions authorized by Rules 8, 9, 18 and 41 are likewise motions of substance; but in the nature of the relief sought, to afford an adversary an automatic delay of at least 7 days is undesirable, thus such motions may be acted upon after notice which is reasonable under the circumstances.

The term "motions for procedural orders" is used in subdivision (b) to describe motions which do not substantially affect the rights of the parties or the ultimate disposition of the appeal. To prevent delay in the disposition of such motions, subdivision (b) provides that they may be acted upon immediately without awaiting a response, subject to the right of any party who is adversely affected by the action to seek reconsideration.

Subdivision (c). Within the general consideration of procedure on motions is the problem of the power of a single circuit judge. Certain powers are granted to a single judge of a court of appeals by statute. Thus, under 28 U.S.C. § 2101(f) a single judge may stay execution and enforcement of a judgment to enable a party aggrieved to obtain certiorari; under 28 U.S.C. § 2251 a judge before whom a habeas corpus proceeding involving a person detained by state authority is pending may stay any proceeding against the person; under 28 U.S.C. § 2253 a single judge may issue a certificate of probably cause. In addition, certain of these rules expressly grant power to a single judge. See Rules 8, 9 and 18.

This subdivision empowers a single circuit judge to act upon virtually all requests for intermediate relief which may be made during the course of an appeal or other proceeding. By its terms he may entertain and act upon any motion other than a motion to dismiss or otherwise determine an appeal or other proceeding. But the relief sought must be "relief which under these rules may properly be sought by motion."

Examples of the power conferred on a single judge by this subdivision are: to extend the time for transmitting the record or docketing the appeal (Rules 11 and 12); to permit intervention in agency cases (Rule 15), or substitution in any case (Rule 43); to permit an appeal in forma pauperis (Rule 24); to enlarge any time period fixed by the rules other than that for initiating a proceeding in the court of appeals (Rule 26(b)); to permit the filing of a brief by amicus curiae (Rule 29); to authorize the filing of a deferred appendix (Rule 30(c)), or dispense with the requirement of an appendix in a specific case (Rule 30(f)), or permit carbon copies of briefs or appendices to be used (Rule 32(a)); to permit the filing of additional briefs (Rule 28(c)), or the filing of briefs of extraordinary length (Rule 28(g)); to postpone oral argument (Rule 34(a)), or grant additional time therefor (Rule 34(b)).

Certain rules require that application for the relief or orders which they authorize be made by petition. Since relief under those rules may not properly be sought by motion, a single judge may not entertain requests for such relief. Thus a single judge may not act upon requests for permission to appeal (see Rules 5 and 6); or for mandamus or other extraordinary writs (see Rule 21), other than for stays or injunctions *pendente lite*, authority to grant which is "expressly conferred by these rules" on a single judge under certain circumstances (see Rules 8 and 18); or upon petitions for rehearing (see Rule 40).

A court of appeals may by order or rule abridge the power of a single judge if it is of the view that a motion or a class of motions should be disposed of by a panel. Exercise of any power granted a single judge is discretionary with the judge. The final sentence in this subdivision makes the disposition of any matter by a single judge subject to review by the court.

1979 Amendment

The proposed amendment would give sanction to local rules in a number of circuits permitting the clerk to dispose of specified types of procedural motions.

1989 Amendment

The amendment is technical. No substantive change is intended.

1994 Amendments

Subdivision (d). The amendment makes it clear that a court may require a different number of copies either by rule or by order in an individual case. The number of copies of any document that a court of appeals needs varies depending upon the way in which the court conducts business. The internal operation of the courts of appeals necessarily varies from circuit to circuit because of differences in the number of judges, the geographic area included within the circuit, and other such factors. Uniformity could be achieved only by setting the number of copies artificially high so that parties in all circuits file enough copies to satisfy the needs of the court requiring the greatest number. Rather than do that, the Committee decided to make it clear that local rules may require a greater or lesser number of copies and that, if the circumstances of a particular case indicate the need for a different number of copies in that case, the court may so order.

1998 Amendments

In addition to amending Rule 27 to conform to uniform drafting standards, several substantive amendments are made. The Advisory Committee had been working on substantive amendments to Rule 27 just prior to completion of this larger project.

Subdivision (a). Paragraph (1) retains the language of the existing rule indicating that an application for an order or other relief is made by filing a motion unless another form is required by some other provision in the rules.

Paragraph (1) also states that a motion must be in writing unless the court permits otherwise. The writing requirement has been implicit in the rule; the Advisory Committee decided to make it explicit. There are, however, instances in which a court may permit oral motions. Perhaps the most common such instance would be a motion made during oral argument in the presence of opposing counsel; for example, a request for permission to submit a supplemental brief on an issue raised by the court for the first time at oral argument. Rather than limit oral motions to those made during oral argument or, conversely, assume the propriety of making even extremely complex motions orally during argument, the Advisory Committee decided that it is better to leave the determination of the propriety of an oral motion to the court's discretion. The provision does not disturb the practice in those circuits that permit certain procedural motions, such as a motion for extension of time for filing a brief, to be made by telephone and ruled upon by the clerk.

Paragraph (2) outlines the contents of a motion. It begins with the general requirement from the current rule that a motion must state with particularity the grounds supporting it and the relief requested. It adds a requirement that all legal arguments should be presented in the body of the motion; a separate brief or memorandum supporting or responding to a motion must not be filed. The Supreme Court uses this single document approach. Sup. Ct. R. 21.1. In furtherance of the requirement that all legal argument must be contained in the body of the motion, paragraph (2) also states that an affidavit that is attached to a motion should contain only factual information and not legal argument.

Paragraph (2) further states that whenever a motion requests substantive relief, a copy of the trial court's opinion or agency's decision must be attached.

Although it is common to present a district court with a proposed order along with the motion requesting relief, that is not the practice in the courts of appeals. A proposed order is not required and is not expected or desired. Nor is a notice of motion required.

Paragraph (3) retains the provisions of the current rule concerning the filing of a response to a motion except that the time for responding has been expanded to 10 days rather than 7 days. Because the time periods in the rule apply to a substantive motion as well as a procedural motion, the longer time period may help reduce the number of motions for extension of time, or at least provide a more realistic time frame within which to make and dispose of such a motion.

A party filing a response in opposition to a motion may also request affirmative relief. It is the Advisory Committee's judgment that it is permissible to combine the response and the new motion in the same document. Indeed, because there may be substantial overlap of arguments in the response and in the request for affirmative relief, a combined document may be preferable. If a request for relief is combined with a response, the caption of the document must alert the court to the request for relief. The time for a response to such a new request and for reply to that response are governed by the general rules regulating responses and replies.

Paragraph (4) is new. Two circuits currently have rules authorizing a reply. As a general matter, a reply should not reargue propositions presented in the motion or present matters that do not relate to the response. Sometimes matters relevant to the motion arise after the motion is filed; treatment of such matters in the reply is appropriate even though strictly speaking it may not relate to the response.

Subdivision (b). The material in this subdivision remains substantively unchanged except to clarify that one may file a motion for reconsideration, etc. of a disposition by either the court or the clerk. A new sentence is added indicating that if a motion is granted in whole or in part before the filing of timely opposition to the motion, the filing of the opposition is not treated as a request for reconsideration, etc., A party wishing to have the court reconsider, vacate, or modify the disposition must file a new motion that addresses the order granting the motion.

Although the rule does not require a court to do so, it would be helpful if, whenever a motion is disposed of before receipt of any response from the opposing party, the ruling indicates that it was issued without awaiting a response. Such a statement will aid the opposing party in deciding whether to request reconsideration. The opposing party may have mailed a response about the time of the ruling and be uncertain whether the court has considered it.

Subdivision (c). The changes in this subdivision are stylistic only. No substantive changes are intended.

Subdivision (d). This subdivision has been substantially revised.

The format requirements have been moved from Rule 32(b) to paragraph (1) of this subdivision. No cover is required, but a caption is needed as well as a descriptive title indicating the purpose of the motion and identifying the party or parties for whom it is filed. Spiral binding or secure stapling at the upper left-hand corner satisfies the binding requirement. But they are not intended to be the exclusive methods of binding.

Paragraph (2) establishes page limits; twenty pages for a motion or a response, and ten pages for a reply. Three circuits have established page limits by local rule. This rule does not establish special page limits for those instances in which a party combines a response to a motion with a new request for affirmative relief. Because a combined document most often will be used when there is substantial overlap in the argument in opposition to the motion and in the argument for the affirmative relief, twenty pages may be sufficient in most instances. If it is not, the party may request additional pages. If ten pages is insufficient for the original movant to both reply to the response, and respond to the new request for affirmative relief, two separate documents may be used or a request for additional pages may be made.

The changes in paragraph (4) are stylistic only. No substantive changes are intended.

Subdivision (e). This new provision makes it clear that there is no right to oral argument on a motion. Seven circuits have local rules stating that oral argument of motions will not be held unless the court orders it.

2002 Amendments

Subdivision (a)(3)(A). Subdivision (a)(3)(A) presently requires that a response to a motion be filed within 10 days after service of the motion. Intermediate Saturdays, Sundays, and legal holidays are counted in computing that 10–day deadline, which means that, except when the 10–day deadline ends on a weekend or legal holiday, parties generally must respond to motions within 10 actual days.

Fed. R. App. P. 26(a)(2) has been amended to provide that, in computing any period of time, a litigant should "[e]xclude intermediate Saturdays, Sundays, and legal holidays when the period is less than 11 days, unless stated in calendar days." This change in the method of computing deadlines means that 10–day deadlines (such as that in subdivision (a)(3)(A)) have been lengthened as a practical matter. Under the new computation method, parties would never have less than 14 actual days to respond to motions, and legal holidays could extend that period to as much as 18 days.

Permitting parties to take two weeks or more to respond to motions would introduce significant and unwarranted delay into appellate proceedings. For that reason, the 10–day deadline in subdivision (a)(3)(A) has been reduced to 8 days. This change will, as a practical matter, ensure that every party will have at least 10 actual days—but, in the absence of a legal holiday, no more than 12 actual days—to respond to motions. The court continues to have discretion to shorten or extend that time in appropriate cases.

Changes Made After Publication and Comments In response to the objections of commentators, the time to respond to a motion was increased from the proposed 7 days to 8 days. No other changes were made to the text of the proposed amendment or to the Committee Note.

Subdivision (a)(4). Subdivision (a)(4) presently requires that a reply to a response to a motion be filed within 7 days after service of the response. Intermediate Saturdays, Sundays, and legal holidays are counted in computing that 7–day deadline, which means that, except when the 7–day deadline ends on a weekend or legal holiday, parties generally must reply to responses to motions within one week.

Fed. R. App. P. 26(a)(2) has been amended to provide that, in computing any period of time, a litigant should "[e]xclude intermediate Saturdays, Sundays, and legal holidays when the period is less than 11 days, unless stated in calendar days." This change in the method of computing deadlines means that 7–day deadlines (such as that in subdivision (a)(4)) have been lengthened as a practical matter. Under the new computation method, parties would never have less than 9 actual days to reply to responses to motions, and legal holidays could extend that period to as much as 13 days.

Permitting parties to take 9 or more days to reply to a response to a motion would introduce significant and unwarranted delay into appellate proceedings. For that reason, the 7–day deadline in subdivision (a)(4) has been reduced to 5 days. This change will, as a practical matter, ensure that every party will have 7 actual days to file replies to responses to motions (in the absence of a legal holiday).

Changes Made After Publication and Comments No changes were made to the text of the proposed amendment or to the Committee Note.

Subdivision (d)(1)(B). A cover is not required on motions, responses to motions, or replies to responses to motions. However, Rule 27(d)(1)(B) has been amended to provide that if a cover is nevertheless used on such a paper, the cover must be white. The amendment is intended to promote uniformity in federal appellate practice.

Changes Made After Publication and Comments No changes were made to the text of the proposed amendment or to the Committee Note.

2005 Amendments

Subdivision (d)(1)(E). A new subdivision (E) has been added to Rule 27(d)(1) to provide that a motion, a response to a motion, and a reply to a response to a motion must comply with the typeface requirements of Rule 32(a)(5) and the typestyle requirements of Rule 32(a)(6). The purpose of the amendment is to promote uniformity in federal appellate practice and to prevent the abuses that might occur if no restrictions were placed on the size of typeface used in motion papers.

Rule 28. Briefs

(a) Appellant's Brief. The appellant's brief must contain, under appropriate headings and in the order indicated:

(1) a corporate disclosure statement if required by Rule 26.1;

(2) a table of contents, with page references;

(3) a table of authorities—cases (alphabetically arranged), statutes, and other authorities—with references to the pages of the brief where they are cited;

(4) a jurisdictional statement, including:

(A) the basis for the district court's or agency's subject-matter jurisdiction, with citations to applicable statutory provisions and stating relevant facts establishing jurisdiction;

(B) the basis for the court of appeals' jurisdiction, with citations to applicable statutory provisions and stating relevant facts establishing jurisdiction;

(C) the filing dates establishing the timeliness of the appeal or petition for review; and

(D) an assertion that the appeal is from a final order or judgment that disposes of all parties' claims, or information establishing the court of appeals' jurisdiction on some other basis;

(5) a statement of the issues presented for review;

(6) a statement of the case briefly indicating the nature of the case, the course of proceedings, and the disposition below;

(7) a statement of facts relevant to the issues submitted for review with appropriate references to the record (see Rule 28(e));

(8) a summary of the argument, which must contain a succinct, clear, and accurate statement of the arguments made in the body of the brief, and which must not merely repeat the argument headings;

(9) the argument, which must contain:

(A) appellant's contentions and the reasons for them, with citations to the authorities and parts of the record on which the appellant relies; and

(B) for each issue, a concise statement of the applicable standard of review (which may appear in the discussion of the issue or under a separate heading placed before the discussion of the issues);

(10) a short conclusion stating the precise relief sought; and

(11) the certificate of compliance, if required by Rule 32(a)(7).

(b) Appellee's Brief. The appellee's brief must conform to the requirements of Rule 28(a)(1)–(9) and (11), except that none of the following need appear unless the appellee is dissatisfied with the appellant's statement:

(1) the jurisdictional statement;

(2) the statement of the issues;

(3) the statement of the case;

(4) the statement of the facts; and

(5) the statement of the standard of review.

(c) Reply Brief. The appellant may file a brief in reply to the appellee's brief. Unless the court permits, no further briefs may be filed. A reply brief must contain a table of contents, with page references, and a table of authorities—cases (alphabetically arranged), statutes, and other authorities—with references to the pages of the reply brief where they are cited.

(d) References to Parties. In briefs and at oral argument, counsel should minimize use of the terms "appellant" and "appellee." To make briefs clear, counsel should use the parties' actual names or the designations used in the lower court or agency proceeding, or such descriptive terms as "the employee," "the injured person," "the taxpayer," "the ship," "the stevedore."

(e) References to the Record. References to the parts of the record contained in the appendix filed with the appellant's brief must be to the pages of the appendix. If the appendix is prepared after the briefs are filed, a party referring to the record must follow one of the methods detailed in Rule 30(c). If the original record is used under Rule 30(f) and is not consecutively paginated, or if the brief refers to an unreproduced part of the record, any reference must be to the page of the original document. For example:

- Answer p. 7;
- Motion for Judgment p. 2;
- Transcript p. 231.

Only clear abbreviations may be used. A party referring to evidence whose admissibility is in controversy must cite the pages of the appendix or of the transcript at which the evidence was identified, offered, and received or rejected.

(f) Reproduction of Statutes, Rules, Regulations, etc. If the court's determination of the issues presented requires the study of statutes, rules, regulations, etc., the relevant parts must be set out in the brief or in an addendum at the end, or may be supplied to the court in pamphlet form.

(g) [Reserved]

(h) [Deleted]

(i) Briefs in a Case Involving Multiple Appellants or Appellees. In a case involving more than one appellant or appellee, including consolidated cases, any number of appellants or appellees may join in a brief, and any party may adopt by reference a part of another's brief. Parties may also join in reply briefs.

(j) Citation of Supplemental Authorities. If pertinent and significant authorities come to a party's attention after the party's brief has been filed—or after oral argument but before decision—a party may promptly advise the circuit clerk by letter, with a copy to all other parties, setting forth the citations. The letter must state the reasons for the supplemental citations, referring either to the page of the brief or to a point argued orally. The body of the letter must not exceed 350 words. Any response must be made promptly and must be similarly limited.

(As amended Apr. 30, 1979, eff. Aug. 1, 1979; Mar. 10, 1986, eff. July 1, 1986; Apr. 25, 1989, eff. Dec. 1, 1989; Apr. 30, 1991, eff. Dec. 1, 1991; Apr. 22, 1993, eff. Dec. 1, 1993; Apr. 29, 1994, eff. Dec. 1, 1994; Apr. 24, 1998, eff. Dec. 1, 1998; Apr. 29, 2002, eff. Dec. 1, 2002; Apr. 25, 2005, eff. Dec. 1, 2005.)

1967 Adoption

This rule is based upon Supreme Court Rule 40. For variations in present circuit rules on briefs see 2d Cir. Rule 17 [rule 17, U.S.Ct. of App. 2d Cir.], 3d Cir. Rule 24 [rule 24, U.S.Ct. of App. 3d Cir.], 5th Cir. Rule 24 [rule 24, U.S.Ct. of App. 5th Cir.], and 7th Cir. Rule 17 [rule 17, U.S.Ct. of App. 7th Cir.]. All circuits now limit the number of pages of briefs, a majority limiting the brief to 50 pages of standard typographic printing. Fifty pages of standard typographic printing is the approximate equivalent of 70 pages of typewritten text, given the page sizes required by Rule 32 and the requirement set out there that text produced by a method other than standard typographic must be double spaced.

1979 Amendments

Subdivision (g). The proposed amendment eliminates the distinction appearing in the present rule between the permissible length in pages of printed and typewritten briefs, investigation of the matter having disclosed that the number of words on the printed page is little if any larger than the number on a page typed in standard elite type.

The provision is made subject to local rule to permit the court of appeals to require that typewritten briefs be typed in larger type and permit a correspondingly larger number of pages.

Subdivision (j). Proposed new Rule 28(j) makes provision for calling the court's attention to authorities that come to the party's attention after the brief has been filed. It is patterned after the practice under local rule in some of the circuits.

1986 Amendments

While Rule 28(g) can be read as requiring that tables of authorities be included in a reply brief, such tables are often not included. Their absence impedes efficient use of the reply brief to ascertain the appellant's response to a particular argument of the appellee or to the appellee's use of a particular authority. The amendment to Rule 28(c) is intended to make it clear that such tables are required in reply briefs.

The amendment to Rule 28(j) is technical. No substantive change is intended.

1989 Amendments

The amendment provides that the corporate disclosure statement required by new Rule 26.1 shall be treated similarly to tables of contents and tables of citations and shall not be counted for purposes of the number of pages allowed in a brief.

1991 Amendments

Subdivision (a). The amendment adds a new subparagraph (2) that requires an appellant to include a specific jurisdictional statement in the appellant's brief to aid the court of appeals in determining whether it has both federal subject matter and appellate jurisdiction.

Subdivision (b). The amendment requires the appellee to include a jurisdictional statement in the appellee's brief except that the appellee need not include the statement if the appellee is satisfied with the appellant's jurisdictional statement.

Subdivision (h). The amendment provides that when more than one party appeals from a judgment or order, the party filing the first appeal is normally treated as the appellant for purposes of this rule and Rules 30 and 31. The party who first files an appeal usually is the principal appellant and should be treated as such. Parties who file a notice of appeal after the first notice often bring protective appeals and they should be treated as cross appellants. Local rules in the Fourth and Federal Circuits now take that approach. If notices of appeal are filed on the same day, the rule follows the old approach of treating the plaintiff below as the appellant. For purposes of this rule, in criminal cases "the plaintiff" means the United States. In those instances where the designations provided by the rule are inappropriate, they may be altered by agreement of the parties or by an order of the court.

1993 Amendments

Note to paragraph (a)(5). The amendment requires an appellant's brief to state the standard of review applicable to each issue on appeal. Five circuits currently require these statements. Experience in those circuits indicates that requiring a statement of the standard of review generally results in arguments that are properly shaped in light of the standard.

1994 Amendments

Subdivision (a). The amendment adds a requirement that an appellant's brief contain a summary of the argument. A number of circuits have local rules requiring a summary and the courts report that they find the summary useful. See, D.C. Cir.R. 11(a)(5); 5th Cir.R. 28.2.2; 8th Cir.R. 28A(i)(6); 11th Cir.R. 28–2(i); and Fed. Cir.R. 28.

Subdivision (b). The amendment adds a requirement that an appellee's brief contain a summary of the argument.

Subdivision (g). The amendment adds proof of service to the list of items in a brief that do not count for purposes of the page limitation. The concurrent amendment to Rule 25(d) requires a certificate of service to list the addresses to which a paper was mailed or at which it was delivered. When a number of parties must be served, the listing of addresses may run to several pages and those pages should not count for purposes of the page limitation.

1998 Amendments

The language and organization of the rule are amended to make the rule more easily understood. In addition to changes made to improve the understanding, the Advisory Committee has changed language to make style and terminology consistent throughout the appellate rules. These changes are intended to by stylistic only.

Several substantive changes are made in this rule, however. Most of them are necessary to confirm Rule 28 with changes recommended in Rule 32.

Subdivision (a). The current rule requires a brief to include a statement of the case which includes a description of the nature of the case, the course of proceedings, the disposition of the case—all of which might be described as the procedural history—as well as a statement of the facts. The amendments separate this into two statements; one procedural, called the statement of the case; and one factual, called the statement of the facts. The Advisory Committee believes that the separation will be helpful to the judges. The table of contents and table of authorities have also been separated into two distinct items.

An additional amendment of subdivision (a) is made to conform it with an amendment being made to Rule 32. Rule 32(a)(7) generally requires a brief to include a certificate of compliance with type-volume limitations contained in that rule. (No certificate is required if a brief does not exceed 30 pages, or 15 pages for a reply brief.) Rule 28(a) is amended to include that certificate in the list of items that must be included in a brief whenever it is required by Rule 32.

Subdivision (g). The amendments delete subdivision (g) that limited a principal brief to 50 pages and a reply brief to 25 pages. The length limitations have been moved to Rule 32. Rule 32 deals generally with the format for a brief or appendix.

Subdivision (h). The amendment requires an appellee's brief to comply with Rule 28(a)(1) through (11) with regard to a cross-appeal. The addition of separate paragraphs requiring a corporate disclosure statement, table of authorities, statement of facts, and certificate of compliance increased the relevant paragraphs of subdivision (a) from (7) to (11). The other changes are stylistic; no substantive changes are intended.

2002 Amendments

Subdivision (j). In the past, Rule 28(j) has required parties to describe supplemental authorities "without argument." Enforcement of this restriction has been lax, in part because of the difficulty of distinguishing "state[ment] . . . [of] the reasons for the supplemental citations," which is required, from "argument" about the supplemental citations, which is forbidden.

As amended, Rule 28(j) continues to require parties to state the reasons for supplemental citations, with reference to the part of a brief or oral argument to which the supplemental citations pertain. But Rule 28(j) no longer forbids "argument." Rather, Rule 28(j) permits parties to decide for themselves what they wish to say about supplemental authorities. The only restriction upon parties is that the body of a

Rule 28(j) letter—that is, the part of the letter that begins with the first word after the salutation and ends with the last word before the complimentary close—cannot exceed 350 words. All words found in footnotes will count toward the 350–word limit.

Changes Made After Publication and Comments No changes were made to the text of the proposed amendment or to the Committee Note, except that the word limit was increased from 250 to 350 in response to the complaint of some commentators that parties would have difficulty bringing multiple supplemental authorities to the attention of the court in one 250–word letter.

2005 Amendments

Subdivision (c). Subdivision (c) has been amended to delete a sentence that authorized an appellee who had cross-appealed to file a brief in reply to the appellant's response. All rules regarding briefing in cases involving cross-appeals have been consolidated into new Rule 28.1.

Subdivision (h). Subdivision (h)—regarding briefing in cases involving cross-appeals—has been deleted. All rules regarding such briefing have been consolidated into new Rule 28.1.

Rule 28.1. Cross–Appeals

(a) Applicability. This rule applies to a case in which a cross-appeal is filed. Rules 28(a)-(c), 31(a)(1), 32(a)(2), and 32(a)(7)(A)-(B) do not apply to such a case, except as otherwise provided in this rule.

(b) Designation of Appellant. The party who files a notice of appeal first is the appellant for the purposes of this rule and Rules 30 and 34. If notices are filed on the same day, the plaintiff in the proceeding below is the appellant. These designations may be modified by the parties' agreement or by court order.

(c) Briefs. In a case involving a cross-appeal:

(1) Appellant's Principal Brief. The appellant must file a principal brief in the appeal. That brief must comply with Rule 28(a).

(2) Appellee's Principal and Response Brief. The appellee must file a principal brief in the cross-appeal and must, in the same brief, respond to the principal brief in the appeal. That appellee's brief must comply with Rule 28(a), except that the brief need not include a statement of the case or a statement of the facts unless the appellee is dissatisfied with the appellant's statement.

(3) Appellant's Response and Reply Brief. The appellant must file a brief that responds to the principal brief in the cross-appeal and may, in the same brief, reply to the response in the appeal. That brief must comply with Rule 28(a)(2)–(9) and (11), except that none of the following need appear unless the appellant is dissatisfied with the appellee's statement in the cross-appeal:

(A) the jurisdictional statement;

(B) the statement of the issues;

(C) the statement of the case;

(D) the statement of the facts; and

(E) the statement of the standard of review.

(4) Appellee's Reply Brief. The appellee may file a brief in reply to the response in the cross-appeal. That brief must comply with Rule 28(a)(2)–(3) and (11) and must be limited to the issues presented by the cross-appeal.

(5) No Further Briefs. Unless the court permits, no further briefs may be filed in a case involving a cross-appeal.

(d) Cover. Except for filings by unrepresented parties, the cover of the appellant's principal brief must be blue; the appellee's principal and response brief, red; the appellant's response and reply brief, yellow; the appellee's reply brief, gray; an intervenor's or amicus curiae's brief, green; and any supplemental brief, tan. The front cover of a brief must contain the information required by Rule 32(a)(2).

(e) Length.

(1) Page Limitation. Unless it complies with Rule 28.1(e)(2) and (3), the appellant's principal brief must not exceed 30 pages; the appellee's principal and response brief, 35 pages; the appellant's response and reply brief, 30 pages; and the appellee's reply brief, 15 pages.

(2) Type-Volume Limitation.

(A) The appellant's principal brief or the appellant's response and reply brief is acceptable if:

(i) it contains no more than 14,000 words; or

(ii) it uses a monospaced face and contains no more than 1,300 lines of text.

(B) The appellee's principal and response brief is acceptable if:

(i) it contains no more than 16,500 words; or

(ii) it uses a monospaced face and contains no more than 1,500 lines of text.

(C) The appellee's reply brief is acceptable if it contains no more than half of the type volume specified in Rule 28.1(e)(2)(A).

(3) Certificate of Compliance. A brief submitted under Rule 28.1(e)(2) must comply with Rule 32(a)(7)(C).

(f) Time to Serve and File a Brief. Briefs must be served and filed as follows:

(1) the appellant's principal brief, within 40 days after the record is filed;

(2) the appellee's principal and response brief, within 30 days after the appellant's principal brief is served;

(3) the appellant's response and reply brief, within 30 days after the appellee's principal and response brief is served; and

(4) the appellee's reply brief, within 14 days after the appellant's response and reply brief is served, but at least 3 days before argument unless the court, for good cause, allows a later filing.

(As added April 25, 2005, eff. Dec. 1, 2005.)

2005 Adoption

The Federal Rules of Appellate Procedure have said very little about briefing in cases involving cross-appeals. This vacuum has frustrated judges, attorneys, and parties who have sought guidance in the rules. More importantly, this vacuum has been filled by conflicting local rules regarding such matters as the number and length of briefs, the colors of the covers of briefs, and the deadlines for serving and filing briefs. These local rules have created a hardship for attorneys who practice in more than one circuit.

New Rule 28.1 provides a comprehensive set of rules governing briefing in cases involving cross-appeals. The few existing provisions regarding briefing in such cases have been moved into new Rule 28.1, and several new provisions have been added to fill the gaps in the existing rules. The new provisions reflect the practices of the large majority of circuits and, to a significant extent, the new provisions have been patterned after the requirements imposed by Rules 28, 31, and 32 on briefs filed in cases that do not involve cross-appeals.

Subdivision (a). Subdivision (a) makes clear that, in a case involving a cross-appeal, briefing is governed by new Rule 28.1, and not by Rules 28(a), 28(b), 28(c), 31(a)(1), 32(a)(2), 32(a)(7)(A), and 32(a)(7)(B), except to the extent that Rule 28.1 specifically incorporates those rules by reference.

Subdivision (b). Subdivision (b) defines who is the "appellant" and who is the "appellee" in a case involving a cross-appeal. Subdivision (b) is taken directly from former Rule 28(h), except that subdivision (b) refers to a party being designated as an appellant "for the purposes of this rule and Rules 30 and 34," whereas former Rule 28(h) also referred to Rule 31. Because the matter addressed by Rule 31(a)(1)—the time to serve and file briefs—is now addressed directly in new Rule 28.1(f), the cross-reference to Rule 31 is no longer necessary. In Rule 31 and in all rules other than Rules 28.1, 30, and 34, references to an "appellant" refer both to the appellant in an appeal and to the cross-appellant in a cross-appeal, and references to an "appellee" refer both to the appellee in an appeal and to the cross-appellee in a cross-appeal. Cf. Rule 31(c).

Subdivision (c). Subdivision (c) provides for the filing of four briefs in a case involving a cross-appeal. This reflects the practice of every circuit except the Seventh. *See* 7th Cir. R. 28(d)(1)(a).

The first brief is the "appellant's principal brief." That brief—like the appellant's principal brief in a case that does not involve a cross-appeal—must comply with Rule 28(a).

The second brief is the "appellee's principal and response brief." Because this brief serves as the appellee's principal brief on the merits of the cross-appeal, as well as the appellee's response brief on the merits of the appeal, it must also comply with Rule 28(a), with the limited exceptions noted in the text of the rule.

The third brief is the "appellant's response and reply brief." Like a response brief in a case that does not involve a cross-appeal—that is, a response brief that does not also serve as a principal brief on the merits of a cross-appeal—the appellant's response and reply brief must comply with Rule 28(a)(2)-(9) and (11), with the exceptions noted in the text of the rule. *See* Rule 28(b). The one difference between the appellant's response and reply brief, on the one hand, and a response brief filed in a case that does not involve a cross-appeal, on the other, is that the latter must include a corporate disclosure statement. *See* Rule 28(a)(1) and (b). An appellant filing a response and reply brief in a case involving a cross-appeal has already filed a corporate disclosure statement with its principal brief on the merits of the appeal.

The fourth brief is the "appellee's reply brief." Like a reply brief in a case that does not involve a cross-appeal, it must comply with Rule 28(c), which essentially restates the requirements of Rule 28(a)(2)–(3) and (11). (Rather than restating the requirements of Rule 28(a)(2)-(3) and (11), as Rule 28(c) does, Rule 28.1(c)(4) includes a direct cross-reference.) The appellee's reply brief must also be limited to the issues presented by the cross-appeal.

Subdivision (d). Subdivision (d) specifies the colors of the covers on briefs filed in a case involving a cross-appeal. It is patterned after Rule 32(a)(2), which does not specifically refer to cross-appeals.

Subdivision (e). Subdivision (e) sets forth limits on the length of the briefs filed in a case involving a cross-appeal. It is patterned after Rule 32(a)(7), which does not specifically refer to cross-appeals. Subdivision (e) permits the appellee's principal and response brief to be longer than a typical principal brief on the merits because this brief serves not only as the principal brief on the merits of the cross-appeal, but also as the response brief on the merits of the appeal. Likewise, subdivision (e) permits the appellant's response and reply brief to be longer than a typical reply brief because this brief serves not only as the reply brief in the appeal, but also as the response brief in the cross-appeal. For purposes of determining the maximum length of an amicus curiae's brief filed in a case involving a cross-appeal, Rule 29(d)'s reference to "the maximum length authorized by these rules for a party's principal brief" should be understood to refer to subdivision (e)'s limitations on the length of an appellant's principal brief.

Subdivision (f). Subdivision (f) provides deadlines for serving and filing briefs in a cross-appeal. It is patterned after Rule 31(a)(1), which does not specifically refer to cross-appeals.

Rule 29. Brief of an Amicus Curiae

(a) When Permitted. The United States or its officer or agency, or a State, Territory, Commonwealth, or the District of Columbia may file an amicus-curiae brief without the consent of the parties or leave of court. Any other amicus curiae may file a brief only by leave of court or if the brief states that all parties have consented to its filing.

(b) Motion for Leave to File. The motion must be accompanied by the proposed brief and state:

(1) the movant's interest; and

(2) the reason why an amicus brief is desirable and why the matters asserted are relevant to the disposition of the case.

(c) Contents and Form. An amicus brief must comply with Rule 32. In addition to the requirements of Rule 32, the cover must identify the party or parties supported and indicate whether the brief supports affirmance or reversal. If an amicus curiae is a corporation, the brief must include a disclosure statement like that required of parties by Rule 26.1. An amicus brief need not comply with Rule 28, but must include the following:

(1) a table of contents, with page references;

(2) a table of authorities—cases (alphabetically arranged), statutes and other authorities—with references to the pages of the brief where they are cited;

(3) a concise statement of the identity of the amicus curiae, its interest in the case, and the source of its authority to file;

(4) an argument, which may be preceded by a summary and which need not include a statement of the applicable standard of review; and

(5) a certificate of compliance, if required by Rule 32(a)(7).

(d) Length. Except by the court's permission, an amicus brief may be no more than one-half the maximum length authorized by these rules for a party's principal brief. If the court grants a party permission to file a longer brief, that extension does not affect the length of an amicus brief.

(e) Time for Filing. An amicus curiae must file its brief, accompanied by a motion for filing when necessary, no later than 7 days after the principal brief of the party being supported is filed. An amicus curiae that does not support either party must file its brief no later than 7 days after the appellant's or petitioner's principal brief is filed. A court may grant leave for later filing, specifying the time within which an opposing party may answer.

(f) Reply Brief. Except by the court's permission, an amicus curiae may not file a reply brief.

(g) Oral Argument. An amicus curiae may participate in oral argument only with the court's permission.

(As amended Apr. 24, 1998, eff. Dec. 1, 1998.)

1967 Adoption

Only five circuits presently regulate the filing of the brief of an amicus curiae. See D.C.Cir. Rule 18(j) [rule 18(j), U.S.Ct. of App.Dist. of Col.Cir., this title]; 1st Cir. Rule 23(10) [rule 23(10), U.S.Ct. of App. 1st Cir.]; 6th Cir. Rule 17(4) [rule 17(4), U.S.Ct. of App. 6th Cir.]; 9th Cir. Rule 18(9) [rule 18(9), U.S.Ct. of App. 9th Cir.]; 10th Cir. Rule 20 [rule 20, U.S.Ct. of App. 10th Cir.]. This rule follows the practice of a majority of circuits in requiring leave of court to file an amicus brief except under the circumstances stated therein. Compare Supreme Court Rule 42.

1998 Amendments

The language and organization of the rule are amended to make the rule more easily understood. In addition to changes made to improve the understanding, the Advisory Committee has changed language to make style and terminology consistent through the appellate rules. These changes are intended to be stylistic only.

Several substantive changes are made in this rule, however.

Subdivision (a). The major change in this subpart is that when a brief is filed with the consent of all parties, it is no longer necessary to obtain the parties' written consent and to file the consents with the brief. It is sufficient to obtain the parties' oral consent and to state in the brief that all parties have consented. It is sometimes difficult to obtain all the written consents by the filing deadline and it is not unusual for counsel to represent that parties have consented; for example, in a motion for extension of time to file a brief it is not unusual for the movant to state that the other parties have been consulted and they do not object to the extension. If a party's consent has been misrepresented, the party will be able to take action before the court considers the amicus brief.

The District of Columbia is added to the list of entities allowed to file an amicus brief without consent of all parties. The other changes in this material are stylistic.

Subdivision (b). The provision in the former rule, granting permission to conditionally file the brief with the motion, is changed to one requiring that the brief accompany the motion. Sup. Ct. R. 37.4 requires that the proposed brief be presented with the motion.

The former rule only required the motion to identify the applicant's interest and to generally state the reasons why an amicus brief is desirable. The amended rule additionally requires that the motion state the relevance of the matters asserted to the disposition of the case. As Sup. Ct. R. 37.1 states:

> An *amicus curiae* brief which brings relevant matter to the attention of the Court that has not already been brought to its attention by the parties is of considerable help to the Court. An *amicus curiae* brief which does not serve this purpose simply burdens the staff and facilities of the Court and its filing is not favored.

Because the relevance of the matters asserted by an amicus is ordinarily the most compelling reason for granting leave to file, the Committee believes that it is helpful to explicitly require such a showing.

Subdivision (c). The provisions in this subdivision are entirely new. Previously there was confusion as to whether an amicus brief must include all of the items listed in Rule 28. Out of caution practitioners in some circuits included all those items. Ordinarily that is unnecessary.

The requirement that the cover identify the party supported and indicate whether the amicus supports affirmance or reversal is an administrative aid.

Paragraph (c)(3) requires an amicus to state the source of its authority to file. The amicus simply must identify which of the provisions in Rule 29(a) provides the basis for the amicus to file its brief.

Subdivision (d). This new provision imposes a shorter page limit for an amicus brief than for a party's brief. This is appropriate for two reasons. First, an amicus may omit certain items that must be included in a party's brief. Second, an amicus brief is supplemental. It need not address all issues or all facets of a case. It should treat only matter not adequately addressed by a party.

Subdivision (e). The time limit for filing is changed. An amicus brief must be filed no later than 7 days after the principal brief of the party being supported is filed. Occasionally, an amicus supports neither party; in such instances, the amendment provides that the amicus brief must be filed no later than 7 days after the appellant's or petitioner's principal brief is filed. Note that in both instances the 7–day period runs from when a brief is filed. The passive voice—"is filed"—is used deliberately. A party or amicus can send its brief to a court for filing and, under Rule 25, the brief is timely if mailed within the filing period. Although the brief is timely if mailed within the filing period, it is not "filed" until the court receives it and file stamps it. "Filing" is done by the court, not by the party. It may be necessary for an amicus to contact the court to ascertain the filing date.

The 7–day stagger was adopted because it is long enough to permit an amicus to review the completed brief of the party being supported and avoid repetitious argument. A 7–day period also is short enough that no adjustment need be made in the opposing party's briefing schedule. The opposing party will have sufficient time to review arguments made by the amicus and address them in the party's responsive pleading. The timetable for filing the parties' briefs is unaffected by this change.

A court may grant permission to file an amicus brief in a context in which the party does not file a "principal brief"; for example, an amicus may be permitted to file in support of a party's petition for rehearing. In such instances the court will establish the filing time for the amicus.

The former rule's statement that a court may, for cause shown, grant leave for later filing is unnecessary. Rule 26(b) grants general authority to enlarge the time prescribed in these rules for good cause shown. This new rule, however, states that when a court grants permission for later filing, the court must specify the period within which an opposing party may answer the arguments of the amicus.

Subdivision (f). This subdivision generally prohibits the filing of a reply brief by an amicus curiae. Sup. Ct. R. 37 and local rules of the D.C., Ninth, and Federal Circuits state that an amicus may not file a reply brief. The role of an amicus should not require the use of a reply brief.

Subdivision (g). The language of this subdivision stating that an amicus will be granted permission to participate in oral argument "only for extraordinary reasons" has been deleted. The change is made to reflect more accurately the current practice in which it is not unusual for a court to permit an amicus to argue when a party is willing to share its argument time with the amicus. The Committee does not intend, however, to suggest that in other instances an amicus will be permitted to argue absent extraordinary circumstances.

Rule 30. Appendix to the Briefs

(a) Appellant's Responsibility.

(1) Contents of the Appendix. The appellant must prepare and file an appendix to the briefs containing:

(A) the relevant docket entries in the proceeding below;

(B) the relevant portions of the pleadings, charge, findings, or opinion;

(C) the judgment, order, or decision in question; and

(D) other parts of the record to which the parties wish to direct the court's attention.

(2) Excluded Material. Memoranda of law in the district court should not be included in the appendix unless they have independent relevance. Parts of the record may be relied on by the court or the parties even though not included in the appendix.

(3) Time to File; Number of Copies. Unless filing is deferred under Rule 30(c), the appellant must file 10 copies of the appendix with the brief and must serve one copy on counsel for each party separately represented. An unrepresented party proceeding in forma pauperis must file 4 legible copies with the clerk, and one copy must be served on counsel for each separately represented party. The court may by local rule or by order in a particular case require the filing or service of a different number.

(b) All Parties' Responsibilities.

(1) Determining the Contents of the Appendix. The parties are encouraged to agree on the contents of the appendix. In the absence of an agreement, the appellant must, within 10 days after the record is filed, serve on the appellee a designation of the parts of the record the appellant intends to include in the appendix and a statement of the issues the appellant intends to present for review. The appellee may, within 10 days after receiving the designation, serve on the appellant a designation of additional parts to which it wishes to direct the court's attention. The appellant must include the designated parts in the appendix. The parties must not engage in unnecessary designation of parts of the record, because the entire record is available to the court. This paragraph applies also to a cross-appellant and a cross-appellee.

(2) Costs of Appendix. Unless the parties agree otherwise, the appellant must pay the cost of the appendix. If the appellant considers parts of the record designated by the appellee to be unnecessary, the appellant may advise the appellee, who must then advance the cost of including those parts. The cost of the appendix is a taxable cost. But if any party causes unnecessary parts of the record to be included in the appendix, the court may impose the cost of those parts on that party. Each circuit must, by local rule, provide for sanctions against attorneys who unreasonably and vexatiously increase litigation costs by including unnecessary material in the appendix.

(c) Deferred Appendix.

(1) Deferral Until After Briefs Are Filed. The court may provide by rule for classes of cases or by order in a particular case that preparation of the appendix may be deferred until after the briefs have been filed and that the appendix may be filed 21 days after the appellee's brief is served. Even though the filing of the appendix may be deferred, Rule 30(b) applies; except that a party must designate the parts of the record it wants included in the appendix when it serves its brief, and need not include a statement of the issues presented.

(2) References to the Record.

(A) If the deferred appendix is used, the parties may cite in their briefs the pertinent pages of the record. When the appendix is prepared, the record pages cited in the briefs must be indicated by inserting record page numbers, in brackets, at places in the appendix where those pages of the record appear.

(B) A party who wants to refer directly to pages of the appendix may serve and file copies of the brief within the time required by Rule 31(a), containing appropriate references to pertinent pages of the record. In that event, within 14 days after the appendix is filed, the party must serve and file copies of the brief, containing references to the pages of the appendix in place of or in addition to the references to the pertinent pages of the record. Except for the correction of typographical errors, no other changes may be made to the brief.

(d) Format of the Appendix. The appendix must begin with a table of contents identifying the page at which each part begins. The relevant docket entries must follow the table of contents. Other parts of the record must follow chronologically. When pages from the transcript of proceedings are placed in the appendix, the transcript page numbers must be shown in brackets immediately before the included pages. Omissions in the text of papers or of the transcript must be indicated by asterisks. Immaterial formal matters (captions, subscriptions, acknowledgments, etc.) should be omitted.

(e) Reproduction of Exhibits. Exhibits designated for inclusion in the appendix may be reproduced in a separate volume, or volumes, suitably indexed. Four copies must be filed with the appendix, and one copy must be served on counsel for each separately represented party. If a transcript of a proceeding before an administrative agency, board, commission, or officer was used in a district-court action and has been designated for inclusion in the appendix, the transcript must be placed in the appendix as an exhibit.

(f) Appeal on the Original Record Without an Appendix. The court may, either by rule for all cases or classes of cases or by order in a particular case, dispense with the appendix and permit an appeal to proceed on the original record with any copies of the record, or relevant parts, that the court may order the parties to file.

(As amended Mar. 30, 1970, eff. July 1, 1970; Mar. 10, 1986, eff. July 1, 1986; Apr. 30, 1991, eff. Dec. 1, 1991; Apr. 29, 1994, eff. Dec. 1, 1994; Apr. 24, 1998. eff. Dec. 1, 1998.)

1967 Adoption

Subdivision (a). Only two circuits presently require a printed record (5th Cir. Rule 23(a) [rule 23(a), U.S.Ct. of App. 5th Cir.]; 8th Cir. Rule 10 [rule 10, U.S.Ct. of App. 8th Cir.] (in civil appeals only)), and the rules and practice in those circuits combine to make the difference between a printed record and the appendix, which is now used in eight circuits and in the Supreme Court in lieu of the printed record, largely nominal. The essential characteristics of the appendix method are: (1) the entire record may not be reproduced; (2) instead, the parties are to set out in an appendix to the briefs those parts of the record which in their judgment the judges must consult in order to determine the issues presented by the appeal; (3) the appendix is not the record but merely a selection therefrom for the convenience of the judges of the court of appeals; the record is the actual trial court record, and the record itself is always available to supply inadvertent omissions from the appendix. These essentials are incorporated, either by rule or by practice, in the circuits that continue to require the printed record rather than the appendix. See 5th Cir. Rule 23(a)(9) [23(a)(9), U.S.Ct. of App. 5th Cir.] and 8th Cir. Rule 10(a)–(d) [rule 10(a)–(d), U.S.Ct. of App. 8th Cir.].

Subdivision (b). Under the practice in six of the eight circuits which now use the appendix method, unless the parties agree to use a single appendix, the appellant files with his brief an appendix containing the parts of the record which he deems it essential that the court read in order to determine the questions presented. If the appellee deems additional parts of the record necessary he must include such parts as an appendix to his brief. The proposed rule differs from that practice. By the new rule a single appendix is to be filed. It is to be prepared by the appellant, who must include therein those parts which he deems essential and those which the appellee designates as essential.

Under the practice by which each party files his own appendix the resulting reproduction of essential parts of the record is often fragmentary; it is not infrequently necessary to piece several appendices together to arrive at a usable reproduction. Too, there seems to be a tendency on the part of some appellants to reproduce less than what is necessary for a determination of the issues presented (see *Moran Towing Corp. v. M. A. Gammino Construction Co.*, 363 F.2d 108 (1st Cir. 1966); *Walters v. Shari Music Publishing*

Corp., 298 F.2d 206 (2d Cir. 1962) and cases cited therein; *Morrison v. Texas Co.*, 289 F.2d 382 (7th Cir. 1961) and cases cited therein), a tendency which is doubtless encouraged by the requirement in present rules that the appellee reproduce in his separately prepared appendix such necessary parts of the record as are not included by the appellant.

Under the proposed rule responsibility for the preparation of the appendix is placed on the appellant. If the appellee feels that the appellant has omitted essential portions of the record, he may require the appellant to include such portions in the appendix. The appellant is protected against a demand that he reproduce parts which he considers unnecessary by the provisions entitling him to require the appellee to advance the costs of reproducing such parts and authorizing denial of costs for matter unnecessarily reproduced.

Subdivision (c). This subdivision permits the appellant to elect to defer the production of the appendix to the briefs until the briefs of both sides are written, and authorizes a court of appeals to require such deferred filing by rule or order. The advantage of this method of preparing the appendix is that it permits the parties to determine what parts of the record need to be reproduced in the light of the issues actually presented by the briefs. Often neither side is in a position to say precisely what is needed until the briefs are completed. Once the argument on both sides is known, it should be possible to confine the matter reproduced in the appendix to that which is essential to a determination of the appeal or review. This method of preparing the appendix is presently in use in the Tenth Circuit (Rule 17) [rule 17, U.S.Ct. of App. 10th Cir.] and in other circuits in review of agency proceedings, and it has proven its value in reducing the volume required to be reproduced. When the record is long, use of this method is likely to result in substantial economy to the parties.

Subdivision (e). The purpose of this subdivision is to reduce the cost of reproducing exhibits. While subdivision (a) requires that 10 copies of the appendix be filed, unless the court requires a lesser number, subdivision (e) permits exhibits necessary for the determination of an appeal to be bound separately, and requires only 4 copies of such a separate volume or volumes to be filed and a single copy to be served on counsel.

Subdivision (f). The subdivision authorizes a court of appeals to dispense with the appendix method of reproducing parts of the record and to hear appeals on the original record and such copies of it as the court may require.

Since 1962 the Ninth Circuit has permitted all appeals to be heard on the original record and a very limited number of copies. Under the practice as adopted in 1962, any party to an appeal could elect to have the appeal heard on the original record and two copies thereof rather than on the printed record theretofore required. The resulting substantial saving of printing costs led to the election of the new practice in virtually all cases, and by 1967 the use of printed records had ceased. By a recent amendment, the Ninth Circuit has abolished the printed record altogether. Its rules now provide that all appeals are to be heard on the original record, and it has reduced the number of copies required to two sets of copies of the transmitted original papers (excluding copies of exhibits, which need not be filed unless specifically ordered). See 9 Cir. Rule 10 [rule 10 U.S.Ct. of App. 9th Cir.], as amended June 2, 1967, effective September 1, 1967. The Eighth Circuit permits appeals in criminal cases and in habeas corpus and 28 U.S.C. § 2255 proceedings to be heard on the original record and two copies thereof. See 8 Cir. Rule 8(i)–(j) [rule 8(i)–(j), U.S.Ct. of App. 8th Cir.]. The Tenth Circuit permits appeals in all cases to be heard on the original record and four copies thereof whenever the record consists of two hundred pages or less. See 10 Cir. Rule 17(a) [rule 17(a), U.S.Ct. of App. 10th Cir.]. This subdivision expressly authorizes the continuation of the practices in the Eighth, Ninth and Tenth Circuits.

The judges of the Court of Appeals for the Ninth Circuit have expressed complete satisfaction with the practice there in use and have suggested that attention be called to the advantages which it offers in terms of reducing cost.

1970 Amendments

Subdivision (a). The amendment of subdivision (a) is related to the amendment of Rule 31(a), which authorizes a court of appeals to shorten the time for filing briefs. By virtue of this amendment, if the time for filing the brief of the appellant is shortened the time for filing the appendix is likewise shortened.

Subdivision (c). As originally written, subdivision (c) permitted the appellant to elect to defer filing of the appendix until 21 days after service of the brief of the appellee. As amended, subdivision (c) requires that an order of court be obtained before filing of the appendix can be deferred, unless a court permits deferred filing by local rule. The amendment should not cause use of the deferred appendix to be viewed with disfavor. In cases involving lengthy records, permission to defer filing of the appendix should be freely granted as an inducement to the parties to include in the appendix only matter that the briefs show to be necessary for consideration by the judges. But the Committee is advised that appellants have elected to defer filing of the appendix in cases involving brief records merely to obtain the 21 day delay. The subdivision is amended to prevent that practice.

1986 Amendments

Subdivision (a). During its study of the separate appendix [see Report of the Advisory Committee on the Federal Appellate Rules on the Operation of Rule 30, FRD (1985)], the Advisory Committee found that this document was frequently encumbered with memoranda submitted to the trial court. *United States v. Noall*, 587 F.2d 123, 125 n. 1 (2nd Cir.1978). See generally *Drewett v. Aetna Cas. & Sur. Co.*, 539 F.2d 496, 500 (5th Cir.1976); *Volkswagenwerk Aktiengesellschaft v. Church*, 413 F.2d 1126, 1128 (9th Cir.1969). Inclusion of such material makes the appendix more bulky and therefore less useful to the appellate panel. It also can increase significantly the costs of litigation.

There are occasions when such trial court memoranda have independent relevance in the appellate litigation. For instance, there may be a dispute as to whether a particular point was raised or whether a concession was made in the district court. In such circumstances, it is appropriate to include pertinent sections of such memoranda in the appendix.

Subdivision (b). The amendment to subdivision (b) is designed to require the circuits, by local rule, to establish a procedural mechanism for the imposition of sanctions against those attorneys who conduct appellate litigation in bad faith.

Both 28 U.S.C. § 1927 and the inherent power of the court authorize such sanctions. See *Brennan v. Local 357, International Brotherhood of Teamsters*, 709 F.2d 611 (9th Cir. 1983). See generally *Roadway Express, Inc. v. Piper*, 447 U.S. 752 (1980). While considerations of uniformity are important and doubtless will be taken into account by the judges of the respective circuits, the Advisory Committee believes that, at this time, the circuits need the flexibility to tailor their approach to the conditions of local practice. The local rule shall provide for notice and opportunity to respond before the imposition of any sanction.

Technical amendments also are made to subdivisions (a), (b) and (c) which are not intended to be substantive changes.

1991 Amendments

Subdivision (b). The amendment requires a cross appellant to serve the appellant with a statement of the issues that the cross appellant intends to pursue on appeal. No later than ten days after the record is filed, the appellant and cross appellant must serve each other with a statement of the issues each intends to present for review and with a designation of the parts of the record that each wants included in the appendix. Within the next ten days, both the appellee and the cross appellee may designate additional materials for inclusion in the appendix. The appellant must then include in the appendix the parts thus designated for both the appeal and any cross appeals. The Committee expects that simultaneous compliance with this subdivision by an appellant and a cross appellant will be feasible in most cases. If a cross appellant cannot fairly be expected to comply until receipt of the appellant's statement of issues, relief may be sought by motion in the court of appeals.

1994 Amendments

Subdivision (a). The only substantive change is to allow a court to require the filing of a greater number of copies of an appendix as well as a lesser number.

1998 Amendments

The language and organization of the new rule are amended to make the rule more easily understood. In addition to changes made to improve the understanding, the Advisory Committee has changed language to make style and terminology consistent throughout the appellate Rules. These changes are intended to be stylistic only.

Subdivision (a). Paragraph (a)(3) is amended so that it is consistent with Rule 31(b). An unrepresented party proceeding in forma pauperis is only required to file 4 copies of the appendix rather than 10.

Subdivision (c). When a deferred appendix is used, a brief must make reference to the original record rather than to the appendix because it does not exist when the briefs are prepared. Unless a party later files an amended brief with direct references to the pages of the appendix (as provided in subparagraph (c)(2)(B)), the material in the appendix must indicate the pages of the original record from which it was drawn so that a reader of the brief can make meaningful use of the appendix. The instructions in the current rule for cross-referencing the appendix materials to the original record are unclear. The language in paragraph (c)(2) has been amended to try to clarify the procedure.

Subdivision (d). In recognition of the fact that use of a typeset appendix is exceedingly rare in the courts of appeals, the last sentence—permitting a question and answer (as from a transcript) to be in a single paragraph—has been omitted.

HISTORICAL NOTES

Taxation of Fees in Appeals in Which Requirement of Appendix is Dispensed With

See item (6) in the Judicial Conference Schedule of Fees note under 28 U.S.C.A. § 1913.

Rule 31. Serving and Filing Briefs

(a) Time to Serve and File a Brief.

(1) The appellant must serve and file a brief within 40 days after the record is filed. The appellee must serve and file a brief within 30 days after the appellant's brief is served. The appellant may serve and file a reply brief within 14 days after service of the appellee's brief but a reply brief must be filed at least 3 days before argument, unless the court, for good cause, allows a later filing.

(2) A court of appeals that routinely considers cases on the merits promptly after the briefs are filed may shorten the time to serve and file briefs, either by local rule or by order in a particular case.

(b) Number of Copies. Twenty-five copies of each brief must be filed with the clerk and 2 copies must be served on each unrepresented party and on counsel for each separately represented party. An unrepresented party proceeding in forma pauperis must file 4 legible copies with the clerk, and one copy must be served on each unrepresented party and on counsel for each separately represented party. The court may by local rule or by order in a particular case require the filing or service of a different number.

(c) Consequence of Failure to File. If an appellant fails to file a brief within the time provided by this rule, or within an extended time, an appellee may move to dismiss the appeal. An appellee who fails to file a brief will not be heard at oral argument unless the court grants permission.

(As amended Mar. 30, 1970, eff. July 1, 1970; Mar. 10, 1986, eff. July 1, 1986; Apr. 29, 1994, eff. Dec. 1, 1994; Apr. 24, 1998, eff. Dec. 1, 1998; Apr. 29, 2002, eff. Dec. 1, 2002.)

1967 Adoption

A majority of the circuits now require the brief of the appellant to be filed within 30 days from the date on which the record is filed. But in those circuits an exchange of designations is unnecessary in the preparation of the appendix. The appellant files with his brief an appendix containing the parts of the record which he deems essential. If the appellee considers other parts essential, he includes those parts in his own appendix. Since the proposed rule requires the appellant to file with his brief an appendix containing necessary parts of the record as designated by both parties, the rule allows the appellant 40 days in order to provide time for the exchange of designations respecting the content of the appendix (see Rule 30(b)).

1970 Amendment

The time prescribed by Rule 31(a) for preparing briefs—40 days to the appellant, 30 days to the appellee—is well within the time that must ordinarily elapse in most circuits before an appeal can be reached for consideration. In those circuits, the time prescribed by the Rule should not be disturbed. But if a court of appeals maintains a current calendar, that is, if an appeal can be heard as soon as the briefs have been filed, or if the practice of the court permits the submission of appeals for preliminary consideration as soon as the briefs have been filed, the court should be free to prescribe shorter periods in the interest of expediting decision.

1986 Amendment

The amendments to Rules 31(a) and (c) are technical. No substantive change is intended.

1994 Amendments

Subdivision (b). The amendment allows a court of appeals to require the filing of a greater, as well as a lesser, number of copies of briefs. The amendment also allows the required number to be prescribed by local rule as well as by order in a particular case.

1998 Amendments

The language and organization of the rule are amended to make the rule more easily understood. In addition to changes made to improve the understanding, the advisory committee has changed language to make style and terminology consistent throughout the appellate rules. These changes are intended to by stylistic only; a substantive change is made, however, in subdivision (b).

Subdivision (a). Paragraph (a)(2) explicitly authorizes a court of appeals to shorten a briefing schedule if the court routinely considers cases on the merits promptly after the briefs are filed. Extensions of the briefing schedule, by order, are permitted under the general provisions of Rule 26(b).

Subdivision (b). The current rules says that a party who is permitted to file "typewritten ribbon and carbon copies of the brief" need only file and original and three copies of the brief. The quoted language, in conjunction with current rule 24(c), means that a party allowed to proceed in forma pauperis need not file 25 copies of the brief. Two changes are made in this subdivision. First, it is anachronistic to refer to a party who is allowed to file a typewritten brief as if that would distinguish the party from all other parties; any party is permitted to file a typewritten brief. The amended rule states directly that it applies to a party to proceed in forma pauperis. Second, the amended rule does not generally permit parties who are represented by counsel to file the lesser number of brief. Inexpensive methods of copying are generally available. Unless it would impose hardship, in which case a motion to file a lesser number should be filed, a represented party must file the usual number of briefs.

2002 Amendments

Subdivision (b). In requiring that two copies of each brief "must be served on counsel for each separately represented party," Rule 31(b) may be read to imply that copies of briefs need not be served on unrepresented parties. The Rule has been amended to clarify that briefs must be served on all parties, including those who are not represented by counsel.

Changes Made After Publication and Comments No changes were made to the text of the proposed amendment or to the Committee Note.

Rule 32. Form of Briefs, Appendices, and Other Papers

(a) Form of a Brief.

(1) Reproduction.

(A) A brief may be reproduced by any process that yields a clear black image on light paper. The paper must be opaque and unglazed. Only one side of the paper may be used.

(B) Text must be reproduced with a clarity that equals or exceeds the output of a laser printer.

(C) Photographs, illustrations, and tables may be reproduced by any method that results in a good copy of the original; a glossy finish is acceptable if the original is glossy.

(2) Cover. Except for filings by unrepresented parties, the cover of the appellant's brief must be blue; the appellee's, red; an intervenor's or amicus curiae's, green; any reply brief, gray; and any supplemental brief, tan. The front cover of a brief must contain:

(A) the number of the case centered at the top;

(B) the name of the court;

(C) the title of the case (see Rule 12(a));

(D) the nature of the proceeding (e.g., Appeal, Petition for Review) and the name of the court, agency, or board below;

(E) the title of the brief, identifying the party or parties for whom the brief is filed; and

(F) the name, office address, and telephone number of counsel representing the party for whom the brief is filed.

(3) Binding. The brief must be bound in any manner that is secure, does not obscure the text, and permits the brief to lie reasonably flat when open.

(4) Paper Size, Line Spacing, and Margins. The brief must be on 8½ by 11 inch paper. The text must be double-spaced, but quotations more than two lines long may be indented and single-spaced. Headings and footnotes may be single-spaced. Margins must be at least one inch on all four sides. Page numbers may be placed in the margins, but no text may appear there.

(5) Typeface. Either a proportionally spaced or a monospaced face may be used.

(A) A proportionally spaced face must include serifs, but sans-serif type may be used in headings and captions. A proportionally spaced face must be 14–point or larger.

(B) A monospaced face may not contain more than 10½ characters per inch.

(6) Type Styles. A brief must be set in a plain, roman style, although italics or boldface may be used for emphasis. Case names must be italicized or underlined.

(7) Length.

(A) Page limitation. A principal brief may not exceed 30 pages, or a reply brief 15 pages, unless it complies with Rule 32(a)(7)(B) and (C).

(B) Type-volume limitation.

(i) A principal brief is acceptable if:

- it contains no more than 14,000 words; or
- it uses a monospaced face and contains no more than 1,300 lines of text.

(ii) A reply brief is acceptable if it contains no more than half of the type volume specified in Rule 32(a)(7)(B)(i).

(iii) Headings, footnotes, and quotations count toward the word and line limitations. The corporate disclosure statement, table of contents, table of citations, statement with respect to oral argument, any addendum containing statutes, rules or regulations, and any certificates of counsel do not count toward the limitation.

(C) Certificate of compliance.

(i) A brief submitted under Rules 28.1(e)(2) or 32(a)(7)(B) must include a certificate by the attorney, or an unrepresented party, that the brief complies with the type-volume limitation. The person preparing the certificate may rely on the word or line count of the word-processing system used to prepare the brief. The certificate must state either:

- the number of words in the brief; or
- the number of lines of monospaced type in the brief.

(ii) Form 6 in the Appendix of Forms is a suggested form of a certificate of compliance. Use of Form 6 must be regarded as sufficient to meet the requirements of Rules 28.1(e)(3) and 32(a)(7)(C)(i).

(b) Form of an Appendix. An appendix must comply with Rule 32(a)(1), (2), (3), and (4), with the following exceptions:

(1) The cover of a separately bound appendix must be white.

(2) An appendix may include a legible photocopy of any document found in the record or of a printed judicial or agency decision.

(3) When necessary to facilitate inclusion of odd-sized documents such as technical drawings, an appendix may be a size other than 8½ by 11 inches, and need not lie reasonably flat when opened.

(c) Form of Other Papers.

(1) Motion. The form of a motion is governed by Rule 27(d).

(2) Other Papers. Any other paper, including a petition for panel rehearing and a petition for hearing or rehearing en banc, and any response to such a petition, must be reproduced in the manner prescribed by Rule 32(a), with the following exceptions:

(A) A cover is not necessary if the caption and signature page of the paper together contain the information required by Rule 32(a)(2). If a cover is used, it must be white.

(B) Rule 32(a)(7) does not apply.

(d) Signature. Every brief, motion, or other paper filed with the court must be signed by the party filing the paper or, if the party is represented, by one of the party's attorneys.

(e) Local Variation. Every court of appeals must accept documents that comply with the form requirements of this rule. By local rule or order in a particular case a court of appeals may accept documents that do not meet all of the form requirements of this rule. (As amended Apr. 24, 1998, eff. Dec. 1, 1998; Apr. 29, 2002, eff. Dec. 1, 2002; Apr. 25, 2005, eff. Dec. 1, 2005.)

1967 Adoption

Only two methods of printing are now generally recognized by the circuits—standard typographic printing and the offset duplicating process (multilith). A third, mimeographing, is permitted in the Fifth Circuit. The District of Columbia, Ninth, and Tenth Circuits permit records to be reproduced by copying processes. The Committee feels that recent and impending advances in the arts of duplicating and copying warrant experimentation with less costly forms of reproduction than those now generally authorized. The proposed rule permits, in effect, the use of any process other than the carbon copy process which produces a clean, readable page. What constitutes such is left in first instance to the parties and ultimately to the court to determine. The final sentence of the first paragraph of subdivision (a) is added to allow the use of multilith, mimeograph, or other forms of copies of the reporter's original transcript whenever such are available.

1998 Amendments

In addition to amending Rule 32 to conform to uniform drafting standards, several substantive amendments are made. The Advisory Committee had been working on substantive amendments to Rule 32 for some time prior to completion of this larger project.

Subdivision (a). Form of a Brief.

Paragraph (a)(1). Reproduction.

The rule permits the use of "light" paper, not just "white" paper. Cream and buff colored paper, including recycled paper, are acceptable. The rule permits printing on only one side of the paper. Although some argue that paper could be saved by allowing double-sided printing, others argue that in order to preserve legibility a heavier weight paper would be needed, resulting in little, if any, paper saving. In addition, the blank sides of a brief are commonly used by judges and their clerks for making notes about the case.

Because photocopying is inexpensive and widely available and because use of carbon paper is now very rare, all references to the use of carbon copies have been deleted.

The rule requires that the text be reproduced with a clarity that equals or exceeds the output of a laser printer. That means that the method used must have a print resolution of 300 dots per inch (dpi) or more. This will ensure the legibility of the brief. A brief produced by a typewriter or a daisy wheel printer, as well as one produced by a laser printer, has a print resolution of 300 dpi or more. But a brief produced by a dot-matrix printer, fax machine, or portable printer that uses head or dye to transfer methods does not. Some ink jet printers are 300 dpi or more, but some are 216 dpi and would not be sufficient.

Photographs, illustrations, and tables may be reproduced by any method that results in a good copy.

Paragraph (a)(2). Cover.

The rule requires that the number of the case be centered at the top of the front cover of a brief. This will aid in identification of the brief. The idea was drawn from a local rule. The rule also requires that the title of the brief identify the party or parties on whose behalf the brief is filed. When there are multiple appellants or appellees, the information is necessary to the court. If, however, the brief is filed on behalf of all appellants or appellees, it may so indicate. Further, it may be possible to identify the class of parties on whose behalf the brief is filed. Otherwise, it may be necessary to name each party. The rule also requires that attorneys' telephone numbers appear on the front cover of a brief or appendix.

Paragraph (a)(3). Binding.

The rule requires a brief to be bound in any manner that is secure, does not obscure the text, and that permits the brief to lie reasonable flat when open. Many judges and most court employees do much of their work at computer keyboards and a brief that lies flat when open is significantly more convenient. One circuit already has such a requirement and another states a preference for it. While a spiral binding would comply with this requirement, it is not intended to be the exclusive method of binding. Stapling a brief at the upper left-hand corner also satisfies this requirement as long as it is sufficiently secure.

Paragraph (a)(4). Paper Size, Line Spacing, and Margins.

The provisions for pamphlet-size briefs are deleted because their use is so rare. If a circuit wishes to authorize their use, it has authority to do so under subdivision (d) of this rule.

Paragraph (a)(5). Typeface.

This paragraph and the next one, governing type style, are new. The existing rule simply states that a brief produced by the standard typographic process must be printed in at least 11 point type, or if produced in any other manner, the lines of text must be double spaced. Today few briefs are produced by commercial printers or by typewriters; most are produced on and printed by computer. The availability of computer fonts in a variety of sizes and styles has given rise to local rules limiting type styles. The Advisory Committee believes that some standards are needed both to ensure that all litigants have an equal opportunity to present their material and to ensure that the briefs are easily legible.

With regard to typeface there are two options; proportionally-spaced typeface or monospaced typeface.

A proportionally-spaced typeface gives a different amount of horizontal space to characters depending upon the width of the character. A capital "M" is given more horizontal space than a lower case "i". The rule requires that a proportionally-spaced typeface have serifs. Serifs are small horizontal or vertical strokes at the ends of the lines that make up the letters and numbers. Studies have shown that long passages of serif type are easier to read and comprehend than long passages of sans-serif type. The rule accordingly limits the principal sections of submissions to serif type although sans-serif type may be used in headings and captions. This is the same approach magazines, newspapers, and commercial printers take. Look at a professionally printed brief; you will find sans–serif type confined to captions, if it is used at all. The next line shows two characters enlarged for detail. The first has serifs, the second does not.

Y Y *

[* For original representation of characters, see House Document 105–269 of the 105th Congress, 2d Session dated May 11, 1998 entitled "Amendments to the Federal Rules of Appellate Procedure .... (Executive Communication No. 9072)."]

So that the type is easily legible, the rule requires a minimum type size of 14 points for proportionally-spaced typeface.

A monospaced typeface is one in which all characters have the same advance width. That means that each character is given the same horizontal space on the line. A wide letter such as a capital "M" and a narrow letter such as a lower case "i" are given the same space. Most typewriters produce mono-spaced type, and most computers also can do so using fonts with names such as "Courier."

This sentence is in a proportionally spaced font; as you can see, the m and i have different widths. *

[* For original representation of characters, see House Document 105–269 of the 105th Congress, 2d Session dated May 11, 1998 entitled "Amendments to the Federal Rules of Appellate Procedure .... (Executive Communication No. 9072)."]

This sentence is in a monospaced font; as you can see, the m and i have the same width. *

[* For original representation of characters, see House Document 105–269 of the 105th Congress, 2d Session dated May 11, 1998 entitled "Amendments to the Federal Rules of Appellate Procedure .... (Executive Communication No. 9072)."]

The rule requires use of a monospaced typeface that produces no more than 10 ½ characters per inch. A standard typewriter with pica type produces a monospaced typeface with 10 characters per inch (cpi). That is the ideal monospaced typeface. The rule permits up to 10 ½ cpi because some computer software programs contain monospaced fonts that purport to produce 10 cpi but that in fact produce slightly more than 10 cpi. In order to avoid the need to reprint a brief produced in good faith reliance upon such a program, the rule permits a bit of leeway. A monospaced typeface with no more than 10 cpi is preferred.

Paragraph (a)(6). Type Styles.

The rule requires use of plain roman, that is not italic or script, type. Italics and boldface may be used for emphasis. Italicizing case names is preferred but underlining may be used.

Paragraph (a)(7). Type-Volume Limitation.

Subparagraph (a)(7)(A) contains a safe-harbor provision. A principal brief that does not exceed 30 pages complies with the type-volume limitation without further question or certification. A reply brief that does not exceed 15 pages is similarly treated. The current limit is 50 pages but that limit was established when most briefs were produced on typewriters. The widespread use of personal computers has made a multitude of printing options available to practitioners. Use of a proportional typeface alone can greatly increase the amount of material per page as compared with use of a monospaced typeface. Even though the rule requires use of 14–point proportional type, there is great variation in the x-height of different 14–point typefaces. Selection of a typeface with a small x-height increases the amount of text per page. Computers also make possible fine gradations in spacing between lines and tight tracking between letters and words. All of this, and more, have made the 50–page limit virtually meaningless. Establishing a safe-harbor of 50 pages would permit a person who makes use of the multitude of printing "tricks" available with most personal computers to file a brief far longer than the "old" 50–page brief. Therefore, as to those briefs not subject to any other volume control than a page limit, a 30–page limit is imposed.

The limits in subparagraph (B) approximate the current 50–page limit and compliance with them is easy even for a person without a personal computer. The aim of these provisions is to create a level playing field. The rule gives every party an equal opportunity to make arguments, without permitting those with the best in-house typesetting an opportunity to expand their submissions.

The length can be determined either by counting words or lines. That is, the length of a brief is determined not by the number of pages but by the number or words or lines in the brief. This gives every party the same opportunity to present an argument without regard to the typeface used and eliminates any incentive to use footnotes or typographical "tricks" to squeeze more material onto a page.

The word counting method can be used with any typeface.

A monospaced brief can meet the volume limitation by using the word or a line count. If the line counting method is used, the number of lines may not exceed 1,300—26 lines per page in a 50–page brief. The number of lines is easily counted manually. Line counting is not sufficient if a proportionally spaced typeface is used, because the amount of material per line can vary widely.

A brief using the type-volume limitations in subparagraph (B) must include a certificate by the attorney, or party proceeding pro se, that the brief complies with the limitation. The rule permits the person preparing the certification to rely upon the word or line count of the word-processing system used to prepare the brief.

Currently, Rule 28(g) governs the length of a brief. Rule 28(g) begins with the words "[e]xcept by permission of the court," signaling that a party may file a motion to exceed the limits established in the rule. The absence of similar language in Rule 32 does not mean that the Advisory Committee intends to prohibit motions to deviate from the requirements of the rule. The Advisory Committee does not believe that any such language is needed to authorize such a motion.

Subdivision (b). Form of an Appendix.

The provisions governing the form of a brief generally apply to an appendix. The rule recognizes, however, that an appendix is usually produced by photocopying existing documents. The rule requires that the photocopies be legible.

The rule permits inclusion not only of documents from the record but also copies of a printed judicial or agency decision. If a decision that is part of the record in the case has been published, it is helpful to provide a copy of the published decision in place of a copy of the decision from the record.

Subdivision (c). Form of Other Papers.

The old rule required a petition for rehearing to be produced in the same manner as a brief or appendix. The new rule also requires that a petition for rehearing en banc and a response to either a petition for panel rehearing or a petition for rehearing en banc be prepared in the same manner. But the length limitations of paragraph (a)(7) do not apply to those documents and a cover is not required if all the formation needed by the court to properly identify the document and the parties is included in the caption or signature page.

Existing subdivision (b) states that other papers may be produced in like manner, or "they may be typewritten upon opaque, unglazed paper 8 ½ by 11 inches in size." The quoted language is deleted but that method of preparing documents is not eliminated because (a)(5)(b) permits use of standard pica type. The only change is that the new rule now specifies margins for typewritten documents.

Subdivision (d). Local Variation.

A brief that complies with the national rule should be acceptable in every court. Local rules may move in one direction only; they may authorize noncompliance with certain of the national norms. For example, a court that wishes to do so may authorize printing of briefs on both sides of the paper, or the use of smaller type size or sans-serif proportional type. A local rules may not, however, impose requirements that are not in the national rule.

2002 Amendments

Subdivision (a)(2). On occasion, a court may permit or order the parties to file supplemental briefs addressing an issue that was not addressed—or adequately addressed—in the principal briefs. Rule 32(a)(2) has been amended to require that tan covers be used on such supplemental briefs. The amendment is intended to promote uniformity in federal appellate practice. At present, the local rules of the circuit courts conflict. *See, e.g.*, D.C. Cir. R. 28(g) (requiring yellow covers on supplemental briefs); 11th Cir. R. 32, I.O.P. 1 (requiring white covers on supplemental briefs).

Changes Made After Publication and Comments No changes were made to the text of the proposed amendment or to the Committee Note.

Subdivision (a)(7)(C). If the principal brief of a party exceeds 30 pages, or if the reply brief of a party exceeds 15 pages, Rule 32(a)(7)(C) provides that the party or the party's attorney must certify that the brief complies with the type-volume limitation of Rule 32(a)(7)(B). Rule 32(a)(7)(C) has been amended to refer to Form 6 (which has been added to the Appendix of Forms) and to provide that a party or attorney who uses Form 6 has complied with Rule 32(a)(7)(C). No court may provide to the contrary, in its local rules or otherwise.

Form 6 requests not only the information mandated by Rule 32(a)(7)(C), but also information that will assist courts in enforcing the typeface requirements of Rule 32(a)(5) and the type style requirements of Rule 32(a)(6). Parties and attorneys are not required to use Form 6, but they are encouraged to do so.

Subdivision (c)(2)(A). Under Rule 32(c)(2)(A), a cover is not required on a petition for panel rehearing, petition for hearing or rehearing en banc, answer to a petition for panel rehearing, response to a petition for hearing or rehearing en banc, or any other paper. Rule 32(d) makes it clear that no court can require that a cover be used on any of these papers. However, nothing prohibits a court from providing in its local rules that if a cover on one of these papers is "voluntarily" used, it must be a particular color. Several circuits have adopted such local rules. *See, e.g.*, Fed. Cir. R. 35(c) (requiring yellow covers on petitions for hearing or rehearing en banc and brown covers on responses to such petitions); Fed. Cir. R. 40(a) (requiring yellow covers on petitions for panel rehearing and brown covers on answers to such petitions); 7th Cir. R. 28 (requiring blue covers on petitions for rehearing filed by appellants or answers to such petitions, and requiring red covers on petitions for rehearing filed by appellees or answers to such petitions); 9th Cir. R. 40–1 (requiring blue covers on petitions for panel rehearing filed by appellants and red covers on answers to such petitions, and requiring red covers on petitions for panel rehearing filed by appellees and blue covers on answers to such petitions); 11th Cir. R. 35–6 (requiring white covers on petitions for hearing or rehearing en banc).

These conflicting local rules create a hardship for counsel who practice in more than one circuit. For that reason, Rule 32(c)(2)(A) has been amended to provide that if a party chooses to use a cover on a paper that is not required to have one, that cover must be white. The amendment is intended to preempt all local rulemaking on the subject of cover colors and thereby promote uniformity in federal appellate practice.

Changes Made After Publication and Comments No changes were made to the text of the proposed amendment or to the Committee Note.

Subdivisions (d) and (e). Former subdivision (d) has been redesignated as subdivision (e), and a new subdivision (d) has been added. The new subdivision (d) requires that every brief, motion, or other paper filed with the court be signed by the attorney or unrepresented party who files it, much as Fed. R. Civ. P. 11(a) imposes a signature requirement on papers filed in district court. Only the original copy of every paper must be signed. An appendix filed with the court does not have to be signed at all.

By requiring a signature, subdivision (d) ensures that a readily identifiable attorney or party takes responsibility for every paper. The courts of appeals already have authority to sanction attorneys and parties who file papers that contain misleading or frivolous assertions, *see, e.g.*, 28 U.S.C. § 1912, Fed. R. App. P. 38 & 46(b)(1)(B), and thus subdivision (d) has not been amended to incorporate provisions similar to those found in Fed. R. Civ. P. 11(b) and 11(c).

Changes Made After Publication and Comments No changes were made to the text of the proposed amendment. A line was added to the Committee Note to clarify that only the original copy of a paper needs to be signed.

2005 Amendments

Subdivision (a)(7)(C). Rule 32(a)(7)(C) has been amended to add cross-references to new Rule 28.1, which governs briefs filed in cases involving cross-appeals. Rule 28.1(e)(2) prescribes type-volume limitations that apply to such briefs, and Rule 28.1(e)(3) requires parties to certify compliance with those type-volume limitations under Rule 32(a)(7)(C).

Rule 32.1. Citing Judicial Dispositions

(a) Citation Permitted. A court may not prohibit or restrict the citation of federal judicial opinions, orders, judgments, or other written dispositions that have been:

(i) designated as "unpublished," "not for publication," "non-precedential," "not precedent," or the like; and

(ii) issued on or after January 1, 2007.

(b) Copies Required. If a party cites a federal judicial opinion, order, judgment, or other written disposition that is not available in a publicly accessible electronic database, the party must file and serve a copy of that opinion, order, judgment, or disposition with the brief or other paper in which it is cited. (Added Apr. 12, 2006, eff. Dec. 1, 2006.)

2006 Adoption

Rule 32.1 is a new rule addressing the citation of judicial opinions, orders, judgments, or other written dispositions that have been designated by a federal court as "unpublished," "not for publication," "non-precedential," "not precedent," or the like. This Committee Note will refer to these dispositions collectively as "unpublished" opinions.

Rule 32.1 is extremely limited. It does not require any court to issue an unpublished opinion or forbid any court from doing so. It does not dictate the circumstances under which a court may choose to designate an opinion as "unpublished" or specify the procedure that a court must follow in making that determination. It says nothing about what effect a court must give to one of its unpublished opinions or to the unpublished opinions of another court. Rule 32.1 addresses only the *citation* of federal judicial dispositions that have been *designated* as "unpublished" or "non-precedential" — whether or not those dispositions have been published in some way or are precedential in some sense.

Subdivision (a). Every court of appeals has allowed unpublished opinions to be cited in some circumstances, such as to support a contention of issue preclusion or claim preclusion. But the circuits have differed dramatically with respect to the restrictions that they have placed on the citation of unpublished opinions for their persuasive value. Some circuits have freely permitted such citation, others have discouraged it but permitted it in limited circumstances, and still others have forbidden it altogether.

Rule 32.1(a) is intended to replace these inconsistent standards with one uniform rule. Under Rule 32.1(a), a court of appeals may not prohibit a party from citing an unpublished opinion of a federal court for its persuasive value or for any other reason. In addition, under Rule 32.1(a), a court may not place any restriction on the citation of such opinions. For example, a court may not instruct parties that the citation of unpublished opinions is discouraged, nor may a court forbid parties to cite unpublished opinions when a published opinion addresses the same issue.

Rule 32.1(a) applies only to unpublished opinions issued on or after January 1, 2007. The citation of unpublished opinions issued before January 1, 2007, will continue to be governed by the local rules of the circuits.

Subdivision (b). Under Rule 32.1(b), a party who cites an opinion of a federal court must provide a copy of that opinion to the court of appeals and to the other parties, unless that opinion is available in a publicly accessible electronic database — such as a commercial database maintained by a legal research service or a database maintained by a court. A party who is required under Rule 32.1(b) to provide a copy of an opinion must file and serve the copy with the brief or other paper in which the opinion is cited. Rule 32.1(b) applies to all unpublished opinions, regardless of when they were issued.

Rule 33. Appeal Conferences

The court may direct the attorneys—and, when appropriate, the parties—to participate in one or more conferences to address any matter that may aid in disposing of the proceedings, including simplifying the issues and discussing settlement. A judge or other person designated by the court may preside over the conference, which may be conducted in person or by telephone. Before a settlement conference, the attorneys must consult with their clients and obtain as much authority as feasible to settle the case. The court may, as a result of the conference, enter an order controlling the course of the proceedings or implementing any settlement agreement.

(As amended Apr. 29, 1994, eff. Dec. 1, 1994; Apr. 24, 1998, eff. Dec. 1, 1998.)

1967 Adoption

The uniform rule for review or enforcement of orders of administrative agencies, boards, commissions or officers (see the general note following Rule 15) authorizes a prehearing conference in agency review proceedings. The same considerations which make a prehearing conference desirable in such proceedings may be present in certain cases on appeal from the district courts. The proposed rule is based upon subdivision 11 of the present uniform rule for review of agency orders.

1994 Amendment

Rule 33 has been entirely rewritten. The new rule makes several changes.

The caption of the rule has been changed from "Prehearing Conference" to "Appeal Conferences" to reflect the fact that occasionally a conference is held after oral argument.

The rule permits the court to require the parties to attend the conference in appropriate cases. The Committee does not contemplate that attendance of the parties will become routine, but in certain instances the parties' presence can be useful. The language of the rule is broad enough to allow a court to determine that an executive or an employee (other than the general counsel) of a corporation or government agency with authority regarding the matter at issue, constitutes "the party."

The rule includes the possibility of settlement among the possible conference topics.

The rule recognizes that conferences are often held by telephone.

The rule allows a judge or other person designated by the court to preside over a conference. A number of local rules permit persons other than judges to preside over conferences. 1st Cir. R. 47.5; 6th Cir. R. 18; 8th Cir. R. 33A; 9th Cir. R. 33–1; and 10th Cir. R. 33.

The rule requires an attorney to consult with his or her client before a settlement conference and obtain as much authority as feasible to settle the case. An attorney can never settle a case without his or her client's consent. Certain entities, especially government entities, have particular difficulty obtaining authority to settle a case. The rule requires counsel to obtain only as much authority "as feasible."

1998 Amendments

The language of the rule is amended to make the rule more easily understood. In addition to changes made to improve the understanding, the Advisory Committee has changed language to make style and terminology consistent throughout the appellate rules. These changes are intended to be stylistic only.

Rule 34. Oral Argument

(a) In General.

(1) Party's Statement. Any party may file, or a court may require by local rule, a statement explaining why oral argument should, or need not, be permitted.

(2) Standards. Oral argument must be allowed in every case unless a panel of three judges who have examined the briefs and record unanimously agrees that oral argument is unnecessary for any of the following reasons:

(A) the appeal is frivolous;

(B) the dispositive issue or issues have been authoritatively decided; or

(C) the facts and legal arguments are adequately presented in the briefs and record, and the decisional process would not be significantly aided by oral argument.

(b) Notice of Argument; Postponement. The clerk must advise all parties whether oral argument will be scheduled, and, if so, the date, time, and place for it, and the time allowed for each side. A motion to postpone the argument or to allow longer argument must be filed reasonably in advance of the hearing date.

(c) Order and Contents of Argument. The appellant opens and concludes the argument. Counsel must not read at length from briefs, records, or authorities.

(d) Cross-Appeals and Separate Appeals. If there is a cross-appeal, Rule 28.1(b) determines which party is the appellant and which is the appellee for purposes of oral argument. Unless the court directs otherwise, a cross-appeal or separate appeal must be argued when the initial appeal is argued. Separate parties should avoid duplicative argument.

(e) Nonappearance of a Party. If the appellee fails to appear for argument, the court must hear appellant's argument. If the appellant fails to appear for argument, the court may hear the appellee's argument. If neither party appears, the case will be decided on the briefs, unless the court orders otherwise.

(f) Submission on Briefs. The parties may agree to submit a case for decision on the briefs, but the court may direct that the case be argued.

(g) Use of Physical Exhibits at Argument; Removal. Counsel intending to use physical exhibits other than documents at the argument must arrange to place them in the courtroom on the day of the argument before the court convenes. After the argument, counsel must remove the exhibits from the courtroom, unless the court directs otherwise. The clerk may destroy or dispose of the exhibits if counsel does not reclaim them within a reasonable time after the clerk gives notice to remove them.

(As amended Apr. 30, 1979, eff. Aug. 1, 1979; Mar. 10, 1986, eff. July 1, 1986; Apr. 30, 1991, eff. Dec. 1, 1991; Apr. 22, 1993, eff. Dec. 1, 1993; Apr. 24, 1998, eff. Dec. 1, 1998; Apr. 25, 2005, eff. Dec. 1, 2005.)

1967 Adoption

A majority of circuits now limit oral argument to thirty minutes for each side, with the provision that additional time may be made available upon request. The Committee is of the view that thirty minutes to each side is sufficient in most cases, but that where additional time is necessary it should be freely granted on a proper showing of cause therefor. It further feels that the matter of time should be left ultimately to each court of appeals, subject to the spirit of the rule that a reasonable time should be allowed for argument. The term "side" is used to indicate that the time allowed by the rule is afforded to opposing interests rather than to individual parties. Thus if multiple appellants or appellees have a common interest, they constitute only a single side. If counsel for multiple parties who constitute a single side feel that additional time is necessary, they may request it. In other particulars this rule follows the usual practice among the circuits. See 3d Cir. Rule 31 [rule 31, U.S.Ct. of App.3rd Cir.]; 6th Cir. Rule 20 [rule 20, U.S.Ct. of App.6th Cir.]; 10th Cir. Rule 23 [rule 23, U.S.Ct. of App.10th Cir.].

1979 Amendment

The proposed amendment, patterned after the recommendations in the Report of the Commission on Revision of the Federal Court Appellate System, *Structure and Internal Procedures: Recommendations for Change*, 1975, created by Public Law 489 of the 92nd Cong.2nd Sess., 86 Stat. 807, sets forth general principles and minimum standards to be observed in formulating any local rule.

1986 Amendment

The amendments to Rules 34(a) and (e) are technical. No substantive change is intended.

1991 Amendment

Subdivision (d). The amendment of subdivision (d) conforms this rule with the amendment of Rule 28(h).

1993 Amendment

Subdivision (c). The amendment deletes the requirement that the opening argument must include a fair statement of the case. The Committee proposed the change because in some circuits the court does not want appellants to give such statements. In those circuits, the rule is not followed and is misleading. Nevertheless, the Committee does not want the deletion of the requirement to indicate disapproval of the practice. Those circuits that desire a statement of the case may continue the practice.

1998 Amendments

The language of the rule is amended to make the rule more easily understood. In addition to changes made to improve the understanding, the Advisory Committee has changed language to make style and terminology consistent throughout the appellate rules. These changes are intended to be stylistic only. Substantive changes are made in subdivision (a).

Subdivision (a). Currently subdivision (a) says that oral argument must be permitted unless, applying a local rule, a panel of three judges unanimously agrees that oral argument is not necessary. Rule 34 then outlines the criteria to be used to determine whether oral argument is needed and requires any local rule to "conform substantially" to the "minimum standard[s]" established in the national rule. The amendments omit the local rule requirement and make the criteria applicable by force of the national rule. The local rule is an unnecessary instrument.

Paragraph (a)(2) states that one reason for deciding that oral argument is unnecessary is that the dispositive issue has been authoritatively decided. the amended language no longer states that the issue must have been "recently" decided. The Advisory Committee does not intend any substantive change, but thinks that the use of "recently" may be misleading.

Subdivision (d). A cross–reference to Rule 28(h) has been substituted for a reiteration of the provisions of Rule 28(h).

2005 Amendments

Subdivision (d). A cross-reference in subdivision (d) has been changed to reflect the fact that, as part of an effort to collect within one rule all provisions regarding briefing in cases involving cross-appeals, former Rule 28(h) has been abrogated and its contents moved to new Rule 28.1(b).

Rule 35. En Banc Determination

(a) When Hearing or Rehearing En Banc May Be Ordered. A majority of the circuit judges who are in regular active service and who are not disqualified may order that an appeal or other proceeding be heard or reheard by the court of appeals en banc. An en banc hearing or rehearing is not favored and ordinarily will not be ordered unless:

(1) en banc consideration is necessary to secure or maintain uniformity of the court's decisions; or

(2) the proceeding involves a question of exceptional importance.

(b) Petition for Hearing or Rehearing En Banc. A party may petition for a hearing or rehearing en banc.

(1) The petition must begin with a statement that either:

(A) the panel decision conflicts with a decision of the United States Supreme Court or of the court to which the petition is addressed (with citation to the conflicting case or cases) and consideration by the full court is therefore necessary to secure and maintain uniformity of the court's decisions; or

(B) the proceeding involves one or more questions of exceptional importance, each of which must be concisely stated; for example, a petition may assert that a proceeding presents a question of exceptional importance if it involves an issue on which the panel decision conflicts with the authoritative decisions of other United States Courts of Appeals that have addressed the issue.

(2) Except by the court's permission, a petition for an en banc hearing or rehearing must not exceed 15 pages, excluding material not counted under Rule 32.

(3) For purposes of the page limit in Rule 35(b)(2), if a party files both a petition for panel rehearing and a petition for rehearing en banc, they are considered a single document even if they are filed separately, unless separate filing is required by local rule.

(c) Time for Petition for Hearing or Rehearing En Banc. A petition that an appeal be heard initially en banc must be filed by the date when the appellee's brief is due. A petition for a rehearing en banc must be filed within the time prescribed by Rule 40 for filing a petition for rehearing.

(d) Number of Copies. The number of copies to be filed must be prescribed by local rule and may be altered by order in a particular case.

(e) Response. No response may be filed to a petition for an en banc consideration unless the court orders a response.

(f) Call for a Vote. A vote need not be taken to determine whether the case will be heard or reheard en banc unless a judge calls for a vote.

(As amended Apr. 30, 1979, eff. Aug. 1, 1979; Apr. 29, 1994, eff. Dec. 1, 1994; Apr. 24, 1998, eff. Dec. 1, 1998; Apr. 25, 2005, eff. Dec. 1, 2005.)

1967 Adoption

Statutory authority for in banc hearings is found in 28 U.S.C. § 46(c). The proposed rule is responsive to the Supreme Court's view in *Western Pacific Ry. Corp. v. Western Pacific Ry. Co.*, 345 U.S. 247, 73 S.Ct. 656, 97 L.Ed. 986 (1953), that litigants should be free to suggest that a particular case is appropriate for consideration by all the judges of a court of appeals. The rule is addressed to the procedure whereby a party may suggest the appropriateness of convening the court in banc. It does not affect the power of a court of appeals to initiate in banc hearings *sua sponte*.

The provision that a vote will not be taken as a result of the suggestion of the party unless requested by a judge of the court in regular active service or by a judge who was a member of the panel that rendered a decision sought to be reheard is intended to make it clear that a suggestion of a party as such does not require any action by the court. See *Western Pacific Ry. Corp. v. Western Pacific Ry. Co.*, supra, 345 U.S. at 262, 73 S.Ct. 656. The rule merely authorizes a suggestion, imposes a time limit on suggestions for rehearings in banc, and provides that suggestions will be directed to the judges of the court in regular active service.

In practice, the suggestion of a party that a case be reheard in banc is frequently contained in a petition for rehearing, commonly styled "petition for rehearing in banc." Such a petition is in fact merely a petition for a rehearing, with a suggestion that the case be reheard in banc. Since no response to the suggestion, as distinguished from the petition for rehearing, is required, the panel which heard the case may quite properly dispose of the petition without reference to the suggestion. In such a case the fact that no response has been made to the suggestion does not affect the finality of the judgment or the issuance of the mandate, and the final sentence of the rule expressly so provides.

1979 Amendment

Under the present rule there is no specific provision for a response to a suggestion that an appeal be heard in banc. This has led to some uncertainty as to whether such a response may be filed. The proposed amendment would resolve this uncertainty.

While the present rule provides a time limit for suggestions for rehearing in banc, it does not deal with the timing of a request that the appeal be heard in banc initially. The proposed amendment fills this gap as well, providing that the suggestion must be made by the date of which the appellee's brief is filed.

Provision is made for circulating the suggestions to members of the panel despite the fact that senior judges on the panel would not be entitled to vote on whether a suggestion will be granted.

1994 Amendment

Subdivision (d). Subdivision (d) is added; it authorizes the courts of appeals to prescribe the number of copies of suggestions for hearing or rehearing in banc that must be filed. Because the number of copies needed depends directly upon the number of judges in the circuit, local rules are the best vehicle for setting the required number of copies.

1998 Amendments

The language and organization of the rule are amended to make the rule more easily understood. In addition to changes made to improve the understanding, the Advisory Committee has changed language to make style and terminology consistent throughout the appellate rules. These changes are intended to be stylistic only.

Several substantive changes are made to this rule, however.

One of the purposes of the substantive amendments is to treat a request for a rehearing en banc like a petition for panel rehearing so that a request for a rehearing en banc will suspend the finality of the court of appeals' judgment and delay the running of the period for filing a petition for writ of certiorari. Companion amendments are made to Rule 41.

Subdivision (a). The title of this subdivision is changed from "When hearing or rehearing in banc *will* be ordered" to "When Hearing or Rehearing En Banc *May* Be Ordered." The change emphasizes the discretion a court has with regard to granting en banc review.

Subdivision (b). The term "petition" for rehearing en banc is substituted for the term "suggestion" for rehearing en banc. The terminology change reflects the Committee's intent to treat similarly a petition for panel rehearing and a request for a rehearing en banc. The terminology change also delays the running of the time for filing a petition for a writ of certiorari because Sur. Ct. R. 13.3 says:

> if a petition for rehearing is timely filed in the lower court by any party, the time to file the petition for a writ of certiorari for all parties...runs from the date of the denial of the petition for rehearing or, if the petition for rehearing is granted, the subsequent entry of judgment.

The amendments also require each petition for en banc consideration to begin with a statement concisely demonstrating that the case meets the usual criteria for en banc consideration. It is the Committee's hope that requiring such a statement will cause the drafter of a petition to focus on the narrow grounds that support en banc consideration and to realize that a petition should not be filed unless the case meets those rigid standards.

Intercircuit conflict is cited as one reason for asserting that a proceeding involves a question of "exceptional importance." Intercircuit conflicts create problems. When the circuits construe the same federal law differently, parties' rights and duties depend upon where a case is litigated. Given the increase in the number of cases decided by the federal courts and the limitation on the number of cases the Supreme Court can hear, conflicts between the circuits may remain unresolved by the Supreme Court for an extended period of time. The existence of an intercircuit conflict often generates additional litigation in the other circuits as well as in the circuits that are already in conflict. Although an en banc proceeding will not necessarily prevent intercircuit conflicts, an en banc proceeding provides a safeguard against unnecessary intercircuit conflicts.

Some circuits have had rules or internal operating procedures that recognize a conflict with another circuit as a legitimate basis for granting a rehearing en banc. An intercircuit conflict may present a question of "exceptional importance" because of the costs that intercircuit conflicts impose on the system as a whole, in addition to the significance of the issues involved. It is not, however, the Committee's intent to make the granting of a hearing or rehearing en banc mandatory whenever there is an intercircuit conflict.

The amendment states that "a petition may assert that a proceeding presents a question of exceptional importance if it involves an issue on which the panel decision conflicts with the authoritative decisions of every other United States Court of Appeals that has addressed the issue." That language contemplates two situations in which a rehearing en banc may be appropriate. The first is when a panel decision creates a conflict. A panel decision creates a conflict when it conflicts with the decisions of all other circuits that have considered the issue. If a panel decision simply joins one side of an already existing conflict, a rehearing en banc may not be as important because it cannot avoid the conflict. The Second situation that may be a strong candidate for a rehearing en banc is one in which the circuit persists in a conflict created by a pre-existing decision of the same circuit and no other circuits have joined on that side of the conflict. The amendment states that the conflict must be with an "authoritative" decision of another circuit. "Authoritative" is used rather than "published" because in some circuits unpublished opinions may be treated as authoritative.

Counsel are reminded that their duty is fully discharged without filing a petition for rehearing en banc unless the case meets the rigid standards of subdivision (a) of this rule and even then the granting of a petition is entirely within the court's discretion.

Paragraph (2) of this subdivision establishes a maximum length for a petition. Fifteen pages is the length currently used in several circuits. Each request for en banc consideration must be studied by every active judge of the court and is a serious call on limited judicial resources. The extraordinary nature of the issue or the threat to uniformity of the court's decision can be established in most cases in less than fifteen pages. A court may shorten the maximum length on a case by case basis but the rule does not permit a circuit to shorten the length by local rule. The Committee has retained page limits rather than using word or line counts similar to those in amended Rule 32 because there has not been a serious enough problem to justify importing the word and line–count and typeface requirement that are applicable to briefs into other contexts.

Paragraph (3), although similar to (2), is separate because it deals with those instances in which a party files both a petition for rehearing en banc under this rule and a petition for panel rehearing under Rule 40.

To improve the clarity of the rule, the material dealing with filing a response to a petition and with voting on a petition have been moved to new subdivisions (e) and (f).

Subdivision (c). Two changes are made in this subdivision. First, the sentence stating that a request for a rehearing en banc does not affect the finality of the judgment or stay the issuance of the mandate is deleted. Second, the language permitting a party to include a request for rehearing en banc in a petition for panel rehearing is deleted. The Committee believes that those circuits that want to require two separate documents should have the option to do so.

Subdivision (e). This is a new subdivision. The substance of the subdivision, however, was drawn from former subdivision (b). The only changes are stylistic; no substantive changes are intended.

Subdivision (f). This is a new subdivision. The substance of the subdivision, however, was drawn from former subdivision (b).

Because of the discretionary nature of the en banc procedure, the filing of a suggestion for rehearing en banc has not required a vote; a vote is taken only when requested by a judge. It is not the Committee's intent to change the discretionary nature of the procedure or to require a vote on a petition for rehearing en banc. The rule continues, therefore, to provide that a court is not obligated to vote on such petitions. It is necessary, however, that each court develop a procedure for disposing of such petitions because they will suspend the finality of the court's judgment and toll the time for filing a petition for certiorari.

Former subdivision (b) contained language directing the clerk to distribute a "suggestion" to certain judges and indicating which judges may call for a vote. New subdivision (f) does not address those issues because they deal with internal court procedures.

2005 Amendments

Subdivision (a). Two national standards—28 U.S.C. § 46(c) and Rule 35(a)—provide that a hearing or rehearing en banc may be ordered by "a majority of the circuit judges who are in regular active service." Although these standards apply to all of the courts of appeals, the circuits are deeply divided over the interpretation of this language when one or more active judges are disqualified.

The Supreme Court has never addressed this issue. In *Shenker v. Baltimore & Ohio R.R. Co.*, 374 U.S. 1 (1963), the Court rejected a petitioner's claim that his rights under § 46(c) had been violated when the Third Circuit refused to rehear his case en banc. The Third Circuit had 8 active judges at the time; 4 voted in favor of rehearing the case, 2 against, and 2 abstained. No judge was disqualified. The Supreme Court ruled against the petitioner, holding, in essence, that § 46(c) did not provide a cause of action, but instead simply gave litigants "the right to know the administrative machinery that will be followed and the right to suggest that the *en banc* procedure be set in motion in his case." *Id.* at 5. *Shenker* did stress that a court of appeals has broad discretion in establishing internal procedures to handle requests for rehearings—or, as *Shenker* put it, " 'to devise its own administrative machinery to provide the *means* whereby a majority may order such a hearing.' " *Id.* (quoting *Western Pac. R.R. Corp. v. Western Pac. R.R. Co.*, 345 U.S. 247, 250 (1953) (emphasis added)). But *Shenker* did not address what is meant by "a majority" in § 46(c) (or Rule 35(a), which did not yet exist)—and *Shenker* certainly did not suggest that the phrase should have different meanings in different circuits.

In interpreting that phrase, 7 of the courts of appeals follow the "absolute majority" approach. *See* Marie Leary, Defining the "Majority" Vote Requirement in Federal Rule of Appellate Procedure 35(a) for Rehearings En Banc in the United States Courts of Appeals 8 tbl.1 (Federal Judicial Center 2002). Under this approach, disqualified judges are counted in the base in calculating whether a majority of judges have voted to hear a case en banc. Thus, in a circuit with 12 active judges, 7 must vote to hear a case en banc. If 5 of the 12 active judges are disqualified, all 7 non-disqualified judges must vote to hear the case en banc. The votes of 6 of the 7 non-disqualified judges are not enough, as 6 is not a majority of 12.

Six of the courts of appeals follow the "case majority" approach. *Id.* Under this approach, disqualified judges are not counted in the base in calculating whether a majority of judges have voted to hear a case en banc. Thus, in a case in which 5 of a circuit's 12 active judges are disqualified, only 4 judges (a majority of the 7 non-disqualified judges) must vote to hear a case en banc. (The First and Third Circuits explicitly qualify the case majority approach by providing that a case cannot be heard en banc unless a majority of all active judges—disqualified and non-disqualified—are eligible to participate.)

Rule 35(a) has been amended to adopt the case majority approach as a uniform national interpretation of § 46(c). The federal rules of practice and procedure exist to "maintain consistency," which Congress has equated with "promot[ing] the interest of justice." 28 U.S.C. § 2073(b). The courts of appeals should not follow two inconsistent approaches in deciding whether sufficient votes exist to hear a case en banc, especially when there is a governing statute and governing rule that apply to all circuits and that use identical terms, and especially when there is nothing about the local conditions of each circuit that justifies conflicting approaches.

The case majority approach represents the better interpretation of the phrase "the circuit judges . . . in regular active service" in the first sentence of § 46(c). The second sentence of § 46(c)—which defines which judges are eligible to participate in a case being heard or reheard en banc—uses the similar expression "all circuit judges in regular active service." It is clear that "all circuit judges in regular active service" in the second sentence does not include disqualified judges, as disqualified judges clearly cannot participate in a case being heard or reheard en banc. Therefore, assuming that two nearly identical phrases appearing in adjacent sentences in a statute should be interpreted in the same way, the best reading of "the circuit judges . . . in regular active service" in the first sentence of § 46(c) is that it, too, does not include disqualified judges.

This interpretation of § 46(c) is bolstered by the fact that the case majority approach has at least two major advantages over the absolute majority approach:

First, under the absolute majority approach, a disqualified judge is, as a practical matter, counted as voting against hearing a case en banc. This defeats the purpose of recusal. To the extent possible, the disqualification of a judge should not result in the equivalent of a vote for or against hearing a case en banc.

Second, the absolute majority approach can leave the en banc court helpless to overturn a panel decision with which almost all of the circuit's active judges disagree. For example, in a case in which 5 of a circuit's 12 active judges are disqualified, the case cannot be heard en banc even if 6 of the 7 non-disqualified judges strongly disagree with the panel opinion. This permits one active judge—perhaps sitting on a panel with a visiting judge—effectively to control circuit precedent, even over the objection of all of his or her colleagues. *See Gulf Power Co. v. FCC*, 226 F.3d 1220, 1222–23 (11th Cir. 2000) (Carnes, J., concerning the denial of reh'g en banc), *rev'd sub nom. National Cable & Telecomm. Ass'n, Inc. v. Gulf Power Co.*, 534 U.S. 327 (2002). Even though the en banc court may, in a future case, be able to correct an erroneous legal interpretation, the en banc court will never be able to correct the injustice inflicted by the panel on the parties to the case. Moreover, it may take many years before sufficient non-disqualified judges can be mustered to overturn the panel's erroneous legal interpretation. In the meantime, the lower courts of the circuit must apply—and the citizens of the circuit must conform their behavior to—an interpretation of the law that almost all of the circuit's active judges believe is incorrect.

The amendment to Rule 35(a) is not meant to alter or affect the quorum requirement of 28 U.S.C. § 46(d). In particular, the amendment is not intended to foreclose the possibility that § 46(d) might be read to require that more than half of all circuit judges in regular active service be eligible to participate in order for the court to hear or rehear a case en banc.

Rule 36. Entry of Judgment; Notice

(a) Entry. A judgment is entered when it is noted on the docket. The clerk must prepare, sign, and enter the judgment:

(1) after receiving the court's opinion—but if settlement of the judgment's form is required, after final settlement; or

(2) if a judgment is rendered without an opinion, as the court instructs.

(b) Notice. On the date when judgment is entered, the clerk must serve on all parties a copy of the opinion—or the judgment, if no opinion was written—and a notice of the date when the judgment was entered.

(As amended Apr. 24, 1998, eff. Dec. 1, 1998; Apr. 29, 2002, eff. Dec. 1, 2002.)

1967 Adoption

This is the typical rule. See 1st Cir. Rule 29 [rule 29, U.S.Ct. of App. 1st Cir.]; 3d Cir. Rule 32 [rule 32, U.S.Ct. of App. 3rd Cir.]; 6th Cir. Rule 21 [rule 21, U.S.Ct. of App. 6th Cir.]. At present, uncertainty exists as to the date of entry of judgment when the opinion directs subsequent settlement of the precise terms of the judgment, a common practice in cases involving enforcement of agency orders. See Stern and Gressman, Supreme Court Practice, p. 203 (3d Ed., 1962). The principle of finality suggests that in such cases entry of judgment should be delayed until approval of the judgment in final form.

1998 Amendments

The language and organization of the rule are amended to make the rule more easily understood. In addition to changes made to improve the understanding, the Advisory Committee has changed language to make style and terminology consistent throughout the appellate rules. These changes are intended to be stylistic only.

2002 Amendments

Subdivision (b). Subdivision (b) has been amended so that the clerk may use electronic means to serve a copy of the opinion or judgment or to serve notice of the date when judgment was entered upon parties who have consented to such service.

Changes Made After Publication and Comments No changes were made to the text of the proposed amendment or to the Committee Note.

Rule 37. Interest on Judgment

(a) When the Court Affirms. Unless the law provides otherwise, if a money judgment in a civil case is affirmed, whatever interest is allowed by law is payable from the date when the district court's judgment was entered.

(b) When the Court Reverses. If the court modifies or reverses a judgment with a direction that a money judgment be entered in the district court, the mandate must contain instructions about the allowance of interest.

(As amended Apr. 24, 1998, eff. Dec. 1, 1998.)

1967 Adoption

The first sentence makes it clear that if a money judgment is affirmed in the court of appeals, the interest which attaches to money judgments by force of law (see 28 U.S.C. § 1961 and § 2411) upon their initial entry is payable as if no appeal had been taken, whether or not the mandate makes mention of interest. There has been some confusion on this point. *See Blair v. Durham*, 139 F.2d 260 (6th Cir., 1943) and cases cited therein.

In reversing or modifying the judgment of the district court, the court of appeals may direct the entry of a money judgment, as, for example, when the court of appeals reverses a judgment notwithstanding the verdict and directs entry of judgment on the verdict. In such a case the question may arise as to whether interest is to run from the date of entry of the judgment directed by the court of appeals or from the date on which the judgment would have been entered in the district court except for the erroneous ruling corrected on appeal. In *Briggs v. Pennsylvania R. Co.*, 334 U.S. 304, 68 S.Ct. 1039, 92 L.Ed. 1403 (1948), the Court held that where the mandate of the court of appeals directed entry of judgment upon a verdict but made no mention of interest from the date of the verdict to the date of the entry of the judgment directed by the mandate, the district court was powerless to add such interest. The second sentence of the proposed rule is a reminder to the court, the clerk and counsel of the *Briggs* rule. Since the rule directs that the matter of interest be disposed of by the mandate, in cases where interest is simply overlooked, a party who conceives himself entitled to interest from a date other than the date of entry of judgment in accordance with the mandate should be entitled to seek recall of the mandate for determination of the question.

1998 Amendments

The language and organization of the rule are amended to make the rule more easily understood. In addition to changes made to improve the understanding, the Advisory Committee has changed language to make style and terminology consistent throughout the appellate rules. These changes are intended to be stylistic only.

Rule 38. Frivolous Appeal—Damages and Costs

If a court of appeals determines that an appeal is frivolous, it may, after a separately filed motion or notice from the court and reasonable opportunity to respond, award just damages and single or double costs to the appellee.

(As amended Apr. 29, 1994, eff. Dec. 1, 1994; Apr. 24, 1998, eff. Dec. 1, 1998.)

1967 Adoption

Compare 28 U.S.C. § 1912. While both the statute and the usual rule on the subject by courts of appeals (Fourth Circuit Rule 20 [rule 20, U.S.Ct. of App. 4th Cir.] is a typical rule) speak of "damages for delay," the courts of appeals quite properly allow damages, attorney's fees and other expenses incurred by an appellee if the appeal is frivolous without requiring a showing that the appeal resulted in delay. See *Dunscombe v. Sayle*, 340 F.2d 311 (5th Cir., 1965), cert. den., 382 U.S. 814, 86 S.Ct. 32, 15 L.Ed.2d 62 (1965); *Lowe v. Willacy*, 239 F.2d 179 (9th Cir., 1956); *Griffin Wellpoint Corp. v. Munro-Langstroth, Inc.*, 269 F.2d 64 (1st Cir., 1959); *Ginsburg v. Stern*, 295 F.2d 698 (3d Cir., 1961). The subjects of interest and damages are separately regulated, contrary to the present practice of combining the two (see Fourth Circuit Rule 20) to make it clear that the awards are distinct and independent. Interest is provided for by law; damages are awarded by the court in its discretion in the case of a frivolous appeal as a matter of justice to the appellee and as a penalty against the appellant.

1994 Amendments

The amendment requires that before a court of appeals may impose sanctions, the person to be sanctioned must have notice and an opportunity to respond. The amendment reflects the basic principle enunciated in the Supreme Court's opinion in *Roadway Express, Inc. v. Piper*, 447 U.S. 752, 767 (1980), that notice and opportunity to respond must precede the imposition of sanctions. A separately filed motion requesting sanctions constitutes notice. A statement inserted in a party's brief that the party moves for sanctions is not sufficient notice. Requests in briefs for sanctions have become so commonplace that it is unrealistic to expect careful responses to such requests without any indication that the court is actually contemplating such measures. Only a motion, the purpose of which is to request sanctions, is sufficient. If there is no such motion filed, notice must come from the court. The form of notice from the court and of the opportunity for comment purposely are left to the court's discretion.

1998 Amendments

Only the caption of this rule has been amended. The changes are intended to be stylistic only.

Rule 39. Costs

(a) Against Whom Assessed. The following rules apply unless the law provides or the court orders otherwise:

(1) if an appeal is dismissed, costs are taxed against the appellant, unless the parties agree otherwise;

(2) if a judgment is affirmed, costs are taxed against the appellant;

(3) if a judgment is reversed, costs are taxed against the appellee;

(4) if a judgment is affirmed in part, reversed in part, modified, or vacated, costs are taxed only as the court orders.

(b) Costs For and Against the United States. Costs for or against the United States, its agency, or officer will be assessed under Rule 39(a) only if authorized by law.

(c) Costs of Copies. Each court of appeals must, by local rule, fix the maximum rate for taxing the cost of producing necessary copies of a brief or appendix, or copies of records authorized by Rule 30(f). The rate must not exceed that generally charged for such work in the area where the clerk's office is located and should encourage economical methods of copying.

(d) Bill of Costs: Objections; Insertion in Mandate.

(1) A party who wants costs taxed must—within 14 days after entry of judgment—file with the circuit clerk, with proof of service, an itemized and verified bill of costs.

(2) Objections must be filed within 10 days after service of the bill of costs, unless the court extends the time.

(3) The clerk must prepare and certify an itemized statement of costs for insertion in the mandate, but issuance of the mandate must not be delayed for taxing costs. If the mandate issues before costs are finally determined, the district clerk must—upon the circuit clerk's request—add the statement of costs, or any amendment of it, to the mandate.

(e) Costs on Appeal Taxable in the District Court. The following costs on appeal are taxable in the district court for the benefit of the party entitled to costs under this rule:

(1) the preparation and transmission of the record;

(2) the reporter's transcript, if needed to determine the appeal;

(3) premiums paid for a supersedeas bond or other bond to preserve rights pending appeal; and

(4) the fee for filing the notice of appeal.

(As amended Apr. 30, 1979, eff. Aug. 1, 1979; Mar. 10, 1986, eff. July 1, 1986; Apr. 24, 1998, eff. Dec. 1, 1998.)

1967 Adoption

Subdivision (a). Statutory authorization for taxation of costs is found in 28 U.S.C. § 1920. The provisions of this subdivision follow the usual practice in the circuits. A few statutes contain specific provisions in derogation of these general provisions. (See 28 U.S.C. § 1928, which forbids the award of costs to a successful plaintiff in a patent infringement action under the circumstances described by the statute). These statutes are controlling in cases to which they apply.

Subdivision (b). The rules of the courts of appeals at present commonly deny costs to the United States except as allowance may be directed by statute. Those rules were promulgated at a time when the United States was generally invulnerable to an award of costs against it, and they appear to be based on the view that if the United States is not subject to costs if it loses, it ought not be entitled to recover costs if it wins.

The number of cases affected by such rules has been greatly reduced by the Act of July 18, 1966, 80 Stat. 308 (1 U.S.Code Cong. & Ad.News, p. 349 (1966), 89th Cong., 2d Sess., which amended 28 U.S.C. § 2412, the former general bar to the award of costs against the United States. Section 2412 as amended generally places the United States on the same footing as private parties with respect to the award of costs in civil cases. But the United States continues to enjoy immunity from costs in certain cases. By its terms amended § 2412 authorizes an award of costs against the United States only in civil actions, and it excepts from its general authorization of an award of costs against the United States cases which are "otherwise specifically provided (for) by statute." Furthermore, the Act of July 18, 1966, *supra*, provides that the amendments of § 2412 which it effects shall apply only to actions filed subsequent to the date of its enactment. The second clause continues in effect, for these and all other cases in which the United States enjoys immunity from costs, the presently prevailing rule that the United States may recover costs as the prevailing party only if it would have suffered them as the losing party.

Subdivision (c). While only five circuits (D.C.Cir. Rule 20(d) [rule 20(d), U.S.Ct. of App. Dist. of Col.]; 1st Cir. Rule 31(4) [rule 31(4), U.S.Ct. of App. 1st Cir.]; 3d Cir. Rule 35(4) [rule 35(4), U.S.Ct. of App. 3rd Cir.]; 4th Cir. Rule 21(4) [rule 21(4) U.S.Ct. of App. 4th Cir.]; 9th Cir. Rule 25 [rule 25, U.S.Ct. of App.9th Cir.], as amended June 2, 1967) presently tax the cost of printing briefs, the proposed rule makes the cost taxable in keeping with the principle of this rule that all cost items expended in the prosecution of a proceeding should be borne by the unsuccessful party.

Subdivision (e). The costs described in this subdivision are costs of the appeal and, as such, are within the undertaking of the appeal bond. They are made taxable in the district court for general convenience. Taxation of the cost of the reporter's transcript is specifically authorized by 28 U.S.C. § 1920, but in the absence of a rule some district courts have held themselves without authority to tax the cost (*Perlman v. Feldmann*, 116 F.Supp. 102 (D. Conn., 1953); *Firtag v. Gendleman*, 152 F.Supp. 226 (D.D.C., 1957); *Todd Atlantic Shipyards Corp. v. The Southport*, 100 F.Supp. 763 (E.D.S.C., 1951). Provision for taxation of the cost of premiums paid for supersedeas bonds is common in the local rules of district courts and the practice is established in the Second, Seventh, and Ninth Circuits. *Berner v. British Commonwealth Pacific Air Lines, Ltd.*, 362 F.2d 799 (2d Cir. 1966); *Land Oberoesterreich v. Gude*, 93 F.2d 292 (2d Cir., 1937); *In re Northern Ind. Oil Co.*, 192 F.2d 139 (7th Cir., 1951); *Lunn v. F. W. Woolworth*, 210 F.2d 159 (9th Cir., 1954).

1979 Amendment

Subdivision (c). The proposed amendment would permit variations among the circuits in regulating the maximum rates taxable as costs for printing or otherwise reproducing briefs, appendices, and copies of records authorized by Rule 30(f). The present rule has had a different effect in different circuits depending upon the size of the circuit, the location of the clerk's office, and the location of other cities. As a consequence there was a growing sense that strict adherence to the rule produces some unfairness in some of the circuits and the matter should be made subject to local rule.

Subdivision (d). The present rule makes no provision for objections to a bill of costs. The proposed amendment would allow 10 days for such objections. Cf. Rule 54(d) of the F.R.C.P. [rule 54(d), Federal Rules of Civil Procedure]. It provides further that the mandate shall not be delayed for taxation of costs.

1986 Amendment

The amendment to subdivision (c) is intended to increase the degree of control exercised by the courts of appeals over rates for printing and copying recoverable as costs. It further requires the courts of appeals to encourage cost-consciousness by requiring that, in fixing the rate, the court consider the most economical methods of printing and copying.

The amendment to subdivision (d) is technical. No substantive change is intended.

1998 Amendments

The language and organization of the rule are amended to make the rule more easily understood. In addition to changes made to improve the understanding, the Advisory Committee has changed language to make style and terminology consistent throughout the appellate rules. These changes are intended to be stylistic only. All references to the cost of "printing" have been deleted from subdivision (c) because commercial printing is so rarely used for preparation of documents filed with a court of appeals.

Rule 40. Petition for Panel Rehearing

(a) Time to File; Contents; Answer; Action by the Court if Granted.

(1) Time. Unless the time is shortened or extended by order or local rule, a petition for panel rehearing may be filed within 14 days after entry of judgment. But in a civil case, if the United States or its officer or agency is a party, the time within which any party may seek rehearing is 45 days after entry of judgment, unless an order shortens or extends the time.

(2) Contents. The petition must state with particularity each point of law or fact that the petitioner believes the court has overlooked or misapprehended and must argue in support of the petition. Oral argument is not permitted.

(3) Answer. Unless the court requests, no answer to a petition for panel rehearing is permitted. But ordinarily rehearing will not be granted in the absence of such a request.

(4) Action by the Court. If a petition for panel rehearing is granted, the court may do any of the following:

(A) make a final disposition of the case without reargument;

(B) restore the case to the calendar for reargument or resubmission; or

(C) issue any other appropriate order.

(b) Form of Petition; Length. The petition must comply in form with Rule 32. Copies must be served and filed as Rule 31 prescribes. Unless the court permits or a local rule provides otherwise, a petition for panel rehearing must not exceed 15 pages.

(As amended Apr. 30, 1979, eff. Aug. 1, 1979; Apr. 29, 1994, eff. Dec. 1, 1994; Apr. 24, 1998, eff. Dec. 1, 1998.)

1967 Adoption

This is the usual rule among the circuits, except that the express prohibition against filing a reply to the petition is found only in the rules of the Fourth, Sixth and Eighth Circuits (it is also contained in Supreme Court Rule 58(3) [rule 58(3), U.S.Sup.Ct.Rules). It is included to save time and expense to the party victorious on appeal. In the very rare instances in which a reply is useful, the court will ask for it.

1979 Amendment

Subdivision (a). The Standing Committee added to the first sentence of Rule 40(a) the words "or by local rule," to conform to current practice in the circuits. The Standing Committee believes the change noncontroversial.

Subdivision (b). The proposed amendment would eliminate the distinction drawn in the present rule between printed briefs and those duplicated from typewritten pages in fixing their maximum length. See Note to Rule 28. Since petitions for rehearing must be prepared in a short time, making typographic printing less likely, the maximum number of pages is fixed at 15, the figure used in the present rule for petitions duplicated by means other than typographic printing.

1994 Amendment

Subdivision (a). The amendment lengthens the time for filing a petition for rehearing from 14 to 45 days in civil cases involving the United States or its agencies or officers. It has no effect upon the time for filing in criminal cases. The amendment makes nation-wide the current practice in the District of Columbia and the Tenth Circuits, *see* D.C. Cir. R. 15 (a), 10th Cir. R. 40.3. This amendment, analogous to the provision in Rule 4(a) extending the time for filing a notice of appeal in cases involving the United States, recognizes that the Solicitor General needs time to conduct a thorough review of the merits of a case before requesting a rehearing. In a case in which a court of appeals believes it necessary to restrict the time for filing a rehearing petition, the amendment provides that the court may do so by order. Although the first sentence of Rule 40 permits a court of appeals to shorten or lengthen the usual 14 day filing period by order or by local rule, the sentence governing appeals in civil cases involving the United States purposely limits a court's power to alter the 45 day period to orders in specific cases. If a court of appeals could adopt a local rule shortening the time for filing a petition for rehearing in all cases involving the United States, the purpose of the amendment would be defeated.

1998 Amendments

The language and organization of the rule are amended to make the rule more easily understood. In addition to changes made to improve the understanding, the Advisory Committee has changed language to make style and terminology consistent throughout the appellate rules. These changes are intended to be stylistic only.

Rule 41. Mandate: Contents; Issuance and Effective Date; Stay

(a) Contents. Unless the court directs that a formal mandate issue, the mandate consists of a certified copy of the judgment, a copy of the court's opinion, if any, and any direction about costs.

(b) When Issued. The court's mandate must issue 7 calendar days after the time to file a petition for rehearing expires, or 7 calendar days after entry of an order denying a timely petition for panel rehearing, petition for rehearing en banc, or motion for stay of mandate, whichever is later. The court may shorten or extend the time.

(c) Effective Date. The mandate is effective when issued.

(d) Staying the Mandate.

(1) On Petition for Rehearing or Motion. The timely filing of a petition for panel rehearing, petition for rehearing en banc, or motion for stay of mandate, stays the mandate until disposition of the petition or motion, unless the court orders otherwise.

(2) Pending Petition for Certiorari.

(A) A party may move to stay the mandate pending the filing of a petition for a writ of certiorari in the Supreme Court. The motion must be served on all parties and must show that the certiorari petition would present a substantial question and that there is good cause for a stay.

(B) The stay must not exceed 90 days, unless the period is extended for good cause or unless the party who obtained the stay files a petition for the writ and so notifies the circuit clerk in writing within the period of the stay. In that case, the stay continues until the Supreme Court's final disposition.

(C) The court may require a bond or other security as a condition to granting or continuing a stay of the mandate.

(D) The court of appeals must issue the mandate immediately when a copy of a Supreme Court order denying the petition for writ of certiorari is filed.

(As amended Apr. 29, 1994, eff. Dec. 1, 1994; Apr. 24, 1998, eff. Dec. 1, 1998; Apr. 29, 2002, eff. Dec. 1, 2002.)

1967 Adoption

The proposed rule follows the rule or practice in a majority of circuits by which copies of the opinion and the judgment serve in lieu of a formal mandate in the ordinary case. Compare Supreme Court Rule 59. Although 28 U.S.C. § 2101(c) permits a writ of certiorari to be filed within 90 days after entry of judgment, seven of the eight circuits which now regulate the matter of stays pending application for certiorari limit the initial stay of the mandate to the 30-day period provided in the proposed rule. Compare D.C.Cir. Rule 27(e) [rule 27(e), U.S.Ct. of App. Dist. of Col.].

1994 Amendment

Subdivision (a). The amendment conforms Rule 41(a) to the amendment made to Rule 40(a). The amendment keys the time for issuance of the mandate to the expiration of the time for filing a petition for rehearing, unless such a petition is filed in which case the mandate issues 7 days after the entry of the order denying the petition. Because the amendment to Rule 40(a) lengthens the time for filing a petition for rehearing in civil cases involving the United States from 14 to 45 days, the rule requiring the mandate to issue 21 days after the entry of judgment would cause the mandate to issue while the government is still considering requesting a rehearing. Therefore, the amendment generally requires the mandate to issue 7 days after the expiration of the time for filing a petition for rehearing.

Subdivision (b). The amendment requires a party who files a motion requesting a stay of mandate to file, at the same time, proof of service on all other parties. The old rule required the party to give notice to the other parties; the amendment merely requires the party to provide the court with evidence of having done so.

The amendment also states that the motion must show that a petition for certiorari would present a substantial question and that there is good cause for a stay. The amendment is intended to alert the parties to the fact that a stay of mandate is not granted automatically and to the type of showing that needs to be made. The Supreme Court has established conditions that must be met before it will stay a mandate. *See* Robert L. Stern et al., Supreme Court Practice § 17.19 (6th ed. 1986).

1998 Amendments

The language and organization of the rule are amended to make the rule more easily understood. In addition to changes made to improve the understanding, the Advisory Committee has changed language to make style and terminology consistent throughout the appellate rules. These changes are intended to be stylistic only.

Several substantive changes are made in this rule, however.

Subdivision (b). The existing rule provides that the mandate issues 7 days after the time to file a petition for panel rehearing expires unless such a petition for rehearing en banc or motion for stay of mandate is filed, the mandate does not issue until 7 days after entry of an order denying the last of all such requests. If a petition for rehearing or a petition for rehearing en banc is granted, the court enters a new judgment after the rehearing and the mandate issues within the normal time after entry of that judgment.

Subdivision (c). Subdivision (c) is new. It provides that the mandate is effective when the court issues it. A court of appeals' judgment or order is not final until issuance of the mandate; at that time the parties' obligations become fixed. This amendment is intended to make it clear that the mandate is effective upon issuance and that its effectiveness is not delayed until receipt of the mandate by the trial court or agency, or until the trial court or agency acts upon it. This amendment is consistent with the current understanding. Unless the court orders that the mandate issue earlier than provided in the rule, the parties can easily calculate the anticipated date of issuance and verify issuance of the mandate, the entry of the order on the docket alerts the parties to that fact.

Subdivision (d). Amended paragraph (1) provides that the filing of a petition for panel rehearing, a petition for rehearing en banc or a motion for a stay of mandate pending petition to the Supreme Court for a writ of certiorari stays the issuance of the mandate until the court disposes of the petition or motion. The provision that a petition for rehearing en banc stays the mandate is a companion to the amendment of Rule 35 that deletes the language stating that a request for a rehearing en banc does not affect the finality of the judgment or stay the issuance of the mandate. The Committee's objective is to treat a request for a rehearing en banc like a petition for panel rehearing so that a request for a rehearing en banc will suspend the finality of the court of appeals' judgment and delay the running of the period for filing a petition for writ of certiorari. Because the filing of a petition for rehearing en banc will stay the mandate, a court of appeals will need to take final action on the petition but the procedure for doing so is left to local practice.

Paragraph (1) also provides that the filing of a motion for a stay of mandate pending petition to the Supreme Court for a writ of certiorari stays the mandate until the court disposes of the motion. If the court denies the motion, the court must issue the mandate 7 days after entering the order denying the motion. If the court grants the motion, the mandate is stayed according to the terms of the order granting the stay. Delaying issuance of the mandate eliminates the need to recall the mandate if the motion for a stay is granted. If, however, the court believes that it would be inappropriate to delay issuance of the mandate until disposition of the motion for a stay, the court may order that the mandate issue immediately.

Paragraph (2). The amendment changes the maximum period for a stay of mandate, absent the court of appeals granting an extension for cause, to 90 days. The presumptive 30–day period was adopted when a party had to file a petition for a writ of certiorari in criminal cases within 30 days after entry of judgment. Supreme Court Rule 13.1 now provides that a party has 90 days after entry of judgment by a court of appeals to file a petition for a writ of certiorari whether the case is civil or criminal.

The amendment does not require a court of appeals to grant a stay of mandate that is coextensive with the period granted for filing a petition for a writ of certiorari. The granting of a stay and the length of the stay remain within the discretion of the court of appeals. The amendment means only that a 90–day stay may be granted without a need to show cause for a stay longer than 30 days.

Subparagraph (C) is not new; it has been moved from the end of the rule to this position.

2002 Amendments

Subdivision (b). Subdivision (b) directs that the mandate of a court must issue 7 days after the time to file a petition for rehearing expires or 7 days after the court denies a timely petition for panel rehearing, petition for rehearing en banc, or motion for stay of mandate, whichever is later. Intermediate Saturdays, Sundays, and legal holidays are counted in computing that 7–day deadline, which means that, except when the 7–day deadline ends on a weekend or legal holiday, the mandate issues exactly one week after the triggering event.

Fed. R. App. P. 26(a)(2) has been amended to provide that, in computing any period of time, one should "[e]xclude intermediate Saturdays, Sundays, and legal holidays when the period is less than 11 days, unless stated in calendar days." This change in the method of computing deadlines means that 7–day deadlines (such as that in subdivision (b)) have been lengthened as a practical matter. Under the new computation method, a mandate would never issue sooner than 9 actual days after a triggering event, and legal holidays could extend that period to as much as 13 days.

Delaying mandates for 9 or more days would introduce significant and unwarranted delay into appellate proceedings. For that reason, subdivision (b) has been amended to require that mandates issue 7 *calendar* days after a triggering event.

Changes Made After Publication and Comments No changes were made to the text of the proposed amendment or to the Committee Note.

Rule 42. Voluntary Dismissal

(a) Dismissal in the District Court. Before an appeal has been docketed by the circuit clerk, the district court may dismiss the appeal on the filing of a stipulation signed by all parties or on the appellant's motion with notice to all parties.

(b) Dismissal in the Court of Appeals. The circuit clerk may dismiss a docketed appeal if the parties file a signed dismissal agreement specifying how costs are to be paid and pay any fees that are due. But no mandate or other process may issue without a court order. An appeal may be dismissed on the appellant's motion on terms agreed to by the parties or fixed by the court.

(As amended Apr. 24, 1998, eff. Dec. 1, 1998.)

1967 Adoption

Subdivision (a). This subdivision is derived from FRCP 73(a) [rule 73(a), Federal Rules of Civil Procedure] without change of substance.

Subdivision (b). The first sentence is a common provision in present circuit rules. The second sentence is added. Compare Supreme Court Rule 60.

1998 Amendments

The language of the rule is amended to make the rule more easily understood. In addition to changes made to improve the understanding, the Advisory Committee has changed language to make style and terminology consistent throughout the appellate rules. These changes are intended to be stylistic only.

Rule 43. Substitution of Parties

(a) Death of a Party.

(1) After Notice of Appeal Is Filed. If a party dies after a notice of appeal has been filed or while a proceeding is pending in the court of appeals, the decedent's personal representative may be substituted as a party on motion filed with the circuit clerk by the representative or by any party. A party's motion must be served on the representative in accordance with Rule 25. If the decedent has no representative, any party may suggest the death on the record, and the court of appeals may then direct appropriate proceedings.

(2) Before Notice of Appeal Is Filed—Potential Appellant. If a party entitled to appeal dies before filing a notice of appeal, the decedent's personal representative—or, if there is no personal representative, the decedent's attorney of record—may file a notice of appeal within the time prescribed by these rules. After the notice of appeal is filed, substitution must be in accordance with Rule 43(a)(1).

(3) Before Notice of Appeal Is Filed—Potential Appellee. If a party against whom an appeal may be taken dies after entry of a judgment or order in the district court, but before a notice of appeal is filed, an appellant may proceed as if the death had not occurred. After the notice of appeal is filed, substitution must be in accordance with Rule 43(a)(1).

(b) Substitution for a Reason Other Than Death. If a party needs to be substituted for any reason other than death, the procedure prescribed in Rule 43(a) applies.

(c) Public Officer: Identification; Substitution.

(1) Identification of Party. A public officer who is a party to an appeal or other proceeding in an official capacity may be described as a party by the public officer's official title rather than by name. But the court may require the public officer's name to be added.

(2) Automatic Substitution of Officeholder. When a public officer who is a party to an appeal or other proceeding in an official capacity dies, resigns, or otherwise ceases to hold office, the action does not abate. The public officer's successor is automatically substituted as a party. Proceedings following the substitution are to be in the name of the substituted party, but any misnomer that does not affect the substantial rights of the parties may be disregarded. An order of substitution may be entered at any time, but failure to enter an order does not affect the substitution.

(As amended Mar. 10, 1986, eff. July 1, 1986; Apr. 24, 1998, eff. Dec. 1, 1998.)

1967 Adoption

Subdivision (a). The first three sentences describe a procedure similar to the rule on substitution in civil actions in the district court. See FRCP 25(a) [rule 25(a), Federal Rules of Civil Procedure]. The fourth sentence expressly authorizes an appeal to be taken against one who has died after the entry of judgment. Compare FRCP 73(b) [rule 73(b), Federal Rules of Civil Procedure], which impliedly authorizes such an appeal.

The sixth sentence authorizes an attorney of record for the deceased to take an appeal on behalf of successors in interest if the deceased has no representative. At present, if a party entitled to appeal dies before the notice of appeal is filed, the appeal can presumably be taken only by his legal representative and must be taken within the time ordinarily prescribed. 13 Cyclopedia of Federal Procedure (3d Ed.) § 63.21. The states commonly make special provision for the even of the death of a party entitled to appeal, usually by extending the time otherwise prescribed. Rules of Civil Procedure for Superior Courts of Arizona, Rule 73(t), 16 A.R.S.; New Jersey Rev.Rules 1:3–3; New York Civil Practice Law and Rules, § 1022; Wisconsin Statutes Ann. 274.01(2). The Provision in the proposed rule is derived from California Code of Civil Procedure, § 941.

Subdivision (c). This subdivision is derived from FRCP 25(d) [rule 25(d), Federal Rules of Civil Procedure] and Supreme Court Rule 48, with appropriate changes.

1986 Amendment

The amendments to Rules 43(a) and (c) are technical. No substantive change is intended.

1998 Amendments

The language and organization of the rule are amended to make the rule more easily understood. In addition to changes made to improve the understanding, the Advisory Committee has changed language to make style and terminology consistent throughout the appellate rules. These changes are intended to be stylistic only.

Rule 44. Case Involving a Constitutional Question When the United States or the Relevant State is Not a Party

(a) Constitutional Challenge to Federal Statute. If a party questions the constitutionality of an Act of Congress in a proceeding in which the United States or its agency, officer, or employee is not a party in an official capacity, the questioning party must give written notice to the circuit clerk immediately upon the filing of the record or as soon as the question is raised in the court of appeals. The clerk must then certify that fact to the Attorney General.

(b) Constitutional Challenge to State Statute. If a party questions the constitutionality of a statute of a State in a proceeding in which that State or its agency, officer, or employee is not a party in an official capacity, the questioning party must give written notice to the circuit clerk immediately upon the filing of the record or as soon as the question is raised in the court of appeals. The clerk must then certify that fact to the attorney general of the State.

(As amended Apr. 24, 1998, eff. Dec. 1, 1998; Apr. 29, 2002, eff. Dec. 1, 2002.)

1967 Adoption

This rule is now found in the rules of a majority of the circuits. It is in response to the Act of August 24, 1937 (28

U.S.C. § 2403), which requires all courts of the United States to advise the Attorney General of the existence of an action or proceeding of the kind described in the rule.

1998 Amendments

The language of the rule is amended to make the rule more easily understood. In addition to changes made to improve the understanding, the Advisory Committee has changed language to make style and terminology consistent throughout the appellate rules. These changes are intended to be stylistic only.

2002 Amendments

Rule 44 requires that a party who "questions the constitutionality of an Act of Congress" in a proceeding in which the United States is not a party must provide written notice of that challenge to the clerk. Rule 44 is designed to implement 28 U.S.C. § 2403(a), which states that:

> In any action, suit or proceeding in a court of the United States to which the United States or any agency, officer or employee thereof is not a party, wherein the constitutionality of any Act of Congress affecting the public interest is drawn in question, the court shall certify such fact to the Attorney General, and shall permit the United States to intervene . . . for argument on the question of constitutionality.

The subsequent section of the statute—§ 2403(*b*)—contains virtually identical language imposing upon the courts the duty to notify the attorney general of a *state* of a constitutional challenge to any statute of that state. But § 2403(b), unlike § 2403(a), was not implemented in Rule 44.

Rule 44 has been amended to correct this omission. The text of former Rule 44 regarding constitutional challenges to federal statutes now appears as Rule 44(a), while new language regarding constitutional challenges to state statutes now appears as Rule 44(b).

Changes Made After Publication and Comments No changes were made to the text of the proposed amendment or to the Committee Note.

Rule 45. Clerk's Duties

(a) General Provisions.

(1) Qualifications. The circuit clerk must take the oath and post any bond required by law. Neither the clerk nor any deputy clerk may practice as an attorney or counselor in any court while in office.

(2) When Court Is Open. The court of appeals is always open for filing any paper, issuing and returning process, making a motion, and entering an order. The clerk's office with the clerk or a deputy in attendance must be open during business hours on all days except Saturdays, Sundays, and legal holidays. A court may provide by local rule or by order that the clerk's office be open for specified hours on Saturdays or on legal holidays other than New Year's Day, Martin Luther King, Jr.'s Birthday, Washington's Birthday, Memorial Day, Independence Day, Labor Day, Columbus Day, Veterans' Day, Thanksgiving Day, and Christmas Day.

(b) Records.

(1) The Docket. The circuit clerk must maintain a docket and an index of all docketed cases in the manner prescribed by the Director of the Administrative Office of the United States Courts. The clerk must record all papers filed with the clerk and all process, orders, and judgments.

(2) Calendar. Under the court's direction, the clerk must prepare a calendar of cases awaiting argument. In placing cases on the calendar for argument, the clerk must give preference to appeals in criminal cases and to other proceedings and appeals entitled to preference by law.

(3) Other Records. The clerk must keep other books and records required by the Director of the Administrative Office of the United States Courts, with the approval of the Judicial Conference of the United States, or by the court.

(c) Notice of an Order or Judgment. Upon the entry of an order or judgment, the circuit clerk must immediately serve a notice of entry on each party, with a copy of any opinion, and must note the date of service on the docket. Service on a party represented by counsel must be made on counsel.

(d) Custody of Records and Papers. The circuit clerk has custody of the court's records and papers. Unless the court orders or instructs otherwise, the clerk must not permit an original record or paper to be taken from the clerk's office. Upon disposition of the case, original papers constituting the record on appeal or review must be returned to the court or agency from which they were received. The clerk must preserve a copy of any brief, appendix, or other paper that has been filed.

(As amended Mar. 1, 1971, eff. July 1, 1971; Mar. 10, 1986, eff. July 1, 1986; Apr. 24, 1998, eff. Dec. 1, 1998; Apr. 29, 2002, eff. Dec. 1, 2002; Apr. 25, 2005, eff. Dec. 1, 2005.)

1967 Adoption

The duties imposed upon clerks of the courts of appeals by this rule are those imposed by rule or practice in a majority of the circuits. The second sentence of subdivision (a) authorizing the closing of the clerk's office on Saturday and non-national legal holidays follows a similar provision respecting the district court clerk's office found in FRCP 77(c) [rule 77(c), Federal Rules of Civil Procedure] and in FRCrP 56 [rule 56, Federal Rules of Criminal Procedure].

1971 Amendment

The amendment adds Columbus Day to the list of legal holidays. See the Note accompanying the amendment of Rule 26(a).

1986 Amendment

The amendment to Rule 45(b) permits the courts of appeals to maintain computerized dockets. The Committee believes that the Administrative Office of the United States Courts ought to have maximum flexibility in prescribing the format of this docket in order to ensure a smooth transition from manual to automated systems and subsequent adaptation to technological improvements.

The amendments to Rules 45(a) and (d) are technical. No substantive change is intended. The Birthday of Martin Luther King, Jr. has been added to the list of national holidays.

1998 Amendments

The language and organization of the rule are amended to make the rule more easily understood. In addition to changes made to improve the understanding, the Advisory Committee has changed language to make style and terminology consistent throughout the appellate rules. These changes are intended to be stylistic only.

2002 Amendments

Subdivision (c). Subdivision (c) has been amended so that the clerk may use electronic means to serve notice of entry of an order or judgment upon parties who have consented to such service.

Changes Made After Publication and Comments No changes were made to the text of the proposed amendment or to the Committee Note.

2005 Amendments

Subdivision (a)(2). Rule 45(a)(2) has been amended to refer to the third Monday in February as "Washington's Birthday." A federal statute officially designates the holiday as "Washington's Birthday," reflecting the desire of Congress specially to honor the first president of the United States. *See* 5 U.S.C. § 6103(a). During the 1998 restyling of the Federal Rules of Appellate Procedure, references to "Washington's Birthday" were mistakenly changed to "Presidents' Day." The amendment corrects that error.

Rule 46. Attorneys

(a) Admission to the Bar.

(1) Eligibility. An attorney is eligible for admission to the bar of a court of appeals if that attorney is of good moral and professional character and is admitted to practice before the Supreme Court of the United States, the highest court of a state, another United States court of appeals, or a United States district court (including the district courts for Guam, the Northern Mariana Islands, and the Virgin Islands).

(2) Application. An applicant must file an application for admission, on a form approved by the court that contains the applicant's personal statement showing eligibility for membership. The applicant must subscribe to the following oath or affirmation:

"I, _____, do solemnly swear [or affirm] that I will conduct myself as an attorney and counselor of this court, uprightly and according to law; and that I will support the Constitution of the United States."

(3) Admission Procedures. On written or oral motion of a member of the court's bar, the court will act on the application. An applicant may be admitted by oral motion in open court. But, unless the court orders otherwise, an applicant need not appear before the court to be admitted. Upon admission, an applicant must pay the clerk the fee prescribed by local rule or court order.

(b) Suspension or Disbarment.

(1) Standard. A member of the court's bar is subject to suspension or disbarment by the court if the member:

(A) has been suspended or disbarred from practice in any other court; or

(B) is guilty of conduct unbecoming a member of the court's bar.

(2) Procedure. The member must be given an opportunity to show good cause, within the time prescribed by the court, why the member should not be suspended or disbarred.

(3) Order. The court must enter an appropriate order after the member responds and a hearing is held, if requested, or after the time prescribed for a response expires, if no response is made.

(c) Discipline. A court of appeals may discipline an attorney who practices before it for conduct unbecoming a member of the bar or for failure to comply with any court rule. First, however, the court must afford the attorney reasonable notice, an opportunity to show cause to the contrary, and, if requested, a hearing.

(As amended Mar. 10, 1986, eff. July 1, 1986; Apr. 24, 1998, eff. Dec. 1, 1998.)

1967 Adoption

Subdivision (a). The basic requirement of membership in the bar of the Supreme Court, or of the highest court of a state, or in another court of appeals or a district court is found, with minor variations, in the rules of ten circuits. The only other requirement in those circuits is that the applicant be of good moral and professional character. In the District of Columbia Circuit applicants other than members of the District of Columbia District bar or the Supreme Court bar must claim membership in the bar of the highest court of a state, territory or possession for three years prior to application for admission (D.C.Cir. Rule 7 [rule 7, U.S.Ct. of App. Dist. of Col.]). Members of the District of Columbia District bar and the Supreme Court bar again excepted, applicants for admission to the District of Columbia Circuit bar must meet precisely defined prelaw and law school study requirements (D.C.Cir. Rule 7½ [rule 7½, U.S.Ct. of App.Dist. of Col.]).

A few circuits now require that application for admission be made by oral motion by a sponsor member in open court.

The proposed rule permits both the application and the motion by the sponsor member to be in writing, and permits action on the motion without the appearance of the applicant or the sponsor, unless the court otherwise orders.

Subdivision (b). The provision respecting suspension or disbarment is uniform. Third Circuit Rule 8(3) [rule 8(3), U.S.Ct. of App. 3rd Cir.] is typical.

Subdivision (c). At present only Fourth Circuit Rule 36 [rule 36, U.S.Ct. of App. 4th Cir.] contains an equivalent provision. The purpose of this provision is to make explicit the power of a court of appeals to impose sanctions less serious than suspension or disbarment for the breach of rules. It also affords some measure of control over attorneys who are not members of the bar of the court. Several circuits permit a non-member attorney to file briefs and motions, membership being required only at the time of oral argument. And several circuits permit argument pro hac vice by non-member attorneys.

1986 Amendments

The amendments to Rules 46(a) and (b) are technical. No substantive change is intended.

1998 Amendments

The language and organization of the rule are amended to make the rule more easily understood. In addition to changes made to improve the understanding, the Advisory Committee has changed language to make style and terminology consistent throughout the appellate rules. These changes are intended to be stylistic only.

HISTORICAL NOTES

Termination of United States District Court for the District of the Canal Zone

For termination of the United States District Court for the District of the Canal Zone at end of the "transition period", being the 30-month period beginning Oct. 1, 1979, and ending midnight Mar. 31, 1982, see Paragraph 5 of Article XI of the Panama Canal Treaty of 1977 and sections 3831 and 3841 to 3843 of Title 22, Foreign Relations and Intercourse.

Rule 47. Local Rules by Courts of Appeals

(a) Local Rules.

(1) Each court of appeals acting by a majority of its judges in regular active service may, after giving appropriate public notice and opportunity for comment, make and amend rules governing its practice. A generally applicable direction to parties or lawyers regarding practice before a court must be in a local rule rather than an internal operating procedure or standing order. A local rule must be consistent with—but not duplicative of—Acts of Congress and rules adopted under 28 U.S.C. § 2072 and must conform to any uniform numbering system prescribed by the Judicial Conference of the United States. Each circuit clerk must send the Administrative Office of the United States Courts a copy of each local rule and internal operating procedure when it is promulgated or amended.

(2) A local rule imposing a requirement of form must not be enforced in a manner that causes a party to lose rights because of a nonwillful failure to comply with the requirement.

(b) Procedure When There Is No Controlling Law. A court of appeals may regulate practice in a particular case in any manner consistent with federal law, these rules, and local rules of the circuit. No sanction or other disadvantage may be imposed for noncompliance with any requirement not in federal law, federal rules, or the local circuit rules unless the alleged violator has been furnished in the particular case with actual notice of the requirement.

(As amended Apr. 27, 1995, eff. Dec. 1, 1995; Apr. 24, 1998, eff. Dec. 1, 1998.)

1967 Adoption

This rule continues the authority now vested in individual courts of appeals by 28 U.S.C. § 2071 to make rules consistent with rules of practice and procedure promulgated by the Supreme Court.

1995 Amendments

Subdivision (a). This rule is amended to require that a generally applicable direction regarding practice before a court of appeals must be in a local rule rather than an internal operating procedure or some other general directive. It is the intent of this rule that a local rule may not bar any practice that these rules explicitly or implicitly permit. Subdivision (b) allows a court of appeals to regulate practice in an individual case by entry of an order in the case. The amendment also reflects the requirement that local rules be consistent not only with the national rules but also with Acts of Congress. The amendment also states that local rules should not repeat national rules and Acts of Congress.

The amendment also requires that the numbering of local rules conform with any uniform numbering system that may be prescribed by the Judicial Conference. Lack of uniform numbering might create unnecessary traps for counsel and litigants. A uniform numbering system would make it easier for an increasingly national bar and for litigants to locate a local rule that applies to a particular procedural issue.

Paragraph (2) is new. Its aim is to protect against loss of rights in the enforcement of local rules relating to matters of form. The proscription of paragraph (2) is narrowly drawn—covering only violations that are not willful and only those involving local rules directed to matters of form. It does not limit the court's power to impose substantive penalties upon a party if it or its attorney stubbornly or repeatedly violates a local rule, even one involving merely a matter of form. Nor does it affect the court's power to enforce local rules that involve more than mere matters of form.

Subdivision (b). This rule provides flexibility to the court in regulating practice in a particular case when there is no controlling law. Specifically, it permits the court to regulate practice in any manner consistent with Acts of Congress, with rules adopted under 28 U.S.C. § 2072, and with the circuit's local rules.

The amendment to this rule disapproves imposing any sanction or other disadvantage on a person for noncompliance with such a directive, unless the alleged violator has been furnished in a particular case with actual notice of the requirement. There should be no adverse consequence to a party or attorney for violating special requirements relating to practice before a particular court unless the party or attorney has actual notice of those requirements.

1998 Amendments

The language of the rule is amended to make the rule more easily understood. In addition to changes made to improve the understanding, the Advisory Committee has changed language to make style and terminology consistent throughout the appellate rules. These changes are intended to be stylistic only.

Rule 48. Masters

(a) Appointment; Powers. A court of appeals may appoint a special master to hold hearings, if necessary, and to recommend factual findings and disposition in matters ancillary to proceedings in the court. Unless the order referring a matter to a master specifies or limits the master's powers, those powers include, but are not limited to, the following:

(1) regulating all aspects of a hearing;

(2) taking all appropriate action for the efficient performance of the master's duties under the order;

(3) requiring the production of evidence on all matters embraced in the reference; and

(4) administering oaths and examining witnesses and parties.

(b) Compensation. If the master is not a judge or court employee, the court must determine the master's compensation and whether the cost is to be charged to any party.

(As amended Apr. 29, 1994, eff. Dec. 1, 1994; Apr. 24, 1998, eff. Dec. 1, 1998.)

1994 Amendments

The text of the existing Rule 48 concerning the title was moved to Rule 1.

This new Rule 48 authorizes a court of appeals to appoint a special master to make recommendations concerning ancillary matters. The courts of appeals have long used masters in contempt proceedings where the issue is compliance with an enforcement order. See *Polish National Alliance v. NLRB*, 159 F.2d 38 (7th Cir. 1946); *NLRB v. Arcade-Sunshine Co.*, 132 F.2d 8 (D.C. Cir. 1942); *NLRB v. Remington Rand, Inc.*, 130 F.2d 919 (2d Cir. 1942). There are other instances when the question before a court of appeals requires a factual determination. An application for fees or eligibility for Criminal Justice Act status on appeal are examples.

Ordinarily when a factual issue is unresolved, a court of appeals remands the case to the district court or agency that originally heard the case. It is not the Committee's intent to alter that practice. However, when factual issues arise in the first instance in the court of appeals, such as fees for representation on appeal, it would be useful to have authority to refer such determinations to a master for a recommendation.

1998 Amendments

The language and organization of the rule are amended to make the rule more easily understood. In addition to changes made to improve the understanding, the Advisory Committee has changed language to make style and terminology consistent throughout the appellate rules. These changes are intended to be stylistic only.

APPENDIX OF FORMS

Form 1. Notice of Appeal to a Court of Appeals From a Judgment or Order of a District Court

United States District Court for the _____
District of _____
File Number _____

A.B., Plaintiff	)	
	)	
v.	)	*Notice of Appeal*
	)	
C.D., Defendant	)	

Notice is hereby given that [___(here name all parties taking the appeal)___, (plaintiffs) (defendants) in the above named case,[1]] hereby appeal to the United States Court of Appeals for the _____ Circuit (from the final judgment) (from an order (describing it)) entered in this action on the _____ day of _____, 20___.

(s)_____
Attorney for [_____]
[Address:_____]

(As amended Apr. 22, 1993, eff. Dec. 1, 1993; Mar. 27, 2003, eff. Dec. 1, 2003.)

[1] See Rule 3(c) for permissible ways of identifying appellants.

Form 2. Notice of Appeal to a Court of Appeals From a Decision of the United States Tax Court

UNITED STATES TAX COURT

Washington, D.C.

A.B., Petitioner	)	
	)	
v.	)	Docket No. _____
	)	
Commissioner of Internal	)	
Revenue, Respondent	)	

Notice of Appeal

Notice is hereby given that [___here name all parties taking the appeal [1]___], hereby appeals to the United States Court of Appeals for the _____ Circuit from (that part of) the decision of this court entered in the above captioned proceeding on the _____ day of _____, 20___ (relating to _____).

(s) _____
Counsel for [_____]
[Address:_____]

(As amended Apr. 22, 1993, eff. Dec. 1, 1993; Mar. 27, 2003, eff. Dec. 1, 2003.)

[1] See Rule 3(c) for permissible ways of identifying appellants.

Form 3. Petition for Review of Order of an Agency, Board, Commission or Officer

United States Court of Appeals
for the _____ Circuit

A.B., Petitioner	)	
	)	
v.	)	Petition for Review
XYZ Commission, Respondent	)	

[___(here name all parties bringing the petition[1])___] hereby petitions the court for review of the Order of the XYZ Commission (describe the order) entered on _____, 20___.

[(s)] _____
Attorney for Petitioners
Address:_____

(As amended Apr. 22, 1993, eff. Dec. 1, 1993; Mar. 27, 2003, eff. Dec. 1, 2003.)

[1] See Rule 15.

Form 4. Affidavit Accompanying Motion for Permission to Appeal In Forma Pauperis

United States District Court
for the
_____ District of _____

A.B., Plaintiff
v. Case No. _____
C.D., Defendant

Affidavit in Support of Motion	**Instructions**
I swear or affirm under penalty of perjury that, because of my poverty, I cannot prepay the docket fees of my appeal or post a bond for them. I believe I am entitled to redress. I swear or affirm under penalty of perjury under United States laws that my answers on this form are true and correct. (28 U.S.C. § 1746; 18 U.S.C. § 1621.)	Complete all questions in this application and then sign it. Do not leave any blanks: if the answer to a question is "0," "none," or "not applicable (N/A)," write in that response. If you need more space to answer a question or to explain your answer, attach a separate sheet of paper identified with your name, your case's docket number, and the question number.

Signed: _____ Date: _____

My issues on appeal are:

1. For both you and your spouse estimate the average amount of money received from each of the following sources during the past 12 months. Adjust any amount that was received weekly, biweekly, quarterly, semiannually, or annually to show the monthly rate. Use gross amounts, that is, amounts before any deductions for taxes or otherwise.

Income source	Average monthly amount during the past 12 months		Amount expected next month	
	You	Spouse	You	Spouse
Employment	$_____	$_____	$_____	$_____
Self-employment	$_____	$_____	$_____	$_____
Income from real property (such as rental income)	$_____	$_____	$_____	$_____
Interest and dividends	$_____	$_____	$_____	$_____
Gifts	$_____	$_____	$_____	$_____
Alimony	$_____	$_____	$_____	$_____
Child support	$_____	$_____	$_____	$_____
Retirement (such as social security, pensions, annuities, insurance)	$_____	$_____	$_____	$_____
Disability (such as social security, insurance payments)	$_____	$_____	$_____	$_____
Unemployment payments	$_____	$_____	$_____	$_____
Public-assistance (such as welfare)	$_____	$_____	$_____	$_____
Other (specify): _	$_____	$_____	$_____	$_____
Total monthly income:	$_____	$_____	$_____	$_____

2. List your employment history, most recent employer first. (Gross monthly pay is before taxes or other deductions.)

Employer	Address	Dates of employment	Gross monthly pay
_____	_____	_____	_____
_____	_____	_____	_____
_____	_____	_____	_____

3. List your spouse's employment history, most recent employer first. (Gross monthly pay is before taxes or other deductions.)

Employer	Address	Dates of employment	Gross monthly pay
_____	_____	_____	_____
_____	_____	_____	_____
_____	_____	_____	_____

4. How much cash do you and your spouse have? $_____

Below, state any money you or your spouse have in bank accounts or in any other financial institution.

Financial institution	Type of account	Amount you have	Amount your spouse has
_____	_____	$_____	$_____
_____	_____	$_____	$_____
_____	_____	$_____	$_____

If you are a prisoner, you must attach a statement certified by the appropriate institutional officer showing all receipts, expenditures, and balances during the last six months in your institutional accounts. If you have multiple accounts, perhaps because you have been in multiple institutions, attach one certified statement of each account.

5. List the assets, and their values, which you own or your spouse owns. Do not list clothing and ordinary household furnishings.

Home	(Value)	**Other real estate**	(Value)	**Motor vehicle #1**	(Value)
_____		_____		Make & year:	_____
_____		_____		Model:	_____
_____		_____		Registration #:	_____

Motor vehicle #2	(Value)	**Other assets**	(Value)	**Other assets**	(Value)
Make & year:	_____	_____		_____	
Model:	_____	_____		_____	
Registration #:	_____	_____		_____	

6. State every person, business, or organization owing you or your spouse money, and the amount owed.

Person owing you or your spouse money	Amount owed to you	Amount owed to your spouse
_____	_____	_____
_____	_____	_____
_____	_____	_____

7. State the persons who rely on you or your spouse for support.

Name	Relationship	Age
_____	_____	_____
_____	_____	_____
_____	_____	_____

8. Estimate the average monthly expenses of you and your family. Show separately the amounts paid by your spouse. Adjust any payments that are made weekly, biweekly, quarterly, semiannually, or annually to show the monthly rate.

	You	Your Spouse
Rent or home-mortgage payment (include lot rented for mobile home)	$_____	$_____
Are real-estate taxes included?	☐ Yes ☐ No	
Is property insurance included?	☐ Yes ☐ No	
Utilities (electricity, heating fuel, water,		

sewer, and Telephone)	$_____	$_____
Home maintenance (repairs and upkeep)	$_____	$_____
Food	$_____	$_____
Clothing	$_____	$_____
Laundry and dry-cleaning	$_____	$_____
Medical and dental expenses	$_____	$_____
Transportation (not including motor vehicle payments)	$_____	$_____
Recreation, entertainment, newspapers, magazines, etc.	$_____	$_____
Insurance (not deducted from wages or included in Mortgage payments)	$_____	$_____
Homeowner's or renter's	$_____	$_____
Life	$_____	$_____
Health	$_____	$_____
Motor Vehicle	$_____	$_____
Other: _____	$_____	$_____
Taxes (not deducted from wages or included in Mortgage payments) (specify): _____	$_____	$_____
Installment payments	$_____	$_____
Motor Vehicle	$_____	$_____
Credit card (name): _____	$_____	$_____
Department store (name): ___	$_____	$_____
Other: _____	$_____	$_____
Alimony, maintenance, and support paid to others	$_____	$_____
Regular expenses for operation of business, profession, or farm (attach detailed statement)	$_____	$_____
Other (specify): ____	$_____	$_____
Total monthly expenses:	$_____	$_____

9. Do you expect any major changes to your monthly income or expenses or in your assets or liabilities during the next 12 months?
☐ Yes ☐ No If yes, describe on an attached sheet.

10. Have you paid—or will you be paying—an attorney any money for services in connection with this case, including the completion of this form? Yes No
If yes, how much? $_____
If yes, state the attorney's name, address, and telephone number:

_____

_____

11. Have you paid—or will you be paying—anyone other than an attorney (such as a paralegal or a typist) any money for services in connection with this case, including the completion of this form?
☐ Yes ☐ No
If yes, how much? $_____
If yes, state the person's name, address, and telephone number:

_____

_____

_____

12. Provide any other information that will help explain why you cannot pay the docket fees for your appeal.

13. State the address of your legal residence.

_____

_____

Your daytime phone number: ___ _____
Your age: _____ Your years of schooling: _____
Your social-security number: _____
(As amended Apr. 24, 1998, eff. Dec. 1, 1998.)

Form 5. Notice of Appeal to a Court of Appeals from a Judgment or Order of a District Court or a Bankruptcy Appellate Panel

United States District Court for the .....
District of .....

In re)
)
.....,)
Debtor)
) File No.....
.....,)
Plaintiff)
)
v.)
)
.....,)
Defendant)

Notice of Appeal to
United States Court of Appeals

for the ..... Circuit
....., the plaintiff [or defendant or other party] appeals to the United States Court of Appeals for the ..... Circuit from the final judgment [or order or decree] of the district court for the district of ..... [or bankruptcy appellate panel of the ..... circuit], entered in this case on ....., 20.... [here describe the judgment, order, or decree] .....

The parties to the judgment [or order or decree] appealed from and the names and addresses of their respective attorneys are as follows:

Dated .....
Signed .....
Attorney for Appellant

Address: .....
.....

(Added Apr. 25, 1989, eff. Dec. 1, 1989; Mar. 27, 2003, eff. Dec. 1, 2003.)

Form 6. Certificate of Compliance with Rule 32(a)

Certificate of Compliance With Type-Volume Limitation, Typeface Requirements, and Type Style Requirements

1. This brief complies with the type-volume limitation of Fed. R. App. P. 32(a)(7)(B) because:

☐ this brief contains [*state the number of*] words, excluding the parts of the brief exempted by Fed. R. App. P. 32(a)(7)(B)(iii), *or*

☐ this brief uses a monospaced typeface and contains [*state the number of*] lines of text, excluding the parts of the brief exempted by Fed. R. App. P. 32(a)(7)(B)(iii).

2. This brief complies with the typeface requirements of Fed. R. App. P. 32(a)(5) and the type style requirements of Fed. R. App. P. 32(a)(6) because:

☐ this brief has been prepared in a proportionally spaced typeface using [*state name and version of word processing program*] in [*state font size and name of type style*], *or*

☐ this brief has been prepared in a monospaced typeface using [*state name and version of word processing program*] with [*state number of characters per inch and name of type style*].

(s)_____

Attorney for _____

Dated: _____

(Added Apr. 29, 2002, eff. Dec. 1, 2002.)

2002 Adoption

Changes Made After Publication and Comments No changes were made to the text of the proposed amendment or to the Committee Note.

RULES OF THE SUPREME COURT OF THE UNITED STATES

Adopted January 11, 1999
Effective May 3, 1999

Amendments received to December 1, 2008

PART I. THE COURT

Rule
1. Clerk.
2. Library.
3. Term.
4. Sessions and Quorum.

PART II. ATTORNEYS AND COUNSELORS

5. Admission to the Bar.
6. Argument *Pro Hac Vice*.
7. Prohibition Against Practice.
8. Disbarment and Disciplinary Action.
9. Appearance of Counsel.

PART III. JURISDICTION ON WRIT OF CERTIORARI

10. Considerations Governing Review on Certiorari.
11. Certiorari to a United States Court of Appeals Before Judgment.
12. Review on Certiorari: How Sought; Parties.
13. Review on Certiorari: Time for Petitioning.
14. Content of a Petition for a Writ of Certiorari.
15. Briefs in Opposition; Reply Briefs; Supplemental Briefs.
16. Disposition of a Petition for a Writ of Certiorari.

PART IV. OTHER JURISDICTION

17. Procedure in an Original Action.
18. Appeal from a United States District Court.
19. Procedure on a Certified Question.
20. Procedure on a Petition for an Extraordinary Writ.

PART V. MOTIONS AND APPLICATIONS

21. Motions to the Court.
22. Applications to Individual Justices.
23. Stays.

PART VI. BRIEFS ON THE MERITS AND ORAL ARGUMENT

24. Briefs on the Merits: In General.

Rule

PART VI. BRIEFS ON THE MERITS AND ORAL ARGUMENT—Cont'd

25. Briefs on the Merits: Number of Copies and Time to File.
26. Joint Appendix.
27. Calendar.
28. Oral Argument.

PART VII. PRACTICE AND PROCEDURE

29. Filing and Service of Documents; Special Notifications; Corporate Listing.
30. Computation and Extension of Time.
31. Translations.
32. Models, Diagrams, Exhibits, and Lodgings.
33. Document Preparation: Booklet Format; 8½- by 11-inch Paper Format.
34. Document Preparation: General Requirements.
35. Death, Substitution, and Revivor; Public Officers.
36. Custody of Prisoners in Habeas Corpus Proceedings.
37. Brief for an Amicus Curiae.
38. Fees.
39. Proceedings *In Forma Pauperis*.
40. Veterans, Seamen, and Military Cases.

PART VIII. DISPOSITION OF CASES

41. Opinions of the Court.
42. Interest and Damages.
43. Costs.
44. Rehearing.
45. Process; Mandates.
46. Dismissing Cases.

PART IX. DEFINITIONS AND EFFECTIVE DATE

47. Reference to "State Court" and "State Law".
48. Effective Date of Rules.

TABLE OF CORRESPONDING SUPREME COURT RULES

This table shows corresponding relationship between the rules effective July 1, 1925, the rules effective July 1, 1928, the rules effective Feb. 27, 1939, the rules effective July 1, 1954, the rules effective Oct. 2, 1967, the rules effective July 1, 1970, and the rules effective June 30, 1980.

1925	1928	1939	1954	1967	1970	1980
1	1	1	1	1	1	1
2	2	2	5, 6, 8	5, 6, 8	5, 6, 8	5, 6, 8
	3	3	7	7	7	7
3	4	4	2	2	2	2
		5	9	9	9	9
4	5					
5	6	6	9, 59	9, 59	9, 59	9, 52
6	7	7	16, 20, 24, 35, 44	16, 20, 24, 35, 44	16, 20, 24, 35, 44	16, 18, 22, 23, 28
7	8	8				
8	9	9				
9	10	10	12	12	12	13
10	11	11	13, 14	13, 14	13, 14	12, 14
	12	12	15, 16	15, 16	15, 16	15, 16
11	13	13	17, 26, 36	17, 26, 36	17, 26, 36	30
12	14	14	37	37	37	31
13	15	15				
14	16	16				
15	17	17	32	32	32	
16	18	18	38	38	38	32
17	19	19	48	48	48	40
18	20	20	35, 43	35, 43	35, 43	37, 42
19	21	21				
20	22	22				
21	23	23				
22	24	24				
23	25	25	45	45	45	38
24	26	26	39	39	39	33
25	27	27	40 to 42	40 to 42	40 to 42	34 to 36
26	28	28	44	44	44	38
27	29	29	55	55	55	48
28	30	30	56	56	56	49
	31	31				
29	32	32	52, 57	52, 57	52, 57	45, 50
30	33	33	58	58	58	51
31	34	34	25, 59	25, 59	25, 59	23, 52
32	35	35	60	60	60	53
33	36	36	18	18	18	44
34	37	37	28	28	28	24
35	38	38	19, 21 to 24, 27, 36	19, 21 to 24, 27, 36	19, 21 to 24, 27, 36	17, 19 to 22, 30, 44
		38½	11, 22	11, 22	11, 22	11, 20
36	39	39	20	20	20	18
37	40	40	28	28	28	24
38	41	41	19	19	19	17
39	42	42	19	19	19	17
40	43	43	25	25	25	23
41	44	44				
42	45	45	49	49	49	41
	46	46				
	46½	47				
		48	46	46	46	10, 19
43	47	49	4	4	4	4
44	48	50	3	3	3	3
45	49	51	61	62	62	55
			62	61	61	54

PART I. THE COURT

Rule 1. Clerk

1. The Clerk receives documents for filing with the Court and has authority to reject any submitted filing that does not comply with these Rules.

2. The Clerk maintains the Court's records and will not permit any of them to be removed from the Court building except as authorized by the Court. Any document filed with the Clerk and made a part of the Court's records may not thereafter be withdrawn from the official Court files. After the conclusion of proceedings in this Court, original records and documents transmitted to this Court by any other court will be returned to the court from which they were received.

3. Unless the Court or the Chief Justice orders otherwise, the Clerk's office is open from 9 a.m. to 5 p.m., Monday through Friday, except on federal legal holidays listed in 5 U.S.C. § 6103.

Rule 2. Library

1. The Court's library is available for use by appropriate personnel of this Court, members of the Bar of this Court, Members of Congress and their legal staffs, and attorneys for the United States and for federal departments and agencies.

2. The library's hours are governed by regulations made by the Librarian with the approval of the Chief Justice or the Court.

3. Library books may not be removed from the Court building, except by a Justice or a member of a Justice's staff.

Rule 3. Term

The Court holds a continuous annual Term commencing on the first Monday in October and ending on the day before the first Monday in October of the following year. See 28 U.S.C. § 2. At the end of each Term, all cases pending on the docket are continued to the next Term.

Rule 4. Sessions and Quorum

1. Open sessions of the Court are held beginning at 10 a.m. on the first Monday in October of each year, and thereafter as announced by the Court. Unless it orders otherwise, the Court sits to hear arguments from 10 a.m. until noon and from 1 p.m. until 3 p.m.

2. Six Members of the Court constitute a quorum. See 28 U.S.C. § 1. In the absence of a quorum on any day appointed for holding a session of the Court, the Justices attending—or if no Justice is present, the Clerk or a Deputy Clerk—may announce that the Court will not meet until there is a quorum.

3. When appropriate, the Court will direct the Clerk or the Marshal to announce recesses.

PART II. ATTORNEYS AND COUNSELORS

Rule 5. Admission to the Bar

1. To qualify for admission to the Bar of this Court, an applicant must have been admitted to practice in the highest court of a State, Commonwealth, Territory or Possession, or the District of Columbia for a period of at least three years immediately before the date of application; must not have been the subject of any adverse disciplinary action pronounced or in effect during that 3-year period; and must appear to the Court to be of good moral and professional character.

2. Each applicant shall file with the Clerk (1) a certificate from the presiding judge, clerk, or other authorized official of that court evidencing the applicant's admission to practice there and the applicant's current good standing, and (2) a completely executed copy of the form approved by this Court and furnished by the Clerk containing (a) the applicant's personal statement, and (b) the statement of two sponsors endorsing the correctness of the applicant's statement, stating that the applicant possesses all the qualifications required for admission, and affirming that the applicant is of good moral and professional character. Both sponsors must be members of the Bar of this Court who personally know, but are not related to, the applicant.

3. If the documents submitted demonstrate that the applicant possesses the necessary qualifications, and if the applicant has signed the oath or affirmation and paid the required fee, the Clerk will notify the applicant of acceptance by the Court as a member of the Bar and issue a certificate of admission. An applicant who so wishes may be admitted in open court on oral motion by a member of the Bar of this Court, provided that all other requirements for admission have been satisfied.

4. Each applicant shall sign the following oath or affirmation: I, ..., do solemnly swear (or affirm) that as an attorney and as a counselor of this Court, I will conduct myself uprightly and according to law, and that I will support the Constitution of the United States.

5. The fee for admission to the Bar and a certificate bearing the seal of the Court is $200, payable to the United States Supreme Court. The Marshal will deposit such fees in a separate fund to be disbursed by the Marshal at the direction of the Chief Justice for the costs of admissions, for the benefit of the Court and its Bar, and for related purposes.

6. The fee for a duplicate certificate of admission to the Bar bearing the seal of the Court is $15, and the fee for a certificate of good standing is $10, payable to the United States Supreme Court. The proceeds will be maintained by the Marshal as provided in paragraph 5 of this Rule.

(As amended Jan. 11, 1999, eff. May 3, 1999; July 17, 2007, eff. Oct. 1, 2007.)

Rule 6. Argument *Pro Hac Vice*

1. An attorney not admitted to practice in the highest court of a State, Commonwealth, Territory or Possession, or the District of Columbia for the requisite three years, but otherwise eligible for admission to practice in this Court under Rule 5.1, may be permitted to argue *pro hac vice*.

2. An attorney qualified to practice in the courts of a foreign state may be permitted to argue *pro hac vice.*

3. Oral argument *pro hac vice* is allowed only on motion of the counsel of record for the party on whose behalf leave is requested. The motion shall state concisely the qualifications of the attorney who is to argue *pro hac vice.* It shall be filed with the Clerk, in the form required by Rule 21, no later than the date on which the respondent's or appellee's brief on the merits is due to be filed, and it shall be accompanied by proof of service as required by Rule 29.

Rule 7. Prohibition Against Practice

No employee of this Court shall practice as an attorney or counselor in any court or before any agency of government while employed by the Court; nor shall any person after leaving such employment participate in any professional capacity in any case pending before this Court or in any case being considered for filing in this Court, until two years have elapsed after separation; nor shall a former employee ever participate in any professional capacity in any case that was pending in this Court during the employee's tenure.

Rule 8. Disbarment and Disciplinary Action

1. Whenever a member of the Bar of this Court has been disbarred or suspended from practice in any court of record, or has engaged in conduct unbecoming a member of the Bar of this Court, the Court will enter an order suspending that member from practice before this Court and affording the member an opportunity to show cause, within 40 days, why a disbarment order should not be entered. Upon response, or if no response is timely filed, the Court will enter an appropriate order.

2. After reasonable notice and an opportunity to show cause why disciplinary action should not be taken, and after a hearing if material facts are in dispute, the Court may take any appropriate disciplinary action against any attorney who is admitted to practice before it for conduct unbecoming a member of the Bar or for failure to comply with these Rules or any Rule or order of the Court.

Rule 9. Appearance of Counsel

1. An attorney seeking to file a document in this Court in a representative capacity must first be admitted to practice before this Court as provided in Rule 5, except that admission to the Bar of this Court is not required for an attorney appointed under the Criminal Justice Act of 1964, see 18 U.S.C. § 3006A(d)(6), or under any other applicable federal statute. The attorney whose name, address, and telephone number appear on the cover of a document presented for filing is considered counsel of record, and a separate notice of appearance need not be filed. If the name of more than one attorney is shown on the cover of the document, the attorney who is counsel of record shall be clearly identified. See Rule 34.1(f).

2. An attorney representing a party who will not be filing a document shall enter a separate notice of appearance as counsel of record indicating the name of the party represented. A separate notice of appearance shall also be entered whenever an attorney is substituted as counsel of record in a particular case. (As amended July 17, 2007, eff. Oct. 1, 2007.)

PART III. JURISDICTION ON WRIT OF CERTIORARI

Rule 10. Considerations Governing Review on Certiorari

Review on a writ of certiorari is not a matter of right, but of judicial discretion. A petition for a writ of certiorari will be granted only for compelling reasons. The following, although neither controlling nor fully measuring the Court's discretion, indicate the character of the reasons the Court considers:

(a) a United States court of appeals has entered a decision in conflict with the decision of another United States court of appeals on the same important matter; has decided an important federal question in a way that conflicts with a decision by a state court of last resort; or has so far departed from the accepted and usual course of judicial proceedings, or sanctioned such a departure by a lower court, as to call for an exercise of this Court's supervisory power;

(b) a state court of last resort has decided an important federal question in a way that conflicts with the decision of another state court of last resort or of a United States court of appeals;

(c) a state court or a United States court of appeals has decided an important question of federal law that has not been, but should be, settled by this Court, or has decided an important federal question in a way that conflicts with relevant decisions of this Court.

A petition for a writ of certiorari is rarely granted when the asserted error consists of erroneous factual findings or the misapplication of a properly stated rule of law.

Rule 11. Certiorari to a United States Court of Appeals Before Judgment

A petition for a writ of certiorari to review a case pending in a United States court of appeals, before judgment is entered in that court, will be granted only upon a showing that the case is of such imperative public importance as to justify deviation from normal appellate practice and to require immediate determination in this Court. See 28 U.S.C. § 2101(e).

Rule 12. Review on Certiorari: How Sought; Parties

1. Except as provided in paragraph 2 of this Rule, the petitioner shall file 40 copies of a petition for a writ of certiorari, prepared as required by Rule 33.1, and shall pay the Rule 38(a) docket fee.

2. A petitioner proceeding *in forma pauperis* under Rule 39 shall file an original and 10 copies of a petition for a writ of certiorari prepared as required by Rule 33.2, together with an original and 10 copies of the motion for leave to proceed *in forma pauperis.* A copy of the motion shall precede and be attached to each copy of the petition. An inmate confined in an institution, if proceeding *in forma pauperis* and not represented by counsel, need file only an original petition and motion.

3. Whether prepared under Rule 33.1 or Rule 33.2, the petition shall comply in all respects with Rule 14 and shall be submitted with proof of service as required by Rule 29. The case then will be placed on the docket. It is the petitioner's duty to notify all respondents promptly, on a form supplied by the Clerk, of the date of filing, the date the case was placed on the docket, and the docket number of the case. The notice shall be served as required by Rule 29.

4. Parties interested jointly, severally, or otherwise in a judgment may petition separately for a writ of certiorari; or any two or more may join in a petition. A party not shown on the petition as joined therein at the time the petition is filed may not later join in that petition. When two or more judgments are sought to be reviewed on a writ of certiorari to the same court and involve identical or closely related questions, a single petition for a writ of certiorari covering all the judgments suffices. A petition for a writ of certiorari may not be joined with any other pleading, except that any motion for leave to proceed *in forma pauperis* shall be attached.

5. No more than 30 days after a case has been placed on the docket, a respondent seeking to file a conditional cross-petition (*i.e.,* a cross-petition that otherwise would be untimely) shall file, with proof of service as required by Rule 29, 40 copies of the cross-petition prepared as required by Rule 33.1, except that a cross-petitioner proceeding *in forma pauperis* under Rule 39 shall comply with Rule 12.2. The cross-petition shall comply in all respects with this Rule and Rule 14, except that material already reproduced in the appendix to the opening petition need not be reproduced again. A cross-petitioning respondent shall pay the Rule 38(a) docket fee or submit a motion for leave to proceed *in forma pauperis.* The cover of the cross-petition shall indicate clearly that it is a conditional cross-petition. The cross-petition then will be placed on the docket, subject to the provisions of Rule 13.4. It is the cross-petitioner's duty to notify all cross-respondents promptly, on a form supplied by the Clerk, of the date of filing, the date the cross-petition was placed on the docket, and the docket number of the cross-petition. The notice shall be served as required by Rule 29. A cross-petition for a writ of certiorari may not be joined with any other pleading, except that any motion for leave to proceed *in forma pauperis* shall be attached. The time to file a conditional cross-petition will not be extended.

6. All parties to the proceeding in the court whose judgment is sought to be reviewed are deemed parties entitled to file documents in this Court, unless the petitioner notifies the Clerk of this Court in writing of the petitioner's belief that one or more of the parties below have no interest in the outcome of the petition. A copy of such notice shall be served as required by Rule 29 on all parties to the proceeding below. A party noted as no longer interested may remain a party by notifying the Clerk promptly, with service on the other parties, of an intention to remain a party. All parties other than the petitioner are considered respondents, but any respondent who supports the position of a petitioner shall meet the petitioner's time schedule for filing documents, except that a response supporting the petition shall be filed within 20 days after the case is placed on the docket, and that time will not be extended. Parties who file no document will not qualify for any relief from this Court.

7. The clerk of the court having possession of the record shall keep it until notified by the Clerk of this Court to certify and transmit it. In any document filed with this Court, a party may cite or quote from the record, even if it has not been transmitted to this Court. When requested by the Clerk of this Court to certify and transmit the record, or any part of it, the clerk of the court having possession of the record shall number the documents to be certified and shall transmit therewith a numbered list specifically identifying each document transmitted. If the record, or stipulated portions, have been printed for the use of the court below, that printed record, plus the proceedings in the court below, may be certified as the record unless one of the parties or the Clerk of this Court requests otherwise. The record may consist of certified copies, but if the lower court is of the view that original documents of any kind should be seen by this

Court, that court may provide by order for the transport, safekeeping, and return of such originals.

Rule 13. Review on Certiorari: Time for Petitioning

1. Unless otherwise provided by law, a petition for a writ of certiorari to review a judgment in any case, civil or criminal, entered by a state court of last resort or a United States court of appeals (including the United States Court of Appeals for the Armed Forces) is timely when it is filed with the Clerk of this Court within 90 days after entry of the judgment. A petition for a writ of certiorari seeking review of a judgment of a lower state court that is subject to discretionary review by the state court of last resort is timely when it is filed with the Clerk within 90 days after entry of the order denying discretionary review.

2. The Clerk will not file any petition for a writ of certiorari that is jurisdictionally out of time. See, *e.g.*, 28 U.S.C. § 2101(c).

3. The time to file a petition for a writ of certiorari runs from the date of entry of the judgment or order sought to be reviewed, and not from the issuance date of the mandate (or its equivalent under local practice). But if a petition for rehearing is timely filed in the lower court by any party, or if the lower court appropriately entertains an untimely petition for rehearing or *sua sponte* considers rehearing, the time to file the petition for a writ of certiorari for all parties (whether or not they requested rehearing or joined in the petition for rehearing) runs from the date of the denial of rehearing or, if rehearing is granted, the subsequent entry of judgment.

4. A cross-petition for a writ of certiorari is timely when it is filed with the Clerk as provided in paragraphs 1, 3, and 5 of this Rule, or in Rule 12.5. However, a conditional cross-petition (which except for Rule 12.5 would be untimely) will not be granted unless another party's timely petition for a writ of certiorari is granted.

5. For good cause, a Justice may extend the time to file a petition for a writ of certiorari for a period not exceeding 60 days. An application to extend the time to file shall set out the basis for jurisdiction in this Court, identify the judgment sought to be reviewed, include a copy of the opinion and any order respecting rehearing, and set out specific reasons why an extension of time is justified. The application must be filed with the Clerk at least 10 days before the date the petition is due, except in extraordinary circumstances. For the time and manner of presenting the application, see Rules 21, 22, 30, and 33.2. An application to extend the time to file a petition for a writ of certiorari is not favored.

(As amended Jan. 11, 1999, eff. May 3, 1999; Jan. 27, 2003, eff. May 1, 2003; Mar. 14, 2005, eff. May 2, 2005.)

Rule 14. Content of a Petition for a Writ of Certiorari

1. A petition for a writ of certiorari shall contain, in the order indicated:

(a) The questions presented for review, expressed concisely in relation to the circumstances of the case, without unnecessary detail. The questions should be short and should not be argumentative or repetitive. If the petitioner or respondent is under a death sentence that may be affected by the disposition of the petition, the notation "capital case" shall precede the questions presented. The questions shall be set out on the first page following the cover, and no other information may appear on that page. The statement of any question presented is deemed to comprise every subsidiary question fairly included therein. Only the questions set out in the petition, or fairly included therein, will be considered by the Court.

(b) A list of all parties to the proceeding in the court whose judgment is sought to be reviewed (unless the caption of the case contains the names of all the parties), and a corporate disclosure statement as required by Rule 29.6.

(c) If the petition exceeds five pages or 1,500 words, a table of contents and a table of cited authorities. The table of contents shall include the items contained in the appendix.

(d) Citations of the official and unofficial reports of the opinions and orders entered in the case by courts or administrative agencies.

(e) A concise statement of the basis for jurisdiction in this Court, showing:

(i) the date the judgment or order sought to be reviewed was entered (and, if applicable, a statement that the petition is filed under this Court's Rule 11);

(ii) the date of any order respecting rehearing, and the date and terms of any order granting an extension of time to file the petition for a writ of certiorari;

(iii) express reliance on Rule 12.5, when a cross-petition for a writ of certiorari is filed under that Rule, and the date of docketing of the petition for a writ of certiorari in connection with which the cross-petition is filed;

(iv) the statutory provision believed to confer on this Court jurisdiction to review on a writ of certiorari the judgment or order in question; and

(v) if applicable, a statement that the notifications required by Rule 29.4(b) or (c) have been made.

(f) The constitutional provisions, treaties, statutes, ordinances, and regulations involved in the case, set out verbatim with appropriate citation. If the provisions involved are lengthy, their citation alone suffices at this point, and their pertinent text shall be set out in the appendix referred to in subparagraph 1(i).

(g) A concise statement of the case setting out the facts material to consideration of the questions presented, and also containing the following:

(i) If review of a state-court judgment is sought, specification of the stage in the proceedings, both in the court of first instance and in the appellate courts, when the federal questions sought to be reviewed were raised; the method or manner of raising them and the way in which they were passed on by those courts; and pertinent quotations of specific portions of the record or summary thereof, with specific reference to the places in the record where the matter appears (*e.g.,* court opinion, ruling on exception, portion of court's charge and exception thereto, assignment of error), so as to show that the federal question was timely and properly raised and that this Court has jurisdiction to review the judgment on a writ of certiorari. When the portions of the record relied on under this subparagraph are voluminous, they shall be included in the appendix referred to in subparagraph 1(i).

(ii) If review of a judgment of a United States court of appeals is sought, the basis for federal jurisdiction in the court of first instance.

(h) A direct and concise argument amplifying the reasons relied on for allowance of the writ. See Rule 10.

(i) An appendix containing, in the order indicated:

(i) the opinions, orders, findings of fact, and conclusions of law, whether written or orally given and transcribed, entered in conjunction with the judgment sought to be reviewed;

(ii) any other relevant opinions, orders, findings of fact, and conclusions of law entered in the case by courts or administrative agencies, and, if reference thereto is necessary to ascertain the grounds of the judgment, of those in companion cases (each document shall include the caption showing the name of the issuing court or agency, the title and number of the case, and the date of entry);

(iii) any order on rehearing, including the caption showing the name of the issuing court, the title and number of the case, and the date of entry;

(iv) the judgment sought to be reviewed if the date of its entry is different from the date of the opinion or order required in sub-subparagraph (i) of this subparagraph;

(v) material required by subparagraphs 1(f) or 1(g)(i); and

(vi) any other material the petitioner believes essential to understand the petition.

If the material required by this subparagraph is voluminous, it may be presented in a separate volume or volumes with appropriate covers.

2. All contentions in support of a petition for a writ of certiorari shall be set out in the body of the petition, as provided in subparagraph 1(h) of this Rule. No separate brief in support of a petition for a writ of certiorari may be filed, and the Clerk will not file any petition for a writ of certiorari to which any supporting brief is annexed or appended.

3. A petition for a writ of certiorari should be stated briefly and in plain terms and may not exceed the word or page limitations specified in Rule 33.

4. The failure of a petitioner to present with accuracy, brevity, and clarity whatever is essential to ready and adequate understanding of the points requiring consideration is sufficient reason for the Court to deny a petition.

5. If the Clerk determines that a petition submitted timely and in good faith is in a form that does not comply with this Rule or with Rule 33 or Rule 34, the Clerk will return it with a letter indicating the deficiency. A corrected petition submitted in accordance with Rule 29.2 no more than 60 days after the date of the Clerk's letter will be deemed timely.

(As amended July 17, 2007, eff. Oct. 1, 2007.)

Rule 15. Briefs in Opposition; Reply Briefs; Supplemental Briefs

1. A brief in opposition to a petition for a writ of certiorari may be filed by the respondent in any case, but is not mandatory except in a capital case, see Rule 14.1(a), or when ordered by the Court.

2. A brief in opposition should be stated briefly and in plain terms and may not exceed the word or page limitations specified in Rule 33. In addition to presenting other arguments for denying the petition, the brief in opposition should address any perceived misstatement of fact or law in the petition that bears on what issues properly would be before the Court if certiorari were granted. Counsel are admonished that they have an obligation to the Court to point out in the brief in opposition, and not later, any perceived misstatement made in the petition. Any objection to consideration of a question presented based on what occurred in the proceedings below, if the objection does not go to jurisdiction, may be deemed waived unless called to the Court's attention in the brief in opposition.

3. Any brief in opposition shall be filed within 30 days after the case is placed on the docket, unless the time is extended by the Court or a Justice, or by the Clerk under Rule 30.4. Forty copies shall be filed, except that a respondent proceeding *in forma pauperis* under Rule 39, including an inmate of an institution, shall file the number of copies required for a petition by such a person under Rule 12.2, together with a motion for leave to proceed *in forma pauperis*, a copy of which shall precede and be attached to each copy of the brief in opposition. If the petitioner is proceeding *in forma pauperis*, the respondent shall prepare its brief in opposition, if any, as required by Rule 33.2, and shall file an original and 10 copies of that brief. Whether prepared under Rule 33.1 or Rule 33.2, the brief in opposition shall comply with the requirements of Rule 24 governing a respondent's brief, except that no summary of the argument is required. A brief in opposition may not be joined with any other pleading, except that any motion for leave to proceed *in forma pauperis* shall be attached. The brief in opposition shall be served as required by Rule 29.

4. No motion by a respondent to dismiss a petition for a writ of certiorari may be filed. Any objections to the jurisdiction of the Court to grant a petition for a writ of certiorari shall be included in the brief in opposition.

5. The Clerk will distribute the petition to the Court for its consideration upon receiving an express waiver of the right to file a brief in opposition, or, if no waiver or brief in opposition is filed, upon the expiration of the time allowed for filing. If a brief in opposition is timely filed, the Clerk will distribute the petition, brief in opposition, and any reply brief to the Court for its consideration no less than 10 days after the brief in opposition is filed.

6. Any petitioner may file a reply brief addressed to new points raised in the brief in opposition, but distribution and consideration by the Court under paragraph 5 of this Rule will not be deferred pending its receipt. Forty copies shall be filed, except that a petitioner proceeding *in forma pauperis* under Rule 39, including an inmate of an institution, shall file the number of copies required for a petition by such a person under Rule 12.2. The reply brief shall be served as required by Rule 29.

7. If a cross-petition for a writ of certiorari has been docketed, distribution of both petitions will be deferred until the cross-petition is due for distribution under this Rule.

8. Any party may file a supplemental brief at any time while a petition for a writ of certiorari is pending, calling attention to new cases, new legislation, or other intervening matter not available at the time of the party's last filing. A supplemental brief shall be restricted to new matter and shall follow, insofar as applicable, the form for a brief in opposition prescribed by this Rule. Forty copies shall be filed, except that a party proceeding *in forma pauperis* under Rule 39, including an inmate of an institution, shall file the number of copies required for a petition by such a person under Rule 12.2. The supplemental brief shall be served as required by Rule 29.

(As amended July 17, 2007, eff. Oct. 1, 2007.)

Rule 16. Disposition of a Petition for a Writ of Certiorari

1. After considering the documents distributed under Rule 15, the Court will enter an appropriate order. The order may be a summary disposition on the merits.

2. Whenever the Court grants a petition for a writ of certiorari, the Clerk will prepare, sign, and enter an order to that effect and will notify forthwith counsel of record and the court whose judgment is to be reviewed. The case then will be scheduled for briefing and oral argument. If the record has not previously been filed in this Court, the Clerk will request the clerk of the court having possession of the record to certify and transmit it. A formal writ will not issue unless specially directed.

3. Whenever the Court denies a petition for a writ of certiorari, the Clerk will prepare, sign, and enter an order to that effect and will notify forthwith counsel of record and the court whose judgment was sought to be reviewed. The order of denial will not be suspended pending disposition of a petition for rehearing except by order of the Court or a Justice.

PART IV. OTHER JURISDICTION

Rule 17. Procedure in an Original Action

1. This Rule applies only to an action invoking the Court's original jurisdiction under Article III of the Constitution of the United States. See also 28 U.S.C. § 1251 and U.S. Const., Amdt. 11. A petition for an extraordinary writ in aid of the Court's appellate jurisdiction shall be filed as provided in Rule 20.

2. The form of pleadings and motions prescribed by the Federal Rules of Civil Procedure is followed. In other respects, those Rules and the Federal Rules of Evidence may be taken as guides.

3. The initial pleading shall be preceded by a motion for leave to file, and may be accompanied by a brief in support of the motion. Forty copies of each document shall be filed, with proof of service. Service shall be as required by Rule 29, except that when an adverse party is a State, service shall be made on both the Governor and the Attorney General of that State.

4. The case will be placed on the docket when the motion for leave to file and the initial pleading are

filed with the Clerk. The Rule 38(a) docket fee shall be paid at that time.

5. No more than 60 days after receiving the motion for leave to file and the initial pleading, an adverse party shall file 40 copies of any brief in opposition to the motion, with proof of service as required by Rule 29. The Clerk will distribute the filed documents to the Court for its consideration upon receiving an express waiver of the right to file a brief in opposition, or, if no waiver or brief is filed, upon the expiration of the time allowed for filing. If a brief in opposition is timely filed, the Clerk will distribute the filed documents to the Court for its consideration no less than 10 days after the brief in opposition is filed. A reply brief may be filed, but consideration of the case will not be deferred pending its receipt. The Court thereafter may grant or deny the motion, set it for oral argument, direct that additional documents be filed, or require that other proceedings be conducted.

6. A summons issued out of this Court shall be served on the defendant 60 days before the return day specified therein. If the defendant does not respond by the return day, the plaintiff may proceed *ex parte.*

7. Process against a State issued out of this Court shall be served on both the Governor and the Attorney General of that State.

Rule 18. Appeal from a United States District Court

1. When a direct appeal from a decision of a United States district court is authorized by law, the appeal is commenced by filing a notice of appeal with the clerk of the district court within the time provided by law after entry of the judgment sought to be reviewed. The time to file may not be extended. The notice of appeal shall specify the parties taking the appeal, designate the judgment, or part thereof, appealed from and the date of its entry, and specify the statute or statutes under which the appeal is taken. A copy of the notice of appeal shall be served on all parties to the proceeding as required by Rule 29, and proof of service shall be filed in the district court together with the notice of appeal.

2. All parties to the proceeding in the district court are deemed parties entitled to file documents in this Court, but a party having no interest in the outcome of the appeal may so notify the Clerk of this Court and shall serve a copy of the notice on all other parties. Parties interested jointly, severally, or otherwise in the judgment may appeal separately, or any two or more may join in an appeal. When two or more judgments involving identical or closely related questions are sought to be reviewed on appeal from the same court, a notice of appeal for each judgment shall be filed with the clerk of the district court, but a single jurisdictional statement covering all the judgments suffices. Parties who file no document will not qualify for any relief from this Court.

3. No more than 60 days after filing the notice of appeal in the district court, the appellant shall file 40 copies of a jurisdictional statement and shall pay the Rule 38 docket fee, except that an appellant proceeding *in forma pauperis* under Rule 39, including an inmate of an institution, shall file the number of copies required for a petition by such a person under Rule 12.2, together with a motion for leave to proceed *in forma pauperis,* a copy of which shall precede and be attached to each copy of the jurisdictional statement. The jurisdictional statement shall follow, insofar as applicable, the form for a petition for a writ of certiorari prescribed by Rule 14, and shall be served as required by Rule 29. The case will then be placed on the docket. It is the appellant's duty to notify all appellees promptly, on a form supplied by the Clerk, of the date of filing, the date the case was placed on the docket, and the docket number of the case. The notice shall be served as required by Rule 29. The appendix shall include a copy of the notice of appeal showing the date it was filed in the district court. For good cause, a Justice may extend the time to file a jurisdictional statement for a period not exceeding 60 days. An application to extend the time to file a jurisdictional statement shall set out the basis for jurisdiction in this Court; identify the judgment sought to be reviewed; include a copy of the opinion, any order respecting rehearing, and the notice of appeal; and set out specific reasons why an extension of time is justified. For the time and manner of presenting the application, see Rules 21, 22, and 30. An application to extend the time to file a jurisdictional statement is not favored.

4. No more than 30 days after a case has been placed on the docket, an appellee seeking to file a conditional cross-appeal (*i.e.,* a cross-appeal that otherwise would be untimely) shall file, with proof of service as required by Rule 29, a jurisdictional statement that complies in all respects (including number of copies filed) with paragraph 3 of this Rule, except that material already reproduced in the appendix to the opening jurisdictional statement need not be reproduced again. A cross-appealing appellee shall pay the Rule 38 docket fee or submit a motion for leave to proceed *in forma pauperis.* The cover of the cross-appeal shall indicate clearly that it is a conditional cross-appeal. The cross-appeal then will be placed on the docket. It is the cross-appellant's duty to notify all cross-appellees promptly, on a form supplied by the Clerk, of the date of filing, the date the cross-appeal was placed on the docket, and the docket number of the cross-appeal. The notice shall be served as required by Rule 29. A cross-appeal may not be joined with any other pleading, except that any

motion for leave to proceed *in forma pauperis* shall be attached. The time to file a cross-appeal will not be extended.

5. After a notice of appeal has been filed in the district court, but before the case is placed on this Court's docket, the parties may dismiss the appeal by stipulation filed in the district court, or the district court may dismiss the appeal on the appellant's motion, with notice to all parties. If a notice of appeal has been filed, but the case has not been placed on this Court's docket within the time prescribed for docketing, the district court may dismiss the appeal on the appellee's motion, with notice to all parties, and may make any just order with respect to costs. If the district court has denied the appellee's motion to dismiss the appeal, the appellee may move this Court to docket and dismiss the appeal by filing an original and 10 copies of a motion presented in conformity with Rules 21 and 33.2. The motion shall be accompanied by proof of service as required by Rule 29, and by a certificate from the clerk of the district court, certifying that a notice of appeal was filed and that the appellee's motion to dismiss was denied. The appellant may not thereafter file a jurisdictional statement without special leave of the Court, and the Court may allow costs against the appellant.

6. Within 30 days after the case is placed on this Court's docket, the appellee may file a motion to dismiss, to affirm, or in the alternative to affirm or dismiss. Forty copies of the motion shall be filed, except that an appellee proceeding *in forma pauperis* under Rule 39, including an inmate of an institution, shall file the number of copies required for a petition by such a person under Rule 12.2, together with a motion for leave to proceed *in forma pauperis,* a copy of which shall precede and be attached to each copy of the motion to dismiss, to affirm, or in the alternative to affirm or dismiss. The motion shall follow, insofar as applicable, the form for a brief in opposition prescribed by Rule 15, and shall comply in all respects with Rule 21.

7. The Clerk will distribute the jurisdictional statement to the Court for its consideration upon receiving an express waiver of the right to file a motion to dismiss or to affirm or, if no waiver or motion is filed, upon the expiration of the time allowed for filing. If a motion to dismiss or to affirm is timely filed, the Clerk will distribute the jurisdictional statement, motion, and any brief opposing the motion to the Court for its consideration no less than 10 days after the motion is filed.

8. Any appellant may file a brief opposing a motion to dismiss or to affirm, but distribution and consideration by the Court under paragraph 7 of this Rule will not be deferred pending its receipt. Forty copies shall be filed, except that an appellant proceeding *in forma pauperis* under Rule 39, including an inmate of an institution, shall file the number of copies required for a petition by such a person under Rule 12.2. The brief shall be served as required by Rule 29.

9. If a cross-appeal has been docketed, distribution of both jurisdictional statements will be deferred until the cross-appeal is due for distribution under this Rule.

10. Any party may file a supplemental brief at any time while a jurisdictional statement is pending, calling attention to new cases, new legislation, or other intervening matter not available at the time of the party's last filing. A supplemental brief shall be restricted to new matter and shall follow, insofar as applicable, the form for a brief in opposition prescribed by Rule 15. Forty copies shall be filed, except that a party proceeding *in forma pauperis* under Rule 39, including an inmate of an institution, shall file the number of copies required for a petition by such a person under Rule 12.2. The supplemental brief shall be served as required by Rule 29.

11. The clerk of the district court shall retain possession of the record until notified by the Clerk of this Court to certify and transmit it. See Rule 12.7.

12. After considering the documents distributed under this Rule, the Court may dispose summarily of the appeal on the merits, note probable jurisdiction, or postpone consideration of jurisdiction until a hearing of the case on the merits. If not disposed of summarily, the case stands for briefing and oral argument on the merits. If consideration of jurisdiction is postponed, counsel, at the outset of their briefs and at oral argument, shall address the question of jurisdiction. If the record has not previously been filed in this Court, the Clerk of this Court will request the clerk of the court in possession of the record to certify and transmit it.

13. If the Clerk determines that a jurisdictional statement submitted timely and in good faith is in a form that does not comply with this Rule or with Rule 33 or Rule 34, the Clerk will return it with a letter indicating the deficiency. If a corrected jurisdictional statement is submitted in accordance with Rule 29.2 no more than 60 days after the date of the Clerk's letter it will be deemed timely.

(As amended July 17, 2007, eff. Oct. 1, 2007.)

Rule 19. Procedure on a Certified Question

1. A United States court of appeals may certify to this Court a question or proposition of law on which it seeks instruction for the proper decision of a case. The certificate shall contain a statement of the nature of the case and the facts on which the question or proposition of law arises. Only questions or propositions of law may be certified, and they shall be stated

separately and with precision. The certificate shall be prepared as required by Rule 33.2 and shall be signed by the clerk of the court of appeals.

2. When a question is certified by a United States court of appeals, this Court, on its own motion or that of a party, may consider and decide the entire matter in controversy. See 28 U.S.C. § 1254(2).

3. When a question is certified, the Clerk will notify the parties and docket the case. Counsel shall then enter their appearances. After docketing, the Clerk will submit the certificate to the Court for a preliminary examination to determine whether the case should be briefed, set for argument, or dismissed. No brief may be filed until the preliminary examination of the certificate is completed.

4. If the Court orders the case briefed or set for argument, the parties will be notified and permitted to file briefs. The Clerk of this Court then will request the clerk of the court in possession of the record to certify and transmit it. Any portion of the record to which the parties wish to direct the Court's particular attention should be printed in a joint appendix, prepared in conformity with Rule 26 by the appellant or petitioner in the court of appeals, but the fact that any part of the record has not been printed does not prevent the parties or the Court from relying on it.

5. A brief on the merits in a case involving a certified question shall comply with Rules 24, 25, and 33.1, except that the brief for the party who is the appellant or petitioner below shall be filed within 45 days of the order requiring briefs or setting the case for argument.

Rule 20. Procedure on a Petition for an Extraordinary Writ

1. Issuance by the Court of an extraordinary writ authorized by 28 U.S.C. § 1651(a) is not a matter of right, but of discretion sparingly exercised. To justify the granting of any such writ, the petition must show that the writ will be in aid of the Court's appellate jurisdiction, that exceptional circumstances warrant the exercise of the Court's discretionary powers, and that adequate relief cannot be obtained in any other form or from any other court.

2. A petition seeking a writ authorized by 28 U.S.C. § 1651(a), § 2241, or § 2254(a) shall be prepared in all respects as required by Rules 33 and 34. The petition shall be captioned "*In re* [name of petitioner]" and shall follow, insofar as applicable, the form of a petition for a writ of certiorari prescribed by Rule 14. All contentions in support of the petition shall be included in the petition. The case will be placed on the docket when 40 copies of the petition are filed with the Clerk and the docket fee is paid, except that a petitioner proceeding *in forma pauperis* under Rule 39, including an inmate of an institution, shall file the number of copies required for a petition by such a person under Rule 12.2, together with a motion for leave to proceed *in forma pauperis*, a copy of which shall precede and be attached to each copy of the petition. The petition shall be served as required by Rule 29 (subject to subparagraph 4(b) of this Rule).

3. **(a)** A petition seeking a writ of prohibition, a writ of mandamus, or both in the alternative shall state the name and office or function of every person against whom relief is sought and shall set out with particularity why the relief sought is not available in any other court. A copy of the judgment with respect to which the writ is sought, including any related opinion, shall be appended to the petition together with any other document essential to understanding the petition.

(b) The petition shall be served on every party to the proceeding with respect to which relief is sought. Within 30 days after the petition is placed on the docket, a party shall file 40 copies of any brief or briefs in opposition thereto, which shall comply fully with Rule 15. If a party named as a respondent does not wish to respond to the petition, that party may so advise the Clerk and all other parties by letter. All persons served are deemed respondents for all purposes in the proceedings in this Court.

4. **(a)** A petition seeking a writ of habeas corpus shall comply with the requirements of 28 U.S.C. §§ 2241 and 2242, and in particular with the provision in the last paragraph of § 2242, which requires a statement of the "reasons for not making application to the district court of the district in which the applicant is held." If the relief sought is from the judgment of a state court, the petition shall set out specifically how and where the petitioner has exhausted available remedies in the state courts or otherwise comes within the provisions of 28 U.S.C. § 2254(b). To justify the granting of a writ of habeas corpus, the petitioner must show that exceptional circumstances warrant the exercise of the Court's discretionary powers, and that adequate relief cannot be obtained in any other form or from any other court. This writ is rarely granted.

(b) Habeas corpus proceedings, except in capital cases, are *ex parte*, unless the Court requires the respondent to show cause why the petition for a writ of habeas corpus should not be granted. A response, if ordered, or in a capital case, shall comply fully with Rule 15. Neither the denial of the petition, without more, nor an order of transfer to a district court under the authority of 28 U.S.C. § 2241(b), is an adjudication on the merits, and therefore does not preclude further application to another court for the relief sought.

5. The Clerk will distribute the documents to the Court for its consideration when a brief in opposition under subparagraph 3(b) of this Rule has been filed,

when a response under subparagraph 4(b) has been ordered and filed, when the time to file has expired, or when the right to file has been expressly waived.

6. If the Court orders the case set for argument, the Clerk will notify the parties whether additional briefs are required, when they shall be filed, and, if the case involves a petition for a common-law writ of certiorari, that the parties shall prepare a joint appendix in accordance with Rule 26.

PART V. MOTIONS AND APPLICATIONS

Rule 21. Motions to the Court

1. Every motion to the Court shall clearly state its purpose and the facts on which it is based and may present legal argument in support thereof. No separate brief may be filed. A motion should be concise and shall comply with any applicable page limits. Rule 22 governs an application addressed to a single Justice.

2. (a) A motion in any action within the Court's original jurisdiction shall comply with Rule 17.3.

(b) A motion to dismiss as moot (or a suggestion of mootness), a motion for leave to file a brief as *amicus curiae*, and any motion the granting of which would dispose of the entire case or would affect the final judgment to be entered (other than a motion to docket and dismiss under Rule 18.5 or a motion for voluntary dismissal under Rule 46) shall be prepared as required by Rule 33.1, and 40 copies shall be filed, except that a movant proceeding *in forma pauperis* under Rule 39, including an inmate of an institution, shall file a motion prepared as required by Rule 33.2, and shall file the number of copies required for a petition by such a person under Rule 12.2. The motion shall be served as required by Rule 29.

(c) Any other motion to the Court shall be prepared as required by Rule 33.2; the moving party shall file an original and 10 copies. The Court subsequently may order the moving party to prepare the motion as required by Rule 33.1; in that event, the party shall file 40 copies.

3. A motion to the Court shall be filed with the Clerk and shall be accompanied by proof of service as required by Rule 29. No motion may be presented in open Court, other than a motion for admission to the Bar, except when the proceeding to which it refers is being argued. Oral argument on a motion will not be permitted unless the Court so directs.

4. Any response to a motion shall be filed as promptly as possible considering the nature of the relief sought and any asserted need for emergency action, and, in any event, within 10 days of receipt, unless the Court or a Justice, or the Clerk under Rule 30.4, orders otherwise. A response to a motion prepared as required by Rule 33.1, except a response to a motion for leave to file an *amicus curiae* brief (see Rule 37.5), shall be prepared in the same manner if time permits. In an appropriate case, the Court may act on a motion without waiting for a response.

Rule 22. Applications to Individual Justices

1. An application addressed to an individual Justice shall be filed with the Clerk, who will transmit it promptly to the Justice concerned if an individual Justice has authority to grant the sought relief.

2. The original and two copies of any application addressed to an individual Justice shall be prepared as required by Rule 33.2, and shall be accompanied by proof of service as required by Rule 29.

3. An application shall be addressed to the Justice allotted to the Circuit from which the case arises. An application arising from the United States Court of Appeals for the Armed Forces shall be addressed to the Chief Justice. When the Circuit Justice is unavailable for any reason, the application addressed to that Justice will be distributed to the Justice then available who is next junior to the Circuit Justice; the turn of the Chief Justice follows that of the most junior Justice.

4. A Justice denying an application will note the denial thereon. Thereafter, unless action thereon is restricted by law to the Circuit Justice or is untimely under Rule 30.2, the party making an application, except in the case of an application for an extension of time, may renew it to any other Justice, subject to the provisions of this Rule. Except when the denial is without prejudice, a renewed application is not favored. Renewed application is made by a letter to the Clerk, designating the Justice to whom the application is to be directed, and accompanied by 10 copies of the original application and proof of service as required by Rule 29.

5. A Justice to whom an application for a stay or for bail is submitted may refer it to the Court for determination.

6. The Clerk will advise all parties concerned, by appropriately speedy means, of the disposition made of an application.

(As amended July 17, 2007, effective Oct. 1, 2007.)

Rule 23. Stays

1. A stay may be granted by a Justice as permitted by law.

2. A party to a judgment sought to be reviewed may present to a Justice an application to stay the enforcement of that judgment. See 28 U.S.C. § 2101(f).

3. An application for a stay shall set out with particularity why the relief sought is not available from any other court or judge. Except in the most extraordinary circumstances, an application for a stay will not be entertained unless the relief requested was first sought in the appropriate court or courts below or from a judge or judges thereof. An application for a stay shall identify the judgment sought to be reviewed and have appended thereto a copy of the order and opinion, if any, and a copy of the order, if any, of the court or judge below denying the relief sought, and shall set out specific reasons why a stay is justified. The form and content of an application for a stay are governed by Rules 22 and 33.2.

4. A judge, court, or Justice granting an application for a stay pending review by this Court may condition the stay on the filing of a supersedeas bond having an approved surety or sureties. The bond will be conditioned on the satisfaction of the judgment in full, together with any costs, interest, and damages for delay that may be awarded. If a part of the judgment sought to be reviewed has already been satisfied, or is otherwise secured, the bond may be conditioned on the satisfaction of the part of the judgment not otherwise secured or satisfied, together with costs, interest, and damages.

PART VI. BRIEFS ON THE MERITS AND ORAL ARGUMENT

Rule 24. Briefs on the Merits: In General

1. A brief on the merits for a petitioner or an appellant shall comply in all respects with Rules 33.1 and 34 and shall contain in the order here indicated:

(a) The questions presented for review under Rule 14.1(a). The questions shall be set out on the first page following the cover, and no other information may appear on that page. The phrasing of the questions presented need not be identical with that in the petition for a writ of certiorari or the jurisdictional statement, but the brief may not raise additional questions or change the substance of the questions already presented in those documents. At its option, however, the Court may consider a plain error not among the questions presented but evident from the record and otherwise within its jurisdiction to decide.

(b) A list of all parties to the proceeding in the court whose judgment is under review (unless the caption of the case in this Court contains the names of all parties). Any amended corporate disclosure statement as required by Rule 29.6 shall be placed here.

(c) If the brief exceeds five pages, a table of contents and a table of cited authorities.

(d) Citations of the official and unofficial reports of the opinions and orders entered in the case by courts and administrative agencies.

(e) A concise statement of the basis for jurisdiction in this Court, including the statutory provisions and time factors on which jurisdiction rests.

(f) The constitutional provisions, treaties, statutes, ordinances, and regulations involved in the case, set out verbatim with appropriate citation. If the provisions involved are lengthy, their citation alone suffices at this point, and their pertinent text, if not already set out in the petition for a writ of certiorari, jurisdictional statement, or an appendix to either document, shall be set out in an appendix to the brief.

(g) A concise statement of the case, setting out the facts material to the consideration of the questions presented, with appropriate references to the joint appendix, *e.g.*, App. 12, or to the record, *e.g.*, Record 12.

(h) A summary of the argument, suitably paragraphed. The summary should be a clear and concise condensation of the argument made in the body of the brief; mere repetition of the headings under which the argument is arranged is not sufficient.

(i) The argument, exhibiting clearly the points of fact and of law presented and citing the authorities and statutes relied on.

(j) A conclusion specifying with particularity the relief the party seeks.

2. A brief on the merits for a respondent or an appellee shall conform to the foregoing requirements, except that items required by subparagraphs 1(a), (b), (d), (e), (f), and (g) of this Rule need not be included unless the respondent or appellee is dissatisfied with their presentation by the opposing party.

3. A brief on the merits may not exceed the word limitations specified in Rule 33.1(g). An appendix to a brief may include only relevant material, and counsel are cautioned not to include in an appendix arguments or citations that properly belong in the body of the brief.

4. A reply brief shall conform to those portions of this Rule applicable to the brief for a respondent or an appellee, but, if appropriately divided by topical headings, need not contain a summary of the argument.

5. A reference to the joint appendix or to the record set out in any brief shall indicate the appropriate page number. If the reference is to an exhibit, the page numbers at which the exhibit appears, at which it was offered in evidence, and at which it was ruled on by the judge shall be indicated, *e.g.*, Pl.Exh. 14, Record 199, 2134.

6. A brief shall be concise, logically arranged with proper headings, and free of irrelevant, immaterial, or scandalous matter. The Court may disregard or strike a brief that does not comply with this paragraph.

(As amended July 17, 2007, eff. Oct. 1, 2007.)

Rule 25. Briefs on the Merits: Number of Copies and Time to File

1. The petitioner or appellant shall file 40 copies of the brief on the merits within 45 days of the order granting the writ of certiorari, noting probable jurisdiction, or postponing consideration of jurisdiction. Any respondent or appellee who supports the petitioner or appellant shall meet the petitioner's or appellant's time schedule for filing documents.

2. The respondent or appellee shall file 40 copies of the brief on the merits within 30 days after the brief for the petitioner or appellant is filed.

3. The petitioner or appellant shall file 40 copies of the reply brief, if any, within 30 days after the brief for the respondent or appellee is filed, but any reply brief must actually be received by the Clerk not later than 2 p.m. one week before the date of oral argument. Any respondent or appellee supporting the petitioner or appellant may file a reply brief.

4. The time periods stated in paragraphs 1, 2, and 3 of this Rule may be extended as provided in Rule 30. An application to extend the time to file a brief on the merits is not favored. If a case is advanced for hearing, the time to file briefs on the merits may be abridged as circumstances require pursuant to an order of the Court on its own motion or that of a party.

5. A party wishing to present late authorities, newly enacted legislation, or other intervening matter that was not available in time to be included in a brief may file 40 copies of a supplemental brief, restricted to such new matter and otherwise presented in conformity with these Rules, up to the time the case is called for oral argument or by leave of the Court thereafter.

6. After a case has been argued or submitted, the Clerk will not file any brief, except that of a party filed by leave of the Court.

7. The Clerk will not file any brief that is not accompanied by proof of service as required by Rule 29.

8. An electronic version of every brief on the merits shall be transmitted to the Clerk of Court and to opposing counsel of record at the time the brief is filed in accordance with guidelines established by the Clerk. The electronic transmission requirement is in addition to the requirement that booklet-format briefs be timely filed.

(As amended Jan. 11, 1999, eff. May 3, 1999; Jan. 27, 2003, eff. May 1, 2003; July 17, 2007, eff. Oct. 1, 2007.)

Rule 26. Joint Appendix

1. Unless the Clerk has allowed the parties to use the deferred method described in paragraph 4 of this Rule, the petitioner or appellant, within 45 days after entry of the order granting the writ of certiorari, noting probable jurisdiction, or postponing consideration of jurisdiction, shall file 40 copies of a joint appendix, prepared as required by Rule 33.1. The joint appendix shall contain: (1) the relevant docket entries in all the courts below; (2) any relevant pleadings, jury instructions, findings, conclusions, or opinions; (3) the judgment, order, or decision under review; and (4) any other parts of the record that the parties particularly wish to bring to the Court's attention. Any of the foregoing items already reproduced in a petition for a writ of certiorari, jurisdictional statement, brief in opposition to a petition for a writ of certiorari, motion to dismiss or affirm, or any appendix to the foregoing, that was prepared as required by Rule 33.1, need not be reproduced again in the joint appendix. The petitioner or appellant shall serve three copies of the joint appendix on each of the other parties to the proceeding as required by Rule 29.

2. The parties are encouraged to agree on the contents of the joint appendix. In the absence of agreement, the petitioner or appellant, within 10 days after entry of the order granting the writ of certiorari, noting probable jurisdiction, or postponing consideration of jurisdiction, shall serve on the respondent or appellee a designation of parts of the record to be included in the joint appendix. Within 10 days after receiving the designation, a respondent or appellee who considers the parts of the record so designated insufficient shall serve on the petitioner or appellant a designation of additional parts to be included in the joint appendix, and the petitioner or appellant shall include the parts so designated. If the Court has permitted the respondent or appellee to proceed *in forma pauperis*, the petitioner or appellant may seek by motion to be excused from printing portions of the record the petitioner or appellant considers unnecessary. In making these designations, counsel should include only those materials the Court should examine; unnecessary designations should be avoided. The record is on file with the Clerk and available to the Justices, and counsel may refer in briefs and in

oral argument to relevant portions of the record not included in the joint appendix.

3. When the joint appendix is filed, the petitioner or appellant immediately shall file with the Clerk a statement of the cost of printing 50 copies and shall serve a copy of the statement on each of the other parties as required by Rule 29. Unless the parties agree otherwise, the cost of producing the joint appendix shall be paid initially by the petitioner or appellant; but a petitioner or appellant who considers that parts of the record designated by the respondent or appellee are unnecessary for the determination of the issues presented may so advise the respondent or appellee, who then shall advance the cost of printing the additional parts, unless the Court or a Justice otherwise fixes the initial allocation of the costs. The cost of printing the joint appendix is taxed as a cost in the case, but if a party unnecessarily causes matter to be included in the joint appendix or prints excessive copies, the Court may impose these costs on that party.

4. (a) On the parties' request, the Clerk may allow preparation of the joint appendix to be deferred until after the briefs have been filed. In that event, the petitioner or appellant shall file the joint appendix no more than 14 days after receiving the brief for the respondent or appellee. The provisions of paragraphs 1, 2, and 3 of this Rule shall be followed, except that the designations referred to therein shall be made by each party when that party's brief is served. Deferral of the joint appendix is not favored.

(b) If the deferred method is used, the briefs on the merits may refer to the pages of the record. In that event, the joint appendix shall include in brackets on each page thereof the page number of the record where that material may be found. A party wishing to refer directly to the pages of the joint appendix may serve and file copies of its brief prepared as required by Rule 33.2 within the time provided by Rule 25, with appropriate references to the pages of the record. In that event, within 10 days after the joint appendix is filed, copies of the brief prepared as required by Rule 33.1 containing references to the pages of the joint appendix in place of, or in addition to, the initial references to the pages of the record, shall be served and filed. No other change may be made in the brief as initially served and filed, except that typographical errors may be corrected.

5. The joint appendix shall be prefaced by a table of contents showing the parts of the record that it contains, in the order in which the parts are set out, with references to the pages of the joint appendix at which each part begins. The relevant docket entries shall be set out after the table of contents, followed by the other parts of the record in chronological order. When testimony contained in the reporter's transcript of proceedings is set out in the joint appendix, the page of the transcript at which the testimony appears shall be indicated in brackets immediately before the statement that is set out. Omissions in the transcript or in any other document printed in the joint appendix shall be indicated by asterisks. Immaterial formal matters (*e.g.*, captions, subscriptions, acknowledgments) shall be omitted. A question and its answer may be contained in a single paragraph.

6. Exhibits designated for inclusion in the joint appendix may be contained in a separate volume or volumes suitably indexed. The transcript of a proceeding before an administrative agency, board, commission, or officer used in an action in a district court or court of appeals is regarded as an exhibit for the purposes of this paragraph.

7. The Court, on its own motion or that of a party, may dispense with the requirement of a joint appendix and may permit a case to be heard on the original record (with such copies of the record, or relevant parts thereof, as the Court may require) or on the appendix used in the court below, if it conforms to the requirements of this Rule.

8. For good cause, the time limits specified in this Rule may be shortened or extended by the Court or a Justice, or by the Clerk under Rule 30.4.

Rule 27. Calendar

1. From time to time, the Clerk will prepare a calendar of cases ready for argument. A case ordinarily will not be called for argument less than two weeks after the brief on the merits for the respondent or appellee is due.

2. The Clerk will advise counsel when they are required to appear for oral argument and will publish a hearing list in advance of each argument session for the convenience of counsel and the information of the public.

3. The Court, on its own motion or that of a party, may order that two or more cases involving the same or related questions be argued together as one case or on such other terms as the Court may prescribe.

Rule 28. Oral Argument

1. Oral argument should emphasize and clarify the written arguments in the briefs on the merits. Counsel should assume that all Justices have read the briefs before oral argument. Oral argument read from a prepared text is not favored.

2. The petitioner or appellant shall open and may conclude the argument. A cross-writ of certiorari or cross-appeal will be argued with the initial writ of certiorari or appeal as one case in the time allowed for that one case, and the Court will advise the parties who shall open and close.

3. Unless the Court directs otherwise, each side is allowed one-half hour for argument. Counsel is not required to use all the allotted time. Any request for additional time to argue shall be presented by motion under Rule 21 in time to be considered at a scheduled Conference prior to the date of oral argument and no later than 7 days after the respondent's or appellee's brief on the merits is filed, and shall set out specifically and concisely why the case cannot be presented within the half-hour limitation. Additional time is rarely accorded.

4. Only one attorney will be heard for each side, except by leave of the Court on motion filed in time to be considered at a scheduled Conference prior to the date of oral argument and no later than 7 days after the respondent's or appellee's brief on the merits is filed. Any request for divided argument shall be presented by motion under Rule 21 and shall set out specifically and concisely why more than one attorney should be allowed to argue. Divided argument is not favored.

5. Regardless of the number of counsel participating in oral argument, counsel making the opening argument shall present the case fairly and completely and not reserve points of substance for rebuttal.

6. Oral argument will not be allowed on behalf of any party for whom a brief has not been filed.

7. By leave of the Court, and subject to paragraph 4 of this Rule, counsel for an *amicus curiae* whose brief has been filed as provided in Rule 37 may argue orally on the side of a party, with the consent of that party. In the absence of consent, counsel for an *amicus curiae* may seek leave of the Court to argue orally by a motion setting out specifically and concisely why oral argument would provide assistance to the Court not otherwise available. Such a motion will be granted only in the most extraordinary circumstances. (As amended July 17, 2007, eff. Oct. 1, 2007.)

PART VII. PRACTICE AND PROCEDURE

Rule 29. Filing and Service of Documents; Special Notifications; Corporate Listing

1. Any document required or permitted to be presented to the Court or to a Justice shall be filed with the Clerk.

2. A document is timely filed if it is received by the Clerk within the time specified for filing; or if it is sent to the Clerk through the United States Postal Service by first-class mail (including express or priority mail), postage prepaid, and bears a postmark, other than a commercial postage meter label, showing that the document was mailed on or before the last day for filing; or if it is delivered on or before the last day for filing to a third-party commercial carrier for delivery to the Clerk within 3 calendar days. If submitted by an inmate confined in an institution, a document is timely filed if it is deposited in the institution's internal mail system on or before the last day for filing and is accompanied by a notarized statement or declaration in compliance with 28 U.S.C. § 1746 setting out the date of deposit and stating that first-class postage has been prepaid. If the postmark is missing or not legible, or if the third-party commercial carrier does not provide the date the document was received by the carrier, the Clerk will require the person who sent the document to submit a notarized statement or declaration in compliance with 28 U.S.C. § 1746 setting out the details of the filing and stating that the filing took place on a particular date within the permitted time.

3. Any document required by these Rules to be served may be served personally, by mail, or by third-party commercial carrier for delivery within 3 calendar days on each party to the proceeding at or before the time of filing. If the document has been prepared as required by Rule 33.1, three copies shall be served on each other party separately represented in the proceeding. If the document has been prepared as required by Rule 33.2, service of a single copy on each other separately represented party suffices. If personal service is made, it shall consist of delivery at the office of the counsel of record, either to counsel or to an employee therein. If service is by mail or third-party commercial carrier, it shall consist of depositing the document with the United States Postal Service, with no less than first-class postage prepaid, or delivery to the carrier for delivery within 3 calendar days, addressed to counsel of record at the proper address. When a party is not represented by counsel, service shall be made on the party, personally, by mail, or by commercial carrier. Ordinarily, service on a party must be by a manner at least as expeditious as the manner used to file the document with the Court.

4. **(a)** If the United States or any federal department, office, agency, officer, or employee is a party to be served, service shall be made on the Solicitor General of the United States, Room 5614, Department of Justice, 950 Pennsylvania Ave., N.W., Washington, DC 20530-0001. When an agency of the United States that is a party is authorized by law to appear before this Court on its own behalf, or when an officer or employee of the United States is a party, the agency, officer, or employee shall be served in addition to the Solicitor General.

(b) In any proceeding in this Court in which the constitutionality of an Act of Congress is drawn into question, and neither the United States nor any federal department, office, agency, officer, or employee is a party, the initial document filed in this Court shall recite that 28 U.S.C. § 2403(a) may apply and shall be served on the Solicitor General of the United States, Room 5614, Department of Justice, 950 Pennsylvania Ave., N.W., Washington, DC 20530-0001. In such a proceeding from any court of the United States, as defined by 28 U.S.C. § 451, the initial document also shall state whether that court, pursuant to 28 U.S.C. § 2403(a), certified to the Attorney General the fact that the constitutionality of an Act of Congress was drawn into question. See Rule 14.1(e)(v).

(c) In any proceeding in this Court in which the constitutionality of any statute of a State is drawn into question, and neither the State nor any agency, officer, or employee thereof is a party, the initial document filed in this Court shall recite that 28 U.S.C. § 2403(b) may apply and shall be served on the Attorney General of that State. In such a proceeding from any court of the United States, as defined by 28 U.S.C. § 451, the initial document also shall state whether that court, pursuant to 28 U.S.C. § 2403(b), certified to the State Attorney General the fact that the constitutionality of a statute of that State was drawn into question. See Rule 14.1(e)(v).

5. Proof of service, when required by these Rules, shall accompany the document when it is presented to the Clerk for filing and shall be separate from it. Proof of service shall contain, or be accompanied by, a statement that all parties required to be served have been served, together with a list of the names, addresses, and telephone numbers of counsel indicating the name of the party or parties each counsel represents. It is not necessary that service on each party required to be served be made in the same manner or evidenced by the same proof. Proof of service may consist of any one of the following:

(a) an acknowledgment of service, signed by counsel of record for the party served, and bearing the address and telephone number of such counsel;

(b) a certificate of service, reciting the facts and circumstances of service in compliance with the appropriate paragraph or paragraphs of this Rule, and signed by a member of the Bar of this Court representing the party on whose behalf service is made or by an attorney appointed to represent that party under the Criminal Justice Act of 1964, see 18 U.S.C. § 3006A(d)(6), or under any other applicable federal statute; or

(c) a notarized affidavit or declaration in compliance with 28 U.S.C. § 1746, reciting the facts and circumstances of service in accordance with the appropriate paragraph or paragraphs of this Rule, whenever service is made by any person not a member of the Bar of this Court and not an attorney appointed to represent a party under the Criminal Justice Act of 1964, see 18 U.S.C. § 3006A(d)(6), or under any other applicable federal statute.

6. Every document, except a joint appendix or *amicus curiae* brief, filed by or on behalf of a nongovernmental corporation shall contain a corporate disclosure statement identifying the parent corporations and listing any publicly held company that owns 10% or more of the corporation's stock. If there is no parent or publicly held company owning 10% or more of the corporation's stock, a notation to this effect shall be included in the document. If a statement has been included in a document filed earlier in the case, reference may be made to the earlier document (except when the earlier statement appeared in a document prepared under Rule 33.2), and only amendments to the statement to make it current need be included in the document being filed.

(As amended Jan. 11, 1999, eff. May 3, 1999; Jan. 27, 2003, eff. May 1, 2003.)

Rule 30. Computation and Extension of Time

1. In the computation of any period of time prescribed or allowed by these Rules, by order of the Court, or by an applicable statute, the day of the act, event, or default from which the designated period begins to run is not included. The last day of the period shall be included, unless it is a Saturday, Sunday, federal legal holiday listed in 5 U.S.C. § 6103, or day on which the Court building is closed by order of the Court or the Chief Justice, in which event the period shall extend until the end of the next day that is not a Saturday, Sunday, federal legal holiday, or day on which the Court building is closed.

2. Whenever a Justice or the Clerk is empowered by law or these Rules to extend the time to file any document, an application seeking an extension shall be filed within the period sought to be extended. An application to extend the time to file a petition for a writ of certiorari or to file a jurisdictional statement must be filed at least 10 days before the specified final filing date as computed under these Rules; if filed less than 10 days before the final filing date, such application will not be granted except in the most extraordinary circumstances.

3. An application to extend the time to file a petition for a writ of certiorari, to file a jurisdictional statement, to file a reply brief on the merits, or to file a petition for rehearing shall be made to an individual Justice and presented and served on all other parties as provided by Rule 22. Once denied, such an application may not be renewed.

4. An application to extend the time to file any document or paper other than those specified in paragraph 3 of this Rule may be presented in the form of a letter to the Clerk setting out specific reasons why an extension of time is justified. The letter shall be served on all other parties as required by Rule 29. The application may be acted on by the Clerk in the first instance, and any party aggrieved by the Clerk's action may request that the application be submitted to a Justice or to the Court. The Clerk will report action under this paragraph to the Court as instructed.

(As amended Jan. 27, 2003, eff. May 1, 2003.)

Rule 31. Translations

Whenever any record to be transmitted to this Court contains material written in a foreign language without a translation made under the authority of the lower court, or admitted to be correct, the clerk of the court transmitting the record shall advise the Clerk of this Court immediately so that this Court may order that a translation be supplied and, if necessary, printed as part of the joint appendix.

Rule 32. Models, Diagrams, Exhibits, and Lodgings

1. Models, diagrams, and exhibits of material forming part of the evidence taken in a case and brought to this Court for its inspection shall be placed in the custody of the Clerk at least two weeks before the case is to be heard or submitted.

2. All models, diagrams, exhibits, and other items placed in the custody of the Clerk shall be removed by the parties no more than 40 days after the case is decided. If this is not done, the Clerk will notify counsel to remove the articles forthwith. If they are not removed within a reasonable time thereafter, the Clerk will destroy them or dispose of them in any other appropriate way.

3. Any party or *amicus curiae* desiring to lodge non-record material with the Clerk must set out in a letter, served on all parties, a description of the material proposed for lodging and the reasons why the non-record material may properly be considered by the Court. The material proposed for lodging may not be submitted until and unless requested by the Clerk.

(As amended Jan. 11, 1999, eff. May 3, 1999; Jan. 27, 2003, eff. May 1, 2003.)

Rule 33. Document Preparation: Booklet Format; 8½- by 11-inch Paper Format

1. **Booklet Format: (a)** Except for a document expressly permitted by these Rules to be submitted on 8½- by 11-inch paper, see, e.g., Rules 21, 22, and 39, every document filed with the Court shall be prepared in a 6⅛- by 9¼-inch booklet format using a standard typesetting process (e.g., hot metal, photocomposition, or computer typesetting) to produce text printed in typographic (as opposed to typewriter) characters. The process used must produce a clear, black image on white paper. The text must be reproduced with a clarity that equals or exceeds the output of a laser printer.

(b) The text of every booklet-format document, including any appendix thereto, shall be typeset in a Century family (e.g., Century Expanded, New Century Schoolbook, or Century Schoolbook) 12-point type with 2-point or more leading between lines. Quotations in excess of 50 words shall be indented. The typeface of footnotes shall be 10-point type with 2-point or more leading between lines. The text of the document must appear on both sides of the page.

(c) Every booklet-format document shall be produced on paper that is opaque, unglazed, and not less than 60 pounds in weight, and shall have margins of at least three-fourths of an inch on all sides. The text field, including footnotes, may not exceed 4⅛ by 7⅛ inches. The document shall be bound firmly in at least two places along the left margin (saddle stitch or perfect binding preferred) so as to permit easy opening, and no part of the text should be obscured by the binding. Spiral, plastic, metal, or string bindings may not be used. Copies of patent documents, except opinions, may be duplicated in such size as is necessary in a separate appendix.

(d) Every booklet-format document shall comply with the word limits shown on the chart in subparagraph 1(g) of this Rule. The word limits do not include the questions presented, the list of parties and the corporate disclosure statement, the table of contents, the table of cited authorities, the listing of counsel at the end of the document, or any appendix. The word limits include footnotes. Verbatim quotations required under Rule 14.1(f), if set out in the text of a brief rather than in the appendix, are also excluded. For good cause, the Court or a Justice may grant leave to file a document in excess of the word limits, but application for such leave is not favored. An application to exceed word limits shall comply with Rule 22 and must be received by the Clerk at least 15 days before the filing date of the document in question, except in the most extraordinary circumstances.

(e) Every booklet-format document shall have a suitable cover consisting of 65-pound weight paper in the color indicated on the chart in subparagraph 1(g) of this Rule. If a separate appendix to any document is filed, the color of its cover shall be the same as that of the cover of the document it supports. The Clerk will furnish a color chart upon request. Counsel shall ensure that there is adequate contrast between the printing and the color of the cover. A document filed by the United States, or by any other federal party represented by the Solicitor General, shall have a gray cover. A joint appendix, answer to a bill of complaint, motion for leave to intervene, and any other document not listed in subparagraph 1(g) of this Rule shall have a tan cover.

(f) Forty copies of a booklet-format document shall be filed.

(g) Word limits and cover colors for booklet-format documents are as follows:

	Type of Document	Word Limits	Color of Cover
(i)	Petition for a Writ of Certiorari (Rule 14); Motion for Leave to File a Bill of Complaint and Brief in Support (Rule 17.3); Jurisdictional Statement (Rule 18.3); Petition for an Extraordinary Writ (Rule 20.2)	9,000	white
(ii)	Brief in Opposition (Rule 15.3); Brief in Opposition to Motion for Leave to File an Original Action (Rule 17.5); Motion to Dismiss or Affirm (Rule 18.6); Brief in Opposition to Mandamus or Prohibition (Rule 20.3(b)); Response to a Petition for Habeas Corpus (Rule 20.4)	9,000	orange
(iii)	Reply to Brief in Opposition (Rules 15.6 and 17.5); Brief Opposing a Motion to Dismiss or Affirm (Rule 18.8)	3,000	tan
(iv)	Supplemental Brief (Rules 15.8, 17, 18.10, and 25.5)	3,000	tan
(v)	Brief on the Merits for Petitioner or Appellant (Rule 24); Exceptions by Plaintiff to Report of Special Master (Rule 17)	15,000	light blue
(vi)	Brief on the Merits for Respondent or Appellee (Rule 24.2); Brief on the Merits for Respondent or Appellee Supporting Petitioner or Appellant (Rule 12.6); Exceptions by Party Other Than Plaintiff to Report of Special Master (Rule 17)	15,000	light red
(vii)	Reply Brief on the Merits (Rule 24.4)	7,500	yellow
(viii)	Reply to Plaintiff's Exceptions to Report of Special Master (Rule 17)	15,000	orange
(ix)	Reply to Exceptions by Party Other Than Plaintiff to Report of Special Master (Rule 17)	15,000	yellow
(x)	Brief for an Amicus Curiae at the Petition Stage or pertaining to a Motion for Leave to file a Bill of Complaint (Rule 37.2)	6,000	cream
(xi)	Brief for an Amicus Curiae in Support of the Plaintiff, Petitioner, or Appellant, or in Support of Neither Party, on the Merits or in an Original Action at the Exceptions Stage (Rule 37.3)	9,000	light green
(xii)	Brief for an Amicus Curiae in Support of the Defendant, Respondent, or Appellee, on the Merits or in an Original Action at the Exceptions Stage (Rule 37.3)	9,000	dark green
(xiii)	Petition for Rehearing (Rule 44)	3,000	tan

(h) A document prepared under Rule 33.1 must be accompanied by a certificate signed by the attorney, the unrepresented party, or the preparer of the document stating that the brief complies with the word limitations. The person preparing the certificate may rely on the word count of the word-processing system used to prepare the document. The word-processing system must be set to include footnotes in the word count. The certificate must state the number of words in the document. The certificate shall accompany the document when it is presented to the Clerk for filing and shall be separate from it. If the certificate is signed by a person other than a member of the Bar of this Court, the counsel of record, or the unrepresented party, it must contain a notarized affidavit or declaration in compliance with 28 U.S.C. § 1746.

2. 8½– by 11–Inch Paper Format: (a) The text of every document, including any appendix thereto, expressly permitted by these Rules to be presented to the Court on 8½– by 11–inch paper shall appear double spaced, except for indented quotations, which shall be single spaced, on opaque, unglazed, white paper. The document shall be stapled or bound at the upper left-hand corner. Copies, if required, shall be produced on the same type of paper and shall be legible. The original of any such document (except a motion to dismiss or affirm under Rule 18.6) shall be signed by the party proceeding pro se or by counsel of record who must be a member of the Bar of this Court or an attorney appointed under the Criminal Justice Act of 1964, see 18 U.S.C. § 3006A(d)(6), or under any other applicable federal statute. Subparagraph 1(g) of this Rule does not apply to documents prepared under this paragraph.

(b) Page limits for documents presented on 8½– by 11–inch paper are: 40 pages for a petition for a writ of certiorari, jurisdictional statement, petition for an extraordinary writ, brief in opposition, or motion to dismiss or affirm; and 15 pages for a reply to a brief in opposition, brief opposing a motion to dismiss or affirm, supplemental brief, or petition for rehearing.

The exclusions specified in subparagraph 1(d) of this Rule apply.

(As amended Jan. 11, 1999, eff. May 3, 1999; July 17, 2007, eff. Oct. 1, 2007.)

Rule 34. Document Preparation: General Requirements

Every document, whether prepared under Rule 33.1 or Rule 33.2, shall comply with the following provisions:

1. Each document shall bear on its cover, in the order indicated, from the top of the page:

(a) the docket number of the case or, if there is none, a space for one;

(b) the name of this Court;

(c) the caption of the case as appropriate in this Court;

(d) the nature of the proceeding and the name of the court from which the action is brought (*e.g.*, "On Petition for Writ of Certiorari to the United States Court of Appeals for the Fifth Circuit"; or, for a merits brief, "On Writ of Certiorari to the United States Court of Appeals for the Fifth Circuit");

(e) the title of the document (*e.g.*, "Petition for Writ of Certiorari," "Brief for Respondent," "Joint Appendix");

(f) the name of the attorney who is counsel of record for the party concerned (who must be a member of the Bar of this Court except as provided in Rule 9.1), and on whom service is to be made, with a notation directly thereunder identifying the attorney as counsel of record and setting out counsel's office address and telephone number. Only one counsel of record may be noted on a single document. The names of other members of the Bar of this Court or of the bar of the highest court of a State acting as counsel, and, if desired, their addresses, may be added, but counsel of record shall be clearly identified. Names of persons other than attorneys admitted to a state bar may not be listed, unless the party is appearing *pro se*, in which case the party's name, address, and telephone number shall appear. The foregoing shall be displayed in an appropriate typographical manner and, except for the identification of counsel, may not be set in type smaller than standard 11–point, if the document is prepared as required by Rule 33.1.

2. Every document exceeding five pages (other than a joint appendix), whether prepared under Rule 33.1 or Rule 33.2, shall contain a table of contents and a table of cited authorities (*i.e.*, cases alphabetically arranged, constitutional provisions, statutes, treatises, and other materials) with references to the pages in the document where such authorities are cited.

3. The body of every document shall bear at its close the name of counsel of record and such other counsel, identified on the cover of the document in conformity with subparagraph 1(f) of this Rule, as may be desired.

(As amended Jan. 11, 1999, eff. May 3, 1999; July 17, 2007, eff. Oct. 1, 2007.)

Rule 35. Death, Substitution, and Revivor; Public Officers

1. If a party dies after the filing of a petition for a writ of certiorari to this Court, or after the filing of a notice of appeal, the authorized representative of the deceased party may appear and, on motion, be substituted as a party. If the representative does not voluntarily become a party, any other party may suggest the death on the record and, on motion, seek an order requiring the representative to become a party within a designated time. If the representative then fails to become a party, the party so moving, if a respondent or appellee, is entitled to have the petition for a writ of certiorari or the appeal dismissed, and if a petitioner or appellant, is entitled to proceed as in any other case of nonappearance by a respondent or appellee. If the substitution of a representative of the deceased is not made within six months after the death of the party, the case shall abate.

2. Whenever a case cannot be revived in the court whose judgment is sought to be reviewed, because the deceased party's authorized representative is not subject to that court's jurisdiction, proceedings will be conducted as this Court may direct.

3. When a public officer who is a party to a proceeding in this Court in an official capacity dies, resigns, or otherwise ceases to hold office, the action does not abate and any successor in office is automatically substituted as a party. The parties shall notify the Clerk in writing of any such successions. Proceedings following the substitution shall be in the name of the substituted party, but any misnomer not affecting substantial rights of the parties will be disregarded.

4. A public officer who is a party to a proceeding in this Court in an official capacity may be described as a party by the officer's official title rather than by name, but the Court may require the name to be added.

(As amended Jan. 11, 1999, eff. May 3, 1999.)

Rule 36. Custody of Prisoners in Habeas Corpus Proceedings

1. Pending review in this Court of a decision in a habeas corpus proceeding commenced before a court, Justice, or judge of the United States, the person having custody of the prisoner may not transfer custody to another person unless the transfer is authorized under this Rule.

2. Upon application by a custodian, the court, Justice, or judge who entered the decision under review may authorize transfer and the substitution of a successor custodian as a party.

3. (a) Pending review of a decision failing or refusing to release a prisoner, the prisoner may be detained in the custody from which release is sought or in other appropriate custody or may be enlarged on personal recognizance or bail, as may appear appropriate to the court, Justice, or judge who entered the decision, or to the court of appeals, this Court, or a judge or Justice of either court.

(b) Pending review of a decision ordering release, the prisoner shall be enlarged on personal recognizance or bail, unless the court, Justice, or judge who entered the decision, or the court of appeals, this Court, or a judge or Justice of either court, orders otherwise.

4. An initial order respecting the custody or enlargement of the prisoner, and any recognizance or surety taken, shall continue in effect pending review in the court of appeals and in this Court unless for reasons shown to the court of appeals, this Court, or a judge or Justice of either court, the order is modified or an independent order respecting custody, enlargement, or surety is entered.

Rule 37. Brief for an Amicus Curiae

1. An *amicus curiae* brief that brings to the attention of the Court relevant matter not already brought to its attention by the parties may be of considerable help to the Court. An *amicus curiae* brief that does not serve this purpose burdens the Court, and its filing is not favored.

2. (a) An *amicus curiae* brief submitted before the Court's consideration of a petition for a writ of certiorari, motion for leave to file a bill of complaint, jurisdictional statement, or petition for an extraordinary writ, may be filed if accompanied by the written consent of all parties, or if the Court grants leave to file under subparagraph 2(b) of this Rule. An *amicus curiae* brief in support of a petitioner or appellant shall be filed within 30 days after the case is placed on the docket or a response is called for by the Court, whichever is later, and that time will not be extended. An *amicus curiae* brief in support of a motion of a plaintiff for leave to file a bill of complaint in an original action shall be filed within 60 days after the case is placed on the docket, and that time will not be extended. An *amicus curiae* brief in support of a respondent, an appellee, or a defendant shall be submitted within the time allowed for filing a brief in opposition or a motion to dismiss or affirm. An *amicus curiae* shall ensure that the counsel of record for all parties receive notice of its intention to file an *amicus curiae* brief at least 10 days prior to the due date for the *amicus curiae* brief, unless the *amicus curiae* brief is filed earlier than 10 days before the due date. Only one signatory to any *amicus curiae* brief filed jointly by more than one *amicus curiae* must timely notify the parties of its intent to file that brief. The *amicus curiae* brief shall indicate that counsel of record received timely notice of the intent to file the brief under this Rule and shall specify whether consent was granted, and its cover shall identify the party supported.

(b) When a party to the case has withheld consent, a motion for leave to file an *amicus curiae* brief before the Court's consideration of a petition for a writ of certiorari, motion for leave to file a bill of complaint, jurisdictional statement, or petition for an extraordinary writ may be presented to the Court. The motion, prepared as required by Rule 33.1 and as one document with the brief sought to be filed, shall be submitted within the time allowed for filing an *amicus curiae* brief, and shall indicate the party or parties who have withheld consent and state the nature of the movant's interest. Such a motion is not favored.

3. (a) An *amicus curiae* brief in a case before the Court for oral argument may be filed if accompanied by the written consent of all parties, or if the Court grants leave to file under subparagraph 3(b) of this Rule. The brief shall be submitted within 7 days after the brief for the party supported is filed, or if in support of neither party, within 7 days after the time allowed for filing the petitioner's or appellant's brief. An electronic version of every *amicus curiae* brief in a case before the Court for oral argument shall be transmitted to the Clerk of Court and to counsel for the parties at the time the brief is filed in accordance with guidelines established by the Clerk. The electronic transmission requirement is in addition to the requirement that booklet-format briefs be timely filed. The *amicus curiae* brief shall specify whether consent was granted, and its cover shall identify the party supported or indicate whether it suggests affirmance or reversal. The Clerk will not file a reply brief for an *amicus curiae,* or a brief for an *amicus curiae* in support of, or in opposition to, a petition for rehearing.

(b) When a party to a case before the Court for oral argument has withheld consent, a motion for leave to file an *amicus curiae* brief may be presented to the Court. The motion, prepared as required by Rule 33.1 and as one document with the brief sought to be filed, shall be submitted within the time allowed for filing an *amicus curiae* brief, and shall indicate the party or parties who have withheld consent and state the nature of the movant's interest.

4. No motion for leave to file an *amicus curiae* brief is necessary if the brief is presented on behalf of the United States by the Solicitor General; on behalf of any agency of the United States allowed by law to appear before this Court when submitted by the agency's authorized legal representative; on behalf of a State, Commonwealth, Territory, or Possession when submitted by its Attorney General; or on behalf of a city, county, town, or similar entity when submitted by its authorized law officer.

5. A brief or motion filed under this Rule shall be accompanied by proof of service as required by Rule 29, and shall comply with the applicable provisions of Rules 21, 24, and 33.1 (except that it suffices to set out in the brief the interest of the *amicus curiae*, the summary of the argument, the argument, and the conclusion). A motion for leave to file may not exceed 1,500 words. A party served with the motion may file an objection thereto, stating concisely the reasons for withholding consent; the objection shall be prepared as required by Rule 33.2.

6. Except for briefs presented on behalf of *amicus curiae* listed in Rule 37.4, a brief filed under this Rule shall indicate whether counsel for a party authored the brief in whole or in part and whether such counsel or a party made a monetary contribution intended to fund the preparation or submission of the brief, and shall identify every person other than the *amicus curiae*, its members, or its counsel, who made such a monetary contribution. The disclosure shall be made in the first footnote on the first page of text.

(As amended July 17, 2007, eff. Oct. 1, 2007.)

Rule 38. Fees

Under 28 U.S.C. § 1911, the fees charged by the Clerk are:

(a) for docketing a case on a petition for a writ of certiorari or on appeal or for docketing any other proceeding, except a certified question or a motion to docket and dismiss an appeal under Rule 18.5, $300;

(b) for filing a petition for rehearing or a motion for leave to file a petition for rehearing, $200;

(c) for reproducing and certifying any record or paper, $1 per page; and for comparing with the original thereof any photographic reproduction of any record or paper, when furnished by the person requesting its certification, $.50 per page;

(d) for a certificate bearing the seal of the Court, $10; and

(e) for a check paid to the Court, Clerk, or Marshal that is returned for lack of funds, $35.

Rule 39. Proceedings *In Forma Pauperis*

1. A party seeking to proceed *in forma pauperis* shall file a motion for leave to do so, together with the party's notarized affidavit or declaration (in compliance with 28 U.S.C. § 1746) in the form prescribed by the Federal Rules of Appellate Procedure, Form 4. The motion shall state whether leave to proceed *in forma pauperis* was sought in any other court and, if so, whether leave was granted. If the United States district court or the United States court of appeals has appointed counsel under the Criminal Justice Act of 1964, 18 U.S.C. § 3006A, or under any other applicable federal statute, no affidavit or declaration is required, but the motion shall cite the statute under which counsel was appointed.

2. If leave to proceed *in forma pauperis* is sought for the purpose of filing a document, the motion, and an affidavit or declaration if required, shall be filed together with that document and shall comply in every respect with Rule 21. As provided in that Rule, it suffices to file an original and 10 copies, unless the party is an inmate confined in an institution and is not represented by counsel, in which case the original, alone, suffices. A copy of the motion, and affidavit or declaration if required, shall precede and be attached to each copy of the accompanying document.

3. Except when these Rules expressly provide that a document shall be prepared as required by Rule 33.1, every document presented by a party proceeding under this Rule shall be prepared as required by Rule 33.2 (unless such preparation is impossible). Every document shall be legible. While making due allowance for any case presented under this Rule by a person appearing *pro se*, the Clerk will not file any document if it does not comply with the substance of these Rules or is jurisdictionally out of time.

4. When the documents required by paragraphs 1 and 2 of this Rule are presented to the Clerk, accompanied by proof of service as required by Rule 29, they will be placed on the docket without the payment of a docket fee or any other fee.

5. The respondent or appellee in a case filed *in forma pauperis* shall respond in the same manner and within the same time as in any other case of the same nature, except that the filing of an original and 10 copies of a response prepared as required by Rule 33.2, with proof of service as required by Rule 29, suffices. The respondent or appellee may challenge the grounds for the motion for leave to proceed *in forma pauperis* in a separate document or in the response itself.

6. Whenever the Court appoints counsel for an indigent party in a case set for oral argument, the briefs on the merits submitted by that counsel, unless otherwise requested, shall be prepared under the Clerk's supervision. The Clerk also will reimburse appointed counsel for any necessary travel expenses to Washington, D.C., and return in connection with the argument.

7. In a case in which certiorari has been granted, probable jurisdiction noted, or consideration of jurisdiction postponed, this Court may appoint counsel to represent a party financially unable to afford an attorney to the extent authorized by the Criminal Justice Act of 1964, 18 U.S.C. § 3006A, or by any other applicable federal statute.

8. If satisfied that a petition for a writ of certiorari, jurisdictional statement, or petition for an extraordinary writ is frivolous or malicious, the Court may deny leave to proceed *in forma pauperis.*

(As amended Jan. 27, 2003, eff. May 1, 2003.)

Rule 40. Veterans, Seamen, and Military Cases

1. A veteran suing under any provision of law exempting veterans from the payment of fees or court costs, may proceed without prepayment of fees or costs or furnishing security therefor and may file a motion for leave to proceed on papers prepared as required by Rule 33.2. The motion shall ask leave to proceed as a veteran and be accompanied by an affidavit or declaration setting out the moving party's veteran status. A copy of the motion shall precede and be attached to each copy of the petition for a writ of certiorari or other substantive document filed by the veteran.

2. A seaman suing under 28 U.S.C. § 1916 may proceed without prepayment of fees or costs or furnishing security therefor and may file a motion for leave to proceed on papers prepared as required by Rule 33.2. The motion shall ask leave to proceed as a seaman and be accompanied by an affidavit or declaration setting out the moving party's seaman status. A copy of the motion shall precede and be attached to each copy of the petition for a writ of certiorari or other substantive document filed by the seaman.

3. An accused person petitioning for a writ of certiorari to review a decision of the United States Court of Appeals for the Armed Forces under 28 U.S.C. § 1259 may proceed without prepayment of fees or costs or furnishing security therefor and without filing an affidavit of indigency, but is not entitled to proceed on papers prepared as required by Rule 33.2, except as authorized by the Court on separate motion under Rule 39.

(As amended July 17, 2007, eff. Oct. 1, 2007.)

PART VIII. DISPOSITION OF CASES

Rule 41. Opinions of the Court

Opinions of the Court will be released by the Clerk immediately upon their announcement from the bench, or as the Court otherwise directs. Thereafter, the Clerk will cause the opinions to be issued in slip form, and the Reporter of Decisions will prepare them for publication in the preliminary prints and bound volumes of the United States Reports.

Rule 42. Interest and Damages

1. If a judgment for money in a civil case is affirmed, any interest allowed by law is payable from the date the judgment under review was entered. If a judgment is modified or reversed with a direction that a judgment for money be entered below, the mandate will contain instructions with respect to the allowance of interest. Interest in cases arising in a state court is allowed at the same rate that similar judgments bear interest in the courts of the State in which judgment is directed to be entered. Interest in cases arising in a court of the United States is allowed at the interest rate authorized by law.

2. When a petition for a writ of certiorari, an appeal, or an application for other relief is frivolous, the Court may award the respondent or appellee just damages, and single or double costs under Rule 43. Damages or costs may be awarded against the petitioner, appellant, or applicant, against the party's counsel, or against both party and counsel.

Rule 43. Costs

1. If the Court affirms a judgment, the petitioner or appellant shall pay costs unless the Court otherwise orders.

2. If the Court reverses or vacates a judgment, the respondent or appellee shall pay costs unless the Court otherwise orders.

3. The Clerk's fees and the cost of printing the joint appendix are the only taxable items in this Court. The cost of the transcript of the record from the court below is also a taxable item, but shall be taxable in that court as costs in the case. The expenses of printing briefs, motions, petitions, or jurisdictional statements are not taxable.

4. In a case involving a certified question, costs are equally divided unless the Court otherwise orders, except that if the Court decides the whole matter in controversy, as permitted by Rule 19.2, costs are allowed as provided in paragraphs 1 and 2 of this Rule.

5. To the extent permitted by 28 U.S.C. § 2412, costs under this Rule are allowed for or against the United States or an officer or agent thereof, unless expressly waived or unless the Court otherwise orders.

6. When costs are allowed in this Court, the Clerk will insert an itemization of the costs in the body of

the mandate or judgment sent to the court below. The prevailing side may not submit a bill of costs.

7. In extraordinary circumstances the Court may adjudge double costs.

Rule 44. Rehearing

1. Any petition for the rehearing of any judgment or decision of the Court on the merits shall be filed within 25 days after entry of the judgment or decision, unless the Court or a Justice shortens or extends the time. The petitioner shall file 40 copies of the rehearing petition and shall pay the filing fee prescribed by Rule 38(b), except that a petitioner proceeding *in forma pauperis* under Rule 39, including an inmate of an institution, shall file the number of copies required for a petition by such a person under Rule 12.2. The petition shall state its grounds briefly and distinctly and shall be served as required by Rule 29. The petition shall be presented together with certification of counsel (or of a party unrepresented by counsel) that it is presented in good faith and not for delay; one copy of the certificate shall bear the signature of counsel (or of a party unrepresented by counsel). A copy of the certificate shall follow and be attached to each copy of the petition. A petition for rehearing is not subject to oral argument and will not be granted except by a majority of the Court, at the instance of a Justice who concurred in the judgment or decision.

2. Any petition for the rehearing of an order denying a petition for a writ of certiorari or extraordinary writ shall be filed within 25 days after the date of the order of denial and shall comply with all the form and filing requirements of paragraph 1 of this Rule, including the payment of the filing fee if required, but its grounds shall be limited to intervening circumstances of a substantial or controlling effect or to other substantial grounds not previously presented. The petition shall be presented together with certification of counsel (or of a party unrepresented by counsel) that it is restricted to the grounds specified in this paragraph and that it is presented in good faith and not for delay; one copy of the certificate shall bear the signature of counsel (or of a party unrepresented by counsel). The certificate shall be bound with each copy of the petition. The Clerk will not file a petition without a certificate. The petition is not subject to oral argument.

3. The Clerk will not file any response to a petition for rehearing unless the Court requests a response. In the absence of extraordinary circumstances, the Court will not grant a petition for rehearing without first requesting a response.

4. The Clerk will not file consecutive petitions and petitions that are out of time under this Rule.

5. The Clerk will not file any brief for an *amicus curiae* in support of, or in opposition to, a petition for rehearing.

6. If the Clerk determines that a petition for rehearing submitted timely and in good faith is in a form that does not comply with this Rule or with Rule 33 or Rule 34, the Clerk will return it with a letter indicating the deficiency. A corrected petition for rehearing submitted in accordance with Rule 29.2 no more than 15 days after the date of the Clerk's letter will be deemed timely.

(As amended Jan. 11, 1999, eff. May 3, 1999; Jan. 27, 2003, eff. May 1, 2003; July 17, 2007, eff. Oct. 1, 2007.)

Rule 45. Process; Mandates

1. All process of this Court issues in the name of the President of the United States.

2. In a case on review from a state court, the mandate issues 25 days after entry of the judgment, unless the Court or a Justice shortens or extends the time, or unless the parties stipulate that it issue sooner. The filing of a petition for rehearing stays the mandate until disposition of the petition, unless the Court orders otherwise. If the petition is denied, the mandate issues forthwith.

3. In a case on review from any court of the United States, as defined by 28 U.S.C. § 451, a formal mandate does not issue unless specially directed; instead, the Clerk of this Court will send the clerk of the lower court a copy of the opinion or order of this Court and a certified copy of the judgment. The certified copy of the judgment, prepared and signed by this Court's Clerk, will provide for costs if any are awarded. In all other respects, the provisions of paragraph 2 of this Rule apply.

Rule 46. Dismissing Cases

1. At any stage of the proceedings, whenever all parties file with the Clerk an agreement in writing that a case be dismissed, specifying the terms for payment of costs, and pay to the Clerk any fees then due, the Clerk, without further reference to the Court, will enter an order of dismissal.

2. **(a)** A petitioner or appellant may file a motion to dismiss the case, with proof of service as required by Rule 29, tendering to the Clerk any fees due and costs payable. No more than 15 days after service thereof, an adverse party may file an objection, limited to the amount of damages and costs in this Court alleged to be payable or to showing that the moving party does not represent all petitioners or appellants. The Clerk will not file any objection not so limited.

(b) When the objection asserts that the moving party does not represent all the petitioners or appellants, the party moving for dismissal may file a reply within 10 days, after which time the matter will be submitted to the Court for its determination.

(c) If no objection is filed—or if upon objection going only to the amount of damages and costs in this Court, the party moving for dismissal tenders the additional damages and costs in full within 10 days of the demand therefor—the Clerk, without further reference to the Court, will enter an order of dismissal. If, after objection as to the amount of damages and costs in this Court, the moving party does not respond by a tender within 10 days, the Clerk will report the matter to the Court for its determination.

3. No mandate or other process will issue on a dismissal under this Rule without an order of the Court.

PART IX. DEFINITIONS AND EFFECTIVE DATE

Rule 47. Reference to "State Court" and "State Law"

The term "state court," when used in these Rules, includes the District of Columbia Court of Appeals, the Supreme Court of the Commonwealth of Puerto Rico, the courts of the Northern Mariana Islands, and the local courts of Guam. References in these Rules to the statutes of a State include the statutes of the District of Columbia, the Commonwealth of Puerto Rico, the Commonwealth of the Northern Mariana Islands, and the Territory of Guam.

(As amended Mar. 14, 2005, eff. May 2, 2005.)

Rule 48. Effective Date of Rules

1. These Rules, adopted July 17, 2007, will be effective October 1, 2007.

2. The Rules govern all proceedings after their effective date except to the extent that, in the opinion of the Court, their application to a pending matter would not be feasible or would work an injustice, in which event the former procedure applies.

3. In any case in which a petition for a writ of certiorari or appeal has been filed before the effective date of these revised Rules, but in which the respondent or appellee has not filed its response prior to that date, all remaining briefs submitted in that case prior to the Court's decision whether to grant review may comply with the May 2, 2005, version of the Rules of the Supreme Court of the United States rather than with these revised Rules. Similarly, in any case in which a petitioner or appellant has filed its brief on the merits prior to the effective date of these revised Rules, all remaining briefs in that case may comply with the May 2, 2005, version of the Rules of the Supreme Court of the United States rather than with these revised Rules.

(As amended July 17, 2007, eff. Oct. 1, 2007.

TITLE 28

JUDICIARY AND JUDICIAL PROCEDURE

Act June 25, 1948, c. 646, § 1, 62 Stat. 869

Part		Section
I.	ORGANIZATION OF COURTS	1
II.	DEPARTMENT OF JUSTICE	501
III.	COURT OFFICERS AND EMPLOYEES	601
IV.	JURISDICTION AND VENUE	1251
V.	PROCEDURE	1651
VI.	PARTICULAR PROCEEDINGS	2201

HISTORICAL AND STATUTORY NOTES

Effective and Applicability Provisions

Section 38 of Act June 25, 1948, c. 646, 62 Stat. 992, provided that: "The provisions of this Act shall take effect on Sept. 1, 1948."

Separability of Provisions

Section 34 of Act June 25, 1948, c. 646, 62 Stat. 991, provided that: "If any part of Title 28, Judiciary and Judicial Procedure, as set out in section 1 of this Act, shall be held invalid, the remainder shall not be affected thereby."

Enactment into Law; Citation

Section 1 of Act June 25, 1948, c. 646, 62 Stat. 869, provided in part: "That title 28 of the United States Code, entitled 'Judicial Code and Judiciary' is hereby revised, codified, and enacted into law, and may be cited as 'Title 28, United States Code, section ___.' "

Miscellaneous Provisions

Sections 2 to 32 of Act June 25, 1948, c. 646, 62 Stat. 985 to 991 contained certain executing provisions and conforming amendments to sections in other titles of the United States Code. For text of sections 2 to 32, see "Act June 25, 1948, c. 646, §§ 2 to 39, 62 Stat. 985 to 991," set out following the last section of Title 28.

Section 35 of Act June 25, 1948, c. 646, 62 Stat. 991, was not classified to the United States Code. For text of section 35, see "Act June 25, 1948, c. 646, §§ 2 to 39, 62 Stat. 985 to 991" set out following the last section of Title 28.

Sections 36 and 37 of Act June 25, 1948, c. 646, 62 Stat. 991, 992, contained certain executing provisions and conforming amendments to sections in other titles of the United States Code. For text of sections 36 and 37, see "Act June 25, 1948, c. 646, §§ 2 to 39, 62 Stat. 985 to 991", set out following the last section of Title 28.

Legislative Construction

Section 33 of Act June 25, 1948, c. 646, 62 Stat. 991, provided that: "No inference of a legislative construction is to be drawn by reason of the chapter in Title 28, Judiciary and Judicial Procedure, as set out in section 1 of this Act, in which any section is placed, nor by reason of the catchlines used in such title."

Repeals; Rights and Liabilities Saved

Section 39 of Act June 25, 1948, c. 646, 62 Stat. 992, repealed the sections or parts thereof of the Revised Statutes of the United States, Statutes at Large, or the Revised Statutes of the District of Columbia covering provisions codified in this title, but saved any rights or liabilities then existing under said sections or parts thereof.

Writs of Error

Act Jan. 31, 1928, c. 14, § 1, 45 Stat. 54 [section 861a of former Title 28, Judicial Code and Judiciary], provided that: "The writ of error in cases, civil and criminal, is abolished. All relief which heretofore [Jan. 31, 1928] could be obtained by writ of error shall hereafter be obtainable by appeal." This provision was omitted from the 1948 Revised Judicial Code as obsolete, and repealed by Act June 25, 1948, c. 646, § 39, 62 Stat. 992.

R.S. § 1012 as affected by Act Mar. 3, 1911, c. 231, § 291, 36 Stat. 1167 [Section 880 of former Title 28, Judicial Code and Judiciary], provided that appeals from district courts shall be subject to the same rules, regulations, and restrictions as are or may be prescribed in law in cases of writs of error. This provision was repealed by Act June 25, 1948, c. 646, § 39, 62 Stat. 992. Section 2 of Act Jan. 31, 1928, c. 14, 45 Stat. 54, as amended Apr. 26, 1928, c. 440, 45 Stat. 466; June 25, 1948, c. 646, § 23, 62 Stat. 990 [section 861b of former Title 28, Judicial Code and Judiciary], provided that: "All Acts of Congress referring to writs of error shall be construed as amended to the extent necessary to substitute appeal for writ of error."

Title 28 as Continuation of Existing Law; Change of Name of Circuit Courts of Appeals

Section 2(b) of Act June 25, 1948, c. 646, 62 Stat. 985, provided that: "The provisions of Title 28, Judiciary and Judicial Procedure, of the United States Code, set out in section 1 of this Act, with respect to the organization of each of the several courts therein provided for and of the Administrative Office of the United States Courts, shall be construed as continuations of existing law, and the tenure of the judges, officers, and employees thereof and of the United States attorneys and marshals and their deputies and assistants, in office on the effective date of this Act [Sept. 1, 1948], shall not be affected by its enactment, but each of them shall continue to serve in the same capacity under the appropriate provisions of title 28, as set out in section 1 of this Act, pursuant to his prior appointment: *Provided, however,* That each circuit court of appeals shall, as in said title 28 set out, hereafter be known as a United States court of appeals. No loss of rights, interruption of jurisdiction, or prejudice to matters pending in any of such courts on the effective date of this Act shall result from its enactment."

PART I—ORGANIZATION OF COURTS

Chapter		Section
1.	**Supreme Court**	1
3.	**Courts of appeals**	41
5.	**District courts**	81
6.	**Bankruptcy judges**	151
7.	**United States Court of Federal Claims**	171
[9.	**Repealed]**	
11.	**Court of International Trade**	251
13.	**Assignment of judges to other courts**	291
15.	**Conferences and councils of judges**	331
16.	**Complaints against judges and judicial discipline**	351
17.	**Resignation and retirement of judges** [1]	371
19.	**Distribution of reports and digests**	411
21.	**General provisions applicable to courts and judges**	451
23.	**Civil justice expense and delay reduction plans**	471

[1] Chapter heading amended by Pub.L. 92–397 without corresponding amendment of analysis.

HISTORICAL AND STATUTORY NOTES

Codifications

Analysis of chapters comprising Part I was amended by Pub.L. 95–598, Title II, § 201(b), Nov. 6, 1978, 92 Stat. 2660, effective June 28, 1984, pursuant to Pub.L. 95–598, Title IV, § 402(b), Nov. 6, 1978, 92 Stat. 2682, as amended by Pub.L. 98–249, § 1(a), Mar. 31, 1984, 98 Stat. 116; Pub.L. 98–271, § 1(a), Apr. 30, 1984, 98 Stat. 163; Pub.L. 98–299, § 1(a), May 25, 1984, 98 Stat. 214; Pub.L. 98–325, § 1(a), June 20, 1984, 98 Stat. 268, by adding:

"6. Bankruptcy courts ..... 151".

Section 402(b) of Pub.L. 95–598 was amended by section 113 of Pub.L. 98–353, Title I, July 10, 1984, 98 Stat. 343, by substituting "shall not be effective" for "shall take effect on June 28, 1984", thereby eliminating the amendment by section 201(b) of Pub.L. 95–598, effective June 27, 1984, pursuant to section 122(c) of Pub.L. 98–353, set out as an Effective Date note under section 151 of the title.

Section 121(a) of Pub.L. 98–353 directed that section 402(b) of Pub.L. 95–598 be amended by substituting "the date of enactment of the Bankruptcy Amendments and Federal Judgeship Act of 1984 [i.e. July 10, 1984]" for "June 28, 1984". This amendment was not executed in view of the prior amendment to section 402(b) of Pub.L. 95–598 by section 113 of Pub.L. 98–353.

CHAPTER 1—SUPREME COURT

Sec.

1. Number of justices; quorum.
2. Terms of court.
3. Vacancy in office of Chief Justice; disability.
4. Precedence of associate justices.
5. Salaries of justices.
6. Records of former court of appeals.

§ 1. Number of justices; quorum

The Supreme Court of the United States shall consist of a Chief Justice of the United States and eight associate justices, any six of whom shall constitute a quorum.

(June 25, 1948, c. 646, 62 Stat. 869.)

HISTORICAL AND STATUTORY NOTES

Short Title

2008 Amendments. Pub.L. 110–406, § 1(a), Oct. 13, 2008, 122 Stat. 4291, provided that: "This Act [enacting 28 U.S.C.A. § 2045, amending 11 U.S.C.A. § 104, 18 U.S.C.A. §§ 3006A, 3152, 3154, 3161, 3563, 3583, 3599, and 3672, and 28 U.S.C.A. §§ 103, 123, 333, 991, 1864, 1866, 1869, 1871, 1875, and 1920, and enacting provisions set out as notes under 28 U.S.C.A. §§ 123 and 1871] may be cited as the 'Judicial Administration and Technical Amendments Act of 2008'."

Pub.L. 110–177, § 1, Jan. 7, 2008, 121 Stat. 2534, provided that: "This Act [enacting 18 U.S.C.A. §§ 119, and 1521, and 42 U.S.C.A. §§ 3702, and 3714a, amending 5 App. U.S.C.A. § 105, 18 U.S.C.A. §§ 111, 115, 930, 1112, 1512, 1513, and 3624, 26 U.S.C.A. § 7456, 28 U.S.C.A. §§ 44, 296, 331, 566, 604, 631, 995, and 2255, 42 U.S.C.A. §§ 3762a, 3762b, 3796*ll*, 13862, and 13867, enacting provisions set out as notes under 5 U.S.C.A. § 8701, 26 U.S.C.A. § 7456, 28 U.S.C.A. §§ 44, 604, 995, and 49 U.S.C.A. § 30301, enacting a table entry set out as a note under 28 U.S.C.A. § 994, and amending provisions set out as a note under 28 U.S.C.A. § 566] may be cited as the 'Court Security Improvement Act of 2007'."

2007 Amendments. Pub.L. 110–34, § 1, June 14, 2007, 121 Stat. 224, provided that: "This Act [amending 28 U.S.C.A. § 546 and enacting provisions set out as a note under 28 U.S.C.A. § 546] may be cited as the 'Preserving United States Attorney Independence Act of 2007'."

2005 Amendments. Pub.L. 109–63, § 1, Sept. 9, 2005, 119 Stat. 1993, provided that: "This Act [amending 28 U.S.C.A. §§ 48, 141, 152, and 636] may be cited as the 'Federal Judiciary Emergency Special Sessions Act of 2005'."

Pub.L. 109–8, Title XII, § 1223(a), April 20, 2005, 119 Stat. 196, provided that: "This section [amending 28 U.S.C.A. § 152 and enacting provisions set out as notes under 28 U.S.C.A. § 152] may be cited as the 'Bankruptcy Judgeship Act of 2005'."

Pub.L. 109–2, § 1(a), Feb. 18, 2005, 119 Stat. 4, provided that: "This Act [enacting 28 U.S.C.A. § 1453 and chapter 114 of this title, 28 U.S.C.A. § 1711 et seq., amending 28 U.S.C.A. §§ 1332, 1335, and 1603, and enacting provisions set out as notes under 28 U.S.C.A. §§ 1332, 1711, 2071, and 2074] may be cited as the 'Class Action Fairness Act of 2005'."

2002 Amendments. Pub.L. 107–273, Div. C, Title I, § 11020(a), Nov. 2, 2002, 116 Stat. 1826, provided that: "This section [enacting 28 U.S.C.A. §§ 1369, 1697, and 1785, amending 28 U.S.C.A. §§ 1391 and 1441, and enacting provisions set out as a note under 28 U.S.C.A. § 1369] may be cited as the 'Multiparty, Multiforum Trial Jurisdiction Act of 2002'."

Pub.L. 107–273, Div. C, Title I, § 11041, Nov. 2, 2002, 116 Stat. 1848, provided that: "This subtitle [Pub.L. 107–273, Div. C, Title I, Subtitle C, §§ 11041 to 11044, Nov. 2, 2002, 116 Stat. 1848, enacting chapter 16 of this title (28 U.S.C.A. § 351 et seq.), amending 28 U.S.C.A. §§ 331, 332, 372, 375, and 604, and 38 U.S.C.A. § 7253, and enacting provisions set out as a note under 28 U.S.C.A. § 351] may be cited as the 'Judicial Improvements Act of 2002'."

2000 Amendments. Pub.L. 106–518, § 1(a), Nov. 13, 2000, 114 Stat. 2410, provided that: "This Act [enacting sections 179 and 613 of this title and provisions set out as notes under sections 613, 996 and 1931 of this title, amending sections 117, 175, 332, 371, 376, 604, 611, 612, 627, 631, 636, 797, 996, 1865, 1930, and 2671 of this title, sections 3102 and 5551 of Title 5, section 1228 of Title 11, sections 3006A and 3401 of Title 18, and section 13n of Title 40, and provisions set out as notes under sections 471, 581, and 1931 of this title, and repealing 2520 of this title] may be cited as the 'Federal Courts Improvement Act of 2000'."

1998 Amendments. Pub.L. 105–315, § 1, Oct. 30, 1998, 112 Stat. 2993, provided that: "This Act [amending sections 651 to 658 of this title, enacting a provision set out as a note under section 651 of this title, and amending a provision set out as a note under section 652 of this title] may be cited as the 'Alternative Dispute Resolution Act of 1998'."

1996 Amendments. Pub.L. 104–317, § 1(a), Oct. 19, 1996, 110 Stat. 3847, provided that: "This Act [enacting sections 258 and 1932 of this title, amending sections 112, 125, 134, 253, 331, 332, 371, 376, 601, 621, 627, 636, 753, 954, 1332, 1404, 1406, 1442, 1446, 1827, 1914, 1931, 1963, and 2511 of this title, sections 3154, 3401, and 3603 of Title 18, Crimes and Criminal Procedure, sections 1983 and 1988 of Title 42, The Public Health and Welfare, and sections 719, 743, 745, 1104, and 1105 of Title 45, Railroads, enacting provisions set out as notes under sections 258, 1332, 1404, 1827, 1914, 1931, and 2412 of this title and section 719 of Title 45, and amending provisions set out as notes under sections 133, 152, 471, and 1913 of this title] may be cited as the 'Federal Courts Improvement Act of 1996'."

1994 Amendments. Pub.L. 103–420, § 1, Oct. 25, 1994, 108 Stat. 4343, provided that: "This Act [amending section 612 of this title, amending provisions set out as notes under sections 471 and 651 of this title, and repealing a provision set out as a note under section 651 of this title] may be cited as the 'Judicial Amendments Act of 1994'."

Pub.L. 103–383, § 1, Oct. 20, 1994, 108 Stat. 4063 provided that: "This Act [enacting section 1738B of this title and a provision set out as a note under section 1738B of this title] may be cited as the 'Full Faith and Credit for Child Support Orders Act'."

Pub.L. 103–270, § 1, June 30, 1994, 108 Stat. 732, provided that: "This Act [amending sections 591 through 596 and 599 of this title and enacting provisions set out as notes under section 591 of this title and section 113 of Title 3, The President] may be cited as the 'Independent Counsel Reauthorization Act of 1994'."

1992 Amendments. Pub.L. 102–572, § 1, Oct. 29, 1992, 106 Stat. 4506, provided that: "This Act [Pub.L. 102–572, Oct. 29, 1992, 106 Stat. 4506, for classifications to which see Tables] may be cited as the 'Federal Courts Administration Act of 1992'."

Pub.L. 102–572, Title IX, § 901, Oct. 29, 1992, 106 Stat. 4516, provided that: "This title [Title IX of Pub.L. 102–572, Oct. 29, 1992, 106 Stat. 4516, for classifications to which see Tables] may be cited as the 'Court of Federal Claims Technical and Procedural Improvements Act of 1992'."

Pub.L. 102–559, § 1, Oct. 28, 1992, 106 Stat. 4227, provided that: "This Act [enacting chapter 178 of this title and provisions set out as a note under section 3701 of this title] may be cited as the 'Professional and Amateur Sports Protection Act'."

Pub.L. 102–417, § 1, Oct. 14, 1992, 106 Stat. 2138, provided that: "This Act [amending section 1821 of this title and enacting provisions set out as a note under section 1821 of this title] may be cited as the 'Incarcerated Witness Fees Act of 1991'."

Pub.L. 102–361, § 1, Aug. 26, 1992, 106 Stat. 965, provided that: "This Act [amending section 152 of this title and enacting provisions set out as a note under section 152 of this title] may be cited as the 'Bankruptcy Judgeship Act of 1992'."

1990 Amendments. Pub.L. 101–650, § 1, Dec. 1, 1990, 104 Stat. 5089, provided: "That this Act [enacting sections 178, 471 to 482, 1367, and 1658 of this title, section 8440b of Title 5, Government Organization and Employees, sections 106A and 120 of Title 17, Copyrights, and section 404c of Title 47, Telegraphs, Telephones, and Radiotelegraphs, amending sections 44, 108, 112, 122, 133, 152, 332, 333, 372, 375, 376, 377, 453, 601, 602, 604, 631, 636, 995, 996, 1334, 1391, 1441, 1452, 1499, 1605, 1610, 1821, 1871, 2072, and 2077 of this title, sections 8331, 8334, 8336, 8339, and 8402 of Title 5, section 104 of Appendix 6 to Title 5, section 502 of Appendix 7 to Title 5, section 305 of Title 11, Bankruptcy, and sections 101, 102, 106, 107, 109, 113, 301, 411, 412, 501, and 506 of Title 17, enacting provisions set out as notes under sections 1, 44, 133, 331, 332, 372, 376, 471, 620, 631, 1367, and 1658 of this title, section 8331 of Title 5, section 307 of Title 11, sections 101, 106A, 109, and 205 of Title 17, and sections 3006A and 3551 of Title 18, Crimes and Criminal Procedure, and amending provisions set out as notes under sections 533 and 581 of this title] may be cited as the 'Judicial Improvements Act of 1990'."

Pub.L. 101–650, Title I, § 101, Dec. 1, 1990, 104 Stat. 5089, provided that: "This title [enacting section 471 to 482 of this title and provisions set out as notes under section 471 of this title] may be cited as the 'Civil Justice Reform Act of 1990'."

Pub.L. 101–650, Title II, § 201, Dec. 1, 1990, 104 Stat. 5098, provided that: "This title [amending sections 44 and 133 of this title and enacting provisions set out as notes under sections 44, 133, and 331 of this title] may be cited as the 'Federal Judgeship Act of 1990'."

Pub.L. 101–650, Title III, § 301, Dec. 1, 1990, 104 Stat. 5104, provided that: "This title [enacting sections 178, 1367, and 1658 of this title and section 8440b of Title 5, Government Organization and Employees, amending sections 108, 112, 122, 133, 152, 158, 332, 333, 375, 376, 377, 601, 602, 604, 631, 636, 995, 996, 1334, 1391, 1441, 1452, 1499, 1605, 1610, 1821, 1871, and 2072 of this title, sections 8331, 8334, 8336,

8339, and 8402 of Title 5, section 502 of Appendix 7 to Title 5, and section 305 of Title 11, Bankruptcy, enacting provisions set out as notes under sections 376, 620, 631, 1367, and 1658 of this title, sections 8331 of Title 5, section 307 of Title 11, and sections 3006A and 3551 of Title 18, Crimes and Criminal Procedure, and amending provisions set out as notes under sections 533 and 581 of this title] may be cited as the 'Federal Courts Study Committee Implementation Act of 1990'."

Pub.L. 101–650, Title IV, § 401, Dec. 1, 1990, 104 Stat. 5122, provided that: "This title [amending sections 332, 372, 453, and 2077 of this title and section 104 of Appendix 6 to Title 5, Government Organization and Employees, and enacting provisions set out as notes under sections 332 and 372 of this title] may be cited as the 'Judicial Discipline and Removal Reform Act of 1990'."

Pub.L. 101–647, Title XXXVI, § 3601, Nov. 29, 1990, 104 Stat. 4933, provided that: "This title [enacting section 2044 and chapter 176 (section 3001 et seq.) of this title, amending sections 550, 1962, 1963 and 2410 of this title, section 523 of Title 11, Bankruptcy, and sections 3142 and 3552 of Title 18, Crimes and Criminal Procedure, and enacting provisions set out as a note under section 3001 of this title] may be cited as the 'Federal Debt Collection Procedures Act of 1990'."

1988 Amendments. Pub. L. 100–702, § 1, Nov. 19, 1988, 102 Stat. 4642, provided that: "This Act [enacting chapter 44 (§§ 651 to 658) and sections 297, 1878, and 2072 to 2074 of this title, 5 U.S.C.A. § 5584, and 9 U.S.C.A. § 15, amending sections 89, 153, 156, 172, 331, 332, 371, 372, 376, 455, 462, 604, 611, 620, 623, 624, 626, 627, 629, 631, 634, 636, 712, 752, 794, 1292, 1295, 1332, 1338, 1391, 1400, 1441, 1446, 1447, 1498, 1827, 1863, 1864, 1865, 1866, 1869, 1963, 2071, 2072, 2077, and 2520 of this title, 5 U.S.C.A. § 5108, 16 U.S.C.A. § 460n–8, 17 U.S.C.A. § 912, 18 U.S.C.A. § 3402, and 42 U.S.C.A. §§ 10702, 10704, 10705, 10706, and 10708, repealing chapter 44 (§§ 651 to 658) and sections 1393, 1963A, 2072, and 2076 of this title, 18 U.S.C.A. §§ 3771 and 3772, and enacting provisions set out as notes under sections 1, 89, 153, 331, 371, 376, 611, 626, 651, 652, 1292, 1332, 1391, 1393, 1827, 1963, 2071, and 2520 of this title and 5 U.S.C.A. § 5584] may be cited as the 'Judicial Improvements and Access to Justice Act'."

Pub. L. 100–702, Title VII, § 701, Nov. 19, 1988, 102 Stat. 4654, provided that: "This title [amending section 1827(a) to (e), (g) to (k) of this title and enacting provisions set out as notes under section 1827 of this title] may be cited as the 'Court Interpreter Amendments Act of 1988'."

Pub. L. 100–694, § 1, Nov. 18, 1988, 102 Stat. 4563, provided that: "This Act [enacting 16 U.S.C.A. § 831c–2, amending sections 2671, 2674, and 2679(b), (d) of this title, and enacting provisions set out as notes under sections 2671 and 2679 of this title] may be cited as the 'Federal Employees Liability Reform and Tort Compensation Act of 1988'."

Pub. L. 100–659, § 1, Nov. 15, 1988, 102 Stat. 3910, provided that: "This Act [which enacted section 377 of this title and section 8440a of Title 5, Government Organization and Employees, amended sections 155, 375, 376, 604, 631, and 636 of this title and sections 8334 and 8402 of Title 5 and enacted provisions set out as notes under sections 376 and 377 of this title] may be cited as the 'Retirement and Survivors' Annuities for Bankruptcy Judges and Magistrates Act of 1988'."

1987 Amendments. Pub.L. 100–191, § 1, Dec. 15, 1987, 101 Stat. 1293, provided that: "This Act [enacting section 599 of this title, amending sections 49 and 591 to 598 of this title, sections 203 and 205 of the Ethics in Government Act of 1978, set out in Appendix 4 to Title 5, Government Organization and Employees, and section 202 of Title 18, Crimes and Criminal Procedure, and enacting provisions set out as a note under section 591 of this title and amending provisions set out as a note under section 591 of this title] may be cited as the 'Independent Counsel Reauthorization Act of 1987'."

1986 Amendments. Pub.L. 99–657, § 1, Nov. 14, 1986, 100 Stat. 3670, provided that: "This Act [amending sections 90 and 121 of this title, and enacting provisions set out as a note under section 121 of this title] may be cited as the 'Judicial Housekeeping Act of 1986'."

Pub.L. 99–570, Title I, § 1151, Oct. 27, 1986, 100 Stat. 3207–12, provided that: "This subtitle [subtitle b (§§ 1151–1153) of Title 1 of amending section 524 of this title, section 1963 of Title 18, Crimes and Criminal Procedure, section 1613a of Title 19, Customs Duties, and section 853 of Title 21, Food and Drugs, and repealing section 1613b of Title 19] may be cited as the 'Department of Justice Assets Forfeiture Fund Amendments Act of 1986'."

Pub.L. 99–363, § 1, July 11, 1986, 100 Stat. 770, provided that: "This Act [amending section 994 of this title] may be cited as the 'Sentencing Guidelines Act of 1986'."

Pub.L. 99–336, § 1, June 19, 1986, 100 Stat. 633, provided that: "This Act [amending sections 376, 620, 1441, 1914, and 2342 of this title, section 288d of Title 2, The Congress, and sections 8706, 8714a, 8714b, and 8714c of Title 5, Government Organization and Employees, and enacting provisions set out as notes under sections 376, 620, 1441, 1914, and 2342 of this title and section 8706 of Title 5] may be cited as the 'Judicial Improvements Act of 1985'."

1984 Amendments. Pub.L. 98–620, Title IV, § 404, Nov. 8, 1984, 98 Stat. 3361, provided that: "This subtitle [subtitle B (sections 404 to 411) of Title IV of Pub.L. 98–620, which amended sections 85, 90, 93, 112, 124, and 126 of this title and enacted provisions set out as notes under sections 85, 90, 93 and 124 of this title] may be cited as the 'Federal District Court Organization Act of 1984'."

Pub.L. 98–620, Title IV, preceding § 412, Nov. 8, 1984, 98 Stat. 3362, provided that: "This subtitle [subtitle C (sections 412 to 416) of Title IV of Pub.L. 98–620, enacting section 798 of this title, amending section 1292 of this title, section 1071 of Title 15, Commerce and Trade, section 1337 of Title 19, Customs Duties, and sections 142 to 144 of Title 35, Patents, and enacting provisions set out as notes under section 713 of this title and section 142 of Title 35] may be cited as the 'Technical Amendments to the Federal Courts Improvement Act of 1982'."

For short title of Pub.L. 98–353, July 10, 1984, 98 Stat. 333 as the "Bankruptcy Amendments and Federal Judgeship Act of 1984", see Short Title of 1984 Amendments note set out under section 151 of this title.

1983 Amendments. Pub.L. 97–409, § 1, Jan. 3, 1983, 96 Stat. 2039, provided: "That this Act [amending sections 49, 591 to 598 of this title and amending provisions set out as a note under section 591 of this title] may be cited as the 'Ethics in Government Act Amendments of 1982'."

1982 Amendments. For provisions authorizing the citation of sections 2–6 of Pub.L. 97–394 as the Indian Claims Limitation Act of 1982, see section 1 of Pub.L. 97–394, as amended, set out as a note under section 2415 of this title.

Pub.L. 97–292, § 1, Oct. 12, 1982, 96 Stat. 1259, provided: "That this Act [amending section 534 of this title] may be cited as the 'Missing Children Act'."

Pub.L. 97–164, § 1, Apr. 2, 1982, 96 Stat. 25, provided: "That this Act [enacting sections 176, 177, 462, 463, 714, 715, 1295, 1296, 1631, 2077, and 2522 of this title, amending sections 41, 44, 45, 46, 48, 136, 160, 171 to 175, 256, 291, 292, 293, 331, 372, 451, 456, 460, 518, 520, 605, 610, 713, 753, 791, 794 to 797, 957, 1291, 1292, 1294, 1336, 1346, 1398, 1402, 1406, 1491, 1492, 1494 to 1503, 1505, 1507, 1926, 1961, 2342, 2411, 2501 to 2517, 2519, 2520, and 2645 of this title, section 308 and rule 1101 in the Appendix to this title, section 356 of Title 2, The Congress, sections 7703, 8332, 8334, 8715, and 8912 of Title 5, Government Organization and Employees, section 2461 of Title 7, Agriculture, section 2273 of Title 10, Armed Forces, sections 714b, 1071, 1121, and 2210 of Title 15, Commerce and Trade, section 831s of Title 16, Conservation, sections 204, 3006A, and 6001 of Title 18, Crimes and Criminal Procedure, sections 1337, 1516, 1516a, 1528, and 2395 of Title 19, Customs Duties, sections 1642b and 2356 of Title 22, Foreign Relations and Intercourse, sections 70v–3, 119, 475a, 652, 1401, and 1402 of Title 25, Indians, sections 6110, 7422, 7428, 7456, and 7482 of Title 26, Internal Revenue Code, section 193a of Title 30, Mineral Lands and Mining, sections 72 and 724a of Title 31, Money and Finance, sections 1321 and 1479 of Title 33, Navigation and Navigable Waters, sections 141 to 146, 183, and 282 of Title 35, Patents, section 330 of Title 40, Public Buildings, Property, and Works, sections 113, 114, 607, and 609 of Title 41, Public Contracts, sections 2182, 2221, 2223, and 2475 of Title 42, The Public Health and Welfare, sections 713, 906, and 1103 of Title 44, Public Printing and Documents, section 87 of Title 45, Railroads, and sections 42, 1213, 1215, 1216, 1218, 1218a, 1224, and 1984 of the Appendix to Title 50, War and National Defense, repealing sections 142, 211 to 216, 415, 792, 831 to 834, 1255, 1256, 1504, 1506, 1541 to 1546, 1584, 2110, 2353, 2518, and 2601–2604 of this title, and enacting provisions set out as notes under sections 44, 45, 171, and 753 of this title, section 7456 of Title 26, and section 3006A of Title 18] may be cited as the 'Federal Courts Improvement Act of 1982'."

1980 Amendments. Pub.L. 96–486, § 1, Dec. 1, 1980, 94 Stat. 2369, provided: "That this Act [amending section 1331 of this title and section 2072 of Title 15, Commerce and Trade, and enacting provisions set out as a note under section 1331 of this title] may be cited as the 'Federal Question Jurisdictional Amendments Act of 1980'."

Pub.L. 96–462, § 1, Oct. 15, 1980, 94 Stat. 2053, provided that: "This Act [amending sections 84, 95, 105, 113, and 124 of this title, and enacting provisions set out as notes under sections 84, 95, 105, and 113 of this title] may be cited as the 'Federal District Court Organization Act of 1980'."

Pub.L. 96–458, § 1, Oct. 15, 1980, 94 Stat. 2035, provided that: "This Act [amending sections 331, 332, 372, and 604 of this title, and enacting provisions set out as notes under section 331 of this title] may be cited as the 'Judicial Councils Reform and Judicial Conduct and Disability Act of 1980'."

Pub.L. 96–452, § 1, Oct. 14, 1980, 94 Stat. 1994, provided: "That this Act [amending sections 41, 44 and 48 of this title, and enacting provisions set out as notes under section 41 of this title] may be cited as the 'Fifth Circuit Court of Appeals Reorganization Act of 1980'."

Pub.L. 96–417, § 1, Oct. 10, 1980, 94 Stat. 1727, provided: "That this Act [which enacted sections 1546, 1581 to 1585, 1876, 1963A, 2603, 2604, and 2631 to 2647 of this title and section 2395 of Title 19, Customs Duties; amended sections 251 to 255, 257, 292, 293, 372, 451, 456, 518, 569, 605, 610, 751, 871 to 873, 1337, 1340, 1352, 1355, 1356, 1491, 1541, 1543, 1862, 1919, 2414, 2601, and 2602 of this title and section 308 of Pub.L. 95–521 in the Appendix of this title, section 791 of Title 16, Conservation, section 6001 of Title 18, Crimes and Criminal Procedure, sections 1305, 1337, 1502, 1503, 1514 to 1516a, 1528, 1592, 1604, and 1641 of Title 19, Customs Duties, section 7443 of Title 26, Internal Revenue Code, and section 906 of Title 44, Public Printing and Documents; repealed sections 405a and 2322 of Title 19, Customs Duties; omitted former sections 1581, 1582, and 2631 to 2639 of this title; and enacted provisions set out as notes under section 251 of this title] may be cited as the 'Customs Courts Act of 1980'."

1979 Amendments. For short title of Pub.L. 96–82, as the "Federal Magistrate Act of 1979", see section 1 of Pub.L. 96–82, set out as a note under section 631 of this title.

1978 Amendments. For short title of Pub.L. 95–572 as the "Jury System Improvements Act of 1978", see section 1 of Pub.L. 95–572, set out as a note under section 1861 of this title.

Pub.L. 95–539, § 1, Oct. 28, 1978, 92 Stat. 2040, provided: "That this Act [enacting sections 1827 and 1828 of this title, amending sections 602 to 604 and 1920 of this title, enacting provisions set out as notes under section 602 of this title, and repealing a provision set out as a note under section 602 of this title] may be cited as the 'Court Interpreters Act'."

Pub.L. 95–408, § 1, Oct. 2, 1978, 92 Stat. 883, provided that: "This Act [amending sections 89, 93, 97, 98, 104, 112, 114, 133 of this title and enacting provisions set out as a note under section 89 of this title] may be cited as the 'Federal District Court Organization Act of 1978'."

1976 Amendments. Pub.L. 94–583, § 1, Oct. 21, 1976, 90 Stat. 2891, provided: "That this Act [enacting sections 1330 and 1602 to 1611 of this title, amending sections 1332, 1391, and 1441 of this title, and enacting provisions set out as notes under section 1602 of this title] may be cited as the 'Foreign Sovereign Immunities Act of 1976'."

Pub.L. 94–554, § 1, Oct. 19, 1976, 90 Stat. 2603, provided: "That this Act [amending this section, and enacting provisions set out as notes under section 376 of this title] may be cited as the 'Judicial Survivors' Annuities Reform Act'."

1970 Amendments. Pub.L. 91–271, Title I, § 101, June 2, 1970, 84 Stat. 274, provided that: "This title [enacting sections 256 and 257 of this title, amending sections 253 to 255, 1541, 1582, 2601, 2602, and 2631 to 2639 of this title, repealing sections 1583 and 2640 to 2642 of this title, and enacting provisions set out as notes under sections 1 and 256 of this title] may be cited as 'The Customs Courts Act of 1970'."

1966 Amendments. Pub.L. 89–504, Title II, § 201, July 18, 1966, 80 Stat. 293, provided that: "This title [enacting provisions set out as notes under sections 603, 604, and 753 of this title] may be cited as the 'Federal Judicial Salary Act of 1966'."

1964 Acts. Pub.L. 88–426, Title IV, § 401, Aug. 14, 1964, 78 Stat. 433, provided that: "This title [amending this section and sections 44, 135, 173, 213, 252, 603 and 792 of this title, section 867 of Title 10, Armed Forces, section 68 of former Title 11, Bankruptcy, and section 7443 of Title 26, Internal

Revenue Code, and enacting provisions set out as notes under sections 603, 604 and 753 of this title] may be cited as the 'Federal Judicial Salary Act of 1964'."

Gifts to the United States Supreme Court

Pub.L. 108–356, § 3, Oct. 21, 2004, 118 Stat. 1416, provided that: "The Chief Justice or his designee is authorized to accept, hold, administer, and utilize gifts and bequests of personal property pertaining to the history of the United States Supreme Court or its justices, but gifts or bequests of money shall be covered into the Treasury."

§ 2. Terms of court

The Supreme Court shall hold at the seat of government a term of court commencing on the first Monday in October of each year and may hold such adjourned or special terms as may be necessary.

(June 25, 1948, c. 646, 62 Stat. 869.)

§ 3. Vacancy in office of Chief Justice; disability

Whenever the Chief Justice is unable to perform the duties of his office or the office is vacant, his powers and duties shall devolve upon the associate justice next in precedence who is able to act, until such disability is removed or another Chief Justice is appointed and duly qualified.

(June 25, 1948, c. 646, 62 Stat. 869.)

§ 4. Precedence of associate justices

Associate justices shall have precedence according to the seniority of their commissions. Justices whose commissions bear the same date shall have precedence according to seniority in age.

(June 25, 1948, c. 646, 62 Stat. 869.)

§ 5. Salaries of justices

The Chief Justice and each associate justice shall each receive a salary at annual rates determined under section 225 of the Federal Salary Act of 1967 (2 U.S.C. 351–361), as adjusted by section 461 of this title.

(June 25, 1948, c. 646, 62 Stat. 870; Mar. 2, 1955, c. 9, § 1(a), 69 Stat. 9; Aug. 14, 1964, Pub.L. 88–426, Title IV, § 403(a), 78 Stat. 434; Aug. 9, 1975, Pub.L. 94–82, Title II, § 205(b)(1), 89 Stat. 422.)

HISTORICAL AND STATUTORY NOTES

References in Text

Section 225 of the Federal Salary Act of 1967, referred to in text, is section 225 of Pub.L. 90–206, Dec. 16, 1967, 81 Stat. 642, as amended, which is classified to chapter 11 (section 351 et seq.) of Title 2, The Congress.

Effective and Applicability Provisions

1964 Acts. Amendment by Pub.L. 88–426 effective on the first day of the first pay period which begins on or after July 1, 1964, except to the extent provided in section 501(c) of Pub.L. 88–426, see section 501 of Pub.L. 88–426.

1955 Acts. Amendment by Act Mar. 2, 1955, effective Mar. 1, 1955, see section 5 of Act Mar. 2, 1955, set out as a note under section 31 of Title 2, The Congress.

Salary Increases

For prior year salary increases per the recommendation of the President, see Prior Salary Recommendations notes under 2 U.S.C.A. § 358.

For miscellaneous provisions dealing with adjustments of pay and limitations on use of funds to pay salaries in prior years, see notes under 5 U.S.C.A. § 5318.

§ 6. Records of former court of appeals

The records and proceedings of the court of appeals, appointed previous to the adoption of the Constitution, shall be kept until deposited with the National Archives of the United States in the office of the clerk of the Supreme Court, who shall furnish copies thereof to any person requiring and paying for them, in the manner provided by law for giving copies of the records and proceedings of the Supreme Court. Such copies shall have the same faith and credit as proceedings of the Supreme Court.

(June 25, 1948, c. 646, 62 Stat. 870; Oct. 25, 1951, c. 562, § 4(7), 65 Stat. 640.)

CHAPTER 3—COURTS OF APPEALS

Sec.

41. Number and composition of circuits.
42. Allotment of Supreme Court justices to circuits.
43. Creation and composition of courts.
44. Appointment, tenure, residence and salary of circuit judges.
45. Chief judges; precedence of judges.
46. Assignment of judges; panels; hearings; quorum.
47. Disqualification of trial judge to hear appeal.
48. Terms of court.
49. Assignment of judges to division to appoint independent counsels.

§ 41. Number and composition of circuits

The thirteen judicial circuits of the United States are constituted as follows:

Circuits	*Composition*
District of Columbia	District of Columbia.
First	Maine, Massachusetts, New Hampshire, Puerto Rico, Rhode Island.
Second	Connecticut, New York, Vermont.

Circuits	*Composition*
Third	Delaware, New Jersey, Pennsylvania, Virgin Islands.
Fourth	Maryland, North Carolina, South Carolina, Virginia, West Virginia.
Fifth	District of the Canal Zone, Louisiana, Mississippi, Texas.
Sixth	Kentucky, Michigan, Ohio, Tennessee.
Seventh	Illinois, Indiana, Wisconsin.
Eighth	Arkansas, Iowa, Minnesota, Missouri, Nebraska, North Dakota, South Dakota.
Ninth	Alaska, Arizona, California, Idaho, Montana, Nevada, Oregon, Washington, Guam, Hawaii.
Tenth	Colorado, Kansas, New Mexico, Oklahoma, Utah, Wyoming.
Eleventh	Alabama, Florida, Georgia.
Federal	All Federal judicial districts.

(June 25, 1948, c. 646, 62 Stat. 870; Oct. 31, 1951, c. 655, § 34, 65 Stat. 723; Oct. 14, 1980, Pub.L. 96–452, § 2, 94 Stat. 1994; Apr. 2, 1982, Pub.L. 97–164, Title I, § 101, 96 Stat. 25.)

HISTORICAL AND STATUTORY NOTES

Effective and Applicability Provisions

1982 Acts. Amendment by Pub.L. 97–164 effective Oct. 1, 1982, see section 402 of Pub.L. 97–164, set out as a note under section 171 of this title.

1980 Acts. Section 12 of Pub.L. 96–452 provided that: "This Act [see Short Title of 1980 Amendments note set out under section 1 of this title] and the amendments made by this Act [amending sections 41, 44, and 48 of this title, and enacting provisions set out as notes under this section] shall take effect on October 1, 1981."

Administrative Action by Fifth Circuit Court of Appeals; Termination of Court

Section 11 of Pub.L. 96–452 provided that: "The court of appeals for the fifth circuit as constituted on the day before the effective date of this Act [Oct. 1, 1981] may take such administrative action as may be required to carry out this Act [see Short Title of 1980 Amendments note set out under section 1 of this title]. Such court shall cease to exist for administrative purposes on July 1, 1984."

Appeals Court Administrative Units

Pub.L. 95–486, § 6, Oct. 20, 1978, 92 Stat. 1633, provided that: "Any court of appeals having more than 15 active judges may constitute itself into administrative units complete with such facilities and staff as may be prescribed by the Administrative Office of the United States Courts, and may perform its en banc function by such number of members of its en banc courts as may be prescribed by rule of the court of appeals."

Assignment of Judges and Procedure For Administration of Pending Cases With Regard to Reorganization of the Fifth Circuit Court of Appeals

Sections 5 to 10 of Pub.L. 96–452 provided that:

"**Sec. 5.** Each circuit judge in regular active service of the former fifth circuit whose official station on the day before the effective date of this Act [Oct. 1, 1981]—

"(1) is in Louisiana, Mississippi, or Texas is assigned as a circuit judge of the new fifth circuit; and

"(2) is in Alabama, Florida, or Georgia is assigned as a circuit judge of the eleventh circuit.

"**Sec. 6.** Each judge who is a senior judge of the former fifth circuit on the day before the effective date of this Act [Oct. 1, 1981] may elect to be assigned to the new fifth circuit or to the eleventh circuit and shall notify the Director of the Administrative Office of the United States Courts of such election.

"**Sec. 7.** The seniority of each judge—

"(1) who is assigned under section 5 of this Act; or

"(2) who elects to be assigned under section 6 of this Act;

shall run from the date of commission of such judge as a judge of the former fifth circuit.

"**Sec. 8.** The eleventh circuit is authorized to hold terms or sessions of court at New Orleans, Louisiana, until such time as adequate facilities for such court are provided in Atlanta, Georgia.

"**Sec. 9.** The provisions of the following paragraphs of this section apply to any case in which, on the day before the effective date of this Act [Oct. 1, 1981], an appeal or other proceeding has been filed with the former fifth circuit:

"(1) If the matter has been submitted for decision, further proceedings in respect of the matter shall be had in the same manner and with the same effect as if this Act [see Short Title of 1980 Amendments note under section 1 of this title] had not been enacted.

"(2) If the matter has not been submitted for decision, the appeal or proceeding, together with the original papers, printed records, and record entries duly certified, shall, by appropriate orders, be transferred to the court to which it would have gone had this Act [see Short Title of 1980 Amendments note under section 1 of this title] been in full force and effect at the time such appeal was taken or other proceeding commenced, and further proceedings in respect of the case shall be had in the same manner and with the same effect as if the appeal or other proceeding had been filed in such court.

"(3) A petition for rehearing or a petition for rehearing en banc in a matter decided before the effective date of this Act [Oct. 1, 1981], or submitted before the effective date of this Act and decided on or after the effective date as provided in paragraph (1) of this section, shall be treated in the same manner and with the same effect as though this Act [see Short Title of 1980 Amendments note under section 1 of this title] had not been enacted. If a petition for rehearing en banc is granted, the matter shall be reheard by a court comprised as though this Act [see Short Title of 1980 Amendments note under section 1 of this title] had not been enacted.

"**Sec. 10.** As used in sections 5, 6, 7, 8, and 9 of this Act, the term—

"(1) 'former fifth circuit' means the fifth judicial circuit of the United States as in existence on the day before the effective date of this Act [Oct. 1, 1981];

"(2) the term 'new fifth circuit' means the fifth judicial circuit of the United States established by the amendment made by section 2(2) of this Act [amending this section]; and

"(3) the term 'eleventh circuit' means the eleventh judicial circuit of the United States established by the amendment made by section 2(3) of this Act [amending this section]."

Commission on Revision of the Federal Appellate System

Pub.L. 92–489, Oct. 13, 1972, 86 Stat. 807, as amended by Pub.L. 93–420, Sept. 19, 1974, 88 Stat. 1153, provided for the establishment, membership, travel expenses, personnel, experts and consultants, administrative and research services, cooperation of other governmental agencies, and appropriations of not to exceed $606,000 of a Commission on Revision of the Federal Court Appellate System which Commission was to study the geographical division of the judicial circuits and the structure and internal procedures of the appellate court system and to report to the President, Congress, and the Chief Justice its recommendations for changes in the geographical boundaries of the circuits to expedite disposition of judicial business and for changes in the appellate court structure to expedite disposition of the appellate court structure to expedite disposition of the appellate courts caseload in a manner consistent with fundamental concepts of fairness and due process. The Commission was to cease existence ninety days after submission of its final report, which report was submitted June 20, 1975.

Commission on Structural Alternatives for the Federal Courts of Appeals

Pub.L. 105–119, Title III, § 305, Nov. 26, 1997, 111 Stat. 2491, provided that:

"**(a) Commission on Structural Alternatives for the Federal Courts of Appeal.—**

"**(1) Establishment and functions of commission.—**

"**(A) Establishment.**—There is established a Commission on Structural Alternatives for the Federal Courts of Appeals (hereinafter referred to as the 'Commission').

"**(B) Functions.**—The functions of the Commission shall be to—

"**(i)** study the present division of the United States into the several judicial circuits;

"**(ii)** study the structure and alignment of the Federal Court of Appeals system, with particular reference to the Ninth Circuit; and

"**(iii)** report to the President and the Congress its recommendations for such changes in circuit boundaries or structure as may be appropriate for the expeditious and effective disposition of the caseload of the Federal Courts of Appeals, consistent with fundamental concepts of fairness and due process.

"**(2) Membership.—**

"**(A) Composition.**—The Commission shall be composed of five members who shall be appointed by the Chief Justice of the United States.

"**(B) Appointment.**—The members of the Commission shall be appointed within 30 days after the date of enactment of this Act.

"**(C) Vacancy.**—Any vacancy in the Commission shall be filled in the same manner as the original appointment.

"**(D) Chair.**—The Commission shall elect a chair and vice chair from among its members.

"**(E) Quorum.**—Three members of the Commission shall constitute a quorum, but two may conduct hearings.

"**(3) Compensation.—**

"**(A) In general.**—Members of the Commission who are officers, or full-time employees, of the United States shall receive no additional compensation for their services, but shall be reimbursed for travel, subsistence, and other necessary expenses incurred in the performance of duties vested in the Commission, but not in excess of the maximum amounts authorized under section 456 of title 28, United States Code.

"**(B) Private members.**—Members of the Commission from private life shall receive $200 for each day (including travel time) during which the member is engaged in the actual performance of duties, but not in excess of the maximum amounts authorized under section 456 of title 28, United States Code.

"**(4) Personnel.—**

"**(A) Executive Director.**—The Commission may appoint an Executive Director who shall receive compensation at a rate not exceeding the rate prescribed for level V of the Executive Schedule under section 5316 of title 5, United States Code.

"**(B) Staff.**—The Executive Director, with the approval of the Commission, may appoint and fix the compensation of such additional personnel as the Executive Director determines necessary, without regard to the provisions of title 5, United States Code, governing appointments in the competitive service or the provisions of chapter 51 [section 5101 et seq. of Title 5] and subchapter III of chapter 53 of such title [section 5331 et seq. of Title 5] relating to classification and General Schedule pay rates. Compensation under this paragraph shall not exceed the annual maximum rate of basic pay for a position above GS–15 of the General Schedule under section 5108 of title 5, United States Code.

"**(C) Experts and consultants.**—The Executive Director may procure personal services of experts and consultants as authorized by section 3109 of title 5, United States Code, at rates not to exceed the highest level payable under the General Schedule pay rates under section 5332 of title 5, United States Code.

"**(D) Services.**—The Administrative Office of the United States Courts shall provide administrative services, including financial and budgeting services, to the Commission on a reimbursable basis. The Federal Judicial Center shall provide necessary research services to the Commission on a reimbursable basis.

"**(5) Information.**—The Commission is authorized to request from any department, agency, or independent instrumentality of the Government any information and assistance the Commission determines necessary to carry out its functions under this section. Each such department, agency, and independent instrumentality is authorized to provide such information and assistance to the extent permitted by law when requested by the chair of the Commission.

"(6) **Report.**—The Commission shall conduct the studies required in this section during the 10-month period beginning on the date on which a quorum of the Commission has been appointed. Not later than 2 months following the completion of such 10-month period, the Commission shall submit its report to the President and the Congress. The Commission shall terminate 90 days after the date of the submission of its report.

"(b) **Authorization of appropriations.**—There are authorized to be appropriated to the Commission such sums, not to exceed $900,000, as may be necessary to carry out the purposes of this section. Such sums as are appropriated shall remain available until expended."

Continuation of Organization of Court

Section 2(b) of Act June 25, 1948, c. 646, 62 Stat. 985, provided in part that the provisions of this title as set out in section 1 of said Act of June 25, 1948, with respect to the organization of each of the several courts therein provided, shall be construed as a continuation of existing law, and the tenure of the judges, officers, and employees in office on Sept. 1, 1948, and of the United States attorneys and marshals and their deputies and assistants in office on that date, shall not be affected by its enactment but each of them shall continue to serve in the same capacity under the appropriate provisions of this title, pursuant to his prior appointment.

Northern Mariana Islands

Pub.L. 95-157, § 1(a), Nov. 8, 1977, 91 Stat. 1265, provided that the Northern Mariana Islands be part of the same judicial circuit as Guam, i.e., the Ninth Circuit. See section 1694(a) of Title 48, Territories and Insular Possessions.

Puerto Rico

The name of the island of "Porto Rico" was changed to "Puerto Rico" by Act May 17, 1932, c. 190, 47 Stat. 158.

Tenth Judicial Circuit

Act Feb. 28, 1929, c. 363, § 1, 45 Stat. 1346, divided the eight judicial circuit and created the tenth judicial circuit. Prior to such division the eighth judicial circuit included, in addition, the states now constituting the tenth judicial circuit.

Termination of United States District Court for the District of the Canal Zone

For termination of the United States District Court for the District of the Canal Zone at end of the "transition period", being the 30-month period beginning Oct. 1, 1979, and ending midnight Mar. 31, 1982, see Paragraph 5 of Article XI of the Panama Canal Treaty of 1977 and sections 3831 and 3841 to 3843 of Title 22, Foreign Relations and Intercourse.

§ 42. Allotment of Supreme Court justices to circuits

The Chief Justice of the United States and the associate justices of the Supreme Court shall from time to time be allotted as circuit justices among the circuits by order of the Supreme Court. The Chief Justice may make such allotments in vacation.

A justice may be assigned to more than one circuit, and two or more justices may be assigned to the same circuit.

(June 25, 1948, c. 646, 62 Stat. 870.)

§ 43. Creation and composition of courts

(a) There shall be in each circuit a court of appeals, which shall be a court of record, known as the United States Court of Appeals for the circuit.

(b) Each court of appeals shall consist of the circuit judges of the circuit in regular active service. The circuit justice and justices or judges designated or assigned shall be competent to sit as judges of the court.

(June 25, 1948, c. 646, 62 Stat. 870; Nov. 13, 1963, Pub.L. 88-176, § 1(a), 77 Stat. 331.)

HISTORICAL AND STATUTORY NOTES

Change of Name of Court

Section 2(b) of Act June 25, 1948, c. 646, 62 Stat. 869, provided in part that each circuit court of appeals should, after Sept. 1, 1948, be known as a United States Court of Appeals, but that the enactment of said Act June 25, 1948 should in no way entail any loss of rights, interruption of jurisdiction, or prejudice to matters pending in any such courts on Sept. 1, 1948.

§ 44. Appointment, tenure, residence and salary of circuit judges

(a) The President shall appoint, by and with the advice and consent of the Senate, circuit judges for the several circuits as follows:

Circuits	Number of Judges
District of Columbia	11
First	6
Second	13
Third	14
Fourth	15
Fifth	17
Sixth	16
Seventh	11
Eighth	11
Ninth	29
Tenth	12
Eleventh	12
Federal	12.

(b) Circuit judges shall hold office during good behavior.

(c) Except in the District of Columbia, each circuit judge shall be a resident of the circuit for which appointed at the time of his appointment and thereafter while in active service. While in active service, each circuit judge of the Federal judicial circuit appointed after the effective date of the Federal Courts Improvement Act of 1982, and the chief judge of the Federal judicial circuit, whenever appointed, shall reside within fifty miles of the District of Columbia. In each circuit (other than the Federal judicial circuit) there shall be at least one circuit judge in regular active service appointed from the residents of each state [1] in that circuit.

(d) Each circuit judge shall receive a salary at an annual rate determined under section 225 of the Federal Salary Act of 1967 (2 U.S.C. 351–361), as adjusted by section 461 of this title.

(June 25, 1948, c. 646, 62 Stat. 871; Aug. 3, 1949, c. 387, § 1, 63 Stat. 493; Feb. 10, 1954, c. 6, § 1, 68 Stat. 8; Mar. 2, 1955, c. 9, § 1(b), 69 Stat. 10; May 19, 1961, Pub.L. 87–36, § 1(b), 75 Stat. 80; Aug. 14, 1964, Pub.L. 88–426, Title IV, § 403(b), 78 Stat. 434; Mar. 18, 1966, Pub.L. 89–372, § 1(b), 80 Stat. 75; June 18, 1968, Pub.L. 90–347, § 3, 82 Stat. 184; Aug. 9, 1975, Pub.L. 94–82, Title II, § 205(b)(2), 89 Stat. 422; Oct. 20, 1978, Pub.L. 95–486, § 3(b), 92 Stat. 1632; Oct. 14, 1980, Pub.L. 96–452, § 3, 94 Stat. 1994; Apr. 2, 1982, Pub.L. 97–164, Title I, § 102, 96 Stat. 25; July 10, 1984, Pub.L. 98–353, Title II, § 201(b), 98 Stat. 346; Dec. 1, 1990, Pub.L. 101–650, Title II, § 202(b), 104 Stat. 5099; Dec. 9, 1991, Pub.L. 102–198, § 10(c), 105 Stat. 1626; Nov. 26, 1997, Pub.L. 105–119, Title III, § 307, 111 Stat. 2493; Jan. 7, 2008, Pub.L. 110–177, Title V, § 509(a), 121 Stat. 2543.)

[1] So in original. Probably should be capitalized.

HISTORICAL AND STATUTORY NOTES

References in Text

The effective date of the Federal Courts Improvement Act of 1982, referred to in subsec. (c), is Oct. 1, 1982. See Effective and Applicability Provisions of 1982 Amendments note set out under section 171 of this title.

Section 225 of the Federal Salary Act of 1967, referred to in subsec. (d), is section 225 of Pub.L. 90–206, Dec. 16, 1967, 81 Stat. 642, as amended, which is classified to chapter 11 (section 351 et seq.) of Title 2, The Congress.

Effective and Applicability Provisions

2008 Acts. Pub.L. 110–177, Title V, § 509(b), Jan. 7, 2008, 121 Stat. 2543, provided that: "The amendments made by subsection (a)(2) [amending this section] shall take effect on January 21, 2009."

1990 Acts. Section 206 of Title II of Pub.L. 101–650 provided that: "This title [amending this section and section 133 of this title and enacting provisions set out as notes under this section and sections 133 and 331 of this title] shall take effect on the date of the enactment of this title [Dec. 1, 1990]."

1982 Acts. Amendment by Pub.L. 97–164 effective Oct. 1, 1982, see section 402 of Pub.L. 97–164, set out as a note under section 171 of this title.

1980 Acts. Amendment by Pub.L. 96–452 effective Oct. 1, 1981, see section 12 of Pub.L. 96–452, set out as a note under section 41 of this title.

1964 Acts. Amendment by Pub.L. 88–426 effective on the first day of the first pay period which begins on or after July 1, 1964, except to the extent provided in section 501(c) of Pub.L. 88–426, see section 501 of Pub.L. 88–426.

1955 Acts. Amendment by Act Mar. 2, 1955, effective Mar. 1, 1955, see section 5 of Act Mar. 2, 1955, set out as a note under section 31 of Title 2, The Congress.

Additional Judges

Since 1925, the appointment of additional judges was authorized by the following acts:

Second circuit. Act May 31, 1938, c. 290, § 1, 52 Stat. 584.

Third circuit. Act Aug. 3, 1949, c. 387, § 1, 63 Stat. 493; Act Dec. 7, 1944, c. 521, § 1, 58 Stat. 796; Act June 10, 1930, c. 438, 46 Stat. 538; Act June 24, 1936, c. 735, § 1, 49 Stat. 1903, repealed by Act May 31, 1938, c. 290, § 3, 52 Stat. 585.

Fifth circuit. Act Dec. 14, 1942, c. 731, 56 Stat. 1050; Act May 31, 1938, c. 290, § 1, 52 Stat. 584; Act June 10, 1930, c. 437, 46 Stat. 538.

Sixth circuit. Act May 24, 1940, c. 209, § 1, 54 Stat. 219; Act May 31, 1938, c. 290, § 1, 52 Stat. 584.

Seventh circuit. Act Aug. 3, 1949, c. 387, § 1, 63 Stat. 493; Act May 31, 1938, c. 290, § 1, 52 Stat. 584.

Eighth circuit. Act May 24, 1940, c. 209, § 1, 54 Stat. 219; Act Mar. 3, 1925, c. 437, 43 Stat. 1116.

Ninth circuit. Act Apr. 14, 1937, c. 80, 50 Stat. 64; Act Aug. 2, 1935, c. 425, § 1, 49 Stat. 508; Act June 16, 1933, c. 102, 48, Stat. 310 (removing limitation on filling of vacancy); Act Mar. 1, 1929, c. 413, 45 Stat. 1414.

Tenth circuit. Act Aug. 3, 1949, c. 387, § 1, 63 Stat. 493.

District of Columbia Court of Appeals. Act Aug. 3, 1949, c. 387, § 1, 63 Stat. 493; Act May 31, 1938, c. 290, § 2, 52 Stat. 584; Act June 19, 1930, c. 538, 46 Stat. 785.

Act Feb. 28, 1929, c. 363, § 2, 45 Stat. 1346, 1347 provided that "There shall be in the sixth, seventh, and tenth circuits, respectively, four circuit judges; and in the second and eighth circuits, respectively, five circuit judges; and in each of the other circuits three circuit judges, to be appointed by the President by and with the advice and consent of the Senate."

Another part of section 1 of Act Feb. 10, 1954, which amended subsec. (a) of this section, provided for the appointment by the President, by and with the advice and consent of the Senate, of the additional judges for the Fifth and Ninth Circuits, provided for in such amendment.

Section 1(a) of Pub.L. 87–36 provided that: "The President shall appoint, by and with the advice and consent of the Senate, three additional circuit judges for the second circuit, one additional circuit judge for the third circuit, two additional circuit judges for the fourth circuit, two additional circuit judges for the fifth circuit, one additional circuit judge for the seventh circuit, and one additional circuit judge for the tenth circuit."

Section 1(a) of Pub.L. 89–372 provided that: "The President shall appoint, by and with the advice and consent of the Senate, two additional circuit judges for the fourth circuit, two additional circuit judges for the sixth circuit, one additional circuit judge for the seventh circuit, and one additional circuit judge for the eighth circuit."

Section 1(c) of Pub.L. 89–372, as amended by Pub.L. 90–347, § 2, June 18, 1968, 82 Stat. 183, provided that: "The President shall appoint, by and with the advice and consent of the Senate, four additional circuit judges for the fifth circuit." The second sentence of section 1(c) of Pub.L. 89–372 which provided that the first four vacancies occurring in the office of circuit judge in the fifth circuit shall not be filled was deleted by section 2 of Pub.L. 90–347, which also made those judgeships permanent and further provided that the present incumbents of such judgeships shall henceforth hold their offices under this section.

Section 1 of Pub.L. 90–347 provided: "That the President shall appoint, by and with the advice and consent of the Senate, one additional circuit judge for the third circuit, two additional circuit judges for the fifth circuit, one additional circuit judge for the sixth circuit, four additional circuit judges for the ninth circuit, and one additional circuit judge for the tenth circuit."

Section 3(a) of Pub.L. 95–486 provided that: "The President shall appoint, by and with the advice and consent of the Senate, one additional circuit judgeship for the first circuit, two additional circuit judgeships for the second circuit, one additional circuit judgeship for the third circuit, three additional circuit judgeships for the fourth circuit, eleven additional circuit judgeships for the fifth circuit, two additional circuit judgeships for the sixth circuit, one additional circuit judgeship for the seventh circuit, one additional circuit judgeship for the eighth circuit, ten additional circuit judgeships for the ninth circuit, one additional circuit judgeship for the tenth circuit, and two additional circuit judgeships for the District of Columbia."

Section 201(a) of Pub.L. 98–353 provided that:

"(1) Subject to the provisions of paragraph (2), the President shall appoint, by and with the advice and consent of the Senate, two additional circuit judges for the first circuit court of appeals, two additional circuit judges for the second circuit court of appeals, two additional circuit judges for the third circuit court of appeals, one additional circuit judge for the fourth circuit court of appeals, two additional circuit judges for the fifth circuit court of appeals, four additional circuit judges for the sixth circuit court of appeals, two additional circuit judges for the seventh circuit court of appeals, one additional circuit judge for the eighth circuit court of appeals, five additional circuit judges for the ninth circuit court of appeals, two additional circuit judges for the tenth circuit court of appeals, and one additional circuit judge for the District of Columbia circuit court of appeals.

"(2) The President shall appoint, by and with the advice and consent of the Senate, no more than 11 of such judges prior to January 21, 1985."

Section 202(a) of Pub.L. 101–650 provided that: "The President shall appoint, by and with the advice and consent of the Senate—

"(1) 2 additional circuit judges for the third circuit court of appeals;

"(2) 4 additional circuit judges for the fourth circuit court of appeals;

"(3) 1 additional circuit judge for the fifth circuit court of appeals;

"(4) 1 additional circuit judge for the sixth circuit court of appeals;

"(5) 1 additional circuit judge for the eighth circuit court of appeals; and

"(6) 2 additional circuit judges for the tenth circuit court of appeals."

Congressional Statement Regarding Appointment of Judges of United States Court of Appeals for the Federal Circuit and United States Claims Court

Section 168 of Pub.L. 97–164 provided that: "The Congress—

"(1) takes notice of the fact that the quality of the Federal judiciary is determined by the competence and experience of its judges; and

"(2) suggests that the President, in nominating individuals to judgeships on the United States Court of Appeals for the Federal Circuit and the United States Claims Court [now the United States Court of Federal Claims], select from a broad range of qualified individuals."

Continued Service of Judges of Court of Claims and Court of Customs and Patent Appeals as Judges of Court of Appeals for the Federal Circuit

Section 165 of Pub.L. 97–164 provided that: "The judges of the United States Court of Claims and of the United States Court of Customs and Patent Appeals in regular active service on the effective date of this Act [Oct. 1, 1982] shall continue in office as judges of the United States Court of Appeals for the Federal Circuit. Senior judges of the United States Court of Claims and of the United States Court of Customs and Patent Appeals on the effective date of this Act [Oct. 1, 1982] shall continue in office as senior judges of the United States Court of Appeals for the Federal Circuit."

Nomination to Federal Judgeship on Nondiscriminatory Basis

Section 211 of Pub.L. 98–353 provided that: "It is the sense of the Congress that the President, in selecting individuals for nomination to the Federal judgeships created by this Act [see Short Title of 1984 Amendments note set out under section 151 of this title], shall give due consideration to qualified individuals without regard to race, color, sex, religion, or national origin."

Salary Increases

For prior year salary increases per the recommendation of the President, see Prior Salary Recommendations notes under 2 U.S.C.A. § 358.

For miscellaneous provisions dealing with adjustments of pay and limitations on use of funds to pay salaries in prior years, see notes under 5 U.S.C.A. § 5318.

§ 45. Chief judges; precedence of judges

(a)(1) The chief judge of the circuit shall be the circuit judge in regular active service who is senior in commission of those judges who—

(A) are sixty-four years of age or under;

(B) have served for one year or more as a circuit judge; and

(C) have not served previously as chief judge.

(2)(A) In any case in which no circuit judge meets the qualifications of paragraph (1), the youngest circuit judge in regular active service who is sixty-five years of age or over and who has served as circuit judge for one year or more shall act as the chief judge.

(B) In any case under subparagraph (A) in which there is no circuit judge in regular active service who has served as a circuit judge for one year or more, the circuit judge in regular active service who is senior in commission and who has not served previously as chief judge shall act as the chief judge.

(3)(A) Except as provided in subparagraph (C), the chief judge of the circuit appointed under paragraph (1) shall serve for a term of seven years and shall serve after expiration of such term until another judge is eligible under paragraph (1) to serve as chief judge of the circuit.

(B) Except as provided in subparagraph (C), a circuit judge acting as chief judge under subparagraph (A) or (B) of paragraph (2) shall serve until a judge has been appointed who meets the qualifications under paragraph (1).

(C) No circuit judge may serve or act as chief judge of the circuit after attaining the age of seventy years unless no other circuit judge is qualified to serve as chief judge of the circuit under paragraph (1) or is qualified to act as chief judge under paragraph (2).

(b) The chief judge shall have precedence and preside at any session of the court which he attends. Other circuit judges of the court in regular active service shall have precedence and preside according to the seniority of their commissions. Judges whose commissions bear the same date shall have precedence according to seniority in age. The circuit justice, however, shall have precedence over all the circuit judges and shall preside at any session which he attends.

(c) If the chief judge desires to be relieved of his duties as chief judge while retaining his active status as circuit judge, he may so certify to the Chief Justice of the United States, and thereafter the chief judge of the circuit shall be such other circuit judge who is qualified to serve or act as chief judge under subsection (a).

(d) If a chief judge is temporarily unable to perform his duties as such, they shall be performed by the circuit judge in active service, present in the circuit and able and qualified to act, who is next in precedence.

(June 25, 1948, c. 646, 62 Stat. 871; Oct. 31, 1951, c. 655, § 35, 65 Stat. 723; Aug. 6, 1958, Pub.L. 85–593, § 1, 72 Stat. 497; Apr. 2, 1982, Pub.L. 97–164, Title II, §§ 201, 204, 96 Stat. 51, 53.)

HISTORICAL AND STATUTORY NOTES

Effective and Applicability Provisions

1982 Acts. Amendment by Pub.L. 97–164 effective Oct. 1, 1982, see section 402 of Pub.L. 97–164, set out as a note under section 171 of this title.

1958 Acts. Section 3 of Pub.L. 85–593, as amended by Pub.L. 95–486, § 4, Oct. 20, 1978, 92 Stat. 1632, provided that: "The amendments to sections 45 and 136 of title 28 of the United States Code [this section and section 136 of this title] made by this Act shall take effect at the expiration of one year from the date of enactment of this Act [Aug. 6, 1958]."

Savings Provisions

Section 203 of part A of Title II of Pub.L. 97–164 provided that:

"**(a)** The amendments to section 45 of title 28, United States Code [this section], and to section 136 of such title [section 136 of this title], made by sections 201 and 202 of this Act, shall not apply to or affect any person serving as chief judge on the effective date of this Act [Oct. 1, 1982].

"**(b)** The provisions of section 45(a) of title 28, United States Code [subsec. (a) of this section], as in effect on the day before the effective date of this Act [Oct. 1, 1982], shall apply to the chief judge of a circuit serving on such effective date. The provisions of section 136(a) of title 28, United States Code [section 136(a) of this title], as in effect on the day before the effective date of this part [Oct. 1, 1982], shall apply to the chief judge of a district court serving on such effective date."

Appointment of Chief Judge of Court of Appeals for the Federal Circuit

Section 166 of Pub.L. 97–164 provided that: "Notwithstanding the provisions of section 45(a) of title 28, United States Code [subsec. (a) of this section], the first chief judge of the United States Court of Appeals for the Federal Circuit shall be the Chief Judge of the United States Court of Claims or the Chief Judge of the United States Court of Customs and Patent Appeals, whoever has served longer as chief judge of his court. Notwithstanding section 45 of title 28, United States Code [this section], whichever of the two chief judges does not become the first chief judge of the United States Court of Appeals for the Federal Circuit under the preceding sentence shall, while in active service, have precedence and be deemed senior in commission over all the circuit judges of the United States Court of Appeals for the Federal Circuit (other than the first chief judge of that circuit). When the person who first serves as chief judge of the United States Court of Appeals for the Federal Circuit vacates that position, the position shall be filled in accordance with section 45(a) of title 28, United States Code [subsec. (a) of this section], as modified by the preceding sentence of this section."

Chief Judge of Court of Appeals for District of Columbia

Section 2(a) of Act June 25, 1948, provided in part that the Chief Justice of the Court of Appeals for the District of Columbia in office on Sept. 1, 1948, shall thereafter be known as the Chief Judge.

§ 46. Assignment of judges; panels; hearings; quorum

(a) Circuit judges shall sit on the court and its panels in such order and at such times as the court directs.

(b) In each circuit the court may authorize the hearing and determination of cases and controversies by separate panels, each consisting of three judges, at least a majority of whom shall be judges of that court, unless such judges cannot sit because recused or disqualified, or unless the chief judge of that court certifies that there is an emergency including, but not limited to, the unavailability of a judge of the court because of illness. Such panels shall sit at the times and places and hear the cases and controversies assigned as the court directs. The United States Court of Appeals for the Federal Circuit shall determine by rule a procedure for the rotation of judges from panel to panel to ensure that all of the judges sit on a representative cross section of the cases heard and, notwithstanding the first sentence of this subsection, may determine by rule the number of judges, not less than three, who constitute a panel.

(c) Cases and controversies shall be heard and determined by a court or panel of not more than three judges (except that the United States Court of Appeals for the Federal Circuit may sit in panels of more than three judges if its rules so provide), unless a hearing or rehearing before the court in banc is ordered by a majority of the circuit judges of the circuit who are in regular active service. A court in banc shall consist of all circuit judges in regular active service, or such number of judges as may be prescribed in accordance with section 6 of Public Law 95–486 (92 Stat. 1633), except that any senior circuit judge of the circuit shall be eligible (1) to participate, at his election and upon designation and assignment pursuant to section 294(c) of this title and the rules of the circuit, as a member of an in banc court reviewing a decision of a panel of which such judge was a member, or (2) to continue to participate in the decision of a case or controversy that was heard or reheard by the court in banc at a time when such judge was in regular active service.

(d) A majority of the number of judges authorized to constitute a court or panel thereof, as provided in paragraph (c), shall constitute a quorum.

(June 25, 1948, c. 646, 62 Stat. 871; Nov. 13, 1963, Pub.L. 88–176, § 1(b), 77 Stat. 331; Oct. 20, 1978, Pub.L. 95–486, § 5(a), (b), 92 Stat. 1633; Apr. 2, 1982, Pub.L. 97–164, Title I, § 103, Title II, § 205, 96 Stat. 25, 53; Aug. 6, 1996, Pub.L. 104–175, § 1, 110 Stat. 1556.)

CHIEF CIRCUIT JUDGE (FIFTH CIRCUIT): ORDER DECLARING AN EMERGENCY UNDER 28 U.S.C. § 46(b)

This court is authorized 17 judges in active service. Today the number of active judges is 14. One of the vacancies has been in existence for two and one-half years. Two nominations have been sent to the Senate for its advice and consent and are pending. In addition, one active judge was recently injured seriously in an automobile accident and will be unavailable to perform his judicial duties for an indefinite period of time needed for his recuperation and rehabilitation. Effectively this places the court's strength at 13 active judges.

As of June 30, 1999, the court's workload is nearly at its historical record, with some 8,325 new filings and 5,430 pending actions.

During the last nine years, the court's filings have increased 65%, but the court has resisted an increase in the number of authorized judgeships, believing that efficiency and economy would thereby be promoted. The result has been an extremely heavy per judge workload even when operating with a full complement of judges. We have now reached the point where we are so far below our authorized strength that the timeliness and quality of our work will be jeopardized if we are unable to enlist the aid of visiting judges in greater numbers.

In sum, the three judicial vacancies, the injury to an active judge and the sustained high level of case filings have created a judicial emergency in the court. Until such time as the injured judge can return to his judicial duties and until the President has nominated and the Congress has advised and consented to the appointment of the number of judges in regular active service provided by law, a judicial emergency exists. This emergency prevents the routine empaneling of three-judge panels consisting of judges at least a majority of whom are judges of this court.

During the continuation of this declared emergency, the hearing and determination of cases and controversies may be conducted by panels of three judges selected without regard to the qualification in 28 U.S.C. § 46(b) that a majority of each panel be composed of judges of this court.

Signed this 28th day of September, 1999.

CAROLYN DINEEN KING
CHIEF JUDGE

Filed: Sept. 28, 1999

CHIEF CIRCUIT JUDGE (FOURTH CIRCUIT): ORDER REGARDING PERFORMANCE OF JUDICIAL DUTIES

Pursuant to the authority set forth in 28 U.S.C. § 46(c) and 28 U.S.C. § 294(c), all senior circuit judges in this circuit are hereby assigned to perform all judicial duties in any case, or in the decision of any matter, such as a motion or any other procedural or administrative matter, which has been properly assigned to them, whether in the ordinary course of business or otherwise. Any senior circuit judge who undertakes the performance of any official duties pursuant to this designation consents to participate (except upon absence from duty station or the like) in the consideration of the same until terminated, including, but not exclusively, participation in in banc consideration of the matter.

ENTERED this 31st day of March, 1993.

SAM J. ERVIN, III
CHIEF CIRCUIT JUDGE

HISTORICAL AND STATUTORY NOTES

References in Text

Section 6 of Public Law 95–486 (92 Stat. 1633), referred to in subsec. (c), is section 6 of Pub.L. 95–486, Oct. 20, 1978, 92 Stat. 1633, which is set out as an Appeals Court Administrative Units note under section 41 of this title.

Effective and Applicability Provisions

1982 Acts. Amendment by Pub.L. 97–164 effective Oct. 1, 1982, see section 402 of Pub.L. 97–164, set out as a note under section 171 of this title.

§ 47. Disqualification of trial judge to hear appeal

No judge shall hear or determine an appeal from the decision of a case or issue tried by him.

(June 25, 1948, c. 646, 62 Stat. 872.)

§ 48. Terms of court

(a) The courts of appeals shall hold regular sessions at the places listed below, and at such other places within the respective circuit as each court may designate by rule.

Circuits	*Places*
District of Columbia	Washington.
First	Boston.
Second	New York.
Third	Philadelphia.
Fourth	Richmond, Asheville.
Fifth	New Orleans, Fort Worth, Jackson.
Sixth	Cincinnati.
Seventh	Chicago.
Eighth	St. Louis, Kansas City, Omaha, St. Paul.
Ninth	San Francisco, Los Angeles, Portland, Seattle.
Tenth	Denver, Wichita, Oklahoma City.
Eleventh	Atlanta, Jacksonville, Montgomery.
Federal	District of Columbia, and in any other place listed above as the court by rule directs.

(b) Each court of appeals may hold special sessions at any place within its circuit as the nature of the business may require, and upon such notice as the court orders. The court may transact any business at a special session which it might transact at a regular session.

(c) Any court of appeals may pretermit any regular session of court at any place for insufficient business or other good cause.

(d) The times and places of the sessions of the Court of Appeals for the Federal Circuit shall be prescribed with a view to securing reasonable opportunity to citizens to appear before the court with as little inconvenience and expense to citizens as is practicable.

(e) Each court of appeals may hold special sessions at any place within the United States outside the circuit as the nature of the business may require and upon such notice as the court orders, upon a finding by either the chief judge of the court of appeals (or, if the chief judge is unavailable, the most senior available active judge of the court of appeals) or the judicial council of the circuit that, because of emergency conditions, no location within the circuit is reasonably available where such special sessions could be held. The court may transact any business at a special session outside the circuit which it might transact at a regular session.

(f) If a court of appeals issues an order exercising its authority under subsection (e), the court—

(1) through the Administrative Office of the United States Courts, shall—

(A) send notice of such order, including the reasons for the issuance of such order, to the Committee on the Judiciary of the Senate and the Committee on the Judiciary of the House of Representatives; and

(B) not later than 180 days after the expiration of such court order submit a brief report to the Committee on the Judiciary of the Senate and the Committee on the Judiciary of the House of Representatives describing the impact of such order, including—

(i) the reasons for the issuance of such order;

(ii) the duration of such order;

(iii) the impact of such order on litigants; and

(iv) the costs to the judiciary resulting from such order; and

(2) shall provide reasonable notice to the United States Marshals Service before the commencement of any special session held pursuant to such order.

(June 25, 1948, c. 646, 62 Stat. 872; Oct. 31, 1951, c. 655, § 36, 65 Stat. 723; Oct. 14, 1980, Pub.L. 96–452, § 4, 94 Stat. 1994; Apr. 2, 1982, Pub.L. 97–164, Title I, § 104, 96 Stat. 26; Oct. 29, 1992, Pub.L. 102–572, Title V, § 501, 106 Stat. 4512; Sept. 9, 2005, Pub.L. 109–63, § 2(a), 119 Stat. 1993.)

HISTORICAL AND STATUTORY NOTES

Effective and Applicability Provisions

1992 Acts. Amendment by Pub.L. 102–572 effective Jan. 1, 1993, see section 1101(a) of Pub.L. 102–572, set out as a note under section 905 of Title 2, The Congress.

1982 Acts. Amendment by Pub.L. 97–164 effective Oct. 1, 1982, see section 402 of Pub.L. 97–164, set out as a note under section 171 of this title.

1980 Acts. Amendment by Pub.L. 96–452 effective Oct. 1, 1981, see section 12 of Pub.L. 96–452, set out as a note under section 41 of this title.

Survey of Judicial Business in Alaska

Section 23(a) of Pub.L. 86–70, June 25, 1959, 73 Stat. 147, provided that: "The Judicial Conference of the United States, with the assistance of the Administrative Office of the United States Courts, shall conduct a study, including a field survey, of the Federal judicial business arising in the State of Alaska with a view toward directing the United States Court of Appeals for the Ninth Circuit to hold such terms of court in Anchorage or such other Alaskan cities as may be necessary for the prompt and efficient administration of justice."

§ 49. Assignment of judges to division to appoint independent counsels

(a) Beginning with the two-year period commencing on the date of the enactment of this section, three judges or justices shall be assigned for each successive two-year period to a division of the United States Court of Appeals for the District of Columbia to be the division of the court for the purpose of appointing independent counsels. The Clerk of the United States Court of Appeals for the District of Columbia Circuit shall serve as the clerk of such division of the court and shall provide such services as are needed by such division of the court.

(b) Except as provided under subsection (f) of this section, assignment to such division of the court shall not be a bar to other judicial assignments during the term of such division.

(c) In assigning judges or justices to sit on such division of the court, priority shall be given to senior circuit judges and retired justices.

(d) The Chief Justice of the United States shall designate and assign three circuit court judges or justices, one of whom shall be a judge of the United States Court of Appeals for the District of Columbia, to such division of the court. Not more than one judge or justice or senior or retired judge or justice may be named to such division from a particular court.

(e) Any vacancy in such division of the court shall be filled only for the remainder of the two-year period in which such vacancy occurs and in the same manner as initial assignments to such division were made.

(f) Except as otherwise provided in chapter 40 of this title, no member of such division of the court who participated in a function conferred on the division under chapter 40 of this title involving an independent counsel shall be eligible to participate in any judicial proceeding concerning a matter which involves such independent counsel while such independent counsel is serving in that office or which involves the exercise of such independent counsel's official duties, regardless of whether such independent counsel is still serving in that office.

(Added Pub.L. 95–521, Title VI, § 602(a), Oct. 26, 1978, 92 Stat. 1873, and amended Pub.L. 97–409, § 2(b)(1), Jan. 3, 1983, 96 Stat. 2039; Pub.L. 99–554, Title I, § 144(g)(3), Oct. 27, 1986, 100 Stat. 3097; Pub.L. 100–191, §§ 4, 5(a), Dec. 15, 1987, 101 Stat. 1307.)

HISTORICAL AND STATUTORY NOTES

References in Text

The date of the enactment of this section, referred to in subsec. (a), means Oct. 26, 1978, the date on which Pub.L. 95–521 was approved.

Effective and Applicability Provisions

1987 Acts. Amendment by Pub.L. 100–191 effective on Dec. 15, 1987, see section 6 of Pub.L. 100–191, set out as a note under section 591 of this title.

1986 Acts. Amendment by Pub.L. 99–554 effective 30 days after Oct. 27, 1986, see section 302(a) of Pub.L. 99–554, as amended, set out as a note under section 581 of this title.

1978 Acts. Section effective Oct. 26, 1978, see section 604 of Pub.L. 95–521, set out as a note under section 591 of this title.

Appointment of Regulatory Independent Counsel

Division of the court described in this section authorized to appoint as independent counsel any individual who, on June 30, 1994, is serving as a regulatory independent counsel under parts 600 and 603 of title 28, Code of Federal Regulations, notwithstanding the restriction in section 593(b)(2) of this title, see section 7(h) of Pub.L. 103–270, set out as an Effective Date of 1994 Acts note under section 591 of this title.

CHAPTER 5—DISTRICT COURTS

Sec.
81. Alabama.
81A. Alaska.
82. Arizona.
83. Arkansas.
84. California.
85. Colorado.
86. Connecticut.
87. Delaware.
88. District of Columbia.
89. Florida.
90. Georgia.
91. Hawaii.
92. Idaho.
93. Illinois.
94. Indiana.
95. Iowa.
96. Kansas.
97. Kentucky.
98. Louisiana.
99. Maine.
100. Maryland.
101. Massachusetts.
102. Michigan.
103. Minnesota.
104. Mississippi.
105. Missouri.
106. Montana.
107. Nebraska.
108. Nevada.
109. New Hampshire.
110. New Jersey.
111. New Mexico.
112. New York.
113. North Carolina.

Sec.
114. North Dakota.
115. Ohio.
116. Oklahoma.
117. Oregon.
118. Pennsylvania.
119. Puerto Rico.
120. Rhode Island.
121. South Carolina.
122. South Dakota.
123. Tennessee.
124. Texas.
125. Utah.
126. Vermont.
127. Virginia.
128. Washington.
129. West Virginia.
130. Wisconsin.
131. Wyoming.
132. Creation and composition of district courts.
133. Appointment and number of district judges.
134. Tenure and residence of district judges.
135. Salaries of district judges.
136. Chief judges; precedence of district judges.
137. Division of business among district judges.
138. Terms abolished.
139. Times for holding regular sessions.
140. Adjournment.
141. Special sessions; places; notice.
[142. Repealed.]
143. Vacant judgeship as affecting proceedings.
144. Bias or prejudice of judge.

HISTORICAL AND STATUTORY NOTES

Short Title

1978 Amendments. For short title of Pub.L. 95–408, Oct. 2, 1978, 92 Stat. 883, as "Federal District Court Organization Act of 1978", see note set out under section 1 of this title.

§ 81. Alabama

Alabama is divided into three judicial districts to be known as the Northern, Middle, and Southern Districts of Alabama.

Northern District

(a) The Northern District comprises seven divisions.

(1) The Northwestern Division comprises the counties of Colbert, Franklin, and Lauderdale.

Court for the Northwestern Division shall be held at Florence.

(2) The Northeastern Division comprises the counties of Cullman, Jackson, Lawrence, Limestone, Madison, and Morgan.

Court for the Northeastern Division shall be held at Huntsville and Decatur.

(3) The Southern Division comprises the counties of Blount, Jefferson, and Shelby.

Court for the Southern Division shall be held at Birmingham.

(4) The Eastern Division comprises the counties of Calhoun, Clay, Cleburne, and Talladega.

Court for the Eastern Division shall be held at Anniston.

(5) The Western Division comprises the counties of Bibb, Greene, Pickens, Sumter, and Tuscaloosa.

Court for the Western Division shall be held at Tuscaloosa.

(6) The Middle Division comprises the counties of Cherokee, De Kalb, Etowah, Marshall, and Saint Clair.

Court for the Middle Division shall be held at Gadsden.

(7) The Jasper Division comprises the counties of Fayette, Lamar, Marion, Walker, and Winston.

Court for the Jasper Division shall be held at Jasper.

Middle District

(b) The Middle District comprises three divisions.

(1) The Northern Division comprises the counties of Autauga, Barbour, Bullock, Butler, Chilton, Coosa, Covington, Crenshaw, Elmore, Lowndes, Montgomery, and Pike.

Court for the Northern Division shall be held at Montgomery.

(2) The Southern Division comprises the counties of Coffee, Dale, Geneva, Henry, and Houston.

Court for the Southern Division shall be held at Dothan.

(3) The Eastern Division comprises the counties of Chambers, Lee, Macon, Randolph, Russell, and Tallapoosa.

Court for the Eastern Division shall be held at Opelika.

Southern District

(c) The Southern District comprises two divisions.

(1) The Northern Division comprises the counties of Dallas, Hale, Marengo, Perry, and Wilcox.

Court for the Northern Division shall be held at Selma.

(2) The Southern Division comprises the counties of Baldwin, Choctaw, Clarke, Conecuh, Escambia, Mobile, Monroe, and Washington.

Court for the Southern Division shall be held at Mobile.

(June 25, 1948, c. 646, 62 Stat. 873; May 19, 1961, Pub.L. 87–36, § 3(a), 75 Stat. 83.)

§ 81A. Alaska

Alaska constitutes one judicial district.

Court shall be held at Anchorage, Fairbanks, Juneau, Ketchikan, and Nome.

(Added Pub.L. 85–508, § 12(b), July 7, 1958, 72 Stat. 348, and amended Pub.L. 86–70, § 23(b), June 25, 1959, 73 Stat. 147.)

HISTORICAL AND STATUTORY NOTES

Effective and Applicability Provisions

1958 Acts. Section 12 of Pub.L. 85–508 provided in part that this section, and the amendments to sections 133, 333, 373, 376, 460, 610, 753, 1252, 1291, 1292, 1294, 1346, 1963, 2072, 2201 and 2410 of this title, former section 341b of Title 5, Government Organization and Employees, and sections 3241, 3401, 3771 and 3772 of Title 18, Crimes and Criminal Procedure, shall be effective upon the admission of Alaska into the Union. Admission as a State was accomplished Jan. 3, 1959 upon issuance of Proc. No. 3269, Jan. 3, 1959, 24 F.R. 81, 73 Stat. c16, as required by sections 1 and 8(c) of Pub.L. 85–508. See notes set out preceding section 21 of Title 48, Territories and Insular Possessions.

Appeals

Section 14 of Pub.L. 85–508 provided that: "All appeals taken from the District Court for the Territory of Alaska to the Supreme Court of the United States or the United States Court of Appeals for the Ninth Circuit, previous to the admission of Alaska as a State, shall be prosecuted to final determination as though this Act had not been passed. All cases in which final judgment has been rendered in such district court, and in which appeals might be had except for the admission of such State, may still be sued out, taken, and prosecuted to the Supreme Court of the United States or the United States Court of Appeals for the Ninth Circuit under the provisions of then existing law, and there held and determined in like manner; and in either case, the Supreme Court of the United States, or the United States Court of Appeals, in the event of reversal, shall remand the said cause to either the State supreme court or other final appellate court of said State, or the United States district court for said district, as the case may require: *Provided*, That the time allowed by existing law for appeals from the district court for said Territory shall not be enlarged thereby."

Continuation of Suits

Section 13 of Pub.L. 85–508 provided that: "No writ, action, indictment, cause, or proceeding pending in the District Court for the Territory of Alaska on the date when said Territory shall become a State, and no case pending in an appellate court upon appeal from the District Court for the Territory of Alaska at the time said Territory shall become a State, shall abate by the admission of the State of Alaska into the Union, but the same shall be transferred and proceeded with as hereinafter provided.

"All civil causes of action and all criminal offenses which shall have arisen or been committed prior to the admission of said State, but as to which no suit, action, or prosecution shall be pending at the date of such admission, shall be subject to prosecution in the appropriate State courts or in the United States District Court for the District of Alaska in like manner, to the same extent, and with like right of appellate review, as if said State had been created and said courts had been established prior to the accrual of said causes of action or the commission of such offenses; and such of said criminal offenses as shall have been committed against the laws of the Territory shall be tried and punished by the appropriate courts of said State, and such as shall have been committed against the laws of the United States shall be tried and punished in the United States District Court for the District of Alaska."

Pending Cases

Section 17 of Pub.L. 85–508 provided that: "All cases pending in the District Court for the Territory of Alaska at the time said Territory becomes a State not transferred to the United States District Court for the District of Alaska shall be proceeded with and determined by the courts created by said State with the right to prosecute appeals to the appellate courts created by said State, and also with the same right to prosecute appeals or writs of certiorari from the final determination in said causes made by the court of last resort created by such State to the Supreme Court of the United States, as now provided by law for appeals and writs of certiorari from the court of last resort of a State to the Supreme Court of the United States."

Schedule of Fees, Mileage, or Other Compensation

Section 23(c) of Pub.L. 86–70, June 25, 1959, 73 Stat. 147, provided that: "Such authority as has been exercised by the Attorney General heretofore, with regard to the Federal court system in Alaska, pursuant to section 30 of the Act of June 6, 1900 (48 U.S.C. 25) [omitted], shall continue to be exercised by him after the court created by section 12(b) of the Act of July 7, 1958 (72 Stat. 339, 348) [this section], providing for the admission of the State of Alaska into the Union, is established."

Succession of Courts

Section 16 of Pub.L. 85–508 provided that: "Jurisdiction of all cases pending or determined in the District Court for the Territory of Alaska not transferred to the United States District Court for the District of Alaska shall devolve upon and be exercised by the courts of original jurisdiction created by said State, which shall be deemed to be the successor of the District Court for the Territory of Alaska with respect to cases not so transferred and, as such, shall take and retain custody of all records, dockets, journals, and files of such court pertaining to such cases. The files and papers in all cases so transferred to the United States district court, together with a transcript of all book entries to complete the record in such particular cases so transferred, shall be in like manner transferred to said district court."

Termination of Jurisdiction of District Court for the Territory of Alaska

Section 18 of Pub.L. 85–508 provided that: "The provisions of the preceding sections with respect to the termination of the jurisdiction of the District Court for the Territory of Alaska, the continuation of suits, the succession of courts, and the satisfaction of rights of litigants in suits before such courts, shall not be effective until three years after the effective date of this Act [see section 8(b) of Pub.L. 85–508, set out as a note preceding section 21 of Title 48, Territories and Insular Possessions] unless the President, by Executive order, shall sooner proclaim that the United States District Court for the District of Alaska, established in accordance with the provisions of this Act, is prepared to assume the functions imposed upon it. During such period of three years or until such Executive order is issued, the United States District Court for the Territory of Alaska shall continue to function as heretofore. The tenure of the judges, the United States attorneys, marshals, and other officers of the United States District Court for the Territory of Alaska shall terminate at such time as that court shall cease to function as provided in this section."

Based on Title 28, U.S.C., 1940 ed., § 216, and District of Columbia Code, 1940 ed., § 11–205 (Acts Feb. 9, 1893, c. 74, § 6, 27 Stat. 435; July 30, 1894, c. 172, § 2, 28 Stat. 161; Mar. 3, 1901, c. 854, § 225, 31 Stat. 1225; Mar. 3, 1911, c. 231, § 120, 36 Stat. 1132).

The provision in section 11–205 of the District of Columbia Code, 1940 ed., that a justice of the district court while on the bench of the Court of Appeals in the District of Columbia shall not sit in review of judgment, order, or decree rendered by him below, was consolidated with a similar provision of section 216 of Title 28 U.S.C., 1940 ed. The consolidation simplifies the language without change of substance.

Transfer of Cases

Section 15 of Pub.L. 85–508 provided that: "All causes pending or determined in the District Court for the Territory of Alaska at the time of the admission of Alaska as a State which are of such nature as to be within the jurisdiction of a district court of the United States shall be transferred to the United States District Court for the District of Alaska for final disposition and enforcement in the same manner as is now provided by law with reference to the judgments and decrees in existing United States district courts. All other causes pending or determined in the District Court for the Territory of Alaska at the time of the admission of Alaska as a State shall be transferred to the appropriate State court of Alaska. All final judgments and decrees rendered upon such transferred cases in the United States District Court for the District of Alaska may be reviewed by the Supreme Court of the United States or by the United States Court of Appeals for the Ninth Circuit in the same manner as is now provided by law with reference to the judgments and decrees in existing United States district courts."

EXECUTIVE ORDERS

EXECUTIVE ORDER NO. 10867

ASSUMPTION OF FUNCTIONS BY UNITED STATES DISTRICT COURT FOR DISTRICT OF ALASKA

WHEREAS the act of July 7, 1958, 72 Stat. 339 [set out as a note preceding section 21 of Title 48, Territories and Insular Possessions], relating to the admission of the State of Alaska into the Union, provides that the United States District Court for the Territory of Alaska shall continue to function as theretofore for a period of three years after the effective date of that act, unless the President, by Executive order, shall sooner proclaim that the United States District Court for the District of Alaska, established in accordance with the provisions of that act, is prepared to assume the functions imposed upon it; and

WHEREAS that act further provides that its provisions relating to the termination of the jurisdiction of the District Court for the Territory of Alaska, the continuation of suits, the succession of courts, and the satisfaction of the rights of litigants in suits before such courts shall not be effective until the expiration of the above-mentioned three-year period or until such Executive order is issued; and that the tenure of the judges, the United States Attorneys, Marshals, and other officers of the United States District Court for the Territory of Alaska shall terminate at such time as that court shall cease to function; and

WHEREAS, I have appointed, by and with the advice and consent of the Senate, and commissioned the Honorable Walter N. Hodge to be United States District Judge for the District of Alaska, and he has taken his oath of office; and

WHEREAS Judge Hodge has appointed an acting United States Attorney, an acting United States Marshal, and other court officers; and

WHEREAS the United States District Court for the District of Alaska is now prepared to assume the functions imposed upon it:

NOW, THEREFORE, by virtue of the authority vested in me by section 18 of the said act of July 7, 1958 [set out as a note under this section], I hereby proclaim that the United States District Court for the District of Alaska is prepared to assume the functions imposed upon it. Accordingly, the jurisdiction of the District Court for the Territory of Alaska and the tenure of the judges, the United States Attorneys, Marshals, and other officers of that court are now terminated.

DWIGHT D. EISENHOWER

§ 82. Arizona

Arizona constitutes one judicial district.

Court shall be held at Globe, Phoenix, Prescott, and Tucson.

(June 25, 1948, c. 646, 62 Stat. 874.)

§ 83. Arkansas

Arkansas is divided into two judicial districts to be known as the Eastern and Western Districts of Arkansas.

Eastern District

(a) The Eastern District comprises five divisions.

(1) The Eastern Division comprises the counties of Cross, Lee, Monroe, Phillips, Saint Francis, and Woodruff.

Court for the Eastern Division shall be held at Helena.

(2) The Western Division comprises the counties of Conway, Faulkner, Lonoke, Perry, Pope, Prairie, Pulaski, Saline, Van Buren, White, and Yell.

Court for the Western Division shall be held at Little Rock.

(3) The Pine Bluff Division comprises the counties of Arkansas, Chicot, Cleveland, Dallas, Desha, Drew, Grant, Jefferson, and Lincoln.

Court for the Pine Bluff Division shall be held at Pine Bluff.

(4) The Northern Division comprises the counties of Cleburne, Fulton, Independence, Izard, Jackson, Sharp, and Stone.

Court for the Northern Division shall be held at Batesville.

(5) The Jonesboro Division comprises the counties of Clay, Craighead, Crittenden, Greene, Lawrence, Mississippi, Poinsett, and Randolph.

Court for the Jonesboro Division shall be held at Jonesboro.

Western District

(b) The Western District comprises six divisions.

(1) The Texarkana Division comprises the counties of Hempstead, Howard, Lafayette, Little River, Miller, Nevada, and Sevier.

Court for the Texarkana Division shall be held at Texarkana, and may be held anywhere within the Federal courthouse in Texarkana that is located astride the State line between Texas and Arkansas.

(2) The El Dorado Division comprises the counties of Ashley, Bradley, Calhoun, Columbia, Ouachita, and Union.

Court for the El Dorado Division shall be held at El Dorado.

(3) The Fort Smith Division comprises the counties of Crawford, Franklin, Johnson, Logan, Polk, Scott, and Sebastian.

Court for the Fort Smith Division shall be held at Fort Smith.

(4) The Harrison Division comprises the counties of Baxter, Boone, Carroll, Marion, Newton, and Searcy.

Court for the Harrison Division shall be held at Harrison.

(5) The Fayetteville Division comprises the counties of Benton, Madison, and Washington.

Court for the Fayetteville Division shall be held at Fayetteville.

(6) The Hot Springs Division comprises the counties of Clark, Garland, Hot Springs, Montgomery, and Pike.

Court for the Hot Springs Division shall be held at Hot Springs.

(June 25, 1948, c. 646, 62 Stat. 874; May 19, 1961, Pub.L. 87–36, § 5, 75 Stat. 84; Dec. 10, 2004, Pub.L. 108–455, § 3, 118 Stat. 3628.)

§ 84. California

California is divided into four judicial districts to be known as the Northern, Eastern, Central, and Southern Districts of California.

Northern District

(a) The Northern District comprises the counties of Alameda, Contra Costa, Del Norte, Humboldt, Lake, Marin, Mendocino, Monterey, Napa, San Benito, Santa Clara, Santa Cruz, San Francisco, San Mateo, and Sonoma.

Court for the Northern District shall be held at Eureka, Oakland, San Francisco, and San Jose.

Eastern District

(b) The Eastern District comprises the counties of Alpine, Amador, Butte, Calaveras, Colusa, El Dorado, Fresno, Glenn, Inyo, Kern, Kings, Lassen, Madera, Mariposa, Merced, Modoc, Mono, Nevada, Placer, Plumas, Sacramento, San Joaquin, Shasta, Sierra, Siskiyou, Solano, Stanislaus, Sutter, Tehama, Trinity, Tulare, Tuolumne, Yolo, and Yuba.

Court for the Eastern District shall be held at Fresno, Redding, and Sacramento.

Central District

(c) The Central District comprises 3 divisions.

(1) The Eastern Division comprises the counties of Riverside and San Bernardino.

Court for the Eastern Division shall be held at a suitable site in the city of Riverside, the city of San Bernardino, or not more than 5 miles from the boundary of either such city.

(2) The Western Division comprises the counties of Los Angeles, San Luis Obispo, Santa Barbara, and Ventura.

Court for the Western Division shall be held at Los Angeles.

(3) The Southern Division comprises Orange County.

Court for the Southern Division shall be held at Santa Ana.

Southern District

(d) The Southern District comprises the counties of Imperial and San Diego.

Court for the Southern District shall be held at San Diego.

(June 25, 1948, c. 646, 62 Stat. 875; Mar. 18, 1966, Pub.L. 89–372, § 3(a), 80 Stat. 75; Oct. 15, 1980, Pub.L. 96–462, § 2, 94 Stat. 2053; Aug. 26, 1992, Pub.L. 102–357, § 2, 106 Stat. 958.)

HISTORICAL AND STATUTORY NOTES

Effective and Applicability Provisions

1992 Acts. Section 3 of Pub.L. 102–357 provided that:

"(a) In general

"This Act and the amendments made by this Act [amending this section and enacting provisions set out as a note under this section] shall take effect 6 months after the date of the enactment of this Act [Aug. 26, 1992].

"(b) Pending cases not affected

"This Act and the amendments made by this Act [amending this section and enacting provisions set out as a note under this section] shall not affect any action commenced before the effective date of this Act and pending in the United States District Court for the Central District of California on such date.

"(c) Juries not affected

"This Act and the amendments made by this Act [amending this section and enacting provisions set out as a note under this section] shall not affect the composition, or preclude the service, of any grand or petit jury summoned, empaneled, or actually serving in the Central Judicial District of California on the effective date of this Act."

1980 Acts. Section 7 of Pub.L. 96–462 provided that:

"(a) This Act and the amendments made by this Act [amending sections 84, 95, 105, 113, and 124 of this title and enacting provisions set out as notes under sections 95, 105, and 113 of this title] shall take effect on October 1, 1981.

"(b) Nothing in this Act shall affect the composition or preclude the service of any grand or petit juror summoned, empaneled, or actually serving in any judicial district on the effective date of this Act [Oct. 1, 1981]."

1966 Acts. Section 3(i) of Pub.L. 89–372 provided that: "The provisions of this section [amending this section and enacting provisions set out as a note under this section and section 133 of this title] shall become effective six months after the date of enactment of this Act [March 18, 1966]."

Congressional Findings Concerning Creation of Three Divisions in Central District

Section 1 of Pub.L. 102–357 provided that:

"The Congress makes the following findings:

"(1) The Federal Government has the responsibility to provide quality services which are readily accessible to the people it serves.

"(2) The court facilities in the Central Judicial District of California are presently inadequate, and current and projected growth exacerbates the problem.

"(3) The population demographics of southern California have changed dramatically over the last decade, as the center of population shifts inland. Between 1980 and 1990, the population of Riverside County increased 76.5 percent, and San Bernardino County's population increased 58.5 percent, to a combined population of 2,600,000.

"(4) In the next 15 years, the population in Riverside and San Bernardino Counties is expected to increase again by 70 percent, and 67 percent, respectively. By the year 2005, Riverside and San Bernardino Counties will have 4,400,000 residents.

"(5) As a result of the population growth, the freeways connecting the Pacific coast and the inland areas are tremendously overburdened, and Federal offices along the coast are no longer accessible to the residents of Riverside and San Bernardino Counties.

"(6) The creation of 3 divisions in the Central Judicial District of California is urgently needed to provide for the delivery of judicial services to all areas and all residents of the Central Judicial District of California."

Creation of Eastern and Central Districts: Transfer of District Judges; Transfer and Appointment of United States Attorneys and United States Marshals

Section 3(b) to (g) of Pub.L. 89–372 provided that:

"(b) The two district judges for the northern district of California holding office on the day before the effective date of this section [see Effective and Applicability Provisions of 1966 Acts note under this section] and whose official station is Sacramento shall, on and after such date, be district judges for the eastern district of California. All other district judges for the northern district of California holding office on the day before the effective date of this section shall, on and after such date, be district judges for the northern district of California.

"(c) The district judge for the southern district of California, residing in the northern division thereof and holding office on the day before the effective date of this section [see Effective and Applicability Provisions of 1966 Acts note under this section], shall, on and after such date, be a district judge for the eastern district of California. The two district judges for the southern district of California holding office on the day before the effective date of this section, and whose official station is San Diego shall, on and after such date, be the district judges for the southern district of California. All other district judges for the southern district of California holding office on the day before the effective date of this section shall, on and after such date, be district judges for the central district of California.

"(d) Nothing in this Act [amending sections 44, 84, and 133 of this title and enacting provisions set out as notes under sections 44, 84, and 133 of this title] shall in any manner affect the tenure of office of the United States attorney and the United States marshal for the northern district of California who are in office on the effective date of this section [see Effective and Applicability Provisions of 1966 Amendments note under this section], and who shall be during the remainder of their present terms of office the United States attorney and marshal for such district as constituted by this Act.

"(e) Nothing in this Act [amending sections 44, 84, and 133 of this title and enacting provisions set out as notes under sections 44, 84, and 133 of this title] shall in any manner affect the tenure of office of the United States attorney and the United States marshal for the southern district of California who are in office on the effective date of this section, and who shall be during the remainder of their present terms of office the United States attorney and marshal for the central district of California.

"(f) The President shall appoint, by and with the advice and consent of the Senate, a United States attorney and a United States marshal for the southern district of California.

"(g) The President shall appoint, by and with the advice and consent of the Senate, a United States attorney and a United States marshal for the eastern district of California."

Study of Judicial Business in Central District, California and Eastern District, New York and Recommendations for Creation of New Judicial Districts

Pub.L. 95–573, § 5, Nov. 2, 1978, 92 Stat. 2458, required the Director of the Administrative Office of the United States

Courts to conduct a study of the judicial business of the Central District of California and the Eastern District of New York, within one year of Nov. 2, 1978, and to make recommendations to Congress with respect to the need for creation of new judicial districts.

§ 85. Colorado

Colorado constitutes one judicial district.

Court shall be held at Boulder, Colorado Springs, Colorado Springs,[1] Denver, Durango, Grand Junction, Montrose, Pueblo, and Sterling.

(June 25, 1948, c. 646, 62 Stat. 875; Nov. 8, 1984, Pub.L. 98–620, Title IV, § 409, 98 Stat. 3362; Dec. 10, 2004, Pub.L. 108–455, § 5, 118 Stat. 3629; Dec. 23, 2004, Pub.L. 108–482, Title III, § 301, 118 Stat. 3918.)

[1] So in original. Pub.L. 108–455, § 5 and Pub.L. 108–482, § 301 both added "Colorado Springs," after "Boulder,".

HISTORICAL AND STATUTORY NOTES

Effective and Applicability Provisions

1984 Acts. Section 411 of Pub.L. 98–620 provided that:

"(a) The amendments made by this subtitle [amending sections 85, 90, 93, 112, 124 and 126 of this title and enacting provisions set out as notes under sections 1, 90, 93, and 124 of this title] shall take effect on January 1, 1985.

"(b) The amendments made by this subtitle shall not affect the composition, or preclude the service, of any grand or petit jury summoned, impaneled, or actually serving on the effective date of this subtitle [Jan. 1, 1985]."

§ 86. Connecticut

Connecticut constitutes one judicial district.

Court shall be held at Bridgeport, Hartford, New Haven, New London, and Waterbury.

(June 25, 1948, c. 646, 62 Stat. 875; May 19, 1961, Pub.L. 87–36, § 3(b), 75 Stat. 83; Sept. 7, 1966, Pub.L. 89–558, 80 Stat. 705.)

§ 87. Delaware

Delaware constitutes one judicial district.

Court shall be held at Wilmington.

(June 25, 1948, c. 646, 62 Stat. 875.)

§ 88. District of Columbia

The District of Columbia constitutes one judicial district.

Court shall be held at Washington.

(June 25, 1948, c. 646, 62 Stat. 875.)

§ 89. Florida

Florida is divided into three judicial districts to be known as the Northern, Middle, and Southern Districts of Florida.

Northern District

(a) The Northern District comprises the counties of Alachua, Bay, Calhoun, Dixie, Escambia, Franklin, Gadsden, Gilchrist, Gulf, Holmes, Jackson, Jefferson, Lafayette, Leon, Levy, Liberty, Madison, Okaloosa, Santa Rosa, Taylor, Wakulla, Walton, and Washington.

Court for the Northern District shall be held at Gainesville, Marianna, Panama City, Pensacola, and Tallahassee.

Middle District

(b) The Middle District comprises the counties of Baker, Bradford, Brevard, Charlotte, Citrus, Clay, Collier, Columbia, De Soto, Duval, Flagler, Glades, Hamilton, Hardee, Hendry, Hernando, Hillsborough, Lake, Lee, Manatee, Marion, Nassau, Orange, Osceola, Pasco, Pinellas, Polk, Putnam, St. Johns, Sarasota, Seminole, Sumter, Suwannee, Union, and Volusia.

Court for the Middle District shall be held at Fernandina, Fort Myers, Jacksonville, Live Oak, Ocala, Orlando, Saint Petersburg, and Tampa.

Southern District

(c) The Southern District comprises the counties of Broward, Dade, Highlands, Indian River, Martin, Monroe, Okeechobee, Palm Beach, and Saint Lucie.

Court for the Southern District shall be held at Fort Lauderdale, Fort Pierce, Key West, Miami, and West Palm Beach.

(June 25, 1948, c. 646, 62 Stat. 876; July 17, 1952, c. 929, 66 Stat. 757; May 19, 1961, Pub.L. 87–36, § 3(f), 75 Stat. 83; July 30, 1962, Pub.L. 87–562, § 1, 76 Stat. 247; June 2, 1970, Pub.L. 91–272, § 10, 84 Stat. 298; Oct. 2, 1978, Pub.L. 95–408, § 4(a), 92 Stat. 884; Nov. 19, 1988, Pub.L. 100–702, Title X, § 1021(a), 102 Stat. 4672.)

HISTORICAL AND STATUTORY NOTES

Effective and Applicability Provisions

1988 Acts. Section 1021(b), (c) of Pub. L. 100–702 provided that:

"**(b) Effective Date.—(1)** The amendments made by this section [amending subsecs. (b) and (c) of this section] shall take effect 90 days after the date of enactment of this title [Nov. 19, 1988].

"**(2)** The amendments made by subsection (a) [amending subsecs. (b) and (c) of this section] shall apply to any action commenced in the United States District Court for the Middle District of Florida, or in the United States District Court for the Southern District of Florida, on or after the effective date of this title [probably should be effective date of this section], and shall not affect any action pending in either such court on such effective date.

"**(c) Juries.**—The amendments made by this section [amending subsecs. (b) and (c) of this section] shall not affect the composition, or preclude the service, of any grand or petit jury summoned, empaneled, or actually serving on the effective date of this title [probably should be effective date of this section]."

1978 Acts. Section 5 of Pub.L. 95–408 provided that:

"(a) The amendments made by this Act [amending sections 89, 93, 97, 98, 104, 112, 114, and 133 of this title and enacting provisions set out as a note under section 81 of this title] shall take effect 180 days after the date of enactment of this Act [Oct. 2, 1978].

"(b) Nothing in this Act [amending sections 89, 93, 97, 98, 104, 112, 114, and 133 of this title and enacting provisions set out as a note under section 81 of this title] shall affect the composition or preclude the service of any grand or petit juror summoned, empaneled, or actually serving in any judicial district on the effective date of this Act."

1962 Acts. Section 5 of Pub.L. 87–562 provided that: "This Act [amending this section and section 133 of this title, and enacting provisions set out as notes under this section and section 142 of this title] shall become effective ninety days after the date of enactment [July 30, 1962]."

District Judges, United States Attorneys, and United States Marshals; Designations; Tenure; Appointments

Section 2 of Pub.L. 87–562 provided that:

"(a) The district judge appointed September 26, 1950, the district judge appointed August 13, 1955, and the district judge appointed March 8, 1961, all for the Southern District of Florida, shall hereafter be designated as district judges for the Middle District of Florida.

"(b) The district judge for the Northern and Southern Districts of Florida shall hereafter be designated as the district judge for the Northern, Middle, and Southern Districts of Florida.

"(c) Nothing in this Act [amending this section and section 133 of this title, and enacting provisions set out as notes under this section and section 142 of this title] shall in any manner affect the tenure of office of the United States Attorney and the United States Marshal for the Northern District of Florida who are in office at the time of the enactment of this Act [July 30, 1962], and who shall be during the remainder of their present terms of office the United States Attorney and Marshal for such district as constituted by this Act.

"(d) Nothing in this Act [amending this section and section 133 of this title, and enacting provisions set out as notes under this section and section 142 of this title] shall in any manner affect the tenure of office of the United States Attorney and the United States Marshal for the Southern District of Florida who are in office at the time of the enactment of this Act [July 30, 1962], and who shall be during the remainder of their present terms of office the United States Attorney and Marshal for the Middle District of Florida as constituted by this Act.

"(e) The President is authorized to appoint, by and with the advice and consent of the Senate, a United States Attorney and a United States Marshal for the Southern District of Florida."

Elimination of District Judgeship for Northern, Middle, and Southern Districts of Florida

District judgeship for northern, middle, and southern districts changed to district judgeship for middle district only, see section (b) of Pub.L. 89–372, set out as a note under section 133 of this title.

§ 90. Georgia

Georgia is divided into three judicial districts to be known as the Northern, Middle, and Southern Districts of Georgia.

Northern District

(a) The Northern District comprises four divisions.

(1) The Gainesville Division comprises the counties of Banks, Barrow, Dawson, Fannin, Forsyth, Gilmer, Habersham, Hall, Jackson, Lumpkin, Pickens, Rabun, Stephens, Towns, Union, and White.

Court for the Gainesville Division shall be held at Gainesville.

(2) The Atlanta Division comprises the counties of Cherokee, Clayton, Cobb, De Kalb, Douglas, Fulton, Gwinnett, Henry, Newton, and Rockdale.

Court for the Atlanta Division shall be held at Atlanta.

(3) The Rome Division comprises the counties of Bartow, Catoosa, Chattooga, Dade, Floyd, Gordon, Murray, Paulding, Polk, Walker, and Whitfield.

Court for the Rome Division shall be held at Rome.

(4) The Newnan Division comprises the counties of Carroll, Coweta, Fayette, Haralson, Heard, Meriwether, Pike, Spalding, and Troup.

Court for the Newnan Division shall be held at Newnan.

Middle District

(b) The Middle District comprises seven divisions.

(1) The Athens Division comprises the counties of Clarke, Elbert, Franklin, Greene, Hart, Madison, Morgan, Oconee, Oglethorpe, and Walton.

Court for the Athens Division shall be held at Athens.

(2) The Macon Division comprises the counties of Baldwin, Bibb, Bleckley, Butts, Crawford, Hancock, Houston, Jasper, Jones, Lamar, Monroe, Peach, Pulaski, Putnam, Twiggs, Upson, Washington, and Wilkinson.

Court for the Macon Division shall be held at Macon.

(3) The Columbus Division comprises the counties of Chattahoochee, Clay, Harris, Marion, Muscogee, Quitman, Randolph, Stewart, Talbot, and Taylor.

Court for the Columbus Division shall be held at Columbus.

(4) The Americus Division comprises the counties of Ben Hill, Crisp, Dooly, Lee, Macon, Schley, Sumter, Terrell, Webster, and Wilcox.

Court for the Americus Division shall be held at Americus.

(5) The Albany Division comprises the counties of Baker, Calhoun, Dougherty, Early, Miller, Mitchell, Turner, and Worth.

Court for the Albany Division shall be held at Albany.

(6) The Valdosta Division comprises the counties of Berrien, Clinch, Cook, Echols, Irwin, Lanier, Lowndes, and Tift.

Court for the Valdosta Division shall be held at Valdosta.

(7) The Thomasville Division comprises the counties of Brooks, Colquitt, Decatur, Grady, Seminole, and Thomas.

Court for the Thomasville Division shall be held at Thomasville.

Southern District

(c) The Southern District comprises six divisions.

(1) The Augusta Division comprises the counties of Burke, Columbia, Glascock, Jefferson, Lincoln, McDuffie, Richmond, Taliaferro, Warren, and Wilkes.

Court for the Augusta Division shall be held at Augusta.

(2) The Dublin Division comprises the counties of Dodge, Johnson, Laurens, Montgomery, Telfair, Treutlen, and Wheeler.

Court for the Dublin Division shall be held at Dublin.

(3) The Savannah Division comprises the counties of Bryan, Chatham, Effingham, and Liberty.

Court for the Savannah Division shall be held at Savannah.

(4) The Waycross Division comprises the counties of Atkinson, Bacon, Brantley, Charlton, Coffee, Pierce, and Ware.

Court for the Waycross Division shall be held at Waycross.

(5) The Brunswick Division comprises the counties of Appling, Camden, Glynn, Jeff Davis, Long, McIntosh, and Wayne.

Court for the Brunswick Division shall be held at Brunswick.

(6) The Statesboro Division comprises the counties of Bulloch, Candler, Emanuel, Evans, Jenkins, Screven, Tattnall, and Toombs.

Court for the Statesboro Division shall be held at Statesboro.

(June 25, 1948, c. 646, 62 Stat. 876; Aug. 16, 1949, c. 444, 63 Stat. 610; Oct. 31, 1951, c. 655, § 36a, 65 Stat. 723; Nov. 8, 1984, Pub.L. 98–620, Title IV, § 408(a)–(c), 98 Stat. 3362; Nov. 14, 1986, Pub.L. 99–657, § 3, 100 Stat. 3670.)

HISTORICAL AND STATUTORY NOTES

Effective and Applicability Provisions

1986 Acts. Amendment by Pub.L. 99–657 effective 90 days after Nov. 14, 1986, and not to affect any action commenced before and pending on such effective date, or to affect the composition, or preclude the service, of any grand or petit jury summoned, empaneled, or actually serving on such date, see section 4 of Pub.L. 99–657, set out as a note under section 121 of this title.

1984 Acts. Section 408(d) of Pub.L. 98–620 provided that: "The amendments made by this section [amending subsecs. (a) and (c) of this section] shall apply to any action commenced in the United States District Court for the Northern District of Georgia on or after the effective date of this subtitle [Jan. 1, 1985], and shall not affect any action pending in such court on such effective date."

Amendment by Pub.L. 98–620 effective Jan. 1, 1985, and not to affect the composition, or preclude the service, of any grand or petit jury summoned, impaneled, or actually serving on that date, see section 411 of Pub.L. 98–620, set out as a note under section 85 of this title.

§ 91. Hawaii

Hawaii constitutes one judicial district which includes the Midway Islands, Wake Island, Johnston Island, Sand Island, Kingman Reef, Palmyra Island, Baker Island, Howland Island, Jarvis Island, Canton Island, and Enderbury Island: *Provided*, That the inclusion of Canton and Enderbury Islands in such judicial district shall in no way be construed to be prejudicial to the claims of the United Kingdom to said Islands in accordance with the agreement of April 6, 1939, between the Governments of the United States and of the United Kingdom to set up a regime for their use in common.

Court shall be held at Honolulu.

(June 25, 1948, c. 646, 62 Stat. 877; May 24, 1949, c. 139, § 64a, 63 Stat. 99; Mar. 18, 1959, Pub.L. 86–3, § 14(i), 73 Stat. 11; July 12, 1960, Pub.L. 86–624, § 19, 74 Stat. 416.)

HISTORICAL AND STATUTORY NOTES

Effective and Applicability Provisions

1959 Acts. Section 14 of Pub.L. 86–3 provided that the amendments of sections 91, 373, 1252, 1293, and 1294 of this title, sections 3771 and 3772 of Title 18, Crimes and Criminal Procedure, and section 644a of Title 48, Territories and Insular Possessions, the repeal of sections 536, 539, 634, 634a, and 645 of title 48, and notes set out under sections 371 and 373 of this title, are effective on admission of the State of Hawaii into the Union. See Admission of Hawaii as State note under this section.

Admission of Hawaii as State

Admission of Hawaii into the Union was accomplished Aug. 21, 1959, upon issuance of Proc. No. 3309, Aug. 21, 1959, 25

F.R. 6868, 73 Stat. c74, as required by sections 1 and 7(c) of Pub.L. 86–3, Mar. 18, 1959, 73 Stat. 4, set out as notes preceding section 491 of Title 48, Territories and Insular Possessions.

Appeals

Section 13 of Pub.L. 86–3 provided that: "Parties shall have the same rights of appeal from and appellate review of final decisions of the United States District Court for the District of Hawaii or the Supreme Court of the Territory of Hawaii in any case finally decided prior to admission of said State into the Union, whether or not an appeal therefrom shall have been perfected prior to such admission, and the United States Court of Appeals for the Ninth Circuit and the Supreme Court of the United States shall have the same jurisdiction therein, as by law provided prior to admission of said State into the Union, and any mandate issued subsequent to the admission of said State shall be to the United States District Court for the District of Hawaii or a court of the State, as may be appropriate. Parties shall have the same rights of appeal from and appellate review of all orders, judgments, and decrees of the United States District Court for the District of Hawaii and of the Supreme Court of the State of Hawaii as successor to the Supreme Court of the Territory of Hawaii, in any case pending at the time of admission of said State into the Union, and the United States Court of Appeals for the Ninth Circuit and the Supreme Court of the United States shall have the same jurisdiction therein, as by law provided in any case arising subsequent to the admission of said State into the Union."

Canton and Enderbury Islands; Sovereignty of Kiribati

By a treaty of friendship, TIAS 10777, which entered into force Sept. 23, 1983, the United States recognized the sovereignty of Kiribati over Canton Island and Enderbury Island.

Continuation of Suits

Section 12 of Pub.L. 86–3 provided that: "No writ, action, indictment, cause, or proceeding pending in any court of the Territory of Hawaii or in the United States District Court for the District of Hawaii shall abate by reason of the admission of said State into the Union, but the same shall be transferred to and proceeded with in such appropriate State courts as shall be established under the constitution of said State, or shall continue in the United States District Court for the District of Hawaii, as the nature of the case may require. And no writ, action, indictment, cause or proceeding shall abate by reason of any change in the courts, but shall be proceeded with in the State or United States courts according to the laws thereof, respectively. And the appropriate State courts shall be the successors of the courts of the Territory as to all cases arising within the limits embraced within the jurisdiction of such courts, respectively, with full power to proceed with the same, and award mesne or final process therein, and all the files, records, indictments, and proceedings relating to any such writ, action, indictment, cause or proceeding shall be transferred to such appropriate State courts and the same shall be proceeded with therein in due course of law.

"All civil causes of action and all criminal offenses which shall have arisen or been committed prior to the admission of said State, but as to which no writ, action, indictment or proceeding shall be pending at the date of such admission, shall be subject to prosecution in the appropriate State courts or in the United States District Court for the District of Hawaii in like manner, to the same extent, and with like right of appellate review, as if said State had been created and said State courts had been established prior to the accrual of such causes of action or the commission of such offenses. The admission of said State shall effect no change in the substantive or criminal law governing such causes of action and criminal offenses which shall have arisen or been committed; and such of said criminal offenses as shall have been committed against the laws of the Territory shall be tried and punished by the appropriate courts of said State, and such as shall have been committed against the laws of the United States shall be tried and punished in the United States District Court for the District of Hawaii."

Court of the United States; District Judges

Section 9(a) of Pub.L. 86–3 provided that: "The United States District Court for the District of Hawaii established by and existing under title 28 of the United States Code shall thenceforth be a court of the United States with judicial power derived from article III, section 1, of the Constitution of the United States: *Provided, however*, That the terms of office of the district judges for the district of Hawaii then in office shall terminate upon the effective date of this section and the President, pursuant to sections 133 and 134 of title 28, United States Code, as amended by this Act, shall appoint, by and with the advice and consent of the Senate, two district judges for the said district who shall hold office during good behavior."

Section 9 of Pub.L. 86–3 provided in part that subsec. (a) of that section shall be effective upon the admission of the State of Hawaii into the Union.

Extension of Jurisdiction of United States District Court for District of Hawaii and of Civil and Criminal Laws to Midway, Wake, Johnson, Sand, etc., Islands

The jurisdiction of the United States District Court for the District of Hawaii and the laws of the United States relating to civil acts or offenses consummated or committed on the high seas on board a vessel belonging to the United States were extended to the Midway Islands, Wake, Johnson, Sand, etc., Islands by section 644a of Title 48, Territories and Insular Possessions.

§ 92. Idaho

Idaho, exclusive of Yellowstone National Park, constitutes one judicial district.

Court shall be held at Boise, Coeur d'Alene, Moscow, and Pocatello.

(June 25, 1948, c. 646, 62 Stat. 877; June 2, 1970, Pub.L. 91–272, § 5, 84 Stat. 297.)

§ 93. Illinois

Illinois is divided into three judicial districts to be known as the Northern, Central, and Southern Districts of Illinois.

Northern District

(a) The Northern District comprises two divisions.

(1) The Eastern Division comprises the counties of Cook, Du Page, Grundy, Kane, Kendall, Lake, La Salle, and Will.

Court for the Eastern Division shall be held at Chicago and Wheaton.

(2) The Western Division comprises the counties of Boone, Carroll, De Kalb, Jo Daviess, Lee, McHenry, Ogle, Stephenson, Whiteside, and Winnebago.

Court for the Western Division shall be held at Freeport and Rockford.

Central District

(b) The Central District comprises the counties of Adams, Brown, Bureau, Cass, Champaign, Christian, Coles, De Witt, Douglas, Edgar, Ford, Fulton, Greene, Hancock, Henderson, Henry, Iroquois, Kankakee, Knox, Livingston, Logan, McDonough, McLean, Macoupin, Macon, Marshall, Mason, Menard, Mercer, Montgomery, Morgan, Moultrie, Peoria, Piatt, Pike, Putnam, Rock Island, Sangamon, Schuyler, Scott, Shelby, Stark, Tazewell, Vermilion, Warren, and Woodford.

Court for the Central District shall be held at Champaign/Urbana, Danville, Peoria, Quincy, Rock Island, and Springfield.

Southern District

(c) The Southern District comprises the counties of Alexander, Bond, Calhoun, Clark, Clay, Clinton, Crawford, Cumberland, Edwards, Effingham, Fayette, Franklin, Gallatin, Hamilton, Hardin, Jackson, Jasper, Jefferson, Jersey, Johnson, Lawrence, Madison, Marion, Massac, Monroe, Perry, Pope, Pulaski, Randolph, Richland, St. Clair, Saline, Union, Wabash, Washington, Wayne, White, and Williamson.

Court for the Southern District shall be held at Alton, Benton, Cairo, and East Saint Louis.

(June 25, 1948, c. 646, 62 Stat. 878; Aug. 10, 1950, c. 675, § 1, 64 Stat. 438; May 19, 1961, Pub.L. 87–36, § 3(c), 75 Stat. 83; June 2, 1970, Pub.L. 91–272, § 8, 84 Stat. 297; Oct. 2, 1978, Pub.L. 95–408, § 4(b) (1), 92 Stat. 884; Nov. 2, 1978, Pub.L. 95–573, § 1, 92 Stat. 2458; Nov. 8, 1984, Pub.L. 98–620, Title IV, § 406(a), (c), 98 Stat. 3361; Dec. 6, 1999, Pub.L. 106–130, § 2, 113 Stat. 1677.)

HISTORICAL AND STATUTORY NOTES

Effective and Applicability Provisions

1984 Acts. Section 406(b) of Pub.L. 98–620 provided that: "The amendments made by subsection (a) of this section [amending subsec. (a) of this section] shall apply to any action commenced in the United States District Court for the Northern District of Illinois on or after the effective date of this subtitle [Jan. 1, 1985], and shall not affect any action pending in such court on such effective date."

Amendment by Pub.L. 98–620 effective Jan. 1, 1985, and not to affect the composition, or preclude the service, of any grand or petit jury summoned, impaneled, or actually serving on that date, see section 411 of Pub.L. 98–620, set out as a note under section 85 of this title.

1978 Acts. Section 6 of Pub.L. 95–573, as amended by Pub.L. 96–4, § 2, Mar. 30, 1979, 93 Stat. 7, provided that:

"(a) Except as provided in subsection (b) of this section, the provisions of this Act [amending sections 93, 99, 112 and 118 of this title and enacting provisions set out as a note under section 84 of this title] shall take effect 180 days after the date of enactment of this Act [Nov. 2, 1978].

"(b)(1) The provisions of section 5 of this Act [set out as a note under section 84 of this title] shall take effect on the date of enactment of this Act [Nov. 2, 1978].

"(2) The provisions of the first section of this Act [amending this section] shall take effect on March 31, 1979.

"(c) Nothing in this Act [amending sections 93, 99, 112, and 118 of this title and enacting provisions set out as a note under section 84 of this title] shall affect the composition or preclude the service of any grand or petit juror summoned, empaneled, or actually serving in any judicial district on the effective date of this Act."

Amendment by Pub.L. 95–408 effective 180 days after Oct. 2, 1978, such amendment not to affect the composition or preclude the service of any grand or petit juror summoned, empaneled, or actually serving in any judicial district on the effective date of this Act, see section 5 of Pub.L. 95–408, set out as a note under section 89 of this title.

District Judges, United States Attorneys, Assistant United States Attorneys, and United States Marshals For Central and Southern Districts; Designation; Tenure; Appointment; Grand Jury

Pub.L. 95–408, § 4(b)(2)–(4), as added Pub.L. 96–4, § 1, Mar. 30, 1979, 93 Stat. 6, provided that:

"(2) The district judge for the Eastern District of Illinois in office on the effective date of this Act [180 days after Oct. 2, 1978] who is senior in commission shall, on and after the effective date of this Act, be a district judge for the Southern District of Illinois. The remaining district judge for the Eastern District of Illinois who is in office on the effective date of this Act and the district judges for the Southern District of Illinois who are in office on the effective date of this Act shall, on and after the effective date of this Act, be district judges for the Central District of Illinois. The President shall appoint, by and with the advice and consent of the Senate, a second district judge for the Southern District of Illinois.

"(3) This section does not in any manner affect the tenure of the United States attorney, the assistant United States attorneys, or the United States marshal for the Eastern District of Illinois or for the Southern District of Illinois who are in office on the effective date of this Act [180 days after Oct. 2, 1978]. The United States attorney, the assistant United States attorneys, and the United States marshal for the Eastern District and for the Southern District of Illinois shall, on the effective date of this Act, become the United States attorney, the assistant United States attorneys, and the United States marshal for the Southern District and for the Central District of Illinois, respectively.

"(4) Notwithstanding section 3240 of title 18, United States Code [section 3240 of Title 18, Crimes and Criminal Procedure], any grand jury impaneled on or after the effective date of this Act [180 days after Oct. 2, 1978] by a district court for the Central District or the Southern District of Illinois may inquire into and return indictments charging offenses against the criminal laws of the United States alleged to have been committed anywhere within the territory of the respective judicial districts as such districts were constituted before or after the effective date of this Act."

§ 94. Indiana

Indiana is divided into two judicial districts to be known as the Northern and Southern Districts of Indiana.

Northern District

(a) The Northern District comprises three divisions.

(1) The Fort Wayne Division comprises the counties of Adams, Allen, Blackford, De Kalb, Grant, Huntington, Jay, Lagrange, Noble, Steuben, Wells, and Whitley.

Court for the Fort Wayne Division shall be held at Fort Wayne.

(2) The South Bend Division comprises the counties of Cass, Elkhart, Fulton, Kosciusko, La Porte, Marshall, Miami, Pulaski, St. Joseph, Starke, and Wabash.

Court for the South Bend Division shall be held at South Bend.

(3) The Hammond Division comprises the counties of Benton, Carroll, Jasper, Lake, Newton, Porter, Tippecanoe, Warren, and White.

Court for the Hammond Division shall be held at Hammond and Lafayette.

Southern District

(b) The Southern District comprises four divisions.

(1) The Indianapolis Division comprises the counties of Bartholomew, Boone, Brown, Clinton, Decatur, Delaware, Fayette, Fountain, Franklin, Hamilton, Hancock, Hendricks, Henry, Howard, Johnson, Madison, Marion, Monroe, Montgomery, Morgan, Randolph, Rush, Shelby, Tipton, Union, and Wayne.

Court for the Indianapolis Division shall be held at Indianapolis and Richmond.

(2) The Terre Haute Division comprises the counties of Clay, Greene, Knox, Owen, Parke, Putnam, Sullivan, Vermilion, and Vigo.

Court for the Terre Haute Division shall be held at Terre Haute.

(3) The Evansville Division comprises the counties of Davies, Dubois, Gibson, Martin, Perry, Pike, Posey, Spencer, Vanderburgh, and Warrick.

Court for the Evansville Division shall be held at Evansville.

(4) The New Albany Division comprises the counties of Clark, Crawford, Dearborn, Floyd, Harrison, Jackson, Jefferson, Jennings, Lawrence, Ohio, Orange, Ripley, Scott, Switzerland, and Washington.

Court for the New Albany Division shall be held at New Albany.

(June 25, 1948, c. 646, 62 Stat. 878; Feb. 10, 1954, c. 6, § 2(b)(7), 68 Stat. 11; June 2, 1970, Pub.L. 91–272, § 9, 84 Stat. 298.)

§ 95. Iowa

Iowa is divided into two judicial districts to be known as the Northern and Southern Districts of Iowa.

Northern District

(a) The Northern District comprises four divisions.

(1) The Cedar Rapids Division comprises the counties of Benton, Cedar, Grundy, Hardin, Iowa, Jones, Linn, and Tama.

Court for the Cedar Rapids Division shall be held at Cedar Rapids.

(2) The Eastern Division comprises the counties of Allamakee, Black Hawk, Bremer, Buchanan, Chickasaw, Clayton, Delaware, Dubuque, Fayette, Floyd, Howard, Jackson, Mitchell, and Winneshiek.

Court for the Eastern Division shall be held at Dubuque and Waterloo.

(3) The Western Division comprises the counties of Buena Vista, Cherokee, Clay, Crawford, Dickinson, Ida, Lyon, Monona, O'Brien, Osceola, Plymouth, Sac, Sioux, and Woodbury.

Court for the Western Division shall be held at Sioux City.

(4) The Central Division comprises the counties of Butler, Calhoun, Carroll, Cerro Gordo, Emmet, Franklin, Hamilton, Hancock, Humboldt, Kossuth, Palo Alto, Pocahontas, Webster, Winnebago, Worth, and Wright.

Court for the Central Division shall be held at Fort Dodge and Mason City.

Southern District

(b) The Southern District comprises six divisions.

(1) The Central Division comprises the counties of Boone, Dallas, Greene, Guthrie, Jasper, Madison, Marion, Marshall, Polk, Poweshiek, Story, and Warren.

Court for the Central Division shall be held at Des Moines.

(2) The Eastern Division comprises the counties of Des Moines, Henry, Lee, Louisa, and Van Buren.

Court for the Eastern Division shall be held at Keokuk.

(3) The Western Division comprises the counties of Audubon, Cass, Fremont, Harrison, Mills, Montgomery, Page, Pottawattamie, and Shelby.

Court for the Western Division shall be held at Council Bluffs.

(4) The Southern Division comprises the counties of Adair, Adams, Clarke, Decatur, Lucas, Ringgold, Taylor, Union, and Wayne.

Court for the Southern Division shall be held at Creston.

(5) The Davenport Division comprises the counties of Clinton, Johnson, Muscatine, Scott, and Washington.

Court for the Davenport Division shall be held at Davenport.

(6) The Ottumwa Division comprises the counties of Appanoose, Davis, Jefferson, Keokuk, Mahaska, Monroe, and Wapello.

Court for the Ottumwa Division shall be held at Ottumwa.

(June 25, 1948, c. 646, 62 Stat. 879; Oct. 15, 1980, Pub.L. 96–462, § 3(a), 94 Stat. 2053.)

HISTORICAL AND STATUTORY NOTES

Effective and Applicability Provisions

1980 Acts. Amendment by Pub.L. 96–462 effective Oct. 1, 1981, but not to affect the composition or preclude the service of any grand or petit juror summoned, empaneled, or actually serving in any judicial district on Oct. 1, 1981, see section 7 of Pub.L. 96–462, set out as a note under section 84 of this title.

Section 3(b) of Pub.L. 96–462 provided that: "The amendments made by subsection (a) [amending subsec. (b)(3), (4) of this section] shall not apply to any action commenced before the effective date of such amendments [Oct. 1, 1981] and pending in the United States District Court for the Southern District of Iowa on such date."

Holding Court for the Southern District of Iowa

Pub.L. 107–273, Div. C, Title I, § 11029, Nov. 2, 2002, 116 Stat. 1836, as amended Pub.L. 108–455, § 1, Dec. 10, 2004, 118 Stat. 3628, provided that: "Notwithstanding any other provision of law, during the period beginning on January 1, 2003, through July 1, 2006, the United States District Court for the Southern District of Iowa may—

"(1) with the consent of the parties in any case filed in the Eastern Division or the Davenport Division of the Southern District of Iowa, hold court on that case in Rock Island, Illinois; and

"(2) summon jurors from the Southern District of Iowa to serve in any case described under paragraph (1)."

§ 96. Kansas

Kansas constitutes one judicial district.

Court shall be held at Kansas City, Lawrence, Leavenworth, Salina, Topeka, Hutchinson, Wichita, Dodge City, and Fort Scott.

(June 25, 1948, c. 646, 62 Stat. 880; Aug. 27, 1949, c. 516, 63 Stat. 666; Oct. 27, 1986, Pub.L. 99–554, Title I, § 141, 100 Stat. 3096.)

HISTORICAL AND STATUTORY NOTES

Effective and Applicability Provisions

1986 Acts. Amendment by Pub.L. 99–554 effective 30 days after Oct. 27, 1986, see section 302(a) of Pub.L. 99–554, set out as a note under section 581 of this title.

§ 97. Kentucky

Kentucky is divided into two judicial districts to be known as the Eastern and Western Districts of Kentucky.

Eastern District

(a) The Eastern District comprises the counties of Anderson, Bath, Bell, Boone, Bourbon, Boyd, Boyle, Bracken, Breathitt, Campbell, Carroll, Carter, Clark, Clay, Elliott, Estill, Fayette, Fleming, Floyd, Franklin, Gallatin, Garrard, Grant, Greenup, Harlan, Harrison, Henry, Jackson, Jessamine, Johnson, Kenton, Knott, Knox, Laurel, Lawrence, Lee, Leslie, Letcher, Lewis, Lincoln, McCreary, Madison, Magoffin, Martin, Mason, Menifee, Mercer, Montgomery, Morgan, Nicholas, Owen, Owsley, Pendleton, Perry, Pike, Powell, Pulaski, Robertson, Rockcastle, Rowan, Scott, Shelby, Trimble, Wayne, Whitley, Wolfe, and Woodford.

Court for the Eastern District shall be held at Ashland, Catlettsburg, Covington, Frankfort, Jackson, Lexington, London, Pikeville, and Richmond.

Western District

(b) The Western District comprises the counties of Adair, Allen, Ballard, Barren, Breckenridge, Bullitt, Butler, Caldwell, Calloway, Carlisle, Casey, Christian, Clinton, Crittenden, Cumberland, Daviess, Edmonson, Fulton, Graves, Grayson, Green, Hancock, Hardin, Hart, Henderson, Hickman, Hopkins, Jefferson, Larue, Livingston, Logan, Lyon, McCracken, McLean, Marion, Marshall, Meade, Metcalfe, Monroe, Muhlenberg, Nelson, Ohio, Oldham, Russell, Simpson, Spencer, Taylor, Todd, Trigg, Union, Warren, Washington, and Webster.

Court for the Western District shall be held at Bowling Green, Louisville, Owensboro, and Paducah.

(June 25, 1948, c. 646, 62 Stat. 880; Oct. 2, 1978, Pub.L. 95–408, § 2(a), 92 Stat. 883.)

HISTORICAL AND STATUTORY NOTES

Effective and Applicability Provisions

1978 Acts. Amendment by Pub.L. 95–408 effective 180 days after Oct. 2, 1978, such amendment not to affect the composition or preclude the service of any grand or petit juror summoned, empaneled, or actually serving in any judicial district on the effective date of this Act, see section 5 of Pub.L. 95–408, set out as a note under section 89 of this title.

§ 98. Louisiana

Louisiana is divided into three judicial districts to be known as the Eastern, Middle, and Western Districts of Louisiana.

Eastern District

(a) The Eastern District comprises the parishes of Assumption, Jefferson, Lafourche, Orleans, Plaquemines, Saint Bernard, Saint Charles, Saint James, Saint John the Baptist, Saint Tammany, Tangipahoa, Terrebonne, and Washington.

Court for the Eastern District shall be held at New Orleans, and Houma.

Middle District

(b) The Middle District comprises the parishes of Ascension, East Baton Rouge, East Feliciana, Iberville, Livingston, Pointe Coupee, Saint Helena, West Baton Rouge, and West Feliciana.

Court for the Middle District shall be held at Baton Rouge.

Western District

(c) The Western District comprises the parishes of Acadia, Allen, Avoyelles, Beauregard, Bienville, Bossier, Caddo, Calcasieu, Caldwell, Cameron, Catahoula, Claiborne, Concordia, Jefferson Davis, De Soto, East Carroll, Evangeline, Franklin, Grant, Iberia, Jackson, Lafayette, La Salle, Lincoln, Madison, Morehouse, Natchitoches, Ouachita, Rapides, Red River, Richland, Sabine, Saint Landry, Saint Martin, Saint Mary, Tensas, Union, Vermilion, Vernon, Webster, West Carroll, and Winn.

Court for the Western District shall be held at Alexandria, Lafayette, Lake Charles, Monroe, Opelousas, and Shreveport.

(June 25, 1948, c. 646, 62 Stat. 881; May 19, 1961, Pub.L. 87–36, § 4, 75 Stat. 83; Dec. 18, 1971, Pub.L. 92–208, § 3(a), 85 Stat. 741; Oct. 2, 1978, Pub.L. 95–408, § 3(a), 92 Stat. 883; July 10, 1984, Pub.L. 98–353, Title II, § 203(b), 98 Stat. 350.)

HISTORICAL AND STATUTORY NOTES

Effective and Applicability Provisions

1978 Acts. Amendment by Pub.L. 95–408 effective 180 days after Oct. 2, 1978, such amendment not to affect the composition or preclude the service of any grand or petit juror summoned, empaneled, or actually serving in any judicial district on the effective date of this Act, see section 5 of Pub.L. 95–408, set out as a note under section 89 of this title.

1971 Acts. Section 3(f) of Pub.L. 92–208 provided that: "The provisions of this section [amending this section and sections 133 and 134 of this title and enacting provisions set out as a note under this section] shall become effective one hundred and twenty days after the date of enactment of this Act [Dec. 18, 1971]."

District Judge, United States Attorney, and United States Marshal For Middle District; Designation; Tenure; Appointment

Section 3(b), (c) of Pub.L. 92–208 provided that:

"**(b)** The district judge for the Eastern District of Louisiana holding office on the day immediately prior to the effective date of this section [see Effective and Applicability Provisions of 1971 Amendments note under this section], and whose official station on such date is Baton Rouge, shall, on and after such date, be the district judge for the Middle District of Louisiana. All other district judges for the Eastern District of Louisiana holding office on the day immediately prior to the effective date of this section shall be district judges for the Eastern District of Louisiana as constituted by this section.

"**(c)(1)** Nothing in this section [amending this section and sections 133 and 134 of this title] shall in any manner affect the tenure of office of the United States attorney and the United States marshal for the Eastern District of Louisiana who are in office on the effective date of this section [see Effective and Applicability Provisions of 1971 Amendments note under this section], and who shall be during the remainder of their present terms of office the United States attorney and marshal for the Eastern District of Louisiana as constituted by this section.

"**(2)** The President shall appoint, by and with the advice and consent of the Senate, a United States attorney and marshal for the Middle District of Louisiana."

§ 99. Maine

Maine constitutes one judicial district.

Court shall be held at Bangor and Portland.

(June 25, 1948, c. 646, 62 Stat. 881; Nov. 2, 1978, Pub.L. 95–573, § 2, 92 Stat. 2458.)

HISTORICAL AND STATUTORY NOTES

Effective and Applicability Provisions

1978 Acts. Amendment by Pub.L. 95–573 effective 180 days after Nov. 2, 1978, except as otherwise provided, except that nothing in this Act shall affect the composition or preclude the service of any grand or petit juror summoned, empaneled, or actually serving in any judicial district on such effective date, see section 6 of Pub.L. 95–573, set out as a note under section 93 of this title.

§ 100. Maryland

Maryland constitutes one judicial district comprising two divisions.

(1) The Northern Division comprises the counties of Allegany, Anne Arundel, Baltimore, Caroline, Carroll, Cecil, Dorchester, Frederick,

Garrett, Harford, Howard, Kent, Queen Anne's, Somerset, Talbot, Washington, Wicomico, and Worcester, and the City of Baltimore.

Court for the Northern Division shall be held at Baltimore, Cumberland, and Denton.

(2) The Southern Division comprises the counties of Calvert, Charles, Montgomery, Prince George's, and St. Mary's.

Court for the Southern Division shall be held at a suitable site in Montgomery or Prince George's County not more than five miles from the boundary of Montgomery and Prince George's Counties.

(June 25, 1948, c. 646, 62 Stat. 882; Dec. 14, 1970, Pub.L. 91–546, § 4, 84 Stat. 1412; Oct. 14, 1988, Pub.L. 100–487, § 1, 102 Stat. 2431.)

HISTORICAL AND STATUTORY NOTES

Effective and Applicability Provisions

1988 Acts. Section 2 of Pub.L. 100–487 provided that:

"(a) **In General.**—This Act [Pub.L. 100–487] and the amendments made by this Act [amending this section] shall take effect 180 days after the date of the enactment of this Act [Oct. 14, 1988].

"(b) **Pending Cases Not Affected.**—This Act [Pub.L. 100–487] and the amendments made by this Act [amending this section] shall not affect any action commenced before the effective date of this Act [180 days after Oct. 14, 1988] and pending in the United States District Court for the District of Maryland on such date.

"(c) **Juries Not Affected.**—This Act [Pub.L. 100–487] and the amendments made by this Act [amending this section] shall not affect the composition, or preclude the service, of any grand or petit jury summoned, empaneled, or actually serving in the Judicial District of Maryland on the effective date of this Act [180 days after Oct. 14, 1988]."

§ 101. Massachusetts

Massachusetts constitutes one judicial district.

Court shall be held at Boston, New Bedford, Springfield, and Worcester.

(June 25, 1948, c. 646, 62 Stat. 882.)

§ 102. Michigan

Michigan is divided into two judicial districts to be known as the Eastern and Western Districts of Michigan.

Eastern District

(a) The Eastern District comprises two divisions.

(1) The Southern Division comprises the counties of Genesee, Jackson, Lapeer, Lenawee, Livingston, Macomb, Monroe, Oakland, Saint Clair, Sanilac, Shiawassee, Washtenaw, and Wayne.

Court for the Southern Division shall be held at Ann Arbor, Detroit, Flint, and Port Huron.

(2) The Northern Division comprises the counties of Alcona, Alpena, Arenac, Bay, Cheboygan, Clare, Crawford, Gladwin, Gratiot, Huron, Iosco, Isabella, Midland, Montmorency, Ogemaw, Oscoda, Otsego, Presque Isle, Roscommon, Saginaw, and Tuscola.

Court for the Northern Division shall be held at Bay City.

Western District

(b) The Western District comprises two divisions.

(1) The Southern Division comprises the counties of Allegan, Antrim, Barry, Benzie, Berrien, Branch, Calhoun, Cass, Charlevoix, Clinton, Eaton, Emmet, Grand Traverse, Hillsdale, Ingham, Ionia, Kalamazoo, Kalkaska, Kent, Lake, Leelanau, Manistee, Mason, Mecosta, Missaukee, Montcalm, Muskegon, Newaygo, Oceana, Osceola, Ottawa, Saint Joseph, Van Buren, and Wexford.

Court for the Southern Division shall be held at Grand Rapids, Kalamazoo, Lansing, and Traverse City.

(2) The Northern Division comprises the counties of Alger, Baraga, Chippewa, Delta, Dickinson, Gogebic, Houghton, Iron, Keweenaw, Luce, Mackinac, Marquette, Menominee, Ontonagon, and Schoolcraft.

Court for the Northern Division shall be held at Marquette and Sault Sainte Marie.

(June 25, 1948, c. 646, 62 Stat. 882; Feb. 10, 1954, c. 6, § 2(b)(8), 68 Stat. 11; May 19, 1961, Pub.L. 87–36, § 3(d), 75 Stat. 83; Oct. 6, 1964, Pub.L. 88–627, 78 Stat. 1003; June 2, 1970, Pub.L. 91–272, § 11, 84 Stat. 298.)

§ 103. Minnesota

Minnesota constitutes one judicial district comprising six divisions.

(1) The First Division comprises the counties of Dodge, Fillmore, Houston, Mower, Olmsted, Steele, Wabasha, and Winona.

Court for the First Division shall be held at Winona.

(2) The Second Division comprises the counties of Blue Earth, Brown, Cottonwood, Faribault, Freeborn, Jackson, Lac qui Parle, Le Sueur, Lincoln, Lyon, Martin, Murray, Nicollet, Nobles, Pipestone, Redwood, Rock, Sibley, Waseca, Watonwan, and Yellow Medicine.

Court for the Second Division shall be held at Mankato.

(3) The Third Division comprises the counties of Chisago, Dakota, Goodhue, Ramsey, Rice, Scott, and Washington.

Court for the Third Division shall be held at Saint Paul.

(4) The Fourth Division comprises the counties of Anoka, Carver, Chippewa, Hennepin, Isanti, Kandiyohi, McLeod, Meeker, Renville, Sherburne, Swift, and Wright.

Court for the Fourth Division shall be held at Minneapolis.

(5) The Fifth Division comprises the counties of Aitkin, Benton, Carlton, Cass, Cook, Crow Wing, Itasca, Kanabec, Koochiching, Lake, Mille Lacs, Morrison, Pine, and Saint Louis.

Court for the Fifth Division shall be held at Duluth.

(6) The Sixth Division comprises the counties of Becker, Beltrami, Big Stone, Clay, Clearwater, Douglas, Grant, Hubbard, Kittson, Lake of the Woods, Mahnomen, Marshall, Norman, Otter Tail, Pennington, Polk, Pope, Red Lake, Roseau, Stearns, Stevens, Todd, Traverse, Wadena, and Wilkin.

Court for the Sixth Division shall be held at Fergus Falls and Bemidji.

(June 25, 1948, c. 646, 62 Stat. 882; Oct. 13, 2008, Pub.L. 110–406, § 18, 122 Stat. 4295.)

§ 104. Mississippi

Mississippi is divided into two judicial districts to be known as the northern and southern districts of Mississippi.

Northern District

(a) The northern district comprises four divisions.

(1) Eastern division comprises the counties of Alcorn, Attala, Chickasaw, Choctaw, Clay, Itawamba, Lee, Lowndes, Monroe, Oktibbeha, Prentiss, Tishomingo, and Winston.

Court for the eastern division shall be held at Aberdeen, Ackerman, and Corinth.

(2) The Western Division comprises the counties of Benton, Calhoun, Grenada, Lafayette, Marshall, Montgomery, Pontotoc, Tippah, Union, Webster, and Yalobusha.

Court for the western division shall be held at Oxford.

(3) The Delta Division comprises the counties of Bolivar, Coahoma, De Soto, Panola, Quitman, Tallahatchie, Tate, and Tunica.

Court for the Delta Division shall be held at Clarksdale and Cleveland.

(4) The Greenville Division comprises the counties of Carroll, Humphreys, Leflore, Sunflower, and Washington.

Court for the Greenville Division shall be held at Greenville.

Southern District

(b) The southern district comprises five divisions.

(1) The Jackson Division comprises the counties of Amite, Copiah, Franklin, Hinds, Holmes, Leake, Lincoln, Madison, Pike, Rankin, Scott, Simpson, and Smith.

Court for the Jackson Division shall be held at Jackson.

(2) The Eastern Division comprises the counties of Clarke, Jasper, Kemper, Lauderdale, Neshoba, Newton, Noxubee, and Wayne.

Court for the Eastern Division shall be held at Meridian.

(3) The western division comprises the counties of Adams, Claiborne, Issaquena, Jefferson, Sharkey, Warren, Wilkinson, and Yazoo.

Court for the western division shall be held at Natchez and Vicksburg.

(4) The southern division comprises the counties of George, Hancock, Harrison, Jackson, Pearl River, and Stone.

Court for the southern division shall be held at Biloxi and Gulfport.

(5) The Hattiesburg division comprises the counties of Covington, Forrest, Greene, Jefferson Davis, Jones, Lamar, Lawrence, Marion, Perry, and Walthall.

Court for the Hattiesburg division shall be held at Hattiesburg.

(June 25, 1948, c. 646, 62 Stat. 883; Aug. 7, 1950, c. 601, 64 Stat. 415; Sept. 27, 1967, Pub.L. 90–92, 81 Stat. 229; Dec. 14, 1970, Pub.L. 91–546, §§ 2, 3, 84 Stat. 1412; Oct. 2, 1978, Pub.L. 95–408, § 2(b), 92 Stat. 883; Dec. 6, 1999, Pub.L. 106–130, § 1, 113 Stat. 1677; Dec. 10, 2004, Pub.L. 108–455, § 2, 118 Stat. 3628.)

HISTORICAL AND STATUTORY NOTES

Effective and Applicability Provisions

1978 Acts. Amendment by Pub.L. 95–408 effective 180 days after Oct. 2, 1978, such amendment not to affect the composition or preclude the service of any grand or petit juror summoned, empaneled, or actually serving in any judicial district on the effective date of this Act, see section 5 of Pub.L. 95–408, set out as a note under section 89 of this title.

§ 105. Missouri

Missouri is divided into two judicial districts to be known as the Eastern and Western Districts of Missouri.

Eastern District

(a) The Eastern District comprises three divisions.

(1) The Eastern Division comprises the counties of Crawford, Dent, Franklin, Gasconade, Iron, Jefferson, Lincoln, Maries, Phelps, Saint Charles, Saint Francois, Saint Genevieve, Saint Louis, Warren, and Washington, and the city of Saint Louis.

Court for the Eastern Division shall be held at Saint Louis.

(2) The Northern Division comprises the counties of Adair, Audrain, Chariton, Clark, Knox, Lewis, Linn, Macon, Marion, Monroe, Montgomery, Pike, Ralls, Randolph, Schuyler, Scotland, and Shelby.

Court for the Northern Division shall be held at Hannibal.

(3) The Southeastern Division comprises the counties of Bollinger, Butler, Cape Girardeau, Carter, Dunklin, Madison, Mississippi, New Madrid, Pemiscot, Perry, Reynolds, Ripley, Scott, Shannon, Stoddard, and Wayne.

Court for the Southeastern Division shall be held at Cape Girardeau.

Western District

(b) The Western District comprises five divisions.

(1) The Western Division comprises the counties of Bates, Carroll, Cass, Clay, Henry, Jackson, Johnson, Lafayette, Ray, Saint Clair, and Saline.

Court for the Western Division shall be held at Kansas City.

(2) The Southwestern Division comprises the counties of Barton, Barry, Jasper, Lawrence, McDonald, Newton, Stone, and Vernon.

Court for the Southwestern Division shall be held at Joplin.

(3) The Saint Joseph Division comprises the counties of Andrew, Atchison, Buchanan, Caldwell, Clinton, Daviess, De Kalb, Gentry, Grundy, Harrison, Holt, Livingston, Mercer, Nodaway, Platte, Putnam, Sullivan, and Worth.

Court for the Saint Joseph Division shall be held at Saint Joseph.

(4) The Central Division comprises the counties of Benton, Boone, Callaway, Camden, Cole, Cooper, Hickory, Howard, Miller, Moniteau, Morgan, Osage, and Pettis.

Court for the Central Division shall be held at Jefferson City.

(5) The Southern Division comprises the counties of Cedar, Christian, Dade, Dallas, Douglas, Greene, Howell, Laclede, Oregon, Ozark, Polk, Pulaski, Taney, Texas, Webster, and Wright.

Court for the Southern Division shall be held at Springfield.

(June 25, 1948, c. 646, 62 Stat. 884; May 31, 1962, Pub.L. 87–461, 76 Stat. 85; Oct. 15, 1980, Pub.L. 96–462, § 4(a), 94 Stat. 2053.)

HISTORICAL AND STATUTORY NOTES

Effective and Applicability Provisions

1980 Acts. Amendment by Pub.L. 96–462 effective Oct. 1, 1981 with that amendment not to affect the composition or preclude the service of any grand or petit juror summoned, empaneled, or actually serving in any judicial district on Oct. 1, 1981, see section 7 of Pub.L. 96–462, set out as a note under section 84 of this title.

Section 4(b) of Pub.L. 96–462 provided that: "The amendments made by subsection (a) [amending subsec. (a)(1), (2) of this section] shall not apply to any action commenced before the effective date of such amendments [Oct. 1, 1981] and pending in the United States District Court for the Eastern District of Missouri on such date."

§ 106. Montana

Montana, exclusive of Yellowstone National Park, constitutes one judicial district.

Court shall be held at Billings, Butte, Glasgow, Great Falls, Havre, Helena, Kalispell, Lewistown, Livingston, Miles City, and Missoula.

(June 25, 1948, c. 646, 62 Stat. 884.)

§ 107. Nebraska

Nebraska constitutes one judicial district.

Court shall be held at Lincoln, North Platte, and Omaha.

(June 25, 1948, c. 646, 62 Stat. 884; Aug. 9, 1955, c. 627, § 1, 69 Stat. 546.)

HISTORICAL AND STATUTORY NOTES

Effective and Applicability Provisions

1955 Acts. Section 2 of Act Aug. 9, 1955, provided that: "The amendment made by the first section of this Act [amending this section] shall take effect on September 1, 1955."

§ 108. Nevada

Nevada constitutes one judicial district.

Court shall be held at Carson City, Elko, Las Vegas, Reno, Ely, and Lovelock.

(June 25, 1948, c. 646, 62 Stat. 885; Dec. 1, 1990, Pub.L. 101–650, Title III, § 324(a)(1), 104 Stat. 5120.)

§ 109. New Hampshire

New Hampshire constitutes one judicial district.

Court shall be held at Concord and Littleton.

(June 25, 1948, c. 646, 62 Stat. 885.)

§ 110. New Jersey

New Jersey constitutes one judicial district.

Court shall be held at Camden, Newark and Trenton.

(June 25, 1948, c. 646, 62 Stat. 885.)

§ 111. New Mexico

New Mexico constitutes one judicial district.

Court shall be held at Albuquerque, Las Cruces, Las Vegas, Roswell, Santa Fe, and Silver City.

(June 25, 1948, c. 646, 62 Stat. 885.)

§ 112. New York

New York is divided into four judicial districts to be known as the Northern, Southern, Eastern, and Western Districts of New York.

Northern District

(a) The Northern District comprises the counties of Albany, Broome, Cayuga, Chenango, Clinton, Columbia, Cortland, Delaware, Essex, Franklin, Fulton, Greene, Hamilton, Herkimer, Jefferson, Lewis, Madison, Montgomery, Oneida, Onondaga, Oswego, Otsego, Rensselaer, Saint Lawrence, Saratoga, Schenectady, Schoharie, Tioga, Tompkins, Ulster, Warren, and Washington.

Court for the Northern District shall be held at Albany, Auburn, Binghamton, Malone, Plattsburgh,[1] Syracuse, Utica, Watertown, and Plattsburgh.[1]

Southern District

(b) The Southern District comprises the counties of Bronx, Dutchess, New York, Orange, Putnam, Rockland, Sullivan, and Westchester and concurrently with the Eastern District, the waters within the Eastern District.

Court for the Southern District shall be held at New York, White Plains, and in the Middletown-Wallkill area of Orange County or such nearby location as may be deemed appropriate.

Eastern District

(c) The Eastern District comprises the counties of Kings, Nassau, Queens, Richmond, and Suffolk and concurrently with the Southern District, the waters within the counties of Bronx and New York.

Court for the Eastern District shall be held at Brooklyn, Hauppauge, Hempstead (including the village of Uniondale), and Central Islip.

Western District

(d) The Western District comprises the counties of Allegany, Cattaraugus, Chautauqua, Chemung, Erie, Genesee, Livingston, Monroe, Niagara, Ontario, Orleans, Schuyler, Seneca, Steuben, Wayne, Wyoming, and Yates.

Court for the Western District shall be held at Buffalo, Canandaigua, Elmira, Jamestown, and Rochester.

(June 25, 1948, c. 646, 62 Stat. 885; Dec. 18, 1967, Pub.L. 90–217, 81 Stat. 662; Dec. 14, 1970, Pub.L. 91–546, § 1, 84 Stat. 1412; Apr. 28, 1978, Pub.L. 95–271, § 1, 92 Stat. 221; Oct. 2, 1978, Pub.L. 95–408, § 4(c), 92 Stat. 885; Nov. 2, 1978, Pub.L. 95–573, § 3, 92 Stat. 2458; Nov. 8, 1984, Pub.L. 98–620, Title IV, § 405, 98 Stat. 3361; Dec. 1, 1990, Pub.L. 101–650, Title III, § 324(a)(2), 104 Stat. 5120; Oct. 19, 1996, Pub.L. 104–317, Title VI, § 609, 110 Stat. 3860; Nov. 29, 1999, Pub.L. 106–113, Div. B, § 1000(a)(1) [Title III, § 306], 113 Stat. 1535, 1501A–37; Dec. 10, 2004, Pub.L. 108–455, § 4, 118 Stat. 3628; Dec. 23, 2004, Pub.L. 108–482, Title III, § 302, 118 Stat. 3918.)

[1] So in original. Pub.L. 108–455, § 4 and Pub.L. 108–482, § 302 both inserted a reference to Plattsburgh in this paragraph.

HISTORICAL AND STATUTORY NOTES

Effective and Applicability Provisions

1984 Acts. Amendment by Pub.L. 98–620 to take effect on Jan. 1, 1985, and not to affect the composition, or preclude the service, of any grand or petit jury summoned, impaneled, or actually serving on that date, see section 411 of Pub.L. 98–620, set out as a note under section 85 of this title.

1978 Acts. Amendment by Pub.L. 95–573 effective 180 days after Nov. 2, 1978, except as otherwise provided, except that nothing in this Act shall affect the composition or preclude the service of any grand or petit juror summoned, empaneled, or actually serving in any judicial district on such effective date, see section 6 of Pub.L. 95–573, set out as a note under section 93 of this title.

Amendment by Pub.L. 95–408 effective 180 days after Oct. 2, 1978, such amendment not to affect the composition or preclude the service of any grand or petit juror summoned, empaneled, or actually serving in any judicial district on the effective date of this Act, see section 5 of Pub.L. 95–408, set out as a note under section 89 of this title.

Pretermission of Regular Session of Court at Hempstead and Holding of Special Session at Westbury; Procedures Applicable, Appropriations, Etc.

Pub.L. 95–271, §§ 2 to 5, Apr. 28, 1978, 92 Stat. 221, provided that:

"**Sec. 2.** The United States District Court for the Eastern District of New York, by order made anywhere within its district, may pretermit the regular session of court at Hempstead until Federal quarters and accommodations are available and ready for occupancy, except that for the entire period and such pretermission, a special session of the court shall be held at Westbury. Pretermission may be ordered without regard to the provisions of section 140(a) of title 28, United States Code [section 140(a) of this title].

"**Sec. 3.** Notwithstanding the provisions of section 142 of title 28, United States Code [section 142 of this title], the

Administrator of General Services, at the request of the Director of the Administrative Office of the United States Courts, shall continue to provide existing quarters and accommodations at Westbury for the duration of the special session held pursuant to section 2 of this Act. Appropriations to the judicial branch of Government shall be available to the Director to make necessary disbursements for such quarters and accommodations, and to pay user charges as required by section 210 of the Federal Property and Administrative Services Act of 1949, as amended (40 U.S.C. 490) [see now 40 U.S.C.A. § 581 et seq.], at rates otherwise authorized by law.

"**Sec. 4.** Notwithstanding the provisions of section 456 of title 28, United States Code [section 456 of this title], any judge, and any officer or employee of the judicial branch, whose official station is, on the day before the date of enactment of this Act [Apr. 28, 1978], Westbury, may maintain that official station for the duration of the special session held pursuant to section 2 of this Act.

"**Sec. 5.** The Director of the Administrative Office of the United States Courts may pay travel and transportation expenses in accordance with subchapter II, chapter 57 of title 5, United States Code [section 5721 et seq. of Title 5, Government Organization and Employees], to any officer or employee of the judicial branch whose official station changes as a consequence of this Act [amending subsec. (c) of this section] and who relocates his residence incident to such change of official station."

§ 113. North Carolina

North Carolina is divided into three judicial districts to be known as the Eastern, Middle, and Western Districts of North Carolina.

Eastern District

(a) The Eastern District comprises the counties of Beaufort, Bertie, Bladen, Brunswick, Camden, Carteret, Chowan, Columbus, Craven, Cumberland, Currituck, Dare, Duplin, Edgecombe, Franklin, Gates, Granville, Greene, Halifax, Harnett, Hertford, Hyde, Johnston, Jones, Lenoir, Martin, Nash, New Hanover, Northampton, Onslow, Pamlico, Pasquotank, Pender, Perquimans, Pitt, Robeson, Sampson, Tyrrell, Vance, Wake, Warren, Washington, Wayne, and Wilson and that portion of Durham County encompassing the Federal Correctional Institution, Butner, North Carolina.

Court for the Eastern District shall be held at Elizabeth City, Fayetteville, Greenville, New Bern, Raleigh, Wilmington, and Wilson.

Middle District

(b) The Middle District comprises the counties of Alamance, Cabarrus, Caswell, Chatham, Davidson, Davie, Durham (excluding that portion of Durham County encompassing the Federal Correctional Institution, Butner, North Carolina), Forsythe, Guilford, Hoke, Lee, Montgomery, Moore, Orange, Person, Randolph, Richmond, Rockingham, Rowan, Scotland, Stanly, Stokes, Surry, and Yadkin.

Court for the Middle District shall be held at Durham, Greensboro, and Winston-Salem.

Western District

(c) The Western District comprises the counties of Alexander, Alleghany, Anson, Ashe, Avery, Buncombe, Burke, Caldwell, Catawba, Cherokee, Clay, Cleveland, Gaston, Graham, Haywood, Henderson, Iredell, Jackson, Lincoln, McDowell, Macon, Madison, Mecklenburg, Mitchell, Polk, Rutherford, Swain, Transylvania, Union, Watauga, Wilkes, and Yancey.

Court for the Western District shall be held at Asheville, Bryson City, Charlotte, Shelby, and Statesville.

(June 25, 1948, c. 646, 62 Stat. 886; Nov. 2, 1965, Pub.L. 89–319, 79 Stat. 1186; Oct. 15, 1980, Pub.L. 96–462, § 5(a)–(c), 94 Stat. 2053, 2054; Apr. 21, 1992, Pub.L. 102–272, 106 Stat. 112.)

HISTORICAL AND STATUTORY NOTES

Effective and Applicability Provisions

1980 Acts. Amendment by Pub.L. 96–462 effective Oct. 1, 1981, with that amendment not to affect the composition or preclude the service of any grand or petit juror summoned, empaneled, or actually serving in any judicial district on Oct. 1, 1981, see section 7 of Pub.L. 96–462, set out as a note under section 84 of this title.

Section 5(d) of Pub.L. 96–462 provided that: "The amendments made by this section [amending this section] shall not apply to any action commenced before the effective date of such amendments [Oct. 1, 1981] and pending in any judicial district of North Carolina on such date."

§ 114. North Dakota

North Dakota constitutes one judicial district comprising four divisions.

(1) The Southwestern Division comprises the counties of Adams, Billings, Bowman, Burleigh, Dunn, Emmons, Golden Valley, Grant, Hettinger, Kidder, Logan, McIntosh, McLean, Mercer, Morton, Oliver, Sioux, Slope, and Stark.

Court for the Southwestern Division shall be held at Bismarck.

(2) The Southeastern Division comprises the counties of Barnes, Cass, Dickey, Eddy, Foster, Griggs, La Moure, Ransom, Richland, Sargent, Steele, and Stutsman.

Court for the Southeastern Division shall be held at Fargo.

(3) The Northeastern Division comprises the counties of Benson, Cavalier, Grand Forks, Nelson, Pembina, Ramsey, Rolette, Towner, Traill, and Walsh.

Court for the Northeastern Division shall be held at Grand Forks.

(4) The Northwestern Division comprises the counties of Bottineau, Burke, Divide, McHenry, McKenzie, Mountrail, Pierce, Renville, Sheridan, Ward, Wells, and Williams.

Court for the Northwestern Division shall be held at Minot.

(June 25, 1948, c. 646, 62 Stat. 886; Oct. 2, 1978, Pub.L. 95–408, § 3(b), 92 Stat. 883.)

HISTORICAL AND STATUTORY NOTES

Effective and Applicability Provisions

1978 Acts. Amendment by Pub.L. 95–408 effective 180 days after Oct. 2, 1978, such amendment not to affect the composition or preclude the service of any grand or petit juror summoned, empaneled, or actually serving in any judicial district on the effective date of this Act, see section 5 of Pub.L. 95–408, set out as a note under section 89 of this title.

§ 115. Ohio

Ohio is divided into two judicial districts to be known as the Northern and Southern Districts of Ohio.

Northern District

(a) The Northern District comprises two divisions.

(1) The Eastern Division comprises the counties of Ashland, Ashtabula, Carroll, Columbiana, Crawford, Cuyahoga, Geauga, Holmes, Lake, Lorain, Mahoning, Medina, Portage, Richland, Stark, Summit, Trumbull, Tuscarawas, and Wayne.

Court for the Eastern Division shall be held at Cleveland, Youngstown, and Akron.

(2) The Western Division comprises the counties of Allen, Auglaize, Defiance, Erie, Fulton, Hancock, Hardin, Henry, Huron, Lucas, Marion, Mercer, Ottawa, Paulding, Putnam, Sandusky, Seneca, Van Wert, Williams, Woods, and Wyandot.

Court for the Western Division shall be held at Lima and Toledo.

Southern District

(b) The Southern District comprises two divisions.

(1) The Western Division comprises the counties of Adams, Brown, Butler, Champaign, Clark, Clermont, Clinton, Darke, Greene, Hamilton, Highland, Lawrence, Miami, Montgomery, Preble, Scioto, Shelby, and Warren.

Court for the Western Division shall be held at Cincinnati and Dayton.

(2) The Eastern Division comprises the counties of Athens, Belmont, Coshocton, Delaware, Fairfield, Fayette, Franklin, Gallia, Guernsey, Harrison, Hocking, Jackson, Jefferson, Knox, Licking, Logan, Madison, Meigs, Monroe, Morgan, Morrow, Muskingum, Noble, Perry, Pickaway, Pike, Ross, Union, Vinton, and Washington.

Court for the Eastern Division shall be held at Columbus[1] St. Clairsville, and Steubenville.

(June 25, 1948, c. 646, 62 Stat. 887; Feb. 10, 1954, c. 6, § 2(b)(9), 68 Stat. 11; Nov. 2, 2002, Pub.L. 107–273, Div. C, Title I, § 11021, 116 Stat. 1829.)

[1] So in original. Probably should be followed by a comma.

§ 116. Oklahoma

Oklahoma is divided into three judicial districts to be known as the Northern, Eastern, and Western Districts of Oklahoma.

Northern District

(a) The Northern District comprises the counties of Craig, Creek, Delaware, Mayes, Nowata, Osage, Ottawa, Pawnee, Rogers, Tulsa, and Washington.

Court for the Northern District shall be held at Bartlesville, Miami, Pawhuska, Tulsa, and Vinita.

Eastern District

(b) The Eastern District comprises the counties of Adair, Atoka, Bryan, Carter, Cherokee, Choctaw, Coal, Haskell, Hughes, Johnston, Latimer, Le Flore, Love, McCurtain, McIntosh, Marshall, Murray, Muskogee, Okfuskee, Okmulgee, Pittsburg, Pontotoc, Pushmataha, Seminole, Sequoyah, and Wagoner.

Court for the Eastern District shall be held at Ada, Ardmore, Durant, Hugo, Muskogee, Okmulgee, Poteau, and S. McAlester.

Western District

(c) The Western District comprises the counties of Alfalfa, Beaver, Beckham, Blaine, Caddo, Canadian, Cimarron, Cleveland, Comanche, Cotton, Custer, Dewey, Ellis, Garfield, Garvin, Grady, Grant, Greer, Harmon, Harper, Jackson, Jefferson, Kay, Kingfisher, Kiowa, Lincoln, Logan, McClain, Major, Noble, Oklahoma, Payne, Pottawatomie, Roger Mills, Stephens, Texas, Tillman, Washita, Woods, and Woodward.

Court for the Western District shall be held at Chickasha, Enid, Guthrie, Lawton, Mangum, Oklahoma City, Pauls Valley, Ponca City, Shawnee, and Woodward.

(June 25, 1948, c. 646, 62 Stat. 887; Aug. 4, 1966, Pub.L. 89–526, § 1, 80 Stat. 335.)

HISTORICAL AND STATUTORY NOTES

Effective and Applicability Provisions

1966 Acts. Section 2 of Pub.L. 89–526 provided that: "The amendments made by this Act [to subsecs. (b) and (c) of this section] shall take effect on the sixtieth day after the date of enactment of this Act [Aug. 4, 1966]."

§ 117. Oregon

Oregon constitutes one judicial district.

Court shall be held at Coquille, Eugene or Springfield, Klamath Falls, Medford, Pendleton, and Portland.

(June 25, 1948, c. 646, 62 Stat. 888; Aug. 3, 1950, c. 514, 64 Stat. 393; June 2, 1970, Pub.L. 91–272, § 7, 84 Stat. 297; Nov. 13, 2000, Pub.L. 106–518, Title V, § 502, 114 Stat. 2422.)

§ 118. Pennsylvania

Pennsylvania is divided into three judicial districts to be known as the Eastern, Middle, and Western Districts of Pennsylvania.

Eastern District

(a) The Eastern District comprises the counties of Berks, Bucks, Chester, Delaware, Lancaster, Lehigh, Montgomery, Northampton, and Philadelphia.

Court for the Eastern District shall be held at Allentown, Easton, Lancaster, Reading, and Philadelphia.

Middle District

(b) The Middle District comprises the counties of Adams, Bradford, Cameron, Carbon, Centre, Clinton, Columbia, Cumberland, Dauphin, Franklin, Fulton, Huntingdon, Juniata, Lackawanna, Lebanon, Luzerne, Lycoming, Mifflin, Monroe, Montour, Northumberland, Perry, Pike, Potter, Schuylkill, Snyder, Sullivan, Susquehanna, Tioga, Union, Wayne, Wyoming, and York.

Court for the Middle District shall be held at Harrisburg, Lewisburg, Scranton, Wilkes-Barre, and Williamsport.

Western District

(c) The Western District comprises the counties of Allegheny, Armstrong, Beaver, Bedford, Blair, Butler, Cambria, Clarion, Clearfield, Crawford, Elk, Erie, Fayette, Forest, Greene, Indiana, Jefferson, Lawrence, McKean, Mercer, Somerset, Venango, Warren, Washington, and Westmoreland.

Court for the Western District shall be held at Erie, Johnstown, and Pittsburgh.

(June 25, 1948, c. 646, 62 Stat. 888; June 2, 1970, Pub.L. 91–272, § 6, 84 Stat. 297; Nov. 2, 1978, Pub.L. 95–573, § 4, 92 Stat. 2458; Oct. 6, 1992, Pub.L. 102–396, Title IX, § 9161, 106 Stat. 1947; Oct. 21, 1998, Pub.L. 105–277, Div. A, § 101(b) [Title VI, § 624(a)], 112 Stat. 2681–116.)

HISTORICAL AND STATUTORY NOTES

Effective and Applicability Provisions

1998 Acts. Pub.L. 105–277, Div. A, § 101(b) [Title VI, § 624(b)], Oct. 21, 1998, 112 Stat. 2681–116, provided that:

"**(b)(1)** This section and the amendments made by this section [amending this section] shall take effect 180 days after the date of the enactment of this Act [Oct. 21, 1998].

"**(2)** This section and the amendments made by this section [amending this section] shall not affect any action commenced before the effective date of this section [Oct. 21, 1998] and pending on such date in the United States District Court for the Eastern District of Pennsylvania.

"**(3)** This section and the amendments made by this section [amending this section] shall not affect the composition, or preclude the service, of any grand or petit jury summoned, impaneled, or actually serving on the effective date of this section [Oct. 21, 1998]."

1978 Acts. Amendment by Pub.L. 95–573 effective 180 days after Nov. 2, 1978, except as otherwise provided, except that nothing in this Act shall affect the composition or preclude the service of any grand or petit juror summoned, empaneled, or actually serving in any judicial district on such effective date, see section 6 of Pub.L. 95–573, set out as a note under section 93 of this title.

§ 119. Puerto Rico

Puerto Rico constitutes one judicial district.

Court shall be held at Mayaguez, Ponce, and San Juan.

(June 25, 1948, c. 646, 62 Stat. 889.)

§ 120. Rhode Island

Rhode Island constitutes one judicial district.

Court shall be held at Providence.

(June 25, 1948, c. 646, 62 Stat. 889.)

§ 121. South Carolina

South Carolina constitutes one judicial district comprising eleven divisions.

(1) The Charleston Division comprises the counties of Berkeley, Charleston, Clarendon, Colleton, Dorchester, and Georgetown.

Court for the Charleston Division shall be held at Charleston.

(2) The Columbia Division comprises the counties of Kershaw, Lee, Lexington, Richland, and Sumter.

Court for the Columbia Division shall be held at Columbia.

(3) The Florence Division comprises the counties of Chesterfield, Darlington, Dillon, Florence, Horry, Marion, Marlboro, and Williamsburg.

Court for the Florence Division shall be held at Florence.

(4) The Aiken Division comprises the counties of Aiken, Allendale, and Barnwell.

Court for the Aiken Division shall be held at Aiken.

(5) The Orangeburg Division comprises the counties of Bamberg, Calhoun, and Orangeburg.

Court for the Orangeburg Division shall be held at Orangeburg.

(6) The Greenville Division comprises the counties of Greenville and Laurens.

Court for the Greenville Division shall be held at Greenville.

(7) The Rock Hill Division comprises the counties of Chester, Fairfield, Lancaster, and York.

Court for the Rock Hill Division shall be held at Rock Hill.

(8) The Greenwood Division comprises the counties of Abbeville, Edgefield, Greenwood, McCormick, Newberry, and Saluda.

Court for the Greenwood Division shall be held at Greenwood.

(9) The Anderson Division comprises the counties of Anderson, Oconee, and Pickens.

Court for the Anderson Division shall be held at Anderson.

(10) The Spartanburg Division comprises the counties of Cherokee, Spartanburg, and Union.

Court for the Spartanburg Division shall be held at Spartanburg.

(11) The Beaufort Division comprises the counties of Beaufort, Hampton, and Jasper.

Court for the Beaufort Division shall be held at Beaufort.

(June 25, 1948, c. 646, 62 Stat. 889; Oct. 7, 1965, Pub.L. 89–242, § 1(a), 79 Stat. 951; Nov. 14, 1986, Pub.L. 99–657, § 2, 100 Stat. 3670; Oct. 28, 1991, Pub.L. 102–140, Title III, § 304, 105 Stat. 810.)

HISTORICAL AND STATUTORY NOTES

Effective and Applicability Provisions

1986 Acts. Section 4 of Pub.L. 99–657 provided that:

"**(a) Effective date.**—(1) The amendments made by sections 2 and 3 [amending this section and section 90 of this title, respectively] take effect 90 days after the date of the enactment of this Act [Nov. 14, 1986].

"(2) The amendment made by section 4 [enacting this note] takes effect on the date of the enactment of this Act [Nov. 14, 1986].

"**(b) Pending actions.**—The amendments made by this Act [amending this section and section 90 of this title, and enacting provisions set out as a note under section 1 of this title] shall not affect any action commenced before the effective date of such amendments and pending on such date.

"**(c) Juries.**—The amendments made by this Act [amending this section and section 90 of this title, and enacting provisions set out as a note under section 1 of this title] shall not affect the composition, or preclude the service, of any grand or petit jury summoned, empaneled, or actually serving on the effective date of such amendments."

1965 Acts. Section 6 of Pub.L. 89–242 provided that: "The provisions of this Act [amending this section and section 133 of this title and enacting provisions set out as notes under this section] shall become effective on the first day of the month following the date of enactment of this Act [Oct. 7, 1965]."

Consolidation of South Carolina Into a Single Judicial District

Sections 2 to 5 of Pub.L. 89–242 provided that:

"**Sec. 2. [Continuity of Judicial Business; Clerk of Court; Records].** In compliance with section 132 of title 28 of the United States Code [section 132 of this title] the District Courts for the Eastern and Western Districts of South Carolina are hereby consolidated into, and shall henceforth constitute, a single District Court for the District of South Carolina. No loss or interruption of the jurisdiction of the consolidated District Court for the District of South Carolina over cases and controversies heretofore decided by or now pending in the District Courts for the Eastern and Western Districts of South Carolina shall result from such consolidation and prosecutions for offenses committed within the Eastern and Western Districts of South Carolina prior to the effective date of this Act [Nov. 1, 1965] shall be commenced and proceeded with the same as if such consolidation had not occurred. For the purpose of the trial of such offenses, the District Courts for the Eastern and Western Districts of South Carolina are continued in existence and the judges of the District Court for the District of South Carolina shall sit as judges in such courts according to assignment made by the chief judge of the United States District Court for the District of South Carolina or the chief judge of the United States Court of Appeals for the Fourth Circuit. The District Court for the District of South Carolina shall appoint a clerk who shall supersede the clerks of the District Courts for the Eastern and Western Districts of South Carolina and who shall maintain his office at Columbia until the court otherwise directs pursuant to sections 457 and 751(c) of title 28 of the United States Code [sections 457 and 751(c) of this title]. The presently existing records of the District Courts for the Eastern and Western Districts of South Carolina shall be placed in his custody.

"**Sec. 3. [United States Attorney].** When the term of office of either the United States attorney for the Eastern District of South Carolina or the United States attorney for the Western District of South Carolina, holding office on the date of enactment of this Act, has expired, the President is authorized to appoint a United States attorney for the District of South Carolina as provided by section 501 of title 28 of the United States Code [section 501 of this title]. Until the United States attorney for the District of South Carolina has been appointed as herein authorized and has qualified, the United States attorney for the Eastern District of South Carolina holding office on the date of enactment of this Act [Oct. 7, 1965] shall continue to serve as a United States attorney and to perform the duties of such office in the Charleston, Columbia, Orangeburg, Florence, and Aiken divisions of the District of South Carolina, and the United States attorney for the Western District of South Carolina holding office on the date of enactment of this Act [Oct. 7, 1965] shall continue to serve as a United States attorney and to perform the duties of such office in the Greenville, Rock Hill, Greenwood, Spartanburg, and Anderson divisions of the District of South Carolina. In the event a vacancy, other than a vacancy resulting from expiration of term, arises in either of such offices prior to the appointment as herein authorized and qualification, of a United States attorney for the District of South Carolina the incumbent of the other such office shall also perform the duties of the office in which the vacancy occurs until such appointment and qualification.

"**Sec. 4. [United States Marshal].** When the term of office of either the United States marshal for the Eastern District of South Carolina or the United States marshal for the Western District of South Carolina, holding office on the date of enactment of this Act [Oct. 7, 1965], has expired, the President is authorized to appoint a United States marshal for the District of South Carolina as provided by section 541(a) of title 28 of the United States Code [section 541(a) of this title]. Until the United States marshal for the District of South Carolina has been appointed as herein authorized and has qualified, the United States marshal for the Eastern District of South Carolina holding office on the date of enactment of this Act [Oct. 7, 1965] shall continue to serve as a United States marshal and to perform the duties of such office in the Charleston, Columbia, Orangeburg, Florence, and Aiken divisions of the District of South Carolina, and the United States marshal for the Western District of South Carolina holding office on the date of enactment of this Act [Oct. 7, 1965] shall continue to serve as a United States marshal and to perform the duties of such office in the Greenville, Rock Hill, Greenwood, Spartanburg, and Anderson divisions of the District of South Carolina. In the event a vacancy, other than a vacancy resulting from expiration of term, arises in either of such offices prior to the appointment as herein authorized and qualification of a United States marshal for the District of South Carolina the incumbent of the other such office shall also perform the duties of the office in which the vacancy occurs until such appointment and qualification.

"**Sec. 5. [Other Court Personnel].** All deputy clerks, clerical assistants, and other employees of the clerks, all court reporters, all probation officers and their clerical assistants, all referees in bankruptcy and their clerical assistants, all United States commissioners and all other presently serving officers and employees of the United States District Courts for the Eastern and Western Districts of South Carolina shall henceforth be officers or employees, as the case may be, of the United States District Court for the District of South Carolina and shall hold their offices or employment under and perform their duties for that court. All presently serving assistant United States attorneys and clerical assistants of the United States attorneys and all presently serving deputy marshals and clerical assistants of the United States marshals appointed for the Eastern or Western District of South Carolina shall henceforth hold their offices or employment for the District of South Carolina."

§ 122. South Dakota

South Dakota constitutes one judicial district comprising four divisions.

(1) The Northern Division comprises the counties of Brown, Campbell, Clark, Codington, Corson, Day, Deuel, Edmonds, Grant, Hamlin, McPherson, Marshall, Roberts, Spink, and Walworth.

Court for the Northern Division shall be held at Aberdeen.

(2) The Southern Division comprises the counties of Aurora, Beadle, Bon Homme, Brookings, Brule, Charles Mix, Clay, Davison, Douglas, Hanson, Hutchinson, Kingsbury, Lake, Lincoln, McCook, Miner, Minnehaha, Moody, Sanborn, Turner, Union, and Yankton.

Court for the Southern Division shall be held at Sioux Falls.

(3) The central division comprises the counties of Buffalo, Dewey, Faulk, Gregory, Haakon, Hand, Hughes, Hyde, Jerauld, Jones, Lyman, Mellette, Potter, Stanley, Sully, Todd, Tripp, and Ziebach.

Court for the Central Division shall be held at Pierre.

(4) The Western Division comprises the counties of Bennett, Butte, Custer, Fall River, Harding, Jackson, Lawrence, Meade, Pennington, Perkins, and Shannon.

Court for the Western Division shall be held at Deadwood and Rapid City.

(June 25, 1948, c. 646, 62 Stat. 889; Oct. 10, 1966, Pub.L. 89–638, 80 Stat. 883; Aug. 10, 1972, Pub.L. 92–376, 86 Stat. 529; Dec. 1, 1990, Pub.L. 101–650, Title III, § 324(b), 104 Stat. 5120.)

§ 123. Tennessee

Tennessee is divided into three judicial districts to be known as the Eastern, Middle, and Western Districts of Tennessee.

Eastern District

(a) The Eastern District comprises four divisions.

(1) The Northern Division comprises the counties of Anderson, Blount, Campbell, Claiborne, Grainger, Jefferson, Knox, Loudon, Monroe, Morgan, Roane, Scott, Sevier, and Union.

Court for the Northern Division shall be held at Knoxville.

(2) The Northeastern Division comprises the counties of Carter, Cocke, Greene, Hamblen, Hancock, Hawkins, Johnson, Sullivan, Unicoi, and Washington.

Court for the Northeastern Division shall be held at Greenville.

(3) The Southern Division comprises the counties of Bledsoe, Bradley, Hamilton, McMinn, Marion, Meigs, Polk, Rhea, and Sequatchie.

Court for the Southern Division shall be held at Chattanooga.

(4) The Winchester Division comprises the counties of Bedford, Coffee, Franklin, Grundy, Lincoln, Moore, Van Buren, and Warren.

Court for the Winchester Division shall be held at Winchester.

Middle District

(b) The Middle District comprises three divisions.

(1) The Nashville Division comprises the counties of Cannon, Cheatham, Davidson, Dickson, Houston, Humphreys, Montgomery, Robertson, Rutherford, Stewart, Sumner, Trousdale, Williamson, and Wilson.

Court for the Nashville Division shall be held at Nashville.

(2) The Northeastern Division comprises the counties of Clay, Cumberland, De Kalb, Fentress, Jackson, Macon, Overton, Pickett, Putnam, Smith, and White.

Court for the Northeastern Division shall be held at Cookeville.

(3) The Columbia Division comprises the counties of Giles, Hickman, Lawrence, Lewis, Marshall, Maury, and Wayne.

Court for the Columbia Division shall be held at Columbia.

Western District

(c) The Western District comprises two divisions.

(1) The Eastern Division comprises the counties of Benton, Carroll, Chester, Crockett, Decatur, Dyer, Gibson, Hardeman, Hardin, Haywood, Henderson, Henry, Lake, McNairy, Madison, Obion, Perry, and Weakley.

The Eastern Division also includes the waters of Tennessee River to low-water mark on the eastern shore wherever such river forms the boundary between the western and middle districts from the north line of Alabama north to the point in Henry County, Tennessee, where the south boundary of Kentucky strikes the east bank of the river.

Court for the Eastern Division shall be held at Jackson and Dyersburg.

(2) The Western Division comprises the counties of Fayette, Lauderdale, Shelby, and Tipton.

Court for the Western Division shall be held at Memphis.

The district judge for the Eastern District in office on November 27, 1940, shall hold court in the Northern and Northeastern Divisions. The other judge of that district shall hold the terms of court in the Southern and Winchester Divisions. Each may appoint and remove all officers and employees of the court whose official headquarters are located in the divisions within which he holds court and whose appointments are vested by law in a district judge or chief judge of a district.

(June 25, 1948, c. 646, 62 Stat. 890; May 19, 1961, Pub.L. 87–36, § 3(e), 75 Stat. 83; July 11, 1961, Pub.L. 87–86, 75 Stat. 203; June 2, 1970, Pub.L. 91–272, § 12, 84 Stat. 298; Oct. 13, 2008, Pub.L. 110–406, § 2(a), 122 Stat. 4291.)

HISTORICAL AND STATUTORY NOTES

Codifications

Section 3(e) of Pub.L. 87–36 provided that "The second sentence of section 123(c)(2), title 18, United States Code, is amended to read as follows:". Pub.L. 87–86 corrected such reference to "title 18" to "title 28."

Effective and Applicability Provisions

2008 Acts. Pub.L. 110–406, § 2(b), Oct. 13, 2008, 122 Stat. 4291, provided that:

"(1) **In general.**—The amendments made by this section [amending this section] shall take effect on the date of enactment of this Act [Oct. 13, 2008].

"(2) **Pending cases not affected.**—The amendments made by this section [amending this section] shall not affect any action commenced before the effective date of this section [Oct. 13, 2008] and pending in the United States District Court for the Western District of Tennessee on such date.

"(3) **Juries not affected.**—The amendments made by this section [amending this section] shall not affect the composition, or preclude the service, of any grand or petit jury summoned, impaneled, or actually serving in the United States District Court for the Western District of Tennessee on the effective date of this section [Oct. 13, 2008]."

§ 124. Texas

Texas is divided into four judicial districts to be known as the Northern, Southern, Eastern, and Western Districts of Texas.

Northern District

(a) The Northern District comprises seven divisions.

(1) The Dallas Division comprises the counties of Dallas, Ellis, Hunt, Johnson, Kaufman, Navarro, and Rockwall.

Court for the Dallas Division shall be held at Dallas.

(2) The Fort Worth Division comprises the counties of Comanche, Erath, Hood, Jack, Palo Pinto, Parker, Tarrant, and Wise.

Court for the Fort Worth Division shall be held at Fort Worth.

(3) The Abilene Division comprises the counties of Callahan, Eastland, Fisher, Haskell, Howard, Jones, Mitchell, Nolan, Shackleford, Stephens, Stonewall, Taylor, and Throckmorton.

Court for the Abilene Division shall be held at Abilene.

(4) The San Angelo Division comprises the counties of Brown, Coke, Coleman, Concho, Crockett, Glasscock, Irion, Menard, Mills, Reagan, Runnels, Schleicher, Sterling, Sutton, and Tom Green.

Court for the San Angelo Division shall be held at San Angelo.

(5) The Amarillo Division comprises the counties of Armstrong, Brisco, Carson, Castro, Childress, Collingsworth, Dallam, Deaf Smith, Donley, Gray, Hall, Hansford, Hartley, Hemphill, Hutchinson, Lipscomb, Moore, Ochiltree, Oldham, Parmer, Potter, Randall, Roberts, Sherman, Swisher, and Wheeler.

Court for the Amarillo Division shall be held at Amarillo.

(6) The Wichita Falls Division comprises the counties of Archer, Baylor, Clay, Cottle, Foard, Hardeman, King, Knox, Montague, Wichita, Wilbarger, and Young.

Court for the Wichita Falls Division shall be held at Wichita Falls.

(7) The Lubbock Division comprises the counties of Bailey, Borden, Cochran, Crosby, Dawson, Dickens, Floyd, Gaines, Garza, Hale, Hockley, Kent, Lamb, Lubbock, Lynn, Motley, Scurry, Terry, and Yoakum.

Court for the Lubbock Division shall be held at Lubbock.

Southern District

(b) The Southern District comprises seven divisions.

(1) The Galveston Division comprises the counties of Brazoria, Chambers, Galveston, and Matagorda.

Court for the Galveston Division shall be held at Galveston.

(2) The Houston Division comprises the counties of Austin, Brazos, Colorado, Fayette, Fort Bend, Grimes, Harris, Madison, Montgomery, San Jacinto, Walker, Waller, and Wharton.

Court for the Houston Division shall be held at Houston.

(3) The Laredo Division comprises the counties of Jim Hogg, La Salle, McMullen, Webb, and Zapata.

Court for the Laredo Division shall be held at Laredo.

(4) The Brownsville Division comprises the counties of Cameron and Willacy.

Court for the Brownsville Division shall be held at Brownsville.

(5) The Victoria Division comprises the counties of Calhoun, DeWitt, Goliad, Jackson, Lavaca, Refugio, and Victoria.

Court for the Victoria Division shall be held at Victoria.

(6) The Corpus Christi Division comprises the counties of Aransas, Bee, Brooks, Duval, Jim Wells, Kenedy, Kleberg, Live Oak, Nueces, and San Patricio.

Court for the Corpus Christi Division shall be held at Corpus Christi.

(7) The McAllen Division comprises the counties of Hidalgo and Starr.

Court for the McAllen Division shall be held at McAllen.

Eastern District

(c) The Eastern District comprises seven divisions.

(1) The Tyler Division comprises the counties of Anderson, Cherokee, Gregg, Henderson, Panola, Rains, Rusk, Smith, Van Zandt, and Wood.

Court for Tyler Division will be held at Tyler.

(2) The Beaumont Division comprises the counties of Hardin, Jasper, Jefferson, Liberty, Newton, and Orange.

Court for the Beaumont Division is to be held at Beaumont.

(3) The Sherman Division comprises the counties of Collin, Cook, Delta, Denton, Fannin, Grayson, Hopkins, and Lamar.

Court for the Sherman Division shall be held at Sherman and Plano.

(4) The Marshall Division comprises the counties of Camp, Cass, Harrison, Marion, Morris, and Upshur.

Court for the Marshall Division shall be held at Marshall.

(5) The Texarkana Division comprises the counties of Bowie, Franklin, Red River, and Titus.

Court for the Texarkana Division shall be held at Texarkana, and may be held anywhere within the Federal courthouse in Texarkana that is located astride the State line between Texas and Arkansas.

(6) The Lufkin Division comprises the counties of Angelina, Houston, Nacogdoches, Polk, Sabine, San Augustine, Shelby, Trinity, and Tyler.

Court for the Lufkin Division shall be held at Lufkin.

Western District

(d) The Western District comprises seven divisions.

(1) The Austin Division comprises the counties of Bastrop, Blanco, Burleson, Burnet, Caldwell, Gillespie, Hays, Kimble, Lampasas, Lee, Llano, Mason, McCulloch, San Saba, Travis, Washington, and Williamson.

Court for the Austin Division shall be held at Austin.

(2) The Waco Division comprises the counties of Bell, Bosque, Coryell, Falls, Freestone, Hamilton, Hill, Leon, Limestone, McLennan, Milam, Robertson, and Somervell.

Court for the Waco Division shall be held at Waco.

(3) The El Paso Division comprises the county of El Paso.

Court for the El Paso Division shall be held at El Paso.

(4) The San Antonio Division comprises the counties of Atascosa, Bandera, Bexar, Comal, Dimmit, Frio, Gonzales, Guadalupe, Karnes, Kendall, Kerr, Medina, Real, and Wilson.

Court for the San Antonio Division shall be held at San Antonio.

(5) The Del Rio Division comprises the counties of Edwards, Kinney, Maverick, Terrell, Uvalde, Val Verde, and Zavalla.

Court for the Del Rio Division shall be held at Del Rio.

(6) The Pecos Division comprises the counties of Brewster, Culberson, Jeff Davis, Hudspeth, Loving, Pecos, Presidio, Reeves, Ward, and Winkler.

Court for the Pecos Division shall be held at Pecos.

(7) The Midland-Odessa Division comprises the counties of Andrews, Crane, Ector, Martin, Midland, and Upton.

Court for the Midland-Odessa Division shall be held at Midland. Court may be held, in the discretion of the court, in Odessa, when courtroom facilities are made available at no expense to the Government.

(June 25, 1948, c. 646, 62 Stat. 891; Feb. 10, 1954, c. 6, § 2(b)(9)(a), (b), 68 Stat. 11; Sept. 4, 1957, Pub.L. 85–298, §§ 1, 2, 71 Stat. 618; Oct. 4, 1961, Pub.L. 87–352, 75 Stat. 772; Mar. 11, 1964, Pub.L. 88–282, 78 Stat. 163; Aug. 30, 1964, Pub.L. 88–512, 78 Stat. 695; Dec. 18, 1967, Pub.L. 90–216, 81 Stat. 661; Oct. 15, 1980, Pub.L. 96–462, § 6, 94 Stat. 2054; Nov. 8, 1984, Pub.L. 98–620, Title IV, § 407(a), 98 Stat. 3362; Dec. 3, 2003, Pub.L. 108–157, § 1(a), 117 Stat. 1947; Dec. 10, 2004, Pub.L. 108–455, § 3, 118 Stat. 3628.)

HISTORICAL AND STATUTORY NOTES

Effective and Applicability Provisions

2003 Acts. Pub.L. 108–157, § 1(b), Dec. 3, 2003, 117 Stat. 1947, provided that:

"(1) **In general.**—This section and the amendments made by this section [amending this section] shall take effect on the date of the enactment of this Act [Dec. 3, 2003].

"(2) **Pending cases not affected.**—This section and the amendments made by this section [amending this section] shall not affect any action commenced before the effective date of this section and pending in the United States District Court for the Eastern District of Texas on such date.

"(3) **Juries not affected.**—This section and the amendments made by this section [amending this section] shall not affect the composition, or preclude the service, of any grand or petit jury summoned, impaneled, or actually serving in the Eastern Judicial District of Texas on the effective date of this section."

1984 Acts. Section 407(b) of Pub.L. 98–620 provided that: "The amendments made by subsection (a) of this section [amending subsec. (b) of this section] shall apply to any action commenced in the United States District Court for the Southern District of Texas on or after the effective date of this subtitle [Jan. 1, 1985], and shall not affect any action pending in such court on such effective date."

Amendment by Pub.L. 98–620 to take effect Jan. 1, 1985, and not to affect the composition, or preclude the service, of any grand or petit jury summoned, impaneled, or actually serving on that date, see section 411 of Pub.L. 98–620, set out as a note under section 85 of this title.

1980 Acts. Amendment by Pub.L. 96–462 effective Oct. 1, 1981, with that amendment not to affect the composition or preclude the service of any grand or petit juror summoned, empaneled, or actually serving in any judicial district on Oct. 1, 1981, see section 7 of Pub.L. 96–462, set out as a note under section 84 of this title.

§ 125. Utah

Utah constitutes one judicial district comprising two divisions.

(1) The Northern Division comprises the counties of Box Elder, Cache, Davis, Morgan, Rich, and Weber.

Court for the Northern Division shall be held at Salt Lake City and Ogden.

(2) The Central Division comprises the counties of Beaver, Carbon, Daggett, Duchesne, Emery, Garfield, Grand, Iron, Juab, Kane, Millard, Piute, Salt Lake, San Juan, Sanpete, Sevier, Summit, Tooele, Uintah, Utah, Wasatch, Washington, and Wayne.

Court for the Central Division shall be held at Salt Lake City, Provo, and St. George.

(June 25, 1948, c. 646, 62 Stat. 893; Oct. 19, 1996, Pub.L. 104–317, Title VI, § 606, 110 Stat. 3859.)

§ 126. Vermont

Vermont constitutes one judicial district.

Court shall be held at Bennington, Brattleboro, Burlington, Montpelier, Rutland, Saint Johnsbury, and Windsor.

(June 25, 1948, c. 646, 62 Stat. 893; May 28, 1964, Pub.L. 88–312, 78 Stat. 201; Nov. 8, 1984, Pub.L. 98–620, Title IV, § 410, 98 Stat. 3362.)

HISTORICAL AND STATUTORY NOTES

Effective and Applicability Provisions

1984 Acts. Amendment by Pub.L. 98–620 to take effect on Jan. 1, 1985, and not to affect the composition, or preclude the service, of any grand or petit jury summoned, impaneled, or actually serving on that date, see section 411 of Pub.L. 98–620, set out as a note under section 85 of this title.

§ 127. Virginia

Virginia is divided into two judicial districts, to be known as the Eastern and Western Districts of Virginia.

Eastern District

(a) The Eastern District comprises the counties of Accomac, Amelia, Arlington, Brunswick, Caroline, Charles City, Chesterfield, Dinwiddie, Elizabeth City, Essex, Fairfax, Fauquier, Gloucester, Goochland, Greensville, Hanover, Henrico, Isle of Wight, James City, King and Queen, King George, King William, Lancaster, Loudoun, Lunenburg, Mathews, Mecklenburg, Middlesex, Nansemond, New Kent, Norfolk, Northampton, Northumberland, Nottoway, Powhatan, Prince Edward, Prince George, Prince William, Princess Anne, Richmond, Southampton, Spotsylvania, Stafford, Surry, Sussex, Warwick, Westmoreland, and York.

Court for the Eastern District shall be held at Alexandria, Newport News, Norfolk, and Richmond.

Western District

(b) The Western District comprises the counties of Albemarle, Alleghany, Amherst, Appomattox, Augusta, Bath, Bedford, Bland, Botetourt, Buchanan, Buckingham, Campbell, Carroll, Charlotte, Clarke, Craig, Culpeper, Cumberland, Dickenson, Floyd, Fluvanna, Franklin, Frederick, Giles, Grayson, Greene, Halifax, Henry, Highland, Lee, Louisa, Madison, Montgomery, Nelson, Orange, Page, Patrick, Pittsylvania, Pulaski, Rappahannock, Roanoke, Rockbridge, Rockingham, Russell, Scott, Shenandoah, Smyth, Tazewell, Warren, Washington, Wise, and Wythe.

Court for the Western District shall be held at Abingdon, Big Stone Gap, Charlottesville, Danville, Harrisonburg, Lynchburg, and Roanoke.

(c) Cities and incorporated towns are included in that district in which are included the counties within the exterior boundaries of which such cities and incorporated towns are geographically located or out of the territory of which they have been incorporated.

(June 25, 1948, c. 646, 62 Stat. 893; July 5, 1968, Pub.L. 90–383, 82 Stat. 292; Dec. 10, 1991, Pub.L. 102–200, § 1, 105 Stat. 1630.)

HISTORICAL AND STATUTORY NOTES

Effective and Applicability Provisions

1991 Acts. Section 2 of Pub.L 102–200 provided that:

"**(a) Pending Actions.**—The amendments made by section 1 [amending subsecs. (a) and (b) of this section] shall not apply to any action commenced before the date of the enactment of this Act [Dec. 10, 1991] and pending in the United States District Court for the Eastern District of Virginia on such date.

"**(b) Juries.**—The amendments made by section 1 [amending subsecs. (a) and (b) of this section] shall not affect the composition, or preclude the service, of any grand or petit jury summoned, empaneled, or actually serving in the Eastern or Western District of Virginia on the date of the enactment of this Act [Dec. 10, 1991]."

§ 128. Washington

Washington is divided into two judicial districts to be known as the Eastern and Western Districts of Washington.

Eastern District

(a) The Eastern District comprises the counties of Adams, Asotin, Benton, Chelan, Columbia, Douglas, Ferry, Franklin, Garfield, Grant, Kittitas, Klickitat, Lincoln, Okanogan, Pend Oreille, Spokane, Stevens, Walla Walla, Whitman, and Yakima.

Court for the Eastern District shall be held at Spokane, Yakima, Walla Walla, and Richland.

Western District

(b) The Western District comprises the counties of Clallam, Clark, Cowlitz, Grays Harbor, Island, Jefferson, King, Kitsap, Lewis, Mason, Pacific, Pierce, San Juan, Skagit, Skamania, Snohomish, Thurston, Wahkiakum, and Whatcom.

Court for the Western District shall be held at Bellingham, Seattle, Tacoma, and Vancouver.

(June 25, 1948, c. 646, 62 Stat. 894; Sept. 25, 1962, Pub.L. 87–699, 76 Stat. 598; June 2, 1970, Pub.L. 91–272, § 4, 84 Stat. 297; Dec. 26, 2007, Pub.L. 110–161, Div. D, Title III, § 308, 121 Stat. 1990.)

§ 129. West Virginia

West Virginia is divided into two judicial districts to be known as the Northern and Southern Districts of West Virginia.

Northern District

(a) The Northern District comprises the counties of Barbour, Berkeley, Braxton, Brooke, Calhoun, Doddridge, Gilmer, Grant, Hampshire, Hancock, Hardy, Harrison, Jefferson, Lewis, Marion, Marshall, Mineral, Monongalia, Morgan, Ohio, Pendleton, Pleasants, Pocahontas, Preston, Randolph, Ritchie, Taylor, Tucker, Tyler, Upshur, Webster, and Wetzel.

Court for the Northern District shall be held at Clarksburg, Elkins, Fairmont, Martinsburg, and Wheeling.

Southern District

(b) The Southern District comprises the counties of Boone, Cabell, Clay, Fayette, Greenbrier, Jackson, Kanawha, Lincoln, Logan, McDowell, Mason, Mercer, Mingo, Monroe, Nicholas, Putnam, Raleigh, Roane, Summers, Wayne, Wirt, Wood, and Wyoming.

Court for the Southern District shall be held at Beckley, Bluefield, Charleston, Huntington, Lewisburg, and Parkersburg.

(June 25, 1948, c. 646, 62 Stat. 894; Jan. 14, 1983, Pub.L. 97–471, § 1, 96 Stat. 2601.)

§ 130. Wisconsin

Wisconsin is divided into two judicial districts to be known as the Eastern and Western districts of Wisconsin.

Eastern District

(a) The Eastern District comprises the counties of Brown, Calumet, Dodge, Door, Florence, Fond du Lac, Forest, Green Lake, Kenosha, Kewaunee, Langlade, Manitowoc, Marinette, Marquette, Menominee, Milwaukee, Oconto, Outagamie, Ozaukee, Racine, Shawano, Sheboygan, Walworth, Washington, Waukesha, Waupaca, Waushara, and Winnebago.

Court for the Eastern District shall be held at Green Bay, Milwaukee, and Oshkosh.

Western District

(b) The Western District comprises the counties of Adams, Ashland, Barron, Bayfield, Buffalo, Burnett, Chippewa, Clark, Columbia, Crawford, Dane, Douglas, Dunn, Eau Claire, Grant, Green, Iowa, Iron, Jackson, Jefferson, Juneau, La Crosse, Lafayette, Lincoln, Marathon, Monroe, Oneida, Pepin, Pierce, Polk, Portage, Price, Richland, Rock, Rusk, Saint Croix, Sauk, Sawyer, Taylor, Trempealeau, Vernon, Vilas, Washburn, and Wood.

Court for the Western District shall be held at Eau Claire, La Crosse, Madison, Superior, and Wausau.

(June 25, 1948, c. 646, 62 Stat. 894; Aug. 6, 1962, Pub.L. 87–573, 76 Stat. 307.)

HISTORICAL AND STATUTORY NOTES

Designation of Judge to Hold Court, Eastern District

Pub.L. 106–553, § 1(a)(2) [Title III, § 305(c)], Dec. 21, 2000, 114 Stat. 2762, 2762A–85, provided that: "The chief judge of the eastern district of Wisconsin shall designate 1 judge who shall hold court for such district in Green Bay, Wisconsin."

§ 131. Wyoming

Wyoming and those portions of Yellowstone National Park situated in Montana and Idaho constitute one judicial district.

Court shall be held at Casper, Cheyenne, Evanston, Lander, Jackson, and Sheridan.

(June 25, 1948, c. 646, 62 Stat. 895; July 10, 1984, Pub.L. 98–353, Title II, § 203(a), 98 Stat. 350.)

§ 132. Creation and composition of district courts

(a) There shall be in each judicial district a district court which shall be a court of record known as the United States District Court for the district.

(b) Each district court shall consist of the district judge or judges for the district in regular active service. Justices or judges designated or assigned shall be competent to sit as judges of the court.

(c) Except as otherwise provided by law, or rule or order of court, the judicial power of a district court with respect to any action, suit or proceeding may be exercised by a single judge, who may preside alone and hold a regular or special session of court at the same time other sessions are held by other judges.

(June 25, 1948, c. 646, 62 Stat. 895; Nov. 13, 1963, Pub.L. 88–176, § 2, 77 Stat. 331.)

HISTORICAL AND STATUTORY NOTES

Continuation of Organization of Court

Section 2(b) of Act June 25, 1948, provided in part that the provisions of this title as set out in section 1 of said Act June 25, 1948, with respect to the organization of the court, shall be construed as a continuation of existing law, and the tenure of the judges, officers, and employees thereof, and of the United States attorneys and marshals and their deputies and assistants, in office on Sept. 1, 1948, shall not be affected by its enactment but each of them shall continue to serve in the same capacity under the appropriate provisions of this title pursuant to his prior appointment.

§ 133. Appointment and number of district judges

(a) The President shall appoint, by and with the advice and consent of the Senate, district judges for the several judicial districts, as follows:

DISTRICTS	JUDGES
Alabama:	
Northern	7
Middle	3

DISTRICTS	JUDGES
Southern	3
Alaska	3
Arizona	12
Arkansas:	
Eastern	5
Western	3
California:	
Northern	14
Eastern	6
Central	27
Southern	13
Colorado	7
Connecticut	8
Delaware	4
District of Columbia	15
Florida:	
Northern	4
Middle	15
Southern	17
Georgia:	
Northern	11
Middle	4
Southern	3
Hawaii	3
Idaho	2
Illinois:	
Northern	22
Central	4
Southern	4
Indiana:	
Northern	5
Southern	5
Iowa:	
Northern	2
Southern	3
Kansas	5
Kentucky:	
Eastern	5
Western	4
Eastern and Western	1
Louisiana:	
Eastern	12
Middle	3
Western	7
Maine	3
Maryland	10
Massachusetts	13
Michigan:	
Eastern	15
Western	4
Minnesota	7
Mississippi:	
Northern	3
Southern	6
Missouri:	
Eastern	6
Western	5
Eastern and Western	2
Montana	3
Nebraska	3
Nevada	7
New Hampshire	3
New Jersey	17
New Mexico	6
New York:	
Northern	5
Southern	28
Eastern	15
Western	4
North Carolina:	
Eastern	4
Middle	4
Western	4
North Dakota	2
Ohio:	
Northern	11
Southern	8
Oklahoma:	
Northern	3
Eastern	1
Western	6
Northern, Eastern, and Western	1
Oregon	6
Pennsylvania:	
Eastern	22
Middle	6
Western	10
Puerto Rico	7
Rhode Island	3
South Carolina	10
South Dakota	3
Tennessee:	
Eastern	5
Middle	4
Western	5
Texas:	
Northern	12
Southern	19
Eastern	7
Western	13
Utah	5
Vermont	2
Virginia:	
Eastern	11
Western	4
Washington:	
Eastern	4
Western	7
West Virginia:	
Northern	3
Southern	5
Wisconsin:	
Eastern	5
Western	2

DISTRICTS	JUDGES
Wyoming	3.

(b)(1) In any case in which a judge of the United States (other than a senior judge) assumes the duties of a full-time office of Federal judicial administration, the President shall appoint, by and with the advice and consent of the Senate, an additional judge for the court on which such judge serves. If the judge who assumes the duties of such full-time office leaves that office and resumes the duties as an active judge of the court, then the President shall not appoint a judge to fill the first vacancy which occurs thereafter in that court.

(2) For purposes of paragraph (1), the term "office of Federal judicial administration" means a position as Director of the Federal Judicial Center, Director of the Administrative Office of the United States Courts, or Counselor to the Chief Justice.

(June 25, 1948, c. 646, 62 Stat. 895; Aug. 3, 1949, c. 387, § 2(a), 63 Stat. 493; Aug. 14, 1950, c. 708, 64 Stat. 443; Aug. 29, 1950, c. 819, § 1, 64 Stat. 562; Sept. 5, 1950, c. 848, § 1, 64 Stat. 578; Feb. 10, 1954, c. 6, § 2(a)(3), 68 Stat. 9; Sept. 7, 1957, Pub.L. 85–310, 71 Stat. 631; July 7, 1958, Pub.L. 85–508, § 12(c), 72 Stat. 348; Mar. 18, 1959, Pub.L. 86–3, § 9(b), 73 Stat. 8; May 19, 1961, Pub.L. 87–36, § 2(d), 75 Stat. 81; July 30, 1962, Pub.L. 87–562, § 3, 76 Stat. 248; Oct. 7, 1965, Pub.L. 89–242, § 1(c), 79 Stat. 951; Mar. 18, 1966, Pub.L. 89–372, § 4, 80 Stat. 77; June 2, 1970, Pub.L. 91–272, § 1(d), 84 Stat. 295; Dec. 18, 1971, Pub.L. 92–208, § 3(d), 85 Stat. 742; Oct. 2, 1978, Pub.L. 95–408, § 4(b)(2), 92 Stat. 883; Oct. 20, 1978, Pub.L. 95–486, § 1(c), 92 Stat. 1630; Jan. 14, 1983, Pub.L. 97–471, § 3, 96 Stat. 2601; July 10, 1984, Pub.L. 98–353, Title II, § 202(e), 98 Stat. 348; Dec. 1, 1990, Pub.L. 101–650, Title II, § 203(d), Title III, § 303, 104 Stat. 5101, 5105; Oct. 6, 1997, Pub.L. 105–53, § 4, 111 Stat. 1174; Nov. 29, 1999, Pub.L. 106–113, Div. B, § 1000(a)(1) [Title III, § 309(b)], 113 Stat. 1535, 1501A–37; Dec. 21, 2000, Pub.L. 106–553, § 1(a)(2) [Title III, § 305(b)], 114 Stat. 2762, 2762A–85; Nov. 2, 2002, Pub.L. 107–273, Div. A, Title III, § 312(a)(2), (b)(2), 116 Stat. 1787, 1788; Oct. 13, 2008, Pub.L. 110–402, § 1(b)(1), 122 Stat. 4254.)

HISTORICAL AND STATUTORY NOTES

Codifications

Section 4(b)(2) of Pub.L. 95–408, set out in the credit of this section, was stricken by Pub.L. 96–4, § 1, Mar. 30, 1979, 93 Stat. 6, and replaced by section 4(b)(2) to (4) of Pub.L. 95–408, as added by Pub.L. 96–4, § 1, Mar. 30, 1979, 93 Stat. 6, which provisions are now set out as a note under section 93 of this title.

Effective and Applicability Provisions

2002 Acts. Pub.L. 107–273, Div. A, Title III, § 312(a)(3), Nov. 2, 2002, 116 Stat. 1787, provided that: "This subsection [amending subsec. (a) of this section and enacting provisions set out as a note under this section] shall take effect on July 15, 2003."

Pub.L. 107–273, Div. A, Title III, § 312(b)(3), Nov. 2, 2002, 116 Stat. 1788, provided that: "With respect to the central or southern district of Illinois, the northern district of New York, or the eastern district of Virginia, this subsection [amending subsec. (a) of this section and enacting provisions set out as notes under this section] shall take effect on the earlier of—

"**(A)** the date on which the first vacancy in the office of district judge occurs in such district; or

"**(B)** July 15, 2003."

1990 Acts. Amendment by section 203(d) of Pub.L. 101–650 effective Dec. 1, 1990, see section 206 of Pub.L. 101–650, set out as a note under section 44 of this title.

1978 Acts. Section 7 of Pub.L. 95–486 provided that:

"**(a)** The first section and section 2 of this Act [amending this section and enacting provisions set out as notes under this section] shall take effect immediately upon the President's promulgation and publication of standards and guidelines for the selection, on the basis of merit, of nominees for United States district court judgeships authorized by this Act [amending this section, sections 44, 46, 1337, and 1445 of this title, section 5108 of Title 5, Government Organization and Employees, enacting provisions set out as notes under this section and sections 41 and 44 of this title, and amending provisions set out as a note under section 45 of this title].

"**(b)** The President may waive such standards and guidelines with respect to any nomination by notifying the Senate of the reasons for such waiver.

"**(c)** Following the promulgation and publication of such standards and guidelines, no nomination or appointment to a United States district court judgeship may be invalidated on the basis of the President's failure to comply with this section or with any standards or guidelines promulgated under this section.

"**(d)** This Act, other than the first section and section 2 [amending this section and enacting provisions set out as notes under this section], shall take effect on the date of enactment of this Act [Oct. 20, 1978]."

Section 11 of Pub.L. 95–486 provided that: "Notwithstanding any other provision of this Act [amending this section, sections 44, 46, 1337 and 1445 of this title, section 5108 of Title 5, Government Organization and Employees, enacting provisions set out as notes under this section, sections 41, 44 of this title, and amending provisions set out as notes under section 45 of this title], the first section and section 2 [amending this section and enacting provisions set out as notes under this section] shall not take effect before November 1, 1978."

Amendment by Pub.L. 95–408 effective 180 days after Oct. 2, 1978, such amendment not to affect the composition or preclude the service of any grand or petit juror summoned, empaneled, or actually serving in any judicial district on the effective date of this Act, see section 5 of Pub.L. 95–408, set out as a note under section 89 of this title.

1971 Acts. Amendment by Pub.L. 92–208 effective one hundred and twenty days after Dec. 18, 1971, see section 3(f) of Pub.L. 92–208, set out as a note under section 98 of this title.

1965 Acts. Amendment by Pub.L. 89–242 effective on the first day of the month following the date of enactment of Pub.L. 89–242, see section 6 of Pub.L. 89–242, set out as a note under section 121 of this title.

1962 Acts. Amendment by Pub.L. 87–562 effective 90 days after July 30, 1962, see section 5 of Pub.L. 87–562, set out as a note under section 89 of this title.

1959 Acts. Section 9 of Pub.L. 86–3 provided in part that the amendment of this section and section 134(a) of this title shall be effective upon the admission of the State of Hawaii into the Union. Admission of Hawaii into the Union was accomplished Aug. 21, 1959, upon issuance of Proc. No. 3309, Aug. 21, 1959, 25 F.R. 6868, 73 Stat. c74, as required by sections 1 and 7(c) of Pub.L. 86–3, Mar. 18, 1959, 73 Stat. 4, set out as notes preceding section 491 of Title 48, Territories and Insular Possessions.

1958 Acts. Amendment by Pub.L. 85–508 effective Jan. 3, 1959, upon admission of Alaska into the Union pursuant to Proc. No. 3269, Jan. 3, 1959, 24 F.R. 81, 73 Stat. c16, as required by sections 1 and 8(c) of Pub.L. 85–508, see notes set out under section 81A of this title and preceding section 21 of Title 48, Territories and Insular Possessions.

Conversion of Temporary Judgeships to Permanent Judgeships

Pub.L. 107–273, Div. A, Title III, § 312(b)(1), Nov. 2, 2002, 116 Stat. 1787, provided that: "The existing district judgeships for the central district and the southern district of Illinois, the northern district of New York, and the eastern district of Virginia authorized by section 203(c) (3), (4), (9), and (12) of the Judicial Improvements Act of 1990 (Public Law 101–650, 28 U.S.C. 133 note) shall be authorized under section 133 of title 28, United States Code [this section], and the incumbents in such offices shall hold the offices under section 133 of title 28, United States Code [this section] (as amended by this section)."

Temporary Judgeships

Pub.L. 107–273, Div. A, Title III, § 312(c), Nov. 2, 2002, 116 Stat. 1788, provided that:

"(1) **In general.**—The President shall appoint, by and with the advice and consent of the Senate—

"(A) 1 additional district judge for the northern district of Alabama;

"(B) 1 additional judge for the district of Arizona;

"(C) 1 additional judge for the central district of California;

"(D) 1 additional judge for the southern district of Florida;

"(E) 1 additional district judge for the district of New Mexico;

"(F) 1 additional district judge for the western district of North Carolina; and

"(G) 1 additional district judge for the eastern district of Texas.

"(2) **Vacancies not filled.**—The first vacancy in the office of district judge in each of the offices of district judge authorized by this subsection [this note], occurring 10 years or more after the confirmation date of the judge named to fill the temporary district judgeship created in the applicable district by this subsection [this note], shall not be filled.

"(3) **Effective date.**—This subsection [this note] shall take effect on July 15, 2003."

Additional Federal Judgeships

Pub.L. 109–115, Div. A, Title IV, § 406, Nov. 30, 2005, 119 Stat. 2470, provided that: "The existing judgeship for the eastern district of Missouri authorized by section 203(c) of the Judicial Improvements Act of 1990 (Public Law 101–650, 104 Stat. 5089) as amended by Public Law 105–53 [set out in a note under this heading], as of the effective date of this Act [Nov. 30, 2005, the effective date of the Transportation, Treasury, Housing and Urban Development, the Judiciary, and Independent Agencies Appropriations Act, 2006, Pub.L. 109–115, Div. A, 119 Stat. 2396, which enacted this note], shall be extended. The first vacancy in the office of district judge in this district occurring 20 years or more after the confirmation date of the judge named to fill the temporary judgeship created by section 203(c) shall not be filled."

Pub.L. 107–273, Div. A, Title III, § 312(a)(1), Nov. 2, 2002, 116 Stat. 1786, provided that: "The President shall appoint, by and with the advice and consent of the Senate—

"(A) 5 additional district judges for the southern district of California;

"(B) 1 additional district judge for the western district of North Carolina; and

"(C) 2 additional district judges for the western district of Texas."

[Pub.L. 107–273, Div. A, Title III, § 312(a)(3), Nov. 2, 2002, 116 Stat. 1787, provided that: "This subsection [amending subsec. (a) of this section and enacting provisions set out as a note under this section] shall take effect on July 15, 2003."]

Pub.L. 106–553, § 1(a)(2) [Title III, § 305(a)], Dec. 21, 2000, 114 Stat. 2762, 2762a–84, provided that:

"(a) **In general**—The President shall appoint, by and with the advice and consent of the Senate—

"(1) 1 additional district judge for the district of Arizona;

"(2) 1 additional district judge for the southern district of Florida;

"(3) 1 additional district judge for the eastern district of Kentucky;

"(4) 1 additional district judge for the district of Nevada;

"(5) 1 additional district judge for the district of New Mexico;

"(6) 1 additional district judge for the district of South Carolina;

"(7) 1 additional district judge for the southern district of Texas;

"(8) 1 additional district judge for the western district of Texas;

"(9) 1 additional district judge for the eastern district of Virginia; and

"(10) 1 additional district judge for the eastern district of Wisconsin."

Pub.L. 106–113, Div. B, § 1000(a)(1) [Title III, § 309(a)], Nov. 29, 1999, 113 Stat. 1535, 1501A–37, provided that:

"(a) The President shall appoint, by and with the advice and consent of the Senate—

"(1) three additional district judges for the district of Arizona;

"(2) four additional district judges for the middle district of Florida; and

"(3) two additional district judges for the district of Nevada."

Section 203(a) to (c) of Title II of Pub.L. 101–650, as amended Pub.L. 104–60, Nov. 28, 1995, 109 Stat. 635; Pub.L. 104–317, Title III, § 304, Oct. 19, 1996, 110 Stat. 3852; Pub.L. 105–53, § 3, Oct. 6, 1997, 111 Stat. 1173; Pub.L. 107–273, Div. A, Title III, § 312(d)(1), Nov. 2, 2002, 116 Stat. 1788; Pub.L. 109–289, Div. B, Title II, § 21056, as added Pub.L. 110–5, § 2, Feb. 15, 2007, 121 Stat. 55; Pub.L. 110–161, Div. D, Title III, § 309, Dec. 26, 2007, 121 Stat. 1990, provided that:

"**(a) In general.**—The President shall appoint, by and with the advice and consent of the Senate—

"**(1)** 1 additional district judge for the western district of Arkansas;

"**(2)** 2 additional district judges for the northern district of California;

"**(3)** 5 additional district judges for the central district of California;

"**(4)** 1 additional district judge for the southern district of California;

"**(5)** 2 additional district judges for the district of Connecticut;

"**(6)** 2 additional district judges for the middle district of Florida;

"**(7)** 1 additional district judge for the northern district of Florida;

"**(8)** 1 additional district judge for the southern district of Florida;

"**(9)** 1 additional district judge for the middle district of Georgia;

"**(10)** 1 additional district judge for the northern district of Illinois;

"**(11)** 1 additional district judge for the southern district of Iowa;

"**(12)** 1 additional district judge for the western district of Louisiana;

"**(13)** 1 additional district judge for the district of Maine;

"**(14)** 1 additional district judge for the district of Massachusetts;

"**(15)** 1 additional district judge for the southern district of Mississippi;

"**(16)** 1 additional district judge for the eastern district of Missouri;

"**(17)** 1 additional district judge for the district of New Hampshire;

"**(18)** 3 additional district judges for the district of New Jersey;

"**(19)** 1 additional district judge for the district of New Mexico;

"**(20)** 1 additional district judge for the southern district of New York;

"**(21)** 3 additional district judges for the eastern district of New York;

"**(22)** 1 additional district judge for the middle district of North Carolina;

"**(23)** 1 additional district judge for the southern district of Ohio;

"**(24)** 1 additional district judge for the northern district of Oklahoma;

"**(25)** 1 additional district judge for the western district of Oklahoma;

"**(26)** 1 additional district judge for the district of Oregon;

"**(27)** 3 additional district judges for the eastern district of Pennsylvania;

"**(28)** 1 additional district judge for the middle district of Pennsylvania;

"**(29)** 1 additional district judge for the district of South Carolina;

"**(30)** 1 additional district judge for the eastern district of Tennessee;

"**(31)** 1 additional district judge for the western district of Tennessee;

"**(32)** 1 additional district judge for the middle district of Tennessee;

"**(33)** 2 additional district judges for the northern district of Texas;

"**(34)** 1 additional district judge for the eastern district of Texas;

"**(35)** 5 additional district judges for the southern district of Texas;

"**(36)** 3 additional district judges for the western district of Texas;

"**(37)** 1 additional district judge for the district of Utah;

"**(38)** 1 additional district judge for the eastern district of Washington;

"**(39)** 1 additional district judge for the northern district of West Virginia;

"**(40)** 1 additional district judge for the southern district of West Virginia; and

"**(41)** 1 additional district judge for the district of Wyoming.

"**(b) Existing judgeships.**—**(1)** The existing district judgeships for the western district of Arkansas, the northern district of Illinois, the northern district of Indiana, the district of Massachusetts, the western district of New York, the eastern district of North Carolina, the northern district of Ohio, and the western district of Washington authorized by section 202(b) of the Bankruptcy Amendments and Federal Judgeship Act of 1984 (Public Law 98–353, 98 Stat. 347–348) [set out as a note under this section] shall, as of the effective date of this title [Dec. 1, 1990], be authorized under section 133 of title 28, United States Code [this section], and the incumbents in those offices shall hold the office under section 133 of title 28, United States Code [this section], as amended by this title.

"**(2)(A)** The existing 2 district judgeships for the eastern and western districts of Arkansas (provided by section 133 of title 28, United States Code [this section], as in effect on the day before the effective date of this title [Dec. 1, 1990]) shall be district judgeships for the eastern district of Arkansas only, and the incumbents of such judgeships shall hold the offices under section 133 of title 28, United States Code [this section], as amended by this title.

"**(B)** The existing district judgeship for the northern and southern districts of Iowa (provided by section 133 of title 28, United States Code [this section], as in effect on the day before the effective date of this title [Dec. 1, 1990]) shall be a district judgeship for the northern district of Iowa only, and the incumbent of such judgeship shall hold the office under section 133 of title 28, United States Code [this section], as amended by this title.

"(C) The existing district judgeship for the northern, eastern, and western districts of Oklahoma (provided by section 133 of title 28, United States Code [this section], as in effect on the day before the effective date of this title [Dec. 1, 1990]) and the occupant of which has his or her official duty station at Oklahoma City on the date of the enactment of this title [Dec. 1, 1990], shall be a district judgeship for the western district of Oklahoma only, and the incumbent of such judgeship shall hold the office under section 133 of title 28, United States Code [this section], as amended by this title.

"(c) **Temporary judgeships.**—The President shall appoint, by and with the advice and consent of the Senate—

"(1) 1 additional district judge for the eastern district of California;

"(2) 1 additional district judge for the district of Hawaii;

"(3) 1 additional district judge for the central district of Illinois;

"(4) 1 additional district judge for the southern district of Illinois;

"(5) 1 additional district judge for the district of Kansas;

"(6) 1 additional district judge for the western district of Michigan;

"(7) 1 additional district judge for the eastern district of Missouri;

"(8) 1 additional district judge for the district of Nebraska;

"(9) 1 additional district judge for the northern district of New York;

"(10) 1 additional district judge for the northern district of Ohio;

"(11) 1 additional district judge for the eastern district of Pennsylvania; and

"(12) 1 additional district judge for the eastern district of Virginia.

"[(13) Redesignated (12)]

Except with respect to the district of Kansas, the western district of Michigan, the eastern district of Pennsylvania, and the northern district of Ohio, the first vacancy in the office of district judge in each of the judicial districts named in this subsection [this note], occurring 10 years or more after the confirmation date of the judge named to fill the temporary judgeship created by this subsection, shall not be filled. The first vacancy in the office of district judge in the district of Kansas occurring 17 years or more after the confirmation date of the judge named to fill the temporary judgeship created for such district under this subsection [this note], shall not be filled. The first vacancy in the office of district judge in the western district of Michigan, occurring after December 1, 1995, shall not be filled. The first vacancy in the office of district judge in the eastern district of Pennsylvania, occurring 5 years or more after the confirmation date of the judge named to fill the temporary judgeship created for such district under this subsection, shall not be filled. The first vacancy in the office of district judge in the northern district of Ohio occurring 17 years or more after the confirmation date of the judge named to fill the temporary judgeship created under this subsection [this note] shall not be filled. For districts named in this subsection [this note] for which multiple judgeships are created by this Act, the last of those judgeships filled shall be the judgeships created under this section."

[Pub.L. 107–273, Div. A, Title III, § 312(d)(2), Nov. 2, 2002, 116 Stat. 1788, provided that: "The amendments made by this subsection [amending this note] shall take effect on the date of enactment of this Act [Nov. 2, 2002]."]

Section 202(a) to (d) of Pub.L. 98–353 provided that:

"(a) Subject to the provisions of subsection (c), the President shall appoint, by and with the advice and consent of the Senate, one additional district judge for the southern district of Alabama, one additional district judge for the district of Alaska, five additional district judges for the central district of California, one additional district judge for the district of Colorado, one additional district judge for the district of Connecticut, one additional district judge for the district of Delaware, three additional district judges for the southern district of Florida, one additional district judge for the middle district of Georgia, one additional district judge for the district of Hawaii, four additional district judges for the northern district of Illinois, one additional district judge for the southern district of Illinois, one additional district judge for the western district of Kentucky, one additional district judge for the western district of Louisiana, one additional district judge for the district of Maryland, one additional district judge for the district of Massachusetts, two additional district judges for the eastern district of Michigan, one additional district judge for the district of Minnesota, one additional district judge for the northern district of Mississippi, two additional district judges for the southern district of Mississippi, one additional district judge for the eastern district of Missouri, one additional district judge for the district of Montana, one additional district judge for the district of Nevada, three additional district judges for the district of New Jersey, one additional district judge for the northern district of New York, two additional district judges for the eastern district of New York, one additional district judge for the southern district of Ohio, one additional district judge for the western district of Oklahoma, one additional district judge for the district of Rhode Island, one additional district judge for the eastern district of Tennessee, one additional district judge for the western district of Tennessee, one additional district judge for the northern district of Texas, two additional district judges for the eastern district of Texas, one additional district judge for the western district of Texas, one additional district judge for the district of Utah, one additional district judge for the eastern district of Virginia, one additional district judge for the eastern district of Washington, one additional district judge for the western district of Washington, and one additional district judge for the district of Wyoming.

"(b) Subject to the provisions of subsection (c) the President shall appoint, by and with the advice and consent of the Senate, one additional district judge for the western district of Arkansas, one additional district judge for the northern district of Illinois, one additional district judge for the northern district of Indiana, one additional district judge for the district of Massachusetts, one additional district judge for the western district of New York, one additional district judge for the eastern district of North Carolina, one additional district judge for the northern district of Ohio, and one additional district judge for the western district of Washington. The first vacancy in each of the offices of district judge authorized by this subsection, occurring five years or more after the effective date of this Act [probably means July 10, 1984], shall not be filled.

"(c) For the judgeships created in subsections (a) and (b), the President shall appoint, by and with the advice and consent of the Senate, no more than twenty-nine of such judges prior to January 21, 1985.

"(d) The existing district judgeship for the district of Minnesota and the existing district judgeship for the northern district of Ohio, heretofore authorized by section 2 of the Act of October 20, 1978 (Public Law 95–486, 92 Stat. 1631) [set out as a note under this section], shall, as of the effective date of this Act [probably means July 10, 1984], be authorized under section 133 of title 28, United States Code [this section], and the incumbents of those offices shall henceforth hold their offices under section 133 [this section], as amended by this Act [Pub.L. 98–353]."

Section 1(a) of Pub.L. 95–486 provided that: "The President shall appoint, by and with the advice and consent of the Senate, three additional district judges for the northern district of Alabama, one additional district judge for the middle district of Alabama, three additional district judges for the district of Arizona, two additional district judges for the eastern district of Arkansas, one additional district judge for the northern district of California, three additional district judges for the eastern district of California, one additional district judge for the central district of California, two additional district judges for the southern district of California, two additional district judges for the district of Colorado, one additional district judge for the district of Connecticut, one additional district judge for the northern district of Florida, three additional district judges for the middle district of Florida, five additional district judges for the southern district of Florida, five additional district judges for the northern district of Georgia, one additional district judge for the southern district of Georgia, three additional district judges for the northern district of Illinois, one additional district judge for the central district of Illinois, one additional district judge for the northern district of Indiana, one additional district judge for the southern district of Indiana, one additional district judge for the southern district of Iowa, one additional district judge for the district of Kansas, two additional district judges for the eastern district of Kentucky, four additional judges for the eastern district of Louisiana, one additional district judge for the middle district of Louisiana, one additional district judge for the western district of Louisiana, one additional district judge for the district of Maine, two additional district judges for the district of Maryland, four additional district judges for the district of Massachusetts, three additional district judges for the eastern district of Michigan, two additional district judges for the western district of Michigan, one additional district judge for the district of Minnesota, one additional district judge for the eastern district of Missouri, two additional district judges for the western district of Missouri, one additional district judge for the district of Nevada, one additional district judge for the district of New Hampshire, two additional district judges for the district of New Jersey, one additional district judge for the district of New Mexico, one additional district judge for the northern district of New York, one additional district judge for the eastern district of New York, one additional district judge for the eastern district of North Carolina, one additional district judge for the middle district of North Carolina, one additional district judge for the western district of North Carolina, one additional district judge for the northern district of Ohio, one additional district judge for the southern district of Ohio, one additional district judge for the western district of Oklahoma, one additional district judge for the northern district of Oklahoma, two additional district judges for the district of Oregon, two additional district judges for the middle district of Pennsylvania, four additional district judges for the district of Puerto Rico, three additional district judges for the district of South Carolina, one additional district judge for the district of South Dakota, one additional district judge for the middle district of Tennessee, three additional district judges for the northern district of Texas, one additional district judge for the eastern district of Texas, five additional district judges for the southern district of Texas, one additional district judge for the western district of Texas, one additional district judge for the district of Utah, two additional district judges for the eastern district of Virginia, two additional district judges for the western district of Virginia, one additional district judge for the eastern district of Washington, one additional district judge for the western district of Washington, one additional district judge for the southern district of West Virginia, one additional district judge for the eastern district of Wisconsin, and one additional district judge for the western district of Wisconsin."

Section 2 of Pub.L. 95–486 provided that: "The President shall appoint, by and with the advice and consent of the Senate, one additional district judge for the eastern district of Kentucky, one additional district judge for the district of Minnesota, one additional district judge for the northern district of Ohio, and one additional district judge for the southern district of West Virginia. The first vacancy in the office of district judge in the judicial districts named in this section occurring five years or more after the effective date of this Act [Oct. 20, 1978] shall not be filled."

Section 1(a) of Pub.L. 91–272 provided that: "The President shall appoint, by and with the advice and consent of the Senate, one additional district judge for the northern district of Alabama, one additional district judge for the middle district of Alabama, one additional district judge for the district of Arizona, two additional district judges for the northern district of California, three additional district judges for the central district of California, three additional district judges for the southern district of California, one additional district judge for the district of Colorado, one additional district judge for the middle district of Florida, two additional district judges for the southern district of Florida, three additional district judges for the northern district of Georgia, one additional district judge for the southern district of Georgia, two additional district judges for the northern district of Illinois, one additional district judge for the eastern district of Kentucky, one additional district judge for the western district of Kentucky, two additional district judges for the eastern district of Louisiana, one additional district judge for the western district of Louisiana, two additional district judges for the district of Maryland, two additional district judges for the eastern district of Michigan, one additional district judge for the eastern district of Missouri, one additional district judge for the district of Nebraska, one additional district judge for the district of New Jersey, one additional district judge for the district of New Mexico, one additional district judge for the eastern district of New York, three additional district judges for the southern district of New York, one additional district judge for the northern district of Ohio, one additional district judge for the southern district of Ohio, six additional district judges for the eastern district of Pennsylvania, two additional district judges for the western district of Pennsylvania, one additional district judge for the district of Puerto Rico, one additional district judge for the district of South Carolina, one additional district judge for the western district of Tennessee, one additional district judge for the northern district of Texas, one additional district judge for the eastern district of Texas, one additional district judge for the southern district of Texas, one additional district judge for the western district of Texas, one additional district judge for the eastern district of Virginia, and one additional district judge for the southern district of West Virginia."

Section 2(a) of Pub.L. 89–372 provided that: "The President shall appoint, by and with the advice and consent of the Senate, one district judge for the middle and southern districts of Alabama, one additional district judge for the district of Arizona, one additional district judge for the northern district of Florida, one additional district judge for the middle district of Florida, two additional district judges for the southern district of Florida, one additional district judge for the northern district of Illinois, one additional district judge for the southern district of Indiana, four additional district judges for the eastern district of Louisiana, one additional district judge for the district of Maryland, one additional district judge for the northern district of Mississippi, one additional district judge for the southern district of Mississippi, one additional district judge for the western district of New York, one additional district judge for the northern district of Ohio, one additional district judge for the southern district of Ohio, one additional district judge for the district of Rhode Island, two additional district judges for the southern district of Texas, one additional district judge for the western district of Texas, two additional district judges for the eastern district of Virginia, and one additional district judge for the district of Vermont."

Section 2(a) of Pub.L. 87–36 provided that: "The President shall appoint, by and with the advice and consent of the Senate, one additional district judge for the northern district of Alabama, one additional district judge for the district of Alaska, one additional district judge for the district of Arizona, one additional district judge for the eastern and western districts of Arkansas, two additional district judges for the northern district of California, two additional district judges for the southern district of California, one additional district judge for the district of Colorado, two additional district judges for the district of Connecticut, two additional district judges for the southern district of Florida, one additional district judge for the northern district of Georgia, two additional district judges for the northern district of Illinois, one additional district judge for the northern district of Indiana, one additional district judge for the southern district of Indiana, one additional district judge for the northern and southern districts of Iowa, one additional district judge for the district of Kansas, two additional district judges for the eastern district of Louisiana, one additional district judge for the western district of Louisiana, two additional district judges for the district of Maryland, one additional district judge for the district of Massachusetts, two additional district judges for the eastern district of Michigan, one additional district judge for the southern district of Mississippi, one additional district judge for the western district of Missouri, one additional district judge for the district of Nevada, one additional district judge for the district of New Jersey, two additional district judges for the eastern district of New York, six additional district judges for the southern district of New York, one additional district judge for the eastern district of North Carolina, one additional district judge for the middle district of North Carolina, one additional district judge for the western district of North Carolina, one additional district judge for the northern district of Ohio, one additional district judge for the northern, eastern, and western districts of Oklahoma, three additional district judges for the eastern district of Pennsylvania, one additional district judge for the middle district of Pennsylvania, two additional district judges for the western district of Pennsylvania, one additional district judge for the district of Puerto Rico, one additional district judge for the eastern and western districts of South Carolina, one additional district judge for the eastern district of Tennessee, one additional district judge for the middle district of Tennessee, one additional district judge for the western district of Tennessee, two additional district judges for the northern district of Texas, one additional district judge for the southern district of Texas, one additional district judge for the western district of Texas, and one additional district judge for the eastern and western districts of Washington."

Subsec. (a)(1) of section 2 of Act Feb. 10, 1954, subsec. (a)(3) of which section amended the table in this section, provided for the appointment by the President, by and with the advice and consent of the Senate, of the additional judges for the districts for which additional permanent judgeships were provided in such amendment.

Alabama.—Section 1(b) of Pub.L. 91–272 provided that: "The existing district judgeship for the middle and southern districts of Alabama, heretofore provided for by section 133 of title 28 of the United States Code [this section], shall hereafter be a district judgeship for the southern district of Alabama only, and the present incumbent of such judgeship shall henceforth hold his office under such section 133, as amended by subsection (d) of this section."

California.—Section 3(h) of Pub.L. 89–372 provided that: "The President shall appoint, by and with the advice and consent of the Senate, three additional district judges for the central district of California, and two additional district judges for the northern district of California."

Delaware.—Act July 24, 1946, c. 602, 60 Stat. 654, which authorized the appointment of an additional judge for the district of Delaware was repealed by section 2 of Act Sept. 5, 1950, cited to text, which by section 1 of said Act Sept. 5, 1950, made the additional judgeship permanent. However, said section 2 also provided that the repeal in no way affected the tenure of the present incumbent.

Florida.—Section 2(b) of Pub.L. 89–372 provided that: "The existing district judgeship for the northern, middle and southern districts of Florida heretofore provided for by section 133 of title 28, United States Code [this section], shall hereafter be a district judgeship for the middle district of Florida only, and the present incumbent of such judgeship shall henceforth hold his office under section 133, as amended by this Act."

Georgia.—Act Mar. 29, 1949, c. 37, 63 Stat. 16, which authorized the appointment of an additional judge for the middle district, was repealed by section 2(b) of Pub.L. 87–36, which made the judgeship permanent and also provided that the incumbent of the judgeship created by Act Mar. 29, 1949, should henceforth hold his office under this section, as amended by Pub.L. 87–36, section 2(d).

Kansas.—Section 5(a) of Pub.L. 89–372, Mar. 18, 1966, 80 Stat. 78, which authorized the appointment of an additional district judge for the eastern district of Kansas and which provided that the first vacancy which occurred in the office of district judge in such district not be filled was repealed by section 1(c) of Pub.L. 91–272, June 2, 1970, 84 Stat. 294, which provided, in part, that such judgeship be a permanent judgeship and that the present incumbent henceforth hold his office under section 133 of title 28, United States Code [this section], as amended by section 1(d) of Pub.L. 91–272.

Missouri.—In connection with the permanent additional judgeship for the Eastern and Western Districts of Missouri, added by section 2(a), (2), (3) of Act Feb. 10, 1954, which previously had been authorized on a temporary basis by Act Dec. 24, 1942, c. 827, 56 Stat. 1083, section 2(b)(10) of Act Feb. 10, 1954, provided: "The present incumbent of the judgeship created by the Act entitled 'An Act to provide for the appointment of an additional district judge for the eastern and western districts of Missouri', approved December 24, 1942 (56 Stat. 1983), shall henceforth hold such office under section 133 of title 28 of the United States Code [this section] as amended by this Act."

Nevada.—Section 2(b)(2) of Act Feb. 10, 1954, provided: "The President shall appoint, by and with the advice and consent of the Senate, one additional district judge for the district of Nevada. The first vacancy occurring in the office of district judge in said district shall not be filled."

New Jersey.—Section 2(a) of Pub.L. 91–272 provided that: "The President shall appoint, by and with the advice and consent of the Senate, one additional district judge for the district of New Jersey. The first vacancy occurring in the office of district judge in that district shall not be filled."

New Mexico.—Act Feb. 10, 1954, c. 6, § 2(b)(1), 68 Stat. 10, which authorized the appointment of an additional judge for the district, was repealed by section 2(b) of Pub.L. 87–36, which made the judgeship permanent and also provided that the incumbent of the judgeship created by Act Feb. 10, 1954, should henceforth hold his office under this section, as amended by Pub.L. 87–36, § 2(d).

North Carolina.—Section 2(c) of Pub.L. 91–272 provided that: "The President shall appoint, by and with the advice and consent of the Senate, one additional district judge for the eastern district of North Carolina. The first vacancy occurring in the office of district judge in that district shall not be filled."

Ohio.—Act May 1, 1941, c. 83, 55 Stat. 148, which provided for the appointment of an additional judge for the northern district was repealed by Act Aug. 3, 1949, c. 387, § 2(e), 63 Stat. 495, which also provided that the incumbent of the judgeship created by said Act May 1, 1941, shall henceforth hold his office under this section, as amended by Act Aug. 3, 1949, § 2(a).

Section 2(e)(1), (2) of Pub.L. 87–36 provided that:

"(1) The President shall appoint, by and with the advice and consent of the Senate, one additional district judge for the southern district of Ohio. The first vacancy occurring in the office of district judge in said district shall not be filled.

"(2) The President shall appoint, by and with the advice and consent of the Senate, one additional district judge for the northern district of Ohio. The first vacancy occurring in the office of district judge in said district shall not be filled."

Oklahoma.—Act May 24, 1940, c. 209, § 2(a), 54 Stat. 219, providing for additional judgeships was amended by Act Aug. 3, 1949, c. 387, 63 Stat. 495, to strike out "western district of Oklahoma", and to make the incumbent of the judgeship created by said Act May 24, 1940, henceforth hold his office under this section, as amended by Act Aug. 3, 1949, § 2(a).

Pennsylvania.—Section 2(b) of Pub.L. 91–272 provided that: "The President shall appoint, by and with the advice and consent of the Senate, one additional district judge for the middle district of Pennsylvania. The first vacancy occurring in the office of district judge in that district shall not be filled."

Section 5(b) of Pub.L. 89–372, Mar. 18, 1966, 80 Stat. 78, as amended by Pub.L. 90–90, Sept. 23, 1967, 81 Stat. 228, which authorized the appointment of three additional district judges for the eastern district of Pennsylvania and which provided that the second, third, and fourth vacancies occurring after Mar. 18, 1966, in the office of district judge in such district not be filled was repealed by section 1(c) of Pub.L. 91–272, June 2, 1970, 84 Stat. 294, which provided, in part, that such judgeships be permanent judgeships and that the present incumbents henceforth hold their offices under section 133 of title 28, United States Code [this section], as amended by section 1(d) of Pub.L. 91–272.

Act Feb. 10, 1954, c. 6, § 2(b)(5), 68 Stat. 10, which authorized the appointment of an additional judge for the western district, was repealed by section 2(b) of Pub.L. 87–36, which made the judgeship permanent and also provided that the incumbent of the judgeship created by Act Feb. 10, 1954, should henceforth hold his office under this section, as amended by Pub.L. 87–36, section 2(d).

Section 2 of Act July 24, 1946, c. 600, 60 Stat. 654, as amended by section 6 of Act Feb. 10, 1954, c. 6, 68 Stat. 14, provided: "The President is authorized to appoint, by and with the advice and consent of the Senate, one additional United States district judge, who shall be an additional district judge for the eastern, middle, and western districts of Pennsylvania. The judge so appointed shall at the time of his appointment be a resident and a citizen of the State of Pennsylvania: *Provided*, That when a vacancy occurs in said office it shall not be filled: *Provided further*, That unless the President shall submit a nomination to the Senate to fill the office hereby created within ninety days after the effective date of this Act [July 24, 1946], then in that event this Act shall be of no force and effect. If a vacancy arises in the office of district judge for the middle district of Pennsylvania while the judge appointed pursuant to this section is holding the office created by this section, such judge shall thereafter be a district judge for the middle district of Pennsylvania."

Section 2(c) of Act Aug. 3, 1949, c. 387, 63 Stat. 495, which provided for an additional temporary judgeship for the western district of Pennsylvania was repealed by section 2 of Act Aug. 29, 1950, which by section 1 of said Act Aug. 29, 1950 made the additional judgeship permanent. However, said section 2 also provided that the repeal in no way affected the tenure of the present incumbent.

South Carolina.—Section 1(b) of Pub.L. 89–242 provided that: "The existing district judgeships for the Eastern District of South Carolina, the Western District of South Carolina, and the Eastern and Western Districts of South Carolina heretofore provided for by section 133 of title 28 of the United States Code [this section] shall hereafter be district judgeships for the District of South Carolina and the present incumbents of such judgeships shall henceforth hold their offices under section 133, as amended by this Act."

South Dakota.—Pub.L. 85–310 provided: "The President is authorized to appoint, by and with the advice and consent of the Senate an additional district judge for the district of South Dakota as authorized by paragraph (3) of section 2(b) of the Act of February 10, 1954 [set out as a note under this section]."

Section 2(b)(3) of Act Feb. 10, 1954, as amended by Pub.L. 85–310, Sept. 7, 1957, 71 Stat. 631, provided: "The President shall appoint, by and with the advice and consent of the Senate, one additional district judge for the district of South Dakota."

Tennessee.—Section 2(b)(4) of Act Feb. 10, 1954, provided: "The President shall appoint, by and with the advice and consent of the Senate, one additional district judge for the middle district of Tennessee. The first vacancy occurring in the office of district judge in said district shall not be filled."

Texas.—In connection with the permanent additional judgeship for the Southern District of Texas, added by section 2(a)(2), (3) of Act Feb. 10, 1954, which previously had been authorized on a temporary basis, section 2(b)(11) of Act Feb. 10, 1954, provided: "The present incumbent of the judgeship for the southern district of Texas created by section 2(d) of the Act entitled 'An Act to provide for the appointment of additional circuit and district judges, and for other purposes', approved August 3, 1949 (63 Stat. 495), shall henceforth hold such office under section 133 of title 28 of the United States Code [this section], as amended by this Act, and section 2(d) of the said Act approved August 3, 1949, is repealed."

Utah.—Act Feb. 10, 1954, c. 6, § 2(b)(6), 68 Stat. 11, which authorized the appointment of an additional judge for the district, was repealed by section 2(b) of Pub.L. 87–36, which made the judgeship permanent and also provided that the incumbent of the judgeship created by Act Feb. 10, 1954, should henceforth hold his office under this section, as amended by Pub.L. 87–36, § 2(d).

Virgin Islands.—Section 3(a) of Pub.L. 91–272 provided that: "The President shall appoint, by and with the advice and consent of the Senate, one additional judge for the District Court of the Virgin Islands, who shall hold office for the term of eight years and until his successor is chosen and qualified, unless sooner removed by the President for cause."

Washington.—Section 1(b) of Pub.L. 95–486 provided that: "The existing district judgeship for the eastern and western districts of Washington, heretofore provided for by section 133 of title 28 of the United States Code [this section], shall hereafter be a district judgeship for the western district of Washington only, and the present incumbent of such judgeship shall henceforth hold his office under section 133 [this section], as amended by this Act [Pub.L. 95–486]."

Section 2(c) of Pub.L. 87–36 provided that: "The existing district judgeship for the eastern and western districts of Washington, heretofore provided for by section 133 of title 28 of the United States Code [this section], shall hereafter be a district judgeship for the western district of Washington only, and the present incumbent of such judgeship shall henceforth hold his office under section 133 [this section], as amended by this Act [Pub.L. 87–36]."

West Virginia.—Section 2 of Pub.L. 97–471 provided that:

"**(a)** The existing district judgeship for the Southern District of West Virginia, authorized by section 2 of the Act entitled 'An Act to provide for the appointment of additional district and circuit judges and for other purposes', approved October 20, 1978 [Pub.L. 95–486] (92 Stat. 1632; 28 U.S.C. 133 note), shall, as of the date of enactment of this Act [Jan. 14, 1983], be authorized under section 133 of title 28 of the United States Code [this section] as a district judgeship for the Northern District of West Virginia, and the incumbent of that office shall henceforth hold office under section 133, as amended by this Act.

"**(b)** The existing district judgeship for the Northern and Southern Districts of West Virginia shall be authorized as the district judgeship for the Southern District."

In connection with the permanent additional judgeship for the Northern and Southern Districts of West Virginia, added by section 2(a)(2), (3) of Act Feb. 10, 1954, which previously had been authorized on a temporary basis by Act June 22, 1936, C. 695, 49 Stat. 1805, section (b)(12) of Act Feb. 10, 1954, provided: "The present incumbent of the judgeship created by the Act entitled 'An Act to provide for the appointment of an additional district judge for the northern and southern districts of West Virginia', approved June 22, 1936 (49 Stat. 1805), shall henceforth hold such office under section 133 of title 28 of the United States Code [this section], as amended by this Act."

Wisconsin.—Section 5(c) of Pub.L. 89–372, Mar. 18, 1966, 80 Stat. 78, which authorized the appointment of an additional district judge for the district of Wisconsin and which provided that the first vacancy occurring in the office of district judge in such district not be filled was repealed by section 1(c) of Pub.L. 91–272, June 2, 1970, 84 Stat. 294, which provided, in part, that such judgeship be a permanent judgeship and that the present incumbent henceforth hold his office under section 133 of title 28, United States Code [this section], as amended by section 1(d) of Pub.L. 91–272.

Nomination of Women and Blacks to Federal Judgeships

Section 8 of Pub.L. 95–486 provided that: "The Congress—

"**(1)** takes notice of the fact that only 1 percent of Federal judges are women and only 4 percent are blacks; and

"**(2)** suggests that the President, in selecting individuals for nomination to the Federal judgeships created by this Act [amending this section, sections 44, 46, 1337, and 1445 of this title, section 5108 of Title 5, Government Organization and Employees, enacting provisions set out as notes under this section, sections 41, 44 of this title, and amending provisions set out as notes under section 45 of this title], give due consideration to qualified individuals regardless of race, color, sex, religion, or national origin."

Residence of Additional Judge for Kansas

Section 2(b)(2) Act Aug. 3, 1949, provided that: "The judge first appointed for the district of Kansas under the authority contained in subsection (a) [amending this section] shall reside at Wichita."

§ 134. Tenure and residence of district judges

(a) The district judges shall hold office during good behavior.

(b) Each district judge, except in the District of Columbia, the Southern District of New York, and the Eastern District of New York, shall reside in the district or one of the districts for which he is appointed. Each district judge of the Southern District of New York and the Eastern District of New York may reside within 20 miles of the district to which he or she is appointed.

(c) If the public interest and the nature of the business of a district court require that a district judge should maintain his abode at or near a particular place for holding court in the district or within a particular part of the district the judicial council of the circuit may so declare and may make an appropriate order. If the district judges of such a district are unable to agree as to which of them shall maintain his abode at or near the place or within the area specified in such an order the judicial council of the circuit may decide which of them shall do so.

(June 25, 1948, c. 646, 62 Stat. 896; Aug. 3, 1949, c. 387, § 2(b)(1), 63 Stat. 495; Feb. 10, 1954, c. 6, § 2(b)(13)(a), 68 Stat. 12; Mar. 18, 1959, Pub.L. 86–3, § 9(c), 73 Stat. 8; May 19, 1961, Pub.L. 87–36, § 2(e)(3), 75 Stat. 83; Sept. 12, 1966, Pub.L. 89–571, § 1, 80 Stat. 764; Dec. 18, 1971, Pub.L. 92–208, § 3(e), 85 Stat. 742; Oct. 19, 1996, Pub.L. 104–317, Title VI, § 607, 110 Stat. 3860.)

HISTORICAL AND STATUTORY NOTES

Effective and Applicability Provisions

1971 Acts. Amendment by Pub.L. 92–208 effective one hundred and twenty days after Dec. 18, 1971, see section 3(f) of Pub.L. 92–208, set out as a note under section 98 of this title.

1959 Acts. Amendment by Pub.L. 86–3 effective upon the admission of Hawaii into the Union, see note set out under Section 133 of this title. Admission of Hawaii into the Union was accomplished Aug. 21, 1959 upon issuance of Proc. No. 3309, Aug. 21, 1959, 25 F.R. 6868, 73 Stat. c74, as required by Sections 1 and 7(c) of Pub.L. 86–3, Mar. 18, 1959, 73 Stat. 4, set out as notes preceding Section 491 of Title 48, Territories and Insular Possessions.

Applicability of Orders under 1954 Amendment

Section 2(b)(13)(b) of Act Feb. 10, 1954, provided: "Orders made by the judicial councils of the circuits under the second sentence of subsection (c) of section 134 of title 28 [this section], as amended by this section, determining that a specified district judge shall maintain his abode at or near a place or within an area which the council has theretofore designated for the abode of a district judge under the first sentence of such subsection, shall be applicable only to district judges appointed after the enactment of this Act [Feb. 10, 1954]."

Tenure and Salary Rights of Judges in Puerto Rico in Office on September 12, 1966

Section 4 of Pub.L. 89–571 provided that: "The amendments made by this section to sections 134 [this section] and 373 of title 28, United States Code [section 373 of this title], shall not affect the tenure of office or right to continue to receive salary after resignation, retirement, or failure of reappointment of any district judge for the district of Puerto Rico who is in office on the date of enactment of this Act [Sept. 12, 1966]."

§ 135. Salaries of district judges

Each judge of a district court of the United States shall receive a salary at an annual rate determined under section 225 of the Federal Salary Act of 1967 (2 U.S.C. 351–361), as adjusted by section 461 of this title.

(June 25, 1948, c. 646, 62 Stat. 897; Mar. 2, 1955, c. 9, § 1(c), 69 Stat. 10; Aug. 14, 1964, Pub.L. 88–426, Title IV, § 403(c), 78 Stat. 434; Aug. 9, 1975, Pub.L. 94–82, Title II, § 205(b)(3), 89 Stat. 422.)

HISTORICAL AND STATUTORY NOTES

References in Text

Section 225 of the Federal Salary Act of 1967, referred to in text, is section 225 of Pub.L. 90–206, Dec. 16, 1967, 81 Stat. 642, as amended, which is classified to Chapter 11 (section 351 et seq.) of Title 2, The Congress.

Effective and Applicability Provisions

1964 Acts. Amendment by Pub.L. 88–426 effective on the first day of the first pay period which begins on or after July 1, 1964, except to the extent provided in section 501(c) of Pub.L. 88–426, see section 501 of Pub.L. 88–426.

1955 Acts. Amendment by Act Mar. 2, 1955, effective Mar. 1, 1955, see section 5 of Act Mar. 2, 1955, set out as a note under section 31 of Title 2, The Congress.

Salary Increases

For prior year salary increases per the recommendation of the President, see Prior Salary Recommendations notes under 2 U.S.C.A. § 358.

For miscellaneous provisions dealing with adjustments of pay and limitations on use of funds to pay salaries in prior years, see notes under 5 U.S.C.A. § 5318.

§ 136. Chief judges; precedence of district judges

(a)(1) In any district having more than one district judge, the chief judge of the district shall be the district judge in regular active service who is senior in commission of those judges who—

(A) are sixty-four years of age or under;

(B) have served for one year or more as a district judge; and

(C) have not served previously as chief judge.

(2)(A) In any case in which no district judge meets the qualifications of paragraph (1), the youngest district judge in regular active service who is sixty-five years of age or over and who has served as district judge for one year or more shall act as the chief judge.

(B) In any case under subparagraph (A) in which there is no district judge in regular active service who has served as a district judge for one year or more, the district judge in regular active service who is senior in commission and who has not served previously as chief judge shall act as the chief judge.

(3)(A) Except as provided in subparagraph (C), the chief judge of the district appointed under paragraph (1) shall serve for a term of seven years and shall serve after expiration of such term until another judge is eligible under paragraph (1) to serve as chief judge of the district.

(B) Except as provided in subparagraph (C), a district judge acting as chief judge under subparagraph (A) or (B) of paragraph (2) shall serve until a judge has been appointed who meets the qualifications under paragraph (1).

(C) No district judge may serve or act as chief judge of the district after attaining the age of seventy years unless no other district judge is qualified to serve as chief judge of the district under paragraph (1) or is qualified to act as chief judge under paragraph (2).

(b) The chief judge shall have precedence and preside at any session which he attends.

Other district judges shall have precedence and preside according to the seniority of their commissions. Judges whose commissions bear the same date shall have precedence according to seniority in age.

(c) A judge whose commission extends over more than one district shall be junior to all district judges except in the district in which he resided at the time he entered upon the duties of his office.

(d) If the chief judge desires to be relieved of his duties as chief judge while retaining his active status as district judge, he may so certify to the Chief Justice of the United States, and thereafter, the chief judge of the district shall be such other district judge who is qualified to serve or act as chief judge under subsection (a).

(e) If a chief judge is temporarily unable to perform his duties as such, they shall be performed by the district judge in active service, present in the district and able and qualified to act, who is next in precedence.

(June 25, 1948, c. 646, 62 Stat. 897; Oct. 31, 1951, c. 655, § 37, 65 Stat. 723; Aug. 6, 1958, Pub.L. 85–593, § 2, 72 Stat. 497; Apr. 2, 1982, Pub.L. 97–164, Title II, § 202, 96 Stat. 52.)

HISTORICAL AND STATUTORY NOTES

Effective and Applicability Provisions

1982 Acts. Amendment by Pub.L. 97–164 effective Oct. 1, 1982, see section 402 of Pub.L. 97–164, set out as a note under section 171 of this title.

1958 Acts. Section 3 of Pub.L. 85–593 provided in part that the amendment to this section by Pub.L. 85–593 shall take effect at the expiration of one year from Aug. 6, 1958, see section 3 of Pub.L. 85–593, as amended, set out as a note under section 45 of this title.

Savings Provisions

Amendment of this section by Pub.L. 97–164 not to apply or affect any person serving as chief judge on the effective date of Pub.L. 97–164 [Oct. 1, 1982], and the provisions of subsec. (a) of this section as in effect on the day before the effective date of part A of Title II of Pub.L. 97–164 [Oct. 1, 1982] to apply to the chief judge of a district court serving on Oct. 1, 1982, see section 203 of Pub.L. 97–164, set out as a note under section 45 of this title.

Chief Justice of District Court for the District of Columbia to be known as Chief Judge

Section 2(a) of Act June 25, 1948, provided in part that the Chief Justice of the District Court for the District of Columbia in office on Sept. 1, 1948, shall thereafter be known as the Chief Judge.

§ 137. Division of business among district judges

The business of a court having more than one judge shall be divided among the judges as provided by the rules and orders of the court.

The chief judge of the district court shall be responsible for the observance of such rules and orders, and shall divide the business and assign the cases so far as such rules and orders do not otherwise prescribe.

If the district judges in any district are unable to agree upon the adoption of rules or orders for that purpose the judicial council of the circuit shall make the necessary orders.

(June 25, 1948, c. 646, 62 Stat. 897.)

§ 138. Terms abolished

The district court shall not hold formal terms.

(June 25, 1948, c. 646, 62 Stat. 897; Oct. 16, 1963, Pub.L. 88–139, § 1, 77 Stat. 248.)

§ 139. Times for holding regular sessions

The times for commencing regular sessions of the district court for transacting judicial business at the places fixed by this chapter shall be determined by the rules or orders of the court. Such rules or orders may provide that at one or more of such places the court shall be in continuous session for such purposes on all business days throughout the year. At other places a session of the court shall continue for such purposes until terminated by order of final adjournment or by commencement of the next regular session at the same place.

(June 25, 1948, c. 646, 62 Stat. 897; Oct. 16, 1963, Pub.L. 88–139, § 1, 77 Stat. 248.)

§ 140. Adjournment

(a) Any district court may, by order made anywhere within its district, adjourn or, with the consent of the judicial council of the circuit, pretermit any regular session of court for insufficient business or other good cause.

(b) If the judge of a district court is unable to attend and unable to make an order of adjournment, the clerk may adjourn the court to the next regular session or to any earlier day which he may determine.

(June 25, 1948, c. 646, 62 Stat. 897; Oct. 16, 1963, Pub.L. 88–139, § 1, 77 Stat. 248.)

§ 141. Special sessions; places; notice

(a)(1) Special sessions of the district court may be held at such places in the district as the nature of the business may require, and upon such notice as the court orders.

(2) Any business may be transacted at a special session which might be transacted at a regular session.

(b)(1) Special sessions of the district court may be held at such places within the United States outside the district as the nature of the business may require and upon such notice as the court orders, upon a finding by either the chief judge of the district court (or, if the chief judge is unavailable, the most senior available active judge of the district court) or the judicial council of the circuit that, because of emergency conditions, no location within the district is reasonably available where such special sessions could be held.

(2) Pursuant to this subsection, any business which may be transacted at a regular session of a district court may be transacted at a special session conducted outside the district, except that a criminal trial may not be conducted at a special session outside the State in which the crime has been committed unless the defendant consents to such a criminal trial.

(3) Notwithstanding any other provision of law, in any case in which special sessions are conducted pursuant to this section, the district court may summon jurors—

(A) in civil proceedings, from any part of the district in which the court ordinarily conducts business or the district in which it is holding a special session; and

(B) in criminal trials, from any part of the district in which the crime has been committed and, if the defendant so consents, from any district in which the court is conducting business pursuant to this section.

(4) If a district court issues an order exercising its authority under paragraph (1), the court—

(A) through the Administrative Office of the United States Courts, shall—

(i) send notice of such order, including the reasons for the issuance of such order, to the Committee on the Judiciary of the Senate and the Committee on the Judiciary of the House of Representatives; and

(ii) not later than 180 days after the expiration of such court order submit a brief report to the Committee on the Judiciary of the Senate and the Committee on the Judiciary of the House of Representatives describing the impact of such order, including—

(I) the reasons for the issuance of such order;

(II) the duration of such order;

(III) the impact of such order on litigants; and

(IV) the costs to the judiciary resulting from such order; and

(B) shall provide reasonable notice to the United States Marshals Service before the commencement of any special session held pursuant to such order.

(5) If a district court issues an order exercising its authority under paragraph (1), the court shall direct the United States marshal of the district where the court is meeting to furnish transportation and subsistence to the same extent as that provided in sections 4282 and 4285 of title 18.

(June 25, 1948, c. 646, 62 Stat. 897; Oct. 16, 1963, Pub.L. 88–139, § 1, 77 Stat. 248; Sept. 9, 2005, Pub.L. 109–63, § 2(b), 119 Stat. 1994; Jan. 5, 2006, Pub.L. 109–162, Title XI, § 1198(a), 119 Stat. 3132.)

[§ 142. Repealed. Pub.L. 97–164, Title I, § 115(c)(3), Apr. 2, 1982, 96 Stat. 32]

HISTORICAL AND STATUTORY NOTES

Section, Acts June 25, 1948, c. 646, 62 Stat. 898; Oct. 9, 1962, Pub.L. 87–764, 76 Stat. 762; Nov. 19, 1977, Pub.L. 95–196, 91 Stat. 1420, related to the providing of accommodations at places for holding court. See section 462 of this title.

Effective Date of Repeal

Repeal effective Oct. 1, 1982, see section 402 of Pub.L. 97–164, set out as an Effective Date of 1982 Amendment note under section 171 of this title.

Waiver of Limitations and Restrictions

The limitations and restrictions contained in this section prior to its repeal were waived with respect to the holding of court at certain places by the following Acts:

Pub. L. 87-833, Oct. 15, 1962, 76 Stat. 959, related to Akron, Ohio.

Pub. L. 87-699, Sept. 25, 1962, 76 Stat. 598, related to Richland, Washington.

Pub. L. 87-562, §4, July 30, 1962, 76 Stat. 248, related to Fort Meyers, Saint Petersburg, Fort Pierce, and West Palm Beach, Florida.

Pub. L. 87-560, July 27, 1962, 76 Stat. 247, related to Marshall, Texas.

Pub. L. 87-559, July 27, 1962, 76 Stat. 246, related to Decatur, Alabama.

Pub. L. 87-553, July 27, 1962, 76 Stat. 222, related to Winchester, Tennessee.

Pub. L. 87-551, July 27, 1962, 76 Stat. 221, related to Bridgeport, Connecticut.

Pub. L. 87-337, Oct. 3, 1961, 75 Stat. 750, related to Lafayette, Louisiana.

Pub. L. 87-36, §3(g), May 19, 1961, 75 Stat. 83, related to Kalamazoo, Michigan; Fayetteville, North Carolina; and Dyersburg, Tennessee.

Pub. L. 86-366, Sept. 22, 1959, 73 Stat. 647, related to Durant, Oklahoma.

Act July 20, 1956, c. 657, 70 Stat. 594, related to Bryson City, North Carolina.

Act Sept. 23, 1950, c. 1006, 64 Stat. 982, related to Klamath Falls, Oregon.

Act Aug. 21, 1950, c. 767, 64 Stat. 469, related to Newnan, Georgia.

Act Aug. 10, 1950, c. 675, § 2, 64 Stat. 438, related to Rock Island, Illinois.

Act Oct. 26, 1949, c. 744, 63 Stat. 923, related to Thomasville, Georgia.

Act Oct. 26, 1949, c. 740, 63 Stat. 921, related to Brunswick, Georgia.

§ 143. Vacant judgeship as affecting proceedings

When the office of a district judge becomes vacant, all pending process, pleadings and proceedings shall, when necessary, be continued by the clerk until a judge is appointed or designated to hold such court. (June 25, 1948, c. 646, 62 Stat. 898.)

§ 144. Bias or prejudice of judge

Whenever a party to any proceeding in a district court makes and files a timely and sufficient affidavit that the judge before whom the matter is pending has a personal bias or prejudice either against him or in favor of any adverse party, such judge shall proceed no further therein, but another judge shall be assigned to hear such proceeding.

The affidavit shall state the facts and the reasons for the belief that bias or prejudice exists, and shall be filed not less than ten days before the beginning of the term at which the proceeding is to be heard, or good cause shall be shown for failure to file it within such time. A party may file only one such affidavit in any case. It shall be accompanied by a certificate of counsel of record stating that it is made in good faith. (June 25, 1948, c. 646, 62 Stat. 898; May 24, 1949, c. 139, § 65, 63 Stat. 99.)

CHAPTER 6—BANKRUPTCY JUDGES

Sec.
151. Designation of bankruptcy courts.
152. Appointment of bankruptcy judges.
153. Salaries; character of service.
154. Division of business; chief judge.[1]
155. Temporary transfer of bankruptcy judges.
156. Staff; expenses.
157. Procedures.
158. Appeals.
159. Bankruptcy statistics.

[1] So in original. Does not conform to section catchline.

HISTORICAL AND STATUTORY NOTES

Codifications

Chapter heading and section analysis of chapter 6, as added by Pub.L. 95–598, Title II, § 201(a), Nov. 6, 1978, 92 Stat. 2657, and amended Pub.L. 97–164, Title I, § 110(d), Apr. 2, 1982, 96 Stat. 29, effective June 28, 1984, pursuant to Pub.L. 95–598, Title IV, § 402(b), Nov. 6, 1978, 92 Stat. 2682, as amended by Pub.L. 98–249, § 1(a), Mar. 31, 1984, 98 Stat. 116; Pub.L. 98–271, § 1(a), Apr. 30, 1984, 98 Stat. 163; Pub.L. 98–299, § 1(a), May 25, 1984, 98 Stat. 214; Pub.L. 98–325, § 1(a), June 20, 1984, 98 Stat. 268, set out as a note preceding section 101 of Title 11, Bankruptcy, read as follows:

CHAPTER 6—BANKRUPTCY COURTS

Sec.
151. Creation and composition of bankruptcy courts.
152. Appointment of bankruptcy judges.
153. Tenure and residence of bankruptcy judges.
154. Salaries of bankruptcy judges.
155. Chief judge; precedence of bankruptcy judges.
156. Division of business among bankruptcy judges.
157. Times of holding court.
158. Accommodations at places for holding court.
159. Vacant judgeship as affecting proceedings.
160. Appellate panels.

Section 402(b) of Pub.L. 95–598 was amended by section 113 of Pub.L. 98–353 by substituting "shall not be effective" for "shall take effect on June 28, 1984", thereby eliminating the addition of the chapter heading and section analysis of chapter 6 by section 201(a) of Pub.L. 95–598, effective June 27, 1984, pursuant to section 122(c) of Pub.L. 98–353, set out as an Effective and Applicability Provisions note under section 151 of this title.

Section 121(a) of Pub.L. 98–353 directed that section 402(b) of Pub.L. 95–598 be amended by substituting "the date of enactment of the Bankruptcy Amendments and Federal Judgeship Act of 1984 [i.e. July 10, 1984]" for "June 28, 1984". This amendment was not executed in view of the prior amendment to section 402(b) of Pub.L. 95–598 by section 113 of Pub.L. 98–353.

Effective and Applicability Provisions

2005 Acts. Amendments by Pub.L. 109–8, Title VI, § 601, effective 18 months after Apr. 20, 2005, see Pub.L. 109–8, § 601(c), set out as a note under 28 U.S.C.A. § 159.

Except as otherwise provided, amendments by Pub.L. 109–8 effective 180 days after April 20, 2005, and inapplicable with respect to cases commenced under Title 11 before the effective date, see Pub.L. 109–8, § 1501, set out as a note under 11 U.S.C.A. § 101.

Courts During Transition

Pub.L. 95–598, Title IV, § 404, Nov. 6, 1978, 92 Stat. 2683, as amended by Pub.L. 98–249, § 1(b), Mar. 31, 1984, 98 Stat. 116; Pub.L. 98–271, § 1(b), Apr. 30, 1984, 98 Stat. 163; Pub.L. 98–299, § 1(b), May 25, 1984, 98 Stat. 214; Pub.L. 98–325, § 1(b), June 20, 1984, 98 Stat. 268; Pub.L. 98–353, Title I, § 121(b), July 10, 1984, 98 Stat. 345, which provided that, for purposes of Pub.L. 95–598, which enacted Title 11, Bankruptcy, and the amendments made by Pub.L. 95–598, the courts of bankruptcy as defined under section 1(10) of former Title 11, created by section 11(a) of former Title 11, and existing on Sept. 30, 1979, continue to be courts of bankruptcy during the transition period beginning Oct. 1, 1979, and ending June 27, 1984, made provision for extension of the term of office of referees in bankruptcy serving on Nov. 6, 1978, and for such a referee to have the title of United States bankruptcy judge, established for each State a merit screening committee to pass on qualifications of such a referee and determine if the term of such referee should be extended, and set forth the rules and provisions applicable to United States bankruptcy judges during the transition period, was repealed by Pub.L. 98–353, Title I, § 114, 122(a), July 10, 1984, 98 Stat. 343, 346, eff. July 10, 1984.

[Section 121(b) of Pub.L. 98–353 purported to amend section 404 of Pub.L. 95–598 by substituting "the day before the date of enactment of the Bankruptcy Amendments and Federal Judgeship Act of 1984 [i.e. July 9, 1984]" for "June 27, 1984" each place it appeared. This amendment was not executed as the probable intent of Congress in view of the repeal of section 404 of Pub.L. 95–598 by section 114 of Pub.L. 98–353.]

Extension and Termination of Term of Office of Bankruptcy Judge Serving on June 27, 1984

Section 121(e) of Pub.L. 98–353 provided that: "The term of office of any bankruptcy judge who was serving on June 27, 1984, is extended to and shall expire at the end of the day of enactment of this Act [July 10, 1984]."

[Section 121(e) of Pub.L. 98–353 effective June 27, 1984, see section 122(c) of Pub.L. 98–353, set out as an Effective and Applicability Provisions note under section 151 of this title.]

For prior extensions of the term of office of bankruptcy judges see:

Pub.L. 98–325, § 2, June 20, 1984, 98 Stat. 268.

Pub.L. 98–299, § 2, May 25, 1984, 98 Stat. 214.

Pub.L. 98–271, § 2, Apr. 30, 1984, 98 Stat. 163.

Pub.L. 98–249, § 2, Mar. 31, 1984, 98 Stat. 116.

Judicial Administration During Transition

Pub.L. 95–598, Title IV, § 407, Nov. 6, 1978, 92 Stat. 2686, which provided that the Director of the Administrative Office of the United States Courts appoint a committee of not fewer than seven United States bankruptcy judges to advise the Director with respect to matters arising during the transition period, or that are relevant to the purposes of the transition period, and directed that during the transition period, the chief judge of each circuit summon at least one bankruptcy judge from each judicial district within the circuit to the judicial conference of such circuit called and held under section 332 of this title, was repealed by Pub.L. 98–353, Title I, §§ 114, 122(a), July 10, 1984, 98 Stat. 343, 346, eff. July 10, 1984.

Transition Study

Pub.L. 95–598, Title IV, § 406, Nov. 6, 1978, 92 Stat. 2686, as amended by Pub.L. 98–249, § 1(c), Mar. 31, 1984, 98 Stat. 116; Pub.L. 98–271, § 1(c), Apr. 30, 1984, 98 Stat. 163; Pub.L. 98–299, § 1(c), May 25, 1984, 98 Stat. 214; Pub.L. 98–325, § 1(c), June 20, 1984, 98 Stat. 268; Pub.L. 98–353, Title I, § 121(c), July 10, 1984, 98 Stat. 346, which provided that during the transition period, Oct. 1, 1979 to June 27, 1984, the Director of the Administrative Office of the United States Courts make continuing studies and surveys in the judicial districts to determine the number of bankruptcy judges needed after June 27, 1984, to provide for the expeditious and effective administration of justice, their regular places of offices, and the places where the court will be held, and that the Director report to the judicial councils of the circuits and the Judicial Conference of the United States his recommendations, the judicial councils advise the Conference stating their recommendations, and the Conference advise the Congress and the President, before Jan. 3, 1983, the number of bankruptcy judges needed after June 27, 1984, and the locations at which they were to serve, was repealed by Pub.L. 98–353, Title I, §§ 114, 122(a), July 10, 1984, 98 Stat. 343, 346 eff. July 10, 1984.

[Section 121(c) of Pub.L. 98–353 purported to amend section 406 of Pub.L. 95–598 by substituting "the day before the date of enactment of the Bankruptcy Amendments and Federal Judgeship Act of 1984 [i.e. July 9, 1984]" for "June 27, 1984" each place it appeared. This amendment was not executed as the probable intent of Congress in view of the repeal of section 406 of Pub.L. 95–598 by section 114 of Pub.L. 98–353.]

§ 151. Designation of bankruptcy courts

In each judicial district, the bankruptcy judges in regular active service shall constitute a unit of the district court to be known as the bankruptcy court for that district. Each bankruptcy judge, as a judicial officer of the district court, may exercise the authority conferred under this chapter with respect to any action, suit, or proceeding and may preside alone and hold a regular or special session of the court, except as otherwise provided by law or by rule or order of the district court.

(Added Pub.L. 98–353, Title I, § 104(a), July 10, 1984, 98 Stat. 336.)

HISTORICAL AND STATUTORY NOTES

Codifications

This section as added by Pub.L. 95–598, Title II, § 201(a), Nov. 6, 1978, 92 Stat. 2657, effective June 28, 1984, pursuant to Pub.L. 95–598, Title IV, § 402(b), Nov. 6, 1978, 92 Stat. 2682, as amended by Pub.L. 98–249, § 1(a), Mar. 31, 1984, 98 Stat. 116; Pub.L. 98–271, § 1(a), Apr. 30, 1984, 98 Stat. 163; Pub.L. 98–299, § 1(a), May 25, 1984, 98 Stat. 214; Pub.L. 98–325, § 1(a), June 20, 1984, 98 Stat. 268, set out as a note preceding section 101 of Title 11, Bankruptcy, read as follows:

§ 151. Creation and composition of bankruptcy courts

(a) There shall be in each judicial district, as an adjunct to the district court for such district, a bankruptcy court which shall be a court of record known as the United States Bankruptcy Court for the district.

(b) Each bankruptcy court shall consist of the bankruptcy judge or judges for the district in regular active service. Justices or judges designated and assigned shall be competent to sit as judges of the bankruptcy court.

(c) Except as otherwise provided by law, or rule or order of court, the judicial power of a bankruptcy court with respect to any action, suit or proceeding may be exercised by a single bankruptcy judge, who may preside alone and hold a regular or special session of court at the same time other sessions are held by other bankruptcy judges.

Section 402(b) of Pub.L. 95–598 was amended by section 113 of Pub.L. 98–353 by substituting "shall not be effective" for "shall take effect on June 28, 1984", thereby eliminating the addition of section 151 by section 201(a) of Pub.L. 95–598, effective June 27, 1984, pursuant to section 122(c) of Pub.L. 98–353, set out as an Effective and Applicability Provisions note under this section.

Section 121(a) of Pub.L. 98–353 directed that section 402(b) of Pub.L. 95–598 be amended by substituting "the date of enactment of the Bankruptcy Amendments and Federal Judgeship Act of 1984 [i.e. July 10, 1984]" for "June 28, 1984". This amendment was not executed in view of the prior amendment to section 402(b) of Pub.L. 95–598 by section 113 of Pub.L. 98–353.

Effective and Applicability Provisions

1984 Acts. Section 122 of Title I of Pub.L. 98–353 provided that:

"**(a)** Except as otherwise provided in this section, this title and the amendments made by this title [Title I of Pub.L. 98–353, enacting this chapter, and sections 1408 to 1412 and 1452 of this title, amending sections 372, 634, 957, 1334, 1360, and 1930 of this title, sections 8331, 8334, 8336, 8339, 8341, and 8344 of Title 5, Government Organization and Employees, and section 105 of Title 11, Bankruptcy, enacting provisions set out as notes preceding section 151 of this title and under sections 151, 152, 153, 634, and 1334 of this title and section 8331 of Title 5, amending provisions set out as notes preceding sections 151 and 1471 of this title and section 101 of Title 11, and repealing provisions set out as notes preceding this section and section 1471 of this title] shall take effect on the date of the enactment of this Act [July 10, 1984].

"**(b)** Section 1334(c)(2) of title 28, United States Code [section 1334(c)(2) of this title], and section 1411(a) of title 28, United States Code, as added by this Act [section 1411(a) of this title], shall not apply with respect to cases under title 11 of the United States Code [Title 11] that are pending on the date of enactment of this Act [July 10, 1984], or to proceedings arising in or related to such cases.

"**(c)** Sections 108(b) [enacting provisions set out as a note under section 634 of this title], 113 [amending section 402(b) of Pub.L. 95–598, set out as a note preceding section 101 of Title 11], and 121(e) [enacting provisions set out as a note preceding section 151 of this title] shall take effect on June 27, 1984."

Separability of Provisions

Section 119 of Pub.L. 98–353 provided that: "If any provision of this Act [see Short Title of 1984 Amendments note set out under this section] or the application thereof to any person or circumstance is held invalid, the remainder of this Act, or the application of that provision to persons or circumstances other than those as to which it is held invalid, is not affected thereby."

Short Title

1984 Amendments. Section 1 of Pub.L. 98–353 provided: That this Act [enacting this chapter and sections 1408 to 1412 and 1452 of this title and sections 557, 558, 559, and 1113 of Title 11, Bankruptcy, amending sections 44, 98, 131, 133, 371, 372, 634, 957, 1334, 1360, and 1930 of this title, sections 8331, 8334, 8336, 8339, 8341, 8344, 8701, 8706, 8714a, and 8714b of Title 5, Government Organization and Employees, and sections 101, 102, 103, 105, 108, 109, 303, 321, 322, 326, 327, 328, 329, 330, 342, 343, 345, 346, 349, 350, 361, 362, 363, 365, 366, 501, 502, 503, 505, 506, 507, 509, 510, 521, 522, 523, 524, 525, 541, 542, 543, 544, 545, 546, 547, 548, 549, 550, 552, 553, 554, 555, 702, 703, 704, 707, 723, 724, 725, 726, 727, 728, 741, 745, 752, 761, 763, 764, 765, 766, 901, 902, 903, 921, 922, 927, 943, 945, 1102, 1103, 1105, 1106, 1107, 1108, 1112, 1121, 1123, 1124, 1125, 1126, 1127, 1129, 1141, 1142, 1144, 1145, 1146, 1166, 1168, 1169, 1170, 1171, 1173, 1301, 1302, 1304, 1307, 1322, 1324, 1325, 1326, 1328, 1329, 15103, and 151302 of Title 11, Bankruptcy Rules 2002 and 3001, Title 11, and Bankruptcy Form No. 1, Title 11, enacting provisions set out as notes preceding section 151 of this title and under sections 44, 133, 151, 152, 153, 371, 634, 1334, and 2075 of this title, sections 8331 and 8706 of Title 5, and preceding section 101 and sections 101, 365, and 1113 of Title 11, amending provisions set out as notes preceding sections 151, 581 and 1471 of this title and section 101 of Title 11, and repealing provisions set out as notes preceding this section and section 1471 of this title] may be cited as the 'Bankruptcy Amendments and Federal Judgeship Act of 1984'."

§ 152. Appointment of bankruptcy judges

(a)(1) Each bankruptcy judge to be appointed for a judicial district, as provided in paragraph (2), shall be appointed by the court of appeals of the United States for the circuit in which such district is located. Such appointments shall be made after considering the recommendations of the Judicial Conference submitted pursuant to subsection (b). Each bankruptcy judge shall be appointed for a term of fourteen years, subject to the provisions of subsection (e). However, upon the expiration of the term, a bankruptcy judge may, with the approval of the judicial council of the circuit, continue to perform the duties of the office until the earlier of the date which is 180 days after the expiration of the term or the date of the appointment of a successor. Bankruptcy judges shall serve as judicial officers of the United States district court established under Article III of the Constitution.

(2) The bankruptcy judges appointed pursuant to this section shall be appointed for the several judicial districts as follows:

Districts	Judges
Alabama:	
Northern	5
Middle	2
Southern	2
Alaska	2
Arizona	7
Arkansas:	
Eastern and Western	3
California:	
Northern	9
Eastern	6
Central	21
Southern	4
Colorado	5
Connecticut	3
Delaware	1
District of Columbia	1
Florida:	
Northern	1
Middle	8
Southern	5
Georgia:	
Northern	8
Middle	3
Southern	2
Hawaii	1
Idaho	2
Illinois:	
Northern	10
Central	3
Southern	1
Indiana:	
Northern	3
Southern	4
Iowa:	
Northern	2
Southern	2
Kansas	4
Kentucky:	
Eastern	2
Western	3
Louisiana:	
Eastern	2
Middle	1
Western	3
Maine	2
Maryland	4
Massachusetts	5
Michigan:	
Eastern	4
Western	3
Minnesota	4
Mississippi:	
Northern	1
Southern	2
Missouri:	
Eastern	3
Western	3
Montana	1
Nebraska	2
Nevada	3
New Hampshire	1
New Jersey	8
New Mexico	2
New York:	
Northern	2
Southern	9
Eastern	6
Western	3
North Carolina:	
Eastern	2
Middle	2
Western	2
North Dakota	1
Ohio:	
Northern	8
Southern	7
Oklahoma:	
Northern	2
Eastern	1
Western	3
Oregon	5
Pennsylvania:	
Eastern	5
Middle	2
Western	4
Puerto Rico	2
Rhode Island	1
South Carolina	2
South Dakota	2
Tennessee:	
Eastern	3
Middle	3
Western	4
Texas:	
Northern	6
Eastern	2
Southern	6
Western	4
Utah	3
Vermont	1
Virginia:	
Eastern	5
Western	3
Washington:	
Eastern	2
Western	5

Districts	Judges
West Virginia:	
Northern	1
Southern	1
Wisconsin:	
Eastern	4
Western	2
Wyoming	1

(3) Whenever a majority of the judges of any court of appeals cannot agree upon the appointment of a bankruptcy judge, the chief judge of such court shall make such appointment.

(4) The judges of the district courts for the territories shall serve as the bankruptcy judges for such courts. The United States court of appeals for the circuit within which such a territorial district court is located may appoint bankruptcy judges under this chapter for such district if authorized to do so by the Congress of the United States under this section.

(b)(1) The Judicial Conference of the United States shall, from time to time, and after considering the recommendations submitted by the Director of the Administrative Office of the United States Courts after such Director has consulted with the judicial council of the circuit involved, determine the official duty stations of bankruptcy judges and places of holding court.

(2) The Judicial Conference shall, from time to time, submit recommendations to the Congress regarding the number of bankruptcy judges needed and the districts in which such judges are needed.

(3) Not later than December 31, 1994, and not later than the end of each 2-year period thereafter, the Judicial Conference of the United States shall conduct a comprehensive review of all judicial districts to assess the continuing need for the bankruptcy judges authorized by this section, and shall report to the Congress its findings and any recommendations for the elimination of any authorized position which can be eliminated when a vacancy exists by reason of resignation, retirement, removal, or death.

(c)(1) Each bankruptcy judge may hold court at such places within the judicial district, in addition to the official duty station of such judge, as the business of the court may require.

(2)(A) Bankruptcy judges may hold court at such places within the United States outside the judicial district as the nature of the business of the court may require, and upon such notice as the court orders, upon a finding by either the chief judge of the bankruptcy court (or, if the chief judge is unavailable, the most senior available bankruptcy judge) or by the judicial council of the circuit that, because of emergency conditions, no location within the district is reasonably available where the bankruptcy judges could hold court.

(B) Bankruptcy judges may transact any business at special sessions of court held outside the district pursuant to this paragraph that might be transacted at a regular session.

(C) If a bankruptcy court issues an order exercising its authority under subparagraph (A), the court—

(i) through the Administrative Office of the United States Courts, shall—

(I) send notice of such order, including the reasons for the issuance of such order, to the Committee on the Judiciary of the Senate and the Committee on the Judiciary of the House of Representatives; and

(II) not later than 180 days after the expiration of such court order submit a brief report to the Committee on the Judiciary of the Senate and the Committee on the Judiciary of the House of Representatives describing the impact of such order, including—

(aa) the reasons for the issuance of such order;

(bb) the duration of such order;

(cc) the impact of such order on litigants; and

(dd) the costs to the judiciary resulting from such order; and

(ii) shall provide reasonable notice to the United States Marshals Service before the commencement of any special session held pursuant to such order.

(d) With the approval of the Judicial Conference and of each of the judicial councils involved, a bankruptcy judge may be designated to serve in any district adjacent to or near the district for which such bankruptcy judge was appointed.

(e) A bankruptcy judge may be removed during the term for which such bankruptcy judge is appointed, only for incompetence, misconduct, neglect of duty, or physical or mental disability and only by the judicial council of the circuit in which the judge's official duty station is located. Removal may not occur unless a majority of all of the judges of such council concur in the order of removal. Before any order of removal may be entered, a full specification of charges shall be furnished to such bankruptcy judge who shall be accorded an opportunity to be heard on such charges.

(Added Pub.L. 98-353, Title I, § 104(a), July 10, 1984, 98 Stat. 336, and amended Pub.L. 99-554, Title I, § 101, Oct. 27, 1986, 100 Stat. 3088; Pub.L. 100-587, Nov. 3, 1988, 102 Stat. 2982; Pub.L. 101-650, Title III, § 304, Dec. 1, 1990, 104 Stat. 5105; Pub.L. 102-361, §§ 2, 4, Aug. 26, 1992, 106 Stat. 965, 966; Pub.L. 109-8, Title XII, § 1223(d), Apr. 20, 2005, 119 Stat. 198; Pub.L. 109-63, § 2(c), Sept. 9, 2005, 119 Stat. 1994.)

HISTORICAL AND STATUTORY NOTES

Codifications

This section as added by Pub.L. 95–598, Title II, § 201(a), Nov. 6, 1978, 92 Stat. 2657, effective June 28, 1984, pursuant to Pub.L. 95–598, Title IV, § 402(b), Nov. 6, 1978, 92 Stat. 2682, as amended by Pub.L. 98–249, § 1(a), Mar. 31, 1984, 98 Stat. 116; Pub.L. 98–271, § 1(a), Apr. 30, 1984, 98 Stat. 163; Pub.L. 98–299, § 1(a), May 25, 1984, 98 Stat. 214; Pub.L. 98–325, § 1(a), June 20, 1984, 98 Stat. 268, set out as a note preceding section 101 of Title 11, Bankruptcy, read as follows:

"§ 152. Appointment of bankruptcy judges

"The President shall appoint, by and with the advice and consent of the Senate, bankruptcy judges for the several judicial districts. In each instance, the President shall give due consideration to the recommended nominee or nominees of the Judicial Council of the Circuit within which an appointment is to be made."

Section 402(b) of Pub.L. 95–598 was amended by section 113 of Pub.L. 98–353 by substituting "shall not be effective" for "shall take effect on June 28, 1984", thereby eliminating the addition of section 152 by section 201(a) of Pub.L. 95–598, effective June 27, 1984, pursuant to section 122(c) of Pub.L. 98–353, set out as an Effective and Applicability Provisions note under 28 U.S.C.A. § 151.

Section 121(a) of Pub.L. 98–353 directed that section 402(b) of Pub.L. 95–598 be amended by substituting "the date of enactment of the Bankruptcy Amendments and Federal Judgeship Act of 1984 [i.e. July 10, 1984]" for "June 28, 1984". This amendment was not executed in view of the prior amendment to section 402(b) of Pub.L. 95–598 by section 113 of Pub.L. 98–353.

Effective and Applicability Provisions

2005 Acts. Pub.L. 109–8, Title XII, § 1223(e), Apr. 20, 2005, 119 Stat. 198, provided that: "The amendments made by this section [amending this section and enacting provisions set out as notes under this section and 28 U.S.C.A. § 1] shall take effect on the date of the enactment of this Act [Apr. 20, 2005]."

Except as otherwise provided, amendments by Pub.L. 109–8 effective 180 days after April 20, 2005, and inapplicable with respect to cases commenced under Title 11 before the effective date, see Pub.L. 109–8, § 1501, set out as a note under 11 U.S.C.A. § 101.

1986 Acts. Amendment by Pub.L. 99–554 effective on Oct. 27, 1986, see section 302(b) of Pub.L. 99–554, set out as a note under section 581 of this title.

1984 Acts. Section effective July 10, 1984, see section 122(a) of Pub.L. 98–353, set out as a note under section 151 of this title.

Termination of Reporting Requirements

For termination of reporting provisions of subsec. (b)(2) of this section, effective May 15, 2000, see Pub.L. 104–66, § 3003, as amended, set out as a note under 31 U.S.C.A. § 1113, and the 16th item on page 12 of House Document No. 103–7.

Temporary Judgeships: Appointments, Vacancies, and Extensions

Pub.L. 109–8, Title XII, § 1223(b), (c), Apr. 20, 2005, 119 Stat. 196, 198, provided that:

"**(b) Temporary Judgeships.**—

"**(1) Appointments.**—The following bankruptcy judges shall be appointed in the manner prescribed in section 152(a)(1) of title 28, United States Code, for the appointment of bankruptcy judges provided for in section 152(a)(2) of such title:

"**(A)** One additional bankruptcy judge for the eastern district of California.

"**(B)** Three additional bankruptcy judges for the central district of California.

"**(C)** Four additional bankruptcy judges for the district of Delaware.

"**(D)** Two additional bankruptcy judges for the southern district of Florida.

"**(E)** One additional bankruptcy judge for the southern district of Georgia.

"**(F)** Three additional bankruptcy judges for the district of Maryland.

"**(G)** One additional bankruptcy judge for the eastern district of Michigan.

"**(H)** One additional bankruptcy judge for the southern district of Mississippi.

"**(I)** One additional bankruptcy judge for the district of New Jersey.

"**(J)** One additional bankruptcy judge for the eastern district of New York.

"**(K)** One additional bankruptcy judge for the northern district of New York.

"**(L)** One additional bankruptcy judge for the southern district of New York.

"**(M)** One additional bankruptcy judge for the eastern district of North Carolina.

"**(N)** One additional bankruptcy judge for the eastern district of Pennsylvania.

"**(O)** One additional bankruptcy judge for the middle district of Pennsylvania.

"**(P)** One additional bankruptcy judge for the district of Puerto Rico.

"**(Q)** One additional bankruptcy judge for the western district of Tennessee.

"**(R)** One additional bankruptcy judge for the eastern district of Virginia.

"**(S)** One additional bankruptcy judge for the district of South Carolina.

"**(T)** One additional bankruptcy judge for the district of Nevada.

"**(2) Vacancies.**—

"**(A) Districts with single appointments.**—Except as provided in subparagraphs (B), (C), (D), and (E), the first vacancy occurring in the office of bankruptcy judge in each of the judicial districts set forth in paragraph (1)—

"**(i)** occurring 5 years or more after the appointment date of the bankruptcy judge appointed under paragraph (1) to such office; and

"**(ii)** resulting from the death, retirement, resignation, or removal of a bankruptcy judge;

shall not be filled.

"**(B) Central district of California.**—The 1st, 2d, and 3d vacancies in the office of bankruptcy judge in the central district of California—

"(i) occurring 5 years or more after the respective 1st, 2d, and 3d appointment dates of the bankruptcy judges appointed under paragraph (1)(B); and

"(ii) resulting from the death, retirement, resignation, or removal of a bankruptcy judge;

shall not be filled.

"**(C) District of Delaware.**—The 1st, 2d, 3d, and 4th vacancies in the office of bankruptcy judge in the district of Delaware—

"(i) occurring 5 years or more after the respective 1st, 2d, 3d, and 4th appointment dates of the bankruptcy judges appointed under paragraph (1)(F); and

"(ii) resulting from the death, retirement, resignation, or removal of a bankruptcy judge;

shall not be filled.

"**(D) Southern district of Florida.**—The 1st and 2d vacancies in the office of bankruptcy judge in the southern district of Florida—

"(i) occurring 5 years or more after the respective 1st and 2d appointment dates of the bankruptcy judges appointed under paragraph (1)(D); and

"(ii) resulting from the death, retirement, resignation, or removal of a bankruptcy judge;

shall not be filled.

"**(E) District of Maryland.**—The 1st, 2d, and 3d vacancies in the office of bankruptcy judge in the district of Maryland—

"(i) occurring 5 years or more after the respective 1st, 2d, and 3d appointment dates of the bankruptcy judges appointed under paragraph (1)(F); and

"(ii) resulting from the death, retirement, resignation, or removal of a bankruptcy judge;

shall not be filled.

"**(c) Extensions.—**

"**(1) In general.**—The temporary office of bankruptcy judges authorized for the northern district of Alabama, the district of Delaware, the district of Puerto Rico, and the eastern district of Tennessee under paragraphs (1), (3), (7), and (9) of section 3(a) of the Bankruptcy Judgeship Act of 1992 (28 U.S.C. 152 note) are extended until the first vacancy occurring in the office of a bankruptcy judge in the applicable district resulting from the death, retirement, resignation, or removal of a bankruptcy judge and occurring 5 years after the date of the enactment of this Act [April 20, 2005].

"**(2) Applicability of other provisions.**—All other provisions of section 3 of the Bankruptcy Judgeship Act of 1992 (28 U.S.C. 152 note) remain applicable to the temporary office of bankruptcy judges referred to in this subsection."

[Amendments by Pub.L. 109–8, § 1223, effective Apr. 20, 2005, see Pub.L. 109–8, § 1223(e), set out as a note under this section.]

Temporary Appointment of Additional Judges

Section 3 of Pub.L. 102–361, as amended Pub.L. 104–317, Title III, § 307, Oct. 19, 1996, 110 Stat. 3852, provided that:

"**(a) Appointments.**—The following bankruptcy judges shall be appointed in the manner prescribed in section 152(a)(1) of title 28, United States Code [subsec. (a)(1) of this section]:

"**(1)** 1 additional bankruptcy judge for the northern district of Alabama.

"**(2)** 1 additional bankruptcy judge for the district of Colorado.

"**(3)** 1 additional bankruptcy judge for the district of Delaware.

"**(4)** 1 additional bankruptcy judge for the southern district of Illinois.

"**(5)** 1 additional bankruptcy judge for the district of New Hampshire.

"**(6)** 1 additional bankruptcy judge for the middle district of North Carolina.

"**(7)** 1 additional bankruptcy judge for the district of Puerto Rico.

"**(8)** 1 additional bankruptcy judge for the district of South Carolina.

"**(9)** 1 additional bankruptcy judge for the eastern district of Tennessee.

"**(10)** 1 additional bankruptcy judge for the western district of Texas.

"**(b) Vacancies.**—The first vacancy in the office of bankruptcy judge in each of the judicial districts set forth in subsection (a), resulting from the death, retirement, resignation, or removal of a bankruptcy judge, and occurring 5 years or more after the appointment date of the judge named to fill the temporary judgeship position shall not be filled. In the case of a vacancy resulting from the expiration of the term of a bankruptcy judge not described in the preceding sentence, that judge shall be eligible for reappointment as a bankruptcy judge in that district."

Appointment to Fill Vacancies; Nominations; Qualifications

Section 120 of Pub.L. 98–353, as amended Pub.L. 99–554, Title I, § 102, Oct. 22, 1986, 100 Stat. 3089; Pub.L. 104–317, Title III, § 303, Oct. 19, 1996, 110 Stat. 3852, provided that:

"**(a)(1)** Whenever a court of appeals is authorized to fill a vacancy that occurs on a bankruptcy court of the United States, such court of appeals shall appoint to fill that vacancy a person whose character, experience, ability, and impartiality qualify such person to serve in the Federal judiciary.

"**(2)** It is the sense of the Congress that the courts of appeals should consider for appointment under section 152 of title 28, United States Code [this section], to the first vacancy which arises after the date of the enactment of this Act [July 10, 1984] in the office of each bankruptcy judge, the bankruptcy judge who holds such office immediately before such vacancy arises, if such bankruptcy judge requests to be considered for such appointment.

"**(3)** When filling vacancies, the court of appeals may consider reappointing incumbent bankruptcy judges under procedures prescribed by regulations issued by the Judicial Conference of the United States.

"**(b)** The judicial council of the circuit involved shall assist the court of appeals by evaluating potential nominees and by recommending to such court for consideration for appointment to each vacancy on the bankruptcy court persons who are qualified to be bankruptcy judges under regulations prescribed by the Judicial Conference of the United States. In the case of the first vacancy which arises after the date of the enactment of this Act [July 10, 1984] in the office of each bankruptcy judge, such potential nominees shall include the bankruptcy judge who holds such office immediately before such vacancy arises, if such bankruptcy judge requests to be considered for such appointment and the judicial council determines that such judge is qualified under subsection (c) of this section to continue to serve. Such potential nominees shall receive consideration equal to that given all other potential nominees for such position. All incumbent nominees seeking reappointment thereafter may be considered for such a reappointment, pursuant to a majority vote of the judges of the appointing court of appeals, under procedures authorized under subsection (a)(3).

"(c) Before transmitting to the court of appeals the names of the persons the judicial council for the circuit deems best qualified to fill any existing vacancy, the judicial council shall have determined that—

"(1) public notice of such vacancy has been given and an effort has been made, in the case of each such vacancy, to identify qualified candidates, without regard to race, color, sex, religion, or national origin,

"(2) such persons are members in good standing of at least one State bar, the District of Columbia bar, or the bar of the Commonwealth of Puerto Rico, and members in good standing of every other bar of which they are members,

"(3) such persons possess, and have a reputation for, integrity and good character,

"(4) such persons are of sound physical and mental health,

"(5) such persons possess and have demonstrated commitment to equal justice under law,

"(6) such persons possess and have demonstrated outstanding legal ability and competence, as evidenced by substantial legal experience, ability to deal with complex legal problems, aptitude for legal scholarship and writing, and familiarity with courts and court processes, and

"(7) such persons [sic] demeanor, character, and personality indicate that they would exhibit judicial temperament if appointed to the position of United States bankruptcy judge."

Extension and Termination of Term of Office of Bankruptcy Judge and Part-Time Bankruptcy Judge Serving on July 10, 1984; Practice of Law by Part-Time Bankruptcy Judge

Section 106 of Pub.L. 98–353 provided that:

"(a) Notwithstanding section 152 of title 28, United States Code, as added by this Act [this section], the term of office of a bankruptcy judge who is serving on the date of enactment of this Act [July 10, 1984] is extended to and expires four years after the date such bankruptcy judge was last appointed to such office or on October 1, 1986, whichever is later.

"(b)(1) Notwithstanding section 153(a) of title 28, United States Code, as added by this Act [section 153(a) of this title], and notwithstanding subsection (a) of this section, a bankruptcy judge serving on a part-time basis on the date of enactment of this Act [July 10, 1984] may continue to serve on such basis for a period not to exceed two years from the date of enactment of this Act [July 10, 1984].

"(2) Notwithstanding the provisions of section 153(b) of title 28, United States Code [section 153(b) of this title], a bankruptcy judge serving on a part-time basis may engage in the practice of law but may not engage in any other practice, business, occupation, or employment inconsistent with the expeditious, proper, and impartial performance of such bankruptcy judge's duties as a judicial officer. The Judicial Conference of the United States may promulgate appropriate rules and regulations to implement this paragraph."

Extension and Termination of Term of Office of Part-Time Bankruptcy Judge Serving on July 2, 1986, In District of Oregon, Western District of Michigan, and Eastern District of Oklahoma

Pub.L. 99–349, Title I, July 2, 1986, 100 Stat. 718, provided that: "Notwithstanding the provisions of section 106(b)(1) of the Bankruptcy Amendments and Federal Judgeship Act of 1984 [section 106(b)(1) of Pub.L. 98–353, set out as a note under this section], a bankruptcy judge serving on a part-time basis on the date of enactment of this Act [July 2, 1986] may continue to serve as a part-time judge for such district until December 31, 1986, or until such time as a full-time bankruptcy judge for such district is appointed, whichever is earlier: *Provided*, That these provisions shall apply only to part-time bankruptcy judges serving in the district of Oregon, the western district of Michigan, and the eastern district of Oklahoma."

§ 153. Salaries; character of service

(a) Each bankruptcy judge shall serve on a full-time basis and shall receive as full compensation for his services, a salary at an annual rate that is equal to 92 percent of the salary of a judge of the district court of the United States as determined pursuant to section 135, to be paid at such times as the Judicial Conference of the United States determines.

(b) A bankruptcy judge may not engage in the practice of law and may not engage in any other practice, business, occupation, or employment inconsistent with the expeditious, proper, and impartial performance of such bankruptcy judge's duties as a judicial officer. The Conference may promulgate appropriate rules and regulations to implement this subsection.

(c) Each individual appointed under this chapter shall take the oath or affirmation prescribed by section 453 of this title before performing the duties of the office of bankruptcy judge.

(d) A bankruptcy judge appointed under this chapter shall be exempt from the provisions of subchapter I of chapter 63 of title 5.

(Added Pub.L. 98–353, Title I, § 104(a), July 10, 1984, 98 Stat. 338, and amended Pub.L. 100–202, § 101(a) [Title IV, § 408(a)], Dec. 22, 1987, 101 Stat. 1329–26; Pub.L. 100–702, Title X, § 1003(a)(1), Nov. 19, 1988, 102 Stat. 4665.)

HISTORICAL AND STATUTORY NOTES

Codifications

This section as added by Pub.L. 95–598, Title II, § 201(a), Nov. 6, 1978, 92 Stat. 2657, effective June 28, 1984, pursuant to Pub.L. 95–598, Title IV, § 402(b), Nov. 6, 1978, 92 Stat. 2682, as amended by Pub.L. 98–249, § 1(a), Mar. 31, 1984, 98 Stat. 116; Pub.L. 98–271, § 1(a), Apr. 30, 1984, 98 Stat. 163; Pub.L. 98–299, § 1(a), May 25, 1984, 98 Stat. 214; Pub.L. 98–325, § 1(a), June 20, 1984, 98 Stat. 268, set out as a note preceding section 101 of Title 11, Bankruptcy, read as follows:

§ 153. Tenure and residence of bankruptcy judges

(a) Each bankruptcy judge shall hold office for a term of 14 years, but may continue to perform the duties of his office until his successor takes office, unless such office has been eliminated.

(b) Removal of a bankruptcy judge during the term for which he is appointed shall be only for incompetency, misconduct, neglect of duty, or physical or mental disability. Removal shall be by the judicial council of the circuit or circuits in which the bankruptcy judge serves, but removal may not occur unless a majority of all the judges of such circuit council or councils concur in the order of removal. Before any order of removal may be entered, a full specification of the charges shall be furnished to the bankruptcy judge, and he shall be accorded an opportunity to be heard on the charges. Any cause for removal of any bankruptcy judge coming to the knowledge of the Director of the Administrative Office of the United States Courts shall be reported by him to the chief judge of the circuit or circuits in which he serves, and a copy of the report shall at the same time be transmitted to the circuit council or councils and to the bankruptcy judge.

(c) Each bankruptcy judge shall reside in the district or one of the districts for which he is appointed, or within 20 miles of his official station.

(d) If the public interest and the nature of the business of a bankruptcy court require that a bankruptcy judge should maintain his abode at or near a particular part of the district the judicial council of the circuit may so declare and may make an appropriate order. If the bankruptcy judges of such a district are unable to agree as to which of them shall maintain his abode at or near the place or within the area specified in such an order the judicial council of the circuit may decide which of them shall do so.

Section 402(b) of Pub.L. 95–598 was amended by section 113 of Pub.L. 98–353 by substituting "shall not be effective" for "shall take effect on June 28, 1984", thereby eliminating the addition of section 153 by section 201(a) of Pub.L. 95–598, effective June 27, 1984, pursuant to section 122(c) of Pub.L. 98–353, set out as an Effective Date note under section 151 of this title.

Section 121(a) of Pub.L. 98–353 directed that section 402(b) of Pub.L. 95–598 be amended by substituting "the date of enactment of the Bankruptcy Amendments and Federal Judgeship Act of 1984 [i.e. July 10, 1984]" for "June 28, 1984". This amendment was not executed in view of the prior amendment to section 402(b) of Pub.L. 95–598 by section 113 of Pub.L. 98–353.

Effective and Applicability Provisions

1987 Acts. Section 101(a) [Title IV, § 408(d)] of Pub.L. 100–202 provided that: "This section [amending this section, section 634 of this title, and section 356 of Title 2, The Congress] shall become effective October 1, 1988, and any salary affected by the provisions of this section shall be adjusted at the beginning of the first applicable pay period commencing on or after such date of enactment [probably should read "such date", meaning Oct. 1, 1988]."

1984 Acts. Section effective July 10, 1984, see section 122(a) of Pub.L. 98–353, set out as a note under section 151 of this title.

Continuation of Salaries of Bankruptcy Judges in Effect on June 27, 1984

Section 105(a) of Pub.L. 98–353 provided that: "The salary of a bankruptcy judge in effect on June 27, 1984, shall remain in effect until changed as a result of a determination or adjustment made pursuant to section 153(a) of title 28, United States Code, as added by this Act [subsec. (a) of this section]."

Increase in Salaries

1988—Salaries of bankruptcy judges continued at $72,500 per annum by Ex. Ord. No. 12622, Dec. 31, 1987, 53 F.R. 222, formerly set out as a note under section 5332 of Title 5, Government Organization and Employees.

1987—Salaries of bankruptcy judges increased to $72,500 per annum, on recommendation of the President of the United States, see note set out under section 358 of Title 2, The Congress.

Salaries of bankruptcy judges increased to $70,500 effective on the first day of the first pay period beginning on or after January 1, 1987, by Ex. Ord. No. 12578, Dec. 31, 1986, 52 F.R. 505, formerly set out as a note under section 5332 of Title 5.

1985—Salaries of bankruptcy judges increased to $68,400 effective on the first day of the first pay period beginning on or after Jan. 1, 1985, by Ex. Ord. No. 12496, Dec. 28, 1984, 50 F.R. 211, as amended by Ex. Ord. No. 12540, Dec. 30, 1985, 51 F.R. 577, formerly set out as a note under section 5332 of Title 5.

1984—Salaries of bankruptcy judges (full-time) and bankruptcy judges (part-time) (maximum rate) increased to $66,100 and $33,100, respectively, effective on the first day of the first pay period beginning on or after Jan. 1, 1984, by Ex. Ord. No. 12456, Dec. 30, 1983, 49 F.R. 347, as amended Ex. Ord. No. 12477, May 23, 1984, 49 F.R. 22041; Ex. Ord. No. 12487, Sept. 14, 1984, 49 F.R. 36493, formerly set out as a note under section 5332 of Title 5.

1982—Salaries of bankruptcy judges and referees in bankruptcy (full-time), or referees in bankruptcy (part-time) (maximum rate) increased to $63,600 and $31,800, respectively, effective on the first day of the first pay period beginning on or after Oct. 1, 1982, by Ex. Ord. No. 12387, Oct. 8, 1982, 47 F.R. 44981, formerly set out as a note under section 5332 of Title 5, Government Organization and Employees. Ex. Ord. No. 12387 further provided that pursuant to section 101(e) of Pub.L. 97–276 funds are not available to pay a salary at a rate which exceeds the rate in effect on Sept. 30, 1982, which was $58,500 for bankruptcy judges and referees in bankruptcy (full-time), and $30,600 for referees in bankruptcy (part-time) (maximum rate).

Maximum rate payable to bankruptcy judges after Dec. 17, 1982, increased from $58,500 to $63,600, see Pub.L. 97–377, Title I, § 129(b)–(d), Dec. 21, 1982, 96 Stat. 1914, set out as a note under section 5318 of Title 5.

1981—Salaries of bankruptcy judges and referees in bankruptcy (full-time), or referees in bankruptcy (part-time) (maximum rate) increased to $61,200 and $30,600, respectively, effective on the first day of the first pay period beginning on or after Oct. 1, 1981, by Ex. Ord. No. 12330, Oct. 15, 1981, 46 F.R. 50921, formerly set out as a note under section 5332 of Title 5. Ex. Ord. No. 12330 further provided that pursuant to section 101(c) of Pub.L. 97–51 funds are not available to pay a salary at a rate which exceeds the rate in effect on Sept. 30, 1981, which was $51,167.50 for bankruptcy judges and referees in bankruptcy (full-time), and $25,583.75 for referees in bankruptcy (part-time) (maximum rate).

1980—Salaries of bankruptcy judges and referees in bankruptcy (full-time), or referees in bankruptcy (part-time) (maximum rate) increased to $58,400 and $29,200, respectively, effective on the first day of the first pay period beginning on or after Oct. 1, 1980, by Ex. Ord. No. 12248, Oct. 16, 1980, 45 F.R. 69199, formerly set out as a note under section 5332 of Title 5. Ex. Ord. No. 12248 further provided that pursuant to section 101(c) of Pub.L. 96–369 funds are not available to pay a salary which exceeds the rate in effect on Sept. 30, 1980, which was $51,167.50 for bankruptcy judges and referees in bankruptcy (full-time), and $25,583.75 for referees in bankruptcy (part-time) (maximum rate).

For limitations on use of funds for period Oct. 1, 1980 through June 5, 1981, appropriated by any Act to pay the salary or pay of any individual in legislative, executive, or judicial branch in position equal to or above level V of the Executive Schedule, see section 101(c) of Pub.L. 96–369 and section 101(c) of Pub.L. 96–536, set out as notes under section 5318 of Title 5.

1979—Salaries of bankruptcy judges increased to $53,500 effective on the first day of the first applicable pay period beginning on or after Oct. 1, 1979, by Ex. Ord. No. 12165, Oct. 9, 1979, 44 F.R. 58671, as amended by Ex. Ord. No. 12200, Mar. 12, 1980, 45 F.R. 16443, formerly set out as a note under section 5332 of Title 5. Ex. Ord. No. 12165 further provided that pursuant to Pub.L. 96–86 funds appropriated for fiscal year 1980 may not be used to pay a salary at a rate which exceeds an increase of 5.5 percent over the applicable rate payable for such position or office in effect on Sept. 30, 1978, which was $51,167.50 for bankruptcy judges.

Part–Time Bankruptcy Judges

For provision that notwithstanding subsecs. (a) and (b) of this section, a bankruptcy judge serving on a part-time basis on July 10, 1984, may continue to serve on such basis for two years from such date, and may engage in the practice of law, see section 106 of Pub.L. 98–353, set out as a note under section 152 of this title.

Transition Provisions

Section 1003(b) of Pub.L. 100–702 provided that:

"(1) If an individual who is exempted from the Leave Act by operation of amendments under this section [amending this section and sections 156, 631, 634, 712, 752, and 794 of this title] and who was previously subject to the provisions of subchapter I of chapter 63 of title 5, United States Code [section 6301 et seq. of Title 5, Government Organization and Employees], without a break in service, again becomes subject to this subchapter on completion of his service as an exempted officer, the unused annual leave and sick leave standing to his credit when he was exempted from this subchapter is deemed to have remained to his credit.

"(2) In computing an annuity under section 8339 of title 5, United States Code [section 8339 of Title 5], the total service of a person specified in paragraph (1) of this subsection who retired on an immediate annuity or dies leaving a survivor or survivors entitled to an annuity includes, without regard to the limitations imposed by subsection (f) of section 8339 of title 5, United States Code [section 8339(f) of Title 5], the days of unused sick leave standing to his credit when he was exempted from subchapter I of chapter 63 of title 5, United States Code [section 6301 et seq. of Title 5], except that these days will not be counted in determining average pay or annuity eligibility."

§ 154. Division of businesses; chief judge

(a) Each bankruptcy court for a district having more than one bankruptcy judge shall by majority vote promulgate rules for the division of business among the bankruptcy judges to the extent that the division of business is not otherwise provided for by the rules of the district court.

(b) In each district court having more than one bankruptcy judge the district court shall designate one judge to serve as chief judge of such bankruptcy court. Whenever a majority of the judges of such district court cannot agree upon the designation as chief judge, the chief judge of such district court shall make such designation. The chief judge of the bankruptcy court shall ensure that the rules of the bankruptcy court and of the district court are observed and that the business of the bankruptcy court is handled effectively and expeditiously.

(Added Pub.L. 98–353, Title I, § 104(a), July 10, 1984, 98 Stat. 339.)

HISTORICAL AND STATUTORY NOTES

Codifications

This section as added by Pub.L. 95–598, Title II, § 201(a), Nov. 6, 1978, 92 Stat. 2657, effective June 28, 1984, pursuant to Pub.L. 95–598, Title IV, § 402(b), Nov. 6, 1978, 92 Stat. 2682, as amended by Pub.L. 98–249, § 1(a), Mar. 31, 1984, 98 Stat. 116; Pub.L. 98–271, § 1(a), Apr. 30, 1984, 98 Stat. 163; Pub.L. 98–299, § 1(a), May 25, 1984, 98 Stat. 214; Pub.L. 98–325, § 1(a), June 20, 1984, 98 Stat. 268, set out as a note preceding section 101 of Title 11, Bankruptcy, read as follows:

§ 154. Salaries of bankruptcy judges

Each judge of a bankruptcy court shall receive a salary at an annual rate of $50,000, subject to adjustment under section 225 of the Federal Salary Act of 1967 (2 U.S.C. 351–361), and section 461 of this title.

Section 402(b) of Pub.L. 95–598 was amended by section 113 of Pub.L. 98–353 by substituting "shall not be effective" for "shall take effect on June 28, 1984", thereby eliminating the addition of section 154 by section 201(a) of Pub.L. 95–598, effective June 27, 1984, pursuant to section 122(c) of Pub.L. 98–353, set out as an Effective Date note under section 151 of this title.

Section 121(a) of Pub.L. 98–353 directed that section 402(b) of Pub.L. 95–598 be amended by substituting "the date of enactment of the Bankruptcy Amendments and Federal

Judgeship Act of 1984 [i.e. July 10, 1984]" for "June 28, 1984". This amendment was not executed in view of the prior amendment to section 402(b) of Pub.L. 95–598 by section 113 of Pub.L. 98–353.

Effective and Applicability Provisions

1984 Acts. Section effective July 10, 1984, see section 122(a) of Pub.L. 98–353, set out as a note under section 151 of this title.

§ 155. Temporary transfer of bankruptcy judges

(a) A bankruptcy judge may be transferred to serve temporarily as a bankruptcy judge in any judicial district other than the judicial district for which such bankruptcy judge was appointed upon the approval of the judicial council of each of the circuits involved.

(b) A bankruptcy judge who has retired may, upon consent, be recalled to serve as a bankruptcy judge in any judicial district by the judicial council of the circuit within which such district is located. Upon recall, a bankruptcy judge may receive a salary for such service in accordance with regulations promulgated by the Judicial Conference of the United States, subject to the restrictions on the payment of an annuity in section 377 of this title or in subchapter III of chapter 83, and chapter 84, of title 5 which are applicable to such judge.

(Added Pub.L. 98–353, Title I, § 104(a), July 10, 1984, 98 Stat. 339, and amended Pub.L. 99–651, Title II, § 202(a), Nov. 14, 1986, 100 Stat. 3648; Pub.L. 100–659, § 4(a), Nov. 15, 1988, 102 Stat. 3918.)

HISTORICAL AND STATUTORY NOTES

Codifications

This section as added by Pub.L. 95–598, Title II, § 201(a), Nov. 6, 1978, 92 Stat. 2658, effective June 28, 1984, pursuant to Pub.L. 95–598, Title IV, § 402(b), Nov. 6, 1978, 92 Stat. 2682, as amended by Pub.L. 98–249, § 1(a), Mar. 31, 1984, 98 Stat. 116; Pub.L. 98–271, § 1(a), Apr. 30, 1984, 98 Stat. 163; Pub.L. 98–299, § 1(a), May 25, 1984, 98 Stat. 214; Pub.L. 98–325, § 1(a), June 20, 1984, 98 Stat. 268, set out as a note preceding section 101 of Title 11, Bankruptcy, read as follows:

§ 155. Chief judge; precedence of bankruptcy judges

(a) In each district having more than one judge the bankruptcy judge in regular active service who is senior in commission and under seventy years of age shall be the chief judge of the bankruptcy court. If all the bankruptcy judges in regular active service are 70 years of age or older the youngest shall act as chief judge until a judge has been appointed and qualified who is under 70 years of age, but a judge may not act as chief judge until he has served as a bankruptcy judge for one year.

(b) The chief judge shall have precedence and preside at any session which he attends.

Other bankruptcy judges shall have precedence and preside according to the seniority of their commissions. Judges whose commissions bear the same date shall have precedence according to seniority in age.

(c) A judge whose commission extends over more than one district shall be junior to all bankruptcy judges except in the district in which he resided at the time he entered upon the duties of his office.

(d) If a chief judge desires to be relieved of his duties as chief judge while retaining his active status as a bankruptcy judge, he may so certify to the chief judge of the court of appeals for the circuit in which the bankruptcy judge serves, and thereafter the bankruptcy judge in active service next in precedence and willing to serve shall be designated by the chief judge of the court of appeals as the chief judge of the bankruptcy court.

(e) If a chief judge is temporarily unable to perform his duties as such, they shall be performed by the bankruptcy judge in active service, present in the district and able and qualified to act, who is next in precedence.

(f) Service as a referee in bankruptcy or as a bankruptcy judge under the Bankruptcy Act shall be taken into account in the determination of seniority of commission under this section.

Section 402(b) of Pub.L. 95–598 was amended by section 113 of Pub.L. 98–353 by substituting "shall not be effective" for "shall take effect on June 28, 1984", thereby eliminating the addition of section 155 by section 201(a) of Pub.L. 95–598, effective June 27, 1984, pursuant to section 122(c) of Pub.L. 98–353, set out as an Effective Date note under section 151 of this title.

Section 121(a) of Pub.L. 98–353 directed that section 402(b) of Pub.L. 95–598 be amended by substituting "the date of enactment of the Bankruptcy Amendments and Federal Judgeship Act of 1984 [i.e. July 10, 1984]" for "June 28, 1984". This amendment was not executed in view of the prior amendment to section 402(b) of Pub.L. 95–598 by section 113 of Pub.L. 98–353.

Effective and Applicability Provisions

1988 Acts. Amendment to this section by Pub.L. 100–659 to take effect on Nov. 15, 1988, and shall apply to bankruptcy judges and magistrates who retire on or after Nov. 15, 1988, with special election provisions for bankruptcy judges, etc., who left office on or after July 31, 1987, and before Nov. 15, 1988, see section 9 of Pub.L. 100–659, set out as a note under section 377 of this title.

1986 Acts. Section 203 of Title II of Pub.L. 99–651 provided that: "This title and the amendments made by this title [enacting section 375 of this title, and amending sections 155, 374, 631, 633, 636, and 797 of this title] take effect on January 1, 1987."

1984 Acts. Section effective July 10, 1984, see section 122(a) of Pub.L. 98–353, set out as a note under section 151 of this title.

§ 156. Staff; expenses

(a) Each bankruptcy judge may appoint a secretary, a law clerk, and such additional assistants as the Director of the Administrative Office of the United States Courts determines to be necessary. A law clerk appointed under this section shall be exempt from the provisions of subchapter I of chapter 63 of title 5, unless specifically included by the appointing judge or by local rule of court.

(b) Upon certification to the judicial council of the circuit involved and to the Director of the Administrative Office of the United States Courts that the number of cases and proceedings pending within the jurisdiction under section 1334 of this title within a judicial district so warrants, the bankruptcy judges for such district may appoint an individual to serve as clerk of such bankruptcy court. The clerk may appoint, with the approval of such bankruptcy judges, and in such number as may be approved by the Director, necessary deputies, and may remove such deputies with the approval of such bankruptcy judges.

(c) Any court may utilize facilities or services, either on or off the court's premises, which pertain to the provision of notices, dockets, calendars, and other administrative information to parties in cases filed under the provisions of title 11, United States Code, where the costs of such facilities or services are paid for out of the assets of the estate and are not charged to the United States. The utilization of such facilities or services shall be subject to such conditions and limitations as the pertinent circuit council may prescribe.

(d) No office of the bankruptcy clerk of court may be consolidated with the district clerk of court office without the prior approval of the Judicial Conference and the Congress.

(e) In a judicial district where a bankruptcy clerk has been appointed pursuant to subsection (b), the bankruptcy clerk shall be the official custodian of the records and dockets of the bankruptcy court.

(f) For purposes of financial accountability in a district where a bankruptcy clerk has been certified, such clerk shall be accountable for and pay into the Treasury all fees, costs, and other monies collected by such clerk except uncollected fees not required by an Act of Congress to be prepaid. Such clerk shall make returns thereof to the Director of the Administrative Office of the United States Courts and the Director of the Executive Office For United States Trustees, under regulations prescribed by such Directors.

(Added Pub.L. 98–353, Title I, § 104(a), July 10, 1984, 98 Stat. 339, and amended Pub.L. 99–554, Title I, §§ 103, 142, 144(a), Oct. 27, 1986, 100 Stat. 3090, 3096; Pub.L. 100–702, Title X, § 1003(a)(3), Nov. 19, 1988, 102 Stat. 4665.)

HISTORICAL AND STATUTORY NOTES

Codifications

This section as added by Pub.L. 95–598, Title II, § 201(a), Nov. 6, 1978, 92 Stat. 2659, effective June 28, 1984, pursuant to Pub.L. 95–598, Title IV, § 402(b), Nov. 6, 1978, 92 Stat. 2682, as amended by Pub.L. 98–249, § 1(a), Mar. 31, 1984, 98 Stat. 116; Pub.L. 98–271, § 1(a), Apr. 30, 1984, 98 Stat. 163; Pub.L. 98–299, § 1(a), May 25, 1984, 98 Stat. 214; Pub.L. 98–325, § 1(a), June 20, 1984, 98 Stat. 268, set out as a note preceding section 101 of Title 11, Bankruptcy, read as follows:

§ 156. Division of business among bankruptcy judges

The business of a bankruptcy court having more than one judge shall be divided among the judges as provided by the rules and orders of the court.

The chief judge of the bankruptcy court shall be responsible for the observance of such rules and orders, and shall divide the business and assign the cases so far as such rules and orders do not otherwise prescribe.

If the bankruptcy judges in any district are unable to agree upon the adoption of rules or orders for that purpose the judicial council of the circuit shall make the necessary orders.

Section 402(b) of Pub.L. 95–598 was amended by section 113 of Pub.L. 98–353 by substituting "shall not be effective" for "shall take effect on June 28, 1984", thereby eliminating the addition of section 156 by section 201(a) of Pub.L. 95–598, effective June 27, 1984, pursuant to section 122(c) of Pub.L. 98–353, set out as an Effective Date note under section 151 of this title.

Section 121(a) of Pub.L. 98–353 directed that section 402(b) of Pub.L. 95–598 be amended by substituting "the date of enactment of the Bankruptcy Amendments and Federal Judgeship Act of 1984 [i.e. July 10, 1984]" for "June 28, 1984". This amendment was not executed in view of the prior amendment to section 402(b) of Pub.L. 95–598 by section 113 of Pub.L. 98–353.

Effective and Applicability Provisions

1986 Acts. Amendment of subsec. (d) by section 103 of Pub.L. 99–554 effective on Oct. 27, 1986, see section 302(b) of Pub.L. 99–554, set out as a note under section 581 of this title.

Enactment of subsecs. (e) and (f) by sections 142 and 144(a) of Pub.L. 99–554 effective 30 days after Oct. 27, 1986, except as otherwise provided for, see section 302(a) of Pub.L. 99–554, set out as a note under section 581 of this title.

1984 Acts. Section effective July 10, 1984, see section 122(a) of Pub.L. 98–353, set out as a note under section 151 of this title.

§ 157. Procedures

(a) Each district court may provide that any or all cases under title 11 and any or all proceedings arising under title 11 or arising in or related to a case under title 11 shall be referred to the bankruptcy judges for the district.

(b)(1) Bankruptcy judges may hear and determine all cases under title 11 and all core proceedings arising under title 11, or arising in a case under title 11, referred under subsection (a) of this section, and may enter appropriate orders and judgments, subject to review under section 158 of this title.

(2) Core proceedings include, but are not limited to—

(A) matters concerning the administration of the estate;

(B) allowance or disallowance of claims against the estate or exemptions from property of the estate, and estimation of claims or interests for the purposes of confirming a plan under chapter 11, 12, or 13 of title 11 but not the liquidation or estimation of contingent or unliquidated personal injury tort or wrongful death claims against the estate for purposes of distribution in a case under title 11;

(C) counterclaims by the estate against persons filing claims against the estate;

(D) orders in respect to obtaining credit;

(E) orders to turn over property of the estate;

(F) proceedings to determine, avoid, or recover preferences;

(G) motions to terminate, annul, or modify the automatic stay;

(H) proceedings to determine, avoid, or recover fraudulent conveyances;

(I) determinations as to the dischargeability of particular debts;

(J) objections to discharges;

(K) determinations of the validity, extent, or priority of liens;

(L) confirmations of plans;

(M) orders approving the use or lease of property, including the use of cash collateral;

(N) orders approving the sale of property other than property resulting from claims brought by the estate against persons who have not filed claims against the estate;

(O) other proceedings affecting the liquidation of the assets of the estate or the adjustment of the debtor-creditor or the equity security holder relationship, except personal injury tort or wrongful death claims; and

(P) recognition of foreign proceedings and other matters under chapter 15 of title 11.

(3) The bankruptcy judge shall determine, on the judge's own motion or on timely motion of a party, whether a proceeding is a core proceeding under this subsection or is a proceeding that is otherwise related to a case under title 11. A determination that a proceeding is not a core proceeding shall not be made solely on the basis that its resolution may be affected by State law.

(4) Non-core proceedings under section 157(b)(2)(B) of title 28, United States Code, shall not be subject to the mandatory abstention provisions of section 1334(c)(2).

(5) The district court shall order that personal injury tort and wrongful death claims shall be tried in the district court in which the bankruptcy case is pending, or in the district court in the district in which the claim arose, as determined by the district court in which the bankruptcy case is pending.

(c)(1) A bankruptcy judge may hear a proceeding that is not a core proceeding but that is otherwise related to a case under title 11. In such proceeding, the bankruptcy judge shall submit proposed findings of fact and conclusions of law to the district court, and any final order or judgment shall be entered by the district judge after considering the bankruptcy judge's proposed findings and conclusions and after reviewing de novo those matters to which any party has timely and specifically objected.

(2) Notwithstanding the provisions of paragraph (1) of this subsection, the district court, with the consent of all the parties to the proceeding, may refer a proceeding related to a case under title 11 to a bankruptcy judge to hear and determine and to enter appropriate orders and judgments, subject to review under section 158 of this title.

(d) The district court may withdraw, in whole or in part, any case or proceeding referred under this section, on its own motion or on timely motion of any party, for cause shown. The district court shall, on timely motion of a party, so withdraw a proceeding if the court determines that resolution of the proceeding requires consideration of both title 11 and other laws of the United States regulating organizations or activities affecting interstate commerce.

(e) If the right to a jury trial applies in a proceeding that may be heard under this section by a bankruptcy judge, the bankruptcy judge may conduct the jury trial if specially designated to exercise such jurisdiction by the district court and with the express consent of all the parties.

(Added Pub.L. 98–353, Title I, § 104(a), July 10, 1984, 98 Stat. 340, and amended Pub.L. 99–554, Title I, §§ 143, 144(b), Oct. 27, 1986, 100 Stat. 3096; Pub.L. 103–394, Title I, § 112, Oct. 22, 1994, 108 Stat. 4117; Pub.L. 109–8, Title VIII, § 802(c)(1), Apr. 20, 2005, 119 Stat. 145.)

HISTORICAL AND STATUTORY NOTES

References in Text

Chapter 11, 12, or 13 of title 11, referred to in subsec. (b)(2)(B), is 11 U.S.C.A. § 1101 et seq., 11 U.S.C.A. § 1201 et seq., or 11 U.S.C.A. § 1301 et seq., respectively.

Chapter 15 of title 11, referred to in subsec. (b)(2)(P), is 11 U.S.C.A. § 1501 et seq.

Codifications

This section as added by Pub.L. 95–598, Title II, § 201(a), Nov. 6, 1978, 92 Stat. 2659, effective June 28, 1984, pursuant to Pub.L. 95–598, Title IV, § 402(b), Nov. 6, 1978, 92 Stat. 2682, as amended by Pub.L. 98–249, § 1(a), Mar. 31, 1984, 98 Stat. 116; Pub.L. 98–271, § 1(a), Apr. 30, 1984, 98 Stat. 163; Pub.L. 98–299, § 1(a), May 25, 1984, 98 Stat. 214; Pub.L. 98–325, § 1(a), June 20, 1984, 98 Stat. 268, set out as a note preceding section 101 of Title 11, Bankruptcy, read as follows:

"§ 157. **Times of holding court**

"(a) The bankruptcy court at each designated location shall be deemed to be in continuous session on all business days throughout the year.

"(b) Each bankruptcy court may establish by local rule or order schedules of court sessions at designated places of holding court other than the headquarters office of the court. Such schedules may be pretermitted by order of the court.

"(c) Bankruptcy court may be held at any place within the territory served, in any case, on order of the bankruptcy court, for the convenience of the parties, on such notice as the bankruptcy court orders."

Section 402(b) of Pub.L. 95–598 was amended by section 113 of Pub.L. 98–353 by substituting "shall not be effective" for "shall take effect on June 28, 1984", thereby eliminating the addition of section 157 by section 201(a) of Pub.L. 95–598, effective June 27, 1984, pursuant to section 122(c) of Pub.L. 98–353, set out as an Effective Date note under section 151 of this title.

Section 121(a) of Pub.L. 98–353 directed that section 402(b) of Pub.L. 95–598 be amended by substituting "the date of enactment of the Bankruptcy Amendments and Federal Judgeship Act of 1984 [i.e. July 10, 1984]" for "June 28, 1984". This amendment was not executed in view of the prior amendment to section 402(b) of Pub.L. 95–598 by section 113 of Pub.L. 98–353.

Effective and Applicability Provisions

2005 Acts. Except as otherwise provided, amendments by Pub.L. 109–8 effective 180 days after April 20, 2005, and inapplicable with respect to cases commenced under Title 11 before the effective date, see Pub.L. 109–8, § 1501, set out as a note under 11 U.S.C.A. § 101.

1994 Acts. Amendment by Pub.L. 103–394 effective on Oct. 22, 1994, and not to apply with respect to cases commenced under Title 11 of the United States Code before Oct. 22, 1994, see section 702 of Pub.L. 103–394, set out as a note under section 101 of Title 11, Bankruptcy.

1986 Acts. Amendment by Pub.L. 99–554 effective 30 days after Oct. 27, 1986, except as otherwise provided for, see section 302(a) of Pub.L. 99–554, set out as a note under section 581 of this title.

1984 Acts. Section effective July 10, 1984, see section 122(a) of Pub.L. 98–353, set out as a note under section 151 of this title.

Separability of Provisions

If any provision of or amendment made by Pub.L. 103–394 or the application of such provision or amendment to any person or circumstance is held to be unconstitutional, the remaining provisions of and amendments made by Pub.L. 103–394 and the application of such provisions and amendments to any person or circumstance shall not be affected thereby, see section 701 of Pub.L. 103–394, set out as a note under section 101 of Title 11, Bankruptcy.

§ 158. Appeals

(a) The district courts of the United States shall have jurisdiction to hear appeals [1]

(1) from final judgments, orders, and decrees;

(2) from interlocutory orders and decrees issued under section 1121(d) of title 11 increasing or reducing the time periods referred to in section 1121 of such title; and

(3) with leave of the court, from other interlocutory orders and decrees;

and, with leave of the court, from interlocutory orders and decrees, of bankruptcy judges entered in cases and proceedings referred to the bankruptcy judges under section 157 of this title. An appeal under this subsection shall be taken only to the district court for the judicial district in which the bankruptcy judge is serving.

(b)(1) The judicial council of a circuit shall establish a bankruptcy appellate panel service composed of bankruptcy judges of the districts in the circuit who are appointed by the judicial council in accordance with paragraph (3), to hear and determine, with the consent of all the parties, appeals under subsection (a) unless the judicial council finds that—

(A) there are insufficient judicial resources available in the circuit; or

(B) establishment of such service would result in undue delay or increased cost to parties in cases under title 11.

Not later than 90 days after making the finding, the judicial council shall submit to the Judicial Conference of the United States a report containing the factual basis of such finding.

(2)(A) A judicial council may reconsider, at any time, the finding described in paragraph (1).

(B) On the request of a majority of the district judges in a circuit for which a bankruptcy appellate panel service is established under paragraph (1), made after the expiration of the 1–year period beginning on the date such service is established, the judicial council of the circuit shall determine whether a circumstance specified in subparagraph (A) or (B) of such paragraph exists.

(C) On its own motion, after the expiration of the 3–year period beginning on the date a bankruptcy appellate panel service is established under paragraph (1), the judicial council of the circuit may determine whether a circumstance specified in subparagraph (A) or (B) of such paragraph exists.

(D) If the judicial council finds that either of such circumstances exists, the judicial council may provide for the completion of the appeals then pending before such service and the orderly termination of such service.

(3) Bankruptcy judges appointed under paragraph (1) shall be appointed and may be reappointed under such paragraph.

(4) If authorized by the Judicial Conference of the United States, the judicial councils of 2 or more circuits may establish a joint bankruptcy appellate panel comprised of bankruptcy judges from the districts within the circuits for which such panel is established, to hear and determine, upon the consent of all the parties, appeals under subsection (a) of this section.

(5) An appeal to be heard under this subsection shall be heard by a panel of 3 members of the bankruptcy appellate panel service, except that a member of such service may not hear an appeal originating in the district for which such member is appointed or designated under section 152 of this title.

(6) Appeals may not be heard under this subsection by a panel of the bankruptcy appellate panel service unless the district judges for the district in which the appeals occur, by majority vote, have authorized such service to hear and determine appeals originating in such district.

(c)(1) Subject to subsections (b) and (d)(2), each appeal under subsection (a) shall be heard by a 3–judge panel of the bankruptcy appellate panel service established under subsection (b)(1) unless—

(A) the appellant elects at the time of filing the appeal; or

(B) any other party elects, not later than 30 days after service of notice of the appeal;

to have such appeal heard by the district court.

(2) An appeal under subsections (a) and (b) of this section shall be taken in the same manner as appeals in civil proceedings generally are taken to the courts of appeals from the district courts and in the time provided by Rule 8002 of the Bankruptcy Rules.

(d)(1) The courts of appeals shall have jurisdiction of appeals from all final decisions, judgments, orders, and decrees entered under subsections (a) and (b) of this section.

(2)(A) The appropriate court of appeals shall have jurisdiction of appeals described in the first sentence of subsection (a) if the bankruptcy court, the district court, or the bankruptcy appellate panel involved, acting on its own motion or on the request of a party to the judgment, order, or decree described in such first sentence, or all the appellants and appellees (if any) acting jointly, certify that—

(i) the judgment, order, or decree involves a question of law as to which there is no controlling decision of the court of appeals for the circuit or of the Supreme Court of the United States, or involves a matter of public importance;

(ii) the judgment, order, or decree involves a question of law requiring resolution of conflicting decisions; or

(iii) an immediate appeal from the judgment, order, or decree may materially advance the progress of the case or proceeding in which the appeal is taken;

and if the court of appeals authorizes the direct appeal of the judgment, order, or decree.

(B) If the bankruptcy court, the district court, or the bankruptcy appellate panel—

(i) on its own motion or on the request of a party, determines that a circumstance specified in clause (i), (ii), or (iii) of subparagraph (A) exists; or

(ii) receives a request made by a majority of the appellants and a majority of appellees (if any) to make the certification described in subparagraph (A);

then the bankruptcy court, the district court, or the bankruptcy appellate panel shall make the certification described in subparagraph (A).

(C) The parties may supplement the certification with a short statement of the basis for the certification.

(D) An appeal under this paragraph does not stay any proceeding of the bankruptcy court, the district court, or the bankruptcy appellate panel from which the appeal is taken, unless the respective bankruptcy court, district court, or bankruptcy appellate panel, or the court of appeals in which the appeal in [2] pending, issues a stay of such proceeding pending the appeal.

(E) Any request under subparagraph (B) for certification shall be made not later than 60 days after the entry of the judgment, order, or decree.

(Added Pub.L. 98–353, Title I, § 104(a), July 10, 1984, 98 Stat. 341, and amended Pub.L. 101–650, Title III, § 305, Dec. 1, 1990, 104 Stat. 5105; Pub.L. 103–394, Title I, §§ 102, 104(c), (d), Oct. 22, 1994, 108 Stat. 4108–4110; Pub.L. 109–8, Title XII, § 1233(a), Apr. 20, 2005, 119 Stat. 202.)

[1] So in original.

[2] So in original. Probably should read "is".

HISTORICAL AND STATUTORY NOTES

Codifications

Amendment by section 102 of Pub.L. 103–394, which directed amendment of subsec. (a) by striking "from" the first place it appeared and all that followed through "decrees," and making a substitution for such language, was executed by striking through "decrees," the first place it appeared, as the probable intent of Congress.

This section (section 158) and section 159 as added by Pub.L. 95–598, Title II, § 201(a), Nov. 6, 1978, 92 Stat. 2659, and section 160, as added by Pub.L. 95–598, Title II, § 201(a), Nov. 6, 1978, 92 Stat. 2659, and amended Pub.L. 97–164, Title I, § 110(d), Apr. 2, 1982, 96 Stat. 29, effective June 28, 1984, pursuant to Pub.L. 95–598, Title IV, § 402(b), Nov. 6, 1978, 92 Stat. 2682, as amended by Pub.L. 98–249, § 1(a), Mar. 31, 1984, 98 Stat. 116; Pub.L. 98–271, § 1(a), Apr. 30, 1984, 98 Stat. 163; Pub.L. 98–299, § 1(a), May 25, 1984, 98 Stat. 214; Pub.L. 98–325, § 1(a), June 20, 1984, 98

Stat. 268, set out as a note preceding section 101 of Title II, Bankruptcy, read as follows:

"§ 158. Accommodations at places for holding court

"Court shall be held only at places where Federal quarters and accommodations are available, or suitable quarters and accommodations are furnished without cost to the United States. The foregoing restrictions shall not, however, preclude the Administrator of General Services, at the request of the Director of the Administrative Office of the United States Courts, from providing such court quarters and accommodations as the Administrator determines can appropriately be made available at places where court is authorized by law to be held, but only if such court quarters and accommodations have been approved as necessary by the judicial council of the appropriate circuit.

"§ 159. Vacant judgeship as affecting proceedings

"When the office of a bankruptcy judge becomes vacant, all pending process, pleadings and proceedings shall, when necessary, be continued by the clerk until a judge is appointed or designated to hold such court.

"§ 160. Appellate panels

"**(a)** If the circuit council of a circuit orders application of this section to a district within such circuit, the chief judge of each circuit shall designate panels of three bankruptcy judges to hear appeals from judgments, orders, and decrees of the bankruptcy court of the United States for such district. Except as provided in section 293(b) of this title, a panel shall be composed only of bankruptcy judges for districts located in the circuit in which the appeal arises. The chief judge shall designate a sufficient number of such panels so that appeals may be heard and disposed of expeditiously.

"**(b)** A panel designated under subsection (a) of this section may not hear an appeal from a judgment, order, or decree entered by a member of the panel.

"**(c)** When hearing an appeal, a panel designated under subsection (a) of this section shall sit at a place convenient to the parties to the appeal."

Section 402(b) of Pub.L. 95–598 was amended by section 113 of Pub.L. 98–353 by substituting "shall not be effective" for "shall take effect on June 28, 1984", thereby eliminating the additions of sections 158 to 160 by section 201(a) of Pub.L. 95–598, effective June 27, 1984, pursuant to section 122(c) of Pub.L. 98–353, set out as an Effective Date note under section 151 of this title.

Section 121(a) of Pub.L. 98–353 directed that section 402(b) of Pub.L. 95–598 be amended by substituting "the date of enactment of the Bankruptcy Amendments and Federal Judgeship Act of 1984 [i.e. July 10, 1984]" for "June 28, 1984". This amendment was not executed in view of the prior amendment to section 402(b) of Pub.L. 95–598 by section 113 of Pub.L. 98–353.

Effective and Applicability Provisions

2005 Acts. Except as otherwise provided, amendments by Pub.L. 109–8 effective 180 days after April 20, 2005, and inapplicable with respect to cases commenced under Title 11 before the effective date, see Pub.L. 109–8, § 1501, set out as a note under 11 U.S.C.A. § 101.

1994 Acts. Amendments by Pub.L. 103–394 effective on Oct. 22, 1994, and not to apply with respect to cases commenced under Title 11 of the United States Code before Oct. 22, 1994, see section 702 of Pub.L. 103–394, set out as a note under 11 U.S.C.A. § 101.

1984 Acts. Section effective July 10, 1984, see section 122(a) of Pub.L. 98–353, set out as a note under 28 U.S.C.A. § 151.

Separability of Provisions

If any provision of or amendment made by Pub.L. 103–394 or the application of such provision or amendment to any person or circumstance is held to be unconstitutional, the remaining provisions of and amendments made by Pub.L. 103–394 and the application of such provisions and amendments to any person or circumstance shall not be affected thereby, see section 701 of Pub.L. 103–394, set out as a note under 11 U.S.C.A. § 101.

Procedural Rules

Pub.L. 109–8, Title XII, § 1233(b), Apr. 20, 2005, 119 Stat. 203, provided that:

"**(1) Temporary application.**—A provision of this subsection shall apply to appeals under section 158(d)(2) of title 28, United States Code, until a rule of practice and procedure relating to such provision and such appeals is promulgated or amended under chapter 131 of such title [28 U.S.C.A. § 2071 et seq.].

"**(2) Certification.**—A district court, a bankruptcy court, or a bankruptcy appellate panel may make a certification under section 158(d)(2) of title 28, United States Code, only with respect to matters pending in the respective bankruptcy court, district court, or bankruptcy appellate panel.

"**(3) Procedure.**—Subject to any other provision of this subsection, an appeal authorized by the court of appeals under section 158(d)(2)(A) of title 28, United States Code, shall be taken in the manner prescribed in subdivisions (a)(1), (b), (c), and (d) of rule 5 of the Federal Rules of Appellate Procedure. For purposes of subdivision (a)(1) of rule 5—

"**(A)** a reference in such subdivision to a district court shall be deemed to include a reference to a bankruptcy court and a bankruptcy appellate panel, as appropriate; and

"**(B)** a reference in such subdivision to the parties requesting permission to appeal to be served with the petition shall be deemed to include a reference to the parties to the judgment, order, or decree from which the appeal is taken.

"**(4) Filing of petition with attachment.**—A petition requesting permission to appeal, that is based on a certification made under subparagraph (A) or (B) of section 158(d)(2) shall—

"**(A)** be filed with the circuit clerk not later than 10 days after the certification is entered on the docket of the bankruptcy court, the district court, or the bankruptcy appellate panel from which the appeal is taken; and

"**(B)** have attached a copy of such certification.

"**(5) References in rule 5.**—For purposes of rule 5 of the Federal Rules of Appellate Procedure—

"**(A)** a reference in such rule to a district court shall be deemed to include a reference to a bankruptcy court and to a bankruptcy appellate panel; and

"**(B)** a reference in such rule to a district clerk shall be deemed to include a reference to a clerk of a bankruptcy court and to a clerk of a bankruptcy appellate panel.

"(6) **Application of rules.**—The Federal Rules of Appellate Procedure [set out in Title 28, Judiciary and Judicial Procedure] shall apply in the courts of appeals with respect to appeals authorized under section 158(d)(2)(A), to the extent relevant and as if such appeals were taken from final judgments, orders, or decrees of the district courts or bankruptcy appellate panels exercising appellate jurisdiction under subsection (a) or (b) of section 158 of title 28, United States Code."

[Except as otherwise provided, amendments by Pub.L. 109–8 effective 180 days after April 20, 2005, and inapplicable with respect to cases commenced under Title 11 before the effective date, see Pub.L. 109–8, § 1501, set out as a note under 11 U.S.C.A. § 101.]

§ 159. Bankruptcy statistics

(a) The clerk of the district court, or the clerk of the bankruptcy court if one is certified pursuant to section 156(b) of this title, shall collect statistics regarding debtors who are individuals with primarily consumer debts seeking relief under chapters 7, 11, and 13 of title 11. Those statistics shall be in a standardized format prescribed by the Director of the Administrative Office of the United States Courts (referred to in this section as the "Director").

(b) The Director shall—

(1) compile the statistics referred to in subsection (a);

(2) make the statistics available to the public; and

(3) not later than July 1, 2008, and annually thereafter, prepare, and submit to Congress a report concerning the information collected under subsection (a) that contains an analysis of the information.

(c) The compilation required under subsection (b) shall—

(1) be itemized, by chapter, with respect to title 11;

(2) be presented in the aggregate and for each district; and

(3) include information concerning—

(A) the total assets and total liabilities of the debtors described in subsection (a), and in each category of assets and liabilities, as reported in the schedules prescribed pursuant to section 2075 of this title and filed by debtors;

(B) the current monthly income, average income, and average expenses of debtors as reported on the schedules and statements that each such debtor files under sections 521 and 1322 of title 11;

(C) the aggregate amount of debt discharged in cases filed during the reporting period, determined as the difference between the total amount of debt and obligations of a debtor reported on the schedules and the amount of such debt reported in categories which are predominantly nondischargeable;

(D) the average period of time between the date of the filing of the petition and the closing of the case for cases closed during the reporting period;

(E) for cases closed during the reporting period—

(i) the number of cases in which a reaffirmation agreement was filed; and

(ii)(I) the total number of reaffirmation agreements filed;

(II) of those cases in which a reaffirmation agreement was filed, the number of cases in which the debtor was not represented by an attorney; and

(III) of those cases in which a reaffirmation agreement was filed, the number of cases in which the reaffirmation agreement was approved by the court;

(F) with respect to cases filed under chapter 13 of title 11, for the reporting period—

(i)(I) the number of cases in which a final order was entered determining the value of property securing a claim in an amount less than the amount of the claim; and

(II) the number of final orders entered determining the value of property securing a claim;

(ii) the number of cases dismissed, the number of cases dismissed for failure to make payments under the plan, the number of cases refiled after dismissal, and the number of cases in which the plan was completed, separately itemized with respect to the number of modifications made before completion of the plan, if any; and

(iii) the number of cases in which the debtor filed another case during the 6–year period preceding the filing;

(G) the number of cases in which creditors were fined for misconduct and any amount of punitive damages awarded by the court for creditor misconduct; and

(H) the number of cases in which sanctions under rule 9011 of the Federal Rules of Bankruptcy Procedure were imposed against debtor's attorney or damages awarded under such Rule.

(Added Pub.L. 109–8, Title VI, § 601(a), Apr. 20, 2005, 119 Stat. 119.)

HISTORICAL AND STATUTORY NOTES

References in Text

Chapters 7 and 11 of title 11, referred to in subsec. (a), are 11 U.S.C.A. § 701 et seq. and 11 U.S.C.A. § 1101 et seq., respectively.

Chapter 13 of title 11, referred to in subsecs. (a) and (c)(3)(F), is 11 U.S.C.A. § 1301 et seq.

The Federal Rules of Bankruptcy Procedure, referred to in subsec. (c)(3)(H), are set out in Title 11.

Effective and Applicability Provisions

2005 Acts. Pub.L. 109–8, Title VI, § 601(c), Apr. 20, 2005, 119 Stat. 120, provided that: "The amendments made by this section [enacting this section] shall take effect 18 months after the date of enactment of this Act [April 20, 2005]."

Except as otherwise provided, amendments by Pub.L. 109–8 effective 180 days after April 20, 2005, and inapplicable with respect to cases commenced under Title 11 before the effective date, see Pub.L. 109–8, § 1501, set out as a note under 11 U.S.C.A. § 101.

CHAPTER 7—UNITED STATES COURT OF FEDERAL CLAIMS

Sec.
171. Appointment and number of judges; character of court; designation of chief judge.
172. Tenure and salaries of judges.
173. Times and places of holding court.
174. Assignment of judges; decisions.
175. Official duty station; residence.
176. Removal from office.
177. Disbarment of removed judges.
178. Retirement of judges of the Court of Federal Claims.
179. Personnel application and insurance programs.
180. [Repealed.]

§ 171. Appointment and number of judges; character of court; designation of chief judge

(a) The President shall appoint, by and with the advice and consent of the Senate, sixteen judges who shall constitute a court of record known as the United States Court of Federal Claims. The court is declared to be a court established under article I of the Constitution of the United States.

(b) The President shall designate one of the judges of the Court of Federal Claims who is less than seventy years of age to serve as chief judge. The chief judge may continue to serve as such until he reaches the age of seventy years or until another judge is designated as chief judge by the President. After the designation of another judge to serve as chief judge, the former chief judge may continue to serve as a judge of the court for the balance of the term to which appointed.

(June 25, 1948, c. 646, 62 Stat. 898; July 28, 1953, c. 253, § 1, 67 Stat. 226; Sept. 3, 1954, c. 1263, § 39(a), 68 Stat. 1240; May 11, 1966, Pub.L. 89–425, § 1(b), 80 Stat. 140; Apr. 2, 1982, Pub.L. 97–164, Title I, § 105(a), 96 Stat. 27; Oct. 29, 1992, Pub.L. 102–572, Title IX, § 902(a), 106 Stat. 4516.)

HISTORICAL AND STATUTORY NOTES

Effective and Applicability Provisions

1992 Acts. Section 911 of Pub.L. 102–572 provided that: "This title and the amendments made by this title [Title IX of Pub.L. 102–572, Oct. 29, 1992, 106 Stat. 4516, for classifications to which see Tables] shall take effect on the date of the enactment of this Act [Oct. 29, 1992]."

1982 Acts. Section 402 of Pub.L. 97–164 provided that: "Unless otherwise specified, the provisions of this Act [see Short Title of 1982 Amendments note set out under section 1 of this title] shall take effect on October 1, 1982."

Change of Name

Section 902(b) of Pub.L. 102–572 provided that:

"Reference in any other Federal law [other than chapters 7, 51, 91, and 165 of this title] or any document to—

"(1) the 'United States Claims Court' shall be deemed to refer to the 'United States Court of Federal Claims'; and

"(2) the 'Claims Court' shall be deemed to refer to the 'Court of Federal Claims'."

Additional Judgeships

Section 1(a) of Pub.L. 89–425 provided that: "The President shall appoint, by and with the advice and consent of the Senate, two additional associate judges for the Court of Claims."

Appointment of United States Court of Federal Claims Judges

For Congressional suggestion that the President select judges of the United States Court of Federal Claims and the Court of Appeals for the Federal Circuit from a broad range of qualified individuals, see section 168 of Pub.L. 97–164, set out as a note under section 44 of this title.

Chief Justice to be known as Chief Judge

Section 2(a) of Act June 25, 1948, provided in part that the Chief Justice of the Court of Claims in office on Sept. 1, 1948, shall be thereafter known as the Chief Judge.

Continuation of Organization of Court

Section 2(b) of Act June 25, 1948, provided in part that the provisions of this title as set out in section 1 of Act June 25, 1948, with respect to the organization of the court, shall be construed as a continuation of existing law, and the tenure of the judges, officers, and employees in office on Sept. 1, 1948, shall not be effected by its enactment but each of them shall continue to serve in the same capacity under the appropriate provisions of this title, pursuant to his prior appointment.

Continued Service of Commissioners of Court of Claims as Judges of United States Claims Court

Section 167 of Pub.L. 97–164 provided that:

"(a) Notwithstanding the provisions of section 171(a) of title 28, United States Code, as amended by this Act [subsec. (a) of this section], a commissioner of the United States Court of Claims serving immediately prior to the effective date of this Act [Oct. 1, 1982] shall become a judge of the United States Claims Court [now the United States Court of Federal Claims] on the effective date of this Act.

"(b) Notwithstanding the provisions of section 172(a) of title 28, United States Code, as amended by this Act [section 172(a) of this title], the initial term of office of a person who becomes a judge of the United States Claims Court under subsection (a) of this section shall expire fifteen years after the date of his or her employment with the United States Court of Claims, or on October 1, 1986, whichever occurs earlier. Any such judge shall continue in office until a successor is sworn or until reappointed. No such individual shall serve as a judge after reaching the age of seventy years.

"(c) Notwithstanding the provisions of section 172(b) of title 28, United States Code [section 172(b) of this title], as amended by this Act, until such time as a change in the salary rate of a judge of the United States Claims Court [now the United States Court of Federal Claims] occurs in accordance with such section 172(b), the salary of such judge shall be equal to the salary of a Commissioner of the Court of Claims."

Tennessee Valley Authority Legal Representation

Section 169 of Pub.L. 97–164 provided that: "Nothing in this Act [see Short Title of 1982 Amendments note set out under section 1 of this title] affects the authority of the Tennessee Valley Authority under the Tennessee Valley Authority Act of 1933 [section 831 et seq. of Title 16, Conservation] to represent itself by attorneys of its choosing."

Transition Provisions; Transfer of Pending Cases

Section 403 of Pub.L. 97–164 provided that:

"(a) Any case pending before the Court of Claims on the effective date of this Act [Oct. 1, 1982] in which a report on the merits has been filed by a commissioner, or in which there is pending a request for review, and upon which the court has not acted, shall be transferred to the United States Court of Appeals for the Federal Circuit.

"(b) Any matter pending before the United States Court of Customs and Patent Appeals on the effective date of this Act [Oct. 1, 1982] shall be transferred to the United States Court of Appeals for the Federal Circuit.

"(c) Any petition for rehearing, reconsideration, alteration, modification, or other change in any decision of the United States Court of Claims or the United States Court of Customs and Patent Appeals rendered prior to the effective date of this Act [Oct. 1, 1982] that has not been determined by either of those courts on that date, or that is filed after that date, shall be determined by the United States Court of Appeals for the Federal Circuit.

"(d) Any matter pending before a commissioner of the United States Court of Claims on the effective date of this Act [Oct. 1, 1982], or any pending dispositive motion that the United States Court of Claims has not determined on that date, shall be determined by the United States Claims Court [now the United States Court of Federal Claims].

"(e) Any case in which a notice of appeal has been filed in a district court of the United States prior to the effective date of this Act [Oct. 1, 1982] shall be decided by the court of appeals to which the appeal was taken."

§ 172. Tenure and salaries of judges

(a) Each judge of the United States Court of Federal Claims shall be appointed for a term of fifteen years.

(b) Each judge shall receive a salary at the rate of pay, and in the same manner, as judges of the district courts of the United States.

(June 25, 1948, c. 646, 62 Stat. 898; Apr. 2, 1982, Pub.L. 97–164, Title I, § 105(a), 96 Stat. 27; Nov. 19, 1988, Pub.L. 100–702, Title X, § 1023, 102 Stat. 4673; Oct. 29, 1992, Pub.L. 102–572, Title IX, § 902(a)(1), 106 Stat. 4516.)

HISTORICAL AND STATUTORY NOTES

Effective and Applicability Provisions

1992 Acts. Amendment by Title IX of Pub.L. 102–572 effective Oct. 29, 1992, see section 911 of Pub.L. 102–572, set out as a note under section 171 of Title 28, Judiciary and Judicial Procedure.

1982 Acts. Amendment by Pub.L. 97–164 effective Oct. 1, 1982, see section 402 of Pub.L. 97–164, set out as a note under section 171 of this title.

Increase in Salaries

1993—Salaries of judges increased to $133,600, effective on the first day of the first applicable pay period beginning on or after Jan. 1, 1993, by Ex. Ord. No. 12826, Dec. 30, 1992, 57 F.R. 62909, set out as a note under section 5332 of Title 5, Government Organization and Employees.

1992—Salaries of judges increased to $129,500, effective on the first day of the first applicable pay period beginning on or after Jan. 1, 1992, by Ex. Ord. No. 12786, Dec. 26, 1991, 56 F.R. 67453, formerly set out as a note under section 5332 of Title 5, Government Organization and Employees.

1991—Salaries of judges increased to $125,100, effective on the first day of the first applicable pay period beginning on or after Jan. 1, 1991, by Ex. Ord. No. 12736, Dec. 12, 1990, 55 F.R. 51385, formerly set out as a note under section 5332 of Title 5, Government Organization and Employees.

1990—Salaries of judges continued at $89,500 per annum, and increased to $96,600, effective on the first day of the first pay period beginning on or after Jan. 31, 1990, by Ex. Ord. No. 12698, Dec. 23, 1989, 54 F.R. 53473, formerly set out as a note under section 5332 of Title 5.

1989—Salaries of judges increased in the amount of 25 percent of their rates (as last in effect before the increase), effective Jan. 1, 1991, see Pub.L. 101–194, Title VII, § 703(a)(3), Nov. 30, 1989, 103 Stat. 1768, set out as a note under section 5318 of Title 5.

Salaries of judges increased to $89,500 per annum by Ex. Ord. No. 12663, Jan. 6, 1989, 54 F.R. 791, formerly set out as a note under section 5332 of Title 5.

1988—Salaries of judges continued at $82,500 per annum by Ex. Ord. No. 12622, Dec. 31, 1987, 53 F.R. 222, formerly set out as a note under section 5332 of Title 5.

1987—Salaries of judges increased to $82,500 per annum, on recommendation of the President of the United States, see note set out under section 358 of Title 2, The Congress.

Salaries of judges increased to $72,300 effective on first day of first pay period beginning on or after January 1, 1987, by Ex. Ord. No. 12578, Dec. 31, 1986, 52 F.R. 505, formerly set out as a note under section 5332 of Title 5.

1985—Salaries of judges increased to $70,200 effective on the first day of the first pay period beginning on or after Jan. 1, 1985, by Ex. Ord. No. 12496, Dec. 28, 1984, 50 F.R. 211, as amended by Ex. Ord. No. 12540, Dec. 30, 1985, 51 F.R. 577, formerly set out as a note under section 5332 of Title 5.

1984—Salaries of judges set at $67,800 effective on the first day of the first pay period beginning on or after Jan. 1, 1984, by Ex. Ord. No. 12456, Dec. 30, 1983, 49 F.R. 347, as amended Ex. Ord. No. 12477, May 23, 1984, 49 F.R. 22041; Ex. Ord. No. 12487, Sept. 14, 1984, 49 F.R. 36493, formerly set out as a note under section 5332 of Title 5.

1982—Salaries of judges set at $65,200 effective on the first day of the first pay period beginning on or after Oct. 1, 1982, by Ex. Ord. No. 12387, Oct. 8, 1982, 47 F.R. 44981, formerly set out as a note under section 5332 of Title 5, Government Organization and Employees. Ex. Ord. No. 12387 further provided that pursuant to section 101(e) of Pub.L. 97–276 funds are not available to pay a salary at a rate which exceeds the rate in effect on Sept. 30, 1982, which was $57,500.

Maximum rate payable after Dec. 17, 1982, increased from $57,500 to $65,200, see Pub.L. 97–377, Title I, § 129(b)–(d), Dec. 21, 1982, 96 Stat. 1914, set out as a note under section 5318 of Title 5.

Limitations on use of funds for fiscal year ending Sept. 30, 1983, appropriated by any Act to pay the salary or pay of any individual in legislative, executive, or judicial branch in position equal to or above level V of the Executive Schedule, see section 101(e) of Pub.L. 97–276, as amended, set out as a note under section 5318 of Title 5.

1981—Salaries of judges increased to $74,300 effective on the first day of the first pay period beginning on or after Oct. 1, 1981, by Ex. Ord. No. 12330, Oct. 15, 1981, 46 F.R. 50921, formerly set out as a note under section 5332 of Title 5.

Limitations on use of funds for fiscal year ending Sept. 30, 1982, appropriated by any Act to pay the salary or pay of any individual in legislative, executive, or judicial branch in position equal to or above level V of the Executive Schedule, see sections 101(g) and 141 of Pub.L. 97–92, set out as a note under section 5318 of Title 5.

1980—Salaries of judges increased to $70,900 effective on the first day of the first pay period beginning on or after Oct. 1, 1980, by Ex. Ord. No. 12248, Oct. 16, 1980, 45 F.R. 69199, formerly set out as a note under section 5332 of Title 5. Ex. Ord. No. 12248 further provided that pursuant to Pub.L. 96–369 funds are not available to pay a salary at a rate which exceeds the rate in effect on Sept. 30, 1980, which was $60,662.50.

Limitations on use of funds for fiscal year ending Sept. 30, 1981, appropriated by any Act to pay the salary or pay of any individual in legislative, executive, or judicial branch in position equal to or above level V of the Executive Schedule, see section 101(c) of Pub.L. 96–536, as amended, set out as a note under section 5318 of Title 5.

1979—Salaries of judges increased to $65,000 effective on the first day of the first applicable pay period beginning on or after Oct. 1, 1979, by Ex. Ord. No. 12165, Oct. 9, 1979, 44 F.R. 58671, as amended by Ex. Ord. No. 12200, Mar. 12, 1980, 45 F.R. 16443, formerly set out as a note under section 5332 of Title 5. Ex. Ord. No. 12165 further provided that pursuant to Pub.L. 96–86 funds appropriated for fiscal year 1980 may not be used to pay a salary at a rate which exceeds an increase of 5.5 percent over the applicable rate payable for such position or office in effect on Sept. 30, 1978, which was $60,662.50.

Applicability to funds appropriated by any Act for fiscal year ending Sept. 30, 1980, of limitation of section 304 of Pub.L. 95–391 on use of funds to pay the salary or pay of any individual in legislative, executive, or judicial branch in position equal to or above level V of the Executive Schedule, see section 101 of Pub.L. 96–86, set out as a note under section 5318 of Title 5.

1978—Salaries of judges increased to $60,700 effective on the first day of the first pay period beginning on or after Oct. 1, 1978, by Ex. Ord. No. 12087, Oct. 7, 1978, 43 F.R. 46823, formerly set out as a note under section 5332 of Title 5. Ex. Ord. No. 12087 further provided that pursuant to the Legislative Branch Appropriation Act, 1979 [Pub.L. 95–391, Title III, § 304, Sept. 30, 1978, 92 Stat. 788, set out as a note under section 5318 of Title 5], funds are not available to pay a salary at a rate which exceeds the rate in effect on Sept. 30, 1978, which was $57,500.

1977—Salaries of judges increased to $57,500 per annum, upon recommendation of the President of the United States, see note set out under section 358 of Title 2, The Congress.

1976—Salaries of judges increased to $46,800 effective on the first day of the first pay period beginning on or after Oct. 1, 1976, see Ex. Ord. No. 11941, Oct. 1, 1976, 41 F.R. 43889, formerly set out as a note under section 5332 of Title 5, Government Organization and Employees. Ex. Ord. No. 11941, further provided that pursuant to the Legislative Branch Appropriation Act, 1977, funds are not available to pay a salary at a rate which exceeds the rate in effect on Sept. 30, 1976, which was $44,600.

1969—Salaries of judges increased from $33,000 to $42,500 per annum, commencing February 14, 1969, on recommendation of the President of the United States, see note set out under section 358 of Title 2, The Congress.

1946—The salaries of the chief judge and associate judges were increased from $12,500 to $17,500 a year by Act July 31, 1946, c. 704, § 1, 60 Stat. 716.

1926—The salary of the Chief Justice, now the chief judge, was increased from $8,000 to $12,500 a year, and the salaries of the associate justices, now judges, were increased from $7,500 to $12,500 a year by Act Dec. 13, 1926, c. 6, § 1, 44 Stat. 919.

1919—The salary of the Chief Justice was increased from $6,500 to $8,000 a year, and the salaries of the associate justices were increased from $6,000 to $7,500 a year by Act Feb. 25, 1919, c. 29, § 1, 40 Stat. 1156.

1911—The salary of the chief justice was set at $6,500, and the salaries of the associate justices were set at $6,000 by the Judicial Code of 1911, Act Mar. 3, 1911, c. 231, § 1, 36 Stat. 1135.

Initial Term of Claims Court Judges; Salaries

For provisions directing that the initial terms of office of former Court of Claims commissioners who become judges of the United States Claims Court [now United States Court of Federal Claims] expire 15 years after the date of his or her employment with the United States Court of Claims or Oct. 1, 1986, whichever occurs earlier, and setting the salary of such judges, see section 167 of Pub.L. 97–164, set out as a note under section 171 of this title.

§ 173. Times and places of holding court

The principal office of the United States Court of Federal Claims shall be in the District of Columbia, but the Court of Federal Claims may hold court at such times and in such places as it may fix by rule of court. The times and places of the sessions of the Court of Federal Claims shall be prescribed with a view to securing reasonable opportunity to citizens to appear before the Court of Federal Claims with as little inconvenience and expense to citizens as is practicable.

(June 25, 1948, c. 646, 62 Stat. 898; Mar. 2, 1955, c. 9, § 1(d), 69 Stat. 10; Aug. 14, 1964, Pub.L. 88–426, Title IV, § 403(d), 78 Stat. 434; Aug. 9, 1975, Pub.L. 94–82, Title II, § 205(b)(4), 89 Stat. 422; Apr. 2, 1982, Pub.L. 97–164, Title I, § 105(a), 96 Stat. 27; Oct. 29, 1992, Pub.L. 102–572, Title IX, § 902(a), 106 Stat. 4516.)

HISTORICAL AND STATUTORY NOTES

Effective and Applicability Provisions

1992 Acts. Amendment by Title IX of Pub.L. 102–572 effective Oct. 29, 1992, see section 911 of Pub.L. 102–572, set out as a note under section 171 of Title 28, Judiciary and Judicial Procedure.

1982 Acts. Amendment by Pub.L. 97–164 effective Oct. 1, 1982, see section 402 of Pub.L. 97–164, set out as a note under section 171 of this title.

1964 Acts. Amendment by Pub.L. 88–426 effective on the first day of the first pay period which begins on or after July 1, 1964, except to the extent provided in section 501(c) of Pub.L. 88–426, see section 501 of Pub.L. 88–426.

1955 Acts. Amendment by Act Mar. 2, 1955, effective Mar. 1, 1955, see section 5 of Act Mar. 2, 1955, set out as a note under section 31 of Title 2, The Congress.

§ 174. Assignment of judges; decisions

(a) The judicial power of the United States Court of Federal Claims with respect to any action, suit, or proceeding, except congressional reference cases, shall be exercised by a single judge, who may preside alone and hold a regular or special session of court at the same time other sessions are held by other judges.

(b) All decisions of the Court of Federal Claims shall be preserved and open to inspection.

(June 25, 1948, c. 646, 62 Stat. 898; Apr. 2, 1982, Pub.L. 97–164, Title I, § 105(a), 96 Stat. 27; Oct. 29, 1992, Pub.L. 102–572, Title IX, § 902(a), 106 Stat. 4516.)

HISTORICAL AND STATUTORY NOTES

Effective and Applicability Provisions

1992 Acts. Amendment by Title IX of Pub.L. 102–572 effective Oct. 29, 1992, see section 911 of Pub.L. 102–572, set out as a note under section 171 of Title 28, Judiciary and Judicial Procedure.

1982 Acts. Amendment by Pub.L. 97–164 effective Oct. 1, 1982, see section 402 of Pub.L. 97–164, set out as a note under section 171 of this title.

§ 175. Official duty station; residence

(a) The official duty station of each judge of the United States Court of Federal Claims is the District of Columbia.

(b) After appointment and while in active service, each judge shall reside within fifty miles of the District of Columbia.

(c) Retired judges of the Court of Federal Claims are not subject to restrictions as to residence. The place where a retired judge maintains the actual abode in which such judge customarily lives shall be deemed to be the judge's official duty station for the purposes of section 456 of this title.

(Added Pub.L. 89–425, § 2, May 11, 1966, 80 Stat. 140, and amended Pub.L. 97–164, Title I, § 105(a), Apr. 2, 1982, 96 Stat. 27; Pub.L. 102–572, Title IX, § 902(a)(1), Oct. 29, 1992, 106 Stat. 4516; Pub.L. 106–518, Title III, § 307, Nov. 13, 2000, 114 Stat. 2419.)

HISTORICAL AND STATUTORY NOTES

Effective and Applicability Provisions

1992 Acts. Amendment by Title IX of Pub.L. 102–572 effective Oct. 29, 1992, see section 911 of Pub.L. 102–572, set out as a note under section 171 of Title 28, Judiciary and Judicial Procedure.

1982 Acts. Amendment by Pub.L. 97–164 effective Oct. 1, 1982, see section 402 of Pub.L. 97–164, set out as a note under section 171 of this title.

Prior Provisions

A prior section 175, Act June 25, 1948, c. 646, 62 Stat. 898, which required three judges of the Court of Claims to constitute a quorum and the concurrence of three judges for any decision, was struck out by section 2 of Pub.L. 89–425.

§ 176. Removal from office

(a) Removal of a judge of the United States Court of Federal Claims during the term for which he is appointed shall be only for incompetency, misconduct, neglect of duty, engaging in the practice of law, or physical or mental disability. Removal shall be by the United States Court of Appeals for the Federal Circuit, but removal may not occur unless a majority of all the judges of such court of appeals concur in the order of removal.

(b) Before any order of removal may be entered, a full specification of the charges shall be furnished to the judge involved, and such judge shall be accorded an opportunity to be heard on the charges.

(c) Any cause for removal of any judge of the United States Court of Federal Claims coming to the knowledge of the Director of the Administrative Office of the United States Courts shall be reported by him to the chief judge of the United States Court of

Appeals for the Federal Circuit, and a copy of the report shall at the same time be transmitted to the judge.

(Added Pub.L. 97–164, Title I, § 105(a), Apr. 2, 1982, 96 Stat. 28, and amended Pub.L. 102–572, Title IX, § 902(a)(1), Oct. 29, 1992, 106 Stat. 4516.)

HISTORICAL AND STATUTORY NOTES

Effective and Applicability Provisions

1992 Acts. Amendment by Title IX of Pub.L. 102–572 effective Oct. 29, 1992, see section 911 of Pub.L. 102–572, set out as a note under section 171 of Title 28, Judiciary and Judicial Procedure.

1982 Acts. Section effective Oct. 1, 1982, see section 402 of Pub.L. 97–164, set out as a note under section 171 of this title.

§ 177. Disbarment of removed judges

A judge of the United States Court of Federal Claims removed from office in accordance with section 176 of this title shall not be permitted at any time to practice before the Court of Federal Claims.

(Added Pub.L. 97–164, Title I, § 105(a), Apr. 2, 1982, 96 Stat. 28, and amended Pub.L. 102–572, Title IX, § 902(a), Oct. 29, 1992, 106 Stat. 4516.)

HISTORICAL AND STATUTORY NOTES

Effective and Applicability Provisions

1992 Acts. Amendment by Title IX of Pub.L. 102–572 effective Oct. 29, 1992, see section 911 of Pub.L. 102–572, set out as a note under section 171 of Title 28, Judiciary and Judicial Procedure.

1982 Acts. Section effective Oct. 1, 1982, see section 402 of Pub.L. 97–164, set out as a note under section 171 of this title.

§ 178. Retirement of judges of the Court of Federal Claims

(a) A judge of the United States Court of Federal Claims who retires from office after attaining the age and meeting the service requirements, whether continuously or otherwise, of this subsection shall, subject to subsection (f), be entitled to receive, during the remainder of the judge's lifetime, an annuity equal to the salary payable to Court of Federal Claims judges in regular active service. The age and service requirements for retirement under this subsection are as follows:

Attained Age:	Years of Service:
65	15
66	14
67	13
68	12
69	11
70	10.

(b) A judge of the Court of Federal Claims who is not reappointed following the expiration of the term of office of such judge, and who retires upon the completion of such term shall, subject to subsection (f), be entitled to receive, during the remainder of such judge's lifetime, an annuity equal to the salary payable to Court of Federal Claims judges in regular active service, if—

(1) such judge has served at least 1 full term as judge of the Court of Federal Claims, and

(2) not earlier than 9 months before the date on which the term of office of such judge expired, and not later than 6 months before such date, such judge advised the President in writing that such judge was willing to accept reappointment as a judge of the Court of Federal Claims.

(c) A judge of the Court of Federal Claims who has served at least 5 years, whether continuously or otherwise, as such a judge, and who retires or is removed from office upon the sole ground of mental or physical disability shall, subject to subsection (f), be entitled to receive, during the remainder of the judge's lifetime—

(1) an annuity equal to 50 percent of the salary payable to Court of Federal Claims judges in regular active service, if before retirement such judge served less than 10 years, or

(2) an annuity equal to the salary payable to Court of Federal Claims judges in regular active service, if before retirement such judge served at least 10 years.

(d) A judge who retires under subsection (a) or (b) may, at or after such retirement, be called upon by the chief judge of the Court of Federal Claims to perform such judicial duties with the Court of Federal Claims as may be requested of the retired judge for any period or periods specified by the chief judge, except that in the case of any such judge—

(1) the aggregate of such periods in any one calendar year shall not (without his or her consent) exceed 90 calendar days; and

(2) he or she shall be relieved of performing such duties during any period in which illness or disability precludes the performance of such duties.

Any act, or failure to act, by an individual performing judicial duties pursuant to this subsection shall have the same force and effect as if it were the act (or failure to act) of a Court of Federal Claims judge in regular active service. Any individual performing judicial duties pursuant to this subsection shall receive the allowances for official travel and other expenses of a judge in regular active service.

(e)(1) Any judge who retires under the provisions of subsection (a) or (b) of this section shall be designated "senior judge".

(2) Any judge who retires under this section shall not be counted as a judge of the Court of Federal Claims for purposes of the number of judgeships authorized by section 171 of this title.

(f)(1) A judge shall be entitled to an annuity under this section if the judge elects an annuity under this section by notifying the Director of the Administrative Office of the United States Courts in writing. Such an election—

(A) may be made only while an individual is a judge of the Court of Federal Claims (except that in the case of an individual who fails to be reappointed as judge at the expiration of a term of office, such election may be made at any time before the day after the day on which his or her successor takes office); and

(B) once made, shall, subject to subsection (k), be irrevocable.

(2) A judge who elects to receive an annuity under this section shall not be entitled to receive—

(A) any annuity to which such judge would otherwise have been entitled under subchapter III of chapter 83, or under chapter 84 (except for subchapters III and VII), of title 5, for service performed as a judge or otherwise;

(B) an annuity or salary in senior status or retirement under section 371 or 372 of this title;

(C) retired pay under section 7447 of the Internal Revenue Code of 1986; or

(D) retired pay under section 7296 of title 38.

(g) For purposes of calculating the years of service of an individual under subsections (a) and (c), only those years of service as a judge of the Court of Federal Claims or a commissioner of the United States Court of Claims shall be credited, and that portion of the aggregate number of years of such service that is a fractional part of 1 year shall not be credited if it is less than 6 months, and shall be credited if it is 6 months or more.

(h) An annuity under this section shall be payable at the times and in the same manner as the salary of a Court of Federal Claims judge in regular active service. Such annuity shall begin to accrue on the day following the day on which the annuitant's salary as a judge in regular active service ceases to accrue.

(i)(1) Payments under this section which would otherwise be made to a judge of the Court of Federal Claims based upon his or her service shall be paid (in whole or in part) by the Director of the Administrative Office of the United States Courts to another person if and to the extent expressly provided for in the terms of any court decree of divorce, annulment, or legal separation, or the terms of any court order or court-approved property settlement agreement incident to any court decree of divorce, annulment, or legal separation. Any payment under this paragraph to a person bars recovery by any other person.

(2) Paragraph (1) shall apply only to payments made by the Director of the Administrative Office of the United States Courts after the date of receipt by the Director of written notice of such decree, order, or agreement, and such additional information as the Director may prescribe.

(3) As used in this subsection, the term "court" means any court of any State, the District of Columbia, the Commonwealth of Puerto Rico, Guam, the Commonwealth of the Northern Mariana Islands, or the Virgin Islands, and any Indian tribal court or court of Indian offense.

(j)(1) Subject to paragraph (4), any judge of the Court of Federal Claims who retires under this section and who thereafter in the practice of law represents (or supervises or directs the representation of) a client in making any civil claim against the United States or any agency thereof shall forfeit all rights to an annuity under this section for all periods beginning on or after the first day on which he engages in any such activity.

(2) Subject to paragraph (4), if a judge of the Court of Federal Claims who retires under this section fails during any calendar year to perform judicial duties required of such judge by subsection (d), such judge shall forfeit all rights to an annuity under this section for the 1-year period which begins on the first day on which he or she so fails to perform such duties.

(3) If a judge of the Court of Federal Claims who retires under this section accepts compensation for civil office or employment under the Government of the United States (other than for the performance of judicial duties under subsection (d)), such judge shall forfeit all rights to an annuity under this section for the period for which such compensation is received.

(4)(A) If a judge makes an election under this paragraph—

(i) paragraphs (1) and (2) (and subsection (d)) shall not apply to such judge beginning on the date such election takes effect, and

(ii) the annuity payable under this section to such judge, for periods beginning on or after the date such election takes effect, shall be equal to the annuity to which such judge is entitled on the day before such effective date.

(B) An election under subparagraph (A)—

(i) may be made by a judge only if such judge meets the age and service requirements for retirement under subsection (a),

(ii) may be made only during the period during which such judge may make an election to receive an annuity under this section or while the judge is receiving an annuity under this section, and

(iii) shall be filed with the Director of the Administrative Office of the United States Courts.

Such an election, once it takes effect, shall be irrevocable.

(C) Any election under this paragraph shall take effect on the first day of the first month following the month in which the election is made.

(k)(1) Notwithstanding subsection (f)(1)(B), an individual who has filed an election under subsection (f) to receive an annuity may revoke such election at any time before the first day on which such annuity would (but for such revocation) begin to accrue with respect to such individual.

(2) Any revocation under this subsection shall be made by filing a notice thereof in writing with the Director of[1] Administrative Office of the United States Courts.

(3) In the case of any revocation under this subsection—

(A) for purposes of this section, the individual shall be treated as not having filed an election under subsection (f) to receive an annuity,

(B) for purposes of section 376 of this title—

(i) the individual shall be treated as not having filed an election under section 376(a)(1), and

(ii) section 376(g) shall not apply, and the amount credited to such individual's account (together with interest at 3 percent per annum, compounded on December 31 of each year to the date on which the revocation is filed) shall be returned to such individual,

(C) no credit shall be allowed for any service as a judge of the Court of Federal Claims or as a commissioner of the United States Court of Claims unless with respect to such service either there has been deducted and withheld the amount required by chapter 83 or 84 (as the case may be) of title 5 or there has been deposited in the Civil Service Retirement and Disability Fund an amount equal to the amount so required, with interest,

(D) the Court of Federal Claims shall deposit in the Civil Service Retirement and Disability Fund an amount equal to the additional amount it would have contributed to such Fund but for the election under subsection (f), and

(E) if subparagraph (D) is complied with, service on the Court of Federal Claims or as a commissioner of the United States Court of Claims shall be treated as service with respect to which deductions and contributions had been made during the period of service.

(*l*)(1) There is established in the Treasury a fund which shall be known as the "Court of Federal Claims Judges Retirement Fund". The Fund is appropriated for the payment of annuities and other payments under this section.

(2) The Secretary of the Treasury shall invest, in interest bearing securities of the United States, such currently available portions of the Court of Federal Claims Judges Retirement Fund as are not immediately required for payments from the Fund. The income derived from these investments constitutes a part of the Fund.

(3)(A) There are authorized to be appropriated to the Court of Federal Claims Judges Retirement Fund amounts required to reduce to zero the unfunded liability of the Fund.

(B) For purposes of subparagraph (A), the term "unfunded liability" means the estimated excess, determined on an annual basis in accordance with the provisions of section 9503 of title 31, of the present value of all benefits payable from the Court of Federal Claims Judges Retirement Fund, over the balance in the Fund as of the date the unfunded liability is determined. In making any determination under this subparagraph, the Comptroller General shall use the applicable information contained in the reports filed pursuant to section 9503 of title 31, with respect to the retirement annuities provided for in this section.

(C) There are authorized to be appropriated such sums as may be necessary to carry out this paragraph.

(Added Pub.L. 101–650, Title III, § 306(a)(1), Dec. 1, 1990, 104 Stat. 5105, and amended Pub.L. 102–40, Title IV, § 402(d)(2), May 7, 1991, 105 Stat. 239; Pub.L. 102–198, § 7(a), Dec. 9, 1991, 105 Stat. 1624; Pub.L. 102–572, Title IX, § 902(a), Oct. 29, 1992, 106 Stat. 4516.)

[1] So in original. Probably should be "of the".

HISTORICAL AND STATUTORY NOTES

References in Text

Section 7447 of the Internal Revenue Code of 1986, referred to in subsec. (f)(2)(C), is classified to section 7447 of Title 26, Internal Revenue Code.

Effective and Applicability Provisions

1992 Acts. Amendment by Title IX of Pub.L. 102–572 effective Oct. 29, 1992, see section 911 of Pub.L. 102–572, set out as a note under section 171 of Title 28, Judiciary and Judicial Procedure.

1990 Acts. Section applicable to judges of, and senior judges in active service with, the United States Court of Federal Claims on or after Dec. 1, 1990, see section 306(f) of Pub.L. 101–650, set out as a note under section 8331 of Title 5, Government Organization and Employees.

§ 179. Personnel application and insurance programs

(a) For purposes of construing and applying title 5, a judge of the United States Court of Federal Claims shall be deemed to be an "officer" under section 2104(a) of such title.

(b)(1)(A) For purposes of construing and applying chapter 89 of title 5, a judge of the United States Court of Federal Claims who—

(i) is retired under subsection (b) of section 178 of this title, and

(ii) at the time of becoming such a retired judge—

(I) was enrolled in a health benefits plan under chapter 89 of title 5, but

(II) did not satisfy the requirements of section 8905(b)(1) of title 5 (relating to eligibility to continue enrollment as an annuitant),

shall be deemed to be an annuitant meeting the requirements of section 8905(b)(1) of title 5, in accordance with the succeeding provisions of this paragraph, if the judge gives timely written notification to the chief judge of the court that the judge is willing to be called upon to perform judicial duties under section 178(d) of this title during the period of continued eligibility for enrollment, as described in subparagraph (B)(ii) or (C)(ii) (whichever applies).

(B) Except as provided in subparagraph (C)—

(i) in order to be eligible for continued enrollment under this paragraph, notification under subparagraph (A) shall be made before the first day of the open enrollment period preceding the calendar year referred to in clause (ii)(II); and

(ii) if such notification is timely made, the retired judge shall be eligible for continued enrollment under this paragraph for the period—

(I) beginning on the date on which eligibility would otherwise cease, and

(II) ending on the last day of the calendar year next beginning after the end of the open enrollment period referred to in clause (i).

(C) For purposes of applying this paragraph for the first time in the case of any particular judge—

(i) subparagraph (B)(i) shall be applied by substituting "the expiration of the term of office of the judge" for the matter following "before"; and

(ii)(I) if the term of office of such judge expires before the first day of the open enrollment period referred to in subparagraph (B)(i), the period of continued eligibility for enrollment shall be as described in subparagraph (B)(ii); but

(II) if the term of office of such judge expires on or after the first day of the open enrollment period referred to in subparagraph (B)(i), the period of continued eligibility shall not end until the last day of the calendar year next beginning after the end of the next full open enrollment period beginning after the date on which the term expires.

(2) In the event that a retired judge remains enrolled under chapter 89 of title 5 for a period of 5 consecutive years by virtue of paragraph (1) (taking into account only periods of coverage as an active judge immediately before retirement and as a retired judge pursuant to paragraph (1)), then, effective as of the day following the last day of that 5-year period—

(A) the provisions of chapter 89 of title 5 shall be applied as if such judge had satisfied the requirements of section 8905(b)(1) [1] on the last day of such period; and

(B) the provisions of paragraph (1) shall cease to apply.

(3) For purposes of this subsection, the term "open enrollment period" refers to a period described in section 8905(g)(1) of title 5.

(c) For purposes of construing and applying chapter 87 of title 5, including any adjustment of insurance rates by regulation or otherwise, a judge of the United States Court of Federal Claims in regular active service or who is retired under section 178 of this title shall be deemed to be a judge of the United States described under section 8701(a)(5) of title 5.

(Added Pub.L. 106–518, Title III, § 309(a), Nov. 13, 2000, 114 Stat. 2419.)

[1] So in original. Probably should be followed by "of title 5".

HISTORICAL AND STATUTORY NOTES

References in Text

Chapter 87 of title 5, referred to in subsec. (c), is 5 U.S.C.A. § 8901 et seq.

[§ 180. Repealed. Pub.L. 106–398, § 1 [Div. A, Title VI, § 654(b)(1)], Oct. 30, 2000, 114 Stat. 1654, 1654A–165.]

HISTORICAL AND STATUTORY NOTES

Section, Pub.L. 102–572, Title IX, § 903(a), Oct. 29, 1992, 106 Stat. 4517, provided for military retirement pay for retired judges of the United States Court of Federal Claims

Effective and Applicability Provisions

2000 Acts. Pub.L. 106–398, § 1 [Div. A, Title VI, § 654(c)], Oct. 30, 2000, 114 Stat. 1654, 1654A–165, provided that: "The amendments made by this section [repealing this section and amending section 371 of this title] shall take effect as of October 1, 1999."

[CHAPTER 9—REPEALED]

[§§ 211 to 216. Repealed. Pub.L. 97–164, Title I, § 106, Apr. 2, 1982, 96 Stat. 28]

HISTORICAL AND STATUTORY NOTES

Section 211, Acts June 25, 1948, c. 646, 62 Stat. 899; Aug. 25, 1958, Pub.L. 85–755, § 1, 72 Stat. 848, provided for the creation of the United States Court of Customs and Patent Appeals under article III of the United States Constitution and for the appointment of a chief judge and four associate judges for that court.

Section 212, Act June 25, 1948, c. 646, 62 Stat. 899, provided for the order of precedence of the chief judge and associate judges of the Court of Customs and Patent Appeals.

Section 213, Acts June 25, 1948, c. 646, 62 Stat. 899; Mar. 2, 1955, c. 9, § 1(e), 69 Stat. 10; Aug. 14, 1964, Pub.L. 88–426, Title IV, § 403(e), 78 Stat. 434; Aug. 9, 1975, Pub.L. 94–82, Title II, § 205(b)(5), 89 Stat. 422, provided for the tenure and salaries of the judges of the Court of Customs and Patent Appeals.

Section 214, Act June 25, 1948, c. 646, 62 Stat. 899, authorized the Court of Customs and Patent Appeals to hold court at such times and places as it might fix by rule.

Section 215, Act June 25, 1948, c. 646, 62 Stat. 899, provided that three judges of the Court of Customs and Patent Appeals constituted a quorum and that the concurrence of three judges was necessary to any decision.

Section 216, Act June 25, 1948, c. 646, 62 Stat. 899, provided for the filing of written opinions by the Court of Customs and Patent Appeals on appeals from decisions of the Patent Office and the recording of those opinions in the Patent Office.

Effective Date of Repeal

Repeal effective Oct. 1, 1982, see section 402 of Pub.L. 97–164, set out as a note under section 171 of this title.

Transfer of Matters and Petitions Pending in United States Court of Customs and Patent Appeals on October 1, 1982

For provisions that any matter pending before the United States Court of Customs and Patent Appeals on Oct. 1, 1982, and any petition for rehearing, reconsideration, alteration, modification, or other change in any decision of the United States Court of Customs and Patent Appeals rendered prior to Oct. 1, 1982, that has not been determined on that date or that is filed after that date, be determined by the United States Court of Appeals for the Federal Circuit, see section 403(b), (c) of Pub.L. 97–164, set out as a note under section 171 of this title.

CHAPTER 11—COURT OF INTERNATIONAL TRADE

Sec.
251. Appointment and number of judges; offices.
252. Tenure and salaries of judges.
253. Duties of chief judge.
254. Single-judge trial.[1]
255. Three-judge trials.
256. Trials at ports other than New York.
257. Publication of decisions.
258. Chief judges; precedence of judges.

[1] So in original. Does not conform to section catchline.

HISTORICAL AND STATUTORY NOTES

History of Court

The United States Customs Court [now Court of International Trade] as "constituted on June 17, 1930", consisted of nine members as provided by Act Sept. 21, 1922, c. 356, Title IV, § 518, 42 Stat. 972, which established the Board of General Appraisers, designated the "United States Customs Court" by Act May 28, 1926, c. 411, § 1, 44 Stat. 669.

Provisions similar to these were contained in Act Sept. 21, 1922, c. 356, Title IV, § 518, 42 Stat. 972. That section was superseded by section 518 of the Tariff Act of 1930, and was repealed by section 651(a)(1) of said 1930 Act.

The sentence in the former first paragraph as to sitting in a case previously participated in, is from Act Aug. 5, 1909, c. 6, § 28, 36 Stat. 98, which combined and amended Customs Administrative Act June 10, 1890, c. 407, § 12, 26 Stat. 136, and section 31, as added by Act May 27, 1908, c. 205, 35 Stat. 406. Section 12 of the Act of 1890 was expressly saved from repeal by Act Sept. 21, 1922, c. 356, Title IV, § 643, 42 Stat. 989, and prior acts, but its provisions, other than the sentence above mentioned, were omitted from the Code.

Provisions for the review of decisions of Boards of General Appraisers by the Circuit Courts, made by section 15 of the Customs Administrative Act of June 10, 1890, c. 407, were superseded by provisions for such review by the Court of Customs Appeals created by section 29 added to that act by the Payne-Aldrich Tariff Act of Aug. 5, 1909, c. 6. The provisions of said new section 29 were incorporated in and superseded by chapter 8 of the Judicial Code of March 3, 1911, incorporated into the Code as former chapter 8 of Title 28, Judicial Code and Judiciary.

R.S. § 2608 provided for the appointment of four appraisers of merchandise, to be employed in visiting ports of entry under the direction of the Secretary of the Treasury, and to assist in the appraisement of merchandise as might be deemed necessary by the Secretary to protect and insure uniformity in the collection of the revenue from customs. It was repealed by Act June 10, 1890, c. 407, § 29, 26 Stat. 141.

R.S. § 2609 provided for the appointment of merchant appraisers. R.S. § 2610 made every merchant refusing to serve as such appraiser liable to a penalty. Both sections were superseded by the provisions relating to appraisers and appraisements of the Customs Administrative Act of June 10, 1890, c. 407, 26 Stat. 131, and subsequent acts, and were repealed by Act Sept. 21, 1922, c. 356, Title IV, § 642, 42 Stat. 989.

R.S. § 2945, which contained a provision similar to that of R.S. § 2610, was repealed, without mention of section 2610, by said Customs Administrative Act of June 10, 1890, c. 407,

§ 29, 26 Stat. 141, and was again repealed by section 642 of Act Sept. 21, 1922.

R.S. § 2725, which prescribed the compensation of merchant appraisers, and section 2726, which prescribed the salary of the general appraiser at New York, were superseded by the provisions relating to general appraisers and appraisers made by the Customs Administrative Act of June 10, 1890, c. 407, §§ 12, 13, 26 Stat. 136, as amended by the Payne-Aldrich Act of Aug. 5, 1909, c. 6, § 28.

R.S. § 2727, fixed the salary of the four general appraisers at the sum of $2,500 a year each, and their actual traveling expenses. It was repealed by Act Feb. 27, 1877, c. 69, 19 Stat. 246.

§ 251. Appointment and number of judges; offices

(a) The President shall appoint, by and with the advice and consent of the Senate, nine judges who shall constitute a court of record to be known as the United States Court of International Trade. Not more than five of such judges shall be from the same political party. The court is a court established under article III of the Constitution of the United States.

(b) The offices of the Court of International Trade shall be located in New York, New York.

(June 25, 1948, c. 646, 62 Stat. 899; July 14, 1956, c. 589, § 1, 70 Stat. 532; Oct. 10, 1980, Pub.L. 96–417, Title I, § 101, 94 Stat. 1727; Oct. 19, 1996, Pub.L. 104–317, Title V, § 501(b)(1), 110 Stat. 3856.)

HISTORICAL AND STATUTORY NOTES

Effective and Applicability Provisions

1980 Acts. Section 701 of Pub.L. 96–417, as amended Pub.L. 96–542, § 1, Dec. 17, 1980, 94 Stat. 3209, provided that:

"**(a)** Except as otherwise provided in this section, the provisions of and amendments made by this Act [see section 1 of Pub.L. 96–417, set out as a Short Title of 1980 Amendments note under section 1 of this title] shall take effect on November 1, 1980 and shall apply with respect to civil actions pending on or commenced on or after such date.

"**(b)(1)** The following sections of title 28, United States Code [this title], shall apply with respect to civil actions commenced on or after the effective date of this Act [Nov. 1, 1980]:

"**(A)** Sections 1581(d), 1581(g), 1581(h), 1581(i), and 1583, as amended by section 201 of this Act.

"**(B)** Sections 2631(d), 2631(g), 2631(h), 2631(i), 2631(j), 2632(a), 2635, 2636, 2637(c), 2639(b), 2640(a)(5), 2640(c), 2640(d), 2643(a), 2643(c)(2), 2643(c)(4), and 2644, as amended by section 301 of this Act.

"**(C)** Section 1876, as added by section 302(a) of this Act.

"**(D)** Sections 2601 and 2602, as amended by section 403 of this Act.

"**(E)** Section 1919, as amended by section 510 of this Act.

"**(F)** Section 1963A, as added by, section 511(a) of this Act.

"**(2)** Sections 337(c) and 641(b) of the Tariff Act of 1930 [sections 1337(c) and 1641(b) of Title 19, Customs Duties], as amended by sections 604 and 611 of this Act, shall apply with respect to civil actions commenced on or after the effective date of this Act [Nov. 1, 1980].

"**(3)** Section 284 of the Trade Act of 1974 [section 2395 of Title 19], as added by section 613 of this Act, shall apply with respect to civil actions commenced on or after the effective date of this Act [Nov. 1, 1980].

"**(c)(1)** The following sections of title 28, United States Code [this title], shall apply with respect to civil actions commenced on or after the 90th day after the effective date of this Act [Nov. 1, 1980]:

"**(A)** Sections 1582, 2639(a)(2), and 2640(a)(6), as amended by sections 201 and 301 of this Act.

"**(B)** Sections 1352, 1355, and 1356, as amended by sections 506, 507, and 508 of this Act.

"**(2)** Section 592(e) of the Tariff Act of 1930 [section 1592(e) of Title 19], as amended by section 609 of this Act, shall apply with respect to civil actions commenced on or after 90th [sic] day after the effective date of this Act [Nov. 1, 1980]."

[Amendment of section 701 of Pub.L. 96–417 by section 1 of Pub.L. 96–542 effective as of Nov. 1, 1980, see section 3 of Pub.L. 96–542, set out as a note under section 1516a of Title 19, Customs Duties.]

Continuation of Organization of Court

Section 2(b) of Act June 25, 1948, provided in part that the provisions of this title as set out in section 1 of Act June 25, 1948, with respect to the organization of the court, shall be construed as continuations of existing law, and the tenure of the judges, officers, and employees, in office on Sept. 1, 1948, shall not be affected by its enactment, but each of them shall continue to serve in the same capacity under the appropriate provisions of this title, pursuant to his prior appointment.

Effect on Customs Court Judges

Section 703 of Pub.L. 96–417 provided that:

"**(a)** Except as provided in subsection (b) of this section, the amendments made by title I of this Act [amending this section and section 293(b), (d) of this title] shall not affect the status of any individual serving as judge or chief judge of the Customs Court on the date of enactment of this Act [Oct. 10, 1980].

"**(b)** The requirement that a person may not continue to serve as chief judge of the Court of International Trade after having reached the age of seventy years, as set forth in the amendment made by section 101 of this Act [amending this section], shall apply to any individual serving as chief judge on or after the date of enactment of this Act [Oct. 10, 1980]."

Effect on Pending Cases

Section 704 of Pub.L. 96–417 provided that: "Nothing in this Act [see section 1 of Pub.L. 96–417, set out as a Short Title of 1980 Amendments note under section 1 of this title] shall cause the dismissal of any action commenced prior to the date of enactment of this Act [Oct. 10, 1980] under jurisdictional statutes relating to the Customs Court or the Court of Customs and Patent Appeals as in effect immediately prior to such date of enactment [Oct. 10, 1980]."

Limitation or Alteration of Jurisdiction

Section 4 of Act July 14, 1956, provided that: "Nothing contained in this Act [amending this section and sections 292(f), 293, and 295 of this title] shall be construed in any way to limit or alter the jurisdiction heretofore conferred upon the United States Customs Court by any provision of law."

References to Certain Courts Deemed References to the United States Court of International Trade

Section 702 of Pub.L. 96–417 provided that: "Any reference in any statute or regulation of the United States to the United States Customs Court, the U.S. Customs Court, or the Customs Court shall be deemed to be a reference to the United States Court of International Trade."

Tennessee Valley Authority Legal Representation

Section 705 of Pub.L. 96–417 provided that: "Nothing in this Act [see section 1 of Pub.L. 96–417, set out as a Short Title of 1980 Amendments note under section 1 of this title] affects the authority of the Tennessee Valley Authority under the Tennessee Valley Authority Act of 1933 [section 831 et seq. of Title 16, Conservation] to represent itself by attorneys of its choosing."

§ 252. Tenure and salaries of judges

Judges of the Court of International Trade shall hold office during good behavior. Each shall receive a salary at an annual rate determined under section 225 of the Federal Salary Act of 1967 (2 U.S.C. 351–361), as adjusted by section 461 of this title.

(June 25, 1948, c. 646, 62 Stat. 899; Mar. 2, 1955, c. 9, § 1(f), 69 Stat. 10; Aug. 14, 1964, Pub.L. 88–426, Title IV, § 403(f), 78 Stat. 434; Aug. 9, 1975, Pub.L. 94–82, Title II, § 205(b)(6), 89 Stat. 423; Oct. 10, 1980, Pub.L. 96–417, Title V, § 502, 94 Stat. 1742.)

HISTORICAL AND STATUTORY NOTES

References in Text

Section 225 of the Federal Salary Act of 1967, referred to in text, is section 225 of Pub.L. 90–206, Dec. 16, 1967, 81 Stat. 642, as amended, which is classified to chapter 11 (section 351 et seq.) of Title 2, The Congress.

Effective and Applicability Provisions

1980 Acts. Amendment by Pub.L. 96–417 effective on Nov. 1, 1980, and applicable with respect to civil actions pending on or commenced on or after such date, see section 701(a) of Pub.L. 96–417, as amended, set out as a note under section 251 of this title.

1964 Acts. Amendment by Pub.L. 88–426 effective on the first day of the first pay period which begins on or after July 1, 1964, except to the extent provided in section 501(c) of Pub.L. 88–426, see section 501 of Pub.L. 88–426.

1955 Acts. Amendment by Act Mar. 2, 1955, effective Mar. 1, 1955, see section 5 of Act Mar. 2, 1955, set out as a note under section 31 of Title 2, The Congress.

Salary Increases

For prior year salary increases per the recommendation of the President, see Prior Salary Recommendations notes under 2 U.S.C.A. § 358.

For miscellaneous provisions dealing with adjustments of pay and limitations on use of funds to pay salaries in prior years, see notes under 5 U.S.C.A. § 5318.

§ 253. Duties of chief judge

(a) The chief judge of the Court of International Trade, with the approval of the court, shall supervise the fiscal affairs and clerical force of the court;[1]

(b) The chief judge shall promulgate dockets.

(c) The chief judge, under rules of the court, may designate any judge or judges of the court to try any case and, when the circumstances so warrant, reassign the case to another judge or judges.

(June 25, 1948, c. 646, 62 Stat. 900; Sept. 9, 1959, Pub.L. 86–243, § 3, 73 Stat. 474; June 2, 1970, Pub.L. 91–271, Title I, § 105, 84 Stat. 276; Oct. 10, 1980, Pub.L. 96–417, Title V, § 501(3), 94 Stat. 1742; Oct. 19, 1996, Pub.L. 104–317, Title V, § 501(b)(2), 110 Stat. 3856.)

[1] So in original. The semicolon probably should be a period.

HISTORICAL AND STATUTORY NOTES

Effective and Applicability Provisions

1980 Acts. Amendment by Pub.L. 96–417 effective on Nov. 1, 1980, and applicable with respect to civil actions pending on or commenced on or after such date, see section 701(a) of Pub.L. 96–417, as amended, set out as a note under section 251 of this title.

1970 Acts. Amendment by Pub.L. 91–271 effective on Oct. 1, 1970, see section 122 of Pub.L. 91–271, set out as a note under section 256 of this title.

Savings Provisions

Amendment by Pub.L. 86–243 not to deprive Customs Court [now Court of International Trade] officers or employees of any rights, privileges, or civil service status, see section 4 of Pub.L. 86–243, set out as a note under section 871 of this title.

§ 254. Single-judge trials

Except as otherwise provided in section 255 of this title, the judicial power of the Court of International Trade with respect to any action, suit or proceeding shall be exercised by a single judge, who may preside alone and hold a regular or special session of court at the same time other sessions are held by other judges.

(June 25, 1948, c. 646, 62 Stat. 900; May 24, 1949, c. 139, § 66, 63 Stat. 99; June 2, 1970, Pub.L. 91–271, Title I, § 106, 84 Stat. 277; Oct. 10, 1980, Pub.L. 96–417, Title V, § 501(4), 94 Stat. 1742.)

HISTORICAL AND STATUTORY NOTES

Effective and Applicability Provisions

1980 Acts. Amendment by Pub.L. 96–417 effective on Nov. 1, 1980, and applicable with respect to civil actions pending on or commenced on or after such date, see section 701(a) of Pub.L. 96–417, as amended, set out as a note under section 251 of this title.

1970 Acts. Amendment by Pub.L. 91–271 effective on Oct. 1, 1970, see section 122 of Pub.L. 91–271, set out as a note under section 256 of this title.

Transfer of Functions

All offices of collector of customs, comptroller of customs, surveyor of customs, and appraiser of merchandise in the Bureau of Customs of the Department of the Treasury to which appointments were required to be made by the President with the advice and consent of the Senate were ordered abolished, with such offices to be terminated not later than December 31, 1966, by Reorg. Plan No. 1 of 1965, eff. May 25, 1965, 30 F.R. 7035, 79 Stat. 1317, set out in Appendix 1 to Title 5, Government Organization and Employees. All functions of the offices eliminated were already vested in the Secretary of the Treasury by Reorg. Plan No. 26 of 1950, eff. July 31, 1950, 15 F.R. 4935, 64 Stat. 1280, set out in Appendix 1 to Title 5.

Prior Provisions

Provisions similar to those relating to the assignment of judges to hear and determine cases, and provisions similar to those authorizing the chief judge to designate judges to hear and determine cases within the jurisdiction of the United States, formerly contained in this section, are now covered by sections 255 and 256(a) of this title, respectively.

§ 255. Three-judge trials

(a) Upon application of any party to a civil action, or upon his own initiative, the chief judge of the Court of International Trade shall designate any three judges of the court to hear and determine any civil action which the chief judge finds: (1) raises an issue of the constitutionality of an Act of Congress, a proclamation of the President or an Executive order; or (2) has broad or significant implications in the administration or interpretation of the customs laws.

(b) A majority of the three judges designated may hear and determine the civil action and all questions pending therein.

(Added Pub.L. 91–271, Title I, § 108, June 2, 1970, 84 Stat. 277, and amended Pub.L. 96–417, Title V, § 501(5), Oct. 10, 1980, 94 Stat. 1742.)

HISTORICAL AND STATUTORY NOTES

Effective and Applicability Provisions

1980 Acts. Amendment by Pub.L. 96–417 effective on Nov. 1, 1980, and applicable with respect to civil actions pending on or commenced on or after such date, see section 701(a) of Pub.L. 96–417, as amended, set out as a note under section 251 of this title.

1970 Acts. Section effective on Oct. 1, 1970, see section 122 of Pub.L. 91–271, set out as a note under section 256 of this title.

Prior Provisions

A prior section 255, relating to the publication of decisions of the Customs Court, formerly contained in this section, was renumbered section 257 of this title.

§ 256. Trials at ports other than New York

(a) The chief judge may designate any judge or judges of the court to proceed, together with necessary assistants, to any port or to any place within the jurisdiction of the United States to preside at a trial or hearing at the port or place.

(b) Upon application of a party or upon his own initiative, and upon a showing that the interests of economy, efficiency, and justice will be served, the chief judge may issue an order authorizing a judge of the court to preside in an evidentiary hearing in a foreign country whose laws do not prohibit such a hearing: *Provided, however,* That an interlocutory appeal may be taken from such an order pursuant to the provisions of section 1292(d)(1) of this title, and the United States Court of Appeals for the Federal Circuit may, in its discretion, consider the appeal.

(Added Pub.L. 91–271, Title I, § 109, June 2, 1970, 84 Stat. 277, and amended Pub.L. 97–164, Title I, § 107, Apr. 2, 1982, 96 Stat. 28.)

HISTORICAL AND STATUTORY NOTES

Effective and Applicability Provisions

1982 Acts. Amendment by Pub.L. 97–164 effective Oct. 1, 1982, see section 402 of Pub.L. 97–164, set out as a note under section 171 of this title.

1970 Acts. Section 122 of Title I of Pub.L. 91–271 provided that:

"**(a)** This title [see Short Title of 1970 Amendments note set out under section 1 of this title] shall become effective on October 1, 1970, and shall thereafter apply to all actions and proceedings in the Customs Court and the Court of Customs and Patent Appeals except those involving merchandise entered before the effective date for which trial has commenced by such effective date.

"**(b)** An appeal for reappraisement timely filed with the Bureau of Customs before the effective date, but as to which trial has not commenced by such date, shall be deemed to have had a summons timely and properly filed under this title. When the judgment or order of the United States Customs Court has become final in this appeal, the papers shall be returned to the appropriate customs officer to decide any remaining matters relating to the entry in accordance with section 500 of the Tariff Act of 1930, as amended [section 1500 of Title 19, Customs Duties]. A protest or summons filed after final decision on an appeal for reappraisement shall not include issues which were raised or could have been raised on the appeal for reappraisement.

"**(c)** A protest timely filed with the Bureau of Customs before the effective date of enactment of this Act [June 2, 1970], which is disallowed before that date, and as to which trial has not commenced by such date, shall be deemed to have had a summons timely and properly filed under this title.

"**(d)** All other provisions of this Act [see Short Title notes set out under section 1 of this title and section 1500 of Title 19] shall apply to appeals and disallowed protests deemed to have had summonses timely and properly filed under this section."

§ 257. Publication of decisions

All decisions of the Court of International Trade shall be preserved and open to inspection. The court shall forward copies of each decision to the Secretary of the Treasury or his designee and to the appropriate customs officer for the district in which the case arose. The Secretary shall publish weekly such decisions as he or the court may designate and abstracts of all other decisions.

(June 25, 1948, c. 646, 62 Stat. 900, § 255; renumbered § 257, and amended June 2, 1970, Pub.L. 91–271, Title I, § 107, 84 Stat. 277; Oct. 10, 1980, Pub.L. 96–417, Title V, § 501(6), 94 Stat. 1742.)

HISTORICAL AND STATUTORY NOTES

Effective and Applicability Provisions

1980 Acts. Amendment by Pub.L. 96–417 effective on Nov. 1, 1980, and applicable with respect to civil actions pending on or commenced on or after such date, see section 701(a) of Pub.L. 96–417, as amended, set out as a note under section 251 of this title.

1970 Acts. Amendment by Pub.L. 91–271 effective on Oct. 1, 1970, see section 122 of Pub.L. 91–271, set out as a note under section 256 of this title.

Transfer of Functions

All offices of collector of customs, comptroller of customs, surveyor of customs, and appraiser of merchandise in the Bureau of Customs of the Department of the Treasury to which appointments were required to be made by the President with the advice and consent of the Senate were ordered abolished, with such offices to be terminated not later than December 31, 1966, by Reorg. Plan No. 1 of 1965, eff. May 25, 1965, 30 F.R. 7035, 79 Stat. 1317, set out in the Appendix to Title 5, Government Organization and Employees. All functions of the offices eliminated were already vested in the Secretary of the Treasury by Reorg. Plan No. 26 of 1950, eff. July 31, 1950, 15 F.R. 4935, 64 Stat. 1280, set out in the Appendix to Title 5.

§ 258. Chief judges; precedence of judges

(a)(1) The chief judge of the Court of International Trade shall be the judge of the court in regular active service who is senior in commission of those judges who—

(A) are 64 years of age or under;

(B) have served for 1 year or more as a judge of the court; and

(C) have not served previously as chief judge.

(2)(A) In any case in which no judge of the court meets the qualifications under paragraph (1), the youngest judge in regular active service who is 65 years of age or over and who has served as a judge of the court for 1 year or more shall act as the chief judge.

(B) In any case under subparagraph (A) in which there is no judge of the court in regular active service who has served as a judge of the court for 1 year or more, the judge of the court in regular active service who is senior in commission and who has not served previously as chief judge shall act as the chief judge.

(3)(A) Except as provided under subparagraph (C), the chief judge serving under paragraph (1) shall serve for a term of 7 years and shall serve after expiration of such term until another judge is eligible under paragraph (1) to serve as chief judge.

(B) Except as provided under subparagraph (C), a judge of the court acting as chief judge under subparagraph (A) or (B) of paragraph (2) shall serve until a judge meets the qualifications under paragraph (1).

(C) No judge of the court may serve or act as chief judge of the court after attaining the age of 70 years unless no other judge is qualified to serve as chief judge under paragraph (1) or is qualified to act as chief judge under paragraph (2).

(b) The chief judge shall have precedence and preside at any session of the court which such judge attends. Other judges of the court shall have precedence and preside according to the seniority of their commissions. Judges whose commissions bear the same date shall have precedence according to seniority in age.

(c) If the chief judge desires to be relieved of the duties as chief judge while retaining active status as a judge of the court, the chief judge may so certify to the Chief Justice of the United States, and thereafter the chief judge of the court shall be such other judge of the court who is qualified to serve or act as chief judge under subsection (a).

(d) If a chief judge is temporarily unable to perform the duties as such, such duties shall be performed by the judge of the court in active service, able and qualified to act, who is next in precedence.

(Added Pub.L. 104–317, Title V, § 501(a), Oct. 19, 1996, 110 Stat. 3855.)

HISTORICAL AND STATUTORY NOTES

Continuance of Position of Chief Judge

Section 501(c) of Pub.L. 104–317 provided that:

"**(1)** Notwithstanding the provisions of section 258(a) of title 28, United States Code (as added by subsection (a) of this section) [subsec. (a) of this section, as added by section 501(a) of Pub.L. 104–317], the chief judge of the United States Court of International Trade who is in office on the day before the date of enactment of this Act [Oct. 19, 1996] shall continue to be such chief judge on or after such date until any one of the following events occurs:

"**(A)** The chief judge is relieved of his duties under section 258(c) of title 28, United States Code [subsec. (c) of this section].

"**(B)** The regular active status of the chief judge is terminated.

"**(C)** The chief judge attains the age of 70 years.

"**(D)** The chief judge has served for a term of 7 years as chief judge.

"**(2)** When the chief judge vacates the position of chief judge under paragraph (1), the position of chief judge of the Court of International Trade shall be filled in accordance with section 258(a) of title 28, United States Code [subsec. (a) of this section]."

CHAPTER 13—ASSIGNMENT OF JUDGES TO OTHER COURTS

Sec.
291. Circuit judges.
292. District judges.
293. Judges of the Court of International Trade.
294. Assignment of retired justices or judges to active duty.[1]
295. Conditions upon designation and assignment.
296. Powers upon designation and assignment.
297. Assignment of judges to courts of the freely associated compact states.

[1] Section catchline amended by Pub.L. 85–755 without corresponding amendment of analysis.

§ 291. Circuit judges

(a) The Chief Justice of the United States may, in the public interest, designate and assign temporarily any circuit judge to act as circuit judge in another circuit upon request by the chief judge or circuit justice of such circuit.

(b) The chief judge of a circuit or the circuit justice may, in the public interest, designate and assign temporarily any circuit judge within the circuit, including a judge designated and assigned to temporary duty therein, to hold a district court in any district within the circuit.

(June 25, 1948, c. 646, 62 Stat. 900; July 28, 1953, c. 253, § 2, 67 Stat. 226; Sept. 3, 1954, c. 1263, § 39(b), 68 Stat. 1240; July 9, 1956, c. 517, § 1(a), 70 Stat. 497; Aug. 25, 1958, Pub.L. 85–755, § 2, 72 Stat. 848; Nov. 6, 1978, Pub.L. 95–598, Title II, § 202, 92 Stat. 2660; Apr. 2, 1982, Pub.L. 97–164, Title I, § 108, 96 Stat. 28; Oct. 29, 1992, Pub.L. 102–572, Title I, § 104, 106 Stat. 4507.)

HISTORICAL AND STATUTORY NOTES

Codifications

Subsec. (c) of this section was amended by Pub.L. 95–598, Title II, § 202, Nov. 6, 1978, 92 Stat. 2660, effective June 28, 1984, pursuant to Pub.L. 95–598, Title IV, § 402(b), Nov. 6, 1978, 92 Stat. 2682, as amended by Pub.L. 98–249, § 1(a), Mar. 31, 1984, 98 Stat. 116; Pub.L. 98–271, § 1(a), Apr. 30, 1984, 98 Stat. 163; Pub.L. 98–299, § 1(a), May 25, 1984, 98 Stat. 214; Pub.L. 98–325, § 1(a), June 20, 1984, 98 Stat. 268, set out as a note preceding section 101 of Title 11, Bankruptcy, by adding "or bankruptcy" after "to hold a district".

Section 402(b) of Pub.L. 95–598 was amended by section 113 of Pub.L. 98–353, Title I, July 10, 1984, 98 Stat. 343, by substituting "shall not be effective" for "shall take effect on June 28, 1984", thereby eliminating the amendment by section 202 of Pub.L. 95–598, effective June 27, 1984, pursuant to section 122(c) of Pub.L. 98–353, set out as an Effective Date note under section 151 of this title.

Section 121(a) of Pub.L. 98–353 directed that section 402(b) of Pub.L. 95–598 be amended by substituting "the date of enactment of the Bankruptcy Amendments and Federal Judgeship Act of 1984 [i.e. July 10, 1984]" for "June 28, 1984". This amendment was not executed in view of the prior amendment to section 402(b) of Pub.L. 95–598 by section 113 of Pub.L. 98–353.

Effective and Applicability Provisions

1992 Acts. Amendment by Pub.L. 102–572 effective Jan. 1, 1993, see section 1101(a) of Pub.L. 102–572, set out as a note under section 905 of Title 2, The Congress.

1982 Acts. Amendment by Pub.L. 97–164 effective Oct. 1, 1982, see section 402 of Pub.L. 97–164, set out as a note under section 171 of this title.

Jurisdiction of United States Court of Customs and Patent Appeals

Section 7 of Pub.L. 85–755 provided that: "Nothing contained in this Act [amending sections 211 and 291 to 295 of this title] shall be construed in any way to limit or alter the jurisdiction heretofore conferred upon the United States Court of Customs and Patent Appeals [now United States Court of Appeals for the Federal Circuit] by any provision of law."

§ 292. District judges

(a) The chief judge of a circuit may designate and assign one or more district judges within the circuit to sit upon the court of appeals or a division thereof whenever the business of that court so requires. Such designations or assignments shall be in conformity with the rules or orders of the court of appeals of the circuit.

(b) The chief judge of a circuit may, in the public interest, designate and assign temporarily any district judge of the circuit to hold a district court in any district within the circuit.

(c) The chief judge of the United States Court of Appeals for the District of Columbia Circuit may, upon presentation of a certificate of necessity by the chief judge of the Superior Court of the District of Columbia pursuant to section 11–908(c) of the District of Columbia Code, designate and assign temporarily any district judge of the circuit to serve as a judge of such Superior Court, if such assignment (1) is approved by the Attorney General of the United States following a determination by him to the effect that such assignment is necessary to meet the ends of justice, and (2) is approved by the chief judge of the United States District Court for the District of Columbia.

(d) The Chief Justice of the United States may designate and assign temporarily a district judge of one circuit for service in another circuit, either in a district court or court of appeals, upon presentation of a certificate of necessity by the chief judge or circuit justice of the circuit wherein the need arises.

(e) The Chief Justice of the United States may designate and assign temporarily any district judge to serve as a judge of the Court of International Trade upon presentation to him of a certificate of necessity by the chief judge of the court.

(June 25, 1948, c. 646, 62 Stat. 901; July 28, 1953, c. 253, § 3, 67 Stat. 226; Sept. 3, 1954, c. 1263, § 39(c), 68 Stat. 1240; July 9, 1956, c. 517, § 1(b), 70 Stat. 497; July 14, 1956, c. 589, § 2, 70 Stat. 532; Aug. 25, 1958, Pub.L. 85–755, § 3, 72 Stat. 848; July 29, 1970, Pub.L. 91–358, Title I, § 172(e), 84 Stat. 591; Nov. 6, 1978, Pub.L. 95–598, Title II, §§ 203, 204, 92 Stat. 2660; Oct. 10, 1980, Pub.L. 96–417, Title V, § 501(7), 94 Stat. 1742; Apr. 2, 1982, Pub.L. 97–164, Title I, § 109, 96 Stat. 28.)

HISTORICAL AND STATUTORY NOTES

Codifications

This section was amended by Pub.L. 95–598, Title II, §§ 203, 204, Nov. 6, 1978, 92 Stat. 2660, effective June 28, 1984, pursuant to Pub.L. 95–598, Title IV, § 402(b), Nov. 6, 1978, 92 Stat. 2682, as amended by Pub.L. 98–249, § 1(a), Mar. 31, 1984, 98 Stat. 116; Pub.L. 98–271, § 1(a), Apr. 30, 1984, 98 Stat. 163; Pub.L. 98–299, § 1(a), May 25, 1984, 98 Stat. 214; Pub.L. 98–325, § 1(a), June 20, 1984, 98 Stat. 268, set out as a note preceding section 101 of Title II, Bankruptcy, in subsec. (b) by substituting "a district court or a bankruptcy court" for "a district court" and in subsec. (d) by substituting "in a bankruptcy court, district court, or court of appeals" for "either in a district court or court of appeals".

Section 402(b) of Pub.L. 95–598 was amended by section 113 of Pub.L. 98–353, Title I, July 10, 1984, 98 Stat. 343, by substituting "shall not be effective" for "shall take effect on June 28, 1984", thereby eliminating the amendments by sections 203 and 204 of Pub.L. 95–598, effective June 27, 1984, pursuant to section 122(c) of Pub.L. 98–353, set out as an Effective Date note under section 151 of this title.

Section 121(a) of Pub.L. 98–353 directed that section 402(b) of Pub.L. 95–598 be amended by substituting "the date of enactment of the Bankruptcy Amendments and Federal Judgeship Act of 1984 [i.e. July 10, 1984]" for "June 28, 1984". This amendment was not executed in view of the prior amendment to section 402(b) of Pub.L. 95–598 by section 113 of Pub.L. 98–353.

Effective and Applicability Provisions

1982 Acts. Amendment by Pub.L. 97–164 effective Oct. 1, 1982, see section 402 of Pub.L. 97–164, set out as a note under section 171 of this title.

1980 Acts. Amendment by Pub.L. 96–417 effective on Nov. 1, 1980, and applicable with respect to civil actions pending on or commenced on or after such date, see section 701(a) of Pub.L. 96–417, as amended, set out as a note under section 251 of this title.

1970 Acts. Amendment by Pub.L. 91–358 effective the first day of the seventh calendar month which begins after July 29, 1970, see section 199(a) of Pub.L. 91–358, set out as a note under section 1257 of this title.

Jurisdiction of United States Court of Customs and Patent Appeals

Amendment by Pub.L. 85–755 not limiting or altering the jurisdiction of the United States Court of Customs and Patent Appeals [now United States Court of Appeals for the Federal Circuit], see section 7 of Pub.L. 85–755, set out as a note under section 291 of this title.

Limitation or Alteration of Jurisdiction

Amendment by Act July 14, 1956, not to be construed as limiting or altering the jurisdiction heretofore conferred upon the Customs Court [now the United States Court of International Trade], see section 4 of Act July 14, 1956, set out as a note under section 251 of this title.

§ 293. Judges of the Court of International Trade

(a)[1] The Chief Justice of the United States may designate and assign temporarily any judge of the Court of International Trade to perform judicial duties in any circuit, either in a court of appeals or district court, upon presentation of a certificate of necessity by the chief judge or circuit justice of the circuit in which the need arises.

(June 25, 1948, c. 646, 62 Stat. 901; July 14, 1956, c. 589, § 3(a), 70 Stat. 532; Aug. 25, 1958, Pub.L. 85–755, § 4, 72 Stat. 848; Nov. 6, 1978, Pub.L. 95–598, Title II, § 205, 92 Stat. 2660; Oct. 10, 1980, Pub.L. 96–417, Title I, § 102, Title V, § 501(8), 94 Stat. 1727, 1742; Apr. 2, 1982, Pub.L. 97–164, Title I, § 110(a), (b), 96 Stat. 29.)

[1] There is no subsec. (b).

HISTORICAL AND STATUTORY NOTES

Codifications

This section was amended by Pub.L. 95–598, Title II, § 205, Nov. 6, 1978, 92 Stat. 2660; Pub.L. 97–164, Title I, § 110(a)(3), Apr. 2, 1982, 96 Stat. 29, effective June 28, 1984, pursuant to Pub.L. 95–598, Title IV, § 402(b), Nov. 6, 1978, 92 Stat. 2682, as amended by Pub.L. 98–249, § 1(a), Mar. 31, 1984, 98 Stat. 116; Pub.L. 98–271, § 1(a), Apr. 30, 1984, 98 Stat. 163; Pub.L. 98–299, § 1(a), May 25, 1984, 98 Stat. 214; Pub.L. 98–325, § 1(a), June 20, 1984, 98 Stat. 268, set out as a note preceding section 101 of Title II, Bankruptcy, by adding a subsec. (b) to read as follows:

(b)(1) The Chief Justice of the United States may designate and assign temporarily a bankruptcy judge of one circuit for service in a bankruptcy court in another circuit upon presentation of a certificate of necessity by the chief judge or circuit justice of the circuit wherein the need arises.

(2) The chief judge of a circuit may, in the public interest, designate and assign temporarily a bankruptcy judge of the circuit to hold a bankruptcy court in any district within the circuit.

Section 402(b) of Pub.L. 95–598 was amended by section 113 of Pub.L. 98–353, Title I, July 10, 1984, 98 Stat. 343, by substituting "shall not be effective" for "shall take effect on June 28, 1984", thereby eliminating the amendment by section 205 of Pub.L. 95–598, effective June 27, 1984, pursuant to section 122(c) of Pub.L. 98–353, set out as an Effective Date note under section 151 of this title.

Section 121(a) of Pub.L. 98–353 directed that section 402(b) of Pub.L. 95–598 be amended by substituting "the date of enactment of the Bankruptcy Amendments and Federal Judgeship Act of 1984 [i.e. July 10, 1984]" for "June 28, 1984". This amendment was not executed in view of the prior amendment to section 402(b) of Pub.L. 95–598 by section 113 of Pub.L. 98–353.

Effective and Applicability Provisions

1982 Acts. Amendment by Pub.L. 97–164 effective Oct. 1, 1982, see section 402 of Pub.L. 97–164, set out as a note under section 171 of this title.

1980 Acts. Amendment by Pub.L. 96–417 effective on Nov. 1, 1980, and applicable with respect to civil actions pending on or commenced on or after such date, see section 701(a) of Pub.L. 96–417, as amended, set out as a note under section 251 of this title.

Jurisdiction of United States Court of Customs and Patent Appeals

Amendment by Pub.L. 85–755 not limiting or altering the jurisdiction of the United States Court of Customs and Patent Appeals [now United States Court of Appeals for the Federal Circuit], see section 7 of Pub.L. 85–755, set out as a note under section 291 of this title.

Limitation or Alteration of Jurisdiction

Amendment by Act July 14, 1956, not to be construed as limiting or altering the jurisdiction heretofore conferred upon the Customs Court [now United States Court of International Trade], see section 4 of Act July 14, 1956, set out as a note under section 251 of this title.

§ 294. Assignment of retired Justices or judges to active duty

(a) Any retired Chief Justice of the United States or Associate Justice of the Supreme Court may be designated and assigned by the Chief Justice of the United States to perform such judicial duties in any circuit, including those of a circuit justice, as he is willing to undertake.

(b) Any judge of the United States who has retired from regular active service under section 371(b) or 372(a) of this title shall be known and designated as a senior judge and may continue to perform such judicial duties as he is willing and able to undertake, when designated and assigned as provided in subsections (c) and (d).

(c) Any retired circuit or district judge may be designated and assigned by the chief judge or judicial council of his circuit to perform such judicial duties within the circuit as he is willing and able to undertake. Any other retired judge of the United States may be designated and assigned by the chief judge of his court to perform such judicial duties in such court as he is willing and able to undertake.

(d) The Chief Justice of the United States shall maintain a roster of retired judges of the United States who are willing and able to undertake special judicial duties from time to time outside their own circuit, in the case of a retired circuit or district judge, or in a court other than their own, in the case of other retired judges, which roster shall be known as the roster of senior judges. Any such retired judge of the United States may be designated and assigned by the Chief Justice to perform such judicial duties as he is willing and able to undertake in a court outside his own circuit, in the case of a retired circuit or district judge, or in a court other than his own, in the case of any other retired judge of the United States. Such designation and assignment to a court of appeals or district court shall be made upon the presentation of a certificate of necessity by the chief judge or circuit justice of the circuit wherein the need arises and to any other court of the United States upon the presentation of a certificate of necessity by the chief judge of such court. No such designation or assignment shall be made to the Supreme Court.

(e) No retired Justice or judge shall perform judicial duties except when designated and assigned.

(June 25, 1948, c. 646, 62 Stat. 901; July 9, 1956, c. 517, § 1(c), 70 Stat. 497; Aug. 29, 1957, Pub.L. 85–219, 71 Stat. 495; Aug. 25, 1958, Pub.L. 85–755, § 5, 72 Stat. 849; Nov. 6, 1978, Pub.L. 95–598, Title II, § 206, 92 Stat. 2660.)

HISTORICAL AND STATUTORY NOTES

Codifications

This section was amended by Pub.L. 95–598, Title II, § 206, Nov. 6, 1978, 92 Stat. 2660, effective June 28, 1984, pursuant to Pub.L. 95–598, Title IV, § 402(b), Nov. 6, 1978, 92 Stat. 2682, as amended by Pub.L. 98–249, § 1(a), Mar. 31, 1984, 98 Stat. 116; Pub.L. 98–271, § 1(a), Apr. 30, 1984, 98 Stat. 163; Pub.L. 98–299, § 1(a), May 25, 1984, 98 Stat. 214; Pub.L. 98–325, § 1(a), June 20, 1984, 98 Stat. 268, set out as a note preceding section 101 of Title II, Bankruptcy, in subsec. (c) by deleting "or district" and inserting "district or bankruptcy judge" and in subsec. (d) by striking out "or district judge" and inserting in lieu thereof ", district judge or bankruptcy judge".

Section 402(b) of Pub.L. 95–598 was amended by section 113 of Pub.L. 98–353, Title I, July 10, 1984, 98 Stat. 343, by substituting "shall not be effective" for "shall take effect on June 28, 1984", thereby eliminating the amendment by section 206 of Pub.L. 95–598, effective June 27, 1984, pursuant to section 122(c) of Pub.L. 98–353, set out as an Effective Date note under section 151 of this title.

Section 121(a) of Pub.L. 98–353 directed that section 402(b) of Pub.L. 95–598 be amended by substituting "the date of enactment of the Bankruptcy Amendments and Federal Judgeship Act of 1984 [i.e. July 10, 1984]" for "June 28, 1984". This amendment was not executed in view of the prior amendment to section 402(b) of Pub.L. 95–598 by section 113 of Pub.L. 98–353.

Jurisdiction of United States Court of Customs and Patent Appeals

Amendment by Pub.L. 85–755 not limiting or altering the jurisdiction of the United States Court of Customs and Patent Appeals [now United States Court of Appeals for the Federal Circuit], see section 7 of Pub.L. 85–755, set out as a note under section 291 of this title.

§ 295. Conditions upon designation and assignment

No designation and assignment of a circuit or district judge in active service shall be made without the consent of the chief judge or judicial council of the circuit from which the judge is to be designated and assigned. No designation and assignment of a judge of any other court of the United States in active service shall be made without the consent of the chief judge of such court.

All designations and assignments of justices and judges shall be filed with the clerks and entered on the minutes of the courts from and to which made.

The Chief Justice of the United States, a circuit justice or a chief judge of a circuit may make new designation and assignments in accordance with the provisions of this chapter and may revoke those previously made by him.

(June 25, 1948, c. 646, 62 Stat. 901; Sept. 3, 1954, c. 1263, § 39(d), 68 Stat. 1240; July 14, 1956, c. 589, § 3(b), 70 Stat. 532; Aug. 25, 1958, Pub.L. 85–755, § 6, 72 Stat. 850; Nov. 6, 1978, Pub.L. 95–598, Title II, § 207, 92 Stat. 2660.)

HISTORICAL AND STATUTORY NOTES

Codifications

This section was amended by Pub.L. 95–598, Title II, § 207, Nov. 6, 1978, 92 Stat. 2660, effective June 28, 1984, pursuant to Pub.L. 95–598, Title IV, § 402(b), Nov. 6, 1978, 92 Stat. 2682, as amended by Pub.L. 98–249, § 1(a), Mar. 31, 1984, 98 Stat. 116; Pub.L. 98–271, § 1(a), Apr. 30, 1984, 98 Stat. 163; Pub.L. 98–299, § 1(a), May 25, 1984, 98 Stat. 214; Pub.L. 98–325, § 1(a), June 20, 1984, 98 Stat. 268, set out as a note preceding section 101 of Title II, Bankruptcy, by substituting "circuit, district, or bankruptcy judge" for "circuit or district judge".

Section 402(b) of Pub.L. 95–598 was amended by section 113 of Pub.L. 98–353, Title I, July 10, 1984, 98 Stat. 343, by substituting "shall not be effective" for "shall take effect on June 28, 1984", thereby eliminating the amendment by section 207 of Pub.L. 95–598, effective June 27, 1984, pursuant to section 122(c) of Pub.L. 98–353, set out as an Effective Date note under section 151 of this title.

Section 121(a) of Pub.L. 98–353 directed that section 402(b) of Pub.L. 95–598 be amended by substituting "the date of enactment of the Bankruptcy Amendments and Federal Judgeship Act of 1984 [i.e. July 10, 1984]" for "June 28, 1984". This amendment was not executed in view of the prior amendment to section 402(b) of Pub.L. 95–598 by section 113 of Pub.L. 98–353.

Jurisdiction of United States Court of Customs and Patent Appeals

Amendment by Pub.L. 85–755 not limiting or altering the jurisdiction of the United States Court of Customs and Patent Appeals [now United States Court of Appeals for the Federal Circuit], see section 7 of Pub.L. 85–755, set out as a note under section 291 of this title.

Limitation or Alteration of Jurisdiction

Amendment by Act July 14, 1956, not to be construed as limiting or altering the jurisdiction heretofore conferred upon the Customs Court [now United States Court of International Trade], see section 4 of Act July 14, 1956, set out as a note under section 251 of this title.

§ 296. Powers upon designation and assignment

A justice or judge shall discharge, during the period of his designation and assignment, all judicial duties for which he is designated and assigned. He may be required to perform any duty which might be required of a judge of the court or district or circuit to which he is designated and assigned.

Such justice or judge shall have all the powers of a judge of the court, circuit or district to which he is designated and assigned, except the power to appoint any person to a statutory position or to designate permanently a depository of funds or a newspaper for publication of legal notices. However, a district judge who has retired from regular active service under section 371(b) of this title, when designated and assigned to the court to which such judge was appointed, having performed in the preceding calendar year an amount of work equal to or greater than the amount of work an average judge in active service on that court would perform in 6 months, and having elected to exercise such powers, shall have the powers of a judge of that court to participate in appointment of court officers and magistrate judges, rulemaking, governance, and administrative matters.

A justice or judge who has sat by designation and assignment in another district or circuit may, notwithstanding his absence from such district or circuit or the expiration of the period of his designation and assignment, decide or join in the decision and final disposition of all matters submitted to him during such period and in the consideration and disposition of applications for rehearing or further proceedings in such matters.

(June 25, 1948, c. 646, 62 Stat. 901; Jan. 7, 2008, Pub.L. 110–177, Title V, § 503, 121 Stat. 2542.)

§ 297. Assignment of judges to courts of the freely associated compact states

(a) The Chief Justice or the chief judge of the United States Court of Appeals for the Ninth Circuit may assign any circuit or district judge of the Ninth Circuit, with the consent of the judge so assigned, to serve temporarily as a judge of any duly constituted court of the freely associated compact states whenever an official duly authorized by the laws of the respective compact state requests such assignment and such assignment is necessary for the proper dispatch of the business of the respective court.

(b) The Congress consents to the acceptance and retention by any judge so authorized of reimbursement from the countries referred to in subsection (a) of all necessary travel expenses, including transportation, and of subsistence, or of a reasonable per diem allowance in lieu of subsistence. The judge shall report to the Administrative Office of the United States Courts any amount received pursuant to this subsection.

(Added Pub.L. 100–702, Title X, § 1022(1), Nov. 19, 1988, 102 Stat. 4672.)

CHAPTER 15—CONFERENCES AND COUNCILS OF JUDGES

Sec.
331. Judicial Conference of the United States.
332. Judicial councils of circuits.
333. Judicial conferences of circuits.
334. Institutes and joint councils on sentencing.
335. Judicial Conference of the Court of International Trade.

§ 331. Judicial Conference of the United States

The Chief Justice of the United States shall summon annually the chief judge of each judicial circuit, the chief judge of the Court of International Trade, and a district judge from each judicial circuit to a conference at such time and place in the United States as he may designate. He shall preside at such conference which shall be known as the Judicial Conference of the United States. Special sessions of the Conference may be called by the Chief Justice at such times and places as he may designate.

The district judge to be summoned from each judicial circuit shall be chosen by the circuit and district judges of the circuit and shall serve as a member of the Judicial Conference of the United States for a term of not less than 3 successive years nor more than 5 successive years, as established by majority vote of all circuit and district judges of the circuit. A district judge serving as a member of the Judicial Conference may be either a judge in regular active service or a judge retired from regular active service under section 371(b) of this title.

If the chief judge of any circuit, the chief judge of the Court of International Trade, or the district judge chosen by the judges of the circuit is unable to attend, the Chief Justice may summon any other circuit or district judge from such circuit or any other judge of the Court of International Trade, as the case may be. Every judge summoned shall attend and, unless excused by the Chief Justice, shall remain throughout the sessions of the conference and advise as to the needs of his circuit or court and as to any matters in respect of which the administration of justice in the courts of the United States may be improved.

The Conference shall make a comprehensive survey of the condition of business in the courts of the United States and prepare plans for assignment of judges to or from circuits or districts where necessary. It shall also submit suggestions and recommendations to the various courts to promote uniformity of management procedures and the expeditious conduct of court business. The Conference is authorized to exercise the authority provided in chapter 16 of this title as the Conference, or through a standing committee. If the Conference elects to establish a standing committee, it shall be appointed by the Chief Justice and all petitions for review shall be reviewed by that committee. The Conference or the standing committee may hold hearings, take sworn testimony, issue subpoenas and subpoenas duces tecum, and make necessary and appropriate orders in the exercise of its authority. Subpoenas and subpoenas duces tecum shall be issued by the clerk of the Supreme Court or by the clerk of any court of appeals, at the direction of the Chief Justice or his designee and under the seal of the court, and shall be served in the manner provided in rule 45(c) of the Federal Rules of Civil Procedure for subpoenas and subpoenas duces tecum issued on behalf of the United States or an officer or any agency thereof. The Conference may also prescribe and modify rules for the exercise of the authority provided in chapter 16 of this title. All judicial officers and employees of the United States shall promptly carry into effect all orders of the Judicial Conference or the standing committee established pursuant to this section.

The Conference shall also carry on a continuous study of the operation and effect of the general rules of practice and procedure now or hereafter in use as prescribed by the Supreme Court for the other courts of the United States pursuant to law. Such changes in and additions to those rules as the Conference may deem desirable to promote simplicity in procedure, fairness in administration, the just determination of litigation, and the elimination of unjustifiable expense and delay shall be recommended by the Conference from time to time to the Supreme Court for its consideration and adoption, modification or rejection, in accordance with law.

The Judicial Conference shall review rules prescribed under section 2071 of this title by the courts, other than the Supreme Court and the district courts, for consistency with Federal law. The Judicial Conference may modify or abrogate any such rule so reviewed found inconsistent in the course of such a review.

The Attorney General shall, upon request of the Chief Justice, report to such Conference on matters relating to the business of the several courts of the United States, with particular reference to cases to which the United States is a party.

The Chief Justice shall submit to Congress an annual report of the proceedings of the Judicial Conference and its recommendations for legislation.

The Judicial Conference shall consult with the Director of United States Marshals Service on a continuing basis regarding the security requirements for the judicial branch of the United States Government, to ensure that the views of the Judicial Conference regarding the security requirements for the judicial branch of the Federal Government are taken into account when determining staffing levels, setting priorities for programs regarding judicial security, and allocating judicial security resources. In this paragraph, the term "judicial security" includes the security of buildings housing the judiciary, the personal security of judicial officers, the assessment of threats made to judicial officers, and the protection of all other judicial personnel. The United States Marshals Service retains final authority regarding security requirements for the judicial branch of the Federal Government.

(June 25, 1948, c. 646, 62 Stat. 902; July 9, 1956, c. 517, § 1(d), 70 Stat. 497; Aug. 28, 1957, Pub.L. 85–202, 71 Stat. 476; July 11, 1958, Pub.L. 85–513, 72 Stat. 356; Sept. 19, 1961, Pub.L. 87–253, §§ 1, 2, 75 Stat. 521; Nov. 6, 1978, Pub.L. 95–598, Title II, § 208, 92 Stat. 2660; Oct. 15, 1980, Pub.L. 96–458, § 4, 94 Stat. 2040; Apr. 2, 1982, Pub.L. 97–164, Title I, § 111, 96 Stat. 29; Oct. 14, 1986, Pub.L. 99–466, § 1, 100 Stat. 1190; Nov. 19, 1988, Pub.L. 100–702, Title IV, § 402(b), 102 Stat. 4650; Oct. 19, 1996, Pub.L. 104–317, Title VI, § 601(a), 110 Stat. 3857; Nov. 2, 2002, Pub.L. 107–273, Div. C, Title I, § 110403(b), 116 Stat. 1855; Jan. 7, 2008, Pub.L. 110–177, Title I, § 101(b), 121 Stat. 2534.)

HISTORICAL AND STATUTORY NOTES

References in Text

Rule 45(c) of the Federal Rules of Civil Procedure, referred to in fourth undesignated paragraph, means rule 45(c), Federal Rules of Civil Procedure, set out in this title.

Codifications

The first three paragraphs of this section were amended by Pub.L. 95–598, Title II, § 208, Nov. 6, 1978, 92 Stat. 2660, effective June 28, 1984, pursuant to Pub.L. 95–598, Title IV, § 402(b), Nov. 6, 1978, 92 Stat. 2682, as amended by Pub.L. 98–249, § 1(a), Mar. 31, 1984, 98 Stat. 116; Pub.L. 98–271, § 1(a), Apr. 30, 1984, 98 Stat. 163; Pub.L. 98–299, § 1(a), May 25, 1984, 98 Stat. 214; Pub.L. 98–325, § 1(a), June 20, 1984, 98 Stat. 268, set out as a note preceding section 101 of Title II, Bankruptcy, to read as follows:

"The Chief Justice of the United States shall summon annually the chief judge of each judicial circuit, a district judge for each judicial circuit, and two bankruptcy judges to a conference at such time and place in the United States as he may designate. He shall preside at such conference which shall be known as the Judicial Conference of the United States. Special sessions of the conference may be called by the Chief Justice at such times and places as he may designate.

"The district judge to be summoned from each judicial circuit shall be chosen by the circuit and district judges of the circuit at the annual judicial conference of the circuit held pursuant to section 333 of this title and shall serve as a member of the conference for three successive years, except that in the year following the enactment of this amended section the circuit and district judges of the first, fourth, seventh, and tenth circuits shall choose a district judge to serve for one year, the circuit and district judges in the second, fifth, and eighth circuits shall choose a district judge to serve for two years and the circuit and district judges in the third, sixth, ninth, and District of Columbia circuits shall choose a district judge to serve for three years. The bankruptcy judges to be summoned shall be chosen at large by all the bankruptcy judges. Each bankruptcy judge chosen shall serve as a member of the conference for three successive years, except that in the year following the effective date of this sentence the bankruptcy judges shall choose one bankruptcy judge to serve for two years.

"If the chief judge of any circuit or the district judge chosen by the judges of the circuit or a bankruptcy judge chosen by the bankruptcy judges is unable to attend, the Chief Justice may summon any other circuit or district judge from such circuit or any other bankruptcy judge. Every judge summoned shall attend and, unless excused by the Chief Justice, shall remain throughout the sessions of the conference and advise as to the needs of his circuit or court and as to any matters in respect of which the administration of justice in the courts of the United States may be improved."

Section 402(b) of Pub.L. 95–598 was amended by section 113 of Pub.L. 98–353, Title I, July 10, 1984, 98 Stat. 343, by substituting "shall not be effective" for "shall take effect on June 28, 1984", thereby eliminating the amendment by section 208 of Pub.L. 95–598, effective June 27, 1984, pursuant to section 122(c) of Pub.L. 98–353, set out as an Effective and Applicability Provisions note under 28 U.S.C.A. § 151.

Section 121(a) of Pub.L. 98–353 directed that section 402(b) of Pub.L. 95–598 be amended by substituting "the date of enactment of the Bankruptcy Amendments and Federal Judgeship Act of 1984 [i.e. July 10, 1984]" for "June 28, 1984". This amendment was not executed in view of the prior amendment to section 402(b) of Pub.L. 95–598 by section 113 of Pub.L. 98–353.

Effective and Applicability Provisions

1988 Acts. Amendment by Pub.L. 100–702 effective Dec. 1, 1988, see section 407 of Pub.L. 100–702, set out as a note under section 2071 of this title.

1986 Acts. Section 4 of Pub.L. 99–466 provided that: "This Act and the amendments made by this Act [enacting section 335 of this title, amending this section and section 569 of this title, repealing former section 872 of this title, and redesignating section 873 of this title as 872] shall take effect 60 days after the date of the enactment of this Act [Oct. 14, 1986]."

1982 Acts. Amendment by Pub.L. 97–164 effective Oct. 1, 1982, see section 402 of Pub.L. 97–164, set out as a note under section 171 of this title.

1980 Acts. Section 7 of Pub.L. 96–458 provided that: "This Act [amending this section and sections 332, 372 and 604 of this title, and enacting provisions set out as notes under this section and section 1 of this title] shall become effective on October 1, 1981".

Termination of Reporting Requirements

For termination, effective May 15, 2000, of provisions in this section relating to requirement that the Chief Justice submit to Congress an annual report of proceedings of the Judicial Conference and recommendations for legislation, see Pub.L. 104–66, § 3003, as amended, set out as a note under 31 U.S.C.A. § 1113 and page 13 of House Document No. 103–7.

Deposit and Use of Fees for Processing Violations Through Central Violations Bureau Cases

Pub.L. 108–447, Div. B, Title III, § 308, Dec. 8, 2004, 118 Stat. 2895, as amended Pub.L. 109–13, Div. A, Title VI, § 6066, May 11, 2005, 119 Stat. 299, provided that: "For fiscal year 2005 and hereafter, such fees as shall be collected for the processing of violations through the Central Violations Bureau cases as prescribed by the Judicial Conference of the United States shall be deposited as offsetting receipts to the fund established under 28 U.S.C. 1931 and shall remain available to the Judiciary until expended to reimburse any appropriation for the amount paid out of such appropriation for expenses of the Courts of Appeals, District Courts, and Other Judicial Services and the Administrative Offices of the United States Courts."

Authorization of Appropriations

Section 6 of Pub.L. 96–458 provided that: "There are authorized to be appropriated such sums as may be necessary to carry out the provisions of this Act [amending this section and sections 332, 372 and 604 of this title, and enacting provisions set out as notes under this section and section 1 of this title]."

Federal Courts Study Committee

Pub.L. 100–702, Title I, Nov. 19, 1988, 102 Stat. 4644, provided that:

"Sec. 101. Short title.

"This title may be cited as the 'Federal Courts Study Act'.

"Sec. 102. Establishment and purposes.

"**(a) Establishment.**—There is hereby established within the Judicial Conference of the United States, a Federal Courts Study Committee on the future of the Federal judiciary (hereafter referred to as the 'Committee').

"**(b) Purposes.**—The purposes of the Committee are to—

"(1) examine problems and issues currently facing the courts of the United States;

"(2) develop a long-range plan for the future of the Federal judiciary, including assessments involving—

"(A) alternative methods of dispute resolution;

"(B) the structure and administration of the Federal court system;

"(C) methods of resolving intracircuit and intercircuit conflicts in the courts of appeals; and

"(D) the types of disputes resolved by the Federal courts; and

"(3) report to the Judicial Conference of the United States, the President, the Congress, the Conference of Chief Justices, and the State Justice Institute on the revisions, if any, in the laws of the United States which the Committee, based on its study and evaluation, deems advisable.

"Sec. 103. Membership of the Committee.

"**(a) Appointments.**—The Committee shall be composed of fifteen members to be appointed by the Chief Justice of the United States, within ten days after the effective date of this title [Jan. 1, 1989].

"**(b) Selection.**—The membership of the Committee shall be selected in such a manner as to be representative of the various interests, needs and concerns which may be affected by the jurisdiction of the Federal courts. The Chief Justice shall designate one of the members of the Committee to serve as Chairman.

"**(c) Term of Office.**—The Committee members shall serve at the pleasure of the Chief Justice.

"**(d) Rules of Procedure.**—Rules of procedure shall be promulgated by vote of a majority of the Committee.

"Sec. 104. Powers of the Committee.

"**(a) Hearings.**—The Committee or, on the authorization of the Committee, any subcommittee thereof may, for the purpose of carrying out its functions and duties, hold such hearings and sit and act at such times and places, as the Committee or any such subcommittee may deem advisable.

"**(b) Information and assistance.**—The Administrative Office of the United States Courts, the Federal Judicial Center, and each department, agency, and instrumentality of the executive branch of the Government, including the National Institute of Justice and independent agencies, shall furnish to the Committee, upon request made by the Chairman, such information and assistance as the Committee may reasonably deem necessary to carry out its functions under this title [Title I of Pub.L. 100–702], consistent with other applicable provisions of law governing the release of such information.

"**(c) Personnel.**—(1) Subject to such rules and regulations as may be adopted by the Committee, the Director of the Administrative Office shall furnish to the Committee necessary staff and technical assistance in response to needs specified.

"(2) [Amendment of section 5108(c)(1) of Title 5, Government Organization and Employees.]

"**(d) Advisory Panels.**—The Committee is authorized, for the purpose of carrying out its functions and duties pursuant to the provisions of this title [Title I of Pub.L. 100–702], to establish advisory panels consisting of Committee members or members of the public. Such panels shall be established to provide expertise and assistance in specific areas, as the Committee deems necessary.

"Sec. 105. Functions and duties.

"The Committee shall—

"(1) make a complete study of the courts of the United States and of the several States and transmit a report to the President, the Chief Justice of the United States, the Congress, the Judicial Conference of the United States, the Conference of Chief Justices, and the State Justice

Institute on such study, within fifteen months after the effective date of this title [Jan. 1. 1989];

"(2) recommend revisions to be made to laws of the United States as the Committee, on the basis of such study, deems advisable;

"(3) develop a long-range plan for the judicial system; and

"(4) make such other recommendations and conclusions it deems advisable.

"Sec. 106. Compensation of members.

"**(a) Employees of the Government.**—A member of the Committee who is an officer or full-time employee of the United States shall receive no additional compensation for his or her services, but shall be reimbursed for travel, subsistence, and other necessary expenses incurred in the performance of duties vested in the Committee, not to exceed the maximum amounts authorized under section 456 of title 28 [section 456 of this title].

"**(b) Private Sector.**—A member of the Committee who is from the private sector shall receive $200 per diem for each day (including travel time) during which he or she is engaged in the actual performance of duties vested in the Committee, plus reimbursement for travel, subsistence, and other necessary expenses incurred in the performance of such duties, not to exceed the maximum amounts authorized under section 456 of title 28 [section 456 of this title].

"Sec. 107. Expiration of the Committee.

"The Committee shall cease to exist on the date 60 days after it transmits the report pursuant to section 105.

"Sec. 108. Authorization of appropriations.

"To carry out the purposes of this title [Title I of Pub.L. 100–702] there are authorized to be appropriated $300,000 for each of the fiscal years 1989 and 1990.

"Sec. 109. Effective date.

"This title [Title I of Pub.L. 100–702] shall become effective on January 1, 1989."

Policies, Procedures, and Methodologies Used in Recommendation For Creation of Additional Federal Judgeships; Study by General Accounting Office [now Government Accountability Office] and Report to Congress

Pub.L. 101–650, Title II, § 205, Dec. 1, 1990, 104 Stat. 5103, provided that:

"**(a) In general.**—The Comptroller General of the United States shall review the policies, procedures, and methodologies used by the Judicial Conference of the United States in recommending to the Congress the creation of additional Federal judgeships. In conducting such review the Comptroller General shall, at a minimum, determine the extent to which such policies, procedures, and methodologies—

"(1) provide an accurate measure of the workload of existing judges;

"(2) are applied consistently to the various circuit courts of appeals and district courts; and

"(3) provide an accurate indicator of the need for additional judgeships.

"**(b) Report to Congress.**—The Comptroller General shall, not later than 18 months after the date of the enactment of this Act [Dec. 1, 1990], report the results of the review conducted under subsection (a) to the Committees on the Judiciary of the House of Representatives and the Senate. The report shall include such recommendations as the Comptroller General considers appropriate for revisions of the policies, procedures, and methodologies used by the Judicial Conference that were reviewed in the report."

§ 332. Judicial councils of circuits

(a)(1) The chief judge of each judicial circuit shall call, at least twice in each year and at such places as he or she may designate, a meeting of the judicial council of the circuit, consisting of the chief judge of the circuit, who shall preside, and an equal number of circuit judges and district judges of the circuit, as such number is determined by majority vote of all such judges of the circuit in regular active service.

(2) Members of the council shall serve for terms established by a majority vote of all judges of the circuit in regular active service.

(3) Except for the chief judge of the circuit, either judges in regular active service or judges retired from regular active service under section 371(b) of this title may serve as members of the council. Service as a member of a judicial council by a judge retired from regular active service under section 371(b) may not be considered for meeting the requirements of section 371(f)(1) (A), (B), or (C).

(4) No more than one district judge from any one district shall serve simultaneously on the council, unless at least one district judge from each district within the circuit is already serving as a member of the council.

(5) In the event of the death, resignation, retirement under section 371(a) or 372(a) of this title, or disability of a member of the council, a replacement member shall be designated to serve the remainder of the unexpired term by the chief judge of the circuit.

(6) Each member of the council shall attend each council meeting unless excused by the chief judge of the circuit.

(b) The council shall be known as the Judicial Council of the circuit.

(c) The chief judge shall submit to the council the semiannual reports of the Director of the Administrative Office of the United States Courts. The council shall take such action thereon as may be necessary.

(d)(1) Each judicial council shall make all necessary and appropriate orders for the effective and expeditious administration of justice within its circuit. Any general order relating to practice and procedure shall be made or amended only after giving appropriate public notice and an opportunity for comment. Any such order so relating shall take effect upon the date specified by such judicial council. Copies of such orders so relating shall be furnished to the Judicial Conference and the Administrative Office of the United States Courts and be made available to the public. Each council is authorized to hold hearings, to take sworn testimony, and to issue subpoenas and subpoenas duces tecum. Subpoenas and subpoenas duces tecum shall be issued by the clerk of the court of appeals, at the direction of the chief judge of the circuit or his designee and under the seal of the court, and shall be served in the manner provided in rule 45(c) of the Federal Rules of Civil Procedure for subpoenas and subpoenas duces tecum issued on behalf of the United States or an officer or agency thereof.

(2) All judicial officers and employees of the circuit shall promptly carry into effect all orders of the judicial council. In the case of failure to comply with an order made under this subsection or a subpoena issued under chapter 16 of this title, a judicial council or a special committee appointed under section 353 of this title may institute a contempt proceeding in any district court in which the judicial officer or employee of the circuit who fails to comply with the order made under this subsection shall be ordered to show cause before the court why he or she should not be held in contempt of court.

(3) Unless an impediment to the administration of justice is involved, regular business of the courts need not be referred to the council.

(4) Each judicial council shall periodically review the rules which are prescribed under section 2071 of this title by district courts within its circuit for consistency with rules prescribed under section 2072 of this title. Each council may modify or abrogate any such rule found inconsistent in the course of such a review.

(e) The judicial council of each circuit may appoint a circuit executive. In appointing a circuit executive, the judicial council shall take into account experience in administrative and executive positions, familiarity with court procedures, and special training. The circuit executive shall exercise such administrative powers and perform such duties as may be delegated to him by the circuit council. The duties delegated to the circuit executive of each circuit may include but need not be limited to:

(1) Exercising administrative control of all nonjudicial activities of the court of appeals of the circuit in which he is appointed.

(2) Administering the personnel system of the court of appeals of the circuit.

(3) Administering the budget of the court of appeals of the circuit.

(4) Maintaining a modern accounting system.

(5) Establishing and maintaining property control records and undertaking a space management program.

(6) Conducting studies relating to the business and administration of the courts within the circuit and preparing appropriate recommendations and reports to the chief judge, the circuit council, and the Judicial Conference.

(7) Collecting, compiling, and analyzing statistical data with a view to the preparation and presentation of reports based on such data as may be directed by the chief judge, the circuit council, and the Administrative Office of the United States Courts.

(8) Representing the circuit as its liaison to the courts of the various States in which the circuit is located, the marshal's office, State and local bar associations, civic groups, news media, and other private and public groups having a reasonable interest in the administration of the circuit.

(9) Arranging and attending meetings of the judges of the circuit and of the circuit council, including preparing the agenda and serving as secretary in all such meetings.

(10) Preparing an annual report to the circuit and to the Administrative Office of the United States Courts for the preceding calendar year, including recommendations for more expeditious disposition of the business of the circuit.

All duties delegated to the circuit executive shall be subject to the general supervision of the chief judge of the circuit.

(f)(1) Each circuit executive shall be paid at a salary to be established by the Judicial Conference of the United States not to exceed the annual rate of level IV of the Executive Schedule pay rates under section 5315 of title 5.

(2) The circuit executive shall serve at the pleasure of the judicial council of the circuit.

(3) The circuit executive may appoint, with the approval of the council, necessary employees in such number as may be approved by the Director of the Administrative Office of the United States Courts.

(4) The circuit executive and his staff shall be deemed to be officers and employees of the judicial branch of the United States Government within the meaning of subchapter III of chapter 83 (relating to civil service retirement), chapter 87 (relating to Federal employees' life insurance program), and chapter 89 (relating to Federal employees' health benefits program) of title 5, United States Code.

(g) No later than January 31 of each year, each judicial council shall submit a report to the Administrative Office of the United States Courts on the number and nature of orders entered under this section during the preceding calendar year that relate to judicial misconduct or disability.

(h)(1) The United States Court of Appeals for the Federal Circuit may appoint a circuit executive, who shall serve at the pleasure of the court. In appointing a circuit executive, the court shall take into account experience in administrative and executive positions, familiarity with court procedures, and special training. The circuit executive shall exercise such administrative powers and perform such duties as may be delegated by the court. The duties delegated to the circuit executive may include the duties specified in subsection (e) of this section, insofar as such duties are applicable to the Court of Appeals for the Federal Circuit.

(2) The circuit executive shall be paid the salary for circuit executives established under subsection (f) of this section.

(3) The circuit executive may appoint, with the approval of the court, necessary employees in such number as may be approved by the Director of the Administrative Office of the United States Courts.

(4) The circuit executive and staff shall be deemed to be officers and employees of the United States within the meaning of the statutes specified in subsection (f)(4).

(5) The court may appoint either a circuit executive under this subsection or a clerk under section 711 of this title, but not both, or may appoint a combined circuit executive/clerk who shall be paid the salary of a circuit executive.

(June 25, 1948, c. 646, 62 Stat. 902; Nov. 13, 1963, Pub.L. 88–176, § 3, 77 Stat. 331; Jan. 5, 1971, Pub.L. 91–647, 84 Stat. 1907; Nov. 6, 1978, Pub.L. 95–598, Title II, § 209, 92 Stat. 2661; Oct. 15, 1980, Pub.L. 96–458, § 2(a) to (d)(1), 94 Stat. 2035, 2036; Oct. 1, 1988, Pub.L. 100–459, Title IV, § 407, 102 Stat. 2213; Nov. 19, 1988, Pub.L. 100–702, Title IV, § 403(a)(2), (b), Title X, §§ 1018, 1020(a)(1), 102 Stat. 4651, 4670, 4671; Dec. 1, 1990, Pub.L. 101–650, Title III, §§ 323, 325(b)(1), Title IV, § 403, 104 Stat. 5120, 5121, 5124; Dec. 9, 1991, Pub.L. 102–198, § 1, 105 Stat. 1623; Oct. 19, 1996, Pub.L. 104–317, Title II, § 208, 110 Stat. 3851; Nov. 13, 2000, Pub.L. 106–518, Title II, § 205, Title III, § 306, 114 Stat. 2414, 2418; Dec. 21, 2000, Pub.L. 106–553, § 1(a)(2) [Title III, § 306], 114 Stat. 2762, 2762A–85; Nov. 2, 2002, Pub.L. 107–273, Div. C, Title I, § 11043(c), 116 Stat. 1855.)

HISTORICAL AND STATUTORY NOTES

References in Text

Section 371(f) of this title, referred to in subsec. (a)(3), was redesignated section 28 U.S.C.A. §371(e) Pub.L. 106–398, § 1 [Div. A, Title VI, Sec. 654(a)(1)(B)], Oct. 30, 2000, 114 Stat. 1654, 1654A–165.

Rule 45(c) of the Federal Rules of Civil Procedure, referred to in subsec. (d)(1), is rule 45(c) of the Federal Rules of Civil Procedure, set out in this title.

Codifications

Subsec. (d) of this section was amended by Pub.L. 95–598, Title II, § 209, Nov. 6, 1978, 92 Stat. 2661, effective June 28, 1984, pursuant to Pub.L. 95–598, Title IV, § 402(b), Nov. 6, 1978, 92 Stat. 2682, as amended by Pub.L. 98–249, § 1(a), Mar. 31, 1984, 98 Stat. 116; Pub.L. 98–271, § 1(a), Apr. 30, 1984, 98 Stat. 163; Pub.L. 98–299, § 1(a), May 25, 1984, 98 Stat. 214; Pub.L. 98–325, § 1(a), June 20, 1984, 98 Stat. 268, set out as a note preceding section 101 of Title 11, Bankruptcy, by inserting "and bankruptcy judges" following "The district judges".

Section 402(b) of Pub.L. 95–598 was amended by section 113 of Pub.L. 98–353, Title I, July 10, 1984, 98 Stat. 343, by substituting "shall not be effective" for "shall take effect on June 28, 1984", thereby eliminating the amendment by section 209 of Pub.L. 95–598, effective June 27, 1984, pursuant to section 122(c) of Pub.L. 98–353, set out as an Effective Date note under section 151 of this title.

Section 121(a) of Pub.L. 98–353 directed that section 402(b) of Pub.L. 95–598 be amended by substituting "the date of enactment of the Bankruptcy Amendments and Federal Judgeship Act of 1984 [i.e. July 10, 1984]" for "June 28, 1984". This amendment was not executed in view of the prior amendment to section 402(b) of Pub.L. 95–598 by section 113 of Pub.L. 98–353.

Effective and Applicability Provisions

1990 Acts. Section 407 of Pub.L. 101–650 provided that: "The amendments made by this subtitle [subtitle I of Title IV of Pub.L. 101–650, amending this section and sections 372, 453, and 2077 of this title and section 104 of Appendix 6 to Title 5, Government Organization and Employees] shall take effect 90 days after the date of the enactment of this Act [Dec. 1, 1990]."

1988 Acts. Amendment of subsec. (d)(1) and enactment of subsec. (d)(4) by Pub.L. 100–702 effective Dec. 1, 1988, see section 407 of Pub.L. 100–702, set out as a note under section 2071 of this title.

1980 Acts. Amendment by Pub.L. 96–458 effective Oct. 1, 1981, see section 7 of Pub.L. 96–458, set out as a note under section 331 of this title.

§ 333. Judicial conferences of circuits

The chief judge of each circuit may summon biennially, and may summon annually, the circuit, district, magistrate, and bankruptcy judges of the circuit, in active service, to a conference at a time and place that he designates, for the purpose of considering the business of the courts and advising means of improving the administration of justice within such circuit. He may preside at such conference, which shall be known as the Judicial Conference of the circuit. The judges of the District Court of Guam, the District Court of the Virgin Islands, and the District Court of the Northern Mariana Islands may also be summoned biennially, and may be summoned annually, to the conferences of their respective circuits.

Every judge summoned may attend.

The court of appeals for each circuit shall provide by its rules for representation and active participation at such conference by members of the bar of such circuit.

(June 25, 1948, c. 646, 62 Stat. 903; Dec. 29, 1950, c. 1185, 64 Stat. 1128; Oct. 31, 1951, c. 655, § 38, 65 Stat. 723; July 7, 1958, Pub.L. 85–508, § 12(e), 72 Stat. 348; Nov. 6, 1978, Pub.L. 95–598, Title II, § 210, 92 Stat. 2661; Dec. 1, 1990, Pub.L. 101–650, Title III, § 320, 104 Stat. 5117; Apr. 26,

1996, Pub.L. 104–134, Title I, § 101[(a)][Title III, § 305], 110 Stat. 1321–36; renumbered Title I May 2, 1996, Pub.L. 104–140, § 1(a), 110 Stat. 1327; Oct. 13, 2008, Pub.L. 110–406, § 9, 122 Stat. 4293.)

HISTORICAL AND STATUTORY NOTES

Effective and Applicability Provisions

1978 Acts. Amendment by Pub.L. 95–598 effective Oct. 1, 1979, see section 402(c) of Pub.L. 95–598, as amended, set out as an Effective Date note preceding section 101 of Title 11, Bankruptcy.

1958 Acts. Amendment by Pub.L. 85–508 effective Jan. 3, 1959, upon admission of Alaska into the Union pursuant to Proc. No. 3269, Jan. 31, 1959, 24 F.R. 81, 73 Stat. c16, as required by sections 1 and 8(c) of Pub.L. 85–508, see notes set out under section 81A of this title and preceding section 21 of Title 48, Territories and Insular Possessions.

Termination of United States District Court for the District of the Canal Zone

For termination of the United States District Court for the District of the Canal Zone at end of the "transition period", being the 30-month period beginning Oct. 1, 1979, and ending midnight Mar. 31, 1982, see Paragraph 5 of Article XI of the Panama Canal Treaty of 1977 and sections 3831 and 3841 to 3843 of Title 22, Foreign Relations and Intercourse.

§ 334. Institutes and joint councils on sentencing

(a) In the interest of uniformity in sentencing procedures, there is hereby authorized to be established under the auspices of the Judicial Conference of the United States, institutes and joint councils on sentencing. The Attorney General and/or the chief judge of each circuit may at any time request, through the Director of the Administrative Office of the United States Courts, the Judicial Conference to convene such institutes and joint councils for the purpose of studying, discussing, and formulating the objectives, policies, standards, and criteria for sentencing those convicted of crimes and offenses in the courts of the United States. The agenda of the institutes and joint councils may include but shall not be limited to: (1) The development of standards for the content and utilization of presentence reports; (2) the establishment of factors to be used in selecting cases for special study and observation in prescribed diagnostic clinics; (3) the determination of the importance of psychiatric, emotional, sociological and physiological factors involved in crime and their bearing upon sentences; (4) the discussion of special sentencing problems in unusual cases such as treason, violation of public trust, subversion, or involving abnormal sex behavior, addiction to drugs or alcohol, and mental or physical handicaps; (5) the formulation of sentencing principles and criteria which will assist in promoting the equitable administration of the criminal laws of the United States.

(b) After the Judicial Conference has approved the time, place, participants, agenda, and other arrangements for such institutes and joint councils, the chief judge of each circuit is authorized to invite the attendance of district judges under conditions which he thinks proper and which will not unduly delay the work of the courts.

(c) The Attorney General is authorized to select and direct the attendance at such institutes and meetings of United States attorneys and other officials of the Department of Justice and may invite the participation of other interested Federal officers. He may also invite specialists in sentencing methods, criminologists, psychiatrists, penologists, and others to participate in the proceedings.

(d) The expenses of attendance of judges shall be paid from applicable appropriations for the judiciary of the United States. The expenses connected with the preparation of the plans and agenda for the conference and for the travel and other expenses incident to the attendance of officials and other participants invited by the Attorney General shall be paid from applicable appropriations of the Department of Justice.

(Added Pub.L. 85–752, § 1, Aug. 25, 1958, 72 Stat. 845.)

HISTORICAL AND STATUTORY NOTES

Sentencing Procedures

Section 7 of Pub.L. 85–752 provided that: "This Act [adding this section and sections 4208 and 4209 of Title 18, Crimes and Criminal Procedure, and provisions set out as a note under section 4208 of Title 18] does not apply to any offense for which there is provided a mandatory penalty."

§ 335. Judicial Conference of the Court of International Trade

(a) The chief judge of the Court of International Trade is authorized to summon annually the judges of such court to a judicial conference, at a time and place that such chief judge designates, for the purpose of considering the business of such court and improvements in the administration of justice in such court.

(b) The Court of International Trade shall provide by its rules for representation and active participation at such conference by members of the bar.

(Added Pub.L. 99–466, § 2(a), Oct. 14, 1986, 100 Stat. 1190.)

HISTORICAL AND STATUTORY NOTES

Effective and Applicability Provisions

1986 Acts. Section effective 60 days after Oct. 14, 1986, see section 4 of Pub.L. 99–466, set out as a note under section 331 of this title.

CHAPTER 16—COMPLAINTS AGAINST JUDGES AND JUDICIAL DISCIPLINE

Sec.
351. Complaints; judge defined.
352. Review of complaint by chief judge.
353. Special committees.
354. Action by judicial council.
355. Action by Judicial Conference.
356. Subpoena power.
357. Review of orders and actions.
358. Rules.
359. Restrictions.
360. Disclosure of information.
361. Reimbursement of expenses.
362. Other provisions and rules not affected.
363. Court of Federal Claims, Court of International Trade, Court of Appeals for the Federal Circuit.
364. Effect of felony conviction.

§ 351. Complaints; judge defined

(a) Filing of complaint by any person.—Any person alleging that a judge has engaged in conduct prejudicial to the effective and expeditious administration of the business of the courts, or alleging that such judge is unable to discharge all the duties of office by reason of mental or physical disability, may file with the clerk of the court of appeals for the circuit a written complaint containing a brief statement of the facts constituting such conduct.

(b) Identifying complaint by chief judge.—In the interests of the effective and expeditious administration of the business of the courts and on the basis of information available to the chief judge of the circuit, the chief judge may, by written order stating reasons therefor, identify a complaint for purposes of this chapter and thereby dispense with filing of a written complaint.

(c) Transmittal of complaint.—Upon receipt of a complaint filed under subsection (a), the clerk shall promptly transmit the complaint to the chief judge of the circuit, or, if the conduct complained of is that of the chief judge, to that circuit judge in regular active service next senior in date of commission (hereafter, for purposes of this chapter only, included in the term "chief judge"). The clerk shall simultaneously transmit a copy of the complaint to the judge whose conduct is the subject of the complaint. The clerk shall also transmit a copy of any complaint identified under subsection (b) to the judge whose conduct is the subject of the complaint.

(d) Definitions.—In this chapter—

(1) the term "judge" means a circuit judge, district judge, bankruptcy judge, or magistrate judge; and

(2) the term "complainant" means the person filing a complaint under subsection (a) of this section.

(Added Pub.L. 107–273, Div. C, Title I, § 11042(a), Nov. 2, 2002, 116 Stat. 1848.)

HISTORICAL AND STATUTORY NOTES

Severability

Pub.L. 107–273, Div. C, Title I, Subtitle C, § 11044, Nov. 2, 2002, 116 Stat. 1856, provided that: "If any provision of this subtitle, an amendment made by this subtitle [enacting this chapter and amending 28 U.S.C.A. §§ 331, 332, 372, 375, and 604, and 38 U.S.C.A. § 7253], or the application of such provision or amendment to any person or circumstance is held to be unconstitutional, the remainder of this subtitle, the amendments made by this subtitle, and the application of the provisions of such to any person or circumstance shall not be affected thereby."

§ 352. Review of complaint by chief judge

(a) Expeditious review; limited inquiry.—The chief judge shall expeditiously review any complaint received under section 351(a) or identified under section 351(b). In determining what action to take, the chief judge may conduct a limited inquiry for the purpose of determining—

(1) whether appropriate corrective action has been or can be taken without the necessity for a formal investigation; and

(2) whether the facts stated in the complaint are either plainly untrue or are incapable of being established through investigation.

For this purpose, the chief judge may request the judge whose conduct is complained of to file a written response to the complaint. Such response shall not be made available to the complainant unless authorized by the judge filing the response. The chief judge or his or her designee may also communicate orally or in writing with the complainant, the judge whose conduct is complained of, and any other person who may have knowledge of the matter, and may review any transcripts or other relevant documents. The chief judge shall not undertake to make findings of fact about any matter that is reasonably in dispute.

(b) Action by chief judge following review.—After expeditiously reviewing a complaint under subsection (a), the chief judge, by written order stating his or her reasons, may—

(1) dismiss the complaint—

(A) if the chief judge finds the complaint to be—

(i) not in conformity with section 351(a);

(ii) directly related to the merits of a decision or procedural ruling; or

(iii) frivolous, lacking sufficient evidence to raise an inference that misconduct has occurred, or containing allegations which are incapable of being established through investigation; or

(B) when a limited inquiry conducted under subsection (a) demonstrates that the allegations in the complaint lack any factual foundation or are conclusively refuted by objective evidence; or

(2) conclude the proceeding if the chief judge finds that appropriate corrective action has been taken or that action on the complaint is no longer necessary because of intervening events.

The chief judge shall transmit copies of the written order to the complainant and to the judge whose conduct is the subject of the complaint.

(c) Review of orders of chief judge.—A complainant or judge aggrieved by a final order of the chief judge under this section may petition the judicial council of the circuit for review thereof. The denial of a petition for review of the chief judge's order shall be final and conclusive and shall not be judicially reviewable on appeal or otherwise.

(d) Referral of petitions for review to panels of the judicial council.—Each judicial council may, pursuant to rules prescribed under section 358, refer a petition for review filed under subsection (c) to a panel of no fewer than 5 members of the council, at least 2 of whom shall be district judges.

(Added Pub.L. 107–273, Div. C, Title I, § 11042(a), Nov. 2, 2002, 116 Stat. 1849.)

HISTORICAL AND STATUTORY NOTES

Severability of Provisions

If any provision of this section or the application of such provision to any person or circumstance is held to be unconstitutional, the remainder of this section and the application thereof to any person or circumstance shall not be affected thereby, see section 11044 of Pub.L. 107–273, set out as a note under 28 U.S.C.A. § 351.

§ 353. Special committees

(a) Appointment.—If the chief judge does not enter an order under section 352(b), the chief judge shall promptly—

(1) appoint himself or herself and equal numbers of circuit and district judges of the circuit to a special committee to investigate the facts and allegations contained in the complaint;

(2) certify the complaint and any other documents pertaining thereto to each member of such committee; and

(3) provide written notice to the complainant and the judge whose conduct is the subject of the complaint of the action taken under this subsection.

(b) Change in status or death of judges.—A judge appointed to a special committee under subsection (a) may continue to serve on that committee after becoming a senior judge or, in the case of the chief judge of the circuit, after his or her term as chief judge terminates under subsection (a)(3) or (c) of section 45. If a judge appointed to a committee under subsection (a) dies, or retires from office under section 371(a), while serving on the committee, the chief judge of the circuit may appoint another circuit or district judge, as the case may be, to the committee.

(c) Investigation by special committee.—Each committee appointed under subsection (a) shall conduct an investigation as extensive as it considers necessary, and shall expeditiously file a comprehensive written report thereon with the judicial council of the circuit. Such report shall present both the findings of the investigation and the committee's recommendations for necessary and appropriate action by the judicial council of the circuit.

(Added Pub.L. 107–273, Div. C, Title I, § 11042(a), Nov. 2, 2002, 116 Stat. 1850.)

HISTORICAL AND STATUTORY NOTES

Severability of Provisions

If any provision of this section or the application of such provision to any person or circumstance is held to be unconstitutional, the remainder of this section and the application thereof to any person or circumstance shall not be affected thereby, see section 11044 of Pub.L. 107–273, set out as a note under 28 U.S.C.A. § 351.

§ 354. Action by judicial council

(a) Actions upon receipt of report.—

(1) Actions.—The judicial council of a circuit, upon receipt of a report filed under section 353(c)—

(A) may conduct any additional investigation which it considers to be necessary;

(B) may dismiss the complaint; and

(C) if the complaint is not dismissed, shall take such action as is appropriate to assure the effective and expeditious administration of the business of the courts within the circuit.

(2) Description of possible actions if complaint not dismissed.—

(A) In general.—Action by the judicial council under paragraph (1)(C) may include—

(i) ordering that, on a temporary basis for a time certain, no further cases be assigned to the judge whose conduct is the subject of a complaint;

(ii) censuring or reprimanding such judge by means of private communication; and

(iii) censuring or reprimanding such judge by means of public announcement.

(B) For Article III judges.—If the conduct of a judge appointed to hold office during good behavior is the subject of the complaint, action by the judicial council under paragraph (1)(C) may include—

(i) certifying disability of the judge pursuant to the procedures and standards provided under section 372(b); and

(ii) requesting that the judge voluntarily retire, with the provision that the length of service requirements under section 371 of this title shall not apply.

(C) For magistrate judges.—If the conduct of a magistrate judge is the subject of the complaint, action by the judicial council under paragraph (1)(C) may include directing the chief judge of the district of the magistrate judge to take such action as the judicial council considers appropriate.

(3) Limitations on judicial council regarding removals.—

(A) Article III judges.—Under no circumstances may the judicial council order removal from office of any judge appointed to hold office during good behavior.

(B) Magistrate and bankruptcy judges.—Any removal of a magistrate judge under this subsection shall be in accordance with section 631 and any removal of a bankruptcy judge shall be in accordance with section 152.

(4) Notice of action to judge.—The judicial council shall immediately provide written notice to the complainant and to the judge whose conduct is the subject of the complaint of the action taken under this subsection.

(b) Referral to Judicial Conference.—

(1) In general.—In addition to the authority granted under subsection (a), the judicial council may, in its discretion, refer any complaint under section 351, together with the record of any associated proceedings and its recommendations for appropriate action, to the Judicial Conference of the United States.

(2) Special circumstances.—In any case in which the judicial council determines, on the basis of a complaint and an investigation under this chapter, or on the basis of information otherwise available to the judicial council, that a judge appointed to hold office during good behavior may have engaged in conduct—

(A) which might constitute one or more grounds for impeachment under article II of the Constitution, or

(B) which, in the interest of justice, is not amenable to resolution by the judicial council,

the judicial council shall promptly certify such determination, together with any complaint and a record of any associated proceedings, to the Judicial Conference of the United States.

(3) Notice to complainant and judge.—A judicial council acting under authority of this subsection shall, unless contrary to the interests of justice, immediately submit written notice to the complainant and to the judge whose conduct is the subject of the action taken under this subsection.

(Added Pub.L. 107–273, Div. C, Title I, § 11042(a), Nov. 2, 2002, 116 Stat. 1850.)

HISTORICAL AND STATUTORY NOTES

Severability of Provisions

If any provision of this section or the application of such provision to any person or circumstance is held to be unconstitutional, the remainder of this section and the application thereof to any person or circumstance shall not be affected thereby, see section 11044 of Pub.L. 107–273, set out as a note under 28 U.S.C.A. § 351.

§ 355. Action by Judicial Conference

(a) In general.—Upon referral or certification of any matter under section 354(b), the Judicial Conference, after consideration of the prior proceedings and such additional investigation as it considers appropriate, shall by majority vote take such action, as described in section 354(a)(1)(C) and (2), as it considers appropriate.

(b) If impeachment warranted.—

(1) In general.—If the Judicial Conference concurs in the determination of the judicial council, or makes its own determination, that consideration of impeachment may be warranted, it shall so certify and transmit the determination and the record of proceedings to the House of Representatives for whatever action the House of Representatives considers to be necessary. Upon receipt of the determination and record of proceedings in the House of Representatives, the Clerk of the House of Representatives shall make available to the public the determination and any reasons for the determination.

(2) In case of felony conviction.—If a judge has been convicted of a felony under State or Federal law and has exhausted all means of obtaining direct review of the conviction, or the time for seeking further direct review of the conviction has passed and no such review has been sought, the Judicial Conference may, by majority vote and without referral or certification under section 354(b), transmit to the House of Representatives a determination that consideration of impeachment may be warranted, together with appropriate court records, for whatever action the House of Representatives considers to be necessary.

(Added Pub.L. 107–273, Div. C, Title I, § 11042(a), Nov. 2, 2002, 116 Stat. 1852.)

HISTORICAL AND STATUTORY NOTES

Severability of Provisions

If any provision of this section or the application of such provision to any person or circumstance is held to be unconstitutional, the remainder of this section and the application thereof to any person or circumstance shall not be affected thereby, see section 11044 of Pub.L. 107–273, set out as a note under 28 U.S.C.A. § 351.

§ 356. Subpoena power

(a) Judicial councils and special committees.—In conducting any investigation under this chapter, the judicial council, or a special committee appointed under section 353, shall have full subpoena powers as provided in section 332(d).

(b) Judicial Conference and standing committees.—In conducting any investigation under this chapter, the Judicial Conference, or a standing committee appointed by the Chief Justice under section 331, shall have full subpoena powers as provided in that section.

(Added Pub.L. 107–273, Div. C, Title I, § 11042(a), Nov. 2, 2002, 116 Stat. 1852.)

HISTORICAL AND STATUTORY NOTES

Severability of Provisions

If any provision of this section or the application of such provision to any person or circumstance is held to be unconstitutional, the remainder of this section and the application thereof to any person or circumstance shall not be affected thereby, see section 11044 of Pub.L. 107–273, set out as a note under 28 U.S.C.A. § 351.

§ 357. Review of orders and actions

(a) Review of action of judicial council.—A complainant or judge aggrieved by an action of the judicial council under section 354 may petition the Judicial Conference of the United States for review thereof.

(b) Action of Judicial Conference.—The Judicial Conference, or the standing committee established under section 331, may grant a petition filed by a complainant or judge under subsection (a).

(c) No judicial review.—Except as expressly provided in this section and section 352(c), all orders and determinations, including denials of petitions for review, shall be final and conclusive and shall not be judicially reviewable on appeal or otherwise.

(Added Pub.L. 107–273, Div. C, Title I, § 11042(a), Nov. 2, 2002, 116 Stat. 1853.)

HISTORICAL AND STATUTORY NOTES

Severability of Provisions

If any provision of this section or the application of such provision to any person or circumstance is held to be unconstitutional, the remainder of this section and the application thereof to any person or circumstance shall not be affected thereby, see section 11044 of Pub.L. 107–273, set out as a note under 28 U.S.C.A. § 351.

§ 358. Rules

(a) In general.—Each judicial council and the Judicial Conference may prescribe such rules for the conduct of proceedings under this chapter, including the processing of petitions for review, as each considers to be appropriate.

(b) Required provisions.—Rules prescribed under subsection (a) shall contain provisions requiring that—

(1) adequate prior notice of any investigation be given in writing to the judge whose conduct is the subject of a complaint under this chapter;

(2) the judge whose conduct is the subject of a complaint under this chapter be afforded an opportunity to appear (in person or by counsel) at proceedings conducted by the investigating panel, to present oral and documentary evidence, to compel the attendance of witnesses or the production of documents, to cross-examine witnesses, and to present argument orally or in writing; and

(3) the complainant be afforded an opportunity to appear at proceedings conducted by the investigating panel, if the panel concludes that the complainant could offer substantial information.

(c) Procedures.—Any rule prescribed under this section shall be made or amended only after giving appropriate public notice and an opportunity for comment. Any such rule shall be a matter of public record, and any such rule promulgated by a judicial council may be modified by the Judicial Conference. No rule promulgated under this section may limit the period of time within which a person may file a complaint under this chapter.

(Added Pub.L. 107–273, Div. C, Title I, § 11042(a), Nov. 2, 2002, 116 Stat. 1853.)

HISTORICAL AND STATUTORY NOTES

Severability of Provisions

If any provision of this section or the application of such provision to any person or circumstance is held to be unconstitutional, the remainder of this section and the application thereof to any person or circumstance shall not be affected thereby, see section 11044 of Pub.L. 107–273, set out as a note under 28 U.S.C.A. § 351.

§ 359. Restrictions

(a) Restriction on individuals who are subject of investigation.—No judge whose conduct is the subject of an investigation under this chapter shall serve upon a special committee appointed under section 353, upon a judicial council, upon the Judicial Conference, or upon the standing committee established under section 331, until all proceedings under this chapter relating to such investigation have been finally terminated.

(b) Amicus curiae.—No person shall be granted the right to intervene or to appear as amicus curiae in any proceeding before a judicial council or the Judicial Conference under this chapter.

(Added Pub.L. 107–273, Div. C, Title I, § 11042(a), Nov. 2, 2002, 116 Stat. 1853.)

HISTORICAL AND STATUTORY NOTES

Severability of Provisions

If any provision of this section or the application of such provision to any person or circumstance is held to be unconstitutional, the remainder of this section and the application thereof to any person or circumstance shall not be affected thereby, see section 11044 of Pub.L. 107–273, set out as a note under 28 U.S.C.A. § 351.

§ 360. Disclosure of information

(a) Confidentiality of proceedings.—Except as provided in section 355, all papers, documents, and records of proceedings related to investigations conducted under this chapter shall be confidential and shall not be disclosed by any person in any proceeding except to the extent that—

(1) the judicial council of the circuit in its discretion releases a copy of a report of a special committee under section 353(c) to the complainant whose complaint initiated the investigation by that special committee and to the judge whose conduct is the subject of the complaint;

(2) the judicial council of the circuit, the Judicial Conference of the United States, or the Senate or the House of Representatives by resolution, releases any such material which is believed necessary to an impeachment investigation or trial of a judge under article I of the Constitution; or

(3) such disclosure is authorized in writing by the judge who is the subject of the complaint and by the chief judge of the circuit, the Chief Justice, or the chairman of the standing committee established under section 331.

(b) Public availability of written orders.—Each written order to implement any action under section 354(a)(1)(C), which is issued by a judicial council, the Judicial Conference, or the standing committee established under section 331, shall be made available to the public through the appropriate clerk's office of the court of appeals for the circuit. Unless contrary to the interests of justice, each such order shall be accompanied by written reasons therefor.

(Added Pub.L. 107–273, Div. C, Title I, § 11042(a), Nov. 2, 2002, 116 Stat. 1854.)

HISTORICAL AND STATUTORY NOTES

Severability of Provisions

If any provision of this section or the application of such provision to any person or circumstance is held to be unconstitutional, the remainder of this section and the application thereof to any person or circumstance shall not be affected thereby, see section 11044 of Pub.L. 107–273, set out as a note under 28 U.S.C.A. § 351.

§ 361. Reimbursement of expenses

Upon the request of a judge whose conduct is the subject of a complaint under this chapter, the judicial council may, if the complaint has been finally dismissed under section 354(a)(1)(B), recommend that the Director of the Administrative Office of the United States Courts award reimbursement, from funds appropriated to the Federal judiciary, for those reasonable expenses, including attorneys' fees, incurred by that judge during the investigation which would not have been incurred but for the requirements of this chapter.

(Added Pub.L. 107–273, Div. C, Title I, § 11042(a), Nov. 2, 2002, 116 Stat. 1854.)

HISTORICAL AND STATUTORY NOTES

Severability of Provisions

If any provision of this section or the application of such provision to any person or circumstance is held to be unconstitutional, the remainder of this section and the application thereof to any person or circumstance shall not be affected thereby, see section 11044 of Pub.L. 107–273, set out as a note under 28 U.S.C.A. § 351.

§ 362. Other provisions and rules not affected

Except as expressly provided in this chapter, nothing in this chapter shall be construed to affect any other provision of this title, the Federal Rules of Civil Procedure, the Federal Rules of Criminal Procedure, the Federal Rules of Appellate Procedure, or the Federal Rules of Evidence.

(Added Pub.L. 107–273, Div. C, Title I, § 11042(a), Nov. 2, 2002, 116 Stat. 1854.)

HISTORICAL AND STATUTORY NOTES

References in Text

The Federal Rules of Civil Procedure, the Federal Rules of Appellate Procedure, and the Federal Rules of Evidence, referred to in text, are all set out in this title.

The Federal Rules of Criminal Procedure, referred to in text, are set out in Title 18, Crimes and Criminal Procedure.

Severability of Provisions

If any provision of this section or the application of such provision to any person or circumstance is held to be unconstitutional, the remainder of this section and the application thereof to any person or circumstance shall not be affected thereby, see section 11044 of Pub.L. 107–273, set out as a note under 28 U.S.C.A. § 351.

§ 363. Court of Federal Claims, Court of International Trade, Court of Appeals for the Federal Circuit

The United States Court of Federal Claims, the Court of International Trade, and the Court of Appeals for the Federal Circuit shall each prescribe rules, consistent with the provisions of this chapter, establishing procedures for the filing of complaints with respect to the conduct of any judge of such court and for the investigation and resolution of such complaints. In investigating and taking action with respect to any such complaint, each such court shall have the powers granted to a judicial council under this chapter.

(Added Pub.L. 107–273, Div. C, Title I, § 11042(a), Nov. 2, 2002, 116 Stat. 1854.)

HISTORICAL AND STATUTORY NOTES

Severability

If any provision of this section or the application of such provision to any person or circumstance is held to be unconstitutional, the remainder of this section and the application thereof to any person or circumstance shall not be affected thereby, see section 11044 of Pub.L. 107–273, set out as a note under 28 U.S.C.A. § 351.

§ 364. Effect of felony conviction

In the case of any judge or judge of a court referred to in section 363 who is convicted of a felony under State or Federal law and has exhausted all means of obtaining direct review of the conviction, or the time for seeking further direct review of the conviction has passed and no such review has been sought, the following shall apply:

(1) The judge shall not hear or decide cases unless the judicial council of the circuit (or, in the case of a judge of a court referred to in section 363, that court) determines otherwise.

(2) Any service as such judge or judge of a court referred to in section 363, after the conviction is final and all time for filing appeals thereof has expired, shall not be included for purposes of determining years of service under section 371(c), 377, or 178 of this title or creditable service under subchapter III of chapter 83, or chapter 84, of title 5.

(Added Pub.L. 107–273, Div. C, Title I, § 11042(a), Nov. 2, 2002, 116 Stat. 1855.)

HISTORICAL AND STATUTORY NOTES

References in Text

Subchapter III of chapter 83 of Title 5, referred to in text, is 5 U.S.C.A. § 8331 et seq.

Chapter 84 of Title 5, referred to in text, is 5 U.S.C.A. § 8401 et seq.

Severability of Provisions

If any provision of this section or the application of such provision to any person or circumstance is held to be unconstitutional, the remainder of this section and the application thereof to any person or circumstance shall not be affected thereby, see section 11044 of Pub.L. 107–273, set out as a note under 28 U.S.C.A. § 351.

CHAPTER 17—RESIGNATION AND RETIREMENT OF JUSTICES AND JUDGES

Sec.
371. Retirement on salary; retirement in senior status.
372. Retirement for disability; substitute judge on failure to retire.
373. Judges in Territories and Possessions.[1]
374. Residence of retired judges; official station.
375. Recall of certain judges and magistrate judges.
376. Annuities for survivors of certain judicial officials of the United States.
377. Retirement of bankruptcy judges and magistrates.

[1] Section catchline amended by Pub.L. 99–396 without corresponding amendment of analysis.

HISTORICAL AND STATUTORY NOTES

Change of Name

"United States magistrate judge" substituted for "United States magistrate" in item 375 pursuant to section 321 of Pub.L. 101–650, set out as a note under 28 U.S.C.A. § 631.

§ 371. Retirement on salary; retirement in senior status

(a) Any justice or judge of the United States appointed to hold office during good behavior may retire from the office after attaining the age and meeting the service requirements, whether continuous or otherwise, of subsection (c) and shall, during the remainder of his lifetime, receive an annuity equal to the salary he was receiving at the time he retired.

(b)(1) Any justice or judge of the United States appointed to hold office during good behavior may retain the office but retire from regular active service after attaining the age and meeting the service requirements, whether continuous or otherwise, of subsection (c) of this section and shall, during the remainder of his or her lifetime, continue to receive the salary of the office if he or she meets the requirements of subsection (e).

(2) In a case in which a justice or judge who retires under paragraph (1) does not meet the requirements of subsection (e), the justice or judge shall continue to receive the salary that he or she was receiving when he or she was last in active service or, if a certification under subsection (e) was made for such justice or judge, when such a certification was last in effect. The salary of such justice or judge shall be adjusted under section 461 of this title.

(c) The age and service requirements for retirement under this section are as follows:

Attained Age:	Years of Service:
65	15
66	14
67	13
68	12

Attained Age:	Years of Service:
69	11
70	10

(d) The President shall appoint, by and with the advice and consent of the Senate, a successor to a justice or judge who retires under this section.

(e)(1) In order to continue receiving the salary of the office under subsection (b), a justice must be certified in each calendar year by the Chief Justice, and a judge must be certified by the chief judge of the circuit in which the judge sits, as having met the requirements set forth in at least one of the following subparagraphs:

(A) The justice or judge must have carried in the preceding calendar year a caseload involving courtroom participation which is equal to or greater than the amount of work involving courtroom participation which an average judge in active service would perform in three months. In the instance of a justice or judge who has sat on both district courts and courts of appeals, the caseload of appellate work and trial work shall be determined separately and the results of those determinations added together for purposes of this paragraph.

(B) The justice or judge performed in the preceding calendar year substantial judicial duties not involving courtroom participation under subparagraph (A), including settlement efforts, motion decisions, writing opinions in cases that have not been orally argued, and administrative duties for the court to which the justice or judge is assigned. Any certification under this subparagraph shall include a statement describing in detail the nature and amount of work and certifying that the work done is equal to or greater than the work described in this subparagraph which an average judge in active service would perform in three months.

(C) The justice or judge has, in the preceding calendar year, performed work described in subparagraphs (A) and (B) in an amount which, when calculated in accordance with such subparagraphs, in the aggregate equals at least 3 months work.

(D) The justice or judge has, in the preceding calendar year, performed substantial administrative duties directly related to the operation of the courts, or has performed substantial duties for a Federal or State governmental entity. A certification under this subparagraph shall specify that the work done is equal to the full-time work of an employee of the judicial branch. In any year in which a justice or judge performs work described under this subparagraph for less than the full year, one-half of such work may be aggregated with work described under subparagraph (A), (B), or (C) of this paragraph for the purpose of the justice or judge satisfying the requirements of such subparagraph.

(E) The justice or judge was unable in the preceding calendar year to perform judicial or administrative work to the extent required by any of subparagraphs (A) through (D) because of a temporary or permanent disability. A certification under this subparagraph shall be made to a justice who certifies in writing his or her disability to the Chief Justice, and to a judge who certifies in writing his or her disability to the chief judge of the circuit in which the judge sits. A justice or judge who is certified under this subparagraph as having a permanent disability shall be deemed to have met the requirements of this subsection for each calendar year thereafter.

(2) Determinations of work performed under subparagraphs (A), (B), (C), and (D) of paragraph (1) shall be made pursuant to rules promulgated by the Judicial Conference of the United States. In promulgating such criteria, the Judicial Conference shall take into account existing standards promulgated by the Conference for allocation of space and staff for senior judges.

(3) If in any year a justice or judge who retires under subsection (b) does not receive a certification under this subsection (except as provided in paragraph (1)(E)), he or she may thereafter receive a certification for that year by satisfying the requirements of subparagraph (A), (B), (C), or (D) of paragraph (1) of this subsection in a subsequent year and attributing a sufficient part of the work performed in such subsequent year to the earlier year so that the work so attributed, when added to the work performed during such earlier year, satisfies the requirements for certification for that year. However, a justice or judge may not receive credit for the same work for purposes of certification for more than 1 year.

(4) In the case of any justice or judge who retires under subsection (b) during a calendar year, there shall be included in the determination under this subsection of work performed during that calendar year all work performed by that justice or judge (as described in subparagraphs (A), (B), (C), and (D) of paragraph (1)) during that calendar year before such retirement.

(June 25, 1948, c. 646, 62 Stat. 903; Oct. 31, 1951, c. 655, § 39, 65 Stat. 724; Feb. 10, 1954, c. 6, § 4(a), 68 Stat. 12; July 10, 1984, Pub.L. 98–353, Title II, § 204(a), 98 Stat. 350; Nov. 19, 1988, Pub.L. 100–702, Title X, § 1005(a), 102 Stat. 4666; Nov. 30, 1989, Pub.L. 101–194, Title VII, § 705(a), 103 Stat. 1770; Oct. 19, 1996, Pub.L. 104–317, Title III, § 301, 110 Stat. 3851; Oct. 30, 2000, Pub.L. 106–398, § 1 [Div. A, Title VI, § 654(a)], 114 Stat. 1654, 1654A–165; Nov. 13, 2000, Pub.L. 106–518, Title III, § 303, 114 Stat. 2417.)

HISTORICAL AND STATUTORY NOTES

Codifications

Pub.L. 106–518, § 303, purported to amend subsec. (e) by inserting ", except such pay as is deductible from the retired or retainer pay as a result of participation in any survivor's benefits plan in connection with the retired pay,". The amendment could not be executed, because, retroactively effective Oct. 1, 1999, former subsec. (e) was struck out by Pub.L. 106–398 [Div. A, Title VI, § 654(a)(1)] which also redesignated former subsec. (f) as subsec. (e).

Effective and Applicability Provisions

2000 Acts. Amendment to subsecs. (b), (e) and (f) by Pub.L. 106–398, § 1 [Div. A, Title VI, § 654(a)] retroactively effective Oct. 1, 1999; see Pub.L. 106–398, § 1 [Div. A, Title VI, § 654(c)], set out as a note under section 180 of this title.

1989 Acts. Section 705(b) of Pub.L. 101–194 provided that:

"**(1) In general.**—The amendments made by subsection (a) [amending this section] shall first apply with respect to work performed on or after January 1, 1990, by a justice or judge of the United States who has retired under section 371(b) of title 28, United States Code [subsec. (b) of this section].

"**(2) Calendar year 1990.**—In the case certifications required by section 371(f) of title 28, United States Code [subsec. (f) of this section], for calendar year 1990—

"**(A)** such certifications shall be based on the 10-month period beginning on January 1, 1990, and ending on October 31, 1990, and shall be completed not later than December 15, 1990;

"**(B)** determinations of work performed under section 371(f) of title 28, United States Code [subsec. (f) of this section], shall be made pro rata on the basis of such 10-month period; and

"**(C)** such certifications shall be deemed to be certifications made in calendar year 1991."

1988 Acts. Section 1005(b) of Pub.L. 100–702 provided that: "The amendment made by this section [enacting subsec. (e) of this section] shall apply to a justice or judge who retires, or has retired, from the judicial office or from regular active service (into senior status) as such justice or judge of the United States on or after the effective date of section 5532(c) of title 5 [effective 90 days after Oct. 13, 1978 (see Effective Date of 1978 Amendment note under section 5532 of Title 5, Government Organization and Employees)], and to whom section 5532(c) would otherwise be applicable."

1984 Acts. Section 204(c) of Pub.L. 98–353 provided that: "The amendments made by this section [amending this section] shall apply with respect to any justice or judge of the United States appointed to hold office during good behavior who retires on or after the date of enactment of this Act [July 10, 1984]."

Computation of Judicial Service, District of Alaska

Pub.L. 89–70, July 8, 1965, 79 Stat. 213, provided: "That, notwithstanding any other provision of law, any service as a judge of the District Court for the Territory of Alaska shall be included in computing under sections 371 and 372 of title 28, United States Code [this section and section 372 of this title], the aggregate years of judicial service of a United States district judge for the district of Alaska."

Judicial Service in Hawaii Included Within Computation of Aggregate Years of Judicial Service

Pub.L. 86–3, § 14(d), Mar. 18, 1959, 73 Stat. 10, provided in part: "That service as a judge of the District Court for the Territory of Hawaii or as a judge of the United States District Court for the District of Hawaii or as a justice of the Supreme Court of the Territory of Hawaii or as a judge of the circuit courts of the Territory of Hawaii shall be included in computing under section 371, 372, or 373 of title 28, United States Code [this section, section 372, or section 373 of this title], the aggregate years of judicial service of any person who is in office as a district judge for the District of Hawaii on the date of enactment of this Act [Mar. 18, 1959]."

§ 372. Retirement for disability; substitute judge on failure to retire

(a) Any justice or judge of the United States appointed to hold office during good behavior who becomes permanently disabled from performing his duties may retire from regular active service, and the President shall, by and with the advice and consent of the Senate, appoint a successor.

Any justice or judge of the United States desiring to retire under this section shall certify to the President his disability in writing.

Whenever an associate justice of the Supreme Court, a chief judge of a circuit or the chief judge of the Court of International Trade, desires to retire under this section, he shall furnish to the President a certificate of disability signed by the Chief Justice of the United States.

A circuit or district judge, desiring to retire under this section, shall furnish to the President a certificate of disability signed by the chief judge of his circuit.

A judge of the Court of International Trade desiring to retire under this section, shall furnish to the President a certificate of disability signed by the chief judge of his court.

Each justice or judge retiring under this section after serving ten years continuously or otherwise shall, during the remainder of his lifetime, receive the salary of the office. A justice or judge retiring under this section who has served less than ten years in all shall, during the remainder of his lifetime, receive one-half the salary of the office.

(b) Whenever any judge of the United States appointed to hold office during good behavior who is eligible to retire under this section does not do so and a certificate of his disability signed by a majority of the members of the Judicial Council of his circuit in the case of a circuit or district judge, or by the Chief Justice of the United States in the case of the Chief Judge of the Court of International Trade, or by the chief judge of his court in the case of a judge of the Court of International Trade, is presented to the President and the President finds that such judge is unable to discharge efficiently all the duties of his office by reason of permanent mental or physical disability and that the appointment of an additional judge is necessary for the efficient dispatch of business, the President may make such appointment by and with the advice and consent of the Senate. Whenever any such additional judge is appointed, the vacancy subsequently caused by the death, resignation, or retirement of the disabled judge shall not be filled. Any judge whose disability causes the appointment of an additional judge shall, for purpose of precedence, service as chief judge, or temporary performance of the duties of that office, be treated as junior in commission to the other judges of the circuit, district, or court.

[(c) Repealed. Pub.L. 107–273, Div. C, Title I, § 11043(a)(1)(B), Nov. 2, 2002, 116 Stat. 1855]

(June 25, 1948, c. 646, 62 Stat. 903; May 24, 1949, c. 139, § 67, 63 Stat. 99; Feb. 10, 1954, c. 6, § 4(a), 68 Stat. 12; Sept. 2, 1957, Pub.L. 85–261, 71 Stat. 586; Oct. 10, 1980, Pub.L. 96–417, Title V, § 501(9), 94 Stat. 1742; Oct. 15, 1980, Pub.L. 96–458, § 3(a), (b), 94 Stat. 2036, 2040; Apr. 2, 1982, Pub.L. 97–164, Title I, § 112, 96 Stat. 29; July 10, 1984, Pub.L. 98–353, Title I, § 107, 98 Stat. 342; Nov. 19, 1988, Pub.L. 100–702, Title IV, § 403(c), 102 Stat. 4651; Dec. 1, 1990, Pub.L. 101–650, Title III, § 321, Title IV, § 402, 104 Stat. 5117, 5122; Oct. 29, 1992, Pub.L. 102–572, Title IX, § 902(b)(1), 106 Stat. 4516; Nov. 2, 2002, Pub.L. 107–273, Div. C, Title I, § 11043(a)(1), 116 Stat. 1855.)

HISTORICAL AND STATUTORY NOTES

Effective and Applicability Provisions

1992 Acts. Amendment by Pub.L. 102–572 effective Oct. 29, 1992, see section 911 of Pub.L. 102–572, set out as a note under section 171 of this title.

1990 Acts. Amendment by section 402 of Pub.L. 101–650 effective 90 days after Dec. 1, 1990, see section 407 of Pub.L. 101–650, set out as a note under section 332 of this title.

1988 Acts. Amendment by Pub.L. 100–702 effective Dec. 1, 1988, see section 407 of Pub.L. 100–702, set out as a note under section 2071 of this title.

1984 Acts. Amendment by Pub.L. 98–353 effective July 10, 1984, see section 122(a) of Pub.L. 98–353, set out as a note under section 151 of this title.

1982 Acts. Amendment by Pub.L. 97–164 effective Oct. 1, 1982, see section 402 of Pub.L. 97–164, set out as a note under section 171 of this title.

1980 Acts. Amendment by Pub.L. 96–458 effective Oct. 1, 1981, see section 7 of Pub.L. 96–458, set out as a note under section 331 of this title.

Amendment by Pub.L. 96–417 effective on Nov. 1, 1980, and applicable with respect to civil actions pending on or commenced on or after such date, see section 701(a) of Pub.L. 96–417, as amended, set out as a note under section 251 of this title.

Change of Name

References to United States Claims Court deemed to refer to United States Court of Federal Claims and references to Claims Court deemed to refer to Court of Federal Claims, see section 902(b) of Pub.L. 102–572, set out as a note under section 171 of Title 28, Judiciary and Judicial Procedure.

"United States magistrate judge" substituted for "United States magistrate" in text pursuant to section 321 of Pub.L. 101–650, set out as a note under 28 U.S.C.A. § 631.

Transfer of Functions

Any reference in any provision of law enacted before Jan. 4, 1995, to a function, duty, or authority of the Clerk of the House of Representatives treated as referring, with respect to that function, duty, or authority, to the officer of the House of Representatives exercising that function, duty, or authority, as determined by the Committee on House Oversight of the House of Representatives, see section 2(1) of Pub.L. 104–14, set out as a note preceding section 21 of Title 2, The Congress.

Computation of Judicial Service, District of Alaska

Inclusion of service as judge of the District Court for the Territory of Alaska in the computation of years of judicial service for judges of the United States District Court for the District of Alaska, see Pub.L. 89–70, July 8, 1965, 79 Stat. 213, set out as a note under section 371 of this title.

Extension of Time For Report by National Commission on Judicial Discipline and Removal

Pub.L. 102–368, Title I, Sept. 23, 1992, 106 Stat. 1118, provided in part that: "Notwithstanding the requirement of section 415 of Public Law 101–650 [set out as a note under this section] to submit the report mandated by said section not later than one year after the date of the Commission's first meeting, the National Commission on Judicial Discipline and Removal shall submit to each House of Congress, the Chief Justice of the United States, and the President, the report mandated in said section no later than August 1, 1993."

Judicial Service in Hawaii

Certain judicial service in Hawaii as included within computation of aggregate years of judicial service, see section 14(d) of Pub.L. 86–3, Mar. 18, 1959, 73 Stat. 10, set out as a note under section 371 of this title.

National Commission on Judicial Discipline and Removal

Subtitle II (sections 408 to 418) of Title IV of Pub.L. 101–650, as amended Pub.L. 102–198, § 8(a),(b)(2), Dec. 9, 1991, 105 Stat. 1625, 1626, provided that:

"Sec. 408. Short Title.

"This subtitle [subtitle II of Title IV of Pub.L. 101–650] may be cited as the 'National Commission on Judicial Discipline and Removal Act'.

"Sec. 409. Establishment.

"There is hereby established a commission to be known as the 'National Commission on Judicial Discipline and Removal' (hereinafter in this subtitle referred to as the 'Commission').

"Sec. 410. Duties of Commission.

"The duties of the Commission are—

"(1) to investigate and study the problems and issues involved in the tenure (including discipline and removal) of an article III judge;

"(2) to evaluate the advisability of proposing alternatives to current arrangements with respect to such problems and issues, including alternatives for discipline or removal of judges that would require amendment to the Constitution; and

"(3) to prepare and submit to the Congress, the Chief Justice of the United States, and the President a report in accordance with section 415.

"Sec. 411. Membership.

"(a) **Number and appointment.**—The Commission shall be composed of 13 members as follows:

"(1) Three appointed by the President pro tempore of the Senate.

"(2) Three appointed by the Speaker of the House of Representatives.

"(3) Three appointed by the Chief Justice of the United States.

"(4) Three appointed by the President.

"(5) One appointed by the Conference of Chief Justices of the States of the United States.

"(b) **Term.**—Members of the Commission shall be appointed for the life of the Commission.

"(c) **Quorum.**—Six members of the Commission shall constitute a quorum, but a lesser number may conduct meetings.

"(d) **Chairman.**—The members of the Commission shall select one of the members to be the Chairman.

"(e) **Vacancy.**—A vacancy on the Commission resulting from the death or resignation of a member shall not affect its powers and shall be filled in the same manner in which the original appointment was made.

"(f) **Continuation of membership.**—If any member of the Commission who was appointed to the Commission as a Member of Congress or as an officer or employee of a government leaves that office, or if any member of the Commission who was appointed from persons who are not officers or employees of a government becomes an officer or employee of a government, the member may continue as a member of the Commission for not longer than the 90-day period beginning on the date the member leaves that office or becomes such an officer or employee, as the case may be.

"Sec. 412. Compensation of the Commission.

"(a) **Pay.**—(1) Except as provided in paragraph (2), each member of the Commission who is not otherwise employed by the United States Government shall be entitled to receive the daily equivalent of the annual rate of basic pay payable for GS-18 of the General Schedule under section 5332 of title 5, United States Code [section 5332 of Title 5, Government Organization and Employees], for each day (including travel time) during which he or she is engaged in the actual performance of duties as a member of the Commission.

"(2) A member of the Commission who is an officer or employee of the United States Government shall serve without additional compensation.

"(b) **Travel.**—All members of the Commission shall be reimbursed for travel, subsistence, and other necessary expenses incurred by them in the performance of their duties.

"Sec. 413. Director and staff of Commission; experts and consultants.

"(a) **Director.**—The Commission shall, without regard to section 5311(b) of title 5, United States Code [section 5311(b) of Title 5], have a Director who shall be appointed by the Chairman and who shall be paid at a rate not to exceed the rate of basic pay payable for level V of the Executive Schedule under section 5316 of such title [section 5316 of Title 5].

"(b) **Staff.**—The Chairman of the Commission may appoint and fix the pay of such additional personnel as the Chairman finds necessary to enable the Commission to carry out its duties. Such personnel may be appointed without regard to the provisions of title 5, United States Code [Title 5], governing appointments in the competitive service, and may be paid without regard to the provisions of chapter 51 and subchapter III of chapter 53 of such title [section 5101 et seq. and section 5331 et seq. of Title 5] relating to classification and General Schedule pay rates, except that the annual rate of pay for any individual so appointed may not exceed a rate equal to the annual rate of basic pay payable for GS-18 of the General Schedule under section 5332 of such title [section 5332 of Title 5].

"(c) **Experts and consultants.**—The Commission may procure temporary and intermittent services of experts and consultants under section 3109(b) of title 5, United States Code [section 3109(b) of Title 5].

"Sec. 414. Powers of Commission.

"(a) **Hearings and sessions.**—The Commission or, on authorization of the Commission, a member of the Commission may, for the purpose of carrying out this subtitle, hold such hearings, sit and act at such times and places, take such testimony, and receive such evidence, as the Commission considers appropriate. The Commission may administer oaths or affirmations to witnesses appearing before it.

"(b) **Obtaining official data.**—The Commission may secure directly from any department, agency, or entity within the executive or judicial branch of the Federal Government information necessary to enable it to carry out this subtitle. Upon request of the Chairman of the Commission, the head of such department or agency shall furnish such information to the Commission.

"(c) **Facilities and support services.**—The Administrator of General Services shall provide to the Commission on a reimbursable basis such facilities and support services as the Commission may request. Upon request of the Commission, the head of any Federal agency is authorized to make any of the facilities and services of such agency available to the Commission to assist the Commission in carrying out its duties under this subtitle.

"(d) **Expenditures and contracts.**—The Commission or, on authorization of the Commission, a member of the Commission may make expenditures and enter into contracts for the procurement of such supplies, services, and property as the Commission or member considers appropriate for the purposes of carrying out the duties of the Commission. Such expenditures and contracts may be made only to such extent or in such amounts as are provided in appropriation Acts.

"(e) **Mails.**—The Commission may use the United States mails in the same manner and under the same conditions as other departments and agencies of the United States.

"(f) **Gifts.**—The Commission may accept, use, and dispose of gifts or donations of services or property.

"Sec. 415. Report.

"The Commission shall submit to each House of Congress, the Chief Justice of the United States, and the President a report not later than one year after the date of its first meeting. The report shall contain a detailed statement of the findings and conclusions of the Commission, together with its recommendations for such legislative or administrative action as it considers appropriate.

"Sec. 416. Termination.

"The Commission shall cease to exist on the date 30 days after the date it submits its report to the President and the Congress under section 415.

"Sec. 417. Authorization of appropriations.

"There is authorized to be appropriated the sum of $750,000 to carry out the provisions of this subtitle.

"Sec. 418. Effective date.

"This subtitle shall take effect on the date of the enactment of this Act [Dec. 1, 1990]."

[References in laws to the rates of pay for GS–16, 17, or 18, or to maximum rates of pay under the General Schedule, to be considered references to rates payable under specified sections of Title 5, Government Organization and Employees, see section 529 [Title I, § 101(c)(1)] of Pub.L. 101–509, set out in a note under section 5376 of Title 5.]

[For provisions extending the time for submission by the National Commission on Judicial Discipline and Removal of the report required by section 415 of Pub.L. 101–650, see Pub.L. 102–368, Title 1, Sept. 23, 1992, 106 Stat. 1118, set out as a note under this section.]

[For termination, effective May 15, 2000, of reporting provisions pertaining to the findings and conclusions of the Commission of Pub.L. 101–650, § 415 set out above, see Pub.L. 104–66, § 3003, as amended, set out as a note under 31 U.S.C.A. § 1113, and the 4th item on page 181 of House Document No. 103–7.]

§ 373. Judges in territories and possessions

(a) Any judge of the District Court of Guam, the District Court of the Northern Mariana Islands, or the District Court of the Virgin Islands who retires from office after attaining the age and meeting the service requirements whether continuous or otherwise, of subsection (b) shall, during the remainder of his lifetime, receive an annuity equal to the salary he is receiving at the time he retires.

(b) The age and service requirements for retirement under subsection (a) of this section are as follows:

Attained Age:	Years of Service:
65	15
66	14
67	13
68	12
69	11
70	10

(c)(1) Any judge or former judge who is receiving an annuity pursuant to this section may elect to become a senior judge of the court upon which he served before retiring.

(2) The chief judge of a judicial circuit may recall any such senior judge, with the judge's consent, to perform, for the court from which he retired, such judicial duties for such periods of time as the chief judge may specify.

(3) Any act or failure to act by a senior judge performing judicial duties pursuant to recall under paragraph (2) of this subsection shall have the same force and effect as if it were an act or failure to act of a judge on active duty; but such senior judge shall not be counted as a judge of the court on which he is serving as a recalled annuitant for purposes of the number of judgeships authorized for that court.

(4) Any senior judge performing judicial duties pursuant to recall under paragraph (2) of this subsection shall be paid, while performing such duties, the same compensation (in lieu of the annuity payable under subsection (a) of this section) and the same allowances for travel and other expenses as a judge on active duty with the court being served.

(5) Any senior judge performing judicial duties pursuant to recall under paragraph (2) of this subsection shall at all times be governed by the code of judicial conduct for United States judges approved by the Judicial Conference of the United States.

(d) Any judge who elects to become a senior judge under subsection (c) of this section and who thereafter—

(1) accepts civil office or employment under the Government of the United States (other than the performance of judicial duties pursuant to recall under subsection (c) of this section);

(2) engages in the practice of law; or

(3) materially violates the code of judicial conduct for United States judges,

shall cease to be a senior judge and to be eligible for recall pursuant to subsection (c) of this section.

(e) Any judge of the District Court of Guam, the District Court of the Northern Mariana Islands, or the District Court of the Virgin Islands who is removed by the President of the United States upon the sole ground of mental or physical disability, or who is not reappointed (as judge of such court), shall be entitled, upon attaining the age of sixty-five years or upon relinquishing office if he is then beyond the age of sixty-five years, (1) if his judicial service, continuous or otherwise, aggregates fifteen years or more, to receive during the remainder of his life an annuity equal to the salary he received when he left office, or (2) if his judicial service, continuous or otherwise, aggregated less than fifteen years but not less than ten years, to receive during the remainder of his life an annuity equal to that proportion of such salary which the aggregate number of his years of his judicial service bears to fifteen.

(f) Service at any time as a judge of the courts referred to in subsection (a) or of any other court of the United States, as defined by section 451 of this title, shall be included in the computation of aggregate years of judicial service for purposes of this section.

(g) Any retired judge who is entitled to receive an annuity under subsection (a) shall be entitled to a cost of living adjustment in the amount payable to him computed as specified in section 8340(b) of title 5, except that in no case may the annuity payable to such retired judge, as increased under this subsection, exceed 95 per centum of the salary of a United States district judge in regular active service.

(June 25, 1948, c. 646, 62 Stat. 904; Oct. 31, 1951, c. 655, § 40, 65 Stat. 724; Feb. 10, 1954, c. 6, § 5, 68 Stat. 13; July 7, 1958, Pub.L. 85–508, § 12(d), 72 Stat. 348; Mar. 18, 1959, Pub.L. 86–3, § 14(d), 73 Stat. 10; Sept. 12, 1966, Pub.L. 89–571, § 2, 80 Stat. 764; Oct. 11, 1976, Pub.L. 94–470, 90 Stat. 2052; Aug. 27, 1986, Pub.L. 99–396, § 21(a), 100 Stat. 844.)

HISTORICAL AND STATUTORY NOTES

Effective and Applicability Provisions

1986 Acts. Section 21(c) of Pub.L. 99–396 provided that: "The amendments made by this section [amending this section and section 376 of this title] shall not affect the amount payable to a judge who retired in accordance with the provisions of section 373 of title 28, United States Code [this section], in effect on the day before the date of enactment of this Act [Aug. 27, 1986]."

1959 Acts. Amendment by Pub.L. 86–3 effective upon the admission of the State of Hawaii into the Union, see note set out under section 91 of this title. Admission of Hawaii into the Union was accomplished Aug. 21, 1959 upon issuance of Proc. No. 3309, Aug. 21, 1959, 25 F.R. 6868, 73 Stat. c74, as required by sections 1 and 7(c) of Pub.L. 86–3, Mar. 18, 1959, 73 Stat. 4, set out as notes preceding 491 of Title 48, Territories and Insular Possessions.

1958 Acts. Amendment by Pub.L. 85–508 effective Jan. 3, 1959 upon admission of Alaska into the Union pursuant to Proc. No. 3269, Jan. 5, 1959, 24 F.R. 81, 73 Stat. c16, as required by sections 1 and 8(c) of Pub.L. 85–508, see notes set out under section 81A of this title and preceding section 21 of Title 48, Territories and Insular Possessions.

Election, Recall, Status, Compensation, Conduct, and Termination of Senior Judges

Pub.L. 98–454, Title X, § 1002, Oct. 5, 1984, 98 Stat. 1745, provided that:

"(a) Any judge or former judge who is receiving, or will upon attaining the age of sixty-five years be entitled to receive, payments pursuant to section 373 of title 28, United States Code[,] [this section] may elect to become a senior judge of the court on which he served while on active duty.

"(b) The chief judge of a judicial circuit may recall any such senior judge of his circuit, with the judge's consent, to perform in the District Court of Guam, the District Court of the Virgin Islands, or the District Court for the Northern Mariana Islands such judicial duties and for such periods of time as the chief judge may specify.

"(c) Any act or failure to act by a senior judge performing judicial duties pursuant to this section shall have the same force and effect as if it were the act or failure to act of a judge on active duty; but such senior judge shall not be counted as a judge of the court on which he is serving for purposes of the number of judgeships authorized for that court.

"(d) Any senior judge shall be paid, while performing duties pursuant to this section, the same compensation (in lieu of payments pursuant to section 373 of title 28, United States Code) [this section] and the same allowances for travel and other expenses as a judge in active service.

"(e) Senior judges under subsection (a) of this section shall at all times be governed by the code of judicial conduct for the United States judges, approved by the Judicial Conference of the United States.

"(f) Any person who has elected to be a senior judge under subsection (a) of this section and who thereafter—

"(1) accepts civil office or employment under the Government of the United States (other than the performance of judicial duties pursuant to subsection (b) of this section);

"(2) engages in the practice of law; or

"(3) materially violated the code of judicial conduct for the United States judges,

shall cease to be a senior judge and to be eligible for recall pursuant to subsection (b) of this section."

Judicial Service in Hawaii

Certain judicial service in Hawaii as included within computation of aggregate years of judicial service, see section 14(d) of Pub.L. 86–3, set out as a note under section 371 of this title.

Preservation of Rights of Retired Judges of the District Court for the District of Hawaii and Justices of the Supreme Court of the Territory of Hawaii

Section 14(d) of Pub.L. 86–3 provided in part: "That the amendments made by this subsection shall not affect the rights of any judge or justice who may have retired before the effective date of this subsection". See Effective and Applicability Provisions of 1959 Amendments note set out under this section.

Preservation of Rights of Retired Judges of the District Court for the Territory of Alaska

Section 12(d) of Pub.L. 85–508 provided in part: "That the amendment made by this subsection [amending this section] shall not affect the rights of any judge who may have retired before it takes effect". See Effective and Applicability Provisions of 1958 Amendments note set out under this section.

Tenure and Salary Rights of Judges in Puerto Rico in Office on September 12, 1966

Amendment by Pub.L. 89–571 not to affect tenure of office or right to continue to receive salary after resignation, retirement, or failure of reappointment of any district judge for the district of Puerto Rico in office on September 12, 1966, see section 4 of Pub.L. 89–571, set out as a note under section 134 of this title.

§ 374. Residence of retired judges; official station

Retired judges of the United States are not subject to restrictions as to residence. The place where a retired judge maintains the actual abode in which he customarily lives shall be deemed to be his official station for the purposes of section 456 of this title.

The place where a judge or magistrate judge recalled under section 155, 375, 636, or 797 of this title maintains the actual abode in which the judge or magistrate judge customarily lives shall be deemed to be the official station of such judge or magistrate judge for purposes of section 604(a)(7) of this title.

(June 25, 1948, c. 646, 62 Stat. 904; Sept. 21, 1959, Pub.L. 86–312, § 1, 73 Stat. 587; Nov. 14, 1986, Pub.L. 99–651, Title II, § 202(b), 100 Stat. 3648; Dec. 1, 1990, Pub.L. 101–650, Title III, § 321, 104 Stat. 5117.)

HISTORICAL AND STATUTORY NOTES

Effective and Applicability Provisions

1986 Acts. Amendment by Pub.L. 99–651 effective Jan. 1, 1987, see section 203 of Pub.L. 99–651, set out as a note under section 155 of this title.

Change of Name

"United States magistrate judge" substituted for "United States magistrate" in text pursuant to section 321 of Pub.L. 101–650, set out as a note under 28 U.S.C.A. § 631.

§ 375. Recall of certain judges and magistrate judges

(a)(1) A bankruptcy judge or a United States magistrate judge appointed under chapter 43 of this title, who has retired under the provisions of section 377 of this title or under the applicable provisions of title 5 upon attaining the age and years of service requirements established in section 371(c) of this title, may agree to be recalled to serve under this section for a period of five years as a bankruptcy judge or magistrate judge, as the case may be, upon certification that substantial service is expected to be performed by such retired judge or magistrate judge during such 5–year period. With the agreement of the judge or magistrate judge involved, a certification under this subsection may be renewed for successive 5–year periods.

(2) For purposes of paragraph (1) of this subsection, a certification may be made, in the case of a bankruptcy judge or a United States magistrate,[1] by the judicial council of the circuit in which the official duty station of the judge or magistrate at the time of retirement was located.

(3) For purposes of this section, the term "bankruptcy judge" means a bankruptcy judge appointed under chapter 6 of this title or serving as a bankruptcy judge on March 31, 1984.

(b) A judge or magistrate judge recalled under this section may exercise all of the powers and duties of the office of judge or magistrate judge held at the time of retirement, including the ability to serve in any other judicial district to the extent applicable, but may not engage in the practice of law or engage in any other business, occupation, or employment inconsistent with the expeditious, proper, and impartial performance of duties as a judicial officer.

(c) During the 5–year period in which a certification under subsection (a) is in effect, the judge or magistrate judge involved shall receive, in addition to the annuity provided under the provisions of section 377 of this title or under the applicable provisions of title 5, an amount equal to the difference between that annuity and the current salary of the office to which the judge or magistrate judge is recalled. The annuity of a bankruptcy judge or magistrate judge who completes that 5–year period of service, whose certification is not renewed, and who retired under section 377 of this title shall be equal to the salary in effect, at the end of that 5–year period, for the office from which he or she retired.

(d) A certification under subsection (a) may be terminated in accordance with chapter 16 of this title, and such a certification shall be terminated upon the death of the recalled judge or magistrate judge involved.

(e) Except as provided in subsection (b), nothing in this section shall affect the right of judges or magistrate judges who retire under the provisions of chapter 83 or chapter 84 of title 5 to serve as reemployed annuitants in accordance with the provisions of title 5. A judge or magistrate judge to whom this section applies may be recalled under section 155, 636(h), or 797 of this title, as the case may be, other than during a 5-year period in which a certification under subsection (a) is in effect with respect to that judge or magistrate judge.

(f) For purposes of determining the years of service requirements in order to be eligible for recall under this section, any service as a bankruptcy judge or a United States magistrate judge, and any prior service as a referee in bankruptcy or a United States commissioner, may be credited.

(g) Except as provided in subsection (c), a judge or magistrate judge recalled under this section who retired under the applicable provisions of title 5 shall be considered to be a reemployed annuitant under chapter 83 or chapter 84, as the case may be, of title 5.

(h) The Judicial Conference of the United States may promulgate regulations to implement this section.

(Added Pub.L. 99–651, Title II, § 201(b)(1), Nov. 14, 1986, 100 Stat. 3647, and amended Pub.L. 100–659, § 4(b), Nov. 15, 1988, 102 Stat. 3918; Pub.L. 101–650, Title III, §§ 321, 325(b)(2), Dec. 1, 1990, 104 Stat. 5117, 5121; Pub.L. 102–572, Title IX, § 904(a), Oct. 29, 1992, 106 Stat. 4517; Pub.L. 107–273, Div. C, Title I, § 11043(d), Nov. 2, 2002, 116 Stat. 1855.)

[1] So in original. Probably should be "United States magistrate judge."

HISTORICAL AND STATUTORY NOTES

Effective and Applicability Provisions

1992 Acts. Amendment by Title IX of Pub.L. 102–572 effective Oct. 29, 1992, see section 911 of Pub.L. 102–572, set out as a note under section 171 of Title 28, Judiciary and Judicial Procedure.

1988 Acts. Amendment to this section by Pub.L. 100–659 to take effect on Nov. 15, 1988, and shall apply to bankruptcy judges and magistrates who retire on or after Nov. 15, 1988, with special election provisions for bankruptcy judges, etc., who left office on or after July 31, 1987, and before Nov. 15, 1988, see section 9 of Pub.L. 100–659, set out as a note under section 377 of this title.

1986 Acts. Section effective Jan. 1, 1987, see section 203 of Pub.L. 99–651, set out as an Effective and Applicability Provisions of 1986 Amendments note under section 155 of this title.

Change of Name

References to United States Claims Court deemed to refer to United States Court of Federal Claims and references to Claims Court deemed to refer to Court of Federal Claims, see section 902(b) of Pub.L. 102–572, set out as a note under section 171 of Title 28, Judiciary and Judicial Procedure.

"United States magistrate judge" substituted for "United States magistrate" in text pursuant to section 321 of Pub.L. 101–650, set out as a note under 28 U.S.C.A. § 631.

Prior Provisions

A prior section 375, added Aug. 28, 1954, c. 1053, § 1, 68 Stat. 918, and amended Aug. 3, 1956, c. 944, § 1(b), 70 Stat. 1021; Aug. 22, 1972, Pub.L. 92–397, § 1, 86 Stat. 579, which provided for annuities to widows of justices, was repealed by Pub.L. 96–504, § 5, Dec. 5, 1980, 94 Stat. 2742.

§ 376. Annuities for survivors of certain judicial officials of the United States

(a) For the purposes of this section—

(1) "judicial official" means:

(A) a Justice or judge of the United States, as defined by section 451 of this title;

(B) a judge of the District Court of Guam, the District Court of the Northern Mariana Islands, or the District Court of the Virgin Islands;

(C) a Director of the Administrative Office of the United States Courts, after he or she has filed a waiver under subsection (a) of section 611 of this title;

(D) a Director of the Federal Judicial Center, after he or she has filed a waiver under subsection (a) of section 627 of this title;

(E) a Counselor to the Chief Justice of the United States, after he or she has filed a waiver in accordance with both subsection (a) of section 677 and subsection (a) of section 611 of this title;

(F) a full-time bankruptcy judge or a full-time United States magistrate judge; or

(G) a judge of the United States Court of Federal Claims;

who notifies the Director of the Administrative Office of the United States Courts in writing of his or her intention to come within the purview of this section within six months after (i) the date upon which he or she takes office, (ii) the date upon which he or she marries, (iii) January 1, 1977, (iv) October 1, 1986, (v) the date of the enactment of the Retirement and Survivors' Annuities for Bankruptcy Judges and Magistrates Act of 1988, in the case of a full-time bankruptcy judge or United States magistrate judge in active service on that date, (vi) the date of the enactment of the Federal Courts Study Committee Implementation Act of 1990, in the case of a full-time judge of the Court of Federal Claims in active service on that date, or (vii) the date of the enactment of the Federal Courts Administration Act of 1992;

(2) "retirement salary" means:

(A) in the case of a Justice or judge of the United States, as defined by section 451 of this title, salary paid (i) after retirement from regular active service under subsection (b) of section 371 or subsection (a) of section 372 of this title, or (ii) after retirement from office by resignation on salary under subsection (a) of section 371 of this title;

(B) in the case of a judge of the District Court of Guam, the District Court of the Northern Mariana Islands, or the District Court of the Virgin Islands, (i) an annuity paid under subsection (a) of section 373 of this title or (ii) compensation paid under paragraph (4) of subsection (c) of section 373 of this title;

(C) in the case of a Director of the Administrative Office of the United States Courts, an annuity paid under subsection (b) or (c) of section 611 of this title;

(D) in the case of a Director of the Federal Judicial Center, an annuity paid under subsection (b) or (c) of section 627 of this title;

(E) in the case of a Counselor to the Chief Justice of the United States, an annuity paid in accordance with both subsection (a) of section 677 and subsection (a) of section 611 of this title;

(F) in the case of a bankruptcy judge or United States magistrate judge, an annuity paid under section 377 of this title; and

(G) in the case of a judge of the United States Court of Federal Claims, an annuity paid under section 178 of this title;

(3) "widow" means the surviving wife of a "judicial official", who:

(A) has been married to him for at least one year on the day of his death; or

(B) is the mother of issue by that marriage;

(4) "widower" means the surviving husband of a "judicial official", who:

(A) has been married to her for at least one year on the day of her death; or

(B) is the father of issue by that marriage;

(5) "child" means:

(A) an unmarried child under eighteen years of age, including (i) an adopted child and (ii) a stepchild or recognized natural child who lived with the judicial official in a regular parent-child relationship;

(B) such unmarried child between eighteen and twenty-two years of age who is a student regularly pursuing a full-time course of study or training in residence in a high school, trade school, technical or vocational institute, junior college, college, university, or comparable educational institution. A child whose twenty-second birthday occurs before July 1, or after August 31, of a calendar year, and while he or she is regularly pursuing such a course of study or training, is deemed to have become twenty-two years of age on the first day of July immediately following that birthday. A child who is a student is deemed not to have ceased being a student during an interim period between school years, if that interim period lasts no longer than five consecutive months and if that child shows, to the satisfaction of the Director of the Administrative Office of the United States Courts, that he or she has a bona fide intention of continuing to pursue a course of study or training in the same or a different school during the school semester, or other period into which the school year is divided, immediately following that interim period; or

(C) such unmarried child, regardless of age, who is incapable of self-support because of a mental or physical disability incurred either (i) before age eighteen, or (ii) in the case of a child who is receiving an annuity as a full-time student under paragraph (5)(B) of this subsection, before the termination of that annuity;

(6) "former spouse" means a former spouse of a judicial official if the former spouse was married to such judicial official for at least 9 months; and

(7) "assassinated" and "assassination" mean the killing of a judicial official described in paragraph (1)(A), (B), (F), or (G) of this subsection that is motivated by the performance by that judicial official of his or her official duties.

(b)(1) Every judicial official who files a written notification of his or her intention to come within the purview of this section, in accordance with paragraph (1) of subsection (a) of this section, shall be deemed thereby to consent and agree to having deducted and withheld from his or her salary a sum equal to 2.2 percent of that salary, and a sum equal to 3.5 percent of his or her retirement salary. The deduction from any retirement salary—

(A) of a justice or judge of the United States retired from regular active service under section 371(b) or section 372(a) of this title,

(B) of a judge of the United States Court of Federal Claims retired under section 178 of this title, or

(C) of a judicial official on recall under section 155(b), 373(c)(4), 375, or 636(h) of this title,

shall be an amount equal to 2.2 percent of retirement salary.

(2) A judicial official who is not entitled to receive an immediate retirement salary upon leaving office but who is eligible to receive a deferred retirement salary on a later date shall file, within 90 days before leaving office, a written notification of his or her intention to remain within the purview of this section under such conditions and procedures as may be determined by the Director of the Administrative Office of the United States Courts. Every judicial official who files a written notification in accordance with this paragraph shall be deemed to consent to contribute, during the period before such a judicial official begins to receive his or her retirement salary, a sum equal to 3.5 percent of the deferred retirement salary which that judicial official is entitled to receive. Any judicial official who fails to file a written notification under this paragraph shall be deemed to have revoked his or her election under subsection (a) of this section.

(3) The amounts deducted and withheld from the salary of each judicial official under paragraphs (1) and (2) of this subsection shall, in accordance with such procedures as may be prescribed by the Comptroller General of the United States, be covered into the Treasury of the United States and credited to the "Judicial Survivors' Annuities Fund" established by section 3 of the Judicial Survivors' Annuities Reform Act. Such fund shall be used for the payment of annuities, refunds, and allowances as provided by this section. Payment of such salary less such deductions (and any deductions made under section 178 or 377 of this title or under subchapter III of chapter 83, or chapter 84, of title 5) shall be a full and complete discharge and acquittance of all claims and demands whatsoever for all services rendered by such judicial official during the period covered by such payment, except the rights to those benefits to which such judicial official, or his or her survivors, shall be entitled under the provisions of this section (and under section 178 or 377 of this title or under subchapter III of chapter 83, or chapter 84, of title 5).

(c)(1) There shall also be deposited to the credit of the Judicial Survivors' Annuities Fund, in accordance with such procedures as the Comptroller General of the United States may prescribe, amounts required to reduce to zero the unfunded liability of the Judicial Survivors' Annuities Fund: *Provided*, That such amounts shall not exceed the equivalent of 9 percent of salary or retirement salary. Such deposits shall, subject to appropriations Acts, be taken from the fund used to pay the compensation of the judicial official, and shall immediately become an integrated part of the Judicial Survivors' Annuities Fund for any use required under this section.

(2) For purposes of paragraph (1), the term "unfunded liability" means the estimated excess, determined on an annual basis in accordance with the provisions of section 9503 of title 31, United States Code, of the present value of all benefits payable from the Judicial Survivors' Annuities Fund, over the sum of—

(A) the present value of deductions to be withheld from the future basic pay of judicial officials; plus

(B) the balance in the Fund as of the date the unfunded liability is determined.

In making any determination under this paragraph, the Comptroller General shall use the applicable information contained in the reports filed pursuant to section 9503 of title 31, United States Code, with respect to the judicial survivors' annuities plan established by this section.

(3) There are authorized to be appropriated such sums as may be necessary to carry out this subsection.

(d) Each judicial official shall deposit, with interest at 4 percent per annum to December 31, 1947, and at 3 percent per annum thereafter, compounded on December 31 of each year, to the credit of the "Judicial Survivors' Annuities Fund":

(1) a sum equal to 3.5 percent of that salary, including "retirement salary", which he or she has received for serving in any of the offices designated in paragraph (1) of subsection (a) of this section prior to the date upon which he or she filed notice of an intention to come within the purview of this section with the Director of the Administrative Office of the United States Courts; and

(2) a sum equal to 3.5 percent of the basic salary, pay, or compensation which he or she has received for serving as a Senator, Representative, Delegate, or Resident Commissioner in Congress, or for serving as an "employee", as that term is defined in subsection (1) of section 8331 of title 5, prior to assuming the responsibilities of any of the offices designated in paragraph (1) of subsection (a) of this section.

The interest otherwise required by this subsection shall not be required for any period during which a judicial official was separated from all such service and was not receiving any retirement salary.

Each such judicial official may elect to make such deposits in installments, during the continuance of his or her service in those offices designated in paragraph (1) of subsection (a) of this section, in such amounts and under such conditions as may be determined in each instance by the Director of the Administrative Office of the United States Courts: *Provided*, That, in each instance in which a judicial official does elect to make such deposits in installments, the Director shall require (i) that the first installment payment made shall be in an amount no smaller than that amount necessary to cover at least the last eighteen months of prior creditable civilian service, and (ii) that at least one additional installment payment shall be made every eighteen months thereafter until the total of all such deposits have been made.

Notwithstanding the failure of any such judicial official to make all such deposits or installment payments, credit shall be allowed for the service rendered, but the annuity of that judicial official's widow or widower shall be reduced by an amount equal to 10 percent of the amount of such deposits, computed as of the date of the death of such judicial official, unless such widow or widower shall elect to eliminate such service entirely from credit under subsection (k) of this section: *Provided*, That no deposit shall be required from any such judicial official for any honorable active duty service in the Army, Navy, Air Force, Marine Corps, or Coast Guard of the United States, or for any other creditable service rendered prior to August 1, 1920.

(e) The amounts deducted and withheld in accordance with subsection (b) of this section, and the amounts deposited in accordance with subsection (d) of this section, shall be credited to individual accounts in the name of each judicial official from whom such amounts are received, for credit to the "Judicial Survivors' Annuities Fund".

(f) The Secretary of the Treasury shall invest, from time to time, in interest bearing securities of the United States or Federal farm loan bonds, those portions of the "Judicial Survivors' Annuities Fund" which in his judgment may not be immediately required for the payment of annuities, refunds, and allowances as provided in this section. The income derived from such investments shall constitute a part of such fund for the purposes of paying annuities and carrying out the provisions of subsections (g), (h), (m), (o), (p), and (q) of this section.

(g) If any judicial official leaves office and is ineligible to receive a retirement salary or leaves office and is entitled to a deferred retirement salary but fails to make an election under subsection (b)(2) of this section, all amounts credited to his or her account established under subsection (e), together with interest at 4 percent per annum to December 31, 1947, and at 3 percent per annum thereafter, compounded on December 31 of each year, to the date of his or her relinquishment of office, minus a sum equal to 2.2

percent of salary for service while deductions were withheld under subsection (b) or for which a deposit was made by the judicial official under subsection (d), shall be returned to that judicial official in a lump-sum payment within a reasonable period of time following the date of his or her relinquishment of office. For the purposes of this section, a "reasonable period of time" shall be presumed to be no longer than 1 year following the date upon which such judicial official relinquishes his or her office.

(h) Annuities payable under this section shall be paid only in accordance with the following provisions:

(1) In any case in which a judicial official dies while in office, while receiving retirement salary, or after filing an election and otherwise complying with the conditions under subsection (b)(2) of this section (A) after having completed at least eighteen months of creditable civilian service, as computed in accordance with subsection (k) of this section, for the last eighteen months of which the salary deductions provided by subsection (b) of this section or, in lieu thereof, the deposits required by subsection (d) of this section have actually been made, or (B) if the death of such judicial official was by assassination, before having satisfied the requirements of clause (A) if, for the period of such service, the deductions provided by subsection (b) or, in lieu thereof, the deposits required by subsection (d) have actually been made—

(i) if such judicial official is survived by a widow or widower, but not by a child, there shall be paid to such widow or widower an annuity, beginning on the day on which such judicial official died, in an amount computed as provided in subsection (*l*) of this section; or

(ii) if such judicial official is survived by a widow or widower and a child or children, there shall be paid to such widow or widower an annuity, beginning on the day on which such judicial official died, in an amount computed as provided in subsection (*l*) of this section, and there shall also be paid to or on behalf of each such child an immediate annuity equal to:

(I) 10 percent of the average annual salary determined under subsection (*l*)(1) of this section; or

(II) 20 percent of such average annual salary, divided by the number of children;

whichever is smallest; or

(iii) if such judicial official leaves no surviving widow or widower, but does leave a surviving child or children, there shall be paid to or on behalf of each such child an immediate annuity equal to:

(I) the amount of the annuity to which the judicial official's widow or widower would have been entitled under clause (i) of this paragraph, had such widow or widower survived the judicial official, divided by the number of children; or

(II) 20 percent of the average annual salary determined under subsection (*l*)(1) of this section; or

(III) 40 percent of such average annual salary amount, divided by the number of children;

whichever is smallest.

(2) An annuity payable to a widow or widower under clause (i) or (ii) of paragraph (1) of this subsection shall be terminated upon his or her death or remarriage before attaining age 55.

(3) An annuity payable to a child under this subsection shall terminate:

(A) if such child is receiving an annuity based upon his or her status under paragraph (5)(A) of subsection (a) of this section, on the last day of the month during which he or she becomes eighteen years of age;

(B) if such child is receiving an annuity based upon his or her status under paragraph (5)(B) of subsection (a) of this section, either (i) on the first day of July immediately following his or her twenty-second birthday or (ii) on the last day of the month during which he or she ceases to be a full-time student in accordance with paragraph (5)(B) of subsection (a) of this section, whichever occurs first: *Provided*, That if such child is rendered incapable of self-support because of a mental or physical disability incurred while receiving that annuity, that annuity shall not terminate, but shall continue without interruption and shall be deemed to have become, as of the date of disability, an annuity based upon his or her status under clause (ii) of paragraph (5)(C) of subsection (a) of this section;

(C) if such child is receiving an annuity based upon his or her status under paragraph (5)(C) of subsection (a) of this section, on the last day of the month during which he or she ceases to be incapable of self-support because of mental or physical disability; or

(D) on the last day of the month during which such child dies or marries.

(4) An annuity payable to a child or children under paragraph (1)(ii) of this subsection shall be recomputed and paid as provided in paragraph (1)(iii) of this subsection upon the death, but not upon the remarriage, of the widow or widower who is receiving an annuity under paragraph (1)(ii) of this subsection.

(5) In any case in which the annuity of a child is terminated, the annuity of each remaining child which is based upon the service of the same judicial official shall be recomputed and paid as though the child whose annuity has been terminated had not survived that judicial official.

(6) In the case of the survivor or survivors of a judicial official to whom paragraph (1)(B) applies, there shall be deducted from the annuities otherwise payable under this section an amount equal to the amount of salary deductions that would have been made if such deductions had been made for 18 months prior to the judicial official's death, subject to subsection (x).

(i)(1) All questions of dependency and disability arising under this section shall be determined by the Director of the Administrative Office of the United States Courts, subject to review only by the Judicial Conference of the United States, and the decision of the Judicial Conference of the United States shall be final and conclusive. The Director may order or direct at any time such medical or other examinations as he deems necessary to determine the facts relative to the nature and degree of disability of any child who is an annuitant, or an applicant for an annuity, under this section, and may suspend or deny any such annuity for failure to submit to any such examination.

(2) The Director of the Administrative Office of the United States Courts shall determine whether the killing of a judicial official was an assassination, subject to review only by the Judicial Conference of the United States. The head of any Federal agency that investigates the killing of a judicial official shall provide information to the Director that would assist the Director in making such determination.

(j) In any case in which a payment under this section is to be made to a minor, or to a person mentally incompetent or under other legal disability, as determined by a court of competent jurisdiction, such payment may be made to the person who is constituted guardian or other fiduciary of such claimant by the laws of the State of residence of such claimant, or to any other person who is otherwise legally vested with the care of the claimant or of the claimant's estate, and need not be made directly to such claimant. The Director of the Administrative Office of the United States Courts may, at his or her discretion, determine whether such payment is made directly to such claimant or to such guardian, fiduciary, or other person legally vested with the care of such claimant or the claimant's estate. Where no guardian or other fiduciary of such minor or such person under legal disability has been appointed under the laws of the State of residence of such claimant, the Director of the Administrative Office of the United States Courts shall determine the person who is otherwise legally vested with the care of the claimant or of the claimant's estate.

(k) The years of service rendered by a judicial official which may be creditable in calculating the amount of an annuity for such judicial official's widow or widower under subsection (*l*) of this section shall include—

(1) those years during which such judicial official served in any of the offices designated in paragraph (1) of subsection (a) of this section, including in the case of a Justice or judge of the United States those years during which he or she continued to hold office following retirement from regular active service under section 371 or subsection (a) of section 372 of this title;

(2) those years during which such judicial official served as a Senator, Representative, Delegate, or Resident Commissioner in Congress, prior to assuming the responsibilities of any of the offices designated in paragraph (1) of subsection (a) of this section;

(3) those years during which such judicial official honorably served on active duty in the Army, Navy, Air Force, Marine Corps, or Coast Guard of the United States, prior to assuming the responsibilities of any of the offices designated in paragraph (1) of subsection (a) of this section: *Provided*, That those years of such military service for which credit has been allowed for the purposes of retirement or retired pay under any other provision of law shall not be included as allowable years of such service under this section;

(4) those years during which such judicial official served as an "employee", as that term is defined in subsection (1) of section 8331 of title 5, prior to assuming the responsibilities of any of the offices designated in paragraph (1) of subsection (a) of this section,[1] and

(5) those years during which such judicial official had deductions withheld from his or her retirement salary in accordance with subsection (b)(1) or (2) of this section.

For the purposes of this subsection the term "years" shall mean full years and twelfth parts thereof, excluding from the aggregate any fractional part of a month which numbers less than fifteen full days and including, as one full month, any fractional part of a month which numbers fifteen full days or more. Nothing in this subsection shall be interpreted as waiving or canceling that reduction in the annuity of a widow or widower which is required by subsection (d) of this section due to the failure of a judicial official to make those deposits required by subsection (d) of this section.

(*l*) The annuity of a widow or widower of a judicial official shall be an amount equal to the sum of—

(1) 1.5 percent of the average annual salary, including retirement salary, which such judicial official received for serving in any of the offices designated in paragraph (1) of subsection (a) of this section (i) during those three years of such service, or during those three years while receiving a retirement salary, in which his or her annual salary or retirement salary was greatest, or (ii) if such judicial official has so served less than three years, then during the total period of such service prior to his or her death, multiplied by the total of:

(A) the number of years of creditable service tabulated in accordance with paragraph (1) of subsection (k) of this section; plus

(B) the number of years of creditable service tabulated in accordance with paragraph (2) of subsection (k) of this section; plus

(C) the number of years of creditable service tabulated in accordance with paragraph (3) of subsection (k) of this section; plus

(D) the number of years during which the judicial official had deductions withheld from his or her retirement salary under subsection (b)(1) or (2) of this section; plus

(E) the number of years up to, but not exceeding, fifteen of creditable service tabulated in accordance with paragraph (4) of subsection (k) of this section,

plus:

(2) three-fourths of 1 percent of such average annual salary, multiplied by the number of years of any prior creditable service, as tabulated in accordance with subsection (k) of this section, not applied under paragraph (1) of this subsection;

except that such annuity shall not exceed an amount equal to 50 percent of such average annual salary, nor be less than an amount equal to 25 percent of such average annual salary. Any annuity determined in accordance with the provisions of this subsection shall be reduced to the extent required by subsection (d) of this section, and by the amount of any annuity payable to a former spouse under subsection (t).

(m) Each time that an increase is made under section 8340(b) of title 5 in annuities paid under subchapter III of chapter 83 of such title, each annuity payable from the Judicial Survivors' Annuities Fund shall be increased at the same time by the same percentage by which annuities are increased under that section.

(n) Each annuity authorized under this section shall accrue monthly and shall be due and payable in monthly installments on the first business day of the month following the month or other period for which the annuity shall have accrued. No annuity authorized under this section shall be assignable, either in law or in equity, except as provided in subsections (s) and (t), or subject to execution, levy, attachment, garnishment, or other legal process.

(*o*)(1) In any case in which a judicial official dies while in office, while receiving retirement salary, or after filing an election and otherwise complying with the conditions under subsection (b)(2) of this section, and;

(A) subject to paragraph (2) of this subsection, before having completed eighteen months of civilian service, computed in accordance with subsection (k) of this section, during which the salary deductions provided by subsection (b) of this section or the deposit required by subsection (d) of this section have actually been made; or

(B) after having completed eighteen months of civilian service, computed in accordance with subsection (k) of this section, during which all such deductions or deposits have been made, but without a survivor or survivors who are entitled to receive the annuity benefits provided by subsection (h) or (t) of this section; or

(C) the rights of all persons entitled to receive the annuity benefits provided by subsection (h) or (t) of this section terminate before a valid claim therefor has been established;

the total amount credited to the individual account of that judicial official, established under subsection (e) of this section, with interest at 4 percent per annum to December 31, 1947, and at 3 percent per annum thereafter, compounded on December 31, of each year, to the date of that judicial official's death, shall be paid, upon the establishment of a valid claim therefor, to the person or persons surviving at the date title to the payment arises, in the following order of precedence:

First, to the beneficiary or beneficiaries whom that judicial official may have designated in a writing received by the Administrative Office of the United States Courts prior to his or her death;

Second, if there be no such beneficiary, to the widow or widower of such judicial official;

Third, if none of the above, to the child or children of such judicial official and the descendants of any deceased children by representation;

Fourth, if none of the above, to the parents of such judicial official or the survivor of them;

Fifth, if none of the above, to the duly appointed executor, executrix, administrator, or administratrix of the estate of such judicial official;

Sixth, if none of the above, to such other next of kin of such judicial official, as may be determined by the Director of the Administrative Office of the United States Courts to be entitled to such payment, under the laws of the domicile of such judicial official, at the time of his or her death.

Such payment shall be a bar to recovery by any other person. For the purposes of this subsection only, a determination that an individual is a widow, widower, or child of a judicial official may be made by the Director of the Administrative Office of the United States Courts without regard to the definitions of those terms contained in paragraphs (3), (4), and (5) of subsection (a) of this section.

(2) In cases in which a judicial official dies as a result of assassination and leaves a survivor or survivors who are entitled to receive the annuity benefits provided by subsection (h) or (t) of this section, paragraph (1)(A) of this subsection shall not apply.

(p) In any case in which all the annuities which are authorized by this section and based upon the service of a given official terminate before the aggregate amount of annuity payments received by the annuitant or annuitants equals the total amount credited to the individual account of such judicial official, established under subsection (e) of this section with interest at 4 percent per annum to December 31, 1947, and at 3 percent per annum thereafter, compounded on December 31, of each year, to the date of that judicial official's death, the difference between such total amount, with such interest, and such aggregate amount shall be paid, upon establishment of a valid claim therefor, in the order of precedence prescribed in subsection (*o*) of this section.

(q) Any accrued annuity benefits remaining unpaid upon the termination of an annuity, other than by the death of an annuitant, shall be paid to that annuitant. Any accrued annuity benefits remaining unpaid upon the death of an annuitant shall be paid, upon the establishment of a valid claim therefor, in the following order of precedence:

First, to the duly appointed executor, executrix, administrator, or administratrix of the estate of such annuitant;

Second, if there is no such executor, executrix, administrator, or administratrix, payments shall be made, after the expiration of sixty days from the date of death of such annuitant, to such individual or individuals as may appear, in the judgment of the Director of the Administrative Office of the United States Courts, to be legally entitled thereto, and such payment shall be a bar to recovery by any other individual.

(r) Nothing contained in this section shall be interpreted to prevent a widow or widower eligible for an annuity under this section from simultaneously receiving such an annuity while also receiving any other annuity to which such widow or widower may also be entitled under any other law without regard to this section: *Provided*, That service used in the computation of the annuity conferred by this section shall not also be credited in computing any such other annuity.

(s) A judicial official who has a former spouse may elect, under procedures prescribed by the Director of the Administrative Office of the United States Courts, to provide a survivor annuity for such former spouse under subsection (t). An election under this subsection shall be made at the time of retirement, or, if later, within 2 years after the date on which the marriage of the former spouse to the judicial official is dissolved. An election under this subsection—

(1) shall not be effective to the extent that it—

(A) conflicts with—

(i) any court order or decree referred to in subsection (t)(1), which was issued before the date of such election, or

(ii) any agreement referred to in such subsection which was entered into before such date; or

(B) would cause the total of survivor annuities payable under subsections (h) and (t) based on the service of the judicial official to exceed 55 percent of the average annual salary (as such term is used in subsection (*l*)) of such official; and

(2) shall not be effective, in the case of a judicial official who is then married, unless it is made with the spouse's written consent.

The Director of the Administrative Office of the United States Courts shall provide by regulation that paragraph (2) of this subsection may be waived if the judicial official establishes to the satisfaction of the Director that the spouse's whereabouts cannot be determined, or that, due to exceptional circumstances, requiring the judicial official to seek the spouse's consent would otherwise be inappropriate.

(t)(1) Subject to paragraphs (2) through (4) of this subsection, a former spouse of a deceased judicial official is entitled to a survivor annuity under this section if and to the extent expressly provided for in an election under subsection (s), or in the terms of any decree of divorce or annulment or any court order or court-approved property settlement agreement incident to such decree.

(2) The annuity payable to a former spouse under this subsection may not exceed the difference between—

(A) the maximum amount that would be payable as an annuity to a widow or widower under subsection (*l*), determined without taking into account any reduction of such annuity caused by payment of an annuity to a former spouse; and

(B) the amount of any annuity payable under this subsection to any other former spouse of the judicial official, based on an election previously made under subsection (s), or a court order previously issued.

(3) The commencement and termination of an annuity payable under this subsection shall be governed by the terms of the applicable order, decree, agreement, or election, as the case may be, except that any such annuity—

(A) shall not commence before—

(i) the day after the judicial official dies, or

(ii) the first day of the second month beginning after the date on which the Director of the Administrative Office of the United States Courts receives written notice of the order, decree, agreement, or election, as the case may be, together with such additional information or documentation as the Director may prescribe,

whichever is later, and

(B) shall terminate no later than the last day of the month before the former spouse remarries before becoming 55 years of age or dies.

(4) For purposes of this section, a modification in a decree, order, agreement, or election referred to in paragraph (1) of this subsection shall not be effective—

(A) if such modification is made after the retirement of the judicial official concerned, and

(B) to the extent that such modification involves an annuity under this subsection.

(u) In the case of a judicial official who is assassinated, an annuity shall be paid under this section notwithstanding a survivor's eligibility for or receipt of benefits under chapter 81 of title 5, except that the annuity for which a surviving spouse is eligible under this section shall be reduced to the extent that the total benefits paid under this section and chapter 81 of title 5 for any year would exceed the current salary for that year of the office of the judicial official.

(v) Subject to the terms of a decree, court order, or agreement described in subsection (t)(1), if any judicial official ceases to be married after making the election under subsection (a), he or she may revoke such election in writing by notifying the Director of the Administrative Office of the United States Courts. The judicial official shall also notify any spouse or former spouse of the application for revocation in accordance with such requirements as the Director of the Administrative Office of the United States Courts shall by regulation prescribe. The Director may provide under such regulations that the notification requirement may be waived with respect to a spouse or former spouse if the judicial official establishes to the satisfaction of the Director that the whereabouts of such spouse or former spouse cannot be determined.

(w) The Comptroller General of the United States shall, at the end of each 3-fiscal year period, determine whether the contributions by judicial officials under subsection (b) during that 3-year period accounted for 50 percent of the costs of the Judicial Survivors' Annuities Fund and if not, then what adjustments in the contribution rates under subsection (b) should be made to achieve that 50 percent figure. The Comptroller General shall report the results of each determination under this subsection to the Congress.

(x) In the case of a widow or widower whose annuity under clause (i) or (ii) of subsection (h)(1) is terminated because of remarriage before attaining 55 years of age, the annuity shall be restored at the same rate commencing on the day the remarriage is dissolved by death, divorce, or annulment, if—

(1) the widow or widower elects to receive this annuity instead of any other survivor annuity to which such widow or widower may be entitled, under this chapter or under another retirement system for Government employees, by reason of the remarriage; and

(2) any payment made to such widow or widower under subsection (*o*) or (p) on termination of the annuity is returned to the Judicial Survivors' Annuities Fund.

(Added Aug. 3, 1956, c. 944, § 2, 70 Stat. 1021, and amended July 7, 1958, Pub.L. 85–508, § 12(n), 72 Stat. 348; Dec. 20, 1967, Pub.L. 90–219, Title II, § 202, 81 Stat. 668; Aug. 8, 1968, Pub.L. 90–466, § 1(a), 82 Stat. 662; Aug. 22, 1972, Pub.L. 92–397, §§ 2, 3(c), 86 Stat. 579, 580; Oct. 19, 1976, Pub.L. 94–554, § 2, 90 Stat. 2603; Nov. 6, 1978, Pub.L. 95–598, Title II, § 211, 92 Stat. 2661; June 19, 1986, Pub.L. 99–336, § 2(a), (d)(1) to (3), (e), 100 Stat. 633, 635 to 637; Aug. 27, 1986, Pub.L. 99–396, § 21(b), 100 Stat. 846; Nov. 15, 1988, Pub.L. 100–659, § 3(a), 102 Stat. 3917; Nov. 19, 1988, Pub.L. 100–702, Title X, § 1017(a), 102 Stat. 4670; Dec. 1, 1990, Pub.L. 101–650, Title III, §§ 306(b), 321, 322(a) to (f), (g)[(h)], 104 Stat. 5109, 5117 to 5120; Oct. 29, 1992, Pub.L. 102–572, Title II, § 201(a) to (i), Title IX, § 902(b), 106 Stat. 4508 to 4510, 4516; Oct. 19, 1996, Pub.L. 104–317, Title III, §§ 302, 308, 110 Stat. 3851, 3853; Nov. 13, 2000, Pub.L. 106–518, Title III, § 312(b), 114 Stat. 2421; Oct. 13, 2008, Pub.L. 110–402, § 1(b)(2), 122 Stat. 4254; Oct. 15, 2008, Pub.L. 110–428, § 3(a), (b), 122 Stat. 4840.)

[1] So in original. Probably should be a semicolon.

HISTORICAL AND STATUTORY NOTES

References in Text

The date of the enactment of the Retirement and Survivors' Annuities for Bankruptcy Judges and Magistrates Act of 1988, referred to in subsec. (a)(1)(v), is the date of the enactment of Pub.L. 100–659 (which amended this section), which was approved Nov. 15, 1988.

The date of the enactment of the Federal Courts Study Committee Implementation Act of 1990, referred to in subsec. (a)(1)(vi), is the date of enactment of Title III of Pub.L. 101–650, which was approved Dec. 1, 1990.

The date of the enactment of the Federal Courts Administration Act of 1992, referred to in subsec. (a)(1)(vii), means the date of enactment of Pub.L. 102–572, which was approved Oct. 29, 1992.

Section 3 of the Judicial Survivors' Annuities Reform Act, referred to in subsec. (b)(3), is section 3 of Pub.L. 94–554, which is set out as a note under this section.

Codifications

Amendments by section 312(b) of Pub.L. 106–518, were executed to subsec. (a) as the probable intent of Congress, despite directory language purporting to amend paragraphs (1)(D) and (2)(D) of section 376 of title 28, leaving out the subsec. (a) identifier from the directory language.

Subsec. (a)(2)(A) of this section was amended by Pub.L. 95–598, Title II, § 211, Nov. 6, 1978, 92 Stat. 2668, effective June 28, 1984, pursuant to Pub.L. 95–598, Title IV, § 402(b), Nov. 6, 1978, 92 Stat. 2682, as amended by Pub.L. 98–249, § 1(a), Mar. 31, 1984, 98 Stat. 116; Pub.L. 98–271, § 1(a), Apr. 30, 1984, 98 Stat. 163; Pub.L. 98–299, § 1(a), May 25, 1984, 98 Stat. 214; Pub.L. 98–325, § 1(a), June 20, 1984, 98 Stat. 268, set out as a note preceding section 101 of Title 11, Bankruptcy, by inserting ", or (iii) in the case of a bankruptcy judge, after retirement under section 337 of this title" following "(ii) after retirement from office by resignation on salary under subsection (a) of section 371 of this title".

Section 402(b) of Pub.L. 95–598 was amended by section 113 of Pub.L. 98–353, Title I, July 10, 1984, 98 Stat. 343, by substituting "shall not be effective" for "shall take effect on June 28, 1984", thereby eliminating the amendment by section 211 of Pub.L. 95–598, effective June 27, 1984, pursuant to section 122(c) of Pub.L. 98–353, set out as an Effective Date note under section 151 of this title.

Section 121(a) of Pub.L. 98–353 directed that section 402(b) of Pub.L. 95–598 be amended by substituting "the date of enactment of the Bankruptcy Amendments and Federal Judgeship Act of 1984 [i.e. July 10, 1984]" for "June 28, 1984". This amendment was not executed in view of the prior amendment to section 402(b) of Pub.L. 95–598 by section 113 of Pub.L. 98–353.

Effective and Applicability Provisions

2008 Acts. Pub.L. 110–428, § 3(c), Oct. 15, 2008, 122 Stat. 4840, provided that:

"**(1) In general.**—This section and the amendments made by this section [enacting subsec. (x) of this section and amending subsec. (h)(2) of this section] shall take effect on the first day of the first month beginning at least 30 days after the date of the enactment of this Act [Oct. 15, 2008] and shall apply in the case of a remarriage which is dissolved by death, divorce, or annulment on or after such first day.

"**(2) Limited retroactive effect.**—

"**(A) In general.**—In the case of a remarriage which is dissolved by death, divorce, or annulment within the 4–year period ending on the day before the effective date of this section, the amendments made by this section [enacting subsec. (x) and amending subsec. (h)(2) of this section] shall apply only if the widow or widower satisfies the requirements of paragraphs (1) and (2) of section 376(x) of title 28, United States Code (as amended by this section) before—

"**(i)** the end of the 1–year period beginning on the effective date of this section; or

"**(ii)** such later date as Director of the Administrative Office of the United States Courts may by regulation prescribe.

"**(B) Restoration.**—If the requirements of paragraph (1) are satisfied, the survivor annuity shall be restored, commencing on the date the remarriage was dissolved by death, annulment, or divorce, at the rate which was in effect when the annuity was terminated.

"**(C) Lump-sum payment.**—Any amounts becoming payable to the widow or widower under this subsection for the period beginning on the date on which the annuity was terminated and ending on the date on which periodic annuity payments resume shall be payable in a lump-sum payment."

1992 Acts. Section 202 of Pub.L. 102–572 provided that: "This title [Title II of Pub.L. 102–572, Oct. 29, 1992, 106 Stat. 4508] and the amendments made by this title [amending this section and enacting provisions set out as notes under this section] shall take effect on the date of the enactment of this Act [Oct. 29, 1992]."

Amendment by section 902(b) of Pub.L. 102–572 effective Oct. 29, 1992, see section 911 of Pub.L. 102–572, set out as a note under section 171 of this title.

1988 Acts. Section 1017(c) of Title X of Pub.L. 100–702 provided that: "The amendment made by subsection (a) [enacting subsec. (m) and deleting former subsec. (m) of this section] shall apply with respect to increases in annuities which are made under section 8340(b) of title 5, United States Code [section 8340(b) of Title 5, Government Organization and Employees], on or after the date of enactment of this title [Nov. 19, 1988]."

Amendment to this section by Pub.L. 100–659 to take effect on Nov. 15, 1988, and shall apply to bankruptcy judges and magistrates who retire on or after Nov. 15, 1988, with special election provisions for bankruptcy judges, etc., who left office on or after July 31, 1987, and before Nov. 15, 1988, see section 9 of Pub.L. 100–659, set out as a note under section 377 of this title.

1986 Acts. Amendment by Pub.L. 99–396 not to affect the amount payable to a judge who retired in accordance with the provisions of section 373 of this title in effect on the day before Aug. 27, 1986, see section 21(c) of Pub.L. 99–396, set out as a note under section 373 of this title.

Section 2(f) of Pub.L. 99–336 provided that: "This section [amending this section and enacting provisions set out as notes under this section] shall take effect on October 1, 1986."

1976 Acts. Section 8 of Pub.L. 94–554 provided: "That this Act [amending this section and enacting provisions set out as notes under this section] shall become effective on the first day of the third month following the month in which it is enacted [Jan. 1, 1977], or on October 1, 1976, whichever occurs last."

1958 Acts. Amendment by Pub.L. 85–508 effective Jan. 3, 1959 upon admission of Alaska into the Union pursuant to Proc. No. 3269, Jan. 5, 1959, 24 F.R. 81, 73 Stat. c16, as required by sections 1 and 8(c) of Pub.L. 85–508, see notes set out under section 81A of this title and preceding section 21 of Title 48, Territories and Insular Possessions.

Change of Name

References to United States Claims Court deemed to refer to United States Court of Federal Claims and references to Claims Court deemed to refer to Court of Federal Claims, see section 902(b) of Pub.L. 102–572, set out as a note under section 171 of Title 28, Judiciary and Judicial Procedure.

"United States magistrate judge" substituted for "United States magistrate" in text pursuant to section 321 of Pub.L. 101–650, set out as a note under 28 U.S.C.A. § 631.

Transfer of Functions

For transfer of authorities, functions, personnel, and assets of the Coast Guard, including the authorities and functions of the Secretary of Transportation relating thereto, to the Department of Homeland Security, and for treatment of related references, see 6 U.S.C.A. §§ 468(b), 551(d), 552(d) and 557, and the Department of Homeland Security Reorganization Plan of November 25, 2002, as modified, set out as a note under 6 U.S.C.A. § 542.

Savings Provisions

Section 6 of Pub.L. 94–554 provided: "That the benefits conferred by this Act shall, on the date upon which this Act becomes effective [see Effective and Applicability Provisions of 1976 Amendments note under this section], immediately become available to any individual then receiving an annuity under section 2 of the Act of August 3, 1956 (70 Stat. 1021) [which enacted this section], as amended: *Provided*, That although the rights of any judicial official electing to come within the purview of section 376 of title 28, United States Code [this section], on or after the date upon which this Act becomes effective, shall be determined exclusively under the provisions of that section as amended by this Act, nothing in this Act shall be interpreted to cancel, abrogate, or diminish any rights to which an individual or his or her survivors may be entitled by virtue of that individuals [sic] having contributed to the judicial survivors annuity fund established by section 2 of the Act of August 3, 1956 (70 Stat. 1021) [which enacted this section], as amended, before the date upon which this Act becomes effective."

Effective and Applicability Provisions of 1990 Amendments; Transition Provisions

Amendment by section 306(b) of Pub.L. 101–650 applicable to judges of, and senior judges in active service with, the United States Court of Federal Claims on or after Dec. 1, 1990, see section 306(f) of Pub.L. 101–650, set out as a note under section 8331 of Title 5, Government Organization and Employees.

Section 322(g) of Pub.L. 101–650 provided that:

"**(1) Effective date.**—Subject to paragraph (2), the amendments made by this Act [probably means section 322 of Pub.L. 101–650, amending this section] shall apply to all judicial officials assassinated on or after May 28, 1979.

"**(2) Rules for retroactive application.—(A)** In the case of a judicial official who was assassinated on or after May 28, 1979, and before the date of the enactment of this Act [Dec. 1, 1990], if the salary deductions provided by subsection (b) of section 376 of title 28, United States Code [subsec. (b) of this section], or the deposits required by subsection (d) of such section [subsec. (d) of this section], have been withdrawn pursuant to subsection (*o*) of such section [subsec. (*o*) of this section], there shall be deducted from the annuities otherwise payable to the survivor or survivors of such judicial official, and the payment authorized by subparagraph (C) of this paragraph, an amount equal to the amount so withdrawn, with interest on the amount withdrawn at 3 percent per annum compounded on December 31 of each year.

"**(B)** In the case of the survivor or survivors of a judicial official to whom this paragraph applies who had less than 18 months of service before being assassinated, there shall be deducted from the annuities otherwise payable to the survivor or survivors of such judicial official, and the payment authorized by subparagraph (C) of this paragraph, an amount equal to the amount of salary deductions that would have been made if such deductions [had] been made for 18 months before the judicial official's death, plus interest as described in subparagraph (A).

"**(C)** Subject to subparagraphs (A) and (B), the survivor or survivors of a judicial official to whom this paragraph applies shall be entitled to the payment of annuities they would have received under section 376 of title 28, United States Code [this section], for the period beginning on the date such judicial official was assassinated and ending the date of the enactment of this Act [Dec. 1, 1990]. The Secretary of the Treasury shall pay into the Judicial Survivors' Annuities fund, out of any money in the Treasury not otherwise appropriated, the amount of the annuities to which the survivor or survivors are entitled under this subparagraph.

"**(3) Definition.**—For purposes of this subsection, the term—

"**(A)** 'assassinated' has the meaning given that term in section 376(a)(7) of title 28, United States Code [subsec. (a) of this section], as added by this section; and

"**(B)** 'judicial official' has the meaning given that term in section 376(a)(1)(A) and (B) of title 28, United States Code [subsec. (a)(1)(A) and (B) of this section]."

Retroactive Effect of 1967 Amendments

The provisions of section 611(a) of this title, the first paragraph of section 611(b) of this title, and subsec. (s) of this section, as added by Pub.L. 90–219, applicable to a Director or former Director of the Administrative Office of the United States Courts who was first appointed prior to Dec. 20, 1967 if at the time such Director or former Director left or leaves such office he had, or shall have, attained the age of sixty-five years and completed fifteen years of service as Director of the Administrative Office of the United States Courts and if, on or before the expiration of six months following Dec. 20, 1967, he makes the election referred to in section 611(a) of this title or subsec. (s) of this section, or both, as the case may be, see section 205(b) of Pub.L. 90–219, set out as a note under section 611 of this title.

Annuity Payment to Surviving Spouses of Judges Who Died Before October 19, 1976

Pub.L. 96–504, § 3, Dec. 5, 1980, 94 Stat. 2741, provided that:

"**(a)** As of the first pay period beginning after the effective date of this Act [see note set out under section 8344 of Title 5, Government Organization and Employees], a surviving spouse, other than a surviving spouse who has remarried, of any Justice of the United States (as defined by section 451 of title 28, United States Code) [section 451 of this title], who died before October 19, 1976, shall be paid an annuity in accordance with the provisions of section 376 of title 28, United States Code [this section], at a rate of $20,000 per year as if such Justice had elected to come within the provisions of, and having made the full deposit required by, section 376(d) of title 28, United States Code [subsec. (d) of this section].

"(b) Notwithstanding the provisions of section 376(h) of title 28, United States Code [subsec. (h) of this section], such annuity shall be payable as provided in section 376(m) of title 28, United States Code [subsec. (m) of this section], until the date of the death of any such spouse."

Appropriations

Section 5 of Act Aug. 3, 1956, c. 944, 70 Stat. 1026, provided that: "Funds necessary to carry out the provisions of this Act [enacting this section and provisions set out as notes hereunder, and amending sections 375, 604(a)(7), and 605 of this title] may be appropriated out of any money in the Treasury not otherwise appropriated."

Audit by General Accounting Office [now Government Accountability Office]

Section 201(*l*) of Pub.L. 102–572 provided that: "The Comptroller General shall—

"(1) conduct an audit of the judicial survivors annuities program under section 376 of title 28, United States Code [this section], for the 3–year period beginning on the date of the enactment of this Act [Oct. 29, 1992]; and

"(2) report to the Congress, not later than 60 days after the end of that 3–year period, on the results of such audit, comparing such program to other survivors annuities programs within the Federal Government."

Compensation for Actuarial Deficiency in the Annuities Fund

Section 4 of Pub.L. 94–554 provided: "That on the date upon which this Act becomes effective [see Effective and Applicability Provisions of 1976 Amendments note under this section] the Secretary of the Treasury shall ascertain from the Director of the Administrative Office of the United States Courts the amount of the actuarial deficiency in the fund transferred by section 3 of this Act [see Judicial Survivors' Annuities Fund note under this section] on the date of that fund's transfer and, at the earliest time thereafter at which appropriated funds in that amount shall become available, the Secretary shall deposit such funds, in a single payment, into the Judicial Survivors' Annuities Fund established by section 3 of this Act. Such funds as are necessary to carry out this section are hereby authorized to be appropriated."

Covered Beneficiaries under Pub.L. 99–336

Section 2(b) of Pub.L. 99–336 provided that: "The benefits conferred by section 376 of title 28, United States Code [this section], by reason of the amendments made by this section [amending this section] shall apply only to individuals who become eligible for annuities under such section on or after the effective date of this section [Oct. 1, 1986], except that—

"(1) such annuities shall be computed in accordance with the provisions of section 376 of title 28, United States Code, as amended by this section [this section], notwithstanding contributions or deposits made in accordance with applicable law at lower rates; and

"(2) no additional liability shall be created with respect to deposits made in accordance with applicable law before the effective date of this section [October 1, 1986], or after such effective date pursuant to an agreement entered into before such effective date."

Credit for Contributions Prior to 1992 Amendment at Higher Rate

Section 201(j) of Pub.L. 102–572 provided that: "Notwithstanding any other provision of law, the contribution under section 376(b)(1) or (2) of title 28, United States Code (as amended by this section) [subsec. (b)(1) or (2) of this section], of any judicial official who is within the purview of such section 376 on the effective date of this title [Oct. 29, 1992] shall be reduced by 0.5 percent for a period of time equal to the number of years of service for which the judicial official has made contributions or deposits before the enactment of this Act [probably means date of enactment of Pub.L. 102–572, which was approved Oct. 29, 1992] to the credit of the Judicial Survivors' Annuities Fund or for 18 months, whichever is less, if such contributions or deposits were never returned to the judicial official. For purposes of this subsection, the term 'years' shall mean full years and twelfth parts thereof."

Increase for Existing Annuitants

Section 1017(b) of Pub.L. 100–702 provided that: "Each annuity payable from the Judicial Survivors' Annuities Fund under section 376 of title 28, United States Code [this section], on the date of the enactment of this title [Nov. 19, 1988] shall be increased by 10 percent, effective on such date of enactment [Nov. 19, 1988]."

Increases in Widows' Annuities Paid under Section 2 of Act August 3, 1956

Section 5 of Pub.L. 94–554 provided: "That on the date upon which this Act becomes effective [see Effective and Applicability Provisions of 1976 Amendments note under this section] each annuity then being paid to a widow from the judicial survivors annuity fund established by section 2 of the Act of August 3, 1956 (70 Stat. 1021) [which enacted this section], as amended, shall be increased by an amount equal to one-fifth of 1 percent of the amount of such annuity multiplied by the number of months which have passed since the commencement of that annuity. For the purposes of this section, any fractional part of a month which numbers less than fifteen full days shall be excluded from the computation of the number of months and any fractional part of a month which numbers fifteen full days or more shall be included in the computation as one full month. Such funds as are necessary to carry out this section are authorized to be appropriated and, upon appropriation, shall be deposited by the Secretary of the Treasury, in a single payment, to credit of the Judicial Survivors' Annuities Fund established by section 3 of this Act [see Judicial Survivors' Annuities Fund note under this section]."

Judge Taking Office on August 8, 1968

Section 1(b) of Pub.L. 90–466 provided that: "For the purpose of the amendment made by subsection (a) [to subsec. (a) of this section], a judge who is in office on the date of enactment of this Act [Aug. 8, 1968] shall be deemed to have taken office on that date [Aug. 8, 1968]."

Judicial Survivors' Annuities Fund

Section 3 of Pub.L. 94–554 provided: "That on the date upon which this Act becomes effective [see Effective and

Applicability Provisions of 1976 Amendments note under this section] there shall be established on the books of the Treasury a fund which shall be known as 'The Judicial Survivors' Annuities Fund,' and all money credited to the judicial survivors annuity fund established by section 2 of the Act of August 3, 1956 (70 Stat. 1021) [which enacted this section], as amended, shall be transferred to the credit of the Judicial Survivors' Annuities Fund established by this section."

Judicial Survivors' Annuity Fund; Authorization of Appropriations

Pub.L. 96–504, § 4, Dec. 5, 1980, 94 Stat. 2742, required the Secretary of the Treasury in consultation with the Director of the Administrative Office of the United States Courts to determine as of Dec. 5, 1980, and deposit as soon as possible thereafter, the amount necessary to offset any actuarial deficiency in the Judicial Survivors Annuities Fund.

Payment of Retirement Salary Pursuant to Court Decree of Divorce, Etc.

Section 2(d)(4) of Pub.L. 99–336 provided that: "Payments of retirement salary as defined in section 376(a)(2) of title 28, United States Code [subsec. (a)(2) of this section], which would otherwise be made to the judicial official upon whose service the retirement salary is based, shall be paid (in whole or in part) to another person if and to the extent expressly provided for in the terms of any court decree of divorce, annulment, or legal separation, or the terms of any court order or court-approved property settlement agreement incident to any court decree of divorce, annulment, or legal separation. Any payment under this paragraph to a person bars recovery by any other person. This paragraph shall apply only to payments made after the date of receipt by the Director of the Administrative Office of [the] United States Courts of written notice of such decree, order, or agreement, and such additional information and documentation as the Director may prescribe. As used in this paragraph, 'court' means any court of any State or the District of Columbia."

Preservation of Rights of Judges of the District Court for the Territory of Alaska

Section 12(n) of Pub.L. 85–508 provided in part that the amendment of subsec. (q) of this section by Pub.L. 85–508 shall not affect the rights under this section of any present or former judge of the District Court for the Territory of Alaska or his survivors.

Prior Death of Judge

Section 7 of Act Aug. 3, 1956, c. 944, 70 Stat. 1021, provided that: "In the case of a living widow of a judge of the United States as defined in section 451 of title 28, United States Code, who died prior to the date of enactment of this Act [Aug. 3, 1956], an annuity shall be paid as provided in section 376 of title 28, United States Code, as added by section 2 of this Act [this section], as if such judge had died on such date and had elected to bring himself within the purview of such section 376 [this section], but had not made the deposit provided for by subsection (c) of the said section: *Provided*, (a) That such widow has not remarried; and (b) that the amount of such annuity and the reduction therein because of such deposit not having been made shall be computed on the basis of the actual length of judicial and other allowable service of such judge: *And provided further*, That notwithstanding the provisions of subsection (g) of such section 376 [this section] such annuity shall be payable even though such judge had not rendered five years of civilian service prior to his death. In the case of a judge of the United States as defined in section 451 of title 28, United States Code, who dies within 6 months after the date of enactment of this Act [August 3, 1956] after having rendered at least 5 years of civilian service computed as prescribed in subsection (o) of section 376 of title 28, United States Code, as added by section 2 of this Act, but without having made an election as provided in such section 376 [this section] to bring himself within the purview of that section, an annuity shall be paid to his widow and surviving dependent children as provided in such section 376 [this section] as if such judge had elected on the day of his death to bring himself within the purview of such section 376 [this section] but had not made the deposit provided for by subsection (c) of the said section. An annuity shall be payable under this section computed on the basis of the actual length of judicial and other allowable service of the judge and subject to the reduction required by subsection (c) of such section 376 even though no deposit has been made, as required by subsection (g) of such section 376 [this section], with respect to any of such service."

Redeposit of Contributions Prior to 1992 Amendment

Section 201(k) of Pub.L. 102–572 provided that: "Any judicial official as defined in section 376(a)(1) of title 28, United States Code [subsec. (a)(1) of this section], who makes an election under section 376(b) of title 28, United States Code [subsec. (b) of this section], may make a redeposit, as required by section 7 of Public Law 94–554 [set out as a note under this section] and section 2(c)(2) of Public Law 99–336 [set out as a note under this section], to the credit of the Judicial Survivors' Annuities Fund in installments, in such amounts and under such conditions as may be determined in each instance by the Director of the Administrative Office of the United States Courts. If a judicial official elects to make a redeposit in installments—

"(1) the Director shall require that the first installment payment made shall be in an amount no smaller than the last 18 months of salary deductions or deposits previously returned to that judicial official in a lump-sum payment; and

"(2) the election under section 376(b) of title 28, United States Code [subsec. (b) of this section], shall be effective upon payment of the first such installment."

Resigned, Removed, and Retired Judges

Section 6 of Act Aug. 3, 1956, c. 944, 70 Stat. 1021, provided that: "A judge who resigned prior to the date of enactment of this Act [Aug. 3, 1956] and who on that date is receiving salary under section 371(a) of title 28, United States Code, or who resigned, was removed or failed of reappointment prior to the date of enactment of this Act [Aug. 3, 1956] and who on that date is receiving salary under section 373 of title 28, United States Code, shall be considered a judge within the meaning of section 376 of title 28, United States Code, as added by section 2 of this Act [this section], and as such shall be entitled within six months after the date of enactment of this Act [Aug. 3, 1956] to make the election authorized by and to receive the benefits of that section. A judge who retired from regular active service under section 260 of the Judicial Code of 1911 or the Act of August 5, 1939, chapter 433, and who is living on the date of enactment of this Act shall be deemed for the purposes of this Act to have retired from regular active service under section 371(b) or 372(a), as the case may be, of title 28, United States Code."

Revocation of Election to Participate in Annuities Program

Section 2(c) of Pub.L. 99–336 provided that:

"(1) Within 180 days after the effective date of this section [Oct. 1, 1986], any judicial official who, before such effective date, made an election under section 376 of title 28, United States Code [this section], to come within the purview of that section, shall be entitled to revoke that election. Such revocation shall constitute a complete withdrawal from the judicial survivors' annuities program provided for in such section 376 [this section]. No such revocation shall be effective unless it is submitted in writing to the Director of the Administrative Office of the United States Courts, and until such writing is received by the Director. Upon receipt by the Director of such writing, any rights to survivorship benefits for the survivors of such judicial official shall terminate, and all amounts credited to the individual account of such judicial official under section 376(e) [subsec. (e) of this section], together with interest at 3 percent per annum, compounded on December 31 of each year to such date of revocation, shall be returned to that judicial official in a lump-sum payment.

"(2) Any judicial official who makes a revocation under paragraph (1) of this subsection and who thereafter becomes eligible to make an election under section 376(b) of title 28, United States Code [subsec. (b) of this section], may make such election only if such judicial official redeposits, to the credit of the Judicial Survivors' Annuities Fund, the full amount of the lump-sum payment made to such judicial official under paragraph (1) of this subsection, together with interest at 3 percent per annum, compounded on December 31 of each year from the date of such revocation until the date upon which that amount is so redeposited.

"(3) Any judicial official who fails to revoke an election in accordance with paragraph (1) of this subsection shall be deemed to have irrevocably waived the right to make that revocation."

Section 7 of Pub.L. 94–554 provided: "That, at any time within one hundred and eighty days after the date upon which this Act becomes effective [see Effective and Applicability Provisions of 1976 Amendments note under this section] any judicial official who has, prior to that date, already participated in the judicial survivors annuity program created by the Act of August 3, 1956 (70 Stat. 1021) [which enacted this section] as amended, shall be entitled to revoke his or her earlier election to participate in that program and thereby completely withdraw from participation in the judicial survivors' annuities program created by this Act: *Provided*, That (a) any such revocation may be effected only by means of a writing filed with the Director of the Administrative Office of the United States Courts, (b) any such writing shall be deemed to have become effective no sooner than the date upon which that writing is received by the Director, (c) upon receipt of such a writing by the Director, any and all rights to survivorship benefits for such judicial official's survivors shall terminate, and all amounts credited to such judicial official's individual account, together with interest at 3 percent per annum, compounded on December 31 of each year to that date of revocation, shall thereafter be returned to that judicial official in a lump-sum refund payment, and (d) any judicial official who effects such a revocation and who subsequently again becomes eligible and elects to join the judicial survivors annuities program created by this Act under the provisions of section 376 of title 28, United States Code [this section] as amended by this Act, shall be permitted to do so only upon the redeposit of the full amount of the refund obtained under this section plus interest at 3 percent per annum, compounded on December 31 of each year from the date of the revocation until the date upon which that amount is redeposited. Any judicial official who fails to effect a revocation in accordance with the right conferred by this section within one hundred and eighty days after the date upon which this Act becomes effective shall be deemed to have irrevocably waived the right to that revocation."

Survivors' Annuities for Incumbents

Section 3(b) of Pub.L. 100–659 provided that: "In the case of a bankruptcy judge or magistrate who elects an annuity under section 2(c) [set out as a note under section 377 of this title], only service for which an annuity under subsection (b) or (c) and subsection (g) of section 377 of title 28, United States Code, as added by section 2 of this Act [section 377(b) or (c) and (g) of this title], is calculated under section 2(c) may be used in the computation of an annuity under section 376 of title 28, United States Code, as amended by subsection (a) of this section."

§ 377. Retirement of bankruptcy judges and magistrate judges

(a) Retirement based on years of service.—A bankruptcy judge or magistrate judge to whom this section applies and who retires from office after attaining the age of 65 years and serving at least 14 years, whether continuously or otherwise, as such bankruptcy judge or magistrate judge shall, subject to subsection (f), be entitled to receive, during the remainder of the judge's or magistrate judge's lifetime, an annuity equal to the salary being received at the time the judge or magistrate judge leaves office.

(b) Retirement upon failure of reappointment.—A bankruptcy judge or magistrate judge to whom this section applies, who is not reappointed following the expiration of the term of office of such judge or magistrate judge, and who retires upon the completion of the term shall, subject to subsection (f), be entitled to receive, upon attaining the age of 65 years and during the remainder of such bankruptcy judge's or magistrate judge's lifetime, an annuity equal to that portion of the salary being received at the time the judge or magistrate judge leaves office which the aggregate number of years of service, not to exceed 14, bears to 14, if—

(1) such judge or magistrate judge has served at least 1 full term as a bankruptcy judge or magistrate judge, and

(2) not earlier than 9 months before the date on which the term of office of such judge or magistrate judge expires, and not later than 6 months before such date, such judge or magistrate judge notified

the appointing authority in writing that such judge or magistrate judge was willing to accept reappointment to the position in which such judge or magistrate judge was serving.

For purposes of this subsection, in the case of a bankruptcy judge, the written notice required by paragraph (2) shall be given to the chief judge of the circuit in which such bankruptcy judge is serving and, in the case of a magistrate judge, such notice shall be given to the chief judge of the district court in which the magistrate judge is serving.

(c) Service of at least 8 years.—A bankruptcy judge or magistrate judge to whom this section applies and who retires after serving at least 8 years, whether continuously or otherwise, as such a bankruptcy judge or magistrate judge shall, subject to subsection (f), be entitled to receive, upon attaining the age of 65 years and during the remainder of the judge's or magistrate judge's lifetime, an annuity equal to that portion of the salary being received at the time the judge or magistrate judge leaves office which the aggregate number of years of service, not to exceed 14, bears to 14. Such annuity shall be reduced by ⅙ of 1 percent for each full month such bankruptcy judge or magistrate judge was under the age of 65 at the time the judge or magistrate judge left office, except that such reduction shall not exceed 20 percent.

(d) Retirement for disability.—A bankruptcy judge or magistrate judge to whom this section applies, who has served at least 5 years, whether continuously or otherwise, as such a bankruptcy judge or magistrate judge, and who retires or is removed from office upon the sole ground of mental or physical disability shall, subject to subsection (f), be entitled to receive, during the remainder of the judge's or magistrate judge's lifetime, an annuity equal to 40 percent of the salary being received at the time of retirement or removal or, in the case of a judge or magistrate judge who has served for at least 10 years, an amount equal to that proportion of the salary being received at the time of retirement or removal which the aggregate number of years of service, not to exceed 14, bears to 14.

(e) Cost-of-living adjustments.—A bankruptcy judge or magistrate judge who is entitled to an annuity under this section is also entitled to a cost-of-living adjustment in such annuity, calculated and payable in the same manner as adjustments under section 8340(b) of title 5, except that any such annuity, as increased under this subsection, may not exceed the salary then payable for the position from which the judge or magistrate judge retired or was removed.

(f) Election; annuity in lieu of other annuities.—A bankruptcy judge or magistrate judge shall be entitled to an annuity under this section if the judge or magistrate judge elects an annuity under this section by notifying the Director of the Administrative Office of the United States Courts. A bankruptcy judge or magistrate judge who elects to receive an annuity under this section shall not be entitled to receive [1]

(1) any annuity to which such judge or magistrate judge would otherwise have been entitled under subchapter III of chapter 83, or under chapter 84 (except for subchapters III and VII), of title 5, for service performed as such a judge or magistrate judge or otherwise;

(2) an annuity or salary in senior status or retirement under section 371 or 372 of this title;

(3) retired pay under section 7447 of the Internal Revenue Code of 1986; or

(4) retired pay under section 7296 of title 38.

(g) Calculation of service.—(1) For purposes of calculating an annuity under this section—

(A) full-time service as a bankruptcy judge or magistrate judge to whom this section applies may be credited; and

(B) each month of service shall be credited as one-twelfth of a year, and the fractional part of any month shall not be credited.

(2)(A) In the case of an individual who is a bankruptcy judge to whom this section applies and who retires under this section or who is removed from office under subsection (d) upon the sole ground of mental or physical disability, any service of that individual as a United States magistrate judge to whom this section applies, and any service of that individual as a full-time judicial officer who performed the duties of a magistrate judge and a bankruptcy judge at the same time, shall be included for purposes of calculating years of service under subsection (a), (b), (c), or (d), as the case may be.

(B) In the case of an individual who is a magistrate judge to whom this section applies and who retires under this section or who is removed from office under subsection (d) upon the sole ground of mental or physical disability, any service of that individual as a bankruptcy judge to whom this section applies, and any service of that individual as a full-time judicial officer who performed the duties of magistrate judge and a bankruptcy judge at the same time, shall be included for purposes of calculating years of service under subsection (a), (b), (c), or (d), as the case may be.

(h) Covered positions and service.—This section applies to—

(1) any bankruptcy judge appointed under—

(A) section 152 of this title;

(B) section 34 of the Bankruptcy Act before the repeal of that Act by section 401 of the Act of

November 6, 1978 (Public Law 95–598; 92 Stat. 2682); or

(C) section 404 of the Act of November 6, 1978 (Public Law 95–598; 92 Stat. 2549); and

(2) any United States magistrate judge appointed under section 631 of this title,

only with respect to service on or after October 1, 1979, as such a bankruptcy judge or magistrate judge.

(i) Payments pursuant to court order.—(1) Payments under this section which would otherwise be made to a bankruptcy judge or magistrate judge based upon his or her service shall be paid (in whole or in part) by the Director of the Administrative Office of the United States Courts to another person if and to the extent expressly provided for in the terms of any court decree of divorce, annulment, or legal separation, or the terms of any court order or court-approved property settlement agreement incident to any court decree of divorce, annulment, or legal separation. Any payment under this paragraph to a person bars recovery by any other person.

(2) Paragraph (1) shall apply only to payments made by the Director of the Administrative Office of the United States Courts after the date of receipt by the Director of written notice of such decree, order, or agreement, and such additional information as the Director may prescribe.

(3) As used in this subsection, the term "court" means any court of any State, the District of Columbia, the Commonwealth of Puerto Rico, Guam, the Northern Mariana Islands, or the Virgin Islands, and any Indian tribal court or courts of Indian offense.

(j) Deductions, contributions, and deposits.—

(1) **Deductions.**—Beginning with the next pay period after the Director of the Administrative Office of the United States Courts receives a notice under subsection (f) that a bankruptcy judge or magistrate judge has elected an annuity under this section, the Director shall deduct and withhold 1 percent of the salary of such bankruptcy judge or magistrate judge. Amounts shall be so deducted and withheld in a manner determined by the Director. Amounts deducted and withheld under this subsection shall be deposited in the Treasury of the United States to the credit of the Judicial Officers' Retirement Fund. Deductions under this subsection from the salary of a bankruptcy judge or magistrate judge shall terminate upon the retirement of the bankruptcy judge or magistrate judge or upon completing 14 years of service for which contributions under this section have been made, whether continuously or otherwise, as calculated under subsection (g), whichever occurs first.

(2) **Consent to deductions; discharge of claims.**—Each bankruptcy judge or magistrate judge who makes an election under subsection (f) shall be deemed to consent and agree to the deductions from salary which are made under paragraph (1). Payment of such salary less such deductions (and any deductions made under section 376 of this title) is a full and complete discharge and acquittance of all claims and demands for all services rendered by such bankruptcy judge or magistrate judge during the period covered by such payment, except the right to those benefits to which the bankruptcy judge or magistrate judge is entitled under this section (and section 376).

(k) Deposits for prior service.—Each bankruptcy judge or magistrate judge who makes an election under subsection (f) may deposit, for service performed before such election for which contributions may be made under this section, an amount equal to 1 percent of the salary received for that service. Credit for any period covered by that service may not be allowed for purposes of an annuity under this section until a deposit under this subsection has been made for that period.

(*l*) Individual retirement records.—The amounts deducted and withheld under subsection (j), and the amounts deposited under subsection (k), shall be credited to individual accounts in the name of each bankruptcy judge or magistrate judge from whom such amounts are received, for credit to the Judicial Officers' Retirement Fund.

(m) Annuities affected in certain cases.—

(1) Practicing law after retirement.—

(A) Forfeiture of annuity.—Subject to subparagraph (B), any bankruptcy judge or magistrate judge who retires under this section and who thereafter practices law shall forfeit all rights to an annuity under this section for all periods beginning on or after the first day on which he or she so practices law.

(B) Forfeiture not to apply where individual elects to freeze amount of annuity.—(i) If a bankruptcy judge or magistrate judge makes an election to practice law after retirement under this section—

(I) subparagraph (A) shall not apply to such bankruptcy judge or magistrate judge beginning on the date such election takes effect, and

(II) the annuity payable under this section to such bankruptcy judge or magistrate judge, for periods beginning on or after the date such election takes effect, shall be equal to the annuity to which such bankruptcy judge or magistrate judge is entitled on the day before such effective date.

(ii) An election under clause (i)—

(I) may be made by a bankruptcy judge or magistrate judge eligible for retirement under this section, and

(II) shall be filed with the Director of the Administrative Office of the United States Courts.

Such an election, once it takes effect, shall be irrevocable.

(iii) Any election under this subparagraph shall take effect on the first day of the first month following the month in which the election is made.

(2) **Recall not permitted.**—Any bankruptcy judge or magistrate judge who retires under this section and who thereafter practices law shall not be eligible for recall under section 155(b), 375, or 636(h) of this title.

(3) **Accepting other employment.**—Any bankruptcy judge or magistrate judge who retires under this section and thereafter accepts compensation for civil office or employment under the United States Government (other than for the performance of functions as a bankruptcy judge or magistrate judge under section 155(b), 375, or 636(h) of this title) shall forfeit all rights to an annuity under this section for the period for which such compensation is received. For purposes of this paragraph, the term "compensation" includes retired pay or salary received in retired status.

(n) Lump-sum payments.—

(1) **Eligibility.**—(A) Subject to paragraph (2), an individual who serves as a bankruptcy judge or magistrate judge and—

(i) who leaves office and is not reappointed as a bankruptcy judge or magistrate judge for at least 31 consecutive days;

(ii) who files an application with the Administrative Office of the United States Courts for payment of the lump-sum credit;

(iii) is not serving as a bankruptcy judge or magistrate judge at the time of filing of the application; and

(iv) will not become eligible to receive an annuity under this section within 31 days after filing the application;

is entitled to be paid the lump-sum credit. Payment of the lump-sum credit voids all rights to an annuity under this section based on the service on which the lump-sum credit is based, until that individual resumes office as a bankruptcy judge or magistrate judge.

(B) Lump-sum benefits authorized by subparagraphs (C), (D), and (E) of this paragraph shall be paid to the person or persons surviving the bankruptcy judge or magistrate judge and alive on the date title to the payment arises, in the order of precedence set forth in subsection (*o*) of section 376 of this title, and in accordance with the last two sentences of that subsection. For purposes of the preceding sentence, the term "judicial official" as used in subsection (*o*) of section 376 shall be deemed to mean "bankruptcy judge or magistrate judge".

(C) If a bankruptcy judge or magistrate judge dies before receiving an annuity under this section, the lump-sum credit shall be paid.

(D) If all annuity rights under this section based on the service of a deceased bankruptcy judge or magistrate judge terminate before the total annuity paid equals the lump-sum credit, the difference shall be paid.

(E) If a bankruptcy judge or magistrate judge who is receiving an annuity under this section dies, annuity accrued and unpaid shall be paid.

(F) Annuity accrued and unpaid on the termination, except by death, of the annuity of a bankruptcy judge or magistrate judge shall be paid to that individual.

(G) Subject to paragraph (2), a bankruptcy judge or magistrate judge who forfeits rights to an annuity under subsection (m)(3) before the total annuity paid equals the lump-sum credit, shall be entitled to be paid the difference if the bankruptcy judge or magistrate judge files an application with the Administrative Office of the United States Courts for payment of that difference. A payment under this subparagraph voids all rights to an annuity on which the payment is based.

(2) **Spouses and former spouses.**—(A) Payment of the lump-sum credit under paragraph (1)(A) or a payment under paragraph (1)(G)—

(i) may be made only if any current spouse and any former spouse of the bankruptcy judge or magistrate judge are notified of the bankruptcy judge's or magistrate judge's application; and

(ii) shall be subject to the terms of a court decree of divorce, annulment, or legal separation or any court or court approved property settlement agreement incident to such decree, if—

(I) the decree, order, or agreement expressly relates to any portion of the lump-sum credit or other payment involved; and

(II) payment of the lump-sum credit or other payment would extinguish entitlement of the bankruptcy judge's or magistrate judge's spouse or former spouse to any portion of an annuity under subsection (i).

(B) Notification of a spouse or former spouse under this paragraph shall be made in accordance with such requirements as the Director of the Administrative Office of the United States Courts shall by regulation prescribe. The Director may provide under such regulations that subparagraph (A)(i) may be waived with respect to a spouse or former spouse if the bankruptcy judge or magistrate judge establishes to the satisfaction of the Director that the whereabouts of such spouse or former spouse cannot be determined.

(C) The Director shall prescribe regulations under which this paragraph shall be applied in any case in which the Director receives two or more orders or decrees described in subparagraph (A).

(3) **Definition.**—For purposes of this subsection, the term "lump-sum credit" means the unrefunded amount consisting of—

(A) retirement deductions made under this section from the salary of a bankruptcy judge or magistrate judge;

(B) amounts deposited under subsection (k) by a bankruptcy judge or magistrate judge covering earlier service; and

(C) interest on the deductions and deposits which, for any calendar year, shall be equal to the overall average yield to the Judicial Officers' Retirement Fund during the preceding fiscal year from all obligations purchased by the Secretary of the Treasury during such fiscal year under subsection (*o*);

but does not include interest—

(i) if the service covered thereby aggregates 1 year or less; or

(ii) for the fractional part of a month in the total service.

(*o*) **Judicial Officers' Retirement Fund.**—

(1) **Establishment.**—There is established in the Treasury a fund which shall be known as the "Judicial Officers' Retirement Fund". The Fund is appropriated for the payment of annuities, refunds, and other payments under this section.

(2) **Investment of Fund.**—The Secretary of the Treasury shall invest, in interest bearing securities of the United States, such currently available portions of the Judicial Officers' Retirement Fund as are not immediately required for payments from the Fund. The income derived from these investments constitutes a part of the Fund.

(3) **Unfunded liability.**—(A) There are authorized to be appropriated to the Judicial Officers' Retirement Fund amounts required to reduce to zero the unfunded liability of the Fund.

(B) For purposes of subparagraph (A), the term "unfunded liability" means the estimated excess, determined on an annual basis in accordance with the provisions of section 9503 of title 31, of the present value of all benefits payable from the Judicial Officers' Retirement Fund over the sum of—

(i) the present value of deductions to be withheld under this section from the future basic pay of bankruptcy judges and magistrate judges; plus

(ii) the balance in the Fund as of the date the unfunded liability is determined.

In making any determination under this subparagraph, the Comptroller General shall use the applicable information contained in the reports filed pursuant to section 9503 of title 31, with respect to the retirement annuities provided for in this section.

(C) There are authorized to be appropriated such sums as may be necessary to carry out this paragraph.

(Added Pub.L. 100–659, § 2(a), Nov. 15, 1988, 102 Stat. 3910, and amended Pub.L. 101–650, Title III, §§ 321, 325(b)(3), Dec. 1, 1990, 104 Stat. 5117, 5121; Pub.L. 102–40, Title IV, § 402(d)(2), May 7, 1991, 105 Stat. 239.)

[1] So in original. Probably should be "receive—"

HISTORICAL AND STATUTORY NOTES

References in Text

Section 7447 of the Internal Revenue Code of 1986, referred to in subsec. (f)(3), is classified to section 7447 of Title 26, Internal Revenue Code.

Section 34 of the Bankruptcy Act, referred to in subsec. (h)(1)(B), was classified to section 62 of former Title 11, Bankruptcy, and was omitted in the enactment of revised Title 11 by Section 101 of Pub.L. 95–598, Nov. 6, 1978, 92 Stat. 2549 the Bankruptcy Act was repealed effective Oct. 1, 1979, by Sections 401(a), 402(a) of Pub.L. 95–598.

Section 404 of the Act of November 6, 1978 (Pub.L. 95–598), referred to in subsec. (h)(1)(C), and formerly set out as a note preceding section 151 of this title, was repealed by Pub.L. 98–353, Title I, § 114, July 10, 1984, 98 Stat. 343.

Effective and Applicability Provisions

1988 Acts. Section 9 of Pub.L. 100–659 provided that:

"(a) **In general.**—Subject to subsection (b), this Act and the amendments made by this Act [enacting this section and section 8440a of Title 5, Government Organization and Employees, amending sections 155, 375, 376, 604, 631, and 636 of this title and sections 8334 and 8402 of Title 5 and enacting provisions set out as notes under this section and sections 1 and 376 of this title] shall take effect on the date of the enactment of this Act [Nov. 15, 1988] and shall apply to bankruptcy judges and magistrates who retire on or after the date of the enactment of this Act.

"(b) **Exception for judges and magistrates retiring on or after July 31, 1987.**—A bankruptcy judge or magistrate who left office on or after July 31, 1987, and before the date of the enactment of this Act [Nov. 15, 1988] may elect to receive an annuity, or to participate in the Judicial Survivors' Annuity System, under the amendments made by this Act if such bankruptcy judge or magistrate, within 60 days after so leaving office, accepted office or employment with the United States Government or a State government or was eligible at the time he or she left office for an immediate annuity under title 5, United States Code. Any election under this subsection shall not be valid unless it is made within 6 months after the date of the enactment of this act [Nov. 15, 1988] and under the same conditions as other persons who may make elections under the amendments made by this Act, except that any such person who makes an election under this subsection shall not receive a lump-sum credit under section

8342 or 8424 of title 5, United States Code [section 8342 or 8424 of Title 5], for prior service and shall not be required to make contributions for prior years of creditable service."

Change of Name

"United States magistrate judge" substituted for "United States magistrate" in text pursuant to section 321 of Pub.L. 101–650, set out as a note under 28 U.S.C.A. § 631.

United States magistrate appointed under section 631 of this title to be known as United States magistrate judge after Dec. 1, 1990, with any reference to United States magistrate or magistrate in this title, in any other Federal statute, etc., deemed a reference to United States magistrate judge appointed under section 631 of this title, see section 321 of Pub.L. 101–650, set out as a note under section 631 of this title.

Qualified Magistrate Judges

Pub.L. 107–116, Title V, § 515, Jan. 10, 2002, 115 Stat. 2220, provided that:

"**(a)** In this section the term 'qualified magistrate judge' means any person who—

"**(1)** retired as a magistrate judge before November 15, 1988; and

"**(2)** On the date of filing an election under subsection (b)—

"**(A)** is serving as a recalled magistrate judge on a full-time basis under section 636(h) of title 28, United States Code [28 U.S.C.A. § 636(h)]; and

"**(B)** has completed at least 5 years of full-time recall service.

"**(b)** The director of the administrative office of the United States courts may accept the election of a qualified magistrate judge to—

"**(1)** receive an annuity under section 377 of title 28, United States Code [this section]; and

"**(2)** come within the purview of section 376 of such title [28 U.S.C.A. § 376].

"**(c)** Full–time recall service performed by a qualified magistrate judge shall be credited for service in calculating an annuity elected under this section.

"**(d)** The Director of the Administrative Office of the United States Courts may promulgate regulations to carry out this section."

Report to Congress on Financial Operation of Retirement Annuity Program

Pub.L. 100–659, § 8, Nov. 15, 1988, 102 Stat. 3920, provided that: "The Director of the Administrative Office of the United States Courts shall, not later than 5 years after the date of the enactment of this Act [Nov. 15, 1988], submit a report to the Congress on the financial operation of the retirement annuity program established under this Act and the amendments made by this Act [see Effective and Applicability Provisions of 1988 Amendments note set out under this section]. The report shall, in particular, include a discussion of the deductions from salary and deposits made for contributions to the annuity program and the need for continuing the deductions at the level established under the amendments made by this Act."

[For termination, effective May 15, 2000, of reporting provisions of Pub.L. 100–659, § 8, set out above, see Pub.L. 104–66, § 3003, as amended, set out as a note under 31 U.S.C.A. § 1113, and the 7th item on page 12 of House Document No. 103–7.]

Retirement Annuities for Incumbent Bankruptcy Judges and Magistrates

Section 2(c) of Pub.L. 100–659 provided that:

"**(1) Retirement annuity under Title 5 and section 377 of Title 28.**—A bankruptcy judge or United States magistrate in active service on the effective date of this Act [Nov. 15, 1988] shall, subject to paragraph (2), be entitled, in lieu of the annuity otherwise provided under the amendments made by this section [enacting this section], to—

"**(A)** an annuity under subchapter III of chapter 83, or under chapter 84, of Title 5, United States Code [section 8331 et seq. or section 8401 et seq. of Title 5, Government Organization and Employees], as the case may be, for creditable service before the date on which service would begin to be credited for purposes of subparagraph (B), and

"**(B)** an annuity calculated under subsection (b) or (c) and subsection (g) of section 377 of title 28, United States Code, as added by this section [subsecs. (b) or (c) and (g) of this section], for any service as a full-time bankruptcy judge or magistrate on or after October 1, 1979 (as specified in the election pursuant to paragraph (2)) for which deductions and deposits are made under subsections (j) and (k) of such section 377 [subsecs. (j) and (k) of this section], as applicable, without regard to the minimum number of years of service as such a bankruptcy judge or magistrate, except that—

"**(i)** in the case of a judge or a magistrate who retires with less than 8 years of service, the annuity under subsection (c) of section 377 of title 28, United States Code [subsec. (c) of this section], shall be equal to that proportion of the salary being received at the time the judge or magistrate leaves office which the years of service bears to 14, subject to a reduction in accordance with subsection (c) of such section 377 if the bankruptcy judge or magistrate is under age 65 at the time he or she leaves office, and

"**(ii)** the aggregate amount of the annuity initially payable on retirement under this subsection may not exceed the rate of pay for the bankruptcy judge or magistrate which is in effect on the day before the retirement becomes effective.

"**(2) Filing of notice of election.**—A bankruptcy judge or magistrate shall be entitled to an annuity under this subsection only if the judge or magistrate files a notice of that election with the Director of the Administrative Office of the United States Courts specifying the date on which service would begin to be credited under section 377 of title 28, United States Code [this section], in lieu of chapter 83 or chapter 84 of title 5, United States Code [section 8331 et seq. or 8401 et seq. of Title 5].

"**(3) Lump-sum credit under Title 5.**—A bankruptcy judge or magistrate who makes an election under paragraph (2) shall be entitled to a lump-sum credit under section 8342 or 8424 of title 5, United States Code [section 8342 or 8424 of Title 5], as the case may be, for any service which is covered under section 377 of title 28, United States Code [this section], as added by this section, pursuant to that election, and with respect to which any contributions were made by the judge or magistrate under the applicable provisions of title 5, United States Code.

"(4) **Recall.**—With respect to any bankruptcy judge or magistrate receiving an annuity under this subsection who is recalled to serve under section 375 of title 28, United States Code [section 375 of this title]—

"(A) the amount of compensation which such recalled judge or magistrate receives under subsection (c) of such section shall be calculated on the basis of the annuity received under this subsection; and

"(B) such recalled judge or magistrate may serve as a reemployed annuitant to the extent permitted by subsection (e) of section 375 of such title [section 375(e) of this title].

Section 377(m)(3) of title 28, United States Code, as added by subsection (a) of this section [subsec. (m)(3) of this section], shall not apply with respect to service as a reemployed annuitant described in subparagraph (B)."

CHAPTER 19—DISTRIBUTION OF REPORTS AND DIGESTS

Sec.
411. Supreme Court reports; printing, binding, and distribution.
412. Sale of Supreme Court reports.
413. Publications; distribution to courts.
414. Transmittal of books to successors.
[415. Repealed.]

§ 411. Supreme Court reports; printing, binding, and distribution

(a) The decisions of the Supreme Court of the United States shall be printed, bound, and distributed in the preliminary prints and bound volumes of the United States Reports as soon as practicable after rendition, to be charged to the proper appropriation for the judiciary. The number and distribution of the copies shall be under the control of the Joint Committee on Printing.

(b) Reports printed prior to June 12, 1926, shall not be furnished the Secretary of the Army, the Secretary of the Navy, or the Secretary of the Air Force.

(c) The Public Printer, or other printer designated by the Supreme Court of the United States, upon request, shall furnish to the Superintendent of Documents the reports required to be distributed under the provisions of this section.

(June 25, 1948, c. 646, 62 Stat. 904; May 24, 1949, c. 139, § 68, 63 Stat. 99; Oct. 31, 1951, c. 655, § 41, 65 Stat. 725; July 10, 1952, c. 632, § 4, 66 Stat. 540.)

§ 412. Sale of Supreme Court reports

The Public Printer, or other printer designated by the Supreme Court of the United States shall print such additional bound volumes and preliminary prints of such reports as may be required for sale to the public. Such additional copies shall be sold by the Superintendent of Documents, as provided by law.

(June 25, 1948, c. 646, 62 Stat. 906; July 10, 1952, c. 632, § 5, 66 Stat. 541.)

§ 413. Publications; distribution to courts

Distribution of publications to Federal courts in accordance with the provisions of this chapter shall not be made to any place where such court is held in a building not owned or controlled by the United States unless such publications are committed to the custody of an officer of the United States at such building.

The Attorney General and the Director in the procurement of law books, books of reference or periodicals may exchange or sell similar items and apply the allowance or proceeds to payment in whole or in part of the cost of the items procured.

(June 25, 1948, c. 646, 62 Stat. 906; May 24, 1949, c. 139, § 69, 63 Stat. 100; July 10, 1952, c. 632, § 6, 66 Stat. 541.)

§ 414. Transmittal of books to successors

All government publications and law books furnished to justices, judges, clerks of courts, and United States attorneys of the United States and its territories and possessions, and other officers of the United States or an agency thereof shall be transmitted to their successors in office. All permanent or bound books and publications furnished under this chapter except those books furnished to the Library of Congress for international exchange shall remain the property of the United States and shall be marked plainly, "The Property of the United States".

(June 25, 1948, c. 646, 62 Stat. 906; Oct. 18, 1962, Pub.L. 87–845, § 7, 76A Stat. 699.)

HISTORICAL AND STATUTORY NOTES

Effective and Applicability Provisions

1962 Acts. Amendment by Pub.L. 87–845 effective Jan. 2, 1963, see section 25 of Pub.L. 87–845, set out as a note under Section 14 of Title 18, Crimes and Criminal Procedure.

[§ 415. Repealed. Pub.L. 97–164, Title I, § 113, Apr. 2, 1982, 96 Stat. 29]

HISTORICAL AND STATUTORY NOTES

Section, Acts June 25, 1948, c. 646, 62 Stat. 906; May 24, 1949, c. 139, § 70, 63 Stat. 100, provided for the distribution of copies of the decisions of the Court of Claims. See section 174(b) of this title.

Effective Date of Repeal

Repeal effective Oct. 1, 1982, see section 402 of Pub.L. 97–164, set out as a note under section 171 of this title.

CHAPTER 21—GENERAL PROVISIONS APPLICABLE TO COURTS AND JUDGES

Sec.
451. Definitions.
452. Courts always open; power unrestricted by expiration of sessions.[1]
453. Oath of justices and judges.[1]
454. Practice of law by justices and judges.
455. Disqualification of justice, judge, or magistrate judge.
456. Traveling expenses of justices and judges; official duty stations.
457. Records; obsolete papers.
458. Relative of justice or judge ineligible to appointment.
459. Administration of oaths and acknowledgments.
460. Application to other courts.
461. Adjustments in certain salaries.
462. Court accommodations.
463. Expenses of litigation.

[1] So in original. Does not conform to section catchline.

HISTORICAL AND STATUTORY NOTES

Change of Name

"United States magistrate judge" substituted for "United States magistrate" in item 455 pursuant to section 321 of Pub.L. 101–650, set out as a note under 28 U.S.C.A. § 631.

§ 451. Definitions

As used in this title:

The term "court of the United States" includes the Supreme Court of the United States, courts of appeals, district courts constituted by chapter 5 of this title, including the Court of International Trade and any court created by Act of Congress the judges of which are entitled to hold office during good behavior.

The terms "district court" and "district court of the United States" mean the courts constituted by chapter 5 of this title.

The term "judge of the United States" includes judges of the courts of appeals, district courts, Court of International Trade and any court created by Act of Congress, the judges of which are entitled to hold office during good behavior.

The term "justice of the United States" includes the Chief Justice of the United States and the associate justices of the Supreme Court.

The term "district" and "judicial district" mean the districts enumerated in Chapter 5 of this title.

The term "department" means one of the executive departments enumerated in section 1 of Title 5, unless the context shows that such term was intended to describe the executive, legislative, or judicial branches of the government.

The term "agency" includes any department, independent establishment, commission, administration, authority, board or bureau of the United States or any corporation in which the United States has a proprietary interest, unless the context shows that such term was intended to be used in a more limited sense.

(June 25, 1948, c. 646, 62 Stat. 907; Mar. 18, 1959, Pub.L. 86–3, § 10, 73 Stat. 9; Sept. 12, 1966, Pub.L. 89–571, § 3, 80 Stat. 764; Nov. 6, 1978, Pub.L. 95–598, Title II, § 213, 92 Stat. 2661; Oct. 10, 1980, Pub.L. 96–417, Title V, § 501(10), 94 Stat. 1742; Apr. 2, 1982, Pub.L. 97–164, Title I, § 114, 96 Stat. 29.)

HISTORICAL AND STATUTORY NOTES

References in Text

Section 1 of Title 5, referred to in text, is section 1 of former Title 5. Executive Departments and Government Officers and Employees, the provisions of which are covered by section 101 of Title 5, Government Organization and Employees.

Codifications

The paragraphs of this section defining the term "court of the United States" and the term "judge of the United States" were amended by Pub.L. 95–598, Title II, § 213, Nov. 6, 1978, 92 Stat. 2668, effective June 28, 1984, pursuant to Pub.L. 95–598, Title IV, § 402(b), Nov. 6, 1978, 92 Stat. 2682, as amended by Pub.L. 98–249, § 1(a), Mar. 31, 1984, 98 Stat. 116; Pub.L. 98–271, § 1(a), Apr. 30, 1984, 98 Stat. 163; Pub.L. 98–299, § 1(a), May 25, 1984, 98 Stat. 214; Pub.L. 98–325, § 1(a), June 20, 1984, 98 Stat. 268, set out as a note preceding section 101 of Title 11, Bankruptcy, to read as follows:

The term "court of the United States" includes the Supreme Court of the United States, courts of appeals, district courts constituted by chapter 5 of this title, including the Court of International Trade and any court created by Act of Congress the judges of which are entitled to hold office during good behavior, and bankruptcy courts, the judges of which are entitled to hold office for a term of 14 years.

The term "judge of the United States" includes judges of the courts of appeals, district courts, Court of International Trade and any court created by Act of Congress, the judges of which are entitled to hold office during good behavior, and judge of the bankruptcy courts, the judges of which are entitled to hold office for a term of 14 years.

Section 402(b) of Pub.L. 95–598 was amended by section 113 of Pub.L. 98–353, Title I, July 10, 1984, 98 Stat. 343, by substituting "shall not be effective" for "shall take effect on June 28, 1984", thereby eliminating the amendment by section 213 of Pub.L. 95–598, effective June 27, 1984, pursuant to section 122(c) of Pub.L. 98–353, set out as an Effective and Applicability Provisions note under section 151 of this title.

Section 121(a) of Pub.L. 98–353 directed that section 402(b) of Pub.L. 95–598 be amended by substituting "the date of enactment of the Bankruptcy Amendments and Federal Judgeship Act of 1984 [i.e. July 10, 1984]" for "June 28, 1984". This amendment was not executed in view of the prior amendment to section 402(b) of Pub.L. 95–598 by section 113 of Pub.L. 98–353.

Effective and Applicability Provisions

1982 Acts. Amendment by Pub.L. 97–164 effective Oct. 1, 1982, see section 402 of Pub.L. 97–164, set out as a note under section 171 of this title.

1980 Acts. Amendment by Pub.L. 96–417 effective on Nov. 1, 1980 and applicable with respect to civil actions pending on or commenced on or after such date, see section 701(a) of Pub.L. 96–417, as amended, set out as a note under section 251 of this title.

1959 Acts. Section 10 of Pub.L. 86–3 provided in part that the amendment of this section shall be effective upon the admission of the State of Hawaii into the Union. Admission of Hawaii into the Union was accomplished Aug. 21, 1959 upon issuance of Proc. No. 3309, Aug. 21, 1959, 25 F.R. 6868, 73 Stat. c74, as required by sections 1 and 7(c) of Pub.L. 86–3, Mar. 18, 1959, 73 Stat. 4, set out as notes preceding Section 491 of Title 48, Territories and Insular Possessions.

"Circuit Court of Appeals;" "Senior Circuit Judge," Etc. Defined

Section 32 of Act June 25, 1948, as amended by Act May 24, 1949, c. 139, § 127, 63 Stat. 107, provided that:

"**(a)** All laws of the United States in force on September 1, 1948, in which reference is made to a 'circuit court of appeals'; 'senior circuit judge'; 'senior district judge'; 'presiding judge'; 'chief justice,' except when reference to the Chief Justice of the United States is intended; or 'justice', except when used with respect to a justice of the Supreme Court of the United States in his capacity as such or as a circuit justice, are hereby amended by substituting 'court of appeals' for 'circuit court of appeals'; 'chief judge of the circuit' for 'senior circuit judge'; 'chief judge of the district court' for 'senior district judge'; 'chief judge' for 'presiding judge'; 'chief judge' for 'chief justice', except when reference to the Chief Justice of the United States is intended; and 'judge' for 'justice', except when the latter term is used with respect to a justice of the Supreme Court of the United States in his capacity as such or as a circuit justice.

"**(b)** All laws of the United States in force on September 1, 1948, in which reference is made to the Supreme Court of the District of Columbia or to the District Court of the United States for the District of Columbia are amended by substituting 'United States District Court for the District of Columbia' for such designations.

"**(c)** All laws of the United States in force on September 1, 1948, in which reference is made to the 'Conference of Senior Circuit Judges', or to the 'Judicial Conference of Senior Circuit Judges' are amended by substituting 'Judicial Conference of the United States' for such designations.

"**(d)** This section shall not be construed to amend historical references to courts or judicial offices which have no present or future application to such courts or offices."

Judges of the United States

Section 2(a) of Act June 25, 1948, c. 646, 62 Stat. 985, amended Sept. 3, 1954, c. 1263, § 51(a), 68 Stat. 1245, provided that: "(a) The Chief Justices of the United States Court of Appeals for the District of Columbia, the District Court of the United States for the District of Columbia, and the Court of Claims [now United States Court of Federal Claims], and the presiding judge of the Court of Customs and Patent Appeals [now United States Court of Appeals for the Federal Circuit], in office on the effective date of this Act shall be the chief judges of their respective courts. The Chief Justice of the United States Court of Appeals for the District of Columbia and the Associate Justices thereof, the Chief Justice of the District Court of the United States for the District of Columbia (formerly named the Supreme Court of the District of Columbia) and the Associate Justices thereof, the Chief Justice of the Court of Claims [now United States Court of Federal Claims], and the presiding judge of the Court of Customs and Patent Appeals [now United States Court of Appeals for the Federal Circuit], in office on the effective date of this Act, shall be judges of the United States within the meaning of Section 451 of Title 28, Judiciary and Judicial Procedure, of the United States Code, set out in Section 1 of this Act. The Chief Justice of the United States Court of Appeals for the District of Columbia and the Associate Justices thereof, in office on the effective date of this Act, shall be circuit judges of the District of Columbia Circuit and vested with all the rights, powers, and duties thereof, and the said Chief Justice of the United States Court of Appeals for the District of Columbia shall be Chief Judge of said Circuit. The Chief Justice of the District Court of the United States for the District of Columbia (formerly named the Supreme Court of the District of Columbia) and the Associate Justices thereof, in office on the effective date of this Act, shall be district judges for the District of Columbia and vested with all the rights, powers, and duties thereof."

Section 51(b) of Act Sept. 3, 1954, provided that this amendment should take effect as of Sept. 1, 1948.

§ 452. Courts always open; powers unrestricted by expiration of sessions

All courts of the United States shall be deemed always open for the purpose of filing proper papers, issuing and returning process, and making motions and orders.

The continued existence or expiration of a session of a court in no way affects the power of the court to do any act or take any proceeding.

(June 25, 1948, c. 646, 62 Stat. 907; Oct. 16, 1963, Pub.L. 88–139, § 2, 77 Stat. 248.)

§ 453. Oaths of justices and judges

Each justice or judge of the United States shall take the following oath or affirmation before performing the duties of his office: "I, _____ _____, do solemnly swear (or affirm) that I will administer justice without respect to persons, and do equal right to the poor and to the rich, and that I will faithfully and impartially discharge and perform all the duties incumbent upon me as _____ under the Constitution and laws of the United States. So help me God."

(June 25, 1948, c. 646, 62 Stat. 907; Dec. 1, 1990, Pub.L. 101–650, Title IV, § 404, 104 Stat. 5124.)

HISTORICAL AND STATUTORY NOTES

Effective and Applicability Provisions

1990 Acts. Amendment by section 404 of Pub.L. 101–650 effective 90 days after Dec. 1, 1990, see section 407 of Pub.L. 101–650, set out as a note under section 332 of this title.

§ 454. Practice of law by justices and judges

Any justice or judge appointed under the authority of the United States who engages in the practice of law is guilty of a high misdemeanor.

(June 25, 1948, c. 646, 62 Stat. 908.)

§ 455. Disqualification of justice, judge, or magistrate judge

(a) Any justice, judge, or magistrate judge of the United States shall disqualify himself in any proceeding in which his impartiality might reasonably be questioned.

(b) He shall also disqualify himself in the following circumstances:

(1) Where he has a personal bias or prejudice concerning a party, or personal knowledge of disputed evidentiary facts concerning the proceeding;

(2) Where in private practice he served as lawyer in the matter in controversy, or a lawyer with whom he previously practiced law served during such association as a lawyer concerning the matter, or the judge or such lawyer has been a material witness concerning it;

(3) Where he has served in governmental employment and in such capacity participated as counsel, adviser or material witness concerning the proceeding or expressed an opinion concerning the merits of the particular case in controversy;

(4) He knows that he, individually or as a fiduciary, or his spouse or minor child residing in his household, has a financial interest in the subject matter in controversy or in a party to the proceeding, or any other interest that could be substantially affected by the outcome of the proceeding;

(5) He or his spouse, or a person within the third degree of relationship to either of them, or the spouse of such a person:

(i) Is a party to the proceeding, or an officer, director, or trustee of a party;

(ii) Is acting as a lawyer in the proceeding;

(iii) Is known by the judge to have an interest that could be substantially affected by the outcome of the proceeding;

(iv) Is to the judge's knowledge likely to be a material witness in the proceeding.

(c) A judge should inform himself about his personal and fiduciary financial interests, and make a reasonable effort to inform himself about the personal financial interests of his spouse and minor children residing in his household.

(d) For the purposes of this section the following words or phrases shall have the meaning indicated:

(1) "proceeding" includes pretrial, trial, appellate review, or other stages of litigation;

(2) the degree of relationship is calculated according to the civil law system;

(3) "fiduciary" includes such relationships as executor, administrator, trustee, and guardian;

(4) "financial interest" means ownership of a legal or equitable interest, however small, or a relationship as director, adviser, or other active participant in the affairs of a party, except that:

(i) Ownership in a mutual or common investment fund that holds securities is not a "financial interest" in such securities unless the judge participates in the management of the fund;

(ii) An office in an educational, religious, charitable, fraternal, or civic organization is not a "financial interest" in securities held by the organization;

(iii) The proprietary interest of a policyholder in a mutual insurance company, of a depositor in a mutual savings association, or a similar proprietary interest, is a "financial interest" in the organization only if the outcome of the proceeding could substantially affect the value of the interest;

(iv) Ownership of government securities is a "financial interest" in the issuer only if the outcome of the proceeding could substantially affect the value of the securities.

(e) No justice, judge, or magistrate judge shall accept from the parties to the proceeding a waiver of any ground for disqualification enumerated in subsection (b). Where the ground for disqualification arises only under subsection (a), waiver may be accepted provided it is preceded by a full disclosure on the record of the basis for disqualification.

(f) Notwithstanding the preceding provisions of this section, if any justice, judge, magistrate judge, or bankruptcy judge to whom a matter has been assigned would be disqualified, after substantial judicial time has been devoted to the matter, because of the appearance or discovery, after the matter was assigned to him or her, that he or she individually or as a fiduciary, or his or her spouse or minor child residing in his or her household, has a financial interest in a party (other than an interest that could be substantially affected by the outcome), disqualification is not required if the justice, judge, magistrate judge, bankruptcy judge, spouse or minor child, as the case may be, divests himself or herself of the interest that provides the grounds for the disqualification.

(June 25, 1948, c. 646, 62 Stat. 908; Dec. 5, 1974, Pub.L. 93–512, § 1, 88 Stat. 1609; Nov. 6, 1978, Pub.L. 95–598, Title II, § 214(a), (b), 92 Stat. 2661; Nov. 19, 1988, Pub.L. 100–702, Title X, § 1007, 102 Stat. 4667; Dec. 1, 1990, Pub.L. 101–650, Title III, § 321, 104 Stat. 5117.)

HISTORICAL AND STATUTORY NOTES

Change of Name

"United States magistrate judge" substituted for "United States magistrate" in text pursuant to section 321 of Pub.L. 101–650, set out as a note under 28 U.S.C.A. § 631.

Effective and Applicability Provisions

1978 Acts. Amendment by Pub.L. 95–598 effective Oct. 1, 1979, see section 402(c) of Pub.L. 95–598, set out as a note preceding section 101 of Title 11, Bankruptcy. For procedures relating to bankruptcy matters during transition period, see note preceding section 151 of this title.

1974 Acts. Section 3 of Pub.L. 93–512 provided that: "This Act [amending this section] shall not apply to the trial of any proceeding commenced prior to the date of this Act [Dec. 5, 1974], nor to appellate review of any proceeding which was fully submitted to the reviewing court prior to the date of this Act."

§ 456. Traveling expenses of justices and judges; official duty stations

(a) The Director of the Administrative Office of the United States Courts shall pay each justice or judge of the United States, and each retired justice or judge recalled or designated and assigned to active duty, while attending court or transacting official business at a place other than his official duty station for any continuous period of less than thirty calendar days (1) all necessary transportation expenses certified by the justice or judge; and (2) payments for subsistence expenses at rates or in amounts which the Director establishes, in accordance with regulations which the Director shall prescribe with the approval of the Judicial Conference of the United States and after considering the rates or amounts set by the Administrator of General Services and the President pursuant to section 5702 of title 5. The Director of the Administrative Office of the United States Courts shall also pay each justice or judge of the United States, and each retired justice or judge recalled or designated and assigned to active duty, while attending court or transacting official business under an assignment authorized under chapter 13 of this title which exceeds in duration a continuous period of thirty calendar days, all necessary transportation expenses and actual and necessary expenses of subsistence actually incurred, notwithstanding the provisions of section 5702 of title 5, in accordance with regulations which the Director shall prescribe with the approval of the Judicial Conference of the United States.

(b) The official duty station of the Chief Justice of the United States, the Justices of the Supreme Court of the United States, and the judges of the United States Court of Appeals for the District of Columbia Circuit, the United States Court of Appeals for the Federal Circuit, and the United States District Court for the District of Columbia shall be the District of Columbia.

(c) The official duty station of the judges of the United States Court of International Trade shall be New York City.

(d) The official duty station of each district judge shall be that place where a district court holds regular sessions at or near which the judge performs a substantial portion of his judicial work, which is nearest the place where he maintains his actual abode in which he customarily lives.

(e) The official duty station of a circuit judge shall be that place where a circuit or district court holds regular sessions at or near which the judge performs a substantial portion of his judicial work, or that place where the Director provides chambers to the judge where he performs a substantial portion of his judicial work, which is nearest the place where he maintains his actual abode in which he customarily lives.

(f) The official duty station of a retired judge shall be established in accordance with section 374 of this title.

(g) Each circuit or district judge whose official duty station is not fixed expressly by this section shall notify the Director of the Administrative Office of the United States Courts in writing of his actual abode and official duty station upon his appointment and from time to time thereafter as his official duty station may change.

(June 25, 1948, c. 646, 62 Stat. 908; Aug. 8, 1953, c. 376, 67 Stat. 488; Aug. 7, 1959, Pub.L. 86–138, 73 Stat. 285; Nov. 6, 1978, Pub.L. 95–598, Title II, § 215, 92 Stat. 2661; Oct. 10, 1980, Pub.L. 96–417, Title V, § 501(11), 94 Stat. 1742; Apr. 2, 1982, Pub.L. 97–164, Title I, § 115(a) (1), 96 Stat. 30; Jan. 2, 1986, Pub.L. 99–234, Title I, § 107(d), 99 Stat. 1759.)

HISTORICAL AND STATUTORY NOTES

Codifications

The amendment by Pub.L. 95–598 in 1978 to be effective Apr. 1, 1984, was never actually executed to text in view of the later amendment of this section by Pub.L. 97–164, eff. Oct. 1, 1982, which completely revised this section both as it would exist just prior to Oct. 1, 1982, and as it would become effective Apr. 1, 1984. See 1978 and 1982 Amendments notes under this section.

Effective and Applicability Provisions

1986 Acts. Amendment by Pub.L. 99–234 effective on the effective date of regulations to be promulgated not later than 150 days after Jan. 2, 1986, or 180 days after Jan. 2, 1986, whichever occurs first, see section 301(a) of Pub.L. 99–234, set out as a note under section 5701 of Title 5, Government Organization and Employees.

1982 Acts. Amendment by Pub.L. 97–164 effective Oct. 1, 1982, see section 402 of Pub.L. 97–164, set out as a note under section 171 of this title.

1980 Acts. Amendment by Pub.L. 96–417 effective on Nov. 1, 1980 and applicable with respect to civil actions pending on or commenced on or after such date, see section 701(a) of Pub.L. 96–417, as amended, set out as a note under section 251 of this title.

Promulgation of Regulations by Director

Director to promulgate regulations effectuating increases in reimbursement for expenses, see section 6 of Pub.L. 87–139, Aug. 14, 1961, 75 Stat. 340, set out as a note under section 604 of this title.

Report on Transportation Needs

Pub.L. 99–550, § 3, Oct. 27, 1986, 100 Stat. 3070, provided that: "Within one year after the date of enactment of this Act [Oct. 27, 1986], the Director of the Administrative Office of the United States Courts shall prepare, in consultation with the Marshal of the Supreme Court of the United States, the Clerk of the United States Court of Military Appeals [now United States Court of Appeals for the Armed Forces] and the Court Administrator of the United States Tax Court, and transmit to the Congress, appropriate recommendations concerning the transportation needs of the judicial branch and of courts established pursuant to Article I of the Constitution [U.S.C.A. Const. Art. I]."

§ 457. Records; obsolete papers

The records of district courts and of courts of appeals shall be kept at one or more of the places where court is held. Such places shall be designated by the respective courts except when otherwise directed by the judicial council of the circuit.

Papers of any court established by Act of Congress which have become obsolete and are no longer necessary or useful, may be disposed of with the approval of the court concerned in the manner provided by sections 366–380 of Title 44 and in accordance with the rules of the Judicial Conference of the United States.

(June 25, 1948, c. 646, 62 Stat. 908; Nov. 6, 1978, Pub.L. 95–598, Title II, § 216, 92 Stat. 2661.)

HISTORICAL AND STATUTORY NOTES

References in Text

Sections 366–380 of Title 44, referred to in text, were repealed and the provisions thereof reenacted as chapter 33 (Section 3301 et seq.) of Title 44, Public Printing and Documents, by Pub.L. 90–620, Oct. 22, 1968, 82 Stat. 1238.

Codifications

The first paragraph of this section was amended by Pub.L. 95–598, Title II, § 216, Nov. 6, 1978, 92 Stat. 261, effective June 28, 1984, pursuant to Pub.L. 95–598, Title IV, § 402(b), Nov. 6, 1978, 92 Stat. 2682, as amended by Pub.L. 98–249, § 1(a), Mar. 31, 1984, 98 Stat. 116; Pub.L. 98–271, § 1(a), Apr. 30, 1984, 98 Stat. 163; Pub.L. 98–299, § 1(a), May 25, 1984, 98 Stat. 214; Pub.L. 98–325, § 1(a), June 20, 1984, 98 Stat. 268, set out as an Effective and Applicability Provisions note preceding section 101 of Title 11, Bankruptcy by substituting "The records of bankruptcy courts, of district courts, and of courts of appeals" for "The records of district courts and of courts of appeals".

Section 402(b) of Pub.L. 95–598 was amended by section 113 of Pub.L. 98–353, Title I, July 10, 1984, 98 Stat. 343, by substituting "shall not be effective" for "shall take effect on June 28, 1984", thereby eliminating the amendment by section 216 of Pub.L. 95–598, effective June 27, 1984, pursuant to section 122(c) of Pub.L. 98–353, set out as an Effective and Applicability Provisions note under section 151 of this title.

Section 121(a) of Pub.L. 98–353 directed that section 402(b) of Pub.L. 95–598 be amended by substituting "the date of enactment of the Bankruptcy Amendments and Federal Judgeship Act of 1984 [i.e. July 10, 1984]" for "June 28, 1984". This amendment was not executed in view of the prior amendment to section 402(b) of Pub.L. 95–598 by section 113 of Pub.L. 98–353.

§ 458. Relative of justice or judge ineligible to appointment

(a)(1) No person shall be appointed to or employed in any office or duty in any court who is related by affinity or consanguinity within the degree of first cousin to any justice or judge of such court.

(2) With respect to the appointment of a judge of a court exercising judicial power under article III of the United States Constitution [U.S.C.A. Const. Art. III] (other than the Supreme Court), subsection (b) shall apply in lieu of this subsection.

(b)(1) In this subsection, the term—

(A) "same court" means—

(i) in the case of a district court, the court of a single judicial district; and

(ii) in the case of a court of appeals, the court of appeals of a single circuit; and

(B) "member"—

(i) means an active judge or a judge retired in senior status under section 371(b); and

(ii) shall not include a retired judge, except as described under clause (i).

(2) No person may be appointed to the position of judge of a court exercising judicial power under article III of the United States Constitution [U.S.C.A. Const. Art. III] (other than the Supreme Court) who is related by affinity or consanguinity within the degree of first cousin to any judge who is a member of the same court.

(June 25, 1948, c. 646, 62 Stat. 908; Oct. 27, 1998, Pub.L. 105–300, § 1(a), 112 Stat. 2836.)

HISTORICAL AND STATUTORY NOTES

Effective and Applicability Provisions

1998 Acts. Section 1(b) of Pub.L. 105–300 provided that: This Act [amending this section] shall take effect on the date of enactment of this Act [Oct. 27, 1998] and shall apply only to any individual whose nomination is submitted to the Senate on or after such date."

§ 459. Administration of oaths and acknowledgments

Each justice or judge of the United States may administer oaths and affirmations and take acknowledgments.

(June 25, 1948, c. 646, 62 Stat. 908.)

§ 460. Application to other courts

(a) Sections 452 through 459 and section 462 of this chapter shall also apply to the United States Court of Federal Claims, to each court created by Act of Congress in a territory which is invested with any jurisdiction of a district court of the United States, and to the judges thereof.

(b) The official duty station of each judge referred to in subsection (a) which is not otherwise established by law shall be that place where the court holds regular sessions at or near which the judge performs a substantial portion of his judicial work, which is nearest the place where he maintains his actual abode in which he customarily lives.

(June 25, 1948, c. 646, 62 Stat. 908; Oct. 31, 1951, c. 655, § 43(a), 65 Stat. 725; July 7, 1958, Pub.L. 85–508, § 12(e), 72 Stat. 348; Nov. 6, 1978, Pub.L. 95–598, Title II, § 217(a), 92 Stat. 2661; Apr. 2, 1982, Pub.L. 97–164, Title I, § 115(b)(1), 96 Stat. 31; Oct. 29, 1992, Pub.L. 102–572, Title IX, § 902(b)(1), 106 Stat. 4516.)

HISTORICAL AND STATUTORY NOTES

Effective and Applicability Provisions

1992 Acts. Amendment by Pub.L. 102–572 effective Oct. 29, 1992, see section 911 of Pub.L. 102–572, set out as a note under section 171 of this title.

1982 Acts. Amendment by Pub.L. 97–164 effective Oct. 1, 1982, see section 402 of Pub.L. 97–164, set out as a note under section 171 of this title.

1978 Acts. Amendment by Pub.L. 95–598 effective Nov. 6, 1978, see section 402(d) of Pub.L. 95–598, set out as a note preceding section 101 of Title 11, Bankruptcy.

1958 Acts. Amendment by Pub.L. 85–508 effective Jan. 3, 1959 upon admission of Alaska into the Union pursuant to Proc. No. 3269, Jan. 3, 1959, 24 F.R. 81, 73 Stat. c16, as required by section 1 and 8(c) of Pub.L. 85–508, see notes set out under section 81A of this title and preceding section 21 of Title 48, Territories and Insular Possessions.

Change of Name

References to United States Claims Court deemed to refer to United States Court of Federal Claims and references to Claims Court deemed to refer to Court of Federal Claims, see section 902(b) of Pub.L. 102–572, set out as a note under section 171 of Title 28, Judiciary and Judicial Procedure.

§ 461. Adjustments in certain salaries

(a)(1) Subject to paragraph (2), effective at the beginning of the first applicable pay period commencing on or after the first day of the month in which an adjustment takes effect under section 5303 of title 5 in the rates of pay under the General Schedule (except as provided in subsection (b)), each salary rate which is subject to adjustment under this section shall be adjusted by an amount, rounded to the nearest multiple of $100 (or if midway between multiples of $100, to the next higher multiple of $100) equal to the percentage of such salary rate which corresponds to the most recent percentage change in the ECI (relative to the date described in the next sentence), as determined under section 704(a)(1) of the Ethics Reform Act of 1989. The appropriate date under this sentence is the first day of the fiscal year in which such adjustment in the rates of pay under the General Schedule takes effect.

(2) In no event shall the percentage adjustment taking effect under paragraph (1) in any calendar year (before rounding), in any salary rate, exceed the percentage adjustment taking effect in such calendar year under section 5303 of title 5 in the rates of pay under the General Schedule.

(b) Subsection (a) shall not apply to the extent it would reduce the salary of any individual whose compensation may not, under section 1 of article III of the Constitution of the United States, be diminished during such individual's continuance in office.

(Added Pub.L. 94–82, Title II, § 205(a)(1), Aug. 9, 1975, 89 Stat. 422, and amended Pub.L. 101–194, Title VII, § 704(a)(2)(A), Nov. 30, 1989, 103 Stat. 1769; Pub.L. 101–509, Title V, § 529 [Title I, § 101(b)(4)(J)], Nov. 5, 1990, 104 Stat. 1427, 1440; Pub.L. 103–356, Title I, § 101(4), Oct. 13, 1994, 108 Stat. 3411.)

HISTORICAL AND STATUTORY NOTES

References in Text

The General Schedule, referred to in subsec. (a), is set out under section 5332 of Title 5, Government Organization and Employees.

Section 704(a)(1) of the Ethics Reform Act of 1989, referred to in subsec. (a), is section 704(a)(1) of Pub.L. 101–194, which is set out as a note under section 5318 of Title 5, Government Organization and Employees.

Effective and Applicability Provisions

1994 Acts. Amendment to this section by section 101(4) of Pub.L. 103–356 effective Dec. 31, 1994, see section 101 of Pub.L. 103–356 set out as a note under section 31 of Title 2, The Congress.

1990 Acts. Amendment to this section (together with any notes enacted or amended hereunder) by the Federal Employees Pay Comparability Act of 1990, as incorporated in section 529 [Title III, § 305] of Pub.L. 101–509, to take effect on May 4, 1991, except that the Office of Personnel Management may establish an earlier effective date, but not earlier than Feb. 3, 1991, for any such provisions with respect to which the Office determines an earlier effective date to be appropriate, see Ex. Ord. No. 12748, Feb. 1, 1991, 56 F.R. 4521, set out as a note under section 5301 of Title 5, Government Organization and Employees.

1989 Acts. Amendment to this section by section 704(a)(2)(A) of Pub.L. 101–194 to take effect Jan. 1, 1991, see section 704(b) of Pub.L. 101–194, set out as a note under section 5318 of Title 5, Government Organization and Employees.

References to "this Act" in Pub.L. 110–161

Pub.L. 110–161, Div. D, Title VII, § 749, Dec. 26, 2007, 121 Stat. 2035, provided that: "Except as expressly provided otherwise, any reference to 'this Act' [Pub. L. 110–161, Div. D, Financial Services and General Government Appropriations Act, 2008, Dec. 26, 2007, 121 Stat. 1972; see Tables for complete classification] contained in any title other than title IV [Pub.L. 110–161, Div. D, Title IV, District of Columbia Appropriations Act, 2008, Dec. 26, 2007, 121 Stat. 1990; see Tables for complete classification] or VIII [Pub.L. 110–161, Div. D, Title VIII, §§ 801 to 828, Dec. 26, 2007, 121 Stat.

2035; see Tables for complete classification] shall not apply to such title IV [Pub.L. 110–161, Div. D, Title IV, District of Columbia Appropriations Act, 2008, Dec. 26, 2007, 121 Stat. 1990; see Tables for complete classification] or VIII [Pub.L. 110–161, Div. D, Title VIII, §§ 801 to 828, Dec. 26, 2007, 121 Stat. 2035; see Tables for complete classification]."

Salary Adjustments for Justices and Judges

Pub.L. 110–161, Div. D, Title III, § 305, Dec. 26, 2007, 121 Stat. 1989, provided that: "Pursuant to section 140 of Public Law 97–92 [Pub.L. 97–92, Title IV, § 140, Dec. 15, 1981, 95 Stat. 1200, as amended, which is set out as a note under this section], and from funds appropriated in this Act [Pub.L. 110–161, Div. D, Financial Services and General Government Appropriations Act, 2008, Dec. 26, 2007, 121 Stat. 1972], Justices and judges of the United States are authorized during fiscal year 2008, to receive a salary adjustment in accordance with 28 U.S.C. 461 [this section]."

Pub.L. 109–115, Div. A, Title IV, § 405, Nov. 30, 2005, 119 Stat. 2470, provided that: "Pursuant to section 140 of Public Law 97–92 [Pub.L. 97–92, Title IV, § 140, Dec. 15, 1981, 95 Stat. 1200, as amended, which is set out as a note under this section], and from funds appropriated in this Act [Pub.L. 109–115, Div. A], Justices and judges of the United States are authorized during fiscal year 2006, to receive a salary adjustment in accordance with 28 U.S.C. 461 [this section]".

Pub.L. 108–491, § 1, Dec. 23, 2004, 118 Stat. 3973, provided that: "Pursuant to section 140 of Public Law 97–92 [Pub.L. 97–92, Title IV, § 140, Dec. 15, 1981, 95 Stat. 1200, as amended, which is set out as a note under this section], Justices and judges of the United States are authorized during fiscal year 2005 to receive a salary adjustment in accordance with section 461 of title 28, United States Code [this section]."

Pub.L. 108–447, Div. B, Title III, § 306, Dec. 8, 2004, 118 Stat. 2895, provided that: "Pursuant to section 140 of Public Law 97–92 [Pub.L. 97–92, Title IV, § 140, Dec. 15, 1981, 95 Stat. 1200, as amended, which is set out as a note under this section], and from funds appropriated in this Act [Departments of Commerce, Justice, and State, the Judiciary, and Related Agencies Appropriations Act, 2005, Pub.L. 108–447, Div. B, Dec. 8, 2004, 118 Stat. 2853; see Tables for classification], Justices and judges of the United States are authorized during fiscal year 2005, to receive a salary adjustment in accordance with 28 U.S.C. 461 [this section]."

Pub.L. 108–167, § 1, Dec. 6, 2003, 117 Stat. 2031, provided that: "Pursuant to section 140 of Public Law 97–92 [Pub.L. 97–92, Title IV, § 140, Dec. 15, 1981, 95 Stat. 1200, as amended, which is set out as a note under this section], Justices and judges of the United States are authorized during fiscal year 2004 to receive a salary adjustment in accordance with section 461 of title 28, United States Code [this section]."

Pub.L. 108–6, § 1, Feb. 13, 2003, 117 Stat. 10, provided that: "Pursuant to section 140 of Public Law 97–92 [Pub.L. 97–92, § 140, Dec. 15, 1981, 95 Stat. 1200, as amended, which is set out as a note under this section], Justices and judges of the United States are authorized during fiscal year 2003 to receive a salary adjustment in accordance with section 461 of title 28, United States Code [this section]."

Pub.L. 107–77, Title III, § 305, Nov. 28, 2001, 115 Stat. 783, provided in part that: "Pursuant to section 140 of Public Law 97–92 [set out as a note under this section], Justices and judges of the United States are authorized during fiscal year 2002, to receive a salary adjustment in accordance with 28 U.S.C. 461."

Pub.L. 106–553, § 1(a)(2) [Title III, § 309], Dec. 21, 2000, 114 Stat. 2762, 2762A–89, provided that: "Pursuant to section 140 of Public Law 97–92 [set out below], Justices and judges of the United States are authorized during fiscal year 2001, to receive a salary adjustment in accordance with 28 U.S.C. 461 [this section], only if for the purposes of each provision of law amended by section 704(a)(2) of the Ethics Reform Act of 1989 (5 U.S.C. 5318 note), adjustments under section 5303 of title 5, United States Code, shall take effect in fiscal year 2001."

Pub.L. 106–113, Div. B, § 1000(a)(1) [Title III, § 304], Nov. 29, 1999, 113 Stat. 1535, 1501A–36, provided in part that: "Pursuant to section 140 of Public Law 97–92 [set out as a note under this section], Justices and judges of the United States are authorized during fiscal year 2000, to receive a salary adjustment in accordance with 28 U.S.C. 461."

Pub.L. 105–119, Title III, § 306, Nov. 26, 1997, 111 Stat. 2493, provided that: "Pursuant to section 140 of Public Law 97–92 [set out as a note under this section], justices and judges of the United States are authorized during fiscal year 1998, to receive a salary adjustment in accordance with 28 U.S.C. 461 [this section]."

Pub.L. 102–395, Title III, § 304, Oct. 6, 1992, 106 Stat. 1859, provided that: "Pursuant to section 140 of Public Law 97–92 [set out as a note under this section], Justices and judges of the United States are authorized during fiscal year 1993, to receive a salary adjustment in accordance with 28 U.S.C. 461 [this section]."

Pub.L. 102–140, Title III, § 305, Oct. 28, 1991, 105 Stat. 810, provided that: "Pursuant to section 140 of Public Law 97–92 [set out as a note under this section], Justices and judges of the United States are authorized during fiscal year 1992, to receive a salary adjustment in accordance with 28 U.S.C. 461 [this section]."

Pub.L. 101–520, Title III, § 321, Nov. 5, 1990, 104 Stat. 2285, provided that: "Pursuant to section 140 of Public Law 97–92 [set out as a note under this section], Justices and judges of the United States are authorized during calendar year 1991 to receive a salary adjustment in accordance with 28 U.S.C. section 461 [this section]."

For provisions that, effective the first day of the first applicable pay period that begins on or after January 1, 1991, the rate of basic pay for the Chief Justice of the United States, an associate justice of the Supreme Court of the United States, a judge of a United States circuit court, a judge of a district court of the United States, and a judge of the United States Court of International Trade shall be increased in the amount of 25 percent of their respective rates (as last in effect before the increase), rounded to the nearest multiple of $100 (or, if midway between multiples of $100, to the next higher multiple of $100), and related provisions, see Pub.L. 101–194, Title VII, § 703, Nov. 30, 1989, 103 Stat. 1768, set out as a note under section 5318 of Title 5, Government Organization and Employees.

For provisions authorizing, for purposes of section 140 of Pub.L. 97–92 (set out as a note under this section), appropriate salary increases for Federal judges and Justices of the Supreme Court, to be determined, effective for pay periods beginning on or after Nov. 30, 1989, as if the provisions of section 620(b) of Pub.L. 100–440 (5 U.S.C. 5305 note) and section 619(b) of Pub.L. 101–136 (5 U.S.C. 5303 note) had never been enacted, together with related provisions, see section 702 of Pub.L. 101–194, set out as a note under section 5303 of Title 5, Government Organization and Employees.

Pub.L. 100–202, § 101(a) [Title IV, § 406], Dec. 22, 1987, 101 Stat. 1329, 1329–26, provided that: "Pursuant to section 140 of Public Law 97–92 [set out as a note under this section], during fiscal year 1988, justices and judges of the United States shall receive the same percentage increase in salary accorded to employees paid under the General Schedule (pursuant to 5 U.S.C. 5305)."

Pub.L. 99–500, Title I, § 101(b) [Title IV, § 406], Oct. 18, 1986, 100 Stat. 1783–39, 1783–64; Pub.L. 99–591, Title I, § 101(b), [Title IV, § 406], Oct. 30, 1986, 100 Stat. 3341–39, 3341–64, provided that: "Pursuant to section 140 of Public Law 97–92 [set out as a note under this section], during fiscal year 1987, justices and judges of the United States shall receive the same percentage increase in salary accorded to employees paid under the General Schedule (pursuant to 5 U.S.C. 5305) [5 U.S.C.A. § 5305]."

Pub.L. 99–88, Title I, § 100, Aug. 15, 1985, 99 Stat. 310, provided in part that: "Effective on the first day of the first applicable pay period commencing on or after January 1, 1985, each rate of pay subject to adjustment by section 461 of title 28, United States Code [this section], shall be increased by an amount, rounded to the nearest multiple of $100 (or if midway between multiples of $100, to the next higher multiple of $100), equal to the overall percentage of the adjustment taking effect under section 5305 of title 5, United States Code [section 5305 of Title 5, Government Organization and Employees], in the rates of pay under the General Schedule during fiscal year 1985."

Pub.L. 98–369, Div.B., Title II, § 2207, July 18, 1984, 98 Stat. 1060, provided that: "Effective on the first day of the first applicable pay period commencing on or after January 1, 1984, each rate of pay subject to adjustment by section 461 of title 28, United States Code [this section], shall be increased by an amount, rounded to the nearest multiple of $100 (or if midway between multiples of $100, to the next higher multiple of $100), equal to the overall percentage of the adjustment taking effect under section 5305 of title 5, United States Code [section 5305 of Title 5, Government Organization of Employees], in the rates of pay under the General Schedule during fiscal year 1984."

Pub.L. 95–66, § 1(3), July 11, 1977, 91 Stat. 270, set out as a note under section 5318 of Title 5, Government Organization and Employees, provided that the first adjustment which, but for the enactment of Pub.L. 95–66, would have been made in the salary and rate of pay of justices, judges, commissioners, and referees under this section after July 11, 1977, would not take effect.

Salary Rate Limitations or Use of Funds

1982—Limitation on the use of funds appropriated or authority made available for the period Oct. 1, 1982, through Sept. 30, 1983, by any Act to pay the salary or pay of any individual in an office or position in the legislative, executive, or judicial branch, or in the government of the District of Columbia, at a rate equal to or greater than Level V of the Executive Schedule, see section 306(a), (b), and (d) of S.2939, Ninety-seventh Congress, 2nd Session, as reported Sept. 22, 1982, which was incorporated by reference in Pub.L. 97–276, § 101(e), Oct. 2, 1982, 96 Stat. 1189, to be effective as if enacted into law, and which is set out as a note under section 5318 of Title 5, Government Organization and Employees.

1981—Limitation on use of funds appropriated for the fiscal year ending Sept. 30, 1982, by any Act to pay the salary or pay of any individual in the legislative, executive, or judicial branch in a position equal or above Level V of the Executive Schedule, see section 305(a), (b), and (d) of H.R. 4120, as reported July 9, 1981, which was incorporated by reference in Pub.L. 97–92, § 101(g), Dec. 15, 1981, 95 Stat. 1190, to be effective as if enacted into law, and section 141 of Pub.L. 97–92, set out as notes under section 5318 of Title 5, Government Organization and Employees.

1980—Limitations on use of funds for fiscal year ending Sept. 30, 1981, appropriated by any Act to pay the salary or pay of any individual in legislative, executive, or judicial branch in position equal to or above level V of the Executive Schedule, see section 101(c) of Pub.L. 96–536, as amended, set out as a note under section 5318 of Title 5.

1979—Applicability to funds appropriated by any Act for fiscal year ending Sept. 30, 1980, of limitation of section 304 of Pub.L. 95–391 on use of funds to pay the salary or pay of any individual in legislative, executive, or judicial branch in position equal to or above level V of the Executive Schedule, see section 101 of Pub.L. 96–86, set out as a note under section 5318 of Title 5.

1978—Limitations on use of funds for fiscal year ending Sept. 30, 1979, appropriated by any Act to pay the salary or pay of any individual in legislative, executive, or judicial branch in position equal or above level V of the Executive Schedule, see section 304 of Pub.L. 95–391 and section 613 of Pub.L. 95–429, set out as a note under section 5318 of Title 5.

Specific Congressional Authorization Required for Salary Increases for Federal Judges and Justices of the Supreme Court

Pub.L. 97–92, § 140, Dec. 15, 1981, 95 Stat. 1200, as amended Pub.L. 107–77, Title VI, § 625, Nov. 28, 2001, 115 Stat. 803, provided that: "Notwithstanding any other provision of law or of this joint resolution [Pub.L. 97–92], none of the funds appropriated by this joint resolution or by any other Act shall be obligated or expended to increase, after the date of enactment of this joint resolution [Dec. 15, 1981], any salary of any Federal judge or Justice of the Supreme Court, except as may be specifically authorized by Act of Congress hereafter enacted: *Provided*, That nothing in this limitation shall be construed to reduce any salary which may be in effect at the time of enactment of this joint resolution [Dec. 15, 1981] nor shall this limitation be construed in any manner to reduce the salary of any Federal judge or of any Justice of the Supreme Court. This section [this note] shall apply to fiscal year 1981 and each fiscal year thereafter."

[For adjustment of pay rates under this section, see the executive order detailing the adjustment of certain rates of pay set out as a note under 5 U.S.C.A. § 5332.]

Salary Increases

For prior year salary increases per the recommendation of the President, see Prior Salary Recommendations notes under 2 U.S.C.A. § 358.

For miscellaneous provisions dealing with adjustments of pay and limitations on use of funds to pay salaries in prior years, see notes under 5 U.S.C.A. § 5318.

§ 462. Court accommodations

(a) Sessions of courts of the United States (except the Supreme Court) shall be held only at places where the Director of the Administrative Office of the United States Courts provides accommodations, or where suitable accommodations are furnished without cost to the judicial branch.

(b) The Director of the Administrative Office of the United States Courts shall provide accommodations, including chambers and courtrooms, only at places where regular sessions of court are authorized by law to be held, but only if the judicial council of the appropriate circuit has approved the accommodations as necessary.

(c) The limitations and restrictions contained in subsection (b) of this section shall not prevent the Director from furnishing chambers to circuit judges at places within the circuit other than where regular sessions of court are authorized by law to be held, when the judicial council of the circuit approves.

(d) The Director of the Administrative Office of the United States Courts shall provide permanent accommodations for the United States Court of Appeals for the Federal Circuit and for the United States Court of Federal Claims only at the District of Columbia. However, each such court may hold regular and special sessions at other places utilizing the accommodations which the Director provides to other courts.

(e) The Director of the Administrative Office of the United States Courts shall provide accommodations for probation officers, pretrial service officers, and Federal Public Defender Organizations at such places as may be approved by the judicial council of the appropriate circuit.

(f) Upon the request of the Director, the Administrator of General Services is authorized and directed to provide the accommodations the Director requests, and to close accommodations which the Director recommends for closure with the approval of the Judicial Conference of the United States.

(Added Pub.L. 97–164, Title I, § 115(c)(1), Apr. 2, 1982, 96 Stat. 31, and amended Pub.L. 100–702, Title X, § 1015, Nov. 19, 1988, 102 Stat. 4669; Pub.L. 102–572, Title IX, § 902(b)(1), Oct. 29, 1992, 106 Stat. 4516.)

HISTORICAL AND STATUTORY NOTES

Effective and Applicability Provisions

1992 Acts. Amendment by Pub.L. 102–572 effective Oct. 29, 1992, see section 911 of Pub.L. 102–572, set out as a note under section 171 of this title.

1982 Acts. Section effective Oct. 1, 1982, see section 402 of Pub.L. 97–164, set out as a note under section 171 of this title.

Change of Name

References to United States Claims Court deemed to refer to United States Court of Federal Claims and references to Claims Court deemed to refer to Court of Federal Claims, see section 902(b) of Pub.L. 102–572, set out as a note under section 171 of Title 28, Judiciary and Judicial Procedure.

§ 463. Expenses of litigation

Whenever a Chief Justice, justice, judge, officer, or employee of any United States court is sued in his official capacity, or is otherwise required to defend acts taken or omissions made in his official capacity, and the services of an attorney for the Government are not reasonably available pursuant to chapter 31 of this title, the Director of the Administrative Office of the United States Courts may pay the costs of his defense. The Director shall prescribe regulations for such payments subject to the approval of the Judicial Conference of the United States.

(Added Pub.L. 97–164, Title I, § 116(a), Apr. 2, 1982, 96 Stat. 32.)

HISTORICAL AND STATUTORY NOTES

Effective and Applicability Provisions

1982 Acts. Section effective Oct. 1, 1982, see section 402 of Pub.L. 97–164, set out as a note under section 171 of this title.

CHAPTER 23—CIVIL JUSTICE EXPENSE AND DELAY REDUCTION PLANS

Sec.
471. Requirement for a district court civil justice expense and delay reduction plan.
472. Development and implementation of a civil justice expense and delay reduction plan.
473. Content of civil justice expense and delay reduction plans.
474. Review of district court action.
475. Periodic district court assessment.
476. Enhancement of judicial information dissemination.
477. Model civil justice expense and delay reduction plan.
478. Advisory groups.
479. Information on litigation management and cost and delay reduction.
480. Training programs.
481. Automated case information.
482. Definitions.

§ 471. Requirement for a district court civil justice expense and delay reduction plan

There shall be implemented by each United States district court, in accordance with this chapter, a civil justice expense and delay reduction plan. The plan may be a plan developed by such district court or a model plan developed by the Judicial Conference of the United States. The purposes of each plan are to facilitate deliberate adjudication of civil cases on the merits, monitor discovery, improve litigation management, and ensure just, speedy, and inexpensive resolutions of civil disputes.

(Added Pub.L. 101–650, Title I, § 103(a), Dec. 1, 1990, 104 Stat. 5090, and amended Pub.L. 102–198, § 2(1), Dec. 9, 1991, 105 Stat. 1623.)

Effect of section requirements

Requirements set forth in this section to remain in effect for seven years after December 1, 1990, see Implementation of Plans note set out under this section.

HISTORICAL AND STATUTORY NOTES

Congressional Statement of Findings

Section 102 of Pub.L. 101–650 provided that: "The Congress makes the following findings:

"(1) The problems of cost and delay in civil litigation in any United States district court must be addressed in the context of the full range of demands made on the district court's resources by both civil and criminal matters.

"(2) The courts, the litigants, the litigants' attorneys, and the Congress and the executive branch, share responsibility for cost and delay in civil litigation and its impact on access to the courts, adjudication of cases on the merits, and the ability of the civil justice system to provide proper and timely judicial relief for aggrieved parties.

"(3) The solutions to problems of cost and delay must include significant contributions by the courts, the litigants, the litigants' attorneys, and by the Congress and the executive branch.

"(4) In identifying, developing, and implementing solutions to problems of cost and delay in civil litigation, it is necessary to achieve a method of consultation so that individual judicial officers, litigants, and litigants' attorneys who have developed techniques for litigation management and cost and delay reduction can effectively and promptly communicate those techniques to all participants in the civil justice system.

"(5) Evidence suggests that an effective litigation management and cost and delay reduction program should incorporate several interrelated principles, including—

"(A) the differential treatment of cases that provides for individualized and specific management according to their needs, complexity, duration, and probable litigation careers;

"(B) early involvement of a judicial officer in planning the progress of a case, controlling the discovery process, and scheduling hearings, trials, and other litigation events;

"(C) regular communication between a judicial officer and attorneys during the pretrial process; and

"(D) utilization of alternative dispute resolution programs in appropriate cases.

"(6) Because the increasing volume and complexity of civil and criminal cases imposes increasingly heavy workload burdens on judicial officers, clerks of court, and other court personnel, it is necessary to create an effective administrative structure to ensure ongoing consultation and communication regarding effective litigation management and cost and delay reduction principles and techniques."

Demonstration Program

Section 104 of Pub.L. 101–650, as amended Pub.L. 104–33, § 1, Oct. 3, 1995, 109 Stat. 292; Pub.L. 104–317, Title VI, § 608(a), Oct. 19, 1996, 110 Stat. 3860, provided that:

"(a) **In general.**—(1) During the 5–year period beginning on January 1, 1991, the Judicial Conference of the United States shall conduct a demonstration program in accordance with subsection (b).

"(2) A district court participating in the demonstration program may also be an Early Implementation District Court under section 103(c) [section 103(c) of Pub.L. 101–650, set out as a note under this section].

"(b) **Program requirement.**—(1) The United States District Court for the Western District of Michigan and the United States District Court for the Northern District of Ohio shall experiment with systems of differentiated case management that provide specifically for the assignment of cases to appropriate processing tracks that operate under distinct and explicit rules, procedures, and time frames for the completion of discovery and for trial.

"(2) The United States District Court for the Northern District of California, the United States District Court for the Northern District of West Virginia, and the United States District Court for the Western District of Missouri shall experiment with various methods of reducing cost and delay in civil litigation, including alternative dispute resolution, that such district courts and the Judicial Conference of the United States shall select.

"(c) **Study of results.**—The Judicial Conference of the United States, in consultation with the Director of the Federal Judicial Center and the Director of the Administrative Office of the United States Courts, shall study the experience of the district courts under the demonstration program.

"(d) **Report.**—Not later than June 30, 1997, the Judicial Conference of the United States shall transmit to the Committees on the Judiciary of the Senate and the House of Representatives a report of the results of the demonstration program."

Implementation of Plans

Section 103(b), (c) of Pub.L. 101–650, as amended Pub.L. 102–572, Title V, § 505, Oct. 29, 1992, 106 Stat. 4513; Pub.L. 105–53, § 2, Oct. 6, 1997, 111 Stat. 1173; Pub.L. 106–518, Title II, § 206, Nov. 13, 2000, 114 Stat. 2414, provided that:

"(b) **Implementation**

"(1) Except as provided in section 105 of this Act [section 105 of Pub.L. 101–650, set out as a note under this section], each United States district court shall, within three years after the date of the enactment of this title [Dec. 1, 1990], implement a civil justice expense and delay reduction plan under section 471 of title 28, United States Code, as added by subsection (a) [this section].

"(2)(A) The requirements set forth in sections 471, 472, 473, 474, 475, 477, and 478 of title 28, United States Code [sections 472, 473, 474, 475, 477, and 478 of this title], as added by subsection (a), shall remain in effect for seven years after the date of the enactment of this title [Dec. 1, 1990].

"(B) The requirements set forth in section 476 of title 28, United States Code, as added by subsection (a), shall remain in effect permanently.

"(c) **Early Implementation District Courts**

"(1) Any United States district court that, no earlier than June 30, 1991, and no later than December 31, 1991, develops and implements a civil justice expense and delay reduction plan under chapter 23 of title 28, United States Code, as added by subsection (a) [this chapter], shall be designated by the Judicial Conference of the United States as an Early Implementation District Court.

"(2) The chief judge of a district so designated may apply to the Judicial Conference for additional resources, including technological and personnel support and information systems, necessary to implement its civil justice expense and delay reduction plan. The Judicial Conference may provide such resources out of funds appropriated pursuant to section 106(a) [section 106(a) of Pub.L. 101–650, not classified to the Code].

"(3) Within 18 months after the date of the enactment of this title [Dec. 1, 1990], the Judicial Conference shall prepare a report on the plans developed and implemented by the Early Implementation District Courts.

"(4) The Director of the Administrative Office of the United States Courts shall transmit to the United States district courts and to the Committees on the Judiciary of the Senate and House of Representatives—

"(A) copies of the plans developed and implemented by the Early Implementation District Courts;

"(B) summaries of the reports submitted by such district courts pursuant to section 472(d) of title 28, United States Code, as added by subsection (a) [section 472(d) of this title]; and

"(C) the report prepared in accordance with paragraph (3) of this subsection."

Pilot Program

Section 105 of Pub.L. 101–650, as amended Pub.L. 103–420, § 4, Oct. 25, 1994, 108 Stat. 4345; Pub.L. 104–317, Title VI, § 608(b), Oct. 19, 1996, 110 Stat. 3860, provided that:

"(a) **In general.**—(1) During the 5–year period beginning on January 1, 1991, the Judicial Conference of the United States shall conduct a pilot program in accordance with subsection (b).

"(2) A district court participating in the pilot program shall be designated as an Early Implementation District Court under section 103(c) [section 103(c) of Pub.L. 101–650, set out as a note under this section].

"(b) **Program requirements.**—(1) Ten district courts (in this section referred to as 'Pilot Districts') designated by the Judicial Conference of the United States shall implement expense and delay reduction plans under chapter 23 of title 28, United States Code (as added by section 103(a)) [this chapter], not later than December 31, 1991. In addition to complying with all other applicable provisions of chapter 23 of title 28, United States Code (as added by section 103(a)) [this chapter], the expense and delay reduction plans implemented by the Pilot Districts shall include the 6 principles and guidelines of litigation management and cost and delay reduction identified in section 473(a) of title 28, United States Code [section 473(a) of this title].

"(2) At least 5 of the Pilot Districts designated by the Judicial Conference shall be judicial districts encompassing metropolitan areas.

"(3) The expense and delay reduction plans implemented by the Pilot Districts shall remain in effect for a period of 4 years. At the end of that 4–year period, the Pilot Districts shall no longer be required to include, in their expense and delay reduction plans, the 6 principles and guidelines of litigation management and cost and delay reduction described in paragraph (1).

"(c) **Program study report.**—(1) Not later than June 30, 1997, the Judicial Conference shall submit to the Committees on the Judiciary of the Senate and House of Representatives a report on the results of the pilot program under this section that includes an assessment of the extent to which costs and delays were reduced as a result of the program. The report shall compare those results to the impact on costs and delays in ten comparable judicial districts for which the application of section 473(a) of title 28, United States Code [section 473(a) of this title], had been discretionary. That comparison shall be based on a study conducted by an independent organization with expertise in the area of Federal court management.

"(2)(A) The Judicial Conference shall include in its report a recommendation as to whether some or all district courts should be required to include, in their expense and delay reduction plans, the 6 principles and guidelines of litigation management and cost and delay reduction identified in section 473(a) of title 28, United States Code [section 473(a) of this title].

"(B) If the Judicial Conference recommends in its report that some or all district courts be required to include such principles and guidelines in their expense and delay reduction plans, the Judicial Conference shall initiate proceedings for the prescription of rules implementing its recommendation, pursuant to chapter 131 of title 28, United States Code [section 2071 et seq. of this title].

"(C) If in its report the Judicial Conference does not recommend an expansion of the pilot program under subparagraph (A), the Judicial Conference shall identify alternative, more effective cost and delay reduction programs that should be implemented in light of the findings of the Judicial Conference in its report, and the Judicial Conference may initiate proceedings for the prescription of rules implementing its recommendation, pursuant to chapter 131 of title 28, United States Code [section 2071 et seq. of this title]."

§ 472. Development and implementation of a civil justice expense and delay reduction plan

(a) The civil justice expense and delay reduction plan implemented by a district court shall be developed or selected, as the case may be, after consideration of the recommendations of an advisory group appointed in accordance with section 478 of this title.

(b) The advisory group of a United States district court shall submit to the court a report, which shall be made available to the public and which shall include—

(1) an assessment of the matters referred to in subsection (c)(1);

(2) the basis for its recommendation that the district court develop a plan or select a model plan;

(3) recommended measures, rules and programs; and

(4) an explanation of the manner in which the recommended plan complies with section 473 of this title.

(c)(1) In developing its recommendations, the advisory group of a district court shall promptly complete a thorough assessment of the state of the court's civil and criminal dockets. In performing the assessment for a district court, the advisory group shall—

(A) determine the condition of the civil and criminal dockets;

(B) identify trends in case filings and in the demands being placed on the court's resources;

(C) identify the principal causes of cost and delay in civil litigation, giving consideration to such potential causes as court procedures and the ways in which litigants and their attorneys approach and conduct litigation; and

(D) examine the extent to which costs and delays could be reduced by a better assessment of the impact of new legislation on the courts.

(2) In developing its recommendations, the advisory group of a district court shall take into account the particular needs and circumstances of the district court, litigants in such court, and the litigants' attorneys.

(3) The advisory group of a district court shall ensure that its recommended actions include significant contributions to be made by the court, the litigants, and the litigants' attorneys toward reducing cost and delay and thereby facilitating access to the courts.

(d) The chief judge of the district court shall transmit a copy of the plan implemented in accordance with subsection (a) and the report prepared in accordance with subsection (b) of this section to—

(1) the Director of the Administrative Office of the United States Courts;

(2) the judicial council of the circuit in which the district court is located; and

(3) the chief judge of each of the other United States district courts located in such circuit.

(Added Pub.L. 101-650, Title I, § 103(a), Dec. 1, 1990, 104 Stat. 5090.)

Effect of section requirements

Requirements set forth in this section to remain in effect for seven years after December 1, 1990, see Implementation of Plans note set out under 28 U.S.C.A. § 471.

§ 473. Content of civil justice expense and delay reduction plans

(a) In formulating the provisions of its civil justice expense and delay reduction plan, each United States district court, in consultation with an advisory group appointed under section 478 of this title, shall consider and may include the following principles and guidelines of litigation management and cost and delay reduction:

(1) systematic, differential treatment of civil cases that tailors the level of individualized and case specific management to such criteria as case complexity, the amount of time reasonably needed to prepare the case for trial, and the judicial and other resources required and available for the preparation and disposition of the case;

(2) early and ongoing control of the pretrial process through involvement of a judicial officer in—

(A) assessing and planning the progress of a case;

(B) setting early, firm trial dates, such that the trial is scheduled to occur within eighteen months after the filing of the complaint, unless a judicial officer certifies that—

(i) the demands of the case and its complexity make such a trial date incompatible with serving the ends of justice; or

(ii) the trial cannot reasonably be held within such time because of the complexity of the case or the number or complexity of pending criminal cases;

(C) controlling the extent of discovery and the time for completion of discovery, and ensuring compliance with appropriate requested discovery in a timely fashion; and

(D) setting, at the earliest practicable time, deadlines for filing motions and a time framework for their disposition;

(3) for all cases that the court or an individual judicial officer determines are complex and any other appropriate cases, careful and deliberate monitoring through a discovery-case management conference or a series of such conferences at which the presiding judicial officer—

(A) explores the parties' receptivity to, and the propriety of, settlement or proceeding with the litigation;

(B) identifies or formulates the principal issues in contention and, in appropriate cases, provides for the staged resolution or bifurcation of issues for trial consistent with Rule 42(b) of the Federal Rules of Civil Procedure;

(C) prepares a discovery schedule and plan consistent with any presumptive time limits that a district court may set for the completion of discovery and with any procedures a district court may develop to—

(i) identify and limit the volume of discovery available to avoid unnecessary or unduly burdensome or expensive discovery; and

(ii) phase discovery into two or more stages; and

(D) sets, at the earliest practicable time, deadlines for filing motions and a time framework for their disposition;

(4) encouragement of cost-effective discovery through voluntary exchange of information among litigants and their attorneys and through the use of cooperative discovery devices;

(5) conservation of judicial resources by prohibiting the consideration of discovery motions unless accompanied by a certification that the moving party has made a reasonable and good faith effort to reach agreement with opposing counsel on the matters set forth in the motion; and

(6) authorization to refer appropriate cases to alternative dispute resolution programs that—

(A) have been designated for use in a district court; or

(B) the court may make available, including mediation, minitrial, and summary jury trial.

(b) In formulating the provisions of its civil justice expense and delay reduction plan, each United States district court, in consultation with an advisory group appointed under section 478 of this title, shall consider and may include the following litigation management and cost and delay reduction techniques:

(1) a requirement that counsel for each party to a case jointly present a discovery-case management plan for the case at the initial pretrial conference, or explain the reasons for their failure to do so;

(2) a requirement that each party be represented at each pretrial conference by an attorney who has the authority to bind that party regarding all matters previously identified by the court for discussion at the conference and all reasonably related matters;

(3) a requirement that all requests for extensions of deadlines for completion of discovery or for postponement of the trial be signed by the attorney and the party making the request;

(4) a neutral evaluation program for the presentation of the legal and factual basis of a case to a neutral court representative selected by the court at a nonbinding conference conducted early in the litigation;

(5) a requirement that, upon notice by the court, representatives of the parties with authority to bind them in settlement discussions be present or available by telephone during any settlement conference; and

(6) such other features as the district court considers appropriate after considering the recommendations of the advisory group referred to in section 472(a) of this title.

(c) Nothing in a civil justice expense and delay reduction plan relating to the settlement authority provisions of this section shall alter or conflict with the authority of the Attorney General to conduct litigation on behalf of the United States, or any delegation of the Attorney General.

(Added Pub.L. 101–650, Title I, § 103(a), Dec. 1, 1990, 104 Stat. 5091.)

Effect of section requirements

Requirements set forth in this section to remain in effect for seven years after December 1, 1990, see Implementation of Plans note set out under 28 U.S.C.A. § 471.

HISTORICAL AND STATUTORY NOTES

References in Text

The Federal Rules of Civil Procedure, referred to in subsec. (a)(3)(B), are set out in this title.

§ 474. Review of district court action

(a)(1) The chief judge of each district court in a circuit and the chief judge of the circuit shall, as a committee—

(A) review each plan and report submitted pursuant to section 472(d) of this title; and

(B) make such suggestions for additional actions or modified actions of that district court as the committee considers appropriate for reducing cost and delay in civil litigation in the district court.

(2) The chief judge of a circuit may designate another judge of the court of appeals of that circuit, and the chief judge of a district court may designate another judge of such court, to perform that chief judge's responsibilities under paragraph (1) of this subsection.

(b) The Judicial Conference of the United States—

(1) shall review each plan and report submitted by a district court pursuant to section 472(d) of this title; and

(2) may request the district court to take additional action if the Judicial Conference determines that such court has not adequately responded to the conditions relevant to the civil and criminal dockets of the court or to the recommendations of the district court's advisory group.

(Added Pub.L. 101–650, Title I, § 103(a), Dec. 1, 1990, 104 Stat. 5093, and amended Pub.L. 102–198, § 2(2), Dec. 9, 1991, 105 Stat. 1623.)

Effect of section requirements

Requirements set forth in this section to remain in effect for seven years after December 1, 1990, see Implementation of Plans note set out under 28 U.S.C.A. § 471.

§ 475. Periodic district court assessment

After developing or selecting a civil justice expense and delay reduction plan, each United States district court shall assess annually the condition of the court's civil and criminal dockets with a view to determining appropriate additional actions that may be taken by the court to reduce cost and delay in civil litigation and to improve the litigation management practices of the court. In performing such assessment, the court shall consult with an advisory group appointed in accordance with section 478 of this title.

(Added Pub.L. 101–650, Title I, § 103(a), Dec. 1, 1990, 104 Stat. 5093.)

Effect of section requirements

Requirements set forth in this section to remain in effect for seven years after December 1, 1990, see Implementation of Plans note set out under 28 U.S.C.A. § 471.

§ 476. Enhancement of judicial information dissemination

(a) The Director of the Administrative Office of the United States Courts shall prepare a semiannual report, available to the public, that discloses for each judicial officer—

(1) the number of motions that have been pending for more than six months and the name of each case in which such motion has been pending;

(2) the number of bench trials that have been submitted for more than six months and the name of each case in which such trials are under submission; and

(3) the number and names of cases that have not been terminated within three years after filing.

(b) To ensure uniformity of reporting, the standards for categorization or characterization of judicial actions to be prescribed in accordance with section 481 of this title shall apply to the semiannual report prepared under subsection (a).

(Added Pub.L. 101–650, Title I, § 103(a), Dec. 1, 1990, 104 Stat. 5093.)

§ 477. Model civil justice expense and delay reduction plan

(a)(1) Based on the plans developed and implemented by the United States district courts designated as Early Implementation District Courts pursuant to section 103(c) of the Civil Justice Reform Act of 1990, the Judicial Conference of the United States may develop one or more model civil justice expense and delay reduction plans. Any such model plan shall be accompanied by a report explaining the manner in which the plan complies with section 473 of this title.

(2) The Director of the Federal Judicial Center and the Director of the Administrative Office of the United States Courts may make recommendations to the Judicial Conference regarding the development of any model civil justice expense and delay reduction plan.

(b) The Director of the Administrative Office of the United States Courts shall transmit to the United States district courts and to the Committees on the Judiciary of the Senate and the House of Representatives copies of any model plan and accompanying report.

(Added Pub.L. 101–650, Title I, § 103(a), Dec. 1, 1990, 104 Stat. 5094.)

Effect of section requirements

Requirements set forth in this section to remain in effect for seven years after December 1, 1990, see Implementation of Plans note set out under 28 U.S.C.A. § 471.

HISTORICAL AND STATUTORY NOTES

References in Text

Section 103(c) of the Civil Justice Reform Act of 1990, referred to in subsec. (a)(1), is section 103(c) of Pub.L. 101–650, as amended, which is set out as a note under section 471 of this title.

§ 478. Advisory groups

(a) Within ninety days after the date of the enactment of this chapter, the advisory group required in each United States district court in accordance with section 472 of this title shall be appointed by the chief judge of each district court, after consultation with the other judges of such court.

(b) The advisory group of a district court shall be balanced and include attorneys and other persons who are representative of major categories of litigants in such court, as determined by the chief judge of such court.

(c) Subject to subsection (d), in no event shall any member of the advisory group serve longer than four years.

(d) Notwithstanding subsection (c), the United States Attorney for a judicial district, or his or her designee, shall be a permanent member of the advisory group for that district court.

(e) The chief judge of a United States district court may designate a reporter for each advisory group, who may be compensated in accordance with guidelines established by the Judicial Conference of the United States.

(f) The members of an advisory group of a United States district court and any person designated as a reporter for such group shall be considered as independent contractors of such court when in the performance of official duties of the advisory group and may not, solely by reason of service on or for the advisory group, be prohibited from practicing law before such court.

(Added Pub.L. 101–650, Title I, § 103(a), Dec. 1, 1990, 104 Stat. 5094.)

Effect of section requirements

Requirements set forth in this section to remain in effect for seven years after December 1, 1990, see Implementation of Plans note set out under 28 U.S.C.A. § 471.

HISTORICAL AND STATUTORY NOTES

References in Text

The date of the enactment of this chapter, referred to in subsec. (a), is the date of enactment of Pub.L. 101–650, which was approved Dec. 1, 1990.

§ 479. Information on litigation management and cost and delay reduction

(a) Within four years after the date of the enactment of this chapter, the Judicial Conference of the United States shall prepare a comprehensive report on all plans received pursuant to section 472(d) of this title. The Director of the Federal Judicial Center and the Director of the Administrative Office of the United States Courts may make recommendations regarding such report to the Judicial Conference during the preparation of the report. The Judicial Conference shall transmit copies of the report to the United States district courts and to the Committees on the Judiciary of the Senate and the House of Representatives.

(b) The Judicial Conference of the United States shall, on a continuing basis—

(1) study ways to improve litigation management and dispute resolution services in the district courts; and

(2) make recommendations to the district courts on ways to improve such services.

(c)(1) The Judicial Conference of the United States shall prepare, periodically revise, and transmit to the United States district courts a Manual for Litigation Management and Cost and Delay Reduction. The Director of the Federal Judicial Center and the Director of the Administrative Office of the United States Courts may make recommendations regarding the preparation of and any subsequent revisions to the Manual.

(2) The Manual shall be developed after careful evaluation of the plans implemented under section 472 of this title, the demonstration program conducted under section 104 of the Civil Justice Reform Act of 1990, and the pilot program conducted under section 105 of the Civil Justice Reform Act of 1990.

(3) The Manual shall contain a description and analysis of the litigation management, cost and delay reduction principles and techniques, and alternative dispute resolution programs considered most effective by the Judicial Conference, the Director of the Federal Judicial Center, and the Director of the Administrative Office of the United States Courts.

(Added Pub.L. 101–650, Title I, § 103(a), Dec. 1, 1990, 104 Stat. 5095.)

HISTORICAL AND STATUTORY NOTES

References in Text

The date of the enactment of this chapter, referred to in subsec. (a), is the date of enactment of Pub.L. 101–650, which was approved Dec. 1, 1990.

Sections 104 and 105 of the Civil Justice Reform Act of 1990, referred to in subsec. (c)(2), are sections 104 and 105 of Pub.L. 101–650, which are set out as notes under section 471 of this title.

§ 480. Training programs

The Director of the Federal Judicial Center and the Director of the Administrative Office of the United States Courts shall develop and conduct comprehensive education and training programs to ensure that all judicial officers, clerks of court, courtroom deputies, and other appropriate court personnel are thoroughly familiar with the most recent available information and analyses about litigation management and other techniques for reducing cost and expediting the resolution of civil litigation. The curriculum of such training programs shall be periodically revised to reflect such information and analyses.

(Added Pub.L. 101–650, Title I, § 103(a), Dec. 1, 1990, 104 Stat. 5095.)

§ 481. Automated case information

(a) The Director of the Administrative Office of the United States Courts shall ensure that each United States district court has the automated capability readily to retrieve information about the status of each case in such court.

(b)(1) In carrying out subsection (a), the Director shall prescribe—

(A) the information to be recorded in district court automated systems; and

(B) standards for uniform categorization or characterization of judicial actions for the purpose of recording information on judicial actions in the district court automated systems.

(2) The uniform standards prescribed under paragraph (1)(B) of this subsection shall include a definition of what constitutes a dismissal of a case and standards for measuring the period for which a motion has been pending.

(c) Each United States district court shall record information as prescribed pursuant to subsection (b) of this section.

(Added Pub.L. 101–650, Title I, § 103(a), Dec. 1, 1990, 104 Stat. 5095.)

§ 482. Definitions

As used in this chapter, the term "judicial officer" means a United States district court judge or a United States magistrate judge.

(Added Pub.L. 101–650, Title I, § 103(a), Title III, § 321, Dec. 1, 1990, 104 Stat. 5096, 5117.)

HISTORICAL AND STATUTORY NOTES

Change of Name

"United States magistrate judge" substituted for "United States magistrate" in text pursuant to section 321 of Pub.L. 101–650, set out as a note under 28 U.S.C.A. § 631.

PART II—DEPARTMENT OF JUSTICE

Chapter		Section
31.	**The Attorney General**	501
33.	**Federal Bureau of Investigation**	531
35.	**United States Attorneys**	541
37.	**United States Marshals Service**	561
39.	**United States Trustees**	581
40.	**Independent Counsel**	591
40A.	**Bureau of Alcohol, Tobacco, Firearms, and Explosives**	2599A [1]

[1] So in original. Should read 599A.

CHAPTER 31—THE ATTORNEY GENERAL

Sec.
501. Executive department.
502. Seal.
503. Attorney General.
504. Deputy Attorney General.
504a. Associate Attorney General.
505. Solicitor General.
506. Assistant Attorneys General.
507. Assistant Attorney General for Administration.
507A. Assistant Attorney General for National Security.
508. Vacancies.
509. Functions of the Attorney General.
509A. National Security Division.
510. Delegation of authority.
511. Attorney General to advise the President.
512. Attorney General to advise heads of executive departments.
513. Attorney General to advise Secretaries of military departments.
514. Legal services on pending claims in departments and agencies.
515. Authority for legal proceedings; commission, oath, and salary for special attorneys.
516. Conduct of litigation reserved to Department of Justice.
517. Interests of United States in pending suits.
518. Conduct and argument of cases.
519. Supervision of litigation.
520. Transmission of petitions in United States Court of Federal Claims or in United States Court of Appeals for the Federal Circuit; statement furnished by departments.
521. Publication and distribution of opinions.
522. Report of business and statistics.
523. Requisitions.
524. Availability of appropriations.
525. Procurement of law books, reference books, and periodicals; sale and exchange.
526. Authority of the Attorney General to investigate United States attorneys, marshals, trustees, clerks of court, and others.[1]
527. Establishment of working capital fund.
528. Disqualification of officers and employees of the Department of Justice.
529. Annual report of Attorney General.
530. Payment of travel and transportation expenses of newly appointed special agents.
530A. Authorization of appropriations for travel and related expenses and for health care of personnel serving abroad.
530B. Ethical standards for attorneys for the Government.
530C. Authority to use available funds.
530D. Report on enforcement of laws.

[1] So in original. Does not conform to section catchline.

HISTORICAL AND STATUTORY NOTES

Change of Name

References to United States Claims Court deemed to refer to United States Court of Federal Claims and references to Claims Court deemed to refer to Court of Federal Claims, see section 902(b) of Pub.L. 102–572, set out as a note under section 171 of Title 28, Judiciary and Judicial Procedure.

§ 501. Executive department

The Department of Justice is an executive department of the United States at the seat of Government. (Added Pub.L. 89–554, § 4(c), Sept. 6, 1966, 80 Stat. 611.)

HISTORICAL AND STATUTORY NOTES

Prior Provisions

A prior section 501, Acts June 25, 1948, c. 646, 62 Stat. 909; Mar. 18, 1959, Pub.L. 86–3, § 11(a), 73 Stat. 9, which related to appointment of United States attorneys, was repealed by Pub.L. 89–554, § 8(a), Sept. 6, 1966, 80 Stat. 632, and reenacted in section 541 of this title by section 4(c) of Pub.L. 89–554.

Office of Justice for Victims of Overseas Terrorism—Establishment

Pub.L. 108–447, Div. B, Title I, § 126, Dec. 8, 2004, 118 Stat. 2872, provided that: "The Department of Justice shall establish an Office of Justice for Victims of Overseas Terrorism."

Specific Authorization of Appropriations Required for Department of Justice

Pub.L. 94–503, Title II, § 204, Oct. 15, 1976, 90 Stat. 2427, provided that: "No sums shall be deemed to be authorized to be appropriated for any fiscal year beginning on or after October 1, 1978, for the Department of Justice (including any bureau, agency, or other similar subdivision thereof) except as specifically authorized by Act of Congress with respect to such fiscal year. Neither the creation of a subdivision in the

Department of Justice, nor the authorization of an activity of the Department, any subdivision, or officer thereof, shall be deemed in itself to be an authorization of appropriations for the Department of Justice, such subdivision, or activity, with respect to any fiscal year beginning on or after October 1, 1978."

§ 502. Seal

The Attorney General shall have a seal for the Department of Justice. The design of the seal is subject to the approval of the President.

(Added Pub.L. 89–554, § 4(c), Sept. 6, 1966, 80 Stat. 611.)

HISTORICAL AND STATUTORY NOTES

Prior Provisions

A prior section 502, Act June 25, 1948, c. 646, 62 Stat. 909, which related to appointment of assistant United States attorneys, was repealed by Pub.L. 89–554, § 8(a), Sept. 6, 1966, 80 Stat. 632, and reenacted in section 542 of this title by section 4(c) of Pub.L. 89–554.

§ 503. Attorney General

The President shall appoint, by and with the advice and consent of the Senate, an Attorney General of the United States. The Attorney General is the head of the Department of Justice.

(Added Pub.L. 89–554, § 4(c), Sept. 6, 1966, 80 Stat. 612.)

HISTORICAL AND STATUTORY NOTES

Prior Provisions

A prior section 503, Act June 25, 1948, c. 646, 62 Stat. 909, which related to appointment of attorneys to assist United States attorneys, was repealed by Pub.L. 89–554, § 8(a), Sept. 6, 1966, 80 Stat. 632, and reenacted in section 543 of this title by section 4(c) of Pub.L. 89–554.

Actions Challenging Appointment of Attorney General on Grounds of Violation of Constitutional Provisions Governing Compensation and Other Emoluments

Pub.L. 93–178, § 2, Dec. 10, 1973, 87 Stat. 697, provided that:

"(a) Any person aggrieved by an action of the Attorney General may bring a civil action in the appropriate district court to contest the constitutionality of the appointment and continuance in office of the Attorney General on the ground that such appointment and continuance in office is in violation of article I, section 6, clause 2, of the Constitution. The United States district courts shall have exclusive jurisdiction, without regard to the sum or value of the matter in controversy, to determine the validity of such appointment and continuance in office.

"(b) Any action brought under this section shall be heard and determined by a panel of three judges in accordance with the provisions of section 2284 of title 28, United States Code [this section]. Any appeal from the action of a court convened pursuant to such section shall lie to the Supreme Court.

"(c) Any judge designated to hear any action brought under this section shall cause such action to be in every way expedited."

§ 504. Deputy Attorneys General

The President may appoint, by and with the advice and consent of the Senate, a Deputy Attorney General and a Deputy Attorney General for Combating Domestic Terrorism.

(Added Pub.L. 89–554, § 4(c), Sept. 6, 1966, 80 Stat. 612, and amended Pub.L. 107–77, Title VI, § 612(b), Nov. 28, 2001, 115 Stat. 800; Pub.L. 107–273, Div. B, Title IV, § 4004(f), Nov. 2, 2002, 116 Stat. 1812.)

HISTORICAL AND STATUTORY NOTES

Prior Provisions

A prior section 504, Acts June 25, 1948, c. 646, 62 Stat. 909; Mar. 18, 1959, Pub.L. 86–3, § 11(b), 73 Stat. 9, which related to tenure and oath of office of United States attorneys, was repealed by Pub.L. 89–554, § 8(a), Sept. 6, 1966, 80 Stat. 632, and reenacted in sections 541 and 544 of this title by section 4(c) of Pub.L. 89–554.

Repeals

Section 612(c) of Pub.L. 107–77, cited in the credit of this section, was repealed by section 4004(f) of Pub.L. 107–273.

Proposal for Combating Domestic Terrorism in Fiscal Year 2003

Pub.L. 107–77, Title VI, § 612, Nov. 28, 2001, 115 Stat. 800, which amended this section and provided that the President shall submit a proposal to Congress regarding the restructuring of the Department of Justice to meet the need for combating domestic terrorism, was repealed by Pub.L. 107–273, Div. B, Title IV, § 4004(f), Nov. 2, 2002, 116 Stat. 1812.

§ 504a. Associate Attorney General

The President may appoint, by and with the advice and consent of the Senate, an Associate Attorney General.

(Added Pub.L. 95–139, § 1(a), Oct. 19, 1977, 91 Stat. 1171.)

§ 505. Solicitor General

The President shall appoint in the Department of Justice, by and with the advice and consent of the Senate, a Solicitor General, learned in the law, to assist the Attorney General in the performance of his duties.

(Added Pub.L. 89–554, § 4(c), Sept. 6, 1966, 80 Stat. 612.)

HISTORICAL AND STATUTORY NOTES

Prior Provisions

A prior section 505, Act June 25, 1948, c. 646, 62 Stat. 909, which related to residence of United States attorneys, was repealed by Pub.L. 89–554, § 8(a), Sept. 6, 1966, 80 Stat. 632, and reenacted in section 545 of this title by section 4(c) of Pub.L. 89–554.

§ 506. Assistant Attorneys General

The President shall appoint, by and with the advice and consent of the Senate, 11 Assistant Attorneys General, who shall assist the Attorney General in the performance of his duties.

(Added Pub.L. 89–554, § 4(c), Sept. 6, 1966, 80 Stat. 612, and amended Pub.L. 95–598, Title II, § 218, Nov. 6, 1978, 92 Stat. 2662; Pub.L. 109–177, Title V, § 506(a)(2), Mar. 9, 2006, 120 Stat. 247.)

HISTORICAL AND STATUTORY NOTES

Effective and Applicability Provisions

1978 Acts. Amendment by Pub.L. 95–598 effective Nov. 6, 1978, see section 402(d) of Pub.L. 95–598, set out as a note preceding section 101 of Title 11, Bankruptcy.

Prior Provisions

A prior section 506, Act June 25, 1948, c. 646, 62 Stat. 909, which related to vacancies in the office of United States attorney, was repealed by Pub.L. 89–554, § 8(a), Sept. 6, 1966, 80 Stat. 632, and reenacted in section 546 of this title by section 4(c) of Pub.L. 89–554.

§ 507. Assistant Attorney General for Administration

(a) The Attorney General shall appoint, with the approval of the President, an Assistant Attorney General for Administration, who shall perform such duties as the Attorney General may prescribe.

(b) The position of Assistant Attorney General for Administration is in the competitive service.

(c) Notwithstanding the provisions of section 901 of title 31, United States Code, the Assistant Attorney General for Administration shall be the Chief Financial Officer of the Department of Justice.

(Added Pub.L. 89–554, § 4(c), Sept. 6, 1966, 80 Stat. 612, and amended Pub.L. 106–113, § 1000(a)(1) [Title I, § 111], Nov. 29, 1999, 113 Stat. 1535, 1501A–20.)

HISTORICAL AND STATUTORY NOTES

Prior Provisions

A prior section 507, Acts June 25, 1948, c. 646, 62 Stat. 910; May 24, 1949, c. 139, § 71, 63 Stat. 100, which related to duties of United States attorneys, and to supervision by the Attorney General, was repealed by Pub.L. 89–554, § 8(a), Sept. 6, 1966, 80 Stat. 632, and reenacted in sections 509 and 547 of this title by section 4(c) of Pub.L. 89–554.

§ 507A. Assistant Attorney General for National Security

(a) Of the Assistant Attorneys General appointed under section 506, one shall serve, upon the designation of the President, as the Assistant Attorney General for National Security.

(b) The Assistant Attorney General for National Security shall—

(1) serve as the head of the National Security Division of the Department of Justice under section 509A of this title;

(2) serve as primary liaison to the Director of National Intelligence for the Department of Justice; and

(3) perform such other duties as the Attorney General may prescribe.

(Added Pub.L. 109–177, Title V, § 506(a)(1), Mar. 9, 2006, 120 Stat. 247.)

§ 508. Vacancies

(a) In case of a vacancy in the office of Attorney General, or of his absence or disability, the Deputy Attorney General may exercise all the duties of that office, and for the purpose of section 3345 of title 5 the Deputy Attorney General is the first assistant to the Attorney General.

(b) When by reason of absence, disability, or vacancy in office, neither the Attorney General nor the Deputy Attorney General is available to exercise the duties of the office of Attorney General, the Associate Attorney General shall act as Attorney General. The Attorney General may designate the Solicitor General and the Assistant Attorneys General, in further order of succession, to act as Attorney General.

(Added Pub.L. 89–554, § 4(c), Sept. 6, 1966, 80 Stat. 612, and amended Pub.L. 95–139, § 2, Oct. 19, 1977, 91 Stat. 1171.)

HISTORICAL AND STATUTORY NOTES

Prior Provisions

A prior section 508, Acts June 25, 1948, c. 646, 62 Stat. 910; Mar. 2, 1955, c. 9, § 2(a), 69 Stat. 10; Oct. 11, 1962, Pub.L. 87–793, § 1003(a), 76 Stat. 865; Aug. 14, 1964, Pub.L. 88–426, Title III, § 306(a)(1), 78 Stat. 428; Oct. 6, 1964, Pub.L. 88–631, § 3(b), 78 Stat. 1008, which related to salaries of United States attorneys, assistant United States attorneys, and special attorneys, was repealed by Pub.L. 89–554, § 8(a), Sept. 6, 1966, 80 Stat. 632, and reenacted in section 548 of this title by section 4(c) of Pub.L. 89–554.

§ 509. Functions of the Attorney General

All functions of other officers of the Department of Justice and all functions of agencies and employees of the Department of Justice are vested in the Attorney General except the functions—

(1) vested by subchapter II of chapter 5 of title 5 in administrative law judges employed by the Department of Justice;

(2) of the Federal Prison Industries, Inc.; and

(3) of the Board of Directors and officers of the Federal Prison Industries, Inc.

(Added Pub.L. 89–554, § 4(c), Sept. 6, 1966, 80 Stat. 612, and amended Pub.L. 95–251, § 2(a)(6), Mar. 27, 1978, 92 Stat. 183; Pub.L. 98–473, Title II, § 228(a), Oct. 12, 1984, 98 Stat. 2030; Pub.L. 107–273, Title II, § 204(d), Title IV, § 4003(b)(1), Nov. 2, 2002, 116 Stat. 1776, 1811.)

HISTORICAL AND STATUTORY NOTES

Effective and Applicability Provisions

1984 Acts. Section 235(a)(1)(B)(ii)(IV) of Pub.L. 98–473 had provided that the amendment made by section 228 of Pub.L. 98–473 was to be effective Oct. 12, 1984. Pub.L. 99–646, § 35(2)(D), Nov. 10, 1986, 100 Stat. 3599, amended section 235(a)(1)(B)(ii)(IV) of Pub.L. 98–473 making it inapplicable to section 228. Amendment by Pub.L. 98–473 effective the first day of the first calendar month beginning 36 months after Oct. 12, 1984, see section 235(a)(1) of Pub.L. 98–473, as amended, set out as a note under section 3551 of Title 18, Crimes and Criminal Procedure.

Transfer of Functions

For transfer of functions, personnel, assets, and liabilities of the Domestic Emergency Support Teams of the Department of Justice, including the functions of the Attorney General relating thereto, to the Secretary of Homeland Security, and for treatment of related references, see 6 U.S.C.A. §§ 313(4), 551(d), 552(d), and 557, and the Department of Homeland Security Reorganization Plan of November 25, 2002, as modified, set out as a note 6 U.S.C.A. § 542.

Prior Provisions

A prior section 509, Act June 25, 1948, c. 646, 62 Stat. 910, which related to expenses of United States attorneys, was repealed by Pub.L. 89–554, § 8(a), Sept. 6, 1966, 80 Stat. 632, and reenacted in section 549 of this title by section 4(c) of Pub.L. 89–554.

Unsolved Civil Rights Crimes

Pub.L. 110–344, §§ 1 to 9, Oct. 7, 2008, 122 Stat. 3934, provided that:

"Sec. 1. Short title.

"This Act [enacting 42 U.S.C.A. § 5780a and this note] may be cited as the 'Emmett Till Unsolved Civil Rights Crime Act of 2007'.

"Sec. 2. Sense of Congress.

"It is the sense of Congress that all authorities with jurisdiction, including the Federal Bureau of Investigation and other entities within the Department of Justice, should—

"(1) expeditiously investigate unsolved civil rights murders, due to the amount of time that has passed since the murders and the age of potential witnesses; and

"(2) provide all the resources necessary to ensure timely and thorough investigations in the cases involved.

"Sec. 3. Deputy Chief of the Criminal Section of the Civil Rights Division.

"**(a) In general.**—The Attorney General shall designate a Deputy Chief in the Criminal Section of the Civil Rights Division of the Department of Justice.

"**(b) Responsibility.**—

"**(1) In general.**—The Deputy Chief shall be responsible for coordinating the investigation and prosecution of violations of criminal civil rights statutes that occurred not later than December 31, 1969, and resulted in a death.

"**(2) Coordination.**—In investigating a complaint under paragraph (1), the Deputy Chief may coordinate investigative activities with State and local law enforcement officials.

"**(c) Study and report.**—

"**(1) Study.**—The Attorney General shall annually conduct a study of the cases under the jurisdiction of the Deputy Chief or under the jurisdiction of the Supervisory Special Agent and, in conducting the study, shall determine—

"**(A)** the number of open investigations within the Department for violations of criminal civil rights statutes that occurred not later than December 31, 1969;

"**(B)** the number of new cases opened pursuant to this Act [enacting 42 U.S.C.A. § 5780a and this note] since the previous year's study;

"**(C)** the number of unsealed Federal cases charged within the study period, including the case names, the jurisdiction in which the charges were brought, and the date the charges were filed;

"**(D)** the number of cases referred by the Department to a State or local law enforcement agency or prosecutor within the study period, the number of such cases that resulted in State charges being filed, the jurisdiction in which such charges were filed, the date the charges were filed, and if a jurisdiction declines to prosecute or participate in an investigation of a case so referred, the fact it did so;

"**(E)** the number of cases within the study period that were closed without Federal prosecution, the case names of unsealed Federal cases, the dates the cases were closed, and the relevant federal statutes;

"**(F)** the number of attorneys who worked, in whole or in part, on any case described in subsection (b)(1); and

"**(G)** the applications submitted for grants under section 5, the award of such grants, and the purposes for which the grant amount were expended.

"**(2) Report.**—Not later than 6 months after the date of enactment of this Act [Oct. 7, 2008], and each year thereafter, the Attorney General shall prepare and submit to Congress a report containing the results of the study conducted under paragraph (1).

"Sec. 4. Supervisory Special Agent in the Civil Rights Unit of the Federal Bureau of Investigation.

"**(a) In general.**—The Attorney General shall designate a Supervisory Special Agent in the Civil Rights Unit of the Federal Bureau of Investigation of the Department of Justice.

"**(b) Responsibility.**—

"**(1) In general.**—The Supervisory Special Agent shall be responsible for investigating violations of criminal civil rights statutes that occurred not later than December 31, 1969, and resulted in a death.

"**(2) Coordination.**—In investigating a complaint under paragraph (1), the Supervisory Special Agent may coordinate the investigative activities with State and local law enforcement officials.

"Sec. 5. Grants to State and local law enforcement.

"**(a) In general.**—The Attorney General may award grants to State or local law enforcement agencies for expenses associated with the investigation and prosecution by them of criminal offenses, involving civil rights, that occurred not later than December 31, 1969, and resulted in a death.

"**(b) Authorization of appropriations.**—There are authorized to be appropriated $2,000,000 for each of the fiscal years 2008 through 2017 to carry out this section.

"Sec. 6. Authorization of appropriations.

"**(a) In general.**—There are authorized to be appropriated, in addition to any other amounts otherwise authorized to be appropriated for this purpose, to the Attorney General

$10,000,000 for each of the fiscal years 2008 through 2017 for the purpose of investigating and prosecuting violations of criminal civil rights statutes that occurred not later than December 31, 1969, and resulted in a death. These funds shall be allocated by the Attorney General to the Deputy Chief of the Criminal Section of the Civil Rights Division and the Supervisory Special Agent of the Civil Rights Unit of the Federal Bureau of Investigation in order to advance the purposes set forth in this Act [enacting 42 U.S.C.A. § 5780a and this note].

"(b) **Community relations service of the Department of Justice.**—In addition to any amounts authorized to be appropriated under title XI of the Civil Rights Act of 1964 (42 U.S.C. 2000h et seq.), there are authorized to be appropriated to the Community Relations Service of the Department of Justice $1,500,000 for fiscal year 2008 and each subsequent fiscal year, to enable the Service (in carrying out the functions described in title X of such Act (42 U.S.C. 2000g et seq.)) to provide technical assistance by bringing together law enforcement agencies and communities in the investigation of violations of criminal civil rights statutes, in cases described in section 4(b).

"Sec. 7. Definition of 'criminal civil rights statutes'.

"In this Act [enacting 42 U.S.C.A. § 5780a and this note], the term 'criminal civil rights statutes' means—

"(1) section 241 of title 18, United States Code (relating to conspiracy against rights);

"(2) section 242 of title 18, United States Code (relating to deprivation of rights under color of law);

"(3) section 245 of title 18, United States Code (relating to federally protected activities);

"(4) sections 1581 and 1584 of title 18, United States Code (relating to involuntary servitude and peonage);

"(5) section 901 of the Fair Housing Act (42 U.S.C. 3631); and

"(6) Any other Federal law that—

"(A) was in effect on or before December 31, 1969; and

"(B) the Criminal Section of the Civil Rights Division of the Department of Justice enforced, before the date of enactment of this Act [Oct. 7, 2008].

"Sec. 8. Sunset.

"Sections 2 through 6 of this Act [set out in this note] shall cease to have effect at the end of fiscal year 2017.

"Sec. 9. [Omitted; enacted 42 U.S.C.A. § 5780a]."

Organized Retail Theft

Pub.L. 109–162, Title XI, § 1105, Jan. 5, 2006, 119 Stat. 3092, as amended Pub.L. 109–271, § 8(a), Aug. 12, 2006, 120 Stat. 766, provided that:

"(a) **National data.**—(1) The Attorney General and the Federal Bureau of Investigation, in consultation with the retail community, shall establish a task force to combat organized retail theft and provide expertise to the retail community for the establishment of a national database or clearinghouse housed and maintained in the private sector to track and identify where organized retail theft type crimes are being committed in the United Sates [sic; probably should be "States"]. The national database shall allow Federal, State, and local law enforcement officials as well as authorized retail companies (and authorized associated retail databases) to transmit information into the database electronically and to review information that has been submitted electronically.

"(2) The Attorney General shall make available funds to provide for the ongoing administrative and technological costs to federal law enforcement agencies participating in the database project.

"(3) The Director of the Bureau of Justice Assistance of the Office of Justice Programs may make grants to help provide for the administrative and technological costs to State and local law enforcement agencies participating in the data base project.

"(b) **Authorization of appropriations.**—There is authorized to be appropriated for each of fiscal years 2006 through 2009, $5,000,000 for educating and training federal law enforcement regarding organized retail theft, for investigating, apprehending and prosecuting individuals engaged in organized retail theft, and for working with the private sector to establish and utilize the database described in subsection (a) [of this note].

"(c) **Definition of organized retail theft.**—For purposes of this section, 'organized retail theft' means—

"(1) the violation of a State prohibition on retail merchandise theft or shoplifting, if the violation consists of the theft of quantities of items that would not normally be purchased for personal use or consumption and for the purpose of reselling the items or for reentering the items into commerce;

"(2) the receipt, possession, concealment, bartering, sale, transport, or disposal of any property that is know [sic] or should be known to have been taken in violation of paragraph (1); or

"(3) the coordination, organization, or recruitment of persons to undertake the conduct described in paragraph (1) or (2)."

United States-Mexico Border Violence Task Force

Pub.L. 109–162, Title XI, § 1106, Jan. 5, 2006, 119 Stat. 3093, provided that:

"(a) **Task Force.**—(1) The Attorney General shall establish the United States-Mexico Border Violence Task Force in Laredo, Texas, to combat drug and firearms trafficking, violence, and kidnapping along the border between the United States and Mexico and to provide expertise to the law enforcement and homeland security agencies along the border between the United States and Mexico. The Task Force shall include personnel from the Bureau of Alcohol, Tobacco, Firearms, and Explosives, Immigration and Customs Enforcement, the Drug Enforcement Administration, Customs and Border Protection, other Federal agencies (as appropriate), the Texas Department of Public Safety, and local law enforcement agencies.

"(2) The Attorney General shall make available funds to provide for the ongoing administrative and technological costs to Federal, State, and local law enforcement agencies participating in the Task Force.

"(b) **Authorization of appropriations.**—There are authorized to be appropriated $10,000,000 for each of the fiscal years 2006 through 2009, for—

"(1) the establishment and operation of the United States-Mexico Border Violence Task Force; and

"(2) the investigation, apprehension, and prosecution of individuals engaged in drug and firearms trafficking, violence, and kidnapping along the border between the United States and Mexico."

Privacy Officer

Pub.L. 109–162, Title XI, § 1174, Jan. 5, 2006, 119 Stat. 3124, provided that:

"(a) **In general.**—The Attorney General shall designate a senior official in the Department of Justice to assume primary responsibility for privacy policy.

"(b) **Responsibilities.**—The responsibilities of such official shall include advising the Attorney General regarding—

"(1) appropriate privacy protections, relating to the collection, storage, use, disclosure, and security of personally identifiable information, with respect to the Department's existing or proposed information technology and information systems;

"(2) privacy implications of legislative and regulatory proposals affecting the Department and involving the collection, storage, use, disclosure, and security of personally identifiable information;

"(3) implementation of policies and procedures, including appropriate training and auditing, to ensure the Department's compliance with privacy-related laws and policies, including section 552a of title 5, United States Code, and Section 208 of the E–Government Act of 2002 (Public Law 107–347 [Pub.L. 107–347, Title II, § 208, Dec. 17, 2002, 116 Stat. 2921, which is set out in a note under 44 U.S.C.A. § 3501]);

"(4) ensuring that adequate resources and staff are devoted to meeting the Department's privacy-related functions and obligations;

"(5) appropriate notifications regarding the Department's privacy policies and privacy-related inquiry and complaint procedures; and

"(6) privacy–related reports from the Department to Congress and the President.

"(c) **Review of privacy related functions, resources, and report.**—Within 120 days of his designation, the privacy official shall prepare a comprehensive report to the Attorney General and to the Committees on the Judiciary of the House of Representatives and of the Senate, describing the organization and resources of the Department with respect to privacy and related information management functions, including access, security, and records management, assessing the Department's current and future needs relating to information privacy issues, and making appropriate recommendations regarding the Department's organizational structure and personnel.

"(d) **Annual report.**—The privacy official shall submit a report to the Committees on the Judiciary of the House of Representatives and of the Senate on an annual basis on activities of the Department that affect privacy, including a summary of complaints of privacy violations, implementation of section 552a of title 5, United States Code, internal controls, and other relevant matters."

Report to Congress on Status of United States Persons or Residents Detained on Suspicion of Terrorism

Pub.L. 109–162, Title XI, § 1176, Jan. 5, 2006, 119 Stat. 3125, provided that:

"Not less often than once every 12 months, the Attorney General shall submit to Congress a report on the status of United States persons or residents detained, as of the date of the report, on suspicion of terrorism. The report shall—

"(1) specify the number of persons or residents so detained; and

"(2) specify the standards developed by the Department of Justice for recommending or determining that a person should be tried as a criminal defendant or should be designated as an enemy combatant."

Federal Bureau of Investigation Use of Translators

Pub.L. 108–458, Title II, § 2006, Dec. 17, 2004, 118 Stat. 3704, provided that:

"Not later than 30 days after the date of the enactment of this Act [Dec. 17, 2004], and annually thereafter, the Attorney General of the United States shall submit to the Committee on the Judiciary of the Senate and the Committee on the Judiciary of the House of Representatives a report that contains, with respect to each preceding 12–month period—

"(1) the number of translators employed, or contracted for, by the Federal Bureau of Investigation or other components of the Department of Justice;

"(2) any legal or practical impediments to using translators employed by the Federal, State, or local agencies on a full-time, part-time, or shared basis;

"(3) the needs of the Federal Bureau of Investigation for the specific translation services in certain languages, and recommendations for meeting those needs;

"(4) the status of any automated statistical reporting system, including implementation and future viability;

"(5) the storage capabilities of the digital collection system or systems utilized;

"(6) a description of the establishment and compliance with audio retention policies that satisfy the investigative and intelligence goals of the Federal Bureau of Investigation; and

"(7) a description of the implementation of quality control procedures and mechanisms for monitoring compliance with quality control procedures."

Authorization for Additional Assistant United States Attorneys for Project Safe Neighborhoods

Pub.L. 107–273, Title I, § 104, Nov. 2, 2002, 116 Stat. 1766, provided that:

"(a) **In general.**—The Attorney General shall establish a program for each United States Attorney to provide for coordination with State and local law enforcement officials in the identification and prosecution of violations of Federal firearms laws including school gun violence and juvenile gun offenses.

"(b) **Authorization for hiring 94 additional assistant United States attorneys.**—There are authorized to be appropriated to carry out this section [this note] $9,000,000 for fiscal year 2002 to hire an additional Assistant United States Attorney in each United States Attorney Office."

Development and Support of Cybersecurity Forensic Capabilities

Pub.L. 107–56, Title VIII, § 816, Oct. 26, 2001, 115 Stat. 385, provided that:

"(a) **In general.**—The Attorney General shall establish such regional computer forensic laboratories as the Attorney General considers appropriate, and provide support to existing computer forensic laboratories, in order that all such computer forensic laboratories have the capability—

"(1) to provide forensic examinations with respect to seized or intercepted computer evidence relating to criminal activity (including cyberterrorism);

"(2) to provide training and education for Federal, State, and local law enforcement personnel and prosecutors regarding investigations, forensic analyses, and prosecutions of computer-related crime (including cyberterrorism);

"(3) to assist Federal, State, and local law enforcement in enforcing Federal, State, and local criminal laws relating to computer-related crime;

"(4) to facilitate and promote the sharing of Federal law enforcement expertise and information about the investigation, analysis, and prosecution of computer-related crime with State and local law enforcement personnel and prosecutors, including the use of multijurisdictional task forces; and

"(5) to carry out such other activities as the Attorney General considers appropriate.

"**(b) Authorization of appropriations.**—

"**(1) Authorization.**—There is hereby authorized to be appropriated in each fiscal year $50,000,000 for purposes of carrying out this section.

"**(2) Availability.**—Amounts appropriated pursuant to the authorization of appropriations in paragraph (1) shall remain available until expended."

Training of Government Officials Regarding Identification and Use of Foreign Intelligence

Pub.L. 107–56, Title IX, § 908, Oct. 26, 2001, 115 Stat. 391, provided that:

"**(a) Program required.**—The Attorney General shall, in consultation with the Director of Central Intelligence, carry out a program to provide appropriate training to officials described in subsection (b) in order to assist such officials in—

"(1) identifying foreign intelligence information in the course of their duties; and

"(2) utilizing foreign intelligence information in the course of their duties, to the extent that the utilization of such information is appropriate for such duties.

"**(b) Officials.**—The officials provided training under subsection (a) are, at the discretion of the Attorney General and the Director, the following:

"(1) Officials of the Federal Government who are not ordinarily engaged in the collection, dissemination, and use of foreign intelligence in the performance of their duties.

"(2) Officials of State and local governments who encounter, or may encounter in the course of a terrorist event, foreign intelligence in the performance of their duties.

"**(c) Authorization of appropriations.**—There is hereby authorized to be appropriated for the Department of Justice such sums as may be necessary for purposes of carrying out the program required by subsection (a)."

First Responders Assistance Act

Pub.L. 107–56, Title X, § 1005, Oct. 26, 2001, 115 Stat. 393, provided that:

"**(a) Grant authorization.**—The Attorney General shall make grants described in subsections (b) and (c) to States and units of local government to improve the ability of State and local law enforcement, fire department and first responders to respond to and prevent acts of terrorism.

"**(b) Terrorism prevention grants.**—Terrorism prevention grants under this subsection may be used for programs, projects, and other activities to—

"(1) hire additional law enforcement personnel dedicated to intelligence gathering and analysis functions, including the formation of full-time intelligence and analysis units;

"(2) purchase technology and equipment for intelligence gathering and analysis functions, including wire-tap, pen links, cameras, and computer hardware and software;

"(3) purchase equipment for responding to a critical incident, including protective equipment for patrol officers such as quick masks;

"(4) purchase equipment for managing a critical incident, such as communications equipment for improved interoperability among surrounding jurisdictions and mobile command posts for overall scene management; and

"(5) fund technical assistance programs that emphasize coordination among neighboring law enforcement agencies for sharing resources, and resources coordination among law enforcement agencies for combining intelligence gathering and analysis functions, and the development of policy, procedures, memorandums of understanding, and other best practices.

"**(c) Antiterrorism training grants.**—Antiterrorism training grants under this subsection may be used for programs, projects, and other activities to address—

"(1) intelligence gathering and analysis techniques;

"(2) community engagement and outreach;

"(3) critical incident management for all forms of terrorist attack;

"(4) threat assessment capabilities;

"(5) conducting followup investigations; and

"(6) stabilizing a community after a terrorist incident.

"**(d) Application.**—

"**(1) In general.**—Each eligible entity that desires to receive a grant under this section [this note] shall submit an application to the Attorney General, at such time, in such manner, and accompanied by such additional information as the Attorney General may reasonably require.

"**(2) Contents.**—Each application submitted pursuant to paragraph (1) shall—

"(A) describe the activities for which assistance under this section is sought; and

"(B) provide such additional assurances as the Attorney General determines to be essential to ensure compliance with the requirements of this section.

"**(e) Minimum amount.**—If all applications submitted by a State or units of local government within that State have not been funded under this section [this note] in any fiscal year, that State, if it qualifies, and the units of local government within that State, shall receive in that fiscal year not less than 0.5 percent of the total amount appropriated in that fiscal year for grants under this section.

"(f) **Authorization of appropriations.**—There are authorized to be appropriated $25,000,000 for each of the fiscal years 2003 through 2007."

Abolition of Interstate Commerce Commission and Transfer of Functions

Interstate Commerce Commission abolished and functions of Commission transferred, except as otherwise provided in Pub.L. 104–88, to Surface Transportation Board effective Jan. 1, 1996, by section 702 of Title 49, Transportation, and section 101 of Pub.L. 104–88, set out as a note under section 701 of Title 49. References to Interstate Commerce Commission deemed to refer to Surface Transportation Board, a member or employee of the Board, or Secretary of Transportation, as appropriate, see section 205 of Pub.L. 104–88, set out as a note under section 701 of Title 49.

Authorization of Appropriations for Humanitarian Expenses Incurred by Federal Bureau of Investigation and Drug Enforcement Administration

Pub.L. 101–647, Title XXXII, § 3201, Nov. 29, 1990, 104 Stat. 4916, as amended Pub.L. 105–277, Div. A, § 101(b) [Title I, § 109(a)], Oct. 21, 1998, 112 Stat. 2681–67, provided that: "Appropriations in this or any other Act hereafter for the Federal Bureau of Investigation, the Drug Enforcement Administration, or the Immigration and Naturalization Service are available, in an amount of not to exceed $25,000 each per fiscal year, to pay humanitarian expenses incurred by or for any employee thereof (or any member of the employee's immediate family) that results from or is incident to serious illness, serious injury, or death occurring to the employee while on official duty or business."

[For abolition of Immigration and Naturalization Service, transfer of functions, and treatment of related references, see note set out under 8 U.S.C.A. § 1551.]

Emergency Preparedness Functions

For assignment of certain emergency preparedness functions to the Attorney General, see Parts 1, 2, and 11 of Ex. Ord. No. 12656, Nov. 18, 1988, 53 F.R. 47491, set out as a note under section 2251 of Title 50, Appendix, War and National Defense.

Expenses of Legal Defense for Federal Government Employees Performing Official Duties; Fees and Expenses of Witnesses

Pub.L. 101–162, Title II, Nov. 21, 1989, 103 Stat. 997, provided in part: "That for fiscal year 1990 and hereafter the Attorney General may enter into reimbursable agreements with other Federal Government agencies or components within the Department of Justice to pay expenses of private counsel to defend Federal Government employees sued for actions while performing their official duties: *Provided further*, That for fiscal year 1990 and hereafter the Attorney General, upon notification to the Committees on Appropriations of the House of Representatives and the Senate in compliance with provisions set forth in section 606 of this Act [Pub.L. 101–162, Title VI, Nov. 21, 1989, 103 Stat. 1031, not classified to the Code], may authorize litigating components to reimburse this account for expert witness expenses when it appears current allocations will be exhausted for cases scheduled for trial in the current fiscal year."

Federal Environmental or Natural Resource Laws; Investigations Respecting, Etc.

Pub.L. 96–132, § 12, Nov. 30, 1979, 93 Stat. 1048, provided that: "The Attorney General may, with the concurrence of any agency or Department with primary enforcement responsibility for an environmental or natural resource law, investigate any violation, of an environmental or natural resource law of the United States, and bring such actions as are necessary to enforce such laws. This section does not affect the criminal law enforcement authority of the Attorney General."

Impact Analysis of Additional Resources to Certain Components of Federal Criminal Justice System; Study by Comptroller General and Report to Congress

Pub.L. 100–690, Title IX, § 9201, Nov. 18, 1988, 102 Stat. 4535, provided that:

"(a) **Study.**—The Comptroller General of the United States shall conduct a study—

"(1) to determine the impact of additional resources to certain components of the Federal criminal justice system on other components of the system and of enhanced or new Federal criminal penalties or laws on the agencies and offices of the Department of Justice, the Federal courts, and other components of the Federal criminal justice system; and

"(2) use the data derived from the impact analysis to develop a model that can be applied by Congress and Federal agencies and departments to help determine appropriate staff and budget responses in order to maintain balance in the Federal criminal justice system and effectively implement changes in resources, laws, or penalties.

"(b) **Report to Congress.**—The Comptroller General shall report the results and recommendations derived from the study required by subsection (a) no later than 1 year after the date of enactment of this Act [Nov. 18, 1988]."

Investigation of Financial Institutions; Assistance of Government Personnel

Pub.L. 101–509, Title V, § 528, Nov. 5, 1990, 104 Stat. 1427, as amended Pub.L. 101–650, Title III, § 321, Dec. 1, 1990, 104 Stat. 5117; Pub.L. 103–322, Title XXXII, § 320923, Sept. 13, 1994, 108 Stat. 2131, provided that:

"(a) Notwithstanding any other law and in any fiscal year—

"(1) The Attorney General shall accept, and Federal departments and agencies, including the United States Secret Service, the Internal Revenue Service, the Resolution Trust Corporation, and the appropriate Federal banking agency, may provide, without reimbursement, the services of attorneys, law enforcement personnel, and other employees of any other departments or agencies of the Federal Government to assist the Department of Justice, subject to the supervision of the Attorney General, in the investigation and prosecution of fraud or other criminal or unlawful activity in or against any federally insured financial institution or the Resolution Trust Corporation;

"(2) any attorney of a department or agency whose services are accepted pursuant to paragraph (1) may, subject to the supervision of the Attorney General, conduct any kind of legal proceeding, civil or criminal, including grand jury proceedings and proceedings before committing magistrate judges, and perform any other investigative or prosecutorial function, which United States attorneys are authorized by law to conduct or perform whether or not the attorney is a resident of the district in which the proceeding is brought; and

"(3) law enforcement personnel of the United States Secret Service are authorized, subject to the supervision of the Attorney General, to conduct or perform any kind of investigation, civil or criminal, related to fraud or other criminal or unlawful activity in or against any federally insured financial institution or the Resolution Trust Corporation, which the Department of Justice law enforcement personnel are authorized by law to conduct or perform: *Provided*, That the Secret Service shall not initiate investigations pursuant to this section independent of the supervision of the Attorney General.

"(b) This section—

"(1) shall not, except as expressly provided herein, alter the authority of any Federal law enforcement agency; and

"(2) shall expire on December 31, 2004.

"(c) This section applies notwithstanding any other provision of law enacted by the 101st Congress after October 15, 1990, that by its terms would grant authority to, or otherwise affect the authority of, the Secret Service or other departments or agencies of the Federal Government to conduct or to assist the Department of Justice in conducting investigations or prosecutions of fraud or other criminal or unlawful activity in or against any federally insured financial institution or the Resolution Trust Corporation, and any other such provision shall not be effective in granting or otherwise affecting any such authority."

[For transfer of the functions, personnel, assets, and obligations of the United States Secret Service, including the functions of the Secretary of the Treasury relating thereto, to the Secretary of Homeland Security, and for treatment of related references, see 6 U.S.C.A. §§ 381, 551(d), 552(d), and 557, and the Department of Homeland Security Reorganization Plan of November 25, 2002, as modified, set out as a note under 6 U.S.C.A. § 542.]

Justice Department Organized Crime and Drug Enforcement Enhancement

Pub.L. 100–690, Title I, Subtitle B, Nov. 18, 1988, 102 Stat. 4189, provided that:

"Sec. 1051. Short Title.

"This subtitle [this note] may be cited as the 'Justice Department Organized Crime and Drug Enforcement Enhancement Act of 1988'.

"Sec. 1052. Findings.

"The Congress finds that—

"(1) organized criminal activity contributes significantly to the importation, distribution, and sale of illegal and dangerous drugs;

"(2) trends in drug trafficking patterns necessitate a response that gives appropriate weight to—

"(A) the prosecution of drug-related crimes; and

"(B) the forfeiture and seizure of assets and other civil remedies used to strike at the inherent strength of the drug networks and organized crime groups;

"(3) law enforcement components of the Department of Justice should give high priority to the enforcement of civil sanctions against drug networks and organized crime groups; and

"(4) the structure of the Department of Justice Criminal Division needs to be reviewed in order to determine the most effective structure to address such drug-related problems.

"Sec. 1053. Civil Enforcement Report.

"(a) **Report.**—Not later than 1 year after the date of the enactment of this title [Nov. 18, 1988], the Director of National Drug Control Policy (the Director) in consultation with the Attorney General, shall report to the Congress on the necessity to establish a new division or make other organizational changes within the Department of Justice in order to promote better civil and criminal law enforcement. In preparing such report, the Director shall consider restructuring and consolidating one or more of the following divisions and programs—

"(1) the Organized Crime and Racketeering Section of the Criminal Division and all subordinate strike forces therein;

"(2) the Narcotic and Dangerous Drug Section of the Criminal Division;

"(3) the Asset Forfeiture Office of the Criminal Division; and

"(4) the Organized Crime Drug Enforcement Task Force Program;[.]

"(b) **Legislative recommendations.**—The report submitted under subsection (a) shall include appropriate legislative recommendations for the Congress.

"Sec. 1054. Civil Enforcement Enhancement.

"(a) **Duty of Attorney General.**—The Attorney General shall insure that each component of the Department of Justice having criminal law enforcement responsibilities with respect to the prosecution of organized crime and controlled substances violations, including each United States Attorney's Office, attaches a high priority to the enforcement of civil statutes creating ancillary sanctions and remedies for such violations, such as civil penalties and actions, forfeitures, injunctions and restraining orders, and collection of fines.

"(b) **Duty of Associate Attorney General.**—The Associate Attorney General shall be responsible for implementing the policy set forth in this subsection.

"(c) **Authorization of appropriations.**—(1) There are authorized to be appropriated $3,000,000 for salaries and expenses to the Department of Justice General Legal Activities Account and $3,000,000 for salaries and expenses for United States Attorneys for fiscal year 1989.

"(2) Any appropriation of funds authorized under paragraph (1) shall be—

"(A) in addition to any appropriations requested by the President in the 1989 fiscal year budget submitted by the President to the Congress on February 18, 1988, or provided in regular appropriations Acts or continuing resolutions for the fiscal year ending September 30, 1989; and

"(B) used to increase the number of field attorneys and related support staff over such personnel levels employed at the Department of Justice on September 30, 1988.

"(3) Any increase in full-time equivalent positions described under paragraph (2)(B) shall be exclusively used for asset forfeiture and civil enforcement and be assigned to appropriate field offices of the Organized Crime and Racketeering Section and the Organized Crime Drug Enforcement Task Forces.

"**(d) Reporting requirement.**—The Attorney General, at the end of each such fiscal year, shall file a report with the Congress setting forth the extent of such enforcement efforts, as well as the need for any enhancements in resources necessary to carry out this policy.

"**Sec. 1055. Expenses of Task Forces.**

"**(a) Appropriations and reimbursements procedure.**—Beginning in fiscal year 1990, the Attorney General in his budget shall submit a separate appropriations request for expenses relating to all Federal agencies participating in the Organized Crime Drug Enforcement Task Forces. Such appropriations shall be made to the Department of Justice's Interagency Law Enforcement Appropriation Account for the Attorney General to make reimbursements to the involved agencies as necessary.

"**(b) Enhancement of field activities.**—The appropriations and reimbursements procedure described under subsection (a) shall—

"(1) provide for the flexibility of the Task Forces which is vital to success;

"(2) permit Federal law enforcement resources to be shifted in response to changing patterns of organized criminal drug activities;

"(3) permit the Attorney General to reallocate resources among the organizational components of the Task Forces and between regions without undue delay; and

"(4) ensure that the Task Forces function as a unit, without the competition for resources among the participating agencies that would undermine the overall effort."

[For termination, effective May 15, 2000, of provisions of law requiring submittal to Congress of any annual, semiannual, or other regular periodic report listed in House Document No. 103–7 (in which a report required under Pub.L. 100–690, § 1054(d), set out in above note, is listed on page 118), see Pub.L. 104–66, § 3003, as amended, set out as a note under 31 U.S.C.A. § 1113.]

Neighborhood Revitalization

Pub.L. 102–395, Title I, Oct. 6, 1992, 106 Stat. 1830, provided in part that: "For fiscal year 1993 and thereafter the Attorney General shall (1) promote neighborhood revitalization by developing a plan for the use of Federal funds appropriated for selected activities in the Departments of Labor, Education, Health and Human Services, Transportation, Agriculture, and Housing and Urban Development; (2) the Attorney General shall solicit from State and local governments plans to revitalize neighborhoods using programs administered by such agencies; and (3) the Attorney General shall review and approve such plans in consultation with the Federal agency to which funds are appropriated."

Overseas Law Enforcement Training Activities

Pub.L. 104–132, Title VIII, § 801, Apr. 24, 1996, 110 Stat. 1304, provided that: "The Attorney General and the Secretary of the Treasury are authorized to support law enforcement training activities in foreign countries, in consultation with the Secretary of State, for the purpose of improving the effectiveness of the United States in investigating and prosecuting transnational offenses."

Positions in Drug Enforcement Administration; Grades Excepted From Competitive Service: Vacancies; Removal, Suspension, or Reduction in Rank or Pay; Rate of Pay

Pub.L. 94–503, Title II, § 201, Oct. 15, 1976, 90 Stat. 2425, provided that:

"(a) Effective beginning one year after date of the enactment of this Act [Oct. 15, 1976], the following positions in the Drug Enforcement Administration (and individuals holding such positions) are hereby excepted from the competitive service:

"(1) positions at GS–16, 17, and 18 of the General Schedule under section 5332(a) of title 5, United States Code [section 5332(a) of Title 5, Government Organization and Employees], and

"(2) positions at GS–15 of the General Schedule which are designated as—

"(A) regional directors,

"(B) office heads, or

"'(C) executive assistants (or equivalent positions) under the immediate supervision of the Administrator (or the Deputy Administrator) of the Drug Enforcement Administration.

"(b) Effective during the one year period beginning on the date of the enactment of this Act [Oct. 15, 1976], vacancies in positions in the Drug Enforcement Administration (other than positions described in subsection (a)) at a grade not lower than GS–14 shall be filled—

"(1) first, from applicants who have continuously held positions described in subsection (a) since the date of the enactment of this Act and who have applied for, and are qualified to fill, such vacancies, and

"(2) then, from other applicants in the order which would have occurred in the absence of this subsection."

Any individual placed in a position under paragraph (1) shall be paid in accordance with subsection (d).

"(c)(1) Effective beginning one year after the date of the enactment of this Act [Oct. 15, 1976], an individual in a position described in subsection (a) may be removed, suspended for more than 30 days, furloughed without pay, or reduced in rank or pay by the Administrator of the Drug Enforcement Administration if—

"(A) such individual has been employed in the Drug Enforcement Administration for less than the one-year period immediately preceding the date of such action, and

"(B) the Administrator determines, in his discretion, that such action would promote the efficiency of the service.

"(2) Effective beginning one year after the date of the enactment of this Act [Oct. 15, 1976], an individual in a position described in subsection (a) may be reduced in rank or pay by the Administrator within the Drug Enforcement Administration if—

"(A) such individual has been continuously employed in such position since the date of the enactment of this Act, and

"(B) the Administrator determines, in his discretion, that such action would promote the efficiency of the service.

Any individual reduced in rank or pay under this paragraph shall be paid in accordance with subsection (d).

"(3) The provisions of sections 7512 and 7701 of title 5, United States Code [sections 7512 and 7701 of Title 5], and otherwise applicable Executive orders, shall not apply with respect to actions taken by the Administrator under paragraph (1) or any reduction in rank or pay (under paragraph (2) or otherwise) of any individual in a position described in subsection (a).

"(d) Any individual whose pay is to be determined in accordance with this subsection shall be paid basic pay at the rate of basic pay he was receiving immediately before he was placed in a position under subsection (b)(1) or reduced in rank or pay under subsection (c)(2), as the case may be, until such time as the rate of basic pay he would receive in the absence of this subsection exceeds such rate of basic pay. The provisions of section 5337 of title 5, United States Code [section 5337 of Title 5], shall not apply in any case in which this subsection applies."

Processing of Name Checks and Background Records for Noncriminal Employment, Licensing, and Humanitarian Purposes

Pub.L. 101–162, Title II, Nov. 21, 1989, 103 Stat. 995, provided in part: "That for fiscal year 1990 and hereafter the Chief, United States National Central Bureau, INTERPOL, may establish and collect fees to process name checks and background records for noncriminal employment, licensing, and humanitarian purposes and, notwithstanding the provisions of 31 U.S.C. 3302 [section 3302 of Title 31, Money and Finance], credit such fees to this appropriation to be used for salaries and other expenses incurred in providing these services."

Procurement of Expert Witnesses Without Regard to Competitive Procurement Procedures

Pub.L. 102–140, Title VI, § 611(a), Oct. 28, 1991, 105 Stat. 832, provided that, notwithstanding any other provision of law: "For fiscal year 1992 and thereafter, the Department of Justice may procure the services of expert witnesses for use in preparing or prosecuting a civil or criminal action, without regard to competitive procurement procedures, including the Commerce Business Daily publication requirements: *Provided*, That no witness shall be paid more than one attendance fee for any calendar day."

Reimbursement of Employees Traveling on Behalf of United States in Temporary Duty Status

Pub.L. 104–208, Div. A, Title I, § 101(a) [Title I, § 115], Sept. 30, 1996, 110 Stat. 3009–22, provided that: "Effective with the enactment of this Act [Pub.L. 104–208, 110 Stat. 3009, which was approved Sept. 30, 1996] and in any fiscal year hereafter, under policies established by the Attorney General, the Department of Justice may reimburse employees who are paid by an appropriation account within the Department of Justice and are traveling on behalf of the United States in temporary duty status to investigate, prosecute, or litigate (including the provision of support therefor) a criminal or civil matter, or for other similar special circumstances, for Federal, State, and local taxes heretofore and hereafter resulting from any reimbursement of travel expenses from an appropriation account within the Department of Justice: *Provided*, That such reimbursement may include an amount equal to all income taxes for which the employee would be liable due to such reimbursement."

Reimbursement by Other Government Agencies of Department of Justice Salaries and Expenses in High–Cost Litigation

Pub.L. 103–317, Title I, § 109, Aug. 26, 1994, 108 Stat. 1735, provided that: "Notwithstanding 31 U.S.C. 3302 [section 3302 of Title 31, Money and Finance] or any other law, in litigation involving unusually high costs, the Department of Justice may receive and retain reimbursement for salaries and expenses, for fiscal year 1995 and thereafter, from any other governmental component being represented in the litigation."

Structural Reforms to Improve Federal Response to Crimes Affecting Financial Institutions

Pub.L. 101–647, Title XXV, §§ 2536 to 2539, Nov. 29, 1990, 104 Stat. 4883, 4884, provided that:

"Sec. 2536. Establishment of Financial Institutions Crime Unit and Office of Special Counsel for Financial Institutions Crime Unit.

"**(a) Establishment.**—There is established within the Office of the Deputy Attorney General in the Department of Justice a Financial Institutions Fraud Unit to be headed by a special counsel (hereafter in this title [probably means this subtitle which is subtitle D [sections 2536–2540] of Title XXV of Pub. L. 101–647, which amended section 1441a of Title 12, Banks and Banking, and enacted this note] referred to as the 'Special Counsel').

"**(b) Responsibility.**—The Financial Institutions Fraud Unit and the Special Counsel shall be responsible to and shall report directly to the Deputy Attorney General.

"**(c) Sunset.**—The provisions of this section shall cease to apply at the end of the 5–year period beginning on the date of the enactment of this Act [Nov. 29, 1990].

"Sec. 2537. Appointment Responsibilities and Compensation of the Special Counsel.

"**(a) Appointment.**—The Special Counsel shall be appointed by the President, by and with the advice and consent of the Senate.

"**(b) Responsibilities.**—The Special Counsel shall—

"(1) supervise and coordinate investigations and prosecutions within the Department of Justice of fraud and other criminal activity in and against the financial services industry, including, to the extent consistent with the independent counsel provision of chapter 40 of title 28, United States Code [section 591 et seq. of this title], any such activity by any current or former elected official or high-level executive branch official or any member of the immediate family of any such official;

"(2) ensure that Federal law relating to civil enforcement, asset seizure and forfeiture, money laundering, and racketeering are used to the fullest extent authorized to recover the proceeds of unlawful activities from persons who have committed crimes in and against the financial services industry; and

"(3) ensure that adequate resources are made available for the investigation and prosecution of fraud and other criminal activity in and against the financial services industry.

"**(c) Compensation.**—The Special Counsel shall be paid at the basic pay payable for level V of the Executive Schedule [see section 5316 of Title 5, Government Organization and Employees].

"Sec. 2538. Assignment of Personnel.

"There shall be assigned to the Financial Institutions Fraud Unit such personnel as the Attorney General deems necessary to provide an appropriate level of enforcement activity in the area of fraud and other criminal activity in and against the financial services industry.

"Sec. 2539. Financial Institutions Fraud Task Forces.

"**(a) Establishment.**—The Attorney General shall establish such financial institutions fraud task forces as the Attorney General deems appropriate to ensure that adequate resources are made available to investigate and prosecute crimes in or against financial institutions and to recover the proceeds of unlawful activities from persons who have committed fraud or have engaged in other criminal activity in or against the financial services industry.

"**(b) Supervision.**—The Attorney General shall determine how each task force shall be supervised and may provide for the supervision of any task force by the Special Counsel.

"**(c) Senior interagency group.**—

"**(1) Establishment.**—The Attorney General shall establish a senior interagency group to assist in identifying the most significant financial institution fraud cases and in allocating investigative and prosecutorial resources where they are most needed.

"**(2) Membership.**—The senior interagency group shall be chaired by the Special Counsel and shall include senior officials from—

"**(A)** the Department of Justice, including representatives of the Federal Bureau of Investigation, the Advisory Committee of United States Attorneys, and other relevant entities;

"**(B)** the Department of the Treasury;

"**(C)** the Office of Thrift Supervision;

"**(D)** the Resolution Trust Corporation;

"**(E)** the Federal Deposit Insurance Corporation;

"**(F)** the Office of the Comptroller of the Currency;

"**(G)** the Board of Governors of the Federal Reserve System; and

"**(H)** the National Credit Union Administration.

"**(3) Duties.**—This senior interagency group shall enhance interagency coordination and assist in accelerating the investigations and prosecution of financial institutions fraud."

Uniforms and Allowances

Pub.L. 101–162, Title II, § 203, Nov. 21, 1989, 103 Stat. 1002, provided that: "For fiscal year 1990 and hereafter, appropriations for 'Salaries and expenses, General Administration', 'Salaries and expenses, United States Marshals Service', 'Salaries and expenses, Federal Bureau of Investigation', 'Salaries and expenses, Drug Enforcement Administration', 'Salaries and expenses, Immigration and Naturalization Service', and 'Salaries and expenses, Federal Prison System', shall be available for uniforms and allowances therefor as authorized by law (5 U.S.C. 5901–5902) [sections 5901 and 5902 of Title 5, Government Organization and Employees]."

[For abolition of Immigration and Naturalization Service (INS), transfer of functions, and treatment of related references, see note set out under 8 U.S.C.A. § 1551.]

EXECUTIVE ORDERS

EXECUTIVE ORDER NO. 12146

MANAGEMENT OF FEDERAL LEGAL RESOURCES

By the authority vested in me as President by the Constitution and statutes of the United States of America, it is hereby ordered as follows:

1–1. Establishment of the Federal Legal Council.

1–101. There is hereby established the Federal Legal Council, which shall be composed of the Attorney General and the representatives of not more than 16 other agencies. The agency representative shall be designated by the head of the agency.

1–102. The initial membership of the Council, in addition to the Attorney General, shall consist of representatives designated by the heads of the following agencies:

(a) The Department of Commerce.

(b) The Department of Defense.

(c) The Department of Energy.

(d) The Environmental Protection Agency.

(e) The Equal Employment Opportunity Commission.

(f) The Federal Trade Commission.

(g) The Department of Health and Human Services.

(h) The Interstate Commerce Commission.

(i) The Department of Labor.

(j) The National Labor Relations Board.

(k) The Securities and Exchange Commission.

(*l*) The Department of State.

(m) The Department of the Treasury.

(*o*) The United States Postal Service and

(p) The Veterans Administration.

1–103. The initial members of the Council shall serve for a term of two years. Thereafter, the agencies which compose the membership shall be designated annually by the Council and at least five positions on the Council, other than that held by the Attorney General, shall rotate annually.

1–104. In addition to the above members, the Directors of the Office of Management and Budget and the Office of Personnel Management, or their designees, shall be advisory members of the Council.

1–105. The Attorney General shall chair the Council and provide staff for its operation. Representatives of agencies that are not members of the Council may serve on or chair subcommittees of the Council.

1–2. Functions of the Council.

1–201. The Council shall promote:

(a) coordination and communication among Federal legal offices;

(b) improved management of Federal lawyers, associated support personnel, and information systems;

(c) improvements in the training provided to Federal lawyers;

(d) the facilitation of the personal donation of pro bono legal services by Federal attorneys;

(e) the use of joint or shared legal facilities in field offices; and

(f) the delegation of legal work to field offices.

1–202. The Council shall study and seek to resolve problems in the efficient and effective management of Federal legal resources that are beyond the capacity or authority of individual agencies to resolve.

1–203. The Council shall develop recommendations for legislation and other actions: (a) to increase the efficient and effective operation and management of Federal legal resources, including those matters specified in Section 1–201, and (b) to avoid inconsistent or unnecessary litigation by agencies.

1–3. Litigation Notice System.

1–301. The Attorney General shall establish and maintain a litigation notice system that provides timely information about all civil litigation pending in the courts in which the Federal Government is a party or has a significant interest.

1–302. The Attorney General shall issue rules to govern operation of the notice system. The rules shall include the following requirement:

(a) All agencies with authority to litigate cases in court shall promptly notify the Attorney General about those cases that fall in classes or categories designated from time to time by the Attorney General.

(b) The Attorney General shall provide all agencies reasonable access to the information collected in the litigation notice system.

1–4. Resolution of Interagency Legal Disputes.

1–401. Whenever two or more Executive agencies are unable to resolve a legal dispute between them, including the question of which has jurisdiction to administer a particular program or to regulate a particular activity, each agency is encouraged to submit the dispute to the Attorney General.

1–402. Whenever two or more Executive agencies whose heads serve at the pleasure of the President are unable to resolve such a legal dispute, the agencies shall submit the dispute to the Attorney General prior to proceeding in any court, except where there is specific statutory vesting of responsibility for a resolution elsewhere.

1–5. Access to Legal Opinions.

1–501. In addition to the disclosure now required by law, all agencies are encouraged to make available for public inspection and copying other opinions of their legal officers that are statements of policy or interpretation that have been adopted by the agency, unless the agency determines that disclosure would result in demonstrable harm.

1–502. All agencies are encouraged to make available on request other legal opinions, when the agency determines that disclosure would not be harmful.

1–6. Automated Legal Research and Information Systems.

1–601. The Attorney General, in coordination with the Secretary of Defense and other agency heads, shall provide for a computerized legal research system that will be available to all Federal law offices on a reimbursable basis. The system may include in its data base such Federal regulations, case briefs, and legal opinions, as the Attorney General deems appropriate.

1–602. The Federal Legal Council shall provide leadership for all Federal legal offices in establishing appropriate word processing and management information systems.

1–7. Responsibilities of the Agencies.

1–701. Each agency shall (a) review the management and operation of its legal activities and report in one year to the Federal Legal Council all steps being taken to improve those operations, and (b) cooperate with the Federal Legal Council and the Attorney General in the performance of the functions provided by this Order.

1–702. To the extent permitted by law, each agency shall furnish the Federal Legal Council and the Attorney General with reports, information and assistance as requested to carry out the provisions of this Order.

JIMMY CARTER

§ 509A. National Security Division

(a) There is a National Security Division of the Department of Justice.

(b) The National Security Division shall consist of the elements of the Department of Justice (other than the Federal Bureau of Investigation) engaged primarily in support of the intelligence and intelligence-related activities of the United States Government, including the following:

(1) The Assistant Attorney General designated as the Assistant Attorney General for National Security under section 507A of this title.

(2) The Office of Intelligence Policy and Review (or any successor organization).

(3) The counterterrorism section (or any successor organization).

(4) The counterespionage section (or any successor organization).

(5) Any other element, component, or office designated by the Attorney General.

(Added Pub.L. 109–177, Title V, § 506(b)(1), Mar. 9, 2006, 120 Stat. 248.)

§ 510. Delegation of authority

The Attorney General may from time to time make such provisions as he considers appropriate authorizing the performance by any other officer, employee, or agency of the Department of Justice of any function of the Attorney General.

(Added Pub.L. 89–554, § 4(c), Sept. 6, 1966, 80 Stat. 612.)

HISTORICAL AND STATUTORY NOTES

Prior Provisions

A prior section 510, Act June 25, 1948, c. 646, 62 Stat. 910, which related to clerical assistants and messengers for United States attorneys, was repealed by Pub.L. 89–554, § 8(a), Sept. 6, 1966, 80 Stat. 632, and reenacted in section 550 of this title by section 4(c) of Pub.L. 89–554.

§ 511. Attorney General to advise the President

The Attorney General shall give his advice and opinion on questions of law when required by the President.

(Added Pub.L. 89–554, § 4(c), Sept. 6, 1966, 80 Stat. 612.)

§ 512. Attorney General to advise heads of executive departments

The head of an executive department may require the opinion of the Attorney General on questions of law arising in the administration of his department.

(Added Pub.L. 89–554, § 4(c), Sept. 6, 1966, 80 Stat. 613.)

§ 513. Attorney General to advise Secretaries of military departments

When a question of law arises in the administration of the Department of the Army, the Department of the Navy, or the Department of the Air Force, the cognizance of which is not given by statute to some other officer from whom the Secretary of the military department concerned may require advice, the Secretary of the military department shall send it to the Attorney General for disposition.

(Added Pub.L. 89–554, § 4(c), Sept. 6, 1966, 80 Stat. 613.)

§ 514. Legal services on pending claims in departments and agencies

When the head of an executive department or agency is of the opinion that the interests of the United States require the service of counsel on the examination of any witness concerning any claim, or on the legal investigation of any claim, pending in the department or agency, he shall notify the Attorney General, giving all facts necessary to enable him to furnish proper professional service in attending the examination or making the investigation, and the Attorney General shall provide for the service.

(Added Pub.L. 89–554, § 4(c), Sept. 6, 1966, 80 Stat. 613.)

§ 515. Authority for legal proceedings; commission, oath, and salary for special attorneys

(a) The Attorney General or any other officer of the Department of Justice, or any attorney specially appointed by the Attorney General under law, may, when specifically directed by the Attorney General, conduct any kind of legal proceeding, civil or criminal, including grand jury proceedings and proceedings before committing magistrate judges, which United States attorneys are authorized by law to conduct, whether or not he is a resident of the district in which the proceeding is brought.

(b) Each attorney specially retained under authority of the Department of Justice shall be commissioned as special assistant to the Attorney General or special attorney, and shall take the oath required by law. Foreign counsel employed in special cases are not required to take the oath. The Attorney General shall fix the annual salary of a special assistant or special attorney.

(Added Pub.L. 89–554, § 4(c), Sept. 6, 1966, 80 Stat. 613, and amended Pub.L. 101–650, Title III, § 321, Dec. 1, 1990, 104 Stat. 5117; Pub.L. 107–273, Div. A, Title II, § 203(b), Nov. 2, 2002, 116 Stat. 1775.)

HISTORICAL AND STATUTORY NOTES

Change of Name

"United States magistrate judge" substituted for "United States magistrate" in text pursuant to section 321 of Pub.L. 101–650, set out as a note under 28 U.S.C.A. § 631.

§ 516. Conduct of litigation reserved to Department of Justice

Except as otherwise authorized by law, the conduct of litigation in which the United States, an agency, or officer thereof is a party, or is interested, and securing evidence therefor, is reserved to officers of the Department of Justice, under the direction of the Attorney General.

(Added Pub.L. 89–554, § 4(c), Sept. 6, 1966, 80 Stat. 613.)

§ 517. Interests of United States in pending suits

The Solicitor General, or any officer of the Department of Justice, may be sent by the Attorney General to any State or district in the United States to attend to the interests of the United States in a suit pending in a court of the United States, or in a court of a State, or to attend to any other interest of the United States.

(Added Pub.L. 89–554, § 4(c), Sept. 6, 1966, 80 Stat. 613.)

§ 518. Conduct and argument of cases

(a) Except when the Attorney General in a particular case directs otherwise, the Attorney General and the Solicitor General shall conduct and argue suits and appeals in the Supreme Court and suits in the United States Court of Federal Claims or in the United States Court of Appeals for the Federal Circuit and in the Court of International Trade in which the United States is interested.

(b) When the Attorney General considers it in the interests of the United States, he may personally conduct and argue any case in a court of the United States in which the United States is interested, or he may direct the Solicitor General or any officer of the Department of Justice to do so.

(Added Pub.L. 89–554, § 4(c), Sept. 6, 1966, 80 Stat. 613, and amended Pub.L. 96–417, Title V, § 503, Oct. 10, 1980, 94 Stat. 1743; Pub.L. 97–164, Title I, § 117, Apr. 2, 1982, 96 Stat. 32; Pub.L. 102–572, Title IX, § 902(b)(1), Oct. 29, 1992, 106 Stat. 4516.)

HISTORICAL AND STATUTORY NOTES

Effective and Applicability Provisions

1992 Acts. Amendment by Pub.L. 102–572 effective Oct. 29, 1992, see section 911 of Pub.L. 102–572, set out as a note under section 171 of this title.

1982 Acts. Amendment by Pub.L. 97–164 effective Oct. 1, 1982, see section 402 of Pub.L. 97–164, set out as a note under section 171 of this title.

1980 Acts. Amendment by Pub.L. 96–417 effective on Nov. 1, 1980 and applicable with respect to civil actions pending on or commenced on or after such date, see section 701(a) of Pub.L. 96–417, as amended, set out as a note under section 251 of this title.

Change of Name

References to United States Claims Court deemed to refer to United States Court of Federal Claims and references to Claims Court deemed to refer to Court of Federal Claims, see section 902(b) of Pub.L. 102–572, set out as a note under section 171 of Title 28, Judiciary and Judicial Procedure.

§ 519. Supervision of litigation

Except as otherwise authorized by law, the Attorney General shall supervise all litigation to which the United States, an agency, or officer thereof is a party, and shall direct all United States attorneys, assistant United States attorneys, and special attorneys appointed under section 543 of this title in the discharge of their respective duties.

(Added Pub.L. 89–554, § 4(c), Sept. 6, 1966, 80 Stat. 614.)

HISTORICAL AND STATUTORY NOTES

Intelligence and National Security Aspects of Espionage Prosecutions

Pub.L. 108–177, Title III, § 341(b), Dec. 13, 2003, 117 Stat. 2615, as amended Pub.L. 108–458, Title I, § 1071(g)(3)(A)(v), Dec. 17, 2004, 118 Stat. 3692; Pub.L. 109–177, Title V, § 506(a)(9), Mar. 9, 2006, 120 Stat. 248, provided that: "The Attorney General, acting through the Assistant Attorney General for National Security, and in consultation with the Director of National Intelligence, acting through the Office of the National Counterintelligence Executive, shall establish policies and procedures to assist the Attorney General in the consideration of intelligence and national security-related equities in the development of charging documents and related pleadings in espionage prosecutions."

[For Determination by President that, except as otherwise provided, provisions in Pub.L. 108–458, Title I [§§ 1001 to 1103] take effect on April 21, 2005, see Memorandum of President of the United States, April 21, 2005, 70 F.R. 23925, set out as a note under 50 U.S.C.A. § 401.]

[Except as otherwise expressly provided, amendments by Pub.L. 108–458, Title I, to take effect not later than six months after Dec. 17, 2004, see Pub.L. 108–458, Title I, § 1097(a), set out in the Transfer, Termination, Implementation, Transition, and Effective Dates of the National Security Intelligence Reform Act of 2004 note under 50 U.S.C.A. § 401.]

Use of Annuity Brokers in Structured Settlements

Pub.L. 107–273, Div. C, Title I, § 11015, Nov. 2, 2002, 116 Stat. 1824, provided that:

"**(a) Establishment and transmission of list of approved annuity brokers.**—Not later than 6 months after the date of enactment of this Act [Nov. 2, 2002], the Attorney General shall establish a list of annuity brokers who meet minimum qualifications for providing annuity brokerage services in connection with structured settlements entered by the United States. This list shall be updated upon request by any annuity broker that meets the minimum qualifications for inclusion on the list. The Attorney General shall transmit such list, and any updates to such list, to all United States Attorneys.

"**(b) Authority to select annuity broker for structured settlements.**—In any structured settlement that is not negotiated exclusively through the Civil Division of the Department of Justice, the United States Attorney (or his designee) involved in any settlement negotiations shall have the exclusive authority to select an annuity broker from the list of such brokers established by the Attorney General, provided that all documents related to any settlement comply with Department of Justice requirements."

Case Management Information and Tracking Systems for Federal Judicial Districts and Divisions of Department; Preparation, Submission, Etc., of Plan

Pub.L. 96–132, § 11, Nov. 30, 1979, 93 Stat. 1047, required the Attorney General, not later than Apr. 15, 1980, after consultation with the Director of the Executive Office of United States Attorneys and such Assistant Attorneys as appropriate, to prepare and submit to the Committees on the Judiciary of the Senate and the House of Representatives a plan for the activation and coordination, within the Department of Justice, of compatible, comprehensive case management information and tracking systems for each of the judicial districts of the United States and for each of the divisions of the Department.

Report to Congress Regarding Provisions of Law Considered Unconstitutional by the Department of Justice; Declaration of Such Position

Pub.L. 96–132, § 21, Nov. 30, 1979, 93 Stat. 1049, required the Attorney General, during the fiscal year ending Sept. 30, 1980, to transmit a report to each House of Congress in any case in which the Attorney General considered the provisions of law enacted by the Congress and at issue to be unconstitutional and in such cases required a representative of the Department of Justice participating in such case to make a declaration that such option of the Attorney General regarding the constitutionality of those provisions of law involved constitutes the opinion of the executive branch of the government with respect to such matter.

Similar provisions were contained in Pub.L. 95–624, § 13, Nov. 9, 1978, 92 Stat. 3464.

Study and Report to Congress on Extent to Which Violations of Federal Criminal Laws Are Not Prosecuted

Pub.L. 95–624, § 17, Nov. 9, 1978, 92 Stat. 3465, provided that the Attorney General undertake a study and make recommendations concerning violations of Federal criminal laws which have not been prosecuted and present such study and recommendations to the Committee on the Judiciary of the Senate and the House of Representatives not later than Oct. 1, 1979.

EXECUTIVE ORDERS

EXECUTIVE ORDER NO. 12778

Ex. Ord. No. 12778, Oct. 23, 1991, 56 F.R. 55195, relating to civil justice reform, was revoked by Ex. Ord. No. 12988,

Feb. 5, 1996, 61 F.R. 4729, set out as a note under this section.

§ 520. Transmission of petitions in United States Court of Federal Claims or in United States Court of Appeals for the Federal Circuit; statement furnished by departments

(a) In suits against the United States in the United States Court of Federal Claims or in the United States Court of Appeals for the Federal Circuit founded on a contract, agreement, or transaction with an executive department or military department, or a bureau, officer, or agent thereof, or when the matter or thing on which the claim is based has been passed on and decided by an executive department, military department, bureau, or officer authorized to adjust it, the Attorney General shall send to the department, bureau, or officer a printed copy of the petition filed by the claimant, with a request that the department, bureau, or officer furnish to the Attorney General all facts, circumstances, and evidence concerning the claim in the possession or knowledge of the department, bureau, or officer.

(b) Within a reasonable time after receipt of the request from the Attorney General, the executive department, military department, bureau, or officer shall furnish the Attorney General with a written statement of all facts, information, and proofs. The statement shall contain a reference to or description of all official documents and papers, if any, as may furnish proof of facts referred to in it, or may be necessary and proper for the defense of the United States against the claim, mentioning the department, office, or place where the same is kept or may be secured. If the claim has been passed on and decided by the department, bureau, or officer, the statement shall briefly state the reasons and principles on which the decision was based. When the decision was founded on an Act of Congress it shall be cited specifically, and if any previous interpretation or construction has been given to the Act, section, or clause by the department, bureau, or officer, it shall be set forth briefly in the statement and a copy of the opinion filed, if any, attached to it. When a decision in the case has been based on a regulation of a department or when a regulation has, in the opinion of the department, bureau, or officer sending the statement, any bearing on the claim, it shall be distinctly quoted at length in the statement. When more than one case or class of cases is pending, the defense of which rests on the same facts, circumstances, and proofs, the department, bureau, or officer may certify and send one statement and it shall be held to apply to all cases as if made out, certified, and sent in each case respectively.

(Added Pub.L. 89–554, § 4(c), Sept. 6, 1966, 80 Stat. 614, and amended Pub.L. 97–164, Title I, § 118(a), Apr. 2, 1982, 96 Stat. 32; Pub.L. 102–572, Title IX, § 902(b)(1), Oct. 29, 1992, 106 Stat. 4516.)

HISTORICAL AND STATUTORY NOTES

Effective and Applicability Provisions

1992 Acts. Amendment by Pub.L. 102–572 effective Oct. 29, 1992, see section 911 of Pub.L. 102–572, set out as a note under section 171 of this title.

1982 Acts. Amendment by Pub.L. 97–164 effective Oct. 1, 1982, see section 402 of Pub.L. 97–164, set out as a note under section 171 of this title.

Change of Name

References to United States Claims Court deemed to refer to United States Court of Federal Claims and references to Claims Court deemed to refer to Court of Federal Claims, see section 902(b) of Pub.L. 102–572, set out as a note under section 171 of Title 28, Judiciary and Judicial Procedure.

§ 521. Publication and distribution of opinions

The Attorney General, from time to time—

(1) shall cause to be edited, and printed in the Government Printing Office, such of his opinions as he considers valuable for preservation in volumes; and

(2) may prescribe the manner for the distribution of the volumes.

Each volume shall contain headnotes, an index, and such footnotes as the Attorney General may approve.

(Added Pub.L. 89–554, § 4(c), Sept. 6, 1966, 80 Stat. 614.)

§ 522. Report of business and statistics

(a) The Attorney General, by April 1 of each year, shall report to Congress on the business of the Department of Justice for the last preceding fiscal year, and on any other matters pertaining to the Department that he considers proper, including—

(1) a statement of the several appropriations which are placed under the control of the Department and the amount appropriated;

(2) the statistics of crime under the laws of the United States; and

(3) a statement of the number of causes involving the United States, civil and criminal, pending during the preceding year in each of the several courts of the United States.

(b) With respect to any data, records, or other information acquired, collected, classified, preserved, or published by the Attorney General for any statistical, research, or other aggregate reporting purpose beginning not later than 1 year after the date of enactment[1] of 21st Century Department of Justice Appropriations Authorization Act and continuing thereafter, and notwithstanding any other provision of law, the same criteria shall be used (and shall be required to be used, as applicable) to classify or categorize offenders and victims (in the criminal context), and to classify or categorize actors and acted upon (in the noncriminal context).

(Added Pub.L. 89–554, § 4(c), Sept. 6, 1966, 80 Stat. 615, and amended Pub.L. 94–273, § 19, Apr. 21, 1976, 90 Stat. 379; Pub.L. 107–273, Div. A, Title II, § 204(b), Nov. 2, 2002, 116 Stat. 1776.)

[1] So in original. Probably should be followed by "the".

HISTORICAL AND STATUTORY NOTES

References in Text

The date of enactment of the 21st Century Department of Justice Appropriations Authorization Act, referred to in subsec. (b), is the date of enactment of Pub.L. 107–273, 116 Stat. 1758, which was approved Nov. 2, 2002.

Termination of Reporting Requirements

Reporting requirement of this section excepted from termination under Pub.L. 104–66, § 3003(a)(1), as amended, set out in a note under 31 U.S.C.A. § 1113, see Pub.L. 106–197, § 1, set out as a note under 31 U.S.C.A. § 1113.

Congressional Oversight

Pub.L. 100–700, § 6, Nov. 19, 1988, 102 Stat. 4634, which required the Attorney General to report annually to Congress on referrals of fraud cases and related matters, terminated, effective May 15, 2000, pursuant to Pub.L. 104–66, § 3003, as amended, set out as a note under 31 U.S.C.A. § 1113. See, also, page 120 of House Document No. 103–7.

Report to Congress on Banking Law Offenses

Pub.L. 101–647, Title XXV, § 2546, Nov. 29, 1990, 104 Stat. 4885, provided that:

"(a) **In general.**—

"(1) **Data collection.**—The Attorney General shall compile and collect data concerning—

"(A) the nature and number of civil and criminal investigations, prosecutions, and related proceedings, and civil enforcement and recovery proceedings, in progress with respect to banking law offenses under sections 981, 1008, 1032, and 3322(d) of title 18, United States Code [18 U.S.C.A. §§ 981, 1008, 1032, and 3322(d)], and section 951 of the Financial Institutions Reform, Recovery, and Enforcement Act of 1989 [12 U.S.C.A. § 1833a] and conspiracies to commit any such offense, including inactive investigations of such offenses;

"(B) the number of—

"(i) investigations, prosecutions, and related proceedings described in subparagraph (A) which are inactive as of the close of the reporting period but have not been closed or declined; and

"(ii) unaddressed referrals which allege criminal misconduct involving offenses described in subparagraph (A),

and the reasons such matters are inactive and the referrals unaddressed;

"(C) the nature and number of such matters closed, settled, or litigated to conclusion; and

"(D) the results achieved, including convictions and pretrial diversions, fines and penalties levied, restitution assessed and collected, and damages recovered, in such matters.

"(2) **Analysis and report.**—The Attorney General shall analyze and report to the Congress on the data described in paragraph (1) and its coordination and other related activities named in section 2539(c)(2) [probably means section 2539(c)(3) of Pub.L. 101–647, set out as a note under 28 U.S.C.A. § 509] and shall provide such report on the data monthly through December 31, 1991, and quarterly after such date.

"(b) **Specifics of Report.**—The report required by subsection (a) shall—

"(1) categorize data as to various types of financial institutions and appropriate dollar loss categories;

"(2) disclose data for each Federal judicial district;

"(3) describe the activities of the Financial Institution Fraud Unit; and

"(4) list—

"(A) the number of institutions, categorized by failed and open institutions, in which evidence of significant fraud, unlawful activity, insider abuse or serious misconduct has been alleged or detected;

"(B) civil, criminal, and administrative enforcement actions, including those of the Federal financial institutions regulatory agencies, brought against offenders;

"(C) any settlements or judgments obtained against offenders;

"(D) indictments, guilty pleas, or verdicts obtained against offenders; and

"(E) the resources allocated in pursuit of investigations, prosecutions, and sentencings (including indictments, guilty pleas, or verdicts obtained against offenders) and related proceedings."

[Reporting requirement of section 2546 of the Comprehensive Thrift and Bank Fraud Prosecution and Taxpayer Recovery Act of 1990, set out above, excepted from termination under Pub.L. 104–66, § 3003(a)(1), as amended, set out as a note under 31 U.S.C.A. § 1113, see Pub.L. 106–569, § 1102, set out as a note under 31 U.S.C.A. § 1113.]

Report to Congress on Robberies and Burglaries Involving Controlled Substances

Pub.L. 98–305, § 4, May 31, 1984, 98 Stat. 222, provided that: "For each of the first three years after the date of enactment of this Act [May 31, 1984], the Attorney General of the United States shall submit an annual report to the Congress with respect to the enforcement activities of the Attorney General relating to the offenses created by the amendment made by section 2 of this Act [enacting section 2118 of Title 18, Crimes and Criminal Procedure]."

Report to Congress on Sexual Exploitation of Children

Pub.L. 98–292, § 9, May 21, 1984, 98 Stat. 206, provided that: "Beginning one hundred and twenty days after the date of enactment of this Act [May 21, 1984], and every year thereafter, the Attorney General shall report to the Congress on prosecutions, convictions, and forfeitures under chapter 110 of title 18 of the United States Code [18 U.S.C.A. § 2251 et seq.]."

[Reporting requirement of section 9 of the Child Protection Act of 1984, set out above, excepted from termination under Pub.L. 104–66, § 3003(a)(1), as amended, set out in a note under 31 U.S.C.A. § 1113, see Pub.L. 106–197, § 1, set out as a note under 31 U.S.C.A. § 1113.]

§ 523. Requisitions

The Attorney General shall sign all requisitions for the advance or payment of moneys appropriated for the Department of Justice, out of the Treasury, subject to the same control as is exercised on like estimates or accounts by the Government Accountability Office.

(Added Pub.L. 89–554, § 4(c), Sept. 6, 1966, 80 Stat. 615, and amended Pub.L. 108–271, § 8(b), July 7, 2004, 118 Stat. 814.)

HISTORICAL AND STATUTORY NOTES

Change of Name

"Government Accountability Office" substituted for "General Accounting Office" in text on authority of Pub.L. 108–271, § 8(b), cited in the credit to this section and set out as a note under 31 U.S.C.A. § 702, which provided that any reference to the General Accounting Office in any law, rule, regulation, certificate, directive, instruction, or other official paper in force on July 17, 2004, to refer and apply to the Government Accountability Office.

§ 524. Availability of appropriations

(a) Appropriations for the Department of Justice are available to the Attorney General for payment of—

(1) notarial fees, including such additional stenographic services as are required in connection therewith in the taking of depositions, and compensation and expenses of witnesses and informants, all at the rates authorized or approved by the Attorney General or the Assistant Attorney General for Administration; and

(2) when ordered by the court, actual expenses of meals and lodging for marshals, deputy marshals, or criers when acting as bailiffs in attendance on juries.

(b) Except as provided in subsection (a) of this section, a claim of not more than $500 for expenses related to litigation that is beyond the control of the Department may be paid out of appropriations currently available to the Department for expenses related to litigation when the Comptroller General settles the payment.

(c)(1) There is established in the United States Treasury a special fund to be known as the Department of Justice Assets Forfeiture Fund (hereafter in this subsection referred to as the "Fund") which shall be available to the Attorney General without fiscal year limitation for the following law enforcement purposes—

(A) the payment, at the discretion of the Attorney General, of any expenses necessary to seize, detain, inventory, safeguard, maintain, advertise, sell, or dispose of property under seizure, detention, or forfeited pursuant to any law enforced or administered by the Department of Justice, or of any other necessary expense incident to the seizure, detention, forfeiture, or disposal of such property including—

(i) payments for—

(I) contract services;

(II) the employment of outside contractors to operate and manage properties or provide other specialized services necessary to dispose of such properties in an effort to maximize the return from such properties; and

(III) reimbursement of any Federal, State, or local agency for any expenditures made to perform the functions described in this clause;

(ii) payments to reimburse any Federal agency participating in the Fund for investigative costs leading to seizures;

(iii) payments for contracting for the services of experts and consultants needed by the Department of Justice to assist in carrying out duties related to asset seizure and forfeiture; and

(iv) payments made pursuant to guidelines promulgated by the Attorney General if such payments are necessary and directly related to seizure and forfeiture program expenses for—

(I) the purchase or lease of automatic data processing systems (not less than a majority of which use will be related to such program);

(II) training;

(III) printing;

(IV) the storage, protection, and destruction of controlled substances; and

(V) contracting for services directly related to the identification of forfeitable assets, and the processing of and accounting for forfeitures;

(B) the payment of awards for information or assistance directly relating to violations of the criminal drug laws of the United States or of sections 1956 and 1957 of title 18, sections 5313 and 5324 of title 31, and section 6050I of the Internal Revenue Code of 1986;

(C) at the discretion of the Attorney General, the payment of awards for information or assistance leading to a civil or criminal forfeiture involving any Federal agency participating in the Fund;

(D) the compromise and payment of valid liens and mortgages against property that has been forfeited pursuant to any law enforced or administered by the Department of Justice, subject to the discretion of the Attorney General to determine the validity of any such lien or mortgage and the amount of payment to be made, and the employment of attorneys and other personnel skilled in State real estate law as necessary;

(E)(i) for disbursements authorized in connection with remission or mitigation procedures relating to property forfeited under any law enforced or administered by the Department of Justice; and

(ii) for payment for—

(I) costs incurred by or on behalf of the Department of Justice in connection with the removal, for purposes of Federal forfeiture and disposition, of any hazardous substance or pollutant or contaminant associated with the illegal manufacture of amphetamine or methamphetamine; and

(II) costs incurred by or on behalf of a State or local government in connection with such removal in any case in which such State or local government has assisted in a Federal prosecution relating to amphetamine or methamphetamine, to the extent such costs exceed equitable sharing payments made to such State or local government in such case;

(F)(i) for equipping for law enforcement functions of any Government-owned or leased vessel, vehicle, or aircraft available for official use by any Federal agency participating in the Fund;

(ii) for equipping any vessel, vehicle, or aircraft available for official use by a State or local law enforcement agency to enable the vessel, vehicle, or aircraft to assist law enforcement functions if the vessel, vehicle, or aircraft will be used in a joint law enforcement operation with a Federal agency participating in the Fund; and

(iii) payments for other equipment directly related to seizure or forfeiture, including laboratory equipment, protective equipment, communications equipment, and the operation and maintenance costs of such equipment;

(G) for purchase of evidence of any violation of the Controlled Substances Act, the Controlled Substances Import and Export Act, chapter 96 of title 18, or sections 1956 and 1957 of title 18;

(H) the payment of State and local property taxes on forfeited real property that accrued between the date of the violation giving rise to the forfeiture and the date of the forfeiture order; and

(I) payment of overtime salaries, travel, fuel, training, equipment, and other similar costs of State or local law enforcement officers that are incurred in a joint law enforcement operation with a Federal law enforcement agency participating in the Fund.

Amounts for paying the expenses authorized by subparagraphs (B), (F), and (G) shall be specified in appropriations Acts and may be used under authorities available to the organization receiving the funds. Amounts for other authorized expenditures and payments from the Fund, including equitable sharing payments, are not required to be specified in appropriations acts. The Attorney General may exempt the procurement of contract services under subparagraph (A) under the Fund from section 3709 of the Revised Statutes of the United States (41 U.S.C. 5), title III of the Federal Property and Administrative Services Act of 1949 (41 U.S.C. 251 and following), and other provisions of law as may be necessary to maintain the security and confidentiality of related criminal investigations.

(2) Any award paid from the Fund, as provided in paragraph (1)(B) or (C), shall be paid at the discretion of the Attorney General or his delegate, under existing departmental delegation policies for the payment of awards, except that the authority to pay an award of $250,000 or more shall not be delegated to any person other than the Deputy Attorney General, the Associate Attorney General, the Director of the Federal Bureau of Investigation, or the Administrator of the Drug Enforcement Administration. Any award pursuant to paragraph (1)(B) shall not exceed $500,000. Any award pursuant to paragraph (1)(C) shall not exceed the lesser of $500,000 or one-fourth of the amount realized by the United States from the property forfeited, without both the personal approval of the Attorney General and written notice within 30 days thereof to the Chairmen and ranking minority members of the Committees on Appropriations and the Judiciary of the Senate and of the House of Representatives.

(3) Any amount under subparagraph (G) of paragraph (1) shall be paid at the discretion of the Attorney General or his delegate, except that the authority to pay $100,000 or more may be delegated only to the respective head of the agency involved.

(4) There shall be deposited in the Fund—

(A) all amounts from the forfeiture of property under any law enforced or administered by the Department of Justice, except all proceeds of forfeitures available for use by the Secretary of the Treasury or the Secretary of the Interior pursuant to section 11(d) of the Endangered Species Act (16 U.S.C. 1540(d)) or section 6(d) of the Lacey Act Amendments of 1981 (16 U.S.C. 3375(d)), or the Postmaster General of the United States pursuant to 39 U.S.C. 2003(b)(7);

(B) all amounts representing the Federal equitable share from the forfeiture of property under any Federal, State, local or foreign law, for any Federal agency participating in the Fund;

(C) all amounts transferred by the Secretary of the Treasury pursuant to section 9703(g)(4)(A)(ii) of title 31; and

(D) all amounts collected—

(i) by the United States pursuant to a reimbursement order under paragraph (2) of section 413(q) of the Controlled Substances Act (21 U.S.C. 853(q)); and

(ii) pursuant to a restitution order under paragraph (1) or (3) of section 413(q) of the Controlled

Substances Act [21 U.S.C.A. § 853(q)] for injuries to the United States.

(5) Amounts in the Fund, and in any holding accounts associated with the Fund, that are not currently needed for the purpose of this section[1] shall be kept on deposit or invested in obligations of, or guaranteed by, the United States and all earnings on such investments shall be deposited in the Fund.

(6)(A) The Attorney General shall transmit to Congress and make available to the public, not later than 4 months after the end of each fiscal year, detailed reports for the prior fiscal year as follows:

(i) A report on total deposits to the Fund by State of deposit.

(ii) A report on total expenses paid from the Fund, by category of expense and recipient agency, including equitable sharing payments.

(iii) A report describing the number, value, and types of properties placed into official use by Federal agencies, by recipient agency.

(iv) A report describing the number, value, and types of properties transferred to State and local law enforcement agencies, by recipient agency.

(v) A report, by type of disposition, describing the number, value, and types of forfeited property disposed of during the year.

(vi) A report on the year-end inventory of property under seizure, but not yet forfeited, that reflects the type of property, its estimated value, and the estimated value of liens and mortgages outstanding on the property.

(vii) A report listing each property in the year-end inventory, not yet forfeited, with an outstanding equity of not less than $1,000,000.

(B) The Attorney General shall transmit to Congress and make available to the public, not later than 2 months after final issuance, the audited financial statements for each fiscal year for the Fund.

(C) Reports under subparagraph (A) shall include information with respect to all forfeitures under any law enforced or administered by the Department of Justice.

(D) The transmittal and publication requirements in subparagraphs (A) and (B) may be satisfied by—

(i) posting the reports on an Internet website maintained by the Department of Justice for a period of not less than 2 years; and

(ii) notifying the Committees on the Judiciary of the House of Representatives and the Senate when the reports are available electronically.

(7) The provisions of this subsection relating to deposits in the Fund shall apply to all property in the custody of the Department of Justice on or after the effective date of the Comprehensive Forfeiture Act of 1983.

(8)(A) There are authorized to be appropriated such sums as necessary for the purposes described in subparagraphs (B), (F), and (G) of paragraph (1).

(B) Subject to subparagraphs (C) and (D), at the end of each of fiscal years 1994, 1995, and 1996, the Attorney General shall transfer from the Fund not more than $100,000,000 to the Special Forfeiture Fund established by section 6073 of the Anti-Drug Abuse Act of 1988.

(C) Transfers under subparagraph (B) may be made only from the excess unobligated balance and may not exceed one-half of the excess unobligated balance for any year. In addition, transfers under subparagraph (B) may be made only to the extent that the sum of the transfers in a fiscal year and one-half of the unobligated balance at the beginning of that fiscal year for the Special Forfeiture Fund does not exceed $100,000,000.

(D) For the purpose of determining amounts available for distribution at year end for any fiscal year, "excess unobligated balance" means the unobligated balance of the Fund generated by that fiscal year's operations, less any amounts that are required to be retained in the Fund to ensure the availability of amounts in the subsequent fiscal year for purposes authorized under paragraph (1).

(E) Subject to the notification procedures contained in section 605 of Public Law 103–121, and after satisfying the transfer requirement in subparagraph (B) of this paragraph, any excess unobligated balance remaining in the Fund on September 30, 1997 and thereafter shall be available to the Attorney General, without fiscal year limitation, for any Federal law enforcement, litigative/prosecutive, and correctional activities, or any other authorized purpose of the Department of Justice. Any amounts provided pursuant to this subparagraph may be used under authorities available to the organization receiving the funds.

(9)(A) Following the completion of procedures for the forfeiture of property pursuant to any law enforced or administered by the Department, the Attorney General is authorized, in her discretion, to warrant clear title to any subsequent purchaser or transferee of such property.

(B) For fiscal years 2002 and 2003, the Attorney General is authorized to transfer, under such terms and conditions as the Attorney General shall specify, real or personal property of limited or marginal value, to a State or local government agency, or its designated contractor or transferee, for use to support drug abuse treatment, drug and crime prevention and education, housing, job skills, and other community-based public health and safety programs. Each such transfer shall be subject to satisfaction by the recipient involved of any outstanding lien against the property transferred, but no such transfer shall create or confer any private right of action in any person against the United States.

(10) The Attorney General shall transfer from the Fund to the Secretary of the Treasury for deposit in the Department of the Treasury Forfeiture Fund amounts appropriate to reflect the degree of participation of the Department of the Treasury law enforcement organizations (described in section 9703(p) of title 31) in the law enforcement effort resulting in the forfeiture pursuant to laws enforced or administered by the Department of Justice.

(11) For purposes of this subsection and notwithstanding section 9703 of title 31 or any other law, property is forfeited pursuant to a law enforced or administered by the Department of Justice if it is forfeited pursuant to—

(A) a judicial forfeiture proceeding when the underlying seizure was made by an officer of a Federal law enforcement agency participating in the Department of Justice Assets Forfeiture Fund or the property was maintained by the United States Marshals Service; or

(B) a civil administrative forfeiture proceeding conducted by a Department of Justice law enforcement component or pursuant to the authority of the Secretary of Commerce.

(d)(1) The Attorney General may accept, hold, administer, and use gifts, devises, and bequests of any property or services for the purpose of aiding or facilitating the work of the Department of Justice.

(2) Gifts, devises, and bequests of money, the proceeds of sale or liquidation of any other property accepted hereunder, and any income accruing from any property accepted hereunder—

(A) shall be deposited in the Treasury in a separate fund and held in trust by the Secretary of the Treasury for the benefit of the Department of Justice; and

(B) are hereby appropriated, without fiscal year limitation, and shall be disbursed on order of the Attorney General.

(3) Upon request of the Attorney General, the Secretary of the Treasury may invest and reinvest the fund described herein in public debt securities with maturities suitable for the needs of the fund and bearing interest at rates determined by the Secretary of the Treasury, taking into consideration the current average market yield on outstanding marketable obligations of the United States or comparable maturities.

(4) Evidences of any intangible personal property (other than money) accepted hereunder shall be deposited with the Secretary of the Treasury, who may hold or liquidate them, except that they shall be liquidated upon the request of the Attorney General.

(5) For purposes of federal income, estate, and gift taxes, property accepted hereunder shall be considered a gift, devise, or bequest to, or for the use of, the United States.

(Added Pub.L. 89–554, § 4(c), Sept. 6, 1966, 80 Stat. 615, and amended Pub.L. 97–258, § 2(g)(1)(B) to (D), Sept. 13, 1982, 96 Stat. 1060; Pub.L. 98–473, Title II, §§ 310, 2303, Oct. 12, 1984, 98 Stat. 2052, 2193; Pub.L. 99–570, Title I, § 1152(a), Oct. 27, 1986, 100 Stat. 3207–12; Pub.L. 99–646, § 27, Nov. 10, 1986, 100 Stat. 3597; Pub.L. 100–202, § 101(a)[Title II, § 210(a)], Dec. 22, 1987, 101 Stat. 1329, 1329–18; Pub.L. 100–690, Title VI, § 6072, Nov. 18, 1988, 102 Stat. 4320; Pub.L. 101–509, Title III, § 1, Nov. 5, 1990, 104 Stat. 1403; Pub.L. 101–647, Title XVI, § 1601, Title XX, §§ 2001(a), 2002, 2005, 2006, Nov. 29, 1990, 104 Stat. 4842, 4854, 4855; Pub.L. 102–27, Title II, § 101, Apr. 10, 1991, 105 Stat. 135; Pub.L. 102–140, Title I, § 112, Oct. 28, 1991, 105 Stat. 795; Pub.L. 102–393, Title VI, § 638(f), Oct. 6, 1992, 106 Stat. 1788; Pub.L. 102–395, Title I, § 114(b), (c), Oct. 6, 1992, 106 Stat. 1845; Pub.L. 102–550, Title XV, § 1529, Oct. 28, 1992, 106 Stat. 4065; Pub.L. 103–121, Title I, § 109, Oct. 27, 1993, 107 Stat. 1164; Pub.L. 103–317, Title I, § 110, Aug. 26, 1994, 108 Stat. 1735; Pub.L. 103–322, Title IX, § 90205(b), Title XXXII, §§ 320301, 320302, 320913(a), Sept. 13, 1994, 108 Stat. 1994, 2114, 2128; Pub.L. 104–66, Title I, § 1091(h), Dec. 21, 1995, 109 Stat. 722; Pub.L. 104–91, Title I, § 101(a), Jan. 6, 1996, 110 Stat. 11; Pub.L. 104–99, Title II, § 211, Jan. 26, 1996, 110 Stat. 37; Pub.L. 104–134, Title I, § 101[(a)][Title I, § 122], Apr. 26, 1996, 110 Stat. 1321–22; renumbered Title I Pub.L. 104–140, § 1(a), May 2, 1996, 110 Stat. 1327, and amended Pub.L. 104–208, Div. A, Title I, § 101(a) [Title I, §§ 108, 114, 116, 117], Sept. 30, 1996, 110 Stat. 3009–18, 3009–22, 3009–23; Pub.L. 105–119, Title I, §§ 108, 124, Title II, § 211(b), Nov. 26, 1997, 111 Stat. 2457, 2471, 2487; Pub.L. 105–272, Title VI, § 605, Oct. 20, 1998, 112 Stat. 2413; Pub.L. 106–185, § 19, Apr. 25, 2000, 114 Stat. 223; Pub.L. 106–310, Div. B, Title XXXVI, §§ 3613(b), 3621(a), Oct. 17, 2000, 114 Stat. 1230; Pub.L. 107–273, Div. A, Title II, § 204(a), Nov. 2, 2002, 116 Stat. 1775.)

[1] So in original. Probably should be followed by a comma.

HISTORICAL AND STATUTORY NOTES

References in Text

The Controlled Substances Act, referred to in subsec. (c)(1)(G), is Title II of Pub.L. 91–513, Oct. 27, 1970, 84 Stat. 1242, as amended, which is classified principally to subchapter I (section 801 et seq.) of chapter 13 of Title 21, Food and Drugs. For complete classification of this Act to the Code, see Short Title note set out under section 801 of Title 21 and Tables.

The Controlled Substances Import and Export Act, referred to in subsec. (c)(1)(G), is Title III of Pub.L. 91–513, Oct. 27, 1970, 84 Stat. 1285, as amended, which is classified principally to subchapter II (section 951 et seq.) of chapter 13 of Title 21. For complete classification of this Act to the Code, see Short Title note set out under section 951 of Title 21 and Tables.

The Federal Property and Administrative Services Act of 1949, referred to in subsec. (c)(1) closing provisions, is Act June 30, 1949, c. 288, 63 Stat. 377, as amended, Title III of which is currently classified to subchapter IV of chapter 4 of Title 41, 41 U.S.C.A. § 251 et seq., and the remainder of which was formerly classified to chapter 10 of former Title 40, 40 U.S.C.A. § 471 et seq., prior to being repealed by Pub.L. 107–217, § 6(b), Aug. 21, 2002, 116 Stat. 1313; see now generally chapter 1 of Title 40, 40 U.S.C.A. § 101 et seq.

The effective date of the Comprehensive Forfeiture Act of 1983, referred to in subsec. (c)(7), probably means the date of enactment of the Comprehensive Forfeiture Act of 1984, chapter III (sections 301 to 323) of title II of Pub.L. 98–473, which was approved Oct. 12, 1984.

Section 6073 of the Anti-Drug Abuse Act of 1988, referred to in subsec. (c)(8)(B), is section 6073 of Pub.L. 100–690, Nov. 18, 1988, 102 Stat. 4323, as amended, which is classified to section 1509 of Title 21, Food and Drugs.

Section 605 of Public Law 103–121, referred to in subsec. (c)(8)(E), was not classified to the Code.

Codifications

Section 101(a) of Pub.L. 104–91, as amended by section 211 of Pub.L. 104–99, provided in part that section 109 of the General Provisions for the Department of Justice in Title I of the Departments of Commerce, Justice, and State, the Judiciary, and Related Agencies Appropriations Act, 1996 (H.R. 2076) as passed by the House of Representatives on Dec. 6, 1995, was enacted into permanent law. Such section 109 of H.R. 2076 directed that subsec. (c)(9) of this section be amended by adding a subpar. (E). However section 110 of Pub.L. 103–317 had previously added a subpar. (E) to former subsec. (c)(9), prior to the redesignation of former subsec. (c)(9) and (10) as subsec. (c)(8) and (9), respectively, by section 1091(h) of Pub.L. 104–66. The subpar. (E) added by section 101(a) of Pub.L. 104–91, as amended, was inserted following the subpar. (E) added by section 110 of Pub.L. 103–317 in subsec. (c)(8), as redesignated, as the probable intent of Congress, because subsec. (c)(9), as redesignated, contained no subpars. (A) through (D). Subpar. (E) as added by Pub.L. 103–317 was subsequently repealed by Pub.L. 104–134, resulting in only one subsec. (c)(8)(E) remaining.

Effective and Applicability Provisions

2000 Acts. Amendments by Pub.L. 106–185, applicable to any forfeiture proceeding commenced on or after the date that is 120 days after April 25, 2000, see section 21 of Pub.L. 106–185, set out as a note under section 1324 of Title 8.

1999 Acts. Pub.L. 106–113, Div. B, § 1000(a)(1) [Title I, § 109], Nov. 29, 1999, 113 Stat. 1535, 1501A–20, provided that: "Sections 115 and 127 of the Departments of Commerce, Justice, and State, the Judiciary, and Related Agencies Appropriations Act, 1999 (as contained in section 101(b) of division A of Public Law 105–277) [enacting a note provision under this section and section 1997e of Title 42, respectively] shall apply to fiscal year 2000 and thereafter."

1994 Acts. Section 320913(b) of Pub.L. 103–322 provided that: "The amendment made by subsection (a) [amending this section] shall apply to all claims pending at the time of or commenced subsequent to the date of enactment of this Act [Sept. 13, 1994]."

1992 Acts. Except as otherwise provided, amendment by Pub.L. 102–550 effective Oct. 28, 1992, see section 2 of Pub.L. 102–550, set out as a note under section 5301 of Title 42, The Public Health and Welfare.

Termination of Reporting Requirements

Reporting requirement of subsec. (c)(6) of this section excepted from termination under Pub.L. 104–66, § 3003(a)(1), as amended, set out in a note under 31 U.S.C.A. § 1113, see Pub.L. 106–197, § 1, set out as a note under 31 U.S.C.A. § 1113.

Transfer of Forfeited Real or Personal Property

Pub.L. 108–199, Div. B, Title I, § 108, Jan. 23, 2004, 118 Stat. 61, provided that:

"**(a)** Hereafter [on or after Jan. 23, 2004], the Attorney General is authorized to transfer, under such terms and conditions as the Attorney General shall specify, forfeited real or personal property of limited or marginal value, as such value is determined by guidelines established by the Attorney General, to a State or local government agency, or its designated contractor or transferee, for use to support drug abuse treatment, drug and crime prevention and education, housing, job skills, and other community-based public health and safety programs.

"**(b)** Any transfer under the preceding proviso shall not create or confer any private right of action in any person against the United States, and shall be treated as a reprogramming under section 605 of this Act [the Departments of Commerce, Justice, and State, the Judiciary, and Related Agencies Appropriations Act, 2004, Pub.L. 108–199, Div. B, Title VI, § 605, Jan. 23, 2004, 118 Stat. 93, which is not classified to the Code]."

Counterterrorism Fund

Pub.L. 107–56, Title I, § 101, Oct. 26, 2001, 115 Stat. 276, provided that:

"**(a) Establishment; availability.**—There is hereby established in the Treasury of the United States a separate fund to be known as the 'Counterterrorism Fund', amounts in which shall remain available without fiscal year limitation—

"**(1)** To reimburse any Department of Justice component for any costs incurred in connection with—

"**(A)** reestablishing the operational capability of an office or facility that has been damaged or destroyed as the result of any domestic or international terrorism incident;

"**(B)** providing support to counter, investigate, or prosecute domestic or international terrorism, including, without limitation, paying rewards in connection with these activities; and

"**(C)** conducting terrorism threat assessments of Federal agencies and their facilities; and

"**(2)** to reimburse any department or agency of the Federal Government for any costs incurred in connection with detaining in foreign countries individuals accused of acts of terrorism that violate the laws of the United States.

"**(b) No effect on prior appropriations.**—Subsection (a) shall not be construed to affect the amount or availability of any appropriation to the Counterterrorism Fund made before the date of the enactment of this Act [Oct. 26, 2001]."

Grant Funds for Pay-to-Stay Programs

Pub.L. 106–553, § 1(a)(2) [Title I, § 117, formerly § 118], Dec. 21, 2000, 114 Stat. 2762, 2762A–69; renumbered § 117, Pub.L. 106–554, § 1(a)(4) [Div. A, § 213(a)(2)], Dec. 21, 2000,

114 Stat. 2763, 2763a–179, provided that: "Notwithstanding any other provision of law, for fiscal 2001 and hereafter, with respect to any grant program for which amounts are made available under this title [the Department of Justice Appropriations Act, 2001, Pub.L. 106–553, § 1(a)(2) [Title I], Dec. 21, 2000, 114 Stat. 2762, 2762A–69; see Tables for complete classification], no grant funds may be made available to any local jail that runs 'pay-to-stay programs'."

Assets Forfeiture Fund

Pub.L. 106–310, Div. B, Title XXXVI, § 3621(c)(1), Oct. 17, 2000, 114 Stat. 1231, provided that: "Any amounts made available from the Department of Justice Assets Forfeiture Fund in a fiscal year by reason of the amendment made by subsection (a) [amending subsec. (c)(1)(E) of this section] shall supplement, and not supplant, any other amounts made available to the Department of Justice in such fiscal year from other sources for payment of costs described in section 524(c)(1)(E)(ii) of title 28, United States Code, as so amended."

Definition of "Tribe", "Indian Tribe" or "Tribal" in Regard to Federal Grant Programs

Pub.L. 105–277, § 101(b) [Title I, § 113], Oct. 21, 1998, 112 Stat. 2681–67, as amended Pub.L. 106–31, § 3028, May 21, 1999, 113 Stat. 102; Pub.L. 106–113, Div. B, § 1000(a)(1) [Title I, § 116], Nov. 29, 1999, 113 Stat. 1535, 1501A–21, provided that: "Notwithstanding any other provision of law for fiscal year 2000 and hereafter, with respect to any grant program for which amounts are made available under this title, the terms 'tribe', 'Indian tribe' or 'tribal' mean of or relating to an Indian tribe as that term is defined in section 4(e) of the Indian Self Determination and Education Assistance Act (Public Law 93–638, as amended; 25 U.S.C. 450b(e) (1998))."

Funds for Counterterrorism Programs, Projects or Activities

Pub.L. 105–277, § 101(b) [Title I, § 115], Oct. 21, 1998, 112 Stat. 2681–68, provided:

"(a)(1) Notwithstanding any other provision of law, for fiscal year 1999, the Attorney General may obligate any funds appropriated for or reimbursed to the Counterterrorism programs, projects or activities of the Department of Justice to purchase or lease equipment or any related items, or to acquire interim services, without regard to any otherwise applicable Federal acquisition rule, if the Attorney General determines that—

"(A) there is an exigent need for the equipment, related items, or services in order to support an ongoing counterterrorism, national security, or computer-crime investigation or prosecution;

"(B) the equipment, related items, or services required are not available within the Department of Justice; and

"(C) adherence to that Federal acquisition rule would—

"(i) delay the timely acquisition of the equipment, related items, or services; and

"(ii) adversely affect an ongoing counterterrorism, national security, or computer-crime investigation or prosecution.

"(2) In this subsection, the term 'Federal acquisition rule' means any provision of title II or IX of the Federal Property and Administrative Services Act of 1949, the Office of Federal Procurement Policy Act, the Small Business Act, the Federal Acquisition Regulation, or any other provision of law or regulation that establishes policies, procedures, requirements, conditions, or restrictions for procurements by the head of a department or agency or the Federal Government.

"(b) The Attorney General shall immediately notify the Committees on Appropriations of the House of Representatives and the Senate in writing of each expenditure under subsection (a), which notification shall include sufficient information to explain the circumstances necessitating the exercise of the authority under that subsection."

Counterterrorism Fund

Pub.L. 104–19, Title III, July 27, 1995, 109 Stat. 249, provided in part that: "There is hereby established the Counterterrorism Fund which shall remain available without fiscal year limitation. For necessary expenses, as determined by the Attorney General, $34,220,000, to remain available until expended, is appropriated to the Counterterrorism Fund to reimburse any Department of Justice organization for the costs incurred in reestablishing the operational capability of an office or facility which has been damaged or destroyed as the result of the bombing of the Alfred P. Murrah Federal Building in Oklahoma City or any domestic or international terrorism event: *Provided*, That funds from this appropriation also may be used to reimburse the appropriation account of any Department of Justice agency engaged in, or providing support to, countering, investigating or prosecuting domestic or international terrorism, including payment of rewards in connection with these activities, and to conduct a terrorism threat assessment of Federal agencies and their facilities: *Provided further*, That any amount obligated from appropriations under this heading may be used under the authorities available to the organization reimbursed from this appropriation: *Provided further*, That amounts in excess of the $10,555,000 made available for extraordinary expenses incurred in the Oklahoma City bombing for fiscal year 1995, shall be available only after the Attorney General notifies the Committees on Appropriations of the House of Representatives and the Senate in accordance with section 605 of Public Law 103–317 [not classified to the Code]: *Provided further*, That the entire amount is designated by Congress as an emergency requirement pursuant to section 251(b)(2)(D)(i) of the Balanced Budget and Emergency Deficit Control Act of 1985 [section 901(b)(2)(D)(i) of Title 2, The Congress], as amended: *Provided further*, That the amount not previously designated by the President as an emergency requirement shall be available only to the extent an official budget request, for a specific dollar amount that includes designation of the entire amount of the request as an emergency requirement, as defined in the Balanced Budget and Emergency Deficit Control Act of 1985, as amended [Pub.L. 99–177, Dec. 12, 1985, 99 Stat. 1037, for classifications of which to the Code see Tables], is transmitted to Congress."

Notice and Approval of Transfer of Subsec. (c)(1)(H) Deposits

Section 101(a) [Title II, § 210(b)] of Pub.L. 100–202 provided that: "Amounts proposed for transfer pursuant to subsection (a) [amending this section] shall be transferred only upon notification by the Attorney General to the Committees on Appropriations of the House of Representatives and the Senate and approval under said Committees' policies concerning the reprogramming of funds."

Unauthorized Transfers from Department of Justice Accounts; Control of Allocation of Funds by Authority Other Than Office of Management and Budget or Department of Justice

Pub.L. 104–91, Title I, § 101(a), Jan. 6, 1996, 110 Stat. 11, as amended Pub.L. 104–99, Title II, § 211, Jan. 26, 1996, 110 Stat. 37, provided, in part, that: "Hereafter, notwithstanding any other provision of law—

"(1) No transfers may be made from Department of Justice accounts other than those authorized in this Act [probably means H.R. 2076, approved by the House of Representatives on Dec. 6, 1995, see bracketed note following this note], or in previous or subsequent appropriations Acts for the Department of Justice, or in part II of title 28 of the United States Code [section 501 et seq. of this title], or in section 10601 of title 42 of the United States Code [section 10601 of Title 42, The Public Health and Welfare]; and

"(2) No appropriation account within the Department of Justice shall have its allocation of funds controlled by other than an apportionment issued by the Office of Management and Budget or an allotment advice issued by the Department of Justice."

[Section 101(a) of Pub.L. 104–91, as amended by section 211 of Pub.L. 104–99, provided in part that section 110 of the General Provisions for the Department of Justice in Title I of the Departments of Commerce, Justice, and State, the Judiciary, and Related Agencies Appropriations Act, 1996 (H.R. 2076) as passed by the House of Representatives on Dec. 6, 1995, was enacted into permanent law. The text of such section 110 of H.R. 2076 is set out in the above note.]

Similar provisions were contained in the following prior appropriation Act:

Pub.L. 103–317, Title I, § 113, Aug. 26, 1994, 108 Stat. 1736.

Use of Deposits Transferred from Assets Forfeiture Fund to Buildings and Facilities Account of Federal Prison System

Section 106 of Pub.L. 103–121 provided that: "For fiscal year 1994 and thereafter, deposits transferred from the Assets Forfeiture Fund to the Buildings and Facilities account of the Federal Prison System may be used for the construction of correctional institutions, and the construction and renovation of Immigration and Naturalization Service and United States Marshals Service detention facilities, and for the authorized purposes of the Cooperative Agreement Program."

[For abolition of Immigration and Naturalization Service, transfer of functions, and treatment of related references, see note set out under 8 U.S.C.A. § 1551.]

§ 525. Procurement of law books, reference books, and periodicals; sale and exchange

In the procurement of law books, reference books, and periodicals, the Attorney General may exchange or sell similar items and apply the exchange allowances or proceeds of such sales in whole or in part payment therefor.

(Added Pub.L. 89–554, § 4(c), Sept. 6, 1966, 80 Stat. 615.)

§ 526. Authority of Attorney General to investigate United States attorneys, marshals, trustees, clerks of court, and others

(a) The Attorney General may investigate the official acts, records, and accounts of—

(1) the United States attorneys, marshals, trustees, including trustees in cases under title 11; and

(2) at the request and on behalf of the Director of the Administrative Office of the United States Courts, the clerks of the United States courts and of the district court of the Virgin Islands, probation officers, United States magistrate judges, and court reporters;

for which purpose all the official papers, records, dockets, and accounts of these officers, without exception, may be examined by agents of the Attorney General at any time.

(b) Appropriations for the examination of judicial officers are available for carrying out this section.

(Added Pub.L. 89–554, § 4(c), Sept. 6, 1966, 80 Stat. 615, and amended Pub.L. 95–598, Title II, §§ 219(a), (b), 220, Nov. 6, 1978, 92 Stat. 2662; Pub.L. 99–554, Title I, § 144(c), Oct. 27, 1986, 100 Stat. 3096; Pub.L. 101–650, Title III, § 321, Dec. 1, 1990, 104 Stat. 5117; Pub.L. 107–273, Div. B, Title IV, §§ 4003(b)(2), Nov. 2, 2002, 116 Stat. 1811.)

HISTORICAL AND STATUTORY NOTES

Codifications

Pub.L. 95–598, Title IV, § 408(c), Nov. 6, 1978, 92 Stat. 2687, as amended by Pub.L. 98–166, Title II, § 200, Nov. 28, 1983, 97 Stat. 1081; Pub.L. 98–353 Title III, § 323, July 10, 1984, 98 Stat. 358; Pub.L. 99–429, Sept. 30, 1986, 100 Stat. 985; Pub.L. 99–500, § 101(b) [Title II, § 200], Oct. 18, 1986, 100 Stat. 1783–39, 1783–45, and Pub.L. 99–591, § 101(b) [Title II, § 200], Oct. 30, 1986, 100 Stat. 3341–39, 3341–45; Pub.L. 99–554, Title III, § 307(a), Oct. 27, 1986, 100 Stat. 3125, which provided for the deletion of any references to United States Trustees in this title at a prospective date, was repealed by Pub.L. 99–554, Title III, § 307(b), Oct. 27, 1986, 100 Stat. 3125.

Effective and Applicability Provisions

1986 Acts. Amendment by Pub.L. 99–554 effective 30 days after Oct. 27, 1986, see section 302(a) of Pub.L. 99–554, set out as a note under section 581 of this title.

1978 Acts. Amendment by Pub.L. 95–598 effective Oct. 1, 1979, see section 402(c) of Pub.L. 95–598, set out as a note preceding section 101 of Title 11, Bankruptcy.

Change of Name

"United States magistrate judge" substituted for "United States magistrate" in text pursuant to section 321 of Pub.L. 101–650, set out as a note under 28 U.S.C.A. § 631.

§ 527. Establishment of working capital fund

There is hereby authorized to be established a working capital fund for the Department of Justice, which shall be available, without fiscal year limitation, for expenses and equipment necessary for maintenance and operations of such administrative services as the Attorney General, with the approval of the Office of Management and Budget, determines may be performed more advantageously as central services. The capital of the fund shall consist of the amount of the fair and reasonable value of such inventories, equipment, and other assets and inventories on order pertaining to the services to be carried on by the fund as the Attorney General may transfer to the fund less related liabilities and unpaid obligations together with any appropriations made for the purpose of providing capital. The fund shall be reimbursed or credited with advance payments from applicable appropriations and funds of the Department of Justice, other Federal agencies, and other sources authorized by law for supplies, materials, and services at rates which will recover the expenses of operations including accrual of annual leave and depreciation of plant and equipment of the fund. The fund shall also be credited with other receipts from sale or exchange of property or in payment for loss or damage to property held by the fund. There shall be transferred into the Treasury as miscellaneous receipts, as of the close of each fiscal year, any net income after making provisions for prior year losses, if any.

(Added Pub.L. 93–613, § 1(1), Jan. 2, 1975, 88 Stat. 1975.)

HISTORICAL AND STATUTORY NOTES

Debt Collection Improvement

Pub.L. 107–273, Div. C, Title I, § 11013(a), Nov. 2, 2002, 116 Stat. 1823, provided that: "Notwithstanding section 3302 of title 31, United States Code, or any other statute affecting the crediting of collections, the Attorney General may credit, as an offsetting collection, to the Department of Justice Working Capital Fund up to 3 percent of all amounts collected pursuant to civil debt collection litigation activities of the Department of Justice. Such amounts in the Working Capital Fund shall remain available until expended and shall be subject to the terms and conditions of that fund, and shall be used first, for paying the costs of processing and tracking civil and criminal debt-collection litigation, and, thereafter, for financial systems and for debt-collection-related personnel, administrative, and litigation expenses."

Capital Equipment Acquisition, Etc., by Income Retained from or Transferred to Working Capital Fund; Amounts and Limitations

Pub.L. 102–140, Title I, Oct. 28, 1991, 105 Stat. 784, provided that:

"Of the total income of the Working Capital Fund in fiscal year 1992 and each fiscal year thereafter, not to exceed 4 percent of the total income may be retained, to remain available until expended, for the acquisition of capital equipment and for the improvement and implementation of the Department's financial management and payroll/personnel systems: *Provided,* That in fiscal year 1992, not to exceed $4,000,000 of the total income retained shall be used for improvements to the Department's data processing operation: *Provided further,* That any proposed use of the retained income in fiscal year 1992 and thereafter, except for the $4,000,000 specified above, shall only be made after notification to the Committees on Appropriations of the House of Representatives and the Senate in accordance with section 606 of this Act [not classified to the Code].

"In addition, for fiscal year 1992 and thereafter, at no later than the end of the fifth fiscal year after the fiscal year for which funds are appropriated or otherwise made available, unobligated balances of appropriations available to the Department of Justice during such fiscal year may be transferred into the capital account of the Working Capital Fund to be available for the department wide acquisition of capital equipment, development and implementation of law enforcement or litigation related automated data processing systems, and for the improvement and implementation of the Department's financial management and payroll/personnel systems: *Provided,* That any proposed use of these transferred funds in fiscal year 1992 and thereafter shall only be made after notification to the Committees on Appropriations of the House of Representatives and the Senate in accordance with section 606 of this Act [not classified to the Code]."

Crediting to Working Capital Fund of Amounts Collected Pursuant to Civil Debt Collection Litigation Activities

Pub.L. 103–121, Title I, § 108, Oct. 27, 1993, 107 Stat. 1164, as amended Pub.L. 107–273, Div. A, Title II, § 204(g), Nov. 2, 2002, 116 Stat. 1776, was repealed by Pub.L. 107–273, Div. C, Title I, § 11013(b), Nov. 2, 2002, 116 Stat. 1823.

§ 528. Disqualification of officers and employees of the Department of Justice

The Attorney General shall promulgate rules and regulations which require the disqualification of any officer or employee of the Department of Justice, including a United States attorney or a member of such attorney's staff, from participation in a particular investigation or prosecution if such participation may result in a personal, financial, or political conflict of interest, or the appearance thereof. Such rules and regulations may provide that a willful violation of any provision thereof shall result in removal from office.

(Added Pub.L. 95–521, Title VI, § 603(a), Oct. 26, 1978, 92 Stat. 1874.)

HISTORICAL AND STATUTORY NOTES

Effective and Applicability Provisions

1978 Acts. Section effective Oct. 26, 1978, see section 604 of Pub.L. 95–521, set out as a note under section 591 of this title.

§ 529. Annual report of Attorney General

(a) Beginning on June 1, 1979, and at the beginning of each regular session of Congress thereafter, the Attorney General shall report to Congress on the activities and operations of the Public Integrity Section or any other unit of the Department of Justice designated to supervise the investigation and prosecution of—

(1) any violation of Federal criminal law by any individual who holds or who at the time of such violation held a position, whether or not elective, as a Federal Government officer, employee, or special employee, if such violation relates directly or indirectly to such individual's Federal Government position, employment, or compensation;

(2) any violation of any Federal criminal law relating to lobbying, conflict of interest, campaigns, and election to public office committed by any person, except insofar as such violation relates to a matter involving discrimination or intimidation on grounds of race, color, religion, or national origin;

(3) any violation of Federal criminal law by any individual who holds or who at the time of such violation held a position, whether or not elective, as a State or local government officer or employee, if such violation relates directly or indirectly to such individual's State or local government position, employment, or compensation; and

(4) such other matters as the Attorney General may deem appropriate.

Such report shall include the number, type, and disposition of all investigations and prosecutions supervised by such Section or such unit, except that such report shall not disclose information which would interfere with any pending investigation or prosecution or which would improperly infringe upon the privacy rights of any individuals.

(b) Notwithstanding any provision of law limiting the amount of management or administrative expenses, the Attorney General shall, not later than May 2, 2003, and of every year thereafter, prepare and provide to the Committees on the Judiciary and Appropriations of each House of the Congress using funds available for the underlying programs—

(1) a report identifying and describing every grant (other than one made to a governmental entity, pursuant to a statutory formula), cooperative agreement, or programmatic services contract that was made, entered into, awarded, or, for which additional or supplemental funds were provided in the immediately preceding fiscal year, by or on behalf of the Office of Justice Programs (including any component or unit thereof, and the Office of Community Oriented Policing Services), and including, without limitation, for each such grant, cooperative agreement, or contract: the term, the dollar amount or value, a description of its specific purpose or purposes, the names of all grantees or parties, the names of each unsuccessful applicant or bidder, and a description of the specific purpose or purposes proposed in each unsuccessful application or bid, and of the reason or reasons for rejection or denial of the same; and

(2) a report identifying and reviewing every grant (other than one made to a governmental entity, pursuant to a statutory formula), cooperative agreement, or programmatic services contract made, entered into, awarded, or for which additional or supplemental funds were provided, after October 1, 2002, by or on behalf of the Office of Justice Programs (including any component or unit thereof, and the Office of Community Oriented Policing Services) that was programmatically and financially closed out or that otherwise ended in the immediately preceding fiscal year (or even if not yet closed out, was terminated or otherwise ended in the fiscal year that ended 2 years before the end of such immediately preceding fiscal year), and including, without limitation, for each such grant, cooperative agreement, or contract: a description of how the appropriated funds involved actually were spent, statistics relating to its performance, its specific purpose or purposes, and its effectiveness, and a written declaration by each non-Federal grantee and each non-Federal party to such agreement or to such contract, that—

(A) the appropriated funds were spent for such purpose or purposes, and only such purpose or purposes;

(B) the terms of the grant, cooperative agreement, or contract were complied with; and

(C) all documentation necessary for conducting a full and proper audit under generally accepted accounting principles, and any (additional) documentation that may have been required under the grant, cooperative agreement, or contract, have been kept in orderly fashion and will be preserved for not less than 3 years from the date of such close out, termination, or end;

except that the requirement of this paragraph shall be deemed satisfied with respect to any such description, statistics, or declaration if such non-Federal grantee or such non-Federal party shall have failed to provide the same to the Attorney General, and the Attorney General notes the fact of such failure and the name of such grantee or such party in the report.

(Added Pub.L. 95–521, Title VI, § 603(a), Oct. 26, 1978, 92 Stat. 1874, and amended Pub.L. 107–273, Div. A, Title II, § 205(a), Div. B, Title IV, § 4003(b)(3), Nov. 2, 2002, 116 Stat. 1777, 1811.)

HISTORICAL AND STATUTORY NOTES

Effective and Applicability Provisions

1978 Acts. Section effective Oct. 26, 1978, see section 604 of Pub.L. 95–521, set out as a note under section 591 of this title.

Termination of Reporting Requirements

Reporting requirement of this section excepted from termination under Pub.L. 104–66, § 3003(a)(1), as amended, set out in a note under 31 U.S.C.A. § 1113, see Pub.L. 106–197, § 1, set out as a note under 31 U.S.C.A. § 1113.

§ 530. Payment of travel and transportation expenses of newly appointed special agents

The Attorney General or the Attorney General's designee is authorized to pay the travel expenses of newly appointed special agents and the transportation expenses of their families and household goods and personal effects from place of residence at time of selection to the first duty station, to the extent such payments are authorized by section 5723 of title 5 for new appointees who may receive payments under that section.

(Added Pub. L. 98–86, § 1, Aug. 26, 1983, 97 Stat. 492.)

§ 530A. Authorization of appropriations for travel and related expenses and for health care of personnel serving abroad

There are authorized to be appropriated, for any fiscal year, for the Department of Justice, such sums as may be necessary—

(1) for travel and related expenses of employees of the Department of Justice serving abroad and their families, to be payable in the same manner as applicable with respect to the Foreign Service under paragraphs (3), (5), (6), (8), (9), (11), and (15) of section 901 of the Foreign Service Act of 1980, and under the regulations issued by the Secretary of State; and

(2) for health care for such employees and families, to be provided under section 904 of that Act.

(Added Pub.L. 100–690, Title VI, § 6281(a), Nov. 18, 1988, 102 Stat. 4368.)

HISTORICAL AND STATUTORY NOTES

References in Text

Section 901 of the Foreign Service Act of 1980, referred to in par. (1), is section 901 of Pub.L. 96–465, Title I, Oct. 17, 1980, 94 Stat. 2124, which is classified to section 4081 of Title 22, Foreign Relations and Intercourse.

Section 904 of the Foreign Service Act of 1980, referred to in par. (2), is section 904 of Pub.L. 96–465, Title I, Oct. 17, 1980, 94 Stat. 2127, which is classified to section 4084 of Title 22, Foreign Relations and Intercourse.

§ 530B. Ethical standards for attorneys for the Government

(a) An attorney for the Government shall be subject to State laws and rules, and local Federal court rules, governing attorneys in each State where such attorney engages in that attorney's duties, to the same extent and in the same manner as other attorneys in that State.

(b) The Attorney General shall make and amend rules of the Department of Justice to assure compliance with this section.

(c) As used in this section, the term "attorney for the Government" includes any attorney described in section 77.2(a) of part 77 of title 28 of the Code of Federal Regulations and also includes any independent counsel, or employee of such a counsel, appointed under chapter 40.

(Added Pub.L. 105–277, Div. A, § 101(b) [Title VIII, § 801(a)], Oct. 21, 1998, 112 Stat. 2681–118.)

HISTORICAL AND STATUTORY NOTES

Effective and Applicability Provisions

1998 Acts. Pub.L. 105–277, Div. A, § 101(b) [Title VIII, § 801(c)], Oct. 21, 1998, 112 Stat. 2681–119, provided that: "The amendments made by this section [enacting this section] shall take effect 180 days after the date of the enactment of this Act [Oct. 21, 1998] and shall apply during that portion of fiscal year 1999 that follows that taking effect, and in each succeeding fiscal year."

§ 530C. Authority to use available funds

(a) In general.—Except to the extent provided otherwise by law, the activities of the Department of Justice (including any bureau, office, board, division, commission, subdivision, unit, or other component thereof) may, in the reasonable discretion of the Attorney General, be carried out through any means, including—

(1) through the Department's own personnel, acting within, from, or through the Department itself;

(2) by sending or receiving details of personnel to other branches or agencies of the Federal Government, on a reimbursable, partially-reimbursable, or nonreimbursable basis;

(3) through reimbursable agreements with other Federal agencies for work, materials, or equipment;

(4) through contracts, grants, or cooperative agreements with non-Federal parties; and

(5) as provided in subsection (b), in section 524, and in any other provision of law consistent herewith, including, without limitation, section 102(b) of Public Law 102–395 (106 Stat. 1838), as incorporated by section 815(d) of Public Law 104–132 (110 Stat. 1315).

(b) Permitted uses.—

(1) General permitted uses.—Funds available to the Attorney General (i.e., all funds available to carry out the activities described in subsection (a)) may be used, without limitation, for the following:

(A) The purchase, lease, maintenance, and operation of passenger motor vehicles, or police-type motor vehicles for law enforcement purposes, without regard to general purchase price limitation for the then-current fiscal year.

(B) The purchase of insurance for motor vehicles, boats, and aircraft operated in official Government business in foreign countries.

(C) Services of experts and consultants, including private counsel, as authorized by section 3109 of title 5, and at rates of pay for individuals not to exceed the maximum daily rate payable from time to time under section 5332 of title 5.

(D) Official reception and representation expenses (i.e., official expenses of a social nature intended in whole or in predominant part to promote goodwill toward the Department or its missions, but excluding expenses of public tours of facilities of the Department of Justice), in accordance with distributions and procedures established, and rules issued, by the Attorney General, and expenses of public tours of facilities of the Department of Justice.

(E) Unforeseen emergencies of a confidential character, to be expended under the direction of the Attorney General and accounted for solely on the certificate of the Attorney General.

(F) Miscellaneous and emergency expenses authorized or approved by the Attorney General, the Deputy Attorney General, the Associate Attorney General, or the Assistant Attorney General for Administration.

(G) In accordance with procedures established and rules issued by the Attorney General—

(i) attendance at meetings and seminars;

(ii) conferences and training; and

(iii) advances of public moneys under section 3324 of title 31: *Provided*, That travel advances of such moneys to law enforcement personnel engaged in undercover activity shall be considered to be public money for purposes of section 3527 of title 31.

(H) Contracting with individuals for personal services abroad, except that such individuals shall not be regarded as employees of the United States for the purpose of any law administered by the Office of Personnel Management.

(I) Payment of interpreters and translators who are not citizens of the United States, in accordance with procedures established and rules issued by the Attorney General.

(J) Expenses or allowances for uniforms as authorized by section 5901 of title 5, but without regard to the general purchase price limitation for the then-current fiscal year.

(K) Expenses of—

(i) primary and secondary schooling for dependents of personnel stationed outside the United States at cost not in excess of those authorized by the Department of Defense for the same area, when it is determined by the Attorney General that schools available in the locality are unable to provide adequately for the education of such dependents; and

(ii) transportation of those dependents between their place of residence and schools serving the area which those dependents would normally attend when the Attorney General, under such regulations as he may prescribe, determines that such schools are not accessible by public means of transportation.

(L) payment of rewards (i.e., payments pursuant to public advertisements for assistance to the Department of Justice), in accordance with procedures and regulations established or issued by the Attorney General: *Provided*, That—

(i) no such reward shall exceed $2,000,000, unless—

(I) the reward is to combat domestic terrorism or international terrorism (as defined in section 2331 of title 18); or

(II) a statute should authorize a higher amount;

(ii) no such reward of $250,000 or more may be made or offered without the personal approval of either the Attorney General or the President;

(iii) the Attorney General shall give written notice to the Chairmen and ranking minority members of the Committees on Appropriations and the Judiciary of the Senate and of the House of Representatives not later than 30 days after the approval of a reward under clause (ii);

(iv) any executive agency or military department (as defined, respectively, in sections 105 and 102 of title 5) may provide the Attorney General with funds for the payment of rewards; and

(v) neither the failure of the Attorney General to authorize a payment nor the amount authorized shall be subject to judicial review.

(2) **Specific permitted uses.—**

(A) **Aircraft and boats.**—Funds available to the Attorney General for United States Attorneys, for the Federal Bureau of Investigation, for the United States Marshals Service, for the Bureau of Alcohol, Tobacco, Firearms and Explosives, for the Drug Enforcement Administration, and for the Immigration and Naturalization Service may be used for the purchase, lease, maintenance, and operation of aircraft and boats, for law enforcement purposes.

(B) **Purchase of ammunition and firearms; firearms competitions.**—Funds available to the Attorney General for United States Attorneys, for the Federal Bureau of Investigation, for the United States Marshals Service, for the Bureau of Alcohol, Tobacco, Firearms and Explosives, for the Drug Enforcement Administration, for the Federal Prison System, for the Office of the Inspector General, and for the Immigration and Naturalization Service may be used for—

(i) the purchase of ammunition and firearms; and

(ii) participation in firearms competitions.

(C) **Construction.**—Funds available to the Attorney General for construction may be used for expenses of planning, designing, acquiring, building, constructing, activating, renovating, converting, expanding, extending, remodeling, equipping, repairing, or maintaining buildings or facilities, including the expenses of acquisition of sites therefor, and all necessary expenses incident or related thereto; but the foregoing shall not be construed to mean that funds generally available for salaries and expenses are not also available for certain incidental or minor construction, activation, remodeling, maintenance, and other related construction costs.

(3) **Fees and expenses of witnesses.**—Funds available to the Attorney General for fees and expenses of witnesses may be used for—

(A) expenses, mileage, compensation, protection, and per diem in lieu of subsistence, of witnesses (including advances of public money) and as authorized by section 1821 or other law, except that no witness may be paid more than 1 attendance fee for any 1 calendar day;

(B) fees and expenses of neutrals in alternative dispute resolution proceedings, where the Department of Justice is a party; and

(C) construction of protected witness safesites.

(4) **Federal Bureau of Investigation.**—Funds available to the Attorney General for the Federal Bureau of Investigation for the detection, investigation, and prosecution of crimes against the United States may be used for the conduct of all its authorized activities.

(5) **Immigration and Naturalization Service.**—Funds available to the Attorney General for the Immigration and Naturalization Service may be used for—

(A) acquisition of land as sites for enforcement fences, and construction incident to such fences;

(B) cash advances to aliens for meals and lodging en route;

(C) refunds of maintenance bills, immigration fines, and other items properly returnable, except deposits of aliens who become public charges and deposits to secure payment of fines and passage money; and

(D) expenses and allowances incurred in tracking lost persons, as required by public exigencies, in aid of State or local law enforcement agencies.

(6) **Federal Prison System.**—Funds available to the Attorney General for the Federal Prison System may be used for—

(A) inmate medical services and inmate legal services, within the Federal prison system;

(B) the purchase and exchange of farm products and livestock;

(C) the acquisition of land as provided in section 4010 of title 18; and

(D) the construction of buildings and facilities for penal and correctional institutions (including prison camps), by contract or force account, including the payment of United States prisoners for their work performed in any such construction;

except that no funds may be used to distribute or make available to a prisoner any commercially published information or material that is sexually explicit or features nudity.

(7) **Detention Trustee.**—Funds available to the Attorney General for the Detention Trustee may be used for all the activities of such Trustee in the exercise of all power and functions authorized by law relating to the detention of Federal prisoners in non-Federal institutions or otherwise in the custody of the United States Marshals Service and to the detention of aliens in the custody of the Immigration and Naturalization Service, including the overseeing of construction of detention facilities or for housing related to such detention, the management of funds appropriated to the Department for the exercise of detention functions, and the direction of the United States Marshals Service and Immigration Service with respect to the exercise of detention policy setting and operations for the Department of Justice.

(c) **Related provisions.**—

(1) **Limitation of compensation of individuals employed as attorneys.**—No funds available to the Attorney General may be used to pay compensation for services provided by an individual employed as an attorney (other than an individual employed to provide services as a foreign attorney in special cases) unless such individual is duly licensed and authorized to practice as an attorney under the law of a State, a territory of the United States, or the District of Columbia.

(2) **Reimbursements paid to governmental entities.**—Funds available to the Attorney General that are paid as reimbursement to a governmental unit of the Department of Justice, to another Federal entity, or to a unit of State or local government, may be used under authorities available to the unit or entity receiving such reimbursement.

(d) **Foreign reimbursements.**—Whenever the Department of Justice or any component participates in a cooperative project to improve law enforcement or national security operations or services with a friendly foreign country on a cost-sharing basis, any reimbursements or contributions received from that foreign country to meet its share of the project may be credited to appropriate current appropriations accounts of the Department of Justice or any component. The amount of a reimbursement or contribution credited shall be available only for payment of the share of the project expenses allocated to the participating foreign country.

(e) Railroad police training fees.—The Attorney General is authorized to establish and collect a fee to defray the costs of railroad police officers participating in a Federal Bureau of Investigation law enforcement training program authorized by Public Law 106–110, and to credit such fees to the appropriation account "Federal Bureau of Investigation, Salaries and Expenses", to be available until expended for salaries and expenses incurred in providing such services.

(f) Warranty work.—In instances where the Attorney General determines that law enforcement-, security-, or mission-related considerations mitigate against obtaining maintenance or repair services from private sector entities for equipment under warranty, the Attorney General is authorized to seek reimbursement from such entities for warranty work performed at Department of Justice facilities, and to credit any payment made for such work to any appropriation charged therefor.

(Added Pub.L. 107–273, Div. A, Title II, § 201(a), Nov. 2, 2002, 116 Stat. 1767, and amended Pub.L. 108–199, Div. B, Title I, Jan. 23, 2004, 118 Stat. 53.)

HISTORICAL AND STATUTORY NOTES

References in Text

Section 102(b) of Public Law 102–395, referred to in subsec. (a)(5), means section 102(b) of the Department of Justice and Related Agencies Appropriations Act, 1993, Pub.L. 102–395, § 102(b), Oct. 6, 1992, 106 Stat. 1838, as incorporated by Public Law 104–132, Title VIII, § 815(d), Apr. 24, 1996, 110 Stat. 1315, as amended, which is set out as a note under 28 U.S.C.A. § 533.

Section 1821, referred to in subsec. (b)(3)(A), probably means section 1821 of this title, 28 U.S.C.A. § 1821.

Public Law 106–110, referred to in subsec. (e), is Pub.L. 106–110, Nov. 24, 1999, 113 Stat. 1497, which is principally classified to 42 U.S.C.A. § 3771.

Use of Federal Training Facilities

Pub.L. 109–162, Title XI, § 1173, Jan. 5, 2006, 119 Stat. 3124, as amended Pub.L. 109–271, § 8(d), Aug. 12, 2006, 120 Stat. 766, provided that:

"**(a) Federal training facilities.**—Unless authorized in writing by the Attorney General, or the Assistant Attorney General for Administration, if so delegated by the Attorney General, the Department of Justice (and each entity within it) shall use for any predominantly internal training or conference meeting only a facility that does not require a payment to a private entity for use of the facility or for meals, lodging, or other expenses related to such internal training or conference meeting.

"**(b) Annual report.**—The Attorney General shall prepare an annual report to the Chairmen and ranking minority members of the Committees on the Judiciary of the Senate and of the House of Representatives that details each training and conference meeting authorized under subsection (a) [of this note]. The report shall include an explanation of why the facility was chosen, and a breakdown of any expenditures incurred in excess of the cost of conducting the training or meeting at a facility that did not require such authorization."

Abolition of Immigration and Naturalization Service and Transfer of Functions

For abolition of Immigration and Naturalization Service (INS), transfer of functions, and treatment of related references, see note set out under 8 U.S.C.A. § 1551.

§ 530D. Report on enforcement of laws

(a) Report.—

(1) In general.—The Attorney General shall submit to the Congress a report of any instance in which the Attorney General or any officer of the Department of Justice—

(A) establishes or implements a formal or informal policy to refrain—

(i) from enforcing, applying, or administering any provision of any Federal statute, rule, regulation, program, policy, or other law whose enforcement, application, or administration is within the responsibility of the Attorney General or such officer on the grounds that such provision is unconstitutional; or

(ii) within any judicial jurisdiction of or within the United States, from adhering to, enforcing, applying, or complying with, any standing rule of decision (binding upon courts of, or inferior to those of, that jurisdiction) established by a final decision of any court of, or superior to those of, that jurisdiction, respecting the interpretation, construction, or application of the Constitution, any statute, rule, regulation, program, policy, or other law whose enforcement, application, or administration is within the responsibility of the Attorney General or such officer;

(B) determines—

(i) to contest affirmatively, in any judicial, administrative, or other proceeding, the constitutionality of any provision of any Federal statute, rule, regulation, program, policy, or other law; or

(ii) to refrain (on the grounds that the provision is unconstitutional) from defending or asserting, in any judicial, administrative, or other proceeding, the constitutionality of any provision of any Federal statute, rule, regulation, program, policy, or other law, or not to appeal or request review of any judicial, administrative, or other determination adversely affecting the constitutionality of any such provision; or

(C) approves (other than in circumstances in which a report is submitted to the Joint Committee on Taxation, pursuant to section 6405 of the Internal Revenue Code of 1986) the settlement or compromise (other than in bankruptcy) of any claim, suit, or other action—

(i) against the United States (including any agency or instrumentality thereof) for a sum that exceeds, or is likely to exceed, $2,000,000, excluding prejudgment interest; or

(ii) by the United States (including any agency or instrumentality thereof) pursuant to an agreement, consent decree, or order (or pursuant to any modification of an agreement, consent decree, or order) that provides injunctive or other nonmonetary relief that exceeds, or is likely to exceed, 3 years in duration: *Provided*, That for purposes of this clause, the term "injunctive or other nonmonetary relief" shall not be understood to include the following, where the same are a matter of public record—

(I) debarments, suspensions, or other exclusions from Government contracts or grants;

(II) mere reporting requirements or agreements (including sanctions for failure to report);

(III) requirements or agreements merely to comply with statutes or regulations;

(IV) requirements or agreements to surrender professional licenses or to cease the practice of professions, occupations, or industries;

(V) any criminal sentence or any requirements or agreements to perform community service, to serve probation, or to participate in supervised release from detention, confinement, or prison; or

(VI) agreements to cooperate with the government in investigations or prosecutions (whether or not the agreement is a matter of public record).

(2) Submission of report to the Congress.—For the purposes of paragraph (1), a report shall be considered to be submitted to the Congress if the report is submitted to—

(A) the majority leader and minority leader of the Senate;

(B) the Speaker, majority leader, and minority leader of the House of Representatives;

(C) the chairman and ranking minority member of the Committee on the Judiciary of the House of Representatives and the chairman and ranking minority member of the Committee on the Judiciary of the Senate; and

(D) the Senate Legal Counsel and the General Counsel of the House of Representatives.

(b) Deadline.—A report shall be submitted—

(1) under subsection (a)(1)(A), not later than 30 days after the establishment or implementation of each policy;

(2) under subsection (a)(1)(B), within such time as will reasonably enable the House of Representatives and the Senate to take action, separately or jointly, to intervene in timely fashion in the proceeding, but in no event later than 30 days after the making of each determination; and

(3) under subsection (a)(1)(C), not later than 30 days after the conclusion of each fiscal-year quarter, with respect to all approvals occurring in such quarter.

(c) Contents.—A report required by subsection (a) shall—

(1) specify the date of the establishment or implementation of the policy described in subsection (a)(1)(A), of the making of the determination described in subsection (a)(1)(B), or of each approval described in subsection (a)(1)(C);

(2) include a complete and detailed statement of the relevant issues and background (including a complete and detailed statement of the reasons for the policy or determination, and the identity of the officer responsible for establishing or implementing such policy, making such determination, or approving such settlement or compromise), except that—

(A) such details may be omitted as may be absolutely necessary to prevent improper disclosure of national-security- or classified information, of any information subject to the deliberative-process-, executive-, attorney- work-product-, or attorney-client privileges, or of any information the disclosure of which is prohibited by section 6103 of the Internal Revenue Code of 1986, or other law or any court order if the fact of each such omission (and the precise ground or grounds therefor) is clearly noted in the statement: *Provided*, That this subparagraph shall not be construed to deny to the Congress (including any House, Committee, or agency thereof) any such omitted details (or related information) that it lawfully may seek, subsequent to the submission of the report; and—

(B) the requirements of this paragraph shall be deemed satisfied—

(i) in the case of an approval described in subsection (a)(1)(C)(i), if an unredacted copy of the entire settlement agreement and consent decree or order (if any) is provided, along with a statement indicating the legal and factual basis or bases for the settlement or compromise (if not apparent on the face of documents provided); and

(ii) in the case of an approval described in subsection (a)(1)(C)(ii), if an unredacted copy of the entire settlement agreement and consent decree or order (if any) is provided, along with a statement indicating the injunctive or other nonmonetary relief (if not apparent on the face of documents provided); and

(3) in the case of a determination described in subsection (a)(1)(B) or an approval described in subsection (a)(1)(C), indicate the nature, tribunal, identifying information, and status of the proceeding, suit, or action.

(d) Declaration.—In the case of a determination described in subsection (a)(1)(B), the representative of the United States participating in the proceeding shall make a clear declaration in the proceeding that any position expressed as to the constitutionality of the provision involved is the position of the executive branch of the Federal Government (or, as applicable, of the President or of any executive agency or military department).

(e) Applicability to the President and to executive agencies and military departments.—The reporting, declaration, and other provisions of this section relating to the Attorney General and other officers of the Department of Justice shall apply to the President (but only with respect to the promulgation of any unclassified Executive order or similar memorandum or order), to the head of each executive agency or military department (as defined, respectively, in sections 105 and 102 of title 5, United States Code) that establishes or implements a policy described in subsection (a)(1)(A) or is authorized to conduct litigation, and to the officers of such executive agency.

(Added Pub.L. 107–273, Div. A, Title II, § 202(a), Nov. 2, 2002, 116 Stat. 1771.)

HISTORICAL AND STATUTORY NOTES

References in Text

Section 6405 of the Internal Revenue Code of 1986, referred to in subsec. (a)(1)(C), is classified to 26 U.S.C.A. § 6405.

Section 6103 of the Internal Revenue Code of 1986, referred to in subsec. (c)(2)(A), is classified to 26 U.S.C.A. § 6103.

Effective and Applicability Provisions

2002 Acts. Pub.L. 107–273, Div. A, Title II, § 202(b)(4), Nov. 2, 2002, 116 Stat. 1774, provided that:

"**(A)** Not later than 90 days after the date of the enactment of this Act [Nov. 2, 2002], the Attorney General (and, as applicable, the President, and the head of any executive agency or military department described in subsection (e) of section 530D of title 28, United States Code [subsec. (e) of this section], as added by subsection (a)) shall submit to Congress a report (in accordance with subsections (a), (c), and (e) of such section [subsecs. (a), (c), and (e) of this section]) on—

"**(i)** all policies of which the Attorney General and applicable official are aware described in subsection (a)(1)(A) of such section [subsec. (a)(1)(A) of this section] that were established or implemented before the date of the enactment of this Act [Nov. 2, 2002] and were in effect on such date; and

"**(ii)** all determinations of which the Attorney General and applicable official are aware described in subsection (a)(1)(B) of such section [subsec. (a)(1)(B) of this section] that were made before the date of the enactment of this Act and were in effect on such date.

"**(B)** If a determination described in subparagraph (A)(ii) [of this note] relates to any judicial, administrative, or other proceeding that is pending in the 90–day period beginning on the date of the enactment of this Act [Nov. 2, 2002], with respect to any such determination, then the report required by this paragraph shall be submitted within such time as will reasonably enable the House of Representatives and the Senate to take action, separately or jointly, to intervene in timely fashion in the proceeding, but not later than 30 days after the date of the enactment of this Act [Nov. 2, 2002]."

Presidential Advisement to Heads of Executive agencies and Military Departments

Pub.L. 107–273, Div. A, Title II, § 202(b)(3), Nov. 2, 2002, 116 Stat. 1774, provided that: "Not later than 30 days after the date of the enactment of this Act [Nov. 2, 2002], the President shall advise the head of each executive agency or military department (as defined, respectively, in sections 105 and 102 of title 5, United States Code) of the enactment of this section [Pub.L. 107–273, Div. A, Title II, § 202, Nov. 2, 2002, 116 Stat. 1771, which enacted this section, amended 2 U.S.C.A. § 288k, and enacted provisions set out as notes under this section]."

CHAPTER 33—FEDERAL BUREAU OF INVESTIGATION

Sec.
531. Federal Bureau of Investigation.
532. Director of the Federal Bureau of Investigation.
533. Investigative and other officials; appointment.
534. Acquisition, preservation, and exchange of identification records and information; appointment of officials.
535. Investigation of crimes involving Government officers and employees; limitations.
536. Positions in excepted service.
537. Expenses of unforeseen emergencies of a confidential character.

Sec.
538. Investigation of aircraft piracy and related violations.
539. Counterintelligence official reception and representation expenses.
540. Investigation of felonious killings of State or local law enforcement officers.
540A. Investigation of violent crimes against travelers.
540B. Investigation of serial killings.
540C. FBI police.

§ 531. Federal Bureau of Investigation

The Federal Bureau of Investigation is in the Department of Justice.

(Added Pub.L. 89–554, § 4(c), Sept. 6, 1966, 80 Stat. 616.)

HISTORICAL AND STATUTORY NOTES

Transfer of Functions

For transfer of functions, personnel, assets, and liabilities of the Federal Bureau of Investigation (FBI), including the functions of the Attorney General relating thereto, to the Secretary of Homeland Security, and for treatment of related references, see 6 U.S.C.A. §§ 121(g)(1), 313(3), 551(d), 552(d), and 557, and the Department of Homeland Security Reorganization Plan of November 25, 2002, as modified, set out as a note under 6 U.S.C.A. § 542.

Enterprise Architecture

Pub.L. 108–458, Title VIII, § 8402, Dec. 17, 2004, 118 Stat. 3869, provided that:

"**(a) Enterprise architecture defined.**—In this section [this note], the term 'enterprise architecture' means a detailed outline or blueprint of the information technology of the Federal Bureau of Investigation that will satisfy the ongoing mission and goals of the Federal Bureau of Investigation and that sets forth specific and identifiable benchmarks.

"**(b) Enterprise architecture.**—The Federal Bureau of Investigation shall—

"(1) continually maintain and update an enterprise architecture; and

"(2) maintain a state of the art and up to date information technology infrastructure that is in compliance with the enterprise architecture of the Federal Bureau of Investigation.

"**(c) Report.**—Subject to subsection (d) [of this note], the Director of the Federal Bureau of Investigation shall, on an annual basis, submit to the Committees on the Judiciary of the Senate and House of Representatives a report on whether the major information technology investments of the Federal Bureau of Investigation are in compliance with the enterprise architecture of the Federal Bureau of Investigation and identify any inability or expectation of inability to meet the terms set forth in the enterprise architecture.

"**(d) Failure to meet terms.**—If the Director of the Federal Bureau of Investigation identifies any inability or expectation of inability to meet the terms set forth in the enterprise architecture in a report under subsection (c) [of this note], the report under subsection (c) [of this note] shall—

"(1) be twice a year until the inability is corrected;

"(2) include a statement as to whether the inability or expectation of inability to meet the terms set forth in the enterprise architecture is substantially related to resources; and

"(3) if the inability or expectation of inability is substantially related to resources, include a request for additional funding that would resolve the problem or a request to reprogram funds that would resolve the problem.

"**(e) Enterprise architecture, agency plans and reports.**—This section [this note] shall be carried out in compliance with the requirements set forth in section 1016(e) and (h) [Pub.L. 108–458, Title I, § 1016(e), (h), Dec. 17, 2004, 118 Stat. 3666, 3669, which is classified to 6 U.S.C.A. § 485(e), (h)]."

Report to Congress

Pub.L. 108–405, Title IV, § 203(f), Oct. 30, 2004, 118 Stat. 2271, provided that: "If the Department of Justice plans to modify or supplement the core genetic markers needed for compatibility with the CODIS system, it shall notify the Judiciary Committee of the Senate and the Judiciary Committee of the House of Representatives in writing not later than 180 days before any change is made and explain the reasons for such change."

Morgan P. Hardiman Child Abduction and Serial Murder Investigative Resources Center

Pub.L. 105–314, Title VII, § 703(a) to (f), Oct. 30, 1998, 112 Stat. 2987 to 2989, provided that:

"**(a) Establishment.**—Not later than 90 days after the date of enactment of this Act [Oct. 30, 1998], the Attorney General shall establish within the Federal Bureau of Investigation a Child Abduction and Serial Murder Investigative Resources Center to be known as the 'Morgan P. Hardiman Child Abduction and Serial Murder Investigative Resources Center' (in this section referred to as the 'CASMIRC').

"**(b) Purpose.**—The CASMIRC shall be managed by the National Center for the Analysis of Violent Crime of the Critical Incident Response Group of the Federal Bureau of Investigation (in this section referred to as the 'NCAVC'), and by multidisciplinary resource teams in Federal Bureau of Investigation field offices, in order to provide investigative support through the coordination and provision of Federal law enforcement resources, training, and application of other multidisciplinary expertise, to assist Federal, State, and local authorities in matters involving child abductions, mysterious disappearances of children, child homicide, and serial murder across the country. The CASMIRC shall be co-located with the NCAVC.

"**(c) Duties of the CASMIRC.**—The CASMIRC shall perform such duties as the Attorney General determines appropriate to carry out the purposes of the CASMIRC, including—

"(1) identifying, developing, researching, acquiring, and refining multidisciplinary information and specialities to provide for the most current expertise available to advance investigative knowledge and practices used in child abduction, mysterious disappearances of children, child homicide, and serial murder investigations;

"(2) providing advice and coordinating the application of current and emerging technical, forensic, and other Federal assistance to Federal, State, and local authorities in child abduction, mysterious disappearances of children, child homicide, and serial murder investigations;

"(3) providing investigative support, research findings, and violent crime analysis to Federal, State, and local authorities in child abduction, mysterious disappearances of children, child homicide, and serial murder investigations;

"(4) providing, if requested by a Federal, State, or local law enforcement agency, on site consultation and advice in child abduction, mysterious disappearances of children, child homicide and serial murder investigations;

"(5) coordinating the application of resources of pertinent Federal law enforcement agencies, and other Federal entities including, but not limited to, the United States Customs Service, the Secret Service, the Postal Inspection Service, and the United States Marshals Service, as appropriate, and with the concurrence of the agency head to support Federal, State, and local law enforcement involved in child abduction, mysterious disappearance of a child, child homicide, and serial murder investigations;

"(6) conducting ongoing research related to child abductions, mysterious disappearances of children, child homicides, and serial murder, including identification and investigative application of current and emerging technologies, identification of investigative searching technologies and methods for physically locating abducted children, investigative use of offender behavioral assessment and analysis concepts, gathering statistics and information necessary for case identification, trend analysis, and case linkages to advance the investigative effectiveness of outstanding abducted children cases, develop investigative systems to identify and track serious serial offenders that repeatedly victimize children for comparison to unsolved cases, and other investigative research pertinent to child abduction, mysterious disappearance of a child, child homicide, and serial murder covered in this section;

"(7) working under the NCAVC in coordination with the National Center For Missing and Exploited Children and the Office of Juvenile Justice and Delinquency Prevention of the Department of Justice to provide appropriate training to Federal, State, and local law enforcement in matters regarding child abductions, mysterious disappearances of children, child homicides; and

"(8) establishing a centralized repository based upon case data reflecting child abductions, mysterious disappearances of children, child homicides and serial murder submitted by State and local agencies, and an automated system for the efficient collection, retrieval, analysis, and reporting of information regarding CASMIRC investigative resources, research, and requests for and provision of investigative support services.

"**(d) Appointment of personnel to the CASMIRC.**—

"**(1) Selection of members of the CASMIRC and participating State and local law enforcement personnel.**—The Director of the Federal Bureau of Investigation shall appoint the members of the CASMIRC. The CASMIRC shall be staffed with Federal Bureau of Investigation personnel and other necessary personnel selected for their expertise that would enable them to assist in the research, data collection, and analysis, and provision of investigative support in child abduction, mysterious disappearances of children, child homicide and serial murder investigations. The Director may, with concurrence of the appropriate State or local agency, also appoint State and local law enforcement personnel to work with the CASMIRC.

"**(2) Status.**—Each member of the CASMIRC (and each individual from any State or local law enforcement agency appointed to work with the CASMIRC) shall remain as an employee of that member's or individual's respective agency for all purposes (including the purpose of performance review), and service with the CASMIRC shall be without interruption or loss of civil service privilege or status and shall be on a nonreimbursable basis, except if appropriate to reimburse State and local law enforcement for overtime costs for an individual appointed to work with the resource team. Additionally, reimbursement of travel and per diem expenses will occur for State and local law enforcement participation in resident fellowship programs at the NCAVC when offered.

"**(3) Training.**—CASMIRC personnel, under the guidance of the Federal Bureau of Investigation's National Center for the Analysis of Violent Crime and in consultation with the National Center For Missing and Exploited Children, shall develop a specialized course of instruction devoted to training members of the CASMIRC consistent with the purpose of this section. The CASMIRC shall also work with the National Center For Missing and Exploited Children and the Office of Juvenile Justice and Delinquency Prevention of the Department of Justice to develop a course of instruction for State and local law enforcement personnel to facilitate the dissemination of the most current multidisciplinary expertise in the investigation of child abductions, mysterious disappearances of children, child homicides, and serial murder of children.

"**(e) Report to Congress.**—One year after the establishment of the CASMIRC, the Attorney General shall submit to Congress a report, which shall include—

"(1) a description of the goals and activities of the CASMIRC; and

"(2) information regarding—

"(A) the number and qualifications of the members appointed to the CASMIRC;

"(B) the provision of equipment, administrative support, and office space for the CASMIRC; and

"(C) the projected resource needs for the CASMIRC.

"**(f) Authorization of appropriations.**—There are authorized to be appropriated to carry out this section such sums as may be necessary for each of fiscal years 1999, 2000, and 2001."

[For transfer of the functions, personnel, assets, and liabilities of the United States Customs Service of the Department of the Treasury, including the functions of the Secretary of the Treasury relating thereto, to the Secretary of Homeland Security, and for treatment of related references, see 6 U.S.C.A. §§ 203(1), 551(d), 552(d) and 557, and the Department of Homeland Security Reorganization Plan of November 25, 2002, as modified, set out as a note under 6 U.S.C.A. § 542.]

[For transfer of the functions, personnel, assets, and obligations of the United States Secret Service, including the functions of the Secretary of the Treasury relating thereto, to the Secretary of Homeland Security, and for treatment of related references, see 6 U.S.C.A. §§ 381, 551(d), 552(d), and 557, and the Department of Homeland Security Reorganization Plan of November 25, 2002, as modified, set out as a note under 6 U.S.C.A. § 542.]

Federal Bureau of Investigation Funding Authorizations

Pub.L. 104–132, Title VIII, § 811, Apr. 24, 1996, 110 Stat. 1312, as amended Pub.L. 106–546, § 6(a), Dec. 19, 2000, 114 Stat. 2733, provided that:

"**(a) In general.**—With funds made available pursuant to subsection (c)—

"**(1)** the Attorney General shall—

"**(A)** provide support and enhance the technical support center and tactical operations of the Federal Bureau of Investigation;

"**(B)** create a Federal Bureau of Investigation counterterrorism and counterintelligence fund for costs associated with the investigation of cases involving cases of terrorism;

"**(C)** expand and improve the instructional, operational support, and construction of the Federal Bureau of Investigation Academy;

"**(D)** construct a Federal Bureau of Investigation laboratory, provide laboratory examination support, and provide for a command center;

"**(E)** make grants to States to carry out the activities described in subsection (b); and

"**(F)** increase personnel to support counterterrorism activities; and

"**(2)** The director of the Federal bureau of investigation shall expand the combined DNA Identification System (CODIS) to include analyses of DNA samples collected from—

"**(A)** individuals convicted of a qualifying Federal offense, as determined under section 3(d) of the DNA Analysis Backlog Elimination Act of 2000 [42 U.S.C.A 14132a(d)];

"**(B)** individuals convicted of a qualifying District of Columbia offense, as determined under section 4(d) of the DNA Analysis Backlog Elimination Act of 2000 [42 U.S.C.A. § 14132b(d)]; and

"**(C)** members of the Armed Forces convicted of a qualifying military offense, as determined under section 1565(d) of Title 10, United States Code. ".

"**(b) State grants.**—

"**(1) Authorization.**—The Attorney General, in consultation with the Director of the Federal Bureau of Investigation, may make grants to each State eligible under paragraph (2) to be used by the chief executive officer of the State, in conjunction with units of local government, other States, or any combination thereof, to carry out all or part of a program to establish, develop, update, or upgrade—

"**(A)** computerized identification systems that are compatible and integrated with the databases of the National Crime Information Center of the Federal Bureau of Investigation;

"**(B)** the capability to analyze deoxyribonucleic acid (DNA) in a forensic laboratory in ways that are compatible and integrated with the combined DNA Identification System (CODIS) of the Federal Bureau of Investigation; and

"**(C)** automated fingerprint identification systems that are compatible and integrated with the Integrated Automated Fingerprint Identification System (IAFIS) of the Federal Bureau of Investigation.

"**(2) Eligibility.**—To be eligible to receive a grant under this subsection, a State shall require that each person convicted of a felony of a sexual nature shall provide to appropriate State law enforcement officials, as designated by the chief executive officer of the State, a sample of blood, saliva, or other specimen necessary to conduct a DNA analysis consistent with the standards established for DNA testing by the Director of the Federal Bureau of Investigation.

"**(3) Interstate compacts.**—A State may enter into a compact or compacts with another State or States to carry out this subsection.

"**(c) Authorization of appropriations.**—

"**(1) In general.**—There are authorized to be appropriated for the activities of the Federal Bureau of Investigation, to help meet the increased demands for activities to combat terrorism—

"**(A)** $114,000,000 for fiscal year 1997;

"**(B)** $166,000,000 for fiscal year 1998;

"**(C)** $96,000,000 for fiscal year 1999; and

"**(D)** $92,000,000 for fiscal year 2000.

"**(2) Availability of funds.**—Funds made available pursuant to paragraph (1), in any fiscal year, shall remain available until expended

"**(3) Allocation.**—

"**(A) In general.**—Of the total amount appropriated to carry out subsection (b) in a fiscal year—

"**(i)** the greater of 0.25 percent of such amount or $500,000 shall be allocated to each eligible State; and

"**(ii)** of the total funds remaining after the allocation under clause (i), there shall be allocated to each State an amount which bears the same ratio to the amount of remaining funds described in this subparagraph as the population of such State bears to the population of all States.

"**(B) Definition.**—For purposes of this paragraph, the term 'State' means any State of the United States, the District of Columbia, the Commonwealth of Puerto Rico, the Virgin Islands, American Samoa, Guam, and the Commonwealth of the Northern Mariana Islands, except that for purposes of the allocation under this subparagraph, American Samoa and the Commonwealth of the Northern Mariana Islands shall be considered as one State and that for these purposes, 67 percent of the amounts allocated shall be allocated to American Samoa, and 33 percent to the Commonwealth of the Northern Mariana Islands."

§ 532. Director of the Federal Bureau of Investigation

The Attorney General may appoint a Director of the Federal Bureau of Investigation. The Director of the Federal Bureau of Investigation is the head of the Federal Bureau of Investigation.

(Added Pub.L. 89–554, § 4(c), Sept. 6, 1966, 80 Stat. 616.)

HISTORICAL AND STATUTORY NOTES

Intelligence Activities of FBI

Pub.L. 108–458, Title II, §§ 2001 to 2003, Dec. 17, 2004, 118 Stat. 3700, provided that:

"Sec. 2001. Improvement of Intelligence Capabilities of the Federal Bureau of Investigation.

"**(a) Findings.**—Congress makes the following findings:

"(1) The National Commission on Terrorist Attacks Upon the United States in its final report stated that, under Director Robert Mueller, the Federal Bureau of Investigation has made significant progress in improving its intelligence capabilities.

"(2) In the report, the members of the Commission also urged that the Federal Bureau of Investigation fully institutionalize the shift of the Bureau to a preventive counterterrorism posture.

"**(b) Improvement of intelligence capabilities.**—The Director of the Federal Bureau of Investigation shall continue efforts to improve the intelligence capabilities of the Federal Bureau of Investigation and to develop and maintain within the Bureau a national intelligence workforce.

"**(c) National intelligence workforce.**—(1) In developing and maintaining a national intelligence workforce under subsection (b), the Director of the Federal Bureau of Investigation shall, develop and maintain a specialized and integrated national intelligence workforce consisting of agents, analysts, linguists, and surveillance specialists who are recruited, trained, and rewarded in a manner which ensures the existence within the Federal Bureau of Investigation an institutional culture with substantial expertise in, and commitment to, the intelligence mission of the Bureau.

"(2) Each agent employed by the Bureau after the date of the enactment of this Act [Dec. 17, 2004] shall receive basic training in both criminal justice matters and national intelligence matters.

"(3) Each agent employed by the Bureau after the date of the enactment of this Act [Dec. 17, 2004] shall, to the maximum extent practicable, be given the opportunity to undergo, during such agent's early service with the Bureau, meaningful assignments in criminal justice matters and in national intelligence matters.

"(4) The Director shall—

"(A) establish career positions in national intelligence matters for agents, analysts, and related personnel of the Bureau; and

"(B) in furtherance of the requirement under subparagraph (A) and to the maximum extent practicable, afford agents, analysts, and related personnel of the Bureau the opportunity to work in the career specialty selected by such agents, analysts, and related personnel over their entire career with the Bureau.

"(5) The Director shall carry out a program to enhance the capacity of the Bureau to recruit and retain individuals with backgrounds in intelligence, international relations, language, technology, and other skills relevant to the intelligence mission of the Bureau.

"(6) The Director shall, to the maximum extent practicable, afford the analysts of the Bureau training and career opportunities commensurate with the training and career opportunities afforded analysts in other elements of the intelligence community.

"(7) Commencing as soon as practicable after the date of the enactment of this Act [Dec. 17, 2004], each direct supervisor of a Field Intelligence Group, and each Bureau Operational Manager at the Section Chief and Assistant Special Agent in Charge (ASAC) level and above, shall be a certified intelligence officer.

"(8) The Director shall, to the maximum extent practicable, ensure that the successful discharge of advanced training courses, and of one or more assignments to another element of the intelligence community, is a precondition to advancement to higher level intelligence assignments within the Bureau.

"**(d) Field office matters.**—(1) In improving the intelligence capabilities of the Federal Bureau of Investigation under subsection (b), the Director of the Federal Bureau of Investigation shall ensure that each Field Intelligence Group reports directly to a field office senior manager responsible for intelligence matters.

"(2) The Director shall provide for such expansion of the secure facilities in the field offices of the Bureau as is necessary to ensure the discharge by the field offices of the intelligence mission of the Bureau.

"(3) The Director shall require that each Field Intelligence Group manager ensures the integration of analysts, agents, linguists, and surveillance personnel in the field.

"**(e) Discharge of improvements.**—(1) The Director of the Federal Bureau of Investigation shall carry out subsections (b) through (d) through the head of the Directorate of Intelligence of the Federal Bureau of Investigation.

"(2) The Director of the Federal Bureau of Investigation shall carry out subsections (b) through (d) under the joint guidance of the Attorney General and the National Intelligence Director in a manner consistent with section 112(e) [sic; there is no section 112(e) in the act which enacted this note].

"**(f) Budget matters.**—The Director of the Federal Bureau of Investigation shall, establish a budget structure of the Federal Bureau of Investigation to reflect the four principal missions of the Bureau as follows:

"(1) Intelligence.

"(2) Counterterrorism and counterintelligence.

"(3) Criminal Enterprises/Federal Crimes.

"(4) Criminal justice services.

"**(g) Reports.**—(1) Not later than 180 days after the date of the enactment of this Act [Dec. 17, 2004], the Director of the Federal Bureau of Investigation shall submit to Congress a report on the progress made as of the date of such report in carrying out the requirements of this section [this note].

"(2) The Director shall include in each annual program review of the Federal Bureau of Investigation that is submitted to Congress a report on the progress made by each field office of the Bureau during the period covered by such review in addressing Bureau and national program priorities.

"(3) Not later than 180 days after the date of the enactment of this Act [Dec. 17, 2004], and every 12 months thereafter, the Director shall submit to Congress a report assessing the qualifications, status, and roles of analysts at Bureau headquarters and in the field offices of the Bureau.

"(4) Not later than 180 days after the date of the enactment of this Act [Dec. 17, 2004], and every 12 months thereafter, the Director shall submit to Congress a report on the progress of the Bureau in implementing information-sharing principles.

"Sec. 2002. Directorate of Intelligence of the Federal Bureau of Investigation.

"(a) **Directorate of Intelligence of Federal Bureau of Investigation.**—The element of the Federal Bureau of Investigation known as of the date of the enactment of this Act [Dec. 17, 2004] as the Office of Intelligence is hereby redesignated as the Directorate of Intelligence of the Federal Bureau of Investigation.

"(b) **Head of Directorate.**—The head of the Directorate of Intelligence shall be the Executive Assistant Director for Intelligence of the Federal Bureau of Investigation.

"(c) **Responsibilities.**—The Directorate of Intelligence shall be responsible for the following:

"(1) Supervision of all national intelligence programs, projects, and activities of the Bureau.

"(2) The discharge by the Bureau of the requirements in section 105B of the National Security Act of 1947 (50 U.S.C. 403–5b).

"(3) The oversight of Bureau field intelligence operations.

"(4) Coordinating human source development and management by the Bureau.

"(5) Coordinating collection by the Bureau against nationally-determined intelligence requirements.

"(6) Strategic analysis.

"(7) Intelligence program and budget management.

"(8) The intelligence workforce.

"(9) Any other responsibilities specified by the Director of the Federal Bureau of Investigation or specified by law.

"(d) **Staff.**—The Directorate of Intelligence shall consist of such staff as the Director of the Federal Bureau of Investigation considers appropriate for the activities of the Directorate.

"Sec. 2003. Federal Bureau of Investigation Intelligence Career Service.

"(a) **Establishment of Federal Bureau of Investigation intelligence career service.**—The Director of the Federal Bureau of Investigation may—

"(1) In consultation with the Director of the Office of Personnel Management—

"(A) establish positions for intelligence analysts, and prescribe standards and procedures for establishing and classifying such positions, without regard to chapter 51 of title 5, United States Code [5 U.S.C.A. § 5101 et seq.]; and

"(B) fix the rate of basic pay for such positions, without regard to subchapter III of chapter 53 of title 5, United States Code [5 U.S.C.A. § 5331 et seq.], if the rate of pay is not greater than the rate of basic pay payable for level IV of the Executive Schedule [see 5 U.S.C.A. § 5315];

"(2) appoint individuals to such positions; and

"(3) establish a performance management system for such individuals with at least one level of performance above a retention standard.

"(b) **Reporting requirement.**—Not less than 60 days before the date of the implementation of authorities authorized under this section [this note], the Director of the Federal Bureau of Investigation shall submit an operating plan describing the Director's intended use of the authorities under this section to the appropriate committees of Congress.

"(c) **Annual report.**—Not later than December 31, 2005, and annually thereafter for 4 years, the Director of the Federal Bureau of Investigation shall submit an annual report of the use of the permanent authorities provided under this section [this note] during the preceding fiscal year to the appropriate committees of Congress.

"(d) **Appropriate committees of Congress defined.**—In this section, the term 'appropriate committees of Congress means' [sic; closing quote mark probably should follow "Congress"]—

"(1) the Committees on Appropriations, Homeland Security and Governmental Affairs, and the Judiciary and the Select Committee on Intelligence of the Senate; and

"(2) the Committees on Appropriations, Government Reform, and the Judiciary and the Permanent Select Committee on Intelligence of the House of Representatives."

Webster Commission Implementation Report

Pub.L. 107–273, Div. C, Title I, § 11023, Nov. 2, 2002, 116 Stat. 1830, provided that:

"(a) **Implementation plan.**—Not later than 6 months after the date of enactment of this Act [Nov. 2, 2002], the Director of the Federal Bureau of Investigation shall submit to the appropriate Committees of Congress a plan for implementation of the recommendations of the Commission for Review of FBI Security Programs, dated March 31, 2002, including the costs of such implementation.

"(b) **Annual reports.**—On the date that is 1 year after the submission of the plan described in subsection (a), and for 2 years thereafter, the Director of the Federal Bureau of Investigation shall submit to the appropriate Committees of Congress a report on the implementation of such plan.

"(c) **Appropriate Committees of Congress.**—For purposes of this section, the term 'appropriate Committees of Congress' means—

"(1) the Committees on the Judiciary of the Senate and the House of Representatives;

"(2) the Committees on Appropriations of the Senate and the House of Representatives;

"(3) the Select Committee on Intelligence of the Senate; and

"(4) the Permanent Select Committee on Intelligence of the House of Representatives."

Employment of Translators by the Federal Bureau of Investigation

Pub.L. 107–56, Title II, § 205, Oct. 26, 2001, 115 Stat. 281, provided that:

"(a) **Authority.**—The Director of the Federal Bureau of Investigation is authorized to expedite the employment of personnel as translators to support counterterrorism investigations and operations without regard to applicable Federal personnel requirements and limitations.

"(b) **Security requirements.**—The Director of the Federal Bureau of Investigation shall establish such security requirements as are necessary for the personnel employed as translators under subsection (a) [of this note].

"(c) **Report.**—The Attorney General shall report to the Committees on the Judiciary of the House of Representatives and the Senate on—

"(1) the number of translators employed by the FBI and other components of the Department of Justice;

"(2) any legal or practical impediments to using translators employed by other Federal, State, or local agencies, on a full, part-time, or shared basis; and

"(3) the needs of the FBI for specific translation services in certain languages, and recommendations for meeting those needs."

Confirmation and Compensation of Director; Term of Service

Pub.L. 90–351, Title VI, § 1101, June 19, 1968, 82 Stat. 236, as amended Pub.L. 94–503, Title II, § 203, Oct. 15, 1976, 90 Stat. 2427, provided that:

"(a) Effective as of the day following the date on which the present incumbent in the office of Director ceases to serve as such, the Director of the Federal Bureau of Investigation shall be appointed by the President, by and with the advice and consent of the Senate, and shall receive compensation at the rate prescribed for level II of the Federal Executive Salary Schedule [section 5313 of Title 5, Government Organization and Employees].

"(b) Effective with respect to any individual appointment by the President, by and with the advice and consent of the Senate, after June 1, 1973, the term of service of the Director of the Federal Bureau of Investigation shall be ten years. A Director may not serve more than one ten-year term. The provisions of subsections (a) through (c) of section 8335 of title 5, United States Code [section 8335(a) through (c) of Title 5], shall apply to any individual appointed under this section."

FBI Critical Skills Scholarship Program

Pub.L. 102–183, Title V, § 501, Dec. 4, 1991, 105 Stat. 1268, provided that:

"(a) **Study.**—The Director of the Federal Bureau of Investigation shall conduct a study relative to the establishment of an undergraduate training program with respect to employees of the Federal Bureau of Investigation that is similar in purpose, conditions, content, and administration to undergraduate training programs administered by the Central Intelligence Agency (under section 8 of the Central Intelligence Agency Act of 1949 (50 U.S.C. 403j) [section 403j of Title 50, War and National Defense]), the National Security Agency (under section 16 of the National Security Agency Act of 1959 (50 U.S.C. 402 (note) [set out as a note under section 402 of Title 50])[)], and the Defense Intelligence Agency (under section 1608 of title 10, United States Code [section 1608 of Title 10, Armed Forces]).

"(b) **Implementation.**—Any program proposed under subsection (a) may be implemented only after the Department of Justice and the Office of Management and Budget review and approve the implementation of such program.

"(c) **Availability of funds.**—Any payment made by the Director of the Federal Bureau of Investigation to carry out any program proposed to be established under subsection (a) may be made in any fiscal year only to the extent that appropriated funds are available for that purpose."

§ 533. Investigative and other officials; appointment

The Attorney General may appoint officials—

(1) to detect and prosecute crimes against the United States;

(2) to assist in the protection of the person of the President; and [1]

(3) to assist in the protection of the person of the Attorney General.[2]

(4) to conduct such other investigations regarding official matters under the control of the Department of Justice and the Department of State as may be directed by the Attorney General.

This section does not limit the authority of departments and agencies to investigate crimes against the United States when investigative jurisdiction has been assigned by law to such departments and agencies. (Added Pub.L. 89–554, § 4(c), Sept. 6, 1966, 80 Stat. 616, and amended Pub.L. 107–273, Div. A, Title II, § 204(e), Nov. 2, 2002, 116 Stat. 1776.)

[1] So in original. The word "and" probably should not appear.

[2] So in original. The period probably should be "; and".

HISTORICAL AND STATUTORY NOTES

Department of Justice Exemption Authority

Pub.L. 104–132, Title VIII, § 815(d), Apr. 24, 1996, 110 Stat. 1315, provided that: "Notwithstanding any other provision of law, section 102(b) of the Department of Justice and Related Agencies Appropriations Act, 1993 (Public Law 102–395) [pars. (5) and (6) of section 102(b) of Pub.L. 102–395, as amended, are set out as a note under this section; pars. (1) to (4) of section 102(b) of such Act were not classified to the Code, see Pub.L. 102–395, Oct. 6, 1992, 106 Stat. 1838], shall remain in effect until specifically repealed, subject to any limitation on appropriations contained in any Department of Justice Appropriation Authorization Act."

FBI Investigations of Espionage by Persons Employed by or Assigned to United States Diplomatic Missions Abroad

Pub.L. 101–193, Title VI, § 603, Nov. 30, 1989, 103 Stat. 1710, provided that: "Subject to the authority of the Attorney General, the FBI shall supervise the conduct of all investigations of violations of the espionage laws of the United States by persons employed by or assigned to United States diplomatic missions abroad. All departments and agencies shall report immediately to the FBI any information concerning such a violation. All departments and agencies shall provide appropriate assistance to the FBI in the conduct of such investigations. Nothing in this provision shall be construed as establishing a defense to any criminal, civil, or administrative action."

Undercover Investigative Operations Conducted by Federal Bureau of Investigation or Drug Enforcement Administration; Annual Report to Congress; Financial Audit

Pub.L. 109–162, Title XI, § 1151(c), Jan. 5, 2006, 119 Stat. 3112, provided that: "**ATFE Undercover Investigative Operations.**—Section 102(b) of the Department of Justice and Related Agencies Appropriations Act, 1993 [Pub.L. 102–395, Title I, § 102(b), Oct. 6, 1992, 106 Stat. 1838, as amended, which is set out under this heading], as in effect pursuant to section 815(d) of the Antiterrorism and Effective Death Penalty Act of 1996 [Pub.L. 104–132, Title VIII, 815(d), Apr. 24, 1996, 110 Stat. 1315, set out as a note under this section] shall apply with respect to the Bureau of Alcohol, Tobacco, Firearms, and Explosives and the undercover investigative operations of the Bureau on the same basis as such section applies with respect to any other agency and the undercover investigative operations of such agency."

Pub.L. 110–161, Div. B, Title II, § 207, Dec. 26, 2007, 121 Stat. 1913, provided that: "Notwithstanding any other provision of law, Public Law 102–395 section 102(b) [Pub.L. 102–395, Title I, § 102(b), Oct. 6, 1992, 106 Stat. 1838, as amended, which is set out as a note under this section] shall extend to the Bureau of Alcohol, Tobacco, Firearms and Explosives in the conduct of undercover investigative operations and shall apply without fiscal year limitation with respect to any undercover investigative operation initiated by the Bureau of Alcohol, Tobacco, Firearms and Explosives that is necessary for the detection and prosecution of crimes against the United States."

Similar provisions were contained in the following prior appropriation Acts:

Pub.L. 109–108, Title I, § 107, Nov. 22, 2005, 119 Stat. 2304.

Pub.L. 108–447, Div. B, Title I, § 116, Dec. 8, 2004, 118 Stat. 2870.

Pub.L. 102–395, Title I, § 102(b), Oct. 6, 1992, 106 Stat. 1838, as amended section 112 of H.R. 2076, One Hundred Fourth Congress, as passed by the House of Representatives on Dec. 6, 1995, and as enacted into law by Pub.L. 104–91, Title I, § 101(a), Jan. 6, 1996, 110 Stat. 11, as amended Pub.L. 104–99, Title II, § 211, Jan. 26, 1996, 110 Stat. 37; Pub.L. 109–177, Title V, § 506(a)(10), Mar. 9, 2006, 120 Stat. 248, provided that:

"(1) During fiscal year 1996, with respect to any undercover investigative operation of the Federal Bureau of Investigation or the Drug Enforcement Administration which is necessary for the detection and prosecution of crimes against the United States or for the collection of foreign intelligence or counterintelligence—

"(A) sums authorized to be appropriated for the Federal Bureau of Investigation and for the Drug Enforcement Administration may be used for purchasing property, buildings, and other facilities, and for leasing space, within the United States, the District of Columbia, and the territories and possessions of the United States, without regard to section 1341 of title 31 of the United States Code [31 U.S.C.A. § 1341], section 3732(a) of the Revised Statutes (41 U.S.C. 11(a)), section 305 of the Act of June 30, 1949 (63 Stat. 396; 41 U.S.C. 255), the third undesignated paragraph under the heading of 'Miscellaneous' of the Act of March 3, 1877 (19 Stat. 370; 40 U.S.C. 34 [see now 40 U.S.C.A. § 8141]), section 3324 of title 31 of the United States Code [31 U.S.C.A. § 3324], section 3741 of the Revised Statutes (41 U.S.C. 22), and subsections (a) and (c) of section 304 of the Federal Property and Administrative Service Act of 1949 (63 Stat. 395; 41 U.S.C. 254(a) and (c)),

"(B) sums authorized to be appropriated for the Federal Bureau of Investigation and for the Drug Enforcement Administration may be used to establish or to acquire proprietary corporations or business entities as part of an undercover investigative operation, and to operate such corporations or business entities on a commercial basis, without regard to section 9102 of title 31 of the United States Code [31 U.S.C.A. § 9102].

"(C) sums authorized to be appropriated for the Federal Bureau of Investigation and for the Drug Enforcement Administration for fiscal years 1996, and the proceeds from such undercover operation, may be deposited in banks or other financial institutions, without regard to section 648 of title 18 of the United States Code [18 U.S.C.A. § 648] and section 3302 of title 31 of the United States Code [31 U.S.C.A. § 3302], and

"(D) proceeds from such undercover operation may be used to offset necessary and reasonable expenses incurred in such operation, without regard to section 3302 of title 31 of the United States Code [31 U.S.C.A. § 3302],

only, in operations designed to detect and prosecute crimes against the United States, upon the written certification of the Director of the Federal Bureau of Investigation (or, if designated by the Director, a member of the Undercover Operations Review Committee established by the Attorney General in the Attorney General's Guidelines on Federal Bureau of Investigation Undercover Operations, as in effect on July 1, 1983) or the Administrator of the Drug Enforcement Administration, as the case may be, and the Attorney General (or, with respect to Federal Bureau of Investigation undercover operations, if designated by the Attorney General, a member of such Review Committee), that any action authorized by subparagraph (A), (B), (C), or (D) is necessary for the conduct of such undercover operation. If the undercover operation is designed to collect foreign intelligence or counterintelligence, the certification that any action authorized by subparagraph (A), (B), (C), or (D) is necessary for the conduct of such undercover operation shall be by the Director of the Federal Bureau of Investigation (or, if designated by the Director, the Assistant Director, Intelligence Division) and the Attorney General (or, if designated by the Attorney General, the Assistant Attorney General for National Security). Such certification shall continue in effect for the duration of such undercover operation, without regard to fiscal years.

"(2) Notwithstanding paragraph (1) [of this note], it shall not be necessary to obtain such certification for an undercover operation in order that proceeds or other money—

"(A) received by an undercover agent from or at the direction of a subject of an investigation, or

"(B) provided to an agent by an individual cooperating with the Government in an investigation, who received the proceeds or money from or at the direction of a subject of the investigation,

may be used as a subject of the investigation directs without regard to section 3302 of title 31 of the United States Code [31 U.S.C.A. § 3302]: Provided, That the Director of the Federal Bureau of Investigation or the Administrator of the Drug Enforcement Administration, or their designees, in advance or as soon as practicable thereafter, make a written determination that such a use would further the investigation: And provided further, That the financial audit requirements of paragraphs (5) and (6) [of this note] shall apply in each investigation where such a determination has been made.

"(3) As soon as the proceeds from an undercover investigative operation with respect to which an action is authorized and carried out under subparagraphs (C) and (D) of paragraph (1) [of this note], or under paragraph (2) [of this note] are no longer necessary for the conduct of such operation, such proceeds or the balance of such proceeds remaining at the time shall be deposited in the Treasury of the United States as miscellaneous receipts.

"(4) If a corporation or business entity established or acquired as part of an undercover operation under subparagraph (B) of paragraph (1) [of this note] with a net value of over $50,000 is to be liquidated, sold, or otherwise disposed of, the Federal Bureau of Investigation or the Drug Enforcement Administration, as much in advance as the Director or the Administrator, or the designee of the Director or the Administrator, determines is practicable, shall report the circumstances to the Attorney General and the Comptroller General. The proceeds of the liquidation, sale, or other disposition, after obligations are met, shall be deposited in the Treasury of the United States as miscellaneous receipts.

"(5)(A) The Federal Bureau of Investigation or the Drug Enforcement Administration, as the case may be, shall conduct a detailed financial audit of each undercover investigative operation which is closed in fiscal year 1996—

"(i) submit the results of such audit in writing to the Attorney General, and

"(ii) not later than 180 days after such undercover operation is closed, submit a report to the Congress concerning such audit.

"(B) The Federal Bureau of Investigation and the Drug Enforcement Administration shall each also submit a report annually to the Congress specifying as to their respective undercover investigative operations—

"(i) the number, by programs, of undercover investigative operations pending as of the end of the one–year period for which such report is submitted,

"(ii) the number, by programs, of undercover investigative operations commenced in the one–year period preceding the period for which such report is submitted, and

"(iii) the number, by programs, of undercover investigative operations closed in the one–year period preceding the period for which such report is submitted and, with respect to each such closed undercover operation, the results obtained. With respect to each such closed undercover operation which involves any of the sensitive circumstances specified in the Attorney General's Guidelines on Federal Bureau of Investigation Undercover Operations, such report shall contain a detailed description of the operation and related matters, including information pertaining to—

"(I) the results,

"(II) any civil claims, and

"(III) identification of such sensitive circumstances involved, that arose at any time during the course of such undercover operation.

"(6) For purposes of paragraph (5) [of this note]—

"(A) the term 'closed' refers to the earliest point in time at which—

"(i) all criminal proceedings (other than appeals) are concluded, or

"(ii) covert activities are concluded, whichever occurs later,

"(B) the term 'employees' means employees, as defined in section 2105 of title 5 of the United States Code [5 U.S.C.A. § 2105], of the Federal Bureau of Investigation, and

"(C) the terms 'undercover investigative operations' and 'undercover operation' mean any undercover investigative operation of the Federal Bureau of Investigation or the Drug Enforcement Administration (other than a foreign counterintelligence undercover investigative operation)—

"(i) in which—

"(I) the gross receipts (excluding interest earned) exceed $50,000, or

"(II) expenditures (other than expenditures for salaries of employees) exceed $150,000, and

"(ii) which is exempt from section 3302 or 9102 of title 31 of the United States Code [31 U.S.C.A. §§ 3302 or 9102],

except that clauses (i) and (ii) shall not apply with respect to the report required under subparagraph (B) of such paragraph."

[Section 101(a) of Pub.L. 104–91, as amended by section 211 of Pub.L. 104–99, provided that the General Provisions for the Department of Justice in Title I of the Departments of Commerce, Justice, and State, the Judiciary, and Related Agencies Appropriations Act, 1996 (H.R. 2076) as passed by the House of Representatives on Dec. 6, 1995, was enacted into permanent law. Section 112 of that bill, cited in the credit to this note, amended subsecs. (b)(1), (b)(1)(C), and (b)(5)(A) of this note.]

[Reporting requirement of section 102(b)(5) of the Department of Justice and Related Agencies Appropriations Act, 1993, set out above, excepted from termination under Pub.L. 104–66, § 3003(a)(1), as amended, set out in a note under 31 U.S.C.A. § 1113, see Pub.L. 106–197, § 1, set out as a note under 31 U.S.C.A. § 1113.]

Similar provisions were contained in the following prior appropriation Acts:

Pub.L. 102–140, Title I, § 102(b)(4), (5), Oct. 28, 1991, 105 Stat. 793.

Pub.L. 101–515, Title II, § 202(b)(4), (5), Nov. 5, 1990, 104 Stat. 2118.

Pub.L. 101–162, Title II, § 204(b)(4), (5), Nov. 21, 1989, 103 Stat. 1004.

Pub.L. 100–459, Title II, § 204(b)(4), (5), Oct. 1, 1988, 102 Stat. 2200, 2201, as amended Pub.L. 101–650, Title III, § 325(c)(2), Dec. 1, 1990, 104 Stat. 5121.

Pub.L. 100–202, § 101(a) [Title II, § 204(b)(4), (5)], Dec. 22, 1987, 101 Stat. 1329–16.

Pub.L. 99–500, Title I, § 101(b) [Title II, § 204(b)(4), (5)], Oct. 18, 1986, 100 Stat. 1783–53 and Pub.L. 99–591, Title I, § 101(b) [Title II, 204(b)(4), (5)], Oct. 30, 1986, 100 Stat. 3341–53.

Pub.L. 99–180, Title II, § 204(b)(4), (5), Dec. 13, 1985, 99 Stat. 1148.

Pub.L. 98–411, Title II, § 203(b)(4), (5), Aug. 30, 1984, 98 Stat. 1560.

Pub.L. 98–166, Title II, § 205(b)(4), (5), Nov. 28, 1983, 97 Stat. 1087.

Pub.L. 96–132, § 7(d), Nov. 30, 1979, 93 Stat. 1046, provided that:

"(1) The Federal Bureau of Investigation shall conduct detailed financial audits of undercover operations closed on or after October 1, 1979, and—

"(A) report the results of each audit in writing to the Department of Justice, and

"(B) report annually to the Congress concerning these audits.

"(2) For the purposes of paragraph (1) [of this note], 'undercover operation' means any undercover operation of the Federal Bureau of Investigation, other than a foreign counterintelligence undercover operation—

"(A) in which the gross receipts exceed $50,000, and

"(B) which is exempted from section 3617 of the Revised Statutes (31 U.S.C. 484) [31 U.S.C.A. § 3302(b)] or section 304(a) of the Government Corporation Control Act (31 U.S.C. 869(a)) [31 U.S.C.A. § 9102]."

Pub.L. 109–162, Title XI, § 1151(c), Jan. 5, 2006, 119 Stat. 3112, provided that: "**ATFE Undercover Investigative Operations.**—Section 102(b) of the Department of Justice and Related Agencies Appropriations Act, 1993 [Pub.L. 102–395, Title I, § 102(b), Oct. 6, 1992, 106 Stat. 1838, as amended, which is set out above under this heading], as in effect pursuant to section 815(d) of the Antiterrorism and Effective Death Penalty Act of 1996 [Pub.L. 104–132, Title VIII, 815(d), Apr. 24, 1996, 110 Stat. 1315, set out as a note under this section] shall apply with respect to the Bureau of Alcohol, Tobacco, Firearms, and Explosives and the undercover investigative operations of the Bureau on the same basis as such section applies with respect to any other agency and the undercover investigative operations of such agency."

§ 534. Acquisition, preservation, and exchange of identification records and information; appointment of officials

(a) The Attorney General shall—

(1) acquire, collect, classify, and preserve identification, criminal identification, crime, and other records;

(2) acquire, collect, classify, and preserve any information which would assist in the identification of any deceased individual who has not been identified after the discovery of such deceased individual;

(3) acquire, collect, classify, and preserve any information which would assist in the location of any missing person (including an unemancipated person as defined by the laws of the place of residence of such person) and provide confirmation as to any entry for such a person to the parent, legal guardian, or next of kin of that person (and the Attorney General may acquire, collect, classify, and preserve such information from such parent, guardian, or next of kin); and

(4) exchange such records and information with, and for the official use of, authorized officials of the Federal Government, including the United States Sentencing Commission, the States, cities, and penal and other institutions.

(b) The exchange of records and information authorized by subsection (a)(4) of this section is subject to cancellation if dissemination is made outside the receiving departments or related agencies.

(c) The Attorney General may appoint officials to perform the functions authorized by this section.

(d) **Indian law enforcement agencies.**—The Attorney General shall permit Indian law enforcement agencies, in cases of domestic violence, dating violence, sexual assault, and stalking, to enter information into Federal criminal information databases and to obtain information from the databases.

(e) For purposes of this section, the term "other institutions" includes—

(1) railroad police departments which perform the administration of criminal justice and have arrest powers pursuant to a State statute, which allocate a substantial part of their annual budget to the administration of criminal justice, and which meet training requirements established by law or ordinance for law enforcement officers; and

(2) police departments of private colleges or universities which perform the administration of criminal justice and have arrest powers pursuant to a State statute, which allocate a substantial part of their annual budget to the administration of criminal justice, and which meet training requirements established by law or ordinance for law enforcement officers.

(f)(1) Information from national crime information databases consisting of identification records, criminal history records, protection orders, and wanted person records may be disseminated to civil or criminal courts for use in domestic violence or stalking cases. Nothing in this subsection shall be construed to permit access to such records for any other purpose.

(2) Federal and State criminal justice agencies authorized to enter information into criminal information databases may include—

(A) arrests, convictions, and arrest warrants for stalking or domestic violence or for violations of protection orders for the protection of parties from stalking or domestic violence; and

(B) protection orders for the protection of persons from stalking or domestic violence, provided such orders are subject to periodic verification.

(3) As used in this subsection—

(A) the term "national crime information databases" means the National Crime Information Center and its incorporated criminal history databases, including the Interstate Identification Index; and

(B) the term "protection order" includes—

(i) any injunction, restraining order, or any other order issued by a civil or criminal court for the purpose of preventing violent or threatening acts or harassment against, sexual violence or contact or communication with or physical proximity to, another person, including any temporary or final orders issued by civil or criminal courts whether obtained by filing an independent action or as a pendente lite order in another proceeding so long as any civil order was issued in response to a complaint, petition, or motion filed by or on behalf of a person seeking protection; and

(ii) any support, child custody or visitation provisions, orders, remedies, or relief issued as part of a protection order, restraining order, or stay away injunction pursuant to State, tribal, territorial, or local law authorizing the issuance of protection orders, restraining orders, or injunctions for the protection of victims of domestic violence, dating violence, sexual assault, or stalking.

(Added Pub.L. 89–554, § 4(c), Sept. 6, 1966, 80 Stat. 616, and amended Pub.L. 97–292, §§ 2, 3(a), Oct. 12, 1982, 96 Stat. 1259; Pub.L. 100–690, Title VII, § 7333, Nov. 18, 1988, 102 Stat. 4469; Pub.L. 103–322, Title IV, § 40601(a), Sept. 13, 1994, 108 Stat. 1950; Pub.L. 107–273, Div. A, Title II, § 204(c), Div. B, Title IV, § 4003(b)(4), Div. C, Title I, § 11004, Nov. 2, 2002, 116 Stat. 1776, 1811, 1816; Pub.L. 109–162, Title I, § 118, Title IX, § 905(a), Jan. 5, 2006, 119 Stat. 2989, 3079; Pub.L. 109–248, Title I, § 153(i), July 27, 2006, 120 Stat. 611.)

HISTORICAL AND STATUTORY NOTES

Additional Reporting on Crime

Pub.L. 110–457, Title II, § 237(a), (b), Dec. 23, 2008, 122 Stat. 5083, provided that:

"(a) **Trafficking offense classification.**—The Director of the Federal Bureau of Investigation shall—

"(1) classify the offense of human trafficking as a Part I crime in the Uniform Crime Reports;

"(2) To the extent feasible, establish subcategories for State sex crimes that involve—

"(A) a person who is younger than 18 years of age;

"(B) the use of force, fraud or coercion; or

"(C) neither of the elements described in subparagraphs (A) and (B); and

"(3) classify the offense of human trafficking as a Group A offense for purpose of the National Incident–Based Reporting System.

"(b) **Additional information.**—The Director of the Federal Bureau of Investigation shall revise the Uniform Crime Reporting System and the National Incident–Based Reporting System to distinguish between reports of—

"(1) Incidents of assisting or promoting prostitution, which shall include crimes committed by persons who—

"(A) do not directly engage in commercial sex acts; and

"(B) direct, manage, or profit from such acts, such as State pimping and pandering crimes;

"(2) incidents of purchasing prostitution, which shall include crimes committed by persons who purchase or attempt to purchase or trade anything of value for commercial sex acts; and

"(3) incidents of prostitution, which shall include crimes committed by persons providing or attempting to provide commercial sex acts."

Tribal Registry

Pub.L. 109–162, Title IX, § 905(b), Jan. 5, 2006, 119 Stat. 3080, provided that:

"(1) **Establishment.**—The Attorney General shall contract with any interested Indian tribe, tribal organization, or tribal nonprofit organization to develop and maintain—

"(A) a national tribal sex offender registry; and

"(B) a tribal protection order registry containing civil and criminal orders of protection issued by Indian tribes and participating jurisdictions.

"(2) **Authorization of appropriations.**—There is authorized to be appropriated to carry out this section [amending this section and enacting this note] $1,000,000 for each of fiscal years 2007 through 2011, to remain available until expended."

National Gang Intelligence Center

Pub.L. 109–162, Title XI, § 1107, Jan. 5, 2006, 119 Stat. 3093, provided that:

"(a) **Establishment.**—The Attorney General shall establish a National Gang Intelligence Center and gang information database to be housed at and administered by the Federal Bureau of Investigation to collect, analyze, and disseminate gang activity information from—

"(1) the Federal Bureau of Investigation;

"(2) the Bureau of Alcohol, Tobacco, Firearms, and Explosives;

"(3) the Drug Enforcement Administration;

"(4) the Bureau of Prisons;

"(5) the United States Marshals Service;

"(6) the Directorate of Border and Transportation Security of the Department of Homeland Security;

"(7) the Department of Housing and Urban Development;

"(8) State and local law enforcement;

"(9) Federal, State, and local prosecutors;

"(10) Federal, State, and local probation and parole offices;

"(11) Federal, State, and local prisons and jails; and

"(12) any other entity as appropriate.

"(b) **Information.**—The Center established under subsection (a) shall make available the information referred to in subsection (a) to—

"(1) Federal, State, and local law enforcement agencies;

"(2) Federal, State, and local corrections agencies and penal institutions;

"(3) Federal, State, and local prosecutorial agencies; and

"(4) any other entity as appropriate.

"(c) **Annual report.**—The Center established under subsection (a) [of this note] shall annually submit to Congress a report on gang activity.

"(d) **Authorization of appropriations.**—There are authorized to be appropriated to carry out this section [this note] $10,000,000 for fiscal year 2006 and for each fiscal year thereafter."

Reviews of Criminal Records of Applicants for Private Security Officer Employment

Pub.L. 108–458, Title VI, § 6402, Dec. 17, 2004, 118 Stat. 3755, provided that:

"(a) **Short title.**—This section [enacting this note] may be cited as the 'Private Security Officer Employment Authorization Act of 2004'.

"(b) **Findings.**—Congress finds that—

"(1) employment of private security officers in the United States is growing rapidly;

"(2) private security officers function as an adjunct to, but not a replacement for, public law enforcement by helping to reduce and prevent crime;

"(3) such private security officers protect individuals, property, and proprietary information, and provide protection to such diverse operations as banks, hospitals, research and development centers, manufacturing facilities, defense and aerospace contractors, high technology businesses, nuclear power plants, chemical companies, oil and gas refineries, airports, communication facilities and operations, office complexes, schools, residential properties, apartment complexes, gated communities, and others;

"(4) sworn law enforcement officers provide significant services to the citizens of the United States in its public areas, and are supplemented by private security officers;

"(5) the threat of additional terrorist attacks requires cooperation between public and private sectors and demands professional, reliable, and responsible security officers for the protection of people, facilities, and institutions;

"(6) the trend in the Nation toward growth in such security services has accelerated rapidly;

"(7) such growth makes available more public sector law enforcement officers to combat serious and violent crimes, including terrorism;

"(8) the American public deserves the employment of qualified, well-trained private security personnel as an adjunct to sworn law enforcement officers; and

"(9) private security officers and applicants for private security officer positions should be thoroughly screened and trained.

"(c) **Definitions.**—In this section [this note]:

"(1) **Employee.**—The term 'employee' includes both a current employee and an applicant for employment as a private security officer.

"(2) **Authorized employer.**—The term 'authorized employer' means any person that—

"(A) employs private security officers; and

"(B) is authorized by regulations promulgated by the Attorney General to request a criminal history record information search of an employee through a State identification bureau pursuant to this section [this note].

"(3) **Private security officer.**—The term 'private security officer'—

"(A) means an individual other than an employee of a Federal, State, or local government, whose primary duty is to perform security services, full or part time, for consideration, whether armed or unarmed and in uniform or plain clothes (except for services excluded from coverage under this Act [this note] if the Attorney General determines by regulation that such exclusion would serve the public interest); but

"(B) Does not include—

"(i) employees whose duties are primarily internal audit or credit functions;

"(ii) employees of electronic security system companies acting as technicians or monitors; or

"(iii) employees whose duties primarily involve the secure movement of prisoners.

"(4) **Security services.**—The term 'security services' means acts to protect people or property as defined by regulations promulgated by the Attorney General.

"(5) **State identification bureau.**—The term 'State identification bureau' means the State entity designated by the Attorney General for the submission and receipt of criminal history record information.

"(d) **Criminal history record information search.**—

"(1) **In general.**—

"(A) **Submission of fingerprints.**—An authorized employer may submit to the State identification bureau of a participating State, fingerprints or other means of positive identification, as determined by the Attorney General, of an employee of such employer for purposes of a criminal history record information search pursuant to this Act [this note].

"(B) **Employee rights.**—

"(i) **Permission.**—An authorized employer shall obtain written consent from an employee to submit to the State identification bureau of the participating State the request to search the criminal history record information of the employee under this Act [this note].

"(ii) **Access.**—An authorized employer shall provide to the employee confidential access to any information relating to the employee received by the authorized employer pursuant to this Act [this note].

"(C) **Providing information to the State identification bureau.**—Upon receipt of a request for a criminal history record information search from an authorized employer pursuant to this Act [this note], submitted through the State identification bureau of a participating State, the Attorney General shall—

"(i) search the appropriate records of the Criminal Justice Information Services Division of the Federal Bureau of Investigation; and

"(ii) promptly provide any resulting identification and criminal history record information to the submitting State identification bureau requesting the information.

"(D) **Use of information.**—

"(i) **In general.**—Upon receipt of the criminal history record information from the Attorney General by the State identification bureau, the information shall be used only as provided in clause (ii).

"(ii) **Terms.**—In the case of—

"(I) A participating State that has no State standards for qualification to be a private security officer, the State shall notify an authorized employer as to the fact of whether an employee has been—

"(aa) convicted of a felony, an offense involving dishonesty or a false statement if the conviction occurred during the previous 10 years, or an offense involving the use or attempted use of physical force against the person of another if the conviction occurred during the previous 10 years; or

"(bb) charged with a criminal felony for which there has been no resolution during the preceding 365 days; or

"(II) a participating State that has State standards for qualification to be a private security officer, the State shall use the information received pursuant to this Act [this note] in applying the State standards and shall only notify the employer of the results of the application of the State standards.

"(E) **Frequency of requests.**—An authorized employer may request a criminal history record information search for an employee only once every 12 months of continuous employment by that employee unless the authorized employer has good cause to submit additional requests.

"(2) **Regulations.**—Not later than 180 days after the date of enactment of this Act [Dec. 17, 2004], the Attorney General shall issue such final or interim final regulations as may be necessary to carry out this Act [this note], including—

"(A) measures relating to the security, confidentiality, accuracy, use, submission, dissemination, destruction of information and audits, and record keeping;

"(B) standards for qualification as an authorized employer; and

"(C) the imposition of reasonable fees necessary for conducting the background checks.

"(3) **Criminal penalties for use of information.**—Whoever knowingly and intentionally uses any information obtained pursuant to this Act [this note] other than for the purpose of determining the suitability of an individual for employment as a private security officer shall be fined under title 18, United States Code [18 U.S.C.A. § 1 et seq.], or imprisoned for not more than 2 years, or both.

"(4) **User fees.**—

"(A) **In general.**—The Director of the Federal Bureau of Investigation may—

"(i) collect fees to process background checks provided for by this Act [this note]; and

"(ii) establish such fees at a level to include an additional amount to defray expenses for the automation of fingerprint identification and criminal justice information services and associated costs.

"(B) **Limitations.**—Any fee collected under this subsection—

"(i) shall, consistent with Public Law 101–515 [Departments of Commerce, Justice, and State, the Judiciary, and Related Agencies Appropriations Act, 1991, Pub.L. 101–515, Nov. 5, 1990, 104 Stat. 2101, see Tables for classifications] and Public Law 104–99 [Balanced Budget Downpayment Act, I, Pub.L. 104–99, Jan. 26, 1996, 110 Stat. 26, see Tables for classification], be credited to the appropriation to be used for salaries and other expenses incurred through providing the services described in such Public Laws and in subparagraph (A);

"(ii) shall be available for expenditure only to pay the costs of such activities and services; and

"(iii) shall remain available until expended.

"(C) **State costs.**—Nothing in this Act [this note] shall be construed as restricting the right of a State to assess a reasonable fee on an authorized employer for the costs to the State of administering this Act [this note].

"(5) **State opt out.**—A State may decline to participate in the background check system authorized by this Act [this note] by enacting a law or issuing an order by the Governor (if consistent with State law) providing that the State is declining to participate pursuant to this subsection."

Criminal Background Checks for Applicants for Employment in Nursing Facilities and Home Health Care Agencies

Pub.L. 105–277, Div. A, § 101(b) [Title I, § 124], Oct. 21, 1998, 112 Stat. 2681–73, provided that:

"(a)(1) A nursing facility or home health care agency may submit a request to the Attorney General to conduct a search and exchange of records described in subsection (b) regarding an applicant for employment if the employment position is involved in direct patient care.

"(2) A nursing facility or home health care agency requesting a search and exchange of records under this section shall submit to the Attorney General through the appropriate State agency or agency designated by the Attorney General a copy of an employment applicant's fingerprints, a statement signed by the applicant authorizing the nursing facility or home health care agency to request the search and exchange of records, and any other identification information not more than 7 days (excluding Saturdays, Sundays, and legal public holidays under section 6103(a) of title 5, United States Code) after acquiring the fingerprints, signed statement, and information.

"(b) Pursuant to any submission that complies with the requirements of subsection (a), the Attorney General shall search the records of the Criminal Justice Information Services Division of the Federal Bureau of Investigation for any criminal history records corresponding to the fingerprints or other identification information submitted. The Attorney General shall provide any corresponding information resulting from the search to the appropriate State agency or agency designated by the Attorney General to receive such information.

"(c) Information regarding an applicant for employment in a nursing facility or home health care agency obtained pursuant to this section may be used only by the facility or agency requesting the information and only for the purpose of determining the suitability of the applicant for employment by the facility or agency in a position involved in direct patient care.

"(d) The Attorney General may charge a reasonable fee, not to exceed $50 per request, to any nursing facility or home health care agency requesting a search and exchange of records pursuant to this section.

"(e) Not later than 2 years after the date of enactment of this Act [Oct. 21, 1998], the Attorney General shall submit a report to Congress on the number of requests for searches and exchanges of records made under this section by nursing facilities and home health care agencies and the disposition of such requests.

"(f) Whoever knowingly uses any information obtained pursuant to this section for a purpose other than as authorized under subsection (c) shall be fined in accordance with title 18, United States Code, imprisoned for not more than 2 years, or both.

"(g) A nursing facility or home health care agency that, in denying employment for an applicant, reasonably relies upon information provided by the Attorney General pursuant to this section shall not be liable in any action brought by the applicant based on the employment determination resulting from the incompleteness or inaccuracy of the information.

"(h) The Attorney General may promulgate such regulations as are necessary to carry out this section, including regulations regarding the security, confidentiality, accuracy, use, destruction, and dissemination of information, audits and recordkeeping, the imposition of fees, and any necessary modifications to the definitions contained in subsection (i).

"(i) In this section:

"(1) The term 'home health care agency' means an agency that provides home health care or personal care services on a visiting basis in a place of residence.

"(2) The term 'nursing facility' means a facility or institution (or a distinct part of an institution) that is primarily engaged in providing to residents of the facility or institution nursing care, including skilled nursing care, and related services for individuals who require medical or nursing care.

"(j) This section shall apply without fiscal year limitation."

Compilation of Statistics Relating to Intimidation of Government Employees

Pub.L. 104–132, Title VIII, § 808, Apr. 24, 1996, 110 Stat. 1310, was repealed by Pub.L. 107–273, Div. A, Title III, § 311(a), Nov. 2, 2002, 116 Stat. 1786.

Family and Domestic Violence; Data Collection and Reporting

Section 7609 of Pub.L. 100–690 provided that:

"(a) **Family violence reporting.**—Under the authority of section 534 of title 28, United States Code [this section], the Attorney General shall require, and include in uniform crime reports, data that indicate—

"(1) the age of the victim; and

"(2) the relationship of the victim to the offender, for crimes of murder, aggravated assault, simple assault, rape, sexual offenses, and offenses against children.

"(b) **National Crime Survey.**—The Director of the Bureau of Justice Statistics, through the annual National Crime Survey, shall collect and publish data that more accurately measures the extent of domestic violence in America, especially the physical and sexual abuse of children and the elderly.

"(c) **Authorization of appropriations.**—There are authorized to be appropriated in fiscal years 1989, 1990, 1991, and 1992, such sums as are necessary to carry out the purposes of this section."

FBI Fees to Process Fingerprint Identification Records and Name Checks

Pub.L. 101–515, Title II, Nov. 5, 1990, 104 Stat. 2112; Pub.L. 104–91, Title I, § 101(a), Jan. 6, 1996, 110 Stat. 11, as amended Pub.L. 104–99, Title II, § 211, Jan. 26, 1996, 110 Stat. 37, provided in part that: "For fiscal year 1991 and hereafter the Director of the Federal Bureau of Investigation may establish and collect fees to process fingerprint identification records and name checks for non-criminal justice, non-law enforcement employment and licensing purposes and for certain employees of private sector contractors with classified Government contracts, and notwithstanding the provisions of 31 U.S.C. 3302 [section 3302 of Title 31, Money and Finance], credit such fees to this appropriation to be used for salaries and other expenses incurred in providing these services, and that the Director of the Federal Bureau of Investigation may establish such fees at a level to include an additional amount to establish a fund to remain available until expended to defray expenses for the automation of fingerprint identification and criminal justice information services and associated costs."

[Section 101(a) of Pub.L. 104–91, as amended by section 211 of Pub.L. 104–99, provided in part that section 113 of the General Provisions for the Department of Justice in Title I of the Departments of Commerce, Justice, and State, the Judiciary, and Related Agencies Appropriations Act, 1996 (H.R. 2076) as passed by the House of Representatives on Dec. 6, 1995, was enacted into permanent law. Such section 113 of H.R. 2076 amended Pub.L. 101–515, set out above.]

Funds for Exchange of Identification Records

Pub.L. 92–544, Title II, § 201, Oct. 25, 1972, 86 Stat. 1115, provided that: "The funds provided for Salaries and Expenses, Federal Bureau of Investigation, may be used hereafter, in addition to those uses authorized thereunder, for the exchange of identification records with officials or federally chartered or insured banking institutions to promote or maintain the security of those institutions, and, if authorized by State statute and approved by the Attorney General, to officials of State and local governments for purposes of employment and licensing, any such exchange to be made only for the official use of any such official and subject to the same restriction with respect to dissemination as that provided for under the aforementioned appropriation."

Hate Crime Statistics

Pub.L. 101–275, Apr. 23, 1990, 104 Stat. 140, as amended Pub.L. 103–322, Title XXXII, § 320926, Sept. 13, 1994, 108 Stat. 2131; Pub.L. 104–155, § 7, July 3, 1996, 110 Stat. 1394, provided:

"That (a) this Act [this note] may be cited as the 'Hate Crime Statistics Act'.

"(b)(1) Under the authority of section 534 of title 28, United States Code [this section], the Attorney General shall acquire data, for each calendar year, about crimes that manifest evidence of prejudice based on race, religion, disability, sexual orientation, or ethnicity, including where appropriate the crimes of murder, non-negligent manslaughter; forcible rape; aggravated assault, simple assault, intimidation; arson; and destruction, damage or vandalism of property.

"(2) The Attorney General shall establish guidelines for the collection of such data including the necessary evidence and criteria that must be present for a finding of manifest prejudice and procedures for carrying out the purposes of this section.

"(3) Nothing in this section creates a cause of action or a right to bring an action, including an action based on discrimination due to sexual orientation. As used in this section, the term 'sexual orientation' means consensual homosexuality or heterosexuality. This subsection does not limit any existing cause of action or right to bring an action, including any action under the Administrative Procedure Act [5 U.S.C.A. §§ 551 et seq., 701 et seq.] or the All Writs Act [28 U.S.C.A. § 1651].

"(4) Data acquired under this section shall be used only for research or statistical purposes and may not contain any information that may reveal the identity of an individual victim of a crime.

"(5) The Attorney General shall publish an annual summary of the data acquired under this section.

"(c) There are authorized to be appropriated such sums as may be necessary to carry out the provisions of this section through fiscal year 2002.

"**Sec. 2.** (a) Congress finds that—

"(1) the American family life is the foundation of American Society,

"(2) Federal policy should encourage the well-being, financial security, and health of the American family,

"(3) schools should not de-emphasize the critical value of American family life.

"(b) Nothing in this Act [this note] shall be construed, nor shall any funds appropriated to carry out the purpose of the Act [this note] be used, to promote or encourage homosexuality."

National Crime Information Center Project 2000

Pub.L. 101–647, Title VI, Subtitle B, Nov. 29, 1990, 104 Stat. 4823, provided that:

"**Sec. 611. Short title.**

"This section [subtitle] may be cited as the 'National Law Enforcement Cooperation Act of 1990'.

"**Sec. 612. Findings.**

"The Congress finds that—

"(1) cooperation among Federal, State and local law enforcement agencies is critical to an effective national response to the problems of violent crime and drug trafficking in the United States;

"(2) the National Crime Information Center, which links more than 16,000 Federal, State and local law enforcement agencies, is the single most important avenue of cooperation among law enforcement agencies;

"(3) major improvements to the National Crime Information Center are needed because the current system is more than twenty years old; carries much greater volumes of enforcement information; and at this time is unable to incorporate technological advances that would significantly improve its performance; and

"(4) the Federal Bureau of Investigation, working with State and local law enforcement agencies and private organizations, has developed a promising plan, 'NCIC 2000', to make the necessary upgrades to the National Crime Information Center that should meet the needs of United States law enforcement agencies into the next century.

"**Sec. 613. Authorization of appropriations.**

"There are authorized to be appropriated the following sums to implement the 'NCIC 2000' project:

"(1) $17,000,000 for fiscal year 1991;

"(2) $25,000,000 for fiscal year 1992;

"(3) $22,000,000 for fiscal year 1993;

"(4) $9,000,000 for fiscal year 1994; and

"(5) such sums as may be necessary for fiscal year 1995.

"**Sec. 614. Report.**

"By February 1 of each fiscal year for which funds for NCIC 2000 are requested, the Director of the Federal Bureau of Investigation shall submit a report to the Committees on the Judiciary of the Senate and House of Representatives that details the progress that has been made in implementing NCIC 2000 and a complete justification for the funds requested in the following fiscal year for NCIC 2000."

Parimutuel Licensing Simplification.

Pub.L. 100–413, Aug. 22, 1988, 102 Stat. 1101, provided that:

"**Section 1. Short title.**

"This Act [this note] may be cited as the 'Parimutuel Licensing Simplification Act of 1988'.

"**Sec. 2. Submission by association of State regulatory officials.**

"**(a) In general.**—An association of State officials regulating parimutuel wagering, designated for the purpose of this section by the Attorney General, may submit fingerprints to the Attorney General on behalf of any applicant for State license to participate in parimutuel wagering. In response to such a submission, the Attorney General may, to the extent provided by law, exchange, for licensing and employment purposes, identification and criminal history records with the State governmental bodies to which such applicant has applied.

"**(b) Definition.**—As used in this section, the term 'State' means a State of the United States, the District of Columbia, the Commonwealth of Puerto Rico, or any territory or possession of the United States.

"**Sec. 3. Effective date.**

"This Act shall take effect on July 1, 1989."

Rulemaking Relating to Authorization of Access to Federal Criminal Information Databases

Section 40601(b) of Pub.L. 103–322 provided that: "The Attorney General may make rules to carry out the subsection added to section 534 of title 28, United States Code, by subsection (a) [subsec. (e) of this section], after consultation with the officials charged with managing the National Crime Information Center and the Criminal Justice Information Services Advisory Policy Board."

Uniform Federal Crime Reporting Act of 1988

Section 7332 of Pub.L. 100–690 provided that:

"**(a) Short Title.**—This section [this note] may be cited as the 'Uniform Federal Crime Reporting Act of 1988'.

"**(b) Definitions.**—For purposes of this section, the term 'Uniform Crime Reports' means the reports authorized under section 534 of title 28, United States Code [this section], and administered by the Federal Bureau of Investigation which compiles nationwide criminal statistics for use in law enforcement administration, operation, and management and to assess the nature and type of crime in the United States.

"**(c) Establishment of system.**—

"**(1) In general.**—The Attorney General shall acquire, collect, classify, and preserve national data on Federal criminal offenses as part of the Uniform Crime Reports.

"(2) **Reporting by Federal agencies.**—All departments and agencies within the Federal government (including the Department of Defense) which routinely investigate complaints of criminal activity, shall report details about crime within their respective jurisdiction to the Attorney General in a uniform manner and on a form prescribed by the Attorney General. The reporting required by this subsection shall be limited to the reporting of those crimes comprising the Uniform Crime Reports.

"(3) **Distribution of data.**—The Attorney General shall distribute data received pursuant to paragraph (2), in the form of annual Uniform Crime Reports for the United States, to the President, Members of the Congress, State governments, and officials of localities and penal and other institutions participating in the Uniform Crime Reports program.

"(d) **Role of Federal Bureau of Investigation.**—The Attorney General may designate the Federal Bureau of Investigation as the lead agency for purposes of performing the functions authorized by this section and may appoint or establish such advisory and oversight boards as may be necessary to assist the Bureau in ensuring uniformity, quality, and maximum use of the data collected.

"(e) **Inclusion of offenses involving illegal drugs.**—The Director of the Federal Bureau of Investigation is authorized to classify offenses involving illegal drugs and drug trafficking as a part I crime in the Uniform Crime Reports.

"(f) **Authorization of appropriations.**—There are authorized to be appropriated $350,000 for fiscal year 1989 and such sums as may be necessary to carry out the provisions of this section after fiscal year 1989.

"(g) **Effective date.**—The provisions of this section shall be effective on January 1, 1989."

§ 535. Investigation of crimes involving Government officers and employees; limitations

(a) The Attorney General and the Federal Bureau of Investigation may investigate any violation of Federal criminal law involving Government officers and employees—

(1) notwithstanding any other provision of law; and

(2) without limiting the authority to investigate any matter which is conferred on them or on a department or agency of the Government.

(b) Any information, allegation, matter, or complaint witnessed, discovered, or received in a department or agency of the executive branch of the Government relating to violations of Federal criminal law involving Government officers and employees shall be expeditiously reported to the Attorney General by the head of the department or agency, or the witness, discoverer, or recipient, as appropriate, unless—

(1) the responsibility to perform an investigation with respect thereto is specifically assigned otherwise by another provision of law; or

(2) as to any department or agency of the Government, the Attorney General directs otherwise with respect to a specified class of information, allegation, or complaint.

(c) This section does not limit—

(1) the authority of the military departments to investigate persons or offenses over which the armed forces have jurisdiction under the Uniform Code of Military Justice (chapter 47 of title 10); or

(2) the primary authority of the Postmaster General to investigate postal offenses.

(Added Pub.L. 89–554, § 4(c), Sept. 6, 1966, 80 Stat. 616, and amended Pub.L. 107–273, Div. A, Title II, § 206, Nov. 2, 2002, 116 Stat. 1779.)

HISTORICAL AND STATUTORY NOTES

Transfer of Functions

The office of Postmaster General of the Post Office Department was abolished and all functions, powers, and duties of the Postmaster General were transferred to the United States Postal Service by Pub.L. 91–375, § 4(a), Aug. 12, 1970, 84 Stat. 773, set out as a note under section 201 of Title 39, Postal Service.

§ 536. Positions in excepted service

All positions in the Federal Bureau of Investigation are excepted from the competitive service, and the incumbents of such positions occupy positions in the excepted service.

(Added Pub.L. 89–554, § 4(c), Sept. 6, 1966, 80 Stat. 617.)

§ 537. Expenses of unforeseen emergencies of a confidential character

Appropriations for the Federal Bureau of Investigation are available for expenses of unforeseen emergencies of a confidential character, when so specified in the appropriation concerned, to be spent under the direction of the Attorney General. The Attorney General shall certify the amount spent that he considers advisable not to specify, and his certification is a sufficient voucher for the amount therein expressed to have been spent.

(Added Pub.L. 89–554, § 4(c), Sept. 6, 1966, 80 Stat. 617.)

§ 538. Investigation of aircraft piracy and related violations

The Federal Bureau of Investigation shall investigate any violation of section 46314 or chapter 465 of title 49.

(Added Pub.L. 103–272, § 4(e)(1), July 5, 1994, 108 Stat. 1361.)

HISTORICAL AND STATUTORY NOTES

References in Text

Chapter 465 of Title 49, referred to in text, is 49 U.S.C.A. § 46501 et seq.

§ 539. Counterintelligence official reception and representation expenses

The Director of the Federal Bureau of Investigation may use funds available to the Federal Bureau of Investigation for counterintelligence programs to pay the expenses of hosting foreign officials in the United States under the auspices of the Federal Bureau of Investigation for consultation on counterintelligence matters.

(Added Pub.L. 99–569, Title IV, § 401(a), Oct. 27, 1986, 100 Stat. 3195.)

§ 540. Investigation of felonious killings of State or local law enforcement officers

The Attorney General and the Federal Bureau of Investigation may investigate felonious killings of officials and employees of a State or political subdivision thereof while engaged in or on account of the performance of official duties relating to the prevention, detection, investigation, or prosecution of an offense against the criminal laws of a State or political subdivision, when such investigation is requested by the head of the agency employing the official or employee killed, and under such guidelines as the Attorney General or his designee may establish.

(Added Pub.L. 100–690, Title VII, § 7331(a), Nov. 18, 1988, 102 Stat. 4468.)

§ 540A. Investigation of violent crimes against travelers

(a) In general.—At the request of an appropriate law enforcement official of a State or political subdivision, the Attorney General and Director of the Federal Bureau of Investigation may assist in the investigation of a felony crime of violence in violation of the law of any State in which the victim appears to have been selected because he or she is a traveler.

(b) Foreign travelers.—In a case in which the traveler who is a victim of a crime described in subsection (a) is from a foreign nation, the Attorney General and Director of the Federal Bureau of Investigation, and, when appropriate, the Secretary of State shall assist the prosecuting and law enforcement officials of a State or political subdivision to the fullest extent possible in securing from abroad such evidence or other information as may be needed for the effective investigation and prosecution of the crime.

(c) Definitions.—In this section—

(1) "felony crime of violence" means an offense punishable by more than one year in prison that has as an element the use, attempted use, or threatened use of physical force against the person of another.

(2) "State" means a State, the District of Columbia, and any commonwealth, territory, or possession of the United States.

(3) "traveler" means a victim of a crime of violence who is not a resident of the State in which the crime of violence occurred.

(Added Pub.L. 103–322, Title XXXII, § 320916(a), Sept. 13, 1994, 108 Stat. 2129, and amended Pub.L. 104–294, Title VI, § 604(b)(21), Oct. 11, 1996, 110 Stat. 3507.)

HISTORICAL AND STATUTORY NOTES

Effective and Applicability Provisions

1996 Acts. Amendment by section 604 of Pub.L. 104–294 effective Sept. 13, 1994, see section 604(d) of Pub.L. 104–294, set out as a note under section 13 of Title 18, Crimes and Criminal Procedure.

§ 540B. Investigation of serial killings

(a) In general.—The Attorney General and the Director of the Federal Bureau of Investigation may investigate serial killings in violation of the laws of a State or political subdivision, if such investigation is requested by the head of a law enforcement agency with investigative or prosecutorial jurisdiction over the offense.

(b) Definitions.—In this section:

(1) **Killing.**—The term "killing" means conduct that would constitute an offense under section 1111 of Title 18, if Federal jurisdiction existed.

(2) **Serial killings.**—The term "serial killings" means a series of three or more killings, not less than one of which was committed within the United States, having common characteristics such as to suggest the reasonable possibility that the crimes were committed by the same actor or actors.

(3) **State.**—The term "State" means a State of the United States, the District of Columbia, and any commonwealth, territory, or possession of the United States.

(Added Pub.L. 105–314, Title VII, § 701(a), Oct. 30, 1998, 112 Stat. 2986.)

§ 540C. FBI Police

(a) Definitions.—In this section:

(1) **Director.**—The term "Director" means the Director of the Federal Bureau of Investigation.

(2) **FBI buildings and grounds.**—

(A) **In general.**—The term "FBI buildings and grounds" means—

(i) the whole or any part of any building or structure which is occupied under a lease or otherwise by the Federal Bureau of Investigation and is subject to supervision and control by the Federal Bureau of Investigation;

(ii) the land upon which there is situated any building or structure which is occupied wholly by the Federal Bureau of Investigation; and

(iii) any enclosed passageway connecting 2 or more buildings or structures occupied in whole or in part by the Federal Bureau of Investigation.

(B) Inclusion.—The term "FBI buildings and grounds" includes adjacent streets and sidewalks not to exceed 500 feet from such property.

(3) FBI police.—The term "FBI police" means the permanent police force established under subsection (b).

(b) Establishment of FBI police; duties.—

(1) In general.—Subject to the supervision of the Attorney General, the Director may establish a permanent police force, to be known as the FBI police.

(2) Duties.—The FBI police shall perform such duties as the Director may prescribe in connection with the protection of persons and property within FBI buildings and grounds.

(3) Uniformed representative.—The Director, or designated representative duly authorized by the Attorney General, may appoint uniformed representatives of the Federal Bureau of Investigation as FBI police for duty in connection with the policing of all FBI buildings and grounds.

(4) Authority.—

(A) In general.—In accordance with regulations prescribed by the Director and approved by the Attorney General, the FBI police may—

(i) police the FBI buildings and grounds for the purpose of protecting persons and property;

(ii) in the performance of duties necessary for carrying out subparagraph (A), make arrests and otherwise enforce the laws of the United States, including the laws of the District of Columbia;

(iii) carry firearms as may be required for the performance of duties;

(iv) prevent breaches of the peace and suppress affrays and unlawful assemblies; and

(v) hold the same powers as sheriffs and constables when policing FBI buildings and grounds.

(B) Exception.—The authority and policing powers of FBI police under this paragraph shall not include the service of civil process.

(5) Pay and benefits.—

(A) In general.—The rates of basic pay, salary schedule, pay provisions, and benefits for members of the FBI police shall be equivalent to the rates of basic pay, salary schedule, pay provisions, and benefits applicable to members of the United States Secret Service Uniformed Division.

(B) Application.—Pay and benefits for the FBI police under subparagraph (A)—

(i) shall be established by regulation;

(ii) shall apply with respect to pay periods beginning after January 1, 2003; and

(iii) shall not result in any decrease in the rates of pay or benefits of any individual.

(c) Authority of Metropolitan Police Force.—This section does not affect the authority of the Metropolitan Police Force of the District of Columbia with respect to FBI buildings and grounds.

(Added Pub.L. 107–273, Div. C, Title I, § 11024(a), Nov. 2, 2002, 116 Stat. 1830.)

HISTORICAL AND STATUTORY NOTES

Codifications

Another section 540C of this title, relating to annual reports on the activities of the Federal Bureau of Investigation personnel outside the United States, was enacted by section 824(a) of Pub.L. 107–306.

Transfer of Functions

For transfer of authorities, functions, personnel, and assets of the Coast Guard, including the authorities and functions of the Secretary of Transportation relating thereto, to the Department of Homeland Security, and for treatment of related references, see 6 U.S.C.A. §§ 468(b), 551(d), 552(d) and 557, and the Department of Homeland Security Reorganization Plan of November 25, 2002, as modified, set out as a note under 6 U.S.C.A. § 542.

Prior Provisions

Another section 540C, added Pub.L. 107–306, Title VIII, § 824(a), Nov. 27, 2002, 116 Stat. 2428, related to annual report on activities of Federal Bureau of Investigation personnel outside the United States. Pub.L. 108–177, Title III, § 361(i), (n), Dec. 13, 2003, 117 Stat. 2625, 2626, which directed the repeal of section 540C of title 28, was executed by repealing the section 540C added by Pub.L. 107–306, to reflect the probable intent of Congress.

CHAPTER 35—UNITED STATES ATTORNEYS

Sec.
541. United States attorneys.
542. Assistant United States attorneys.
543. Special attorneys.
544. Oath of office.
545. Residence.
546. Vacancies.
547. Duties.
548. Salaries.
549. Expenses.
550. Clerical assistants, messengers, and private process servers.

§ 541. United States attorneys

(a) The President shall appoint, by and with the advice and consent of the Senate, a United States attorney for each judicial district.

(b) Each United States attorney shall be appointed for a term of four years. On the expiration of his term, a United States attorney shall continue to perform the duties of his office until his successor is appointed and qualifies.

(c) Each United States attorney is subject to removal by the President.

(Added Pub.L. 89–554, § 4(c), Sept. 6, 1966, 80 Stat. 617.)

HISTORICAL AND STATUTORY NOTES

Prior Provisions

A prior Section 541, Acts June 25, 1948, c. 646, 62 Stat. 910; Mar. 18, 1959, Pub.L. 86–3, § 11(c), (d), 73 Stat. 9, which related to appointment, residence and tenure of marshals, was repealed by Pub.L. 89–554, § 8(a), Sept. 6, 1966, 80 Stat. 632, and reenacted in Section 561 of this title by Section 4(c) of Pub.L. 89–554.

§ 542. Assistant United States attorneys

(a) The Attorney General may appoint one or more assistant United States attorneys in any district when the public interest so requires.

(b) Each assistant United States attorney is subject to removal by the Attorney General.

(Added Pub.L. 89–554, § 4(c), Sept. 6, 1966, 80 Stat. 618.)

HISTORICAL AND STATUTORY NOTES

1948 Acts. Prior Section 502.—Based on Title 28, U.S.C., 1940, ed., §§ 483, 594 (May 28, 1896, c. 252, § 8, 29 Stat. 181; July 19, 1919, c. 24, § 1, 41 Stat. 209; Mar. 4, 1923, c. 295, 42 Stat. 1560; June 25, 1936, c. 804, 49 Stat. 1921).

Section consolidates sections 483 and 594 of Title 28, U.S.C., 1940 ed., relating to appointment of assistant United States attorneys.

Words "United States attorneys" were substituted for "district attorneys." (See reviser's note [now Revision Notes and Legislative Reports] under section 501 [now 541] of this title).

The exception of Alaska from the operation of such section 483 was omitted as covered by section 109 of Title 48, U.S.C., 1940 ed., Territories and Insular Possessions, authorizing appointment of assistant United States attorneys in Alaska.

Reference in such section 483 to "District of Columbia" was omitted. (See reviser's note [now Revision Notes and Legislative Reports] under section 501 [now 541] of this title).

The provisions of sections 483 and 594 of Title 28, U.S.C., 1940 ed., requiring the judges and United States attorneys to certify or evidence in writing the necessity for assistant United States attorneys in their respective districts, and specifying that such opinion of the judge shall state to the Attorney General the facts as distinguished from conclusions, showing the necessity therefor, were omitted. The Attorney General, as chief law enforcement officer, is in a better position to determine such necessity.

The salary provisions of such section 594 were omitted as covered by section 508 [now 548] of this title.

Changes were made in phraseology. 80th Congress House Report No. 308.

1966 Acts

Derivation:	United States Code	Revised Statutes and Statutes at Large
(a)	28 U.S.C. 502	[None]
(b)	28 U.S.C. 504(b) (2d sentence, as applicable to assistant United States attorneys)	[None]

In subsection (b), the word "is" is substituted for "shall be".

Prior Provisions

A prior section 542, Act June 25, 1948, c. 646, 62 Stat. 911, which related to appointment and tenure of deputies and assistants for United States marshals, was repealed by Pub.L. 89–554, § 8(a), Sept. 6, 1966, 80 Stat. 632, and reenacted in section 562 of this title by section 4(c) of Pub.L. 89–554.

§ 543. Special attorneys

(a) The Attorney General may appoint attorneys to assist United States attorneys when the public interest so requires.

(b) Each attorney appointed under this section is subject to removal by the Attorney General.

(Added Pub.L. 89–554, § 4(c), Sept. 6, 1966, 80 Stat. 618.)

HISTORICAL AND STATUTORY NOTES

Prior Provisions

A prior section 543, Act June 25, 1948, c. 646, 62 Stat. 911, which related to oath of office for United States Marshals, was repealed by Pub.L. 89–554, § 8(a), Sept. 6, 1966, 80 Stat. 632, and reenacted in section 563 of this title by section 4(c) of Pub.L. 89–554.

§ 544. Oath of office

Each United States attorney, assistant United States attorney, and attorney appointed under section 543 of this title, before taking office, shall take an oath to execute faithfully his duties.

(Added Pub.L. 89–554, § 4(c), Sept. 6, 1966, 80 Stat. 618.)

HISTORICAL AND STATUTORY NOTES

Prior Provisions

A prior section 544, Acts June 25, 1948, c. 646, 62 Stat. 911; Sept. 2, 1958, Pub.L. 85–856, 72 Stat. 1104, which related to bonds of United States marshals, was repealed by Pub.L. 89–554, § 8(a), Sept. 6, 1966, 80 Stat. 632, and reenacted in section 564 of this title by section 4(c) of Pub.L. 89–554.

§ 545. Residence

(a) Each United States attorney shall reside in the district for which he is appointed, except that these officers of the District of Columbia, the Southern District of New York, and the Eastern District of New York may reside within 20 miles thereof. Each assistant United States attorney shall reside in the district for which he or she is appointed or within 25 miles thereof. The provisions of this subsection shall not apply to any United States attorney or assistant United States attorney appointed for the Northern Mariana Islands who at the same time is serving in the same capacity in another district. Pursuant to an order from the Attorney General or his designee, a United States attorney or an assistant United States attorney may be assigned dual or additional responsibilities that exempt such officer from the residency requirement in this subsection for a specific period as established by the order and subject to renewal.

(b) The Attorney General may determine the official stations of United States attorneys and assistant United States attorneys within the districts for which they are appointed.

(Added Pub.L. 89–554, § 4(c), Sept. 6, 1966, 80 Stat. 618, and amended Pub.L. 95–530, § 1, Oct. 27, 1978, 92 Stat. 2028; Pub.L. 96–91, Oct. 25, 1979, 93 Stat. 700; Pub.L. 103–322, Title XXXII, § 320932, Sept. 13, 1994, 108 Stat. 2135; Pub.L. 109–177, Title V, § 501(a), Mar. 9, 2006, 120 Stat. 246.)

HISTORICAL AND STATUTORY NOTES

Effective and Applicability Provisions

2006 Acts. Pub.L. 109–177, Title V, § 501(b), Mar. 9, 2006, 120 Stat. 246, provided that: "The amendment made by subsection (a) [amending this section] shall take effect as of February 1, 2005."

Prior Provisions

A prior section 545, Act June 25, 1948, c. 646, 62 Stat. 911, which related to vacancies in the office of the United States Marshal, was repealed by Pub.L. 89–554, § 8(a), Sept. 6, 1966, 80 Stat. 632, and reenacted in section 565 of this title by section 4(c) of Pub.L. 89–554.

§ 546. Vacancies

(a) Except as provided in subsection (b), the Attorney General may appoint a United States attorney for the district in which the office of United States attorney is vacant.

(b) The Attorney General shall not appoint as United States attorney a person to whose appointment by the President to that office the Senate refused to give advice and consent.

(c) A person appointed as United States attorney under this section may serve until the earlier of—

(1) the qualification of a United States attorney for such district appointed by the President under section 541 of this title; or

(2) the expiration of 120 days after appointment by the Attorney General under this section.

(d) If an appointment expires under subsection (c)(2) of this section, the district court for such district may appoint a United States attorney to serve until the vacancy is filled. The order of appointment by the court shall be filed with the clerk of the court.

(Added Pub.L. 89–554, § 4(c), Sept. 6, 1966, 80 Stat. 618, and amended Pub.L. 99–646, § 69, Nov. 10, 1986, 100 Stat. 3616; Pub.L. 109–177, Title V, § 502, Mar. 9, 2006, 120 Stat. 246; Pub.L. 110–34, § 2, June 14, 2007, 121 Stat. 224.)

HISTORICAL AND STATUTORY NOTES

Effective and Applicability Provisions

2007 Acts. Pub.L. 110–34, § 3, June 14, 2007, 121 Stat. 224, provided that:

"**(a) In general.**—The amendments made by this Act [Pub.L. 110–34, June 14, 2007, 121 Stat. 224, which amended this section and enacted provisions set out as a note under 28 U.S.C.A. § 1] shall take effect on the date of enactment of this Act [June 14, 2007].

"**(b) Application.**—

"**(1) In general.**—Any person serving as a United States attorney on the day before the date of enactment of this Act [June 14, 2007] who was appointed under section 546 of title 28, United States Code, may serve until the earlier of—

"**(A)** the qualification of a United States attorney for such district appointed by the President under section 541 of that title; or

"**(B)** 120 days after the date of enactment of this Act [June 14, 2007].

"**(2) Expired appointments.**—If an appointment expires under paragraph (1), the district court for that district may appoint a United States attorney for that district under section 546(d) of title 28, United States Code, as added by this Act [Pub.L. 110–34, June 14, 2007, 121 Stat. 224, § 2, which amended this section]."

Prior Provisions

A prior section 546, Act June 25, 1948, c. 646, 62 Stat. 911, which related to the death of a marshal, was repealed by Pub.L. 89–554, § 8(a), Sept. 6, 1966, 80 Stat. 632, and reenacted in section 566 of this title by section 4(c) of Pub.L. 89–554.

§ 547. Duties

Except as otherwise provided by law, each United States attorney, within his district, shall—

(1) prosecute for all offenses against the United States;

(2) prosecute or defend, for the Government, all civil actions, suits or proceedings in which the United States is concerned;

(3) appear in behalf of the defendants in all civil actions, suits or proceedings pending in his district against collectors, or other officers of the revenue or customs for any act done by them or for the recovery of any money exacted by or paid to these officers, and by them paid into the Treasury;

(4) institute and prosecute proceedings for the collection of fines, penalties, and forfeitures incurred for violation of any revenue law, unless satisfied on investigation that justice does not require the proceedings; and

(5) make such reports as the Attorney General may direct.

(Added Pub.L. 89–554, § 4(c), Sept. 6, 1966, 80 Stat. 618.)

HISTORICAL AND STATUTORY NOTES

Prior Provisions

A prior section 547, Acts June 25, 1948, c. 646, 62 Stat. 912; Oct. 18, 1962, Pub.L. 87–845, § 8, 76A Stat. 699, which related to powers and duties of marshals, was repealed by Pub.L. 89–554, § 8(a), Sept. 6, 1966, 80 Stat. 632, and reenacted in section 569 of this title, by section 4(c) of Pub.L. 89–554.

§ 548. Salaries

Subject to sections 5315 through 5317 of title 5, the Attorney General shall fix the annual salaries of United States attorneys, assistant United States attorneys, and attorneys appointed under section 543 of this title at rates of compensation not in excess of the rate of basic compensation provided for Executive Level IV of the Executive Schedule set forth in section 5315 of title 5, United States Code.

(Added Pub.L. 89–554, § 4(c), Sept. 6, 1966, 80 Stat. 618, and amended Pub.L. 98–473, Title II, § 1701(a), Oct. 12, 1984, 98 Stat. 2184.)

HISTORICAL AND STATUTORY NOTES

Prior Provisions

A prior section 548, Act June 25, 1948, c. 646, 62 Stat. 912, which related to administration of oaths by marshals, was repealed by Pub.L. 89–554, § 8(a), Sept. 6, 1966, 80 Stat. 632.

Alaska, Canal Zone and Virgin Islands

Act Mar. 2, 1955, c. 9, § 2(b), 69 Stat. 10, provided that: "The salaries of United States attorneys and assistant United States attorneys for the districts of Alaska, Canal Zone, and the Virgin Islands are subject to the provisions of section 508 of title 28, United States Code [now this section]."

Compensation of Incumbent United States Attorneys and Assistant United States Attorneys

Pub.L. 88–426, § 306(a)(2), Aug. 14, 1962, 78 Stat. 428, as amended by Pub.L. 88–631, § 3(c), Oct. 6, 1964, 78 Stat. 1008, provided that: "Subject to section 303(f) and (g) of this Act [see sections 5315 to 5317 of Title 5, Government Organization and Employees], each incumbent United States attorney and assistant United States attorney shall be paid compensation at a rate equal to that of attorneys of comparable responsibility and professional qualifications, as determined by the Attorney General, whose compensation is prescribed in the General Schedule of the Classification Act of 1949, as amended [now covered by Chapter 51 and subchapter III of Chapter 53 of Title 5]."

Salary Increases

1969—Increase in the rates of pay of United States Attorneys and Assistant United States Attorneys whose annual salaries are fixed pursuant to this section, effective on the first day of the first pay period which begins on or after Dec. 27, 1969, by amounts equal, as nearly as may be practicable, to the increases provided pursuant to section 2 of Pub.L. 91–231, which raised corresponding rates by 6 percent, see Pub.L. 91–231, set out as a note under section 5332 of Title 5, Government Organization and Employees.

1967—Pub.L. 90–206, Title II, § 211(a), Dec. 16, 1967, 81 Stat. 633, provided that: "The rates of basic pay of United States attorneys and assistant United States attorneys whose annual salaries are fixed pursuant to section 548 of title 28, United States Code [this section] shall be increased, effective on the effective date of section 202 of this title [see Effective and Applicability Provisions of 1967 Amendments note under section 5332 of Title 5], by amounts equal, as nearly as may be practicable, to the increases provided by section 202(a) of this title [see section 5332(a) of Title 5] for corresponding rates of basic pay."

Section 211(a) of Pub.L. 90–206 effective as of the beginning of the first pay period which begins on or after Oct. 1, 1967, see section 220(a)(2) of Pub.L. 90–206, set out as a note under section 5332 of Title 5, Government Organization and Employees.

1966—Pub.L. 89–504, Title I, § 108(a), July 18, 1966, 80 Stat. 293, provided that: "The rates of basic compensation of assistant United States attorneys whose basic salaries are fixed pursuant to section 508 of title 28, United States Code [now this section], shall be increased, effective on the effective date of section 102 of this title [first of the first pay period beginning on or after July 1, 1966], by amounts equal, as nearly as may be practicable, to the increases provided by section 102(a) of this title [see section 5332(a) of Title 5] for corresponding rates of compensation."

Provision effective July 18, 1966, see section 109(1) of Pub.L. 89–504.

1965—Pub.L. 89–301, § 15(a), Oct. 29, 1965, 79 Stat. 1122, provided that: "The rates of basic compensation of assistant United States attorneys whose basic salaries are fixed pursuant to section 508 of title 28, United States Code [now this section], shall be increased by 3.6 per centum effective on the first day of the first pay period which begins on or after October 1, 1965."

1962—Pub.L. 87–793, § 1003(b), Oct. 11, 1962, 76 Stat. 866, provided that: "The rates of basic compensation of assistant United States attorneys whose basic salaries are fixed by section 508 of title 28, United States Code [now this section], shall be increased by 7½ per centum effective on the first day of the first pay period which begins on or after the date of enactment of this Act [Oct. 11, 1962]."

Salary Limitations

Acts Aug. 5, 1953, C. 328, Title II, § 202, 67 Stat. 375; July 2, 1954, C. 456, Title II, § 202, 68 Stat. 421, which prescribed salary limitations, were repealed by Pub.L. 89–554, § 8(a), Sept. 6, 1966, 80 Stat. 657.

§ 549. Expenses

Necessary office expenses of United States attorneys shall be allowed when authorized by the Attorney General.

(Added Pub.L. 89–554, § 4(c), Sept. 6, 1966, 80 Stat. 618.)

HISTORICAL AND STATUTORY NOTES

Prior Provisions

A prior section 549, Act June 25, 1948, c. 646, 62 Stat. 912, which related to the marshal's power as a sheriff, was repealed by Pub.L. 89–554, § 8(a), Sept. 6, 1966, 80 Stat. 632, and reenacted in section 570 of this title by section 4(c) of Pub.L. 89–554.

§ 550. Clerical assistants, messengers, and private process servers

The United States attorneys may employ clerical assistants, messengers, and private process servers on approval of the Attorney General.

(Added Pub.L. 89–554, § 4(c), Sept. 6, 1966, 80 Stat. 619, and amended Pub.L. 101–647, Title XXXVI, § 3626(a), Nov. 29, 1990, 104 Stat. 4965.)

HISTORICAL AND STATUTORY NOTES

Effective and Applicability Provisions

1990 Acts. Amendment by section 3626(a) of Pub.L. 101–647 effective 183 days after Nov. 29, 1990, see section 3631 of Pub.L. 101–647, set out as a note under section 3001 of this title.

Prior Provisions

A prior section 550, Acts June 25, 1948, c. 646, 62 Stat. 912; Sept. 9, 1959, Pub.L. 86–243, § 2, 73 Stat. 474, which related to disbursement of salaries and expenses, was repealed by Pub.L. 89–554, § 8(a), Sept. 6, 1966, 80 Stat. 632, and reenacted in section 571 of this title by section 4(c) of Pub.L. 89–554.

A prior section 551, Act June 25, 1948, c. 646, 62 Stat. 912, which related to the collection of fees by United States marshals, was repealed by Pub.L. 89–554, § 8(a), Sept. 6, 1966, 80 Stat. 632, and reenacted in section 572 of this title by section 4(c) of Pub.L. 89–554.

A prior section 552, Act June 25, 1948, c. 646, 62 Stat. 912, which related to the fixing of salaries of United States marshals, their deputies and assistants, by the Attorney General, was repealed by Pub.L. 89–554, § 8(a), Sept. 6, 1966, 80 Stat. 632, and reenacted in section 571 of this title by section 4(c) of Pub.L. 89–554.

A prior section 553, Acts June 25, 1948, c. 646, 62 Stat. 912; May 24, 1949, c. 139, § 72, 63 Stat. 100; Aug. 4, 1955, c. 550, 69 Stat. 492; Aug. 14, 1961, Pub.L. 87–139, § 5, 75 Stat. 340, which related to expenses of marshal, was repealed by Pub.L. 89–554, § 8(a), Sept. 6, 1966, 80 Stat. 632, and reenacted in section 567 of this title by section 4(c) of Pub.L. 89–554.

A prior section 554, Act June 25, 1948, c. 646, 62 Stat. 913, which related to the delivery of prisoners to the successor marshal, was repealed by Pub.L. 89–554, § 8(a), Sept. 6, 1966, 80 Stat. 632, and reenacted in section 573 of this title by section 4(c) of Pub.L. 89–554.

A prior section 555, Act June 25, 1948, c. 646, 62 Stat. 913, which related to the delivery of all unserved process to the successor marshal or his deputies, was repealed by Pub.L. 89–554, § 8(a), Sept. 6, 1966, 80 Stat. 632, and reenacted in section 574 of this title by section 4(c) of Pub.L. 89–554.

A prior section 556, Act June 25, 1948, c. 646, 62 Stat. 913, which related to the prohibition of the practice of law by a marshal or deputy marshal, was repealed by Pub.L. 89–554, § 8(a), Sept. 6, 1966, 80 Stat. 632, and reenacted in section 575 of this title by section 4(c) of Pub.L. 89–554.

CHAPTER 37—UNITED STATES MARSHALS SERVICE

Sec.
561. United States Marshals Service.
562. Vacancies.
563. Oath of office.
564. Powers as sheriff.
565. Expenses of the Service.
566. Powers and duties.
567. Collection of fees; accounting.
568. Practice of law prohibited.
569. Reemployment rights.
[570, 571. Repealed.]
[572. Renumbered.]
[572a to 574. Repealed.]
[575, 576. Renumbered.]

§ 561. United States Marshals Service

(a) There is hereby established a United States Marshals Service as a bureau within the Department of Justice under the authority and direction of the Attorney General. There shall be at the head of the United States Marshals Service (hereafter in this chapter referred to as the "Service") a Director who shall be appointed by the President, by and with the advice and consent of the Senate.

(b) The Director of the United States Marshals Service (hereafter in this chapter referred to as the "Director") shall, in addition to the powers and duties set forth in this chapter, exercise such other functions as may be delegated by the Attorney General.

(c) The President shall appoint, by and with the advice and consent of the Senate, a United States marshal for each judicial district of the United States and for the Superior Court of the District of Columbia, except that any marshal appointed for the Northern Mariana Islands may at the same time serve as marshal in another judicial district. Each United States marshal shall be an official of the Service and shall serve under the direction of the Director.

(d) Each marshal shall be appointed for a term of four years. A marshal shall, unless that marshal has resigned or been removed by the President, continue to perform the duties of that office after the end of that 4–year term until a successor is appointed and qualifies.

(e) The Director shall designate places within a judicial district for the official station and offices of each marshal. Each marshal shall reside within the district for which such marshal is appointed, except that—

(1) the marshal for the District of Columbia, for the Superior Court of the District of Columbia, and for the Southern District of New York may reside within 20 miles of the district for which the marshal is appointed; and

(2) any marshal appointed for the Northern Mariana Islands who at the same time is serving as marshal in another district may reside in such other district.

(f) The Director is authorized to appoint and fix the compensation of such employees as are necessary to carry out the powers and duties of the Service and may designate such employees as law enforcement officers in accordance with such policies and procedures as the Director shall establish pursuant to the applicable provisions of title 5 and regulations issued thereunder.

(g) The Director shall supervise and direct the United States Marshals Service in the performance of its duties.

(h) The Director may administer oaths and may take affirmations of officials and employees of the Service, but shall not demand or accept any fee or compensation therefor.

(i) Each marshal appointed under this section should have—

(1) a minimum of 4 years of command-level law enforcement management duties, including personnel, budget, and accountable property issues, in a police department, sheriff's office or Federal law enforcement agency;

(2) experience in coordinating with other law enforcement agencies, particularly at the State and local level;

(3) college–level academic experience; and

(4) experience in or with county, State, and Federal court systems or experience with protection of court personnel, jurors, and witnesses.

(Added Pub.L. 100–690, Title VII, § 7608(a)(1), Nov. 18, 1988, 102 Stat. 4512, and amended Pub.L. 107–273, Div. A, Title III, § 301(b), Nov. 2, 2002, 116 Stat. 1781; Pub.L. 109–177, Title V, § 505, Mar. 9, 2006, 120 Stat. 247.)

HISTORICAL AND STATUTORY NOTES

Prior Provisions

A prior section 561, added Pub.L. 89–554, § 4(c), Sept. 6, 1966, 80 Stat. 619, and amended Pub.L. 95–530, § 2, Oct. 27, 1978, 92 Stat. 2028, which related to appointment, term, and residence of United States marshals, was repealed by Pub.L. 100–690, Title VII, § 7608(a)(1), Nov. 18, 1988, 102 Stat. 4512.

§ 562. Vacancies

(a) In the case of a vacancy in the office of a United States marshal, the Attorney General may designate a person to perform the functions of and act as marshal, except that the Attorney General may not designate to act as marshal any person who was appointed by the President to that office but with respect to such appointment the Senate has refused to give its advice and consent.

(b) A person designated by the Attorney General under subsection (a) may serve until the earliest of the following events:

(1) The entry into office of a United States marshal appointed by the President, pursuant to section 561(c).

(2) The expiration of the thirtieth day following the end of the next session of the Senate.

(3) If such designee of the Attorney General is appointed by the President pursuant to section 561(c), but the Senate refuses to give its advice and consent to the appointment, the expiration of the thirtieth day following such refusal.

(Added Pub.L. 100–690, Title VII, § 7608(a)(1), Nov. 18, 1988, 102 Stat. 4513.)

HISTORICAL AND STATUTORY NOTES

Prior Provisions

A prior section 562, added Pub.L. 89–554, § 4(c), Sept. 6, 1966, 80 Stat. 619, which related to appointment of deputy marshals and clerical assistants, was repealed by Pub.L. 100–690, Title VII, § 7608(a)(1), Nov. 18, 1988, 102 Stat. 4512. See section 561(f) of this title.

§ 563. Oath of office

The Director and each United States marshal and law enforcement officer of the Service, before taking office, shall take an oath or affirmation to faithfully execute the duties of that office.

(Added Pub.L. 100–690, Title VII, § 7608(a)(1), Nov. 18, 1988, 102 Stat. 4513.)

HISTORICAL AND STATUTORY NOTES

Prior Provisions

A prior section 563, added Pub.L. 89–554, § 4(c), Sept. 6, 1966, 80 Stat. 619, which specifically stated the oath of office to be taken, was repealed by Pub.L. 100–690, Title VII, § 7608(a)(1), Nov. 18, 1988, 102 Stat. 4512. See section 561(h) of this title.

§ 564. Powers as sheriff

United States marshals, deputy marshals and such other officials of the Service as may be designated by the Director, in executing the laws of the United States within a State, may exercise the same powers which a sheriff of the State may exercise in executing the laws thereof.

(Added Pub.L. 100–690, Title VII, § 7608(a)(1), Nov. 18, 1988, 102 Stat. 4513.)

HISTORICAL AND STATUTORY NOTES

Prior Provisions

A prior section 564, added Pub.L. 89–554, § 4(c), Sept. 6, 1966, 80 Stat. 619, which related to bonds of United States marshals, was repealed by Pub.L. 92–310, Title II, § 206(a)(1), June 6, 1972, 86 Stat. 203.

§ 565. Expenses of the Service

The Director is authorized to use funds appropriated for the Service to make payments for expenses incurred pursuant to personal services contracts and cooperative agreements, authorized by the Attorney General, for security guards and for the service of summons on complaints, subpoenas, and notices in lieu of services by United States marshals and deputy marshals.

(Added Pub.L. 100–690, Title VII, § 7608(a)(1), Nov. 18, 1988, 102 Stat. 4513.)

HISTORICAL AND STATUTORY NOTES

Prior Provisions

A prior section 565, added Pub.L. 89–554, § 4(c), Sept. 6, 1966, 80 Stat. 620, which related to filling vacancies, was repealed by Pub.L. 100–690, Title VII, § 7608(a)(1), Nov. 18, 1988, 102 Stat. 4512. See section 562 of this title.

§ 566. Powers and duties

(a) It is the primary role and mission of the United States Marshals Service to provide for the security and to obey, execute, and enforce all orders of the United States District Courts, the United States Courts of Appeals, the Court of International Trade, and the United States Tax Court, as provided by law.

(b) The United States marshal of each district is the marshal of the district court and of the court of appeals when sitting in that district, and of the Court of International Trade holding sessions in that district, and may, in the discretion of the respective courts, be required to attend any session of court.

(c) Except as otherwise provided by law or Rule of Procedure, the United States Marshals Service shall execute all lawful writs, process, and orders issued under the authority of the United States, and shall command all necessary assistance to execute its duties.

(d) Each United States marshal, deputy marshal, and any other official of the Service as may be designated by the Director may carry firearms and make arrests without warrant for any offense against the United States committed in his or her presence, or for any felony cognizable under the laws of the United States if he or she has reasonable grounds to believe that the person to be arrested has committed or is committing such felony.

(e)(1) The United States Marshals Service is authorized to—

(A) provide for the personal protection of Federal jurists, court officers, witnesses, and other threatened persons in the interests of justice where criminal intimidation impedes on the functioning of the judicial process or any other official proceeding; and

(B) investigate such fugitive matters, both within and outside the United States, as directed by the Attorney General.

(2) Nothing in paragraph (1)(B) shall be construed to interfere with or supersede the authority of other Federal agencies or bureaus.

(f) In accordance with procedures established by the Director, and except for public money deposited under section 2041 of this title, each United States marshal shall deposit public moneys that the marshal collects into the Treasury, subject to disbursement by the marshal. At the end of each accounting period, the earned part of public moneys accruing to the United States shall be deposited in the Treasury to the credit of the appropriate receipt accounts.

(g) Prior to resignation, retirement, or removal from office—

(1) a United States marshal shall deliver to the marshal's successor all prisoners in his custody and all unserved process; and

(2) a deputy marshal shall deliver to the marshal all process in the custody of the deputy marshal.

(h) The United States marshals shall pay such office expenses of United States Attorneys as may be directed by the Attorney General.

(i) The Director of the United States Marshals Service shall consult with the Judicial Conference of the United States on a continuing basis regarding the security requirements for the judicial branch of the United States Government, to ensure that the views of the Judicial Conference regarding the security requirements for the judicial branch of the Federal Government are taken into account when determining staffing levels, setting priorities for programs regarding judicial security, and allocating judicial security resources. In this paragraph, the term "judicial security" includes the security of buildings housing the judiciary, the personal security of judicial officers, the assessment of threats made to judicial officers, and the protection of all other judicial personnel. The United States Marshals Service retains final authority regarding security requirements for the judicial branch of the Federal Government.

(Added Pub.L. 100–690, Title VII, § 7608(a)(1), Nov. 18, 1988, 102 Stat. 4514, and amended Pub.L. 110–177, Title I, §§ 101(a), 102(a), Jan. 7, 2008, 121 Stat. 2534, 2535.)

HISTORICAL AND STATUTORY NOTES

Prior Provisions

A prior section 566, added Pub.L. 89–554, § 4(c), Sept. 6, 1966, 80 Stat. 620, and amended Pub.L. 92–310, Title II, § 206(b), June 6, 1972, 86 Stat. 203, which provided that upon death of a marshal his deputy or deputies perform his duties until a successor is appointed and qualifies, was repealed by Pub.L. 100–690, Title VII, § 7608(a)(1), Nov. 18, 1988, 102 Stat. 4512.

Fugitive Apprehension Task Forces

Pub.L. 106–544, § 6, Dec. 19, 2000, 114 Stat. 2718, as amended Pub.L. 110–177, Title V, § 507, Jan. 7, 2008, 121 Stat. 2543, provided that:

"**(a) In general.**—The Attorney General shall, upon consultation with appropriate Department of Justice and Department of the Treasury law enforcement components, establish permanent Fugitive Apprehension Task Forces consisting of Federal, State, and local law enforcement authorities in designated regions of the United States, to be directed and coordinated by the United States Marshals Service, for the purpose of locating and apprehending fugitives.

"**(b) Authorization of appropriations.**—There are authorized to be appropriated to the Attorney General for the United States Marshals Service to carry out the provisions of this section $30,000,000 for the fiscal year 2001, $5,000,000 for fiscal year 2002, $5,000,000 for fiscal year 2003, and $10,000,000 for each of fiscal years 2008 through 2012.

"**(c) Other existing applicable law.**—Nothing in this section shall be construed to limit any existing authority under any other provision of Federal or State law for law enforcement agencies to locate or apprehend fugitives through task forces or any other means."

§ 567. Collection of fees; accounting

(a) Each United States marshal shall collect, as far as possible, his lawful fees and account for the same as public moneys.

(b) The marshal's accounts of fees and costs paid to a witness or juror on certificate of attendance issued as provided by sections 1825 and 1871 of this title may not be reexamined to charge him for an erroneous payment of the fees or costs.

(Added Pub.L. 89–554, § 4(c), Sept. 6, 1966, 80 Stat. 621, § 572; renumbered, § 567, Pub.L. 100–690, Title VII, § 7608(a)(2)(B), Nov. 18, 1988, 102 Stat. 4514.)

HISTORICAL AND STATUTORY NOTES

Prior Provisions

A prior section 567, added Pub.L. 89–554, § 4(c), Sept. 6, 1966, 80 Stat. 620, which related to expenses of marshals, was repealed by Pub.L. 100–690, Title VII, § 7608(a)(1), Nov. 18, 1988, 102 Stat. 4512. See section 565 of this title.

§ 568. Practice of law prohibited

A United States marshal or deputy marshal may not practice law in any court of the United States.

(Added Pub.L. 89–554, § 4(c), Sept. 6, 1966, 80 Stat. 621, § 575; renumbered § 568, Pub.L. 100–690, Title VII, § 7608(a)(2)(B), Nov. 18, 1988, 102 Stat. 4514.)

HISTORICAL AND STATUTORY NOTES

Prior Provisions

A prior section 568, added Pub.L. 89–554, § 4(c), Sept. 6, 1966, 80 Stat. 620, which related to availability of appropriations for transfer of prisoners to narcotic farms, was repealed by Pub.L. 100–690, Title VII, § 7608(a)(1), Nov. 18, 1988, 102 Stat. 4512.

§ 569. Reemployment rights

(a) A United States marshal for a judicial district who was appointed from a position in the competitive service (as defined in section 2102 of title 5) in the United States Marshals Service and who, for reasons other than misconduct, neglect of duty, or malfeasance, is removed from such office, is entitled to be reemployed in any vacant position in the competitive service in the United States Marshals Service at the same grade or pay level, or lower, as the individual's former position if—

(1) the individual is qualified for the vacant position; and

(2) the individual has made application for the position not later than ninety days after being removed from office as a United States marshal.

Such individual shall be so reemployed within thirty days after making such application or after being removed from office, whichever is later. An individual denied reemployment under this section in a position because the individual is not qualified for that position may appeal that denial to the Merit Systems Protection Board under section 7701 of title 5.

(b) Any United States marshal serving on the effective date of this section shall continue to serve for the remainder of the term for which such marshal was appointed, unless sooner removed by the President.

(Added Pub.L. 98–473, Title II, § 1211(a), Oct. 12, 1984, 98 Stat. 2163, § 576; renumbered § 569, Pub.L. 100–690, Title VII, § 7608(a)(2)(B), Nov. 18, 1988, 102 Stat. 4514.)

HISTORICAL AND STATUTORY NOTES

References in Text

The effective date of this section, referred to in subsec. (b), is Oct. 1, 1984. See Effective and Applicability Provisions note set out under this section.

Effective and Applicability Provisions

1984 Acts. Section 1212 of Pub.L. 98–473 provided that: "The amendments made by this subpart [subpart B (sections 1211, 1212) of part F of chapter XII of Title II of Pub.L. 98–473, which enacted this section] shall take effect on October 1, 1984."

Prior Provisions

A prior section 569, added Pub.L. 89–554, § 4(c), Sept. 6, 1966, 80 Stat. 620, and amended Pub.L. 95–598, Title II,

§ 221, Nov. 6, 1978, 92 Stat. 2662; Pub.L. 96–417, Title V, § 501(12), Oct. 10, 1980, 94 Stat. 1742; Pub.L. 99–466, § 3(a), Oct. 14, 1986, 100 Stat. 1191, which related to powers and duties generally and supervision by the Attorney General, was repealed by Pub.L. 100–690, Title VII, § 7608(a)(1), Nov. 18, 1988, 102 Stat. 4512. See section 566 of this title.

[§§ 570, 571. Repealed. Pub.L. 100–690, Title VII, § 7608(a)(1), Nov. 18, 1988, 102 Stat. 4512]

HISTORICAL AND STATUTORY NOTES

Section 570, added Pub.L. 89–554, § 4(c), Sept. 6, 1966, 80 Stat. 620, granted United States marshals the power of a sheriff in executing the laws of the United States in a State. See section 564 of this title.

Section 571, added Pub.L. 89–554, § 4(c), Sept. 6, 1966, 80 Stat. 621, and amended Pub.L. 95–598, Title II, §§ 222, 223, Nov. 6, 1978, 92 Stat. 2662; Pub.L. 97–258, § 2(g)(2), Sept. 13, 1982, 96 Stat. 1060, related to disbursement of salaries and moneys.

[§ 572. Renumbered § 567]

[§§ 572a to 574. Repealed. Pub.L. 100–690, Title VII, § 7608(a)(2)(A), Nov. 18, 1988, 102 Stat. 4514]

HISTORICAL AND STATUTORY NOTES

Section 572a, added Pub.L. 97–258, § 2(g)(3)(B), Sept. 13, 1982, 96 Stat. 1060, related to depositing of public moneys. See section 566(f) of this title.

Section 573, added Pub.L. 89–554, § 4(c), Sept. 6, 1966, 80 Stat. 621, related to delivery of prisoners to a successor. See section 566(g)(1) of this title.

Section 574, added Pub.L. 89–554, § 4(c), Sept. 6, 1966, 80 Stat. 621, related to delivery of unserved process to a successor. See section 566(g)(2) of this title.

[§§ 575, 576. Renumbered §§ 568, 569]

CHAPTER 39—UNITED STATES TRUSTEES

Sec.
581. United States trustees.
582. Assistant United States trustees.
583. Oath of office.
584. Official stations.
585. Vacancies.
586. Duties; supervision by Attorney General.
587. Salaries.
588. Expenses.
589. Staff and other employees.
589a. United States Trustee System Fund.
589b. Bankruptcy data.

HISTORICAL AND STATUTORY NOTES

Effective and Applicability Provisions

2005 Acts. Except as otherwise provided, amendments by Pub.L. 109–8 effective 180 days after April 20, 2005, and inapplicable with respect to cases commenced under Title 11 before the effective date, see Pub.L. 109–8, § 1501, set out as a note under 11 U.S.C.A. § 101.

United States Trustee Pilot; Repeal of Bankruptcy Provisions Relating to United States Trustees

Pub.L. 95–598, Title IV, § 408, Nov. 6, 1978, 92 Stat. 2686, as amended Pub.L. 98–166, Title II, § 200, Nov. 28, 1983, 97 Stat. 1081; Pub.L. 98–353, Title III, § 323, July 10, 1984, 98 Stat. 358; Pub.L. 99–429, Sept. 30, 1986, 100 Stat. 985; Pub.L. 99–500, Title I, § 101(b) [Title II, § 200], Oct. 18, 1986, 100 Stat. 1783–39, 1783–45, and Pub.L. 99–591, Title I, § 101(b), [Title II, § 2001, Oct. 30, 1986, 100 Stat. 3341–45; Pub.L. 99–554, Title III, § 307(a), Oct. 27, 1986, 100 Stat. 3125, which provided that the Attorney General conduct such studies and surveys as necessary to evaluate the needs, feasibility, and effectiveness of the United States trustee system, and report the result of such studies and surveys to the Congress, the President, and the Judicial Conference of the United States, beginning on or before January 3, 1980, and annually thereafter during the transition period; that not later than January 3, 1984, the Attorney General report to the Congress, the President, and the Judicial Conference of the United States, as to the feasibility, projected annual cost and effectiveness of the United States trustee system, as determined on the basis of the studies and surveys respecting the operation of the United States trustee system in the districts, together with recommendations as to the desirability and method of proceeding with implementation of the United States trustee system in all judicial districts of the United States; and that chapter 15 of title 11 of the United States Code [section 1501 et seq. of Title 11, Bankruptcy] and chapter 39 of title 28 of the United States Code [this chapter] are repealed, and all references to the United States trustee contained in title 28 of the United States Code [this title] are deleted, as of 30 days after the effective date of the Bankruptcy Judges, United States Trustees, and Family Farmer Bankruptcy Act of 1986 [see section 302 of Pub.L. 99–554, set out as a note under 28 U.S.C.A. § 581], with service of any United States trustee, of any assistant United States trustee, and of any employee employed or appointed under the authority of such chapter 39 is terminated on such date, was repealed by Pub.L. 99–554, Title III, § 307(b), Oct. 27, 1986, 100 Stat. 3125 [set out as a note under 28 U.S.C.A. § 581].

§ 581. United States trustees

(a) The Attorney General shall appoint one United States trustee for each of the following regions composed of Federal judicial districts (without regard to section 451):

(1) The judicial districts established for the States of Maine, Massachusetts, New Hampshire, and Rhode Island.

(2) The judicial districts established for the States of Connecticut, New York, and Vermont.

(3) The judicial districts established for the States of Delaware, New Jersey, and Pennsylvania.

(4) The judicial districts established for the States of Maryland, North Carolina, South Carolina, Virginia, and West Virginia and for the District of Columbia.

(5) The judicial districts established for the States of Louisiana and Mississippi.

(6) The Northern District of Texas and the Eastern District of Texas.

(7) The Southern District of Texas and the Western District of Texas.

(8) The judicial districts established for the States of Kentucky and Tennessee.

(9) The judicial districts established for the States of Michigan and Ohio.

(10) The Central District of Illinois and the Southern District of Illinois; and the judicial districts established for the State of Indiana.

(11) The Northern District of Illinois; and the judicial districts established for the State of Wisconsin.

(12) The judicial districts established for the States of Minnesota, Iowa, North Dakota, and South Dakota.

(13) The judicial districts established for the States of Arkansas, Nebraska, and Missouri.

(14) The District of Arizona.

(15) The Southern District of California; and the judicial districts established for the State of Hawaii, and for Guam and the Commonwealth of the Northern Mariana Islands.

(16) The Central District of California.

(17) The Eastern District of California and the Northern District of California; and the judicial district established for the State of Nevada.

(18) The judicial districts established for the States of Alaska, Idaho (exclusive of Yellowstone National Park), Montana (exclusive of Yellowstone National Park), Oregon, and Washington.

(19) The judicial districts established for the States of Colorado, Utah, and Wyoming (including those portions of Yellowstone National Park situated in the States of Montana and Idaho).

(20) The judicial districts established for the States of Kansas, New Mexico, and Oklahoma.

(21) The judicial districts established for the States of Alabama, Florida, and Georgia and for the Commonwealth of Puerto Rico and the Virgin Islands of the United States.

(b) Each United States trustee shall be appointed for a term of five years. On the expiration of his term, a United States trustee shall continue to perform the duties of his office until his successor is appointed and qualifies.

(c) Each United States trustee is subject to removal by the Attorney General.

(Added Pub.L. 95–598, Title II, § 224(a), Nov. 6, 1978, 92 Stat. 2662, and amended Pub.L. 99–554, Title I, § 111(a) to (c), Oct. 27, 1986, 100 Stat. 3090, 3091.)

HISTORICAL AND STATUTORY NOTES

Codifications

Section 408(c) of Pub.L. 95–598, as amended, which provided for the repeal of this section and the deletion of any references to United States Trustees in this title at a prospective date, was repealed by section 307(b) of Pub.L. 99–554. See note set out preceding this section.

Effective and Applicability Provisions

1978 Acts. Section effective Oct. 1, 1979, see section 402(c) of Pub.L. 95–598, as amended, set out as a note preceding 11 U.S.C.A. § 101.

Effective and Applicability Provisions of 1986 Amendments; Transition and Administrative Provisions

Pub.L. 99–554, Title III, Oct. 27, 1986, 100 Stat. 3118, as amended Pub.L. 101–650, Title III, § 317(a), (c), Dec. 1, 1990, 104 Stat. 5115, 5116; Pub.L. 103–65, § 1, Aug. 6, 1993, 107 Stat. 311; Pub.L. 106–518, Title V, § 501, Nov. 13, 2000, 114 Stat. 2421; Pub.L. 109–8, Title X, § 1001(c), Apr. 20, 2005, 119 Stat. 186, provided that:

"Sec. 301. Incumbent United States Trustees.

"(a) Area for which appointed. Notwithstanding any paragraph of section 581(a) of title 28, United States Code, as in effect before the effective date of this Act, a United States trustee serving in such office on the effective date of this Act shall serve the remaining term of such office as United States trustee for the region specified in a paragraph of such section, as amended by this Act, that includes the site at which the primary official station of the United States trustee is located immediately before the effective date of this Act.

"(b) Term of office. Notwithstanding section 581(b) of title 28, United States Code [28 U.S.C.A. § 581(b)], as in effect before the effective date of this Act, the term of office of any United States trustee serving in such office on the date of the enactment of this Act [Oct. 27, 1986] shall expire—

"(1) 2 years after the expiration date of such term of office under such section, as so in effect, or

"(2) 4 years after the date of the enactment of this Act [Oct. 27, 1986],

whichever occurs first.

"Sec. 302. Effective dates; Application of Amendments.

"(a) General effective date. Except as provided in subsections (b), (c), (d), (e), and (f), this Act and the amendments made by this Act [see Short Title of 1986 Amendment note set out under this section] shall take effect 30 days after the date of the enactment of this Act [Oct. 27, 1986].

"(b) Amendments relating to bankruptcy judges and incumbent United States trustees. Subtitle A of title I [amending 28 U.S.C.A. §§ 152 and 156 and provisions set out as a note under 28 U.S.C.A. § 152], and sections 301 [set out as a note under 28 U.S.C.A. § 581] and 307(a) [amending provisions formerly set out as a note preceding 28 U.S.C.A. § 581], shall take effect on the date of the enactment of this Act [Oct. 27, 1986].

"**(c) Amendments relating to family farmers.** (1) The amendments made by subtitle B of title II [enacting 11 U.S.C.A. §§ 1201 to 1231, and amending 11 U.S.C.A. §§ 101, 103, 108, 109, 303, 321, 322, 327, 329, 330, 346, 347, 348, 362, 363, 364, 365, 502, 523, 524, 546, 557, 706, 726, 727, 728, 1106, 1112, 1306, and 1307] shall not apply with respect to cases commenced under title 11 of the United States Code before the effective date of this Act.

"(2) Section 1202 of title 11 of the United States Code [11 U.S.C.A. § 1202] (as added by the amendment made by section 255 of this Act) shall take effect on the effective date of this Act and before the amendment made by section 227 of this Act [amending 11 U.S.C.A. § 1202].

"(3) Until the amendments made by subtitle A of title II of this Act [enacting 11 U.S.C.A. § 307, amending 11 U.S.C.A. §§ 101, 102, 105, 303, 321, 322, 324, 326, 327, 330, 341, 343, 345, 701, 703, 704, 705, 707, 727, 1102, 1104, 1105, 1112, 1129, 1163, 1202, 1302, 1307, and 1326, and repealing 11 U.S.C.A. §§ 1501 to 151326] become effective in a district and apply to a case, for purposes of such case—

"(A)(i) any reference in section 326(b) of title 11 of the United States Code [11 U.S.C.A. § 326(b)] to chapter 13 of title 11 of the United States Code [11 U.S.C.A. § 1301 et seq.] shall be deemed to be a reference to chapter 12 or chapter 13 of title 11 of the United States Code [11 U.S.C.A. § 1201 et seq. or 1301 et seq.],

"(ii) any reference in such section 326(b) to section 1302(d) of title 11 of the United States Code [11 U.S.C.A. §§ 326(b) to 1302(d)] shall be deemed to be a reference to section 1302(d) of title 11 of the United States Code [11 U.S.C.A. § 1302(d)] or section 586(b) of title 28 of the United States Code [28 U.S.C.A. § 586(b)], and

"(iii) any reference in such section 326(b) to section 1302(a) of title 11 of the United States Code [11 U.S.C.A. §§ 326(b) to 1302(a)] shall be deemed to be a reference to section 1202(a) or section 1302(a) of title 11 of the United States Code [11 U.S.C.A. § 1202(a) or 1302(a)], and

"(B)(i) the first two references in section 1202(a) of title 11 of the United States Code [11 U.S.C.A. § 1202(a)] (as added by the amendment made by section 255 of this Act) to the United States trustee shall be deemed to be a reference to the court, and

"(ii) any reference in such section 1202(a) [11 U.S.C.A. § 1202(a)] to section 586(b) of title 28 of the United States Code [28 U.S.C.A. § 586(b)] shall be deemed to be a reference to section 1202(c) of title 11 of the United States Code [11 U.S.C.A. § 1202(c)] (as so added).

"**(d) Application of amendments to judicial districts.**

"**(1) Certain regions not currently served by United States trustees.** (A) The amendments made by subtitle A of title II of this Act [enacting 11 U.S.C.A. § 307, amending 11 U.S.C.A. §§ 101, 102, 105, 303, 321, 322, 324, 326, 327, 330, 341, 343, 345, 701, 703, 704, 705, 707, 727, 1102, 1104, 1105, 1112, 1129, 1163, 1202, 1302, 1307, and 1326, and repealing 11 U.S.C.A. §§ 1501 to 151326], and section 1930(a)(6) of title 28 of the United States Code [28 U.S.C.A. § 1930(a)(6)] (as added by section 117(4) of this Act), shall not—

"(i) become effective in or with respect to a judicial district specified in subparagraph (B) until, or

"(ii) apply to cases while pending in such district before,

the expiration of the 270–day period beginning on the effective date of this Act or of the 30–day period beginning on the date the Attorney General certifies under section 303 of this Act the region specified in a paragraph of section 581(a) of Title 28, United States Code [subsec. (a) of this section], as amended by section 111(a) of this Act, that includes such district, whichever occurs first.

"(B) Subparagraph (A) applies to the following:

"(i) The judicial district established for the Commonwealth of Puerto Rico.

"(ii) The District of Connecticut.

"(iii) The judicial districts established for the State of New York (other than the Southern District of New York).

"(iv) The District of Vermont.

"(v) The judicial districts established for the State of Pennsylvania.

"(vi) The judicial district established for the Virgin Islands of the United States.

"(vii) The District of Maryland.

"(viii) The judicial districts established for the State of North Carolina.

"(ix) The District of South Carolina.

"(x) The judicial districts established for the State of West Virginia.

"(xi) The Western District of Virginia.

"(xii) The Eastern District of Texas.

"(xiii) The judicial districts established for the State of Wisconsin.

"(xiv) The judicial districts established for the State of Iowa.

"(xv) The judicial districts established for the State of New Mexico.

"(xvi) The judicial districts established for the State of Oklahoma.

"(xvii) The District of Utah.

"(xviii) The District of Wyoming (including those portions of Yellowstone National Park situated in the States of Montana and Idaho).

"(xix) The judicial districts established for the State of Alabama.

"(xx) The judicial districts established for the State of Florida.

"(xxi) The judicial districts established for the State of Georgia.

"**(2) Certain remaining judicial districts not currently served by United States trustees.** (A) The amendments made by subtitle A of title II of this Act [enacting 11 U.S.C.A. § 307, amending 11 U.S.C.A. §§ 101, 102, 105, 303, 321, 322, 324, 326, 327, 330, 341, 343, 345, 701, 703, 704, 705, 707, 727, 1102, 1104, 1105, 1112, 1129, 1163, 1202, 1302, 1307, and 1326, and repealing 11 U.S.C.A. §§ 1501 to 151326], and section 1930(a)(6) of title 28 of the United States Code [28 U.S.C.A. § 1930(a)(6)] (as added by section 117(4) of this Act), shall not—

"(i) become effective in or with respect to a judicial district specified in subparagraph (B) until, or

"(ii) apply to cases while pending in such district before,

the expiration of the 2-year period beginning on the effective date of this Act or of the 30-day period beginning on the date the Attorney General certifies under section 303 of this Act the region specified in a paragraph of section 581(a) of title 28, United States Code [subsec. (a) of this section], as amended by section 111(a) of this Act, that includes such district, whichever occurs first.

"(B) Subparagraph (A) applies to the following:

"(i) The judicial districts established for the State of Louisiana.

"(ii) The judicial districts established for the State of Mississippi.

"(iii) The Southern District of Texas and the Western District of Texas.

"(iv) The judicial districts established for the State of Kentucky.

"(v) The judicial districts established for the State of Tennessee.

"(vi) The judicial districts established for the State of Michigan.

"(vii) The judicial districts established for the State of Ohio.

"(viii) The judicial districts established for the State of Illinois (other than the Northern District of Illinois).

"(ix) The judicial districts established for the State of Indiana.

"(x) The judicial districts established for the State of Arkansas.

"(xi) The judicial districts established for the State of Nebraska.

"(xii) The judicial districts established for the State of Missouri.

"(xiii) The District of Arizona.

"(xiv) The District of Hawaii.

"(xv) The judicial district established for Guam.

"(xvi) The judicial district established for the Commonwealth of the Northern Mariana Islands.

"(xvii) The judicial districts established for the State of California (other than the Central District of California).

"(xviii) The District of Nevada.

"(xix) The District of Alaska.

"(xx) The District of Idaho.

"(xxi) The District of Montana.

"(xxii) The District of Oregon.

"(xxiii) The judicial districts established for the State of Washington.

"(3) **Judicial districts for the States of Alabama and North Carolina.** (A) Notwithstanding paragraphs (1) and (2), and any other provision of law, the amendments made by subtitle A of title II of this Act [enacting 11 U.S.C.A. § 307, amending 11 U.S.C.A. §§ 101, 102, 105, 303, 321, 322, 324, 326, 327, 330, 341, 343, 345, 701, 703, 704, 705, 707, 727, 1102, 1104, 1105, 1112, 1129, 1163, 1202, 1302, 1307, and 1326, and repealing 11 U.S.C.A. §§ 1501 to 151326], and section 1930(a)(6) of title 28 of the United States Code [28 U.S.C.A. § 1930(a)(6)] (as added by section 117(4) of this Act), shall not—

"(i) become effective in or with respect to a judicial district specified in subparagraph (E) until, or

"(ii) apply to cases while pending in such district before,

such district elects to be included in a bankruptcy region established in section 581(a) of Title 28, United States Code [subsec. (a) of this section], as amended by section 111(a) of this Act, except that the amendment to section 105(a) of title 11, United States Code [11 U.S.C.A. § 105(a)], shall become effective as of the date of the enactment of the Federal Courts Study Committee Implementation Act of 1990 [Dec. 1, 1990].

"(B) Any election under subparagraph (A) shall be made upon a majority vote of the chief judge of such district and each bankruptcy judge in such judicial district in favor of such election.

"(C) Notice that an election has been made under subparagraph (A) shall be given, not later than 10 days after such election, to the Attorney General and the appropriate Federal Circuit Court of Appeals for such district.

"(D) Any election made under subparagraph (A) shall become effective on the date the amendments made by subtitle A of title II of this Act become effective in the region that includes such district or 30 days after the Attorney General receives the notice required under subparagraph (C), whichever occurs later.

"(E) Subparagraph (A) applies to the following:

"(i) The judicial districts established for the State of Alabama.

"(ii) The judicial districts established for the State of North Carolina.

"(F)(i) Subject to clause (ii), with respect to cases under chapters 7, 11, 12, and 13 of title 11, United States Code [11 U.S.C.A. §§ 701 et seq., 1101 et seq., 1201 et seq., and 1301 et seq., respectively]—

"(I) commenced before the effective date of this Act, and

"(II) pending in a judicial district in the State of Alabama or the State of North Carolina before any election made under subparagraph (A) by such district becomes effective,

the amendments made by section 113 [amending 28 U.S.C.A. § 586] and subtitle A of title II of this Act, and section 1930(a)(6) of title 28 of the United States Code [28 U.S.C.A. § 1930(a)(6)] (as added by section 117(4) of this Act), shall not apply until the expiration of the 1-year period beginning on the date such election becomes effective.

"(ii) For purposes of clause (i), the amendments made by section 113 [amending 28 U.S.C.A. § 586] and subtitle A of title II of this Act, and section 1930(a)(6) of title 28 of the United States Code [28 U.S.C.A. § 1930(a)(6)] (as added by section 117(4) of this Act), shall not apply with respect to a case under chapter 7, 11, 12, or 13 of title 11, United States Code [11 U.S.C.A. § 701 et seq., 1101 et seq., 1201 et seq., or 1301 et seq., respectively], if—

"(I) the trustee in the case files the final report and account of administration of the estate, required under section 704 of such title [11 U.S.C.A. § 704], or

"(II) a plan is confirmed under section 1129, 1225, or 1325 of such title [11 U.S.C.A. § 1129, 1225, or 1325, respectively], before the expiration of the 1–year period beginning on the date such election becomes effective.

"(G) Notwithstanding section 589a of title 28, United States Code [28 U.S.C.A. § 589a], as added by section 115 of this Act, funds collected as a result of the amendments made by section 117 of this Act [amending 28 U.S.C.A. § 1930] in a judicial district in the State of Alabama or the State of North Carolina under section 1930(a) of title 28, United States Code [28 U.S.C.A. § 1930(a)], before the date the amendments made by subtitle A of title II of this Act take effect in such district shall be deposited in the general receipts of the Treasury.

"(H) The repeal made by section 231 of this Act [repealing chapter 15 of Title 11] shall not apply in or with respect to the Northern District of Alabama until March 1, 1987, or the effective date of any election made under subparagraph (A) by such district, whichever occurs first.

"(I) In any judicial district in the State of Alabama or the State of North Carolina that has not made the election described in subparagraph (A), any person who is appointed under regulations issued by the Judicial Conference of the United States to administer estates in cases under title 11 of the United States Code [11 U.S.C.A. § 101 et seq.] may—

"(i) establish, maintain, and supervise a panel of private trustees that are eligible and available to serve as trustees in cases under title 11, United States Code, and

"(ii) supervise the administration of cases and trustees in cases under chapters 7, 11, 12, and 13 of title 11, United States Code [11 U.S.C.A. §§ 701 et seq., 1101 et seq., 1201 et seq., and 1301 et seq., respectively],

until the amendments made by subtitle A of title II take effect in such district.

"(e) Application of United States Trustee System and quarterly fees to certain cases.

"(1) **In general.** Subject to paragraph (2), with respect to cases under chapters 7, 11, 12, and 13 of title 11, United States Code [11 U.S.C.A. §§ 701 et seq., 1101 et seq., 1201 et seq., and 1301 et seq., respectively]—

"(A) commenced before the effective date of this Act, and

"(B) pending in a judicial district referred to in section 581(a)of title 28, United States Code [subsec. (a) of this section], as amended by section 111(a) of this Act, for which a United States trustee is not authorized before the effective date of this Act to be appointed,

the amendments made by section 113 [amending 28 U.S.C.A. § 586] and subtitle A of title II of this Act [enacting 11 U.S.C.A. § 307, amending 11 U.S.C.A. §§ 101, 102, 105, 303, 321, 322, 324, 326, 327, 330, 341, 343, 345, 701, 703, 704, 705, 707, 727, 1102, 1104, 1105, 1112, 1129, 1163, 1202, 1302, 1307, and 1326, and repealing 11 U.S.C.A. § 1501 to 151326], and section 1930(a)(6) of title 28 of the United States Code [28 U.S.C.A. § 1930(a)(6)] (as added by section 117(4) of this Act), shall not apply until the expiration of the 3–year period beginning on the effective date of this Act, or of the 1–year period beginning on the date the Attorney General certifies under section 303 of this Act the region specified in a paragraph of such section 581(a) [subsec. (a) of this section], as so amended, that includes such district, whichever occurs first.

"(2) **Amendments inapplicable.** For purposes of paragraph (1), the amendments made by section 113 [amending 28 U.S.C.A. § 586] and subtitle A of title II of this Act, and section 1930(a)(6) of title 28 of the United States Code [28 U.S.C.A. § 1930(a)(6)] (as added by section 117(4) of this Act), shall not apply with respect to a case under chapter 7, 11, 12, or 13 of title 11, United States Code [11 U.S.C.A. § 701 et seq., 1101 et seq., 1201 et seq., or 1301 et seq., respectively], if—

"(A) the trustee in the case files the final report and account of administration of the estate, required under section 704 of such title [11 U.S.C.A. § 704], or

"(B) a plan is confirmed under section 1129, 1225, or 1325 of such title [11 U.S.C.A. § 1129, 1225, or 1325, respectively],

before the expiration of the 3–year period, or the expiration of the 1–year period, specified in paragraph (1), whichever occurs first.

"(3) **Rule of construction regarding fees for cases.** This Act [see Short Title of 1986 Amendments note set out under this section] and the amendments made by section 117(4) of this Act [amending 28 U.S.C.A. § 1930] shall not be construed to require the payment of a fee under paragraph (6) of section 1930(a) of Title 28, United States Code [28 U.S.C.A. § 1930(a)], in a case under Title 11 of the United States Code for any conduct or period occurring before such paragraph becomes effective in the district in which such case is pending.

"(f) [Repealed. Pub.L. 109–8, Title X, § 1001(c), Apr. 20, 2005, 119 Stat. 186.]

"Sec. 303.—Certification of judicial districts; notice and publication of certification.

"(a) Certification by Attorney General. The Attorney General may certify in writing a region specified in a paragraph of section 581(a) of title 28, United States Code [subsec. (a) of this section] (other than paragraph (16)), as amended by section 111(a) of this Act, to the appropriate court of appeals of the United States, for the purpose of informing such court that certain amendments made by this Act will become effective in accordance with section 302 of this Act [section 302 of this note].

"(b) Notice and publication of certification. Whenever the Attorney General transmits a certification under subsection (a), the Attorney General shall simultaneously—

"(1) transmit a copy of such certification to the Speaker of the House of Representatives and to the President pro tempore of the Senate, and

"(2) publish such certification in the Federal Register.

"Sec. 304. Administrative provisions.

"(a) Cooperative arrangements. The Attorney General and the Director of the Administrative Office of the United States Courts may enter into agreements under which United States trustees may—

"(1) use—

"(A) the services, equipment, personnel, records, reports, and data compilations, in any form, of the courts of the United States, and

"(B) the facilities of such courts, and

"(2) cooperate in the use by the courts of the United States of—

"(A) the services, equipment, personnel, records, reports, and data compilations, in any form, of United States trustees, and

"(B) the facilities of such trustees,

to prevent duplication during the 2-year period beginning on the effective date of this Act.

"(b) **Information and documents relating to bankruptcy cases and United States trustees.** The Director of the Administrative Office of the United States Courts shall make available to United States trustees, at the request of the Attorney General and on a continuing basis, all records, reports, and data compilations relating to—

"(1) cases and proceedings under title 11 of the United States Code [11 U.S.C.A. § 101 et seq.], and

"(2) the duties of United States trustees under titles 11 and 28 of the United States Code.

"Sec. 305. Application of certain Bankruptcy Rules.

"(a) **Rules relating to the United States Trustee System.** If a United States trustee is not authorized, before the effective date of this Act to be appointed for a judicial district referred to in section 581(a) of title 28, United States Code [subsec. (a) of this section], as amended by section 111(a) of this Act, then part X of the Bankruptcy Rules [set out in Title 11, Bankruptcy] shall not apply to cases in such district until the amendments made by subtitle A of title II of this Act [Pub.L. 99-554, Title II, §§ 201 to 231; see Tables for classification] become effective under section 302 of this Act [section 302 of this note] in such district.

"(b) **Rules relating to Chapter 12 of Title 11.** The rules prescribed under section 2075 of title 28, United States Code [28 U.S.C.A. § 2075], and in effect on the date of the enactment of this Act [Oct. 27, 1986] shall apply to cases filed under chapter 12 of title 11, United States Code [11 U.S.C.A. § 1201 et seq.], to the extent practicable and not inconsistent with the amendments made by title II of this Act [Pub.L. 99-554, Title II, §§ 201 to 283; see Tables for classification].

"Sec. 306. Salary of incumbent United States trustees.

"For service as a United States trustee in the period beginning on the effective date of this Act and ending on the expiration under section 301 of this Act of their respective terms of office, the salary payable to United States trustees serving in such offices on the effective date of this Act shall be fixed in accordance with section 587 of title 28, United States Code [28 U.S.C.A. § 587], as amended by section 114(a) of this Act.

"Sec. 307. Preservation of United States Trustee System during pendency of legislation; repealer.

"(a) **Temporary delay of Repeal of United States Trustee System.** Effective immediately before November 10, 1986, section 408(c) of the Act of November 6, 1978 (Pub.L. 95-598; 92 Stat. 2687) [formerly set out as a note preceding this section], is amended by striking out 'November 10, 1986' and inserting in lieu thereof '30 days after the effective date of the Bankruptcy Judges, United States Trustees, and Family Farmer Bankruptcy Act of 1986 [Pub.L. 99-554]'.

"(b) **Conforming amendment.** Section 408 of the Act of November 6, 1978 (Pub.L. 95-598; 92 Stat. 2687) [formerly set out as a note preceding this section], is repealed.

[Section 302(b) of Pub.L. 99-554 provided in part that the amendment by subsec. (a) is effective Oct. 27, 1986.]

"Sec. 308. Consideration of current private trustees for appointment by United States trustees.

"(a) **Trustees in bankruptcy cases under Chapter 7.** It is the sense of the Congress that individuals who are serving before the effective date of this Act, as trustees in cases under chapter 7 of title 11, United States Code [11 U.S.C.A. § 701 et seq.], should be considered by United States trustees for appointment under section 586(a)(1) of title 28, United States Code [28 U.S.C.A. § 586(a)(1)], to the panels of private trustees that are established as a result of the amendments made by this Act [see Short Title of 1986 Amendments note under this section].

"(b) **Standing trustees in bankruptcy cases under Chapter 13.** It is the sense of the Congress that individuals who are serving before the effective date of this Act, as standing trustees in cases under chapter 13 of title 11, United States Code [11 U.S.C.A. § 1301 et seq.], should be considered by the United States trustees for appointment under section 586(b) of title 28, United States Code [28 U.S.C.A. § 586(b)], as standing trustees who are appointed as a result of the amendments made by this Act [see Short Title of 1986 Amendments note set out under this section].

"Sec. 309. Appointment of United States trustees by the Attorney General.

"It is the sense of the Congress that individuals otherwise qualified who are serving, before the effective date of this Act, as estate administrators under title 11 of the United States Code [11 U.S.C.A. § 101 et seq.] should be considered by the Attorney General for appointment under sections 581 and 582 of title 28, United States Code [this section and 28 U.S.C.A. § 582], to new positions of United States trustee and assistant United States trustee resulting from the amendments made by this Act [see Short Title of 1986 Amendments note set out under this section].

"Sec. 310. Electronic case management demonstration project.

"(a) **Establishment of project.** Not later than 1 year after the effective date of this Act, the Director of the Executive Office for United States Trustees, in consultation with the Director of the Administrative Office of the United States Courts, shall establish an electronic case management demonstration project to be carried out in 3 Federal judicial districts that have a sufficiently large and varied bankruptcy caseload so as to provide a meaningful evaluation of the cost and effectiveness of such system. A contract for such project shall be awarded—

"(1) on the basis of competitive bids submitted by qualified nongovernmental entities that are able to design an automated joint information system for use by the United States courts and by United States trustees, and

"(2) in accordance with the Federal Property and Administrative Services Act of 1949 [see Short Title note under 40 U.S.C.A. § 471], the Office of Federal Procurement Policy Act [see Short Title note under 41 U.S.C.A. § 401], and title 31 of the United States Code.

"(b) **Study by General Accounting Office [now Government Accountability Office].** Not later than 1 year after the electronic case management system begins to operate in all of the judicial districts participating in the demonstration project carried out under subsection (a), the General Accounting Office [now Government Accountability Office] shall conduct a study to compare the cost and effectiveness of such system with the cost and effectiveness of case management systems used in Federal judicial districts that are not participating in such project.

"(c) **Term of project.** The demonstration project required by subsection (a) shall be carried out until—

"(1) the expiration of the 2–year period beginning on the date the electronic case management system begins to operate in all of the judicial districts participating in such project, or

"(2) legislation is enacted to extend, expand, modify, or terminate the operation of such project,

whichever occurs first.

"(d) **Use by clerks of the courts.** The electronic case management system demonstrated under the project required by subsection (a) shall provide the clerk of court in each district in which such system is operated, with a means of—

"(1) maintaining a complete electronic case file of all relevant information contained in petitions and schedules (and any amendments thereto) relating to debtors in cases under title 11 of the United States Code [11 U.S.C.A. § 101 et seq.], including—

"(A) a complete list of creditors in each such case, as listed by the debtor,

"(B) a complete list of assets scheduled by the debtor, the value of such asset, and any action taken by the trustee or debtor in possession with regard to such asset during the pendency of such case,

"(C) a complete list of debts and, with respect to each debt—

"(i) any priority of such debt under title 11 of the United States Code [11 U.S.C.A. § 101 et seq.],

"(ii) whether such debt is secured or unsecured, and

"(iii) whether such debt is contingent or noncontingent, and

"(D) the debtor's statements of current expenses and income, and

"(2) maintaining all calendars and dockets and producing all notices required to be sent in cases under title 11 of the United States Code [11 U.S.C.A. § 101 et seq.].

"(e) **Use by United States trustees.** The electronic case management system demonstrated under the project required by subsection (a) shall provide, at a minimum, the United States trustee in each district in which such system is operated with—

"(1) complete electronic case files which contain, in addition to the information listed in subsection (d), records of case openings, case closings, hearings, and the filing of all motions, trustee appointments, pleadings, and responses, as well as a record of the responses by the United States trustee to those motions, trustee appointments, and pleadings,

"(2) a means to generate standardized forms for motions, appointments, pleadings, and responses,

"(3) a means to generate standard management reports and letters on an exception basis,

"(4) a means to maintain accounting records, reports, and information required to be maintained by debtors in possession and trustees in cases under title 11 of the United States Code [11 U.S.C.A. § 101 et seq.],

"(5) a means to calculate and record distribution to creditors, final applications and orders for distribution, and final case closing reports, and

"(6) a means to monitor the payment of filing and other required fees.

"(f) **Availability to certain governmental entities.** Unlimited access to information maintained in the electronic case management system demonstrated under the project required by subsection (a) shall be provided at no charge to the following:

"(1) The Congress.

"(2) The Executive Office for the United States Trustees.

"(3) The Administrative Office of the United States Courts.

"(4) The clerks of the courts in judicial districts in which such system is operated and persons who review case information, in accordance with section 107(a) of title 11, United States Code [11 U.S.C.A. § 107(a)], in the offices of the clerks.

"(5) The judges on the bankruptcy and district courts in districts in which such system is operated.

"(6) Trustees in cases pending in districts in which such system is operated.

"(g) **Fees for other users.** (1) The entity which is awarded a contract to provide the electronic case management system demonstrated under this project may, under guidelines established by the Director of the Executive Office for the United States Trustees in the provisions of such contract, collect reasonable fees from assets of the estate of the debtor in bankruptcy for providing notices and services to the court and trustees under the demonstration project.

"(2) Access to information maintained in electronic case files pursuant to the demonstration project may be provided to persons other than those specified in subsection (f), but such access shall be limited to viewing such information only. A reasonable charge for such access may be collected by the entity which is awarded a contract under this section, in accordance with the guidelines established by the Director of the Executive Office for the United States Trustees in such contract. A reasonable portion of any charge so collected may be required by the Director to be remitted to the Executive Office for United States Trustees and deposited in the United States Trustee System Fund established in section 589a of title 28, United States Code [28 U.S.C.A. § 589a].

"(h) **Security.** Access provided under subsection (f) to an entity or an individual shall be subject to such security limitations as may be imposed by the Congress or the head of the affected entity.

"**Sec. 311. Cases pending under the Bankruptcy Act.**

"At the end of one calendar year following the date the amendments made by subtitle A of title II of this Act [amendments by Pub.L. 99–554, Title II, §§ 201 to 231, which were approved Oct. 27, 1986; see Tables for classification] take effect in a district in which any case is still pending under the Bankruptcy Act [section 1 et seq. of former Title 11, Bankruptcy, see notes set out preceding 11 U.S.C.A. § 101], the district court shall withdraw the reference of any such case and, after notice and a hearing, determine the status of the case. Such case shall be remanded to the bankruptcy judge with such instructions as are necessary for the prompt closing of the case and with a requirement that a progress report on the case be provided by the bankruptcy judge after such interval as the district court deems appropriate."

[For termination of reporting provisions pertaining to certification of judicial districts, effective May 15, 2000, see Pub.L. 104–66, § 3003, as amended, set out as a note under 31 U.S.C.A. § 1113, and the 13th item on page 117 of House Document No. 103–7.]

[Amendments by Pub.L. 109–8 effective, except as otherwise provided, 180 days after April 20, 2005, and inapplicable with respect to cases commenced under Title 11 before the effective date, see Pub.L. 109–8, § 1501, set out as a note under 11 U.S.C.A. § 101.]

Short Title

1986 Amendments. Section 1 of Pub.L. 99–554 provided: "That this Act [enacting section 589a of this title and sections 307, and 1201 to 1231 of Title 11, Bankruptcy, amending sections 49, 96, 152, 156, 157, 528, 581, 582, 584 to 587, 604, 1334, and 1930 of this title and sections 101 to 103, 105, 108, 109, 303, 321, 322, 324, 326, 327, 329, 330, 341, 343, 345 to 348, 362 to 365, 502, 503, 521 to 524, 546 to 549, 554, 557, 701, 703 to 707, 724, 726 to 728, 743, 1102, 1104 to 1106, 1112, 1121, 1129, 1163, 1202, 1302, 1306, 1307, and 1324 to 1326 of Title 11, Bankruptcy Form No. 1, set out in the Appendix to Title 11, repealing sections 1201 to 1231 and 1501 to 151326 of Title 11, enacting provisions set out as notes under sections 581 and 589 of this title, amending provisions set out as a note under section 152 of this title and preceding section 581 of this title, and repealing provisions set out as notes under preceding section 581 of this title] may be cited as the 'Bankruptcy Judges, United States Trustees, and Family Farmer Bankruptcy Act of 1986'."

Bankruptcy Crimes

Pub.L. 109–162, Title XI, § 1175, Jan. 5, 2006, 119 Stat. 3125, provided that:

"The Director of the Executive Office for United States Trustees shall prepare an annual report to the Congress detailing—

"(1) the number and types of criminal referrals made by the United States Trustee Program;

"(2) the outcomes of each criminal referral;

"(3) for any year in which the number of criminal referrals is less than for the prior year, an explanation of the decrease; and

"(4) the United States Trustee Program's efforts to prevent bankruptcy fraud and abuse, particularly with respect to the establishment of uniform internal controls to detect common, higher risk frauds, such as a debtor's failure to disclose all assets."

§ 582. Assistant United States trustees

(a) The Attorney General may appoint one or more assistant United States trustees in any region when the public interest so requires.

(b) Each assistant United States trustee is subject to removal by the Attorney General.

(Added Pub.L. 95–598, Title II, § 224(a), Nov. 6, 1978, 92 Stat. 2663, and amended Pub.L. 99–554, Title I, § 111(d), Oct. 27, 1986, 100 Stat. 3091.)

HISTORICAL AND STATUTORY NOTES

Codifications

Section 408(c) of Pub.L. 95–598, as amended, which provided for the repeal of this section and the deletion of any references to United States Trustees in this title at a prospective date, was repealed by section 307(b) of Pub.L. 99–554. See note set out preceding section 581 of this title.

Effective and Applicability Provisions

1986 Acts. Amendment by Pub.L. 99–554 effective 30 days after Oct. 27, 1986, except as otherwise provided, see section 302(a) of Pub.L. 99–554, as amended, set out as a note under section 581 of this title.

1978 Acts. Section effective Oct. 1, 1979, see section 402(c) of Pub.L. 95–598, as amended, set out as a note preceding section 101 of Title 11, Bankruptcy.

Appointment of United States Trustees by Attorney General

Appointment of United States Trustees by the Attorney General of individuals otherwise qualified, serving as estate administrators under Title 11, Bankruptcy, before effective date of Pub.L. 99–554, see section 309 of Pub.L. 99–554, as amended; set out as a note under section 581 of this title.

§ 583. Oath of office

Each United States trustee and assistant United States trustee, before taking office, shall take an oath to execute faithfully his duties.

(Added Pub.L. 95–598, Title II, § 224(a), Nov. 6, 1978, 92 Stat. 2663.)

HISTORICAL AND STATUTORY NOTES

Codifications

Section 408(c) of Pub.L. 95–598, as amended, which provided for the repeal of this section and the deletion of any references to United States Trustees in this title at a prospective date, was repealed by section 307(b) of Pub.L. 99–554. See note set out preceding section 581 of this title.

Effective and Applicability Provisions

1978 Acts. Section effective Oct. 1, 1979, see section 402(c) of Pub.L. 95–598, as amended, set out as a note preceding section 101 of Title 11, Bankruptcy.

§ 584. Official stations

The Attorney General may determine the official stations of the United States trustees and assistant United States trustees within the regions for which they were appointed.

(Added Pub.L. 95–598, Title II, § 224(a), Nov. 6, 1978, 92 Stat. 2663, and amended Pub.L. 99–554, Title I, § 144(d), Oct. 27, 1986, 100 Stat. 3096.)

HISTORICAL AND STATUTORY NOTES

Codifications

Section 408(c) of Pub.L. 95–598, as amended, which provided for the repeal of this section and the deletion of any references to United States Trustees in this title at a prospective date, was repealed by section 307(b) of Pub.L. 99–554. See note set out preceding section 581 of this title.

Effective and Applicability Provisions

1986 Acts. Amendment by Pub.L. 99–554 effective 30 days after Oct. 27, 1986, except as otherwise provided, see section 302(a) of Pub.L. 99–554, as amended, set out as a note under section 581 of this title.

1978 Acts. Section effective Oct. 1, 1979, see section 402(c) of Pub.L. 95–598, as amended, set out as a note preceding section 101 of Title 11, Bankruptcy.

§ 585. Vacancies

(a) The Attorney General may appoint an acting United States trustee for a region in which the office of the United States trustee is vacant. The individual so appointed may serve until the date on which the vacancy is filled by appointment under section 581 of this title or by designation under subsection (b) of this section.

(b) The Attorney General may designate a United States trustee to serve in not more than two regions for such time as the public interest requires.

(Added Pub.L. 95–598, Title II, § 224(a), Nov. 6, 1978, 92 Stat. 2663, and amended Pub.L. 99–554, Title I, § 112, Oct. 27, 1986, 100 Stat. 3091.)

HISTORICAL AND STATUTORY NOTES

Codifications

Section 408(c) of Pub.L. 95–598, as amended, which provided for the repeal of this section and the deletion of any references to United States Trustees in this title at a prospective date, was repealed by section 307(b) of Pub.L. 99–554. See note set out preceding section 581 of this title.

Effective and Applicability Provisions

1986 Acts. Amendment by Pub.L. 99–554 effective 30 days after Oct. 27, 1986, except as otherwise provided, see section 302(a) of Pub.L. 99–554, as amended, set out as a note under section 581 of this title.

1978 Acts. Section effective Oct. 1, 1979, see section 402(c) of Pub.L. 95–598, as amended, set out as a note preceding section 101 of Title 11, Bankruptcy.

§ 586. Duties; supervision by Attorney General

(a) Each United States trustee, within the region for which such United States trustee is appointed, shall—

(1) establish, maintain, and supervise a panel of private trustees that are eligible and available to serve as trustees in cases under chapter 7 of title 11;

(2) serve as and perform the duties of a trustee in a case under title 11 when required under title 11 to serve as trustee in such a case;

(3) supervise the administration of cases and trustees in cases under chapter 7, 11, 12, 13, or 15 of title 11 by, whenever the United States trustee considers it to be appropriate—

(A)(i) reviewing, in accordance with procedural guidelines adopted by the Executive Office of the United States Trustee (which guidelines shall be applied uniformly by the United States trustee except when circumstances warrant different treatment), applications filed for compensation and reimbursement under section 330 of title 11; and

(ii) filing with the court comments with respect to such application and, if the United States Trustee considers it to be appropriate, objections to such application.[1]

(B) monitoring plans and disclosure statements filed in cases under chapter 11 of title 11 and filing with the court, in connection with hearings under sections 1125 and 1128 of such title, comments with respect to such plans and disclosure statements;

(C) monitoring plans filed under chapters 12 and 13 of title 11 and filing with the court, in connection with hearings under sections 1224, 1229, 1324, and 1329 of such title, comments with respect to such plans;

(D) taking such action as the United States trustee deems to be appropriate to ensure that all reports, schedules, and fees required to be filed under title 11 and this title by the debtor are properly and timely filed;

(E) monitoring creditors' committees appointed under title 11;

(F) notifying the appropriate United States attorney of matters which relate to the occurrence of any action which may constitute a crime under the laws of the United States and, on the request of the United States attorney, assisting the United States attorney in carrying out prosecutions based on such action;

(G) monitoring the progress of cases under title 11 and taking such actions as the United States trustee deems to be appropriate to prevent undue delay in such progress;

(H) in small business cases (as defined in section 101 of title 11), performing the additional duties specified in title 11 pertaining to such cases; and

(I) monitoring applications filed under section 327 of title 11 and, whenever the United States trustee deems it to be appropriate, filing with the court comments with respect to the approval of such applications;

(4) deposit or invest under section 345 of title 11 money received as trustee in cases under title 11;

(5) perform the duties prescribed for the United States trustee under title 11 and this title, and such duties consistent with title 11 and this title as the Attorney General may prescribe;

(6) make such reports as the Attorney General directs, including the results of audits performed under section 603(a) of the Bankruptcy Abuse Prevention and Consumer Protection Act of 2005;

(7) in each of such small business cases—

(A) conduct an initial debtor interview as soon as practicable after the date of the order for relief but before the first meeting scheduled under section 341(a) of title 11, at which time the United States trustee shall—

(i) begin to investigate the debtor's viability;

(ii) inquire about the debtor's business plan;

(iii) explain the debtor's obligations to file monthly operating reports and other required reports;

(iv) attempt to develop an agreed scheduling order; and

(v) inform the debtor of other obligations;

(B) if determined to be appropriate and advisable, visit the appropriate business premises of the debtor, ascertain the state of the debtor's books and records, and verify that the debtor has filed its tax returns; and

(C) review and monitor diligently the debtor's activities, to identify as promptly as possible whether the debtor will be unable to confirm a plan; and

(8) in any case in which the United States trustee finds material grounds for any relief under section 1112 of title 11, the United States trustee shall apply promptly after making that finding to the court for relief.

(b) If the number of cases under chapter 12 or 13 of title 11 commenced in a particular region so warrants, the United States trustee for such region may, subject to the approval of the Attorney General, appoint one or more individuals to serve as standing trustee, or designate one or more assistant United States trustees to serve in cases under such chapter. The United States trustee for such region shall supervise any such individual appointed as standing trustee in the performance of the duties of standing trustee.

(c) Each United States trustee shall be under the general supervision of the Attorney General, who shall provide general coordination and assistance to the United States trustees.

(d)(1) The Attorney General shall prescribe by rule qualifications for membership on the panels established by United States trustees under paragraph (a)(1) of this section, and qualifications for appointment under subsection (b) of this section to serve as standing trustee in cases under chapter 12 or 13 of title 11. The Attorney General may not require that an individual be an attorney in order to qualify for appointment under subsection (b) of this section to serve as standing trustee in cases under chapter 12 or 13 of title 11.

(2) A trustee whose appointment under subsection (a)(1) or under subsection (b) is terminated or who ceases to be assigned to cases filed under title 11, United States Code, may obtain judicial review of the final agency decision by commencing an action in the district court of the United States for the district for which the panel to which the trustee is appointed under subsection (a)(1), or in the district court of the United States for the district in which the trustee is appointed under subsection (b) resides, after first exhausting all available administrative remedies, which if the trustee so elects, shall also include an administrative hearing on the record. Unless the trustee elects to have an administrative hearing on the record, the trustee shall be deemed to have exhausted all administrative remedies for purposes of this paragraph if the agency fails to make a final agency decision within 90 days after the trustee requests administrative remedies. The Attorney General shall prescribe procedures to implement this paragraph. The decision of the agency shall be affirmed by the district court unless it is unreasonable and without cause based on the administrative record before the agency.

(e)(1) The Attorney General, after consultation with a United States trustee that has appointed an individual under subsection (b) of this section to serve as standing trustee in cases under chapter 12 or 13 of title 11, shall fix—

(A) a maximum annual compensation for such individual consisting of—

(i) an amount not to exceed the highest annual rate of basic pay in effect for level V of the Executive Schedule; and

(ii) the cash value of employment benefits comparable to the employment benefits provided by the United States to individuals who are employed by the United States at the same rate of basic pay to perform similar services during the same period of time; and

(B) a percentage fee not to exceed—

(i) in the case of a debtor who is not a family farmer, ten percent; or

(ii) in the case of a debtor who is a family farmer, the sum of—

(I) not to exceed ten percent of the payments made under the plan of such debtor, with respect to payments in an aggregate amount not to exceed $450,000; and

(II) three percent of payments made under the plan of such debtor, with respect to payments made after the aggregate amount of payments made under the plan exceeds $450,000;

based on such maximum annual compensation and the actual, necessary expenses incurred by such individual as standing trustee.

(2) Such individual shall collect such percentage fee from all payments received by such individual under plans in the cases under chapter 12 or 13 of title 11 for which such individual serves as standing trustee. Such individual shall pay to the United States trustee, and the United States trustee shall deposit in the United States Trustee System Fund—

(A) any amount by which the actual compensation of such individual exceeds 5 per centum upon all payments received under plans in cases under chapter 12 or 13 of title 11 for which such individual serves as standing trustee; and

(B) any amount by which the percentage for all such cases exceeds—

(i) such individual's actual compensation for such cases, as adjusted under subparagraph (A) of paragraph (1); plus

(ii) the actual, necessary expenses incurred by such individual as standing trustee in such cases. Subject to the approval of the Attorney General, any or all of the interest earned from the deposit of payments under plans by such individual may be utilized to pay actual, necessary expenses without regard to the percentage limitation contained in subparagraph (d)(1)(B) of this section.

(3) After first exhausting all available administrative remedies, an individual appointed under subsection (b) may obtain judicial review of final agency action to deny a claim of actual, necessary expenses under this subsection by commencing an action in the district court of the United States for the district where the individual resides. The decision of the agency shall be affirmed by the district court unless it is unreasonable and without cause based upon the administrative record before the agency.

(4) The Attorney General shall prescribe procedures to implement this subsection.

(f)(1) The United States trustee for each district is authorized to contract with auditors to perform audits in cases designated by the United States trustee, in accordance with the procedures established under section 603(a) of the Bankruptcy Abuse Prevention and Consumer Protection Act of 2005.

(2)(A) The report of each audit referred to in paragraph (1) shall be filed with the court and transmitted to the United States trustee. Each report shall clearly and conspicuously specify any material misstatement of income or expenditures or of assets identified by the person performing the audit. In any case in which a material misstatement of income or expenditures or of assets has been reported, the clerk of the district court (or the clerk of the bankruptcy court if one is certified under section 156(b) of this title) shall give notice of the misstatement to the creditors in the case.

(B) If a material misstatement of income or expenditures or of assets is reported, the United States trustee shall—

(i) report the material misstatement, if appropriate, to the United States Attorney pursuant to section 3057 of title 18; and

(ii) if advisable, take appropriate action, including but not limited to commencing an adversary proceeding to revoke the debtor's discharge pursuant to section 727(d) of title 11.

(Added Pub.L. 95–598, Title II, § 224(a), Nov. 6, 1978, 92 Stat. 2663, and amended Pub.L. 99–554, Title I, § 113, Oct. 27, 1986, 100 Stat. 3091; Pub.L. 101–509, Title V, § 529 [Title I, § 110(a)], Nov. 5, 1990, 104 Stat. 1427, 1452; Pub.L. 103–394, Title II, § 224(a), Title V, § 502, Oct. 22, 1994, 108 Stat. 4130, 4147; Pub.L. 109–8, Title IV, § 439, Title VI, § 603(b), Title VIII, § 802(c)(3), Title XII, § 1231, Apr. 20, 2005, 119 Stat. 113, 122, 146, 201.)

[1] So in original. The period probably should be a semicolon.

HISTORICAL AND STATUTORY NOTES

References in Text

Chapter 12 or 13 of title 11, referred to in text, is 11 U.S.C.A. § 1201 et seq. or 11 U.S.C.A. § 1301 et seq., respectively.

Chapter 7, 11, 12, 13, or 15 of title 11, referred to in subsec. (a)(3), is 11 U.S.C.A. § 701 et seq., 11 U.S.C.A. § 1101 et seq., 11 U.S.C.A. § 1201 et seq., 11 U.S.C.A. § 1301 et seq., or 11 U.S.C.A. § 1501 et seq., respectively.

Level V of the Executive Schedule, referred to in subsec. (e)(1)(A)(i), is set out in section 5316 of Title 5, Government Organization and Employees.

Section 603(a) of the Bankruptcy Abuse Prevention and Consumer Protection Act of 2005, referred to in subsecs. (a)(6) and (f)(1), is Pub.L. 109–8, Title VII, § 603(a), Apr. 20, 2005, 119 Stat. 122, which is set out as a note under this section.

Codifications

Section 408(c) of Pub.L. 95–598, as amended, which provided for the repeal of this section and the deletion of any references to United States Trustees in this title at a prospective date, was repealed by section 307(b) of Pub.L. 99–554. See note set out preceding section 581 of this title.

Effective and Applicability Provisions

2005 Acts. Amendments by Pub.L. 109–8, § 603, effective 18 months after Apr. 20, 2005, see Pub.L. 109–8, § 603(e), set out as a note under 11 U.S.C.A. 521.

Except as otherwise provided, amendments by Pub.L. 109–8 effective 180 days after April 20, 2005, and inapplicable with respect to cases commenced under Title 11 before the effective date, see Pub.L. 109–8, § 1501, set out as a note under 11 U.S.C.A. § 101.

1994 Acts. Amendments by Pub.L. 103–394 effective on Oct. 22, 1994, and not to apply with respect to cases commenced under Title 11 of the United States Code before Oct. 22, 1994, see section 702 of Pub.L. 103–394, set out as a note under section 101 of Title 11, Bankruptcy.

1990 Acts. Amendment by Pub.L. 101–509 effective on such date as the President shall determine, but not earlier than 90 days, and not later than 180 days, after Nov. 5, 1990, see section 529 [Title III, § 305] of Pub.L. 101–509, set out as a note under section 5301 of Title 5, Government Organization and Employees. [See also related provisions in Ex. Ord. No. 12748, Feb. 1, 1991, 56 F.R. 4521, set out under that section.]

1986 Acts. Effective date and applicability of amendment by Pub.L. 99–554 dependent upon the judicial district involved, see section 302(d), (e) of Pub.L. 99–554, set out as a note under section 581 of this title.

1978 Acts. Section effective Oct. 1, 1979, see section 402(c) of Pub.L. 95–598, as amended, set out as a note preceding section 101 of Title 11, Bankruptcy.

Separability of Provisions

If any provision of or amendment made by Pub.L. 103–394 or the application of such provision or amendment to any person or circumstance is held to be unconstitutional, the remaining provisions of and amendments made by Pub.L. 103–394 and the application of such provisions and amendments to any person or circumstance shall not be affected thereby, see section 701 of Pub.L. 103–394, set out as a note under section 101 of Title 11, Bankruptcy.

Audit Procedures

Pub.L. 109–8, Title VI, § 603(a), Apr. 20, 2005, 119 Stat. 122, provided that:

"**(a) In general.—**

"**(1) Establishment of procedures.**—The Attorney General (in judicial districts served by United States trustees) and the Judicial Conference of the United States (in judicial districts served by bankruptcy administrators) shall establish procedures to determine the accuracy, veracity, and completeness of petitions, schedules, and other information that the debtor is required to provide under sections 521 and 1322 of title 11, United States Code, and, if applicable, section 111 of such title [11 U.S.C.A. § 111], in cases filed under chapter 7 or 13 of such title [11 U.S.C.A. § 701 or 1301 et seq.] in which the debtor is an individual. Such audits shall be in accordance with generally accepted auditing standards and performed by independent certified public accountants or independent licensed public accountants, provided that the Attorney General and the Judicial Conference, as appropriate, may develop alternative auditing standards not later than 2 years after the date of enactment of this Act [April 20, 2005].

"**(2) Procedures.**—Those procedures required by paragraph (1) shall—

"**(A)** establish a method of selecting appropriate qualified persons to contract to perform those audits;

"**(B)** establish a method of randomly selecting cases to be audited, except that not less than 1 out of every 250 cases in each Federal judicial district shall be selected for audit;

"**(C)** require audits of schedules of income and expenses that reflect greater than average variances from the statistical norm of the district in which the schedules were filed if those variances occur by reason of higher income or higher expenses than the statistical norm of the district in which the schedules were filed; and

"**(D)** establish procedures for providing, not less frequently than annually, public information concerning the aggregate results of such audits including the percentage of cases, by district, in which a material misstatement of income or expenditures is reported."

[Enactment of this note by Pub.L. 109–8, § 603, effective 18 months after Apr. 20, 2005, see Pub.L. 109–8, § 603(e), set out as a note under 11 U.S.C.A. § 521.]

[Except as otherwise provided, amendments by Pub.L. 109–8 effective 180 days after April 20, 2005, and inapplicable with respect to cases commenced under Title 11 before the effective date, see Pub.L. 109–8, § 1501, set out as a note under 11 U.S.C.A. § 101.]

Application to All Standing Trustees

Section 529 [Title I, § 110(b)] of Pub.L. 101–509 provided that: "The amendment made by subsection (a) [amending this section] shall apply to any trustee to whom the provisions of section 302(d)(3) of the Bankruptcy Judges, United States Trustees, and Family Farmer Bankruptcy Act of 1986 (Public Law 99–54 [Pub.L. 99–554]; 100 Stat. 3121) [set out in a note under section 581 of this title] apply."

§ 587. Salaries

Subject to sections 5315 through 5317 of title 5, the Attorney General shall fix the annual salaries of United States trustees and assistant United States trustees at rates of compensation not in excess of the rate of basic compensation provided for Executive Level IV of the Executive Schedule set forth in section 5315 of title 5, United States Code.

(Added Pub.L. 95–598, Title II, § 224(a), Nov. 6, 1978, 92 Stat. 2664, and amended Pub.L. 99–554, Title I, § 114(a), Oct. 27, 1986, 100 Stat. 3093.)

HISTORICAL AND STATUTORY NOTES

Codifications

Section 408(c) of Pub.L. 95–598, as amended, which provided for the repeal of this section and the deletion of any references to United States Trustees in this title at a prospective date, was repealed by section 307(b) of Pub.L. 99–554. See note set out preceding section 581 of this title.

Effective and Applicability Provisions

1986 Acts. Amendment by Pub.L. 99–554 effective 30 days after Oct. 27, 1986, except as otherwise provided, see section 302(a) of Pub.L. 99–554, as amended, set out as a note under section 581 of this title.

1978 Acts. Section effective Oct. 1, 1979, see section 402(c) of Pub.L. 95–598, as amended, set out as a note preceding section 101 of Title 11, Bankruptcy.

§ 588. Expenses

Necessary office expenses of the United States trustee shall be allowed when authorized by the Attorney General.

(Added Pub.L. 95–598, Title II, § 224(a), Nov. 6, 1978, 92 Stat. 2664.)

HISTORICAL AND STATUTORY NOTES

Codifications

Section 408(c) of Pub.L. 95–598, as amended, which provided for the repeal of this section and the deletion of any references to United States Trustees in this title at a prospective date, was repealed by section 307(b) of Pub.L. 99–554. See note set out preceding section 581 of this title.

Effective and Applicability Provisions

1978 Acts. Section effective Oct. 1, 1979, see section 402(c) of Pub.L. 95–598, as amended, set out as a note preceding section 101 of Title 11, Bankruptcy.

§ 589. Staff and other employees

The United States trustee may employ staff and other employees on approval of the Attorney General. (Added Pub.L. 95–598, Title II, § 224(a), Nov. 6, 1978, 92 Stat. 2664.)

HISTORICAL AND STATUTORY NOTES

Codifications

Section 408(c) of Pub.L. 95–598, as amended, which provided for the repeal of this section and the deletion of any references to United States Trustees in this title at a prospective date, was repealed by section 307(b) of Pub.L. 99–554. See note set out preceding section 581 of this title.

Effective and Applicability Provisions

1978 Acts. Section effective Oct. 1, 1979, see section 402(c) of Pub.L. 95–598, as amended, set out as a note preceding section 101 of Title 11, Bankruptcy.

Temporary Suspension of Limitation on Appointments

Pub.L. 99–554, Title I, § 114(b), Oct. 27, 1986, 100 Stat. 3093, provided that: "During the period beginning on the effective date of this Act [see section 302 of Pub.L. 99–554, as amended, set out as a note under section 581 of this title], and ending on October 1, 1989, the provisions of title 5 of the United States Code [Title 5, Government Organization and Employees] governing appointments in the competitive service shall not apply with respect to appointments under section 589 of title 28, United States Code [this section]."

§ 589a. United States Trustee System Fund

(a) There is hereby established in the Treasury of the United States a special fund to be known as the "United States Trustee System Fund" (hereinafter in this section referred to as the "Fund"). Monies in the Fund shall be available to the Attorney General without fiscal year limitation in such amounts as may be specified in appropriations Acts for the following purposes in connection with the operations of United States trustees—

(1) salaries and related employee benefits;

(2) travel and transportation;

(3) rental of space;

(4) communication, utilities, and miscellaneous computer charges;

(5) security investigations and audits;

(6) supplies, books, and other materials for legal research;

(7) furniture and equipment;

(8) miscellaneous services, including those obtained by contract; and

(9) printing.

(b) For the purpose of recovering the cost of services of the United States Trustee System, there shall be deposited as offsetting collections to the appropriation "United States Trustee System Fund", to remain available until expended, the following—

(1)(A) 40.46 percent of the fees collected under section 1930(a)(1)(A); and

(B) 28.33 percent of the fees collected under section 1930(a)(1)(B);

(2) 55 percent of the fees collected under section 1930(a)(3) of this title;

(3) one-half of the fees collected under section 1930(a)(4) of this title;

(4) one-half of the fees collected under section 1930(a)(5) of this title;

(5) 100 percent of the fees collected under section 1930(a)(6) of this title;

(6) three-fourths of the fees collected under the last sentence of section 1930(a) of this title;

(7) the compensation of trustees received under section 330(d) of title 11 by the clerks of the bankruptcy courts;

(8) excess fees collected under section 586(e)(2) of this title;

(9) interest earned on Fund investment; and

(10) fines imposed under section 110(*l*) of title 11, United States Code.

(c) Amounts in the Fund which are not currently needed for the purposes specified in subsection (a) shall be kept on deposit or invested in obligations of, or guaranteed by, the United States.

(d) The Attorney General shall transmit to the Congress, not later than 120 days after the end of each fiscal year, a detailed report on the amounts deposited in the Fund and a description of expenditures made under this section.

(e) There are authorized to be appropriated to the Fund for any fiscal year such sums as may be necessary to supplement amounts deposited under subsection (b) for the purposes specified in subsection (a). (Added Pub.L. 99–554, Title I, § 115(a), Oct. 27, 1986, 100 Stat. 3094, and amended Pub.L. 101–162, Title IV, § 406(c), Nov. 21, 1989, 103 Stat. 1016; Pub.L. 102–140, Title I, § 111(b), (c), Oct. 28, 1991, 105 Stat. 795; Pub.L. 103–121, Title I, § 111(a)(2), (b)(2), (3), Oct. 27, 1993, 107 Stat. 1164; Pub.L. 104–91, Title I, § 101(a), Jan. 6, 1996, 110 Stat. 11, as amended Pub.L. 104–99, Title II, § 211, Jan. 26, 1996, 110

Stat. 37; Pub.L. 104–208, Div. A, Title I, § 101(a) [Title I, § 109(b)], Sept. 30, 1996, 110 Stat. 3009–18; Pub.L. 106–113, Div. B, § 1000(a)(1) [Title I, § 113], Nov. 29, 1999, 113 Stat. 1535, 1501A–6, 1501A–20; Pub.L. 109–8, Title III, § 325(b), Apr. 20, 2005, 119 Stat. 99; Pub.L. 109–13, Div. A, Title VI, § 6058(a), May 11, 2005, 119 Stat. 297; Pub.L. 110–161, Div. B, Title II, § 212(a), Dec. 26, 2007, 121 Stat. 1914.)

HISTORICAL AND STATUTORY NOTES

Codifications

Section 101(a) of Pub.L. 104–91, as amended by section 211 of Pub.L. 104–99, provided in part that section 111(b) and (c) of the General Provisions for the Department of Justice in Title I of the Departments of Commerce, Justice, and State, the Judiciary, and Related Agencies Appropriations Act, 1996 (H.R. 2076) as passed by the House of Representatives on Dec. 6, 1995, was enacted into permanent law. Such section 111(b) and (c) of H.R. 2076 amended subsecs. (b) and (f) of this section. See 1996 Amendments notes set out under this section.

Effective and Applicability Provisions

2005 Acts. Pub.L. 109–13, Div. A, Title VI, § 6058(b), May 11, 2005, 119 Stat. 297, provided that: "This section [amending this section and 28 U.S.C.A. § 1930, enacting provisions set out as a note under this section, and amending provisions set out as notes under this section and 28 U.S.C.A. §§ 1930 and 1931] and the amendment made by this section shall take effect immediately after the enactment of the Bankruptcy Abuse Prevention and Consumer Protection Act of 2005 [Pub.L. 109–8, approved Apr. 20, 2005]."

Except as otherwise provided, amendments by Pub.L. 109–8 effective 180 days after April 20, 2005, and inapplicable with respect to cases commenced under Title 11 before the effective date, see Pub.L. 109–8, § 1501, set out as a note under 11 U.S.C.A. § 101.

1999 Acts. Pub.L. 106–113, Div. B, § 1000(a)(1), [Title I, § 113], Nov. 29, 1999, 113 Stat. 1535, 1501A–20, provided in part that section 113 (amending this section and section 1930 of this title and provisions set out as a note under section 1931 of this title) is "[e]ffective 30 days after the enactment of this Act [Department of Commerce, Justice, and State, the Judiciary and Related Agencies Appropriations Act, 2000, Pub.L. 106–113, Div. B, § 1000(a)(1), Nov. 29, 1999, 113 Stat. 1535, 1501A–3; see Tables for complete classification]".

1996 Acts. Pub.L. 104–208, Div. A, Title I, § 101(a) [Title I, § 109(c)], Sept. 30, 1996, 110 Stat. 3009–19, provided that: "Notwithstanding any other provision of law or of this Act [Pub.L. 104–208, Sept. 30, 1996, 110 Stat. 3009, see Tables for classification] the amendments to 28 U.S.C. 589a [this section] made by subsection (b) of this section shall take effect upon enactment of this Act [probably means the date of enactment of Pub.L. 104–208, 110 Stat. 3009, which was approved Sept. 30, 1996]."

1993 Acts. Section 111(a) of Pub.L. 103–121 provided in part that amendment by section 111(a)(2) of Pub.L. 103–121, amending subsec. (b)(1) of this section, is effective 30 days after Oct. 27, 1993.

Section 111(b) of Pub.L. 103–121 provided in part that amendment by section 111(b)(2) and (3) of Pub.L. 103–121, amending subsecs. (b)(2) and (f)(1) of this section, is effective 30 days after Oct. 27, 1993.

1991 Acts. Section 111 of Pub.L. 102–140 provided that the amendment made by that section is effective 60 days after Oct. 28, 1991.

1986 Acts. Enactment by Pub.L. 99–554 effective 30 days after Oct. 27, 1986, except as otherwise provided, see section 302(a) of Pub.L. 99–554, as amended, set out as a note under section 581 of this title.

Sunset Provisions

Pub.L. 109–8, Title III, § 325(d), Apr. 20, 2005, 119 Stat. 99, as amended Pub.L. 109–13, Div. A, Title VI, § 6058(b), May 11, 2005, 119 Stat. 297, which set forth a two-year effective period for the original amendments by Pub.L. 109–8 to this section, has been omitted. The amendment by Pub.L. 109–13, § 6058(a), to Pub.L. 109–8, § 325, omitted this note in the reenactment of the section, to take effect immediately after the enactment of the Bankruptcy Abuse Prevention and Consumer Protection Act of 2005 [Pub.L. 109–8, Apr. 20, 2005, 119 Stat. 23], see Pub.L. 109–13, § 6058(b), set out as an Effective and Applicability Provisions note under this section.

Termination of Reporting Requirements

For termination of reporting provisions of this section, effective May 15, 2000, see Pub.L. 104–66, § 3003, as amended, set out as a note under 31 U.S.C.A. § 1113, and the 9th item on page 119 of House Document No. 103–7.

Reporting requirement of subsec. (d) of this section excepted from termination under Pub.L. 104–66, § 3003(a)(1), as amended, set out in a note under 31 U.S.C.A. § 1113, see Pub.L. 106–197, § 1, set out as a note under 31 U.S.C.A. § 1113.

§ 589b. Bankruptcy data

(a) Rules.—The Attorney General shall, within a reasonable time after the effective date of this section, issue rules requiring uniform forms for (and from time to time thereafter to appropriately modify and approve)—

(1) final reports by trustees in cases under chapters 7, 12, and 13 of title 11; and

(2) periodic reports by debtors in possession or trustees in cases under chapter 11 of title 11.

(b) Reports.—Each report referred to in subsection (a) shall be designed (and the requirements as to place and manner of filing shall be established) so as to facilitate compilation of data and maximum possible access of the public, both by physical inspection at one or more central filing locations, and by electronic access through the Internet or other appropriate media.

(c) Required information.—The information required to be filed in the reports referred to in subsection (b) shall be that which is in the best interests of debtors and creditors, and in the public interest in reasonable and adequate information to evaluate the efficiency and practicality of the Federal bankruptcy system. In issuing rules proposing the forms referred to in subsection (a), the Attorney General shall strike the best achievable practical balance between—

(1) the reasonable needs of the public for information about the operational results of the Federal bankruptcy system;

(2) economy, simplicity, and lack of undue burden on persons with a duty to file reports; and

(3) appropriate privacy concerns and safeguards.

(d) Final reports.—The uniform forms for final reports required under subsection (a) for use by trustees under chapters 7, 12, and 13 of title 11 shall, in addition to such other matters as are required by law or as the Attorney General in the discretion of the Attorney General shall propose, include with respect to a case under such title—

(1) information about the length of time the case was pending;

(2) assets abandoned;

(3) assets exempted;

(4) receipts and disbursements of the estate;

(5) expenses of administration, including for use under section 707(b), actual costs of administering cases under chapter 13 of title 11;

(6) claims asserted;

(7) claims allowed; and

(8) distributions to claimants and claims discharged without payment,

in each case by appropriate category and, in cases under chapters 12 and 13 of title 11, date of confirmation of the plan, each modification thereto, and defaults by the debtor in performance under the plan.

(e) Periodic reports.—The uniform forms for periodic reports required under subsection (a) for use by trustees or debtors in possession under chapter 11 of title 11 shall, in addition to such other matters as are required by law or as the Attorney General in the discretion of the Attorney General shall propose, include—

(1) information about the industry classification, published by the Department of Commerce, for the businesses conducted by the debtor;

(2) length of time the case has been pending;

(3) number of full-time employees as of the date of the order for relief and at the end of each reporting period since the case was filed;

(4) cash receipts, cash disbursements and profitability of the debtor for the most recent period and cumulatively since the date of the order for relief;

(5) compliance with title 11, whether or not tax returns and tax payments since the date of the order for relief have been timely filed and made;

(6) all professional fees approved by the court in the case for the most recent period and cumulatively since the date of the order for relief (separately reported, for the professional fees incurred by or on behalf of the debtor, between those that would have been incurred absent a bankruptcy case and those not); and

(7) plans of reorganization filed and confirmed and, with respect thereto, by class, the recoveries of the holders, expressed in aggregate dollar values and, in the case of claims, as a percentage of total claims of the class allowed.

(Added Pub.L. 109–8, Title VI, § 602(a), Apr. 20, 2005, 119 Stat. 120.)

HISTORICAL AND STATUTORY NOTES

References in Text

The effective date of this section, referred to in subsec. (a), means 180 days after April 20, 2005. See Pub.L. 109–8, § 1501, set out as an Effective and Applicability Provisions note for 2005 Acts under 11 U.S.C.A. § 101.

Chapters 7, 12, and 13 of title 11, referred to in subsecs. (a)(1) and (d), are 11 U.S.C.A. § 701 et seq., 11 U.S.C.A. § 1201 et seq., and 11 U.S.C.A. § 1301 et seq., respectively.

Chapter 11 of title 11, referred to in subsecs. (a)(2) and (e), is 11 U.S.C.A. § 1101 et seq.

Effective and Applicability Provisions

2005 Acts. Except as otherwise provided, amendments by Pub.L. 109–8 effective 180 days after April 20, 2005, and inapplicable with respect to cases commenced under Title 11 before the effective date, see Pub.L. 109–8, § 1501, set out as a note under 11 U.S.C.A. § 101.

CHAPTER 40—INDEPENDENT COUNSEL

Sec.
591. Applicability of provisions of this chapter.
592. Preliminary investigation and application for appointment of an independent counsel.
593. Duties of the division of the court.
594. Authority and duties of an independent counsel.
595. Congressional oversight.
596. Removal of an independent counsel; termination of office.
597. Relationship with Department of Justice.
598. Severability.
599. Termination of effect of chapter.

§ 591. Applicability of provisions of this chapter

(a) Preliminary investigation with respect to certain covered persons.—The Attorney General shall conduct a preliminary investigation in accordance with section 592 whenever the Attorney General receives information sufficient to constitute grounds to investigate whether any person described in subsection (b) may have violated any Federal criminal law other than a violation classified as a Class B or C misdemeanor or an infraction.

(b) Persons to whom subsection (a) applies.—The persons referred to in subsection (a) are—

(1) the President and Vice President;

(2) any individual serving in a position listed in section 5312 of title 5;

(3) any individual working in the Executive Office of the President who is compensated at a rate of pay at or above level II of the Executive Schedule under section 5313 of title 5;

(4) any Assistant Attorney General and any individual working in the Department of Justice who is compensated at a rate of pay at or above level III of the Executive Schedule under section 5314 of title 5;

(5) the Director of Central Intelligence, the Deputy Director of Central Intelligence, and the Commissioner of Internal Revenue;

(6) the chairman and treasurer of the principal national campaign committee seeking the election or reelection of the President, and any officer of that committee exercising authority at the national level, during the incumbency of the President; and

(7) any individual who held an office or position described in paragraph (1), (2), (3), (4), or (5) for 1 year after leaving the office or position.

(c) Preliminary investigation with respect to other persons.—

(1) In general.—When the Attorney General determines that an investigation or prosecution of a person by the Department of Justice may result in a personal, financial, or political conflict of interest, the Attorney General may conduct a preliminary investigation of such person in accordance with section 592 if the Attorney General receives information sufficient to constitute grounds to investigate whether that person may have violated Federal criminal law other than a violation classified as a Class B or C misdemeanor or an infraction.

(2) Members of Congress.—When the Attorney General determines that it would be in the public interest, the Attorney General may conduct a preliminary investigation in accordance with section 592 if the Attorney General receives information sufficient to constitute grounds to investigate whether a Member of Congress may have violated any Federal criminal law other than a violation classified as a Class B or C misdemeanor or an infraction.

(d) Examination of information to determine need for preliminary investigation.—

(1) Factors to be considered.—In determining under subsection (a) or (c) (or section 592(c)(2)) whether grounds to investigate exist, the Attorney General shall consider only—

(A) the specificity of the information received; and

(B) the credibility of the source of the information.

(2) Time period for making determination.—The Attorney General shall determine whether grounds to investigate exist not later than 30 days after the information is first received. If within that 30–day period the Attorney General determines that the information is not specific or is not from a credible source, then the Attorney General shall close the matter. If within that 30–day period the Attorney General determines that the information is specific and from a credible source, the Attorney General shall, upon making that determination, commence a preliminary investigation with respect to that information. If the Attorney General is unable to determine, within that 30–day period, whether the information is specific and from a credible source, the Attorney General shall, at the end of that 30–day period, commence a preliminary investigation with respect to that information.

(e) Recusal of Attorney General.—

(1) When recusal is required.—**(A)** If information received under this chapter involves the Attorney General, the next most senior official in the Department of Justice who is not also recused shall perform the duties assigned under this chapter to the Attorney General.

(B) If information received under this chapter involves a person with whom the Attorney General has a personal or financial relationship, the Attorney General shall recuse himself or herself by designating the next most senior official in the Department of Justice who is not also recused to perform the duties assigned under this chapter to the Attorney General.

(2) Requirements for recusal determination.—Before personally making any other determination under this chapter with respect to information received under this chapter, the Attorney General shall determine under paragraph (1)(B) whether recusal is necessary. The Attorney General shall set forth this determination in writing, identify the facts considered by the Attorney General, and set forth the reasons for the recusal. The Attorney General shall file this determination with any notification or application submitted to the division of the court under this chapter with respect to such information.

(Added Pub.L. 95–521, Title VI, § 601(a), Oct. 26, 1978, 92 Stat. 1867, and amended Pub.L. 97–409, §§ 3, 4(a), Jan. 3, 1983, 96 Stat. 2039, 2040; Pub.L. 98–473, Title II, § 228(b), Oct. 12, 1984, 98 Stat. 2030; Pub.L. 100–191, § 2, Dec. 15, 1987, 101 Stat. 1293; Pub.L. 103–270, §§ 3(j), (k), 4, June 30, 1994, 108 Stat. 735, 736.)

HISTORICAL AND STATUTORY NOTES

Effective and Applicability Provisions

1994 Acts. Section 7 of Pub.L. 103–270 provided that:

"**(a) In general.**—Except as provided in this section, the amendments made by this Act [amending this section and sections 592 through 596 and 599 of this title and enacting provisions set out as notes under this section and section 113 of Title 3, The President] shall apply with respect to independent counsels appointed before, on, or after the date of enactment of this Act [June 30, 1994].

"**(b) Assignment of employee to certify expenditures.**—An independent counsel appointed prior to the date of enactment of this Act [June 30, 1994] shall assign to an employee the duty of certifying expenditures, as required by section 594(*l*) of title 28, United States Code, as added by section 3(a) [section 594(*l*) of this title], by the date that is 30 days after the date of enactment of this Act.

"**(c) Office space.**—The Administrator of General Services, in applying section 594(*l*)(3) of title 28, United States Code, as added by section 3(a) [section 594(*l*)(3) of this title], to determine whether the office of an independent counsel appointed prior to the date of enactment of this Act [June 30, 1994] should be moved to a Federal building, shall take into account the moving, legal, and other expenses that might arise if the office were moved.

"**(d) Travel and subsistence expenses.**—For purposes of the restrictions on reimbursement of travel and subsistence expenses of an independent counsel and employees of an office of independent counsel contained in paragraph (3) of section 594(b) of title 28, United States Code, as amended by section 3(b) [section 594(b)(3) of this title], as applied to the office of an independent counsel appointed before the date of enactment of this Act [June 30, 1994], the 1–year service period shall begin on the date of enactment of this Act.

"**(e) Rates of compensation.**—The limitation on rates of compensation of employees of an office of independent counsel contained in the last sentence of section 594(c) of title 28, United States Code, as amended by section 3(c) [section 594(c) of this title], shall not be applied to cause a reduction in the rate of compensation of an employee appointed before the date of enactment of this Act [June 30, 1994].

"**(f) Periodic reappointment.**—The determinations by the division of the court contained in the last sentence of section 596(b)(2) of title 28, United States Code, as amended by section 3(h) [section 596(b)(2) of this title], shall, for the office of an independent counsel appointed before the date of enactment of this Act [June 30, 1994], be required no later than 1 year after the date of enactment of this Act and at the end of each succeeding 1–year period.

"**(g) Reporting requirements.**—No amendment made by this Act [amending this section and sections 592 through 596 and 599 of this title and enacting provisions set out as notes under this section and section 113 of Title 3] that establishes or modifies a requirement that any person submit a report to any other person with respect to an activity occurring during any time period shall be construed to require that a report submitted prior to the date of enactment of this Act [June 30, 1994], with respect to that time period be supplemented to include information with respect to such activity.

"**(h) Regulatory independent counsel.**—Notwithstanding the restriction in section 593(b)(2) of title 28, United States Code [section 593(b)(2) of this title], the division of the court described in section 49 of that title [section 49 of this title] may appoint as an independent counsel any individual who, on the date of enactment of this Act [June 30, 1994], is serving as a regulatory independent counsel under parts 600 and 603 of title 28, Code of Federal Regulations. If such an individual is so appointed, such an independent counsel shall comply with chapter 40 of title 28, United States Code, as amended by this Act [this chapter], in the same manner and to the same extent as an independent counsel appointed before the date of enactment of this Act is required to comply with that chapter, except that subsection (f) of this section shall not apply to such an independent counsel.

"**(i) White House personnel report.**—Section 6 [enacting provisions set out as a note under section 113 of Title 3] shall take effect on January 1, 1995."

1987 Acts. Section 6 of Pub.L. 100–191 provided that:

"**(a) In general.**— Subject to subsection (b), the amendments made by this Act [enacting section 599 of this title, amending sections 49 and 591 to 598 of this title, sections 203 and 205 of Pub.L. 95–521 set out in Appendix 4 to Title 5, Government Organization and Employees, and section 202 of Title 18, Crimes and Criminal Procedure, enacting provisions set out as a note under section 1 of this title, and amending provisions set out as a note under this section] take effect on the date of the enactment of this Act [Dec. 15, 1987].

"**(b) Pending proceedings.**— With respect to any proceeding under chapter 39 of title 28, United States Code (before the redesignation of such chapter as chapter 40 by section 144(g) of Public Law 99–554) [this chapter], or under chapter 40 of such title (after such redesignation) [this chapter], which is pending on the date of the enactment of this Act [Dec. 15, 1987], the following shall apply:

"**(1)** Except as provided in paragraphs (2) and (3), the provisions of chapter 40 of such title [this chapter] as in effect on the day before such date of enactment [Dec. 15, 1987] shall, in lieu of the amendments made by this Act, continue to apply on or after such date to such proceeding until such proceeding is terminated in accordance with such chapter.

"**(2)** The following provisions shall apply to such proceeding on or after such date of enactment:

"**(A)** Section 593(f) of title 28, United States Code, as amended by section 2 of this Act [section 593(f) of this title] relating to the award of attorneys' fees.

"**(B)** Section 594(d)(2) of such title, as added by section 2 of this Act [section 594(d)(2) of this title], to the extent that such section 594(d)(2) relates to reports by the Attorney General on expenditures by independent counsel, except that the first such report shall be made only with respect to expenditures on or after the date of the enactment of this Act [Dec. 15, 1987].

"**(C)** Section 594(h)(1)(A) of such title, as added by section 2 of this Act [section 594(h)(1)(A) of this title], relating to reports by independent counsel, except that the 6–month periods described in such section

594(h)(1)(A) shall be calculated from the date of the enactment of this Act [Dec. 15, 1987].

"(D) Section 594(i) of such title, as added by section 2 of this Act [section 594(i) of this title], relating to the independence of the office of independent counsel for certain purposes.

"(E) Section 594(k) of such title, as added by section 2 of this Act [section 594(u) of this title], relating to custody of records of independent counsel.

"(F) Section 596(a)(3) of such title, as amended by section 2 of this Act [section 596(a)(3) of this title], relating to judicial review of the removal of an independent counsel from office.

"(G) Section 596(c) of such title, as added by section 2 of this Act [section 596(c) of this title], relating to audits of expenditures of independent counsel.

"(H) The amendments made by section 3 of this Act [amending section 202(a) of Title 18, Crimes and Criminal Procedure, and sections 203 and 205 of Pub.L. 95–521, set out in Appendix 4 to Title 5, Government Organization and Employees], relating to the status of independent counsel and their appointees as special government employees and to their financial disclosure requirements.

"(3) Section 594(j) of title 28, United States Code, as added by section 2 of this Act [section 594(j) of this title], relating to certain standards of conduct shall, 90 days after the date of the enactment of this Act [Dec. 15, 1987], apply to a pending proceeding described in this subsection."

1984 Acts. Section 235(a)(1)(B)(ii)(IV) of Pub.L. 98–473 had provided that the amendment made by section 228 of Pub.L. 98–473 was to be effective Oct. 12, 1984. Pub.L. 99–646, § 35(2)(D), Nov. 10, 1986, 100 Stat. 3599, amended section 235(a)(1)(B)(ii)(IV) of Pub.L. 98–473 making it inapplicable to section 228. Amendment by Pub.L. 98–473 effective the first day of the first calendar month beginning 36 months after Oct. 12, 1984, see section 235(a)(1) of Pub.L. 98–473, as amended, set out as a note under section 3551 of Title 18, Crimes and Criminal Procedure.

1978 Acts. Section 604 of Pub.L. 95–521 provided that: "Except as provided in this section, the amendments made by this title [enacting this chapter and sections 49, 528, and 529 of this title] shall take effect on the date of the enactment of this Act [Oct. 26, 1978]. The provisions of chapter 39 of title 28 of the United States Code, as added by section 601 of this Act, shall not apply to specific information received by the Attorney General pursuant to section 591 of such title 28, if the Attorney General determines that—

"(1) such specific information is directly related to a prosecution pending at the time such specific information is received by the Attorney General;

"(2) such specific information is related to a matter which has been presented to a grand jury and is received by the Attorney General within one hundred and eighty days of the date of the enactment of this Act [Oct. 26, 1978]; or

"(3) such specific information is related to an investigation that is pending at the time such specific information is received by the Attorney General, and such specific information is received by the Attorney General within ninety days of the date of the enactment of this Act [Oct. 26, 1978]."

Change of Name

Reference to the Director of Central Intelligence or the Director of the Central Intelligence Agency in the Director's capacity as the head of the intelligence community deemed to be a reference to the Director of National Intelligence. Reference to the Director of Central Intelligence or the Director of the Central Intelligence Agency in the Director's capacity as the head of the Central Intelligence Agency deemed to be a reference to the Director of the Central Intelligence Agency. See section 1081(a), (b) of Pub.L. 108–458, set out as a note under 50 U.S.C.A. § 401.

Contingency Fund for Independent Counsels

Section 601(c) of Pub.L. 95–521, as amended Pub.L. 97–409, § 2(c)(2), Jan. 3, 1983, 96 Stat. 2039; Pub.L. 100–191, § 5(b), Dec. 15, 1987, 101 Stat. 1307, provided that: "There are authorized to be appropriated for each fiscal year such sums as may be necessary, to be held by the Department of Justice as a contingent fund for the use of any independent counsels appointed under chapter 40 (relating to independent counsel) of title 28 of the United States Code [this chapter] in the carrying out of functions under such chapter."

Permanent Appropriation for Expenses of Independent Counsels

Pub.L. 100–202, § 101(a) [Title II], Dec. 22, 1987, 101 Stat. 1329–9, provided in part "That a permanent indefinite appropriation is established within the Department of Justice to pay all necessary expenses of investigations and prosecutions by independent counsel appointed pursuant to the provisions of 28 U.S.C. 591 et seq. [this chapter] or other law: *Provided further,* That the Comptroller General shall perform semiannual financial reviews of expenditures from the Independent Counsel permanent indefinite appropriation, and report their findings to the Committees on Appropriations of the House and Senate".

[For termination, effective May 15, 2000, of provisions of Pub.L. 100–202, (Title II), § 101(a), set out above, which require the Comptroller General to report findings of semiannual financial reviews to the Committees on Appropriations of the House and Senate, see Pub.L. 104–66, § 3003, as amended, set out as a note under 31 U.S.C.A. § 1113, and page 9 of House Document No. 103–7.]

§ 592. Preliminary investigation and application for appointment of an independent counsel

(a) Conduct of preliminary investigation.—

(1) In general.—A preliminary investigation conducted under this chapter shall be of such matters as the Attorney General considers appropriate in order to make a determination, under subsection (b) or (c), on whether further investigation is warranted, with respect to each potential violation, or allegation of a violation, of criminal law. The Attorney General shall make such determination not later than 90 days after the preliminary investigation is commenced, except that, in the case of a preliminary investigation commenced after a congressional request under subsection (g), the Attorney General shall make such determination not later than 90 days after the request is received. The Attorney General shall promptly notify the division of the court specified in section 593(a) of the commencement of such preliminary investigation and the date of such commencement.

(2) Limited authority of Attorney General.—(A) In conducting preliminary investigations under this chapter, the Attorney General shall have no authority to convene grand juries, plea bargain, grant immunity, or issue subpoenas.

(B)(i) The Attorney General shall not base a determination under this chapter that information with respect to a violation of criminal law by a person is not specific and from a credible source upon a determination that such person lacked the state of mind required for the violation of criminal law.

(ii) The Attorney General shall not base a determination under this chapter that there are no reasonable grounds to believe that further investigation is warranted, upon a determination that such person lacked the state of mind required for the violation of criminal law involved, unless there is clear and convincing evidence that the person lacked such state of mind.

(3) Extension of time for preliminary investigation.—The Attorney General may apply to the division of the court for a single extension, for a period of not more than 60 days, of the 90–day period referred to in paragraph (1). The division of the court may, upon a showing of good cause, grant such extension.

(b) Determination that further investigation not warranted.—

(1) Notification of division of the court.—If the Attorney General, upon completion of a preliminary investigation under this chapter, determines that there are no reasonable grounds to believe that further investigation is warranted, the Attorney General shall promptly so notify the division of the court, and the division of the court shall have no power to appoint an independent counsel with respect to the matters involved.

(2) Form of notification.—Such notification shall contain a summary of the information received and a summary of the results of the preliminary investigation.

(c) Determination that further investigation is warranted.—

(1) Application for appointment of independent counsel.—The Attorney General shall apply to the division of the court for the appointment of an independent counsel if—

(A) the Attorney General, upon completion of a preliminary investigation under this chapter, determines that there are reasonable grounds to believe that further investigation is warranted; or

(B) the 90–day period referred to in subsection (a)(1), and any extension granted under subsection (a)(3), have elapsed and the Attorney General has not filed a notification with the division of the court under subsection (b)(1).

In determining under this chapter whether reasonable grounds exist to warrant further investigation, the Attorney General shall comply with the written or other established policies of the Department of Justice with respect to the conduct of criminal investigations.

(2) Receipt of additional information.—If, after submitting a notification under subsection (b)(1), the Attorney General receives additional information sufficient to constitute grounds to investigate the matters to which such notification related, the Attorney General shall—

(A) conduct such additional preliminary investigation as the Attorney General considers appropriate for a period of not more than 90 days after the date on which such additional information is received; and

(B) otherwise comply with the provisions of this section with respect to such additional preliminary investigation to the same extent as any other preliminary investigation under this section.

(d) Contents of application.—Any application for the appointment of an independent counsel under this chapter shall contain sufficient information to assist the division of the court in selecting an independent counsel and in defining that independent counsel's prosecutorial jurisdiction so that the independent counsel has adequate authority to fully investigate and prosecute the subject matter and all matters related to that subject matter.

(e) Disclosure of information.—Except as otherwise provided in this chapter or as is deemed necessary for law enforcement purposes, no officer or employee of the Department of Justice or an office of independent counsel may, without leave of the division of the court, disclose to any individual outside the Department of Justice or such office any notification, application, or any other document, materials, or memorandum supplied to the division of the court under this chapter. Nothing in this chapter shall be construed as authorizing the withholding of information from the Congress.

(f) Limitation on judicial review.—The Attorney General's determination under this chapter to apply to the division of the court for the appointment of an independent counsel shall not be reviewable in any court.

(g) Congressional request.—

(1) By Judiciary Committee or members thereof.—The Committee on the Judiciary of either House of the Congress, or a majority of majority party members or a majority of all nonmajority party members of either such committee, may request in writing that the Attorney General apply for the appointment of an independent counsel.

(2) Report by Attorney General pursuant to request.—Not later than 30 days after the receipt of a request under paragraph (1), the Attorney General shall submit, to the committee making the request, or to the committee on which the persons making the request serve, a report on whether the Attorney General has begun or will begin a preliminary investigation under this chapter of the matters with respect to which the request is made, in accordance with subsection (a) or (c) of section 591, as the case may be. The report shall set forth the reasons for the Attorney General's decision regarding such preliminary investigation as it relates to each of the matters with respect to which the congressional request is made. If there is such a preliminary investigation, the report shall include the date on which the preliminary investigation began or will begin.

(3) Submission of information in response to congressional request.—At the same time as any notification, application, or any other document, material, or memorandum is supplied to the division of the court pursuant to this section with respect to a preliminary investigation of any matter with respect to which a request is made under paragraph (1), such notification, application, or other document, material, or memorandum shall be supplied to the committee making the request, or to the committee on which the persons making the request serve. If no application for the appointment of an independent counsel is made to the division of the court under this section pursuant to such a preliminary investigation, the Attorney General shall submit a report to that committee stating the reasons why such application was not made, addressing each matter with respect to which the congressional request was made.

(4) Disclosure of information.—Any report, notification, application, or other document, material, or memorandum supplied to a committee under this subsection shall not be revealed to any third party, except that the committee may, either on its own initiative or upon the request of the Attorney General, make public such portion or portions of such report, notification, application, document, material, or memorandum as will not in the committee's judgment prejudice the rights of any individual.

(Added Pub.L. 95–521, Title VI, § 601(a), Oct. 26, 1978, 92 Stat. 1868, and amended Pub.L. 97–409, §§ 2(a)(1), 4(b)–(e), Jan. 3, 1983, 96 Stat. 2039–2041; Pub.L. 100–191, § 2, Dec. 15, 1987, 101 Stat. 1295; Pub.L. 103–270, § 3(*l*), June 30, 1994, 108 Stat. 736.)

HISTORICAL AND STATUTORY NOTES

Effective and Applicability Provisions

1994 Acts. Amendment by Pub.L. 103–270 applicable with respect to independent counsels appointed before, on, or after June 30, 1994, see section 7(a) of Pub.L. 103–270, set out as a note under section 591 of this title.

1987 Acts. Amendment by Pub.L. 100–191 to take effect on Dec. 15, 1987, and to apply only to new independent counsel proceedings and to new independent counsels coming into existence on and after Dec. 15, 1987, see section 6 of Pub.L. 100–191, set out as a note under section 591 of this title.

1978 Acts. Section effective Oct. 26, 1978, except for specific information received by the Attorney General pursuant to section 591 of this title based on determinations made by the Attorney General respecting such information, see section 604 of Pub.L. 95–521, set out as a note under section 591 of this title.

Termination of Reporting Requirements

For termination of reporting provisions of this section pertaining to response to Congressional request for appointment of independent counsel, effective May 15, 2000, see Pub.L. 104–66, § 3003, as amended, set out as a note under 31 U.S.C.A. § 1113, and page 117 of House Document No. 103–7.

§ 593. Duties of the division of the court

(a) Reference to division of the court.—The division of the court to which this chapter refers is the division established under section 49 of this title.

(b) Appointment and jurisdiction of independent counsel.—

(1) Authority.—Upon receipt of an application under section 592(c), the division of the court shall appoint an appropriate independent counsel and shall define that independent counsel's prosecutorial jurisdiction.

(2) Qualifications of independent counsel.—The division of the court shall appoint as independent counsel an individual who has appropriate experience and who will conduct the investigation and any prosecution in a prompt, responsible, and cost-effective manner. The division of the court shall seek to appoint as independent counsel an individual who will serve to the extent necessary to complete the investigation and any prosecution without undue delay. The division of the court may not appoint as an independent counsel any person who holds any office of profit or trust under the United States.

(3) Scope of prosecutorial jurisdiction.—In defining the independent counsel's prosecutorial jurisdiction, the division of the court shall assure that the independent counsel has adequate authority to fully investigate and prosecute the subject matter with respect to which the Attorney General has requested the appointment of the independent counsel, and all matters related to that subject matter. Such jurisdiction shall also include the authority to investigate and prosecute Federal crimes, other than those classified as Class B or C misdemeanors or infractions, that may arise out of the investigation or prosecution of the matter with respect to which the Attorney General's request was made, including perjury, obstruction of justice, destruction of evidence, and intimidation of witnesses.

(4) Disclosure of identity and prosecutorial jurisdiction.—An independent counsel's identity and prosecutorial jurisdiction (including any expansion under subsection (c)) may not be made public except upon the request of the Attorney General or upon a determination of the division of the court that disclosure of the identity and prosecutorial jurisdiction of such independent counsel would be in the best interests of justice. In any event, the identity and prosecutorial jurisdiction of such independent counsel shall be made public when any indictment is returned, or any criminal information is filed, pursuant to the independent counsel's investigation.

(c) Expansion of jurisdiction.—

(1) In general.—The division of the court, upon the request of the Attorney General, may expand the prosecutorial jurisdiction of an independent counsel, and such expansion may be in lieu of the appointment of another independent counsel.

(2) Procedure for request by independent counsel.—(A) If the independent counsel discovers or receives information about possible violations of criminal law by persons as provided in section 591, which are not covered by the prosecutorial jurisdiction of the independent counsel, the independent counsel may submit such information to the Attorney General. The Attorney General shall then conduct a preliminary investigation of the information in accordance with the provisions of section 592, except that such preliminary investigation shall not exceed 30 days from the date such information is received. In making the determinations required by section 592, the Attorney General shall give great weight to any recommendations of the independent counsel.

(B) If the Attorney General determines, after according great weight to the recommendations of the independent counsel, that there are no reasonable grounds to believe that further investigation is warranted, the Attorney General shall promptly so notify the division of the court and the division of the court shall have no power to expand the jurisdiction of the independent counsel or to appoint another independent counsel with respect to the matters involved.

(C) If—

(i) the Attorney General determines that there are reasonable grounds to believe that further investigation is warranted; or

(ii) the 30-day period referred to in subparagraph (A) elapses without a notification to the division of the court that no further investigation is warranted,

the division of the court shall expand the jurisdiction of the appropriate independent counsel to include the matters involved or shall appoint another independent counsel to investigate such matters.

(d) Return for further explanation.—Upon receipt of a notification under section 592 or subsection (c)(2)(B) of this section from the Attorney General that there are no reasonable grounds to believe that further investigation is warranted with respect to information received under this chapter, the division of the court shall have no authority to overrule this determination but may return the matter to the Attorney General for further explanation of the reasons for such determination.

(e) Vacancies.—If a vacancy in office arises by reason of the resignation, death, or removal of an independent counsel, the division of the court shall appoint an independent counsel to complete the work of the independent counsel whose resignation, death, or removal caused the vacancy, except that in the case of a vacancy arising by reason of the removal of an independent counsel, the division of the court may appoint an acting independent counsel to serve until any judicial review of such removal is completed.

(f) Attorneys' fees.—

(1) Award of fees.—Upon the request of an individual who is the subject of an investigation conducted by an independent counsel pursuant to this chapter, the division of the court may, if no indictment is brought against such individual pursuant to that investigation, award reimbursement for those reasonable attorneys' fees incurred by that individual during that investigation which would not have been incurred but for the requirements of this chapter. The division of the court shall notify the the [1] independent counsel who conducted the investigation and Attorney [2] General of any request for attorneys' fees under this subsection.

(2) Evaluation of fees.—The division of the court shall direct such independent counsel and the Attorney General to file a written evaluation of any request for attorneys' fees under this subsection, addressing—

(A) the sufficiency of the documentation;

(B) the need or justification for the underlying item;

(C) whether the underlying item would have been incurred but for the requirements of this chapter; and

(D) the reasonableness of the amount of money requested.

(g) Disclosure of information.—The division of the court may, subject to section 594(h)(2), allow the disclosure of any notification, application, or any other document, material, or memorandum supplied to the division of the court under this chapter.

(h) Amicus curiae briefs.—When presented with significant legal issues, the division of the court may disclose sufficient information about the issues to permit the filing of timely amicus curiae briefs.

(Added Pub.L. 95–521, Title VI, § 601(a), Oct. 26, 1978, 92 Stat. 1869, and amended Pub.L. 97–409, §§ 2(a)(1), 5, Jan. 3, 1983, 96 Stat. 2039, 2041; Pub.L. 100–191, § 2, Dec. 15, 1987, 101 Stat. 1297; Pub.L. 103–270, § 3(n), June 30, 1994, 108 Stat. 736.)

1 So in original.

2 So in original. Probably should be preceded by "the".

HISTORICAL AND STATUTORY NOTES

Effective and Applicability Provisions

1994 Acts. Amendment by Pub.L. 103–270 applicable with respect to independent counsels appointed before, on, or after June 30, 1994, with provisions directing that no amendment made by Pub.L. 103–270 establishing or modifying a reporting requirement shall be construed to require that a report submitted prior to June 30, 1994 be supplemented to include information with respect to activity occurring during any time period, and that the division of the court described in section 49 of this title is authorized to appoint as an independent counsel any individual who, on June 30, 1994, is serving as a regulatory independent counsel under parts 600 and 603 of title 28, Code of Federal Regulations, notwithstanding the restriction in subsec. (b)(2) of this section, see section 7(a), (g), (h) of Pub.L. 103–270, set out as a note under section 591 of this title.

1987 Acts. Amendment by Pub.L. 100–191 to take effect on Dec. 15, 1987, and to apply only to new independent counsel proceedings and to new independent counsels coming into existence on and after Dec. 15, 1987, but with subsec. (f) applicable to previously initiated proceedings still pending on Dec. 15, 1987, see section 6 of Pub.L. 100–191, set out as a note under section 591 of this title.

1978 Acts. Section effective Oct. 26, 1978, except for specific information received by the Attorney General pursuant to section 591 of this title based on determinations made by the Attorney General respecting such information, see section 604 of Pub.L. 95–521, set out as a note under section 591 of this title.

§ 594. Authority and duties of an independent counsel

(a) Authorities.—Notwithstanding any other provision of law, an independent counsel appointed under this chapter shall have, with respect to all matters in such independent counsel's prosecutorial jurisdiction established under this chapter, full power and independent authority to exercise all investigative and prosecutorial functions and powers of the Department of Justice, the Attorney General, and any other officer or employee of the Department of Justice, except that the Attorney General shall exercise direction or control as to those matters that specifically require the Attorney General's personal action under section 2516 of title 18. Such investigative and prosecutorial functions and powers shall include—

(1) conducting proceedings before grand juries and other investigations;

(2) participating in court proceedings and engaging in any litigation, including civil and criminal matters, that such independent counsel considers necessary;

(3) appealing any decision of a court in any case or proceeding in which such independent counsel participates in an official capacity;

(4) reviewing all documentary evidence available from any source;

(5) determining whether to contest the assertion of any testimonial privilege;

(6) receiving appropriate national security clearances and, if necessary, contesting in court (including, where appropriate, participating in in camera proceedings) any claim of privilege or attempt to withhold evidence on grounds of national security;

(7) making applications to any Federal court for a grant of immunity to any witness, consistent with applicable statutory requirements, or for warrants, subpoenas, or other court orders, and, for purposes of sections 6003, 6004, and 6005 of title 18, exercising the authority vested in a United States attorney or the Attorney General;

(8) inspecting, obtaining, or using the original or a copy of any tax return, in accordance with the applicable statutes and regulations, and, for purposes of section 6103 of the Internal Revenue Code of 1986 and the regulations issued thereunder, exercising the powers vested in a United States attorney or the Attorney General;

(9) initiating and conducting prosecutions in any court of competent jurisdiction, framing and signing indictments, filing informations, and handling all aspects of any case, in the name of the United States; and

(10) consulting with the United States attorney for the district in which any violation of law with respect to which the independent counsel is appointed was alleged to have occurred.

(b) Compensation.—

(1) In general.—An independent counsel appointed under this chapter shall receive compensation at the per diem rate equal to the annual rate of basic pay payable for level IV of the Executive Schedule under section 5315 of title 5.

(2) Travel expenses.—Except as provided in paragraph (3), an independent counsel and persons appointed under subsection (c) shall be entitled to the payment of travel expenses as provided by subchapter I of chapter 57 of title 5, United States Code, including travel, per diem, and subsistence expenses in accordance with section 5703 of title 5.

(3) Travel to primary office.—

(A) In general.—After 1 year of service under this chapter, an independent counsel and persons appointed under subsection (c) shall not be entitled to the payment of travel, per diem, or subsistence expenses under subchapter I of chapter 57 of title 5, United States Code, for the purpose of commuting to or from the city in which the primary office of the independent counsel or person is located. The 1-year period may be extended for successive 6-month periods if the independent counsel and the division of the court certify that the payment is in the public interest to carry out the purposes of this chapter.

(B) Relevant factors.—In making any certification under this paragraph with respect to travel and subsistence expenses of an independent counsel or person appointed under subsection (c), such employee shall consider, among other relevant factors—

(i) the cost to the Government of reimbursing such travel and subsistence expenses;

(ii) the period of time for which the independent counsel anticipates that the activities of the independent counsel or person, as the case may be, will continue;

(iii) the personal and financial burdens on the independent counsel or person, as the case may be, of relocating so that such travel and subsistence expenses would not be incurred; and

(iv) the burdens associated with appointing a new independent counsel, or appointing another person under subsection (c), to replace the individual involved who is unable or unwilling to so relocate.

(c) Additional personnel.—For the purposes of carrying out the duties of an office of independent counsel, such independent counsel may appoint, fix the compensation, and assign the duties of such employees as such independent counsel considers necessary (including investigators, attorneys, and part-time consultants). The positions of all such employees are exempted from the competitive service. Such employees shall be compensated at levels not to exceed those payable for comparable positions in the Office of United States Attorney for the District of Columbia under sections 548 and 550, but in no event shall any such employee be compensated at a rate greater than the rate of basic pay payable for level ES-4 of the Senior Executive Service Schedule under section 5382 of title 5, as adjusted for the District of Columbia under section 5304 of that title regardless of the locality in which an employee is employed.

(d) Assistance of Department of Justice.—

(1) In carrying out functions.—An independent counsel may request assistance from the Department of Justice in carrying out the functions of the independent counsel, and the Department of Justice shall provide that assistance, which may include access to any records, files, or other materials relevant to matters within such independent counsel's prosecutorial jurisdiction, and the use of the resources and personnel necessary to perform such independent counsel's duties. At the request of an independent counsel, prosecutors, administrative personnel, and other employees of the Department of Justice may be detailed to the staff of the independent counsel.

(2) Payment of and reports on expenditures of independent counsel.—The Department of Justice shall pay all costs relating to the establishment and operation of any office of independent counsel. The Attorney General shall submit to the Congress, not later than 30 days after the end of each fiscal year, a report on amounts paid during that fiscal year for expenses of investigations and prosecutions by independent counsel. Each such report shall include a statement of all payments made for activities of independent counsel but may not reveal the identity or prosecutorial jurisdiction of any independent counsel which has not been disclosed under section 593(b)(4).

(e) Referral of other matters to an independent counsel.—An independent counsel may ask the Attorney General or the division of the court to refer to the independent counsel matters related to the independent counsel's prosecutorial jurisdiction, and the Attorney General or the division of the court, as the case may be, may refer such matters. If the Attorney General refers a matter to an independent counsel on the Attorney General's own initiative, the independent counsel may accept such referral if the matter relates to the independent counsel's prosecutorial jurisdiction. If the Attorney General refers any matter to the independent counsel pursuant to the independent counsel's request, or if the independent counsel accepts a referral made by the Attorney General on the Attorney General's own initiative, the independent counsel shall so notify the division of the court.

(f) Compliance with policies of the Department of Justice.—

(1) In general.—An independent counsel shall, except to the extent that to do so would be inconsistent with the purposes of this chapter, comply with the written or other established policies of the

Department of Justice respecting enforcement of the criminal laws. To determine these policies and policies under subsection (*l*)(1)(B), the independent counsel shall, except to the extent that doing so would be inconsistent with the purposes of this chapter, consult with the Department of Justice.

(2) National security.—An independent counsel shall comply with guidelines and procedures used by the Department in the handling and use of classified material.

(g) Dismissal of matters.—The independent counsel shall have full authority to dismiss matters within the independent counsel's prosecutorial jurisdiction without conducting an investigation or at any subsequent time before prosecution, if to do so would be consistent with the written or other established policies of the Department of Justice with respect to the enforcement of criminal laws.

(h) Reports by independent counsel.—

(1) Required reports.—An independent counsel shall—

(A) file with the division of the court, with respect to the 6-month period beginning on the date of his or her appointment, and with respect to each 6-month period thereafter until the office of that independent counsel terminates, a report which identifies and explains major expenses, and summarizes all other expenses, incurred by that office during the 6-month period with respect to which the report is filed, and estimates future expenses of that office; and

(B) before the termination of the independent counsel's office under section 596(b), file a final report with the division of the court, setting forth fully and completely a description of the work of the independent counsel, including the disposition of all cases brought.

(2) Disclosure of information in reports.—The division of the court may release to the Congress, the public, or any appropriate person, such portions of a report made under this subsection as the division of the court considers appropriate. The division of the court shall make such orders as are appropriate to protect the rights of any individual named in such report and to prevent undue interference with any pending prosecution. The division of the court may make any portion of a final report filed under paragraph (1)(B) available to any individual named in such report for the purposes of receiving within a time limit set by the division of the court any comments or factual information that such individual may submit. Such comments and factual information, in whole or in part, may, in the discretion of the division of the court, be included as an appendix to such final report.

(3) Publication of reports.—At the request of an independent counsel, the Public Printer shall cause to be printed any report previously released to the public under paragraph (2). The independent counsel shall certify the number of copies necessary for the public, and the Public Printer shall place the cost of the required number to the debit of such independent counsel. Additional copies shall be made available to the public through the depository library program and Superintendent of Documents sales program pursuant to sections 1702 and 1903 of title 44.

(i) Independence from Department of Justice.—Each independent counsel appointed under this chapter, and the persons appointed by that independent counsel under subsection (c), are separate from and independent of the Department of Justice for purposes of sections 202 through 209 of title 18.

(j) Standards of conduct applicable to independent counsel, persons serving in the office of an independent counsel, and their law firms.—

(1) Restrictions on employment while independent counsel and appointees are serving.—(A) During the period in which an independent counsel is serving under this chapter—

(i) such independent counsel, and

(ii) any person associated with a firm with which such independent counsel is associated,

may not represent in any matter any person involved in any investigation or prosecution under this chapter.

(B) During the period in which any person appointed by an independent counsel under subsection (c) is serving in the office of independent counsel, such person may not represent in any matter any person involved in any investigation or prosecution under this chapter.

(2) Post employment restrictions on independent counsel and appointees.—(A) Each independent counsel and each person appointed by that independent counsel under subsection (c) may not, for 3 years following the termination of the service under this chapter of that independent counsel or appointed person, as the case may be, represent any person in any matter if that individual was the subject of an investigation or prosecution under this chapter that was conducted by that independent counsel.

(B) Each independent counsel and each person appointed by that independent counsel under subsection (c) may not, for 1 year following the termination of the service under this chapter of that independent counsel or appointed person, as the case may be, represent any person in any matter involving any investigation or prosecution under this chapter.

(3) One-year ban on representation by members of firms of independent counsel.—Any person who is associated with a firm with which an independent counsel is associated or becomes associated after termination of the service of that independent counsel under this chapter may not, for 1 year following such termination, represent any person in any matter involving any investigation or prosecution under this chapter.

(4) Definitions.—For purposes of this subsection—

(A) the term "firm" means a law firm whether organized as a partnership or corporation; and

(B) a person is "associated" with a firm if that person is an officer, director, partner, or other member or employee of that firm.

(5) Enforcement.—The Attorney General and the Director of the Office of Government Ethics have authority to enforce compliance with this subsection.

(k) Custody of records of an independent counsel.—

(1) Transfer of records.—Upon termination of the office of an independent counsel, that independent counsel shall transfer to the Archivist of the United States all records which have been created or received by that office. Before this transfer, the independent counsel shall clearly identify which of these records are subject to rule 6(e) of the Federal Rules of Criminal Procedure as grand jury materials and which of these records have been classified as national security information. Any records which were compiled by an independent counsel and, upon termination of the independent counsel's office, were stored with the division of the court or elsewhere before the enactment of the Independent Counsel Reauthorization Act of 1987, shall also be transferred to the Archivist of the United States by the division of the court or the person in possession of such records.

(2) Maintenance, use, and disposal of records.—Records transferred to the Archivist under this chapter shall be maintained, used, and disposed of in accordance with chapters 21, 29, and 33 of title 44.

(3) Access to records.—

(A) In general.—Subject to paragraph (4), access to the records transferred to the Archivist under this chapter shall be governed by section 552 of title 5.

(B) Access by Department of Justice.—The Archivist shall, upon written application by the Attorney General, disclose any such records to the Department of Justice for purposes of an ongoing law enforcement investigation or court proceeding, except that, in the case of grand jury materials, such records shall be so disclosed only by order of the court of jurisdiction under rule 6(e) of the Federal Rules of Criminal Procedure.

(C) Exception.—Notwithstanding any restriction on access imposed by law, the Archivist and persons employed by the National Archives and Records Administration who are engaged in the performance of normal archival work shall be permitted access to the records transferred to the Archivist under this chapter.

(4) Records provided by Congress.—Records of an investigation conducted by a committee of the House of Representatives or the Senate which are provided to an independent counsel to assist in an investigation or prosecution conducted by that independent counsel—

(A) shall be maintained as a separate body of records within the records of the independent counsel; and

(B) shall, after the records have been transferred to the Archivist under this chapter, be made available, except as provided in paragraph (3)(B) and (C), in accordance with the rules governing release of the records of the House of Congress that provided the records to the independent counsel.

Subparagraph (B) shall not apply to those records which have been surrendered pursuant to grand jury or court proceedings.

(*l*) Cost controls and administrative support.—

(1) Cost controls.—

(A) In general.—An independent counsel shall—

(i) conduct all activities with due regard for expense;

(ii) authorize only reasonable and lawful expenditures; and

(iii) promptly, upon taking office, assign to a specific employee the duty of certifying that expenditures of the independent counsel are reasonable and made in accordance with law.

(B) Liability for invalid certification.—An employee making a certification under subparagraph (A)(iii) shall be liable for an invalid certification to the same extent as a certifying official certifying a voucher is liable under section 3528 of title 31.

(C) Department of justice policies.—An independent counsel shall comply with the established policies of the Department of Justice respecting expenditures of funds, except to the extent that compliance would be inconsistent with the purposes of this chapter.

(2) Administrative support.—The Director of the Administrative Office of the United States Courts shall provide administrative support and guidance to each independent counsel. No officer or employee of the Administrative Office of the United States Courts shall disclose information related to an independent counsel's expenditures, personnel, or administrative acts or arrangements without the authorization of the independent counsel.

(3) Office space.—The Administrator of General Services, in consultation with the Director of the Administrative Office of the United States Courts, shall promptly provide appropriate office space for each independent counsel. Such office space shall be within a Federal building unless the Administrator of General Services determines that other arrangements would cost less. Until such office space is provided, the Administrative Office of the United States Courts shall provide newly appointed independent counsels immediately upon appointment with appropriate, temporary office space, equipment, and supplies.

(Added Pub.L. 95–521, Title VI, § 601(a), Oct. 26, 1978, 92 Stat. 1869, and amended Pub.L. 97–409, §§ 2(a)(1), 6(a) to (c), Jan. 3, 1983, 96 Stat. 2039, 2041; Pub.L. 99–514, § 2, Oct. 22, 1986, 100 Stat. 2095; Pub.L. 100–191, § 2, Dec. 15, 1987, 101 Stat. 1300; Pub.L. 103–270, § 3(a) to (f), (m), (*o*), June 30, 1994, 108 Stat. 732 to 734, 736; Pub.L. 104–208, Div. A, Title I, § 101(a) [Title I, § 118], Sept. 30, 1996, 110 Stat. 3009–23.)

HISTORICAL AND STATUTORY NOTES

References in Text

Section 6103 of the Internal Revenue Code of 1986, referred to in subsec. (a)(8), is classified to section 6103 of Title 26, Internal Revenue Code.

The Federal Rules of Criminal Procedure, referred to in subsec. (k)(1), (3)(B), are set out in Title 18, Crimes and Criminal Procedure.

The enactment of the Independent Counsel Reauthorization Act of 1987, referred to in subsec. (k)(1), is the enactment of Pub.L. 100–191, which was approved Dec. 15, 1987.

Termination of Reporting Requirements

Reporting requirement of this section excepted from termination under Pub.L. 104–66, § 3003(a)(1), as amended, set out in a note under 31 U.S.C.A. § 1113, see Pub.L. 106–197, § 1, set out as a note under 31 U.S.C.A. § 1113.

References in Other Laws to GS–16, 17, or 18 Pay Rates

References in laws to the rates of pay for GS–16, 17, or 18, or to maximum rates of pay under the General Schedule, to be considered references to rates payable under specified sections of Title 5, Government Organization and Employees, see section 529 [Title I, § 101(c)(1)] of Pub.L. 101–509, set out in a note under section 5376 of Title 5.

Codifications

Pub.L. 104–208, Div. A, Title I, § 101(a) [Title I, § 118(c)], Sept. 30, 1996, 110 Stat. 3009–23, which directed that the second sentence of subsec. (b)(3)(A) of this section be amended by substituting "the independent counsel" and "the division of the court" for "such employee", could not be executed to text, as second sentence of subsec. (b)(3)(A) did not contain phrase "such employee".

Effective and Applicability Provisions

1994 Acts. Amendment by Pub.L. 103–270 applicable with respect to independent counsels appointed before, on, or after June 30, 1994, with transition provisions relating to assignment of employee to certify expenditures, and relating to office space, travel and subsistence expenses, and rates of compensation under this section, and with provision directing that no amendment made by Pub.L. 103–270 establishing or modifying a reporting requirement be construed to require that a report submitted prior to June 30, 1994 be supplemented to include information with respect to activity occurring during any time period, see section 7(a) to (e), (g) of Pub.L. 103–270, set out as a note under section 591 of this title.

1987 Acts. Amendment by Pub.L. 100–191 effective Dec. 15, 1987, and applicable to proceedings initiated and independent counsels appointed on and after Dec. 15, 1987, but with the following provisions applicable to previously initiated proceedings pending on Dec. 15, 1987: subsec. (d)(2) (relating to reports by Attorney General on expenditures by independent counsel, except that the first such report shall be made only with respect to expenditures on or after Dec. 15, 1987), subsec. (h)(1)(A) except that the 6–month periods described in subsec. (h)(1)(A) of this section shall be calculated from Dec. 15, 1987, subsec. (i), subsec. (k) of this section, and 90 days after Dec. 15, 1987, subsec. (j), see section 6 of Pub.L. 100–191, set out as a note under section 591 of this title.

1978 Acts. Section effective Oct. 26, 1978, except for specific information received by the Attorney General pursuant to section 591 of this title based on determinations made by the Attorney General respecting such information, see section 604 of Pub.L. 95–521, set out as a note under section 591 of this title.

§ 595. Congressional oversight

(a) Oversight of conduct of independent counsel.—

(1) Congressional oversight.—The appropriate committees of the Congress shall have oversight jurisdiction with respect to the official conduct of any independent counsel appointed under this chapter, and such independent counsel shall have the duty to cooperate with the exercise of such oversight jurisdiction.

(2) Reports to Congress.—An independent counsel appointed under this chapter shall submit to the Congress annually a report on the activities of the independent counsel, including a description of the progress of any investigation or prosecution conducted by the independent counsel. Such report may omit any matter that in the judgment of the independent counsel should be kept confidential, but shall provide information adequate to justify the expenditures that the office of the independent counsel has made.

(b) Oversight of conduct of Attorney General.—Within 15 days after receiving an inquiry about a particular case under this chapter, which is a matter of public knowledge, from a committee of the Congress with jurisdiction over this chapter, the Attorney General shall provide the following information to that committee with respect to that case:

(1) When the information about the case was received.

(2) Whether a preliminary investigation is being conducted, and if so, the date it began.

(3) Whether an application for the appointment of an independent counsel or a notification that further investigation is not warranted has been filed with the division of the court, and if so, the date of such filing.

(c) Information relating to impeachment.—An independent counsel shall advise the House of Representatives of any substantial and credible information which such independent counsel receives, in carrying out the independent counsel's responsibilities under this chapter, that may constitute grounds for an impeachment. Nothing in this chapter or section 49 of this title shall prevent the Congress or either House thereof from obtaining information in the course of an impeachment proceeding.

(Added Pub.L. 95–521, Title VI, § 601(a), Oct. 26, 1978, 92 Stat. 1871, and amended Pub.L. 97–409, § 2(a)(1), Jan. 3, 1983, 96 Stat. 2039; Pub.L. 100–191, § 2, Dec. 15, 1987, 101 Stat. 1304; Pub.L. 103–270, § 3(g), June 30, 1994, 108 Stat. 734.)

HISTORICAL AND STATUTORY NOTES

Effective and Applicability Provisions

1994 Acts. Amendment by Pub.L. 103–270 applicable with respect to independent counsels appointed before, on, or after June 30, 1994, with provision directing that no amendment made by Pub.L. 103–270 establishing or modifying a reporting requirement be construed to require that a report submitted prior to June 30, 1994 be supplemented to include information with respect to any time period, see section 7(a), (g) of Pub.L. 103–270, set out as a note under section 591 of this title.

1987 Acts. Amendment by Pub.L. 100–191 effective Dec. 15, 1987, and applicable to proceedings initiated and independent counsels appointed on and after Dec. 15, 1987, see section 6 of Pub.L. 100–191, set out as a note under section 591 of this title.

1978 Acts. Section effective Oct. 26, 1978, except for specific information received by the Attorney General pursuant to section 591 of this title based on determinations made by the Attorney General respecting such information, see section 604 of Pub.L. 95–521, set out as a note under section 591 of this title.

Termination of Reporting Requirements

For termination of reporting provisions of this section pertaining to response to inquiry from oversight committee on particular case involving independent counsel, effective May 15, 2000, see Pub.L. 104–66, § 3003, as amended, set out as a note under 31 U.S.C.A. § 1113, and the last item on page 117 of House Document No. 103–7.

For termination of reporting provisions of subsecs. (a) and (c) of this section, effective May 15, 2000, see Pub.L. 104–66, § 3003, as amended, set out as a note under 31 U.S.C.A. § 1113, and the 4th and last items on page 122 of House Document No. 103–7.

§ 596. Removal of an independent counsel; termination of office

(a) Removal; report on removal.—

(1) Grounds for removal.—An independent counsel appointed under this chapter may be removed from office, other than by impeachment and conviction, only by the personal action of the Attorney General and only for good cause, physical or mental disability (if not prohibited by law protecting persons from discrimination on the basis of such a disability),,[1] or any other condition that substantially impairs the performance of such independent counsel's duties.

(2) Report to division of the court and Congress.—If an independent counsel is removed from office, the Attorney General shall promptly submit to the division of the court and the Committees on the Judiciary of the Senate and the House of Representatives a report specifying the facts found and the ultimate grounds for such removal. The committees shall make available to the public such report, except that each committee may, if necessary to protect the rights of any individual named in the report or to prevent undue interference with any pending prosecution, postpone or refrain from publishing any or all of the report. The division of the court may release any or all of such report in accordance with section 594(h)(2).

(3) Judicial review of removal.—An independent counsel removed from office may obtain judicial review of the removal in a civil action commenced in the United States District Court for the District of Columbia. A member of the division of the court may not hear or determine any such civil action or any appeal of a decision in any such civil action. The independent counsel may be reinstated or granted other appropriate relief by order of the court.

(b) Termination of office.—

(1) Termination by action of independent counsel.—An office of independent counsel shall terminate when—

(A) the independent counsel notifies the Attorney General that the investigation of all matters within the prosecutorial jurisdiction of such independent counsel or accepted by such independent counsel under section 594(e), and any resulting prosecutions, have been completed or so substantially completed that it would be appropriate for the Department of Justice to complete such investigations and prosecutions; and

(B) the independent counsel files a final report in compliance with section 594(h)(1)(B).

(2) Termination by division of the court.—The division of the court, either on its own motion or upon the request of the Attorney General, may terminate an office of independent counsel at any time, on the ground that the investigation of all matters within the prosecutorial jurisdiction of such independent counsel or accepted by such independent counsel under section 594(e), and any resulting prosecutions, have been completed or so substantially completed that it would be appropriate for the Department of Justice to complete such investigations and prosecutions. At the time of such termination, the independent counsel shall file the final report required by section 594(h)(1)(B). If the Attorney General has not made a request under this paragraph, the division of the court shall determine on its own motion whether termination is appropriate under this paragraph no later than 2 years after the appointment of an independent counsel, at the end of the succeeding 2-year period, and thereafter at the end of each succeeding 1-year period.

(c) Audits.—(1) On or before June 30 of each year, an independent counsel shall prepare a statement of expenditures for the 6 months that ended on the immediately preceding March 31. On or before December 31 of each year, an independent counsel shall prepare a statement of expenditures for the fiscal year that ended on the immediately preceding September 30. An independent counsel whose office is terminated prior to the end of the fiscal year shall prepare a statement of expenditures on or before the date that is 90 days after the date on which the office is terminated.

(2) The Comptroller General shall—

(A) conduct a financial review of a mid-year statement and a financial audit of a year-end statement and statement on termination; and

(B) report the results to the Committee on the Judiciary, Committee on Governmental Affairs, and Committee on Appropriations of the Senate and the Committee on the Judiciary, Committee on Government Operations, and Committee on Appropriations of the House of Representatives not later than 90 days following the submission of each such statement.

(Added Pub.L. 95–521, Title VI, § 601(a), Oct. 26, 1978, 92 Stat. 1872, and amended Pub.L. 97–409, §§ 2(a)(1), 6(d), Jan. 3, 1983, 96 Stat. 2039, 2042; Pub.L. 98–620, Title IV, § 402(29)(A), Nov. 8, 1984, 98 Stat. 3359; Pub.L. 100–191, § 2, Dec. 15, 1987, 101 Stat. 1304; Pub.L. 103–270, §§ 3(h), (i), 5, June 30, 1994, 108 Stat. 735, 737.)

[1] So in original.

HISTORICAL AND STATUTORY NOTES

Effective and Applicability Provisions

1994 Acts. Amendment by Pub.L. 103–270 applicable with respect to independent counsels appointed before, on, or after June 30, 1994, with provisions directing that determinations by the division of the court contained in the last sentence of subsec. (b)(2) of this section shall, for the office of an independent counsel appointed before June 30, 1994, be required no later than 1 year after June 30, 1994, and at the end of each succeeding 1-year period, and provisions directing that no amendment made by Pub.L. 103–270 establishing or modifying a reporting requirement be construed to require that a report submitted prior to June 30, 1994 be supplemented to include information with respect to activity occurring during any time period, see section 7(a), (f), (g) of Pub.L. 103–270, set out as a note under section 591 of this title.

1987 Acts. Amendment by Pub.L. 100–191 effective Dec. 15, 1987, and applicable to proceedings initiated and independent counsels appointed on and after Dec. 15, 1987, but with subsecs. (a)(3) and (c) applicable to previously initiated proceedings pending on Dec. 15, 1987, see section 6 of Pub.L. 100–191, set out as a note under section 591 of this title.

1984 Acts. Amendment by Pub.L. 98–620 not to apply to cases pending on Nov. 8, 1984, see section 403 of Pub.L. 98–620, set out as a note under section 1657 of this title.

1978 Acts. Section effective Oct. 26, 1978, except for specific information received by the Attorney General pursuant to section 591 of this title based on determinations made by the Attorney General respecting such information, see section 604 of Pub.L. 95–521, set out as a note under section 591 of this title.

Termination of Reporting Requirements

For termination of reporting provisions of this section pertaining to removal of an independent counsel, effective May 15, 2000, see Pub.L. 104–66, § 3003, as amended, set out as a note under 31 U.S.C.A. § 1113, and page 119 of House Document No. 103–7.

Change of Name

Committee on Governmental Affairs of Senate changed to Committee on Homeland Security and Governmental Affairs of Senate, effective Jan. 4, 2005, by Senate Resolution No. 445, One Hundred Eighth Congress, Oct. 9, 2004.

Committee on Government Operations of House of Representatives treated as referring to Committee on Government Reform and Oversight of House of Representatives by section 1(a) of Pub.L. 104–14, set out as a note preceding 2 U.S.C.A. § 21. Committee on Government Reform and Oversight of House of Representatives changed to Committee on Government Reform of House of Representatives by House Resolution No. 5, One Hundred Sixth Congress, Jan. 6, 1999.

Any reference in any provision of law enacted before Jan. 4, 1995, to the Committee on Government Operations of the House of Representatives treated as referring to the Committee on Government Reform and Oversight of the House of Representatives, except that any reference in any provision of law enacted before Jan. 4, 1995, to the Committee on Government Operations of the House of Representatives treated as referring to the Committee on the Budget of the House of Representatives in the case of a provision of law relating to the establishment, extension, and enforcement of special controls over the Federal budget, see section 1(a)(6) and (c)(2) of Pub.L. 104–14, set out as a note preceding section 21 of Title 2, The Congress.

§ 597. Relationship with Department of Justice

(a) Suspension of other investigations and proceedings.—Whenever a matter is in the prosecutorial jurisdiction of an independent counsel or has been accepted by an independent counsel under section 594(e), the Department of Justice, the Attorney General, and all other officers and employees of the Department of Justice shall suspend all investigations and proceedings regarding such matter, except to the extent required by section 594(d)(1), and except insofar as such independent counsel agrees in writing that such investigation or proceedings may be continued by the Department of Justice.

(b) Presentation as amicus curiae permitted.—Nothing in this chapter shall prevent the Attorney General or the Solicitor General from making a presentation as amicus curiae to any court as to issues of law raised by any case or proceeding in which an independent counsel participates in an official capacity or any appeal of such a case or proceeding.

(Added Pub.L. 95–521, Title VI, § 601(a), Oct. 26, 1978, 92 Stat. 1872, and amended Pub.L. 97–409, § 2(a)(1)(A), Jan. 3, 1983, 96 Stat. 2039; Pub.L. 100–191, § 2, Dec. 15, 1987, 101 Stat. 1306.)

HISTORICAL AND STATUTORY NOTES

Effective and Applicability Provisions

1987 Acts. Amendment by Pub.L. 100–191 effective Dec. 15, 1987, and applicable to proceedings initiated and independent counsels appointed on and after Dec. 15, 1987, section 6 of Pub.L. 100–191, set out as a note under section 591 of this title.

1978 Acts. Section effective Oct. 26, 1978, except for specific information received by the Attorney General pursuant to section 591 of this title based on determinations made by the Attorney General respecting such information, see section 604 of Pub.L. 95–521, set out as a note under section 591 of this title.

§ 598. Severability

If any provision of this chapter or the application thereof to any person or circumstance is held invalid, the remainder of this chapter and the application of such provision to other persons not similarly situated or to other circumstances shall not be affected by such invalidation.

(Added Pub.L. 95–521, Title VI, § 601(a), Oct. 26, 1978, 92 Stat. 1873, and amended Pub.L. 97–409, §§ 2(a)(1)(A), 7, Jan. 3, 1983, 96 Stat. 2039, 2042; Pub.L. 100–191, § 2, Dec. 15, 1987, 101 Stat. 1306.)

HISTORICAL AND STATUTORY NOTES

Effective and Applicability Provisions

1987 Acts. Amendment by Pub.L. 100–191 effective Dec. 15, 1987, and to apply only to new independent counsel proceedings and to new independent counsels coming into existence on and after Dec. 15, 1987, see section 6 of Pub.L. 100–191, set out as a note under section 591 of this title.

1978 Acts. Section effective Oct. 26, 1978, except for specific information received by the Attorney General pursuant to section 591 of this title based on determinations made by the Attorney General respecting such information, see section 604 of Pub.L. 95–521, set out as a note under section 591 of this title.

§ 599. Termination of effect of chapter

This chapter shall cease to be effective five years after the date of the enactment of the Independent Counsel Reauthorization Act of 1994, except that this chapter shall continue in effect with respect to then pending matters before an independent counsel that in the judgment of such counsel require such continuation until that independent counsel determines such matters have been completed.

(Added Pub.L. 100–191, § 2, Dec. 15, 1987, 101 Stat. 1306, and amended Pub.L. 103–270, § 2, June 30, 1994, 108 Stat. 732.)

HISTORICAL AND STATUTORY NOTES

References in Text

The date of the enactment of the Independent Counsel Reauthorization Act of 1994, referred to in text, is the date of the enactment of Pub.L. 103–270, which was approved June 30, 1994.

Effective and Applicability Provisions

1994 Acts. Amendment by Pub.L. 103–270 applicable with respect to independent counsels appointed before, on, or after June 30, 1994, see section 7(a) of Pub.L. 103–270, set out as a note under section 591 of this title.

1987 Acts. Section effective Dec. 15, 1987, see section 6 of Pub.L. 100–191, set out as a note under section 591 of this title.

CHAPTER 40A—BUREAU OF ALCOHOL, TOBACCO, FIREARMS, AND EXPLOSIVES

Sec.

599A. Bureau of Alcohol, Tobacco, Firearms, and Explosives[1]

599B. Personnel management demonstration project[1]

[1] So in original. Does not correspond to section name line.

§ 599A. Bureau of alcohol, tobacco, firearms, and Explosives [1]

(a) Establishment.—

(1) In general.—There is established within the Department of Justice under the general authority of the Attorney General the Bureau of Alcohol, Tobacco, Firearms, and Explosives (in this section referred to as the "Bureau").

(2) Director.—There shall be at the head of the Bureau a Director, Bureau of Alcohol, Tobacco, Firearms, and Explosives (in this part referred to as the "Director"). The Director shall be appointed by the President, by and with the advice and consent of the Senate and shall perform such functions as the Attorney General shall direct. The Director shall receive compensation at the rate prescribed by law under section 5314 of title V, United States Code,[2] for positions at level III of the Executive Schedule.

(3) Coordination.—The Attorney General, acting through the Director and such other officials of the Department of Justice as the Attorney General may designate, shall provide for the coordination of all firearms, explosives, tobacco enforcement, and arson enforcement functions vested in the Attorney General so as to assure maximum cooperation between and among any officer, employee, or agency of the Department of Justice involved in the performance of these and related functions.

(4) Performance of transferred functions.—The Attorney General may make such provisions as the Attorney General determines appropriate to authorize the performance by any officer, employee, or agency of the Department of Justice of any function transferred to the Attorney General under this section.

(b) Responsibilities.—Subject to the direction of the Attorney General, the Bureau shall be responsible for investigating—

(1) criminal and regulatory violations of the Federal firearms, explosives, arson, alcohol, and tobacco smuggling laws;

(2) the functions transferred by subsection (c) of section 1111 of the Homeland Security Act of 2002 (as enacted on the date of the enactment of such Act); and

(3) any other function related to the investigation of violent crime or domestic terrorism that is delegated to the Bureau by the Attorney General.

(c) Transfer of authorities, functions, personnel, and assets to the Department of Justice.—

(1) In general.—Subject to paragraph (2), but notwithstanding any other provision of law, there are transferred to the Department of Justice the authorities, functions, personnel, and assets of the Bureau of Alcohol, Tobacco and Firearms, which shall be maintained as a distinct entity within the Department of Justice, including the related functions of the Secretary of the Treasury.

(3) [3] **Building prospectus.**—Prospectus PDC–98W10, giving the General Services Administration the authority for site acquisition, design, and construction of a new headquarters building for the Bureau of Alcohol, Tobacco [4] and Firearms, is transferred, and deemed to apply, to the Bureau of Alcohol, Tobacco, Firearms, and Explosives established in the Department of Justice under subsection (a).

(Added and amended Pub.L. 109–162, Title XI, § 1187(b), (c)(1), Jan. 5, 2006, 119 Stat. 3127.)

[1] So in original. Does not correspond to analysis, which reads: "Bureau of Alcohol, Tobacco, Firearms, and Explosives".

[2] So in original. Probably should be "Title 5, United States Code,".

[3] So in original. There is no par. (2).

[4] So in original. Probably should be a comma.

HISTORICAL AND STATUTORY NOTES

References in Text

This subtitle, referred to in subsec. (a)(2), meant subtitle B (§§ 1111–1115) of Title XI of Pub.L. 107–296, Nov. 25, 2002, 116 Stat. 2274, when subsec. (a) was originally included in section 1111 of Pub.L. 107–296. See Codifications note below. There are no subtitles in this title of the Code. Subtitle B of title XI of Pub.L. 107–296 enacted part B (§ 531 et seq.) of subchapter XI of chapter 1 of Title 6, and 18 U.S.C.A. § 3051, amended 28 U.S.C.A. § 2006, sections 8D and 9 of the Inspector General Act of 1978, Pub.L. 95–452, set out in the Appendix to Title 5, 7 U.S.C.A. § 1445–3, 8 U.S.C.A. § 1701, 15 U.S.C.A. § 2223b, 18 U.S.C.A. §§ 841 to 847, 921 to 923, 925, 926, 1261, 1952, 2341, 2343, and 2346, 26 U.S.C.A. §§ 6103 and 7801, 31 U.S.C.A. §§ 713 and 9703, 42 U.S.C.A. §§ 10502 and 13921, 49 U.S.C.A. §§ 80303 and 80304, and provisions set out as a note under 18 U.S.C.A. § 921. For complete classification of subtitle B to the Code, see Tables.

Subsection (c) of section 1111 of the Homeland Security Act of 2002 (as enacted on the date of the enactment of such Act), referred to in subsec. (b)(2), is section 1111(c) of Pub.L. 107–296, Title XI, Nov. 25, 2002, 116 Stat. 2275, which was classified to 6 U.S.C.A. § 531(c), prior to transfer of subsec. (c)(1), (3) of such section to subsec. (c)(1), (3) of this section.

Paragraph (2), referred to in subsec. (c)(1), meant paragraph (2) of section 1111(c) of Pub.L. 107–296, when subsec. (c)(1) of this section was originally included in section 1111 of Pub.L. 107–296. See Codifications note below. Section 1111(c)(2) of Pub.L. 107–296 is classified to 6 U.S.C.A. § 531(c)(2).

Codifications

The section catchline and text of subsecs. (a) to (c)(1), (3) of section 1111 of Pub.L. 107–296, formerly classified to 6 U.S.C.A. § 531, which were transferred to this chapter, redesignated as this section, and amended by Pub.L. 109–162, § 1187(b), (c)(1), were based on Pub.L. 107–296, Title XI, § 1111(a) to (c)(1), (3), Nov. 25, 2002, 116 Stat. 2274, 2275.

Pub.L. 109–177, Title V, § 504, March 9, 2006, 120 Stat. 247, which directed that "The second sentence of section 1111(a)(2) of the Homeland Security Act of 2002 (6 U.S.C. 531(a)(2)) is amended by striking 'Attorney General' the first place it appears and inserting 'President, by and with the advice and consent of the Senate' ", was executed to subsec. (a)(2) of this section, as the probable intent of Congress, in view of the transfer of section 531 of Title 6 to this section by Pub.L. 109–162, § 1187.

Effective and Applicability Provisions

2002 Acts. Section 1111 of Pub.L. 107–296, set out in part as this section, effective 60 days after Nov. 25, 2002, see Pub.L. 107–296, § 4, set out as a note under 6 U.S.C.A. § 101.

§ 599B. Personnel Management demonstration [1] project [1]

Notwithstanding any other provision of law, the Personnel Management Demonstration Project established under section 102 of title I of division C of the Omnibus Consolidated and Emergency Supplemental Appropriations Act for Fiscal Year 1999 (Public Law 105–277; 122 [2] Stat. 2681–585) shall be transferred to the Attorney General of the United States for continued use by the Bureau of Alcohol, Tobacco, Firearms, and Explosives, Department of Justice, and the Secretary of the Treasury for continued use by the Tax and Trade Bureau.

(Added and amended Pub.L. 109–162, Title XI, § 1187(b), (c)(2), Jan. 5, 2006, 119 Stat. 3127, 3128.)

[1] So in original. Probably should be capitalized.

[2] So in original. Probably should be "112".

HISTORICAL AND STATUTORY NOTES

References in Text

Section 102 of title I of division C of the Omnibus Consolidated and Emergency Supplemental Appropriations Act for Fiscal Year 1999, referred to in text, probably means section 102 of title I of div. C of the Omnibus Consolidated and Emergency Supplemental Appropriations Act, 1999, Pub.L. 105–277, which amended Pub. L. 105–119, § 122, which is classified as a note under 5 U.S.C.A. § 3104.

Codifications

The text of section 1115 of Pub.L. 107–296, formerly classified as 6 U.S.C.A. § 533, which was transferred to this chapter, redesignated as this section, and amended by Pub.L. 109–162, § 1187(b), (c)(2), was based on Pub.L. 107–296, Title XI, § 1115, Nov. 25, 2002, 116 Stat. 2280.

Effective and Applicability Provisions

2002 Acts. This section effective 60 days after Nov. 25, 2002, see Pub.L. 107–296, § 4, set out as a note under 6 U.S.C.A. § 101.

PART III—COURT OFFICERS AND EMPLOYEES

Chapter		Section
41.	**Administrative Office of United States Courts**	601
42.	**Federal Judicial Center**	620
43.	**United States Magistrate Judges**	631
44.	**Alternative Dispute Resolution**	651
45.	**Supreme Court**	671
47.	**Courts of Appeals**	711
49.	**District Courts**	751
51.	**United States Court of Federal Claims**	791
[53.	**Repealed]**	
55.	**Court of International Trade**	871
57.	**General Provisions Applicable to Court Officers and Employees**	951
58.	**United States Sentencing Commission**	991

HISTORICAL AND STATUTORY NOTES

Codifications

The analysis of chapters comprising Part III was amended by Pub.L. 95–598, Title II, § 233(b) Nov. 6, 1978, 92 Stat. 2667 effective June 28, 1984, pursuant to Pub.L. 95–598, Title IV, § 402(b), Nov. 6, 1978, 92 Stat. 2682, as amended by Pub.L. 98–249, § 1(a), Mar. 31, 1984, 98 Stat. 116; Pub.L. 98–271, § 1(a), Apr. 30, 1984, 98 Stat. 163; Pub.L. 98–299, § 1(a), May 25, 1984, 98 Stat. 214; Pub.L. 98–325, § 1(a), June 20, 1984, 98 Stat. 268, set out as an Effective and Applicability Provisions note preceding section 101 of Title 11, Bankruptcy, by adding:

"50. Bankruptcy Courts ..... 771."

Senate Revision Amendment

Chapter 59 was renumbered as Chapter 57 but without change in its section numbers, by Senate amendment. See 80th Congress Senate Report No. 1559.

Change of Name

"United States magistrate judge" substituted for "United States magistrate" in item 43 pursuant to section 321 of Pub.L. 101–650, set out as a note under 28 U.S.C.A. § 631.

CHAPTER 41—ADMINISTRATIVE OFFICE OF UNITED STATES COURTS

Sec.
601. Creation; Director and Deputy Director.
602. Employees.
603. Salaries.
604. Duties of Director generally.
605. Budget estimates.
606. Duties of Deputy Director.
607. Practice of law prohibited.
608. Seal.
609. Courts' appointive power unaffected.
610. Courts defined.
611. Retirement of Director.
612. Judiciary Automation Fund.
613. Disbursing and certifying officers.

HISTORICAL AND STATUTORY NOTES

Codifications

Section 5602(b)(1) of Pub.L. 104–106, Div. E, Title LVI, Feb. 10, 1996, 110 Stat. 699, directed the substitution of "Judiciary Information Technology Fund" for "Judiciary Automation Fund" as the heading of section 612 of this title with no conforming amendment to item 612 of the section analysis. Section 5701 of Pub.L. 104–106, Div. E, Title LVII, Feb. 10, 1996, 110 Stat. 702, provided that the amendment to section 612 of this title is effective 180 days after Feb. 10, 1996.

§ 601. Creation; Director and Deputy Director

The Administrative Office of the United States Courts shall be maintained at the seat of government. It shall be supervised by a Director and a Deputy Director appointed and subject to removal by the Chief Justice of the United States, after consulting with the Judicial Conference. The Director and Deputy Director shall be deemed to be officers for purposes of title 5, United States Code.

(June 25, 1948, c. 646, 62 Stat. 913; Sept. 23, 1959, Pub.L. 86–370, § 5(a)(1), 73 Stat. 652; Dec. 1, 1990, Pub.L. 101–650, Title III, § 307, 104 Stat. 5112; Oct. 19, 1996, Pub.L. 104–317, Title VI, § 602, 110 Stat. 3857.)

HISTORICAL AND STATUTORY NOTES

Effective and Applicability Provisions

1959 Acts. Amendment by Pub.L. 86–370 effective Sept. 23, 1959, see section 7(a) of Pub.L. 86–370.

Judicial Branch Appointments

Pub.L. 105–339, § 4(d), Oct. 31, 1998, 112 Stat. 3186, provided that:

"**(1) In general.**—Subject to paragraphs (2) and (3), the Judicial Conference of the United States shall prescribe procedures to provide for—

"**(A)** veterans' preference in the consideration of applicants for employment, and in the conduct of any reductions in force, within the judicial branch; and

"**(B)** redress for alleged violations of any rights provided for under subparagraph (A).

"**(2) Procedures.**—Under the procedures, a preference eligible (as defined by section 2108 of title 5, United States Code) shall be afforded preferences in a manner and to the extent consistent with preferences afforded to preference eligibles in the executive branch.

"**(3) Exclusions.**—Nothing in the procedures shall apply with respect to an applicant or employee—

"(A) whose appointment is made by the President with the advice and consent of the Senate;

"(B) whose appointment is as a judicial officer;

"(C) whose appointment is required by statute to be made by or with the approval of a court or judicial officer; or

"(D) whose appointment is to a position, the duties of which are equivalent to those of a Senior Executive Service position (within the meaning of section 3132(a)(2) of title 5, United States Code).

"(4) **Definitions.**—For purposes of this subsection [this note], the term "judicial officer" means a justice, judge, or magistrate judge listed in subparagraph (A), (B), (F), or (G) of section 376(a)(1) of title 28, United States Code.

"(5) **Submission to Congress; effective date.**—

"(A) **Submission to Congress.**—Not later than 12 months after the date of enactment of this Act [Oct. 31, 1998], the Judicial Conference of the United States shall submit a copy of the procedures prescribed under this subsection [this note] to the Committee on Government Reform and Oversight and the Committee on the Judiciary of the House of Representatives and the Committee on Governmental Affairs and the Committee on the Judiciary of the Senate.

"(B) **Effective date.**—The procedures prescribed under this subsection [this note] shall take effect 13 months after the date of enactment of this Act [Oct. 31, 1998]."

Continuation of Law Existing on Sept. 1, 1948

Section 2(b) of Act June 25, 1948, provided that: "The provisions of Title 28, Judiciary and Judicial Procedure, of the United States Code, set out in section 1 of this Act, with respect to the organization of each of the several courts therein provided for and of the Administrative Office of the United States Courts, shall be construed as continuations of existing law, and the tenure of the judges, officers, and employees thereof and of the United States attorneys and marshals and their deputies and assistants, in office on the effective date of this Act [Sept. 1, 1948], shall not be affected by its enactment, but each of them shall continue to serve in the same capacity under the appropriate provisions of title 28, as set out in section 1 of this Act, pursuant to his prior appointment: *Provided, however*, That each circuit court of appeals shall, as in said title 28 set out, hereafter be known as a United States court of appeals. No loss of rights, interruption of jurisdiction, or prejudice to matters pending in any of such courts on the effective date of this Act shall result from its enactment."

Reference to Assistant Director Deemed Reference to Deputy Director

Section 5(a)(4) of Pub.L. 86–370 provided that: "Whenever the Assistant Director of the Administrative Office of the United States Courts is referred to in any other law, such reference shall be deemed to be to the Deputy Director of the Administrative Office of the United States Courts."

§ 602. Employees

(a) The Director shall appoint and fix the compensation of necessary employees of the Administrative Office in accordance with the Administrative Office of the United States Courts Personnel Act of 1990.

(b) Notwithstanding any other law, the Director may appoint certified interpreters in accordance with section 604(a)(16)(B) of this title without regard to the provisions of chapter 51 and subchapter III of chapter 53 of title 5, relating to classification and General Schedule pay rates, but the compensation of any person appointed under this subsection shall not exceed the appropriate equivalent of the highest rate of pay payable for the highest grade established in the General Schedule, section 5332 of title 5.

(c) The Director may obtain personal services as authorized by section 3109 of title 5, at rates not to exceed the appropriate equivalent of the highest rate of pay payable for the highest grade established in the General Schedule, section 5332 of title 5.

(d) All functions of other officers and employees of the Administrative Office and all functions of organizational units of the Administrative Office are vested in the Director. The Director may delegate any of the Director's functions, powers, duties, and authority (except the authority to promulgate rules and regulations) to such officers and employees of the judicial branch of Government as the Director may designate, and subject to such terms and conditions as the Director may consider appropriate; and may authorize the successive redelegation of such functions, powers, duties, and authority as the Director may deem desirable. All official acts performed by such officers and employees shall have the same force and effect as though performed by the Director in person.

(June 25, 1948, c. 646, 62 Stat. 913; Oct. 28, 1978, Pub.L. 95–539, § 5, 92 Stat. 2044; Oct. 30, 1990, Pub.L. 101–474, § 5(a), (q), 104 Stat. 1099, 1101; Dec. 1, 1990, Pub.L. 101–650, Title III, § 325(b)(4), 104 Stat. 5121.)

HISTORICAL AND STATUTORY NOTES

References in Text

The Administrative Office of the United States Courts Personnel Act of 1990, referred to in subsec. (a), is Pub.L. 101–474, Oct. 30, 1990, 104 Stat. 1097, which is principally classified as a note under this section. For complete classification of this Act to the Code, see Administrative Office of United States Courts Personnel note set out under this section and Tables.

References in Other Laws to GS–16, 17, or 18 Pay Rates

References in laws to the rates of pay for GS–16, 17, or 18, or to maximum rates of pay under the General Schedule, to be considered references to rates payable under specified sections of Title 5, Government Organization and Employees, see section 529 [Title I, § 101 (c)(1)] of Pub.L. 101–509, set out in a note under section 5376 of Title 5.

Effective and Applicability Provisions

1978 Acts. Section 10 of Pub.L. 95–539 provided that:

"(a) Except as provided in subsection (b), this Act [enacting sections 1827 and 1828 of this title, amending sections 602, 603, 604, and 1920 of this title, enacting provisions set out as notes under this section and section 1 of this title, and repealing a provision set out as a note under this section] shall take effect on the date of the enactment of this Act [Oct. 28, 1978].

"(b) Section 2 of this Act [enacting sections 1827 and 1828 of this title] shall take effect ninety days after the date of the enactment of this Act [Oct. 28, 1978]."

Administrative Office of United States Courts Personnel

Sections 1 to 4 and 6 of Pub.L. 101–474 provided that:

"Section 1. Short title.

"This Act [enacting this note and amending sections 602, 603, and 604 of this title and sections 2301, 2302, 4301, 4501, 4701, 5102, 5108, 5349, 5595, 5596, 8331, 8347, 8401, and 8402 of Title 5, Government Organization and Employees] may be cited as the 'Administrative Office of the United States Courts Personnel Act of 1990'.

"Sec. 2. General personnel authority.

"The Director of the Administrative Office of the United States Courts (hereinafter in this Act referred to as the 'Director') may appoint, fix the compensation of, assign, and direct such personnel as the Director determines necessary to discharge the duties and functions of the Administrative Office.

"Sec. 3. Establishment of personnel management system.

"(a) The Director shall, by regulation, establish a personnel management system for the Administrative Office which provides for the appointment, pay, promotion, and assignment of all employees on the basis of merit, but without regard to the provisions of title 5, United States Code [Title 5, Government Organization and Employees], governing appointments and other personnel actions in the competitive service, or the provisions of chapter 51 and subchapter III of chapter 53 of such title, relating to classification and General Schedule pay rates. The system shall apply to all Administrative Office employees except those referred to in section 603 of title 28, United States Code [section 603 of this title], and shall, at a minimum—

"(1) provide for a schedule of pay rates applicable to all employees; except as provided in paragraph (10), the basic pay of any person appointed under this section shall not exceed the rate of basic pay for level V of the Executive Schedule;

"(2) incorporate pay comparability principles as set forth in section 5301(a) of title 5, United States Code [section 5301(a) of Title 5];

"(3) provide for the adjustment of the pay of employees at the same time and in the same percentage amount as rates of basic pay are adjusted for General Schedule and prevailing rate employees, as appropriate;

"(4) establish procedures for employee evaluations, the granting of periodic pay adjustments, incentive awards, and resolution of employee grievances;

"(5) establish procedures for disciplinary actions, including reduction in grade or pay, suspension, and removal, based on unacceptable performance or misconduct, except that—

"(A) such procedures shall be consistent with—

"(i) section 4303 of title 5, United States Code [section 4303 of Title 5], to the extent that they relate to adverse actions based on unacceptable performance; and

"(ii) chapter 75 of title 5, United States Code [section 7501 et seq. of Title 5], to the extent that they relate to adverse actions covered by such chapter; and

"(B) the Director may exempt from these procedures positions of a confidential or policy-determining character, not to exceed 4 percent of the authorized positions of the Administrative Office;

"(6) establish procedures for premium pay (including overtime), except that the Director may at his discretion implement flexible and compressed work schedules and may exempt the hours constituting such schedules from premium pay to the extent he deems necessary to implement such schedules;

"(7) include the principles set forth in section 2301(b) of title 5, United States Code [section 2301(b) of Title 5];

"(8) prohibit personnel practices prohibited under section 2302(b) of title 5, United States Code [section 2302(b) of Title 5];

"(9) prohibit discrimination on the basis of race, color, religion, age, sex, national origin, political affiliation, marital status, or handicapping condition; the Director must promulgate regulations providing procedures for resolving complaints of discrimination by employees and applicants for employment;

"(10) provide for the basic pay of not more than 5 percent of the authorized positions of the Administrative Office (excluding the positions referred to in section 603 of title 28, United States Code [section 603 of this title]) to be set at rates not to exceed the rate of basic pay for positions at level IV of the Executive Schedule; the aggregate pay (including basic pay and incentive awards) of any individual whose basic pay is set under this subsection may not exceed the salary of the Director; and

"(11) in the case of any individual who would be a preference eligible in the executive branch, provide preference for that individual in a manner and to an extent consistent with preference accorded to preference eligibles in the executive branch.

"(b) The Director may apply the provisions of sections 5723 and 6304(f) of title 5, United State Code [sections 5723 and 6304(f) of Title 5, Government Organization and Employees], to the positions referred to in subsection (a)(10) and in section 603 of title 28, United States Code [section 603 of this title], including the Deputy Director.

"(c) The Director may provide for incentive awards for the positions referred to in section 603 of title 28, United States Code [section 603 of this title], including the Deputy Director, subject to the aggregate pay limitation in subsection (a)(10).

"(d) The Chief Justice of the United States or the Judicial Conference of the United States may grant incentive awards to the Director, except that the Director's aggregate pay for any fiscal year, including salary and incentive awards, may not exceed the salary of a United States circuit judge. The Chief Justice or the Judicial Conference may authorize application of section 5723 of title 5, United States Code [section 5723 of Title 5, Government Organization and Employees], to the Director.

"(e) The Director may develop and conduct programs to meet the short- and long-range training needs of the agency.

"(f) Notwithstanding any other provision of law, an individual who is an employee of the Administrative Office on the day before the effective date of this section and who, as of that day, was entitled to—

"(1) appeal a reduction in grade or removal to the Merit Systems Protection Board under chapter 43 of title 5, United States Code [section 4301 et seq. of Title 5],

"(2) appeal an adverse action to the Merit Systems Protection Board under chapter 75 of title 5, United State Code [section 7501 et seq. of Title 5], or

"(3) file an appeal with the Equal Employment Opportunity Commission under part 1613 of title 29 of the Code of Federal Regulations,

shall continue to be entitled to file such appeal so long as the individual remains an employee of the Administrative Office, except that this provision shall not apply to employees in positions referred to in section 603 of title 28, United States Code, or in positions of a confidential or policy-determining character referred to in subsection (a)(10).

"(g) Nothing in this Act shall be construed to abolish or diminish any right or remedy granted to employees of or applicants for employment in the Administrative Office by any law prohibiting discrimination in Federal employment on the basis of race, color, religion, age, sex, national origin, political affiliation, marital status, or handicapping condition, except that, with respect to any such employees and applicants for employment, any authority granted under any such law to the Equal Employment Opportunity Commission, the Office of Personnel Management, the Merit Systems Protection Board, or any other agency in the executive branch, shall be exercised by the Administrative Office.

"Sec. 4. Noncompetitive appointments.

"(a) Notwithstanding any other provision of law, any employee of the Administrative Office who has completed at least 1 year of continuous service under a nontemporary appointment under the personnel system established pursuant to section 3 acquires a competitive status for appointment to any position in the competitive service for which the employee possesses the required qualifications.

"(b) A period of continuous service performed as a nontemporary employee of the Administrative Office immediately before the personnel system under section 3 takes effect shall, for purposes of subsection (a), be treated as if it had been performed under such system.

"Sec. 6. Authorization.

"There are authorized to be appropriated for fiscal year 1990 and for each fiscal year thereafter such sums as may be necessary to carry out the provisions of this Act."

Contract Limitations

Section 11 of Pub.L. 95–539 provided that: "Any contracts entered into under this Act or any of the amendments made by this Act [enacting sections 1827 and 1828 of this title, amending sections 602, 603, 604, and 1920 of this title, enacting provisions set out as notes under this section and section 1 of this title, and repealing a provision set out as a note under this section] shall be limited to such extent or in such amounts as are provided in advance in appropriation Acts."

Employment of Experts or Consultants: Rates

Pub.L. 86–370, § 5(b), Sept. 23, 1959, 73 Stat. 652, which authorized the Director of the Administrative Office of the United States Courts to procure the temporary or intermittent services of experts or consultants, was repealed by Pub.L. 95–539, § 8, Oct. 28, 1978, 92 Stat. 2044.

§ 603. Salaries

The salary of the Director shall be the same as the salary of a district judge. Notwithstanding any other provision of law, the Director shall not be deemed to be an "employee" for the purpose of subchapter I of chapter 63 of title 5. The salary of the Deputy Director shall be 92 percent of the salary of the Director. The salaries of six additional positions shall be fixed by the Director at rates not to exceed the annual rate of basic pay for positions at level IV of the Executive Schedule under section 5315 of title 5.

(June 25, 1948, c. 646, 62 Stat. 913; Oct. 15, 1949, c. 695, §§ 5(b), 6(b), 63 Stat. 881; Oct. 31, 1951, c. 655, § 43(b), 65 Stat. 725; Sept. 23, 1959, Pub.L. 86–370, § 5(a)(1), 73 Stat. 652; Aug. 14, 1964, Pub.L. 88–426, Title IV, § 403(g), 78 Stat. 434; Dec. 16, 1967, Pub.L. 90–206, Title II, § 213(d), 81 Stat. 635; Oct. 28, 1978, Pub.L. 95–539, § 6, 92 Stat. 2044; Dec. 22, 1987, Pub.L. 100–202, § 101(a) [Title IV § 409], 101 Stat. 1329–27; Oct. 1, 1988, Pub.L. 100–459, Title IV, § 406, 102 Stat. 2213; Oct. 30, 1990, Pub.L. 101–474, § 5(b), 104 Stat. 1099.)

HISTORICAL AND STATUTORY NOTES

Effective and Applicability Provisions

1978 Acts. Amendment by Pub.L. 95–539 effective Oct. 28, 1978, see section 10(a) of Pub.L. 95–539, set out as a note under section 602 of this title.

1967 Acts. Section 220(a)(3) of Pub.L. 90–206 provided, except as otherwise expressly provided, that: "Sections 213(d) and (e) [which amended this section and section 792 of this title], 214(j), (k), (*l*), (n), and (*o*) [which amended sections 60j and 61–1 of Title 2, The Congress, and section 5533 of Title 5, Government Organization and Employees], 215 [which amended sections 5314 to 5316 of Title 5], 217 [which amended section 5545 of Title 5], 219 [which amended sections 136a and 136a–1 of Title 2, sections 42a and 51a of former Title 31, Money and Finance, sections 162a, 166b, and 166b–1 of former Title 40, Public Buildings, Property and Works, and section 39a of Title 44, Public Printing and Documents], and 224(c) [which amended provisions set out as a note under section 102 of Title 2], shall become effective at the beginning of the first pay period which begins on or after the date of enactment of this title [Dec. 16, 1967]."

1964 Acts. Amendment by Pub.L. 88–426 effective on the first day of the first pay period which begins on or after July 1, 1964, except to the extent provided in section 501(c) of Pub.L. 88–426, see section 501(a) of Pub.L. 88–426.

1959 Acts. Amendment by Pub.L. 86–370 effective Sept. 23, 1959, see section 7(a) of Pub.L. 86–370.

1949 Acts. The increased compensation provided for by Act Oct. 15, 1949, took effect on the first day of the first pay period which began after Oct. 15, 1949 by the provisions of section 9 of said Act Oct. 15, 1949 which is set out as a note under section 273 of Title 2, The Congress.

Reference to Assistant Director Deemed Reference to Deputy Director

References in any other law to Assistant Director of the Administrative Office of the United States Courts deemed to be reference to the Deputy Director of the Administrative Office of the United States Courts, see section 5(a)(4) of Pub.L. 86–370 set out as a note under section 601 of this title.

Salary Increases

1987—Salaries of the Director and Deputy Director increased respectively to $89,500 and $72,500 per annum, on recommendation of the President of the United States, see note set out under section 358 of Title 2, The Congress.

1977—Salaries of the Director and Deputy Director increased respectively to $54,500 and $48,500 per annum, upon recommendation of the President of the United States, see note set out under section 358 of Title 2, The Congress.

1969—Salaries of the Director and Deputy Director increased respectively from $30,000 and $28,000 to $40,000 and $36,000 per annum, commencing February 14, 1969, on recommendation of the President of the United States, see note set out under section 358 of Title 2.

1967—Section 213(a) of Pub.L. 90–206 provided that: "The rates of basic compensation of officers and employees in or under the judicial branch of the Government whose rates of compensation are fixed by or pursuant to paragraph (2) of subdivision a of section 62 of the Bankruptcy Act (11 U.S.C. 102(a)(2) [section 102(a)(2) of Title 11, Bankruptcy]), section 3656 of title 18, United States Code [section 3656 of Title 18, Crimes and Criminal Procedure], the third sentence of section 603, sections 671 to 675, inclusive, or section 604(a)(5), of title 28, United States Code [sections 603, 671 to 675, or 604(a)(5) of this Title], insofar as the latter section applies to graded positions, are hereby increased by amounts reflecting the respective applicable increases provided by section 202(a) of this title [amending section 5332(a) of Title 5, Government Organization and Employees] in corresponding rates of compensation for officers and employees subject to section 5332 of title 5, United States Code [section 5332 of Title 5]. The rates of basic compensation of officers and employees holding ungraded positions and whose salaries are fixed pursuant to such section 604(a)(5) [section 604(a)(5) of this title] may be increased by the amounts reflecting the respective applicable increases provided by section 202(a) of this title [amending section 5332(a) of Title 5] in corresponding rates of compensation for officers and employees subject to section 5332 of title 5, United States Code [section 5332 of Title 5]."

Section 213(a) of Pub.L. 90–206 effective as of the beginning of the first pay period which begins on or after Oct. 1, 1967, see section 220(a)(2) of Pub.L. 90–206, set out as a note under section 5332 of Title 5, Government Organization and Employees.

1966—Pub.L. 89–504, Title II, § 202(a), July 18, 1966, 80 Stat. 293, provided that: "The rates of basic compensation of officers and employees in or under the judicial branch of the Government whose rates of compensations are fixed by or pursuant to paragraph (2) of subdivision a of section 62 of the Bankruptcy Act (11 U.S.C. 102(a)(2) [section 102(a)(2) of Title 11, Bankruptcy]), section 3656 of title 18, United States Code [section 3656 of Title 18, Crimes and Criminal Procedure], the third sentence of section 603, sections 671 to 675, inclusive or section 604(a)(5), of title 28, United States Code [sections 603, 671 to 675, or 604(a)(5) of this title], insofar as the latter section applies to graded positions, are hereby increased by amounts reflecting the respective applicable increases provided by section 102(a) of title I of this Act [amending section 1113(b) of former Title 5, Executive Departments and Government Officers and Employees], in corresponding rates of compensation for officers and employees subject to the Classification Act of 1949, as amended [chapter 51 and subchapter III of chapter 53 of Title 5, Government Organization and Employees]. The rates of basic compensation of officers and employees holding ungraded positions and whose salaries are fixed pursuant to such section 604(a)(5) [section 604(a)(5) of this title] may be increased by the amounts reflecting the respective applicable increases provided by section 102(a) of title I of this Act in corresponding rates of compensation for officers and employees subject to the Classification Act of 1949, as amended [chapter 51 and subchapter III of chapter 53 of Title 5]."

Section 203 of Title II of Pub.L. 89–504 provided that:

"This title [sections 201 to 203 of Pub.L. 89–504] shall become effective as follows:

"(1) This section and section 201 [enacting provisions set out as a note under section 1 of this title] shall become effective on the date of enactment of this Act [July 18, 1966].

"(2) Section 202 [enacting provisions set out as note under this section and sections 604 and 753 of this title] shall become effective on the first day of the first pay period which begins on or after July 1, 1966."

1965—Pub.L. 89–301, § 12(a), Oct. 29, 1965, 79 Stat. 1121, provided that: "The rates of basic compensation of officers and employees in or under the judicial branch of the Government whose rates of compensation are fixed by or pursuant to paragraph (2) of subdivision a of section 62 of the Bankruptcy Act (11 U.S.C. 102(a)(2) [section 102(a)(2) of Title 11, Bankruptcy]), section 3656 of title 18, United States Code [section 3656 of Title 18, Crimes and Criminal Procedure], the third sentence of section 603, sections 671 to 675, inclusive, or section 604(a)(5), of title 28, United States Code [sections 603, 671 to 675, or section 604(a)(5) of this title], insofar as the latter section applies to graded positions, are hereby increased by amounts reflecting the respective applicable increases provided by section 2(a) of this Act [amending section 1113(b) of former Title 5, Executive Departments and Government Officers and Employees] in corresponding rates of compensation for officers and employees subject to the Classification Act of 1949, as amended [chapter 51 and subchapter III of chapter 53 of Title 5, Government Organization and Employees]. The rates of basic compensation of officers and employees holding ungraded positions and whose salaries are fixed pursuant to such section 604(a)(5) [section 604(a)(5) of this title] may be increased by the amounts reflecting the respective applicable increases provided by section 2(a) of this Act in corresponding rates of compensation for officers and employees subject to the Classification Act of 1949, as amended [chapter 51 and subchapter III of chapter 53 of Title 5]."

1964—Section 402(a) of Pub.L. 88–426 provided that: "The rates of basic compensation of officers and employees in or under the judicial branch of the Government whose rates of compensation are fixed by or pursuant to paragraph (2) of subdivision a of section 62 of the Bankruptcy Act (11 U.S.C. 102(a)(2) [section 102(a)(2) of Title 11, Bankruptcy]), section 3656 of title 18, United States Code [section 3656 of Title 18, Crimes and Criminal Procedure], the third sentence of section 603, sections 672 to 675, inclusive, or section 604(a)(5), of title 28, United States Code [sections 603, 672 to 675, or 604(a)(5) of this title], insofar as the latter section applies to graded positions, are hereby increased by amounts reflecting the respective applicable increases provided by title I of this Act in corresponding rates of compensation for officers and employees subject to the Classification Act of 1949, as amended [chapter 51 and subchapter III of chapter 53 of Title 5, Government Organization and Employees]. The rates of basic compensation of officers and employees holding ungraded positions and whose salaries are fixed pursuant to section 604(a)(5) [section 604(a)(5) of this title] may be increased by the amounts reflecting the respective applicable increases provided by title I of this Act in corresponding rates of compensation for officers and employees subject to the Classification Act of 1949, as amended [chapter 51 and subchapter III of chapter 53 of Title 5]."

1962—Pub.L. 87–793, Title VI, § 1004(a), Oct. 11, 1962, 76 Stat. 866, provided that: "The rates of basic compensation of officers and employees in or under the judicial branch of the Government whose rates of compensation are fixed by or pursuant to paragraph (2) of subdivision a of section 62 of the Bankruptcy Act (11 U.S.C. 102(a)(2) [section 102(a)(2) of Title 11, Bankruptcy]), section 3656 of title 18 of the United States Code [section 3656 of Title 18, Crimes and Criminal Procedure], the third sentence of section 603, section 604(a)(5), or section 672 to 675 inclusive, of title 28 of the United States Code [sections 603, 604(a)(5), or 672 to 675 of this title], or section 107(a)(6) of the Act of July 31, 1956, as amended (5 U.S.C. 2206(a)(6) [section 2206(a)(6) of former Title 5, Executive Departments and Government Officers and Employees]), are hereby increased by two amounts, the first amount to be effective for the period beginning as of the first day of the first pay period which begins on or after the date of enactment of this Act [Oct. 11, 1962], and ending immediately prior to the first day of the first pay period which begins on or after January 1, 1964, and the second amount to be effective on the first day of the first pay period which begins on or after January 1, 1964, and thereafter, which reflect the respective applicable increases provided by title II of this part in corresponding rates of compensation for officers and employees subject to the Classification Act of 1949, as amended [chapter 51 and subchapter III of chapter 53 of Title 5, Government Organization and Employees]."

1960—Pub.L. 86–568, Title I, § 116(a), July 1, 1960, 74 Stat. 303, provided that: "The rates of basic compensation of officers and employees in or under the judicial branch of the Government whose rates of compensation are fixed by or pursuant to paragraph (2) of subdivision a of section 62 of the Bankruptcy Act (11 U.S.C. 102(a)(2) [section 102(a)(2) of Title 11, Bankruptcy]), section 3656 of title 18 of the United States Code [section 3656 of Title 18, Crimes and Criminal Procedure], the third sentence of section 603, section 604(a)(5), or sections 672 to 675, inclusive, of title 28 of the United States Code [sections 603, 604(a)(5), or sections 672 to 675 of this title], or section 107(a)(6) of the Act of July 31, 1956, as amended (5 U.S.C. 2206(a)(6) [section 2206(a)(6) of former Title 5, Executive Departments and Government Officers and Employees]), are hereby increased by amounts equal to the increases provided by section 612 [112] of this part [amending former section 1113(b) of Title 5] in corresponding rates of compensation paid to officers and employees subject to the Classification Act of 1949, as amended [chapter 51 and subchapter III of chapter 53 of Title 5, Government Organization and Employees]."

Pub.L. 87–367, Title III, § 302(d), Oct. 4, 1961, 75 Stat. 793, provided that: "On and after the effective date of this subsection, section 116(a) of the Federal Employees Salary Increase Act of 1960 (Part B of the Act of July 1, 1960; 74 Stat. 303; Public Law 86–568) [set out as a note under this section] shall not be applicable with respect to the Deputy Director of the Administrative Office of the United States Courts."

1958—Pub.L. 85–462, § 3(a), June 20, 1958, 72 Stat. 207, provided that: "The rates of basic compensation of officers and employees in or under the judicial branch of the Government whose rates of compensation are fixed pursuant to paragraph (2) of subdivision a of section 62 of the Bankruptcy Act (11 U.S.C. 102(a)(2) [section 102(a)(2) of Title 11, Bankruptcy]), section 3656 of title 18 of the United States Code [section 3656 of Title 18, Crimes and Criminal Procedure], the third sentence of section 603, section 604(a)(5), or sections 672 to 675, inclusive, of title 28 of the United States Code [sections 603, 604(a)(5), or 672 to 675 of this title] are hereby increased by amounts equal to the increases provided by section 2 of this Act [amending section 1113(b) of former Title 5, Executive Departments and Government Officers and Employees] in corresponding rates of compensation paid to officers and employees subject to the Classification Act of 1949, as amended [chapter 51 and subchapter III of Chapter 33 of Title 5, Government Organization and Employees]."

1955—Act June 28, 1955, c. 189, § 3(a), 69 Stat. 175, provided that: "The rates of basic compensation of officers and employees in or under the judicial branch of the Government whose rates of compensation are fixed pursuant to paragraph (2) of subdivision a of section 62 of the Bankruptcy Act (11 U.S.C., sec. 102(a)(2) [section 102(a)(2) of Title 11, Bankruptcy]), section 3656 of title 18 of the United States Code [section 3656 of Title 18, Crimes and Criminal Procedure], the second and third sentences of section 603, section 604(a)(5), or sections 672 to 675, inclusive, of title 28 of the United States Code [sections 603, 604(a)(5) or 672 to 675 of this title] are hereby increased by amounts equal to the increases provided by section 2 of this Act in corresponding rates of compensation paid to officers and employees subject to the Classification Act of 1949, as amended [chapter 51 and subchapter III of chapter 53 of Title 5, Government Organization and Employees]."

1951—Act Oct. 24, 1951, c. 554, § 1(c), 65 Stat. 613, provided that: "The rates of basic compensation of officers and employees in or under the judicial branch of the Government whose rates of compensation are fixed pursuant to section 62(2) of the Bankruptcy Act (11 U.S.C. 102(a)(2) [section 102(a)(2) of Title 11, Bankruptcy]), section 3656 of Title 18 of the United States Code [section 3656 of Title 18, Crimes and Criminal Procedure], the second and third sentences of section 603, section 604(5), or sections 672 to 675, inclusive, of title 28 of the United States Code [sections 603, 604(a)(5) or 672 to 675 of this title], or who are appointed pursuant to section 792(b) of title 28 of the United States Code [section 792(b) this title], are hereby increased by amounts equal to the increases provided by subsections (a) and (b) in corresponding rates of compensation paid to officers and employees subject to the Classification Act of 1949 [chapter 51 and subchapter III of chapter 53 of Title 5, Government Organization and Employees]."

§ 604. Duties of Director generally

(a) The Director shall be the administrative officer of the courts, and under the supervision and direction of the Judicial Conference of the United States, shall:

(1) Supervise all administrative matters relating to the offices of clerks and other clerical and administrative personnel of the courts;

(2) Examine the state of the dockets of the courts; secure information as to the courts' need of assistance; prepare and transmit semiannually to the chief judges of the circuits, statistical data and reports as to the business of the courts;

(3) Submit to the annual meeting of the Judicial Conference of the United States, at least two weeks prior thereto, a report of the activities of the Administrative Office and the state of the business of the courts, together with the statistical data submitted to the chief judges of the circuits under paragraph (a)(2) of this section, and the Director's recommendations, which report, data and recommendations shall be public documents.

(4) Submit to Congress and the Attorney General copies of the report, data and recommendations required by paragraph (a)(3) of this section;

(5) Fix the compensation of clerks of court, deputies, librarians, criers, messengers, law clerks, secretaries, stenographers, clerical assistants, and other employees of the courts whose compensation is not otherwise fixed by law, and, notwithstanding any other provision of law, pay on behalf of Justices and judges of the United States appointed to hold office during good behavior magistrate judges appointed under section 631 of this title,,[1] aged 65 or over, any increases in the cost of Federal Employees' Group Life Insurance imposed after April 24, 1999, including any expenses generated by such payments, as authorized by the Judicial Conference of the United States;

(6) Determine and pay necessary office expenses of courts, judges, and those court officials whose expenses are by law allowable, and the lawful fees of United States magistrate judges;

(7) Regulate and pay annuities to widows and surviving dependent children of justices and judges of the United States, judges of the United States Court of Federal Claims, bankruptcy judges, United States magistrate judges, Directors of the Federal Judicial Center, and Directors of the Administrative Office, and necessary travel and subsistence expenses incurred by judges, court officers and employees, and officers and employees of the Administrative Office, and the Federal Judicial Center, while absent from their official stations on official business, without regard to the per diem allowances and amounts for reimbursement of actual and necessary expenses established by the Administrator of General Services under section 5702 of title 5, except that the reimbursement of subsistence expenses may not exceed that authorized by the Director for judges of the United States under section 456 of this title;

(8) Disburse appropriations and other funds for the maintenance and operation of the courts;

(9) Establish pretrial services pursuant to section 3152 of title 18, United States Code;

(10) (A) Purchase, exchange, transfer, distribute, and assign the custody of lawbooks, equipment, supplies, and other personal property for the judicial branch of Government (except the Supreme Court unless otherwise provided pursuant to paragraph (17)); (B) provide or make available readily to each court appropriate equipment for the interpretation of proceedings in accordance with section 1828 of this title; and (C) enter into and perform contracts and other transactions upon such terms as the Director may deem appropriate as may be necessary to the conduct of the work of the judicial branch of Government (except the Supreme Court unless otherwise provided pursuant to paragraph (17)), and contracts for nonpersonal services providing pretrial services, agencies for the interpretation of proceedings, and for the provision of special interpretation services pursuant to section 1828 of this title may be awarded without regard to section 3709 of the Revised Statutes of the United States (41 U.S.C. 5);

(11) Audit vouchers and accounts of the courts, the Federal Judicial Center, the offices providing pretrial services, and their clerical and administrative personnel;

(12) Provide accommodations for the courts, the Federal Judicial Center, the offices providing pretrial services and their clerical and administrative personnel;

(13) Lay before Congress, annually, statistical tables that will accurately reflect the business transacted by the several bankruptcy courts, and all other pertinent data relating to such courts;

(14) Pursuant to section 1827 of this title, establish a program for the certification and utilization of interpreters in courts of the United States;

(15) Pursuant to section 1828 of this title, establish a program for the provision of special interpretation services in courts of the United States;

(16) (A) In those districts where the Director considers it advisable based on the need for interpreters, authorize the full-time or part-time employment by the court of certified interpreters; (B) where the Director considers it advisable based on the need for interpreters, appoint certified inter-

preters on a full-time or part-time basis, for services in various courts when he determines that such appointments will result in the economical provision of interpretation services; and (C) pay out of moneys appropriated for the judiciary interpreters' salaries, fees, and expenses, and other costs which may accrue in accordance with the provisions of sections 1827 and 1828 of this title;

(17) In the Director's discretion, (A) accept and utilize voluntary and uncompensated (gratuitous) services, including services as authorized by section 3102(b) of title 5, United States Code; and (B) accept, hold, administer, and utilize gifts and bequests of personal property for the purpose of aiding or facilitating the work of the judicial branch of Government, but gifts or bequests of money shall be covered into the Treasury;

(18) Establish procedures and mechanisms within the judicial branch for processing fines, restitution, forfeitures of bail bonds or collateral, and assessments;

(19) Regulate and pay annuities to bankruptcy judges and United States magistrate judges in accordance with section 377 of this title and paragraphs (1)(B) and (2) of section 2(c) of the Retirement and Survivors' Annuities for Bankruptcy Judges and Magistrates Act of 1988;

(20) Periodically compile—

(A) the rules which are prescribed under section 2071 of this title by courts other than the Supreme Court;

(B) the rules which are prescribed under section 358 of this title; and

(C) the orders which are required to be publicly available under section 360(b) of this title;

so as to provide a current record of such rules and orders;

(21) Establish a program of incentive awards for employees of the judicial branch of the United States Government, other than any judge who is entitled to hold office during good behavior;

(22) Receive and expend, either directly or by transfer to the United States Marshals Service or other Government agency, funds appropriated for the procurement, installation, and maintenance of security equipment and protective services for the United States Courts in courtrooms and adjacent areas, including building ingress/egress control, inspection of packages, directed security patrols, and other similar activities;

(23) Regulate and pay annuities to judges of the United States Court of Federal Claims in accordance with section 178 of this title; and

(24) Perform such other duties as may be assigned to him by the Supreme Court or the Judicial Conference of the United States.

(b) The clerical and administrative personnel of the courts shall comply with all requests by the Director for information or statistical data as to the state of court dockets.

(c) Inspection of court dockets outside the continental United States may be made through United States officials residing within the jurisdiction where the inspection is made.

(d) The Director, under the supervision and direction of the conference, shall:

(1) supervise all administrative matters relating to the offices of the United States magistrate judges;

(2) gather, compile, and evaluate all statistical and other information required for the performance of his duties and the duties of the conference with respect to such officers;

(3) lay before Congress annually statistical tables and other information which will accurately reflect the business which has come before the various United States magistrate judges, including (A) the number of matters in which the parties consented to the exercise of jurisdiction by a magistrate judge, (B) the number of appeals taken pursuant to the decisions of magistrate judges and the disposition of such appeals, and (C) the professional background and qualifications of individuals appointed under section 631 of this title to serve as magistrate judges;

(4) prepare and distribute a manual, with annual supplements and periodic revisions, for the use of such officers, which shall set forth their powers and duties, describe all categories of proceedings that may arise before them, and contain such other information as may be required to enable them to discharge their powers and duties promptly, effectively, and impartially.

(e) The Director may promulgate appropriate rules and regulations approved by the conference and not inconsistent with any provision of law, to assist him in the performance of the duties conferred upon him by subsection (d) of this section. Magistrate judges shall keep such records and make such reports as are specified in such rules and regulations.

(f) The Director may make, promulgate, issue, rescind, and amend rules and regulations (including regulations prescribing standards of conduct for Administrative Office employees) as may be necessary to carry out the Director's functions, powers, duties, and authority. The Director may publish in the Federal Register such rules, regulations, and notices for the judicial branch of Government as the Director determines to be of public interest; and the Director of the Federal Register hereby is authorized to accept and shall publish such materials.

(g)(1) When authorized to exchange personal property, the Director may exchange or sell similar items and may apply the exchange allowance or proceeds of sale in such cases in whole or in part payment for the property acquired, but any transaction carried out under the authority of this subsection shall be evidenced in writing.

(2) The Director hereby is authorized to enter into contracts for public utility services and related terminal equipment for periods not exceeding ten years.

(3)(A) In order to promote the recycling and reuse of recyclable materials, the Director may provide for the sale or disposal of recyclable scrap materials from paper products and other consumable office supplies held by an entity within the judicial branch.

(B) The sale or disposal of recyclable materials under subparagraph (A) shall be consistent with the procedures provided in sections 541–555 of title 40 for the sale of surplus property.

(C) Proceeds from the sale of recyclable materials under subparagraph (A) shall be deposited as offsetting collections to the fund established under section 1931 of this title and shall remain available until expended to reimburse any appropriations for the operation and maintenance of the judicial branch.

(4) The Director is hereby authorized:

(A) to enter into contracts for the acquisition of severable services for a period that begins in one fiscal year and ends in the next fiscal year to the same extent as the head of an executive agency under the authority of section 253l of title 41, United States Code;

(B) to enter into contracts for multiple years for the acquisition of property and services to the same extent as executive agencies under the authority of section 254c of title 41, United States Code; and

(C) to make advance, partial, progress or other payments under contracts for property or services to the same extent as executive agencies under the authority of section 255 of title 41, United States Code.

(h)(1) The Director shall, out of funds appropriated for the operation and maintenance of the courts, provide facilities and pay necessary expenses incurred by the judicial councils of the circuits and the Judicial Conference under chapter 16 of this title, including mileage allowance and witness fees, at the same rate as provided in section 1821 of this title. Administrative and professional assistance from the Administrative Office of the United States Courts may be requested by each judicial council and the Judicial Conference for purposes of discharging their duties under chapter 16 of this title.

(2) The Director of the Administrative Office of the United States Courts shall include in his annual report filed with the Congress under this section a summary of the number of complaints filed with each judicial council under chapter 16 of this title, indicating the general nature of such complaints and the disposition of those complaints in which action has been taken.

(June 25, 1948, c. 646, 62 Stat. 914; Aug. 3, 1956, c. 944, § 3, 70 Stat. 1026; Dec. 20, 1967, Pub.L. 90–219, Title II, § 203, 81 Stat. 669; Oct. 17, 1968, Pub.L. 90–578, Title II, § 201, Title IV, § 402(b)(2), 82 Stat. 1114, 1118; Aug. 22, 1972, Pub.L. 92–397, § 4, 86 Stat. 580; Jan. 3, 1975, Pub.L. 93–619, Title II, § 204, 88 Stat. 2089; Oct. 28, 1978, Pub.L. 95–539, §§ 3, 4, 92 Stat. 2043; Nov. 6, 1978, Pub.L. 95–598, Title II, § 225, 92 Stat. 2664; Oct. 10, 1979, Pub.L. 96–82, § 5, 93 Stat. 645; Oct. 15, 1980, Pub.L. 96–458, § 5, 94 Stat. 2040; Dec. 12, 1980, Pub.L. 96–523, § 1(c)(1), 94 Stat. 3040; Sept. 27, 1982, Pub.L. 97–267, § 7, 96 Stat. 1139; Oct. 27, 1986, Pub.L. 99–554, Title I, § 116, 100 Stat. 3095; Dec. 11, 1987, Pub.L. 100–185, § 2, 101 Stat. 1279; Nov. 15, 1988, Pub.L. 100–659, § 6(a), 102 Stat. 3918; Nov. 19, 1988, Pub.L. 100–702, Title IV, § 402(a), Title X, §§ 1008, 1010, 1011, 1020(a)(2), 102 Stat. 4650, 4667, 4668, 4671; Oct. 30, 1990, Pub.L. 101–474, § 5(r), 104 Stat. 1101; Nov. 29, 1990, Pub.L. 101–647, Title XXV, § 2548, 104 Stat. 4888; Dec. 1, 1990, Pub.L. 101–650, Title III, §§ 306(e)(1), 321, 325(c)(1), 104 Stat. 5111, 5117, 5121; Oct. 29, 1992, Pub.L. 102–572, Title V, § 503, Title IX, § 902(b)(1), 106 Stat. 4513, 4516; Nov. 29, 1999, Pub.L. 106–113, § 1000(a)(1) [Title III, § 305], 113 Stat. 1535, 1501A–37; Nov. 13, 2000, Pub.L. 106–518, Title II, § 204, Title III, § 304(d), 114 Stat. 2414, 2418; Aug. 21, 2002, Pub.L. 107–217, § 3(g)(1), 116 Stat. 1299; Nov. 2, 2002, Pub.L. 107–273, Div. C, Title I, § 11043(e), 116 Stat. 1855; Nov. 30, 2005, Pub.L. 109–115, Div. A, Title IV, § 407(a), 119 Stat. 2470; Jan. 7, 2008, Pub.L. 110–177, Title V, § 502(a), 121 Stat. 2542.)

[1] So in original.

HISTORICAL AND STATUTORY NOTES

References in Text

Section 2(c) of the Retirement and Survivors' Annuities for Bankruptcy Judges and Magistrates Act of 1988, referred to in subsec. (a)(19), is section 2(c) of Pub.L. 100–659, Nov. 15, 1988, 102 Stat. 3916, which is set out as a note under section 377 of this title.

Codifications

Pub.L. 101–650, § 306(e)(1)(A), directing amendment of Pub.L. 100–702, § 402(1), probably intended amendment of section 402(a)(1) of pub.L. 100–702, which provided for redesignation of subsec. (a)(19) to be subsec. (a)(23) of this section, redesignated as subsec. (a)(24) by Pub.L. 101–650, § 306(e)(1)(B)(ii).

Amendment by Pub.L. 109–115, Div. A, § 407(a), which directed that this section is amended by adding "section (4) at the end of section '(g)' " was executed by adding par. (4) to the end of subsec. (g), as the probable intent of Congress.

Effective and Applicability Provisions

2008 Acts. Pub.L. 110–177, Title V, § 502(c), Jan. 7, 2008, 121 Stat. 2542, provided that: "Subsection (b) [enacting provisions set out as a note under 5 U.S.C.A. § 8701] and the amendment made by subsection (a) [amending this section] shall apply with respect to any payment made on or after the first day of the first applicable pay period beginning on or after the date of enactment of this Act [Jan. 7, 2008]."

1992 Acts. Amendment by section 902(b)(1) of Pub.L. 102–572 effective Oct. 29, 1992, see section 911 of Pub.L. 102–572, set out as a note under section 171 of this title.

Amendment by Pub.L. 102–572 effective Jan. 1, 1993, see section 1101(a) of Pub.L. 102–572, set out as a note under section 905 of Title 2, The Congress.

1990 Acts. Amendment by section 306(e)(1) of Pub.L. 101–650 applicable to judges of, and senior judges in active service with, the United States Court of Federal Claims on or after Dec. 1, 1990, see section 306(f) of Pub.L. 101–650, set out as a note under section 8331 of Title 5, Government Organization and Employees.

1988 Acts. Amendment by section 402(a) of Pub.L. 100–702 effective Dec. 1, 1988, see section 407 of Pub.L. 100–702, set out as a note under section 2071 of this title.

Amendment to this section by Pub.L. 100–659 to take effect on Nov. 15, 1988, and shall apply to bankruptcy judges and magistrates who retire on or after Nov. 15, 1988, with special election provisions for bankruptcy judges, etc., who left office on or after July 31, 1987, and before Nov. 15, 1988, see section 9 of Pub.L. 100–659, set out as a note under section 377 of this title.

1986 Acts. Amendment by Pub.L. 99–554 effective 30 days after Oct. 27, 1986, except as otherwise provided, see section 302(a) of Pub.L. 99–554, as amended, set out as a note under section 581 of this title.

1980 Acts. Amendment by Pub.L. 96–523 effective sixty days after Dec. 12, 1980, see section 3 of Pub.L. 96–523, set out as a note under section 3102 of Title 5, Government Organization and Employees.

Amendment by Pub.L. 96–458 effective Oct. 1, 1981, see section 7 of Pub.L. 96–458, set out as a note under section 331 of this title.

1978 Acts. Amendment by Pub.L. 95–598 effective Oct. 1, 1979, see section 402(c) of Pub.L. 95–598, as amended, set out as a note preceding section 101 of Title 11, Bankruptcy.

Amendment by Pub.L. 95–539 effective Oct. 28, 1978, see section 10(a) of Pub.L. 95–539, set out as a note under section 602 of this title.

1968 Acts. Amendment by Pub.L. 90–578 effective Oct. 17, 1968, except when a later effective date is applicable, which is the earlier of date when implementation of amendment by appointment of magistrates and assumption of office takes place or third anniversary of enactment of Pub.L. 90–578 on Oct. 17, 1968, see section 403 of Pub.L. 90–578, set out as a note under section 631 of this title.

Termination of Authority

Pub.L. 109–115, Div. A, Title IV, § 407(c), Nov. 30, 2005, 119 Stat. 2471, provided that: "The authorities granted in this section [Pub.L. 109–115, Div. A, Title IV, § 407, 119 Stat. 2470, which amended subsec. (g)(4) of this section and 28 U.S.C.A. § 612] shall expire on September 30, 2010."

Termination of Reporting Requirements

For termination, effective May 15, 2000, of provisions in subsecs. (a)(4), (d)(3), and (h)(2) of this section relating to reporting certain information annually to Congress, see Pub.L. 104–66, § 3003, as amended, set out as a note under 31 U.S.C.A. § 1113 and page 12 of House Document No. 103–7.

Change of Name

References to United States Claims Court deemed to refer to United States Court of Federal Claims and references to Claims Court deemed to refer to Court of Federal Claims, see section 902(b) of Pub.L. 102–572, set out as a note under section 171 of Title 28, Judiciary and Judicial Procedure.

"United States magistrate judge" substituted for "United States magistrate" in text pursuant to section 321 of Pub.L. 101–650, set out as a note under 28 U.S.C.A. § 631. Previously, United States commissioners, referred to in text, were replaced by United States magistrates pursuant to Pub.L. 90–578, Oct. 17, 1968, 82 Stat. 1118. See chapter 43 of Title 28, 28 U.S.C.A. § 631 et seq.

Compensation and Appointment of Secretaries and Law Clerks

Provisions authorizing the appointment and compensation of secretaries and law clerks to circuit and district judges in such number and at such rates of compensation as may be determined by the Judicial Conference of the United States were contained in the following appropriation Acts:

Dec. 12, 1985, Pub.L. 99–180, Title IV, § 400, 99 Stat. 1154.

Aug. 30, 1984, Pub.L. 98–411, Title IV, § 400, 98 Stat. 1571.

Nov. 28, 1983, Pub.L. 98–166, Title IV, § 400, 97 Stat. 1099.

Dec. 21, 1982, Pub.L. 97–377, § 101(d) [S. 2956, Title IV, § 400], 96 Stat. 1866.

Dec. 15, 1981, Pub.L. 97–92, § 101(h) [incorporating Pub.L. 96–536, § 101(*o*); H.R. 7584, Title IV, § 400], 95 Stat. 1190.

Dec. 16, 1980, Pub.L. 96–536, § 101(*o*) [H.R. 7584, Title IV, § 400], 94 Stat. 3169.

Sept. 24, 1979, Pub.L. 96–68, Title IV, § 400, 93 Stat. 428.

Oct. 10, 1978, Pub.L. 95–431, Title IV, § 401, 92 Stat. 1037.

Aug. 2, 1977, Pub.L. 95–86, Title IV, § 401, 91 Stat. 435.

July 14, 1976, Pub.L. 94–362, Title IV, § 401, 90 Stat. 953.

Oct. 21, 1975, Pub.L. 94–121, Title IV, § 401, 89 Stat. 630.

Oct. 5, 1974, Pub.L. 93–433, Title IV, § 401, 88 Stat. 1202.

Nov. 27, 1973, Pub.L. 93–162, Title IV, § 401, 87 Stat. 651.

Oct. 25, 1972, Pub.L. 92–544, Title IV, § 401, 86 Stat. 1126.

Aug. 10, 1971, Pub.L. 92–77, Title IV, § 401, 85 Stat. 262.

Oct. 21, 1970, Pub.L. 91–472, Title IV, § 401, 84 Stat. 1056.

Dec. 24, 1969, Pub.L. 91–153, Title IV, § 401, 83 Stat. 419.

Aug. 9, 1968, Pub.L. 90–470, Title IV, § 401, 82 Stat. 685.

Nov. 8, 1967, Pub.L. 90–133, Title IV, § 401, 81 Stat. 427.

Nov. 8, 1966, Pub.L. 89–797, Title IV, § 401, 80 Stat. 1499.

Sept. 2, 1965, Pub.L. 89–164, Title IV, § 401, 79 Stat. 638.

Aug. 31, 1964, Pub.L. 88–527, Title IV, § 401, 78 Stat. 729.

Dec. 30, 1963, Pub.L. 88–245, Title IV, § 401, 77 Stat. 795.

Oct. 18, 1962, Pub.L. 87–843, Title IV, § 401, 76 Stat. 1099.

Sept. 21, 1961, Pub.L. 87–264, Title III, § 301, 75 Stat. 555.

Aug. 31, 1960, Pub.L. 86–678, Title III, § 301, 74 Stat. 566.

July 13, 1959, Pub.L. 86–84, Title III, § 301, 73 Stat. 192.

June 30, 1958, Pub.L. 85–474, Title III, § 301, 72 Stat. 254.

June 11, 1957, Pub.L. 85–40, Title III, § 301, 70 Stat. 65.

June 20, 1956, c. 414, Title III, § 301, 70 Stat. 310.

July 7, 1955, c. 279, Title III, § 301, 69 Stat. 276.

July 2, 1954, c. 455, Title II, § 201, 68 Stat. 410.

Aug. 1, 1953, c. 304, Title II, § 201, 67 Stat. 334.

July 10, 1952, c. 651, Title IV, § 401, 66 Stat. 569.

Oct. 22, 1951, c. 533, Title IV, § 401, 65 Stat. 596.

Sept. 6, 1950, c. 896, ch. III, Title IV, § 401, 64 Stat. 631.

Increases in Compensation Rates

Increases in rates of basic compensation fixed pursuant to subsec. (a)(5) of this section, see notes under section 603 of this title.

Limitation on Aggregate Salaries of Secretaries and Law Clerks

1967—Pub.L. 90–206, Title II, § 213(b), Dec. 16, 1967, 81 Stat. 635, provided that: "The limitations provided by applicable law on the effective date of this section [see Effective and Applicability Provisions of 1967 amendments note set out under section 5332 of Title 5, Government Organization and Employees] with respect to the aggregate salaries payable to secretaries and law clerks of circuit and district judges are hereby increased by amounts which reflect the respective applicable increases provided by section 202(a) of this title [amending section 5332(a) of Title 5] in corresponding rates of compensation for officers and employees subject to section 5332 of title 5, United States Code [section 5332 of Title 5]."

Section 213(b) of Pub.L. 90–206 effective as of the beginning of the first pay period which begins on or after Oct. 1, 1967, see section 220(a)(2) of Pub.L. 90–206, set out as a note under section 5332 of Title 5, Government Organization and Employees.

1966—Pub.L. 89–504, Title II, § 202(b), July 18, 1966, 80 Stat. 294, provided that: "The limitations provided by applicable law on the effective date of this section with respect to the aggregate salaries payable to secretaries and law clerks of circuit and district judges are hereby increased by amounts which reflect the respective applicable increases provided by section 102(a) of title I of this Act [amending section 1113(b) of former Title 5, Executive Departments and Government Officers and Employees] in corresponding rates of compensation for officers and employees subject to the Classification Act of 1949, as amended [chapter 51 and subchapter III of chapter 53 of Title 5, Government Organization and Employees]."

Provision effective the first day of the first pay period which begins on or after July 1, 1966, see section 203 of Pub.L. 89–504, set out as a note under section 603 of this title.

1965—Pub.L. 89–301, § 12(b), Oct. 29, 1965, 79 Stat. 1122, provided that: "The limitations provided by applicable law on the effective date of this section with respect to the aggregate salaries payable to secretaries and law clerks of circuit and district judges are hereby increased by amounts which reflect the respective applicable increases provided by section 2(a) of this Act [amending section 1113(b) of former Title 5, Executive Departments and Government Officers and Employees] in corresponding rates of compensation for officers and employees subject to the Classification Act of 1949, as amended [chapter 51 and subchapter III of chapter 53 of Title 5, Government Organization and Employees]."

1964—Pub.L. 88–426, Title IV, § 402(b), Aug. 14, 1964, 78 Stat. 433, provided that: "The limitations provided by applicable law on the effective date of this section with respect to the aggregate salaries payable to secretaries and law clerks of circuit and district judges are hereby increased by amounts which reflect the respective applicable increases provided by title I of this Act in corresponding rates of compensation for officers and employees subject to the Classification Act of 1949, as amended [chapter 51 and subchapter III of chapter 53 of Title 5, Government Organization and Employees]."

1962—Pub.L. 87–793, Title VI, § 1004(b), Oct. 11, 1962, 76 Stat. 866, provided that: "The limitations provided by applicable law on the effective date of this section with respect to the aggregate salaries payable to secretaries and law clerks of circuit and district judges are hereby increased by two amounts, the first amount to be effective for the period beginning as of the first day of the first pay period which begins on or after the date of enactment of this Act [Oct. 11, 1962], and ending immediately prior to the first day of the first pay period which begins on or after January 1, 1964, and the second amount to be effective on the first day of the first pay period which begins on or after January 1, 1964, and thereafter, which reflect the respective applicable increases provided by title II of this part in corresponding rates of compensation for officers and employees subject to the Classification Act of 1949, as amended [chapter 51 and subchapter III of chapter 53 of Title 5, Government Organization and Employees]."

1960—Pub.L. 86–568, Title I, § 116(b), July 1, 1960, 74 Stat. 303, provided that: "The limitations provided by applicable law on the effective date of this section with respect to the aggregate salaries payable to secretaries and law clerks of circuit and district judges are hereby increased by the amounts necessary to pay the additional basic compensation provided by this part."

Words "this part", referred to in section 116(b) of Pub.L. 86–568 [this note], means Part B of Pub.L. 86–568, which enacted section 932e of former Title 5, Executive Departments and Government Officers and Employees, amended section 753 of this title, sections 1113, 2091, 2252 and 3002 of former Title 5, sections 867 and 870 of Title 22, Foreign Relations and Intercourse, and sections 4103, 4107 and 4108 of Title 38, Veterans' Benefits and enacted notes set out under sections 603 and 604 of this title, sections 60a and 60f of Title 2, The Congress, sections 1113 and 2252 of former Title 5, section 590h of Title 16, Conservation, and section 867 of Title 22.

1958—Pub.L. 85–462, § 3(b), June 20, 1958, 72 Stat. 207, provided that: "The limitations of $13,485 and $18,010 with respect to the aggregate salaries payable to secretaries and law clerks of circuit and district judges, contained in the paragraph designated "Salaries of supporting personnel" in the Judiciary Appropriation Act, 1958 (71 Stat. 65; Public Law 85–49), or any subsequent appropriation Act, shall be increased by the amounts necessary to pay the additional basic compensation provided by this Act."

1955—Act June 28, 1955, c. 189, § 3(b), 69 Stat. 175, provided that: "The limitations of $10,560 and $14,355 with respect to the aggregate salaries payable to secretaries and law clerks of circuit and district judges, contained in the paragraph under the heading 'SALARIES OF SUPPORTING PERSONNEL' in the Judiciary Appropriation Act, 1955 (Public Law 470, Eighty-third Congress), or in any subsequent appropriation Act, shall be increased by the amounts necessary to pay the additional basic compensation provided by this Act."

1951—Act Oct. 24, 1951, c. 554, § 1(d), 65 Stat. 613, provided that: "The limitations of $9,600 and $13,050 with respect to the aggregate salaries payable to secretaries and law clerks of circuit and district judges, contained in the sixteenth paragraph under the head 'Miscellaneous salaries' in the Judiciary Appropriation Act, 1951 (Public Law 759, Eighty-first Congress), or in any subsequent appropriation Act, shall be increased by the amounts necessary to pay the additional basic compensation provided by this Act."

The particular paragraph of the "Judiciary Appropriation Act, 1951 (Public Law 759, Eighty-first Congress)", referred to in section 1(d) of Act Oct. 24, 1951, c. 554 [this note], is Act Sept. 6, 1950, c. 896, ch. III, Title IV, § 401 (part), 64 Stat. 631. The salary limitations therein, also referred to above, were identical with those in the Judiciary Appropriation Act, 1952 (Act Oct. 22, 1951, c. 533, Title IV, § 401 (part), 65 Stat. 596).

1970 Increase in Pay Rates of Judicial Branch Employees Whose Rates of Pay Are Fixed by Administrative Action

Adjustment of rates of pay of judicial branch employees whose rates of pay are fixed by administrative action by not to exceed the amounts of the adjustment for corresponding rates for employees subject to section 2(a) of Pub.L. 91–231, which raised corresponding rates by 6 percent, effective on the first day of the first pay period which begins on or after Dec. 27, 1969, see Pub.L. 91–231, set out as a note under section 5332 of Title 5, Government Organization and Employees.

Reports by Director of Administrative Office of United States Courts

For requirement that Director of Administrative Office of the United States Courts include statistical information about implementation of chapter 44 of this title in annual report under section 604(a)(3) of this title, see section 903(a) of Pub.L. 100–702, set out as a note under section 651 of this title.

Travel and Subsistence Expenses

Pub.L. 87–139, § 6, Aug. 14, 1961, 75 Stat. 340, provided that: "The Director of the Administrative Office of the United States Courts shall promulgate, in accordance with section 604(a)(7) and section 456 of title 28 of the United States Code [subsec. (a)(7) of this section and section 456 of this title], such regulations as he may deem necessary to effectuate the increases provided by this Act [amending section 553 of this title, section 68b of Title 2, The Congress, sections 73b–2, 836 and 837 of former Title 5, Executive Departments and Government Officers and Employees, and sections 287o, 287q and 1471 of Title 22, Foreign Relations and Intercourse]."

§ 605. Budget estimates

The Director, under the supervision of the Judicial Conference of the United States, shall submit to the Office of Management and Budget annual estimates of the expenditures and appropriations necessary for the maintenance and operation of the courts and the Administrative Office and the operation of the judicial survivors annuity fund, and such supplemental and deficiency estimates as may be required from time to time for the same purposes, according to law. The Director shall cause periodic examinations of the judicial survivors annuity fund to be made by an actuary, who may be an actuary employed by another department of the Government temporarily assigned for the purpose, and whose findings and recommendations shall be transmitted by the Director to the Judicial Conference.

Such estimates shall be approved, before presentation to the Office of Management and Budget, by the Judicial Conference of the United States, except that the estimate with respect to the Court of International Trade shall be approved by such court and the estimate with respect to the United States Court of Appeals for the Federal Circuit shall be approved by such court.

(June 25, 1948, c. 646, 62 Stat. 915; July 9, 1956, c. 517, § 1(e), 70 Stat. 497; Aug. 3, 1956, c. 944, § 4, 70 Stat. 1026; Sept. 19, 1961, Pub.L. 87–253, § 3, 75 Stat. 521; Oct. 10, 1980, Pub.L. 96–417, Title V, § 501(14), 94 Stat. 1742; Apr. 2, 1982, Pub.L. 97–164, Title I, § 119(a), 96 Stat. 33; Sept. 13, 1982, Pub.L. 97–258, § 5(b), 96 Stat. 1068, 1085.)

HISTORICAL AND STATUTORY NOTES

Effective and Applicability Provisions

1982 Acts. Amendment by Pub.L. 97–164 effective Oct. 1, 1982, see section 402 of Pub.L. 97–164, set out as a note under section 171 of this title.

1980 Acts. Amendment by Pub.L. 96–417 effective on Nov. 1, 1980 and applicable with respect to civil actions pending on or commenced on or after such date, see section 701(a) of Pub.L. 96–417, as amended, set out as a note under section 251 of this title.

§ 606. Duties of Deputy Director

The Deputy Director shall perform the duties assigned to him by the Director, and shall act as Director during the absence or incapacity of the Director or when the Director's office is vacant.

(June 25, 1948, c. 646, 62 Stat. 915; Sept. 23, 1959, Pub.L. 86–370, § 5(a)(1), 73 Stat. 652.)

HISTORICAL AND STATUTORY NOTES

Effective and Applicability Provisions

1959 Acts. Amendment by Pub.L. 86–370 effective Sept. 23, 1959, see section 7(a) of Pub.L. 86–370.

Reference to Assistant Director Deemed Reference to Deputy Director

References in any other law to Assistant Director of the Administrative Office of the United States Courts deemed to be reference to the Deputy Director of the Administrative Office of the United States Courts, see section 5(a)(4) of Pub.L. 86–370, set out as a note under section 601 of this title.

§ 607. Practice of law prohibited

An officer or employee of the Administrative Office shall not engage directly or indirectly in the practice of law in any court of the United States.

(June 25, 1948, c. 646, 62 Stat. 915.)

§ 608. Seal

The Director shall use a seal approved by the Supreme Court. Judicial notice shall be taken of such seal.

(June 25, 1948, c. 646, 62 Stat. 915.)

§ 609. Courts' appointive power unaffected

The authority of the courts to appoint their own administrative or clerical personnel shall not be limited by any provisions of this chapter.

(June 25, 1948, c. 646, 62 Stat. 915.)

§ 610. Courts defined

As used in this chapter the word "courts" includes the courts of appeals and district courts of the United States, the United States District Court for the District of the Canal Zone, the District Court of Guam, the District Court of the Virgin Islands, the United States Court of Federal Claims, and the Court of International Trade.

(June 25, 1948, c. 646, 62 Stat. 915; Oct. 31, 1951, c. 655, § 44, 65 Stat. 725; July 7, 1958, Pub.L. 85–508, § 12(e), 72 Stat. 348; Nov. 6, 1978, Pub.L. 95–598, Title II, § 226, 92 Stat. 2665; Oct. 10, 1980, Pub.L. 96–417, Title V, § 501(15), 94 Stat. 1742; Apr. 2, 1982, Pub.L. 97–164, Title I, § 120(a), 96 Stat. 33; Oct. 29, 1992, Pub.L. 102–572, Title IX, § 902(b)(1), 106 Stat. 4516.)

HISTORICAL AND STATUTORY NOTES

Codifications

This section was amended by Pub.L. 95–598, Title II, § 226, Nov. 6, 1978, 92 Stat. 2665, effective June 28, 1984, pursuant to Pub.L. 95–598, Title IV, § 402(b), Nov. 6, 1978, 92 Stat. 2682, as amended by Pub.L. 98–249, § 1(a), Mar. 31, 1984, 98 Stat. 116; Pub.L. 98–271, § 1(a), Apr. 30, 1984, 98 Stat. 163; Pub.L. 98–299, § 1(a), May 25, 1984, 98 Stat. 214; Pub.L. 98–325, § 1(a), June 20, 1984, 98 Stat. 268, set out as an Effective and Applicability Provisions note preceding section 101 of Title II, Bankruptcy, by substituting ", district courts, and bankruptcy courts" for "and district courts."

Section 402(b) of Pub.L. 95–598 was amended by section 113 of Pub.L. 98–353, Title I, July 10, 1984, 98 Stat. 343, by substituting "shall not be effective" for "shall take effect on June 28, 1984", thereby eliminating the amendment by section 226 of Pub.L. 95–598, effective June 27, 1984, pursuant to section 122(c) of Pub.L. 98–353, set out as an Effective Date, note under section 151 of this title.

Section 121(a) of Pub.L. 98–353 directed that section 402(b) of Pub.L. 95–598 be amended by substituting "the date of enactment of the Bankruptcy Amendments and Federal Judgeship Act of 1984 [i.e. July 10, 1984]" for "June 28, 1984". This amendment was not executed in view of the prior amendment to section 402(b) of Pub.L. 95–598 by section 113 of Pub.L. 98–353.

Effective and Applicability Provisions

1982 Acts. Amendment by Pub.L. 97–164 effective Oct. 1, 1982, see section 402 of Pub.L. 97–164, set out as a note under section 171 of this title.

1980 Acts. Amendment by Pub.L. 96–417 effective on Nov. 1, 1980 and applicable with respect to civil actions pending on or commenced on or after such date, see section 701(a) of Pub.L. 96–417, as amended, set out as a note under section 251 of this title.

1958 Acts. Amendment by Pub.L. 85–508 effective Jan. 3, 1959, upon admission of Alaska into the Union pursuant to Proc. No. 3269, Jan. 3, 1959, 24 F.R. 81, 73 Stat. c16, as required by sections 1 and 8(c) of Pub.L. 85–508, see notes set out under section 81A of this title and preceding section 21 of Title 48, Territories and Insular Possessions.

Termination of United States District Court for the District of the Canal Zone

For termination of the United States District Court for the District of the Canal Zone at end of the "transition period", being the 30–month period beginning Oct. 1, 1979, and ending midnight Mar. 31, 1982, see Paragraph 5 of Article XI of the Panama Canal Treaty of 1977 and sections 3831 and 3841 to 3843 of Title 22, Foreign Relations and Intercourse.

§ 611. Retirement of Director

(a) The Director may, by written election filed with the Chief Justice of the United States within 6 months after the date on which he takes office, waive coverage under chapter 83 of title 5, subchapter III (the Civil Service Retirement System) or chapter 84 of title 5 (the Federal Employees' Retirement System), whichever is applicable, and bring himself within the purview of this section. A Director who elects coverage under this section shall be deemed an "employee" for purposes of chapter 84 of title 5, subchapter III, regardless of whether he has waived the coverage of chapter 83, subchapter III, or chapter 84. Waiver of coverage under chapter 83, subchapter III, and election of this section shall not operate to foreclose to the Director, upon separation from service other than by retirement, such opportunity as the law may provide to secure retirement credit under chapter 83 for service as Director by depositing with interest the amount required by section 8334 of title 5. A Director who waives coverage under chapter 84 and elects this section may secure retirement credit under chapter 84 for service as Director by depositing with interest 1.3 percent of basic pay for service from January 1, 1984, through December 31, 1986, and the amount referred to in section 8422(a) of title 5, for service after December 31, 1986. Interest shall be computed under section 8334(e) of title 5.

(b) Upon the retirement of a Director who has elected coverage under this section and who has at least fifteen years of service and has attained the age of sixty-five years the Administrative Office of the United States Courts shall pay him an annuity for life equal to 80 per centum of the salary of the office at the time of his retirement.

Upon the retirement of a Director who has elected coverage under this section and who has at least ten years of service, but who is not eligible to receive an annuity under the first paragraph of this subsection, the Administrative Office of the United States Courts shall pay him an annuity for life equal to that proportion of 80 per centum of the salary of the office at the time of his retirement that the number of years of his service bears to fifteen, reduced by one-quarter of 1 per centum for each full month, if any, he is under the age of sixty-five at the time of separation from service.

(c) A Director who has elected coverage under this section and who becomes permanently disabled to perform the duties of his office shall be retired and shall receive an annuity for life equal to 80 per centum of the salary of the office at the time of his retirement if he has at least fifteen years of service, or equal to that proportion of 80 percentum of such salary that the aggregate number of years of his service bears to fifteen if he has less than fifteen years of service, but in no event less than 50 per centum of such salary.

(d) For the purpose of this section, "service" means service, whether or not continuous, as Director of the Administrative Office of the United States Courts, and any service, not to exceed five years, as a judge of the United States, a Senator or Representative in Congress, a congressional employee in the capacity of primary administrative assistant to a Member of Congress or in the capacity of staff director or chief counsel for the majority or the minority of a committee or subcommittee of the Senate or House of Representatives, or a civilian official appointed by the President, by and with the advice and consent of the Senate.

(e) Each annuity payable under this section shall be increased by the same percentage amount and effective on the same date as annuities payable under chapter 83 of title 5, are increased as provided by section 8340 of title 5.

(Added Pub.L. 90–219, Title II, § 201(a), Dec. 20, 1967, 81 Stat. 668, and amended Pub.L. 100–702, Title X, §§ 1004(a), 1006(a)(1), Nov. 19, 1988, 102 Stat. 4665, 4666; Pub.L. 106–518, Title III, § 301(a), Nov. 13, 2000, 114 Stat. 2416.)

HISTORICAL AND STATUTORY NOTES

Effective and Applicability Provisions

1988 Acts. Section 1004(b) of Title X of Pub.L. 100–702 provided that: "The amendments made by this section [amending this section and section 627 of this title] shall apply to cost-of-living increases that go into effect on or after the date of enactment of this title [Nov. 19, 1988] with respect to any annuity being paid or becoming payable on or after such date."

Section 1006(b) of Pub.L. 100–702 provided that: "The amendments made by this section [amending this section and section 627 of this title] shall apply to persons holding the offices of Director of the Administrative Office of the United States Courts, Director of the Federal Judicial Center, and Administrative Assistant to the Chief Justice on the date of enactment of this title [Nov. 19, 1988]."

Retroactive Effect

Section 205 of Pub.L. 90–219 provided that:

"**(a)** Except as provided in subsection (b), the amendments made by this title [enacting this section and amending sections 376 and 604 of this title], insofar as they relate to retirement and survivorship benefits of the Director of the Administrative Office of the United States Courts, shall be applicable only with respect to persons first appointed to such office after the date of enactment of this Act [Dec. 20, 1967].

"**(b)** The provisions of section 611(a), the first paragraph of section 611(b), and section 376(s), of title 28, United States Code, as added by such amendments [subsecs. (a) and (b) of this section, and section 376(s) of this title], shall be applicable to a Director or former Director of the Administrative Office of the United States Courts who was first appointed prior to the date of enactment of this Act [Dec. 20, 1967] if at the time such Director or former Director left or leaves such office he had, or shall have, attained the age of sixty-five years and completed fifteen years of service as Director of the Administrative Office of the United States Courts and if, on or before the expiration of six months following the date of enactment of this Act [Dec. 20, 1967], he makes the election referred to in section 611(a) or section 376(s) [subsec. (a) of this section or section 376(s) of this title], or both, as the case may be."

§ 612. Judiciary Information Technology Fund

(a) Establishment and availability of Fund.—There is hereby established in the Treasury of the United States a special fund to be known as the

"Judiciary Information Technology Fund" (hereafter in this section referred to as the "Fund"). Moneys in the Fund shall be available to the Director without fiscal year limitation for the procurement (by lease, purchase, exchange, transfer, or otherwise) of information technology resources for program activities included in the courts of appeals, district courts, and other judicial services account of the judicial branch of the United States. The Fund shall also be available for expenses, including personal services, support personnel in the courts and in the Administrative Office of the United States Courts, and other costs, for the effective management, coordination, operation, and use of information technology resources purchased by the Fund. In addition, all agencies of the judiciary may make deposits into the Fund to meet their information technology needs in accordance with subsections (b) and (c)(2).

(b) Plan for meeting information technology needs.—

(1) Development of plan.—The Director shall develop and annually revise, with the approval of the Judicial Conference of the United States, a long range plan for meeting the information technology resources needs of the activities funded under subsection (a) and shall include an annual estimate of any fees that may be collected under section 404 of the Judiciary Appropriations Act, 1991 (Public Law 101–515; 104 Stat. 2133). Such plan and revisions shall be submitted to Congress.

(2) Expenditures consistent with plan.—The Director may use amounts in the Fund to procure information technology resources for the activities funded under subsection (a) only in accordance with the plan developed under paragraph (1).

(c) Deposits into Fund.—

(1) Deposits.—There shall be deposited in the Fund—

(A) all proceeds resulting from activities conducted under subsection (a), including net proceeds of disposal of excess or surplus property, all fees collected after the date of the enactment of the Judicial Amendments Act of 1994 by the judiciary under section 404 of the Judiciary Appropriations Act, 1991 (Public Law 101–515; 104 Stat. 2133) and receipts from carriers and others for loss of or damage to property;

(B) amounts available for activities described in subsection (a) from funds appropriated to the judiciary; and

(C) any advances and reimbursements required by paragraph (2).

(2) Advances and reimbursements.—Whenever the Director procures information technology resources for any entity in the judicial branch other than the courts or the Administrative Office, that entity shall advance or reimburse the Fund, whichever the Director considers appropriate, for the costs of the information technology resources, from appropriations available to that entity.

(d) Authorization of appropriations.—There are authorized to be appropriated to the Fund for any fiscal year such sums as are required to supplement amounts deposited under subsection (c) in order to conduct activities under subsection (a).

(e) Contract authority.—

(1) For each fiscal year.—In fiscal year 1990, and in each succeeding fiscal year, the Director may enter into contracts for the procurement of information technology resources in amounts which, in the aggregate, do not exceed amounts estimated to be collected under subsection (c) for that fiscal year in advance of the availability of amounts in the Fund for such contracts.

(2) Multiyear contracts.—In conducting activities under subsection (a), the Director is authorized to enter into multiyear contracts for information technology resources for periods of not more than five years for any contract, if—

(A) funds are available and adequate for payment of the costs of such contract for the first fiscal year and for payment of any costs of cancellation or termination of the contract;

(B) such contract is in accordance with the Director's authority in section 604(g) of 28 U.S.C.; and,[1]

(C) the Director determines that—

(i) the need for the information technology resources being provided will continue over the period of the contract; and

(ii) the use of the multi-year contract will yield substantial cost savings when compared with other methods of providing the necessary resources.

(3) Cancellation costs of multiyear contract.—Any cancellation costs incurred with respect to a contract entered into under paragraph (2) shall be paid from currently available amounts in the Fund.

(f) Authority of Administrator of General Services.—Nothing in this section shall be construed to limit the authority of the Administrator of General Services under sections 501–505 of title 40.

(g) Annual report.—

(1) In general.—The Director shall submit to the Congress an annual report on the operation of the Fund, including on the inventory, use, and acquisition of information technology resources from the Fund and the consistency of such acquisition with the plan prepared under subsection (b). The report shall set forth the amounts deposited into the Fund under subsection (c).

(2) Additional contents of report.—The annual report submitted under this subsection shall include—

(A) the specific actions taken and the progress made to improve the plan developed under subsection (b) and the long range automation plan and strategic business plan developed under subsection (k); and

(B) a comparison of planned Fund expenditures and accomplishments with actual Fund expenditures and accomplishments, and the reasons for any delays in scheduled systems development, or budget overruns.

(h) Reprogramming.—The Director of the Administrative Office of the United States Courts, under the supervision of the Judicial Conference of the United States, may transfer amounts up to $1,000,000 from the Fund into the account to which the funds were originally appropriated. Any amounts transferred from the Fund in excess of $1,000,000 in any fiscal year may only be transferred by following reprogramming procedures in compliance with section 606 of the Departments of Commerce, Justice, and State, the Judiciary, and Related Agencies Appropriations Act, 1989 (Public Law 100–459; 102 Stat. 2227).

(i) Appropriations into the Fund.—If the budget request of the judiciary is appropriated in full, the amount deposited into the Fund during any fiscal year under the authority of subsection (c)(1)(B) will be the same as the amount of funds requested by the judiciary for activities described in subsection (a). If an amount to be deposited is not specified in statute by Congress and if the full request is not appropriated, the amount to be deposited under subsection (c)(1)(B) will be set by the spending priorities established by the Judicial Conference.

(j) Long range management and business plans.—The Director of the Administrative Office of the United States Court shall—

(1) develop an overall strategic business plan which would identify the judiciary's missions, goals, and objectives;

(2) develop a long range automation plan based on the strategic business plan and user needs assessments;

(3) establish effective Administrative Office oversight of court automation efforts to ensure the effective operation of existing systems and control over developments of future systems;

(4) expedite efforts to complete the development and implementation of life cycle management standards;

(5) utilize the standards in developing the next generation of case management and financial systems; and

(6) assess the current utilization and future user requirements of the data communications network.

(Added Pub.L. 101–162, Title IV, § 404(b)(1), Nov. 21, 1989, 103 Stat. 1013, and amended Pub.L. 103–420, § 2, Oct. 25, 1994, 108 Stat. 4343; Pub.L. 104–106, Div. E, Title LVI, § 5602, Feb. 10, 1996, 110 Stat. 699; Pub.L. 104–208, Div. A, Title I, §§ 101(a) [Title III, § 305], 101(f) [Title VIII, § 808(c)], Sept. 30, 1996, 110 Stat. 3009–45, 3009–394; Pub.L. 105–85, Div. A, Title X, § 1073(h)(2), Nov. 18, 1997, 111 Stat. 1907; Pub.L. 105–119, Title III, § 304, Nov. 26, 1997, 111 Stat. 2491; Pub.L. 106–518, Title I, § 101, Nov. 13, 2000, 114 Stat. 2411; Pub.L. 107–217, § 3(g)(2), Aug. 21, 2002, 116 Stat. 1299; Pub.L. 109–115, Div. A, Title IV, § 407(b), Nov. 30, 2005, 119 Stat. 2471.)

[1] So in original. The comma probably should not appear.

HISTORICAL AND STATUTORY NOTES

References in Text

"Section 404 of the Judiciary Appropriations Act, 1991 (Public Law 101–515; 104 Stat. 2133)", referred to in subsecs. (b)(1) and (c)(1)(A), is Pub.L. 101–515, Title IV, § 404, Nov. 5, 1990, 104 Stat. 2132, which was formerly set out as a note under 28 U.S.C.A. § 913.

The date of the enactment of the Judicial Amendments Act of 1994, referred to in subsec. (c)(1)(A), is the date of enactment of Pub.L. 103–420, 108 Stat. 4343, which was approved Oct. 25, 1994.

Section 606 of the Departments of Commerce, Justice, and State, the Judiciary, and Related Agencies Appropriations Act, 1989 (Public Law 100–459, 108 Stat. 2227), referred to in subsec. (h), is Pub.L. 100–459, Title VI, § 606, Oct. 1, 1988, 102 Stat. 2227, which is not classified to the Code.

Effective and Applicability Provisions

1996 Acts. Amendment by section 5602 of Pub.L. 104–106 effective 180 days after Feb. 10, 1996, see section 5701 of Pub.L. 104–106, set out as a note under 40 U.S.C.A. § 1401.

Termination of Authority

Authority granted by Pub.L. 109–115, § 407, which amended subsec. (e)(2)(B) of this section, expires on Sept. 30, 2010, see Pub.L. 109–115, § 407(c), set out as a note under 28 U.S.C.A. § 604.

Termination of Reporting Requirements

For termination, effective May 15, 2000, of provisions of law requiring submittal to Congress of any annual, semiannual, or other regular periodic report listed in House Document No. 103–7 (in which a report required under subsec. (g) of this section is listed on page 143), see Pub.L. 104–66, § 3003, as amended, set out as a note under 31 U.S.C.A. § 1113.

Coordination with Other Amendments

Amendments by section 1073 of Pub.L. 105–85 to be treated as having been enacted immediately before the other provisions of Pub.L. 105–85, see section 1073(i) of Pub.L. 105–85, set out as a note under section 5315 of Title 5, Government Organization and Employees.

§ 613. Disbursing and certifying officers

(a) Disbursing officers.—The Director may designate in writing officers and employees of the judicial branch of the Government, including the courts as defined in section 610 other than the Supreme Court, to be disbursing officers in such numbers and locations as the Director considers necessary. Such disbursing officers shall—

(1) disburse moneys appropriated to the judicial branch and other funds only in strict accordance with payment requests certified by the Director or in accordance with subsection (b);

(2) examine payment requests as necessary to ascertain whether they are in proper form, certified, and approved; and

(3) be held accountable for their actions as provided by law, except that such a disbursing officer shall not be held accountable or responsible for any illegal, improper, or incorrect payment resulting from any false, inaccurate, or misleading certificate for which a certifying officer is responsible under subsection (b).

(b) Certifying officers.—

(1) In general.—The Director may designate in writing officers and employees of the judicial branch of the Government, including the courts as defined in section 610 other than the Supreme Court, to certify payment requests payable from appropriations and funds. Such certifying officers shall be responsible and accountable for—

(A) the existence and correctness of the facts recited in the certificate or other request for payment or its supporting papers;

(B) the legality of the proposed payment under the appropriation or fund involved; and

(C) the correctness of the computations of certified payment requests.

(2) Liability.—The liability of a certifying officer shall be enforced in the same manner and to the same extent as provided by law with respect to the enforcement of the liability of disbursing and other accountable officers. A certifying officer shall be required to make restitution to the United States for the amount of any illegal, improper, or incorrect payment resulting from any false, inaccurate, or misleading certificates made by the certifying officer, as well as for any payment prohibited by law or which did not represent a legal obligation under the appropriation or fund involved.

(c) Rights.—A certifying or disbursing officer—

(1) has the right to apply for and obtain a decision by the Comptroller General on any question of law involved in a payment request presented for certification; and

(2) is entitled to relief from liability arising under this section in accordance with title 31.

(d) Other authority not affected.—Nothing in this section affects the authority of the courts with respect to moneys deposited with the courts under chapter 129 of this title.

(Added Pub.L. 106–518, Title III, § 304(a), Nov. 13, 2000, 114 Stat. 2417.)

HISTORICAL AND STATUTORY NOTES

References in Text

Chapter 129 of this title, referred to in subsec. (d), is 28 U.S.C.A. § 2041 et seq.

Designation of Disbursing and Certifying Officers

Pub.L. 106–553, § 1(a)(2) [Title III, § 304], Dec. 21, 2000, 114 Stat. 2762, 2762A–83, provided that:

"**(a)** The Director of the Administrative Office of the United States Courts (the Director) may designate in writing officers and employees of the judicial branch of the United States Government, including the courts as defined in section 610 of title 28, United States Code, but excluding the Supreme Court, to be disbursing officers in such numbers and locations as the Director considers necessary. These disbursing officers will: (1) disburse moneys appropriated to the judicial branch and other funds only in strict accordance with payment requests certified by the Director or in accordance with subsection (b) of this section; (2) examine payment requests as necessary to ascertain whether they are in proper form, certified, and approved; and (3) be held accountable as provided by law. However, a disbursing officer will not be held accountable or responsible for any illegal, improper, or incorrect payment resulting from any false, inaccurate, or misleading certificate for which a certifying officer is responsible under subsection (b) of this section.

"**(b)(1)** The Director may designate in writing officers and employees of the judicial branch of the United States Government, including the courts as defined in section 610 of title 28, United States Code, but excluding the Supreme Court, to certify payment requests payable from appropriations and funds. These certifying officers will be responsible and accountable for: (A) the existence and correctness of the facts recited in the certificate or other request for payment or its supporting papers; (B) the legality of the proposed payment under the appropriation or fund involved; and (C) the correctness of the computations of certified payment requests.

"**(2)** The liability of a certifying officer will be enforced in the same manner and to the same extent as provided by law with respect to the enforcement of the liability of disbursing and other accountable officers. A certifying officer shall be required to make restitution to the United States for the amount of any illegal, improper, or incorrect payment resulting from any false, inaccurate, or misleading certificates made by the certifying officer, as well as for any payment prohibited by law or which did not represent a legal obligation under the appropriation or fund involved.

"**(c)** A certifying or disbursing officer: (1) has the right to apply for and obtain a decision by the Comptroller General on any question of law involved in a payment request presented for certification; and (2) is entitled to relief from liability arising under this section as provided by law.

"**(d)** The Director shall disburse, directly or through officials designated pursuant to this section, appropriations and other funds for the maintenance and operation of the courts.

"(e) Nothing in this section affects the authority of the courts to receive or disburse moneys in accordance with chapter 129 of title 28, United States Code [28 U.S.C.A. § 2041 et seq.].

"(f) This section shall be effective for fiscal year 2001 and hereafter."

Rule of Construction

Pub.L. 106–518, § 304(c), Nov. 13, 2000, 114 Stat. 2418, provided that: "The amendment made by subsection (a) [enacting this section] shall not be construed to authorize the hiring of any Federal officer or employee."

CHAPTER 42—FEDERAL JUDICIAL CENTER

Sec.
620. Federal Judicial Center.
621. Board; composition, tenure of members, compensation.
622. Meetings; conduct of business.
623. Duties of the Board.
624. Powers of the Board.
625. Director and staff.
626. Compensation of the Director and Deputy Director.
627. Retirement; employee benefits.
628. Appropriations and accounting.
629. Federal Judicial Center Foundation.

§ 620. Federal Judicial Center

(a) There is established within the judicial branch of the Government a Federal Judicial Center, whose purpose it shall be to further the development and adoption of improved judicial administration in the courts of the United States.

(b) The Center shall have the following functions:

(1) to conduct research and study of the operation of the courts of the United States, and to stimulate and coordinate such research and study on the part of other public and private persons and agencies;

(2) to develop and present for consideration by the Judicial Conference of the United States recommendations for improvement of the administration and management of the courts of the United States;

(3) to stimulate, create, develop, and conduct programs of continuing education and training for personnel of the judicial branch of the Government and other persons whose participation in such programs would improve the operation of the judicial branch, including, but not limited to, judges, United States magistrate judges, clerks of court, probation officers, and persons serving as mediators and arbitrators;

(4) insofar as may be consistent with the performance of the other functions set forth in this section, to provide staff, research, and planning assistance to the Judicial Conference of the United States and its committees;

(5) Insofar[1] as may be consistent with the performance of the other functions set forth in this section, to cooperate with the State Justice Institute in the establishment and coordination of research and programs concerning the administration of justice; and

(6) insofar as may be consistent with the performance of the other functions set forth in this section, to cooperate with and assist agencies of the Federal Government and other appropriate organizations in providing information and advice to further improvement in the administration of justice in the courts of foreign countries and to acquire information about judicial administration in foreign countries that may contribute to performing the other functions set forth in this section.

(Added Pub.L. 90–219, Title I, § 101, Dec. 20, 1967, 81 Stat. 664, and amended Pub.L. 95–598, Title II, § 227, Nov. 6, 1978, 92 Stat. 2665; Pub.L. 98–620, Title II, § 214, Nov. 8, 1984, 98 Stat. 3346; Pub.L. 99–336, § 6(b), June 19, 1986, 100 Stat. 639; Pub.L. 100–702, Title III, § 303, Nov. 19, 1988, 102 Stat. 4648; Pub.L. 101–650, Title III, § 321, Dec. 1, 1990, 104 Stat. 5117; Pub.L. 102–572, Title VI, § 602(a), Oct. 29, 1992, 106 Stat. 4514.)

[1] So in original. Probably should not be capitalized.

HISTORICAL AND STATUTORY NOTES

Codifications

Subsec. (b)(3) of this section was amended by Pub.L. 95–598, Title II, § 227, Nov. 6, 1978, 92 Stat. 2665, effective June 28, 1984, pursuant to Pub.L. 95–598, Title IV, § 402(b), Nov. 6, 1978, 92 Stat. 2682, as amended by Pub.L. 98–249, § 1(a), Mar. 31, 1984, 98 Stat. 116; Pub.L. 98–271, § 1(a), Apr. 30, 1984, 98 Stat. 163; Pub.L. 98–299, § 1(a), May 25, 1984, 98 Stat. 214; Pub.L. 98–325, § 1(a), June 20, 1984, 98 Stat. 268, set out as an Effective Date note preceding section 101 of Title 11, Bankruptcy, by substituting "magistrates" for "commissioners" and striking out "referees" following "judges,".

Section 402(b) of Pub.L. 95–598 was amended by section 113 of Pub.L. 98–353, Title I, July 10, 1984, 98 Stat. 343, by substituting "shall not be effective" for "shall take effect on June 28, 1984", thereby eliminating the amendment by section 227 of Pub.L. 95–598, effective June 27, 1984, pursuant to section 122(c) of Pub.L. 98–353, set out as an Effective Date note under section 151 of this title.

Section 121(a) of Pub.L. 98–353 directed that section 402(b) of Pub.L. 95–598 be amended by substituting "the date of enactment of the Bankruptcy Amendments and Federal Judgeship Act of 1984 [i.e. July 10, 1984]" for "June 28, 1984". This amendment was not executed in view of the prior amendment to section 402(b) of Pub.L. 95–598 by section 113 of Pub.L. 98–353.

Effective and Applicability Provisions

1992 Acts. Amendment by Pub.L. 102–572 effective Jan. 1, 1993, see section 1101(a) of Pub.L. 102–572, set out as a note under section 905 of Title 2, The Congress.

1986 Acts. Section 6(c) of Pub.L. 99–336 provided that: "The amendments made by this section [amending this section and section 288d of Title 2, The Congress, and redesignating former section 1364, set out second, and former section 1364, set out third, as sections 1365 and 1366 of this title, respectively] shall take effect on the date of the enactment of this Act [June 19, 1986]."

1984 Acts. Amendment by Pub.L. 98–620 to take effect Oct. 1, 1985, see section 216 of Pub.L. 98–620, set out as a note under section 10701 of Title 42, The Public Health and Welfare.

Change of Name

"United States magistrate judge" substituted for "United States magistrate" in text pursuant to section 321 of Pub.L. 101–650, set out as a note under 28 U.S.C.A. § 631.

Study of Intercircuit Conflicts and Structural Alternatives For Courts of Appeals by Federal Judicial Center

Pub.L. 101–650, Title III, § 302, Dec. 1, 1990, 104 Stat. 5104, as amended Pub.L. 102–572, Title V, § 502(c), Oct. 29, 1992, 106 Stat. 4513, provided that:

"**(a) Intercircuit conflicts.**—The Board of the Federal Judicial Center is requested to conduct a study and submit to the Congress a report by January 1, 1992, on the number and frequency of conflicts among the judicial circuits in interpreting the law that remain unresolved because they are not heard by the Supreme Court.

"**(b) Factors to consider in study.**—In conducting such a study, the Center should consider, to the extent feasible, all relevant factors, such as whether the conflict—

"(1) imposes economic costs or other harm on persons engaging in interstate commerce;

"(2) encourages forum shopping among circuits;

"(3) creates unfairness to litigants in different circuits, as in allowing Federal benefits in one circuit that are denied in other circuits; or

"(4) encourages nonacquiescence by Federal agencies in the holdings of the courts of appeals for different circuits, "but is unlikely to be resolved by the Supreme Court.

"**(c) Structural alternatives for the Courts of Appeals.**—The Board of the Federal Judicial Center is requested to study the full range of structural alternatives for the Federal Courts of Appeals and submit a report on the study to the Congress and the Judicial Conference of the United States, no later than 2 years and 9 months after the date of the enactment of this Act [Dec. 1, 1990]."

[For termination, effective May 15, 2000, of reporting provisions of Pub.L. 101–650, § 302(a), (c), set out above, see Pub.L. 104–66, § 3003, as amended, set out as a note under 31 U.S.C.A. § 1113, and the 9th and 10th items on page 12 of House Document No. 103–7.]

§ 621. Board; composition, tenure of members, compensation

(a) The activities of the Center shall be supervised by a Board to be composed of—

(1) the Chief Justice of the United States, who shall be the permanent Chairman of the Board;

(2) two circuit judges, three district judges, one bankruptcy judge, and one magistrate judge, elected by vote of the members of the Judicial Conference of the United States, except that any circuit or district judge so elected may be either a judge in regular active service or a judge retired from regular active service under section 371(b) of this title but shall not be a member of the Judicial Conference of the United States; and

(3) the Director of the Administrative Office of the United States Courts, who shall be a permanent member of the Board.

(b) The term of office of each elected member of the Board shall be four years. A member elected to serve for an unexpired term arising by virtue of the death, disability, retirement pursuant to section 371(a) or section 372(a) of this title, or resignation of a member shall be elected only for such unexpired term.

(c) No member elected for a four-year term shall be eligible for reelection to the Board.

(d) Members of the Board shall serve without additional compensation, but shall be reimbursed for actual and necessary expenses incurred in the performance of their official duties.

(Added Pub.L. 90–219, Title I, § 101, Dec. 20, 1967, 81 Stat. 664, and amended Pub.L. 95–598, Title II, §§ 228, 229, Nov. 6, 1978, 92 Stat. 2665; Pub.L. 104–317, Title VI, § 601(b), Oct. 19, 1996, 110 Stat. 3857.)

HISTORICAL AND STATUTORY NOTES

Effective and Applicability Provisions

1978 Acts. Amendment by Pub.L. 95–598 effective Oct. 1, 1979, see section 402(c) of Pub.L. 95–598, set out as a note preceding section 101 of Title 11, Bankruptcy.

§ 622. Meetings; conduct of business

(a) Regular meetings of the Board shall be held quarterly. Special meetings shall be held from time to time upon the call of the Chairman, acting at his own discretion or pursuant to the petition of any four members.

(b) Each member of the Board shall be entitled to one vote. A simple majority of the membership shall constitute a quorum for the conduct of business. The Board shall act upon the concurrence of a simple majority of the members present and voting.

(Added Pub.L. 90–219, Title I, § 101, Dec. 20, 1967, 81 Stat. 665.)

§ 623. Duties of the Board

(a) In its direction and supervision of the activities of the Federal Judicial Center, the Board shall—

(1) establish such policies and develop such programs for the Federal Judicial Center as will further achievement of its purpose and performance of its functions;

(2) formulate recommendations for improvements in the administration of the courts of the United States, in the training of the personnel of those courts, and in the management of their resources;

(3) submit to the Judicial Conference of the United States, at least one month in advance of its annual meeting, a report of the activities of the Center and such recommendations as the Board may propose for the consideration of the Conference;

(4) present to other government departments, agencies, and instrumentalities whose programs or activities relate to the administration of justice in the courts of the United States the recommendations of the Center for the improvement of such programs or activities;

(5) study and determine ways in which automatic data processing and systems procedures may be applied to the administration of the courts of the United States, and include in the annual report required by paragraph (3) of this subsection details of the results of the studies and determinations made pursuant to this paragraph;

(6) consider and recommend to both public and private agencies aspects of the operation of the courts of the United States deemed worthy of special study; and

(7) conduct, coordinate, and encourage programs relating to the history of the judicial branch of the United States Government.

(b) The Board shall transmit to Congress and to the Attorney General of the United States copies of all reports and recommendations submitted to the Judicial Conference of the United States. The Board shall also keep the Committees on the Judiciary of the United States Senate and House of Representatives fully and currently informed with respect to the activities of the Center.

(Added Pub.L. 90–219, Title I, § 101, Dec. 20, 1967, 81 Stat. 665, and amended Pub.L. 100–702, Title III, § 302, Nov. 19, 1988, 102 Stat. 4648.)

HISTORICAL AND STATUTORY NOTES

Termination of Reporting Requirements

For termination, effective May 15, 2000, of provisions in subsec. (b) of this section relating to requirement that the Board transmit to Congress copies of all reports and recommendations submitted to the Judicial Conference of the United States, see Pub.L. 104–66, § 3003, as amended, set out as a note under 31 U.S.C.A. § 1113, and page 12 of House Document No. 103–7.

§ 624. Powers of the Board

The Board is authorized—

(1) to appoint and fix the duties of the Director and the Deputy Director of the Federal Judicial Center, who shall serve at the pleasure of the Board;

(2) to request from any department, agency, or independent instrumentality of the Government any information it deems necessary to the performance of the functions of the Federal Judicial Center set forth in this chapter, and each such department, agency, or instrumentality is directed to cooperate with the Board and, to the extent permitted by law, to furnish such information to the Center upon request of the Chairman or upon request of the Director when the Board has delegated this authority to him;

(3) to contract with and compensate government and private agencies or persons for research projects and other services, without regard to section 3709 of the Revised Statutes, as amended (41 U.S.C. 5), and to delegate such contract authority to the Director of the Federal Judicial Center, who is hereby empowered to exercise such delegated authority.

(Added Pub.L. 90–219, Title I, § 101, Dec. 20, 1967, 81 Stat. 666, and amended Pub.L. 100–702, Title III, § 304(a), Nov. 19, 1988, 102 Stat. 4648.)

§ 625. Director and staff

(a) The Director shall supervise the activities of persons employed by the Center and perform other duties assigned to him by the Board.

(b) The Director shall appoint and fix the compensation of such additional professional personnel as the Board may deem necessary, without regard to the provisions of title 5, United States Code, governing appointments in competitive service, or the provisions of chapter 51 and subchapter III of chapter 53 of such title, relating to classification and General Schedule pay rates: *Provided, however*, That the compensation of any person appointed under this subsection shall not exceed the annual rate of basic pay of level V of the Executive Schedule pay rates, section 5316, title 5, United States Code: *And provided further*, That the salary of a reemployed annuitant under the Civil Servive [1] Retirement Act shall be adjusted pursuant to the provisions of section 8344, title 5, United States Code.

(c) The Director shall appoint and fix the compensation of such secretarial and clerical personnel as he may deem necessary, subject to the provisions of title 5, United States Code, governing appointments in competitive service without regard to the provisions of chapter 51 and subchapter III of chapter 53 of such title, relating to classification and General Schedule pay rates.

(d) The Director may procure personal services as authorized by section 3109 of title 5, United States Code, at rates not to exceed the daily equivalent of the highest rate payable under General Schedule pay rates, section 5332, title 5, United States Code.

(e) The Director is authorized to incur necessary travel and other miscellaneous expenses incident to the operation of the Center.

(Added Pub.L. 90–219, Title I, § 101, Dec. 20, 1967, 81 Stat. 666, and amended Pub.L. 102–572, Title VI, § 602(b), Oct. 29, 1992, 106 Stat. 4514.)

[1] So in original. Probably should be "Service".

HISTORICAL AND STATUTORY NOTES

References in Text

The General Schedule, referred to in subsec. (b), is set out under section 5332 of Title 5, Government Organization and Employees.

The Civil Service Retirement Act, referred to in subsec. (b), is Act May 29, 1930, c. 349, 46 Stat. 468, as amended by Act July 31, 1956, c. 804, § 401, 70 Stat. 743, which was repealed by Pub.L. 89–554, § 8(a), Sept. 6, 1966, 80 Stat. 632, and reenacted by the first section thereof as subchapter III (section 8331 et seq.) of chapter 83 of Title 5.

References in Other Laws to GS–16, 17, or 18 Pay Rates

References in laws to the rates of pay for GS–16, 17, or 18, or to maximum rates of pay under the General Schedule, to be considered references to rates payable under specified sections of Title 5, Government Organization and Employees, see section 529 [Title I, § 101(c)(1)] of Pub.L. 101–509, set out in a note under section 5376 of Title 5.

Effective and Applicability Provisions

1992 Acts. Amendment by Pub.L. 102–572 effective Jan. 1, 1993, see section 1101 of Pub.L. 102–572, set out as a note under section 905 of Title 2, The Congress.

§ 626. Compensation of the Director and Deputy Director

The compensation of the Director of the Federal Judicial Center shall be the same as that of the Director of the Administrative Office of the United States Courts, and his appointment and salary shall not be subject to the provisions of title 5, United States Code, governing appointments in competitive service, or the provisions of chapter 51 and subchapter III of chapter 53 of such title, relating to classification and General Schedule pay rates: *Provided, however,* That any Director who is a justice or judge of the United States in active or retired status shall serve without additional compensation. The compensation of the Deputy Director of the Federal Judicial Center shall be the same as that of the Deputy Director of the Administrative Office of the United States Courts.

(Added Pub.L. 90–219, Title I, § 101, Dec. 20, 1967, 81 Stat. 666, and amended Pub.L. 100–702, Title III, § 304(b)(1), Nov. 19, 1988, 102 Stat. 4648.)

HISTORICAL AND STATUTORY NOTES

References in Text

The General Schedule, referred to in text, is set out under section 5332 of Title 5, Government Organization and Employees.

Effective and Applicability Provisions

1988 Acts. Section 304(c) of Pub.L. 100–702 provided that: "The amendment made by subsection (b) [amending this section] shall be effective for fiscal years beginning on or after October 1, 1988."

§ 627. Retirement; employee benefits

(a) The Director, Deputy Director, the professional staff, and the clerical and secretarial employees of the Federal Judicial Center shall be deemed to be officers and employees of the judicial branch of the United States Government within the meaning of subchapter III of chapter 83 (relating to civil service retirement), chapter 84 (relating to the Federal Employees' Retirement System), chapter 87 (relating to Federal employees' life insurance program), and chapter 89 (relating to Federal employees' health benefits program) of title 5, United States Code: *Provided, however,* That the Director, upon written notice filed with the Director of the Administrative Office of the United States Courts within 6 months after the date on which he takes office, may waive coverage under chapter 83 of title 5, subchapter III (the Civil Service Retirement System) or chapter 84 of title 5 (the Federal Employees' Retirement System), whichever is applicable, and elect coverage under the retirement and disability provisions of this section. A Director who elects coverage under this section shall be deemed an "employee" for purposes of chapter 84 of title 5, subchapter III, regardless of whether he has waived the coverage of chapter 83, subchapter III, or chapter 84: *And provided further,* That upon his nonretirement separation from the Federal Judicial Center, waiver of coverage under chapter 83, subchapter III, and election of this section shall not operate to foreclose to the Director such opportunity as the law may provide to secure retirement credit under chapter 83 for service as Director by depositing with interest the amount required by section 8334 of title 5. A Director who waives coverage under chapter 84 and elects this section may secure retirement credit under chapter 84 for service as Director by depositing with interest 1.3 percent of basic pay for service from January 1, 1984, through December 31, 1986, and the amount referred to in section 8422(a) of title 5, for service after December 31, 1986. Interest shall be computed under section 8334(e) of title 5.

(b) Upon the retirement of a Director who has elected coverage under this section and who has at least fifteen years of service and has attained the age of sixty-five years the Director of the Administrative Office of the United States Courts shall pay him an annuity for life equal to 80 per centum of the salary of the office at the time of his retirement.

Upon the retirement of a Director who has elected coverage under this section and who has at least ten years of service, but who is not eligible to receive an annuity under the first paragraph of this subsection, the Administrative Office of the United States Courts shall pay him an annuity for life equal to that proportion of 80 per centum of the salary of the office at the time of his retirement that the number of years of his service bears to fifteen, reduced by one-quarter of 1 per centum for each full month, if any, he is under the age of sixty-five at the time of separation from service.

(c) A Director who has elected coverage under this section and who becomes permanently disabled to perform the duties of his office shall be retired and shall receive an annuity for life equal to 80 per centum of the salary of the office at the time of his retirement if he has at least fifteen years of service, or equal to that proportion of 80 per centum of such salary that the aggregate number of years of his service bears to fifteen if he has less than fifteen years of service, but in no event less than 50 per centum of such salary.

(d) For the purpose of this section, "service" means service, whether or not continuous, as Director of the Federal Judicial Center, and any service, not to exceed five years, as a judge of the United States, a Senator or Representative in Congress, a congressional employee in the capacity of primary administrative assistant to a Member of Congress or in the capacity of staff director or chief counsel for the majority or the minority of a committee or subcommittee of the Senate or House of Representatives, or a civilian official appointed by the President, by and with the advice and consent of the Senate.

(e) Each annuity payable under this section shall be increased by the same percentage amount and effective on the same date as annuities payable under chapter 83 of title 5, are increased as provided by section 8340 of title 5.

(Added Pub.L. 90–219, Title I, § 101, Dec. 20, 1967, 81 Stat. 666, and amended Pub.L. 100–702, Title X, §§ 1004(a), 1006(a)(2), Nov. 19, 1988, 102 Stat. 4665, 4666; Pub.L. 104–317, Title VI, § 604, Oct. 19, 1996, 110 Stat. 3857; Pub.L. 106–518, Title III, §§ 301(b), 312(a), Nov. 13, 2000, 114 Stat. 2416, 2421.)

HISTORICAL AND STATUTORY NOTES

Effective and Applicability Provisions

1988 Acts. Amendment by section 1004(a) of Pub.L. 100–702 applicable to cost-of-living increases that go into effect on or after Nov. 19, 1988, with respect to any annuity being paid or becoming payable on or after such date, see section 1004(b) of Pub.L. 100–702, set out as a note under section 611 of this title.

Amendment by section 1006(a)(2) of Pub.L. 100–702 applicable to persons holding the offices of Director of the Administrative Office of the United States Courts, Director of the Federal Judicial Center, and Administrative Assistant to the Chief Justice on Nov. 19, 1988, see section 1006(b) of Pub.L. 100–702, set out as a note under section 611 of this title.

§ 628. Appropriations and accounting

There are hereby authorized to be appropriated such sums as may be necessary to carry out the provisions of this chapter. The Administrative Office of the United States Courts shall provide accounting, disbursing, auditing, and other fiscal services for the Federal Judicial Center.

(Added Pub.L. 90–219, Title I, § 101, Dec. 20, 1967, 81 Stat. 667.)

§ 629. Federal Judicial Center Foundation

(a) There is established a private nonprofit corporation which shall be known as the Federal Judicial Center Foundation (hereafter in this section referred to as the "Foundation") and which shall be incorporated in the District of Columbia. The purpose of the Foundation shall be to have sole authority to accept and receive gifts of real and personal property and services made for the purpose of aiding or facilitating the work of the Federal Judicial Center. The Foundation shall not accept conditional or otherwise restricted gifts, except gifts that are designated for the support of specific projects previously approved by the Board of the Center may be accepted. The Foundation shall have no authority to administer or otherwise determine the use of gifts accepted under this section.

(b) The business of the Foundation shall be conducted by a Board that shall have seven members, including a chairman. Three members, including the chairman, shall be appointed by the Chief Justice of the United States, two by the President Pro Tempore of the Senate, and two by the Speaker of the House of Representatives. The term of office of each member of the Board shall be 5 years, except that the initial terms shall be 5 years for the chairman, one member appointed by the President Pro Tempore and one member appointed by the Speaker, 3 years for the other member appointed by the President Pro Tempore and the other member appointed by the Speaker, and two years for the two other members appointed by the Chief Justice. Members of the Board shall serve without compensation but, upon authorization of the Director of the Center, shall be reimbursed by the Federal Judicial Center for actual and necessary expenses incurred in the performance of their official duties. No person who is a Federal or State judge in regular active service or otherwise eligible to perform judicial duties shall be eligible for membership on the

Board. The Center shall provide all administrative support and facilities necessary for the operation of the Board.

(c) The Federal Judicial Center is authorized to administer and use gifts received by the Foundation under this section. The gifts shall be used to further the goals of the Center as determined by the Board of the Center.

(d) Gifts of money and proceeds from sales of other property received as gifts shall be deposited in a separate fund in the Treasury of the United States and disbursed on the order of the Director of the Center, in accordance with policies established by the Board of the Center.

(e) The Board of the Foundation shall, not later than October 1 of each year, submit to the Committees on the Judiciary of the United States Senate and House of Representatives a report with respect to gifts received under this section during the preceding 12-month period, including the source of each such gift, the amount of each gift of cash or cash equivalent, and a description of any other gift. The Center shall include in its annual report of the activities of the Center under section 623(a)(3) a description of the purposes for which gifts were used during the year covered by the report.

(f) For the purpose of Federal income, estate, and gift taxes, property accepted under this section shall be considered as a gift or bequest to or for the use of the United States.

(Added Pub.L. 100-702, Title III, § 301(a), Nov. 19, 1988, 102 Stat. 4647.)

HISTORICAL AND STATUTORY NOTES

Prior Provisions

A prior section 629, added Pub.L. 90-219, Title I, § 101, Dec. 20, 1967, 81 Stat. 667, which related to organization provisions for the Board, was repealed by Pub.L. 95-598, Title II, § 230(1), Nov. 6, 1978, 92 Stat. 2665, effective Nov. 6, 1978, pursuant to section 402(d) of Pub.L. 95-598, as amended, set out as an Effective and Applicability Provisions note preceding section 101 of Title 11, Bankruptcy.

CHAPTER 43—UNITED STATES MAGISTRATE JUDGES

Sec.
631. Appointment and tenure.
632. Character of service.
633. Determination of number, locations, and salaries of magistrates.
634. Compensation.
635. Expenses.
636. Jurisdiction, powers, and temporary assignment.
637. Training.
638. Dockets and forms; United States Code; seals.
639. Definitions.

HISTORICAL AND STATUTORY NOTES

Change of Name

"United States magistrate judge" substituted for "United States magistrate" in the chapter heading pursuant to section 321 of Pub.L. 101-650, set out as a note under 28 U.S.C.A. § 631.

§ 631. Appointment and tenure

(a) The judges of each United States district court and the district courts of the Virgin Islands, Guam, and the Northern Mariana Islands (including any judge in regular active service and any judge who has retired from regular active service under section 371(b) of this title, when designated and assigned to the court to which such judge was appointed) shall appoint United States magistrate judges in such numbers and to serve at such locations within the judicial districts as the Judicial Conference may determine under this chapter. In the case of a magistrate judge appointed by the district court of the Virgin Islands, Guam, or the Northern Mariana Islands, this chapter shall apply as though the court appointing such a magistrate judge were a United States district court. Where there is more than one judge of a district court, the appointment, whether an original appointment or a reappointment, shall be by the concurrence of a majority of all the judges of such district court, and when there is no such concurrence, then by the chief judge. Where the conference deems it desirable, a magistrate judge may be designated to serve in one or more districts adjoining the district for which he is appointed. Such a designation shall be made by the concurrence of a majority of the judges of each of the district courts involved and shall specify the duties to be performed by the magistrate judge in the adjoining district or districts.

(b) No individual may be appointed or reappointed to serve as a magistrate judge under this chapter unless:

(1) He has been for at least five years a member in good standing of the bar of the highest court of a State, the District of Columbia, the Commonwealth of Puerto Rico, the Territory of Guam, the Commonwealth of the Northern Mariana Islands, or the Virgin Islands of the United States, except that an individual who does not meet the bar membership requirements of this paragraph may be appointed and serve as a part-time magistrate judge if the appointing court or courts and the conference find that no qualified individual who is a member of the bar is available to serve at a specific location;

(2) He is determined by the appointing district court or courts to be competent to perform the duties of the office;

(3) In the case of an individual appointed to serve in a national park, he resides within the exterior boundaries of that park, or at some place reasonably adjacent thereto;

(4) He is not related by blood or marriage to a judge of the appointing court or courts at the time of his initial appointment; and

(5) He is selected pursuant to standards and procedures promulgated by the Judicial Conference of the United States. Such standards and procedures shall contain provision for public notice of all vacancies in magistrate judge positions and for the establishment by the district courts of merit selection panels, composed of residents of the individual judicial districts, to assist the courts in identifying and recommending persons who are best qualified to fill such positions.

(c) A magistrate judge may hold no other civil or military office or employment under the United States: *Provided, however*, That, with the approval of the conference, a part-time referee in bankruptcy or a clerk or deputy clerk of a court of the United States may be appointed and serve as a part-time United States magistrate judge, but the conference shall fix the aggregate amount of compensation to be received for performing the duties of part-time magistrate judge and part-time referee in bankruptcy, clerk or deputy clerk: *And provided further*, That retired officers and retired enlisted personnel of the Regular and Reserve components of the Army, Navy, Air Force, Marine Corps, and Coast Guard, members of the Reserve components of the Army, Navy, Air Force, Marine Corps, and Coast Guard, and members of the Army National Guard of the United States, the Air National Guard of the United States, and the Naval Militia and of the National Guard of a State, territory, or the District of Columbia, except the National Guard disbursing officers who are on a full-time salary basis, may be appointed and serve as United States magistrate judges.

(d) Except as otherwise provided in sections 375 and 636(h) of this title, no individual may serve under this chapter after having attained the age of seventy years: *Provided, however*, That upon a majority vote of all the judges of the appointing court or courts, which is taken upon the magistrate judge's attaining age seventy and upon each subsequent anniversary thereof, a magistrate judge who has attained the age of seventy years may continue to serve and may be reappointed under this chapter.

(e) The appointment of any individual as a full-time magistrate judge shall be for a term of eight years, and the appointment of any individuals as a part-time magistrate judge shall be for a term of four years, except that the term of a full-time or part-time magistrate judge appointed under subsection (k) shall expire upon—

(1) the expiration of the absent magistrate judge's term,

(2) the reinstatement of the absent magistrate judge in regular service in office as a magistrate judge,

(3) the failure of the absent magistrate judge to make timely application under subsection (j) of this section for reinstatement in regular service in office as a magistrate judge after discharge or release from military service,

(4) the death or resignation of the absent magistrate judge, or

(5) the removal from office of the absent magistrate judge pursuant to subsection (i) of this section,

whichever may first occur.

(f) Upon the expiration of his term, a magistrate judge may, by a majority vote of the judges of the appointing district court or courts and with the approval of the judicial council of the circuit, continue to perform the duties of his office until his successor is appointed, or for 180 days after the date of the expiration of the magistrate judge's term, whichever is earlier.

(g) Each individual appointed as a magistrate judge under this section shall take the oath or affirmation prescribed by section 453 of this title before performing the duties of his office.

(h) Each appointment made by a judge or judges of a district court shall be entered of record in such court, and notice of such appointment shall be given at once by the clerk of that court to the Director.

(i) Removal of a magistrate judge during the term for which he is appointed shall be only for incompetency, misconduct, neglect of duty, or physical or mental disability, but a magistrate judge's office shall be terminated if the conference determines that the services performed by his office are no longer needed. Removal shall be by the judges of the district court for the judicial district in which the magistrate judge serves; where there is more than one judge of a district court, removal shall not occur unless a majority of all the judges of such court concur in the order of removal; and when there is a tie vote of the judges of the district court on the question of the removal or retention in office of a magistrate judge, then removal shall be only by a concurrence of a majority of all the judges of the council. In the case of a magistrate judge appointed under the third sentence of subsection (a) of this section, removal shall not occur unless a majority of all the judges of the appointing district courts concur in the order of removal; and where there is a tie vote on the question of the removal or retention in office of a magistrate judge, then removal shall be only by a concurrence of a majority of all the judges of the council or councils. Before any order or removal shall be entered, a full specification of the charges shall be furnished to the magistrate judge, and he shall be accorded by the judge or judges of the removing court, courts, council, or councils an opportunity to be heard on the charges.

(j) Upon the grant by the appropriate district court or courts of a leave of absence to a magistrate judge entitled to such relief under chapter 43 of title 38, such court or courts may proceed to appoint, in the manner specified in subsection (a) of this section, another magistrate judge, qualified for appointment and service under subsections (b), (c), and (d) of this section, who shall serve for the period specified in subsection (e) of this section.

(k) A United States magistrate judge appointed under this chapter shall be exempt from the provisions of subchapter I of chapter 63 of title 5.

(June 25, 1948, c. 646, 62 Stat. 915; May 24, 1949, c. 139, § 73, 63 Stat. 100; July 9, 1952, c. 609, § 1, 66 Stat. 509; July 25, 1956, c. 722, 70 Stat. 642; Oct. 17, 1968, Pub.L. 90–578, Title I, § 101, 82 Stat. 1108; Oct. 17, 1976, Pub.L. 94–520, § 2, 90 Stat. 2458; Nov. 6, 1978, Pub.L. 95–598, Title II, § 231, 92 Stat. 2665; Oct. 10, 1979, Pub.L. 96–82, § 3(a)–(d), 93 Stat. 644, 645; Aug. 6, 1982, Pub.L. 97–230, 96 Stat. 255; Nov. 14, 1986, Pub.L. 99–651, Title II, § 201(a)(1), 100 Stat. 3646; Nov. 15, 1988, Pub.L. 100–659, § 5, 102 Stat. 3918; Nov. 19, 1988, Pub.L. 100–702, Title X, § 1003(a)(2), 102 Stat. 4665; June 30, 1989, Pub.L. 101–45, Title II, § 104, 103 Stat. 122; Dec. 1, 1990, Pub.L. 101–650, Title III, §§ 308(b), 321, 104 Stat. 5112, 5117; Oct. 13, 1994, Pub.L. 103–353, § 2(c), 108 Stat. 3169; Nov. 13, 2000, Pub.L. 106–518, Title II, § 201, 114 Stat. 2412; Jan. 7, 2008, Pub.L. 110–177, Title V, § 504, 121 Stat. 2542.)

HISTORICAL AND STATUTORY NOTES

References in Text

Subsections (j) and (k) of this section, referred to in subsec. (e), probably mean subsecs. (j) and (k) prior to amendment by Pub.L. 103–353, § 2(c)(1), (2), Oct. 13, 1994, 108 Stat. 3169, which redesignated subsec. (k) as (j) and struck out former subsec. (j).

Codifications

Subsec. (c) of this section was amended by Pub.L. 95–598, Title II, § 231, Nov. 6, 1978, 92 Stat. 2665, effective June 28, 1984, pursuant to Pub.L. 95–598, Title IV, § 402(b), Nov. 6, 1978, 92 Stat. 2682, as amended by Pub.L. 98–249, § 1(a), Mar. 31, 1984, 98 Stat. 116; Pub.L. 98–271, § 1(a), Apr. 30, 1984, 98 Stat. 163; Pub.L. 98–299, § 1(a), May 25, 1984, 98 Stat. 214; Pub.L. 98–325, § 1(a), June 20, 1984, 98 Stat. 268, set out as an Effective Date note preceding section 101 of Title 11, Bankruptcy, by striking out "a part-time referee in bankruptcy or" following "of the conference," and "part-time referee in bankruptcy," following "magistrate and".

Section 402(b) of Pub.L. 95–598 was amended by section 113 of Pub.L. 98–353, Title I, July 10, 1984, 98 Stat. 343, by substituting "shall not be effective" for "shall take effect on June 28, 1984", thereby eliminating the amendment by section 231 of Pub.L. 95–598, effective June 27, 1984, pursuant to section 122(c) of Pub.L. 98–353, set out as an Effective Date note under section 151 of this title.

Section 121(a) of Pub.L. 98–353 directed that section 402(b) of Pub.L. 95–598 be amended by substituting "the date of enactment of the Bankruptcy Amendments and Federal Judgeship Act of 1984 [i.e. July 10, 1984]" for "June 28, 1984". This amendment was not executed in view of the prior amendment to section 402(b) of Pub.L. 95–598 by section 113 of Pub.L. 98–353.

Effective and Applicability Provisions

1994 Acts. Amendment by section 2(c) of Pub.L. 103–353 effective with respect to reemployments initiated on or after the first day after the 60–day period beginning on Oct. 13, 1994, except as otherwise provided, see section 8 of Pub.L. 103–353, set out as a note under section 4301 of Title 38, Veterans' Benefits.

1988 Acts. Amendment by Pub.L. 100–659 effective Nov. 15, 1988, and applicable to bankruptcy judges and magistrates who retire on or after Nov. 15, 1988, with exception for judges and magistrates retiring on or after July 31, 1987, see section 9 of Pub.L. 100–659, set out as an Effective Date note under section 377 of this title.

1986 Acts. Amendment by Pub.L. 99–651 effective Jan. 1, 1987, see section 203 of Pub.L. 99–651, set out as a note under section 155 of this title.

1979 Acts. Section 3(g) of Pub.L. 96–82 provided that: "The amendment made by subsection (c) of this section [enacting subsec. (b)(5) of this section] shall not take effect until 30 days after the meeting of the Judicial Conference of the United States next following the effective date of this Act [Oct. 10, 1979]." [The meeting of the Judicial Conference took place on Mar. 5 and 6, 1980.]

1968 Acts. Section 403 of Pub.L. 90–578 provided that: "Except as otherwise provided by sections 401 and 402 of this title [set out as Appointment of Magistrate and Applicable Law notes under this section], this Act [which amended this chapter and sections 202, 3006A, 3041, 3043, 3045, 3060, 3102, 3116, 3184, 3191, 3195, 3401, 3402, 3569, and 3771 of Title 18, Crimes and Criminal Procedure, and enacted provisions set out as notes under this section] shall take effect on the date of its enactment [Oct. 17, 1968]."

Change of Name

Section 321 of Pub.L. 101–650 provided that: "After the enactment of this Act [Dec. 1, 1990], each United States magistrate appointed under section 631 of title 28, United States Code [this section], shall be known as a United States magistrate judge, and any reference to any United States magistrate or magistrate that is contained in title 28, United States Code [this title], in any other Federal statute, or in any regulation of any department or agency of the United States in the executive branch that was issued before the enactment of this Act [Dec. 1, 1990], shall be deemed to refer to a United States magistrate judge appointed under section 631 of title 28, United States Code [this section]."

Transfer of Functions

For transfer of authorities, functions, personnel, and assets of the Coast Guard, including the authorities and functions of the Secretary of Transportation relating thereto, to the Department of Homeland Security, and for treatment of related references, see 6 U.S.C.A. §§ 468(b), 551(d), 552(d) and 557, and the Department of Homeland Security Reorganization Plan of November 25, 2002, as modified, set out as a note under 6 U.S.C.A. § 542.

Severability of Provisions

Section 501 of Pub.L. 90–578 provided that: "If any provision of this Act [which amended this chapter and sections 202, 3006A, 3041, 3043, 3045, 3060, 3102, 3116, 3184, 3191, 3195, 3401, 3402, 3569, and 3771 of Title 18, Crimes and Criminal Procedure, and enacted provisions set out as notes under this section] or the application thereof to any person or circumstances is held invalid, the validity of the remainder of the Act [such sections] and of its application to other persons and circumstances shall not be affected."

Short Title

1979 Amendments. Section 1 of Pub.L. 96–82 provided: "That this Act [amending this section, sections 604, 633, 634, 635, 636, and 1915 of this title, and section 3401 of Title 18, Crimes and Criminal Procedure, and enacting provisions set out as notes under this section] may be cited as the 'Federal Magistrate Act of 1979'."

1968 Acts. Section 1 of Pub.L. 90–578 provided: "That this Act [which amended this chapter and sections 202, 3006A, 3041, 3043, 3045, 3060, 3102, 3116, 3184, 3191, 3195, 3401, 3402, 3569, and 3771 of Title 18, Crimes and Criminal Procedure, and enacted provisions set out as notes under this section] may be cited as the 'Federal Magistrates Act'."

Applicable Law

Section 402 of Pub.L. 90–578 provided that:

"**(a)** All provisions of law relating to the powers, duties, jurisdiction, functions, service, compensation, and facilities of United States commissioners, as such provisions existed on the day preceding the date of enactment of this Act [Oct. 17, 1968], shall continue in effect in each judicial district until but not on or after (1) the date on which the first United States magistrate [now United States magistrate judge] assumes office within such judicial district pursuant to section 631 of chapter 43, title 28, United States Code, as amended by this Act [this section], or (2) the third anniversary of the date of enactment of this Act [Oct. 17, 1968], whichever date is earlier.

"**(b)** On and after the date on which the first United States magistrate assumes office within any judicial district pursuant to section 631 of chapter 43, title 28, United States Code, as amended by this Act [this section], or the third anniversary of the date of enactment of this Act [Oct. 17, 1968], whichever date is earlier—

"**(1)** the provisions of chapter 43, title 28, United States Code, as amended by this Act [this chapter], shall be effective within such judicial district except as otherwise specifically provided by section 401(b) of this title [set out as Appointment of Magistrates note under this section]; and

"**(2)** within such judicial district every reference to a United States commissioner contained in any previously enacted statute of the United States (other than sections 8331(1)(E), 8332(i), 8701(a)(7), and 8901(1)(G) of title 5), any previously promulgated rule of any court of the United States, or any previously promulgated regulation of any executive department or agency of the United States, shall be deemed to be a reference to a United States magistrate duly appointed under section 631 of chapter 43, title 28, United States Code, as amended by this Act [this section].

"**(c)** The administrative powers and duties of the Director of the Administrative Office of the United States Courts with respect to United States commissioners under the provisions of chapter 41, title 28, United States Code, as such provisions existed on the day preceding the date of enactment of this Act [Oct. 17, 1968], shall continue in effect until no United States commissioner remains in service."

Appointment of Magistrates

Section 401 of Pub.L. 90–578 provided that:

"**(a)** No individual may serve as a United States commissioner within any judicial district after the date on which a United States magistrate assumes office in such judicial district.

"**(b)** An individual serving as a United States commissioner within any judicial district on the date of enactment of this Act [Oct. 17, 1968] who is a member in good standing of the bar of the highest court of any State may be appointed to the office of United States magistrate for an initial term, and may be reappointed to such office for successive terms, notwithstanding his failure to meet the bar membership qualification imposed by section 631(b)(1) of chapter 43, title 28, United States Code [subsec. (b)(1) of this section]: *Provided, however*, That any appointment or reappointment of such an individual must be by unanimous vote of all the judges of the appointing district court or courts."

Authorization of Appropriations

Section 10 of Pub.L. 96–82 provided that: "Such sums as may be necessary to carry out the purposes of this Act [see Short Title of 1979 Amendments note under this section] are hereby authorized to be appropriated for expenditure on or after October 1, 1979."

Due Consideration by Merit Selection Panels of Women, Blacks, Hispanics, and Other Minorities

Section 3(e) of Pub.L. 96–82 provided that: "The merit selection panels established under section 631(b)(5) of title 28, United States Code [subsec. (b)(5) of this section], in recommending persons to the district court, shall give due consideration to all qualified individuals, especially such groups as women, blacks, Hispanics, and other minorities."

Judicial Conference Study of the Future of the Magistrate System

Section 9 of Pub.L. 96–82 provided for a study by the Judicial Conference of the United States to begin within 90 days after the effective date of Pub.L. 96–82, which was approved Oct. 10, 1979, and to be completed and made available to Congress within 24 months thereafter respecting the future of the magistrate system.

Jurisdictional Limitation of Commissioner Holding Office on July 9, 1952

Section 2 of Act July 9, 1952, provided that: "The jurisdiction of the United States commissioner holding office as commissioner of the Great Smoky Mountains National Park on the date of enactment of this Act [July 9, 1952] shall be limited to the portion of the park situated in North Carolina."

Magistrates Serving Prior to Promulgation of Magistrate Selection Standards and Procedures by Judicial Conference; Reappointment; Certification as Qualified

Section 3(f) of Pub.L. 96–82 provided that: "Magistrates serving prior to the promulgation of magistrate selection standards and procedures by the Judicial Conference of the United States may only exercise the jurisdiction conferred under the amendment made by section 2 of this Act [enacting section 636(c) of this title] after having been reappointed under such standards and procedures or after having been certified as qualified to exercise such jurisdiction by the judicial council of the circuit in which the magistrate serves."

Special Commissioner for Grand Canyon National Park; Appointment; Jurisdiction; Compensation

Pub.L. 86–258, Sept. 14, 1959, 73 Stat. 546, provided: "That the United States District Court for the District of Arizona shall appoint a special commissioner for the Grand Canyon National Park, Arizona. The commissioner shall hold office for four years, unless sooner removed by the district court, and he shall be subject to the general laws and requirements applicable to United States commissioners.

"**Sec. 2.** The jurisdiction of the commissioner in adjudicating cases brought before him shall be limited to the trial, and sentencing upon conviction, of persons charged with the commission of those misdemeanors classified as petty offenses (18 U.S.C. 1) [section 1 of Title 18, Crimes and Criminal Procedure] relating to the violation of Federal laws or regulations applicable within the park: *Provided*, That any person charged with a petty offense may elect to be tried in the district court of the United States; and the commissioner shall apprise the defendant of his right to make such election, but shall not proceed to try the case unless the defendant, after being so apprised, signs a written consent to be tried before the commissioner. The exercise of additional functions by the commissioner shall be consistent with and be carried out in accordance with the authority, laws, and regulations of general application to United States commissioners. The rules of procedure set forth in title 18, section 3402, of the United States Code [section 3402 of Title 18], shall be followed in the handling of cases by such commissioner. The probation laws shall be applicable to persons tried by the commissioner and he shall have power to grant probation.

"**Sec. 3.** The commissioner shall receive an annual salary to be fixed by the district court with the approval of the Judicial Conference of the United States and shall account for all fees, fines, and costs collected by him as public moneys. He shall reside within the boundary of the park or at some place reasonably adjacent thereto designated by the Secretary of the Interior with the approval of the district court."

§ 632. Character of service

(a) Full-time United States magistrate judges may not engage in the practice of law, and may not engage in any other business, occupation, or employment inconsistent with the expeditious, proper, and impartial performance of their duties as judicial officers.

(b) Part-time United States magistrate judges shall render such service as judicial officers as is required by law. While so serving they may engage in the practice of law, but may not serve as counsel in any criminal action in any court of the United States, nor act in any capacity that is, under such regulations as the conference may establish, inconsistent with the proper discharge of their office. Within such restrictions, they may engage in any other business, occupation, or employment which is not inconsistent with the expeditious, proper, and impartial performance of their duties as judicial officers.

(June 25, 1948, c. 646, 62 Stat. 916; Oct. 17, 1968, Pub.L. 90–578, Title I, § 101, 82 Stat. 1110; Pub.L. 101–650, Title III, § 321, Dec. 1 1990, 104 Stat. 5117.)

HISTORICAL AND STATUTORY NOTES

Effective and Applicability Provisions

1968 Acts. Amendment by Pub.L. 90–578 effective Oct. 17, 1968, except when a later effective date is applicable, which is the earlier of date when implementation of amendment by appointment of magistrates and assumption of office takes place or third anniversary of enactment of Pub.L. 90–578 on Oct. 17, 1968, see section 403 of Pub.L. 90–578, set out as a note under section 631 of this title.

Change of Name

"United States magistrate judge" substituted for "United States magistrate" in text pursuant to section 321 of Pub.L. 101–650, set out as a note under 28 U.S.C.A. § 631.

§ 633. Determination of number, locations, and salaries of magistrate judges

(a) Surveys by the Director.—

(1) The Director shall, within one year immediately following the date of the enactment of the Federal Magistrates Act, make a careful survey of conditions in judicial districts to determine (A) the number of appointments of full-time magistrates and part-time magistrates required to be made under this chapter to provide for the expeditious and effective administration of justice, (B) the locations at which such officers shall serve, and (C) their respective salaries under section 634 of this title. Thereafter, the Director shall, from time to time, make such surveys, general or local, as the conference shall deem expedient.

(2) In the course of any survey, the Director shall take into account local conditions in each judicial district, including the areas and the populations to be served, the transportation and communications facilities available, the amount and distribution of business of the type expected to arise before officers appointed under this chapter (including such matters as may be assigned under section 636(b) of this chapter), and any other material factors. The Director shall give consideration to suggestions from any interested parties, including district judges, United States magistrate judges or officers appointed under this chapter, United States attorneys, bar associations, and other parties having relevant experience or information.

(3) The surveys shall be made with a view toward creating and maintaining a system of full-time United States magistrate judges. However, should the Director find, as a result of any such surveys, areas in which the employment of a full-time magistrate judge would not be feasible or desirable, he shall recommend the appointment of part-time United States magistrate judges in such numbers and at such locations as may be required to permit prompt and efficient issuance of process and to permit individuals charged with criminal offenses against the United States to be brought before a judicial officer of the United States promptly after arrest.

(b) Determination by the conference.—Upon the completion of the initial surveys required by subsection (a) of this section, the Director shall report to the district courts, the councils, and the conference his recommendations concerning the number of full-time magistrates and part-time magistrates, their respective locations, and the amount of their respective salaries under section 634 of this title. The district courts shall advise their respective councils, stating their recommendations and the reasons therefor; the councils shall advise the conference, stating their recommendations and the reasons therefor, and shall also report to the conference the recommendations of the district courts. The conference shall determine, in the light of the recommendations of the Director, the district courts, and the councils, the number of full-time United States magistrates and part-time United States magistrates, the locations at which they shall serve, and their respective salaries. Such determinations shall take effect in each judicial district at such time as the district court for such judicial district shall determine, but in no event later than one year after they are promulgated.

(c) Changes in number, locations, and salaries.—Except as otherwise provided in this chapter, the conference may, from time to time, in the light of the recommendations of the Director, the district courts, and the councils, change the number, locations, and salaries of full-time and part-time magistrate judges, as the expeditious administration of justice may require.

(June 25, 1948, c. 646, 62 Stat. 916; Aug. 13, 1954, c. 728, § 1(a), (b), 68 Stat. 703, 704; Sept. 2, 1957, Pub.L. 85–276, §§ 1, 2, 71 Stat. 600; Oct. 17, 1968, Pub.L. 90–578, Title I, § 101, 82 Stat. 1111; Oct. 10, 1979, Pub.L. 96–82, § 4, 93 Stat. 645; Nov. 14, 1986, Pub.L. 99–651, Title II, § 202(d), 100 Stat. 3648; Dec. 1, 1990, Pub.L. 101–650, Title III, § 321, 104 Stat. 5117.)

HISTORICAL AND STATUTORY NOTES

References in Text

Date of the enactment of the Federal Magistrates Act, referred to in subsec. (a)(1), means Oct. 17, 1968, the date of enactment of Pub.L. 90–578.

Effective and Applicability Provisions

1986 Acts. Amendment by Pub.L. 99–651 effective Jan. 1, 1987, see section 203 of Pub.L. 99–651, set out as a note under section 155 of this title.

1968 Acts. Amendment by Pub.L. 90–578 effective Oct. 17, 1968, except when a later effective date is applicable, which is the earlier of date when implementation of amendment by appointment of magistrates and assumption of office takes place or third anniversary of enactment of Pub.L. 90–578 on Oct. 17, 1968, see section 403 of Pub.L. 90–578, set out as a note under section 631 of this title.

Change of Name

"United States magistrate judge" substituted for "United States magistrate" in the section headings, and subsecs. (a)(2), (a)(3), and (c) pursuant to section 321 of Pub.L. 101–650, set out as a note under 28 U.S.C.A. § 631. Previously, United States commissioners, referred to in text, were replaced by United States magistrates pursuant to Pub.L. 90–578, Oct. 17, 1968, 82 Stat. 1118. See chapter 43 of Title 28, 28 U.S.C.A. § 631 et seq.

United States magistrate appointed under section 631 of this title to be known as United States magistrate judge after Dec. 1, 1990, with any reference to United States magistrate or magistrate in this title, in any other Federal statute, etc., deemed a reference to United States magistrate judge appointed under section 631 of this title, see section 321 of Pub.L. 101–650, set out as a note under section 631 of this title.

§ 634. Compensation

(a) Officers appointed under this chapter shall receive, as full compensation for their services, salaries to be fixed by the conference pursuant to section 633, at rates for full-time United States magistrate judges up to an annual rate equal to 92 percent of the salary of a judge of the district court of the United States, as determined pursuant to section 135, and at rates for part-time magistrate judges of not less than an annual salary of $100, nor more than one-half the maximum salary payable to a full-time magistrate judge. In fixing the amount of salary to be paid to any officer appointed under this chapter, consideration shall be given to the average number and the nature of matters that have arisen during the immediately preceding period of five years, and that may be expected thereafter to arise, over which such officer would have jurisdiction and to such other factors as may be material. Disbursement of salaries shall be made by or pursuant to the order of the Director.

(b) Except as provided by section 8344, title 5, relating to reductions of the salaries of reemployed annuitants under subchapter III of chapter 83 of such title and unless the office has been terminated as provided in this chapter, the salary of a full-time United States magistrate judge shall not be reduced, during the term in which he is serving, below the salary fixed for him at the beginning of that term.

(c) All United States magistrate judges, effective upon their taking the oath or affirmation of office, and all necessary legal, clerical, and secretarial assistants employed in the offices of full-time United States magistrate judges shall be deemed to be officers and employees in the judicial branch of the United States Government within the meaning of subchapter III (relating to civil service retirement) of chapter 83, chapter 87 (relating to Federal employees' group life insurance), and chapter 89 (relating to Federal employees' health benefits program) of title 5. Part-time magistrate judges shall not be excluded from coverage under these chapters solely for lack of a prearranged regular tour of duty. A legal assistant appointed under this section shall be exempt from the provisions of subchapter I of chapter 63 of title 5, unless specifically included by the appointing judge or by local rule of court.

(June 25, 1948, c. 646, 62 Stat. 917; Oct. 17, 1968, Pub.L. 90–578, Title I, § 101, 82 Stat. 1112; Sept. 21, 1972, Pub.L. 92–428, 86 Stat. 721; Oct. 17, 1976, Pub.L. 94–520, § 1, 90 Stat. 2458; Nov. 6, 1978, Pub.L. 95–598, Title II, § 232, 92 Stat. 2665; Oct. 10, 1979, Pub.L. 96–82, § 8(b), 93 Stat. 647; July 10, 1984, Pub.L. 98–353, Title I, § 108(a), Title II, § 210, 98 Stat. 342, 351; Dec. 22, 1987, Pub.L. 100–202, § 101(a) [Title IV, § 408 (b)], 101 Stat. 1329, 1329–27; Nov. 19, 1988, Pub.L. 100–702, Title X, § 1003(a)(4), 102 Stat. 4665; Dec. 1, 1990, Pub.L. 101–650, Title III, § 321, 104 Stat. 5117.)

HISTORICAL AND STATUTORY NOTES

Codifications

Subsec. (a) of this section was amended by Pub.L. 95–598, Title II, § 232, Nov. 6, 1978, 92 Stat. 2665, effective June 28, 1984, pursuant to Pub.L. 95–598, Title IV, § 402(b), Nov. 6, 1978, 92 Stat. 2682, as amended by Pub.L. 98–249, § 1(a), Mar. 31, 1984, 98 Stat. 116; Pub.L. 98–271, § 1(a), Apr. 30, 1984, 98 Stat. 163; Pub.L. 98–299, § 1(a), May 25, 1984, 98 Stat. 214; Pub.L. 98–325, § 1(a), June 20, 1984, 98 Stat. 268, set out as an Effective Date note preceding section 101 of Title 11, Bankruptcy, to read as follows:

"**(a)** Officers appointed under this chapter shall receive as full compensation for their services salaries to be fixed by the conference pursuant to section 633 of this title, at rates not to exceed $48,500 per annum, subject to adjustment in accordance with section 225 of the Federal Salary Act of 1967 and section 461 of this title, except that the salary of a part-time United States magistrate shall not be less than $100 nor more than one-half the maximum salary payable to a full-time magistrate. In fixing the amount of salary to be paid to any officer appointed under this chapter, consideration shall be given to the average number and the nature of matters that have arisen during the immediately preceding period of five years, and that may be expected thereafter to arise, over which such officer would have jurisdiction and to such other factors as may be material. Disbursement of salaries shall be made by or pursuant to the order of the Director."

Section 402(b) of Pub.L. 95–598 was amended by section 113 of Pub.L. 98–353, Title I, July 10, 1984, 98 Stat. 343, by substituting "shall not be effective" for "shall take effect on June 28, 1984", thereby eliminating the amendment by section 232 of Pub.L. 95–598, effective June 27, 1984, pursuant to section 122(c) of Pub.L. 98–353, set out as an Effective Date note under section 151 of this title.

Section 121(a) of Pub.L. 98–353 directed that section 402(b) of Pub.L. 95–598 be amended by substituting "the date of enactment of the Bankruptcy Amendments and Federal Judgeship Act of 1984 [i.e. July 10, 1984] " for "June 28, 1984". This amendment was not executed in view of the prior amendment to section 402(b) of Pub.L. 95–598 by section 113 of Pub.L. 98–353.

Effective and Applicability Provisions

1987 Acts. Amendment by section 101(a) [Title IV, § 408(b)] of Pub.L. 100–202 (amending subsec. (a) of this section) effective Oct. 1, 1988, and any salary affected by its provisions to be adjusted at the beginning of the first applicable pay period commencing on or after such date, see section 101(a) [Title IV, § 408(d)] of Pub.L. 100–202, set out as a note under section 153 of this title.

1984 Acts. Amendment by section 108(a) of Pub.L. 98–353 effective July 10, 1984, see section 122(a) of Pub.L. 98–353, set out as a note under section 151 of this title.

1968 Acts. Amendment by Pub.L. 90–578 effective Oct. 17, 1968, except when a later effective date is applicable, which is the earlier of date when implementation of amendment by appointment of magistrates and assumption of office takes place or third anniversary of enactment of Pub.L. 90–578 on Oct. 17, 1968, see section 403 of Pub.L. 90–578, set out as a note under section 631 of this title.

Change of Name

"United States magistrate judge" substituted for "United States magistrate" in text pursuant to section 321 of Pub.L. 101–650, set out as a note under 28 U.S.C.A. § 631.

Continuation of Maximum Rates of Salary of Full-Time and Part-Time United States Magistrates in Effect on June 27, 1984

Section 108(b) of Pub.L. 98–353 provided that: "The maximum rates for salary of full-time and part-time United States magistrates in effect on June 27, 1984, shall remain in effect until changed as a result of a determination made under section 634(a) of title 28, United States Code [subsec. (a) of this section], as amended by this Act."

[Section 108(b) of Pub.L. 98–353 effective June 27, 1984, see section 122(c) of Pub.L. 98–353, set out as an Effective and Applicability Provisions note under section 151 of this title.]

Salary Increases of 1987

Maximum salaries of U.S. magistrates (full-time) and U.S. magistrates (part-time) increased respectively to $72,500 and $36,200 per annum, on recommendation of the President of the United States, see note set out under section 358 of Title 2, The Congress.

§ 635. Expenses

(a) Full-time United States magistrate judges serving under this chapter shall be allowed their actual and necessary expenses incurred in the performance of their duties, including the compensation of such legal assistants as the Judicial Conference, on the basis of the recommendations of the judicial councils of the circuits, considers necessary, and the compensation of necessary clerical and secretarial assistance. Such expenses and compensation shall be determined and paid by the Director under such regulations as the Director shall prescribe with the approval of the conference. The Administrator of General Services shall provide such magistrate judges with necessary courtrooms, office space, furniture and facilities within United States courthouses or office buildings owned or occupied by departments or agencies of the United States, or should suitable courtroom and office space not be available within any such courthouse or office building, the Administrator of General Services, at the request of the Director, shall procure and pay for suitable courtroom and office space, furniture and facilities for such magistrate judge in another building, but only if such request has been approved as necessary by the judicial council of the appropriate circuit.

(b) Under such regulations as the Director shall prescribe with the approval of the conference, the Director shall reimburse part-time magistrate judges for actual expenses necessarily incurred by them in the performance of their duties under this chapter. Such reimbursement may be made, at rates not exceeding those prescribed by such regulations, for expenses incurred by such part-time magistrate judges for clerical and secretarial assistance, stationery, telephone and other communications services, travel, and such other expenses as may be determined to be necessary for the proper performance of the duties of such officers: *Provided, however*, That no reimbursement shall be made for all or any portion of the expense incurred by such part-time magistrate judges for the procurement of office space.

(June 25, 1948, c. 646, 62 Stat. 917; Oct. 17, 1968, Pub.L. 90–578, Title I, § 101, 82 Stat. 1112; Oct. 10, 1979, Pub.L. 96–82, § 8(a), 93 Stat. 646; Dec. 1, 1990, Pub.L. 101–650, title III, § 321, 104 Stat. 5117.)

HISTORICAL AND STATUTORY NOTES

Effective and Applicability Provisions

1968 Acts. Amendment by Pub.L. 90–578 effective Oct. 17, 1968, except when a later effective date is applicable, which is the earlier of date when implementation of amendment by appointment of magistrates and assumption of office takes place or third anniversary of enactment of Pub.L. 90–578 on Oct. 17, 1968, see section 403 of Pub.L. 90–578, set out as a note under section 631 of this title.

Change of Name

"United States magistrate judge" substituted for "United States magistrate" in text pursuant to section 321 of Pub.L. 101–650, set out as a note under 28 U.S.C.A. § 631.

§ 636. Jurisdiction, powers, and temporary assignment

(a) Each United States magistrate judge serving under this chapter shall have within the district in which sessions are held by the court that appointed the magistrate judge, at other places where that court may function, and elsewhere as authorized by law—

(1) all powers and duties conferred or imposed upon United States commissioners by law or by the Rules of Criminal Procedure for the United States District Courts;

(2) the power to administer oaths and affirmations, issue orders pursuant to section 3142 of title 18 concerning release or detention of persons pending trial, and take acknowledgements, affidavits, and depositions;

(3) the power to conduct trials under section 3401, title 18, United States Code, in conformity with and subject to the limitations of that section;

(4) the power to enter a sentence for a petty offense; and

(5) the power to enter a sentence for a class A misdemeanor in a case in which the parties have consented.

(b)(1) Notwithstanding any provision of law to the contrary—

(A) a judge may designate a magistrate judge to hear and determine any pretrial matter pending before the court, except a motion for injunctive relief, for judgment on the pleadings, for summary judgment, to dismiss or quash an indictment or information made by the defendant, to suppress evidence in a criminal case, to dismiss or to permit maintenance of a class action, to dismiss for failure to state a claim upon which relief can be granted, and to involuntarily dismiss an action. A judge of the court may reconsider any pretrial matter under this subparagraph (A) where it has been shown that the magistrate judge's order is clearly erroneous or contrary to law.

(B) a judge may also designate a magistrate judge to conduct hearings, including evidentiary hearings, and to submit to a judge of the court proposed findings of fact and recommendations for the disposition, by a judge of the court, of any motion excepted in subparagraph (A), of applications for posttrial[1] relief made by individuals convicted of criminal offenses and of prisoner petitions challenging conditions of confinement.

(C) the magistrate judge shall file his proposed findings and recommendations under subparagraph (B) with the court and a copy shall forthwith be mailed to all parties.

Within ten days after being served with a copy, any party may serve and file written objections to such proposed findings and recommendations as provided by rules of court. A judge of the court shall make a de novo determination of those portions of the report or specified proposed findings or recommendations to which objection is made. A judge of the court may accept, reject, or modify, in whole or in part, the findings or recommendations made by the magistrate judge. The judge may also receive further evidence or recommit the matter to the magistrate judge with instructions.

(2) A judge may designate a magistrate judge to serve as a special master pursuant to the applicable provisions of this title and the Federal Rules of Civil Procedure for the United States district courts. A judge may designate a magistrate judge to serve as a special master in any civil case, upon consent of the parties, without regard to the provisions of rule 53(b) of the Federal Rules of Civil Procedure for the United States district courts.

(3) A magistrate judge may be assigned such additional duties as are not inconsistent with the Constitution and laws of the United States.

(4) Each district court shall establish rules pursuant to which the magistrate judges shall discharge their duties.

(c) Notwithstanding any provision of law to the contrary—

(1) Upon the consent of the parties, a full-time United States magistrate judge or a part-time United States magistrate judge who serves as a full-time judicial officer may conduct any or all proceedings in a jury or nonjury civil matter and order the entry of judgment in the case, when specially designated to exercise such jurisdiction by the district court or courts he serves. Upon the consent of the parties, pursuant to their specific written request, any other part-time magistrate judge may exercise such jurisdiction, if such magistrate judge meets the bar membership requirements set forth in section 631(b)(1) and the chief judge of the district court certifies that a full-time magistrate judge is not reasonably available in accordance with guidelines established by the judicial council of the circuit. When there is more than one judge of a district court, designation under this paragraph shall be by the concurrence of a majority of all the judges of such district court, and when there is no such concurrence, then by the chief judge.

(2) If a magistrate judge is designated to exercise civil jurisdiction under paragraph (1) of this subsection, the clerk of court shall, at the time the action is filed, notify the parties of the availability of a magistrate judge to exercise such jurisdiction. The decision of the parties shall be communicated to the clerk of court. Thereafter, either the district court judge or the magistrate judge may again advise the parties of the availability of the magistrate judge, but in so doing, shall also advise the parties that they are free to withhold consent without adverse substantive consequences. Rules of court for the reference of civil matters to magistrate judges shall include procedures to protect the voluntariness of the parties' consent.

(3) Upon entry of judgment in any case referred under paragraph (1) of this subsection, an aggrieved party may appeal directly to the appropriate United States court of appeals from the judgment of the magistrate judge in the same manner as an appeal from any other judgment of a district court. The consent of the parties allows a magistrate judge designated to exercise civil jurisdiction under paragraph (1) of this subsection to direct the entry of a judgment of the district court in accordance with the Federal Rules of Civil Procedure. Nothing in this paragraph shall be construed as a limitation of any party's right to seek review by the Supreme Court of the United States.

(4) The court may, for good cause shown on its own motion, or under extraordinary circumstances shown by any party, vacate a reference of a civil matter to a magistrate judge under this subsection.

(5) The magistrate judge shall, subject to guidelines of the Judicial Conference, determine whether the record taken pursuant to this section shall be taken by electronic sound recording, by a court reporter, or by other means.

(d) The practice and procedure for the trial of cases before officers serving under this chapter shall conform to rules promulgated by the Supreme Court pursuant to section 2072 of this title.

(e) Contempt authority.—

(1) In general.—A United States magistrate judge serving under this chapter shall have within the territorial jurisdiction prescribed by the appointment of such magistrate judge the power to exercise contempt authority as set forth in this subsection.

(2) Summary criminal contempt authority.—A magistrate judge shall have the power to punish summarily by fine or imprisonment, or both, such contempt of the authority of such magistrate judge constituting misbehavior of any person in the magistrate judge's presence so as to obstruct the administration of justice. The order of contempt shall be issued under the Federal Rules of Criminal Procedure.

(3) Additional criminal contempt authority in civil consent and misdemeanor cases.—In any case in which a United States magistrate judge presides with the consent of the parties under subsection (c) of this section, and in any misdemeanor case proceeding before a magistrate judge under section 3401 of title 18, the magistrate judge shall have the power to punish, by fine or imprisonment, or both, criminal contempt constituting disobedience or resistance to the magistrate judge's lawful writ, process, order, rule, decree, or command. Disposition of such contempt shall be conducted upon notice and hearing under the Federal Rules of Criminal Procedure.

(4) Civil contempt authority in civil consent and misdemeanor cases.—In any case in which a United States magistrate judge presides with the consent of the parties under subsection (c) of this section, and in any misdemeanor case proceeding before a magistrate judge under section 3401 of title 18, the magistrate judge may exercise the civil contempt authority of the district court. This paragraph shall not be construed to limit the authority of a magistrate judge to order sanctions under any other statute, the Federal Rules of Civil Procedure, or the Federal Rules of Criminal Procedure.

(5) Criminal contempt penalties.—The sentence imposed by a magistrate judge for any criminal contempt provided for in paragraphs (2) and (3) shall not exceed the penalties for a Class C misdemeanor as set forth in sections 3581(b)(8) and 3571(b)(6) of title 18.

(6) Certification of other contempts to the district court.—Upon the commission of any such act—

(A) in any case in which a United States magistrate judge presides with the consent of the parties under subsection (c) of this section, or in any misdemeanor case proceeding before a magistrate judge under section 3401 of title 18, that may, in the opinion of the magistrate judge, constitute a serious criminal contempt punishable by penalties exceeding those set forth in paragraph (5) of this subsection, or

(B) in any other case or proceeding under subsection (a) or (b) of this section, or any other statute, where—

(i) the act committed in the magistrate judge's presence may, in the opinion of the magistrate judge, constitute a serious criminal contempt punishable by penalties exceeding those set forth in paragraph (5) of this subsection,

(ii) the act that constitutes a criminal contempt occurs outside the presence of the magistrate judge, or

(iii) the act constitutes a civil contempt,

the magistrate judge shall forthwith certify the facts to a district judge and may serve or cause to be served, upon any person whose behavior is brought into question under this paragraph, an order requiring such person to appear before a district judge upon a day certain to show cause why that person should not be adjudged in contempt by reason of the facts so certified. The district judge shall thereupon hear the evidence as to the act or conduct complained of and, if it is such as to warrant punishment, punish such person in the same manner and to the same extent as for a contempt committed before a district judge.

(7) Appeals of magistrate judge contempt orders.—The appeal of an order of contempt under this subsection shall be made to the court of appeals in cases proceeding under subsection (c) of this section. The appeal of any other order of contempt issued under this section shall be made to the district court.

(f) In an emergency and upon the concurrence of the chief judges of the districts involved, a United States magistrate judge may be temporarily assigned to perform any of the duties specified in subsection (a), (b), or (c) of this section in a judicial district other than the judicial district for which he has been appointed. No magistrate judge shall perform any of such duties in a district to which he has been temporarily assigned until an order has been issued by the chief judge of such district specifying (1) the emergency by reason of which he has been transferred, (2) the duration of his assignment, and (3) the duties which he is authorized to perform. A magistrate judge so assigned shall not be entitled to additional compensation but shall be reimbursed for actual and necessary expenses incurred in the performance of his duties in accordance with section 635.

(g) A United States magistrate judge may perform the verification function required by section 4107 of title 18, United States Code. A magistrate judge may be assigned by a judge of any United States district court to perform the verification required by section 4108 and the appointment of counsel authorized by section 4109 of title 18, United States Code, and may perform such functions beyond the territorial limits of the United States. A magistrate judge assigned such functions shall have no authority to perform any other function within the territory of a foreign country.

(h) A United States magistrate judge who has retired may, upon the consent of the chief judge of the district involved, be recalled to serve as a magistrate judge in any judicial district by the judicial council of the circuit within which such district is located. Upon recall, a magistrate judge may receive a salary for such service in accordance with regulations promulgated by the Judicial Conference, subject to the restrictions on the payment of an annuity set forth in section 377 of this title or in subchapter III of chapter 83, and chapter 84, of title 5 which are applicable to such magistrate judge. The requirements set forth in subsections (a), (b)(3), and (d) of section 631, and paragraph (1) of subsection (b) of such section to the extent such paragraph requires membership of the bar of the location in which an individual is to serve as a magistrate judge, shall not apply to the recall of a retired magistrate judge under this subsection or section 375 of this title. Any other requirement set forth in section 631(b) shall apply to the recall of a retired magistrate judge under this subsection or section 375 of this title unless such retired magistrate judge met such requirement upon appointment or reappointment as a magistrate judge under section 361.

(June 25, 1948, c. 646, 62 Stat. 917; Oct. 17, 1968, Pub.L. 90–578, Title I, § 101, 82 Stat. 1113; Mar. 1, 1972, Pub.L. 92–239, §§ 1, 2, 86 Stat. 47; Oct. 21, 1976, Pub.L. 94–577, § 1, 90 Stat. 2729; Oct. 28, 1977, Pub.L. 95–144, § 2, 91 Stat. 1220; Oct. 10, 1979, Pub.L. 96–82, § 2, 93 Stat. 643; Oct. 12, 1984, Pub.L. 98–473, Title II, § 208, 98 Stat. 1986; Nov. 8, 1984, Pub.L. 98–620, Title IV, § 402(29)(B), 98 Stat. 3359; Nov. 14, 1986, Pub.L. 99–651, Title II, § 201(a)(2), 100 Stat. 3647; Nov. 15, 1988, Pub.L. 100–659, § 4(c), 102 Stat. 3918; Nov. 18, 1988, Pub.L. 100–690, Title VII, § 7322, 102 Stat. 4467; Nov. 19, 1988, Pub.L. 100–702, Title IV, § 404(b)(1), Title X, § 1014, 102 Stat. 4651, 4669; Dec. 1, 1990, Pub.L. 101–650, Title III, §§ 308(a), 321, 104 Stat. 5112, 5117; Oct. 19, 1996, Pub.L. 104–317, Title II, §§ 201, 202(b), 207, 110 Stat. 3848, 3849, 3851; Nov. 13, 2000, Pub.L. 106–518, Title II, §§ 202, 203(b), 114 Stat. 2412, 2414; Nov. 2, 2002, Pub.L. 107–273, Div. B, Title III, § 3002(b), 116 Stat. 1805; Sept. 9, 2005, Pub.L. 109–63, § 2(d), 119 Stat. 1995.)

[1] So in original. Probably should be "post-trial".

HISTORICAL AND STATUTORY NOTES

References in Text

The Rules of Criminal Procedure for the United States District Courts, referred to in subsec. (a)(1), are classified to Title 18, Crimes and Criminal Procedure.

The Federal Rules of Civil Procedure for the United States district courts, referred to in subsec. (b)(2) and (c)(3), are classified to this title.

Effective and Applicability Provisions

1988 Acts. Amendment by section 404(b)(1) of Pub.L. 100–702 effective Dec. 1, 1988, see section 407 of Pub.L. 100–702, set out as a note under section 2071 of this title.

Amendment to this section by Pub.L. 100–659 to take effect on Nov. 15, 1988, and shall apply to bankruptcy judges and magistrates who retire on or after Nov. 15, 1988, with special election provisions for bankruptcy judges, etc., who left office on or after July 31, 1987, and before Nov. 15, 1988, see section 9 of Pub.L. 100–659, set out as a note under section 377 of this title.

1986 Acts. Amendment by Pub.L. 99–651 effective Jan. 1, 1987, see section 203 of Pub.L. 99–651, set out as a note under section 155 of this title.

1984 Acts. Amendment by Pub.L. 98–620 not to apply to cases pending on Nov. 8, 1984, see section 403 of Pub.L. 98–620, set out as a note under section 1657 of this title.

1968 Acts. Amendment by Pub.L. 90–578 effective Oct. 17, 1968, except when a later effective date is applicable, which is the earlier of date when implementation of amendment by appointment of magistrates and assumption of office takes place or third anniversary of enactment of Pub.L. 90–578 on Oct. 17, 1968, see section 403 of Pub.L. 90–578, set out as a note under section 631 of this title.

Change of Name

"United States magistrate judge" substituted for "United States magistrate" in text pursuant to section 321 of Pub.L. 101–650, set out as a note under 28 U.S.C.A. § 631.

§ 637. Training

The Federal Judicial Center shall conduct periodic training programs and seminars for both full-time and part-time United States magistrate judges, including an introductory training program for new magistrate judges, to be held within one year after initial appointment.

(June 25, 1948, c. 646, 62 Stat. 917; Oct. 17, 1968, Pub.L. 90–578, Title I, § 101, 82 Stat. 1114; Dec. 1, 1990, Pub.L. 101–650, Title III, § 321, 104 Stat. 5117.)

HISTORICAL AND STATUTORY NOTES

Effective and Applicability Provisions

1968 Acts. Amendment by Pub.L. 90–578 effective Oct. 17, 1968, except when a later effective date is applicable, which is the earlier of date when implementation of amendment by appointment of magistrates and assumption of office takes place or third anniversary of enactment of Pub.L. 90–578 on Oct. 17, 1968, see section 403 of Pub.L. 90–578, set out as a note under section 631 of this title.

Change of Name

"United States magistrate judge" substituted for "United States magistrate" in text pursuant to section 321 of Pub.L. 101–650, set out as a note under 28 U.S.C.A. § 631.

§ 638. Dockets and forms; United States Code; seals

(a) The Director shall furnish to United States magistrate judges adequate docket books and forms prescribed by the Director. The Director shall also furnish to each such officer a copy of the current edition of the United States Code.

(b) All property furnished to any such officer shall remain the property of the United States and, upon the termination of his term of office, shall be transmitted to his successor in office or otherwise disposed of as the Director orders.

(c) The Director shall furnish to each United States magistrate judge appointed under this chapter an official impression seal in a form prescribed by the conference. Each such officer shall affix his seal to every jurat or certificate of his official acts without fee.

(June 25, 1948, c. 646, 62 Stat. 917; Oct. 17, 1968, Pub.L. 90–578, Title I, § 101, 82 Stat. 1114; Dec. 1, 1990, Pub.L. 101–650, Title III, § 321, 104 Stat. 5117.)

HISTORICAL AND STATUTORY NOTES

Effective and Applicability Provisions

1968 Acts. Amendment by Pub.L. 90–578 effective Oct. 17, 1968, except when a later effective date is applicable, which is the earlier of date when implementation of amendment by appointment of magistrates and assumption of office takes place or third anniversary of enactment of Pub.L. 90–578 on Oct. 17, 1968, see section 403 of Pub.L. 90–578, set out as a note under section 631 of this title.

Change of Name

"United States magistrate judge" substituted for "United States magistrate" in text pursuant to section 321 of Pub.L. 101–650, set out as a note under 28 U.S.C.A. § 631.

§ 639. Definitions

As used in this chapter—

(1) "Conference" shall mean the Judicial Conference of the United States;

(2) "Council" shall mean the Judicial Council of the Circuit;

(3) "Director" shall mean the Director of the Administrative Office of the United States Courts;

(4) "Full-time magistrate judge" shall mean a full-time United States magistrate judge;

(5) "Part-time magistrate judge" shall mean a part-time United States magistrate judge; and

(6) "United States magistrate judge" and "magistrate judge" shall mean both full-time and part-time United States magistrate judges.

(June 25, 1948, c. 646, 62 Stat. 917; Oct. 17, 1968, Pub.L. 90–578, Title I, § 101, 82 Stat. 1114; Dec. 1, 1990, Pub.L. 101–650, Title III, § 321, 104 Stat. 5117.)

HISTORICAL AND STATUTORY NOTES

Effective and Applicability Provisions

1968 Acts. Amendment by Pub.L. 90–578 effective Oct. 17, 1968, except when a later effective date is applicable, which is the earlier of date when implementation of amendment by appointment of magistrates and assumption of office takes place or third anniversary of enactment of Pub.L. 90–578 on Oct. 17, 1968, see section 403 of Pub.L. 90–578, set out as a note under section 631 of this title.

Change of Name

"United States magistrate judge" substituted for "United States magistrate" in text pursuant to section 321 of Pub.L. 101–650, set out as a note under 28 U.S.C.A. § 631.

CHAPTER 44—ALTERNATIVE DISPUTE RESOLUTION

Sec.
651. Authorization of alternative dispute resolution.
652. Jurisdiction.
653. Neutrals.
654. Arbitration.
655. Arbitrators.
656. Subpoenas.
657. Arbitration award and judgment.
658. Compensation of arbitrators and neutrals.

§ 651. Authorization of alternative dispute resolution

(a) Definition.—For purposes of this chapter, an alternative dispute resolution process includes any process or procedure, other than an adjudication by a presiding judge, in which a neutral third party participates to assist in the resolution of issues in controversy, through processes such as early neutral evaluation, mediation, minitrial, and arbitration as provided in sections 654 through 658.

(b) Authority.—Each United States district court shall authorize, by local rule adopted under section 2071(a), the use of alternative dispute resolution processes in all civil actions, including adversary proceedings in bankruptcy, in accordance with this chapter, except that the use of arbitration may be authorized only as provided in section 654. Each United States district court shall devise and implement its own alternative dispute resolution program, by local rule adopted under section 2071(a), to encourage and promote the use of alternative dispute resolution in its district.

(c) Existing alternative dispute resolution programs.—In those courts where an alternative dispute resolution program is in place on the date of the enactment of the Alternative Dispute Resolution Act of 1998, the court shall examine the effectiveness of that program and adopt such improvements to the program as are consistent with the provisions and purposes of this chapter [28 U.S.C.A. § 651 et seq.].

(d) Administration of alternative dispute resolution programs.—Each United States district court shall designate an employee, or a judicial officer, who is knowledgeable in alternative dispute resolution practices and processes to implement, administer, oversee, and evaluate the court's alternative dispute resolution program. Such person may also be responsible for recruiting, screening, and training attorneys to serve as neutrals and arbitrators in the court's alternative dispute resolution program.

(e) Title 9 not affected.—This chapter [28 U.S.C.A. § 651 et seq.] shall not affect title 9, United States Code.

(f) Program support.—The Federal Judicial Center and the Administrative Office of the United States Courts are authorized to assist the district courts in the establishment and improvement of alternative dispute resolution programs by identifying particular practices employed in successful programs and providing additional assistance as needed and appropriate. (Added Pub.L. 100–702, Title IX, § 901(a), Nov. 19, 1988, 102 Stat. 4659, and amended Pub.L. 105–315, § 3, Oct. 30, 1998, 112 Stat. 2993.)

HISTORICAL AND STATUTORY NOTES

References in Text

The enactment of the Alternative Dispute Resolution Act of 1998, referred to in subsec. (c), is the enactment of Pub.L. 105–315, 112 Stat. 2993, which was approved Oct. 30, 1998.

Effective and Applicability Provisions

1988 Acts. Section 906 of Title IX of Pub.L. 100–702, as amended Pub.L. 103–192, § 1(a), Dec. 14, 1993, 107 Stat. 2292, which provided that, effective December 31, 1994, this chapter, as added by section 901 of Pub.L. 100–702, and the item relating to this chapter in the table of chapters at the beginning of part III of this title, were repealed, except that the provisions of this chapter were to continue to apply through final disposition of all actions in which referral to arbitration was made before the date of repeal, was itself repealed by Pub.L. 103–420, § 3(b), Oct. 25, 1994, 108 Stat. 4345.

Section 907 of Title IX of Pub.L. 100–702 provided that: "This title and the amendments made by this title [enacting this chapter, provisions set out as notes under this section and section 652 of this title] shall take effect 180 days after the date of enactment of this Act [Nov. 19, 1988]."

Findings and Declaration of Policy

Pub.L. 105–315, § 2, Oct. 30, 1998, 112 Stat. 2993, provided that:

"Congress finds that—

"(1) alternative dispute resolution, when supported by the bench and bar, and utilizing properly trained neutrals in a program adequately administered by the court, has the potential to provide a variety of benefits, including greater satisfaction of the parties, innovative methods of resolving disputes, and greater efficiency in achieving settlements;

"(2) certain forms of alternative dispute resolution, including mediation, early neutral evaluation, minitrials, and voluntary arbitration, may have potential to reduce the large backlog of cases now pending in some Federal courts throughout the United States, thereby allowing the courts to process their remaining cases more efficiently; and

"(3) the continued growth of Federal appellate court-annexed mediation programs suggests that this form of alternative dispute resolution can be equally effective in resolving disputes in the Federal trial courts; therefore, the district courts should consider including mediation in their local alternative dispute resolution programs."

Authorization of Appropriations

Pub.L. 105–315, § 11, Oct. 30, 1998, 112 Stat. 2998, provided that: "There are authorized to be appropriated for each fiscal year such sums as may be necessary to carry out chapter 44 of title 28, United States Code [28 U.S.C.A. § 651 et seq.], as amended by this Act [Alternative Dispute Resolution Act of 1998, Pub.L. 105–315, Oct. 30, 1998, 112 Stat. 2993, amending sections 651 to 658 of this title, amending a provision set out as a note under section 652 of this title, and enacting notes set out under this section]."

Section 905 of Title IX of Pub.L. 100–702, as amended Pub.L. 103–192, § 1(b), Dec. 14, 1993, 107 Stat. 2292; Pub.L. 103–420, § 3(a), Oct. 25, 1994, 108 Stat. 4345; Pub.L. 105–53, § 1, Oct. 6, 1997, 111 Stat. 1173, provided that: "There are authorized to be appropriated for each fiscal year to the judicial branch such sums as may be necessary to carry out the purposes of chapter 44 [this chapter], as added by section 901 of this Act. Funds appropriated under this section shall be allocated by the Administrative Office of the United States Courts to Federal judicial districts and the Federal Judicial Center. The funds so appropriated are authorized to remain available until expended."

Effect on Judicial Rulemaking Powers

Section 904 of Title IX of Pub.L. 100–702 provided that: "Nothing in this title [enacting this chapter and provisions set out as notes under this section and section 652 of this title], or in chapter 44 [this chapter], as added by section 901 of this Act, is intended to abridge, modify, or enlarge the rule making powers of the Federal judiciary."

Model Procedures

Section 902 of Title IX of Pub.L. 100–702 provided that: "The Judicial Conference of the United States may develop model rules relating to procedures for arbitration under chapter 44 [this chapter], as added by section 901 of this Act. No model rule may supersede any provision of such chapter 44, this title [enacting this chapter and provisions set out as notes under this section and section 652 of this title], or any law of the United States."

Reports by Director of Administrative Office of United States Courts and by Federal Judicial Center

Pub.L. 100–702, Title IX, § 903, Nov. 19, 1988, 102 Stat. 4663, provided that:

"**(a) Annual Report by Director of Administrative Office of the United States Courts.**—The Director of the Administrative Office of the United States Courts shall include in the annual report of the activities of the Administrative Office required under section 604(a)(3) [section 604(a)(3) of this title], statistical information about the implementation of chapter 44 [this chapter], as added by section 901 of this Act."

"**(b) Report by Federal Judicial Center.**—Not later than 5 years after the date of enactment of this Act [Nov. 19, 1988], the Federal Judicial Center, in consultation with the Director of the Administrative Office of the United States Courts, shall submit to the Congress a report on the implementation of chapter 44 [this chapter], as added by section 901 of this Act, which shall include the following:

"(1) A description of the arbitration programs authorized by such chapter, as conceived and as implemented in the judicial districts in which such programs are authorized.

"(2) A determination of the level of satisfaction with the arbitration programs in those judicial districts by a sampling of court personnel, attorneys, and litigants whose cases have been referred to arbitration.

"(3) A summary of those program features that can be identified as being related to program acceptance both within and across judicial districts.

"(4) A description of the levels of satisfaction relative to the cost per hearing of each program.

"(5) Recommendations to the Congress on whether to terminate or continue chapter 44, or alternatively, to enact an arbitration provision in title 28, United States Code [this title], authorizing arbitration in all Federal district courts."

[For termination, effective May 15, 2000, of reporting provisions of this note, see Pub.L. 104–66, § 3003, as amended, set out as a note under 31 U.S.C.A. § 1113, and the 11th item on page 12 of House Document No. 103–7.]

Treatment of Expired Provisions

Pub.L. 103–192, § 2, Dec. 14, 1993, 107 Stat. 2292, provided that: "Chapter 44 of title 28, United States Code [this chapter], and the item relating to that chapter in the table of chapters at the beginning of part III of such title [analysis preceding section 601 of this title], shall be effective on or after the date of the enactment of this Act [Dec. 14, 1993] as if such chapter and item had not been repealed by section 906 of the Judicial Improvements and Access to Justice Act [section 906 of Pub.L. 100–702, set out as an Effective Date of Repeal note under this section] as such section was in effect on the day before the date of the enactment of this Act [Dec. 14, 1993]."

§ 652. Jurisdiction

(a) Consideration of alternative dispute resolution in appropriate cases.—Notwithstanding any provision of law to the contrary and except as provided in subsections (b) and (c), each district court shall, by local rule adopted under section 2071(a), require that litigants in all civil cases consider the use of an alternative dispute resolution process at an appropriate stage in the litigation. Each district court shall provide litigants in all civil cases with at least one alternative dispute resolution process, including, but not limited to, mediation, early neutral evaluation, minitrial, and arbitration as authorized in sections 654 through 658. Any district court that elects to require the use of alternative dispute resolution in certain cases may do so only with respect to mediation, early neutral evaluation, and, if the parties consent, arbitration.

(b) Actions exempted from consideration of alternative dispute resolution.—Each district court may exempt from the requirements of this section specific cases or categories of cases in which use of alternative dispute resolution would not be appropriate. In defining these exemptions, each district court shall consult with members of the bar, including the United States Attorney for that district.

(c) Authority of the Attorney General.—Nothing in this section shall alter or conflict with the authority of the Attorney General to conduct litigation on behalf of the United States, with the authority of any Federal agency authorized to conduct litigation in the United States courts, or with any delegation of litigation authority by the Attorney General.

(d) Confidentiality provisions.—Until such time as rules are adopted under chapter 131 of this title [28 U.S.C.A. § 2071 et seq.] providing for the confidentiality of alternative dispute resolution processes under this chapter [28 U.S.C.A. § 651 et seq.], each district court shall, by local rule adopted under section 2071(a), provide for the confidentiality of the alternative dispute resolution processes and to prohibit disclosure of confidential dispute resolution communications.

(Added Pub.L. 100–702, Title IX, § 901(a), Nov. 19, 1988, 102 Stat. 4659, and amended Pub.L. 105–315, § 4, Oct. 30, 1998, 112 Stat. 2994.)

HISTORICAL AND STATUTORY NOTES

Effective and Applicability Provisions

1988 Acts. Section 906 of Pub.L. 100–702, as amended, which provided that, effective Dec. 31, 1994, this section was repealed, with certain exceptions, was itself repealed by Pub.L. 103–420, § 3(b), Oct. 25, 1994, 108 Stat. 4345. See section 906 of Pub.L. 100–702, set out as a note under section 651 of this title.

Section effective 180 days after Nov. 19, 1988, see section 907 of Pub.L. 100–702, set out as a note under section 651 of this title.

Treatment of Expired Provisions

This section to continue to be effective on or after Dec. 14, 1993 as if it had not been repealed by section 906 of Pub.L. 100–702, as such section was in effect on the day before such date, see Treatment of Expired Provisions note set out under section 651 of this title.

Exception to Limitation on Money Damages

Section 901(c) of Pub.L. 100–702, which provided that notwithstanding this section a district court listed in section 658 of this title whose local rule on Nov. 19, 1988 provided for a limitation on money damages with respect to cases referred to arbitration of not more than $150,000 may continue to apply the higher limitation, was repealed by Pub.L. 105–315, § 12(a), Oct. 30, 1998, 112 Stat. 2998.

§ 653. Neutrals

(a) Panel of neutrals.—Each district court that authorizes the use of alternative dispute resolution processes shall adopt appropriate processes for making neutrals available for use by the parties for each category of process offered. Each district court shall promulgate its own procedures and criteria for the selection of neutrals on its panels.

(b) Qualifications and training.—Each person serving as a neutral in an alternative dispute resolution process should be qualified and trained to serve as a neutral in the appropriate alternative dispute resolution process. For this purpose, the district court may use, among others, magistrate judges who have been trained to serve as neutrals in alternative dispute resolution processes, professional neutrals from the private sector, and persons who have been trained to serve as neutrals in alternative dispute resolution processes. Until such time as rules are adopted under chapter 131 of this title [28 U.S.C.A. § 2071 et seq.] relating to the disqualification of neutrals, each district court shall issue rules under section 2071(a) relating to the disqualification of neutrals (including, where appropriate, disqualification under section 455 of this title, other applicable law, and professional responsibility standards).

(Added Pub.L. 100–702, Title IX, § 901(a), Nov. 19, 1988, 102 Stat. 4660, and amended Pub.L. 105–315, § 5, Oct. 30, 1998, 112 Stat. 2995.)

HISTORICAL AND STATUTORY NOTES

Effective and Applicability Provisions

1988 Acts. Section 906 of Pub.L. 100–702, as amended, which provided that, effective Dec. 31, 1994, this section was repealed, with certain exceptions, was itself repealed by Pub.L. 103–420, § 3(b), Oct. 25, 1994, 108 Stat. 4345. See section 906 of Pub.L. 100–702, set out as a note under section 651 of this title.

Section effective 180 days after Nov. 19, 1988, see section 907 of Pub.L. 100–702, set out as a note under section 651 of this title.

Treatment of Expired Provisions

This section to continue to be effective on or after Dec. 14, 1993 as if it had not been repealed by section 906 of Pub.L. 100–702 as such section was in effect on the day before such date, see Treatment of Expired Provisions note set out under section 651 of this title.

§ 654. Arbitration

(a) Referral of actions to arbitration.—Notwithstanding any provision of law to the contrary and except as provided in subsections (a), (b), and (c) of section 652 and subsection (d) of this section, a district court may allow the referral to arbitration of any civil action (including any adversary proceeding in bankruptcy) pending before it when the parties consent, except that referral to arbitration may not be made where—

(1) the action is based on an alleged violation of a right secured by the Constitution of the United States;

(2) jurisdiction is based in whole or in part on section 1343 of this title; or

(3) the relief sought consists of money damages in an amount greater than $150,000.

(b) Safeguards in consent cases.—Until such time as rules are adopted under chapter 131 of this title relating to procedures described in this subsection, the district court shall, by local rule adopted under section 2071(a), establish procedures to ensure that any civil action in which arbitration by consent is allowed under subsection (a)—

(1) consent to arbitration is freely and knowingly obtained; and

(2) no party or attorney is prejudiced for refusing to participate in arbitration.

(c) Presumptions.—For purposes of subsection (a)(3), a district court may presume damages are not in excess of $150,000 unless counsel certifies that damages exceed such amount.

(d) Existing programs.—Nothing in this chapter is deemed to affect any program in which arbitration is conducted pursuant to section [1] title IX of the Judicial Improvements and Access to Justice Act (Public Law 100–702), as amended by section 1 of Public Law 105–53.

(Added Pub.L. 100–702, Title IX, § 901(a), Nov. 19, 1988, 102 Stat. 4660, and amended Pub.L. 105–315, § 6, Oct. 30, 1998, 112 Stat. 2995.)

[1] So in original. The word "section" probably should not appear.

HISTORICAL AND STATUTORY NOTES

References in Text

Title IX of the Judicial Improvements and Access to Justice Act, referred to in subsec. (d), is Pub.L. 100–702, Title IX, Nov. 19, 1988, 102 Stat. 4663. See Codifications note under this section.

Codifications

Section title IX of the Judicial Improvements and Access to Justice Act, referred to in subsec. (d), probably should read section 905 of title IX of the Judicial Improvements and Access to Justice Act, which is Pub.L. 100–702, Title IX, § 905, Nov. 19, 1988, 102 Stat. 4663, set out as a note under section 651 of this title.

Effective and Applicability Provisions

1988 Acts. Section 906 of Pub.L. 100–702, as amended, which provided that, effective Dec. 31, 1994, this section was repealed, with certain exceptions, was itself repealed by Pub.L. 103–420, § 3(b), Oct. 25, 1994, 108 Stat. 4345. See section 906 of Pub.L. 100–702, set out as a note under section 651 of this title.

Section effective 180 days after Nov. 19, 1988, see section 907 of Pub.L. 100–702, set out as a note under section 651 of this title.

Treatment of Expired Provisions

This section to continue to be effective on or after Dec. 14, 1993 as if it had not been repealed by section 906 of Pub.L. 100–702 as such section was in effect on the day before such date, see Treatment of Expired Provisions note set out under section 651 of this title.

§ 655. Arbitrators

(a) Powers of arbitrators.—An arbitrator to whom an action is referred under section 654 shall have the power, within the judicial district of the district court which referred the action to arbitration—

(1) to conduct arbitration hearings;

(2) to administer oaths and affirmations; and

(3) to make awards.

(b) Standards for certification.—Each district court that authorizes arbitration shall establish standards for the certification of arbitrators and shall certify arbitrators to perform services in accordance with such standards and this chapter. The standards shall include provisions requiring that any arbitrator—

(1) shall take the oath or affirmation described in section 453; and

(2) shall be subject to the disqualification rules under section 455.

(c) Immunity.—All individuals serving as arbitrators in an alternative dispute resolution program under this chapter are performing quasi-judicial functions and are entitled to the immunities and protections that the law accords to persons serving in such capacity.

(Added Pub.L. 100–702, Title IX, § 901(a), Nov. 19, 1988, 102 Stat. 4661, and amended Pub.L. 105–315, § 7, Oct. 30, 1998, 112 Stat. 2996.)

HISTORICAL AND STATUTORY NOTES

Effective and Applicability Provisions

1988 Acts. Section 906 of Pub.L. 100–702, as amended, which provided that, effective Dec. 31, 1994, this section was repealed, with certain exceptions, was itself repealed by Pub.L. 103–420, § 3(b), Oct. 25, 1994, 108 Stat. 4345. See section 906 of Pub.L. 100–702, set out as a note under section 651 of this title.

Section effective 180 days after Nov. 19, 1988, see section 907 of Pub.L. 100–702, set out as a note under section 651 of this title.

Treatment of Expired Provisions

This section to continue to be effective on or after Dec. 14, 1993 as if it had not been repealed by section 906 of Pub.L. 100–702 as such section was in effect on the day before such date, see Treatment of Expired Provisions note set out under section 651 of this title.

§ 656. Subpoenas

Rule 45 of the Federal Rules of Civil Procedure (relating to subpoenas) applies to subpoenas for the attendance of witnesses and the production of documentary evidence at an arbitration hearing under this chapter.

(Added Pub.L. 100–702, Title IX, § 901(a), Nov. 19, 1988, 102 Stat. 4662, and amended Pub.L. 105–315, § 8, Oct. 30, 1998, 112 Stat. 2996.)

HISTORICAL AND STATUTORY NOTES

Effective and Applicability Provisions

1988 Acts. Section 906 of Pub.L. 100–702, as amended, which provided that, effective Dec. 31, 1994, this section was repealed, with certain exceptions, was itself repealed by Pub.L. 103–420, § 3(b), Oct. 25, 1994, 108 Stat. 4345. See section 906 of Pub.L. 100–702, set out as a note under section 651 of this title.

Section effective 180 days after Nov. 19, 1988, see section 907 of Pub.L. 100–702, set out as a note under section 651 of this title.

Treatment of Expired Provisions

This section to continue to be effective on or after Dec. 14, 1993 as if it had not been repealed by section 906 of Pub.L. 100–702 as such section was in effect on the day before such date, see Treatment of Expired Provisions note set out under section 651 of this title.

§ 657. Arbitration award and judgment

(a) Filing and effect of arbitration award.—An arbitration award made by an arbitrator under this chapter, along with proof of service of such award on the other party by the prevailing party or by the plaintiff, shall be filed promptly after the arbitration hearing is concluded with the clerk of the district court that referred the case to arbitration. Such award shall be entered as the judgment of the court after the time has expired for requesting a trial de novo. The judgment so entered shall be subject to the same provisions of law and shall have the same force and effect as a judgment of the court in a civil action, except that the judgment shall not be subject to review in any other court by appeal or otherwise.

(b) Sealing of arbitration award.—The district court shall provide, by local rule adopted under section 2071(a), that the contents of any arbitration award made under this chapter shall not be made known to any judge who might be assigned to the case until the district court has entered final judgment in the action or the action has otherwise terminated.

(c) Trial de novo of arbitration awards.—

(1) **Time for filing demand.**—Within 30 days after the filing of an arbitration award with a district court under subsection (a), any party may file a written demand for a trial de novo in the district court.

(2) **Action restored to court docket.**—Upon a demand for a trial de novo, the action shall be restored to the docket of the court and treated for all purposes as if it had not been referred to arbitration.

(3) **Exclusion of evidence of arbitration.**—The court shall not admit at the trial de novo any evidence that there has been an arbitration proceeding, the nature or amount of any award, or any other matter concerning the conduct of the arbitration proceeding, unless—

(A) the evidence would otherwise be admissible in the court under the Federal Rules of Evidence; or

(B) the parties have otherwise stipulated.

(Added Pub.L. 100–702, Title IX, § 901(a), Nov. 19, 1988, 102 Stat. 4662, and amended Pub.L. 105–315, § 9, Oct. 30, 1998, 112 Stat. 2997.)

HISTORICAL AND STATUTORY NOTES

Effective and Applicability Provisions

1988 Acts. Section 906 of Pub.L. 100–702, as amended, which provided that, effective Dec. 31, 1994, this section was repealed, with certain exceptions, was itself repealed by Pub.L. 103–420, § 3(b), Oct. 25, 1994, 108 Stat. 4345. See section 906 of Pub.L. 100–702, set out as a note under section 651 of this title.

Section effective 180 days after Nov. 19, 1988, see section 907 of Pub.L. 100–702, set out as a note under section 651 of this title.

Treatment of Expired Provisions

This section to continue to be effective on or after Dec. 14, 1993 as if it had not been repealed by section 906 of Pub.L. 100–702 as such section was in effect on the day before such date, see Treatment of Expired Provisions note set out under section 651 of this title.

§ 658. Compensation of arbitrators and neutrals

(a) Compensation.—The district court shall, subject to regulations approved by the Judicial Conference of the United States, establish the amount of compensation, if any, that each arbitrator or neutral shall receive for services rendered in each case under this chapter.

(b) Transportation allowances.—Under regulations prescribed by the Director of the Administrative Office of the United States Courts, a district court may reimburse arbitrators and other neutrals for actual transportation expenses necessarily incurred in the performance of duties under this chapter.

(Added Pub.L. 100–702, Title IX, § 901(a), Nov. 19, 1988, 102 Stat. 4662, and amended Pub.L. 105–315, § 10, Oct. 30, 1998, 112 Stat. 2997.)

HISTORICAL AND STATUTORY NOTES

Effective and Applicability Provisions

1988 Acts. Section 906 of Pub.L. 100–702, as amended, which provided that, effective Dec. 31, 1994, this section was repealed, with certain exceptions, was itself repealed by Pub.L. 103–420, § 3(b), Oct. 25, 1994, 108 Stat. 4345. See section 906 of Pub.L. 100–702, set out as a note under section 651 of this title.

Section effective 180 days after Nov. 19, 1988, see section 907 of Pub.L. 100–702, set out as a note under section 651 of this title.

Treatment of Expired Provisions

This section to continue to be effective on or after Dec. 14, 1993 as if it had not been repealed by section 906 of Pub.L. 100–702 as such section was in effect on the day before such date, see Treatment of Expired Provisions note set out under section 651 of this title.

CHAPTER 45—SUPREME COURT

Sec.
671. Clerk.
672. Marshal.
673. Reporter.
674. Librarian.
675. Law clerks and secretaries.
676. Printing and binding.
677. Counselor to the Chief Justice.

§ 671. Clerk

(a) The Supreme Court may appoint and fix the compensation of a clerk and one or more deputy clerks. The clerk shall be subject to removal by the Court. Deputy clerks shall be subject to removal by the clerk with the approval of the Court or the Chief Justice of the United States.

[**(b)** Repealed. Pub.L. 92–310, Title II, § 206(c), June 6, 1972, 86 Stat. 203.]

(c) The clerk may appoint and fix the compensation of necessary assistants and messengers with the approval of the Chief Justice of the United States.

(d) The clerk shall pay into the Treasury all fees, costs, and other moneys collected by him. He shall make annual returns thereof to the Court under regulations prescribed by it.

(June 25, 1948, c. 646, 62 Stat. 918; Mar. 10, 1964, Pub.L. 88–279, § 1, 78 Stat. 158; June 6, 1972, Pub.L. 92–310, Title II, § 206(c), 86 Stat. 203.)

HISTORICAL AND STATUTORY NOTES

Effective and Applicability Provisions

1964 Acts. Section 4 of Pub.L. 88–279 provided that: "The amendments proposed in this Act [amending subsecs. (c) and (d) of this section and section 672 of this title] shall become effective only when funds have been appropriated and are available to pay the salaries and other expenses of the clerk's office."

Appropriations

Section 3 of Pub.L. 88–279 provided that: "There are hereby authorized to be appropriated annually such sums as are necessary to carry out the provisions of this Act [amending subsecs. (c) and (d) of this section and section 672 of this title]."

§ 672. Marshal

(a) The Supreme Court may appoint a marshal, who shall be subject to removal by the Court, and may fix his compensation.

(b) The marshal may, with the approval of the Chief Justice of the United States, appoint and fix the compensation of necessary assistants and other employees to attend the Court, and necessary custodial employees.

(c) The marshal shall:

(1) Attend the Court at its sessions;

(2) Serve and execute all process and orders issued by the Court or a member thereof;

(3) Take charge of all property of the United States used by the Court or its members;

(4) Disburse funds appropriated for work upon the Supreme Court building and grounds under the jurisdiction of the Architect of the Capitol upon certified vouchers submitted by the Architect;

(5) Disburse funds appropriated for the purchase of books, pamphlets, periodicals and other publications, and for their repair, binding, and rebinding, upon vouchers certified by the librarian of the Court;

(6) Pay the salaries of the Chief Justice, Associate Justices, and all officers and employees of the Court and disburse other funds appropriated for disbursement, under the direction of the Chief Justice;

(7) Pay the expenses of printing briefs and travel expenses of attorneys in behalf of persons whose motions to appear in forma pauperis in the Supreme Court have been approved and when counsel have been appointed by the Supreme Court, upon vouchers certified by the clerk of the Court;

(8) Oversee the Supreme Court Police.

(June 25, 1948, c. 646, 62 Stat. 918; Mar. 10, 1964, Pub.L. 88–279, § 2, 78 Stat. 158; Dec. 29, 1982, Pub.L. 97–390, § 2, 96 Stat. 1958.)

HISTORICAL AND STATUTORY NOTES

Effective and Applicability Provisions

1964 Acts. Amendment of subsec. (c) of this section by Pub.L. 88–279 effective upon appropriation and availability of funds to pay salaries and other expenses of the clerk's office, see section 4 of Pub.L. 88–279, set out as a note under section 671 of this title.

Appropriations

Annual appropriations to carry out amendment of subsec. (c) of this section by Pub.L. 88–279, see section 3 of Pub.L. 88–279, set out as a note under section 671 of this title.

Increases in Compensation Rates

For increases in rates of basic compensation fixed pursuant to this section, see notes under section 603 of this title.

§ 673. Reporter

(a) The Supreme Court may appoint and fix the compensation of a reporter of its decisions who shall be subject to removal by the Court.

(b) The reporter may appoint and fix the compensation of necessary professional and clerical assistants and other employees, with the approval of the Court or the Chief Justice of the United States.

(c) The reporter shall, under the direction of the Court or the Chief Justice, prepare the decisions of the Court for publication in bound volumes and advance copies in pamphlet installments.

The reporter shall determine the quality and size of the paper, type, format, proofs and binding subject to the approval of the Court or the Chief Justice.

(June 25, 1948, c. 646, 62 Stat. 919.)

HISTORICAL AND STATUTORY NOTES

Increases in Compensation Rates

For increases in rates of basic compensation fixed pursuant to this section, see notes under section 603 of this title.

§ 674. Librarian

(a) The Supreme Court may appoint a librarian, whose salary it shall fix, and who shall be subject to removal by the Court.

(b) The librarian shall, with the approval of the Chief Justice, appoint necessary assistants and fix their compensation and make rules governing the use of the library.

(c) He shall select and acquire by purchase, gift, bequest, or exchange, such books, pamphlets, periodicals, microfilm and other processed copy as may be required by the Court for its official use and for the reasonable needs of its bar.

(d) The librarian shall certify to the marshal for payment vouchers covering expenditures for the purchase of such books and other material, and for binding, rebinding and repairing the same.

(June 25, 1948, c. 646, 62 Stat. 919; June 6, 1972, Pub.L. 92–310, Title II, § 206(d), 86 Stat. 203.)

HISTORICAL AND STATUTORY NOTES

Increases in Compensation Rates

For increases in rates of basic compensation fixed pursuant to this section, see notes under section 603 of this title.

§ 675. Law clerks and secretaries

The Chief Justice of the United States, and the associate justices of the Supreme Court may appoint law clerks and secretaries whose salaries shall be fixed by the Court.

(June 25, 1948, c. 646, 62 Stat. 919.)

HISTORICAL AND STATUTORY NOTES

Increases in Compensation Rates

For increases in rates of basic compensation fixed pursuant to this section, see notes under section 603 of this title.

§ 676. Printing and binding

(a) The printing and binding for the Supreme Court, including the printing and binding of individual copies, advance pamphlet installments, and bound volumes, of its decisions, whether requisitioned or ordered by the Court or any of its officers or by any other office or agency, and whether paid for by, or charged to the appropriation for, the Court or any other office or agency, shall be done by the printer or printers whom the Court or the Chief Justice of the United States may select, unless it shall otherwise order.

(b) Whenever advance pamphlet installments and bound volumes of the Court's decisions are printed by a private printer, an adequate number of copies for distribution in accordance with the requirements of section 411 of this title and for sale to the public shall be provided and made available for these purposes in such manner and at such prices as may be determined from time to time by the Supreme Court or the Chief Justice of the United States, in lieu of compliance by the Public Printer and the Superintendent of Documents with the requirements of sections 411 and 412 of this title with respect to such copies. Pending distribution or sale, such copies shall be the property of the United States and shall be held in the custody of the marshal or such other person, organization, or agency, as the Supreme Court or the Chief Justice of the United States may designate.

(June 25, 1948, c. 646, 62 Stat. 919; May 24, 1949, c. 139, § 74, 63 Stat. 100; Oct. 31, 1951, c. 655, § 45, 65 Stat. 725.)

§ 677. Counselor to the Chief Justice

(a) The Chief Justice of the United States may appoint a Counselor who shall serve at the pleasure of the Chief Justice and shall perform such duties as may be assigned to him by the Chief Justice. The salary payable to the Counselor shall be fixed by the Chief Justice at a rate which shall not exceed the salary payable to the Director of the Administrative Office of the United States Courts. The Counselor may elect to bring himself within the same retirement program available to the Director of the Administrative Office of the United States Courts, as provided by section 611 of this title, by filing a written election with the Chief Justice within the time and in the manner prescribed by section 611.

(b) The Counselor, with the approval of the Chief Justice, may appoint and fix the compensation of necessary employees. The Counselor and his employees shall be deemed employees of the Supreme Court.

(c)(1) Notwithstanding section 1342 of title 31, the Counselor, with the approval of the Chief Justice, may accept voluntary personal services to assist with public and visitor programs.

(2) No person may volunteer personal services under this subsection unless the person has first agreed, in writing, to waive any claim against the United States arising out of or in connection with such services, other than a claim under chapter 81 of title 5 [5 U.S.C.A. § 8101 et seq.].

(3) No person volunteering personal services under this subsection shall be considered an employee of the United States for any purpose other than for purposes of—

(A) chapter 81 of title 5 [5 U.S.C.A. § 8101 et seq.]; or

(B) chapter 171 of this title [28 U.S.C.A. § 2671 et seq.].

(4) In the administration of this subsection, the Counselor shall ensure that the acceptance of personal services shall not result in the reduction of pay or displacement of any employee of the Supreme Court.

(Added Pub.L. 92–238, § 1, Mar. 1, 1972, 86 Stat. 46, and amended Pub.L. 105–233, § 1, Aug. 13, 1998, 112 Stat. 1535; Pub.L. 110–402, § 1(b)(3)(A), Oct. 13, 2008, 122 Stat. 4254.)

CHAPTER 47—COURTS OF APPEALS

Sec.
711. Clerks and employees.
712. Law clerks and secretaries.
713. Librarians.
714. Criers and messengers.
715. Staff attorneys and technical assistants.

§ 711. Clerks and employees

(a) Each court of appeals may appoint a clerk who shall be subject to removal by the court.

(b) The clerk, with the approval of the court, may appoint necessary deputies, clerical assistants and employees in such number as may be approved by the Director of the Administrative Office of the United States Courts. Such deputies, clerical assistants and employees shall be subject to removal by the clerk with the approval of the court.

(c) The clerk shall pay into the Treasury all fees, costs and other moneys collected by him and make returns thereof to the Director of the Administrative Office of the United States Courts under regulations prescribed by him.

(June 25, 1948, c. 646, 62 Stat. 920.)

§ 712. Law clerks and secretaries

Circuit judges may appoint necessary law clerks and secretaries. A law clerk appointed under this section shall be exempt from the provisions of subchapter I of chapter 63 of title 5, unless specifically included by the appointing judge or by local rule of court.

(June 25, 1948, c. 646, 62 Stat. 920; Nov. 19, 1988, Pub.L. 100–702, Title X, § 1003(a)(3), 102 Stat. 4665.)

§ 713. Librarians

(a) Each court of appeals may appoint a librarian who shall be subject to removal by the court.

(b) The librarian, with the approval of the court, may appoint necessary library assistants in such numbers as the Director of the Administrative Office of the United States Courts may approve. The librarian may remove such library assistants with the approval of the court.

(June 25, 1948, c. 646, 62 Stat. 920; May 24, 1949, c. 139, § 75, 63 Stat. 100; Apr. 2, 1982, Pub.L. 97–164, Title I, § 120(b)(1), 96 Stat. 33.)

HISTORICAL AND STATUTORY NOTES

Effective and Applicability Provisions

1982 Acts. Amendment by Pub.L. 97–164 effective Oct. 1, 1982, see section 402 of Pub.L. 97–164, set out as a note under section 171 of this title.

Continuation of Service of Marshal for Court of Appeals for District of Columbia; Applicability of Other Law to Court During Such Individual's Service

Pub.L. 98–620, Title IV, § 415, Nov. 8, 1984, 98 Stat. 3364, provided that: "Any individual who, on the date of the enactment of the Federal Courts Improvement Act of 1982 [Pub.L. 97–164, enacted Apr. 2, 1982], was serving as marshal for the Court of Appeals for the District of Columbia under section 713(c) of title 28, United States Code [subsec. (c) of this section], may, after the date of the enactment of this Act [Nov. 8, 1984], so serve under that section as in effect on the date of the enactment of the Federal Courts Improvement Act of 1982. While such individual so serves, the provisions of section 714(a) of title 28, United States Code [section 714(a) of this title], shall not apply to the Court of Appeals for the District of Columbia."

§ 714. Criers and messengers

(a) Each court of appeals may appoint a crier who shall be subject to removal by the court.

(b) The crier, with the approval of the court, may appoint necessary messengers in such number as the Director of the Administrative Office of the United States Courts may approve. The crier may remove such messengers with the approval of the court. The crier shall also perform the duties of bailiff and messenger.

(Added Pub.L. 97–164, Title I, § 120(c)(1), Apr. 2, 1982, 96 Stat. 33.)

HISTORICAL AND STATUTORY NOTES

Effective and Applicability Provisions

1982 Acts. Section effective Oct. 1, 1982, see section 402 of Pub.L. 97–164, set out as a note under section 171 of this title.

Applicability of This Section to Court of Appeals for District of Columbia During Continued Service of Marshal for Court in Office on Apr. 2, 1982

Subsec. (a) of this section not to apply to the Court of Appeals for the District of Columbia during the continued service as Marshal for such Court of any individual who was serving in such office under section 713(c) of this title as of Apr. 2, 1982, see section 415 of Pub.L. 98–620, set out as a note under section 713 of this title.

§ 715. Staff attorneys and technical assistants

(a) The chief judge of each court of appeals, with the approval of the court, may appoint a senior staff attorney, who shall be subject to removal by the chief judge with the approval of the court.

(b) The senior staff attorney, with the approval of the chief judge, may appoint necessary staff attorneys and secretarial and clerical employees in such numbers as the Director of the Administrative Office of the United States Courts may approve, but in no event may the number of staff attorneys exceed the number of positions expressly authorized in an annual appropriation Act. The senior staff attorney may remove such staff attorneys and secretarial and clerical employees with the approval of the chief judge.

(c) The chief judge of the Court of Appeals for the Federal Circuit, with the approval of the court, may appoint a senior technical assistant who shall be subject to removal by the chief judge with the approval of the court.

(d) The senior technical assistant, with the approval of the court, may appoint necessary technical assistants in such number as the Director of the Administrative Office of the United States Courts may approve, but in no event may the number of technical assistants in the Court of Appeals for the Federal Circuit exceed the number of circuit judges in regular active service within such circuit. The senior technical assistant may remove such technical assistants with the approval of the court.

(Added Pub.L. 97–164, Title I, § 120(c)(1), Apr. 2, 1982, 96 Stat. 34.)

HISTORICAL AND STATUTORY NOTES

Effective and Applicability Provisions

1982 Acts. Section effective Oct. 1, 1982, see section 402 of Pub.L. 97–164, set out as a note under section 171 of this title.

CHAPTER 49—DISTRICT COURTS

Sec.
751. Clerks.
752. Law clerks and secretaries.

Sec.
753. Reporters.
754. Receivers of property in different districts.
755. Criers and bailiffs.
756. Power to appoint.

§ 751. Clerks

(a) Each district court may appoint a clerk who shall be subject to removal by the court.

(b) The clerk may appoint, with the approval of the court, necessary deputies, clerical assistants and employees in such number as may be approved by the Director of the Administrative Office of the United States Courts. Such deputies, clerical assistants and employees shall be subject to removal by the clerk with the approval of the court.

(c) The clerk of each district court shall reside in the district for which he is appointed, except that the clerk of the district court for the District of Columbia and the Southern District of New York may reside within twenty miles thereof. The district court may designate places within the district for the offices of the clerk and his deputies, and their official stations.

(d) A clerk of a district court or his deputy or assistant shall not receive any compensation or emoluments through any office or position to which he is appointed by the court, other than that received as such clerk, deputy or assistant, whether from the United States or from private litigants.

This subsection shall not apply to clerks or deputy clerks appointed as United States magistrate judges pursuant to section 631 of this title.

(e) The clerk of each district court shall pay into the Treasury all fees, costs and other moneys collected by him, except naturalization fees listed in section 742 of Title 8 and uncollected fees not required by Act of Congress to be prepaid.

He shall make returns thereof to the Director of the Administrative Office of the United States Courts under regulations prescribed by him.

(f) When the Court of International Trade is sitting in a judicial district, other than the Southern District or Eastern District of New York, the clerk of the district court of such judicial district or an authorized deputy clerk, upon the request of the chief judge of the Court of International Trade and with the approval of such district court, shall act in the district as clerk of the Court of International Trade, as prescribed by the rules and orders of the Court of International Trade for all purposes relating to the civil action then pending before such court.

(June 25, 1948, c. 646, 62 Stat. 920; Oct. 17, 1968, Pub.L. 90–578, Title IV, § 402(b)(2), 82 Stat. 1118; Oct. 10, 1980, Pub.L. 96–417, Title V, § 504, 94 Stat. 1743; Dec. 1, 1990, Pub.L. 101–650, Title III, § 321, 104 Stat. 5117.)

HISTORICAL AND STATUTORY NOTES

References in Text

Section 742 of Title 8, referred to in subsec. (e), was repealed by Act June 27, 1952, c. 477, Title IV, § 403(a)(42), 66 Stat. 280 eff. Dec. 24, 1952, and is now covered by section 1455 of Title 8, Aliens and Nationality.

Effective and Applicability Provisions

1980 Acts. Amendment by Pub.L. 96–417 effective on Nov. 1, 1980 and applicable with respect to civil actions pending on or commenced on or after such date, see section 701(a) of Pub.L. 96–417, as amended, set out as a note under section 251 of this title.

Change of Name

"United States magistrate judge" substituted for "United States magistrate" in text pursuant to section 321 of Pub.L. 101–650, set out as a note under 28 U.S.C.A. § 631. Previously, United States commissioners, referred to in text, were replaced by United States magistrates pursuant to Pub.L. 90–578, Oct. 17, 1968, 82 Stat. 1118. See chapter 43 of Title 28, 28 U.S.C.A. § 631 et seq.

§ 752. Law clerks and secretaries

District judges may appoint necessary law clerks and secretaries subject to any limitation on the aggregate salaries of such employees which may be imposed by law. A law clerk appointed under this section shall be exempt from the provisions of subchapter I of chapter 63 of title 5, unless specifically included by the appointing judge or by local rule of court.

(June 25, 1948, c. 646, 62 Stat. 921; Sept. 1, 1959, Pub.L. 86–221, 73 Stat. 452; Nov. 19, 1988, Pub.L. 100–702, Title X, § 1003(a)(3), 102 Stat. 4665.)

§ 753. Reporters

(a) Each district court of the United States, the United States District Court for the District of the Canal Zone, the District Court of Guam, and the District Court of the Virgin Islands shall appoint one or more court reporters.

The number of reporters shall be determined by the Judicial Conference of the United States.

The qualifications of such reporters shall be determined by standards formulated by the Judicial Conference. Each reporter shall take an oath faithfully to perform the duties of his office.

Each such court, with the approval of the Director of the Administrative Office of the United States Courts, may appoint additional reporters for temporary service not exceeding three months, when there is more reporting work in the district than can be performed promptly by the authorized number of reporters and the urgency is so great as to render it impracticable to obtain the approval of the Judicial Conference.

If any such court and the Judicial Conference are of the opinion that it is in the public interest that the duties of reporter should be combined with those of any other employee of the court, the Judicial Conference may authorize such a combination and fix the salary for the performance of the duties combined.

(b) Each session of the court and every other proceeding designated by rule or order of the court or by one of the judges shall be recorded verbatim by shorthand, mechanical means, electronic sound recording, or any other method, subject to regulations promulgated by the Judicial Conference and subject to the discretion and approval of the judge. The regulations promulgated pursuant to the preceding sentence shall prescribe the types of electronic sound recording or other means which may be used. Proceedings to be recorded under this section include (1) all proceedings in criminal cases had in open court; (2) all proceedings in other cases had in open court unless the parties with the approval of the judge shall agree specifically to the contrary; and (3) such other proceedings as a judge of the court may direct or as may be required by rule or order of court as[1] may be requested by any party to the proceeding.

The reporter or other individual designated to produce the record shall attach his official certificate to the original shorthand notes or other original records so taken and promptly file them with the clerk who shall preserve them in the public records of the court for not less than ten years.

The reporter or other individual designated to produce the record shall transcribe and certify such parts of the record of proceedings as may be required by any rule or order of court, including all arraignments, pleas, and proceedings in connection with the imposition of sentence in criminal cases unless they have been recorded by electronic sound recording as provided in this subsection and the original records so taken have been certified by him and filed with the clerk as provided in this subsection. He shall also transcribe and certify such other parts of the record of proceedings as may be required by rule or order of court. Upon the request of any party to any proceeding which has been so recorded who has agreed to pay the fee therefor, or of a judge of the court, the reporter or other individual designated to produce the record shall promptly transcribe the original records of the requested parts of the proceedings and attach to the transcript his official certificate, and deliver the same to the party or judge making the request.

The reporter or other designated individual shall promptly deliver to the clerk for the records of the court a certified copy of any transcript so made.

The transcript in any case certified by the reporter or other individual designated to produce the record shall be deemed prima facie a correct statement of the testimony taken and proceedings had. No transcripts of the proceedings of the court shall be considered as official except those made from the records certified by the reporter or other individual designated to produce the record.

The original notes or other original records and the copy of the transcript in the office of the clerk shall be open during office hours to inspection by any person without charge.

(c) The reporters shall be subject to the supervision of the appointing court and the Judicial Conference in the performance of their duties, including dealings with parties requesting transcripts.

(d) The Judicial Conference shall prescribe records which shall be maintained and reports which shall be filed by the reporters. Such records shall be inspected and audited in the same manner as the records and accounts of clerks of the district courts, and may include records showing:

(1) the quantity of transcripts prepared;

(2) the fees charged and the fees collected for transcripts;

(3) any expenses incurred by the reporters in connection with transcripts;

(4) the amount of time the reporters are in attendance upon the courts for the purpose of recording proceedings; and

(5) such other information as the Judicial Conference may require.

(e) Each reporter shall receive an annual salary to be fixed from time to time by the Judicial Conference of the United States. For the purposes of subchapter III of chapter 83 of title 5 and chapter 84 of such title, a reporter shall be considered a full-time employee during any pay period for which a reporter receives a salary at the annual salary rate fixed for a full-time reporter under the preceding sentence. All supplies shall be furnished by the reporter at his own expense.

(f) Each reporter may charge and collect fees for transcripts requested by the parties, including the United States, at rates prescribed by the court subject to the approval of the Judicial Conference. He shall not charge a fee for any copy of a transcript delivered to the clerk for the records of court. Fees for transcripts furnished in criminal proceedings to persons proceeding under the Criminal Justice Act (18 U.S.C. 3006A), or in habeas corpus proceedings to persons allowed to sue, defend, or appeal in forma pauperis, shall be paid by the United States out of moneys appropriated for those purposes. Fees for transcripts furnished in proceedings brought under section 2255 of this title to persons permitted to sue or appeal in forma pauperis shall be paid by the United States out of money appropriated for that purpose if the trial judge or a circuit judge certifies that the suit or appeal is not frivolous and that the transcript is needed to decide the issue presented by the suit or appeal. Fees for transcripts furnished in other proceedings to persons permitted to appeal in forma pauperis shall also be paid by the United States if the trial judge or a circuit judge certifies that the appeal is not frivolous (but presents a substantial question). The reporter may require any party requesting a transcript to prepay the estimated fee in advance except as to transcripts that are to be paid for by the United States.

(g) If, upon the advice of the chief judge of any district court within the circuit, the judicial council of any circuit determines that the number of court reporters provided such district court pursuant to subsection (a) of this section is insufficient to meet temporary demands and needs and that the services of additional court reporters for such district court should be provided the judges of such district court (including the senior judges thereof when such senior judges are performing substantial judicial services for such court) on a contract basis, rather than by appointment of court reporters as otherwise provided in this section, and such judicial council notifies the Director of the Administrative Office, in writing, of such determination, the Director of the Administrative Office is authorized to and shall contract, without regard to section 3709 of the Revised Statutes of the United States, as amended (41 U.S.C. 5), with any suitable person, firm, association, or corporation for the providing of court reporters to serve such district court under such terms and conditions as the Director of the Administrative Office finds, after consultation with the chief judge of the district court, will best serve the needs of such district court.

(June 25, 1948, c. 646, 62 Stat. 921; Oct. 31, 1951, c. 655, § 46, 65 Stat. 726; June 28, 1955, c. 189, § 3(c), 69 Stat. 176; June 20, 1958, Pub.L. 85–462, § 3(c), 72 Stat. 207; July 7, 1958, Pub.L. 85–508, § 12(e), 72 Stat. 348; July 1, 1960, Pub.L. 86–568, Title I, § 116(c), 74 Stat. 303; Sept. 2, 1965, Pub.L. 89–163, 79 Stat. 619; Sept. 2, 1965, Pub.L. 89–167, 79 Stat. 647; June 2, 1970, Pub.L. 91–272, § 14, 84 Stat. 298; Dec. 11, 1970, Pub.L. 91–545, 84 Stat. 1412; Apr. 2, 1982, Pub.L. 97–164, Title IV, § 401(a), 96 Stat. 56; Oct. 19, 1996, Pub.L. 104–317, Title III, § 305, 110 Stat. 3852.)

[1] So in original. Probably should be "or as".

HISTORICAL AND STATUTORY NOTES

References in Text

The Criminal Justice Act (18 U.S.C. 3006A), referred to in subsec. (f), probably means Pub.L. 88–455, Aug. 20, 1964, 78 Stat. 552, as amended, known as the Criminal Justice Act of 1964, which is classified to section 3006A of Title 18, Crimes and Criminal Procedure, and provisions set out as notes under that section.

Effective and Applicability Provisions

1982 Acts. Amendment by Pub.L. 97–164 effective Oct. 1, 1982, see section 402 of Pub.L. 97–164, set out as a note under section 171 of this title.

1960 Acts. Amendment by Pub.L. 86–568 effective on the first day of the first pay period which begins on or after July 1, 1960, see section 122 of Pub.L. 86–568.

1958 Acts. Amendment by Pub.L. 85–508 effective Jan. 3, 1959, upon admission of Alaska into the Union pursuant to Proc. No. 3269, Jan. 3, 1959, 24 F.R. 81, 73 Stat. c16, as required by sections 1 and 8(c) of Pub.L. 85–508, see notes set out under section 81A of this title and preceding section 21 of Title 48, Territories and Insular Possessions.

Savings Provisions

Section 401(b) of Pub.L. 97–164 provided that: "The regulations promulgated by the Judicial Conference pursuant to subsection (b) of section 753 of title 28 [subsec. (b) of this section], as amended by subsection (a) of this section, shall not take effect before one year after the effective date of this Act [Oct. 1, 1982]. During the one-year period after the date of the enactment of this Act [Apr. 2, 1982], the Judicial Conference shall experiment with the different methods of recording court proceedings. Prior to the effective date of such regulations, the law and regulations in effect the day before the date of enactment of this Act [Apr. 2, 1982] shall remain in full force and effect."

Salary Limitation For Court Reporters

1967—Pub.L. 90–206, Title II, § 213(c), Dec. 16, 1967, 81 Stat. 635, inserted a new salary limitation for court reporters effective the first pay period which begins on or after Oct. 1, 1967, which reflected the respective applicable pay increases provided by section 202(a) of Pub.L. 90–206 in corresponding rates of compensation for particular officers and employees of the government.

1966—Pub.L. 89–504, Title II, § 202(c), July 18, 1966, 80 Stat. 294, inserted a new salary limitation for court reporters effective the first pay period which begins on or after July 1, 1966, which reflected the respective applicable pay increases provided by section 102(a) of title I of Pub.L. 89–504 in corresponding rates of compensation for particular officers and employees of the government.

1965—Pub.L. 89–301, § 12(c), Oct. 29, 1965, 79 Stat. 1122, inserted a new salary limitation for court reporters which reflected the applicable pay increases provided by section 2(a) of Pub.L. 89–301 in corresponding rates of compensation for particular government officers and employees.

1964—Pub.L. 88–426, Title IV, § 402(c), Aug. 14, 1964, 78 Stat. 434, inserted a new salary limitation for court reporters which reflected the applicable pay increases provided by Title I of Pub.L. 88–426 in corresponding rates of compensation for particular government officers and employees.

1962—Pub.L. 87–793, Title VI, § 1004(c), Oct. 11, 1962, 76 Stat. 866, inserted a new salary limitation for court reporters effective for the pay period beginning on or after Oct. 11, 1962, and ending immediately prior to the first pay period beginning on or after Jan. 1, 1964, and provided for a second salary limitation effective for the first pay period beginning on or after Jan. 1, 1964, which reflected applicable pay increases provided by Title II of Pub.L. 87–793 in corresponding rates of compensation for particular government officers and employees.

Termination of United States District Court For The District Of The Canal Zone

For termination of the United States District Court for the District of the Canal Zone at end of the "transition period", being the 30-month period beginning Oct. 1, 1979, and ending midnight Mar. 31, 1982, see Paragraph 5 of Article XI of the Panama Canal Treaty of 1977 and sections 3831 and 3841 to 3843 of Title 22, Foreign Relations and Intercourse.

§ 754. Receivers of property in different districts

A receiver appointed in any civil action or proceeding involving property, real, personal or mixed, situated in different districts shall, upon giving bond as required by the court, be vested with complete jurisdiction and control of all such property with the right to take possession thereof.

He shall have capacity to sue in any district without ancillary appointment, and may be sued with respect thereto as provided in section 959 of this title.

Such receiver shall, within ten days after the entry of his order of appointment, file copies of the complaint and such order of appointment in the district court for each district in which property is located. The failure to file such copies in any district shall divest the receiver of jurisdiction and control over all such property in that district.

(June 25, 1948, c. 646, 62 Stat. 922.)

§ 755. Criers and bailiffs

Each district judge may appoint a crier for the court in which he presides who shall perform also the duties of bailiff and messenger. A crier may perform also the duties of law clerk if he is qualified to do so and the district judge who appointed him designates him to serve as a crier-law clerk. A crier designated to serve as a crier-law clerk shall receive the compensation of a law clerk, but only so much of that compensation as is in excess of the compensation to which he would be entitled as a crier shall be deemed the compensation of a law clerk for the purposes of any limitation imposed by law upon the aggregate salaries of law clerks and secretaries appointed by a district judge.

Each United States marshal may employ, with the approval of the judge, not exceeding four bailiffs as the district judge may determine, to attend the court, maintain order, wait upon the grand and petit juries, and perform such other necessary duties as the judge or marshal may direct.

If the position of crier or bailiff is to be filled by the appointment of a person who has not previously served as either crier or bailiff, preference in the appointment shall be given to a person who has served in the military or naval forces of the United States in time of war and who has been honorably discharged therefrom, if in the opinion of the appointing officer such person is as well qualified as any other available person to perform to the satisfaction of the appointing officer all the duties of the position.

(June 25, 1948, c. 646, 62 Stat. 923; Oct. 21, 1965, Pub.L. 89-281, 79 Stat. 1012; Nov. 18, 1988, Pub.L. 100-690, Title VII, § 7608(b), 102 Stat. 4515.)

§ 756. Power to appoint

Whenever a majority of the district judges of any district court cannot agree upon the appointment of any officer of such court, the chief judge shall make such appointment.

(June 25, 1948, c. 646, 62 Stat. 923.)

HISTORICAL AND STATUTORY NOTES

District of Columbia Register of Wills

Pub.L. 88-241, § 21(b), Dec. 23, 1963, 77 Stat. 628, repealed sections 3 and 4 of Act Aug. 2, 1949, c. 383, 63 Stat. 491, which provided for the appointment and removal of the Register of Wills by the United States District Court for the District of Columbia and made the office of Register of Wills a part of the United States District Court for the District of Columbia. See D.C.Code 1961 Ed., § 11-504(a).

CHAPTER 50—BANKRUPTCY COURTS [OMITTED]

§§ 771 to 775. Omitted.

HISTORICAL AND STATUTORY NOTES

Chapter 50, consisted of sections 771 to 775, as added by Pub.L. 95-598, Title II, § 233(a), Nov. 6, 1978, 92 Stat. 2666, 2667, effective June 28, 1984, pursuant to Pub.L. 95-598, Title IV, § 402(b), Nov. 6, 1978, 92 Stat. 2682, as amended by Pub.L. 98-249, § 1(a), Mar. 31, 1984, 98 Stat. 116; Pub.L. 98-271, § 1(a), Apr. 30, 1984, 98 Stat. 163; Pub.L. 98-299, § 1(a), May 25, 1984, 98 Stat. 214; Pub.L. 98-325, § 1(a), June 20, 1984, 98 Stat. 268.

Section 402(b) of Pub.L. 95-598 was amended by section 113 of Pub.L. 98-353, Title I, July 10, 1984, 98 Stat. 343, by substituting "shall not be effective" for "shall take effect on June 28 1984", thereby eliminating the addition of the chapter heading, section analysis, and sections 771 to 775 by section 233(a) of Pub.L. 95-598, effective June 27, 1984, pursuant to section 122(c) of Pub.L. 98-353, set out as an Effective Date note under section 151 of this title.

Section 121(a) of Pub.L. 98-353 directed that section 402(b) of Pub.L. 95-598 be amended by substituting "the date of enactment of the Bankruptcy Amendments and Federal Judgeship Act of 1984 [i.e. July 10, 1984]" for "June 28, 1984". This amendment was not executed in view of the prior amendment to section 402(b) of Pub.L. 95-598 by section 113 of Pub.L. 98-353.

Sections 771 to 775 read as follows:

CHAPTER 50—BANKRUPTCY COURTS

Sec.
771. Clerks.
772. Other employees.
773. Records of proceedings; reporters.
774. Power to appoint.
775. Salaries of employees.

§ 771. Clerks

(a) Based on need each bankruptcy court may appoint a clerk who shall be subject to removal only by the court.

(b) The clerk may appoint, with the approval of the court, necessary deputies, clerical assistants, and employees in such number as may be approved by the Director of the Administrative Office of the United States Courts. Such deputies, clerical assistants, and employees shall be subject to removal only by the clerk with the approval of the court. If there is no clerk, the Bankruptcy Judge shall perform the duties of this subsection.

(c) The clerk of each bankruptcy court shall reside in the district for which he is appointed. The bankruptcy court may designate places within the district for the offices of the clerk and his deputies, and their official stations.

(d) A clerk of a bankruptcy court or his deputy or assistant shall not receive any compensation or emoluments through any office or position to which he is appointed by the court, other than that received as such clerk, deputy or assistant, whether from the United States or from private litigants.

(e) The clerk of each bankruptcy court shall pay into the Treasury all fees, costs and other moneys collected by him, except uncollected fees not required by Act of Congress to be prepaid.

He shall make returns thereof to the Director of the Administrative Office of the United States Courts under regulations prescribed by him.

§ 772. Other employees

Bankruptcy judges may appoint necessary other employees, including law clerks and secretaries, subject to any limitation on the aggregate salaries of such employees which may be imposed by law.

§ 773. Records of proceedings; reporters

(a) The bankruptcy court shall require a record to be made, whenever practicable, of all proceedings in cases had in open court. The Judicial Conference shall prescribe that the record be taken by electronic sound recording means, by a court reporter appointed or employed by such bankruptcy court to take a verbatim record by shorthand or mechanical means, or by an employee of such court designated by such court to take such a verbatim record.

(b) On the request of a party to a proceeding that has been recorded who has agreed to pay the fee for a transcript, or a judge of the bankruptcy court, a transcript of the original record of the requested parts of such proceeding shall be made and delivered promptly to such party or judge. Any such transcript that is certified shall be deemed prima facie a correct statement of the testimony taken and proceedings had. No transcript of the proceedings of the bankruptcy court shall be considered as official except those made from certified records.

(c) Fees for transcripts furnished in proceedings to persons permitted to appeal in forma pauperis shall be paid by the United States out of money appropriated for that purpose if the trial judge or a circuit judge certifies that the appeal is not frivolous (but presents a substantial question).

§ 774. Power to appoint

Whenever a majority of the bankruptcy judges of any bankruptcy court cannot agree upon the appointment of any officer of such court, the chief judge shall make such appointment.

§ 775. Salaries of employees

The salary of an individual appointed or employed under section 771(a), 772, or 773(a) of this title shall be the same as the salary of an individual appointed or employed under section 751(a), 752, or 753(a) of this title, as the case may be. The salaries of individuals appointed under section 771(b) of this title shall be comparable to the salaries of individuals appointed under section 751(b) of this title.

CHAPTER 51—UNITED STATES COURT OF FEDERAL CLAIMS

Sec.
791. Clerk.
[792, 793. Repealed.]
794. Law clerks and secretaries.
795. Bailiffs and messengers.
796. Reporting of court proceedings.
797. Recall of retired judges.
798. Places of holding court; appointment of special masters.

§ 791. Clerk

(a) The United States Court of Federal Claims may appoint a clerk, who shall be subject to removal by the court. The clerk, with the approval of the court, may appoint necessary deputies and employees in such numbers as may be approved by the Director of the Administrative Office of the United States Courts. Such deputies and employees shall be subject to removal by the clerk with the approval of the court.

(b) The clerk shall pay into the Treasury all fees, costs and other moneys collected by him. He shall make returns thereof to the Director of the Administrative Office of the United States Courts under regulations prescribed by him.

(c) On the first day of every regular session of Congress, the clerk shall transmit to Congress a full and complete statement of all the judgments rendered by the court during the previous year, showing the dates and amounts thereof and the parties in whose favor they were rendered, together with a brief synopsis of the nature of the claims upon which they were rendered, and a statement of the costs taxed in each case.

(June 25, 1948, c. 646, 62 Stat. 923; Apr. 2, 1982, Pub.L. 97–164, Title I, § 121(a), 96 Stat. 34; Oct. 29, 1992, Pub.L. 102–572, Title IX, § 902(a)(1), 106 Stat. 4516.)

HISTORICAL AND STATUTORY NOTES

Effective and Applicability Provisions

1992 Acts. Amendment by Title IX of Pub.L. 102–572 effective Oct. 29, 1992, see section 911 of Pub.L 102–572, set out as a note under section 171 of Title 28, Judiciary and Judicial Procedure.

1982 Acts. Amendment by Pub.L. 97–164 effective Oct. 1, 1982, see section 402 of Pub.L. 97–164, set out as a note under section 171 of this title.

Termination of Reporting Requirements

For termination, effective May 15, 2000, of provisions in subsec. (c) of this section requiring transmittal to Congress of an annual statement relating to judgments rendered by the court, see Pub.L. 104–66, § 3003, as amended, set out as a note under 31 U.S.C.A. § 1113 and page 13 of House Document No. 103–7.

[§ 792. Repealed. Pub.L. 97–164, Title I, § 121(b), Apr. 2, 1982, 96 Stat. 34]

HISTORICAL AND STATUTORY NOTES

Section, Acts June 25, 1948, c. 646, 62 Stat. 923; July 28, 1953, c. 253, § 4(a), 67 Stat. 226; Sept. 3, 1954, c. 1263, § 41, 68 Stat. 1240; Aug. 14, 1964, Pub.L. 88–426, Title IV, § 403(h), 78 Stat. 434; Oct. 15, 1966, Pub.L. 89–681, § 3, 80 Stat. 959; Dec. 16, 1967, Pub.L. 90–206, Title II, § 213(e), 81 Stat. 635; Aug. 9, 1975, Pub.L. 94–82, Title II, § 205(b)(7), 89 Stat. 423; July 20, 1977, Pub.L. 95–69, § 3, 91 Stat. 274, provided for the appointment by the Court of Claims and compensation of sixteen commissioners of the Court of Claims.

Effective Date of Repeal

Repeal effective Oct. 1, 1982, see section 402 of Pub.L. 97–164, set out as an Effective and Applicability Provisions of 1992 Amendments note under section 171 of this title.

[§ 793. Repealed. July 28, 1953, c. 253, § 6, 67 Stat. 226]

HISTORICAL AND STATUTORY NOTES

Section, Act June 25, 1948, c. 646, 62 Stat. 924, related to the appointment of reporter-commissioners by the Court of Claims, and the employment of stenographers therefor.

§ 794. Law clerks and secretaries

The judges of the United States Court of Federal Claims may appoint necessary law clerks and secretaries, in such numbers as the Judicial Conference of the United States may approve for district judges, subject to any limitation of the aggregate salaries of such employees which may be imposed by law. A law clerk appointed under this section shall be exempt from the provisions of subchapter I of chapter 63 of title 5, unless specifically included by the appointing judge or by local rule of court.

(June 25, 1948, c. 646, 62 Stat. 924; Apr. 2, 1982, Pub.L. 97–164, Title I, § 121(c)(1), 96 Stat. 34; Nov. 19, 1988, Pub.L. 100–702, Title X, § 1003(a)(3), 102 Stat. 4665; Oct. 29, 1992, Pub.L. 102–572, Title IX, §§ 902(a)(1), 905, 106 Stat. 4516, 4517.)

HISTORICAL AND STATUTORY NOTES

Effective and Applicability Provisions

1992 Acts. Amendment by Title IX of Pub.L. 102–572 effective Oct. 29, 1992, see section 911 of Pub.L. 102–572, set out as a note under section 171 of Title 28, Judiciary and Judicial Procedure.

1982 Acts. Amendment by Pub.L. 97–164 effective Oct. 1, 1982, see section 402 of Pub.L. 97–164, set out as a note under section 171 of this title.

§ 795. Bailiffs and messengers

The chief judge of [1] United States Court of Federal Claims, with the approval of the court, may appoint necessary bailiffs and messengers, in such numbers as the Director of the Administrative Office of the United States Courts may approve, each of whom shall be subject to removal by the chief judge, with the approval of the court.

(June 25, 1948, c. 646, 62 Stat. 924; Apr. 2, 1982, Pub.L. 97–164, Title I, § 121(d)(1), 96 Stat. 35; Oct. 29, 1992, Pub.L. 102–572, Title IX, § 902(a)(1), 106 Stat. 4516.)

[1] So in original. "The" probably should follow "judge of".

HISTORICAL AND STATUTORY NOTES

Effective and Applicability Provisions

1992 Acts. Amendment by Title IX of Pub.L. 102–572 effective Oct. 29, 1992, see section 911 of Pub.L. 102–572, set out as a note under section 171 of Title 28, Judiciary and Judicial Procedure.

1982 Acts. Amendment by Pub.L. 97–164 effective Oct. 1, 1982, see section 402 of Pub.L. 97–164, set out as a note under section 171 of this title.

§ 796. Reporting of court proceedings

Subject to the approval of the United States Court of Federal Claims, the Director of the Administrative Office of the United States Courts is authorized to contract for the reporting of all proceedings had in open court, and in such contract to fix the terms and conditions under which such reporting services shall be performed, including the terms and conditions under which transcripts shall be supplied by the contractor to the court and to other persons, departments, and agencies.

(Added Pub.L. 91–272, § 15(a), June 2, 1970, 84 Stat. 298, and amended Pub.L. 97–164, Title I, § 121(e), Apr. 2, 1982,

96 Stat. 35; Pub.L. 102–572, Title IX, § 902(a)(1), Oct. 29, 1992, 106 Stat. 4516.)

HISTORICAL AND STATUTORY NOTES

Effective and Applicability Provisions

1992 Acts. Amendment by Title IX of Pub.L. 102–572 effective Oct. 29, 1992, see section 911 of Pub.L. 102–572, set out as a note under section 171 of Title 28, Judiciary and Judicial Procedure.

1982 Acts. Amendment by Pub.L. 97–164 effective Oct. 1, 1982, see section 402 of Pub.L. 97–164, set out as a note under section 171 of this title.

§ 797. Recall of retired judges

(a)(1) Any judge of the United States Court of Federal Claims who has retired from regular active service under subchapter III of chapter 83, or chapter 84, of title 5 shall be known and designated as a senior judge and may perform duties as a judge when recalled pursuant to subsection (b) of this section.

(2) Any judge of the Court of Federal Claims receiving an annuity under section 178(c) of this title (pertaining to disability) who, in the estimation of the chief judge, has recovered sufficiently to render judicial service, shall be known and designated as a senior judge and may perform duties as a judge when recalled under subsection (b) of this section.

(b) The chief judge of the Court of Federal Claims may, whenever he deems it advisable, recall any senior judge, with such judge's consent, to perform such duties as a judge and for such period of time as the chief judge may specify.

(c) Any senior judge performing duties pursuant to this section shall not be counted as a judge for purposes of the number of judgeships authorized by section 171 of this title.

(d) Any senior judge, while performing duties pursuant to this section, shall be paid the same allowances for travel and other expenses as a judge in active service. Such senior judge shall also receive from the Court of Federal Claims supplemental pay in an amount sufficient, when added to his retirement annuity, to equal the salary of a judge in active service for the same period or periods of time. Such supplemental pay shall be paid in the same manner as the salary of a judge.

(Added Pub.L. 92–375, § 2, Aug. 10, 1972, 86 Stat. 529, and amended Pub.L. 97–164, Title I, § 121(f)(1), Apr. 2, 1982, 96 Stat. 35; Pub.L. 99–651, Title II, § 202(c), Nov. 14, 1986, 100 Stat. 3648; Pub.L. 102–572, Title IX, §§ 902(a), 904(b), Oct. 29, 1992, 106 Stat. 4516, 4517; Pub.L. 106–518, Title III, § 308, Nov. 13, 2000, 114 Stat. 2419.)

HISTORICAL AND STATUTORY NOTES

Effective and Applicability Provisions

1992 Acts. Amendment by Title IX of Pub.L. 102–572 effective Oct. 29, 1992, see section 911 of Pub.L. 102–572, set out as a note under section 171 of Title 28, Judiciary and Judicial Procedure.

1986 Acts. Amendment by Pub.L. 99–651 effective Jan. 1, 1987, see section 203 of Pub.L. 99–651, set out as a note under section 155 of this title.

1982 Acts. Amendment by Pub.L. 97–164 effective Oct. 1, 1982, see section 402 of Pub.L. 97–164, set out as a note under section 171 of this title.

§ 798. Places of holding court; appointment of special masters

(a) The United States Court of Federal Claims is authorized to use facilities and hold court in Washington, District of Columbia, and throughout the United States (including its territories and possessions) as necessary for compliance with sections 173 and 2503(c) of this title. The facilities of the Federal courts, as well as other comparable facilities administered by the General Services Administration, shall be made available for trials and other proceedings outside of the District of Columbia.

(b) Upon application of a party or upon the judge's own initiative, and upon a showing that the interests of economy, efficiency, and justice will be served, the chief judge of the Court of Federal Claims may issue an order authorizing a judge of the court to conduct proceedings, including evidentiary hearings and trials, in a foreign country whose laws do not prohibit such proceedings, except that an interlocutory appeal may be taken from such an order pursuant to section 1292(d)(2) of this title, and the United States Court of Appeals for the Federal Circuit may, in its discretion, consider the appeal.

(c) The chief judge of the Court of Federal Claims may appoint special masters to assist the court in carrying out its functions. Any special masters so appointed shall carry out their responsibilities and be compensated in accordance with procedures set forth in the rules of the court.

(Added Pub.L. 98–620, Title IV, § 416(a), Nov. 8, 1984, 98 Stat. 3364, and amended Pub.L. 102–572, Title IX, §§ 902(a)(2), 906(a), (b), Oct. 29, 1992, 106 Stat. 4516–4518.)

HISTORICAL AND STATUTORY NOTES

Effective and Applicability Provisions

1992 Acts. Amendment by Title IX of Pub.L. 102–572 effective Oct. 29, 1992, see section 911 of Pub.L. 102–572, set out as a note under section 171 of Title 28, Judiciary and Judicial Procedure.

[CHAPTER 53—REPEALED]

[§§ 831 to 834. Repealed. Pub.L. 97–164, Title I, § 122(a), Apr. 2, 1982, 96 Stat. 36]

HISTORICAL AND STATUTORY NOTES

Section 831, Act June 25, 1948, c. 646, 62 Stat. 924, authorized the Court of Customs and Patent Appeals to appoint a clerk, assistant clerks, stenographic law clerks, clerical assistants, and other necessary employees, and set out duties of clerk.

Section 832, Acts June 25, 1948, c. 646, 62 Stat. 924; May 24, 1949, c. 139, § 76, 63 Stat. 101, authorized the Court of Customs and Patent Appeals to appoint a marshal and set out the duties of that marshal.

Section 833, Act June 25, 1948, c. 646, 62 Stat. 925, authorized the Court of Customs and Patent Appeals to appoint a reporter and set out duties of that reporter.

Section 834, Act June 25, 1948, c. 646, 62 Stat. 925, authorized the Court of Customs and Patent Appeals to appoint necessary bailiffs and messengers and set out the duties of those bailiffs and messengers.

Effective Date of Repeal

Repeal effective Oct. 1, 1982, see section 402 of Pub.L. 97–164, set out as a note under section 171 of this title.

CHAPTER 55—COURT OF INTERNATIONAL TRADE

Sec.
871. Clerk, chief deputy clerk, assistant clerk, deputies, assistants, and other employees.
872. Criers, bailiffs, and messengers.

§ 871. Clerk, chief deputy clerk, assistant clerk, deputies, assistants, and other employees

The Court of International Trade may appoint a clerk, a chief deputy clerk, an assistant clerk, deputy clerks, and such deputies, assistants, and other employees as may be necessary for the effective dispatch of the business of the court, who shall be subject to removal by the court.

(June 25, 1948, c. 646, 62 Stat. 925; Sept. 9, 1959, Pub.L. 86–243, § 1, 73 Stat. 474; Oct. 10, 1980, Pub.L. 96–417, Title V, § 501(17), 94 Stat. 1742.)

HISTORICAL AND STATUTORY NOTES

Effective and Applicability Provisions

1980 Acts. Amendment by Pub.L. 96–417 effective on Nov. 1, 1980 and applicable with respect to civil actions pending on or commenced on or after such date, see section 701(a) of Pub.L. 96–417, as amended, set out as a note under section 251 of this title.

Savings Provisions

Section 4 of Pub.L. 86–243 provided that: "Nothing contained in the amendments made by this Act [enacting section 873 and amending sections 253, 550, 871 and 872 of this title] shall be construed to deprive any person serving on the date of enactment of this Act [Sept. 9, 1959] as an officer or employee of the Customs Court of any rights, privileges, or civil service status, if any, to which such person is entitled under the laws of the United States or regulations thereunder."

§ 872. Criers, bailiffs, and messengers

The Court of International Trade may appoint such criers as it may require for said court, which criers shall also perform the duties of bailiffs and messengers and such other duties as the court directs and shall be subject to removal by the court.

(Added Pub.L. 86–243, § 1, Sept. 9, 1959, 73 Stat. 474, § 873, and amended Pub.L. 96–417, Title V, § 501(19), Oct. 10, 1980, 94 Stat. 1742; renumbered § 872, Pub.L. 99–466, § 3(b)(2), Oct. 14, 1986, 100 Stat. 1191.)

HISTORICAL AND STATUTORY NOTES

Effective and Applicability Provisions

1980 Acts. Amendment by Pub.L. 96–417 effective on Nov. 1, 1980 and applicable with respect to civil actions pending on or commenced on or after such date, see section 701(a) of Pub.L. 96–417, as amended, set out as a note under section 251 of this title.

Savings Provisions

Enactment of section by Pub.L. 86–243 as not depriving Customs Court officers or employees of any rights, privileges, or civil service status, see section 4 of Pub.L. 86–243, set out as a note under section 871 of this title.

Prior Provisions

A prior section 872, Acts June 25, 1948, c. 646, 62 Stat. 925; May 24, 1949, c. 139, § 78, 63 Stat. 101; Sept. 9, 1959, Pub.L. 86–243, § 1, 73 Stat. 474; Oct. 10, 1980, Pub.L. 96–417, Title V, § 501(18), 94 Stat. 1742, which related to appointment and duties of a marshal and deputy marshals, was repealed by Pub.L. 99–466, § 3(b)(1), Oct. 14, 1986, 100 Stat. 1191, effective 60 days after Oct. 14, 1986, pursuant to section 4 of Pub.L. 99–466, set out as a note under section 331 of this title.

CHAPTER 57—GENERAL PROVISIONS APPLICABLE TO COURT OFFICERS AND EMPLOYEES

Sec.
951. Oath of office of clerks and deputies.
[952. Repealed.]
953. Administration of oaths and acknowledgments.
954. Vacancy in clerk position; absence of clerk.
955. Practice of law restricted.
956. Powers and duties of clerks and deputies.
957. Clerks ineligible for certain offices.
958. Persons ineligible as receivers.
959. Trustees and receivers suable; management; State laws.
960. Tax liability.
961. Office expenses of clerks.
[962. Repealed.]
963. Courts defined.

§ 951. Oath of office of clerks and deputies

Each clerk of court and his deputies shall take the following oath or affirmation before entering upon their duties: "I, _____ _____, having been appointed _____, do solemnly swear (or affirm) that I will truly and faithfully enter and record all orders, decrees, judgments and proceedings of such court, and will faithfully and impartially discharge all other duties of my office according to the best of my abilities and understanding. So help me God."

(June 25, 1948, c. 646, 62 Stat. 925.)

[§ 952. Repealed. Pub.L. 92–310, Title II, § 206(e)(1), June 6, 1972, 86 Stat. 203]

HISTORICAL AND STATUTORY NOTES

Section, Act June 25, 1948, c. 646, 62 Stat. 926, related to bonds of clerks and deputies.

§ 953. Administration of oaths and acknowledgments

Each clerk of court and his deputies may administer oaths and affirmations and take acknowledgments.

(June 25, 1948, c. 646, 62 Stat. 926.)

§ 954. Vacancy in clerk position; absence of clerk

When the office of clerk is vacant, the deputy clerks shall perform the duties of the clerk in the name of the last person who held that office. When the clerk is incapacitated, absent, or otherwise unavailable to perform official duties, the deputy clerks shall perform the duties of the clerk in the name of the clerk. The court may designate a deputy clerk to act temporarily as clerk of the court in his or her own name.

(June 25, 1948, c. 646, 62 Stat. 926; June 6, 1972, Pub.L. 92–310, Title II, § 206(f), 86 Stat. 203; Oct. 19, 1996, Pub.L. 104–317, Title II, § 204(a), 110 Stat. 3850.)

§ 955. Practice of law restricted

The clerk of each court and his deputies and assistants shall not practice law in any court of the United States.

(June 25, 1948, c. 646, 62 Stat. 926.)

§ 956. Powers and duties of clerks and deputies

The clerk of each court and his deputies and assistants shall exercise the powers and perform the duties assigned to them by the court.

(June 25, 1948, c. 646, 62 Stat. 926.)

§ 957. Clerks ineligible for certain offices

A clerk of a court or any of his deputies shall not be appointed a commissioner, master, referee or receiver in any case, unless there are special reasons requiring such appointment which are recited in the order of appointment.

(June 25, 1948, c. 646, 62 Stat. 926; Nov. 6, 1978, Pub.L. 95–598, Title II, § 234, 92 Stat. 2667; Apr. 2, 1982, Pub.L. 97–164, Title I, § 122(b), 96 Stat. 36; July 10, 1984, Pub.L. 98–353, Title I, § 109, 98 Stat. 342.)

HISTORICAL AND STATUTORY NOTES

Codifications

Subsec. (a) of this section was amended by Pub.L. 95–598, Title II, § 234, Nov. 6, 1978, 92 Stat. 2667, effective June 28, 1984, pursuant to Pub.L. 95–598, Title IV, § 402(b), Nov. 6, 1978, 92 Stat. 2682, as amended by Pub.L. 98–249, § 1(a), Mar. 31, 1984, 98 Stat. 116; Pub.L. 98–271, § 1(a), Apr. 30, 1984, 98 Stat. 163; Pub.L. 98–299, § 1(a), May 25, 1984, 98 Stat. 214; Pub.L. 98–325, § 1(a), June 20, 1984, 98 Stat. 268, set out as an Effective and Applicability Provisions note preceding section 101 at T. 11, Bankruptcy, by inserting "or bankruptcy court" after "district court".

Section 402(b) of Pub.L. 95–598 was amended by section 113 of Pub.L. 98–353 by substituting "shall not be effective" for "shall take effect on June 28, 1984", thereby eliminating the amendment by section 234 of Pub.L. 95–598, effective June 27, 1984, pursuant to section 122(c) of Pub.L. 98–353, set out as an Effective and Applicability Provisions note under section 151 of this title.

Section 121(a) of Pub.L. 98–353 directed that section 402(b) of Pub.L. 95–598 be amended by substituting "the date of enactment of the Bankruptcy Amendments and Federal Judgeship Act of 1984 [i.e. July 10, 1984]" for "June 28, 1984". This amendment was not executed in view of the prior amendment to section 402(b) of Pub.L. 95–598 by section 113 of Pub.L. 98–353.

Effective and Applicability Provisions

1984 Acts. Amendment by Pub.L. 98–353 effective July 10, 1984, see section 122(a) of Pub.L. 98–353, set out as an Effective and Applicability Provisions note under section 151 of this title.

1982 Acts. Amendment by Pub.L. 97–164 effective Oct. 1, 1982, see section 402 of Pub.L. 97–164, set out as a note under section 171 of this title.

§ 958. Persons ineligible as receivers

A person holding any civil or military office or employment under the United States or employed by any justice or judge of the United States shall not at the same time be appointed a receiver in any case in any court of the United States.

(June 25, 1948, c. 646, 62 Stat. 926.)

§ 959. Trustees and receivers suable; management; State laws

(a) Trustees, receivers or managers of any property, including debtors in possession, may be sued, without leave of the court appointing them, with respect to any of their acts or transactions in carrying on business connected with such property. Such actions shall be subject to the general equity power of such court so far as the same may be necessary to the ends of justice, but this shall not deprive a litigant of his right to trial by jury.

(b) Except as provided in section 1166 of title 11, a trustee, receiver or manager appointed in any cause pending in any court of the United States, including a debtor in possession, shall manage and operate the property in his possession as such trustee, receiver or manager according to the requirements of the valid laws of the State in which such property is situated, in the same manner that the owner or possessor thereof would be bound to do if in possession thereof.

(June 25, 1948, c. 646, 62 Stat. 926; Nov. 6, 1978, Pub.L. 95–598, Title II, § 235, 92 Stat. 2667.)

HISTORICAL AND STATUTORY NOTES

Effective and Applicability Provisions

1978 Acts. Amendment by Pub.L. 95–598 effective Oct. 1, 1979, see section 402(c) of Pub.L. 95–598, as amended, set out as a note preceding section 101 of Title 11, Bankruptcy.

§ 960. Tax liability

(a) Any officers and agents conducting any business under authority of a United States court shall be subject to all Federal, State and local taxes applicable to such business to the same extent as if it were conducted by an individual or corporation.

(b) A tax under subsection (a) shall be paid on or before the due date of the tax under applicable nonbankruptcy law, unless—

(1) the tax is a property tax secured by a lien against property that is abandoned under section 554 of title 11, within a reasonable period of time after the lien attaches, by the trustee in a case under title 11; or

(2) payment of the tax is excused under a specific provision of title 11.

(c) In a case pending under chapter 7 of title 11, payment of a tax may be deferred until final distribution is made under section 726 of title 11, if—

(1) the tax was not incurred by a trustee duly appointed or elected under chapter 7 of title 11; or

(2) before the due date of the tax, an order of the court makes a finding of probable insufficiency of funds of the estate to pay in full the administrative expenses allowed under section 503(b) of title 11 that have the same priority in distribution under section 726(b) of title 11 as the priority of that tax.

(June 25, 1948, c. 646, 62 Stat. 927; Apr. 20, 2005, Pub.L. 109–8, Title VII, § 712(a), 119 Stat. 127.)

HISTORICAL AND STATUTORY NOTES

References in Text

Chapter 7 of title 11, referred to in subsec. (c), is 11 U.S.C.A. § 701 et seq.

Effective and Applicability Provisions

2005 Acts. Except as otherwise provided, amendments by Pub.L. 109–8 effective 180 days after April 20, 2005, and inapplicable with respect to cases commenced under Title 11 before the effective date, see Pub.L. 109–8, § 1501, set out as a note under 11 U.S.C.A. § 101.

§ 961. Office expenses of clerks

Each clerk of court shall be allowed his necessary office expenses when authorized by the Director of the Administrative Office of the United States Courts.

(June 25, 1948, c. 646, 62 Stat. 927.)

[§ 962. Repealed. Pub.L. 89–554, § 8(a), Sept. 6, 1966, 80 Stat. 663]

HISTORICAL AND STATUTORY NOTES

Section, Act June 25, 1948, c. 646, 62 Stat. 927, related to traveling expenses and subsistence for officers and employees of the courts of the United States and of the Administrative Office of the United States Courts and is now covered by section 5701 et seq. of Title 5, Government Organization and Employees.

§ 963. Courts defined

As used in this chapter, unless the context indicates otherwise, the words "court" and "courts" include the Supreme Court of the United States and the courts enumerated in section 610 of this title.

(June 25, 1948, c. 646, 62 Stat. 927.)

CHAPTER 58—UNITED STATES SENTENCING COMMISSION

Sec.
991. United States Sentencing Commission; establishment and purposes.
992. Terms of office; compensation.
993. Powers and duties of Chair.
994. Duties of the Commission.
995. Powers of the Commission.
996. Director and staff.
997. Annual report.
998. Definitions.

§ 991. United States Sentencing Commission; establishment and purposes

(a) There is established as an independent commission in the judicial branch of the United States a United States Sentencing Commission which shall consist of seven voting members and one nonvoting member. The President, after consultation with representatives of judges, prosecuting attorneys, defense attorneys, law enforcement officials, senior citizens, victims of crime, and others interested in the criminal justice process, shall appoint the voting members of the Commission, by and with the advice and consent of the Senate, one of whom shall be appointed, by and with the advice and consent of the Senate, as the Chair and three of whom shall be designated by the President as Vice Chairs. At least 3 of the members shall be Federal judges selected after considering a list of six judges recommended to the President by the Judicial Conference of the United States. Not more than four of the members of the Commission shall be members of the same political party, and of the three Vice Chairs, no more than two shall be members of the same political party. The Attorney General, or the Attorney General's designee, shall be an ex officio, nonvoting member of the Commission. The Chair, Vice Chairs, and members of the Commission shall be subject to removal from the Commission by the President only for neglect of duty or malfeasance in office or for other good cause shown.

(b) The purposes of the United States Sentencing Commission are to—

(1) establish sentencing policies and practices for the Federal criminal justice system that—

(A) assure the meeting of the purposes of sentencing as set forth in section 3553(a)(2) of title 18, United States Code;

(B) provide certainty and fairness in meeting the purposes of sentencing, avoiding unwarranted sentencing disparities among defendants with similar records who have been found guilty of similar criminal conduct while maintaining sufficient flexibility to permit individualized sentences when warranted by mitigating or aggravating factors not taken into account in the establishment of general sentencing practices; and

(C) reflect, to the extent practicable, advancement in knowledge of human behavior as it relates to the criminal justice process; and

(2) develop means of measuring the degree to which the sentencing, penal, and correctional practices are effective in meeting the purposes of sentencing as set forth in section 3553(a)(2) of title 18, United States Code.

(Added Pub.L. 98–473, Title II, § 217(a), Oct. 12, 1984, 98 Stat. 2017, and amended Pub.L. 99–22, § 1(1), Apr. 15, 1985, 99 Stat. 46; Pub.L. 103–322, Title XXVIII, § 280005(a), (c)(1), (2), Sept. 13, 1994, 108 Stat. 2096, 2097; Pub.L. 104–294, Title VI, § 604(b)(11), Oct. 11, 1996, 110 Stat. 3507; Pub.L. 108–21, Title IV, § 401(n)(1), Apr. 30, 2003, 117 Stat. 676; Pub.L. 110–406, § 16, Oct. 13, 2008, 122 Stat. 4295.)

HISTORICAL AND STATUTORY NOTES

Effective and Applicability Provisions

2003 Acts. Pub.L. 108–21, Title IV, § 401(n)(2), Apr. 30, 2003, 117 Stat. 676, provided that: "The amendment made under paragraph (1) [amending subsec. (a) of this section] shall not apply to any person who is serving, or who has been nominated to serve, as a member of the Sentencing Commission on the date of enactment of this Act [Apr. 30, 2003]."

1996 Acts. Amendment by section 604 of Pub.L. 104–294 effective Sept. 13, 1994, see section 604(d) of Pub.L. 104–294, set out as a note under section 13 of Title 18, Crimes and Criminal Procedure.

1984 Acts. Section effective Oct. 12, 1984, see section 235(a)(1)(B)(i) of Pub.L. 98–473, as amended, set out as a note under section 3551 of Title 18, Crimes and Criminal Procedure.

Composition of Members of Commission During First Five-Year Period

For provisions directing that, notwithstanding the provisions of this section, during the five-year period following Oct. 12, 1984, the United States Sentencing Commission shall consist of nine members, including two ex officio, nonvoting members, see section 235(b)(5) of Pub.L. 98–473, set out as an Effective Date note under section 3551 of Title 18, Crimes and Criminal Procedure.

§ 992. Terms of office; compensation

(a) The voting members of the United States Sentencing Commission shall be appointed for six-year terms, except that the initial terms of the first members of the Commission shall be staggered so that—

(1) two members, including the Chair, serve terms of six years;

(2) three members serve terms of four years; and

(3) two members serve terms of two years.

(b)(1) Subject to paragraph (2)—

(A) no voting member of the Commission may serve more than two full terms; and

(B) a voting member appointed to fill a vacancy that occurs before the expiration of the term for which a predecessor was appointed shall be appointed only for the remainder of such term.

(2) A voting member of the Commission whose term has expired may continue to serve until the earlier of—

(A) the date on which a successor has taken office; or

(B) the date on which the Congress adjourns sine die to end the session of Congress that commences after the date on which the member's term expired.

(c) The Chair and Vice Chairs of the Commission shall hold full-time positions and shall be compensated during their terms of office at the annual rate at which judges of the United States courts of appeals are compensated. The voting members of the Commission, other than the Chair and Vice Chairs, shall hold full-time positions until the end of the first six years after the sentencing guidelines go into effect pursuant to section 235(a)(1)(B)(ii) of the Sentencing Reform Act of 1984, and shall be compensated at the annual rate at which judges of the United States courts of appeals are compensated. Thereafter, the voting members of the Commission, other than the Chair and Vice Chairs,,[1] shall hold part-time positions and shall be paid at the daily rate at which judges of the United States courts of appeals are compensated. A Federal judge may serve as a member of the Commission without resigning the judge's appointment as a Federal judge.

(d) Sections 44(c) and 134(b) of this title (relating to the residence of judges) do not apply to any judge holding a full-time position on the Commission under subsection (c) of this section.

(Added Pub.L. 98–473, Title II, § 217(a), Oct. 12, 1984, 98 Stat. 2018, and amended Pub.L. 99–646, §§ 4, 6(a), Nov. 10, 1986, 100 Stat. 3592; Pub.L. 102–349, § 1, Aug. 26, 1992, 106 Stat. 933; Pub.L. 103–322, Title XXVIII, § 280005(b), (c)(1), (3), Sept. 13, 1994, 108 Stat. 2096, 2097.)

[1] So in original.

HISTORICAL AND STATUTORY NOTES

References in Text

Section 235(a)(1)(B)(ii) of the Sentencing Reform Act of 1984, referred to in subsec. (c), is section 235(a)(1)(B)(ii) of Pub.L. 98–473, which is set out as a note under section 3551 of Title 18, Crimes and Criminal Procedure.

Effective and Applicability Provisions

1984 Acts. Section effective Oct. 12, 1984, see section 235(a)(1)(B)(i) of Pub.L. 98–473, as amended, set out as a note under section 3551 of Title 18, Crimes and Criminal Procedure.

Commencement of Terms of First Members of Commission

For provisions directing that, for purposes of subsec. (a) of this section, the terms of the first members of the United States Sentencing Commission shall not begin to run until the sentencing guidelines go into effect pursuant to section 235(a)(1)(B)(ii) of Pub.L. 98–473, set out as an Effective Date note under section 3551 of Title 18, Crimes and Criminal Procedure, see section 235(a)(2) of Pub.L. 98–473, as amended, set out as an Effective Date note under section 3551 of Title 18.

§ 993. Powers and duties of Chair

The Chair shall—

(a) call and preside at meetings of the Commission, which shall be held for at least two weeks in each quarter after the members of the Commission hold part-time positions; and

(b) direct—

(1) the preparation of requests for appropriations for the Commission; and

(2) the use of funds made available to the Commission.

(Added Pub.L. 98–473, Title II, § 217(a), Oct. 12, 1984, 98 Stat. 2019, and amended Pub.L. 99–22, § 1(2), Apr. 15, 1985, 99 Stat. 46; Pub.L. 99–646, § 5, Nov. 10, 1986, 100 Stat. 3592; Pub.L. 103–322, Title XXVIII, § 280005(c)(1), Sept. 13, 1994, 108 Stat. 2097.)

HISTORICAL AND STATUTORY NOTES

Effective and Applicability Provisions

1984 Acts. Section effective Oct. 12, 1984, see section 235(a)(1)(B)(i) of Pub.L. 98–473, as amended, set out as a note under section 3551 of Title 18, Crimes and Criminal Procedure.

§ 994. Duties of the Commission

(a) The Commission, by affirmative vote of at least four members of the Commission, and pursuant to its rules and regulations and consistent with all pertinent provisions of any Federal statute shall promulgate and distribute to all courts of the United States and to the United States Probation System—

(1) guidelines, as described in this section, for use of a sentencing court in determining the sentence to be imposed in a criminal case, including—

(A) a determination whether to impose a sentence to probation, a fine, or a term of imprisonment;

(B) a determination as to the appropriate amount of a fine or the appropriate length of a term of probation or a term of imprisonment;

(C) a determination whether a sentence to a term of imprisonment should include a requirement that the defendant be placed on a term of supervised release after imprisonment, and, if so, the appropriate length of such a term;

(D) a determination whether multiple sentences to terms of imprisonment should be ordered to run concurrently or consecutively; and

(E) a determination under paragraphs (6) and (11) of section 3563(b) of title 18;

(2) general policy statements regarding application of the guidelines or any other aspect of sentencing or sentence implementation that in the view of the Commission would further the purposes set forth in section 3553(a)(2) of title 18, United States Code, including the appropriate use of—

(A) the sanctions set forth in sections 3554, 3555, and 3556 of title 18;

(B) the conditions of probation and supervised release set forth in sections 3563(b) and 3583(d) of title 18;

(C) the sentence modification provisions set forth in sections 3563(c), 3564, 3573, and 3582(c) of title 18;

(D) the fine imposition provisions set forth in section 3572 of title 18;

(E) the authority granted under rule 11(e)(2) of the Federal Rules of Criminal Procedure to accept or reject a plea agreement entered into pursuant to rule 11(e)(1); and

(F) the temporary release provisions set forth in section 3622 of title 18, and the prerelease custody provisions set forth in section 3624(c) of title 18; and

(3) guidelines or general policy statements regarding the appropriate use of the provisions for revocation of probation set forth in section 3565 of title 18, and the provisions for modification of the term or conditions of supervised release and revocation of supervised release set forth in section 3583(e) of title 18.

(b)(1) The Commission, in the guidelines promulgated pursuant to subsection (a)(1), shall, for each category of offense involving each category of defendant, establish a sentencing range that is consistent with all pertinent provisions of title 18, United States Code.

(2) If a sentence specified by the guidelines includes a term of imprisonment, the maximum of the range established for such a term shall not exceed the minimum of that range by more than the greater of 25 percent or 6 months, except that, if the minimum term of the range is 30 years or more, the maximum may be life imprisonment.

(c) The Commission, in establishing categories of offenses for use in the guidelines and policy statements governing the imposition of sentences of probation, a fine, or imprisonment, governing the imposition of other authorized sanctions, governing the size of a fine or the length of a term of probation, imprisonment, or supervised release, and governing the conditions of probation, supervised release, or imprisonment, shall consider whether the following matters, among others, have any relevance to the nature, extent, place of service, or other incidents [1] of an appropriate sentence, and shall take them into account only to the extent that they do have relevance—

(1) the grade of the offense;

(2) the circumstances under which the offense was committed which mitigate or aggravate the seriousness of the offense;

(3) the nature and degree of the harm caused by the offense, including whether it involved property, irreplaceable property, a person, a number of persons, or a breach of public trust;

(4) the community view of the gravity of the offense;

(5) the public concern generated by the offense;

(6) the deterrent effect a particular sentence may have on the commission of the offense by others; and

(7) the current incidence of the offense in the community and in the Nation as a whole.

(d) The Commission in establishing categories of defendants for use in the guidelines and policy statements governing the imposition of sentences of probation, a fine, or imprisonment, governing the imposition of other authorized sanctions, governing the size of a fine or the length of a term of probation, imprisonment, or supervised release, and governing the conditions of probation, supervised release, or imprisonment, shall consider whether the following matters, among others, with respect to a defendant, have any relevance to the nature, extent, place of service, or other incidents [1] of an appropriate sentence, and shall take them into account only to the extent that they do have relevance—

(1) age;

(2) education;

(3) vocational skills;

(4) mental and emotional condition to the extent that such condition mitigates the defendant's culpability or to the extent that such condition is otherwise plainly relevant;

(5) physical condition, including drug dependence;

(6) previous employment record;

(7) family ties and responsibilities;

(8) community ties;

(9) role in the offense;

(10) criminal history; and

(11) degree of dependence upon criminal activity for a livelihood.

The Commission shall assure that the guidelines and policy statements are entirely neutral as to the race, sex, national origin, creed, and socioeconomic status of offenders.

(e) The Commission shall assure that the guidelines and policy statements, in recommending a term of imprisonment or length of a term of imprisonment, reflect the general inappropriateness of considering the education, vocational skills, employment record, family ties and responsibilities, and community ties of the defendant.

(f) The Commission, in promulgating guidelines pursuant to subsection (a)(1), shall promote the purposes set forth in section 991(b)(1), with particular attention to the requirements of subsection 991(b)(1)(B) for providing certainty and fairness in sentencing and reducing unwarranted sentence disparities.

(g) The Commission, in promulgating guidelines pursuant to subsection (a)(1) to meet the purposes of sentencing as set forth in section 3553(a)(2) of title 18, United States Code, shall take into account the nature and capacity of the penal, correctional, and other facilities and services available, and shall make recommendations concerning any change or expansion in the nature or capacity of such facilities and services that might become necessary as a result of the guidelines promulgated pursuant to the provisions of this chapter. The sentencing guidelines prescribed under this chapter shall be formulated to minimize the likelihood that the Federal prison population will exceed the capacity of the Federal prisons, as determined by the Commission.

(h) The Commission shall assure that the guidelines specify a sentence to a term of imprisonment at or near the maximum term authorized for categories of defendants in which the defendant is eighteen years old or older and—

(1) has been convicted of a felony that is—

(A) a crime of violence; or

(B) an offense described in section 401 of the Controlled Substances Act (21 U.S.C. 841), sections 1002(a), 1005, and 1009 of the Controlled Substances Import and Export Act (21 U.S.C. 952(a), 955, and 959), and chapter 705 of title 46; and

(2) has previously been convicted of two or more prior felonies, each of which is—

(A) a crime of violence; or

(B) an offense described in section 401 of the Controlled Substances Act (21 U.S.C. 841), sections 1002(a), 1005, and 1009 of the Controlled Substances Import and Export Act (21 U.S.C. 952(a), 955, and 959), and chapter 705 of title 46.

(i) The Commission shall assure that the guidelines specify a sentence to a substantial term of imprisonment for categories of defendants in which the defendant—

(1) has a history of two or more prior Federal, State, or local felony convictions for offenses committed on different occasions;

(2) committed the offense as part of a pattern of criminal conduct from which the defendant derived a substantial portion of the defendant's income;

(3) committed the offense in furtherance of a conspiracy with three or more persons engaging in a pattern of racketeering activity in which the defendant participated in a managerial or supervisory capacity;

(4) committed a crime of violence that constitutes a felony while on release pending trial, sentence, or appeal from a Federal, State, or local felony for which he was ultimately convicted; or

(5) committed a felony that is set forth in section 401 or 1010 of the Comprehensive Drug Abuse Prevention and Control Act of 1970 (21 U.S.C. 841 and 960), and that involved trafficking in a substantial quantity of a controlled substance.

(j) The Commission shall insure that the guidelines reflect the general appropriateness of imposing a sentence other than imprisonment in cases in which the defendant is a first offender who has not been convicted of a crime of violence or an otherwise serious offense, and the general appropriateness of imposing a term of imprisonment on a person convicted of a crime of violence that results in serious bodily injury.

(k) The Commission shall insure that the guidelines reflect the inappropriateness of imposing a sentence to a term of imprisonment for the purpose of rehabilitating the defendant or providing the defendant with needed educational or vocational training, medical care, or other correctional treatment.

(*l*) The Commission shall insure that the guidelines promulgated pursuant to subsection (a)(1) reflect—

(1) the appropriateness of imposing an incremental penalty for each offense in a case in which a defendant is convicted of—

(A) multiple offenses committed in the same course of conduct that result in the exercise of ancillary jurisdiction over one or more of the offenses; and

(B) multiple offenses committed at different times, including those cases in which the subsequent offense is a violation of section 3146 (penalty for failure to appear) or is committed while the person is released pursuant to the provisions of section 3147 (penalty for an offense committed while on release) of title 18; and

(2) the general inappropriateness of imposing consecutive terms of imprisonment for an offense of conspiring to commit an offense or soliciting com-

mission of an offense and for an offense that was the sole object of the conspiracy or solicitation.

(m) The Commission shall insure that the guidelines reflect the fact that, in many cases, current sentences do not accurately reflect the seriousness of the offense. This will require that, as a starting point in its development of the initial sets of guidelines for particular categories of cases, the Commission ascertain the average sentences imposed in such categories of cases prior to the creation of the Commission, and in cases involving sentences to terms of imprisonment, the length of such terms actually served. The Commission shall not be bound by such average sentences, and shall independently develop a sentencing range that is consistent with the purposes of sentencing described in section 3553(a)(2) of title 18, United States Code.

(n) The Commission shall assure that the guidelines reflect the general appropriateness of imposing a lower sentence than would otherwise be imposed, including a sentence that is lower than that established by statute as a minimum sentence, to take into account a defendant's substantial assistance in the investigation or prosecution of another person who has committed an offense.

(o) The Commission periodically shall review and revise, in consideration of comments and data coming to its attention, the guidelines promulgated pursuant to the provisions of this section. In fulfilling its duties and in exercising its powers, the Commission shall consult with authorities on, and individual and institutional representatives of, various aspects of the Federal criminal justice system. The United States Probation System, the Bureau of Prisons, the Judicial Conference of the United States, the Criminal Division of the United States Department of Justice, and a representative of the Federal Public Defenders shall submit to the Commission any observations, comments, or questions pertinent to the work of the Commission whenever they believe such communication would be useful, and shall, at least annually, submit to the Commission a written report commenting on the operation of the Commission's guidelines, suggesting changes in the guidelines that appear to be warranted, and otherwise assessing the Commission's work.

(p) The Commission, at or after the beginning of a regular session of Congress, but not later than the first day of May, may promulgate under subsection (a) of this section and submit to Congress amendments to the guidelines and modifications to previously submitted amendments that have not taken effect, including modifications to the effective dates of such amendments. Such an amendment or modification shall be accompanied by a statement of the reasons therefor and shall take effect on a date specified by the Commission, which shall be no earlier than 180 days after being so submitted and no later than the first day of November of the calendar year in which the amendment or modification is submitted, except to the extent that the effective date is revised or the amendment is otherwise modified or disapproved by Act of Congress.

(q) The Commission and the Bureau of Prisons shall submit to Congress an analysis and recommendations concerning maximum utilization of resources to deal effectively with the Federal prison population. Such report shall be based upon consideration of a variety of alternatives, including—

(1) modernization of existing facilities;

(2) inmate classification and periodic review of such classification for use in placing inmates in the least restrictive facility necessary to ensure adequate security; and

(3) use of existing Federal facilities, such as those currently within military jurisdiction.

(r) The Commission, not later than two years after the initial set of sentencing guidelines promulgated under subsection (a) goes into effect, and thereafter whenever it finds it advisable, shall recommend to the Congress that it raise or lower the grades, or otherwise modify the maximum penalties, of those offenses for which such an adjustment appears appropriate.

(s) The Commission shall give due consideration to any petition filed by a defendant requesting modification of the guidelines utilized in the sentencing of such defendant, on the basis of changed circumstances unrelated to the defendant, including changes in—

(1) the community view of the gravity of the offense;

(2) the public concern generated by the offense; and

(3) the deterrent effect particular sentences may have on the commission of the offense by others.

(t) The Commission, in promulgating general policy statements regarding the sentencing modification provisions in section 3582(c)(1)(A) of title 18, shall describe what should be considered extraordinary and compelling reasons for sentence reduction, including the criteria to be applied and a list of specific examples. Rehabilitation of the defendant alone shall not be considered an extraordinary and compelling reason.

(u) If the Commission reduces the term of imprisonment recommended in the guidelines applicable to a particular offense or category of offenses, it shall specify in what circumstances and by what amount the sentences of prisoners serving terms of imprisonment for the offense may be reduced.

(v) The Commission shall ensure that the general policy statements promulgated pursuant to subsection (a)(2) include a policy limiting consecutive terms of imprisonment for an offense involving a violation of a general prohibition and for an offense involving a violation of a specific prohibition encompassed within the general prohibition.

(w)(1) The Chief Judge of each district court shall ensure that, within 30 days following entry of judgment in every criminal case, the sentencing court submits to the Commission, in a format approved and required by the Commission, a written report of the sentence, the offense for which it is imposed, the age, race, sex of the offender, and information regarding factors made relevant by the guidelines. The report shall also include—

(A) the judgment and commitment order;

(B) the written statement of reasons for the sentence imposed (which shall include the reason for any departure from the otherwise applicable guideline range and which shall be stated on the written statement of reasons form issued by the Judicial Conference and approved by the United States Sentencing Commission);

(C) any plea agreement;

(D) the indictment or other charging document;

(E) the presentence report; and

(F) any other information as the Commission finds appropriate.

The information referred to in subparagraphs (A) through (F) shall be submitted by the sentencing court in a format approved and required by the Commission.

(2) The Commission shall, upon request, make available to the House and Senate Committees on the Judiciary, the written reports and all underlying records accompanying those reports described in this section, as well as other records received from courts.

(3) The Commission shall submit to Congress at least annually an analysis of these documents, any recommendations for legislation that the Commission concludes is warranted by that analysis, and an accounting of those districts that the Commission believes have not submitted the appropriate information and documents required by this section.

(4) The Commission shall make available to the Attorney General, upon request, such data files as the Commission itself may assemble or maintain in electronic form as a result of the information submitted under paragraph (1). Such data files shall be made available in electronic form and shall include all data fields requested, including the identity of the sentencing judge.

(x) The provisions of section 553 of title 5, relating to publication in the Federal Register and public hearing procedure, shall apply to the promulgation of guidelines pursuant to this section.

(y) The Commission, in promulgating guidelines pursuant to subsection (a)(1), may include, as a component of a fine, the expected costs to the Government of any imprisonment, supervised release, or probation sentence that is ordered.

(Added Pub.L. 98–473, Title II, § 217(a), Oct. 12, 1984, 98 Stat. 2019, and amended Pub.L. 99–217, § 3, Dec. 26, 1985, 99 Stat. 1728; Pub.L. 99–363, § 2, July 11, 1986, 100 Stat. 770; Pub.L. 99–570, Title I, §§ 1006(b), 1008, Oct. 27, 1986, 100 Stat. 3207–7; Pub.L. 99–646, §§ 6(b), 56, Nov. 10, 1986, 100 Stat. 3592, 3611; Pub.L. 100–182, §§ 16(b), 23, Dec. 7, 1987, 101 Stat. 1269, 1271; Pub.L. 100–690, Title VII, §§ 7083, 7103(b), 7109, Nov. 18, 1988, 102 Stat. 4408, 4417, 4419; Pub.L. 103–322, Title II, § 20403(b), Title XXVIII, § 280005(c)(4), Title XXXIII, § 330003(f)(1), Sept. 13, 1994, 108 Stat. 1825, 2097, 2141; Pub.L. 108–21, Title IV, § 401(h), (k), Apr. 30, 2003, 117 Stat. 672, 674; Pub.L. 109–177, Title VII, § 735, Mar. 9, 2006, 120 Stat. 271; Pub.L. 109–304, § 17(f)(1), Oct. 6, 2006, 120 Stat. 1708.)

[1] So in original. Probably should be "incidence".

Application of Sentencing Guidelines

See Blakely v. Washington, 124 S.Ct. 2531 (2004); U.S. v. Booker, U.S. v. Fanfan, 125 S.Ct. 738 (2005).

HISTORICAL AND STATUTORY NOTES

References in Text

Paragraphs (6) and (11) of section 3563(b) of Title 18, referred to in subsec. (a)(1)(E), were renumbered paragraphs (5) and (10), respectively, of section 3563(b) by Pub.L. 104–132, Title II, § 203(2)(B), Apr. 24, 1996, 110 Stat. 1227.

The Federal Rules of Criminal Procedure, referred to in subsec. (a)(2)(E), are set out in Title 18, Crimes and Criminal Procedure.

Chapter 705 of Title 46, referred to in subsecs. (h)(1)(B), (2)(B), is Maritime Drug Law Enforcement, 46 U.S.C.A. § 70501 et seq.

Codifications

Amendment by Pub.L. 99–646 to subsec. (t) of this section has been executed to subsec. (u) as the probable intent of Congress in view of prior redesignation of subsec. (t) as (u) by Pub.L. 99–570.

Effective and Applicability Provisions

1987 Acts. Amendment by Pub.L. 100–182 applicable with respect to offenses committed after Dec. 7, 1987, see section 26 of Pub.L. 100–182, set out as a note under section 3006A of Title 18, Crimes and Criminal Procedure.

1984 Acts. Section effective Oct. 12, 1984, see section 235(a)(1)(B)(i) of Pub.L. 98–473, as amended, set out as a note under section 3551 of Title 18, Crimes and Criminal Procedure.

Termination of Reporting Requirements

For termination of reporting provisions of subsec. (p) of this section, relating to amendments to guidelines in determining the sentence to be imposed in a criminal case, effective May 15, 2000, see Pub.L. 104–66, § 3003, as amended, set out as a note under 31 U.S.C.A. § 1113, and the 13th item on page 13 of House Document No. 103–7, which references subsec. (*o*) of this section, which was subsequently renumbered subsec. (p) of this section.

For termination, effective May 15, 2000, of reporting provisions of this section, pertaining to the U.S. Sentencing Commission, Bureau of Prisons, analysis and recommendations concerning maximum utilization of resources to deal with Federal prison population, see Pub.L. 104–66, § 3003, as amended, set out as a note under 31 U.S.C.A. § 1113, and the 9th item on page 147 of House Document No. 103–7, which references subsec. (p) of this section, which was subsequently renumbered as subsec. (q).

For termination, effective May 15, 2000, of provisions in subsec. (w) of this section relating to requirement that the Commission submit to Congress at least annually an analysis of reports and recommendations for legislation that the Commission concludes is warranted by that analysis, see Pub.L. 104–66, § 3003, as amended, set out as a note under 31 U.S.C.A. § 1113 and House Document No. 103–7, page 13.

Short Title

1997 Amendments. Pub.L. 105–101, § 1, Nov. 19, 1997, 111 Stat. 2202, provided that: "This Act [enacting a provision set out as a note under this section] may be cited as the 'Veterans' Cemetery Protection Act of 1997'."

1995 Acts. Pub.L. 104–71, § 1, Dec. 23, 1995, 109 Stat. 774, provided that: "This Act [amending section 2423 of Title 18, Crimes and Criminal Procedure, and enacting provisions set out as a note under this section] may be cited as the 'Sex Crimes Against Children Prevention Act of 1995'."

Provisions for Review, Promulgation, or Amendment of Federal Sentencing Guidelines

Pub.L. 110–457, Title II, § 222(g), Dec. 23, 2008, 122 Stat. 5071.—Convictions of alien harboring to ensure conformity with sentencing guidelines applicable to convictions of promoting a commercial sex act if harboring was committed in furtherance of prostitution and the defendant to be sentenced is an organizer, leader, manager, or supervisor of the criminal activities.

Pub.L. 110–425, § 3(k)(2), Oct. 15, 2008, 122 Stat. 4833.—Offenses involving controlled substances.

Pub.L. 110–407, Title I, § 103, Oct. 13, 2008, 122 Stat. 4298.—Offenses involving knowingly operating by any means or embarking in any submersible vessel or semi-submersible vessel in violation of 18 U.S.C.A. § 2285.

Pub.L. 110–384, Oct. 10, 2008, 122 Stat. 4094.—Offenses involving desecration, theft, or trafficking in, a grave marker, headstone, monument, or other object, intended to permanently mark a veteran's grave.

Pub.L. 110–326, Title II, § 209, Sept. 26, 2008, 122 Stat. 3564.—Offenses involving computer crime, and theft or misuse of personally identifying data punishable under 18 U.S.C.A. §§ 1028, 1028A, 1030, 2511, and 2701.

Pub.L. 110–179, § 5, Jan. 7, 2008, 121 Stat. 2557.—Offenses involving fraud or theft in connection with a major disaster declaration under section 401 of the Robert T. Stafford Disaster Relief and Emergency Assistance Act (42 U.S.C. 5170) or an emergency declaration under section 501 of the Robert T. Stafford Disaster Relief and Emergency Assistance Act (42 U.S.C. 5191).

Pub.L. 110–177, Title II, § 209, Jan. 7, 2008, 121 Stat. 2538.—Threats punishable under 18 U.S.C.A. § 115, Influencing, impeding, or retaliating against a Federal official by threatening or injuring a family member, that occur over the Internet.

Pub.L. 109–476, § 4, Jan. 12, 2007, 120 Stat. 3571.—Offenses involving obtaining confidential phone records information by fraud or related activity.

Pub.L. 109–295, Title V, § 551(d), Oct. 4, 2006, 120 Stat. 1390, as amended Pub.L. 110–161, Div. E, Title V, § 553(c), Dec. 26, 2007, 121 Stat. 2082.—Offenses involving border tunnels and passages under 18 U.S.C.A. § 555.

Pub.L. 109–248, Title I, § 141(b), July 27, 2006, 120 Stat. 602.—Offenses involving failure to register as a sex offender.

Pub.L. 109–181, § 1(c), Mar. 16, 2006, 120 Stat. 287.—Offenses involving trafficking in counterfeit labels, illicit labels, counterfeit documentation or packaging, or counterfeit goods or services.

Pub.L. 109–177, Title III, § 307(c), Mar. 9, 2006, 120 Stat. 240.—Goods or chattel within interstate or foreign shipment or commerce (any offense under 18 U.S.C.A. § 659 or 2311).

Pub.L. 109–162, Title XI, § 1191(c), Jan. 5, 2006, 119 Stat. 3129.—Offenses committed while wearing illicitly received public employee insignia or uniform.

Pub.L. 109–9, Title I, § 105, Apr. 27, 2005, 119 Stat. 222.—Intellectual property rights crimes, including any offense under 17 U.S.C.A. §§ 506, 1201, or 1202, or 18 U.S.C.A. §§ 2318, 2319, 2319A, 2319B, or 2320.

Pub.L. 108–482, Title II, § 204(b), Dec. 23, 2004, 118 Stat. 3917.—Felony offense carried out online that may be facilitated through use of a domain name registered with materially false contact information.

Pub.L. 108–458, Title VI, § 6703(b), Dec. 17, 2004, 118 Stat. 3766.—Offenses involving international or domestic terrorism.

Pub.L. 108–358, § 3, Oct. 22, 2004, 118 Stat. 1664.—Offenses involving anabolic steroids.

Pub.L. 108–275, § 5, July 15, 2004, 118 Stat. 833.—Identity theft offenses involving an abuse of position.

Pub.L. 108–187, § 4(b), Dec. 16, 2003, 117 Stat. 2705.—Electronic mail fraud.

Pub.L. 108–21, Title I, § 104(a), Apr. 30, 2003, 117 Stat. 653.—Kidnapping.

Pub.L. 108–21, Title IV, § 401(b), (g), (i), (j)(1) to (4), and (m), Apr. 30, 2003, 117 Stat. 668 to 675.—Child crimes and sexual offenses, child pornography, downward departures, and acceptance of responsibility.

Pub.L. 108–21, Title V, § 504(c)(2), Apr. 30, 2003, 117 Stat. 682.—Offenses involving obscene visual representations of sexual abuse of children.

Pub.L. 108–21, Title V, § 512, Apr. 30, 2003, 117 Stat. 685.—Offenses involving interstate travel to engage in sexual act with a juvenile.

Pub.L. 108–21, Title V, § 513(c), Apr. 30, 2003, 117 Stat. 685.—Offenses involving distribution of images, whether real or computer generated, that contain, or appear to contain, obscene visual depictions of a minor engaging in sexually explicit conduct.

Pub.L. 108–21, Title VI, § 608(e), Apr. 30, 2003, 117 Stat. 691.—Offenses involving gamma hydroxybutyric acid (GHB).

Pub.L. 107–296, Title II, § 225(b), Nov. 25, 2002, 116 Stat. 2156.—Computer fraud and abuse.

Pub.L. 107–273, Div. C, Title I, § 11008(e), Nov. 2, 2002, 116 Stat. 1819.—Threats.

Pub.L. 107–204, Title VIII, § 805, July 30, 2002, 116 Stat. 802.—Destruction, alteration, or falsification of records.

Pub.L. 107–204, Title IX, § 905, July 30, 2002, 116 Stat. 805.—White-collar crimes.

Pub.L. 107–204, Title XI, § 1104, July 30, 2002, 116 Stat. 808.—Securities and accounting fraud and related offenses.

Pub.L. 107–155, § 314, Mar. 27, 2002, 116 Stat. 107.—Violations of Federal Election Campaign Act of 1971 and related election laws.

Pub.L. 107–56, Title VIII, § 814(f), Oct. 26, 2001, 115 Stat. 384.—Computer fraud and abuse.

Pub.L. 106–420, § 3, Nov. 1, 2000, 114 Stat. 1868.—Higher education financial assistance fraud.

Pub.L. 106–386, Div. B, Title I, § 1107(b)(2), Oct. 28, 2000, 114 Stat. 1498.—Interstate stalking.

Pub.L. 106–310, Div. B, Title XXXVI, § 3611, Oct. 17, 2000, 114 Stat. 1228.—Manufacture of and trafficking in amphetamine.

Pub.L. 106–310, Div. B, Title XXXVI, § 3612, Oct. 17, 2000, 114 Stat. 1228.—Manufacture of amphetamine or methamphetamine.

Pub.L. 106–310, Div. B, Title XXXVI, § 3651, Oct. 17, 2000, 114 Stat. 1238.—Trafficking in list I chemicals.

Pub.L. 106–310, Div. B, Title XXXVI, §§ 3663, 3664, Oct. 17, 2000, 114 Stat. 1242, 1244.—Manufacture of or trafficking in Ecstasy.

Pub.L. 106–160, § 3, Dec. 9, 1999, 113 Stat. 1774.—Electronic theft offenses.

Pub.L. 105–318, § 4, Oct. 30, 1998, 112 Stat. 3009.—Crimes against intellectual property.

Pub.L. 105–314, Title V, Oct. 30, 1998, 112 Stat. 2980.—Sexual abuse, transportation for illegal sexual activity, and distribution of pornography.

Pub.L. 105–184, § 6, June 23, 1998, 112 Stat. 521.—Telemarketing fraud.

Pub.L. 105–172, § 2(e), Apr. 24, 1998, 112 Stat. 55.—Wireless telephone cloning.

Pub.L. 105–147, § 2(g), Dec. 16, 1997, 111 Stat. 2680.—Crimes against intellectual property.

Pub.L. 105–101, Nov. 19, 1997, 111 Stat. 2202; Pub. L. 105–368, Title IV, § 403(d)(1), Nov. 11, 1998, 112 Stat. 3339.—Offenses against property at national cemeteries.

Pub.L. 104–305, § 2(b)(3), Oct. 13, 1996, 110 Stat. 3808.—Offenses involving flunitrazepam.

Pub.L. 104–237, Title II, § 203(b), Oct. 3, 1996, 110 Stat. 3102.—Manufacture of methamphetamine.

Pub.L. 104–237, Title III, § 301, Oct. 3, 1996, 110 Stat. 3105.—Manufacture of and trafficking in methamphetamine.

Pub.L. 104–237, Title III, § 302(c), Oct. 3, 1996, 110 Stat. 3105.—Offenses involving list I chemicals.

Pub.L. 104–237, Title III, § 303, Oct. 3, 1996, 110 Stat. 3106.—Dangerous handling of controlled substances.

Pub.L. 104–208, Div. C, Title II, § 203(e), Sept. 30, 1996, 110 Stat. 3009–566.—Smuggling, transporting, harboring, and inducing aliens.

Pub.L. 104–208, Div. C, Title II, § 211(b), Sept. 30, 1996, 110 Stat. 3009–569.—Fraudulent acquisition and use of government-issued documents.

Pub.L. 104–208, Div. C, Title II, § 218(b), (c), Sept. 30, 1996, 110 Stat. 3009–573, 3009–574.—Involuntary servitude.

Pub.L. 104–208, Div. C, Title III, § 333, Sept. 30, 1996, 110 Stat. 3009–634.—Conspiring with or assisting an alien to import, export, possess, manufacture, or distribute a controlled substance.

Pub.L. 104–208, Div. C, Title III, § 334, Sept. 30, 1996, 110 Stat. 3009–635.—Failure to depart, illegal reentry, and passport and visa fraud.

Pub.L. 104–201, Div. A, Title XIV, § 1423, Sept. 23, 1996, 110 Stat. 2725; Pub. L. 105–261, Div. A, Title X, § 1069(c)(1), Oct. 17, 1998, 112 Stat. 2136.—Offenses relating to importation and exportation of nuclear, biological, or chemical weapons or technologies.

Pub.L. 104–132, Title II, § 208, Apr. 24, 1996, 110 Stat. 1240.—Mandatory victim restitution.

Pub.L. 104–132, Title VII, § 730, Apr. 24, 1996, 110 Stat. 1303.—International terrorism.

Pub.L. 104–132, Title VIII, § 805, Apr. 24, 1996, 110 Stat. 1305.—Terrorist activity damaging Federal interest computer.

Pub.L. 104–132, Title VIII, § 807(h), Apr. 24, 1996, 110 Stat. 1308.—International counterfeiting of United States currency; codified at 18 U.S.C.A. § 470 note.

Pub.L. 104–71, §§ 1–4, Dec. 23, 1995, 109 Stat. 774.—Sex crimes against children.

Pub.L. 103–322, Title IV, § 40111(b), Sept. 13, 1994, 108 Stat. 1903.—Sexual abuse by repeat sex offender.

Pub.L. 103–322, Title IV, § 40112, Sept. 13, 1994, 108 Stat. 1903.—Aggravated sexual abuse or sexual abuse.

Pub.L. 103–322, Title IV, § 40503(c), Sept. 13, 1994, 108 Stat. 1947.—Intentional transmission of HIV; codified at 42 U.S.C.A. § 10607(c).

Pub.L. 103–322, Title VIII, § 80001(b), Sept. 13, 1994, 108 Stat. 1986.—Importing, exporting, possessing, manufacturing, and distributing a controlled substance.

Pub.L. 103–322, Title IX, § 90102, Sept. 13, 1994, 108 Stat. 1987.—Drug-dealing in "drug-free" zones; codified at 42 U.S.C.A. § 14051.

Pub.L. 103–322, Title IX, § 90103(b), Sept. 13, 1994, 108 Stat. 1987.—Use or distribution of illegal drugs in the Federal prisons; codified at 42 U.S.C.A. § 14052(b).

Pub.L. 103–322, Title XI, § 110501, Sept. 13, 1994, 108 Stat. 2015.—Use of semiautomatic firearm during crime of violence or drug trafficking.

Pub.L. 103–322, Title XI, § 110502, Sept. 13, 1994, 108 Stat. 2015.—Second offense of using explosive to commit felony.

Pub.L. 103–322, Title XI, § 110512, Sept. 13, 1994, 108 Stat. 2019.—Using firearm in commission of counterfeiting or forgery.

Pub.L. 103–322, Title XI, § 110513, Sept. 13, 1994, 108 Stat. 2019.—Firearms possession by violent felons and serious drug offenders.

Pub.L. 103–322, Title XII, § 120004, Sept. 13, 1994, 108 Stat. 2022.—Felonies promoting international terrorism.

Pub.L. 103–322, Title XIV, § 140008, Sept. 13, 1994, 108 Stat. 2033.—Solicitation of minor to commit crime.

Pub.L. 103–322, Title XVIII, § 180201(c), Sept. 13, 1994, 108 Stat. 2047.—Possession or distribution of drugs at truck stops or safety rest areas.

Pub.L. 103–322, Title XXIV, § 240002, Sept. 13, 1994, 108 Stat. 2081, as amended Pub.L. 104–294, Title VI, § 604(b)(10), Oct. 11, 1996, 110 Stat. 3507.—Crimes against elderly victims.

Pub.L. 103–322, Title XXV, § 250003, Sept. 13, 1994, 108 Stat. 2085.—Fraud against older victims.

Pub.L. 103–322, Title XXVIII, § 280003, Sept. 13, 1994, 108 Stat. 2096.—Hate crimes.

Pub.L. 102–141, Title VI, § 632, Oct. 28, 1991, 105 Stat. 876.—Sexual abuse or exploitation of minors.

Pub.L. 101–647, Title III, § 321, Nov. 29, 1990, 104 Stat. 4817.—Sexual crimes against children.

Pub.L. 101–647, Title XXV, § 2507, Nov. 29, 1990, 104 Stat. 4862.—Major bank crimes.

Pub.L. 101–647, Title XXVII, § 2701, Nov. 29, 1990, 104 Stat. 4912.—Methamphetamine offenses.

Pub.L. 101–73, Title IX, § 961(m), Aug. 9, 1989, 103 Stat. 501.—Offenses substantially jeopardizing safety and soundness of federally insured financial institutions.

Pub.L. 100–700, § 2(b), Nov. 19, 1988, 102 Stat. 4631.—Major fraud against the United States.

Pub.L. 100–690, Title VI, § 6453, Nov. 18, 1988, 102 Stat. 4371.—Importation of controlled substances by aircraft and other vessels.

Pub.L. 100–690, Title VI, § 6454, Nov. 18, 1988, 102 Stat. 4372.—Drug offenses involving children.

Pub.L. 100–690, Title VI, § 6468(c), (d), Nov. 18, 1988, 102 Stat. 4376.—Drug offenses within Federal prisons.

Pub.L. 100–690, Title VI, § 6482(c), Nov. 18, 1988, 102 Stat. 4382.—Common carrier operation under influence of alcohol or drugs.

[Except as otherwise provided, amendments by Pub.L. 107–155 generally effective Nov. 6, 2002, see Pub.L. 107–155, § 402, set out as a note under 2 U.S.C.A. § 431, for effective date provisions, modification of contribution limits applicability to run off elections, applicability and transitional rules for spending of soft money of national political parties and promulgation of regulation provisions.]

[Amendments by Pub.L. 108–187 effective Jan. 1, 2004, see section 16 of Pub.L. 108–187, set out as a note under 15 U.S.C.A. § 7701.]

Provision of Emergency Amendment Authority for Sentencing Commission

Pub.L. 109–76, § 3, Sept. 29, 2005, 119 Stat. 2035.—False testimony and obstruction of Justice involving international or domestic terrorism or anabolic steroids.

Cocaine and Crack Sentences and Sentences for Money Laundering and Other Unlawful Activity; Reduction of Sentencing Disparities

Pub.L. 104–38, Oct. 30, 1995, 109 Stat. 334, provided that:

"Section 1. Disapproval of Amendments Relating to Lowering of Crack Sentences and Sentences for Money Laundering and Transactions in Property Derived From Unlawful Activity.

"In accordance with section 994(p) of title 28, United States Code [subsec. (p) of this section], amendments numbered 5 and 18 of the 'Amendments to the Sentencing Guidelines, Policy Statements, and Official Commentary', submitted by the United States Sentencing Commission to Congress on May 1, 1995, are hereby disapproved and shall not take effect.

"Sec. 2. Reduction of Sentencing Disparity.

"(a) Recommendations.—

"**(1) In general.**—The United States Sentencing Commission shall submit to Congress recommendations (and an explanation therefor), regarding changes to the statutes and sentencing guidelines governing sentences for unlawful manufacturing, importing, exporting, and trafficking of cocaine, and like offenses, including unlawful possession, possession with intent to commit any of the forgoing offenses, and attempt and conspiracy to commit any of the forgoing offenses. The recommendations shall reflect the following considerations—

"**(A)** the sentence imposed for trafficking in a quantity of crack cocaine should generally exceed the sentence imposed for trafficking in a like quantity of powder cocaine;

"**(B)** high-level wholesale cocaine traffickers, organizers, and leaders, of criminal activities should generally receive longer sentences than low-level retail cocaine traffickers and those who played a minor or minimal role in such criminal activity;

"**(C)** if the Government establishes that a defendant who traffics in powder cocaine has knowledge that such cocaine will be converted into crack cocaine prior to its distribution to individual users, the defendant should be treated at sentencing as though the defendant had trafficked in crack cocaine; and

"**(D)** an enhanced sentence should generally be imposed on a defendant who, in the course of an offense described in this subsection—

"**(i)** murders or causes serious bodily injury to an individual;

"**(ii)** uses a dangerous weapon;

"**(iii)** uses or possesses a firearm;

"**(iv)** involves a juvenile or a woman who the defendant knows or should know to be pregnant;

"**(v)** engages in a continuing criminal enterprise or commits other criminal offenses in order to facilitate his drug trafficking activities;

"**(vi)** knows, or should know, that he is involving an unusually vulnerable person;

"**(vii)** restrains a victim;

"**(viii)** traffics in cocaine within 500 feet of a school;

"**(ix)** obstructs justice;

"**(x)** has a significant prior criminal record; or

"(xi) is an organizer or leader of drug trafficking activities involving five or more persons.

"(2) **Ratio.**—The recommendations described in the preceding subsection shall propose revision of the drug quantity ratio of crack cocaine to powder cocaine under the relevant statutes and guidelines in a manner consistent with the ratios set for other drugs and consistent with the objectives set forth in section 3553(a) of title 28 United States Code [reference to section 3553(a) of Title 18, Crimes and Criminal Procedure, was probably intended].

"(b) **Study.**—No later than May 1, 1996, the Department of Justice shall submit to the Judiciary Committees of the Senate and House of Representatives a report on the charging and plea practices of Federal prosecutors with respect to the offense of money laundering. Such study shall include an account of the steps taken or to be taken by the Justice Department to ensure consistency and appropriateness in the use of the money laundering statute. The Sentencing Commission shall submit to the Judiciary Committees comments on the study prepared by the Department of Justice."

Emergency Guidelines Promulgation Authority

Pub.L. 100–182, § 21, Dec. 7, 1987, 101 Stat. 1271, provided that:

"(a) **In general.**—In the case of—

"(1) an invalidated sentencing guideline;

"(2) the creation of a new offense or amendment of an existing offense; or

"(3) any other reason relating to the application of a previously established sentencing guideline, and determined by the United States Sentencing Commission to be urgent and compelling;

the Commission, by affirmative vote of at least four members of the Commission, and pursuant to its rules and regulations and consistent with all pertinent provisions of title 28 and title 18, United States Code, shall promulgate and distribute to all courts of the United States and to the United States Probation System a temporary guideline or amendment to an existing guideline, to remain in effect until and during the pendency of the next report to Congress under section 994(p) of title 28, United States Code [subsec. (p) of this section].

"(b) **Expiration of authority.**—The authority of the Commission under paragraphs (1) and (2) of subsection (a) shall expire on November 1, 1989. The authority of the Commission to promulgate and distribute guidelines under paragraph (3) of subsection (a) shall expire on May 1, 1988."

Submission to Congress of Initial Sentencing Guidelines

Provisions directing that the United States Sentencing Commission submit to Congress within 30 months of Oct. 12, 1984, the initial sentencing guidelines promulgated pursuant to subsec. (a)(1) of this section, see section 235(a)(1)(B)(i) of Pub.L. 98–473, as amended, set out as an Effective Date note under 18 U.S.C.A. § 3551.

Effective Date of Sentencing Guidelines

Sentencing guidelines promulgated pursuant to this section effective when U.S. Sentencing Commission has submitted the initial set of sentencing guidelines to Congress, the General Accounting Office has studied and reported to Congress on the guidelines, Congress has examined the guidelines, and section 212(a)(2) of Pub.L. 98–473 takes effect [Nov. 1, 1987], see section 235(a)(1)(B)(ii) of Pub.L. 98–473, as amended, set out as an Effective and Applicability Provisions note under 18 U.S.C.A. § 3551.

Studies of Impact and Operation of Sentencing Guideline System; Reporting Requirements

Pub.L. 98–473, Title II, § 236, Oct. 11, 1984, 98 Stat. 2033, provided that:

"(a)(1) Four years after the sentencing guidelines promulgated pursuant to section 994(a)(1) [subsec. (a)(1) of this section], and the provisions of sections 3581, 3583, and 3624 of title 18, United States Code, go into effect, the General Accounting Office [now Government Accountability Office] shall undertake a study of the guidelines in order to determine their impact and compare the guidelines system with the operation of the previous sentencing and parole release system, and, within six months of the undertaking of such study, report to the Congress the results of its study.

"(2) Within one month of the start of the study required under subsection (a), the United States Sentencing Commission shall submit a report to the General Accounting Office [now Government Accountability Office], all appropriate courts, the Department of Justice, and the Congress detailing the operation of the sentencing guideline system and discussing any problems with the system or reforms needed. The report shall include an evaluation of the impact of the sentencing guidelines on prosecutorial discretion, plea bargaining, disparities in sentencing, and the use of incarceration, and shall be issued by affirmative vote of a majority of the voting members of the Commission.

"(b) The Congress shall review the study submitted pursuant to subsection (a) in order to determine—

"(1) whether the sentencing guideline system has been effective;

"(2) whether any changes should be made in the sentencing guideline system; and

"(3) whether the parole system should be reinstated in some form and the life of the Parole Commission extended."

[For termination, effective May 15, 2000, of reporting provisions of above note, see Pub.L. 104–66, § 3003, as amended, set out as a note under 31 U.S.C.A. § 1113, and the 12th item on page 13 of House Document No. 103–7.]

§ 995. Powers of the Commission

(a) The Commission, by vote of a majority of the members present and voting, shall have the power to—

(1) establish general policies and promulgate such rules and regulations for the Commission as are necessary to carry out the purposes of this chapter;

(2) appoint and fix the salary and duties of the Staff Director of the Sentencing Commission, who shall serve at the discretion of the Commission and who shall be compensated at a rate not to exceed the highest rate now or hereafter prescribed for Level 6 of the Senior Executive Service Schedule (5 U.S.C. 5382);

(3) deny, revise, or ratify any request for regular, supplemental, or deficiency appropriations prior to

any submission of such request to the Office of Management and Budget by the Chair;

(4) procure for the Commission temporary and intermittent services to the same extent as is authorized by section 3109(b) of title 5, United States Code;

(5) utilize, with their consent, the services, equipment, personnel, information, and facilities of other Federal, State, local, and private agencies and instrumentalities with or without reimbursement therefor;

(6) without regard to 31 U.S.C. 3324, enter into and perform such contracts, leases, cooperative agreements, and other transactions as may be necessary in the conduct of the functions of the Commission, with any public agency, or with any person, firm, association, corporation, educational institution, or non-profit organization;

(7) accept and employ, in carrying out the provisions of this title, voluntary and uncompensated services, notwithstanding the provisions of 31 U.S.C. 1342, however, individuals providing such services shall not be considered Federal employees except for purposes of chapter 81 of title 5, United States Code, with respect to job-incurred disability and title 28, United States Code, with respect to tort claims;

(8) request such information, data, and reports from any Federal agency or judicial officer as the Commission may from time to time require and as may be produced consistent with other law;

(9) monitor the performance of probation officers with regard to sentencing recommendations, including application of the Sentencing Commission guidelines and policy statements;

(10) issue instructions to probation officers concerning the application of Commission guidelines and policy statements;

(11) arrange with the head of any other Federal agency for the performance by such agency of any function of the Commission, with or without reimbursement;

(12) establish a research and development program within the Commission for the purpose of—

(A) serving as a clearinghouse and information center for the collection, preparation, and dissemination of information on Federal sentencing practices; and

(B) assisting and serving in a consulting capacity to Federal courts, departments, and agencies in the development, maintenance, and coordination of sound sentencing practices;

(13) collect systematically the data obtained from studies, research, and the empirical experience of public and private agencies concerning the sentencing process;

(14) publish data concerning the sentencing process;

(15) collect systematically and disseminate information concerning sentences actually imposed, and the relationship of such sentences to the factors set forth in section 3553(a) of title 18, United States Code;

(16) collect systematically and disseminate information regarding effectiveness of sentences imposed;

(17) devise and conduct, in various geographical locations, seminars and workshops providing continuing studies for persons engaged in the sentencing field;

(18) devise and conduct periodic training programs of instruction in sentencing techniques for judicial and probation personnel and other persons connected with the sentencing process;

(19) study the feasibility of developing guidelines for the disposition of juvenile delinquents;

(20) make recommendations to Congress concerning modification or enactment of statutes relating to sentencing, penal, and correctional matters that the Commission finds to be necessary and advisable to carry out an effective, humane and rational sentencing policy;

(21) hold hearings and call witnesses that might assist the Commission in the exercise of its powers or duties;

(22) perform such other functions as are required to permit Federal courts to meet their responsibilities under section 3553(a) of title 18, United States Code, and to permit others involved in the Federal criminal justice system to meet their related responsibilities;

(23) retain private attorneys to provide legal advice to the Commission in the conduct of its work, or to appear for or represent the Commission in any case in which the Commission is authorized by law to represent itself, or in which the Commission is representing itself with the consent of the Department of Justice; and the Commission may in its discretion pay reasonable attorney's fees to private attorneys employed by it out of its appropriated funds. When serving as officers or employees of the United States, such private attorneys shall be considered special government employees as defined in section 202(a) of title 18; and

(24) grant incentive awards to its employees pursuant to chapter 45 of title 5, United States Code.

(b) The Commission shall have such other powers and duties and shall perform such other functions as may be necessary to carry out the purposes of this chapter, and may delegate to any member or designated person such powers as may be appropriate other than the power to establish general policy statements and guidelines pursuant to section 994(a)(1) and (2), the issuance of general policies and promulgation of rules and regulations pursuant to subsection (a)(1) of this section, and the decisions as to the factors to be considered in establishment of categories of offenses and offenders pursuant to section 994(b). The Commission shall, with respect to its activities under subsections (a)(9), (a)(10), (a)(11), (a)(12), (a)(13), (a)(14), (a)(15), (a)(16), (a)(17), and (a)(18), to the extent practicable, utilize existing resources of the Administrative Office of the United States Courts and the Federal Judicial Center for the purpose of avoiding unnecessary duplication.

(c) Upon the request of the Commission, each Federal agency is authorized and directed to make its services, equipment, personnel, facilities, and information available to the greatest practicable extent to the Commission in the execution of its functions.

(d) A simple majority of the membership then serving shall constitute a quorum for the conduct of business. Other than for the promulgation of guidelines and policy statements pursuant to section 994, the Commission may exercise its powers and fulfill its duties by the vote of a simple majority of the members present.

(e) Except as otherwise provided by law, the Commission shall maintain and make available for public inspection a record of the final vote of each member on any action taken by it.

(f) The Commission may—

(1) use available funds to enter into contracts for the acquisition of severable services for a period that begins in 1 fiscal year and ends in the next fiscal year, to the same extent as executive agencies may enter into such contracts under the authority of section 303L of the Federal Property and Administrative Services Act of 1949 (41 U.S.C. 253l);

(2) enter into multi-year contracts for the acquisition of property or services to the same extent as executive agencies may enter into such contracts under the authority of section 304B of the Federal Property and Administrative Services Act of 1949 (41 U.S.C. 254c); and

(3) make advance, partial, progress, or other payments under contracts for property or services to the same extent as executive agencies may make such payments under the authority of section 305 of the Federal Property and Administrative Services Act of 1949 (41 U.S.C. 255).

(Added Pub.L. 98–473, Title II, § 217(a), Oct. 12, 1984, 98 Stat. 2024, and amended Pub.L. 100–690, Title VII, §§ 7104, 7105, 7106(b), Nov. 18, 1988, 102 Stat. 4418; Pub.L. 101–650, Title III, § 325(b)(5), Dec. 1, 1990, 104 Stat. 5121; Pub.L. 103–322, Title XXVIII, § 280005(c)(1), Sept. 13, 1994, 108 Stat. 2097; Pub.L. 110–177, Title V, § 501(a), Jan. 7, 2008, 121 Stat. 2541.)

Termination of Subsec. (f)

For termination of subsec. (f) on September 30, 2010, see Pub.L. 110–177, § 501(b), set out as a Sunset Provisions note under this section.

HISTORICAL AND STATUTORY NOTES

References in Text

The provisions of title 28, United States Code, with respect to tort claims, referred to in subsec. (a)(7), are classified generally to section 1346(b) and chapter 171 (section 2671 et seq.) of this title.

Effective and Applicability Provisions

1984 Acts. Section effective Oct. 12, 1984, see section 235(a)(1)(B)(i) of Pub.L. 98–473, as amended, set out as a note under section 3551 of Title 18, Crimes and Criminal Procedure.

Sunset Provisions

Pub.L. 110–177, Title V, § 501(b), Jan. 7, 2008, 121 Stat. 2542, provided that: "The amendment made by subsection (a) [enacting subsec. (f) of this section] shall cease to have force and effect on September 30, 2010.".

§ 996. Director and staff

(a) The Staff Director shall supervise the activities of persons employed by the Commission and perform other duties assigned to the Staff Director by the Commission.

(b) The Staff Director shall, subject to the approval of the Commission, appoint such officers and employees as are necessary in the execution of the functions of the Commission. The officers and employees of the Commission shall be exempt from the provisions of part III of title 5, except the following: chapters 45 (Incentive Awards), 63 (Leave), 81 (Compensation for Work Injuries), 83 (Retirement), 85 (Unemployment Compensation), 87 (Life Insurance), and 89 (Health Insurance), and subchapter VI of chapter 55 (Payment for accumulated and accrued leave).

(Added Pub.L. 98–473, Title II, § 217(a), Oct. 12, 1984, 98 Stat. 2026, and amended Pub.L. 100–690, Title VII, § 7106(c), Nov. 18, 1988, 102 Stat. 4418; Pub.L. 101–650, Title III, § 325(b)(6), Dec. 1, 1990, 104 Stat. 5121; Pub.L. 103–322, Title XXVIII, § 280005(c)(5), Sept. 13, 1994, 108 Stat. 2097; Pub.L. 106–518, Title III, § 302(a), Nov. 13, 2000, 114 Stat. 2416.)

HISTORICAL AND STATUTORY NOTES

References in Text

Part III of title 5, referred to in subsec. (b), is 5 U.S.C.A. § 2101 et seq.

Chapter 45 of title 5, referred to in subsec. (b), is 5 U.S.C.A. § 4501 et seq.

Chapter 63 of title 5, referred to in subsec. (b), is 5 U.S.C.A. § 6301 et seq.

Chapter 81 of title 5, referred to in subsec. (b), is 5 U.S.C.A. § 8101 et seq.

Chapter 83 of title 5, referred to in subsec. (b), is 5 U.S.C.A. § 8301 et seq.

Chapter 85 of title 5, referred to in subsec. (b), is 5 U.S.C.A. § 8501 et seq.

Chapter 87 of title 5, referred to in subsec. (b), is 5 U.S.C.A. § 8701 et seq.

Chapter 89 of title 5, referred to in subsec. (b), is 5 U.S.C.A. § 8901 et seq.

Subchapter VI of chapter 55, referred to in subsec. (b), is 5 U.S.C.A. § 5551 et seq.

Effective and Applicability Provisions

1984 Acts. Section effective Oct. 12, 1984, see section 235(a)(1)(B)(i) of Pub.L. 98–473, as amended, set out as a note under section 3551 of Title 18, Crimes and Criminal Procedure.

Accrued or Accumulated Leave

Pub.L. 106–518, § 302(b), Nov. 13, 2000, 114 Stat. 2417, provided that: "Any leave that an individual accrued or accumulated (or that otherwise became available to such individual) under the leave system of the United States Sentencing Commission and that remains unused as of the date of the enactment of this Act shall, on and after such date, be treated as leave accrued or accumulated (or that otherwise became available to such individual) under chapter 63 of title 5, United States Code [5 U.S.C.A. § 6301 et seq.]."

§ 997. Annual report

The Commission shall report annually to the Judicial Conference of the United States, the Congress, and the President of the United States on the activities of the Commission.

(Added Pub.L. 98–473, Title II, § 217(a), Oct. 12, 1984, 98 Stat. 2026.)

HISTORICAL AND STATUTORY NOTES

Effective and Applicability Provisions

1984 Acts. Section effective Oct. 12, 1984, see section 235(a)(1)(B)(i) of Pub.L. 98–473, as amended, set out as a note under section 3551 of Title 18, Crimes and Criminal Procedure.

Termination of Reporting Requirements

For termination, effective May 15, 2000, of provisions of this section relating to requirement to report annually to Congress, see Pub.L. 104–66, § 3003, as amended, set out as a note under 31 U.S.C.A. § 1113, and page 13 of House Document No. 103–7.

§ 998. Definitions

As used in this chapter—

(a) "Commission" means the United States Sentencing Commission;

(b) "Commissioner" means a member of the United States Sentencing Commission;

(c) "guidelines" means the guidelines promulgated by the Commission pursuant to section 994(a) of this title; and

(d) "rules and regulations" means rules and regulations promulgated by the Commission pursuant to section 995 of this title.

(Added Pub.L. 98–473, Title II, § 217(a), Oct. 12, 1984, 98 Stat. 2026.)

HISTORICAL AND STATUTORY NOTES

Effective and Applicability Provisions

1984 Acts. Section effective Oct. 12, 1984, see section 235(a)(1)(B)(i) of Pub.L. 98–473, as amended, set out as a note under section 3551 of Title 18, Crimes and Criminal Procedure.

PART IV—JURISDICTION AND VENUE

Chapter	Section
81. Supreme Court	1251
83. Courts of Appeals	1291
85. District Courts; Jurisdiction	1331 [1]
87. District Courts; Venue	1391
89. District Courts; Removal of Cases from State Courts	1441
[90. District Courts and Bankruptcy Courts] [Omitted]	1471
91. United States Court of Federal Claims	1491
[93. Repealed]	
95. Court of International Trade	1581
97. Jurisdictional Immunities of Foreign States	1602
99. General Provisions	1631

[1] So in original. Probably should be "1330".

HISTORICAL AND STATUTORY NOTES

Codifications

The analysis of chapters comprising Part IV was amended by Pub.L. 95–598, Title II, § 241(b), Nov. 6, 1978, 92 Stat. 2671, effective June 28, 1984, pursuant to Pub.L. 95–598, Title IV, § 402(b), Nov. 6, 1978, 92 Stat. 2682, as amended by Pub.L. 98–249, § 1(a), Mar. 31, 1984, 98 Stat. 116; Pub.L. 98–271, § 1(a), Apr. 30, 1984, 98 Stat. 163; Pub.L. 98–299, § 1(a), May 25, 1984, 98 Stat. 214; Pub.L. 98–325, § 1(a), June 20, 1984, 98 Stat. 268, set out as an Effective Date note preceding section 101 of Title 11, Bankruptcy, by adding:

Section 402(b) of Pub.L. 95–598 was amended by section 113 of Pub.L. 98–353, Title I, July 10, 1984, 98 Stat. 343, by substituting "shall not be effective" for "shall take effect on June 28, 1984", thereby eliminating the amendment by section 241(b) of Pub.L. 95–598, effective June 27, 1984, pursuant to section 122(c) of Pub.L. 98–353, set out as an Effective and Applicability Provisions note under section 151 of this title.

Section 121(a) of Pub.L. 98–353 directed that section 402(b) of Pub.L. 95–598 be amended by substituting "the date of enactment of the Bankruptcy Amendments and Federal Judgeship Act of 1984 [i.e. July 10, 1984]" for "June 28, 1984". This amendment was not executed in view of the prior amendment to section 402(b) of Pub.L. 95–598 by section 113 of Pub.L. 98–353.

Change of Name

References to United States Claims Court deemed to refer to United States Court of Federal Claims and references to Claims Court deemed to refer to Court of Federal Claims, see section 902(b) of Pub.L. 102–572, set out as a note under section 171 of Title 28, Judiciary and Judicial Procedure.

CHAPTER 81—SUPREME COURT

Sec.
1251. Original jurisdiction.
[1252. Repealed.]
1253. Direct appeals from decisions of three-judge courts.
1254. Courts of appeals; certiorari; certified questions.
[1255, 1256. Repealed.]
1257. State courts; certiorari.
1258. Supreme Court of Puerto Rico; certiorari.
1259. Court of Appeals for the Armed Forces; certiorari.

HISTORICAL AND STATUTORY NOTES

Definitions of Courts and Judges

Section 32 of Act June 25, 1948, as amended by Act May 24, 1949, c. 139, § 127, 63 Stat. 107, provided:

"(a) All laws of the United States in force on September 1, 1948, in which reference is made to a 'circuit court of appeals'; 'senior circuit judge'; 'senior district judge'; 'presiding judge'; 'chief justice', except when reference to the Chief Justice of the United States is intended; or 'justice', except when used with respect to a justice of the Supreme Court of the United States in his capacity as such or as a circuit justice, are hereby amended by substituting 'court of appeals' for 'circuit court of appeals'; 'chief judge of the circuit' for 'senior circuit judge'; 'chief judge of the district court' for 'senior district judge'; 'chief judge' for 'presiding judge'; 'chief judge' for 'chief justice', except when reference to the Chief Justice of the United States is intended; and 'judge' for 'justice', except when the latter term is used with respect to a justice of the Supreme Court of the United States in his capacity as such or as a circuit justice.

"(b) All laws of the United States in force on September 1, 1948, in which reference is made to the Supreme Court of the District of Columbia or to the District Court of the United States for the District of Columbia are amended by substituting 'United States District Court for the District of Columbia' for such designations.

"(c) All laws of the United States in force on September 1, 1948, in which reference is made to the 'Conference of Senior Circuit Judges', or to the 'Judicial Conference of Senior Circuit Judges' are amended by substituting 'Judicial Conference of the United States' for such designations.

"(d) This section shall not be construed to amend historical references to courts or judicial offices which have no present or future application to such courts or offices."

§ 1251. Original jurisdiction

(a) The Supreme Court shall have original and exclusive jurisdiction of all controversies between two or more States.

(b) The Supreme Court shall have original but not exclusive jurisdiction of:

(1) All actions or proceedings to which ambassadors, other public ministers, consuls, or vice consuls of foreign states are parties;

(2) All controversies between the United States and a State;

(3) All actions or proceedings by a State against the citizens of another State or against aliens.

(June 25, 1948, c. 646, 62 Stat. 927; Sept. 30, 1978, Pub.L. 95–393, § 8(b), 92 Stat. 810.)

HISTORICAL AND STATUTORY NOTES

Effective and Applicability Provisions

1978 Acts. Amendment by Pub.L. 95–393 effective at the end of the 90-day period beginning on Sept. 30, 1978, see section 9 of Pub.L. 95–393, set out as a note under section 254a of Title 22, Foreign Relations and Intercourse.

Statutes Governing Writs of Error to Apply to Appeals

Act Jan. 31, 1928, c. 14, § 2, 45 Stat. 54, amended Apr. 26, 1928, c. 440, 45 Stat. 466; June 25, 1948, c. 646, § 23, 62 Stat. 990, provided that: "All Acts of Congress referring to writs of error shall be construed as amended to the extent necessary to substitute appeal for writ of error." See, also, notes preceding section 1 of this title.

[§ 1252. Repealed. Pub.L. 100–352, § 1, June 27, 1988, 102 Stat. 662]

HISTORICAL AND STATUTORY NOTES

Section, Acts June 25, 1948, c. 646, 62 Stat. 928; Oct. 31, 1951, c. 655, § 47, 65 Stat. 726; July 7, 1958, Pub.L. 85–508, § 12(e), (f), 72 Stat. 348; Mar. 18, 1959, Pub.L. 86–3, § 14(a), 73 Stat. 10, provided for direct appeals to Supreme Court from decisions invalidating Acts of Congress.

Effective Date of Repeal

Repeal of section effective ninety days after June 27, 1988, except that such repeal shall not apply to cases pending in the Supreme Court on such effective date or affect the right to review or the manner of reviewing the judgment or decree of a court which was entered before such effective date, see section 7 of Pub.L. 100–352, set out as a note under section 1254 of this title.

§ 1253. Direct appeals from decisions of three-judge courts

Except as otherwise provided by law, any party may appeal to the Supreme Court from an order granting or denying, after notice and hearing, an interlocutory or permanent injunction in any civil action, suit or proceeding required by any Act of Congress to be heard and determined by a district court of three judges.

(June 25, 1948, c. 646, 62 Stat. 928.)

§ 1254. Courts of appeals; certiorari; certified questions

Cases in the courts of appeals may be reviewed by the Supreme Court by the following methods:

(1) By writ of certiorari granted upon the petition of any party to any civil or criminal case, before or after rendition of judgment or decree;

(2) By certification at any time by a court of appeals of any question of law in any civil or criminal case as to which instructions are desired, and upon such certification the Supreme Court may give binding instructions or require the entire record to be sent up for decision of the entire matter in controversy.

(June 25, 1948, c. 646, 62 Stat. 928; June 27, 1988, Pub.L. 100–352, § 2(a), (b), 102 Stat. 662.)

HISTORICAL AND STATUTORY NOTES

Effective and Applicability Provisions

1988 Acts. Section 7 of Pub.L. 100–352 provided that: "The amendments made by this Act [amending this section by striking out 'appeal;' in heading and by striking out par. (2) and redesignating former par. (3) as (2), and amending sections 1257, 1258, 2101, 2104, and 2350 of this title, section 437h of Title 2, The Congress, section 136w of Title 7, Agriculture, section 1631e of Title 22, Foreign Relations and Intercourse, section 652 of Title 25, Indians, section 988 of Title 33, Navigation and Navigable Waters, section 1652 of Title 43, Public Lands, and sections 719, 743, and 1105 of Title 45, Railroads, and repealing sections 1252 and 2103 of this title] shall take effect ninety days after the date of the enactment of this Act [June 27, 1988], except that such amendments shall not apply to cases pending in the Supreme Court on the effective date of such amendments or affect the right to review or the manner of reviewing the judgment or decree of a court which was entered before such effective date."

[§§ 1255, 1256. Repealed. Pub.L. 97–164, Title I, § 123, Apr. 2, 1982, 96 Stat. 36]

HISTORICAL AND STATUTORY NOTES

Section 1255, Act June 25, 1948, c. 646, 62 Stat. 928, authorized the Supreme Court to review cases in the Court of Claims by writ of certiorari and by certification of questions of law.

Section 1256, Act June 25, 1948, c. 646, 62 Stat. 928, authorized the Supreme Court to review cases in the Court of Customs and Patent Appeals by writ of certiorari.

Effective Date of Repeal

Repeal effective Oct. 1, 1982, see section 402 of Pub.L. 97–164, set out as Effective and Applicability Provisions of 1982 Amendments note under section 171 of this title.

§ 1257. State courts; certiorari

(a) Final judgments or decrees rendered by the highest court of a State in which a decision could be had, may be reviewed by the Supreme Court by writ of certiorari where the validity of a treaty or statute of the United States is drawn in question or where the validity of a statute of any State is drawn in question on the ground of its being repugnant to the Constitution, treaties, or laws of the United States, or where any title, right, privilege, or immunity is specially set up or claimed under the Constitution or the treaties or statutes of, or any commission held or authority exercised under, the United States.

(b) For the purposes of this section, the term "highest court of a State" includes the District of Columbia Court of Appeals.

(June 25, 1948, c. 646, 62 Stat. 929; July 29, 1970, Pub.L. 91–358, Title I, § 172(a)(1), 84 Stat. 590; June 27, 1988, Pub.L. 100–352, § 3, 102 Stat. 662.)

HISTORICAL AND STATUTORY NOTES

Effective and Applicability Provisions

1988 Acts. Amendment by section 3 of Pub.L. 100–352 effective ninety days after June 27, 1988, except that such amendment not to apply to cases pending in the Supreme Court on such effective date or affect the right to review or the manner of reviewing the judgment or decree of a court which was entered before such effective date, see section 7 of Pub.L. 100–352, set out as a note under section 1254 of this title.

1970 Acts. Section 199(a) of Title 1 of Pub.L. 91–358 provided that: "The effective date of this title (and the amendments made by this title) [which enacted sections 1363, 1451, and 2113 of this title, and amended this section and sections 292 and 1869 of this title, section 5102 of Title 5, Government Organization and Employees, and section 260a of Title 42, the Public Health and Welfare] shall be the first day of the seventh calendar month which begins after the date of the enactment of this Act [July 29, 1970]."

§ 1258. Supreme Court of Puerto Rico; certiorari

Final judgments or decrees rendered by the Supreme Court of the Commonwealth of Puerto Rico may be reviewed by the Supreme Court by writ of certiorari where the validity of a treaty or statute of the United States is drawn in question or where the validity of a statute of the Commonwealth of Puerto Rico is drawn in question on the ground of its being repugnant to the Constitution, treaties, or laws of the United States, or where any title, right, privilege, or immunity is specially set up or claimed under the Constitution or the treaties or statutes of, or any commission held or authority exercised under, the United States.

(Added Pub.L. 87–189, § 1, Aug. 30, 1961, 75 Stat. 417, and amended, Pub.L. 100–352, § 4, June 27, 1988, 102 Stat. 662.)

HISTORICAL AND STATUTORY NOTES

Effective and Applicability Provisions

1988 Acts. Amendment by section 4 of Pub.L. 100–352 effective ninety days after June 27, 1988, except that such amendment not to apply to cases pending in the Supreme Court on such effective date or affect the right to review or the manner of reviewing the judgment or decree of a court which was entered before such effective date, pursuant to section 7 of Pub.L. 100–352, set out as a note under section 1254 of this title.

§ 1259. Court of Appeals for the Armed Forces; certiorari

Decisions of the United States Court of Appeals for the Armed Forces may be reviewed by the Supreme Court by writ of certiorari in the following cases:

(1) Cases reviewed by the Court of Appeals for the Armed Forces under section 867(a)(1) of title 10.

(2) Cases certified to the Court of Appeals for the Armed Forces by the Judge Advocate General under section 867(a)(2) of title 10.

(3) Cases in which the Court of Appeals for the Armed Forces granted a petition for review under section 867(a)(3) of title 10.

(4) Cases, other than those described in paragraphs (1), (2), and (3) of this subsection, in which the Court of Appeals for the Armed Forces granted relief.

(Added Pub.L. 98–209, § 10(a)(1), Dec. 6, 1983, 97 Stat. 1405, and amended Pub.L. 101–189, Div. A, Title XIII, § 1304(b)(3), Nov. 29, 1989, 103 Stat. 1577; Pub.L. 103–337, Div. A, Title IX, § 924(d)(1)(C), (2)(A), Oct. 5, 1994, 108 Stat. 2832.)

HISTORICAL AND STATUTORY NOTES

Effective and Applicability Provisions

1983 Acts. Section effective on the first day of the eighth calendar month beginning after Dec. 6, 1983, see section 12(a)(1) of Pub.L 98–209, set out as a note under section 801 of Title 10, Armed Forces.

CHAPTER 83—COURTS OF APPEALS

Sec.
1291. Final decisions of district courts.
1292. Interlocutory decisions.
[1293. Repealed.]
1294. Circuits in which decisions reviewable.
1295. Jurisdiction of the United States Court of Appeals for the Federal Circuit.
1296. Review of certain agency actions.

HISTORICAL AND STATUTORY NOTES

Codifications

The table of sections for chapter 83 was amended by Pub.L. 95–598, Title II, § 236(b), Nov. 6, 1978, 92 Stat. 2667, effective June 28, 1984, pursuant to Pub.L. 95–598, Title IV, § 402(b), Nov. 6, 1978, 92 Stat. 2682, as amended by Pub.L. 98–249, § 1(a), Mar. 31, 1984, 98 Stat. 116; Pub.L. 98–271, § 1(a), Apr. 30, 1984, 98 Stat. 163; Pub.L. 98–299, § 1(a), May 25, 1984, 98 Stat. 214; Pub.L. 98–325, § 1(a), June 20, 1984, 98 Stat. 268, set out as an Effective and Applicability Provisions note preceding section 101 of Title 11, Bankruptcy, by adding:

"1293. Bankruptcy appeals.".

Section 402(b) of Pub.L. 95–598 was amended by section 113 of Pub.L. 98–353, Title I, July 10, 1984, 98 Stat. 343, by substituting "shall not be effective" for "shall take effect on June 28, 1984", thereby eliminating the amendment by section 236(a) of Pub.L. 95–598, effective June 27, 1984, pursuant to section 122(c) of Pub.L. 98–353, set out as an Effective and Applicability Provisions note under section 151 of this title.

Section 121(a) of Pub.L. 98–353 directed that section 402(b) of Pub.L. 95–598 be amended by substituting "the date of enactment of the Bankruptcy Amendments and Federal Judgeship Act of 1984 [i.e. July 10, 1984]" for "June 28, 1984". This amendment was not executed in view of the prior amendment to section 402(b) of Pub.L. 95–598 by section 113 of Pub.L. 98–353.

§ 1291. Final decisions of district courts

The courts of appeals (other than the United States Court of Appeals for the Federal Circuit) shall have jurisdiction of appeals from all final decisions of the district courts of the United States, the United States District Court for the District of the Canal Zone, the District Court of Guam, and the District Court of the Virgin Islands, except where a direct review may be had in the Supreme Court. The jurisdiction of the United States Court of Appeals for the Federal Circuit shall be limited to the jurisdiction described in sections 1292(c) and (d) and 1295 of this title.

(June 25, 1948, c. 646, 62 Stat. 929; Oct. 31, 1951, c. 655, § 48, 65 Stat. 726; July 7, 1958, Pub.L. 85–508, § 12(e), 72 Stat. 348; Apr. 2, 1982, Pub.L. 97–164, Title I, § 124, 96 Stat. 36.)

HISTORICAL AND STATUTORY NOTES

Effective and Applicability Provisions

1982 Acts. Amendment by Pub.L. 97–164 effective Oct. 1, 1982, see section 402 of Pub.L. 97–164, set out as a note under section 171 of this title.

1958 Acts. Amendment of section by Pub.L. 85–508 effective Jan. 3, 1959, upon admission of Alaska into the Union pursuant to Proc. No. 3269, Jan. 3, 1959, 24 F.R. 81, 73 Stat. c16, as required by sections 1 and 8(c) of Pub.L. 85–508, see notes set out under section 81A of this title and preceding section 21 of Title 48, Territories and Insular Possessions.

Termination of United States District Court for the District of the Canal Zone

For termination of the United States District Court for the District of the Canal Zone at end of the "transition period", being the 30-month period beginning Oct. 1, 1979, and ending midnight Mar. 31, 1982, see Paragraph 5 of Article XI of the Panama Canal Treaty of 1977 and sections 3831 and 3841 to 3843 of Title 22, Foreign Relations and Intercourse.

§ 1292. Interlocutory decisions

(a) Except as provided in subsections (c) and (d) of this section, the courts of appeals shall have jurisdiction of appeals from:

(1) Interlocutory orders of the district courts of the United States, the United States District Court for the District of the Canal Zone, the District Court of Guam, and the District Court of the Virgin Islands, or of the judges thereof, granting, continuing, modifying, refusing or dissolving injunctions, or refusing to dissolve or modify injunctions, except where a direct review may be had in the Supreme Court;

(2) Interlocutory orders appointing receivers, or refusing orders to wind up receiverships or to take steps to accomplish the purposes thereof, such as directing sales or other disposals of property;

(3) Interlocutory decrees of such district courts or the judges thereof determining the rights and liabilities of the parties to admiralty cases in which appeals from final decrees are allowed.

(b) When a district judge, in making in a civil action an order not otherwise appealable under this section, shall be of the opinion that such order involves a controlling question of law as to which there is substantial ground for difference of opinion and that an immediate appeal from the order may materially advance the ultimate termination of the litigation, he shall so state in writing in such order. The Court of Appeals which would have jurisdiction of an appeal of such action may thereupon, in its discretion, permit an appeal to be taken from such order, if application is made to it within ten days after the entry of the order: *Provided, however,* That application for an appeal hereunder shall not stay proceedings in the district court unless the district judge or the Court of Appeals or a judge thereof shall so order.

(c) The United States Court of Appeals for the Federal Circuit shall have exclusive jurisdiction—

(1) of an appeal from an interlocutory order or decree described in subsection (a) or (b) of this section in any case over which the court would have jurisdiction of an appeal under section 1295 of this title; and

(2) of an appeal from a judgment in a civil action for patent infringement which would otherwise be appealable to the United States Court of Appeals for the Federal Circuit and is final except for an accounting.

(d)(1) When the chief judge of the Court of International Trade issues an order under the provisions of section 256(b) of this title, or when any judge of the Court of International Trade, in issuing any other interlocutory order, includes in the order a statement that a controlling question of law is involved with respect to which there is a substantial ground for difference of opinion and that an immediate appeal from that order may materially advance the ultimate termination of the litigation, the United States Court of Appeals for the Federal Circuit may, in its discretion, permit an appeal to be taken from such order, if application is made to that Court within ten days after the entry of such order.

(2) When the chief judge of the United States Court of Federal Claims issues an order under section 798(b) of this title, or when any judge of the United States Court of Federal Claims, in issuing an interlocutory order, includes in the order a statement that a controlling question of law is involved with respect to which there is a substantial ground for difference of opinion and that an immediate appeal from that order may materially advance the ultimate termination of the litigation, the United States Court of Appeals for the Federal Circuit may, in its discretion, permit an appeal to be taken from such order, if application is made to that Court within ten days after the entry of such order.

(3) Neither the application for nor the granting of an appeal under this subsection shall stay proceedings in the Court of International Trade or in the Court of Federal Claims, as the case may be, unless a stay is ordered by a judge of the Court of International Trade or of the Court of Federal Claims or by the United States Court of Appeals for the Federal Circuit or a judge of that court.

(4)(A) The United States Court of Appeals for the Federal Circuit shall have exclusive jurisdiction of an appeal from an interlocutory order of a district court of the United States, the District Court of Guam, the District Court of the Virgin Islands, or the District Court for the Northern Mariana Islands, granting or denying, in whole or in part, a motion to transfer an action to the United States Court of Federal Claims under section 1631 of this title.

(B) When a motion to transfer an action to the Court of Federal Claims is filed in a district court, no further proceedings shall be taken in the district court until 60 days after the court has ruled upon the motion. If an appeal is taken from the district court's grant or denial of the motion, proceedings shall be further stayed until the appeal has been decided by the Court of Appeals for the Federal Circuit. The stay of proceedings in the district court shall not bar the granting of preliminary or injunctive relief, where appropriate and where expedition is reasonably necessary. However, during the period in which proceedings are stayed as provided in this subparagraph, no transfer to the Court of Federal Claims pursuant to the motion shall be carried out.

(e) The Supreme Court may prescribe rules, in accordance with section 2072 of this title, to provide for an appeal of an interlocutory decision to the courts of appeals that is not otherwise provided for under subsection (a), (b), (c), or (d).

(June 25, 1948, c. 646, 62 Stat. 929; Oct. 31, 1951, c. 655, § 49, 65 Stat. 726; July 7, 1958, Pub.L. 85–508, § 12(e), 72 Stat. 348; Sept. 2, 1958, Pub.L. 85–919, 72 Stat. 1770; Apr. 2, 1982, Pub.L. 97–164, Title I, § 125, 96 Stat. 36; Nov. 8, 1984, Pub.L. 98–620, Title IV, § 412, 98 Stat. 3362; Nov. 19, 1988, Pub.L. 100–702, Title V, § 501, 102 Stat. 4652; Oct. 29, 1992, Pub.L. 102–572, Title I, § 101, Title IX, §§ 902(b), 906(c), 106 Stat. 4506, 4516, 4518.)

HISTORICAL AND STATUTORY NOTES

Effective and Applicability Provisions

1992 Acts. Amendment by sections 902(b) and 906(c) of Pub.L. 102–572 effective Oct. 29, 1992, see section 911 of Pub.L. 102–572, set out as a note under section 171 of this title.

Amendment by section 906(c) of Pub.L. 102–572 effective Oct. 29, 1992, see section 911 of Pub.L. 102–572, set out as a note under section 171 of Title 28, Judiciary and Judicial Procedure.

Amendment by section 101 of Pub.L. 102–572 effective Jan. 1, 1993, see section 1101(a) of Pub.L. 102–572, set out as a note under section 905 of Title 2, The Congress.

1988 Acts. Section 502 of Title V of Pub.L. 100–702 provided that: "The amendment made by section 501 [enacting subsec. (d)(4) of this section] shall apply to any action commenced in the district court on or after the date of enactment of this title [Nov. 19, 1988]."

1982 Acts. Amendment by Pub.L. 97–164 effective Oct. 1, 1982, see section 402 of Pub.L. 97–164, set out as a note under section 171 of this title.

1958 Acts. Amendment of section by Pub.L. 85–508 effective Jan. 3, 1959, upon admission of Alaska into the Union pursuant to Proc. No. 3269, Jan. 3, 1959, 24 F.R. 81, 73 Stat. c16, as required by Section 1 and 8(c) of Pub.L. 85–508, see notes set out under Section 81A of this title and preceding Section 21 of Title 48, Territories and Insular Possessions.

Change of Name

References to United States Claims Court deemed to refer to United States Court of Federal Claims and references to Claims Court deemed to refer to Court of Federal Claims, see section 902(b) of Pub.L. 102–572, set out as a note under section 171 of Title 28, Judiciary and Judicial Procedure.

Termination of United States District Court for the District of the Canal Zone

For termination of the United States District Court for the District of the Canal Zone at end of the "transition period", being the 30–month period beginning Oct. 1, 1979, and ending midnight Mar. 31, 1982, see Paragraph 5 of Article XI of the Panama Canal Treaty of 1977 and sections 3831 and 3841 to 3843 of Title 22, Foreign Relations and Intercourse.

[§ 1293. Repealed. Pub.L. 87–189, § 3, Aug. 30, 1961, 75 Stat. 417]

HISTORICAL AND STATUTORY NOTES

Section, Acts June 25, 1948, c. 646, 62 Stat. 929; Mar. 18, 1959, Pub.L. 86–3, § 14(b), 73 Stat. 10, provided for appeal from supreme court of Puerto Rico to court of appeals for first circuit. See section 1258 of this title.

Codifications

A subsequent section 1293, as added by Pub.L. 95–598, Title II, § 236a, Nov. 6, 1978, 92 Stat. 2667, effective June 28, 1984, pursuant to Pub.L. 95–598, Title IV, § 402(b), Nov. 6, 1978, 92 Stat. 2682, as amended by Pub.L. 98–249, § 1(a), Mar. 31, 1984, 98 Stat. 116; Pub.L. 98–271, § 1(a), Apr. 30,

1984, 98 Stat. 163; Pub.L. 98–299, § 1(a), May 25, 1984, 98 Stat. 214; Pub.L. 98–325, § 1(a), June 20, 1984, 98 Stat. 268, set out as an Effective and Applicability Provisions note preceding section 101 of Title 11, Bankruptcy, read as follows:

§ 1293. Bankruptcy appeals

(a) The courts of appeals shall have jurisdiction of appeals from all final decisions of panels designated under section 160(a) of this title.

(b) Notwithstanding section 1482 of this title, a court of appeals shall have jurisdiction of an appeal from a final judgment, order, or decree of an appellate panel created under section 160 or a District court of the United States or from a final judgment, order, or decree of a bankruptcy court of the United States if the parties to such appeal agree to a direct appeal to the court of appeals.

Section 402(b) of Pub.L. 95–598 was amended by section 113 of Pub.L. 98–353, Title I, July 10, 1984, 98 Stat. 343, by substituting "shall not be effective" for "shall take effect on June 28, 1984", thereby eliminating the addition of subsequent section 1293 by section 236(a) of Pub.L. 95–598, effective June 27, 1984, pursuant to section 122(c) of Pub.L. 98–353, set out as an Effective and Applicability Provisions note under section 151 of this title.

Section 121(a) of Pub.L. 98–353 directed that section 402(b) of Pub.L. 95–598 be amended by substituting "the date of enactment of the Bankruptcy Amendments and Federal Judgeship Act of 1984 [i.e. July 10, 1984]" for "June 28, 1984". This amendment was not executed in view of the prior amendment to section 402(b) of Pub.L. 95–598 by section 113 of Pub.L. 98–353.

§ 1294. Circuits in which decisions reviewable

Except as provided in sections 1292(c), 1292(d), and 1295 of this title, appeals from reviewable decisions of the district and territorial courts shall be taken to the courts of appeals as follows:

(1) From a district court of the United States to the court of appeals for the circuit embracing the district;

(2) From the United States District Court for the District of the Canal Zone, to the Court of Appeals for the Fifth Circuit;

(3) From the District Court of the Virgin Islands, to the Court of Appeals for the Third Circuit;

(4) From the District Court of Guam, to the Court of Appeals for the Ninth Circuit.

(June 25, 1948, c. 646, 62 Stat. 930; Oct. 31, 1951, c. 655, § 50(a), 65 Stat. 727; July 7, 1958, Pub.L. 85–508, § 12(g), 72 Stat. 348; Mar. 18, 1959, Pub.L. 86–3, § 14(c), 73 Stat. 10; Aug. 30, 1961, Pub.L. 87–189, § 5, 75 Stat. 417; Nov. 6, 1978, Pub.L. 95–598, Title II, § 237, 92 Stat. 2667; Apr. 2, 1982, Pub.L. 97–164, Title I, § 126, 96 Stat. 37.)

HISTORICAL AND STATUTORY NOTES

Codifications

This section was amended by Pub.L. 95–598, Title II, § 237, Nov. 6, 1978, 92 Stat. 2667, effective June 28, 1984, pursuant to Pub.L. 95–598, Title IV, § 402(b), Nov. 6, 1978, 92 Stat. 2682, as amended by Pub.L. 98–249, § 1(a), Mar. 31, 1984, 98 Stat. 116; Pub.L. 98–271, § 1(a), Apr. 30, 1984, 98 Stat. 163; Pub.L. 98–299, § 1(a), May 25, 1984, 98 Stat. 214; Pub.L. 98–325, § 1(a), June 20, 1984, 98 Stat. 268, set out as an Effective and Applicability Provisions note preceding section 101 of Title II, Bankruptcy, to read as follows:

§ 1294. Circuits in which decisions reviewable

Except as provided in sections 1292(c), 1292(d), and 1295 of this title, appeals from reviewable decisions of the district, bankruptcy, and territorial courts shall be taken to the courts of appeals as follows:

(1) From a district court of the United States to the court of appeals for the circuit embracing the district;

(2) From the United States District Court for the District of the Canal Zone, to the Court of Appeals for the Fifth Circuit;

(3) From the District Court of the Virgin Islands, to the Court of Appeals for the Third Circuit;

(4) From the District Court of Guam, to the Court of Appeals for the Ninth Circuit;

(5) From a panel designated under section 160(a) of this title to the court of appeals for the circuit in which the panel was so designated;

(6) From a bankruptcy court of the United States to the court of appeals for the circuit embracing the district in which the bankruptcy court is located.

Section 402(b) of Pub.L. 95–598 was amended by section 113 of Pub.L. 98–353, Title I, July 10, 1984, 98 Stat. 343, by substituting "shall not be effective" for "shall take effect on June 28, 1984", thereby eliminating the amendment by section 237 of Pub.L. 95–598, effective June 27, 1984, pursuant to section 122(c) of Pub.L. 98–353, set out as an Effective and Applicability Provisions note under section 151 of this title.

Section 121(a) of Pub.L. 98–353 directed that section 402(b) of Pub.L. 95–598 be amended by substituting "the date of enactment of the Bankruptcy Amendments and Federal Judgeship Act of 1984 [i.e. July 10, 1984]" for "June 28, 1984". This amendment was not executed in view of the prior amendment to section 402(b) of Pub.L. 95–598 by section 113 of Pub.L. 98–353.

Effective and Applicability Provisions

1982 Acts. Amendment by Pub.L. 97–164 effective Oct. 1, 1982, see section 402 of Pub.L. 97–164, set out as a note under section 171 of this title.

1959 Acts. Amendment of section by Pub.L. 86–3 effective upon the admission of the State of Hawaii into the Union, see note set out under section 91 of this title. Admission of Hawaii into the Union was accomplished Aug. 21, 1959 upon issuance of Proc. No. 3309, Aug. 21, 1959, 25 F.R. 6868, 73 Stat. c74, as required by sections 1 and 7(c) of Pub.L. 86–3, Mar. 18, 1959, 73 Stat. 4, set out as notes preceding section 491 of Title 48, Territories and Insular Possessions.

1958 Acts. Amendment of section by Pub.L. 85–508 effective Jan. 3, 1959, upon admission of Alaska into the Union pursuant to Proc. No. 3269, Jan. 3, 1959, 24 F.R. 81, 73 Stat. c16, as required by sections 1 and 8(c) of Pub.L. 85–508, see notes set out under section 81A of this title and preceding section 21 of Title 48, Territories and Insular Possessions.

Termination of United States District Court for the District of the Canal Zone

For termination of the United States District Court for the District of the Canal Zone at end of the "transition period", being the 30-month period beginning Oct. 1, 1979, and ending midnight Mar. 31, 1982, see Paragraph 5 of Article XI of the Panama Canal Treaty of 1977 and sections 3831 and 3841 to 3843 of Title 22, Foreign Relations and Intercourse.

§ 1295. Jurisdiction of the United States Court of Appeals for the Federal Circuit

(a) The United States Court of Appeals for the Federal Circuit shall have exclusive jurisdiction—

(1) of an appeal from a final decision of a district court of the United States, the United States District Court for the District of the Canal Zone, the District Court of Guam, the District Court of the Virgin Islands, or the District Court for the Northern Mariana Islands, if the jurisdiction of that court was based, in whole or in part, on section 1338 of this title, except that a case involving a claim arising under any Act of Congress relating to copyrights, exclusive rights in mask works, or trademarks and no other claims under section 1338(a) shall be governed by sections 1291, 1292, and 1294 of this title;

(2) of an appeal from a final decision of a district court of the United States, the United States District Court for the District of the Canal Zone, the District Court of Guam, the District Court of the Virgin Islands, or the District Court for the Northern Mariana Islands, if the jurisdiction of that court was based, in whole or in part, on section 1346 of this title, except that jurisdiction of an appeal in a case brought in a district court under section 1346(a)(1), 1346(b), 1346(e), or 1346(f) of this title or under section 1346(a)(2) when the claim is founded upon an Act of Congress or a regulation of an executive department providing for internal revenue shall be governed by sections 1291, 1292, and 1294 of this title;

(3) of an appeal from a final decision of the United States Court of Federal Claims;

(4) of an appeal from a decision of—

(A) the Board of Patent Appeals and Interferences of the United States Patent and Trademark Office with respect to patent applications and interferences, at the instance of an applicant for a patent or any party to a patent interference, and any such appeal shall waive the right of such applicant or party to proceed under section 145 or 146 of title 35;

(B) the Under Secretary of Commerce for Intellectual Property and Director of the United States Patent and Trademark Office or the Trademark Trial and Appeal Board with respect to applications for registration of marks and other proceedings as provided in section 21 of the Trademark Act of 1946 (15 U.S.C. 1071); or

(C) a district court to which a case was directed pursuant to section 145, 146, or 154(b) of title 35;

(5) of an appeal from a final decision of the United States Court of International Trade;

(6) to review the final determinations of the United States International Trade Commission relating to unfair practices in import trade, made under section 337 of the Tariff Act of 1930 (19 U.S.C. 1337);

(7) to review, by appeal on questions of law only, findings of the Secretary of Commerce under U.S. note 6 to subchapter X of chapter 98 of the Harmonized Tariff Schedule of the United States (relating to importation of instruments or apparatus);

(8) of an appeal under section 71 of the Plant Variety Protection Act (7 U.S.C. 2461);

(9) of an appeal from a final order or final decision of the Merit Systems Protection Board, pursuant to sections 7703(b)(1) and 7703(d) of title 5;

(10) of an appeal from a final decision of an agency board of contract appeals pursuant to section 8(g)(1) of the Contract Disputes Act of 1978 (41 U.S.C. 607(g)(1));

(11) of an appeal under section 211 of the Economic Stabilization Act of 1970;

(12) of an appeal under section 5 of the Emergency Petroleum Allocation Act of 1973;

(13) of an appeal under section 506(c) of the Natural Gas Policy Act of 1978; and

(14) of an appeal under section 523 of the Energy Policy and Conservation Act.

(b) The head of any executive department or agency may, with the approval of the Attorney General, refer to the Court of Appeals for the Federal Circuit for judicial review any final decision rendered by a board of contract appeals pursuant to the terms of any contract with the United States awarded by that department or agency which the head of such department or agency has concluded is not entitled to finality pursuant to the review standards specified in section 10(b) of the Contract Disputes Act of 1978 (41 U.S.C. 609(b)). The head of each executive department or agency shall make any referral under this section within one hundred and twenty days after the receipt of a copy of the final appeal decision.

(c) The Court of Appeals for the Federal Circuit shall review the matter referred in accordance with the standards specified in section 10(b) of the Contract Disputes Act of 1978. The court shall proceed with judicial review on the administrative record made before the board of contract appeals on matters so referred as in other cases pending in such court, shall determine the issue of finality of the appeal decision, and shall, if appropriate, render judgment thereon, or remand the matter to any administrative or executive body or official with such direction as it may deem proper and just.

(Added Pub.L. 97–164, Title I, § 127(a), Apr. 2, 1982, 96 Stat. 37, and amended Pub.L. 98–622, Title II, § 205(a), Nov. 8, 1984, 98 Stat. 3388; Pub.L. 100–418, Title I, § 1214(a)(3), Aug. 23, 1988, 102 Stat. 1156; Pub.L. 100–702, Title X, § 1020(a)(3), Nov. 19, 1988, 102 Stat. 4671; Pub.L. 102–572, Title I, § 102(c), Title IX, § 902(b)(1), Oct. 29, 1992, 106 Stat. 4507, 4516; Pub.L. 106–113, Div. B, § 1000(a)(9) [Title IV, §§ 4402(b)(2), 4732(b)(14)], Nov. 29, 1999, 113 Stat. 1536, 1501A–560, 1501A–584.)

HISTORICAL AND STATUTORY NOTES

References in Text

The Harmonized Tariff Schedule of the United States, referred to in subsec. (a)(7), is not carried in the Code. See Publication of Harmonized Tariff Schedule note set out under section 1202 of Title 19, Customs Duties.

Section 211 of the Economic Stabilization Act of 1970, referred to in subsec. (a)(11), is section 211 of Pub.L. 91–379, Title II, Aug. 15, 1970, as added Pub.L. 92–210, § 2, Dec. 22, 1971, 85 Stat. 743, as amended, which is set out as a note under TECA Rule 3, this title, and in codified form under section 1904 of Title 12, Banks and Banking.

Section 5 of the Emergency Petroleum Allocation Act of 1973, referred to in subsec. (a)(12), is section 5 of Pub.L. 93–159, Nov. 27, 1973, 87 Stat. 633, as amended, which was classified to section 754 of Title 15, Commerce and Trade, prior to the omission of such section pursuant to section 760g of Title 15.

Section 506(c) of the Natural Gas Policy Act of 1978, referred to in subsec. (a)(13), is section 506(c) of Pub.L. 95–621, Title V, Nov. 9, 1978, 92 Stat. 3404, which is classified to section 3416(c) of Title 15, Commerce and Trade.

Section 523 of the Energy Policy and Conservation Act, referred to in subsec. (a)(14), is section 523 of Pub.L. 94–163, Title V, Dec. 22, 1975, 89 Stat. 962, which is classified to section 6393 of Title 42, The Public Health and Welfare.

Effective and Applicability Provisions

1999 Acts. Amendment by Pub.L. 106–113 [§ 4732], effective 4 months after Nov. 29, 1999, see Pub.L. 106–113 [§ 4731], set out as a note under section 1 of Title 35.

Amendment by Pub.L. 106–113 [§ 4402], to take effect on the date that is six months after Nov. 29, 1999 and, except for a design patent application filed under chapter 16 of Title 35, to be applicable to any application filed on or after the date that is six months after Nov. 29, 1999, see Pub.L. 106–113 [§ 4405], set out as a note under section 154 of Title 35.

1992 Acts. Amendment by section 902(b)(1) of Pub.L. 102–572 effective Oct. 29, 1992, see section 911 of Pub.L. 102–572, set out as a note under section 171 of this title.

Amendment by Pub.L. 102–572 effective Jan. 1, 1993, see section 1101(a) of Pub.L. 102–572, set out as a note under section 905 of Title 2, The Congress.

1988 Acts. Amendment by Pub.L. 100–418 effective Jan. 1, 1989, and applicable with respect to articles entered on or after such date, see section 1217(b)(1) of Pub.L. 100–418, set out as an Effective and Applicability Provisions note under section 3001 of Title 19, Customs Duties.

1984 Acts. Amendment by Pub.L. 98–622 applicable to all United States patents granted before, on, or after Nov. 8, 1984, and to all applications for United States patents pending on or filed after that date, except as otherwise provided, see section 106 of Pub.L. 98–622, set out as a note under section 103 of Title 35, Patents.

Amendment by Pub.L. 98–622, effective three months after Nov. 8, 1984, see section 207 of Pub.L. 98–622, set out as a note under section 7 of Title 35, Patents.

1982 Acts. Section effective Oct. 1, 1982, see section 402 of Pub.L. 97–164, set out as a note under section 171 of this title.

Abolition of Temporary Emergency Court of Appeals

Section 102(d), (e) of Pub.L. 102–572 provided that:

"**(d) Abolition of Court.**—The Temporary Emergency Court of Appeals created by section 211(b) of the Economic Stabilization Act of 1970 [set out as a note under TECA Rule 3, this title] is abolished, effective 6 months after the date of the enactment of this Act [Oct. 29, 1992].

"**(e) Pending cases.—(1)** Any appeal which, before the effective date of abolition described in subsection (d), is pending in the Temporary Emergency Court of Appeals but has not been submitted to a panel of such court as of that date shall be assigned to the United States Court of Appeals for the Federal Circuit as though the appeal had originally been filed in that court.

"**(2)** Any case which, before the effective date of abolition described in subsection (d), has been submitted to a panel of the Temporary Emergency Court of Appeals and as to which the mandate has not been issued as of that date shall remain with that panel for all purposes and, notwithstanding the provisions of sections 291 and 292 of title 28, United States Code [sections 291 and 292 of this title], that panel shall be assigned to the United States Court of Appeals for the Federal Circuit for the purpose of deciding such case."

Termination of United States District Court for the District of the Canal Zone

For termination of the United States District Court for the District of the Canal Zone at end of the "transition period", being the 30–month period beginning Oct. 1, 1979, and ending midnight Mar. 31, 1982, see Paragraph 5 of Article XI of the Panama Canal Treaty of 1977 and sections 3831 and 3841 to 3843 of Title 22, Foreign Relations and Intercourse.

Transfer of Cases and Petitions Pending in Court of Claims and in Court of Customs and Patent Appeals on October 1, 1982

For provisions directing that any case pending before the Court of Claims on Oct. 1, 1982, in which a report on the merits has been filed by a commissioner, or in which there is pending a request for review, and upon which the court has not acted, and any matter pending before the United States Court of Customs and Patent Appeals on Oct. 1, 1982, be transferred to the United States Court of Appeals for the Federal Circuit, and that any petition for rehearing, reconsideration, alteration, modification, or other change in any decision of the United States Court of Claims or the United States Court of Customs and Patent Appeals rendered prior to Oct. 1, 1982, that has not been determined by either of those courts on that date, or that is filed after that date, be determined by the United States Court of Appeals for the Federal Circuit, see section 403(a)–(c) of Pub.L. 97–164, set out as a note under section 171 of this title.

§ 1296. Review of certain agency actions

(a) Jurisdiction.—Subject to the provisions of chapter 179, the United States Court of Appeals for the Federal Circuit shall have jurisdiction over a petition for review of a final decision under chapter 5 of title 3 of—

(1) an appropriate agency (as determined under section 454 of title 3);

(2) the Federal Labor Relations Authority made under part D of subchapter II of chapter 5 of title 3, notwithstanding section 7123 of title 5; or

(3) the Secretary of Labor or the Occupational Safety and Health Review Commission, made under part C of subchapter II of chapter 5 of title 3.

(b) Filing of petition.—Any petition for review under this section must be filed within 30 days after the date the petitioner receives notice of the final decision.

(Added Pub.L. 104–331, § 3(a)(1), Oct. 26, 1996, 110 Stat. 4069.)

HISTORICAL AND STATUTORY NOTES

Effective and Applicability Provisions

1996 Acts. Section 3(d) of Pub.L. 104–331 provided that: "The amendments made by this section [enacting this section, sections 1413, and 3901 to 3908 of this title, and amending sections 1346 and 2402 of this title] shall take effect on October 1, 1997."

Prior Provisions

A prior section 1296, Pub.L. 97–164, Title I, § 127(a), Apr. 2, 1982, 96 Stat. 39, relating to precedence of cases in the United States Court of Appeals for the Federal Circuit, was repealed by Pub.L. 98–620, Title IV, § 402(29)(C), Nov. 8, 1984, 98 Stat. 3359.

CHAPTER 85—DISTRICT COURTS; JURISDICTION

Sec.
1330. Actions against foreign states.
1331. Federal question.
1332. Diversity of citizenship; amount in controversy; costs.
1333. Admiralty, maritime and prize cases.
1334. Bankruptcy cases and proceedings.
1335. Interpleader.
1336. Surface Transportation Board's orders.
1337. Commerce and antitrust regulations; amount in controversy, costs.
1338. Patents, plant variety protection, copyrights, mask works, designs, trademarks, and unfair competition.
1339. Postal matters.
1340. Internal revenue; customs duties.
1341. Taxes by States.
1342. Rate orders of State agencies.
1343. Civil rights and elective franchise.
1344. Election disputes.
1345. United States as plaintiff.
1346. United States as defendant.
1347. Partition action where United States is joint tenant.
1348. Banking association as party.
1349. Corporation organized under federal law as party.
1350. Alien's action for tort.
1351. Consuls, vice consuls, and members of a diplomatic mission as defendant.
1352. Bonds executed under federal law.
1353. Indian allotments.
1354. Land grants from different states.
1355. Fine, penalty or forfeiture.
1356. Seizures not within admiralty and maritime jurisdiction.
1357. Injuries under Federal laws.
1358. Eminent domain.
1359. Parties collusively joined or made.
Sec.
1360. State civil jurisdiction in actions to which Indians are parties.
1361. Action to compel an officer of the United States to perform his duty.
1362. Indian tribes.
1363. Jurors' employment rights.
1364. Direct actions against insurers of members of diplomatic missions and their families.
1365. Senate actions.
1366. Construction of references to laws of the United States or Acts of Congress.
1367. Supplemental jurisdiction.
1368. Counterclaims in unfair practices in international trade.
1369. Multiparty, multiforum jurisdiction.

HISTORICAL AND STATUTORY NOTES

Codifications

The table of sections for chapter 85 was amended by Pub.L. 95–598, Title II, § 238(b), Nov. 6, 1978, 92 Stat. 2668, effective June 28, 1984, pursuant to Pub.L. 95–598, Title IV, § 402(b), Nov. 6, 1978, 92 Stat. 2682, as amended by Pub.L. 98–249, § 1(a), Mar. 31, 1984, 98 Stat. 116; Pub.L. 98–271, § 1(a), Apr. 30, 1984, 98 Stat. 163; Pub.L. 98–299, § 1(a), May 25, 1984, 98 Stat. 214; Pub.L. 98–325, § 1(a), June 20, 1984, 98 Stat. 268, by substituting "1334. Bankruptcy appeals." for "1334. Bankruptcy matters and proceedings.".

Section 402(b) of Pub.L. 95–598 was amended by section 113 of Pub.L. 98–353, Title I, July 10, 1984, 98 Stat. 343, by substituting "shall not be effective" for "shall take effect on June 28, 1984", thereby eliminating the amendment by section 238(b) of Pub.L. 95–598, effective June 27, 1984, pursuant to section 122(c) of Pub.L. 98–353, set out as an Effective Date note under section 151 of this title.

Section 121(a) of Pub.L. 98–353 directed that section 402(b) of Pub.L. 95–598 be amended by substituting "the date of enactment of the Bankruptcy Amendments and Federal Judgeship Act of 1984 [i.e. July 10, 1984]" for "June 28, 1984". This amendment was not executed in view of the prior amendment to section 402(b) of Pub.L. 95–598 by section 113 of Pub.L. 98–353.

§ 1330. Actions against foreign states

(a) The district courts shall have original jurisdiction without regard to amount in controversy of any nonjury civil action against a foreign state as defined in section 1603(a) of this title as to any claim for relief in personam with respect to which the foreign state is not entitled to immunity either under sections 1605–1607 of this title or under any applicable international agreement.

(b) Personal jurisdiction over a foreign state shall exist as to every claim for relief over which the district courts have jurisdiction under subsection (a) where service has been made under section 1608 of this title.

(c) For purposes of subsection (b), an appearance by a foreign state does not confer personal jurisdiction with respect to any claim for relief not arising out of any transaction or occurrence enumerated in sections 1605–1607 of this title.

(Added Pub.L. 94–583, § 2(a), Oct. 21, 1976, 90 Stat. 2891.)

HISTORICAL AND STATUTORY NOTES

Effective and Applicability Provisions

1976 Acts. Section effective 90 days after Oct. 21, 1976, see section 8 of Pub.L. 94–583, set out as a note under section 1602 of this title.

§ 1331. Federal question

The district courts shall have original jurisdiction of all civil actions arising under the Constitution, laws, or treaties of the United States.

(June 25, 1948, c. 646, 62 Stat. 930; July 25, 1958, Pub.L. 85–554, § 1, 72 Stat. 415; Oct. 21, 1976, Pub.L. 94–574, § 2, 90 Stat. 2721; Dec. 1, 1980, Pub.L. 96–486, § 2(a), 94 Stat. 2369.)

HISTORICAL AND STATUTORY NOTES

Effective and Applicability Provisions

1980 Acts. Section 4 of Pub.L. 96–486 provided: "This Act [amending this section and section 2072 of Title 15, Commerce and Trade, and enacting provisions set out as a note under section 1 of this title] shall apply to any civil action pending on the date of enactment of this Act [Dec. 1, 1980]."

1958 Acts. Section 3 of Pub.L. 85–554 provided that: "This Act [amending this section and sections 1332 and 1445 of this title] shall apply only in the case of actions commenced after the date of the enactment of this Act [July 25, 1958]."

§ 1332. Diversity of citizenship; amount in controversy; costs

(a) The district courts shall have original jurisdiction of all civil actions where the matter in controversy exceeds the sum or value of $75,000, exclusive of interest and costs, and is between—

(1) citizens of different States;

(2) citizens of a State and citizens or subjects of a foreign state;

(3) citizens of different States and in which citizens or subjects of a foreign state are additional parties; and

(4) a foreign state, defined in section 1603(a) of this title, as plaintiff and citizens of a State or of different States.

For the purposes of this section, section 1335, and section 1441, an alien admitted to the United States for permanent residence shall be deemed a citizen of the State in which such alien is domiciled.

(b) Except when express provision therefor is otherwise made in a statute of the United States, where the plaintiff who files the case originally in the Federal courts is finally adjudged to be entitled to recover less than the sum or value of $75,000, computed without regard to any setoff or counterclaim to which the defendant may be adjudged to be entitled, and exclusive of interest and costs, the district court may deny costs to the plaintiff and, in addition, may impose costs on the plaintiff.

(c) For the purposes of this section and section 1441 of this title—

(1) a corporation shall be deemed to be a citizen of any State by which it has been incorporated and of the State where it has its principal place of business, except that in any direct action against the insurer of a policy or contract of liability insurance, whether incorporated or unincorporated, to which action the insured is not joined as a party-defendant, such insurer shall be deemed a citizen of the State of which the insured is a citizen, as well as of any State by which the insurer has been incorporated and of the State where it has its principal place of business; and

(2) the legal representative of the estate of a decedent shall be deemed to be a citizen only of the same State as the decedent, and the legal representative of an infant or incompetent shall be deemed to be a citizen only of the same State as the infant or incompetent.

(d)(1) In this subsection—

(A) the term "class" means all of the class members in a class action;

(B) the term "class action" means any civil action filed under rule 23 of the Federal Rules of Civil

Procedure or similar State statute or rule of judicial procedure authorizing an action to be brought by 1 or more representative persons as a class action;

(C) the term "class certification order" means an order issued by a court approving the treatment of some or all aspects of a civil action as a class action; and

(D) the term "class members" means the persons (named or unnamed) who fall within the definition of the proposed or certified class in a class action.

(2) The district courts shall have original jurisdiction of any civil action in which the matter in controversy exceeds the sum or value of $5,000,000, exclusive of interest and costs, and is a class action in which—

(A) any member of a class of plaintiffs is a citizen of a State different from any defendant;

(B) any member of a class of plaintiffs is a foreign state or a citizen or subject of a foreign state and any defendant is a citizen of a State; or

(C) any member of a class of plaintiffs is a citizen of a State and any defendant is a foreign state or a citizen or subject of a foreign state.

(3) A district court may, in the interests of justice and looking at the totality of the circumstances, decline to exercise jurisdiction under paragraph (2) over a class action in which greater than one-third but less than two-thirds of the members of all proposed plaintiff classes in the aggregate and the primary defendants are citizens of the State in which the action was originally filed based on consideration of—

(A) whether the claims asserted involve matters of national or interstate interest;

(B) whether the claims asserted will be governed by laws of the State in which the action was originally filed or by the laws of other States;

(C) whether the class action has been pleaded in a manner that seeks to avoid Federal jurisdiction;

(D) whether the action was brought in a forum with a distinct nexus with the class members, the alleged harm, or the defendants;

(E) whether the number of citizens of the State in which the action was originally filed in all proposed plaintiff classes in the aggregate is substantially larger than the number of citizens from any other State, and the citizenship of the other members of the proposed class is dispersed among a substantial number of States; and

(F) whether, during the 3-year period preceding the filing of that class action, 1 or more other class actions asserting the same or similar claims on behalf of the same or other persons have been filed.

(4) A district court shall decline to exercise jurisdiction under paragraph (2)—

(A)(i) over a class action in which—

(I) greater than two-thirds of the members of all proposed plaintiff classes in the aggregate are citizens of the State in which the action was originally filed;

(II) at least 1 defendant is a defendant—

(aa) from whom significant relief is sought by members of the plaintiff class;

(bb) whose alleged conduct forms a significant basis for the claims asserted by the proposed plaintiff class; and

(cc) who is a citizen of the State in which the action was originally filed; and

(III) principal injuries resulting from the alleged conduct or any related conduct of each defendant were incurred in the State in which the action was originally filed; and

(ii) during the 3-year period preceding the filing of that class action, no other class action has been filed asserting the same or similar factual allegations against any of the defendants on behalf of the same or other persons; or

(B) two-thirds or more of the members of all proposed plaintiff classes in the aggregate, and the primary defendants, are citizens of the State in which the action was originally filed.

(5) Paragraphs (2) through (4) shall not apply to any class action in which—

(A) the primary defendants are States, State officials, or other governmental entities against whom the district court may be foreclosed from ordering relief; or

(B) the number of members of all proposed plaintiff classes in the aggregate is less than 100.

(6) In any class action, the claims of the individual class members shall be aggregated to determine whether the matter in controversy exceeds the sum or value of $5,000,000, exclusive of interest and costs.

(7) Citizenship of the members of the proposed plaintiff classes shall be determined for purposes of paragraphs (2) through (6) as of the date of filing of the complaint or amended complaint, or, if the case stated by the initial pleading is not subject to Federal jurisdiction, as of the date of service by plaintiffs of an amended pleading, motion, or other paper, indicating the existence of Federal jurisdiction.

(8) This subsection shall apply to any class action before or after the entry of a class certification order by the court with respect to that action.

(9) Paragraph (2) shall not apply to any class action that solely involves a claim—

(A) concerning a covered security as defined under 16(f)(3) [1] of the Securities Act of 1933 (15 U.S.C. 78p(f)(3)[2]) and section 28(f)(5)(E) of the Securities Exchange Act of 1934 (15 U.S.C. 78bb(f)(5)(E));

(B) that relates to the internal affairs or governance of a corporation or other form of business enterprise and that arises under or by virtue of the laws of the State in which such corporation or business enterprise is incorporated or organized; or

(C) that relates to the rights, duties (including fiduciary duties), and obligations relating to or created by or pursuant to any security (as defined under section 2(a)(1) of the Securities Act of 1933 (15 U.S.C. 77b(a)(1)) and the regulations issued thereunder).

(10) For purposes of this subsection and section 1453, an unincorporated association shall be deemed to be a citizen of the State where it has its principal place of business and the State under whose laws it is organized.

(11)(A) For purposes of this subsection and section 1453, a mass action shall be deemed to be a class action removable under paragraphs (2) through (10) if it otherwise meets the provisions of those paragraphs.

(B)(i) As used in subparagraph (A), the term "mass action" means any civil action (except a civil action within the scope of section 1711(2)) in which monetary relief claims of 100 or more persons are proposed to be tried jointly on the ground that the plaintiffs' claims involve common questions of law or fact, except that jurisdiction shall exist only over those plaintiffs whose claims in a mass action satisfy the jurisdictional amount requirements under subsection (a).

(ii) As used in subparagraph (A), the term "mass action" shall not include any civil action in which—

(I) all of the claims in the action arise from an event or occurrence in the State in which the action was filed, and that allegedly resulted in injuries in that State or in States contiguous to that State;

(II) the claims are joined upon motion of a defendant;

(III) all of the claims in the action are asserted on behalf of the general public (and not on behalf of individual claimants or members of a purported class) pursuant to a State statute specifically authorizing such action; or

(IV) the claims have been consolidated or coordinated solely for pretrial proceedings.

(C)(i) Any action(s) removed to Federal court pursuant to this subsection shall not thereafter be transferred to any other court pursuant to section 1407, or the rules promulgated thereunder, unless a majority of the plaintiffs in the action request transfer pursuant to section 1407.

(ii) This subparagraph will not apply—

(I) to cases certified pursuant to rule 23 of the Federal Rules of Civil Procedure; or

(II) if plaintiffs propose that the action proceed as a class action pursuant to rule 23 of the Federal Rules of Civil Procedure.

(D) The limitations periods on any claims asserted in a mass action that is removed to Federal court pursuant to this subsection shall be deemed tolled during the period that the action is pending in Federal court.

(e) The word "States", as used in this section, includes the Territories, the District of Columbia, and the Commonwealth of Puerto Rico.

(June 25, 1948, c. 646, 62 Stat. 930; July 26, 1956, c. 740, 70 Stat. 658; July 25, 1958, Pub.L. 85–554, § 2, 72 Stat. 415; Aug. 14, 1964, Pub.L. 88–439, § 1, 78 Stat. 445; Oct. 21, 1976, Pub.L. 94–583, § 3, 90 Stat. 2891; Nov. 19, 1988, Pub.L. 100–702, Title II, §§ 201(a), 202(a), 203(a), 102 Stat. 4646; Oct. 19, 1996, Pub.L. 104–317, Title II, § 205(a), 110 Stat. 3850; Feb. 18, 2005, Pub.L. 109–2, § 4(a), 119 Stat. 9.)

[1] So in original. Reference to "16(f)(3)" probably should be preceded by "section".

[2] So in original. Probably should be "77p(f)(3)".

HISTORICAL AND STATUTORY NOTES

References in Text

Rule 23 of the Federal Rules of Civil Procedure, referred to in subsec. (d)(1)(B) and (11)(C)(ii), is set out following the code sections of this title.

Section 16(f) of the Securities Act of 1933, referred to in subsec. (d)(9)(A), does not contain a par. (3). See Act May 27, 1933, c. 38, Title I, § 16(f), 48 Stat. 84, as amended, which is classified to 15 U.S.C.A. § 78p(f).

Section 28(f)(5)(E) of the Securities Exchange Act of 1934, referred to in subsec. (d)(9)(A), is May 27, 1933, c. 38, Title I, § 2(f)(5)(E), 48 Stat. 74, as amended, which is classified to 15 U.S.C.A. § 78bb(f)(5)(E).

Section 2(a)(1) of the Securities Act of 1933, referred to in subsec. (d)(9)(C), is May 27, 1933, c. 38, Title I, § 2(a)(1), 48 Stat. 74, as amended, which is classified to 15 U.S.C.A. § 77b(a)(1).

Effective and Applicability Provisions

2005 Acts. Pub.L. 109–2, § 9, Feb. 18, 2005, 119 Stat. 14, provided that: "The amendments made by this Act [enacting 28 U.S.C.A. § 1453 and chapter 114 of this title (28 U.S.C.A. §§ 1711 to 1715), and amending this section and 28 U.S.C.A. §§ 1335, and 1603 of this title] shall apply to any civil action commenced on or after the date of enactment of this Act [Feb. 18, 2005]."

1996 Acts. Section 205(b) of Pub.L. 104–317 provided that: "The amendment made by this section [amending this section] shall take effect 90 days after the date of enactment of this Act [Oct. 19, 1996]."

1988 Acts. Section 201(b) of Title II of Pub.L. 100–702 provided that: "The amendments made by this section [amending amount in controversy in subsecs. (a) and (b) of this section] shall apply to any civil action commenced on or after the 180th day after the date of enactment of this title [Nov. 19, 1988]."

Section 202(b) of Title II of Pub.L. 100–702 provided that: "The amendment made by this section [amending subsec. (c) of this section] shall apply to any civil action commenced in or removed to a United States district court on or after the 180th day after the date of enactment of this title [Nov. 19, 1988]."

Section 203(b) of Title II of Pub.L. 100–702 provided that: "The amendment made by this section [amending subsec. (a) of this section by enacting citizenship of permanent resident alien provision] shall apply to claims in civil actions commenced in or removed to the United States district courts on or after the 180th day after the date of enactment of this title [Nov. 19, 1988]."

1976 Acts. Amendment by Pub.L. 94–583 effective 90 days after Oct. 21, 1976, see section 8 of Pub.L. 94–583, set out as a note under section 1602 of this title.

1964 Acts. Section 2 of Pub.L. 88–439 provided that: "The amendment made by this Act to section 1332(c), title 28, United States Code [subsec. (c) of this section], applies only to causes of action arising after the date of enactment of this Act [Aug. 14, 1964]."

1958 Acts. Amendment of section by Pub.L. 85–554 applicable only in the case of actions commenced after July 25, 1958, see section 3 of Pub.L. 85–554, set out as a note under section 1331 of this title.

§ 1333. Admiralty, maritime and prize cases

The district courts shall have original jurisdiction, exclusive of the courts of the States, of:

(1) Any civil case of admiralty or maritime jurisdiction, saving to suitors in all cases all other remedies to which they are otherwise entitled.

(2) Any prize brought into the United States and all proceedings for the condemnation of property taken as prize.

(June 25, 1948, c. 646, 62 Stat. 931; May 24, 1949, c. 139, § 79, 63 Stat. 101.)

§ 1334. Bankruptcy cases and proceedings

(a) Except as provided in subsection (b) of this section, the district courts shall have original and exclusive jurisdiction of all cases under title 11.

(b) Except as provided in subsection (e)(2), and notwithstanding any Act of Congress that confers exclusive jurisdiction on a court or courts other than the district courts, the district courts shall have original but not exclusive jurisdiction of all civil proceedings arising under title 11, or arising in or related to cases under title 11.

(c)(1) Except with respect to a case under chapter 15 of title 11, nothing in this section prevents a district court in the interest of justice, or in the interest of comity with State courts or respect for State law, from abstaining from hearing a particular proceeding arising under title 11 or arising in or related to a case under title 11.

(2) Upon timely motion of a party in a proceeding based upon a State law claim or State law cause of action, related to a case under title 11 but not arising under title 11 or arising in a case under title 11, with respect to which an action could not have been commenced in a court of the United States absent jurisdiction under this section, the district court shall abstain from hearing such proceeding if an action is commenced, and can be timely adjudicated, in a State forum of appropriate jurisdiction.

(d) Any decision to abstain or not to abstain made under subsection (c) (other than a decision not to abstain in a proceeding described in subsection (c)(2)) is not reviewable by appeal or otherwise by the court of appeals under section 158(d), 1291, or 1292 of this title or by the Supreme Court of the United States under section 1254 of this title. Subsection (c) and this subsection shall not be construed to limit the applicability of the stay provided for by section 362 of title 11, United States Code, as such section applies to an action affecting the property of the estate in bankruptcy.

(e) The district court in which a case under title 11 is commenced or is pending shall have exclusive jurisdiction—

(1) of all the property, wherever located, of the debtor as of the commencement of such case, and of property of the estate; and

(2) over all claims or causes of action that involve construction of section 327 of title 11, United States Code, or rules relating to disclosure requirements under section 327.

(June 25, 1948, c. 646, 62 Stat. 931; Nov. 6, 1978, Pub.L. 95–598, Title II, § 238(a), 92 Stat. 2667; July 10, 1984, Pub.L. 98–353, Title I, § 101(a), 98 Stat. 333; Oct. 27, 1986, Pub.L. 99–554, Title I, § 144(e), 100 Stat. 3096; Dec. 1, 1990, Pub.L. 101–650, Title III, § 309(b), 104 Stat. 5113; Oct. 22, 1994, Pub.L. 103–394, Title I, § 104(b), 108 Stat. 4109; Apr. 20, 2005, Pub.L. 109–8, Title III, § 324(a), Title VIII, § 802(c)(2), Title XII, § 1219, 119 Stat. 98, 145, 195.)

HISTORICAL AND STATUTORY NOTES

References in Text

Chapter 15 of title 11, referred to in subsec. (c), is 11 U.S.C.A. § 1501 et seq.

Codifications

This section was amended by Pub.L. 95–598, Title II, § 238(a), Nov. 6, 1978, 92 Stat. 2668, effective June 28, 1984, pursuant to Pub.L. 95–598, Title IV, § 402(b), Nov. 6, 1978, 92 Stat. 2682, as amended by Pub.L. 98–249, § 1(a), Mar. 31, 1984, 98 Stat. 116; Pub.L. 98–271, § 1(a), Apr. 30, 1984, 98 Stat. 163; Pub.L. 98–299, § 1(a), May 25, 1984, 98 Stat. 214; Pub.L. 98–325, § 1(a), June 20, 1984, 98 Stat. 268, set out as an Effective and Applicability Provisions note preceding section 101 of Title 11, Bankruptcy, to read as follows:

"§ 1334. **Bankruptcy appeals**

"(a) The district courts for districts for which panels have not been ordered appointed under section 160 of this title shall have jurisdiction of appeals from all final judgments, orders, and decrees of bankruptcy courts.

"(b) The district courts for such districts shall have jurisdiction of appeals from interlocutory orders and decrees of bankruptcy courts, but only by leave of the district court to which the appeal is taken.

"(c) A district court may not refer an appeal under that section to a magistrate or to a special master."

Section 402(b) of Pub.L. 95–598 was amended by section 113 of Pub.L. 98–353 by substituting "shall not be effective" for "shall take effect on June 28, 1984", thereby eliminating the amendment by section 238(a) of Pub.L. 95–598, effective June 27, 1984, pursuant to section 122(c) of Pub.L. 98–353, set out as an Effective and Applicability Provisions note under 28 U.S.C.A. § 151.

Section 121(a) of Pub.L. 98–353 directed that section 402(b) of Pub.L. 95–598 be amended by substituting "the date of enactment of the Bankruptcy Amendments and Federal Judgeship Act of 1984 [i.e. July 10, 1984]" for "June 28, 1984". This amendment was not executed in view of the prior amendment to section 402(b) of Pub.L. 95–598 by section 113 of Pub.L. 98–353.

Effective and Applicability Provisions

2005 Acts. Pub.L. 109–8, Title III, § 324(b), Apr. 20, 2005, 119 Stat. 98, provided that: "This section [amending subsecs. (b) and (e) of this section] shall only apply to cases filed after the date of enactment of this Act [Apr. 20, 2005]."

Except as otherwise provided, amendments by Pub.L. 109–8 effective 180 days after April 20, 2005, and inapplicable with respect to cases commenced under Title 11 before the effective date, see Pub.L. 109–8, § 1501, set out as a note under 11 U.S.C.A. § 101.

1994 Acts. Amendment by Pub.L. 103–394 effective on Oct. 22, 1994, and not to apply with respect to cases commenced under Title 11 of the United States Code before Oct. 22, 1994, see section 702 of Pub.L. 103–394, set out as a note under section 101 of Title 11, Bankruptcy.

1986 Acts. Amendment by Pub.L. 99–554 effective 30 days after Oct. 27, 1986, except as otherwise provided for, see section 302(a) of Pub.L. 99–554, as amended, set out as a note under section 581 of this title.

1984 Acts. Amendment by Pub.L. 98–353, except for subsec. (c)(2), effective July 10, 1984, see section 122(a) of Pub.L. 98–353, set out as a note under section 151 of this title.

Subsec. (c)(2) not applicable with respect to cases under Title 11, Bankruptcy, that are pending on July 10, 1984, or to proceedings arising in or related to such cases, see section 122(b) of Pub.L. 98–353, set out as a note under section 151 of this title.

Separability of Provisions

If any provision of or amendment made by Pub.L. 103–394 or the application of such provision or amendment to any person or circumstance is held to be unconstitutional, the remaining provisions of and amendments made by Pub.L. 103–394 and the application of such provisions and amendments to any person or circumstance shall not be affected thereby, see section 701 of Pub.L. 103–394, set out as a note under section 101 of Title 11, Bankruptcy.

Jurisdiction Over and Transfer of Bankruptcy Cases and Proceedings

Section 115 of Pub.L. 98–353 provided that:

"(a) On the date of the enactment of this Act [July 10, 1984] the appropriate district court of the United States shall have jurisdiction of—

"(1) cases, and matters and proceedings in cases, under the Bankruptcy Act [former Title 11, Bankruptcy] that are pending immediately before such date in the bankruptcy courts continued by section 404(a) of the Act of November 6, 1978 (Public Law 95–598; 92 Stat. 2687) [Pub.L. 95–598, Title IV, § 404(a), Nov. 6, 1978, 92 Stat. 2683, formerly set out as a note preceding section 151 of this title], and

"(2) cases under title 11 of the United States Code [Title 11, Bankruptcy], and proceedings arising under title 11 of the United States Code or arising in or related to cases under title 11 of the United States Code, that are pending immediately before such date in the bankruptcy courts continued by section 404(a) of the Act of November 6, 1978 (Public Law 95–598; 92 Stat. 2687).

"(b) On the date of the enactment of this Act [July 10, 1984], there shall be transferred to the appropriate district court of the United States appeals from final judgments, orders, and decrees of the bankruptcy courts pending immediately before such date in the bankruptcy appellate panels appointed under section 405(c) of the Act of November 6, 1978 (Public Law 95–598; 92 Stat. 2685) [formerly set out as a note preceding section 1471 of this title]."

§ 1335. Interpleader

(a) The district courts shall have original jurisdiction of any civil action of interpleader or in the nature of interpleader filed by any person, firm, or corporation, association, or society having in his or its custody or possession money or property of the value of $500 or more, or having issued a note, bond, certificate, policy of insurance, or other instrument of value or amount of $500 or more, or providing for the delivery or payment or the loan of money or property of such amount or value, or being under any obligation written or unwritten to the amount of $500 or more, if

(1) Two or more adverse claimants, of diverse citizenship as defined in subsection (a) or (d) of section 1332 of this title, are claiming or may claim to be entitled to such money or property, or to any one or more of the benefits arising by virtue of any note, bond, certificate, policy or other instrument, or arising by virtue of any such obligation; and if (2) the plaintiff has deposited such money or property or has paid the amount of or the loan or other value of such instrument or the amount due under such obligation into the registry of the court, there to abide the judgment of the court, or has given bond payable to the clerk of the court in such amount and with such surety as the court or judge may deem proper, conditioned upon the compliance by the plaintiff with the future order or judgment of the court with respect to the subject matter of the controversy.

(b) Such an action may be entertained although the titles or claims of the conflicting claimants do not have a common origin, or are not identical, but are adverse to and independent of one another.

(June 25, 1948, c. 646, 62 Stat. 931; Feb. 18, 2005, Pub.L. 109–2, § 4(b)(1), 119 Stat. 12.)

HISTORICAL AND STATUTORY NOTES

Effective and Applicability Provisions

2005 Acts. Amendments by Class Action Fairness Act of 2005, Pub.L. 109–2, Feb. 18, 2005, 119 Stat. 4, applicable to any civil action commenced on or after Feb. 18, 2005, see Pub.L. 109–2, § 9, set out as a note under 28 U.S.C.A. § 1332.

§ 1336. Surface Transportation Board's orders

(a) Except as otherwise provided by Act of Congress, the district courts shall have jurisdiction of any civil action to enforce, in whole or in part, any order of the Surface Transportation Board, and to enjoin or suspend, in whole or in part, any order of the Surface Transportation Board for the payment of money or the collection of fines, penalties, and forfeitures.

(b) When a district court or the United States Court of Federal Claims refers a question or issue to the Surface Transportation Board for determination, the court which referred the question or issue shall have exclusive jurisdiction of a civil action to enforce, enjoin, set aside, annul, or suspend, in whole or in part, any order of the Surface Transportation Board arising out of such referral.

(c) Any action brought under subsection (b) of this section shall be filed within 90 days from the date that the order of the Surface Transportation Board becomes final.

(June 25, 1948, c. 646, 62 Stat. 931; Aug. 30, 1964, Pub.L. 88–513, § 1, 78 Stat. 695; Jan. 2, 1975, Pub.L. 93–584, § 1, 88 Stat. 1917; Apr. 2, 1982, Pub.L. 97–164, Title I, § 128, 96 Stat. 39; Oct. 29, 1992, Pub.L. 102–572, Title IX, § 902(b)(1), 106 Stat. 4516; Dec. 29, 1995, Pub.L. 104–88, Title III, § 305(a)(1), (2), 109 Stat. 944.)

HISTORICAL AND STATUTORY NOTES

Effective and Applicability Provisions

1995 Acts. Amendment by Pub.L. 104–88 effective Jan. 1, 1996, see section 2 of Pub.L. 104–88, set out as a note under section 701 of Title 49, Transportation.

1992 Acts. Amendment by Pub.L. 102–572 effective Oct. 29, 1992, see section 911 of Pub.L. 102–572, set out as a note under section 171 of this title.

1982 Acts. Amendment by Pub.L. 97–164 effective Oct. 1, 1982, see section 402 of Pub.L. 97–164, set out as a note under section 171 of this title.

1975 Acts. Amendment by Pub.L. 93–584 not applicable to actions commenced on or before the last day of the first month beginning after Jan. 2, 1975, and actions to enjoin or suspend orders of the Interstate Commerce Commission which are pending when this amendment becomes effective shall not be affected thereby, but shall proceed to final disposition under the law existing on the date they were commenced, see section 10 of Pub.L. 93–584, set out as a note under section 2321 of this title.

§ 1337. Commerce and antitrust regulations; amount in controversy, costs

(a) The district courts shall have original jurisdiction of any civil action or proceeding arising under any Act of Congress regulating commerce or protecting trade and commerce against restraints and monopolies: *Provided, however*, That the district courts shall have original jurisdiction of an action brought under section 11706 or 14706 of title 49, only if the matter in controversy for each receipt or bill of lading exceeds $10,000, exclusive of interest and costs.

(b) Except when express provision therefor is otherwise made in a statute of the United States, where a plaintiff who files the case under section 11706 or 14706 of title 49, originally in the Federal courts is finally adjudged to be entitled to recover less than the sum or value of $10,000, computed without regard to any setoff or counterclaim to which the defendant may be adjudged to be entitled, and exclusive of any interest and costs, the district court may deny costs to the plaintiff and, in addition, may impose costs on the plaintiff.

(c) The district courts shall not have jurisdiction under this section of any matter within the exclusive jurisdiction of the Court of International Trade under chapter 95 of this title.

(June 25, 1948, c. 646, 62 Stat. 931; Oct. 20, 1978, Pub.L. 95–486, § 9(a), 92 Stat. 1633; Oct. 10, 1980, Pub.L. 96–417, Title V, § 505, 94 Stat. 1743; Jan. 12, 1983, Pub.L. 97–449, § 5(f), 96 Stat. 2442; Dec. 29, 1995, Pub.L. 104–88, Title III, § 305(a)(3), 109 Stat. 944.)

HISTORICAL AND STATUTORY NOTES

Effective and Applicability Provisions

1995 Acts. Amendment by Pub.L. 104–88 effective Jan. 1, 1996, see section 2 of Pub.L. 104–88, set out as a note under section 701 of Title 49, Transportation.

1980 Acts. Amendment by Pub.L. 96–417 effective on Nov. 1, 1980 and applicable with respect to civil actions pending on or commenced on or after such date, see section 701(a) of Pub.L. 96–417, as amended, set out as a note under section 251 of this title.

§ 1338. Patents, plant variety protection, copyrights, mask works, designs, trademarks, and unfair competition

(a) The district courts shall have original jurisdiction of any civil action arising under any Act of Congress relating to patents, plant variety protection, copyrights and trademarks. Such jurisdiction shall be exclusive of the courts of the states in patent, plant variety protection and copyright cases.

(b) The district courts shall have original jurisdiction of any civil action asserting a claim of unfair competition when joined with a substantial and related claim under the copyright, patent, plant variety protection or trademark laws.

(c) Subsections (a) and (b) apply to exclusive rights in mask works under chapter 9 of title 17, and to exclusive rights in designs under chapter 13 of title 17, to the same extent as such subsections apply to copyrights.

(June 25, 1948, c. 646, 62 Stat. 931; Dec. 24, 1970, Pub.L. 91–577, Title III, § 143(b), 84 Stat. 1559; Nov. 19, 1988, Pub.L. 100–702, Title X, § 1020(a)(4), 102 Stat. 4671; Oct. 28, 1998, Pub.L. 105–304, Title V, § 503(b)(1), (2)(A), 112 Stat. 2917; Nov. 29, 1999, Pub.L. 106–113, Div. B, § 1000(a)(9) [Title III, § 3009(1)], 113 Stat. 1536, 1501A–551.)

HISTORICAL AND STATUTORY NOTES

Effective and Applicability Provisions

1998 Acts. Amendment by Pub.L. 105–304, effective Oct. 28, 1998, see section 505 of Pub.L. 105–304, set out as a note under section 1301 of Title 17, Copyrights.

1970 Acts. Amendment by Pub.L. 91–577 effective Dec. 24, 1970, see section 141 of Pub.L. 91–577, set out as a note under section 2321 of Title 7, Agriculture.

§ 1339. Postal matters

The district courts shall have original jurisdiction of any civil action arising under any Act of Congress relating to the postal service.

(June 25, 1948, c. 646, 62 Stat. 932.)

§ 1340. Internal revenue; customs duties

The district courts shall have original jurisdiction of any civil action arising under any Act of Congress providing for internal revenue, or revenue from imports or tonnage except matters within the jurisdiction of the Court of International Trade.

(June 25, 1948, c. 646, 62 Stat. 932; Oct. 10, 1980, Pub.L. 96–417, Title V, § 501(21), 94 Stat. 1742.)

HISTORICAL AND STATUTORY NOTES

Effective and Applicability Provisions

1980 Acts. Amendment by Pub.L. 96–417 effective on Nov. 1, 1980 and applicable with respect to civil actions pending on or commenced on or after such date, see section 701(a) of Pub.L. 96–417, as amended, set out as a note under section 251 of this title.

§ 1341. Taxes by States

The district courts shall not enjoin, suspend or restrain the assessment, levy or collection of any tax under State law where a plain, speedy and efficient remedy may be had in the courts of such State.

(June 25, 1948, c. 646, 62 Stat. 932.)

HISTORICAL AND STATUTORY NOTES

Short Title

1948 Acts. This section is commonly known as the Tax Injunction Act.

§ 1342. Rate orders of State agencies

The district courts shall not enjoin, suspend or restrain the operation of, or compliance with, any order affecting rates chargeable by a public utility and made by a State administrative agency or a ratemaking body of a State political subdivision, where:

(1) Jurisdiction is based solely on diversity of citizenship or repugnance of the order to the Federal Constitution; and,

(2) The order does not interfere with interstate commerce; and,

(3) The order has been made after reasonable notice and hearing; and,

(4) A plain, speedy and efficient remedy may be had in the courts of such State.

(June 25, 1948, c. 646, 62 Stat. 932.)

§ 1343. Civil rights and elective franchise

(a) The district courts shall have original jurisdiction of any civil action authorized by law to be commenced by any person:

(1) To recover damages for injury to his person or property, or because of the deprivation of any right or privilege of a citizen of the United States, by any act done in furtherance of any conspiracy mentioned in section 1985 of Title 42;

(2) To recover damages from any person who fails to prevent or to aid in preventing any wrongs mentioned in section 1985 of Title 42 which he had knowledge were about to occur and power to prevent;

(3) To redress the deprivation, under color of any State law, statute, ordinance, regulation, custom or usage, of any right, privilege or immunity secured by the Constitution of the United States or by any Act of Congress providing for equal rights of citizens or of all persons within the jurisdiction of the United States;

(4) To recover damages or to secure equitable or other relief under any Act of Congress providing for the protection of civil rights, including the right to vote.

(b) For purposes of this section—

(1) the District of Columbia shall be considered to be a State; and

(2) any Act of Congress applicable exclusively to the District of Columbia shall be considered to be a statute of the District of Columbia.

(June 25, 1948, c. 646, 62 Stat. 932; Sept. 3, 1954, c. 1263, § 42, 68 Stat. 1241; Sept. 9, 1957, Pub.L. 85–315, Part III, § 121, 71 Stat. 637; Dec. 29, 1979, Pub.L. 96–170, § 2, 93 Stat. 1284.)

HISTORICAL AND STATUTORY NOTES

Effective and Applicability Provisions

1979 Acts. Section 3 of Pub.L. 96–170 provided that: "The amendments made by this Act [amending this section and section 1983 of Title 42, The Public Health and Welfare] shall apply with respect to any deprivation of rights, privileges, or immunities secured by the Constitution and laws occurring after the date of the enactment of this Act [Dec. 29, 1979]."

§ 1344. Election disputes

The district courts shall have original jurisdiction of any civil action to recover possession of any office, except that of elector of President or Vice President, United States Senator, Representative in or delegate to Congress, or member of a state legislature, authorized by law to be commenced, wherein it appears that the sole question touching the title to office arises out of denial of the right to vote, to any citizen offering to vote, on account of race, color or previous condition of servitude.

The jurisdiction under this section shall extend only so far as to determine the rights of the parties to office by reason of the denial of the right, guaranteed by the Constitution of the United States and secured by any law, to enforce the right of citizens of the United States to vote in all the States.

(June 25, 1948, c. 646, 62 Stat. 932.)

§ 1345. United States as plaintiff

Except as otherwise provided by Act of Congress, the district courts shall have original jurisdiction of all civil actions, suits or proceedings commenced by the United States, or by any agency or officer thereof expressly authorized to sue by Act of Congress.

(June 25, 1948, c. 646, 62 Stat. 933.)

§ 1346. United States as defendant

(a) The district courts shall have original jurisdiction, concurrent with the United States Court of Federal Claims, of:

(1) Any civil action against the United States for the recovery of any internal-revenue tax alleged to have been erroneously or illegally assessed or collected, or any penalty claimed to have been collected without authority or any sum alleged to have been excessive or in any manner wrongfully collected under the internal-revenue laws;

(2) Any other civil action or claim against the United States, not exceeding $10,000 in amount, founded either upon the Constitution, or any Act of Congress, or any regulation of an executive department, or upon any express or implied contract with the United States, or for liquidated or unliquidated damages in cases not sounding in tort, except that the district courts shall not have jurisdiction of any civil action or claim against the United States founded upon any express or implied contract with the United States or for liquidated or unliquidated damages in cases not sounding in tort which are subject to sections 8(g)(1) and 10(a)(1) of the Contract Disputes Act of 1978. For the purpose of this paragraph, an express or implied contract with the Army and Air Force Exchange Service, Navy Exchanges, Marine Corps Exchanges, Coast Guard Exchanges, or Exchange Councils of the National Aeronautics and Space Administration shall be considered an express or implied contract with the United States.

(b)(1) Subject to the provisions of chapter 171 of this title, the district courts, together with the United States District Court for the District of the Canal Zone and the District Court of the Virgin Islands, shall have exclusive jurisdiction of civil actions on claims against the United States, for money damages, accruing on and after January 1, 1945, for injury or loss of property, or personal injury or death caused by the negligent or wrongful act or omission of any employee of the Government while acting within the scope of his office or employment, under circumstances where the United States, if a private person, would be liable to the claimant in accordance with the law of the place where the act or omission occurred.

(2) No person convicted of a felony who is incarcerated while awaiting sentencing or while serving a sentence may bring a civil action against the United States or an agency, officer, or employee of the Government, for mental or emotional injury suffered while in custody without a prior showing of physical injury.

(c) The jurisdiction conferred by this section includes jurisdiction of any set-off, counterclaim, or other claim or demand whatever on the part of the United States against any plaintiff commencing an action under this section.

(d) The district courts shall not have jurisdiction under this section of any civil action or claim for a pension.

(e) The district courts shall have original jurisdiction of any civil action against the United States provided in section 6226, 6228(a), 7426, or 7428 (in the case of the United States district court for the District of Columbia) or section 7429 of the Internal Revenue Code of 1986.

(f) The district courts shall have exclusive original jurisdiction of civil actions under section 2409a to quiet title to an estate or interest in real property in which an interest is claimed by the United States.

(g) Subject to the provisions of chapter 179, the district courts of the United States shall have exclusive jurisdiction over any civil action commenced under section 453(2) of title 3, by a covered employee under chapter 5 of such title.

(June 25, 1948, c. 646, 62 Stat. 933; Apr. 25, 1949, c. 92, § 2(a), 63 Stat. 62; May 24, 1949, c. 139, § 80(a), (b), 63 Stat. 101; Oct. 31, 1951, c. 655, § 50(b), 65 Stat. 727; July 30, 1954, c. 648, § 1, 68 Stat. 589; July 7, 1958, Pub.L. 85–508, § 12(e), 72 Stat. 348; Aug. 30, 1964, Pub.L. 88–519, 78 Stat. 699; Nov. 2, 1966, Pub.L. 89–719, Title II, § 202(a), 80 Stat. 1148; July 23, 1970, Pub.L. 91–350, § 1(a), 84 Stat. 449; Oct.

25, 1972, Pub.L. 92–562, § 1, 86 Stat. 1176; Oct. 4, 1976, Pub.L. 94–455, Title XII, § 1204(c) (1), Title XIII, § 1306(b) (7), 90 Stat. 1697, 1719; Nov. 1, 1978, Pub.L. 95–563, § 14(a), 92 Stat. 2389; Apr. 2, 1982, Pub.L. 97–164, Title I, § 129, 96 Stat. 39; Sept. 3, 1982, Pub.L. 97–248, Title IV, § 402(c) (17), 96 Stat. 669; Oct. 22, 1986, Pub.L. 99–514, § 2, 100 Stat. 2095; Oct. 29, 1992, Pub.L. 102–572, Title IX, § 902(b)(1), 106 Stat. 4516; Apr. 26, 1996, Pub.L. 104–134, Title I, § 101[(a)][Title VIII, § 806], 110 Stat. 1321–75; renumbered Title I May 2, 1996, Pub.L. 104–140, § 1(a), 110 Stat. 1327, and amended Oct. 26, 1996, Pub.L. 104–331, § 3(b)(1), 110 Stat. 4069.)

HISTORICAL AND STATUTORY NOTES

Senate Revision Amendment

The provisions of Title 28, U.S.C., section 932, which related to application of the Federal Rules of Civil Procedure, were originally set out in section 2676 of this revised title, but such section 2676 was eliminated by Senate amendment. See 80th Congress Senate Report No. 1559, amendment No. 61.

1949 Acts. This section corrects typographical errors in section 1346(a)(1) of Title 28, U.S.C., and in section 1346(b) of such title.

House Report No. 276, see 1949 U.S. Code Cong. Service, p. 1226.

Senate Report No. 303 and House Report No. 352, see 1949 U.S.Code Cong.Service, p. 1248.

1951 Acts. Senate Report No. 1020, see 1951 U.S. Code Cong. and Adm. Service, p. 2578.

1954 Acts. House Report No. 659 and Conference Report No. 2276, see 1954 U.S. Code Cong. and Adm. News, p. 2716.

1958 Acts. House Report No. 624, see 1958 U.S. Code Cong. and Adm. News, p. 2933.

1964 Acts. Senate Report No. 1390, see 1964 U.S. Code Cong. and Adm. News, p. 3254.

1966 Acts. Senate Report No. 1708, see 1966 U.S. Code Cong. and Adm. News, p. 3722.

1970 Acts. House Report No. 91–933, see 1970 U.S. Code Cong. and Adm. News, p. 3477.

1972 Acts. House Report No. 92–1559, see 1972 U.S. Code Cong. and Adm. News, p. 4547.

1976 Acts. House Report Nos. 94–658 and 94–1380, Senate Report No. 94–938(Parts I and II), and House Conference Report No. 94–1515, see 1976 U.S. Code Cong. and Adm. News, p. 2897.

1978 Acts. Senate Report No. 95–1118, see 1978 U.S. Code Cong. and Adm. News, p. 5235.

1982 Acts. Senate Report No. 97–275, see 1982 U.S. Code Cong. and Adm. News, p. 11.

Senate Report No. 97–494, House Conference Report No. 97–760 and Statements by Legislative Leaders, see 1982 U.S. Code Cong. and Adm. News, p. 781.

1996 Acts. House Report No. 104–820, see 1996 U.S. Code Cong. and Adm. News, p. 4348.

References in Text

The internal-revenue laws, referred to in subsec. (a)(1), are classified generally to Title 26, Internal Revenue Code.

Sections 8(g)(1) and 10(a)(1) of the Contract Disputes Act of 1978, referred to in subsec. (a)(2), are sections 8(g)(1) and 10(a)(1) of Pub.L. 95–563, Nov. 1, 1978, 92 Stat. 2387, 2388, which are classified to sections 607(g)(1) and 609(a)(1) of Title 41, Public Contracts.

Sections 6226, 6228(a), 7426, 7428, and 7429 of the Internal Revenue Code of 1986, referred to in subsec. (e), are classified to sections 6226, 6228(a), 7426, 7428, and 7429, respectively, of Title 26, Internal Revenue Code.

Effective and Applicability Provisions

1996 Acts. Amendment by Pub.L. 104–331 effective October 1, 1997, see section 3(d) of Pub.L. 104–331, set out as a note under section 1296 of this title.

1992 Acts. Amendment by Pub.L. 102–572 effective Oct. 29, 1992, see section 911 of Pub.L. 102–572, set out as a note under section 171 of this title.

1982 Acts. Amendment by Pub.L. 97–248 applicable to partnership taxable years beginning after Sept. 3, 1982, with provision for the applicability of the amendment to any partnership taxable year ending after Sept. 3, 1982, if the partnership, each partner, and each indirect partner requests such application and the Secretary of the Treasury or his delegate consents to such application, see section 407(a) (1) and (3) of Pub.L. 97–248, as amended, set out as a note under section 6221 of Title 26, Internal Revenue Code.

Amendment by Pub.L. 97–164 effective Oct. 1, 1982, see section 402 of Pub.L. 97–164, set out as a note under section 171 of this title.

1978 Acts. Amendment by Pub.L. 95–563 effective with respect to contracts entered into 120 days after Nov. 1, 1978 and, at the election of the contractor, with respect to any claim pending at such time before the contracting officer or initiated thereafter, see section 16 of Pub.L. 95–563, set out as a note under section 601 of Title 41, Public Contracts.

1970 Acts. Section 2 of Pub.L. 91–350 provided that:

"**(a)** In addition to granting jurisdiction over suits brought after the date of enactment of this Act [July 23, 1970], the provisions of this Act [amending this section and section 1491 of this title and section 724a of former Title 31, Money and Finance], shall also apply to claims and civil actions dismissed before or pending on the date of enactment of this Act if the claim or civil action is based upon a transaction, omission, or breach that occurred not more than six years prior to the date of enactment of this Act [July 23, 1970].

"**(b)** The provisions of subsection (a) of this section shall apply notwithstanding a determination or judgment made prior to the date of enactment of this Act that the United States district courts or the United States Court of Claims [now United States Court of Federal Claims] did not have jurisdiction to entertain a suit on an express or implied contract with a nonappropriated fund instrumentality of the United States described in section 1 of this Act."

1966 Acts. Section 203 of Title II of Pub.L. 89–719 provided that: "The amendments made by this title [amending this section and sections 1402 and 2410 of this title] shall apply after the date of the enactment of this Act [Nov. 2, 1966]."

1958 Acts. Amendment of section by Pub.L. 85–508 effective Jan. 3, 1959, upon admission of Alaska into the Union pursuant to Proc. No. 3269, Jan. 3, 1959, 24 F.R. 81, 73 Stat. c16, as required by sections 1 and 8(c) of Pub.L. 85–508, see notes set out under section 81A of this title and preceding former section 21 of Title 48, Territories and Insular Possessions.

Transfer of Functions

For transfer of authorities, functions, personnel, and assets of the Coast Guard, including the authorities and functions of the Secretary of Transportation relating thereto, to the Department of Homeland Security, and for treatment of related references, see 6 U.S.C.A. §§ 468(b), 551(d), 552(d) and 557, and the Department of Homeland Security Reorganization Plan of November 25, 2002, as modified, set out as a note under 6 U.S.C.A. § 542.

Savings Clause for Act Oct. 31, 1951

Act June 4, 1956, c. 363, 70 Stat. 246, which was formerly set out as a note under this section, and which conferred jurisdiction on district courts of certain actions to recover pay of employees who had been dismissed, was repealed by Pub.L. 89–554, § 8(a), Sept. 6, 1966, 80 Stat. 658.

Severability of Provisions

If any provision of section 101[a] [Title VIII] of Pub.L. 104–134, an amendment made by such Title, or the application of such provision or amendment to any person or circumstance is held to be unconstitutional, the remainder of such Title, the amendments made by such Title, and the application of the provisions of such Title to any person or circumstance not affected thereby, see section 101[a] [Title VIII, § 810] of Pub.L. 104–134, set out as a note under section 3626 of Title 18, Crimes and Criminal Procedure.

Termination of United States District Court for the District of the Canal Zone

For termination of the United States District Court for the District of the Canal Zone at end of the "transition period", being the 30–month period beginning Oct. 1, 1979, and ending midnight Mar. 31, 1982, see Paragraph 5 of Article XI of the Panama Canal Treaty of 1977 and sections 3831 and 3841 to 3843 of Title 22, Foreign Relations and Intercourse.

§ 1347. Partition action where United States is joint tenant

The district courts shall have original jurisdiction of any civil action commenced by any tenant in common or joint tenant for the partition of lands where the United States is one of the tenants in common or joint tenants.

(June 25, 1948, c. 646, 62 Stat. 933.)

§ 1348. Banking association as party

The district courts shall have original jurisdiction of any civil action commenced by the United States, or by direction of any officer thereof, against any national banking association, any civil action to wind up the affairs of any such association, and any action by a banking association established in the district for which the court is held, under chapter 2 of Title 12, to enjoin the Comptroller of the Currency, or any receiver acting under his direction, as provided by such chapter.

All national banking associations shall, for the purposes of all other actions by or against them, be deemed citizens of the States in which they are respectively located.

(June 25, 1948, c. 646, 62 Stat. 933.)

HISTORICAL AND STATUTORY NOTES

Exception as to Transfer of Functions

Functions vested by any provision of law in the Comptroller of the Currency, referred to in this section, were not included in the transfer of functions of officers, agencies and employees of the Department of the Treasury to the Secretary of the Treasury, made by 1950 Reorg. Plan No. 26, § 1, eff. July 31, 1950, 15 F.R. 4935, 64 Stat. 1280, set out in Appendix 1 to Title 5, Government Organization and Employees. See section 321(c)(2) of Title 31 Money and Fiance.

§ 1349. Corporation organized under federal law as party

The district courts shall not have jurisdiction of any civil action by or against any corporation upon the ground that it was incorporated by or under an Act of Congress, unless the United States is the owner of more than one-half of its capital stock.

(June 25, 1948, c. 646, 62 Stat. 934.)

§ 1350. Alien's action for tort

The district courts shall have original jurisdiction of any civil action by an alien for a tort only, committed in violation of the law of nations or a treaty of the United States.

(June 25, 1948, c. 646, 62 Stat. 934.)

HISTORICAL AND STATUTORY NOTES

Torture Victim Protection

Pub.L. 102–256, Mar. 12, 1992, 106 Stat. 73, provided that:

"Section 1. Short Title.

"This Act may be cited as the 'Torture Victim Protection Act of 1991'.

"Sec. 2. Establishment of civil action.

"**(a) Liability.**—An individual who, under actual or apparent authority, or color of law, of any foreign nation—

"(1) subjects an individual to torture shall, in a civil action, be liable for damages to that individual; or

"(2) subjects an individual to extrajudicial killing shall, in a civil action, be liable for damages to the individual's legal representative, or to any person who may be a claimant in an action for wrongful death.

"**(b) Exhaustion of remedies.**—A court shall decline to hear a claim under this section if the claimant has not exhausted adequate and available remedies in the place in which the conduct giving rise to the claim occurred.

"**(c) Statute of limitations.**—No action shall be maintained under this section unless it is commenced within 10 years after the cause of action arose.

"Sec. 3. Definitions.

"**(a) Extrajudicial killing.**—For the purposes of this Act, the term 'extrajudicial killing' means a deliberated killing not authorized by a previous judgment pronounced by a regularly constituted court affording all the judicial guarantees which are recognized as indispensable by civilized peoples. Such term, however, does not include any such killing that, under international law, is lawfully carried out under the authority of a foreign nation.

"(b) **Torture.**—For the purposes of this Act—

"(1) the term 'torture' means any act, directed against an individual in the offender's custody or physical control, by which severe pain or suffering (other than pain or suffering arising only from or inherent in, or incidental to, lawful sanctions), whether physical or mental, is intentionally inflicted on that individual for such purposes as obtaining from that individual or a third person information or a confession, punishing that individual for an act that individual or a third person has committed or is suspected of having committed, intimidating or coercing that individual or a third person, or for any reason based on discrimination of any kind; and

"(2) mental pain or suffering refers to prolonged mental harm caused by or resulting from—

"(A) the intentional infliction or threatened infliction of severe physical pain or suffering;

"(B) the administration or application, or threatened administration or application, of mind altering substances or other procedures calculated to disrupt profoundly the senses or the personality;

"(C) the threat of imminent death; or

"(D) the threat that another individual will imminently be subjected to death, severe physical pain or suffering, or the administration or application of mind altering substances or other procedures calculated to disrupt profoundly the senses or personality."

§ 1351. Consuls, vice consuls, and members of a diplomatic mission as defendant

The district courts shall have original jurisdiction, exclusive of the courts of the States, of all civil actions and proceedings against—

(1) consuls or vice consuls of foreign states; or

(2) members of a mission or members of their families (as such terms are defined in section 2 of the Diplomatic Relations Act).

(June 25, 1948, c. 646, 62 Stat. 934; May 24, 1949, c. 139, § 80(c), 63 Stat. 101; Sept. 30, 1978, Pub.L. 95–393, § 8(a)(1), 92 Stat. 810.)

HISTORICAL AND STATUTORY NOTES

References in Text

Section 2 of the Diplomatic Relations Act, referred to in par. (2), is section 2 of Pub.L. 95–393, Sept. 30, 1978, 92 Stat. 808, which is classified to section 254a of Title 22, Foreign Relations and Intercourse.

Effective and Applicability Provisions

1978 Acts. Amendment by Pub.L. 95–393 effective at the end of the 90-day period beginning on Sept. 30, 1978, see section 9 of Pub.L. 95–393, set out as a note under section 254a of Title 22, Foreign Relations and Intercourse.

§ 1352. Bonds executed under federal law

The district courts shall have original jurisdiction, concurrent with State courts, of any action on a bond executed under any law of the United States, except matters within the jurisdiction of the Court of International Trade under section 1582 of this title.

(June 25, 1948, c. 646, 62 Stat. 934; Oct. 10, 1980, Pub.L. 96–417, Title V, § 506, 94 Stat. 1743.)

HISTORICAL AND STATUTORY NOTES

Effective and Applicability Provisions

1980 Acts. Amendment by Pub.L. 96–417 applicable with respect to civil actions commenced on or after the 90th day after Nov. 1, 1980, see section 701(c)(1)(B) of Pub.L. 96–417, as amended, set out as a note under section 251 of this title.

§ 1353. Indian allotments

The district courts shall have original jurisdiction of any civil action involving the right of any person, in whole or in part of Indian blood or descent, to any allotment of land under any Act of Congress or treaty.

The judgment in favor of any claimant to an allotment of land shall have the same effect, when properly certified to the Secretary of the Interior, as if such allotment had been allowed and approved by him; but this provision shall not apply to any lands held on or before December 21, 1911, by either of the Five Civilized Tribes, the Osage Nation of Indians, nor to any of the lands within the Quapaw Indian Agency.

(June 25, 1948, c. 646, 62 Stat. 934.)

§ 1354. Land grants from different states

The district courts shall have original jurisdiction of actions between citizens of the same state claiming lands under grants from different states.

(June 25, 1948, c. 646, 62 Stat. 934.)

§ 1355. Fine, penalty or forfeiture

(a) The district courts shall have original jurisdiction, exclusive of the courts of the States, of any action or proceeding for the recovery or enforcement of any fine, penalty, or forfeiture, pecuniary or otherwise, incurred under any Act of Congress, except matters within the jurisdiction of the Court of International Trade under section 1582 of this title.

(b)(1) A forfeiture action or proceeding may be brought in—

(A) the district court for the district in which any of the acts or omissions giving rise to the forfeiture occurred, or

(B) any other district where venue for the forfeiture action or proceeding is specifically provided for in section 1395 of this title or any other statute.

(2) Whenever property subject to forfeiture under the laws of the United States is located in a foreign country, or has been detained or seized pursuant to legal process or competent authority of a foreign government, an action or proceeding for forfeiture may be brought as provided in paragraph (1), or in the United States District court[1] for the District of Columbia.

(c) In any case in which a final order disposing of property in a civil forfeiture action or proceeding is appealed, removal of the property by the prevailing party shall not deprive the court of jurisdiction. Upon motion of the appealing party, the district court or the court of appeals shall issue any order necessary to preserve the right of the appealing party to the full value of the property at issue, including a stay of the judgment of the district court pending appeal or requiring the prevailing party to post an appeal bond.

(d) Any court with jurisdiction over a forfeiture action pursuant to subsection (b) may issue and cause to be served in any other district such process as may be required to bring before the court the property that is the subject of the forfeiture action.

(June 25, 1948, c. 646, 62 Stat. 934; Oct. 10, 1980, Pub.L. 96–417, Title V, § 507, 94 Stat. 1743; Oct. 28, 1992, Pub.L. 102–550, Title XV, § 1521, 106 Stat. 4062.)

[1] So in original. Probably should be capitalized.

HISTORICAL AND STATUTORY NOTES

Effective and Applicability Provisions

1992 Acts. Except as otherwise provided, amendment by Pub.L. 102–550 effective Oct. 28, 1992, see section 2 of Pub.L. 102–550, set out as a note under section 5301 of Title 42, The Public Health and Welfare.

1980 Acts. Amendment by Pub.L. 96–417 applicable with respect to civil actions commenced on or after the 90th day after Nov. 1, 1980, see section 701(c)(1)(B) of Pub.L. 96–417, as amended, set out as a note under section 251 of this title.

§ 1356. Seizures not within admiralty and maritime jurisdiction

The district courts shall have original jurisdiction, exclusive of the courts of the States, of any seizure under any law of the United States on land or upon waters not within admiralty and maritime jurisdiction, except matters within the jurisdiction of the Court of International Trade under section 1582 of this title.

(June 25, 1948, c. 646, 62 Stat. 934; Oct. 10, 1980, Pub.L. 96–417, Title V, § 508, 94 Stat. 1743.)

HISTORICAL AND STATUTORY NOTES

Effective and Applicability Provisions

1980 Acts. Amendment by Pub.L. 96–417 applicable with respect to civil actions commenced on or after the 90th day after Nov. 1, 1980, see section 701(c)(1)(B) of Pub.L. 96–417, as amended, set out as a note under section 251 of this title.

§ 1357. Injuries under Federal laws

The district courts shall have original jurisdiction of any civil action commenced by any person to recover damages for any injury to his person or property on account of any act done by him, under any Act of Congress, for the protection or collection of any of the revenues, or to enforce the right of citizens of the United States to vote in any State.

(June 25, 1948, c. 646, 62 Stat. 934.)

§ 1358. Eminent domain

The district courts shall have original jurisdiction of all proceedings to condemn real estate for the use of the United States or its departments or agencies.

(June 25, 1948, c. 646, 62 Stat. 935.)

§ 1359. Parties collusively joined or made

A district court shall not have jurisdiction of a civil action in which any party, by assignment or otherwise, has been improperly or collusively made or joined to invoke the jurisdiction of such court.

(June 25, 1948, c. 646, 62 Stat. 935.)

§ 1360. State civil jurisdiction in actions to which Indians are parties

(a) Each of the States listed in the following table shall have jurisdiction over civil causes of action between Indians or to which Indians are parties which arise in the areas of Indian country listed opposite the name of the State to the same extent that such State has jurisdiction over other civil causes of action, and those civil laws of such State that are of general application to private persons or private property shall have the same force and effect within such Indian country as they have elsewhere within the State:

State of	*Indian country affected*
Alaska	All Indian country within the State
California	All Indian country within the State
Minnesota	All Indian country within the State, except the Red Lake Reservation
Nebraska	All Indian country within the State
Oregon	All Indian country within the State, except the Warm Springs Reservation
Wisconsin	All Indian country within the State

(b) Nothing in this section shall authorize the alienation, encumbrance, or taxation of any real or personal property, including water rights, belonging to any Indian or any Indian tribe, band, or community that is held in trust by the United States or is subject to a restriction against alienation imposed by the United States; or shall authorize regulation of the use of such property in a manner inconsistent with any Federal treaty, agreement, or statute or with any regulation made pursuant thereto; or shall confer jurisdiction upon the State to adjudicate, in probate proceedings or otherwise, the ownership or right to possession of such property or any interest therein.

(c) Any tribal ordinance or custom heretofore or hereafter adopted by an Indian tribe, band, or community in the exercise of any authority which it may possess shall, if not inconsistent with any applicable civil law of the State, be given full force and effect in the determination of civil causes of action pursuant to this section.

(Added Aug. 15, 1953, c. 505, § 4, 67 Stat. 589, and amended Aug. 24, 1954, c. 910, § 2, 68 Stat. 795; Aug. 8, 1958, Pub.L. 85–615, § 2, 72 Stat. 545; Nov. 6, 1978, Pub.L. 95–598, Title II, § 239, 92 Stat. 2668; July 10, 1984, Pub.L. 98–353, Title I, § 110, 98 Stat. 342.)

HISTORICAL AND STATUTORY NOTES

Codifications

Subsec. (a) of this section was amended by Pub.L. 95–598, Title II, § 239, Nov. 6, 1978, 92 Stat. 2668, effective June 28, 1984, pursuant to Pub.L. 95–598, Title IV, § 402(b), Nov. 6, 1978, 92 Stat. 2682, as amended by Pub.L. 98–249, § 1(a), Mar. 31, 1984, 98 Stat. 116; Pub.L. 98–271, § 1(a), Apr. 30, 1984, 98 Stat. 163; Pub.L. 98–299, § 1(a), May 25, 1984, 98 Stat. 214; Pub.L. 98–325, § 1(a), June 20, 1984, 98 Stat. 268, set out as an Effective and Applicability Provisions note preceding section 101 of Title 11, Bankruptcy, by substituting "Alaska ..... All Indian country within the State" for "Alaska ..... All Indian country within the Territory".

Section 402(b) of Pub.L. 95–598 was amended by section 113 of Pub.L. 98–353 by substituting "shall not be effective" for "shall take effect on June 28, 1984", thereby eliminating the amendment by section 239 of Pub.L. 95–598, effective June 27, 1984, pursuant to section 122(c) of Pub.L. 98–353, set out as an Effective and Applicability Provisions note under section 151 of this title.

Section 121(a) of Pub.L. 98–353 directed that section 402(b) of Pub.L. 95–598 be amended by substituting "the date of enactment of the Bankruptcy Amendments and Federal Judgeship Act of 1984 [i.e. July 10, 1984]" for "June 28, 1984". This amendment was not executed in view of the prior amendment to section 402(b) of Pub.L. 95–598 by section 113 of Pub.L. 98–353.

Effective and Applicability Provisions

1984 Acts. Amendment by Pub.L. 98–353 effective July 10, 1984, see section 122(a) of Pub.L. 98–353, set out as a note under section 151 of this title.

Admission of Alaska as State

Admission of Alaska into the Union was accomplished Jan. 3, 1959 upon issuance of Proc. No. 3269, Jan. 3, 1959, 24 F.R. 81, 73 Stat. c16, as required by sections 1 and 8(c) of Pub.L. 85–508, July 7, 1958, 72 Stat. 339, set out as notes preceding former section 21 of Title 48, Territories and Insular Possessions.

Amendment of State Constitutions to Remove Legal Impediment; Effective Date

Section 6 of Act Aug. 15, 1953, provided that: "Notwithstanding the provisions of any Enabling Act for the admission of a State, the consent of the United States is hereby given to the people of any State to amend, where necessary, their State constitution or existing statutes, as the case may be, to remove any legal impediment to the assumption of civil and criminal jurisdiction in accordance with the provisions of this Act [adding section 1360 of this title and section 1162 of Title 18]: *Provided*, That the provisions of this Act shall not become effective with respect to such assumption of jurisdiction by any such State until the people thereof have appropriately amended their State constitution or statutes as the case may be."

Consent of United States to Other States to Assume Jurisdiction

Act Aug. 15, 1953, c. 505, § 7, 67 Stat. 590, which gave consent of the United States to any other State not having jurisdiction with respect to criminal offenses or civil causes of action, or with respect to both, as provided for in this section and section 1162 of Title 18, Crimes and Criminal Procedure, to assume jurisdiction at such time and in such manner as the people of the State shall, by legislative action, obligate and bind the State to assumption thereof, was repealed by section 403(b) of Pub.L. 90–284, Title IV, Apr. 11, 1968, 82 Stat. 79, such repeal not to affect any cession of jurisdiction made pursuant to such section prior to its repeal.

Retrocession by State of jurisdiction acquired by State pursuant to section 7 of Act Aug. 15, 1953, prior to its repeal, see section 1323 of Title 25, Indians.

§ 1361. Action to compel an officer of the United States to perform his duty

The district courts shall have original jurisdiction of any action in the nature of mandamus to compel an officer or employee of the United States or any agency thereof to perform a duty owed to the plaintiff.

(Added Pub.L. 87–748, § 1(a), Oct. 5, 1962, 76 Stat. 744.)

§ 1362. Indian tribes

The district courts shall have original jurisdiction of all civil actions, brought by any Indian tribe or band with a governing body duly recognized by the Secretary of the Interior, wherein the matter in controversy arises under the Constitution, laws, or treaties of the United States.

(Added Pub.L. 89–635, § 1, Oct. 10, 1966, 80 Stat. 880.)

§ 1363. Jurors' employment rights

The district courts shall have original jurisdiction of any civil action brought for the protection of jurors' employment under section 1875 of this title.

(Added Pub.L. 95–572, § 6(b)(1), Nov. 2, 1978, 92 Stat. 2457.)

HISTORICAL AND STATUTORY NOTES

Effective and Applicability Provisions

1978 Acts. Section 7 of Pub.L. 95–572 provided that:

"**(a)** Except as provided in subsection (b) of this section, the amendments made by this Act [enacting sections 1363 and 1875, renumbering as section 1364 prior section 1363, and amending sections 1863, 1865, 1866, 1869, and 1871 of this title] shall apply with respect to any grand or petit juror summoned for service or actually serving on or after the date of enactment of this Act [Nov. 2, 1978].

"**(b)** The amendment made by section 5 of this Act [to section 1871 of this title] shall apply with respect to any grand or petit juror serving on or after the sixtieth day following the date of enactment of this Act [Nov. 2, 1978]."

Prior Provisions

A prior section 1363 was renumbered 1366.

§ 1364. Direct actions against insurers of members of diplomatic missions and their families

(a) The district courts shall have original and exclusive jurisdiction, without regard to the amount in controversy, of any civil action commenced by any person against an insurer who by contract has insured an individual, who is, or was at the time of the tortious act or omission, a member of a mission (within the meaning of section 2(3) of the Diplomatic Relations Act (22 U.S.C. 254a(3))) or a member of the family of such a member of a mission, or an individual described in section 19 of the Convention on Privileges and Immunities of the United Nations of February 13, 1946, against liability for personal injury, death, or damage to property.

(b) Any direct action brought against an insurer under subsection (a) shall be tried without a jury, but shall not be subject to the defense that the insured is immune from suit, that the insured is an indispensable party, or in the absence of fraud or collusion, that the insured has violated a term of the contract, unless the contract was cancelled before the claim arose.

(Added Pub.L. 95–393, § 7(a), Sept. 30, 1978, 92 Stat. 809, and amended Pub.L. 97–241, Title II, § 203(b)(4), Aug. 24, 1982, 96 Stat. 291; Pub.L. 100–204, Title I, § 138(a), Dec. 22, 1987, 101 Stat. 1347.)

HISTORICAL AND STATUTORY NOTES

Codifications

Two other sections 1364 were renumbered sections 1365 and 1366 of this title.

Effective and Applicability Provisions

1987 Acts. Section 138(b) of Pub.L. 100–204 provided that: "The amendment made by subsection (a) [amending subsec. (a) of this section] shall apply to the first tortious act or omission occurring after the date of enactment of this Act [Dec. 22, 1987]."

1982 Acts. Amendment by Pub.L. 97–241 effective Oct. 1, 1982, see section 204 of Pub.L. 97–241, set out as a note under section 4301 of Title 22, Foreign Relations and Intercourse.

1978 Acts. Section effective at the end of the 90 day period beginning on Sept. 30, 1978, see section 9 of Pub.L. 95–393, set out as a note under section 254a of Title 22, Foreign Relations and Intercourse.

§ 1365. Senate actions

(a) The United States District Court for the District of Columbia shall have original jurisdiction, without regard to the amount in controversy, over any civil action brought by the Senate or any authorized committee or subcommittee of the Senate to enforce, to secure a declaratory judgment concerning the validity of, or to prevent a threatened refusal or failure to comply with, any subpena or order issued by the Senate or committee or subcommittee of the Senate to any entity acting or purporting to act under color or authority of State law or to any natural person to secure the production of documents or other materials of any kind or the answering of any deposition or interrogatory or to secure testimony or any combination thereof. This section shall not apply to an action to enforce, to secure a declaratory judgment concerning the validity of, or to prevent a threatened refusal to comply with, any subpena or order issued to an officer or employee of the executive branch of the Federal Government acting within his or her official capacity, except that this section shall apply if the refusal to comply is based on the assertion of a personal privilege or objection and is not based on a governmental privilege or objection the assertion of which has been authorized by the executive branch of the Federal Government.

(b) Upon application by the Senate or any authorized committee or subcommittee of the Senate, the district court shall issue an order to an entity or person refusing, or failing to comply with, or threatening to refuse or not to comply with, a subpena or order of the Senate or committee or subcommittee of the Senate requiring such entity or person to comply forthwith. Any refusal or failure to obey a lawful order of the district court issued pursuant to this section may be held by such court to be a contempt thereof. A contempt proceeding shall be commenced by an order to show cause before the court why the entity or person refusing or failing to obey the court order should not be held in contempt of court. Such contempt proceeding shall be tried by the court and shall be summary in manner. The purpose of sanctions imposed as a result of such contempt proceeding shall be to compel obedience to the order of the court. Process in any such action or contempt proceeding may be served in any judicial district wherein the entity or party refusing, or failing to comply, or threatening to refuse or not to comply, resides, transacts business, or may be found, and subpenas for witnesses who are required to attend such proceeding may run into any other district. Nothing in this section shall confer upon such court jurisdiction to affect by injunction or otherwise the issuance or effect of any subpena or order of the Senate or any committee or subcommittee of the Senate or to review, modify, suspend, terminate, or set aside any such subpena or order. An action, contempt proceeding, or sanction brought or imposed pursuant to this section shall not abate upon adjournment sine die by the Senate at the end of a Congress if the Senate or the committee or subcommittee of the Senate which issued the subpena or order certifies to the court that it maintains its interest in securing the documents, answers, or testimony during such adjournment.

[**(c)** Repealed. Pub.L. 98–620, Title IV, § 402(29)(D), Nov. 8, 1984, 98 Stat. 3359]

(d) The Senate or any committee or subcommittee of the Senate commencing and prosecuting a civil action or contempt proceeding under this section may be represented in such action by such attorneys as the Senate may designate.

(e) A civil action commenced or prosecuted under this section, may not be authorized pursuant to the Standing Order of the Senate "authorizing suits by Senate Committees" (S. Jour. 572, May 28, 1928).

(f) For the purposes of this section the term "committee" includes standing, select, or special committees of the Senate established by law or resolution.

(Added Pub.L. 95–521, Title VII, § 705(f)(1), Oct. 26, 1978, 92 Stat. 1879, § 1364, and amended Pub.L. 98–620, Title IV, § 402(29)(D), Nov. 8, 1984, 98 Stat. 3359; renumbered § 1365, Pub.L. 99–336, § 6(a)(1)(B), June 19, 1986, 100 Stat. 638; Pub.L. 104–292, § 4, Oct. 11, 1996, 110 Stat. 3460.)

HISTORICAL AND STATUTORY NOTES

Effective and Applicability Provisions

1984 Acts. Amendment by Pub.L. 98–620 not to apply to cases pending on Nov. 8, 1984, see section 403 of Pub.L. 98–620, set out as a note under section 1657 of this title.

1978 Acts. Section effective Jan. 3, 1979, see section 717 of Pub.L. 95–521, set out as a note under section 288 of Title 2, The Congress.

§ 1366. Construction of references to laws of the United States or Acts of Congress

For the purposes of this chapter, references to laws of the United States or Acts of Congress do not include laws applicable exclusively to the District of Columbia.

(Added Pub.L. 91–358, Title I, § 172(c)(1), July 29, 1970, 84 Stat. 590, § 1363; renumbered § 1364, Pub.L. 95–572, § 6(b)(1), Nov. 2, 1978, 92 Stat. 2456; renumbered § 1366, Pub.L. 99–336, § 6(a)(1)(C), June 19, 1986, 100 Stat. 639.)

HISTORICAL AND STATUTORY NOTES

Effective and Applicability Provisions

1970 Acts. Section effective first day of seventh calendar month which begins after July 29, 1970, see section 199(a) of Pub.L. 91–358, set out as a note under section 1257 of this title.

§ 1367. Supplemental jurisdiction

(a) Except as provided in subsections (b) and (c) or as expressly provided otherwise by Federal statute, in any civil action of which the district courts have original jurisdiction, the district courts shall have supplemental jurisdiction over all other claims that are so related to claims in the action within such original jurisdiction that they form part of the same case or controversy under Article III of the United States Constitution. Such supplemental jurisdiction shall include claims that involve the joinder or intervention of additional parties.

(b) In any civil action of which the district courts have original jurisdiction founded solely on section 1332 of this title, the district courts shall not have supplemental jurisdiction under subsection (a) over claims by plaintiffs against persons made parties under Rule 14, 19, 20, or 24 of the Federal Rules of Civil Procedure, or over claims by persons proposed to be joined as plaintiffs under Rule 19 of such rules, or seeking to intervene as plaintiffs under Rule 24 of such rules, when exercising supplemental jurisdiction over such claims would be inconsistent with the jurisdictional requirements of section 1332.

(c) The district courts may decline to exercise supplemental jurisdiction over a claim under subsection (a) if—

(1) the claim raises a novel or complex issue of State law,

(2) the claim substantially predominates over the claim or claims over which the district court has original jurisdiction,

(3) the district court has dismissed all claims over which it has original jurisdiction, or

(4) in exceptional circumstances, there are other compelling reasons for declining jurisdiction.

(d) The period of limitations for any claim asserted under subsection (a), and for any other claim in the same action that is voluntarily dismissed at the same time as or after the dismissal of the claim under subsection (a), shall be tolled while the claim is pending and for a period of 30 days after it is dismissed unless State law provides for a longer tolling period.

(e) As used in this section, the term "State" includes the District of Columbia, the Commonwealth of Puerto Rico, and any territory or possession of the United States.

(Added Pub.L. 101–650, Title III, § 310(a), Dec. 1, 1990, 104 Stat. 5113.)

HISTORICAL AND STATUTORY NOTES

References in Text

The Federal Rules of Civil Procedure, referred to in subsec. (b), are set out in this title.

Effective and Applicability Provisions

1990 Acts. Section 310(c) of Pub.L. 101–650 provided that: "The amendments made by this section [enacting this section] shall apply to civil actions commenced on or after the date of the enactment of this Act [Dec. 1, 1990]."

§ 1368. Counterclaims in unfair practices in international trade.

The district courts shall have original jurisdiction of any civil action based on a counterclaim raised pursuant to section 337(c) of the Tariff Act of 1930, to the extent that it arises out of the transaction or occurrence that is the subject matter of the opposing party's claim in the proceeding under section 337(a) of that Act.

(Added Pub.L. 103–465, Title III, § 321(b)(3)(A), Dec. 8, 1994, 108 Stat. 4946.)

HISTORICAL AND STATUTORY NOTES

References in Text

Section 337 of the Tariff Act of 1930, referred to in text, is section 337 of Act June 17, 1930, c. 497, Title III, 46 Stat. 703, which is classified to section 1337 of Title 19, Customs Duties.

Effective and Applicability Provisions

1994 Acts. Section applicable with respect to complaints filed under section 1337 of Title 19, Customs Duties, on or after the date on which the WTO Agreement enters into force with respect to the United States, Jan. 1, 1995, or in cases under section 1337 of Title 19 in which no complaint is filed, with respect to investigations initiated under such section on or after such date, see section 322 of Pub.L. 103–465, set out as a note under section 1337 of Title 19.

§ 1369. Multiparty, multiforum jurisdiction

(a) In general.—The district courts shall have original jurisdiction of any civil action involving minimal diversity between adverse parties that arises from a single accident, where at least 75 natural persons have died in the accident at a discrete location, if—

(1) a defendant resides in a State and a substantial part of the accident took place in another State or other location, regardless of whether that defendant is also a resident of the State where a substantial part of the accident took place;

(2) any two defendants reside in different States, regardless of whether such defendants are also residents of the same State or States; or

(3) substantial parts of the accident took place in different States.

(b) Limitation of jurisdiction of district courts.—The district court shall abstain from hearing any civil action described in subsection (a) in which—

(1) the substantial majority of all plaintiffs are citizens of a single State of which the primary defendants are also citizens; and

(2) the claims asserted will be governed primarily by the laws of that State.

(c) Special rules and definitions.—For purposes of this section—

(1) minimal diversity exists between adverse parties if any party is a citizen of a State and any adverse party is a citizen of another State, a citizen or subject of a foreign state, or a foreign state as defined in section 1603(a) of this title;

(2) a corporation is deemed to be a citizen of any State, and a citizen or subject of any foreign state, in which it is incorporated or has its principal place of business, and is deemed to be a resident of any State in which it is incorporated or licensed to do business or is doing business;

(3) the term "injury" means—

(A) physical harm to a natural person; and

(B) physical damage to or destruction of tangible property, but only if physical harm described in subparagraph (A) exists;

(4) the term "accident" means a sudden accident, or a natural event culminating in an accident, that results in death incurred at a discrete location by at least 75 natural persons; and

(5) the term "State" includes the District of Columbia, the Commonwealth of Puerto Rico, and any territory or possession of the United States.

(d) Intervening parties.—In any action in a district court which is or could have been brought, in whole or in part, under this section, any person with a claim arising from the accident described in subsection (a) shall be permitted to intervene as a party plaintiff in the action, even if that person could not have brought an action in a district court as an original matter.

(e) Notification of judicial panel on multidistrict litigation.—A district court in which an action under this section is pending shall promptly notify the judicial panel on multidistrict litigation of the pendency of the action.

(Added Pub.L. 107–273, Div. C, Title I, § 11020(b)(1)(A), Nov. 2, 2002, 116 Stat. 1826.)

HISTORICAL AND STATUTORY NOTES

Effective and Applicability Provisions

2002 Acts. Pub.L. 107–273, Div. C, Title I, § 11020(c), Nov. 2, 2002, 116 Stat. 1829, provided that: "The amendments made by subsection (b) [enacting this section and 28 U.S.C.A. §§ 1697 and 1785 and amending 28 U.S.C.A. §§ 1391 and 1441] shall apply to a civil action if the accident giving rise to the cause of action occurred on or after the 90th day after the date of the enactment of this Act [Nov. 2, 2002]."

CHAPTER 87—DISTRICT COURTS; VENUE

Sec.
1391. Venue generally.
1392. Defendants or property in different districts in same State.
[1393. Repealed.]

Sec.
1394. Banking association's action against Comptroller of Currency.
1395. Fine, penalty or forfeiture.
1396. Internal revenue taxes.
1397. Interpleader.
1398. Interstate Commerce Commission's orders.
1399. Partition action involving United States.
1400. Patents and copyrights.[1]
1401. Stockholder's derivative action.
1402. United States as defendant.
1403. Eminent domain.
1404. Change of venue.
1405. Creation or alteration of district or division.
1406. Cure or waiver of defects.
1407. Multidistrict litigation.
1408. Venue of cases under title 11.
1409. Venue of proceedings arising under title 11 or arising in or related to cases under title 11.
1410. Venue of cases ancillary to foreign proceedings.
1411. Jury trials.
1412. Change of venue.
1413. Venue of cases under chapter 5 of title 3.

[1] So in original. Does not conform to section nameline.

HISTORICAL AND STATUTORY NOTES

Codifications

Amendment by Pub.L. 104–331, § 3(b)(2)(B), Oct. 26, 1996, 110 Stat. 4069, which directed the addition of item 1413 to the end of chapter 37 of this title, was executed by adding item 1413 to the end of this chapter, as the probable intent of Congress.

The table of sections for chapter 87 was amended by Pub.L. 95–598, Title II, § 240(b), Nov. 6, 1978, 92 Stat. 2668, effective June 28, 1984, pursuant to Pub.L. 95–598, Title IV, § 402(b), Nov. 6, 1978, 92 Stat. 2682, as amended by Pub.L. 98–249, § 1(a), Mar. 31, 1984, 98 Stat. 116; Pub.L. 98–271, § 1(a), Apr. 30, 1984, 98 Stat. 163; Pub.L. 98–299, § 1(a), May 25, 1984, 98 Stat. 214; Pub.L. 98–325, § 1(a), June 20, 1984, 98 Stat. 268, set out as an effective dates note preceding section 101 of Title 11, Bankruptcy, by adding "1408, Bankruptcy appeals."

Section 402(b) of Pub.L. 95–598 was amended by section 113 of Pub.L. 98–353, Title 1, July 10, 1984, 98 Stat. 343, by substituting "shall not be effective" for "shall take effect on June 28, 1984," thereby eliminating the amendment by section 240(b) of Pub.L. 95–598, effective June 27, 1984, pursuant to section 122(e) of Pub.L. 98–353, set out as an Effective Date, note under section 151 of this title.

Section 121(a) of Pub.L. 98–353 directed that section 402(b) of Pub.L. 95–598 be amended by substituting "the date of enactment of the Bankruptcy Amendments and Federal Judgeship Act of 1984 [i.e. July 10, 1984]" for "June 28, 1984". This amendment was not executed in view of the prior amendment to section 402(b) of Pub.L. 95–598 by section 113 of Pub.L. 98–353.

Effective and Termination Dates

Pub.L. 105–304, Title V, §§ 502(c)(3), 505, Oct. 28, 1998, 112 Stat. 2917, 2918, provided that effective Oct. 28, 1998 and remaining in effect until the end of the 2-year period beginning on Oct. 28, 1998, the item relating to section 1400 is amended by inserting ", mask works, and designs" after "Patents and copyrights".

§ 1391. Venue generally

(a) A civil action wherein jurisdiction is founded only on diversity of citizenship may, except as otherwise provided by law, be brought only in (1) a judicial district where any defendant resides, if all defendants reside in the same State, (2) a judicial district in which a substantial part of the events or omissions giving rise to the claim occurred, or a substantial part of property that is the subject of the action is situated, or (3) a judicial district in which any defendant is subject to personal jurisdiction at the time the action is commenced, if there is no district in which the action may otherwise be brought.

(b) A civil action wherein jurisdiction is not founded solely on diversity of citizenship may, except as otherwise provided by law, be brought only in (1) a judicial district where any defendant resides, if all defendants reside in the same State, (2) a judicial district in which a substantial part of the events or omissions giving rise to the claim occurred, or a substantial part of property that is the subject of the action is situated, or (3) a judicial district in which any defendant may be found, if there is no district in which the action may otherwise be brought.

(c) For purposes of venue under this chapter, a defendant that is a corporation shall be deemed to reside in any judicial district in which it is subject to personal jurisdiction at the time the action is commenced. In a State which has more than one judicial district and in which a defendant that is a corporation is subject to personal jurisdiction at the time an action is commenced, such corporation shall be deemed to reside in any district in that State within which its contacts would be sufficient to subject it to personal jurisdiction if that district were a separate State, and, if there is no such district, the corporation shall be deemed to reside in the district within which it has the most significant contacts.

(d) An alien may be sued in any district.

(e) A civil action in which a defendant is an officer or employee of the United States or any agency thereof acting in his official capacity or under color of legal authority, or an agency of the United States, or the United States, may, except as otherwise provided by law, be brought in any judicial district in which (1) a defendant in the action resides, (2) a substantial part of the events or omissions giving rise to the claim occurred, or a substantial part of property that is the subject of the action is situated, or (3) the plaintiff resides if no real property is involved in the action. Additional persons may be joined as parties to any such action in accordance with the Federal Rules of Civil Procedure and with such other venue requirements as would be applicable if the United States or one of its officers, employees, or agencies were not a party.

The summons and complaint in such an action shall be served as provided by the Federal Rules of Civil Procedure except that the delivery of the summons and complaint to the officer or agency as required by the rules may be made by certified mail beyond the territorial limits of the district in which the action is brought.

(f) A civil action against a foreign state as defined in section 1603(a) of this title may be brought—

(1) in any judicial district in which a substantial part of the events or omissions giving rise to the claim occurred, or a substantial part of property that is the subject of the action is situated;

(2) in any judicial district in which the vessel or cargo of a foreign state is situated, if the claim is asserted under section 1605(b) of this title;

(3) in any judicial district in which the agency or instrumentality is licensed to do business or is doing business, if the action is brought against an agency or instrumentality of a foreign state as defined in section 1603(b) of this title; or

(4) in the United States District Court for the District of Columbia if the action is brought against a foreign state or political subdivision thereof.

(g) A civil action in which jurisdiction of the district court is based upon section 1369 of this title may be brought in any district in which any defendant resides or in which a substantial part of the accident giving rise to the action took place.

(June 25, 1948, c. 646, 62 Stat. 935; Oct. 5, 1962, Pub.L. 87–748, § 2, 76 Stat. 744; Dec. 23, 1963, Pub.L. 88–234, 77 Stat. 473; Nov. 2, 1966, Pub.L. 89–714, §§ 1, 2, 80 Stat. 1111; Oct. 21, 1976, Pub.L. 94–574, § 3, 90 Stat. 2721; Oct. 21, 1976, Pub.L. 94–583, § 5, 90 Stat. 2897; Nov. 19, 1988, Pub.L. 100–702, Title X, § 1013(a), 102 Stat. 4669; Dec. 1, 1990, Pub.L. 101–650, Title III, § 311, 104 Stat. 5114; Dec. 9, 1991, Pub.L. 102–198, § 3, 105 Stat. 1623; Oct. 29, 1992, Pub.L. 102–572, Title V, § 504, 106 Stat. 4513; Oct. 3, 1995, Pub.L. 104–34, § 1, 109 Stat. 293; Nov. 2, 2002, Pub.L. 107–273, Div. C, Title I, § 11020(b)(2), 116 Stat. 1827.)

HISTORICAL AND STATUTORY NOTES

References in Text

The Federal Rules of Civil Procedure, referred to in subsec. (e), are set out in this title.

Effective and Applicability Provisions

2002 Acts. Amendments by section 11020(b) of Pub.L. 107–273 shall apply to a civil action if the accident giving rise to the cause of action occurred on or after the 90th day after Nov. 2, 2002, see section 11020(c) of Pub.L. 107–273, set out as a note under 28 U.S.C.A. § 1369.

1992 Acts. Amendment by Pub.L. 102–572 effective Jan. 1, 1993, see section 1101(a) of Pub.L. 102–572, set out as a note under section 905 of Title 2, The Congress.

1988 Acts. Section 1013(b) of Title X of Pub.L. 100–702 provided that: "The amendment made by this section [amending this section] takes effect 90 days after the date of enactment of this title [Nov. 19, 1988]."

1976 Acts. Amendment by Pub.L. 94–583 effective 90 days after Oct. 21, 1976, see section 8 of Pub.L. 94–583, set out as a note under section 1602 of this title.

§ 1392. Defendants or property in different districts in same State

Any civil action, of a local nature, involving property located in different districts in the same State, may be brought in any of such districts.

(June 25, 1948, c. 646, 62 Stat. 935; Oct. 1, 1996, Pub.L. 104–220, § 1, 110 Stat. 3023.)

[§ 1393. Repealed. Pub.L. 100–702, Title X, § 1001(a), Nov. 19, 1988, 102 Stat. 4664]

HISTORICAL AND STATUTORY NOTES

Section, Act June 25, 1948, c. 646, 62 Stat. 935, related to divisional venue in civil cases of a single defendant or defendants in different divisions.

Effective Date of Repeal

Section 1001(b) of Pub.L. 100–702 provided that "The amendments made by this section [repealing this section] take effect 90 days after the date of enactment of this Act [Nov. 19, 1988]."

§ 1394. Banking association's action against Comptroller of Currency

Any civil action by a national banking association to enjoin the Comptroller of the Currency, under the provisions of any Act of Congress relating to such associations, may be prosecuted in the judicial district where such association is located.

(June 25, 1948, c. 646, 62 Stat. 935.)

HISTORICAL AND STATUTORY NOTES

Exception as to Transfer of Functions

Functions vested by any provision of law in the Comptroller of the Currency, referred to in this section, were not included in the transfer of functions of officers, agencies and employees of the Department of the Treasury to the Secretary of the Treasury, made by Reorg. Plan No. 26 of 1950, § 1, eff. July 31, 1950, 15 F.R. 4935, 64 Stat. 1280. See section 321(c)(2) of Title 31, Money and Finance.

§ 1395. Fine, penalty or forfeiture

(a) A civil proceeding for the recovery of a pecuniary fine, penalty or forfeiture may be prosecuted in the district where it accrues or the defendant is found.

(b) A civil proceeding for the forfeiture of property may be prosecuted in any district where such property is found.

(c) A civil proceeding for the forfeiture of property seized outside any judicial district may be prosecuted in any district into which the property is brought.

(d) A proceeding in admiralty for the enforcement of fines, penalties and forfeitures against a vessel may be brought in any district in which the vessel is arrested.

(e) Any proceeding for the forfeiture of a vessel or cargo entering a port of entry closed by the President in pursuance of law, or of goods and chattels coming from a State or section declared by proclamation of the President to be in insurrection, or of any vessel or vehicle conveying persons or property to or from such State or section or belonging in whole or in part to a resident thereof, may be prosecuted in any district into which the property is taken and in which the proceeding is instituted.

(June 25, 1948, c. 646, 62 Stat. 936.)

HISTORICAL AND STATUTORY NOTES

Senate Revision Amendment

While section 3745(c) of Title 26, U.S.C., Internal Revenue Code, is one of the sources of this section, it was eliminated from the schedule of repeals by Senate amendment. Therefore, such section 3745(c) remains in Title 26. See 80th Congress Senate Report No. 1559.

Said section 3745(c) was subsequently repealed by Act May 24, 1949, c. 139, § 142, 63 Stat. 110.

§ 1396. Internal revenue taxes

Any civil action for the collection of internal revenue taxes may be brought in the district where the liability for such tax accrues, in the district of the taxpayer's residence, or in the district where the return was filed.

(June 25, 1948, c. 646, 62 Stat. 936.)

HISTORICAL AND STATUTORY NOTES

Senate Revision Amendment

While section 3744 of Title 26, U.S.C., Internal Revenue Code [1939], is one of the sources of this section, it was eliminated from the schedule of repeals by Senate amendment. Therefore, it remains in Title 26 [I.R.C.1939]. See 80th Congress Senate Report No. 1559.

Said section 3744 was subsequently repealed by Act May 24, 1949, c. 139, § 142, 63 Stat. 110.

§ 1397. Interpleader

Any civil action of interpleader or in the nature of interpleader under section 1335 of this title may be brought in the judicial district in which one or more of the claimants reside.

(June 25, 1948, c. 646, 62 Stat. 936.)

§ 1398. Interstate Commerce Commission's orders

(a) Except as otherwise provided by law, a civil action brought under section 1336(a) of this title shall be brought only in a judicial district in which any of the parties bringing the action resides or has its principal office.

(b) A civil action to enforce, enjoin, set aside, annul, or suspend, in whole or in part, an order of the Interstate Commerce Commission made pursuant to the referral of a question or issue by a district court or by the United States Court of Federal Claims, shall be brought only in the court which referred the question or issue.

(June 25, 1948, c. 646, 62 Stat. 936; Aug. 30, 1964, Pub.L. 88–513, § 2, 78 Stat. 695; Jan. 2, 1975, Pub.L. 93–584, § 2, 88 Stat. 1917; Apr. 2, 1982, Pub.L. 97–164, Title I, § 130, 96 Stat. 39; Oct. 29, 1992, Pub.L. 102–572, Title IX, § 902(b)(1), 106 Stat. 4516.)

HISTORICAL AND STATUTORY NOTES

Effective and Applicability Provisions

1992 Acts. Amendment by Pub.L. 102–572 effective Oct. 29, 1992, see section 911 of Pub.L. 102–572, set out as a note under section 171 of this title.

1982 Acts. Amendment by Pub.L. 97–164 effective Oct. 1, 1982, see section 402 of Pub.L. 97–164, set out as a note under section 171 of this title.

1975 Acts. Amendment by Pub.L. 93–584 not applicable to actions commenced on or before the last day of the first month beginning after Jan. 2, 1975, and actions to enjoin or suspend orders of the Interstate Commerce Commission which are pending when this amendment becomes effective shall not be affected thereby, but shall proceed to final disposition under the law existing on the date they were commenced, see section 10 of Pub.L. 93–584, set out as a note under section 2321 of this title.

Abolition of Interstate Commerce Commission and Transfer of Functions

Interstate Commerce Commission abolished and functions of Commission transferred, except as otherwise provided in Pub.L. 104–88, to Surface Transportation Board effective Jan. 1, 1996, by sections 702 of Title 49, Transportation, and section 101 of Pub.L. 104–88, set out as a note under section 701 of title 49. References to Interstate Commerce Commission deemed to refer to Surface Transportation Board, a member or employee of the Board, or Secretary of Transportation, as appropriate, see section 205 of Pub.L. 104–88, set out as a note under section 701 of Title 49.

§ 1399. Partition action involving United States

Any civil action by any tenant in common or joint tenant for the partition of lands, where the United States is one of the tenants in common or joint tenants, may be brought only in the judicial district where such lands are located or, if located in different districts in the same State, in any of such districts.

(June 25, 1948, c. 646, 62 Stat. 936.)

§ 1400. Patents and copyrights, mask works, and designs

(a) Civil actions, suits, or proceedings arising under any Act of Congress relating to copyrights or exclusive rights in mask works or designs may be instituted in the district in which the defendant or his agent resides or may be found.

(b) Any civil action for patent infringement may be brought in the judicial district where the defendant resides, or where the defendant has committed acts of infringement and has a regular and established place of business.

(June 25, 1948, c. 646, 62 Stat. 936; Nov. 19, 1988, Pub.L. 100–702, Title X, § 1020(a)(5), 102 Stat. 4671; Oct. 28, 1998, Pub.L. 105–304, Title V, § 503(c)(1), (2), 112 Stat. 2917; Aug. 5, 1999, Pub.L. 106–44, § 2(a), 113 Stat. 223.)

HISTORICAL AND STATUTORY NOTES

Senate Revision Amendment

Title 17 of the United States Code was enacted into positive law by Act July 30, 1947, c. 391, 61 Stat. 652, and, in such enactment, section 35 of the prior title became section 111 of the new title, and all Acts from which sections of the prior title had been derived, were repealed. Therefore, this paragraph should read: "Based on Title 28, U.S.C., 1940 ed., § 109 (Mar. 3, 1911, c. 231, § 48, 36 Stat. 1100), and section 111 of Title 17, U.S.C., 1946 ed., Copyrights." By Senate amendment, section 111 of Title 17 U.S.C., is included in the schedule of repeals. See 80th Congress Senate Report No. 1559.

1988 Acts. House Report No. 100–889, see 1988 U.S. Code Cong. and Adm. News, p. 5982.

1998 Acts. House Conference Report No. 105–796 and Statement by President, see 1998 U.S. Code Cong. and Adm. News, p. 645.

Effective and Applicability Provisions

1998 Acts. Amendment by Pub.L. 105–304, effective Oct. 28, 1998, see section 505 of Pub.L. 105–304, set out as a note under section 1301 of Title 17, Copyrights.

§ 1401. Stockholder's derivative action

Any civil action by a stockholder on behalf of his corporation may be prosecuted in any judicial district where the corporation might have sued the same defendants.

(June 25, 1948, c. 646, 62 Stat. 936.)

§ 1402. United States as defendant

(a) Any civil action in a district court against the United States under subsection (a) of section 1346 of this title may be prosecuted only:

(1) Except as provided in paragraph (2), in the judicial district where the plaintiff resides;

(2) In the case of a civil action by a corporation under paragraph (1) of subsection (a) of section 1346, in the judicial district in which is located the principal place of business or principal office or agency of the corporation; or if it has no principal place of business or principal office or agency in any judicial district (A) in the judicial district in which is located the office to which was made the return of the tax in respect of which the claim is made, or (B) if no return was made, in the judicial district in which lies the District of Columbia. Notwithstanding the foregoing provisions of this paragraph a district court, for the convenience of the parties and witnesses, in the interest of justice, may transfer any such action to any other district or division.

(b) Any civil action on a tort claim against the United States under subsection (b) of section 1346 of this title may be prosecuted only in the judicial district where the plaintiff resides or wherein the act or omission complained of occurred.

(c) Any civil action against the United States under subsection (e) of section 1346 of this title may be prosecuted only in the judicial district where the property is situated at the time of levy, or if no levy is made, in the judicial district in which the event occurred which gave rise to the cause of action.

(d) Any civil action under section 2409a to quiet title to an estate or interest in real property in which an interest is claimed by the United States shall be brought in the district court of the district where the property is located or, if located in different districts, in any of such districts.

(June 25, 1948, c. 646, 62 Stat. 937; Sept. 2, 1958, Pub.L. 85–920, 72 Stat. 1770; Nov. 2, 1966, Pub.L. 89–719, Title II, § 202(b), 80 Stat. 1149; Oct. 25, 1972, Pub.L. 92–562, § 2, 86 Stat. 1176; Apr. 2, 1982, Pub.L. 97–164, Title I, § 131, 96 Stat. 39.)

HISTORICAL AND STATUTORY NOTES

Effective and Applicability Provisions

1982 Acts. Amendment by Pub.L. 97–164 effective Oct. 1, 1982, see section 402 of Pub.L. 97–164, set out as a note under section 171 of this title.

1966 Acts. Subsec. (c) of this section applicable after Nov. 2, 1966, see section 203 of Pub.L. 89–719, set out as a note under section 1346 of this title.

§ 1403. Eminent domain

Proceedings to condemn real estate for the use of the United States or its departments or agencies shall be brought in the district court of the district where the land is located or, if located in different districts in the same State, in any of such districts.

(June 25, 1948, c. 646, 62 Stat. 937.)

§ 1404. Change of venue

(a) For the convenience of parties and witnesses, in the interest of justice, a district court may transfer any civil action to any other district or division where it might have been brought.

(b) Upon motion, consent or stipulation of all parties, any action, suit or proceeding of a civil nature or any motion or hearing thereof, may be transferred, in the discretion of the court, from the division in which pending to any other division in the same district. Transfer of proceedings in rem brought by or on behalf of the United States may be transferred under this section without the consent of the United States where all other parties request transfer.

(c) A district court may order any civil action to be tried at any place within the division in which it is pending.

(d) As used in this section, the term "district court" includes the District Court of Guam, the District Court for the Northern Mariana Islands, and the District Court of the Virgin Islands, and the term "district" includes the territorial jurisdiction of each such court.

(June 25, 1948, c. 646, 62 Stat. 937; Oct. 18, 1962, Pub.L. 87–845, § 9, 76A Stat. 699; Oct. 19, 1996, Pub.L. 104–317, Title VI, § 610(a), 110 Stat. 3860.)

HISTORICAL AND STATUTORY NOTES

Effective and Applicability Provisions

1996 Acts. Section 610(c) of Pub.L. 104–317 provided that: "The amendments made by this section [amending this section and section 1406 of this title] apply to cases pending on the date of the enactment of this Act [Oct. 19, 1996] and to cases commenced on or after such date."

1962 Acts. Amendment of section by Pub.L. 87–845 effective Jan. 2, 1963, see section 25 of Pub.L. 87–845, set out as a note under section 14 of Title 18, Crimes and Criminal Procedure.

Termination of United States District Court for the District of the Canal Zone

For termination of the United States District Court for the District of the Canal Zone at end of the "transition period", being the 30-month period beginning Oct. 1, 1979, and ending midnight Mar. 31, 1982, see Paragraph 5 of Article XI of the Panama Canal Treaty of 1977 and sections 3831 and 3841 to 3843 of Title 22, Foreign Relations and Intercourse.

§ 1405. Creation or alteration of district or division

Actions or proceedings pending at the time of the creation of a new district or division or transfer of a county or territory from one division or district to another may be tried in the district or division as it existed at the institution of the action or proceeding, or in the district or division so created or to which the county or territory is so transferred as the parties shall agree or the court direct.

(June 25, 1948, c. 646, 62 Stat. 937.)

§ 1406. Cure or waiver of defects

(a) The district court of a district in which is filed a case laying venue in the wrong division or district shall dismiss, or if it be in the interest of justice, transfer such case to any district or division in which it could have been brought.

(b) Nothing in this chapter shall impair the jurisdiction of a district court of any matter involving a party who does not interpose timely and sufficient objection to the venue.

(c) As used in this section, the term "district court" includes the District Court of Guam, the District Court for the Northern Mariana Islands, and the District Court of the Virgin Islands, and the term "district" includes the territorial jurisdiction of each such court.

(June 25, 1948, c. 646, 62 Stat. 937; May 24, 1949, c. 139, § 81, 63 Stat. 101; Sept. 13, 1960, Pub.L. 86–770, § 1, 74 Stat. 912; Oct. 18, 1962, Pub.L. 87–845, § 10, 76A Stat. 699; Apr. 2, 1982, Pub.L. 97–164, Title I, § 132, 96 Stat. 39; Oct. 19, 1996, Pub.L. 104–317, Title VI, § 610(b), 110 Stat. 3860.)

HISTORICAL AND STATUTORY NOTES

Effective and Applicability Provisions

1996 Acts. Amendment by section 610(b) of Pub.L. 104–317 to apply to cases pending on Oct. 19, 1996, and to cases commenced on or after such date, see section 610(c) of Pub.L. 104–317, set out as a note under section 1404 of this title.

1982 Acts. Amendment by Pub.L. 97–164 effective Oct. 1, 1982, see section 402 of Pub.L. 97–164, set out as a note under section 171 of this title.

1962 Acts. Amendment of section by Pub.L. 87–845 effective Jan. 2, 1963, see section 25 of Pub.L. 87–845, set out as a note under section 14 of Title 18, Crimes and Criminal Procedure.

1960 Acts. Section 4 of Pub.L. 86–770 provided in part that: "The amendments made by sections 1 and 2 of this Act [adding subsec. (c) of this section and section 1506 of this title] shall apply to any case or proceeding pending on, or brought after, the date of enactment of this Act [Sept. 13, 1960] in the district courts or the Court of Claims."

Termination of United States District Court for the District of the Canal Zone

For termination of the United States District Court for the District of the Canal Zone at end of the "transition period", being the 30-month period beginning Oct. 1, 1979, and ending midnight Mar. 31, 1982, see Paragraph 5 of Article XI of the Panama Canal Treaty of 1977 and sections 3831 and 3841 to 3843 of Title 22, Foreign Relations and Intercourse.

§ 1407. Multidistrict litigation

(a) When civil actions involving one or more common questions of fact are pending in different districts, such actions may be transferred to any district for coordinated or consolidated pretrial proceedings. Such transfers shall be made by the judicial panel on multidistrict litigation authorized by this section upon its determination that transfers for such proceedings will be for the convenience of parties and witnesses and will promote the just and efficient conduct of such actions. Each action so transferred shall be remanded by the panel at or before the conclusion of such pretrial proceedings to the district from which it was transferred unless it shall have been previously terminated: *Provided, however*, That the panel may separate any claim, cross-claim, counter-claim, or third-party claim and remand any of such claims before the remainder of the action is remanded.

(b) Such coordinated or consolidated pretrial proceedings shall be conducted by a judge or judges to whom such actions are assigned by the judicial panel on multidistrict litigation. For this purpose, upon request of the panel, a circuit judge or a district judge may be designated and assigned temporarily for service in the transferee district by the Chief Justice of the United States or the chief judge of the circuit, as may be required, in accordance with the provisions of chapter 13 of this title. With the consent of the transferee district court, such actions may be assigned by the panel to a judge or judges of such district. The judge or judges to whom such actions are assigned, the members of the judicial panel on multidistrict litigation, and other circuit and district judges designated when needed by the panel may exercise the powers of a district judge in any district for the purpose of conducting pretrial depositions in such coordinated or consolidated pretrial proceedings.

(c) Proceedings for the transfer of an action under this section may be initiated by—

(i) the judicial panel on multidistrict litigation upon its own initiative, or

(ii) motion filed with the panel by a party in any action in which transfer for coordinated or consolidated pretrial proceedings under this section may be appropriate. A copy of such motion shall be filed in the district court in which the moving party's action is pending.

The panel shall give notice to the parties in all actions in which transfers for coordinated or consolidated pretrial proceedings are contemplated, and such notice shall specify the time and place of any hearing to determine whether such transfer shall be made. Orders of the panel to set a hearing and other orders of the panel issued prior to the order either directing or denying transfer shall be filed in the office of the clerk of the district court in which a transfer hearing is to be or has been held. The panel's order of transfer shall be based upon a record of such hearing at which material evidence may be offered by any party to an action pending in any district that would be affected by the proceedings under this section, and shall be supported by findings of fact and conclusions of law based upon such record. Orders of transfer and such other orders as the panel may make thereafter shall be filed in the office of the clerk of the district court of the transferee district and shall be effective when thus filed. The clerk of the transferee district court shall forthwith transmit a certified copy of the panel's order to transfer to the clerk of the district court from which the action is being transferred. An order denying transfer shall be filed in each district wherein there is a case pending in which the motion for transfer has been made.

(d) The judicial panel on multidistrict litigation shall consist of seven circuit and district judges designated from time to time by the Chief Justice of the United States, no two of whom shall be from the same circuit. The concurrence of four members shall be necessary to any action by the panel.

(e) No proceedings for review of any order of the panel may be permitted except by extraordinary writ pursuant to the provisions of title 28, section 1651, United States Code. Petitions for an extraordinary writ to review an order of the panel to set a transfer hearing and other orders of the panel issued prior to the order either directing or denying transfer shall be filed only in the court of appeals having jurisdiction over the district in which a hearing is to be or has been held. Petitions for an extraordinary writ to review an order to transfer or orders subsequent to transfer shall be filed only in the court of appeals having jurisdiction over the transferee district. There shall be no appeal or review of an order of the panel denying a motion to transfer for consolidated or coordinated proceedings.

(f) The panel may prescribe rules for the conduct of its business not inconsistent with Acts of Congress and the Federal Rules of Civil Procedure.

(g) Nothing in this section shall apply to any action in which the United States is a complainant arising under the antitrust laws. "Antitrust laws" as used herein include those acts referred to in the Act of October 15, 1914, as amended (38 Stat. 730; 15 U.S.C. 12), and also include the Act of June 19, 1936 (49 Stat. 1526; 15 U.S.C. 13, 13a, and 13b) and the Act of September 26, 1914, as added March 21, 1938 (52 Stat. 116, 117; 15 U.S.C. 56); but shall not include section 4A of the Act of October 15, 1914, as added July 7, 1955 (69 Stat. 282; 15 U.S.C. 15a).

(h) Notwithstanding the provisions of section 1404 or subsection (f) of this section, the judicial panel on multidistrict litigation may consolidate and transfer with or without the consent of the parties, for both pretrial purposes and for trial, any action brought under section 4C of the Clayton Act.

(Added Pub.L. 90–296, § 1, Apr. 29, 1968, 82 Stat. 109, and amended Pub.L. 94–435, Title III, § 303, Sept. 30, 1976, 90 Stat. 1396.)

HISTORICAL AND STATUTORY NOTES

References in Text

The Federal Rules of Civil Procedure, referred to in subsec. (f), are set out in this title.

Section 4C of the Clayton Act, referred to in subsec. (h), is section 4C of Act Oct. 15, 1914, c. 323, as added by Pub.L. 94–435, Title III, § 301, Sept. 30, 1976, 90 Stat. 1394, which is classified to section 15c of Title 15, Commerce and Trade.

CROSS REFERENCES

Rules of Procedure of the Judicial Panel on Multidistrict Litigation are set out ante, following the Federal Rules of Civil Procedure for the United States District Courts.

§ 1408. Venue of cases under title 11

Except as provided in section 1410 of this title, a case under title 11 may be commenced in the district court for the district—

(1) in which the domicile, residence, principal place of business in the United States, or principal assets in the United States, of the person or entity that is the subject of such case have been located for the one hundred and eighty days immediately preceding such commencement, or for a longer portion of such one-hundred-and-eighty-day period than the domicile, residence, or principal place of business, in the United States, or principal assets in the United States, of such person were located in any other district; or

(2) in which there is pending a case under title 11 concerning such person's affiliate, general partner, or partnership.

(Added Pub.L. 98–353, Title I, § 102(a), July 10, 1984, 98 Stat. 334.)

HISTORICAL AND STATUTORY NOTES

Effective and Applicability Provisions

1984 Acts. Section effective July 10, 1984, see section 122(a) of Pub.L. 98–353, set out as a note under section 151 of this title.

Prior Provisions

A prior section 1408, added by Pub.L. 95–598, Title II, § 240(a), Nov. 6, 1978, 92 Stat. 2668, which related to bankruptcy appeals, did not become effective pursuant to section 402(b) of Pub.L. 95–598, as amended, set out as an Effective and Applicability Provisions note preceding section 101 of Title 11, Bankruptcy.

§ 1409. Venue of proceedings arising under title 11 or arising in or related to cases under title 11

(a) Except as otherwise provided in subsections (b) and (d), a proceeding arising under title 11 or arising in or related to a case under title 11 may be commenced in the district court in which such case is pending.

(b) Except as provided in subsection (d) of this section, a trustee in a case under title 11 may commence a proceeding arising in or related to such case to recover a money judgment of or property worth less than $1,100 [1] or a consumer debt of less than $16,425 [1], or a debt (excluding a consumer debt) against a noninsider of less than $10,950 [1], only in the district court for the district in which the defendant resides.

(c) Except as provided in subsection (b) of this section, a trustee in a case under title 11 may commence a proceeding arising in or related to such case as statutory successor to the debtor or creditors under section 541 or 544(b) of title 11 in the district court for the district where the State or Federal court sits in which, under applicable nonbankruptcy venue provisions, the debtor or creditors, as the case may be, may have commenced an action on which such proceeding is based if the case under title 11 had not been commenced.

(d) A trustee may commence a proceeding arising under title 11 or arising in or related to a case under title 11 based on a claim arising after the commencement of such case from the operation of the business of the debtor only in the district court for the district where a State or Federal court sits in which, under applicable nonbankruptcy venue provisions, an action on such claim may have been brought.

(e) A proceeding arising under title 11 or arising in or related to a case under title 11, based on a claim arising after the commencement of such case from the operation of the business of the debtor, may be commenced against the representative of the estate in such case in the district court for the district where the State or Federal court sits in which the party commencing such proceeding may, under applicable nonbankruptcy venue provisions, have brought an action on such claim, or in the district court in which such case is pending.

(Added Pub.L. 98–353, Title I, § 102(a), July 10, 1984, 98 Stat. 334, and amended Pub.L. 109–8, Title IV, § 410, Apr. 20, 2005, 119 Stat. 106.)

[1] Dollar amount as adjusted by the Judicial Conference of the United States. See Adjustment of Dollar Amounts notes set out under this section and 11 U.S.C.A. § 104.

HISTORICAL AND STATUTORY NOTES

Effective and Applicability Provisions

2007 Acts. Increase of dollar amounts by Judicial Conference of the United States by notice published Feb. 14, 2007, 72 F.R. 7082 effective April 1, 2007, and increase not applicable to cases commenced before the effective date of the adjustments, i.e., April 1, 2007. See Adjustment of Dollar Amounts notes under 11 U.S.C.A. § 104 and this section.

2005 Acts. Except as otherwise provided, amendments by Pub.L. 109–8 effective 180 days after April 20, 2005, and inapplicable with respect to cases commenced under Title 11 before the effective date, see Pub.L. 109–8, § 1501, set out as a note under 11 U.S.C.A. § 101.

1984 Acts. Section effective July 10, 1984, see section 122(a) of Pub.L. 98–353, set out as a note under section 151 of this title.

Adjustment of Dollar Amounts

For adjustment of dollar amounts specified in subsec. (b) of this section by the Judicial Conference of the United States, effective Apr. 1, 2007, see note set out under 11 U.S.C.A. § 104.

By notice published Feb. 14, 2007, 72 F.R. 7082, the Judicial Conference of the United States adjusted the dollar amounts in provisions specified in subsec. (b) of this section, effective Apr. 1, 2007, as follows:

Adjusted $1,000 to $1,100.

Adjusted $15,000 to $16,425.

Adjusted $10,000 to $10,950.

§ 1410. Venue of cases ancillary to foreign proceedings

A case under chapter 15 of title 11 may be commenced in the district court of the United States for the district—

(1) in which the debtor has its principal place of business or principal assets in the United States;

(2) if the debtor does not have a place of business or assets in the United States, in which there is pending against the debtor an action or proceeding in a Federal or State court; or

(3) in a case other than those specified in paragraph (1) or (2), in which venue will be consistent with the interests of justice and the convenience of the parties, having regard to the relief sought by the foreign representative.

(Added Pub.L. 98–353, Title I, § 102(a), July 10, 1984, 98 Stat. 335, and amended Pub.L. 109–8, Title VIII, § 802(c)(4), Apr. 20, 2005, 119 Stat. 146.)

HISTORICAL AND STATUTORY NOTES

References in Text

Chapter 15 of title 11, referred to in text, is 11 U.S.C.A. § 1501 et seq.

Effective and Applicability Provisions

2005 Acts. Except as otherwise provided, amendments by Pub.L. 109–8 effective 180 days after April 20, 2005, and inapplicable with respect to cases commenced under Title 11 before the effective date, see Pub.L. 109–8, § 1501, set out as a note under 11 U.S.C.A. § 101.

1984 Acts. Section effective July 10, 1984, see section 122(a) of Pub.L. 98–353, set out as a note under section 151 of this title.

§ 1411. Jury trials

(a) Except as provided in subsection (b) of this section, this chapter and title 11 do not affect any right to trial by jury that an individual has under applicable nonbankruptcy law with regard to a personal injury or wrongful death tort claim.

(b) The district court may order the issues arising under section 303 of title 11 to be tried without a jury.

(Added Pub.L. 98–353, Title I, § 102(a), July 10, 1984, 98 Stat. 335.)

HISTORICAL AND STATUTORY NOTES

Effective and Applicability Provisions

1984 Acts. Section, except subsec. (a), effective July 10, 1984, see section 122(a) of Pub.L. 98–353, set out as a note under section 151 of this title.

Subsec. (a) not applicable with respect to cases under Title 11, Bankruptcy, that are pending on July 10, 1984, or to proceedings arising in or related to such cases, see section 122(b) of Pub.L. 98–353, set out as a note under section 151 of this title.

§ 1412. Change of venue

A district court may transfer a case or proceeding under title 11 to a district court for another district, in the interest of justice or for the convenience of the parties.

(Added Pub.L. 98–353, Title I, § 102(a), July 10, 1984, 98 Stat. 335.)

HISTORICAL AND STATUTORY NOTES

Effective and Applicability Provisions

1984 Acts. Section effective July 10, 1984, see section 122(a) of Pub.L. 98–353, set out as a note under section 151 of this title.

§ 1413. Venue of cases under chapter 5 of title 3

Notwithstanding the preceding provisions of this chapter, a civil action under section 1346(g) may be brought in the United States district court for the district in which the employee is employed or in the United States District Court for the District of Columbia.

(Added Pub.L. 104–331, § 3(b)(2)(A), Oct. 26, 1996, 110 Stat. 4069.)

HISTORICAL AND STATUTORY NOTES

Codifications

Amendment by Pub.L. 104–331, § 3(b)(2)(A), which directed the addition of this section to the end of chapter 37 of this title, was executed by adding this section to the end of this chapter, as the probable intent of Congress.

Effective and Applicability Provisions

1996 Acts. Amendment by Pub.L. 104–331, § 3(b)(2)(B), effective October 1, 1997, see section 3(d) of Pub.L. 104–331, set out as a note under section 1296 of this title.

CHAPTER 89—DISTRICT COURTS; REMOVAL OF CASES FROM STATE COURTS

Sec.
1441. Actions removable generally.
1442. Federal officers and agencies sued or prosecuted.[1]
1442a. Members of armed forces sued or prosecuted.
1443. Civil rights cases.
1444. Foreclosure action against United States.
1445. Nonremovable actions.

Sec.
1446. Procedure for removal.
1447. Procedure after removal generally.
1448. Process after removal.
1449. State court record supplied.
1450. Attachment or sequestration; securities.
1451. Definitions.
1452. Removal of claims related to bankruptcy cases.
1453. Removal of class actions.

[1] So in original. Does not conform to section catchline.

§ 1441. Actions removable generally

(a) Except as otherwise expressly provided by Act of Congress, any civil action brought in a State court of which the district courts of the United States have original jurisdiction, may be removed by the defendant or the defendants, to the district court of the United States for the district and division embracing the place where such action is pending. For purposes of removal under this chapter, the citizenship of defendants sued under fictitious names shall be disregarded.

(b) Any civil action of which the district courts have original jurisdiction founded on a claim or right arising under the Constitution, treaties or laws of the United States shall be removable without regard to the citizenship or residence of the parties. Any other such action shall be removable only if none of the parties in interest properly joined and served as defendants is a citizen of the State in which such action is brought.

(c) Whenever a separate and independent claim or cause of action within the jurisdiction conferred by section 1331 of this title is joined with one or more otherwise non-removable claims or causes of action, the entire case may be removed and the district court may determine all issues therein, or, in its discretion, may remand all matters in which State law predominates.

(d) Any civil action brought in a State court against a foreign state as defined in section 1603(a) of this title may be removed by the foreign state to the district court of the United States for the district and division embracing the place where such action is pending. Upon removal the action shall be tried by the court without jury. Where removal is based upon this subsection, the time limitations of section 1446(b) of this chapter may be enlarged at any time for cause shown.

(e)(1) Notwithstanding the provisions of subsection (b) of this section, a defendant in a civil action in a State court may remove the action to the district court of the United States for the district and division embracing the place where the action is pending if—

(A) the action could have been brought in a United States district court under section 1369 of this title; or

(B) the defendant is a party to an action which is or could have been brought, in whole or in part, under section 1369 in a United States district court and arises from the same accident as the action in State court, even if the action to be removed could not have been brought in a district court as an original matter.

The removal of an action under this subsection shall be made in accordance with section 1446 of this title, except that a notice of removal may also be filed before trial of the action in State court within 30 days after the date on which the defendant first becomes a party to an action under section 1369 in a United States district court that arises from the same accident as the action in State court, or at a later time with leave of the district court.

(2) Whenever an action is removed under this subsection and the district court to which it is removed or transferred under section 1407(j) has made a liability determination requiring further proceedings as to damages, the district court shall remand the action to the State court from which it had been removed for the determination of damages, unless the court finds that, for the convenience of parties and witnesses and in the interest of justice, the action should be retained for the determination of damages.

(3) Any remand under paragraph (2) shall not be effective until 60 days after the district court has issued an order determining liability and has certified its intention to remand the removed action for the determination of damages. An appeal with respect to the liability determination of the district court may be taken during that 60–day period to the court of appeals with appellate jurisdiction over the district court. In the event a party files such an appeal, the remand shall not be effective until the appeal has been finally disposed of. Once the remand has become effective, the liability determination shall not be subject to further review by appeal or otherwise.

(4) Any decision under this subsection concerning remand for the determination of damages shall not be reviewable by appeal or otherwise.

(5) An action removed under this subsection shall be deemed to be an action under section 1369 and an action in which jurisdiction is based on section 1369 of this title for purposes of this section and sections 1407, 1697, and 1785 of this title.

(6) Nothing in this subsection shall restrict the authority of the district court to transfer or dismiss an action on the ground of inconvenient forum.

(f) The court to which a civil action is removed under this section is not precluded from hearing and determining any claim in such civil action because the State court from which such civil action is removed did not have jurisdiction over that claim.

(June 25, 1948, c. 646, 62 Stat. 937; Oct. 21, 1976, Pub.L. 94–583, § 6, 90 Stat. 2898; June 19, 1986, Pub.L. 99–336, § 3(a), 100 Stat. 637; Nov. 19, 1988, Pub.L. 100–702, Title X, § 1016(a), 102 Stat. 4669; Dec. 1, 1990, Pub.L. 101–650, Title III, § 312, 104 Stat. 5114; Dec. 9, 1991, Pub.L. 102–198, § 4, 105 Stat. 1623; Nov. 2, 2002, Pub.L. 107–273, Div. C, Title I, § 11020(b)(3), 116 Stat. 1827.)

HISTORICAL AND STATUTORY NOTES

References in Text

Section 1407(j) of Title 28, referred to in subsec. (e)(2), does not exist.

Effective and Applicability Provisions

2002 Acts. Amendments by section 11020(b) of Pub.L. 107–273 shall apply to a civil action if the accident giving rise to the cause of action occurred on or after the 90th day after Nov. 2, 2002, see section 11020(c) of Pub.L. 107–273, set out as a note under 28 U.S.C.A. § 1369.

1986 Acts. Section 3(b) of Pub.L. 99–336 provided that: "The amendment made by this section [amending this section] shall apply with respect to claims in civil actions commenced in State courts on or after the date of the enactment of this section [June 19, 1986]."

1976 Acts. Amendment by Pub.L. 94–583 effective 90 days after Oct. 21, 1976, see section 8 of Pub.L. 94–583, set out as a note under section 1602 of this title.

§ 1442. Federal officers or agencies sued or prosecuted

(a) A civil action or criminal prosecution commenced in a State court against any of the following may be removed by them to the district court of the United States for the district and division embracing the place wherein it is pending:

(1) The United States or any agency thereof or any officer (or any person acting under that officer) of the United States or of any agency thereof, sued in an official or individual capacity for any act under color of such office or on account of any right, title or authority claimed under any Act of Congress for the apprehension or punishment of criminals or the collection of the revenue.

(2) A property holder whose title is derived from any such officer, where such action or prosecution affects the validity of any law of the United States.

(3) Any officer of the courts of the United States, for any act under color of office or in the performance of his duties;

(4) Any officer of either House of Congress, for any act in the discharge of his official duty under an order of such House.

(b) A personal action commenced in any State court by an alien against any citizen of a State who is, or at the time the alleged action accrued was, a civil officer of the United States and is a nonresident of such State, wherein jurisdiction is obtained by the State court by personal service of process, may be removed by the defendant to the district court of the United States for the district and division in which the defendant was served with process.

(June 25, 1948, c. 646, 62 Stat. 938; Oct. 19, 1996, Pub.L. 104–317, Title II, § 206(a), 110 Stat. 3850.)

§ 1442a. Members of armed forces sued or prosecuted

A civil or criminal prosecution in a court of a State of the United States against a member of the armed forces of the United States on account of an act done under color of his office or status, or in respect to which he claims any right, title, or authority under a law of the United States respecting the armed forces thereof, or under the law of war, may at any time before the trial or final hearing thereof be removed for trial into the district court of the United States for the district where it is pending in the manner prescribed by law, and it shall thereupon be entered on the docket of the district court, which shall proceed as if the cause had been originally commenced therein and shall have full power to hear and determine the cause.

(Added Aug. 10, 1956, c. 1041, § 19(a), 70A Stat. 626.)

HISTORICAL AND STATUTORY NOTES

Codifications

Section was from the Uniform Code of Military Justice, Act May 5, 1950, c. 169, § 9, 64 Stat. 146, which was based on Article 117, Articles of War, Act June 4, 1920, c. 227, subch. II, § 1, 41 Stat. 811, as amended June 24, 1948, c. 625, Title II, § 242, 62 Stat. 642.

§ 1443. Civil rights cases

Any of the following civil actions or criminal prosecutions, commenced in a State court may be removed by the defendant to the district court of the United States for the district and division embracing the place wherein it is pending:

(1) Against any person who is denied or cannot enforce in the courts of such State a right under any law providing for the equal civil rights of citizens of the United States, or of all persons within the jurisdiction thereof;

(2) For any act under color of authority derived from any law providing for equal rights, or for refusing to do any act on the ground that it would be inconsistent with such law.

(June 25, 1948, c. 646, 62 Stat. 938.)

§ 1444. Foreclosure action against United States

Any action brought under section 2410 of this title against the United States in any State court may be removed by the United States to the district court of the United States for the district and division in which the action is pending.

(June 25, 1948, c. 646, 62 Stat. 938; May 24, 1949, c. 139, § 82, 63 Stat. 101.)

§ 1445. Nonremovable actions

(a) A civil action in any State court against a railroad or its receivers or trustees, arising under sections 1–4 and 5–10 of the Act of April 22, 1908 (45 U.S.C. 51–54, 55–60), may not be removed to any district court of the United States.

(b) A civil action in any State court against a carrier or its receivers or trustees to recover damages for delay, loss, or injury of shipments, arising under section 11706 or 14706 of title 49, may not be removed to any district court of the United States unless the matter in controversy exceeds $10,000, exclusive of interest and costs.

(c) A civil action in any State court arising under the workmen's compensation laws of such State may not be removed to any district court of the United States.

(d) A civil action in any State court arising under section 40302 of the Violence Against Women Act of 1994 may not be removed to any district court of the United States.

(June 25, 1948, c. 646, 62 Stat. 939; July 25, 1958, Pub.L. 85–554, § 5, 72 Stat. 415; Oct. 17, 1978, Pub.L. 95–473, § 2(a)(3)(A), 92 Stat. 1465; Oct. 20, 1978, Pub.L. 95–486, § 9(b), 92 Stat. 1634; Sept. 13, 1994, Pub.L. 103–322, Title IV, § 40302(e)(5), 108 Stat. 1942; Dec. 29, 1995, Pub.L. 104–88, Title III, § 305(b), 109 Stat. 944; Oct. 11, 1996, Pub.L. 104–287, § 3, 110 Stat. 3388.)

HISTORICAL AND STATUTORY NOTES

References in Text

The Act of April 22, 1908, referred to in subsec. (a), popularly referred to as the [second] Employers' Liability Act, is Act Apr. 22, 1908, c. 149, 35 Stat. 65, as amended, which is classified generally to chapter 2 (section 51 et seq.) of Title 45, Railroads. For complete classification of this Act to the Code, see Short Title note set out under section 51 of Title 45 and Tables.

Section 40302 of the Violence Against Women Act of 1994, referred to in subsec. (d), means section 40302 of Pub.L. 103–322, the Violent Crime Control and Law Enforcement Act of 1994 (Title IV of such Act is the Violence Against Women Act of 1994), which is classified to section 13981 of Title 42, The Public Health and Welfare.

Effective and Applicability Provisions

1996 Acts. Amendment by section 3 of Pub.L. 104–287 effective on July 5, 1994, see section 8(1) of Pub.L. 104–287, set out as a note under section 5303 of Title 49, Transportation.

1995 Acts. Amendment by Pub.L. 104–88 effective Jan. 1, 1996, see section 2 of Pub.L. 104–88, set out as a note under section 701 of Title 49, Transportation.

1958 Acts. Amendment of section by Pub.L. 85–554 applicable only in the case of actions commenced after July 25, 1958, see section 3 of Pub.L. 85–554, set out as a note under section 1331 of this title.

§ 1446. Procedure for removal

(a) A defendant or defendants desiring to remove any civil action or criminal prosecution from a State court shall file in the district court of the United States for the district and division within which such action is pending a notice of removal signed pursuant to Rule 11 of the Federal Rules of Civil Procedure and containing a short and plain statement of the grounds for removal, together with a copy of all process, pleadings, and orders served upon such defendant or defendants in such action.

(b) The notice of removal of a civil action or proceeding shall be filed within thirty days after the receipt by the defendant, through service or otherwise, of a copy of the initial pleading setting forth the claim for relief upon which such action or proceeding is based, or within thirty days after the service of summons upon the defendant if such initial pleading has then been filed in court and is not required to be served on the defendant, whichever period is shorter.

If the case stated by the initial pleading is not removable, a notice of removal may be filed within thirty days after receipt by the defendant, through service or otherwise, of a copy of an amended pleading, motion, order or other paper from which it may first be ascertained that the case is one which is or has become removable, except that a case may not be removed on the basis of jurisdiction conferred by section 1332 of this title more than 1 year after commencement of the action.

(c)(1) A notice of removal of a criminal prosecution shall be filed not later than thirty days after the arraignment in the State court, or at any time before trial, whichever is earlier, except that for good cause shown the United States district court may enter an order granting the defendant or defendants leave to file the notice at a later time.

(2) A notice of removal of a criminal prosecution shall include all grounds for such removal. A failure to state grounds which exist at the time of the filing of the notice shall constitute a waiver of such grounds, and a second notice may be filed only on grounds not existing at the time of the original notice. For good cause shown, the United States district court may grant relief from the limitations of this paragraph.

(3) The filing of a notice of removal of a criminal prosecution shall not prevent the State court in which such prosecution is pending from proceeding further, except that a judgment of conviction shall not be entered unless the prosecution is first remanded.

(4) The United States district court in which such notice is filed shall examine the notice promptly. If it clearly appears on the face of the notice and any exhibits annexed thereto that removal should not be permitted, the court shall make an order for summary remand.

(5) If the United States district court does not order the summary remand of such prosecution, it shall order an evidentiary hearing to be held promptly and after such hearing shall make such disposition of the prosecution as justice shall require. If the United States district court determines that removal shall be permitted, it shall so notify the State court in which prosecution is pending, which shall proceed no further.

(d) Promptly after the filing of such notice of removal of a civil action the defendant or defendants shall give written notice thereof to all adverse parties and shall file a copy of the notice with the clerk of such State court, which shall effect the removal and the State court shall proceed no further unless and until the case is remanded.

(e) If the defendant or defendants are in actual custody on process issued by the State court, the district court shall issue its writ of habeas corpus, and the marshal shall thereupon take such defendant or defendants into his custody and deliver a copy of the writ to the clerk of such State court.

(f) With respect to any counterclaim removed to a district court pursuant to section 337(c) of the Tariff Act of 1930, the district court shall resolve such counterclaim in the same manner as an original complaint under the Federal Rules of Civil Procedure, except that the payment of a filing fee shall not be required in such cases and the counterclaim shall relate back to the date of the original complaint in the proceeding before the International Trade Commission under section 337 of that Act.

(June 25, 1948, c. 646, 62 Stat. 939; May 24, 1949, c. 139, § 83, 63 Stat. 101; Sept. 29, 1965, Pub.L. 89–215, 79 Stat. 887; July 30, 1977, Pub.L. 95–78, § 3, 91 Stat. 321; Nov. 19, 1988, Pub.L. 100–702, Title X, § 1016(b), 102 Stat. 4669; Dec. 9, 1991, Pub.L. 102–198, § 10(a), 105 Stat. 1626; Dec. 8, 1994, Pub.L. 103–465, Title III, § 321(b)(2), 108 Stat. 4946; Oct. 19, 1996, Pub.L. 104–317, Title VI, § 603, 110 Stat. 3857.)

HISTORICAL AND STATUTORY NOTES

References in Text

The Federal Rules of Civil Procedure, referred to in subsec. (a), are set out in this title.

Codifications

Section 10(a)(5)(A) of Pub.L. 102–198, which directed that subsec. (d) of this section be amended by substituting "removal" for "the removal", was executed by making such substitution at the first appearance of the term "the removal", as the probable intent of Congress.

1994 Acts

House Report No. 103–826 (Parts I and II) and Statement of Administrative Action, see 1994 U.S. Code Cong. and Adm. News, p. 3773.

Effective and Applicability Provisions

1994 Acts. Amendment by section 321(b)(2) of Pub.L. 103–465 applicable with respect to complaints filed under section 1337 of Title 19, Customs Duties, on or after the date on which the WTO Agreement enters into force with respect to the United States, Jan. 1, 1995, or in cases under section 1337 of Title 19 in which no complaint is filed, with respect to investigations initiated under such section on or after such date, see section 322 of Pub.L. 103–465, set out as a note under section 1337 of Title 19.

1977 Acts. Amendment by Pub.L. 95–78 effective Oct. 1, 1977, see section 4 of Pub.L. 95–78, set out as a note under section 3771 of Title 18, Crimes and Criminal Procedure.

§ 1447. Procedure after removal generally

(a) In any case removed from a State court, the district court may issue all necessary orders and process to bring before it all proper parties whether served by process issued by the State court or otherwise.

(b) It may require the removing party to file with its clerk copies of all records and proceedings in such State court or may cause the same to be brought before it by writ of certiorari issued to such State court.

(c) A motion to remand the case on the basis of any defect other than lack of subject matter jurisdiction must be made within 30 days after the filing of the notice of removal under section 1446(a). If at any time before final judgment it appears that the district court lacks subject matter jurisdiction, the case shall be remanded. An order remanding the case may require payment of just costs and any actual expenses, including attorney fees, incurred as a result of the removal. A certified copy of the order of remand shall be mailed by the clerk to the clerk of the State court. The State court may thereupon proceed with such case.

(d) An order remanding a case to the State court from which it was removed is not reviewable on appeal or otherwise, except that an order remanding a case to the State court from which it was removed pursuant to section 1443 of this title shall be reviewable by appeal or otherwise.

(e) If after removal the plaintiff seeks to join additional defendants whose joinder would destroy subject matter jurisdiction, the court may deny joinder, or permit joinder and remand the action to the State court.

(June 25, 1948, c. 646, 62 Stat. 939; May 24, 1949, c. 139, § 84, 63 Stat. 102; July 2, 1964, Pub.L. 88–352, Title IX, § 901, 78 Stat. 266; Nov. 19, 1988, Pub.L. 100–702, Title X, § 1016(c), 102 Stat. 4670; Dec. 9, 1991, Pub.L. 102–198, § 10(b), 105 Stat. 1626; Oct. 1, 1996, Pub.L. 104–219, § 1, 110 Stat. 3022.)

HISTORICAL AND STATUTORY NOTES

Exception to Subsection (d)

Section 3(c) of Act Aug. 4, 1947, c. 458, 61 Stat. 732, provided in part that the United States shall have the right to appeal from any order of remand entered in any case removed to a United States district court pursuant to the provisions of Act Apr. 12, 1926, c. 115, 44 Stat. 239. These Acts referred to herein relate to restrictions on land of the Five Civilized Tribes of Oklahoma and are set out as notes under section 355 of Title 25, Indians.

§ 1448. Process after removal

In all cases removed from any State court to any district court of the United States in which any one or more of the defendants has not been served with process or in which the service has not been perfected prior to removal, or in which process served proves to be defective, such process or service may be completed or new process issued in the same manner as in cases originally filed in such district court.

This section shall not deprive any defendant upon whom process is served after removal of his right to move to remand the case.

(June 25, 1948, c. 646, 62 Stat. 940.)

§ 1449. State court record supplied

Where a party is entitled to copies of the records and proceedings in any suit or prosecution in a State court, to be used in any district court of the United States, and the clerk of such State court, upon demand, and the payment or tender of the legal fees, fails to deliver certified copies, the district court may, on affidavit reciting such facts, direct such record to be supplied by affidavit or otherwise. Thereupon such proceedings, trial, and judgment may be had in such district court, and all such process awarded, as if certified copies had been filed in the district court.

(June 25, 1948, c. 646, 62 Stat. 940; May 24, 1949, c. 139, § 85, 63 Stat. 102.)

§ 1450. Attachment or sequestration; securities

Whenever any action is removed from a State court to a district court of the United States, any attachment or sequestration of the goods or estate of the defendant in such action in the State court shall hold the goods or estate to answer the final judgment or decree in the same manner as they would have been held to answer final judgment or decree had it been rendered by the State court.

All bonds, undertakings, or security given by either party in such action prior to its removal shall remain valid and effectual notwithstanding such removal.

All injunctions, orders, and other proceedings had in such action prior to its removal shall remain in full force and effect until dissolved or modified by the district court.

(June 25, 1948, c. 646, 62 Stat. 940.)

§ 1451. Definitions

For purposes of this chapter—

(1) The term "State court" includes the Superior Court of the District of Columbia.

(2) The term "State" includes the District of Columbia.

(Added Pub.L. 91–358, Title I, § 172(d)(1), July 29, 1970, 84 Stat. 591.)

HISTORICAL AND STATUTORY NOTES

Effective and Applicability Provisions

1970 Acts. Section effective the first day of the seventh calendar month which begins after July 29, 1970, see section 199(a) of Pub.L. 91–358, set out as a note under section 1257 of this title.

§ 1452. Removal of claims related to bankruptcy cases

(a) A party may remove any claim or cause of action in a civil action other than a proceeding before the United States Tax Court or a civil action by a governmental unit to enforce such governmental unit's police or regulatory power, to the district court for the district where such civil action is pending, if such district court has jurisdiction of such claim or cause of action under section 1334 of this title.

(b) The court to which such claim or cause of action is removed may remand such claim or cause of action on any equitable ground. An order entered under this subsection remanding a claim or cause of action, or a decision to not remand, is not reviewable by appeal or otherwise by the court of appeals under section 158(d), 1291, or 1292 of this title or by the Supreme Court of the United States under section 1254 of this title.

(Added Pub.L. 98–353, Title I, § 103(a), July 10, 1984, 98 Stat. 335, and amended Pub.L. 101–650, Title III, § 309(c), Dec. 1, 1990, 104 Stat. 5113.)

HISTORICAL AND STATUTORY NOTES

Effective and Applicability Provisions

1984 Acts. Section effective July 10, 1984, see section 122(a) of Pub.L. 98–353, set out as a note under section 151 of this title.

§ 1453. Removal of class actions

(a) Definitions.—In this section, the terms "class", "class action", "class certification order", and "class member" shall have the meanings given such terms under section 1332(d)(1).

(b) In general.—A class action may be removed to a district court of the United States in accordance with section 1446 (except that the 1-year limitation under section 1446(b) shall not apply), without regard to whether any defendant is a citizen of the State in which the action is brought, except that such action may be removed by any defendant without the consent of all defendants.

(c) Review of remand orders.—

(1) In general.—Section 1447 shall apply to any removal of a case under this section, except that notwithstanding section 1447(d), a court of appeals may accept an appeal from an order of a district court granting or denying a motion to remand a class action to the State court from which it was removed if application is made to the court of appeals not less than 7 days after entry of the order.

(2) Time period for judgment.—If the court of appeals accepts an appeal under paragraph (1), the court shall complete all action on such appeal, including rendering judgment, not later than 60 days after the date on which such appeal was filed, unless an extension is granted under paragraph (3).

(3) Extension of time period.—The court of appeals may grant an extension of the 60–day period described in paragraph (2) if—

(A) all parties to the proceeding agree to such extension, for any period of time; or

(B) such extension is for good cause shown and in the interests of justice, for a period not to exceed 10 days.

(4) Denial of appeal.—If a final judgment on the appeal under paragraph (1) is not issued before the end of the period described in paragraph (2), including any extension under paragraph (3), the appeal shall be denied.

(d) Exception.—This section shall not apply to any class action that solely involves—

(1) a claim concerning a covered security as defined under section 16(f)(3) of the Securities Act of 1933 (15 U.S.C. 78p(f)(3)[1]) and section 28(f)(5)(E) of the Securities Exchange Act of 1934 (15 U.S.C. 78bb(f)(5)(E));

(2) a claim that relates to the internal affairs or governance of a corporation or other form of business enterprise and arises under or by virtue of the laws of the State in which such corporation or business enterprise is incorporated or organized; or

(3) a claim that relates to the rights, duties (including fiduciary duties), and obligations relating to or created by or pursuant to any security (as defined under section 2(a)(1) of the Securities Act of 1933 (15 U.S.C. 77b(a)(1)) and the regulations issued thereunder).

(Added Pub.L. 109–2, § 5(a), Feb. 18, 2005, 119 Stat. 12.)

[1] So in original. Probably should be "77p(f)(3)".

HISTORICAL AND STATUTORY NOTES

References in Text

Section 16(f)(3) of the Securities Act of 1933, referred to in subsec. (d)(1), is May 27, 1933, c. 38, Title I, § 16(f)(3), 48 Stat. 84, as amended, which is classified to 15 U.S.C.A. § 78p(f)(3).

Section 28(f)(5)(E) of the Securities Exchange Act of 1934, referred to in subsec. (d)(1), is May 27, 1933, c. 38, Title I, § 2(f)(5)(E), 48 Stat. 74, as amended, which is classified to 15 U.S.C.A. § 78bb(f)(5)(E).

Section 2(a)(1) of the Securities Act of 1933, referred to in subsec. (d)(3), is May 27, 1933, c. 38, Title I, § 2(a)(1), 48 Stat. 74, as amended, which is classified to 15 U.S.C.A. § 77b(a)(1).

Effective and Applicability Provisions

2005 Acts. Amendments by Class Action Fairness Act of 2005, Pub.L. 109–2, Feb. 18, 2005, 119 Stat. 4, applicable to any civil action commenced on or after Feb. 18, 2005, see Pub.L. 109–2, § 9, set out as a note under 28 U.S.C.A. § 1332.

[CHAPTER 90—DISTRICT COURTS AND BANKRUPTCY COURTS] [OMITTED]

HISTORICAL AND STATUTORY NOTES

Codifications

Chapter 90, consisting of sections 1471 to 1482, which was added by Pub.L.95–598, Title II, § 241(a), Nov. 6, 1978, 92 Stat. 2668, and which related to district courts and bankruptcy courts, did not become effective pursuant to section 402(b) of Pub.L. 95–598, as amended, set out as an Effective and Applicability Provisions note preceding section 101 of Title 11, Bankruptcy.

Transition to New Court System

Pub.L. 95–598, Title IV, § 409, Nov. 6, 1978, 92 Stat. 2687, as amended by Pub.L. 98–249, § 1(d), Mar. 31, 1984, 98 Stat. 116; Pub.L. 98–271, § 1(d), Apr. 30, 1984, 98 Stat. 163; Pub.L. 98–299, § 1(d), May 25, 1984, 98 Stat. 214; Pub.L. 98–325, § 1(d), June 20, 1984, 98 Stat. 268; Pub.L. 98–353, Title I, § 121(d), July 10, 1984, 98 Stat. 346, was repealed by Pub.L. 98–353, Title I, §§ 114, 122(a), July 10, 1984, 98 Stat. 343, 346, eff. July 10, 1984. The repealed section had provided for transfer to the new court system of 1) cases, and matters and proceedings in cases, under the Bankruptcy Act [former Title 11] pending at the end of Sept. 30, 1983, in the courts of bankruptcy continued under section 404(a) of Pub.L. 95–598, with certain exceptions, and 2) cases and proceedings arising under or related to cases under Title 11 pending at the end of July 9, 1984, in the courts of bankruptcy continued under section 404(a) of Pub.L. 95–598, and directed that civil actions pending on July 9, 1984, over which a bankruptcy court had jurisdiction on July 9, 1984, not abate, that actions not finally determined before Apr. 1, 1985, be removed to a bankruptcy court under this chapter, and that all law books, publications, etc., furnished bankruptcy judges as of July 9, 1984, be transferred to the United States bankruptcy courts under the supervision of the Director of the Administrative Office of the United States Courts.

[§§ 1471 to 1482. Omitted]

CHAPTER 91—UNITED STATES COURT OF FEDERAL CLAIMS

Sec.
1491. Claims against United States generally; actions involving Tennessee Valley Authority.
1492. Congressional reference cases.
[1493. Repealed.]
1494. Accounts of officers, agents or contractors.
1495. Damages for unjust conviction and imprisonment; claim against United States.
1496. Disbursing officers' claims.
1497. Oyster growers' damages from dredging operations.
1498. Patent and copyright cases.
1499. Liquidated damages withheld from contractors under chapter 37 of title 40.
1500. Pendency of claims in other courts.
1501. Pensions.
1502. Treaty cases.
1503. Set-offs.
[1504. Repealed.]
1505. Indian claims.
[1506. Repealed.]
1507. Jurisdiction for certain declaratory judgments.
1508. Jurisdiction for certain partnership proceedings.
1509. No jurisdiction in cases involving refunds of tax shelter promoter and understatement penalties.

§ 1491. Claims against United States generally; actions involving Tennessee Valley Authority

(a)(1) The United States Court of Federal Claims shall have jurisdiction to render judgment upon any claim against the United States founded either upon the Constitution, or any Act of Congress or any regulation of an executive department, or upon any express or implied contract with the United States, or for liquidated or unliquidated damages in cases not sounding in tort. For the purpose of this paragraph, an express or implied contract with the Army and Air Force Exchange Service, Navy Exchanges, Marine Corps Exchanges, Coast Guard Exchanges, or Exchange Councils of the National Aeronautics and Space Administration shall be considered an express or implied contract with the United States.

(2) To provide an entire remedy and to complete the relief afforded by the judgment, the court may, as an incident of and collateral to any such judgment, issue orders directing restoration to office or position, placement in appropriate duty or retirement status, and correction of applicable records, and such orders may be issued to any appropriate official of the United States. In any case within its jurisdiction, the court shall have the power to remand appropriate matters to any administrative or executive body or official with such direction as it may deem proper and just. The Court of Federal Claims shall have jurisdiction to render judgment upon any claim by or against, or dispute with, a contractor arising under section 10(a)(1) of the Contract Disputes Act of 1978, including a dispute concerning termination of a contract, rights in tangible or intangible property, compliance with cost accounting standards, and other nonmonetary disputes on which a decision of the contracting officer has been issued under section 6 of that Act.

(b)(1) Both the Unites[1] States Court of Federal Claims and the district courts of the United States shall have jurisdiction to render judgment on an action by an interested party objecting to a solicitation by a Federal agency for bids or proposals for a proposed contract or to a proposed award or the award of a contract or any alleged violation of statute or regulation in connection with a procurement or a proposed procurement. Both the United States Court of Federal Claims and the district courts of the United States shall have jurisdiction to entertain such an action without regard to whether suit is instituted before or after the contract is awarded.

(2) To afford relief in such an action, the courts may award any relief that the court considers proper, including declaratory and injunctive relief except that any monetary relief shall be limited to bid preparation and proposal costs.

(3) In exercising jurisdiction under this subsection, the courts shall give due regard to the interests of national defense and national security and the need for expeditious resolution of the action.

(4) In any action under this subsection, the courts shall review the agency's decision pursuant to the standards set forth in section 706 of title 5.

(5) If an interested party who is a member of the private sector commences an action described in paragraph (1) with respect to a public-private competition conducted under Office of Management and Budget Circular A–76 regarding the performance of an activity or function of a Federal agency, or a decision to convert a function performed by Federal employees to private sector performance without a competition under Office of Management and Budget Circular A–76, then an interested party described in section 3551(2)(B) of title 31 shall be entitled to intervene in that action.

(c) Nothing herein shall be construed to give the United States Court of Federal Claims jurisdiction of any civil action within the exclusive jurisdiction of the Court of International Trade, or of any action against, or founded on conduct of, the Tennessee Valley Authority, or to amend or modify the provisions of the Tennessee Valley Authority Act of 1933 with respect to actions by or against the Authority.

(June 25, 1948, c. 646, 62 Stat. 940; July 28, 1953, c. 253, § 7, 67 Stat. 226; Sept. 3, 1954, c. 1263, § 44(a), (b), 68 Stat. 1241; July 23, 1970, Pub.L. 91–350, § 1(b), 84 Stat. 449; Aug. 29, 1972, Pub.L. 92–415, § 1, 86 Stat. 652; Nov. 1, 1978, Pub.L. 95–563, § 14(i), 92 Stat. 2391; Oct. 10, 1980, Pub.L. 96–417, Title V, § 509, 94 Stat. 1743; Apr. 2, 1982, Pub.L. 97–164, Title I, § 133(a), 96 Stat. 39; Oct. 29, 1992, Pub.L. 102–572, Title IX, §§ 902(a), 907(b)(1), 106 Stat. 4516, 4519; Oct. 19, 1996, Pub.L. 104–320, § 12(a), 110 Stat. 3874; Dec. 26, 2007, Pub.L. 110–161, Div. D, Title VII, § 739(c)(2), 121 Stat. 2031; Jan. 28, 2008, Pub.L. 110–181, Div. A, Title III, § 326(c), 122 Stat. 63; Oct. 14, 2008, Pub.L. 110–417, Div. A, Title X, § 1061(d), 122 Stat. 4613.)

[1] So in original.

HISTORICAL AND STATUTORY NOTES

References in Text

The Contracts Disputes Act of 1978, referred to in subsec. (a)(2), is Pub.L. 95–563, Nov. 1, 1978, 92 Stat. 2383, which is classified principally to chapter 9 (section 601 et seq.) of Title 41, Public Contracts. Sections 6 and 10(a)(1) of such Act are classified to sections 605 and 609(a)(1), respectively, of Title 41. For complete classification of this Act to the Code, see Short Title note set out under section 601 of Title 41 and Tables.

The Tennessee Valley Authority Act of 1933, referred to in subsec. (c), is Act May 18, 1933, c. 32, 48 Stat. 58, as amended, which is classified generally to chapter 12A (section 831 et seq.) of Title 16, Conservation. For complete classification of this Act to the Code, see section 831 of Title 16 and Tables.

Effective and Applicability Provisions

2008 Acts. Pub.L. 110–181, Div. A, Title III, § 326(d), Jan. 28, 2008, 122 Stat. 63, provided that:

"Subparagraph (B) of section 3551(2) of title 31, United States Code (as added by subsection (a) [amending 31 U.S.C.A. § 3551]), and paragraph (5) of section 1491(b) of title 28, United States Code (as added by subsection (c) [enacting subsec. (b)(5) of this section]), shall apply to—

"(1) a protest or civil action that challenges final selection of the source of performance of an activity or function of a Federal agency that is made pursuant to a study initiated under Office of Management and Budget Circular A–76 on or after January 1, 2004; and

"(2) any other protest or civil action that relates to a public-private competition initiated under Office of Management and Budget Circular A–76, or to a decision to convert a function performed by Federal employees to private sector performance without a competition under Office of Management and Budget Circular A–76, on or after the date of the enactment of this Act [Jan. 28, 2008]."

2007 Acts. Amendments by Pub.L. 110–161, Div. D, § 739, applicable to protests and civil actions that challenge final selections of sources of performance of an activity or function of a Federal agency that are made pursuant to studies initiated under Office of Management and Budget Circular A–76 on or after Jan. 1, 2004; any other protests and civil actions that relate to public-private competitions initiated under Office of Management and Budget Circular A–76, or a decision to convert a function performed by Federal employees to private sector performance without a competition under Office of Management and Budget Circular A–76, on or after Dec. 26, 2007, see Pub.L. 110–161, Div. D, § 739(c)(3), set out as a note under 31 U.S.C.A. § 501.

Amendments made by Pub.L. 110–161, Div. D, § 739(c)(2), applicable with respect to fiscal year 2008 and each succeeding fiscal year, see Pub.L. 110–61, Div. D, § 739(e), set out as a note under 31 U.S.C.A. § 501.

1996 Acts. Section 12(b) of Pub.L. 104–320 provided that: "This section and the amendments made by this section [amending subsecs. (a)(3), (b), and (c) of this section] shall take effect on December 31, 1996 and shall apply to all actions filed on or after that date."

1992 Acts. Amendments by section 902(a) of Pub.L. 102–572 effective Oct. 29, 1992, see section 911 of Pub.L. 102–572, set out as a note under section 171 of this title.

Section 907(b)(2) of Pub.L. 102–572 provided that: "The amendment made by paragraph (1) [amending subsec. (a)(2) of this section] shall be effective with respect to all actions filed before, on, or after the date of the enactment of this Act [Oct. 29, 1992], except for those actions which, before such date of enactment, have been the subject of—

"(A) a final judgment of the United States Claims Court, if the time for appeal of that judgment has expired without an appeal having been filed, or

"(B) a final judgment of the Court of Appeals for the Federal Circuit."

1982 Acts. Amendment by Pub.L. 97–164 effective Oct. 1, 1982, see section 402 of Pub.L. 97–164, set out as a note under section 171 of this title.

1980 Acts. Amendment by Pub.L. 96–417 effective Nov. 1, 1980 and applicable with respect to civil actions pending on or commenced on or after such date, see section 701(a) of Pub.L. 96–417, as amended, set out as a note under section 251 of this title.

1978 Acts. Amendment by Pub.L. 95–563 effective with respect to contracts entered into 120 days after Nov. 1, 1978, and, at the election of the contractor, with respect to any claim pending at such time before the contracting officer or initiated thereafter, see section 16 of Pub.L. 95–563, set out as a note under section 601 of Title 41, Public Contracts.

1972 Acts. Section 2 of Pub.L. 92–415 provided that: "This Act [amending this section] shall be applicable to all judicial proceedings pending on or instituted after the date of its enactment [Aug. 29, 1972]."

1970 Acts. Amendment by Pub.L. 91–350 applicable to claims and civil actions dismissed before or pending on July 23, 1970, if the claim or civil action was based upon a transaction, omission, or breach that occurred not more than six years prior to July 23, 1970, notwithstanding a determination or judgment made prior to July 23, 1970, that the United States district courts or the United States Court of Claims did not have jurisdiction to entertain a suit on an express or implied contract with a nonappropriated fund instrumentality of the United States, see section 2 of Pub.L. 91–350, set out as a note under section 1346 of this title.

Transfer of Functions

For transfer of authorities, functions, personnel, and assets of the Coast Guard, including the authorities and functions of the Secretary of Transportation relating thereto, to the Department of Homeland Security, and for treatment of related references, see 6 U.S.C.A. §§ 468(b), 551(d), 552(d) and 557, and the Department of Homeland Security Reorganization Plan of November 25, 2002, as modified, set out as a note under 6 U.S.C.A. § 542.

Sunset Provisions

Section 12(d) of Pub.L. 104–320 provided that: "The jurisdiction of the district courts of the United States over the actions described in section 1491(b)(1) of title 28, United States Code [subsec. (b)(1) of this section] (as amended by subsection (a) of this section) shall terminate on January 1, 2001 unless extended by Congress. The savings provisions in subsection (e) [section 12(e) of Pub.L. 104–320, set out as a note under this section] shall apply if the bid protest jurisdiction of the district courts of the United States terminates under this subsection [this note]."

Savings Provisions

Section 12(e) of Pub.L. 104–320 provided that:

"**(1) Orders.**—A termination under subsection (d) [section 12(d) of Pub.L. 104–320, set out as a note under this section] shall not terminate the effectiveness of orders that have been issued by a court in connection with an action within the jurisdiction of that court on or before December 31, 2000. Such orders shall continue in effect according to their terms until modified, terminated, superseded, set aside, or revoked by a court of competent jurisdiction or by operation of law.

"**(2) Proceedings and applications.—(A)** a [sic] termination under subsection (d) shall not affect the jurisdiction of a court of the United States to continue with any proceeding that is pending before the court on December 31, 2000.

"**(B)** Orders may be issued in any such proceeding, appeals may be taken therefrom, and payments may be made pursuant to such orders, as if such termination had not occurred. An order issued in any such proceeding shall continue in effect until modified, terminated, superseded, set aside, or revoked by a court of competent jurisdiction or by operation of law.

"**(C)** Nothing in this paragraph prohibits the discontinuance or modification of any such proceeding under the same terms and conditions and to the same extent that proceeding could have been discontinued or modified absent such termination."

Study on Concurrent Jurisdiction

Section 12(c) of Pub.L. 104–320 provided that: "No earlier than 2 years after the effective date of this section [see section 12(b) of Pub.L. 104–320, set out as a note under this section], the United States General Accounting Office [now Government Accountability Office] shall undertake a study regarding the concurrent jurisdiction of the district courts of the United States and the Court of Federal Claims over bid protests to determine whether concurrent jurisdiction is necessary. Such a study shall be completed no later than December 31, 1999, and shall specifically consider the effect of any proposed change on the ability of small businesses to challenge violations of Federal procurement law."

§ 1492. Congressional reference cases

Any bill, except a bill for a pension, may be referred by either House of Congress to the chief judge of the United States Court of Federal Claims for a report in conformity with section 2509 of this title.

(June 25, 1948, c. 646, 62 Stat. 941; Oct. 15, 1966, Pub.L. 89–681, § 1, 80 Stat. 958; Apr. 2, 1982, Pub.L. 97–164, Title I, § 133(b), 96 Stat. 40; Oct. 29, 1992, Pub.L. 102–572, Title IX, § 902(a)(1), 106 Stat. 4516.)

HISTORICAL AND STATUTORY NOTES

Effective and Applicability Provisions

1992 Acts. Amendment by Title IX of Pub.L. 102–572 effective Oct. 29, 1992, see section 911 of Pub.L. 102–572, set out as a note under section 171 of this title.

1982 Acts. Amendment by Pub.L. 97–164 effective Oct. 1, 1982, see section 402 of Pub.L. 97–164, set out as a note under section 171 of this title.

[§ 1493. Repealed. July 28, 1953, c. 253, § 8, 67 Stat. 226]

HISTORICAL AND STATUTORY NOTES

Section, Act June 25, 1948, c. 646, 62 Stat. 941, authorized the Court of Claims to give legal advice to the heads of executive departments in matters referred to it by such heads, if the Court had jurisdiction over such matters.

§ 1494. Accounts of officers, agents or contractors

The United States Court of Federal Claims shall have jurisdiction to determine the amount, if any, due to or from the United States by reason of any unsettled account of any officer or agent of, or contractor with, the United States, or a guarantor, surety or personal representative of any such officer, agent or contractor, and to render judgment thereof,[1] where—

(1) claimant or the person he represents has applied to the proper department of the Government for settlement of the account;

(2) three years have elapsed from the date of such application without settlement; and

(3) no suit upon the same has been brought by the United States.

(June 25, 1948, c. 646, 62 Stat. 941; July 28, 1953, c. 253, § 9, 67 Stat. 226; Sept. 3, 1954, c. 1263, § 44(c), 68 Stat. 1242; Apr. 2, 1982, Pub.L. 97–164, Title I, § 133(c)(1), 96 Stat. 40; Oct. 29, 1992, Pub.L. 102–572, Title IX, § 902(a)(1), 106 Stat. 4516.)

[1] So in original. Probably should be "thereon".

HISTORICAL AND STATUTORY NOTES

Effective and Applicability Provisions

1992 Acts. Amendment by Title IX of Pub.L. 102–572 effective Oct. 29, 1992, see section 911 of Pub.L. 102–572, set out as a note under section 171 of this title.

1982 Acts. Amendment by Pub.L. 97–164 effective Oct. 1, 1982, see section 402 of Pub.L. 97–164, set out as a note under section 171 of this title.

§ 1495. Damages for unjust conviction and imprisonment; claim against United States

The United States Court of Federal Claims shall have jurisdiction to render judgment upon any claim for damages by any person unjustly convicted of an offense against the United States and imprisoned.

(June 25, 1948, c. 646, 62 Stat. 941; Apr. 2, 1982, Pub.L. 97–164, Title I, § 133(c) (1), 96 Stat. 40; Oct. 29, 1992, Pub.L. 102–572, Title IX, § 902(a)(1), 106 Stat. 4516.)

HISTORICAL AND STATUTORY NOTES

Effective and Applicability Provisions

1992 Acts. Amendment by Title IX of Pub.L. 102–572 effective Oct. 29, 1992, see section 911 of Pub.L. 102–572, set out as a note under section 171 of this title.

1982 Acts. Amendment by Pub.L. 97–164 effective Oct. 1, 1982, see section 402 of Pub.L. 97–164, set out as a note under section 171 of this title.

§ 1496. Disbursing officers' claims

The United States Court of Federal Claims shall have jurisdiction to render judgment upon any claim by a disbursing officer of the United States or by his administrator or executor for relief from responsibility for loss, in line of duty, of Government funds, vouchers, records or other papers in his charge.

(June 25, 1948, c. 646, 62 Stat. 941; Apr. 2, 1982, Pub.L. 97–164, Title I, § 133(c)(1), 96 Stat. 40; Oct. 29, 1992, Pub.L. 102–572, Title IX, § 902(a)(1), 106 Stat. 4516.)

HISTORICAL AND STATUTORY NOTES

Effective and Applicability Provisions

1992 Acts. Amendment by Title IX of Pub.L. 102–572 effective Oct. 29, 1992, see section 911 of Pub.L. 102–572, set out as a note under section 171 of this title.

1982 Acts. Amendment by Pub.L. 97–164 effective Oct. 1, 1982, see section 402 of Pub.L. 97–164, set out as a note under section 171 of this title.

§ 1497. Oyster growers' damages from dredging operations

The United States Court of Federal Claims shall have jurisdiction to render judgment upon any claim for damages to oyster growers on private or leased lands or bottoms arising from dredging operations or use of other machinery and equipment in making river and harbor improvements authorized by Act of Congress.

(June 25, 1948, c. 646, 62 Stat. 941; Apr. 2, 1982, Pub.L. 97–164, Title I, § 133(c), 96 Stat. 40; Oct. 29, 1992, Pub.L. 102–572, Title IX, § 902(a)(1), 106 Stat. 4516.)

HISTORICAL AND STATUTORY NOTES

Effective and Applicability Provisions

1992 Acts. Amendment by Title IX of Pub.L. 102–572 effective Oct. 29, 1992, see section 911 of Pub.L. 102–572, set out as a note under section 171 of this title.

1982 Acts. Amendment by Pub.L. 97–164 effective Oct. 1, 1982, see section 402 of Pub.L. 97–164, set out as a note under section 171 of this title.

§ 1498. Patent and copyright cases

(a) Whenever an invention described in and covered by a patent of the United States is used or manufactured by or for the United States without license of the owner thereof or lawful right to use or manufacture the same, the owner's remedy shall be by action against the United States in the United States Court of Federal Claims for the recovery of his reasonable and entire compensation for such use and manufacture. Reasonable and entire compensation shall include the owner's reasonable costs, including reasonable fees for expert witnesses and attorneys, in pursuing the action if the owner is an independent inventor, a nonprofit organization, or an entity that had no more than 500 employees at any time during the 5–year period preceding the use or manufacture of the patented invention by or for the United States. Nothwithstanding[1] the preceding sentences, unless the action has been pending for more than 10 years from the time of filing to the time that the owner applies for such costs and fees, reasonable and entire compensation shall not include such costs and fees if the court finds that the position of the United States was substantially justified or that special circumstances make an award unjust.

For the purposes of this section, the use or manufacture of an invention described in and covered by a patent of the United States by a contractor, a subcontractor, or any person, firm, or corporation for the Government and with the authorization or consent of the Government, shall be construed as use or manufacture for the United States.

The court shall not award compensation under this section if the claim is based on the use or manufacture by or for the United States of any article owned, leased, used by, or in the possession of the United States prior to July 1, 1918.

A Government employee shall have the right to bring suit against the Government under this section except where he was in a position to order, influence, or induce use of the invention by the Government. This section shall not confer a right of action on any patentee or any assignee of such patentee with respect to any invention discovered or invented by a person while in the employment or service of the United States, where the invention was related to the official functions of the employee, in cases in which such functions included research and development, or in the making of which Government time, materials or facilities were used.

(b) Hereafter, whenever the copyright in any work protected under the copyright laws of the United States shall be infringed by the United States, by a corporation owned or controlled by the United States, or by a contractor, subcontractor, or any person, firm, or corporation acting for the Government and with the authorization or consent of the Government, the exclusive action which may be brought for such infringement shall be an action by the copyright owner against the United States in the Court of Federal Claims for the recovery of his reasonable and entire compensation as damages for such infringement, including the minimum statutory damages as set forth in section 504(c) of title 17, United States Code: *Provided*, That a Government employee shall have a right of action against the Government under this subsection except where he was in a position to order, influence, or induce use of the copyrighted work by the Government: *Provided, however*, That this subsection shall not confer a right of action on any copyright owner or any assignee of such owner with respect to any copyrighted work prepared by a person while in the employment or service of the United States, where the copyrighted work was prepared as a part of the official functions of the employee, or in the preparation of which Government time, material, or facilities were used: *And provided further*, That before such action against the United States has been instituted the appropriate corporation owned or controlled by the United States or the head of the appropriate department or agency of the Government, as the case may be, is authorized to enter into an agreement with the copyright owner in full settlement and compromise for the damages accruing to him by reason of such infringement and to settle the claim administratively out of available appropriations.

Except as otherwise provided by law, no recovery shall be had for any infringement of a copyright covered by this subsection committed more than three years prior to the filing of the complaint or counterclaim for infringement in the action, except that the period between the date of receipt of a written claim for compensation by the Department or agency of the Government or corporation owned or controlled by the United States, as the case may be, having authority to settle such claim and the date of mailing by the Government of a notice to the claimant that his claim has been denied shall not be counted as a part of the three years, unless suit is brought before the last-mentioned date.

(c) The provisions of this section shall not apply to any claim arising in a foreign country.

(d) Hereafter, whenever a plant variety protected by a certificate of plant variety protection under the laws of the United States shall be infringed by the United States, by a corporation owned or controlled by the United States, or by a contractor, subcontractor, or any person, firm, or corporation acting for the Government, and with the authorization and consent of the Government, the exclusive remedy of the owner of such certificate shall be by action against the United States in the Court of Federal Claims for the recovery of his reasonable and entire compensation as damages for such infringement: *Provided*, That a Government employee shall have a right of action against the Government under this subsection except where he was in a position to order, influence, or induce use of the protected plant variety by the Government: *Provided, however*, That this subsection shall not confer a right of action on any certificate owner or any assignee of such owner with respect to any protected plant variety made by a person while in the employment or service of the United States, where such variety was prepared as a part of the official functions of the employee, or in the preparation of which Government time, material, or facilities were used: *And provided further*, That before such action against the United States has been instituted, the appropriate corporation owned or controlled by the United States or the head of the appropriate agency of the Government, as the case may be, is authorized to enter into an agreement with the certificate owner in full settlement and compromise, for the damages accrued to him by reason of such infringement and to settle the claim administratively out of available appropriations.

(e) Subsections (b) and (c) of this section apply to exclusive rights in mask works under chapter 9 of title 17, and to exclusive rights in designs under chapter 13 of title 17 [17 U.S.C.A. § 1301 et seq.], to the same extent as such subsections apply to copyrights.

(June 25, 1948, c. 646, 62 Stat. 941; May 24, 1949, c. 139, § 87, 63 Stat. 102; Oct. 31, 1951, c. 655, § 50(c), 65 Stat. 727; July 17, 1952, c. 930, 66 Stat. 757; Sept. 8, 1960, Pub.L. 86–726, §§ 1, 4, 74 Stat. 855, 856; Dec. 24, 1970, Pub.L. 91–577, Title III, § 143(d), 84 Stat. 1559; Oct. 19, 1976, Pub.L. 94–553, Title I, § 105(c), 90 Stat. 2599; Apr. 2, 1982, Pub.L. 97–164, Title I, § 133(d), 96 Stat. 40; Nov. 19, 1988, Pub.L. 100–702, Title X, § 1020(a)(6), 102 Stat. 4671; Oct. 29, 1992, Pub.L. 102–572, Title IX, § 902(a), 106 Stat. 4516; Oct. 19, 1996, Pub.L. 104–308, § 1(a), 110 Stat. 3814; Dec. 16, 1997, Pub.L. 105–147, § 3, 111 Stat. 2680; Oct. 28, 1998, Pub.L. 105–304, Title V, § 503(d), 112 Stat. 2917.)

[1] So in original. Probably should be "Notwithstanding".

HISTORICAL AND STATUTORY NOTES

References in Text

Hereafter, referred to in subsec. (b), probably means the date of enactment of Pub. L. 86–726 [which, among other changes, added subsec. (b)], which was approved on Sept. 8, 1960.

The copyright laws of the United States, referred to in subsec. (b), are classified generally to Title 17, Copyrights.

The "hereafter" set out at the beginning of subsec. (d) probably means after Dec. 24, 1970, the date of enactment of Pub.L. 91–577 which added subsec. (d).

Effective and Applicability Provisions

1998 Acts. Amendment by Pub.L. 105–304, effective Oct. 28, 1998, see section 505 of Pub.L. 105–304, set out as a note under section 1301 of Title 17, Copyrights.

1996 Acts. Section 1(b) of Pub.L. 104–308 provided that: "The amendment made by subsection (a) [amending subsec. (a) of this section] shall apply to actions under section 1498(a) of title 28, United States Code [subsec. (a) of this section], that are pending on, or brought on or after, the date of the enactment of this Act [Oct. 19, 1996]."

1992 Acts. Amendments by Title IX of Pub.L. 102–572 effective Oct. 29, 1992, see section 911 of Pub.L. 102–572, set out as a note under section 171 of Title 28, Judiciary and Judiciary Procedure.

1982 Acts. Amendment by Pub.L. 97–164 effective Oct. 1, 1982, see section 402 of Pub.L. 97–164, set out as a note under section 171 of this title.

1976 Acts. Amendment by Pub.L. 94–553 effective Jan. 1, 1978, see section 102 of Pub.L. 94–553, set out as a note preceding section 101 of Title 17, Copyrights.

1970 Acts. Amendment by Pub.L. 91–577 effective Dec. 24, 1970, see section 141 of Pub.L. 91–577, set out as a note under section 2321 of Title 7, Agriculture.

Waiver of Immunity for Members of Congress

Section 2 of Pub.L. 86–726 provided that: "Nothing in this Act [amending this section and section 2386 of Title 10, Armed Forces] shall be construed to in any way waive any immunity provided for Members of Congress under article I of section 6 of the Constitution of the United States."

§ 1499. Liquidated damages withheld from contractors under chapter 37 of title 40

The United States Court of Federal Claims shall have jurisdiction to render judgment upon any claim for liquidated damages withheld from a contractor or subcontractor under section 3703 of title 40.

(June 25, 1948, c. 646, 62 Stat. 942; Aug. 13, 1962, Pub.L. 87–581, Title II, § 202(a), 76 Stat. 360; Apr. 2, 1982, Pub.L. 97–164, Title I, § 133(e) (1), (2) (A), 96 Stat. 40, 41; Dec. 1, 1990, Pub.L. 101–650, Title III, § 325(b)(7), 104 Stat. 5121; Oct. 29, 1992, Pub.L. 102–572, Title IX, § 902(a)(1), 106 Stat. 4516; Aug. 21, 2002, Pub.L. 107–217, § 3(g)(3), 116 Stat. 1299; Sept. 27, 2006, Pub.L. 109–284, § 4(2), 120 Stat. 1211.)

HISTORICAL AND STATUTORY NOTES

References in Text

Chapter 37 of Title 40, referred to in the section heading, is Contract Work Hours and Safety Standards, 40 U.S.C.A. § 3701 et seq.

Effective and Applicability Provisions

1992 Acts. Amendment by Title IX of Pub.L. 102–572 effective Oct. 29, 1992, see section 911 of Pub.L. 102–572, set out as a note under section 171 of Title 28, Judiciary and Judicial Procedure.

1982 Acts. Amendment by Pub.L. 97–164 effective Oct. 1, 1982, see section 402 of Pub.L. 97–164, set out as a note under section 171 of this title.

1962 Acts. Amendment of section by Pub.L. 87–581 effective 60 days after Aug. 13, 1962, but shall not affect contracts existing or thereafter entered into pursuant to invitations for bids outstanding on Aug. 13, 1962, see section 204 of Pub.L. 87–581, set out as a note under section 327 of former Title 40, Public Buildings, Property and Works.

Continued Jurisdiction Upon Claims Under Section 324 of Title 40

Pub.L. 87–581, Title II, § 202(a), Aug. 13, 1962, 76 Stat. 360 provided that: "The Court of Claims [now Court of Federal Claims] shall continue to have jurisdiction to render judgment upon any claim for a penalty withheld from a contractor or subcontractor under section 324 of title 40, United States Code [repealed], in connection with any contract subject to said section existing on the effective date of this Act [60 days after Aug. 13, 1962; see Pub.L. 87–581, Title II, § 204, Aug. 13, 1962, 76 Stat. 360, repealed Pub.L. 107–217, § 6(b), Aug. 21, 2002, 116 Stat. 1316], or thereafter entered into pursuant to invitations for bids that are outstanding at the time of the enactment of this Act [Aug. 13, 1962]."

§ 1500. Pendency of claims in other courts

The United States Court of Federal Claims shall not have jurisdiction of any claim for or in respect to which the plaintiff or his assignee has pending in any other court any suit or process against the United States or any person who, at the time when the cause of action alleged in such suit or process arose, was, in respect thereto, acting or professing to act, directly or indirectly under the authority of the United States.

(June 25, 1948, c. 646, 62 Stat. 942; Apr. 2, 1982, Pub.L. 97–164, Title I, § 133(e) (1), 96 Stat. 40; Oct. 29, 1992, Pub.L. 102–572, Title IX, § 902(a)(1), 106 Stat. 4516.)

HISTORICAL AND STATUTORY NOTES

Effective and Applicability Provisions

1992 Acts. Amendment by Title IX of Pub.L. 102–572 effective Oct. 29, 1992, see section 911 of Pub.L. 102–572 , set out as a note under section 171 of this title.

1982 Acts. Amendment by Pub.L. 97–164 effective Oct. 1, 1982, see section 402 of Pub.L. 97–164, set out as a note under section 171 of this title.

§ 1501. Pensions

The United States Court of Federal Claims shall not have jurisdiction of any claim for a pension.

(June 25, 1948, c. 646, 62 Stat. 942; Apr. 2, 1982, Pub.L. 97–164, Title I, § 133(e) (1), 96 Stat. 40; Oct. 29, 1992, Pub.L. 102–572, Title IX, § 902(a)(1), 106 Stat. 4516.)

HISTORICAL AND STATUTORY NOTES

Effective and Applicability Provisions

1992 Acts. Amendment by Title IX of Pub.L. 102–572 effective Oct. 29, 1992, see section 911 of Pub.L. 102–572, set out as a note under section 171 of this title.

1982 Acts. Amendment by Pub.L. 97–164 effective Oct. 1, 1982, see section 402 of Pub.L. 97–164, set out as a note under section 171 of this title.

§ 1502. Treaty cases

Except as otherwise provided by Act of Congress, the United States Court of Federal Claims shall not have jurisdiction of any claim against the United States growing out of or dependent upon any treaty entered into with foreign nations.

(June 25, 1948, c. 646, 62 Stat. 942; May 24, 1949, c. 139, § 88, 63 Stat. 102; Apr. 2, 1982, Pub.L. 97–164, Title I, § 133(e) (1), 96 Stat. 40; Oct. 29, 1992, Pub.L. 102–572, Title IX, § 902(a)(1), 106 Stat. 4516.)

HISTORICAL AND STATUTORY NOTES

Effective and Applicability Provisions

1992 Acts. Amendment by Title IX of Pub.L. 102–572 effective Oct. 29, 1992, see section 911 of Pub.L. 102–572, set out as a note under section 171 of this title.

1982 Acts. Amendment by Pub.L. 97–164 effective Oct. 1, 1982, see section 402 of Pub.L. 97–164, set out as a note under section 171 of this title.

§ 1503. Set-offs

The United States Court of Federal Claims shall have jurisdiction to render judgment upon any set-off or demand by the United States against any plaintiff in such court.

(June 25, 1948, c. 646, 62 Stat. 942; Apr. 2, 1982, Pub.L. 97–164, Title I, § 133(e) (1), 96 Stat. 40; Oct. 29, 1992, Pub.L. 102–572, Title IX, § 902(a)(1), 106 Stat. 4516.)

HISTORICAL AND STATUTORY NOTES

Effective and Applicability Provisions

1992 Acts. Amendment by Title IX of Pub.L. 102–572 effective Oct. 29, 1992, see section 911 of Pub.L. 102–572, set out as a note under section 171 of this title.

1982 Acts. Amendment by Pub.L. 97–164 effective Oct. 1, 1982, see section 402 of Pub.L. 97–164, set out as a note under section 171 of this title.

[§ 1504. Repealed. Pub.L. 97–164, Title I, § 133(f), Apr. 2, 1982, 96 Stat. 41]

HISTORICAL AND STATUTORY NOTES

Section, Act June 25, 1948, c. 646, 62 Stat. 942, directed that the Court of Claims [now Court of Federal Claims] have jurisdiction to review by appeal final judgments in the district courts in civil actions based on tort claims brought under section 1346(b) of this title if the notice of appeal filed in the district court had affixed to it a written consent on behalf of the appellees that the appeal be taken to the Court of Claims.

Effective Date of Repeal

Repeal effective Oct. 1, 1982, see section 402 of Pub.L. 97–164, set out as an Effective and Applicability Provisions of 1982 Amendments note under section 171 of this title.

§ 1505. Indian claims

The United States Court of Federal Claims shall have jurisdiction of any claim against the United States accruing after August 13, 1946, in favor of any tribe, band, or other identifiable group of American Indians residing within the territorial limits of the United States or Alaska whenever such claim is one arising under the Constitution, laws or treaties of the United States, or Executive orders of the President, or is one which otherwise would be cognizable in the Court of Federal Claims if the claimant were not an Indian tribe, band or group.

(Added May 24, 1949, c. 139, § 89(a), 63 Stat. 102, and amended Apr. 2, 1982, Pub.L. 97–164, Title I, § 133(g), 96 Stat. 41; Oct. 29, 1992, Pub.L. 102–572, Title IX, § 902(a), 106 Stat. 4516.)

HISTORICAL AND STATUTORY NOTES

Effective and Applicability Provisions

1992 Acts. Amendment by Title IX of Pub.L. 102–572 effective Oct. 29, 1992, see section 911 of Pub.L. 102–572, set out as a note under section 171 of this title.

1982 Acts. Amendment by Pub.L. 97–164 effective Oct. 1, 1982, see section 402 of Pub.L. 97–164, set out as a note under section 171 of this title.

[§ 1506. Repealed. Pub.L. 97–164, Title I, § 133(h), Apr. 2, 1982, 96 Stat. 41]

HISTORICAL AND STATUTORY NOTES

Section, added Pub.L. 86–770, § 2(a), Sept. 13, 1960, 74 Stat. 912, provided that if a case within the exclusive jurisdiction of the district courts was filed in the Court of Claims [now Court of Federal Claims], the Court of Claims, if it were in the interest of justice, had to transfer such case to any district court in which it could have been brought at the time such case was filed, where the case would proceed as if it had been filed in the district court on the date it was filed in the Court of Claims.

Effective Date of Repeal

Repeal effective Oct. 1, 1982, see section 402 of Pub.L. 97–164, set out as a note under section 171 of this title.

§ 1507. Jurisdiction for certain declaratory judgments

The United States Court of Federal Claims shall have jurisdiction to hear any suit for and issue a declaratory judgment under section 7428 of the Internal Revenue Code of 1986.

(Added Pub.L. 94–455, Title XIII, § 1306(b)(9)(A), Oct. 4, 1976, 90 Stat. 1720, and amended Pub.L. 97–164, Title I, § 133(i), Apr. 2, 1982, 96 Stat. 41; Pub.L. 99–514, § 2, Oct. 22, 1986, 100 Stat. 2095; Pub.L. 102–572, Title IX, § 902(a)(1), Oct. 29, 1992, 106 Stat. 4516.)

HISTORICAL AND STATUTORY NOTES

References in Text

Section 7428 of the Internal Revenue Code of 1986, referred to in text, is classified to section 7428 of Title 26, Internal Revenue Code.

Effective and Applicability Provisions

1992 Acts. Amendment by Title IX of Pub.L. 102–572 effective Oct. 29, 1992, see section 911 of Pub.L. 102–572, set out as a note under section 171 of this title.

1982 Acts. Amendment by Pub.L. 97–164 effective Oct. 1, 1982, see section 402 of Pub.L. 97–164, set out as a note under section 171 of this title.

1976 Acts. Section applicable with respect to pleadings filed with the United States Tax Court, the district court of the United States for the District of Columbia, or the United States Court of Claims more than 6 months after Oct. 4, 1976, but only with respect to determinations (or requests for determinations) made after Jan. 1, 1976, see section 1306(c) of Pub.L. 94–455, set out as a note under section 7428 of Title 26, Internal Revenue Code.

§ 1508. Jurisdiction for certain partnership proceedings

The Court of Federal Claims shall have jurisdiction to hear and to render judgment upon any petition under section 6226 or 6228(a) of the Internal Revenue Code of 1986.

(Added Pub.L. 97–248, Title IV, § 402(c)(18)(A), Sept. 3, 1982, 96 Stat. 669, and amended Pub.L. 99–514, § 2, Oct. 22, 1986, 100 Stat. 2095; Pub.L. 102–572, Title IX, § 902(a)(2), Oct. 29, 1992, 106 Stat. 4516.)

HISTORICAL AND STATUTORY NOTES

References in Text

Sections 6226 and 6228(a) of the Internal Revenue Code of 1986, referred to in text, are classified to sections 6226 and 6228(a) of Title 26, Internal Revenue Code.

Effective and Applicability Provisions

1992 Acts. Amendment by Title IX of Pub.L. 102–572 effective Oct. 29, 1992, see section 911 of Pub.L. 102–572, set out as a note under section 171 of this title.

1982 Acts. Section applicable to partnership taxable years beginning after Sept. 3, 1982, with provision for the applicability of this section to any partnership taxable year ending after Sept. 3, 1982, if the partnership, each partner, and each indirect partner requests such application and the Secretary of the Treasury or his delegate consents to such application, see section 407(a) (1) and (3) of Pub.L. 97–248, set out as a note under section 6221 of Title 26, Internal Revenue Code.

§ 1509. No jurisdiction in cases involving refunds of tax shelter promoter and understatement penalties

The United States Court of Federal Claims shall not have jurisdiction to hear any action or proceeding for any refund or credit of any penalty imposed under section 6700 of the Internal Revenue Code of 1986 (relating to penalty for promoting abusive tax shelters, etc.) or section 6701 of such Code (relating to penalties for aiding and abetting understatement of tax liability).

(Added Pub.L. 98–369, Div. A, Title VII, § 714(g)(2), July 18, 1984, 98 Stat. 962, and amended Pub.L. 99–514, § 2, Oct. 22, 1986, 100 Stat. 2095; Pub.L. 102–572, Title IX, § 902(a)(1), Oct. 29, 1992, 106 Stat. 4516.)

HISTORICAL AND STATUTORY NOTES

References in Text

Sections 6700 and 6701 of the Internal Revenue Code of 1986, referred to in text, are classified to sections 6700 and 6701, respectively, of Title 26, Internal Revenue Code.

Effective and Applicability Provisions

1992 Acts. Amendment by Title IX of Pub.L. 102–572 effective Oct. 29, 1992, see section 911 of Pub.L. 102–572, set out as a note under section 171 of this title.

1984 Acts. Section 714(g)(4) of Pub.L. 98–369 provided that: "The amendments made by this subsection [enacting this section and amending section 7422 of Title 26, Internal Revenue Code] shall apply to any claim for refund or credit filed after the date of the enactment of this Act [July 18, 1984]."

[CHAPTER 93—REPEALED]

[§§ 1541 to 1546. Repealed. Pub.L. 97–164, Title I, § 134, Apr. 2, 1982, 96 Stat. 41]

HISTORICAL AND STATUTORY NOTES

Section 1541, Acts June 25, 1948, c. 646, 62 Stat. 942; June 2, 1970, Pub.L. 91–271, Title I, § 102, 84 Stat. 274; July 26, 1979, Pub.L. 96–39, Title X, § 1001(b) (4) (A), 93 Stat. 305; Oct. 10, 1980, Pub.L. 96–417, Title IV, § 401(a), Title V, § 501(23), (24), 94 Stat. 1740, 1742, gave the Court of Customs and Patent Appeals exclusive jurisdiction of appeals from all final decisions of the Court of International Trade and from interlocutory orders of the Court of International Trade granting, continuing, modifying, refusing, or dissolving injunctions, or refusing to dissolve or modify injunctions, and with discretion to entertain appeals from certain orders of the Court of International Trade. See section 1295(a) (5) of this title.

Section 1542, Acts June 25, 1948, c. 646, 62 Stat. 942; May 24, 1949, c. 139, § 89(b), 63 Stat. 102, gave the Court of Customs and Patent Appeals jurisdiction of appeals from decisions of the Board of Appeals and the Board of Interference Examiners of the Patent Office as to patent applications and interferences, at the instance of an applicant for a patent or any party to a patent interference, with such appeal by an applicant to waive his right to proceed under section 63 of Title 35, and the Commissioner of Patents as to trade-mark applications and proceedings as provided in section 1071 of Title 15. See section 1295(a) (4) of this title.

Section 1543, Acts June 25, 1948, c. 646, 62 Stat. 943; Oct. 10, 1980, Pub.L. 96–417, Title IV, § 401(b) (1), 94 Stat. 1740, gave the Court of Customs and Patent Appeals jurisdiction to review final determinations of the United States International Trade Commission made under section 337 of the Tariff Act of 1930 relating to unfair trade practices in import trade. See section 1295(a) (6) of this title.

Section 1544, added Pub.L. 89–651, § 8(c)(1), Oct. 14, 1966, 80 Stat. 901, gave the Court of Customs and Patent Appeals jurisdiction to review, by appeal on questions of law only, findings of the Secretary of Commerce under headnote 6 to schedule 8, part 4, of the Tariff Schedules of the United States (relating to importation of instruments or apparatus). See section 1295(a)(7) of this title.

Section 1545, added Pub.L. 91–577, Title III, § 143(a), Dec. 24, 1970, 84 Stat. 1558, gave the Court of Customs and Patent Appeals nonexclusive jurisdiction of appeals under section 71 of the Plant Variety Protection Act, classified to section 2461 of Title 7, Agriculture. See section 1295(a)(8) of this title.

Section 1546, added Pub.L. 96–417, Title IV, § 402(a), Oct. 10, 1980, 94 Stat. 1740, gave the Court of Customs and Patent Appeals all of the powers in law and in equity of, or conferred by statute upon, a court of appeals of the United States.

Effective Date of Repeal

Repeal effective Oct. 1, 1982, see section 402 of Pub.L. 97–164, set out as a note under section 171 of this title.

CHAPTER 95—COURT OF INTERNATIONAL TRADE

Sec.
1581. Civil actions against the United States and agencies and officers thereof.
1582. Civil actions commenced by the United States.
1583. Counterclaims, cross-claims, and third-party actions.
1584. Civil actions under the North American Free Trade Agreement or the United States–Canada Free-Trade Agreement.
1585. Powers in law and equity.

HISTORICAL AND STATUTORY NOTES

Prior Provisions

A prior Chapter 95—Customs Court, comprising sections 1581 and 1582, was omitted from the Code upon the general revision of this chapter by Pub.L. 96–417, Title II, § 201, Oct. 10, 1980, 94 Stat. 1728.

§ 1581. Civil actions against the United States and agencies and officers thereof

(a) The Court of International Trade shall have exclusive jurisdiction of any civil action commenced to contest the denial of a protest, in whole or in part, under section 515 of the Tariff Act of 1930.

(b) The Court of International Trade shall have exclusive jurisdiction of any civil action commenced under section 516 of the Tariff Act of 1930.

(c) The Court of International Trade shall have exclusive jurisdiction of any civil action commenced under section 516A of the Tariff Act of 1930.

(d) The Court of International Trade shall have exclusive jurisdiction of any civil action commenced to review—

(1) any final determination of the Secretary of Labor under section 223 of the Trade Act of 1974 with respect to the eligibility of workers for adjustment assistance under such Act;

(2) any final determination of the Secretary of Commerce under section 251 of the Trade Act of 1974 with respect to the eligibility of a firm for adjustment assistance under such Act; and

(3) any final determination of the Secretary of Commerce under section 271 of the Trade Act of 1974 with respect to the eligibility of a community for adjustment assistance under such Act.

(e) The Court of International Trade shall have exclusive jurisdiction of any civil action commenced to review any final determination of the Secretary of the Treasury under section 305(b)(1) of the Trade Agreements Act of 1979.

(f) The Court of International Trade shall have exclusive jurisdiction of any civil action involving an application for an order directing the administering authority or the International Trade Commission to make confidential information available under section 777(c)(2) of the Tariff Act of 1930.

(g) The Court of International Trade shall have exclusive jurisdiction of any civil action commenced to review—

(1) any decision of the Secretary of the Treasury to deny a customs broker's license under section 641(b)(2) or (3) of the Tariff Act of 1930, or to deny a customs broker's permit under section 641(c)(1) of such Act, or to revoke a license or permit under section 641(b)(5) or (c)(2) of such Act;

(2) any decision of the Secretary of the Treasury to revoke or suspend a customs broker's license or permit, or impose a monetary penalty in lieu thereof, under section 641(d)(2)(B) of the Tariff Act of 1930; and

(3) any decision or order of the Customs Service to deny, suspend, or revoke accreditation of a private laboratory under section 499(b) of the Tariff Act of 1930.

(h) The Court of International Trade shall have exclusive jurisdiction of any civil action commenced to review, prior to the importation of the goods involved, a ruling issued by the Secretary of the Treasury, or a refusal to issue or change such a ruling, relating to classification, valuation, rate of duty, marking, restricted merchandise, entry requirements, drawbacks, vessel repairs, or similar matters, but only if the party commencing the civil action demonstrates to the court that he would be irreparably harmed unless given an opportunity to obtain judicial review prior to such importation.

(i) In addition to the jurisdiction conferred upon the Court of International Trade by subsections (a)–(h) of this section and subject to the exception set forth in subsection (j) of this section, the Court of International Trade shall have exclusive jurisdiction of any civil action commenced against the United States, its agencies, or its officers, that arises out of any law of the United States providing for—

(1) revenue from imports or tonnage;

(2) tariffs, duties, fees, or other taxes on the importation of merchandise for reasons other than the raising of revenue;

(3) embargoes or other quantitative restrictions on the importation of merchandise for reasons other than the protection of the public health or safety; or

(4) administration and enforcement with respect to the matters referred to in paragraphs (1)–(3) of this subsection and subsections (a)–(h) of this section.

This subsection shall not confer jurisdiction over an antidumping or countervailing duty determination which is reviewable either by the Court of International Trade under section 516A(a) of the Tariff Act of 1930 or by a binational panel under article 1904 of the North American Free Trade Agreement or the United States–Canada Free–Trade Agreement and section 516A(g) of the Tariff Act of 1930.

(j) The Court of International Trade shall not have jurisdiction of any civil action arising under section 305 of the Tariff Act of 1930.

(Added Pub.L. 96–417, Title II, § 201, Oct. 10, 1980, 94 Stat. 1728, and amended Pub.L. 98–573, Title II, § 212(b)(1), Oct. 30, 1984, 98 Stat. 2983; Pub.L. 99–514, Title XVIII, § 1891(1), Oct. 22, 1986, 100 Stat. 2926; Pub.L. 100–449, Title IV, § 402(a), Sept. 28, 1988, 102 Stat. 1883; Pub.L. 103–182, Title IV, § 414(a)(1), Title VI, § 684(a)(1), Dec. 8, 1993, 107 Stat. 2147, 2219.)

Termination of Amendments

For provisions directing that, except for transition provisions relating to proceedings regarding protective orders and undertakings, and binational panel and extraordinary challenge committee reviews, the amendment to this section by Title IV of Pub.L. 103–182 shall cease to have effect with respect to any country on the date on which such country ceases to be a NAFTA country, see 19 U.S.C.A. § 3451.

Termination of United States–Canada Free–Trade Agreement

For provisions directing that the amendments made by Pub.L. 100–449, which amended this section, shall cease to have effect on the date on which the United States–Canada Free–Trade Agreement ceases to be in force, see section 501(c) of Pub.L. 100–449, set out in the note under 19 U.S.C.A. § 2112.

Articles 1906 and 2106 of the Agreement authorize either the United States or Canada to terminate the Agreement on 6–month notice if, at the end of the 7–year period following the date of the entry into effect of the Agreement, no agreement has been entered into between the United States and Canada on a substitute system of antidumping and countervailing duties.

HISTORICAL AND STATUTORY NOTES

References in Text

Sections 515 and 516 of the Tariff Act of 1930, referred to in subsecs. (a) and (b), respectively, are classified, respectively, to sections 1515 and 1516 of Title 19, Customs Duties.

The Trade Act of 1974, referred to in subsec. (d)(1) to (3), is Pub.L. 93–618, Jan. 3, 1975, 88 Stat.1978, as amended, which is classified principally to chapter 12 (section 2101 et seq.) of Title 19. Sections 223, 251, and 271 of the Trade Act of 1974 are classified to sections 2273, 2341, and 2371, respectively, of Title 19. For complete classification of this Act to the Code, see References in Text note set out under section 2101 of Title 19 and Tables.

Section 305(b)(1) of the Trade Agreements Act of 1979, referred to in subsec. (e), is classified to section 2515(b)(1) of Title 19, Customs Duties.

Sections 777(c)(2), 641(b), (c), (d), and 305 of the Tariff Act of 1930, referred to in subsecs. (f), (g), and (j), are classified to sections 1677f(c)(2), 1641, (b), (c), (d), and 1305, respectively, of Title 19, Customs Duties.

Section 499(b) of the Tariff Act of 1930, referred to in subsec. (g)(3), is classified to section 1499(b) of Title 19, Customs Duties.

Section 516A of the Tariff Act of 1930, referred to in subsec. (i), is classified to section 1516a of Title 19.

The United States–Canada Free–Trade Agreement, referred to in subsec. (i), was entered into on Jan. 2, 1988. The Agreement is not set out in the Code.

Effective and Applicability Provisions

1993 Acts. Amendment by section 414 of Pub.L. 103–182 effective on the date the North American Free Trade Agreement enters into force with respect to the United States [Jan. 1, 1994], but not to apply to any final determination described in section 1516a(a)(1)(B) or (2)(B)(i), (ii), or (iii) of Title 19, Customs Duties, notice of which is published in the Federal Register before such date, or to a determination described in section 1516a(a)(2)(B)(vi) of Title 19 notice of which is received by the Government of Canada or Mexico before such date, or to any binational panel review under the United States-Canada Free-Trade Agreement, or to any extraordinary challenge arising out of any such review that was commenced before such date, see section 416 of Pub.L. 103–182, set out as a note under section 3431 of Title 19.

Amendment by section 684(a)(1) of Pub.L. 103–182 effective Dec. 8, 1993, see section 692 of Pub.L. 103–182, set out as a note under section 58c of Title 19, Customs Duties.

1988 Acts. Amendment by Pub.L. 100–449 effective on the date the United States–Canada Free–Trade Agreement enters into force, (Jan. 1, 1989), and to cease to have effect on the date the Agreement ceases to be in force, see section 501(a), (c) of Pub.L. 100–449, set out in a note under section 2112 of Title 19, Customs Duties. [A Presidential Memorandum on the Canada–United States Free–Trade Agreement, dated Dec. 31, 1988, directing the Secretary of State to exchange notes with the Government of Canada to provide for the entry into force of the Agreement on Jan. 1, 1989, is set out in 24 Weekly Compilation of Presidential Documents 1688, Jan. 2, 1989.]

1984 Acts. Amendment by Pub.L. 98–573 to take effect on the close of the 180th day after Oct. 30, 1984, see section 214(d) of Pub.L. 98–573, set out as a note under section 1304 of Title 19, Customs Duties.

1980 Acts. Section effective on Nov. 1, 1980, and applicable with respect to civil actions pending on or commenced on or after such date, see section 701(a) of Pub.L. 96–417, as amended, set out as a note under section 251 of this title.

Subsecs. (d) and (g) to (i) of this section applicable with respect to civil actions commenced on or after Nov. 1, 1980, see section 701(b)(1)(A) of Pub.L. 96–417, as amended, set out as a note under section 251 of this title.

Transfer of Functions

For transfer of the functions, personnel, assets, and liabilities of the United States Customs Service of the Department of the Treasury, including the functions of the Secretary of the Treasury relating thereto, to the Secretary of Homeland Security, and for treatment of related references, see 6 U.S.C.A. §§ 203(1), 551(d), 552(d) and 557, and the Department of Homeland Security Reorganization Plan of November 25, 2002, as modified, set out as a note under 6 U.S.C.A. § 542.

Prior Provisions

A prior section 1581, Act June 25, 1948, c. 646, 62 Stat. 943, related to powers of the Customs Court generally and was omitted in the general revision of this chapter by Pub.L. 96–417. See section 1585 of this title.

Application of Amendments Relating to Accreditation of Private Laboratories

Section 684(b) of Pub.L. 103–182 provided that: "For purposes of applying the amendments made by subsection (a) [amending subsec. (g) of this section, and sections 2631, 2636, 2640 and 2642 of this title], any decision or order of the Customs Service denying, suspending, or revoking the accreditation of a private laboratory on or after the date of the enactment of this Act [Dec. 8, 1993] and before regulations to implement section 499(b) of the Tariff Act of 1930 [section 1499(b) of Title 19, Customs Duties] are issued shall be treated as having been denied, suspended, or revoked under such section 499(b)."

Prior History of Court

The United States Customs Court, the predecessor of the Court of International Trade, was omitted in the general revision of this chapter by Pub.L. 96–417.

The predecessor of the United States Customs Court was the Board of General Appraisers which was created by the Customs Administrative Act of June 10, 1890. The Board was under the administrative supervision of the Secretary of the Treasury.

From 1890 to 1926, the Board of General Appraisers had jurisdiction over all protests from decisions of the collectors of customs and appeals for reappraisement under sections 13 and 14 of the Customs Administrative Act of June 10, 1890, c. 407, 26 Stat. 136.

The Customs Court was established by Act May 28, 1926, c. 411, §§ 1, 2, 44 Stat. 669, sections 405a and 405b of Title 19, Customs Duties, and said act transferred to it all the jurisdiction and powers of the former Board of General Appraisers. The Tariff Act of June 1930, c. 497, Title IV, § 518, 46 Stat. 737, section 1518 of Title 19, continued the Customs Court as constituted on June 17, 1930 with, however, several important changes.

§ 1582. Civil actions commenced by the United States

The Court of International Trade shall have exclusive jurisdiction of any civil action which arises out of an import transaction and which is commenced by the United States—

(1) to recover a civil penalty under section 592, 593A, 641(b)(6), 641(d)(2)(A), 704(i)(2), or 734(i)(2) of the Tariff Act of 1930;

(2) to recover upon a bond relating to the importation of merchandise required by the laws of the United States or by the Secretary of the Treasury; or

(3) to recover customs duties.

(Added Pub.L. 96–417, Title II, § 201, Oct. 10, 1980, 94 Stat. 1729, and amended Pub.L. 98–573, Title II, § 212(b)(2), Oct. 30, 1984, 98 Stat. 2983; Pub.L. 99–514, Title XVIII, § 1891(2), Oct. 22, 1986, 100 Stat. 2926; Pub.L. 103–182, Title VI, § 684(c), Dec. 8, 1993, 107 Stat. 2219.)

HISTORICAL AND STATUTORY NOTES

References in Text

Sections 592, 593A, 641(b)(2), 641(d)(2)(A), 704(i)(2), and 734(i)(2) of the Tariff Act of 1930, referred to in par. (1), are classified to sections 1592, 1593a, 1641(b)(6), 1641(d)(2)(A), 1671c(i)(2), and 1673c(i)(2) of Title 19, Customs Duties.

Effective and Applicability Provisions

1993 Acts. Amendment by section 684(c) of Pub.L. 103–182 effective Dec. 8, 1993, see section 692 of Pub.L. 103–182, set out as a note under section 58c of Title 19, Customs Duties.

1984 Acts. Amendment by Pub.L. 98–573 to take effect on the close of the 180th day after Oct. 30, 1984, see section 214(d) of Pub.L. 98–573, set out as a note under section 1304 of Title 19, Customs Duties.

1980 Acts. Section applicable with respect to civil actions commenced on or after the 90th day after Nov. 1, 1980, see section 701(c)(1)(A) of Pub.L. 96–417, as amended, set out as a note under section 251 of this title.

Prior Provisions

A prior section 1582, Acts June 25, 1948, c. 646, 62 Stat. 943; June 2, 1970, Pub.L. 91–271, Title I, § 110, 84 Stat. 278;

July 26, 1979, Pub.L. 96–39, Title X, § 1001(b)(4)(B), 93 Stat. 305, related to the jurisdiction of the Customs Court and was omitted in the general revision of this chapter by Pub.L. 96–417.

§ 1583. Counterclaims, cross-claims, and third-party actions

In any civil action in the Court of International Trade, the court shall have exclusive jurisdiction to render judgment upon any counterclaim, cross-claim, or third-party action of any party, if (1) such claim or action involves the imported merchandise that is the subject matter of such civil action, or (2) such claim or action is to recover upon a bond or customs duties relating to such merchandise.

(Added Pub.L. 96–417, Title II, § 201, Oct. 10, 1980, 94 Stat. 1729.)

HISTORICAL AND STATUTORY NOTES

Effective and Applicability Provisions

1980 Acts. Section applicable with respect to civil actions commenced on or after Nov. 1, 1980, see section 701(b)(1)(A) of Pub.L. 96–417, as amended, set out as a note under section 251 of this title.

Prior Provisions

A prior section 1583, Act June 25, 1948, c. 646, 62 Stat. 943, related to certain cases of exclusive jurisdiction of the Customs Court and was repealed by Pub.L. 91–271, Title I, § 111, June 2, 1970, 84 Stat. 278.

§ 1584. Civil actions under the North American Free Trade Agreement or the United States–Canada Free–Trade Agreement

The United States Court of International Trade shall have exclusive jurisdiction of any civil action which arises under section 777(f) of the Tariff Act of 1930 and is commenced by the United States to enforce administrative sanctions levied for violation of a protective order or an undertaking.

(Added Pub.L. 100–449, Title IV, § 402(d)(1), Sept. 28, 1988, 102 Stat. 1884, and amended Pub.L. 103–182, Title IV, § 414(a)(2), Dec. 8, 1993, 107 Stat. 2147.)

Termination of Amendments

For provisions directing that, except for transition provisions relating to proceedings regarding protective orders and undertakings, and binational panel and extraordinary challenge committee reviews, the amendment to this section by Title IV of Pub.L. 103–182 shall cease to have effect with respect to any country on the date on which such country ceases to be a NAFTA country, see 19 U.S.C.A. § 3451.

Termination of United States–Canada Free–Trade Agreement

For provisions directing that the amendments made by Pub.L. 100–449, which enacted this section, shall cease to have effect on the date on which the United States–Canada Free–Trade Agreement ceases to be in force, see section 501(c) of Pub.L. 100–449, set out in the note under 19 U.S.C.A. § 2112.

Articles 1906 and 2106 of the Agreement authorize either the United States or Canada to terminate the Agreement on 6–month notice if, at the end of the 7–year period following the date of the entry into effect of the Agreement, no agreement has been entered into between the United States and Canada on a substitute system of antidumping and countervailing duties.

HISTORICAL AND STATUTORY NOTES

References in Text

Section 777(f) of the Tariff Act of 1930, referred to in text, is classified to section 1677f(f) of Title 19, Customs Duties.

Effective and Applicability Provisions

1993 Acts. Amendment by section 414 of Pub.L. 103–182 effective on the date the North American Free Trade Agreement enters into force with respect to the United States [Jan. 1, 1994], but not to apply to any final determination described in section 1516a(a)(1)(B) or (2)(B)(i), (ii), or (iii) of Title 19, Customs Duties, notice of which is published in the Federal Register before such date, or to a determination described in section 1516a(a)(2)(B)(vi) of Title 19 notice of which is received by the Government of Canada or Mexico before such date, or to any binational panel review under the United States-Canada Free-Trade Agreement, or to any extraordinary challenge arising out of any such review that was commenced before such date, see section 416 of Pub.L. 103–182, set out as a note under section 3431 of Title 19.

1988 Acts. Section effective on the date the United States–Canada Free–Trade Agreement enters into force (Jan. 1, 1989), and to cease to have effect on the date the Agreement ceases to be in force, see section 501(a), (c), of Pub.L. 100–449, set out in a note under section 2112 of Title 19, Customs Duties. [A Presidential Memorandum on the Canada–United States Free–Trade Agreement, dated Dec. 31, 1988, directing the Secretary of State to exchange notes with the Government of Canada to provide for the entry into force of the Agreement on Jan. 1, 1989, is set out in 24 Weekly Compilation of Presidential Documents 1688, Jan. 2, 1989.]

Prior Provisions

A prior section 1584, added Pub.L. 96–417, Title II, § 201, Oct. 10, 1980, 94 Stat. 1729, which provided that if a civil action within the exclusive jurisdiction of the Court of International Trade were commenced in a district court of the United States, the district court, in the interest of justice, would transfer such civil action to the Court of International Trade, where such action proceeded as if it had been commenced in the Court of International Trade in the first instance, and that if a civil action within the exclusive jurisdiction of a district court, a court of appeals, or the Court of Customs and Patent Appeals were commenced in the Court of International Trade, the Court of International Trade, in the interest of justice, would transfer such civil action to the appropriate district court or court of appeals or to the Court of Customs and Patent Appeals where such action proceeded as if it had been commenced in such court in the first instance, was repealed by Pub.L. 97–164, Title I, § 135, Apr. 2, 1982, 96 Stat. 41, eff. Oct. 1, 1982.

§ 1585. Powers in law and equity

The Court of International Trade shall possess all the powers in law and equity of, or as conferred by statute upon, a district court of the United States.

(Added Pub.L. 96–417, Title II, § 201, Oct. 10, 1980, 94 Stat. 1730.)

CHAPTER 97—JURISDICTIONAL IMMUNITIES OF FOREIGN STATES

Sec.
1602. Findings and declaration of purpose.
1603. Definitions.
1604. Immunity of a foreign state from jurisdiction.
1605. General exceptions to the jurisdictional immunity of a foreign state.
1605A. Terrorism exception to the jurisdictional immunity of a foreign state.
1606. Extent of liability.
1607. Counterclaims.
1608. Service; time to answer default.[1]
1609. Immunity from attachment and execution of property of a foreign state.
1610. Exceptions to the immunity from attachment or execution.
1611. Certain types of property immune from execution.

[1] So in original. Does not conform to section catchline.

§ 1602. Findings and declaration of purpose

The Congress finds that the determination by United States courts of the claims of foreign states to immunity from the jurisdiction of such courts would serve the interests of justice and would protect the rights of both foreign states and litigants in United States courts. Under international law, states are not immune from the jurisdiction of foreign courts insofar as their commercial activities are concerned, and their commercial property may be levied upon for the satisfaction of judgments rendered against them in connection with their commercial activities. Claims of foreign states to immunity should henceforth be decided by courts of the United States and of the States in conformity with the principles set forth in this chapter.

(Added Pub.L. 94–583, § 4(a), Oct. 21, 1976, 90 Stat. 2892.)

HISTORICAL AND STATUTORY NOTES

Effective and Applicability Provisions

1976 Acts. Section 8 of Pub.L. 94–583 provided that: "This Act [enacting this chapter and section 1330 of this title, amending sections 1332, 1391, and 1441 of this title, and enacting provisions set out as notes under this section] shall take effect ninety days after the date of its enactment [Oct. 21, 1976]."

Separability of Provisions

Section 7 of Pub.L. 94–583 provided that: "If any provision of this Act [enacting this chapter and section 1330 of this title, amending sections 1332, 1391, and 1441 of this title, and enacting provisions set out as notes under this section and section 1 of this title] or the application thereof to any foreign state is held invalid, the invalidity does not affect other provisions or applications of the Act which can be given effect without the invalid provision or application, and to this end the provisions of this Act are severable."

Short Title

1976 Acts. Authorization to cite Pub.L. 94–583, which enacted this chapter, as the "Foreign Sovereign Immunities Act of 1976", see section 1 of Pub.L. 94–583, set out as a note under section 1 of this title.

§ 1603. Definitions

For purposes of this chapter—

(a) A "foreign state", except as used in section 1608 of this title, includes a political subdivision of a foreign state or an agency or instrumentality of a foreign state as defined in subsection (b).

(b) An "agency or instrumentality of a foreign state" means any entity—

(1) which is a separate legal person, corporate or otherwise, and

(2) which is an organ of a foreign state or political subdivision thereof, or a majority of whose shares or other ownership interest is owned by a foreign state or political subdivision thereof, and

(3) which is neither a citizen of a State of the United States as defined in section 1332(c) and (e) of this title, nor created under the laws of any third country.

(c) The "United States" includes all territory and waters, continental or insular, subject to the jurisdiction of the United States.

(d) A "commercial activity" means either a regular course of commercial conduct or a particular commercial transaction or act. The commercial character of an activity shall be determined by reference to the nature of the course of conduct or particular transaction or act, rather than by reference to its purpose.

(e) A "commercial activity carried on in the United States by a foreign state" means commercial activity carried on by such state and having substantial contact with the United States.

(Added Pub.L. 94–583, § 4(a), Oct. 21, 1976, 90 Stat. 2892, and amended Pub.L. 109–2, § 4(b)(2), Feb. 18, 2005, 119 Stat. 12.)

HISTORICAL AND STATUTORY NOTES

Effective and Applicability Provisions

2005 Acts. Amendments by Class Action Fairness Act of 2005, Pub.L. 109–2, Feb. 18, 2005, 119 Stat. 4, applicable to any civil action commenced on or after Feb. 18, 2005, see Pub.L. 109–2, § 9, set out as a note under 28 U.S.C.A. § 1332.

1976 Acts. Section effective 90 days after Oct. 21, 1976, see section 8 of Pub.L. 94–583, set out as a note under section 1602 of this title.

§ 1604. Immunity of a foreign state from jurisdiction

Subject to existing international agreements to which the United States is a party at the time of enactment of this Act a foreign state shall be immune from the jurisdiction of the courts of the United States and of the States except as provided in sections 1605 to 1607 of this chapter.

(Added Pub.L. 94–583, § 4(a), Oct. 21, 1976, 90 Stat. 2892.)

HISTORICAL AND STATUTORY NOTES

References in Text

The time of enactment of this Act, referred to in text, probably means the time of enactment of Pub.L. 94–583, which was approved on Oct. 21, 1976.

Effective and Applicability Provisions

1976 Acts. Section effective 90 days after Oct. 21, 1976, see section 8 of Pub.L. 94–583, set out as a note under section 1602 of this title.

§ 1605. General exceptions to the jurisdictional immunity of a foreign state

(a) A foreign state shall not be immune from the jurisdiction of courts of the United States or of the States in any case—

(1) in which the foreign state has waived its immunity either explicitly or by implication, notwithstanding any withdrawal of the waiver which the foreign state may purport to effect except in accordance with the terms of the waiver;

(2) in which the action is based upon a commercial activity carried on in the United States by the foreign state; or upon an act performed in the United States in connection with a commercial activity of the foreign state elsewhere; or upon an act outside the territory of the United States in connection with a commercial activity of the foreign state elsewhere and that act causes a direct effect in the United States;

(3) in which rights in property taken in violation of international law are in issue and that property or any property exchanged for such property is present in the United States in connection with a commercial activity carried on in the United States by the foreign state; or that property or any property exchanged for such property is owned or operated by an agency or instrumentality of the foreign state and that agency or instrumentality is engaged in a commercial activity in the United States;

(4) in which rights in property in the United States acquired by succession or gift or rights in immovable property situated in the United States are in issue;

(5) not otherwise encompassed in paragraph (2) above, in which money damages are sought against a foreign state for personal injury or death, or damage to or loss of property, occurring in the United States and caused by the tortious act or omission of that foreign state or of any official or employee of that foreign state while acting within the scope of his office or employment; except this paragraph shall not apply to—

(A) any claim based upon the exercise or performance or the failure to exercise or perform a discretionary function regardless of whether the discretion be abused, or

(B) any claim arising out of malicious prosecution, abuse of process, libel, slander, misrepresentation, deceit, or interference with contract rights; or

(6) in which the action is brought, either to enforce an agreement made by the foreign state with or for the benefit of a private party to submit to arbitration all or any differences which have arisen or which may arise between the parties with respect to a defined legal relationship, whether contractual or not, concerning a subject matter capable of settlement by arbitration under the laws of the United States, or to confirm an award made pursuant to such an agreement to arbitrate, if (A) the arbitration takes place or is intended to take place in the United States, (B) the agreement or award is or may be governed by a treaty or other international agreement in force for the United States calling for the recognition and enforcement of arbitral awards, (C) the underlying claim, save for the agreement to arbitrate, could have been brought in a United States court under this section or section 1607, or (D) paragraph (1) of this subsection is otherwise applicable.

(7) Repealed. Pub.L. 110–181, Div. A, § 1083(b)(1)(A)(iii), Jan. 28, 2008, 122 Stat. 341

(b) A foreign state shall not be immune from the jurisdiction of the courts of the United States in any case in which a suit in admiralty is brought to enforce a maritime lien against a vessel or cargo of the foreign state, which maritime lien is based upon a commercial activity of the foreign state: *Provided*, That—

(1) notice of the suit is given by delivery of a copy of the summons and of the complaint to the person, or his agent, having possession of the vessel or cargo against which the maritime lien is asserted;

and if the vessel or cargo is arrested pursuant to process obtained on behalf of the party bringing the suit, the service of process of arrest shall be deemed to constitute valid delivery of such notice, but the party bringing the suit shall be liable for any damages sustained by the foreign state as a result of the arrest if the party bringing the suit had actual or constructive knowledge that the vessel or cargo of a foreign state was involved; and

(2) notice to the foreign state of the commencement of suit as provided in section 1608 of this title is initiated within ten days either of the delivery of notice as provided in paragraph (1) of this subsection or, in the case of a party who was unaware that the vessel or cargo of a foreign state was involved, of the date such party determined the existence of the foreign state's interest.

(c) Whenever notice is delivered under subsection (b)(1), the suit to enforce a maritime lien shall thereafter proceed and shall be heard and determined according to the principles of law and rules of practice of suits in rem whenever it appears that, had the vessel been privately owned and possessed, a suit in rem might have been maintained. A decree against the foreign state may include costs of the suit and, if the decree is for a money judgment, interest as ordered by the court, except that the court may not award judgment against the foreign state in an amount greater than the value of the vessel or cargo upon which the maritime lien arose. Such value shall be determined as of the time notice is served under subsection (b)(1). Decrees shall be subject to appeal and revision as provided in other cases of admiralty and maritime jurisdiction. Nothing shall preclude the plaintiff in any proper case from seeking relief in personam in the same action brought to enforce a maritime lien as provided in this section.

(d) A foreign state shall not be immune from the jurisdiction of the courts of the United States in any action brought to foreclose a preferred mortgage, as defined in section 31301 of title 46. Such action shall be brought, heard, and determined in accordance with the provisions of chapter 313 of title 46 and in accordance with the principles of law and rules of practice of suits in rem, whenever it appears that had the vessel been privately owned and possessed a suit in rem might have been maintained.

(e), (f) Repealed. Pub.L. 110–181, Div. A, Title X, § 1083(b)(1)(B), Jan. 28, 2008, 122 Stat. 341

(g) Limitation on discovery.—

(1) In general.—(A) Subject to paragraph (2), if an action is filed that would otherwise be barred by section 1604, but for section 1605A, the court, upon request of the Attorney General, shall stay any request, demand, or order for discovery on the United States that the Attorney General certifies would significantly interfere with a criminal investigation or prosecution, or a national security operation, related to the incident that gave rise to the cause of action, until such time as the Attorney General advises the court that such request, demand, or order will no longer so interfere.

(B) A stay under this paragraph shall be in effect during the 12–month period beginning on the date on which the court issues the order to stay discovery. The court shall renew the order to stay discovery for additional 12–month periods upon motion by the United States if the Attorney General certifies that discovery would significantly interfere with a criminal investigation or prosecution, or a national security operation, related to the incident that gave rise to the cause of action.

(2) Sunset.—(A) Subject to subparagraph (B), no stay shall be granted or continued in effect under paragraph (1) after the date that is 10 years after the date on which the incident that gave rise to the cause of action occurred.

(B) After the period referred to in subparagraph (A), the court, upon request of the Attorney General, may stay any request, demand, or order for discovery on the United States that the court finds a substantial likelihood would—

(i) create a serious threat of death or serious bodily injury to any person;

(ii) adversely affect the ability of the United States to work in cooperation with foreign and international law enforcement agencies in investigating violations of United States law; or

(iii) obstruct the criminal case related to the incident that gave rise to the cause of action or undermine the potential for a conviction in such case.

(3) Evaluation of evidence.—The court's evaluation of any request for a stay under this subsection filed by the Attorney General shall be conducted ex parte and in camera.

(4) Bar on motions to dismiss.—A stay of discovery under this subsection shall constitute a bar to the granting of a motion to dismiss under rules 12(b)(6) and 56 of the Federal Rules of Civil Procedure.

(5) Construction.—Nothing in this subsection shall prevent the United States from seeking protective orders or asserting privileges ordinarily available to the United States.

(Added Pub.L. 94–583, § 4(a), Oct. 21, 1976, 90 Stat. 2892, and amended Pub.L. 100–640, § 1, Nov. 9, 1988, 102 Stat. 3333; Pub.L. 100–669, § 2, Nov. 16, 1988, 102 Stat. 3969; Pub.L. 101–650, Title III, § 325(b)(8), Dec. 1, 1990, 104 Stat. 5121; Pub.L. 104–132, Title II, § 221(a), Apr. 24, 1996, 110 Stat. 1241; Pub.L. 105–11, Apr. 25, 1997, 111 Stat. 22; Pub.L. 107–77, Title VI, § 626(c), Nov. 28, 2001, 115 Stat.

803; Pub.L. 107–117, Div. B, Ch. 2, § 208, Jan. 10, 2002, 115 Stat. 2299; Pub.L. 109–304, § 17(f)(2), Oct. 6, 2006, 120 Stat. 1708; Pub.L. 110–181, Title X, § 1083(b)(1), Jan. 28, 2008, 122 Stat. 341.)

HISTORICAL AND STATUTORY NOTES

References in Text

Section 101(a)(22) of the Immigration and Nationality Act, referred to in subsec. (a)(7)(B)(ii), is classified to section 1101(a)(22) of Title 8, Aliens and Nationality.

Chapter 313 of Title 46, referred to in subsec. (d), is Commercial Instruments and Maritime Liens, 46 U.S.C.A. § 31301 et seq.

Section 3 of the Torture Victim Protection Act of 1991, referred to in subsec. (e)(1), is section 3 of Pub.L. 102–256, Mar. 12, 1992, 106 Stat. 73, set out in a note under section 1350 of this title.

Effective and Applicability Provisions

1997 Acts. Section 1 of Pub.L. 105–11 provided in part that the amendment of subsec. (a)(7)(B)(ii) by Pub.L. 105–11 is effective with respect to any cause of action arising before, on, or after April 25, 1997.

1996 Acts. Section 221(c) of Pub.L. 104–132 provided that: "The amendments made by this subtitle [amending this section and section 1610 of this title] shall apply to any cause of action arising before, on, or after the date of the enactment of this Act [Apr. 24, 1996]."

1988 Acts. Section 3 of Pub.L. 100–640 provided that: "The amendments made by this Act [amending this section and section 1610 of this title] shall apply to actions commenced on or after the date of the enactment of this Act [Nov. 9, 1988]."

1976 Acts. Section effective 90 days after Oct. 21, 1976, see section 8 of Pub.L. 94–583, set out as a note under section 1602 of this title.

Application of Pub.L. 110–181, Div. A, § 1083 to Pending Cases

For application of amendments made by Pub.L. 110–181, Div. A, § 1083 to pending cases and treatment of prior actions, see Pub.L. 110–181, Div. A, § 1083(c), set out as a note under 28 U.S.C.A. § 1605A.

Application of Pub.L. 110–181, Div. A, § 1083 to Iraq

For application of amendments made by Pub.L. 110–181, Div. A, § 1083 to Iraq, see Pub.L. 110–181, Div. A, § 1083(d), set out as a note under 28 U.S.C.A. § 1605A.

Severability

If any provision of Pub.L. 110–181, Div. A, § 1083, or the amendments made by that section, or the application of such provision to any person or circumstance, is held invalid, the remainder of that section and such amendments, and the application of such provision to other persons not similarly situated or to other circumstances, shall not be affected by such invalidation, see Pub.L. 110–181, Div. A, § 1083(e), set out as a note under 28 U.S.C.A. § 1605A.

Civil Liability for Acts of State Sponsored Terrorism

Pub.L. 104–208, Div. A, Title I, § 101(c) [Title V, § 589], Sept. 30, 1996, 110 Stat. 3009–172, provided that:

"**(a)** An official, employee, or agent of a foreign state designated as a state sponsor of terrorism designated under section 6(j) of the Export Administration Act of 1979 [section 2405(j) of the Appendix to Title 50, War and National Defense] while acting within the scope of his or her office, employment, or agency shall be liable to a United States national or the national's legal representative for personal injury or death caused by acts of that official, employee, or agent for which the courts of the United States may maintain jurisdiction under section 1605(a)(7) of title 28, United States Code [subsec. (a)(7) of this section] for money damages which may include economic damages, solatium, pain, and suffering, and punitive damages if the acts were among those described in section 1605(a)(7) [subsec. (a)(7) of this section].

"**(b)** Provisions related to statute of limitations and limitations on discovery that would apply to an action brought under 28 U.S.C. 1605(f) and (g) [subsecs. (f) and (g) of this section] shall also apply to actions brought under this section. No action shall be maintained under this action [SIC] if an official, employee, or agent of the United States, while acting within the scope of his or her office, employment, or agency would not be liable for such acts if carried out within the United States."

§ 1605A. Terrorism exception to the jurisdictional immunity of a foreign state

(a) In general.—

(1) No immunity.—A foreign state shall not be immune from the jurisdiction of courts of the United States or of the States in any case not otherwise covered by this chapter in which money damages are sought against a foreign state for personal injury or death that was caused by an act of torture, extrajudicial killing, aircraft sabotage, hostage taking, or the provision of material support or resources for such an act if such act or provision of material support or resources is engaged in by an official, employee, or agent of such foreign state while acting within the scope of his or her office, employment, or agency.

(2) Claim heard.—The court shall hear a claim under this section if—

(A)(i)(I) the foreign state was designated as a state sponsor of terrorism at the time the act described in paragraph (1) occurred, or was so designated as a result of such act, and, subject to subclause (II), either remains so designated when the claim is filed under this section or was so designated within the 6–month period before the claim is filed under this section; or

(II) in the case of an action that is refiled under this section by reason of section 1083(c)(2)(A) of the National Defense Authorization Act for Fiscal Year 2008 or is filed under this section by reason of section 1083(c)(3) of that Act, the foreign state was designated as a state sponsor of terrorism when the original action or the related action under section 1605(a)(7) (as in effect before the enactment of this section) or section 589 of the Foreign Operations, Export Financing, and Related Programs Appropriations Act, 1997 (as contained in section 101(c) of division A of Public Law 104–208) was filed;

(ii) the claimant or the victim was, at the time the act described in paragraph (1) occurred—

(I) a national of the United States;

(II) a member of the armed forces; or

(III) otherwise an employee of the Government of the United States, or of an individual performing a contract awarded by the United States Government, acting within the scope of the employee's employment; and

(iii) in a case in which the act occurred in the foreign state against which the claim has been brought, the claimant has afforded the foreign state a reasonable opportunity to arbitrate the claim in accordance with the accepted international rules of arbitration; or

(B) the act described in paragraph (1) is related to Case Number 1:00CV03110 (EGS) in the United States District Court for the District of Columbia.

(b) Limitations.—An action may be brought or maintained under this section if the action is commenced, or a related action was commenced under section 1605(a)(7) (before the date of the enactment of this section) or section 589 of the Foreign Operations, Export Financing, and Related Programs Appropriations Act, 1997 (as contained in section 101(c) of division A of Public Law 104–208) not later than the latter of—

(1) 10 years after April 24, 1996; or

(2) 10 years after the date on which the cause of action arose.

(c) Private right of action.—A foreign state that is or was a state sponsor of terrorism as described in subsection (a)(2)(A)(i), and any official, employee, or agent of that foreign state while acting within the scope of his or her office, employment, or agency, shall be liable to—

(1) a national of the United States,

(2) a member of the armed forces,

(3) an employee of the Government of the United States, or of an individual performing a contract awarded by the United States Government, acting within the scope of the employee's employment, or

(4) the legal representative of a person described in paragraph (1), (2), or (3),

for personal injury or death caused by acts described in subsection (a) (1) of that foreign state, or of an official, employee, or agent of that foreign state, for which the courts of the United States may maintain jurisdiction under this section for money damages. In any such action, damages may include economic damages, solatium, pain and suffering, and punitive damages. In any such action, a foreign state shall be vicariously liable for the acts of its officials, employees, or agents.

(d) Additional damages.—After an action has been brought under subsection (c), actions may also be brought for reasonably foreseeable property loss, whether insured or uninsured, third party liability, and loss claims under life and property insurance policies, by reason of the same acts on which the action under subsection (c) is based.

(e) Special masters.—

(1) In general.—The courts of the United States may appoint special masters to hear damage claims brought under this section.

(2) Transfer of funds.—The Attorney General shall transfer, from funds available for the program under section 1404C of the Victims of Crime Act of 1984 (42 U.S.C. 10603c), to the Administrator of the United States district court in which any case is pending which has been brought or maintained under this section such funds as may be required to cover the costs of special masters appointed under paragraph (1). Any amount paid in compensation to any such special master shall constitute an item of court costs.

(f) Appeal.—In an action brought under this section, appeals from orders not conclusively ending the litigation may only be taken pursuant to section 1292(b) of this title.

(g) Property disposition.—

(1) In general.—In every action filed in a United States district court in which jurisdiction is alleged under this section, the filing of a notice of pending action pursuant to this section, to which is attached a copy of the complaint filed in the action, shall have the effect of establishing a lien of lis pendens upon any real property or tangible personal property that is—

(A) subject to attachment in aid of execution, or execution, under section 1610;

(B) located within that judicial district; and

(C) titled in the name of any defendant, or titled in the name of any entity controlled by any defendant if such notice contains a statement listing such controlled entity.

(2) Notice.—A notice of pending action pursuant to this section shall be filed by the clerk of the district court in the same manner as any pending action and shall be indexed by listing as defendants all named defendants and all entities listed as controlled by any defendant.

(3) Enforceability.—Liens established by reason of this subsection shall be enforceable as provided in chapter 111 of this title.

(h) Definitions.—For purposes of this section—

(1) the term "aircraft sabotage" has the meaning given that term in Article 1 of the Convention for the Suppression of Unlawful Acts Against the Safety of Civil Aviation;

(2) the term "hostage taking" has the meaning given that term in Article 1 of the International Convention Against the Taking of Hostages;

(3) the term "material support or resources" has the meaning given that term in section 2339A of title 18;

(4) the term "armed forces" has the meaning given that term in section 101 of title 10;

(5) the term "national of the United States" has the meaning given that term in section 101(a)(22) of the Immigration and Nationality Act (8 U.S.C. 1101(a)(22));

(6) the term "state sponsor of terrorism" means a country the government of which the Secretary of State has determined, for purposes of section 6(j) of the Export Administration Act of 1979 (50 U.S.C. App. 2405(j)), section 620A of the Foreign Assistance Act of 1961 (22 U.S.C. 2371), section 40 of the Arms Export Control Act (22 U.S.C. 2780), or any other provision of law, is a government that has repeatedly provided support for acts of international terrorism; and

(7) the terms "torture" and "extrajudicial killing" have the meaning given those terms in section 3 of the Torture Victim Protection Act of 1991 (28 U.S.C. 1350 note).

(Added Pub.L. 110–181, Div. A, Title X, § 1083(a)(1), Jan. 28, 2008, 122 Stat. 338.)

HISTORICAL AND STATUTORY NOTES

References in Text

Section 1083(c) of the National Defense Authorization Act for Fiscal Year 2008, referred to in subsec. (a)(2)(A)(II), is Pub.L. 110–181, Div. A, Title X, § 1083(c), Jan. 28, 2008, 122 Stat. 342, which is set out as a note under this section.

The enactment of this section, and the date of the enactment of this section, referred to in subsecs. (a)(2)(A)(II), (b), is Jan. 28, 2008, the approval date of Pub.L. 110–181, 122 Stat. 3, which enacted this section.

The Foreign Operations, Export Financing, and Related Programs Appropriations Act, 1997, referred to in subsecs. (a)(2)(A)(II), (b), is Pub.L. 104–208, Div. A, Title I, § 101(c), [Title I to V], Sept. 30, 1996, 110 Stat. 3009. Section 589 of the Act is not classified to the Code; see Tables for complete classification.

The Victims of Crime Act of 1984, referred to in subsec. (e)(2), is Pub.L. 98–473, Title II, ch. XIV, Oct. 12, 1984, 98 Stat. 2170, which is principally classified to Chapter 112 of Title 42, 42 U.S.C.A. § 10601 et seq. Section 1404C of the Act is classified to 42 U.S.C.A. § 10603c. For complete classification, see Short Title note set out under 42 U.S.C.A. § 10601 and Tables.

Chapter 111 of this title, referred to in subsec. (g)(3), is 28 U.S.C.A. § 1651 et seq.

The Immigration and Nationality Act, referred to in subsec. (h)(5), is Act June 27, 1952, c. 477, 66 Stat. 163, as amended, also known as the INA, the McCarran Act, and the McCarran-Walter Act, which is classified principally to chapter 12 of Title 8, 8 U.S.C.A. § 1101 et seq. Section 101 of the Act is classified to 8 U.S.C.A. § 1101. For complete classification, see Short Title note set out under 8 U.S.C.A. § 1101 and Tables.

The Export Administration Act of 1979, referred to in subsec. (h)(6), is Pub.L. 96–72, Sept. 29, 1979, 93 Stat. 503, which is classified principally to 50 App. U.S.C.A. §§ 2401 to 2420. Section 6 of the Act is classified to 50 App. U.S.C.A. § 2405. See Tables for complete classification.

The Foreign Assistance Act of 1961, referred to in subsec. (h)(6), is Pub.L. 87–195, Sept. 4, 1961, 75 Stat. 424, as amended, also known as the Act for International Development of 1961 and the FAA, which is classified principally to chapter 32 of Title 22, 22 U.S.C.A. § 2151 et seq. Section 620A of the Act is classified to 22 U.S.C.A. § 2371. For complete classification, see Short Title note set out under 22 U.S.C.A. § 2151 and Tables.

The Arms Export Control Act, referred to in subsec. (h)(6), is Pub.L. 90–629, Oct. 22, 1968, 82 Stat. 1320, as amended, also known as the AECA and the Foreign Military Sales Act, which is classified principally to chapter 39 of Title 22, 22 U.S.C.A. § 2751 et seq. Section 40 of the Act is classified to 22 U.S.C.A. § 2780. For complete classification, see Short Title note set out under 22 U.S.C.A. § 2751 and Tables.

Section 3 of the Torture Victim Protection Act of 1991, referred to in subsec. (h)(7), is section 3 of Pub.L. 102–256, Mar. 12, 1992, 106 Stat. 73, set out in a note under section 28 U.S.C.A. § 1350.

Libyan Claims Resolution Act

Pub.L. 110–301, Aug. 4, 2008, 122 Stat. 2999, provided that:

"Section 1. Short title.

"This Act [enacting this note] may be cited as the 'Libyan Claims Resolution Act'.

"Sec. 2. Definitions.

"In this Act—

"(1) the term 'appropriate congressional committees' means the Committee on Foreign Relations and the Committee on the Judiciary of the Senate and the Committee on Foreign Affairs and the Committee on the Judiciary of the House of Representatives;

"(2) the term 'claims agreement' means an international agreement between the United States and Libya, binding under international law, that provides for the settlement of terrorism-related claims of nationals of the United States against Libya through fair compensation;

"(3) the term 'national of the United States' has the meaning given that term in section 101(a)(22) of the Immigration and Nationality Act (8 U.S.C. 1101(a)(22));

"(4) the term 'Secretary' means the Secretary of State; and

"(5) the term 'state sponsor of terrorism' means a country the government of which the Secretary has determined, for purposes of section 6(j) of the Export Administration Act of 1979 (50 U.S.C. App. 2405(j)), section 620A of the Foreign Assistance Act of 1961 (22 U.S.C. 2371), section 40 of the Arms Export Control Act (22 U.S.C. 2780), or any other provision of law, is a government that has repeatedly provided support for acts of international terrorism.

"Sec. 3. Sense of Congress.

"Congress supports the President in his efforts to provide fair compensation to all nationals of the United States who have terrorism-related claims against Libya through a comprehensive settlement of claims by such nationals against Libya pursuant to an international agreement between the United States and Libya as a part of the process of restoring normal relations between Libya and the United States.

"Sec. 4. Entity to assist in implementation of claims agreement.

"**(a) Designation of entity.**—

"**(1) Designation.**—The Secretary, by publication in the Federal Register, may, after consultation with the appropriate congressional committees, designate 1 or more entities to assist in providing compensation to nationals of the United States, pursuant to a claims agreement.

"**(2) Authority of the Secretary.**—The designation of an entity under paragraph (1) is within the sole discretion of the Secretary, and may not be delegated. The designation shall not be subject to judicial review.

"**(b) Immunity.**—

"**(1) Property.**—

"**(A) In general.**—Notwithstanding any other provision of law, if the Secretary designates any entity under subsection (a)(1), any property described in subparagraph (B) of this paragraph shall be immune from attachment or any other judicial process. Such immunity shall be in addition to any other applicable immunity.

"**(B) Property described.**—The property described in this subparagraph is any property that—

"**(i)** relates to the claims agreement; and

"**(ii)** For the purpose of implementing the claims agreement, is—

"**(I)** held by an entity designated by the Secretary under subsection (a)(1);

"**(II)** transferred to the entity; or

"**(III)** transferred from the entity.

"**(2) Other acts.**—An entity designated by the Secretary under subsection (a)(1), and any person acting through or on behalf of such entity, shall not be liable in any Federal or State court for any action taken to implement a claims agreement.

"**(c) Nonapplicability of the Government Corporation Control Act.**—An entity designated by the Secretary under subsection (a)(1) shall not be subject to chapter 91 of title 31, United States Code [31 U.S.C.A. § 9101 et seq.] (commonly known as the 'Government Corporation Control Act').

"Sec. 5. Receipt of adequate funds; immunities of Libya.

"**(a) Immunity.**—

"**(1) In general.**—Notwithstanding any other provision of law, upon submission of a certification described in paragraph (2)—

"**(A)** Libya, an agency or instrumentality of Libya, and the property of Libya or an agency or instrumentality of Libya, shall not be subject to the exceptions to immunity from jurisdiction, liens, attachment, and execution contained in section 1605A, 1605(a)(7), or 1610 (insofar as section 1610 relates to a judgment under such section 1605A or 1605(a)(7)) of title 28, United States Code;

"**(B)** section 1605A(c) of title 28, United States Code, section 1083(c) of the National Defense Authorization Act for Fiscal Year 2008 (Public Law 110–181; 122 Stat. 342; 28 U.S.C. 1605A note), section 589 of the Foreign Operations, Export Financing, and Related Programs Appropriations Act, 1997 (28 U.S.C. 1605 note), and any other private right of action relating to acts by a state sponsor of terrorism arising under Federal, State, or foreign law shall not apply with respect to claims against Libya, or any of its agencies, instrumentalities, officials, employees, or agents in any action in a Federal or State court; and

"**(C)** any attachment, decree, lien, execution, garnishment, or other judicial process brought against property of Libya, or property of any agency, instrumentality, official, employee, or agent of Libya, in connection with an action that would be precluded by subparagraph (A) or (B) shall be void.

"**(2) Certification.**—A certification described in this paragraph is a certification—

"**(A)** by the Secretary to the appropriate congressional committees; and

"**(B)** Stating that the United States Government has received funds pursuant to the claims agreement that are sufficient to ensure—

"**(i)** payment of the settlements referred to in section 654(b) of division J of the Consolidated Appropriations Act, 2008 (Public Law 110–161; 121 Stat. 2342); and

"**(ii)** fair compensation of claims of nationals of the United States for wrongful death or physical injury in cases pending on the date of enactment of this Act against Libya arising under section 1605A of title 28, United States Code (including any action brought under section 1605(a)(7) of title 28, United States Code, or section 589 of the Foreign Operations, Export Financing, and Related Programs Appropriations Act, 1997 (28 U.S.C. 1605 note), that has been given effect as if the action had originally been filed under 1605A(c) of title 28, United States Code, pursuant to section 1083(c) of the National Defense Authorization Act for Fiscal Year 2008 (Public Law 110–181; 122 Stat. 342; 28 U.S.C. 1605A note)).

"**(b) Temporal scope.**—Subsection (a) shall apply only with respect to any conduct or event occurring before June 30, 2006, regardless of whether, or the extent to which, application of that subsection affects any action filed before, on, or after that date.

"**(c) Authority of the Secretary.**—The certification by the Secretary referred to in subsection (a)(2) may not be delegated, and shall not be subject to judicial review."

Application of Pub.L. 110–181, Div. A, § 1083 to Pending Cases

Pub.L. 110–181, Div. A, Title X, § 1083(c), Jan. 28, 2008, 122 Stat. 342, provided that:

"**(1) In general.**—The amendments made by this section [enacting this section and amending 28 U.S.C.A. §§ 1605,

1607, 1610, and 42 U.S.C.A. § 10603c] shall apply to any claim arising under section 1605A of title 28, United States Code [this section].

"(2) **Prior actions.**—

"(A) **In general.**—With respect to any action that—

"(i) was brought under section 1605(a)(7) of title 28, United States Code, or section 589 of the Foreign Operations, Export Financing, and Related Programs Appropriations Act, 1997 (as contained in section 101(c) of division A of Public Law 104–208) [not classified to the Code], before the date of the enactment of this Act [Jan. 28, 2008],

"(ii) relied upon either such provision as creating a cause of action,

"(iii) has been adversely affected on the grounds that either or both of these provisions fail to create a cause of action against the state, and

"(iv) as of such date of enactment [Jan. 28, 2008], is before the courts in any form, including on appeal or motion under rule 60(b) of the Federal Rules of Civil Procedure,

that action, and any judgment in the action shall, on motion made by plaintiffs to the United States district court where the action was initially brought, or judgment in the action was initially entered, be given effect as if the action had originally been filed under section 1605A(c) of title 28, United States Code [subsec. (c) of this section].

"(B) **Defenses waived.**—The defenses of res judicata, collateral estoppel, and limitation period are waived—

"(i) in any action with respect to which a motion is made under subparagraph (A), or

"(ii) in any action that was originally brought, before the date of the enactment of this Act [Jan. 28, 2008], under section 1605(a)(7) of title 28, United States Code, or section 589 of the Foreign Operations, Export Financing, and Related Programs Appropriations Act, 1997 (as contained in section 101(c) of division A of Public Law 104–208) [not classified to the Code], and is refiled under section 1605A(c) of title 28, United States Code [subsec. (c) of this section],

to the extent such defenses are based on the claim in the action.

"(C) **Time limitations.**—A motion may be made or an action may be refiled under subparagraph (A) only—

"(i) If the original action was commenced not later than the latter of—

"(I) 10 years after April 24, 1996; or

"(II) 10 years after the cause of action arose; and

"(ii) within the 60–day period beginning on the date of the enactment of this Act [Jan. 28, 2008].

"(3) **Related actions.**—If an action arising out of an act or incident has been timely commenced under section 1605(a)(7) of title 28, United States Code, or section 589 of the Foreign Operations, Export Financing, and Related Programs Appropriations Act, 1997 (as contained in section 101(c) of division A of Public Law 104–208), any other action arising out of the same act or incident may be brought under section 1605A of title 28, United States Code [this section], if the action is commenced not later than the latter of 60 days after—

"(A) the date of the entry of judgment in the original action; or

"(B) the date of the enactment of this Act [Jan. 28, 2008].

"(4) **Preserving the jurisdiction of the courts.**—Nothing in section 1503 of the Emergency Wartime Supplemental Appropriations Act, 2003 (Public Law 108–11, 117 Stat. 579 [not classified to the Code]) has ever authorized, directly or indirectly, the making inapplicable of any provision of chapter 97 of title 28, United States Code [28 U.S.C.A. § 1602 et seq.], or the removal of the jurisdiction of any court of the United States."

[If any provision of Pub.L. 110–181, Div. A, § 1083, or the amendments made by that section, or the application of such provision to any person or circumstance, is held invalid, the remainder of that section and such amendments, and the application of such provision to other persons not similarly situated or to other circumstances, shall not be affected by such invalidation, see Pub.L. 110–181, Div. A, § 1083(e), set out as a note under this section.]

Application of Pub.L. 110–181, Div. A, § 1083 to Iraq

Pub.L. 110–181, Div. A, Title X, § 1083(d), Jan. 28, 2008, 122 Stat. 343, provided that:

"(1) **Applicability.**—The President may waive any provision of this section [enacting this section, amending 28 U.S.C.A. §§ 1605, 1607, 1610, and 42 U.S.C.A. § 10603c, and enacting provisions set out as notes under this section] with respect to Iraq, insofar as that provision may, in the President's determination, affect Iraq or any agency or instrumentality thereof, if the President determines that—

"(A) the waiver is in the national security interest of the United States;

"(B) the waiver will promote the reconstruction of, the consolidation of democracy in, and the relations of the United States with, Iraq; and

"(C) Iraq continues to be a reliable ally of the United States and partner in combating acts of international terrorism.

"(2) **Temporal scope.**—The authority under paragraph (1) shall apply—

"(A) with respect to any conduct or event occurring before or on the date of the enactment of this Act [Jan. 28, 2008];

"(B) with respect to any conduct or event occurring before or on the date of the exercise of that authority; and

"(C) regardless of whether, or the extent to which, the exercise of that authority affects any action filed before, on, or after the date of the exercise of that authority or of the enactment of this Act [Jan. 28, 2008].

"(3) **Notification to Congress.**—A waiver by the President under paragraph (1) shall cease to be effective 30 days after it is made unless the President has notified Congress in writing of the basis for the waiver as determined by the President under paragraph (1).

"(4) **Sense of Congress.**—It is the sense of the Congress that the President, acting through the Secretary of State, should work with the Government of Iraq on a state-to-state basis to ensure compensation for any meritorious claims based on terrorist acts committed by the Saddam Hussein regime against individuals who were United States nationals or members of the United States Armed Forces at the time of those terrorist acts and whose claims cannot be addressed in courts in the United States due to the exercise of the waiver authority under paragraph (1)."

[If any provision of Pub.L. 110–181, Div. A, § 1083, or the amendments made by that section, or the application of such provision to any person or circumstance, is held invalid, the remainder of that section and such amendments, and the application of such provision to other persons not similarly situated or to other circumstances, shall not be affected by such invalidation, see Pub.L. 110–181, Div. A, § 1083(e), set out as a note under this section.]

Severability

Pub.L. 110–181, Div. A, Title X, § 1083(e), Jan. 28, 2008, 122 Stat. 344, provided that: "If any provision of this section or the amendments made by this section [enacting this section, amending 28 U.S.C.A. §§ 1605, 1607, 1610, and 42 U.S.C.A. § 10603e, and enacting provisions set out as notes under this section], or the application of such provision to any person or circumstance, is held invalid, the remainder of this section and such amendments, and the application of such provision to other persons not similarly situated or to other circumstances, shall not be affected by such invalidation."

§ 1606. Extent of liability

As to any claim for relief with respect to which a foreign state is not entitled to immunity under section 1605 or 1607 of this chapter, the foreign state shall be liable in the same manner and to the same extent as a private individual under like circumstances; but a foreign state except for an agency or instrumentality thereof shall not be liable for punitive damages; if, however, in any case wherein death was caused, the law of the place where the action or omission occurred provides, or has been construed to provide, for damages only punitive in nature, the foreign state shall be liable for actual or compensatory damages measured by the pecuniary injuries resulting from such death which were incurred by the persons for whose benefit the action was brought.

(Added Pub.L. 94–583, § 4(a), Oct. 21, 1976, 90 Stat. 2894, and amended Pub.L. 105–277, Div. A, § 101(h) [Title I, § 117(b)], Oct. 21, 1998, 112 Stat. 2681–491; Pub.L. 106–386, Div. C, § 2002(f)(2), Oct. 28, 2000, 114 Stat. 1543; Pub.L. 107–297, Title II, § 201(c)(3), Nov. 26, 2002, 116 Stat. 2337.)

HISTORICAL AND STATUTORY NOTES

Effective and Applicability Provisions

1998 Acts. Amendment by section 117(b) of Pub.L. 105–277 to apply to any claim for which a foreign state is not immune under section 1605(a)(7) of this title arising before, on, or after Oct. 21, 1998, see Pub.L. 105–277, Div. A, § 101(h) [Title I, § 117(c)], set out as a note under section 1610 of this title.

1976 Acts. Section effective 90 days after Oct. 21, 1976, see section 8 of Pub.L. 94–583, set out as a note under section 1602 of this title.

Waiver of Exception to Immunity from Attachment or Execution

Provisions formerly authorizing the President to waive the requirements of section 117(b) of Pub.L. 105–277 [Div. A, § 101(h), Title I], (which amended this section) in the interest of national security, set out in Pub.L. 105–277, Div. A, § 101(h) [Title I, § 117(d)], Oct. 21, 1998, 112 Stat. 2681–491, which formerly appeared as a note under section 1610 of this title, were repealed by Pub.L. 106–386, Div. C, § 2002(f)(2), Oct. 28, 2000, 114 Stat. 1543.

§ 1607. Counterclaims

In any action brought by a foreign state, or in which a foreign state intervenes, in a court of the United States or of a State, the foreign state shall not be accorded immunity with respect to any counterclaim—

(a) for which a foreign state would not be entitled to immunity under section 1605 or 1605A of this chapter had such claim been brought in a separate action against the foreign state; or

(b) arising out of the transaction or occurrence that is the subject matter of the claim of the foreign state; or

(c) to the extent that the counterclaim does not seek relief exceeding in amount or differing in kind from that sought by the foreign state.

(Added Pub.L. 94–583, § 4(a), Oct. 21, 1976, 90 Stat. 2894, and amended Pub.L. 110–181, Div. A, Title X, § 1083(b)(2), Jan. 28, 2008, 122 Stat. 341.)

HISTORICAL AND STATUTORY NOTES

Effective and Applicability Provisions

1976 Acts. Section effective 90 days after Oct. 21, 1976, see section 8 of Pub.L. 94–583, set out as a note under section 1602 of this title.

Application of Pub.L. 110–181, Div. A, § 1083 to Pending Cases

For application of amendments made by Pub.L. 110–181, Div. A, § 1083 to pending cases and treatment of prior actions, see Pub.L. 110–181, Div. A, § 1083(c), set out as a note under 28 U.S.C.A. § 1605A.

Application of Pub.L. 110–181, Div. A, § 1083 to Iraq

For application of amendments made by Pub.L. 110–181, Div. A, § 1083 to Iraq, see Pub.L. 110–181, Div. A, § 1083(d), set out as a note under 28 U.S.C.A. § 1605A.

Severability

If any provision of Pub.L. 110–181, Div. A, § 1083, or the amendments made by that section, or the application of such provision to any person or circumstance, is held invalid, the remainder of that section and such amendments, and the application of such provision to other persons not similarly situated or to other circumstances, shall not be affected by such invalidation, see Pub.L. 110–181, Div. A, § 1083(e), set out as a note under 28 U.S.C.A. § 1605A.

§ 1608. Service; time to answer; default

(a) Service in the courts of the United States and of the States shall be made upon a foreign state or political subdivision of a foreign state:

(1) by delivery of a copy of the summons and complaint in accordance with any special arrangement for service between the plaintiff and the foreign state or political subdivision; or

(2) if no special arrangement exists, by delivery of a copy of the summons and complaint in accordance with an applicable international convention on service of judicial documents; or

(3) if service cannot be made under paragraphs (1) or (2), by sending a copy of the summons and complaint and a notice of suit, together with a translation of each into the official language of the foreign state, by any form of mail requiring a signed receipt, to be addressed and dispatched by the clerk of the court to the head of the ministry of foreign affairs of the foreign state concerned, or

(4) if service cannot be made within 30 days under paragraph (3), by sending two copies of the summons and complaint and a notice of suit, together with a translation of each into the official language of the foreign state, by any form of mail requiring a signed receipt, to be addressed and dispatched by the clerk of the court to the Secretary of State in Washington, District of Columbia, to the attention of the Director of Special Consular Services—and the Secretary shall transmit one copy of the papers through diplomatic channels to the foreign state and shall send to the clerk of the court a certified copy of the diplomatic note indicating when the papers were transmitted.

As used in this subsection, a "notice of suit" shall mean a notice addressed to a foreign state and in a form prescribed by the Secretary of State by regulation.

(b) Service in the courts of the United States and of the States shall be made upon an agency or instrumentality of a foreign state:

(1) by delivery of a copy of the summons and complaint in accordance with any special arrangement for service between the plaintiff and the agency or instrumentality; or

(2) if no special arrangement exists, by delivery of a copy of the summons and complaint either to an officer, a managing or general agent, or to any other agent authorized by appointment or by law to receive service of process in the United States; or in accordance with an applicable international convention on service of judicial documents; or

(3) if service cannot be made under paragraphs (1) or (2), and if reasonably calculated to give actual notice, by delivery of a copy of the summons and complaint, together with a translation of each into the official language of the foreign state—

(A) as directed by an authority of the foreign state or political subdivision in response to a letter rogatory or request or

(B) by any form of mail requiring a signed receipt, to be addressed and dispatched by the clerk of the court to the agency or instrumentality to be served, or

(C) as directed by order of the court consistent with the law of the place where service is to be made.

(c) Service shall be deemed to have been made—

(1) in the case of service under subsection (a)(4), as of the date of transmittal indicated in the certified copy of the diplomatic note; and

(2) in any other case under this section, as of the date of receipt indicated in the certification, signed and returned postal receipt, or other proof of service applicable to the method of service employed.

(d) In any action brought in a court of the United States or of a State, a foreign state, a political subdivision thereof, or an agency or instrumentality of a foreign state shall serve an answer or other responsive pleading to the complaint within sixty days after service has been made under this section.

(e) No judgment by default shall be entered by a court of the United States or of a State against a foreign state, a political subdivision thereof, or an agency or instrumentality of a foreign state, unless the claimant establishes his claim or right to relief by evidence satisfactory to the court. A copy of any such default judgment shall be sent to the foreign state or political subdivision in the manner prescribed for service in this section.

(Added Pub.L. 94–583, § 4(a), Oct. 21, 1976, 90 Stat. 2894.)

HISTORICAL AND STATUTORY NOTES

Effective and Applicability Provisions

1976 Acts. Section effective 90 days after Oct. 21, 1976, see section 8 of Pub.L. 94–583, set out as a note under section 1602 of this title.

§ 1609. Immunity from attachment and execution of property of a foreign state

Subject to existing international agreements to which the United States is a party at the time of enactment of this Act the property in the United States of a foreign state shall be immune from attachment arrest and execution except as provided in sections 1610 and 1611 of this chapter.

(Added Pub.L. 94–583, § 4(a), Oct. 21, 1976, 90 Stat. 2895.)

HISTORICAL AND STATUTORY NOTES

References in Text

The time of enactment of this Act, referred to in text, probably means the time of enactment of Pub.L. 94–583, which was approved on Oct. 21, 1976.

Effective and Applicability Provisions

1976 Acts. Section effective 90 days after Oct. 21, 1976, see section 8 of Pub.L. 94–583, set out as a note under section 1602 of this title.

§ 1610. Exceptions to the immunity from attachment or execution

(a) The property in the United States of a foreign state, as defined in section 1603(a) of this chapter, used for a commercial activity in the United States, shall not be immune from attachment in aid of execution, or from execution, upon a judgment entered by a court of the United States or of a State after the effective date of this Act, if—

(1) the foreign state has waived its immunity from attachment in aid of execution or from execution either explicitly or by implication, notwithstanding any withdrawal of the waiver the foreign state may purport to effect except in accordance with the terms of the waiver, or

(2) the property is or was used for the commercial activity upon which the claim is based, or

(3) the execution relates to a judgment establishing rights in property which has been taken in violation of international law or which has been exchanged for property taken in violation of international law, or

(4) the execution relates to a judgment establishing rights in property—

(A) which is acquired by succession or gift, or

(B) which is immovable and situated in the United States: *Provided,* That such property is not used for purposes of maintaining a diplomatic or consular mission or the residence of the Chief of such mission, or

(5) the property consists of any contractual obligation or any proceeds from such a contractual obligation to indemnify or hold harmless the foreign state or its employees under a policy of automobile or other liability or casualty insurance covering the claim which merged into the judgment, or

(6) the judgment is based on an order confirming an arbitral award rendered against the foreign state, provided that attachment in aid of execution, or execution, would not be inconsistent with any provision in the arbitral agreement, or

(7) the judgment relates to a claim for which the foreign state is not immune under section 1605A, regardless of whether the property is or was involved with the act upon which the claim is based.

(b) In addition to subsection (a), any property in the United States of an agency or instrumentality of a foreign state engaged in commercial activity in the United States shall not be immune from attachment in aid of execution, or from execution, upon a judgment entered by a court of the United States or of a State after the effective date of this Act, if—

(1) the agency or instrumentality has waived its immunity from attachment in aid of execution or from execution either explicitly or implicitly, notwithstanding any withdrawal of the waiver the agency or instrumentality may purport to effect except in accordance with the terms of the waiver, or

(2) the judgment relates to a claim for which the agency or instrumentality is not immune by virtue of section 1605(a) (2), (3), or (5), 1605(b), or 1605A of this chapter, regardless of whether the property is or was involved in the act upon which the claim is based.

(c) No attachment or execution referred to in subsections (a) and (b) of this section shall be permitted until the court has ordered such attachment and execution after having determined that a reasonable period of time has elapsed following the entry of judgment and the giving of any notice required under section 1608(e) of this chapter.

(d) The property of a foreign state, as defined in section 1603(a) of this chapter, used for a commercial activity in the United States, shall not be immune from attachment prior to the entry of judgment in any action brought in a court of the United States or of a State, or prior to the elapse of the period of time provided in subsection (c) of this section, if—

(1) the foreign state has explicitly waived its immunity from attachment prior to judgment, notwithstanding any withdrawal of the waiver the foreign state may purport to effect except in accordance with the terms of the waiver, and

(2) the purpose of the attachment is to secure satisfaction of a judgment that has been or may ultimately be entered against the foreign state, and not to obtain jurisdiction.

(e) The vessels of a foreign state shall not be immune from arrest in rem, interlocutory sale, and execution in actions brought to foreclose a preferred mortgage as provided in section 1605(d).

(f)(1)(A) Notwithstanding any other provision of law, including but not limited to section 208(f) of the Foreign Missions Act (22 U.S.C. 4308(f)), and except as provided in subparagraph (B), any property with respect to which financial transactions are prohibited or regulated pursuant to section 5(b) of the Trading with the Enemy Act (50 U.S.C. App. 5(b)), section 620(a) of the Foreign Assistance Act of 1961 (22 U.S.C. 2370(a)), sections 202 and 203 of the International Emergency Economic Powers Act (50 U.S.C. 1701–1702), or any other proclamation, order, regulation, or license issued pursuant thereto, shall be subject to execution or attachment in aid of execution of any judgment relating to a claim for which a foreign state (including any agency or instrumentality or such state) claiming such property is not immune under section 1605(a)(7) (as in effect before the enactment of section 1605A) or section 1605A.

(B) Subparagraph (A) shall not apply if, at the time the property is expropriated or seized by the foreign state, the property has been held in title by a natural person or, if held in trust, has been held for the benefit of a natural person or persons.

(2)(A) At the request of any party in whose favor a judgment has been issued with respect to a claim for which the foreign state is not immune under section 1605(a)(7) (as in effect before the enactment of section 1605A) or section 1605A, the Secretary of the Treasury and the Secretary of State should make every effort to fully, promptly, and effectively assist any judgment creditor or any court that has issued any such judgment in identifying, locating, and executing against the property of that foreign state or any agency or instrumentality of such state.

(B) In providing such assistance, the Secretaries—

(i) may provide such information to the court under seal; and

(ii) should make every effort to provide the information in a manner sufficient to allow the court to direct the United States Marshall's office to promptly and effectively execute against that property.

(3) Waiver.—The President may waive any provision of paragraph (1) in the interest of national security.

(g) Property in certain actions.—

(1) In general.—Subject to paragraph (3), the property of a foreign state against which a judgment is entered under section 1605A, and the property of an agency or instrumentality of such a state, including property that is a separate juridical entity or is an interest held directly or indirectly in a separate juridical entity, is subject to attachment in aid of execution, and execution, upon that judgment as provided in this section, regardless of—

(A) the level of economic control over the property by the government of the foreign state;

(B) whether the profits of the property go to that government;

(C) the degree to which officials of that government manage the property or otherwise control its daily affairs;

(D) whether that government is the sole beneficiary in interest of the property; or

(E) whether establishing the property as a separate entity would entitle the foreign state to benefits in United States courts while avoiding its obligations.

(2) United States sovereign immunity inapplicable.—Any property of a foreign state, or agency or instrumentality of a foreign state, to which paragraph (1) applies shall not be immune from attachment in aid of execution, or execution, upon a judgment entered under section 1605A because the property is regulated by the United States Government by reason of action taken against that foreign state under the Trading With the Enemy Act or the International Emergency Economic Powers Act.

(3) Third-party joint property holders.—Nothing in this subsection shall be construed to supersede the authority of a court to prevent appropriately the impairment of an interest held by a person who is not liable in the action giving rise to a judgment in property subject to attachment in aid of execution, or execution, upon such judgment.

(Added Pub.L. 94–583, § 4(a), Oct. 21, 1976, 90 Stat. 2896, and amended Pub.L. 100–640, § 2, Nov. 9, 1988, 102 Stat. 3333; Pub.L. 100–669, § 3, Nov. 16, 1988, 102 Stat. 3969; Pub.L. 101–650, Title III, § 325(b)(9), Dec. 1, 1990, 104 Stat. 5121; Pub.L. 104–132, Title II, § 221(b), Apr. 24, 1996, 110 Stat. 1243; Pub.L. 105–277, Div. A, § 101(h) [Title I, § 117(a)], Oct. 21, 1998, 112 Stat. 2681–491; Pub.L. 106–386, Div. C, § 2002(g)(1), Oct. 28, 2000, 114 Stat. 1543; Pub.L. 107–297, Title II, § 201(c)(3), Nov. 26, 2002, 116 Stat. 2337; Pub.L. 110–181, Div. A, Title X, § 1083(b)(3), Jan. 28, 2008, 122 Stat. 341.)

HISTORICAL AND STATUTORY NOTES

References in Text

The effective date of this Act, referred to in subsecs. (a) and (b), is 90 days after Oct. 21, 1976, see section 8 of Pub.L. 94–583, set out as an Effective and Applicability Provisions note under section 1602 of this title.

The enactment of section 1605A, referred to in subsec. (f), is Jan. 28, 2008, the approval date of National Defense Authorization Act for Fiscal Year 2008, Pub.L. 110–181, 122 Stat. 3, which enacted 28 U.S.C.A. § 1605A.

Effective and Applicability Provisions

1998 Acts. Pub.L. 105–277, § 101(h) [Title I, § 117(c)], provided that: "The amendments made by subsections (a) and (b) [amending this section and section 1606 of this title] shall apply to any claim for which a foreign state is not immune under section 1605(a)(7) of title 28, United States Code, arising before, on, or after the date of enactment of this Act [Oct. 21, 1998]."

1996 Acts. Amendment by Pub.L. 104–132 to apply to any cause of action arising before, on, or after Apr. 24, 1996, see section 221(c) of Pub.L. 104–132, set out as a note under section 1605 of this title.

1988 Acts. Amendment to this section by section 2 of Pub.L. 100–640, enacting subsec. (e) of this section, to apply to actions commenced on or after Nov. 9, 1988, see section 3 of Pub.L. 100–640, set out as a note under section 1605 of this title.

1976 Acts. Section effective 90 days after Oct. 21, 1976, see section 8 of Pub.L. 94–583, set out as a note under section 1602 of this title.

Application of Pub.L. 110–181, Div. A, § 1083 to Pending Cases

For application of amendments made by Pub.L. 110–181, Div. A, § 1083 to pending cases and treatment of prior actions, see Pub.L. 110–181, Div. A, § 1083(c), set out as a note under 28 U.S.C.A. § 1605A.

Application of Pub.L. 110–181, Div. A, § 1083 to Iraq

For application of amendments made by Pub.L. 110–181, Div. A, § 1083 to Iraq, see Pub.L. 110–181, Div. A, § 1083(d), set out as a note under 28 U.S.C.A. § 1605A.

Severability

If any provision of Pub.L. 110–181, Div. A, § 1083, or the amendments made by that section, or the application of such provision to any person or circumstance, is held invalid, the remainder of that section and such amendments, and the application of such provision to other persons not similarly situated or to other circumstances, shall not be affected by such invalidation, see Pub.L. 110–181, Div. A, § 1083(e), set out as a note under 28 U.S.C.A. § 1605A.

Treatment of Terrorist Assets

Pub.L. 107–297, Title II, § 201(a), (b), (d), Nov. 26, 2002, 116 Stat. 2337, provided that:

"**(a) In general.**—Notwithstanding any other provision of law, and except as provided in subsection (b) [of this note], in every case in which a person has obtained a judgment against a terrorist party on a claim based upon an act of terrorism, or for which a terrorist party is not immune under section 1605(a)(7) of title 28, United States Code, the blocked assets of that terrorist party (including the blocked assets of any agency or instrumentality of that terrorist party) shall be subject to execution or attachment in aid of execution in order to satisfy such judgment to the extent of any compensatory damages for which such terrorist party has been adjudged liable.

"**(b) Presidential waiver.**—

"**(1) In general.**—Subject to paragraph (2), upon determining on an asset-by-asset basis that a waiver is necessary in the national security interest, the President may waive the requirements of subsection (a) [of this note] in connection with (and prior to the enforcement of) any judicial order directing attachment in aid of execution or execution against any property subject to the Vienna Convention on Diplomatic Relations or the Vienna Convention on Consular Relations.

"**(2) Exception.**—A waiver under this subsection shall not apply to—

"**(A)** property subject to the Vienna Convention on Diplomatic Relations or the Vienna Convention on Consular Relations that has been used by the United States for any nondiplomatic purpose (including use as rental property), or the proceeds of such use; or

"**(B)** the proceeds of any sale or transfer for value to a third party of any asset subject to the Vienna Convention on Diplomatic Relations or the Vienna Convention on Consular Relations."

"**(d) Definitions.**—In this section [this note] the following definitions shall apply:

"**(1) Act of terrorism.**—The term 'act of terrorism' means—

"**(A)** any act or event certified under section 102(1) [Pub.L. 107–297, Title I, § 102(1), Nov. 26, 2002, 116 Stat. 2323, which is set out in a note under 15 U.S.C.A. § 6701]; or

"**(B)** to the extent not covered by subparagraph (A), any terrorist activity (as defined in section 212(a)(3)(B)(iii) of the Immigration and Nationality Act (8 U.S.C. 1182(a)(3)(B)(iii))).

"**(2) Blocked asset.**—The term 'blocked asset' means—

"**(A)** any asset seized or frozen by the United States under section 5(b) of the Trading With the Enemy Act (50 U.S.C. App. 5(b)) or under sections 202 and 203 of the International Emergency Economic Powers Act (50 U.S.C. 1701; 1702); and

"**(B)** Does not include property that—

"**(i)** is subject to a license issued by the United States Government for final payment, transfer, or disposition by or to a person subject to the jurisdiction of the United States in connection with a transaction for which the issuance of such license has been specifically required by statute other than the International Emergency Economic Powers Act (50 U.S.C. 1701 et seq.) or the United Nations Participation Act of 1945 (22 U.S.C. 287 et seq.); or

"**(ii)** in the case of property subject to the Vienna Convention on Diplomatic Relations or the Vienna Convention on Consular Relations, or that enjoys equivalent privileges and immunities under the law of the United States, is being used exclusively for diplomatic or consular purposes.

"**(3) Certain property.**—The term 'property subject to the Vienna Convention on Diplomatic Relations or the Vienna Convention on Consular Relations' and the term 'asset subject to the Vienna Convention on Diplomatic Relations or the Vienna Convention on Consular Relations' mean any property or asset, respectively, the attachment in aid of execution or execution of which would result in a violation of an obligation of the United States under the Vienna Convention on Diplomatic Relations or the Vienna Convention on Consular Relations, as the case may be.

"**(4) Terrorist party.**—The term 'terrorist party' means a terrorist, a terrorist organization (as defined in section 212(a)(3)(B)(vi) of the Immigration and Nationality Act (8 U.S.C. 1182(a)(3)(B)(vi))), or a foreign state designated as a state sponsor of terrorism under section 6(j) of the Export Administration Act of 1979 (50 U.S.C. App. 2405(j)) or section 620A of the Foreign Assistance Act of 1961 (22 U.S.C. 2371)."

Waiver of Exception to Immunity from Attachment or Execution

Pub.L. 105–277, Div. A, § 101(h) [Title I, § 117(d)], Oct. 21, 1998, 112 Stat. 2681–491, which had provided authority for the President to waive the requirements of section 117 of Pub.L. 105–277 [amending this section and section 1606 of this title and enacting provisions set out as notes under this section] in the interest of national security, was repealed by Pub.L. 106–386, Div. C, § 2002(g)(2), Oct. 28, 2000, 114 Stat. 1543; Pub.L. 107–297, Title II, § 201(c)(3), Nov. 26, 2002, 116 Stat. 2337.

§ 1611. Certain types of property immune from execution

(a) Notwithstanding the provisions of section 1610 of this chapter, the property of those organizations designated by the President as being entitled to enjoy the privileges, exemptions, and immunities provided by the International Organizations Immunities Act shall not be subject to attachment or any other judicial process impeding the disbursement of funds to, or on the order of, a foreign state as the result of an action brought in the courts of the United States or of the States.

(b) Notwithstanding the provisions of section 1610 of this chapter, the property of a foreign state shall be immune from attachment and from execution, if—

(1) the property is that of a foreign central bank or monetary authority held for its own account, unless such bank or authority, or its parent foreign government, has explicitly waived its immunity from attachment in aid of execution, or from execution, notwithstanding any withdrawal of the waiver which the bank, authority or government may purport to effect except in accordance with the terms of the waiver; or

(2) the property is, or is intended to be, used in connection with a military activity and

(A) is of a military character, or

(B) is under the control of a military authority or defense agency.

(c) Notwithstanding the provisions of section 1610 of this chapter, the property of a foreign state shall be immune from attachment and from execution in an action brought under section 302 of the Cuban Liberty and Democratic Solidarity (LIBERTAD) Act of 1996 to the extent that the property is a facility or installation used by an accredited diplomatic mission for official purposes.

(Added Pub.L. 94–583, § 4(a), Oct. 21, 1976, 90 Stat. 2897, and amended Pub.L. 104–114, Title III, § 302(e), Mar. 12, 1996, 110 Stat. 818.)

HISTORICAL AND STATUTORY NOTES

References in Text

The International Organizations Immunities Act, referred to in subsec. (a), is Act Dec. 29, 1945, c. 652, Title I, 59 Stat. 669, as amended, which is classified principally to section 288 et seq. of Title 22, Foreign Relations and Intercourse. For complete classification of this Act to the Code, see Short Title note set out under section 288 of Title 22 and Tables.

Section 302 of the Cuban Liberty and Democratic Solidarity (LIBERTAD) Act of 1996, referred to in subsec. (c), is Pub.L. 104–114, Title III, § 302, Mar. 12, 1996, 110 Stat. 815, which is classified to section 6082 of Title 22, Foreign Relations and Intercourse.

Effective and Applicability Provisions

1996 Acts. Amendment by section 302(e) of Pub.L. 104–114 effective Aug. 1, 1996, except as otherwise provided, see section 6085 of Title 22, Foreign Relations and Intercourse.

1976 Acts. Section effective 90 days after Oct. 21, 1976, see section 8 of Pub.L. 94–583, set out as a note under section 1602 of this title.

CHAPTER 99—GENERAL PROVISIONS

Sec.
1631. Transfer to cure want of jurisdiction.

§ 1631. Transfer to cure want of jurisdiction

Whenever a civil action is filed in a court as defined in section 610 of this title or an appeal, including a petition for review of administrative action, is noticed for or filed with such a court and that court finds that there is a want of jurisdiction, the court shall, if it is in the interest of justice, transfer such action or appeal to any other such court in which the action or appeal could have been brought at the time it was filed or noticed, and the action or appeal shall proceed as if it had been filed in or noticed for the court to which it is transferred on the date upon which it was actually filed in or noticed for the court from which it is transferred.

(Added Pub.L. 97–164, Title III, § 301(a), Apr. 2, 1982, 96 Stat. 55.)

HISTORICAL AND STATUTORY NOTES

Effective and Applicability Provisions

1982 Acts. Section effective Oct. 1, 1982, see section 402 of Pub.L. 97–164, set out as a note under section 171 of this title.

PART V—PROCEDURE

Chapter		Section
111.	General Provisions	1651
113.	Process	1691
114.	Class Actions	1711
115.	Evidence; Documentary	1731
117.	Evidence; Depositions	1781
119.	Evidence; Witnesses	1821
121.	Juries; Trial by Jury	1861
123.	Fees and Costs	1911
125.	Pending Actions and Judgments	1961
127.	Executions and Judicial Sales	2001
129.	Moneys Paid into Court	2041
131.	Rules of Courts	2071
133.	Review—Miscellaneous Provisions	2101

CHAPTER 111—GENERAL PROVISIONS

Sec.
1651. Writs.
1652. State laws as rules of decision.
1653. Amendment of pleadings to show jurisdiction.
1654. Appearance personally or by counsel.
1655. Lien enforcement; absent defendants.
1656. Creation of new district or division or transfer of territory; lien enforcement.
1657. Priority of civil actions.
1658. Time limitations on the commencement of civil actions arising under Acts of Congress.
1659. Stay of certain actions pending disposition of related proceedings before the United States International Trade Commission.

§ 1651. Writs

(a) The Supreme Court and all courts established by Act of Congress may issue all writs necessary or appropriate in aid of their respective jurisdictions and agreeable to the usages and principles of law.

(b) An alternative writ or rule nisi may be issued by a justice or judge of a court which has jurisdiction.

(June 25, 1948, c. 646, 62 Stat. 944; May 24, 1949, c. 139, § 90, 63 Stat. 102.)

HISTORICAL AND STATUTORY NOTES

Writ of Error

Act Jan. 31, 1928, c. 14, § 2, 45 Stat. 54, as amended Apr. 26, 1928, c. 440, 45 Stat. 466; June 25, 1948, c. 646, § 23, 62 Stat. 990, provided that: "All Acts of Congress referring to writs of error shall be construed as amended to the extent necessary to substitute appeal for writ of error."

§ 1652. State laws as rules of decision

The laws of the several states, except where the Constitution or treaties of the United States or Acts of Congress otherwise require or provide, shall be regarded as rules of decision in civil actions in the courts of the United States, in cases where they apply.

(June 25, 1948, c. 646, 62 Stat. 944.)

§ 1653. Amendment of pleadings to show jurisdiction

Defective allegations of jurisdiction may be amended, upon terms, in the trial or appellate courts.

(June 25, 1948, c. 646, 62 Stat. 944.)

§ 1654. Appearance personally or by counsel

In all courts of the United States the parties may plead and conduct their own cases personally or by counsel as, by the rules of such courts, respectively, are permitted to manage and conduct causes therein.

(June 25, 1948, c. 646, 62 Stat. 944; May 24, 1949, c. 139, § 91, 63 Stat. 103.)

§ 1655. Lien enforcement; absent defendants

In an action in a district court to enforce any lien upon or claim to, or to remove any incumbrance or lien or cloud upon the title to, real or personal property within the district, where any defendant cannot be served within the State, or does not voluntarily appear, the court may order the absent defendant to appear or plead by a day certain.

Such order shall be served on the absent defendant personally if practicable, wherever found, and also upon the person or persons in possession or charge of such property, if any. Where personal service is not practicable, the order shall be published as the court may direct, not less than once a week for six consecutive weeks.

If an absent defendant does not appear or plead within the time allowed, the court may proceed as if the absent defendant had been served with process within the State, but any adjudication shall, as regards the absent defendant without appearance, affect only the property which is the subject of the action. When a part of the property is within another district, but within the same state, such action may be brought in either district.

Any defendant not so personally notified may, at any time within one year after final judgment, enter his appearance, and thereupon the court shall set aside the judgment and permit such defendant to plead on payment of such costs as the court deems just.

(June 25, 1948, c. 646, 62 Stat. 944.)

§ 1656. Creation of new district or division or transfer of territory; lien enforcement

The creation of a new district or division or the transfer of any territory to another district or division shall not affect or divest any lien theretofore acquired in a district court upon property within such district, division or territory.

To enforce such lien, the clerk of the court in which the same is acquired, upon the request and at the cost of the party desiring the same, shall make a certified copy of the record thereof, which, when filed in the proper court of the district or division in which such property is situated after such creation or transfer shall be evidence in all courts and places equally with the original thereof; and, thereafter like proceedings shall be had thereon, and with the same effect, as though the case or proceeding had been originally instituted in such court.

(June 25, 1948, c. 646, 62 Stat. 944; Nov. 6, 1978, Pub.L. 95–598, Title II, § 242, 92 Stat. 2671.)

HISTORICAL AND STATUTORY NOTES

Codifications

This section, was amended by Pub.L. 95–598, Title II, § 242, Nov. 6, 1978, 92 Stat. 2671, effective June 28, 1984, pursuant to Pub.L. 95–598, Title IV, § 402(b), Nov. 6, 1978, 92 Stat. 2682, as amended by Pub.L. 98–249, § 1(a), Mar. 31, 1984, 98 Stat. 116; Pub.L. 98–271, § 1(a), Apr. 30, 1984, 98 Stat. 163; Pub.L. 98–299, § 1(a), May 25, 1984, 98 Stat. 214; Pub.L. 98–325, § 1(a), June 20, 1984, 98 Stat. 268, set out as an Effective and Applicability Provisions note preceding section 101 of Title 11, Bankruptcy, by inserting "or in a bankruptcy court" following "a district court".

Section 402(b) of Pub.L. 95–598 was amended by section 113 of Pub.L. 98–353, Title I, July 10, 1984, 98 Stat. 343, by substituting "shall not be effective" for "shall take effect on June 28, 1984", thereby eliminating the amendment by section 242 of Pub.L. 95–598, effective June 27, 1984, pursuant to section 122(c) of Pub.L. 98–353, set out as an Effective and Applicability Provisions note under section 151 of this title.

Section 121(a) of Pub.L. 98–353 directed that section 402(b) of Pub.L. 95–598 be amended by substituting "the date of enactment of the Bankruptcy Amendments and Federal Judgeship Act of 1984 [i.e. July 10, 1984]" for "June 28, 1984". This amendment was not executed in view of the prior amendment to section 402(b) of Pub.L. 95–598 by section 113 of Pub.L. 98–353.

§ 1657. Priority of civil actions

(a) Notwithstanding any other provision of law, each court of the United States shall determine the order in which civil actions are heard and determined, except that the court shall expedite the consideration of any action brought under chapter 153 or section 1826 of this title, any action for temporary or preliminary injunctive relief, or any other action if good cause therefor is shown. For purposes of this subsection, "good cause" is shown if a right under the Constitution of the United States or a Federal Statute (including rights under section 552 of title 5) would be maintained in a factual context that indicates that a request for expedited consideration has merit.

(b) The Judicial Conference of the United States may modify the rules adopted by the courts to determine the order in which civil actions are heard and determined, in order to establish consistency among the judicial circuits.

(Added Pub.L. 98–620, Title IV, § 401(a), Nov. 8, 1984, 98 Stat. 3356.)

HISTORICAL AND STATUTORY NOTES

Codifications

Pub.L. 101–647, Title XXV, § 2527(b), Nov. 29, 1990, 104 Stat. 4877, purported to amend section 1657 of Title 18, Crimes and Criminal Procedure, by inserting "section 11, 12, or 13 of the Federal Deposit Insurance Act" after "consideration of any action brought under", which amendment could not be executed to the text of section 1657 of Title 18. Such amendment was probably intended to amend this section.

Effective and Applicability Provisions

1984 Acts. Section 403 of Pub.L. 98–620 provided that: "The amendments made by this subtitle [subtitle A of Title IV of Pub.L. 98–620, enacting this section, amending sections 596, 636, 1364, 2284, and 2349 of this title, sections 437g, 437h and 687 of Title 2, The Congress, section 552 of Title 5, Government Organization and Employees, sections 8, 136d, 136h, 136n, 136w, 194, 1366, 1600 and 1601 of Title 7, Agriculture, section 1464 of Title 12, Banks and Banking, sections 18a, 21, 45, 57a–1, 78k–1, 687a, 687c, 719h, 1415, 2003 and 2622 of Title 15, Commerce and Trade, sections 1463a, 1910, 3117, and 3168 of Title 16, Conservation, sections 1964 and 1966 of Title 18, Crimes and Criminal Procedure, sections 346a and 348 of Title 21, Food and Drugs, section 618 of Title 22, Foreign Relations and Intercourse, section 640d–3 of Title 25, Indians, sections 3310, 6110, 6363, 7609, 9010 and 9011 of Title 26, Internal Revenue Code, sections 110, 160, 660 and 1303 of Title 29, Labor, section 816 of Title 30, Mineral Lands and Mining, section 2022 of Title 38, Veterans' Benefits, section 3628 of Title 39, Postal Service, sections 300j–9, 504, 6508 and 8514 of Title 42, The Public Health and Welfare, sections 1062, 1349, 1652 and 2011 of Title 43, Public Lands, sections 355, 745, 1018 and 1205 of Title 45, Railroads, section 402 of Title 47, Telegraphs, Telephones, and Radiotelegraphs, section 2305 of Title 49 Appendix, Transportation, section 792a of Title 50, War and National Defense, sections 462 and 1984 of the Appendix to Title 50, repealing sections 1296 and 2647 of this title, section 28 of Title 15, Commerce and Trade, and section 3614 of Title 42, The Public Health and Welfare, and amending provisions set out as a note under section 2304 of Title 10, Armed Forces] shall not apply to cases pending on the date of the enactment of this subtitle [Nov. 8, 1984]."

§ 1658. Time limitations on the commencement of civil actions arising under Acts of Congress

(a) Except as otherwise provided by law, a civil action arising under an Act of Congress enacted after the date of the enactment of this section may not be commenced later than 4 years after the cause of action accrues.

(b) Notwithstanding subsection (a), a private right of action that involves a claim of fraud, deceit, manipulation, or contrivance in contravention of a regulatory requirement concerning the securities laws, as defined in section 3(a)(47) of the Securities Exchange Act of 1934 (15 U.S.C. 78c(a)(47)), may be brought not later than the earlier of—

(1) 2 years after the discovery of the facts constituting the violation; or

(2) 5 years after such violation.

(Added Pub.L. 101–650, Title III, § 313(a), Dec. 1, 1990, 104 Stat. 5114, and amended Pub.L. 107–204, Title VIII, § 804(a), July 30, 2002, 116 Stat. 801.)

HISTORICAL AND STATUTORY NOTES

References in Text

The date of the enactment of this section, referred to in text, is the date of enactment of this section by section 313(a) of Pub.L. 101–650, which was approved Dec. 1, 1990.

Effective and Applicability Provisions

2002 Acts. Pub.L. 107–204, Title VIII, § 804(b), July 30, 2002, 116 Stat. 801, provided that: "The limitations period provided by section 1658(b) of title 28, United States Code [subsec. (b) of this section], as added by this section [section 804 of Pub.L. 107–204, which amended this section], shall apply to all proceedings addressed by this section that are commenced on or after the date of enactment of this Act [July 30, 2002]."

1990 Acts. Section 313(c) of Pub.L. 101–650 provided that: "The amendments made by this section [enacting this section] shall apply with respect to causes of action accruing on or after the date of the enactment of this Act [Dec. 1, 1990]."

No Creation of Actions

Pub.L. 107–204, Title VIII, § 804(c), July 30, 2002, 116 Stat. 801, provided that: "Nothing in this section [Pub.L. 107–204, Title VIII, § 804, July 30, 2002, 116 Stat. 801, which amended this section and enacted provisions set out as a note under this section] shall create a new, private right of action."

§ 1659. Stay of certain actions pending disposition of related proceedings before the United States International Trade Commission

(a) Stay.—In a civil action involving parties that are also parties to a proceeding before the United States International Trade Commission under section 337 of the Tariff Act of 1930, at the request of a party to the civil action that is also a respondent in the proceeding before the Commission, the district court shall stay, until the determination of the Commission becomes final, proceedings in the civil action with respect to any claim that involves the same issues involved in the proceeding before the Commission, but only if such request is made within—

(1) 30 days after the party is named as a respondent in the proceeding before the Commission, or

(2) 30 days after the district court action is filed,

whichever is later.

(b) Use of Commission record.—Notwithstanding section 337(n)(1) of the Tariff Act of 1930, after dissolution of a stay under subsection (a), the record of the proceeding before the United States International Trade Commission shall be transmitted to the district court and shall be admissible in the civil action, subject to such protective order as the district court determines necessary, to the extent permitted under the Federal Rules of Evidence and the Federal Rules of Civil Procedure.

(Added Pub.L. 103–465, Title III, § 321(b)(1)(A), Dec. 8, 1994, 108 Stat. 4945.)

HISTORICAL AND STATUTORY NOTES

References in Text

Section 337 of the Tariff Act of 1930, referred to in text, is section 337 of Act June 17, 1930, c. 497, Title III, 46 Stat. 703, which is classified to section 1337 of Title 19, Customs Duties.

Effective and Applicability Provisions

1994 Acts. Section applicable with respect to complaints filed under section 1337 of Title 19, Customs Duties, on or after the date on which the WTO Agreement enters into force with respect to the United States, Jan. 1, 1995, or in cases under section 1337 of Title 19 in which no complaint is filed, with respect to investigations initiated under such section on or after such date, see section 322 of Pub.L. 103–465, set out as a note under section 1337 of Title 19.

CHAPTER 113—PROCESS

Sec.
1691. Seal and teste of process.
1692. Process and orders affecting property in different districts.
1693. Place of arrest in civil action.
1694. Patent infringement action.
1695. Stockholder's derivative action.
1696. Service in foreign and international litigation.
1697. Service in multiparty, multiforum actions.

§ 1691. Seal and teste of process

All writs and process issuing from a court of the United States shall be under the seal of the court and signed by the clerk thereof.

(June 25, 1948, c. 646, 62 Stat. 945.)

HISTORICAL AND STATUTORY NOTES

Immunity from Seizure under Judicial Process of Cultural Objects Imported for Temporary Exhibition or Display

Presidential determination of cultural significance of objects and exhibition or display thereof in the national interest, see section 2459 of Title 22, Foreign Relations and Intercourse.

§ 1692. Process and orders affecting property in different districts

In proceedings in a district court where a receiver is appointed for property, real, personal, or mixed, situated in different districts, process may issue and be executed in any such district as if the property lay wholly within one district, but orders affecting the property shall be entered of record in each of such districts.

(June 25, 1948, c. 646, 62 Stat. 945.)

§ 1693. Place of arrest in civil action

Except as otherwise provided by Act of Congress, no person shall be arrested in one district for trial in another in any civil action in a district court.

(June 25, 1948, c. 646, 62 Stat. 945.)

§ 1694. Patent infringement action

In a patent infringement action commenced in a district where the defendant is not a resident but has a regular and established place of business, service of process, summons or subpoena upon such defendant may be made upon his agent or agents conducting such business.

(June 25, 1948, c. 646, 62 Stat. 945.)

§ 1695. Stockholder's derivative action

Process in a stockholder's action in behalf of his corporation may be served upon such corporation in any district where it is organized or licensed to do business or is doing business.

(June 25, 1948, c. 646, 62 Stat. 945.)

§ 1696. Service in foreign and international litigation

(a) The district court of the district in which a person resides or is found may order service upon him of any document issued in connection with a proceeding in a foreign or international tribunal. The order may be made pursuant to a letter rogatory issued, or request made, by a foreign or international tribunal or upon application of any interested person and shall direct the manner of service. Service pursuant to this subsection does not, of itself, require the recognition or enforcement in the United States of a judgment, decree, or order rendered by a foreign or international tribunal.

(b) This section does not preclude service of such a document without an order of court.

(Added Pub.L. 88–619, § 4(a), Oct. 3, 1964, 78 Stat. 995.)

HISTORICAL AND STATUTORY NOTES

Treaties and Conventions; Service Abroad of Judicial and Extrajudicial Documents in Civil or Commercial Matters; Observance On and After Feb. 10, 1969, by United States and Citizens and Persons Subject to Jurisdiction of United States

For text of Convention, see provisions set out as a note under Rule 4, Federal Rules of Civil Procedure, 28 U.S.C.A.

§ 1697. Service in multiparty, multiforum actions

When the jurisdiction of the district court is based in whole or in part upon section 1369 of this title, process, other than subpoenas, may be served at any place within the United States, or anywhere outside the United States if otherwise permitted by law.

(Added Pub.L. 107–273, Div. C, Title I, § 11020(b)(4)(A)(i), Nov. 2, 2002, 116 Stat. 1828.)

HISTORICAL AND STATUTORY NOTES

Effective and Applicability Provisions

2002 Acts. Amendments by section 11020(b) of Pub.L. 107–273 shall apply to a civil action if the accident giving rise to the cause of action occurred on or after the 90th day after Nov. 2, 2002, see section 11020(c) of Pub.L. 107–273, set out as a note under 28 U.S.C.A. § 1369.

CHAPTER 114—CLASS ACTIONS

Sec.
1711. Definitions.
1712. Coupon settlements.
1713. Protection against loss by class members.
1714. Protection against discrimination based on geographic location.
1715. Notifications to appropriate Federal and State officials.

§ 1711. Definitions

In this chapter:

(1) Class.—The term "class" means all of the class members in a class action.

(2) Class action.—The term "class action" means any civil action filed in a district court of the United States under rule 23 of the Federal Rules of Civil Procedure or any civil action that is removed to a district court of the United States that was originally filed under a State statute or rule of judicial procedure authorizing an action to be brought by 1 or more representatives as a class action.

(3) Class counsel.—The term "class counsel" means the persons who serve as the attorneys for the class members in a proposed or certified class action.

(4) Class members.—The term "class members" means the persons (named or unnamed) who fall within the definition of the proposed or certified class in a class action.

(5) Plaintiff class action.—The term "plaintiff class action" means a class action in which class members are plaintiffs.

(6) Proposed settlement.—The term "proposed settlement" means an agreement regarding a class action that is subject to court approval and that, if approved, would be binding on some or all class members.

(Added Pub.L. 109–2, § 3(a), Feb. 18, 2005, 119 Stat. 5.)

HISTORICAL AND STATUTORY NOTES

References in Text

Rule 23 of the Federal Rules of Civil Procedure, referred to in par. (2), is set out following the code sections of this title.

Effective and Applicability Provisions

2005 Acts. Enactment of this section by Class Action Fairness Act of 2005, Pub.L. 109–2, Feb. 18, 2005, 119 Stat. 4, applicable to any civil action commenced on or after Feb. 18, 2005, see Pub.L. 109–2, § 9, set out as a note under 28 U.S.C.A. § 1332.

Findings and Purposes

Pub.L. 109–2, § 2, Feb. 18, 2005, 119 Stat. 4, provided that:

"(a) **Findings.**—Congress finds the following:

"(1) Class action lawsuits are an important and valuable part of the legal system when they permit the fair and efficient resolution of legitimate claims of numerous parties by allowing the claims to be aggregated into a single action against a defendant that has allegedly caused harm.

"(2) Over the past decade, there have been abuses of the class action device that have—

"(A) harmed class members with legitimate claims and defendants that have acted responsibly;

"(B) adversely affected interstate commerce; and

"(C) undermined public respect for our judicial system.

"(3) Class members often receive little or no benefit from class actions, and are sometimes harmed, such as where—

"(A) counsel are awarded large fees, while leaving class members with coupons or other awards of little or no value;

"(B) unjustified awards are made to certain plaintiffs at the expense of other class members; and

"(C) confusing notices are published that prevent class members from being able to fully understand and effectively exercise their rights.

"(4) Abuses in class actions undermine the National judicial system, the free flow of interstate commerce, and the concept of diversity jurisdiction as intended by the framers of the United States constitution, in that State and local courts are—

"(A) keeping cases of national importance out of Federal court;

"(B) sometimes acting in ways that demonstrate bias against out-of-State defendants; and

"(C) making judgments that impose their view of the law on other States and bind the rights of the residents of those States.

"(b) **Purposes.**—The purposes of this Act [the Class Action Fairness Act of 2005, which enacted this note, this chapter, and 28 U.S.C.A. § 1453, amended 28 U.S.C.A. §§ 1332, 1335, and 1603, and enacted provisions set out as notes under 28 U.S.C.A. §§ 1332, 2071, and 2074] are to—

"(1) assure fair and prompt recoveries for class members with legitimate claims;

"(2) restore the intent of the framers of the United States Constitution by providing for Federal court consideration of interstate cases of national importance under diversity jurisdiction; and

"(3) benefit society by encouraging innovation and lowering consumer prices."

[Enactment of this note by Class Action Fairness Act of 2005, Pub.L. 109–2, Feb. 18, 2005, 119 Stat. 4, applicable to any civil action commenced on or after Feb. 18, 2005, see Pub.L. 109–2, § 9, set out as a note under 28 U.S.C.A. § 1332.]

§ 1712. Coupon settlements

(a) Contingent fees in coupon settlements.—If a proposed settlement in a class action provides for a recovery of coupons to a class member, the portion of any attorney's fee award to class counsel that is attributable to the award of the coupons shall be based on the value to class members of the coupons that are redeemed.

(b) Other attorney's fee awards in coupon settlements.—

(1) In general.—If a proposed settlement in a class action provides for a recovery of coupons to class members, and a portion of the recovery of the coupons is not used to determine the attorney's fee to be paid to class counsel, any attorney's fee award shall be based upon the amount of time class counsel reasonably expended working on the action.

(2) Court approval.—Any attorney's fee under this subsection shall be subject to approval by the court and shall include an appropriate attorney's fee, if any, for obtaining equitable relief, including an injunction, if applicable. Nothing in this subsection shall be construed to prohibit application of a lodestar with a multiplier method of determining attorney's fees.

(c) Attorney's fee awards calculated on a mixed basis in coupon settlements.—If a proposed settlement in a class action provides for an award of coupons to class members and also provides for equitable relief, including injunctive relief—

(1) that portion of the attorney's fee to be paid to class counsel that is based upon a portion of the recovery of the coupons shall be calculated in accordance with subsection (a); and

(2) that portion of the attorney's fee to be paid to class counsel that is not based upon a portion of the recovery of the coupons shall be calculated in accordance with subsection (b).

(d) Settlement valuation expertise.—In a class action involving the awarding of coupons, the court may, in its discretion upon the motion of a party, receive expert testimony from a witness qualified to provide information on the actual value to the class members of the coupons that are redeemed.

(e) Judicial scrutiny of coupon settlements.—In a proposed settlement under which class members would be awarded coupons, the court may approve the proposed settlement only after a hearing to determine whether, and making a written finding that, the settlement is fair, reasonable, and adequate for class members. The court, in its discretion, may also require that a proposed settlement agreement provide for the distribution of a portion of the value of unclaimed coupons to 1 or more charitable or governmental organizations, as agreed to by the parties. The distribution and redemption of any proceeds under this subsection shall not be used to calculate attorneys' fees under this section.

(Added Pub.L. 109–2, § 3(a), Feb. 18, 2005, 119 Stat. 6.)

HISTORICAL AND STATUTORY NOTES

Effective and Applicability Provisions

2005 Acts. Enactment of this section by Class Action Fairness Act of 2005, Pub.L. 109–2, Feb. 18, 2005, 119 Stat. 4, applicable to any civil action commenced on or after Feb. 18, 2005, see Pub.L. 109–2, § 9, set out as a note under 28 U.S.C.A. § 1332.

§ 1713. Protection against loss by class members

The court may approve a proposed settlement under which any class member is obligated to pay sums to class counsel that would result in a net loss to the class member only if the court makes a written finding that nonmonetary benefits to the class member substantially outweigh the monetary loss.

(Added Pub.L. 109–2, § 3(a), Feb. 18, 2005, 119 Stat. 7.)

HISTORICAL AND STATUTORY NOTES

Effective and Applicability Provisions

2005 Acts. Enactment of this section by Class Action Fairness Act of 2005, Pub.L. 109–2, Feb. 18, 2005, 119 Stat. 4, applicable to any civil action commenced on or after Feb. 18, 2005, see Pub.L. 109–2, § 9, set out as a note under 28 U.S.C.A. § 1332.

§ 1714. Protection against discrimination based on geographic location

The court may not approve a proposed settlement that provides for the payment of greater sums to some class members than to others solely on the basis that the class members to whom the greater sums are to be paid are located in closer geographic proximity to the court.

(Added Pub.L. 109–2, § 3(a), Feb. 18, 2005, 119 Stat. 7.)

HISTORICAL AND STATUTORY NOTES

Effective and Applicability Provisions

2005 Acts. Enactment of this section by Class Action Fairness Act of 2005, Pub.L. 109–2, Feb. 18, 2005, 119 Stat. 4, applicable to any civil action commenced on or after Feb. 18, 2005, see Pub.L. 109–2, § 9, set out as a note under 28 U.S.C.A. § 1332.

§ 1715. Notifications to appropriate Federal and State officials

(a) Definitions.—

(1) Appropriate Federal official.—In this section, the term "appropriate Federal official" means—

(A) the Attorney General of the United States; or

(B) in any case in which the defendant is a Federal depository institution, a State depository institution, a depository institution holding company, a foreign bank, or a nondepository institution subsidiary of the foregoing (as such terms are defined in section 3 of the Federal Deposit Insurance Act (12 U.S.C. 1813)), the person who has the primary Federal regulatory or supervisory responsibility with respect to the defendant, if some or all of the matters alleged in the class action are subject to regulation or supervision by that person.

(2) Appropriate State official.—In this section, the term "appropriate State official" means the person in the State who has the primary regulatory or supervisory responsibility with respect to the defendant, or who licenses or otherwise authorizes the defendant to conduct business in the State, if some or all of the matters alleged in the class action are subject to regulation by that person. If there is no primary regulator, supervisor, or licensing authority, or the matters alleged in the class action are not subject to regulation or supervision by that person, then the appropriate State official shall be the State attorney general.

(b) In general.—Not later than 10 days after a proposed settlement of a class action is filed in court, each defendant that is participating in the proposed settlement shall serve upon the appropriate State official of each State in which a class member resides and the appropriate Federal official, a notice of the proposed settlement consisting of—

(1) a copy of the complaint and any materials filed with the complaint and any amended complaints (except such materials shall not be required to be served if such materials are made electronically available through the Internet and such service includes notice of how to electronically access such material);

(2) notice of any scheduled judicial hearing in the class action;

(3) any proposed or final notification to class members of—

(A)(i) the members' rights to request exclusion from the class action; or

(ii) if no right to request exclusion exists, a statement that no such right exists; and

(B) a proposed settlement of a class action;

(4) any proposed or final class action settlement;

(5) any settlement or other agreement contemporaneously made between class counsel and counsel for the defendants;

(6) any final judgment or notice of dismissal;

(7)(A) if feasible, the names of class members who reside in each State and the estimated proportionate share of the claims of such members to the entire settlement to that State's appropriate State official; or

(B) if the provision of information under subparagraph (A) is not feasible, a reasonable estimate of the number of class members residing in each State and the estimated proportionate share of the claims of such members to the entire settlement; and

(8) any written judicial opinion relating to the materials described under subparagraphs (3) through (6).

(c) Depository institutions notification.—

(1) Federal and other depository institutions.—In any case in which the defendant is a Federal depository institution, a depository institution holding company, a foreign bank, or a nondepository institution subsidiary of the foregoing, the notice requirements of this section are satisfied by serving the notice required under subsection (b) upon the person who has the primary Federal regulatory or supervisory responsibility with respect to the defendant, if some or all of the matters alleged in the class action are subject to regulation or supervision by that person.

(2) State depository institutions.—In any case in which the defendant is a State depository institution (as that term is defined in section 3 of the Federal Deposit Insurance Act (12 U.S.C. 1813)), the notice requirements of this section are satisfied by serving the notice required under subsection (b) upon the State bank supervisor (as that term is defined in section 3 of the Federal Deposit Insurance Act (12 U.S.C. 1813)) of the State in which the defendant is incorporated or chartered, if some or all of the matters alleged in the class action are subject to regulation or supervision by that person, and upon the appropriate Federal official.

(d) Final approval.—An order giving final approval of a proposed settlement may not be issued earlier than 90 days after the later of the dates on which the appropriate Federal official and the appropriate State official are served with the notice required under subsection (b).

(e) Noncompliance if notice not provided.—

(1) In general.—A class member may refuse to comply with and may choose not to be bound by a settlement agreement or consent decree in a class action if the class member demonstrates that the notice required under subsection (b) has not been provided.

(2) Limitation.—A class member may not refuse to comply with or to be bound by a settlement agreement or consent decree under paragraph (1) if the notice required under subsection (b) was directed to the appropriate Federal official and to either the State attorney general or the person that has primary regulatory, supervisory, or licensing authority over the defendant.

(3) Application of rights.—The rights created by this subsection shall apply only to class members or any person acting on a class member's behalf, and shall not be construed to limit any other rights affecting a class member's participation in the settlement.

(f) Rule of construction.—Nothing in this section shall be construed to expand the authority of, or impose any obligations, duties, or responsibilities upon, Federal or State officials.

(Added Pub.L. 109–2, § 3(a), Feb. 18, 2005, 119 Stat. 7.)

HISTORICAL AND STATUTORY NOTES

References in Text

Section 3 of the Federal Deposit Insurance Act, referred to in subsecs. (a)(1)(B) and (c)(2), is Act Sept. 21, 1950, c. 967, § 2[3], 64 Stat. 873, as amended, which is classified to 12 U.S.C.A. § 1813. A Federal depository institution is defined in 12 U.S.C.A. § 1813(c)(4); a State depository institution, in 12 U.S.C.A. § 1813(c)(5); a depository institution holding company, in 12 U.S.C.A. § 1813(w)(1); a foreign bank, in 12 U.S.C.A. § 1813(s)(1); and State bank supervisor, in 12 U.S.C.A. § 1813(r)(1).

Effective and Applicability Provisions

2005 Acts. Enactment of this section by Class Action Fairness Act of 2005, Pub.L. 109–2, Feb. 18, 2005, 119 Stat. 4, applicable to any civil action commenced on or after Feb. 18, 2005, see Pub.L. 109–2, § 9, set out as a note under 28 U.S.C.A. § 1332.

CHAPTER 115—EVIDENCE; DOCUMENTARY

Sec.
1731. Handwriting.
1732. Record made in regular course of business; photographic copies.
1733. Government records and papers; copies.
1734. Court record lost or destroyed generally.[1]
1735. Court record lost or destroyed where United States interested.
1736. Congressional Journals.
1737. Copy of officer's bond.
1738. State and Territorial statutes and judicial proceedings; full faith and credit.
1738A. Full faith and credit given to child custody determinations.
1738B. Full faith and credit for child support orders.
1738C. Certain acts, records, and proceedings and the effect thereof.
1739. State and Territorial nonjudicial records; full faith and credit.
1740. Copies of consular papers.
1741. Foreign official documents.
[1742. Repealed.]
1743. Demand on postmaster.
1744. Copies of United States Patent and Trademark Office documents generally.[1]
1745. Copies of foreign patent documents.
1746. Unsworn declarations under penalty of perjury.

[1] So in original. Does not conform to section catchline.

§ 1731. Handwriting

The admitted or proved handwriting of any person shall be admissible, for purposes of comparison, to determine genuineness of other handwriting attributed to such person.

(June 25, 1948, c. 646, 62 Stat. 945.)

§ 1732. Record made in regular course of business; photographic copies

If any business, institution, member of a profession or calling, or any department or agency of government, in the regular course of business or activity has kept or recorded any memorandum, writing, entry, print, representation or combination thereof, of any act, transaction, occurrence, or event, and in the regular course of business has caused any or all of the same to be recorded, copied, or reproduced by any photographic, photostatic, microfilm, micro-card, miniature photographic, or other process which accurately reproduces or forms a durable medium for so reproducing the original, the original may be destroyed in the regular course of business unless its preservation is required by law. Such reproduction, when satisfactorily identified, is as admissible in evidence as the original itself in any judicial or administrative proceeding whether the original is in existence or not and an enlargement or facsimile of such reproduction is likewise admissible in evidence if the original reproduction is in existence and available for inspection under direction of court. The introduction of a reproduced record, enlargement, or facsimile does not preclude admission of the original. This subsection[1] shall not be construed to exclude from evidence any document or copy thereof which is otherwise admissible under the rules of evidence.

(June 25, 1948, c. 646, 62 Stat. 945; Aug. 28, 1951, c. 351, §§ 1, 3, 65 Stat. 205, 206; Aug. 30, 1961, Pub.L. 87–183, 75 Stat. 413; Jan. 2, 1975, Pub.L. 93–595, § 2(b), 88 Stat. 1949.)

[1] Probably should be read as "section". Section formerly was subsec. (b) of this section.

§ 1733. Government records and papers; copies

(a) Books or records of account or minutes of proceedings of any department or agency of the United States shall be admissible to prove the act, transaction or occurrence as a memorandum of which the same were made or kept.

(b) Properly authenticated copies or transcripts of any books, records, papers or documents of any department or agency of the United States shall be admitted in evidence equally with the originals thereof.

(c) This section does not apply to cases, actions, and proceedings to which the Federal Rules of Evidence apply.

(June 25, 1948, c. 646, 62 Stat. 946; Jan. 2, 1975, Pub.L. 93–595, § 2(c), 88 Stat. 1949.)

HISTORICAL AND STATUTORY NOTES

References in Text

The Federal Rules of Evidence, referred to in subsec. (c), are set out in this title.

§ 1734. Court record lost or destroyed, generally

(a) A lost or destroyed record of any proceeding in any court of the United States may be supplied on application of any interested party not at fault, by substituting a copy certified by the clerk of any court in which an authentic copy is lodged.

(b) Where a certified copy is not available, any interested person not at fault may file in such court a verified application for an order establishing the lost or destroyed record.

Every other interested person shall be served personally with a copy of the application and with notice of hearing on a day stated, not less than sixty days after service. Service may be made on any nonresident of the district anywhere within the jurisdiction of the United States or in any foreign country.

Proof of service in a foreign country shall be certified by a minister or consul of the United States in such country, under his official seal.

If, after the hearing, the court is satisfied that the statements contained in the application are true, it shall enter an order reciting the substance and effect of the lost or destroyed record. Such order, subject to intervening rights of third persons, shall have the same effect as the original record.

(June 25, 1948, c. 646, 62 Stat. 946.)

§ 1735. Court record lost or destroyed where United States interested

(a) When the record of any case or matter in any court of the United States to which the United States is a party, is lost or destroyed, a certified copy of any official paper of a United States attorney, United States marshal or clerk or other certifying or recording officer of any such court, made pursuant to law, on file in any department or agency of the United States and relating to such case or matter, shall, on being filed in the court to which it relates, have the same effect as an original paper filed in such court. If the copy so filed discloses the date and amount of a judgment or decree and the names of the parties thereto, the court may enforce the judgment or decree as though the original record had not been lost or destroyed.

(b) Whenever the United States is interested in any lost or destroyed records or files of a court of the United States, the clerk of such court and the United States attorney for the district shall take the steps necessary to restore such records or files, under the direction of the judges of such court.

(June 25, 1948, c. 646, 62 Stat. 946.)

§ 1736. Congressional Journals

Extracts from the Journals of the Senate and the House of Representatives, and from the Executive Journal of the Senate when the injunction of secrecy is removed, certified by the Secretary of the Senate or the Clerk of the House of Representatives shall be received in evidence with the same effect as the originals would have.

(June 25, 1948, c. 646, 62 Stat. 947.)

HISTORICAL AND STATUTORY NOTES

Transfer of Functions

Any reference in any provision of law enacted before Jan. 4, 1995, to a function, duty, or authority of the Clerk of the House of Representatives treated as referring, with respect to that function, duty, or authority, to the officer of the House of Representatives exercising that function, duty, or authority, as determined by the Committee on House Oversight of the House of Representatives, see section 2(1) of Pub.L. 104–14, set out as a note preceding section 21 of Title 2, The Congress.

§ 1737. Copy of officer's bond

Any person to whose custody the bond of any officer of the United States has been committed shall, on proper request and payment of the fee allowed by any Act of Congress, furnish certified copies thereof, which shall be prima facie evidence in any court of the execution, filing and contents of the bond.

(June 25, 1948, c. 646, 62 Stat. 947.)

§ 1738. State and Territorial statutes and judicial proceedings; full faith and credit

The Acts of the legislature of any State, Territory, or Possession of the United States, or copies thereof, shall be authenticated by affixing the seal of such State, Territory or Possession thereto.

The records and judicial proceedings of any court of any such State, Territory or Possession, or copies thereof, shall be proved or admitted in other courts within the United States and its Territories and Possessions by the attestation of the clerk and seal of the court annexed, if a seal exists, together with a certificate of a judge of the court that the said attestation is in proper form.

Such Acts, records and judicial proceedings or copies thereof, so authenticated, shall have the same full faith and credit in every court within the United States and its Territories and Possessions as they have by law or usage in the courts of such State, Territory or Possession from which they are taken.

(June 25, 1948, c. 646, 62 Stat. 947.)

§ 1738A. Full faith and credit given to child custody determinations

(a) The appropriate authorities of every State shall enforce according to its terms, and shall not modify except as provided in subsections (f), (g), and (h) of this section, any custody determination or visitation determination made consistently with the provisions of this section by a court of another State.

(b) As used in this section, the term—

(1) "child" means a person under the age of eighteen;

(2) "contestant" means a person, including a parent or grandparent, who claims a right to custody or visitation of a child;

(3) "custody determination" means a judgment, decree, or other order of a court providing for the custody of a child, and includes permanent and temporary orders, and initial orders and modifications;

(4) "home State" means the State in which, immediately preceding the time involved, the child lived with his parents, a parent, or a person acting as parent, for at least six consecutive months, and in the case of a child less than six months old, the State in which the child lived from birth with any of such persons. Periods of temporary absence of any of such persons are counted as part of the six-month or other period;

(5) "modification" and "modify" refer to a custody or visitation determination which modifies, replaces, supersedes, or otherwise is made subsequent to, a prior custody or visitation determination concerning the same child, whether made by the same court or not;

(6) "person acting as a parent" means a person, other than a parent, who has physical custody of a child and who has either been awarded custody by a court or claims a right to custody;

(7) "physical custody" means actual possession and control of a child;

(8) "State" means a State of the United States, the District of Columbia, the Commonwealth of Puerto Rico, or a territory or possession of the United States; and

(9) "visitation determination" means a judgment, decree, or other order of a court providing for the visitation of a child and includes permanent and temporary orders and initial orders and modifications.

(c) A child custody or visitation determination made by a court of a State is consistent with the provisions of this section only if—

(1) such court has jurisdiction under the law of such State; and

(2) one of the following conditions is met:

(A) such State (i) is the home State of the child on the date of the commencement of the proceeding, or (ii) had been the child's home State within six months before the date of the commencement of the proceeding and the child is absent from such State because of his removal or retention by a contestant or for other reasons, and a contestant continues to live in such State;

(B) (i) it appears that no other State would have jurisdiction under subparagraph (A), and (ii) it is in the best interest of the child that a court of such State assume jurisdiction because (I) the child and his parents, or the child and at least one contestant, have a significant connection with such State other than mere physical presence in such State, and (II) there is available in such State substantial evidence concerning the child's present or future care, protection, training, and personal relationships;

(C) the child is physically present in such State and (i) the child has been abandoned, or (ii) it is necessary in an emergency to protect the child because the child, a sibling, or parent of the child has been subjected to or threatened with mistreatment or abuse;

(D) (i) it appears that no other State would have jurisdiction under subparagraph (A), (B), (C), or (E), or another State has declined to exercise jurisdiction on the ground that the State whose jurisdiction is in issue is the more appropriate forum to determine the custody or visitation of the child, and (ii) it is in the best interest of the child that such court assume jurisdiction; or

(E) the court has continuing jurisdiction pursuant to subsection (d) of this section.

(d) The jurisdiction of a court of a State which has made a child custody or visitation determination consistently with the provisions of this section continues as long as the requirement of subsection (c)(1) of this section continues to be met and such State remains the residence of the child or of any contestant.

(e) Before a child custody or visitation determination is made, reasonable notice and opportunity to be heard shall be given to the contestants, any parent whose parental rights have not been previously terminated and any person who has physical custody of a child.

(f) A court of a State may modify a determination of the custody of the same child made by a court of another State, if—

(1) it has jurisdiction to make such a child custody determination; and

(2) the court of the other State no longer has jurisdiction, or it has declined to exercise such jurisdiction to modify such determination.

(g) A court of a State shall not exercise jurisdiction in any proceeding for a custody or visitation determination commenced during the pendency of a proceeding in a court of another State where such court of that other State is exercising jurisdiction consistently with the provisions of this section to make a custody or visitation determination.

(h) A court of a State may not modify a visitation determination made by a court of another State unless the court of the other State no longer has jurisdiction to modify such determination or has declined to exercise jurisdiction to modify such determination.

(Added Pub.L. 96–611, § 8(a), Dec. 28, 1980, 94 Stat. 3569, and amended Pub.L. 105–374, § 1, Nov. 12, 1998, 112 Stat. 3383; Pub.L. 106–386, Div. B, Title III, § 1303(d), Oct. 28, 2000, 114 Stat. 1512.)

HISTORICAL AND STATUTORY NOTES

Report on Effects of Parental Kidnapping Laws in Domestic Violence Cases

Pub.L. 106–386, Div. B, Title III, § 1303(a) to (c), Oct. 28, 2000, 114 Stat. 1512, provided that:

"(a) **In general.**—The Attorney General shall—

"(1) conduct a study of Federal and State laws relating to child custody, including custody provisions in protection orders, the Uniform Child Custody Jurisdiction and Enforcement Act adopted by the National Conference of Commissioners on Uniform State Laws in July 1997, the Parental Kidnaping Prevention Act of 1980 [Pub.L. 96–611, Dec. 28, 1980, 94 Stat. 3568] and the amendments made by that Act, and the effect of those laws on child custody cases in which domestic violence is a factor; and

"(2) submit to Congress a report describing the results of that study, including the effects of implementing or applying model State laws, and the recommendations of the Attorney General to reduce the incidence or pattern of violence against women or of sexual assault of the child.

"(b) **Sufficiency of defenses.**—In carrying out subsection (a) with respect to the Parental Kidnaping Prevention Act of 1980 [Pub.L. 96–611, Dec. 28, 1980, 94 Stat. 3568] and the amendments made by that Act [see Tables for classification], the Attorney General shall examine the sufficiency of defenses to parental abduction charges available in cases involving domestic violence, and the burdens and risks encountered by victims of domestic violence arising from jurisdictional requirements of that Act and the amendments made by that Act.

"(c) **Authorization of appropriations.**—There is authorized to be appropriated to carry out this section $200,000 for fiscal year 2001."

Congressional Findings and Declaration of Purpose

Section 7 of Pub.L. 96–611 provided that:

"(a) The Congress finds that—

"(1) there is a large and growing number of cases annually involving disputes between persons claiming rights of custody and visitation of children under the laws, and in the courts, of different States, the District of Columbia, the Commonwealth of Puerto Rico, and the territories and possessions of the United States;

"(2) the laws and practices by which the courts of those jurisdictions determine their jurisdiction to decide such disputes, and the effect to be given the decisions of such disputes by the courts of other jurisdictions, are often inconsistent and conflicting;

"(3) those characteristics of the law and practice in such cases, along with the limits imposed by a Federal system on the authority of each such jurisdiction to conduct investigations and take other actions outside its own boundaries, contribute to a tendency of parties involved in such disputes to frequently resort to the seizure, restraint, concealment, and interstate transportation of children, the disregard of court orders, excessive relitigation of cases, obtaining of conflicting orders by the courts of various jurisdictions, and interstate travel and communication that is so expensive and time consuming as to disrupt their occupations and commercial activities; and

"(4) among the results of those conditions and activities are the failure of the courts of such jurisdictions to give full faith and credit to the judicial proceedings of the other jurisdictions, the deprivation of rights of liberty and property without due process of law, burdens on commerce among such jurisdictions and with foreign nations, and harm to the welfare of children and their parents and other custodians.

"(b) For those reasons it is necessary to establish a national system for locating parents and children who travel from one such jurisdiction to another and are concealed in connection with such disputes, and to establish national standards under which the courts of such jurisdictions will determine their jurisdiction to decide such disputes and the effect to be given by each such jurisdiction to such decisions by the courts of other such jurisdictions.

"(c) The general purposes of sections 6 to 10 of this Act [enacting this section and sections 654(17) and 663 of Title 42, The Public Health and Welfare, amending section 655(a) of Title 42, and enacting provisions set out as notes under this section and sections 663 and 1305 of Title 42 and 1073 of Title 18, Crimes and Criminal Procedure] are to—

"(1) promote cooperation between State courts to the end that a determination of custody and visitation is rendered in the State which can best decide the case in the interest of the child;

"(2) promote and expand the exchange of information and other forms of mutual assistance between States which are concerned with the same child;

"(3) facilitate the enforcement of custody and visitation decrees of sister States;

"(4) discourage continuing interstate controversies over child custody in the interest of greater stability of home environment and of secure family relationships for the child;

"(5) avoid jurisdictional competition and conflict between State courts in matters of child custody and visitation which have in the past resulted in the shifting of children from State to State with harmful effects on their well-being; and

"(6) deter interstate abductions and other unilateral removals of children undertaken to obtain custody and visitation awards."

State Court Proceedings for Custody Determinations; Priority Treatment; Fees, Costs, and Other Expenses

Section 8(c) of Pub.L. 96–611 provided that: "In furtherance of the purposes of section 1738A of title 28, United States Code [this section], as added by subsection (a) of this section, State courts are encouraged to—

"(1) afford priority to proceedings for custody determinations; and

"(2) award to the person entitled to custody or visitation pursuant to a custody determination which is consistent with the provisions of such section 1738A [this section], necessary travel expenses, attorneys' fees, costs of private investigations, witness fees or expenses, and other expenses incurred in connection with such custody determination in any case in which—

"(A) a contestant has, without the consent of the person entitled to custody or visitation pursuant to a custody determination which is consistent with the provisions of such section 1738A [this section], (i) wrongfully removed the child from the physical custody of such person, or (ii) wrongfully retained the child after a visit or other temporary relinquishment of physical custody; or

"(B) the court determines it is appropriate."

§ 1738B. Full faith and credit for child support orders

(a) General rule.—The appropriate authorities of each State—

(1) shall enforce according to its terms a child support order made consistently with this section by a court of another State; and

(2) shall not seek or make a modification of such an order except in accordance with subsections (e), (f), and (i).

(b) Definitions.—In this section:

"child" means—

(A) a person under 18 years of age; and

(B) a person 18 or more years of age with respect to whom a child support order has been issued pursuant to the laws of a State.

"child's State" means the State in which a child resides.

"child's home State" means the State in which a child lived with a parent or a person acting as parent for at least 6 consecutive months immediately preceding the time of filing of a petition or comparable pleading for support and, if a child is less than 6 months old, the State in which the child lived from birth with any of them. A period of temporary absence of any of them is counted as part of the 6-month period.

"child support" means a payment of money, continuing support, or arrearages or the provision of a benefit (including payment of health insurance, child care, and educational expenses) for the support of a child.

"child support order"—

(A) means a judgment, decree, or order of a court requiring the payment of child support in periodic amounts or in a lump sum; and

(B) includes—

(i) a permanent or temporary order; and

(ii) an initial order or a modification of an order.

"contestant" means—

(A) a person (including a parent) who—

(i) claims a right to receive child support;

(ii) is a party to a proceeding that may result in the issuance of a child support order; or

(iii) is under a child support order; and

(B) a State or political subdivision of a State to which the right to obtain child support has been assigned.

"court" means a court or administrative agency of a State that is authorized by State law to establish the amount of child support payable by a contestant or make a modification of a child support order.

"modification" means a change in a child support order that affects the amount, scope, or duration of the order and modifies, replaces, supersedes, or otherwise is made subsequent to the child support order.

"State" means a State of the United States, the District of Columbia, the Commonwealth of Puerto Rico, the territories and possessions of the United States, and Indian country (as defined in section 1151 of title 18).

(c) Requirements of child support orders.—A child support order made by a court of a State is made consistently with this section if—

(1) a court that makes the order, pursuant to the laws of the State in which the court is located and subsections (e), (f), and (g)—

(A) has subject matter jurisdiction to hear the matter and enter such an order; and

(B) has personal jurisdiction over the contestants; and

(2) reasonable notice and opportunity to be heard is given to the contestants.

(d) Continuing jurisdiction.—A court of a State that has made a child support order consistently with this section has continuing, exclusive jurisdiction over the order if the State is the child's State or the residence of any individual contestant unless the court of another State, acting in accordance with subsections (e) and (f), has made a modification of the order.

(e) Authority to modify orders.—A court of a State may modify a child support order issued by a court of another State if—

(1) the court has jurisdiction to make such a child support order pursuant to subsection (i); and

(2)(A) the court of the other State no longer has continuing, exclusive jurisdiction of the child support order because that State no longer is the child's State or the residence of any individual contestant; or

(B) each individual contestant has filed written consent with the State of continuing, exclusive jurisdiction for a court of another State to modify the order and assume continuing, exclusive jurisdiction over the order.

(f) Recognition of child support orders.—If 1 or more child support orders have been issued with regard to an obligor and a child, a court shall apply the following rules in determining which order to recognize for purposes of continuing, exclusive jurisdiction and enforcement:

(1) If only 1 court has issued a child support order, the order of that court must be recognized.

(2) If 2 or more courts have issued child support orders for the same obligor and child, and only 1 of the courts would have continuing, exclusive jurisdiction under this section, the order of that court must be recognized.

(3) If 2 or more courts have issued child support orders for the same obligor and child, and more than 1 of the courts would have continuing, exclusive jurisdiction under this section, an order issued by a court in the current home State of the child must be recognized, but if an order has not been issued in the current home State of the child, the order most recently issued must be recognized.

(4) If 2 or more courts have issued child support orders for the same obligor and child, and none of the courts would have continuing, exclusive jurisdiction under this section, a court having jurisdiction over the parties shall issue a child support order, which must be recognized.

(5) The court that has issued an order recognized under this subsection is the court having continuing, exclusive jurisdiction under subsection (d).

(g) Enforcement of modified orders.—A court of a State that no longer has continuing, exclusive jurisdiction of a child support order may enforce the order with respect to nonmodifiable obligations and unsatisfied obligations that accrued before the date on which a modification of the order is made under subsections (e) and (f).

(h) Choice of law.—

(1) In general.—In a proceeding to establish, modify, or enforce a child support order, the forum State's law shall apply except as provided in paragraphs (2) and (3).

(2) Law of State of issuance of order.—In interpreting a child support order including the duration of current payments and other obligations of support, a court shall apply the law of the State of the court that issued the order.

(3) Period of limitation.—In an action to enforce arrears under a child support order, a court shall apply the statute of limitation of the forum State or the State of the court that issued the order, whichever statute provides the longer period of limitation.

(i) Registration for modification.—If there is no individual contestant or child residing in the issuing State, the party or support enforcement agency seeking to modify, or to modify and enforce, a child support order issued in another State shall register that order in a State with jurisdiction over the nonmovant for the purpose of modification.

(Added Pub.L. 103–383, § 3(a), Oct. 22, 1994, 108 Stat. 4064, and amended Pub.L. 104–193, Title III, § 322, Aug. 22, 1996, 110 Stat. 2221; Pub.L. 105–33, Title V, § 5554, Aug. 5, 1997, 111 Stat. 636.)

HISTORICAL AND STATUTORY NOTES

Effective and Applicability Provisions

1997 Acts. Amendments by Pub.L. 105–33 made by sections 5531 to 5556 to take effect as if included in the enactment of Title III of the Personal Responsibility and Work Opportunity Reconciliation Act of 1996 (Pub.L. 104–193, Aug. 22, 1996, 110 Stat. 2105), except for amendments made by section 5532(b)(2) (amending section 608(a)(3)(A) of Title 42, The Public Health and Welfare), see section 5557 of Pub.L. 105–33, set out as a note under section 608 of Title 42, The Public Health and Welfare.

1996 Acts. For effective date of Title III of Pub.L. 104–193, see section 395(a) to (c) of Pub.L. 104–193, set out as a note under section 654 of Title 42, The Public Health and Welfare.

Congressional Findings and Declaration of Purpose

Section 2 of Pub.L. 103–383 provided that:

"**(a) Findings.**—The Congress finds that—

"(1) there is a large and growing number of child support cases annually involving disputes between parents who reside in different States;

"(2) the laws by which the courts of different jurisdictions determine their authority to establish child support orders are not uniform;

"(3) those laws, along with the limits imposed by the Federal system on the authority of each State to take certain actions outside its own boundaries—

"(A) encourage noncustodial parents to relocate outside the States where their children and the custodial parents reside to avoid the jurisdiction of the courts of such States, resulting in an increase in the amount of interstate travel and communication required to establish and collect on child support orders and a burden on custodial parents that is expensive, time consuming, and disruptive of occupations and commercial activity;

"(B) contribute to the pressing problem of relatively low levels of child support payments in interstate cases and to inequities in child support payments levels that are based solely on the noncustodial parent's choice of residence;

"(C) encourage a disregard of court orders resulting in massive arrearages nationwide;

"(D) allow noncustodial parents to avoid the payment of regularly scheduled child support payments for extensive periods of time, resulting in substantial hardship for the children for whom support is due and for their custodians; and

"(E) lead to the excessive relitigation of cases and to the establishment of conflicting orders by the courts of various jurisdictions, resulting in confusion, waste of judicial resources, disrespect for the courts, and a diminution of public confidence in the rule of law; and

"(4) among the results of the conditions described in this subsection are—

"(A) the failure of the courts of the States to give full faith and credit to the judicial proceedings of the other States;

"(B) the deprivation of rights of liberty and property without due process of law;

"(C) burdens on commerce among the States; and

"(D) harm to the welfare of children and their parents and other custodians.

"(b) **Statement of policy.**—In view of the findings made in subsection (a), it is necessary to establish national standards under which the courts of the various States shall determine their jurisdiction to issue a child support order and the effect to be given by each State to child support orders issued by the courts of other States.

"(c) **Purposes.**—The purposes of this Act [enacting this section and a provision set out as a note under section 1 of this title] are—

"(1) to facilitate the enforcement of child support orders among the States;

"(2) to discourage continuing interstate controversies over child support in the interest of greater financial stability and secure family relationships for the child; and

"(3) to avoid jurisdictional competition and conflict among State courts in the establishment of child support orders."

§ 1738C. Certain acts, records, and proceedings and the effect thereof

No State, territory, or possession of the United States, or Indian tribe, shall be required to give effect to any public act, record, or judicial proceeding of any other State, territory, possession, or tribe respecting a relationship between persons of the same sex that is treated as a marriage under the laws of such other State, territory, possession, or tribe, or a right or claim arising from such relationship.

(Added Pub.L. 104–199, § 2(a), Sept. 21, 1996, 110 Stat. 2419.)

§ 1739. State and Territorial nonjudicial records; full faith and credit

All nonjudicial records or books kept in any public office of any State, Territory, or Possession of the United States, or copies thereof, shall be proved or admitted in any court or office in any other State, Territory, or Possession by the attestation of the custodian of such records or books, and the seal of his office annexed, if there be a seal, together with a certificate of a judge of a court of record of the county, parish, or district in which such office may be kept, or of the Governor, or secretary of state, the chancellor or keeper of the great seal, of the State, Territory, or Possession that the said attestation is in due form and by the proper officers.

If the certificate is given by a judge, it shall be further authenticated by the clerk or prothonotary of the court, who shall certify, under his hand and the seal of his office, that such judge is duly commissioned and qualified; or, if given by such Governor, secretary, chancellor, or keeper of the great seal, it shall be under the great seal of the State, Territory, or Possession in which it is made.

Such records or books, or copies thereof, so authenticated, shall have the same full faith and credit in every court and office within the United States and its Territories and Possessions as they have by law or usage in the courts or offices of the State, Territory, or Possession from which they are taken.

(June 25, 1948, c. 646, 62 Stat. 947.)

§ 1740. Copies of consular papers

Copies of all official documents and papers in the office of any consul or vice consul of the United States, and of all official entries in the books or records of any such office, authenticated by the consul or vice consul, shall be admissible equally with the originals.

(June 25, 1948, c. 646, 62 Stat. 947.)

§ 1741. Foreign official documents

An official record or document of a foreign country may be evidenced by a copy, summary, or excerpt authenticated as provided in the Federal Rules of Civil Procedure.

(June 25, 1948, c. 646, 62 Stat. 948; May 24, 1949, c. 139, § 92(b), 63 Stat. 103; Oct. 3, 1964, Pub.L. 88–619, § 5(a), 78 Stat. 996.)

HISTORICAL AND STATUTORY NOTES

Treaties and Conventions; Taking of Evidence Abroad in Civil or Commercial Matters; Observance On and After Oct. 7, 1972, by United States and Citizens and Persons Subject to Jurisdiction of United States

For text of Convention, see provisions set out as a note under section 1781 of this title.

[§ 1742. Repealed. Pub.L. 88–619, § 6(a), Oct. 3, 1964, 78 Stat. 996]

HISTORICAL AND STATUTORY NOTES

Section, Act June 25, 1948, c. 646, 62 Stat. 948, related to authentication and certification of copies of documents relating to land titles, by persons having custody of such of any foreign government or its agents, certification by an American minister or consul that they be true copies of the originals, the recording of such copies in the office of the General Counsel for the Department of the Treasury, and to the evidentiary value of such copies.

§ 1743. Demand on postmaster

The certificate of the Postmaster General or the Government Accountability Office of the mailing to a postmaster of a statement of his account and that payment of the balance stated has not been received shall be sufficient evidence of a demand notwithstanding any allowances or credits subsequently made. A copy of such statement shall be attached to the certificate.

(June 25, 1948, c. 646, 62 Stat. 948; July 7, 2004, Pub.L. 108–271, § 8(b), 118 Stat. 814.)

HISTORICAL AND STATUTORY NOTES

Transfer of Functions

The office of Postmaster General of the Post Office Department was abolished and all functions, powers, and duties of the Postmaster General were transferred to the United States Postal Service by Pub.L. 91–375, § 4(a), Aug. 12, 1970, 84 Stat. 773, set out as a note under section 201 of Title 39, Postal Service.

§ 1744. Copies of United States Patent and Trademark Office documents, generally

Copies of letters patent or of any records, books, papers, or drawings belonging to the United States Patent and Trademark Office and relating to patents, authenticated under the seal of the United States Patent and Trademark Office and certified by the Under Secretary of Commerce for Intellectual Property and Director of the United States Patent and Trademark Office, or by another officer of the United States Patent and Trademark Office authorized to do so by the Director, shall be admissible in evidence with the same effect as the originals.

Any person making application and paying the required fee may obtain such certified copies.

(June 25, 1948, c. 646, 62 Stat. 948; May 24, 1949, c. 139, § 92(c), 63 Stat. 103; Nov. 29, 1999, Pub.L. 106–113, Div. B, § 1000(a)(9) [Title IV, § 4732(b)(15)(B), (C)], 113 Stat. 1536, 1501A–584.)

HISTORICAL AND STATUTORY NOTES

Effective and Applicability Provisions

1999 Acts. Amendment by Pub.L. 106–113 [§ 4732], effective 4 months after Nov. 29, 1999, see Pub.L. 106–113 [§ 4731], set out as a note under section 1 of Title 35.

Change of Name

Patent Office and Commissioner of Patents redesignated Patent and Trademark Office and Commissioner of Patents and Trademarks, respectively, by section 3 of Pub.L. 93–596, Jan. 2, 1975, 88 Stat. 1949, set out as a note under section 1 of Title 35, Patents.

Transfer of Functions

The functions of all officers of the Department of Commerce and all functions of all agencies and employees of such Department, were, with a few exceptions, transferred to the Secretary of Commerce, with power vested in him to authorize their performance or the performance of any of his functions by any of such officers, agencies, and employees, by 1950 Reorg. Plan No. 5, §§ 1, 2, eff. May 24, 1950, 15 F.R. 3174, 64 Stat. 1263, set out in Appendix 1 to Title 5, Government Organization and Employees. The Patent Office [now Patent and Trademark Office], referred to in this section, is an agency of the Department of Commerce, and the Commissioner of Patents [now Commissioner of Patents and Trademarks], referred to in this section, is an officer of such Department.

§ 1745. Copies of foreign patent documents

Copies of the specifications and drawings of foreign letters patent, or applications for foreign letters patent, and copies of excerpts of the official journals and other official publications of foreign patent offices belonging to the United States Patent and Trademark Office, certified in the manner provided by section 1744 of this title are prima facie evidence of their contents and of the dates indicated on their face.

(June 25, 1948, c. 646, 62 Stat. 948, § 1746; renumbered § 1745 and amended May 24, 1949, c. 139, § 92(d), (e), 63 Stat. 103; Oct. 3, 1964, Pub.L. 88–619, § 7(a), 78 Stat. 996; Nov. 29, 1999, Pub.L. 106–113, Div. B, § 1000(a)(9) [Title IV, § 4732(b)(16)], 113 Stat. 1536, 1501A–585.)

HISTORICAL AND STATUTORY NOTES

Effective and Applicability Provisions

1999 Acts. Amendment by Pub.L. 106–113 [§ 4732], effective 4 months after Nov. 29, 1999, see Pub.L. 106–113 [§ 4731], set out as a note under section 1 of Title 35.

Change of Name

Patent Office redesignated Patent and Trademark Office by section 3 of Pub.L. 93–596, Jan. 2, 1975, 88 Stat. 1949, set out as a note under section 1 of Title 35, Patents.

Prior Provisions

A prior section 1745, Act June 25, 1948, c. 646, 62 Stat. 948, related to printed copies of patent specifications and drawings, prior to repeal by Act May 24, 1949, c. 139, § 92(d), 63 Stat. 103.

§ 1746. Unsworn declarations under penalty of perjury

Wherever, under any law of the United States or under any rule, regulation, order, or requirement made pursuant to law, any matter is required or permitted to be supported, evidenced, established, or proved by the sworn declaration, verification, certificate, statement, oath, or affidavit, in writing of the person making the same (other than a deposition, or an oath of office, or an oath required to be taken before a specified official other than a notary public), such matter may, with like force and effect, be supported, evidenced, established, or proved by the unsworn declaration, certificate, verification, or statement, in writing of such person which is subscribed by him, as true under penalty of perjury, and dated, in substantially the following form:

(1) If executed without the United States: "I declare (or certify, verify, or state) under penalty of perjury under the laws of the United States of America that the foregoing is true and correct. Executed on (date).

(Signature)".

(2) If executed within the United States, its territories, possessions, or commonwealths: "I declare (or certify, verify, or state) under penalty of perjury that the foregoing is true and correct. Executed on (date).

(Signature)".

(Added Pub.L. 94–550, § 1(a), Oct. 18, 1976, 90 Stat. 2534.)

HISTORICAL AND STATUTORY NOTES

Prior Provisions

A prior section 1746 was renumbered section 1745 of this title by Act May 24, 1949.

CHAPTER 117—EVIDENCE; DEPOSITIONS

Sec.
1781. Transmittal of letter rogatory or request.
1782. Assistance to foreign and international tribunals and to litigants before such tribunals.
1783. Subpoena of person in foreign country.
1784. Contempt.
1785. Subpoenas in multiparty, multiforum actions.

HISTORICAL AND STATUTORY NOTES

Deposition in Admiralty Cases

Prior to the general unification of civil and admiralty procedure and the rescission of the Admiralty Rules on July 1, 1966, Revised Statutes, §§ 863 to 865, as amended, which related to depositions de bene esse, when and how taken, notice, mode of taking, and transmission to court, provided as follows:

"**Sec. 863.** The testimony of any witness may be taken in any civil cause depending in a district court by deposition de bene esse, when the witness lives at a greater distance from the place of trial than one hundred miles, or is bound on a voyage to sea, or is about to go out of the United States, or out of the district in which the case is to be tried, and to a greater distance than one hundred miles from the place of trial, before the time of trial, or when he is ancient and infirm. The deposition may be taken before any judge of any court of the United States, or any clerk of a district court, or any chancellor, justice, or judge of a supreme or superior court, mayor or chief magistrate of a city, judge of a county court or court of common pleas of any of the United States, or any notary public, not being of counsel or attorney to either of the parties, nor interested in the event of the cause. Reasonable notice must first be given in writing by the party or his attorney proposing to take such deposition, to the opposite party or his attorney of record, as either may be nearest, which notice shall state the name of the witness and the time and place of the taking of his deposition; and in all cases in rem, the person having the agency or possession of the property at the time of seizure shall be deemed the adverse party, until a claim shall have been put in; and whenever, by reason of the absence from the district and want of an attorney of record or other reason, the giving of the notice herein required shall be impracticable, it shall be lawful to take such depositions as there shall be urgent necessity for taking, upon such notice as any judge authorized to hold courts in such district shall think reasonable and direct. Any person may be compelled to appear and depose as provided by this section, in the same manner as witnesses may be compelled to appear and testify in court.

"**Sec. 864.** Every person deposing as provided in the preceding section [R.S. § 863] shall be cautioned and sworn to testify the whole truth, and carefully examined.

"His testimony shall be reduced to writing or typewriting by the officer taking the deposition, or by some person under his personal supervision, or by the deponent himself in the officer's presence, and by no other person, and shall, after it has been reduced to writing or typewriting, be subscribed by the deponent. [As amended May 23, 1900, c. 541, 31 Stat. 182.]

"**Sec. 865.** Every deposition taken under the two preceding sections [R.S. §§ 863, 864] shall be retained by the magistrate taking it, until he delivers it with his own hand into the court for which it is taken; or it shall, together with a certificate of the reasons as aforesaid of taking it and of the notice, if any, given to the adverse party, be by him sealed up and directed to such court, and remain under his seal until opened in court. But unless it appears to the satisfaction of the court that the witness is then dead, or gone out of the United States, or to a greater distance than one hundred miles from the place where the court is sitting, or that, by reason of age, sickness, bodily infirmity, or imprisonment, he is unable to travel and appear at court, such deposition shall not be used in the cause."

R.S. §§ 863 to 865, as amended, quoted above, were applicable to admiralty proceedings only. Proceedings in bankruptcy and copyright are governed by Rule 26 et seq. of Federal Rules of Civil Procedure. See also Rules of Bankruptcy Procedure set out in Title 11, Bankruptcy.

§ 1781. Transmittal of letter rogatory or request

(a) The Department of State has power, directly, or through suitable channels—

(1) to receive a letter rogatory issued, or request made, by a foreign or international tribunal, to transmit it to the tribunal, officer, or agency in the United States to whom it is addressed, and to receive and return it after execution; and

(2) to receive a letter rogatory issued, or request made, by a tribunal in the United States, to transmit it to the foreign or international tribunal, officer, or agency to whom it is addressed, and to receive and return it after execution.

(b) This section does not preclude—

(1) the transmittal of a letter rogatory or request directly from a foreign or international tribunal to the tribunal, officer, or agency in the United States to whom it is addressed and its return in the same manner; or

(2) the transmittal of a letter rogatory or request directly from a tribunal in the United States to the foreign or international tribunal, officer, or agency to whom it is addressed and its return in the same manner.

(June 25, 1948, c. 646, 62 Stat. 949; Oct. 3, 1964, Pub.L. 88–619, § 8(a), 78 Stat. 996.)

TREATIES AND CONVENTIONS

CONVENTION ON THE TAKING OF EVIDENCE ABROAD IN CIVIL OR COMMERCIAL MATTERS

The States signatory to the present Convention,

Desiring to facilitate the transmission and execution of Letters of Request and to further the accommodation of the different methods which they use for this purpose.

Desiring to improve mutual judicial co-operation in civil or commercial matters.

Have resolved to conclude a Convention to this effect and have agreed upon the following provisions—

* * * * * * *

CHAPTER I—LETTERS OF REQUEST

Article 1

In civil or commercial matters a judicial authority of a Contracting State may, in accordance with the provisions of the law of that State, request the competent authority of another Contracting State, by means of a Letter of Request, to obtain evidence, or to perform some other judicial act.

A Letter shall not be used to obtain evidence which is not intended for use in judicial proceedings, commenced or contemplated.

The expression "other judicial act" does not cover the service of judicial documents or the issuance of any process by which judgments or orders are executed or enforced, or orders for provisional or protective measures.

Article 2

A Contracting State shall designate a Central Authority which will undertake to receive Letters of Request coming from a judicial authority of another Contracting State and to transmit them to the authority competent to execute them. Each State shall organize the Central Authority in accordance with its own law.

Letters shall be sent to the Central Authority of the State of execution without being transmitted through any other authority of that State.

Article 3

A Letter of Request shall specify—

(a) the authority requesting its execution and the authority requested to execute it, if known to the requesting authority;

(b) the names and addresses of the parties to the proceedings and their representatives, if any;

(c) the nature of the proceedings for which the evidence is required, giving all necessary information in regard thereto;

(d) the evidence to be obtained or other judicial act to be performed.

Where appropriate, the Letter shall specify, inter alia—

(e) the names and addresses of the persons to be examined;

(f) the questions to be put to the persons to be examined or a statement of the subject-matter about which they are to be examined;

(g) the documents or other property, real or personal, to be inspected;

(h) any requirement that the evidence is to be given on oath or affirmation, and any special form to be used;

(i) any special method or procedure to be followed under Article 9.

A Letter may also mention any information necessary for the application of Article 11.

No legalization or other like formality may be required.

Article 4

A Letter of Request shall be in the language of the authority requested to execute it or be accompanied by a translation into that language.

Nevertheless, a Contracting State shall accept a Letter in either English or French, or a translation into one of these languages, unless it has made the reservation authorized by Article 33.

A Contracting State which has more than one official language and cannot, for reasons of internal law, accept Letters in one of these languages for the whole of its territory, shall, by declaration, specify the language in which the Letter or translation thereof shall be expressed for execution in the specified parts of its territory. In case of failure to comply with this declaration, without justifiable excuse, the costs of translation into the required language shall be borne by the State of origin.

A Contracting State may, by declaration, specify the language or languages other than those referred to in the preceding paragraphs, in which a Letter may be sent to its Central Authority.

Any translation accompanying a Letter shall be certified as correct, either by a diplomatic officer or consular agent or by a sworn translator or by any other person so authorized in either State.

Article 5

If the Central Authority considers that the request does not comply with the provisions of the present Convention, it shall promptly inform the authority of the State of origin which transmitted the Letter of Request, specifying the objections to the Letter.

Article 6

If the authority to whom a Letter of Request has been transmitted is not competent to execute it, the Letter shall be sent forthwith to the authority in the same State which is competent to execute it in accordance with the provisions of its own law.

Article 7

The requesting authority shall, if it so desires, be informed of the time when, and the place where, the proceedings will take place, in order that the parties concerned, and their representatives, if any, may be present. This information shall be sent directly to the parties or their representatives when the authority of the State of origin so requests.

Article 8

A Contracting State may declare that members of the judicial personnel of the requesting authority of another Contracting State may be present at the execution of a Letter of Request. Prior authorization by the competent authority designated by the declaring State may be required.

Article 9

The judicial authority which executes a Letter of Request shall apply its own law as to the methods and procedures to be followed.

However, it will follow a request of the requesting authority that a special method or procedure be followed, unless this is incompatible with the internal law of the State of execution or is impossible of performance by reason of its internal practice and procedure or by reason of practical difficulties.

A Letter of Request shall be executed expeditiously.

Article 10

In executing a Letter of Request the requested authority shall apply the appropriate measures of compulsion in the instances and to the same extent as are provided by its internal law for the execution of orders issued by the authorities of its own country or of requests made by parties in internal proceedings.

Article 11

In the execution of a Letter of Request the person concerned may refuse to give evidence in so far as he has a privilege or duty to refuse to give the evidence—

(a) under the law of the State of execution; or

(b) under the law of the State of origin, and the privilege or duty has been specified in the Letter, or, at the instance of the requested authority, has been otherwise confirmed to that authority by the requesting authority.

A Contracting State may declare that, in addition, it will respect privileges and duties existing under the law of States other than the State of origin and the State of execution, to the extent specified in that declaration.

Article 12

The execution of a Letter of Request may be refused only to the extent that—

(a) in the State of execution the execution of the Letter does not fall within the functions of the judiciary; or

(b) the State addressed considers that its sovereignty or security would be prejudiced thereby.

Execution may not be refused solely on the ground that under its internal law the State of execution claims exclusive jurisdiction over the subject-matter of the action or that its internal law would not admit a right of action on it.

Article 13

The documents establishing the execution of the Letter of Request shall be sent by the requested authority to the requesting authority by the same channel which was used by the latter.

In every instance where the Letter is not executed in whole or in part, the requesting authority shall be informed immediately through the same channel and advised of the reasons.

Article 14

The execution of the Letter of Request shall not give rise to any reimbursement of taxes or costs of any nature.

Nevertheless, the State of execution has the right to require the State of origin to reimburse the fees paid to experts and interpreters and the costs occasioned by the use of a special procedure requested by the State of origin under Article 9, paragraph 2.

The requested authority whose law obliges the parties themselves to secure evidence, and which is not able itself to execute the Letter, may, after having obtained the consent of the requesting authority, appoint a suitable person to do so. When seeking this consent the requested authority shall indicate the approximate costs which would result from this procedure. If the requesting authority gives its consent it shall reimburse any costs incurred; without such consent the requesting authority shall not be liable for the costs.

CHAPTER II—TAKING OF EVIDENCE BY DIPLOMATIC OFFICERS, CONSULAR AGENTS AND COMMISSIONERS

Article 15

In a civil or commercial matter, a diplomatic officer or consular agent of a Contracting State may, in the territory of another Contracting State and within the area where he exercises his functions, take the evidence without compulsion of nationals of a State which he represents in aid of proceedings commenced in the courts of a State which he represents.

A Contracting State may declare that evidence may be taken by a diplomatic officer or consular agent only if permission to that effect is given upon application made by him or on his behalf to the appropriate authority designated by the declaring State.

Article 16

A diplomatic officer or consular agent of a Contracting State may, in the territory of another Contracting State and within the area where he exercises his functions, also take the evidence, without compulsion, of nationals of the State in which he exercises his functions or of a third State, in aid of proceedings commenced in the courts of a State which he represents, if—

(a) a competent authority designated by the State in which he exercises his functions has given its permission either generally or in the particular case, and

(b) he complies with the conditions which the competent authority has specified in the permission.

A Contracting State may declare that evidence may be taken under this Article without its prior permission.

Article 17

In a civil or commercial matter, a person duly appointed as a commissioner for the purpose may, without compulsion, take evidence in the territory of a Contracting State in aid of proceedings commenced in the courts of another Contracting State if—

(a) a competent authority designated by the State where the evidence is to be taken has given its permission either generally or in the particular case; and

(b) he complies with the conditions which the competent authority has specified in the permission.

A Contracting State may declare that evidence may be taken under this Article without its prior permission.

Article 18

A Contracting State may declare that a diplomatic officer, consular agent or commissioner authorized to take evidence under Articles 15, 16 or 17, may apply to the competent authority designated by the declaring State for appropriate assistance to obtain the evidence by compulsion. The declaration may contain such conditions as the declaring State may see fit to impose.

If the authority grants the application it shall apply any measures of compulsion which are appropriate and are prescribed by its law for use in internal proceedings.

Article 19

The competent authority, in giving the permission referred to in Articles 15, 16 or 17, or in granting the application referred to in Article 18, may lay down such conditions as it deems fit, *inter alia*, as to the time and place of the taking of the evidence. Similarly it may require that it be given reasonable advance notice of the time, date and place of the taking of the evidence; in such a case a representative of the authority shall be entitled to be present at the taking of the evidence.

Article 20

In the taking of evidence under any Article of this Chapter persons concerned may be legally represented.

Article 21

Where a diplomatic officer, consular agent or commissioner is authorized under Articles 15, 16 or 17 to take evidence—

(a) he may take all kinds of evidence which are not incompatible with the law of the State where the evidence is taken or contrary to any permission granted pursuant to the above Articles, and shall have power within such limits to administer an oath or take an affirmation;

(b) a request to a person to appear or to give evidence shall, unless the recipient is a national of the State where the action is pending, be drawn up in the language of the place where the evidence is taken or be accompanied by a translation into such language;

(c) the request shall inform the person that he may be legally represented and, in any State that has not filed a declaration under Article 18, shall also inform him that he is not compelled to appear or to give evidence;

(d) the evidence may be taken in the manner provided by the law applicable to the court in which the action is pending provided that such manner is not forbidden by the law of the State where the evidence is taken;

(e) a person requested to give evidence may invoke the privileges and duties to refuse to give the evidence contained in Article 11.

Article 22

The fact that an attempt to take evidence under the procedure laid down in this Chapter has failed, owing to the refusal of a person to give evidence, shall not prevent an application being subsequently made to take the evidence in accordance with Chapter I.

CHAPTER III—GENERAL CLAUSES

Article 23

A Contracting State may at the time of signature, ratification or accession, declare that it will not execute Letters of Request issued for the purpose of obtaining pretrial discovery of documents as known in Common Law countries.

Article 24

A Contracting State may designate other authorities in addition to the Central Authority and shall determine the extent of their competence. However, Letters of Request may in all cases be sent to the Central Authority.

Federal States shall be free to designate more than one Central Authority.

Article 25

A Contracting State which has more than one legal system may designate the authorities of one of such systems, which shall have exclusive competence to execute Letters of Request pursuant to this Convention.

Article 26

A Contracting State, if required to do so because of constitutional limitations, may request the reimbursement by the State of origin of fees and costs, in connection with the execution of Letters of Request, for the service of process necessary to compel the appearance of a person to give evidence, the costs of attendance of such persons, and the cost of any transcript of the evidence.

Where a State has made a request pursuant to the above paragraph, any other Contracting State may request from that State the reimbursement of similar fees and costs.

Article 27

The provisions of the present Convention shall not prevent a Contracting State from—

(a) declaring that Letters of Request may be transmitted to its judicial authorities through channels other than those provided for in Article 2;

(b) permitting, by internal law or practice, any act provided for in this Convention to be performed upon less restrictive conditions;

(c) permitting, by internal law or practice, methods of taking evidence other than those provided for in this Convention.

Article 28

The present Convention shall not prevent an agreement between any two or more Contracting States to derogate from—

(a) the provisions of Article 2 with respect to methods of transmitting Letters of Request;

(b) the provisions of Article 4 with respect to the languages which may be used;

(c) the provisions of Article 8 with respect to the presence of judicial personnel at the execution of Letters;

(d) the provisions of Article 11 with respect to the privileges and duties of witnesses to refuse to give evidence;

(e) the provisions of Article 13 with respect to the methods of returning executed Letters to the requesting authority;

(f) the provisions of Article 14 with respect to fees and costs;

(g) the provisions of Chapter II.

Article 29

Between Parties to the present Convention who are also Parties to one or both of the Conventions on Civil Procedure signed at the Hague on the 17th of July 1905 [99 British Foreign and State Papers 990] and the 1st of March 1954 [286 UNTS 265], this Convention shall replace Articles 8–16 of the earlier Conventions.

Article 30

The present Convention shall not affect the application of Article 23 of the Convention of 1905, or of Article 24 of the Convention of 1954.

Article 31

Supplementary Agreements between Parties to the Conventions of 1905 and 1954 shall be considered as equally applicable to the present Convention unless the Parties have otherwise agreed.

Article 32

Without prejudice to the provisions of Articles 29 and 31, the present Convention shall not derogate from conventions containing provisions on the matters covered by this Convention to which the Contracting States are, or shall become Parties.

Article 33

A State may, at the time of signature, ratification or accession exclude, in whole or in part, the application of the provisions of paragraph 2 of Article 4 and of Chapter II. No other reservation shall be permitted.

Each Contracting State may at any time withdraw a reservation it has made; the reservation shall cease to have effect on the sixtieth day after notification of the withdrawal.

When a State has made a reservation, any other State affected thereby may apply the same rule against the reserving State.

Article 34

A State may at any time withdraw or modify a declaration.

Article 35

A Contracting State shall, at the time of the deposit of its instrument of ratification or accession, or at a later date, inform the Ministry of Foreign Affairs of the Netherlands of the designation of authorities, pursuant to Articles 2, 8, 24 and 25.

A Contracting State shall likewise inform the Ministry, where appropriate, of the following—

(a) the designation of the authorities to whom notice must be given, whose permission may be required, and whose assistance may be invoked in the taking of evidence by diplomatic officers and consular agents, pursuant to Articles 15, 16 and 18 respectively;

(b) the designation of the authorities whose permission may be required in the taking of evidence by commissioners pursuant to Article 17 and of those who may grant the assistance provided for in Article 18;

(c) declarations pursuant to Articles 4, 8, 11, 15, 16, 17, 18, 23 and 27;

(d) any withdrawal or modification of the above designations and declarations;

(e) the withdrawal of any reservation.

Article 36

Any difficulties which may arise between Contracting States in connection with the operation of this Convention shall be settled through diplomatic channels.

Article 37

The present Convention shall be open for signature by the States represented at the Eleventh Session of the Hague Conference on Private International Law.

It shall be ratified, and the instruments of ratification shall be deposited with the Ministry of Foreign Affairs of the Netherlands.

Article 38

The present Convention shall enter into force on the sixtieth day after the deposit of the third instrument of ratification referred to in the second paragraph of Article 37.

The Convention shall enter into force for each signatory State which ratifies subsequently on the sixtieth day after the deposit of its instrument of ratification.

Article 39

Any State not represented at the Eleventh Session of the Hague Conference on Private International Law which is a Member of this Conference or of the United Nations or of a specialized agency of that Organization, or a Party to the Statute of the International Court of Justice may accede to the present Convention after it has entered into force in accordance with the first paragraph of Article 38.

The instrument of accession shall be deposited with the Ministry of Foreign Affairs of the Netherlands.

The Convention shall enter into force for a State acceding to it on the sixtieth day after the deposit of its instrument of accession.

The accession will have effect only as regards the relations between the acceding State and such Contracting States as will have declared their acceptance of the accession. Such declaration shall be deposited at the Ministry of Foreign Affairs of the Netherlands; this Ministry shall forward, through diplomatic channels, a certified copy to each of the Contracting States.

The Convention will enter into force as between the acceding State and the State that has declared its acceptance of the accession on the sixtieth day after the deposit of the declaration of acceptance.

Article 40

Any State may, at the time of signature, ratification or accession, declare that the present Convention shall extend to all the territories for the international relations of which it is responsible, or to one or more of them. Such a declaration shall take effect on the date of entry into force of the Convention for the State concerned.

At any time thereafter, such extensions shall be notified to the Ministry of Foreign Affairs of the Netherlands.

The Convention shall enter into force for the territories mentioned in such an extension on the sixtieth day after the notification indicated in the preceding paragraph.

Article 41

The present Convention shall remain in force for five years from the date of its entry into force in accordance with the first paragraph of Article 38, even for States which have ratified it or acceded to it subsequently.

If there has been no denunciation, it shall be renewed tacitly every five years.

Any denunciation shall be notified to the Ministry of Foreign Affairs of the Netherlands at least six months before the end of the five year period.

It may be limited to certain of the territories to which the Convention applies.

The denunciation shall have effect only as regards the State which has notified it. The Convention shall remain in force for the other Contracting States.

Article 42

The Ministry of Foreign Affairs of the Netherlands shall give notice to the States referred to in Article 37, and to the States which have acceded in accordance with Article 39, of the following—

(a) the signatures and ratifications referred to in Article 37;

(b) the date on which the present Convention enters into force in accordance with the first paragraph of Article 38;

(c) the accessions referred to in Article 39 and the dates on which they take effect;

(d) the extensions referred to in Article 40 and the dates on which they take effect;

(e) the designations, reservations and declarations referred to in Articles 33 and 35;

(f) the denunciations referred to in the third paragraph of Article 41.

IN WITNESS WHEREOF the undersigned, being duly authorized thereto, have signed the present Convention.

DONE at The Hague, on the 18th day of March 1970, in the English and French languages, both texts being equally authentic, in a single copy which shall be deposited in the archives of the Government of the Netherlands, and of which a certified copy shall be sent, through the diplomatic channel, to each of the States represented at the Eleventh Session of the Hague Conference on Private International Law. [Signatures omitted.]

Convention on the taking of evidence abroad in civil or commercial matters. Done at The Hague March 18, 1970; entered into force for the United States October 7, 1972. TIAS 7444; 23 UST 2555

Annotations to the Convention

"Report of the U.S. Delegation on the Evidence Convention", 8 Int'l Legal Materials 804 (1969).

Amram, "Explanatory Report on the Convention on the Taking of Evidence Abroad in Civil and Commercial Matters—Message from the President of the United States", Sen.Exec. A, 92nd Cong., 2d Sess. (Feb. 1, 1972).

Edwards, "Taking of Evidence Abroad in Civil or Commercial Matters", 18 Int'l and Comp.L.Q. 646 (1969).

Amram, "U.S. Ratification of the Hague Convention on the Taking of Evidence Abroad" 67 Am.J. Int'l L. (1973).

Model for Letters of Request Recommended for Use in Applying the Hague Convention of 18 March 1970 on the Taking of Evidence Abroad in Civil or Commercial Matters

Request for International Judicial Assistance Pursuant to the Hague Convention of 18 March 1970 on the Taking of Evidence in Civil or Commercial Matters

N.B. Under the first paragraph of article 4, the Letter of Request shall be in the language of the authority requested to execute it or be accompanied by a translation into that language. However, the provisions of the second and third paragraphs may permit use of other languages.

In order to avoid confusion, please spell out the name of the month in each date.

I. *(Items to be included in all Letters of Request.)*

1. Sender _____*(identity and address)*_____
_____
_____

2. Central Authority of the Requested State _____*(identity and address)*_____

3. Person to whom the executed request is to be returned _____ *(identity and address)* _____

II. *(Items to be included in all Letters of Request.)*

4. In conformity with article 3 of the Convention, the undersigned applicant has the honour to submit the following request:

5. a. Requesting judicial authority (article 3, a) _____ *(identity and address)* _____

b. To the competent authority of (article 3, a) _____ *(the requested State)* _____

6. Names and addresses of the parties and their representatives (article 3, b)

a. Plaintiff

b. Defendant

c. Other parties

7. Nature and purpose of the proceedings and summary of the facts (article 3, c)

8. Evidence to be obtained or other judicial act to be performed (article 3, d)

III. *(Items to be completed where applicable.)*

9. Identity and address of any person to be examined (article 3, e)

10. Questions to be put to the persons to be examined or statement of the subject-matter about which they are to be examined (article 3, f) _____ *(or see attached list)* _____

11. Documents or other property to be inspected (article 3, g) _____ *(specify whether it is to be produced, copied, valued, etc.)* _____

12. Any requirement that the evidence be given on oath or affirmation and any special form to be used (article 3, h) _____ *(In the event that the evidence cannot be taken in the manner requested, specify whether it is to be taken in such manner as provided by local law for the formal taking of evidence.)* _____

13. Special methods or procedure to be followed (articles 3, i and 9) _____
14. Request for notification of the time and place for the execution of the Request and identity and address of any person to be notified (article 7) _____
15. Request for attendance or participation of judicial personnel of the requesting authority at the execution of the letter of Request _____
16. Specification of privilege or duty to refuse to give evidence under the law of the State of origin (article 11, b) _____
17. The fees and costs incurred which are reimbursable under the second paragraph of article 14 or under article 26 of the Convention will be borne by _____*(identity and address)*_____

IV. *(Items to be included in all Letters of Request.)*

18. Date of request _____
19. Signature and seal of the requesting authority _____

TREATIES AND CONVENTIONS

INTER-AMERICAN CONVENTION ON LETTERS ROGATORY

The Governments of the Member States of the Organization of American States, desirous of concluding a convention on letters rogatory, have agreed as follows:

I. USE OF TERMS

Article 1

For the purposes of this Convention the terms "exhortos" and "cartas rogatorias" are synonymous in the Spanish text. The terms "letters rogatory", "commissions rogatoires", and "cartas rogatórias" used in the English, French and Portuguese texts, respectively, cover both "exhortos" and "cartas rogatorias".

II. SCOPE OF THE CONVENTION

Article 2

This Convention shall apply to letters rogatory, issued in conjunction with proceedings in civil and commercial matters held before the appropriate judicial or other adjudicatory authority of one of the States Parties to this Convention, that have as their purpose:

a. The performance of procedural acts of a merely formal nature, such as service of process, summonses or subpoenas abroad;

b. The taking of evidence and the obtaining of information abroad, unless a reservation is made in this respect.

Article 3

This Convention shall not apply to letters rogatory relating to procedural acts other than those specified in the preceding article; and in particular it shall not apply to acts involving measures of compulsion.

III. TRANSMISSION OF LETTERS ROGATORY

Article 4

Letters rogatory may be transmitted to the authority to which they are addressed by the interested parties, through judicial channels, diplomatic or consular agents, or the Central Authority of the State of origin or of the State of destination, as the case may be.

Each State Party shall inform the General Secretariat of the Organization of American States of the Central Authority competent to receive and distribute letters rogatory.

IV. REQUIREMENTS FOR EXECUTION

Article 5

Letters rogatory shall be executed in the States Parties provided they meet the following requirements:

a. The letter rogatory is legalized, except as provided for in Articles 6 and 7 of this Convention. The letter rogatory shall be presumed to be duly legalized in the State of origin when legalized by the competent consular or diplomatic agent;

b. The letter rogatory and the appended documentation are duly translated into the official language of the State of destination.

Article 6

Whenever letters rogatory are transmitted through consular or diplomatic channels or through the Central Authority, legalization shall not be required.

Article 7

Courts in border areas of the States Parties may directly execute the letters rogatory contemplated in this Convention and such letters shall not require legalization.

Article 8

Letters rogatory shall be accompanied by the following documents to be delivered to the person on whom process, summons or subpoena is being served:

a. An authenticated copy of the complaint with its supporting documents, and of other exhibits or rulings that serve as the basis for the measure requested;

b. Written information identifying the judicial or other adjudicatory authority issuing the letter, indicating the time-limits allowed the person affected to act upon the request, and warning of the consequences of failure to do so;

c. Where appropriate, information on the existence and address of the court-appointed defense counsel or of competent legal-aid societies in the State of origin.

Article 9

Execution of letters rogatory shall not imply ultimate recognition of the jurisdiction of the judicial or other adjudicatory authority issuing the letter rogatory or a commitment to recognize the validity of the judgment it may render or to execute it.

V. EXECUTION

Article 10

Letters rogatory shall be executed in accordance with the laws and procedural rules of the State of destination.

At the request of the judicial or other adjudicatory authority issuing the letter rogatory, the authority of the State of destination may execute the letter through a special procedure, or accept the observance of additional formalities in performing the act requested, provided this procedure or the observance of those formalities is not contrary to the law of the State of destination.

Article 11

The authority of the State of destination shall have jurisdiction to determine any issue arising as a result of the execution of the measure requested in the letter rogatory.

Should such authority find that it lacks jurisdiction to execute the letter rogatory, it shall ex officio forward the documents and antecedents of the case to the authority of the State which has jurisdiction.

Article 12

The costs and other expenses involved in the processing and execution of letters rogatory shall be borne by the interested parties.

The State of destination may, in its discretion, execute a letter rogatory that does not indicate the person to be held responsible for costs and other expenses when incurred. The identity of the person empowered to represent the applicant for legal purposes may be indicated in the letter rogatory or in the documents relating to its execution.

The effects of a declaration in forma pauperis shall be regulated by the law of the State of destination.

Article 13

Consular or diplomatic agents of the States Parties to this Convention may perform the acts referred to in Article 2 in the State in which they are accredited, provided the performance of such acts is not contrary to the laws of that State. In so doing, they shall not perform any acts involving measures of compulsion.

VI. GENERAL PROVISIONS

Article 14

States Parties belonging to economic integration systems may agree directly between themselves upon special methods and procedures more expeditious than those provided for in this Convention. These agreements may be extended to include other States in the manner in which the parties may agree.

Article 15

This Convention shall not limit any provisions regarding letters rogatory in bilateral or multilateral agreements that may have been signed or may be signed in the future by the States Parties or preclude the continuation of more favorable practices in this regard that may be followed by these States.

Article 16

The States Parties to this Convention may declare that its provisions cover the execution of letters rogatory in criminal, labor, and "contentious-administrative" cases, as well as in arbitrations and other matters within the jurisdiction of special courts. Such declarations shall be transmitted to the General Secretariat of the Organization of American States.

Article 17

The State of destination may refuse to execute a letter rogatory that is manifestly contrary to its public policy ("ordre public").

Article 18

The States Parties shall inform the General Secretariat of the Organization of American States of the requirements stipulated in their laws for the legalization and the translation of letters rogatory.

VII. FINAL PROVISIONS

Article 19

This Convention shall be open for signature by the Member States of the Organization of American States.

Article 20

This Convention is subject to ratification. The instruments of ratification shall be deposited with the General Secretariat of the Organization of American States.

Article 21

This Convention shall remain open for accession by any other State. The instrument of accession shall be deposited with the General Secretariat of the Organization of American States.

Article 22

This Convention shall enter into force on the thirtieth day following the date of deposit of the second instrument of ratification.

For each State ratifying or acceding to the Convention after the deposit of the second instrument of ratification, the Convention shall enter into force on the thirtieth day after deposit by such State of its instrument of ratification or accession.

Article 23

If a State Party has two or more territorial units in which different systems of law apply in relation to the matters dealt with in this Convention, it may, at the time of signature, ratification or accession, declare that this Convention shall extend to all its territorial units or only to one or more of them.

Such declaration may be modified by subsequent declarations, which shall expressly indicate the territorial unit or units to which the Convention applies. Such subsequent declarations shall be transmitted to the General Secretariat of the Organization of American States, and shall become effective thirty days after the date of their receipt.

Article 24

This Convention shall remain in force indefinitely, but any of the States Parties may denounce it. The instrument of denunciation shall be deposited with the General Secretariat of the Organization of American States. After one year from the date of deposit of the instrument of denunciation, the Convention shall no longer be in effect for the denouncing State, but shall remain in effect for the other States Parties.

Article 25

The original instrument of this Convention, the English, French, Portuguese and Spanish texts of which are equally authentic, shall be deposited with the General Secretariat of the Organization of American States. The Secretariat shall notify the Member States of the Organization of American States and the States that have acceded to the Convention of the signatures, deposits of instruments of ratification, accession, and denunciation as well as of reservations, if any. It shall also transmit the information mentioned in the second paragraph of Article 4 and in Article 18 and the declarations referred to in Articles 16 and 23 of this Convention.

IN WITNESS WHEREOF the undersigned Plenipotentiaries, being duly authorized thereto by their respective Governments, have signed this Convention.

DONE AT PANAMA CITY, Republic of Panama, this thirtieth day of January one thousand nine hundred and seventy-five.

[Signatures omitted]

Inter–American Convention on Letters Rogatory.
Done at Panama January 30, 1975; entered into force for the United States August 27, 1988.

ADDITIONAL PROTOCOL TO THE INTER–AMERICAN CONVENTION ON LETTERS ROGATORY

The Governments of the Member States of the Organization of American States, desirous of strengthening and facilitating international cooperation in judicial procedures as provided for in the Inter–American Convention on Letters Rogatory done in Panama on January 30, 1975, have agreed as follows:

I. SCOPE OF PROTOCOL

Article 1

This Protocol shall apply only to those procedural acts set forth in Article 2(a) of the Inter–American Convention on Letters Rogatory, hereinafter referred to as "the Convention". For the purposes of this Protocol, such acts shall be understood to mean procedural acts (pleadings, motions, orders, and subpoenas) that are served and requests for information that are made by a judicial or other adjudicatory authority of a State Party to a judicial or administrative authority of another State Party and are transmitted by a letter rogatory from the Central Authority of the State of origin to the Central Authority of the State of destination.

II. CENTRAL AUTHORITY

Article 2

Each State Party shall designate a central authority that shall perform the functions assigned to it in the Convention and in this Protocol. At the time of deposit of their instruments of ratification or accession to this Protocol, the States Parties shall communicate the designations to the General Secretariat of the Organization of American States, which shall distribute to the States Parties to the Convention a list containing the designations received. The Central Authority designated by a State Party in accordance with Article 4 of the Convention may be changed at any time. The State Party shall inform the above-mentioned Secretariat of such change as promptly as possible.

III. PREPARATION OF LETTERS ROGATORY

Article 3

Letters rogatory shall be prepared on forms that are printed in the four official languages of the Organization of

American States or in the languages of the State of origin and of the State of destination and conform to Form A contained in the Annex to this Protocol.

Letters rogatory shall be accompanied by the following:

a. Copy of the complaint or pleading that initiated the action in which the letter rogatory was issued, as well as a translation thereof into the language of the State of destination;

b. Untranslated copy of the documents attached to the complaint or pleading;

c. Untranslated copy of any rulings ordering issuance of the letter rogatory;

d. Form conforming to Form B annexed to this Protocol and containing essential information for the person to be served or the authority to receive the documents; and

e. Certificate conforming to Form C annexed to this Protocol on which the Central Authority of the State of destination shall attest to execution or non-execution of the letter rogatory.

The copies shall be regarded as authenticated for the purposes of Article 8(a) of the Convention if they bear the seal of the judicial or other adjudicatory authority that issued the letter rogatory.

A copy of the letter rogatory together with Form B and the copies referred to in items a, b, and c of this Article shall be delivered to the person notified or to the authority to which the request is addressed. One of the copies of the letter rogatory and the documents attached to it shall remain in the possession of the State of destination; the untranslated original, the certificate of execution and the documents attached to them shall be returned to the Central Authority of the State of origin through appropriate channels.

If a State Party has more than one official language, it shall, at the time of signature, ratification or accession to this Protocol, declare which language or languages shall be considered official for the purposes of the Convention and of this Protocol. If a State Party comprises territorial units that have different official languages, it shall, at the time of signature, ratification or accession to this Protocol, declare which language or languages in each territorial unit shall be considered official for the purposes of the Convention and of this Protocol. The General Secretariat of the Organization of American States shall distribute to the States Parties to this Protocol the information contained in such declarations.

IV. TRANSMISSION AND PROCESSING OF LETTERS ROGATORY

Article 4

Upon receipt of a letter rogatory from the Central Authority in another State Party, the Central Authority in the State of destination shall transmit the letter rogatory to the appropriate judicial or administrative authority for processing in accordance with the applicable local law.

Upon execution of the letter rogatory, the judicial or administrative authority or authorities that processed it shall attest to the execution thereof in the manner prescribed in their local law, and shall transmit it with the relevant documents to the Central Authority. The Central Authority of the State Party of destination shall certify execution of the letter rogatory to the Central Authority of the State Party of origin on a form conforming to Form C of the Annex, which shall not require legalization. In addition, the Central Authority of the State of destination shall return the letter rogatory and attached documents to the Central Authority of the State of origin for delivery to the judicial or other adjudicatory authority that issued it.

V. COSTS AND EXPENSES

Article 5

The processing of letters rogatory by the Central Authority of the State Party of destination and its judicial or administrative authorities shall be free of charge. However, this State Party may seek payment by parties requesting execution of letters rogatory for those services which, in accordance with its local law, are required to be paid for directly by those parties.

The party requesting the execution of a letter rogatory shall, at its election, either select and indicate in the letter rogatory the person who is responsible in the State of destination for the cost of such services or, alternatively, shall attach to the letter rogatory a check for the fixed amount that is specified in Article 6 of this Protocol for its processing by the State of destination and will cover the cost of such services or a document proving that such amount has been transferred by some other means to the Central Authority of the State of destination.

The fact that the cost of such services ultimately exceeds the fixed amount shall not delay or prevent the processing or execution of the letter rogatory by the Central Authority or the judicial or administrative authorities of the State of destination. Should the cost exceed that amount, the Central Authority of the State of destination may, when returning the executed letter rogatory, seek payment of the outstanding amount due from the party requesting execution of the letter rogatory.

Article 6

At the time of deposit of its instrument of ratification or accession to this Protocol with the General Secretariat of the Organization of American States, each State Party shall attach a schedule of the services and the costs and other expenses that, in accordance with its local law, shall be paid directly by the party requesting execution of the letter rogatory. In addition, each State Party shall specify in the above-mentioned schedule the single amount which it considers will reasonably cover the cost of such services, regardless of the number or nature thereof. This amount shall be paid when the person requesting execution of the letter rogatory has not designated a person responsible for the payment of such services in the State of destination but has decided to pay for them directly in the manner provided for in Article 5 of this Protocol.

The General Secretariat of the Organization of American States shall distribute the information received to the States Parties to this Protocol. A State Party may at any time notify the General Secretariat of the Organization of American States of changes in the above-mentioned schedules, which shall be communicated by the General Secretariat to the other States Parties to this Protocol.

Article 7

States Parties may declare in the schedules mentioned in the foregoing articles that, provided there is reciprocity, they will not charge parties requesting execution of letters rogatory for the services necessary for executing them, or will accept in complete satisfaction of the cost of such services either the single fixed amount specified in Article 6 or another specified amount.

Article 8

This Protocol shall be open for signature and subject to ratification or accession by those Member States of the Organization of American States that have signed, ratified, or acceded to the Inter-American Convention on Letters Rogatory signed in Panama on January 30, 1975.

This Protocol shall remain open for accession by any other State that accedes or has acceded to the Inter-American Convention on Letters Rogatory, under the conditions set forth in this article.

The instruments of ratification and accession shall be deposited with the General Secretariat of the Organization of American States.

Article 9

This Protocol shall enter into force on the thirtieth day following the date on which two States Parties to the Convention have deposited their instruments of ratification or accession to this Protocol.

For each State ratifying or acceding to the Protocol after its entry into force, the Protocol shall enter into force on the thirtieth day following deposit by such State of its instrument of ratification or accession, provided that such State is a Party to the Convention.

Article 10

If a State Party has two or more territorial units in which different systems of law apply in relation to matters dealt with in this Protocol, it may, at the time of signature, ratification or accession, declare that this Protocol shall extend to all its territorial units or only to one or more of them.

Such declaration may be modified by subsequent declarations that shall expressly indicate the territorial unit or units to which this Protocol applies. Such subsequent declarations shall be transmitted to the General Secretariat of the Organization of American States, and shall become effective thirty days after the date of their receipt.

Article 11

This Protocol shall remain in force indefinitely, but any of the States Parties may denounce it. The instrument of denunciation shall be deposited with the General Secretariat of the Organization of American States. After one year from the date of deposit of the instrument of denunciation, the Protocol shall no longer be in effect for the denouncing State, but shall remain in effect for the other States Parties.

Article 12

The original instrument of this Protocol and its Annex (Forms A, B and C), the English, French, Portuguese and Spanish texts of which are equally authentic, shall be deposited with the General Secretariat of the Organization of American States, which will forward an authenticated copy of the text to the Secretariat of the United Nations for registration and publication in accordance with Article 102 of its Charter. The General Secretariat of the Organization of American States shall notify the Member States of that Organization and the States that have acceded to the Protocol of the signatures, deposits of instruments of ratification, accession and denunciation, as well as of reservations, if any. It shall also transmit to them the information mentioned in Article 2, the last paragraph of Article 3, and Article 6 and the declarations referred to in Article 10 of this Protocol.

IN WITNESS WHEREOF the undersigned Plenipotentiaries, being duly authorized thereto by their respective Governments, have signed this Protocol.

DONE AT MONTEVIDEO, Republic of Uruguay, this eighth day of May, one thousand nine hundred and seventy-nine.

[Signatures omitted]

ANNEX TO THE ADDITIONAL PROTOCOL
TO THE INTER-AMERICAN CONVENTION ON LETTERS ROGATORY
FORM A

LETTER ROGATORY [1]

1	2
REQUESTING JUDICIAL OR OTHER ADJUDICATORY AUTHORITY Name Address	CASE: DOCKET No.:
3	4
CENTRAL AUTHORITY OF THE STATE OF ORIGIN Name Address	CENTRAL AUTHORITY OF THE STATE OF DESTINATION Name Address

5	6
REQUESTING PARTY	COUNSEL TO THE REQUESTING PARTY
Name	Name
Address	Address

PERSON DESIGNATED TO ACT IN CONNECTION WITH THE LETTER ROGATORY

Name

Address

Is this person responsible for costs and expenses?
YES ☐ NO ☐

*If not, check in the amount of _____ is attached
*Or proof of payment is attached

The Central Authority signing this letter rogatory has the honor to transmit to you in triplicate the documents listed below and, in conformity with the Protocol to the Inter-American Convention on Letters Rogatory:

* A. Requests their prompt service on:

_____

_____

_____

The undersigned authority requests that service be carried out in the following manner:

* (1). In accordance with the special procedure or additional formalities that are described below, as provided for in the second paragraph of Article 10 of the above-mentioned Convention; or

_____

_____

_____

* (2). By service personally on the identified addressee or, in the case of a legal entity, on its authorized agent; or

* (3). If the person or the authorized agent of the entity to be served is not found, service shall be made in accordance with the law of the State of destination.

* B. Requests the delivery of the documents listed below to the following judicial or administrative authority:
Authority _____

_____

_____

* C. Requests the Central Authority of the State of destination to return to the Central Authority of the State of origin one copy of the documents listed below and attached to this letter rogatory, and an executed Certificate on the attached Form C.
Done at _____ this _____ date of _____, 19___.

Signature and stamp of the judicial or other adjudicatory authority of the State of origin	Signature and stamp of the Central Authority of the State of origin

Title or other identification of each document to be delivered:

_____

_____

(Attach additional pages, if necessary.)

1 Complete the original and two copies of this form; if A(1) is applicable, attach the original and two copies of the translation of this item in the language of the State of destination.
* Delete if inapplicable.

ANNEX TO THE ADDITIONAL PROTOCOL
TO THE INTER-AMERICAN CONVENTION ON LETTERS ROGATORY

FORM B

ESSENTIAL INFORMATION FOR THE ADDRESSEE [1]

To (Name and address of the person being served)_____

You are hereby informed that (Brief statement of nature of service) _____

A copy of the letter rogatory that gives rise to the service or delivery of these documents is attached to this document. This copy also contains essential information for you. Also attached are copies of the complaint or pleading initiating the action in which the letter rogatory was issued, of the documents attached to the complaint or pleading, and of any rulings that ordered the issuance of the letter rogatory.

ADDITIONAL INFORMATION

I*

FOR SERVICE

A. The document being served on you (original or copy) concerns the following:

B. The remedies sought or the amount in dispute is as follows:

C. By this service, you are requested:

D. * In case of service on you as a defendant you can answer the complaint before the judicial or other adjudicatory authority specified in Form A, Box 1 (State place, date and hour):

* You are being summoned to appear as: _____

* If some other action is being requested of the person served, please describe: _____

E. If you fail to comply, the consequences might be: _____

F. You are hereby informed that a defense counsel appointed by the Court or the following legal aid societies are available to you at the place where the proceeding is pending.
Name: _____

Address: _____

The documents listed in Part III are being furnished to you so that you may better understand and defend your interests.

II *

FOR INFORMATION FROM JUDICIAL OR ADMINISTRATIVE AUTHORITY

To: _____

_____

_____

(Name and address of the judicial or administrative authority)

You are respectfully requested to furnish the undersigned authority with the following information:

_____

_____

_____

_____

The documents listed in Part III are being furnished to you to facilitate your reply.

III

LIST OF ATTACHED DOCUMENTS

_____

_____

_____

_____

_____

_____

_____

_____

(Attach additional pages if necessary.)

Done at _____ this _____ day of _____, 19___

_____	_____
Signature and stamp of the judicial or other adjudicatory authority of the State of origin	Signature and stamp of the Central Authority of the State of Origin

1 Complete the original and two copies of this form in the language of the State of origin and two copies in the language of the State of destination.

* Delete if inapplicable.

ANNEX TO THE ADDITIONAL PROTOCOL
TO THE INTER-AMERICAN CONVENTION ON LETTERS ROGATORY

FORM C

CERTIFICATE OF EXECUTION1

To: _____

_____

_____

(Name and address of judicial or other adjudicatory authority that issued the letter rogatory)

In conformity with the Additional Protocol to the Inter-American Convention on Letters Rogatory, signed at Montevideo on May 8, 1979, and in accordance with the attached original letter rogatory, the undersigned Central Authority has the honor to certify the following:

*A. That one copy of the documents attached to this Certificate has been served or delivered as follows:

Date: _____

At (Address) _____

By one of the following methods authorized by the Convention.

*(1) In accordance with the special procedure or additional formalities that are described below, as provided for in the second paragraph of Article 10 of the above-mentioned Convention, or

_____

_____

_____

*(2) By service personally on the identified addressee or, in the case of a legal entity, on its authorized agent, or

*(3) If the person or the authorized agent of the entity to be served was not found, in accordance with the law of the State of destination: (Specify method used)

_____
_____
_____
_____

*B. That the documents referred to in the letter rogatory have been delivered to:

Identity of person _____
_____
_____

Relationship to the addressee _____
(family, business or other)
_____
_____

*C. That the documents attached to the Certificate have not been served or delivered for the following reason(s):

_____
_____
_____
_____

*D. In conformity with the Protocol, the party requesting execution of the letter rogatory is requested to pay the outstanding balance of costs in the amount indicated in the attached statement.

Done at _____ the _____ day of _____ 19___

_____
Signature and stamp of Central Authority of the State of destination

Where appropriate, attach originals or copies of any additional documents proving service or delivery, and identify them.
1 Complete the original and one copy in the language of the State of destination.
* Delete if inapplicable.

Additional Protocol to the Inter–American Convention on Letters Rogatory, with Annex. Done at Montevideo May 8, 1979; entered into force for the United States August 27, 1988.

§ 1782. Assistance to foreign and international tribunals and to litigants before such tribunals

(a) The district court of the district in which a person resides or is found may order him to give his testimony or statement or to produce a document or other thing for use in a proceeding in a foreign or international tribunal, including criminal investigations conducted before formal accusation. The order may be made pursuant to a letter rogatory issued, or request made, by a foreign or international tribunal or upon the application of any interested person and may direct that the testimony or statement be given, or the document or other thing be produced, before a person appointed by the court. By virtue of his appointment, the person appointed has power to administer any necessary oath and take the testimony or statement. The order may prescribe the practice and procedure, which may be in whole or part the practice and procedure of the foreign country or the international tribunal, for taking the testimony or statement or producing the document or other thing. To the extent that the order does not prescribe otherwise, the testimony or statement shall be taken, and the document or other thing produced, in accordance with the Federal Rules of Civil Procedure.

A person may not be compelled to give his testimony or statement or to produce a document or other thing in violation of any legally applicable privilege.

(b) This chapter does not preclude a person within the United States from voluntarily giving his testimony or statement, or producing a document or other thing, for use in a proceeding in a foreign or international tribunal before any person and in any manner acceptable to him.

(June 25, 1948, c. 646, 62 Stat. 949; May 24, 1949, c. 139, § 93, 63 Stat. 103; Oct. 3, 1964, Pub.L. 88–619, § 9(a), 78 Stat. 997; Feb. 10, 1996, Pub.L. 104–106, Div. A, Title XIII, § 1342(b), 110 Stat. 486.)

HISTORICAL AND STATUTORY NOTES

References in Text

The Federal Rules of Civil Procedure, referred to in subsec. (a), are set out in this title.

§ 1783. Subpoena of person in foreign country

(a) A court of the United States may order the issuance of a subpoena requiring the appearance as a witness before it, or before a person or body designated by it, of a national or resident of the United States who is in a foreign country, or requiring the production of a specified document or other thing by him, if the court finds that particular testimony or the production of the document or other thing by him is necessary in the interest of justice, and, in other than a criminal action or proceeding, if the court finds, in addition, that it is not possible to obtain his testimony in admissible form without his personal appearance or to obtain the production of the document or other thing in any other manner.

(b) The subpoena shall designate the time and place for the appearance or for the production of the document or other thing. Service of the subpoena and any order to show cause, rule, judgment, or decree authorized by this section or by section 1784 of this title shall be effected in accordance with the provisions of the Federal Rules of Civil Procedure relating to service of process on a person in a foreign country. The person serving the subpoena shall tender to the person to whom the subpoena is addressed his estimated necessary travel and attendance expenses, the amount of which shall be determined by the court and stated in the order directing the issuance of the subpoena.

(June 25, 1948, c. 646, 62 Stat. 949; Oct. 3, 1964, Pub.L. 88–619, § 10(a), 78 Stat. 997.)

HISTORICAL AND STATUTORY NOTES

References in Text

The Federal Rules of Civil Procedure, referred to in subsec. (b), are set out in this title.

§ 1784. Contempt

(a) The court of the United States which has issued a subpoena served in a foreign country may order the person who has failed to appear or who has failed to produce a document or other thing as directed therein to show cause before it at a designated time why he should not be punished for contempt.

(b) The court, in the order to show cause, may direct that any of the person's property within the United States be levied upon or seized, in the manner provided by law or court rules governing levy or seizure under execution, and held to satisfy any judgment that may be rendered against him pursuant to subsection (d) of this section if adequate security, in such amount as the court may direct in the order, be given for any damage that he might suffer should he not be found in contempt. Security under this subsection may not be required of the United States.

(c) A copy of the order to show cause shall be served on the person in accordance with section 1783(b) of this title.

(d) On the return day of the order to show cause or any later day to which the hearing may be continued, proof shall be taken. If the person is found in contempt, the court, notwithstanding any limitation upon its power generally to punish for contempt, may fine him not more than $100,000 and direct that the fine and costs of the proceedings be satisfied by a sale of the property levied upon or seized, conducted upon the notice required and in the manner provided for sales upon execution.

(June 25, 1948, c. 646, 62 Stat. 949; Oct. 3, 1964, Pub.L. 88–619, § 11, 78 Stat. 998.)

§ 1785. Subpoenas in multiparty, multiforum actions

When the jurisdiction of the district court is based in whole or in part upon section 1369 of this title, a subpoena for attendance at a hearing or trial may, if authorized by the court upon motion for good cause shown, and upon such terms and conditions as the court may impose, be served at any place within the United States, or anywhere outside the United States if otherwise permitted by law.

(Added Pub.L. 107–273, Div. C, Title I, § 11020(b)(4)(B)(i), Nov. 2, 2002, 116 Stat. 1828.)

HISTORICAL AND STATUTORY NOTES

Effective and Applicability Provisions

2002 Acts. Amendments by section 11020(b) of Pub.L. 107–273 shall apply to a civil action if the accident giving rise to the cause of action occurred on or after the 90th day after Nov. 2, 2002, see section 11020(c) of Pub.L. 107–273, set out as a note under 28 U.S.C.A. § 1369.

Prior Provisions

A prior section 1785, Act June 25, 1948, c. 646, 62 Stat. 950, relating to the privilege against self-incrimination on examination under letters rogatory (see section 1782(a) of this title), was repealed by Pub.L. 88–619, § 12(a), Oct. 3, 1964, 78 Stat. 998.

CHAPTER 119—EVIDENCE; WITNESSES

Sec.
1821. Per diem and mileage generally; subsistence.
1822. Competency of interested persons; share of penalties payable.

Sec.
[1823. Repealed.]
1824. Mileage fees under summons as both witness and juror.
1825. Payment of fees.
1826. Recalcitrant witnesses.
1827. Interpreters in courts of the United States.
1828. Special interpretation services.

§ 1821. Per diem and mileage generally; subsistence

(a)(1) Except as otherwise provided by law, a witness in attendance at any court of the United States, or before a United States Magistrate Judge, or before any person authorized to take his deposition pursuant to any rule or order of a court of the United States, shall be paid the fees and allowances provided by this section.

(2) As used in this section, the term "court of the United States" includes, in addition to the courts listed in section 451 of this title, any court created by Act of Congress in a territory which is invested with any jurisdiction of a district court of the United States.

(b) A witness shall be paid an attendance fee of $40 per day for each day's attendance. A witness shall also be paid the attendance fee for the time necessarily occupied in going to and returning from the place of attendance at the beginning and end of such attendance or at any time during such attendance.

(c)(1) A witness who travels by common carrier shall be paid for the actual expenses of travel on the basis of the means of transportation reasonably utilized and the distance necessarily traveled to and from such witness's residence by the shortest practical route in going to and returning from the place of attendance. Such a witness shall utilize a common carrier at the most economical rate reasonably available. A receipt or other evidence of actual cost shall be furnished.

(2) A travel allowance equal to the mileage allowance which the Administrator of General Services has prescribed, pursuant to section 5704 of title 5, for official travel of employees of the Federal Government shall be paid to each witness who travels by privately owned vehicle. Computation of mileage under this paragraph shall be made on the basis of a uniformed table of distances adopted by the Administrator of General Services.

(3) Toll charges for toll roads, bridges, tunnels, and ferries, taxicab fares between places of lodging and carrier terminals, and parking fees (upon presentation of a valid parking receipt), shall be paid in full to a witness incurring such expenses.

(4) All normal travel expenses within and outside the judicial district shall be taxable as costs pursuant to section 1920 of this title.

(d)(1) A subsistence allowance shall be paid to a witness when an overnight stay is required at the place of attendance because such place is so far removed from the residence of such witness as to prohibit return thereto from day to day.

(2) A subsistence allowance for a witness shall be paid in an amount not to exceed the maximum per diem allowance prescribed by the Administrator of General Services, pursuant to section 5702(a) of title 5, for official travel in the area of attendance by employees of the Federal Government.

(3) A subsistence allowance for a witness attending in an area designated by the Administrator of General Services as a high-cost area shall be paid in an amount not to exceed the maximum actual subsistence allowance prescribed by the Administrator, pursuant to section 5702(c)(B) of title 5, for official travel in such area by employees of the Federal Government.

(4) When a witness is detained pursuant to section 3144 of title 18 for want of security for his appearance, he shall be entitled for each day of detention when not in attendance at court, in addition to his subsistence, to the daily attendance fee provided by subsection (b) of this section.

(e) An alien who has been paroled into the United States for prosecution, pursuant to section 212(d)(5) of the Immigration and Nationality Act (8 U.S.C. 1182(d)(5)), or an alien who either has admitted belonging to a class of aliens who are deportable or has been determined pursuant to section 240 of such Act (8 U.S.C. 1252(b) [1]) to be deportable, shall be ineligible to receive the fees or allowances provided by this section.

(f) Any witness who is incarcerated at the time that his or her testimony is given (except for a witness to whom the provisions of section 3144 of title 18 apply) may not receive fees or allowances under this section, regardless of whether such a witness is incarcerated at the time he or she makes a claim for fees or allowances under this section.

(June 25, 1948, c. 646, 62 Stat. 950; May 10, 1949, c. 96, 63 Stat. 65; May 24, 1949, c. 139, § 94, 63 Stat. 103; Oct. 31, 1951, c. 655, § 51(a), 65 Stat. 727; Sept. 3, 1954, c. 1263, § 45, 68 Stat. 1242; Aug. 1, 1956, c. 826, 70 Stat. 798; Mar. 27, 1968, Pub.L. 90–274, § 102(b), 82 Stat. 62; Oct. 27, 1978, Pub.L. 95–535, § 1, 92 Stat. 2033; Dec. 1, 1990, Pub.L. 101–650, Title III, §§ 314(a), 321, 104 Stat. 5115, 5117; Oct. 14, 1992, Pub.L. 102–417, § 2(a)–(c), 106 Stat. 2138; Sept. 30, 1996, Pub.L. 104–208, Div. C, Title III, § 308(g)(5)(E), 110 Stat. 3009–623.)

[1] So in original. Reference in parenthesis should probably be "(8 U.S.C. 1229a)".

HISTORICAL AND STATUTORY NOTES

References in Text

Clause (B) of section 5702(c) of title 5, referred to in subsec. (d)(3), was redesignated clause (2) by Pub.L. 96–54, § 2(a)(36), Aug. 14, 1979, 93 Stat. 383. Thereafter subsec. (c) of section 5702 of Title 5, which related to conditions under which an employee could be reimbursed for actual and necessary expenses of official travel when the maximum per diem allowance was less than these expenses, was struck out in its entirety, and subsec. (e) of that section was redesignated as subsec. (c) thereof, by Pub.L. 99–234, Title I, § 102, Jan. 2, 1986, 99 Stat. 1756. Both amendments were made without any conforming amendments to this section.

Effective and Applicability Provisions

1996 Acts. Amendment by section 308(g)(5)(E) of Div. C of Pub.L. 104–208, effective, with certain exceptions and subject to certain transitional rules, on the first day of the first month beginning more than 180 days after Sept. 30, 1996, see section 309 of Pub.L. 104–208, set out as a note under section 1101 of Title, Aliens and Nationality.

1992 Acts. Section 2(d) of Pub.L. 102–417 provided that: "The amendments made by this section [amending this section] shall be effective on and after the date of the enactment of this act [Oct. 14, 1992] and shall apply to any witness who testified before such date and has not received any fee or allowance under section 1821 of title 28, United States Code [this section], relating to such testimony."

1978 Acts. Section 2 of Pub.L. 95–535 provided that: "The amendments made by this Act [amending this section] shall take effect on October 1, 1978, or on the date of enactment [Oct. 27, 1978], whichever occurs later."

1968 Acts. Amendment by Pub.L. 90–274 effective 270 days after Mar. 27, 1968, except as to cases in which an indictment has been returned or a petit jury empaneled prior to such effective date, see section 104 of Pub.L. 90–274, set out as a note under section 1861 of this title.

Change of Name

"United States magistrate judge" substituted for "United States magistrate" in text pursuant to section 321 of Pub.L. 101–650, set out as a note under 28 U.S.C.A. § 631.

Severability of Provisions

If any provision of Division C of Pub.L. 104–208 or the application of such provision to any person or circumstances is held to be unconstitutional, the remainder of Division C of Pub.L. 104–208 and the application of the provisions of Division C of Pub.L. 104–208 to any person or circumstance not to be affected thereby, see section 1(e) of Pub.L. 104–208, set out as a note under section 1101 of Title 8, Aliens and Nationality.

Payment of Fact Witness Fee to Incarcerated Person Prohibited

Pub.L. 102–395, Title I, § 108, Oct. 6, 1992, 106 Stat. 1841, provided that: "Notwithstanding 28 U.S.C. 1821 [this section], no funds appropriated to the Department of Justice in fiscal year 1993 or any prior fiscal year, or any other funds available from the Treasury of the United States, shall be obligated or expended to pay a fact witness fee to a person who is incarcerated testifying as a fact witness in a court of the United States, as defined in 28 U.S.C. 1821(a)(2) [subsec. (a)(2) of this section]."

Similar provisions were contained in the following prior appropriations Acts:

Pub.L. 102–140, Title I, § 110, Oct. 28, 1991, 105 Stat. 795.

Pub.L. 102–27, Title II, § 102, Apr. 10, 1991, 105 Stat. 136.

§ 1822. Competency of interested persons; share of penalties payable

Any person interested in a share of any fine, penalty or forfeiture incurred under any Act of Congress, may be examined as a witness in any proceeding for the recovery of such fine, penalty or forfeiture by any party thereto. Such examination shall not deprive the witness of his share.

(June 25, 1948, c. 646, 62 Stat. 950.)

[§ 1823. Repealed. Pub.L. 91–563, § 5(a), Dec. 19, 1970, 84 Stat. 1478]

HISTORICAL AND STATUTORY NOTES

Section, Acts June 25, 1948, c. 646, 62 Stat. 950; May 24, 1949, c. 139, § 95, 63 Stat. 103; Oct. 5, 1949, c. 601, 63 Stat. 704; July 7, 1952, c. 581, 66 Stat. 439; July 28, 1955, c. 424, § 3, 69 Stat. 394, related to payment of witness fees to officers and employees of the United States, and is now covered by sections 5515, 5537, 5751, and 6322 of Title 5, Government Organization and Employees.

§ 1824. Mileage fees under summons as both witness and juror

No constructive or double mileage fees shall be allowed by reason of any person being summoned both as a witness and a juror.

(June 25, 1948, c. 646, 62 Stat. 951.)

§ 1825. Payment of fees

(a) In any case in which the United States or an officer or agency of the United States is a party, the United States marshal for the district shall pay all fees of witnesses on the certificate of the United States attorney or assistant United States attorney, and in the proceedings before a United States magistrate judge, on the certificate of such magistrate judge, except that any fees of defense witnesses, other than experts, appearing pursuant to subpoenas issued upon approval of the court, shall be paid by the United States marshal for the district—

(1) on the certificate of a Federal public defender or assistant Federal public defender, in a criminal case in which the defendant is represented by such Federal public defender or assistant Federal public defender, and

(2) on the certificate of the clerk of the court upon the affidavit of such witnesses' attendance given by other counsel appointed pursuant to section 3006A of title 18, in a criminal case in which a defendant is represented by such other counsel.

(b) In proceedings in forma pauperis for a writ of habeas corpus, and in proceedings in forma pauperis under section 2255 of this title, the United States marshal for the district shall pay, on the certificate of the district judge, all fees of witnesses for the party authorized to proceed in forma pauperis, except that any fees of witnesses for such party, other than experts, appearing pursuant to subpoenas issued upon approval of the court, shall be paid by the United States marshal for the district—

(1) on the certificate of a Federal public defender or assistant Federal public defender, in any such proceedings in which a party is represented by such Federal public defender or assistant Federal public defender, and

(2) on the certificate of the clerk of the court upon the affidavit of such witnesses' attendance given by other counsel appointed pursuant to section 3006A of title 18, in any such proceedings in which a party is represented by such other counsel.

(c) Fees and mileage need not be tendered to a witness upon service of a subpoena issued on behalf of the United States or an officer or agency of the United States, upon service of a subpoena issued on behalf of a defendant represented by a Federal public defender, assistant Federal public defender, or other attorney appointed pursuant to section 3006A of title 18, or upon service of a subpoena issued on behalf of a party authorized to proceed in forma pauperis, if the payment of such fees and mileage is to be made by the United States marshal under this section.

(June 25, 1948, c. 646, 62 Stat. 951; Sept. 2, 1965, Pub.L. 89–162, 79 Stat. 618; Nov. 14, 1986, Pub.L. 99–651, Title I, § 104, 100 Stat. 3645; Dec. 1, 1990, Pub.L. 101–650, Title III, § 321, 104 Stat. 5117.)

HISTORICAL AND STATUTORY NOTES

Effective and Applicability Provisions

1986 Acts. Amendment to this section by section 104 of Pub.L. 99–651 to take effect one hundred and twenty days after Nov. 14, 1986, see section 105 of Pub.L. 99–651, set out as a note under section 3006A of Title 18, Crimes and Criminal Procedure.

Change of Name

"United States magistrate judge" substituted for "United States magistrate" in text pursuant to section 321 of Pub.L. 101–650, set out as a note under 28 U.S.C.A. § 631.

§ 1826. Recalcitrant witnesses

(a) Whenever a witness in any proceeding before or ancillary to any court or grand jury of the United States refuses without just cause shown to comply with an order of the court to testify or provide other information, including any book, paper, document, record, recording or other material, the court, upon such refusal, or when such refusal is duly brought to its attention, may summarily order his confinement at a suitable place until such time as the witness is willing to give such testimony or provide such information. No period of such confinement shall exceed the life of—

(1) the court proceeding, or

(2) the term of the grand jury, including extensions,

before which such refusal to comply with the court order occurred, but in no event shall such confinement exceed eighteen months.

(b) No person confined pursuant to subsection (a) of this section shall be admitted to bail pending the determination of an appeal taken by him from the order for his confinement if it appears that the appeal is frivolous or taken for delay. Any appeal from an order of confinement under this section shall be disposed of as soon as practicable, but not later than thirty days from the filing of such appeal.

(c) Whoever escapes or attempts to escape from the custody of any facility or from any place in which or to which he is confined pursuant to this section or section 4243 of title 18, or whoever rescues or attempts to rescue or instigates, aids, or assists the escape or attempt to escape of such a person, shall be subject to imprisonment for not more than three years, or a fine of not more than $10,000, or both.

(Added Pub.L. 91–452, Title III, § 301(a), Oct. 15, 1970, 84 Stat. 932, and amended Pub.L. 98–473, Title II, § 1013, Oct. 12, 1984, 98 Stat. 2142.)

§ 1827. Interpreters in courts of the United States

(a) The Director of the Administrative Office of the United States Courts shall establish a program to facilitate the use of certified and otherwise qualified interpreters in judicial proceedings instituted by the United States.

(b)(1) The Director shall prescribe, determine, and certify the qualifications of persons who may serve as certified interpreters, when the Director considers certification of interpreters to be merited, for the hearing impaired (whether or not also speech impaired) and persons who speak only or primarily a language other than the English language, in judicial proceedings instituted by the United States. The Director may certify interpreters for any language if the Director determines that there is a need for certified interpreters in that language. Upon the request of the Judicial Conference of the United States for certified interpreters in a language, the Director shall certify interpreters in that language. Upon such a request from the judicial council of a circuit and the approval of the Judicial Conference, the Director shall certify interpreters for that circuit in the language requested. The judicial council of a circuit shall identify and evaluate the needs of the districts within a circuit. The Director shall certify interpreters based on the results of criterion-referenced performance examinations. The Director shall issue regulations to carry out this paragraph within 1 year after the date of the enactment of the Judicial Improvements and Access to Justice Act.

(2) Only in a case in which no certified interpreter is reasonably available as provided in subsection (d) of this section, including a case in which certification of interpreters is not provided under paragraph (1) in a particular language, may the services of otherwise qualified interpreters be used. The Director shall provide guidelines to the courts for the selection of otherwise qualified interpreters, in order to ensure that the highest standards of accuracy are maintained in all judicial proceedings subject to the provisions of this chapter.

(3) The Director shall maintain a current master list of all certified interpreters and otherwise qualified interpreters and shall report periodically on the use and performance of both certified and otherwise qualified interpreters in judicial proceedings instituted by the United States and on the languages for which interpreters have been certified. The Director shall prescribe, subject to periodic review, a schedule of reasonable fees for services rendered by interpreters, certified or otherwise, used in proceedings instituted by the United States, and in doing so shall consider the prevailing rate of compensation for comparable service in other governmental entities.

(c)(1) Each United States district court shall maintain on file in the office of the clerk, and each United States attorney shall maintain on file, a list of all persons who have been certified as interpreters by the Director in accordance with subsection (b) of this section. The clerk shall make the list of certified interpreters for judicial proceeding available upon request.

(2) The clerk of the court, or other court employee designated by the chief judge, shall be responsible for securing the services of certified interpreters and otherwise qualified interpreters required for proceedings initiated by the United States, except that the United States attorney is responsible for securing the services of such interpreters for governmental witnesses.

(d)(1) The presiding judicial officer, with the assistance of the Director of the Administrative Office of the United States Courts, shall utilize the services of the most available certified interpreter, or when no certified interpreter is reasonably available, as determined by the presiding judicial officer, the services of an otherwise qualified interpreter, in judicial proceedings instituted by the United States, if the presiding judicial officer determines on such officer's own motion or on the motion of a party that such party (including a defendant in a criminal case), or a witness who may present testimony in such judicial proceedings—

(A) speaks only or primarily a language other than the English language; or

(B) suffers from a hearing impairment (whether or not suffering also from a speech impairment)

so as to inhibit such party's comprehension of the proceedings or communication with counsel or the presiding judicial officer, or so as to inhibit such witness' comprehension of questions and the presentation of such testimony.

(2) Upon the motion of a party, the presiding judicial officer shall determine whether to require the electronic sound recording of a judicial proceeding in which an interpreter is used under this section. In making this determination, the presiding judicial officer shall consider, among other things, the qualifications of the interpreter and prior experience in interpretation of court proceedings; whether the language to be interpreted is not one of the languages for which the Director has certified interpreters, and the complexity or length of the proceeding. In a grand jury proceeding, upon the motion of the accused, the presiding judicial officer shall require the electronic sound recording of the portion of the proceeding in which an interpreter is used.

(e)(1) If any interpreter is unable to communicate effectively with the presiding judicial officer, the United States attorney, a party (including a defendant in a criminal case), or a witness, the presiding judicial officer shall dismiss such interpreter and obtain the services of another interpreter in accordance with this section.

(2) In any judicial proceedings instituted by the United States, if the presiding judicial officer does not appoint an interpreter under subsection (d) of this section, an individual requiring the services of an interpreter may seek assistance of the clerk of court or the Director of the Administrative Office of the United States Courts in obtaining the assistance of a certified interpreter.

(f)(1) Any individual other than a witness who is entitled to interpretation under subsection (d) of this section may waive such interpretation in whole or in part. Such a waiver shall be effective only if approved by the presiding judicial officer and made expressly by such individual on the record after opportunity to consult with counsel and after the presiding judicial officer has explained to such individual, utilizing the services of the most available certified interpreter, or when no certified interpreter is reasonably available, as determined by the presiding judicial officer, the services of an otherwise competent interpreter, the nature and effect of the waiver.

(2) An individual who waives under paragraph (1) of this subsection the right to an interpreter may utilize the services of a noncertified interpreter of such individual's choice whose fees, expenses, and costs shall be paid in the manner provided for the payment of such fees, expenses, and costs of an interpreter appointed under subsection (d) of this section.

(g)(1) There are authorized to be appropriated to the Federal judiciary, and to be paid by the Director of the Administrative Office of the United States Courts, such sums as may be necessary to establish a program to facilitate the use of certified and otherwise qualified interpreters, and otherwise fulfill the provisions of this section and the Judicial Improvements and Access to Justice Act, except as provided in paragraph (3).

(2) Implementation of the provisions of this section is contingent upon the availability of appropriated funds to carry out the purposes of this section.

(3) Such salaries, fees, expenses, and costs that are incurred with respect to Government witnesses (including for grand jury proceedings) shall, unless direction is made under paragraph (4), be paid by the Attorney General from sums appropriated to the Department of Justice.

(4) Upon the request of any person in any action for which interpreting services established pursuant to subsection (d) are not otherwise provided, the clerk of the court, or other court employee designated by the chief judge, upon the request of the presiding judicial officer, shall, where possible, make such services available to that person on a cost-reimbursable basis, but the judicial officer may also require the prepayment of the estimated expenses of providing such services.

(5) If the Director of the Administrative Office of the United States Courts finds it necessary to develop and administer criterion-referenced performance examinations for purposes of certification, or other examinations for the selection of otherwise qualified interpreters, the Director may prescribe for each examination a uniform fee for applicants to take such examination. In determining the rate of the fee for each examination, the Director shall consider the fees charged by other organizations for examinations that are similar in scope or nature. Notwithstanding section 3302(b) of title 31, the Director is authorized to provide in any contract or agreement for the development or administration of examinations and the collection of fees that the contractor may retain all or a portion of the fees in payment for the services. Notwithstanding paragraph (6) of this subsection, all fees collected after the effective date of this paragraph and not retained by a contractor shall be deposited in the fund established under section 1931 of this title and shall remain available until expended.

(6) Any moneys collected under this subsection may be used to reimburse the appropriations obligated and disbursed in payment for such services.

(h) The presiding judicial officer shall approve the compensation and expenses payable to interpreters, pursuant to the schedule of fees prescribed by the Director under subsection (b)(3).

(i) The term "presiding judicial officer" as used in this section refers to any judge of a United States district court, including a bankruptcy judge, a United States magistrate judge, and in the case of grand jury proceedings conducted under the auspices of the United States attorney, a United States attorney.

(j) The term "judicial proceedings instituted by the United States" as used in this section refers to all proceedings, whether criminal or civil, including pretrial and grand jury proceedings (as well as proceedings upon a petition for a writ of habeas corpus initiated in the name of the United States by a relator) conducted in, or pursuant to the lawful authority and jurisdiction of a United States district court. The term "United States district court" as used in this subsection includes any court which is created by an Act of Congress in a territory and is invested with any jurisdiction of a district court established by chapter 5 of this title.

(k) The interpretation provided by certified or otherwise qualified interpreters pursuant to this section shall be in the simultaneous mode for any party to a judicial proceeding instituted by the United States and in the consecutive mode for witnesses, except that the presiding judicial officer, sua sponte or on the motion of a party, may authorize a simultaneous, or consecutive interpretation when such officer determines after a hearing on the record that such interpretation will aid in the efficient administration of justice. The presiding judicial officer, on such officer's motion or on the motion of a party, may order that special interpretation services as authorized in section 1828 of this title be provided if such officer determines that the provision of such services will aid in the efficient administration of justice.

(*l*) Notwithstanding any other provision of this section or section 1828, the presiding judicial officer may appoint a certified or otherwise qualified sign language interpreter to provide services to a party, witness, or other participant in a judicial proceeding, whether or not the proceeding is instituted by the United States, if the presiding judicial officer determines, on such officer's own motion or on the motion of a party or other participant in the proceeding, that such individual suffers from a hearing impairment. The presiding judicial officer shall, subject to the availability of appropriated funds, approve the compensation and expenses payable to sign language interpreters appointed under this section in accordance with the schedule of fees prescribed by the Director under subsection (b)(3) of this section.

(Added Pub.L. 95–539, § 2(a), Oct. 28, 1978, 92 Stat. 2040, and amended Pub.L. 100–702, Title VII, §§ 702–710, Nov. 19, 1988, 102 Stat. 4654–4657; Pub.L. 101–650, Title III, § 321, Dec. 1, 1990, 104 Stat. 5117; Pub.L. 104–317, Title III, § 306, Title IV, § 402(a), Oct. 19, 1996, 110 Stat. 3852, 3854.)

HISTORICAL AND STATUTORY NOTES

References in Text

The date of the enactment of the Judicial Improvements and Access to Justice Act, referred to in subsec. (b)(1), is the date of enactment of Pub.L. 100–702, which was approved Nov. 19, 1988.

The Judicial Improvements and Access to Justice Act, referred to in subsec. (g)(1), is Pub.L. 100–702, Nov. 19, 1988, 102 Stat. 4642. For complete classification of this Act to the Code, see Short Title note set out under section 1 of this title and Tables.

The effective date of this paragraph, referred to in subsec. (g)(5), probably means the date of enactment of Pub.L. 104–317, which was approved Oct. 19, 1996.

Effective and Applicability Provisions

1988 Acts. Section 712 of Title VII of Pub.L. 100–702 provided that: "This title [amending subsecs. (a) to (e) and (g) to (k) of this section and enacting provisions set out as notes under this section and section 1 of this title] shall become effective upon the date of enactment [Nov. 19, 1988]."

1978 Acts. Section effective 90 days after Oct. 28, 1978, see section 10(b) of Pub.L. 95–539, set out as a note under section 602 of this title.

Change of Name

"United States magistrate judge" substituted for "United States magistrate" in text pursuant to section 321 of Pub.L. 101–650, set out as a note under 28 U.S.C.A. § 631.

Short Title

1978 Acts. For Short title of Pub.L. 95–539 as "Court Interpreters Act", see section 1 of Pub.L. 95–539, set out as a note under section 1 of this title.

Impact on Existing Programs

Section 711 of Title VII of Pub.L. 100–702 provided that: "Nothing in this title [amending subsecs. (a) to (e) and (g) to (k) of this section and enacting provisions set out as notes under this section and section 1 of this title] shall be construed to terminate or diminish existing programs for the certification of interpreters."

Payment for Contractual Services

Section 402(b) of Pub.L. 104–317 provided that: "Notwithstanding sections 3302(b), 1341, and 1517 of title 31, United States Code [sections 3302(b), 1341, and 1517 of Title 31, Money and Finance], the Director of the Administrative Office of the United States Courts may include in any contract for the development or administration of examinations for interpreters (including such a contract entered into before the date of the enactment of this Act [Oct. 19, 1996]) a provision which permits the contractor to collect and retain fees in payment for contractual services in accordance with section 1827(g)(5) of title 28, United States Code [subsec. (g)(5) of this section]."

§ 1828. Special interpretation services

(a) The Director of the Administrative Office of the United States Courts shall establish a program for the provision of special interpretation services in criminal actions and in civil actions initiated by the United States (including petitions for writs of habeas corpus initiated in the name of the United States by relators) in a United States district court. The program shall provide a capacity for simultaneous interpretation services in multidefendant criminal actions and multidefendant civil actions.

(b) Upon the request of any person in any action for which special interpretation services established pursuant to subsection (a) are not otherwise provided, the Director, with the approval of the presiding judicial officer, may make such services available to the person requesting the services on a reimbursable basis at rates established in conformity with section 9701 of title 31, but the Director may require the prepayment of the estimated expenses of providing the services by the person requesting them.

(c) Except as otherwise provided in this subsection, the expenses incident to providing services under subsection (a) of this section shall be paid by the Director from sums appropriated to the Federal judiciary. A presiding judicial officer, in such officer's discretion, may order that all or part of the expenses shall be apportioned between or among the parties or shall be taxed as costs in a civil action, and any moneys collected as a result of such order may be used to reimburse the appropriations obligated and disbursed in payment for such services.

(d) Appropriations available to the Director shall be available to provide services in accordance with subsection (b) of this section, and moneys collected by the Director under that subsection may be used to reimburse the appropriations charged for such services. A presiding judicial officer, in such officer's discretion, may order that all or part of the expenses shall be apportioned between or among the parties or shall be taxed as costs in the action.

(Added Pub.L. 95–539, § 2(a), Oct. 28, 1978, 92 Stat. 2042, and amended Pub.L. 97–258, § 3(g), Sept. 13, 1982, 96 Stat. 1065.)

HISTORICAL AND STATUTORY NOTES

Effective and Applicability Provisions

1978 Acts. Section effective 90 days after Oct. 28, 1978, see section 10(b) of Pub.L. 95–539, set out as a note under section 602 of this title.

CHAPTER 121—JURIES; TRIAL BY JURY

Sec.
1861. Declaration of policy.
1862. Discrimination prohibited.
1863. Plan for random jury selection.
1864. Drawing of names from the master jury wheel; completion of juror qualification form.
1865. Qualifications for jury service.
1866. Selection and summoning of jury panels.
1867. Challenging compliance with selection procedures.
1868. Maintenance and inspection of records.
1869. Definitions.
1870. Challenges.
1871. Fees.
1872. Issues of fact in Supreme Court.
1873. Admiralty and maritime cases.
1874. Actions on bonds and specialties.
1875. Protection of jurors' employment.
1876. Trial by jury in the Court of International Trade.
1877. Protection of jurors.
1878. Optional use of a one-step summoning and qualification procedure.

§ 1861. Declaration of policy

It is the policy of the United States that all litigants in Federal courts entitled to trial by jury shall have the right to grand and petit juries selected at random from a fair cross section of the community in the district or division wherein the court convenes. It is further the policy of the United States that all citizens shall have the opportunity to be considered for service on grand and petit juries in the district courts of the United States, and shall have an obligation to serve as jurors when summoned for that purpose.

(June 25, 1948, c. 646, 62 Stat. 951; Sept. 9, 1957, Pub.L. 85–315, Part V, § 152, 71 Stat. 638; Mar. 27, 1968, Pub.L. 90–274, § 101, 82 Stat. 54.)

HISTORICAL AND STATUTORY NOTES

Effective and Applicability Provisions

1968 Acts. Section 104 of Pub.L. 90–274 provided that: "This Act [amending this section and sections 1821, 1862–1869, and 1871 of this title, repealing section 867 of Title 48, Territories and Insular Possessions, and enacting provisions set out as notes under this section] shall become effective two hundred and seventy days after the date of enactment [Mar. 27, 1968]: *Provided* That this Act shall not apply in any case in which an indictment has been returned or petit jury empaneled prior to such effective date."

Short Title

1978 Acts. Pub.L. 95–572, § 1, Nov. 2, 1978, 92 Stat. 2453, provided that: "This Act [which enacted sections 1363 and 1875 of this title, renumbered as section 1364 prior section 1363 of this title, amended sections 1863, 1865, 1866, 1869, and 1871 of this title, and enacted provisions set out as a note under section 1363 of this title] may be cited as the 'Jury System Improvements Act of 1978'."

1968 Acts. Section 1 of Pub.L. 90–274 provided: "That this Act [amending this section and sections 1821, 1862–1869, and 1871 of this title, repealing section 867 of Title 48, Territories and Insular Possessions, and enacting material set out as notes under this section] may be cited as the 'Jury Selection and Service Act of 1968'."

§ 1862. Discrimination prohibited

No citizen shall be excluded from service as a grand or petit juror in the district courts of the United States or in the Court of International Trade on account of race, color, religion, sex, national origin, or economic status.

(June 25, 1948, c. 646, 62 Stat. 952; Mar. 27, 1968, Pub.L. 90–274, § 101, 82 Stat. 54; Oct. 10, 1980, Pub.L. 96–417, Title III, § 302(c), 94 Stat. 1739.)

HISTORICAL AND STATUTORY NOTES

Effective and Applicability Provisions

1980 Acts. Amendment by Pub.L. 96–417 effective on Nov. 1, 1980 and applicable with respect to civil actions pending on or commenced on or after such date, see section 701(a) of Pub.L. 96–417, as amended, set out as a note under section 251 of this title.

1968 Acts. Amendment by Pub.L. 90–274 effective 270 days after Mar. 27, 1968, except as to cases in which an indictment has been returned or a petit jury empaneled prior to such effective date, see section 104 of Pub.L. 90–274, set out as a note under section 1861 of this title.

§ 1863. Plan for random jury selection

(a) Each United States district court shall devise and place into operation a written plan for random selection of grand and petit jurors that shall be designed to achieve the objectives of sections 1861 and 1862 of this title, and that shall otherwise comply with the provisions of this title. The plan shall be placed into operation after approval by a reviewing panel consisting of the members of the judicial council of the circuit and either the chief judge of the district whose plan is being reviewed or such other active district judge of that district as the chief judge of the district may designate. The panel shall examine the plan to ascertain that it complies with the provisions of this title. If the reviewing panel finds that the plan does not comply, the panel shall state the particulars in which the plan fails to comply and direct the district court to present within a reasonable time an alternative plan remedying the defect or defects. Separate plans may be adopted for each division or combination of divisions within a judicial district. The district court may modify a plan at any time and it shall modify the plan when so directed by the reviewing panel. The district court shall promptly notify the panel, the Administrative Office of the United States Courts, and the Attorney General of the United States, of the initial adoption and future modifications of the plan by filing copies therewith. Modifications of the plan made at the instance of the district court shall become effective after approval by the panel. Each district court shall submit a report on the jury selection process within its jurisdiction to the Administrative Office of the United States Courts in such form and at such times as the Judicial Conference of the United States may specify. The Judicial Conference of the United States may, from time to time, adopt rules and regulations governing the provisions and the operation of the plans formulated under this title.

(b) Among other things, such plan shall—

(1) either establish a jury commission, or authorize the clerk of the court, to manage the jury selection process. If the plan establishes a jury commission, the district court shall appoint one citizen to serve with the clerk of the court as the jury commission: *Provided, however*, That the plan for the District of Columbia may establish a jury commission consisting of three citizens. The citizen jury commissioner shall not belong to the same political party as the clerk serving with him. The clerk or the jury commission, as the case may be, shall act under the supervision and control of the chief judge of the district court or such other judge of the district court as the plan may provide. Each jury commissioner shall, during his tenure in office, reside in the judicial district or division for which he is appointed. Each citizen jury commissioner shall receive compensation to be fixed by the district court plan at a rate not to exceed $50 per day for each day necessarily employed in the performance of his duties, plus reimbursement for travel, subsistence, and other necessary expenses incurred by him in the performance of such duties. The Judicial Conference of the United States may establish standards for allowance of travel, subsistence, and other necessary expenses incurred by jury commissioners.

(2) specify whether the names of prospective jurors shall be selected from the voter registration lists or the lists of actual voters of the political subdivisions within the district or division. The plan shall prescribe some other source or sources of names in addition to voter lists where necessary to foster the policy and protect the rights secured by sections 1861 and 1862 of this title. The plan for the District of Columbia may require the names of prospective jurors to be selected from the city directory rather than from voter lists. The plans for the districts of Puerto Rico and the Canal Zone may prescribe some other source or sources of names of prospective jurors in lieu of voter lists, the use of which shall be consistent with the policies declared and rights secured by sections 1861 and 1862 of this title. The plan for the district of Massachusetts may require the names of prospective jurors to be selected from the resident list provided for in chapter 234A, Massachusetts General Laws, or comparable authority, rather than from voter lists.

(3) specify detailed procedures to be followed by the jury commission or clerk in selecting names from the sources specified in paragraph (2) of this subsection. These procedures shall be designed to ensure the random selection of a fair cross section of the persons residing in the community in the district or division wherein the court convenes. They shall ensure that names of persons residing in each of the counties, parishes, or similar political subdivisions within the judicial district or division are placed in a master jury wheel; and shall ensure that each county, parish, or similar political subdivision within the district or division is substantially proportionally represented in the master jury wheel for that judicial district, division, or combination of divisions. For the purposes of determining proportional representation in the master jury wheel, either the number of actual voters at the last general election in each county, parish, or similar political subdivision, or the number of registered voters if registration of voters is uniformly required throughout the district or division, may be used.

(4) provide for a master jury wheel (or a device similar in purpose and function) into which the names of those randomly selected shall be placed. The plan shall fix a minimum number of names to be placed initially in the master jury wheel, which shall be at least one-half of 1 per centum of the total number of persons on the lists used as a source of names for the district or division; but if this number of names is believed to be cumbersome and unnecessary, the plan may fix a smaller number of names to be placed in the master wheel, but in no event less than one thousand. The chief judge of the district court, or such other district court judge as the plan may provide, may order additional names to be placed in the master jury wheel from time to time as necessary. The plan shall provide for periodic emptying and refilling of the master jury wheel at specified times, the interval for which shall not exceed four years.

(5)(A) except as provided in subparagraph (B), specify those groups of persons or occupational classes whose members shall, on individual request therefor, be excused from jury service. Such groups or classes shall be excused only if the district court finds, and the plan states, that jury service by such class or group would entail undue hardship or extreme inconvenience to the members thereof, and excuse of members thereof would not be inconsistent with sections 1861 and 1862 of this title.

(B) specify that volunteer safety personnel, upon individual request, shall be excused from jury service. For purposes of this subparagraph, the term "volunteer safety personnel" means individuals serving a public agency (as defined in section 1203(6) of title I of the Omnibus Crime Control and Safe Streets Act of 1968) in an official capacity, without compensation, as firefighters or members of a rescue squad or ambulance crew.

(6) specify that the following persons are barred from jury service on the ground that they are exempt: (A) members in active service in the Armed Forces of the United States; (B) members of the fire or police departments of any State, the District of Columbia, any territory or possession of the United States, or any subdivision of a State, the District of Columbia, or such territory or possession; (C) public officers in the executive, legislative, or judicial branches of the Government of the United States, or of any State, the District of Columbia, any territory or possession of the United States, or any subdivision of a State, the District of Columbia, or such territory or possession, who are actively engaged in the performance of official duties.

(7) fix the time when the names drawn from the qualified jury wheel shall be disclosed to parties and to the public. If the plan permits these names to be made public, it may nevertheless permit the chief judge of the district court, or such other district court judge as the plan may provide, to keep these names confidential in any case where the interests of justice so require.

(8) specify the procedures to be followed by the clerk or jury commission in assigning persons whose names have been drawn from the qualified jury wheel to grand and petit jury panels.

(c) The initial plan shall be devised by each district court and transmitted to the reviewing panel specified in subsection (a) of this section within one hundred and twenty days of the date of enactment of the Jury Selection and Service Act of 1968. The panel shall approve or direct the modification of each plan so submitted within sixty days thereafter. Each plan or modification made at the direction of the panel shall become effective after approval at such time thereafter as the panel directs, in no event to exceed ninety days from the date of approval. Modifications made at the instance of the district court under subsection (a) of this section shall be effective at such time thereafter as the panel directs, in no event to exceed ninety days from the date of modification.

(d) State, local, and Federal officials having custody, possession, or control of voter registration lists, lists of actual voters, or other appropriate records shall make such lists and records available to the jury commission or clerks for inspection, reproduction, and copying at all reasonable times as the commission or clerk may deem necessary and proper for the performance of duties under this title. The district courts shall have jurisdiction upon application by the Attorney General of the United States to compel compliance with this subsection by appropriate process.

(June 25, 1948, c. 646, 62 Stat. 952; Mar. 27, 1968, Pub.L. 90–274, § 101, 82 Stat. 54; Apr. 6, 1972, Pub.L. 92–269, § 2, 86 Stat. 117; Nov. 2, 1978, Pub.L. 95–572, § 2(a), 92 Stat. 2453; Nov. 19, 1988, Pub.L. 100–702, Title VIII, § 802(b), (c), 102 Stat. 4657, 4658; Oct. 29, 1992, Pub.L. 102–572, Title IV, § 401, 106 Stat. 4511.)

HISTORICAL AND STATUTORY NOTES

References in Text

Section 1203(6) of title I of the Omnibus Crime Control and Safe Streets Act of 1968, referred to in subsec. (b)(5)(B), was successively renumbered and redesignated as section 1204(8) of the Act which is classified to 42 U.S.C.A. § 3796b(8).

The date of enactment of the Jury Selection and Service Act of 1968, referred to in subsec. (c), is the date of enactment of Pub.L. 90–274, which was approved on Mar. 27, 1968.

Effective and Applicability Provisions

1992 Acts. Amendment by Pub.L. 102–572 effective Jan. 1, 1993, see section 1101(a) of Pub.L. 102–572, set out as a note under section 905 of Title 2, The Congress.

1978 Acts. Amendment by Pub.L. 95–572 applicable with respect to any grand or petit juror summoned for service or actually serving on or after Nov. 2, 1978, see section 7(a) of Pub.L. 95–572, set out as a note under section 1363 of this title.

1968 Acts. Amendment by Pub.L. 90–274 effective 270 days after Mar. 27, 1968, except as to cases in which an indictment has been returned or a petit jury empaneled prior to such effective date, see section 104 of Pub.L. 90–274, set out as a note under section 1861 of this title.

Refilling of Master Jury Wheel Not Later Than September 1, 1973; Refilling of Qualified Jury Wheel Not Later Than October 1, 1973; Retroactive Effect

Sections 3 and 4 of Pub.L. 92–269 provided that:

"**Sec. 3.** **(a)** Each judicial district and each division or combination of divisions within a judicial district, for which a separate plan for random selection of jurors has been adopted pursuant to section 1863 of title 28, United States Code [this section], other than the District of Columbia and the districts of Puerto Rico and the Canal Zone, shall not later than September 1, 1973, refill its master jury wheel with names obtained from the voter registration lists for, or the lists of actual voters in, the 1972 general election.

"**(b)** The District of Columbia and the judicial districts of Puerto Rico and the Canal Zone shall not later than September 1, 1973, refill their master jury wheels from sources which include the names of persons eighteen years of age or older.

"**(c)** The qualified jury wheel in each judicial district, and in each division or combination of divisions in a judicial district for which a separate plan for random selection of jurors has been adopted, shall be refilled from the master jury wheel not later than October 1, 1973.

"Sec. 4. (a) Nothing in this Act [amending this section and section 1865 of this title] shall affect the composition of any master jury wheel or qualified jury wheel prior to the date on which it is first refilled in compliance with the terms of section 3.

"(b) Nothing in this Act shall affect the composition or preclude the service of any jury empaneled on or before the date on which the qualified jury wheel from which the jurors' names were drawn is refilled in compliance with the provisions of section 3."

§ 1864. Drawing of names from the master jury wheel; completion of juror qualification form

(a) From time to time as directed by the district court, the clerk or a district judge shall draw at random from the master jury wheel the names of as many persons as may be required for jury service. The clerk or jury commission shall post a general notice for public review in the clerk's office and on the court's website explaining the process by which names are periodically and randomly drawn. The clerk or jury commission may, upon order of the court, prepare an alphabetical list of the names drawn from the master jury wheel. Any list so prepared shall not be disclosed to any person except pursuant to the district court plan or pursuant to section 1867 or 1868 of this title. The clerk or jury commission shall mail to every person whose name is drawn from the master wheel a juror qualification form accompanied by instructions to fill out and return the form, duly signed and sworn, to the clerk or jury commission by mail within ten days. If the person is unable to fill out the form, another shall do it for him, and shall indicate that he has done so and the reason therefor. In any case in which it appears that there is an omission, ambiguity, or error in a form, the clerk or jury commission shall return the form with instructions to the person to make such additions or corrections as may be necessary and to return the form to the clerk or jury commission within ten days. Any person who fails to return a completed juror qualification form as instructed may be summoned by the clerk or jury commission forthwith to appear before the clerk or jury commission to fill out a juror qualification form. A person summoned to appear because of failure to return a juror qualification form as instructed who personally appears and executes a juror qualification form before the clerk or jury commission may, at the discretion of the district court, except where his prior failure to execute and mail such form was willful, be entitled to receive for such appearance the same fees and travel allowances paid to jurors under section 1871 of this title. At the time of his appearance for jury service, any person may be required to fill out another juror qualification form in the presence of the jury commission or the clerk or the court, at which time, in such cases as it appears warranted, the person may be questioned, but only with regard to his responses to questions contained on the form. Any information thus acquired by the clerk or jury commission may be noted on the juror qualification form and transmitted to the chief judge or such district court judge as the plan may provide.

(b) Any person summoned pursuant to subsection (a) of this section who fails to appear as directed shall be ordered by the district court forthwith to appear and show cause for his failure to comply with the summons. Any person who fails to appear pursuant to such order or who fails to show good cause for noncompliance with the summons may be fined not more than $1,000, imprisoned not more than three days, ordered to perform community service, or any combination thereof. Any person who willfully misrepresents a material fact on a juror qualification form for the purpose of avoiding or securing service as a juror may be fined not more than $1,000, imprisoned not more than three days, ordered to perform community service, or any combination thereof.

(June 25, 1948, c. 646, 62 Stat. 952; Mar. 27, 1968, Pub.L. 90–274, § 101, 82 Stat. 57; Nov. 19, 1988, Pub.L. 100–702, Title VIII, § 803(a), 102 Stat. 4658; Oct. 13, 2008, Pub.L. 110–406, §§ 5(a), 17(a), 122 Stat. 4292, 4295.)

HISTORICAL AND STATUTORY NOTES

Effective and Applicability Provisions

1968 Acts. Amendment by Pub.L. 90–274 effective 270 days after Mar. 27, 1968, except as to cases in which an indictment has been returned or a petit jury empaneled prior to such effective date, see section 104 of Pub.L. 90–274, set out as a note under section 1861 of this title.

§ 1865. Qualifications for jury service

(a) The chief judge of the district court, or such other district court judge as the plan may provide, on his initiative or upon recommendation of the clerk or jury commission, or the clerk under supervision of the court if the court's jury selection plan so authorizes, shall determine solely on the basis of information provided on the juror qualification form and other competent evidence whether a person is unqualified for, or exempt, or to be excused from jury service. The clerk shall enter such determination in the space provided on the juror qualification form and in any alphabetical list of names drawn from the master jury wheel. If a person did not appear in response to a summons, such fact shall be noted on said list.

(b) In making such determination the chief judge of the district court, or such other district court judge as the plan may provide, or the clerk if the court's jury selection plan so provides, shall deem any person qualified to serve on grand and petit juries in the district court unless he—

(1) is not a citizen of the United States eighteen years old who has resided for a period of one year within the judicial district;

(2) is unable to read, write, and understand the English language with a degree of proficiency sufficient to fill out satisfactorily the juror qualification form;

(3) is unable to speak the English language;

(4) is incapable, by reason of mental or physical infirmity, to render satisfactory jury service; or

(5) has a charge pending against him for the commission of, or has been convicted in a State or Federal court of record of, a crime punishable by imprisonment for more than one year and his civil rights have not been restored.

(June 25, 1948, c. 646, 62 Stat. 952; Mar. 27, 1968, Pub.L. 90–274, § 101, 82 Stat. 58; Apr. 6, 1972, Pub.L. 92–269, § 1, 86 Stat. 117; Nov. 2, 1978, Pub.L. 95–572, § 3(a), 92 Stat. 2453; Nov. 19, 1988, Pub.L. 100–702, Title VIII, § 803(b), 102 Stat. 4658; Nov. 13, 2000, Pub.L. 106–518, Title III, § 305, 114 Stat. 2418.)

HISTORICAL AND STATUTORY NOTES

Effective and Applicability Provisions

1978 Acts. Amendment by Pub.L. 95–572 applicable with respect to any grand or petit juror summoned for service or actually serving on or after Nov. 2, 1978, see section 7(a) of Pub.L. 95–572, set out as a note under section 1363 of this title.

1968 Acts. Amendment by Pub.L. 90–274 effective 270 days after Mar. 27, 1968, except as to cases in which an indictment has been returned or a petit jury empaneled prior to such effective date, see section 104 of Pub.L. 90–274, set out as a note under section 1861 of this title.

§ 1866. Selection and summoning of jury panels

(a) The jury commission, or in the absence thereof the clerk, shall maintain a qualified jury wheel and shall place in such wheel names of all persons drawn from the master jury wheel who are determined to be qualified as jurors and not exempt or excused pursuant to the district court plan. From time to time, the jury commission or the clerk shall draw at random from the qualified jury wheel such number of names of persons as may be required for assignment to grand and petit jury panels. The clerk or jury commission shall post a general notice for public review in the clerk's office and on the court's website explaining the process by which names are periodically and randomly drawn. The jury commission or the clerk shall prepare a separate list of names of persons assigned to each grand and petit jury panel.

(b) When the court orders a grand or petit jury to be drawn, the clerk or jury commission or their duly designated deputies shall issue summonses for the required number of jurors.

Each person drawn for jury service may be served personally, or by registered, certified, or first-class mail addressed to such person at his usual residence or business address.

If such service is made personally, the summons shall be delivered by the clerk or the jury commission or their duly designated deputies to the marshal who shall make such service.

If such service is made by mail, the summons may be served by the marshal or by the clerk, the jury commission or their duly designated deputies, who shall make affidavit of service and shall attach thereto any receipt from the addressee for a registered or certified summons.

(c) Except as provided in section 1865 of this title or in any jury selection plan provision adopted pursuant to paragraph (5) or (6) of section 1863(b) of this title, no person or class of persons shall be disqualified, excluded, excused, or exempt from service as jurors: *Provided*, That any person summoned for jury service may be (1) excused by the court, or by the clerk under supervision of the court if the court's jury selection plan so authorizes, upon a showing of undue hardship or extreme inconvenience, for such period as the court deems necessary, at the conclusion of which such person either shall be summoned again for jury service under subsections (b) and (c) of this section or, if the court's jury selection plan so provides, the name of such person shall be reinserted into the qualified jury wheel for selection pursuant to subsection (a) of this section, or (2) excluded by the court on the ground that such person may be unable to render impartial jury service or that his service as a juror would be likely to disrupt the proceedings, or (3) excluded upon peremptory challenge as provided by law, or (4) excluded pursuant to the procedure specified by law upon a challenge by any party for good cause shown, or (5) excluded upon determination by the court that his service as a juror would be likely to threaten the secrecy of the proceedings, or otherwise adversely affect the integrity of jury deliberations. No person shall be excluded under clause (5) of this subsection unless the judge, in open court, determines that such is warranted and that exclusion of the person will not be inconsistent with sections 1861 and 1862 of this title. The number of persons excluded under clause (5) of this subsection shall not exceed one per centum of the number of persons who return executed jury qualification forms during the period, specified in the plan, between two consecutive fillings of the master jury wheel. The names of persons excluded under clause (5) of this subsection, together with detailed explanations for the exclusions, shall be forwarded immediately to the judicial council of the circuit, which shall have the power to make any appropriate order, prospective or retroactive, to redress any misapplication of clause (5) of this subsection, but otherwise exclusions effectuated under such clause shall not be subject to challenge under the provisions of this title. Any person excluded from a particular jury under clause (2), (3), or (4) of this subsection shall be eligible to sit on another jury if the basis for his initial exclusion would not be relevant to his ability to serve on such other jury.

(d) Whenever a person is disqualified, excused, exempt, or excluded from jury service, the jury commission or clerk shall note in the space provided on his juror qualification form or on the juror's card drawn from the qualified jury wheel the specific reason therefor.

(e) In any two-year period, no person shall be required to (1) serve or attend court for prospective service as a petit juror for a total of more than thirty days, except when necessary to complete service in a particular case, or (2) serve on more than one grand jury, or (3) serve as both a grand and petit juror.

(f) When there is an unanticipated shortage of available petit jurors drawn from the qualified jury wheel, the court may require the marshal to summon a sufficient number of petit jurors selected at random from the voter registration lists, lists of actual voters, or other lists specified in the plan, in a manner ordered by the court consistent with sections 1861 and 1862 of this title.

(g) Any person summoned for jury service who fails to appear as directed may be ordered by the district court to appear forthwith and show cause for failure to comply with the summons. Any person who fails to show good cause for noncompliance with a summons may be fined not more than $1,000, imprisoned not more than three days, ordered to perform community service, or any combination thereof.

(June 25, 1948, c. 646, 62 Stat. 952; May 24, 1949, c. 139, § 96, 63 Stat. 103; Mar. 27, 1968, Pub.L. 90–274, § 101, 82 Stat. 58; Dec. 11, 1970, Pub.L. 91–543, 84 Stat. 1408; Nov. 2, 1978, Pub.L. 95–572, § 2(b), 92 Stat. 2453; Jan. 12, 1983, Pub.L. 97–463, § 2, 96 Stat. 2531; Nov. 19, 1988, Pub.L. 100–702, Title VIII, § 801, 102 Stat. 4657; Oct. 13, 2008, Pub.L. 110–406, §§ 4, 5(b), 17(b), 122 Stat. 4292, 4295.)

HISTORICAL AND STATUTORY NOTES

Effective and Applicability Provisions

1978 Acts. Amendment by Pub.L. 95–572 applicable with respect to any grand or petit juror summoned for service or actually serving on or after Nov. 2, 1978, see section 7(a) of Pub.L. 95–572, set out as a note under section 1363 of this title.

1968 Acts. Amendment by Pub.L. 90–274 effective 270 days after Mar. 27, 1968, except as to cases in which an indictment has been returned or a petit jury empaneled prior to such effective date, see section 104 of Pub.L. 90–274, set out as a note under section 1861 of this title.

§ 1867. Challenging compliance with selection procedures

(a) In criminal cases, before the voir dire examination begins, or within seven days after the defendant discovered or could have discovered, by the exercise of diligence, the grounds therefor, whichever is earlier, the defendant may move to dismiss the indictment or stay the proceedings against him on the ground of substantial failure to comply with the provisions of this title in selecting the grand or petit jury.

(b) In criminal cases, before the voir dire examination begins, or within seven days after the Attorney General of the United States discovered or could have discovered, by the exercise of diligence, the grounds therefor, whichever is earlier, the Attorney General may move to dismiss the indictment or stay the proceedings on the ground of substantial failure to comply with the provisions of this title in selecting the grand or petit jury.

(c) In civil cases, before the voir dire examination begins, or within seven days after the party discovered or could have discovered, by the exercise of diligence, the grounds therefor, whichever is earlier, any party may move to stay the proceedings on the ground of substantial failure to comply with the provisions of this title in selecting the petit jury.

(d) Upon motion filed under subsection (a), (b), or (c) of this section, containing a sworn statement of facts which, if true, would constitute a substantial failure to comply with the provisions of this title, the moving party shall be entitled to present in support of such motion the testimony of the jury commission or clerk, if available, any relevant records and papers not public or otherwise available used by the jury commissioner or clerk, and any other relevant evidence. If the court determines that there has been a substantial failure to comply with the provisions of this title in selecting the grand jury, the court shall stay the proceedings pending the selection of a grand jury in conformity with this title or dismiss the indictment, whichever is appropriate. If the court determines that there has been a substantial failure to comply with the provisions of this title in selecting the petit jury, the court shall stay the proceedings pending the selection of a petit jury in conformity with this title.

(e) The procedures prescribed by this section shall be the exclusive means by which a person accused of a Federal crime, the Attorney General of the United States or a party in a civil case may challenge any jury on the ground that such jury was not selected in conformity with the provisions of this title. Nothing in this section shall preclude any person or the United States from pursuing any other remedy, civil or criminal, which may be available for the vindication or enforcement of any law prohibiting discrimination on account of race, color, religion, sex, national origin or economic status in the selection of persons for service on grand or petit juries.

(f) The contents of records or papers used by the jury commission or clerk in connection with the jury selection process shall not be disclosed, except pursuant to the district court plan or as may be necessary in the preparation or presentation of a motion under subsection (a), (b), or (c) of this section, until after the master jury wheel has been emptied and refilled pursuant to section 1863(b)(4) of this title and all persons selected to serve as jurors before the master wheel was emptied have completed such service. The parties in a case shall be allowed to inspect, reproduce, and copy such records or papers at all reasonable times during the preparation and pendency of such a motion. Any person who discloses the contents of any record or paper in violation of this subsection may be fined not more than $1,000 or imprisoned not more than one year, or both.

(June 25, 1948, c. 646, 62 Stat. 953; Sept. 2, 1957, Pub.L. 85–259, 71 Stat. 583; Mar. 27, 1968, Pub.L. 90–274, § 101, 82 Stat. 59.)

HISTORICAL AND STATUTORY NOTES

Effective and Applicability Provisions

1968 Acts. Amendment by Pub.L. 90–274 effective 270 days after Mar. 27, 1968, except as to cases in which an indictment has been returned or a petit jury empaneled prior to such effective date, see section 104 of Pub.L. 90–274, set out as a note under section 1861 of this title.

§ 1868. Maintenance and inspection of records

After the master jury wheel is emptied and refilled pursuant to section 1863(b)(4) of this title, and after all persons selected to serve as jurors before the master wheel was emptied have completed such service, all records and papers compiled and maintained by the jury commission or clerk before the master wheel was emptied shall be preserved in the custody of the clerk for four years or for such longer period as may be ordered by a court, and shall be available for public inspection for the purpose of determining the validity of the selection of any jury.

(June 25, 1948, c. 646, 62 Stat. 953; Mar. 27, 1968, Pub.L. 90–274, § 101, 82 Stat. 60.)

HISTORICAL AND STATUTORY NOTES

Effective and Applicability Provisions

1968 Acts. Amendment by Pub.L. 90–274 effective 270 days after Mar. 27, 1968, except as to cases in which an indictment has been returned or a petit jury empaneled prior to such effective date, see section 104 of Pub.L. 90–274, set out as a note under section 1861 of this title.

§ 1869. Definitions

For purposes of this chapter—

(a) "clerk" and "clerk of the court" shall mean the clerk of the district court of the United States, any authorized deputy clerk, and any other person authorized by the court to assist the clerk in the performance of functions under this chapter;

(b) "chief judge" shall mean the chief judge of any district court of the United States;

(c) "voter registration lists" shall mean the official records maintained by State or local election officials of persons registered to vote in either the most recent State or the most recent Federal general election, or, in the case of a State or political subdivision thereof that does not require registration as a prerequisite to voting, other official lists of persons qualified to vote in such election. The term shall also include the list of eligible voters maintained by any Federal examiner pursuant to the Voting Rights Act of 1965 where the names on such list have not been included on the official registration lists or other official lists maintained by the appropriate State or local officials. With respect to the districts of Guam and the Virgin Islands, "voter registration lists" shall mean the official records maintained by territorial election officials of persons registered to vote in the most recent territorial general election;

(d) "lists of actual voters" shall mean the official lists of persons actually voting in either the most recent State or the most recent Federal general election;

(e) "division" shall mean: (1) one or more statutory divisions of a judicial district; or (2) in statutory divisions that contain more than one place of holding court, or in judicial districts where there are no statutory divisions, such counties, parishes, or similar political subdivisions surrounding the places where court is held as the district court plan shall determine: *Provided*, That each county, parish, or similar political subdivision shall be included in some such division;

(f) "district court of the United States", "district court", and "court" shall mean any district court established by chapter 5 of this title, and any court which is created by Act of Congress in a territory and is invested with any jurisdiction of a district court established by chapter 5 of this title;

(g) "jury wheel" shall include any device or system similar in purpose or function, such as a properly programed electronic data processing system or device;

(h) "juror qualification form" shall mean a form prescribed by the Administrative Office of the United States Courts and approved by the Judicial Conference of the United States, which shall elicit the name, address, age, race, occupation, education, length of residence within the judicial district, distance from residence to place of holding court, prior jury service, and citizenship of a potential juror, and whether he should be excused or exempted from jury service, has any physical or mental infirmity impairing his capacity to serve as juror, is able to read, write, speak, and understand the English language, has pending against him any charge for the commission of a State or Federal criminal offense punishable by imprisonment for more than one year, or has been convicted in any State or Federal court of record of a crime punishable by imprisonment for more than one year and has not had his civil rights restored. The form shall request, but not require, any other information not inconsistent with the provisions of this title and required by the district court plan in the interests of the sound administration of justice. The form shall also elicit the sworn statement that his responses are true to the best of his knowledge. Notarization shall not be required. The form shall contain words clearly informing the person that the furnishing of any information with respect to his religion, national origin, or economic status is not a prerequisite to his qualification for jury service, that such information need not be furnished if the person finds it objectionable to do so, and that information concerning race is required solely to enforce nondiscrimination in jury selection and has no bearing on an individual's qualification for jury service.

(i) "public officer" shall mean a person who is either elected to public office or who is directly appointed by a person elected to public office;

(j) "undue hardship or extreme inconvenience", as a basis for excuse from immediate jury service under section 1866(c)(1) of this chapter, shall mean great distance, either in miles or traveltime, from the place of holding court, grave illness in the family or any other emergency which outweighs in immediacy and urgency the obligation to serve as a juror when summoned, or any other factor which the court determines to constitute an undue hardship or to create an extreme inconvenience to the juror; and in addition, in situations where it is anticipated that a trial or grand jury proceeding may require more than thirty days of service, the court may consider, as a further basis for temporary excuse, severe economic hardship to an employer which would result from the absence of a key employee during the period of such service; and

(k) "jury summons" shall mean a summons issued by a clerk of court, jury commission, or their duly designated deputies, containing either a preprinted or stamped seal of court, and containing the name of the issuing clerk imprinted in preprinted, type, or facsimile manner on the summons or the envelopes transmitting the summons.

(June 25, 1948, c. 646, 62 Stat. 953; Oct. 16, 1963, Pub.L. 88–139, § 2, 77 Stat. 248; Mar. 27, 1968, Pub.L. 90–274, § 101, 82 Stat. 61; July 29, 1970, Pub.L. 91–358, Title I, § 172(b), 84 Stat. 590; Sept. 29, 1972, Pub.L. 92–437, § 1, 86 Stat. 740; Nov. 2, 1978, Pub.L. 95–572, §§ 3(b), (4), 92 Stat. 2453; Nov. 6, 1978, Pub.L. 95–598, Title II, § 243, 92 Stat. 2671; Nov. 14, 1986, Pub.L. 99–650, § 3, 100 Stat. 3641; Nov. 19, 1988, Pub.L. 100–702, Title VIII, §§ 802(a), 804, 102 Stat. 4657, 4658; Oct. 13, 2008, Pub.L. 110–406, § 5(c), 122 Stat. 4292.)

HISTORICAL AND STATUTORY NOTES

References in Text

The Voting Rights Act of 1965, referred to in subsec. (c), is Pub.L. 89–110, Aug. 6, 1965, 79 Stat. 437, as amended, which is classified generally to subchapters I–A (Section 1973 et seq.), I–B (Section 1973aa et seq.), and I–C (Section 1973bb et seq.) of chapter 20 of Title 42, The Public Health and Welfare. For complete classification of this Act to the Code, see Short Title note set out under section 1973 of Title 42 and Tables.

Codifications

Subsec. (f) of this section was amended by Pub.L. 95–598, Title II, § 243, Nov. 6, 1978, 92 Stat. 2671, effective June 28, 1984, pursuant to Pub.L. 95–598, Title IV, § 402(b), Nov. 6, 1978, 92 Stat. 2682, as amended by Pub.L. 98–249, § 1(a), Mar. 31, 1984, 98 Stat. 116; Pub.L. 98–271, § 1(a), Apr. 30, 1984, 98 Stat. 163; Pub.L. 98–299, § 1(a), May 25, 1984, 98 Stat. 214; Pub.L. 98–325, § 1(a), June 20, 1984, 98 Stat. 268, set out as an Effective and Applicability Provisions note preceding section 101 of Title 11, Bankruptcy, by inserting "chapter 6 of title 28, United States Code," following "chapter 5 of title 28, United States Code,".

Section 402(b) of Pub.L. 95–598 was amended by section 113 of Pub.L. 98–353, Title I, July 10, 1984, 98 Stat. 343, by substituting "shall not be effective" for "shall take effect on June 28, 1984", thereby eliminating the amendment by section 243 of Pub.L. 95–598, effective June 27, 1984, pursuant to section 122(c) of Pub.L. 98–353, set out as an Effective and Applicability Provisions note under section 151 of this title.

Section 121(a) of Pub.L. 98–353 directed that section 402(b) of Pub.L. 95–598 be amended by substituting "the date of enactment of the Bankruptcy Amendments and Federal Judgeship Act of 1984 [i.e. July 10, 1984]" for "June 28, 1984". This amendment was not executed in view of the prior amendment to section 402(b) of Pub.L. 95–598 by section 113 of Pub.L. 98–353.

Effective and Applicability Provisions

1986 Acts. Section 4(a) of Pub.L. 99–650 provided in part that: "The provisions of this Act [amending this section] shall take effect 180 days after the date of enactment of this Act [Nov. 14, 1986]".

1978 Acts. Amendment by Pub.L. 95–572 applicable with respect to any grand or petit juror summoned for service or actually serving on or after Nov. 2, 1978, see section 7(a) of Pub.L. 95–572, set out as a note under section 1363 of this title.

1972 Acts. Section 2 of Pub.L. 92–437 provided that: "This Act [amending subsec. (h) of this section] shall take effect on the sixtieth day after the date of its enactment [Sept. 29, 1972]".

1970 Acts. Amendment by Pub.L. 91–358 effective the first day of the seventh calendar month which begins after

July 29, 1970, see section 199(a) of Pub.L. 91–358, set out as a note under section 1257 of this title.

1968 Acts. Amendment by Pub.L. 90–274 effective 270 days after Mar. 27, 1968, except as to cases in which an indictment has been returned or a petit jury empaneled prior to such effective date, see section 104 of Pub.L. 90–274, set out as a note under section 1861 of this title.

Termination of United States District Court for the District of the Canal Zone

For termination of the United States District Court for the District of the Canal Zone at end of the "transition period", being the 30–month period beginning Oct. 1, 1979, and ending midnight Mar. 31, 1982, see Paragraph 5 of Article XI of the Panama Canal Treaty of 1977 and sections 3831 and 3841 to 3843 of Title 22, Foreign Relations and Intercourse.

§ 1870. Challenges

In civil cases, each party shall be entitled to three peremptory challenges. Several defendants or several plaintiffs may be considered as a single party for the purposes of making challenges, or the court may allow additional peremptory challenges and permit them to be exercised separately or jointly.

All challenges for cause or favor, whether to the array or panel or to individual jurors, shall be determined by the court.

(June 25, 1948, c. 646, 62 Stat. 953; Sept. 16, 1959, Pub.L. 86–282, 73 Stat. 565.)

§ 1871. Fees

(a) Grand and petit jurors in district courts appearing pursuant to this chapter shall be paid the fees and allowances provided by this section. The requisite fees and allowances shall be disbursed on the certificate of the clerk of court in accordance with the procedure established by the Director of the Administrative Office of the United States Courts. Attendance fees for extended service under subsection (b) of this section shall be certified by the clerk only upon the order of a district judge.

(b)(1) A juror shall be paid an attendance fee of $40 per day for actual attendance at the place of trial or hearing. A juror shall also be paid the attendance fee for the time necessarily occupied in going to and returning from such place at the beginning and end of such service or at any time during such service.

(2) A petit juror required to attend more than thirty days in hearing one case may be paid, in the discretion of the trial judge, an additional fee, not exceeding $10 more than the attendance fee, for each day in excess of thirty days on which he is required to hear such case.

(3) A grand juror required to attend more than forty-five days of actual service may be paid, in the discretion of the district judge in charge of the particular grand jury, an additional fee, not exceeding $10 more than the attendance fee, for each day in excess of forty-five days of actual service.

(4) A grand or petit juror required to attend more than ten days of actual service may be paid, in the discretion of the judge, the appropriate fees at the end of the first ten days and at the end of every ten days of service thereafter.

(5) Certification of additional attendance fees may be ordered by the judge to be made effective commencing on the first day of extended service, without reference to the date of such certification.

(c)(1) A travel allowance not to exceed the maximum rate per mile that the Director of the Administrative Office of the United States Courts has prescribed pursuant to section 604(a)(7) of this title for payment to supporting court personnel in travel status using privately owned automobiles shall be paid to each juror, regardless of the mode of transportation actually employed. The prescribed rate shall be paid for the distance necessarily traveled to and from a juror's residence by the shortest practical route in going to and returning from the place of service. Actual mileage in full at the prescribed rate is payable at the beginning and at the end of a juror's term of service.

(2) The Director shall promulgate rules regulating interim travel allowances to jurors. Distances traveled to and from court should coincide with the shortest practical route.

(3) Toll charges for toll roads, bridges, tunnels, and ferries shall be paid in full to the juror incurring such charges. In the discretion of the court, reasonable parking fees may be paid to the juror incurring such fees upon presentation of a valid parking receipt. Parking fees shall not be included in any tabulation of mileage cost allowances.

(4) Any juror who travels to district court pursuant to summons in an area outside of the contiguous forty-eight States of the United States shall be paid the travel expenses provided under this section, or actual reasonable transportation expenses subject to the discretion of the district judge or clerk of court as circumstances indicate, exercising due regard for the mode of transportation, the availability of alternative modes, and the shortest practical route between residence and court.

(5) A grand juror who travels to district court pursuant to a summons may be paid the travel expenses provided under this section or, under guidelines established by the Judicial Conference, the actual reasonable costs of travel by aircraft when travel by other means is not feasible and when certified by the chief judge of the district court in which the grand juror serves.

(d)(1) A subsistence allowance covering meals and lodging of jurors shall be established from time to time by the Director of the Administrative Office of the United States Courts pursuant to section 604(a)(7) of this title, except that such allowance shall not exceed the allowance for supporting court personnel in travel status in the same geographical area. Claims for such allowance shall not require itemization.

(2) A subsistence allowance shall be paid to a juror when an overnight stay is required at the place of holding court, and for the time necessarily spent in traveling to and from the place of attendance if an overnight stay is required.

(3) A subsistence allowance for jurors serving in district courts outside of the contiguous forty-eight States of the United States shall be allowed at a rate not to exceed that per diem allowance which is paid to supporting court personnel in travel status in those areas where the Director of the Administrative Office of the United States Courts has prescribed an increased per diem fee pursuant to section 604(a)(7) of this title.

(e) During any period in which a jury is ordered to be kept together and not to separate, the actual cost of subsistence shall be paid upon the order of the court in lieu of the subsistence allowances payable under subsection (d) of this section. Such allowance for the jurors ordered to be kept separate or sequestered shall include the cost of meals, lodging, and other expenditures ordered in the discretion of the court for their convenience and comfort.

(f) A juror who must necessarily use public transportation in traveling to and from court, the full cost of which is not met by the transportation expenses allowable under subsection (c) of this section on account of the short distance traveled in miles, may be paid, in the discretion of the court, the actual reasonable expense of such public transportation, pursuant to the methods of payment provided by this section. Jurors who are required to remain at the court beyond the normal business closing hour for deliberation or for any other reason may be transported to their homes, or to temporary lodgings where such lodgings are ordered by the court, in a manner directed by the clerk and paid from funds authorized under this section.

(g) The Director of the Administrative Office of the United States Courts shall promulgate such regulations as may be necessary to carry out his authority under this section.

(June 25, 1948, c. 646, 62 Stat. 953; May 24, 1949, c. 139, § 97, 63 Stat. 103; July 14, 1949, c. 333, 63 Stat. 411; Sept. 7, 1957, Pub.L. 85–299, 71 Stat. 618; Sept. 2, 1965, Pub.L. 89–165, 79 Stat. 645; Mar. 27, 1968, Pub.L. 90–274, § 102(a), 82 Stat. 62; Nov. 2, 1978, Pub.L. 95–572, § 5, 92 Stat. 2454; Dec. 1, 1990, Pub.L. 101–650, Title III, § 314(b), 104 Stat. 5115; Oct. 29, 1992, Pub.L. 102–572, Title IV, § 402, 106 Stat. 4511.)

Amendment of Subsection (b)(2)

Pub.L. 110–406, § 3, Oct. 13, 2008, 122 Stat. 4292, provided that, effective Oct. 1, 2009, subsec. (b)(2) is amended by striking out "thirty" in each place it occurs and inserting "ten".

HISTORICAL AND STATUTORY NOTES

Effective and Applicability Provisions

2008 Acts. Pub.L. 110–406, § 3(b), Oct. 13, 2008, 122 Stat. 4292, provided that: "The amendments made by this section [amending this section] shall take effect on October 1, 2009."

1992 Acts. Amendment by Pub.L. 102–572 effective Jan. 1, 1993, see section 1101(a) of Pub.L. 102–572, set out as a note under section 905 of Title 2, The Congress.

1978 Acts. Amendment by Pub.L. 95–572 applicable with respect to any grand or petit juror serving on or after the sixtieth day following Nov. 2, 1978, see section 7(b) of Pub.L. 95–572, set out as a note under section 1363 of this title.

1968 Acts. Amendment by Pub.L. 90–274 effective 270 days after Mar. 27, 1968, except as to cases in which an indictment has been returned or a petit jury empaneled prior to such effective date, see section 104 of Pub.L. 90–274, set out as a note under section 1861 of this title.

Refreshment of Jurors

Pub.L. 101–162, Title IV, Nov. 21, 1989, 103 Stat. 1012, provided in part: "That for fiscal year 1990 and hereafter, funds appropriated under this heading [Courts of Appeals, District Courts and Other Judicial Services and Fees of Jurors and Commissioners] shall be available for refreshment of jurors."

§ 1872. Issues of fact in Supreme Court

In all original actions at law in the Supreme Court against citizens of the United States, issues of fact shall be tried by a jury.

(June 25, 1948, c. 646, 62 Stat. 953.)

§ 1873. Admiralty and maritime cases

In any case of admiralty and maritime jurisdiction relating to any matter of contract or tort arising upon or concerning any vessel of twenty tons or upward, enrolled and licensed for the coasting trade, and employed in the business of commerce and navigation between places in different states upon the lakes and navigable waters connecting said lakes, the trial of all issues of fact shall be by jury if either party demands it.

(June 25, 1948, c. 646, 62 Stat. 953.)

§ 1874. Actions on bonds and specialties

In all actions to recover the forfeiture annexed to any articles of agreement, covenant, bond, or other specialty, wherein the forfeiture, breach, or nonperformance appears by default or confession of the defendant, the court shall render judgment for the plaintiff for such amount as is due. If the sum is

uncertain, it shall, upon request of either party, be assessed by a jury.
(June 25, 1948, c. 646, 62 Stat. 953.)

§ 1875. Protection of jurors' employment

(a) No employer shall discharge, threaten to discharge, intimidate, or coerce any permanent employee by reason of such employee's jury service, or the attendance or scheduled attendance in connection with such service, in any court of the United States.

(b) Any employer who violates the provisions of this section—

(1) shall be liable for damages for any loss of wages or other benefits suffered by an employee by reason of such violation;

(2) may be enjoined from further violations of this section and ordered to provide other appropriate relief, including but not limited to the reinstatement of any employee discharged by reason of his jury service; and

(3) shall be subject to a civil penalty of not more than $5,000 for each violation as to each employee, and may be ordered to perform community service.

(c) Any individual who is reinstated to a position of employment in accordance with the provisions of this section shall be considered as having been on furlough or leave of absence during his period of jury service, shall be reinstated to his position of employment without loss of seniority, and shall be entitled to participate in insurance or other benefits offered by the employer pursuant to established rules and practices relating to employees on furlough or leave of absence in effect with the employer at the time such individual entered upon jury service.

(d)(1) An individual claiming that his employer has violated the provisions of this section may make application to the district court for the district in which such employer maintains a place of business and the court shall, upon finding probable merit in such claim, appoint counsel to represent such individual in any action in the district court necessary to the resolution of such claim. Such counsel shall be compensated and necessary expenses repaid to the extent provided by section 3006A of title 18, United States Code.

(2) In any action or proceeding under this section, the court may award a prevailing employee who brings such action by retained counsel a reasonable attorney's fee as part of the costs. The court may tax a defendant employer, as costs payable to the court, the attorney fees and expenses incurred on behalf of a prevailing employee, where such costs were expended by the court pursuant to paragraph (1) of this subsection. The court may award a prevailing employer a reasonable attorney's fee as part of the costs only if the court finds that the action is frivolous, vexatious, or brought in bad faith.

(Added Pub.L. 95–572, § 6(a) (1), Nov. 2, 1978, 92 Stat. 2456, and amended Pub.L. 97–463, § 1, Jan. 12, 1983, 96 Stat. 2531; Pub.L. 110–406, § 19, Oct. 13, 2008, 122 Stat. 4295.)

HISTORICAL AND STATUTORY NOTES

Effective and Applicability Provisions

1978 Acts. Section applicable with respect to any grand or petit juror summoned for service or actually serving on or after Nov. 2, 1978, see section 7(a) of Pub.L. 95–572, set out as a note under section 1363 of this title.

§ 1876. Trial by jury in the Court of International Trade

(a) In any civil action in the Court of International Trade which is to be tried before a jury, the jury shall be selected in accordance with the provisions of this chapter and under the procedures set forth in the jury selection plan of the district court for the judicial district in which the case is to be tried.

(b) Whenever the Court of International Trade conducts a jury trial—

(1) the clerk of the district court for the judicial district in which the Court of International Trade is sitting, or an authorized deputy clerk, shall act as clerk of the Court of International Trade for the purposes of selecting and summoning the jury;

(2) the qualifications for jurors shall be the same as those established by section 1865(b) of this title for jurors in the district courts of the United States;

(3) each party shall be entitled to challenge jurors in accordance with section 1870 of this title; and

(4) jurors shall be compensated in accordance with section 1871 of this title.

(Added Pub.L. 96–417, Title III, § 302(a), Oct. 10, 1980, 94 Stat. 1739.)

HISTORICAL AND STATUTORY NOTES

Effective and Applicability Provisions

1980 Acts. Section applicable with respect to civil actions commenced on or after Nov. 1, 1980, see section 701(b) (1) (C) of Pub.L. 96–417, as amended, set out as a note under section 251 of this title.

§ 1877. Protection of jurors

(a) Subject to the provisions of this section and title 5 of the United States Code, subchapter 1 of chapter 81, title 5, United States Code, applies to a Federal grand or petit juror, except that entitlement to disability compensation payments does not commence until the day after the date of termination of service as a juror.

(b) In administering this section with respect to a juror covered by this section—

(1) a juror is deemed to receive monthly pay at the minimum rate for grade GS–2 of the General

Schedule unless his actual pay as a Government employee while serving on court leave is higher, in which case monthly pay is determined in accordance with section 8114 of title 5, United States Code, and

(2) performance of duty as a juror includes that time when a juror is (A) in attendance at court pursuant to a summons, (B) in deliberation, (C) sequestered by order of a judge, or (D) at a site, by order of the court, for the taking of a view.

(Added Pub.L. 97–463, § 3(1), Jan. 12, 1983, 96 Stat. 2531.)

HISTORICAL AND STATUTORY NOTES

References in Text

The General Schedule, referred to in subsec. (b)(1), is set out under 5 U.S.C.A. § 5332.

§ 1878. Optional use of a one-step summoning and qualification procedure

(a) At the option of each district court, jurors may be summoned and qualified in a single procedure, if the court's jury selection plan so authorizes, in lieu of the two separate procedures otherwise provided for by this chapter. Courts shall ensure that a one-step summoning and qualification procedure conducted under this section does not violate the policies and objectives set forth in sections 1861 and 1862 of this title.

(b) Jury selection conducted under this section shall be subject to challenge under section 1867 of this title for substantial failure to comply with the provisions of this title in selecting the jury. However, no challenge under section 1867 of this title shall lie solely on the basis that a jury was selected in accordance with a one-step summoning and qualification procedure authorized by this section.

(Added Pub.L. 100–702, Title VIII, § 805(a), Nov. 19, 1988, 102 Stat. 4658, and amended Pub.L. 102–572, Title IV, § 403(a), Oct. 29, 1992, 106 Stat. 4512.)

HISTORICAL AND STATUTORY NOTES

Effective and Applicability Provisions

1992 Acts. Amendment by Pub.L. 102–572 effective Jan. 1, 1993, see section 1101(a) of Pub.L. 102–572, set out as a note under section 905 of Title 2, The Congress.

Savings Provisions

Section 403(c) of Pub.L. 102–572 provided that: "For courts participating in the experiment authorized under section 1878 of title 28, United States Code [this section] (as in effect before the effective date of this section [see Effective and Applicability Provisions of 1992 Amendments note set out under this section]), the amendment made by subsection (a) of this section [amending this section] shall be effective on and after January 1, 1992."

CHAPTER 123—FEES AND COSTS

Sec.
1911. Supreme Court.
1912. Damages and costs on affirmance.
1913. Courts of appeals.
1914. District court; filing and miscellaneous fees; rules of court.
1915. Proceedings in forma pauperis.
1915A. Screening.
1916. Seamen's suits.
1917. District courts; fee on filing notice of or petition for appeal.
1918. District courts; fines, forfeitures and criminal proceedings.
1919. Dismissal for lack of jurisdiction.
1920. Taxation of costs.
1921. United States marshal's fees.
1922. Witness fees before United States magistrate judges.
1923. Docket fees and costs of briefs.
1924. Verification of bill of costs.
1925. Admiralty and maritime cases.
1926. Court of Federal Claims.
1927. Counsel's liability for excessive costs.
1928. Patent infringement action; disclaimer not filed.
1929. Extraordinary expenses not expressly authorized.
1930. Bankruptcy fees.
1931. Disposition of filing fees.
1932.[1] Judicial Panel on Multidistrict Litigation.
1932.[1] Revocation of earned release credit.

[1] Two sections 1932 have been enacted.

HISTORICAL AND STATUTORY NOTES

Codifications

Amendment by section 111(c) of Pub.L. 98–353, Title I, July 10, 1984, 98 Stat. 343, purported to amend the table of sections for chapter 125. The amendment was executed to this chapter as the probable intent of Congress. Section 111(c) substituted "Bankruptcy fees" for "Bankruptcy courts" in item 1930.

Change of Name

"United States magistrate judge" substituted for "United States magistrate" in text pursuant to section 321 of Pub.L. 101–650, set out as a note under 28 U.S.C.A. § 631. Previously, United States commissioners, referred to in text, were replaced by United States magistrates pursuant to Pub.L. 90–578, Oct. 17, 1968, 82 Stat. 1118. See chapter 43 of Title 28, 28 U.S.C.A. § 631 et seq.

§ 1911. Supreme Court

The Supreme Court may fix the fees to be charged by its clerk.

The fees of the clerk, cost of serving process, and other necessary disbursements incidental to any case before the court, may be taxed against the litigants as the court directs.

(June 25, 1948, c. 646, 62 Stat. 954.)

§ 1912. Damages and costs on affirmance

Where a judgment is affirmed by the Supreme Court or a court of appeals, the court in its discretion may adjudge to the prevailing party just damages for his delay, and single or double costs.

(June 25, 1948, c. 646, 62 Stat. 954.)

§ 1913. Courts of appeals

The fees and costs to be charged and collected in each court of appeals shall be prescribed from time to time by the Judicial Conference of the United States. Such fees and costs shall be reasonable and uniform in all the circuits.

(June 25, 1948, c. 646, 62 Stat. 954.)

JUDICIAL CONFERENCE SCHEDULE OF FEES

Court of Appeals Miscellaneous Fee Schedule

(Issued in accordance with 28 U.S.C. § 1913)

(Effective 01/01/2009)

The fees included in the Court of Appeals Miscellaneous Fee Schedule are to be charged for services provided by the courts of appeals.

- The United States should not be charged fees under this schedule, except as prescribed in Items 2, 4, and 5 when the information requested is available through remote electronic access.
- Federal agencies or programs that are funded from judiciary appropriations (agencies, organizations, and individuals providing services authorized by the Criminal Justice Act, 18 U.S.C. § 3006A, and bankruptcy administrators) should not be charged any fees under this schedule.

(1) For docketing a case on appeal or review, or docketing any other proceeding, $450.

- Each party filing a notice of appeal pays a separate fee to the district court, but parties filing a joint notice of appeal pay only one fee.
- There is no docketing fee for an application for an interlocutory appeal under 28 U.S.C. § 1292(b) or other petition for permission to appeal under FED. R. APP. P. 5, unless the appeal is allowed.
- There is no docketing fee for a direct bankruptcy appeal or a direct bankruptcy cross appeal, when the fee has been collected by the bankruptcy court in accordance with item 14 of the Bankruptcy Court Miscellaneous Fee Schedule.

(2) For conducting a search of the court of appeals records, $26 per name or item searched. This fee applies to services rendered on behalf of the United States if the information requested is available through remote electronic access.

(3) For certification of any document, $9.

(4) For reproducing any document, $.50 per page. This fee applies to services rendered on behalf of the United States if the document requested is available through remote electronic access.

(5) For reproducing recordings of proceedings, regardless of the medium, $26, including the cost of materials. This fee applies to services rendered on behalf of the United States if the recording is available through remote electronic access.

(6) For reproducing the record in any appeal in which the court of appeals does not require an appendix pursuant to FED. R. APP. P.30(f), $71.

(7) For retrieving a record from a Federal Records Center, National Archives, or other storage location removed from the place of business of the court, $45.

(8) For a check paid into the court which is returned for lack of funds, $45.

(9) For copies of opinions, a fee commensurate with the cost of printing, as fixed by each court.

(10) For copies of the local rules of court, a fee commensurate with the cost of distributing the copies. The court may also distribute copies of the local rules without charge.

(11) For filing:

- Any separate or joint notice of appeal or application for appeal from the Bankruptcy Appellate Panel, $5.
- A notice of the allowance of an appeal from the Bankruptcy Appellate Panel, $5.

(12) For counsel's requested use of the court's videoconferencing equipment in connection with each oral argument, the court may charge and collect a fee of $200 per remote location.

(13) For original admission of an attorney to practice, including a certificate of admission, $150. For a duplicate certificate of admission or certificate of good standing, $15.

ELECTRONIC PUBLIC ACCESS FEE SCHEDULE (eff. 3/11/2008)

As directed by Congress, the Judicial Conference has determined that the following fees are necessary to reimburse expenses incurred by the judiciary in providing electronic public access to court records. These fees shall apply to the United States unless otherwise stated. No fees under this schedule shall be charged to federal agencies or programs which are funded from judiciary appropriations, including, but not limited to, agencies, organizations, and individuals providing services authorized by the Criminal Justice Act, 18 U.S.C. § 3006A, and bankruptcy administrator programs.

I. For electronic access to court data via a federal judiciary Internet site: 8 cents per page, with the total for any document, docket sheet, or case-specific report not to exceed the fee for 30 pages—provided however that transcripts of federal court proceedings shall not be subject to the 30–page fee limit. Attorneys of record and parties in a case (including pro se litigants) receive one free electronic copy of all documents filed electronically, if receipt is required by law or directed by the filer. No fee is owed under this provision until an account holder accrues charges of more than $10 in a calendar year. Consistent with Judicial Conference policy, courts may, upon a showing of cause, exempt indigents, bankruptcy case trustees, individual researchers associated with educational institutions, courts, section 501(c)(3) not-for-profit organizations, court appointed pro bono attorneys, and pro bono ADR neutrals from payment of these fees. Courts must find that parties from the classes of persons or entities listed above seeking exemption have demonstrated that an exemption is necessary in order to avoid unreasonable burdens and to promote public access to information. Any user granted an exemption agrees not to sell for profit the data obtained as a result. Any transfer of data obtained as the result of a fee exemption is prohibited unless expressly authorized by the court. Exemptions may be granted for a definite period of time and may be revoked at the discretion of the court granting the exemption.

II. For printing copies of any record or document accessed electronically at a public terminal in the courthouse: 10 cents per page. This fee shall apply to services rendered on behalf of the United States if the record requested is remotely available through electronic access.

III. For every search of court records conducted by the PACER Service Center, $26 per name or item searched.

IV. For the PACER Service Center to reproduce on paper any record pertaining to a PACER account, if this information is remotely available through electronic access, 50 cents per page.

V. For a check paid to the PACER Service Center which is returned for lack of funds, $45.

JUDICIAL CONFERENCE POLICY NOTES

Courts should not exempt local, state or federal government agencies, members of the media, attorneys or others not members of one of the groups listed above. Exemptions should be granted as the exception, not the rule. A court may not use this exemption language to exempt all users. An exemption applies only to access related to the case or purpose for which it was given. The prohibition on transfer of information received without fee is not intended to bar a quote or reference to information received as a result of a fee exemption in a scholarly or other similar work.

The electronic public access fee applies to electronic court data viewed remotely from the public records of individual cases in the court, including filed documents and the docket sheet. Electronic court data may be viewed free at public terminals at the courthouse and courts may provide other local court information at no cost. Examples of information that can be provided at no cost include: local rules, court forms, news items, court calendars, opinions, and other information—such as court hours, court location, telephone listings—determined locally to benefit the public and the court.

Miscellaneous Fee Schedules

Registry Fund Fees

Effective June 12, 1989, a fee will be assessed for handling funds deposited in noncriminal proceedings with the court and held in interest bearing accounts or instruments pursuant to 28 U.S.C. § 2041 and Federal Rules of Civil Procedure rule 67. For new accounts, i.e., investments made on or after June 12, 1989, the fee will be equal to the first 45 days income earned on the deposit. Each subsequent deposit of new principal in the same case or proceeding will be subject to the fee. Reinvestment of prior deposits will not be subject to the fee. For existing accounts, i.e., investments held by the court prior to June 12, 1989, a fee will be assessed equal to the first 45 days of income earned beginning 30 days after June 12, 1989. Subsequent deposits of new principal in the same account will be subject to the fee. Subsequent reinvestment of existing deposits will not be subject to the fee.

The fee will apply only once to each sum deposited regardless of the length of time deposits are held and will not exceed income actually earned on the account.

The fee does not apply in the District Courts of Guam, Northern Mariana Islands, the Virgin Islands, the United States Claims Court, or other courts whose fees are not set under 28 U.S.C. §§ 1913, 1914, and 1930.

Registry Fund Fees—Item 12
(55 F.R. 42867, October 24, 1990)

Effective December 1, 1990, the registry fee assessment provisions were revised and converted from a one-time charge equal to all income earned in the first 45 days of the investment to a charge of 10 percent of the income earned while funds are held in the court registry. Additionally, the fee was extended to any funds placed in the court's registry and invested regardless of the nature of the action underlying the deposit.

The new method will not be applied on investments in cases from which a fee has been exacted based on the prior method (interest earned in the first 45 days the funds were invested or the first 45 days following July 12, 1989). The new method will also not be applied in cases where the investment instrument has a maturity date greater than one year, but where a fee under the prior method applies but has not been deducted.

The fee does not apply in the District Courts of Guam, the Northern Mariana Islands, the Virgin Islands, the United States Claims Court, or any other federal court whose fees are not set under 28 U.S.C. §§ 1913, 1914, and 1930.

Registry Fund Fees—Item 12
(56 F.R. 56356, November 4, 1991)

Effective February 3, 1992, the registry fee assessment provisions are revised and converted from a charge equal to 10 percent of the income earned while funds are held in the court's registry to a variable rate based on the amount deposited with the court and, in certain cases, the length of time funds are held in the court's registry.

The revised fee will be a fee of 10 percent of the total income received during each income period from investments of less than $100,000,000 of registry funds in income-bearing accounts. On investments exceeding $100,000,000 the 10 percent fee shall be reduced by one percent for each increment of $50,000,000 over the initial $100,000,000. For those deposits where funds are placed in the registry by court order for a time certain, for example, by the terms of an adjudicated trust, the fee will be further reduced. This further reduction will amount to 2.5 percent for each five-year interval or part thereof. The total minimum fee to be charged will be no less than two percent of the income on investments.

The following table sets out the fee schedule promulgated by this notice:

REGISTRY—SCHEDULE OF FEES

[% of income earned]

Amount of deposit *	0–5 yrs.	>5–10 yrs.	>10–15 yrs.	>15 yrs.
less than 100M	10	7.5	5.0	2.5
100M–<150M	9	6.5	4.0	2.0
150M–<200M	8	5.5	3.0	2.0
200M–<250M	7	4.5	2.0	2.0
250M–<300M	6	3.5	2.0	2.0
300M–<350M	5	2.5	2.0	2.0
350M–<400M	4	2.0	2.0	2.0
400M–<450M	3	2.0	2.0	2.0
over 450M	2	2.0	2.0	2.0

* Except where otherwise authorized by the Director, each deposit into any account is treated separately in determining the fee.

The new fee applies to all earnings applied to investments on and after the effective date of this change, except for earnings on investments in cases being administered under the provisions of the May 11, 1989 notice [54 FR 20407], i.e., to which the fee equal to the first 45 days income is applicable.

The fee, as modified herein, will continue to apply to any case where the court has authorized the investment of funds placed in its custody or held by it in trust in its registry regardless of the nature of the underlying action.

The fee does not apply in the District Court of Guam, the Northern Mariana Islands, the Virgin Islands, the United States Claims Court, or any other Federal court whose fees are not set under 28 U.S.C. §§ 1913, 1914, and 1930.

HISTORICAL AND STATUTORY NOTES

Appeals Filed in Courts of Appeals

Pub.L. 109–171, Title X, § 10001(b), Feb. 8, 2006, 120 Stat. 183, provided that: "The $250 fee for docketing a case on appeal or review, or docketing any other proceeding, in a court of appeals, as prescribed by the Judicial Conference, effective as of January 1, 2005, under section 1913 of title 28, United States Code [this section], shall be increased to $450."

[This note effective 60 days after Feb. 8, 2006, see Pub.L. 109–171, § 10001(d), set out as a note under 28 U.S.C.A. § 1914]

Court Fees for Electronic Access to Information

Pub.L. 102–140, Title III, § 303, Oct. 28, 1991, 105 Stat. 810, as amended Pub.L. 104–317, Title IV, § 403(b), Oct. 19, 1996, 110 Stat. 3854; Pub.L. 107–347, Title II, § 205(e), Dec. 17, 2002, 116 Stat. 2915, provided that:

"(a) The Judicial Conference may, only to the extent necessary, prescribe reasonable fees, pursuant to sections 1913, 1914, 1926, 1930, and 1932 of title 28, United States Code [this section and sections 1914, 1926, 1930, and 1932 of this title], for collection by the courts under those sections for access to information available through automatic data processing equipment. These fees may distinguish between classes of persons, and shall provide for exempting persons or classes of persons from the fees, in order to avoid unreasonable burdens and to promote public access to such information. The Director of the Administrative Office of the United States Courts, under the direction of the Judicial Conference of the United States, shall prescribe a schedule of reasonable fees for electronic access to information which the Director is required to maintain and make available to the public.

"(b) The Judicial Conference and the Director shall transmit each schedule of fees prescribed under paragraph (a) to the Congress at least 30 days before the schedule becomes effective. All fees hereafter collected by the Judiciary under paragraph (a) as a charge for services rendered shall be deposited as offsetting collections to the Judiciary Automation Fund pursuant to 28 U.S.C. 612(c)(1)(A) [section 612(c)(1)(A) of this title] to reimburse expenses incurred in providing these services."

[Amendment by Pub.L. 107–347, § 205, effective 120 days after Dec. 17, 2002, see section 402(a) of Pub.L. 107–347, set out as a note under 44 U.S.C.A. § 3601.]

Similar provisions were contained in the following prior appropriation Act:

Pub.L. 101–515, Title IV, § 404, Nov. 5, 1990, 104 Stat. 2132.

§ 1914. District court; filing and miscellaneous fees; rules of court

(a) The clerk of each district court shall require the parties instituting any civil action, suit or proceeding in such court, whether by original process, removal or otherwise, to pay a filing fee of $350, except that on application for a writ of habeas corpus the filing fee shall be $5.

(b) The clerk shall collect from the parties such additional fees only as are prescribed by the Judicial Conference of the United States.

(c) Each district court by rule or standing order may require advance payment of fees.

(June 25, 1948, c. 646, 62 Stat. 954; Nov. 6, 1978, Pub.L. 95–598, Title II, § 244, 92 Stat. 2671; June 19, 1986, Pub.L. 99–336, § 4(a), 100 Stat. 637; Oct. 18, 1986, Pub.L. 99–500, Title I, § 101(b) [Title IV, § 407(a)], 100 Stat. 1783–39, 1783–64, and Oct. 30, 1986, Pub.L. 99–591, Title I, § 101(b) [Title IV, § 407(a)], 100 Stat. 3341–39, 3341–64; Oct. 19, 1996, Pub.L. 104–317, Title IV, § 401(a), 110 Stat. 3853; Pub.L. 108–447, Div. B, Title III, § 307(a), Dec. 8, 2004, 118 Stat. 2895; Feb. 8, 2006, Pub.L. 109–171, Title X, § 10001(a), 120 Stat. 183.)

JUDICIAL CONFERENCE SCHEDULE OF FEES

District Court Miscellaneous Fee Schedule

[The Judicial Conference of the United States, at its session on March 7–9, 1979, set forth the schedule of fees to be charged in the United States district courts pursuant to this section. That new schedule became effective on October 1, 1979. At its March 1987 meeting, the Judicial Conference amended the schedule of fees to be effective May 1, 1987. Amendments to this revision of the schedule of fees were adopted at the September, 1988 and March, 1990 meetings of the Judicial Conference. At its 1991 meeting, the Judicial Conference amended its schedule of fees to be effective Feb. 3, 1992. At its March 1991 meeting, the Judicial Conference amended the schedule of fees to be effective Oct. 19, 1992, with later implementation. At its March, 1993 meeting, the Judicial Conference amended its schedule of fees to be effective May 6, 1993. At its September, 1993 meeting, the Judicial Conference amended its schedule of fees to be effective October 1, 1993. At its 1994 meeting, the Judicial Conference amended its schedule of fees to be effective January 1, 1995. At its March 15, 1995 meeting, the Judicial Conference amended its schedule of fees to be effective April 18, 1995, and at its 1996 meetings it adopted amendments to be effective April 1, 1996 and December 18, 1996. At its 1997 meeting, the Judicial Conference amended its schedule of fees to be effective January 1, 1998. At its 1999 meeting, the Judicial Conference amended its schedule of fees to be effective October 1, 1999. The Judicial Conference subsequently adopted amendments to its fee schedule effective February 1, 2001. At its March 2001 meeting, the Judicial Conference amended its schedule of fees to be effective July 1, 2001. The Judicial Conference adopted amendments to its fee schedule effective November 1, 2003. The Judicial Conference at its March 16, 2004 meeting adopted amendments to its fee schedule to be effective June 1, 2004.]

[The Administrative Office of the United States Courts provided for Registry Fund Fees effective June 12, 1989.]

Following are fees to be charged for services provided by the district courts. No fees are to be charged for services rendered on behalf of the United States, with the exception of those specifically prescribed in items 2, 4 and 5. No fees under this schedule shall be charged to federal agencies or programs which are funded from judiciary appropriations, including, but not limited to, agencies, organizations, and individuals providing services authorized by the Criminal Justice Act, 18 U.S.C. § 3006A, and Bankruptcy Administrator programs.

(1) For filing or indexing any document not in a case or proceeding for which a filing fee has been paid, $39.

(2) For every search of the records of the district court conducted by the clerk of the district court or a deputy clerk, $26 per name or item searched. This fee shall apply to services rendered on behalf of the United States if the information requested is available through electronic access.

(3) For certification of any document or paper, whether the certification is made directly on the document or by separate instrument, $9. For exemplification of any document or paper, twice the amount of the fee for certification.

(4) For reproducing any record or paper, $.50 per page. This fee shall apply to paper copies made from either: (1) original documents; or (2) microfiche or microfilm reproductions of the original records. This fee shall apply to services rendered on behalf of the United States if the record or paper requested is available through electronic access.

(5) For reproduction of recordings of proceedings, regardless of the medium, $26, including the cost of materials. This fee shall apply to services rendered on behalf of the United States, if the reproduction of the recording is available electronically.

(6) For each microfiche sheet of film or microfilm jacket copy of any court record, where available, $5.

(7) For retrieval of a record from a Federal Records Center, National Archives, or other storage location removed from the place of business of the court, $45.

(8) For a check paid into the court which is returned for lack of funds, $45.

(9) For an appeal to a district judge from a judgment of conviction by a magistrate in a misdemeanor case, $32.

(10) For original admission of attorneys to practice, $150 each, including a certificate of admission. For a duplicate certificate of admission or certificate of good standing, $15.

(11) The court may charge and collect fees commensurate with the cost of providing copies of the local rules of court. The court may also distribute copies of the local rules without charge.

(12) The clerk shall assess a charge for the handling of registry funds deposited with the court, to be assessed from interest earnings and in accordance with the detailed fee schedule issued by the Director of the Administrative Office of the United States Courts.

(13) For filing an action brought under Title III of the Cuban Liberty and Democratic Solidarity (LIBERTAD) Act of 1996, P.L. 104–114, 110 Stat. 785 (1996), $5,431. (This fee is in addition to the filing fee prescribed in 28 U.S.C. § 1914(a) for instituting any civil action other than a writ of habeas corpus.)

ELECTRONIC PUBLIC ACCESS FEE SCHEDULE (eff. 3/11/2008)

As directed by Congress, the Judicial Conference has determined that the following fees are necessary to reimburse expenses incurred by the judiciary in providing electronic public access to court records. These fees shall apply to the United States unless otherwise stated. No fees under this schedule shall be charged to federal agencies or programs which are funded from judiciary appropriations, including, but not limited to, agencies, organizations, and individuals providing services authorized by the Criminal Justice Act, 18 U.S.C. § 3006A, and bankruptcy administrator programs.

I. For electronic access to court data via a federal judiciary Internet site: 8 cents per page, with the total for any document, docket sheet, or case-specific report not to exceed the fee for 30 pages—provided however that transcripts of federal court proceedings shall not be subject to the 30–page fee limit. Attorneys of record and parties in a case (including pro se litigants) receive one free electronic copy of all documents filed electronically, if receipt is required by law or directed by the filer. No fee is owed under this provision until an account holder accrues charges of more than $10 in a calendar year. Consistent with Judicial Conference policy, courts may, upon a showing of cause, exempt indigents, bankruptcy case trustees, individual researchers associated with educational institutions, courts, section 501(c)(3) not-for-profit organizations, court appointed pro bono attorneys, and pro bono ADR neutrals from payment of these fees. Courts must find that parties from the classes of persons or entities listed above seeking exemption have demonstrated that an exemption is necessary in order to avoid unreasonable burdens and to promote public access to information. Any user granted an exemption agrees not to sell for profit the data obtained as a result. Any transfer of data obtained as the result of a fee exemption is prohibited unless expressly authorized by the court. Exemptions may be granted for a definite period of time and may be revoked at the discretion of the court granting the exemption.

II. For printing copies of any record or document accessed electronically at a public terminal in the courthouse: 10 cents per page. This fee shall apply to services rendered on behalf of the United States if the record requested is remotely available through electronic access.

III. For every search of court records conducted by the PACER Service Center, $26 per name or item searched.

IV. For the PACER Service Center to reproduce on paper any record pertaining to a PACER account, if this information is remotely available through electronic access, 50 cents per page.

V. For a check paid to the PACER Service Center which is returned for lack of funds, $45.

JUDICIAL CONFERENCE POLICY NOTES

Courts should not exempt local, state or federal government agencies, members of the media, attorneys or others not members of one of the groups listed above. Exemptions should be granted as the exception, not the rule. A court may not use this exemption language to exempt all users. An exemption applies only to access related to the case or purpose for which it was given. The prohibition on transfer of information received without fee is not intended to bar a quote or reference to information received as a result of a fee exemption in a scholarly or other similar work.

The electronic public access fee applies to electronic court data viewed remotely from the public records of individual cases in the court, including filed documents and the docket sheet. Electronic court data may be viewed free at public terminals at the courthouse and courts may provide other local court information at no cost. Examples of information that can be provided at no cost include: local rules, court forms, news items, court calendars, opinions, and other information—such as court hours, court location, telephone listings—determined locally to benefit the public and the court.

Registry Fund Fees—Item 13
(54 F.R 20407, May 11, 1989)

Effective June 12, 1989, a fee will be assessed for handling funds deposited in noncriminal proceedings with the court and held in interest bearing accounts or instruments pursuant to 28 U.S.C. § 2041 and Federal Rules of Civil Procedure rule 67. For new accounts, i.e, investments made on or after June 12, 1989, the fee will be equal to the first 45 days income earned on the deposit. Each subsequent deposit of new principal in the same case or proceeding will be subject to the fee. Reinvestment of prior deposits will not be subject to the fee. For existing accounts, i.e., investments held by the court prior to June 12, 1989, a fee will be assessed equal to the first 45 days of income earned beginning 30 days after June 12, 1989. Subsequent deposits of new principal in the same account will be subject to the fee. Subsequent reinvestment of existing deposits will not be subject to the fee.

The fee will apply only once to each sum deposited regardless of the length of time deposits are held and will not exceed income actually earned on the account.

The fee does not apply in the District Courts of Guam, Northern Mariana Islands, the Virgin Islands, the United States Claims Court, or other courts whose fees are not set under 28 U.S.C. § 1914.

Registry Fund Fees—Item 13
(55 F.R. 42867, October 24, 1990)

Effective December 1, 1990, the registry fee assessment provisions were revised and converted from a one-time charge equal to all income earned in the first 45 days of the investment to a charge of 10 percent of the income earned while funds are held in the court registry. Additionally, the fee was extended to any funds placed in the court's registry and invested regardless of the nature of the action underlying the deposit.

The new method will not be applied on investments in cases from which a fee has been exacted based on the prior method (interest earned in the first 45 days the funds were invested or the first 45 days following July 12, 1989). The new method will also not be applied in cases where the investment instrument has a maturity date greater than one year, but where a fee under the prior method applies but has not been deducted.

The fee does not apply in the District Courts of Guam, the Northern Mariana Islands, the Virgin Islands, the United States Claims Court, or any other federal court whose fees are not set under 28 U.S.C. §§ 1913, 1914, and 1930.

Registry Fund Fees—Item 13
(56 F.R. 56356, November 4, 1991)

Effective February 3, 1992, the registry fee assessment provisions are revised and converted from a charge equal to 10 percent of the income earned while funds are held in the court's registry to a variable rate based on the amount deposited with the court and, in certain cases, the length of time funds are held in the court's registry.

The revised fee will be a fee of 10 percent of the total income received during each income period from investments of less than $100,000,000 of registry funds in income-bearing accounts. On investments exceeding $100,000,000 the 10 percent fee shall be reduced by one percent for each increment of $50,000,000 over the initial $100,000,000. For those deposits where funds are placed in the registry by court order for a time certain, for example, by the terms of an adjudicated trust, the fee will be further reduced. This further reduction will amount to 2.5 percent for each five-year interval or part thereof. The total minimum fee to be charged will be no less than two percent of the income on investments.

The following table sets out the fee schedule promulgated by this notice:

REGISTRY—SCHEDULE OF FEES

[% of income earned]

Amount of deposit *	0–5 yrs.	>5–10 yrs.	>10–15 yrs.	>15 yrs.
less than 100M	10	7.5	5.0	2.5
100M–<150M	9	6.5	4.0	2.0
150M–<200M	8	5.5	3.0	2.0
200M–<250M	7	4.5	2.0	2.0
250M–<300M	6	3.5	2.0	2.0
300M–<350M	5	2.5	2.0	2.0
350M–<400M	4	2.0	2.0	2.0
400M–<450M	3	2.0	2.0	2.0
over 450M	2	2.0	2.0	2.0

* Except where otherwise authorized by the Director, each deposit into any account is treated separately in determining the fee.

The new fee applies to all earnings applied to investments on and after the effective date of this change, except for earnings on investments in cases being administered under the provisions of the May 11, 1989 notice [54 FR 20407], i.e., to which the fee equal to the first 45 days income is applicable.

The fee, as modified herein, will continue to apply to any case where the court has authorized the investment of funds placed in its custody or held by it in trust in its registry regardless of the nature of the underlying action.

The fee does not apply in the District Court of Guam, the Northern Mariana Islands, the Virgin Islands, the United States Claims Court, or any other Federal court whose fees are not set under 28 U.S.C. §§ 1913, 1914, and 1930.

HISTORICAL AND STATUTORY NOTES

Codifications

Pub.L. 99–591 is a corrected version of Pub.L. 99–500.

Effective and Applicability Provisions

2006 Acts. Pub.L. 109–171, Title X, § 10001(d), Feb. 8, 2006, 120 Stat. 184, provided that: "This section and the amendment made by this section [amending this section and enacting provisions set out as notes under 28 U.S.C.A.

§§ 1913 and 1931] shall take effect 60 days after the date of the enactment of this Act [Feb. 8, 2006]."

2004 Acts. Pub.L. 108–447, Div. B, Title III, § 307(c), Dec. 8, 2004, 118 Stat. 2895, provided that: "This section [amending subsec. (a) of this section and subsecs. (a) and (b) of 28 U.S.C.A. § 1931] shall take effect 60 days after the date of the enactment of this Act [Dec. 8, 2004]."

1996 Acts. Section 401(c) of Pub.L. 104–317 provided that: "This section [amending this section and section 1931 of this title] shall take effect 60 days after the date of the enactment of this Act [Oct. 19, 1996]."

1986 Acts. Section 4(c) of Pub.L. 99–336 provided that: "The amendments made by this section [amending this section and provisions of the District of Columbia Code not classified to this Code] shall apply with respect to any civil action, suit, or proceeding instituted on or after the date of the enactment of this Act [June 19, 1986]."

1978 Acts. Amendment by Pub.L. 95–598 effective Oct. 1, 1979, see section 402(c) of Pub.L. 95–598, set out as a note preceding section 101 of Title 11, Bankruptcy.

Court Fees for Electronic Access to Information

Judicial Conference to prescribe reasonable fees for collection by courts under this section for access to information available through automatic data processing equipment and fees to be deposited in Judiciary Automation Fund, see section 303 of Pub.L. 102–140, set out as a note under section 1913 of this title.

§ 1915. Proceedings in forma pauperis

(a)(1) Subject to subsection (b), any court of the United States may authorize the commencement, prosecution or defense of any suit, action or proceeding, civil or criminal, or appeal therein, without prepayment of fees or security therefor, by a person who submits an affidavit that includes a statement of all assets such prisoner possesses that the person is unable to pay such fees or give security therefor. Such affidavit shall state the nature of the action, defense or appeal and affiant's belief that the person is entitled to redress.

(2) A prisoner seeking to bring a civil action or appeal a judgment in a civil action or proceeding without prepayment of fees or security therefor, in addition to filing the affidavit filed under paragraph (1), shall submit a certified copy of the trust fund account statement (or institutional equivalent) for the prisoner for the 6–month period immediately preceding the filing of the complaint or notice of appeal, obtained from the appropriate official of each prison at which the prisoner is or was confined.

(3) An appeal may not be taken in forma pauperis if the trial court certifies in writing that it is not taken in good faith.

(b)(1) Notwithstanding subsection (a), if a prisoner brings a civil action or files an appeal in forma pauperis, the prisoner shall be required to pay the full amount of a filing fee. The court shall assess and, when funds exist, collect, as a partial payment of any court fees required by law, an initial partial filing fee of 20 percent of the greater of—

(A) the average monthly deposits to the prisoner's account; or

(B) the average monthly balance in the prisoner's account for the 6–month period immediately preceding the filing of the complaint or notice of appeal.

(2) After payment of the initial partial filing fee, the prisoner shall be required to make monthly payments of 20 percent of the preceding month's income credited to the prisoner's account. The agency having custody of the prisoner shall forward payments from the prisoner's account to the clerk of the court each time the amount in the account exceeds $10 until the filing fees are paid.

(3) In no event shall the filing fee collected exceed the amount of fees permitted by statute for the commencement of a civil action or an appeal of a civil action or criminal judgment.

(4) In no event shall a prisoner be prohibited from bringing a civil action or appealing a civil or criminal judgment for the reason that the prisoner has no assets and no means by which to pay the initial partial filing fee.

(c) Upon the filing of an affidavit in accordance with subsections (a) and (b) and the prepayment of any partial filing fee as may be required under subsection (b), the court may direct payment by the United States of the expenses of (1) printing the record on appeal in any civil or criminal case, if such printing is required by the appellate court; (2) preparing a transcript of proceedings before a United States magistrate judge in any civil or criminal case, if such transcript is required by the district court, in the case of proceedings conducted under section 636(b) of this title or under section 3401(b) of title 18, United States Code; and (3) printing the record on appeal if such printing is required by the appellate court, in the case of proceedings conducted pursuant to section 636(c) of this title. Such expenses shall be paid when authorized by the Director of the Administrative Office of the United States Courts.

(d) The officers of the court shall issue and serve all process, and perform all duties in such cases. Witnesses shall attend as in other cases, and the same remedies shall be available as are provided for by law in other cases.

(e)(1) The court may request an attorney to represent any person unable to afford counsel.

(2) Notwithstanding any filing fee, or any portion thereof, that may have been paid, the court shall dismiss the case at any time if the court determines that—

(A) the allegation of poverty is untrue; or

(B) the action or appeal—

(i) is frivolous or malicious;

(ii) fails to state a claim on which relief may be granted; or

(iii) seeks monetary relief against a defendant who is immune from such relief.

(f)(1) Judgment may be rendered for costs at the conclusion of the suit or action as in other proceedings, but the United States shall not be liable for any of the costs thus incurred. If the United States has paid the cost of a stenographic transcript or printed record for the prevailing party, the same shall be taxed in favor of the United States.

(2)(A) If the judgment against a prisoner includes the payment of costs under this subsection, the prisoner shall be required to pay the full amount of the costs ordered.

(B) The prisoner shall be required to make payments for costs under this subsection in the same manner as is provided for filing fees under subsection (a)(2).

(C) In no event shall the costs collected exceed the amount of the costs ordered by the court.

(g) In no event shall a prisoner bring a civil action or appeal a judgment in a civil action or proceeding under this section if the prisoner has, on 3 or more prior occasions, while incarcerated or detained in any facility, brought an action or appeal in a court of the United States that was dismissed on the grounds that it is frivolous, malicious, or fails to state a claim upon which relief may be granted, unless the prisoner is under imminent danger of serious physical injury.

(h) As used in this section, the term "prisoner" means any person incarcerated or detained in any facility who is accused of, convicted of, sentenced for, or adjudicated delinquent for, violations of criminal law or the terms and conditions of parole, probation, pretrial release, or diversionary program.

(June 25, 1948, c. 646, 62 Stat. 954; May 24, 1949, c. 139, § 98, 63 Stat. 104; Oct. 31, 1951, c. 655, § 51(b), (c), 65 Stat. 727; Sept. 21, 1959, Pub.L. 86–320, 73 Stat. 590; Oct. 10, 1979, Pub.L. 96–82, § 6, 93 Stat. 645; Dec. 1, 1990, Pub.L. 101–650, Title III, § 321, 104 Stat. 5117; Apr. 26, 1996, Pub.L. 104–134, Title I, § 101[(a)] [Title VIII, § 804(a), (c) to (e)], 110 Stat. 1321–73, 1321–74, 1321–75; renumbered Title I May 2, 1996, Pub.L. 104–140, § 1(a), 110 Stat. 1327.)

HISTORICAL AND STATUTORY NOTES

Change of Name

"United States magistrate judge" substituted for "United States magistrate" in text pursuant to section 321 of Pub.L. 101–650, set out as a note under 28 U.S.C.A. § 631.

Severability of Provisions

If any provision of section 101[a] [Title VIII] of Pub.L. 104–134, an amendment made by such Title, or the application of such provision or amendment to any person or circumstance is held to be unconstitutional, the remainder of such Title, the amendments made by such Title, and the application of the provisions of such Title to any person or circumstance not affected thereby, see section 101[a] [Title VIII, § 810] of Pub.L. 104–134, set out as a note under section 3626 of Title 18, Crimes and Criminal Procedure.

§ 1915A. Screening

(a) Screening.—The court shall review, before docketing, if feasible or, in any event, as soon as practicable after docketing, a complaint in a civil action in which a prisoner seeks redress from a governmental entity or officer or employee of a governmental entity.

(b) Grounds for dismissal.—On review, the court shall identify cognizable claims or dismiss the complaint, or any portion of the complaint, if the complaint—

(1) is frivolous, malicious, or fails to state a claim upon which relief may be granted; or

(2) seeks monetary relief from a defendant who is immune from such relief.

(c) Definition.—As used in this section, the term "prisoner" means any person incarcerated or detained in any facility who is accused of, convicted of, sentenced for, or adjudicated delinquent for, violations of criminal law or the terms and conditions of parole, probation, pretrial release, or diversionary program.

(Added Pub.L. 104–134, Title I, § 101[(a)][Title VIII, § 805(a)], Apr. 26, 1996, 110 Stat. 1321–75; renumbered Title I Pub.L. 104–140, § 1(a), May 2, 1996, 110 Stat. 1327.)

HISTORICAL AND STATUTORY NOTES

Severability of Provisions

If any provision of section 101[a] [Title VIII] of Pub.L. 104–134, an amendment made by such Title, or the application of such provision or amendment to any person or circumstance is held to be unconstitutional, the remainder of such Title, the amendments made by such Title, and the application of the provisions of such Title to any person or circumstance not affected thereby, see section 101[a] [Title VIII, § 810] of Pub.L. 104–134, set out as a note under section 3626 of Title 18, Crimes and Criminal Procedure.

§ 1916. Seamen's suits

In all courts of the United States, seamen may institute and prosecute suits and appeals in their own names and for their own benefit for wages or salvage or the enforcement of laws enacted for their health or safety without prepaying fees or costs or furnishing security therefor.

(June 25, 1948, c. 646, 62 Stat. 955.)

§ 1917. District courts; fee on filing notice of or petition for appeal

Upon the filing of any separate or joint notice of appeal or application for appeal or upon the receipt of any order allowing, or notice of the allowance of, an appeal or of a writ of certiorari $5 shall be paid to the clerk of the district court, by the appellant or petitioner.

(June 25, 1948, c. 646, 62 Stat. 955.)

§ 1918. District courts; fines, forfeitures and criminal proceedings

(a) Costs shall be included in any judgment, order, or decree rendered against any person for the violation of an Act of Congress in which a civil fine or forfeiture of property is provided for.

(b) Whenever any conviction for any offense not capital is obtained in a district court, the court may order that the defendant pay the costs of prosecution.

(June 25, 1948, c. 646, 62 Stat. 955.)

§ 1919. Dismissal for lack of jurisdiction

Whenever any action or suit is dismissed in any district court, the Court of International Trade, or the Court of Federal Claims for want of jurisdiction, such court may order the payment of just costs.

(June 25, 1948, c. 646, 62 Stat. 955; Oct. 10, 1980, Pub.L. 96–417, Title V, § 510, 94 Stat. 1743; Oct. 29, 1992, Pub.L. 102–572, Title IX, § 908(a), (b)(1), 106 Stat. 4519.)

HISTORICAL AND STATUTORY NOTES

Effective and Applicability Provisions

1992 Acts. Amendment by Title IX of Pub.L. 102–572 effective Oct. 29, 1992, see section 911 of Pub.L. 102–572, set out as a note under section 171 of this title.

1980 Acts. Amendment by Pub.L. 96–417 applicable with respect to civil actions commenced on or after Nov. 1, 1980, see section 701(b)(1)(E) of Pub.L. 96–417, as amended, set out as a note under section 251 of this title.

§ 1920. Taxation of costs

A judge or clerk of any court of the United States may tax as costs the following:

(1) Fees of the clerk and marshal;

(2) Fees for printed or electronically recorded transcripts necessarily obtained for use in the case;

(3) Fees and disbursements for printing and witnesses;

(4) Fees for exemplification and the costs of making copies of any materials where the copies are necessarily obtained for use in the case;

(5) Docket fees under section 1923 of this title;

(6) Compensation of court appointed experts, compensation of interpreters, and salaries, fees, expenses, and costs of special interpretation services under section 1828 of this title.

A bill of costs shall be filed in the case and, upon allowance, included in the judgment or decree.

(June 25, 1948, c. 646, 62 Stat. 955; Oct. 28, 1978, Pub.L. 95–539, § 7, 92 Stat. 2044; Oct. 13, 2008, Pub.L. 110–406, § 6, 122 Stat. 4292.)

HISTORICAL AND STATUTORY NOTES

Effective and Applicability Provisions

1978 Acts. Amendment by Pub.L. 95–539 effective Oct. 28, 1978, see section 10(a) of Pub.L. 95–539, set out as a note under section 602 of this title.

§ 1921. United States marshal's fees

(a)(1) The United States marshals or deputy marshals shall routinely collect, and a court may tax as costs, fees for the following:

(A) Serving a writ of possession, partition, execution, attachment in rem, or libel in admiralty, warrant, attachment, summons, complaints, or any other writ, order or process in any case or proceeding.

(B) Serving a subpoena or summons for a witness or appraiser.

(C) Forwarding any writ, order, or process to another judicial district for service.

(D) The preparation of any notice of sale, proclamation in admiralty, or other public notice or bill of sale.

(E) The keeping of attached property (including boats, vessels, or other property attached or libeled), actual expenses incurred, such as storage, moving, boat hire, or other special transportation, watchmen's or keepers' fees, insurance, and an hourly rate, including overtime, for each deputy marshal required for special services, such as guarding, inventorying, and moving.

(F) Copies of writs or other papers furnished at the request of any party.

(G) Necessary travel in serving or endeavoring to serve any process, writ, or order, except in the District of Columbia, with mileage to be computed from the place where service is returnable to the place of service or endeavor.

(H) Overtime expenses incurred by deputy marshals in the course of serving or executing civil process.

(2) The marshals shall collect, in advance, a deposit to cover the initial expenses for special services required under paragraph (1)(E), and periodically thereafter such amounts as may be necessary to pay such expenses until the litigation is concluded. This paragraph applies to all private litigants, including seamen proceeding pursuant to section 1916 of this title.

(3) For purposes of paragraph (1)(G), if two or more services or endeavors, or if an endeavor and a service, are made in behalf of the same party in the same case on the same trip, mileage shall be computed to the place of service or endeavor which is most remote from the place where service is returnable, adding thereto any additional mileage traveled in serving or endeavoring to serve in behalf of the party. If two or more writs of any kind, required to be

served in behalf of the same party on the same person in the same case or proceeding, may be served at the same time, mileage on only one such writ shall be collected.

(b) The Attorney General shall from time to time prescribe by regulation the fees to be taxed and collected under subsection (a). Such fees shall, to the extent practicable, reflect the actual and reasonable cost of the service provided.

(c)(1) The United States Marshals Service shall collect a commission of 3 percent of the first $1,000 collected and 1½ percent on the excess of any sum over $1,000, for seizing or levying on property (including seizures in admiralty), disposing of such property by sale, setoff, or otherwise, and receiving and paying over money, except that the amount of commission shall be within the range set by the Attorney General. if[1] the property is not disposed of by marshal's sale, the commission shall be in such amount, within the range set by the Attorney General, as may be allowed by the court. In any case in which the vessel or other property is sold by a public auctioneer, or by some party other than a marshal or deputy marshal, the commission authorized under this subsection shall be reduced by the amount paid to such auctioneer or other party. This subsection applies to any judicially ordered sale or execution sale, without regard to whether the judicial order of sale constitutes a seizure or levy within the meaning of State law. This subsection shall not apply to any seizure, forfeiture, sale, or other disposition of property pursuant to the applicable provisions of law amended by the Comprehensive Forfeiture Act of 1984 (98 Stat. 2040).

(2) The Attorney General shall prescribe from time to time regulations which establish a minimum and maximum amount for the commission collected under paragraph (1).

(d) The United States marshals may require a deposit to cover the fees and expenses prescribed under this section.

(e) Notwithstanding section 3302 of title 31, the United States Marshals Service is authorized, to the extent provided in advance in appropriations Acts—

(1) to credit to such Service's appropriation all fees, commissions, and expenses collected by such Service for—

(A) the service of civil process, including complaints, summonses, subpoenas, and similar process; and

(B) seizures, levies, and sales associated with judicial orders of execution; and

(2) to use such credited amounts for the purpose of carrying out such activities.

(June 25, 1948, c. 646, 62 Stat. 955; Sept. 9, 1950, c. 937, 64 Stat. 824; Aug. 31, 1962, Pub.L. 87–621, § 1, 76 Stat. 417; Nov. 10, 1986, Pub.L. 99–646, § 39(a), 100 Stat. 3600; Nov. 18, 1988, Pub.L. 100–690, Title VII, § 7608(c), 102 Stat. 4515; Nov. 29, 1990, Pub.L. 101–647, Title XII, § 1212, 104 Stat. 4833.)

[1] So in original. Probably should be capitalized.

HISTORICAL AND STATUTORY NOTES

References in Text

The Comprehensive Forfeiture Act of 1984, referred to in subsec. (c)(1), is chapter III (sections 301 to 322) of Title II of Pub.L. 98–473, Oct. 12, 1984, 98 Stat. 2040, as amended. For complete classification of this Act to the Code, see Short Title of 1984 Amendments note set out under section 1961 of Title 18, Crimes and Criminal Procedure, and Tables.

Effective and Applicability Provisions

1986 Acts. Section 39(b) of Pub.L. 99–646 provided that: "The amendments made by this section [amending this section] shall take effect 30 days after the date of enactment of this Act [Nov. 10, 1986]."

1962 Acts. Section 3 of Pub.L. 87–621 provided that: "This Act [amending this section] shall become effective ninety days after enactment [Aug. 31, 1962]."

Collection and Disposition of Fees and Expenses for Services

Pub.L. 101–162, Title II, Nov. 21, 1989, 103 Stat. 997, provided in part: "That notwithstanding the provisions of title 31 U.S.C. 3302 [section 3302 of Title 31, Money and Finance], for fiscal year 1990 and hereafter the Director of the United States Marshals Service may collect fees and expenses for the services authorized by 28 U.S.C. 1921 as amended by Public Law 100–690 [this section], and credit such fees to this appropriation to be used for salaries and other expenses incurred in providing these services."

§ 1922. Witness fees before United States magistrate judges

The fees of more than four witnesses shall not be taxed against the United States, in the examination of any criminal case before a United States magistrate judge, unless their materiality and importance are first approved and certified to by the United States attorney for the district in which the examination is had.

(June 25, 1948, c. 646, 62 Stat. 956; Oct. 17, 1968, Pub.L. 90–578, Title IV, § 402(b)(2), 82 Stat. 1118; Dec. 1, 1990, Pub.L. 101–650, Title III, § 321, 104 Stat. 5117.)

HISTORICAL AND STATUTORY NOTES

Change of Name

"United States magistrate judge" substituted for "United States magistrate" in text pursuant to section 321 of Pub.L. 101–650, set out as a note under 28 U.S.C.A. § 631. Previously, United States commissioners, referred to in text, were replaced by United States magistrates pursuant to Pub.L. 90–578, Oct. 17, 1968, 82 Stat. 1118. See chapter 43 of Title 28, 28 U.S.C.A. § 631 et seq.

§ 1923. Docket fees and costs of briefs

(a) Attorney's and proctor's docket fees in courts of the United States may be taxed as costs as follows:

$20 on trial or final hearing (including a default judgment whether entered by the court or by the clerk) in civil, criminal, or admiralty cases, except that in cases of admiralty and maritime jurisdiction where the libellant recovers less than $50 the proctor's docket fee shall be $10;

$20 in admiralty appeals involving not over $1,000;

$50 in admiralty appeals involving not over $5,000;

$100 in admiralty appeals involving more than $5,000;

$5 on discontinuance of a civil action;

$5 on motion for judgment and other proceedings on recognizances;

$2.50 for each deposition admitted in evidence.

(b) The docket fees of United States attorneys and United States trustees shall be paid to the clerk of court and by him paid into the Treasury.

(c) In admiralty appeals the court may allow as costs for printing the briefs of the successful party not more than:

$25 where the amount involved is not over $1,000;

$50 where the amount involved is not over $5,000;

$75 where the amount involved is over $5,000.

(June 25, 1948, c. 646, 62 Stat. 956; June 18, 1954, c. 304, 68 Stat. 253; Nov. 6, 1978, Pub.L. 95–598, Title II, § 245, 92 Stat. 2671.)

HISTORICAL AND STATUTORY NOTES

Codifications

Section 408(c) of Pub.L. 95–598, Nov. 6, 1978, 92 Stat. 2687, as amended by Pub.L. 98–166, Title II, § 200, Nov. 28, 1983, 97 Stat. 1081; Pub.L. 98–353, Title III, § 323, July 10, 1984, 98 Stat. 358; Pub.L. 99–429, Sept. 30, 1986, 100 Stat. 985; Pub.L. 99–500, § 101(b) [title II, § 200], Oct. 18, 1986, 100 Stat. 1783–39, 1783–45, and Pub.L. 99–591, § 101(b) [Title II, § 200], Oct. 30, 1986, 100 Stat. 3341–39, 3341–45; Pub.L. 99–554, Title III, § 307(a), Oct. 27, 1986, 100 Stat. 3125, which provided for the deletion of any references to United States Trustees in this title at a prospective date, was repealed by Pub.L. 99–554, Title III, § 307(b), Oct. 27, 1986, 100 Stat. 3125.

[For effective date of repeal, see section 302 of Pub.L. 99–554, set out as a note under section 581 of Title 28.]

Effective and Applicability Provisions

1978 Acts. Amendment by Pub.L. 95–598 effective Oct. 1, 1979, see section 402(c) of Pub.L. 95–598, set out as a note preceding section 101 of Title 11, Bankruptcy.

§ 1924. Verification of bill of costs

Before any bill of costs is taxed, the party claiming any item of cost or disbursement shall attach thereto an affidavit, made by himself or by his duly authorized attorney or agent having knowledge of the facts, that such item is correct and has been necessarily incurred in the case and that the services for which fees have been charged were actually and necessarily performed.

(June 25, 1948, c. 646, 62 Stat. 957.)

§ 1925. Admiralty and maritime cases

Except as otherwise provided by Act of Congress, the allowance and taxation of costs in admiralty and maritime cases shall be prescribed by rules promulgated by the Supreme Court.

(June 25, 1948, c. 646, 62 Stat. 957.)

§ 1926. Court of Federal Claims

(a) The Judicial Conference of the United States shall prescribe from time to time the fees and costs to be charged and collected in the United States Court of Federal Claims.

(b) The court and its officers shall collect only such fees and costs as the Judicial Conference prescribes. The court may require advance payment of fees by rule.

(June 25, 1948, c. 646, 62 Stat. 957; Apr. 2, 1982, Pub.L. 97–164, Title I, § 139(p)(1), 96 Stat. 44; Oct. 29, 1992, Pub.L. 102–572, Title IX, § 902(b), 106 Stat. 4516.)

JUDICIAL CONFERENCE SCHEDULE OF FEES

United States Court of Federal Claims Fee Schedule
Issued in Accordance with 28 U.S.C. § 1926(a)

(Effective 12/08/2005)

[The Federal Courts Improvement Act of 1982 [Pub.L. 97–164, Apr. 2, 1982, 96 Stat. 25] added a new Sec. 1926 to Title 28, United States Code [this section], authorizing the Judicial Conference to prescribe from time to time the fees and costs to be charged and collected in the United States Claims Court [now Court of Federal Claims]. A fee schedule was approved, effective October 1, 1982. At its March 1987 meeting, the Judicial Conference amended the schedule of fees to be effective May 1, 1987. Amendments to this revision of the schedule of fees were adopted at the September, 1988 and March, 1990 meetings of the Judicial Conference. The Judicial Conference amended the schedule of fees at its September, 1992 meeting to be effective Nov. 15, 1992. The Judicial Conference amended the schedule of fees at its March 15, 1995 meeting to be effective April 18, 1995. The Judicial Conference amended the schedule of fees at its 1996 meeting to be effective April 15, 1996. The Judicial Conference amended the schedule of fees at its 1999 meeting to be effective October 1, 1999. The Judicial Conference subsequently adopted amendments to its fee schedule effective February 1, 2001. The Judicial Conference amended the schedule of fees at its March 2001 meeting to be effective July 1, 2001 The Judicial Conference adopted amendments to its fee schedule effective November 1, 2003. The Judicial Conference at its March 16, 2004 meeting adopted amendments to its fee schedule to be effective June 1, 2004. The Judicial Conference amended the schedule of fees effective December 8, 2005]

Following are fees to be charged for services provided by the United States Court of Federal Claims. No fees are to be charged for services rendered on behalf of the United States, with the exception of those specifically prescribed in items 2 and 8. No fees under this schedule shall be charged to federal agencies or programs which are funded from judiciary appropriations, including, but not limited to, agencies, organizations, and individuals providing services authorized by the Criminal Justice Act, 18 U.S.C. § 3006A, and Bankruptcy Administrator programs.

(1) For filing a civil action or proceeding, $250.[1]

(2) For reproducing any record or paper, $.50 per page. This fee shall apply to paper copies made from either: (a) original documents; or (b) microfiche or microfilm reproduction of the original records. This fee shall apply to services rendered on behalf of the United States if the record or paper requested is available through electronic access.

(3) For certification of any document or paper, whether the certification is made directly on the document or by separate instrument, $9. For exemplification of any document or paper, twice the amount of the charge for certification.

(4) For admission of attorneys to practice, $250 each, including a certificate of admission.[2] For a duplicate certificate of admission or certificate of good standing, $15.

(5) For receipt of a monthly listing of court orders and opinions, $19 per year.

(6) The court may charge and collect fees commensurate with the cost of providing copies of the local rules of court. The court may also distribute copies of the local rules without charge.

(7) For a check paid into the court which is returned for lack of funds, $45.

(8) For every search of the records of the Court of Federal Claims conducted by the clerk of the court or a deputy clerk, $26 per name or item searched. This fee shall apply to services rendered on behalf of the United States if the information requested is available through electronic access.

1 Filing fee increase effective April 4, 2005.

2 Admission of attorneys to practice fee increase effective September 18, 2005.

ELECTRONIC PUBLIC ACCESS FEE SCHEDULE (eff. 3/11/2008)

As directed by Congress, the Judicial Conference has determined that the following fees are necessary to reimburse expenses incurred by the judiciary in providing electronic public access to court records. These fees shall apply to the United States unless otherwise stated. No fees under this schedule shall be charged to federal agencies or programs which are funded from judiciary appropriations, including, but not limited to, agencies, organizations, and individuals providing services authorized by the Criminal Justice Act, 18 U.S.C. § 3006A, and bankruptcy administrator programs.

I. For electronic access to court data via a federal judiciary Internet site: 8 cents per page, with the total for any document, docket sheet, or case-specific report not to exceed the fee for 30 pages—provided however that transcripts of federal court proceedings shall not be subject to the 30–page fee limit. Attorneys of record and parties in a case (including pro se litigants) receive one free electronic copy of all documents filed electronically, if receipt is required by law or directed by the filer. No fee is owed under this provision until an account holder accrues charges of more than $10 in a calendar year. Consistent with Judicial Conference policy, courts may, upon a showing of cause, exempt indigents, bankruptcy case trustees, individual researchers associated with educational institutions, courts, section 501(c)(3) not-for-profit organizations, court appointed pro bono attorneys, and pro bono ADR neutrals from payment of these fees. Courts must find that parties from the classes of persons or entities listed above seeking exemption have demonstrated that an exemption is necessary in order to avoid unreasonable burdens and to promote public access to information. Any user granted an exemption agrees not to sell for profit the data obtained as a result. Any transfer of data obtained as the result of a fee exemption is prohibited unless expressly authorized by the court. Exemptions may be granted for a definite period of time and may be revoked at the discretion of the court granting the exemption.

II. For printing copies of any record or document accessed electronically at a public terminal in the courthouse: 10 cents per page. This fee shall apply to services rendered on behalf of the United States if the record requested is remotely available through electronic access.

III. For every search of court records conducted by the PACER Service Center, $26 per name or item searched.

IV. For the PACER Service Center to reproduce on paper any record pertaining to a PACER account, if this information is remotely available through electronic access, 50 cents per page.

V. For a check paid to the PACER Service Center which is returned for lack of funds, $45.

JUDICIAL CONFERENCE POLICY NOTES

Courts should not exempt local, state or federal government agencies, members of the media, attorneys or others not members of one of the groups listed above. Exemptions should be granted as the exception, not the rule. A court may not use this exemption language to exempt all users. An exemption applies only to access related to the case or purpose for which it was given. The prohibition on transfer of information received without fee is not intended to bar a quote or reference to information received as a result of a fee exemption in a scholarly or other similar work.

The electronic public access fee applies to electronic court data viewed remotely from the public records of individual cases in the court, including filed documents and the docket sheet. Electronic court data may be viewed free at public terminals at the courthouse and courts may provide other local court information at no cost. Examples of information that can be provided at no cost include: local rules, court forms, news items, court calendars, opinions, and other information—such as court hours, court location, telephone listings—determined locally to benefit the public and the court.

HISTORICAL AND STATUTORY NOTES

Effective and Applicability Provisions

1992 Acts. Amendment by Pub.L. 102–572 effective Oct. 29, 1992, see section 911 of Pub.L. 102–572, set out as a note under section 171 of this title.

1982 Acts. Amendment by Pub.L. 97–164 effective Oct. 1, 1982, see section 402 of Pub.L. 97–164, set out as a note under section 171 of this title.

Court Fees for Electronic Access to Information

Judicial Conference to prescribe reasonable fees for collection by courts under this section for access to information available through automatic data processing equipment and fees to be deposited in Judiciary Automation Fund, see section 303 of Pub.L. 102–140, set out as a note under section 1913 of this title.

§ 1927. Counsel's liability for excessive costs

Any attorney or other person admitted to conduct cases in any court of the United States or any Territory thereof who so multiplies the proceedings in any case unreasonably and vexatiously may be required by the court to satisfy personally the excess costs, expenses, and attorneys' fees reasonably incurred because of such conduct.

(June 25, 1948, c. 646, 62 Stat. 957; Sept. 12, 1980, Pub.L. 96–349, § 3, 94 Stat. 1156.)

§ 1928. Patent infringement action; disclaimer not filed

Whenever a judgment is rendered for the plaintiff in any patent infringement action involving a part of a patent and it appears that the patentee, in his specifications, claimed to be, but was not, the original and first inventor or discoverer of any material or substantial part of the thing patented, no costs shall be included in such judgment, unless the proper disclaimer has been filed in the United States Patent and Trademark Office prior to the commencement of the action.

(June 25, 1948, c. 646, 62 Stat. 957; Nov. 29, 1999, Pub.L. 106–113, Div. B, § 1000(a)(9) [Title IV, § 4732(b)(17)], 113 Stat. 1536, 1501A–585.)

HISTORICAL AND STATUTORY NOTES

Effective and Applicability Provisions

1999 Acts. Amendment by Pub.L. 106–113 [§ 4732], effective 4 months after Nov. 29, 1999, see Pub.L. 106–113 [§ 4731], set out as a note under section 1 of Title 35.

Change of Name

Patent Office redesignated Patent and Trademark Office by section 3 of Pub.L. 93–596, Jan. 2, 1975, 88 Stat. 1949, set out as a note under section 1 of Title 35, Patents.

§ 1929. Extraordinary expenses not expressly authorized

Where the ministerial officers of the United States incur extraordinary expense in executing Acts of Congress, the payment of which is not specifically provided for, the Attorney General may allow the payment thereof.

(June 25, 1948, c. 646, 62 Stat. 957.)

§ 1930. Bankruptcy fees

(a) The parties commencing a case under title 11 shall pay to the clerk of the district court or the clerk of the bankruptcy court, if one has been certified pursuant to section 156(b) of this title, the following filing fees:

(1) For a case commenced under—

(A) chapter 7 of title 11, $245, and

(B) chapter 13 of title 11, $235.

(2) For a case commenced under chapter 9 of title 11, equal to the fee specified in paragraph (3) for filing a case under chapter 11 of title 11. The amount by which the fee payable under this paragraph exceeds $300 shall be deposited in the fund established under section 1931 of this title.

(3) For a case commenced under chapter 11 of title 11 that does not concern a railroad, as defined in section 101 of title 11, $1,000.

(4) For a case commenced under chapter 11 of title 11 concerning a railroad, as so defined, $1,000.

(5) For a case commenced under chapter 12 of title 11, $200.

(6) In addition to the filing fee paid to the clerk, a quarterly fee shall be paid to the United States trustee, for deposit in the Treasury, in each case under chapter 11 of title 11 for each quarter (including any fraction thereof) until the case is converted or dismissed, whichever occurs first. The fee shall be $325 for each quarter in which disbursements total less than $15,000; $650 for each quarter in which disbursements total $15,000 or more but less than $75,000; $975 for each quarter in which disbursements total $75,000 or more but less than $150,000; $1,625 for each quarter in which disbursements total $150,000 or more but less than $225,000; $1,950 for each quarter in which disbursements total $225,000 or more but less than $300,000; $4,875 for each quarter in which disbursements total $300,000 or more but less than $1,000,000; $6,500 for each quarter in which disbursements total $1,000,000 or more but less than $2,000,000; $9,750 for each quarter in which disbursements total $2,000,000 or more but less than $3,000,000; $10,400 for each quarter in which disbursements total $3,000,000 or more but less than $5,000,000; $13,000 for each quarter in which disbursements total $5,000,000 or more but less than $15,000,000; $20,000 for each quarter in which disbursements total $15,000,000 or more but less than $30,000,000; $30,000 for each quarter in which disbursements total more than $30,000,000. The fee shall be payable on the last day of the calendar month following the calendar quarter for which the fee is owed.

(7) In districts that are not part of a United States trustee region as defined in section 581 of this title, the Judicial Conference of the United States may require the debtor in a case under chapter 11 of title 11 to pay fees equal to those imposed by paragraph (6) of this subsection. Such fees shall be deposited as offsetting receipts to the

fund established under section 1931 of this title and shall remain available until expended.

An individual commencing a voluntary case or a joint case under title 11 may pay such fee in installments. For converting, on request of the debtor, a case under chapter 7, or 13 of title 11, to a case under chapter 11 of title 11, the debtor shall pay to the clerk of the district court or the clerk of the bankruptcy court, if one has been certified pursuant to section 156(b) of this title, a fee of the amount equal to the difference between the fee specified in paragraph (3) and the fee specified in paragraph (1).

(b) The Judicial Conference of the United States may prescribe additional fees in cases under title 11 of the same kind as the Judicial Conference prescribes under section 1914(b) of this title.

(c) Upon the filing of any separate or joint notice of appeal or application for appeal or upon the receipt of any order allowing, or notice of the allowance of, an appeal or a writ of certiorari $5 shall be paid to the clerk of the court, by the appellant or petitioner.

(d) Whenever any case or proceeding is dismissed in any bankruptcy court for want of jurisdiction, such court may order the payment of just costs.

(e) The clerk of the court may collect only the fees prescribed under this section.

(f)(1) Under the procedures prescribed by the Judicial Conference of the United States, the district court or the bankruptcy court may waive the filing fee in a case under chapter 7 of title 11 for an individual if the court determines that such individual has income less than 150 percent of the income official poverty line (as defined by the Office of Management and Budget, and revised annually in accordance with section 673(2) of the Omnibus Budget Reconciliation Act of 1981) applicable to a family of the size involved and is unable to pay that fee in installments. For purposes of this paragraph, the term "filing fee" means the filing fee required by subsection (a), or any other fee prescribed by the Judicial Conference under subsections (b) and (c) that is payable to the clerk upon the commencement of a case under chapter 7.

(2) The district court or the bankruptcy court may waive for such debtors other fees prescribed under subsections (b) and (c).

(3) This subsection does not restrict the district court or the bankruptcy court from waiving, in accordance with Judicial Conference policy, fees prescribed under this section for other debtors and creditors.

(Added Pub.L. 95–598, Title II, § 246(a), Nov. 6, 1978, 92 Stat. 2671, and amended Pub.L. 98–353, Title I, § 111(a), (b), July 10, 1984, 98 Stat. 342; Pub.L. 99–500, Title I, § 101(b) [Title IV, § 407(b)], Oct. 18, 1986, 100 Stat. 1783–64; Pub.L. 99–554, Title I, §§ 117, 144(f), Oct. 27, 1986, 100 Stat. 3095, 3097; Pub.L. 99–591, Title I, § 101(b) [Title IV, § 407(b)], Oct. 30, 1986, 100 Stat. 3341–64; Pub.L. 101–162, Title IV, § 406(a), Nov. 21, 1989, 103 Stat. 1016; Pub.L. 102–140, Title I, § 111(a), Oct. 28, 1991, 105 Stat. 795; Pub.L. 103–121, Title I, § 111(a)(1), (b)(1), Oct. 27, 1993, 107 Stat. 1164; Pub.L. 104–91, Title I, § 101(a), Jan. 6, 1996, 110 Stat. 11; Pub.L. 104–99, Title II, § 211, Jan. 26, 1996, 110 Stat. 37; Pub.L. 104–208, Div. A, Title I, § 101(a) [Title I, § 109(a)], Sept. 30, 1996, 110 Stat. 3009–18; Pub.L. 106–113, Div. B, § 1000(a)(1) [Title I, § 113], Nov. 29, 1999, 113 Stat. 1535, 1501A–20; Pub.L. 106–518, Title I, §§ 103 to 105, Nov. 13, 2000, 114 Stat. 2411; Pub.L. 109–8, Title III, § 325(a), Title IV, § 418, Apr. 20, 2005, 119 Stat. 98, 108; Pub.L. 109–13, Div. A, Title VI, § 6058(a), May 11, 2005, 119 Stat. 297; Pub.L. 109–171, Title X, § 10101(a), Feb. 8, 2006, 120 Stat. 184; Pub.L. 110–161, Div. B, Title II, § 213(a), Dec. 26, 2007, 121 Stat. 1914.)

JUDICIAL CONFERENCE SCHEDULE OF FEES

Bankruptcy Court Miscellaneous Fee Schedule

(Issued in accordance with 28 U.S.C. § 1930(b))

(Effective 10/1/2008)

[The Judicial Conference of the United States at its session on March 7–9, 1979, set forth the schedule of fees to be charged in bankruptcy courts pursuant to this section. That schedule became effective on October 1, 1979. At its sessions in March and September 1980, March, 1981, March, 1987, and March and September, 1988, the Judicial Conference amended the schedule of fees. The Administrative Office of the United States Courts provided for Registry Fund Fees effective June 12, 1989. At its September, 1989 meeting, the Judicial Conference again amended the schedule of fees, such amendments effective pursuant to 1989 Judicial Conference Statement. The schedule of fees was again amended by the Judicial Conference at its March, 1990 and September, 1990 meetings. At its 1991 meeting, the Judicial Conference amended the schedule of fees to be effective Feb. 3, 1992. At its March 1991 meeting the Judicial Conference adopted Item 23 to be effective Oct. 19, 1992, with later implementation. At its September, 1992 meeting the Judicial Conference amended Item 8 to be effective Dec. 1, 1992. At its March, 1993 meeting the Judicial Conference amended its fee schedule effective May 6, 1993. At its September, 1993 meeting the Judicial Conference amended its fee schedule to be effective November 8, 1993. At its 1994 meeting, the Judicial Conference amended its fee schedule to be effective January 1, 1995. At its September, 1995 meeting the Judicial Conference amended its fee schedule to be effective November 9, 1995, and at its 1996 meetings it adopted amendments to be effective April 1, 1996 and October 28, 1996. At its 1997 meeting the Judicial Conference amended its fee schedule to be effective January 1, 1998. At its 1999 meeting the Judicial Conference amended its fee schedule to be effective October 1, 1999. The Judicial Conference subsequently adopted amendments to its fee schedule effective February 1, 2001. At its March 2001 meeting the Judicial Conference amended its fee schedule to be effective July 1, 2001. The Judicial Conference adopted amendments to its fee schedule effective January 1, 2002; and effective November 1, 2003. The Judicial Conference at its March 16, 2004 meeting adopted amendments to its fee schedule to be effective June 1, 2004. The Judicial Conference adopted amendments to its fee schedule effective January 1, 2005; and effective September 20, 2005; and effective

October 17, 2005; and effective January 1, 2007; and effective October 1, 2008.]

The fees included in the Bankruptcy Court Miscellaneous Fee Schedule are to be charged for services provided by the bankruptcy courts.

- The United States should not be charged fees under this schedule, with the exception of those specifically prescribed in Items 1, 3 and 5 when the information requested is available through remote electronic access.
- Federal agencies or programs that are funded from judiciary appropriations (agencies, organizations, and individuals providing services authorized by the Criminal Justice Act, 18 U.S.C. § 3006A, and bankruptcy administrators) should not be charged any fees under this schedule.

(1) For reproducing any document, $.50 per page. This fee applies to services rendered on behalf of the United States if the document requested is available through electronic access.

(2) For certification of any document, $9.

For exemplification of any document, $18.

(3) For reproduction of an audio recording of a court proceeding, $26. This fee applies to services rendered on behalf of the United States if the recording is available electronically.

(4) For filing an amendment to the debtor's schedules, lists of creditors, or mailing list, $26, except:

- The bankruptcy judge may, for good cause, waive the charge in any case.
- This fee must not be charged if—
  - the amendment is to change the address of a creditor or an attorney for a creditor listed on the schedules; or
  - the amendment is to add the name and address of an attorney for a creditor listed on the schedules.

(5) For conducting a search of the bankruptcy court records, $26 per name or item searched. This fee applies to services rendered on behalf of the United States if the information requested is available through electronic access.

(6) For filing a complaint, $250, except:

- If the trustee or debtor-in-possession files the complaint, the fee should be paid by the estate, if there is an estate.
- This fee must not be charged if—
  - the debtor is the plaintiff; or
  - a child support creditor or representative files the complaint and submits the form required by § 304(g) of the Bankruptcy Reform Act of 1994.

(7) For filing any document that is not related to a pending case or proceeding, $39.

(8) Administrative fee for filing a case under Title 11 or when a motion to divide a joint case under Title 11 is filed, $39.

(9) For payment to trustees pursuant to 11 U.S.C. § 330(b)(2), a $15 fee applies in the following circumstances:

- For filing a petition under Chapter 7.
- For filing a motion to reopen a Chapter 7 case.
- For filing a motion to divide a joint Chapter 7 case.
- For filing a motion to convert a case to a Chapter 7 case.
- For filing a notice of conversion to a Chapter 7 case.

(10) In addition to any fees imposed under Item 9, above, the following fees must be collected:

- For filing a motion to convert a Chapter 12 case to a Chapter 7 case or a notice of conversion pursuant to 11 U.S.C. § 1208(a), $45.
- For filing a motion to convert a Chapter 13 case to a Chapter 7 case or a notice of conversion pursuant to 11 U.S.C. § 1307(a), $10.

The fee amounts in this item are derived from the fees prescribed in 28 U. S.C. § 1930(a).

If the trustee files the motion to convert, the fee is payable only from the estate that exists prior to conversion.

If the filing fee for the chapter to which the case is requested to be converted is less than the fee paid at the commencement of the case, no refund may be provided.

(11) For filing a motion to reopen, the following fees apply:

- For filing a motion to reopen a Chapter 7 case, $245.
- For filing a motion to reopen a Chapter 9 case, $1000.
- For filing a motion to reopen a Chapter 11 case, $1000.
- For filing a motion to reopen a Chapter 12 case, $200.
- For filing a motion to reopen a Chapter 13 case, $235.
- For filing a motion to reopen a Chapter 15 case, $1000.

The fee amounts in this item are derived from the fees prescribed in 28 U. S.C. § 1930(a).

The reopening fee must be charged when a case has been closed without a discharge being entered.

The court may waive this fee under appropriate circumstances or may defer payment of the fee from trustees pending discovery of additional assets. If payment is deferred, the fee should be waived if no additional assets are discovered.

The reopening fee must not be charged in the following situations:

- to permit a party to file a complaint to obtain a determination under Rule 4007(b); or
- when a debtor files a motion to reopen a case based upon an alleged violation of the terms of the discharge under 11 U.S.C. § 524.

(12) For retrieval of a record from a Federal Records Center, National Archives, or other storage location removed from the place of business of the court, $45.

(13) For a check paid into the court which is returned for lack of funds, $45.

(14) For filing an appeal or cross appeal from a final judgment, $250.

This fee is collected in addition to the statutory fee of $5 that is collected under 28 U.S.C. § 1930(c) when a notice of appeal is filed.

Parties filing a joint notice of appeal should pay only one fee.

If a trustee or debtor in possession is the appellant, the fee must be payable only from the estate and to the extent there is any estate realized.

Upon notice from the court of appeals that a direct appeal or direct cross appeal has been authorized, an additional fee of $200 must be collected.

(15) For filing a case under Chapter 15 of the Bankruptcy Code, $1000.

This fee is derived from and equal to the fee prescribed in 28 U.S.C. § 1930(a)(4) for filing a case commenced under Chapter 11 of Title 11.

(16) The court may charge and collect fees commensurate with the cost of providing copies of the local rules of court. The court may also distribute copies of the local rules without charge.

(17) The clerk shall assess a charge for the handling of registry funds deposited with the court, to be assessed from interest earnings and in accordance with the detailed fee schedule issued by the Director of the Administrative Office of the United States Courts.

(18) For filing a motion to divide a joint case filed under 11 U.S.C. § 302, the following fees apply:

- For filing a motion to divide a joint Chapter 7 case, $245.
- For filing a motion to divide a joint Chapter 11 case, $1000.
- For filing a motion to divide a joint Chapter 12 case, $200.
- For filing a motion to divide a joint Chapter 13 case, $235.

These fees are derived from and equal to the filing fees prescribed in 28 U.S.C. § 1930(a).

(19) For filing the following motions, $150:

- To terminate, annul, modify or condition the automatic stay;
- To compel abandonment of property of the estate pursuant to Rule 6007(b) of the Federal Rules of Bankruptcy Procedure; or
- To withdraw the reference of a case or proceeding under 28 U.S.C. § 157(d).

This fee must not be collected in the following situations:

- For a motion for relief from the co-debtor stay;
- For a stipulation for court approval of an agreement for relief from a stay; or
- For a motion filed by a child support creditor or its representative, if the form required by § 304(g) of the Bankruptcy Reform Act of 1994 is filed.

ELECTRONIC PUBLIC ACCESS FEE SCHEDULE (eff. 3/11/2008)

As directed by Congress, the Judicial Conference has determined that the following fees are necessary to reimburse expenses incurred by the judiciary in providing electronic public access to court records. These fees shall apply to the United States unless otherwise stated. No fees under this schedule shall be charged to federal agencies or programs which are funded from judiciary appropriations, including, but not limited to, agencies, organizations, and individuals providing services authorized by the Criminal Justice Act, 18 U.S.C. § 3006A, and bankruptcy administrator programs.

I. For electronic access to court data via a federal judiciary Internet site: 8 cents per page, with the total for any document, docket sheet, or case-specific report not to exceed the fee for 30 pages—provided however that transcripts of federal court proceedings shall not be subject to the 30-page fee limit. Attorneys of record and parties in a case (including pro se litigants) receive one free electronic copy of all documents filed electronically, if receipt is required by law or directed by the filer. No fee is owed under this provision until an account holder accrues charges of more than $10 in a calendar year. Consistent with Judicial Conference policy, courts may, upon a showing of cause, exempt indigents, bankruptcy case trustees, individual researchers associated with educational institutions, courts, section 501(c)(3) not-for-profit organizations, court appointed pro bono attorneys, and pro bono ADR neutrals from payment of these fees. Courts must find that parties from the classes of persons or entities listed above seeking exemption have demonstrated that an exemption is necessary in order to avoid unreasonable burdens and to promote public access to information. Any user granted an exemption agrees not to sell for profit the data obtained as a result. Any transfer of data obtained as the result of a fee exemption is prohibited unless expressly authorized by the court. Exemptions may be granted for a definite period of time and may be revoked at the discretion of the court granting the exemption.

II. For printing copies of any record or document accessed electronically at a public terminal in the courthouse: 10 cents per page. This fee shall apply to services rendered on behalf of the United States if the record requested is remotely available through electronic access.

III. For every search of court records conducted by the PACER Service Center, $26 per name or item searched.

IV. For the PACER Service Center to reproduce on paper any record pertaining to a PACER account, if this information is remotely available through electronic access, 50 cents per page.

V. For a check paid to the PACER Service Center which is returned for lack of funds, $45.

JUDICIAL CONFERENCE POLICY NOTES

Courts should not exempt local, state or federal government agencies, members of the media, attorneys or others not members of one of the groups listed above. Exemptions should be granted as the exception, not the rule. A court may not use this exemption language to exempt all users. An exemption applies only to access related to the case or purpose for which it was given. The prohibition on transfer of information received without fee is not intended to bar a quote or reference to information received as a result of a fee exemption in a scholarly or other similar work.

The electronic public access fee applies to electronic court data viewed remotely from the public records of individual cases in the court, including filed documents and the docket sheet. Electronic court data may be viewed free at public terminals at the courthouse and courts may provide other local court information at no cost. Examples of information that can be provided at no cost include: local rules, court forms, news items, court calendars, opinions, and other information—such as court hours, court location, telephone listings—determined locally to benefit the public and the court.

STATEMENT RESPECTING 1988 AMENDMENTS FROM ADMINISTRATIVE OFFICE OF UNITED STATES COURTS

The Director of the Administrative Office of the United States Courts in a memorandum to the Chief Judges of the United States Courts of Appeals, United States District Courts, and United States Bankruptcy Courts, dated April

19, 1988, provided in part that: "The amendment establishing a fee for filing a petition ancillary to a foreign proceeding under § 304 of the Bankruptcy Code will become effective May 1, 1988. The amendment expanding the exemption for services rendered 'to the United States' to include services rendered to bankruptcy administrators simply expresses a policy which has been in effect since the creation of the bankruptcy administrator program by Congress in the Bankruptcy Judges, United States Trustees and Family Farmer Bankruptcy Act of 1986. [Pub.L. No. 99–554, § 302(d)(3)(I).]"

Statement from 1989 Meeting of Judicial Conference

The Judicial Conference, at the September 20, 1989 meeting, provided in part that Item 21 takes effect on December 21, 1989. The Conference further provided that: "The remaining fees, Items 20 and 22, take effect on January 11, 1990, pending approval of the Appropriations Committees."

Registry Fund Fees—Item 19
(54 FR 20407, May 11, 1989)

Effective June 12, 1989, a fee will be assessed for handling funds deposited in noncriminal proceedings with the court and held in interest bearing accounts or instruments pursuant to 28 U.S.C. § 2041 and Federal Rules of Civil Procedure rule 67. For new accounts, i.e., investments made on or after June 12, 1989, the fee will be equal to the first 45 days income earned on the deposit. Each subsequent deposit of new principal in the same case or proceeding will be subject to the fee. Reinvestment of prior deposits will not be subject to the fee. For existing accounts, i.e., investments held by the court prior to June 12, 1989, a fee will be assessed equal to the first 45 days of income earned beginning 30 days after June 12, 1989. Subsequent deposits of new principal in the same account will be subject to the fee. Subsequent reinvestment of existing deposits will not be subject to the fee.

The fee will apply only once to each sum deposited regardless of the length of time deposits are held and will not exceed income actually earned on the account.

The fee does not apply in the District Courts of Guam, Northern Mariana Islands, the Virgin Islands, the United States Claims Court, or other courts whose fees are not set under 28 U.S.C. § 1930.

Registry Fund Fees—Item 19
(55 F.R. 42867, October 24, 1990)

Effective December 1, 1990, the registry fee assessment provisions were revised and converted from a one-time charge equal to all income earned in the first 45 days of the investment to a charge of 10 percent of the income earned while funds are held in the court registry. Additionally, the fee was extended to any funds placed in the court's registry and invested regardless of the nature of the action underlying the deposit.

The new method will not be applied on investments in cases from which a fee has been exacted based on the prior method (interest earned in the first 45 days the funds were invested or the first 45 days following July 12, 1989). The new method will also not be applied in cases where the investment instrument has a maturity date greater than one year, but where a fee under the prior method applies but has not been deducted.

The fee does not apply in the District Courts of Guam, the Northern Mariana Islands, the Virgin Islands, the United States Claims Court, or any other federal court whose fees are not set under 28 U.S.C. §§ 1913, 1914, and 1930.

Registry Fund Fees—Item 19
(56 F.R. 56356, November 4, 1991)

Effective February 3, 1992, the registry fee assessment provisions are revised and converted from a charge equal to 10 percent of the income earned while funds are held in the court's registry to a variable rate based on the amount deposited with the court and, in certain cases, the length of time funds are held in the court's registry.

The revised fee will be a fee of 10 percent of the total income received during each income period from investments of less than $100,000,000 of registry funds in income-bearing accounts. On investments exceeding $100,000,000 the 10 percent fee shall be reduced by one percent for each increment of $50,000,000 over the initial $100,000,000. For those deposits where funds are placed in the registry by court order for a time certain, for example, by the terms of an adjudicated trust, the fee will be further reduced. This further reduction will amount to 2.5 percent for each five-year interval or part thereof. The total minimum fee to be charged will be no less than two percent of the income on investments.

The following table sets out the fee schedule promulgated by this notice:

REGISTRY—SCHEDULE OF FEES

[% of income earned]

Amount of deposit *	0–5 yrs.	>5–10 yrs.	>10–15 yrs.	>15 yrs.
less than 100M	10	7.5	5.0	2.5
100M–<150M	9	6.5	4.0	2.0
150M–<200M	8	5.5	3.0	2.0
200M–<250M	7	4.5	2.0	2.0
250M–<300M	6	3.5	2.0	2.0
300M–<350M	5	2.5	2.0	2.0
350M–<400M	4	2.0	2.0	2.0
400M–<450M	3	2.0	2.0	2.0
over 450M	2	2.0	2.0	2.0

* Except where otherwise authorized by the Director, each deposit into any account is treated separately in determining the fee.

The new fee applies to all earnings applied to investments on and after the effective date of this change, except for earnings on investments in cases being administered under the provisions of the May 11, 1989 notice [54 FR 20407], i.e., to which the fee equal to the first 45 days income is applicable.

The fee, as modified herein, will continue to apply to any case where the court has authorized the investment of funds placed in its custody or held by it in trust in its registry regardless of the nature of the underlying action.

The fee does not apply in the District Court of Guam, the Northern Mariana Islands, the Virgin Islands, the United States Claims Court, or any other Federal court whose fees are not set under 28 U.S.C. §§ 1913, 1914, and 1930.

HISTORICAL AND STATUTORY NOTES

References in Text

Chapter 7, 11, 12, or 13 of title 11, referred to in text, is 11 U.S.C.A. § 701 et seq., 11 U.S.C.A. § 1101 et seq., 11 U.S.C.A. § 1201 et seq., or 11 U.S.C.A. § 1301 et seq., respectively.

Section 673(2) of the Omnibus Budget Reconciliation Act of 1981, referred to in subsec. (f)(1), is Pub.L. 97–35, Title VI, § 673(2), Aug. 13, 1981, as added Pub.L. 105–285, Title II, § 201, Oct. 27, 1998, 112 Stat. 2729, which is classified to 42 U.S.C.A. § 9902(2).

Codifications

Pub.L. 99–591 is a corrected version of Pub.L. 99–500.

The Chapter 11 filing fee will not change from its current amount of $1,000. It appears that Congress intended to increase chapter 11 filing fees from $1,000 to $2,750. However, there is a drafting error in the language of the Deficit Reduction Act of 2005 which references the incorrect statutory subsection [Pub.L. 109–171, Title X, § 10101(a)(2), Feb. 8, 2006, 120 Stat. 184]. Thus, the chapter 11 fee, at this time, is unaltered. See 2006 Amendments note set out under this section.

Section 101(a) of Pub.L. 104–91, as amended by section 211 of Pub.L. 104–99, provided in part that section 111(a) of the General Provisions for the Department of Justice in Title I of the Departments of Commerce, Justice, and State, the Judiciary, and Related Agencies Appropriations Act, 1996 (H.R. 2076) as passed by the House of Representatives on Dec. 6, 1995, was enacted into permanent law. Such section 111(a) of H.R. 2076 amended subsec. (a)(6) of this section. See 1996 Amendments note set out under this section.

Effective and Applicability Provisions

2007 Acts. Pub.L. 110–161, Div. B, Title II, § 213(b), Dec. 26, 2007, 121 Stat. 1914, provided that: "This section and the amendment made by this section [amending this section] shall take effect January 1, 2008, or the date of the enactment of this Act [Dec. 26, 2007], whichever is later."

2006 Acts. Pub.L. 109–171, Title X, § 10101(c), Feb. 8, 2006, 120 Stat. 184, provided that: "This section and the amendments made by this section [amending this section and enacting provisions set out as a note under 28 U.S.C.A. § 1931] shall take effect 60 days after the date of the enactment of this Act [Feb. 8, 2006]."

2005 Acts. Amendment by Pub.L. 109–13, § 6058(a), amending Pub.L. 109–8, § 325, which amended this section, effective immediately after the enactment of the Bankruptcy Abuse Prevention and Consumer Protection Act of 2005 [Pub.L. 109–8, Apr. 20, 2005, 119 Stat. 23], see Pub.L. 109–13, § 6058(b), set out as a note under 28 U.S.C.A. § 589a.

Except as otherwise provided, amendments by Pub.L. 109–8 effective 180 days after April 20, 2005, and inapplicable with respect to cases commenced under Title 11 before the effective date, see Pub.L. 109–8, § 1501, set out as a note under 11 U.S.C.A. § 101.

1999 Acts. Amendment by Pub.L. 106–113, [§ 113], effective 30 days after Nov. 29, 1999, see Pub.L. 106–113, [§ 113], set out as a note under section 589a of this title.

1993 Acts. Section 111(a) of Pub.L. 103–121 provided in part that amendment by section 111(a)(1) of Pub.L. 103–121, amending subsec. (a)(1) of this section, is effective 30 days after Oct. 27, 1993.

Section 111(b) of Pub.L. 103–121 provided in part that amendment by section 111(b)(1) of Pub.L. 103–121, amending subsec. (a)(3) of this section, is effective 30 days after Oct. 27, 1993.

1991 Acts. Amendment by Pub.L. 102–140 effective 60 days after the date of the enactment of Pub.L. 102–140, which was approved Oct. 28, 1991, see section 111(a) of Pub.L. 102–140, set out as a note under section 589a of this title.

1986 Acts. Amendment by Pub.L. 99–554 effective 30 days after Oct. 27, 1986, except as otherwise provided for, see section 302(a) of Pub.L. 99–554, set out as a note under section 581 of this title.

Amendment by Pub.L. 99–554, § 117(4), not to become effective in or with respect to certain specified judicial districts until, or apply to cases while pending in such district before, the expiration of the 270-day period beginning 30 days after Oct. 27, 1986, or of the 30-day period beginning on the date the Attorney General certifies under section 303 of Pub.L. 99–554 the region specified in a paragraph of section 581(a) of Title 28, as amended by section 111(a) of Pub.L. 99–554, that includes such district, whichever occurs first, see section 302(d)(1) of Pub.L. 99–554, set out as a note under section 581 of this title.

Amendment by Pub.L. 99–554, § 117(4), not to become effective in or with respect to certain specified judicial districts until, or apply to cases while pending in such district before, the expiration of the 2-year period beginning 30 days after Oct. 27, 1986, or of the 30-day period beginning on the date the Attorney General certifies under section 303 of Pub.L. 99–554 the region specified in a paragraph of section 581(a) of Title 28, as amended by section 111(a) of Pub.L. 99–554, that includes such district, whichever occurs first, see section 302(d)(2) of Pub.L. 99–554, set out as a note under section 581 of this title.

Amendment by Pub.L. 99–554, § 117(4), not to become effective in or with respect to judicial districts established for the States of Alabama and North Carolina until, or apply to cases while pending in such district before, such district elects to be included in a bankruptcy region established in section 581(a) of Title 28, as amended by section 111(a) of Pub.L. 99–554, or Oct. 1, 2002, whichever occurs first, and, except as otherwise provided for, with respect to cases under chapters 7, 11, 12, and 13 of Title 11 commenced before 30 days after Oct. 27, 1986, and pending in a judicial district in the States of Alabama or North Carolina before any election made under section 302(d)(3)(A) of Pub.L. 99–554 by such district becomes effective or Oct. 1, 2002, whichever occurs first, amendments by Pub.L. 99–554 not to apply until Oct. 1, 2003, or the expiration of the 1-year period beginning on the date such election becomes effective, whichever occurs first, and further, in any judicial district in Alabama or North Carolina not making the election described in section 302(d)(3)(A) of Pub.L. 99–554, any person appointed under regulations issued by the Judicial Conference to administer estates in cases under Title 11 authorized to establish, etc., a panel of private trustees, and to supervise cases and trustees in cases under chapters 7, 11, 12, and 13 of Title 11, until amendments by sections 201 to 231 of Pub.L. 99–554 effective in such district, see section 302(d)(3)(A) to (F), (H), (I) of Pub.L. 99–554, set out as a note under section 581 of this title.

Deposit in the general receipts of the Treasury of funds collected as a result of the amendments made by section 117 of Pub.L. 99–554 in a judicial district in the States of Alabama or North Carolina under section 1930(a) of Title 28 before the date the amendments made by sections 201 to 231 of Pub.L. 99–554 take effect in such districts, and notwithstanding section 589a of Title 28, see section 302(d)(3)(G) of Pub.L. 99–554, set out as a note under section 581 of this title.

Amendment by Pub.L. 99–554, § 117(4), except as otherwise provided, with respect to cases under chapters 7, 11, 12, and 13 of Title 11 commenced before 30 days after Oct. 27, 1986, and pending in a judicial district referred to in section 581(a) of Title 28, as amended by section 111(a) of Pub.L. 99–554, for which a United States trustee is not authorized before 30 days after Oct. 27, 1986 to be appointed, not applicable until the expiration of the 3-year period beginning on Oct. 27, 1986, or of the 1-year period beginning on the date the Attorney General certifies under section 303 of Pub.L. 99–554 the region specified in a paragraph of such section 581(a) that includes, such district, whichever occurs first, see section 302(e)(1), (2) of Pub.L. 99–554, set out as a note under section 581 of this title.

Rule of construction regarding fees for cases under Title 11 for any conduct or period occurring before section 1930(a)(6) of Title 28 becomes effective in the district in which such case is pending, see section 302(e)(3) of Pub.L. 99–554, set out as a note under section 581 of this title.

1984 Acts. Amendment by Pub.L. 98–353 effective July 10, 1984, see section 122(a) of Pub.L. 98–353, set out as a note under section 151 of this title.

1979 Acts. Section effective Oct. 1, 1979, see section 402(c) of Pub.L. 95–598, set out as a note preceding section 101 of Title 11, Bankruptcy.

Use of Increased Receipts

Pub.L. 109–8, Title III, § 325(e), Apr. 20, 2005, 119 Stat. 99, which pertained to the use of increased receipts from fees under subsec. (a) of this section, was omitted in the general amendment of Pub.L. 109–8, § 325, by Pub.L. 109–13, Div. A, Title VI, § 6058(a), May 11, 2005, 119 Stat. 297. Such amendment by Pub.L. 109–13, § 6058(a), effective immediately after the enactment of the Bankruptcy Abuse Prevention and Consumer Protection Act of 2005 [Pub.L. 109–8, Apr. 20, 2005, 119 Stat. 23], see Pub.L. 109–13, § 6058(b), set out as a note under 28 U.S.C.A. § 589a.

[Except as otherwise provided, amendments by Pub.L. 109–8 effective 180 days after April 20, 2005, and inapplicable with respect to cases commenced under Title 11 before the effective date, see Pub.L. 109–8, § 1501, set out as a note under 11 U.S.C.A. § 101.]

Effective and Applicability Provisions of 1989 Amendments; Miscellaneous Fees

Section 406(a) of Pub.L. 101–162 provided in part that: "Pursuant to section 1930(b) of title 28 [subsec. (b) of this section] the Judicial Conference of the United States shall prescribe a fee of $60 on motions seeking relief from the automatic stay under 11 U.S.C. section 362(b) [section 362(b) of Title 11, Bankruptcy] and motions to compel abandonment of property of the estate. The fees established pursuant to the preceding two sentences shall take effect 30 days after the enactment of this Act [Nov. 21, 1989]."

Accrual and Payment of Quarterly Fees in Chapter 11 Cases After Jan. 27, 1996; Confirmation Status of Plans

Section 101(a) of Pub.L. 104–91, as amended Pub.L. 104–99, Title II, § 211, Jan. 26, 1996, 110 Stat. 37; Pub.L. 104–208, Div. A, Title I, § 101(a) [Title I, § 109(d)], Sept. 30, 1996, 110 Stat. 3009–19, provided, in part: "That, notwithstanding any other provision of law, the fees under 28 U.S.C. 1930(a)(6) [subsec. (a)(6) of this section] shall accrue and be payable from and after January 27, 1996, in all cases (including, without limitation, any cases pending as of that date), regardless of confirmation status of their plans."

Collection and Disposition of Fees in Bankruptcy Cases

Section 404(a) of Pub. L. 101–162 provided that: "For fiscal year 1990 and hereafter, such fees as shall be collected for the preparation and mailing of notices in bankruptcy cases as prescribed by the Judicial Conference of the United States pursuant to 28 U.S.C. 1930(b) [subsec. (b) of this section] shall be deposited to the 'Courts of Appeals, District Courts, and Other Judicial Services, Salaries and Expenses' appropriation to be used for salaries and other expenses incurred in providing these services."

Court Fees for Electronic Access to Information

Judicial Conference to prescribe reasonable fees for collection by courts under this section for access to information available through automatic data processing equipment and fees to be deposited in Judiciary Automation Fund, see section 303 of Pub.L. 102–140, set out as a note under section 1913 of this title.

Issuance of Notices to Creditors and Other Interested Parties

Section 403 of Pub.L. 101–162 provided that: "Notwithstanding any other provision of law, for fiscal year 1990 and hereafter, (a) The Administrative Office of the United States Courts, or any other agency or instrumentality of the United States, is prohibited from restricting solely to staff of the Clerks of the United States Bankruptcy Courts the issuance of notices to creditors and other interested parties. (b) The Administrative Office shall permit and encourage the preparation and mailing of such notices to be performed by or at the expense of the debtors, trustees or such other interested parties as the Court may direct and approve. (c) The Director of the Administrative Office of the United States Courts shall make appropriate provisions for the use of and accounting for any postage required pursuant to such directives."

Report on Bankruptcy Fees

Section 111(d) of Pub.L. 103–121 provided that:

"**(1) Report required.**—Not later than March 31, 1998, the Judicial Conference of the United States shall submit to the Committees on the Judiciary of the House of Representatives and the Senate, a report relating to the bankruptcy fee system and the impact of such system on various participants in bankruptcy cases.

"**(2) Contents of report.**—Such report shall include—

"**(A)(i)** an estimate of the costs and benefits that would result from waiving bankruptcy fees payable by debtors who are individuals, and

"**(ii)** recommendations regarding various revenue sources to offset the net cost of waiving such fees; and

"**(B)(i)** an evaluation of the effects that would result in cases under chapters 11 and 13 of title 11, United States Code [sections 1101 et seq. and 1301 et seq., respectively, of Title 11, Bankruptcy], from using a graduated bankruptcy fee system based on assets, liabilities, or both of the debtor, and

"(ii) recommendations regarding various methods to implement such a graduated bankruptcy fee system.

"(3) **Waiver of fees in selected districts.**—For purposes of carrying out paragraphs (1) and (2), the Judicial Conference of the United States shall carry out in not more than six judicial districts, throughout the 3-year period beginning on October 1, 1994, a program under which fees payable under section 1930 of title 28, United States Code [this section], may be waived in cases under chapter 7 of title 11, United States Code [section 701 et seq. of Title 11], for debtors who are individuals unable to pay such fees in installments.

"(4) **Study of graduated fee system.**—For purposes of carrying out paragraphs (1) and (2), the Judicial Conference of the United States shall carry out, in not fewer than six judicial districts, a study to estimate the results that would occur in cases under chapters 11 and 13 of title 11, United States Code [sections 1101 et seq. and 1301 et seq., respectively, of Title 11], if filing fees payable under section 1930 of title 28, United States Code [this section], were paid on a graduated scale based on assets, liabilities, or both of the debtor."

§ 1931. Disposition of filing fees

(a) Of the amounts paid to the clerk of court as a fee under section 1914(a) or as part of a judgment for costs under section 2412(a)(2) of this title, $190 shall be deposited into a special fund of the Treasury to be available to offset funds appropriated for the operation and maintenance of the courts of the United States.

(b) If the court authorizes a fee under section 1914(a) or an amount included in a judgment for costs under section 2412(a)(2) of this title of less than $250, the entire fee or amount, up to $190, shall be deposited into the special fund provided in this section.

(Added Pub.L. 99–500, Title I, § 101(b) [Title IV, § 407(c)], Oct. 18, 1986, 100 Stat. 1783–64, and Pub.L. 99–591, Title I, § 101(b) [Title IV, § 407(c)], Oct. 30, 1986, 100 Stat. 3341–64, and amended Pub.L. 101–162, Title IV, § 406(d), Nov. 21, 1989, 103 Stat. 1016; Pub.L. 102–572, Title III, § 301(b), Oct. 29, 1992, 106 Stat. 4511; Pub.L. 104–317, Title IV, § 401(b), Oct. 19, 1996, 110 Stat. 3853; Pub.L. 108–447, Div. B, Title III, § 307(b), Dec. 8, 2004, 118 Stat. 2895.)

HISTORICAL AND STATUTORY NOTES

Codifications

Pub.L. 99–591 is a corrected version of Pub.L. 99–500.

Effective and Applicability Provisions

2004 Acts. Amendments by Pub.L. 108–447, Div. B, § 307(b), shall take effect 60 days after December 8, 2004, see Pub.L. 108–447, Div. B, § 307(c), set out as a note under 28 U.S.C.A. § 1914.

1996 Acts. Amendment by section 401(b) of Pub.L. 104–317 effective 60 days after Oct. 19, 1996, see section 401(c) of Pub.L. 104–317, set out as a note under section 1914 of this title.

1992 Acts. Amendment by Pub.L. 102–572 effective Jan. 1, 1993, see section 1101(a) of Pub.L. 102–572, set out as a note under section 905 of Title 2, The Congress.

Expenditure Limitation

Pub.L. 109–171, Title X, § 10001(c), Feb. 8, 2006, 120 Stat. 183, provided that: "Incremental amounts collected by reason of the enactment of this section [Pub.L. 109–171, Title X, § 10001, Feb. 8, 2006, 120 Stat. 183, which amended 28 U.S.C.A. § 1914 and enacted this note and provisions set out as notes under 28 U.S.C.A. §§ 1913 and 1914] shall be deposited in a special fund in the Treasury to be established after the enactment of this Act [Feb. 8, 2006]. Such amounts shall be available for the purposes specified in section 1931(a) of title 28, United States Code [subsec. (a) of this section], but only to the extent specifically appropriated by an Act of Congress enacted after the enactment of this Act [Feb. 8, 2006]."

[This note effective 60 days after Feb. 8, 2006, see Pub.L. 109–171, § 10001(d), set out as a note under 28 U.S.C.A. § 1914]

Pub.L. 109–171, Title X, § 10101(b), Feb. 8, 2006, 120 Stat. 184, provided that: "Incremental amounts collected by reason of the amendments made by subsection (a) [amending 28 U.S.C.A. § 1930] shall be deposited in a special fund in the Treasury to be established after the enactment of this Act [Feb. 8, 2006]. Such amounts shall be available for the purposes specified in section 1931(a) of title 28, United States Code [subsec. (a) of this section], but only to the extent specifically appropriated by an Act of Congress enacted after the enactment of this Act [Feb. 8, 2006]."

[This note effective 60 days after Feb. 8, 2006, see Pub.L. 109–171, § 10101(c), set out as a note under 28 U.S.C.A. § 1930]

Disposition of Miscellaneous Fees

Pub.L. 106–518, Title I, § 102, Nov. 13, 2000, 114 Stat. 2411, provided that: "For fiscal year 2001 and each fiscal year thereafter, any portion of miscellaneous fees collected as prescribed by the Judicial Conference of the United States under sections 1913 [this section], 1914(b), 1926(a), 1930(b), and 1932 of title 28, United States Code, exceeding the amount of such fees in effect on September 30, 2000, shall be deposited into the special fund of the Treasury established under section 1931 of title 28, United States Code [this section]."

Collection and Deposit of Miscellaneous Bankruptcy Fees

Section 406(b) of Pub.L. 101–162, as amended Pub.L. 103–121, Title I, § 111(a)(3), (b)(4), Oct. 27, 1993, 107 Stat. 1164; Pub.L. 106–113, Div. B, § 1000(a)(1) [Title I, § 113], Nov. 29, 1999, 113 Stat. 1535, 1501A–20; Pub.L. 106–518, Title II, § 209(a), Nov. 13, 2000, 114 Stat. 2415; Pub.L. 109–8, Title III, § 325(c), Apr. 20, 2005, 119 Stat. 99; Pub.L. 109–13, Div. A, Title VI, § 6058(a), May 11, 2005, 119 Stat. 297, provided that: "All fees as shall be hereafter collected for any service not of a kind described in any of the items enumerated as items 1 through 7 and as items 9 through 18, as in effect on November 21, 1989, of the bankruptcy miscellaneous fee schedule prescribed by the Judicial Conference of the United States under section 1930(b) of title 28, United States Code [28 U.S.C.A. § 1930(b)], 28.87 percent of the fees collected under section 1930(a)(1)(A) of that title [28 U.S.C.A. § 1930(a)(1)(A)], 35.00 percent of the fees collected under section 1930(a)(1)(B) of that title [28 U.S.C.A. § 1930(a)(1)(B)], and 25 percent of the fees collected under section 1930(a)(3) of that title [28 U.S.C.A. § 1930(a)(3)] shall be deposited as offsetting receipts to the fund established under section 1931 of that title [this section] and shall remain available to the Judiciary until expended to reimburse any appropriation for the amount paid out of such appropriation for expenses of the Courts of Appeals, District Courts, and other Judicial Services and the Administrative Office of the United States Courts. The Judicial Conference shall report to the Committees on Appropriations of the House of Representatives and the Senate on a quarterly basis beginning on the first day of each fiscal year regarding the sums deposited in said fund."

[Pub.L. 109–8, § 325(c), as amended by Pub.L. 109–13, § 6058(a), amended this note effective immediately after the enactment of the Bankruptcy Abuse Prevention and Consumer Protection Act of 2005 [Pub.L. 109–8, Apr. 20, 2005, 119 Stat. 23], see Pub.L. 109–13, § 6058(b), set out as an Effective and Applicability Provisions note under 28 U.S.C.A. § 589a.]

[Amendment of this note by Pub.L. 109–8, § 325(c), to become effective during the 2–year period beginning on Apr. 20, 2005, under the terms of Pub.L. 109–8, § 325(d), but was omitted in the amendment of Pub.L. 109–8, § 325 by Pub.L. 109–13, § 6058(a); see Pub.L. 109–8, § 325(d), as amended by Pub.L. 109–13, § 6058(a), set out as a Sunset Provisions note under 28 U.S.C.A. § 589a.]

[For termination, effective May 15, 2000, of provisions relating to a quarterly report to the Committees on Appropriations of the House of Representatives and the Senate in section 406(b) of Pub.L. 101–162, as amended, set out as a note above, see Pub.L. 104–66, § 3003, as amended, set out as a note under 31 U.S.C.A. § 1113 and page 12 of House Document No. 103–7.]

[Amendment of this note by Pub.L. 106–113, [§ 113], effective 30 days after Nov. 29, 1999, see Pub.L. 106–113, [§ 113], set out as a note under section 589a of this title.]

[Pub.L. 106–518, Title II, § 209(b), Nov. 13,, 2000, 114 Stat. 2415, provided that: "The amendment made by subsection (a) [amending this note] shall not apply with respect to fees collected before the date of enactment of this Act [Nov. 13, 2000]."

[Section 111(a) of Pub.L. 103–121 provided in part that amendment of this note by section 111(a)(3) of Pub.L. 103–121 is effective 30 days after Oct. 27, 1993.]

[Section 111(b) of Pub.L. 103–121 provided in part that amendment of this note by section 111(b)(4) of Pub.L. 103–121 is effective 30 days after Oct. 27, 1993.]

Disposition of Fees

Section 404 of Pub.L. 104–317 provided that:

"**(a) Disposition of attorney admission fees.**—For each fee collected for admission of an attorney to practice, as prescribed by the Judicial Conference of the United States pursuant to section 1914 of title 28, United States Code [section 1914 of this title], $30 of that portion of the fee exceeding $20 shall be deposited into the special fund of the Treasury established under section 1931 of title 28, United States Code [this section]. Any portion exceeding $5 of the fee for a duplicate certificate of admission or certificate of good standing, as prescribed by the Judicial Conference of the United States pursuant to section 1914 of title 28, United States Code [section 1914 of this title], shall be deposited into the special fund of the Treasury established under section 1931 of title 28, United States Code [this section].

"**(b) Disposition of bankruptcy complaint filing fees.**—For each fee collected for filing an adversary complaint in a bankruptcy proceeding, as established in Item 6 of the Bankruptcy Court Miscellaneous Fee Schedule prescribed by the Judicial Conference of the United States [set out under section 1930 of this title] pursuant to section 1930(b) of title 28, United States Code [section 1930(b) of this title], the portion of the fee exceeding $120 shall be deposited into the special fund of the Treasury established under section 1931 of title 28, United States Code [this section].

"**(c) Effective date.**—This section shall take effect 60 days after the date of the enactment of this Act [Oct. 19, 1996]."

§ 1932.[1] Judicial Panel on Multidistrict Litigation

The Judicial Conference of the United States shall prescribe from time to time the fees and costs to be charged and collected by the Judicial Panel on Multidistrict Litigation.

(Added Pub.L. 104–317, Title IV, § 403(a)(1), Oct. 19, 1996, 110 Stat. 3854.)

[1] Another section 1932 is set out post.

JUDICIAL CONFERENCE SCHEDULE OF FEES

Judicial Panel on Multidistrict Litigation Fee Schedule

[The Judicial Conference of the United States issued pursuant to this section the schedule of the fees to be charged and collected by the Judicial Panel on Multidistrict Litigation effective October 1, 1999. The Judicial Conference at its March 2001 meeting adopted amendments to its fee schedule to be effective July 1, 2001. The Judicial Conference adopted amendments to its fee schedule effective January 1, 2002; and effective November 1, 2003. The Judicial Conference at its March 16, 2004 meeting adopted amendments to its fee schedule to be effective June 1, 2004.]

Following are fees to be charged for services provided by the Judicial Panel on Multidistrict Litigation. No fees are to be charged for services rendered on behalf of the United States, with the exception of those specifically prescribed in items 1 and 3. No fees under this schedule shall be charged to federal agencies or programs which are funded from judiciary appropriations, including, but not limited to, agencies, organizations, and individuals providing services authorized by the Criminal Justice Act, 18 U.S.C. § 3006A.

(1) For every search of the records of the court conducted by the clerk of the court or a deputy clerk, $26 per name or item searched. This fee shall apply to services rendered on behalf of the United States if the information requested is available through electronic access.

(2) For certification of any document or paper, whether the certification is made directly on the document or by separate instrument, $9.

(3) For reproducing any record or paper, $.50 per page. This fee shall apply to paper copies made from either: (1)

original documents; or (2) microfiche or microfilm reproductions of the original records. This fee shall apply to services rendered on behalf of the United States if the record or paper requested is available through electronic access.

(4) For retrieval of a record from a Federal Records Center, National Archives, or other storage location removed from the place of business of the court, $45.

(5) For a check paid into the Panel which is returned for lack of funds, $45.

ELECTRONIC PUBLIC ACCESS FEE SCHEDULE (eff. 3/11/2008)

As directed by Congress, the Judicial Conference has determined that the following fees are necessary to reimburse expenses incurred by the judiciary in providing electronic public access to court records. These fees shall apply to the United States unless otherwise stated. No fees under this schedule shall be charged to federal agencies or programs which are funded from judiciary appropriations, including, but not limited to, agencies, organizations, and individuals providing services authorized by the Criminal Justice Act, 18 U.S.C. § 3006A, and bankruptcy administrator programs.

I. For electronic access to court data via a federal judiciary Internet site: 8 cents per page, with the total for any document, docket sheet, or case-specific report not to exceed the fee for 30 pages—provided however that transcripts of federal court proceedings shall not be subject to the 30-page fee limit. Attorneys of record and parties in a case (including pro se litigants) receive one free electronic copy of all documents filed electronically, if receipt is required by law or directed by the filer. No fee is owed under this provision until an account holder accrues charges of more than $10 in a calendar year. Consistent with Judicial Conference policy, courts may, upon a showing of cause, exempt indigents, bankruptcy case trustees, individual researchers associated with educational institutions, courts, section 501(c)(3) not-for-profit organizations, court appointed pro bono attorneys, and pro bono ADR neutrals from payment of these fees. Courts must find that parties from the classes of persons or entities listed above seeking exemption have demonstrated that an exemption is necessary in order to avoid unreasonable burdens and to promote public access to information. Any user granted an exemption agrees not to sell for profit the data obtained as a result. Any transfer of data obtained as the result of a fee exemption is prohibited unless expressly authorized by the court. Exemptions may be granted for a definite period of time and may be revoked at the discretion of the court granting the exemption.

II. For printing copies of any record or document accessed electronically at a public terminal in the courthouse: 10 cents per page. This fee shall apply to services rendered on behalf of the United States if the record requested is remotely available through electronic access.

III. For every search of court records conducted by the PACER Service Center, $26 per name or item searched.

IV. For the PACER Service Center to reproduce on paper any record pertaining to a PACER account, if this information is remotely available through electronic access, 50 cents per page.

V. For a check paid to the PACER Service Center which is returned for lack of funds, $45.

JUDICIAL CONFERENCE POLICY NOTES

Courts should not exempt local, state or federal government agencies, members of the media, attorneys or others not members of one of the groups listed above. Exemptions should be granted as the exception, not the rule. A court may not use this exemption language to exempt all users. An exemption applies only to access related to the case or purpose for which it was given. The prohibition on transfer of information received without fee is not intended to bar a quote or reference to information received as a result of a fee exemption in a scholarly or other similar work.

The electronic public access fee applies to electronic court data viewed remotely from the public records of individual cases in the court, including filed documents and the docket sheet. Electronic court data may be viewed free at public terminals at the courthouse and courts may provide other local court information at no cost. Examples of information that can be provided at no cost include: local rules, court forms, news items, court calendars, opinions, and other information—such as court hours, court location, telephone listings—determined locally to benefit the public and the court.

§ 1932.[1] Revocation of earned release credit

In any civil action brought by an adult convicted of a crime and confined in a Federal correctional facility, the court may order the revocation of such earned good time credit under section 3624(b) of title 18, United States Code, that has not yet vested, if, on its own motion or the motion of any party, the court finds that—

(1) the claim was filed for a malicious purpose;

(2) the claim was filed solely to harass the party against which it was filed; or

(3) the claimant testifies falsely or otherwise knowingly presents false evidence or information to the court.

(Added Pub.L. 104–134, Title I, § 101[(a)][Title VIII, § 809(a)], Apr. 26, 1996, 110 Stat. 1321–76; renumbered Title I Pub.L. 104–140, § 1(a), May 2, 1996, 110 Stat. 1327.)

[1] Another section 1932 is set out ante.

HISTORICAL AND STATUTORY NOTES

Severability of Provisions

If any provision of section 101[a] [Title VIII] of Pub.L. 104–134, an amendment made by such Title, or the application of such provision or amendment to any person or circumstance is held to be unconstitutional, the remainder of such Title, the amendments made by such Title, and the application of the provisions of such Title to any person or circumstance not affected thereby, see section 101[a] [Title VIII, § 810] of Pub.L. 104–134, set out as a note under section 3626 of Title 18, Crimes and Criminal Procedure.

CHAPTER 125—PENDING ACTIONS AND JUDGMENTS

Sec.
1961. Interest.
1962. Lien.
1963. Registration of judgments for enforcement in other districts.
[1963A. Repealed.]
1964. Constructive notice of pending actions.

§ 1961. Interest

(a) Interest shall be allowed on any money judgment in a civil case recovered in a district court. Execution therefor may be levied by the marshal, in any case where, by the law of the State in which such court is held, execution may be levied for interest on judgments recovered in the courts of the State. Such interest shall be calculated from the date of the entry of the judgment, at a rate equal to the weekly average 1–year constant maturity Treasury yield, as published by the Board of Governors of the Federal Reserve System, for the calendar week preceding.[1] the date of the judgment. The Director of the Administrative Office of the United States Courts shall distribute notice of that rate and any changes in it to all Federal judges.

(b) Interest shall be computed daily to the date of payment except as provided in section 2516(b) of this title and section 1304(b) of title 31, and shall be compounded annually.

(c)(1) This section shall not apply in any judgment of any court with respect to any internal revenue tax case. Interest shall be allowed in such cases at the underpayment rate or overpayment rate (whichever is appropriate) established under section 6621 of the Internal Revenue Code of 1986.

(2) Except as otherwise provided in paragraph (1) of this subsection, interest shall be allowed on all final judgments against the United States in the United States Court of Appeals for the Federal circuit,[2] at the rate provided in subsection (a) and as provided in subsection (b).

(3) Interest shall be allowed, computed, and paid on judgments of the United States Court of Federal Claims only as provided in paragraph (1) of this subsection or in any other provision of law.

(4) This section shall not be construed to affect the interest on any judgment of any court not specified in this section.

(June 25, 1948, c. 646, 62 Stat. 957; Apr. 2, 1982, Pub.L. 97–164, Title III, § 302(a), 96 Stat. 55; Sept. 13, 1982, Pub.L. 97–258, § 2(m)(1), 96 Stat. 1062; Jan. 12, 1983, Pub.L. 97–452, § 2(d)(1), 96 Stat. 2478; Oct. 22, 1986, Pub.L. 99–514, § 2, Title XV, § 1511(c)(17), 100 Stat. 2095, 2745; Oct. 29, 1992, Pub.L. 102–572, Title IX, § 902(b)(1), 106 Stat. 4516; Dec. 21, 2000, Pub.L. 106–554, § 1(a)(7) [Title III, § 307(d)(1)], 114 Stat. 2763, 2763A–636.)

[1] So in original. The period probably should not appear.
[2] So in original. Probably should be "Circuit,".

HISTORICAL AND STATUTORY NOTES

References in Text

Section 6621 of the Internal Revenue Code of 1986, referred to in subsec. (c)(1), is section 6621 of Title 26, Internal Revenue Code.

Codifications

Amendment of subsec. (b) by Pub.L. 97–452, substituting "section 1304(b) of title 31" for "section 1302 of the Act of July 27, 1956 (31 U.S.C. 724a)" was executed without reference to the intervening amendment by Pub.L. 97–258, as the probable intent of Congress.

Effective and Applicability Provisions

1992 Acts. Amendment by Pub.L. 102–572 effective Oct. 29, 1992, see section 911 of Pub.L. 102–572, set out as a note under section 171 of this title.

1986 Acts. Amendment by section 1511(c)(17) of Pub.L. 99–514 applicable for purposes of determining interest for periods after Dec. 31, 1986, see section 1511(d) of Pub.L. 99–514, set out as a note under section 47 of Title 26, Internal Revenue Code.

1982 Acts. Section 2(m) of Pub.L. 97–258 provided in part that the amendment to subsec. (b) would be effective on Oct. 1, 1982.

Amendment by Pub.L. 97–164 effective Oct. 1, 1982, see section 402 of Pub.L. 97–164, set out as a note under section 171 of this title.

Calculation of Interest

The method of calculation of interest on money judgments in civil cases recovered in district courts changed as of December 21, 2000, the date of enactment of Pub.L. 106–554, § 1(a)(7) [Title III, § 307(d)(1)] which amended subsec. (a) of this section. It was formerly calculated at a rate equal to the coupon issue yield equivalent (as determined by the Secretary of the Treasury) of the average accepted auction price for the last auction of fifty-two week United States Treasury bills (for past rates, see Table set out below). It is now calculated at a rate equal to the weekly average 1-year constant maturity Treasury yield, as published by the Board of Governors of the Federal Reserve System. For information regarding weekly releases, see *www.federalreserve.gov.*

52–WEEK T–BILL RATE TABLE OF CHANGES

Date of Auction	Equivalent Coupon Issue Yield
12/11/74	7.07%
01/08/75	6.80%
02/05/75	5.61%
03/05/75	5.99%
04/02/75	6.92%
04/30/75	6.84%
05/28/75	6.17%
06/24/75	6.72%
07/24/75	7.27%
08/20/75	7.89%

Date of Auction	Equivalent Coupon Issue Yield
09/17/75	7.90%
10/18/75	7.07%
11/13/75	6.40%
12/10/75	6.88%
01/07/76	5.92%
02/04/76	5.92%
03/03/76	6.29%
03/31/76	6.13%
04/29/76	5.98%
05/26/76	6.72%
06/23/76	6.47%
07/21/76	6.25%
08/19/76	5.97%
09/15/76	5.89%
10/13/76	5.41%
11/09/76	5.49%
12/08/76	4.95%
01/05/77	4.97%
02/02/77	5.65%
03/02/77	5.52%
03/30/77	5.44%
04/27/77	5.45%
05/25/77	5.71%
06/22/77	5.72%
07/20/77	5.98%
08/17/77	6.49%
09/14/77	6.55%
10/12/77	7.07%
11/09/77	6.98%
12/07/77	6.99%
01/04/78	6.99%
02/01/78	7.29%
03/01/78	7.34%
03/29/78	7.36%
04/26/78	7.58%
05/24/78	7.97%
06/21/78	8.27%
07/19/78	8.43%
08/16/78	8.50%
09/13/78	8.59%
10/12/78	8.90%
11/08/78	10.17%
12/06/78	10.17%
01/03/79	10.51%
01/31/79	10.21%
02/28/79	10.40%
04/04/79	10.09%
04/25/79	10.10%
05/23/79	10.01%
06/20/79	9.63%
07/18/79	9.70%
08/15/79	10.05%
09/12/79	10.88%
10/10/79	12.83%
11/07/79	13.18%
12/05/79	11.98%
01/02/80	12.25%
01/30/80	12.45%
02/27/80	15.28%
03/26/80	16.46%
04/23/80	11.45%
05/21/80	9.02%
06/18/80	8.08%
07/16/80	8.25%
08/13/80	9.75%
09/10/80	10.93%
10/08/80	13.33%
10/30/80	13.67%
11/26/80	14.97%
12/23/80	13.49%
01/22/81	14.68%
02/19/81	14.39%
03/19/81	12.76%
04/16/81	14.63%
05/14/81	16.70%
06/11/81	14.82%
07/09/81	15.57%
08/07/81	16.60%
09/03/81	17.26%
10/01/81	16.55%
10/29/81	14.84%
11/25/81	11.58%
12/23/81	14.02%
01/21/82	14.92%
02/18/82	14.87%
03/18/82	14.03%
04/15/82	14.30%
05/13/82	13.64%
06/10/82	13.61%
07/08/82	13.79%
08/05/82	12.41%
09/02/82	11.32%
09/30/82	10.41%
10/28/82	9.29%
11/24/82	9.07%
12/23/82	8.75%
01/20/83	8.65%
02/17/83	8.99%
03/17/83	9.16%
04/14/83	8.98%
05/12/83	8.72%
06/09/83	9.59%
07/07/83	10.25%
08/09/83	10.74%
09/01/83	10.58%
09/29/83	9.98%
11/01/83	9.86%
11/23/83	9.93%
12/22/83	10.10%
01/19/84	9.87%
02/16/84	10.11%
03/15/84	10.60%
04/12/84	10.81%
05/15/84	11.74%
06/07/84	12.08%
07/10/84	12.17%
08/02/84	11.93%
08/30/84	11.98%
09/27/84	11.36%
10/25/84	10.33%
11/27/84	9.50%
12/20/84	9.08%
01/17/85	9.09%
02/14/85	9.17%

Date of Auction	Equivalent Coupon Issue Yield
03/14/85	10.08%
04/11/85	9.15%
05/14/85	8.57%
06/06/85	7.70%
07/09/85	7.60%
08/01/85	8.18%
08/29/85	7.91%
09/26/85	7.87%
10/24/85	8.08%
11/26/85	7.87%
12/19/85	7.57%
01/16/86	7.85%
02/13/86	7.71%
03/13/86	7.06%
04/10/86	6.31%
05/13/86	6.56%
06/05/86	7.03%
07/08/86	6.35%
07/31/86	6.18%
08/28/86	5.63%
09/25/86	5.79%
10/23/86	5.75%
11/20/86	5.77%
12/23/86	5.93%
01/15/87	5.75%
02/12/87	6.09%
03/12/87	6.04%
04/09/87	6.30%
05/12/87	7.02%
06/04/87	7.00%
07/02/87	6.64%
08/04/87	6.98%
09/01/87	7.22%
09/30/87	7.88%
10/22/87	6.90%
11/19/87	6.93%
12/17/87	7.22%
01/14/88	7.14%
02/11/88	6.59%
03/10/88	6.71%
04/07/88	7.01%
05/05/88	7.20%
06/02/88	7.59%
06/30/88	7.54%
07/28/88	7.95%
08/25/88	8.32%
09/22/88	8.04%
10/20/88	8.15%
11/17/88	8.55%
12/15/88	9.20%
01/12/89	9.16%
02/15/89	9.32%
03/09/89	9.43%
04/06/89	9.31%
05/04/89	9.15%
06/01/89	8.85%
06/29/89	8.16%
07/27/89	7.75%
08/24/89	8.27%
09/21/89	8.19%
10/19/89	7.90%
11/16/89	7.69%
12/14/89	7.66%
01/11/90	7.74%
02/13/90	7.97%
03/08/90	8.36%
04/05/90	8.32%
05/03/90	8.70%
05/31/90	8.24%
06/28/90	8.09%
07/26/90	7.88%
08/23/90	7.95%
09/20/90	7.78%
10/26/90	7.51%
11/15/90	7.28%
12/13/90	7.02%
01/10/91	6.62%
02/12/91	6.21%
03/07/91	6.46%
04/04/91	6.26%
05/02/91	6.07%
05/30/91	6.09%
06/27/91	6.39%
07/25/91	6.26%
08/22/91	5.68%
09/19/91	5.57%
10/17/91	5.42%
11/14/91	4.98%
12/12/91	4.41%
01/09/92	4.02%
02/06/92	4.21%
03/05/92	4.58%
04/02/92	4.55%
04/30/92	4.40%
05/28/92	4.26%
06/25/92	4.11%
07/23/92	3.51%
08/20/92	3.41%
09/17/92	3.13%
10/15/92	3.24%
11/17/92	3.76%
12/10/92	3.72%
01/07/93	3.67%
02/04/93	3.45%
03/04/93	3.21%
04/06/93	3.37%
04/30/93	3.25%
05/27/93	3.54%
06/24/93	3.54%
07/22/93	3.58%
08/19/93	3.43%
09/16/93	3.40%
10/14/93	3.38%
11/16/93	3.57%
12/09/93	3.61%
01/06/94	3.67%
02/03/94	3.74%
03/03/94	4.22%
03/31/94	4.51%
04/28/94	5.02%
5/26/94	5.28%
6/23/94	5.31%
7/21/94	5.49%
8/18/94	5.67%

Date of Auction	Equivalent Coupon Issue Yield
9/15/94	5.69%
10/13/94	6.06%
11/10/94	6.482%
12/08/94	7.22%
1/5/95	7.34%
2/2/95	7.03%
3/2/95	6.57%
3/30/95	6.41%
4/27/95	6.28%
5/25/95	5.88%
6/22/95	5.53%
7/20/95	5.70%
8/17/95	5.89%
9/14/95	5.52%
10/12/95	5.62%
11/15/95	5.45%
12/7/95	5.35%
1/4/96	5.16%
2/1/96	4.89%
2/29/96	5.25%
4/2/96	5.46%
4/25/96	5.60%
5/23/96	5.62%
6/20/96	5.89%
7/18/96	5.81%
8/15/96	5.67%
9/12/96	5.90%
10/10/96	5.64%
11/7/96	5.49%
12/5/96	5.45%
1/2/97	5.61%
1/30/97	5.64%
2/27/97	5.67%
3/26/97	6.00%
4/24/97	6.06%
5/22/97	5.88%
6/19/97	5.65%
7/17/97	5.56%
8/14/97	5.58%
9/11/97	5.60%
10/9/97	5.49%
11/6/97	5.42%
12/4/97	5.468%
1/6/98	5.341%
1/29/98	5.232%
2/26/98	5.407%
3/26/98	5.391%
4/23/98	5.407%
5/21/98	5.434%
6/18/98	5.413%
7/16/98	5.375%
8/18/98	5.271%
9/15/98	4.730%
10/13/98	4.242%
11/9/98	4.616%
12/8/98	4.513%
1/5/99	4.545%
2/2/99	4.584%
3/2/99	4.918%
3/30/99	4.732%
4/27/99	4.727%
5/25/99	4.879%
6/22/99	5.163%
7/20/99	4.966%
8/17/99	5.224%
9/14/99	5.285%
10/13/99	5.411%
11/9/99	5.471%
12/7/99	5.670%
1/4/00	5.997%
2/1/00	6.287%
2/29/00	6.197%
5/31/00	6.375%
8/29/00	6.241%
11/28/00	6.052%

§ 1962. Lien

Every judgment rendered by a district court within a State shall be a lien on the property located in such State in the same manner, to the same extent and under the same conditions as a judgment of a court of general jurisdiction in such State, and shall cease to be a lien in the same manner and time. This section does not apply to judgments entered in favor of the United States. Whenever the law of any State requires a judgment of a State court to be registered, recorded, docketed or indexed, or any other act to be done, in a particular manner, or in a certain office or county or parish before such lien attaches, such requirements shall apply only if the law of such State authorizes the judgment of a court of the United States to be registered, recorded, docketed, indexed or otherwise conformed to rules and requirements relating to judgments of the courts of the State. (June 25, 1948, c. 646, 62 Stat. 958; Nov. 29, 1990, Pub.L. 101–647, Title XXXVI, § 3627, 104 Stat. 4965.)

HISTORICAL AND STATUTORY NOTES

Effective and Applicability Provisions

1990 Acts. Amendment by section 3627 of Pub.L. 101–647 effective 180 days after Nov. 29, 1990, see section 3631 of Pub.L. 101–647, set out as a note under section 3001 of this title.

§ 1963. Registration of judgments for enforcement in other districts

A judgment in an action for the recovery of money or property entered in any court of appeals, district court, bankruptcy court, or in the Court of International Trade may be registered by filing a certified copy of the judgment in any other district or, with respect to the Court of International Trade, in any judicial district, when the judgment has become final by appeal or expiration of the time for appeal or when ordered by the court that entered the judgment for good cause shown. Such a judgment entered in favor of the United States may be so registered any time after judgment is entered. A judgment so registered shall have the same effect as a judgment of the district court of the district where registered and may be enforced in like manner.

A certified copy of the satisfaction of any judgment in whole or in part may be registered in like manner in any district in which the judgment is a lien.

The procedure prescribed under this section is in addition to other procedures provided by law for the enforcement of judgments.

(June 25, 1948, c. 646, 62 Stat. 958; Aug. 23, 1954, c. 837, 68 Stat. 772; July 7, 1958, Pub.L. 85–508, § 12(*o*), 72 Stat. 349; Nov. 19, 1988, Pub.L. 100–702, Title X, § 1002(a), (b)(1), 102 Stat. 4664; Nov. 29, 1990, Pub.L. 101–647, Title XXXVI, § 3628, 104 Stat. 4965; Oct. 19, 1996, Pub.L. 104–317, Title II, § 203(a), 110 Stat. 3849.)

HISTORICAL AND STATUTORY NOTES

Effective and Applicability Provisions

1990 Acts. Amendment by section 3628 of Pub.L. 101–647 effective 180 days after Nov. 29, 1990, see section 3631 of Pub.L. 101–647, set out as a note under section 3001 of this title.

1988 Acts. Section 1002(c) of Title X of Pub.L. 100–702 provided that: "The amendments made by this section [amending this section and repealing section 1963A of this title] take effect 90 days after the date of enactment of this title [Nov. 19, 1988]."

1958 Acts. Amendment by Pub.L. 85–508 as effective Jan. 3, 1959, upon admission of Alaska into the Union pursuant to Proc. No. 3269, Jan. 3, 1959, 24 F.R. 81, as required by sections 1 and 8(c) of Pub.L. 85–508, see notes set out under section 81A of this title and preceding section 21 of Title 48, Territories and Insular Possessions.

[§ 1963A. Repealed. Pub.L. 100–702, Title X, § 1002(b)(2), Nov. 19, 1988, 102 Stat. 4664]

HISTORICAL AND STATUTORY NOTES

Section, added Pub.L. 96–417, Title V, § 511(a), Oct. 10, 1980, 94 Stat. 1743, provided for registration of judgments of the Court of International Trade. See section 1963 of this title.

Effective Date of Repeal

Section repealed 90 days after Nov. 19, 1988, see section 1002(c) of Pub.L. 100–702, set out as a note under section 1963 of this title.

§ 1964. Constructive notice of pending actions

Where the law of a State requires a notice of an action concerning real property pending in a court of the State to be registered, recorded, docketed, or indexed in a particular manner, or in a certain office or county or parish in order to give constructive notice of the action as it relates to the real property, and such law authorizes a notice of an action concerning real property pending in a United States district court to be registered, recorded, docketed, or indexed in the same manner, or in the same place, those requirements of the State law must be complied with in order to give constructive notice of such an action pending in a United States district court as it relates to real property in such State.

(Added Pub.L. 85–689, § 1(a), Aug. 20, 1958, 72 Stat. 683.)

HISTORICAL AND STATUTORY NOTES

Effective and Applicability Provisions

1958 Acts. Section 2 of Pub.L. 85–689 provided that: "The amendments made by this Act [adding this section] shall only be effective with respect to actions commenced in United States district courts more than one hundred and eighty days after the date of enactment of this Act [Aug. 20, 1958]."

CHAPTER 127—EXECUTIONS AND JUDICIAL SALES

Sec.
2001. Sale of realty generally.
2002. Notice of sale of realty.
2003. Marshal's incapacity after levy on or sale of realty.
2004. Sale of personalty generally.
2005. Appraisal of goods taken on execution.
2006. Execution against revenue officer.
2007. Imprisonment for debt.

§ 2001. Sale of realty generally

(a) Any realty or interest therein sold under any order or decree of any court of the United States shall be sold as a whole or in separate parcels at public sale at the courthouse of the county, parish, or city in which the greater part of the property is located, or upon the premises or some parcel thereof located therein, as the court directs. Such sale shall be upon such terms and conditions as the court directs.

Property in the possession of a receiver or receivers appointed by one or more district courts shall be sold at public sale in the district wherein any such receiver was first appointed, at the courthouse of the county, parish, or city situated therein in which the greater part of the property in such district is located, or on the premises or some parcel thereof located in such county, parish, or city, as such court directs, unless the court orders the sale of the property or one or more parcels thereof in one or more ancillary districts.

(b) After a hearing, of which notice to all interested parties shall be given by publication or otherwise as the court directs, the court may order the sale of such realty or interest or any part thereof at private sale for cash or other consideration and upon such terms and conditions as the court approves, if it finds that the best interests of the estate will be conserved thereby. Before confirmation of any private sale, the court shall appoint three disinterested persons to appraise such property or different groups of three appraisers each to appraise properties of different classes or situated in different localities. No private sale shall be confirmed at a price less than two-thirds of the appraised value. Before confirmation of any private sale, the terms thereof shall be published in such newspaper or newspapers of general circulation as the court directs at least ten days before confirmation. The private sale shall not be confirmed if a bona fide offer is made, under conditions prescribed by the court, which guarantees at least a 10 per centum increase over the price offered in the private sale.

(c) This section shall not apply to sales and proceedings under Title 11 or by receivers or conservators of banks appointed by the Comptroller of the Currency.

(June 25, 1948, c. 646, 62 Stat. 958; May 24, 1949, c. 139, § 99, 63 Stat. 104.)

§ 2002. Notice of sale of realty

A public sale of realty or interest therein under any order, judgment or decree of any court of the United States shall not be made without notice published once a week for at least four weeks prior to the sale in at least one newspaper regularly issued and of general circulation in the county, state, or judicial district of the United States wherein the realty is situated.

If such realty is situated in more than one county, state, district or circuit, such notice shall be published in one or more of the counties, states, or districts wherein it is situated, as the court directs. The notice shall be substantially in such form and contain such description of the property by reference or otherwise as the court approves. The court may direct that the publication be made in other newspapers.

This section shall not apply to sales and proceedings under Title 11 or by receivers or conservators of banks appointed by the Comptroller of the Currency.

(June 25, 1948, c. 646, 62 Stat. 959; May 24, 1949, c. 139, § 100, 63 Stat. 104.)

§ 2003. Marshal's incapacity after levy on or sale of realty

Whenever a United States marshal dies, is removed from office, or the term of his commission expires, after levying on realty or any interest therein under a writ of execution issued by a court of the United States, and before sale or other final disposition thereof, like process shall issue to the succeeding marshal and the same proceedings shall be had as if such contingency had not occurred.

Whenever any such contingency arises after a marshal has sold any realty or interest therein and before a deed is executed, the court may, on application by the purchaser, or the plaintiff in whose action the sale was made, setting forth the facts of the case and the reason why the title was not perfected by such marshal, order the succeeding marshal to perfect the title and execute a deed to the purchaser, upon payment of the purchase money and unpaid costs.

(June 25, 1948, c. 646, 62 Stat. 959; May 24, 1949, c. 139, § 101, 63 Stat. 104.)

§ 2004. Sale of personalty generally

Any personalty sold under any order or decree of any court of the United States shall be sold in accordance with section 2001 of this title, unless the court orders otherwise.

This section shall not apply to sales and proceedings under Title 11 or by receivers or conservators of banks appointed by the Comptroller of the Currency.

(June 25, 1948, c. 646, 62 Stat. 959.)

§ 2005. Appraisal of goods taken on execution

Whenever State law requires that goods taken on execution be appraised before sale, goods taken under execution issued from a court of the United States shall be appraised in like manner.

The United States marshal shall summon the appraisers in the same manner as the sheriff is required to summon appraisers under State law.

If the appraisers fail to attend and perform their required duties, the marshal may sell the goods without an appraisal. Appraisers attending and performing their duties, shall receive the fees allowed for appraisals under State law.

(June 25, 1948, c. 646, 62 Stat. 959.)

§ 2006. Execution against revenue officer

Execution shall not issue against a collector or other revenue officer on a final judgment in any proceeding against him for any of his acts, or for the recovery of any money exacted by or paid to him and subsequently paid into the Treasury, in performing his official duties, if the court certifies that:

(1) probable cause existed; or

(2) the officer acted under the directions of the Secretary of the Treasury, the Director, Bureau of Alcohol, Tobacco, Firearms, and Explosives, Department of Justice, or other proper Government officer.

When such certificate has been issued, the amount of the judgment shall be paid out of the proper appropriation by the Treasury.

(June 25, 1948, c. 646, 62 Stat. 960; Nov. 25, 2002, Pub.L. 107–296, Title XI, § 1112(*l*), 116 Stat. 2277.)

HISTORICAL AND STATUTORY NOTES

Effective and Applicability Provisions

2002 Acts. Amendment to this section by Pub.L. 107–296 effective 60 days after Nov. 25, 2002, see Pub.L. 107–296, § 4, set out as a note under 6 U.S.C.A. § 101.

§ 2007. Imprisonment for debt

(a) A person shall not be imprisoned for debt on a writ of execution or other process issued from a court of the United States in any State wherein imprisonment for debt has been abolished. All modifications, conditions, and restrictions upon such imprisonment provided by State law shall apply to any writ of execution or process issued from a court of the United States in accordance with the procedure applicable in such State.

(b) Any person arrested or imprisoned in any State on a writ of execution or other process issued from any court of the United States in a civil action shall have the same jail privileges and be governed by the same regulations as persons confined in like cases on process issued from the courts of such State. The same requirements governing discharge as are applicable in such State shall apply. Any proceedings for discharge shall be conducted before a United States magistrate judge for the judicial district wherein the defendant is held.

(June 25, 1948, c. 646, 62 Stat. 960; Oct. 17, 1968, Pub.L. 90–578, Title IV, § 402(b)(2), 82 Stat. 1118; Dec. 1, 1990, Pub.L. 101–650, Title III, § 321, 104 Stat. 5117.)

HISTORICAL AND STATUTORY NOTES

Change of Name

"United States magistrate judge" substituted for "United States magistrate" in text pursuant to section 321 of Pub.L. 101–650, set out as a note under 28 U.S.C.A. § 631. Previously, United States commissioners, referred to in text, were replaced by United States magistrates pursuant to Pub.L. 90–578, Oct. 17, 1968, 82 Stat. 1118. See chapter 43 of Title 28, 28 U.S.C.A. § 631 et seq.

CHAPTER 129—MONEYS PAID INTO COURT

Sec.
2041. Deposit of moneys in pending or adjudicated cases.
2042. Withdrawal.
2043. Deposit of other moneys.
2044. Payment of fine with bond money.
2045. Investment of court registry funds.

§ 2041. Deposit of moneys in pending or adjudicated cases

All moneys paid into any court of the United States, or received by the officers thereof, in any case pending or adjudicated in such court, shall be forthwith deposited with the Treasurer of the United States or a designated depositary, in the name and to the credit of such court.

This section shall not prevent the delivery of any such money to the rightful owners upon security, according to agreement of parties, under the direction of the court.

(June 25, 1948, c. 646, 62 Stat. 960; Sept. 13, 1982, Pub.L. 97–258, § 2(g) (4) (C), 96 Stat. 1061.)

HISTORICAL AND STATUTORY NOTES

Registry Administration Account

Pub.L. 100–459, Title IV, Oct. 1, 1988, 102 Stat. 2211, provided in part: "That any funds hereafter collected by the Judiciary as a charge for services rendered in administering accounts kept in a court's registry shall be deposited into a separate account entitled 'Registry Administration Account' in the Treasury of the United States. Such funds shall remain available to the Judiciary until expended to reimburse any appropriation for the amount paid out of such appropriation for expenses of the Courts of Appeals, District Courts and Other Judicial Services and the Administrative Office of the United States Courts."

§ 2042. Withdrawal

No money deposited under section 2041 of this title shall be withdrawn except by order of court.

In every case in which the right to withdraw money deposited in court under section 2041 has been adjudicated or is not in dispute and such money has remained so deposited for at least five years unclaimed by the person entitled thereto, such court shall cause such money to be deposited in the Treasury in the name and to the credit of the United States. Any claimant entitled to any such money may, on petition to the court and upon notice to the United States attorney and full proof of the right thereto, obtain an order directing payment to him.

(June 25, 1948, c. 646, 62 Stat. 960; Sept. 13, 1982, Pub.L. 97–258, § 2(g) (4) (D), 96 Stat. 1061.)

§ 2043. Deposit of other moneys

Except for public moneys deposited under section 2041 of this title, each clerk of the United States courts shall deposit public moneys that the clerk collects into a checking account in the Treasury, subject to disbursement by the clerk. At the end of each accounting period, the earned part of public moneys accruing to the United States shall be deposited in the Treasury to the credit of the appropriate receipt accounts.

(Added Pub.L. 97–258, § 2(g) (4) (E), Sept. 13, 1982, 96 Stat. 1061.)

§ 2044. Payment of fine with bond money

On motion of the United States attorney, the court shall order any money belonging to and deposited by or on behalf of the defendant with the court for the purposes of a criminal appearance bail bond (trial or appeal) to be held and paid over to the United States attorney to be applied to the payment of any assessment, fine, restitution, or penalty imposed upon the defendant. The court shall not release any money deposited for bond purposes after a plea or a verdict of the defendant's guilt has been entered and before sentencing except upon a showing that an assessment, fine, restitution or penalty cannot be imposed for the offense the defendant committed or that the defendant would suffer an undue hardship. This section shall not apply to any third party surety.

(Added Pub.L. 101–647, Title XXXVI, § 3629(a), Nov. 29, 1990, 104 Stat. 4966.)

HISTORICAL AND STATUTORY NOTES

Effective and Applicability Provisions

1990 Acts. Section to take effect 180 days after Nov. 29, 1990, see section 3631 of Pub.L. 101–647, set out as a note under section 3001 of this title.

§ 2045. Investment of court registry funds

(a) The Director of the Administrative Office of the United States Courts, or the Director's designee under subsection (b), may request the Secretary of the Treasury to invest funds received under section 2041 in public debt securities with maturities suitable to the needs of the funds, as determined by the Director or the Director's designee, and bearing interest at a rate determined by the Secretary of the Treasury, taking into consideration current market yields on outstanding marketable obligations of the United States of comparable maturity.

(b) The Director may designate the clerk of a court described in section 610 to exercise the authority conferred by subsection (a).

(Added Pub.L. 110–406, § 8(a), Oct. 13, 2008, 122 Stat. 4293.)

CHAPTER 131—RULES OF COURTS

Sec.
2071. Rule-making power generally.
2072. Rules of procedure and evidence; power to prescribe.
2073. Rules of procedure and evidence; method of prescribing.
2074. Rules of procedure and evidence; submission to Congress; effective date.
2075. Bankruptcy rules.
[2076. Repealed.]
2077. Publication of rules; advisory committees.

§ 2071. Rule-making power generally

(a) The Supreme Court and all courts established by Act of Congress may from time to time prescribe rules for the conduct of their business. Such rules shall be consistent with Acts of Congress and rules of practice and procedure prescribed under section 2072 of this title.

(b) Any rule prescribed by a court, other than the Supreme Court, under subsection (a) shall be prescribed only after giving appropriate public notice and an opportunity for comment. Such rule shall take effect upon the date specified by the prescribing court and shall have such effect on pending proceedings as the prescribing court may order.

(c)(1) A rule of a district court prescribed under subsection (a) shall remain in effect unless modified or abrogated by the judicial council of the relevant circuit.

(2) Any other rule prescribed by a court other than the Supreme Court under subsection (a) shall remain in effect unless modified or abrogated by the Judicial Conference.

(d) Copies of rules prescribed under subsection (a) by a district court shall be furnished to the judicial council, and copies of all rules prescribed by a court other than the Supreme Court under subsection (a) shall be furnished to the Director of the Administrative Office of the United States Courts and made available to the public.

(e) If the prescribing court determines that there is an immediate need for a rule, such court may proceed under this section without public notice and opportunity for comment, but such court shall promptly thereafter afford such notice and opportunity for comment.

(f) No rule may be prescribed by a district court other than under this section.

(June 25, 1948, c. 646, 62 Stat. 961; May 24, 1949, c. 139, § 102, 63 Stat. 104; Nov. 19, 1988, Pub.L. 100–702, Title IV, § 403(a)(1), 102 Stat. 4650.)

HISTORICAL AND STATUTORY NOTES

Senate Revision Amendment

By Senate amendment, all provisions relating to the Tax Court were eliminated. Therefore, section 1111 of Title 26, U.S.C., Internal Revenue Code, was not one of the sources of this section as finally enacted. However, no change in the text of this section was necessary. See 80th Congress Senate Report No. 1559.

1949 Acts. This amendment clarifies section 2071 of Title 28, U.S.C., by giving express recognition to the power of the Supreme Court to prescribe its own rules and by giving a better description of its procedural rules.

1988 Acts. House Report No. 100–889, see 1988 U.S. Code Cong. and Adm. News, p. 5982.

Effective and Applicability Provisions

1988 Acts. Section 407 of Title IV of Pub.L. 100–702 provided that: "This title [enacting sections 332(d)(4), 604(a)(19) [redesignated (a)(20)], 2071(b)–(f), and 2072–2074 of this title; amending sections 331, 332(d)(1), 372(c)(11), 636(d), 2071(a) [formerly designated 2071], and 2077(b) of this title and sections 460n–8 of Title 16, Conservation and 3402 of Title 18, Crimes and Criminal Procedure; redesignating as 604(a)(23) former section 604(a)(18) of this title; repealing former section 2072 and section 2076 of this title and sections 3771 and 3772 of Title 18; and enacting provisions set out as notes under this section] shall take effect on December 1, 1988."

1983 Acts. Pub.L. 97–462, § 4, Jan. 12, 1983, 96 Stat. 2530, provided: "The amendments made by this Act [which amended Rule 4 of the Federal Rules of Civil Procedure, added Form 18–A, Appendix of Forms, enacted provisions set out as notes under this section, and amended section 951 of Title 18, Crimes and Criminal Procedure] shall take effect 45 days after the enactment of this Act [Jan. 12, 1983]."

Savings Provisions

Section 406 of Title IV of Pub.L. 100–702 provided that: "The rules prescribed in accordance with law before the effective date of this title [Dec. 1, 1988] and in effect on the date of such effective date [Dec. 1, 1988] shall remain in force until changed pursuant to the law as amended by this title [see Effective and Applicability Provisions of 1988 Amendments note under this section]."

Short Title

1983 Acts. Pub.L. 97–462, § 1, Jan. 12, 1983, 96 Stat. 2527, provided: "That this Act [which amended Rule 4 of the Federal Rules of Civil Procedure, enacted Form 18–A, Appendix of Forms, enacted provisions set out as notes under this section, and amended section 951 of Title 18, Crimes and Criminal Procedure] may be cited as the 'Federal Rules of Civil Procedure Amendments Act of 1982'."

Rulemaking Authority of Supreme Court and Judicial Conference

Pub.L. 109–2, § 8, Feb. 18, 2005, 119 Stat. 14, provided that: "Nothing in this Act [the Class Action Fairness Act of 2005, which enacted this note and 28 U.S.C.A. §§ 1453 and 1711 to 1715, amended 28 U.S.C.A. §§ 1332, 1335, and 1603, and enacted provisions set out as notes under 28 U.S.C.A. §§ 1332, 1711, and 2074] shall restrict in any way the authority of the Judicial Conference and the Supreme Court to propose and prescribe general rules of practice and procedure under chapter 131 of title 28, United States Code [this chapter]."

[Enactment of this note by Class Action Fairness Act of 2005, Pub.L. 109–2, Feb. 18, 2005, 119 Stat. 4, applicable to any civil action commenced on or after Feb. 18, 2005, see Pub.L. 109–2, § 9, set out as a note under 28 U.S.C.A. § 1332.]

Admiralty Rules

The Rules of Practice in Admiralty and Maritime Cases, promulgated by the Supreme Court on Dec. 20, 1920, effective Mar. 7, 1921, as revised, amended, and supplemented, were rescinded, effective July 1, 1966, in accordance with the general unification of civil and admiralty procedure which became effective July 1, 1966. Provision for certain distinctively maritime remedies were preserved however in the Supplemental Rules for Certain Admiralty and Maritime Claims, Rules A to F, Federal Rules of Civil Procedure.

Tax Court Rulemaking Not Affected

Section 405 of Title IV of Pub.L. 100–702 provided that: "The amendments made by this title [see Effective and Applicability Provisions of 1988 Amendments note set out under this section] shall not affect the authority of the Tax Court to prescribe rules under section 7453 of the Internal Revenue Code of 1986 [section 7453 of Title 26, Internal Revenue Code]."

§ 2072. Rules of procedure and evidence; power to prescribe

(a) The Supreme Court shall have the power to prescribe general rules of practice and procedure and rules of evidence for cases in the United States district courts (including proceedings before magistrate judges thereof) and courts of appeals.

(b) Such rules shall not abridge, enlarge or modify any substantive right. All laws in conflict with such rules shall be of no further force or effect after such rules have taken effect.

(c) Such rules may define when a ruling of a district court is final for the purposes of appeal under section 1291 of this title.

(Added Pub.L. 100–702, Title IV, § 401(a), Nov. 19, 1988, 102 Stat. 4648, and amended Pub.L. 101–650, Title III, §§ 315, 321, Dec. 1, 1990, 104 Stat. 5115, 5117.)

HISTORICAL AND STATUTORY NOTES

Effective and Applicability Provisions

1988 Acts. Section effective Dec. 1, 1988, see section 407 of Pub.L. 100–702, set out as a note under section 2071 of this title.

Change of Name

"United States magistrate judge" substituted for "United States magistrate" in text pursuant to section 321 of Pub.L. 101–650, set out as a note under 28 U.S.C.A. § 631.

Prior Provisions

A prior section 2072, Acts June 25, 1948, c. 646, 62 Stat. 961; May 24, 1949, c. 139, § 103, 63 Stat. 104; July 18, 1949, c. 343, § 2, 63 Stat. 446; May 10, 1950, c. 174, § 2, 64 Stat. 158; July 7, 1958, Pub.L. 85–508, § 12(m), 72 Stat. 348; Nov. 6, 1966, Pub.L. 89–773, § 1, 80 Stat. 1323, which authorized the Supreme Court to prescribe rules of civil procedure, was repealed by Pub.L. 100–702, Title IV, §§ 401(a), 407, Nov. 19, 1988, 102 Stat. 4648, 4652, effective Dec. 1, 1988.

Admiralty Rules

The Rules of Practice in Admiralty and Maritime Cases, promulgated by the Supreme Court on Dec. 20, 1920, effective Mar. 7, 1921, as revised, amended, and supplemented, were rescinded, effective July 1, 1966, in accordance with the general unification of civil and admiralty procedure which became effective July 1, 1966. Provision for certain distinctively maritime remedies were preserved however, in the Supplemental Rules for Certain Admiralty and Maritime Claims, Rules A to F, Federal Rules of Civil Procedure, this title.

Applicability to Virgin Islands

Rules of civil procedure promulgated under this section as applicable to the District Court of the Virgin Islands, see section 1614 of Title 48, Territories and Insular Possessions.

§ 2073. Rules of procedure and evidence; method of prescribing

(a)(1) The Judicial Conference shall prescribe and publish the procedures for the consideration of proposed rules under this section.

(2) The Judicial Conference may authorize the appointment of committees to assist the Conference by recommending rules to be prescribed under sections 2072 and 2075 of this title. Each such committee shall consist of members of the bench and the professional bar, and trial and appellate judges.

(b) The Judicial Conference shall authorize the appointment of a standing committee on rules of practice, procedure, and evidence under subsection (a) of this section. Such standing committee shall review each recommendation of any other committees so appointed and recommend to the Judicial Conference rules of practice, procedure, and evidence and such changes in rules proposed by a committee appointed under subsection (a)(2) of this section as may be necessary to maintain consistency and otherwise promote the interest of justice.

(c)(1) Each meeting for the transaction of business under this chapter by any committee appointed under this section shall be open to the public, except when the committee so meeting, in open session and with a majority present, determines that it is in the public interest that all or part of the remainder of the meeting on that day shall be closed to the public, and states the reason for so closing the meeting. Minutes of each meeting for the transaction of business under this chapter shall be maintained by the committee and made available to the public, except that any portion of such minutes, relating to a closed meeting and made available to the public, may contain such deletions as may be necessary to avoid frustrating the purposes of closing the meeting.

(2) Any meeting for the transaction of business under this chapter, by a committee appointed under this section, shall be preceded by sufficient notice to enable all interested persons to attend.

(d) In making a recommendation under this section or under section 2072 or 2075, the body making that recommendation shall provide a proposed rule, an explanatory note on the rule, and a written report explaining the body's action, including any minority or other separate views.

(e) Failure to comply with this section does not invalidate a rule prescribed under section 2072 or 2075 of this title.

(Added Pub.L. 100–702, Title IV, § 401(a), Nov. 19, 1988, 102 Stat. 4649, and amended Pub.L. 103–394, Title I, § 104(e), Oct. 22, 1994, 108 Stat. 4110.)

HISTORICAL AND STATUTORY NOTES

Effective and Applicability Provisions

1994 Acts. Amendment by Pub.L. 103–394 effective on Oct. 22, 1994, and not to apply with respect to cases commenced under Title 11 of the United States Code before Oct. 22, 1994, see section 702 of Pub.L. 103–394, set out as a note under section 101 of Title 11, Bankruptcy.

1988 Acts. Section effective Dec. 1, 1988, see section 407 of Pub.L. 100–702, set out as a note under section 2071 of this title.

Separability of Provisions

If any provision of or amendment made by Pub.L. 103–394 or the application of such provision or amendment to any person or circumstance is held to be unconstitutional, the remaining provisions of and amendments made by Pub.L. 103–394 and the application of such provisions and amendments to any person or circumstance shall not be affected thereby, see section 701 of Pub.L. 103–394, set out as a note under section 101 of Title 11, Bankruptcy.

Prior Provisions

A prior section 2073, Acts June 25, 1948, c. 646, 62 Stat. 961; May 24, 1949, c. 139, § 104, 63 Stat. 104; May 10, 1950, c. 174, § 3, 64 Stat. 158, which empowered the Supreme Court to prescribe, by general rules, the practice and procedure in admiralty and maritime cases in the district courts, was repealed by Pub.L. 89–773, § 2, Nov. 6, 1966, 80 Stat. 1323, which provided in part that the repeal of section 2073 should not operate to invalidate or repeal rules adopted under the authority of such section prior to the enactment of Pub.L. 89–773, which rules should remain in effect until superseded by rules prescribed under the authority of former section 2072 of this title as amended by Pub.L. 89–773. See sections 2071 to 2074 of this title.

More Complete Information Regarding Assets of the Estate

Pub.L. 109–8, Title IV, § 419, Apr. 20, 2005, 119 Stat. 109, provided that:

"**(a) In general.—**

"**(1) Disclosure.**—The Judicial Conference of the United States, in accordance with section 2075 of title 28 of the United States Code and after consideration of the views of the Director of the Executive Office for United States Trustees, shall propose amended Federal Rules of Bankruptcy Procedure and in accordance with rule 9009 of the Federal Rules of Bankruptcy Procedure [set out in Title 11] shall prescribe official bankruptcy forms directing debtors under chapter 11 of title 11 of United States Code [11 U.S.C.A. § 1101 et seq.], to disclose the information described in paragraph (2) by filing and serving periodic financial and other reports designed to provide such information.

"**(2) Information.**—The information referred to in paragraph (1) is the value, operations, and profitability of any closely held corporation, partnership, or of any other entity in which the debtor holds a substantial or controlling interest.

"(b) **Purpose.**—The purpose of the rules and reports under subsection (a) [of this note] shall be to assist parties in interest taking steps to ensure that the debtor's interest in any entity referred to in subsection (a)(2) [of this note] is used for the payment of allowed claims against debtor."

[Except as otherwise provided, amendments by Pub.L. 109–8 effective 180 days after April 20, 2005, and inapplicable with respect to cases commenced under Title 11 before the effective date, see Pub.L. 109–8, § 1501, set out as a note under 11 U.S.C.A. § 101.]

Standard Form Disclosure Statement and Plan

Pub.L. 109–8, Title IV, § 433, Apr. 20, 2005, 119 Stat. 110, provided that: "Within a reasonable period of time after the date of enactment of this Act [Apr. 20,. 2005], the Judicial Conference of the United States shall prescribe in accordance with rule 9009 of the Federal Rules of Bankruptcy Procedure [set out in Title 11] official standard form disclosure statements and plans of reorganization for small business debtors (as defined in section 101 of title 11, United States Code, as amended by this Act), designed to achieve a practical balance between—

"(1) the reasonable needs of the courts, the United States trustee, creditors, and other parties in interest for reasonably complete information; and

"(2) economy and simplicity for debtors."

[Except as otherwise provided, amendments by Pub.L. 109–8 effective 180 days after April 20, 2005, and inapplicable with respect to cases commenced under Title 11 before the effective date, see Pub.L. 109–8, § 1501, set out as a note under 11 U.S.C.A. § 101.]

Uniform Reporting Rules and Forms for Small Business Cases

Pub.L. 109–8, Title IV, § 435, Apr. 20, 2005, 119 Stat. 111, provided that:

"(a) **Proposal of rules and forms.**—The Judicial Conference of the United States shall propose in accordance with section 2073 of title 28 of the United States Code [this section] amended Federal Rules of Bankruptcy Procedure, and shall prescribe in accordance with rule 9009 of the Federal Rules of Bankruptcy Procedure [set out in Title 11] official bankruptcy forms, directing small business debtors to file periodic financial and other reports containing information, including information relating to—

"(1) the debtor's profitability;

"(2) the debtor's cash receipts and disbursements; and

"(3) whether the debtor is timely filing tax returns and paying taxes and other administrative expenses when due.

"(b) **Purpose.**—The rules and forms proposed under subsection (a) [of this note] shall be designed to achieve a practical balance among—

"(1) the reasonable needs of the bankruptcy court, the United States trustee, creditors, and other parties in interest for reasonably complete information;

"(2) a small business debtor's interest that required reports be easy and inexpensive to complete; and

"(3) the interest of all parties that the required reports help such debtor to understand such debtor's financial condition and plan the [sic] such debtor's future."

[Except as otherwise provided, amendments by Pub.L. 109–8 effective 180 days after April 20, 2005, and inapplicable with respect to cases commenced under Title 11 before the effective date, see Pub.L. 109–8, § 1501, set out as a note under 11 U.S.C.A. § 101.]

§ 2074. Rules of procedure and evidence; submission to Congress; effective date

(a) The Supreme Court shall transmit to the Congress not later than May 1 of the year in which a rule prescribed under section 2072 is to become effective a copy of the proposed rule. Such rule shall take effect no earlier than December 1 of the year in which such rule is so transmitted unless otherwise provided by law. The Supreme Court may fix the extent such rule shall apply to proceedings then pending, except that the Supreme Court shall not require the application of such rule to further proceedings then pending to the extent that, in the opinion of the court in which such proceedings are pending, the application of such rule in such proceedings would not be feasible or would work injustice, in which event the former rule applies.

(b) Any such rule creating, abolishing, or modifying an evidentiary privilege shall have no force or effect unless approved by Act of Congress.

(Added Pub.L. 100–702, Title IV, § 401(a), Nov. 19, 1988, 102 Stat. 4649.)

HISTORICAL AND STATUTORY NOTES

Effective and Applicability Provisions

1988 Acts. Section effective Dec. 1, 1988, see section 407 of Pub.L. 100–702, set out as a note under section 2071 of this title.

Prior Provisions

A prior section 2074, Act July 27, 1954, c. 583, § 1, 68 Stat. 567, which empowered the Supreme Court to prescribe rules for review of decisions of the Tax Court of the United States, was repealed by Pub.L. 89–773, § 2, Nov. 6, 1966, 80 Stat. 1323, which provided in part that the repeal of section 2074 of this title should not operate to invalidate or repeal rules adopted under the authority of such section prior to the enactment of Pub.L. 89–773, which rules should remain in effect until superseded by rules prescribed under the authority of former section 2072 of this title as amended by Pub.L. 89–773. See sections 2071 to 2074 of this title.

Amendments to Civil Rules Proposed March 27, 2003

Pub.L. 109–2, § 7, Feb. 18, 2005, 119 Stat. 13, provided that: "Notwithstanding any other provision of law, the amendments to rule 23 of the Federal Rules of Civil Procedure, which are set forth in the order entered by the Supreme Court of the United States on March 27, 2003, shall take effect on the date of enactment of this Act [Feb. 18, 2005] or on December 1, 2003 (as specified in that order), whichever occurs first."

[Enactment of this note by Class Action Fairness Act of 2005, Pub.L. 109–2, Feb. 18, 2005, 119 Stat. 4, applicable to any civil action commenced on or after Feb. 18, 2005, see Pub.L. 109–2, § 9, set out as a note under 28 U.S.C.A. § 1332.]

Amendments to Criminal Rules Proposed April 29, 2002

Pub.L. 107–273, Div. C, Title I, § 11019(a), Nov. 2, 2002, 116 Stat. 1825, provided that: "The proposed amendments to the Federal Rules of Criminal Procedure that are embraced by an order entered by the Supreme Court of the United States on April 29, 2002, shall take effect on December 1, 2002, as otherwise provided by law, but with the amendments made in subsection (b) [amending Rule 16 of the Federal Rules of Criminal Procedure]."

Amendments to Criminal Rules Proposed April 29, 1994

Pub.L. 103–322, Title XXIII, § 230101, Sept. 13, 1994, 108 Stat. 2077, provided that:

"**(a) Modification of proposed amendments.**—The proposed amendments to the Federal Rules of Criminal Procedure which are embraced by an order entered by the Supreme Court of the United States on April 29, 1994, shall take effect on December 1, 1994, as otherwise provided by law, but with the following amendments:

"**(b) In general.**—Rule 32 of the Federal Rules of Criminal Procedure is amended by—

"**(1)** striking 'and' following the semicolon in subdivision (c)(3)(C);

"**(2)** striking the period at the end of subdivision (c)(3)(D) and inserting '; and';

"**(3)** inserting after subdivision (c)(3)(D) the following:

" '**(E)** if sentence is to be imposed for a crime of violence or sexual abuse, address the victim personally if the victim is present at the sentencing hearing and determine if the victim wishes to make a statement or present any information in relation to the sentence.';

"**(4)** in subdivision (c)(3)(D), striking 'equivalent opportunity' and inserting in lieu thereof 'opportunity equivalent to that of the defendant's counsel';

"**(5)** in the last sentence of subdivision (c)(4), striking 'and (D)' and inserting '(D), and (E)';

"**(6)** in the last sentence of subdivision (c)(4), inserting 'the victim,' before 'or the attorney for the Government.'; and

"**(7)** adding at the end the following:

" '**(f) Definitions.**—For purposes of this rule—

" '**(1)** "victim" means any individual against whom an offense has been committed for which a sentence is to be imposed, but the right of allocution under subdivision (c)(3)(E) may be exercised instead by—

" '**(A)** a parent or legal guardian if the victim is below the age of eighteen years or incompetent; or

" '**(B)** one or more family members or relatives designated by the court if the victim is deceased or incapacitated;

if such person or persons are present at the sentencing hearing, regardless of whether the victim is present; and

" '**(2)** "crime of violence or sexual abuse" means a crime that involved the use or attempted or threatened use of physical force against the person or property of another, or a crime under chapter 109A of title 18, United States Code.'

"**(c) Effective date.**—The amendments made by subsection (b) [amending Rule 32 of the Federal Rules of Criminal Procedure] shall become effective on December 1, 1994."

Amendments to Civil Rules Proposed April 30, 1991

Pub.L. 102–198, § 11, Dec. 9, 1991, 105 Stat. 1626, provided that:

"**(a) Technical amendment.**—Rule 15(c)(3) of the Federal Rules of Civil Procedure for the United States Courts, as transmitted to the Congress by the Supreme Court pursuant to section 2074 of title 28, United States Code [this section], to become effective on December 1, 1991, is amended by striking 'Rule 4(m)' and inserting 'Rule 4(j)'.

"**(b) Amendment to Forms.**—Form 1–A, Notice of Lawsuit and Request for Waiver of Service of Summons, and Form 1–B, Waiver of Service of Summons, included in the transmittal by the Supreme Court described in subsection (a), shall not be effective and Form 18–A, Notice and Acknowledgment for Service by Mail, abrogated by the Supreme Court in such transmittal, effective December 1, 1991, shall continue in effect on or after that date."

Amendments to Civil Rules Proposed April 28, 1982

Pub.L. 97–462, § 5, Jan. 12, 1983, 96 Stat. 2530, provided: "The amendments to the Federal Rules of Civil Procedure [Rule 4], the effective date [Aug. 1, 1982] of which was delayed [to Oct. 1, 1983] by the Act [Pub.L. 97–227] entitled 'An Act to delay the effective date of proposed amendments to rule 4 of the Federal Rules of Civil Procedure', [proposed by the Supreme Court of the United States and transmitted to the Congress by the Chief Justice on Apr. 28, 1982], approved August 2, 1982 (96 Stat. 246), shall not take effect."

Pub.L. 97–227, Aug. 2, 1982, 96 Stat. 246, provided: "That notwithstanding the provisions of section 2072 of title 28, United States Code, [section 2072 of this title] the amendments to rule 4 of the Federal Rules of Civil Procedure as proposed by the Supreme Court of the United States and transmitted to the Congress by the Chief Justice on April 28, 1982, shall take effect on October 1, 1983, unless previously approved, disapproved, or modified by Act of Congress.

"**Sec. 2.** This Act shall be effective as of August 1, 1982, but shall not apply to the service of process that takes place between August 1, 1982, and the date of enactment of this Act [Aug. 2, 1982]."

Amendments to Criminal Rules and Rules of Evidence Proposed April 30, 1979; Postponement of Effective Date

Pub.L. 96–42, July 31, 1979, 93 Stat. 326, provided: "That notwithstanding any provision of section 3771 or 3772 of title 18 of the United States Code [section 3771 or 3772 of Title 18, Crimes and Criminal Procedure] or of section 2072, 2075, or 2076 of title 28 of the United States Code [sections 2072, 2075 and 2076 of this title] to the contrary—

"**(1)** the amendments proposed by the United States Supreme Court and transmitted by the Chief Justice on April 30, 1979, to the Federal Rules of Criminal Procedure affecting rules 11(e)(6), 17(h), 32(f), and 44(c), and adding new rules 26.2 and 32.1, and the amendment so proposed and transmitted to the Federal Rules of Evidence affecting rule 410, shall not take effect until December 1, 1980, or until and then only to the extent approved by Act of Congress, whichever is earlier; and

"**(2)** the amendment proposed by the United States Supreme Court and transmitted by the Chief Justice on April 30, 1979, affecting rule 40 of the Federal Rules of Criminal Procedure shall take effect on August 1, 1979, with the following amendments:

"(A) In the matter designated as paragraph (1) of subdivision (d), strike out 'in accordance with Rule 32.1(a).'

"(B) In the matter designated as paragraph (2) of subdivision (d), strike out 'in accordance with Rule 32.1(a)(1)'."

Approval and Effective Date of Amendments Proposed November 20, 1972 and December 18, 1972

Pub.L. 93–595, § 3, Jan. 2, 1975, 88 Stat. 1949, provided that: "The Congress expressly approves the amendments to the Federal Rules of Civil Procedure [Rules 30(c), 32(c), 43 and 44.1] and the amendments to the Federal Rules of Criminal Procedure [Rules 26, 26.1 and 28], which are embraced by the orders entered by the Supreme Court of the United States on November 20, 1972, and December 18, 1972, and such amendments shall take effect on the one hundred and eightieth day beginning after the date of the enactment of this Act [Jan. 2, 1975]."

Approval and Effective Date of Rules Governing Section 2254 Cases and Section 2255 Proceedings for United States District Courts

Pub.L. 94–426, § 1, Sept. 28, 1976, 90 Stat. 1334, provided: "That the rules governing section 2254 cases in the United States district courts and the rules governing section 2255 proceedings for the United States district courts, as proposed by the United States Supreme Court, which were delayed by the Act entitled 'An Act to delay the effective date of certain proposed amendments to the Federal Rules of Criminal Procedure and certain other rules promulgated by the United States Supreme Court' (Public Law 94–349), are approved with the amendments set forth in section 2 of this Act and shall take effect as so amended, with respect to petitions under section 2254 and motions under section 2255 of title 28 of the United States Code [sections 2254 and 2255 of this title] filed on or after February 1, 1977."

Amendments to Rules of Evidence Proposed on April 29, 1994

Pub.L. 103–322, Title IV, § 40141, Sept. 13, 1994, 108 Stat. 1918, provided that:

"**(a) Modification of proposed amendment.**—The proposed amendments to the Federal Rules of Evidence that are embraced by an order entered by the Supreme Court of the United States on April 29, 1994, shall take effect on December 1, 1994, as otherwise provided by law, but with the amendment made by subsection (b).

"**(b) Rule.**—Rule 412 of the Federal Rules of Evidence is amended to read as follows:

"'**Rule 412. Sex Offense Cases; Relevance of Alleged Victim's Past Sexual Behavior or Alleged Sexual Predisposition**

"'**(a) Evidence generally inadmissible.**—The following evidence is not admissible in any civil or criminal proceeding involving alleged sexual misconduct except as provided in subdivisions (b) and (c):

"'(1) Evidence offered to prove that any alleged victim engaged in her sexual behavior.

"'(2) Evidence offered to prove any alleged victim's sexual predisposition.

"'**(b) Exceptions.**—

"'(1) In a criminal case, the following evidence is admissible, if otherwise admissible under these rules:

"'(A) evidence of specific instances of sexual behavior by the alleged victim offered to prove that a person other than the accused was the source of semen, injury or other physical evidence;

"'(B) evidence of specific instances of sexual behavior by the alleged victim with respect to the person accused of the sexual misconduct offered by the accused to prove consent or by the prosecution; and

"'(C) evidence the exclusion of which would violate the constitutional rights of the defendant.

"'(2) In a civil case, evidence offered to prove the sexual behavior or sexual predisposition of any alleged victim is admissible if it is otherwise admissible under these rules and its probative value substantially outweighs the danger of harm to any victim and of unfair prejudice to any party. Evidence of an alleged victim's reputation is admissible only if it has been placed in controversy by the alleged victim.

"'**(c) Procedure to determine admissibility.**—

"'(1) A party intending to offer evidence under subdivision (b) must—

"'(A) file a written motion at least 14 days before trial specifically describing the evidence and stating the purpose for which it is offered unless the court, for good cause requires a different time for filing or permits filing during trial; and

"'(B) serve the motion on all parties and notify the alleged victim or, when appropriate, the alleged victim's guardian or representative.

"'(2) Before admitting evidence under this rule the court must conduct a hearing in camera and afford the victim and parties a right to attend and be heard. The motion, related papers, and the record of the hearing must be sealed and remain under seal unless the court orders otherwise.'

"**(c) Technical amendment.**—The table of contents for the Federal Rules of Evidence is amended by amending the item relating to rule 412 to read as follows:

"'**412. Sex Offense Cases; Relevance of Alleged Victim's Past Sexual Behavior or Alleged Sexual Predisposition:**

"'(a) Evidence generally inadmissible.

"'(b) Exceptions.

"'(c) Procedure to determine admissibility.'"

Congressional Approval Requirement for Proposed Rules of Evidence for United States Courts and Amendments to Federal Rules of Civil Procedure and Criminal Procedure; Suspension of Effectiveness of Such Rules

Pub.L. 93–12, Mar. 30, 1973, 87 Stat. 9, provided: "That notwithstanding any other provisions of law, the Rules of Evidence for United States Courts and Magistrates, the Amendments to the Federal Rules of Civil Procedure, and the Amendments to the Federal Rules of Criminal Procedure, which are embraced by the orders entered by the Supreme Court of the United States on Monday, November 20, 1972, and Monday, December 18, 1972, shall have no force or effect except to the extent, and with such amendments, as they may be expressly approved by Act of Congress."

Postponement of Effective Date of Proposed Rules and Forms Governing Proceedings Under Sections 2254 and 2255 of this Title

Pub.L. 94–349, § 2, July 8, 1976, 90 Stat. 822, provided: "That, notwithstanding the provisions of section 2072 of title 28 of the United States Code [section 2072 of this title], the rules and forms governing section 2254 [section 2254 of this title] cases in the United States district courts and the rules and forms governing section 2255 [section 2255 of this title] proceedings in the United States district courts which are embraced by the order entered by the United States Supreme Court on April 26, 1976, and which were transmitted to the Congress on or about April 26, 1976, shall not take effect until thirty days after the adjournment sine die of the 94th Congress, or until and to the extent approved by Act of Congress, whichever is earlier."

§ 2075. Bankruptcy rules

The Supreme Court shall have the power to prescribe by general rules, the forms of process, writs, pleadings, and motions, and the practice and procedure in cases under title 11.

Such rules shall not abridge, enlarge, or modify any substantive right.

The Supreme Court shall transmit to Congress not later than May 1 of the year in which a rule prescribed under this section is to become effective a copy of the proposed rule. The rule shall take effect no earlier than December 1 of the year in which it is transmitted to Congress unless otherwise provided by law.

The bankruptcy rules promulgated under this section shall prescribe a form for the statement required under section 707(b)(2)(C) of title 11 and may provide general rules on the content of such statement.

(Added Pub.L. 88–623, § 1, Oct. 3, 1964, 78 Stat. 1001, and amended Pub.L. 95–598, Title II, § 247, Nov. 6, 1978, 92 Stat. 2672; Pub.L. 103–394, Title I, § 104(f), Oct. 22, 1994, 108 Stat. 4110; Pub.L. 109–8, Title XII, § 1232, Apr. 20, 2005, 119 Stat. 202.)

HISTORICAL AND STATUTORY NOTES

Effective and Applicability Provisions

2005 Acts. Except as otherwise provided, amendments by Pub.L. 109–8 effective 180 days after April 20, 2005, and inapplicable with respect to cases commenced under Title 11 before the effective date, see Pub.L. 109–8, § 1501, set out as a note under 11 U.S.C.A. § 101.

1994 Acts. Amendment by Pub.L. 103–394 effective on Oct. 22, 1994, and not to apply with respect to cases commenced under Title 11 of the United States Code before Oct. 22, 1994, see section 702 of Pub.L. 103–394, set out as a note under section 101 of Title 11, Bankruptcy.

1978 Acts. Amendment by Pub.L. 95–598 effective Nov. 6, 1978, see section 402(d) of Pub.L. 95–598, set out as a note preceding section 101 of Title 11, Bankruptcy.

Separability of Provisions

If any provision of or amendment made by Pub.L. 103–394 or the application of such provision or amendment to any person or circumstance is held to be unconstitutional, the remaining provisions of and amendments made by Pub.L. 103–394 and the application of such provisions and amendments to any person or circumstance shall not be affected thereby, see section 701 of Pub.L. 103–394, set out as a note under section 101 of Title 11, Bankruptcy.

Additional Rulemaking Power

Pub.L. 95–598, Title IV, § 410, Nov. 6, 1978, 92 Stat. 2687, provided that: "The Supreme Court may issue such additional rules of procedure, consistent with Acts of Congress, as may be necessary for the orderly transfer of functions and records and the orderly transition to the new bankruptcy court system created by this Act [see Tables for complete classification of Pub.L. 95–598]."

Applicability of Rules to Cases Under Title 11

Pub.L. 95–598, Title IV, § 405(d), Nov. 6, 1978, 92 Stat. 2685, provided that: "The rules prescribed under section 2075 of title 28 of the United States Code and in effect on September 30, 1979, shall apply to cases under title 11, to the extent not inconsistent with the amendments made by this Act, or with this Act [see Tables for complete classification of Pub.L. 95–598], until such rules are repealed or superseded by rules prescribed and effective under such section, as amended by section 248 of this Act."

Rules Promulgated by Supreme Court

Pub.L. 98–353, Title III, § 320, July 10, 1984, 98 Stat. 357, provided that: "The Supreme Court shall prescribe general rules implementing the practice and procedure to be followed under section 707(b) of title 11, United States Code [section 707(b) of Title 11, Bankruptcy]. Section 2075 of title 28, United States Code [this section], shall apply with respect to the general rules prescribed under this section."

[§ 2076. Repealed. Pub.L. 100–702, Title IV, § 401(c), Nov. 19, 1988, 102 Stat. 4650]

HISTORICAL AND STATUTORY NOTES

Section, added Pub.L. 93–595, § 2(a)(1), Jan. 2, 1975, 88 Stat. 1948, and amended Pub.L. 94–149, § 2, Dec. 12, 1975, 89 Stat. 806, related to Federal Rules of Evidence prescribed by the Supreme Court and amendment thereof. See sections 2072 to 2074 of this title.

Effective Date of Repeal

Section repealed effective Dec. 1, 1988, see section 407 of Pub.L. 100–702, set out as a note under section 2071 of this title.

§ 2077. Publication of rules; advisory committees

(a) The rules for the conduct of the business of each court of appeals, including the operating procedures of such court, shall be published. Each court of appeals shall print or cause to be printed necessary copies of the rules. The Judicial Conference shall prescribe the fees for sales of copies under section 1913 of this title, but the Judicial Conference may provide for free distribution of copies to members of the bar of each court and to other interested persons.

(b) Each court, except the Supreme Court, that is authorized to prescribe rules of the conduct of such court's business under section 2071 of this title shall appoint an advisory committee for the study of the rules of practice and internal operating procedures of such court and, in the case of an advisory committee appointed by a court of appeals, of the rules of the judicial council of the circuit. The advisory committee shall make recommendations to the court concerning such rules and procedures. Members of the committee shall serve without compensation, but the Director may pay travel and transportation expenses in accordance with section 5703 of title 5.

(Added Pub.L. 97–164, Title II, § 208(a), Apr. 2, 1982, 96 Stat. 54, and amended Pub.L. 100–702, Title IV, § 401(b), Nov. 19, 1988, 102 Stat. 4650; Pub.L. 101–650, Title IV, § 406, Dec. 1, 1990, 104 Stat. 5124.)

HISTORICAL AND STATUTORY NOTES

Effective and Applicability Provisions

1990 Acts. Amendment by section 406 of Pub.L. 101–650 effective 90 days after Dec. 1, 1990, see section 407 of Pub.L. 101–650, set out as a note under section 332 of this title.

1988 Acts. Amendment by Pub.L. 100–702 effective Dec. 1, 1988, see section 407 of Pub.L. 100–702, set out as a note under section 2071 of this title.

1982 Acts. Section effective Oct. 1, 1982, see section 402 of Pub.L. 97–164, set out as a note under section 171 of this title.

CHAPTER 133—REVIEW—MISCELLANEOUS PROVISIONS

Sec.
2101. Supreme Court; time for appeal or certiorari; docketing; stay.
2102. Priority of criminal case on appeal from State court.
[2103. Repealed.]
2104. Reviews of State court decisions.
2105. Scope of review; abatement.
2106. Determination.
2107. Time for appeal to court of appeals.
2108. Proof of amount in controversy.
2109. Quorum of Supreme Court justices absent.
[2110. Repealed.]
2111. Harmless error.
2112. Record on review and enforcement of agency orders.
2113. Definition.

§ 2101. Supreme Court; time for appeal or certiorari; docketing; stay

(a) A direct appeal to the Supreme Court from any decision under section 1253 of this title, holding unconstitutional in whole or in part, any Act of Congress, shall be taken within thirty days after the entry of the interlocutory or final order, judgment or decree. The record shall be made up and the case docketed within sixty days from the time such appeal is taken under rules prescribed by the Supreme Court.

(b) Any other direct appeal to the Supreme Court which is authorized by law, from a decision of a district court in any civil action, suit or proceeding, shall be taken within thirty days from the judgment, order or decree, appealed from, if interlocutory, and within sixty days if final.

(c) Any other appeal or any writ of certiorari intended to bring any judgment or decree in a civil action, suit or proceeding before the Supreme Court for review shall be taken or applied for within ninety days after the entry of such judgment or decree. A justice of the Supreme Court, for good cause shown, may extend the time for applying for a writ of certiorari for a period not exceeding sixty days.

(d) The time for appeal or application for a writ of certiorari to review the judgment of a State court in a criminal case shall be as prescribed by rules of the Supreme Court.

(e) An application to the Supreme Court for a writ of certiorari to review a case before judgment has been rendered in the court of appeals may be made at any time before judgment.

(f) In any case in which the final judgment or decree of any court is subject to review by the Supreme Court on writ of certiorari, the execution and enforcement of such judgment or decree may be stayed for a reasonable time to enable the party aggrieved to obtain a writ of certiorari from the Supreme Court. The stay may be granted by a judge of the court rendering the judgment or decree or by a justice of the Supreme Court, and may be conditioned on the giving of security, approved by such judge or justice, that if the aggrieved party fails to make application for such writ within the period allotted therefor, or fails to obtain an order granting his application, or fails to make his plea good in the Supreme Court, he shall answer for all damages and costs which the other party may sustain by reason of the stay.

(g) The time for application for a writ of certiorari to review a decision of the United States Court of Appeals for the Armed Forces shall be as prescribed by rules of the Supreme Court.

(June 25, 1948, c. 646, 62 Stat. 961; May 24, 1949, c. 139, § 106, 63 Stat. 104; Dec. 6, 1983, Pub.L. 98–209, § 10(b), 97 Stat. 1406; June 27, 1988, Pub.L. 100–352, § 5(b), 102 Stat. 663; Oct. 5, 1994, Pub.L. 103–337, Div. A, Title IX, § 924(d)(1)(C), 108 Stat. 2832.)

HISTORICAL AND STATUTORY NOTES

Effective and Applicability Provisions

1988 Acts. Amendment by section 5(b) of Pub.L. 100–352, which substituted "section 1253" for "sections 1252, 1253 and

2282" in subsec. (a), effective ninety days after June 27, 1988, except that such amendment not to apply to cases pending in the Supreme Court on such effective date or affect the right to review or the manner of reviewing the judgment or decree of a court which was entered before such effective date, see section 7 of Pub.L. 100–352, set out as a note under section 1254 of this title.

1983 Acts. Amendment by Pub.L. 98–209 effective on the first day of the eighth calendar month beginning after Dec. 6, 1983, see section 12(a)(1) of Pub.L. 98–209, set out as a note under section 801 of Title 10, Armed Forces.

§ 2102. Priority of criminal case on appeal from State court

Criminal cases on review from State courts shall have priority, on the docket of the Supreme Court, over all cases except cases to which the United States is a party and such other cases as the court may decide to be of public importance.

(June 25, 1948, c. 646, 62 Stat. 962.)

[§ 2103. Repealed. Pub.L. 100–352, § 5(c), June 27, 1988, 102 Stat. 663]

HISTORICAL AND STATUTORY NOTES

Section, Acts June 25, 1948, c. 646, 62 Stat. 962; Sept. 19, 1962, Pub.L. 87–669, § 1, 76 Stat. 556, provided that appeal from State court or from a United States court of appeals improvidently taken be regarded as petition for writ of certiorari.

Effective Date of Repeal

Repeal of section effective ninety days after June 27, 1988, except that such repeal not to apply to cases pending in the Supreme Court on such effective date or affect the right to review or the manner of reviewing the judgment or decree of a court which was entered before such effective date, see section 7 of Pub.L. 100–352, set out as a note under section 1254 of this title.

§ 2104. Reviews of State court decisions

A review by the Supreme Court of a judgment or decree of a State court shall be conducted in the same manner and under the same regulations, and shall have the same effect, as if the judgment or decree reviewed had been rendered in a court of the United States.

(June 25, 1948, c. 646, 62 Stat. 962; June 27, 1988, Pub.L. 100–352, § 5(d)(1), 102 Stat. 663.)

HISTORICAL AND STATUTORY NOTES

Effective and Applicability Provisions

1988 Acts. Amendment by section 5(d)(1) of Pub.L. 100–352 effective ninety days after June 27, 1988, except that such amendment not to apply to cases pending in the Supreme Court on such effective date or affect the right to review or the manner of reviewing the judgment or decree of a court which was entered before such effective date, see section 7 of Pub.L. 100–352, set out as a note under section 1254 of this title.

§ 2105. Scope of review; abatement

There shall be no reversal in the Supreme Court or a court of appeals for error in ruling upon matters in abatement which do not involve jurisdiction.

(June 25, 1948, c. 646, 62 Stat. 963.)

§ 2106. Determination

The Supreme Court or any other court of appellate jurisdiction may affirm, modify, vacate, set aside or reverse any judgment, decree, or order of a court lawfully brought before it for review, and may remand the cause and direct the entry of such appropriate judgment, decree, or order, or require such further proceedings to be had as may be just under the circumstances.

(June 25, 1948, c. 646, 62 Stat. 963.)

§ 2107. Time for appeal to court of appeals

(a) Except as otherwise provided in this section, no appeal shall bring any judgment, order or decree in an action, suit or proceeding of a civil nature before a court of appeals for review unless notice of appeal is filed, within thirty days after the entry of such judgment, order or decree.

(b) In any such action, suit or proceeding in which the United States or an officer or agency thereof is a party, the time as to all parties shall be sixty days from such entry.

(c) The district court may, upon motion filed not later than 30 days after the expiration of the time otherwise set for bringing appeal, extend the time for appeal upon a showing of excusable neglect or good cause. In addition, if the district court finds—

(1) that a party entitled to notice of the entry of a judgment or order did not receive such notice from the clerk or any party within 21 days of its entry, and

(2) that no party would be prejudiced,

the district court may, upon motion filed within 180 days after entry of the judgment or order or within 7 days after receipt of such notice, whichever is earlier, reopen the time for appeal for a period of 14 days from the date of entry of the order reopening the time for appeal.

(d) This section shall not apply to bankruptcy matters or other proceedings under Title 11.

(June 25, 1948, c. 646, 62 Stat. 963; May 24, 1949, c. 139, §§ 107, 108, 63 Stat. 104; Nov. 6, 1978, Pub.L. 95–598, Title II, § 248, 92 Stat. 2672; Dec. 9, 1991, Pub.L. 102–198, § 12, 105 Stat. 1627.)

HISTORICAL AND STATUTORY NOTES

Senate Revision Amendment

By Senate amendment, all provisions relating to the Tax Court were eliminated. Therefore, section 1142 of Title 26, U.S.C., Internal Revenue Code, was not one of the sources of this section as finally enacted. However, no change in the text of this section was necessary. See 80th Congress Senate Report No. 1559.

1949 Acts. This amendment to section 2107 of Title 28, U.S.C., restores the former 15-day limitation of time within which to appeal from an interlocutory order in admiralty.

This amendment eliminates as surplusage the words "in any such action, suit or proceeding," from the fourth paragraph of section 2107 of Title 28, U.S.C., and corrects a typographical error in the same paragraph.

1991 Acts. House Report No. 102–322, see 1991 U.S. Code Cong. and Adm. News, p. 1303.

Codifications

This section was amended by Pub.L. 95–598, Title II, § 248, Nov. 6, 1978, 92 Stat. 2672, effective June 28, 1984, pursuant to Pub.L. 95–598, Title IV, § 402(b), Nov. 6, 1978, 92 Stat. 2682, as amended by Pub.L. 98–249, § 1(a), Mar. 31, 1984, 98 Stat. 116; Pub.L. 98–271, § 1(a), Apr. 30, 1984, 98 Stat. 163; Pub.L. 98–299, § 1(a), May 25, 1984, 98 Stat. 214; Pub.L. 98–325, § 1(a), June 20, 1984, 98 Stat. 268 [set out as an Effective and Applicability Provisions note preceding section 101 of Title 11, Bankruptcy], by adding "or the bankruptcy court" following "district court" and by striking out the final paragraph relating to nonapplicability to bankruptcy matters or other proceedings under Title 11.

Section 402(b) of Pub.L. 95–598 was amended by section 113 of Pub.L. 98–353, Title I, July 10, 1984, 98 Stat. 343, by substituting "shall not be effective" for "shall take effect on June 28, 1984", thereby eliminating the amendment by section 248 of Pub.L. 95–598, effective June 27, 1984, pursuant to section 122(c) of Pub.L. 98–353, set out as an Effective Date note under section 151 of this title.

Section 121(a) of Pub.L. 98–353 directed that section 402(b) of Pub.L. 95–598 be amended by substituting "the date of enactment of the Bankruptcy Amendments and Federal Judgeship Act of 1984 [i.e. July 10, 1984]" for "June 28, 1984". This amendment was not executed in view of the prior amendment to section 402(b) of Pub.L. 95–598 by section 113 of Pub.L. 98–353.

§ 2108. Proof of amount in controversy

Where the power of any court of appeals to review a case depends upon the amount or value in controversy, such amount or value, if not otherwise satisfactorily disclosed upon the record, may be shown and ascertained by the oath of a party to the case or by other competent evidence.

(June 25, 1948, c. 646, 62 Stat. 963.)

§ 2109. Quorum of Supreme Court justices absent

If a case brought to the Supreme Court by direct appeal from a district court cannot be heard and determined because of the absence of a quorum of qualified justices, the Chief Justice of the United States may order it remitted to the court of appeals for the circuit including the district in which the case arose, to be heard and determined by that court either sitting in banc or specially constituted and composed of the three circuit judges senior in commission who are able to sit, as such order may direct. The decision of such court shall be final and conclusive. In the event of the disqualification or disability of one or more of such circuit judges, such court shall be filled as provided in chapter 15 of this title.

In any other case brought to the Supreme Court for review, which cannot be heard and determined because of the absence of a quorum of qualified justices, if a majority of the qualified justices shall be of opinion that the case cannot be heard and determined at the next ensuing term, the court shall enter its order affirming the judgment of the court from which the case was brought for review with the same effect as upon affirmance by an equally divided court.

(June 25, 1948, c. 646, 62 Stat. 963.)

[§ 2110. Repealed. Pub.L. 97–164, Title I, § 136, Apr. 2, 1982, 96 Stat. 41]

HISTORICAL AND STATUTORY NOTES

Section, Act June 25, 1948, c. 646, 62 Stat. 964; May 24, 1949, c. 139, § 109, 63 Stat. 105, provided that appeals to the Court of Claims in tort claims cases, as provided in section 1504 of this title, be taken within 90 days after the entry of the final judgment of the district court.

Effective Date of Repeal

Repeal effective Oct. 1, 1982, see section 402 of Pub.L. 97–164, set out as a note under section 171 of this title.

§ 2111. Harmless error

On the hearing of any appeal or writ of certiorari in any case, the court shall give judgment after an examination of the record without regard to errors or defects which do not affect the substantial rights of the parties.

(Added May 24, 1949, c. 139, § 110, 63 Stat. 105.)

§ 2112. Record on review and enforcement of agency orders

(a) The rules prescribed under the authority of section 2072 of this title may provide for the time and manner of filing and the contents of the record in all proceedings instituted in the courts of appeals to enjoin, set aside, suspend, modify, or otherwise review or enforce orders of administrative agencies, boards, commissions, and officers. Such rules may authorize the agency, board, commission, or officer to file in the court a certified list of the materials comprising the record and retain and hold for the court all such materials and transmit the same or any part thereof to the court, when and as required by it, at any time prior to the final determination of the proceeding, and such filing of such certified list of the materials comprising the record and such subsequent transmittal of any such materials when and as required shall be deemed full compliance with any provision of law requiring the filing of the record in the court. The record in such proceedings shall be certified and filed in or held for and transmitted to the court of appeals by the agency, board, commission, or officer concerned within the time and in the manner prescribed by such rules. If proceedings are instituted in two or more courts of appeals with respect to the same order, the following shall apply:

(1) If within ten days after issuance of the order the agency, board, commission, or officer concerned receives, from the persons instituting the proceedings, the petition for review with respect to proceedings in at least two courts of appeals, the agency, board, commission, or officer shall proceed in accordance with paragraph (3) of this subsection. If within ten days after the issuance of the order the agency, board, commission, or officer concerned receives, from the persons instituting the proceedings, the petition for review with respect to proceedings in only one court of appeals, the agency, board, commission, or officer shall file the record in that court notwithstanding the institution in any other court of appeals of proceedings for review of that order. In all other cases in which proceedings have been instituted in two or more courts of appeals with respect to the same order, the agency, board, commission, or officer concerned shall file the record in the court in which proceedings with respect to the order were first instituted.

(2) For purposes of paragraph (1) of this subsection, a copy of the petition or other pleading which institutes proceedings in a court of appeals and which is stamped by the court with the date of filing shall constitute the petition for review. Each agency, board, commission, or officer, as the case may be, shall designate by rule the office and the officer who must receive petitions for review under paragraph (1).

(3) If an agency, board, commission, or officer receives two or more petitions for review of an order in accordance with the first sentence of paragraph (1) of this subsection, the agency, board, commission, or officer shall, promptly after the expiration of the ten-day period specified in that sentence, so notify the judicial panel on multidistrict litigation authorized by section 1407 of this title, in such form as that panel shall prescribe. The judicial panel on multidistrict litigation shall, by means of random selection, designate one court of appeals, from among the courts of appeals in which petitions for review have been filed and received within the ten-day period specified in the first sentence of paragraph (1), in which the record is to be filed, and shall issue an order consolidating the petitions for review in that court of appeals. The judicial panel on multidistrict litigation shall, after providing notice to the public and an opportunity for the submission of comments, prescribe rules with respect to the consolidation of proceedings under this paragraph. The agency, board, commission, or officer concerned shall file the record in the court of appeals designated pursuant to this paragraph.

(4) Any court of appeals in which proceedings with respect to an order of an agency, board, commission, or officer have been instituted may, to the extent authorized by law, stay the effective date of the order. Any such stay may thereafter be modified, revoked, or extended by a court of appeals designated pursuant to paragraph (3) with respect to that order or by any other court of appeals to which the proceedings are transferred.

(5) All courts in which proceedings are instituted with respect to the same order, other than the court in which the record is filed pursuant to this subsection, shall transfer those proceedings to the court in which the record is so filed. For the convenience of the parties in the interest of justice, the court in which the record is filed may thereafter transfer all the proceedings with respect to that order to any other court of appeals.

(b) The record to be filed in the court of appeals in such a proceeding shall consist of the order sought to be reviewed or enforced, the findings or report upon which it is based, and the pleadings, evidence, and proceedings before the agency, board, commission, or officer concerned, or such portions thereof (1) as the rules prescribed under the authority of section 2072 of this title may require to be included therein, or (2) as the agency, board, commission, or officer concerned, the petitioner for review or respondent in enforcement, as the case may be, and any intervenor in the court proceeding by written stipulation filed with the agency, board, commission, or officer concerned or in the court in any such proceeding may consistently with the rules prescribed under the authority of section 2072 of this title designate to be included therein, or (3) as the court upon motion of a party or, after a prehearing conference, upon its own motion may by order in any such proceeding designate to be included therein. Such a stipulation or order may provide in an appropriate case that no record need be filed in the court of appeals. If, however, the correctness of a finding of fact by the agency, board, commission, or officer is in question all of the evidence before the agency, board, commission, or officer shall be included in the record except such as the agency, board, commission, or officer concerned, the petitioner for review or respondent in enforcement, as the case may be, and any intervenor in the court proceeding by written stipulation filed with the agency, board, commission, or officer concerned or in the court agree to omit as wholly immaterial to the questioned finding. If there is omitted from the record any portion of the proceedings before the agency, board, commission, or officer which the court subsequently determines to be proper for it to consider to enable it to review or enforce the order in question the court may direct that such additional portion of the proceedings be filed as a supplement to the record. The agency, board, commission, or officer concerned may, at its option and without regard to the foregoing provisions of this subsection, and if so requested by the petitioner for review or respondent in enforcement shall, file in the court the entire record of the proceedings before it without abbreviation.

(c) The agency, board, commission, or officer concerned may transmit to the court of appeals the original papers comprising the whole or any part of the record or any supplemental record, otherwise true copies of such papers certified by an authorized officer or deputy of the agency, board, commission, or officer concerned shall be transmitted. Any original papers thus transmitted to the court of appeals shall be returned to the agency, board, commission, or officer concerned upon the final determination of the review or enforcement proceeding. Pending such final determination any such papers may be returned by the court temporarily to the custody of the agency, board, commission, or officer concerned if needed for the transaction of the public business. Certified copies of any papers included in the record or any supplemental record may also be returned to the agency, board, commission, or officer concerned upon the final determination of review or enforcement proceedings.

(d) The provisions of this section are not applicable to proceedings to review decisions of the Tax Court of the United States or to proceedings to review or enforce those orders of administrative agencies, boards, commissions, or officers which are by law reviewable or enforceable by the district courts.

(Added Pub.L. 85–791, § 2, Aug. 28, 1958, 72 Stat. 941, and amended Pub.L. 89–773, § 5(a), (b), Nov. 6, 1966, 80 Stat. 1323; Pub.L. 100–236, § 1, Jan. 8, 1988, 101 Stat. 1731.)

HISTORICAL AND STATUTORY NOTES

Effective and Applicability Provisions

1988 Acts. Section 3 of Pub.L. 100–236 provided that: "The amendments made by this Act [amending subsec. (a) of this section and section 1369(b) of Title 33, Navigation and Navigable Waters] take effect 180 days after the date of the enactment of this Act [Jan. 8, 1988], except that the judicial panel on multidistrict litigation may issue rules pursuant to subsection (a)(3) of section 2112 of title 28, United States Code (as added by section 1) [subsec. (a)(3) of this section], on or after such date of enactment."

Savings Provisions

Section 5(c) of Pub.L. 89–773 provided that: "The amendments of section 2112 of title 28 of the United States Code [this section] made by this Act shall not operate to invalidate or repeal rules adopted under the authority of that section prior to the enactment of this Act [Nov. 6, 1966], which rules shall remain in effect until superseded by rules prescribed under the authority of section 2072 of title 28 of the United States Code [section 2072 of this title] as amended by this Act."

§ 2113. Definition

For purposes of this chapter, the terms "State court", "State courts", and "highest court of a State" include the District of Columbia Court of Appeals.

(Added Pub.L. 91–358, Title I, § 172(a)(2)(A), July 29, 1970, 84 Stat. 590.)

HISTORICAL AND STATUTORY NOTES

Effective and Applicability Provisions

1970 Acts. Section effective the first day of the seventh calendar month which begins after July 29, 1970, see section 199(a) of Pub.L. 91–358, set out as a note under section 1257 of this title.

PART VI—PARTICULAR PROCEEDINGS

Chapter		Section
151.	Declaratory Judgments	2201
153.	Habeas Corpus	2241
154.	Special Habeas Corpus Procedures in Capital Cases	2261.[1]
155.	Injunctions; Three-Judge Courts	2281
157.	Surface Transportation Board Orders; Enforcement and Review	2321
158.	Orders of Federal Agencies; Review	2341
159.	Interpleader	2361
161.	United States as Party Generally	2401
163.	Fines, Penalties and Forfeitures	2461
165.	United States Court of Federal Claims Procedure	2501
[167.	Repealed]	
169.	Court of International Trade Procedure	2631
171.	Tort Claims Procedure	2671
173.	Attachment in Postal Suits	2710
[175.	Repealed]	
176.	Federal Debt Collection Procedure	3001
178.	Professional and Amateur Sports Protection	3701
179.	Judicial Review of Certain Actions by Presidential Offices	3901
180.	Assumption of Certain Contractual Obligations	4001

[1] So in original. The period probably should not appear.

HISTORICAL AND STATUTORY NOTES

Effective and Applicability Provisions

1996 Acts. Amendment of analysis by section 3(e) of Pub.L. 104–331, effective Oct. 1, 1997, see section 3(d) of Pub.L. 104–331, set out as a note under section 1296 of this title.

CHAPTER 151—DECLARATORY JUDGMENTS

Sec.
2201. Creation of remedy.
2202. Further relief.

§ 2201. Creation of remedy

(a) In a case of actual controversy within its jurisdiction, except with respect to Federal taxes other than actions brought under section 7428 of the Internal Revenue Code of 1986, a proceeding under section 505 or 1146 of title 11, or in any civil action involving an antidumping or countervailing duty proceeding regarding a class or kind of merchandise of a free trade area country (as defined in section 516A(f)(10) of the Tariff Act of 1930), as determined by the administering authority, any court of the United States, upon the filing of an appropriate pleading, may declare the rights and other legal relations of any interested party seeking such declaration, whether or not further relief is or could be sought. Any such declaration shall have the force and effect of a final judgment or decree and shall be reviewable as such.

(b) For limitations on actions brought with respect to drug patents see section 505 or 512 of the Federal Food, Drug, and Cosmetic Act.

(June 25, 1948, c. 646, 62 Stat. 964; May 24, 1949, c. 139, § 111, 63 Stat. 105; Aug. 28, 1954, c. 1033, 68 Stat. 890; July 7, 1958, Pub.L. 85–508, § 12(p), 72 Stat. 349; Oct. 4, 1976, Pub.L. 94–455, Title XIII, § 1306(b)(8), 90 Stat. 1719; Nov. 6, 1978, Pub.L. 95–598, Title II, § 249, 92 Stat. 2672; Sept. 24, 1984, Pub.L. 98–417, Title I, § 106, 98 Stat. 1597; Sept. 28, 1988, Pub.L. 100–449, Title IV, § 402(c), 102 Stat. 1884; Nov. 16, 1988, Pub.L. 100–670, Title I, § 107(b), 102 Stat. 3984; Dec. 8, 1993, Pub.L. 103–182, Title IV, § 414(b), 107 Stat. 2147.)

Termination of Amendments

For provisions directing that, except for transition provisions relating to proceedings regarding protective orders and undertakings, and binational panel and extraordinary challenge committee reviews, the amendment to this section by Title IV of Pub.L. 103–182 shall cease to have effect with respect to any country on the date on which such country ceases to be a NAFTA country, see 19 U.S.C.A. § 3451.

For provisions directing that the amendments made by Pub.L. 100–449, which amended this section, shall cease to have effect on the date on which the United States-Canada Free-Trade Agreement ceases to be in force, see section 501(c) of Pub.L. 100–449, set out in the note under 19 U.S.C.A. § 2112.

Articles 1906 and 2106 of the Agreement authorize either the United States or Canada to terminate the Agreement on 6–month notice if, at the end of the 7–year period following the date of the entry into effect of the Agreement, no agreement has been entered into between the United States and Canada on a substitute system of antidumping and countervailing duties.

HISTORICAL AND STATUTORY NOTES

References in Text

Section 7428 of the Internal Revenue Code of 1986, referred to in subsec. (a), is classified to section 7428 of Title 26, Internal Revenue Code.

Section 516A(f)(10) of the Tariff Act of 1930, referred to in subsec. (a), is classified to section 1516a(f)(10) of Title 19, Customs Duties.

Sections 505 and 512 of the Federal Food, Drug, and Cosmetic Act, referred to in subsec. (b), are classified to sections 355 and 360b, respectively, of Title 21, Food and Drugs.

Effective and Applicability Provisions

1993 Acts. Amendment of this section by section 414 of Pub.L. 103–182 to take effect on the date the North American Free Trade Agreement enters into force with respect to the United States, but not to apply to any final determination described in section 1516a(a)(1)(B) or (2)(B)(i), (ii), or (iii) of Title 19, Customs Duties, notice of which is published in the Federal Register before such date, or to a determination described in section 1516a(a)(2)(B)(vi) of Title 19 notice of which is received by the Government of Canada or Mexico before such date, or to any binational panel review under the United States-Canada Free-Trade Agreement, or to any extraordinary challenge arising out of any such review that was commenced before such date, see section 416 of Pub.L. 103–182, set out as a note under section 3431 of Title 19.

1988 Acts. Amendment by Pub.L. 100–449 effective on the date the United States-Canada Free-Trade Agreement enters into force (Jan. 1, 1989), and to cease to have effect on the date the Agreement ceases to be in force, see section 501(a), (c) of Pub.L. 100–449, set out in a note under section 2112 of Title 19, Customs Duties. [A Presidential Memorandum on the Canada-United States Free-Trade Agreement, dated Dec. 31, 1988, directing the Secretary of State to exchange notes with the Government of Canada to provide for the entry into force of the Agreement on Jan. 1, 1989, is set out in 24 Weekly Compilation of Presidential Documents 1688, Jan. 2, 1989.]

1978 Acts. Amendment by Pub.L. 95–598 effective Oct. 1, 1979, see section 402(c) of Pub.L. 95–598, set out as a note preceding section 101 of Title 11, Bankruptcy.

1976 Acts. Amendment by Pub.L. 94–455 applicable with respect to pleadings filed with the United States Tax Court, the District Court of the United States for the District of Columbia, or the United States Court of Claims more than 6 months after Oct. 4, 1976, but only with respect to determinations (or requests for determinations) made after Jan. 1, 1976, see section 1306(c) of Pub.L. 94–455, set out as a note under section 7428 of Title 26, Internal Revenue Code.

1958 Acts. Amendment by Pub.L. 85–508 effective Jan. 3, 1959, upon admission of Alaska into the Union pursuant to Proc. No. 3269, Jan. 3, 1959, 24 F.R. 81, 73 Stat. c. 16, as required by sections 1 and 8(c) of Pub.L. 85–508, see notes set out under section 81A of this title and preceding section 21 of Title 48, Territories and Insular Possessions.

Amount in Controversy

Jurisdictional amount increased from $3,000 to $50,000 in diversity of citizenship cases, see section 1332 of this title.

§ 2202. Further relief

Further necessary or proper relief based on a declaratory judgment or decree may be granted, after reasonable notice and hearing, against any adverse party whose rights have been determined by such judgment.

(June 25, 1948, c. 646, 62 Stat. 964.)

CHAPTER 153—HABEAS CORPUS

Sec.
2241. Power to grant writ.
2242. Application.
2243. Issuance of writ; return; hearing; decision.
2244. Finality of determination.
2245. Certificate of trial judge admissible in evidence.
2246. Evidence; depositions; affidavits.
2247. Documentary evidence.
2248. Return or answer; conclusiveness.
2249. Certified copies of indictment, plea and judgment; duty of respondent.
2250. Indigent petitioner entitled to documents without cost.
2251. Stay of State court proceedings.
2252. Notice.
2253. Appeal.
2254. State custody; remedies in Federal courts.
2255. Federal custody; remedies on motion attacking sentence.
[2256. Omitted.]

HISTORICAL AND STATUTORY NOTES

Codifications

The table of sections for chapter 153 was amended by Pub.L. 95–598, Title II, § 250(b), Nov. 6, 1978, 92 Stat. 2672, effective June 28, 1984, pursuant to Pub.L. 95–598, Title IV, § 402(b), Nov. 6, 1978, 92 Stat. 2682, as amended by Pub.L. 98–249, § 1(a), Mar. 31, 1984, 98 Stat. 116; Pub.L. 98–271, § 1(a), Apr. 30, 1984, 98 Stat. 163; Pub.L. 98–299, § 1(a), May 25, 1984, 98 Stat. 214; Pub.L. 98–325, § 1(a), June 20, 1984, 98 Stat. 268, set out as an Effective and Applicability Provisions note preceding section 101 of Title 11, Bankruptcy, by adding:

"2256. Habeas corpus from bankruptcy courts.".

Section 402(b) of Pub.L. 95–598 was amended by section 113 of Pub.L. 98–353, Title I, July 10, 1984, 98 Stat. 343, by substituting "shall not be effective" for "shall take effect on June 28, 1984", thereby eliminating the amendment by section 250(b) of Pub.L. 95–598, effective June 27, 1984, pursuant to section 122(c) of Pub.L. 98–353, set out as an Effective and Applicability Provisions note under section 151 of this title.

Section 121(a) of Pub.L. 98–353 directed that section 402(b) of Pub.L. 95–598 be amended by substituting "the date of enactment of the Bankruptcy Amendments and Federal Judgeship Act of 1984 [i.e. July 10, 1984]" for "June 28, 1984". This amendment was not executed in view of the prior amendment to section 402(b) of Pub.L. 95–598 by section 113 of Pub.L. 98–353.

§ 2241. Power to grant writ

(a) Writs of habeas corpus may be granted by the Supreme Court, any justice thereof, the district courts and any circuit judge within their respective jurisdictions. The order of a circuit judge shall be entered in the records of the district court of the district wherein the restraint complained of is had.

(b) The Supreme Court, any justice thereof, and any circuit judge may decline to entertain an application for a writ of habeas corpus and may transfer the application for hearing and determination to the district court having jurisdiction to entertain it.

(c) The writ of habeas corpus shall not extend to a prisoner unless—

(1) He is in custody under or by color of the authority of the United States or is committed for trial before some court thereof; or

(2) He is in custody for an act done or omitted in pursuance of an Act of Congress, or an order, process, judgment or decree of a court or judge of the United States; or

(3) He is in custody in violation of the Constitution or laws or treaties of the United States; or

(4) He, being a citizen of a foreign state and domiciled therein is in custody for an act done or omitted under any alleged right, title, authority, privilege, protection, or exemption claimed under the commission, order or sanction of any foreign state, or under color thereof, the validity and effect of which depend upon the law of nations; or

(5) It is necessary to bring him into court to testify or for trial.

(d) Where an application for a writ of habeas corpus is made by a person in custody under the judgment and sentence of a State court of a State which contains two or more Federal judicial districts, the application may be filed in the district court for the district wherein such person is in custody or in the district court for the district within which the State court was held which convicted and sentenced him and each of such district courts shall have concurrent jurisdiction to entertain the application. The district court for the district wherein such an application is filed in the exercise of its discretion and in furtherance of justice may transfer the application to the other district court for hearing and determination.

(e)(1) No court, justice, or judge shall have jurisdiction to hear or consider an application for a writ of habeas corpus filed by or on behalf of an alien detained by the United States who has been determined by the United States to have been properly detained as an enemy combatant or is awaiting such determination.

(2) Except as provided in paragraphs (2) and (3) of section 1005(e) of the Detainee Treatment Act of 2005 (10 U.S.C. 801 note), no court, justice, or judge shall have jurisdiction to hear or consider any other action against the United States or its agents relating to any aspect of the detention, transfer, treatment, trial, or conditions of confinement of an alien who is or was detained by the United States and has been determined by the United States to have been properly detained as an enemy combatant or is awaiting such determination.

(June 25, 1948, c. 646, 62 Stat. 964; May 24, 1949, c. 139, § 112, 63 Stat. 105; Sept. 19, 1966, Pub.L. 89–590, 80 Stat. 811; Dec. 30, 2005, Pub.L. 109–148, Div. A, Title X, § 1005(e)(1), 119 Stat. 2741; Jan. 6, 2006, Pub.L. 109–163, Div. A, Title XIV, § 1405(e)(1), 119 Stat. 3477; Oct. 17, 2006, Pub.L. 109–366, § 7(a), 120 Stat. 2635; Jan. 28, 2008, Pub.L. 110–181, Div. A, Title X, § 1063(f), 122 Stat. 323.)

HISTORICAL AND STATUTORY NOTES

References in Text

Section 1005(e) of the Detainee Treatment Act of 2005, referred to in subsec. (e)(2), probably means Pub.L. 109–148, Div. A, Title X, § 1005, Dec. 30, 2005, 119 Stat. 2740, which is set out in a note under 10 U.S.C.A. § 801 note. Pub.L. 109–163, Div. A, Title XIV, Jan. 6, 2006, 119 Stat. 3474, also enacted a "Detainee Treatment Act of 2005", see Short Title note under 42 U.S.C.A. § 2000dd and Tables, but that Act contains no section 1005(e).

Effective and Applicability Provisions

2006 Acts. Pub.L. 109–366, § 7(b), Oct. 17, 2006, 120 Stat. 2635, provided that: "The amendment made by subsection (a) [amending this section] shall take effect on the date of the enactment of this Act [Oct. 17, 2006], and shall apply to all cases, without exception, pending on or after the date of the enactment of this Act which relate to any aspect of the detention, transfer, treatment, trial, or conditions of detention of an alien detained by the United States since September 11, 2001."

Treaty Obligations not Establishing Grounds for Certain Claims

Pub.L. 109–366, § 5, Oct. 17, 2006, 120 Stat. 2631, provided that:

"(a) **In general.**—No person may invoke the Geneva Conventions or any protocols thereto in any habeas corpus or other civil action or proceeding to which the United States, or a current or former officer, employee, member of the Armed Forces, or other agent of the United States is a party as a source of rights in any court of the United States or its States or territories.

"(b) **Geneva conventions defined.**—In this section, the term 'Geneva Conventions' means—

"(1) the Convention for the Amelioration of the Condition of the Wounded and Sick in Armed Forces in the Field, done at Geneva August 12, 1949 (6 UST 3114);

"(2) the Convention for the Amelioration of the Condition of the Wounded, Sick, and Shipwrecked Members of the Armed Forces at Sea, done at Geneva August 12, 1949 (6 UST 3217);

"(3) the Convention Relative to the Treatment of Prisoners of War, done at Geneva August 12, 1949 (6 UST 3316); and

"(4) the Convention Relative to the Protection of Civilian Persons in Time of War, done at Geneva August 12, 1949 (6 UST 3516)."

§ 2242. Application

Application for a writ of habeas corpus shall be in writing signed and verified by the person for whose relief it is intended or by someone acting in his behalf.

It shall allege the facts concerning the applicant's commitment or detention, the name of the person who has custody over him and by virtue of what claim or authority, if known.

It may be amended or supplemented as provided in the rules of procedure applicable to civil actions.

If addressed to the Supreme Court, a justice thereof or a circuit judge it shall state the reasons for not making application to the district court of the district in which the applicant is held.

(June 25, 1948, c. 646, 62 Stat. 965.)

§ 2243. Issuance of writ; return; hearing; decision

A court, justice or judge entertaining an application for a writ of habeas corpus shall forthwith award the writ or issue an order directing the respondent to show cause why the writ should not be granted, unless it appears from the application that the applicant or person detained is not entitled thereto.

The writ, or order to show cause shall be directed to the person having custody of the person detained. It shall be returned within three days unless for good cause additional time, not exceeding twenty days, is allowed.

The person to whom the writ or order is directed shall make a return certifying the true cause of the detention.

When the writ or order is returned a day shall be set for hearing, not more than five days after the return unless for good cause additional time is allowed.

Unless the application for the writ and the return present only issues of law the person to whom the writ is directed shall be required to produce at the hearing the body of the person detained.

The applicant or the person detained may, under oath, deny any of the facts set forth in the return or allege any other material facts.

The return and all suggestions made against it may be amended, by leave of court, before or after being filed.

The court shall summarily hear and determine the facts, and dispose of the matter as law and justice require.

(June 25, 1948, c. 646, 62 Stat. 965.)

§ 2244. Finality of determination

(a) No circuit or district judge shall be required to entertain an application for a writ of habeas corpus to inquire into the detention of a person pursuant to a judgment of a court of the United States if it appears that the legality of such detention has been determined by a judge or court of the United States on a prior application for a writ of habeas corpus, except as provided in section 2255.

(b)(1) A claim presented in a second or successive habeas corpus application under section 2254 that was presented in a prior application shall be dismissed.

(2) A claim presented in a second or successive habeas corpus application under section 2254 that was not presented in a prior application shall be dismissed unless—

(A) the applicant shows that the claim relies on a new rule of constitutional law, made retroactive to cases on collateral review by the Supreme Court, that was previously unavailable; or

(B)(i) the factual predicate for the claim could not have been discovered previously through the exercise of due diligence; and

(ii) the facts underlying the claim, if proven and viewed in light of the evidence as a whole, would be sufficient to establish by clear and convincing evidence that, but for constitutional error, no reasonable factfinder would have found the applicant guilty of the underlying offense.

(3)(A) Before a second or successive application permitted by this section is filed in the district court, the applicant shall move in the appropriate court of appeals for an order authorizing the district court to consider the application.

(B) A motion in the court of appeals for an order authorizing the district court to consider a second or successive application shall be determined by a three-judge panel of the court of appeals.

(C) The court of appeals may authorize the filing of a second or successive application only if it determines that the application makes a prima facie showing that the application satisfies the requirements of this subsection.

(D) The court of appeals shall grant or deny the authorization to file a second or successive application not later than 30 days after the filing of the motion.

(E) The grant or denial of an authorization by a court of appeals to file a second or successive application shall not be appealable and shall not be the subject of a petition for rehearing or for a writ of certiorari.

(4) A district court shall dismiss any claim presented in a second or successive application that the court of appeals has authorized to be filed unless the applicant shows that the claim satisfies the requirements of this section.

(c) In a habeas corpus proceeding brought in behalf of a person in custody pursuant to the judgment of a State court, a prior judgment of the Supreme Court of the United States on an appeal or review by a writ of certiorari at the instance of the prisoner of the decision of such State court, shall be conclusive as to all issues of fact or law with respect to an asserted denial of a Federal right which constitutes ground for discharge in a habeas corpus proceeding, actually adjudicated by the Supreme Court therein, unless the applicant for the writ of habeas corpus shall plead and the court shall find the existence of a material and controlling fact which did not appear in the record of the proceeding in the Supreme Court and the court shall further find that the applicant for the writ of habeas corpus could not have caused such fact to appear in such record by the exercise of reasonable diligence.

(d)(1) A 1-year period of limitation shall apply to an application for a writ of habeas corpus by a person in custody pursuant to the judgment of a State court. The limitation period shall run from the latest of—

(A) the date on which the judgment became final by the conclusion of direct review or the expiration of the time for seeking such review;

(B) the date on which the impediment to filing an application created by State action in violation of the Constitution or laws of the United States is removed, if the applicant was prevented from filing by such State action;

(C) the date on which the constitutional right asserted was initially recognized by the Supreme Court, if the right has been newly recognized by the Supreme Court and made retroactively applicable to cases on collateral review; or

(D) the date on which the factual predicate of the claim or claims presented could have been discovered through the exercise of due diligence.

(2) The time during which a properly filed application for State post-conviction or other collateral review with respect to the pertinent judgment or claim is pending shall not be counted toward any period of limitation under this subsection.

(June 25, 1948, c. 646, 62 Stat. 965; Nov. 2, 1966, Pub.L. 89–711, § 1, 80 Stat. 1104; Apr. 24, 1996, Pub.L. 104–132, Title I, §§ 101, 106, 110 Stat. 1217, 1220.)

§ 2245. Certificate of trial judge admissible in evidence

On the hearing of an application for a writ of habeas corpus to inquire into the legality of the detention of a person pursuant to a judgment the certificate of the judge who presided at the trial resulting in the judgment, setting forth the facts occurring at the trial, shall be admissible in evidence. Copies of the certificate shall be filed with the court in which the application is pending and in the court in which the trial took place.

(June 25, 1948, c. 646, 62 Stat. 966.)

§ 2246. Evidence; depositions; affidavits

On application for a writ of habeas corpus, evidence may be taken orally or by deposition, or, in the discretion of the judge, by affidavit. If affidavits are admitted any party shall have the right to propound written interrogatories to the affiants, or to file answering affidavits.

(June 25, 1948, c. 646, 62 Stat. 966.)

§ 2247. Documentary evidence

On application for a writ of habeas corpus documentary evidence, transcripts of proceedings upon arraignment, plea and sentence and a transcript of the oral testimony introduced on any previous similar application by or in behalf of the same petitioner, shall be admissible in evidence.

(June 25, 1948, c. 646, 62 Stat. 966.)

§ 2248. Return or answer; conclusiveness

The allegations of a return to the writ of habeas corpus or of an answer to an order to show cause in a habeas corpus proceeding, if not traversed, shall be accepted as true except to the extent that the judge finds from the evidence that they are not true.

(June 25, 1948, c. 646, 62 Stat. 966.)

§ 2249. Certified copies of indictment, plea and judgment; duty of respondent

On application for a writ of habeas corpus to inquire into the detention of any person pursuant to a judgment of a court of the United States, the respondent shall promptly file with the court certified copies of the indictment, plea of petitioner and the judgment, or such of them as may be material to the questions raised, if the petitioner fails to attach them to his petition, and same shall be attached to the return to the writ, or to the answer to the order to show cause.

(June 25, 1948, c. 646, 62 Stat. 966.)

§ 2250. Indigent petitioner entitled to documents without cost

If on any application for a writ of habeas corpus an order has been made permitting the petitioner to prosecute the application in forma pauperis, the clerk of any court of the United States shall furnish to the petitioner without cost certified copies of such documents or parts of the record on file in his office as may be required by order of the judge before whom the application is pending.

(June 25, 1948, c. 646, 62 Stat. 966.)

§ 2251. Stay of State court proceedings

(a) In general.—

(1) Pending matters.—A justice or judge of the United States before whom a habeas corpus proceeding is pending, may, before final judgment or after final judgment of discharge, or pending appeal, stay any proceeding against the person detained in any State court or by or under the authority of any State for any matter involved in the habeas corpus proceeding.

(2) Matter not pending.—For purposes of this section, a habeas corpus proceeding is not pending until the application is filed.

(3) Application for appointment of counsel.—If a State prisoner sentenced to death applies for appointment of counsel pursuant to section 3599(a)(2) of title 18 in a court that would have jurisdiction to entertain a habeas corpus application regarding that sentence, that court may stay execution of the sentence of death, but such stay shall terminate not later than 90 days after counsel is appointed or the application for appointment of counsel is withdrawn or denied.

(b) No further proceedings.—After the granting of such a stay, any such proceeding in any State court or by or under the authority of any State shall be void. If no stay is granted, any such proceeding shall be as valid as if no habeas corpus proceedings or appeal were pending.

(June 25, 1948, c. 646, 62 Stat. 966; Mar. 9, 2006, Pub.L. 109–177, Title V, § 507(f), 120 Stat. 251.)

HISTORICAL AND STATUTORY NOTES

Application to Pending Cases

Pub.L. 109–177, Title V, § 507(d), Mar. 9, 2006, 120 Stat. 251, provided that:

"**(1) In general.**—This section and the amendments made by this section [enacting 28 U.S.C.A. § 2265, amending 28 U.S.C.A. §§ 2251, 2261, and 2266, and repealing 28 U.S.C.A. § 2265] shall apply to cases pending on or after the date of enactment of this Act [Mar. 9, 2006].

"**(2) Time limits.**—In a case pending on the date of enactment of this Act [Mar. 9, 2006], if the amendments made by this section [enacting 28 U.S.C.A. § 2265, amending 28 U.S.C.A. §§ 2251, 2261, and 2266, and repealing 28 U.S.C.A. § 2265] establish a time limit for taking certain action, the period of which began on the date of an event that occurred prior to the date of enactment of this Act [Mar. 9, 2006], the period of such time limit shall instead begin on the date of enactment of this Act [Mar. 9, 2006]."

§ 2252. Notice

Prior to the hearing of a habeas corpus proceeding in behalf of a person in custody of State officers or by virtue of State laws notice shall be served on the attorney general or other appropriate officer of such State as the justice or judge at the time of issuing the writ shall direct.

(June 25, 1948, c. 646, 62 Stat. 967.)

§ 2253. Appeal

(a) In a habeas corpus proceeding or a proceeding under section 2255 before a district judge, the final order shall be subject to review, on appeal, by the court of appeals for the circuit in which the proceeding is held.

(b) There shall be no right of appeal from a final order in a proceeding to test the validity of a warrant to remove to another district or place for commitment or trial a person charged with a criminal offense against the United States, or to test the validity of such person's detention pending removal proceedings.

(c)(1) Unless a circuit justice or judge issues a certificate of appealability, an appeal may not be taken to the court of appeals from—

(A) the final order in a habeas corpus proceeding in which the detention complained of arises out of process issued by a State court; or

(B) the final order in a proceeding under section 2255.

(2) A certificate of appealability may issue under paragraph (1) only if the applicant has made a substantial showing of the denial of a constitutional right.

(3) The certificate of appealability under paragraph (1) shall indicate which specific issue or issues satisfy the showing required by paragraph (2).

(June 25, 1948, c. 646, 62 Stat. 967; May 24, 1949, c. 139, § 113, 63 Stat. 105; Oct. 31, 1951, c. 655, § 52, 65 Stat. 727; Apr. 24, 1996, Pub.L. 104–132, Title I, § 102, 110 Stat. 1217.)

§ 2254. State custody; remedies in Federal courts

(a) The Supreme Court, a Justice thereof, a circuit judge, or a district court shall entertain an application for a writ of habeas corpus in behalf of a person in custody pursuant to the judgment of a State court only on the ground that he is in custody in violation of the Constitution or laws or treaties of the United States.

(b)(1) An application for a writ of habeas corpus on behalf of a person in custody pursuant to the judgment of a State court shall not be granted unless it appears that—

(A) the applicant has exhausted the remedies available in the courts of the State; or

(B)(i) there is an absence of available State corrective process; or

(ii) circumstances exist that render such process ineffective to protect the rights of the applicant.

(2) An application for a writ of habeas corpus may be denied on the merits, notwithstanding the failure of the applicant to exhaust the remedies available in the courts of the State.

(3) A State shall not be deemed to have waived the exhaustion requirement or be estopped from reliance upon the requirement unless the State, through counsel, expressly waives the requirement.

(c) An applicant shall not be deemed to have exhausted the remedies available in the courts of the State, within the meaning of this section, if he has the right under the law of the State to raise, by any available procedure, the question presented.

(d) An application for a writ of habeas corpus on behalf of a person in custody pursuant to the judgment of a State court shall not be granted with respect to any claim that was adjudicated on the merits in State court proceedings unless the adjudication of the claim—

(1) resulted in a decision that was contrary to, or involved an unreasonable application of, clearly established Federal law, as determined by the Supreme Court of the United States; or

(2) resulted in a decision that was based on an unreasonable determination of the facts in light of the evidence presented in the State court proceeding.

(e)(1) In a proceeding instituted by an application for a writ of habeas corpus by a person in custody pursuant to the judgment of a State court, a determination of a factual issue made by a State court shall be presumed to be correct. The applicant shall have the burden of rebutting the presumption of correctness by clear and convincing evidence.

(2) If the applicant has failed to develop the factual basis of a claim in State court proceedings, the court shall not hold an evidentiary hearing on the claim unless the applicant shows that—

(A) the claim relies on—

(i) a new rule of constitutional law, made retroactive to cases on collateral review by the Supreme Court, that was previously unavailable; or

(ii) a factual predicate that could not have been previously discovered through the exercise of due diligence; and

(B) the facts underlying the claim would be sufficient to establish by clear and convincing evidence that but for constitutional error, no reasonable factfinder would have found the applicant guilty of the underlying offense.

(f) If the applicant challenges the sufficiency of the evidence adduced in such State court proceeding to support the State court's determination of a factual issue made therein, the applicant, if able, shall produce that part of the record pertinent to a determination of the sufficiency of the evidence to support such determination. If the applicant, because of indigency or other reason is unable to produce such part of the record, then the State shall produce such part of the record and the Federal court shall direct the State to do so by order directed to an appropriate State official. If the State cannot provide such pertinent part of the record, then the court shall determine under the existing facts and circumstances what weight shall be given to the State court's factual determination.

(g) A copy of the official records of the State court, duly certified by the clerk of such court to be a true and correct copy of a finding, judicial opinion, or other reliable written indicia showing such a factual determination by the State court shall be admissible in the Federal court proceeding.

(h) Except as provided in section 408 of the Controlled Substances Act, in all proceedings brought under this section, and any subsequent proceedings on review, the court may appoint counsel for an applicant who is or becomes financially unable to afford counsel, except as provided by a rule promulgated by the Supreme Court pursuant to statutory authority. Appointment of counsel under this section shall be governed by section 3006A of title 18.

(i) The ineffectiveness or incompetence of counsel during Federal or State collateral post-conviction proceedings shall not be a ground for relief in a proceeding arising under section 2254.

(June 25, 1948, c. 646, 62 Stat. 967; Nov. 2, 1966, Pub.L. 89–711, § 2, 80 Stat. 1105; Apr. 24, 1996, Pub.L. 104–132, Title I, § 104, 110 Stat. 1218.)

HISTORICAL AND STATUTORY NOTES

Senate Revision Amendments

Senate amendment to this section, Senate Report No. 1559, amendment No. 47, has three declared purposes, set forth as follows:

"The first is to eliminate from the prohibition of the section applications in behalf of prisoners in custody under authority of a State officer but whose custody has not been directed by the judgment of a State court. If the section were applied to applications by persons detained solely under authority of a State officer it would unduly hamper Federal courts in the protection of Federal officers prosecuted for acts committed in the course of official duty.

"The second purpose is to eliminate, as a ground of Federal jurisdiction to review by habeas corpus judgments of State courts, the proposition that the State court has denied a prisoner a 'fair adjudication of the legality of his detention under the Constitution and laws of the United States.' The Judicial Conference believes that this would be an undesirable ground for Federal jurisdiction in addition to exhaustion of State remedies or lack of adequate remedy in the State courts because it would permit proceedings in the Federal court on this ground before the petitioner had exhausted his State remedies. This ground would, of course, always be open to a petitioner to assert in the Federal court after he had exhausted his State remedies or if he had no adequate State remedy.

"The third purpose is to substitute detailed and specific language for the phrase 'no adequate remedy available.' That phrase is not sufficiently specific and precise, and its meaning should, therefore, be spelled out in more detail in the section as is done by the amendment."

1966 Acts. Senate Report No. 1797, see 1966 U.S. Code Cong. and Adm. News, p. 3663.

References in Text

Section 408 of the Controlled Substances Act, referred to in subsec. (h), is classified to section 848 of Title 21, Food and Drugs.

Approval and Effective Date of Rules Governing Section 2254 Cases and Section 2255 Proceedings for United States District Courts

Pub.L. 94–426, § 1, Sept. 28, 1976, 90 Stat. 1334, provided: "That the rules governing section 2254 cases in the United States district courts and the rules governing section 2255 proceedings for the United States district courts, as proposed by the United States Supreme Court, which were delayed by the Act entitled 'An Act to delay the effective date of certain proposed amendments to the Federal Rules of Criminal Procedure and certain other rules promulgated by the United States Supreme Court' (Public Law 94–349), are approved with the amendments set forth in section 2 of this Act and shall take effect as so amended, with respect to petitions under section 2254 and motions under section 2255 of title 28 of the United States Code filed on or after February 1, 1977."

Postponement of Effective Date of Proposed Rules Governing Proceedings Under Sections 2254 and 2255 of this Title

Rules and forms governing proceedings under sections 2254 and 2255 of this title proposed by Supreme Court order of Apr. 26, 1976, effective 30 days after adjournment sine die of 94th Congress, or until and to the extent approved by Act of Congress, whichever is earlier, see section 2 of Pub.L. 94–349, set out as a note under section 2074 of this title.

CROSS REFERENCES

Rules Governing Section 2254 Cases in the United States District Courts are set out ante, following the Rules of Procedure of the Judicial Panel on Multidistrict Litigation.

§ 2255. Federal custody; remedies on motion attacking sentence

(a) A prisoner in custody under sentence of a court established by Act of Congress claiming the right to be released upon the ground that the sentence was imposed in violation of the Constitution or laws of the United States, or that the court was without jurisdiction to impose such sentence, or that the sentence was in excess of the maximum authorized by law, or is otherwise subject to collateral attack, may move the court which imposed the sentence to vacate, set aside or correct the sentence.

(b) Unless the motion and the files and records of the case conclusively show that the prisoner is entitled to no relief, the court shall cause notice thereof to be served upon the United States attorney, grant a prompt hearing thereon, determine the issues and make findings of fact and conclusions of law with respect thereto. If the court finds that the judgment was rendered without jurisdiction, or that the sentence imposed was not authorized by law or otherwise open to collateral attack, or that there has been such a denial or infringement of the constitutional rights of the prisoner as to render the judgment vulnerable to collateral attack, the court shall vacate and set the judgment aside and shall discharge the prisoner or resentence him or grant a new trial or correct the sentence as may appear appropriate.

(c) A court may entertain and determine such motion without requiring the production of the prisoner at the hearing.

(d) An appeal may be taken to the court of appeals from the order entered on the motion as from a final judgment on application for a writ of habeas corpus.

(e) An application for a writ of habeas corpus in behalf of a prisoner who is authorized to apply for relief by motion pursuant to this section, shall not be entertained if it appears that the applicant has failed to apply for relief, by motion, to the court which sentenced him, or that such court has denied him relief, unless it also appears that the remedy by motion is inadequate or ineffective to test the legality of his detention.

(f) A 1-year period of limitation shall apply to a motion under this section. The limitation period shall run from the latest of—

(1) the date on which the judgment of conviction becomes final;

(2) the date on which the impediment to making a motion created by governmental action in violation of the Constitution or laws of the United States is removed, if the movant was prevented from making a motion by such governmental action;

(3) the date on which the right asserted was initially recognized by the Supreme Court, if that right has been newly recognized by the Supreme Court and made retroactively applicable to cases on collateral review; or

(4) the date on which the facts supporting the claim or claims presented could have been discovered through the exercise of due diligence.

(g) Except as provided in section 408 of the Controlled Substances Act, in all proceedings brought under this section, and any subsequent proceedings on review, the court may appoint counsel, except as provided by a rule promulgated by the Supreme Court pursuant to statutory authority. Appointment of counsel under this section shall be governed by section 3006A of title 18.

(h) A second or successive motion must be certified as provided in section 2244 by a panel of the appropriate court of appeals to contain—

(1) newly discovered evidence that, if proven and viewed in light of the evidence as a whole, would be sufficient to establish by clear and convincing evidence that no reasonable factfinder would have found the movant guilty of the offense; or

(2) a new rule of constitutional law, made retroactive to cases on collateral review by the Supreme Court, that was previously unavailable.

(June 25, 1948, c. 646, 62 Stat. 967; May 24, 1949, c. 139, § 114, 63 Stat. 105; Apr. 24, 1996, Pub.L. 104–132, Title I, § 105, 110 Stat. 1220; Jan. 7, 2008, Pub.L. 110–177, Title V, § 511, 121 Stat. 2545.)

HISTORICAL AND STATUTORY NOTES

References in Text

Section 408 of the Controlled Substances Act, referred to in text, is classified to section 848 of Title 21, Food and Drugs.

Approval and Effective Date of Rules Governing Section 2254 Cases and Section 2255 Proceedings For United States District Courts

Pub.L. 94–426, § 1, Sept. 28, 1976, 90 Stat. 1334, provided: "That the rules governing section 2254 cases in the United States district courts and the rules governing section 2255 proceedings for the United States district courts, as proposed by the United States Supreme Court, which were delayed by the Act entitled 'An Act to delay the effective date of certain proposed amendments to the Federal Rules of Criminal Procedure and certain other rules promulgated by the United States Supreme Court' (Public Law 94–349), are approved with the amendments set forth in section 2 of this Act and shall take effect as so amended, with respect to petitions under section 2254 and motions [sections 2254 and 2255 of this title] under section 2255 of title 28 of the United States Code filed on or after February 1, 1977."

Postponement of Effective Date of Proposed Rules and Forms Governing Proceedings Under Sections 2254 and 2255 of this Title

Rules and forms governing proceedings under this section and section 2254 of this title proposed by Supreme Court order of Apr. 26, 1976, effective 30 days after adjournment sine die of 94th Congress, or until and to the extent approved by Act of Congress, whichever is earlier, see section 2 of Pub.L. 94–349, set out as a note under section 2074 of this title.

CROSS REFERENCES

Rules Governing Section 2255 Proceedings in the United States District Courts are set out ante, following the Rules Governing Section 2254 Cases in the United States District Courts.

[§ 2256. Omitted]

HISTORICAL AND STATUTORY NOTES

Codifications

This section as added by Pub. L. 95–598, Title II, § 250(a), Nov. 6, 1978, 92 Stat. 2672, effective June 28, 1984, pursuant to Pub. L. 95–598, Title IV, § 402(b), Nov. 6, 1978, 92 Stat. 2682, as amended by Pub. L. 98–249, § 1(a), Mar. 31, 1984, 98 Stat. 116; Pub. L. 98–271, § 1(a), Apr. 30, 1984, 98 Stat. 163; Pub. L. 98–299, § 1(a), May 25, 1984, 98 Stat. 214; Pub. L. 98–325, § 1(a), June 20, 1984, 98 Stat. 268 [set out as an Effective and Applicability Provisions note preceding section 101 of Title 11, Bankruptcy], read as follows:

§ 2256. Habeas corpus from bankruptcy courts

A bankruptcy court may issue a writ of habeas corpus—

(1) when appropriate to bring a person before the court—

(A) for examination;

(B) to testify; or

(C) to perform a duty imposed on such person under this title; or

(2) ordering the release of a debtor in a case under title 11 in custody under the judgment of a Federal or State court if—

(A) such debtor was arrested or imprisoned on process in any civil action;

(B) such process was issued for the collection of a debt—

(i) dischargeable under title 11; or

(ii) that is or will be provided for in a plan under chapter 11 or 13 of title 11; and

(C) before the issuance of such writ, notice and a hearing have been afforded the adverse party of such debtor in custody to contest the issuance of such writ.

Section 402(b) of Pub. L. 95–598 was amended by section 113 of Pub. L. 98–353 Title I, July 10, 1984, 98 Stat. 343, by substituting "shall not be effective" for "shall take effect on June 28, 1984", thereby eliminating the amendment by section 250(a) of Pub. L. 95–598, effective June 27, 1984, pursuant to section 122(c) of Pub. L. 98–353, set out as an Effective and Applicability Provisions note under section 151 of this title.

Section 121(a) of Pub. L. 98–353 directed that section 402(b) of Pub. L. 95–598 be amended by substituting "the date of enactment of the Bankruptcy Amendments and Federal Judgeship Act of 1984 [i.e. July 10, 1984]" for "June 28 1984". This amendment was not executed in view of the prior amendment to section 402(b) of Pub. L. 95–598 by section 113 of Pub. L. 98–353.

Prior Provisions

A prior section 2256, added Pub. L. 95–144, § 3, Oct. 28, 1977, 91 Stat. 1220, which related to jurisdiction of proceedings relating to transferred offenders, was transferred to section 3244 of Title 18, Crimes and Criminal Procedure, by Pub. L. 95–598, Title III, § 314(j), Nov. 6, 1978, 92 Stat. 2677.

CHAPTER 154—SPECIAL HABEAS CORPUS PROCEDURES IN CAPITAL CASES

Sec.
2261. Prisoners in State custody subject to capital sentence; appointment of counsel; requirement of rule of court or statute; procedures for appointment.
2262. Mandatory stay of execution; duration; limits on stays of execution; successive petitions.
2263. Filing of habeas corpus application; time requirements; tolling rules.
2264. Scope of Federal review; district court adjudications.
2265. Certification and judicial review.
2266. Limitation periods for determining applications and motions.

§ 2261. Prisoners in State custody subject to capital sentence; appointment of counsel; requirement of rule of court or statute; procedures for appointment

(a) This chapter shall apply to cases arising under section 2254 brought by prisoners in State custody who are subject to a capital sentence. It shall apply only if the provisions of subsections (b) and (c) are satisfied.

(b) Counsel.—This chapter is applicable if—

(1) the Attorney General of the United States certifies that a State has established a mechanism for providing counsel in postconviction proceedings as provided in section 2265; and

(2) counsel was appointed pursuant to that mechanism, petitioner validly waived counsel, petitioner retained counsel, or petitioner was found not to be indigent.

(c) Any mechanism for the appointment, compensation, and reimbursement of counsel as provided in subsection (b) must offer counsel to all State prisoners under capital sentence and must provide for the entry of an order by a court of record—

(1) appointing one or more counsels to represent the prisoner upon a finding that the prisoner is indigent and accepted the offer or is unable competently to decide whether to accept or reject the offer;

(2) finding, after a hearing if necessary, that the prisoner rejected the offer of counsel and made the decision with an understanding of its legal consequences; or

(3) denying the appointment of counsel upon a finding that the prisoner is not indigent.

(d) No counsel appointed pursuant to subsections (b) and (c) to represent a State prisoner under capital sentence shall have previously represented the prisoner at trial in the case for which the appointment is made unless the prisoner and counsel expressly request continued representation.

(e) The ineffectiveness or incompetence of counsel during State or Federal post-conviction proceedings in a capital case shall not be a ground for relief in a proceeding arising under section 2254. This limitation shall not preclude the appointment of different counsel, on the court's own motion or at the request of the prisoner, at any phase of State or Federal post-conviction proceedings on the basis of the ineffectiveness or incompetence of counsel in such proceedings.

(Added Pub.L. 104–132, Title I, § 107(a), Apr. 24, 1996, 110 Stat. 1221, and amended Pub.L. 109–177, Title V, § 507(a), (b), Mar. 9, 2006, 120 Stat. 250.)

HISTORICAL AND STATUTORY NOTES

Effective and Applicability Provisions

1996 Acts. Section 107(c) of Pub.L. 104–132 provided that: "Chapter 154 of title 28, United States Code (as added by subsection (a)) [this chapter] shall apply to cases pending on or after the date of enactment of this Act [Apr. 24, 1996]."

§ 2262. Mandatory stay of execution; duration; limits on stays of execution; successive petitions

(a) Upon the entry in the appropriate State court of record of an order under section 2261(c), a warrant or order setting an execution date for a State prisoner shall be stayed upon application to any court that would have jurisdiction over any proceedings filed under section 2254. The application shall recite that the State has invoked the post-conviction review procedures of this chapter and that the scheduled execution is subject to stay.

(b) A stay of execution granted pursuant to subsection (a) shall expire if—

(1) a State prisoner fails to file a habeas corpus application under section 2254 within the time required in section 2263;

(2) before a court of competent jurisdiction, in the presence of counsel, unless the prisoner has competently and knowingly waived such counsel, and after having been advised of the consequences, a State prisoner under capital sentence waives the right to pursue habeas corpus review under section 2254; or

(3) a State prisoner files a habeas corpus petition under section 2254 within the time required by section 2263 and fails to make a substantial showing of the denial of a Federal right or is denied relief in the district court or at any subsequent stage of review.

(c) If one of the conditions in subsection (b) has occurred, no Federal court thereafter shall have the authority to enter a stay of execution in the case,

unless the court of appeals approves the filing of a second or successive application under section 2244(b).
(Added Pub.L. 104–132, Title I, § 107(a), Apr. 24, 1996, 110 Stat. 1222.)

HISTORICAL AND STATUTORY NOTES

Effective and Applicability Provisions

1996 Acts. Section applicable to cases pending on or after Apr. 24, 1996, see section 107(c) of Pub.L. 104–132, set out as a note under section 2261 of this title.

§ 2263. Filing of habeas corpus application; time requirements; tolling rules

(a) Any application under this chapter for habeas corpus relief under section 2254 must be filed in the appropriate district court not later than 180 days after final State court affirmance of the conviction and sentence on direct review or the expiration of the time for seeking such review.

(b) The time requirements established by subsection (a) shall be tolled—

(1) from the date that a petition for certiorari is filed in the Supreme Court until the date of final disposition of the petition if a State prisoner files the petition to secure review by the Supreme Court of the affirmance of a capital sentence on direct review by the court of last resort of the State or other final State court decision on direct review;

(2) from the date on which the first petition for post-conviction review or other collateral relief is filed until the final State court disposition of such petition; and

(3) during an additional period not to exceed 30 days, if—

(A) a motion for an extension of time is filed in the Federal district court that would have jurisdiction over the case upon the filing of a habeas corpus application under section 2254; and

(B) a showing of good cause is made for the failure to file the habeas corpus application within the time period established by this section.

(Added Pub.L. 104–132, Title I, § 107(a), Apr. 24, 1996, 110 Stat. 1223.)

HISTORICAL AND STATUTORY NOTES

Effective and Applicability Provisions

1996 Acts. Section applicable to cases pending on or after Apr. 24, 1996, see section 107(c) of Pub.L. 104–132, set out as a note under section 2261 of this title.

§ 2264. Scope of Federal review; district court adjudications

(a) Whenever a State prisoner under capital sentence files a petition for habeas corpus relief to which this chapter applies, the district court shall only consider a claim or claims that have been raised and decided on the merits in the State courts, unless the failure to raise the claim properly is—

(1) the result of State action in violation of the Constitution or laws of the United States;

(2) the result of the Supreme Court's recognition of a new Federal right that is made retroactively applicable; or

(3) based on a factual predicate that could not have been discovered through the exercise of due diligence in time to present the claim for State or Federal post-conviction review.

(b) Following review subject to subsections (a), (d), and (e) of section 2254, the court shall rule on the claims properly before it.
(Added Pub.L. 104–132, Title I, § 107(a), Apr. 24, 1996, 110 Stat. 1223.)

HISTORICAL AND STATUTORY NOTES

Effective and Applicability Provisions

1996 Acts. Section applicable to cases pending on or after Apr. 24, 1996, see section 107(c) of Pub.L. 104–132, set out as a note under section 2261 of this title.

§ 2265. Certification and judicial review

(a) Certification.—

(1) In general.—If requested by an appropriate State official, the Attorney General of the United States shall determine—

(A) whether the State has established a mechanism for the appointment, compensation, and payment of reasonable litigation expenses of competent counsel in State postconviction proceedings brought by indigent prisoners who have been sentenced to death;

(B) the date on which the mechanism described in subparagraph (A) was established; and

(C) whether the State provides standards of competency for the appointment of counsel in proceedings described in subparagraph (A).

(2) Effective date.—The date the mechanism described in paragraph (1)(A) was established shall be the effective date of the certification under this subsection.

(3) Only express requirements.—There are no requirements for certification or for application of this chapter other than those expressly stated in this chapter.

(b) Regulations.—The Attorney General shall promulgate regulations to implement the certification procedure under subsection (a).

(c) Review of certification.—

(1) In general.—The determination by the Attorney General regarding whether to certify a State under this section is subject to review exclusively as provided under chapter 158 of this title.

(2) Venue.—The Court of Appeals for the District of Columbia Circuit shall have exclusive jurisdiction over matters under paragraph (1), subject to review by the Supreme Court under section 2350 of this title.

(3) Standard of review.—The determination by the Attorney General regarding whether to certify a State under this section shall be subject to de novo review.

(Added Pub.L. 109–177, Title V, § 507(c)(1), Mar. 9, 2006, 120 Stat. 250.)

HISTORICAL AND STATUTORY NOTES

References in Text

Chapter 158 of this title, referred to in subsec. (c)(1), is Orders of Federal Agencies; Review, 28 U.S.C.A. § 2341 et seq.

Prior Provisions

A prior section 2265, added Pub.L. 104–132, Title I, § 107(a), Apr. 24, 1996, 110 Stat. 1223, relating to application to State unitary review procedure, was repealed by Pub.L. 109–177, Title V, § 507(c)(1), Mar. 9, 2006, 120 Stat. 250.

§ 2266. Limitation periods for determining applications and motions

(a) The adjudication of any application under section 2254 that is subject to this chapter, and the adjudication of any motion under section 2255 by a person under sentence of death, shall be given priority by the district court and by the court of appeals over all noncapital matters.

(b)(1)(A) A district court shall render a final determination and enter a final judgment on any application for a writ of habeas corpus brought under this chapter in a capital case not later than 450 days after the date on which the application is filed, or 60 days after the date on which the case is submitted for decision, whichever is earlier.

(B) A district court shall afford the parties at least 120 days in which to complete all actions, including the preparation of all pleadings and briefs, and if necessary, a hearing, prior to the submission of the case for decision.

(C)(i) A district court may delay for not more than one additional 30–day period beyond the period specified in subparagraph (A), the rendering of a determination of an application for a writ of habeas corpus if the court issues a written order making a finding, and stating the reasons for the finding, that the ends of justice that would be served by allowing the delay outweigh the best interests of the public and the applicant in a speedy disposition of the application.

(ii) The factors, among others, that a court shall consider in determining whether a delay in the disposition of an application is warranted are as follows:

(I) Whether the failure to allow the delay would be likely to result in a miscarriage of justice.

(II) Whether the case is so unusual or so complex, due to the number of defendants, the nature of the prosecution, or the existence of novel questions of fact or law, that it is unreasonable to expect adequate briefing within the time limitations established by subparagraph (A).

(III) Whether the failure to allow a delay in a case that, taken as a whole, is not so unusual or so complex as described in subclause (II), but would otherwise deny the applicant reasonable time to obtain counsel, would unreasonably deny the applicant or the government continuity of counsel, or would deny counsel for the applicant or the government the reasonable time necessary for effective preparation, taking into account the exercise of due diligence.

(iii) No delay in disposition shall be permissible because of general congestion of the court's calendar.

(iv) The court shall transmit a copy of any order issued under clause (i) to the Director of the Administrative Office of the United States Courts for inclusion in the report under paragraph (5).

(2) The time limitations under paragraph (1) shall apply to—

(A) an initial application for a writ of habeas corpus;

(B) any second or successive application for a writ of habeas corpus; and

(C) any redetermination of an application for a writ of habeas corpus following a remand by the court of appeals or the Supreme Court for further proceedings, in which case the limitation period shall run from the date the remand is ordered.

(3)(A) The time limitations under this section shall not be construed to entitle an applicant to a stay of execution, to which the applicant would otherwise not be entitled, for the purpose of litigating any application or appeal.

(B) No amendment to an application for a writ of habeas corpus under this chapter shall be permitted after the filing of the answer to the application, except on the grounds specified in section 2244(b).

(4)(A) The failure of a court to meet or comply with a time limitation under this section shall not be a ground for granting relief from a judgment of conviction or sentence.

(B) The State may enforce a time limitation under this section by petitioning for a writ of mandamus to the court of appeals. The court of appeals shall act on the petition for a writ of mandamus not later than 30 days after the filing of the petition.

(5)(A) The Administrative Office of the United States Courts shall submit to Congress an annual report on the compliance by the district courts with the time limitations under this section.

(B) The report described in subparagraph (A) shall include copies of the orders submitted by the district courts under paragraph (1)(B)(iv).

(c)(1)(A) A court of appeals shall hear and render a final determination of any appeal of an order granting or denying, in whole or in part, an application brought under this chapter in a capital case not later than 120 days after the date on which the reply brief is filed, or if no reply brief is filed, not later than 120 days after the date on which the answering brief is filed.

(B)(i) A court of appeals shall decide whether to grant a petition for rehearing or other request for rehearing en banc not later than 30 days after the date on which the petition for rehearing is filed unless a responsive pleading is required, in which case the court shall decide whether to grant the petition not later than 30 days after the date on which the responsive pleading is filed.

(ii) If a petition for rehearing or rehearing en banc is granted, the court of appeals shall hear and render a final determination of the appeal not later than 120 days after the date on which the order granting rehearing or rehearing en banc is entered.

(2) The time limitations under paragraph (1) shall apply to—

(A) an initial application for a writ of habeas corpus;

(B) any second or successive application for a writ of habeas corpus; and

(C) any redetermination of an application for a writ of habeas corpus or related appeal following a remand by the court of appeals en banc or the Supreme Court for further proceedings, in which case the limitation period shall run from the date the remand is ordered.

(3) The time limitations under this section shall not be construed to entitle an applicant to a stay of execution, to which the applicant would otherwise not be entitled, for the purpose of litigating any application or appeal.

(4)(A) The failure of a court to meet or comply with a time limitation under this section shall not be a ground for granting relief from a judgment of conviction or sentence.

(B) The State may enforce a time limitation under this section by applying for a writ of mandamus to the Supreme Court.

(5) The Administrative Office of the United States Courts shall submit to Congress an annual report on the compliance by the courts of appeals with the time limitations under this section.

(Added Pub.L. 104–132, Title I, § 107(a), Apr. 24, 1996, 110 Stat. 1224, and amended Pub.L. 109–177, Title V, § 507(e), Mar. 9, 2006, 120 Stat. 251.)

HISTORICAL AND STATUTORY NOTES

Effective and Applicability Provisions

1996 Acts. Section applicable to cases pending on or after Apr. 24, 1996, see section 107(c) of Pub.L. 104–132, set out as a note under section 2261 of this title.

CHAPTER 155—INJUNCTIONS; THREE-JUDGE COURTS

Sec.
[2281, 2282. Repealed.]
2283. Stay of State court proceedings.
2284. Three-judge district court; when required; composition; procedure.[1]

[1] So in original. Does not conform to section catchline.

[§ 2281. Repealed. Pub.L. 94–381, § 1, Aug. 12, 1976, 90 Stat. 1119]

HISTORICAL AND STATUTORY NOTES

Section, Act June 25, 1948, c. 646, 62 Stat. 968, provided that an interlocutory or permanent injunction restraining the enforcement, operation or execution of a State statute on grounds of unconstitutionality should not be granted unless the application has been heard and determined by a three-judge district court.

Effective Date of Repeal

Repeal by Pub.L. 94–381 not applicable to any action commenced on or before Aug. 12, 1976, see section 7 of Pub.L. 94–381, set out as an Effective and Applicability Provisions of 1976 Amendments note under section 2284 of this title.

[§ 2282. Repealed. Pub.L. 94–381, § 2, Aug. 12, 1976, 90 Stat. 1119]

HISTORICAL AND STATUTORY NOTES

Section, Act June 25, 1948, c. 646, 62 Stat. 968, provided that an interlocutory or permanent injunction restraining the enforcement, operation or execution of any Act of Congress on grounds of unconstitutionality should not be granted unless the application therefor has been heard and determined by a three-judge district court.

Effective Date of Repeal

Repeal by Pub.L. 94–381 not applicable to any action commenced on or before Aug. 12, 1976, see section 7 of Pub.L. 94–381, set out as an Effective and Applicability Provisions of 1976 Amendments note under section 2284 of this title.

§ 2283. Stay of State court proceedings

A court of the United States may not grant an injunction to stay proceedings in a State court except as expressly authorized by Act of Congress, or where necessary in aid of its jurisdiction, or to protect or effectuate its judgments.

(June 25, 1948, c. 646, 62 Stat. 968.)

§ 2284. Three-judge court; when required; composition; procedure

(a) A district court of three judges shall be convened when otherwise required by Act of Congress, or when an action is filed challenging the constitutionality of the apportionment of congressional districts or the apportionment of any statewide legislative body.

(b) In any action required to be heard and determined by a district court of three judges under subsection (a) of this section, the composition and procedure of the court shall be as follows:

(1) Upon the filing of a request for three judges, the judge to whom the request is presented shall, unless he determines that three judges are not required, immediately notify the chief judge of the circuit, who shall designate two other judges, at least one of whom shall be a circuit judge. The judges so designated, and the judge to whom the request was presented, shall serve as members of the court to hear and determine the action or proceeding.

(2) If the action is against a State, or officer or agency thereof, at least five days' notice of hearing of the action shall be given by registered or certified mail to the Governor and attorney general of the State.

(3) A single judge may conduct all proceedings except the trial, and enter all orders permitted by the rules of civil procedure except as provided in this subsection. He may grant a temporary restraining order on a specific finding, based on evidence submitted, that specified irreparable damage will result if the order is not granted, which order, unless previously revoked by the district judge, shall remain in force only until the hearing and determination by the district court of three judges of an application for a preliminary injunction. A single judge shall not appoint a master, or order a reference, or hear and determine any application for a preliminary or permanent injunction or motion to vacate such an injunction, or enter judgment on the merits. Any action of a single judge may be reviewed by the full court at any time before final judgment.

(June 25, 1948, c. 646, 62 Stat. 968; June 11, 1960, Pub.L. 86–507, § 1(19), 74 Stat. 201; Aug. 12, 1976, Pub.L. 94–381, § 3, 90 Stat. 1119; Nov. 8, 1984, Pub.L. 98–620, Title IV, § 402(29)(E), 98 Stat. 3359.)

HISTORICAL AND STATUTORY NOTES

References in Text

The rules of civil procedure, referred to in subsec. (b)(3), are classified generally to this title.

Effective and Applicability Provisions

1984 Acts. Amendment by Pub.L. 98–620 not to apply to cases pending on Nov. 8, 1984, see section 403 of Pub.L. 98–620, set out as a note under section 1657 of this title.

1976 Acts. Section 7 of Pub.L. 94–381 provided that: "This Act [amending this section and section 2403 of this title and repealing sections 2281 and 2282 of this title] shall not apply to any action commenced on or before the date of enactment [Aug. 12, 1976]."

CHAPTER 157—SURFACE TRANSPORTATION BOARD ORDERS; ENFORCEMENT AND REVIEW

Sec.
2321. Judicial review of Board's orders and decisions; procedure generally; process.
2322. United States as party.
2323. Duties of Attorney General; intervenors.
[2324, 2325. Repealed.]

§ 2321. Judicial review of Board's orders and decisions; procedure generally; process

(a) Except as otherwise provided by an Act of Congress, a proceeding to enjoin or suspend, in whole or in part, a rule, regulation, or order of the Surface Transportation Board shall be brought in the court of appeals as provided by and in the manner prescribed in chapter 158 of this title.

(b) The procedure in the district courts in actions to enforce, in whole or in part, any order of the Surface Transportation Board other than for payment of money or the collection of fines, penalties, and forfeitures, shall be as provided in this chapter.

(c) The orders, writs, and process of the district courts may, in the cases specified in subsection (b) and in enforcement actions and actions to collect civil penalties under subtitle IV of title 49, run, be served and be returnable anywhere in the United States.

(June 25, 1948, c. 646, 62 Stat. 969; May 24, 1949, c. 139, § 115, 63 Stat. 105; Jan. 2, 1975, Pub.L. 93–584, § 5, 88 Stat. 1917; Oct. 17, 1978, Pub.L. 95–473, § 2(a)(3)(B), 92 Stat. 1465; Dec. 29, 1995, Pub.L. 104–88, Title III, § 305(c)(1)(B), (C), 109 Stat. 945.)

HISTORICAL AND STATUTORY NOTES

Effective and Applicability Provisions

1995 Acts. Amendment by Pub.L. 104–88 effective Jan. 1, 1996, see section 2 of Pub.L. 104–88, set out as a note under section 701 of Title 49, Transportation.

1975 Acts. Section 10 of Pub.L. 93–584 provided that: "This Act [amending this section and sections 1336, 1398, 2323, 2341, and 2342 of this title and section 305 of former Title 49, Transportation, and repealing sections 2324 and 2325 of this title] shall not apply to any action commenced on or before the last day of the first month beginning after the date of enactment [Jan. 2, 1975]. However, actions to enjoin or suspend orders of the Interstate Commerce Commission [now Surface Transportation Board] which are pending when this Act becomes effective shall not be affected thereby, but shall proceed to final disposition under the law existing on the date they were commenced."

[Interstate Commerce Commission abolished and functions of Commission transferred, except as otherwise provided in Pub.L. 104–88, to Surface Transportation Board effective Jan. 1, 1996, by sections 702 of Title 49, Transportation, and section 101 of Pub.L. 104–88, set out as a note under section 701 of title 49. References to Interstate Commerce Commission deemed to refer to Surface Transportation Board, a member or employee of the Board, or Secretary of Transportation, as appropriate, see section 205 of Pub.L. 104–88, set out as a note under section 701 of Title 49.]

§ 2322. United States as party

All actions specified in section 2321 of this title shall be brought by or against the United States.

(June 25, 1948, c. 646, 62 Stat. 969.)

§ 2323. Duties of Attorney General; intervenors

The Attorney General shall represent the Government in the actions specified in section 2321 of this title and in enforcement actions and actions to collect civil penalties under subtitle IV of title 49.

The Surface Transportation Board and any party or parties in interest to the proceeding before the Board, in which an order or requirement is made, may appear as parties of their own motion and as of right, and be represented by their counsel, in any action involving the validity of such order or requirement or any part thereof, and the interest of such party.

Communities, associations, corporations, firms, and individuals interested in the controversy or question before the Board, or in any action commenced under the aforesaid sections may intervene in said action at any time after commencement thereof.

The Attorney General shall not dispose of or discontinue said action or proceeding over the objection of such party or intervenor, who may prosecute, defend, or continue said action or proceeding unaffected by the action or nonaction of the Attorney General therein.

(June 25, 1948, c. 646, 62 Stat. 970; May 24, 1949, c. 139, § 116, 63 Stat. 105; Jan. 2, 1975, Pub.L. 93–584, § 6, 88 Stat. 1917; Oct. 17, 1978, Pub.L. 95–473, § 2(a)(3)(C), 92 Stat. 1465; Dec. 29, 1995, Pub.L. 104–88, Title III, § 305(c)(1)(C), (D), 109 Stat. 945.)

HISTORICAL AND STATUTORY NOTES

Effective and Applicability Provisions

1995 Acts. Amendment by Pub.L. 104–88 effective Jan. 1, 1996, see section 2 of Pub.L. 104–88, set out as a note under section 701 of Title 49, Transportation.

1975 Acts. Amendment by Pub.L. 93–584 not applicable to actions commenced on or before the last day of the first month beginning after Jan. 2, 1975, and actions to enjoin or suspend orders of the Interstate Commerce Commission [now Surface Transportation Board] which are pending when this amendment becomes effective shall not be affected thereby, but shall proceed to final disposition under the law existing on the date they were commenced, see section 10 of Pub.L. 93–584, set out as a note under section 2321 of this title.

[Interstate Commerce Commission abolished and functions of Commission transferred, except as otherwise provided in Pub.L. 104–88, to Surface Transportation Board effective Jan. 1, 1996, by sections 702 of Title 49, Transportation, and section 101 of Pub.L. 104–88, set out as a note under section 701 of title 49. References to Interstate Commerce Commission deemed to refer to Surface Transportation Board, a member or employee of the Board, or Secretary of Transportation, as appropriate, see section 205 of Pub.L. 104–88, set out as a note under section 701 of Title 49.]

[§§ 2324, 2325. Repealed. Pub.L. 93–584, § 7, Jan. 2, 1975, 88 Stat. 1918]

HISTORICAL AND STATUTORY NOTES

Section 2324, Act June 25, 1948, c. 646, 62 Stat. 970, related to the power of the court to restrain or suspend the operation of orders of Interstate Commerce Commission pending the final hearing and determination of the action.

Section 2325, Act June 25, 1948, c. 646, 62 Stat. 970, related to the requirement of a three-judge district court to hear and determine interlocutory or permanent injunctions restraining the enforcement, operation or execution of orders of Interstate Commerce Commission.

Effective Date of Repeal

Repeal of sections not applicable to actions commenced on or before the last day of the first month beginning after Jan. 2, 1975, and actions to enjoin or suspend orders of the Interstate Commerce Commission which are pending when this repeal becomes effective shall not be affected thereby, but shall proceed to final disposition under the law existing on the date they were commenced, see section 10 of Pub.L. 93–584, set out as an Effective and Applicability Provisions of 1975 Amendments note under section 2321 of this title.

CHAPTER 158—ORDERS OF FEDERAL AGENCIES; REVIEW

Sec.
2341. Definitions.
2342. Jurisdiction of court of appeals.

Sec.
2343. Venue.
2344. Review of orders; time; notice; contents of petitions; service.[1]
2345. Prehearing conference.
2346. Certification of record on review.
2347. Petitions to review; proceedings.
2348. Representation in proceeding; intervention.
2349. Jurisdiction of the proceeding.
2350. Review in Supreme Court on certiorari or certification.
2351. Enforcement of orders by district courts.
[2352, 2353. Repealed.]

[1] So in original. Does not conform to section catchline.

§ 2341. Definitions

As used in this chapter—

(1) "clerk" means the clerk of the court in which the petition for the review of an order, reviewable under this chapter, is filed;

(2) "petitioner" means the party or parties by whom a petition to review an order, reviewable under this chapter, is filed; and

(3) "agency" means—

(A) the Commission, when the order sought to be reviewed was entered by the Federal Communications Commission, the Federal Maritime Commission, or the Atomic Energy Commission, as the case may be;

(B) the Secretary, when the order was entered by the Secretary of Agriculture or the Secretary of Transportation;

(C) the Administration, when the order was entered by the Maritime Administration;

(D) the Secretary, when the order is under section 812 of the Fair Housing Act; and

(E) the Board, when the order was entered by the Surface Transportation Board.

(Added Pub.L. 89–554, § 4(e), Sept. 6, 1966, 80 Stat. 622, and amended Pub.L. 93–584, § 3, Jan. 2, 1975, 88 Stat. 1917; Pub.L. 100–430, § 11(b), Sept. 13, 1988, 102 Stat. 1635; Pub.L. 102–365, § 5(c)(1), Sept. 3, 1992, 106 Stat. 975; Pub.L. 104–88, Title III, § 305(d)(1) to (4), Dec. 29, 1995, 109 Stat. 945.)

HISTORICAL AND STATUTORY NOTES

References in Text

Section 812 of the Fair Housing Act, referred to in par. (3)(D), is classified to section 3612 of Title 42, The Public Health and Welfare.

Effective and Applicability Provisions

1995 Acts. Amendment by Pub.L. 104–88 effective Jan. 1, 1996, see section 2 of Pub.L. 104–88, set out as a note under section 701 of Title 49, Transportation.

1988 Acts. Amendment by Pub.L. 100–430 effective on the 180th day beginning after Sept. 13, 1988, see section 13(a) of Pub.L. 100–430, set out as a note under section 3601 of Title 42, The Public Health and Welfare.

1975 Acts. Amendment by Pub.L. 93–584 not applicable to actions commenced on or before the last day of the first month beginning after Jan. 2, 1975, and actions to enjoin or suspend orders of the Interstate Commerce Commission [now Surface Transportation Board] which are pending when this amendment becomes effective shall not be affected thereby, but shall proceed to final disposition under the law existing on the date they were commenced, see section 10 of Pub.L. 93–584, set out as a note under section 2321 of this title.

[Interstate Commerce Commission abolished and functions of Commission transferred, except as otherwise provided in Pub.L. 104–88, to Surface Transportation Board effective Jan. 1, 1996, by sections 702 of Title 49, Transportation, and section 101 of Pub.L. 104–88, set out as a note under section 701 of title 49. References to Interstate Commerce Commission deemed to refer to Surface Transportation Board, a member or employee of the Board, or Secretary of Transportation, as appropriate, see section 205 of Pub.L. 104–88, set out as a note under section 701 of Title 49.]

Transfer of Functions

The Atomic Energy Commission was abolished and all functions of the Commission, the Chairman, the members of the Commission, and the officers and components of the Commission were transferred to and vested in the Administrator of the Energy Research and Development Administration, with certain exceptions, by Pub.L. 93–438, Oct. 11, 1974, 88 Stat. 1233. See section 5814 of Title 42, The Public Health and Welfare. The Energy Research and Development Administration was terminated and functions vested by law in the Administrator of the Energy Research and Development Administration were transferred to and vested in the Secretary of Energy (unless otherwise specifically provided) by Pub.L. 95–91, Title III, § 301(a), Title VII, § 703, Aug. 4, 1977, 91 Stat. 577, 606. See sections 7151(a), 7293 of Title 42.

§ 2342. Jurisdiction of court of appeals

The court of appeals (other than the United States Court of Appeals for the Federal Circuit) has exclusive jurisdiction to enjoin, set aside, suspend (in whole or in part), or to determine the validity of—

(1) all final orders of the Federal Communications Commission made reviewable by section 402(a) of title 47;

(2) all final orders of the Secretary of Agriculture made under chapters 9 and 20A of title 7, except orders issued under sections 210(e), 217a, and 499g(a) of title 7;

(3) all rules, regulations, or final orders of—

(A) the Secretary of Transportation issued pursuant to section 50501, 50502, 56101–56104, or 57109 of title 46 or pursuant to part B or C of subtitle IV, subchapter III of chapter 311, chapter 313, or chapter 315 of title 49; and

(B) the Federal Maritime Commission issued pursuant to section 305, 41304, 41308, or 41309 or chapter 421 or 441 of title 46;

(4) all final orders of the Atomic Energy Commission made reviewable by section 2239 of title 42;

(5) all rules, regulations, or final orders of the Surface Transportation Board made reviewable by section 2321 of this title;

(6) all final orders under section 812 of the Fair Housing Act; and

(7) all final agency actions described in section 20114(c) of title 49.

Jurisdiction is invoked by filing a petition as provided by section 2344 of this title.

(Added Pub.L. 89–554, § 4(e), Sept. 6, 1966, 80 Stat. 622, and amended Pub.L. 93–584, § 4, Jan. 2, 1975, 88 Stat. 1917; Pub.L. 95–454, Title II, § 206, Oct. 13, 1978, 92 Stat. 1144; Pub.L. 96–454, § 8(b)(2), Oct. 15, 1980, 94 Stat. 2021; Pub.L. 97–164, Title I, § 137, Apr. 2, 1982, 96 Stat. 41; Pub.L. 98–554, Title II, § 227(a)(4), Oct. 30, 1984, 98 Stat. 2852; Pub.L. 99–336, § 5(a), June 19, 1986, 100 Stat. 638; Pub.L. 100–430, § 11(a), Sept. 13, 1988, 102 Stat. 1635; Pub.L. 102–365, § 5(c)(2), Sept. 3, 1992, 106 Stat. 975; Pub.L. 103–272, § 5(h), July 5, 1994, 108 Stat. 1375; Pub.L. 104–88, Title III, § 305(d)(5) to (8), Dec. 29, 1995, 109 Stat. 945; Pub.L. 104–287, § 6(f)(2), Oct. 11, 1996, 110 Stat. 3399; Pub.L. 109–59, Title IV, § 4125(a), Aug. 10, 2005, 119 Stat. 1738; Pub.L. 109–304, § 17(f)(3), Oct. 6, 2006, 120 Stat. 1708.)

HISTORICAL AND STATUTORY NOTES

References in Text

Part B or C of subtitle IV, subchapter III of chapter 311, chapter 313, or chapter 315 of title 49, referred to in par. (3)(A), is 49 U.S.C.A. § 13101 et seq. or 15101 et seq., 49 U.S.C.A. § 31131 et seq., 49 U.S.C.A. § 31301 et seq., or 49 U.S.C.A. § 31501 et seq., respectively.

Chapter 421 or 441 of title 46, referred to in par. (3)(B), are Regulations Affecting Shipping in Foreign Trade, 46 U.S.C.A. § 42101 et seq., and Evidence of Financial Responsibility for Passenger Transportation, 46 U.S.C.A. § 44101 et seq.

Section 812 of the Fair Housing Act, referred to in par. (6), is classified to section 3612 of Title 42, The Public Health and Welfare.

Effective and Applicability Provisions

1996 Acts. Section 6(f) of Pub.L. 104–287 provided in part that amendments made by such section 6(f) to this section, sections 744 and 797*l* of Title 45, Railroads, and section 30166 of Title 49, Transportation, were effective Dec. 29, 1995.

1995 Acts. Amendment by Pub.L. 104–88 effective Jan. 1, 1996, see section 2 of Pub.L. 104–88, set out as a note under section 701 of Title 49, Transportation.

1988 Acts. Amendment by Pub.L. 100–430 effective on the 180th day beginning after Sept. 13, 1988, see section 13(a) of Pub.L. 100–430, set out as a note under section 3601 of Title 42, The Public Health and Welfare.

1986 Acts. Section 5(b) of Pub.L. 99–336 provided that: "The amendment made by this section [amending this section] shall apply with respect to any rule, regulation, or final order described in such amendment which is issued on or after the date of the enactment of this Act [June 19, 1986]."

1982 Acts. Amendment by Pub.L. 97–164 effective Oct. 1, 1982, see section 402 of Pub.L. 97–164, set out as a note under section 171 of this title.

1978 Acts. Amendment by Pub.L. 95–454 effective 90 days after Oct. 13, 1978, see section 907 of Pub.L. 95–454, set out as a note under section 1101 of Title 5, Government Organization and Employees.

1975 Acts. Amendment by Pub.L. 93–584 not applicable to actions commenced on or before the last day of the first month beginning after Jan. 2, 1975, and actions to enjoin or suspend orders of the Interstate Commerce Commission [now Surface Transportation Board] which are pending when this amendment becomes effective shall not be affected thereby, but shall proceed to final disposition under the law existing on the date they were commenced, see section 10 of Pub.L. 93–584, set out as a note under section 2321 of this title.

[Interstate Commerce Commission abolished and functions of Commission transferred, except as otherwise provided in Pub.L. 104–88, to Surface Transportation Board effective Jan. 1, 1996, by section 702 of Title 49, Transportation, and section 101 of Pub.L. 104–88, set out as a note under section 701 of Title 49. References to Interstate Commerce Commission deemed to refer to Surface Transportation Board, a member or employee of the Board, or Secretary of Transportation, as appropriate, see section 205 of Pub.L. 104–88, set out as a note under section 701 of Title 49.]

Transfer of Functions

The Atomic Energy Commission was abolished and all functions of the Commission, the Chairman, the members of the Commission, and the officers and components of the Commission were transferred to and vested in the Administrator of the Energy Research and Development Administration, with certain exceptions, by Pub.L. 93–438, Oct. 11, 1974, 88 Stat. 1233. See section 5814 of Title 42, The Public Health and Welfare. The Energy Research and Development Administration was terminated and functions vested by law in the Administration of the Energy Research and Development Administration were transferred to and vested in the Secretary of Energy (unless otherwise specifically provided) by Pub.L. 95–91, Title III, § 301(a), Title VII, § 703, Aug. 4, 1977, 91 Stat. 577, 606. See sections 7151(a), 7293 of Title 42.

§ 2343. Venue

The venue of a proceeding under this chapter is in the judicial circuit in which the petitioner resides or has its principal office, or in the United States Court of Appeals for the District of Columbia Circuit.

(Added Pub.L. 89–554, § 4(e), Sept. 6, 1966, 80 Stat. 622.)

§ 2344. Review of orders; time; notice; contents of petition; service

On the entry of a final order reviewable under this chapter, the agency shall promptly give notice thereof by service or publication in accordance with its rules. Any party aggrieved by the final order may, within 60 days after its entry, file a petition to review the order in the court of appeals wherein venue lies. The action shall be against the United States. The petition shall contain a concise statement of—

(1) the nature of the proceedings as to which review is sought;

(2) the facts on which venue is based;

(3) the grounds on which relief is sought; and

(4) the relief prayed.

The petitioner shall attach to the petition, as exhibits, copies of the order, report, or decision of the agency. The clerk shall serve a true copy of the petition on the agency and on the Attorney General by registered mail, with request for a return receipt.

(Added Pub.L. 89–554, § 4(e), Sept. 6, 1966, 80 Stat. 622.)

§ 2345. Prehearing conference

The court of appeals may hold a prehearing conference or direct a judge of the court to hold a prehearing conference.

(Added Pub.L. 89–554, § 4(e), Sept. 6, 1966, 80 Stat. 622.)

§ 2346. Certification of record on review

Unless the proceeding has been terminated on a motion to dismiss the petition, the agency shall file in the office of the clerk the record on review as provided by section 2112 of this title.

(Added Pub.L. 89–554, § 4(e), Sept. 6, 1966, 80 Stat. 623.)

§ 2347. Petitions to review; proceedings

(a) Unless determined on a motion to dismiss, petitions to review orders reviewable under this chapter are heard in the court of appeals on the record of the pleadings, evidence adduced, and proceedings before the agency, when the agency has held a hearing whether or not required to do so by law.

(b) When the agency has not held a hearing before taking the action of which review is sought by the petition, the court of appeals shall determine whether a hearing is required by law. After that determination, the court shall—

(1) remand the proceedings to the agency to hold a hearing, when a hearing is required by law;

(2) pass on the issues presented, when a hearing is not required by law and it appears from the pleadings and affidavits filed by the parties that no genuine issue of material fact is presented; or

(3) transfer the proceedings to a district court for the district in which the petitioner resides or has its principal office for a hearing and determination as if the proceedings were originally initiated in the district court, when a hearing is not required by law and a genuine issue of material fact is presented. The procedure in these cases in the district court is governed by the Federal Rules of Civil Procedure.

(c) If a party to a proceeding to review applies to the court of appeals in which the proceeding is pending for leave to adduce additional evidence and shows to the satisfaction of the court that—

(1) the additional evidence is material; and

(2) there were reasonable grounds for failure to adduce the evidence before the agency;

the court may order the additional evidence and any counterevidence the opposite party desires to offer to be taken by the agency. The agency may modify its findings of fact, or make new findings, by reason of the additional evidence so taken, and may modify or set aside its order, and shall file in the court the additional evidence, the modified findings or new findings, and the modified order or the order setting aside the original order.

(Added Pub.L. 89–554, § 4(e), Sept. 6, 1966, 80 Stat. 623.)

HISTORICAL AND STATUTORY NOTES

References in Text

The Federal Rules of Civil Procedure, referred to in subsec. (b)(3), are classified generally to this title.

§ 2348. Representation in proceeding; intervention

The Attorney General is responsible for and has control of the interests of the Government in all court proceedings under this chapter. The agency, and any party in interest in the proceeding before the agency whose interests will be affected if an order of the agency is or is not enjoined, set aside, or suspended, may appear as parties thereto of their own motion and as of right, and be represented by counsel in any proceeding to review the order. Communities, associations, corporations, firms, and individuals, whose interests are affected by the order of the agency, may intervene in any proceeding to review the order. The Attorney General may not dispose of or discontinue the proceeding to review over the objection of any party or intervenor, but any intervenor may prosecute, defend, or continue the proceeding unaffected by the action or inaction of the Attorney General.

(Added Pub.L. 89–554, § 4(e), Sept. 6, 1966, 80 Stat. 623.)

§ 2349. Jurisdiction of the proceeding

(a) The court of appeals has jurisdiction of the proceeding on the filing and service of a petition to review. The court of appeals in which the record on review is filed, on the filing, has jurisdiction to vacate stay orders or interlocutory injunctions previously granted by any court, and has exclusive jurisdiction to make and enter, on the petition, evidence, and proceedings set forth in the record on review, a judgment determining the validity of, and enjoining, setting aside, or suspending, in whole or in part, the order of the agency.

(b) The filing of the petition to review does not of itself stay or suspend the operation of the order of the agency, but the court of appeals in its discretion may restrain or suspend, in whole or in part, the operation of the order pending the final hearing and determination of the petition. When the petitioner makes application for an interlocutory injunction restraining or suspending the enforcement, operation, or execution of, or setting aside, in whole or in part, any order reviewable under this chapter, at least 5 days' notice of the hearing thereon shall be given to the agency and to the Attorney General. In a case in which irreparable damage would otherwise result to the petitioner, the court of appeals may, on hearing, after reasonable notice to the agency and to the Attorney General, order a temporary stay or suspension, in whole or in part, of the operation of the order of the agency for not more than 60 days from the date of the order pending the hearing on the application for the interlocutory injunction, in which case the order of the court of appeals shall contain a specific finding, based on evidence submitted to the court of appeals, and identified by reference thereto, that irreparable damage would result to the petitioner and specifying the nature of the damage. The court of appeals, at the time of hearing the application for an interlocutory injunction, on a like finding, may continue the temporary stay or suspension, in whole or in part, until decision on the application.

(Added Pub.L. 89–554, § 4(e), Sept. 6, 1966, 80 Stat. 624, and amended Pub.L. 98–620, Title IV, § 402(29)(F), Nov. 8, 1984, 98 Stat. 3359.)

HISTORICAL AND STATUTORY NOTES

Effective and Applicability Provisions

1984 Acts. Amendment by Pub.L. 98–620 not to apply to cases pending on Nov. 8, 1984, see section 403 of Pub.L. 98–620, set out as a note under section 1657 of this title.

§ 2350. Review in Supreme Court on certiorari or certification

(a) An order granting or denying an interlocutory injunction under section 2349(b) of this title and a final judgment of the court of appeals in a proceeding to review under this chapter are subject to review by the Supreme Court on a writ of certiorari as provided by section 1254(1) of this title. Application for the writ shall be made within 45 days after entry of the order and within 90 days after entry of the judgment, as the case may be. The United States, the agency, or an aggrieved party may file a petition for a writ of certiorari.

(b) The provisions of section 1254(2) of this title, regarding certification, and of section 2101(f) of this title, regarding stays, also apply to proceedings under this chapter.

(Added Pub.L. 89–554, § 4(e), Sept. 6, 1966, 80 Stat. 624, and amended Pub.L. 100–352, § 5(e), June 27, 1988, 102 Stat. 663.)

HISTORICAL AND STATUTORY NOTES

Effective and Applicability Provisions

1988 Acts. Amendment by Pub.L. 100–352 effective ninety days after June 27, 1988, except that such amendment not to apply to cases pending in the Supreme Court on such effective date or affect the right to review or the manner of reviewing the judgment or decree of a court which was entered before such effective date, see section 7 of Pub.L. 100–352, set out as a note under section 1254 of this title.

§ 2351. Enforcement of orders by district courts

The several district courts have jurisdiction specifically to enforce, and to enjoin and restrain any person from violating any order issued under section 193 of title 7.

(Added Pub.L. 89–554, § 4(e), Sept. 6, 1966, 80 Stat. 624.)

[§ 2352. Repealed. Pub.L. 89–773, § 4, Nov. 6, 1966, 80 Stat. 1323]

HISTORICAL AND STATUTORY NOTES

Section, Pub.L. 89–554, § 4(e), Sept. 6, 1966, 80 Stat. 624, directed the several courts of appeals to adopt and promulgate rules, subject to the approval of the Judicial Conference of the United States, governing the practice and procedure, including prehearing conference procedure, in proceedings to review orders under this chapter. See section 2072 of this title.

Savings Provisions

Section 4 of Pub.L. 89–773 provided in part that the repeal of this section shall not operate to invalidate or repeal rules adopted under the authority of this section prior to the enactment of Pub.L. 89–773, which rules shall remain in effect until superseded by rules prescribed under authority of section 2072 of this title as amended by Pub.L. 89–773.

[§ 2353. Repealed. Pub.L 97–164, Title I, § 138, Apr. 2, 1982, 96 Stat. 42]

HISTORICAL AND STATUTORY NOTES

Section, added Pub.L. 91–577, Title III, § 143(c), Dec. 24, 1970, 84 Stat. 1559, gave the court of appeals nonexclusive jurisdiction to hear appeals under section 71 of the Plant Variety Protection Act [7 U.S.C.A. § 2461]. See section 1295(a) (8) of this title.

Effective Date of Repeal

Repeal effective Oct. 1, 1982, see section 402 of Pub.L. 97–164, set out as a note under section 171 of this title.

CHAPTER 159—INTERPLEADER

Sec.
2361. Process and procedure.

§ 2361. Process and procedure

In any civil action of interpleader or in the nature of interpleader under section 1335 of this title, a district court may issue its process for all claimants and enter its order restraining them from instituting or prosecuting any proceeding in any State or United States court affecting the property, instrument or obligation involved in the interpleader action until further order of the court. Such process and order shall be returnable at such time as the court or judge thereof directs, and shall be addressed to and served by the United States marshals for the respective districts where the claimants reside or may be found.

Such district court shall hear and determine the case, and may discharge the plaintiff from further liability, make the injunction permanent, and make all appropriate orders to enforce its judgment.

(June 25, 1948, c. 646, 62 Stat. 970; May 24, 1949, c. 139, § 117, 63 Stat. 105.)

CHAPTER 161—UNITED STATES AS PARTY GENERALLY

Sec.
2401. Time for commencing action against United States.
2402. Jury trial in actions against United States.
2403. Intervention by United States or a State; constitutional question.
2404. Death of defendant in damage action.
2405. Garnishment.
2406. Credits in actions by United States; prior disallowance.
2407. Delinquents for public money; judgment at return term; continuance.
2408. Security not required of United States.
2409. Partition actions involving United States.
2409a. Real property quiet title actions.
2410. Actions affecting property on which United States has lien.
2411. Interest.
2412. Costs and fees.
2413. Executions in favor of United States.
2414. Payment of judgments and compromise settlements.
2415. Time for commencing actions brought by the United States.
2416. Time for commencing actions brought by the United States—Exclusions.

§ 2401. Time for commencing action against United States

(a) Except as provided by the Contract Disputes Act of 1978, every civil action commenced against the United States shall be barred unless the complaint is filed within six years after the right of action first accrues. The action of any person under legal disability or beyond the seas at the time the claim accrues may be commenced within three years after the disability ceases.

(b) A tort claim against the United States shall be forever barred unless it is presented in writing to the appropriate Federal agency within two years after such claim accrues or unless action is begun within six months after the date of mailing, by certified or registered mail, of notice of final denial of the claim by the agency to which it was presented.

(June 25, 1948, c. 646, 62 Stat. 971; Apr. 25, 1949, c. 92, § 1, 63 Stat. 62; Sept. 8, 1959, Pub.L. 86–238, § 1(3), 73 Stat. 472; July 18, 1966, Pub.L. 89–506, § 7, 80 Stat. 307; Nov. 1, 1978, Pub.L. 95–563, § 14(b), 92 Stat. 2389.)

HISTORICAL AND STATUTORY NOTES

Senate Revision Amendment

Subsection (b) amended in the Senate to insert the 1 year limitation on the bringing of tort actions and to include the limitation upon the time in which tort claims not exceeding $1000 must be presented to the appropriate Federal agencies for administrative disposition. 80th Congress Senate Report No. 1559, Amendment No. 48.

1949 Acts. House Report No. 276, see 1949 U.S. Code Cong. Service, p. 1226.

1959 Acts. Senate Report No. 797, see 1959 U.S. Code Cong. and Adm. News, p. 2272.

1966 Acts. Senate Report No. 1327, see 1966 U.S. Code Cong. and Adm. News, p. 2515.

1978 Acts. Senate Report No. 95–1118, see 1978 U.S. Code Cong. and Adm. News, p. 5235.

References in Text

The Contract Disputes Act of 1978, referred to in subsec. (a), is Pub.L. 95–563, Nov. 1, 1978, 92 Stat. 2383, as amended, which is classified principally to chapter 9 (section 601 et seq.) of Title 41, Public Contracts. For complete classification of this Act to the Code, see Short Title note set out under section 601 of Title 41 and Tables.

Effective and Applicability Provisions

1978 Acts. Amendment by Pub.L. 95–563 effective with respect to contracts entered into 120 days after Nov. 1, 1978 and, at the election of the contractor, with respect to any claim pending at such time before the contracting officer or initiated thereafter, see section 16 of Pub.L. 95–563, set out as a note under section 601 of Title 41, Public Contracts.

1966 Acts. Amendment by Pub.L. 89–506 applicable to claims accruing six months or more after July 18, 1966, see section 10 of Pub.L. 89–506, set out as a note under section 2672 of this title.

§ 2402. Jury trial in actions against United States

Subject to chapter 179 of this title, any action against the United States under section 1346 shall be tried by the court without a jury, except that any action against the United States under section 1346(a)(1) shall, at the request of either party to such action, be tried by the court with a jury.

(June 25, 1948, c. 646, 62 Stat. 971; July 30, 1954, c. 648, § 2(a), 68 Stat. 589; Oct. 26, 1996, Pub.L. 104–331, § 3(b)(3), 110 Stat. 4069.)

HISTORICAL AND STATUTORY NOTES

Effective and Applicability Provisions

1996 Acts. Amendment by section 3(b)(3) of Pub.L. 104–331, effective Oct. 1, 1997, see section 3(d) of Pub.L. 104–331, set out as a note under section 1296 of this title.

§ 2403. Intervention by United States or a State; constitutional question

(a) In any action, suit or proceeding in a court of the United States to which the United States or any agency, officer or employee thereof is not a party, wherein the constitutionality of any Act of Congress affecting the public interest is drawn in question, the court shall certify such fact to the Attorney General, and shall permit the United States to intervene for presentation of evidence, if evidence is otherwise admissible in the case, and for argument on the question of constitutionality. The United States shall, subject to the applicable provisions of law, have all the rights of a party and be subject to all liabilities of a party as to court costs to the extent necessary for a proper presentation of the facts and law relating to the question of constitutionality.

(b) In any action, suit, or proceeding in a court of the United States to which a State or any agency, officer, or employee thereof is not a party, wherein the constitutionality of any statute of that State affecting the public interest is drawn in question, the court shall certify such fact to the attorney general of the State, and shall permit the State to intervene for presentation of evidence, if evidence is otherwise admissible in the case, and for argument on the question of constitutionality. The State shall, subject to the applicable provisions of law, have all the rights of a party and be subject to all liabilities of a party as to court costs to the extent necessary for a proper presentation of the facts and law relating to the question of constitutionality.

(June 25, 1948, c. 646, 62 Stat. 971; Aug. 12, 1976, Pub.L. 94–381, § 5, 90 Stat. 1120.)

HISTORICAL AND STATUTORY NOTES

Effective and Applicability Provisions

1976 Acts. Amendment by Pub.L. 94–381 not applicable to any action commenced on or before Aug. 12, 1976, see section 7 of Pub.L. 94–381, set out as a note under section 2284 of this title.

§ 2404. Death of defendant in damage action

A civil action for damages commenced by or on behalf of the United States or in which it is interested shall not abate on the death of a defendant but shall survive and be enforceable against his estate as well as against surviving defendants.

(June 25, 1948, c. 646, 62 Stat. 971.)

§ 2405. Garnishment

In any action or suit commenced by the United States against a corporation for the recovery of money upon a bill, note, or other security, the debtors of the corporation may be summoned as garnishees. Any person so summoned shall appear in open court and depose in writing to the amount of his indebtedness to the corporation at the time of the service of the summons and at the time of making the deposition, and judgment may be entered in favor of the United States for the sum admitted by the garnishee to be due the corporation as if it had been due the United States. A judgment shall not be entered against any garnishee until after judgment has been rendered against the corporation, nor until the sum in which the garnishee is indebted is actually due.

When any garnishee deposes in open court that he is not and was not at the time of the service of the summons indebted to the corporation, an issue may be tendered by the United States upon such deposition. If, upon the trial of that issue, a verdict is rendered against the garnishee, judgment shall be entered in favor of the United States, pursuant to such verdict, with costs.

Any garnishee who fails to appear at the term to which he is summoned shall be subject to attachment for contempt.

(June 25, 1948, c. 646, 62 Stat. 971.)

§ 2406. Credits in actions by United States; prior disallowance

In an action by the United States against an individual, evidence supporting the defendant's claim for a credit shall not be admitted unless he first proves that such claim has been disallowed, in whole or in part, by the Government Accountability Office, or that he has, at the time of the trial, obtained possession of vouchers not previously procurable and has been prevented from presenting such claim to the Government Accountability Office by absence from the United States or unavoidable accident.

(June 25, 1948, c. 646, 62 Stat. 972; July 7, 2004, Pub.L. 108–271, § 8(b), 118 Stat. 814.)

§ 2407. Delinquents for public money; judgment at return term; continuance

In an action by the United States against any person accountable for public money who fails to pay into the Treasury the sum reported due the United States, upon the adjustment of his account the court shall grant judgment upon motion unless a continuance is granted as specified in this section.

A continuance may be granted if the defendant, in open court and in the presence of the United States attorney, states under oath that he is equitably entitled to credits which have been disallowed by the Government Accountability Office prior to the commencement of the action, specifying each particular claim so rejected, and stating that he cannot safely come to trial.

A continuance may also be granted if such an action is commenced on a bond or other sealed instrument and the court requires the original instrument to be produced.

(June 25, 1948, c. 646, 62 Stat. 972; Pub.L. 108–271, § 8(b), July 7, 2004, 118 Stat. 814.)

§ 2408. Security not required of United States

Security for damages or costs shall not be required of the United States, any department or agency thereof or any party acting under the direction of any such department or agency on the issuance of process or the institution or prosecution of any proceeding.

Costs taxable, under other Acts of Congress, against the United States or any such department, agency or party shall be paid out of the contingent fund of the department or agency which directed the proceedings to be instituted.

(June 25, 1948, c. 646, 62 Stat. 972.)

§ 2409. Partition actions involving United States

Any civil action by any tenant in common or joint tenant owning an undivided interest in lands, where the United States is one of such tenants in common or joint tenants, against the United States alone or against the United States and any other of such owners, shall proceed, and be determined, in the same manner as would a similar action between private persons.

Whenever in such action the court orders a sale of the property or any part thereof the Attorney General may bid for the same in behalf of the United States. If the United States is the purchaser, the amount of the purchase money shall be paid from the Treasury upon a warrant drawn by the Secretary of the Treasury on the requisition of the Attorney General.

(June 25, 1948, c. 646, 62 Stat. 972.)

§ 2409a. Real property quiet title actions

(a) The United States may be named as a party defendant in a civil action under this section to adjudicate a disputed title to real property in which the United States claims an interest, other than a security interest or water rights. This section does not apply to trust or restricted Indian lands, nor does it apply to or affect actions which may be or could have been brought under sections 1346, 1347, 1491, or 2410 of this title, sections 7424, 7425, or 7426 of the Internal Revenue Code of 1986, as amended (26 U.S.C. 7424, 7425, and 7426), or section 208 of the Act of July 10, 1952 (43 U.S.C. 666).

(b) The United States shall not be disturbed in possession or control of any real property involved in any action under this section pending a final judgment or decree, the conclusion of any appeal therefrom, and sixty days; and if the final determination shall be adverse to the United States, the United States nevertheless may retain such possession or control of the real property or of any part thereof as it may elect, upon payment to the person determined to be entitled thereto of an amount which upon such election the district court in the same action shall determine to be just compensation for such possession or control.

(c) No preliminary injunction shall issue in any action brought under this section.

(d) The complaint shall set forth with particularity the nature of the right, title, or interest which the plaintiff claims in the real property, the circumstances under which it was acquired, and the right, title, or interest claimed by the United States.

(e) If the United States disclaims all interest in the real property or interest therein adverse to the plaintiff at any time prior to the actual commencement of the trial, which disclaimer is confirmed by order of the court, the jurisdiction of the district court shall cease unless it has jurisdiction of the civil action or suit on ground other than and independent of the authority conferred by section 1346(f) of this title.

(f) A civil action against the United States under this section shall be tried by the court without a jury.

(g) Any civil action under this section, except for an action brought by a State, shall be barred unless it is commenced within twelve years of the date upon which it accrued. Such action shall be deemed to have accrued on the date the plaintiff or his predecessor in interest knew or should have known of the claim of the United States.

(h) No civil action may be maintained under this section by a State with respect to defense facilities (including land) of the United States so long as the lands at issue are being used or required by the United States for national defense purposes as determined by the head of the Federal agency with jurisdiction over the lands involved, if it is determined that the State action was brought more than twelve years after the State knew or should have known of the claims of the United States. Upon cessation of such use or requirement, the State may dispute title to such lands pursuant to the provisions of this section. The decision of the head of the Federal agency is not subject to judicial review.

(i) Any civil action brought by a State under this section with respect to lands, other than tide or submerged lands, on which the United States or its lessee or right-of-way or easement grantee has made substantial improvements or substantial investments or on which the United States has conducted substantial activities pursuant to a management plan such as range improvement, timber harvest, tree planting, mineral activities, farming, wildlife habitat improvement, or other similar activities, shall be barred unless the action is commenced within twelve years after the date the State received notice of the Federal claims to the lands.

(j) If a final determination in an action brought by a State under this section involving submerged or tide lands on which the United States or its lessee or right-of-way or easement grantee has made substantial improvements or substantial investments is adverse to the United States and it is determined that the State's action was brought more than twelve years after the State received notice of the Federal claim to the lands, the State shall take title to the lands subject to any existing lease, easement, or right-of-way. Any compensation due with respect to such lease, easement, or right-of-way shall be determined under existing law.

(k) Notice for the purposes of the accrual of an action brought by a State under this section shall be—

(1) by public communications with respect to the claimed lands which are sufficiently specific as to be reasonably calculated to put the claimant on notice of the Federal claim to the lands, or

(2) by the use, occupancy, or improvement of the claimed lands which, in the circumstances, is open and notorious.

(*l*) For purposes of this section, the term "tide or submerged lands" means "lands beneath navigable waters" as defined in section 2 of the Submerged Lands Act (43 U.S.C. 1301).

(m) Not less than one hundred and eighty days before bringing any action under this section, a State shall notify the head of the Federal agency with jurisdiction over the lands in question of the State's intention to file suit, the basis therefor, and a description of the lands included in the suit.

(n) Nothing in this section shall be construed to permit suits against the United States based upon adverse possession.

(Added Pub.L. 92–562, § 3(a), Oct. 25, 1972, 86 Stat. 1176, and amended Pub.L. 99–514, § 2, Oct. 22, 1986, 100 Stat. 2095; Pub.L. 99–598, Nov. 4, 1986, 100 Stat. 3351.)

HISTORICAL AND STATUTORY NOTES

References in Text

Section 208 of the Act July 10, 1952, referred to in subsec. (a), is section 208 (a) to (d) of Act July 10, 1952, c. 651, 66 Stat. 560. Section 208 (a) to (c) is classified to section 666 of Title 43, Public Lands. Section 208(d) is not classified to the Code.

§ 2410. Actions affecting property on which United States has lien

(a) Under the conditions prescribed in this section and section 1444 of this title for the protection of the United States, the United States may be named a party in any civil action or suit in any district court, or in any State court having jurisdiction of the subject matter—

(1) to quiet title to,

(2) to foreclose a mortgage or other lien upon,

(3) to partition,

(4) to condemn, or

(5) of interpleader or in the nature of interpleader with respect to,

real or personal property on which the United States has or claims a mortgage or other lien.

(b) The complaint or pleading shall set forth with particularity the nature of the interest or lien of the United States. In actions or suits involving liens arising under the internal revenue laws, the complaint or pleading shall include the name and address of the taxpayer whose liability created the lien and, if a notice of the tax lien was filed, the identity of the internal revenue office which filed the notice, and the date and place such notice of lien was filed. In actions in the State courts service upon the United States shall be made by serving the process of the court with a copy of the complaint upon the United States attorney for the district in which the action is brought or upon an assistant United States attorney or clerical employee designated by the United States attorney in writing filed with the clerk of the court in which the action is brought and by sending copies of the process and complaint, by registered mail, or by certified mail, to the Attorney General of the United States at Washington, District of Columbia. In such actions the United States may appear and answer, plead or demur within sixty days after such service or such further time as the court may allow.

(c) A judgment or decree in such action or suit shall have the same effect respecting the discharge of the property from the mortgage or other lien held by the United States as may be provided with respect to such matters by the local law of the place where the court is situated. However, an action to foreclose a mortgage or other lien, naming the United States as a party under this section, must seek judicial sale. A sale to satisfy a lien inferior to one of the United States shall be made subject to and without disturbing the lien of the United States, unless the United States consents that the property may be sold free of its lien and the proceeds divided as the parties may be entitled. Where a sale of real estate is made to satisfy a lien prior to that of the United States, the United States shall have one year from the date of sale within which to redeem, except that with respect to a lien arising under the internal revenue laws the period shall be 120 days or the period allowable for redemption under State law, whichever is longer, and in any case in which, under the provisions of section 505 of the Housing Act of 1950, as amended (12 U.S.C. 1701k), and subsection (d) of section 3720 of title 38 of the United States Code, the right to redeem does not arise, there shall be no right of redemption. In any case where the debt owing the United States is due, the United States may ask, by way of affirmative relief, for the foreclosure of its own lien and where property is sold to satisfy a first lien held by the United States, the United States may bid at the sale such sum, not exceeding the amount of its claim with expenses of sale, as may be directed by the head (or his delegate) of the department or agency of the United States which has charge of the administration of the laws in respect to which the claim of the United States arises. In any case where the United States is a bidder at the judicial sale, it may credit the amount determined to be due it against the amount it bids at such sales.

(d) In any case in which the United States redeems real property under this section or section 7425 of the Internal Revenue Code of 1986, the amount to be paid for such property shall be the sum of—

(1) the actual amount paid by the purchaser at such sale (which, in the case of a purchaser who is the holder of the lien being foreclosed, shall include the amount of the obligation secured by such lien to the extent satisfied by reason of such sale),

(2) interest on the amount paid (as determined under paragraph (1)) at 6 percent per annum from the date of such sale, and

(3) the amount (if any) equal to the excess of (A) the expenses necessarily incurred in connection with such property, over (B) the income from such property plus (to the extent such property is used by the purchaser) a reasonable rental value of such property.

(e) Whenever any person has a lien upon any real or personal property, duly recorded in the jurisdiction in which the property is located, and a junior lien, other than a tax lien, in favor of the United States attaches to such property, such person may make a written request to the officer charged with the administration of the laws in respect of which the lien of the United States arises, to have the same extinguished. If after appropriate investigation, it appears to such officer that the proceeds from the sale of the property would be insufficient to wholly or partly satisfy the lien of the United States, or that the claim of the United States has been satisfied or by lapse of time or otherwise has become unenforceable, such officer may issue a certificate releasing the property from such lien.

(June 25, 1948, c. 646, 62 Stat. 972; May 24, 1949, c. 139, § 119, 63 Stat. 105; July 7, 1958, Pub.L. 85–508, § 12(h), 72 Stat. 348; June 11, 1960, Pub.L. 86–507, § 1(20), 74 Stat. 201; Nov. 2, 1966, Pub.L. 89–719, Title II, § 201, 80 Stat. 1147; Oct. 22, 1986, Pub.L. 99–514, § 2, 100 Stat. 2095; Nov. 29, 1990, Pub.L. 101–647, Title XXXVI, § 3630, 104 Stat. 4966; Aug. 6, 1991, Pub.L. 102–83, § 5(c)(2), 105 Stat. 406; Oct. 19, 1996, Pub.L. 104–316, Title I, § 114, 110 Stat. 3834.)

HISTORICAL AND STATUTORY NOTES

References in Text

The internal revenue laws, referred to in subsec. (b), are classified generally to Title 26, Internal Revenue Code.

Section 7425 of the Internal Revenue Code of 1986, referred to in subsec. (d), is classified to section 7425 of Title 26, Internal Revenue Code.

Effective and Applicability Provisions

1996 Acts. Amendment by Pub.L. 104–316 effective Oct. 19, 1996, see section 101(e) of Pub.L. 104–316, set out as a note under section 130c of Title 2, The Congress.

1990 Acts. Amendment by section 3630 of Pub.L. 101–647 effective 180 days after Nov. 29, 1990, see section 3631 of Pub.L. 101–647, set out as a note under section 3001 of this title.

1966 Acts. Amendment of section by Pub.L. 89–719 applicable after Nov. 2, 1966, see section 203 of Pub.L. 89–719, set out as a note under section 1346 of this title.

1958 Acts. Amendment of section by Pub.L. 85–508 effective Jan. 3, 1959, upon admission of Alaska into the Union pursuant to Proc. No. 3269, Jan. 3, 1959, 24 F.R. 81, 73 Stat. c16, as required by sections 1 and 8(c) of Pub.L. 85–508, see notes set out under section 81A of this title and preceding section 21 of Title 48, Territories and Insular Possessions.

§ 2411. Interest

In any judgment of any court rendered (whether against the United States, a collector or deputy collector of internal revenue, a former collector or deputy collector, or the personal representative in case of death) for any overpayment in respect of any internal-revenue tax, interest shall be allowed at the overpayment rate established under section 6621 of the Internal Revenue Code of 1986 upon the amount of the overpayment, from the date of the payment or collection thereof to a date preceding the date of the refund check by not more than thirty days, such date to be determined by the Commissioner of Internal Revenue. The Commissioner is authorized to tender by check payment of any such judgment, with interest as herein provided, at any time after such judgment becomes final, whether or not a claim for such payment has been duly filed, and such tender shall stop the running of interest, whether or not such refund check is accepted by the judgment creditor.

(June 25, 1948, c. 646, 62 Stat. 973; May 24, 1949, c. 139, § 120, 63 Stat. 106; Jan. 3, 1975, Pub.L. 93–625, § 7(a)(2), 88 Stat. 2115; Apr. 2, 1982, Pub.L. 97–164, Title III, § 302(b), 96 Stat. 56; Oct. 22, 1986, Pub.L. 99–514, § 2, Title XV, § 1511(c)(18), 100 Stat. 2095, 2746.)

HISTORICAL AND STATUTORY NOTES

References in Text

Section 6621 of the Internal Revenue Code of 1986, referred to in text, is classified to section 6621 of Title 26, Internal Revenue Code.

Effective and Applicability Provisions

1986 Acts. Amendment by section 1511(c)(18) of Pub.L. 99–514 applicable for purposes of determining interest for periods after Dec. 31, 1986, see section 1511(d) of Pub.L. 99–514, set out as a note under section 47 of Title 26, Internal Revenue Code.

1982 Acts. Amendment by Pub.L. 97–164 effective Oct. 1, 1982, see section 402 of Pub.L. 97–164, set out as a note under section 171 of this title.

1975 Acts. Amendment by Pub.L. 93–625 effective July 1, 1975, and applicable to amounts outstanding on such date or arising thereafter, see section 7(e) of Pub.L. 93–625, set out as a note under section 6621 of Title 26, Internal Revenue Code.

§ 2412. Costs and fees

(a)(1) Except as otherwise specifically provided by statute, a judgment for costs, as enumerated in section 1920 of this title, but not including the fees and expenses of attorneys, may be awarded to the prevailing party in any civil action brought by or against the United States or any agency or any official of the United States acting in his or her official capacity in any court having jurisdiction of such action. A judgment for costs when taxed against the United States shall, in an amount established by statute, court rule, or order, be limited to reimbursing in whole or in part the prevailing party for the costs incurred by such party in the litigation.

(2) A judgment for costs, when awarded in favor of the United States in an action brought by the United States, may include an amount equal to the filing fee prescribed under section 1914(a) of this title. The preceding sentence shall not be construed as requiring the United States to pay any filing fee.

(b) Unless expressly prohibited by statute, a court may award reasonable fees and expenses of attorneys, in addition to the costs which may be awarded pursuant to subsection (a), to the prevailing party in any civil action brought by or against the United States or any agency or any official of the United States acting in his or her official capacity in any court having jurisdiction of such action. The United States shall be liable for such fees and expenses to the same extent that any other party would be liable under the common law or under the terms of any statute which specifically provides for such an award.

(c)(1) Any judgment against the United States or any agency and any official of the United States acting in his or her official capacity for costs pursuant to subsection (a) shall be paid as provided in sections 2414 and 2517 of this title and shall be in addition to any relief provided in the judgment.

(2) Any judgment against the United States or any agency and any official of the United States acting in his or her official capacity for fees and expenses of attorneys pursuant to subsection (b) shall be paid as provided in sections 2414 and 2517 of this title, except that if the basis for the award is a finding that the United States acted in bad faith, then the award shall be paid by any agency found to have acted in bad faith and shall be in addition to any relief provided in the judgment.

(d)(1)(A) Except as otherwise specifically provided by statute, a court shall award to a prevailing party other than the United States fees and other expenses, in addition to any costs awarded pursuant to subsection (a), incurred by that party in any civil action (other than cases sounding in tort), including proceedings for judicial review of agency action, brought by or against the United States in any court having jurisdiction of that action, unless the court finds that the position of the United States was substantially justified or that special circumstances make an award unjust.

(B) A party seeking an award of fees and other expenses shall, within thirty days of final judgment in the action, submit to the court an application for fees and other expenses which shows that the party is a prevailing party and is eligible to receive an award under this subsection, and the amount sought, including an itemized statement from any attorney or expert witness representing or appearing in behalf of the party stating the actual time expended and the rate at which fees and other expenses were computed. The party shall also allege that the position of the United States was not substantially justified. Whether or not the position of the United States was substantially justified shall be determined on the basis of the record (including the record with respect to the action or failure to act by the agency upon which the civil action is based) which is made in the civil action for which fees and other expenses are sought.

(C) The court, in its discretion, may reduce the amount to be awarded pursuant to this subsection, or deny an award, to the extent that the prevailing party during the course of the proceedings engaged in conduct which unduly and unreasonably protracted the final resolution of the matter in controversy.

(D) If, in a civil action brought by the United States or a proceeding for judicial review of an adversary adjudication described in section 504(a)(4) of title 5, the demand by the United States is substantially in excess of the judgment finally obtained by the United States and is unreasonable when compared with such judgment, under the facts and circumstances of the case, the court shall award to the party the fees and other expenses related to defending against the excessive demand, unless the party has committed a willful violation of law or otherwise acted in bad faith, or special circumstances make an award unjust. Fees and expenses awarded under this subparagraph shall be paid only as a consequence of appropriations provided in advance.

(2) For the purposes of this subsection—

(A) "fees and other expenses" includes the reasonable expenses of expert witnesses, the reasonable cost of any study, analysis, engineering report, test, or project which is found by the court to be necessary for the preparation of the party's case, and reasonable attorney fees (The amount of fees awarded under this subsection shall be based upon prevailing market rates for the kind and quality of the services furnished, except that (i) no expert witness shall be compensated at a rate in excess of the highest rate of compensation for expert witnesses paid by the United States; and (ii) attorney fees shall not be awarded in excess of $125 per hour unless the court determines that an increase in the cost of living or a special factor, such as the limited availability of qualified attorneys for the proceedings involved, justifies a higher fee.);

(B) "party" means (i) an individual whose net worth did not exceed $2,000,000 at the time the civil action was filed, or (ii) any owner of an unincorporated business, or any partnership, corporation, association, unit of local government, or organization, the net worth of which did not exceed $7,000,000 at the time the civil action was filed, and which had not more than 500 employees at the time the civil action was filed; except that an organization described in section 501(c)(3) of the Internal Revenue Code of 1986 (26 U.S.C. 501(c)(3)) exempt from taxation under section 501(a) of such Code, or a cooperative association as defined in section 15(a) of the Agricultural Marketing Act (12 U.S.C. 1141j(a)), may be a party regardless of the net worth of such organization or cooperative association or for purposes of subsection (d)(1)(D), a small entity as defined in section 601 of Title 5;

(C) "United States" includes any agency and any official of the United States acting in his or her official capacity;

(D) "position of the United States" means, in addition to the position taken by the United States in the civil action, the action or failure to act by the agency upon which the civil action is based; except that fees and expenses may not be awarded to a party for any portion of the litigation in which the party has unreasonably protracted the proceedings;

(E) "civil action brought by or against the United States" includes an appeal by a party, other than the United States, from a decision of a contracting officer rendered pursuant to a disputes clause in a contract with the Government or pursuant to the Contract Disputes Act of 1978;

(F) "court" includes the United States Court of Federal Claims and the United States Court of Appeals for Veterans Claims;

(G) "final judgment" means a judgment that is final and not appealable, and includes an order of settlement;

(H) "prevailing party", in the case of eminent domain proceedings, means a party who obtains a final judgment (other than by settlement), exclusive of interest, the amount of which is at least as close to the highest valuation of the property involved that is attested to at trial on behalf of the property owner as it is to the highest valuation of the property involved that is attested to at trial on behalf of the Government; and

(I) "demand" means the express demand of the United States which led to the adversary adjudication, but shall not include a recitation of the maximum statutory penalty (i) in the complaint, or (ii) elsewhere when accompanied by an express demand for a lesser amount.

(3) In awarding fees and other expenses under this subsection to a prevailing party in any action for judicial review of an adversary adjudication, as defined in subsection (b)(1)(C) of section 504 of title 5, United States Code, or an adversary adjudication subject to the Contract Disputes Act of 1978, the court shall include in that award fees and other expenses to the same extent authorized in subsection (a) of such section, unless the court finds that during such adversary adjudication the position of the United States was substantially justified, or that special circumstances make an award unjust.

(4) Fees and other expenses awarded under this subsection to a party shall be paid by any agency over

which the party prevails from any funds made available to the agency by appropriation or otherwise.

(e) The provisions of this section shall not apply to any costs, fees, and other expenses in connection with any proceeding to which section 7430 of the Internal Revenue Code of 1986 applies (determined without regard to subsections (b) and (f) of such section). Nothing in the preceding sentence shall prevent the awarding under subsection (a) of section 2412 of title 28, United States Code, of costs enumerated in section 1920 of such title (as in effect on October 1, 1981).

(f) If the United States appeals an award of costs or fees and other expenses made against the United States under this section and the award is affirmed in whole or in part, interest shall be paid on the amount of the award as affirmed. Such interest shall be computed at the rate determined under section 1961(a) of this title, and shall run from the date of the award through the day before the date of the mandate of affirmance.

(June 25, 1948, c. 646, 62 Stat. 973; July 18, 1966, Pub.L. 89–507, § 1, 80 Stat. 308; Oct. 21, 1980, Pub. L. 96–481, Title II, § 204(a), (c), 94 Stat. 2327, 2329; Sept. 3, 1982, Pub. L. 97–248, Title II, § 292(c), 96 Stat. 574; Aug. 5, 1985, Pub. L. 99–80, §§ 2, 6(a), (b)(2), 99 Stat. 184, 186; Oct. 22, 1986, Pub.L. 99–514, § 2, 100 Stat. 2095; Oct. 29, 1992, Pub.L. 102–572, Title III, § 301(a), Title V, §§ 502(b), 506(a), Title IX, § 902(b)(1), 106 Stat. 4511–4513, 4516; Dec. 21, 1995, Pub.L. 104–66, Title I, § 1091(b), 109 Stat. 722; Mar. 29, 1996, Pub.L. 104–121, Title II, § 232, 110 Stat. 863; Pub.L. 105–368, Title V, § 512(b)(1)(B), Nov. 11, 1998, 112 Stat. 3342.)

HISTORICAL AND STATUTORY NOTES

References in Text

The Contract Disputes Act of 1978, referred to in subsec. (d)(2)(E), (3), is Pub. L. 95–563, Nov. 1, 1978, 92 Stat. 2383, as amended, which is classified principally to chapter 9 (section 601 et seq.) of Title 41, Public Contracts. For complete classification of this Act to the Code, see Short Title note set out under section 601 of Title 41 and Tables.

Section 7430 of the Internal Revenue Code of 1986, referred to in subsec. (e), is classified to section 7430 of Title 26, Internal Revenue Code.

Effective and Applicability Provisions

1998 Acts. Amendment by Pub.L. 105–368 effective on the first day of the first month beginning more than 90 days after Nov. 11, 1998, see section 513 of Pub.L. 105–368, set out as a note under section 7251 of Title 38.

1996 Acts. Amendment by Pub.L. 104–121 applicable to civil actions and adversary adjudications commenced on or after March 29, 1996, see section 233 of Pub.L. 104–121, set out as a note under section 504 of Title 5, Government Organization and Employees.

1992 Acts. Section 506(b) of Pub.L. 102–572 provided that: "The amendment made by subsection (a) [amending subsec. (d)(2)(F) of this section] shall apply to any case pending before the United States Court of Veterans Appeals on the date of the enactment of this Act [Oct. 29, 1992], to any appeal filed in that court on or after such date, and to any appeal from that court that is pending on such date in the United States Court of Appeals for the Federal Circuit."

Section 506(d) of Pub.L. 102–572 provided that: "This section, and the amendment made by this section [amending subsec. (d)(2)(F) of this section and enacting provisions set out as notes under this section], shall take effect on the date of the enactment of this Act [Oct. 29, 1992]."

Amendment by section 902(b)(1) of Pub.L. 102–572 effective Oct. 29, 1992, see section 911 of Pub.L. 102–572, set out as a note under section 171 of this title.

Amendments by sections 301(a) and 502(b) of Pub.L. 102–572 effective Jan. 1, 1993, see section 1101(a) of Pub.L. 102–572, set out as a note under section 905 of Title 2, The Congress.

1985 Acts. Amendment by Pub. L. 99–80 applicable to cases pending on or commenced on or after Aug. 5, 1985, but with provision for additional applicability to certain prior cases and to prior board of contracts appeals cases, see section 7 of Pub. L. 99–80, set out as a note under section 504 of Title 5, Government Organization and Employees.

1982 Acts. Amendment by Pub.L. 97–248 applicable to civil actions or proceedings commenced after Feb. 28, 1983, see section 292(e)(1) of Pub.L. 97–248, as amended, set out as a note under section 7430 of Title 26, Internal Revenue Code.

1980 Acts. Amendment by section 204(a) of Pub.L. 96–481 to take effect on Oct. 1, 1981, and applicable to any adversary adjudication, as defined in section 504(b)(1)(C) of Title 5, and to civil actions and adversary adjudications described in this section, which are pending on, or commenced on or after, Oct. 1, 1981, see section 208 of Pub.L. 96–481, as amended, set out as a note under section 504 of Title 5, Government Organization and Employees.

Section 204(c) of Pub.L. 96–481 which provided in part that effective Oct. 1, 1984, subsec. (d) of this section is repealed, except that the provisions of subsec. (d) shall continue to apply through final disposition of any adversary adjudication initiated before the date of repeal, was repealed by Pub.L. 99–80, § 6(b)(2), Aug. 5, 1985, 99 Stat. 186.

1966 Acts. Section 3 of Pub.L. 89–507 provided that: "These amendments [to this section and section 2520 of this title] shall apply only to judgments entered in actions filed subsequent to the date of enactment of this Act [July 18, 1966]. These amendments [to this section and section 2520 of this title] shall not authorize the reopening or modification of judgments entered prior to the enactment of this Act [July 18, 1966]."

Fees Awarded to Non-attorney Practitioners

Pub.L. 107–330, Title IV, § 403, Dec. 6, 2002, 116 Stat. 2833, provided that: "The authority of the United States Court of Appeals for Veterans Claims to award reasonable fees and expenses of attorneys under section 2412(d) of title 28, United States Code [Subsec. (d) of this section], shall include authority to award fees and expenses, in an amount determined appropriate by the United States Court of Appeals for Veterans Claims, of individuals admitted to practice before the Court as non-attorney practitioners under subsection (b) or (c) of Rule 46 of the Rules of Practice and Procedure of the United States Court of Appeals for Veterans Claims."

Savings Provisions

Section 206 of Pub.L. 96–481, as amended by Pub.L. 99–80, § 3, Aug. 5, 1985, 99 Stat. 186, provided that:

"(a) Except as provided in subsection (b), nothing in section 2412(d) of title 28, United States Code, as added by section 204(a) of this title [subsec. (d) of this section], alters, modifies, repeals, invalidates, or supersedes any other provision of Federal law which authorizes an award of such fees and other expenses to any party other than the United States that prevails in any civil action brought by or against the United States.

"(b) Section 206(b) of the Social Security Act (42 U.S.C. 406(b)(1)) [section 406(b) of Title 42, The Public Health and Welfare] shall not prevent an award of fees and other expenses under section 2412(d) of title 28, United States Code [subsec. (d) of this section]. Section 206(b)(2) of the Social Security Act [section 406(b)(2) of Title 42] shall not apply with respect to any such award but only if, where the claimant's attorney receives fees for the same work under both section 206(b) of that Act [section 406(b) of Title 42] and section 2412(d) of title 28, United States Code [subsec. (d) of this section], the claimant's attorney refunds to the claimant the amount of the smaller fee."

Congressional Findings and Purposes

For Congressional findings and purposes relating to 1980 amendment of this section, see section 202 of Pub.L. 96–481, set out as a note under section 504 of Title 5, Government Organization and Employees.

Fee Agreements

Section 506(c) of Pub.L. 102–572 provided that: "Section 5904(d) of title 38, United States Code [section 5904(d) of Title 38, Veterans' Benefits], shall not prevent an award of fees and other expenses under section 2412(d) of title 28, United States Code [subsec. (d) of this section]. Section 5904(d) of title 38, United States Code, shall not apply with respect to any such award but only if, where the claimant's attorney receives fees for the same work under both section 5904 of title 38, United States Code, and section 2412(d) of title 28, United States Code, the claimant's attorney refunds to the claimant the amount of the smaller fee."

Nonliability of Judicial Officers for Costs

Pub.L. 104–317, Title III, § 309(a), Oct. 19, 1996, 110 Stat. 3853, provided that: "Notwithstanding any other provision of law, no judicial officer shall be held liable for any costs, including attorney's fees, in any action brought against such officer for an act or omission taken in such officer's judicial capacity, unless such action was clearly in excess of such officer's jurisdiction."

Revival of Previously Repealed Provisions

For revival of subsec. (d) of this section effective on or after Aug. 5, 1985, as if it had not been repealed by section 204(c) of Pub.L. 96–481, and repeal of section 204(c) of Pub.L. 96–481, see section 6 of Pub.L. 99–80, set out as a note under section 504 of Title 5, Government Organization and Employees.

§ 2413. Executions in favor of United States

A writ of execution on a judgment obtained for the use of the United States in any court thereof shall be issued from and made returnable to the court which rendered the judgment, but may be executed in any other State, in any Territory, or in the District of Columbia.

(June 25, 1948, c. 646, 62 Stat. 974.)

§ 2414. Payment of judgments and compromise settlements

Except as provided by the Contract Disputes Act of 1978, payment of final judgments rendered by a district court or the Court of International Trade against the United States shall be made on settlements by the Secretary of the Treasury. Payment of final judgments rendered by a State or foreign court or tribunal against the United States, or against its agencies or officials upon obligations or liabilities of the United States, shall be made on settlements by the Secretary of the Treasury after certification by the Attorney General that it is in the interest of the United States to pay the same.

Whenever the Attorney General determines that no appeal shall be taken from a judgment or that no further review will be sought from a decision affirming the same, he shall so certify and the judgment shall be deemed final.

Except as otherwise provided by law, compromise settlements of claims referred to the Attorney General for defense of imminent litigation or suits against the United States, or against its agencies or officials upon obligations or liabilities of the United States, made by the Attorney General or any person authorized by him, shall be settled and paid in a manner similar to judgments in like causes and appropriations or funds available for the payment of such judgments are hereby made available for the payment of such compromise settlements.

(June 25, 1948, c. 646, 62 Stat. 974; Aug. 30, 1961, Pub.L. 87–187, § 1, 75 Stat. 415; Nov. 1, 1978, Pub.L. 95–563, § 14(d), 92 Stat. 2390; Oct. 10, 1980, Pub.L. 96–417, Title V, § 512, 94 Stat. 1744; Oct. 19, 1996, Pub.L. 104–316, Title II, § 202(k), 110 Stat. 3843.)

HISTORICAL AND STATUTORY NOTES

References in Text

The Contract Disputes Act of 1978, referred to in first paragraph, is Pub.L. 95–563, Nov. 1, 1978, 92 Stat. 2383, as amended, which is classified principally to chapter 9 (section 601 et seq.) of Title 41, Public Contracts. For complete classification of this Act to the Code, see Short Title note set out under section 601 of Title 41 and Tables.

Effective and Applicability Provisions

1980 Acts. Amendment by Pub.L. 96–417 effective on Nov. 1, 1980, and applicable with respect to civil actions pending on or commenced on or after such date, see section 701(a) of Pub.L. 96–417, as amended, set out as a note under section 251 of this title.

1978 Acts. Amendment by Pub.L. 95–563 effective with respect to contracts entered into 120 days after Nov. 1, 1978, and, at the election of the contractor, with respect to any claim pending at such time before the contracting officer or initiated thereafter, see section 16 of Pub.L. 95–563, set out as a note under section 601 of Title 41, Public Contracts.

Transfer of Functions

Effective June 30, 1996, the functions of the Comptroller General under this section to be transferred to the Director of the Office of Management and Budget, contingent upon the additional transfer to the Office of Management and Budget of such personnel, budget authority, records, and property of the General Accounting Office relating to such functions as the Comptroller General and the Director jointly determine to be necessary, see section 211 of Pub.L. 104–53, set out as a note under section 501 of Title 31, Money and Finance.

§ 2415. Time for commencing actions brought by the United States

(a) Subject to the provisions of section 2416 of this title, and except as otherwise provided by Congress, every action for money damages brought by the United States or an officer or agency thereof which is founded upon any contract express or implied in law or fact, shall be barred unless the complaint is filed within six years after the right of action accrues or within one year after final decisions have been rendered in applicable administrative proceedings required by contract or by law, whichever is later: *Provided,* That in the event of later partial payment or written acknowledgment of debt, the right of action shall be deemed to accrue again at the time of each such payment or acknowledgment: *Provided further,* That an action for money damages brought by the United States for or on behalf of a recognized tribe, band or group of American Indians shall not be barred unless the complaint is filed more than six years and ninety days after the right of action accrued: *Provided further,* That an action for money damages which accrued on the date of enactment of this Act in accordance with subsection (g) brought by the United States for or on behalf of a recognized tribe, band, or group of American Indians, or on behalf of an individual Indian whose land is held in trust or restricted status, shall not be barred unless the complaint is filed sixty days after the date of publication of the list required by section 4(c) of the Indian Claims Limitation Act of 1982: *Provided,* That, for those claims that are on either of the two lists published pursuant to the Indian Claims Limitation Act of 1982, any right of action shall be barred unless the complaint is filed within (1) one year after the Secretary of the Interior has published in the Federal Register a notice rejecting such claim or (2) three years after the date the Secretary of the Interior has submitted legislation or legislative report to Congress to resolve such claim or more than two years after a final decision has been rendered in applicable administrative proceedings required by contract or by law, whichever is later.

(b) Subject to the provisions of section 2416 of this title, and except as otherwise provided by Congress, every action for money damages brought by the United States or an officer or agency thereof which is founded upon a tort shall be barred unless the complaint is filed within three years after the right of action first accrues: *Provided,* That an action to recover damages resulting from a trespass on lands of the United States; an action to recover damages resulting from fire to such lands; an action to recover for diversion of money paid under a grant program; and an action for conversion of property of the United States may be brought within six years after the right of action accrues, except that such actions for or on behalf of a recognized tribe, band or group of American Indians, including actions relating to allotted trust or restricted Indian lands, may be brought within six years and ninety days after the right of action accrues, except that such actions for or on behalf of a recognized tribe, band, or group of American Indians, including actions relating to allotted trust or restricted Indian lands, or on behalf of an individual Indian whose land is held in trust or restricted status which accrued on the date of enactment of this Act in accordance with subsection (g) may be brought on or before sixty days after the date of the publication of the list required by section 4(c) of the Indian Claims Limitation Act of 1982: *Provided,* That, for those claims that are on either of the two lists published pursuant to the Indian Claims Limitation Act of 1982, any right of action shall be barred unless the complaint is filed within (1) one year after the Secretary of the Interior has published in the Federal Register a notice rejecting such claim or (2) three years after the Secretary of the Interior has submitted legislation or legislative report to Congress to resolve such claim.

(c) Nothing herein shall be deemed to limit the time for bringing an action to establish the title to, or right of possession of, real or personal property.

(d) Subject to the provisions of section 2416 of this title and except as otherwise provided by Congress, every action for the recovery of money erroneously paid to or on behalf of any civilian employee of any agency of the United States or to or on behalf of any member or dependent of any member of the uniformed services of the United States, incident to the employment or services of such employee or member, shall be barred unless the complaint is filed within six years after the right of action accrues: *Provided,* That in the event of later partial payment or written acknowledgment of debt, the right of action shall be deemed to accrue again at the time of each such payment or acknowledgment.

(e) In the event that any action to which this section applies is timely brought and is thereafter dismissed without prejudice, the action may be recommenced within one year after such dismissal, regardless of whether the action would otherwise then be barred by this section. In any action so recommenced the defendant shall not be barred from interposing any claim which would not have been barred in the original action.

(f) The provisions of this section shall not prevent the assertion, in an action against the United States or an officer or agency thereof, of any claim of the United States or an officer or agency thereof against an opposing party, a co-party, or a third party that arises out of the transaction or occurrence that is the subject matter of the opposing party's claim. A claim of the United States or an officer or agency thereof that does not arise out of the transaction or occurrence that is the subject matter of the opposing party's claim may, if time-barred, be asserted only by way of offset and may be allowed in an amount not to exceed the amount of the opposing party's recovery.

(g) Any right of action subject to the provisions of this section which accrued prior to the date of enactment of this Act shall, for purposes of this section, be deemed to have accrued on the date of enactment of this Act.

(h) Nothing in this Act shall apply to actions brought under the Internal Revenue Code or incidental to the collection of taxes imposed by the United States.

(i) The provisions of this section shall not prevent the United States or an officer or agency thereof from collecting any claim of the United States by means of administrative offset, in accordance with section 3716 of title 31.

(Added Pub.L. 89–505, § 1, July 18, 1966, 80 Stat. 304, and amended Pub.L. 92–353, July 18, 1972, 86 Stat. 499; Pub.L. 92–485, Oct. 13, 1972, 86 Stat. 803; Pub.L. 95–64, July 11, 1977, 91 Stat. 268; Pub.L. 95–103, Aug. 15, 1977, 91 Stat. 842; Pub.L. 96–217, § 1, Mar. 27, 1980, 94 Stat. 126; Pub.L. 97–365, § 9, Oct. 25, 1982, 96 Stat. 1754; Pub.L. 97–394, Title I, § 2, Dec. 30, 1982, 96 Stat. 1976; Pub.L. 97–452, § 2(d)(2), Jan. 12, 1983, 96 Stat. 2478; Pub.L. 98–250, § 4(a), Apr. 3, 1984, 98 Stat. 118.)

HISTORICAL AND STATUTORY NOTES

References in Text

The date of enactment of this Act, referred to in subsecs. (a), (b), and (g), means the date of enactment of Pub.L. 89–505, which was approved on July 18, 1966.

The Indian Claims Limitation Act of 1982, referred to in subsecs. (a) and (b), is Pub.L. 97–394, Title I, §§ 2–6, Dec. 30, 1982, 96 Stat. 1976–1978, which amended this section and enacted provisions set out as notes under this section. For complete classification of this Act to the Code, see Short Title of 1982 Amendments note set out under this section and Tables.

This Act, referred to in subsec. (h), means Pub.L. 89–505, July 18, 1966, 80 Stat. 304, which enacted this section and section 2416 of this title. For complete classification of this Act to the Code see Tables.

Short Title

1982 Amendments. Section 1 of Pub.L. 97–394, as amended by Pub.L. 98–250, § 4(b), Apr. 3, 1984, 98 Stat. 119, provided that: "Sections 2 through 6 of this Act [sections 2–6 of Pub.L. 97–394, which amended this section and enacted provisions set out as a note under this section] may be cited as the 'Indian Claims Limitation Act of 1982'."

Legislative Proposals Respecting Appropriateness of Resolution By Litigation of Unresolved Indian Claims

Section 2 of Pub.L. 96–217 provided that: "Not later than June 30, 1981, the Secretary of the Interior, after consultation with the Attorney General, shall submit to the Congress legislative proposals to resolve those Indian claims subject to the amendments made by the first section of this Act [amending this section] that the Secretary of the Interior or the Attorney General believes are not appropriate to resolve by litigation."

Publication of List of Indian Claims; Additional Claims; Time to Commence Action; Rejection of Claims; Claims Resolved By Legislation

Sections 3 to 6 of Pub.L. 97–394 provided that:

"**Sec. 3.** **(a)** Within ninety days after the enactment of this Act [Dec. 30, 1982], the Secretary of the Interior (hereinafter referred to as the 'Secretary') shall publish in the Federal Register a list of all claims accruing to any tribe, band or group of Indians or individual Indian on or before July 18, 1966, which have at any time been identified by or submitted to the Secretary under the 'Statute of Limitation Project' undertaken by the Department of the Interior and which, but for the provisions of this Act [sections 2–6 of Pub.L. 97–394; see Short Title of 1982 Amendments note set out under this section] would be barred by the provisions of section 2415 of title 28, United States Code [this section]: *Provided,* That the Secretary shall have the discretion to exclude from such list any matter which was erroneously identified as a claim and which has no legal merit whatsoever.

"**(b)** Such list shall group the claims on a reservation-by-reservation, tribe-by-tribe, or State-by-State basis, as appropriate, and shall state the nature and geographic location of each claim and only such other additional information as may be needed to identify specifically such claims.

"**(c)** Within thirty days after the publication of this list, the Secretary shall provide a copy of the Indian Claims Limitation Act of 1982 [sections 2–6 of Pub.L. 97–394; see short title of 1982 Amendments note under this section] and a copy of the Federal Register containing this list, or such parts as may be pertinent, to each Indian tribe, band or group whose rights or the rights of whose members could be affected by the provisions of section 2415 of title 28, United States Code [this section].

"**Sec. 4.** **(a)** Any tribe, band or group of Indians or any individual Indian shall have one hundred and eighty days after the date of the publication in the Federal Register of the list provided for in section 3 of this Act [section 3 of Pub.L. 97–394] to submit to the Secretary any additional specific claim or claims which such tribe, band or group of Indians or individual Indian believes may be affected by section 2415 of title 28, United States Code [this section], and desires to have considered for litigation or legislation by the United States.

"(b) Any such claim submitted to the Secretary shall be accompanied by a statement identifying the nature of the claim, the date when the right of action allegedly accrued, the names of the potential plaintiffs and defendants, if known, and such other information needed to identify and evaluate such claim.

"(c) Not more than thirty days after the expiration of the one hundred and eighty day period provided for in subsection (a) of this section, the Secretary shall publish in the Federal Register a list containing the additional claims submitted during such period: *Provided*, That the Secretary shall have the discretion to exclude from such list any matter which has not been sufficiently identified as a claim.

"**Sec. 5.** (a) Any right of action shall be barred sixty days after the date of the publication of the list required by section 4(c) of this Act [section 4(c) of Pub.L. 97–394] for those pre-1966 claims which, but for the provisions of this Act [sections 2–6 of Pub.L. 97–394; see Short Title of 1982 Amendments note set out under this section] would have been barred by section 2415 of title 28, United States Code [this section], unless such claims are included on either of the lists required by section 3 or 4(c) of this Act [section 3 or 4(c) of Pub.L. 97–394].

"(b) If the Secretary decides to reject for litigation any of the claims or groups or categories of claims contained on either of the lists required by section 3 or 4(c) of this Act [section 3 or 4(c) of Pub.L. 97–394], he shall send a report to the appropriate tribe, band, or group of Indians, whose rights or the rights of whose members could be affected by such rejection, advising them of his decision. The report shall identify the nature and geographic location of each rejected claim and the name of the potential plaintiffs and defendants if they are known or can be reasonably ascertained and shall, briefly, state the reasons why such claim or claims were rejected for litigation. Where the Secretary knows or can reasonably ascertain the identity of any of the potential individual Indian plaintiffs and their present addresses, he shall provide them with written notice of such rejection. Upon the request of any Indian claimant, the Secretary shall, without undue delay, provide to such claimant any nonprivileged research materials or evidence gathered by the United States in the documentation of such claim.

"(c) The Secretary, as soon as possible, after providing the report required by subsection (b) of this section, shall publish a notice in the Federal Register identifying the claims covered in such report. With respect to any claim covered by such report, any right of action shall be barred unless the complaint is filed within one year after the date of publication in the Federal Register.

"**Sec. 6.** (a) If the Secretary determines that any claim or claims contained in either of the lists as provided in sections 3 or 4(c) of this Act [sections 3 or 4(c) of Pub.L. 97–394] is not appropriate for litigation, but determines that such claims may be appropriately resolved by legislation, he shall submit to the Congress legislation to resolve such claims or shall submit to Congress a report setting out options for legislative resolution of such claims.

"(b) Any right of action on claims covered by such legislation or report shall be barred unless the complaint is filed within 3 years after the date of submission of such legislation or legislative report to Congress."

[For termination of reporting provisions pertaining to proposed legislation to resolve Indian claims, effective May 15, 2000, see Pub.L. 104–66, § 3003, as amended, set out as a note under 31 U.S.C.A. § 1113, and the last item on page 113 of House Document No. 103–7.]

§ 2416. Time for commencing actions brought by the United States—Exclusions

For the purpose of computing the limitations periods established in section 2415, there shall be excluded all periods during which—

(a) the defendant or the res is outside the United States, its territories and possessions, the District of Columbia, or the Commonwealth of Puerto Rico; or

(b) the defendant is exempt from legal process because of infancy, mental incompetence, diplomatic immunity, or for any other reason; or

(c) facts material to the right of action are not known and reasonably could not be known by an official of the United States charged with the responsibility to act in the circumstances; or

(d) the United States is in a state of war declared pursuant to article I, section 8, of the Constitution of the United States.

(Added Pub.L. 89–505, § 1, July 18, 1966, 80 Stat. 305.)

CHAPTER 163—FINES, PENALTIES AND FORFEITURES

Sec.
2461. Mode of recovery.
2462. Time for commencing proceedings.
2463. Property taken under revenue law not repleviable.
2464. Security; special bond.
2465. Return of property to claimant; liability for wrongful seizure; attorney fees, costs, and interest.
2466. Fugitive disentitlement.
2467. Enforcement of foreign judgment.

§ 2461. Mode of recovery

(a) Whenever a civil fine, penalty or pecuniary forfeiture is prescribed for the violation of an Act of Congress without specifying the mode of recovery or enforcement thereof, it may be recovered in a civil action.

(b) Unless otherwise provided by Act of Congress, whenever a forfeiture of property is prescribed as a penalty for violation of an Act of Congress and the seizure takes place on the high seas or on navigable waters within the admiralty and maritime jurisdiction of the United States, such forfeiture may be enforced by libel in admiralty but in cases of seizures on land the forfeiture may be enforced by a proceeding by libel which shall conform as near as may be to proceedings in admiralty.

(c) If a person is charged in a criminal case with a violation of an Act of Congress for which the civil or criminal forfeiture of property is authorized, the Government may include notice of the forfeiture in the indictment or information pursuant to the Federal Rules of Criminal Procedure. If the defendant is convicted of the offense giving rise to the forfeiture, the court shall order the forfeiture of the property as part of the sentence in the criminal case pursuant to to the Federal Rules of Criminal Procedure and section 3554 of title 18, United States Code. The procedures in section 413 of the Controlled Substances Act (21 U.S.C. 853) apply to all stages of a criminal forfeiture proceeding, except that subsection (d) of such section applies only in cases in which the defendant is convicted of a violation of such Act.

(June 25, 1948, c. 646, 62 Stat. 974; Apr. 25, 2000, Pub.L. 106–185, § 16, 114 Stat. 221; Mar. 9, 2006, Pub.L. 109–177, Title IV, § 410, 120 Stat. 246.)

HISTORICAL AND STATUTORY NOTES

References in Text

The Federal Rules of Criminal Procedure, referred to in subsec. (c), are set out in Title 18, Rules of Criminal Procedure, Fed.Rules Cr.Proc., Rule 1 et seq., 18 U.S.C.A.

Section 413 of the Controlled Substances Act, referred to in subsec. (c), is Pub.L. 91–513, Title II, § 413, as added Pub.L. 98–473, Title II, § 303, Oct. 12, 1984, 98 Stat. 2044, as amended, which is classified to 21 U.S.C.A. § 853. The Controlled Substances Act (CSA), is title II of Pub.L. 91–513, Oct. 27, 1970, 84 Stat. 1242, as amended, which is classified principally to subchapter I of chapter 13, of Title 21, 21 U.S.C.A. § 801 et seq. For complete classification of Title II to the Code, see Short Title note set out under 21 U.S.C.A. § 801 and Tables.

Effective and Applicability Provisions

2000 Acts. Amendments by Pub.L. 106–185, applicable to any forfeiture proceeding commenced on or after the date that is 120 days after April 25, 2000, see section 21 of Pub.L. 106–185, set out as a note under section 1324 of Title 8.

Federal Civil Penalties Inflation Adjustment

Pub.L. 101–410, Oct. 5, 1990, 104 Stat. 890, as amended Pub.L. 104–134, Title III, § 31001(s)(1), Apr. 26, 1996, 110 Stat. 1321–373; Pub.L. 105–362, Title XIII, § 1301(a), Nov. 10, 1998, 112 Stat. 3293, provided that:

"SHORT TITLE

"**Section 1.** This Act may be cited as the 'Federal Civil Penalties Inflation Adjustment Act of 1990'.

"FINDINGS AND PURPOSE

"**Sec. 2.** (a) **Findings.**—The Congress finds that—

"(1) the power of Federal agencies to impose civil monetary penalties for violations of Federal law and regulations plays an important role in deterring violations and furthering the policy goals embodied in such laws and regulations;

"(2) the impact of many civil monetary penalties has been and is diminished due to the effect of inflation;

"(3) by reducing the impact of civil monetary penalties, inflation has weakened the deterrent effect of such penalties; and

"(4) the Federal Government does not maintain comprehensive, detailed accounting of the efforts of Federal agencies to assess and collect civil monetary penalties.

"(b) **Purpose.**—The purpose of this Act is to establish a mechanism that shall—

"(1) allow for regular adjustment for inflation of civil monetary penalties;

"(2) maintain the deterrent effect of civil monetary penalties and promote compliance with the law; and

"(3) improve the collection by the Federal Government of civil monetary penalties.

"DEFINITIONS

"**Sec. 3.** For purposes of this Act, the term—

"(1) 'agency' means an Executive agency as defined under section 105 of title 5, United States Code [5 U.S.C.A. § 105], and includes the United States Postal Service;

"(2) 'civil monetary penalty' means any penalty, fine, or other sanction that—

"(A)(i) is for a specific monetary amount as provided by Federal law; or

"(ii) has a maximum amount provided for by Federal law; and

"(B) is assessed or enforced by an agency pursuant to Federal law; and

"(C) is assessed or enforced pursuant to an administrative proceeding or a civil action in the Federal courts; and

"(3) 'Consumer Price Index' means the Consumer Price Index for all-urban consumers published by the Department of Labor.

"CIVIL MONETARY PENALTY INFLATION ADJUSTMENT REPORTS

"**Sec. 4.** The head of each agency shall, not later than 180 days after the date of enactment of the Debt Collection Improvement Act of 1996 [Apr. 26, 1996], and at least once every 4 years thereafter—

"(1) by regulation adjust each civil monetary penalty provided by law within the jurisdiction of the Federal agency, except for any penalty (including any addition to tax and additional amount) under the Internal Revenue Code of 1986 [26 U.S.C.A. § 1 et seq.], the Tariff Act of 1930 [19 U.S.C.A. § 1202 et seq.], the Occupational Safety and Health Act of 1970 [29 U.S.C.A. § 651 et seq.], or the Social Security Act [42 U.S.C.A. § 301 et seq.], by the inflation adjustment described under section 5 of this Act; and

"(2) publish each such regulation in the Federal Register.

"COST-OF-LIVING ADJUSTMENTS OF CIVIL MONETARY PENALTIES

"**Sec. 5. (a) Adjustment.**—The inflation adjustment under section 4 shall be determined by increasing the maximum civil monetary penalty or the range of minimum and maximum civil monetary penalties, as applicable, for each civil monetary penalty by the cost-of-living adjustment. Any increase determined under this subsection shall be rounded to the nearest—

"(1) multiple of $10 in the case of penalties less than or equal to $100;

"(2) multiple of $100 in the case of penalties greater than $100 but less than or equal to $1,000;

"(3) multiple of $1,000 in the case of penalties greater than $1,000 but less than or equal to $10,000;

"(4) multiple of $5,000 in the case of penalties greater than $10,000 but less than or equal to $100,000;

"(5) multiple of $10,000 in the case of penalties greater than $100,000 but less than or equal to $200,000; and

"(6) multiple of $25,000 in the case of penalties greater than $200,000.

"**(b) Definition.**—For purposes of subsection (a), the term 'cost-of-living adjustment' means the percentage (if any) for each civil monetary penalty by which—

"(1) the Consumer Price Index for the month of June of the calendar year preceding the adjustment, exceeds

"(2) the Consumer Price Index for the month of June of the calendar year in which the amount of such civil monetary penalty was last set or adjusted pursuant to law.

"ANNUAL REPORT

"**Sec. 6.** Any increase under this Act in a civil monetary penalty shall apply only to violations which occur after the date the increase takes effect."

[Former Sec. 6 repealed by Pub.L. 105–362, Title XIII, § 1301(a)(1), Nov. 10, 1998, 112 Stat. 3293.]

"**Sec. 7. [Redesignated as Sec. 6.** Pub.L. 105–362, Title XIII, § 1301(a)(2), Nov. 10, 1998, 112 Stat. 3293.]

[Pub.L. 104–134, Title III, § 31001(s)(2), Apr. 26, 1996, 110 Stat. 1321–373, provided that: "The first adjustment of a civil monetary penalty made pursuant to the amendment made by paragraph (1) [amending Pub.L. 101–410, set out as a note under this section] may not exceed 10 percent of such penalty."]

[Any reference in any provision of law enacted before Jan. 4, 1995, to the Committee on Government Operations of the House of Representatives treated as referring to the Committee on Government Reform and Oversight of the House of Representatives, except that any reference in any provision of law enacted before Jan. 4, 1995, to the Committee on Government Operations of the House of Representatives treated as referring to the Committee on the Budget of the House of Representatives in the case of a provision of law relating to the establishment, extension, and enforcement of special controls over the Federal budget, see section 1(a)(6) and (c)(2) of Pub.L. 104–14, set out as a note preceding section 21 of Title 2, The Congress.]

Memorandum of President of the United States, May 3, 1991, 56 F.R. 21911, delegated to Director of Office of Management and Budget responsibility of President for submitting reports on civil monetary penalties to Committee on Governmental Affairs of the Senate and Committee on Government Operations of the House of Representatives and to Congress as required by sections 4 and 6 of the Federal Civil Penalties Inflation Adjustment Act of 1990, Pub.L. 101–410, set out as a note under this section.

§ 2462. Time for commencing proceedings

Except as otherwise provided by Act of Congress, an action, suit or proceeding for the enforcement of any civil fine, penalty, or forfeiture, pecuniary or otherwise, shall not be entertained unless commenced within five years from the date when the claim first accrued if, within the same period, the offender or the property is found within the United States in order that proper service may be made thereon.

(June 25, 1948, c. 646, 62 Stat. 974.)

§ 2463. Property taken under revenue law not repleviable

All property taken or detained under any revenue law of the United States shall not be repleviable, but shall be deemed to be in the custody of the law and subject only to the orders and decrees of the courts of the United States having jurisdiction thereof.

(June 25, 1948, c. 646, 62 Stat. 974.)

§ 2464. Security; special bond

(a) Except in cases of seizures for forfeiture under any law of the United States, whenever a warrant of arrest or other process in rem is issued in any admiralty case, the United States marshal shall stay the execution of such process, or discharge the property arrested if the process has been levied, on receiving from the respondent or claimant of the property a bond or stipulation in double the amount claimed by the libellant, with sufficient surety, to be approved by the judge of the district court where the case is pending, or, in his absence, by the collector of the port, conditioned to answer the decree of the court in such case. Such bond or stipulation shall be returned to the court, and judgment or decree thereon, against both the principal and sureties, may be secured at the time of rendering the decree in the original case. The owner of any vessel may deliver to the marshal a bond or stipulation, with sufficient surety, to be approved by the judge of the district court, conditioned to answer the decree of such court in all or any cases that are brought thereafter in such court against the vessel. Thereupon the execution of all such process against such vessel shall be stayed so long as the amount secured by such bond or stipulation is at least double the aggregate amount claimed by libellants in such suits which are begun and pending against such vessel. Similar judgments or decrees and remedies may be had on such bond or stipulation as if a special bond or stipulation had been filed in each of such suits.

(b) The court may make necessary orders to carry this section into effect, particularly in giving proper notice of any such suit. Such bond or stipulation shall be indorsed by the clerk with a minute of the suits wherein process is so stayed. Further security may be required by the court at any time.

(c) If a special bond or stipulation in the particular case is given under this section, the liability as to said case on the general bond or stipulation shall cease. The parties may stipulate the amount of the bond or stipulation for the release of a vessel or other property to be not more than the amount claimed in the libel, with interest, plus an allowance for libellant's costs. In the event of the inability or refusal of the parties to so stipulate, the court shall fix the amount, but if not so fixed then a bond shall be required in the amount prescribed in this section.

(June 25, 1948, c. 646, 62 Stat. 974.)

HISTORICAL AND STATUTORY NOTES

Transfer of Functions

All offices of Collector of Customs, Comptroller of Customs, Surveyor of Customs, and Appraiser of Merchandise in the Bureau of Customs of the Department of the Treasury to which appointments were required to be made by the President with the advice and consent of the Senate were ordered abolished, with such offices to be terminated not later than December 31, 1966, by 1965 Reorg. Plan No. 1, eff. May 25, 1965, 30 F.R. 7035, 79 Stat. 1317, set out in Appendix 1 to Title 5, Government Organization and Employees. All functions of the offices eliminated were already vested in the Secretary of the Treasury by 1950 Reorg. Plan No. 26, eff. July 31, 1950, 15 F.R. 4935, 64 Stat. 1280, set out in Appendix 1 to Title 5.

§ 2465. Return of property to claimant; liability for wrongful seizure; attorney fees, costs, and interest

(a) Upon the entry of a judgment for the claimant in any proceeding to condemn or forfeit property seized or arrested under any provision of Federal law—

(1) such property shall be returned forthwith to the claimant or his agent; and

(2) if it appears that there was reasonable cause for the seizure or arrest, the court shall cause a proper certificate thereof to be entered and, in such case, neither the person who made the seizure or arrest nor the prosecutor shall be liable to suit or judgment on account of such suit or prosecution, nor shall the claimant be entitled to costs, except as provided in subsection (b).

(b)(1) Except as provided in paragraph (2), in any civil proceeding to forfeit property under any provision of Federal law in which the claimant substantially prevails, the United States shall be liable for—

(A) reasonable attorney fees and other litigation costs reasonably incurred by the claimant;

(B) post-judgment interest, as set forth in section 1961 of this title; and

(C) in cases involving currency, other negotiable instruments, or the proceeds of an interlocutory sale—

(i) interest actually paid to the United States from the date of seizure or arrest of the property that resulted from the investment of the property in an interest-bearing account or instrument; and

(ii) an imputed amount of interest that such currency, instruments, or proceeds would have earned at the rate applicable to the 30–day Treasury Bill, for any period during which no interest was paid (not including any period when the property reasonably was in use as evidence in an official proceeding or in conducting scientific tests for the purpose of collecting evidence), commencing 15 days after the property was seized by a Federal law enforcement agency, or was turned over to a Federal law enforcement agency by a State or local law enforcement agency.

(2)(A) The United States shall not be required to disgorge the value of any intangible benefits nor make any other payments to the claimant not specifically authorized by this subsection.

(B) The provisions of paragraph (1) shall not apply if the claimant is convicted of a crime for which the interest of the claimant in the property was subject to forfeiture under a Federal criminal forfeiture law.

(C) If there are multiple claims to the same property, the United States shall not be liable for costs and attorneys fees associated with any such claim if the United States—

(i) promptly recognizes such claim;

(ii) promptly returns the interest of the claimant in the property to the claimant, if the property can be divided without difficulty and there are no competing claims to that portion of the property;

(iii) does not cause the claimant to incur additional, reasonable costs or fees; and

(iv) prevails in obtaining forfeiture with respect to one or more of the other claims.

(D) If the court enters judgment in part for the claimant and in part for the Government, the court shall reduce the award of costs and attorney fees accordingly.

(June 25, 1948, c. 646, 62 Stat. 975; Apr. 25, 2000, Pub.L. 106–185, § 4(a), 114 Stat. 211.)

HISTORICAL AND STATUTORY NOTES

Effective and Applicability Provisions

2000 Acts. Amendments by Pub.L. 106–185, applicable to any forfeiture proceeding commenced on or after the date that is 120 days after April 25, 2000, see section 21 of Pub.L. 106–185, set out as a note under section 1324 of Title 8.

§ 2466. Fugitive disentitlement

(a) A judicial officer may disallow a person from using the resources of the courts of the United States in furtherance of a claim in any related civil forfeiture action or a claim in third party proceedings in any related criminal forfeiture action upon a finding that such person—

(1) after notice or knowledge of the fact that a warrant or process has been issued for his apprehension, in order to avoid criminal prosecution—

(A) purposely leaves the jurisdiction of the United States;

(B) declines to enter or reenter the United States to submit to its jurisdiction; or

(C) otherwise evades the jurisdiction of the court in which a criminal case is pending against the person; and

(2) is not confined or held in custody in any other jurisdiction for commission of criminal conduct in that jurisdiction.

(b) Subsection (a) may be applied to a claim filed by a corporation if any majority shareholder, or individual filing the claim on behalf of the corporation is a person to whom subsection (a) applies.

(Added Pub.L. 106–185, § 14(a), Apr. 25, 2000, 114 Stat. 219, and amended Pub.L. 107–56, Title III, § 322, Oct. 26, 2001, 115 Stat. 315; Pub.L. 109–162, Title XI, § 1171(c), Jan. 5, 2006, 119 Stat. 3123; Pub.L. 109–177, Title IV, § 406(a)(1), Mar. 9, 2006, 120 Stat. 244.)

HISTORICAL AND STATUTORY NOTES

Codifications

Pub.L. 109–177, § 406(a)(1), which directed the amendment of directory language of Pub.L. 107–56, § 322, was incapable of execution due to prior identical amendment by Pub.L. 109–162, 1171(c). See 2006 Amendments notes under this section.

Effective and Applicability Provisions

2006 Acts. Pub.L. 109–162, Title XI, § 1171(c), Jan. 5, 2006, 119 Stat. 3123, provided in part that the amendment of the directory language of Pub.L. 107–56, § 322 was "effective on the date of enactment of that section [Oct. 26, 2001]".

2000 Acts. Pub.L. 106–185, § 14(c), Apr. 25, 2000, 114 Stat. 219, provided that: "The amendments made by this section [adding this section] shall apply to any case pending on or after the date of the enactment of this Act [Apr. 25, 2000]."

4–Year Congressional Review; Expedited Consideration

Effective on and after the first day of fiscal year 2005, amendments by Title III (§§ 301 to 377) of Pub.L. 107–56 shall terminate if Congress enacts a joint resolution, and such resolution shall be given expedited consideration, see Pub.L. 107–56, Title III, § 303, Oct. 26, 2001, 115 Stat. 298, set out as a note under 31 U.S.C.A. § 5311.

§ 2467. Enforcement of foreign judgment

(a) Definitions.—In this section—

(1) the term "foreign nation" means a country that has become a party to the United Nations Convention Against Illicit Traffic in Narcotic Drugs and Psychotropic Substances (referred to in this section as the "United Nations Convention") or a foreign jurisdiction with which the United States has a treaty or other formal international agreement in effect providing for mutual forfeiture assistance; and

(2) the term "forfeiture or confiscation judgment" means a final order of a foreign nation compelling a person or entity—

(A) to pay a sum of money representing the proceeds of an offense described in Article 3, Paragraph 1, of the United Nations Convention, any violation of foreign law that would constitute a violation or an offense for which property could be forfeited under Federal law if the offense were committed in the United States, or any foreign offense described in section 1956(c)(7)(B) of title 18, or property the value of which corresponds to such proceeds; or

(B) to forfeit property involved in or traceable to the commission of such offense.

(b) Review by attorney general.—

(1) In general.—A foreign nation seeking to have a forfeiture or confiscation judgment registered and enforced by a district court of the United States under this section shall first submit a request to the Attorney General or the designee of the Attorney General, which request shall include—

(A) a summary of the facts of the case and a description of the proceedings that resulted in the forfeiture or confiscation judgment;

(B) certified [1] copy of the forfeiture or confiscation judgment;

(C) an affidavit or sworn declaration establishing that the foreign nation took steps, in accordance with the principles of due process, to give notice of the proceedings to all persons with an interest in the property in sufficient time to enable such persons to defend against the charges and that the judgment rendered is in force and is not subject to appeal; and

(D) such additional information and evidence as may be required by the Attorney General or the designee of the Attorney General.

(2) Certification of request.—The Attorney General or the designee of the Attorney General shall determine whether, in the interest of justice, to certify the request, and such decision shall be final and not subject to either judicial review or review under subchapter II of chapter 5, or chapter 7, of title 5 (commonly known as the "Administrative Procedure Act").

(c) Jurisdiction and venue.—

(1) In general.—If the Attorney General or the designee of the Attorney General certifies a request under subsection (b), the United States may file an application on behalf of a foreign nation in district court of the United States seeking to enforce the foreign forfeiture or confiscation judgment as if the judgment had been entered by a court in the United States.

(2) Proceedings.—In a proceeding filed under paragraph (1)—

(A) the United States shall be the applicant and the defendant or another person or entity affected by the forfeiture or confiscation judgment shall be the respondent;

(B) venue shall lie in the district court for the District of Columbia or in any other district in which the defendant or the property that may be the basis for satisfaction of a judgment under this section may be found; and

(C) the district court shall have personal jurisdiction over a defendant residing outside of the United States if the defendant is served with process in accordance with rule 4 of the Federal Rules of Civil Procedure.

(d) Entry and enforcement of judgment.—

(1) In general.—The district court shall enter such orders as may be necessary to enforce the judgment on behalf of the foreign nation unless the court finds that—

(A) the judgment was rendered under a system that provides tribunals or procedures incompatible with the requirements of due process of law;

(B) the foreign court lacked personal jurisdiction over the defendant;

(C) the foreign court lacked jurisdiction over the subject matter;

(D) the foreign nation did not take steps, in accordance with the principles of due process, to give notice of the proceedings to a person with an interest in the property of the proceedings [2] in sufficient time to enable him or her to defend; or

(E) the judgment was obtained by fraud.

(2) Process.—Process to enforce a judgment under this section shall be in accordance with rule 69(a) of the Federal Rules of Civil Procedure.

(3) Preservation of property.—

(A) In general.—To preserve the availability of property subject to a foreign forfeiture or confiscation judgment, the Government may apply for, and the court may issue, a restraining order pursuant to section 983(j) of title 18, at any time before or after an application is filed pursuant to subsection (c)(1) of this section.

(B) Evidence.—The court, in issuing a restraining order under subparagraph (A)—

(i) may rely on information set forth in an affidavit describing the nature of the proceeding or investigation underway in the foreign country, and setting forth a reasonable basis to believe that the property to be restrained will be named in a judgment of forfeiture at the conclusion of such proceeding; or

(ii) may register and enforce a restraining order that has been issued by a court of competent jurisdiction in the foreign country and certified by the Attorney General pursuant to subsection (b)(2).

(C) Limit on grounds for objection.—No person may object to a restraining order under subparagraph (A) on any ground that is the subject of parallel litigation involving the same property that is pending in a foreign court.

(e) Finality of foreign findings.—In entering orders to enforce the judgment, the court shall be bound by the findings of fact to the extent that they are stated in the foreign forfeiture or confiscation judgment.

(f) Currency conversion.—The rate of exchange in effect at the time the suit to enforce is filed by the foreign nation shall be used in calculating the amount stated in any forfeiture or confiscation judgment requiring the payment of a sum of money submitted for registration.

(Added Pub.L. 106–185, § 15(a), Apr. 25, 2000, 114 Stat. 219, and amended Pub.L. 107–56, Title III, § 323, Oct. 26, 2001, 115 Stat. 315.)

[1] So in original. Probably should be preceded by "a".

[2] So in original. The phrase "of the proceedings" probably should not appear.

HISTORICAL AND STATUTORY NOTES

References in Text

Rule 4 of the Federal Rules of Civil Procedure, referred to in subsec. (c)(2)(C), is set out in this title.

Effective and Applicability Provisions

2000 Acts. Enactment by Pub.L. 106–185, applicable to any forfeiture proceeding commenced on or after the date that is 120 days after April 25, 2000, see section 21 of Pub.L. 106–185, set out as a note under section 1324 of Title 8.

4–Year Congressional Review; Expedited Consideration

Effective on and after the first day of fiscal year 2005, amendments by Title III (§§ 301 to 377) of Pub.L. 107–56 shall terminate if Congress enacts a joint resolution to that effect; such resolution shall be given expedited consideration, see Pub.L. 107–56, Title III, § 303, Oct. 26, 2001, 115 Stat. 298, set out as a note under 31 U.S.C.A. § 5311.

CHAPTER 165—UNITED STATES COURT OF FEDERAL CLAIMS PROCEDURE

Sec.
2501. Time for filing suit.
2502. Aliens' privilege to sue.
2503. Proceedings generally.
2504. Plaintiff's testimony.
2505. Trial before judges.
2506. Interest of witness.
2507. Calls and discovery.
2508. Counterclaim or set-off.[1]
2509. Congressional reference cases.
2510. Referral of cases by Comptroller General.
2511. Accounts of officers, agents or contractors.
2512. Disbursing officers; relief.
2513. Unjust conviction and imprisonment.
2514. Forfeiture of fraudulent claims.
2515. New trial, stay of judgment.[1]
2516. Interest on claims and judgments.
2517. Payment of judgments.
[2518. Repealed.]
2519. Conclusiveness of judgment.
[2520. Repealed.]
2521. Subpoenas and incidental powers.
2522. Notice of appeal.

[1] So in original. Does not conform to section catchline.

§ 2501. Time for filing suit

Every claim of which the United States Court of Federal Claims has jurisdiction shall be barred unless the petition thereon is filed within six years after such claim first accrues.

Every claim under section 1497 of this title shall be barred unless the petition thereon is filed within two years after the termination of the river and harbor improvements operations on which the claim is based.

A petition on the claim of a person under legal disability or beyond the seas at the time the claim accrues may be filed within three years after the disability ceases.

A suit for the fees of an officer of the United States shall not be filed until his account for such fees has been finally acted upon, unless the Government Accountability Office fails to act within six months after receiving the account.

(June 25, 1948, c. 646, 62 Stat. 976; Sept. 3, 1954, c. 1263, § 52, 68 Stat. 1246; Apr. 2, 1982, Pub.L. 97–164, Title I, § 139(a), 96 Stat. 42; Oct. 29, 1992, Pub.L. 102–572, Title IX, § 902(a)(1), 106 Stat. 4516; July 7, 2004, Pub.L. 108–271, § 8(b), 118 Stat. 814.)

HISTORICAL AND STATUTORY NOTES

Effective and Applicability Provisions

1992 Acts. Amendment by Title IX of Pub.L. 102–572 effective Oct. 29, 1992, see section 911 of Pub.L. 102–572, set out as a note under section 171 of Title 28, Judiciary and Judicial Procedure.

1982 Acts. Amendment by Pub.L. 97–164 effective Oct. 1, 1982, see section 402 of Pub.L. 97–164, set out as a note under section 171 of this title.

§ 2502. Aliens' privilege to sue

(a) Citizens or subjects of any foreign government which accords to citizens of the United States the right to prosecute claims against their government in its courts may sue the United States in the United States Court of Federal Claims if the subject matter of the suit is otherwise within such court's jurisdiction.

(b) See section 7422(f) of the Internal Revenue Code of 1986 for exception with respect to suits involving internal revenue taxes.

(June 25, 1948, c. 646, 62 Stat. 976; Nov. 2, 1966, Pub.L. 89–713, § 3(b), 80 Stat. 1108; Apr. 2, 1982, Pub.L. 97–164, Title I, § 139(a), 96 Stat. 42; Oct. 22, 1986, Pub.L. 99–514, § 2, 100 Stat. 2095; Oct. 29, 1992, Pub.L. 102–572, Title IX, § 902(a)(1), 106 Stat. 4516.)

HISTORICAL AND STATUTORY NOTES

References in Text

Section 7422(f) of the Internal Revenue Code of 1986, referred to in subsec. (b), is classified to section 7422(f) of Title 26, Internal Revenue Code.

Effective and Applicability Provisions

1992 Acts. Amendment by Title IX of Pub.L. 102–572 effective Oct. 29, 1992, see section 911 of Pub.L. 102–572, set out as a note under section 171 of Title 28, Judiciary and Judicial Procedure.

1982 Acts. Amendment by Pub.L. 97–164 effective Oct. 1, 1982, see section 402 of Pub.L. 97–164, set out as a note under section 171 of this title.

1966 Acts. Amendment by Pub.L. 89–713, which added subsec. (b) to this section, applicable to suits brought against officers, employees, or personal representatives instituted 90 days or more after Nov. 2, 1966, see section 3(d) of Pub.L. 89–713, set out as a note under section 7422 of Title 26, Internal Revenue Code.

§ 2503. Proceedings generally

(a) Parties to any suit in the United States Court of Federal Claims may appear before a judge of that court in person or by attorney, produce evidence, and examine witnesses.

(b) The proceedings of the Court of Federal Claims shall be in accordance with such rules of practice and procedure (other than the rules of evidence) as the Court of Federal Claims may prescribe and in accordance with the Federal Rules of Evidence.

(c) The judges of the Court of Federal Claims shall fix times for trials, administer oaths or affirmations, examine witnesses, receive evidence, and enter dispositive judgments. Hearings shall, if convenient, be held in the counties where the witnesses reside.

(d) For the purpose of construing sections 1821, 1915, 1920, and 1927 of this title, the United States Court of Federal Claims shall be deemed to be a court of the United States.

(June 25, 1948, c. 646, 62 Stat. 976; Sept. 3, 1954, c. 1263, § 53, 68 Stat. 1246; Apr. 2, 1982, Pub.L. 97–164, Title I, § 139(b) (1), 96 Stat. 42; Oct. 29, 1992, Pub.L. 102–572, Title IX, §§ 902(a), 909, 106 Stat. 4516, 4519.)

HISTORICAL AND STATUTORY NOTES

References in Text

The Federal Rules of Evidence, referred to in subsec. (b), are set out in this title.

Effective and Applicability Provisions

1992 Acts. Amendment by Title IX of Pub.L. 102–572 effective Oct. 29, 1992, see section 911 of Pub.L. 102–572, set out as a note under section 171 of Title 28, Judiciary and Judicial Procedure.

1982 Acts. Amendment by Pub.L. 97–164 effective Oct. 1, 1982, see section 402 of Pub.L. 97–164, set out as a note under section 171 of this title.

§ 2504. Plaintiff's testimony

The United States Court of Federal Claims may, at the instance of the Attorney General, order any plaintiff to appear, upon reasonable notice, before any judge of the court and be examined on oath as to all matters pertaining to his claim. Such examination shall be reduced to writing by the judge, and shall be returned to and filed in the court, and may, at the discretion of the attorneys for the United States, be read and used as evidence on the trial. If any plaintiff, after such order is made and due and reasonable notice thereof is given to him, fails to appear, or refuses to testify or answer fully as to all material matters within his knowledge, the court may order that the case shall not be tried until he fully complies with such order.

(June 25, 1948, c. 646, 62 Stat. 976; Apr. 2, 1982, Pub.L. 97–164, Title I, § 139(c), 96 Stat. 42; Oct. 29, 1992, Pub.L. 102–572, Title IX, § 902(a)(1), 106 Stat. 4516.)

HISTORICAL AND STATUTORY NOTES

Effective and Applicability Provisions

1992 Acts. Amendment by Title IX of Pub.L. 102–572 effective Oct. 29, 1992, see section 911 of Pub.L. 102–572, set out as a note under section 171 of Title 28, Judiciary and Judicial Procedure.

1982 Acts. Amendment by Pub.L. 97–164 effective Oct. 1, 1982, see section 402 of Pub.L. 97–164, set out as a note under section 171 of this title.

§ 2505. Trial before judges

Any judge of the United States Court of Federal Claims may sit at any place within the United States to take evidence and enter judgment.

(June 25, 1948, c. 646, 62 Stat. 976; Sept. 3, 1954, c. 1263, § 54(a), (b), 68 Stat. 1246; Apr. 2, 1982, Pub.L. 97–164, Title I, § 139(d), 96 Stat. 42; Oct. 29, 1992, Pub.L. 102–572, Title IX, § 902(a)(1), 106 Stat. 4516.)

HISTORICAL AND STATUTORY NOTES

Effective and Applicability Provisions

1992 Acts. Amendment by Title IX of Pub.L. 102–572 effective Oct. 29, 1992, see section 911 of Pub.L. 102–572, set out as a note under section 171 of Title 28, Judiciary and Judicial Procedure.

1982 Acts. Amendment by Pub.L. 97–164 effective Oct. 1, 1982, see section 402 of Pub.L. 97–164, set out as a note under section 171 of this title.

§ 2506. Interest of witness

A witness in a suit in the United States Court of Federal Claims shall not be exempt or disqualified because he is a party to or interested in such suit.

(June 25, 1948, c. 646, 62 Stat. 977; Apr. 2, 1982, Pub.L. 97–164, Title I, § 139(e), 96 Stat. 42; Oct. 29, 1992, Pub.L. 102–572, Title IX, § 902(a)(1), 106 Stat. 4516.)

HISTORICAL AND STATUTORY NOTES

Effective and Applicability Provisions

1992 Acts. Amendment by Title IX of Pub.L. 102–572 effective Oct. 29, 1992, see section 911 of Pub.L. 102–572, set out as a note under section 171 of Title 28, Judiciary and Judicial Procedure.

1982 Acts. Amendment by Pub.L. 97–164 effective Oct. 1, 1982, see section 402 of Pub.L. 97–164, set out as a note under section 171 of this title.

§ 2507. Calls and discovery

(a) The United States Court of Federal Claims may call upon any department or agency of the United States or upon any party for any information or papers, not privileged, for purposes of discovery or for use as evidence. The head of any department or agency may refuse to comply with a call issued pursuant to this subsection when, in his opinion, compliance will be injurious to the public interest.

(b) Without limitation on account of anything contained in subsection (a) of this section, the court may, in accordance with its rules, provide additional means for the discovery of any relevant facts, books, papers, documents or tangible things, not privileged.

(c) The Court of Federal Claims may use all recorded and printed reports made by the committees of the Senate or House of Representatives.

(June 25, 1948, c. 646, 62 Stat. 977; Sept. 3, 1954, c. 1263, § 55(a)–(c), 68 Stat. 1247; Apr. 2, 1982, Pub.L. 97–164, Title I, § 139(f), 96 Stat. 42; Oct. 29, 1992, Pub.L. 102–572, Title IX, § 902(a), 106 Stat. 4516.)

HISTORICAL AND STATUTORY NOTES

Effective and Applicability Provisions

1992 Acts. Amendment by Title IX of Pub.L. 102–572 effective Oct. 29, 1992, see section 911 of Pub.L. 102–572, set out as a note under section 171 of Title 28, Judiciary and Judicial Procedure.

1982 Acts. Amendment by Pub.L. 97–164 effective Oct. 1, 1982, see section 402 of Pub.L. 97–164, set out as a note under section 171 of this title.

§ 2508. Counterclaim or set-off; registration of judgment

Upon the trial of any suit in the United States Court of Federal Claims in which any setoff, counterclaim, claim for damages, or other demand is set up on the part of the United States against any plaintiff making claim against the United States in said court, the court shall hear and determine such claim or demand both for and against the United States and plaintiff.

If upon the whole case it finds that the plaintiff is indebted to the United States it shall render judgment to that effect, and such judgment shall be final and reviewable.

The transcript of such judgment, filed in the clerk's office of any district court, shall be entered upon the records and shall be enforceable as other judgments. (June 25, 1948, c. 646, 62 Stat. 977; July 28, 1953, c. 253, § 10, 67 Stat. 227; Sept. 3, 1954, c. 1263, § 47(a), 68 Stat. 1243; Apr. 2, 1982, Pub.L. 97–164, Title I, § 139(g), 96 Stat. 42; Oct. 29, 1992, Pub.L. 102–572, Title IX, § 902(a)(1), 106 Stat. 4516.)

HISTORICAL AND STATUTORY NOTES

Effective and Applicability Provisions

1992 Acts. Amendment by Title IX of Pub.L. 102–572 effective Oct. 29, 1992, see section 911 of Pub.L. 102–572, set out as a note under section 171 of Title 28, Judiciary and Judicial Procedure.

1982 Acts. Amendment by Pub.L. 97–164 effective Oct. 1, 1982, see section 402 of Pub.L. 97–164, set out as a note under section 171 of this title.

§ 2509. Congressional reference cases

(a) Whenever a bill, except a bill for a pension, is referred by either House of Congress to the chief judge of the United States Court of Federal Claims pursuant to section 1492 of this title, the chief judge shall designate a judge as hearing officer for the case and a panel of three judges of the court to serve as a reviewing body. One member of the review panel shall be designated as presiding officer of the panel.

(b) Proceedings in a congressional reference case shall be under rules and regulations prescribed for the purpose by the chief judge who is hereby authorized and directed to require the application of the pertinent rules of practice of the Court of Federal Claims insofar as feasible. Each hearing officer and each review panel shall have authority to do and perform any acts which may be necessary or proper for the efficient performance of their duties, including the power of subpena and the power to administer oaths and affirmations. None of the rules, rulings, findings, or conclusions authorized by this section shall be subject to judicial review.

(c) The hearing officer to whom a congressional reference case is assigned by the chief judge shall proceed in accordance with the applicable rules to determine the facts, including facts relating to delay or laches, facts bearing upon the question whether the bar of any statute of limitation should be removed, or facts claimed to excuse the claimant for not having resorted to any established legal remedy. He shall append to his findings of fact conclusions sufficient to inform Congress whether the demand is a legal or equitable claim or a gratuity, and the amount, if any, legally or equitably due from the United States to the claimant.

(d) The findings and conclusions of the hearing officer shall be submitted by him, together with the record in the case, to the review panel for review by it pursuant to such rules as may be provided for the purpose, which shall include provision for submitting the report of the hearing officer to the parties for consideration, exception, and argument before the panel. The panel, by majority vote, shall adopt or modify the findings or the conclusions of the hearing officer.

(e) The panel shall submit its report to the chief judge for transmission to the appropriate House of Congress.

(f) Any act or failure to act or other conduct by a party, a witness, or an attorney which would call for the imposition of sanctions under the rules of practice of the Court of Federal Claims shall be noted by the panel or the hearing officer at the time of occurrence thereof and upon failure of the delinquent or offending party, witness, or attorney to make prompt compliance with the order of the panel or the hearing officer a full statement of the circumstances shall be incorporated in the report of the panel.

(g) The Court of Federal Claims is hereby authorized and directed, under such regulations as it may prescribe, to provide the facilities and services of the office of the clerk of the court for the filing, processing, hearing, and dispatch of congressional reference cases and to include within its annual appropriations the costs thereof and other costs of administration, including (but without limitation to the items herein listed) the salaries and traveling expenses of the judges serving as hearing officers and panel members, mailing and service of process, necessary physical facilities, equipment, and supplies, and personnel (including secretaries and law clerks).

(June 25, 1948, c. 646, 62 Stat. 977; Oct. 15, 1966, Pub.L. 89–681, § 2, 80 Stat. 958; Apr. 2, 1982, Pub.L. 97–164, Title I, § 139(h), 96 Stat. 42; Oct. 29, 1992, Pub.L. 102–572, Title IX, § 902(a), 106 Stat. 4516.)

HISTORICAL AND STATUTORY NOTES

Effective and Applicability Provisions

1992 Acts. Amendment by Title IX of Pub.L. 102–572 effective Oct. 29, 1992, see section 911 of Pub.L. 102–572, set out as a note under section 171 of Title 28, Judiciary and Judicial Procedure.

1982 Acts. Amendment by Pub.L. 97–164 effective Oct. 1, 1982, see section 402 of Pub.L. 97–164, set out as a note under section 171 of this title.

Termination of Reporting Requirements

For termination of reporting provisions of this section, effective May 15, 2000, see Pub.L. 104–66, § 3003, as amended, set out as a note under 31 U.S.C.A. § 1113, and page 13 of House Document No. 103–7.

§ 2510. Referral of cases by Comptroller General

(a) The Comptroller General may transmit to the United States Court of Federal Claims for trial and adjudication any claim or matter of which the Court of Federal Claims might take jurisdiction on the voluntary action of the claimant, together with all vouchers, papers, documents, and proofs pertaining thereto.

(b) The Court of Federal Claims shall proceed with the claims or matters so referred as in other cases pending in such Court and shall render judgment thereon.

(June 25, 1948, c. 646, 62 Stat. 977; July 28, 1953, c. 253, § 11, 67 Stat. 227; Sept. 3, 1954, c. 1263, § 47(b), 68 Stat. 1243; Nov. 1, 1978, Pub.L. 95–563, § 14(h)(1), (2)(A), 92 Stat. 2390; Apr. 2, 1982, Pub.L. 97–164, Title I, § 139(i)(1), 96 Stat. 43; Oct. 29, 1992, Pub.L. 102–572, Title IX, § 902(a), 106 Stat. 4516.)

HISTORICAL AND STATUTORY NOTES

Effective and Applicability Provisions

1992 Acts. Amendment by Title IX of Pub.L. 102–572 effective Oct. 29, 1992, see section 911 of Pub.L. 102–572, set out as a note under section 171 of Title 28, Judiciary and Judicial Procedure.

1982 Acts. Amendment by Pub.L. 97–164 effective Oct. 1, 1982, see section 402 of Pub.L. 97–164, set out as a note under section 171 of this title.

1978 Acts. Amendment by Pub.L. 95–563 effective with respect to contracts entered into 120 days after Nov. 1, 1978, and, at the election of the contractor, with respect to any claim pending at such time before the contracting officer or initiated thereafter, see section 16 of Pub.L. 95–563, set out as a note under section 601 of Title 41, Public Contracts.

§ 2511. Accounts of officers, agents or contractors

Notice of suit under section 1494 of this title shall be given to the Attorney General, to the Comptroller General, and to the head of the department requested to settle the account in question.

The judgment of the United States Court of Federal Claims in such suit shall be conclusive upon the parties, and payment of the amount found due shall discharge the obligation.

The transcript of such judgment, filed in the clerk's office of any district court, shall be entered upon the records, and shall be enforceable as other judgments.

(June 25, 1948, c. 646, 62 Stat. 977; July 28, 1953, c. 253, § 12, 67 Stat. 227; Apr. 2, 1982, Pub.L. 97–164, Title I, § 139(j), 96 Stat. 43; Oct. 29, 1992, Pub.L. 102–572, Title IX, § 902(a)(1), 106 Stat. 4516.)

HISTORICAL AND STATUTORY NOTES

Effective and Applicability Provisions

1992 Acts. Amendment by Title IX of Pub. L. 102–572 effective Oct. 29, 1992, see section 911 of Pub.L. 102–572, set out as a note under section 171 of Title 28, Judiciary and Judicial Procedure.

1982 Acts. Amendment by Pub.L. 97–164 effective Oct. 1, 1982, see section 402 of Pub.L. 97–164, set out as a note under section 171 of this title.

Termination of Reporting Requirements

For termination of reporting provisions of subsec. (i) of this section, effective May 15, 2000, see Pub.L. 104–66, § 3003, as amended, set out as a note under 31 U.S.C.A. § 1113, and the 1st provision on page 14 of House Document No. 103–7.

§ 2512. Disbursing officers; relief

Whenever the United States Court of Federal Claims finds that any loss by a disbursing officer of the United States was without his fault or negligence, it shall render a judgment setting forth the amount thereof, and the Government Accountability Office shall allow the officer such amount as a credit in the settlement of his accounts.

(June 25, 1948, c. 646, 62 Stat. 978; Apr. 2, 1982, Pub.L. 97–164, Title I, § 139(j)(2), 96 Stat. 43; Oct. 29, 1992, Pub.L. 102–572, Title IX, § 902(a)(1), 106 Stat. 4516; Pub.L. 108–271, § 8(b), July 7, 2004, 118 Stat. 814.)

HISTORICAL AND STATUTORY NOTES

Effective and Applicability Provisions

1992 Acts. Amendment by Title IX of Pub.L. 102–572 effective Oct. 29, 1992, see section 911 of Pub.L. 102–572, set out as a note under section 171 of Title 28, Judiciary and Judicial Procedure.

1982 Acts. Amendment by Pub.L. 97–164 effective Oct. 1, 1982, see section 402 of Pub.L. 97–164, set out as a note under section 171 of this title.

§ 2513. Unjust conviction and imprisonment

(a) Any person suing under section 1495 of this title must allege and prove that:

(1) His conviction has been reversed or set aside on the ground that he is not guilty of the offense of which he was convicted, or on new trial or rehearing he was found not guilty of such offense, as appears from the record or certificate of the court setting aside or reversing such conviction, or that he has been pardoned upon the stated ground of innocence and unjust conviction and

(2) He did not commit any of the acts charged or his acts, deeds, or omissions in connection with such charge constituted no offense against the United States, or any State, Territory or the District of Columbia, and he did not by misconduct or neglect cause or bring about his own prosecution.

(b) Proof of the requisite facts shall be by a certificate of the court or pardon wherein such facts are alleged to appear, and other evidence thereof shall not be received.

(c) No pardon or certified copy of a pardon shall be considered by the United States Court of Federal Claims unless it contains recitals that the pardon was granted after applicant had exhausted all recourse to the courts and that the time for any court to exercise its jurisdiction had expired.

(d) The Court may permit the plaintiff to prosecute such action in forma pauperis.

(e) The amount of damages awarded shall not exceed $100,000 for each 12–month period of incarceration for any plaintiff who was unjustly sentenced to death and $50,000 for each 12–month period of incarceration for any other plaintiff.

(June 25, 1948, c. 646, 62 Stat. 978; Sept. 3, 1954, c. 1263, § 56, 68 Stat. 1247; Apr. 2, 1982, Pub.L. 97–164, Title I, § 139(j)(2), 96 Stat. 43; Oct. 29, 1992, Pub.L. 102–572, Title IX, § 902(a)(1), 106 Stat. 4516; Oct. 30, 2004, Pub.L. 108–405, Title IV, § 431, 118 Stat. 2293.)

HISTORICAL AND STATUTORY NOTES

Effective and Applicability Provisions

1992 Acts. Amendment by Title IX of Pub.L. 102–572 effective Oct. 29, 1992, see section 911 of Pub.L. 102–572, set out as a note under section 171 of Title 28, Judiciary and Judicial Procedure.

1982 Acts. Amendment by Pub.L. 97–164 effective Oct. 1, 1982, see section 402 of Pub.L. 97–164, set out as a note under section 171 of this title.

§ 2514. Forfeiture of fraudulent claims

A claim against the United States shall be forfeited to the United States by any person who corruptly practices or attempts to practice any fraud against the United States in the proof, statement, establishment, or allowance thereof.

In such cases the United States Court of Federal Claims shall specifically find such fraud or attempt and render judgment of forfeiture.

(June 25, 1948, c. 646, 62 Stat. 978; Apr. 2, 1982, Pub.L. 97–164, Title I, § 139(j)(2), 96 Stat. 43; Oct. 29, 1992, Pub.L. 102–572, Title IX, § 902(a)(1), 106 Stat. 4516.)

HISTORICAL AND STATUTORY NOTES

Effective and Applicability Provisions

1992 Acts. Amendment by Title IX of Pub.L. 102–572 effective Oct. 29, 1992, see section 911 of Pub.L. 102–572, set out as a note under section 171 of Title 28, Judiciary and Judicial Procedure.

1982 Acts. Amendment by Pub.L. 97–164 effective Oct. 1, 1982, see section 402 of Pub.L. 97–164, set out as a note under section 171 of this title.

§ 2515. New trial; stay of judgment

(a) The United States Court of Federal Claims may grant a plaintiff a new trial on any ground established by rules of common law or equity applicable as between private parties.

(b) Such court, at any time while any suit is pending before it, or after proceedings for review have been instituted, or within two years after the final disposition of the suit, may grant the United States a new trial and stay the payment of any judgment upon satisfactory evidence, cumulative or otherwise, that any fraud, wrong, or injustice has been done the United States.

(June 25, 1948, c. 646, 62 Stat. 978; Apr. 2, 1982, Pub.L. 97–164, Title I, § 139(j)(2), 96 Stat. 43; Oct. 29, 1992, Pub.L. 102–572, Title IX, § 902(a)(1), 106 Stat. 4516.)

HISTORICAL AND STATUTORY NOTES

Effective and Applicability Provisions

1992 Acts. Amendment by Title IX of Pub.L. 102–572 effective Oct. 29, 1992, see section 911 of Pub.L. 102–572, set out as a note under section 171 of Title 28, Judiciary and Judicial Procedure.

1982 Acts. Amendment by Pub.L. 97–164 effective Oct. 1, 1982, see section 402 of Pub.L. 97–164, set out as a note under section 171 of this title.

§ 2516. Interest on claims and judgments

(a) Interest on a claim against the United States shall be allowed in a judgment of the United States Court of Federal Claims only under a contract or Act of Congress expressly providing for payment thereof.

(b) Interest on a judgment against the United States affirmed by the Supreme Court after review on petition of the United States is paid at a rate equal to the weekly average 1–year constant maturity Treasury yield, as published by the Board of Governors of the Federal Reserve System, for the calendar week preceding the date of the judgment.

(June 25, 1948, c. 646, 62 Stat. 978; Sept. 3, 1954, c. 1263, § 57, 68 Stat. 1248; Apr. 2, 1982, Pub.L. 97–164, Title I, § 139(j)(2), Title III, § 302(d), 96 Stat. 43, 56; Sept. 13, 1982, Pub.L. 97–258, § 2(g)(5), (m)(3), 96 Stat. 1061, 1062; Oct. 29, 1992, Pub.L. 102–572, Title IX, § 902(a)(1), 106 Stat. 4516; Dec. 21, 2000, Pub.L. 106–554, § 1(a)(7) [Title III, § 307(d)(2)], 114 Stat. 2763, 2763A–636.)

HISTORICAL AND STATUTORY NOTES

Effective and Applicability Provisions

1992 Acts. Amendment by Title IX of Pub.L. 102–572 effective Oct. 29, 1992, see section 911 of Pub.L. 102–572, set out as a note under section 171 of Title 28, Judiciary and Judicial Procedure.

1982 Acts. Section 2(g)(5) of Pub.L. 97–258 provided in part that the amendment made to subsec. (b) would become effective on Oct. 1, 1982.

Amendment by Pub.L. 97–164 effective Oct. 1, 1982, see section 402 of Pub.L. 97–164, set out as a note under section 171 of this title.

Repeals

Section 302(d) of Pub.L. 97–164, set out in the credit of this section, was repealed by Pub.L. 97–258, § 2(m)(3), Sept. 13, 1982, 96 Stat. 1062, effective Oct. 1, 1982.

§ 2517. Payment of judgments

(a) Except as provided by the Contract Disputes Act of 1978, every final judgment rendered by the United States Court of Federal Claims against the United States shall be paid out of any general appropriation therefor, on presentation to the Secretary of the Treasury of a certification of the judgment by the clerk and chief judge of the court.

(b) Payment of any such judgment and of interest thereon shall be a full discharge to the United States of all claims and demands arising out of the matters involved in the case or controversy, unless the judgment is designated a partial judgment, in which event only the matters described therein shall be discharged.

(June 25, 1948, c. 646, 62 Stat. 979; Nov. 1, 1978, Pub.L. 95–563, § 14(e), (f), 92 Stat. 2390; Apr. 2, 1982, Pub.L. 97–164, Title I, § 139(k), 96 Stat. 43; Oct. 29, 1992, Pub.L. 102–572, Title IX, § 902(a)(1), 106 Stat. 4516; Oct. 19, 1996, Pub.L. 104–316, Title II, § 202(*l*), 110 Stat. 3843.)

HISTORICAL AND STATUTORY NOTES

References in Text

The Contract Disputes Act of 1978, referred to in subsec. (a), is Pub.L. 95–563, Nov. 1, 1978, 92 Stat. 2383, as amended, which is classified principally to chapter 9 (section 601 et seq.) of Title 41, Public Contracts. For complete classification of this Act to the Code, see Short Title note set out under section 601 of Title 41 and Tables.

Effective and Applicability Provisions

1992 Acts. Amendment by Title IX of Pub.L. 102–572 effective Oct. 29, 1992, see section 911 of Pub.L. 102–572, set out as a note under section 171 of Title 28, Judiciary and Judicial Procedure.

1982 Acts. Amendment by Pub.L. 97–164 effective Oct. 1, 1982, see section 402 of Pub.L. 97–164, set out as a note under section 171 of this title.

1978 Acts. Amendment by Pub.L. 95–563 effective with respect to contracts entered into 120 days after Nov. 1, 1978, and, at the election of the contractor, with respect to any claim pending at such time before the contracting officer or initiated thereafter, see section 16 of Pub.L. 95–563, set out as a note under section 601 of Title 41, Public Contracts.

Transfer of Functions

Effective June 30, 1996, the functions of the Comptroller General under this section to be transferred to the Director of the Office of Management and Budget, contingent upon the additional transfer to the Office of Management and Budget of such personnel, budget authority, records, and property of the General Accounting Office relating to such functions as the Comptroller General and the Director jointly determine to be necessary, see section 211 of Pub.L. 104–53, set out as a note under section 501 of Title 31, Money and Finance.

[§ 2518. Repealed. Pub.L. 97–164, Title I, § 139(*l*), Apr. 2, 1982, 96 Stat. 43]

HISTORICAL AND STATUTORY NOTES

Section, Act June 25, 1948, c. 646, 62 Stat. 979, directed the Secretary of the Treasury to certify to Congress for appropriation only such judgments of the Court of Claims as were not to be reviewed or were entered upon the mandate of the Supreme Court.

Effective Date of Repeal

Repeal effective Oct. 1, 1982, see section 402 of Pub.L. 97–164, set out as an Effective Date of 1982 Amendment note under section 171 of this title.

§ 2519. Conclusiveness of judgment

A final judgment of the United States Court of Federal Claims against any plaintiff shall forever bar any further claim, suit, or demand against the United States arising out of the matters involved in the case or controversy.

(June 25, 1948, c. 646, 62 Stat. 979; Apr. 2, 1982, Pub.L. 97–164, Title I, § 139(m), 96 Stat. 43; Oct. 29, 1992, Pub.L. 102–572, Title IX, § 902(a)(1), 106 Stat. 4516.)

HISTORICAL AND STATUTORY NOTES

Effective and Applicability Provisions

1992 Acts. Amendment by Title IX of Pub.L. 102–572 effective Oct. 29, 1992, see section 911 of Pub.L. 102–572, set out as a note under section 171 of Title 28, Judiciary and Judicial Procedure.

1982 Acts. Amendment by Pub.L. 97–164 effective Oct. 1, 1982, see section 402 of Pub.L. 97–164, set out as a note under section 171 of this title.

[§ 2520. Repealed. Pub.L. 106–518, Title II, § 207, Nov. 13, 2000, 114 Stat. 2414]

HISTORICAL AND STATUTORY NOTES

Section, Act June 25, 1948, c. 646, 62 Stat. 979; Sept. 3, 1954, c. 1263, § 58, 68 Stat. 1248; July 18, 1966, Pub.L. 89–507, § 2, 80 Stat. 308; Apr. 2, 1982, Pub.L. 97–164, Title I, § 139(n) (1)–(3), 96 Stat. 43, 44; Nov. 19, 1988, Pub.L. 100–702, Title X, § 1012(a)(1), 102 Stat. 4668; Oct. 29, 1992, Pub.L. 102–572, Title IX, § 902(a)(1), 106 Stat. 4516 related to fees for the filing of any petition.

Effective and Applicability Provisions

1988 Acts. Section 1012(a)(2) of Title X of Pub.L. 100–702 provided that: "The amendment made by this subsection [amending this section] shall take effect 30 days after the date of enactment of this title [Nov. 19, 1988]."

§ 2521. Subpoenas and incidental powers

(a) Subpoenas requiring the attendance of parties or witnesses and subpoenas requiring the production of books, papers, documents or tangible things by any party or witness having custody or control thereof, may be issued for purposes of discovery or for use of the things produced as evidence in accordance with the rules and orders of the court. Such subpoenas shall be issued and served and compliance therewith shall be compelled as provided in the rules and orders of the court.

(b) The United States Court of Federal Claims shall have power to punish by fine or imprisonment, at its discretion, such contempt of its authority as—

(1) misbehavior of any person in its presence or so near thereto as to obstruct the administration of justice;

(2) misbehavior of any of its officers in their official transactions; or

(3) disobedience or resistance to its lawful writ, process, order, rule, decree, or command.

(c) The United States Court of Federal Claims shall have such assistance in the carrying out of its lawful writ, process, order, rule, decree, or command as is available to a court of the United States. The United States marshal for any district in which the Court of Federal Claims is sitting shall, when requested by the chief judge of the Court of Federal Claims, attend any session of the Court of Federal Claims in such district.

(Added Sept. 3, 1954, c. 1263, § 59(a), 68 Stat. 1248, and amended Oct. 29, 1992, Pub.L. 102–572, Title IX, § 910(a), 106 Stat. 4519.)

HISTORICAL AND STATUTORY NOTES

Effective and Applicability Provisions

1992 Acts. Amendment by Title IX of Pub.L. 102–572 effective Oct. 29, 1992, see section 911 of Pub.L. 102–572, set out as a note under section 171 of Title 28, Judiciary and Judicial Procedure.

§ 2522. Notice of appeal

Review of a decision of the United States Court of Federal Claims shall be obtained by filing a notice of appeal with the clerk of the Court of Federal Claims within the time and in the manner prescribed for appeals to United States courts of appeals from the United States district courts.

(Added Pub.L. 97–164, Title I, § 139(q)(1), Apr. 2, 1982, 96 Stat. 44, and amended Pub.L. 102–572, Title IX, § 902(a), Oct. 29, 1992, 106 Stat. 4516.)

HISTORICAL AND STATUTORY NOTES

Effective and Applicability Provisions

1992 Acts. Amendment by Title IX of Pub.L. 102–572 effective Oct. 29, 1992, see section 911 of Pub.L. 102–572, set out as a note under section 171 of Title 28, Judiciary and Judicial Procedure.

1982 Acts. Section effective Oct. 1, 1982, see section 402 of Pub.L. 97–164, set out as a note under section 171 of this title.

[CHAPTER 167—REPEALED]

[§§ 2601 to 2604. Repealed. Pub.L. 97–164, Title I, § 140, Apr. 2, 1982, 96 Stat. 44]

HISTORICAL AND STATUTORY NOTES

Section 2601, Acts June 25, 1948, c. 646, 62 Stat. 979; June 2, 1970, Pub.L. 91–271, Title I, § 103, 84 Stat. 275; Oct. 10, 1980, Pub.L. 96–417, Title IV, § 403(a)–(d), Title V, § 501(27), (28), 94 Stat. 1740–1742, provided for appeals to the Court of Customs and Patent Appeals from final judgments or orders of the Court of International Trade and for the procedures to be followed in such appeals. See section 1295(a)(5) of this title.

Section 2602, Acts June 25, 1948, c. 646, 62 Stat. 980; Oct. 14, 1966, Pub.L. 89–651, § 8(c)(3), 80 Stat. 902; June 2, 1970, Pub.L. 91–271, Title I, § 104, 84 Stat. 276; Oct. 10, 1980, Pub.L. 96–417, Title IV, § 403(e)(1), 94 Stat. 1741, provided for the precedence of enumerated civil cases in the Court of Customs and Patent Appeals. See note set out under former section 1296 of this title.

Section 2603, added Pub.L. 96–417, Title IV, § 404(a), Oct. 10, 1980, 94 Stat. 1741, provided that, except as provided in section 2639 or 2641(b) of this title or in the rules prescribed by the court, the Federal Rules of Evidence would apply in the Court of Customs and Patent Appeals in any appeal from the Court of International Trade.

Section 2604, added Pub.L. 96–417, Title IV, § 405(a), Oct. 10, 1980, 94 Stat. 1741, authorized the chief judge of the Court of Customs and Patent Appeals to summon annually the judges of the court to a judicial conference for the purpose of considering the business of the court and improvements in the administration of justice of the court.

Effective Date of Repeal

Repeal effective Oct. 1, 1982, see section 402 of Pub.L. 97–164, set out as a note under section 171 of this title.

CHAPTER 169—COURT OF INTERNATIONAL TRADE PROCEDURE

Sec.
2631. Persons entitled to commence a civil action.
2632. Commencement of a civil action.
2633. Procedure and fees.
2634. Notice.
2635. Filing of official documents.
2636. Time for commencement of action.
2637. Exhaustion of administrative remedies.
2638. New grounds in support of a civil action.
2639. Burden of proof; evidence of value.
2640. Scope and standard of review.
2641. Witnesses; inspection of documents.
2642. Analysis of imported merchandise.
2643. Relief.
2644. Interest.
2645. Decisions.
2646. Retrial or rehearing.
[2647. Repealed.]

§ 2631. Persons entitled to commence a civil action

(a) A civil action contesting the denial of a protest, in whole or in part, under section 515 of the Tariff Act of 1930 may be commenced in the Court of International Trade by the person who filed the protest pursuant to section 514 of such Act, or by a surety on the transaction which is the subject of the protest.

(b) A civil action contesting the denial of a petition under section 516 of the Tariff Act of 1930 may be commenced in the Court of International Trade by the person who filed such petition.

(c) A civil action contesting a determination listed in section 516A of the Tariff Act of 1930 may be commenced in the Court of International Trade by any interested party who was a party to the proceeding in connection with which the matter arose.

(d)(1) A civil action to review any final determination of the Secretary of Labor under section 223 of the Trade Act of 1974 with respect to the eligibility of workers for adjustment assistance under such Act may be commenced in the Court of International Trade by a worker, group of workers, certified or recognized union, or authorized representative of such worker or group that applies for assistance under such Act and is aggrieved by such final determination.

(2) A civil action to review any final determination of the Secretary of Commerce under section 251 of the Trade Act of 1974 with respect to the eligibility of a firm for adjustment assistance under such Act may be commenced in the Court of International Trade by a firm or its representative that applies for assistance under such Act and is aggrieved by such final determination, or by any other interested domestic party that is aggrieved by such final determination.

(3) A civil action to review any final determination of the Secretary of Commerce under section 271 of the Trade Act of 1974 with respect to the eligibility of a community for adjustment assistance under such Act may be commenced in the Court of International Trade by a community that applies for assistance under such Act and is aggrieved by such final determination, or by any other interested domestic party that is aggrieved by such final determination.

(e) A civil action to review a final determination made under section 305(b)(1) of the Trade Agreements Act of 1979 may be commenced in the Court of International Trade by any person who was a party-at-interest with respect to such determination.

(f) A civil action involving an application for the issuance of an order directing the administering authority or the International Trade Commission to make confidential information available under section 777(c)(2) of the Tariff Act of 1930 may be commenced in the Court of International Trade by any interested party whose application for disclosure of such confidential information was denied under section 777(c)(1) of such Act.

(g)(1) A civil action to review any decision of the Secretary of the Treasury to deny a customs broker's license under section 641(b)(2) or (3) of the Tariff Act of 1930, or to deny a customs broker's permit under section 641(c)(1) of such Act, or to revoke such license or permit under section 641(b)(5) or (c)(2) of such Act, may be commenced in the Court of International Trade by the person whose license or permit was denied or revoked.

(2) A civil action to review any decision of the Secretary of the Treasury to revoke or suspend a customs broker's license or permit or impose a monetary penalty in lieu thereof under section 641(d)(2)(B) of the Tariff Act of 1930 may be commenced in the Court of International Trade by the person against whom the decision was issued.

(3) A civil action to review any decision or order of the Customs Service to deny, suspend, or revoke accreditation of a private laboratory under section 499(b) of the Tariff Act of 1930 may be commenced in the Court of International Trade by the person whose accreditation was denied, suspended, or revoked.

(h) A civil action described in section 1581(h) of this title may be commenced in the Court of International Trade by the person who would have standing to bring a civil action under section 1581(a) of this title if he imported the goods involved and filed a protest which was denied, in whole or in part, under section 515 of the Tariff Act of 1930.

(i) Any civil action of which the Court of International Trade has jurisdiction, other than an action specified in subsections (a)–(h) of this section, may be commenced in the court by any person adversely affected or aggrieved by agency action within the meaning of section 702 of title 5.

(j)(1) Any person who would be adversely affected or aggrieved by a decision in a civil action pending in the Court of International Trade may, by leave of court, intervene in such action, except that—

(A) no person may intervene in a civil action under section 515 or 516 of the Tariff Act of 1930;

(B) in a civil action under section 516A of the Tariff Act of 1930, only an interested party who was a party to the proceeding in connection with which the matter arose may intervene, and such person may intervene as a matter of right; and

(C) in a civil action under section 777(c)(2) of the Tariff Act of 1930, only a person who was a party to the investigation may intervene, and such person may intervene as a matter of right.

(2) In those civil actions in which intervention is by leave of court, the Court of International Trade shall consider whether the intervention will unduly delay or prejudice the adjudication of the rights of the original parties.

(k) In this section—

(1) "interested party" has the meaning given such term in section 771(9) of the Tariff Act of 1930; and

(2) "party-at-interest" means—

(A) a foreign manufacturer, producer, or exporter, or a United States importer, of merchandise which is the subject of a final determination under section 305(b)(1) of the Trade Agreements Act of 1979;

(B) a manufacturer, producer, or wholesaler in the United States of a like product;

(C) United States members of a labor organization or other association of workers whose members are employed in the manufacture, production, or wholesale in the United States of a like product;

(D) a trade or business association a majority of whose members manufacture, produce, or wholesale a like product in the United States,[1] and

(E) an association composed of members who represent parties-at-interest described in subparagraph (B), (C), or (D).

(Added Pub.L. 96–417, Title III, § 301, Oct. 10, 1980, 94 Stat. 1730, and amended Pub.L. 98–573, Title II, § 212(b)(3), Title VI, § 612(b)(3), Oct. 30, 1984, 98 Stat. 2983, 3034; Pub.L. 103–182, Title VI, § 684(a)(2), Dec. 8, 1993, 107 Stat. 2219.)

[1] So in original. The comma probably should be a semicolon.

HISTORICAL AND STATUTORY NOTES

References in Text

Sections 514, 515, 516, and 516A of the Tariff Act of 1930, referred to in subsecs. (a) and/or (b), (c), (h), and (j)(1)(A), (B), are classified to sections 1514, 1515, 1516, and 1516a of Title 19, Customs Duties.

The Trade Act of 1974, referred to in subsec. (d)(1) to (3), is Pub.L. 93–618, Jan. 3, 1975, 88 Stat. 1978, as amended, which is classified principally to chapter 12 (section 2101 et seq.) of Title 19. Sections 223, 251, and 271 of the Trade Act of 1974 are classified to sections 2273, 2341, and 2371, respectively, of Title 19. For complete classification of this Act to the Code, see References in Text note set out under section 2101 of Title 19 and Tables.

Section 305(b)(1) of the Trade Agreements Act of 1979, referred to in subsecs. (e) and (k)(2)(A), is classified to section 2515(b)(1) of Title 19.

Section 777 of the Tariff Act of 1930, referred to in subsecs. (f) and (j)(1)(C), is classified to section 1677f of Title 19.

Section 641 of the Tariff Act of 1930, referred to in subsec. (g)(1), (2), is classified to section 1641 of Title 19.

Section 499(b) of the Tariff Act of 1930, referred to in subsec. (g)(3), is classified to section 1499(b) of Title 19, Customs Duties.

Section 771(9) of the Tariff Act of 1930, referred to in subsec. (k)(1), is classified to section 1677(9) of Title 19.

Effective and Applicability Provisions

1993 Acts. Amendment by section 684(a)(2) of Pub.L. 103–182 effective Dec. 8, 1993, see section 692 of Pub.L. 103–182, set out as a note under section 58c of Title 19, Customs Duties.

1984 Acts. Amendment by section 212(b)(3) of Pub.L. 98–573 to take effect on the close of the 180th day after Oct. 30, 1984, see section 214(d) of Pub.L. 98–573, set out as a note under section 1304 of Title 19, Customs Duties.

Amendment by section 612(b)(3) of Pub.L. 98–573 applicable with respect to investigations initiated by petition or by the administering authority under subtitle A or B of Title VII of the Tariff Act of 1930 (19 U.S.C. 1671 et seq., 1673 et seq.), and to reviews begun under section 751 of that Act (19 U.S.C. 1675), on or after Oct. 30, 1984, see section 626(b)(1) of Pub.L. 98–573, as amended, set out as a note under section 1671 of Title 19.

1980 Acts. Subsecs. (d) and (g) to (j) of this section applicable with respect to civil actions commenced on or after Nov. 1, 1980, see section 701(b)(1)(B) of Pub.L. 96–417, as amended, set out as a note under section 251 of this title.

Remainder of this section effective on Nov. 1, 1980 and applicable with respect to civil actions pending on or commenced or on after such date, see section 701(a) of Pub.L. 96–417, as amended, set out as a note under section 251 of this title.

Transfer of Functions

For transfer of the functions, personnel, assets, and liabilities of the United States Customs Service of the Department of the Treasury, including the functions of the Secretary of the Treasury relating thereto, to the Secretary of Homeland Security, and for treatment of related references, see 6

U.S.C.A. §§ 203(1), 551(d), 552(d) and 557, and the Department of Homeland Security Reorganization Plan of November 25, 2002, as modified, set out as a note under 6 U.S.C.A. § 542.

Prior Provisions

A prior section 2631, Acts June 25, 1948, c. 646, 62 Stat. 980; May 24, 1949, c. 139, § 122, 63 Stat. 106; June 2, 1970, Pub. L. 91–271, Title I, § 112, 84 Stat. 278; Jan. 3, 1975, Pub. L. 93–618, Title III, § 321(f)(2), 88 Stat. 2048, related to time for commencement of action and was omitted from the Code in the general revision of this chapter by Pub. L. 96–417. See section 2636 of this title.

Application of Amendments Relating to Accreditation of Private Laboratories

For purposes of applying amendments relating to accreditation of private laboratories, any decision or order of the Customs Service denying, suspending, or revoking the accreditation of a private laboratory on or after Dec. 8, 1993 and before regulations to implement section 1499(b) of Title 19, Customs Duties, are issued shall be treated as having been denied, suspended, or revoked under such section 1499(b) of Title 19. See section 684(b) of Pub.L. 103–182 set out as a note under section 1581 of this title.

§ 2632. Commencement of a civil action

(a) Except for civil actions specified in subsections (b) and (c) of this section, a civil action in the Court of International Trade shall be commenced by filing concurrently with the clerk of the court a summons and complaint, with the content and in the form, manner, and style prescribed by the rules of the court.

(b) A civil action in the Court of International Trade under section 515 or section 516 of the Tariff Act of 1930 shall be commenced by filing with the clerk of the court a summons, with the content and in the form, manner, and style prescribed by the rules of the court.

(c) A civil action in the Court of International Trade under section 516A of the Tariff Act of 1930 shall be commenced by filing with the clerk of the court a summons or a summons and a complaint, as prescribed in such section, with the content and in the form, manner, and style prescribed by the rules of the court.

(d) The Court of International Trade may prescribe by rule that any summons, pleading, or other paper mailed by registered or certified mail properly addressed to the clerk of the court with the proper postage affixed and return receipt requested shall be deemed filed as of the date of mailing.

(Added Pub.L. 96–417, Title III, § 301, Oct. 10, 1980, 94 Stat. 1732.)

HISTORICAL AND STATUTORY NOTES

References in Text

Sections 515 and 516 of the Tariff Act of 1930, referred to in subsec. (b), are classified to sections 1515 and 1516 of Title 19, Customs Duties.

Section 516A of the Tariff Act of 1930, referred to in subsec. (c), is classified to section 1516a of Title 19.

Effective and Applicability Provisions

1980 Acts. Subsec. (a) of this section applicable with respect to civil actions commenced on or after Nov. 1, 1980, see section 701(b)(1)(B) of Pub.L. 96–417, as amended, set out as a note under section 251 of this title.

Remainder of this section effective on Nov. 1, 1980 and applicable with respect to civil actions pending on or commenced on or after such date, see section 701(a) of Pub.L. 96–417, as amended, set out as a note under section 251 of this title.

Prior Provisions

A prior section 2632, Acts June 25, 1948, c. 646, 62 Stat. 980; June 2, 1970, Pub. L. 91–271, Title I, § 113, 84 Stat. 279; Jan. 3, 1975, Pub. L. 93–618, Title III, § 321(f)(3), 88 Stat. 2048; July 26, 1979, Pub. L. 96–39, Title X, § 1001(b)(4)(C), 93 Stat. 306, related to Customs Court procedure and fees and was omitted from the Code in the general revision of this chapter by Pub. L. 96–417. See section 2633 of this title.

§ 2633. Procedure and fees

(a) A filing fee shall be payable to the clerk of the Court of International Trade upon the commencement of a civil action in such court. The amount of the fee shall be prescribed by the rules of the court, but shall be not less than $5 nor more than the filing fee for commencing a civil action in a district court of the United States. The court may fix all other fees to be charged by the clerk of the court.

(b) The Court of International Trade shall prescribe rules governing the summons, pleadings, and other papers, for their amendment, service, and filing, for consolidations, severances, suspensions of cases, and for other procedural matters.

(c) All summons, pleadings, and other papers filed in the Court of International Trade shall be served on all parties in accordance with rules prescribed by the court. When the United States, its agencies, or its officers are adverse parties, service of the summons shall be made upon the Attorney General and the head of the Government agency whose action is being contested. When injunctive relief is sought, the summons, pleadings, and other papers shall also be served upon the named officials sought to be enjoined.

(Added Pub.L. 96–417, Title III, § 301, Oct. 10, 1980, 94 Stat. 1732.)

HISTORICAL AND STATUTORY NOTES

Effective and Applicability Provisions

1980 Acts. Section effective on Nov. 1, 1980 and applicable with respect to civil actions pending on or commenced on or after such date, see section 701(a) of Pub.L. 96–417, as amended, set out as a note under section 251 of this title.

Prior Provisions

A prior section 2633, Acts June 25, 1948, c. 646, 62 Stat. 980; June 2, 1970, Pub.L. 91–271, Title I, § 114, 84 Stat. 279; July 26, 1979, Pub.L. 96–39, Title X, § 1001(b)(4)(D), 93 Stat. 306, related to precedence of cases and was omitted from the Code in the general revision of this chapter by Pub.L. 96–417. See note set out under former section 2647 of this title.

§ 2634. Notice

Reasonable notice of the time and place of trial or hearing before the Court of International Trade shall be given to all parties to any civil action, as prescribed by the rules of the court.

(Added Pub.L. 96–417, Title III, § 301, Oct. 10, 1980, 94 Stat. 1733.)

HISTORICAL AND STATUTORY NOTES

Effective and Applicability Provisions

1980 Acts. Section effective on Nov. 1, 1980 and applicable with respect to civil actions pending on or commenced on or after such date, see section 701(a) of Pub.L. 96–417, as amended, set out as a note under section 251 of this title.

Prior Provisions

A prior section 2634, Acts June 25, 1948, c. 646, 62 Stat. 981; June 2, 1970, Pub.L. 91–271, Title I, § 115, 84 Stat. 280, related to notice and was omitted from the Code in the general revision of this chapter by Pub.L. 96–417.

§ 2635. Filing of official documents

(a) In any action commenced in the Court of International Trade contesting the denial of a protest under section 515 of the Tariff Act of 1930 or the denial of a petition under section 516 of such Act, the Customs Service, as prescribed by the rules of the court, shall file with the clerk of the court, as part of the official record, any document, paper, information or data relating to the entry of merchandise and the administrative determination that is the subject of the protest or petition.

(b)(1) In any civil action commenced in the Court of International Trade under section 516A of the Tariff Act of 1930, within forty days or within such other period of time as the court may specify, after the date of service of a complaint on the administering authority established to administer title VII of the Tariff Act of 1930 or the United States International Trade Commission, the administering authority or the Commission shall transmit to the clerk of the court the record of such action, as prescribed by the rules of the court. The record shall, unless otherwise stipulated by the parties, consist of—

(A) a copy of all information presented to or obtained by the administering authority or the Commission during the course of the administrative proceedings, including all governmental memoranda pertaining to the case and the record of ex parte meetings required to be maintained by section 777(a)(3) of the Tariff Act of 1930; and

(B) (i) a copy of the determination and the facts and conclusions of law upon which such determination was based, (ii) all transcripts or records of conferences or hearings, and (iii) all notices published in the Federal Register.

(2) The administering authority or the Commission shall identify and transmit under seal to the clerk of the court any document, comment, or information that is accorded confidential or privileged status by the Government agency whose action is being contested and that is required to be transmitted to the clerk under paragraph (1) of this subsection. Any such document, comment, or information shall be accompanied by a nonconfidential description of the nature of the material being transmitted. The confidential or privileged status of such material shall be preserved in the civil action, but the court may examine the confidential or privileged material in camera and may make such material available under such terms and conditions as the court may order.

(c) Within fifteen days, or within such other period of time as the Court of International Trade may specify, after service of a summons and complaint in a civil action involving an application for an order directing the administering authority or the International Trade Commission to make confidential information available under section 777(c)(2) of the Tariff Act of 1930, the administering authority or the Commission shall transmit under seal to the clerk of the Court of International Trade, as prescribed by its rules, the confidential information involved, together with pertinent parts of the record. Such information shall be accompanied by a nonconfidential description of the nature of the information being transmitted. The confidential status of such information shall be preserved in the civil action, but the court may examine the confidential information in camera and may make such information available under a protective order consistent with section 777(c)(2) of the Tariff Act of 1930.

(d)(1) In any other civil action in the Court of International Trade in which judicial review is to proceed upon the basis of the record made before an agency, the agency shall, within forty days or within such other period of time as the court may specify, after the date of service of the summons and complaint upon the agency, transmit to the clerk of the court, as prescribed by its rules—

(A) a copy of the contested determination and the findings or report upon which such determination was based;

(B) a copy of any reported hearings or conferences conducted by the agency; and

(C) any documents, comments, or other papers filed by the public, interested parties, or governments with respect to the agency's action.

(2) The agency shall identify and transmit under seal to the clerk of the court any document, comment, or other information that was obtained on a confidential basis and that is required to be transmitted to the clerk under paragraph (1) of this subsection. Any such document, comment, or information shall include a nonconfidential description of the nature of the material being transmitted. The confidential or privileged status of such material shall be preserved in the civil action, but the court may examine such material in camera and may make such material available under such terms and conditions as the court may order.

(3) The parties may stipulate that fewer documents, comments, or other information than those specified in paragraph (1) of this subsection shall be transmitted to the clerk of the court.

(Added Pub.L. 96–417, Title III, § 301, Oct. 10, 1980, 94 Stat. 1733, and amended Pub.L. 103–182, Title VI, § 684(d), Dec. 8, 1993, 107 Stat. 2219.)

HISTORICAL AND STATUTORY NOTES

References in Text

The Tariff Act of 1930, referred to in subsecs. (a), (b)(1), (b)(1)(A), and (c), is Act June 17, 1930, c. 497, 46 Stat. 590, as amended. Title VII of the Tariff Act of 1930 is classified generally to subtitle IV (section 1671 et seq.) of chapter 4 of Title 19, Customs Duties. Sections 515, 516, 516A and 777 of the Tariff Act of 1930 are classified to sections 1515, 1516, 1516a, and 1677f, respectively, of Title 19. For complete classification of this Act to the Code, see section 1654 of Title 19 and Tables.

Effective and Applicability Provisions

1993 Acts. Amendment by section 684(d) of Pub.L. 103–182 effective Dec. 8, 1993, see section 692 of Pub.L. 103–182, set out as a note under section 58c of Title 19, Customs Duties.

1980 Acts. Section applicable with respect to civil actions commenced on or after Nov. 1, 1980, see section 701(b)(1)(B) of Pub.L. 96–417, as amended, set out as a note under section 251 of this title.

Transfer of Functions

For transfer of functions, personnel, assets, and liabilities of the United States Customs Service of the Department of the Treasury, including functions of the Secretary of the Treasury relating thereto, to the Secretary of Homeland Security, and for treatment of related references, see 6 U.S.C.A. §§ 203(1), 551(d), 552(d), and 557, and the Department of Homeland Security Reorganization Plan of November 25, 2002, as modified, set out as a note under 6 U.S.C.A. § 542.

Prior Provisions

A prior section 2635, Acts June 25, 1948, c. 646, 62 Stat. 981; June 2, 1970, Pub. L. 91–271, Title I, § 116, 84 Stat. 280, related to burden of proof and evidence of value and was omitted from the Code in the general revision of this chapter by Pub. L. 96–417. See section 2639 of this title.

§ 2636. Time for commencement of action

(a) A civil action contesting the denial, in whole or in part, of a protest under section 515 of the Tariff Act of 1930 is barred unless commenced in accordance with the rules of the Court of International Trade—

(1) within one hundred and eighty days after the date of mailing of notice of denial of a protest under section 515(a) of such Act; or

(2) within one hundred and eighty days after the date of denial of a protest by operation of law under the provisions of section 515(b) of such Act.

(b) A civil action contesting the denial of a petition under section 516 of the Tariff Act of 1930 is barred unless commenced in accordance with the rules of the Court of International Trade within thirty days after the date of mailing of a notice pursuant to section 516(c) of such Act.

(c) A civil action contesting a reviewable determination listed in section 516A of the Tariff Act of 1930 is barred unless commenced in accordance with the rules of the Court of International Trade within the time specified in such section.

(d) A civil action contesting a final determination of the Secretary of Labor under section 223 of the Trade Act of 1974 or a final determination of the Secretary of Commerce under section 251 or section 271 of such Act is barred unless commenced in accordance with the rules of the Court of International Trade within sixty days after the date of notice of such determination.

(e) A civil action contesting a final determination made under section 305(b)(1) of the Trade Agreements Act of 1979 is barred unless commenced in accordance with the rules of the Court of International Trade within thirty days after the date of the publication of such determination in the Federal Register.

(f) A civil action involving an application for the issuance of an order making confidential information available under section 777(c)(2) of the Tariff Act of 1930 is barred unless commenced in accordance with the rules of the Court of International Trade within ten days after the date of the denial of the request for such confidential information.

(g) A civil action contesting the denial or revocation by the Secretary of the Treasury of a customs broker's license or permit under subsection (b) or (c) of section 641 of the Tariff Act of 1930, or the revocation or suspension of such license or permit or the imposition of a monetary penalty in lieu thereof by such Secretary under section 641(d) of such Act, is barred unless commenced in accordance with the rules of the Court of International Trade within sixty days after the date of the entry of the decision or order of such Secretary.

(h) A civil action contesting the denial, suspension, or revocation by the Customs Service of a private laboratory's accreditation under section 499(b) of the Tariff Act of 1930 is barred unless commenced in accordance with the rules of the Court of International Trade within 60 days after the date of the decision or order of the Customs Service.

(i) A civil action of which the Court of International Trade has jurisdiction under section 1581 of this title, other than an action specified in subsections (a)–(h) of this section, is barred unless commenced in accordance with the rules of the court within two years after the cause of action first accrues.

(Added Pub.L. 96–417, Title III, § 301, Oct. 10, 1980, 94 Stat. 1734, and amended Pub.L. 98–573, Title II, § 212(b)(4), Title VI, § 623(b)(1), Oct. 30, 1984, 98 Stat. 2984, 3041; Pub.L. 103–182, Title VI, § 684(a)(3), Dec. 8, 1993, 107 Stat. 2219.)

HISTORICAL AND STATUTORY NOTES

References in Text

Section 515 of the Tariff Act of 1930, referred to in subsec. (a), is is classified to section 1515 of Title 19, Customs Duties.

Section 516 of the Tariff Act of 1930, referred to in subsec. (b), is classified to section 1516 of Title 19.

Section 516A of the Tariff Act of 1930, referred to in subsec. (c), is classified to section 1516a of Title 19.

Sections 223, 251, and 271 of the Trade Act of 1974, referred to in subsec. (d), are classified to sections 2273, 2341, and 2371 of Title 19.

Section 305(b)(1) of the Trade Agreements Act of 1979, referred to in subsec. (e), is classified to section 2515(b)(1) of Title 19.

Section 777(c)(2) of the Tariff Act of 1930, referred to in subsec. (f), is classified to section 1677f(c)(2) of Title 19.

Section 641 of the Tariff Act of 1930, referred to in subsec. (g), is classified to section 1641 of Title 19.

Section 499(b) of the Tariff Act of 1930, referred to in subsec. (h), is classified to section 1499(b) of Title 19, Customs Duties.

Effective and Applicability Provisions

1993 Acts. Amendment by section 684(a)(3) of Pub.L. 103–182 effective Dec. 8, 1993, see section 692 of Pub.L. 103–182, set out as a note under section 58c of Title 19, Customs Duties.

1984 Acts. Amendment by section 212(b)(4) of Pub.L. 98–573 to take effect on the close of the 180th day after Oct. 30, 1984, see section 214(d) of Pub.L. 98–573, set out as a note under section 1304 of Title 19, Customs Duties.

Amendment by section 623(b)(1) of Pub.L. 98–573 applicable with respect to civil actions pending on, or filed on or after, Oct. 30, 1984, see section 626(b)(2) of Pub.L. 98–573, as amended, set out as a note under section 1671 of Title 19.

1980 Acts. Section applicable with respect to civil actions commenced on or after Nov. 1, 1980, see section 701(b)(1)(B) of Pub.L. 96–417, as amended, set out as a note under section 251 of this title.

Transfer of Functions

For transfer of functions, personnel, assets, and liabilities of the United States Customs Service of the Department of the Treasury, including functions of the Secretary of the Treasury relating thereto, to the Secretary of Homeland Security, and for treatment of related references, see 6 U.S.C.A. §§ 203(1), 551(d), 552(d), and 557, and the Department of Homeland Security Reorganization Plan of November 25, 2002, as modified, set out as a note under 6 U.S.C.A. § 542.

Prior Provisions

A prior section 2636, Acts June 25, 1948, c. 646, 62 Stat. 981; June 2, 1970, Pub.L. 91–271, Title I, § 117, 84 Stat. 280, related to analysis of imported merchandise and was omitted from the Code in the general revision of this chapter by Pub.L. 96–417. See section 2642 of this title.

Application of Amendments Relating to Accreditation of Private Laboratories

For purposes of applying amendments relating to accreditation of private laboratories, any decision or order of the Customs Service denying, suspending, or revoking the accreditation of a private laboratory on or after Dec. 8, 1993 and before regulations to implement section 1499(b) of Title 19, Customs Duties, are issued shall be treated as having been denied, suspended, or revoked under such section 1499(b) of Title 19. See section 684(b) of Pub.L. 103–182 set out as a note under section 1581 of this title.

§ 2637. Exhaustion of administrative remedies

(a) A civil action contesting the denial of a protest under section 515 of the Tariff Act of 1930 may be commenced in the Court of International Trade only if all liquidated duties, charges, or exactions have been paid at the time the action is commenced, except that a surety's obligation to pay such liquidated duties, charges, or exactions is limited to the sum of any bond related to each entry included in the denied protest.

(b) A civil action contesting the denial of a petition under section 516 of the Tariff Act of 1930 may be commenced in the Court of International Trade only by a person who has first exhausted the procedures set forth in such section.

(c) A civil action described in section 1581(h) of this title may be commenced in the Court of International Trade prior to the exhaustion of administrative remedies if the person commencing the action makes the demonstration required by such section.

(d) In any civil action not specified in this section, the Court of International Trade shall, where appropriate, require the exhaustion of administrative remedies.

(Added Pub.L. 96–417, Title III, § 301, Oct. 10, 1980, 94 Stat. 1735.)

HISTORICAL AND STATUTORY NOTES

References in Text

Sections 515 and 516 of the Tariff Act of 1930, referred to in subsecs. (a) and (b), respectively, are classified to sections 1515 and 1516, respectively, of Title 19, Customs Duties.

Effective and Applicability Provisions

1980 Acts. Subsec. (c) of this section applicable with respect to civil actions commenced on or after Nov. 1, 1980, see section 701(b)(1)(B) of Pub.L. 96–417, as amended, set out as a note under section 251 of this title.

Remainder of this section effective on Nov. 1, 1980 and applicable with respect to civil actions pending on or commenced on or after such date, see section 701(a) of Pub.L. 96–417, as amended, set out as a note under section 251 of this title.

Prior Provisions

A prior section 2637, Acts June 25, 1948, c. 646, 62 Stat. 982; June 2, 1970, Pub.L. 91–271, Title I, § 118, 84 Stat. 280; July 26, 1979, Pub.L. 96–39, Title X, § 1001(b)(4)(E), 93 Stat. 306, related to witnesses and inspection of documents and was omitted from the Code in the general revision of this chapter by Pub.L. 96–417. See section 2641 of this title.

§ 2638. New grounds in support of a civil action

In any civil action under section 515 of the Tariff Act of 1930 in which the denial, in whole or in part, of a protest is a precondition to the commencement of a civil action in the Court of International Trade, the court, by rule, may consider any new ground in support of the civil action if such new ground—

(1) applies to the same merchandise that was the subject of the protest; and

(2) is related to the same administrative decision listed in section 514 of the Tariff Act of 1930 that was contested in the protest.

(Added Pub.L. 96–417, Title III, § 301, Oct. 10, 1980, 94 Stat. 1736.)

HISTORICAL AND STATUTORY NOTES

References in Text

Sections 515 and 514 of the Tariff Act of 1930, referred to in the introductory text and cl. (2), respectively, are classified to sections 1515 and 1514, respectively, of Title 19, Customs Duties.

Effective and Applicability Provisions

1980 Acts. Section effective on Nov. 1, 1980 and applicable with respect to civil actions pending on or commenced on or after such date, see section 701(a) of Pub.L. 96–417, as amended, set out as a note under section 251 of this title.

Prior Provisions

A prior section 2638, Acts June 25, 1948, c. 646, 62 Stat. 982; June 2, 1970, Pub.L. 91–271, Title I, § 119, 84 Stat. 281, related to decisions, findings of fact and conclusions of law, and effect of opinions and was omitted from the Code in the general revision of this chapter by Pub.L. 96–417. See section 2645(a) and (c) of this title.

§ 2639. Burden of proof; evidence of value

(a)(1) Except as provided in paragraph (2) of this subsection, in any civil action commenced in the Court of International Trade under section 515, 516, or 516A of the Tariff Act of 1930, the decision of the Secretary of the Treasury, the administering authority, or the International Trade Commission is presumed to be correct. The burden of proving otherwise shall rest upon the party challenging such decision.

(2) The provisions of paragraph (1) of this subsection shall not apply to any civil action commenced in the Court of International Trade under section 1582 of this title.

(b) In any civil action described in section 1581(h) of this title, the person commencing the action shall have the burden of making the demonstration required by such section by clear and convincing evidence.

(c) Where the value of merchandise or any of its components is in issue in any civil action in the Court of International Trade—

(1) reports or depositions of consuls, customs officers, and other officers of the United States, and depositions and affidavits of other persons whose attendance cannot reasonably be had, may be admitted into evidence when served upon the opposing party as prescribed by the rules of the court; and

(2) price lists and catalogs may be admitted in evidence when duly authenticated, relevant, and material.

(Added Pub.L. 96–417, Title III, § 301, Oct. 10, 1980, 94 Stat. 1736.)

HISTORICAL AND STATUTORY NOTES

References in Text

Sections 515, 516, and 516A of the Tariff Act of 1930, referred to in subsec. (a)(1), are classified to sections 1515, 1516, and 1516a, respectively, of Title 19, Customs Duties.

Effective and Applicability Provisions

1980 Acts. Subsec. (a)(2) of this section applicable with respect to civil actions commenced on or after the 90th day after Nov. 1, 1980, see section 701(c)(1)(A) of Pub.L. 96–417, as amended, set out as a note under section 251 of this title.

Subsec. (b) of this section applicable with respect to civil actions commenced on or after Nov. 1, 1980, see section 701(b) (1) (B) of Pub.L. 96–417, as amended, set out as a note under section 251 of this title.

Remainder of this section effective on Nov. 1, 1980 and applicable with respect to civil actions pending on or commenced on or after such date, see section 701(a) of Pub.L. 96–417, as amended, set out as a note under section 251 of this title.

Prior Provisions

A prior section 2639, Acts June 25, 1948, c. 646, 62 Stat. 982; June 2, 1970, Pub.L. 91–271, Title I, § 120, 84 Stat. 281, provided for retrial or rehearing and was omitted from the Code in the general revision of this chapter by Pub.L. 96–417. See section 2646 of this title.

§ 2640. Scope and standard of review

(a) The Court of International Trade shall make its determinations upon the basis of the record made before the court in the following categories of civil actions:

(1) Civil actions contesting the denial of a protest under section 515 of the Tariff Act of 1930.

(2) Civil actions commenced under section 516 of the Tariff Act of 1930.

(3) Civil actions commenced to review a final determination made under section 305(b)(1) of the Trade Agreements Act of 1979.

(4) Civil actions commenced under section 777(c)(2) of the Tariff Act of 1930.

(5) Civil actions commenced to review any decision of the Secretary of the Treasury under section 641 of the Tariff Act of 1930, with the exception of decisions under section 641(d)(2)(B), which shall be governed by subdivision (d) of this section.

(6) Civil actions commenced under section 1582 of this title.

(b) In any civil action commenced in the Court of International Trade under section 516A of the Tariff Act of 1930, the court shall review the matter as specified in subsection (b) of such section.

(c) In any civil action commenced in the Court of International Trade to review any final determination of the Secretary of Labor under section 223 of the Trade Act of 1974 or any final determination of the Secretary of Commerce under section 251 or section 271 of such Act, the court shall review the matter as specified in section 284 of such Act.

(d) In any civil action commenced to review any order or decision of the Customs Service under section 499(b) of the Tariff Act of 1930, the court shall review the action on the basis of the record before the Customs Service at the time of issuing such decision or order.

(e) In any civil action not specified in this section, the Court of International Trade shall review the matter as provided in section 706 of title 5.

(Added Pub.L. 96–417, Title III, § 301, Oct. 10, 1980, 94 Stat. 1736, and amended Pub.L. 98–573, Title II, § 212(b)(5), Oct. 30, 1984, 98 Stat. 2984; Pub.L. 103–182, Title VI, § 684(a)(4), Dec. 8, 1993, 107 Stat. 2219.)

HISTORICAL AND STATUTORY NOTES

References in Text

Sections 515 and 516 of the Tariff Act of 1930, referred to in subsec. (a)(1) and (2), are classified to sections 1515 and 1516, respectively, of Title 19, Customs Duties.

Section 305(b)(1) of the Trade Agreements Act of 1979, referred to in subsec. (a)(3), is classified to section 2515(b)(1) of Title 19.

Section 777(c)(2) of the Tariff Act of 1930, referred to in subsec. (a)(4), is classified to section 1677f(c)(2) of Title 19.

Section 641 of the Tariff Act of 1930, referred to in subsec. (a)(5), is classified to section 1641 of Title 19.

Section 516A of the Tariff Act of 1930, referred to in subsec. (b), is classified to section 1516a of Title 19.

Sections 223, 251, 271, and 284 of the Trade Act of 1974, referred to in subsec. (c), are classified to sections 2273, 2341, 2371, and 2395 of Title 19.

Section 499(b) of the Tariff Act of 1930, referred to in subsec. (d), is classified to section 1499(b) of Title 19, Customs Duties.

Effective and Applicability Provisions

1993 Acts. Amendment by section 684(a)(4) of Pub.L. 103–182 effective Dec. 8, 1993, see section 692 of Pub.L. 103–182, set out as a note under section 58c of Title 19, Customs Duties.

1984 Acts. Amendment by Pub.L. 98–573 to take effect on the close of the 180th day after Oct. 30, 1984, see section 214(d) of Pub.L. 98–573, set out as a note under section 1304 of Title 19, Customs Duties.

1980 Acts. Subsecs. (a)(5), (c), and (d) of this section applicable with respect to civil actions commenced on or after Nov. 1, 1980, see section 701(b)(1)(B) of Pub.L. 96–417, as amended, set out as a note under section 251 of this title.

Subsec. (a)(6) of this section applicable with respect to civil actions commenced on or after the 90th day after Nov. 1, 1980, see section 701(c)(1)(A) of Pub.L. 96–417, as amended, set out as a note under section 251 of this title.

Remainder of this section effective on Nov. 1, 1980 and applicable with respect to civil actions pending on or commenced on or after such date, see section 701(a) of Pub.L. 96–417, as amended, set out as a note under section 251 of this title.

Transfer of Functions

For transfer of functions, personnel, assets, and liabilities of the United States Customs Service of the Department of the Treasury, including functions of the Secretary of the Treasury relating thereto, to the Secretary of Homeland Security, and for treatment of related references, see 6 U.S.C.A. §§ 203(1), 551(d), 552(d), and 557, and the Department of Homeland Security Reorganization Plan of November 25, 2002, as modified, set out as a note under 6 U.S.C.A. § 542.

Prior Provisions

A prior section 2640, Act June 25, 1948, c. 646, 62 Stat. 982, authorized the division which had decided a case or the single judge who had decided an appeal for a reappraisement to grant a rehearing or retrial and was repealed by Pub.L. 91–271, Title I, § 121, June 2, 1970, 84 Stat. 281. See section 2646 of this title.

Application of Amendments Relating to Accreditation of Private Laboratories

For purposes of applying amendments relating to accreditation of private laboratories, any decision or order of the Customs Service denying, suspending, or revoking the accreditation of a private laboratory on or after Dec. 8, 1993 and before regulations to implement section 1499(b) of Title 19, Customs Duties, are issued shall be treated as having been denied, suspended, or revoked under such section 1499(b) of Title 19. See section 684(b) of Pub.L. 103–182 set out as a note under section 1581 of this title.

§ 2641. Witnesses; inspection of documents

(a) Except as otherwise provided by law, in any civil action in the Court of International Trade, each party and its counsel shall have an opportunity to introduce evidence, to hear and cross-examine the witnesses of the other party, and to inspect all samples and papers admitted or offered as evidence, as prescribed by the rules of the court. Except as provided in section 2639 of this title, subsection (b) of this section, or the rules of the court, the Federal Rules of Evidence shall apply to all civil actions in the Court of International Trade.

(b) The Court of International Trade may order that trade secrets and commercial or financial information which is privileged and confidential, or any information provided to the United States by any foreign government or foreign person, may be disclosed to a party, its counsel, or any other person under such terms and conditions as the court may order.

(Added Pub.L. 96–417, Title III, § 301, Oct. 10, 1980, 94 Stat. 1737.)

HISTORICAL AND STATUTORY NOTES

References in Text

The Federal Rules of Evidence, referred to in subsec. (a), are set out in this title.

Effective and Applicability Provisions

1980 Acts. Section effective on Nov. 1, 1980 and applicable with respect to civil actions pending on or commenced on or after such date, see section 701(a) of Pub.L. 96–417, as amended, set out as a note under section 251 of this title.

Prior Provisions

A prior section 2641, Act June 25, 1948, c. 646, 62 Stat. 982, authorized the Customs Court to assess a penalty of not less than $5 nor more than $250 against any person filing a frivolous protest or appeal and was repealed by Pub.L. 91–271, Title I, § 121, June 2, 1970, 84 Stat. 281.

§ 2642. Analysis of imported merchandise

The Court of International Trade may order an analysis of imported merchandise and reports thereon by laboratories or agencies of the United States or laboratories accredited by the Customs Service under section 499(b) of the Tariff Act of 1930.

(Added Pub.L. 96–417, Title III, § 301, Oct. 10, 1980, 94 Stat. 1737, and amended Pub.L. 103–182, Title VI, § 684(a)(5), Dec. 8, 1993, 107 Stat. 2219.)

HISTORICAL AND STATUTORY NOTES

References in Text

Section 499(b) of the Tariff Act of 1930, referred to in text, is classified to section 1499(b) of Title 19, Customs Duties.

Effective and Applicability Provisions

1993 Acts. Amendment by section 684(a)(5) of Pub.L. 103–182 effective Dec. 8, 1993, see section 692 of Pub.L. 103–182, set out as a note under section 58c of Title 19, Customs Duties.

1980 Acts. Section effective on Nov. 1, 1980 and applicable with respect to civil actions pending on or commenced on or after such date, see section 701(a) of Pub.L. 96–417, as amended, set out as a note under section 251 of this title.

Transfer of Functions

For transfer of functions, personnel, assets, and liabilities of the United States Customs Service of the Department of the Treasury, including functions of the Secretary of the Treasury relating thereto, to the Secretary of Homeland Security, and for treatment of related references, see 6 U.S.C.A. §§ 203(1), 551(d), 552(d), and 557, and the Department of Homeland Security Reorganization Plan of November 25, 2002, as modified, set out as a note under 6 U.S.C.A. § 542.

Prior Provisions

A prior section 2642, Act May 24, 1949, c. 139, § 123, 63 Stat. 106, authorized the Customs Court under its rules and in its discretion to permit the amendment of protests, appeals and pleadings and was repealed by Pub.L. 91–271, Title I, § 121, June 2, 1970, 84 Stat. 281. See section 2633(b) of this title.

Application of Amendments Relating to Accreditation of Private Laboratories

For purposes of applying amendments relating to accreditation of private laboratories, any decision or order of the Customs Service denying, suspending, or revoking the accreditation of a private laboratory on or after Dec. 8, 1993 and before regulations to implement section 1499(b) of Title 19, Customs Duties, are issued shall be treated as having been denied, suspended, or revoked under such section 1499(b) of Title 19. See section 684(b) of Pub.L. 103–182 set out as a note under section 1581 of this title.

§ 2643. Relief

(a) The Court of International Trade may enter a money judgment—

(1) for or against the United States in any civil action commenced under section 1581 or 1582 of this title; and

(2) for or against the United States or any other party in any counterclaim, cross-claim, or third-party action under section 1583 of this title.

(b) If the Court of International Trade is unable to determine the correct decision on the basis of the evidence presented in any civil action, the court may order a retrial or rehearing for all purposes, or may order such further administrative or adjudicative procedures as the court considers necessary to enable it to reach the correct decision.

(c)(1) Except as provided in paragraphs (2), (3), (4), and (5) of this subsection, the Court of International Trade may, in addition to the orders specified in subsections (a) and (b) of this section, order any other form of relief that is appropriate in a civil action, including, but not limited to, declaratory judgments, orders of remand, injunctions, and writs of mandamus and prohibition.

(2) The Court of International Trade may not grant an injunction or issue a writ of mandamus in any civil action commenced to review any final determination of the Secretary of Labor under section 223 of the Trade Act of 1974, or any final determination of the Secretary of Commerce under section 251 or section 271 of such Act.

(3) In any civil action involving an application for the issuance of an order directing the administering authority or the International Trade Commission to make confidential information available under section 777(c)(2) of the Tariff Act of 1930, the Court of International Trade may issue an order of disclosure only with respect to the information specified in such section.

(4) In any civil action described in section 1581(h) of this title, the Court of International Trade may only order the appropriate declaratory relief.

(5) In any civil action involving an antidumping or countervailing duty proceeding regarding a class or kind of merchandise of a free trade area country (as defined in section 516A(f)(10) of the Tariff Act of 1930), as determined by the administering authority, the Court of International Trade may not order declaratory relief.

(d) If a surety commences a civil action in the Court of International Trade, such surety shall recover only the amount of the liquidated duties, charges, or exactions paid on the entries included in such action. The excess amount of any recovery shall be paid to the importer of record.

(e) In any proceeding involving assessment or collection of a monetary penalty under section 641(b)(6) or 641(d)(2)(A) of the Tariff Act of 1930, the court may not render judgment in an amount greater than that sought in the initial pleading of the United States, and may render judgment in such lesser amount as shall seem proper and just to the court.

(Added Pub.L. 96–417, Title III, § 301, Oct. 10, 1980, 94 Stat. 1737, and amended Pub.L. 98–573, Title II, § 212(b)(6), Oct. 30, 1984, 98 Stat. 2984; Pub.L. 100–449, Title IV, § 402(b), Sept. 28, 1988, 102 Stat. 1884; Pub.L. 103–182, Title IV, § 414(b), Dec. 8, 1993, 107 Stat. 2147.)

Termination of Amendments

For provisions directing that, except for transition provisions relating to proceedings regarding protective orders and undertakings, and binational panel and extraordinary challenge committee reviews, the amendment to this section by Title IV of Pub.L. 103–182 shall cease to have effect with respect to any country on the date on which such country ceases to be a NAFTA country, see 19 U.S.C.A. § 3451.

For provisions directing that the amendments made by Pub.L. 100–449, which amended this section, shall cease to have effect on the date on which the United States–Canada Free–Trade Agreement ceases to be in force, see section 501(c) of Pub.L. 100–449, set out in a note under 19 U.S.C.A. § 2112.

Articles 1906 and 2106 of the Agreement authorize either the United States or Canada to terminate the Agreement on 6–month notice if, at the end of the 7–year period following the date of the entry into effect of the Agreement, no agreement has been entered into between the United States and Canada on a substitute system of antidumping and countervailing duties.

HISTORICAL AND STATUTORY NOTES

References in Text

Section 223 of the Trade Act of 1974 and sections 251, 271 of such Act, referred to in subsec. (c)(2), are classified to sections 2273 and 2341, 2371, respectively, of Title 19, Customs Duties.

Section 777(c)(2) of the Tariff Act of 1930, referred to in subsec. (c)(3), is classified to section 1677f(c)(2) of Title 19.

Section 516A(f)(10) of the Tariff Act of 1930, referred to in subsec. (c)(5), is classified to section 1516a(f)(10) of Title 19, Customs Duties.

Section 641 of the Tariff Act of 1930, referred to in subsec. (e), is classified to section 1641 of Title 19.

Effective and Applicability Provisions

1993 Acts. Amendment by section by section 414 of Pub.L. 103–182 to take effect on the date the North American Free Trade Agreement enters into force with respect to the United States [Jan. 1, 1994], but not to apply to any final determination described in section 1516a(a)(1)(B) or (2)(B)(i), (ii), or (iii) of Title 19, Customs Duties, notice of which is published in the Federal Register before such date, or to a determination described in section 1516a(a)(2)(B)(vi) of Title 19 notice of which is received by the Government of Canada or Mexico before such date, or to any binational panel review under the United States–Canada Free–Trade Agreement, or to any extraordinary challenge arising out of any such review that was commenced before such date, see section 416 of Pub.L. 103–182, set out as a note under section 3431 of Title 19.

1988 Acts. Amendment by Pub.L. 100–449 effective on the date the United States–Canada Free–Trade Agreement enters into force (Jan. 1, 1989) and to cease to have effect on the date the Agreement ceases to be in force, see section 501(a), (c), of Pub.L. 100–449, set out in a note under section 2112 of Title 19, Customs Duties. [A Presidential Memorandum on the Canada–United States Free–Trade Agreement, dated Dec. 31, 1988, directing the Secretary of State to exchange notes with the Government of Canada to provide for the entry into force of the Agreement on Jan. 1, 1989, is set out in 24 Weekly Compilation of Presidential Documents 1688, Jan. 2, 1989.]

1984 Acts. Amendment by Pub.L. 98–573 to take effect on the close of the 180th day after Oct. 30, 1984, see section 214(d) of Pub.L. 98–573, set out as a note under section 1304 of Title 19, Customs Duties.

1980 Acts. Subsecs. (a) and (c)(2), (4) of this section applicable with respect to civil actions commenced on or after Nov. 1, 1980, see section 701(b)(1)(B) of Pub.L. 96–417, as amended, set out as a note under section 251 of this title.

Remainder of this section effective on Nov. 1, 1980 and applicable with respect to civil actions pending on or commenced on or after such date, see section 701(a) of Pub.L. 96–417, as amended, set out as a note under section 251 of this title.

§ 2644. Interest

If, in a civil action in the Court of International Trade under section 515 of the Tariff Act of 1930, the plaintiff obtains monetary relief by a judgment or under a stipulation agreement, interest shall be allowed at an annual rate established under section 6621 of the Internal Revenue Code of 1986. Such interest shall be calculated from the date of the filing of the summons in such action to the date of the refund.

(Added Pub.L. 96–417, Title III, § 301, Oct. 10, 1980, 94 Stat. 1738, and amended Pub.L. 99–514, § 2, Oct. 22, 1986, 100 Stat. 2095.)

HISTORICAL AND STATUTORY NOTES

References in Text

Section 515 of the Tariff Act of 1930, referred to in text, is classified to section 1515 of Title 19, Customs Duties.

Section 6621 of the Internal Revenue Code of 1986, referred to in the text, refers to section 6621 of Title 26, Internal Revenue Code.

Effective and Applicability Provisions

1980 Acts. Section applicable with respect to civil actions commenced on or after Nov. 1, 1980, see section 701(b)(1)(B) of Pub.L. 96–417, as amended, set out as a note under section 251 of this title.

§ 2645. Decisions

(a) A final decision of the Court of International Trade in a contested civil action or a decision granting or refusing a preliminary injunction shall be supported by—

(1) a statement of findings of fact and conclusions of law; or

(2) an opinion stating the reasons and facts upon which the decision is based.

(b) After the Court of International Trade has rendered a judgment, the court may, upon the motion of a party or upon its own motion, amend its findings or make additional findings and may amend the decision and judgment accordingly. A motion of a party or the court shall be made not later than thirty days after the date of entry of the judgment.

(c) A decision of the Court of International Trade is final and conclusive, unless a retrial or rehearing is granted pursuant to section 2646 of this title or an appeal is taken to the Court of Appeals for the Federal Circuit by filing a notice of appeal with the clerk of the Court of International Trade within the time and in the manner prescribed for appeals to United States courts of appeals from the United States district courts.

(Added Pub.L. 96–417, Title III, § 301, Oct. 10, 1980, 94 Stat. 1738, and amended Pub.L. 97–164, Title I, § 141, Apr. 2, 1982, 96 Stat. 45.)

HISTORICAL AND STATUTORY NOTES

Effective and Applicability Provisions

1982 Acts. Amendment by Pub.L. 97–164 effective Oct. 1, 1982, see section 402 of Pub.L. 97–164, set out as a note under section 171 of this title.

1980 Acts. Section effective on Nov. 1, 1980 and applicable with respect to civil actions pending on or commenced on or after such date, see section 701(a) of Pub.L. 96–417, as amended, set out as a note under section 251 of this title.

§ 2646. Retrial or rehearing

After the Court of International Trade has rendered a judgment or order, the court may, upon the motion of a party or upon its own motion, grant a retrial or rehearing, as the case may be. A motion of a party or the court shall be made not later than thirty days after the date of entry of the judgment or order.

(Added Pub.L. 96–417, Title III, § 301, Oct. 10, 1980, 94 Stat. 1739.)

HISTORICAL AND STATUTORY NOTES

Effective and Applicability Provisions

1980 Acts. Section effective on Nov. 1, 1980 and applicable with respect to civil actions pending on or commenced on or after such date, see section 701(a) of Pub.L. 96–417, as amended, set out as a note under section 251 of this title.

[§ 2647. Repealed. Pub.L. 98–620, Title IV, § 402(29)(G), Nov. 8, 1984, 98 Stat. 3359]

HISTORICAL AND STATUTORY NOTES

Section, added Pub.L. 96–417, Title III, § 301, Oct. 10, 1980, 94 Stat. 1739, and amended Pub.L. 98–573, Title VI, § 623(b)(2), Oct. 30, 1984, 98 Stat. 3041, related to precedence of cases.

Effective Date of Repeal

Repeal not to apply to cases pending on Nov. 8, 1984, see section 403 of Pub.L. 98–620, set out as a note under section 1657 of this title.

CHAPTER 171—TORT CLAIMS PROCEDURE

Sec.
2671. Definitions.
2672. Administrative adjustment of claims.
2673. Reports to Congress.
2674. Liability of United States.
2675. Disposition by federal agency as prerequisite; evidence.
2676. Judgment as bar.
2677. Compromise.
2678. Attorney fees; penalty.
2679. Exclusiveness of remedy.
2680. Exceptions.

§ 2671. Definitions

As used in this chapter and sections 1346(b) and 2401(b) of this title, the term "Federal agency" includes the executive departments, the judicial and legislative branches, the military departments, independent establishments of the United States, and corporations primarily acting as instrumentalities or agencies of the United States, but does not include any contractor with the United States.

"Employee of the government" includes (1) officers or employees of any federal agency, members of the military or naval forces of the United States, members of the National Guard while engaged in training or duty under section 115, 316, 502, 503, 504, or 505 of title 32, and persons acting on behalf of a federal agency in an official capacity, temporarily or permanently in the service of the United States, whether with or without compensation, and (2) any officer or employee of a Federal public defender organization, except when such officer or employee performs professional services in the course of providing representation under section 3006A of title 18.

"Acting within the scope of his office or employment", in the case of a member of the military or naval forces of the United States or a member of the National Guard as defined in section 101(3) of title 32, means acting in line of duty.

(June 25, 1948, c. 646, 62 Stat. 982; May 24, 1949, c. 139, § 124, 63 Stat. 106; July 18, 1966, Pub.L. 89–506, § 8, 80 Stat. 307; Dec. 29, 1981, Pub.L. 97–124, § 1, 95 Stat. 1666; Nov. 18, 1988, Pub.L. 100–694, § 3, 102 Stat. 4564; Oct. 30, 2000, Pub.L. 106–398, § 1 [Div. A, Title VI, § 665(b)], 114 Stat. 1654, 1654A–169; Nov. 13, 2000, Pub.L. 106–518, Title IV, § 401, 114 Stat. 2421.)

HISTORICAL AND STATUTORY NOTES

Effective and Applicability Provisions

2000 Acts. Pub.L. 106–398, § 1 [Div. A, Title VI, § 665(c)(2)], Oct. 30, 2000, 114 Stat. 1654, 1654A–169, provided that: "The amendment made by subsection (b) [amending this section] shall apply with respect to acts and omissions occurring before, on, or after the date of the enactment of this Act [Oct. 30, 2000]."

1988 Acts. Amendment by Pub.L 100–694 effective Nov. 18, 1988, and applicable to all claims, civil actions, and proceedings pending on, or filed on or after, Nov. 18, 1988, see section 8 of Pub.L. 100–694, set out as a note under section 2679 of this title.

1981 Acts. Amendment by Pub.L. 97–124 applicable only with respect to claims arising on or after Dec. 29, 1981, see section 4 of Pub.L. 97–124, set out as a note under section 1089 of Title 10, Armed Forces.

1966 Acts. Amendment of section by Pub.L. 89–506 applicable to claims accruing six months or more after July 18, 1966, see section 10 of Pub.L. 89–506, set out as a note under section 2672 of this title.

Severability of Provisions

Section 7 of Pub.L. 100–694 provided that: "If any provision of this Act or the amendments made by this Act [enacting section 831c–2 of Title 16, Conservation, amending sections 2671, 2674, and 2679 of this title, and enacting provisions set out as notes under sections 1, 2671, and 2679 of this title] or the application of the provision to any person or circumstance is held invalid, the remainder of this Act and such amendments and the application of the provision to any other person or circumstance shall not be affected by that invalidation."

Law Enforcement Officer Acting Within Scope of Office or Employment

Pub.L. 105–277, § 101(h) [Title VI, § 627], 112 Stat. 2681–519, as amended Pub.L. 106–58, Title VI, § 623, Sept. 29, 1999, 113 Stat. 471, provided that:

"**(a) Definitions.**—In this section—

"(1) the term 'crime of violence' has the meaning given that term in section 16 of title 18, United States Code; and

"(2) the term 'law enforcement officer' means any employee described in subparagraph (A), (B), or (C) of section 8401(17) of title 5, United States Code; and any special in the Diplomatic Security Service of the Department of State.

"**(b) Rules of construction.**—Effective on the date of enactment of this Act [Oct. 21, 1998] and thereafter, and notwithstanding any other provision of law, for purposes of chapter 171 of title 28, United States Code, or any other provision of law relating to tort liability, a law enforcement officer shall be construed to be acting within the scope of his or her office or employment, if the officer takes reasonable action, including the use of force, to—

"(1) protect an individual in the presence of the officer from a crime of violence;

"(2) provide immediate assistance to an individual who has suffered or who is threatened with bodily harm; or

"(3) prevent the escape of any individual who the officer reasonably believes to have committed in the presence of the officer a crime of violence."

Congressional Findings and Purposes

Section 2 of Pub.L. 100–694 provided that:

"**(a) Findings.**—the Congress finds and declares the following:

"(1) For more than 40 years the Federal Tort Claims Act [28 U.S.C.A. §§ 1346(b), 2671 et seq.] has been the legal mechanism for compensating persons injured by negligent or wrongful acts of Federal employees committed within the scope of their employment.

"(2) The United States, through the Federal Tort Claims Act, is responsible to injured persons for the common law torts of its employees in the same manner in which the common law historically has recognized the responsibility of an employer for torts committed by its employees within the scope of their employment.

"(3) Because Federal employees for many years have been protected from personal common law tort liability by a broad based immunity, the Federal Tort Claims Act has served as the sole means for compensating persons injured by the tortious conduct of Federal employees.

"(4) Recent judicial decisions, and particularly the decision of the United States Supreme Court in Westfall v. Erwin [1988, 108 S.Ct. 580], have seriously eroded the common law tort immunity previously available to Federal employees.

"(5) This erosion of immunity of Federal employees from common law tort liability has created an immediate crisis involving the prospect of personal liability and the threat of protracted personal tort litigation for the entire Federal workforce.

"(6) The prospect of such liability will seriously undermine the morale and well being of Federal employees, impede the ability of agencies to carry out their missions, and diminish the vitality of the Federal Tort Claims Act as the proper remedy for Federal employee torts.

"(7) In its opinion in Westfall v. Erwin [1988, 108 S.Ct. 580], the Supreme Court indicated that the Congress is in the best position to determine the extent to which Federal employees should be personally liable for common law torts, and that legislative consideration of this matter would be useful.

"(b) **Purpose.**—It is the purpose of this Act [enacting section 831c–2 of Title 16, Conservation, amending sections 2671, 2674, and 2679 of this title, and enacting provisions set out as notes under sections 1, 2671, and 2679 of this title] to protect Federal employees from personal liability for common law torts committed within the scope of their employment, while providing persons injured by the common law torts of Federal employees with an appropriate remedy against the United States."

§ 2672. Administrative adjustment of claims

The head of each Federal agency or his designee, in accordance with regulations prescribed by the Attorney General, may consider, ascertain, adjust, determine, compromise, and settle any claim for money damages against the United States for injury or loss of property or personal injury or death caused by the negligent or wrongful act or omission of any employee of the agency while acting within the scope of his office or employment, under circumstances where the United States, if a private person, would be liable to the claimant in accordance with the law of the place where the act or omission occurred: *Provided*, That any award, compromise, or settlement in excess of $25,000 shall be effected only with the prior written approval of the Attorney General or his designee. Notwithstanding the proviso contained in the preceding sentence, any award, compromise, or settlement may be effected without the prior written approval of the Attorney General or his or her designee, to the extent that the Attorney General delegates to the head of the agency the authority to make such award, compromise, or settlement. Such delegations may not exceed the authority delegated by the Attorney General to the United States attorneys to settle claims for money damages against the United States. Each Federal agency may use arbitration, or other alternative means of dispute resolution under the provisions of subchapter IV of chapter 5 of title 5, to settle any tort claim against the United States, to the extent of the agency's authority to award, compromise, or settle such claim without the prior written approval of the Attorney General or his or her designee.

Subject to the provisions of this title relating to civil actions on tort claims against the United States, any such award, compromise, settlement, or determination shall be final and conclusive on all officers of the Government, except when procured by means of fraud.

Any award, compromise, or settlement in an amount of $2,500 or less made pursuant to this section shall be paid by the head of the Federal agency concerned out of appropriations available to that agency. Payment of any award, compromise, or settlement in an amount in excess of $2,500 made pursuant to this section or made by the Attorney General in any amount pursuant to section 2677 of this title shall be paid in a manner similar to judgments and compromises in like causes and appropriations or funds available for the payment of such judgments and compromises are hereby made available for the payment of awards, compromises, or settlements under this chapter.

The acceptance by the claimant of any such award, compromise, or settlement shall be final and conclusive on the claimant, and shall constitute a complete release of any claim against the United States and against the employee of the government whose act or omission gave rise to the claim, by reason of the same subject matter.

(June 25, 1948, c. 646, 62 Stat. 983; Apr. 25, 1949, c. 92, § 2(b), 63 Stat. 62; May 24, 1949, c. 139, § 125, 63 Stat. 106; Sept. 23, 1950, c. 1010, § 9, 64 Stat. 987; Sept. 8, 1959, Pub.L. 86–238, § 1(1), 73 Stat. 471; July 18, 1966, Pub.L. 89–506, §§ 1, 9(a), 80 Stat. 306, 308; Nov. 15, 1990, Pub.L. 101–552, § 8(a), 104 Stat. 2746.)

HISTORICAL AND STATUTORY NOTES

Effective and Applicability Provisions

1990 Acts. The termination of amendments by Pub.L. 101–552 and authority to use dispute resolution proceedings on Oct. 1, 1995, provided by section 11 of Pub.L. 101–552, set out as a note under section 571 of Title 5, Government Organization and Employees, was repealed by section 9 of Pub.L. 104–320.

1966 Acts. Section 10 of Pub.L. 89–506 provided that: "This Act [amending this section and sections 2401(b), 2671, 2675, 2677, 2678, and 2679(b) of this title, section 724a of former Title 31, Money and Finance, and section 4116(a) of Title 38, Veteran's Benefits (see Section 7316 of Title 38)] shall apply to claims accruing six months or more after the date of its enactment [July 18, 1966]."

Laws Unaffected

Section 424(b) of Act Aug. 2, 1946, c. 753, Title IV, 60 Stat. 847, provided that: "Nothing contained herein shall be deemed to repeal any provision of law authorizing any Federal agency to consider, ascertain, adjust, settle, determine, or pay any claim on account of damage to or loss of property or on account of personal injury or death, in cases in which such damage, loss, injury, or death was not caused by any negligent or wrongful act or omission of an employee of the Government while acting within the scope of his office or employment, or any other claim not cognizable under part 2 of this title."

§ 2673. Reports to Congress

The head of each federal agency shall report annually to Congress all claims paid by it under section 2672 of this title, stating the name of each claimant, the amount claimed, the amount awarded, and a brief description of the claim.

(June 25, 1948, c. 646, 62 Stat. 983.)

Repeal

Section 1(1) of Pub.L. 89–348, Nov. 8, 1965, 79 Stat. 1310, repealed the requirement that an annual report to Congress be made of the administrative adjustment of tort claims of $2,500 or less, stating the name of each claimant, the amount claimed, the amount awarded, and a brief description of the claim.

§ 2674. Liability of United States

The United States shall be liable, respecting the provisions of this title relating to tort claims, in the same manner and to the same extent as a private individual under like circumstances, but shall not be liable for interest prior to judgment or for punitive damages.

If, however, in any case wherein death was caused, the law of the place where the act or omission complained of occurred provides, or has been construed to provide, for damages only punitive in nature, the United States shall be liable for actual or compensatory damages, measured by the pecuniary injuries resulting from such death to the persons respectively, for whose benefit the action was brought, in lieu thereof.

With respect to any claim under this chapter, the United States shall be entitled to assert any defense based upon judicial or legislative immunity which otherwise would have been available to the employee of the United States whose act or omission gave rise to the claim, as well as any other defenses to which the United States is entitled.

With respect to any claim to which this section applies, the Tennessee Valley Authority shall be entitled to assert any defense which otherwise would have been available to the employee based upon judicial or legislative immunity, which otherwise would have been available to the employee of the Tennessee Valley Authority whose act or omission gave rise to the claim as well as any other defenses to which the Tennessee Valley Authority is entitled under this chapter.

(June 25, 1948, c. 646, 62 Stat. 983; Nov. 18, 1988, Pub.L. 100–694, §§ 4, 9(c), 102 Stat. 4564, 4567.)

HISTORICAL AND STATUTORY NOTES

Effective and Applicability Provisions

1988 Acts. Amendment by Pub.L. 100–694 effective Nov. 18, 1988, and applicable to all claims, civil actions, and proceedings pending on, or filed on or after, Nov. 18, 1988, see section 8 of Pub.L. 100–694 set out as a note under section 2679 of this title.

§ 2675. Disposition by federal agency as prerequisite; evidence

(a) An action shall not be instituted upon a claim against the United States for money damages for injury or loss of property or personal injury or death caused by the negligent or wrongful act or omission of any employee of the Government while acting within the scope of his office or employment, unless the claimant shall have first presented the claim to the appropriate Federal agency and his claim shall have been finally denied by the agency in writing and sent by certified or registered mail. The failure of an agency to make final disposition of a claim within six months after it is filed shall, at the option of the claimant any time thereafter, be deemed a final denial of the claim for purposes of this section. The provisions of this subsection shall not apply to such claims as may be asserted under the Federal Rules of Civil Procedure by third party complaint, cross-claim, or counterclaim.

(b) Action under this section shall not be instituted for any sum in excess of the amount of the claim presented to the federal agency, except where the increased amount is based upon newly discovered evidence not reasonably discoverable at the time of presenting the claim to the federal agency, or upon allegation and proof of intervening facts, relating to the amount of the claim.

(c) Disposition of any claim by the Attorney General or other head of a federal agency shall not be competent evidence of liability or amount of damages.

(June 25, 1948, c. 646, 62 Stat. 983; May 24, 1949, c. 139, § 126, 63 Stat. 107; July 18, 1966, Pub.L. 89–506, § 2, 80 Stat. 306.)

HISTORICAL AND STATUTORY NOTES

References in Text

The Federal Rules of Civil Procedure, referred to in subsec. (a), are set out in the Appendix to this title.

Effective and Applicability Provisions

1966 Acts. Amendment of section by Pub.L. 89–506 applicable to claims accruing six months or more after July 18, 1966, see section 10 of Pub.L. 89–506, set out as a note under section 2672 of this title.

§ 2676. Judgment as bar

The judgment in an action under section 1346(b) of this title shall constitute a complete bar to any action by the claimant, by reason of the same subject matter, against the employee of the government whose act or omission gave rise to the claim.

(June 25, 1948, c. 646, 62 Stat. 984.)

§ 2677. Compromise

The Attorney General or his designee may arbitrate, compromise, or settle any claim cognizable under section 1346(b) of this title, after the commencement of an action thereon.

(June 25, 1948, c. 646, 62 Stat. 984; July 18, 1966, Pub.L. 89–506, § 3, 80 Stat. 307.)

HISTORICAL AND STATUTORY NOTES

Effective and Applicability Provisions

1966 Acts. Amendment of section by Pub.L. 89–506 applicable to claims accruing six months or more after July 18, 1966, see section 10 of Pub.L. 89–506, set out as a note under section 2672 of this title.

§ 2678. Attorney fees; penalty

No attorney shall charge, demand, receive, or collect for services rendered, fees in excess of 25 per centum of any judgment rendered pursuant to section 1346(b) of this title or any settlement made pursuant to section 2677 of this title, or in excess of 20 per centum of any award, compromise, or settlement made pursuant to section 2672 of this title.

Any attorney who charges, demands, receives, or collects for services rendered in connection with such claim any amount in excess of that allowed under this section, if recovery be had, shall be fined not more than $2,000 or imprisoned not more than one year, or both.

(June 25, 1948, c. 646, 62 Stat. 984; July 18, 1966, Pub.L. 89–506, § 4, 80 Stat. 307.)

HISTORICAL AND STATUTORY NOTES

Effective and Applicability Provisions

1966 Acts. Amendment of section by Pub.L. 89–506 applicable to claims accruing six months or more after July 18, 1966, see section 10 of Pub.L. 89–506, set out as a note under section 2672 of this title.

§ 2679. Exclusiveness of remedy

(a) The authority of any federal agency to sue and be sued in its own name shall not be construed to authorize suits against such federal agency on claims which are cognizable under section 1346(b) of this title, and the remedies provided by this title in such cases shall be exclusive.

(b)(1) The remedy against the United States provided by sections 1346(b) and 2672 of this title for injury or loss of property, or personal injury or death arising or resulting from the negligent or wrongful act or omission of any employee of the Government while acting within the scope of his office or employment is exclusive of any other civil action or proceeding for money damages by reason of the same subject matter against the employee whose act or omission gave rise to the claim or against the estate of such employee. Any other civil action or proceeding for money damages arising out of or relating to the same subject matter against the employee or the employee's estate is precluded without regard to when the act or omission occurred.

(2) Paragraph (1) does not extend or apply to a civil action against an employee of the Government—

(A) which is brought for a violation of the Constitution of the United States, or

(B) which is brought for a violation of a statute of the United States under which such action against an individual is otherwise authorized.

(c) The Attorney General shall defend any civil action or proceeding brought in any court against any employee of the Government or his estate for any such damage or injury. The employee against whom such civil action or proceeding is brought shall deliver within such time after date of service or knowledge of service as determined by the Attorney General, all process served upon him or an attested true copy thereof to his immediate superior or to whomever was designated by the head of his department to receive such papers and such person shall promptly furnish copies of the pleadings and process therein to the United States attorney for the district embracing the place wherein the proceeding is brought, to the Attorney General, and to the head of his employing Federal agency.

(d)(1) Upon certification by the Attorney General that the defendant employee was acting within the scope of his office or employment at the time of the incident out of which the claim arose, any civil action or proceeding commenced upon such claim in a United States district court shall be deemed an action against the United States under the provisions of this title and all references thereto, and the United States shall be substituted as the party defendant.

(2) Upon certification by the Attorney General that the defendant employee was acting within the scope of his office or employment at the time of the incident out of which the claim arose, any civil action or proceeding commenced upon such claim in a State court shall be removed without bond at any time before trial by the Attorney General to the district court of the United States for the district and division embracing the place in which the action or proceeding is pending. Such action or proceeding shall be deemed to be an action or proceeding brought against the United States under the provisions of this title and all references thereto, and the United States shall be substituted as the party defendant. This certification of the Attorney General shall conclusively establish scope of office or employment for purposes of removal.

(3) In the event that the Attorney General has refused to certify scope of office or employment under this section, the employee may at any time before trial petition the court to find and certify that the employee was acting within the scope of his office or employment. Upon such certification by the court, such action or proceeding shall be deemed to be an action or proceeding brought against the United States under the provisions of this title and all references thereto, and the United States shall be substituted as the party defendant. A copy of the petition shall be served upon the United States in accordance with the provisions of Rule 4(d)(4) of the Federal Rules of Civil Procedure. In the event the petition is filed in a civil action or proceeding pending in a State court, the action or proceeding may be removed without bond by the Attorney General to the district court of the United States for the district and division embracing the place in which it is pending. If, in considering the petition, the district court determines that the employee was not acting within the scope of his office or employment, the action or proceeding shall be remanded to the State court.

(4) Upon certification, any action or proceeding subject to paragraph (1), (2), or (3) shall proceed in the same manner as any action against the United States filed pursuant to section 1346(b) of this title and shall be subject to the limitations and exceptions applicable to those actions.

(5) Whenever an action or proceeding in which the United States is substituted as the party defendant under this subsection is dismissed for failure first to present a claim pursuant to section 2675(a) of this title, such a claim shall be deemed to be timely presented under section 2401(b) of this title if—

(A) the claim would have been timely had it been filed on the date the underlying civil action was commenced, and

(B) the claim is presented to the appropriate Federal agency within 60 days after dismissal of the civil action.

(e) The Attorney General may compromise or settle any claim asserted in such civil action or proceeding in the manner provided in section 2677, and with the same effect.

(June 25, 1948, c. 646, 62 Stat. 984; Sept. 21, 1961, Pub.L. 87–258, § 1, 75 Stat. 539; July 18, 1966, Pub.L. 89–506, § 5(a), 80 Stat. 307; Nov. 18, 1988, Pub.L. 100–694, §§ 5, 6, 102 Stat. 4564.)

HISTORICAL AND STATUTORY NOTES

References in Text

The Federal Rules of Civil Procedures referred to in subsec. (d)(3), are set out in this title.

Effective and Applicability Provisions

1988 Acts. Section 8 of Pub.L. 100–694 provided that:

"**(a) General rule.**—This Act and the amendments made by this Act [enacting section 831c–2 of Title 16, Conservation; amending sections 2671, 2674, and 2679(b), (d) of this title, and enacting provisions set out as notes under this section and sections 1 and 2671 of this title] shall take effect on the date of the enactment of this Act [Nov. 18, 1988].

"**(b) Applicability to proceedings.**—The amendments made by this Act [amending sections 2671, 2674, and 2679 of this title] shall apply to all claims, civil actions, and proceedings pending on, or filed on or after, the date of the enactment of this Act [Nov. 18, 1988].

"**(c) Pending State proceedings.**—With respect to any civil action or proceeding pending in a State court to which the amendments made by this Act apply, and as to which the period for removal under section 2679(d) of title 28, United States Code [subsec. (d) of this section] (as amended by section 6 of this Act), has expired, the Attorney General shall have 60 days after the date of the enactment of this Act [Nov. 18, 1988] during which to seek removal under such section 2679(d) [subsec. (d) of this section].

"**(d) Claims accruing before enactment.**—With respect to any civil action or proceeding to which the amendments made by this Act apply in which the claim accrued before the date of the enactment of this Act [Nov. 18, 1988], the period during which the claim shall be deemed to be timely presented under section 2679(d)(5) of title 28, United States Code [subsec. (d)(5) of this section] (as amended by section 6 of this Act) shall be that period within which the claim could have been timely filed under applicable State law, but in no event shall such period exceed two years from the date of the enactment of this Act [Nov. 18, 1988]."

1966 Acts. Amendment of section by Pub.L. 89–506 applicable to claims accruing six months or more after July 18, 1966, see section 10 of Pub.L. 89–506, set out as a note under section 2672 of this title.

1961 Acts. Section 2 of Pub.L. 87–258 provided that: "The amendments made by this Act [adding subsecs. (b)–(e) of this section] shall be deemed to be in effect six months after the enactment hereof [Sept. 21, 1961] but any rights or liabilities then existing shall not be affected."

§ 2680. Exceptions

The provisions of this chapter and section 1346(b) of this title shall not apply to—

(a) Any claim based upon an act or omission of an employee of the Government, exercising due care, in the execution of a statute or regulation, whether or not such statute or regulation be valid, or based upon the exercise or performance or the failure to exercise or perform a discretionary function or duty on the part of a federal agency or an employee of the Government, whether or not the discretion involved be abused.

(b) Any claim arising out of the loss, miscarriage, or negligent transmission of letters or postal matter.

(c) Any claim arising in respect of the assessment or collection of any tax or customs duty, or the detention of any goods, merchandise, or other property by any officer of customs or excise or any other law enforcement officer, except that the provisions of this chapter and section 1346(b) of this title apply to any claim based on injury or loss of goods, merchandise, or other property, while in the possession of any officer of customs or excise or any other law enforcement officer, if—

(1) the property was seized for the purpose of forfeiture under any provision of Federal law providing for the forfeiture of property other than as a sentence imposed upon conviction of a criminal offense;

(2) the interest of the claimant was not forfeited;

(3) the interest of the claimant was not remitted or mitigated (if the property was subject to forfeiture); and

(4) the claimant was not convicted of a crime for which the interest of the claimant in the property was subject to forfeiture under a Federal criminal forfeiture law..[1]

(d) Any claim for which a remedy is provided by chapter 309 or 311 of title 46 relating to claims or suits in admiralty against the United States.

(e) Any claim arising out of an act or omission of any employee of the Government in administering the provisions of sections 1–31 of Title 50, Appendix.

(f) Any claim for damages caused by the imposition or establishment of a quarantine by the United States.

[(g) Repealed. Sept. 26, 1950, c. 1049, § 13(5), 64 Stat. 1043.]

(h) Any claim arising out of assault, battery, false imprisonment, false arrest, malicious prosecution, abuse of process, libel, slander, misrepresentation, deceit, or interference with contract rights: *Provided*, That, with regard to acts or omissions of investigative or law enforcement officers of the United States Government, the provisions of this chapter and section 1346(b) of this title shall apply to any claim arising, on or after the date of the enactment of this proviso, out of assault, battery, false imprisonment, false arrest, abuse of process, or malicious prosecution. For the purpose of this subsection, "investigative or law enforcement officer" means any officer of the United States who is empowered by law to execute searches, to seize evidence, or to make arrests for violations of Federal law.

(i) Any claim for damages caused by the fiscal operations of the Treasury or by the regulation of the monetary system.

(j) Any claim arising out of the combatant activities of the military or naval forces, or the Coast Guard, during time of war.

(k) Any claim arising in a foreign country.

(*l*) Any claim arising from the activities of the Tennessee Valley Authority.

(m) Any claim arising from the activities of the Panama Canal Company.

(n) Any claim arising from the activities of a Federal land bank, a Federal intermediate credit bank, or a bank for cooperatives.

(June 25, 1948, c. 646, 62 Stat. 984; July 16, 1949, c. 340, 63 Stat. 444; Sept. 26, 1950, c. 1049, §§ 2(a)(2), 13(5), 64 Stat. 1038, 1043; Aug. 18, 1959, Pub.L. 86–168, Title II, § 202(b), 73 Stat. 389; Mar. 16, 1974, Pub.L. 93–253, § 2, 88 Stat. 50; Apr. 25, 2000, Pub.L. 106–185, § 3(a), 114 Stat. 211; Oct. 6, 2006, Pub.L. 109–304, § 17(f)(4), 120 Stat. 1708.)

[1] So in original. Second period probably should not appear.

HISTORICAL AND STATUTORY NOTES

References in Text

Chapter 309 or 311 of title 46, referred to in subsec. (d), are Suits in Admiralty Against the United States, 46 U.S.C.A. § 30901 et seq., and Commercial Instruments and Maritime Liens, 46 U.S.C.A. § 31101 et seq.

Sections 1–31 of Title 50, Appendix, referred to in subsec. (e), was in the original source of this section (section 943 [of Title 28, which was section 421] of Act Aug. 2, 1946) a reference to the Trading with the Enemy Act, as amended. The Trading with the Enemy Act is now comprised of sections 1 to 43, which are classified to sections 1 to 6, 7 to 39, and 41 to 44 of Title 50, Appendix, War and National Defense.

Date of the enactment of this proviso, referred to in subsec. (h), means Mar. 16, 1974, the date on which Pub.L. 93–253, enacting the proviso, was approved.

Panama Canal Company, referred to in subsec. (m), deemed to refer to Panama Canal Commission, see section 3602(b)(5) of Title 22, Foreign Relations and Intercourse.

Effective and Applicability Provisions

2000 Acts. Amendments by Pub.L. 106–185, applicable to any forfeiture proceeding commenced on or after the date that is 120 days after April 25, 2000, see section 21 of Pub.L. 106–185, set out as a note under section 1324 of Title 8.

1959 Acts. Amendment by Pub.L. 86–168 effective Jan. 1, 1960, pursuant to section 203(c) of Pub.L. 86–168.

1950 Acts. Section 14 of Act Sept. 26, 1950, provided that the repeal of subsec. (g) and amendment of subsec. (m) of this section by such Act shall take effect upon the effective date of the transfer to the Panama Canal Company, pursuant to the provisions of section 256 of the Canal Zone Code, as added by section 10 of such Act, of the Panama Canal together with the facilities and appurtenances related thereto.

Transfer of Functions

The Coast Guard was transferred to the Department of Transportation and all functions, powers, and duties, relating to the Coast Guard, of the Secretary of the Treasury and of all other offices and officers of the Department of the Treasury were transferred to the Secretary of Transportation by Pub.L. 89–670, § 6(b)(1), Oct. 15, 1966, 80 Stat. 938. Section 6(b)(2) of Pub.L. 89–670, however, provided that notwithstanding such transfer of functions, the Coast Guard shall operate as part of the Navy in time of war or when the President directs as provided in section 3 of Title 14, Coast Guard. See section 108 of Title 49, Transportation.

For transfer of certain functions relating to claims and litigation, insofar as they pertain to the Air Force, from the Secretary of the Army to the Secretary of the Air Force, see Secretary of Defense Transfer Order No. 34 [§ 1a(2)(4)], eff. July 1, 1949.

Applicability of Subsec. (j)

Section 1(a)(32) of Joint Res. July 3, 1952, c. 570, 66 Stat. 333, as amended by Joint Res. Mar. 31, 1953, c. 13, § 1, 67 Stat. 18 and Joint Res. June 30, 1953, c. 172, 67 Stat. 132, provided that subsec. (j) of this section should continue in force until six months after the termination of the national emergency proclaimed by the President on Dec. 16, 1950, by 1950 Proc. No. 2914, 15 F.R. 9029, set out as a note preceding section 1 of the Appendix to Title 50, War and National Defense, or such earlier date or dates as may be provided for by Congress, but in no event beyond Aug. 1, 1953. Section 7 of Joint Res. July 3, 1952, provided that it should become effective June 16, 1952.

Section 6 of Joint Res. July 3, 1952, c. 570, § 6, 66 Stat. 334, repealed Joint Res. Apr. 14, 1952, c. 204, 66 Stat. 54 as amended by Joint Res. May 28, 1952, c. 339, 66 Stat. 96; Joint Res. June 14, 1952, c. 437, 66 Stat. 137; Joint Res. June 30, 1952, c. 526, 66 Stat. 296, which continued provisions of subsection (j) of this section (see note above) until July 3, 1952. This repeal was made effective June 16, 1952, by section 7 of Joint Res. July 3, 1952.

Northern Mariana Islands as Foreign Country With Respect to Claims Accruing No More than Two Years Prior to Oct. 19, 1982

Pub.L. 97–357, Title II, § 204, Oct. 19, 1982, 96 Stat. 1708, provided: "That the Northern Mariana Islands shall not be considered a foreign country for purposes of subsection (k) of section 2680 of Title 28, United States Code [subsec. (k) of this section], with respect to claims which accrued no more than two years prior to the effective date of this Act [Oct. 19, 1982]."

Termination of National Emergency

Declaration of national emergency in effect on Sept. 14, 1976, was terminated two years from that date by Section 1601 of Title 50, War and National Defense.

CHAPTER 173—ATTACHMENT IN POSTAL SUITS

Sec.
2710. Right of attachment.
2711. Application for warrant.
2712. Issue of warrant.
2713. Trial of ownership of property.
2714. Investment of proceeds of attached property.
2715. Publication.
2716. Personal notice.
2717. Discharge.
2718. Interest on balances due department.

§ 2710. Right of attachment

(a) Where debts are due from a defaulting or delinquent postmaster, contractor, or other officer, agent or employee of the Post Office Department, a warrant of attachment may issue against all property and legal and equitable rights belonging to him, and his sureties, or either of them, where he—

(1) is a nonresident of the district where he was appointed, or has departed from that district for the purpose of permanently residing outside thereof, or of avoiding the service of civil process; and

(2) has conveyed away, or is about to convey away any of his property, or has removed or is about to remove the same from the district wherein it is situated, with intent to defraud the United States.

(b) When the property has been removed, the marshal of the district into which it has been removed, upon receipt of certified copies of the warrant, may seize the property and convey it to a convenient place within the jurisdiction of the court which issued the warrant. Alias warrants may be issued upon due application. The warrant first issued remains valid until the return day thereof.

(Added Pub.L. 86–682, § 9, Sept. 2, 1960, 74 Stat. 706.)

HISTORICAL AND STATUTORY NOTES

Codifications

Section was derived from R.S. § 924, which was originally classified to section 737 of former Title 28. Following the general revision and enactment of Title 28 by Act June 25, 1948, R.S. § 924 was reclassified to section 837 of Title 39. R.S. § 924 was repealed by section 12(c) of Pub.L. 86–682 (section 1 of which revised and enacted Title 39), and reenacted by section 9 thereof as section 2710 of Title 28, Judiciary and Judicial Procedure.

Effective and Applicability Provisions

1960 Acts. Section 11 of Pub.L. 86–682, Sept. 2, 1960, 74 Stat. 708, provided that this chapter shall be effective on Sept. 1, 1960.

Change of Name

References to the Post Office Department, the Postal Service, the Postal Field Service, the Field Postal Service, or the Departmental Service or the Departmental Headquarters of the Post Office Department to be considered references to the United States Postal Service pursuant to Pub.L. 91–375, § 6(*o*), Aug. 12, 1970, 84 Stat. 783, set out as a Cross Reference note preceding section 101 of Title 39, Postal Service.

§ 2711. Application for warrant

A United States attorney or assistant United States attorney or a person authorized by the Attorney General—

(1) upon his own affidavit or that of another credible person, stating the existence of either of the grounds of attachments enumerated in section 2710 of this title and

(2) upon production of legal evidence of the debt

may apply for a warrant of attachment to a judge, or, in his absence, to the clerk of any court of the United States having original jurisdiction of the cause of action.

(Added Pub.L. 86–682, § 9, Sept. 2, 1960, 74 Stat. 707.)

HISTORICAL AND STATUTORY NOTES

Codifications

Section was derived from R.S. § 925, which was originally classified to section 738 of former Title 28. Following the general revision and enactment of Title 28 by Act June 25, 1948, R.S. § 925 was reclassified to section 838 of Title 39. R.S. § 925 was repealed by section 12(c) of Pub.L. 86–682 (section 1 of which revised and enacted Title 39), and reenacted by section 9 thereof as section 2711 of Title 28, Judiciary and Judicial Procedure.

§ 2712. Issue of warrant

Upon an order of a judge of a court, or, in his absence and upon the clerk's own initiative, the clerk shall issue a warrant for the attachment of the property belonging to the person specified in the affidavit. The marshal shall execute the warrant forthwith and take the property attached, if personal, in his custody, subject to the interlocutory or final orders of the court.

(Added Pub.L. 86–682, § 9, Sept. 2, 1960, 74 Stat. 707.)

HISTORICAL AND STATUTORY NOTES

Codifications

Section was derived from R.S. § 926, which was originally classified to section 739 of former Title 28. Following the general revision and enactment of Title 28 by Act June 25, 1948, R.S. § 926 was reclassified to section 839 of Title 39. R.S. § 926 was repealed by section 12(c) of Pub.L. 86–682 (section 1 of which revised and enacted Title 39), and reenacted by section 9 thereof as section 2712 of Title 28. Judiciary and Judicial Procedure.

§ 2713. Trial of ownership of property

Not later than twenty days before the return day of a warrant issued under section 2712 of this title, the party whose property is attached, on notice to the United States Attorney, may file a plea in abatement, denying the allegations of the affidavit, or denying ownership in the defendant of the property attached. The court, upon application of either party, shall order a trial by jury of the issues. Where the parties, by consent, waive a trial by jury, the court shall decide the issues. A party claiming ownership of the property attached and seeking its return is limited to the remedy afforded by this section, but his right to an action of trespass, or other action for damages, is not impaired.

(Added Pub.L. 86–682, § 9, Sept. 2, 1960, 74 Stat. 707.)

HISTORICAL AND STATUTORY NOTES

Codifications

Section was derived from R.S. § 927, which was originally classified to section 740 of former Title 28. Following the general revision and enactment of Title 28 by Act June 25, 1948, R.S. § 927 was reclassified to section 840 of Title 39. R.S. § 927 was repealed by section 12(c) of Pub.L. 86–682 (section 1 of which revised and enacted Title 39), and reenacted by section 9 thereof as section 2713 of Title 28, Judiciary and Judicial Procedure.

§ 2714. Investment of proceeds of attached property

When the property attached is sold on an interlocutory order or is producing revenue, the money arising from the sale or revenue shall be invested, under the order of the court, in securities of the United States. The accretions therefrom are subject to the order of the court.

(Added Pub.L. 86–682, § 9, Sept. 2, 1960, 74 Stat. 707.)

HISTORICAL AND STATUTORY NOTES

Codifications

Section was derived from R.S. § 928, which was originally classified to section 741 of former Title 28. Following the general revision and enactment of Title 28 by Act June 25, 1948, R.S. § 928 was reclassified to section 841 of Title 39. R.S. § 928 was repealed by section 12(c) of Pub.L. 86–682 (section 1 of which revised and enacted Title 39), and reenacted by section 9 thereof as section 2714 of Title 28, Judiciary and Judicial Procedure.

§ 2715. Publication

The marshal shall cause publication of an executed warrant of attachment—

(1) for two months in case of an absconding debtor, and

(2) for four months in case of a nonresident debtor

in a newspaper published in the district where the property is situated pursuant to the details of the order under which the warrant is issued.

(Added Pub.L. 86–682, § 9, Sept. 2, 1960, 74 Stat. 707.)

HISTORICAL AND STATUTORY NOTES

Codifications

Section was derived from R.S. § 929, which was originally classified to section 742 of former Title 28. Following the general revision and enactment of Title 28 by Act June 25, 1948, R.S. § 929 was reclassified to section 842 of Title 39. R.S. § 929 was repealed by section 12(c) of Pub.L. 86–682 (section 1 of which revised and enacted Title 39), and reenacted by section 9 thereof as section 2715 of Title 28, Judiciary and Judicial Procedure.

§ 2716. Personal notice

After the first publication of the notice of attachment, a person indebted to, or having possession of property of a defendant and having knowledge of the notice, shall answer for the amount of his debt or the value of the property. Any disposal or attempted disposal of the property, to the injury of the United States, is unlawful. When the person indebted to, or having possession of the property of a defendant, is known to the United States attorney or marshal, the officer shall cause a personal notice of the attachment to be served upon him, but the lack of the notice does not invalidate the attachment.

(Added Pub.L. 86–682, § 9, Sept. 2, 1960, 74 Stat. 707.)

HISTORICAL AND STATUTORY NOTES

Codifications

Section was derived from R.S. § 930, which was originally classified to section 743 of former Title 28. Following the general revision and enactment of Title 28 by Act June 25, 1948, R.S. § 930 was reclassified to section 843 of Title 39. R.S. § 930 was repealed by section 12(c) of Pub.L. 86–682 (section 1 of which revised and enacted Title 39), and reenacted by section 9 thereof as section 2716 of Title 28, Judiciary and Judicial Procedure.

§ 2717. Discharge

The court, or a judge thereof, upon—

(1) application of the party when property has been attached and

(2) execution to the United States of a penal bond, approved by a judge, in double the value of the property attached and conditioned upon the return of the property or the payment of any judgment rendered by the court

may discharge the warrant of attachment as to the property of the applicant.

(Added Pub.L. 86–682, § 9, Sept. 2, 1960, 74 Stat. 708.)

HISTORICAL AND STATUTORY NOTES

Codifications

Section was derived from R.S. § 931, which was originally classified to section 744 of former Title 28. Following the general revision and enactment of Title 28 by Act June 25, 1948, R.S. § 931 was reclassified to section 844 of Title 39. R.S. § 931 was repealed by section 12(c) of Pub.L. 86–682 (section 1 of which revised and enacted Title 39), and reenacted by section 9 thereof as section 2717 of Title 28, Judiciary and Judicial Procedure.

§ 2718. Interest on balances due department

In suits for balances due the Post Office Department may recover interest at the rate of 6 per centum per year from the time of default.

(Added Pub.L. 86–682, § 9, Sept. 2, 1960, 74 Stat. 708.)

HISTORICAL AND STATUTORY NOTES

Codifications

Section was derived from R.S. § 964, which was originally classified to section 788 of former Title 28. Following the general revision and enactment of Title 28 by Act June 25, 1948, R.S. § 964 was reclassified to section 846 of Title 39. R.S. § 964 was repealed by section 12(c) of Pub.L. 86–682 (section 1 of which revised and enacted Title 39), and reenacted by section 9 thereof as section 2718 of Title 28, Judiciary and Judicial Procedure.

Change of Name

References to the Post Office Department, the Postal Service, the Postal Field Service, the Field Postal Service, or the Departmental Service or the Departmental Headquarters of the Post Office Department to be considered references to the United States Postal Service pursuant to Pub.L. 91–375, § 6(*o*), Aug. 12, 1970, 84 Stat. 783, set out as a Cross References note preceding section 101 of Title 39, Postal Service.

CHAPTER 175—CIVIL COMMITMENT AND REHABILITATION OF NARCOTIC ADDICTS [REPEALED]

[§§ 2901 to 2906. Repealed. Pub.L. 106–310, Div. B, Title XXXIV, § 3405(c)(1), Oct. 17, 2000, 114 Stat. 1221]

HISTORICAL AND STATUTORY NOTES

Section 2901, added Pub.L. 89–793, Title I, § 101, Nov. 8, 1966, 80 Stat. 1438, and amended Pub.L. 91–513, Title III, § 1102(*l*), Oct. 27, 1970, 84 Stat. 1293; Pub.L. 92–420, § 2, Sept. 16, 1972, 86 Stat. 677; Pub.L. 98–473, Title II, § 228(c), Oct. 12, 1984, 98 Stat. 2030, related to definitions under this chapter.

Section 2902, added Pub.L. 89–793, Title I, § 101, Nov. 8, 1966, 80 Stat. 1439, related to discretionary authority of court; examination, report, and determination by court; termination of civil commitment.

Section 2903, added Pub.L. 89–793, Title I, § 101, Nov. 8, 1966, 80 Stat. 1440, related to authority and responsibilities of the Surgeon General; institutional custody; aftercare; maximum period of civil commitment; credit toward sentence.

Section 2904, added Pub.L. 89–793, Title I, § 101, Nov. 8, 1966, 80 Stat. 1441, related to civil commitment not a conviction; use of test results.

Section 2905, added Pub.L. 89–793, Title I, § 101, Nov. 8, 1966, 80 Stat. 1441, related to delegation of functions by Surgeon General; use of Federal, State, and private facilities.

Section 2906, added Pub.L. 89–793, Title I, § 101, Nov. 8, 1966, 80 Stat. 1441, provided that absence of offer by the court to a defendant of an election under section 2902(a) or any determination as to civil commitment, not reviewable on appeal or otherwise.

Effective and Applicability Provisions

1972 Acts. Section 5 of Pub.L. 92–420 provided that: "This Act [amending section 2901(d) of this title, section 4251(c) of Title 18, and section 3411(b) of Title 42] shall take effect immediately upon enactment [Sept. 16, 1972]. Sections 2 and 3 [amending section 4251(c) of Title 18 and section 3411(b) of Title 42, respectively] shall apply to any case pending in a district court of the United States in which an appearance has not been made prior to the effective date [Sept. 16, 1972]."

CHAPTER 176—FEDERAL DEBT COLLECTION PROCEDURE

Subchapter	Section[1]
A. Definitions and general provisions	3001
B. Prejudgment remedies	3101
C. Postjudgments remedies[2]	3201
D. Fraudulent transfers[2]	3301

1 Editorially supplied.

2 So in original. Does not conform to subchapter heading.

SUBCHAPTER A—DEFINITIONS AND GENERAL PROVISIONS

Sec.
3001. Applicability of chapter.
3002. Definitions.
3003. Rules of construction.
3004. Service of process; enforcement; notice.
3005. Application of chapter to judgments.
3006. Affidavit requirements.
3007. Perishable personal property.
3008. Proceedings before United States magistrate judges.
3009. United States marshals' authority to designate keeper.
3010. Co-owned property.
3011. Assessment of surcharge on a debt.
3012. Joinder of additional defendant.
3013. Modification or protective order; supervision of enforcement.
3014. Exempt property.
3015. Discovery as to debtor's financial condition.

§ 3001. Applicability of chapter

(a) In general.—Except as provided in subsection (b), the[1] chapter provides the exclusive civil procedures for the United States—

(1) to recover a judgment on a debt; or

(2) to obtain, before judgment on a claim for a debt, a remedy in connection with such claim.

(b) Limitation.—To the extent that another Federal law specifies procedures for recovering on a claim or a judgment for a debt arising under such law, those procedures shall apply to such claim or judgment to the extent those procedures are inconsistent with this chapter.

(c) Amounts owing other than debts.—This chapter shall not apply with respect to an amount owing that is not a debt or to a claim for an amount owing that is not a debt.

(Added Pub.L. 101–647, Title XXXVI, § 3611, Nov. 29, 1990, 104 Stat. 4933.)

1 So in original. Probably should be "this".

HISTORICAL AND STATUTORY NOTES

Effective and Applicability Provisions

1990 Acts. Section 3631 of Title XXXVI of Pub.L. 101–647 provided that:

"(a) Except as provided in subsection (b), this Act and the amendments made by this Act [Pub.L. 101–647, Title XXXVI, Nov. 29, 1990, 104 Stat. 4933, popularly known as the Federal Debt Collection Procedures Act of 1990. For distribution of this Act to the Code, see Short Title note set out under section 1 of this title and Tables] shall take effect 180 days after the date of the enactment of this Act [Nov. 29, 1990].

"(b)(1) The amendments made by title I of this Act [probably means subtitle A of Title XXXVI of Pub.L. 101–647, which enacted this chapter] shall apply with respect to actions pending on the effective date of this Act [180 days after Nov. 29, 1990] in any court on—

"(A) a claim for a debt; or

"(B) a judgment for a debt.

"(2) All notices, writs, orders, and judgments in effect in such actions shall continue in effect until superseded or modified in an action under chapter 176 of title 28 of the United States Code, as added by title I of this Act [this chapter].

"(3) For purposes of this subsection—

"(A) the term 'court' means a Federal, State, or local court, and

"(B) the term 'debt' has the meaning given such term in section and 3002(3) of such chapter [probably means section 3002(3) of this title]."

§ 3002. Definitions

As used in this chapter:

(1) "Counsel for the United States" means—

(A) a United States attorney, an assistant United States attorney designated to act on behalf of the United States attorney, or an attorney with the United States Department of Justice or with a Federal agency who has litigation authority; and

(B) any private attorney authorized by contract made in accordance with section 3718 of title 31 to conduct litigation for collection of debts on behalf of the United States.

(2) "Court" means any court created by the Congress of the United States, excluding the United States Tax Court.

(3) "Debt" means—

(A) an amount that is owing to the United States on account of a direct loan, or loan insured or guaranteed, by the United States; or

(B) an amount that is owing to the United States on account of a fee, duty, lease, rent, service, sale of real or personal property, overpayment, fine, assessment, penalty, restitution, damages, interest, tax, bail bond forfeiture, reimbursement, recovery of a cost incurred by the United States, or other source of indebtedness to the United States, but that is not owing under the terms of a contract originally entered into by only persons other than the United States;

and includes any amount owing to the United States for the benefit of an Indian tribe or individual Indian, but excludes any amount to which the United States is entitled under section 3011(a).

(4) "Debtor" means a person who is liable for a debt or against whom there is a claim for a debt.

(5) "Disposable earnings" means that part of earnings remaining after all deductions required by law have been withheld.

(6) "Earnings" means compensation paid or payable for personal services, whether denominated as wages, salary, commission, bonus, or otherwise, and includes periodic payments pursuant to a pension or retirement program.

(7) "Garnishee" means a person (other than the debtor) who has, or is reasonably thought to have, possession, custody, or control of any property in which the debtor has a substantial nonexempt interest, including any obligation due the debtor or to become due the debtor, and against whom a garnishment under section 3104 or 3205 is issued by a court.

(8) "Judgment" means a judgment, order, or decree entered in favor of the United States in a court and arising from a civil or criminal proceeding regarding a debt.

(9) "Nonexempt disposable earnings" means 25 percent of disposable earnings, subject to section 303 of the Consumer Credit Protection Act.

(10) "Person" includes a natural person (including an individual Indian), a corporation, a partnership, an unincorporated association, a trust, or an estate, or any other public or private entity, including a State or local government or an Indian tribe.

(11) "Prejudgment remedy" means the remedy of attachment, receivership, garnishment, or sequestration authorized by this chapter to be granted before judgment on the merits of a claim for a debt.

(12) "Property" includes any present or future interest, whether legal or equitable, in real, personal (including choses in action), or mixed property, tangible or intangible, vested or contingent, wherever located and however held (including community property and property held in trust (including spendthrift and pension trusts)), but excludes—

(A) property held in trust by the United States for the benefit of an Indian tribe or individual Indian; and

(B) Indian lands subject to restrictions against alienation imposed by the United States.

(13) "Security agreement" means an agreement that creates or provides for a lien.

(14) "State" means any of the several States, the District of Columbia, the Commonwealth of Puerto Rico, the Commonwealth of the Northern Marianas, or any territory or possession of the United States.

(15) "United States" means—

(A) a Federal corporation;

(B) an agency, department, commission, board, or other entity of the United States; or

(C) an instrumentality of the United States.

(16) "United States marshal" means a United States marshal, a deputy marshal, or an official of the United States Marshals Service designated under section 564.

(Added Pub.L. 101-647, Title XXXVI, § 3611, Nov. 29, 1990, 104 Stat. 4933.)

HISTORICAL AND STATUTORY NOTES

References in Text

Section 303 of the Consumer Credit Protection Act, referred to in par. (9), is classified to section 1673 of Title 15, Commerce and Trade.

Effective and Applicability Provisions

1990 Acts. Section to take effect 180 days after Nov. 29, 1990, except as otherwise provided, see section 3631 of Pub.L. 101-647, set out as a note under section 3001 of this title.

§ 3003. Rules of construction

(a) Terms.—For purposes of this chapter—

(1) the terms "includes" and "including" are not limiting;

(2) the term "or" is not exclusive; and

(3) the singular includes the plural.

(b) Effect on rights of the United States.—This chapter shall not be construed to curtail or limit the right of the United States under any other Federal law or any State law—

(1) to collect taxes or to collect any other amount collectible in the same manner as a tax;

(2) to collect any fine, penalty, assessment, restitution, or forfeiture arising in a criminal case;

(3) to appoint or seek the appointment of a receiver; or

(4) to enforce a security agreement.

(c) Effect on other laws.—This chapter shall not be construed to supersede or modify the operation of—

(1) title 11;

(2) admiralty law;

(3) section 3713 of title 31;

(4) section 303 of the Consumer Credit Protection Act (15 U.S.C. 1673);

(5) a statute of limitation applicable to a criminal proceeding;

(6) the common law or statutory rights to set-off or recoupment;

(7) any Federal law authorizing, or any inherent authority of a court to provide, injunctive relief;

(8) the authority of a court—

(A) to impose a sanction under the Federal Rules of Civil Procedure;

(B) to appoint a receiver to effectuate its order; or

(C) to exercise the power of contempt under any Federal law;

(9) any law authorizing the United States to obtain partition, or to recover possession, of property in which the United States holds title; or

(10) any provision of any other chapter of this title, except to the extent such provision is inconsistent with this chapter.

(d) Preemption.—This chapter shall preempt State law to the extent such law is inconsistent with a provision of this chapter.

(e) Effect on rights of the United States under foreign and international law.—This chapter shall not be construed to curtail or limit the rights of the United States under foreign law, under a treaty or an international agreement, or otherwise under international law.

(f) Applicability of Federal Rules of Civil Procedure.—Except as provided otherwise in this chapter, the Federal Rules of Civil Procedure shall apply with respect to actions and proceedings under this chapter.

(Added Pub.L. 101-647, Title XXXVI, § 3611, Nov. 29, 1990, 104 Stat. 4935.)

HISTORICAL AND STATUTORY NOTES

References in Text

The Federal Rules of Civil Procedure, referred to in subsecs. (c)(8)(A) and (f), are set out in this title.

Effective and Applicability Provisions

1990 Acts. Section to take effect 180 days after Nov. 29, 1990, except as otherwise provided, see section 3631 of Pub.L. 101-647, set out as a note under section 3001 of this title.

§ 3004. Service of process; enforcement; notice

(a) Manner of service.—A complaint, notice, writ, or other process required to be served in an action or proceeding under this chapter shall be served in accordance with the Federal Rules of Civil Procedure unless otherwise provided in this chapter.

(b) Nationwide enforcement.—(1) Except as provided in paragraph (2)—

(A) any writ, order, judgment, or other process, including a summons and complaint, filed under this chapter may be served in any State; and

(B) such writ, order, or judgment may be enforced by the court issuing the writ, order, or process, regardless of where the person is served with the writ, order, or process.

(2) If the debtor so requests, within 20 days after receiving the notice described in section 3101(d) or 3202(b), the action or proceeding in which the writ,

order, or judgment was issued shall be transferred to the district court for the district in which the debtor resides.

(c) Notice and other process.—At such time as counsel for the United States considers appropriate, but not later than the time a prejudgment or postjudgment remedy is put into effect under this chapter, counsel for the United States shall exercise reasonable diligence to serve on the debtor and any person who the United States believes, after exercising due diligence, has possession, custody, or control of the property, a copy of the application for such remedy, the order granting such remedy, and the notice required by section 3101(d) or 3202(b).

(Added Pub.L. 101–647, Title XXXVI, § 3611, Nov. 29, 1990, 104 Stat. 4936.)

HISTORICAL AND STATUTORY NOTES

References in Text

The Federal Rules of Civil Procedure, referred to in subsec. (a), are set out in this title.

Effective and Applicability Provisions

1990 Acts. Section to take effect 180 days after Nov. 29, 1990, except as otherwise provided, see section 3631 of Pub.L. 101–647, set out as a note under section 3001 of this title.

§ 3005. Application of chapter to judgments

This chapter shall not apply with respect to a judgment on a debt if such judgment is entered more than 10 years before the effective date of this chapter.

(Added Pub.L. 101–647, Title XXXVI, § 3611, Nov. 29, 1990, 104 Stat. 4936.)

HISTORICAL AND STATUTORY NOTES

References in Text

For effective date of this chapter, referred to in text, see section 3631 of Pub.L. 101–647, set out as an Effective Date note under section 3001 of this title.

Effective and Applicability Provisions

1990 Acts. Section to take effect 180 days after Nov. 29, 1990, except as otherwise provided, see section 3631 of Pub.L. 101–647, set out as a note under section 3001 of this title.

§ 3006. Affidavit requirements

Any affidavit required of the United States by this chapter may be made on information and belief, if reliable and reasonably necessary, establishing with particularity, to the court's satisfaction, facts supporting the claim of the United States.

(Added Pub.L. 101–647, Title XXXVI, § 3611, Nov. 29, 1990, 104 Stat. 4936.)

HISTORICAL AND STATUTORY NOTES

Effective and Applicability Provisions

1990 Acts. Section to take effect 180 days after Nov. 29, 1990, except as otherwise provided, see section 3631 of Pub.L. 101–647, set out as a note under section 3001 of this title.

§ 3007. Perishable personal property

(a) Authority to sell.—If at any time during any action or proceeding under this chapter the court determines on its own initiative or upon motion of any party, that any seized or detained personal property is likely to perish, waste, or be destroyed, or otherwise substantially depreciate in value during the pendency of the proceeding, the court shall order a commercially reasonable sale of such property.

(b) Deposit of sale proceeds.—Within 5 days after such sale, the proceeds shall be deposited with the clerk of the court, accompanied by a statement in writing and signed by the United States marshal, to be filed in the action or proceeding, stating the time and place of sale, the name of the purchaser, the amount received, and an itemized account of expenses.

(c) Presumption.—For purposes of liability on the part of the United States, there shall be a presumption that the price paid at a sale under subsection (a) is the fair market value of the property or portion.

(Added Pub.L. 101–647, Title XXXVI, § 3611, Nov. 29, 1990, 104 Stat. 4937.)

HISTORICAL AND STATUTORY NOTES

Effective and Applicability Provisions

1990 Acts. Section to take effect 180 days after Nov. 29, 1990, except as otherwise provided, see section 3631 of Pub.L. 101–647, set out as a note under section 3001 of this title.

§ 3008. Proceedings before United States magistrate judges

A district court of the United States may assign its duties in proceedings under this chapter to a United States magistrate judge to the extent not inconsistent with the Constitution and laws of the United States.

(Added Pub.L. 101–647, Title XXXVI, § 3611, Nov. 29, 1990, 104 Stat. 4937, and amended Pub.L. 101–650, Title III, § 321, Dec. 1, 1990, 104 Stat. 5117.)

HISTORICAL AND STATUTORY NOTES

Effective and Applicability Provisions

1990 Acts. Section to take effect 180 days after Nov. 29, 1990, except as otherwise provided, see section 3631 of Pub.L. 101–647, set out as a note under section 3001 of this title.

Change of Name

"United States magistrate judges" substituted for "United States magistrates" in the catchline and "United States magistrate judge" substituted for "United States magistrate" in text pursuant to section 321 of Pub.L. 101–650, set out as a note under 28 U.S.C.A. § 631.

§ 3009. United States marshals' authority to designate keeper

Whenever a United States marshal is authorized to seize property pursuant to this chapter, the United States marshal may designate another person or Federal agency to hold for safekeeping such property seized.

(Added Pub.L. 101–647, Title XXXVI, § 3611, Nov. 29, 1990, 104 Stat. 4937.)

HISTORICAL AND STATUTORY NOTES

Effective and Applicability Provisions

1990 Acts. Section to take effect 180 days after Nov. 29, 1990, except as otherwise provided, see section 3631 of Pub.L. 101–647, set out as a note under section 3001 of this title.

§ 3010. Co-owned property

(a) Limitation.—The remedies available to the United States under this chapter may be enforced against property which is co-owned by a debtor and any other person only to the extent allowed by the law of the State where the property is located. This section shall not be construed to limit any right or interest of a debtor or co-owner in a retirement system for Federal military or civilian personnel established by the United States or any agency thereof or in a qualified retirement arrangement.

(b) Definitions.—For purposes of subsection (a)—

(1) the term "retirement system for Federal military or civilian personnel" means a pension or annuity system for Federal military or civilian personnel of more than one agency, or for some or all of such personnel of a single agency, established by statute or by regulation pursuant to statutory authority; and

(2) the term "qualified retirement arrangement" means a plan qualified under section 401(a), 403(a), or 409 of the Internal Revenue Code of 1986 or a plan that is subject to the requirements of section 205 of the Employee Retirement Income Security Act of 1974.

(Added Pub.L. 101–647, Title XXXVI, § 3611, Nov. 29, 1990, 104 Stat. 4937.)

HISTORICAL AND STATUTORY NOTES

References in Text

Sections 401(a), 403(a) and 409 of the Internal Revenue Code of 1986, referred to in subsec. (b)(2), are set out in sections 401(a), 403(a) and 409, respectively, of Title 26, Internal Revenue Code.

Section 205 of the Employee Retirement Income Security Act of 1974, referred to in subsec. (b)(2), is classified to section 1055 of Title 29, Labor.

Effective and Applicability Provisions

1990 Acts. Section to take effect 180 days after Nov. 29, 1990, except as otherwise provided, see section 3631 of Pub.L. 101–647, set out as a note under section 3001 of this title.

§ 3011. Assessment of surcharge on a debt

(a) Surcharge authorized.—In an action or proceeding under subchapter B or C, and subject to subsection (b), the United States is entitled to recover a surcharge of 10 percent of the amount of the debt in connection with the recovery of the debt, to cover the cost of processing and handling the litigation and enforcement under this chapter of the claim for such debt.

(b) Limitation.—Subsection (a) shall not apply if—

(1) the United States receives an attorney's fee in connection with the enforcement of the claim; or

(2) the law pursuant to which the action on the claim is based provides any other amount to cover such costs.

(Added Pub.L. 101–647, Title XXXVI, § 3611, Nov. 29, 1990, 104 Stat. 4937.)

HISTORICAL AND STATUTORY NOTES

Effective and Applicability Provisions

1990 Acts. Section to take effect 180 days after Nov. 29, 1990, except as otherwise provided, see section 3631 of Pub.L. 101–647, set out as a note under section 3001 of this title.

§ 3012. Joinder of additional defendant

The United States or the debtor may join as an additional defendant in an action or proceeding under this chapter any person reasonably believed to owe money (including money owed on account of a requirement to provide goods or services pursuant to a loan or loan guarantee extended under Federal law) to the debtor arising out of the transaction or occurrence giving rise to a debt.

(Added Pub.L. 101–647, Title XXXVI, § 3611, Nov. 29, 1990, 104 Stat. 4938.)

HISTORICAL AND STATUTORY NOTES

Effective and Applicability Provisions

1990 Acts. Section to take effect 180 days after Nov. 29, 1990, except as otherwise provided, see section 3631 of Pub.L. 101–647, set out as a note under section 3001 of this title.

§ 3013. Modification or protective order; supervision of enforcement

The court may at any time on its own initiative or the motion of any interested person, and after such notice as it may require, make an order denying, limiting, conditioning, regulating, extending, or modifying the use of any enforcement procedure under this chapter.

(Added Pub.L. 101–647, Title XXXVI, § 3611, Nov. 29, 1990, 104 Stat. 4938.)

HISTORICAL AND STATUTORY NOTES

Effective and Applicability Provisions

1990 Acts. Section to take effect 180 days after Nov. 29, 1990, except as otherwise provided, see section 3631 of Pub.L. 101–647, set out as a note under section 3001 of this title.

§ 3014. Exempt property

(a) Election to exempt property.—An individual debtor may, in an action or proceeding under this chapter, elect to exempt property listed in either paragraph (1) or, in the alternative, paragraph (2). If such action or proceeding is against debtors who are husband and wife, one debtor may not elect to exempt property listed in paragraph (1) and the other debtor elect to exempt property listed in paragraph (2). If the debtors cannot agree on the alternative to be elected, they shall be deemed to elect paragraph (1). Such property is either—

(1) property that is specified in section 522(d) of title 11, as amended from time to time; or

(2)(A) any property that is exempt under Federal law, other than paragraph (1), or State or local law that is applicable on the date of the filing of the application for a remedy under this chapter at the place in which the debtor's domicile has been located for the 180 days immediately preceding the date of the filing of such application, or for a longer portion of such 180–day period than in any other place; and

(B) any interest in property in which the debtor had, immediately before the filing of such application, an interest as a tenant by the entirety or joint tenant, or an interest in a community estate, to the extent that such interest is exempt from process under applicable nonbankruptcy law.

(b) Effect on assertion and manner of determination.—

(1) Statement.—A court may order the debtor to file a statement with regard to any claimed exemption. A copy of such statement shall be served on counsel for the United States. Such statement shall be under oath and shall describe each item of property for which exemption is claimed, the value and the basis for such valuation, and the nature of the debtor's ownership interest.

(2) Hearing.—The United States or the debtor, by application to the court in which an action or proceeding under this chapter is pending, may request a hearing on the applicability of any exemption claimed by the debtor. The court shall determine the extent (if any) to which the exemption applies. Unless it is reasonably evident that the exemption applies, the debtor shall bear the burden of persuasion.

(3) Stay of disposition.—Assertion of an exemption shall prevent the United States from selling or otherwise disposing of the property for which such exemption is claimed until the court determines whether the debtor has a substantial nonexempt interest in such property. The United States may not take possession of, dispose of, sell, or otherwise interfere with the debtor's normal use and enjoyment of an interest in property the United States knows or has reason to know is exempt.

(c) Debtors in joint cases.—Subject to the limitation in subsection (a), this section shall apply separately with respect to each debtor in a joint case.

(Added Pub.L. 101–647, Title XXXVI, § 3611, Nov. 29, 1990, 104 Stat. 4938.)

HISTORICAL AND STATUTORY NOTES

Effective and Applicability Provisions

1990 Acts. Section to take effect 180 days after Nov. 29, 1990, except as otherwise provided, see section 3631 of Pub.L. 101–647, set out as a note under section 3001 of this title.

§ 3015. Discovery as to debtor's financial condition

(a) In general.—Except as provided in subsection (b), in an action or proceeding under subchapter B or C, the United States may have discovery regarding the financial condition of the debtor in the manner in which discovery is authorized by the Federal Rules of Civil Procedure in an action on a claim for a debt.

(b) Limitation.—Subsection (a) shall not apply with respect to an action or proceeding under subchapter B unless there is a reasonable likelihood that the debt involved exceeds $50,000.

(Added Pub.L. 101–647, Title XXXVI, § 3611, Nov. 29, 1990, 104 Stat. 4939.)

HISTORICAL AND STATUTORY NOTES

References in Text

The Federal Rules of Civil Procedure, referred to in subsec. (a), are set out in this title.

Effective and Applicability Provisions

1990 Acts. Section to take effect 180 days after Nov. 29, 1990, except as otherwise provided, see section 3631 of Pub.L. 101–647, set out as a note under section 3001 of this title.

SUBCHAPTER B—PREJUDGMENT REMEDIES

Sec.

3101. Prejudgment remedies.
3102. Attachment.
3103. Receivership.
3104. Garnishment.
3105. Sequestration.

§ 3101. Prejudgment remedies

(a) Application.—(1) The United States may, in a proceeding in conjunction with the complaint or at any time after the filing of a civil action on a claim for a debt, make application under oath to a court to issue any prejudgment remedy.

(2) Such application shall be filed with the court and shall set forth the factual and legal basis for each prejudgment remedy sought.

(3) Such application shall—

(A) state that the debtor against whom the prejudgment remedy is sought shall be afforded an opportunity for a hearing; and

(B) set forth with particularity that all statutory requirements under this chapter for the issuance of the prejudgment remedy sought have been satisfied.

(b) Grounds.—Subject to section 3102, 3103, 3104, or 3105, a prejudgment remedy may be granted by any court if the United States shows reasonable cause to believe that—

(1) the debtor—

(A) is about to leave the jurisdiction of the United States with the effect of hindering, delaying, or defrauding the United States in its effort to recover a debt;

(B) has or is about to assign, dispose, remove, conceal, ill treat, waste, or destroy property with the effect of hindering, delaying, or defrauding the United States;

(C) has or is about to convert the debtor's property into money, securities, or evidence of debt in a manner prejudicial to the United States with the effect of hindering, delaying, or defrauding the United States; or

(D) has evaded service of process by concealing himself or has temporarily withdrawn from the jurisdiction of the United States with the effect of hindering, delaying, or defrauding the United States; or

(2) a prejudgment remedy is required to obtain jurisdiction within the United States and the prejudgment remedy sought will result in obtaining such jurisdiction.

(c) Affidavit.—(1) The application under subsection (a) shall include an affidavit establishing with particularity to the court's satisfaction facts supporting the probable validity of the claim for a debt and the right of the United States to recover what is demanded in the application.

(2) The affidavit shall state—

(A) specifically the amount of the debt claimed by the United States and any interest or costs attributable to such debt;

(B) one or more of the grounds specified in subsection (b); and

(C) the requirements of section 3102(b), 3103(a), 3104(a), or 3105(b), as the case may be.

(3) No bond is required of the United States.

(d) Notice and hearing.—(1) On filing an application by the United States as provided in this section, the counsel for the United States shall prepare, and the clerk shall issue, a notice for service on the debtor against whom the prejudgment remedy is sought and on any other person whom the United States reasonably believes, after exercising due diligence, has possession, custody, or control of property affected by such remedy. Three copies of the notice shall be served on each such person. The form and content of such notice shall be approved jointly by a majority of the chief judges of the Federal districts in the State in which the court is located and shall be in substantially the following form:

"NOTICE

"You are hereby notified that this [property] is being taken by the United States Government ('the Government'), which says that [name of debtor] owes it a debt of $ [amount] for [reason for debt] and has filed a lawsuit to collect this debt. The Government says it must take this property at this time because [recite the pertinent ground or grounds from section 3101(b)]. The Government wants to make sure [name of debtor] will pay if the court determines that this money is owed.

"In addition, you are hereby notified that there are exemptions under the law which may protect some of this property from being taken by the Government if [name of debtor] can show that the exemptions apply. Below is a summary of the major exemptions which apply in most situations in the State of [State where property is located]:

"[A statement summarizing in plain and understandable English the election available with respect to such State under section 3014 and the types of property that may be exempted under each of the alternatives specified in paragraphs (1) and (2) of section 3014(a), and a statement that different property may be so exempted with respect to the State in which the debtor resides.]

"If you are [name of debtor] and you disagree with the reason the Government gives for taking your property now, or if you think you do not owe the money to the Government that it says you do, or if you think the property the Government is taking qualifies under one of the above exemptions, you have a right to ask the court to return your property to you.

"If you want a hearing, you must promptly notify the court. You must make your request in writing, and either mail it or deliver it in person to the clerk of the court at [address]. If you wish, you may use this notice to request the hearing by checking the box below and mailing this notice to the court clerk. You must also send a copy of your request to the Government at [address], so the Government will know you want a hearing. The hearing will take place within 5 days after the clerk receives your request, if you ask for it to take place that quickly, or as soon after that as possible.

"At the hearing you may explain to the judge why you think you do not owe the money to the Government, why you disagree with the reason the Government says it must take your property at this time, or why you believe the property the Government has taken is exempt or belongs to someone else. You may make any or all of these explanations as you see fit.

"If you think you live outside the Federal judicial district in which the court is located, you may request, not later than 20 days after you receive this notice, that this proceeding to take your property be transferred by the court to the Federal judicial district in which you reside. You must make your request in writing, and either mail it or deliver it in person to the clerk of the court at [address]. You must also send a copy of your request to the Government at [address], so the Government will know you want the proceeding to be transferred.

"Be sure to keep a copy of this notice for your own records. If you have any questions about your rights or about this procedure, you should contact a lawyer, an office of public legal assistance, or the clerk of the court. The clerk is not permitted to give legal advice, but can refer you to other sources of information."

(2) By requesting, at any time before judgment on the claim for a debt, the court to hold a hearing, the debtor may move to quash the order granting such remedy. The court shall hold a hearing on such motion as soon as practicable, or, if requested by the debtor, within 5 days after receiving the request for a hearing or as soon thereafter as possible. The issues at such hearing shall be limited to—

(A) the probable validity of the claim for the debt for which such remedy was granted and of any defense or claim of exemption asserted by such person;

(B) compliance with any statutory requirement for the issuance of the prejudgment remedy granted;

(C) the existence of any ground set forth in subsection (b); and

(D) the inadequacy of alternative remedies (if any) to protect the interests of the United States.

(e) Issuance of writ.—On the court's determination that the requirements of subsections (a), (b), and (c) have been met, the court shall issue all process sufficient to put into effect the prejudgment remedy sought.

(Added Pub.L. 101–647, Title XXXVI, § 3611, Nov. 29, 1990, 104 Stat. 4939.)

HISTORICAL AND STATUTORY NOTES

Effective and Applicability Provisions

1990 Acts. Section to take effect 180 days after Nov. 29, 1990, except as otherwise provided, see section 3631 of Pub.L. 101–647, set out as a note under section 3001 of this title.

§ 3102. Attachment

(a) Property subject to attachment.—(1) Any property in the possession, custody, or control of the debtor and in which the debtor has a substantial nonexempt interest, except earnings, may be attached pursuant to a writ of attachment in an action or proceeding against a debtor on a claim for a debt and may be held as security to satisfy such judgment, and interest and costs, as the United States may recover on such claim.

(2) The value of property attached shall not exceed the amount by which the sum of the amount of the debt claimed by the United States and the amount of interest and costs reasonably likely to be assessed against the debtor by the court exceeds the aggregate value of the nonexempt interest of the debtor in any—

(A) property securing the debt; and

(B) property garnished or in receivership, or income sequestered, under this subchapter.

(b) Availability of attachment.—If the requirements of section 3101 are satisfied, a court shall issue a writ authorizing the United States to attach property in which the debtor has a substantial nonexempt interest, as security for such judgment (and interest and costs) as the United States may recover on a claim for a debt—

(1) in an action on a contract, express or implied, against the debtor for payment of money, only if the United States shows reasonable cause to believe that—

(A) the contract is not fully secured by real or personal property; or

(B) the value of the original security is substantially diminished, without any act of the United States or the person to whom the security was given, below the amount of the debt;

(2) in an action against the debtor for damages in tort;

(3) if the debtor resides outside the jurisdiction of the United States; or

(4) in an action to recover a fine, penalty, or tax.

(c) Issuance of writ; contents.—(1) Subject to subsections (a) and (b), a writ of attachment shall be issued by the court directing the United States marshal of the district where property described in subsection (a) is located to attach the property.

(2) Several writs of attachment may be issued at the same time, or in succession, and sent to different judicial districts until sufficient property is attached.

(3) The writ of attachment shall contain—

(A) the date of the issuance of the writ;

(B) the identity of the court, the docket number of the action, and the identity of the cause of action;

(C) the name and last known address of the debtor;

(D) the amount to be secured by the attachment; and

(E) a reasonable description of the property to be attached.

(d) Levy of attachment.—(1) The United States marshal receiving the writ shall proceed without delay to levy upon the property specified for attachment if found within the district. The marshal may not sell property unless ordered by the court.

(2) In performing the levy, the United States marshal may enter any property owned, occupied, or controlled by the debtor, except that the marshal may not enter a residence or other building unless the writ expressly authorizes the marshal to do so or upon specific order of the court.

(3) Levy on real property is made by entering the property and posting the writ and notice of levy in a conspicuous place upon the property.

(4) Levy on personal property is made by taking possession of it. Levy on personal property not easily taken into possession or which cannot be taken into possession without great inconvenience or expense may be made by affixing a copy of the writ and notice of levy on it or in a conspicuous place in the vicinity of it describing in the notice of levy the property by quantity and with sufficient detail to identify the property levied on.

(5) The United States marshal shall file a copy of the notice of levy in the same manner as provided for judgments in section 3201(a)(1). The United States marshal shall serve a copy of the writ and notice of levy on—

(A) the debtor against whom the writ is issued; and

(B) the person who has possession of the property subject to the writ;

in the same manner that a summons is served in a civil action and make the return thereof.

(e) Return of writ; duties of marshal; further return.—(1) A United States marshal executing a writ of attachment shall return the writ with the marshal's action endorsed thereon or attached thereto and signed by the marshal, to the court from which it was issued, within 5 days after the date of the levy.

(2) The return shall describe the property attached with sufficient certainty to identify it and shall state the location where it was attached, the date and time it was attached, and the disposition made of the property. If no property was attached, the return shall so state.

(3) If the property levied on is claimed, replevied under subsection (j)(2), or sold under section 3007 after the return, the United States marshal shall immediately make a further return to the clerk of the court showing the disposition of the property.

(4) If personal property is replevied, the United States marshal shall deliver the replevin bond to the clerk of the court to be filed in the action.

(f) Levy of attachment as lien on property; satisfaction of lien.—(1) A levy on property under a writ of attachment under this section creates a lien in favor of the United States on the property or, in the case of perishable property sold under section 3007, on the proceeds of the sale.

(2) Such lien shall be ranked ahead of any other security interests perfected after the later of the time of levy and the time a copy of the notice of levy is filed under subsection (d)(5).

(3) Such lien shall arise from the time of levy and shall continue until a judgment in the action is obtained or denied, or the action is otherwise dismissed. The death of the debtor whose property is attached does not terminate the attachment lien. Upon issuance of a judgment in the action and registration under this chapter, the judgment lien so created relates back to the time of levy.

(g) Reduction or dissolution of attachment.—(1) If an excessive or unreasonable attachment is made, the debtor may submit a motion to the court for a reduction of the amount of the attachment or its dissolution. Notice of such motion shall be served on the United States.

(2) The court shall order a part of the property to be released, if after a hearing the court finds that the amount of the attachment is excessive or unreasonable or if the attachment is for an amount larger than the sum of the liquidated or ascertainable amount of the debt and the amount of interest and costs likely to be taxed.

(3) The court shall dissolve the attachment if the amount of the debt is unliquidated and unascertainable by calculation.

(4) If any property claimed to be exempt is levied on, the debtor may, at any time after such levy, request that the court vacate such levy. If it appears to the court that the property so levied upon is exempt, the court shall order the levy vacated and the property returned to the debtor.

(h) Replevin of attached property by debtor; bond.—If attached property is not sold before judgment, the debtor may replevy such property or any part thereof by giving a bond approved by counsel for the United States or the court and payable to the United States in double the reasonable value of the property to be replevied or double the value of the claim, whichever is less.

(i) Preservation of personal property under attachment.—If personal property in custody of the United States marshal under a writ of attachment is not replevied, claimed, or sold, the court may make such order for its preservation or use as appears to be in the interest of the parties.

(j) Judgment and disposition of attached property.—

(1) Judgment for the United States.—On entry of judgment for the United States, the court shall order the proceeds of personal property sold pursuant to section 3007 to be applied to the satisfaction of the judgment, and shall order the sale of any remaining personal property and any real property levied on to the extent necessary to satisfy the judgment.

(2) Judgment for the United States when personal property replevied.—With respect to personal property under attachment that is replevied, the judgment which may be entered shall be against the debtor against whom the writ of attachment is issued and also against the sureties on the debtor's replevin bond for the value of the property.

(3) Restoration of property and exoneration of replevin bond.—If the attachment is vacated or if the judgment on the claim for the debt is for the person against whom the writ attachment is issued, the court shall order the property, or proceeds of perishable property sold under section 3007, restored to the debtor and shall exonerate any replevin bond.

(Added Pub.L. 101-647, Title XXXVI, § 3611, Nov. 29, 1990, 104 Stat. 4942.)

HISTORICAL AND STATUTORY NOTES

Effective and Applicability Provisions

1990 Acts. Section to take effect 180 days after Nov. 29, 1990, except as otherwise provided, see section 3631 of Pub.L. 101-647, set out as a note under section 3001 of this title.

§ 3103. Receivership

(a) Appointment of a receiver.—If the requirements of section 3101 are satisfied, a court may appoint a receiver for property in which the debtor has a substantial nonexempt interest if the United States shows reasonable cause to believe that there is a substantial danger that the property will be removed from the jurisdiction of the court, lost, concealed, materially injured or damaged, or mismanaged.

(b) Powers of receiver.—(1) The appointing court may authorize a receiver—

(A) to take possession of real and personal property and sue for, collect, and sell obligations upon such conditions and for such purposes as the court shall direct; and

(B) to administer, collect, improve, lease, repair or sell pursuant to section 3007 such real and personal property as the court shall direct.

A receiver appointed to manage residential or commercial property shall have demonstrable expertise in the management of these types of property.

(2) Unless expressly authorized by order of the court, a receiver shall have no power to employ attorneys, accountants, appraisers, auctioneers, or other professional persons.

(c) Duration of receivership.—A receivership shall not continue past the entry of judgment, or the conclusion of an appeal of such judgment, unless the court orders it continued under section 3203(e) or unless the court otherwise directs its continuation.

(d) Accounts; requirement to report.—A receiver shall keep written accounts itemizing receipts and expenditures, describing the property and naming the depository of receivership funds. The receiver's accounts shall be open to inspection by any person having an apparent interest in the property. The receiver shall file reports at regular intervals as directed by the court and shall serve the debtor and the United States with a copy thereof.

(e) Modification of powers; removal.—On motion of the receiver or on its own initiative, the court which appointed the receiver may remove the receiver or modify the receiver's powers at any time.

(f) Priority.—If more than one court appoints a receiver for particular property, the receiver first qualifying under law shall be entitled to take possession, control, or custody of the property.

(g) Compensation of receivers.—(1) A receiver is entitled to such commissions, not exceeding 5 percent of the sums received and disbursed by him, as the court allows unless the court otherwise directs.

(2) If, at the termination of a receivership, there are no funds in the hands of a receiver, the court may fix the compensation of the receiver in accordance

with the services rendered and may direct the party who moved for the appointment of the receiver to pay such compensation in addition to the necessary expenditures incurred by the receiver which remain unpaid.

(3) At the termination of a receivership, the receiver shall file a final accounting of the receipts and disbursements and apply for compensation setting forth the amount sought and the services rendered by the receiver.

(Added Pub.L. 101–647, Title XXXVI, § 3611, Nov. 29, 1990, 104 Stat. 4944.)

HISTORICAL AND STATUTORY NOTES

Effective and Applicability Provisions

1990 Acts. Section to take effect 180 days after Nov. 29, 1990, except as otherwise provided, see section 3631 of Pub.L. 101–647, set out as a note under section 3001 of this title.

§ 3104. Garnishment

(a) In general.—If the requirements of section 3101 are satisfied, a court may issue a writ of garnishment against property (excluding earnings) in which the debtor has a substantial nonexempt interest and which is in the possession, custody, or control of a person other than the debtor in order to satisfy a claim for a debt. Co-owned property shall be subject to garnishment to the same extent as co-owned property is subject to garnishment under the law of the State in which such property is located. A court may issue simultaneous separate writs of garnishment to several garnishees. A writ of garnishment issued under this subsection shall be continuing and shall terminate only as provided in section 3205(c)(10).

(b) Writ.—(1) Subsections (b)(2) and (c) of section 3205 shall apply with respect to garnishment under this section, except that for purposes of this section—

(A) earnings of the debtor shall not be subject to garnishment; and

(B) a reference in such subsections to a judgment debtor shall be deemed to be a reference to a debtor.

(2) The United States shall include in its application for a writ of garnishment—

(A) the amount of the claim asserted by the United States for a debt; and

(B) the date the writ is issued.

(c) Limitation.—The value of property garnished shall not exceed the amount by which the sum of the amount of the debt claimed by the United States and the amount of interest and costs reasonably likely to be assessed against the debtor by the court exceeds the aggregate value of the nonexempt interest of the debtor in any—

(1) property securing the debt; and

(2) property attached or in receivership, or income sequestered, under this subchapter.

(Added Pub.L. 101–647, Title XXXVI, § 3611, Nov. 29, 1990, 104 Stat. 4945.)

HISTORICAL AND STATUTORY NOTES

Effective and Applicability Provisions

1990 Acts. Section to take effect 180 days after Nov. 29, 1990, except as otherwise provided, see section 3631 of Pub.L. 101–647, set out as a note under section 3001 of this title.

§ 3105. Sequestration

(a) Property subject to sequestration.—(1) Any income from property in which the debtor has a substantial nonexempt interest may be sequestered pursuant to a writ of sequestration in an action or proceeding against a debtor on a claim for a debt and may be held as security to satisfy such judgment, and interest and costs, as the United States may recover on such claim.

(2) The amount of income sequestered shall not exceed the amount by which the sum of the amount of the debt claimed by the United States and the amount of interest and costs reasonably likely to be assessed against the debtor by the court exceeds the aggregate value of the nonexempt interest of the debtor in any—

(A) property securing the debt; and

(B) property attached, garnished, or in receivership under this subchapter.

(b) Availability of sequestration.—If the requirements of section 3101 are satisfied, a court shall issue a writ authorizing the United States to sequester income from property in which the debtor has a substantial nonexempt interest, as security for such judgment (and interest and costs) as the United States may recover on a claim for a debt—

(1) in an action on a contract, express or implied, against the debtor for payment of money, only if the United States shows reasonable cause to believe that—

(A) the contract is not fully secured by real or personal property; or

(B) the value of the original security is substantially diminished, without any act of the United States or the person to whom the security was given, below the amount of the debt;

(2) in an action against the debtor for damages in tort;

(3) if the debtor resides outside the jurisdiction of the United States; or

(4) in an action to recover a fine, penalty, or tax.

(c) Issuance of writ; contents.—(1) Subject to subsections (a) and (b), a writ of sequestration shall be issued by the court directing the United States marshal of the district where income described in subsection (a) is located to sequester the income.

(2) Several writs of sequestration may be issued at the same time, or in succession, and sent to different judicial districts until sufficient income is sequestered.

(3) The writ of sequestration shall contain—

(A) the date of the issuance of the writ;

(B) the identity of the court, the docket number of the action, and the identity of the cause of action;

(C) the name and last known address of the debtor;

(D) the amount to be secured by the sequestration; and

(E) a reasonable description of the income to be sequestered.

(d) Execution of writ.—(1) The United States marshal receiving the writ shall proceed without delay to execute the writ.

(2) The United States marshal shall file a copy of the notice of sequestration in the same manner as provided for judgments in section 3201(a)(1). The United States marshal shall serve a copy of the writ and notice of sequestration on—

(A) the debtor against whom the writ is issued; and

(B) the person who has possession of the income subject to the writ;

in the same manner that a summons is served in a civil action and make the return thereof.

(e) Deposit of sequestered income.—A person who has possession of the income subject to a writ of sequestration shall deposit such income with the clerk of the court, accompanied by a statement in writing stating the person's name, the name of the debtor, the amount of such income, the property from which such income is produced, and the period during which such income is produced.

(f) Return of writ; duties of marshal; further return.—(1) A United States marshal executing a writ of sequestration shall return the writ with the marshal's action endorsed thereon or attached thereto and signed by the marshal, to the court from which it was issued, within 5 days after the date of the execution.

(2) The return shall describe the income sequestered with sufficient certainty to identify it and shall state the location where it was sequestered, and the date and time it was sequestered. If no income was sequestered, the return shall so state.

(3) If sequestered income is claimed after the return, the United States marshal shall immediately make a further return to the clerk of the court showing the disposition of the income.

(g) Reduction or dissolution of sequestration.—(1) If an excessive or unreasonable sequestration is made, the debtor may submit a motion to the court for a reduction of the amount of the sequestration or its dissolution. Notice of such motion shall be served on the United States.

(2) The court shall order a part of the income to be released, if after a hearing the court finds that the amount of the sequestration is excessive or unreasonable or if the sequestration is for an amount larger than the sum of the liquidated or ascertainable amount of the debt and the amount of interest and costs likely to be taxed.

(3) The court shall dissolve the sequestration if the amount of the debt is unliquidated and unascertainable by calculation.

(h) Preservation of income under sequester.—If personal property in custody of the United States marshal under a writ of sequestration is not claimed, the court may make such order for its preservation or use as appears to be in the interest of the parties.

(i) Judgment and disposition of sequestered income.—

(1) **Judgment for the United States.**—On entry of judgment for the United States, the court shall order the sequestered income to be applied to the satisfaction of the judgment.

(2) **Restoration of income.**—If the sequestration is vacated or if the judgment on the claim for the debt is for the person against whom the writ of sequestration is issued, the court shall order the income restored to the debtor.

(Added Pub.L. 101–647, Title XXXVI, § 3611, Nov. 29, 1990, 104 Stat. 4946.)

HISTORICAL AND STATUTORY NOTES

Effective and Applicability Provisions

Section to take effect 180 days after Nov. 29, 1990, except as otherwise provided, see section 3631 of Pub.L. 101–647, set out as a note under section 3001 of this title.

SUBCHAPTER C—POSTJUDGMENT REMEDIES

Sec.
3201. Judgment liens.
3202. Enforcement of judgments.
3203. Execution.
3204. Installment payment order.
3205. Garnishment.
3206. Discharge.

§ 3201. Judgment liens

(a) Creation.—A judgment in a civil action shall create a lien on all real property of a judgment debtor on filing a certified copy of the abstract of the judgment in the manner in which a notice of tax lien would be filed under paragraphs (1) and (2) of section 6323(f) of the Internal Revenue Code of 1986. A lien created under this paragraph is for the amount necessary to satisfy the judgment, including costs and interest.

(b) Priority of lien.—A lien created under subsection (a) shall have priority over any other lien or encumbrance which is perfected later in time.

(c) Duration of lien; renewal.—(1) Except as provided in paragraph (2), a lien created under subsection (a) is effective, unless satisfied, for a period of 20 years.

(2) Such lien may be renewed for one additional period of 20 years upon filing a notice of renewal in the same manner as the judgment is filed and shall relate back to the date the judgment is filed if—

(A) the notice of renewal is filed before the expiration of the 20–year period to prevent the expiration of the lien; and

(B) the court approves the renewal of such lien under this paragraph.

(d) Release of judgment lien.—A judgment lien shall be released on the filing of a satisfaction of judgment or release of lien in the same manner as the judgment is filed to obtain the lien.

(e) Effect of lien on eligibility for Federal grants, loans or programs.—A debtor who has a judgment lien against the debtor's property for a debt to the United States shall not be eligible to receive any grant or loan which is made, insured, guaranteed, or financed directly or indirectly by the United States or to receive funds directly from the Federal Government in any program, except funds to which the debtor is entitled as beneficiary, until the judgment is paid in full or otherwise satisfied. The agency of the United States that is responsible for such grants and loans may promulgate regulations to allow for waiver of this restriction on eligibility for such grants, loans, and funds.

(f) Sale of property subject to judgment lien.—(1) On proper application to a court, the court may order the United States to sell, in accordance with sections 2001 and 2002, any real property subject to a judgment lien in effect under this section.

(2) This subsection shall not preclude the United States from using an execution sale pursuant to section 3203(g) to sell real property subject to a judgment lien.

(Added Pub.L. 101–647, Title XXXVI, § 3611, Nov. 29, 1990, 104 Stat. 4948.)

HISTORICAL AND STATUTORY NOTES

References in Text

Section 6323(f) of the Internal Revenue Code of 1986, referred to in subsec. (a), is classified to section 6323(f) of Title 26, Internal Revenue Code.

Effective and Applicability Provisions

1990 Acts. Section to take effect 180 days after Nov. 29, 1990, except as otherwise provided, see section 3631 of Pub.L. 101–647, set out as a note under section 3001 of this title.

§ 3202. Enforcement of judgments

(a) Enforcement remedies.—A judgment may be enforced by any of the remedies set forth in this subchapter. A court may issue other writs pursuant to section 1651 of title 28, United States Code, as necessary to support such remedies, subject to rule 81(b) of the Federal Rules of Civil Procedure.

(b) Notice.—On the commencement by the United States of an action or proceeding under this subchapter to obtain a remedy, the counsel for the United States shall prepare, and clerk of the court shall issue, a notice in substantially the following form:

"NOTICE

"You are hereby notified that this [property] is being taken by the United States Government, which has a court judgment in [case docket number and jurisdiction of court] of $[amount] for [reason of debt].

"In addition, you are hereby notified that there are exemptions under the law which may protect some of this property from being taken by the United States Government if [name of judgment debtor] can show that the exemptions apply. Below is a summary of the major exemptions which apply in most situations in the State of [State where property is located]:

"[A statement summarizing in plain and understandable English the election available with respect to such State under section 3014 and the types of property that may be exempted under each of the alternatives specified in paragraphs (1) and (2) of section 3014(a) and a statement that different property may be so exempted with respect to the State in which the debtor resides.]

"If you are [name of judgment debtor], you have a right to ask the court to return your property to you if you think the property the Government is taking qualifies under one of the above exemptions [For a default judgment:] or if you think you do not owe the money to the United States Government that it says you do.

"If you want a hearing, you must notify the court within 20 days after you receive this notice. You must make your request in writing, and either mail it or deliver it in person to the clerk of the court at [address]. If you wish, you may use this notice to request the hearing by checking the box below and mailing this notice to the court clerk. You must also send a copy of your request to the Government at [address], so the Government will know you want a hearing. The hearing will take place within 5 days after the clerk receives your request, if you ask for it to take place that quickly, or as soon after that as possible.

"At the hearing you may explain to the judge why you believe the property the Government has taken is exempt [For a default judgment:] or why you think you do not owe the money to the Government. [For a writ of execution:] If you do not request a hearing within 20 days of receiving this notice, your [property] may be sold at public auction and the payment used toward the money you owe the Government.

"If you think you live outside the Federal judicial district in which the court is located, you may request, not later than 20 days after your[1] receive this notice, that this proceeding to take your property be transferred by the court to the Federal judicial district in which you reside. You must make your request in writing, and either mail it or deliver it in person to the clerk of the court at [address]. You must also send a copy of your request to the Government at [address], so the Government will know you want the proceeding to be transferred.

"Be sure to keep a copy of this notice for your own records. If you have any questions about your rights or about this procedure, you should contact a lawyer, an office of public legal assistance, or the clerk of the court. The clerk is not permitted to give legal advice, but can refer you to other sources of information."

(c) Service.—A copy of the notice and a copy of the application for granting a remedy under this subchapter shall be served by counsel for the United States on the judgment debtor against whom such remedy is sought and on each person whom the United States, after diligent inquiry, has reasonable cause to believe has an interest in property to which the remedy is directed.

(d) Hearing.—By requesting, within 20 days after receiving the notice described in section 3202(b), the court to hold a hearing, the judgment debtor may move to quash the order granting such remedy. The court that issued such order shall hold a hearing on such motion as soon as practicable, or, if so requested by the judgment debtor, within 5 days after receiving the request or as soon thereafter as possible. The issues at such hearing shall be limited—

(1) to the probable validity of any claim of exemption by the judgment debtor;

(2) to compliance with any statutory requirement for the issuance of the postjudgment remedy granted; and

(3) if the judgment is by default and only to the extent that the Constitution or another law of the United States provides a right to a hearing on the issue, to—

(A) the probable validity of the claim for the debt which is merged in the judgment; and

(B) the existence of good cause for setting aside such judgment.

This subparagraph shall not be construed to afford the judgment debtor the right to more than one such hearing except to the extent that the Constitution or another law of the United States provides a right to more than one such hearing.

(e) Sale of property.—The property of a judgment debtor which is subject to sale to satisfy the judgment may be sold by judicial sale, pursuant to sections 2001, 2002, and 2004 or by execution sale pursuant to section 3203(g). If a hearing is requested pursuant to subsection (d), property with respect to which the request relates shall not be sold before such hearing. (Added Pub.L. 101–647, Title XXXVI, § 3611, Nov. 29, 1990, 104 Stat. 4949.)

[1] So in original. Probably should be "you".

HISTORICAL AND STATUTORY NOTES

Effective and Applicability Provisions

1990 Acts. Section to take effect 180 days after Nov. 29, 1990, except as otherwise provided, see section 3631 of Pub.L. 101–647, set out as a note under section 3001 of this title.

§ 3203. Execution

(a) Property subject to execution.—All property in which the judgment debtor has a substantial nonexempt interest shall be subject to levy pursuant to a writ of execution. The debtor's earnings shall not be subject to execution while in the possession, custody, or control of the debtor's employer. Co-owned property shall be subject to execution to the extent such property is subject to execution under the law of the State in which it is located.

(b) Creation of execution lien.—A lien shall be created in favor of the United States on all property levied on under a writ of execution and shall date from the time of the levy. Such lien shall have priority over all subsequent liens and shall be for the aggregate amount of the judgment, costs, and interest. The execution lien on any real property as to which the United States has a judgment lien shall relate back to the judgment lien date.

(c) Writ of execution.—

(1) Issuance.—On written application of counsel for the United States, the court may issue a writ of execution. Multiple writs may issue simultaneously, and successive writs may issue before the return date of a writ previously issued.

(2) Form of writ.—

(A) General contents.—A writ of execution shall specify the date that the judgment is entered, the court in which it is entered, the amount of the judgment if for money, the amount of the costs, the amount of interest due, the sum due as of the date the writ is issued, the rate of post-judgment interest, the name of the judgment debtor, and the judgment debtor's last known address.

(B) Additional contents.—(i) Except as provided in clauses (ii) and (iii), the writ shall direct the United States marshal to satisfy the judgment by levying on and selling property in which the judgment debtor has a substantial nonexempt interest, but not to exceed property reasonably equivalent in value to the aggregate amount of the judgment, costs, and interest.

(ii) A writ of execution issued on a judgment for the delivery to the United States of the possession of personal property, or for the delivery of the possession of real property, shall particularly describe the property, and shall require the marshal to deliver the possession of the property to the United States.

(iii) A writ of execution on a judgment for the recovery of personal property or its value shall direct the marshal, in case a delivery of the specific property cannot be had, to levy and collect such value out of any property in which the judgment debtor has a substantial nonexempt interest.

(d) Levy of execution.—

(1) In general.—Levy on property pursuant to a writ of execution issued under this section shall be made in the same manner as levy on property is made pursuant to a writ of attachment issued under section 3102(d).

(2) Death of judgment debtor.—The death of the judgment debtor after a writ of execution is issued stays the execution proceedings, but any lien acquired by levy of the writ shall be recognized and enforced by the court for the district in which the estate of the deceased is located. The execution lien may be enforced—

(A) against the executor, administrator, or personal representative of the estate of the deceased; or

(B) if there be none, against the deceased's property coming to the heirs or devisees or at their option against cash in their possession, but only to the extent of the value of the property coming to them.

(3) Records of United States marshal.—(A) A United States marshal receiving a writ of execution shall endorse thereon the exact hour and date of receipt.

(B) The United States marshal shall make a written record of every levy, specify the property on which levy is made, the date on which levy is made, and the marshal's costs, expenses, and fees.

(C) The United States marshal shall make a written return to the court on each writ of execution stating concisely what is done pursuant to the writ and shall deliver a copy to counsel for the United States who requests the writ. The writ shall be returned not more than—

(i) 90 days after the date of issuance if levy is not made; or

(ii) 10 days after the date of sale of property on which levy is made.

(e) Appointment of receiver.—Pending the levy of execution, the court may appoint a receiver to manage property described in such writ if there is a substantial danger that the property will be removed from the jurisdiction of the court, lost, materially injured or damaged, or mismanaged.

(f) Replevy; redemption.—

(1) Before execution sale.—(A) Before execution sale, the United States marshal may return property[1] to the judgment debtor any personal property taken in execution, on—

(i) satisfaction of the judgment, interest, and costs, and any costs incurred in connection with scheduling the sale; or

(ii) receipt from the judgment debtor of a bond—

(I) payable to the United States, with 2 or more good and sufficient sureties to be approved by the marshal, conditioned on the delivery of the property to the marshal at the time and place named in the bond to be sold under subsection (g); or

(II) for the payment to the marshal of a fair value thereof which shall be stated in the bond.

(B) A judgment debtor who sells or disposes of property replevied under subparagraph (A) shall pay the United States marshal the stipulated value of such property.

(C) If the judgment debtor fails to deliver such property to the United States marshal pursuant to the terms of the delivery described in subparagraph (A)(ii)(I) and fails to pay the United States marshal the stipulated value of such property, the United States marshal shall endorse the bond "forfeited" and return it to the court from which the writ of execution issued. If the judgment is not fully satisfied, the court shall issue a writ of execution against the judgment debtor and the sureties on the bond for the amount due, not exceeding the stipulated value of the property, on which execution no delivery bond shall be taken, which instruction shall be endorsed on the writ.

(2) After execution sale.—The judgment debtor shall not be entitled to redeem the property after the execution sale.

(g) Execution sale.—

(1) General procedures.—An execution sale under this section shall be conducted in a commercially reasonable manner—

(A) Sale of real property.—

(i) In general.—**(I)** Except as provided in clause (ii), real property, or any interest therein, shall be sold, after the expiration of the 90–day period beginning on the date of levy under subsection (d), for cash at public auction at the courthouse of the county, parish, or city in which the greater part of the property is located or on the premises or some parcel thereof.

(II) The court may order the sale of any real property after the expiration of the 30–day period beginning on the date of levy under subsection (d) if the court determines that such property is likely to perish, waste, be destroyed, or otherwise substantially depreciate in value during the 90–day period beginning on the date of levy.

(III) The time and place of sale of real property, or any interest therein, under execution shall be advertised by the United States marshal, by publication of notice, once a week for at least 3 weeks prior to the sale, in at least one newspaper of general circulation in the county or parish where the property is located. The first publication shall appear not less than 25 days preceding the day of sale. The notice shall contain a statement of the authority by which the sale is to be made, the time of levy, the time and place of sale, and a brief description of the property to be sold, sufficient to identify the property (such as a street address for urban property and the survey identification and location for rural property), but it shall not be necessary for the notice to contain field notes. Such property shall be open for inspection and appraisal, subject to the judgment debtor's reasonable objections, for a reasonable period before the day of sale.

(IV) The United States marshal shall serve written notice of public sale by personal delivery, or certified or registered mail, to each person whom the marshal has reasonable cause to believe, after a title search is conducted by the United States, has an interest in property under execution, including lienholders, co-owners, and tenants, at least 25 days before the day of sale, to the last known address of each such person.

(ii) Sale of city lots.—If the real property consists of several lots, tracts, or parcels in a city or town, each lot, tract, or parcel shall be offered for sale separately, unless not susceptible to separate sale because of the character of improvements.

(iii) Sale of rural property.—If the real property is not located in a city or town, the judgment debtor may—

(I) divide the property into lots of not less than 50 acres or in such greater or lesser amounts as ordered by the court;

(II) furnish a survey of such prepared by a registered surveyor; and

(III) designate the order in which those lots shall be sold.

When a sufficient number of lots are sold to satisfy the amount of the execution and costs of sale, the marshal shall stop the sale.

(B) Sale of personal property.—**(i)** Personal property levied on shall be offered for sale on the premises where it is located at the time of levy, at the courthouse of the county, parish or city wherein it is located, or at another location if ordered by the court. Personal property susceptible of being exhibited shall not be sold unless it is present and subject to the view of those attending the sale unless—

(I) the property consists of shares of stock in corporations;

(II) by reason of the nature of the property, it is impractical to exhibit it; or

(III) the debtor's interest in the property does not include the right to the exclusive possession.

(ii)(I) Except as provided in subclause (II), personal property, or any interest therein, shall be sold after the expiration of the 30–day period beginning on the date of levy under subsection (d).

(II) The court may order the sale of any personal property before the expiration of such 30–day period if the court determines that such property is likely to perish, waste, be destroyed, or otherwise substantially depreciate in value during such 30–day period.

(iii) Notice of the time and place of the sale of personal property shall be given by the United States marshal by posting notice thereof for not less than 10 days successively immediately before the day of sale at the courthouse of any county, parish, or city, and at the place where the sale is to be made.

(iv) The United States marshal shall serve written notice of public sale by personal delivery, or registered or certified mail at their last known addresses, on the judgment debtor and other persons who the marshal has reasonable cause to believe, after diligent inquiry, have a substantial interest in the property.

(2) Postponement of sale.—The United States marshal may postpone an execution sale from time to time by continuing the required posting or publication of notice until the date to which the sale is postponed, and appending, at the foot of each such notice of a current copy of the following:

"The above sale is postponed until the _____ day of _____, 19____, at ____ o'clock ____.M., _____, United States Marshal for the District of _____, by _____, Deputy, dated _____."

(3) Sale procedures.—

(A) Bidding requirements.—A bidder at an execution sale of property, may be required by the United States marshal to make a cash deposit of as much as 20 percent of the sale price proposed before the bid is accepted.

(B) Resale of property.—If the terms of the sale are not complied with by the successful bidder, the United States marshal shall proceed to sell the property again on the same day if there is sufficient time. If there is insufficient time, the marshal shall schedule and notice a subsequent sale of the property as provided in paragraphs (1) and (2).

(4) Rights and liabilities of purchasers.—

(A) Transfer of title after sale.—

(i) If property is sold under this subsection and the successful bidder complies with the terms of the sale, the United States marshal shall execute and deliver all documents necessary to transfer to the successful bidder, without warranty, all the rights, titles, interests, and claims of the judgment debtor in the property.

(ii) If the successful bidder dies before execution and delivery of the documents needed to transfer ownership, the United States marshal shall execute and deliver them to the successful bidder's estate. Such delivery to the estate shall have the same effect as if accomplished during the lifetime of the purchaser.

(B) Purchaser considered innocent purchaser without notice.—The purchaser of property sold under execution shall be deemed to be an innocent purchaser without notice if the purchaser would have been considered an innocent purchaser without notice had the sale been made voluntarily and in person by the judgment debtor.

(C) Liability of successful bidder who fails to comply.—A successful bidder at an execution sale who fails to comply with the terms of the sale shall forfeit to the United States the cash deposit or, at the election of the United States, shall be liable to the United States, on a subsequent sale of the property, for all net losses incurred by the United States as a result of such failure.

(h) Disposition of proceeds; further levy.—

(1) Distribution of sale proceeds.—(A) The United States marshal shall first deliver to the judgment debtor such amounts to which the judgment debtor is entitled from the sale of partially exempt property.

(B) The United States marshal shall next deduct from the proceeds of an execution sale of property an amount equal to the reasonable expenses incurred in making the levy of execution and in keeping and maintaining the property.

(C) Except as provided in subparagraph (D), the United States marshal shall deliver the balance of the proceeds to the counsel for the United States as soon as practicable.

(D) If more proceeds are received from the execution sale than is necessary to satisfy the executions held by the United States marshal, the marshal shall pay the surplus to the judgment debtor.

(2) Further levy if execution not satisfied.—If the proceeds of the execution sale of the property levied on are insufficient to satisfy the execution, the United States marshal shall proceed on the same writ of execution to levy other property of the judgment debtor.

(Added Pub.L. 101–647, Title XXXVI, § 3611, Nov. 29, 1990, 104 Stat. 4950.)

[1] So in original. The word "property" probably should not appear.

HISTORICAL AND STATUTORY NOTES

Effective and Applicability Provisions

1990 Acts. Section to take effect 180 days after Nov. 29, 1990, except as otherwise provided, see section 3631 of Pub.L. 101–647, set out as a note under section 3001 of this title.

§ 3204. Installment payment order

(a) Authority to issue order.—Subject to subsection (c), if it is shown that the judgment debtor—

(1) is receiving or will receive substantial nonexempt disposable earnings from self employment that are not subject to garnishment; or

(2) is diverting or concealing substantial earnings from any source, or property received in lieu of earnings;

then upon motion of the United States and notice to the judgment debtor, the court may, if appropriate, order that the judgment debtor make specified installment payments to the United States. Notice of the motion shall be served on the judgment debtor in the same manner as a summons or by registered or certified mail, return receipt requested. In fixing the amount of the payments, the court shall take into consideration after a hearing, the income, resources, and reasonable requirements of the judgment debtor and the judgment debtor's dependents, any other payments to be made in satisfaction of judgments against the judgment debtor, and the amount due on the judgment in favor of the United States.

(b) Modification of order.—On motion of the United States or the judgment debtor, and upon a showing that the judgment debtor's financial circumstances have changed or that assets not previously disclosed by the judgment debtor have been discovered, the court may modify the amount of payments, alter their frequency, or require full payment.

(c) Limitation.—(1) An order may not be issued under subsection (a), and if so issued shall have no force or effect, against a judgment debtor with respect to whom there is in effect a writ of garnishment of earnings issued under this chapter and based on the same debt.

(2) An order may not be issued under subsection (a) with respect to any earnings of the debtor except nonexempt disposable earnings.

(Added Pub.L. 101-647, Title XXXVI, § 3611, Nov. 29, 1990, 104 Stat. 4955.)

HISTORICAL AND STATUTORY NOTES

Effective and Applicability Provisions

1990 Acts. Section to take effect 180 days after Nov. 29, 1990, except as otherwise provided, see section 3631 of Pub.L. 101-647, set out as a note under section 3001 of this title.

§ 3205. Garnishment

(a) In general.—A court may issue a writ of garnishment against property (including nonexempt disposable earnings) in which the debtor has a substantial nonexempt interest and which is in the possession, custody, or control of a person other than the debtor, in order to satisfy the judgment against the debtor. Co-owned property shall be subject to garnishment to the same extent as co-owned property is subject to garnishment under the law of the State in which such property is located. A court may issue simultaneous separate writs of garnishment to several garnishees. A writ of garnishment issued under this subsection shall be continuing and shall terminate only as provided in subsection (c)(10).

(b) Writ.—

(1) General requirements.—The United States shall include in its application for a writ of garnishment—

(A) the judgment debtor's name, social security number (if known), and last known address;

(B) the nature and amount of the debt owed and the facts that not less than 30 days has elapsed since demand on the debtor for payment of the debt was made and the judgment debtor has not paid the amount due; and

(C) that the garnishee is believed to have possession of property (including nonexempt disposable earnings) in which the debtor has a substantial nonexempt interest.

(2) Proper garnishee for particular property.—

(A) If the property consists of a right to or share in the stock of an association or corporation, or interests or profits therein, for which a certificate of stock or other negotiable instrument is not outstanding, the corporation, or the president or treasurer of the association shall be the garnishee.

(B) If the property consists of an interest in a partnership interest, any partner other than the debtor shall be the garnishee on behalf of the partnership.

(C) If the property or a debt is evidenced by a negotiable instrument for the payment of money, a negotiable document of title or a certificate of stock of an association or corporation, the instrument, document, or certificate shall be treated as property capable of delivery and the person holding it shall be the garnishee, except that—

(i) subject to clause (ii), in the case of a security which is transferable in the manner set forth in State law, the entity that carries on its books an account in the name of the debtor in which is reflected such security shall be the garnishee; and

(ii) notwithstanding clause (i), the pledgee shall be the garnishee if such security is pledged.

(c) Procedures applicable to writ.—

(1) Court determination.—If the court determines that the requirements of this section are satisfied, the court shall issue an appropriate writ of garnishment.

(2) Form of writ.—The writ shall state—

(A) The nature and amount of the debt, and any cost and interest owed with respect to the debt.

(B) The name and address of the garnishee.

(C) The name and address of counsel for the United States.

(D) The last known address of the judgment debtor.

(E) That the garnishee shall answer the writ within 10 days of service of the writ.

(F) That the garnishee shall withhold and retain any property in which the debtor has a substantial nonexempt interest and for which the garnishee is or may become indebted to the judgment debtor pending further order of the court.

(3) Service of writ.—The United States shall serve the garnishee and the judgment debtor with a copy of the writ of garnishment and shall certify to the court that this service was made. The writ shall be accompanied by—

(A) an instruction explaining the requirement that the garnishee submit a written answer to the writ; and

(B) instructions to the judgment debtor for objecting to the answer of the garnishee and for obtaining a hearing on the objections.

(4) **Answer of the garnishee.**—In its written answer to the writ of garnishment, the garnishee shall state under oath—

(A) whether the garnishee has custody, control or possession of such property;

(B) a description of such property and the value of such interest;

(C) a description of any previous garnishments to which such property is subject and the extent to which any remaining property is not exempt; and

(D) the amount of the debt the garnishee anticipates owing to the judgment debtor in the future and whether the period for payment will be weekly or another specified period.

The garnishee shall file the original answer with the court issuing the writ and serve a copy on the debtor and counsel for the United States.

(5) **Objections to answer.**—Within 20 days after receipt of the answer, the judgment debtor or the United States may file a written objection to the answer and request a hearing. The party objecting shall state the grounds for the objection and bear the burden of proving such grounds. A copy of the objection and request for a hearing shall be served on the garnishee and all other parties. The court shall hold a hearing within 10 days after the date the request is received by the court, or as soon thereafter as is practicable, and give notice of the hearing date to all the parties.

(6) **Garnishee's failure to answer or pay.**—If a garnishee fails to answer the writ of garnishment or to withhold property in accordance with the writ, the United States may petition the court for an order requiring the garnishee to appear before the court to answer the writ and to so withhold property before the appearance date. If the garnishee fails to appear, or appears and fails to show good cause why the garnishee failed to comply with the writ, the court shall enter judgment against the garnishee for the value of the judgment debtor's nonexempt interest in such property (including nonexempt disposable earnings). The court may award a reasonable attorney's fee to the United States and against the garnishee if the writ is not answered within the time specified therein and a petition requiring the garnishee to appear is filed as provided in this section.

(7) **Disposition order.**—After the garnishee files an answer and if no hearing is requested within the required time period, the court shall promptly enter an order directing the garnishee as to the disposition of the judgment debtor's nonexempt interest in such property. If a hearing is timely requested, the order shall be entered within 5 days after the hearing, or as soon thereafter as is practicable.

(8) **Priorities.**—Judicial orders and garnishments for the support of a person shall have priority over a writ of garnishment issued under this section. As to any other writ of garnishment or levy, a garnishment issued under this section shall have priority over writs which are issued later in time.

(9) **Accounting.**—(A) While a writ of garnishment is in effect under this section, the United States shall give an annual accounting on the garnishment to the judgment debtor and the garnishee.

(B) Within 10 days after the garnishment terminates, the United States shall give a cumulative written accounting to the judgment debtor and garnishee of all property it receives under a writ of garnishment. Within 10 days after such accounting is received, the judgment debtor or garnishee may file a written objection to the accounting and a request for hearing. The party objecting shall state grounds for the objection. The court shall hold a hearing on the objection within 10 days after the court receives the request for a hearing, or as soon thereafter as is practicable.

(10) **Termination of garnishment.**—A garnishment under this chapter is terminated only by—

(A) a court order quashing the writ of garnishment;

(B) exhaustion of property in the possesion,[1] custody, or control of the garnishee in which the debtor has a substantial nonexempt interest (including nonexempt disposable earnings), unless the garnishee reinstates or reemploys the judgment debtor within 90 days after the judgment debtor's dismissal or resignation; or

(C) satisfaction of the debt with respect to which the writ is issued.

(Added Pub.L. 101–647, Title XXXVI, § 3611, Nov. 29, 1990, 104 Stat. 4956.)

[1] So in original. Probably should be "possession,".

HISTORICAL AND STATUTORY NOTES

Effective and Applicability Provisions

1990 Acts. Section to take effect 180 days after Nov. 29, 1990, except as otherwise provided, see section 3631 of Pub.L. 101–647, set out as a note under section 3001 of this title.

§ 3206. Discharge

A person who pursuant to an execution or order issued under this chapter by a court pays or delivers to the United States, a United States marshal, or a receiver, money or other personal property in which a judgment debtor has or will have an interest, or so pays a debt such person owes the judgment debtor, is discharged from such debt to the judgment debtor to the extent of the payment or delivery.

(Added Pub.L. 101-647, Title XXXVI, § 3611, Nov. 29, 1990, 104 Stat. 4959.)

HISTORICAL AND STATUTORY NOTES

Effective and Applicability Provisions

1990 Acts. Section to take effect 180 days after Nov. 29, 1990, except as otherwise provided, see section 3631 of Pub.L. 101-647, set out as a note under section 3001 of this title.

SUBCHAPTER D—FRAUDULENT TRANSFERS INVOLVING DEBTS

Sec.
3301. Definitions.
3302. Insolvency.
3303. Value for a transfer or obligation.[1]
3304. Transfer fraudulent as to a debt to the United States.
3305. When transfer is made or obligation is incurred.
3306. Remedies of the United States.
3307. Defenses, liability and protection of transferee.[1]
3308. Supplementary provision.

[1] So in original. Does not conform to section catchline.

§ 3301. Definitions

As used in this subchapter:

(1) "Affiliate" means—

(A) a person who directly or indirectly owns, controls, or holds with power to vote, 20 percent or more of the outstanding voting securities of the debtor, other than a person who holds the securities—

(i) as a fiduciary or agent without sole discretionary power to vote the securities; or

(ii) solely to secure a debt, if the person has not exercised the power to vote;

(B) a corporation 20 percent or more of whose outstanding voting securities are directly or indirectly owned, controlled, or held with power to vote, by the debtor or a person who directly or indirectly owns, controls, or holds with power to vote, 20 percent or more of the outstanding voting securities of the debtor, other than the person who holds securities—

(i) as a fiduciary or agent without sole power to vote the securities; or

(ii) solely to secure a debt, if the person has not in fact exercised the power to vote;

(C) a person whose business is operated by the debtor under a lease or other agreement, or a person substantially all of whose assets are controlled by the debtor; or

(D) a person who operates the debtor's business under a lease or other agreement or controls substantially all of the debtor's assets.

(2) "Asset" means property of a debtor, but does not include—

(A) property to the extent it is encumbered by a valid lien;

(B) property to the extent it is generally exempt under nonbankruptcy law; or

(C) an interest in real property held in tenancy by the entirety, or as part of a community estate, to extent such interest is not subject to process by the United States holding a claim against only one tenant or co-owner.

(3) "Claim" means a right to payment, whether or not the right is reduced to judgment, liquidated, unliquidated, fixed, contingent, matured, unmatured, disputed, undisputed, legal, equitable, secured, or unsecured.

(4) "Creditor" means a person who has a claim.

(5) "Insider" includes—

(A) if the debtor is an individual—

(i) a relative of the debtor or of a general partner of the debtor;

(ii) a partnership in which the debtor is a general partner;

(iii) a general partner in a partnership described in clause (ii); or

(iv) a corporation of which the debtor is a director, officer, or person in control;

(B) if the debtor is a corporation—

(i) a director of the debtor;

(ii) an officer of the debtor;

(iii) a person in control of the debtor;

(iv) a partnership in which the debtor is a general partner;

(v) a general partner in a partnership described in clause (iv); or

(vi) a relative of a general partner, director, officer, or person in control of the debtor;

(C) if the debtor is a partnership—

(i) a general partner in the debtor;

(ii) a relative of a general partner in, a general partner of, or a person in control of the debtor;

(iii) another partnership in which the debtor is a general partner;

(iv) a general partner in a partnership described in clause (iii); or

(v) a person in control of the debtor.[1]

(D) an affiliate, or an insider of an affiliate as if the affiliate were the debtor; and

(E) a managing agent of the debtor.

(4)[2] "Lien" means a charge against or an interest in property to secure payment of a debt and includes a security interest created by agreement, a judicial lien obtained by legal or equitable process or proceedings, a common law lien, or a statutory lien.

(5)[3] "Relative" means an individual related, by consanguinity or adoption, within the third degree as determined by the common law, a spouse, or an individual so related to a spouse within the third degree as so determined.

(6)[4] "Transfer" means every mode, direct or indirect, absolute or conditional, voluntary or involuntary, of disposing of or parting with an asset or an interest in an asset, and includes payment of money, release, lease, and creation of a lien or other encumbrance.

(7)[5] "Valid lien" means a lien that is effective against the holder of a judicial lien subsequently obtained in legal or equitable proceeding.

(Added Pub.L. 101–647, Title XXXVI, § 3611, Nov. 29, 1990, 104 Stat. 4959.)

[1] So in original. The period probably should be a semicolon.
[2] So in original. Probably should be "(6)".
[3] So in original. Probably should be "(7)".
[4] So in original. Probably should be "(8)".
[5] So in original. Probably should be "(9)".

HISTORICAL AND STATUTORY NOTES

Effective and Applicability Provisions

1990 Acts. Section to take effect 180 days after Nov. 29, 1990, except as otherwise provided, see section 3631 of Pub.L. 101–647, set out as a note under section 3001 of this title.

§ 3302. Insolvency

(a) In general.—Except as provided in subsection (c), a debtor is insolvent if the sum of the debtor's debts is greater than all of the debtor's assets at a fair valuation.

(b) Presumption.—A debtor who is generally not paying debts as they become due is presumed to be insolvent.

(c) Calculation.—A partnership is insolvent under subsection (a) if the sum of the partnership's debts is greater than the aggregate, at a fair valuation, of—

(1) all of the partnership's assets; and

(2) the sum of the excess of the value of each general partner's non-partnership assets over the partner's non-partnership debts.

(d) Assets.—For purposes of this section, assets do not include property that is transferred, concealed, or removed with intent to hinder, delay, or defraud creditors or that has been transferred in a manner making the transfer voidable under this subchapter.

(e) Debts.—For purposes of this section, debts do not include an obligation to the extent such obligation is secured by a valid lien on property of the debtor not included as an asset.

(Added Pub.L. 101–647, Title XXXVI, § 3611, Nov. 29, 1990, 104 Stat. 4961.)

HISTORICAL AND STATUTORY NOTES

Effective and Applicability Provisions

1990 Acts. Section to take effect 180 days after Nov. 29, 1990, except as otherwise provided, see section 3631 of Pub.L. 101–647, set out as a note under section 3001 of this title.

§ 3303. Value for transfer or obligation

(a) Transaction.—Value is given for a transfer or an obligation if, in exchange for the transfer or obligation, property is transferred or an antecedent debt is secured or satisfied, but value does not include an unperformed promise made otherwise than in the ordinary course of the promisor's business to furnish support to the debtor or another person.

(b) Reasonably equivalent value.—For the purposes of sections 3304 and 3307, a person gives a reasonably equivalent value if the person acquires an interest of the debtor in an asset pursuant to a regularly conducted, noncollusive foreclosure sale or execution of a power of sale for the acquisition or disposition of such interest upon default under a mortgage, deed of trust, or security agreement.

(c) Present value.—A transfer is made for present value if the exchange between the debtor and the transferee is intended by them to be contemporaneous and is in fact substantially contemporaneous.

(Added Pub.L. 101–647, Title XXXVI, § 3611, Nov. 29, 1990, 104 Stat. 4961.)

HISTORICAL AND STATUTORY NOTES

Effective and Applicability Provisions

1990 Acts. Section to take effect 180 days after Nov. 29, 1990, except as otherwise provided, see section 3631 of Pub.L. 101–647, set out as a note under section 3001 of this title.

§ 3304. Transfer fraudulent as to a debt to the United States

(a) Debt arising before transfer.—Except as provided in section 3307, a transfer made or obligation incurred by a debtor is fraudulent as to a debt to the United States which arises before the transfer is made or the obligation is incurred if—

(1)(A) the debtor makes the transfer or incurs the obligation without receiving a reasonably equivalent value in exchange for the transfer or obligation; and

(B) the debtor is insolvent at that time or the debtor becomes insolvent as a result of the transfer or obligation; or

(2)(A) the transfer was made to an insider for an antecedent debt, the debtor was insolvent at the time; and

(B) the insider had reasonable cause to believe that the debtor was insolvent.

(b) Transfers without regard to date of judgment.—(1) Except as provided in section 3307, a transfer made or obligation incurred by a debtor is fraudulent as to a debt to the United States, whether such debt arises before or after the transfer is made or the obligation is incurred, if the debtor makes the transfer or incurs the obligation—

(A) with actual intent to hinder, delay, or defraud a creditor; or

(B) without receiving a reasonably equivalent value in exchange for the transfer or obligation if the debtor—

(i) was engaged or was about to engage in a business or a transaction for which the remaining assets of the debtor were unreasonably small in relation to the business or transaction; or

(ii) intended to incur, or believed or reasonably should have believed that he would incur, debts beyond his ability to pay as they became due.

(2) In determining actual intent under paragraph (1), consideration may be given, among other factors, to whether—

(A) the transfer or obligation was to an insider;

(B) the debtor retained possession or control of the property transferred after the transfer;

(C) the transfer or obligation was disclosed or concealed;

(D) before the transfer was made or obligation was incurred, the debtor had been sued or threatened with suit;

(E) the transfer was of substantially all the debtor's assets;

(F) the debtor absconded;

(G) the debtor removed or concealed assets;

(H) the value of the consideration received by the debtor was reasonably equivalent to the value of the asset transferred or the amount of the obligation incurred;

(I) the debtor was insolvent or became insolvent shortly after the transfer was made or the obligation was incurred;

(J) the transfer occurred shortly before or shortly after a substantial debt was incurred; and

(K) the debtor transferred the essential assets of the business to a lienor who transferred the assets to an insider of the debtor.

(Added Pub.L. 101–647, Title XXXVI, § 3611, Nov. 29, 1990, 104 Stat. 4961.)

HISTORICAL AND STATUTORY NOTES

Effective and Applicability Provisions

1990 Acts. Section to take effect 180 days after Nov. 29, 1990, except as otherwise provided, see section 3631 of Pub.L. 101–647, set out as a note under section 3001 of this title.

§ 3305. When transfer is made or obligation is incurred

For the purposes of this subchapter:

(1) A transfer is made—

(A) with respect to an asset that is real property (other than a fixture, but including the interest of a seller or purchaser under a contract for the sale of the asset), when the transfer is so far perfected that a good-faith purchaser of the asset from the debtor against whom applicable law permits the transfer to be perfected cannot acquire an interest in the asset that is superior to the interest of the transferee; and

(B) with respect to an asset that is not real property or that is a fixture, when the transfer is so far perfected that a creditor on a simple contract cannot acquire, otherwise than under this subchapter, a judicial lien that is superior to the interest of the transferee.

(2) If applicable law permits the transfer to be perfected as approved in paragraph (1) and the transfer is not so perfected before the commencement of an action or proceeding for relief under this subchapter, the transfer is deemed made immediately before the commencement of the action or proceeding.

(3) If applicable law does not permit the transfer to be perfected as provided in paragraph (1), the transfer is made when it becomes effective between the debtor and the transferee.

(4) A transfer is not made until the debtor has acquired rights in the asset transferred.

(5) An obligation is incurred—

(A) if oral, when it becomes effective between the parties; or

(B) if evidenced by a writing executed by the obligor, when such writing is delivered to or for the benefit of the obligee.

(Added Pub.L. 101–647, Title XXXVI, § 3611, Nov. 29, 1990, 104 Stat. 4962.)

HISTORICAL AND STATUTORY NOTES

Effective and Applicability Provisions

1990 Acts. Section to take effect 180 days after Nov. 29, 1990, except as otherwise provided, see section 3631 of Pub.L. 101–647, set out as a note under section 3001 of this title.

§ 3306. Remedies of the United States

(a) In general.—In an action or proceeding under this subchapter for relief against a transfer or obligation, the United States, subject to section 3307 and to applicable principles of equity and in accordance with the Federal Rules of Civil Procedure, may obtain—

(1) avoidance of the transfer or obligation to the extent necessary to satisfy the debt to the United States;

(2) a remedy under this chapter against the asset transferred or other property of the transferee; or

(3) any other relief the circumstances may require.

(b) Limitation.—A claim for relief with respect to a fraudulent transfer or obligation under this subchapter is extinguished unless action is brought—

(1) under section 3304(b)(1)(A) within 6 years after the transfer was made or the obligation was incurred or, if later, within 2 years after the transfer or obligation was or could reasonably have been discovered by the claimant;

(2) under subsection (a)(1) or (b)(1)(B) of section 3304 within 6 years after the transfer was made or the obligation was incurred; or

(3) under section 3304(a)(2) within 2 years after the transfer was made or the obligation was incurred.

(Added Pub.L. 101–647, Title XXXVI, § 3611, Nov. 29, 1990, 104 Stat. 4963.)

HISTORICAL AND STATUTORY NOTES

References in Text

The Federal Rules of Civil Procedure, referred to in subsec. (a), are set out in this title.

Effective and Applicability Provisions

1990 Acts. Section to take effect 180 days after Nov. 29, 1990, except as otherwise provided, see section 3631 of Pub.L. 101–647, set out as a note under section 3001 of this title.

§ 3307. Defenses, liability, and protection of transferee

(a) Good faith transfer.—A transfer or obligation is not voidable under section 3304(b) with respect to a person who took in good faith and for a reasonably equivalent value or against any transferee or obligee subsequent to such person.

(b) Limitation.—Except as provided in subsection (d), to the extent a transfer is voidable in an action or proceeding by the United States under section 3306(a)(1), the United States may recover judgment for the value of the asset transferred, but not to exceed the judgment on a debt. The judgment may be entered against—

(1) the first transferee of the asset or the person for whose benefit the transfer was made; or

(2) any subsequent transferee, other than a good faith transferee who took for value or any subsequent transferee of such good-faith transferee.

(c) Value of asset.—For purposes of subsection (b), the value of the asset is the value of the asset at the time of the transfer, subject to adjustment as the equities may require.

(d) Rights of good faith transferees and obligees.—Notwithstanding voidability of a transfer or an obligation under this subchapter, a good-faith transferee or obligee is entitled, to the extent of the value given the debtor for the transfer or obligation, to—

(1) a lien on or a right to retain any interest in the asset transferred;

(2) enforcement of any obligation incurred; or

(3) a reduction in the amount of the liability on the judgment.

(e) Exceptions.—A transfer is not voidable under section 3304(a) or section 3304(b)(2) if the transfer results from—

(1) termination of a lease upon default by the debtor when the termination is pursuant to the lease and applicable law; or

(2) enforcement of a security interest in compliance with article 9 of the Uniform Commercial Code or its equivalent in effect in the State where the property is located.

(f) Limitation of voidability.—A transfer is not voidable under section 3304(a)(2)—

(1) to the extent the insider gives new value to or for the benefit of the debtor after the transfer is made unless the new value is secured by a valid lien;

(2) if made in the ordinary course of business or financial affairs of the debtor and the insider; or

(3) if made pursuant to a good-faith effort to rehabilitate the debtor and the transfer secured both present value given for that purpose and an antecedent debt of the debtor.

(Added Pub.L. 101–647, Title XXXVI, § 3611, Nov. 29, 1990, 104 Stat. 4963.)

HISTORICAL AND STATUTORY NOTES

Effective and Applicability Provisions

1990 Acts. Section to take effect 180 days after Nov. 29, 1990, except as otherwise provided, see section 3631 of Pub.L. 101–647, set out as a note under section 3001 of this title.

§ 3308. Supplementary provision

Except as provided in this subchapter, the principles of law and equity, including the law merchant and the law relating to principal and agent, estoppel, laches, fraud, misrepresentation, duress, coercion, mistake, insolvency, or other validating or invalidating cause shall apply to actions and proceedings under this subchapter.

(Added Pub.L. 101–647, Title XXXVI, § 3611, Nov. 29, 1990, 104 Stat. 4964.)

HISTORICAL AND STATUTORY NOTES

Effective and Applicability Provisions

1990 Acts. Section to take effect 180 days after Nov. 29, 1990, except as otherwise provided, see section 3631 of Pub.L. 101–647, set out as a note under section 3001 of this title.

CHAPTER 178—PROFESSIONAL AND AMATEUR SPORTS PROTECTION

Sec.
3701. Definitions.
3702. Unlawful sports gambling.
3703. Injunctions.
3704. Applicability.

§ 3701. Definitions

For purposes of this chapter—

(1) the term "amateur sports organization" means—

(A) a person or governmental entity that sponsors, organizes, schedules, or conducts a competitive game in which one or more amateur athletes participate, or

(B) a league or association of persons or governmental entities described in subparagraph (A),

(2) the term "governmental entity" means a State, a political subdivision of a State, or an entity or organization, including an entity or organization described in section 4(5) of the Indian Gaming Regulatory Act (25 U.S.C. 2703(5)), that has governmental authority within the territorial boundaries of the United States, including on lands described in section 4(4) of such Act (25 U.S.C. 2703(4)),

(3) the term "professional sports organization" means—

(A) a person or governmental entity that sponsors, organizes, schedules, or conducts a competitive game in which one or more professional athletes participate, or

(B) a league or association of persons or governmental entities described in subparagraph (A),

(4) the term "person" has the meaning given such term in section 1 of title 1, and

(5) the term "State" means any of the several States, the District of Columbia, the Commonwealth of Puerto Rico, the Commonwealth of the Northern Mariana Islands, Palau, or any territory or possession of the United States.

(Added Pub.L. 102–559, § 2(a), Oct. 28, 1992, 106 Stat. 4227.)

HISTORICAL AND STATUTORY NOTES

Effective and Applicability Provisions

1992 Acts. Section 3 of Pub.L. 102–559 provided that: "This Act [enacting this chapter and enacting provisions set out as a note under section 1 of this title] shall take effect on January 1, 1993."

§ 3702. Unlawful sports gambling

It shall be unlawful for—

(1) a governmental entity to sponsor, operate, advertise, promote, license, or authorize by law or compact, or

(2) a person to sponsor, operate, advertise, or promote, pursuant to the law or compact of a governmental entity,

a lottery, sweepstakes, or other betting, gambling, or wagering scheme based, directly or indirectly (through the use of geographical references or otherwise), on one or more competitive games in which amateur or professional athletes participate, or are intended to participate, or on one or more performances of such athletes in such games.

(Added Pub.L. 102–559, § 2(a), Oct. 28, 1992, 106 Stat. 4228.)

HISTORICAL AND STATUTORY NOTES

Effective and Applicability Provisions

1992 Acts. Section effective Jan. 1, 1993, see section 3 of Pub.L. 102–559, set out as a note under section 3701 of this title.

§ 3703. Injunctions

A civil action to enjoin a violation of section 3702 may be commenced in an appropriate district court of the United States by the Attorney General of the United States, or by a professional sports organization or amateur sports organization whose competitive game is alleged to be the basis of such violation.

(Added Pub.L. 102–559, § 2(a), Oct. 28, 1992, 106 Stat. 4228.)

HISTORICAL AND STATUTORY NOTES

Effective and Applicability Provisions

1992 Acts. Section effective Jan. 1, 1993, see section 3 of Pub.L. 102–559, set out as a note under section 3701 of this title.

§ 3704. Applicability

(a) Section 3702 shall not apply to—

(1) a lottery, sweepstakes, or other betting, gambling, or wagering scheme in operation in a State or other governmental entity, to the extent that the

scheme was conducted by that State or other governmental entity at any time during the period beginning January 1, 1976, and ending August 31, 1990;

(2) a lottery, sweepstakes, or other betting, gambling, or wagering scheme in operation in a State or other governmental entity where both—

(A) such scheme was authorized by a statute as in effect on October 2, 1991; and

(B) a scheme described in section 3702 (other than one based on parimutuel animal racing or jai-alai games) actually was conducted in that State or other governmental entity at any time during the period beginning September 1, 1989, and ending October 2, 1991, pursuant to the law of that State or other governmental entity;

(3) a betting, gambling, or wagering scheme, other than a lottery described in paragraph (1), conducted exclusively in casinos located in a municipality, but only to the extent that—

(A) such scheme or a similar scheme was authorized, not later than one year after the effective date of this chapter, to be operated in that municipality; and

(B) any commercial casino gaming scheme was in operation in such municipality throughout the 10-year period ending on such effective date pursuant to a comprehensive system of State regulation authorized by that State's constitution and applicable solely to such municipality; or

(4) parimutuel animal racing or jai-alai games.

(b) Except as provided in subsection (a), section 3702 shall apply on lands described in section 4(4) of the Indian Gaming Regulatory Act (25 U.S.C. 2703(4)).

(Added Pub.L. 102–559, § 2(a), Oct. 28, 1992, 106 Stat. 4228.)

HISTORICAL AND STATUTORY NOTES

References in Text

The effective date of this chapter, referred to in subsec. (a)(3)(A), is Jan. 1, 1993, see section 3 of Pub.L. 102–559, set out as an Effective and Applicability Provisions note under section 3701 of this title.

Effective and Applicability Provisions

1992 Acts. Section effective Jan. 1, 1993, see section 3 of Pub.L. 102–559, set out as a note under section 3701 of this title.

CHAPTER 179—JUDICIAL REVIEW OF CERTAIN ACTIONS BY PRESIDENTIAL OFFICES

Sec.
3901. Civil actions.
3902. Judicial review of regulations.
3903. Effect of failure to issue regulations.
3904. Expedited review of certain appeals.
3905. Attorney's fees and interest.
3906. Payments.
3907. Other judicial review prohibited.
3908. Definitions.

§ 3901. Civil actions

(a) Parties.—In an action under section 1346(g) of this title, the defendant shall be the employing office alleged to have committed the violation involved.

(b) Jury trial.—In an action described in subsection (a), any party may demand a jury trial where a jury trial would be available in an action against a private defendant under the relevant law made applicable by chapter 5 of title 3. In any case in which a violation of section 411 of title 3 is alleged, the court shall not inform the jury of the maximum amount of compensatory damages available under section 411(b)(1) or 411(b)(3) of title 3.

(Added Pub.L. 104–331, § 3(c), Oct. 26, 1996, 110 Stat. 4070.)

HISTORICAL AND STATUTORY NOTES

Effective and Applicability Provisions

1996 Acts. Enactment of this section by section 3(c) of Pub.L. 104–331, effective Oct. 1, 1997, see section 3(d) of Pub.L. 104–331, set out as a note under section 1296 of this title.

§ 3902. Judicial review of regulations

In any proceeding under section 1296 or 1346(g) of this title in which the application of a regulation issued under chapter 5 of title 3 is at issue, the court may review the validity of the regulation in accordance with the provisions of subparagraphs (A) through (D) of section 706(2) of title 5. If the court determines that the regulation is invalid, the court shall apply, to the extent necessary and appropriate, the most relevant substantive executive agency regulation promulgated to implement the statutory provisions with respect to which the invalid regulation was issued. Except as provided in this section, the validity of regulations issued under this chapter is not subject to judicial review.

(Added Pub.L. 104–331, § 3(c), Oct. 26, 1996, 110 Stat. 4070.)

HISTORICAL AND STATUTORY NOTES

Effective and Applicability Provisions

1996 Acts. Enactment of this section by section 3(c) of Pub.L. 104–331, effective Oct. 1, 1997, see section 3(d) of Pub.L. 104–331, set out as a note under section 1296 of this title.

§ 3903. Effect of failure to issue regulations

In any proceeding under section 1296 or 1346(g) of this title, if the President, the designee of the President, or the Federal Labor Relations Authority has not issued a regulation on a matter for which chapter 5 of title 3 requires a regulation to be issued, the court shall apply, to the extent necessary and appropriate, the most relevant substantive executive agency regulation promulgated to implement the statutory provision at issue in the proceeding.

(Added Pub.L. 104–331, § 3(c), Oct. 26, 1996, 110 Stat. 4070.)

HISTORICAL AND STATUTORY NOTES

Effective and Applicability Provisions

1996 Acts. Enactment of this section by section 3(c) of Pub.L. 104–331, effective Oct. 1, 1997, see section 3(d) of Pub.L. 104–331, set out as a note under section 1296 of this title.

§ 3904. Expedited review of certain appeals

(a) In general.—An appeal may be taken directly to the Supreme Court of the United States from any interlocutory or final judgment, decree, or order of a court upon the constitutionality of any provision of chapter 5 of title 3.

(b) Jurisdiction.—The Supreme Court shall, if it has not previously ruled on the question, accept jurisdiction over the appeal referred to in subsection (a), advance the appeal on the docket, and expedite the appeal to the greatest extent possible.

(Added Pub.L. 104–331, § 3(c), Oct. 26, 1996, 110 Stat. 4070.)

HISTORICAL AND STATUTORY NOTES

Effective and Applicability Provisions

1996 Acts. Enactment of this section by section 3(c) of Pub.L. 104–331, effective Oct. 1, 1997, see section 3(d) of Pub.L. 104–331, set out as a note under section 1296 of this title.

§ 3905. Attorney's fees and interest

(a) Attorney's fees.—If a covered employee, with respect to any claim under chapter 5 of title 3, or a qualified person with a disability, with respect to any claim under section 421 of title 3, is a prevailing party in any proceeding under section 1296 or section 1346(g), the court may award attorney's fees, expert fees, and any other costs as would be appropriate if awarded under section 706(k) of the Civil Rights Act of 1964.

(b) Interest.—In any proceeding under section 1296 or section 1346(g), the same interest to compensate for delay in payment shall be made available as would be appropriate if awarded under section 717(d) of the Civil Rights Act of 1964.

(c) Punitive damages.—Except as otherwise provided in chapter 5 of title 3, no punitive damages may be awarded with respect to any claim under chapter 5 of title 3.

(Added Pub.L. 104–331, § 3(c), Oct. 26, 1996, 110 Stat. 4070.)

HISTORICAL AND STATUTORY NOTES

References in Text

The Civil Rights Act of 1964, referred to in subsecs. (a) and (b), is Pub.L. 88–352, July 2, 1964, 78 Stat. 252, as amended. Title VII of such Act is classified generally to subchapter VI (section 2000e et seq.) of chapter 21 of Title 42, The Public Health and Welfare. Sections 706 and 717 of such Act are classified to sections 2000e–5 and 2000e–16, respectively, of Title 42. For complete classification of this Act to the Code, see Short Title note set out under section 2000a of Title 42 and Tables.

Effective and Applicability Provisions

1996 Acts. Enactment of this section by section 3(c) of Pub.L. 104–331, effective Oct. 1, 1997, see section 3(d) of Pub.L. 104–331, set out as a note under section 1296 of this title.

§ 3906. Payments

A judgment, award, or compromise settlement against the United States under this chapter (including any interest and costs) shall be paid—

(1) under section 1304 of title 31, if it arises out of an action commenced in a district court of the United States (or any appeal therefrom); or

(2) out of amounts otherwise appropriated or available to the office involved, if it arises out of an appeal from an administrative proceeding under chapter 5 of title 3.

(Added Pub.L. 104–331, § 3(c), Oct. 26, 1996, 110 Stat. 4071.)

HISTORICAL AND STATUTORY NOTES

Effective and Applicability Provisions

1996 Acts. Enactment of this section by section 3(c) of Pub.L. 104–331, effective Oct. 1, 1997, see section 3(d) of Pub.L. 104–331, set out as a note under section 1296 of this title.

§ 3907. Other judicial review prohibited

Except as expressly authorized by this chapter and chapter 5 of title 3, the compliance or noncompliance with the provisions of chapter 5 of title 3, and any action taken pursuant to chapter 5 of title 3, shall not be subject to judicial review.

(Added Pub.L. 104–331, § 3(c), Oct. 26, 1996, 110 Stat. 4071.)

HISTORICAL AND STATUTORY NOTES

Effective and Applicability Provisions

1996 Acts. Enactment of this section by section 3(c) of Pub.L. 104–331, effective Oct. 1, 1997, see section 3(d) of Pub.L. 104–331, set out as a note under section 1296 of this title.

§ 3908. Definitions

For purposes of applying this chapter, the terms "employing office" and "covered employee" have the meanings given those terms in section 401 of title 3.

(Added Pub.L. 104–331, § 3(c), Oct. 26, 1996, 110 Stat. 4071.)

HISTORICAL AND STATUTORY NOTES

Effective and Applicability Provisions

1996 Acts. Enactment of this section by section 3(c) of Pub.L. 104–331, effective Oct. 1, 1997, see section 3(d) of Pub.L. 104–331, set out as a note under section 1296 of this title.

CHAPTER 180—ASSUMPTION OF CERTAIN CONTRACTUAL OBLIGATIONS

Sec.
4001. Assumption of contractual obligations related to transfers of rights in motion pictures.

§ 4001. Assumption of contractual obligations related to transfers of rights in motion pictures

(a) Assumption of obligations.—(1) In the case of a transfer of copyright ownership under United States law in a motion picture (as the terms "transfer of copyright ownership" and "motion picture" are defined in section 101 of title 17) that is produced subject to 1 or more collective bargaining agreements negotiated under the laws of the United States, if the transfer is executed on or after the effective date of this chapter and is not limited to public performance rights, the transfer instrument shall be deemed to incorporate the assumption agreements applicable to the copyright ownership being transferred that are required by the applicable collective bargaining agreement, and the transferee shall be subject to the obligations under each such assumption agreement to make residual payments and provide related notices, accruing after the effective date of the transfer and applicable to the exploitation of the rights transferred, and any remedies under each such assumption agreement for breach of those obligations, as those obligations and remedies are set forth in the applicable collective bargaining agreement, if—

(A) the transferee knows or has reason to know at the time of the transfer that such collective bargaining agreement was or will be applicable to the motion picture; or

(B) in the event of a court order confirming an arbitration award against the transferor under the collective bargaining agreement, the transferor does not have the financial ability to satisfy the award within 90 days after the order is issued.

(2) For purposes of paragraph (1)(A), "knows or has reason to know" means any of the following:

(A) Actual knowledge that the collective bargaining agreement was or will be applicable to the motion picture.

(B)(i) Constructive knowledge that the collective bargaining agreement was or will be applicable to the motion picture, arising from recordation of a document pertaining to copyright in the motion picture under section 205 of title 17 or from publication, at a site available to the public on-line that is operated by the relevant union, of information that identifies the motion picture as subject to a collective bargaining agreement with that union, if the site permits commercially reasonable verification of the date on which the information was available for access.

(ii) Clause (i) applies only if the transfer referred to in subsection (a)(1) occurs—

(I) after the motion picture is completed, or

(II) before the motion picture is completed and—

(aa) within 18 months before the filing of an application for copyright registration for the motion picture under section 408 of title 17, or

(bb) if no such application is filed, within 18 months before the first publication of the motion picture in the United States.

(C) Awareness of other facts and circumstances pertaining to a particular transfer from which it is apparent that the collective bargaining agreement was or will be applicable to the motion picture.

(b) Scope of exclusion of transfers of public performance rights.—For purposes of this section, the exclusion under subsection (a) of transfers of copyright ownership in a motion picture that are limited to public performance rights includes transfers to a terrestrial broadcast station, cable system, or programmer to the extent that the station, system, or programmer is functioning as an exhibitor of the motion picture, either by exhibiting the motion picture on its own network, system, service, or station, or by initiating the transmission of an exhibition that is carried on another network, system, service, or station. When a terrestrial broadcast station, cable system, or programmer, or other transferee, is also functioning otherwise as a distributor or as a producer of the motion picture, the public performance exclusion does not affect any obligations imposed on the transferee to the extent that it is engaging in such functions.

(c) Exclusion for grants of security interests.—Subsection (a) shall not apply to—

(1) a transfer of copyright ownership consisting solely of a mortgage, hypothecation, or other security interest; or

(2) a subsequent transfer of the copyright ownership secured by the security interest described in paragraph (1) by or under the authority of the secured party, including a transfer through the exercise of the secured party's rights or remedies as a secured party, or by a subsequent transferee.

The exclusion under this subsection shall not affect any rights or remedies under law or contract

(d) Deferral pending resolution of bona fide dispute.—A transferee on which obligations are imposed under subsection (a) by virtue of paragraph (1) of that subsection may elect to defer performance of such obligations that are subject to a bona fide dispute between a union and a prior transferor until that dispute is resolved, except that such deferral shall not stay accrual of any union claims due under an applicable collective bargaining agreement.

(e) Scope of obligations determined by private agreement.—Nothing in this section shall expand or diminish the rights, obligations, or remedies of any person under the collective bargaining agreements or assumption agreements referred to in this section.

(f) Failure to notify.—If the transferor under subsection (a) fails to notify the transferee under subsection (a) of applicable collective bargaining obligations before the execution of the transfer instrument, and subsection (a) is made applicable to the transferee solely by virtue of subsection (a)(1)(B), the transferor shall be liable to the transferee for any damages suffered by the transferee as a result of the failure to notify.

(g) Determination of disputes and claims.—Any dispute concerning the application of subsections (a) through (f) shall be determined by an action in United States district court, and the court in its discretion may allow the recovery of full costs by or against any party and may also award a reasonable attorney's fee to the prevailing party as part of the costs.

(h) Study.—The Comptroller General, in consultation with the Register of Copyrights, shall conduct a study of the conditions in the motion picture industry that gave rise to this section, and the impact of this section on the motion picture industry. The Comptroller General shall report the findings of the study to the Congress within 2 years after the effective date of this chapter.

(Added Pub.L. 105–304, Title IV, § 406(a), Oct. 28, 1998, 112 Stat. 2902.)

HISTORICAL AND STATUTORY NOTES

Effective and Applicability Provisions

1998 Acts. Amendments by Title IV of Pub.L. 105–304 effective Oct. 28, 1998, except as otherwise provided, see section 407 of Pub.L. 105–304, set out as a note under section 108 of Title 17, Copyrights.

MISCELLANEOUS PROVISIONS

Act June 25, 1948, c. 646, §§ 2 to 39, 62 Stat. 985 to 991, as amended

Sec. 2. **(a)** The Chief Justices of the United States Court of Appeals for the District of Columbia, the District Court of the United States for the District of Columbia, and the Court of Claims, and the presiding judge of the Court of Customs and Patent Appeals, in office on the effective date of this Act shall be the chief judges of their respective courts. The Chief Justice of the United States Court of Appeals for the District of Columbia and the Associate Justices thereof, the Chief Justice of the District Court of the United States for the District of Columbia (formerly named the Supreme Court of the District of Columbia) and the Associate Justices thereof, the Chief Justice of the Court of Claims, and the presiding judge of the Court of Customs and Patent Appeals, in office on the effective date of this Act, shall be judges of the United States within the meaning of Section 451 of Title 28, Judiciary and Judicial Procedure, of the United States Code, set out in Section 1 of this Act. The Chief Justice of the United States Court of Appeals for the District of Columbia and the Associate Justices thereof, in office on the effective date of this Act, shall be circuit judges of the District of Columbia Circuit and vested with all the rights, powers, and duties thereof, and the said Chief Justice of the United States Court of Appeals for the District of Columbia shall be Chief Judge of said Circuit. The Chief Justice of the District Court of the United States for the District of Columbia (formerly named the Supreme Court of the District of Columbia) and the Associate Justices thereof, in office on the effective date of this Act shall be district judges for the District of Columbia and vested with all the rights, powers, and duties thereof.

(b) The provisions of title 28, Judiciary and Judicial Procedure, of the United States Code, set out in section 1 of this Act, with respect to the organization of each of the several courts therein provided for and of the Administrative Office of the United States Courts, shall be construed as continuations of existing law, and the tenure of the judges, officers, and employees thereof and of the United States attorneys and marshals and their deputies and assistants, in office on the effective date of this Act, shall not be affected by its enactment, but each of them shall continue to serve in the same capacity under the appropriate provisions of title 28, as set out in section 1 of this Act, pursuant to his prior appointment: *Provided, however,* That each circuit court of appeals shall, as in said title 28 set out, hereafter be known as a United States court of appeals. No loss of rights, interruption of jurisdiction, or prejudice to matters pending in any of such courts on the effective date of this Act shall result from its enactment.

(c) The sum of $7,500 specified in this Act as the salary which the Assistant Director of the Administrative Office of the United States Courts shall receive, and the sum of $7,500 specified in this Act as the salary which each commissioner whom the Court of Claims may appoint shall receive, shall each respectively be that basic compensation on which shall be computed and paid the additional basic compensation mentioned in section 521 of the Act of June 30, 1945 (ch. 212, 59 Stat. 301), as amended by the Act of May 24, 1946 (ch. 270, sec. 6, 60 Stat. 217).

(d) Anything in this Act to the contrary notwithstanding, the provisions of section 14 of the Act of July 1, 1944 (ch. 358, 58 Stat. 663) are not hereby repealed.

Sec. 3. Section 366 of the Revised Statutes (5 U.S.C., section 315), as amended, is amended to read as follows:

"**Sec. 366.** Every attorney specially retained under authority of the Department of Justice shall be commissioned as special assistant to the Attorney General or special attorney and shall take the oath required by law. Foreign counsel employed in special cases shall not be required to take such oath".

Sec. 4. Section 5261 of the Revised Statutes (45 U.S.C., section 87), is amended to read as follows:

"**Sec. 5261.** Any railroad company from whom payments for freight and transportation have been withheld under the provisions of section 5260 may bring suit in the Court of Claims to recover the price of such freight and transportation.".

Sec. 5. Section 3 of the Act approved February 28, 1887 (chapter 210, 24 Stat. 409, 410; 21 U.S.C., section 193) is amended by striking out the present third sentence thereof, and by striking out the final sentence thereof and substituting in lieu of such final sentence the following:

"Every package of opium or package containing opium, either in whole or in part, brought, taken, or transported, trafficked, or dealt in contrary to the provisions of this section, shall be forfeited to the United States, for the benefit of China.".

Sec. 6. Section 1 of the Act approved August 1, 1888 (chapter 728, 25 Stat. 357; 40 U.S.C., sec. 257) is amended to read as follows:

"That in every case in which the Secretary of the Treasury or any other officer of the Government has been, or hereafter shall be, authorized to procure real estate for the erection of a public building or for other public uses, he may acquire the same for the United States by condemnation, under judicial process, whenever in his opinion it is necessary or advantageous to the Government to do so, and the Attorney General of the United States, upon every application of the Secretary of the Treasury, under this Act, or such other officer, shall cause proceedings to be commenced for condemnation within thirty days from receipt of the application at the Department of Justice.".

Sec. 7. Section 13 of the Act approved July 31, 1894 (chapter 174, 28 Stat. 210) is hereby amended by striking out the second paragraph thereof (5 U.S.C., section 321), and by amending the first paragraph thereof (31 U.S.C., section 84) to read as follows:

"**Sec. 13.** Before transmission to the General Accounting Office, the accounts of United States attorneys, assistant attorneys, and marshals, made out and approved as required by law, and accounts relating to prisoners convicted or held for trial in any court of the United States, and all other accounts relating to the Department of Justice, shall be sent with their vouchers to the Attorney General and examined under his supervision. Before transmission to the General Accounting Office, the accounts of United States Commissioners, clerks of court and other officers of the courts of the United States, except the Supreme Court of the United States and consular courts, made out and approved as required by law, shall be sent with their vouchers to the Director of the Administrative Office of the United States Courts and examined under his supervision."

Sec. 8. Section 86 of the Act approved April 30, 1900 (chapter 339, 31 Stat. 158; 48 U.S.C., secs. 641, 642, 643–645), as amended, is amended to read as follows:

"**Sec. 86.** The laws of the United States relating to removal of causes, appeals and other matters and proceedings as between the courts of the United States and the courts of the several States shall govern in such matters and proceedings as between the courts of the United States and the courts of the Territory of Hawaii."

Sec. 9. The first paragraph of section 4 of the Act approved June 6, 1900 (chapter 786, 31 Stat. 322; 48 U.S.C., section 101, first paragraph), as amended, is amended to read as follows:

"**Sec. 4.** There is hereby established a district court for the District of Alaska, with the jurisdiction of district courts of the United States and with general jurisdiction in civil, criminal, equity, and admiralty causes; and four district judges shall be appointed for the district, each at an annual salary of $15,000, who shall during their terms of office reside in the divisions of the district to which they may be respectively assigned by the President. The court shall consist of four divisions, which shall also be recording divisions.".

Sec. 10. Section 7 of the Act approved June 6, 1900 (chapter 786, 31 Stat. 324; 48 U.S.C., section 106), as amended, is amended by striking out the words "Attorney General" wherever such words appear in such section, and substituting in lieu thereof the words "Director of the Administrative Office of the United States Courts"; also by striking out the seventh sentence thereof (such sentence being the third sentence after the proviso in such section) and substituting in lieu of such sentence the following: "He may appoint necessary deputies and employ other necessary clerical assistance to aid him in the expeditious discharge of the duties of his office, with the approval of the court or judge, and, subject to the approval of the Director of the Administrative Office of the United States Courts, fix the compensation of such deputies and the compensation for such clerical assistance."

Sec. 11. Section 8 of the Act approved June 6, 1900 (chapter 786, 31 Stat. 324; 48 U.S.C., section 109), as amended by the Act approved March 3, 1909, ch. 269, § 4, 35 Stat. 841, is amended to read as follows:

"**Sec. 8.** Four district attorneys shall be appointed for the district, one of whom shall be assigned to each division and shall reside at such place in the division as the Attorney General shall direct. They shall each perform the duties required to be performed by United States attorneys in other districts, and such other duties as may be required by law. The Attorney General shall fix the salaries of such district attorneys, and such attorneys shall not while in office accept retainers or engage in any other law business in the district than that pertaining to the duties of their office. The Attorney General may, upon the recommendation of the district attorney, appoint and at pleasure remove one or more assistant district attorneys and one or more clerical assistants, who shall receive such compensation as the Attorney General shall fix, to be paid as assistant United States attorneys and clerical assistants in other districts are paid. In the case of the death or disability of a district attorney the judge may appoint a suitable person to fill the office until his successor is appointed and qualified or until the disability is removed.".

Sec. 12. The first paragraph of section 9 of the Act approved June 6, 1900 (chapter 786, 31 Stat. 324; 48 U.S.C., section 110, part) is amended to read as follows:

"**Sec. 9.** Four United States marshals shall be appointed for the district, at salaries which shall be fixed by the Attorney General, one of whom shall be assigned to each division, and shall reside at such place in the division as the Attorney General shall direct. Each marshal shall have authority and be required to appoint, subject to the approval of the Attorney General, such deputy marshals as he may deem necessary for the efficient execution of the law and the orders of the court and of the commissioners appointed as herein provided.".

Sec. 13. Section 10 of the Act approved June 6, 1900 (chapter 786, 31 Stat. 325; 48 U.S.C., sections 62, 63, 107, 110, 112, 113, 114) is amended to read as follows:

"**Sec. 10.** The governor, attorneys, judges, and the marshals provided for in this Act shall be appointed by the President, by and with the advice and consent of the Senate, and shall hold their respective offices for the term of four years and until their successors are appointed and qualified, unless sooner removed by the President for cause.

"The governor shall receive an annual salary of $10,000, payable from the Treasury of the United States.

"The salaries of the judges, marshals, clerks, and district attorneys shall be payable from the Treasury of the United States, as like officers are paid in other districts.

"Each clerk shall collect all money arising from the fees of his office or on any other account authorized by law to be paid to or collected by him, and shall report the same and the disposition thereof in detail, under oath, quarterly, or more frequently if required, to the court, the Director of the Administrative Office of the United States Courts, and the Secretary of the Treasury, and all public money received by him and his deputies for fees or on any other account shall be paid out by the clerk on the order of the court, duly made and signed by the judge, and any balance remaining in his hands after all payments ordered by the court shall have been made shall be by him covered into the Treasury of the United States at such times and under such rules and regulations as the Secretary of the Treasury may prescribe. The clerk may employ, with the approval of the court, necessary clerical assistants and other employees in such number as may be approved by the Director of the Administrative Office of the United States Courts.

"The governor shall, in addition to his salary, be paid his actual traveling and subsistence expenses when traveling in the discharge of his official duties. The judges shall be entitled to the same travel and subsistence allowances as those of United States District Judges in other districts. The marshals, clerks of court, and district attorneys shall, in addition to their salaries, be paid their actual traveling and subsistence expenses in accordance with the Subsistence Expense Act of 1926 (chapter 457, 44 Stat. 688), as amended, and government travel regulations, when traveling in the discharge of their official duties.

"Accounts for such expenses of judges, marshals, district attorneys, and clerks shall be rendered and paid as are accounts of judges, marshals, district attorneys, and clerks for like expenses in other districts.".

Sec. 14. [Repealed. Pub.L. 88–241, § 21, Dec. 23, 1963, 77 Stat. 628.]

Sec. 15. [Repealed. Pub.L. 88–241, § 21, Dec. 23, 1963, 77 Stat. 628.]

Sec. 16. [Repealed. Pub.L. 88–241, § 21, Dec. 23, 1963, 77 Stat. 628.]

Sec. 17. Section 2 of the Act approved February 11, 1903 (chapter 544, 32 Stat. 823; 15 U.S.C., sec. 29, 49 U.S.C., sec. 45), as amended, is amended to read as follows:

"**Sec. 2.** In every civil action brought in any district court of the United States under any of said Acts, wherein the United States is complainant, an appeal from the final judgment of the district court will lie only to the Supreme Court.".

Sec. 18. The second sentence of the second paragraph of section 6 of the Act approved April 22, 1908 (chapter 149, 35 Stat. 65, 66; 45 U.S.C., section 56), as added by the Act approved April 5, 1910 (chapter 143, section 1, 36 Stat. 291), is amended to read as follows:

"The jurisdiction of the courts of the United States under this Act shall be concurrent with that of the courts of the several States.".

Sec. 19. The final sentence of section 1 of the Act approved June 19, 1912 (chapter 174, 37 Stat. 137; 40 U.S.C., section 324) is amended to read as follows:

"Any contractor or subcontractor aggrieved by the withholding of any penalty as hereinbefore provided shall have the right within six months thereafter to appeal to the head of the department making the contract on behalf of the United States or the Territory, and in the case of a contract made by the District of Columbia to the Commissioners thereof, who shall have power to review the action imposing the penalty, and in all such appeals from such final order whereby a contractor or subcontractor may be aggrieved by the imposition of the penalty hereinbefore provided, such contractor or subcontractor may, within six months after decision by such head of a department or the Commissioners of the District of Columbia, file a claim in the Court of Claims.".

Sec. 20. Section 41 of the Act approved March 2, 1917 (chapter 145, 39 Stat. 965; 48 U.S.C., section 863), as amended, is amended to read as follows:

"**Sec. 41.** The United States District Court for the District of Puerto Rico shall, in addition to its other jurisdiction, have jurisdiction for the naturalization of aliens and Puerto Ricans, and, for this purpose, residence in Puerto Rico shall be counted in the same manner as residence elsewhere in the United States. Said district court shall have jurisdiction of all controversies where all of the parties on either side of the controversy are citizens or subjects of a foreign State or States, or citizens of a State, Territory, or District of the United States not domiciled in Puerto Rico, wherein the matter in dispute exceeds, exclusive of interest or cost, the sum or value of $3,000, and of all controversies in which there is a separable controversy involving such jurisdictional amount and in which all of the parties on either side of such separable controversy are citizens or subjects of the character aforesaid. The salaries of the judge and officials of the United States District Court for the District of Puerto Rico, together with the court expenses, shall be paid from the United States revenues in the same manner as in other United States district courts. In case of vacancy or of the death, absence, or other legal disability on the part of the judge of the said United States District Court for the District of Puerto Rico, the President of the United States is authorized to designate one of the judges of the Supreme Court of Puerto Rico to discharge the duties of judge of said court until such absence or disability shall be removed, and thereupon such judge so designated for said service shall be fully authorized and empowered to perform the duties of said office during such absence or disability of such regular judge, and to sign all necessary papers and records as the acting judge of said court without extra compensation.".

Sec. 21. Section 42 of the Act approved March 2, 1917 (ch. 145, 39 Stat. 966; 48 U.S.C., section 864) is amended to read as follows:

"**Sec. 42.** The laws of the United States relating to appeals, certiorari, removal of causes, and other matters or proceedings as between the courts of the United States and the courts of the several States shall govern in such matters and proceedings as between the United States District Court for the District of Puerto Rico and the courts of Puerto Rico.

"All pleadings and proceedings in the District Court of the United States for Puerto Rico shall be conducted in the English language.".

Sec. 22. Section 1 of the Act approved May 28, 1926 (chapter 411, 44 Stat. 669; 19 U.S.C., section 405a), is amended to read as follows:

"That the Board of General Appraisers shall hereafter be known as the United States Customs Court and the members thereof shall hereafter be known as the judges of the United States Customs Court.".

Sec. 23. Section 2 of the Act approved January 31, 1928 (chapter 14, 45 Stat. 54), as amended, is amended to read as follows:

"**Sec. 2.** All Acts of Congress referring to writs of error shall be construed as amended to the extent necessary to substitute appeal for writ of error.".

Sec. 24. [Repealed. Pub.L. 88–241, § 21, Dec. 23, 1963, 77 Stat. 628.]

Sec. 25. Subsection (a) of section 501 of the Act approved June 17, 1930 (chapter 497, Title IV, 46 Stat. 730; 19 U.S.C., section 1501(a)), as amended, is amended by striking out the fourth sentence thereof and inserting in lieu of such sentence the following: "Every such appeal shall be transmitted with the entry and the accompanying papers by the collector to the United States Customs Court."

Sec. 26. Section 509 of the Act approved June 17, 1930 (chapter 497, Title IV, 46 Stat. 733; 19 U.S.C., section 1509) is amended by striking out the words, "Collectors, appraisers, and judges and divisions of the United States Customs Court" at the beginning of such section, and inserting in lieu thereof the words, "Collectors and appraisers".

Sec. 27. Section 3 of the Act approved May 7, 1934 (chapter 222, 48 Stat. 668; 40 U.S.C., section 13c) is amended to read as follows:

"**Sec. 3.** All other duties and work required for the operation, domestic care, and custody of the building shall be performed under the direction of the Marshal of the Supreme Court of the United States, who shall be superintendent of the United States Supreme Court Building.".

Sec. 28. Section 26 of the Act approved June 22, 1936 (chapter 699, section 26, 49 Stat. 1813), as amended by the Act approved August 5, 1939 (chapter 430, 53 Stat. 1203; U.S.C., 48 U.S.C., section 1405y) is amended by adding to the first paragraph thereof, the following:

"In the case of a vacancy in the office of district attorney, the District Court of the Virgin Islands may appoint a district attorney to serve until the vacancy is filled. The order of appointment by the court shall be filed with the clerk of court".

Sec. 29. Section 5 of the Act approved June 26, 1936 (chapter 831, 49 Stat. 1968; 25 U.S.C., section 505) as amended by striking out the third, fourth, and fifth sentences thereof, and substituting in lieu of such sentences the following sentence: "Within thirty days after such service or within such extended time as the trial court may permit, the Secretary of the Interior may intervene in such action or may remove such action to the United States district court."

Sec. 30. Section 3 of the Act approved May 24, 1940 (chapter 209, 54 Stat. 220; 28 U.S.C., 1940 edition, section 5a) is amended to read as follows:

"**Sec. 3.** The salary of the judge of the District Court of the Virgin Islands of the United States shall be at the rate of $15,000 per year.".

Sec. 31. [Repealed. Pub.L. 87–845, § 26(b), Oct. 18, 1962, 76A Stat. 702.]

Sec. 32. **(a)** All laws of the United States in force on September 1, 1948, in which reference is made to a 'circuit court of appeals'; 'senior circuit judge'; 'senior district judge'; 'presiding judge'; 'chief justice', except when reference to the Chief Justice of the United States is intended; or 'justice', except when used with respect to a justice of the Supreme Court of the United States in his capacity as such or as a circuit justice, are hereby amended by substituting 'court of appeals' for 'circuit court of appeals'; 'chief judge of the circuit' for 'senior circuit judge'; 'chief judge of the district court' for 'senior district judge'; 'chief judge' for 'presiding judge'; 'chief judge' for 'chief justice', except when reference to the Chief Justice of the United States is intended; and 'judge' for 'justice', except when the latter term is used with respect to a justice of the Supreme Court of the United States in his capacity as such or as a circuit justice. As amended May 24, 1949, c. 139, § 127, 63 Stat. 107.

(b) All laws of the United States in force on September 1, 1948, in which reference is made to the Supreme Court of the District of Columbia or to the District Court of the United States for the District of Columbia are amended by substituting 'United States District Court for the District of Columbia' for such designations.

(c) All laws of the United States in force on September 1, 1948, in which reference is made to the 'Conference of Senior Circuit Judges', or to the 'Judicial Conference of Senior Circuit Judges' are amended by substituting 'Judicial Conference of the United States' for such designations.

(d) This section shall not be construed to amend historical references to courts or judicial offices which have no present or future application to such courts or offices.

Sec. 33. No inference of a legislative construction is to be drawn by reason of the chapter in Title 28, Judiciary and Judicial Procedure, as set out in section 1 of this Act, in which any section is placed, nor by reason of the catchlines used in such title.

Sec. 34. If any part of Title 28, Judiciary and Judicial Procedure, as set out in section 1 of this Act, shall be held invalid, the remainder shall not be affected thereby.

Sec. 35. Sections 61 and 62 of Title 7 of the Canal Zone Code are hereby repealed.

Sec. 36. Section 1141(a) of the Internal Revenue Code is hereby amended to read as follows:

"The circuit courts of appeals and the United States Court of Appeals for the District of Columbia shall have exclusive jurisdiction to review the decisions of the Tax Court, except as provided in section 1254 of title 28 of the United States Code, in the same manner and to the same extent as decisions of the district courts in civil actions tried without a jury; and the judgment of any such court shall be final, except that it shall be subject to review by the Supreme Court of the United States upon certiorari, in the manner provided in section 1254 of title 28 of the United States Code."

Sec. 37. Section 6 of the Act approved August 7, 1946 (ch. 864, 60 Stat. 903), is amended to read as follows:

"**Sec. 6.** Whenever any claimant under this Act is dissatisfied with the action of a department or agency of the Government in either granting or denying his claim, such claimant shall have the right within six months to file a petition with the Court of Claims or, if the claim does not exceed $10,000 in amount or suit has heretofore been brought or is brought within thirty days after the enactment of this amendatory act, with any Federal district court of competent jurisdiction, asking a determination by the court of the equities involved in such claim; and upon the filing of such a petition, the court, sitting as a court of equity, shall have jurisdiction to determine the amount, if any, to which such claimant and petitioner may be equitably entitled (not exceeding the amount which might have been allowed by the department or agency concerned under the terms of this Act) and to enter an order directing such department or agency to settle the claim in accordance with the finding of the court; and thereafter either party may appeal from the decision if it was rendered by a district court or petition the Supreme Court for a writ of certiorari if it was rendered by the court of claims, as in other cases. Any case heretofore brought in a district court under this section may, at the election of the petitioner to be exercised within thirty days after the enactment of this amendatory Act, be transferred to the Court of Claims for original disposition in that court."

Sec. 38. The provisions of this Act shall take effect on September 1, 1948.

Sec. 39. The sections or parts thereof of the Revised Statutes of the District of Columbia, Revised Statutes of the United States or Statutes at Large enumerated in the following schedules* are hereby repealed. Any rights or liabilities now existing under such sections or parts thereof shall not be affected by this repeal.

*For schedules, see the volume of U.S.C.A. covering the end of Title 28, Judiciary and Judicial Procedure.

APPENDIX

JUDICIAL PERSONNEL FINANCIAL DISCLOSURE REQUIREMENTS

Pub.L. 95–521, Title III, §§ 301 to 309, Oct. 26, 1978, 92 Stat. 1851, as amended

[§§ 301 to 309. Transferred]

HISTORICAL AND STATUTORY NOTES

Codifications

Title III (§§ 301 to 309) of Pub.L. 95–521, Oct. 26, 1978, 92 Stat. 1851, as amended Pub.L. 96–19, §§ 2(a)(3), (c)(3), 3(a)(3), (b), 4(c), 6, 7(a) to (c), (d)(2), (e), (f), 8(c), 9(c)(3), (d), (j), (p) to (r), June 13, 1979, 93 Stat. 37 to 43; Pub.L. 96–417, Title VI, § 601(9), Oct. 10, 1980, 94 Stat. 1744; Pub.L. 96–579, § 13(c), Dec. 23, 1980, 94 Stat. 3369; Pub.L. 97–164, Title I, § 163(a)(6), Apr. 2, 1982, 96 Stat. 49; Pub.L. 98–150, § 10, Nov. 11, 1983, 97 Stat. 962; Pub.L. 99–514, § 2, Oct. 22, 1986, 100 Stat. 2095; Pub.L. 99–573, § 6, Oct. 28, 1986, 100 Stat. 3231; Pub.L. 101–237, Title VI, § 602(a)(1), Dec. 18, 1989, 103 Stat. 2094, which related to judicial personnel financial disclosure requirements, was repealed by Pub.L. 101–194, Title II, § 201, Nov. 30, 1989, 103 Stat. 1724. See Title I of the Ethics in Government Act of 1978, Pub.L. 95–521, as amended, relating to financial disclosure requirements of Federal personnel, set out in Appendix 4 to Title 5, Government Organization and Employees.

Effective Date of Repeal

The repeal of Pub.L. 95–521, Title III, by Pub.L. 101–194, Title II, § 201, Nov. 30, 1989, 103 Stat. 1724, as effective Jan. 1, 1991, see Pub.L. 101–194, Title II, § 204, as added Pub.L. 101–280, § 3(10)(B), May 4, 1990, 104 Stat. 157, set out as an Effective Date of 1989 Amendment note under section 101 of Pub.L. 95–521 in Appendix 4 to Title 5, Government Organization and Employees.

Provisions of Title III of Pub.L. 95–521, as in effect prior to Nov. 30, 1989, to be effective until Jan. 1, 1991, as if Pub.L. 101–194 had not been enacted, and nothing in Title III, of Pub.L. 101–194 to be construed to prevent prosecution of civil actions against individuals for violating Title III of Pub.L. 95–521 before Jan. 1, 1991, see section 3(10)(C) and (D) of Pub.L. 101–280, set out as notes under section 101 of Pub.L. 95–521 in Appendix 4 to Title 5, Government Organization and Employees.

DEVELOPMENT OF MECHANISMS FOR RESOLVING MINOR DISPUTES

Pub.L. 96–190, Feb. 12, 1980, 94 Stat. 17

HISTORICAL AND STATUTORY NOTES

Codifications

Pub.L. 96–190, Feb. 12, 1980, 94 Stat. 17, known as the Dispute Resolution Act, provided for the establishment and maintenance of mechanisms for resolving minor disputes, established the Dispute Resolution Resource Center and Dispute Resolution Advisory Board, prescribed duties for the Center and Board, authorized appropriations for the Center and Board of $1,000,000 for each of the fiscal years 1980, 1981, 1982, 1983, and 1984, directed that financial assistance to eligible applicants be in the form of grants, prescribed conditions for such grants, authorized appropriations for such grants of $10,000,000 for each of the fiscal years 1981, 1982, 1983, and 1984, and required an annual report by the Attorney General to the President and Congress relating to the administration of Pub.L. 96–190. For termination of reporting provisions of Pub.L. 96–190, § 9(d), effective May 15, 2000, see Pub.L. 104–66, § 3003, as amended, set out as a note under 31 U.S.C.A. § 1113, and page 117 of House Document No. 103–7.

CONSTITUTION OF THE UNITED STATES

PREAMBLE

WE THE PEOPLE of the United States, in Order to form a more perfect Union, establish Justice, insure domestic Tranquility, provide for the common defence, promote the general Welfare, and secure the Blessings of Liberty to ourselves and our Posterity, do ordain and establish this CONSTITUTION for the United States of America.

ARTICLE I

Section. 1. All legislative Powers herein granted shall be vested in a Congress of the United States, which shall consist of a Senate and House of Representatives.

Section. 2. The House of Representatives shall be composed of Members chosen every second Year by the People of the several States, and the Electors in each State shall have the Qualifications requisite for Electors of the most numerous Branch of the State Legislature.

No Person shall be a Representative who shall not have attained to the Age of twenty five Years, and been seven Years a Citizen of the United States, and who shall not, when elected, be an Inhabitant of that State in which he shall be chosen.

[Representatives and direct Taxes shall be apportioned among the several States which may be included within this Union, according to their respective Numbers, which shall be determined by adding to the whole Number of free Persons, including those bound to Service for a Term of Years, and excluding Indians not taxed, three fifths of all other Persons.] [1] The actual Enumeration shall be made within three Years after the first Meeting of the Congress of the United States, and within every subsequent Term of ten Years, in such Manner as they shall by Law direct. The Number of Representatives shall not exceed one for every thirty Thousand, but each State shall have at Least one Representative; and until such enumeration shall be made, the State of New Hampshire shall be entitled to chuse three, Massachusetts eight, Rhode-Island and Providence Plantations one, Connecticut five, New-York six, New Jersey four, Pennsylvania eight, Delaware one, Maryland six, Virginia ten, North Carolina five, South Carolina five, and Georgia three.

When vacancies happen in the Representation from any State, the Executive Authority thereof shall issue Writs of Election to fill such Vacancies.

The House of Representatives shall chuse their Speaker and other Officers; and shall have the sole Power of Impeachment.

[1] The clause of this paragraph inclosed in brackets was amended, as to the mode of apportionment of representatives among the several states, by the Fourteenth Amendment, § 2, and as to taxes on incomes without apportionment, by the Sixteenth Amendment.

Section. 3. [The Senate of the United States shall be composed of two Senators from each State, chosen by the Legislature thereof, for six Years; and each Senator shall have one Vote.] [1]

Immediately after they shall be assembled in Consequence of the first Election, they shall be divided as equally as may be into three Classes. The Seats of the Senators of the first Class shall be vacated at the Expiration of the second Year, of the second Class at the Expiration of the fourth Year, and of the third Class at the Expiration of the sixth Year, so that one third may be chosen every second Year; [and if Vacancies happen by Resignation, or otherwise, during the Recess of the Legislature of any State, the Executive thereof may make temporary Appointments until the next Meeting of the Legislature, which shall then fill such Vacancies.] [2]

No Person shall be a Senator who shall not have attained to the Age of thirty Years, and been nine Years a Citizen of the United States, and who shall not, when elected, be an Inhabitant of that State for which he shall be chosen.

The Vice President of the United States shall be President of the Senate, but shall have no Vote, unless they be equally divided.

The Senate shall chuse their other Officers, and also a President pro tempore, in the Absence of the Vice

President, or when he shall exercise the Office of President of the United States.

The Senate shall have the sole Power to try all Impeachments. When sitting for that Purpose, they shall be on Oath or Affirmation. When the President of the United States is tried, the Chief Justice shall preside: And no Person shall be convicted without the Concurrence of two thirds of the Members present.

Judgment in Cases of Impeachment shall not extend further than to removal from Office, and disqualification to hold and enjoy any Office of honor, Trust or Profit under the United States: but the Party convicted shall nevertheless be liable and subject to Indictment, Trial, Judgment and Punishment, according to Law.

1 This paragraph, inclosed in brackets, was superseded by the Seventeenth Amendment.

2 The clause of this paragraph inclosed in brackets was superseded by the Seventeenth Amendment.

Section. 4. The Times, Places and Manner of holding Elections for Senators and Representatives, shall be prescribed in each State by the Legislature thereof; but the Congress may at any time by Law make or alter such Regulations, except as to the Places of chusing Senators.

The Congress shall assemble at least once in every Year, and such Meeting shall be on the [first Monday in December],[1] unless they shall by Law appoint a different Day.

1 The clause of this paragraph inclosed in brackets was superseded by the Twentieth Amendment.

Section. 5. Each House shall be the Judge of the Elections, Returns and Qualifications of its own Members, and a Majority of each shall constitute a Quorum to do Business; but a smaller Number may adjourn from day to day, and may be authorized to compel the Attendance of absent Members, in such Manner, and under such Penalties as each House may provide.

Each House may determine the Rules of its Proceedings, punish its Members for disorderly Behaviour, and, with the Concurrence of two thirds, expel a Member.

Each House shall keep a Journal of its Proceedings, and from time to time publish the same, excepting such Parts as may in their Judgment require Secrecy; and the Yeas and Nays of the Members of either House on any question shall, at the Desire of one fifth of those Present, be entered on the Journal.

Neither House, during the Session of Congress, shall, without the Consent of the other, adjourn for more than three days, nor to any other Place than that in which the two Houses shall be sitting.

Section. 6. The Senators and Representatives shall receive a Compensation for their Services, to be ascertained by Law, and paid out of the Treasury of the United States. They shall in all Cases, except Treason, Felony and Breach of the Peace, be privileged from Arrest during their Attendance at the Session of their respective Houses, and in going to and returning from the same; and for any Speech or Debate in either House, they shall not be questioned in any other Place.

No Senator or Representative shall, during the Time for which he was elected, be appointed to any civil Office under the Authority of the United States, which shall have been created, or the Emoluments whereof shall have been encreased during such time; and no Person holding any Office under the United States, shall be a Member of either House during his Continuance in Office.

Section. 7. All Bills for raising Revenue shall originate in the House of Representatives; but the Senate may propose or concur with Amendments as on other Bills.

Every Bill which shall have passed the House of Representatives and the Senate, shall, before it becomes a Law, be presented to the President of the United States; If he approve he shall sign it, but if not he shall return it, with his Objections to that House in which it shall have originated, who shall enter the Objections at large on their Journal, and proceed to reconsider it. If after such Reconsideration two thirds of that House shall agree to pass the Bill, it shall be sent, together with the Objections, to the other House, by which it shall likewise be reconsidered, and if approved by two thirds of that House, it shall become a Law. But in all such Cases the Votes of both Houses shall be determined by Yeas and Nays, and the Names of the Persons voting for and against the Bill shall be entered on the Journal of each House respectively. If any Bill shall not be returned by the President within ten Days (Sundays excepted) after it shall have been presented to him, the Same shall be a Law, in like Manner as if he had signed it, unless the Congress by their Adjournment prevent its Return, in which Case it shall not be a Law.

Every Order, Resolution, or Vote to which the Concurrence of the Senate and House of Representatives may be necessary (except on a question of Adjournment) shall be presented to the President of the United States; and before the Same shall take Effect, shall be approved by him, or being disapproved by him, shall be repassed by two thirds of the Senate and House of Representatives, according to the Rules and Limitations prescribed in the Case of a Bill.

Section. 8. The Congress shall have Power To lay and collect Taxes, Duties, Imposts and Excises, to pay the Debts and provide for the common Defence and general Welfare of the United States; but all Duties, Imposts and Excises shall be uniform throughout the United States;

To borrow Money on the credit of the United States;

To regulate Commerce with foreign Nations, and among the several States, and with the Indian Tribes;

To establish an uniform Rule of Naturalization, and uniform Laws on the subject of Bankruptcies throughout the United States;

To coin Money, regulate the Value thereof, and of foreign Coin, and fix the Standard of Weights and Measures;

To provide for the Punishment of counterfeiting the Securities and current Coin of the United States;

To establish Post Offices and post Roads;

To promote the Progress of Science and useful Arts, by securing for limited Times to Authors and Inventors the exclusive Right to their respective Writings and Discoveries;

To constitute Tribunals inferior to the supreme Court;

To define and punish Piracies and Felonies committed on the high Seas, and Offences against the Law of Nations;

To declare War, grant Letters of Marque and Reprisal, and make Rules concerning Captures on Land and Water;

To raise and support Armies, but no Appropriation of Money to that Use shall be for a longer Term than two Years;

To provide and maintain a Navy;

To make Rules for the Government and Regulation of the land and naval Forces;

To provide for calling forth the Militia to execute the Laws of the Union, suppress Insurrections and repel Invasions;

To provide for organizing, arming, and disciplining, the Militia, and for governing such Part of them as may be employed in the Service of the United States, reserving to the States respectively, the Appointment of the Officers, and the Authority of training the Militia according to the discipline prescribed by Congress;

To exercise exclusive Legislation in all Cases whatsoever, over such District (not exceeding ten Miles square) as may, by Cession of particular States, and the Acceptance of Congress, become the Seat of the Government of the United States, and to exercise like Authority over all Places purchased by the Consent of the Legislature of the State in which the Same shall be, for the Erection of Forts, Magazines, Arsenals, dock-Yards, and other needful Buildings;—And

To make all Laws which shall be necessary and proper for carrying into Execution the foregoing Powers, and all other Powers vested by this Constitution in the Government of the United States, or in any Department or Officer thereof.

Section. 9. The Migration or Importation of such Persons as any of the States now existing shall think proper to admit, shall not be prohibited by the Congress prior to the Year one thousand eight hundred and eight, but a Tax or duty may be imposed on such Importation, not exceeding ten dollars for each Person.

The Privilege of the Writ of Habeas Corpus shall not be suspended, unless when in Cases of Rebellion or Invasion the public Safety may require it.

No Bill of Attainder or ex post facto Law shall be passed.

No Capitation, or other direct, Tax shall be laid, unless in Proportion to the Census or Enumeration herein before directed to be taken.[1]

No Tax or Duty shall be laid on Articles exported from any State.

No Preference shall be given by any Regulation of Commerce or Revenue to the Ports of one State over those of another; nor shall Vessels bound to, or from, one State, be obliged to enter, clear, or pay Duties in another.

No Money shall be drawn from the Treasury, but in Consequence of Appropriations made by Law; and a regular Statement and Account of the Receipts and Expenditures of all public Money shall be published from time to time.

No Title of Nobility shall be granted by the United States: And no Person holding any Office of Profit or Trust under them, shall, without the Consent of the Congress, accept of any present, Emolument, Office, or Title, of any kind whatever, from any King, Prince, or foreign State.

[1] This paragraph has been affected by the Sixteenth Amendment.

Section. 10. No State shall enter into any Treaty, Alliance, or Confederation; grant Letters of Marque and Reprisal; coin Money; emit Bills of Credit; make any Thing but gold and silver Coin a Tender in Payment of Debts; pass any Bill of Attainder, ex post facto Law, or Law impairing the Obligation of Contracts, or grant any Title of Nobility.

No State shall, without the Consent of the Congress, lay any Imposts or Duties on Imports or Exports, except what may be absolutely necessary for executing it's inspection Laws: and the net Produce of all Duties and Imposts, laid by any State on Imports or Exports, shall be for the Use of the Treasury of the United States; and all such Laws shall be subject to the Revision and Controul of the Congress.

No State shall, without the Consent of Congress, lay any Duty of Tonnage, keep Troops, or Ships of War in time of Peace, enter into any Agreement or Compact with another State, or with a foreign Power, or engage in War, unless actually invaded, or in such imminent Danger as will not admit of delay.

ARTICLE II

Section. 1. The executive Power shall be vested in a President of the United States of America. He shall hold his Office during the Term of four Years, and, together with the Vice President, chosen for the same Term, be elected, as follows:

Each State shall appoint, in such Manner as the Legislature thereof may direct, a Number of Electors, equal to the whole Number of Senators and Representatives to which the State may be entitled in the Congress: but no Senator or Representative, or Person holding an Office of Trust or Profit under the United States, shall be appointed an Elector.

[The Electors shall meet in their respective States, and vote by Ballot for two Persons, of whom one at least shall not be an Inhabitant of the same State with themselves. And they shall make a List of all the Persons voted for, and of the Number of Votes for each; which List they shall sign and certify, and transmit sealed to the Seat of the Government of the United States, directed to the President of the Senate. The President of the Senate shall, in the Presence of the Senate and House of Representatives, open all the Certificates, and the Votes shall then be counted. The Person having the greatest Number of Votes shall be the President, if such Number be a Majority of the whole Number of Electors appointed; and if there be more than one who have such Majority, and have an equal Number of Votes, then the House of Representatives shall immediately chuse by Ballot one of them for President; and if no Person have a Majority, then from the five highest on the List the said House shall in like Manner chuse the President. But in chusing the President, the Votes shall be taken by States, the Representation from each State having one Vote; A quorum for this Purpose shall consist of a Member or Members from two thirds of the States, and a Majority of all the States shall be necessary to a Choice. In every Case, after the Choice of the President, the Person having the greatest Number of Votes of the Electors shall be the Vice President. But if there should remain two or more who have equal Votes, the Senate shall chuse from them by Ballot the Vice President.] [1]

The Congress may determine the Time of chusing the Electors, and the Day on which they shall give their Votes; which Day shall be the same throughout the United States.

No Person except a natural born Citizen, or a Citizen of the United States, at the time of the Adoption of this Constitution, shall be eligible to the Office of President; neither shall any Person be eligible to that Office who shall not have attained to the Age of thirty five Years, and been fourteen Years a Resident within the United States.

In Case of the Removal of the President from Office, or of his Death, Resignation, or Inability to discharge the Powers and Duties of the said Office, the Same shall devolve on the Vice President, and the Congress may by Law provide for the Case of Removal, Death, Resignation or Inability, both of the President and Vice President, declaring what Officer shall then act as President, and such Officer shall act accordingly, until the Disability be removed, or a President shall be elected.

The President shall, at stated Times, receive for his Services, a Compensation, which shall neither be encreased nor diminished during the Period for which he shall have been elected, and he shall not receive within that Period any other Emolument from the United States, or any of them.

Before he enter on the Execution of his Office, he shall take the following Oath or Affirmation:—"I do solemnly swear (or affirm) that I will faithfully execute the Office of President of the United States, and will to the best of my Ability, preserve, protect and defend the Constitution of the United States."

[1] This paragraph, inclosed in brackets, was superseded by the Twelfth Amendment, post.

Section. 2. The President shall be Commander in Chief of the Army and Navy of the United States, and of the Militia of the several States, when called into the actual Service of the United States; he may require the Opinion, in writing, of the principal Officer in each of the executive Departments, upon any Subject relating to the Duties of their respective Offices, and he shall have Power to grant Reprieves and Pardons for Offences against the United States, except in Cases of Impeachment.

He shall have Power, by and with the Advice and Consent of the Senate, to make Treaties, provided two thirds of the Senators present concur; and he shall nominate, and by and with the Advice and Consent of the Senate, shall appoint Ambassadors, other public Ministers and Consuls, Judges of the supreme Court, and all other Officers of the United States, whose Appointments are not herein otherwise provided for, and which shall be established by Law: but the Congress may by Law vest the Appointment of such inferior Officers, as they think proper, in the President alone, in the Courts of Law, or in the Heads of Departments.

The President shall have Power to fill up all Vacancies that may happen during the Recess of the Senate, by granting Commissions which shall expire at the End of their next Session.

Section. 3. He shall from time to time give to the Congress Information of the State of the Union, and recommend to their Consideration such Measures as he shall judge necessary and expedient; he may, on extraordinary Occasions, convene both Houses, or either of them, and in Case of Disagreement between them, with Respect to the Time of Adjournment, he may adjourn them to such Time as he shall think proper; he shall receive Ambassadors and other public Ministers; he shall take Care that the Laws be faithfully executed, and shall Commission all the Officers of the United States.

Section. 4. The President, Vice President and all civil Officers of the United States, shall be removed from Office on Impeachment for, and Conviction of, Treason, Bribery, or other high Crimes and Misdemeanors.

ARTICLE III

Section. 1. The judicial Power of the United States, shall be vested in one supreme Court, and in such inferior Courts as the Congress may from time to time ordain and establish. The Judges, both of the supreme and inferior Courts, shall hold their Offices during good Behaviour, and shall, at stated Times, receive for their Services, a Compensation, which shall not be diminished during their Continuance in Office.

Section. 2. The judicial Power shall extend to all Cases, in Law and Equity, arising under this Constitution, the Laws of the United States, and Treaties made, or which shall be made, under their Authority;—to all Cases affecting Ambassadors, other public Ministers and Consuls;—to all Cases of admiralty and maritime Jurisdiction;—to Controversies to which the United States shall be a Party;—to Controversies between two or more States;—between a State and Citizens of another State;—between citizens of different States;—between Citizens of the same State claiming Lands under Grants of different States, and between a State, or the Citizens thereof, and foreign States, Citizens or Subjects.[1]

In all Cases affecting Ambassadors, other public Ministers and Consuls, and those in which a State shall be Party, the supreme Court shall have original Jurisdiction. In all the other Cases before mentioned, the supreme Court shall have appellate Jurisdiction, both as to Law and Fact, with such Exceptions, and under such Regulations as the Congress shall make.

The Trial of all Crimes, except in Cases of Impeachment, shall be by Jury; and such Trial shall be held in the State where the said Crimes shall have been committed; but when not committed within any State, the Trial shall be at such Place or Places as the Congress may by Law have directed.

[1] This section has been affected by the Eleventh Amendment.

Section. 3. Treason against the United States, shall consist only in levying War against them, or in adhering to their Enemies, giving them Aid and Comfort. No Person shall be convicted of Treason unless on the Testimony of two Witnesses to the same overt Act, or on Confession in open Court.

The Congress shall have Power to declare the Punishment of Treason, but no Attainder of Treason shall work Corruption of Blood, or Forfeiture except during the Life of the Person attainted.

ARTICLE IV

Section. 1. Full Faith and Credit shall be given in each State to the public Acts, Records, and judicial Proceedings of every other State. And the Congress may by general Laws prescribe the Manner in which such Acts, Records and Proceedings shall be proved, and the Effect thereof.

Section. 2. The Citizens of each State shall be entitled to all Privileges and Immunities of Citizens in the several States.

A Person charged in any State with Treason, Felony, or other Crime, who shall flee from Justice, and be found in another State, shall on Demand of the executive Authority of the State from which he fled, be delivered up, to be removed to the State having Jurisdiction of the Crime.

No Person held to Service or Labour in one State, under the Laws thereof, escaping into another, shall, in Consequence of any Law or Regulation therein, be discharged from such Service or Labour, but shall be delivered up on Claim of the Party to whom such Service or Labour may be due.[1]

[1] This clause was affected by the Thirteenth Amendment.

Section. 3. New States may be admitted by the Congress into this Union; but no new State shall be formed or erected within the Jurisdiction of any other State; nor any State be formed by the Junction of two or more States, or Parts of States, without the Consent of the Legislatures of the States concerned as well as of the Congress.

The Congress shall have Power to dispose of and make all needful Rules and Regulations respecting the Territory or other Property belonging to the United States; and nothing in this Constitution shall be so construed as to Prejudice any Claims of the United States, or of any particular State.

Section. 4. The United States shall guarantee to every State in this Union a Republican Form of Government, and shall protect each of them against Invasion; and on Application of the Legislature, or of the Executive (when the Legislature cannot be convened) against domestic Violence.

ARTICLE V

The Congress, whenever two thirds of both Houses shall deem it necessary, shall propose Amendments to this Constitution, or, on the Application of the Legislatures of two thirds of the several States, shall call a Convention for proposing Amendments, which, in either Case, shall be valid to all Intents and Purposes, as Part of this Constitution, when ratified by the Legislatures of three fourths of the several States, or by Conventions in three fourths thereof, as the one or the other Mode of Ratification may be proposed by the Congress; Provided that no Amendment which may be made prior to the Year One thousand eight hundred and eight shall in any Manner affect the first and fourth Clauses in the Ninth Section of the first Article; and that no State, without its Consent, shall be deprived of its equal Suffrage in the Senate.

ARTICLE VI

All Debts contracted and Engagements entered into, before the Adoption of this Constitution, shall be as valid against the United States under this Constitution, as under the Confederation.

This Constitution, and the Laws of the United States which shall be made in Pursuance thereof; and all Treaties made, or which shall be made, under the Authority of the United States, shall be the supreme Law of the Land; and the Judges in every State shall be bound thereby, any Thing in the Constitution or Laws of any State to the Contrary notwithstanding.

The Senators and Representatives before mentioned, and the Members of the several State Legislatures, and all executive and judicial Officers, both of the United States and of the several States, shall be bound by Oath or Affirmation, to support this Constitution; but no religious Test shall ever be required as a Qualification to any Office or public Trust under the United States.

ARTICLE VII

The Ratification of the Conventions of nine States, shall be sufficient for the Establishment of this Constitution between the States so ratifying the Same.

DONE in Convention by the Unanimous Consent of the States present the Seventeenth Day of September in the Year of Our Lord one thousand seven hundred and Eighty seven and of the Independence of the United States of America the Twelfth. IN WITNESS whereof We have hereunto subscribed our Names.

Go. WASHINGTON—*Presidt.*
and deputy from Virginia

Attest WILLIAM JACKSON *Secretary*

New Hampshire

JOHN LANGDON
NICHOLAS GILMAN

Massachusetts

NATHANIEL GORHAM
RUFUS KING

Connecticut

WM. SAML. JOHNSON
ROGER SHERMAN

New York

ALEXANDER HAMILTON

New Jersey

WIL: LIVINGSTON
WM. PATERSON.
DAVID BREARLEY.
JONA: DAYTON

Pennsylvania

B FRANKLIN
THOS. FITZSIMONS
THOMAS MIFFLIN
JARED INGERSOLL
ROBT MORRIS
JAMES WILSON
GEO. CLYMER
GOUV MORRIS

Delaware

GEO: READ
RICHARD BASSETT
GUNNING BEDFORD jun
JACO: BROOM
JOHN DICKINSON

Maryland

JAMES MCHENRY
DANL CARROLL
DAN OF ST THOS. JENIFER

Virginia
JOHN BLAIR— JAMES MADISON JR.
North Carolina
WM. BLOUNT HU WILLIAMSON
RICHD. DOBBS SPAIGHT

South Carolina
J. RUTLEDGE CHARLES PINCKNEY
CHARLES COTESWORTH PINCKNEY PIERCE BUTLER
Georgia
WILLIAM FEW ABR BALDWIN

Articles in Addition to, and Amendment of, the Constitution of the United States of America, Proposed by Congress, and Ratified by the Legislatures of the Several States Pursuant to the Fifth Article of the Original Constitution

ARTICLE [I]

Congress shall make no law respecting an establishment of religion, or prohibiting the free exercise thereof; or abridging the freedom of speech, or of the press; or the right of the people peaceably to assemble, and to petition the Government for a redress of grievances.

ARTICLE [II]

A well regulated Militia, being necessary to the security of a free State, the right of the people to keep and bear Arms, shall not be infringed.

ARTICLE [III]

No Soldier shall, in time of peace be quartered in any house, without the consent of the Owner, nor in time of war, but in a manner to be prescribed by law.

ARTICLE [IV]

The right of the people to be secure in their persons, houses, papers, and effects, against unreasonable searches and seizures, shall not be violated, and no Warrants shall issue, but upon probable cause, supported by Oath or affirmation, and particularly describing the place to be searched, and the persons or things to be seized.

ARTICLE [V]

No person shall be held to answer for a capital, or otherwise infamous crime, unless on a presentment or indictment of a Grand Jury, except in cases arising in the land or naval forces, or in the Militia, when in actual service in time of War or public danger; nor shall any person be subject for the same offence to be twice put in jeopardy of life or limb; nor shall be compelled in any criminal case to be a witness against himself, nor be deprived of life, liberty, or property, without due process of law; nor shall private property be taken for public use, without just compensation.

ARTICLE [VI]

In all criminal prosecutions, the accused shall enjoy the right to a speedy and public trial, by an impartial jury of the State and district wherein the crime shall have been committed, which district shall have been previously ascertained by law, and to be informed of the nature and cause of the accusation; to be confronted with the witnesses against him; to have compulsory process for obtaining witnesses in his favor, and to have the Assistance of Counsel for his defence.

ARTICLE [VII]

In Suits at common law, where the value in controversy shall exceed twenty dollars, the right of trial by jury shall be preserved, and no fact tried by a jury, shall be otherwise reexamined in any Court of the United States, than according to the rules of the common law.

ARTICLE [VIII]

Excessive bail shall not be required, nor excessive fines imposed, nor cruel and unusual punishments inflicted.

ARTICLE [IX]

The enumeration in the Constitution, of certain rights, shall not be construed to deny or disparage others retained by the people.

ARTICLE [X]

The powers not delegated to the United States by the Constitution, nor prohibited by it to the States, are reserved to the States respectively, or to the people.

ARTICLE [XI]

The Judicial power of the United States shall not be construed to extend to any suit in law or equity, commenced or prosecuted against one of the United States by Citizens of another State, or by Citizens or Subjects of any Foreign State.

ARTICLE [XII]

The Electors shall meet in their respective states, and vote by ballot for President and Vice-President, one of whom, at least, shall not be an inhabitant of the same state with themselves; they shall name in their ballots the person voted for as President, and in distinct ballots the person voted for as Vice-President, and they shall make distinct lists of all persons voted for as President, and of all persons voted for as Vice-President, and of the number of votes for each, which lists they shall sign and certify, and transmit sealed to the seat of the government of the United States, directed to the President of the Senate;—The President of the Senate shall, in the presence of the Senate and House of Representatives, open all the certificates and the votes shall then be counted;—The person having the greatest number of votes for President, shall be the President, if such number be a majority of the whole number of Electors appointed; and if no person have such majority, then from the persons having the highest numbers not exceeding three on the list of those voted for as President, the House of Representatives shall choose immediately, by ballot, the President. But in choosing the President, the votes shall be taken by states, the representation from each state having one vote; a quorum for this purpose shall consist of a member or members from two-thirds of the states, and a majority of all the states shall be necessary to a choice. And if the House of Representatives shall not choose a President whenever the right of choice shall devolve upon them, before the fourth day of March next following, then the Vice-President shall act as President, as in the case of the death or other constitutional disability of the President.—The person having the greatest number of votes as Vice-President, shall be the Vice-President, if such number be a majority of the whole number of Electors appointed, and if no person have a majority, then from the two highest numbers on the list, the Senate shall choose the Vice-President; a quorum for the purpose shall consist of two-thirds of the whole number of Senators, and a majority of the whole number shall be necessary to a choice. But no person constitutionally ineligible to the office of President shall be eligible to that of Vice-President of the United States.[1]

[1] This Amendment was affected by the Twentieth Amendment.

ARTICLE XIII

Section 1. Neither slavery nor involuntary servitude, except as a punishment for crime whereof the party shall have been duly convicted, shall exist within the United States, or any place subject to their jurisdiction.

Section 2. Congress shall have power to enforce this article by appropriate legislation.

ARTICLE XIV

Section 1. All persons born or naturalized in the United States, and subject to the jurisdiction thereof, are citizens of the United States and of the State wherein they reside. No State shall make or enforce any law which shall abridge the privileges or immunities of citizens of the United States; nor shall any State deprive any person of life, liberty, or property, without due process of law; nor deny to any person within its jurisdiction the equal protection of the laws.

Section 2. Representatives shall be apportioned among the several States according to their respective numbers, counting the whole number of persons in each State, excluding Indians not taxed. But when the right to vote at any election for the choice of electors for President and Vice President of the United States, Representatives in Congress, the Executive and Judicial officers of a State, or the members of the Legislature thereof, is denied to any of the male inhabitants of such State, being twenty-one years of age, and citizens of the United States, or in any way abridged, except for participation in rebellion, or other crime, the basis of representation therein shall be reduced in the proportion which the number of such male citizens shall bear to the whole number of male citizens twenty-one years of age in such State.

Section 3. No person shall be a Senator or Representative in Congress, or elector of President and Vice President, or hold any office, civil or military, under the United States, or under any State, who, having previously taken an oath, as a member of Congress, or as an officer of the United States, or as a member of any State legislature, or as an executive or judicial officer of any State, to support the Constitution of the United States, shall have engaged in insurrection or rebellion against the same, or given aid or comfort to the enemies thereof. But Congress may by a vote of two-thirds of each House, remove such disability.

Section 4. The validity of the public debt of the United States, authorized by law, including debts incurred for payment of pensions and bounties for services in suppressing insurrection or rebellion, shall not be questioned. But neither the United States nor any State shall assume or pay any debt or obligation incurred in aid of insurrection or rebellion against the United States, or any claim for the loss or emancipation of any slave; but all such debts, obligations and claims shall be held illegal and void.

Section 5. The Congress shall have power to enforce, by appropriate legislation, the provisions of this article.

ARTICLE XV

Section 1. The right of citizens of the United States to vote shall not be denied or abridged by the United States or by any State on account of race, color, or previous condition of servitude.

Section 2. The Congress shall have power to enforce this article by appropriate legislation.

ARTICLE XVI

The Congress shall have power to lay and collect taxes on incomes, from whatever source derived, without apportionment among the several States, and without regard to any census or enumeration.

ARTICLE [XVII]

The Senate of the United States shall be composed of two Senators from each state, elected by the people thereof, for six years; and each Senator shall have one vote. The electors in each State shall have the qualifications requisite for electors of the most numerous branch of the State legislatures.

When vacancies happen in the representation of any State in the Senate, the executive authority of such State shall issue writs of election to fill such vacancies: *Provided,* That the legislature of any State may empower the executive thereof to make temporary appointments until the people fill the vacancies by election as the legislature may direct.

This amendment shall not be so construed as to affect the election or term of any Senator chosen before it becomes valid as part of the Constitution.

ARTICLE [XVIII] [Repealed. See Article XXI]

Section 1. After one year from the ratification of this article the manufacture, sale, or transportation of intoxicating liquors within, the importation thereof into, or the exportation thereof from the United States and all territory subject to the jurisdiction thereof for beverage purposes is hereby prohibited.

Section 2. The Congress and the several States shall have concurrent power to enforce this article by appropriate legislation.

Section 3. This article shall be inoperative unless it shall have been ratified as an amendment to the Constitution by the legislatures of the several States, as provided in the Constitution, within seven years from the date of the submission hereof to the States by the Congress.

ARTICLE [XIX]

The right of citizens of the United States to vote shall not be denied or abridged by the United States or by any State on account of sex.

Congress shall have power to enforce this article by appropriate legislation.

ARTICLE [XX]

Section 1. The terms of the President and Vice President shall end at noon on the 20th day of January, and the terms of Senators and Representatives at noon on the 3d day of January, of the years in which such terms would have ended if this article had not been ratified; and the terms of their successors shall then begin.

Sec. 2. The Congress shall assemble at least once in every year, and such meeting shall begin at noon on the 3d day of January, unless they shall by law appoint a different day.

Sec. 3. If, at the time fixed for the beginning of the term of the President, the President elect shall have died, the Vice President elect shall become President. If a President shall not have been chosen before the time fixed for the beginning of his term, or if the President elect shall have failed to qualify, then the Vice President elect shall act as President until a President shall have qualified; and the Congress may by law provide for the case wherein neither a President elect nor a Vice President elect shall have qualified, declaring who shall then act as President, or the manner in which one who is to act shall be selected, and such person shall act accordingly until a President or Vice President shall have qualified.

Sec. 4. The Congress may by law provide for the case of the death of any of the persons from whom the House of Representatives may choose a President whenever the right of choice shall have devolved upon them, and for the case of the death of any of the persons from whom the Senate may choose a Vice President whenever the right of choice shall have devolved upon them.

Sec. 5. Sections 1 and 2 shall take effect on the 15th day of October following the ratification of this article.

Sec. 6. This article shall be inoperative unless it shall have been ratified as an amendment to the Constitution by the legislatures of three-fourths of the several States within seven years from the date of its submission.

ARTICLE [XXI]

Section 1. The eighteenth article of amendment to the Constitution of the United States is hereby repealed.

Sec. 2. The transportation or importation into any State, Territory, or possession of the United States for delivery or use therein of intoxicating liquors, in violation of the laws thereof, is hereby prohibited.

Sec. 3. This article shall be inoperative unless it shall have been ratified as an amendment to the Constitution by conventions in the several States, as provided in the Constitution, within seven years from the date of the submission hereof to the States by the Congress.

ARTICLE [XXII]

Section 1. No person shall be elected to the office of the President more than twice, and no person who has held the office of President, or acted as President, for more than two years of a term to which some other person was elected President shall be elected to the office of the President more than once. But this Article shall not apply to any person holding the office of President when this Article was proposed by the Congress, and shall not prevent any person who may be holding the office of President, or acting as President, during the term within which this Article becomes operative from holding the office of President or acting as President during the remainder of such term.

Sec. 2. This Article shall be inoperative unless it shall have been ratified as an amendment to the Constitution by the legislatures of three-fourths of the several States within seven years from the date of its submission to the States by the Congress.

ARTICLE [XXIII]

Section 1. The District constituting the seat of Government of the United States shall appoint in such manner as the Congress may direct:

A number of electors of President and Vice President equal to the whole number of Senators and Representatives in Congress to which the District would be entitled if it were a State, but in no event more than the least populous State; they shall be in addition to those appointed by the States, but they shall be considered, for the purposes of the election of President and Vice President, to be electors appointed by a State; and they shall meet in the District and perform such duties as provided by the twelfth article of amendment.

Sec. 2. The Congress shall have power to enforce this article by appropriate legislation.

ARTICLE [XXIV]

Section 1. The right of citizens of the United States to vote in any primary or other election for President or Vice President, for electors for President or Vice President, or for Senator or Representative in Congress, shall not be denied or abridged by the United States or any State by reason of failure to pay any poll tax or other tax.

Sec. 2. The Congress shall have power to enforce this article by appropriate legislation.

ARTICLE [XXV]

Section 1. In case of the removal of the President from office or of his death or resignation, the Vice President shall become President.

Sec. 2. Whenever there is a vacancy in the office of the Vice President, the President shall nominate a Vice President who shall take office upon confirmation by a majority vote of both Houses of Congress.

Sec. 3. Whenever the President transmits to the President pro tempore of the Senate and the Speaker of the House of Representatives his written declaration that he is unable to discharge the powers and duties of his office, and until he transmits to them a written declaration to the contrary, such powers and duties shall be discharged by the Vice President as Acting President.

Sec. 4. Whenever the Vice President and a majority of either the principal officers of the executive departments or of such other body as Congress may by law provide, transmit to the President pro tempore of the Senate and the Speaker of the House of Representatives their written declaration that the President is unable to discharge the powers and duties of his office, the Vice President shall immediately assume the powers and duties of the office as Acting President.

Thereafter, when the President transmits to the President pro tempore of the Senate and the Speaker of the House of Representatives his written declaration that no inability exists, he shall resume the powers and duties of his office unless the Vice President and a majority of either the principal officers of the executive department or of such other body as Congress may by law provide, transmit within four days to the President pro tempore of the Senate and the Speaker of the House of Representatives their written declaration that the President is unable to discharge the powers and duties of his office. Thereupon Congress shall decide the issue, assembling within forty-eight hours for that purpose if not in session. If the Congress, within twenty-one days after receipt of the latter written declaration, or, if Congress is not in session, within twenty-one days after Congress is required to assemble, determines by two-thirds vote of both Houses that the President is unable to discharge the powers and duties of his office, the Vice President shall continue to discharge the same as Acting President; otherwise, the President shall resume the powers and duties of his office.

ARTICLE [XXVI]

Section 1. The right of citizens of the United States, who are eighteen years of age or older, to vote shall not be denied or abridged by the United States or by any State on account of age.

Sec. 2. The Congress shall have power to enforce this article by appropriate legislation.

ARTICLE [XXVII][1]

No law, varying the compensation for the services of the Senators and Representatives, shall take effect, until an election of Representatives shall have intervened.

1 "Article [XXVII]" editorially added. Originally read "Article the second".

TITLE 5
GOVERNMENT ORGANIZATION AND EMPLOYEES
APPENDIX 4
ETHICS IN GOVERNMENT ACT OF 1978 [1]

[1] Number and order of Appendixes editorially supplied.

TITLE I—FINANCIAL DISCLOSURE REQUIREMENTS OF FEDERAL PERSONNEL

Sec.
101. Persons required to file.
102. Contents of reports.
103. Filing of reports.
104. Failure to file or filing false reports.
105. Custody of and public access to reports.
106. Review of reports.
107. Confidential reports and other additional requirements.
108. Authority of Comptroller General.
109. Definitions.
110. Notice of actions taken to comply with ethics agreements.
111. Administration of provisions.
[112. Repealed.]

[TITLE II—REPEALED]

[201 to 212. Repealed.]

[TITLE III—REPEALED]

[301 to 309. Repealed.]

TITLE I—FINANCIAL DISCLOSURE REQUIREMENTS OF FEDERAL PERSONNEL

HISTORICAL AND STATUTORY NOTES

Codifications

Title I of Pub.L. 95–521 was classified to chapter 18 (section 701 et seq.) of Title 2, The Congress, prior to general amendment of Title I by Pub.L. 101–194, Title II, § 202, Nov. 30, 1989, 103 Stat. 1724.

§ 101. Persons required to file

(a) Within thirty days of assuming the position of an officer or employee described in subsection (f), an individual shall file a report containing the information described in section 102(b) unless the individual has left another position described in subsection (f) within thirty days prior to assuming such new position or has already filed a report under this title with respect to nomination for the new position or as a candidate for the position.

(b)(1) Within five days of the transmittal by the President to the Senate of the nomination of an individual (other than an individual nominated for appointment to a position as a Foreign Service Officer or a grade or rank in the uniformed services for which the pay grade prescribed by section 201 of title 37, United States Code, is O–6 or below) to a position, appointment to which requires the advice and consent of the Senate, such individual shall file a report containing the information described in section 102(b). Such individual shall, not later than the date of the first hearing to consider the nomination of such individual, make current the report filed pursuant to this paragraph by filing the information required by section 102(a)(1)(A) with respect to income and honoraria received as of the date which occurs five days before the date of such hearing. Nothing in this Act shall prevent any Congressional committee from requesting, as a condition of confirmation, any additional financial information from any Presidential nominee whose nomination has been referred to that committee.

(2) An individual whom the President or the President-elect has publicly announced he intends to nominate to a position may file the report required by paragraph (1) at any time after that public announcement, but not later than is required under the first sentence of such paragraph.

(c) Within thirty days of becoming a candidate as defined in section 301 of the Federal Campaign Act of 1971, in a calendar year for nomination or election to the office of President, Vice President, or Member of Congress, or on or before May 15 of that calendar year, whichever is later, but in no event later than 30 days before the election, and on or before May 15 of each successive year an individual continues to be a candidate, an individual other than an incumbent President, Vice President, or Member of Congress shall file a report containing the information described in section 102(b). Notwithstanding the preceding sentence, in any calendar year in which an individual continues to be a candidate for any office but all elections for such office relating to such candidacy were held in prior calendar years, such individual need not file a report unless he becomes a candidate for another vacancy in that office or another office during that year.

(d) Any individual who is an officer or employee described in subsection (f) during any calendar year and performs the duties of his position or office for a period in excess of sixty days in that calendar year shall file on or before May 15 of the succeeding year a report containing the information described in section 102(a).

(e) Any individual who occupies a position described in subsection (f) shall, on or before the thirtieth day after termination of employment in such position, file a report containing the information described in section 102(a) covering the preceding calendar year if the report required by subsection (d) has not been filed and covering the portion of the calendar year in which such termination occurs up to the date the individual left such office or position, unless such individual has accepted employment in another position described in subsection (f).

(f) The officers and employees referred to in subsections (a), (d), and (e) are—

(1) the President;

(2) the Vice President;

(3) each officer or employee in the executive branch, including a special Government employee as defined in section 202 of title 18, United States Code, who occupies a position classified above GS–15 of the General Schedule or, in the case of positions not under the General Schedule, for which the rate of basic pay is equal to or greater than 120 percent of the minimum rate of basic pay payable for GS–15 of the General Schedule; each member of a uniformed service whose pay grade is at or in excess of O–7 under section 201 of title 37, United States Code; and each officer or employee in any other position determined by the Director of the Office of Government Ethics to be of equal classification;

(4) each employee appointed pursuant to section 3105 of title 5, United States Code;

(5) any employee not described in paragraph (3) who is in a position in the executive branch which is excepted from the competitive service by reason of being of a confidential or policymaking character, except that the Director of the Office of Government Ethics may, by regulation, exclude from the application of this paragraph any individual, or group of individuals, who are in such positions, but only in cases in which the Director determines such exclusion would not affect adversely the integrity of the Government or the public's confidence in the integrity of the Government;

(6) the Postmaster General, the Deputy Postmaster General, each Governor of the Board of Governors of the United States Postal Service and each officer or employee of the United States Postal Service or Postal Regulatory Commission who occupies a position for which the rate of basic pay is equal to or greater than 120 percent of the minimum rate of basic pay payable for GS–15 of the General Schedule;

(7) the Director of the Office of Government Ethics and each designated agency ethics official;

(8) any civilian employee not described in paragraph (3), employed in the Executive Office of the President (other than a special government[1] employee) who holds a commission of appointment from the President;

(9) a Member of Congress as defined under section 109(12);

(10) an officer or employee of the Congress as defined under section 109(13);

(11) a judicial officer as defined under section 109(10); and

(12) a judicial employee as defined under section 109(8).

(g)(1) Reasonable extensions of time for filing any report may be granted under procedures prescribed by the supervising ethics office for each branch, but the total of such extensions shall not exceed ninety days.

(2)(A) In the case of an individual who is serving in the Armed Forces, or serving in support of the Armed Forces, in an area while that area is designated by the President by Executive order as a combat zone for purposes of section 112 of the Internal Revenue Code of 1986, the date for the filing of any report shall be extended so that the date is 180 days after the later of—

(i) the last day of the individual's service in such area during such designated period; or

(ii) the last day of the individual's hospitalization as a result of injury received or disease contracted while serving in such area.

(B) The Office of Government Ethics, in consultation with the Secretary of Defense, may prescribe procedures under this paragraph.

(h) The provisions of subsections (a), (b), and (e) shall not apply to an individual who, as determined by the designated agency ethics official or Secretary concerned (or in the case of a Presidential appointee under subsection (b), the Director of the Office of Government Ethics), the congressional ethics committees, or the Judicial Conference, is not reasonably expected to perform the duties of his office or position for more than sixty days in a calendar year, except that if such individual performs the duties of his office or position for more than sixty days in a calendar year—

(1) the report required by subsections (a) and (b) shall be filed within fifteen days of the sixtieth day, and

(2) the report required by subsection (e) shall be filed as provided in such subsection.

(i) The supervising ethics office for each branch may grant a publicly available request for a waiver of any reporting requirement under this section for an individual who is expected to perform or has performed the duties of his office or position less than one hundred and thirty days in a calendar year, but only if the supervising ethics office determines that—

(1) such individual is not a full-time employee of the Government,

(2) such individual is able to provide services specially needed by the Government,

(3) it is unlikely that the individual's outside employment or financial interests will create a conflict of interest, and

(4) public financial disclosure by such individual is not necessary in the circumstances.

(Pub.L. 95–521, Title I, § 101, Oct. 26, 1978, 92 Stat. 1824; Pub.L. 96–19, §§ 2(a)(1), (b), (c)(1), 4(b)(1), (d) to (f), 5, June 13, 1979, 93 Stat. 37, 38, 40; Pub.L. 101–194, Title II, § 202, Nov. 30, 1989, 103 Stat. 1725; Pub.L. 101–280, § 3(1), (2), May 4, 1990, 104 Stat. 152; Pub.L. 102–25, Title VI, § 605(a), Apr. 6, 1991, 105 Stat. 110; Pub.L. 102–378, § 4(a)(1), Oct. 2, 1992, 106 Stat. 1356; Pub.L. 109–435, Title VI, § 604(c), Dec. 20, 2006, 120 Stat. 3241.)

[1] So in original. Probably should be capitalized.

HISTORICAL AND STATUTORY NOTES

References in Text

This Act, referred to in subsec. (b)(1), is Pub.L. 95–521, Oct. 26, 1978, 92 Stat. 1824, as amended, known as the Ethics in Government Act of 1978. For complete classification of this Act to the Code, see Short Title note set out under this section and Tables.

Section 301 of the Federal Campaign Act of 1971, referred to in subsec. (c), probably means section 301 of Pub.L. 92–225, Feb. 7, 1972, 86 Stat. 3, as amended, known as the Federal Election Campaign Act of 1971, which is classified to section 431 of Title 2, The Congress.

The General Schedule, referred to in subsec. (f)(3), (6), is set out under section 5332 of Title 5, Government Organization and Employees.

Section 112 of the Internal Revenue Code, referred to in subsec. (g)(2), is classified to section 112 of Title 26, Internal Revenue Code.

Codifications

Section was formerly classified to section 701 of Title 2, The Congress.

Effective and Applicability Provisions

1992 Acts. Amendment by Pub.L. 102–378 effective Oct. 2, 1992, see section 9(a) of Pub.L. 102–378, set out as a note under section 6303 of this title.

1991 Acts. Section 605(b) of Pub.L. 102–25 provided that: "The amendments made by subsection (a) [amending this section] shall apply with respect to reports required to be filed after January 17, 1991."

1990 Acts. Section 11 of Pub.L. 101–280 provided that: "Except as otherwise provided in this joint resolution, this Act and the amendments made by this joint resolution [amending sections 101 to 106, 109 to 111, former section 202, and sections 501 to 503 of Pub.L. 95–521, set out in this Appendix, sections 3393, 7351, 7353, and 7701 of this title, sections 31–1, 31–2, and 441i of Title 2, The Congress, sections 1601 and 2397a of Title 10, Armed Forces, sections 202, 203, 205, 207, 207 note, 208, 208 note, and 216 of Title 18, Crimes and Criminal Procedure, section 3945 of Title 22, Foreign Relations and Intercourse, section 1043 of Title 26, Internal Revenue Code, and sections 1353, 1344 note, and 3730 of Title 31, Money and Finance, repealing section 112 of Pub.L. 95–521, set out in this Appendix, renumbering section 1352 of Title 31 as section 1353, and enacting provisions set out as notes under sections 101 and 105 of Pub.L. 95–521, set out in this Appendix, and under section 2397a of Title 10 and section 1043 of Title 26] take effect on the date of the enactment of this joint resolution [May 4, 1990]."

1989 Acts. Section 204 of Pub.L. 101–194, as added Pub.L. 101–280, § 3(10)(B), May 4, 1990, 104 Stat. 157, provided that: "The amendments made by this title [enacting sections 110 to 112 of Pub.L. 95–521, set out in this Appendix, amending sections 101 to 109 of Pub.L. 95–521, set out in this Appendix, but formerly classified to sections 701 to 709 of Title 2, The Congress] and the repeal made by section 201 [repealing sections 201 to 212 of Pub.L. 95–521, formerly set out under the heading Executive Personnel Financial Disclosure Requirements in this Appendix, and sections 301 to 309 of Pub.L. 95–521, formerly set out under the heading Judicial Personnel Financial Disclosure Requirements in the Appendix to Title 28, Judiciary and Judicial Procedure] shall take effect on January 1, 1991, except that the provisions of section 102(f)(4)(B) of the Ethics in Government Act of 1978, as amended by this title [section 102(f)(4)(B) of Pub.L. 95–521, set out in this Appendix], shall be effective as of January 1, 1990."

Section 3(10)(C), (D) of Pub.L. 101–280 provided that:

"(C) The provisions of titles I [formerly classified to section 701 et seq. of Title 2, The Congress], II [formerly set out under the heading Executive Personnel Financial Disclosure Requirements in this Appendix], and III [formerly set out under the heading Judicial Personnel Financial Disclosure Requirements in the Appendix to Title 28, Judiciary and Judicial Procedure] of the Ethics in Government Act of 1978 [Pub.L. 95–521] as in effect on the day before the date of the enactment of the Ethics Reform Act of 1989 [Nov. 30, 1989], shall be effective for the period beginning on November 30, 1989, and ending on January 1, 1991, as if the Ethics Reform Act of 1989 [Pub.L. 101–194] had not been enacted, except that the provisions of section 202(f)(4)(B) of the Ethics in Government Act of 1978 [section 202(f)(4)(B) of Pub.L. 95–521] shall be repealed as of January 1, 1990.

"(D) "Nothing in title II of the Ethics Reform Act of 1989 or the amendments made by such title [title II of Pub.L. 101–194, amending title I of Pub.L. 95–521, set out in this Appendix, but formerly classified to sections 701 to 709 of Title 2, The Congress, and repealing title II of Pub.L. 95–521, formerly set out in this Appendix, and title III of Pub.L. 95–521, formerly set out in the Appendix to Title 28, Judiciary and Judicial Procedure] shall be construed to prevent the prosecution of civil actions against individuals for violations of the Ethics in Government Act of 1978 [Pub.L. 95–521] before January 1, 1991."

Short Title

2007 Amendments. Pub.L. 110–24, § 1, May 3, 2007, 121 Stat. 100, provided that: "This Act [amending 5 U.S.C.A. App. 4 § 105] may be cited as the 'Judicial Disclosure Responsibility Act'."

2002 Amendments. Pub.L. 107–119, § 1, Jan. 15, 2002, 115 Stat. 2382, provided that: "This Act [amending section 405 of this Appendix] may be cited as the 'Office of Government Ethics Authorization Act of 2001'."

1996 Amendments. Pub.L. 104–179, § 1, Aug. 6, 1996, 110 Stat. 1566, provided that: "This Act [amending sections 401, 403, 405, and 408 of Pub.L. 95–521, set out in this Appendix, section 1822 of Title 12, Banks and Banking, and section 207 of Title 18, Crimes and Criminal Procedure, and repealing a provision set out as a note under section 7301 of this title] may be cited as the 'Office of Government Ethics Authorization Act of 1996'."

1992 Amendments. Pub.L. 102–506, § 1, Oct. 24, 1992, 106 Stat. 3280, provided that: "This Act [amending section 405 of Pub.L. 95–521, set out in this Appendix] may be cited as the 'Office of Government Ethics Amendment of 1992'."

1990 Amendments. Pub.L. 101–334, § 1, July 16, 1990, 104 Stat. 318, provided that: "This Act [amending section 405 of Pub.L. 95–521, set out in this Appendix] may be cited as the 'Ethics in Government Act Amendment of 1990'."

1989 Amendments. Section 1 of Pub.L. 101–194 provided that: "This Act [see table for classification] may be cited as the 'Ethics Reform Act of 1989'."

1978 Acts. Section 1 of Pub.L. 95–521 provided: "That this Act [enacting provisions set out in this Appendix, sections 118a, 288 to 288m of Title 2, The Congress, sections 49, 528, 529, 591 to 598, 1364 of Title 28, Judiciary and Judicial Procedure, amending section 5316 of this title, section 207 of Title 18, Crimes and Criminal Procedure, and sections 3210, 3216, and 3219 of Title 39, Postal Service, and enacting provisions set out as notes under section 288 of Title 2, section 207 of Title 18, and section 591 of Title 28] may be cited as the 'Ethics in Government Act of 1978'."

Declaration of Purpose of 1990 Amendments

Section 1 of Pub.L. 101–280 provided that: "It is the purpose of this joint resolution to make technical corrections in the Ethics Reform Act of 1989 [Pub.L. 101–194, see Short Title of 1989 Amendments note set out under this section and Tables for classification]."

Rulemaking Power of Congress

Pub.L. 102–90, Title III, § 314(f), Aug. 14, 1991, 105 Stat. 470, provided that: "The provisions of this section [amending sections 102 and 505 of Pub.L. 95–521, set out in this Appendix, section 31–2 of Title 2, The Congress, and section 7701 of Title 26, Internal Revenue Code, and enacting provisions set out as a note under section 31–2 of Title 2] that are applicable to Members, officers, or employees of the legislative branch are enacted by the Congress—

"(1) as an exercise of the rulemaking power of the House of Representatives and the Senate, respectively, and as such they shall be considered as part of the rules of each House, respectively, or of that House to which they specifically apply, and such rules shall supersede other rules only to the extent that they are inconsistent therewith; and

"(2) with full recognition of the constitutional right of either House to change such rules (so far as relating to such House) at any time, in the same manner, and to the same extent as in the case of any other rule of such House."

Section 1001 of Pub.L. 101–194 provided that: "The provisions of this Act [see Short Title of 1989 Amendments note set out under this section] that are applicable to Members, officers, or employees of the legislative branch are enacted by the Congress—

"(1) as an exercise of the rulemaking power of the House of Representatives and the Senate, respectively, and as such they shall be considered as part of the rules of each House, respectively, or of that House to which they specifically apply, and such rules shall supersede other rules only to the extent that they are inconsistent therewith; and

"(2) with full recognition of the constitutional right of either House to change such rules (so far as relating to such House) at any time, in the same manner, and to the same extent as in the case of any other rule of such House."

§ 102. Contents of reports

(a) Each report filed pursuant to section 101(d) and (e) shall include a full and complete statement with respect to the following:

(1)(A) The source, type, and amount or value of income (other than income referred to in subparagraph (B)) from any source (other than from current employment by the United States Government), and the source, date, and amount of honoraria from any source, received during the preceding calendar year, aggregating $200 or more in value and, effective January 1, 1991, the source, date, and amount of payments made to charitable organizations in lieu of honoraria, and the reporting individual shall simultaneously file with the applicable supervising ethics office, on a confidential basis, a corresponding list of recipients of all such payments, together with the dates and amounts of such payments.

(B) The source and type of income which consists of dividends, rents, interest, and capital gains, received during the preceding calendar year which exceeds $200 in amount or value, and an indication of which of the following categories the amount or value of such item of income is within:

(i) not more than $1,000,

(ii) greater than $1,000 but not more than $2,500,

(iii) greater than $2,500 but not more than $5,000,

(iv) greater than $5,000 but not more than $15,000,

(v) greater than $15,000 but not more than $50,000,

(vi) greater than $50,000 but not more than $100,000,

(vii) greater than $100,000 but not more than $1,000,000,

(viii) greater than $1,000,000 but not more than $5,000,000, or

(ix) greater than $5,000,000.

(2)(A) The identity of the source, a brief description, and the value of all gifts aggregating more than the minimal value as established by section 7342(a)(5) of title 5, United States Code, or $250, whichever is greater, received from any source other than a relative of the reporting individual during the preceding calendar year, except that any food, lodging, or entertainment received as personal hospitality of an individual need not be reported, and any gift with a fair market value of $100 or less, as adjusted at the same time and by the same percentage as the minimal value is adjusted, need not be aggregated for purposes of this subparagraph.

(B) The identity of the source and a brief description (including a travel itinerary, dates, and nature of expenses provided) of reimbursements received from any source aggregating more than the minimal value as established by section 7342(a)(5) of title 5, United States Code, or $250, whichever is greater and received during the preceding calendar year.

(C) In an unusual case, a gift need not be aggregated under subparagraph (A) if a publicly available request for a waiver is granted.

(3) The identity and category of value of any interest in property held during the preceding calendar year in a trade or business, or for investment or the production of income, which has a fair market value which exceeds $1,000 as of the close of the preceding calendar year, excluding any personal liability owed to the reporting individual by a spouse,,[1] or by a parent, brother, sister, or child of the reporting individual or of the reporting individual's spouse, or any deposits aggregating $5,000 or less in a personal savings account. For purposes of this paragraph, a personal savings account shall include any certificate of deposit or any other form of deposit in a bank, savings and loan association, credit union, or similar financial institution.

(4) The identity and category of value of the total liabilities owed to any creditor other than a spouse, or a parent, brother, sister, or child of the reporting individual or of the reporting individual's spouse which exceed $10,000 at any time during the preceding calendar year, excluding—

(A) any mortgage secured by real property which is a personal residence of the reporting individual or his spouse; and

(B) any loan secured by a personal motor vehicle, household furniture, or appliances, which loan does not exceed the purchase price of the item which secures it.

With respect to revolving charge accounts, only those with an outstanding liability which exceeds $10,000 as of the close of the preceding calendar year need be reported under this paragraph.

(5) Except as provided in this paragraph, a brief description, the date, and category of value of any purchase, sale or exchange during the preceding calendar year which exceeds $1,000—

(A) in real property, other than property used solely as a personal residence of the reporting individual or his spouse; or

(B) in stocks, bonds, commodities futures, and other forms of securities.

Reporting is not required under this paragraph of any transaction solely by and between the reporting individual, his spouse, or dependent children.

(6)(A) The identity of all positions held on or before the date of filing during the current calendar year (and, for the first report filed by an individual, during the two-year period preceding such calendar year) as an officer, director, trustee, partner, proprietor, representative, employee, or consultant of any corporation, company, firm, partnership, or other business enterprise, any nonprofit organization, any labor organization, or any educational or other institution other than the United States. This subparagraph shall not require the reporting of positions held in any religious, social, fraternal, or political entity and positions solely of an honorary nature.

(B) If any person, other than the United States Government, paid a nonelected reporting individual compensation in excess of $5,000 in any of the two calendar years prior to the calendar year during which the individual files his first report under this title, the individual shall include in the report—

(i) the identity of each source of such compensation; and

(ii) a brief description of the nature of the duties performed or services rendered by the reporting individual for each such source.

The preceding sentence shall not require any individual to include in such report any information which is considered confidential as a result of a privileged relationship, established by law, between such individual and any person nor shall it require an individual to report any information with respect to any person for whom services were provided by any firm or association of which such individual was a member, partner, or employee unless such individual was directly involved in the provision of such services.

(7) A description of the date, parties to, and terms of any agreement or arrangement with respect to (A) future employment; (B) a leave of absence during the period of the reporting individual's Government service; (C) continuation of payments by a former employer other than the United States Government; and (D) continuing participation in an employee welfare or benefit plan maintained by a former employer.

(8) The category of the total cash value of any interest of the reporting individual in a qualified blind trust, unless the trust instrument was executed prior to July 24, 1995 and precludes the beneficiary from receiving information on the total cash value of any interest in the qualified blind trust.

(b)(1) Each report filed pursuant to subsections (a), (b), and (c) of section 101 shall include a full and complete statement with respect to the information required by—

(A) paragraph (1) of subsection (a) for the year of filing and the preceding calendar year,

(B) paragraphs (3) and (4) of subsection (a) as of the date specified in the report but which is less than thirty-one days before the filing date, and

(C) paragraphs (6) and (7) of subsection (a) as of the filing date but for periods described in such paragraphs.

(2)(A) In lieu of filling out one or more schedules of a financial disclosure form, an individual may supply the required information in an alternative format, pursuant to either rules adopted by the supervising ethics office for the branch in which such individual serves or pursuant to a specific written determination by such office for a reporting individual.

(B) In lieu of indicating the category of amount or value of any item contained in any report filed under this title, a reporting individual may indicate the exact dollar amount of such item.

(c) In the case of any individual described in section 101(e), any reference to the preceding calendar year shall be considered also to include that part of the calendar year of filing up to the date of the termination of employment.

(d)(1) The categories for reporting the amount or value of the items covered in paragraphs (3), (4), (5), and (8) of subsection (a) are as follows:

(A) not more than $15,000;

(B) greater than $15,000 but not more than $50,000;

(C) greater than $50,000 but not more than $100,000;

(D) greater than $100,000 but not more than $250,000;

(E) greater than $250,000 but not more than $500,000;

(F) greater than $500,000 but not more than $1,000,000;

(G) greater than $1,000,000 but not more than $5,000,000;

(H) greater than $5,000,000 but not more than $25,000,000;

(I) greater than $25,000,000 but not more than $50,000,000; and

(J) greater than $50,000,000.

(2) For the purposes of paragraph (3) of subsection (a) if the current value of an interest in real property (or an interest in a real estate partnership) is not ascertainable without an appraisal, an individual may list (A) the date of purchase and the purchase price of the interest in the real property, or (B) the assessed value of the real property for tax purposes, adjusted to reflect the market value of the property used for the assessment if the assessed value is computed at less than 100 percent of such market value, but such individual shall include in his report a full and complete description of the method used to determine such assessed value, instead of specifying a category of value pursuant to paragraph (1) of this subsection. If the current value of any other item required to be reported under paragraph (3) of subsection (a) is not ascertainable without an appraisal, such individual may list the book value of a corporation whose stock is not publicly traded, the net worth of a business partnership, the equity value of an individually owned business, or with respect to other holdings, any recognized indication of value, but such individual shall include in his report a full and complete description of the method used in determining such value. In lieu of any value referred to in the preceding sentence, an individual may list the assessed value of the item for tax purposes, adjusted to reflect the market value of the item used for the assessment if the assessed value is computed at less than 100 percent of such market value, but a full and complete description of the method used in determining such assessed value shall be included in the report.

(e)(1) Except as provided in the last sentence of this paragraph, each report required by section 101 shall also contain information listed in paragraphs (1) through (5) of subsection (a) of this section respecting the spouse or dependent child of the reporting individual as follows:

(A) The source of items of earned income earned by a spouse from any person which exceed $1,000 and the source and amount of any honoraria received by a spouse, except that, with respect to earned income (other than honoraria), if the spouse is self-employed in business or a profession, only the nature of such business or profession need be reported.

(B) All information required to be reported in subsection (a)(1)(B) with respect to income derived by a spouse or dependent child from any asset held by the spouse or dependent child and reported pursuant to subsection (a)(3).

(C) In the case of any gifts received by a spouse or dependent child which are not received totally independent of the relationship of the spouse or dependent child to the reporting individual, the identity of the source and a brief description of gifts of transportation, lodging, food, or entertainment and a brief description and the value of other gifts.

(D) In the case of any reimbursements received by a spouse or dependent child which are not received totally independent of the relationship of the spouse or dependent child to the reporting individual, the identity of the source and a brief description of each such reimbursement.

(E) In the case of items described in paragraphs (3) through (5) of subsection (a), all information required to be reported under these paragraphs other than items (i) which the reporting individual certifies represent the spouse's or dependent child's sole financial interest or responsibility and which the reporting individual has no knowledge of, (ii) which are not in any way, past or present, derived from the income, assets, or activities of the reporting individual, and (iii) from which the reporting individual neither derives, nor expects to derive, any financial or economic benefit.

(F) For purposes of this section, categories with amounts or values greater than $1,000,000 set forth in sections 102(a)(1)(B) and 102(d)(1) shall apply to the income, assets, or liabilities of spouses and dependent children only if the income, assets, or liabilities are held jointly with the reporting individual. All other income, assets, or liabilities of the spouse or dependent children required to be reported under this section in an amount or value greater than $1,000,000 shall be categorized only as an amount or value greater than $1,000,000.

Reports required by subsections (a), (b), and (c) of section 101 shall, with respect to the spouse and dependent child of the reporting individual, only contain information listed in paragraphs (1), (3), and (4) of subsection (a), as specified in this paragraph.

(2) No report shall be required with respect to a spouse living separate and apart from the reporting individual with the intention of terminating the marriage or providing for permanent separation; or with respect to any income or obligations of an individual arising from the dissolution of his marriage or the permanent separation from his spouse.

(f)(1) Except as provided in paragraph (2), each reporting individual shall report the information required to be reported pursuant to subsections (a), (b), and (c) of this section with respect to the holdings of and the income from a trust or other financial arrangement from which income is received by, or with respect to which a beneficial interest in principal or income is held by, such individual, his spouse, or any dependent child.

(2) A reporting individual need not report the holdings of or the source of income from any of the holdings of—

(A) any qualified blind trust (as defined in paragraph (3));

(B) a trust—

(i) which was not created directly by such individual, his spouse, or any dependent child, and

(ii) the holdings or sources of income of which such individual, his spouse, and any dependent child have no knowledge of; or

(C) an entity described under the provisions of paragraph (8),

but such individual shall report the category of the amount of income received by him, his spouse, or any dependent child from the trust or other entity under subsection (a)(1)(B) of this section.

(3) For purposes of this subsection, the term "qualified blind trust" includes any trust in which a reporting individual, his spouse, or any minor or dependent child has a beneficial interest in the principal or income, and which meets the following requirements:

(A)(i) The trustee of the trust and any other entity designated in the trust instrument to perform fiduciary duties is a financial institution, an attorney, a certified public accountant, a broker, or an investment advisor who—

(I) is independent of and not associated with any interested party so that the trustee or other person cannot be controlled or influenced in the administration of the trust by any interested party; and

(II) is not and has not been an employee of or affiliated with any interested party and is not a partner of, or involved in any joint venture or other investment with, any interested party; and

(III) is not a relative of any interested party.

(ii) Any officer or employee of a trustee or other entity who is involved in the management or control of the trust—

(I) is independent of and not associated with any interested party so that such officer or employee cannot be controlled or influenced in the administration of the trust by any interested party;

(II) is not a partner of, or involved in any joint venture or other investment with, any interested party; and

(III) is not a relative of any interested party.

(B) Any asset transferred to the trust by an interested party is free of any restriction with respect to its transfer or sale unless such restriction is expressly approved by the supervising ethics office of the reporting individual.

(C) The trust instrument which establishes the trust provides that—

(i) except to the extent provided in subparagraph (B) of this paragraph, the trustee in the exercise of his authority and discretion to manage and control the assets of the trust shall not consult or notify any interested party;

(ii) the trust shall not contain any asset the holding of which by an interested party is prohibited by any law or regulation;

(iii) the trustee shall promptly notify the reporting individual and his supervising ethics office when the holdings of any particular asset transferred to the trust by any interested party are disposed of or when the value of such holding is less than $1,000;

(iv) the trust tax return shall be prepared by the trustee or his designee, and such return and any information relating thereto (other than the trust income summarized in appropriate categories necessary to complete an interested party's tax return), shall not be disclosed to any interested party;

(v) an interested party shall not receive any report on the holdings and sources of income of the trust, except a report at the end of each calendar quarter with respect to the total cash value of the interest of the interested party in the trust or the net income or loss of the trust or any reports necessary to enable the interested party to complete an individual tax return required by law or to provide the information required by subsection (a)(1) of this section, but such report shall not identify any asset or holding;

(vi) except for communications which solely consist of requests for distributions of cash or other unspecified assets of the trust, there shall be no direct or indirect communication between the trustee and an interested party with respect to the trust unless such communication is in writing and unless it relates only (I) to the general financial interest and needs of the interested party (including, but not limited to, an interest in maximizing income or long-term capital gain), (II) to the notification of the trustee of a law or regulation subsequently applicable to the reporting individual which prohibits the interested party from holding an asset, which notification directs that the asset not be held by the trust, or (III) to directions to the trustee to sell all of an asset initially placed in the trust by an interested party which in the determination of the reporting individual creates a conflict of interest or the appearance thereof due to the subsequent assumption of duties by the reporting individual (but nothing herein shall require any such direction); and

(vii) the interested parties shall make no effort to obtain information with respect to the holdings of the trust, including obtaining a copy of any trust tax return filed or any information relating thereto except as otherwise provided in this subsection.

(D) The proposed trust instrument and the proposed trustee is approved by the reporting individual's supervising ethics office.

(E) For purposes of this subsection, "interested party" means a reporting individual, his spouse, and any minor or dependent child; "broker" has the meaning set forth in section 3(a)(4) of the Securities and Exchange Act of 1934 (15 U.S.C. 78c(a)(4)); and "investment adviser" includes any investment adviser who, as determined under regulations prescribed by the supervising ethics office, is generally involved in his role as such an adviser in the management or control of trusts.

(F) Any trust qualified by a supervising ethics office before the effective date of title II of the Ethics Reform Act of 1989 shall continue to be governed by the law and regulations in effect immediately before such effective date.

(4)(A) An asset placed in a trust by an interested party shall be considered a financial interest of the reporting individual, for the purposes of any applicable conflict of interest statutes, regulations, or rules of the Federal Government (including section 208 of title 18, United States Code), until such time as the reporting individual is notified by the trustee that such asset has been disposed of, or has a value of less than $1,000.

(B)(i) The provisions of subparagraph (A) shall not apply with respect to a trust created for the benefit of a reporting individual, or the spouse, dependent child, or minor child of such a person, if the supervising ethics office for such reporting individual finds that—

(I) the assets placed in the trust consist of a well-diversified portfolio of readily marketable securities;

(II) none of the assets consist of securities of entities having substantial activities in the area of the reporting individual's primary area of responsibility;

(III) the trust instrument prohibits the trustee, notwithstanding the provisions of paragraphs (3)(C)(iii) and (iv) of this subsection, from making public or informing any interested party of the sale of any securities;

(IV) the trustee is given power of attorney, notwithstanding the provisions of paragraph (3)(C)(v) of this subsection, to prepare on behalf of any interested party the personal income tax returns and similar returns which may contain information relating to the trust; and

(V) except as otherwise provided in this paragraph, the trust instrument provides (or in the case of a trust established prior to the effective date of this Act which by its terms does not permit amendment, the trustee, the reporting individual, and any other interested party agree in writing) that the trust shall be administered in accordance with the requirements of this subsection and the trustee of such trust meets the requirements of paragraph (3)(A).

(ii) In any instance covered by subparagraph (B) in which the reporting individual is an individual whose nomination is being considered by a congressional committee, the reporting individual shall inform the congressional committee considering his nomination before or during the period of such individual's confirmation hearing of his intention to comply with this paragraph.

(5)(A) The reporting individual shall, within thirty days after a qualified blind trust is approved by his supervising ethics office, file with such office a copy of—

(i) the executed trust instrument of such trust (other than those provisions which relate to the testamentary disposition of the trust assets), and

(ii) a list of the assets which were transferred to such trust, including the category of value of each asset as determined under subsection (d) of this section.

This subparagraph shall not apply with respect to a trust meeting the requirements for being considered a qualified blind trust under paragraph (7) of this subsection.

(B) The reporting individual shall, within thirty days of transferring an asset (other than cash) to a previously established qualified blind trust, notify his supervising ethics office of the identity of each such asset and the category of value of each asset as determined under subsection (d) of this section.

(C) Within thirty days of the dissolution of a qualified blind trust, a reporting individual shall—

(i) notify his supervising ethics office of such dissolution, and

(ii) file with such office a copy of a list of the assets of the trust at the time of such dissolution and the category of value under subsection (d) of this section of each such asset.

(D) Documents filed under subparagraphs (A), (B), and (C) of this paragraph and the lists provided by the trustee of assets placed in the trust by an interested party which have been sold shall be made available to the public in the same manner as a report is made available under section 105 and the provisions of that section shall apply with respect to such documents and lists.

(E) A copy of each written communication with respect to the trust under paragraph (3)(C)(vi) shall be filed by the person initiating the communication with the reporting individual's supervising ethics office within five days of the date of the communication.

(6)(A) A trustee of a qualified blind trust shall not knowingly and willfully, or negligently, (i) disclose any information to an interested party with respect to such trust that may not be disclosed under paragraph (3) of this subsection; (ii) acquire any holding the ownership of which is prohibited by the trust instrument; (iii) solicit advice from any interested party with respect to such trust, which solicitation is prohibited by paragraph (3) of this subsection or the trust agreement; or (iv) fail to file any document required by this subsection.

(B) A reporting individual shall not knowingly and willfully, or negligently, (i) solicit or receive any information with respect to a qualified blind trust of which he is an interested party that may not be disclosed under paragraph (3)(C) of this subsection or (ii) fail to file any document required by this subsection.

(C)(i) The Attorney General may bring a civil action in any appropriate United States district court against any individual who knowingly and willfully violates the provisions of subparagraph (A) or (B) of this paragraph. The court in which such action is brought may assess against such individual a civil penalty in any amount not to exceed $10,000.

(ii) The Attorney General may bring a civil action in any appropriate United States district court against any individual who negligently violates the provisions of subparagraph (A) or (B) of this paragraph. The court in which such action is brought may assess against such individual a civil penalty in any amount not to exceed $5,000.

(7) Any trust may be considered to be a qualified blind trust if—

(A) the trust instrument is amended to comply with the requirements of paragraph (3) or, in the case of a trust instrument which does not by its terms permit amendment, the trustee, the reporting individual, and any other interested party agree in writing that the trust shall be administered in accordance with the requirements of this subsection and the trustee of such trust meets the requirements of paragraph (3)(A); except that in the case of any interested party who is a dependent child, a parent or guardian of such child may execute the agreement referred to in this subparagraph;

(B) a copy of the trust instrument (except testamentary provisions) and a copy of the agreement referred to in subparagraph (A), and a list of the assets held by the trust at the time of approval by the supervising ethics office, including the category of value of each asset as determined under subsection (d) of this section, are filed with such office and made available to the public as provided under paragraph (5)(D) of this subsection; and

(C) the supervising ethics office determines that approval of the trust arrangement as a qualified blind trust is in the particular case appropriate to assure compliance with applicable laws and regulations.

(8) A reporting individual shall not be required to report the financial interests held by a widely held investment fund (whether such fund is a mutual fund, regulated investment company, pension or deferred compensation plan, or other investment fund), if—

(A)(i) the fund is publicly traded; or

(ii) the assets of the fund are widely diversified; and

(B) the reporting individual neither exercises control over nor has the ability to exercise control over the financial interests held by the fund.

(g) Political campaign funds, including campaign receipts and expenditures, need not be included in any report filed pursuant to this title.

(h) A report filed pursuant to subsection (a), (d), or (e) of section 101 need not contain the information described in subparagraphs (A), (B), and (C) of subsection (a)(2) with respect to gifts and reimbursements received in a period when the reporting individual was not an officer or employee of the Federal Government.

(i) A reporting individual shall not be required under this title to report—

(1) financial interests in or income derived from—

(A) any retirement system under title 5, United States Code (including the Thrift Savings Plan under subchapter III of chapter 84 of such title); or

(B) any other retirement system maintained by the United States for officers or employees of the United States, including the President, or for members of the uniformed services; or

(2) benefits received under the Social Security Act [42 U.S.C.A. § 301 et seq.].

(Pub.L. 95–521, Title I, § 102, Oct. 26, 1978, 92 Stat. 1825; Pub.L. 96–19, §§ 3(a)(1), (b), 6(a), 7(a) to (d)(1), (f), 9(b), (c)(1), (j), June 13, 1979, 93 Stat. 39 to 43; Pub.L. 97–51, § 130(b), Oct. 1, 1981, 95 Stat. 966; Pub.L. 98–150, § 10, Nov. 11, 1983, 97 Stat. 962; Pub.L. 101–194, Title II, § 202, Nov. 30, 1989, 103 Stat. 1727; Pub.L. 101–280, § 3(3), May 4, 1990, 104 Stat. 152; Pub.L. 102–90, Title III, § 314(a), Aug. 14, 1991, 105 Stat. 469; Pub.L. 104–65, §§ 20, 22(a), (b), Dec. 19, 1995, 109 Stat. 704, 705.)

[1] So in original.

HISTORICAL AND STATUTORY NOTES

References in Text

The effective date of title II of the Ethics Reform Act of 1989, referred to in subsec. (f)(3)(F) is Jan. 1, 1991. See section 204 of Pub.L. 101–194, set out as an Effective Date of 1989 Acts note under section 101 of this Appendix.

The effective date of this Act, referred to in subsec. (f)(4)(B)(i)(V), probably refers to the effective date of title II of the Ethics Reform Act of 1989, which is Jan. 1, 1991. See section 204 of Pub.L. 101–194, set out as an Effective Date of 1989 Acts note under section 101 of this Appendix.

The Social Security Act, referred to in subsec. (i)(2), is Act Aug. 14, 1935, c. 531, 49 Stat. 620, as amended, which is classified generally to chapter 7 (section 301 et seq.) of Title 42, The Public Health and Welfare. For complete classification of this Act to the Code, see section 1305 of Title 42 and Tables.

Codifications

Section was formerly classified to section 702 of Title 2, The Congress.

Effective and Applicability Provisions

1995 Acts. Amendment by section 20 of Pub.L. 104–65 effective Jan. 1, 1996, see section 24 of Pub.L. 104–65, set out as a note under section 1601 of Title 2, The Congress.

Section 22(c) of Pub.L. 104–65 provided that: "The amendment made by this section [enacting par. (8) of subsec. (a) of this section and amending subsec. (d)(1) of this section] shall apply with respect to reports filed under title I of the Ethics in Government Act of 1978 [Title I of this Appendix] for calendar year 1996 and thereafter."

1991 Acts. Amendment by Pub.L. 102–90 effective Jan. 1, 1993, see section 314(g)(2) of Pub.L. 102–90, as amended, set out as a note under section 31–2 of Title 2, The Congress.

1990 Acts. Amendment of the text of this section by Pub.L. 101–280 effective May 4, 1990, see section 11 of Pub.L. 101–280, set out as a note under section 101 of this Appendix. The text as thus amended to be effective Jan. 1, 1991, see section 204 of Pub.L. 101–194 set out as a note under section 101 of this Appendix.

1989 Acts. Amendment by Pub.L. 101–194 effective Jan. 1, 1991, except that subsec. (f)(4)(B) of this section as amended by Pub.L. 101–194 is effective Jan. 1, 1990, see section 204 of Pub.L. 101–194, as added Pub.L. 101–280, § 3(10)(B), May 4, 1990, 104 Stat. 157, set out as a note under section 101 of this Appendix.

1983 Acts. Section 13 of Pub.L. 98–150 provided that: "The amendments made by this Act [enacting sections 211

and 407 of Pub.L. 95–521, set out in this Appendix, amending sections 102, 201 to 203, 210, 302, and 401 to 405 of Pub.L. 95–521, set out in this Appendix, and enacting provisions set out as a note under section 402 of this Appendix] shall take effect on October 1, 1983."

§ 103. Filing of reports

(a) Except as otherwise provided in this section, the reports required under this title shall be filed by the reporting individual with the designated agency ethics official at the agency by which he is employed (or in the case of an individual described in section 101(e), was employed) or in which he will serve. The date any report is received (and the date of receipt of any supplemental report) shall be noted on such report by such official.

(b) The President, the Vice President, and independent counsel and persons appointed by independent counsel under chapter 40 of title 28, United States Code, shall file reports required under this title with the Director of the Office of Government Ethics.

(c) Copies of the reports required to be filed under this title by the Postmaster General, the Deputy Postmaster General, the Governors of the Board of Governors of the United States Postal Service, designated agency ethics officials, employees described in section 105(a)(2)(A) or (B), 106(a)(1)(A) or (B), or 107(a)(1)(A) or (b)(1)(A)(i), of title 3, United States Code, candidates for the office of President or Vice President and officers and employees in (and nominees to) offices or positions which require confirmation by the Senate or by both Houses of Congress other than individuals nominated to be judicial officers and those referred to in subsection (f) shall be transmitted to the Director of the Office of Government Ethics. The Director shall forward a copy of the report of each nominee to the congressional committee considering the nomination.

(d) Reports required to be filed under this title by the Director of the Office of Government Ethics shall be filed in the Office of Government Ethics and, immediately after being filed, shall be made available to the public in accordance with this title.

(e) Each individual identified in section 101(c) who is a candidate for nomination or election to the Office of President or Vice President shall file the reports required by this title with the Federal Election Commission.

(f) Reports required of members of the uniformed services shall be filed with the Secretary concerned.

(g) Each supervising ethics office shall develop and make available forms for reporting the information required by this title.

(h)(1) The reports required under this title shall be filed by a reporting individual with—

(A)(i)(I) the Clerk of the House of Representatives, in the case of a Representative in Congress, a Delegate to Congress, the Resident Commissioner from Puerto Rico, an officer or employee of the Congress whose compensation is disbursed by the Chief Administrative Officer of the House of Representatives, an officer or employee of the Architect of the Capitol, United States Capitol Police, the United States Botanic Garden, the Congressional Budget Office, the Government Printing Office, the Library of Congress, or the Copyright Royalty Tribunal (including any individual terminating service, under section 101(e), in any office or position referred to in this subclause), or an individual described in section 101(c) who is a candidate for nomination or election as a Representative in Congress, a Delegate to Congress, or the Resident Commissioner from Puerto Rico; and

(II) the Secretary of the Senate, in the case of a Senator, an officer or employee of the Congress whose compensation is disbursed by the Secretary of the Senate, an officer or employee of the Government Accountability Office, the Office of Technology Assessment, or the Office of the Attending Physician (including any individual terminating service, under section 101(e), in any office or position referred to in this subclause), or an individual described in section 101(c) who is a candidate for nomination or election as a Senator; and

(ii) in the case of an officer or employee of the Congress as described under section 101(f)(10) who is employed by an agency or commission established in the legislative branch after the date of the enactment of the Ethics Reform Act of 1989—

(I) the Secretary of the Senate or the Clerk of the House of Representatives, as the case may be, as designated in the statute establishing such agency or commission; or

(II) if such statute does not designate such committee, the Secretary of the Senate for agencies and commissions established in even numbered calendar years, and the Clerk of the House of Representatives for agencies and commissions established in odd numbered calendar years; and

(B) the Judicial Conference with regard to a judicial officer or employee described under paragraphs (11) and (12) of section 101(f) (including individuals terminating service in such office or position under section 101(e) or immediately preceding service in such office or position).

(2) The date any report is received (and the date of receipt of any supplemental report) shall be noted on such report by such committee.

(i) A copy of each report filed under this title by a Member or an individual who is a candidate for the office of Member shall be sent by the Clerk of the

House of Representatives or Secretary of the Senate, as the case may be, to the appropriate State officer designated under section 316(a) of the Federal Election Campaign Act of 1971 of the State represented by the Member or in which the individual is a candidate, as the case may be, within the 30-day period beginning on the day the report is filed with the Clerk or Secretary.

(j)(1) A copy of each report filed under this title with the Clerk of the House of Representatives shall be sent by the Clerk to the Committee on Standards of Official Conduct of the House of Representatives within the 7-day period beginning on the day the report is filed.

(2) A copy of each report filed under this title with the Secretary of the Senate shall be sent by the Secretary to the Select Committee on Ethics of the Senate within the 7-day period beginning on the day the report is filed.

(k) In carrying out their responsibilities under this title with respect to candidates for office, the Clerk of the House of Representatives and the Secretary of the Senate shall avail themselves of the assistance of the Federal Election Commission. The Commission shall make available to the Clerk and the Secretary on a regular basis a complete list of names and addresses of all candidates registered with the Commission, and shall cooperate and coordinate its candidate information and notification program with the Clerk and the Secretary to the greatest extent possible.

(Pub.L. 95-521, Title I, § 103, Oct. 26, 1978, 92 Stat. 1831; Pub.L. 96-19, §§ 4(b)(2), 9(a), June 13, 1979, 93 Stat. 40, 42; Pub.L. 101-194, Title II, § 202, Nov. 30, 1989, 103 Stat. 1736; Pub.L. 101-280, § 3(1), (4), May 4, 1990, 104 Stat. 152, 153; Pub.L. 102-90, Title III, § 313(1), Aug. 14, 1991, 105 Stat. 469; Pub.L. 104-186, Title II, § 216(1), Aug. 20, 1996, 110 Stat. 1747; Pub.L. 108-271, § 8(b), July 7, 2004, 118 Stat. 814; Pub.L. 109-55, Title I, § 1003(a), Aug. 2, 2005, 119 Stat. 572.)

HISTORICAL AND STATUTORY NOTES

References in Text

The date of the enactment of the Ethics Reform Act of 1989, referred to in subsec. (h)(1)(A)(ii), is the date of the enactment of Pub.L. 101-194, Nov. 30, 1989, 103 Stat. 1716, which was approved Nov. 30, 1989.

Section 316(a) of the Federal Election Campaign Act of 1971, referred to in subsec. (i), was probably intended to be a reference to section 312(a) of the Federal Election Campaign Act of 1971, Pub.L. 92-225, which is classified to section 439(a) of Title 2, The Congress, which directs the chief executive officer of each State to designate a State officer to receive reports and statements filed by persons under the Federal Election Campaign Act of 1971.

Codifications

Section was formerly classified to section 703 of Title 2, The Congress.

Effective and Applicability Provisions

2005 Acts. Pub.L. 109-55, Title I, § 1003(b), Aug. 2, 2005, 119 Stat. 572, provided that: "The amendment made by subsection (a) [amending this section] shall apply with respect to reports filed under the Ethics in Government Act of 1978 [Pub.L. 95-521, set out in this Appendix] for calendar year 2005 and each succeeding calendar year."

1990 Acts. Amendment of the text of this section by Pub.L. 101-280 effective May 4, 1990, see section 11 of Pub.L. 101-280, set out as a note under section 101 of this Appendix. The text as thus amended to be effective Jan. 1, 1991, see section 204 of Pub.L. 101-194 set out as a note under section 101 of this Appendix.

1989 Acts. Amendment by Pub.L. 101-194 effective Jan. 1, 1991, see section 204 of Pub.L. 101-194, as added Pub.L. 101-280, § 3(10)(B), May 4, 1990, 104 Stat. 157, set out as a note under section 101 of this Appendix.

Termination of Reporting Requirements

For termination, effective May 15, 2000, of reporting provisions of subsec. (d) of this section, see Pub.L. 104-66, § 3003, as amended, set out as a note under 31 U.S.C.A. § 1113, and the 6th item on page 1 of House Document No. 103-7, which references 2 U.S.C. § 703(d)(1), which was subsequently redesignated as subsec. (d) of this section.

Transfer of Functions

Any reference in any provision of law enacted before Jan. 4, 1995, to a function, duty, or authority of the Clerk of the House of Representatives treated as referring, with respect to that function, duty, or authority, to the officer of the House of Representatives exercising that function, duty, or authority, as determined by the Committee on House Oversight of the House of Representatives, see section 2(1) of Pub.L. 104-14, set out as a note preceding section 21 of Title 2, The Congress.

§ 104. Failure to file or filing false reports

(a)(1) The Attorney General may bring a civil action in any appropriate United States district court against any individual who knowingly and willfully falsifies or who knowingly and willfully fails to file or report any information that such individual is required to report pursuant to section 102. The court in which such action is brought may assess against such individual a civil penalty in any amount, not to exceed $50,000.

(2)(A) It shall be unlawful for any person to knowingly and willfully—

(i) falsify any information that such person is required to report under section 102; and

(ii) fail to file or report any information that such person is required to report under section 102.

(B) Any person who—

(i) violates subparagraph (A)(i) shall be fined under title 18, United States Code, imprisoned for not more than 1 year, or both; and

(ii) violates subparagraph (A)(ii) shall be fined under title 18, United States Code.

(b) The head of each agency, each Secretary concerned, the Director of the Office of Government Ethics, each congressional ethics committee, or the Judicial Conference, as the case may be, shall refer to the Attorney General the name of any individual which such official or committee has reasonable cause to believe has willfully failed to file a report or has willfully falsified or willfully failed to file information required to be reported. Whenever the Judicial Conference refers a name to the Attorney General under this subsection, the Judicial Conference also shall notify the judicial council of the circuit in which the named individual serves of the referral.

(c) The President, the Vice President, the Secretary concerned, the head of each agency, the Office of Personnel Management, a congressional ethics committee, and the Judicial Conference, may take any appropriate personnel or other action in accordance with applicable law or regulation against any individual failing to file a report or falsifying or failing to report information required to be reported.

(d)(1) Any individual who files a report required to be filed under this title more than 30 days after the later of—

(A) the date such report is required to be filed pursuant to the provisions of this title and the rules and regulations promulgated thereunder; or

(B) if a filing extension is granted to such individual under section 101(g), the last day of the filing extension period,

shall, at the direction of and pursuant to regulations issued by the supervising ethics office, pay a filing fee of $200. All such fees shall be deposited in the miscellaneous receipts of the Treasury. The authority under this paragraph to direct the payment of a filing fee may be delegated by the supervising ethics office in the executive branch to other agencies in the executive branch..[1]

(2) The supervising ethics office may waive the filing fee under this subsection in extraordinary circumstances.

(Pub.L. 95–521, Title I, § 104, Oct. 26, 1978, 92 Stat. 1832; Pub.L. 96–19, § 8(a), June 13, 1979, 93 Stat. 41; Pub.L. 101–194, Title II, § 202, Nov. 30, 1989, 103 Stat. 1737; Pub.L. 101–280, § 3(1), (5), May 4, 1990, 104 Stat. 152, 154; Pub.L. 101–650, Title IV, § 405, Dec. 1, 1990, 104 Stat. 5124; Pub.L. 110–81, Title VII, § 702, Sept. 14, 2007, 121 Stat. 775.)

[1] So in original.

HISTORICAL AND STATUTORY NOTES

Codifications

Section was formerly classified to section 704 of Title 2, The Congress.

Effective Date

1990 Acts. Amendment by section 405 of Pub.L. 101–650 effective 90 days after Dec. 1, 1990, see section 407 of Pub.L. 101–650, set out as a note under section 332 of Title 28, Judiciary and Judicial Procedure.

Amendment of the text of this section by Pub.L. 101–280 effective May 4, 1990, see section 11 of Pub.L. 101–280, set out as a note under section 101 of this Appendix. The text as thus amended to be effective Jan. 1, 1991, see section 204 of Pub.L. 101–194 set out as a note under section 101 of this Appendix.

1989 Acts. Amendment by Pub.L. 101–194 effective Jan. 1, 1991, see section 204 of Pub.L. 101–194, as added Pub.L. 101–280, § 3(10)(B), May 4, 1990, 104 Stat. 157, set out as a note under section 101 of this Appendix.

Rule of Construction

Nothing in the amendments made by Pub.L. 110–81, shall prohibit any expressive conduct protected from legal prohibition by, or any activities protected by the free speech, free exercise, or free association clauses of the Constitution, First Amendment, see Pub. L. 110–81, Title VII, § 703, set out as a note under 2 U.S.C.A. § 1601.

§ 105. Custody of and public access to reports

(a) Each agency, each supervising ethics office in the executive or judicial branch, the Clerk of the House of Representatives, and the Secretary of the Senate shall make available to the public, in accordance with subsection (b), each report filed under this title with such agency or office or with the Clerk or the Secretary of the Senate, except that—

(1) this section does not require public availability of a report filed by any individual in the Office of the Director of National Intelligence, the Central Intelligence Agency, the Defense Intelligence Agency, the National Geospatial–Intelligence Agency, or the National Security Agency, or any individual engaged in intelligence activities in any agency of the United States, if the President finds or has found that, due to the nature of the office or position occupied by such individual, public disclosure of such report would, be [1] revealing the identity of the individual or other sensitive information, compromise the national interest of the United States; and such individuals may be authorized, notwithstanding section 104(a), to file such additional reports as are necessary to protect their identity from public disclosure if the President first finds or has found that such filing is necessary in the national interest; and

(2) any report filed by an independent counsel whose identity has not been disclosed by the division of the court under chapter 40 of title 28, United States Code, and any report filed by any person appointed by that independent counsel under such chapter, shall not be made available to the public under this title.

(b)(1) Except as provided in the second sentence of this subsection, each agency, each supervising ethics office in the executive or judicial branch, the Clerk of the House of Representatives, and the Secretary of the Senate shall, within thirty days after any report is received under this title by such agency or office or by the Clerk or the Secretary of the Senate, as the case may be,,[2] permit inspection of such report by or furnish a copy of such report to any person requesting such inspection or copy. With respect to any report required to be filed by May 15 of any year, such report shall be made available for public inspection within 30 calendar days after May 15 of such year or within 30 days of the date of filing of such a report for which an extension is granted pursuant to section 101(g). The agency, office, Clerk, or Secretary of the Senate, as the case may be [3] may require a reasonable fee to be paid in any amount which is found necessary to recover the cost of reproduction or mailing of such report excluding any salary of any employee involved in such reproduction or mailing. A copy of such report may be furnished without charge or at a reduced charge if it is determined that waiver or reduction of the fee is in the public interest.

(2) Notwithstanding paragraph (1), a report may not be made available under this section to any person nor may any copy thereof be provided under this section to any person except upon a written application by such person stating—

(A) that person's name, occupation and address;

(B) the name and address of any other person or organization on whose behalf the inspection or copy is requested; and

(C) that such person is aware of the prohibitions on the obtaining or use of the report.

Any such application shall be made available to the public throughout the period during which the report is made available to the public.

(3)(A) This section does not require the immediate and unconditional availability of reports filed by an individual described in section 109(8) or 109(10) of this Act if a finding is made by the Judicial Conference, in consultation with United States Marshall [4] Service, that revealing personal and sensitive information could endanger that individual or a family member of that individual.

(B) A report may be redacted pursuant to this paragraph only—

(i) to the extent necessary to protect the individual who filed the report or a family member of that individual; and

(ii) for as long as the danger to such individual exists.

(C) The Administrative Office of the United States Courts shall submit to the Committees on the Judiciary of the House of Representatives and of the Senate an annual report with respect to the operation of this paragraph including—

(i) the total number of reports redacted pursuant to this paragraph;

(ii) the total number of individuals whose reports have been redacted pursuant to this paragraph;

(iii) the types of threats against individuals whose reports are redacted, if appropriate;

(iv) the nature or type of information redacted;

(v) what steps or procedures are in place to ensure that sufficient information is available to litigants to determine if there is a conflict of interest;

(vi) principles used to guide implementation of redaction authority; and

(vii) any public complaints received relating to redaction.

(D) The Judicial Conference, in consultation with the Department of Justice, shall issue regulations setting forth the circumstances under which redaction is appropriate under this paragraph and the procedures for redaction.

(E) This paragraph shall expire on December 31, 2011, and apply to filings through calendar year 2011.

(c)(1) It shall be unlawful for any person to obtain or use a report—

(A) for any unlawful purpose;

(B) for any commercial purpose, other than by news and communications media for dissemination to the general public;

(C) for determining or establishing the credit rating of any individual; or

(D) for use, directly or indirectly, in the solicitation of money for any political, charitable, or other purpose.

(2) The Attorney General may bring a civil action against any person who obtains or uses a report for any purpose prohibited in paragraph (1) of this subsection. The court in which such action is brought may assess against such person a penalty in any amount not to exceed $10,000. Such remedy shall be in addition to any other remedy available under statutory or common law.

(d) Any report filed with or transmitted to an agency or supervising ethics office or to the Clerk of the House of Representatives or the Secretary of the Senate pursuant to this title shall be retained by such agency or office or by the Clerk or the Secretary of the Senate, as the case may be. Such report shall be made available to the public for a period of six years after receipt of the report. After such six-year period the report shall be destroyed unless needed in an ongoing investigation, except that in the case of an individual who filed the report pursuant to section 101(b) and was not subsequently confirmed by the Senate, or who filed the report pursuant to section 101(c) and was not subsequently elected, such reports shall be destroyed one year after the individual either is no longer under consideration by the Senate or is no longer a candidate for nomination or election to the Office of President, Vice President, or as a Member of Congress, unless needed in an ongoing investigation. (Pub.L. 95–521, Title I, § 105, Oct. 26, 1978, 92 Stat. 1833; Pub.L. 101–194, Title II, § 202, Nov. 30, 1989, 103 Stat. 1737; Pub.L. 101–280, § 3(6), May 4, 1990, 104 Stat. 154; Pub.L. 102–90, Title III, § 313(2), Aug. 14, 1991, 105 Stat. 469; Pub.L. 103–359, Title V, § 501(m), Oct. 14, 1994, 108 Stat. 3430; Pub.L. 104–201, Div. A, Title XI, § 1122(b)(2), Sept. 23, 1996, 110 Stat. 2687; Pub.L. 105–318, § 7, Oct. 30, 1998, 112 Stat. 3011; Pub.L. 107–126, Jan. 16, 2002, 115 Stat. 2404; Pub.L. 108–458, Title I, § 1079(c), Dec. 17, 2004, 118 Stat. 3696; Pub.L. 110–24, §§ 2, 3, May 3, 2007, 121 Stat. 100; Pub.L. 110–177, Title I, § 104, Jan. 7, 2008, 121 Stat. 2535; Pub.L. 110–417, Div. A, Title IX, § 931(b)(1), Oct. 14, 2008, 122 Stat. 4575.)

[1] So in original. Probably should be "by".

[2] So in original.

[3] So in original. Probably should be followed by a comma.

[4] So in original. Probably should be "Marshal".

HISTORICAL AND STATUTORY NOTES

Codifications

Pub.L. 110–417, Div. A, Title IX, § 931(b)(1), which purported to amend subsec. (a)(1) of this section by striking "National Imagery and Mapping Agency" and inserting "National Geospatial-Intelligence Agency" was incapable of execution, due to prior identical amendment by Pub.L. 108–136. See 2008 Amendments note set out below.

Paragraph (3)(E) of subsection (b) of this section, prior to amendment by Pub.L. 110–24, provided that the paragraph expired by its own terms on December 31, 2005, and applied to filings through calendar year 2005. Pub.L. 110–24, §§ 2, 3, May 3, 2007, 121 Stat. 100 and Pub.L. 110–177, § 104, Jan. 7, 2008, 121 Stat. 2535, subsequently amended provisions in paragraph (3). See 2007 and 2008 Amendments notes set out under this section.

Section was formerly classified to 2 U.S.C.A. § 705.

Effective and Applicability Provisions

2004 Acts. For Determination by President that, except as otherwise provided, provisions in Pub.L. 108–458, Title I [§§ 1001 to 1103] take effect on April 21, 2005, see Memorandum of President of the United States, April 21, 2005, 70 F.R. 23925, set out as a note under 50 U.S.C.A. § 401.

Except as otherwise expressly provided, amendments by Pub.L. 108–458, Title I, to take effect not later than six months after Dec. 17, 2004, see Pub.L. 108–458, Title I, § 1097(a), set out in the Transfer, Termination, Implementation, Transition, and Effective Dates of the National Security Intelligence Reform Act of 2004 note under 50 U.S.C.A. § 401.

1990 Acts. Amendment of the text of this section by Pub.L. 101–280 effective May 4, 1990, see section 11 of Pub.L. 101–280, set out as a note under section 101 of this Appendix. The text as thus amended to be effective Jan. 1, 1991, see section 204 of Pub.L. 101–194 set out as a note under section 101 of this Appendix.

1989 Acts. Amendment by Pub.L. 101–194 effective Jan. 1, 1991, see section 204 of Pub.L. 101–194, as added Pub.L. 101–280, § 3(10)(B), May 4, 1990, 104 Stat. 157, set out as a note under section 101 of this Appendix.

Transfer of Functions

Any reference in any provision of law enacted before Jan. 4, 1995, to a function, duty, or authority of the Clerk of the House of Representatives treated as referring, with respect to that function, duty, or authority, to the officer of the House of Representatives exercising that function, duty, or authority, as determined by the Committee on House Oversight of the House of Representatives, see section 2(1) of Pub.L. 104–14, set out as a note preceding section 21 of Title 2, The Congress.

Certain functions of Clerk of House of Representatives transferred to Director of Non-legislative and Financial Services by section 7 of House Resolution No. 423, One Hundred Second Congress, Apr. 9, 1992. Any reference in any provision of law enacted before Jan. 4, 1995, to a function, duty, or authority of the Director of Non-legislative and Financial Services treated as referring, with respect to that function, duty, or authority, to the officer of the House of Representatives exercising that function, duty, or authority, as determined by the Committee on House Oversight of the House of Representatives, see section 2(4) of Pub.L. 104–14, set out as a note preceding section 21 of Title 2, The Congress.

Public Availability of Reports Filed Under Pre–1991 Ethics in Government Act Provisions

Section 9 of Pub.L. 101–280 provided that: "Those reports filed under title I [formerly classified to section 701 et seq. of Title 2, The Congress], II [formerly set out under the heading Executive Personnel Financial Disclosure Requirements in this Appendix], or III [formerly set out under the heading Judicial Personnel Financial Disclosure Requirements in the Appendix to Title 28, Judiciary and Judicial Procedure] of the Ethics in Government Act of 1978 [Pub.L. 95–521], as in effect before January 1, 1991, shall be made available to the public on or after such date in accordance with section 105 of that Act [this section], as amended by the Ethics Reform Act of 1989 [Pub.L. 101–194], and the provisions of such section shall apply with respect to those reports."

§ 106. Review of reports

(a)(1) Each designated agency ethics official or Secretary concerned shall make provisions to ensure that each report filed with him under this title is reviewed within sixty days after the date of such filing, except that the Director of the Office of Government Ethics shall review only those reports required to be transmitted to him under this title within sixty days after the date of transmittal.

(2) Each congressional ethics committee and the Judicial Conference shall make provisions to ensure that each report filed under this title is reviewed within sixty days after the date of such filing.

(b)(1) If after reviewing any report under subsection (a), the Director of the Office of Government Ethics, the Secretary concerned, the designated agency ethics official, a person designated by the congressional ethics committee, or a person designated by the Judicial Conference, as the case may be, is of the opinion that on the basis of information contained in such report the individual submitting such report is in compliance with applicable laws and regulations, he shall state such opinion on the report, and shall sign such report.

(2) If the Director of the Office of Government Ethics, the Secretary concerned, the designated agency ethics official, a person designated by the congressional ethics committee, or a person designated by the Judicial Conference, after reviewing any report under subsection (a)—

(A) believes additional information is required to be submitted, he shall notify the individual submitting such report what additional information is required and the time by which it must be submitted, or

(B) is of the opinion, on the basis of information submitted, that the individual is not in compliance with applicable laws and regulations, he shall notify the individual, afford a reasonable opportunity for a written or oral response, and after consideration of such response, reach an opinion as to whether or not, on the basis of information submitted, the individual is in compliance with such laws and regulations.

(3) If the Director of the Office of Government Ethics, the Secretary concerned, the designated agency ethics official, a person designated by a congressional ethics committee, or a person designated by the Judicial Conference, reaches an opinion under paragraph (2)(B) that an individual is not in compliance with applicable laws and regulations, the official or committee shall notify the individual of that opinion and, after an opportunity for personal consultation (if practicable), determine and notify the individual of which steps, if any, would in the opinion of such official or committee be appropriate for assuring compliance with such laws and regulations and the date by which such steps should be taken. Such steps may include, as appropriate—

(A) divestiture,

(B) restitution,

(C) the establishment of a blind trust,

(D) request for an exemption under section 208(b) of title 18, United States Code, or

(E) voluntary request for transfer, reassignment, limitation of duties, or resignation.

The use of any such steps shall be in accordance with such rules or regulations as the supervising ethics office may prescribe.

(4) If steps for assuring compliance with applicable laws and regulations are not taken by the date set under paragraph (3) by an individual in a position in the executive branch (other than in the Foreign Service or the uniformed services), appointment to which requires the advice and consent of the Senate, the matter shall be referred to the President for appropriate action.

(5) If steps for assuring compliance with applicable laws and regulations are not taken by the date set under paragraph (3) by a member of the Foreign Service or the uniformed services, the Secretary concerned shall take appropriate action.

(6) If steps for assuring compliance with applicable laws and regulations are not taken by the date set under paragraph (3) by any other officer or employee, the matter shall be referred to the head of the appropriate agency, the congressional ethics committee, or the Judicial Conference, for appropriate action; except that in the case of the Postmaster General or Deputy Postmaster General, the Director of the Office of Government Ethics shall recommend to the Governors of the Board of Governors of the United States Postal Service the action to be taken.

(7) Each supervising ethics office may render advisory opinions interpreting this title within its respective jurisdiction. Notwithstanding any other provision of law, the individual to whom a public advisory opinion is rendered in accordance with this paragraph, and any other individual covered by this title who is involved in a fact situation which is indistinguishable in all material aspects, and who acts in good faith in accordance with the provisions and findings of such advisory opinion shall not, as a result of such act, be subject to any penalty or sanction provided by this title.

(Pub.L. 95–521, Title I, § 106, Oct. 26, 1978, 92 Stat. 1833; Pub.L. 101–194, Title II, § 202, Nov. 30, 1989, 103 Stat. 1739; Pub.L. 101–280, § 3(1), (7), May 4, 1990, 104 Stat. 152, 155.)

HISTORICAL AND STATUTORY NOTES

Codifications

Section was formerly classified to section 706 of Title 2, The Congress.

Effective and Applicability Provisions

1990 Acts. Amendment of the text of this section by Pub.L. 101–280 effective May 4, 1990, see section 11 of Pub.L. 101–280, set out as a note under section 101 of this Appendix. The text as thus amended to be effective Jan. 1, 1991, see section 204 of Pub.L. 101–194 set out as a note under section 101 of this Appendix.

1989 Acts. Amendment by Pub.L. 101–194 effective Jan. 1, 1991, see section 204 of Pub.L. 101–194, as added Pub.L.

101–280, § 3(10)(B), May 4, 1990, 104 Stat. 157, set out as a note under section 101 of this Appendix.

§ 107. Confidential reports and other additional requirements

(a)(1) Each supervising ethics office may require officers and employees under its jurisdiction (including special Government employees as defined in section 202 of title 18, United States Code) to file confidential financial disclosure reports, in such form as the supervising ethics office may prescribe. The information required to be reported under this subsection by the officers and employees of any department or agency shall be set forth in rules or regulations prescribed by the supervising ethics office, and may be less extensive than otherwise required by this title, or more extensive when determined by the supervising ethics office to be necessary and appropriate in light of sections 202 through 209 of title 18, United States Code, regulations promulgated thereunder, or the authorized activities of such officers or employees. Any individual required to file a report pursuant to section 101 shall not be required to file a confidential report pursuant to this subsection, except with respect to information which is more extensive than information otherwise required by this title. Subsections (a), (b), and (d) of section 105 shall not apply with respect to any such report.

(2) Any information required to be provided by an individual under this subsection shall be confidential and shall not be disclosed to the public.

(3) Nothing in this subsection exempts any individual otherwise covered by the requirement to file a public financial disclosure report under this title from such requirement.

(b) The provisions of this title requiring the reporting of information shall supersede any general requirement under any other provision of law or regulation with respect to the reporting of information required for purposes of preventing conflicts of interest or apparent conflicts of interest. Such provisions of this title shall not supersede the requirements of section 7342 of title 5, United States Code.

(c) Nothing in this Act requiring reporting of information shall be deemed to authorize the receipt of income, gifts, or reimbursements; the holding of assets, liabilities, or positions; or the participation in transactions that are prohibited by law, Executive order, rule, or regulation.

(Pub.L. 95–521, Title I, § 107, Oct. 26, 1978, 92 Stat. 1834; Pub.L. 96–19, § 9(d), (g), June 13, 1979, 93 Stat. 42, 43; Pub.L. 101–194, Title II, § 202, Nov. 30, 1989, 103 Stat. 1740.)

HISTORICAL AND STATUTORY NOTES

References in Text

This Act, referred to in subsec. (c), is Pub.L. 95–521, Oct. 26, 1978, 92 Stat. 1824, as amended, known as the Ethics in Government Act of 1978. For complete classification of this Act to the Code, see Short Title note set out under section 101 of this Appendix and Tables.

Codifications

Section was formerly classified to section 707 of Title 2, The Congress.

Effective and Applicability Provisions

1989 Acts. Amendment by Pub.L. 101–194 effective Jan. 1, 1991, see section 204 of Pub.L. 101–194, as added Pub.L. 101–280, § 3(10)(B), May 4, 1990, 104 Stat. 157, set out as a note under section 101 of this Appendix.

§ 108. Authority of Comptroller General

(a) The Comptroller General shall have access to financial disclosure reports filed under this title for the purposes of carrying out his statutory responsibilities.

(b) No later than December 31, 1992, and regularly thereafter, the Comptroller General shall conduct a study to determine whether the provisions of this title are being carried out effectively.

(Pub.L. 95–521, Title I, § 108, Oct. 26, 1978, 92 Stat. 1835; Pub.L. 96–19, § 9(t), June 13, 1979, 93 Stat. 44; Pub.L. 101–194, Title II, § 202, Nov. 30, 1989, 103 Stat. 1741.)

HISTORICAL AND STATUTORY NOTES

Codifications

Section was formerly classified to section 708 of Title 2, The Congress.

Effective and Applicability Provisions

1989 Acts. Amendment by Pub.L. 101–194 effective Jan. 1, 1991, see section 204 of Pub.L. 101–194, as added Pub.L. 101–280, § 3(10)(B), May 4, 1990, 104 Stat. 157, set out as a note under section 101 of this Appendix.

§ 109. Definitions

For the purposes of this title, the term—

(1) "congressional ethics committees" means the Select Committee on Ethics of the Senate and the Committee on Standards of Official Conduct of the House of Representatives;

(2) "dependent child" means, when used with respect to any reporting individual, any individual who is a son, daughter, stepson, or stepdaughter and who—

(A) is unmarried and under age 21 and is living in the household of such reporting individual; or

(B) is a dependent of such reporting individual within the meaning of section 152 of the Internal Revenue Code of 1986 [26 U.S.C.A. § 152];

(3) "designated agency ethics official" means an officer or employee who is designated to administer the provisions of this title within an agency;

(4) "executive branch" includes each Executive agency (as defined in section 105 of title 5, United States Code), other than the Government Accountability Office, and any other entity or administrative unit in the executive branch;

(5) "gift" means a payment, advance, forbearance, rendering, or deposit of money, or any thing of value, unless consideration of equal or greater value is received by the donor, but does not include—

(A) bequest and other forms of inheritance;

(B) suitable mementos of a function honoring the reporting individual;

(C) food, lodging, transportation, and entertainment provided by a foreign government within a foreign country or by the United States Government, the District of Columbia, or a State or local government or political subdivision thereof;

(D) food and beverages which are not consumed in connection with a gift of overnight lodging;

(E) communications to the offices of a reporting individual, including subscriptions to newspapers and periodicals; or

(F) consumable products provided by home-State businesses to the offices of a reporting individual who is an elected official, if those products are intended for consumption by persons other than such reporting individual;

(6) "honoraria" has the meaning given such term in section 505 of this Act;

(7) "income" means all income from whatever source derived, including but not limited to the following items: compensation for services, including fees, commissions, and similar items; gross income derived from business (and net income if the individual elects to include it); gains derived from dealings in property; interest; rents; royalties; dividends; annuities; income from life insurance and endowment contracts; pensions; income from discharge of indebtedness; distributive share of partnership income; and income from an interest in an estate or trust;

(8) "judicial employee" means any employee of the judicial branch of the Government, of the United States Sentencing Commission, of the Tax Court, of the Court of Federal Claims, of the Court of Appeals for Veterans Claims, or of the United States Court of Appeals for the Armed Forces, who is not a judicial officer and who is authorized to perform adjudicatory functions with respect to proceedings in the judicial branch, or who occupies a position for which the rate of basic pay is equal to or greater than 120 percent of the minimum rate of basic pay payable for GS–15 of the General Schedule;

(9) "Judicial Conference" means the Judicial Conference of the United States;

(10) "judicial officer" means the Chief Justice of the United States, the Associate Justices of the Supreme Court, and the judges of the United States courts of appeals, United States district courts, including the district courts in Guam, the Northern Mariana Islands, and the Virgin Islands, Court of Appeals for the Federal Circuit, Court of International Trade, Tax Court, Court of Federal Claims, Court of Appeals for Veterans Claims, United States Court of Appeals for the Armed Forces, and any court created by Act of Congress, the judges of which are entitled to hold office during good behavior;

(11) "legislative branch" includes—

(A) the Architect of the Capitol;

(B) the Botanic Gardens;

(C) the Congressional Budget Office;

(D) the Government Accountability Office;

(E) the Government Printing Office;

(F) the Library of Congress;

(G) the United States Capitol Police;

(H) the Office of Technology Assessment; and

(I) any other agency, entity, office, or commission established in the legislative branch;

(12) "Member of Congress" means a United States Senator, a Representative in Congress, a Delegate to Congress, or the Resident Commissioner from Puerto Rico;

(13) "officer or employee of the Congress" means—

(A) any individual described under subparagraph (B), other than a Member of Congress or the Vice President, whose compensation is disbursed by the Secretary of the Senate or the Chief Administrative Officer of the House of Representatives;

(B)(i) each officer or employee of the legislative branch (except any officer or employee of the Government Accountability Office) who, for at least 60 days, occupies a position for which the rate of basic pay is equal to or greater than 120 percent of the minimum rate of basic pay payable for GS–15 of the General Schedule;

(ii) each officer or employee of the Government Accountability Office who, for at least 60 consecutive days, occupies a position for which the rate of basic pay, minus the amount of locality pay that would have been authorized under section 5304 of title 5, United States Code (had the officer or employee been paid under the General

Schedule) for the locality within which the position of such officer or employee is located (as determined by the Comptroller General), is equal to or greater than 120 percent of the minimum rate of basic pay payable for GS–15 of the General Schedule; and

(iii) at least one principal assistant designated for purposes of this paragraph by each Member who does not have an employee who occupies a position for which the rate of basic pay is equal to or greater than 120 percent of the minimum rate of basic pay payable for GS–15 of the General Schedule;

(14) "personal hospitality of any individual" means hospitality extended for a nonbusiness purpose by an individual, not a corporation or organization, at the personal residence of that individual or his family or on property or facilities owned by that individual or his family;

(15) "reimbursement" means any payment or other thing of value received by the reporting individual, other than gifts, to cover travel-related expenses of such individual other than those which are—

(A) provided by the United States Government, the District of Columbia, or a State or local government or political subdivision thereof;

(B) required to be reported by the reporting individual under section 7342 of title 5, United States Code; or

(C) required to be reported under section 304 of the Federal Election Campaign Act of 1971 (2 U.S.C. 434);

(16) "relative" means an individual who is related to the reporting individual, as father, mother, son, daughter, brother, sister, uncle, aunt, great aunt, great uncle, first cousin, nephew, niece, husband, wife, grandfather, grandmother, grandson, granddaughter, father-in-law, mother-in-law, son-in-law, daughter-in-law, brother-in-law, sister-in-law, stepfather, stepmother, stepson, stepdaughter, stepbrother, stepsister, half brother, half sister, or who is the grandfather or grandmother of the spouse of the reporting individual, and shall be deemed to include the fiance or fiancee of the reporting individual;

(17) "Secretary concerned" has the meaning set forth in section 101(a)(9) of title 10, United States Code, and, in addition, means—

(A) the Secretary of Commerce, with respect to matters concerning the National Oceanic and Atmospheric Administration;

(B) the Secretary of Health and Human Services, with respect to matters concerning the Public Health Service; and

(C) the Secretary of State, with respect to matters concerning the Foreign Service;

(18) "supervising ethics office" means—

(A) the Select Committee on Ethics of the Senate, for Senators, officers and employees of the Senate, and other officers or employees of the legislative branch required to file financial disclosure reports with the Secretary of the Senate pursuant to section 103(h) of this title;

(B) the Committee on Standards of Official Conduct of the House of Representatives, for Members, officers and employees of the House of Representatives and other officers or employees of the legislative branch required to file financial disclosure reports with the Clerk of the House of Representatives pursuant to section 103(h) of this title;

(C) the Judicial Conference for judicial officers and judicial employees; and

(D) the Office of Government Ethics for all executive branch officers and employees; and

(19) "value" means a good faith estimate of the dollar value if the exact value is neither known nor easily obtainable by the reporting individual.

(Pub.L. 95–521, Title I, § 109, Oct. 26, 1978, 92 Stat. 1836; Pub.L. 101–194, Title II, § 202, Nov. 30, 1989, 103 Stat. 1741; Pub.L. 101–280, § 3(1), (8), May 4, 1990, 104 Stat. 152, 155; Pub.L. 102–378, § 4(a)(2), Oct. 2, 1992, 106 Stat. 1357; Pub.L. 102–572, Title IX, § 902(b)(2), Oct. 29, 1992, 106 Stat. 4516; Pub.L. 103–160, Div. A, Title XI, § 1182(d)(3), Nov. 30, 1993, 107 Stat. 1773; Pub.L. 103–337, Div. A, Title IX, § 924(d)(3), Oct. 5, 1994, 108 Stat. 2832; Pub.L. 104–186, Title II, § 216(2), Aug. 20, 1996, 110 Stat. 1747; Pub.L. 105–368, Title V, § 512(b)(1)(D), Nov. 11, 1998, 112 Stat. 3342; Pub.L. 108–271, § 8(b), July 7, 2004, 118 Stat. 814; Pub.L. 110–323, § 7, Sept. 22, 2008, 122 Stat. 3547.)

HISTORICAL AND STATUTORY NOTES

References in Text

The General Schedule, referred to in pars. (8) and (13)(B), is set out under section 5332 of this title.

The General Schedule, referred to in par. (13)(B)(ii), is set out under 5 U.S.C.A. § 5332.

Codifications

Section was formerly classified to section 709 of Title 2, The Congress.

Effective and Applicability Provisions

1998 Acts. Amendment by Pub.L. 105–368 effective on the first day of the first month beginning more than 90 days after Nov. 11, 1998, see section 513 of Pub.L. 105–368, set out as a note under section 7251 of Title 38.

1992 Acts. Amendment by Pub.L. 102–572 effective Oct. 29, 1992, see section 911 of Pub.L. 102–572, set out as a note under section 171 of Title 28, Judiciary and Judicial Procedure.

Amendment by Pub.L. 102–378 effective Oct. 2, 1992, see section 9(a) of Pub.L. 102–378, set out as a note under section 6303 of this title.

1990 Acts. Amendment of the text of this section by Pub.L. 101–280 effective May 4, 1990, see section 11 of

Pub.L. 101–280, set out as a note under section 101 of this Appendix. The text as thus amended to be effective Jan. 1, 1991, see section 204 of Pub.L. 101–194 set out as a note under section 101 of this Appendix.

1989 Acts. Amendment by Pub.L. 101–194 effective Jan. 1, 1991, see section 204 of Pub.L. 101–194, as added Pub.L. 101–280, § 3(10)(B), May 4, 1990, 104 Stat. 157, set out as a note under section 101 of this Appendix.

Termination of Reporting Requirements

For termination, effective May 15, 2000, of reporting provisions of this section, see Pub.L. 104–66, § 3003, as amended, set out as a note under 31 U.S.C.A. § 1113, the 7th item on page 1 of House Document No. 103–7, and the 7th item on page 5 of House Document No. 103–7, which references 2 U.S.C. § 709, which was subsequently redesignated as this section.

Transfer of Functions

Statutory functions, duties, or authority of Chief Administrative Officer of the House of Representatives or Secretary of the Senate as disbursing officers for the Capitol Police transferred to Chief of the Capitol Police, and references in any law or resolution before Feb. 20, 2003, to funds paid or disbursed by Chief Administrative Officer of the House of Representatives and Secretary of the Senate relating to pay and allowances of Capitol Police employees deemed to refer to Chief of the Capitol Police. See 2 U.S.C.A. § 1907(a).

Any reference in any provision of law enacted before Jan. 4, 1995, to a function, duty, or authority of the Clerk of the House of Representatives treated as referring, with respect to that function, duty, or authority, to the officer of the House of Representatives exercising that function, duty, or authority, as determined by the Committee on House Oversight of the House of Representatives, see section 2(1) of Pub.L. 104–14, set out as a note preceding section 21 of Title 2, The Congress.

Certain functions of Clerk of House of Representatives transferred to Director of Non-legislative and Financial Services by section 7 of House Resolution No. 423, One Hundred Second Congress, Apr. 9, 1992. Any reference in any provision of law enacted before Jan. 4, 1995, to a function, duty, or authority of the Director of Non-legislative and Financial Services treated as referring, with respect to that function, duty, or authority, to the officer of the House of Representatives exercising that function, duty, or authority, as determined by the Committee on House Oversight of the House of Representatives, see section 2(4) of Pub.L. 104–14, set out as a note preceding section 21 of Title 2, The Congress.

Prior Provisions

Provisions similar to those comprising this section were contained in section 107 prior to the general revision of this title by Pub.L. 101–194.

Provision similar to that comprising par. (11) of this section was contained in section 101(e) prior to the general revision of this title by Pub.L. 101–194.

§ 110. Notice of actions taken to comply with ethics agreements

(a) In any case in which an individual agrees with that individual's designated agency ethics official, the Office of Government Ethics, a Senate confirmation committee, a congressional ethics committee, or the Judicial Conference, to take any action to comply with this Act or any other law or regulation governing conflicts of interest of, or establishing standards of conduct applicable with respect to, officers or employees of the Government, that individual shall notify in writing the designated agency ethics official, the Office of Government Ethics, the appropriate committee of the Senate, the congressional ethics committee, or the Judicial Conference, as the case may be, of any action taken by the individual pursuant to that agreement. Such notification shall be made not later than the date specified in the agreement by which action by the individual must be taken, or not later than three months after the date of the agreement, if no date for action is so specified.

(b) If an agreement described in subsection (a) requires that the individual recuse himself or herself from particular categories of agency or other official action, the individual shall reduce to writing those subjects regarding which the recusal agreement will apply and the process by which it will be determined whether the individual must recuse himself or herself in a specific instance. An individual shall be considered to have complied with the requirements of subsection (a) with respect to such recusal agreement if such individual files a copy of the document setting forth the information described in the preceding sentence with such individual's designated agency ethics official or the appropriate supervising ethics office within the time prescribed in the last sentence of subsection (a).

(Pub.L. 95–521, Title I, § 110, as added Pub.L. 101–194, Title II, § 202, Nov. 30, 1989, 103 Stat. 1744, and amended Pub.L. 101–280, § 3(1), May 4, 1990, 104 Stat. 152.)

HISTORICAL AND STATUTORY NOTES

References in Text

This Act, referred to in subsec. (a), is Pub.L. 95–521, Oct. 26, 1978, 92 Stat. 1824, as amended, known as the Ethics in Government Act of 1978. For complete classification of this Act to the Code, see Short Title note set out under section 101 of this Appendix and Tables.

Effective and Applicability Provisions

1990 Acts. Amendment of the text of this section by Pub.L. 101–280 effective May 4, 1990, see section 11 of Pub.L. 101–280, set out as a note under section 101 of this Appendix. The text as thus amended to be effective Jan. 1, 1991, see section 204 of Pub.L. 101–194 set out as a note under section 101 of this Appendix.

1989 Acts. Section effective Jan. 1, 1991, see section 204 of Pub.L. 101–194, set out as a note under section 101 of this Appendix.

§ 111. Administration of provisions

The provisions of this title shall be administered by—

(1) the Director of the Office of Government Ethics, the designated agency ethics official, or the Secretary concerned, as appropriate, with regard to officers and employees described in paragraphs (1) through (8) of section 101(f);

(2) the Select Committee on Ethics of the Senate and the Committee on Standards of Official Conduct of the House of Representatives, as appropriate, with regard to officers and employees described in paragraphs (9) and (10) of section 101(f); and

(3) the Judicial Conference in the case of an officer or employee described in paragraphs (11) and (12) of section 101(f).

The Judicial Conference may delegate any authority it has under this title to an ethics committee established by the Judicial Conference.

(Pub.L. 95–521, Title I, § 111, as added Pub.L. 101–194, Title II, § 202, Nov. 30, 1989, 103 Stat. 1744, and amended Pub.L. 101–280, § 3(1), (9), May 4, 1990, 104 Stat. 152, 157.)

HISTORICAL AND STATUTORY NOTES

Effective and Applicability Provisions

1990 Acts. Amendment of the text of this section by Pub.L. 101–280 effective May 4, 1990, see section 11 of Pub.L. 101–280, set out as a note under section 101 of this Appendix. The text as thus amended to be effective Jan. 1, 1991, see section 204 of Pub.L. 101–194 set out as a note under section 101 of this Appendix.

1989 Acts. Section effective Jan. 1, 1991, see section 204 of Pub.L. 101–194, set out as a note under section 101 of this Appendix.

Transmittal of Financial Disclosure Reports

Section 902 of Pub.L. 101–194 provided that:

"(a) The Select Committee on Ethics shall transmit a copy of each report filed with it under title I of the Ethics in Government Act of 1978 [sections 101 to 112 of Pub.L. 95–521, set out in this Appendix] (other than a report filed by a Member of Congress) to the head of the employing office of the individual filing the report.

"(b) For purposes of this section, the head of the employing office shall be—

"(A) in the case of an employee of a Member, the Member by whom that person is employed;

"(B) in the case of an employee of a Committee, the chairman and ranking minority member of such Committee;

"(C) in the case of an employee on the leadership staff, the Member of the leadership on whose staff such person serves; and

"(D) in the case of any other employee of the legislative branch, the head of the office in which such individual serves."

[§ 112. Repealed. Pub.L. 101–280, § 3(10)(A), May 4, 1990, 104 Stat. 157]

HISTORICAL AND STATUTORY NOTES

Section, Pub.L. 95–521, Title I, § 112, as added Pub.L. 101–194, Title II, § 202, Nov. 30, 1989, 103 Stat. 1744, directed that the provisions made by title I of Pub.L. 95–521 [sections 101 to 112 of Pub.L. 95–521, set out in this Appendix] take effect on January 1, 1990, and be applicable to reports filed under such title after January 1, 1991. See section 3(10)(C) of Pub.L. 101–280 and section 204 of Pub.L. 101–194, as added by section 3(10)(B) of Pub.L. 101–280, set out as notes under section 101 of this Appendix.

Effective Date of Repeal

Repeal effective May 4, 1990, see section 11 of Pub.L. 101–280, set out as a note under section 101 of this Appendix.

[TITLE II—REPEALED]

[§§ 201 to 212. Repealed. Pub.L. 101–194, Title II, § 201, Nov. 30, 1989, 103 Stat. 1724]

HISTORICAL AND STATUTORY NOTES

Sections 201 to 212 of Pub.L. 95–521, Title II, Oct. 26, 1978, 92 Stat. 1836, as amended Pub.L. 96–19, §§ 2(a)(2), (c)(2), 3(a)(2), (b), 4(a), (d), (g), 5, 6, 7(a) to (c), (d)(2), (e), (f), 8(b), 9(c)(2), (d), (f), (h) to (o), June 13, 1979, 93 Stat. 37 to 43; Pub.L. 98–150, §§ 6 to 11, Nov. 11, 1983, 97 Stat. 960 to 962; Pub.L. 99–190, § 148(b), Dec. 19, 1985, 99 Stat. 1325; Pub.L. 100–191, § 3(b), Dec. 15, 1987, 101 Stat. 1306, related to executive personnel financial disclosure requirements.

Effective Date of Repeal

Repeal effective Jan. 1, 1991, see section 204 of Pub.L. 101–194, as added Pub.L. 101–280, § 3(10)(B), May 4, 1990, 104 Stat. 157, set out as an Effective Date of 1989 Amendment note under section 101 of the Appendix.

See section 3(10)(C) and (D) of Pub.L. 101–280, May 4, 1990, 104 Stat. 157, set out as notes under section 101 of this Appendix, for provisions directing that Title II of Pub.L. 95–521, as in effect prior to Nov. 30, 1989, are effective until Jan. 1, 1991, as if Pub.L. 101–194 had not been enacted, and except that section 202(F)(4)(B) of Pub.L. 95–521 repealed effective Jan. 1, 1990, except that nothing in Title II of Pub.L. 101–194 shall be construed to prevent the prosecution of civil actions against individuals for violations of Title II of Pub.L. 95–521, before Jan. 1, 1991.

Prior Provisions

Prior to repeal, sections 201 to 212 of Pub.L. 95–521, Title II, Oct. 26, 1978, 92 Stat. 1836, read as follows:

§ 201. Persons required to file

(a) Within thirty days of assuming the position of an officer or employee described in subsection (f), an individual shall file a report containing the information described in section 202(b) unless the individual has left another position described in subsection (f) within thirty days prior to assuming such new position or has already filed a report under this title [sections 201 to 212 of this Act] with respect to nomination for the new position or as a candidate for the position.

(b)(1) Within five days of the transmittal by the President to the Senate of the nomination of an individual (other than an individual covered by section 301(b) or an individual nominated for appointment to a grade or rank in the uniformed services for which the pay grade prescribed by section 201 of title 37, United States Code, is O–6 or below) to a position, appointment to which requires the advice and consent of the Senate, such individual shall file a report containing the information described in section 202(b). Such individual shall, not later than the date of the first hearing to consider the nomination of such individual, make current the report filed pursuant to this paragraph by filing the information required by section 202(a)(1)(A) with respect to income and honoraria received as of the date which occurs five days before the date of such hearing. Nothing in this Act shall prevent any Congressional committee from requesting, as a condition of confirmation, any additional financial information from any Presidential nominee whose nomination has been referred to that committee.

(2) An individual whom the President or the President-elect has publicly announced he intends to nominate to a position may file the report required by paragraph (1) at any time after that public announcement but not later than is required under the first sentence of such paragraph.

(c) Within thirty days of becoming a candidate in a calendar year for nomination or election to the office of President or Vice President, as determined by the Federal Election Commission, or on or before May 15 of that calendar year, whichever is later, and on or before May 15 of each successive year an individual continues to be a candidate, an individual other than an incumbent President or Vice President shall file a report containing the information described in section 202(b). Notwithstanding the preceding sentence, in any calendar year in which an individual continues to be a candidate for any office but all elections for such office relating to such candidacy were held in prior calendar years, such individual need not file a report unless he becomes a candidate for another vacancy in that office or another office during that year.

(d) Any individual who is an officer or employee described in subsection (f) during any calendar year and performs the duties of his position or office for a period in excess of sixty days in that calendar year shall file on or before May 15 of the succeeding year a report containing the information described in section 202(a).

(e) Any individual who occupies a position described in subsection (f) shall, on or before the thirtieth day after termination of employment in such position, file a report containing the information described in section 202(a) covering the preceding calendar year if the report required by subsection (d) has not been filed and covering the portion of the calendar year in which such termination occurs up to the date the individual left such office or position, unless such individual has accepted employment in another position described in subsection (f).

(f) The officers and employees referred to in subsections (a), (d), and (e) are—

(1) the President;

(2) the Vice President;

(3) each officer or employee in the executive branch, including a special Government employee as defined in section 202 of title 18, United States Code, whose position is classified at GS–16 or above of the General Schedule prescribed by section 5332 of title 5, United States Code, or the rate of basic pay for which is fixed (other than under the General Schedule) at a rate equal to or greater than the minimum rate of basic pay fixed for GS–16; each member of a uniformed service whose pay grade is at or in excess of O–7 under section 201 of title 37, United States Code; and each officer or employee in any other position determined by the Director of the Office of Government Ethics to be of equal classification;

(4) each employee appointed pursuant to section 3105 of title 5, United States Code;

(5) any employee not described in paragraph (3) who is in a position in the executive branch which is excepted from the competitive service by reason of being of a confidential or policymaking character, except that the Director of the Office of Government Ethics may, by regulation, exclude from the application of this paragraph any individual, or group of individuals, who are in such positions, but only in cases in which the Director determines such exclusion would not affect adversely the integrity of the Government or the public's confidence in the integrity of the Government;

(6) the Postmaster General, the Deputy Postmaster General, each Governor of the Board of Governors of the United States Postal Service and each officer or employee of the United States Postal Service or Postal Rate Commission whose basic rate of pay is equal to or greater than the minimum rate of basic pay fixed for GS–16; and

(7) the Director of the Office of Government Ethics and each designated agency official.

(g) Reasonable extensions of time for filing any report may be granted under procedures prescribed by the Director of the Office of Government Ethics, but the total of such extensions shall not exceed ninety days.

(h) The provisions of subsections (a), (b), and (e) shall not apply to an individual who, as determined by the designated agency official or Secretary concerned (or in the case of a Presidential appointee under subsection (b), the Director of the Office of Government Ethics), is not reasonably expected to perform the duties of his office or position for more than sixty days in a calendar year, except that if such individual performs the duties of his office or position for more than sixty days in a calendar year—

(1) the report required by subsections (a) and (b) shall be filed within fifteen days of the sixtieth day, and

(2) the report required by subsection (e) shall be filed as provided in such subsection.

(i) The Director of the Office of Government Ethics may grant a publicly available request for a waiver of any reporting requirement under this section for an individual who is expected to perform or has performed the duties of his office or position less than one hundred and thirty days in a calendar year, but only if the Director determines that—

(1) such individual is not a full-time employee of the Government,

(2) such individual is able to provide services specially needed by the Government,

(3) it is unlikely that the individual's outside employment or financial interests will create a conflict of interest, and

(4) public financial disclosure by such individual is not necessary in the circumstances.

(j)(1) Any individual who performs staff functions in support of an advisory committee which is composed, in whole or in part, of special Government employees shall be subject to the provisions of this title [sections 201 to 212 of this Act] as if that individual were such a special Government employee.

(2) For purposes of paragraph (1)—

(A) the term "advisory committee" means any committee, board, commission, council, conference, panel, task force, or other similar group which is established—

(i) by statute or reorganization plan,

(ii) by the President, or

(iii) by one or more agencies,

in the interest of obtaining advice or recommendations for the President or one or more agencies or officers of the Federal Government; such term includes any subcommittee or other subgroup of an advisory committee, but does not include the Advisory Commission on Intergovernmental Relations and the Commission on Government Procurement;

(B) the term "staff functions in support of an advisory committee" means such activities as the Director of the Office of Government Ethics by regulation prescribes which are carried out with respect to those functions for which the advisory committee was established as described in subparagraph (A) of this paragraph;

(C) the term "special Government employee" has the meaning given that term by section 202 of title 18, United States Code; and

(D) the term "agency" has the meaning given that term by section 551(1) of title 5, United States Code.

(3) The Director of the Office of Government Ethics shall prescribe such regulations as may be necessary to carry out this subsection.

(Pub.L. 95–521, Title II, § 201, Oct. 26, 1978, 92 Stat. 1836; Pub.L. 96–19, §§ 2(a)(2), (c)(2), 4(d), (g), 5, 9(h), (i), June 13, 1979, 93 Stat. 37, 38, 40, 43; Pub.L. 98–150, §§ 8, 11, Nov. 11, 1983, 97 Stat. 961, 962.)

§ 202. Contents of reports

(a) Each report filed pursuant to section 201(d) shall include a full and complete statement with respect to the following:

(1)(A) The source, type, and amount or value of income (other than income referred to in subparagraph (B)) from any source (other than from current employment by the United States Government), and the source, date, and amount of honoraria from any source, received during the preceding calendar year, aggregating $100 or more in value.

(B) The source and type of income which consists of dividends, rents, interest, and capital gains, received during the preceding calendar year which exceeds $100 in amount or value, and an indication of which of the following categories the amount or value of such item of income is within:

(i) not more than $1,000,

(ii) greater than $1,000 but not more than $2,500,

(iii) greater than $2,500 but not more than $5,000,

(iv) greater than $5,000 but not more than $15,000,

(v) greater than $15,000 but not more than $50,000,

(vi) greater than $50,000 but not more than $100,000, or

(vii) greater than $100,000.

(2)(A) The identity of the source and a brief description of any gifts of transportation, lodging, food, or entertainment aggregating $250 or more in value received from any source other than a relative of the reporting individual during the preceding calendar year, except that any food, lodging, or entertainment received as personal hospitality of any individual need not be reported, and any gift with a fair market value of $35 or less need not be aggregated for purposes of this subparagraph.

(B) The identity of the source, a brief description, and the value of all gifts other than transportation, lodging, food, or entertainment aggregating $100 or more in value received from any source other than a relative of the reporting individual during the preceding calendar year, except that any gift with a fair market value of $35 or less need not be aggregated for purposes of this subparagraph.

(C) The identity of the source and a brief description of reimbursements received from any source aggregating $250 or more in value and received during the preceding calendar year.

(D) In an unusual case, a gift need not be aggregated under subparagraph (A) or (B) if a publicly available request for a waiver is granted.

(3) The identity and category of value of any interest in property held during the preceding calendar year in a trade or business, or for investment or the production of income, which has a fair market value which exceeds $1,000 as of the close of the preceding calendar year, excluding any personal liability owed to the reporting individual by a relative or any deposits aggregating $5,000 or less in a personal savings account. For purposes of this paragraph, a personal savings account shall include any certificate of deposit or any other form of deposit in a bank, savings and loan association, credit union, or similar financial institution.

(4) The identity and category of value of the total liabilities owed to any creditor other than a relative which exceed $10,000 at any time during the preceding calendar year, excluding—

(A) any mortgage secured by real property which is a personal residence of the reporting individual or his spouse; and

(B) any loan secured by a personal motor vehicle, household furniture, or appliances, which loan does not exceed the purchase price of the item which secures it.

With respect to revolving charge accounts, only those with an outstanding liability which exceeds $10,000 as of the close of the preceding calendar year need be reported under this paragraph.

(5) Except as provided in this paragraph, a brief description, the date, and category of value of any purchase, sale or exchange during the preceding calendar year which exceeds $1,000—

(A) in real property, other than property used solely as a personal residence of the reporting individual or his spouse; or

(B) in stocks, bonds, commodities futures, and other forms of securities.

Reporting is not required under this paragraph of any transaction solely by and between the reporting individual, his spouse, or dependent children.

(6)(A) The identity of all positions held on or before the date of filing during the current calendar year (and, for the first report filed by an individual, during the two-year period preceding such calendar year) as an officer, director, trustee, partner, proprietor, representative, employee, or consultant of any corporation, company, firm, partnership, or other business enterprise, any nonprofit organization, any labor organization, or any educational or other institution other than the United States. This subparagraph shall not require the reporting of positions held in any religious, social, fraternal, or political entity and positions solely of an honorary nature.

(B) If any person, other than the United States Government, paid a nonelected reporting individual compensation in excess of $5,000 in any of the two calendar years prior to the calendar year during which the individual files his first report under this title [sections 201 to 212 of this Act], the individual shall include in the report—

(i) the identity of each source of such compensation; and

(ii) a brief description of the nature of the duties performed or services rendered by the reporting individual for each such source.

The preceding sentence shall not require any individual to include in such report any information which is considered confidential as a result of a privileged relationship, established by law, between such individual and any person nor shall it require an individual to report any information with respect to any person for whom services were provided by any firm or association of which such individual was a member, partner, or employee unless such individual was directly involved in the provision of such services.

(7) A description of the date, parties to, and terms of any agreement or arrangement with respect to (A) future employment; (B) a leave of absence during the period of the reporting individual's Government service; (C) continuation of payments by a former employer other than the United States Government; and (D) continuing participation in an employee welfare or benefit plan maintained by a former employer.

(b) Each report filed pursuant to subsections (a), (b), and (c) of section 201 shall include a full and complete statement with respect to the information required by—

(1) paragraph (1) of subsection (a) for the year of filing and the preceding calendar year,

(2) paragraphs (3) and (4) of subsection (a) as of the date specified in the report but which is less than thirty-one days before the filing date, and

(3) paragraphs (6) and (7) of subsection (a) as of the filing date but for periods described in such paragraphs.

(c) In the case of any individual described in section 201(e), any reference to the preceding calendar year shall be considered also to include that part of the calendar year of filing up to the date of the termination of employment.

(d)(1) The categories for reporting the amount or value of the items covered in paragraphs (3), (4), and (5) of subsection (a) are as follows:

(A) not more than $5,000;

(B) greater than $5,000 but not more than $15,000;

(C) greater than $15,000 but not more than $50,000;

(D) greater than $50,000 but not more than $100,000;

(E) greater than $100,000 but not more than $250,000; and

(F) greater than $250,000.

(2) For the purposes of paragraph (3) of subsection (a) if the current value of an interest in real property (or an interest in a real estate partnership) is not ascertainable without an appraisal, an individual may list (A) the date of purchase and the purchase price of the interest in the real property, or (B) the assessed value of the real property for tax purposes, adjusted to reflect the market value of the property used for the assessment if the assessed value is computed at less than 100 percent of such market value, but such individual shall include in his report a full and complete description of the method used to determine such assessed value, instead of specifying a category of value pursuant to paragraph (1) of this subsection. If the current value of any other item required to be reported under paragraph (3) of subsection (a) is not ascertainable without an appraisal, such individual may list the book value of a corporation whose stock is not publicly traded, the net worth of a business partnership, the equity value of an individually owned business, or with respect to other holdings, any recognized indication of value, but such individual shall include in his report a full and complete description of the method used in determining such value. In lieu of any value referred to in the preceding sentence, an individual may list the assessed value of the item for tax purposes, adjusted to reflect the market value of the item used for the assessment if the assessed value is computed at less than 100 percent of such market value, but a full and complete description of the method used in determining such assessed value shall be included in the report.

(e)(1) Except as provided in the last sentence of this paragraph, each report required by subsection (a), (b), or (c) shall also contain information listed in paragraphs (1) through (5) of subsection (a) respecting the spouse or dependent child of the reporting individual as follows:

(A) The source of items of earned income earned by a spouse from any person which exceed $1,000 and, with respect to a spouse or dependent child, all information required to be reported in subsection (a)(1)(B) with respect to income derived from any asset held by the spouse or dependent child and reported pursuant to paragraph (3). With respect to earned income, if the spouse is self-employed in business or a profession, only the nature of such business or profession need be reported.

(B) In the case of any gifts received by a spouse which are not received totally independent of the spouse's relationship to the reporting individual, the identity of the source and a brief description of gifts of transportation, lodging, food, or entertainment and a brief description and the value of other gifts.

(C) In the case of any reimbursements received by a spouse which are not received totally independent of the spouse's relationship to the reporting individual, the identity of the source and a brief description of each such reimbursement.

(D) In the case of items described in paragraphs (3) through (5), all information required to be reported under these paragraphs other than items (i) which the reporting individual certifies represent the spouse's or dependent child's sole financial interest or responsibility and which the reporting individual has no knowledge of, (ii) which are not in any way, past or present, derived from the income, assets, or activities of the reporting individual, and (iii) from which the reporting individual neither derives, nor expects to derive, any financial or economic benefit.

Each report referred to in subsection (b) of this section shall, with respect to the spouse and dependent child of the reporting individual, only contain information listed in paragraphs (1), (3), and (4) of subsection (a), as specified in this paragraph.

(2) No report shall be required with respect to a spouse living separate and apart from the reporting individual with the intention of terminating the marriage or providing for permanent separation; or with respect to any income or obligations of an individual arising from the dissolution of his marriage or the permanent separation from his spouse.

(f)(1) Except as provided in paragraph (2), each reporting individual shall report the information required to be reported pursuant to subsections (a), (b), and (c) of this section with respect to the holdings of and the income from a trust or other financial arrangement from which income is received by, or with respect to which a beneficial interest in principal or income is held by, such individual, his spouse, or any dependent child.

(2) A reporting individual need not report the holdings of or the source of income from any of the holdings of—

(A) any qualified blind trust (as defined in paragraph (3)); or

(B) a trust—

(i) which was not created directly by such individual, his spouse, or any dependent child, and

(ii) the holdings or sources of income of which such individual, his spouse, and any dependent child have no knowledge of,

but such individual shall report the category of the amount of income received by him, his spouse, or any dependent child from the trust under subsection (a)(1)(B) of this subsection.[1]

(3) For purposes of this subsection, the term "qualified blind trust" includes any trust in which a reporting individual, his spouse, or any dependent child has a beneficial interest in the principal or income, and which meets the following requirements:

(A) The trustee of the trust is a financial institution, an attorney, a certified public accountant, a broker, or an investment adviser, who (in the case of a financial institution or investment company, any officer or employee involved in the management or control of the trust who)—

(i) is independent of and unassociated with any interested party so that the trustee cannot be controlled or influenced in the administration of the trust by any interested party,

(ii) is not or has not been an employee of any interested party, or any organization affiliated with any interested party and is not a partner of, or involved in any joint venture or other investment with, any interested party, and

(iii) is not a relative of any interested party.

(B) Any asset transferred to the trust by an interested party is free of any restriction with respect to its transfer or sale unless such restriction is expressly approved by the supervising ethics office of the reporting individual.

(C) The trust instrument which establishes the trust provides that—

(i) except to the extent provided in subparagraph (B) of this paragraph, the trustee in the exercise of his authority and discretion to manage and control the assets of the trust shall not consult or notify any interested party;

(ii) the trust shall not contain any asset the holding of which by an interested party is prohibited by any law or regulation;

(iii) the trustee shall promptly notify the reporting individual and his supervising ethics office when the holdings of any particular asset transferred to the trust by any interested party are disposed of or when the value of such holding is less than $1,000;

(iv) the trust tax return shall be prepared by the trustee or his designee, and such return and any information relating thereto (other than the trust income summarized in appropriate categories necessary to complete an interested party's tax return), shall not be disclosed to any interested party;

(v) an interested party shall not receive any report on the holdings and sources of income of the trust, except a report at the end of each calendar quarter with respect to the total cash value of the interest of the interested party in the trust or the net income or loss of the trust or any reports necessary to enable the interested party to complete an individual tax return required by law or to provide the information required by subsection (a)(1)(B) of this section, but such report shall not identify any asset or holding;

(vi) except for communications which solely consist of requests for distributions of cash or other unspecified assets of the trust, there shall be no direct or indirect communication between the trustee and an interested party with respect to the trust unless such communication is in writing and unless it relates only (I) to the general financial interest and needs of the interested party (including, but not limited to, an interest in maximizing income or long-term capital gain), (II) to the notification of the trustee of a law or regulation subsequently applicable to the reporting individual which prohibits the interested party from holding an asset, which notification directs that the asset not be held by the trust, or (III) to directions to the trustee to sell all of an asset initially placed in the trust by an interested party which in the determination of the reporting individual creates a conflict of interest or the appearance thereof due to the subsequent assumption of duties by the reporting individual (but nothing herein shall require any such direction); and

(vii) the interested parties shall make no effort to obtain information with respect to the holdings of the trust, including obtaining a copy of any trust tax return filed or any information relating thereto except as otherwise provided in this subsection.

(D) The proposed trust instrument and the proposed trustee is approved by the reporting individual's supervising ethics office.

For purposes of this subsection, "interested party" means a reporting individual, his spouse, and any dependent child if the reporting individual, his spouse, or dependent child has a beneficial interest in the principal or income of a qualified blind trust; "broker" has the meaning set forth in section 3(a)(4) of the Securities and Exchange Act of 1934 (15 U.S.C. 78c(a)(4)); "investment adviser" includes any investment adviser who, as determined under regulations prescribed by the supervising ethics office, is generally involved in his role as such an adviser in the management or control of trusts; and "supervising ethics office" means the Office of Government Ethics.

(4)(A) An asset placed in a trust by an interested party shall be considered a financial interest of the reporting individual, for the purposes of section 208 of title 18, United States Code, and any other conflict of interest statutes or regulations of the Federal Government, until such time as the reporting individual is notified by the trustee that such asset has been disposed of, or has a value of less than $1,000.

(B) Repealed. Pub.L. 101–280, § 3(10)(C), May 4, 1990, 104 Stat. 157

(5)(A) The reporting individual shall, within thirty days after a qualified blind trust is approved by his supervising ethics office, file with such office a copy of—

(i) the executed trust instrument of such trust (other than those provisions which relate to the testamentary disposition of the trust assets), and

(ii) a list of the assets which were transferred to such trust, including the category of value of each asset as determined under subsection (d) of this section.

This subparagraph shall not apply with respect to a trust meeting the requirements for being considered a qualified blind trust under paragraph (7) of this subsection.

(B) The reporting individual shall, within thirty days of transferring an asset (other than cash) to a previously established qualified blind trust, notify his supervising ethics office of the identity of each such asset and the category of value of each asset as determined under subsection (d) of this section.

(C) Within thirty days of the dissolution of a qualified blind trust, a reporting individual shall—

(i) notify his supervising ethics office of such dissolution, and

(ii) file with such office a copy of a list of the assets of the trust at the time of such dissolution and the category of value under subsection (d) of this section of each such asset.

(D) Documents filed under subparagraphs (A), (B), and (C) of this paragraph and the lists provided by the trustee of assets placed in the trust by an interested party which have been sold shall be made available to the public in the same manner as a report is made available under section 205 and the provisions of that section shall apply with respect to such documents and lists.

(E) A copy of each written communication with respect to the trust under paragraph (3)(C)(vi) shall be filed by the person initiating the communication with the reporting individual's supervising ethics office within five days of the date of the communication.

(6)(A) A trustee of a qualified blind trust shall not knowingly or negligently (i) disclose any information to an interested party with respect to such trust that may not be disclosed under paragraph (3) of this subsection, (ii) acquire any holding the ownership of which is prohibited by the trust instrument; (iii) solicit advice from any interested party with respect to such trust, which solicitation is prohibited by paragraph (3) of this subsection or the trust agreement; or (iv) fail to file any document required by this subsection.

(B) A reporting individual shall not knowingly or negligently (i) solicit or receive any information with respect to a qualified blind trust of which he is an interested party that may not be disclosed under paragraph (3)(C) of this subsection or (ii) fail to file any document required by this subsection.

(C)(i) The Attorney General may bring a civil action in any appropriate United States District Court against any individual who knowingly and willfully violates the provisions of subparagraph (A) or (B) of this paragraph. The court in which such action is brought may assess against such individual a civil penalty in any amount not to exceed $5,000.

(ii) The Attorney General may bring a civil action in any appropriate United States District Court against any individual who negligently violates the provisions of subparagraph (A) or (B) of this paragraph. The court in which such action is brought may assess against such individual a civil penalty in any amount not to exceed $1,000.

(7) Any trust may be considered to be a qualified blind trust if—

(A) the trust instrument is amended to comply with the requirements of paragraph (3) or, in the case of a trust instrument which does not by its terms permit amendment, the trustee, the reporting individual, and any other interested party agree in writing that the trust shall be administered in accordance with the requirements of this subsection and the trustee of such trust meets the requirements of paragraph (3)(A); except that in the case of any interested party who is a dependent child, a parent or guardian of such child may execute the agreement referred to in this subparagraph;

(B) a copy of the trust instrument (except testamentary provisions) and a copy of the agreement referred to in subparagraph (A), and a list of the assets held by the trust at the time of approval by the supervising ethics office, including the category of value of each asset as determined under subsection (d) of this section, are filed with such office and made available to the public as provided under paragraph (5)(D) of this subsection; and

(C) the supervising ethics office determines that approval of the trust arrangement as a qualified blind trust is in the particular case appropriate to assure compliance with applicable laws and regulations.

(g) Political campaign funds, including campaign receipts and expenditures, need not be included in any report filed pursuant to this title [sections 201 to 212 of this Act].

(h) A report filed pursuant to subsection (d) or (e) of section 201 need not contain the information described in subparagraphs (A), (B), and (C) of subsection (a)(2) with respect to gifts and reimbursements received in a period when the reporting individual was not an officer or employee of the Federal Government.

(Pub.L. 95–521, Title II, § 202, Oct. 26, 1978, 92 Stat. 1837; Pub.L. 96–19, §§ 3(a)(2), (b), 6, 7(a) to (c), (d)(2), (e), (f), 9(c)(2), (j), June 13, 1979, 93 Stat. 39–43; Pub.L. 98–150, § 10, Nov. 11, 1983, 97 Stat. 962; Pub.L. 101–280, § 3(10)(C), May 4, 1990, 104 Stat. 157.)

[1] So in original. Probably should be "section".

§ 203. Filing of reports

(a) Except as otherwise provided in this subsection, the reports required under this title shall be filed by the reporting individual with the designated agency official at the agency by which he is employed (or in the case of an individual described in section 201(e), was employed) or in which he will serve. The date any report is received (and the date of receipt of any supplemental report) shall be noted on such report by such official.

(b) The President, the Vice President, and independent counsel and persons appointed by independent counsel under chapter 40 of title 28 shall file reports required under this title with the Director of the Office of Government Ethics.

(c) Copies of the reports required to be filed under this title by the Postmaster General, the Deputy Postmaster General, the Governors of the Board of Governors of the United States Postal Service, designated agency officials, employees described in section 105(a)(2)(A) or (B), 106(a)(1)(A) or (B), or 107(a)(1)(A) or (b)(1)(A)(i), of title 3, United States Code, candidates for the office of President or Vice President and officers and employees in (and nominees to) offices or positions which require confirmation by the Senate or by both Houses of Congress other than those referred to in subsection (f) shall be transmitted to the Director of the Office of Government Ethics. The Director shall forward a copy of the report of each nominee to the congressional committee considering the nomination.

(d) Reports required to be filed under this title [sections 201 to 212 of this Act] by the Director shall be filed in the Office of Government Ethics and, immediately after being filed, shall be made available to the public in accordance with this title, except that any report filed by an independent counsel whose identity has not been disclosed by the division of the court under chapter 40 of title 28, and any report filed by any person appointed by that independent counsel under such chapter, shall not be made available to the public under this title.

(e) Each individual identified in section 201(c) shall file the reports required by this title with the Federal Elections Commission.

(f) Reports required of members of the uniformed services shall be filed with the Secretary concerned.

(g) The Office of Government Ethics shall develop and make available forms for reporting the information required by this title [sections 201 to 212 of this Act].

(Pub.L. 95–521, Title II, § 203, Oct. 26, 1978, 92 Stat. 1845; Pub.L. 96–19, § 9(k), June 13, 1979, 93 Stat. 43; Pub.L. 98–150, § 6, Nov. 11, 1983, 97 Stat. 960; Pub.L. 100–191, § 3(b)(1), (2)(A), Dec. 15, 1987, 101 Stat. 1306.)

§ 204. Failure to file or filing false reports

(a) The Attorney General may bring a civil action in any appropriate United States District Court against any individual who knowingly and willfully falsifies or who knowingly or willfully fails to file or report any information that such individual is required to report pursuant to section 202. The court in which such action is brought may assess against such individual a civil penalty in any amount, not to exceed $5,000.

(b) The head of each agency, each Secretary concerned, or the Director of the Office of Government Ethics, as the case may be, shall refer to the Attorney General the name of any individual he has reasonable cause to believe has willfully failed to file a report or has willfully falsified or willfully failed to file information required to be reported.

(c) The President, the Vice President, the Secretary concerned, the head of each agency, and the Office of Personnel Management, may take any appropriate personnel or other action in accordance with applicable law or regulation against any individual failing to file a report or falsifying or failing to report information required to be reported.

(Pub.L. 95–521, Title II, § 204, Oct. 26, 1978, 92 Stat. 1846; Pub.L. 96–19, § 9(f), June 13, 1979, 93 Stat. 43.)

§ 205. Custody of and public access to reports

(a) Except as provided in section 203(d) of this Act, each agency shall make each report filed with it under this title [sections 201 to 212 of this Act] available to the public in accordance with the provisions of subsection (b) of this section, together with a copy of the official position description of the Government office or position held by the reporting individual involved (if available) which shall be added to such report by such individual's designated agency official or by the Secretary concerned, except that this section does not require public availability of the report filed by any individual in the Central Intelligence Agency, the Defense Intelligence Agency, or the National Security Agency, or any individual engaged in intelligence activities in any agency of the United States, if the President finds that, due to the nature of the office or position occupied by such individual, public disclosure of such report would, by revealing the identity of the individual or other sensitive information, compromise the national interest of the United States. In addition, such individuals may be authorized, notwithstanding section 204(a), to file such additional reports as are necessary to protect their identity from public disclosure if the President first finds that such filing is necessary in the national interest.

(b)(1) Each agency shall, within fifteen days after any report is received by the agency under this title [sections 201 to 212 of this Act], permit inspection of such report by or furnish a copy of such report to any person requesting such inspection or copy. The agency may require a reasonable fee to be paid in any amount which is found necessary to recover the cost of reproduction or mailing of such report excluding any salary of any employee involved in such reproduction or mailing. A copy of such report may be furnished without charge or at a reduced charge if it is determined that waiver or reduction of the fee is in the public interest.

(2) Notwithstanding paragraph (1), a report may not be made available under this section to any person nor may any copy thereof be provided under this section to any person except upon a written application by such person stating—

(A) that person's name, occupation and address;

(B) the name and address of any other person or organization on whose behalf the inspection or copy is requested; and

(C) that such person is aware of the prohibitions on the obtaining or use of the report.

Any such application shall be made available to the public throughout the period during which the report is made available to the public.

(c)(1) It shall be unlawful for any person to obtain or use a report—

(A) for any unlawful purpose;

(B) for any commercial purpose, other than by news and communications media for dissemination to the general public;

(C) for determining or establishing the credit rating of any individual; or

(D) for use, directly or indirectly, in the solicitation of money for any political, charitable, or other purpose.

(2) The Attorney General may bring a civil action against any person who obtains or uses a report for any purpose prohibited in paragraph (1) of this subsection. The court in which such action is brought may assess against such person a penalty in any amount not to exceed $5,000. Such remedy shall be in addition to any other remedy available under statutory or common law.

(d) Any report filed with an agency, or transmitted to the Director of the Office of Government Ethics, pursuant to this title [sections 201 to 212 of this Act] shall be retained by such agency or the Office of Government Ethics, or both, as the case may be. Such report shall be made available to the public for a period of six years after receipt of the report. After such six-year period the report shall be destroyed unless needed in an ongoing investigation, except that in the case of an individual who filed the report pursuant to section 201(b) and was not subsequently confirmed by the Senate, or who filed the report pursuant to section 201(c) and was not subsequently elected, such reports shall be destroyed one year after the individual either is no longer under consideration by the Senate or is no longer a candidate for nomination or election to the Office of President or Vice President unless needed in an ongoing investigation.

(Pub.L. 95–521, Title II, § 205, Oct. 26, 1978, 92 Stat. 1846; Pub.L. 96–19, §§ 8(b), 9(*l*), June 13, 1979, 93 Stat. 41, 43; Pub.L. 100–191, § 3(b)(2)(B), Dec. 15, 1987, 101 Stat. 1307.)

§ 206. Review of reports

(a) Each designated agency official or Secretary concerned shall make provisions to ensure that each report filed with him under this title [sections 201 to 212 of this Act] is reviewed within sixty days after the date of such filing, except that the Director of the Office of Government Ethics shall review only those reports transmitted to him under this title within sixty days after the date of transmittal.

(b)(1) If after reviewing any report under subsection (a), the Director of the Office of Government Ethics, Secretary concerned, or designated agency official, as the case may be, is of the opinion that on the basis of information contained in such report the individual submitting such report is in compliance with applicable laws and regulations, he shall state such opinion on the report, and shall sign such report.

(2) If the Director of the Office of Government Ethics, Secretary concerned, or designated agency official, after reviewing any report under subsection (a)—

(A) believes additional information is required to be submitted, he shall notify the individual submitting such report what additional information is required and the time by which it must be submitted, or

(B) is of the opinion, on the basis of information submitted, that the individual is not in compliance with applicable laws and regulations, he shall notify the individual, afford him a reasonable opportunity for a written or oral response, and after consideration of such response, reach an opinion as to whether or not, on the basis of information submitted, the individual is in compliance with such laws and regulations.

(3) If the Director of the Office of Government Ethics, Secretary concerned, or designated agency official reaches an opinion under paragraph (2)(B) that an individual is not in compliance with applicable laws and regulations, he shall notify the individual of that opinion and, after an opportunity for personal consultation (if practicable), determine and notify the individual of which steps, if any, would in his opinion be appropriate for assuring compliance with such laws and regulations and the date by which such steps should be taken. Such steps may include, as appropriate—

(A) divestiture,

(B) restitution,

(C) the establishment of a blind trust,

(D) request for an exemption under section 208(b) of title 18, United States Code, or

(E) voluntary request for transfer, reassignment, limitation of duties, or resignation.

The use of any such steps shall be in accordance with such regulations as the Director of the Office of Government Ethics or a Secretary concerned, as the case may be, may prescribe.

(4) If steps for assuring compliance with applicable laws and regulations are not taken by the date set under paragraph (3) by an individual in a position (other than in the uniformed services), appointment to which requires the advice and consent of the Senate, the matter shall be referred to the President for appropriate action.

(5) If steps for assuring compliance with applicable laws and regulations are not taken by the date set under paragraph (3) by a member of the uniformed services, the Secretary concerned shall take appropriate action.

(6) If steps for assuring compliance with applicable laws and regulations are not taken by the date set under paragraph (3) by any other officer or employee the matter shall be referred to the head of the appropriate agency for appropriate action; except that in the case of the Postmaster General or Deputy Postmaster General, the Director of the Office of Government Ethics shall recommend to the Governors of the Board of Governors of the United States Postal Service the action to be taken.

(7) For purposes of assisting employees in avoiding situations in which they would not be in compliance with applicable laws and regulations, each Secretary concerned and designated agency official (including the President in the case of the individuals employed in the Executive Office of the President) shall maintain a list of those circumstances or situations which have resulted or may result in noncompliance with such laws or regulations. Such list shall be periodically published, and shall be furnished to those individuals employed within the agency who are required to file reports under this title [sections 201 to 212 of this Act]. The absence of any situation or circumstance from such a list shall not be construed as an indication that an individual in such circumstance or situation would be in compliance with such laws or regulations.

(8) The preceding provisions of this subsection shall not apply in the case of the President or Vice President, or a candidate or nominee for such office.

(Pub.L. 95–521, Title II, § 206, Oct. 26, 1978, 92 Stat. 1847; Pub.L. 96–19, § 9(m), June 13, 1979, 93 Stat. 43.)

§ 207. Confidential reports and other additional requirements

(a)(1) The President may require officers and employees in the executive branch (including the United States Postal Service, the Postal Rate Commission, members of the uniformed services, and special Government employees as defined in section 202 of title 18, United States Code) to file a confidential financial disclosure report, in such form as the President may prescribe. The information required to be reported under this subsection by the officers and employees of any department or agency shall be set forth in regulations prescribed by the President, and may be less extensive than otherwise required by this title [sections 201 to 212 of this Act], or more extensive when determined by the President to be necessary and appropriate in light of sections 202 through 209 of title 18, United States Code, regulations promulgated thereunder, or the authorized activities of any such department or agency. Any individual required to file a report pursuant to section 201 shall not be required to file a confidential report pursuant to this subsection, except with respect to information which is more extensive than information otherwise required by this title [sections 201 to 212 of this Act]. Subsections (a), (b), and (d) of section 205 shall not apply with respect to any such report.

(2) Any information required to be provided by an individual under this subsection shall be confidential and shall not be disclosed to the public.

(b) The Director of the Office of Government Ethics may by rule require disclosure, in the reports filed pursuant to subsections (a) and (c) of section 202, of gifts received by a dependent child of a reporting individual if the information required to be disclosed does not exceed that which must be reported by a spouse of a reporting individual under this title [sections 201 to 212 of this Act].

(c) The provisions of this title [sections 201 to 212 of this Act] requiring the reporting of information shall supersede any general requirement under any other provision of law or regulation with respect to the reporting of information required for purposes of preventing conflicts of interest or apparent conflicts of interest. Such provisions of this title shall not supersede the requirements of section 7342 of title 5, United States Code.

(d) Nothing in this Act requiring reporting of information shall be deemed to authorize the receipt of income, gifts, or reimbursements; the holding of assets, liabilities, or positions; or the participation in transactions that are prohibited by law, Executive order, or regulation.

(Pub.L. 95–521, Title II, § 207, Oct. 26, 1978, 92 Stat. 1848; Pub.L. 96–19, § 9(n), June 13, 1979, 93 Stat. 43; Pub.L. 99–190, § 148(b), Dec. 19, 1985, 99 Stat. 1325.)

§ 208. Authority of Comptroller General

The Comptroller General shall have access to financial disclosure reports filed under this title [sections 201 to 212 of this Act] for the purposes of carrying out his statutory responsibilities.

(Pub.L. 95–521, Title II, § 208, Oct. 26, 1978, 92 Stat. 1849.)

§ 209. Definitions

For the purposes of this title [sections 201 to 212 of this Act], the term—

(1) "income" means all income from whatever source derived, including but not limited to the following items: compensation for services, including fees, commissions, and similar items; gross income derived from business (and net income if the individual elects to include it); gains derived from dealings in property; interest; rents; royalties; dividends; annuities; income from life insurance and endowment contracts; pensions; income from discharge of indebtedness; distributive share of partnership income; and income from an interest in an estate or trust;

(2) "relative" means an individual who is related to the reporting individual, as father, mother, son, daughter, brother, sister, uncle, aunt, great aunt, great uncle, first cousin, nephew, niece, husband, wife, grandfather, grandmother, grandson, granddaughter, father-in-law, mother-in-law, son-in-law, daughter-in-law, brother-in-law, sister-in-law, stepfather, stepmother, stepson, stepdaughter, stepbrother, stepsister, half brother, half sister, or who is the grandfather or grandmother of the spouse of the reporting individual, and shall be deemed to include the fiance or fiancee of the reporting individual;

(3) "gift" means a payment, advance, forbearance, rendering, or deposit of money, or any thing of value, unless consideration of equal or greater value is received by the donor, but does not include—

(A) bequest and other forms of inheritance;

(B) suitable mementos of a function honoring the reporting individual;

(C) food, lodging, transportation, and entertainment provided by a foreign government within a foreign country or by the United States Government;

(D) food and beverages consumed at banquets, receptions, or similar events; or

(E) communications to the offices of a reporting individual including subscriptions to newspapers and periodicals;

(4) "honoraria" has the meaning given such term in the Federal Election Campaign Act of 1971 [2 U.S.C. 431 et seq.].[2]

(5) "value" means a good faith estimate of the dollar value if the exact value is neither known nor easily obtainable by the reporting individual;

(6) "personal hospitality of any individual" means hospitality extended for a nonbusiness purpose by an individual, not a corporation or organization, at the personal residence of that individual or his family or on property or facilities owned by that individual or his family;

(7) "dependent child" means, when used with respect to any reporting individual, any individual who is a son, daughter, stepson, or stepdaughter and who—

(A) is unmarried and under age 21 and is living in the household of such reporting individual; or

(B) is a dependent of such reporting individual within the meaning of section 152 of the Internal Revenue Code of 1986 [26 U.S.C. 152];

(8) "reimbursement" means any payment or other thing of value received by the reporting individual, other than gifts, to cover travel-related expenses of such individual other than those which are—

(A) provided by the United States Government;

(B) required to be reported by the reporting individual under section 7342 of title 5, United States Code; or

(C) required to be reported under section 304 of the Federal Election Campaign Act of 1971 (2 U.S.C. 434);

(9) "Secretary concerned" has the meaning set forth in section 101(8) of title 10, United States Code, and, in addition, means—

(A) the Secretary of Commerce, with respect to matters concerning the National Oceanic and Atmospheric Administration; and

(B) the Secretary of Health and Human Services, with respect to matters concerning the Public Health Service;

(10) "designated agency official" means an officer or employee who is designated to administer the provisions of this title within an agency; and

(11) "executive branch" includes each Executive agency (as defined in section 105 of title 5, United States Code) and any other entity or administrative unit in the executive branch unless such agency, entity, or unit is specifically included in the coverage of title I or III of this Act.

(Pub.L. 95–521, Title II, § 209, Oct. 26, 1978, 92 Stat. 1849; Pub.L. 96–19, §§ 4(a), 9(d), (o), June 13, 1979, 93 Stat. 39, 42, 43; Pub.L. 96–88, title V, § 509, Oct. 17, 1979, 93 Stat. 695; Pub.L. 99–514, § 2, Oct. 22, 1986, 100 Stat. 2095.)

2 So in original. The period probably should be a semicolon.

§ 210. Outside earned income

Except where the employee's agency or department shall have more restrictive limitations on outside earned income, all employees covered by this title [sections 201 to 212 of this Act]—

(1) who are compensated at a pay grade in the General Schedule of grade GS–16 or above and who occupy nonjudicial full-time positions, appointments to which are required to be made by the President by and with the advice and consent of the Senate, or

(2) who are employees of the White House Office and are compensated at rates equivalent to level II of the Executive Schedule under section 5313 of title 5, United States Code,

may not have in any calendar year outside earned income attributable to such calendar year which is in excess of 15 percent of their salary.

(Pub.L. 95–521, Title II, § 210, Oct. 26, 1978, 92 Stat. 1850; Pub.L. 98–150, § 7, Nov. 11, 1983, 97 Stat. 961.)

§ 211. Notice of actions taken to comply with ethics agreements

(a) In any case in which an individual agrees with that individual's designated agency official, the Office of Government Ethics, or a Senate confirmation committee to take any action to comply with this Act or any other law or regulation governing conflicts of interest of, or establishing standards of conduct applicable with respect to, officers or employees of the Government, that individual shall notify in writing the designated agency official, the Office of Government Ethics, or the appropriate committee of the Senate, as the case may be, of any action taken by the individual pursuant to that agreement. Such notification shall be made not later than the date specified in the agreement by which action by the individual must be taken, or not later than three months after the date of the agreement, if no date for action is so specified.

(b) If an agreement described in subsection (a) requires that the individual recuse himself or herself from particular categories of agency or other official action, the individual shall reduce to writing those subjects regarding which the recusal agreement will apply and the process by which it will be determined whether the individual must recuse himself or herself in a specific instance. An individual shall be considered to have complied with the requirements of subsection (a) with respect to such recusal agreement if such individual files a copy of the document setting forth the information described in the preceding sentence with such individual's designated agency official, the Office of Government Ethics, or the appropriate committee of the Senate, as the case may be, within the time prescribed in the last sentence of subsection (a).

(Pub.L. 95–521, title II, § 211, as added Pub.L. 98–150, § 9(2), Nov. 11, 1983, 97 Stat. 961.)

§ 212. Effective date

The provisions made by this title [sections 201 to 212 of this Act] shall take effect on January 1, 1979, and the reports filed under section 201(d) on May 15, 1979, shall include information for calendar year 1978.

(Pub.L. 95–521, title II, § 212, formerly § 211, Oct. 26, 1978, 92 Stat. 1850, renumbered Pub.L. 98–150, § 9(1), Nov. 11, 1983, 97 Stat. 961.)

[TITLE III—REPEALED]

[§§ 301 to 309. Repealed. Pub.L. 101–194, Title II, § 201, Nov. 30, 1989, 103 Stat. 1724]

HISTORICAL AND STATUTORY NOTES

Sections 301 to 309 of Pub.L. 95–521, Title III, Oct. 26, 1978, 92 Stat. 1851, as amended Pub.L. 96–19, §§ 2(a)(3), (c)(3), 3(a)(3), (b), 4(c), 6, 7(a) to (c), (d)(2), (e), (f), 8(c), 9(c)(3), (d), (j), (p) to (r), June 13, 1979, 93 Stat. 37 to 43; Pub.L. 96–417, Title VI, § 601(9), Oct. 10, 1980, 94 Stat. 1744; Pub.L. 96–579, § 13(c), Dec. 23, 1980, 94 Stat. 3369; Pub.L. 97–164, Title I, § 163(a)(6), Apr. 2, 1982, 96 Stat. 49; Pub.L. 98–150, § 10, Nov. 11, 1983, 97 Stat. 962; Pub.L. 99–573, § 6, Oct. 28, 1986, 100 Stat. 3231; Pub.L. 101–237, Title VI, § 602(a)(1), Dec. 18, 1989, 103 Stat. 2094, related to judicial personnel financial disclosure requirements.

Effective Date of Repeal

Repeal effective Jan. 1, 1991, see section 204 of Pub.L. 101–194, as added Pub.L. 101–280, § 3(10)(B), May 4, 1990, 104 Stat. 157, set out as a Effective Date of 1989 Amendment note under section 101 of this Appendix.

See section 3(10)(C) and (D) of Pub.L. 101–280, May 4, 1990, 104 Stat. 157, set out as notes under section 101 of this Appendix, for provisions directing that the provisions of Title III of Pub.L. 95–521, as in effect prior to Nov. 30, 1989, are effective until Jan. 1, 1991, as if Pub.L. 101–194 had not been enacted, and that nothing in Title III of Pub.L. 101–194 shall be construed to prevent the prosecution of civil actions against individuals for violations of Title III of Pub.L. 95–521 before Jan. 1, 1991.

Prior Provisions

Prior to repeal, sections 301 to 309 of Pub.L. 95–521, Title III, Oct. 26, 1978, 92 Stat. 1851, read as follows:

§ 301. Persons required to file

(a) Within thirty days of assuming the position of a judicial employee, an individual shall file a report containing the information described in section 302(b).

(b) Within five days of the transmittal by the President to the Senate of the nomination of an individual to be a judicial officer, such individual shall file a report containing the information described in section 302(b). Nothing in this Act shall prevent any Congressional committee from requesting, as a condition of confirmation, any additional financial information from any Presidential nominee whose nomination has been referred to that committee.

(c) Any individual who is a judicial officer or employee during any calendar year and performs the duties of his position or office for a period in excess of sixty days in that calendar year shall file on or before May 15 of the succeeding year a report containing the information described in section 302(a).

(d) Any individual who occupies a position as a judicial officer or employee shall, on or before the thirtieth day after termination of employment in such position, file a report containing the information described in section 302(a) covering the preceding calendar year if the report required by subsection (c) of this subsection[1] has not been filed and covering the portion of the calendar year in which such termination occurs up to the date the individual left such office or position, unless such individual has accepted employment in another position as a judicial officer or employee.

(e) Reasonable extensions of time for filing any report may be granted under procedures prescribed by the Judicial Ethics Committee established pursuant to section 303(a) of this title (hereinafter in this title referred to as the "Committee"), but the total of such extensions shall not exceed ninety days.

(f) The provisions of subsections (a) and (d) of this section shall not apply to an individual who, as determined by the Judicial Ethics Committee, is not reasonably expected to perform the duties of his office or position for more than sixty days in a calendar year, except that if such individual performs the duties of his office or position for more than sixty days in a calendar year—

(1) the report required by subsection (a) of this section shall be filed within fifteen days of the sixtieth day, and

(2) the report required by subsection (d) of this section shall be filed as provided in such subsection.

(g) The Committee may grant a publicly available request for a waiver of any reporting requirement under this section for an individual who is expected to perform or has performed the duties of his office or position less than one hundred and thirty days in a calendar year but only if the Committee determines that—

(1) such individual is not a full-time employee of the Government,

(2) such individual is able to provide services specially needed by the Government,

(3) it is unlikely that the individual's outside employment or financial interests will create a conflict of interest, and

(4) public financial disclosure by such individual is not necessary in the circumstances.

(h) The provisions of this Act shall not apply to any judicial officer or employee of the Superior Court of the District of Columbia or the District of Columbia Court of Appeals or any other employee of the District of Columbia court system.

(Pub.L. 95–521, Title III, § 301, Oct. 26, 1978, 92 Stat. 1851; Pub.L. 96–19, §§ 2(a)(3), (c)(3), 9(p), June 13, 1979, 93 Stat. 37, 38, 43; Pub.L. 99–573, § 6(a), Oct. 28, 1986, 100 Stat. 3231.)

[1] So in original. Probably should be "section".

§ 302. Contents of reports

(a) Each report filed pursuant to section 301(c) shall include a full and complete statement with respect to the following:

(1)(A) The source, type, and amount or value of income (other than income referred to in subparagraph (B)) from any source (other than from current employment by the United States Government), and the source, date, and amount of honoraria from any source, received during the preceding calendar year, aggregating $100 or more in value.

(B) The source and type of income which consists of dividends, rent, interest, and capital gains received during the preceding calendar year which exceeds $100 in amount or value, and an indication of which of the following categories the amount or value of such item of income is within—

(i) not more than $1,000,

(ii) greater than $1,000 but not more than $2,500,

(iii) greater than $2,500 but not more than $5,000,

(iv) greater than $5,000 but not more than $15,000,

(v) greater than $15,000 but not more than $50,000,

(vi) greater than $50,000 but not more than $100,000, or

(vii) greater than $100,000.

(2)(A) The identity of the source and a brief description of any gifts of transportation, lodging, food, or entertainment aggregating $250 or more in value received from any source other than a relative of the reporting individual during the preceding calendar year, except that any food, lodging, or entertainment received as personal hospitality of any individual need not be reported, and any gift with a fair market value of $35 or less need not be aggregated for purposes of this subparagraph.

(B) The identity of the source, a brief description, and the value of all gifts other than transportation, lodging, food, or entertainment aggregating $100 or more in value received from any source other than a relative of the reporting individual during the preceding calendar year, except that any gift with a fair market value of $35 or less need not be aggregated for purposes of this subparagraph.

(C) The identity of the source and a brief description of reimbursements received from any source aggregating $250 or more in value and received during the preceding calendar year.

(D) In an unusual case, a gift need not be aggregated under subparagraph (A) or (B) if a publicly available request for a waiver is granted.

(3) The identity and category of value of any interest in property held during the preceding calendar year in a trade or business, or for investment or the production of income, which has a fair market value which exceeds $1,000 as of the close of the preceding calendar year, excluding any personal liability owed to the reporting individual by a relative or any deposits aggregating $5,000 or less in a personal savings account. For purposes of this paragraph, a personal savings account shall include any certificate of deposit or any other form of deposit in a bank, savings and loan association, credit union, or similar financial institution.

(4) The identity and category of value of the total liabilities owed to any creditor other than a relative which exceed $10,000 at any time during the preceding calendar year, excluding—

(A) any mortgage secured by real property which is a personal residence of the reporting individual or his spouse; and

(B) any loan secured by a personal motor vehicle, household furniture, or appliances, which loan does not exceed the purchase price of the item which secures it.

With respect to revolving charge accounts, only those with an outstanding liability which exceeds $10,000 as of the close of the preceding calendar year need be reported under this paragraph.

(5) Except as provided in this paragraph, a brief description, the date, and category of value of any purchase, sale, or exchange during the preceding calendar year which exceeds $1,000—

(A) in real property, other than property used solely as a personal residence of the reporting individual or his spouse; or

(B) in stocks, bonds, commodities futures, and other forms of securities.

Reporting is not required under this paragraph of any transactions solely by and between the reporting individual, his spouse, or dependent children.

(6) The identity of all positions held on or before the date of filing during the current calendar year as an officer, director, trustee, partner, proprietor, representative, employee, or consultant of any corporation, company, firm, partnership, or other business enterprise, any nonprofit organization, any labor organization, or any educational or other institution other than the United States. This paragraph shall not require the reporting of positions held in any religious, social, fraternal, or political entity and positions solely of an honorary nature.

(7) A description of the date, parties to, and terms of any agreement or arrangement with respect to (A) future employment; (B) a leave of absence during the period of the reporting individual's Government service; (C) continuation of payments by a former employer other than the United States Government; and (D) continuing participation in an employee welfare or benefit plan maintained by a former employer.

(b) Each report filed pursuant to subsections (a) and (b) of section 301 shall include a full and complete statement with respect to the information required by—

(1) paragraph (1) of subsection (a) of this section for the year of filing and the preceding calendar year,

(2) paragraphs (3) and (4) of subsection (a) of this section as of the date specified in the report but which is less than thirty-one days before the filing date, and

(3) paragraphs (6) and (7) of subsection (a) of this section as of the filing date but for periods described in such paragraphs.

(c) In the case of any individual described in section 301(d) of this title, any reference to the preceding calendar year shall be considered also to include that part of the calendar year of filing up to the date of the termination of employment.

(d)(1) The categories for reporting the amount or value of the items covered in paragraphs (3), (4), and (5) of subsection (a) of this section are as follows:

(A) not more than $5,000;

(B) greater than $5,000 but not more than $15,000;

(C) greater than $15,000 but not more than $50,000;

(D) greater than $50,000 but not more than $100,000;

(E) greater than $100,000 but not more than $250,000; and

(F) greater than $250,000.

(2) For the purposes of paragraph (3) of subsection (a) of this section if the current value of an interest in real property (or an interest in a real estate partnership) is not ascertainable without an appraisal, an individual may list (A) the date of purchase and the purchase price of the interest in the real property, or (B) the assessed value of the real property for tax purposes, adjusted to reflect the market value of the property used for the assessment if the assessed value is computed at less than 100 percent of such market value, but such individual shall include in his report a full and complete description of the method used to determine such assessed value, instead of specifying a category of value pursuant to paragraph (1) of this subsection. If the current value of any other item required to be reported under paragraph (3) of subsection (a) of this section is not ascertainable without an appraisal, such individual may list the book value of a corporation whose stock is not publicly traded, the net worth of a business partnership, the equity value of an individually owned business, or with respect to other holdings, any recognized indication of value, but such individual shall include in his report a full and complete description of the method used in determining such value. In lieu of any value referred to in the preceding sentence, an individual may list the assessed value of the item for tax purposes, adjusted to reflect the market value of the item used for the assessment if the assessed value is computed at less than 100 percent of such market value, but a full and complete description of the method used in determining such assessed value shall be included in the report.

(e)(1) Except as provided in the last sentence of this paragraph, each report required by subsection (a), (b), or (c) of this section shall also contain information listed in paragraphs (1) through (5) of subsection (a) of this section respecting the spouse or dependent child of the reporting individual as follows:

(A) The source of items of earned income earned by a spouse from any person which exceed $1,000 and, with respect to his spouse or dependent child, all information required to be reported in subsection (a)(1)(B) of this section with respect to income derived from any asset held by the spouse or dependent child and reported pursuant to paragraph (3). With respect to earned income, if the spouse is self-employed in business or a profession, only the nature of such business or profession need be reported.

(B) In the case of any gifts received by a spouse which are not received totally independent of the spouse's relationship to the reporting individual, the identity of the source and a brief description of gifts of transportation, lodging, food, or entertainment or the value of other gifts.

(C) In the case of any reimbursements received by a spouse which are not received totally independent of the spouse's relationship to the reporting individual, the identity of the source and a brief description of each such reimbursement.

(D) In the case of items described in paragraphs (3) through (5), all information required to be reported under these paragraphs other than items (i) which the reporting individual certifies represent the spouse's or dependent child's sole financial interest or responsibility and which the reporting individual has no knowledge of, (ii) which are not in any way, past or present, derived from the income, assets, or activities of the reporting individual, and (iii) from which the reporting individual neither derives, nor expects to derive, any financial or economic benefit.

Each report referred to in subsection (b) of this section shall, with respect to the spouse and dependent child of the reporting individual, only contain information listed in paragraphs (1), (3), and (4) of subsection (a) of this section, as specified in this paragraph.

(2) No report shall be required with respect to a spouse living separate and apart from the reporting individual with the intention of terminating the marriage or providing for permanent separation; or with respect to any income or obligations of an individual arising from the dissolution of his marriage or the permanent separation from his spouse.

(f)(1) Except as provided in paragraph (2), each reporting individual shall report the information required to be reported pursuant to subsections (a), (b), and (c) of this subsection [1] with respect to the holdings of and the income from a trust or other financial arrangement from which income is received by, or with respect to which a beneficial interest in principal or income is held by, such individual, his spouse, or any dependent child.

(2) A reporting individual other than a judicial officer of the United States need not report the holdings of or the source of income from any of the holdings of—

(A) any qualified blind trust (as defined in paragraph (3)); or

(B) a trust—

(i) which was not created directly by such individual, his spouse, or any dependent child, and

(ii) the holding or sources of income of which such individual, his spouse, and any dependent child have no knowledge of,

but such individual shall report the category of the amount of income received by him, his spouse, or any dependent child from the trust under subsection (a)(1)(B) of this section.

(3) For purposes of this subsection, the term "qualified blind trust" includes any trust in which a reporting individual, his spouse, or any dependent child has a beneficial interest in the principal or income, and which meets the following requirements:

(A) The trustee of the trust is a financial institution, an attorney, a certified public accountant, a broker, or an investment adviser, who (in the case of a financial institution or investment company, any officer or employee involved in the management or control of the trust who)—

(i) is independent of and unassociated with any interested party so that the trustee cannot be controlled or influenced in the administration of the trust by any interested party,

(ii) is not or has not been an employee of any interested party, or any organization affiliated with any interested party and is not a partner of, or involved in any joint venture or other investment with, any interested party, and

(iii) is not a relative of any interested party.

(B) Any asset transferred to the trust by an interested party is free of any restriction with respect to its transfer or sale unless such restriction is expressly approved by the supervising ethics office of the reporting individual.

(C) The trust instrument which establishes the trust provides that—

(i) except to the extent provided in subparagraph (B) of this paragraph, the trustee in the exercise of his authority and discretion to manage and control the assets of the trust shall not consult or notify any interested party;

(ii) the trust shall not contain any asset the holding of which by an interested party is prohibited by any law or regulation;

(iii) the trustee shall promptly notify the reporting individual and his supervising ethics office when the holdings of any particular asset transferred to the trust by any interested party are disposed of or when the value of such holding is less than $1,000;

(iv) the trust tax return shall be prepared by the trustee or his designee, and such return and any information relating thereto (other than the trust income summarized in appropriate categories necessary to complete an interested party's tax return), shall not be disclosed to any interested party;

(v) an interested party shall not receive any report on the holdings and sources of income of the trust, except a report at the end of each calendar quarter with respect to the total cash value of the interest of the interested party in the trust or the net income or loss of the trust or any reports necessary to enable the interested party to complete an individual tax return required by law or to provide the information required by subsection (a)(1)(B) of this section, but such report shall not identify any asset or holding;

(vi) except for communications which solely consist of requests for distributions of cash or other unspecified assets of the trust, there shall be no direct or indirect communication between the trustee and an interested party with respect to the trust unless such communication is in writing and unless it relates only (I) to the general financial interest and needs of the interested party (including, but not limited to, an interest in maximizing income or long-term capital gain), (II) to the notification of the trustee of a law or regulation subsequently applicable to the reporting individual which prohibits the interested party from holding an asset, which notification directs that the asset not be held by the trust, or (III) to directions to the trustee to sell all of an asset initially placed in the trust by an interested party which in the determination of the reporting individual creates a conflict of interest or the appearance thereof due to the subsequent assumption of duties by the reporting individual (but nothing herein shall require any such direction); and

(vii) the interested parties shall make no effort to obtain information with respect to the holdings of the trust, including obtaining a copy of any trust tax return filed or any information relating thereto except as otherwise provided in this subsection.

(D) The proposed trust instrument and the proposed trustee is approved by the reporting individual's supervising ethics office.

For purposes of this subsection "interested party" means a reporting individual, his spouse, and any dependent child if the reporting individual, his spouse, or dependent child has a beneficial interest in the principal or income of a qualified blind trust; "broker" has the meaning set forth in section 78c(a)(4) of title 15; "investment adviser" includes any investment adviser who, as determined under regulations prescribed by the supervising ethics office, is generally involved in his role as such an adviser in the management or control of trusts; and "supervising ethics office" means the Judicial Ethics Committee.

(4) An asset placed in a trust by an interested party shall be considered a financial interest of the reporting individual, for the purpose of section 208 of title 28,[2] and any other conflict of interest statutes or regulations of the Federal Government, until such time as the reporting individual is notified by the trustee that such asset has been disposed of, or has a value of less than $1,000.

(5)(A) The reporting individual shall, within thirty days after a qualified blind trust is approved by his supervising ethics office, file with such office a copy of—

(i) the executed trust instrument of such trust (other than those provisions which relate to the testamentary disposition of the trust assets), and

(ii) a list of the assets which were transferred to such trust, including the category of value of each asset as determined under subsection (d) of this section.

This subparagraph shall not apply with respect to a trust meeting the requirements for being considered a qualified blind trust under paragraph (7) of this subsection.

(B) The reporting individual shall, within thirty days of transferring an asset (other than cash) to a previously established qualified blind trust, notify his supervising ethics office of the identity of each such asset and the category of value of each asset as determined under subsection (d) of this section.

(C) Within thirty days of the dissolution of a qualified blind trust, a reporting individual shall—

(i) notify his supervising ethics office of such dissolution, and

(ii) file with such office a copy of a list of the assets of the trust at the time of such dissolution and the category of value under subsection (d) of this section of each such asset.

(D) Documents filed under subparagraphs (A), (B), and (C) of this paragraph and the lists provided by the trustee of assets placed in the trust by an interested party which have been sold shall be made available to the public in the same manner as a report is made available under section 305 and the provisions of that section shall apply with respect to such documents and lists.

(E) A copy of each written communication with respect to the trust under paragraph (3)(C)(vi) shall be filed by the person initiating the communication with the reporting individual's supervising ethics office within five days of the date of the communication.

(6)(A) A trustee of a qualified blind trust shall not knowingly or negligently (i) disclose any information to an interested party with respect to such trust that may not be disclosed under paragraph (3) of this subsection; (ii) acquire any holding the ownership of which is prohibited by the trust instrument; (iii) solicit advice from any interested party with respect to such trust, which solicitation is prohibited by paragraph (3) of this subsection or the trust agreement; or (vi)[3] fail to file any document required by this subsection.

(B) A reporting individual shall not knowingly or negligently (i) solicit or receive any information with respect to a qualified blind trust of which he is an interested party that may not be disclosed under paragraph (3)(C) of this subsection, or (ii) fail to file any document required by this subsection.

(C)(i) The Attorney General may bring a civil action in any appropriate United States District Court against any individual who knowingly and willfully violates the provisions of subparagraph (A) or (B) of this paragraph. The court in which such action is brought may assess against such individual a civil penalty in any amount not to exceed $5,000.

(ii) The Attorney General may bring a civil action in any appropriate United States District Court against any individual who negligently violates the provisions of subparagraph (A) or (B) of this paragraph. The court in which such action is brought may assess against such individual a civil penalty in any amount not to exceed $1,000.

(7) Any trust may be considered to be a qualified blind trust if—

(A) the trust instrument is amended to comply with the requirements of paragraph (3) or, in the case of a trust instrument which does not by its terms permit amendment, the trustee, the reporting individual, and any other interested party agree in writing that the trust shall be administered in accordance with the requirements of this subsection and the trustee of such trust meets the requirements of paragraph (3)(A); except that in the case of any interested party who is a dependent child, a parent or guardian of such child may execute the agreement referred to in this subparagraph;

(B) a copy of the trust instrument (except testamentary provisions) and a copy of the agreement referred to in subparagraph (A), and a list of the assets held by the trust at the time of approval by the supervising ethics office, including the category of value of each asset as determined under subsection (d) of this section, are filed with such office and made available to the public as provided under paragraph (5)(D) of this subsection; and

(C) the supervising ethics office determines that approval of the trust arrangement as a qualified blind trust is in the particular case appropriate to assure compliance with applicable laws and regulations.

(g) Political campaign funds, including campaign receipts and expenditures, need not be included in any report filed pursuant to this title.

(h) A report filed pursuant to subsection (c) or (d) of section 301 need not contain the information described in subparagraphs (A), (B), and (C) of subsection (a)(2) of this section with respect to gifts and reimbursements received in a period when the reporting individual was not an officer or employee of the Federal Government.

(Pub.L. 95–521, Title III, § 302, Oct. 26, 1978, 92 Stat. 851; Pub.L. 96–19, §§ 3(a)(3), (b), 6, 7(a) to (c), (d)(2), (e), (f), 9(c)(3), (j), (q), June 13, 1979, 93 Stat. 39, 40–43; Pub.L. 98–150, § 10, Nov. 11, 1983, 97 Stat. 962.)

[1] So in original. Probably should be "section".

[2] So in original. Probably should be "title 18,".

[3] So in original. Probably should be "(iv)".

§ 303. Filing of reports

(a) The Judicial Conference of the United States shall establish a Judicial Ethics Committee which shall be responsible for developing the forms for reporting the information required by this title and for receiving and making available, in accordance with the provisions of this title, the reports described in section 301.

(b) Each judicial officer and judicial employee shall file the report required by this title with the Committee and shall file a copy of such report as a public document with the clerk of the court on which he sits or serves.

(c) In the performance of its functions under this title, the Committee, with the approval of the Judicial Conference of the United States, shall—

(1) develop the necessary forms and promulgate such rules and regulations as may be necessary;

(2) monitor and investigate compliance with the requirements of this title;

(3) provide for the availability of reports as required by section 305;

(4) conduct, or cause to be conducted, the reviews required by section 306;

(5) cooperate with the Attorney General in enforcing the requirements of this title;

(6) submit to the Congress and the President recommendations for legislative revision of this title; and

(7) perform such other functions as may be assigned by the Judicial Conference of the United States.

(d) The Committee shall, within one hundred and twenty days after October 26, 1978, develop and, with the approval of the Judicial Conference of the United States, promulgate a regulation establishing a method or methods for readily determining, without the necessity for expert appraisal, the fair market value of assets required to be disclosed by this title.

(Pub.L. 95–521, Title III, § 303, Oct. 26, 1978, 92 Stat. 1858; Pub.L. 96–19, § 9(r), June 13, 1979, 93 Stat. 43.)

§ 304. Failure to file or falsifying reports

(a) The Attorney General may bring a civil action in any appropriate United States District Court against any individual who knowingly and willfully falsifies or who knowingly or willfully fails to file or report any information that such individual is required to report pursuant to section 302. The court in which such action is brought may assess against such individual a civil penalty in any amount not to exceed $5,000.

(b) The Committee shall refer to the Attorney General the name of any individual the Committee has reasonable cause to believe has willfully failed to file a report or has willfully falsified or failed to file information required to be reported.

(Pub.L. 95–521, Title III, § 304, Oct. 26, 1978, 92 Stat. 1858.)

§ 305. Custody of and public access to reports

(a) The Committee shall make each report filed with it under this title available to the public in accordance with subsection (b) of this section.

(b)(1) The Committee shall, within fifteen days after any report is received by the Committee under this title, permit inspection by or furnish a copy of such report to any person requesting such inspection or copy. The Committee may require the requesting person to pay a reasonable fee in any amount which is found necessary to recover the cost of reproduction or mailing of such report excluding any salary of any employee involved in such reproduction or mailing. A copy of such report may be furnished without charge or at a reduced charge if it is determined that waiver or reduction of the fee is in the public interest.

(2) Notwithstanding paragraph (1), a report may not be made available under this section to any person nor may any copy thereof be provided under this section to any person except upon a written application by such person stating—

(A) that person's name, occupation and address;

(B) the name and address of any other person or organization on whose behalf the inspection or copy is requested; and

(C) that such person is aware of the prohibitions on the obtaining or use of the report.

Any such application shall be made available to the public throughout the period during which the report is made available to the public.

(c)(1) It shall be unlawful for any person to obtain or use a report—

(A) for any unlawful purpose;

(B) for any commercial purpose other than by news and communications media for dissemination to the general public;

(C) for determining or establishing the credit rating of any individual; or

(D) for use, directly or indirectly, in the solicitation of money for any political, charitable, or other purpose.

(2) The Attorney General may bring a civil action against any person who obtains or uses a report for any purpose prohibited in paragraph (1). The court in which such action is brought may assess against such person a penalty in any amount not to exceed $5,000. Such remedy shall be in addition to any other remedy available under statutory or common law.

(d) Any report received by the Committee shall be held in its custody and be made available to the public for a period of six years after receipt of the report. After such six-year period the report shall be destroyed unless needed in an ongoing investigation, except that in the case of an individual who filed the report pursuant to section 301(b) and was not subsequently confirmed by the Senate, such reports shall be destroyed one year after the individual is no longer under consideration by the Senate unless needed in an ongoing investigation.

(Pub.L. 95–521, Title III, § 305, Oct. 26, 1978, 92 Stat. 1859; Pub.L. 96–19, § 8(c), June 13, 1979, 93 Stat. 41.)

§ 306. Compliance procedures

(a) The Committee shall establish procedures for the review of reports filed with it under this title to determine whether the reports are filed in a timely manner, are complete, and are in proper form. In the event a determination is made that a report is not so filed, the Committee shall so inform the reporting individual and direct him to take all necessary corrective action.

(b) Such procedures shall include provisions for conducting a review each year of financial statements filed in that year by judicial officers and employees to determine whether such statements reveal possible violations of applicable conflict of interest laws or regulations and recommending appropriate action to correct any conflict of interest or ethical problems revealed by such review.

(Pub.L. 95–521, Title III, § 306, Oct. 26, 1978, 92 Stat. 1859.)

§ 307. Additional requirements

(a) Nothing in this title shall be construed to prevent the Committee, with the approval of the Judicial Conference of the United States, from requiring officers or employees of the judicial branch not covered by this title to submit confidential financial statements.

(b) The Committee, with the approval of the Judicial Conference, may require disclosure, in the reports filed pursuant to subsections (a) and (c) of section 302, of gifts received by a dependent child of a reporting individual if the information required to be disclosed does not exceed that which must be reported by a spouse of a reporting individual under this title.

(c) Nothing in this Act requiring reporting of information shall be deemed to authorize the receipt of income, gifts, or reimbursements; the holding of assets, liabilities, or positions; or the participation in transactions that are prohibited by law or regulation.

(d) The provisions of this title requiring the reporting of information shall not supersede the requirements of section 7342 of title 5.

(Pub.L. 95–521, Title III, § 307, Oct. 26, 1978, 92 Stat. 1860.)

§ 308. Definitions

For the purposes of this title, the term—

(1) "income" means all income from whatever source derived, including but not limited to the following items: compensation for services, including fees, commissions, and similar items; gross income derived from business (and net income if the individual elects to include it); gains derived from dealings in property; interest; rents; royalties; dividends; annuities; income from life insurance and endowment contracts; pensions; income from discharge of indebtedness; distributive share of partnership income; and income from an interest in an estate or trust;

(2) "relative" means an individual who is related to the reporting individual, as father, mother, son, daughter, brother, sister, uncle, aunt, great aunt, great uncle, first cousin, nephew, niece, husband, wife, grandfather, grandmother, grandson, granddaughter, father-in-law, mother-in-law, son-in-law, daughter-in-law, brother-in-law, sister-in-law, stepfather, stepmother, stepson, stepdaughter, stepbrother, stepsister, half brother, half sister, or who is the grandfather or grandmother of the spouse of the reporting individual, and shall be deemed to include the fiance or fiancee of the reporting individual;

(3) "gift" means a payment, advance, forebearance, rendering, or deposit of money, or any thing of value, unless consideration of equal or greater value is received by the donor, but does not include—

(A) bequest and other forms of inheritance;

(B) suitable mementos of a function honoring the reporting individual;

(C) food, lodging, transportation, and entertainment provided by a foreign government within a foreign country or by the United States Government;

(D) food and beverages consumed at banquets, receptions, or similar events; or

(E) communications to the offices of a reporting individual including subscriptions to newspapers and periodicals;

(4) "honoraria" has the meaning given such term in the Federal Election Campaign Act of 1971 [2 U.S.C.A. § 431 et seq.].

(5) "value" means a good faith estimate of the dollar value if the exact value is neither known nor easily obtainable by the reporting individual;

(6) "personal hospitality of any individual" means hospitality extended for a nonbusiness purpose by an individual, not a corporation or organization, at the personal residence of that individual or his family or on property or facilities owned by that individual or his family;

(7) "dependent child" means, when used with respect to any reporting individual, any individual who is a son, daughter, stepson, or stepdaughter and who—

(A) is unmarried and under age 21 and is living in the household of such reporting individual; or

(B) is a dependent of such reporting individual within the meaning of section 152 of title 26;

(8) "reimbursement" means any payment or other thing of value received by the reporting individual, other than gifts, to cover travel-related expenses of such individual other than those which are—

(A) provided by the United States Government;

(B) required to be reported by the reporting individual under section 7342 of title 5; or

(C) required to be reported under section 434 of title 2;

(9) "judicial officer" means the Chief Justice of the United States, the Associate Justices of the Supreme Court, and the judges of the United States courts of appeals; United States district courts, including the district courts in the Canal Zone, Guam, and the Virgin Islands; Court of Claims; Court of Appeals for the Federal Circuit; Court of International Trade; Tax Court; United States Court of Military Appeals [now United States Court of Appeals for the Armed Forces]; United States Court of Veterans Appeals; and any court created by Act of Congress, the judges of which are entitled to hold office during good behavior; and

(10) "judicial employee" means any employee of the judicial branch of the Government, of the Tax Court, of the United States Court of Military Appeals [now United States Court of Appeals for the Armed Forces], or of the United States Court of Veterans Appeals who is not a judicial officer and who is authorized to perform adjudicatory functions with respect to proceedings in the judicial branch, or who receives compensation at a rate at or in excess of the minimum rate prescribed for grade 16 of the General Schedule under section 5332 of title 5.

(Pub.L. 95–521, Title III, § 308, Oct. 26, 1978, 92 Stat. 1860; Pub.L. 96–19, §§ 4(c), 9(d), June 13, 1979, 93 Stat. 40, 42; Pub.L. 96–417, title VI, § 601(9), Oct. 10, 1980, 94 Stat. 1744; Pub.L. 96–579, § 12(c), Dec. 23, 1980, 94 Stat. 3369; Pub.L. 97–164, title I, § 163(a)(6), Apr. 2, 1982, 96 Stat. 49; Pub.L. 99–514, § 2, Oct. 22, 1986, 100 Stat. 2095; Pub.L. 99–573, § 6(b), Oct. 28, 1986, 100 Stat. 3231; Pub.L. 101–237, title VI, § 602(a)(1), Dec. 18, 1989, 103 Stat. 2094.)

§ 309. Effective Date

This title shall take effect on January 1, 1979, and the reports filed under section 301(c) on May 15, 1979, shall include information for calendar year 1978.

(Pub.L. 95–521, Title III, § 309, Oct. 26, 1978, 92 Stat. 1861.)

Filing of Reports by Judges, Judicial Nominees, and Employees of United States Court of Veterans Appeals

Pub.L. 101–237, Title VI, § 602(a)(2), Dec. 18, 1989, 103 Stat. 2095, provided that: "Not later than 30 days after the date of the enactment of this Act [Dec. 18, 1989], each person who, on that date, is a judge of the United States Court of Veterans Appeals or a judicial employee of such court and each person who, before that date, has been nominated by the President to be a judge on such court shall file a report containing the information described in section 302(b) of the Ethics in Government Act of 1978 (28 U.S.C.App. 302(b)) [former section 302(b) of this Appendix]. Subsections (e), (f), and (g) of section 302 of such Act [former section 302(e), (f) and (g) of this Appendix] shall apply to the requirement in the preceding sentence."

FEDERAL CIVIL JUDICIAL PROCEDURE AND RULES INDEX

References are to United States Code Annotated unless otherwise noted.

Constitution of the United States (See text following Appendix.)

CITATION ABBREVIATIONS

FRCVP	**Federal Rules of Civil Procedure**
MDL	**Rules of Procedure of the Judicial Panel on Multidistrict Litigation**
HCR	**Rules Governing Section 2254 Cases (Habeas Corpus)**
MAS	**Rules Governing Section 2255 Proceedings (Motion Attacking Sentence)**
FRE	**Federal Rules of Evidence**
FRAP	**Federal Rules of Appellate Procedure**
SCR	**Rules of the Supreme Court of the United States**
EON	**Executive Order Number**
nt	**Note**

ABATEMENT AND REVIVAL
Appellate courts, errors, reversals, **28 § 2105**
Death, parties, United States, **28 § 2404**
United States, death, parties, **28 § 2404**

ABDUCTION
Kidnapping, generally, this index

ABOLITION
See specific index headings

ABSENCE AND ABSENTEES
Rules of Evidence, this index

ABSTENTION
Bankruptcy, this index

ABUSE
Sexual Abuse, generally, this index
Tort Claims Act, abuse of process, **28 § 2680**

ACCESS
See specific index headings

ACCIDENTS
Definitions, district courts, multiparty and multiforum, **28 § 1369**
Unavoidable accidents, United States, actions and proceedings, **28 § 2406**

ACCOMMODATIONS
See specific index headings

ACCOUNTABILITY
See specific index headings

ACCOUNTS AND ACCOUNTING
Audits and Auditors, generally, this index
Carriers, this index
Comptroller General, generally, this index
Federal Officers and Employees, this index
Government Accountability Office, generally, this index
Judicial Center, services, **28 § 628**
Justice Department, this index
Rules of Civil Procedure, this index

ACETIC ANHYDRIDE
Controlled Substances, generally, this index

ACETONE
Controlled Substances, generally, this index

ACETORPHINE
Controlled Substances, generally, this index

ACETYLDIHYDROCODEINE
Controlled Substances, generally, this index

ACETYLMETHADOL
Controlled Substances, generally, this index

ACIDS
Controlled Substances, generally, this index
DNA (Deoxyribonucleic Acid), generally, this index
Drugs and Medicine, generally, this index

ACKNOWLEDGMENTS
Clerks of courts, **28 § 953**
Judges or justices, **28 § 459**

ACTIONS AND PROCEEDINGS
Abatement and Revival, generally, this index
Administrative Law and Procedure, generally, this index
Admiralty, generally, this index
Aircraft, this index
Aliens, this index
Ambassadors, **28 § 1251**
Appeal and Review, generally, this index
Arbitration, generally, this index
Attachment, generally, this index
Attorney General, this index
Bankruptcy, this index
Bonds, this index
Civil justice reform, **28 § 519 nt, EON 12988**
Civil Rights, this index
Claims, generally, this index
Class Actions, generally, this index
Constitution of the United States, this index
Copyrights, this index
Corporations, this index
Correctional Institutions, this index
Counterclaim. Set-Off and Counterclaim, generally, this index
Covenants, **28 § 1874**
Customs Duties, this index
Damages, generally, this index
Declaratory Judgments and Decrees, generally, this index
Depositions, generally, this index
Derivative Actions, generally, this index
Detention, generally, this index
Dismissal and Nonsuit, generally, this index
District Courts, generally, this index
Dockets and Docketing, generally, this index
Eminent Domain, generally, this index
Equity, generally, this index
Evidence, generally, this index
Execution, generally, this index
Executive Departments, this index
Exports and Imports, this index
Federal Agencies, this index
Federal Debt Collection, this index
Federal Legal Council, **28 § 509 nt, EON 12146**
Federal Officers and Employees, this index
Foreign Countries, this index
Forma Pauperis, generally, this index
Government Accountability Office, this index

ACTIONS AND PROCEEDINGS
—Cont'd
Hawaii, this index
In Rem, generally, this index
Independent Counsel, generally, this index
Indian Lands and Reservations, this index
Indians, this index
Injunctions, generally, this index
Internal Revenue Service, this index
International Trade Commission, this index
Interpleader, generally, this index
Intervention, generally, this index
Judges or justices, disqualification, **28 § 455**
Judgments and Decrees, generally, this index
Judicial Panel On Multidistrict Litigation, generally, this index
Judicial review. Appeal and Review, generally, this index
Jurisdiction, generally, this index
Justice Department, this index
Limitation of Actions, generally, this index
Ministers of foreign states, **28 § 1251**
Money, this index
Monopolies and Combinations, this index
Motor Carriers, this index
Nonsuit. Dismissal and Nonsuit, generally, this index
Parties, generally, this index
Pending actions,
  Court of Federal Claims, this index
  District courts, multiparty and multiforum, **28 § 1369**
  Judicial Panel on Multidistrict Litigation, **28 § 1369**
  Real estate, registration, **28 § 1964**
  Reports, **28 § 522**
Place of arrest, civil action, **28 § 1693**
Postal Service, this index
Process, generally, this index
Quieting Title, generally, this index
Receivers and Receivership, generally, this index
Release, generally, this index
Remand, generally, this index
Removal of Cases or Causes, generally, this index
Rules of Civil Procedure, generally, this index
Rules of Evidence, this index
Seamen, this index
Searches and Seizures, generally, this index
Security, this index
Senate, this index
Set-Off and Counterclaim, generally, this index
States, this index
Stay of Proceedings, generally, this index
Summons, generally, this index
Surface Transportation Board, this index

ACTIONS AND PROCEEDINGS
—Cont'd
Survival of actions and proceedings. Abatement and Revival, generally, this index
Tax Liens, this index
Terrorists and Terrorism, this index
Torts, generally, this index
Torture, **28 § 1350 nt**
Trespass, generally, this index
Trial, generally, this index
Trusts and trustees, **28 § 959**
United States, this index
United States attorneys, **28 § 547**
Venue, generally, this index
War, this index
Witnesses, generally, this index
Writs, generally, this index

ACTS OF CONGRESS
Statutes, generally, this index

ADDRESSES
See specific index headings

ADJOURNMENT
See specific index headings

ADJUSTMENTS
See specific index headings

ADMINISTRATION
See specific index headings

ADMINISTRATION OF ESTATES
Executors and Administrators, generally, this index

ADMINISTRATIVE CONFERENCE OF UNITED STATES
Civil justice reform, **28 § 519 nt, EON 12988**

ADMINISTRATIVE EXPENSES
See specific index headings

ADMINISTRATIVE LAW AND PROCEDURE
Adjudications, civil justice reform, **28 § 519 nt, EON 12988**
Alternative dispute resolution,
Attorney General, **28 § 2672**
Civil justice, reforms, **28 § 519 nt, EON 12988**
Federal tort claims, **28 § 2672**
Torts, **28 § 2672**
Attorneys, fees, **28 § 2412**
Bias, administrative adjudications, civil justice reform, **28 § 519 nt, EON 12988**
Civil justice reform, **28 § 519 nt, EON 12988**
Costs, **28 § 2412**
Court, definitions, **28 § 2412**
Definitions, attorneys, fees, **28 § 2412**
Demand, definitions, **28 § 2412**
Disclosure, civil justice, reform, **28 § 519 nt, EON 12988**

ADMINISTRATIVE LAW AND PROCEDURE—Cont'd
Document search, guidelines, civil justice reform, **28 § 519 nt, EON 12988**
Education, this index
Excessive demands, attorneys, fees, **28 § 2412**
Fees, attorneys, **28 § 2412**
Final judgment, definitions, **28 § 2412**
Guidelines, civil justice reform, **28 § 519 nt, EON 12988**
Hearings, fees, **28 § 2412**
Interest, awards, **28 § 2412**
International Trade Court, this index
Legislation, civil justice reform, **28 § 519 nt, EON 12988**
Military Departments, this index
Notice, civil justice reform, **28 § 519 nt, EON 12988**
Parties, attorneys, fees, **28 § 2412**
Payment, fees, prevailing parties, **28 § 2412**
Position of the United States, definitions, **28 § 2412**
Prevailing parties, attorneys, fees, **28 § 2412**
Rules and regulations, civil justice reform, **28 § 519 nt, EON 12988**
Rules of Appellate Procedure, this index
Settlement, guidelines, civil justice reform, **28 § 519 nt, EON 12988**
United States, definitions, **28 § 2412**
Witnesses, fees, **28 § 2412**

ADMINISTRATIVE LAW JUDGES
Attorney General, **28 § 509**

ADMINISTRATIVE OFFICE OF UNITED STATES COURTS
Generally, **28 § 601 et seq.**
Actions and proceedings, expenses and expenditures, payment, **28 § 463**
Annuities, **28 §§ 376, 604, 611**
Appointments,
Director, **28 § 601**
Officers and employees, **28 § 602 nt**
Appropriations, Judiciary Information Technology Fund, **28 § 612**
Assistant Director, **28 § 601 nt**
Bankruptcy, this index
Circuit Executive, **28 § 332**
Civil service, **28 § 602**
Retirement and pensions, waiver, **28 §§ 376, 611**
Clerical court assistants, accounts and accounting, **28 § 604**
Clerks of Courts, generally, this index
Compensation and salaries,
Deputy Director, post
Director, post
Officers and employees, post
Computers, Judiciary Information Technology Fund, **28 § 612**
Contracts, Director, **28 § 604**
Court of Federal Claims, this index
Courts of appeals, facilities, **28 § 41 nt**

ADMINISTRATIVE OFFICE OF UNITED STATES COURTS—Cont'd
Definitions,
Director, **28 § 611**
Office of Federal Judicial Administration, **28 § 133**
Deputy Director,
Compensation and salaries, **28 § 603**
Powers and duties, **28 § 606**
Removal, **28 § 601**
Salary, **28 § 603**
Supervision, **28 § 601**
Director, **28 § 601 et seq.**
Accommodations, **28 §§ 462, 604**
Annuities, **28 §§ 376, 604, 611**
Appointments, **28 § 601**
Audits and auditors, **28 § 604**
Books and papers, **28 § 413**
Budget, **28 § 605**
Compensation and salaries, **28 § 602 et seq.**
Contracts, **28 § 604**
Definitions, **28 § 611**
Delegation of authority, **28 § 602**
Deputy Director, generally, ante
Disbursements, **28 § 604**
Jury, **28 § 1871**
District courts, reporters, **28 § 753**
Dockets and docketing, **28 § 604**
Equal employment opportunity, **28 § 463**
Expenses and expenditures, **28 § 604**
Fees, **28 § 1913 nt**
Fines, penalties and forfeitures, **28 § 604**
In forma pauperis, **28 § 1915**
Independent Counsel, **28 § 594**
Investigations, **28 § 526**
Judgments and decrees, interest, **28 § 1961**
Judicial Conference,
Judiciary Information Technology Fund, **28 § 612**
Supervision, **28 § 604**
Judicial Survivors Annuity Fund, **28 § 605**
Leave of absence, **28 § 603**
Librarians, compensation and salaries, **28 § 604**
Library assistants, courts of appeals, **28 § 713**
Long range management and business plans, **28 § 612**
Messengers, **28 § 714**
Notice,
Judges or justices, domicile and residence, **28 § 456**
United States magistrates, appointments, **28 § 631**
Office of Management and Budget, estimates, **28 § 605**
Personnel Management System, **28 § 602 nt**
Powers and duties, **28 § 604**
Probation officers, accommodations, **28 § 462**

ADMINISTRATIVE OFFICE OF UNITED STATES COURTS—Cont'd
Director—Cont'd
Recycling, **28 § 604**
Removal, **28 § 601**
Reports, **28 § 604**
Funds, **28 § 612**
Reprogramming, **28 § 612**
Restitution, **28 § 604**
Retirement and pensions, **28 §§ 376, 611**
Seal (official seals), **28 § 608**
Secretaries, compensation and salaries, **28 § 604**
Sentence and punishment, joint councils, **28 § 334**
Staff, **28 § 715**
Statistics, **28 § 604**
Stenographers, compensation fixed by, **28 § 604**
Supervision, **28 §§ 601, 604**
Supplies, **28 § 604**
Technical assistants, courts of appeals, **28 § 715**
Transportation, passenger carriers, **28 § 456**
Traveling expenses, **28 § 604**
United States magistrate judges, powers and duties, **28 §§ 604, 631 et seq.**
Vacancies in office, **28 § 606**
Waiver, Civil Service retirement, **28 §§ 376, 611**
Employees. Officers and employees, generally, post
Exchange, personal property, **28 § 604**
Expenses and expenditures, actions and proceedings, payment, **28 § 463**
Federal Public Defender Organizations, accommodations, **28 § 462**
Fees, Director, **28 § 1913 nt**
Habeas corpus, capital cases, reports, **28 § 2266**
Incentive pay or awards, **28 §§ 602 nt, 604**
Information, Judiciary Information Technology Fund, **28 § 612**
Judiciary Information Technology Fund, **28 § 612**
Jury,
Forms, qualification, **28 § 1869**
Selection, notice, **28 § 1863**
Librarians, compensation and salaries, **28 § 604**
Notice,
Domicile and residence, **28 § 456**
Jury, selection, **28 § 1863**
Office of Federal Judicial Administration, definitions, **28 § 133**
Officers and employees, **28 § 602**
Appointments, **28 § 602 nt**
Compensation and salaries,
Additional positions, **28 § 603**
Increases, **28 § 603 nt**
Personnel Management System, **28 § 602 nt**

ADMINISTRATIVE OFFICE OF UNITED STATES COURTS—Cont'd
Officers and employees—Cont'd
Grievances, **28 § 602 nt**
Incentive pay or awards, **28 §§ 602 nt, 604**
Personnel Management System, **28 § 602 nt**
Practice of law, **28 § 607**
Personnel Management System, **28 § 602 nt**
Pretrial services. Crimes and Offenses, this index
Public utilities, contracts, **28 § 604**
Reports,
Director, ante
Habeas corpus, capital cases, **28 § 2266**
Jury, selection, **28 § 1863**
Retirement and pensions. Civil service, ante
Rules and regulations,
Judges or justices, litigation, expenses and expenditures, payment, **28 § 463**
Publication, **28 § 604**
Traveling expenses, **28 § 604 nt**
Secretaries, compensation and salaries, **28 §§ 603 nt, 604**
Stenographers, compensation and salaries, **28 §§ 603 nt, 604**
Technology, Judiciary Information Technology Fund, **28 § 612**
Terminal equipment, contracts, **28 § 604**
Traveling expenses,
Director, **28 § 604**
Judges or justices, **28 § 456**
Jury, **28 § 1871**
Volunteers, **28 § 604**

ADMINISTRATORS
See specific index headings

ADMIRALTY
Appeal and review,
Docket fees, taxation as costs, **28 § 1923**
Interlocutory decisions, district courts, **28 § 1292**
Printing, briefs, taxation as costs, **28 § 1923**
Arrest,
Property, discharge, **28 § 2464**
Stay of proceedings, **28 § 2464**
Bonds (officers and fiduciaries), stay of proceedings, **28 § 2464**
Briefs, appeals, taxation of printing as costs, **28 § 1923**
Costs, **28 § 1925**
Docket fees, **28 § 1923**
U.S. marshal, **28 § 1921**
District courts, original jurisdiction, **28 § 1333**
Docket fees, taxation as costs, **28 § 1923**
Fines, penalties and forfeitures,
High seas, **28 § 2461**
Venue, **28 § 1395**

ADMIRALTY—Cont'd
International Trade Court, this index
Jurisdiction, district court, **28 § 1333**
Jury trial, **28 § 1873**
Libel (proceedings),
Forfeitures, **28 § 2461**
U.S. Marshals, fees, **28 § 1921**
Maritime lien, Foreign States, privileges and immunities, **28 § 1605**
Orders of court, process, stay of proceedings, **28 § 2464**
Printing, appellate briefs, costs, **28 § 1923**
Process, stay of proceedings, **28 § 2464**
Review. Appeal and review, generally, ante
Rules of Civil Procedure, this index
Sale of vessels, fees of U.S. Marshal, **28 § 1921**
Searches and seizures, **28 § 2461**
Secretary of Navy,
Forfeitures, **28 § 2461**
Jurisdiction, **28 § 1356**
Special bonds, stay of proceedings, **28 § 2464**
Stipulations, **28 § 2464**
Tort Claims Act, **28 § 2680**
United States Marshals, fees, **28 § 1921**
Venue, fines, penalties and forfeitures, **28 § 1395**
Warrants, stay of proceedings, **28 § 2464**

ADMISSIBILITY IN EVIDENCE
Evidence, generally, this index

ADMISSIONS
See specific index headings

ADR
Alternative Dispute Resolution, generally, this index

ADVANCES
Justice Department, **28 § 523**

ADVERSE POSSESSION
Quieting title, **28 § 2409a**

ADVISORY COMMITTEES
Courts of appeals, **28 § 2077**

AERONAUTICS AND SPACE
Aircraft, generally, this index

AFFIDAVITS
Attachment, Postal Service, **28 § 2711**
Costs, this index
Customs Duties, this index
District judges, bias or prejudice, **28 § 144**
Federal Agencies, this index
Federal Debt Collection, this index
Forma pauperis, **28 § 1915**
Habeas corpus, **28 § 2246**
International Trade Court, this index
Jury, summons, **28 § 1866**
Postal Service, attachment, **28 § 2711**
Removal of case, **28 § 1449**

AFFIDAVITS—Cont'd
Rules of Appellate Procedure, this index
Rules of Civil Procedure, this index

AFFILIATES
Bankruptcy, this index

AFFINITY
Relatives, generally, this index

AFFIRMATIONS
Oaths and Affirmations, generally, this index

AFFIRMATIVE DEFENSES
Rules of Civil Procedure, this index

AFRICA
Libya, generally, this index

AFRICAN AMERICANS
Black Persons, generally, this index

AGE
Court of Federal Claims, this index
International Trade Court, this index
Judges or Justices, this index
Rules of Civil Procedure, this index

AGED PERSONS
Crimes and offenses, guidelines, **28 § 994 nt**
Fraud, sentencing guidelines, **28 § 994 nt**
Long term care. Nursing Homes, generally, this index
Nursing Homes, generally, this index
Retirement and Pensions, generally, this index
Sentence and punishment, **28 § 994 nt**

AGENT FOR SERVICE OF PROCESS
Process, this index

AGENTS AND AGENCIES
Administrative Law and Procedure, generally, this index
Bill of costs, affidavit verifying, **28 § 1924**
Disbursing Officials, Clerks, and Agents, generally, this index
Executive Agencies, generally, this index
Federal Agencies, generally, this index
Judicial Agencies, generally, this index
Justice Department, this index
Patent infringement action, defendant not resident of district, service of process, on agent, **28 § 1694**
Rules of Civil Procedure, this index

AGREEMENTS
Contracts, generally, this index

AGRICULTURAL ASSOCIATIONS AND ORGANIZATIONS
Attorneys, fees, **28 § 2412**

AGRICULTURAL COOPERATIVE MARKETING
Attorneys, fees, **28 § 2412**

AGRICULTURAL CREDIT
Damages, Federal agencies, **28 § 2408**

AGRICULTURAL PRODUCTS
Correctional institutions, funds, **28 § 530C**
Secretary of Agriculture, generally, this index

AGRICULTURE
Secretary of Agriculture, generally, this index

AGRICULTURE DEPARTMENT
Community development, neighborhood revitalization plan, **28 § 509 nt**
Plant Variety Protection, generally, this index
Secretary of Agriculture, generally, this index

AGRICULTURE SECRETARY
Secretary of Agriculture, generally, this index

AIR CARRIERS
Aircraft, generally, this index

AIR FORCE
Cemeteries and dead bodies. National Cemeteries, generally, this index
Commissary stores. Armed Forces, this index
Justice. Military Justice Code, generally, this index
Military Justice Code, generally, this index
National Cemeteries, generally, this index
Reserves,
National Cemeteries, generally, this index
Retirement and pensions, United States magistrate judges, appointment, eligibility, **28 § 631**
United States magistrate judges, appointment, eligibility, **28 § 631**
Retirement and pensions,
Enlisted members, United States magistrate judges, **28 § 631**
United States magistrate judges, **28 § 631**
Tort Claims Act, **28 § 2680**
United States magistrate judges, retirees, eligibility, **28 § 631**

AIR FORCE DEPARTMENT
Attorney General, advice, **28 § 513**

AIR FORCE RESERVE
Reserves. Air Force, this index

AIR NATIONAL GUARD
Cemeteries and dead bodies. National Cemeteries, generally, this index
National Cemeteries, generally, this index

AIR SERVICE
Air Force, generally, this index

AIRCRAFT
Actions and proceedings,
Sabotage, **28 § 1605A**
Terrorists and terrorism, **28 § 1605A**
Damages,
Foreign countries, sabotage, **28 § 1605A**
Sabotage, **28 § 1605A**
Terrorists and terrorism, **28 § 1605A**
Definitions. Terrorists and terrorism, post
Drug Enforcement Administration, funds, **28 § 530C**
Federal Bureau of Investigation,
Funds, **28 § 530C**
Piracy, **28 § 538**
Foreign countries,
Damages, sabotage, **28 § 1605A**
Sabotage, damages, **28 § 1605A**
Immigration, this index
Justice Department, funds, **28 § 530C**
Privileges and immunities, terrorists and terrorism, **28 § 1605A**
Sabotage,
Actions and proceedings, **28 § 1605A**
Damages, **28 § 1605A**
Foreign countries, damages, **28 § 1605A**
Security. Terrorists and terrorism, generally, post
Terrorists and terrorism,
Actions and proceedings, **28 § 1605A**
Damages, **28 § 1605A**
Definitions, privileges and immunities, **28 § 1605A**
Privileges and immunities, **28 § 1605A**
United States attorneys, funds, **28 § 530C**
United States Marshals Service, funds, **28 § 530C**

AIRLINES
Aircraft, generally, this index

ALABAMA
Bankruptcy, judges or justices, appointments, **28 § 152**
District courts, **28 § 81**
Judges or justices, **28 § 133**
Judicial circuit, **28 § 41**
Judicial districts, **28 § 81**
Bankruptcy, **28 § 581 nt**
Numbers and numbering, **28 § 133**
United States trustees of judicial districts, appointment, **28 § 581**

ALASKA
Admission, Statehood, **28 § 373 nt**
Bankruptcy, judges or justices, appointments, **28 § 152**
Court of Appeals for Ninth Circuit, generally, this index
District courts, **28 § 81A**
Appeal and review, **28 § 81A nt**
Final judgments, **28 § 81A nt**
Location, **28 § 81A**
Pending cases, **28 § 81A nt**

ALASKA—Cont'd
District courts—Cont'd
Powers and duties, **28 § 81A nt, EON 10867**
Statehood, **28 § 81A nt**
Successors, state courts, **28 § 81A nt**
Term of office, judges or justices, **28 § 81A nt, EON 10867**
Termination, **28 § 81A nt, EON 10867**
Territorial district courts, transfer of cases or causes, **28 § 81A nt**
Transfer of cases or causes, **28 § 81A nt**
Districts. Judicial districts, generally, post
Indians,
Jurisdiction, **28 § 1360**
U.S. Court of Federal Claims, **28 § 1505**
Judges or justices, **28 § 133**
Retirement and pensions, **28 § 371 nt**
Statehood, **28 §§ 373 nt, 376 nt**
Term of office, **28 § 81A nt, EON 10867**
Judicial circuit, **28 § 41**
Judicial districts, **28 § 81A**
Bankruptcy, **28 § 581 nt**
Judges or justices, **28 § 133**
Jurisdiction, Indians, **28 § 1360**
Marshals, **28 § 81A nt, EON 10867**
President of the United States, this index
United States attorneys, **28 § 81A nt, EON 10867**
United States trustees, judicial districts, appointments, **28 § 581**

ALCOHOLIC BEVERAGES
Bureau of Alcohol, Tobacco, Firearms, and Explosives, generally, this index

ALCOHOLICS AND ALCOHOLISM
Common carriers, sentence and punishment, **28 § 994 nt**
Controlled Substances, generally, this index

ALIAS WARRANTS
Postal Service, attachment, **28 § 2710**

ALIEN ENEMIES
Enemies. Aliens, this index

ALIENS
Actions and proceedings,
Court of Federal Claims, **28 § 2502**
Removal of cases or causes, **28 § 1442**
Supreme Court, jurisdiction, **28 § 1251**
Torts, jurisdiction, **28 § 1350**
Torture, **28 § 1350 nt**
United States Court of Federal Claims, **28 § 2502**
Venue, **28 § 1391**
Bringing in aliens, sentence and punishment, **28 § 994 nt**
Combatants, enemy combatants, **28 § 2241**

ALIENS—Cont'd
Controlled substances, United States Sentencing Commission, guidelines, **28 § 994 nt**
Court of Federal Claims, this index
Crimes and offenses, detention. Immigration, this index
Detention. Immigration, this index
District courts, torts, **28 § 1350**
Enemies, combatants, detention, **28 § 2241**
Fences. Immigration, this index
Green card, permanent residence. Immigration, this index
Harboring, sentence and punishment, **28 § 994 nt**
Immigration and Naturalization Service, generally, this index
Income tax, refunds, **28 § 2502**
Lodging, funds, **28 § 530C**
Military Justice Code, detention, **28 § 2241**
Parole, witnesses, fees, **28 § 1821**
Passports, fraud, sentencing guidelines, **28 § 994 nt**
Permanent residence. Immigration, this index
Proceedings. Actions and proceedings, generally, ante
Real estate, fences, funds, **28 § 530C**
Sentence and punishment,
Bringing in and harboring aliens, guidelines, **28 § 994 nt**
Guidelines, sentencing, **28 § 994 nt**
Smuggling, sentence and punishment, **28 § 994 nt**
States, this index
Supreme Court, jurisdiction, State against aliens, **28 § 1251**
Terrorists and Terrorism, this index
Torts, **28 § 1350**
Torture, actions and proceedings, **28 § 1350 nt**
United States Court of Federal Claims, actions and proceedings, **28 § 2502**
United States Sentencing Commission, guidelines, **28 § 994 nt**
Venue, **28 § 1391**

ALLIANCES
Treaties, generally, this index

ALLOTMENTS
See specific index headings

ALLOWANCES
See specific index headings

ALLYLPRODINE
Controlled Substances, generally, this index

ALPHACETYLMATHADOL
Controlled Substances, generally, this index

ALPHAMEPRODINE
Controlled Substances, generally, this index

ALPHAMETHADOL
Controlled Substances, generally, this index

ALPHAPRODINE
Controlled Substances, generally, this index

ALTERATION OF INSTRUMENTS
Counterfeiting, generally, this index

ALTERATIONS
See specific index headings

ALTERNATIVE DISPUTE RESOLUTION
Generally, **28 § 651 et seq.**
Administration, **28 § 651**
Administrative Law and Procedure, this index
Confidential or privileged information, **28 § 652**
Consent, arbitration referrals, **28 § 654**
Damages, arbitration referrals, **28 § 654**
Definitions, **28 § 651**
Exemptions, **28 § 652**
Jurisdiction, **28 § 652**
Neutrals, **28 § 653**
Referrals, arbitration referrals, **28 § 654**

ALTERNATIVE WRITS
Power to issue, **28 § 1651**

AMATEUR SPORTS AND ATHLETIC ORGANIZATIONS
Attorneys, fees, prevailing parties, **28 § 2412**
Definitions, gambling, **28 § 3701**
Gambling, **28 § 3701 et seq.**

AMBASSADORS AND CONSULS
Foreign Diplomatic and Consular Officers, generally, this index

AMENDMENTS
See specific index headings

AMICUS CURIAE
See specific index headings

AMMUNITION
Correctional institutions, funds, **28 § 530C**
Drug Enforcement Administration, funds, **28 § 530C**
Federal Bureau of Investigation, funds, **28 § 530C**
Immigration and Naturalization Service, funds, **28 § 530C**
Justice Department, funds, **28 § 530C**
United States attorneys, funds, **28 § 530C**
United States Marshals Service, funds, **28 § 530C**

AMOUNT IN CONTROVERSY
District Courts, this index

AMPHETAMINES
Controlled Substances, generally, this index

ANALOGUES
Controlled Substances, generally, this index
Drugs and Medicine, generally, this index

ANALYSTS
See specific index headings

ANCESTRY
Discrimination, generally, this index

ANCIENT DOCUMENTS
Rules of Evidence, this index

ANILERIDINE
Controlled Substances, generally, this index

ANNUITIES
Administrative Office of United States Courts, **28 §§ 376, 604, 611**
Judges or Justices, this index
Judicial Center, director of, **28 §§ 376, 627**
Judicial Survivors Annuity Fund, generally, this index

ANNULMENT
See specific index headings

ANTHRANILIC ACID
Controlled Substances, generally, this index

ANTIDUMPING DUTIES
Customs Duties, this index
International Trade Court, this index

ANTITERRORISM
Terrorists and Terrorism, generally, this index

ANTITRUST LAWS
Monopolies and Combinations, generally, this index

APPEAL AND REVIEW
Admiralty, this index
Amendment, pleading, jurisdiction, **28 § 1653**
Annuities to survivors of justices and judges, **28 § 376**
Attorney General, this index
Bankruptcy, this index
Certificates and certification,
Appeal in good faith, in forma pauperis proceeding, **28 § 1915**
Attorney General, no appeal from judgment against U.S., **28 § 2414**
Congressional reference cases, **28 § 2509**
Court of Appeals for First Circuit, generally, this index

APPEAL AND REVIEW—Cont'd
Court of Appeals for Second Circuit, generally, this index
Court of Appeals for Third Circuit, generally, this index
Court of Appeals for Fourth Circuit, generally, this index
Court of Appeals for Fifth Circuit, generally, this index
Court of Appeals for Sixth Circuit, generally, this index
Court of Appeals for Seventh Circuit, generally, this index
Court of Appeals for Eighth Circuit, generally, this index
Court of Appeals for Ninth Circuit, generally, this index
Court of Appeals for Tenth Circuit, generally, this index
Court of Appeals for Eleventh Circuit, generally, this index
Court of Appeals for the District of Columbia, generally, this index
Court of Appeals for the Federal Circuit, generally, this index
Court of Federal Claims, this index
Courts of Appeals, generally, this index
Crimes and Offenses, this index
Customs Duties, this index
Declaratory judgments, **28 § 2201**
Disqualification, judges or justices, **28 § 455**
District Courts, this index
Docket fees, taxation as costs, **28 § 1923**
Exports and Imports, this index
Extension, time for appeal, **28 § 2107**
Fair Housing, this index
Federal Agencies, this index
Federal Maritime Commission, this index
Federal Officers and Employees, this index
Fees,
Docket fee, **28 § 1923**
Forma pauperis proceeding, **28 § 1915**
Seamen, **28 § 1916**
Forma Pauperis, this index
Habeas Corpus, this index
Harmless error, judgment, **28 § 2111**
Hawaii, this index
Independent Counsel, this index
Injunctions,
Direct appeal to Supreme Court from three-judge court decisions, **28 § 1253**
Interlocutory, orders of district courts to courts of appeals, **28 § 1292**
International Trade Court, this index
Judges or Justices, this index
Judicial Panel On Multidistrict Litigation, this index
Merit Systems Protection Board, this index
Modification of judgment, powers of Supreme Court, courts of appeals, **28 § 2106**

APPEAL AND REVIEW—Cont'd
Notice,
District courts, **28 § 1917**
Federal agency orders, **28 §§ 2344, 2349**
Plant Variety Protection, this index
Presidential and Executive Office Accountability, this index
Quieting title, **28 § 2409a**
Receivers and receivership, interlocutory orders, **28 § 1292**
Remand, generally, this index
Removal of cases or causes, state courts, **28 § 1447**
Reopening, **28 § 2107**
Rules of Appellate Procedure, generally, this index
Rules of Civil Procedure, this index
Seamen, this index
Secretary of Agriculture, this index
Supreme Court, this index
Surface Transportation Board, this index
Telecommunications, this index
Territorial courts, review of decisions by courts of appeals, **28 § 1294**
Terrorists and Terrorism, this index
Three judge court, **28 § 2284**
Time,
Court of appeals, **28 § 2107**
Supreme Court, **28 § 2101**
Transfer, to cure want of jurisdiction, appeals or petitions for review of administrative action, **28 § 1631**
United States, this index
United States Magistrate Judges, this index
United States Tax Court, this index
Vacating or setting aside, **28 § 2106**
Virgin Islands, this index
Want of jurisdiction, transfer to cure, **28 § 1631**

APPEARANCES
See specific index headings

APPELLATE PROCEDURE RULES
Rules of Appellate Procedure, generally, this index

APPENDICES
See specific index headings

APPLICATIONS
See specific index headings

APPOINTMENTS
See specific index headings

APPRAISAL AND APPRAISERS
Execution, goods, wares and merchandise, **28 § 2005**
Exports and imports, U.S. Court of International Trade, **28 § 1582**
Fees,
Goods, wares and merchandise, execution, **28 § 2005**
United States Marshals, **28 § 1921**
International Trade Court, this index

APPRAISAL AND APPRAISERS
—Cont'd
Real Estate, this index
Summons,
Goods, wares and merchandise, execution, **28 § 2005**
U.S. Marshals, fees, **28 § 1921**
United States Marshal, fees, **28 § 1921**

APPRAISERS
Appraisal and Appraisers, generally, this index

APPROPRIATIONS
Attorney General, this index
Civil Rights, this index
Court of Federal Claims, this index
Drugs and Medicine, this index
Federal Bureau of Investigation, this index
Hate crimes, statistics, **28 § 534 nt**
Institutes and joint councils on sentencing, **28 § 334**
Judgments against U.S., **28 § 2414**
Judicial Center, **28 § 628**
Judicial Officers, examination, **28 § 526**
Judicial Survivors Annuity Fund, authorization of, **28 § 376 nt**
Jury, this index
Justice Department, this index
National Crime Information Center Project 2000, **28 § 534 nt**

APPROPRIATIONS COMMITTEE (SENATE OR HOUSE OF REPRESENTATIVES)
Congressional Committees, this index

ARBITRATION
Arbitrators,
Certificates and certification, **28 § 655**
Compensation and salaries, **28 § 658**
Disqualification, **28 § 655**
Privileges and immunities, **28 § 655**
Referrals, **28 § 655**
Training, Federal Judicial Center, **28 § 620**
Attorney General, Federal tort claims, **28 § 2672**
Awards,
Referrals, **28 §§ 655, 657**
Sealing, **28 § 657**
Bankruptcy, this index
Certificates and certification,
Arbitrators, **28 § 655**
Foreign judgments, **28 § 1963**
Compensation and salaries, **28 § 658**
Disqualification, arbitrators, **28 § 655**
Dockets and docketing, new trial, **28 § 657**
Federal Judicial Center, training, **28 § 620**
Federal tort claims, **28 § 2672**
Hearings, referrals, **28 § 655**
Judgments and decrees, **28 § 657**
Neutrals, compensation and salaries, **28 § 658**

ARBITRATION—Cont'd
New trial, **28 § 657**
Oaths and affirmations, **28 § 655**
Powers and duties, arbitrators, **28 § 655**
Privileges and immunities, arbitrators, **28 § 655**
Process, awards, **28 § 657**
Production of books and papers, **28 § 656**
Referrals, **28 §§ 654, 655**
Registration, foreign judgments, **28 § 1963**
Rules of Civil Procedure, this index
Sealing, awards, **28 § 657**
Subpoenas, **28 § 656**
Time, new trial, **28 § 657**
Torts, **28 §§ 2672, 2677**
Training, Federal Judicial Center, **28 § 620**
Traveling expenses, **28 § 658**
Trial de novo, **28 § 657**
United States attorneys, **28 § 2672**

ARBITRATORS
Arbitration, this index

ARCHITECT OF THE CAPITOL
Supreme Court Buildings and Grounds, this index

ARGUMENTS
See specific index headings

ARIZONA
Bankruptcy, judges or justices, appointments, **28 § 152**
Court of Appeals for Ninth Circuit, generally, this index
District courts,
Additional, **28 § 133 nt**
Cities, held at, **28 § 82**
Judges, **28 § 133**
Places of holding, **28 § 82**
Judicial Circuit of U.S., **28 § 41**
Judicial districts, **28 § 82**
Bankruptcy, **28 § 581 nt**
Number of district judges, **28 § 133**
United States trustees of judicial districts, appointment, **28 § 581**

ARKANSAS
Bankruptcy, judges or justices, appointments, **28 § 152**
District courts,
Cities, **28 § 83**
Judges, **28 § 133**
Places of holding, **28 § 83**
Judicial Circuit of U.S., **28 § 41**
Judicial districts, **28 § 83**
Bankruptcy, **28 § 581 nt**
Number of district judges, **28 § 133**
United States trustees of judicial districts, appointment, **28 § 581**

ARMED FORCES
Air Force, generally, this index

ARMED FORCES—Cont'd
Appeal and review. Court of Appeals for the Armed Forces, generally, this index
Army, generally, this index
Cemeteries and dead bodies. National Cemeteries, generally, this index
Combat zones, Tort Claims Act, **28 § 2680**
Commissary stores,
Claims, contracts, **28 § 1346**
Contracts,
Claims, **28 § 1346**
Jurisdiction, **28 § 1491**
Jurisdiction, contracts, **28 § 1491**
Court of Appeals for the Armed Forces, generally, this index
Crimes and offenses,
Military Justice Code, generally, this index
State courts, removal, **28 § 1442a**
Departments. Military Departments, generally, this index
District court crier or bailiff, preference, **28 § 755**
Foreign Service, generally, this index
Judges or justices, survivors annuities, deposits, **28 § 376**
Jury, active service exemption, **28 § 1863**
Justice code. Military Justice Code, generally, this index
Marine Corps, generally, this index
Military Departments, generally, this index
Military Justice Code, generally, this index
National Cemeteries, generally, this index
National Guard, generally, this index
Navy, generally, this index
Negligence, wrongful acts, of members, claims against U.S., procedure, **28 § 2671 et seq.**
Newly democratic nations, retired members, **28 § 2671 et seq.**
Removal of cases, **28 § 1442a**
Reserves,
Air Force, this index
Army, this index
Marine Corps, this index
National Cemeteries, generally, this index
Navy, this index

ARMED SERVICES
Armed Forces, generally, this index

ARMY
Air Force, generally, this index
Ammunition, generally, this index
Cemeteries and dead bodies. National Cemeteries, generally, this index
Commissary stores. Armed Forces, this index
Explosives. Ammunition, generally, this index
Honorable discharges,
Bailiffs, **28 § 755**

ARMY—Cont'd
Honorable discharges—Cont'd
Court criers, **28 § 755**
Justice code. Military Justice Code, generally, this index
Marine Corps, generally, this index
Military Justice Code, generally, this index
Munitions. Ammunition, generally, this index
National Cemeteries, generally, this index
Reserves,
National Cemeteries, generally, this index
Retirement and pensions, United States magistrate judges, appointment, **28 § 631**
United States magistrate judges, appointment, eligibility, **28 § 631**
Retirement and pensions, United States Magistrate Judge, appointments, **28 § 631**
Supplies. Ammunition, generally, this index
Tort Claims Act, **28 § 2680**
United States magistrate judges, appointments, **28 § 631**

ARMY AND AIR FORCE EXCHANGE SERVICE
Commissary stores. Armed Forces, this index

ARMY DEPARTMENT
Attorney General, advice, **28 § 513**

ARMY NATIONAL GUARD
Cemeteries and dead bodies. National Cemeteries, generally, this index
National Cemeteries, generally, this index

ARMY RESERVE
Reserves. Army, this index

ARRAIGNMENT
District courts, records and recordation, **28 § 753**
Habeas corpus, **28 § 2247**

ARREST
Admiralty, this index
Fugitives from justice, task forces, **28 § 566 nt**
Rules of Civil Procedure, this index
Task forces, fugitives from justice, **28 § 566 nt**
United States Magistrate Judges, this index
United States Marshals Service, this index

ARSON
Bureau of Alcohol, Tobacco, Firearms, and Explosives, generally, this index

ARTICLES OF WAR
Military Justice Code, generally, this index

ARTILLERY
Ammunition, generally, this index

ASHEVILLE, NC
Court of Appeals for Fourth Circuit, generally, this index

ASSAULT AND BATTERY
Domestic Violence, generally, this index
Husband and wife. Domestic Violence, generally, this index
Tort Claims Act, exemptions, **28 § 2680**

ASSESSMENTS
Income Tax, this index

ASSETS
See specific index headings

ASSIGNEES AND ASSIGNORS
Assignments, generally, this index

ASSIGNMENTS
Congressional reference cases, **28 § 2509**
Copyrights, this index
Court of Federal Claims, this index
District Judges, this index
Judges or Justices, this index
Jury panels, **28 § 1866**
Public Defenders, generally, this index
Supreme Court, this index
United States magistrate judges, **28 § 636**

ASSISTANCE
See specific index headings

ASSISTANTS
See specific index headings

ASSOCIATE ATTORNEY GENERAL
Attorney General, this index

ASSOCIATIONS AND SOCIETIES
Attorneys, fees, prevailing parties, **28 § 2412**
Carriers, generally, this index
Federal agencies, intervention, **28 § 2348**
Interpleader, **28 § 1335**
Intervention, **28 § 2348**
Religious Organizations and Societies, generally, this index
Rules of Civil Procedure, this index
Surface Transportation Board, **28 § 2323**

AT-RISK YOUTH
Juvenile Delinquents and Dependents, generally, this index

ATFE
Bureau of Alcohol, Tobacco, Firearms, and Explosives, generally, this index

ATHLETICS
Amateur Sports and Athletic Organizations, generally, this index
Crimes and offenses, gambling, **28 § 3701 et seq.**
Gambling, this index

ATHLETICS—Cont'd
Injunctions, gambling, **28 § 3703**

ATOMIC ENERGY
Atomic Energy Commission, orders, **28 § 2341 et seq.**

ATOMIC ENERGY COMMISSION
Atomic Energy, this index

ATROPINE SULFATE
Controlled Substances, generally, this index

ATTACHMENT
Clerks of courts, postmasters and postal officers, **28 §§ 2711, 2712**
Coastal suits, **28 § 2710 et seq.**
Contempt, nonappearance, **28 § 2405**
Deposits, U.S. marshal, **28 § 1921**
Federal debt collection, **28 § 3102**
Fees, U.S. marshal, **28 § 1921**
Foreign countries, privileges and immunities, **28 § 1609 et seq.**
Foreign States, privileges and immunities, **28 § 1609 et seq.**
Justices and judges, survivors annuities, exemptions, **28 § 376**
Postal Service, this index
Privileges and immunities, terrorists and terrorism, waiver, **28 § 1610 nt, PD 2001–03**
Removal of cases or causes, **28 § 1450**
Rules of Civil Procedure, this index
Terrorists and terrorism, waiver, **28 § 1610 nt, PD 2001–03**
United States Marshal, fees, **28 § 1921**
Waiver, terrorists and terrorism, **28 § 1610 nt, PD 2001–03**

ATTACKING SENTENCE
Sentence and Punishment, this index

ATTENDANCE
See specific index headings

ATTESTATION
Possessions, records and recordation, **28 §§ 1738, 1739**
States, records and recordation, **28 §§ 1738, 1739**
Territories, records and recordation, **28 §§ 1738, 1739**

ATTORNEY FEES
Attorneys, this index

ATTORNEY GENERAL
Generally, **28 § 502 et seq.**
Absence and absentees, vacancies in office, **28 § 508**
Actions and proceedings,
Pending actions, notice, **28 § 509 nt, EON 12146**
Powers and duties, **28 § 519 nt, EON 12988**
Supervision, **28 § 519**
Administrative expenses, **28 § 524**

ATTORNEY GENERAL—Cont'd
Administrative law and procedure, enforcement, reports, **28 § 530D**
Administrative Office of United States Courts, cooperative agreements and arrangements, **28 § 581 nt**
Advice, **28 § 511 et seq.**
Annuities, compromise and settlement, brokers, **28 § 519 nt**
Appeal and review,
Appointment, **28 § 503 nt**
Orders, **28 §§ 2344, 2348**
Appointment, **28 § 503 et seq.**
Assistant Attorneys General, **28 §§ 506, 507**
Contests, **28 § 503 nt**
Deputy Attorney General, **28 § 504**
FBI, Director, **28 § 532**
Investigations, **28 § 533**
Records and recordation, **28 § 534**
Special attorney, **28 § 515**
Appropriations,
Deputy Attorney General for Combating Domestic Terrorism, **28 § 504**
Examinations and examiners, Judicial Officers, **28 § 526**
Judicial Officers, examinations and examiners, **28 § 526**
Argument, oral argument, **28 § 518**
Associate Attorney General,
Appointment, **28 § 504a**
Drugs and medicine, **28 § 509 nt**
Succession, **28 § 508**
Attachment, postmasters, **28 § 2711**
Automated legal research and information systems, **28 § 509 nt, EON 12146**
Bankruptcy, this index
Books and papers, **28 § 413**
Brokers, compromise and settlement, annuities, **28 § 519 nt**
Cases, oral argument, **28 § 518**
Certificates and certification,
Act of Congress, constitutionality, **28 § 2403**
Appeal and review, judgment against U.S., **28 § 2414**
Contract Disputes Act of 1978, **28 § 2414**
Foreign judgments, payment, **28 § 2414**
United States trustees, judicial districts, **28 § 581 nt**
Civil justice reform, **28 § 519 nt, EON 12988**
Clerks of court, investigations, official acts, **28 § 526**
Community Development, this index
Compensation and salaries,
Special Assistants, **28 § 515**
Special attorneys, **28 § 515**
Competitive service, **28 § 507**
Complaints, pre-filing requirements, civil justice reform, **28 § 519 nt, EON 12988**

ATTORNEY GENERAL—Cont'd
Compromise and settlement,
Brokers, annuities, **28 § 519 nt**
Reports, **28 § 530D**
United States, claims, **28 § 2414**
Conduct, **28 § 516**
Cases, **28 § 518**
Conflict of interest, **28 § 528**
Constitution of United States, appointment, **28 § 503 nt**
Continuance in office, **28 § 503 nt**
Corporate Fraud Task Force, **28 § 509 nt, EON 13271**
Correctional Institutions, this index
Counterterrorism Fund, **28 § 524 nt**
Court reporters, investigations, **28 § 526**
Crimes and offenses,
Actions and proceedings, **28 § 515**
Federal officers and employees, reports, **28 § 535**
Federally insured financial institutions, **28 § 509 nt**
Reports, Federal officers and employees, **28 § 535**
Statistics, **28 § 522**
Decisions. Opinions and decisions, generally, post
Delegation of authority, **28 § 510**
Department of Justice Assets Forfeiture Fund, **28 § 524**
Deputies,
Appointments, **28 § 504 et seq.**
Chief Financial Officer, Justice Department, **28 § 507**
Notarial fees, **28 § 524**
Succession, **28 § 508**
Director,
Administrative Office of U.S. Courts, reports, **28 § 604**
Federal Bureau of Investigation, appointments, **28 § 532**
Disability, vacancies in office, **28 § 508**
Disqualification, officers and employees, conflicts of interest, **28 § 528**
Distribution, opinions, **28 § 521**
District Courts, this index
Drug Enforcement Administration, undercover operations, **28 § 533 nt**
Drugs and medicine, powers and duties, **28 § 509 nt**
Enforcement, statutes, reports, **28 § 530D**
Environment, violations, **28 § 509 nt**
Espionage, **28 § 519 nt**
Examinations and examiners,
Official papers, **28 § 526**
Witnesses, **28 § 514**
Exchange, books and papers, **28 § 525**
Executive departments, pending claims, **28 § 514**
Extraordinary expenses, **28 § 1929**
Federal Agencies, this index
Federal Bureau of Investigation,
Counterterrorism, powers and duties, **28 § 531 nt**
Undercover operations, **28 § 533 nt**

ATTORNEY GENERAL—Cont'd
Federal Environmental and Natural Resource Laws, investigations, **28 § 509 nt**
Federal Legal Council, **28 § 509 nt, EON 12146**
Federally insured financial institutions, investigations, **28 § 509 nt**
Financial institutions, fraud task forces, **28 § 509 nt**
Fines, penalties and forfeitures,
Information, **28 § 524**
Title to property, **28 § 524**
Grand jury, **28 § 515**
Grants, reports, **28 § 529**
Guidelines,
Civil justice reform, **28 § 519 nt, EON 12988**
Law enforcement officers, felonious killings, **28 § 540**
Hate crimes, statistics, **28 § 534 nt**
Identification records, preservation, **28 § 534**
Independent Counsel, generally, this index
Injunctions, enforcement, reports, **28 § 530D**
Institutes on Sentencing, powers and duties, **28 § 334**
Interagency legal disputes, **28 § 509 nt, EON 12146**
Interception of wire, oral, or electronic communications, special prosecutors, **28 § 594**
Investigations,
Appointments, **28 § 533**
Government officers and employees, **28 § 535**
Law enforcement officers, felonious killings, **28 § 540**
Official acts, **28 § 526**
Pending claims, **28 § 514**
Protection, **28 § 533**
Serial killings, **28 § 540B**
United States trustees, **28 § 526**
Joint councils on sentencing, **28 § 334**
Judicial Center Board, **28 § 623**
Judicial Conference of the United States, reports, **28 § 331**
Jury selection procedures, **28 § 1867**
Law books, **28 § 525**
Law enforcement, training, overseas, **28 § 509 nt**
Military departments, advice, **28 § 513**
Murder, this index
Notice,
Federal agencies, orders, **28 § 2349**
Random jury selection plan, **28 § 1863**
Three judge court, States, **28 § 2284**
Oaths and affirmations, **28 § 515**
Opinions and decisions,
Distribution, **28 § 521**
Enforcement, reports, **28 § 530D**
Executive departments, **28 § 512**
President of the United States, **28 § 511**

ATTORNEY GENERAL—Cont'd
Opinions and decisions—Cont'd
Publication, **28 § 521**
Overseas law enforcement training, **28 § 509 nt**
Parimutuel betting, licenses and permits, **28 § 534 nt**
Periodicals, **28 § 525**
Powers and duties, **28 § 509 et seq.**
President of the United States,
Advice, **28 § 511**
Appointments, **28 § 503 et seq.**
Assistant Attorneys General, **28 §§ 506, 507**
Associate Attorney General, **28 § 504a**
Deputy Attorney General, **28 § 504**
Opinions, **28 § 511**
Probation officers, investigations, official acts, **28 § 526**
Protection, investigations, **28 § 533**
Public Contracts, this index
Public policy, statutes, enforcement, reports, **28 § 530D**
Publication, opinions, **28 § 521**
Questions of Law or Fact, this index
Reference books, **28 § 525**
Reform, civil litigation reform, **28 § 519 nt, EON 12988**
Reports,
Banking offenses, **28 § 522 nt**
Crimes and offenses, ante
Federal agencies, disputes, **28 § 509 nt, EON 12146**
Fines, penalties and forfeitures, **28 § 524**
Forfeited property transactions, **28 § 524**
Fraud, **28 § 522 nt**
Public Integrity Section, **28 § 529**
Searches and seizures, **28 § 524**
Statutes, enforcement, **28 § 530D**
Requisitions,
Advances, **28 § 523**
Partition, **28 § 2409**
Review. Appeal and review, generally, ante
Rules and regulations, conflicts of interest, **28 § 528**
Rules of Civil Procedure, this index
Sales, books and papers, **28 § 525**
Seal (official seal), **28 § 502**
Senior interagency group, financial institution fraud, **28 § 509 nt**
Serial killings, investigations and investigators, **28 § 540B**
Settlement. Compromise and settlement, generally, ante
Solicitor General, assistance, **28 § 505**
Special agents, **28 § 530**
Special Assistants, **28 §§ 515, 519**
Special prosecutor. Independent Counsel, generally, this index
Statements,
Facts, **28 § 520**
Pending causes, **28 § 522**
States, this index

ATTORNEY GENERAL—Cont'd
Statistics, hate crimes, **28 § 534 nt**
Statutes, enforcement, reports, **28 § 530D**
Supervision of litigation, **28 § 519**
Civil justice reform, **28 § 519 nt, EON 12988**
Supreme Court, this index
Surface Transportation Board, **28 § 2323**
Tax liens, **28 § 2410**
Terrorists and Terrorism, this index
Torts, **28 § 2672 et seq.**
Compromise and settlement, **28 §§ 2677, 2679**
Damages, **28 § 2675**
Defense, **28 § 2679**
Removal of cases or causes, **28 § 2679**
Transmission, petitions, **28 § 520**
Trusts and trustees, bankruptcy, investigations, official acts, **28 § 526**
Undercover operations, **28 § 533 nt**
Unemancipated persons, missing persons, information, **28 § 534**
United States,
Oral argument, **28 § 518**
Pending actions, **28 § 517**
United States Attorneys, generally, this index
United States Court of Appeals for the Federal Circuit, petitions, **28 § 520**
United States Marshals Service, this index
United States Sentencing Commission, **28 § 991**
Vacancies in office, **28 § 508**

ATTORNEYS
Administrative Office of U.S. Courts, practice of law, **28 § 607**
Admission to practice, fees, disposition, **28 § 1931 nt**
Agricultural cooperative marketing, **28 § 2412**
Appearance, **28 § 1654**
Assignments. Public Defenders, generally, this index
Attorney General, generally, this index
Bad faith. Fees, post
Bankruptcy, this index
Bill of costs, affidavit verifying, **28 § 1924**
Certificates and certification, bias or prejudice, district judges, **28 § 144**
Charities, this index
Civil justice reform, **28 § 519 nt, EON 12988**
Claims, this index
Class actions, **28 § 1711 et seq.**
Clerks of courts, practice of law, **28 § 955**
Colleges and Universities, this index
Compensation and salaries. Fees, generally, post
Convention on the Taking of Evidence Abroad in Civil or Commercial Matters, **28 § 1781 nt**
Copyrights, this index

ATTORNEYS—Cont'd
Corporations, this index
Correctional institutions, funds, **28 § 530C**
Costs, docket fees, taxation as costs, **28 § 1923**
Court of Appeals for Veterans Claims, this index
Court of Federal Claims, this index
District Courts, this index
Docket fees, taxation as costs, **28 § 1923**
Ethics, Justice Department, **28 § 530B**
Federal Agencies, this index
Federal Debt Collection, this index
Federal Legal Council, **28 § 509 nt, EON 12146**
Federal Officers and Employees, this index
Federal Public Defender. Public Defenders, generally, this index
Fees,
Administrative law and procedure, **28 § 2412**
Agricultural cooperative marketing, **28 § 2412**
Bad faith, district courts, **28 § 1927**
Class actions, **28 § 1712 et seq.**
Colleges and Universities, this index
Copyrights, this index
Federal Agencies, this index
Federal Officers and Employees, this index
Fines, penalties and forfeitures, claims, **28 § 2465**
Independent Counsel, **28 § 593**
Judges or justices, discipline, **28 § 372**
Jury, labor and employment, discharge, **28 § 1875**
Labor and Employment, this index
Parental Kidnapping Prevention Act, **28 § 1738A nt**
Presidential and Executive Office Accountability, appeal and review, **28 § 3905**
Prevailing parties, **28 § 2412**
Rules of Civil Procedure, this index
Safety, **28 § 2412**
Searches and seizures, claims, **28 § 2465**
Social security, **28 § 2412 nt**
Torts, Federal tort claims, **28 § 2678**
United States, this index
United States Court of Federal Claims, sanctions, **28 § 1927**
United States magistrate judges, **28 § 372**
Unreasonable lawsuits, **28 § 1927**
Vexatious lawsuits, **28 § 1927**
Fines, penalties and forfeitures, claims, **28 § 2465**
Forma pauperis proceedings, **28 § 1915**
Habeas Corpus, this index
Independent Counsel, generally, this index
International Trade Court, this index

ATTORNEYS—Cont'd
Judges or justices,
Disqualification, **28 § 455**
High misdemeanors, **28 § 454**
Judicial Conference of Circuit, **28 § 333**
Justice Department, ethics, **28 § 530B**
Labor and Employment, this index
Military Departments, this index
Money laundering, Special Counsel, **28 § 509 nt**
Presidential and Executive Office Accountability, fees, appeal and review, **28 § 3905**
Public Defenders, generally, this index
Review, orders, certain Federal agencies, representation, **28 § 2348**
Rules of Appellate Procedure, this index
Rules of Civil Procedure, this index
Safety, fees, **28 § 2412**
Salaries. Fees, generally, ante
Searches and seizures, claims, **28 § 2465**
Social Security, this index
Supreme Court, this index
Surface Transportation Board, this index
United States, this index
United States Attorneys, generally, this index
United States magistrate judges, practice of law, **28 § 632**
United States Marshals, practice of law, **28 § 568**
United States Tax Court, this index

AUCTIONS AND AUCTIONEERS
Sale of vessel by public auctioneer, commissions of U.S. marshal, **28 § 1921**

AUDITS AND AUDITORS
Administrative Office of U.S. Courts, **28 § 604**
Bankruptcy, this index
Comptroller General, generally, this index
Drug Enforcement Administration, undercover operations, **28 § 533 nt**
Federal Bureau of Investigation, undercover operations, **28 § 533 nt**
Government Accountability Office, generally, this index
Independent Counsel, **28 § 596**
Judicial Center, services provided for, **28 § 628**
Rules of Civil Procedure, this index

AUNTS AND UNCLES
Relatives, generally, this index

AUTHENTICATION
Acts of legislature, **28 § 1738**
Consular officers, **28 § 1740 et seq.**
Legislature, acts of legislature, **28 § 1738**
Patents, **28 § 1744 et seq.**
Rules of Evidence, this index
States, **28 §§ 1738, 1739**
Territories, **28 §§ 1738, 1739**
United States possessions, **28 §§ 1738, 1739**

AUTHORS
Copyrights, generally, this index

AUTOMATED DATA PROCESSING
Computers, generally, this index

AVIATION
Aircraft, generally, this index

AWARDS
Arbitration, this index
Incentive Pay or Awards, generally, this index

BACKGROUND CHECKS
Criminal Background Checks, generally, this index

BAIL
Bonds, fines, penalties and forfeitures, payment, **28 § 2044**
Fines, penalties and forfeitures, bonds, payment, **28 § 2044**
Motion for judgment, **28 § 1923**
Witnesses, **28 § 1826**

BAILIFFS
Appointment,
District courts, **28 § 755**
United States Court of Federal Claims, **28 § 795**
Appropriations, **28 § 524**
Courts of appeals, **28 § 714**
District courts, appointment, **28 § 755**
Jury, this index
United States Court of Federal Claims, **28 § 795**
United States Court of International Trade, **28 § 872**

BAKER ISLAND
Judicial District of Hawaii, **28 § 91**

BANKRUPTCY
Abstention,
Comity, **28 § 1334**
Reciprocity, **28 § 1334**
Actions and proceedings,
Alternative dispute resolution, **28 § 651 et seq.**
Core proceedings, **28 § 157**
Foreign countries, generally, post
Governmental units, **28 § 1452**
Joint proceedings, generally, post
Managers and management, **28 § 959**
Noncore proceedings, abstention, **28 § 157**
Original jurisdiction, **28 § 1334**
References, generally, post
Transfers, **28 nt prec § 1471**
Trusts and trustees, post
Adjustments,
Core proceedings, **28 § 157**
Individual debtors. Chapter 13 proceedings, generally, post
Administration, **28 § 604**
Transition, **28 § 151; 28 nt prec § 151**

BANKRUPTCY—Cont'd
Administrative Office of United States Courts,
Judges or justices,
Assistants, appointments, **28 § 156**
Official stations, recommendations, **28 § 152**
Notice, **28 § 1930 nt**
Returns, **28 § 156**
Studies, transition studies, **28 nt prec § 151**
United States trustees, information, **28 § 581 nt**
Affiliates, chapter 11 proceedings, venue, **28 § 1408**
Agriculture. Chapter 12 proceedings, generally, post
Allowances. Claims, post
Alternative dispute resolution, **28 § 651 et seq.**
Amendments, Bankruptcy Amendments and Federal Judgeship Act of 1984, **28 § 151 nt**
Ancillary cases. Foreign countries, generally, post
Appeal and review,
Bankruptcy appellate panels, generally, post
Claims, removal, **28 § 1452**
Direct appeals, **28 § 158**
Jurisdiction, **28 §§ 158, 1334**
Notice, filing, fees, **28 § 1930**
Orders of court, **28 § 157**
Taxation, declaratory judgments, **28 § 2201**
Venue, **28 § 1408**
Appellate panel. Bankruptcy appellate panels, generally, post
Appointments,
Temporary judges, **28 § 152 nt**
Trusts and trustees, post
United States trustees, post
Arbitration, reference, **28 § 654**
Assistants,
Judges or justices, appointments, **28 § 156**
United States trustees, post
Attorney General,
Appointments, United States trustees, **28 § 581 nt**
Audits and auditors, **28 § 586 nt**
Forms, **28 § 589b**
Attorneys, judges or justices, practice of law, **28 §§ 152 nt, 153**
Audits and auditors,
Attorney General, **28 § 586 nt**
Judicial Conference of the United States, **28 § 586 nt**
United States trustees, **28 § 586**
Bankruptcy Amendments and Federal Judgeship Act of 1984, **28 § 151 nt**
Bankruptcy appellate panels, **28 § 158**
Joint appellate panels, **28 § 158**
Judgments and decrees, transfers, **28 § 1334 nt**

BANKRUPTCY—Cont'd
Books and papers, United States trustees, **28 § 581 nt**
Buildings, **28 § 156**
Expenses and expenditures, **28 § 156**
Business and commerce,
Foreign countries, post
Taxation, payment, **28 § 960**
Certiorari, fees, receipts, **28 § 1930**
Changes, venue, **28 § 1412**
Chapter 7 proceedings,
Conversion, chapter 11 proceedings, **28 § 1930**
Fees, filing, **28 § 1930**
Filing, fees, **28 § 1930**
Panel, trusts and trustees, **28 § 586**
Supervision, **28 § 586**
United States trustees, post
Waiver, fees, filing, **28 § 1930**
Chapter 9 proceedings,
Filing, fees, payment, **28 § 1930**
Plans and specifications, core proceeding, **28 § 157**
Chapter 11 proceedings,
Declaratory judgments, taxation, **28 § 2201**
Foreign countries, venue, **28 § 1408**
Jurisdiction, **28 § 1334**
Managers and management, **28 § 959**
Powers and duties, United States trustees, **28 § 586**
United States trustees, post
Venue, **28 §§ 1408, 1409**
Chapter 12 proceedings,
Claims, allowances, **28 § 157**
Fees, filing, **28 § 1930**
Filing, fees, **28 § 1930**
United States trustees, post
Chapter 13 proceedings,
Conversion, reorganization, **28 § 1930**
Filing,
Fees, payment, **28 § 1930**
Payment, fees, **28 § 1930**
Plans and specifications, core proceedings, **28 § 157**
Trusts and trustees, standing trustees, compensation and salaries, **28 § 586**
United States trustees, post
Chapter 15 proceedings. Foreign countries, generally, post
Chief Judge. Judges or justices, post
Claims,
Allowances, core proceeding, **28 § 157**
Removal, **28 § 1452**
Trusts and trustees, post
Clerks of courts,
Appointments, **28 § 156**
Fees, **28 § 1930**
Fraud, notice, **28 § 586**
Statistics, **28 § 159**
Collection, fees, **28 § 1930 nt**
Comity, abstention, **28 § 1334**
Compensation and salaries,
Judges or justices, post
Retired judges, recall, **28 § 155**

BANKRUPTCY—Cont'd
Compensation and salaries—Cont'd
United States trustees, post
Computers,
Fees, records and recordation, **28 § 1930 nt**
Records and recordation, fees, **28 § 1930 nt**
Conferences. Judicial Conference of the United States, generally, post
Confirmation of plan, core proceedings, **28 § 157**
Conflict of interest. Judges or justices, post
Consent, arbitration, alternative dispute resolution, referrals, **28 § 654**
Conversion,
Chapter 7 proceedings, ante
Chapter 13 proceedings, ante
Core proceedings, **28 § 157**
Corporations,
Chapter 11 proceedings, generally, ante
Reorganization. Chapter 11 proceedings, generally, ante
Costs, dismissal and nonsuit, **28 § 1930**
Councils. Judicial Council, generally, post
Courts,
Emergencies, special sessions, **28 § 152**
Judges or justices, generally, post
Jurisdiction, generally, post
Location, **28 § 152**
Orders of court, generally, post
Courts of appeals,
Judges or justices, appointments, **28 § 152**
Jurisdiction, **28 § 158**
Credit (payment of indebtedness), core proceedings, orders of court, **28 § 157**
Crimes and offenses,
Reports, **28 § 581 nt**
United States trustees, reports, **28 § 581 nt**
Cross border cases. Foreign countries, generally, post
Damages. Taxation, post
Debtors in possession, actions and proceedings, **28 § 959**
Declaratory judgments and decrees, reorganization, taxation, **28 § 2201**
Deposits, interest, **28 § 589a**
Deputies, clerks, **28 § 156**
Direct appeals, **28 § 158**
Directors, Administrative Office of United States Courts, powers and duties, **28 § 604**
Discharge, core proceedings, objections and exceptions, **28 § 157**
Dismissal and nonsuit, costs, **28 § 1930**
Dispute resolution, **28 § 651 et seq.**
Disqualification, judges or justices, **28 § 455**
District of Columbia, judges or justices, appointments, **28 § 152**

BANKRUPTCY—Cont'd
Dockets and docketing, custodians, **28 § 156**
Domicile and residence, chapter 11 proceedings, **28 § 1408**
Emergencies, courts, special sessions, **28 § 152**
Equity security holders, core proceedings, **28 § 157**
Exclusive jurisdiction, **28 § 1334**
Exemptions,
Fees, **28 § 1930 nt**
Joint proceedings, post
Support, **28 § 1930 nt**
Wrongful death, **28 § 157**
Expenses and expenditures, **28 § 604**
Buildings, **28 § 156**
United States trustees, **28 §§ 586, 588**
Farmers. Chapter 12 proceedings, generally, ante
Fees, **28 § 1930**
Administrators, **28 § 1930**
Automatic stay, motions, **28 § 1930 nt**
Chapter 7 proceedings, ante
Child support, **28 § 1930 nt**
Collection, **28 § 1930 nt**
Computers, records and recordation, **28 § 1930 nt**
Exemptions, **28 § 1930 nt**
Filing, post
Judicial Conference of the United States, **28 § 1930**
Reports, **28 § 1930 nt**
Schedules, **28 § 1930 nt**
Treasury of United States, post
United States trustees, post
Fiduciaries. Trusts and trustees, generally, post
Filing,
Chapter 7 proceedings, ante
Chapter 9 proceedings, ante
Chapter 12 proceedings, ante
Chapter 13 proceedings, ante
Fees, **28 § 1930**
Disposition, **28 § 1931 nt**
Foreign countries, post
Financial statements and reports, forms, **28 § 589b**
Fish and game,
Commercial fishing. Chapter 12 proceedings, generally, ante
Family fishermen. Chapter 12 proceedings, generally, ante
Foreign countries,
Business and commerce, venue, **28 § 1410**
Chapter 11 proceedings, venue, **28 § 1408**
Core proceedings, **28 § 157**
Fees, filing, **28 § 1930**
Filing, fees, **28 § 1930**
Pending actions, venue, **28 § 1410**
United States trustees, **28 § 586**
Venue, **28 § 1410**
Chapter 11 proceedings, **28 § 1408**

BANKRUPTCY—Cont'd
Forms,
Attorney General, **28 § 589b**
Financial statements and reports, **28 § 589b**
Motions, post
Reports, **28 § 589b**
Small businesses, **28 § 2073 nt**
Statistics, **28 § 159**
Fraud,
Clerks of courts, notice, **28 § 586**
United States trustees, reports, **28 § 586**
Fraudulent conveyances, judges or justices, **28 § 157**
Handicapped persons, judges or justices, **28 § 152**
Hearings, **28 § 157**
Judges or justices, removal, **28 § 152**
Panels, bankruptcy appellate panels, **28 § 158**
Individual debtors. Chapter 13 proceedings, generally, ante
Information, **28 § 581 nt**
Installments,
Joint proceedings, **28 § 1930**
Voluntary proceedings, **28 § 1930**
Interest, deposits, **28 § 589a**
Interlocutory orders, **28 § 158**
Internet, reports, **28 § 589b**
Interpreters, **28 § 1827**
Interstate commerce, **28 § 157**
Joint appellate panels, **28 § 158**
Joint proceedings,
Exemptions,
Fees, filing, **28 § 1930**
Filing, fees, **28 § 1930**
Fees, filing, exemptions, **28 § 1930**
Filing, fees, exemptions, **28 § 1930**
Judges or justices, **28 § 151 et seq.**
Adjacent districts, **28 § 152**
Annual leave, **28 § 153**
Appeal and review, **28 § 158**
Appellate panels, **28 § 158; 28 nt prec § 151**
Appointments, **28 § 152**
Bankruptcy Amendments and Federal Judgeship Act of 1984, **28 § 151 nt**
Chief Judge, **28 § 154**
Court of appeals, **28 § 152**
Compensation and salaries, **28 § 153**
Retired judges, recall, **28 §§ 155, 375**
Conflict of interest, **28 §§ 152 nt, 153**
Core proceedings, **28 § 157**
Definitions, **28 § 375**
Discipline, **28 § 372**
Discrimination, nominees, **28 § 44 nt**
Disqualification, **28 § 455**
Expenses and expenditures, **28 § 604**
Fraudulent conveyances, **28 § 157**
Incumbents, appointments, **28 § 152 nt**
Judicial Center, board, membership, **28 § 621**

BANKRUPTCY—Cont'd
Judges or justices—Cont'd
Judicial Conference of the Circuit, **28 § 333**
Law clerks, **28 § 156**
Leave of absence, **28 §§ 152 nt, 153**
Mental health, **28 § 152**
Nominees, **28 § 44 nt**
Oaths and affirmations, **28 § 153**
Official duty station, **28 § 152**
Part time judges, **28 § 152 nt**
Practice of law, **28 § 153**
Part time judges, **28 § 152 nt**
President of the United States, nominees, **28 § 44 nt**
Puerto Rico, appointments, **28 § 152**
Recall, **28 §§ 155, 375, 377**
References, generally, post
Removal from office, **28 § 372**
Grounds, **28 § 152**
Retirement and pensions, **28 § 376 et seq.**
Recall, **28 § 155**
Secretaries, **28 § 156**
Sick leave, **28 § 153**
Staff, **28 § 156**
Temporary judges, **28 § 152 nt**
Terms of office, **28 § 152; 28 nt prec § 151**
Extension of time, **28 § 151 nt**
Territories, **28 § 152**
Transfers, **28 § 155**
Vacancies in office, **28 § 152**
Judgments and decrees, **28 § 157**
Declaratory judgments and decrees, reorganization, taxation, **28 § 2201**
Judicial Conference of the Circuit, **28 § 333**
Judicial Conference of the United States, **28 § 152 et seq.**
Assessments, reports, **28 § 152**
Audits and auditors, **28 § 586 nt**
Compensation and salaries, retired judges, **28 § 155**
Fees, **28 § 1930**
Filing, fees, **28 § 1930**
Merger and consolidation, **28 § 156**
Payment, **28 § 153**
Reports,
Assessments, **28 § 152**
Fees, **28 § 1930 nt**
Retired judges, compensation and salaries, **28 § 155**
Schedules, fees, **28 § 1930 nt**
Judicial Council,
Appellate panels, **28 § 158**
Appointments, **28 § 156**
Civil service, retirement and pensions, recall, **28 § 375**
Joint appellate panels, **28 § 158**
Recall, **28 §§ 155, 375**
Removal, judges or justices, **28 §§ 152, 372, 375**
Reports,
Appellate panels, **28 § 158**
Transition, **28 nt prec § 151**

BANKRUPTCY—Cont'd
Judicial Council—Cont'd
Transition, reports, **28 nt prec § 151**
Vacancies in office, **28 § 152 nt**
Judicial districts, United States trustees, appointments, **28 § 581**
Judicial Panel On Multidistrict Litigation, generally, this index
Judicial review. Appeal and review, generally, ante
Jurisdiction, **28 § 1334**
Abstention, **28 § 1334**
Appeal and review, **28 § 158**
Chapter 11 proceedings, **28 § 1334**
Dismissal and nonsuit, **28 § 1930**
Jury, **28 § 157**
Pending proceedings, **28 § 1334 nt**
Transfers, **28 § 1631**
Transition, **28 nt prec § 1471**
Jury, **28 § 157**
Personal injuries, **28 § 1411**
Wrongful death, **28 § 1411**
Justices. Judges or justices, generally, ante
Law clerks, **28 § 156**
Leases, orders of court, **28 § 157**
Leave of absence,
Judges or justices, **28 § 153**
Law clerks, **28 § 156**
Liens and incumbrances, validation, **28 § 157**
Liquidations. Chapter 7 proceedings, generally, ante
Location, courts, **28 § 152**
Managers and management,
Actions and proceedings, **28 § 959**
Chapter 11 proceedings, ante
Mental health, judges or justices, **28 § 152**
Money, orders of court, **28 § 157**
Motions,
Core proceedings, **28 § 157**
Forms, **28 § 2075**
State laws, claims, abstention, **28 § 1334**
Withdrawal, **28 § 157**
Noncore proceedings, abstention, **28 § 157**
Notice,
Appeal and review, ante
Courts, emergencies, special sessions, **28 § 152**
Mailing, **28 § 1930 nt**
United States trustees, post
Oaths and affirmations, judges or justices, **28 § 153**
Officers and employees,
Trusts and trustees, generally, post
United States trustees, generally, post
Official bankruptcy forms. Forms, generally, ante
Official stations, courts, judges or justices, **28 § 152**
Orders of court, **28 § 157**
Jury, **28 § 1411**
Sales, **28 § 157**

BANKRUPTCY—Cont'd
Orders of court—Cont'd
Sessions, **28 § 151**
Torts, **28 § 157**
Original jurisdiction, **28 § 1334**
Panel trustees, **28 § 586**
Panels. Bankruptcy appellate panels, generally, ante
Partnership, chapter 11 proceedings, venue, **28 § 1408**
Payment. Taxation, post
Pending actions,
Foreign countries, ante
Jurisdiction, **28 § 1334 nt**
Personal injuries,
Jury, **28 § 1411**
Liquidation, exemptions, **28 § 157**
Place of business, venue, **28 §§ 1408, 1410**
Plans and specifications,
Chapter 9 proceedings, ante
Chapter 13 proceedings, ante
Pleading, forms, **28 § 2075**
Political subdivisions,
Actions and proceedings, **28 § 1452**
Taxation, generally, post
Powers and duties,
Administrative Office of United States Courts, directors, **28 § 604**
Chapter 11 proceedings, ante
President of the United States, judges or justices, appointments, **28 § 44 nt**
Procedures, **28 § 157; 28 nt prec § 1471**
Proceedings. Actions and proceedings, generally, ante
Puerto Rico, judges or justices, appointments, **28 § 152**
Qualifications, judges or justices, **28 § 152 nt**
Recall, judges or justices, **28 §§ 155, 375, 377**
Receivers and receivership, **28 § 959**
Reciprocity, abstention, **28 § 1334**
Records and recordation, custodians, **28 § 156**
Referees. References, generally, post
References, **28 § 157**
Alternative dispute resolution, **28 § 654**
Appellate panels, **28 § 158**
Arbitration, **28 § 654**
Chapter 11 proceedings, **28 § 157**
Interpreters, **28 § 1827**
Sessions, **28 § 151**
Term of office, **28 nt prec § 151**
Referrals. References, generally, ante
Remand, **28 § 1452**
Removal from office. Judges or justices, ante
Removal of cases or causes,
Claims, **28 § 1452**
Grounds, **28 § 152**
Reorganization,
Chapter 11 proceedings, generally, ante

BANKRUPTCY—Cont'd
Reorganization—Cont'd
Chapter 12 proceedings, generally, ante
Reports,
Crimes and offenses, **28 § 581 nt**
Fees, **28 § 1930 nt**
Forms, **28 § 589b**
Internet, **28 § 589b**
Statistics, **28 § 159**
United States trustees, post
Representatives and representation, chapter 11 proceedings, venue, **28 § 1409**
Retirement and pensions. Judges or justices, ante
Review. Appeal and review, generally, ante
Revocation or suspension, trusts and trustees, **28 § 586**
Rules of Appellate Procedure, this index
Rules of Civil Procedure, this index
Sales, orders of court, **28 § 157**
Schedules, fees, **28 § 1930 nt**
Secretaries, judges or justices, **28 § 156**
Set-off and counterclaim, hearings, **28 § 157**
Shares and shareholders, United States trustees, **28 § 586**
Small businesses,
Forms, **28 § 2073 nt**
United States trustees, **28 § 586**
Special sessions, courts, emergencies, **28 § 152**
Standing trustees. United States trustees, post
States,
Chapter 11 proceedings, managers and management, **28 § 959**
Core proceedings, **28 § 157**
Managers and management, chapter 11 proceedings, **28 § 959**
Statistics, **28 § 159**
Stay of proceedings, core proceedings, **28 § 157**
Straight bankruptcy. Chapter 7 proceedings, generally, ante
Studies, graduated fee system, **28 § 1930 nt**
Successors. Trusts and trustees, post
Supervision, **28 § 586**
Support, exemptions, **28 § 1930 nt**
Supreme Court, **28 § 2075**
Taxation,
Business and commerce, ante
Damages, judgments and decrees, **28 § 2201**
Declaratory judgments, **28 § 2201**
Judgments and decrees, damages, **28 § 2201**
Payment, business and commerce, **28 § 960**
Temporary judges, **28 § 152 nt**
Termination, trusts and trustees, **28 § 586**
Terms of office. Judges or justices, ante

BANKRUPTCY—Cont'd
Time, venue, **28 § 1408**
Transfers,
Actions and proceedings, **28 nt prec § 1471**
Appeal and review, **28 § 1334 nt**
Courts, **28 nt prec § 1471**
Judges or justices, **28 § 155**
Jurisdiction, **28 § 1631**
Transition, **28 nt prec § 151**
Jurisdiction, **28 nt prec § 1471**
Reform Act of 1978, **28 nt prec §§ 151, 1471**
Treasury of United States,
Fees, **28 § 156**
Standing trustees, **28 § 586**
Standing trustees, fees, **28 § 586**
Trustees. Trusts and trustees, generally, post
Trusts and trustees,
Actions and proceedings, **28 § 959**
Appointments, standing trustees, **28 § 586**
Chapter 13 proceedings, ante
Claims, business and commerce, venue, **28 § 1409**
Investigations, **28 § 526**
Money, judgments and decrees, venue, **28 § 1409**
Revocation or suspension, **28 § 586**
Standing trustees. United States trustees, post
Statutory successors, **28 § 1409**
Successors, statutory successors, **28 § 1409**
Termination, **28 § 586**
United States trustees, generally, post
Venue, **28 § 1409**
United States Tax Court, this index
United States trustees, **28 § 581 et seq.**
Applications, compensation and salaries, **28 § 586**
Appointments, **28 § 581**
Standing trustees, **28 § 586**
Appropriations, System Fund, **28 § 589a**
Assistants,
Appointments, **28 § 582**
Compensation and salaries, limitation, **28 § 587**
Official stations, **28 § 584**
Removal from office, **28 § 582**
Audits and auditors, **28 § 586**
Chapter 7 proceedings, **28 § 581 nt**
Chapter 11 proceedings, **28 § 586**
Chapter 12 proceedings, compensation and salaries, **28 § 586**
Chapter 13 proceedings, **28 § 581 nt**
Powers and duties, **28 § 586**
Compensation and salaries, **28 § 581 nt**
Assistants, **28 § 587**
Standing trustees, **28 § 586**
Costs, recovery, deposits, **28 § 589a**
Crimes and offenses, reports, **28 § 581 nt**

BANKRUPTCY—Cont'd
United States trustees—Cont'd
Deposits, **28 § 586**
Districts, regions, appointments, **28 § 581**
Executive Office, Director, **28 § 156**
Expenses and expenditures, **28 §§ 586, 588**
Fees,
Percentage fee, **28 § 586**
Quarterly fees, **28 § 1930**
Foreign countries, **28 § 586**
Fraud, reports, **28 § 586**
Incumbent trustees, **28 § 581 nt**
Information, **28 § 581 nt**
Interest, deposits, System Fund, **28 § 589a**
Investigations, **28 § 526**
Judicial districts, appointments, **28 § 581**
Notice, judicial districts, **28 § 581 nt**
Oaths and affirmations, **28 § 583**
Officers and employees, **28 § 589**
Official stations, **28 § 584**
Panel trustees, **28 § 586**
Powers and duties, **28 § 581 et seq.**
Private trustees, **28 § 586**
Publication, judicial districts, **28 § 581 nt**
Quarterly fees, payment, **28 § 1930**
Regions, judicial districts, appointments, **28 § 581**
Removal from office, **28 § 581**
Reports, **28 § 586**
Crimes and offenses, **28 § 581 nt**
System Fund, deposits, **28 § 589a**
Small businesses, **28 § 586**
Standing trustees, qualifications, **28 § 586**
Supervision, standing trustees, **28 § 586**
System Fund, investments, **28 § 589a**
Terms of office, **28 § 581**
Treasury of United States,
Quarterly fees, deposits, **28 § 1930**
System Fund, **28 § 589a**
Vacancies in office, **28 § 585**
Vacancies in office, judges or justices, **28 § 152**
Validation, liens and incumbrances, **28 § 157**
Venue, **28 § 1408 et seq.**
Change of venue, **28 § 1412**
Chapter 11 proceedings, **28 §§ 1408, 1409**
Foreign countries, ante
Place of business, **28 §§ 1408, 1410**
Voluntary proceedings, fees, filing, payment, **28 § 1930**
Wage earners bankruptcy. Chapter 13 proceedings, generally, ante
Waiver,
Chapter 7 proceedings, ante
Fees, reports, **28 § 1930 nt**
Withdrawal, **28 § 157**
Writs, **28 § 2075**

BANKRUPTCY—Cont'd
Wrongful death,
Exemptions, **28 § 157**
Jury, **28 § 1411**

BANKS AND BANKING
Conservators, **28 § 2001 et seq.**
National Banks, this index
Financial assistance. Colleges and Universities, this index
Fraud,
Financial institutions fraud task forces, **28 § 509 nt**
Sentence and punishment, **28 § 994 nt**
Task forces, **28 § 509 nt**
National Banks, generally, this index
Parties, district courts, **28 § 1348**
Receivers and receivership,
National Banks, this index
Personal property, sales, **28 § 2004**
Real estate, sales, **28 §§ 2001, 2002**
Resolution Trust Corporation, generally, this index
Sentence and punishment, major bank crime cases, **28 § 994 nt**
Venue, comptroller of currency, **28 § 1394**

BANKS FOR COOPERATIVES
Tort Claims Act, **28 § 2680**

BARBADOS
Convention on the Taking of Evidence Abroad in Civil or Commercial Matters, **28 § 1781 nt**

BARBITAL
Controlled Substances, generally, this index

BARBITURIC ACID
Controlled Substances, generally, this index

BATTERED WOMEN AND CHILDREN
Domestic Violence, generally, this index

BENZETHIDINE
Controlled Substances, generally, this index

BENZILATE
Controlled Substances, generally, this index

BENZYL CHLORIDE
Controlled Substances, generally, this index

BENZYL CYANIDE
Controlled Substances, generally, this index

BENZYLMORPHINE
Controlled Substances, generally, this index

BEST EVIDENCE RULE
Rules of Evidence, this index

BETACETYLMETHADOL
Controlled Substances, generally, this index

BETAMEPRODINE
Controlled Substances, generally, this index

BETAMETHADOL
Controlled Substances, generally, this index

BETAPRODINE
Controlled Substances, generally, this index

BETTING
Gambling, generally, this index

BEZITRAMIDE
Controlled Substances, generally, this index

BIAS AND PREJUDICE
Discrimination, generally, this index
District judges, **28 § 144**
Hate Crimes, generally, this index
Judges or justices, **28 § 455**
Rules of Evidence, this index

BILLS OF LADING
Jurisdiction, amounts, **28 § 1337**

BLACK AMERICANS
Black Persons, generally, this index

BLACK PERSONS
Civil Rights, generally, this index
Elections, jurisdiction, **28 § 1344**
Fair Housing, generally, this index
Housing. Fair Housing, generally, this index
Judges or justices, nominations, **28 § 133 nt**
United States magistrate judges, merit selection panels, **28 § 631 nt**

BLIND PERSONS
Discrimination, generally, this index

BLOOD RELATIONSHIP
Relatives, generally, this index

BLUEPRINTS
Plans and Specifications, generally, this index

BOARD OF PATENT APPEALS AND INTERFERENCES
Patents, this index

BOARDS AND COMMISSIONS
Atomic Energy Commission. Atomic Energy, this index
Citizens Commission On Public Service and Compensation, generally, this index
Clerks of courts, **28 § 957**

BOARDS AND COMMISSIONS
—Cont'd
Federal Maritime Commission, generally, this index
International Trade Commission, generally, this index
Judicial Center, this index
Jury Commission, generally, this index
Maritime Commission. Federal Maritime Commission, generally, this index
Merit Systems Protection Board, generally, this index
Rules of Civil Procedure, this index
Structural Alternatives for the Federal Courts of Appeals, **28 § 41 nt**
Surface Transportation Board, generally, this index
United States Commissioner, generally, this index
United States Sentencing Commission. Sentence and Punishment, this index

BOATS AND BOATING
Drug Enforcement Administration, funds, **28 § 530C**
Federal Bureau of Investigation, funds, **28 § 530C**
Immigration and Naturalization Service, funds, **28 § 530C**
Justice Department, funds, **28 § 530C**
United States attorneys, funds, **28 § 530C**
United States Marshals Service, funds, **28 § 530C**

BONDS
Actions and proceedings,
Execution under Federal law, jurisdiction of District Court, **28 § 1352**
Stay of execution of process in rem in admiralty, **28 § 2464**
Bail, this index
Evidence, Federal officers, **28 § 1737**
Fiduciaries. Bonds (Officers and Fiduciaries), generally, this index
Interpleader proceedings, district court, **28 § 1335**
Jurisdiction, **28 § 1352**
Interpleader, **28 § 1335**
Officers and employees. Bonds (Officers and Fiduciaries), generally, this index
Performance bonds. Bonds (Officers and Fiduciaries), generally, this index
Receivers and receivership, district court, **28 § 754**
Removal of cases or causes, **28 § 1450**
Securities, generally, this index

BONDS (OFFICERS AND FIDUCIARIES)
Admiralty, this index
Customs Duties, this index
District courts,
Interpleader, **28 § 1335**

BONDS (OFFICERS AND FIDUCIARIES)—Cont'd
District courts—Cont'd
Jurisdiction, **28 § 1352**
Documentary evidence, **28 § 1737**
Federal debt collection, prejudgment remedies, **28 § 3102**
International Trade Court, this index
Jury, **28 § 1874**
Postal Service, this index
Rules of Appellate Procedure, this index
Rules of Civil Procedure, this index
Ships and Shipping, this index

BOOKS AND PAPERS
Attorney General, **28 § 413**
Audits and Auditors, generally, this index
Authentication, generally, this index
Bankruptcy, this index
Consuls, evidence, **28 § 1740**
Court of Federal Claims, this index
Director of Administrative Office of U.S. Courts, **28 § 413**
Disbursing officers, U.S. Court of Federal Claims, **28 § 1496**
Documentary Evidence, generally, this index
Executive Departments, this index
Federal Agencies, this index
Foreign Documents, generally, this index
Grand Jury, this index
International Trade Court, this index
Law Books, generally, this index
Patent and Trademark Office, **28 § 1744**
Possessions of U.S., evidence, **28 § 1739**
Production of Books and Papers, generally, this index
Rules of Appellate Procedure, this index
Rules of Civil Procedure, this index
Rules of Evidence, this index
States, evidence, **28 § 1739**
Supreme Court, this index
Territories, this index
Vice Consuls, evidence, **28 § 1740**
Witnesses, recalcitrant witnesses, **28 § 1826**

BORDER CROSSING POINTS
Customs Duties, generally, this index

BOSTON, MA
Court of Appeals for First Circuit, generally, this index

BOUNDARIES
Mexico, this index
Rules of Evidence, this index

BOUNTIES
Customs Duties, this index

BREEDERS AND BREEDING
Plant Variety Protection, generally, this index

BRIEFS
See specific index headings

BRINGING IN ALIENS
Aliens, this index

BROTHERS AND SISTERS
Relatives, generally, this index

BUDGET
Administrative Office of U.S. Courts, estimates, **28 § 605**
Estimates, Administrative Office of U.S. Courts, **28 § 605**
Federal Bureau of Investigation, **28 § 532 nt**
United States Court of International Trade, estimates, approval of, **28 § 605**

BUFOTENINE
Controlled Substances, generally, this index

BUILDINGS
Bankruptcy, this index
Federal Bureau of Investigation, police, **28 § 540C**
Justice Department, construction, funds, **28 § 530C**

BULLETS
Ammunition, generally, this index

BURDEN OF PROOF
Habeas corpus, **28 § 2254**
United States Court of International Trade, **28 § 2639**

BUREAU OF ALCOHOL, TOBACCO, FIREARMS, AND EXPLOSIVES
Generally, **28 § 599A et seq.**
Compensation and salaries, directors, **28 § 599A**
Coordination, **28 § 599A**
Demonstration projects or programs, personnel management demonstration project, **28 § 599B**
Directors, **28 § 599A**
Investigations, undercover investigations, **28 § 533 nt**
Officers and employees,
Personnel management demonstration project, **28 § 599B**
Transfer of powers and duties, **28 § 599A**
Reports, undercover investigations, **28 § 533 nt**
Transfer of powers and duties, **28 § 599A**
Undercover investigations, **28 § 533 nt**

BUREAU OF INTERNAL REVENUE
Internal Revenue Service, generally, this index

BUREAU OF INVESTIGATION
Federal Bureau of Investigation, generally, this index

BUREAU OF PRISONS
Drug addicts. Correctional Institutions, this index

BUREAU OF TAX AND TRADE
Tax and Trade Bureau. Treasury Department, this index

BURLINGTON, VT
District court, **28 § 126**

BUSINESS AND COMMERCE
Bankruptcy, this index
Carriers, generally, this index
Corporations, generally, this index
Exports and Imports, generally, this index
International Trade Court, generally, this index
Jurisdiction, carriers, **28 § 1337**
Monopolies and Combinations, generally, this index
Securities, generally, this index
Telecommunications, generally, this index
Writings, this index

BUSINESS CORPORATIONS
Corporations, generally, this index

BUTYL NITRITE
Controlled Substances, generally, this index

C CORPORATIONS
Corporations, generally, this index

CABOOSES
Railroads, generally, this index

CALENDARS
See specific index headings

CALIFORNIA
Bankruptcy, judges or justices, appointments, **28 § 152**
Court of Appeals for Ninth Circuit, generally, this index
District courts,
Cities, held at, **28 § 84**
Congressional findings, **28 § 84 nt**
Judges or justices, **28 § 133**
Transfer of, **28 § 84 nt**
Places of holding, **28 § 84**
Indians, civil jurisdiction of actions to which Indians are parties, **28 § 1360**
Judicial Circuit of U.S., **28 § 41**
Judicial districts,
Bankruptcy, **28 § 581 nt**
Number of district judges, **28 § 133**
United States attorneys, transfer and appointment, **28 § 84 nt**
United States Marshals, transfer and appointment, **28 § 84 nt**
United States trustees of judicial districts, **28 § 581**

CALLS
Court of Federal Claims, this index

CANAL ZONE
Court, definitions, **28 § 1869**
Grand jury, **28 § 1861 et seq.**
Judicial Circuit of U.S., **28 § 41**
Jury, **28 § 1861 et seq.**
Fees, **28 § 1871**
Refilling master jury wheel, **28 § 1863 nt**
Tort Claims Act, exemptions, **28 § 2680**

CANALS
Canal Zone, generally, this index
Zones. Canal Zone, generally, this index

CANTON ISLAND
Judicial District of Hawaii, **28 § 91**

CAPACITY
See specific index headings

CAPITAL STOCK
Shares and Shareholders, generally, this index

CAPTIONS
See specific index headings

CARGO
Customs Duties, generally, this index

CARRIERS
Accounts and accounting, Surface Transportation Board, **28 § 2321 et seq.**
Aircraft, generally, this index
Customs Duties, generally, this index
Damages,
District courts, **28 § 1337**
Nonremovable actions, **28 § 1445**
Trusts and trustees, **28 § 1445**
Delivery, delay, **28 § 1445**
Initial carriers, liability, **28 §§ 1337, 2321 et seq.**
Injuries, nonremovable actions, **28 § 1445**
Losses, **28 §§ 1337, 1445**
Mandamus, equal facilities, **28 § 2321 et seq.**
Motor Carriers, generally, this index
Nonremovable actions, **28 § 1445**
Orders, Surface Transportation Board, **28 § 2321 et seq.**
Railroads, generally, this index
Receivers and receivership, nonremovable actions, **28 § 1445**
Records and recordation, Surface Transportation Board, **28 § 2321 et seq.**
Reports, Surface Transportation Board, **28 § 2321 et seq.**
Ships and Shipping, generally, this index
Telecommunications, generally, this index
Traveling expenses, witnesses, U.S. courts, **28 § 1821**
Trusts and trustees, damages, **28 § 1445**
Vessels. Ships and Shipping, generally, this index

CARRYING AWAY
Kidnapping, generally, this index

CARS
Railroads, generally, this index

CASH
Money, generally, this index

CASINOS
Gambling, generally, this index

CATALOGUES AND CATALOGING
United States Court of International Trade, evidence, **28 § 2639**

CEASE AND DESIST
Plant Variety Protection, this index

CELLULAR TELEPHONES
Telecommunications, this index

CEMETERIES AND DEAD BODIES
National Cemeteries, generally, this index

CENSURE
See specific index headings

CENTRAL INTELLIGENCE AGENCY
Director, Independent Counsel, appointment, **28 § 591**
Independent Counsel, appointment, **28 § 591**

CERTIFICATES AND CERTIFICATION
See specific index headings

CERTIFICATES OF PUBLIC CONVENIENCE AND NECESSITY
Judges or justices, **28 § 291 et seq.**

CERTIFIED COPIES
Bonds (officers and fiduciaries), **28 § 1737**
Clerks of Courts, this index
Clerks of District Courts, this index
Court of Federal Claims, this index
Courts, **28 § 1734 et seq.**
Evidence, this index
Federal agencies, appeal and review, **28 § 2112**
Habeas Corpus, this index
International Trade Court, this index
Judgments and Decrees, this index
Patent and Trademark Office, **28 § 1744**
Postal Service, attachment, **28 § 2710**
Remand, **28 § 1447**
Removal of cases or causes, **28 § 1449**

CERTIFIED OR REGISTERED MAIL
Jury, summons, **28 § 1866**
Process, this index
Service of process. Process, this index
Tax liens, **28 § 2410**
Three-Judge Courts, district courts, **28 § 2284**
United States,
Claims, **28 § 2675**
Liens and incumbrances, **28 § 2410**

CERTIFIED QUESTIONS
Generally, **28 § 1254**
Federal agencies, **28 § 2350**
Intervention, **28 § 2403**

CERTIFYING OFFICER
Courts, privileges and immunities, **28 § 613**

CERTIORARI
Court of Appeals for Fourth Circuit, this index
District courts,
Notice of allowance of certiorari, fees, **28 § 1917**
State court, bring up records and proceedings on removal of case, **28 § 1447**
Harmless error, judgment, **28 § 2111**
Rules of Appellate Procedure, this index
State Courts, this index
Supreme Court, this index

CHALLENGES
Jury, this index

CHAMBERS
See specific index headings

CHANCELLORS
Certificates and certification, records and recordation, **28 § 1739**
Records and recordation, certificates and certification, **28 § 1739**

CHANCERY
Equity, generally, this index

CHANGE OF VENUE
Venue, this index

CHANNELS
Harbors and Ports, generally, this index

CHAPTER 7 PROCEEDINGS
Bankruptcy, this index

CHAPTER 9 PROCEEDINGS
Bankruptcy, this index

CHAPTER 11 PROCEEDINGS
Bankruptcy, this index

CHAPTER 12 PROCEEDINGS
Bankruptcy, this index

CHAPTER 13 PROCEEDINGS
Bankruptcy, this index

CHARACTER AND REPUTATION
Rules of Evidence, this index

CHARITIES
Attorneys, fees, prevailing party, United States, **28 § 2412**
Disqualification, judges or justices, **28 § 455**
Judges or justices, disqualification, **28 § 455**

CHATTEL MORTGAGES
Foreclosure, United States, **28 § 2410**

CHECKS
Internal Revenue Service, this index
Judgments and decrees, Internal Revenue Service, **28 § 2411**

CHICAGO, IL
Court of Appeals for Seventh Circuit, generally, this index

CHIEF FINANCIAL OFFICER
See specific index headings

CHIEF JUDGE OR JUSTICE
Court of Appeals for Third Circuit, this index
Court of Appeals for the District of Columbia, this index
Court of Appeals for the Federal Circuit, this index
Court of Federal Claims, this index
Courts of Appeals, this index
District Judges, this index
International Trade Court, this index
Jury Selection and Service Act, **28 § 1869**
Office of Federal Judicial Administration, **28 § 133**
Sentence and punishment, **28 § 334**
Supreme Court, this index

CHILD
Children and Minors, generally, this index

CHILD ABUSE AND NEGLECT
Crime victims, sentence and punishment, **28 § 994 nt**
Sentencing guidelines, **28 § 994 nt**

CHILD SUPPORT
Support, generally, this index

CHILDREN AND MINORS
Abduction. Kidnapping, generally, post
Annuities, justices and judges, payments, **28 § 376**
Annuities to surviving dependent children of justices and judges, **28 § 376**
Crimes and offenses. Sexual exploitation, generally, post
Definitions, judges or justices, annuities for survivors, **28 § 376**
Disqualification, judges or justices, **28 § 455**
Exploitation. Sexual exploitation, generally, post
Federal Bureau of Investigation, this index
Fines, penalties and forfeitures, exploitation, **28 § 994 nt**
Internet. Sexual exploitation, post
Judges or justices, disqualification, **28 § 455**
Juvenile Delinquents and Dependents, generally, this index

CHILDREN AND MINORS—Cont'd
Kidnapping,
Centers, Child Abduction and Serial Murder Investigative Resources Center, **28 § 531 nt**
Definitions, parental kidnapping, **28 § 1738A**
Parental kidnapping, **28 § 1738A**
Definitions, **28 § 1738A**
Limitation of actions, United States, **28 § 2416**
Parental kidnapping. Kidnapping, ante
Rules of Civil Procedure, this index
Sentence and punishment. Sexual exploitation, post
Sexual exploitation,
Internet, sentence and punishment, **28 § 994 nt**
Sentence and punishment, **28 § 994 nt**
Transportation, **28 § 994 nt**
Solicitation of minor to commit crime, sentence enhancement, **28 § 994 nt**
Support, generally, this index
Transportation. Sexual exploitation, ante
United States, limitation of actions, **28 § 2416**

CHIPS
Semiconductors, generally, this index

CHLORAL BETAINE
Controlled Substances, generally, this index

CHLORAL HYDRATE
Controlled Substances, generally, this index

CHORHEXADOL
Controlled Substances, generally, this index

CHRONIC DISEASES
Nursing Homes, generally, this index

CHURCHES
Attorneys, fees, prevailing parties, **28 § 2412**

CINCINNATI, OH
Court of Appeals for Sixth Circuit, generally, this index

CIRCUIT EXECUTIVE
Courts of appeals, **28 § 332**

CIRCUITS
Judicial Circuits, generally, this index
Semiconductors, generally, this index

CITATIONS
See specific index headings

CITIZENS AND CITIZENSHIP
Civil Rights, generally, this index
District Courts, this index
Juror qualification form, **28 § 1869**

CITIZENS AND CITIZENSHIP—Cont'd
National banks, actions and proceedings, **28 § 1348**
Removal of cases or causes, **28 § 1441**
Rules of Civil Procedure, this index
Subpoenas, foreign countries, **28 §§ 1783, 1784**
Supreme Court, actions and proceedings, **28 § 1251**

CITIZENS COMMISSION ON PUBLIC SERVICE AND COMPENSATION
Judges or justices, pay rates, **28 §§ 5, 132, 252**

CITIZENSHIP
Citizens and Citizenship, generally, this index

CIVIL ACTIONS
Actions and Proceedings, generally, this index

CIVIL AIRCRAFT
Aircraft, generally, this index

CIVIL FORFEITURES
Fines, Penalties and Forfeitures, generally, this index

CIVIL NONCONTRACTUAL WRONGS
Torts, generally, this index

CIVIL PENALTY
Fines, Penalties and Forfeitures, generally, this index

CIVIL PROCEDURE
Rules of Civil Procedure, generally, this index

CIVIL RIGHTS
Actions and proceedings, removal of cases or causes, **28 § 1443**
Appropriations, unsolved crimes, investigations, **28 § 509 nt**
Conspiracy, jurisdiction, **28 § 1343**
Crimes and offenses, unsolved crimes, investigations, **28 § 509 nt**
Discrimination, generally, this index
District courts, jurisdiction, **28 § 1343**
Fair Housing, generally, this index
Investigations, unsolved crimes, **28 § 509 nt**
Jurisdiction, **28 § 1343**
District court, **28 §§ 1343, 1344**
Elections disputes, **28 § 1344**
Jury,
Qualification for service, **28 § 1865**
Qualification form, contents concerning, **28 § 1869**
Privileges and immunities, **28 § 1343**
Removal of cases or causes, **28 § 1443**
Torture, **28 § 1350 nt**
Unsolved crimes, investigations, **28 § 509 nt**

CIVIL SERVICE
Administrative Office of United States Courts, this index
Boards and commissions. Merit Systems Protection Board, generally, this index
Competitive service,
Assistant Attorney General for Administration, **28 § 507**
Judicial Center, **28 § 625**
Court of Appeals for the Federal Circuit, this index
Merit system. Merit Systems Protection Board, generally, this index
Retirement and pensions,
Administrative Office of United States Courts, this index
Judges or Justices, this index
Judicial Center, **28 §§ 625, 627**
United States Court of Federal Claims, **28 § 797**
United States Court of International Trade, **28 § 871 nt**

CLAIMS
Attorneys, claims against U.S., fees, **28 § 2678**
Bankruptcy, this index
Banks for cooperatives, Tort Claims Act, **28 § 2680**
Constitution of the United States, this index
Copyrights, this index
Court of Federal Claims, generally, this index
Credits in actions by U.S., **28 § 2406**
Disbursing Officials, Clerks, and Agents, this index
District Courts, generally, this index
Federal Debt Collection, generally, this index
Federal intermediate credit banks, Tort Claims Act, **28 § 2680**
Federal land banks, Tort Claims Act, **28 § 2680**
Federal Officers and Employees, this index
Fraud, forfeitures, **28 § 2514**
Indians, this index
Interest, claims against U.S., **28 § 2516**
International Trade Court, this index
Military Departments, this index
National Guard, this index
Patents, this index
Quieting title, **28 § 2409a**
Time, **28 § 2401**
Torts, generally, this index
United States, this index

CLAIMS COURT
Court of Federal Claims, generally, this index

CLASS ACTION FAIRNESS ACT OF 2005
Generally, **28 §§ 1 nt, 1711 et seq.**

CLASS ACTIONS
Attorneys, **28 § 1711 et seq.**
Compromise and settlement, **28 § 1711 et seq.**
Coupons, **28 § 1712**
Definitions, fairness, **28 §§ 1332, 1711, 1715**
Depository institutions, notice, **28 § 1715**
Discrimination, **28 § 1714**
District courts, **28 § 1332**
Fairness, **28 § 1711 et seq.**
Fees, attorneys, **28 § 1712 et seq.**
Interstate class actions, **28 § 1711 et seq.**
Losses, compromise and settlement, **28 § 1713**
Notice, fairness, **28 § 1715**
Removal of cases or causes, **28 § 1453**
Rules of Civil Procedure, this index
Time, removal of cases or causes, **28 § 1453**

CLASSIFICATION
See specific index headings

CLASSROOMS
Colleges and Universities, generally, this index

CLEARINGHOUSES
Stores, organized retail theft task force, **28 § 509 nt**

CLERK OF HOUSE OF REPRESENTATIVES
Certificates and certification, journals, **28 § 1736**
Journals, certificates and certification, **28 § 1736**

CLERKS OF COURTS
Generally, **28 § 951 et seq.**
Absence, **28 § 954**
Acknowledgments, **28 § 953**
Assistants, **28 § 955 et seq.**
Attachment, postmasters and postal officers, **28 §§ 2711, 2712**
Attestation, States, records and recordation, **28 § 1738**
Authentication, States, records and recordation, **28 § 1739**
Bankruptcy, this index
Certified copies,
Habeas corpus, indigents, **28 § 2250**
Lost or destroyed documents, **28 §§ 1734, 1735**
Commissioners, appointments, **28 § 957**
Compensation and salaries,
Deputies, **28 §§ 603 nt, 604**
Director of Administrative Office of U.S. Courts, **28 § 604**
Increases, **28 § 603 nt**
Copies,
Certified copies, generally, ante
Former court of appeals, records and recordation, **28 § 6**
Costs, **28 § 1920**
Habeas corpus, indigents, **28 § 2250**

CLERKS OF COURTS—Cont'd
Court of Federal Claims, this index
Courts of Appeals, this index
Definitions, Jury Selection and Service Act, **28 § 1869**
Deposits, **28 § 2043**
Deputies, **28 § 951 et seq.**
Acknowledgments, **28 § 953**
Compensation and salaries, **28 §§ 603 nt, 604**
Oaths and affirmations, **28 § 951**
Powers and duties, **28 § 956**
Practice of law, **28 § 955**
Supreme Court, **28 § 671**
United States magistrate judges, **28 § 631**
Vacancies in office, **28 § 954**
Director of Administrative Office of U.S. Courts, supervision, **28 § 604**
Disclosure, financial disclosures, **5 App. 4 § 111**
District courts. Clerks of District Courts, generally, this index
Dockets and docketing, fees, **28 § 1923**
Evidence,
Attestation, States, records and recordation, **28 § 1738**
Authentication, States, records and recordation, **28 § 1739**
Certified copies, lost or destroyed documents, **28 §§ 1734, 1735**
Expenses and expenditures, offices, **28 § 961**
Fees,
Dockets and docketing, **28 § 1923**
State courts, removal of cases or causes, **28 § 1449**
Financial disclosures, **5 App. 4 § 111**
Habeas corpus, certified copies, indigents, **28 § 2250**
Incentive pay or awards, **28 § 604**
International Trade Court, this index
Investigations, Attorney General, **28 § 526**
Judicial Center, training, **28 § 620**
Judicial Panel On Multidistrict Litigation, this index
Law books, **28 § 414**
Masters, appointments, **28 § 957**
Naturalization, this index
Oaths and affirmations, **28 § 951**
Administration, **28 § 953**
Offices, expenses and expenditures, **28 § 961**
Part-time Magistrate Judge, appointment, **28 § 631**
Payment,
Dockets and docketing, **28 § 1923**
Supreme Court, **28 § 671**
Powers and duties, **28 § 956**
Practice of law, restrictions, **28 § 955**
Process, **28 § 143**
Signatures, **28 § 1691**
Receivers and receivership, appointments, **28 § 957**

CLERKS OF COURTS—Cont'd
Records and recordation,
Attestation, States, **28 § 1738**
Authentication, States, **28 § 1739**
Certified copies, lost or destroyed documents, **28 §§ 1734, 1735**
Former court of appeals, **28 § 6**
Referees, appointments, **28 § 957**
Returns, fees, **28 § 671**
Rules of Appellate Procedure, this index
Rules of Civil Procedure, this index
Salaries. Compensation and salaries, generally, ante
Signatures, writs, **28 § 1691**
State Courts, this index
Subpoenas, **28 § 1825**
Supervision, Director of Administrative Office of U.S. Courts, **28 § 604**
Supreme Court, this index
Training, Judicial Center, **28 § 620**
United States magistrate judges, **28 § 631**
United States Tax Court, this index
Vacancies in office, **28 § 954**
Writs, signatures, **28 § 1691**

CLERKS OF DISTRICT COURTS
Generally, **28 § 751**
Appointment, **28 § 751**
United States attorneys, **28 § 546**
Certificates and certification, jury, fees, **28 § 1871**
Certified copies,
Liens and incumbrances, **28 § 1656**
Transcripts, **28 § 753**
Compensation and salaries,
Deputies, **28 § 751**
Director of Administrative Office of U.S. Courts, **28 § 604**
Increases, **28 § 603 nt**
Restrictions, **28 § 751**
United States magistrate judges, **28 § 751**
Costs, **28 § 751**
Deposits, **28 § 751**
Deputies, **28 § 751**
Director of Administrative Office of U.S. Courts,
Compensation and salaries, **28 § 604**
Powers and duties, **28 § 751**
Domicile and residence, **28 § 751**
Fees, **28 § 1914**
Appeal and review, **28 § 1917**
Filing, **28 § 1931**
Jury, **28 § 1871**
Returns, **28 § 751**
Transcripts, **28 § 753**
United States, awards, **28 § 1931**
Filing,
Fees, **28 § 1931**
Removal of cases or causes, **28 § 1447**
Grand Jury, this index
Incentive pay or awards, **28 § 604**
Jury, fees, **28 § 1871**
Notice, United States Magistrate Judge, appointments, **28 § 631**

CLERKS OF DISTRICT COURTS—Cont'd
Offices, **28 § 751**
Official stations, **28 § 751**
Orders,
Adjournment, **28 § 140**
Judicial Panel on Multidistrict Litigation, **28 § 1407**
Original records, access, **28 § 753**
Payment,
Costs, **28 § 751**
Jury, **28 § 1871**
Practice of law, **28 § 955**
Preservation, original records, **28 § 753**
Process, **28 § 143**
Records and recordation,
Liens and incumbrances, **28 § 1656**
Removal of cases or causes, **28 § 1447**
Transcripts, **28 § 753**
Removal, deputies, assistants or employees, **28 § 751**
Removal from office, **28 § 751**
Removal of cases or causes, **28 § 1447**
Reporters, transcripts, certified copies, **28 § 753**
Residence, **28 § 751**
Returns,
Costs, **28 § 751**
Fees, **28 § 751**
Salaries. Compensation and salaries, generally, ante
Transcripts, **28 § 753**
United States attorneys, appointments, **28 § 546**
United States Court of Federal Claims, judgments and decrees, transcripts, **28 §§ 2508, 2511**
United States District Court for District of Columbia, **28 § 751**
United States Magistrate Judges, this index

CLONING
Wireless telephones, **28 § 994 nt**

CLONITAZENE
Controlled Substances, generally, this index

CLOSINGS
See specific index headings

CLOTHING
Uniforms, generally, this index

CLOUD ON TITLE
Removal, district courts, **28 § 1655**

COAST GUARD
Commissary stores. Armed Forces, this index
Military Justice Code, generally, this index
Retirement and pensions, United States magistrate judges, **28 § 631**
Torts, exemptions, **28 § 2680**

COAST GUARD RESERVE
Retirement and pensions, United States magistrate judges, appointment, eligibility, **28 § 631**
United States magistrate judges, appointment, eligibility, **28 § 631**

COASTWISE VOYAGES
Ships and Shipping, this index

CODE
Military Justice Code, generally, this index

CODEINE
Controlled Substances, generally, this index

COERCION AND DURESS
Terrorists and Terrorism, generally, this index

COLLECTION
See specific index headings

COLLECTIVE BARGAINING
Labor Disputes, this index

COLLEGES AND UNIVERSITIES
Attorneys,
Fees, prevailing parties, **28 § 2412**
Prevailing parties, fees, **28 § 2412**
Disqualification, judges or justices, **28 § 455**
Financial assistance,
Fraud, sentence and punishment, **28 § 994 nt**
Sentence and punishment, fraud, **28 § 994 nt**
Judges or justices, disqualification, **28 § 455**
Loans,
Fraud, sentence and punishment, **28 § 994 nt**
Sentence and punishment, fraud, **28 § 994 nt**

COLLUSION
Joinder of parties, **28 § 1359**

COLOR
Race, Color, and Previous Condition of Servitude, generally, this index

COLORADO
Bankruptcy, judges or justices, appointments, **28 § 152**
District courts,
Cities, **28 § 85**
Judges or justices, **28 § 133**
Judicial Circuit of U.S., **28 § 41**
Judicial districts, **28 § 85**
Number of district judges, **28 § 133**

COLUMBIA, TN
District court held at, **28 § 123**

COMBAT ZONES
Armed Forces, this index

COMBATANTS
Enemy combatants, detention, **28 § 2241**

COMBINATIONS
Monopolies and Combinations, generally, this index

COMMANDER-IN-CHIEF
President of the United States, generally, this index

COMMERCE DEPARTMENT
Patent and Trademark Office, generally, this index
Trademark office. Patent and Trademark Office, generally, this index

COMMERCIAL MOTOR VEHICLES
Motor Carriers, generally, this index

COMMERCIAL VEHICLES
Motor Carriers, generally, this index

COMMERCIAL VESSELS
Harbors and Ports, generally, this index
Ships and Shipping, generally, this index

COMMISSARY STORES
Armed Forces, this index

COMMISSION ON EXECUTIVE, LEGISLATIVE, AND JUDICIAL SALARIES
Citizens Commission On Public Service and Compensation, generally, this index

COMMISSIONS (COMPENSATION)
Compensation and Salaries, generally, this index

COMMISSIONS OF OFFICERS
Attorney General, Special Assistants, **28 § 515**
Circuit judges, **28 § 45**
District judges, **28 § 136**
Supreme Court, associate Justices, **28 § 4**

COMMITMENT
Habeas Corpus, generally, this index
Witnesses, recalcitrant witnesses, **28 § 1826**

COMMITTEES
Congressional Committees, generally, this index
Judges or Justices, this index

COMMODITIES
Brokers, liquidation, **28 § 586**

COMMON CARRIERS
Carriers, generally, this index

COMMON STOCK
Shares and Shareholders, generally, this index

COMMONWEALTH
Northern Mariana Islands, generally, this index
Puerto Rico, generally, this index

COMMUNICATIONS
Telecommunications, generally, this index

COMMUNITIES
Development. Community Development, generally, this index
Federal agencies, intervention, **28 § 2348**
Intervention, Federal agencies, **28 § 2348**
Surface Transportation Board, intervention, **28 § 2323**

COMMUNITY CHESTS
Attorneys fees, **28 § 2412**

COMMUNITY DEVELOPMENT
Attorney General, neighborhood revitalization plans, **28 § 509 nt**
Neighborhood revitalization, **28 § 509 nt**
Plans and specifications, neighborhood revitalization, **28 § 509 nt**

COMPELLING PRODUCTION OF EVIDENCE OR DOCUMENTS
Production of Books and Papers, generally, this index

COMPENSATION AND SALARIES
Administrative Office of United States Courts, this index
Arbitration, **28 § 658**
Attorney General, this index
Bankruptcy, this index
Bureau of Alcohol, Tobacco, Firearms, and Explosives, this index
Circuit court executives, **28 § 332**
Citizens Commission On Public Service and Compensation, generally, this index
Clerks of Courts, this index
Clerks of District Courts, this index
Condemnation. Eminent Domain, generally, this index
Court Criers, this index
Courts of Appeals, this index
Crime Victims, this index
District Courts, this index
District Judges, this index
Drug Enforcement Administration, this index
Federal Bureau of Investigation, this index
Federal Officers and Employees, this index
Garnishment, generally, this index
Grand jurors, **28 § 1871**
Incentive Pay or Awards, generally, this index
International Trade Court, this index
Interpreters, this index
Judges or Justices, this index
Judicial Center, this index
Law Clerks, this index

COMPENSATION AND SALARIES
—Cont'd
Libraries, this index
Marshals, Supreme Court, **28 § 672**
Messengers, courts, **28 §§ 603 nt, 604**
Per Diem, generally, this index
Reporters, this index
Retirement and Pensions, generally, this index
Rules of Civil Procedure, this index
Special attorney to Attorney General, **28 § 515**
Stenographers, this index
Subsistence, generally, this index
Supreme Court, this index
United States attorneys, **28 § 548**
United States Magistrate Judges, this index
United States Marshals Service, this index

COMPETENCY
See specific index headings

COMPETITIVE SERVICE
Civil Service, this index

COMPLAINTS
Correctional institutions, frivolous complaints, inmates, **28 § 1915A**
Court of Appeals for Sixth Circuit, this index
Federal Officers and Employees, this index
Fees, U.S. Marshals, process, **28 § 1921**
Indictment and Information, generally, this index
International Trade Court, this index
Judges or Justices, this index
Liens and incumbrances, United States, **28 § 2410**
Quieting title, **28 § 2409a**
Rules of Civil Procedure, this index
Tax liens, **28 § 2410**
United States, liens and incumbrances, **28 § 2410**

COMPROMISE AND SETTLEMENT
Attorney General, this index
Award for negligence, wrongful acts, of employee of Government, **28 § 2672**
Civil justice reform, **28 § 519 nt, EON 12988**
Class actions, **28 § 1711 et seq.**
Copyright cases, damages for infringement, actions against U.S., **28 § 1498**
Executive Agencies, this index
Federal Agencies, this index
Government officers and employees, negligence, **28 § 2672**
International Trade Court, this index
Libya, terrorists and terrorism, United States nationals, **28 § 1605A nt**
Military Departments, this index
Rules of Appellate Procedure, this index
Rules of Civil Procedure, this index

COMPROMISE AND SETTLEMENT
—Cont'd
Secretary of the Treasury, contract disputes, **28 § 2414**
Torts, this index
United States, this index
United States Court of Federal Claims, **28 § 1494**

COMPTROLLER GENERAL
Financial disclosure reports, **5 App. 4 § 108**
Independent Counsel, **28 § 596**
Judges and justices, annuities, survivors, **28 § 376**
Reports,
Financial disclosure reports, **5 App. 4 § 108**
Judicial Survivors Annuities Program, **28 § 376 nt**
Studies, financial disclosures, Federal officers and employees, **5 App. 4 § 108**
United States Court of Federal Claims,
Notice, lawsuits, **28 § 2511**
Referrals, **28 § 2510**

COMPTROLLER OF THE CURRENCY
Injunctions, **28 §§ 1348, 1394**

COMPUTATION
See specific index headings

COMPUTER FORENSIC LABORATORIES
Generally, **28 § 509 nt**

COMPUTERS
Bankruptcy, this index
Federal Bureau of Investigation, this index
Forensic laboratories, computer forensic laboratories, **28 § 509 nt**
Semiconductors, generally, this index
Sexual abuse, children and minors, sentence enhancement, **28 § 994 nt**
Sexual exploitation of children, **28 § 994 nt**

CONCLUSIONS OF LAW
See specific index headings

CONCURRENT JURISDICTION
District Courts, this index

CONDEMNATION
Eminent Domain, generally, this index

CONDUCT
See specific index headings

CONFERENCES
Civil justice, reforms, **28 § 519 nt, EON 12988**
Judicial Conference of the United States, generally, this index
Justice Department, funds, **28 § 530C**

CONFERENCES—Cont'd
United States, compromise and settlement, guidelines, **28 § 519 nt, EON 12988**

CONFESSION OF JUDGMENT
Generally, **28 § 1874**

CONFIDENTIAL OR PRIVILEGED INFORMATION
Alternative dispute resolution, **28 § 652**
Civil justice, reforms, **28 § 519 nt, EON 12988**
District courts, alternative dispute resolution, **28 § 652**
Federal Officers and Employees, this index
Home health care and services, criminal background checks, labor and employment, **28 § 534 nt**
International Trade Court, this index
Judges or justices, complaints, **28 § 360**
Justice Department, funds, **28 § 530C**
Nursing homes, criminal background checks, labor and employment, **28 § 534 nt**

CONFINEMENT
Kidnapping, generally, this index
Recalcitrant witness, **28 § 1826**
Witnesses, recalcitrant witnesses, **28 § 1826**

CONFISCATION
Searches and Seizures, generally, this index

CONFLICT OF INTEREST
Bankruptcy, this index
Federal Officers and Employees, this index
Judges or justices, disqualification, **28 § 455**
Justice Department, this index
United States Magistrate Judges, this index

CONGRESS
Committees. Congressional Committees, generally, this index
Congressional Committees, generally, this index
Court of Federal Claims, this index
Government Accountability Office, generally, this index
Journals, evidence, **28 § 1736**
Judges, recommendations, **28 § 133 nt**
Judicial Center, reports, **28 § 623**
Notice, Judiciary Information Technology Fund, **28 § 612**
Officers and employees, removal, **28 § 1442**
Removal of cases or causes, **28 § 1442**
Reports,
Administrative Office of U.S. Courts, transportation, needs, **28 § 456 nt**
Congressional reference cases, **28 § 2509**

CONGRESS—Cont'd
Reports—Cont'd
Department of Justice Assets Forfeiture Fund, **28 § 524**
Judicial Center, **28 § 623**
Judicial Conference of the United States, **28 § 331**
Rules of civil procedure, **28 § 2072**
Sentencing guidelines, **28 § 994 nt**
Undercover operations, **28 § 533 nt**
United States Sentencing Commission, **28 §§ 994 nt, 997**
Rules of civil procedure, reports, **28 § 2072**
Rules of Evidence, this index
Undercover operations, **28 § 533 nt**

CONGRESSIONAL COMMITTEES
Appropriations Committee (Senate or House of Representatives),
Bankruptcy, fees, **28 § 1931 nt**
Judiciary Information Technology Fund, **28 § 612**
Judiciary Committee,
Bankruptcy, fees, **28 § 1930 nt**
Federal Judicial Center Foundation, **28 § 629**
Judicial Center Board, **28 § 623**
Money laundering, **28 § 994 nt**
Reports, U.S. Court of Federal Claims, **28 § 2507**

CONGRESSIONAL DISTRICTS
Three judge court, apportionments, **28 § 2284**

CONNECTICUT
Bankruptcy, judges or justices, appointments, **28 § 152**
District courts, **28 § 86**
Judges or justices, **28 § 133**
Judicial circuit, **28 § 41**
Judicial districts,
Bankruptcy, **28 § 581 nt**
Judges or justices, **28 § 133**
United States trustees, appointments, **28 § 581**
United States trustees, judicial districts, appointments, **28 § 581**

CONSANGUINITY
Relatives, generally, this index

CONSENT
See specific index headings

CONSERVATORS
Banks and Banking, this index
National Banks, this index

CONSIDERATION
See specific index headings

CONSOLIDATIONS AND MERGERS
International Trade Court, this index

CONSPIRACY
Civil Rights, this index

CONSTITUTION OF THE UNITED STATES
Actions and proceedings,
Jurisdiction, generally, post
United States, **28 § 2402**
Certificates and certification, intervention, **28 § 2403**
Claims,
Court of Federal Claims, **28 § 1491**
District courts, **28 § 1346**
Venue, **28 § 1402**
Court of Federal Claims, this index
Full Faith and Credit, generally, this index
International Trade Court, **28 § 251**
Jurisdiction,
Civil rights, **28 § 1343**
Claims, **28 § 1346**
District courts, **28 § 1331**
Indians, **28 § 1362**
Questions of law or fact,
Congressional districts, **28 § 2284**
Intervention, **28 § 2403**
States, **28 § 1257**
Supreme Court, Puerto Rico, **28 § 1258**
States,
Certificates and certification, intervention, **28 § 2403**
Rates and charges, jurisdiction, **28 § 1342**
Statutes,
Appeal and review, **28 § 1257**
Opinions and decisions, **28 § 1652**

CONSTITUTIONAL QUESTIONS
District courts, **28 § 1331**

CONSTITUTIONS
United States. Constitution of the United States, generally, this index

CONSTRUCTION
Correctional Institutions, this index
Justice Department, buildings, funds, **28 § 530C**

CONSULAR AGENTS
Foreign Service, this index

CONSULS AND CONSULAR OFFICERS
Foreign Diplomatic and Consular Officers, generally, this index

CONSULTANTS
Federal Court Appellate System Revision Commission, **28 § 41 nt**
Judicial Conference of the United States, security, **28 § 331**
Justice Department, this index
Secretary of Defense, this index
United States Marshals Service, security, **28 § 566**

CONSUMER CREDIT PROTECTION
Garnishment, generally, this index

CONSUMER PRICE INDEX
Federal agencies, fines, penalties and forfeitures, **28 § 2461 nt**
Fines, penalties and forfeitures, Federal agencies, **28 § 2461 nt**

CONSUMER PROTECTION
Monopolies and Combinations, generally, this index

CONTEMPT
Attachment, this index
Court of Federal Claims, this index
Crimes and offenses, United States magistrate judges, **28 § 636**
Foreign nationals, **28 § 1784**
Judicial Council, **28 § 332**
Rules of Civil Procedure, this index
Security, witnesses, foreign countries, **28 § 1784**
United States magistrate judges, **28 § 636**

CONTESTS
Customs Duties, this index

CONTINUANCES
Public money, delinquencies, **28 § 2407**

CONTRABAND
Counterfeiting, generally, this index
Trafficking, generally, this index

CONTRACTORS
Patents, **28 § 1498**
United States Court of Federal Claims, accounts and accounting, **28 §§ 1494, 2511**

CONTRACTS
Actions against U.S., trial by court, **28 § 2402**
Administrative Office of United States Courts, this index
Admiralty cases, jury trial, **28 § 1873**
Annuities, generally, this index
Court of Federal Claims, this index
District courts,
Reporters, **28 § 753**
United States, **28 §§ 1346, 2414**
Executive agencies. Public Contracts, this index
Federal agencies. Public Contracts, generally, this index
Handicapped Persons, this index
Information technology, Judiciary Information Technology Fund, **28 § 612**
Interference with contract rights, exception of claim from Tort Claims Act, **28 § 2680**
Interpreters, this index
Judicial Center Board, research projects and other services, **28 § 624**
Long term care. Nursing Homes, generally, this index
Maritime matters, jury trial, **28 § 1873**
Nursing Homes, generally, this index
Patents, generally, this index

CONTRACTS—Cont'd
Public Contracts, generally, this index
Quieting title, **28 § 2409a**
Restraint of trade. Monopolies and Combinations, generally, this index
United States, this index

CONTROLLED SUBSTANCES
Civil enforcement enhancement, **28 § 509 nt**
Crank. Methamphetamines, generally, post
Crimes and offenses. Sentence and punishment, generally, post
Drug Enforcement Administration, generally, this index
Ecstasy. Methamphetamines, generally, post
Exports and imports, methamphetamines, **28 § 994 nt**
Hazardous substances and waste, methamphetamine, removal, **28 § 524**
Laboratories,
Methamphetamines, post
Sentence and punishment, **28 § 994 nt**
List I chemicals, sentence and punishment, guidelines, **28 § 994 nt**
MDMA. Methamphetamines, generally, post
Methamphetamines,
Exports and imports, **28 § 994 nt**
Hazardous substances and waste, removal, **28 § 524**
Laboratories, operators, sentence and punishment, **28 § 994 nt**
Sentence and punishment, **28 § 994 nt**
Trafficking, sentence and punishment, **28 § 994 nt**
Operators, laboratories, sentence and punishment, guidelines, **28 § 994 nt**
Punishment. Sentence and punishment, generally, post
Removal, methamphetamine, hazardous substances and waste, **28 § 524**
Sentence and punishment,
Ecstasy, trafficking, guidelines, **28 § 994 nt**
Laboratories, operators, guidelines, **28 § 994 nt**
List I chemicals, guidelines, **28 § 994 nt**
Methamphetamines, ante
Trafficking. Methamphetamines, ante

CONVENTIONS
Evidence, Convention on the Taking of Evidence Abroad in Civil or Commercial Matters, **28 § 1781 nt**
Israel, evidence, Convention on the Taking of Evidence Abroad in Civil or Commercial Matters, **28 § 1781 nt**
Taking of Evidence Abroad in Civil or Commercial Matters, **28 § 1781 nt**

CONVERSION
United States, property, **28 §§ 2415, 2416**

CONVICTION OF CRIME
Crimes and Offenses, this index

CONVICTS
Correctional Institutions, generally, this index

COORDINATION
See specific index headings

COPIES
See specific index headings

COPYRIGHTS
Actions and proceedings,
Semiconductors, this index
Venue, **28 § 1400**
Assignments, Government employees, **28 § 1498**
Attorneys,
Fees, motion pictures, **28 § 4001**
Motion pictures, **28 § 4001**
Claims, foreign countries, **28 § 1498**
Collective bargaining agreements, motion pictures, transfers, **28 § 4001**
Costs, motion pictures, **28 § 4001**
Court of Federal Claims, infringement, **28 § 1498**
Damages. Infringement, post
District courts, **28 § 1338**
Exemptions, motion pictures, transfers, **28 § 4001**
Federal officers and employees, claims, **28 § 1498**
Fees. Attorneys, ante
Films. Motion Pictures, this index
Immunities, Congress, **28 § 1498 nt**
Infringement,
Damages, United States, **28 § 1498**
Limitation of actions, **28 § 1498**
Jurisdiction, **28 § 1338**
Semiconductors, this index
Limitation of actions, infringement, **28 § 1498**
Mask work cases, semiconductor chip products, **28 §§ 1338, 1498**
Mask works. Semiconductors, this index
Motion Pictures, this index
Notice, motion pictures, transfers, **28 § 4001**
Privileges and immunities, Congress, **28 § 1498 nt**
Reasonable and entire compensation, definitions, **28 § 1498**
Rules of Civil Procedure, this index
Security interest, motion pictures, transfers, **28 § 4001**
Semiconductors, this index
Transfers, motion pictures, collective bargaining agreements, **28 § 4001**
United States, this index
Venue, **28 § 1400**

CORPORATIONS
Actions and proceedings, **28 § 1349**
Shares and shareholders, **28 § 1695**
Attorneys, prevailing parties, **28 § 2412**

CORPORATIONS—Cont'd
Banks and Banking, generally, this index
Capital stock. Shares and Shareholders, generally, this index
District courts,
Citizens and and citizenship, **28 § 1332**
Jurisdiction, **28 § 1349**
Shareholders derivative actions, **28 § 1695**
Federal agencies, review of orders, right to intervene, **28 § 2348**
Federal Corporations, generally, this index
Federal prison industries. Correctional Institutions, this index
Fraud, task forces, **28 § 509 nt, EON 13271**
Garnishment, United States, **28 § 2405**
Income tax, refunds, venue, **28 § 1402**
Interpleader, filing, district courts, jurisdiction, **28 § 1335**
Intervention, review, orders, certain Federal agencies, **28 § 2348**
Jurisdiction, diversity of citizenship, **28 § 1332**
National Banks, generally, this index
Process, stockholder's derivative action, **28 § 1695**
Railroads, generally, this index
Refunds. Income tax, ante
Residence for venue purposes, **28 § 1391**
Resolution Trust Corporation, generally, this index
Rules of Civil Procedure, this index
Shares and Shareholders, generally, this index
Stock and stockholders. Shares and Shareholders, generally, this index
Surface Transportation Board, intervention, **28 § 2323**
Task forces, fraud, **28 § 509 nt, EON 13271**
Venue, **28 § 1391**
Shares and shareholders, **28 § 1401**
Tax refunds, **28 § 1402**

CORRECTIONAL INSTITUTIONS
Actions and proceedings,
Against Government, court screening and review, dismissal, grounds, **28 § 1915A**
District courts, **28 § 1346**
Forma Pauperis, generally, this index
Trust funds, **28 § 1915**
Agricultural products, funds, **28 § 530C**
Ammunition, funds, **28 § 530C**
Arrest or imprisonment on writ of execution or other process, privileges, **28 § 2007**
Attorney General, building and facilities account, **28 § 524**
Attorneys, funds, **28 § 530C**
Building and facilities account, Assets Forfeiture Fund, **28 § 524**
Complaints, frivolous complaints, inmates, **28 § 1915A**

CORRECTIONAL INSTITUTIONS
—Cont'd
Construction,
Assets Forfeiture Fund, **28 § 524 nt**
Funds, **28 § 530C**
Use of deposits transferred from Assets Forfeiture Fund to buildings and facilities account of Federal prison system, **28 § 524**
Criminal and other identification records, exchange with authorized officials, **28 § 534**
Dismissal and nonsuit, frivolous actions, inmates, **28 § 1915A**
Drug addicts, sentencing guidelines, **28 § 994 nt**
Federal prison industries, exceptions, **28 § 509**
Fees, fact witnesses, payment prohibition, **28 § 1821 nt**
Forma Pauperis, generally, this index
Frivolous actions, **28 § 1915A**
Dismissal, **28 § 1915**
Good time allowances, revocation, **28 § 1932**
Habeas Corpus, generally, this index
Indigent persons. Forma Pauperis, generally, this index
Juvenile Delinquents and Dependents, generally, this index
Labor and employment, funds, **28 § 530C**
Medical care and treatment, funds, **28 § 530C**
Probation, generally, this index
Proceedings. Actions and proceedings, generally, ante
Real estate, funds, **28 § 530C**
Revocation or suspension, earned release or good time credits, **28 § 1932**
Rules of Appellate Procedure, this index
Rules of Civil Procedure, this index
Trusts and trustees, funds, **28 § 530C**
Uniforms, allowances, **28 § 509 nt**
Weapons, funds, **28 § 530C**

CORRECTIONS
See specific index headings

COST OF LIVING
District judges, retirement and pensions, **28 § 373**
Federal agencies, fines, penalties and forfeitures, **28 § 2461 nt**

COSTS
Administrative Law and Procedure, this index
Admiralty, this index
Affidavits, bill of costs, **28 § 1924**
Amount in controversy,
Carriers, removal of cases or causes, **28 § 1445**
District courts, **28 § 1332**
Appeal, forma pauperis proceeding, **28 § 1915**
Attorneys, this index

COSTS—Cont'd
Bankruptcy, this index
Bill of costs, filing and inclusion in judgment or decree, **28 § 1920**
Briefs, admiralty appeals taxation of printing as costs, **28 § 1923**
Clerks of Courts, this index
Contempt, foreign nationals, subpoenas, **28 § 1784**
Convention on the Taking of Evidence Abroad in Civil or Commercial Matters, **28 § 1781 nt**
Copies of papers, taxation as costs, **28 § 1920**
Copyrights, this index
Court clerk's fees, taxation as costs, **28 § 1920**
Court interpreters, services, taxation as, **28 §§ 1827, 1828**
Court of Federal Claims, this index
Court reporter, fees, taxation as costs, **28 § 1920**
Courts of Appeals, this index
Criminal proceedings, in district court, **28 § 1918**
District Courts, this index
Docket fees, **28 §§ 1920, 1923**
Taxation, **28 §§ 1920, 1923**
Executive departments, **28 §§ 2408, 2412**
Exemplification of papers, fees, taxation as costs, **28 § 1920**
Experts, compensation of court appointed experts, taxation as costs, **28 § 1920**
Federal Agencies, this index
Federal Officers and Employees, this index
Fines, penalties and forfeitures,
Claims, **28 § 2465**
Violation of provisions, **28 § 1918**
Garnishment by U.S., **28 § 2405**
International Trade Court, this index
Interpreters,
Court interpreters, taxation as, **28 §§ 1827, 1828**
Special interpretation services, taxation as costs, **28 § 1920**
Patent infringement action, **28 § 1928**
Patents, this index
Printing fees, taxation as costs, **28 § 1920**
Removal of cases, remand of case removed, **28 § 1447**
Rules of Appellate Procedure, this index
Rules of Civil Procedure, this index
Seamen, this index
Searches and seizures, claims, **28 § 2465**
Stay of execution and enforcement of judgment to obtain certiorari, **28 § 2101**
Supreme Court, this index
Taxation, **28 §§ 1920, 1922**
United States marshal's fees, **28 § 1921**
Transcripts, this index
United States, this index
Witnesses, this index

COUNCILS
Federal Legal Council, **28 § 509 nt, EON 12146**
Judicial Council, generally, this index

COUNSELORS
Attorneys, generally, this index

COUNTERCLAIMS
Set-Off and Counterclaim, generally, this index

COUNTERFEITING
Emblems and insignia, public officers and employees, **28 § 994 nt**
Federal officers and employees, emblems and insignia, **28 § 994 nt**
Political subdivisions, officers and employees, emblems and insignia, **28 § 994 nt**
Sentence and punishment, amendments, **28 § 994 nt**
States, officers and employees, emblems and insignia, **28 § 994 nt**
Uniforms, public officers and employees, **28 § 994 nt**

COUNTERINTELLIGENCE
Intelligence, generally, this index

COUNTERTERRORISM
Terrorists and Terrorism, generally, this index

COUNTERTERRORISM FUND
Generally, **28 § 524 nt**

COUNTERVAILING DUTIES
Customs Duties, this index
International Trade Court, this index

COUPONS
Class actions, **28 § 1712**

COURT CRIERS
Compensation and salaries,
Director of Administrative Office of U.S. Courts, **28 § 604**
Increase, **28 § 603 nt**
Courts of appeals, appointment and removal, **28 § 714**
Director of Administrative Office of U.S. Courts, compensation and salaries, **28 § 604**
District courts, crier-law clerks, appointment, **28 § 755**
Meals and lodging when acting as bailiffs, appropriations, **28 § 524**
United States Court of International Trade, appointment, duties, **28 § 872**

COURT INTERPRETERS ACT
Generally, **28 §§ 1 nt, 602 et seq., 1827, 1828, 1920**

COURT OF APPEALS
Courts of Appeals, generally, this index

COURT OF APPEALS FOR FIRST CIRCUIT
Generally, **28 § 41 et seq.**
Chief Judge, priorities and preferences, **28 § 45**
Discipline, complaints, **28 § 372**
Emergencies, special sessions, **28 § 48**
Judges or justices,
Appointments, tenure, **28 § 44**
Assignments, **28 § 46**
Disqualification, **28 § 47**
Numbers and numbering, **28 § 44**
Jurisdiction, **28 § 41**
Sessions, **28 § 48**
Special sessions, **28 § 48**

COURT OF APPEALS FOR SECOND CIRCUIT
Generally, **28 § 41 et seq.**
Chief Judge, priorities and preferences, **28 § 45**
Emergencies, special sessions, **28 § 48**
Judges or justices,
Appointments, **28 § 44**
Assignments, **28 § 46**
Chief Judge, priorities and preferences, **28 § 45**
Complaints, **28 § 372**
Disqualification, **28 § 47**
Numbers and numbering, **28 § 44**
Jurisdiction, **28 § 41**
New York City, sessions, **28 § 48**
Numbers and numbering, judges or justices, **28 § 44**
Sessions, **28 § 48**
Terms of court, **28 § 48**

COURT OF APPEALS FOR THIRD CIRCUIT
Generally, **28 § 41 et seq.**
Chief Judge or Justice, precedence, **28 § 45**
Discipline, judges or justices, complaints, **28 § 372**
Emergencies, special sessions, **28 § 48**
Judges or justices,
Appointments, **28 § 44**
Numbers and numbering, **28 § 44**
Jurisdiction, **28 § 41**
Special sessions, **28 § 48**
Special terms, **28 § 48**
Terms of court, **28 § 48**
Virgin Islands, **28 § 1294**

COURT OF APPEALS FOR FOURTH CIRCUIT
Generally, **28 § 41 et seq.**
Certiorari, precedence, **28 § 45**
Emergencies, special sessions, **28 § 48**
Judges or justices,
Appointments, **28 § 44**
Assignments, **28 § 46**
Chief Judge, precedence, **28 § 45**
Complaints, **28 § 372**
Disqualification, **28 § 47**
Numbers and numbering, **28 § 44**
Judicial Council, **28 § 41**

COURT OF APPEALS FOR FOURTH CIRCUIT—Cont'd
Sessions, **28 § 48**
Special sessions, **28 § 48**
Special terms, **28 § 48**
Terms, court, **28 § 48**

COURT OF APPEALS FOR FIFTH CIRCUIT
Generally, **28 § 41 et seq.**
Assignments. Judges or justices, post
Emergencies,
Orders of court, **28 § 46**
Special sessions, **28 § 48**
Judges or justices,
Appointments, **28 § 44**
Assignments, **28 §§ 41 nt, 46**
Complaints, **28 § 372**
Priorities and preferences, **28 § 45**
Jurisdiction, **28 § 41**
New Fifth Circuit, definitions, Reorganization Act of 1980, **28 § 41 nt**
Orders of court, emergencies, **28 § 46**
Panels, emergencies, **28 § 46**
Sessions, **28 § 48**
Special sessions and terms, **28 § 48**
Terms, **28 § 48**

COURT OF APPEALS FOR SIXTH CIRCUIT
Generally, **28 § 41 et seq.**
Assignments, judges or justices, **28 § 46**
Chief Judge, **28 § 45**
Complaints, judges or justices, **28 § 372**
Emergencies, special sessions, **28 § 48**
Judges or justices,
Appointment, **28 § 44**
Assignments, **28 § 46**
Chief Judge, **28 § 45**
Complaints, **28 § 372**
Disability, complaints, **28 § 372**
Disqualification, **28 § 47**
Misconduct, **28 § 372**
Numbers and numbering, **28 § 44**
Location, **28 § 48**
Misconduct. Judges or justices, ante
Organization, **28 § 41**
Sessions, **28 § 48**
Special sessions, **28 § 48**
Terms, **28 § 48**

COURT OF APPEALS FOR SEVENTH CIRCUIT
Generally, **28 § 41 et seq.**
Emergencies, special sessions, **28 § 48**
Judges or justices,
Appointments, **28 § 44**
Assignments, **28 § 46**
Complaints, **28 § 372**
Disqualification, **28 § 47**
Numbers and numbering, **28 § 44**
Jurisdiction, **28 § 41**
Sessions, **28 § 48**
Terms of court, **28 § 48**

COURT OF APPEALS FOR EIGHTH CIRCUIT
Generally, **28 § 41 et seq.**
Chief Judge or Justice, priorities and preferences, **28 § 45**
Emergencies, special sessions, **28 § 48**
Judges or justices,
Appointment, **28 § 44**
Assignments, **28 § 46**
Discipline, **28 § 372**
Disqualification, **28 § 47**
Number, **28 § 44**
Jurisdiction, **28 § 41**
Kansas City, MO, sessions, **28 § 48**
Omaha NB, sessions, **28 § 48**
Saint Louis, MO, sessions, **28 § 48**
Saint Paul, MN, sessions, **28 § 48**
Sessions, **28 § 48**
Special sessions, **28 § 48**
Special terms, **28 § 48**
Terms of court, **28 § 48**

COURT OF APPEALS FOR NINTH CIRCUIT
Generally, **28 § 41 et seq.**
Emergencies, special sessions, **28 § 48**
Judges or justices, complaints, **28 § 372**

COURT OF APPEALS FOR TENTH CIRCUIT
Generally, **28 § 41 et seq.**
Emergencies, special sessions, **28 § 48**
Judges or justices, **28 § 44**
Assignments, **28 § 46**
Complaints, **28 § 372**
Disqualification, **28 § 47**
Jurisdiction, **28 § 41**
Location, **28 § 48**
Sessions, **28 § 48**
Special sessions, **28 § 48**

COURT OF APPEALS FOR ELEVENTH CIRCUIT
Generally, **28 § 41 et seq.**
Chief Judge or Justice, **28 § 45**
Emergencies, special sessions, **28 § 48**
Judges or justices,
Appointments, **28 § 44**
Assignments, **28 §§ 41 nt, 46**
Complaints, **28 § 372**
Judicial circuit, **28 § 41**
Montgomery AL, location, **28 § 48**
Special sessions, **28 § 48**
Special terms, **28 § 48**
Terms of court, **28 § 48**

COURT OF APPEALS FOR THE ARMED FORCES
Certiorari, writ of, Supreme Court, **28 § 1259**
Supreme Court, writ of certiorari, **28 § 1259**
Time, certiorari, application, **28 § 2101**
Transportation, **28 § 456 nt**

COURT OF APPEALS FOR THE DISTRICT OF COLUMBIA
Generally, **28 § 1651 et seq.**
Chief Judge or Justice, **28 §§ 45, 451 nt**
Emergencies, special sessions, **28 § 48**
Evidence, **28 § 1731 et seq.**
Independent Counsel, **28 § 49**
Judges or justices,
Appointments, terms of office, **28 § 44**
Assignments, **28 § 46**
Disqualification, **28 § 47**
Domicile and residence, exemptions, **28 § 44**
Numbers and numbering, **28 § 44**
Official duty station, **28 § 456**
Jurisdiction, **28 § 41**
Marshals, **28 § 713 nt**
Numbers and numbering, judges or justices, **28 § 44**
Orders of court, Federal agencies, venue, **28 § 2343**
Retirement and pensions, judges or justices, assignments, **28 § 49**
Sessions, **28 § 48**
Special sessions, **28 § 48**
Special terms, **28 § 48**
Terms, **28 § 48**
Traveling expenses, judges or justices, **28 § 456**
Washington, city of, sessions, **28 § 48**

COURT OF APPEALS FOR THE FEDERAL CIRCUIT
Accommodations, **28 § 462**
Appointments, Chief Judge or Justice, **28 § 45 nt**
Black persons, judges or justices, **28 § 133 nt**
Budget, **28 § 605**
Chief Judge or Justice, **28 § 45**
Domicile and residence, **28 § 44**
Removal from office, **28 § 176**
Civil service, opinions and decisions, **28 § 1295**
Complaints. Judges or justices, post
Copyrights, **28 § 1295**
District of Columbia, sessions, **28 § 48**
Domicile and residence, judges or justices, **28 § 44**
Economic stabilization, opinions and decisions, **28 § 1295**
Emergencies,
Oil and gas, **28 § 1295**
Special sessions, **28 § 48**
Executive departments,
Opinions and decisions, **28 § 1295**
Petitions, **28 § 520**
Executive offices, **28 § 1296**
Exemptions, jurisdiction, **28 § 2342**
Foreign countries, orders of court, **28 § 256**
Guam, **28 § 1295**
Harmonized Tariff Schedules, **28 § 1295**
Interest, judgments and decrees, **28 § 1961**

COURT OF APPEALS FOR THE FEDERAL CIRCUIT—Cont'd
Interlocutory proceedings, **28 § 1292**
Foreign countries, evidence, **28 § 256**
Jurisdiction, **28 § 1292**
International Trade Commission, unfair trade practices, **28 § 1295**
International Trade Court, **28 § 2645**
Investigations, judges or justices, complaints, **28 § 351 et seq.**
Judges or justices,
Appointments, **28 § 44**
Assignments, **28 § 46**
Chief Judge or Justice, generally, ante
Compensation and salaries, **28 § 371**
Complaints, **28 § 351 et seq.**
Domicile and residence, **28 § 44**
Former judges or justices, **28 § 44 nt**
Official duty station, **28 § 456**
Panels, **28 § 46**
Removal from office, **28 § 176**
Retirement and pensions, **28 § 371**
Senior judges, **28 § 44 nt**
Successors, **28 § 371**
Women, **28 § 133 nt**
Judgments and decrees, interest, **28 § 1961**
Judicial district, **28 § 41**
Jurisdiction, **28 §§ 41, 291 nt, 1291 et seq.**
Exemptions, **28 § 2342**
Northern Mariana Islands, **28 § 1295**
Official duty station, judges, **28 § 456**
Oil and gas, **28 § 1295**
Oral argument, **28 § 518**
Solicitor General, **28 § 518**
Panels,
Judges or justices, **28 § 46**
Quorum, **28 § 46**
Rotation, **28 § 46**
Patents,
Infringement, **28 § 1292**
Interference, **28 § 1295**
Jurisdiction, **28 § 1295**
Petitions,
Rehearing, post
Transportation, **28 § 520**
Plant variety protection, **28 § 1295**
Presidential Offices, **28 § 1296**
Quorum, panels, **28 § 46**
Rehearing, petitions, **28 § 171 nt**
Removal from office, judges or justices, **28 § 176**
Sessions, **28 § 48**
Solicitor General, **28 § 518**
Special sessions, **28 § 48**
Special terms, **28 § 48**
Stay of proceedings, interlocutory appeal, **28 § 1292**
Terms, **28 § 48**
Time, sessions, **28 § 48**
Trademarks and trade names, jurisdiction, **28 § 1295**
Transfers, Court of Claims, **28 § 171 nt**
Transportation, petitions, **28 § 520**
United States, jurisdiction, **28 § 1295**

COURT OF APPEALS FOR THE FEDERAL CIRCUIT—Cont'd
Vacancies in office, Chief Judge or Justice, **28 § 45 nt**
Virgin Islands, **28 § 1295**
Women, judges or justices, **28 § 133 nt**

COURT OF APPEALS FOR VETERANS CLAIMS
Attorneys,
Federal agencies, fees, **28 § 2412**
Fees,
Federal agencies, **28 § 2412**
United States, **28 § 2412**
United States, fees, **28 § 2412**
Federal agencies, attorneys, fees, **28 § 2412**
Fees, nonattorney practitioners, **28 § 2412 nt**
Nonattorney practitioners, **28 § 2412 nt**
United States, attorneys, fees, **28 § 2412**

COURT OF CLAIMS
Court of Federal Claims, generally, this index

COURT OF FEDERAL CLAIMS
Generally, **28 § 2501 et seq.**
Accommodations, **28 § 462**
Act of Congress, jurisdiction, **28 § 1491**
Administrative Office of United States Courts,
Annuities, **28 § 604**
Bailiffs, **28 § 795**
Deputies, **28 § 791**
Admissions. Attorneys, post
Age, judges, **28 § 171 nt**
Agreements. Contracts, generally, post
Aliens, **28 § 2502**
Appeal and review,
Congressional reference cases, **28 § 2509**
Indebtedness, **28 § 2508**
Interest, **28 § 2516**
Interlocutory orders, **28 § 1292**
Judges, discipline, **28 § 372**
Jurisdiction, **28 § 1295**
New trial, **28 § 2515**
Notice, **28 § 2522**
Appearances, **28 § 2503**
Plaintiffs, **28 § 2504**
Application of law, **28 § 460**
Appointment,
Bailiffs, **28 § 795**
Clerks, **28 § 791**
Judges, **28 § 171**
Law clerks, **28 § 794**
Messengers, **28 § 795**
Secretaries, **28 § 794**
Appropriations, congressional reference cases, **28 § 2509**
Arguments, **28 § 518**
Army, contracts, **28 § 1491**
Assignments,
Congressional reference cases, **28 § 2509**
Judges or justices, post

COURT OF FEDERAL CLAIMS
—Cont'd
Assignments—Cont'd
Patents, **28 § 1498**
Attorneys,
Admissions, fees, **28 § 1926 nt**
Fees, vexatious procedures, **28 § 1927**
Bailiffs, **28 § 795**
Black persons, judges, **28 § 133 nt**
Books and papers,
Federal agencies, **28 § 2507**
Fees, **28 § 1926 nt**
Referrals, **28 § 2510**
Reproduction, **28 § 1926 nt**
Calls, Federal agencies, **28 § 2507**
Certificates and certification,
Attorneys, **28 § 1926 nt**
Books and papers, **28 § 1926 nt**
Judgments and decrees, **28 § 2517**
Unjust convictions, **28 § 2513**
Certified copies, pardons, **28 § 2513**
Chief Judge or Justice, **28 § 171**
Assignments, **28 § 174**
Bailiffs, **28 § 795**
Congress, bills, references, **28 §§ 1492, 2509**
Foreign countries, **28 § 798**
Judgments and decrees, **28 § 2517**
Messengers, **28 § 795**
Special masters, **28 § 798**
United States Marshals Service, **28 § 2521**
Clerks of courts,
Appointment, **28 § 791**
Removal from office, **28 § 791**
Coast Guard Exchanges, contracts, jurisdiction, **28 § 1491**
Commissioners, **28 § 171 nt**
Compensation and salaries. Judges or justices, post
Complaints. Judges or justices, post
Conclusions of law, congressional reference cases, **28 § 2509**
Concurrent jurisdiction, **28 § 1346**
Conduct, **28 § 518**
Congress,
Chief Judge, bills, references, **28 §§ 1492, 2509**
Judgments and decrees, **28 §§ 791, 2516**
Patents, **28 § 1498 nt**
Reference cases, **28 § 2509**
Constitution of the United States, jurisdiction, **28 § 1491**
Contempt, **28 § 2521**
Contracts,
Interest, **28 § 2516**
Jurisdiction, **28 § 1491**
Reporters, **28 § 796**
Copyrights, infringement, **28 § 1498**
Costs, **28 § 2503**
Congress, **28 §§ 791, 2509**
Dismissal and nonsuit, **28 § 1919**
Excesses, **28 § 1927**
Judicial Conference, **28 § 1926**
Payment, **28 § 791**

COURT OF FEDERAL CLAIMS
—Cont'd
Damages, **28 § 2508**
Imprisonment, **28 § 2513**
Jurisdiction, **28 § 1491**
Oysters, growers, **28 § 1497**
Declaratory judgments and decrees, income tax, exemptions, **28 § 1507**
Decrees. Judgments and decrees, generally, post
Demand, **28 § 2508**
Deputy clerks, **28 § 791**
Disbursing officials, clerks, and agents, losses, **28 §§ 1496, 2512**
Discipline, judges or justices, **28 § 372**
Discovery, **28 § 2507**
Subpoenas, **28 § 2521**
Dismissal and nonsuit,
Costs, **28 § 1919**
Jurisdiction, **28 § 1919**
District of Columbia,
Judges or justices, official duty station, **28 § 175**
Location, **28 § 798**
Principal office, **28 § 173**
Domicile and residence, judges or justices, **28 § 175**
Electronically stored information, fees, **28 § 1926 nt**
Employees. Officers and employees, generally, post
Entry. Judgments and decrees, post
Evidence, **28 § 2503**
Federal agencies, **28 §§ 2503, 2507**
Fraud,
Forfeitures, **28 § 2514**
New trial, **28 § 2515**
Imprisonment, **28 § 2513**
Location, **28 § 2505**
Executive departments,
Books and papers, **28 § 2507**
Petitions, **28 § 520**
Records and recordation, **28 § 1491**
Expenses and expenditures, judges or justices, retirement and pensions, **28 § 797**
Fees,
Advances, **28 § 1926**
Attorneys, ante
Judicial Conference of the United States, post
Payment, **28 § 791**
Schedules, **28 § 1926 nt**
Filing, schedules, **28 § 1926 nt**
Findings of fact,
Congressional reference cases, **28 § 2509**
Fraud, **28 § 2514**
Fines, penalties and forfeitures,
Contempt, **28 § 2521**
Unreasonable conduct, **28 § 1927**
Vexatious conduct, **28 § 1927**
Forma pauperis proceedings, **28 § 2503**

COURT OF FEDERAL CLAIMS
—Cont'd
Former court, **28 § 171 nt**
U.S. Court of Appeals for the Federal Circuit, judges or justices, **28 §§ 44 nt, 45 nt**
Fraud, **28 § 2514**
Evidence,
Forfeitures, **28 § 2514**
New trial, **28 § 2515**
New trial, fraud against U.S., **28 § 2515**
Hearings, witnesses, domicile and residence, **28 § 2503**
Hours of labor, contractors, **28 § 1499**
In forma pauperis, imprisonment, damages, **28 § 2513**
Income tax,
Aliens, refunds, objections and exceptions, **28 § 2502**
Declaratory judgments and decrees, **28 § 1507**
Partnership, jurisdiction, **28 § 1508**
Indians,
Jurisdiction, **28 § 1505**
Treaties, jurisdiction, **28 § 1505**
Insurance, judges, retirement and pensions, **28 § 179**
Interest, judgments and decrees, **28 § 2516**
Rates and charges, **28 § 1961**
Interlocutory proceedings, appeal and review, **28 § 1292**
Intervention, **28 § 1491**
Investigations, judges or justices, complaints, **28 § 351 et seq.**
Judges or justices,
Age, **28 § 171 nt**
Appointment, **28 § 171**
Law clerks and secretaries, **28 § 794**
Assignments, **28 § 174**
Certificates and certification, substantial service, recall, **28 § 375**
Chief Judge or Justice, generally, ante
Commissioner of former U.S. Court of Claims, **28 § 171 nt**
Compensation and salaries, **28 § 171 nt**
Adjustments, **28 § 172**
Resignation, **28 § 371**
Retirement and pensions, supplemental pay, **28 §§ 375, 797**
Complaints, **28 § 351 et seq.**
Appeal and review, **28 § 372**
Discipline, **28 § 372**
Congressional reference cases, **28 § 2509**
Discipline, **28 § 372**
Domicile and residence, **28 § 175**
Entry of judgment, **28 § 2505**
Insurance, retirement and pensions, **28 § 179**
Law books, successors, **28 § 414**
Law clerks,
Appointment, **28 § 794**

COURT OF FEDERAL CLAIMS
—Cont'd
Judges or justices—Cont'd
Law clerks—Cont'd
Leaves of absence, objections and exceptions, **28 § 794**
Number, **28 § 171**
Official duty station, District of Columbia, **28 § 175**
Powers and duties, **28 § 2503**
Recall, **28 § 375**
Removal from office, **28 § 176**
Disbarment, **28 § 177**
Resignation, age, **28 § 371**
Retirement and pensions,
Age, **28 §§ 178, 371**
Annuities, **28 § 178**
Payment, **28 § 604**
Survivors, **28 § 376**
Definitions, **28 § 178**
Insurance, **28 § 179**
Payments, **28 § 178**
Recall, **28 §§ 375, 797**
Retirement Fund, **28 § 178**
Service, **28 § 178**
Secretaries, appointment, **28 § 794**
Selection, nomination, **28 § 133 nt**
Senior retired judges, recall, **28 § 797**
Successor, appointment, **28 § 371**
Term of office, **28 §§ 171 nt, 172**
Judgments and decrees,
Conclusiveness, **28 § 2519**
Contractors, unsettled accounts, payment, **28 § 2511**
Disbursing officers, relief, **28 § 2512**
Entry, **28 § 2505**
Indebtedness, **28 § 2508**
Interest, **28 § 2516**
Allowance, computation, **28 § 1961**
Judges, powers and duties, **28 § 2503**
Labor and employment, **28 § 1491**
Opinions and decisions, inspection and inspectors, **28 § 174**
Payment, **28 § 2517**
Interest, **28 § 2516**
Referrals, **28 § 2510**
Statements, **28 § 791**
Transcripts, post
Judicial Conference of the United States, fees, **28 § 1926**
Jurisdiction,
Appeal and review, **28 § 1295**
Concurrent jurisdiction, **28 § 1346**
Contractors, **28 §§ 1494, 1499**
Contracts, **28 § 1491**
Copyright, **28 § 1498**
Disbursing officers, **28 § 1496**
Imprisonment, damages, **28 § 1495**
Indians, ante
Lack of, dismissal and nonsuit, **28 § 1919**
Mask work cases, semiconductor chip products, **28 § 1498**
Oysters, growers, dredging, **28 § 1497**
Pendency, claims in other courts, **28 § 1500**

COURT OF FEDERAL CLAIMS
—Cont'd
Jurisdiction—Cont'd
Pensions, **28 § 1501**
Set-off and counterclaim, **28 § 1503**
Transfer to cure want of jurisdiction, **28 § 1631**
Treaties, **28 § 1502**
Labor and employment, records and recordation, **28 § 1491**
Law clerks, **28 § 794**
Liability. Damages, generally, ante
Limitation of actions, **28 § 2501**
Filing, **28 § 2501**
New trial, **28 § 2515**
Lists, monthly listing of opinions and orders, **28 § 1926 nt**
Location, **28 § 798**
Marine Corps Exchanges, contracts, **28 § 1491**
Mask work cases, semiconductor chip products, jurisdiction, **28 § 1498**
Messengers, appointment and removal, **28 § 795**
Misrepresentation. Fraud, generally, ante
Motions. Stay of proceedings, post
National Aeronautics and Space Administration Exchange Councils, contracts, jurisdiction, **28 § 1491**
Navy, exchanges, contracts, jurisdiction, **28 § 1491**
New trial, **28 § 2515**
Nominations, judges, minorities, **28 § 133 nt**
Notice,
Appeal and review, ante
Contractors, **28 § 2511**
Federal officers and employees, contractors, unsettled accounts, **28 § 2511**
Plaintiffs, oaths and affirmations, **28 § 2504**
Numbers and numbering, judges, **28 § 171**
Oaths and affirmations,
Judges, administration, **28 § 2503**
Plaintiffs, examinations and examiners, **28 § 2504**
Officers and employees,
Accounts and accounting, jurisdiction, **28 § 1494**
Appointment, **28 § 791**
Information, refusal, **28 § 2507**
Labor and employment, remand, **28 § 1491**
Patents, jurisdiction, **28 § 1498**
Removal, **28 § 791**
Unsettled accounts, notice, **28 § 2511**
Opinions and decisions, fees, schedule, lists, **28 § 1926 nt**
Orders of court,
Fees, schedule, **28 § 1926 nt**
Labor and employment, records and recordation, **28 § 1491**

COURT OF FEDERAL CLAIMS
—Cont'd
Orders of court—Cont'd
Plaintiffs, examinations and examiners, **28 § 2504**
Postponement, plaintiffs, appearances, **28 § 2504**
Subpoenas, **28 § 2521**
Oysters, growers, dredging, damages, **28 § 1497**
Papers. Books and papers, generally, ante
Pardon,
Consideration, **28 § 2513**
Unjust conviction and imprisonment, evidence, **28 § 2513**
Parties,
Examinations and examiners, oaths and affirmations, **28 § 2504**
Information, **28 § 2507**
Subpoenas, **28 § 2521**
Witnesses, exemptions, **28 § 2506**
Partnership. Income tax, ante
Patents,
Jurisdiction, **28 § 1498**
Privileges and immunities, Member of Congress, **28 § 1498 nt**
Payment. Judgments and decrees, ante
Penalties. Fines, penalties and forfeitures, generally, ante
Pending actions, **28 § 1500**
Pensions. Retirement and pensions, generally, post
Petitions, **28 § 520**
Attorney General, transmission, **28 § 520**
Plant variety protection, infringement, **28 § 1498**
Pleading, convictions, unjust, **28 § 2513**
President of the United States, judges, appointment, **28 § 171**
Privileges and immunities, patents, **28 § 1498 nt**
Proof. Evidence, generally, ante
Punishment. Sentence and punishment, generally, post
Reasonable and entire compensation, definitions, copyright, **28 § 1498**
Records and recordation, **28 § 171**
Fees, reproduction, **28 § 1926 nt**
Labor and employment, **28 § 1491**
References, **28 § 2510**
Refunds. Taxation, post
Refusal, plea or answer, **28 § 2504**
Remand, labor and employment, **28 § 1491**
Removal, judges or justices, **28 § 176**
Removal of cases or causes,
Bailiffs, **28 § 795**
Clerks, **28 § 791**
Judges or justices, **28 § 177**
Jurisdiction, **28 § 1631**
Messengers, **28 § 795**
Reporters,
Contracts, **28 § 796**
Transcripts, generally, post

COURT OF FEDERAL CLAIMS
—Cont'd
Reports,
Bills, reference, **28 §§ 1492, 2509**
Congressional reference cases, **28 § 2509**
Reproduction, fees, **28 § 1926 nt**
Retirement and pensions,
Chief judges, bills, **28 §§ 1492, 2509**
Federal agencies, **28 § 1491**
Judges or justices, ante
Jurisdiction, **28 § 1501**
Status, **28 § 1491**
Returns, funds, **28 § 791**
Review. Appeal and review, generally, ante
Sanctions. Fines, penalties and forfeitures, generally, ante
Schedules, fees, Judicial Conference, **28 § 1926 nt**
Secretaries, appointment, **28 § 794**
Sentence and punishment,
Contempt, **28 § 2521**
Unjust imprisonment, damages, **28 §§ 1495, 2513**
Set-off and counterclaim, **28 § 2508**
Jurisdiction, **28 § 1503**
Solicitor General, conduct and argument of cases, **28 § 518**
Special masters, appointment, **28 § 798**
Statements, Congress, **28 § 791**
Statute of limitations. Limitation of actions, generally, ante
Stay of proceedings,
Interlocutory appeal, **28 § 1292**
Judgments and decrees, **28 § 2515**
Motions, transfers, **28 § 1292**
Studies, concurrent jurisdiction, **28 § 1491 nt**
Subpoenas, parties, attendance, **28 § 2521**
Supersedeas bond. Stay of proceedings, generally, ante
Supreme Court, judgments and decrees, interest, **28 § 2516**
Surface Transportation Board, orders,
Jurisdiction, **28 § 1336**
Venue, **28 § 1398**
Taxation,
Costs, generally, ante
Refunds, tax shelters, **28 § 1509**
Terms of office, judges, **28 § 171**
Time,
Holding court, **28 § 173**
Limitation of actions, **28 § 2501**
Torts, damages, **28 § 1491**
Transcripts, judgments and decrees, **28 § 2508**
Federal officers and employees, contractors, **28 § 2511**
Interest, **28 § 2516**
Transfer of cases or causes. Removal of cases or causes, generally, ante
Transmission, petitions, **28 § 520**
Treaties, jurisdiction, **28 § 1502**

COURT OF FEDERAL CLAIMS
—Cont'd
Understatement penalties, refunds, jurisdiction, **28 § 1509**
United States Marshals Service, attendance, **28 § 2521**
Unjust conviction and imprisonment,
Damages, **28 § 1495**
Evidence, **28 § 2513**
Vouchers,
Disbursing officers, **28 § 1496**
Referrals, books and papers, **28 § 2510**
Witnesses,
Disqualification, **28 § 2506**
Examinations and examiners, oaths and affirmations, **28 § 2503**
Per diem, **28 § 1821**
Subpoenas, **28 § 2521**
Subsistence allowance, **28 § 1821**
Women, judges, nominations, **28 § 133 nt**

COURT REPORTERS
Reporters, generally, this index

COURT RULES
Rules of Court, generally, this index

COURTHOUSES AND COURTROOMS
Administrative Office of United States Courts, generally, this index
Sales, **28 § 2001**
United States Court of International Trade, **28 § 251**

COURTS
Generally, **28 § 1 et seq.**
Accommodations, **28 §§ 462, 604**
Administrative Office of United States Courts, generally, this index
Agents and agencies. Judicial Agencies, generally, this index
Always open, **28 § 452**
Appeal and Review, generally, this index
Application of law, **28 nt prec § 1**
Appointments, **28 § 609**
Attorney General, **28 § 518**
Attorneys, generally, this index
Audits and auditors, **28 § 604**
Bail, generally, this index
Bailiffs, generally, this index
Bankruptcy, this index
Budget estimate, **28 § 605**
Calendars. Dockets and Docketing, generally, this index
Certificates and certification,
Certifying officers, **28 § 613**
Revenue officers, **28 § 2006**
Certified copies, **28 § 1734 et seq.**
Circuits. Judicial Circuits, generally, this index
Clerical assistants,
Compensation and salaries, **28 §§ 603 nt, 604**
Salaries, **28 §§ 603 nt, 604**
Clerks of Courts, generally, this index

COURTS—Cont'd
Compensation and salaries. Officers and employees, post
Construction of Act relating to, **28 nt prec § 1**
Contempt, generally, this index
Court of Appeals for First Circuit, generally, this index
Court of Appeals for Second Circuit, generally, this index
Court of Appeals for Third Circuit, generally, this index
Court of Appeals for Fourth Circuit, generally, this index
Court of Appeals for Fifth Circuit, generally, this index
Court of Appeals for Sixth Circuit, generally, this index
Court of Appeals for Seventh Circuit, generally, this index
Court of Appeals for Eighth Circuit, generally, this index
Court of Appeals for Ninth Circuit, generally, this index
Court of Appeals for Tenth Circuit, generally, this index
Court of Appeals for Eleventh Circuit, generally, this index
Court of Appeals for the Armed Forces, generally, this index
Court of Appeals for the District of Columbia, generally, this index
Court of Appeals for the Federal Circuit, generally, this index
Court of Appeals for Veterans Claims, generally, this index
Court of Federal Claims, generally, this index
Courts of Appeals, generally, this index
Criers. Court Criers, generally, this index
Definitions, **28 § 451**
Depositions, generally, this index
Deposits, **28 § 296**
Fines, penalties and forfeitures, **28 § 2044**
Interpleader, **28 § 1335**
Investments, pending actions, **28 § 2045**
Treasury Department, powers and duties, **28 §§ 2041, 2043**
Withdrawals, **28 § 2042**
Detention, generally, this index
Disbursing officials, clerks, and agents, **28 § 613**
District Courts, generally, this index
District Judges, generally, this index
Dockets and Docketing, generally, this index
Employees. Officers and employees, generally, post
Evidence. Rules of Evidence, generally, this index
Federal Rules of Evidence. Rules of Evidence, generally, this index
Fees, **28 § 1931 nt**

COURTS—Cont'd
Foreign Courts or Tribunals, generally, this index
Funds. Deposits, generally, ante
Grand Jury, generally, this index
Guam, this index
Incentive pay or awards, **28 § 604**
Independent Counsel, generally, this index
Inspection and inspectors, overseas, dockets and docketing, **28 § 604**
Insular Possessions and Dependencies, this index
International Trade Court, generally, this index
International tribunals. Foreign Courts or Tribunals, generally, this index
Interpreters, generally, this index
Investments, deposits, pending actions, **28 § 2045**
Judges or Justices, generally, this index
Judgments and Decrees, generally, this index
Judicial Center, generally, this index
Judicial Circuits, generally, this index
Judicial Conference of the United States, generally, this index
Judicial Districts, generally, this index
Judicial review. Appeal and Review, generally, this index
Judicial Sales, generally, this index
Jurisdiction, generally, this index
Jury, generally, this index
Justice Department, services, **28 § 518**
Law Books, generally, this index
Law Clerks, generally, this index
Libraries. Law Libraries, generally, this index
Machinery and equipment, **28 § 604**
Magistrates. United States Magistrate Judges, generally, this index
Marshals. United States Marshals Service, generally, this index
Messengers, compensation and salaries, **28 §§ 603 nt, 604**
Minutes, assignments of justices and judges, **28 § 295**
Obsolete papers, disposal, **28 § 457**
Office expenses, payment, **28 § 604**
Officers and employees,
Administrative personnel, **28 § 609**
Certifying officers, **28 § 613**
Citizens Commission On Public Service and Compensation, generally, this index
Clerical assistants, generally, ante
Compensation and salaries, **28 § 602 et seq.**
Increases, **28 § 603 nt**
Court Criers, generally, this index
Disbursing officials, clerks, and agents, **28 § 613**
Forma pauperis proceedings, **28 § 1915**
Incentive pay or awards, **28 § 604**
Jury service, exemptions, **28 § 1863**

COURTS—Cont'd
Officers and employees—Cont'd
Receivers and receivership, **28 § 958**
Removal of cases or causes, **28 § 1442**
Taxation, liability, **28 § 960**
United States Marshals Service, generally, this index
Orders of Court, generally, this index
Payment. Deposits, generally, ante
Pending actions,
Deposits, investments, **28 § 2045**
Statements, **28 § 522**
Personal appearances, **28 § 1654**
Priorities and preferences, civil cases, **28 § 1657**
Publications, distribution, **28 § 413**
Records and recordation,
Copies, former courts, **28 § 6**
Disqualification, judges or justices, **28 § 455**
Former courts, **28 § 6**
Habeas corpus, indigents, costs, **28 § 2250**
Judges or justices, disqualification, **28 § 455**
Lost or destroyed records, **28 § 1735**
Property, different districts, orders, **28 § 1692**
Release, generally, this index
Remand, generally, this index
Removal of Cases or Causes, generally, this index
Reporters, generally, this index
Rules of Civil Procedure, generally, this index
Rules of Court, generally, this index
Seals (Official Seals), this index
Secretaries, compensation and salaries, **28 §§ 603 nt, 604**
Security, **28 § 604**
Separability, **28 nt prec § 1**
Sessions, generally, this index
Solicitor General, services, **28 § 518**
Speedy trial. Trial, this index
State Courts, generally, this index
State laws, rules of decision, **28 § 1652**
Stenographers, compensation and salaries, **28 §§ 603 nt, 604**
Subpoenas, foreign countries, **28 § 1783**
Supplies, **28 § 604**
Supreme Court, generally, this index
Tax Court. United States Tax Court, generally, this index
Taxation, officers and employees, liability, **28 § 960**
Territories, this index
United States courts of appeals. Courts of Appeals, generally, this index
United States Magistrate Judges, generally, this index
United States Marshals Service, generally, this index
United States Tax Court, generally, this index
Venue, generally, this index
Witnesses, generally, this index

COURTS-MARTIAL
Appeal and review. Court of Appeals for the Armed Forces, generally, this index

COURTS OF APPEALS
Administrative Office of United States Courts, **28 § 41 nt**
Admiralty, **28 § 1292**
Advisory committees, **28 § 2077**
Age, Chief Judge or Justice, **28 § 45**
Agriculture, **28 § 2342**
Amount in controversy, **28 § 2108**
Appearance, **28 § 1654**
Appointments,
Clerks of courts, **28 § 711**
Federal Courts of Appeals Commission, **28 § 41 nt**
Judges or justices, post
Assignments. Chief Judge or Justice, post
Atomic Energy Commission, **28 § 2342**
Bailiffs, **28 § 714**
Bankruptcy, this index
Black persons, judges or justices, **28 § 133 nt**
Certificates and certification,
Federal agencies, **28 §§ 2112, 2346**
Habeas corpus, **28 § 2253**
Certified Questions, generally, this index
Certiorari. Supreme Court, this index
Chief Judge or Justice, **28 § 45 et seq.**
Age, **28 § 45**
Appointments, **28 § 45**
Assignments, **28 § 292 et seq.**
Consent, **28 § 295**
Multidistrict litigation, **28 § 1407**
Retired judges or justices, **28 § 294**
Revocation, **28 § 295**
Disability, **28 §§ 45, 372**
Federal Courts Improvement Act of 1982, amendments, **28 § 45 nt**
Illnesses, **28 § 46**
Judicial Conference of the Circuit, **28 § 333**
Judicial Conference of the United States, **28 § 331**
Judicial Council, **28 § 332**
Retired judges or justices, **28 §§ 294, 371**
Senior circuit judges, **28 § 451 nt**
Senior staff attorneys, **28 §§ 604 nt, 715**
Senior technical assistants, **28 § 715**
Sentence and punishment, **28 § 334**
Status, circuit judges, **28 § 45**
Temporary assignments, **28 § 292**
Terms of office, **28 § 45**
Three judge court, **28 § 2284**
Circuit Executive, **28 § 332**
Circuits, **28 § 41 et seq.**
Clerks of courts,
Appointments, **28 § 711**
Assistants, **28 § 711**
Compensation and salaries, **28 § 604 nt**

COURTS OF APPEALS—Cont'd
Clerks of courts—Cont'd
Costs, **28 § 711**
Deputies, **28 § 711**
Fees, **28 § 711**
Compensation and salaries,
Federal Courts of Appeals Commission, **28 § 41 nt**
Judges or justices, post
Law clerks, **28 §§ 603 nt, 604**
Secretaries, **28 §§ 603 nt, 604**
Costs, **28 § 1912**
Clerks of courts, **28 § 711**
Judicial Conference, **28 § 1913**
Court of Appeals for Veterans Claims, generally, this index
Criers, **28 § 714**
Damages, **28 § 1912**
Deputies, clerks of courts, **28 § 711**
District of Columbia. Court of Appeals for the District of Columbia, generally, this index
Divisions, **28 § 292**
Domicile and residence. Judges or justices, post
Eighth Circuit. Court of Appeals for Eighth Circuit, generally, this index
Elections, en banc, **28 § 46**
Eleventh Circuit. Court of Appeals for Eleventh Circuit, generally, this index
Emergencies, special sessions, **28 § 48**
En banc (courts), **28 §§ 41 nt, 46**
Evidence, **28 § 1731 et seq.**
Amount in controversy, **28 § 2108**
Federal agencies, records and recordation, **28 § 2112**
Rules of Evidence, generally, this index
Extension of time, **28 § 2107**
Extradition, **28 § 2253**
Federal agencies, **28 §§ 2112, 2346 et seq.**
Federal Circuit. Court of Appeals for the Federal Circuit, generally, this index
Federal Communications Commission, **28 § 2342**
Federal Maritime Commission, jurisdiction, **28 § 2342**
Federal Rules of Evidence. Rules of Evidence, generally, this index
Fees,
Clerks of courts, **28 § 711**
Judicial Conference, **28 § 1913 nt**
Fifth Circuit. Court of Appeals for Fifth Circuit, generally, this index
First Circuit. Court of Appeals for First Circuit, generally, this index
Fourth Circuit. Court of Appeals for Fourth Circuit, generally, this index
Habeas Corpus, generally, this index
Hearings, **28 § 46 et seq.**
Hours, **28 § 452**
Incentive pay or awards, **28 § 604**

COURTS OF APPEALS—Cont'd
Injunctions, **28 § 1292**
Federal agencies, **28 §§ 2112, 2342, 2349 et seq.**
Interlocutory orders, **28 § 1292**
Interstate Commerce Commission, **28 § 2342**
Judges or justices, **28 §§ 43 et seq., 291 et seq.**
Acknowledgments, **28 § 459**
Additional judges, **28 § 372**
Age, **28 § 45**
Annuities, **28 § 376**
Appointments, **28 § 44 et seq.**
Black persons, **28 § 133 nt**
Chambers, **28 § 462**
Chief Judge or Justice, generally, ante
Compensation and salaries, **28 § 44**
Annuities, **28 § 376**
Disability, **28 § 372**
Disability, **28 § 372**
Discrimination, **28 § 44 nt**
Disqualification, **28 § 46 et seq.**
Domicile and residence, **28 § 44**
Official duty station, **28 § 456**
Retired judges, **28 § 374**
Judicial Center, **28 § 621**
Judicial Council, **28 § 332**
Judicial Panel on Multidistrict Litigation, **28 § 1407**
Law books, **28 § 414**
Law clerks, **28 § 712**
Multidistrict litigation, **28 § 1407**
Oaths and affirmations, **28 §§ 453, 459**
Official duty station, **28 § 456**
Powers and duties, **28 § 296**
Practice of law, **28 § 454**
Quorum, **28 § 46**
Relatives, appointments, **28 § 458**
Retirement and pensions, **28 § 294**
Assignments, **28 § 49**
Disability, **28 § 372**
Offices, **28 § 374**
Secretaries, **28 § 712**
Senior circuit judges, **28 §§ 46, 49**
Temporary assignment, **28 § 291**
Three judge court, **28 § 2284**
Traveling expenses, **28 § 456**
Vacancies in office, **28 § 372**
Women, **28 § 133 nt**
Judicial circuits, **28 § 41 et seq.**
Judicial Conference of the Circuit, judges or justices, **28 § 333**
Judicial Conference of the United States,
Costs, **28 § 1913**
Fees, **28 § 1913**
Judges or justices, **28 § 331**
Judiciary Automation Fund, **28 § 1913 nt**
Rules of practice, **28 § 2077**
Judicial Council, generally, this index
Judicial Sales, generally, this index
Jurisdiction, **28 § 1291 et seq.**
Justices. Judges or justices, generally, ante
Law clerks, **28 §§ 604 nt, 712**

COURTS OF APPEALS—Cont'd
Libraries, **28 § 713**
Messengers, **28 § 714**
Military appeals. Court of Appeals for the Armed Forces, generally, this index
Names, **28 nt prec § 1**
Ninth Circuit. Court of Appeals for Ninth Circuit, generally, this index
Nominations, judges or justices, **28 § 133 nt**
Notice, **28 § 2107**
Special sessions, **28 § 48**
Oaths and affirmations,
Amount in controversy, **28 § 2108**
Judges or justices, ante
Obsolete papers, **28 § 457**
Officers and employees, **28 § 711 et seq.**
Incentive pay or awards, **28 § 604**
Omissions, **28 § 2112**
Opinions and decisions, **28 § 1291 et seq.**
Panels, **28 § 46**
Per diem, Federal Courts of Appeals Commission, **28 § 41 nt**
Pleadings, **28 § 2112**
Prehearing conferences, **28 § 2345**
President of the United States, judges or justices, **28 § 44**
Procedure, **28 § 1651 et seq.**
Quorum, **28 § 46**
Receivers and receivership, **28 § 1292**
Records and recordation, **28 § 457**
Supreme Court, **28 § 6**
Recusal, **28 § 46**
Rehearings, **28 § 46**
Remand, **28 § 2106**
Federal agencies, **28 § 2347**
Reports,
Administrative Office of U.S. Courts, **28 § 604**
Federal Courts of Appeals Commission, **28 § 41 nt**
Retirement and pensions. Judges or justices, ante
Rules of Appellate Procedure, generally, this index
Rules of Civil Procedure, this index
Second Circuit. Court of Appeals for Second Circuit, generally, this index
Secretaries, **28 §§ 604 nt, 712, 715**
Senate, appointments, **28 § 44**
Senior staff attorneys, **28 § 715**
Senior technical assistants, **28 § 715**
Sessions, **28 §§ 48, 452**
Seventh Circuit. Court of Appeals for Seventh Circuit, generally, this index
Sixth Circuit. Court of Appeals for Sixth Circuit, generally, this index
Special sessions, **28 § 48**
Staff attorneys, **28 § 715**
Stipulations, **28 § 2112**
Structural alternatives, **28 § 41 nt**
Studies, structural alternatives, **28 § 41 nt**
Supplements, records and recordation, **28 § 2112**

COURTS OF APPEALS—Cont'd
Surface Transportation Board, **28 § 2342**
Technical assistants, **28 § 715**
Tenth Circuit. Court of Appeals for Tenth Circuit, generally, this index
Term of office, **28 § 45**
Territorial courts, **28 § 1294**
Third Circuit. Court of Appeals for Third Circuit, generally, this index
Time, **28 § 2101 et seq.**
Transfers,
Federal agencies, **28 §§ 2112, 2347**
Jurisdiction, **28 § 1631**
United States Court of International Trade, **28 § 293**
United States magistrate judges, **28 § 604**
Veterans. Court of Appeals for Veterans Claims, generally, this index
Women, judges or justices, **28 § 133 nt**

COVENANTS
Actions and proceedings, **28 § 1874**

CRACK (COCAINE)
Controlled Substances, generally, this index

CREDIT (PAYMENT OF INDEBTEDNESS)
Bankruptcy, this index
Garnishment, generally, this index

CREDITOR
See specific index headings

CREDITS
Full Faith and Credit, generally, this index
Justice Department, working capital funds, **28 § 527 nt**
United States, this index

CREW
Seamen, generally, this index

CRIERS OF COURTS
Court Criers, generally, this index

CRIME VICTIMS
Child Abuse and Neglect, this index
Compensation and salaries, United States Sentencing Commission, guidelines, **28 § 994 nt**
Domestic Violence, generally, this index
Impact statements, **28 § 994**
Offices, Justice for Victims of Overseas Terrorism Office, **28 § 501 nt**
Restitution, generally, this index
Sentence and punishment, impact statements, **28 § 994**
Terrorists and terrorism, Office of Justice for Victims of Overseas Terrorism, **28 § 501 nt**
Torture, **28 § 1350 nt**
United States Sentencing Commission, compensation and salaries, guidelines, **28 § 994 nt**

CRIMES AND OFFENSES
Aged Persons, this index
Appeal and review, state courts, **28 § 2102**
Application of law, civil justice, **28 § 519 nt, EON 12988**
Apprehension of criminals, Federal officers and employees, **28 § 1442**
Armed Forces, this index
Athletics, gambling, **28 § 3701 et seq.**
Attorney General, this index
Background checks. Criminal Background Checks, generally, this index
Bail, generally, this index
Bankruptcy, this index
Certiorari, Supreme Court, **28 § 1254**
Civil Rights, this index
Contempt, this index
Conviction of crime,
Costs, **28 § 1918**
Criminal Background Checks, generally, this index
Juror, competency, **28 §§ 1861, 1869**
Rules of Evidence, this index
Unjust convictions, damages, **28 §§ 1495, 2513**
Correctional Institutions, generally, this index
Counterfeiting, generally, this index
Crime of violence, definitions, violent crime control, protection for the elderly, **28 § 994 nt**
Crime Victims, generally, this index
Criminal Background Checks, generally, this index
Detention, generally, this index
Disclosure of Federal Campaign Funds, this index
District Courts, this index
District Judges, this index
Domestic Violence, generally, this index
Emblems and insignia, **28 § 994 nt**
Environmental or natural resource laws, violations, **28 § 509 nt**
Espionage, generally, this index
Executive Agencies, this index
Executive Departments, this index
False swearing. Perjury, generally, this index
Federal Officers and Employees, this index
Financial Institutions, this index
Foreign Countries, this index
Forfeitures. Fines, Penalties and Forfeitures, generally, this index
Forma pauperis, proceedings in, **28 § 1915**
Fraud, generally, this index
Gambling, this index
Gangs, generally, this index
Grand Jury, generally, this index
Guards, labor and employment, **28 § 534 nt**
Hate Crimes, generally, this index

CRIMES AND OFFENSES—Cont'd
History record information. Criminal Background Checks, generally, this index
Homicide. Murder, generally, this index
Identity and Identification, this index
Imprisonment. Sentence and Punishment, generally, this index
Independent Counsel, generally, this index
Indians, this index
Indictment and Information, generally, this index
Information,
Indictment and Information, generally, this index
National Crime Information Center, generally, this index
Investigations. Criminal Background Checks, generally, this index
Judges or Justices, this index
Judgment, on conviction. Sentence and Punishment, generally, this index
Jury, this index
Juvenile Delinquents and Dependents, generally, this index
Kidnapping, generally, this index
Law Enforcement Officers, this index
Military Justice Code, generally, this index
Murder, generally, this index
National cemeteries, **28 § 994 nt**
National Crime Information Center, generally, this index
Penal institutions. Correctional Institutions, generally, this index
Pending actions, reports, **28 § 522**
Perjury, generally, this index
Pretrial services,
Accommodations, **28 § 604**
Administrative Office of United States Courts, Director, **28 §§ 462, 604**
Administrative personnel, **28 § 604**
Federal Public Defender, **28 § 462**
Judicial Conference of the United States, **28 § 604**
Law books, **28 § 604**
Pretrial service officers, **28 § 462**
Supplies, **28 § 604**
Vouchers, audits and auditing, **28 § 604**
Priority, criminal cases on appeal from State court, **28 § 2102**
Prisons. Correctional Institutions, generally, this index
Probation, generally, this index
Punishment. Sentence and Punishment, generally, this index
Records and recordation. Criminal Background Checks, generally, this index
Removal of Cases or Causes, generally, this index
Reports,
Banking law offenses, **28 § 522 nt**
Statistics, **28 § 522**

CRIMES AND OFFENSES—Cont'd
Restitution, generally, this index
Rules of Appellate Procedure, this index
Rules of Criminal Procedure, generally, this index
Rules of Evidence, this index
Second and subsequent offenses. Sentence and Punishment, this index
Service in criminal cases, fee of U.S. Marshal, **28 § 1921**
Sexual Abuse, generally, this index
Speedy trial. Trial, this index
States, this index
Task forces, United States-Mexico Border Violence Task Force, **28 § 509 nt**
Telecommunications, this index
Torture, generally, this index
Trafficking, generally, this index
Trespass, generally, this index
Trial, generally, this index
United States Attorneys, this index
United States Marshals Service, this index
United States-Mexico Border Violence Task Force, **28 § 509 nt**
United States Sentencing Commission. Sentence and Punishment, this index
Unjust convictions, claims, **28 § 2513**
Victims. Crime Victims, generally, this index
Witnesses, generally, this index
Women, this index

CRIMINAL BACKGROUND CHECKS
Exchanges, **28 § 534**
Federal Officers and Employees, this index
Guards, labor and employment, **28 § 534 nt**
Home health care and services, labor and employment, **28 § 534 nt**
International Criminal Police Organization, **28 § 509 nt**
Municipal Corporations, this index
Nursing homes, labor and employment, **28 § 534 nt**
Parimutuel betting, licenses and permits, **28 § 534 nt**
Sentencing Commission, **28 § 534**

CRIMINAL CODE
Crimes and Offenses, generally, this index

CRIMINAL DIVISION
Justice Department, this index

CRIMINAL HISTORY RECORDS
Criminal Background Checks, generally, this index

CRIMINAL JUSTICE SYSTEM
Crimes and Offenses, generally, this index

CRIMINAL PROCEDURE
Crimes and Offenses, generally, this index
Rules of Criminal Procedure, generally, this index

CRIMINOLOGISTS
Sentence and punishment, **28 § 334**

CRIPPLED PERSONS
Handicapped Persons, generally, this index

CROSS APPEALS
Rules of Appellate Procedure, this index

CROSS CLAIMS
International Trade Court, this index
Rules of Civil Procedure, this index

CROSS EXAMINATION
International Trade Court, this index
Rules of Evidence, this index

CRUELTY
Attorneys, fees, prevailing parties, **28 § 2412**

CURRENCY
Money, generally, this index

CUSTODY
Detention, generally, this index
Habeas Corpus, generally, this index
Kidnapping, generally, this index

CUSTOMS BROKERS
International Trade Court, this index

CUSTOMS COURT
Generally, **28 §§ 253 et seq., 1582, 2631 et seq.**
International Trade Court, this index

CUSTOMS DUTIES
Actions and proceedings,
Appeal and review, generally, post
Brokers, licenses and permits, **28 § 2636**
Jurisdiction, generally, post
Laboratories, accreditation, **28 § 2631**
Protests, generally, post
Affidavits,
Fraud, **28 § 2639**
Merchandise, valuation, **28 § 2639**
Analysis, **28 §§ 2636, 2642**
Antidumping duties,
Burden of proof, actions and proceedings, **28 § 2639**
Information,
Disclosure, **28 § 1581**
NAFTA, **28 § 1584**
NAFTA, actions and proceedings, disclosure, **28 § 1584**
Orders, disclosure, **28 §§ 1581, 1582**
Protective orders, **28 §§ 1581, 1582**
Standards, appeal and review, **28 § 2640**
Standing to sue, **28 § 2631**

CUSTOMS DUTIES—Cont'd
Antidumping duties—Cont'd
Time, contests, **28 § 2636**
United States-Canada Free-Trade Agreement, **28 § 1584**
Appeal and review,
Brokers, licenses and permits, **28 § 2631**
Protests, post
Regulations, **28 § 1581 nt**
Rules and regulations, **28 § 1581 nt**
Bonds (officers and fiduciaries), actions and proceedings, **28 § 1582**
Bounties, payments, **28 § 2631**
Catalogs, valuation, **28 § 2639**
Classification,
Commencement of action, **28 § 2631**
Declaratory relief, **28 § 2643**
Exclusive jurisdiction, **28 § 1582**
Exhaustion of administration remedies, **28 § 2637**
Valuation, **28 § 2639**
Confidential or privileged information. Countervailing duties, post
Contests,
Countervailing duties, post
Limitation of actions, **28 § 2631**
Valuation, **28 § 2632**
Countervailing duties,
Burden of proof, **28 § 2639**
Confidential or privileged information, disclosure, **28 § 1581**
Contests, bounties, **28 §§ 2631, 2632**
Information, NAFTA, **28 § 1584**
Limitation of actions, **28 § 2636**
NAFTA, post
Protective orders, U.S. Court of International Trade, **28 § 1581**
Standards,
Appeal and review, **28 § 2640**
Judicial review, **28 § 2640**
Standing to sue, **28 § 2631**
Time, civil actions, **28 § 2636**
United States Canada Agreement, **28 § 1584**
Declaratory judgments and decrees, **28 § 2201**
Depositions, valuation, **28 § 2639**
District courts, jurisdiction, **28 § 1340**
Dumping. Antidumping duties, generally, ante
Entry. Reliquidation, post
Evidence, valuation, **28 § 2639**
Exclusion,
Limitation of actions, **28 § 2631**
Protests, **28 § 1582**
Filing, civil actions, fees, **28 § 2632**
Fines, penalties and forfeitures,
Brokers, **28 § 2643**
International Trade Court, **28 § 1582**
U.S. Court of International Trade, **28 § 1582**
Foreign manufacturers, country of origin, appeal and review, **28 § 1581**
Forfeitures. Fines, penalties and forfeitures, generally, ante

CUSTOMS DUTIES—Cont'd
Fraud, customs brokers, **28 § 1582**
Grants,
Contests, **28 §§ 2631, 2632**
Limitation of actions, **28 § 2631**
Gross negligence, customs brokers, **28 § 1582**
Information,
Antidumping duties, ante
Countervailing duties, ante
International Trade Court, this index
Jurisdiction,
Customs brokers, **28 § 1581**
District courts, **28 § 1340**
Private laboratories, accreditation, **28 §§ 1581, 2631**
Rates and charges, **28 §§ 1582, 2631**
Licenses and permits,
Actions and proceedings, **28 § 2631**
Revocation or suspension, **28 § 1581**
Limitation of actions, **28 § 2631**
Countervailing duties, **28 § 2636**
Free trade area country merchandise, declaratory judgments, **28 § 2201**
Protests, **28 § 2636**
Manufacturers and manufacturing, country of origin, **28 § 1581**
Modifications, entry, actions and proceedings, **28 §§ 1582, 2631**
NAFTA,
Antidumping duties, ante
Countervailing duties, disclosure, **28 § 1584**
Negligence, customs brokers, **28 § 1582**
Orders. Antidumping duties, ante
Penalties. Fines, penalties and forfeitures, generally, ante
Petitions,
Burden of proof, **28 § 2639**
Domestic interested persons, **28 §§ 2636, 2637, 2640**
Presumptions, correctness, **28 § 2639**
Prices, lists, evidence, **28 § 2639**
Private laboratories, accreditation, **28 § 2636**
Producers, country of origin, appeal and review, **28 § 1581**
Protests,
Appeal and review, standards, **28 § 2640**
Burden of proof, **28 § 2639**
Exclusive jurisdiction, **28 § 1582**
Exhaustion of administrative remedies, **28 § 2637**
Limitation of actions, **28 § 2636**
New grounds, **28 § 2638**
Standing to sue, **28 § 2631**
Rates and charges, jurisdiction, **28 §§ 1582, 2631**
Records and recordation, jurisdiction, **28 § 1581**
Recovery, civil actions, **28 § 1583**
Reliquidation, entry,
Jurisdiction, **28 § 1582**
Limitation of actions, **28 § 2631**
Reports, valuation, **28 § 2639**

CUSTOMS DUTIES—Cont'd
Review. Appeal and review, generally, ante
Secretary of Commerce, U.S. Court of Appeals for the Federal Circuit, **28 § 1295**
Standards,
Countervailing duties, ante
Customs brokers, **28 § 2640**
Standing to sue, **28 § 2631**
Statute of limitations. Limitation of actions, generally, ante
Suspension, customs brokers, **28 § 1581**
Time,
Antidumping duties, ante
Countervailing duties, ante
Designated actions, **28 § 2631**
Limitation of actions, generally, ante
Tort Claims Act, exceptions, **28 § 2680**
Trade associations, country of origin, **28 § 1581**
Unions, country of origin, **28 § 1581**
United States attorneys, **28 § 547**
Valuation,
Evidence, **28 § 2635**
Reports, **28 § 2639**

CUSTOMS HOUSES
Brokers, licenses and permits, **28 § 2640**
Licenses and permits, brokers, **28 § 2640**

CUSTOMS LAWS
Customs Duties, generally, this index

CUSTOMS OFFICERS
Bonds (officers and fiduciaries), admiralty, **28 § 2464**
International Trade Court, this index
Protests, jurisdiction, **28 § 1582**

CYPRENORPHINE
Controlled Substances, generally, this index

CZECHOSLOVAKIA
Convention on the Taking of Evidence Abroad in Civil or Commercial Matters, **28 § 1781 nt**

DAGGERS
Weapons, generally, this index

DAMAGES
Agricultural Credit, this index
Aircraft, this index
Bankruptcy, this index
Carriers, this index
Conspiracy, civil rights, **28 § 1343**
Court of appeals, affirmance of judgment, **28 § 1912**
Court of Federal Claims, this index
Death,
Federal officers and employees, claims, **28 § 1346**
United States, **28 § 2404**
District Courts, this index
Executive Departments, this index
Federal Agencies, this index

DAMAGES—Cont'd
Federal Employers Liability Act, **28 § 1445**
Federal Officers and Employees, this index
Foreign countries, support of terrorism, **28 § 1605A**
Foreign States, **28 § 1606**
Hostages, terrorists and terrorism, Foreign States, **28 § 1605A**
Indians, this index
Internal Revenue Service, this index
Plant Variety Protection, this index
Postal Service, this index
Presidential and Executive Office Accountability, this index
Property, this index
Punitive Damages, generally, this index
Quieting title, **28 § 2409a**
Rules of Civil Procedure, this index
Ships and Shipping, this index
Supreme Court, this index
Terrorists and Terrorism, this index
Torture, terrorists and terrorism, Foreign States, **28 § 1605A**
United States, this index
Voting, **28 § 1357**

DANGEROUS DRUGS
Controlled Substances, generally, this index

DATA PROCESSING
Computers, generally, this index

DATING VIOLENCE
Domestic Violence, generally, this index

DC
District of Columbia, generally, this index

DEA
Drug Enforcement Administration, generally, this index

DEATH
Abatement and Revival, this index
Federal Officers and Employees, this index
Foreign Countries, this index
Foreign States, privileges and immunities, **28 § 1605**
International Trade Court, this index
Judicial Center Board, **28 § 621**
Justices or judges,
Annuities, **28 § 376**
Vacancies in office, **28 § 372**
Quieting title, **28 § 2409a**
Rules of Civil Procedure, this index
Supreme Court, this index
Terrorists and Terrorism, this index
Torts, United States, **28 §§ 1346, 2672**
United States Marshals, levies, **28 § 2003**

DEATH PENALTY
Habeas Corpus, this index

DEBENTURES
Bonds, generally, this index

DEBT
See specific index headings

DEBTORS IN POSSESSION
Bankruptcy, this index

DECEIT
Fraud, generally, this index

DECEPTIVE ACT OR PRACTICE
Fraud, generally, this index

DECLARATORY JUDGMENTS AND DECREES
Generally, **28 § 2201 et seq.**
Bankruptcy, taxation, liability, **28 § 2201**
Court of Federal Claims, this index
Drugs and medicine, new drugs, **28 § 2201**
International Trade Court, this index
Rules of Civil Procedure, this index
Senate, subpoenas, **28 § 1365**

DECORATIONS, MEDALS, AND BADGES
Seals (Official Seals), generally, this index

DECREES
Judgments and Decrees, generally, this index

DEEDS AND CONVEYANCES
Judicial sales, **28 § 2003**

DEFAULT
Judgments. Default Judgment, generally, this index
Rules of Appellate Procedure, this index

DEFAULT JUDGMENT
Generally, **28 § 1874**
Costs, **28 § 1923**
Dockets and docketing, fees, **28 § 1923**
Foreign States, privileges and immunities, **28 § 1608**
Rules of Civil Procedure, this index

DEFENDER ORGANIZATIONS
Public Defenders, generally, this index

DEFENSE DEPARTMENT
Security, generally, this index

DEFENSE OF MARRIAGE ACT
Generally, **28 § 1738C**

DEFENSE SECRETARY
Secretary of Defense, generally, this index

DEFENSES
See specific index headings

DEFINITIONS
Words and Phrases, generally, this index

DELAWARE
Bankruptcy, judges or justices, appointments, **28 § 152**
District courts, **28 § 87**
Judges, **28 § 133**
Judicial circuit, **28 § 41**
United States trustees of judicial districts, appointment, **28 § 581**

DELAYS
See specific index headings

DELEGATE TO CONGRESS
Judicial Survivors Annuity Fund, **28 § 376**
Jurisdiction, possession of office, **28 § 1344**

DELEGATION OF AUTHORITY
See specific index headings

DELINQUENCIES
See specific index headings

DELINQUENTS
Juvenile Delinquents and Dependents, generally, this index

DELIVERY
See specific index headings

DEMAND
See specific index headings

DEMONSTRATION PROJECTS OR PROGRAMS
Bureau of Alcohol, Tobacco, Firearms, and Explosives, this index

DENIAL
See specific index headings

DENMARK
Convention on the Taking of Evidence Abroad in Civil or Commercial Matters, **28 § 1781 nt**

DENVER, CO
Court of Appeals for Tenth Circuit, generally, this index

DEOXYRIBONUCLEIC ACID
DNA (Deoxyribonucleic Acid), generally, this index

DEPARTMENTS
See specific index headings

DEPENDENCIES OF UNITED STATES
Insular Possessions and Dependencies, generally, this index

DEPENDENTS
Juvenile Delinquents and Dependents, generally, this index

DEPOSITARIES
Clerk of U.S. courts, **28 § 2043**
Depository Institutions, generally, this index

DEPOSITARIES—Cont'd
Pending actions, **28 §§ 2041, 2044**

DEPOSITIONS
Docket fees, **28 § 1923**
Fees, docket fees, **28 § 1923**
Foreign Service, this index
Garnishment, **28 § 2405**
Habeas corpus, **28 § 2246**
International Trade Court, this index
Justice Department, **28 § 524**
Letters Rogatory, generally, this index
Per diem, **28 § 1821**
Rules of Civil Procedure, this index
Senate, **28 § 1365**
Traveling expenses, **28 § 1821**

DEPOSITORY INSTITUTIONS
Class actions, notice, **28 § 1715**
Clerk of U.S. courts, deposits of other moneys into checking account in Treasury, **28 § 2043**
Notice, class actions, **28 § 1715**
Pending or adjudicated cases, moneys paid into court, deposit, **28 § 2041**
Payment of fine, with bond money, **28 § 2044**

DEPOSITS
Bankruptcy, this index
Courts, this index
Judges or justices, annuities, survivors, **28 § 376**
Rules of Civil Procedure, this index
United States Marshal, **28 § 1921**

DEPUTIES
See specific index headings

DERIVATIVE ACTIONS
Process, **28 § 1695**
Service of process, **28 § 1695**
Venue, **28 § 1401**

DESCENT AND DISTRIBUTION
Executors and Administrators, generally, this index

DESIGNS
Justice Department, seals, **28 § 502**

DESOMORPHINE
Controlled Substances, generally, this index

DESTRUCTION
See specific index headings

DETENTION
Aliens. Immigration, this index
Appearances, witnesses, **28 § 1821**
Bail, generally, this index
Combatants, enemy combatants, **28 § 2241**
Correctional Institutions, generally, this index
Enemy combatants, **28 § 2241**
Habeas Corpus, generally, this index

DETENTION—Cont'd
Immigration, this index
Military Justice Code, this index
Pending judicial proceedings, United States magistrate judges, **28 § 636**
Terrorists and Terrorism, this index
United States, this index
Witnesses, appearances, **28 § 1821**

DETRICHLORAL
Controlled Substances, generally, this index

DEVELOPMENT
See specific index headings

DEVELOPMENTALLY DISABLED INDIVIDUALS OR PERSONS
Incompetency, generally, this index

DEXTROMETHORPHAN
Controlled Substances, generally, this index

DEXTROMORAMIDE
Controlled Substances, generally, this index

DEXTRORPHAN
Controlled Substances, generally, this index

DIAMPROMIDE
Controlled Substances, generally, this index

DIETHYLTHIAMBUTENE
Controlled Substances, generally, this index

DIETHYLTRYPTAMINE
Controlled Substances, generally, this index

DIHYDROCODEINE
Controlled Substances, generally, this index

DIHYDROCODEINONE
Controlled Substances, generally, this index

DIHYDROMORPHINE
Controlled Substances, generally, this index

DIMENOXADOL
Controlled Substances, generally, this index

DIMEPHEPTANOL
Controlled Substances, generally, this index

DIMETHYLTHIAMBUTENE
Controlled Substances, generally, this index

DIMETHYLTRYPTAMINE
Controlled Substances, generally, this index

DIOXAPHETYL BUTYRATE
Controlled Substances, generally, this index

DIPHENOXYLATE
Controlled Substances, generally, this index

DIPIPANONE
Controlled Substances, generally, this index

DIPLOMATIC SECURITY
Crimes and offenses, **28 § 2671 nt**
Diplomatic Security Service, torts, **28 § 2671 nt**
Escape, Diplomatic Security Service, **28 § 2671 nt**
Torts, Diplomatic Security Service, **28 § 2671 nt**

DIPLOMATIC SECURITY SERVICE
Diplomatic Security, this index

DIPLOMATS
Foreign Diplomatic and Consular Officers, generally, this index

DIRECT APPEALS
Supreme Court, this index

DIRECTORS
See specific index headings

DIRKS
Weapons, generally, this index

DISABILITIES
Handicapped Persons, generally, this index

DISABLED PERSONS
Handicapped Persons, generally, this index

DISALLOWANCE
See specific index headings

DISASTERS
Terrorists and Terrorism, generally, this index

DISBURSEMENTS
See specific index headings

DISBURSING OFFICIALS, CLERKS, AND AGENTS
Administrative Office of U.S. Courts, **28 § 604**
Claims, jurisdiction, **28 § 1496**
Comptroller General, generally, this index
Court of Federal Claims, losses, **28 §§ 1496, 2512**
Courts, **28 § 613**

DISBURSING OFFICIALS, CLERKS, AND AGENTS—Cont'd
Losses, U.S. Court of Federal Claims, **28 §§ 1496, 2512**
Supreme Court Marshal, **28 § 672**

DISCHARGE
See specific index headings

DISCIPLINE
Court of Appeals for First Circuit, this index
Court of Appeals for Third Circuit, this index
Court of Federal Claims, this index
International Trade Court, this index
Justice Department, this index

DISCLAIMERS
Patents, this index
Quieting title, **28 § 2409a**

DISCLOSURE
Administrative Law and Procedure, this index
Clerks of courts, financial disclosures, **5 App. 4 § 111**
Federal campaign funds. Disclosure of Federal Campaign Funds, generally, this index
Grand Jury, this index
International Trade Court, this index
Judges or justices, complaints, confidential or privileged information, **28 § 360**
Jury, this index
Rules of Civil Procedure, this index

DISCLOSURE OF FEDERAL CAMPAIGN FUNDS
Crimes and offenses, Federal officers and employees, reports, **28 § 529**
Federal officers and employees, crimes and offenses, reports, **28 § 529**
Reports, Federal officers and employees, crimes and offenses, **28 § 529**
Traveling expenses, Federal officers and employees, **5 App. 4 § 109**

DISCOVERY
Civil justice reform, **28 § 519 nt, EON 12988**
Convention on the Taking of Evidence Abroad in Civil or Commercial Matters, **28 § 1781 nt**
Court of Federal Claims, this index
Depositions, generally, this index
Rules of Civil Procedure, this index
Subpoenas, **28 § 2521**

DISCRETION OF COURT
See specific index headings

DISCRIMINATION
Class actions, **28 § 1714**
Elections, this index
Fair Housing, generally, this index

DISCRIMINATION—Cont'd
Federal Officers and Employees, this index
Jury, **28 § 1862 et seq.**
Merit Systems Protection Board, this index
President of the United States, this index
United States Court of International Trade, jurors, **28 § 1862**

DISEASES
Drugs and Medicine, generally, this index

DISMISSAL AND NONSUIT
Bankruptcy, this index
Correctional institutions, frivolous actions, inmates, **28 § 1915A**
Court of Federal Claims, this index
District courts, lack of jurisdiction, costs, **28 § 1919**
In forma pauperis proceeding, appeals, **28 § 1915**
Indictment and Information, this index
International Trade Court, this index
Judges or justices, complaints, **28 § 354**
Rules of Civil Procedure, this index
Three judge court, **28 § 2284**
Venue laid in wrong division or district, **28 § 1406**

DISPUTE RESOLUTION
Alternative Dispute Resolution, generally, this index
Arbitration, generally, this index

DISQUALIFICATION
See specific index headings

DISSOLUTION
See specific index headings

DISTRIBUTION
See specific index headings

DISTRICT ATTORNEYS
United States Attorneys, generally, this index

DISTRICT COURT OF UNITED STATES FOR DISTRICT OF COLUMBIA
United States District Court for District of Columbia, generally, this index

DISTRICT COURTS
Generally, **28 § 81 et seq.**
Abolition of terms, **28 § 138**
Act of Congress, **28 § 1346**
Adjournment, **28 §§ 139, 140**
Admiralty, original jurisdiction, **28 § 1333**
Affidavit of bias or prejudice, **28 § 144**
Alabama, this index
Alaska, this index
Aliens, this index
Alternative Dispute Resolution, generally, this index

DISTRICT COURTS—Cont'd
Always open, designated purposes, **28 § 452**
Amount in controversy, **28 § 1330 et seq.**
Carriers, **28 § 1337**
Diversity of citizenship, **28 § 1332**
Interpleader, **28 § 1335**
United States, **28 § 2402**
Appeal and review,
Courts of Appeals, generally, this index
Federal agencies, **28 §§ 2112, 2347**
Fees, **28 § 1917**
Appearance, **28 §§ 1654, 1655**
Appointments,
Bailiff, **28 § 755**
Crier, **28 § 755**
Officers and employees, **28 § 756**
Receivers and receivership, **28 § 754**
Reporters, **28 § 753**
Arbitration, referrals, **28 § 654**
Arizona, this index
Arkansas, this index
Army and Air Force Exchange Service, contracts, claims, **28 § 1346**
Arrest in one district for trial in another district, civil actions, **28 § 1693**
Assignments, cases, **28 § 137**
Assistance, international tribunals, **28 § 1782**
Attorney General,
Appointments, challenges, **28 § 503 nt**
Financial disclosures, **5 App. 4 § 102**
Attorneys, fees, labor and employment, dismissal, jury service, **28 § 1875**
Bailiffs, **28 § 755**
Bankruptcy, generally, this index
Bids and bidding, protests, concurrent jurisdiction, **28 § 1491**
Bonds (officers and fiduciaries),
Interpleader, **28 § 1335**
Jurisdiction, **28 § 1352**
California, this index
Carriers, jurisdiction, **28 § 1337**
Certificates and certification,
Affidavit of bias or prejudice, good faith, **28 § 144**
Interpleader, **28 § 1335**
Reporters, **28 § 753**
Certiorari, this index
Chief Judge or Justice. District Judges, this index
Circuit court judges, temporary assignments, **28 § 291**
Citizens and citizenship, **28 § 1332**
Diverse citizenship, generally, post
Civil justice expense and delay reduction plans, **28 § 471 et seq.**
Civil Rights, this index
Class actions, **28 § 1332**
Clerks of District Courts, generally, this index
Coast Guard Exchanges, contracts, **28 § 1346**
Collusive joinder of parties, **28 § 1359**
Colorado, this index

DISTRICT COURTS—Cont'd
Compensation and salaries,
Crier-law clerks, **28 § 755**
Reporters, **28 § 753**
Composition, **28 § 132**
Concurrent jurisdiction,
Bonds, **28 § 1352**
United States Court of Federal Claims, **28 § 1346**
Connecticut, this index
Conspiracy, civil rights, **28 § 1343**
Constitutional questions, **28 § 1331**
Constructive notice, real estate, pending actions, **28 § 1964**
Consuls, jurisdiction, **28 § 1351**
Contempt, generally, this index
Contracts, this index
Corporations, this index
Costs,
Amount in controversy, **28 § 1332**
Carriers, **28 § 1337**
Civil justice expense and delay reduction plans, **28 § 471 et seq.**
Criminal proceedings, **28 § 1918**
Dismissal for lack of jurisdiction, **28 § 1919**
Diversity of citizenship, **28 § 1332**
Federal question, **28 §§ 1331, 1332**
Labor and employment, jurors, protection, **28 § 1875**
Creation, **28 § 132**
Crier-law clerks, **28 § 755**
Criers, **28 § 755**
Crimes and offenses, reporters, **28 § 753**
Customs duties, jurisdiction, **28 § 1340**
Damages,
Alternative dispute resolution, **28 § 654**
Civil rights, **28 § 1343**
Contract Disputes Act of 1978, **28 § 1346**
Revenue, collection, **28 § 1357**
United States, **28 §§ 1346, 1402**
Voting rights, **28 § 1357**
Definitions,
Alternative dispute resolution, **28 § 651**
Multiparty and multiforum, **28 § 1369**
Delaware, this index
Delays, civil justice expense and delay reduction plans, **28 § 471 et seq.**
Deposits, interpleader, **28 § 1335**
District Judges, generally, this index
District of Columbia. United States District Court for District of Columbia, generally, this index
Diverse citizenship,
Amount in controversy, **28 § 1332**
Class actions, **28 § 1332**
Corporations, **28 § 1332**
Estates, **28 § 1332**
Incompetents, **28 § 1332**
Infants, **28 § 1332**
Interpleader, **28 § 1335**
Liability insurance, **28 § 1332**
Permanent resident aliens, **28 § 1332**

DISTRICT COURTS—Cont'd
Diverse citizenship—Cont'd
Representative parties, **28 § 1332**
State agencies, orders, **28 § 1342**
Elections, **28 § 1343 et seq.**
Civil rights, **28 § 1343**
Damages, **28 § 1357**
Electric utility companies, **28 § 753**
Emergencies, special sessions, **28 § 141**
Eminent domain,
Jurisdiction, **28 § 1358**
Prize (vessels), **28 § 1333**
Evidence, **28 § 1731 et seq.**
International Trade Commission, **28 § 1659**
Rules of Evidence, generally, this index
Transcripts, **28 § 753**
Exclusive jurisdiction,
Admiralty, **28 § 1333**
Copyrights, **28 § 1338**
Fines, penalties and forfeitures, **28 § 1355**
Maritime cases, **28 § 1333**
Mask work cases, **28 § 1338**
Patents, **28 § 1338**
Prize cases, **28 § 1333**
Searches and seizures, **28 § 1356**
Surface Transportation Board, **28 § 1336**
Torts, United States, **28 § 1346**
Executive departments, **28 § 1346**
Exemptions, alternative dispute resolution, **28 § 652**
Expenses and expenditures,
Civil justice expense and delay reduction plans, **28 § 471 et seq.**
Reporters, **28 § 753**
Exports and Imports, this index
Federal officers and employees, **28 §§ 1345, 1361**
Federal question, jurisdiction, **28 § 1331**
Federal Rules of Evidence. Rules of Evidence, generally, this index
Fees, **28 § 1914**
Attorneys, labor and employment, dismissal, jury service, **28 § 1875**
Certiorari, notice of allowance, **28 § 1917**
Electronic access to court data, exemptions, **28 § 1914 nt**
Filing, disposition, **28 § 1931**
Habeas corpus,
Filing, **28 § 1914**
Transcripts, **28 § 753**
Judicial Conference of U.S., **28 § 1914**
Notice of allowance, **28 § 1917**
Reporters, **28 § 753**
Schedule, **28 § 1914 nt**
Transcripts, **28 § 753**
Fines, penalties and forfeitures, jurisdiction, **28 § 1355**
Florida, this index
Foreign diplomatic mission, jurisdiction, **28 §§ 1351, 1364**
Foreign States, jurisdiction, **28 §§ 1330, 1332**

DISTRICT COURTS—Cont'd
Formal terms, **28 § 138**
Georgia, this index
Grand Jury, this index
Guam, this index
Habeas Corpus, generally, this index
Hawaii, this index
Idaho, this index
Illinois, this index
Improper joinder of party, **28 § 1359**
Indiana, this index
Indians, this index
Injunctions, **28 § 1292**
Packers and Stockyards Act, **28 § 2351**
State agencies, rates and charges, **28 § 1342**
States, taxation, **28 § 1341**
Surface Transportation Board, **28 § 1336**
Three judge court, **28 § 2284**
Inspection and inspectors, records and recordation, **28 § 753**
Insurance, interpleader, jurisdiction, **28 § 1335**
Interest, judgments and decrees, **28 § 1961**
Interlocutory orders, **28 § 1292**
International litigation, process, **28 § 1696**
International Trade Commission, **28 § 1659**
International Trade Court, this index
Interpleader,
Bonds, **28 § 1335**
Jurisdiction, **28 § 1335**
Interpreters, generally, this index
Intervention, multiparty and multiforum, **28 § 1369**
Iowa, this index
Judges. District Judges, generally, this index
Judgments and decrees, **28 § 1961 et seq.**
Interest, **28 § 1961**
Liens and incumbrances, absent defendants, **28 § 1655**
United States, payment, **28 § 2414**
Judicial Council,
Reporters, **28 § 753**
Sessions, **28 § 140**
Judicial districts, **28 § 133**
Alabama, **28 § 81**
Alaska, **28 § 81A**
Arizona, **28 § 82**
Arkansas, **28 § 83**
California, **28 § 84**
Colorado, **28 § 85**
Connecticut, **28 § 86**
Delaware, **28 § 87**
District of Columbia, **28 § 88**
Florida, **28 § 89**
Georgia, **28 § 90**
Hawaii, **28 § 91**
Idaho, **28 § 92**
Illinois, **28 § 93**
Indiana, **28 § 94**
Iowa, **28 § 95**

DISTRICT COURTS—Cont'd
Judicial districts—Cont'd
Kansas, **28 § 96**
Kentucky, **28 § 97**
Louisiana, **28 § 98**
Maine, **28 § 99**
Maryland, **28 § 100**
Massachusetts, **28 § 101**
Michigan, **28 § 102**
Minnesota, **28 § 103**
Mississippi, **28 § 104**
Missouri, **28 § 105**
Montana, **28 § 106**
Nebraska, **28 § 107**
Nevada, **28 § 108**
New Hampshire, **28 § 109**
New Jersey, **28 § 110**
New Mexico, **28 § 111**
New York, **28 § 112**
North Carolina, **28 § 113**
North Dakota, **28 § 114**
Ohio, **28 § 115**
Oklahoma, **28 § 116**
Oregon, **28 § 117**
Pennsylvania, **28 § 118**
Puerto Rico, **28 § 119**
Rhode Island, **28 § 120**
South Carolina, **28 § 121**
South Dakota, **28 § 122**
Tennessee, **28 § 123**
Texas, **28 § 124**
Utah, **28 § 125**
Vermont, **28 § 126**
Virginia, **28 § 127**
Washington, **28 § 128**
West Virginia, **28 § 129**
Wisconsin, **28 § 130**
Wyoming, **28 § 131**
Judicial Panel On Multidistrict Litigation, generally, this index
Judicial Sales, generally, this index
Jurisdiction, **28 § 1330 et seq.**
Aliens, torts, **28 § 1350**
Alternative dispute resolution, **28 § 652**
Amount in controversy, generally, ante
Attorney General, appointment, challenges, **28 § 503 nt**
Bonds, **28 § 1352**
Business and commerce, **28 § 1337**
Civil rights, **28 § 1343**
Class actions, **28 § 1332**
Collusive joinder of parties, **28 § 1359**
Congressional Acts, **28 § 1366**
Consuls, **28 § 1351**
Corporations, **28 § 1349**
Customs duties, **28 § 1340**
Dismissal for want of jurisdiction, **28 § 1919**
Diverse citizenship, generally, ante
Elections, **28 § 1344**
Eminent domain, **28 § 1358**
Exclusive jurisdiction, generally, ante
Federal agencies, **28 § 1345**
Federal question, **28 § 1331**

DISTRICT COURTS—Cont'd
Jurisdiction—Cont'd
Fines, penalties and forfeitures, **28 § 1355**
Foreign diplomatic relations, **28 §§ 1351, 1364**
Foreign States, **28 §§ 1330, 1332**
Improper joinder of party, **28 § 1359**
Internal Revenue Service, **28 § 1340**
Internet Tax Freedom Acts, **28 § 1447**
Interpleader, **28 § 1335**
Land grants, **28 § 1354**
Maritime cases, **28 § 1333**
Mask work cases, **28 § 1338**
Multiparty and multiforum, generally, post
Original jurisdiction, generally, post
Packers and Stockyards Act, **28 § 2351**
Partition, **28 § 1347**
Patents, **28 § 1338**
Possession of office, **28 § 1344**
Postal matters, **28 § 1339**
Prize (vessels), **28 § 1333**
Restraints of trade, **28 § 1337**
Revenue, collection, **28 § 1357**
State agencies, rate orders, **28 § 1342**
Supplemental jurisdiction, **28 § 1367**
Surface Transportation Board, **28 § 1336**
Taxation, States, **28 § 1341**
Trademarks and trade names, **28 § 1338**
Transfer to cure want of jurisdiction, **28 § 1631**
Unfair competition, **28 § 1338**
Vice Consuls, **28 § 1351**
Voting, enforcement of right of citizens, **28 § 1357**
Voting rights, **28 § 1357**
Jury, this index
Kansas, this index
Kentucky, this index
Land grants, **28 § 1354**
Liability insurance, **28 § 1332**
Liens and Incumbrances, this index
Loans, interpleader, jurisdiction, **28 § 1335**
Location, special sessions, **28 § 141**
Louisiana, this index
Maine, this index
Mandamus, Federal officers and employees, **28 § 1361**
Marine Corps Exchanges, contracts, claims, **28 § 1346**
Maryland, this index
Mask work cases, semiconductor chip products, jurisdiction, **28 § 1338**
Massachusetts, this index
Messenger, crier, **28 § 755**
Michigan, this index
Minnesota, this index
Mississippi, this index
Missouri, this index
Money, interpleader, jurisdiction, **28 § 1335**
Monopolies and Combinations, this index

DISTRICT COURTS—Cont'd
Montana, this index
Motions, multidistrict litigation, pretrial proceedings, **28 § 1407**
Multiparty and multiforum, **28 §§ 1 nt, 1369**
Process, **28 § 1697**
Removal of cases or causes, **28 § 1441**
Subpoenas, **28 § 1785**
Venue, **28 § 1391**
National Aeronautics and Space Administration Exchange Councils, contracts, **28 § 1346**
Navy exchanges, contracts, **28 § 1346**
Nebraska, this index
Neutrals, alternative dispute resolution, **28 § 653**
Nevada, this index
New Hampshire, this index
New Jersey, this index
New Mexico, this index
New York, this index
North Carolina, this index
North Dakota, this index
Northern Mariana Islands, this index
Notes, interpleader, jurisdiction, **28 § 1335**
Notice,
Federal Courts Improvement Act of 1982, appeal and review, **28 § 171 nt**
Multiparty and multiforum, pending actions, **28 § 1369**
Special sessions, **28 § 141**
State agencies, rate orders, **28 § 1342**
Obsolete papers, disposition, **28 § 457**
Officers and employees, appointments, **28 § 756**
Ohio, this index
Oklahoma, this index
Open court, records and recordation, **28 § 753**
Orders of court, **28 § 137**
Adjournment, **28 § 140**
Advances, fees, **28 § 1914**
Contempt, generally, this index
Filing, complaint and order of appointment of receiver, **28 § 754**
International litigation, process, **28 § 1696**
International tribunals, assistance, **28 § 1782**
Interpleader, **28 § 2361**
Judicial Council, **28 § 332**
Liens and incumbrances, absent defendants, **28 § 1655**
Surface Transportation Board, enforcement, **28 § 2321 et seq.**
Transcripts, **28 § 753**
Oregon, this index
Original jurisdiction, **28 § 1330 et seq.**
Admiralty, **28 § 1333**
Aliens, torts, **28 § 1350**
Amount in controversy, **28 § 1332**
Civil rights, **28 § 1343**
Copyrights, **28 § 1338**

DISTRICT COURTS—Cont'd
Original jurisdiction—Cont'd
Customs duties, **28 § 1340**
Diversity of citizenship, **28 § 1332**
Elections, **28 §§ 1343, 1344**
Eminent domain, **28 § 1358**
Federal officers and employees, **28 § 1361**
Federal question, **28 § 1331**
Fines, penalties and forfeitures, **28 § 1355**
Indians, **28 §§ 1353, 1362**
Injuries, **28 § 1357**
Internal Revenue Service, **28 § 1340**
Interpleader, **28 § 1335**
Jurors, labor and employment, protection, **28 § 1363**
Land grants, **28 § 1354**
Maritime cases, **28 § 1333**
Mask works, **28 § 1338**
Partition, **28 § 1347**
Patents, **28 § 1338**
Possession of office, **28 § 1344**
Postal matters, **28 § 1339**
Prize cases, **28 § 1333**
Seizures not within admiralty and maritime jurisdiction, **28 § 1356**
Trademarks and trade names, **28 § 1338**
Treaties, **28 § 1331**
Unfair competition, **28 § 1338**
United States, **28 §§ 1331, 1345 et seq.**
Packers and Stockyards Act, jurisdiction, enforcement, **28 § 2351**
Parties. Multiparty and multiforum, generally, ante
Partition, jurisdiction, **28 § 1347**
Patents,
Infringement, **28 §§ 1292, 1694**
Jurisdiction, **28 § 1338**
Pending actions, multiparty and multiforum, notice, **28 § 1369**
Pennsylvania, this index
Personal injuries, civil rights, **28 § 1343**
Plans and specifications, civil justice expense and delay reduction plans, **28 § 471 et seq.**
Plant variety protection, **28 § 1338**
Possession of office, **28 § 1344**
Pretrial services. Crimes and Offenses, this index
Priorities and preferences, **28 § 1657**
Procedure, **28 § 1651 et seq.**
Process, generally, this index
Property, interpleader, jurisdiction, **28 § 1335**
Public contracts, **28 § 1346**
Quieting title, **28 § 2409a**
Receivers and Receivership, this index
Records and recordation, **28 § 457**
Court of record, **28 § 132**
Inspection and inspectors, **28 § 753**
Property in different districts, orders, **28 § 1692**
Reporters, **28 § 753**

DISTRICT COURTS—Cont'd
Records and recordation—Cont'd
United States magistrate judges, **28 § 631**
Reduction, civil justice expense and delay reduction plans, **28 § 471 et seq.**
Referrals, arbitration, **28 § 654**
Regular sessions, **28 §§ 132, 139**
Removal of Cases or Causes, generally, this index
Reporters, **28 § 753**
Compensation and salaries, **28 § 753 nt**
Retirement and pensions, United States, **28 § 1346**
Revenue, jurisdiction, **28 § 1357**
Review. Appeal and review, generally, ante
Rhode Island, this index
Rules of Appellate Procedure, this index
Rules of Civil Procedure, this index
Rules of Evidence, generally, this index
Searches and seizures, admiralty, **28 § 1356**
Security, **28 § 604**
Sentence and Punishment, this index
Sessions,
Adjournment, **28 § 140**
Affidavit of bias or prejudice, **28 § 144**
Chief judges, **28 § 136**
Judicial Council, pretermitting, **28 § 140**
Powers and duties, **28 § 452**
Records and recordation, **28 §§ 753, 1692**
Regular sessions, **28 §§ 132, 139**
Single judge, **28 § 132**
Special sessions, **28 § 141**
Termination, **28 § 139**
Set-off and counterclaim, United States, **28 § 1346**
Shareholders derivative actions, **28 § 1695**
Shorthand, sessions of court, **28 § 753**
South Carolina, this index
South Dakota, this index
Special sessions, **28 § 141**
Standing orders, advance payments, **28 § 1914**
State, definitions, **28 § 1367**
State agencies, rate orders, jurisdiction, **28 § 1342**
Stay of proceedings, in rem, **28 § 2464**
Studies, concurrent jurisdiction, Federal Claims Court, **28 § 1491 nt**
Subpoenas, generally, this index
Subsistence, special sessions, **28 § 141**
Supervision, reporters, **28 § 753**
Supplemental jurisdiction, **28 § 1367**
Supreme Court, this index
Surface Transportation Board, this index
Taxes by States, jurisdiction, **28 § 1341**
Tennessee, this index
Terms of court,
Abolishment, **28 § 138**
Formal terms, **28 § 138**

DISTRICT COURTS—Cont'd
Terms of court—Cont'd
Sessions, generally, ante
Territories, this index
Texas, this index
Three Judge Court, generally, this index
Time, sessions, **28 § 139**
Torts,
States, removal or transfer of causes, **28 § 2679**
United States, claims, **28 § 1346**
Torture, **28 § 1350 nt**
Trademarks and trade names, jurisdiction, **28 § 1338**
Transcripts, **28 § 753**
Transfer to cure want of jurisdiction, **28 § 1631**
Transportation, special sessions, **28 § 141**
Treaties, original jurisdiction, **28 § 1331**
Unfair competition, jurisdiction, **28 § 1338**
United States, **28 § 1345 et seq.**
Indebtedness, United States Court of Federal Claims, **28 § 2508**
Judgments and decrees, payment, **28 § 2414**
Liens and incumbrances, **28 § 2410**
Partition, **28 § 1347**
United States District Court for District of Columbia, generally, this index
United States laws, original jurisdiction, **28 § 1331**
United States Magistrate Judges, generally, this index
Utah, this index
Vice Consuls, **28 § 1351**
Virgin Islands, this index
Virginia, this index
Washington (State), this index
West Virginia, this index
Wisconsin, this index
Witnesses,
Foreign tribunals, assistance, **28 § 1782**
International tribunals, assistance, **28 § 1782**
Wyoming, this index

DISTRICT JUDGES
Acknowledgments, **28 § 459**
Affidavits of bias or prejudice, **28 § 144**
Annuities, survivors, **28 § 376**
Appointment, **28 § 133**
Additional judges, **28 § 133 nt**
Chief judges, **28 § 136**
Crier, **28 § 755**
Disability, **28 § 372**
Disagreements, **28 § 756**
Law clerks, **28 § 752**
Relatives, **28 § 458**
Assignments, **28 § 132**
Affidavit of bias or prejudice, **28 § 144**
Conditions, **28 § 295**
Cost of living, **28 § 373**
Judicial Conference of the United States, **28 § 331**

DISTRICT JUDGES—Cont'd
Assignments—Cont'd
Multidistrict litigation, pretrial proceedings, **28 § 1407**
Ninth Circuit, **28 § 297**
Powers and duties, **28 § 296**
Pretrial proceedings, multidistrict litigation, **28 § 1407**
Retired judges, **28 § 294**
Temporary assignments, **28 § 292**
Bailiffs, **28 § 755**
Bias and prejudice, **28 § 144**
Black persons, **28 § 133 nt**
Certificates and certification,
Appeal and review, **28 § 753**
Assignments, **28 § 292**
Disability, **28 § 372**
Habeas corpus, **28 § 1825**
Jury, fees, **28 § 1871**
Chief Judge or Justice,
Age, **28 § 136**
Appointment, **28 § 136**
Officers and employees, **28 § 756**
Assignments, **28 § 137**
Retired judge, **28 § 294**
Senior district judges, **28 § 451 nt**
Successors, **28 § 136**
United States magistrate judges, assignments, **28 § 636**
Circuit judge, assignments, **28 § 291**
Compensation and salaries,
Adjustments, **28 § 135**
Deductions, annuities, **28 § 376**
Disability, **28 § 372**
Secretaries, **28 § 604**
Territories, **28 § 373**
Crier, appointment, **28 § 755**
Crimes and offenses, practice of law, **28 § 454**
Disability. Handicapped persons, generally, post
Discipline, **28 § 372**
Domicile and residence, **28 § 134**
Official duty stations, **28 § 456**
Retired judges, **28 § 374**
Expenses and expenditures,
Joint council on sentencing, **28 § 334**
Office expenses, retired judges, **28 § 374**
Retired judges, office expenses, **28 § 374**
Fees, jury, **28 § 1871**
Habeas corpus, **28 §§ 2244, 2253**
Handicapped persons,
Appointments, **28 §§ 371, 372**
Retirement and pensions, **28 § 372**
Interest, judgments and decrees, **28 § 1961**
Joint council on sentencing, **28 § 334**
Judgments and decrees, interest, **28 § 1961**
Judicial Center, **28 § 621**
Judicial Conference of the Circuit, **28 § 333**
Judicial Conference of the United States, **28 § 331**

DISTRICT JUDGES—Cont'd
Judicial Council, generally, this index
Judicial Panel on Multidistrict Litigation, **28 § 1407**
Junior judges, **28 § 136**
Law books, **28 § 414**
Law clerks,
Appointment, **28 § 752**
Compensation and salaries, **28 §§ 603 nt, 604**
Leave of absence, **28 § 752**
Merit selection, **28 §§ 133 nt, 631**
Nominations, **28 § 133 nt**
Numbers, **28 § 133**
Oaths and affirmations, **28 §§ 453, 459**
Office expenses, retired judges, **28 § 374**
Official duty station, **28 § 456**
Orders, Judicial Council, **28 § 332**
Possessions, **28 § 373**
Powers and duties, **28 § 132**
Practice of law, **28 § 454**
Precedence, **28 § 136**
Disability, **28 § 372**
President of the United States,
Appointment, **28 § 133**
Discrimination, **28 § 44 nt**
Merit selection, **28 § 133 nt**
Presiding judges, **28 § 136**
Race, merit selection, **28 § 44 nt**
Records and recordation, **28 § 753**
Regular active service, **28 § 132**
Regular sessions, **28 § 132**
Relatives, appointments, **28 § 458**
Residence. Domicile and residence, generally, ante
Resignation,
Disability, **28 § 372**
Possessions, **28 § 373**
Territories, **28 § 373**
Salaries. Compensation and salaries, generally, ante
Secretaries, **28 § 752**
Senate, appointments, **28 § 133 nt**
Seniority, **28 § 136**
Sessions, **28 §§ 132, 136**
Sex, merit selection, **28 § 44 nt**
Standards, merit selection, **28 § 133 nt**
Supreme Court, this index
Tables, numbers and numbering, **28 § 133**
Temporary assignments, **28 § 292**
Temporary judgeships, **28 § 133 nt**
Tenure, **28 § 134**
Chief judges, **28 § 136**
Territories, **28 § 373**
Three Judge Court, generally, this index
Time,
Affidavit of bias or prejudice, **28 § 144**
Temporary judgeships, **28 § 133 nt**
Traveling expenses, **28 § 456**
United States Magistrate Judges, generally, this index
Vacancies in office, **28 § 372**
Pending proceedings, **28 § 143**
Waiver, nominations, **28 § 133 nt**
Women, nominations, **28 § 133 nt**

DISTRICT OF COLUMBIA
Acts of Congress, application of law, **28 § 1343**
Bankruptcy, this index
Civil Rights, generally, this index
Court of Federal Claims, this index
Courts,
Appeal and review. Court of Appeals for the District of Columbia, generally, this index
United States District Court for District of Columbia, generally, this index
District court. United States District Court for District of Columbia, generally, this index
Diversity of citizenship, district courts, jurisdiction, **28 § 1332**
Executions, United States, **28 § 2413**
Federal Judicial Center Foundation, incorporation, **28 § 629**
Grand jury, **28 § 1861 et seq.**
Judicial circuit, **28 § 41**
Judicial districts, **28 § 88**
Judges or justices, **28 § 133**
Jurisdiction, diversity of citizenship, **28 § 1332**
Jury, **28 § 1861 et seq.**
National Guard, this index
United States attorneys, domicile and residence, **28 § 545**
United States magistrate judges, **28 § 631**
United States Marshals Service,
Domicile and residence, **28 § 561**
Mileage, **28 § 1921**
United States trustees, judicial districts, **28 § 581**

DISTRICTS
Columbia. District of Columbia, generally, this index
District Courts, generally, this index
Firefighters, jury, exemptions, **28 § 1863**
Judicial Districts, generally, this index
Officers and employees, jury, exemptions, **28 § 1863**
Pending suits, attending to interests of U.S. in, **28 § 517**
Police, jury, exemptions, **28 § 1863**

DIVERSE CITIZENSHIP
District Courts, this index

DIVISIONS
See specific index headings

DNA (DEOXYRIBONUCLEIC ACID)
Core genetic markers, reports, **28 § 531 nt**
Indexes, tests, **28 § 531 nt**
Reports, core genetic markers, **28 § 531 nt**

DOCKETS AND DOCKETING
Administrative Office of U.S. Courts, information, **28 § 604**

DOCKETS AND DOCKETING—Cont'd
Arbitration, this index
Armed Forces, removal of cases, **28 § 1442a**
Attorneys, fees, **28 § 1923**
Bankruptcy, this index
Examinations and examiners, **28 § 604**
Fees, **28 § 1920**
United States attorneys, **28 § 1923**
United States trustees, **28 § 1923**
Information, Administrative Office of U.S. Courts, **28 § 604**
Liens and incumbrances, **28 § 1962**
Real estate, pending actions, constructive notice, **28 § 1964**
Rules of Appellate Procedure, this index
Rules of Civil Procedure, this index
Supreme Court, this index
United States attorneys, fees, **28 § 1923**
United States magistrate judges, **28 § 638**
United States trustees, fees, **28 § 1923**

DOCUMENTARY EVIDENCE
Generally, **28 § 1731 et seq.**
Acts of legislature, **28 § 1738**
Authentication, generally, this index
Bonds (officers and fiduciaries), **28 § 1737**
Business and commerce, **28 § 1732**
Congressional Journals, **28 § 1736**
Consular officers, **28 § 1740**
Convention on the Taking of Evidence Abroad in Civil or Commercial Matters, **28 § 1781 nt**
Copies, **28 § 1732**
Courts, **28 §§ 1734, 1738**
Federal agencies, **28 § 1733**
Foreign countries, **28 §§ 1741, 1745**
Foreign diplomatic and consular officers, **28 § 1740**
Habeas corpus, **28 § 2247**
Handwriting, **28 § 1731**
Insular possessions and dependencies, **28 §§ 1738, 1739**
Lost or destroyed property, courts, **28 § 1734**
Patent and Trademark Office, **28 §§ 1744, 1745**
Photographs and photography, business and commerce, **28 § 1732**
Production of Books and Papers, generally, this index
Reproductions, **28 § 1732**
States, **28 §§ 1738, 1739**
Territories, **28 §§ 1738, 1739**
Vice Consuls, **28 § 1740**

DOCUMENTS
Books and Papers, generally, this index

DOG RACES
Unlawful sports gambling, **28 § 3704**

DOLLAR
Money, generally, this index

DOMESTIC ABUSE
Domestic Violence, generally, this index

DOMESTIC CORPORATIONS
Corporations, generally, this index

DOMESTIC SECURITY
Security, generally, this index

DOMESTIC VIOLENCE
Kidnapping, parental kidnapping, reports, **28 § 1738A nt**
Parental kidnapping, reports, **28 § 1738A nt**
Reports,
Kidnapping, parental kidnapping, **28 § 1738A nt**
Parental kidnapping, **28 § 1738A nt**

DOMICILE AND RESIDENCE
Bankruptcy, this index
Circuit judges, **28 § 44**
Clerk of district court, **28 § 751**
Court of Federal Claims, this index
District Judges, this index
Judges or Justices, this index
Jurors, **28 §§ 1865, 1869**
Jury commissioner, **28 § 1863**
Nonresidents, generally, this index
United States attorneys, **28 § 545**
United States Court of Appeals for the Federal Circuit, judges or justices, **28 § 44**
United States Marshals, **28 § 561**

DOMICILIARY CARE
Nursing Homes, generally, this index

DONATIONS
Gifts, generally, this index

DOUBLE MILEAGE FEES
Summons, **28 § 1824**

DRAWBACKS
International Trade Court, this index

DRAWINGS
Copyrights, generally, this index
Foreign letters patent, copies, evidence, **28 § 1745**
Patent and Trademark Office, evidence, **28 § 1744**

DREDGES AND DREDGING
Harbors and Ports, generally, this index
Oysters, this index

DRUG ADDICTS
Correctional Institutions, this index

DRUG ENFORCEMENT ADMINISTRATION
Administrative forfeitures, **28 § 524**
Aircraft, this index
Ammunition, funds, **28 § 530C**
Assets Forfeiture Fund. Justice Department, this index

DRUG ENFORCEMENT ADMINISTRATION—Cont'd
Attorney General, undercover investigations, **28 § 533 nt**
Boats and boating, funds, **28 § 530C**
Compensation and salaries, **28 § 509 nt**
Definitions, undercover operations, **28 § 533 nt**
Grades or rank, **28 § 509 nt**
Humanitarian assistance and relief, **28 § 509 nt**
Officers and employees, suspension, **28 § 509 nt**
Reduction in rank or pay, **28 § 509 nt**
Removal, **28 § 509 nt**
Reports, undercover operations, **28 § 533 nt**
Suspension, officers and employees, **28 § 509 nt**
Undercover operations, reports, **28 § 533 nt**
Uniforms, **28 § 509 nt**
Vacancies in office, **28 § 509 nt**
Weapons, funds, **28 § 530C**

DRUGS AND MEDICINE
Appropriations, Justice Department, **28 § 509 nt**
Controlled Substances, generally, this index
Declaratory judgments and decrees, new drugs, **28 § 2201**
New drugs, declaratory judgments and decrees, **28 § 2201**
Patents, declaratory judgments and decrees, **28 § 2201**

DUE PROCESS OF LAW
Parental Kidnapping Prevention Act, **28 § 1738A nt**

DUPLICATES
See specific index headings

EARNINGS
Compensation and Salaries, generally, this index

ECONOMIC DEVELOPMENT
Community Development, generally, this index

ECONOMIC STATUS
Jurors,
Discrimination, **28 §§ 1862, 1867**
Qualification, **28 § 1869**

EDUCATION
Administrative law and procedure, civil justice reform, **28 § 519 nt, EON 12988**
Colleges and Universities, generally, this index
Federal agencies, civil justice reform, **28 § 519 nt, EON 12988**
Judges or justices, annuities for survivors, continued status as child, **28 § 376**
Judicial Center, personnel, **28 § 620**

EDUCATION—Cont'd
Juror qualification form, **28 § 1869**

EDUCATION DEPARTMENT
Community development, neighborhood revitalization plan, **28 § 509 nt**

ELDERLY PERSONS
Aged Persons, generally, this index

ELECTIONS
Candidates, expenses and expenditures. Disclosure of Federal Campaign Funds, generally, this index
Courts of Appeals, this index
Damages, right to vote, **28 § 1357**
Denial, jurisdiction, **28 § 1344**
Disclosure of Federal Campaign Funds, generally, this index
Discrimination,
Lists, registration, **28 § 1869**
Registration, lists, **28 § 1869**
District Courts, this index
Expenses and expenditures. Disclosure of Federal Campaign Funds, generally, this index
House of Representatives, this index
Judges or Justices, this index
Nominations. Judges or Justices, this index
Quieting title, **28 § 2409a**
Race, color, and previous condition of servitude, **28 § 1344**
Recall, generally, this index
Registration,
Jury, selection, **28 §§ 1863, 1866, 1869**
Lists, jury, selection, **28 §§ 1863, 1866, 1869**

ELECTRONIC CIRCUITRY
Semiconductors, generally, this index

ELECTRONIC COMMUNICATIONS
Telecommunications, generally, this index

ELECTRONIC DATA PROCESSING
Computers, generally, this index

ELECTRONIC FILING
Rules of Appellate Procedure, this index

ELECTRONICALLY STORED INFORMATION
See specific index headings

ELEEMOSYNARY INSTITUTIONS
Charities, generally, this index

EMBASSIES
Foreign Diplomatic and Consular Officers, generally, this index
Foreign Service, generally, this index

EMBLEMS AND INSIGNIA
Counterfeiting, public officers and employees, **28 § 994 nt**
Crimes and offenses, **28 § 994 nt**

EMBLEMS AND INSIGNIA—Cont'd
Federal Officers and Employees, this index
Political subdivisions, officers and employees, counterfeiting, **28 § 994 nt**
Sentence and punishment, **28 § 994 nt**
States, this index

EMERGENCIES
Bankruptcy, this index
Bureau of Investigation, expenses and expenditures, **28 § 537**
Court of Appeals for First Circuit, this index
Court of Appeals for Second Circuit, this index
Court of Appeals for Third Circuit, this index
Court of Appeals for Fourth Circuit, this index
Court of Appeals for Fifth Circuit, this index
Court of Appeals for Sixth Circuit, this index
Court of Appeals for Seventh Circuit, special sessions, **28 § 48**
Court of Appeals for Eighth Circuit, this index
Court of Appeals for Ninth Circuit, this index
Court of Appeals for Tenth Circuit, this index
Court of Appeals for Eleventh Circuit, this index
Court of Appeals for the District of Columbia, this index
Court of Appeals for the Federal Circuit, this index
Courts of appeals, special sessions, **28 § 48**
District Courts, this index
Justice Department, this index
United States magistrate judges, assignments, **28 § 636**

EMERGENCY FEDERAL LAW ENFORCEMENT ASSISTANCE
Definitions, **28 § 509 nt**
Investigations, Federally insured financial institutions, **28 § 509 nt**

EMERGENCY MEDICAL SERVICES
Assistance, **28 § 509 nt**
Terrorists and Terrorism, this index

EMIGRATION
Immigration, generally, this index

EMINENT DOMAIN
District Courts, this index
Federal Agencies, this index
Jurisdiction, district court, **28 § 1358**
Liens and incumbrances, **28 § 2410**
Rules of Civil Procedure, this index
United States, jurisdiction of District Court, **28 § 1358**
Venue, proceeding by U.S., **28 § 1403**

EMMETT TILL UNSOLVED CIVIL RIGHTS CRIME ACT OF 2007
Generally, **28 § 509 nt**

EMOLUMENTS
Compensation and Salaries, generally, this index

EMPLOYMENT
Labor and Employment, generally, this index

EN BANC
See specific index headings

ENCUMBRANCES
Liens and Incumbrances, generally, this index

ENDERBURY ISLANDS
Judicial District of Hawaii, **28 § 91**

ENEMIES
Aliens, this index
Detention, enemy combatants, **28 § 2241**
Military Justice Code, this index

ENFORCEMENT
See specific index headings

ENFORCEMENT ACT (TARIFF)
Customs Duties, generally, this index

ENGINEHOUSES
Railroads, generally, this index

ENGLISH LANGUAGE
Jurors, **28 §§ 1865, 1869**

ENTERPRISE ARCHITECTURE
Federal Bureau of Investigation, computers, **28 § 531 nt**

ENTRY
See specific index headings

ENTRY UPON LAND
Rules of Civil Procedure, this index
Trespass, generally, this index

ENVIRONMENT
Federal Agencies, this index

ENVOYS EXTRAORDINARY
Foreign Service, generally, this index

EQUITY
Receivers and receivership, **28 § 959**
Rules of Civil Procedure, this index
Trusts and trustees, **28 § 959**
United States Court of International Trade, **28 § 1585**

EQUITY SECURITY HOLDERS
Bankruptcy, this index

ERGONOVINE
Controlled Substances, generally, this index

ERGOTIMINE
Controlled Substances, generally, this index

ERROR
See specific index headings

ERROR CORAM NOBIS, WRIT OF
Sentence and Punishment, generally, this index

ESCAPE
Fines, penalties and forfeitures, custody, civil commitment, **28 § 1826**
Sentence and punishment, custody, civil commitment, **28 § 1826**

ESPIONAGE
Attorney General, **28 § 519 nt**
National Counterintelligence Executive Office, **28 § 519 nt**
Pleading, **28 § 519 nt**

ESTATE TAX
United States Tax Court, generally, this index

ESTIMATES
See specific index headings

ETHCHLORVYNOL
Controlled Substances, generally, this index

ETHICS
Attorneys, Justice Department, **28 § 530B**
Federal Officers and Employees, this index
Government Accountability Office, officers and employees, **5 App. 4 § 109**
Independent Counsel, **28 §§ 530B, 594**

ETHINAMATE
Controlled Substances, generally, this index

ETHYL ETHER
Controlled Substances, generally, this index

ETHYLMETHYLTHIAMBUTENE
Controlled Substances, generally, this index

ETHYLMORPHINE
Controlled Substances, generally, this index

ETONITAZENE
Controlled Substances, generally, this index

ETORPHINE
Controlled Substances, generally, this index

ETOXERIDINE
Controlled Substances, generally, this index

EVIDENCE
Generally, **28 § 1731 et seq.**
Amount in controversy, court of appeals, **28 § 2108**
Authentication, generally, this index
Bonds (officers and fiduciaries), **28 § 1737**
Certificates and certification, habeas corpus, **28 § 2245**
Certified copies,
Courts, **28 § 1734**
Liens and incumbrances, **28 § 1656**
Pardons, **28 § 2513**
Patent and Trademark Office, **28 § 1744**
Trademarks and trade names, **28 § 1735**
Clerks of Courts, this index
Compelling production. Production of Books and Papers, generally, this index
Congressional Journals, **28 § 1736**
Consular papers, **28 § 1740**
Contempt, subpoenas, foreign residents, **28 § 1784**
Convention on the Taking of Evidence Abroad in Civil or Commercial Matters, **28 § 1781 nt**
Court of Federal Claims, this index
Courts of Appeals, this index
Customs Duties, this index
Depositions, generally, this index
Deposits in court, **28 § 2042**
Discovery, generally, this index
District Courts, this index
Documentary Evidence, generally, this index
Federal Agencies, this index
Federal Rules of Evidence. Rules of Evidence, generally, this index
Foreign Diplomatic and Consular Officers, this index
Foreign Documents, generally, this index
Government Accountability Office, this index
Grand Jury, this index
Habeas Corpus, this index
Handwriting, **28 § 1731**
International Trade Court, this index
Intervention, constitutional questions, **28 § 2403**
Judges or justices, complaints, **28 § 358**
Jury, this index
Justice Department, officers and employees, **28 § 516**
Microfilm, **28 § 1732**
Multidistrict litigation, pretrial proceedings, **28 § 1407**
Oaths and affirmations, unsworn declarations, **28 § 1746**
Patents, this index
Perjury, unsworn declarations, **28 § 1746**
Photographs, **28 § 1732**
Photostatic copies, **28 § 1732**
Possessions of U.S., nonjudicial records, **28 § 1739**

EVIDENCE—Cont'd
Postal Service, this index
Postmasters, **28 § 1743**
Production of Books and Papers, generally, this index
Questions of Law or Fact, generally, this index
Records and recordation,
Business records, **28 § 1732**
Consuls, **28 § 1740**
Court records, **28 § 1734 et seq.**
Courts of appeals, **28 § 2112**
Federal agencies, **28 § 1733**
Foreign countries, authentication, **28 § 1741**
Liens and incumbrances, **28 § 1656**
Microfilm, **28 § 1732**
Patent and Trademark Office, **28 § 1744**
Photographs, **28 § 1732**
Possessions of U.S., **28 § 1739**
Regular course of business, **28 § 1732**
States, **28 §§ 1738, 1739**
Territories, **28 § 1739**
Vice Consuls, **28 § 1740**
Rules of Appellate Procedure, this index
Rules of Civil Procedure, this index
Rules of Evidence, generally, this index
State courts, **28 § 1738**
State laws, **28 § 1738**
State nonjudicial records, **28 § 1739**
Supreme Court, district courts, rules of court, **28 § 2072**
Territories, **28 §§ 1738, 1739**
Three judge court, **28 § 2284**
Unsworn declarations, **28 § 1746**
Virgin Islands, this index
Witnesses, generally, this index

EX PARTE PROCEEDINGS
See specific index headings

EXAMINATIONS AND EXAMINERS
Judicial Officers, appropriations, **28 § 526**
Judicial Survivors Annuity Fund, **28 § 605**
Jurors, random selection, **28 § 1863**
Rules of Civil Procedure, this index

EXCEPTIONS
See specific index headings

EXCHANGE
See specific index headings

EXCHANGE OF PROPERTY
Attorney General, books and papers, **28 § 525**
Identification and criminal identification records, **28 § 534**
Supreme Court, books, pamphlets, **28 § 674**

EXCLUSIVE JURISDICTION
District Courts, this index

EXCUSE
See specific index headings

EXECUTION
Appraisals and appraisers, **28 § 2005**
Exemptions, judges or justices, annuities, **28 § 376**
Federal Debt Collection, this index
Foreign countries, privileges and immunities, **28 § 1609 et seq.**
Foreign States, privileges and immunities, **28 § 1609 et seq.**
Goods, wares and merchandise, **28 § 2005**
Imprisonment, **28 § 2007**
Interest, **28 § 1961**
Internal Revenue Service, this index
Judges or justices, annuities, exemptions, **28 § 376**
Privileges and immunities, terrorists and terrorism, waiver, **28 § 1610 nt, PD 2001–03**
Revenue officers, **28 § 2006**
Rules of Civil Procedure, this index
Terrorists and terrorism, **28 §§ 1605A, 1610**
United States, **28 § 2413**
United States Marshals Service, this index
Waiver, terrorists and terrorism, immunity, **28 § 1610 nt, PD 2001–03**

EXECUTIVE AGENCIES
Accountability. Presidential and Executive Office Accountability, generally, this index
Administrative law and procedure, enforcement, reports, **28 § 530D**
Attorney General, legal services, pending claims in, **28 § 514**
Attorneys, fees, prevailing parties, **28 § 2412**
Civil justice reform, **28 § 519 nt, EON 12988**
Compromise and settlement, enforcement, reports, **28 § 530D**
Contracts. Public Contracts, this index
Costs, prevailing party, **28 § 2412**
Crimes and offenses, reports, **28 § 535**
Enforcement, statutes, reports, **28 § 530D**
Espionage, reports, **28 § 533 nt**
General Services Administration, generally, this index
Hearings, witnesses, fees, **28 § 2412**
Injunctions, enforcement, reports, **28 § 530D**
Interagency legal disputes, **28 § 509 nt, EON 12146**
Investigations, **28 § 533**
Motor vehicles. Federal Agencies, this index
Opinions and decisions, enforcement, reports, **28 § 530D**
Public Contracts, this index
Public policy, statutes, enforcement, reports, **28 § 530D**

EXECUTIVE AGENCIES—Cont'd
Purchasers and purchasing. Federal Agencies, this index
Reports, statutes, enforcement, **28 § 530D**
Statutes, enforcement, reports, **28 § 530D**

EXECUTIVE BRANCH
See specific index headings

EXECUTIVE DEPARTMENTS
Accounts and accounting. Government Accountability Office, generally, this index
Actions and proceedings, district courts, **28 § 1346**
Attorney General, pending claims, **28 § 514**
Attorneys, fees, prevailing parties, **28 § 2412**
Books and papers,
Evidence, **28 § 1733**
Regular course of business, admissibility, **28 § 1732**
Budget, generally, this index
Civil Service, generally, this index
Commissions of Officers, generally, this index
Comptroller General, generally, this index
Condemnation, real estate,
Jurisdiction, **28 § 1358**
Venue, **28 § 1403**
Costs, **28 §§ 2408, 2412**
Court of Appeals for the Federal Circuit, this index
Court of Federal Claims, this index
Crimes and offenses, officers and employees, **28 § 535**
Damages, **28 § 2408**
Espionage, reports, **28 § 533 nt**
Foreign Service, generally, this index
Government Accountability Office, generally, this index
Investigations, **28 § 533**
Justice Department, generally, this index
National budget. Budget, generally, this index
Officers and employees, jury service, **28 § 1863**
President of the United States, generally, this index
Rules and regulations,
Actions and proceedings, **28 § 2402**
Venue, **28 § 1402**
Secretary of Agriculture, generally, this index
Secretary of the Treasury, generally, this index
State Department, generally, this index
Torts, **28 § 2671 et seq.**

EXECUTIVE ORDERS
Indians, U.S. Court of Federal Claims, **28 § 1505**

EXECUTIVE PROTECTIVE SERVICE
Secret Service, generally, this index

EXECUTORS AND ADMINISTRATORS
Annuities, judges or justices, survivors, **28 § 376**
Disbursing officers, claims against U.S., jurisdiction of U.S. Court of Federal Claims, **28 § 1496**
Disqualification, judges or justices, **28 § 455**
Judges or justices, disqualification, **28 § 455**

EXEMPTIONS
Bankruptcy, this index
Copyrights, this index
Court of Appeals for the Federal Circuit, this index
Execution, this index
Federal Debt Collection, this index
Foreign Countries, this index
Garnishment, this index
Jury, this index
Multidistrict litigation, antitrust laws, **28 § 1407**
Rules of Civil Procedure, this index
Terrorists and Terrorism, this index
Trading With the Enemy, this index
United States attorneys, domicile and residence, **28 § 545**
Witnesses, U.S. Court of Federal Claims, **28 § 2506**

EXHAUSTION OF REMEDIES
See specific index headings

EXHIBITS
Federal agencies, **28 § 2344**
Rules of Appellate Procedure, this index
Rules of Civil Procedure, this index

EXONERATION
See specific index headings

EXPENSES AND EXPENDITURES
Administrative Office of U.S. Courts, **28 § 604**
Bankruptcy, this index
Bureau of Investigation, unforeseen emergencies, **28 § 537**
Clerks of courts, offices, **28 § 961**
Court of Federal Claims, this index
Court officers and employees, payment, Administrative Office of U.S. Courts, **28 § 604**
Disclosure of Federal Campaign Funds, generally, this index
District Courts, this index
District Judges, this index
Institutes and joint councils on sentencing, **28 § 334**
Judges or Justices, this index
Jury commissioners, **28 § 1863**
Justice Department, conferences, reports, **28 § 530C nt**
Ministerial officers, **28 § 1929**
Rules of Civil Procedure, this index

EXPENSES AND EXPENDITURES
—Cont'd
Subsistence, generally, this index
Traveling Expenses, generally, this index
United States attorneys, **28 § 549**
United States Magistrate Judges, this index
United States Marshals Service, this index

EXPERTS
Justice Department, funds, **28 § 530C**
Rules of Civil Procedure, this index

EXPLOITATION
See specific index headings

EXPLOSIVES
Bureau of Alcohol, Tobacco, Firearms, and Explosives, generally, this index
Sentence and punishment, second or subsequent offenses, **28 § 994 nt**

EXPORTS AND IMPORTS
Actions and proceedings,
Firms, assistance, **28 § 2636**
Government procurement, **28 §§ 2631, 2636**
Labor and employment, **28 § 2636**
Appeal and review, labor and employment, **28 § 2640**
Boards and commissions. International Trade Commission, generally, this index
Controlled Substances, this index
Courts. International Trade Court, generally, this index
Customs Duties, generally, this index
District courts, unfair practices, **28 § 1368**
Duties. Customs Duties, generally, this index
Employment. Labor and employment, generally, post
Firms,
Actions and proceedings, assistance, **28 § 2636**
Injunctions, assistance, **28 § 2643**
Standing to sue, **28 § 2631**
Government procurement,
Actions and proceedings, **28 §§ 2631, 2636**
Rules of origin, appeal and review, **28 §§ 1581, 1582**
Injunctions, labor and employment, **28 § 2643**
International Trade Commission, generally, this index
International Trade Court, generally, this index
ITC. International Trade Commission, generally, this index
Jurisdiction, monopolies and combinations, **28 § 1368**
Labor and employment,
Actions and proceedings, **28 § 2636**
Appeal and review, **28 § 2640**

EXPORTS AND IMPORTS—Cont'd
Labor and employment—Cont'd
Injunctions, **28 § 2643**
Standing to sue, **28 § 2631**
Monopolies and combinations,
Jurisdiction, **28 § 1368**
Removal of cases or causes, **28 § 1446**
Proceedings. Actions and proceedings, generally, ante
Procurement. Government procurement, generally, ante
Purchasers and purchasing. Government procurement, generally, ante
Records and recordation, ITC, **28 § 1659**
Removal of cases or causes, monopolies and combinations, **28 § 1446**
Rules of origin. Government procurement, ante
Stay of proceedings, **28 § 1659**
Trade representative, Independent Counsel, **28 § 592 et seq.**
United States International Trade Commission. International Trade Commission, generally, this index

EXTENDED CARE SERVICES
Nursing Homes, generally, this index

EXTENSION OF TIME
See specific index headings

EXTRADITION
Habeas corpus, appeal and proceeding to test validity of warrant of removal, **28 § 2253**

EXTRAJUDICIAL KILLING
Definitions, **28 § 1350 nt**

FACTS
Questions of Law or Fact, generally, this index

FAIR HOUSING
Appeal and review, **28 § 2341 et seq.**
Enforcement, private persons, **28 § 2341**
Jurisdiction, **28 § 2342**
Orders, **28 § 2341 et seq.**
Private persons, enforcement, **28 § 2341**

FAIR LABOR STANDARDS
Labor and Employment, generally, this index

FAITH
Full Faith and Credit, generally, this index

FALSE ARREST
Tort Claims Act, **28 § 2680**

FALSE IMPRISONMENT
Tort Claims Act, **28 § 2680**

FALSE PRETENSES
Fraud, generally, this index

FALSE REPRESENTATIONS
Fraud, generally, this index

FALSE STATEMENTS
Fraud, generally, this index

FAMILY
Domestic Violence, generally, this index
Foreign Missions, this index
Relatives, generally, this index

FATHERS
Children and Minors, generally, this index

FBI
Federal Bureau of Investigation, generally, this index

FEDERAL AGENCIES
Actions and proceedings,
Civil justice reform, **28 § 519 nt, EON 12988**
Federal Legal Council, **28 § 509 nt, EON 12146**
Interagency legal disputes, **28 § 509 nt, EON 12146**
Justice Department,
Compensation and salaries, **28 § 509 nt**
Parties, **28 § 516**
Negligence, **28 § 2672**
Wrongful acts, **28 § 2679**
Administrative adjudications, civil justice reform, **28 § 519 nt, EON 12988**
Administrative Law and Procedure, generally, this index
Affidavits, court of appeals, **28 § 2347**
Alternative dispute resolution, civil justice reform, guidelines, **28 § 519 nt, EON 12988**
Annuities, compromise and settlement, brokers, **28 § 519 nt**
Appeal and review, **28 § 2341 et seq.**
Attorney General, **28 § 2348**
Certification of record, **28 § 2346**
Clerks, **28 § 2341**
Copies, orders, **28 § 2344**
Definitions, **28 § 2341**
Evidence, **28 § 2347**
Hearings, post
Injunctions, **28 §§ 2349, 2350**
Intervention, **28 § 2348**
Jurisdiction, **28 §§ 2342, 2349**
Lists, **28 § 2112**
Notice, **28 §§ 2344, 2349**
Packers, **28 § 2351**
Petitions, **28 § 2341 et seq.**
Prehearing conferences, **28 § 2345**
Record on review, **28 § 2112**
Representation, **28 § 2348**
Service of petition, **28 § 2344**
Supreme Court, **28 § 2350**
Time, **28 § 2344**
Venue, **28 §§ 1391, 2343**
Arbitration, generally, this index
Assets Forfeiture Fund, Justice Department, **28 § 524**
Assistance. Federal Aid, generally, this index

FEDERAL AGENCIES—Cont'd
Attorney General,
Civil justice reform, **28 § 519 nt, EON 12988**
Fraud, **28 § 509 nt**
Pending claims, **28 § 514**
Reimbursement, private counsel, **28 § 509 nt**
Attorneys,
Civil justice reform, **28 § 519 nt, EON 12988**
Fees, prevailing parties, **28 § 2412**
Fraud, **28 § 509 nt**
Prevailing parties, fees, **28 § 2412**
Pro bono service, **28 § 519 nt, EON 12988**
Books and papers, evidence, **28 § 1733**
Civil justice reform, guidelines, litigation, **28 § 519 nt, EON 12988**
Civil Service, generally, this index
Compelling performance, **28 § 1361**
Compensation and salaries. Federal Officers and Employees, this index
Compromise and settlement, annuities, brokers, **28 § 519 nt**
Contracts. Public Contracts, generally, this index
Costs, **28 §§ 2408, 2412**
Damages, **28 § 2349**
Security, **28 § 2408**
Disbursing Officials, Clerks, and Agents, generally, this index
Discovery, civil justice reform, guidelines, **28 § 519 nt, EON 12988**
Documents, civil justice reform, guidelines, **28 § 519 nt, EON 12988**
Drug Enforcement Administration, generally, this index
Education, this index
Eminent domain,
Jurisdiction, **28 § 1358**
Venue, **28 § 1403**
Environment, actions and proceedings, **28 § 509 nt**
Espionage, reports, **28 § 533 nt**
Evidence, injunctions, **28 § 2349**
Federal Aid, generally, this index
Federal Legal Council, actions and proceedings, **28 § 509 nt, EON 12146**
Fees,
Attorneys, ante
Witnesses, post
Financial aid. Federal Aid, generally, this index
Government Accountability Office, generally, this index
Hearings, appeal and review,
Court of appeals, **28 § 2347**
Injunctions, **28 § 2349**
Information. Purchasers and purchasing, post
Interagency legal disputes, **28 § 509 nt, EON 12146**
Intervention, orders, **28 § 2348**
Investigations, **28 § 533**

FEDERAL AGENCIES—Cont'd
Judgments and decrees, payment, **28 § 2414**
Judicial Center Board,
Recommendations, **28 § 623**
Research, **28 § 624**
Justice Department,
Assets Forfeiture Fund, **28 § 524**
Reimbursement, funds, **28 § 530C**
Law books, successors, **28 § 414**
Legislation, civil justice reform, **28 § 519 nt, EON 12988**
Limitation of actions, **28 §§ 2415, 2416**
Lists, appeal and review, **28 § 2112**
Motions, civil justice reform, discovery guidelines, **28 § 519 nt, EON 12988**
Motor vehicles, scope of employment, defense, **28 § 2679**
Notice,
Bankruptcy, debtors and creditors, **28 § 1930 nt**
Civil justice reform, complaints, **28 § 519 nt, EON 12988**
Officers and employees. Federal Officers and Employees, generally, this index
Parties, **28 § 1345**
Patent and Trademark Office, generally, this index
Payment,
Disbursing Officials, Clerks, and Agents, generally, this index
Negligence, **28 § 2672**
Pleading,
Court of appeals, **28 § 2347**
Record on review, **28 § 2112**
Pro bono services, civil justice reform, guidelines, **28 § 519 nt, EON 12988**
Proceedings. Actions and proceedings, generally, ante
Public Contracts, generally, this index
Purchasers and purchasing, information, Judiciary Information Technology Fund, **28 § 612**
Records and recordation,
Business records, admissibility in evidence, **28 § 1732**
Evidence, **28 § 1733**
Removal of cases or causes, **28 § 1442**
Review. Appeal and review, generally, ante
Rules and regulations,
Administrative Law and Procedure, this index
Civil justice, **28 § 519 nt, EON 12988**
Rules of Civil Procedure, this index
Rules of Evidence, this index
Sanctions, civil justice reform, guidelines, **28 § 519 nt, EON 12988**
Settlements, civil justice reform, **28 § 519 nt, EON 12988**
Subpoenas, fees, **28 § 1825**
Torts, **28 §§ 2671, 2672**
Limitation of actions, **28 § 2401**
Transcripts, evidence, **28 § 1733**

FEDERAL AGENCIES—Cont'd
United States magistrate judges, **28 § 631**
Witnesses, fees, **28 §§ 1825, 2412**

FEDERAL AID
Diversion of money under programs, action by U.S. for recovery, limitations, **28 §§ 2415, 2416**
Federal debt collection, postjudgment remedies, **28 § 3201**

FEDERAL BUREAU OF INVESTIGATION
Generally, **28 § 531 et seq.**
Aircraft, this index
Ammunition, funds, **28 § 530C**
Analysts, intelligence, **28 § 532 nt**
Appointments, directors, **28 § 532**
Appropriations,
Counterterrorism, **28 § 531 nt**
Humanitarian expenses, **28 § 509 nt**
Unforeseen emergencies, confidential character, **28 § 537**
Uniform Crime Reports, **28 § 534 nt**
Assets Forfeiture Fund. Justice Department, this index
Attorney General, this index
Audits and auditors, undercover operations, **28 § 533 nt**
Automation, fingerprints and fingerprinting, **28 § 534 nt**
Boats and boating, funds, **28 § 530C**
Budget, **28 § 532 nt**
Buildings, police, **28 § 540C**
Children and minors, centers, Child Abduction and Serial Murder Investigative Resources Center, **28 § 531 nt**
Civil service, **28 § 536**
Compensation and salaries,
Director, **28 § 532 nt**
Police, **28 § 540C**
Computers,
Enterprise architecture, **28 § 531 nt**
Reports, enterprise architecture, **28 § 531 nt**
Confirmation of Director, **28 § 532 nt**
Counterintelligence. Intelligence, generally, post
Counterterrorism, funds, **28 § 531 nt**
Critical Skills Scholarship Program, **28 § 532 nt**
Definitions,
Police, **28 § 540C**
Undercover operations, **28 § 533 nt**
Director,
Appointments, **28 § 532**
Compensation, **28 § 532 nt**
Confirmation, **28 § 532 nt**
Drug abuse prevention, **28 § 524**
Head of Bureau, **28 § 532**
Racketeer influence and corrupt organizations, forfeitures, **28 § 524**
Term of service, **28 § 532 nt**
Undergraduate Training Program, **28 § 532 nt**
Directorate of Intelligence, **28 § 532 nt**

FEDERAL BUREAU OF INVESTIGATION—Cont'd
Employees. Officers and employees, generally, post
Enterprise architecture, computers, **28 § 531 nt**
Espionage, generally, this index
Exchange, records and recordation, **28 § 534 nt**
Expenses and expenditures, unforeseen emergencies, confidential character, **28 § 537**
Expungement, DNA (Deoxyribonucleic Acid), indexes, tests, **28 § 531 nt**
Federal officers and employees, crimes and offenses, investigations, **28 § 535**
Felony crime of violence, definitions, **28 § 540A**
Field intelligence groups, **28 § 532 nt**
Fingerprints and fingerprinting, automation, **28 § 534 nt**
Funds, **28 § 530C**
Homicide, serial killings, investigations and investigators, **28 § 540B**
Humanitarian expenses, appropriations, authorization, **28 § 509 nt**
Improvements, intelligence, **28 § 532 nt**
Intelligence,
Analysts, **28 § 532 nt**
Budget, **28 § 532 nt**
Directorate of Intelligence, **28 § 532 nt**
Expenses and expenditures, **28 § 539**
Field intelligence groups, **28 § 532 nt**
Funds, **28 § 531 nt**
Improvements, **28 § 532 nt**
National intelligence workforce, **28 § 532 nt**
Interpreters,
Reports, **28 § 509 nt**
Terrorists and terrorism, **28 § 532 nt**
Local government, records and recordation, exchanges, **28 § 534 nt**
Morgan P. Hardiman Child Abduction and Serial Murder Investigative Resources Center, **28 § 531 nt**
Murder, serial killings, investigations and investigators, **28 § 540B**
National intelligence workforce, **28 § 532 nt**
Officers and employees,
Analysts, intelligence, **28 § 532 nt**
Directorate of Intelligence, **28 § 532 nt**
National intelligence workforce, **28 § 532 nt**
Police, **28 § 540C**
Organization, **28 § 531**
Police, **28 § 540C**
Powers and duties, police, **28 § 540C**
Records and recordation,
DNA (Deoxyribonucleic Acid), tests, **28 § 531 nt**
Exchange, **28 § 534 nt**

FEDERAL BUREAU OF INVESTIGATION—Cont'd
Reports,
Computers, enterprise architecture, **28 § 531 nt**
Enterprise architecture, computers, **28 § 531 nt**
Interpreters, **28 § 509 nt**
National Crime Information Center Project 2000, **28 § 534 nt**
Security, **28 § 532 nt**
Translators, **28 § 509 nt**
Undercover operations, **28 § 533 nt**
Uniform Crime Reports, **28 § 534 nt**
Security, reports, **28 § 532 nt**
Serial killings,
Child Abduction and Serial Murder Investigative Resources Center, **28 § 531 nt**
Investigations and investigators, **28 § 540B**
States,
Counterterrorism, **28 § 531 nt**
Definitions, **28 § 540A**
Records and recordation, exchange, **28 § 534 nt**
Term of service of Director, **28 § 532 nt**
Terrorists and Terrorism, this index
Translators,
Reports, **28 § 509 nt**
Terrorists and terrorism, **28 § 532 nt**
Travelers, **28 § 540A**
Undercover operations, reports, **28 § 533 nt**
Undergraduate Training Program, **28 § 532 nt**
Uniform Crime Reports, **28 § 534 nt**
Uniforms,
Allowances, **28 § 509 nt**
Police, **28 § 540C**
Weapons, funds, **28 § 530C**

FEDERAL CIVIL PENALTIES INFLATION ADJUSTMENT ACT OF 1990
Generally, **28 § 2461 nt**

FEDERAL CLAIMS COURT
Court of Federal Claims, generally, this index

FEDERAL CORPORATIONS
Civil Service, generally, this index
Copyrights, **28 § 1498**
Federal prison industries. Correctional Institutions, this index
Jurisdiction, **28 § 1349**
Patents, **28 § 1498**
Torts, **28 § 2671 et seq.**

FEDERAL DEBT COLLECTION
Generally, **28 § 3001 et seq.**
Actions and proceedings, **28 § 3004**
Joinder of defendants, **28 § 3012**
Postjudgment remedies, generally, post
Prejudgment remedies, generally, post
Surcharges, **28 § 3011**

FEDERAL DEBT COLLECTION—Cont'd
Actions and proceedings—Cont'd
United States magistrates, **28 § 3008**
Affidavits, **28 § 3006**
Prejudgment remedies, **28 § 3101**
Application of law, **28 § 3001**
Judgments and decrees, **28 § 3005**
Assessments, surcharges, **28 § 3011**
Attachment, **28 § 3102**
Attorneys,
Definitions, **28 § 3002**
Notice, **28 § 3004**
Prejudgment remedies, **28 § 3101**
Bonds (officers and fiduciaries), prejudgment remedies, **28 § 3102**
Coowned property, **28 § 3010**
Garnishment, **28 § 3104**
Court, definitions, **28 § 3002**
Debt, definitions, **28 § 3002**
Debtor, definitions, **28 § 3002**
Deceit. Fraud, generally, post
Decrees. Judgments and decrees, generally, post
Definitions, **28 § 3002**
Deposits, proceeds, perishable property, **28 § 3007**
Discovery, **28 § 3015**
Disposable earnings, definitions, **28 § 3002**
Dissolution, prejudgment remedies, **28 §§ 3102, 3105**
Earnings, definitions, **28 § 3002**
Elections, exemptions, **28 § 3014**
Enforcement, **28 §§ 3004, 3013**
Execution,
Postjudgment remedies, **28 § 3203**
Prejudgment remedies, **28 § 3105**
Exemptions, **28 § 3014**
Exoneration, prejudgment remedies, **28 § 3102**
Federal Rules of Civil Procedure, **28 §§ 3003, 3004**
Foreign laws, **28 § 3003**
Fraud, **28 § 3301 et seq.**
Actions and proceedings, **28 § 3306**
Affiliates, definitions, **28 § 3301**
Application of law, **28 § 3308**
Assets,
Definitions, **28 § 3301**
Valuation, **28 § 3307**
Claim, definitions, **28 § 3301**
Creditor, definitions, **28 § 3301**
Definitions, **28 § 3301**
Exemptions, transfers, voidability, **28 § 3307**
Federal Rules of Civil Procedure, **28 § 3306**
Good faith, transfers, **28 § 3307**
Insider, definitions, **28 § 3301**
Insolvency, **28 § 3302**
Intent, transfers, **28 § 3304**
Judgment date, transfers, **28 § 3304**
Lien, definitions, **28 § 3301**
Prejudgment remedies, **28 § 3101**
Presumptions, insolvency, **28 § 3302**

FEDERAL DEBT COLLECTION—Cont'd
Fraud—Cont'd
Relative, definitions, **28 § 3301**
Time, **28 §§ 3304, 3305**
Transfers, **28 § 3301 et seq.**
Valid lien, definitions, **28 § 3301**
Valuation, **28 §§ 3303, 3307**
Voidability, transfers, **28 § 3307**
Fraudulent conveyances, **28 § 3301 et seq.**
Garnishment,
Definitions, **28 § 3002**
Postjudgment remedies, **28 § 3205**
Prejudgment remedies, **28 § 3104**
Hearings,
Exemptions, **28 § 3014**
Postjudgment remedies, **28 § 3202**
Prejudgment remedies, **28 §§ 3101, 3105**
Incumbrances. Liens and incumbrances, generally, post
Interference, prejudgment remedies, **28 § 3101**
Joinder of defendants, **28 § 3012**
Joint cases, exemptions, **28 § 3014**
Judgments and decrees,
Application of law, **28 § 3005**
Definitions, **28 § 3002**
Prejudgment remedies, **28 §§ 3102, 3105**
Judicial sales, **28 § 3201 et seq.**
Levy,
Postjudgment remedies, **28 § 3203**
Prejudgment remedies, **28 § 3102**
Liens and incumbrances,
Postjudgment remedies, **28 §§ 3201, 3203**
Prejudgment remedies, **28 § 3102**
Misrepresentation. Fraud, generally, ante
Modification, enforcement, **28 § 3013**
Nonexempt disposable earnings, definitions, **28 § 3002**
Notice,
Enforcement, **28 § 3004**
Prejudgment remedies, **28 § 3101 et seq.**
Perishable goods, presumptions, **28 § 3007**
Person, definitions, **28 § 3002**
Personal property,
Perishable goods, presumptions, **28 § 3007**
Prejudgment remedies, **28 § 3102**
Postjudgment remedies, **28 § 3201 et seq.**
Attorneys, notice, **28 § 3202**
Commencement, **28 § 3202**
Coowned property,
Execution, **28 § 3203**
Garnishment, **28 § 3205**
Discharge, **28 § 3206**
Execution, **28 § 3203**
Garnishment, **28 § 3205**
Hearings, **28 § 3202**
Installment payment orders, **28 § 3204**

FEDERAL DEBT COLLECTION
—Cont'd
Postjudgment remedies—Cont'd
Judicial sales, **28 § 3201 et seq.**
Levy, **28 § 3203**
Liens and incumbrances, **28 §§ 3201, 3203**
Modification, installment payment orders, **28 § 3204**
Notice, **28 §§ 3202, 3203**
Priorities and preferences, **28 §§ 3201, 3205**
Proceeds, **28 § 3203**
Process, **28 §§ 3202, 3205**
Receivers and receivership, **28 § 3203**
Records and recordation, **28 § 3203**
Redemption, **28 § 3203**
Release, judgment liens, **28 § 3201**
Renewal, judgment liens, **28 § 3201**
Replevin, **28 § 3203**
Rural areas, **28 § 3203**
Sales, **28 § 3201 et seq.**
Service of process, **28 §§ 3202, 3205**
Stay of proceedings, **28 § 3203**
Termination, **28 § 3205**
Waiver, **28 § 3201**
Preemption, **28 § 3003**
Preferences. Priorities and preferences, generally, post
Prejudgment remedies, **28 § 3101 et seq.**
Accounts and accounting, receivers and receivership, **28 § 3103**
Affidavits, **28 § 3101**
Applications, **28 §§ 3101, 3104**
Appointments, receivers and receivership, **28 § 3103**
Attachment, **28 § 3102**
Attorneys, **28 § 3101**
Bonds (officers and fiduciaries), **28 § 3102**
Compensation and salaries, receivers and receivership, **28 § 3103**
Coowned property, garnishment, **28 § 3104**
Definitions, **28 § 3002**
Deposits, **28 § 3105**
Dissolution, **28 §§ 3102, 3105**
Execution, **28 § 3105**
Exoneration, **28 § 3102**
Fraud, **28 § 3101**
Garnishment, **28 § 3104**
Hearings, **28 §§ 3101, 3105**
Interference, **28 § 3101**
Judgments and decrees, **28 §§ 3102, 3105**
Levy, **28 § 3102**
Liens and incumbrances, **28 § 3102**
Notice, **28 § 3101 et seq.**
Personal property, **28 § 3102**
Priorities and preferences, receivers and receivership, **28 § 3103**
Receivers and receivership, **28 § 3103**
Removal, receivers and receivership, **28 § 3103**
Replevin, **28 § 3102**

FEDERAL DEBT COLLECTION
—Cont'd
Prejudgment remedies—Cont'd
Reports, receivers and receivership, **28 § 3103**
Sequestration, **28 § 3105**
Termination, **28 § 3103**
Presumptions, perishable property, **28 § 3007**
Priorities and preferences,
Postjudgment remedies, **28 §§ 3201, 3205**
Prejudgment remedies, **28 § 3103**
Proceedings. Actions and proceedings, generally, ante
Proceeds, postjudgment remedies, **28 § 3203**
Process, **28 § 3004**
Postjudgment remedies, **28 §§ 3202, 3205**
Property, definitions, **28 § 3002**
Qualified retirement arrangement, definitions, **28 § 3010**
Receivers and receivership,
Postjudgment remedies, **28 § 3203**
Prejudgment remedies, **28 § 3103**
Records and recordation, postjudgment remedies, **28 § 3203**
Redemption, postjudgment remedies, **28 § 3203**
Release, judgment liens, **28 § 3201**
Renewal, judgment liens, **28 § 3201**
Replevin, **28 § 3203**
Reports, receivers and receivership, **28 § 3103**
Retirement system for Federal military or civilian personnel, definitions, **28 § 3010**
Rural areas, postjudgment remedies, **28 § 3203**
Sales,
Perishable property, presumptions, **28 § 3007**
Postjudgment remedies, **28 § 3201 et seq.**
Searches and seizures, **28 § 3009**
Security agreement, definitions, **28 § 3002**
Sequestration, prejudgment remedies, **28 § 3105**
Service of process. Process, generally, ante
Stay of proceedings, **28 § 3014**
Postjudgment remedies, **28 § 3203**
Surcharges, **28 § 3011**
Termination,
Postjudgment remedies, **28 § 3205**
Prejudgment remedies, **28 § 3103**
Transfers, fraud, **28 § 3301 et seq.**
United States magistrates, **28 § 3008**
United States Marshals Service,
Definitions, **28 § 3002**
Postjudgment remedies, generally, ante
Prejudgment remedies, generally, ante
Searches and seizures, **28 § 3009**

FEDERAL DEBT COLLECTION
—Cont'd
Waiver, postjudgment remedies, **28 § 3201**

FEDERAL GOVERNMENT
United States, generally, this index

FEDERAL INTERMEDIATE CREDIT BANKS
Tort Claims Act, **28 § 2680**

FEDERAL LAND BANKS
Tort Claims Act, **28 § 2680**

FEDERAL LANDS
Public Lands, generally, this index

FEDERAL LEGAL COUNCIL
Generally, **28 § 509 nt, EON 12146**

FEDERAL MARITIME COMMISSION
Appeal and review, orders, **28 § 2341 et seq.**
Jurisdiction, **28 § 2342**
Orders, appeal and review, **28 § 2341 et seq.**

FEDERAL OFFICERS AND EMPLOYEES
Access, financial statements and reports, **5 App. 4 § 105**
Accounts and accounting, U.S. Court of Federal Claims, compromise and settlement, **28 § 1494**
Actions and proceedings,
Claims, fees, **28 § 2501**
Compelling performance of duty, **28 § 1361**
Administration, financial statements and reports, **5 App. 4 § 111**
Appeal and review,
Financial statements and reports, **5 App. 4 § 106**
Records and recordation, **28 § 2112**
Appointment, powers and duties, **28 § 756**
Attorneys, fees, **28 §§ 509 nt, 2412**
Basic pay. Compensation and salaries, post
Civil Service, generally, this index
Claims,
Heads of departments, post
Personal injuries, **28 § 2672**
Commissions of Officers, generally, this index
Compelling performance of duty, **28 § 1361**
Compensation and salaries,
Basic pay, Judicial Branch, increase, **28 § 603 nt**
Citizens Commission On Public Service and Compensation, generally, this index
Complaints, crimes and offenses, reports, **28 § 535**
Comptroller General, generally, this index

FEDERAL OFFICERS AND EMPLOYEES—Cont'd
Confidential or privileged information, financial statements and reports, **5 App. 4 § 107**
Conflict of interest, disclosure, **5 App. 4 §§ 101, 107**
Costs, **28 § 2412**
Counterfeiting, emblems and insignia, **28 § 994 nt**
Crimes and offenses,
Emblems and insignia, post
Investigations, **28 §§ 509 nt, 535**
Removal of action or prosecution against for acts under color of office, **28 § 1442**
Uniforms, **28 § 994 nt**
Criminal background checks, **28 § 534 et seq.**
Damages, district courts, **28 § 1346**
Death,
Actions and proceedings, **28 § 2402**
Administrative law and procedure, **28 § 2675**
Damages, administrative adjustments, **28 § 2672**
District courts, **28 § 1346**
Punitive damages, **28 § 2674**
Definitions,
Financial statements and reports, **5 App. 4 § 109**
Jury Selection and Service Act, **28 § 1869**
Disbursing Officials, Clerks, and Agents, generally, this index
Disclosure. Financial statements and reports, post
Discrimination, judicial review, decisions of Merit Systems Protection Board, United States Court of Appeals for the Federal Circuit, jurisdiction, **28 § 1295**
Disqualification, judges or justices, **28 § 455**
District Courts, this index
Emblems and insignia,
Aggravating factor, counterfeiting, **28 § 994 nt**
Counterfeiting, **28 § 994 nt**
Crimes and offenses, counterfeiting, **28 § 994 nt**
Ethics, financial statements and reports, **5 App. 4 § 101 et seq.**
Extraordinary expenses, **28 § 1929**
Fees,
Attorneys, ante
Claims, filing, **28 § 2501**
Felonies. Crimes and offenses, generally, ante
Filing, financial statements and reports, **5 App. 4 § 101 et seq.**
Financial statements and reports,
Access, **5 App. 4 § 105**
Administration, **5 App. 4 § 111**
Appeal and review, **5 App. 4 § 106**

FEDERAL OFFICERS AND EMPLOYEES—Cont'd
Financial statements and reports —Cont'd
Comptroller General, powers and duties, **5 App. 4 § 108**
Definitions, **5 App. 4 § 109**
Disclosure, **5 App. 4 § 101 et seq.**
Access, **5 App. 4 § 105**
Administration, **5 App. 4 § 111**
Appeal and review, **5 App. 4 § 106**
Comptroller General, powers and duties, **5 App. 4 § 108**
Confidential or privileged information, **5 App. 4 § 107**
Definitions, **5 App. 4 § 109**
Filing, **5 App. 4 § 101 et seq.**
Fraud, **5 App. 4 § 104**
Notice, **5 App. 4 § 110**
Ethics, **5 App. 4 § 101 et seq.**
Filing, **5 App. 4 § 101 et seq.**
Fraud, **5 App. 4 § 104**
Notice, **5 App. 4 § 110**
Foreign Diplomatic and Consular Officers, generally, this index
Fraud,
Financial statements and reports, **5 App. 4 § 104**
Investigations, **28 § 509 nt**
Group health insurance, Judicial Center, Director, professional staff, as officers and employees within meaning of provisions, **28 § 627**
Group life insurance, Judicial Center, Director, professional staff, as officers and employees within meaning of provisions, **28 § 627**
Handicapped persons. Workers compensation, post
Heads of departments,
Attorneys, **28 § 514**
Claims,
Notice, contractors, **28 § 2511**
Production of books and papers, **28 § 2507**
Judicial sales, **28 § 2410**
Notice, pending claims, **28 § 514**
Questions of law, **28 § 512**
Witnesses, fees, **28 § 2412**
Independent Counsel, generally, this index
Insignia. Emblems and insignia, generally, ante
Institutes and joint councils on sentencing, attendance by Federal officers, **28 § 334**
Judges or justices, disqualification, **28 § 455**
Judgments and decrees, payment, **28 § 2414**
Jury,
Exemptions, **28 § 1863**
Workers compensation, **28 § 1877**
Law books, successors, **28 § 414**
Limitation of actions, **28 § 2415**

FEDERAL OFFICERS AND EMPLOYEES—Cont'd
Litigation where a party, conducting reserved to Justice Department, **28 § 516**
Motor vehicles. Federal Agencies, this index
Negligence,
Administration, **28 § 2672**
Arbitration, **28 § 2677**
Attorney General, **28 § 2677**
Attorneys, fees, **28 § 2678**
Claims against U.S., **28 § 2672**
Disposition by agency, **28 § 2675**
District courts, **28 § 1346**
Exceptions, **28 § 2680**
Excessive fees, attorneys, **28 § 2678**
Exclusiveness of remedy, **28 § 2679**
Res judicata, **28 § 2676**
Trial, **28 § 2402**
Notice,
Financial statements and reports, **5 App. 4 § 110**
Heads of departments, ante
Offenses. Crimes and offenses, generally, ante
Parties,
Appeal and review, time, **28 § 2107**
Plaintiffs, **28 § 1345**
Political activities, crimes and offenses, **28 § 529**
President of the United States, generally, this index
Purchasers and purchasing. Federal Agencies, this index
Quieting title, **28 § 2409a**
Receivers and receivership, ineligibility to appointment as receivers, **28 § 958**
Recovery of money erroneously paid to, action by U.S., limitation, **28 §§ 2415, 2416**
Removal, action or prosecution against, **28 § 1442**
Reports,
Crimes and offenses, **28 § 535**
Financial statements and reports, generally, ante
Rules of Civil Procedure, this index
Secretary of Agriculture, generally, this index
Sentence and punishment,
Assault and battery, threats, guidelines, **28 § 994 nt**
Threats, guidelines, **28 § 994 nt**
Subpoenas, **28 § 1825**
Territories, this index
Threats, sentence and punishment, guidelines, **28 § 994 nt**
Transmittal of letter rogatory or request to, **28 § 1781**
Uniforms,
Aggravating factor, crimes and offenses, **28 § 994 nt**
Allowances, **28 § 509 nt**
Crimes and offenses, **28 § 994 nt**

FEDERAL OFFICERS AND EMPLOYEES—Cont'd
United States Attorneys, generally, this index
United States Marshals Service, generally, this index
Venue, **28 § 1391**
Actions against, **28 § 1391**
Witnesses, payment, **28 § 1825**
Workers compensation,
Handicapped persons, juror, entitlement, termination of service as, **28 § 1877**
Jurors, protection of, applicability of provisions, **28 § 1877**

FEDERAL PRISON INDUSTRIES
Correctional Institutions, this index

FEDERAL PRISONS
Correctional Institutions, generally, this index

FEDERAL PUBLIC DEFENDER
Public Defenders, generally, this index

FEDERAL QUESTION JURISDICTIONAL AMENDMENTS ACT OF 1980
Generally, **28 §§ 1 nt, 1331**

FEDERAL RECORDS
Records and Recordation, this index

FEDERAL REGISTER
Administrative Office of United States Courts, rules and regulations, **28 § 604**
Indians, this index

FEDERAL RESERVE BANKS
National Banks, generally, this index

FEDERAL RULES OF APPELLATE PROCEDURE
Rules of Appellate Procedure, generally, this index

FEDERAL TORT CLAIMS ACT
Torts, generally, this index

FEDERAL TRADE COMMISSION
Monopolies and Combinations, generally, this index

FEES
See specific index headings

FELONIES
Crimes and Offenses, generally, this index

FEMALES
Women, generally, this index

FENCES
Aliens. Immigration, this index
Immigration, this index

FENTANYL
Controlled Substances, generally, this index

FERRIES
Jurors, tolls, **28 § 1871**
Tolls, jurors, **28 § 1871**

FIDELITY BONDS
Bonds (Officers and Fiduciaries), generally, this index

FIDUCIARIES
Disqualification, judges or justices, **28 § 455**
Executors and Administrators, generally, this index
Guardian and Ward, generally, this index
Judges or justices, disqualification, **28 § 455**
Receivers and Receivership, generally, this index

FIELD INTELLIGENCE GROUPS
Federal Bureau of Investigation, **28 § 532 nt**

FIFTH CIRCUIT COURT OF APPEALS REORGANIZATION ACT OF 1980
Generally, **28 §§ 1 nt, 41, 44, 48**

FILING
See specific index headings

FINALITY
See specific index headings

FINANCE
Money, generally, this index

FINANCIAL ASSISTANCE
Federal Aid, generally, this index

FINANCIAL INSTITUTIONS
Banks and Banking, generally, this index
Crimes and offenses, Financial Institutions Fraud Unit, **28 § 509 nt**
National Banks, generally, this index
Sentence and punishment, federally insured institutions, **28 § 994 nt**

FINANCIAL STATEMENTS AND REPORTS
Bankruptcy, this index
Federal Officers and Employees, this index

FINDING TOOLS
Indexes, generally, this index

FINDINGS
See specific index headings

FINES, PENALTIES AND FORFEITURES
Generally, **28 § 2461 et seq.**
Admiralty, this index
Attorney General, this index
Attorneys, this index

FINES, PENALTIES AND FORFEITURES—Cont'd
Bail, bonds, payment, **28 § 2044**
Children and Minors, this index
Contempt, generally, this index
Costs, claims, **28 § 2465**
Court of Federal Claims, this index
Customs Duties, this index
District Courts, this index
Escape, this index
Foreign countries, **28 § 2467**
Foreign currency, **28 § 2467**
Forgery, this index
Fraud, this index
Fugitives from justice, **28 § 2466**
Grand Jury, this index
Guards, labor and employment, **28 § 534 nt**
Home health care and services, criminal background checks, labor and employment, **28 § 534 nt**
Indictment and Information, this index
Interest, returns, **28 § 2465**
Internal Revenue Service, this index
International Trade Court, this index
Jurisdiction, **28 § 1355**
Foreign countries, **28 § 2467**
Jury, **28 § 1864 et seq.**
Limitation of Actions, this index
Military Justice Code, generally, this index
Mode of recovery, **28 § 2461**
Modification, guidelines, **28 § 994**
Nursing Homes, this index
Oceans, this index
Orders of court, **28 § 994**
Perjury, generally, this index
Privileges and immunities, **28 § 2465**
Process, this index
Reasonable cause certificates, **28 § 2465**
Reports, Attorney General, **28 § 524**
Restitution, generally, this index
Returns, **28 § 2465**
Revenue laws, **28 § 2463**
Rules of Civil Procedure, this index
Sexual Abuse, generally, this index
Ships and Shipping, this index
Stay of proceedings, execution of process in admiralty, **28 § 2464**
Telecommunications, this index
Terrorists and Terrorism, this index
Time, enforcement, **28 § 2462**
Tort claims against U.S., excessive attorneys' fees, **28 § 2678**
Trafficking, generally, this index
Venue, **28 § 1395**
Foreign countries, **28 § 2467**
Internal Revenue Service, **28 § 1402**

FINGERPRINTS AND FINGERPRINTING
Criminal Background Checks, generally, this index
Federal Bureau of Investigation, this index

FINLAND
Convention on the Taking of Evidence Abroad in Civil or Commercial Matters, party to, **28 § 1781 nt**

FIREARMS
Weapons, generally, this index

FIREFIGHTERS AND FIRE DEPARTMENTS
Grants, training, **28 § 509 nt**
Jury service, exemption, **28 § 1863**
Terrorists and terrorism, training, **28 § 509 nt**
Training,
Grants, **28 § 509 nt**
Terrorists and terrorism, **28 § 509 nt**

FIREMEN
Firefighters and Fire Departments, generally, this index

FIRES AND FIRE PROTECTION
Bureau of Alcohol, Tobacco, Firearms, and Explosives, generally, this index
Indian Lands and Reservations, this index
Public Lands, this index

FIRMS
See specific index headings

FIRST RESPONDERS ASSISTANCE ACT
Generally, **28 § 509 nt**

FISH AND WILDLIFE SERVICE
United States magistrate judges, **28 § 631**

FIVE CIVILIZED TRIBES
Judgment in favor of claimant to allotment, exception, **28 § 1353**

FLIGHTS
Aircraft, generally, this index

FLORIDA
Bankruptcy, judges or justices, appointments, **28 § 152**
District courts, **28 § 89**
Judges or justices, **28 § 133**
Designation of, **28 § 89 nt**
Jury, composition, **28 § 89 nt**
Location, **28 § 89**
Judicial Circuit of U.S., **28 § 41**
Number of district judges, **28 § 133**
Judicial districts,
Bankruptcy, **28 § 581 nt**
Number of district judges, **28 § 133**
United States,
Attorneys, tenure and appointment, **28 § 89 nt**
Trustees of judicial districts, appointment, **28 § 581**

FORCE
See specific index headings

FORCES
Armed Forces, generally, this index

FORECLOSURE
Tax liens, **28 § 2410**

FOREIGN AND INTERNATIONAL RELATIONS
Conventions, generally, this index
Foreign Service, generally, this index
Intelligence, generally, this index
State Department, generally, this index
Treaties, generally, this index

FOREIGN COUNTRIES
Actions and proceedings,
Jurisdiction, **28 § 1330**
Removal of action, **28 § 1441**
Venue, **28 § 1391**
Aircraft, this index
Aliens, generally, this index
Assistance, foreign tribunals and to litigants before such tribunals, **28 § 1782**
Attachment, privileges and immunities, **28 § 1609 et seq.**
Bankruptcy, this index
Conventions, generally, this index
Crimes and offenses, travelers, violent crimes, investigations, **28 § 540A**
Damages, support of terrorism, **28 § 1605A**
Death, damages, support of terrorism, **28 § 1605A**
Diplomatic Security, generally, this index
Documents. Foreign Documents, generally, this index
Embassies. Foreign Diplomatic and Consular Officers, generally, this index
Execution, privileges and immunities, **28 § 1609 et seq.**
Exemptions, privileges and immunities, **28 §§ 1605, 1605A**
Exports and Imports, generally, this index
Fines, penalties and forfeitures, **28 § 2467**
Justice Department Assets Forfeiture Fund, **28 § 524**
Notice, **28 § 2467**
Forfeitures. Fines, penalties and forfeitures, generally, ante
Immigration, generally, this index
Immunities. Privileges and immunities, generally, post
Imports. Exports and Imports, generally, this index
Injunctions, **28 § 2467**
International Trade Court, this index
Iraq, generally, this index
Judgments and decrees,
Fines, penalties and forfeitures, **28 § 2467**
Payment of final judgment against U.S., exception, **28 § 2414**
Jurisdiction, **28 § 1330**
Diversity of citizenship, **28 § 1332**

FOREIGN COUNTRIES—Cont'd
Justice Department, reimbursements, funds, **28 § 530C**
Letters rogatory or request, transmittal to foreign tribunal, **28 § 1781**
Libya, generally, this index
Missions. Foreign Missions, generally, this index
Notice, fines, penalties and forfeitures, **28 § 2467**
Official records, authentication, **28 § 1741**
Patents. Foreign Patents, generally, this index
Privileges and immunities, **28 § 1602 et seq.**
Admiralty suits, **28 § 1605**
Answers, time, **28 § 1608**
Attachment, **28 § 1609 et seq.**
Attorney General, discovery, **28 § 1605**
Business and commerce, **28 §§ 1603, 1605**
Counterclaims, **28 § 1607**
Cuba, **28 § 1611**
Death, **28 § 1605**
Declaration of purpose, **28 § 1602**
Default, **28 § 1608**
Definitions, **28 § 1603**
Discovery, **28 § 1605**
District courts, **28 § 1330**
Execution, **28 § 1609 et seq.**
Exemptions, **28 §§ 1605, 1605A**
International agreements, **28 § 1604**
Maritime liens, **28 § 1605**
Notice, **28 § 1608**
Personal injuries, **28 § 1605**
Process, **28 § 1608**
Property damage, **28 § 1605**
Punitive damages, **28 § 1606**
Removal of cases or causes, **28 § 1441**
Service of process, **28 § 1608**
Stay of proceedings, **28 § 1605**
Terrorists and terrorism, **28 § 1605A**
Time, answers, **28 § 1608**
Venue, **28 § 1391**
Waiver, **28 § 1605**
Process, **28 § 1696**
Privileges and immunities, **28 § 1608**
Rules of Civil Procedure, this index
Subpoenas, **28 §§ 1783, 1784**
Supreme Court, jurisdiction of actions involving ambassadors, ministers, **28 § 1251**
Terrorists and Terrorism, generally, this index
Tort Claims Act, exemptions, **28 § 2680**
Treaties, generally, this index
Tribunals, service of document issued in connection with proceeding in, **28 § 1696**
Voluntary witnesses, **28 § 1782**
Waiver. Privileges and immunities, ante

FOREIGN COURTS OR TRIBUNALS
Assistance, **28 § 1782**

FOREIGN COURTS OR TRIBUNALS —Cont'd
Civil justice reform, **28 § 519 nt, EON 12988**
Exports and imports. International Trade Court, generally, this index
Judgments and decrees, United States, payment, **28 § 2414**
Letters rogatory, **28 § 1781**
Process, **28 § 1696**
Witnesses, **28 § 1782**

FOREIGN CURRENCY
Fines, penalties and forfeitures, **28 § 2467**

FOREIGN DIPLOMATIC AND CONSULAR OFFICERS
Convention on the Taking of Evidence Abroad in Civil or Commercial Matters, **28 § 1781 nt**
District courts, jurisdiction, **28 § 1351**
Evidence, **28 § 1740**
Convention on the Taking of Evidence Abroad in Civil or Commercial Matters, **28 § 1781 nt**
Jurisdiction,
District courts, **28 § 1351**
Supreme Court, **28 § 1251**
Missions. Foreign Missions, generally, this index
Rules of Civil Procedure, this index
Security. Diplomatic Security, generally, this index
Supreme Court, jurisdiction, **28 § 1251**
Vice Consuls, evidence, **28 § 1740**

FOREIGN DOCUMENTS
Authentication, copies, **28 § 1741**
Copies, authentication, **28 § 1741**
Process, **28 § 1696**

FOREIGN EMBASSIES
Foreign Diplomatic and Consular Officers, generally, this index

FOREIGN GOVERNMENTS
Foreign Countries, generally, this index

FOREIGN INTELLIGENCE
Intelligence, generally, this index

FOREIGN LANGUAGES
Interpreters, generally, this index

FOREIGN LEGATIONS
Foreign Diplomatic and Consular Officers, generally, this index

FOREIGN MERCHANDISE
Customs Duties, generally, this index

FOREIGN MISSIONS
District courts, **28 § 1364**
Espionage, **28 § 533 nt**
Family, insurance, **28 § 1364**
Insurance, **28 § 1364**

FOREIGN MISSIONS—Cont'd
Privileges and immunities, insurance, **28 § 1364**
Security. Diplomatic Security, generally, this index

FOREIGN NATIONS
Foreign Countries, generally, this index

FOREIGN OFFICIALS
Diplomatic Security, generally, this index
Murder, this index

FOREIGN PATENTS
Applications, copies, **28 § 1745**
Copies, applications, **28 § 1745**
Documents, evidence, **28 § 1745**
Evidence, **28 § 1745**
Journals, evidence, **28 § 1745**
Specifications and drawings, evidence, **28 § 1745**

FOREIGN SERVICE
Ambassadors and consuls. Foreign Diplomatic and Consular Officers, generally, this index
Consular agents, Convention on the Taking of Evidence Abroad in Civil or Commercial Matters, **28 § 1781 nt**
Depositions, United States Court of International Trade, **28 § 2639**
Diplomatic Security, generally, this index
Foreign Diplomatic and Consular Officers, generally, this index
Missions. Foreign Missions, generally, this index
Officers and employees. Foreign Diplomatic and Consular Officers, generally, this index
Privileges and immunities, **28 § 2416**
Reports, United States Court of International Trade, merchandise, valuation, **28 § 2639**
Security. Diplomatic Security, generally, this index
Vice Consuls. Foreign Diplomatic and Consular Officers, this index

FOREIGN SOVEREIGN IMMUNITIES ACT OF 1976
Generally, **28 §§ 1 nt, 1330, 1332, 1391, 1441, 1602 et seq.**

FOREIGN STATES
Execution, **28 § 1609 et seq.**
Foreign Countries, generally, this index

FOREIGNERS
Aliens, generally, this index

FORENSIC LABORATORIES
Computer forensic laboratories, **28 § 509 nt**

FORFEITURES
Fines, Penalties and Forfeitures, generally, this index

FORGERY
Fines, penalties and forfeitures, weapons, **28 § 994 nt**

FORMA PAUPERIS
Generally, **28 § 1915**
Affidavits, assets, **28 § 1915**
Appeal and review, **28 § 1915**
Fees, transcripts, **28 § 753**
Transcripts, fees, **28 § 753**
Assets, affidavits, **28 § 1915**
Attorneys, capital cases, habeas corpus, **28 § 2261**
Capital cases, habeas corpus, attorneys, **28 § 2261**
Costs, **28 § 1915**
Definitions, fees, **28 § 1915**
Fees,
Transcripts, **28 § 753**
Witnesses, habeas corpus, **28 § 1825**
Frivolous actions, **28 § 1915**
Habeas Corpus, this index
Judgments and decrees, **28 § 1915**
Malicious pleadings, **28 § 1915**
Prison trust fund account statements, fees, **28 § 1915**
Review. Appeal and review, generally, ante
Standing to sue, **28 § 1915**
Successive claims, **28 § 1915**
Supreme Court, expenses and expenditures, **28 § 672**
Transcripts, fees, **28 § 753**
United States Court of Federal Claims, **28 § 2513**
Witnesses, habeas corpus, fees, **28 § 1825**

FORMS
Judicial Panel On Multidistrict Litigation, this index
Juror qualification form, **28 § 1864 et seq.**
Rules of Appellate Procedure, this index
Rules of Civil Procedure, this index
Sentence and punishment, reports, **28 § 994**

FORMULARIES
Drugs and Medicine, generally, this index

FORT WORTH, TX
Court of Appeals for Fifth Circuit, generally, this index

FORUM NON CONVENIENS
Venue, generally, this index

FOUNDATIONS
Federal Judicial Center, **28 § 629**

4-METHYLENEDIOXYPHENYL-2-PROPANONE
Controlled Substances, generally, this index

FRANCE
Evidence, Convention on the Taking of Evidence Abroad in Civil or Commercial Matters, **28 § 1781 nt**

FRATERNAL ASSOCIATIONS AND SOCIETIES
Disqualification, judges or justices, **28 § 455**
Judges or justices, disqualification, **28 § 455**

FRAUD
Aged Persons, this index
Bankruptcy, this index
Banks and Banking, this index
Claims, this index
Corporations, this index
Court of Federal Claims, this index
Customs Duties, this index
Federal Debt Collection, this index
Federal Officers and Employees, this index
Federally insured financial institutions, **28 § 509 nt**
Fines, penalties and forfeitures, United States, **28 § 2514**
Resolution Trust Corporation, this index
Rules of Civil Procedure, this index
Scholarships, this index
Secret Service, this index
Securities, this index
Sentence and punishment,
Telemarketing, **28 § 994 nt**
Victims, aged persons, **28 § 994 nt**
Telecommunications, this index
Terrorists and Terrorism, this index
Tort Claims Act, exemptions, **28 § 2680**
United States, this index
Visas, this index

FRAUDULENT CONVEYANCES
Bankruptcy, this index
Federal debt collection, **28 § 3301 et seq.**
Postal Service, attachment, **28 § 2710**
Rules of Civil Procedure, this index

FREE BASE (COCAINE)
Controlled Substances, generally, this index

FREIGHT
Motor Carriers, generally, this index
Ships and Shipping, generally, this index

FREIGHT FORWARDERS
Surface Transportation Board, generally, this index

FRIVOLOUS ACTIONS
Correctional Institutions, this index
Judges or justices, complaints, **28 § 352**

FUGITIVES APPREHENSION TASK FORCES
Generally, **28 § 566 nt**

FUGITIVES FROM JUSTICE
Arrest, task forces, **28 § 566 nt**
Task forces, arrest, **28 § 566 nt**

FULL FAITH AND CREDIT
Child support orders, **28 § 1738B**
Parental Kidnapping Prevention Act, **28 § 1738A nt**
States, this index
Support, **28 § 1738B**

FULL FAITH AND CREDIT FOR CHILD SUPPORT ORDERS ACT
Generally, **28 § 1738B**

FUNDS
Appropriations, generally, this index
Counterterrorism Fund, **28 § 524 nt**
Department of Justice Assets Forfeiture Fund, **28 § 524**
Depositaries, generally, this index
Disbursing officers, U.S. Court of Federal Claims, relief, **28 § 1496**
Disclosure of Federal Campaign Funds, generally, this index
Immigration, this index
Judges or Justices, this index
Judiciary Automation Fund, **28 § 1913 nt**
Judiciary Information Technology Fund, **28 § 612**
Justice Department, this index
Terrorists and Terrorism, this index

FURETHIDINE
Controlled Substances, generally, this index

GAMBLING
Amateur sports and athletic organizations, **28 § 3701 et seq.**
Athletics, **28 § 3701 et seq.**
Application of law, **28 § 3704**
Definitions, **28 § 3701**
Injunctions, **28 § 3703**
Crimes and offenses, athletics, **28 § 3701 et seq.**
Definitions, athletics, **28 § 3701**
Dog races, unlawful sports gambling, **28 § 3704**
Governmental entity, definitions, **28 § 3701**
Jai alai, **28 § 3704**
Person, definitions, **28 § 3701**
Professional sports, **28 § 3701 et seq.**
States, definitions, **28 § 3701**

GANGS
Intelligence, national gang intelligence center, **28 § 534 nt**
National gang intelligence center, **28 § 534 nt**
Reports, national gang intelligence center, **28 § 534 nt**

GAO
Government Accountability Office, generally, this index

GARNISHMENT
Exemptions, judges or justices, annuities, **28 § 376**
Federal Debt Collection, this index
Judges or justices, annuities, exemptions, **28 § 376**
Rules of Civil Procedure, this index
United States, **28 § 2405**

GENDER
Discrimination, generally, this index

GENERAL ACCOUNTING OFFICE
Government Accountability Office, generally, this index

GENERAL ELECTIONS
Elections, generally, this index

GENERAL SERVICES ADMINISTRATION
Administrators,
Administrative Office of U.S. Courts, **28 § 462**
Independent Counsel, **28 § 594**
United States magistrate judges, courtrooms, **28 § 635**
Witnesses, subsistence allowances, **28 § 1821**

GENERAL STORES
Stores, generally, this index

GENEVA CONVENTIONS OF 1949
Definitions, habeas corpus, **28 § 2241 nt**
Habeas corpus, **28 § 2241 nt**

GEORGIA
Bankruptcy, judges or justices, appointments, **28 § 152**
District courts,
Cities, held at, **28 § 90**
Judges, **28 § 133**
Places of holding, **28 § 90**
Judicial Circuit of U.S., **28 § 41**
Judicial districts, **28 § 90**
Bankruptcy, **28 § 581 nt**
Number of district judges, **28 § 133**

GERMANY
Conventions, evidence, **28 § 1781 nt**

GI
Armed Forces, generally, this index

GIFT TAX
Federal Judicial Center Foundation, **28 § 629**
United States Tax Court, generally, this index

GIFTS
Charities, generally, this index
Disclosure of Federal Campaign Funds, generally, this index
Federal Judicial Center Foundation, **28 § 629**
Supreme Court, **28 § 674**
History, **28 § 1 nt**

GLUTETHIMIDE
Controlled Substances, generally, this index

GOOD CAUSE
See specific index headings

GOOD FAITH
Judges or justices, district judges, affidavits, **28 § 144**

GOODS, WARES AND MERCHANDISE
Exports and Imports, generally, this index
Stores, generally, this index

GOVERNMENT
States, generally, this index
United States, generally, this index

GOVERNMENT ACCOUNTABILITY OFFICE
Actions and proceedings,
Allowances, **28 § 2512**
Credits, **28 § 2406**
Disallowance, **28 § 2407**
Fees, **28 § 2501**
Allowances, claims, **28 § 2512**
Certificates and certification, mail and mailing, evidence, **28 § 1743**
Claims. Actions and proceedings, generally, ante
Credits, claims, **28 § 2406**
Disallowance, **28 § 2407**
Disallowance, claims, credits, **28 § 2407**
Ethics, officers and employees, **5 App. 4 § 109**
Evidence, mail and mailing, certificates and certification, **28 § 1743**
Federal officers and employees, claims, fees, **28 § 2501**
Fees, Federal officers and employees, claims, **28 § 2501**
Mail and mailing, evidence, certificates and certification, **28 § 1743**
Officers and employees, ethics, **5 App. 4 § 109**
Proceedings. Actions and proceedings, generally, ante
Reports, United States Sentencing Commission, **28 § 994 nt**
Sentencing guidelines, studies, **28 § 994 nt**
Transcripts, judgments and decrees, claims, **28 § 2516**
United States Sentencing Commission, reports, **28 § 994 nt**

GOVERNMENT BONDS
Counterfeiting, generally, this index
Postmasters, **28 § 2714**

GOVERNMENT CORPORATIONS
Federal Corporations, generally, this index

GOVERNMENT EMPLOYEES
Federal Officers and Employees, generally, this index

GOVERNMENT LANDS
Public Lands, generally, this index

GOVERNMENT OFFICERS AND EMPLOYEES
Federal Officers and Employees, generally, this index

GOVERNMENT PRINTING OFFICE
Attorney General, opinions, **28 § 521**

GOVERNOR
Books and papers, certificates and certification, **28 § 1739**
Certificates and certification, books and papers, **28 § 1739**
Three judge court, notice, **28 § 2284**

GRAND JURY
Generally, **28 § 1861 et seq.**
Additional attendance fee, certification, time for payment, **28 § 1871**
Adverse effect upon deliberations, exclusion from service, **28 § 1866**
Affidavits, service of summons for jury service by registered or certified mail, **28 § 1866**
Age, **28 § 1865**
Alphabetical list, names drawn from master jury wheel, **28 § 1864**
Entry, determination, qualifications for service, **28 § 1865**
Assignment,
Names to panels, **28 § 1866**
Persons drawn, **28 § 1863**
Attendance fees, time for payment, **28 § 1871**
Attorney General, conducting, authority, **28 § 515**
Attorneys, fees, award, protection of jurors' employment, **28 § 1875**
Bailiffs, employment to wait upon, **28 § 755**
Books and papers,
Maintenance and inspection, **28 § 1868**
Nondisclosure, **28 § 1867**
Voter registration lists and records, generally, post
Certificate for payment of fees, travel and subsistence allowances, **28 § 1871**
Chief judge of district court,
Chief Judge, as meaning, **28 § 1869**
Duties, **28 § 1863 et seq.**
Citizenship requirement for service, **28 § 1865**
Civil penalty, discharge of employee for jury service, **28 § 1875**
Clerks of district courts,
Clerk and clerk of the court, as meaning, **28 § 1869**
Duties, **28 § 1863 et seq.**

GRAND JURY—Cont'd
Commission. Jury Commission, generally, this index
Conditions, ineligibility for service, **28 § 1865**
Court, definitions, **28 § 1869**
Court interpreters, use of electronic sound recordings, in addition to, **28 § 1827**
Criminal charge, pending or conviction, freedom from, requirement for service, **28 § 1865**
Declaration of policy, **28 § 1861**
Definitions, **28 § 1869**
Deputy clerks of district courts, summons for jury service, duties concerning, **28 § 1866**
Disclosure, names drawn,
Master jury wheel, **28 § 1864**
Time, **28 § 1863**
Discrimination, **28 §§ 1862, 1867**
Disqualification from service, **28 §§ 1863, 1865, 1866**
Disruption of proceedings, exclusion from service, **28 § 1866**
District courts,
Contiguous 48 States, jurors serving outside of, amount, subsistence allowance, **28 § 1871**
Definitions, **28 § 1869**
Division, definitions, **28 § 1869**
Drawing, names from master jury wheel, **28 §§ 1864, 1866**
Effective date, plan for random selection, **28 § 1863**
Electronic sound recordings, where interpreters are used, **28 § 1827**
Evidence,
Challenging compliance with selection procedures, **28 § 1867**
Qualifications for service, **28 § 1865**
Examination, plan for random selection, **28 § 1863**
Exclusion, from service, **28 §§ 1863, 1865, 1866**
Prohibition on account of race, color, religion, **28 § 1862**
Excuse or exemption from service, **28 §§ 1863, 1866**
Determination, **28 § 1865**
Exemption from service, juror qualification form contents, **28 § 1869**
Fees, **28 § 1871**
Attendance in excess of 45 days, additional payment in discretion of district judge, **28 § 1871**
Qualification form, completion, **28 § 1864**
Ferries, payment of toll charges for, **28 § 1871**
Fines, penalties and forfeitures,
Failure to appear pursuant to summons to complete qualification form, **28 § 1864**
Noncompliance with summons for service, **28 § 1866**

GRAND JURY—Cont'd
Fines, penalties and forfeitures—Cont'd
Willful misrepresentation of facts on qualification form, **28 § 1864**
First-class mail, service of summons for jury service, **28 § 1866**
Grounds for excuse or exemption from service, **28 § 1863**
Groups of persons or occupational classes excused or exempt from service, **28 § 1863**
Illinois, indictments, **28 § 93 nt**
Impartial service, inability to render, exclusion from service, **28 § 1866**
Imprisonment. Sentence and punishment, generally, post
Independent Counsel, generally, this index
Indictment and Information, generally, this index
Inspection of records and papers, **28 § 1868**
Interim travel allowances, **28 § 1871**
Jurisdiction, district court, compelling availability of voter registration lists and records, **28 § 1863**
Juror qualification form,
Completion, **28 § 1864**
Contents, **28 § 1869**
Definitions, **28 § 1869**
Entry, determination of qualifications, **28 § 1865**
Information, determination of qualifications, **28 § 1865**
Reasons for exclusion from service, notations on, **28 § 1866**
Jury summons, definitions, **28 § 1869**
Jury wheel,
Definitions, **28 § 1869**
Master jury wheel, generally, post
Limitation, number of persons excluded from service, **28 § 1866**
List,
Names assigned to panels, **28 § 1866**
Voter registration lists and records, generally, post
Lists of actual voters, definitions, **28 § 1869**
Literacy requirement for service, **28 § 1865**
Mail and mailing,
Qualification, forms, **28 § 1864**
Summons, **28 § 1866**
Maintenance, records and papers, **28 § 1868**
Master jury wheel,
Determination, proportional representation in, **28 § 1863**
Drawing of names from, **28 § 1864**
Nondisclosure, records or papers, until after emptying and refilling, **28 § 1867**
Providing for and placing names in, **28 § 1863**
Meals and lodging,
Refreshment of jurors, **28 § 1871 nt**

GRAND JURY—Cont'd
Meals and lodging—Cont'd
Subsistence allowance, itemization not required, **28 § 1871**
Mental or physical capacity requirement for service, **28 § 1865**
Mileage, **28 § 1871**
Modification, plan for random selection, **28 § 1863**
Motions, challenging compliance with selection procedures, **28 § 1867**
Noncompliance of recalcitrant witness to court's order to provide information, **28 § 1826**
Nondisclosure, records or papers, selection process, **28 § 1867**
Notice, adoption or modification of plan for random selection, **28 § 1863**
Opportunity for service on, declaration of policy, **28 § 1861**
Orders of court,
Appearance upon failure to appear after being summoned, **28 § 1866**
Failure to appear pursuant to summons to complete qualification form, penalties, **28 § 1864**
Noncompliance of recalcitrant witness in testifying or providing information, **28 § 1826**
Original jurisdiction of district courts, jurors' employment rights, **28 § 1363**
Overnight stay, subsistence allowance paid to juror, **28 § 1871**
Parking fees, payment to juror, presentation of valid parking receipt, **28 § 1871**
Penalties. Fines, penalties and forfeitures, generally, ante
Period of service, **28 § 1866**
Personal service, summons for jury service, **28 § 1866**
Preservation of records and papers, **28 § 1868**
Procedure for selection of names, **28 § 1863**
Prohibition, payment, fees for interim or daily travel exceeding subsistence allowance, **28 § 1871**
Protection,
Compensation for work injuries, Federal employees, **28 § 1877**
Employment, **28 § 1875**
Federal employees' compensation for work injuries, applicability of provisions, **28 § 1877**
Public officer, definitions, **28 § 1869**
Public policy, **28 § 1861**
Publicly draw, definitions, **28 § 1869**
Punishment. Sentence and punishment, generally, post
Qualifications for service, **28 § 1865**
Qualified jury wheel, drawing names from, assignment to panels, **28 § 1866**
Random drawing of names from master jury wheel, **28 §§ 1864, 1866**

GRAND JURY—Cont'd
Random selection,
Challenging compliance with procedures, **28 § 1867**
Declaration of policy, **28 § 1861**
Plan for, **28 § 1863**
Recalcitrant witnesses, **28 § 1826**
Registered or certified mail, service of summons for jury service, **28 § 1866**
Reinstatement, discharge by employer for employee's jury service, **28 § 1875**
Reports, selection process, **28 § 1863**
Residence requirement for service, **28 § 1865**
Restoration of civil rights, qualifications for service, **28 § 1865**
Return, qualification form, error, **28 § 1864**
Reviewing panel, plan for random selection, approval, **28 § 1863**
Rules of Evidence, this index
Secrecy of proceedings threatened, exclusion from service, **28 § 1866**
Selection, panels, **28 § 1866**
Challenging compliance with procedures, **28 § 1867**
Random selection, generally, ante
Sentence and punishment,
Disclosure, records or papers, violations, **28 § 1867**
Failure to appear pursuant to summons to complete qualification form, **28 § 1864**
Noncompliance with summons for service, **28 § 1866**
Willful misrepresentation of facts on qualification form, **28 § 1864**
Separation of jurors, orders, payment, actual cost of subsistence, **28 § 1871**
Sequestration of jurors, orders, payment, actual cost of subsistence, **28 § 1871**
Service of summons for jury service, **28 § 1866**
Sources of names for selection, specification in plan, **28 § 1863**
Stay of proceedings, noncompliance with selection procedures, **28 § 1867**
Subsistence allowance, meals and lodging, itemization not required, **28 § 1871**
Summons,
Failure to return completed qualification form, **28 § 1864**
Panels, **28 § 1866**
Time,
Challenging compliance with selection procedures, **28 § 1867**
Preservation, records and papers, **28 § 1868**
Tolls for roads, tunnels, and bridges, fees, **28 § 1871**
Transmittal of plan for random selection, time, **28 § 1863**

GRAND JURY—Cont'd
Traveling expenses, **28 § 1871**
Qualification form, completion, **28 § 1864**
Summons in area outside contiguous 48 States, **28 § 1871**
Undue hardship or extreme inconvenience, definitions, **28 § 1869**
United States Marshal, payment of fees, **28 § 1871**
Voter registration lists and records,
Availability for inspection, **28 § 1863**
Definitions, **28 § 1869**
Random selection where shortage, **28 § 1866**
Witnesses, recalcitrant witness, **28 § 1826**

GRANTOR AND GRANTEE
Grants, generally, this index

GRANTS
Attorney General, this index
Customs Duties, this index
Diversions, recovery, **28 §§ 2415, 2416**
Firefighters and Fire Departments, this index
First responders, terrorists and terrorism, **28 § 509 nt**
Law Enforcement Agencies or Instrumentalities, this index
Terrorists and Terrorism, this index

GRAPHIC ART
Copyrights, generally, this index

GREAT BRITAIN
Convention on the Taking of Evidence Abroad in Civil or Commercial Matters, **28 § 1781 nt**
Judicial District of Hawaii, **28 § 91**

GREAT SEAL
Seals (Official Seals), generally, this index

GREEN BAY, WI
District courts, **28 § 130 nt**

GRENADES
Weapons, generally, this index

GROSS NEGLIGENCE
Customs Duties, this index

GROUNDS
See specific index headings

GSA
General Services Administration, generally, this index

GUAM
Bankruptcy, **28 § 610**
Courts, Jury Selection and Service Act, **28 § 1869**
District courts,
Administrative Office of U.S. Courts, **28 § 610**
Appeal and review, **28 § 1294**

GUAM—Cont'd
District courts—Cont'd
Courts of appeals, **28 § 1294**
Evidence, **28 § 1731 et seq.**
Interlocutory orders, **28 § 1292**
Judges or justices,
Annuities, survivors, **28 § 376**
Circuit conferences, **28 § 333**
Compensation and salaries, **28 § 373**
Relatives, **28 § 458**
Senior judges, **28 § 373 nt**
Jury, **28 § 1869**
Obsolete papers, **28 § 457**
Procedure, **28 § 1651 et seq.**
Records and recordation, **28 § 457**
Reporters, **28 § 753**
Rulemaking, **28 § 2071**
U.S. Court of Appeals for the Federal Circuit, **28 § 1295**
Grand jury, **28 § 1861 et seq.**
Judges or justices. District courts, ante
Judicial circuit, **28 § 41**
Judicial district, bankruptcy, **28 § 581 nt**
Jurisdiction,
Court of appeals, **28 §§ 1291, 1292**
Transfers, **28 § 1631**
Jury, **28 § 1861 et seq.**
United States Court of Appeals for the Federal Circuit, **28 § 1295**
United States trustees of judicial districts, **28 § 581**

GUARANTY
Court of Federal Claims, **28 § 1494**

GUARDIAN AND WARD
Annuities, judges or justices, **28 § 376**
Children and minors, missing persons, information, **28 § 534**
Disqualification, judges or justices, **28 § 455**
Judges or justices, disqualification, **28 § 455**

GUARDS
Crimes and offenses, labor and employment, **28 § 534 nt**
Criminal background checks, labor and employment, **28 § 534 nt**
Definitions, criminal background checks, labor and employment, **28 § 534 nt**
Fees, criminal background checks, labor and employment, **28 § 534 nt**
Fines, penalties and forfeitures, labor and employment, **28 § 534 nt**
Labor and employment, criminal background checks, **28 § 534 nt**

GUIDELINES
See specific index headings

GUILTY
Sentence and Punishment, generally, this index

GUNS
Weapons, generally, this index

HABEAS CORPUS
Generally, **28 § 2241 et seq.; HCR 1 et seq.**
Act of Congress, **28 § 2241**
Ad prosequendum, **28 § 2241**
Ad testificandum, **28 § 2241**
Administrative Office of the United States Courts, death penalty, reports, **28 § 2266**
Affidavits, **28 § 2246**
Amendments, returns, **28 § 2243**
Answer,
Rules governing section 2254 cases, **HCR 5**
Show cause orders, **28 §§ 2248, 2249**
Appeal and review, **28 § 2253**
Stay of proceedings, **28 § 2251**
Applications, **28 § 2242**
Death penalty, post
Attorneys,
Appointment, **28 § 2254**
Death penalty, **28 §§ 2261, 2265**
Forma pauperis, death penalty, **28 §§ 2261, 2265**
Capital cases. Death penalty, generally, post
Certificates and certification,
Appeal and review, **28 § 2253**
Copies, **28 § 2249**
Death penalty, forma pauperis, **28 § 2265**
Certified copies,
Indigent persons, **28 § 2250**
Judgments and decrees, **28 § 2249**
State courts, **28 § 2254**
Citizens and citizenship, **28 § 2241**
Civil procedure rules, rules governing section 2254 cases, **HCR 11**
Costs, indigent persons, **28 § 2250**
Court interpreters, **28 §§ 1827, 1828**
Death penalty, **28 § 2261 et seq.**
Administrative Office of the United States Courts, reports, **28 § 2266**
Applications, **28 § 2263**
Limitation of actions, **28 § 2266**
Attorneys, **28 §§ 2261, 2265**
Certificates and certification, forma pauperis, **28 § 2265**
Forma pauperis, attorneys, **28 §§ 2261, 2265**
Motions, **28 § 2266**
Reports, Administrative Office of the United States Courts, **28 § 2266**
Stay of proceedings, **28 § 2262**
Venue, forma pauperis, **28 § 2265**
Depositions, **28 § 2246**
Discovery, rules governing section 2254 cases, **HCR 6**
Enemy combatants, **28 § 2241**
Evidence, **28 § 2245 et seq.**
Answer, **28 § 2248**
Burden of proof, **28 § 2254**
Certificates and certification, **28 § 2245**
Documents, **28 § 2247**
Returns, **28 § 2248**

HABEAS CORPUS—Cont'd
Evidence—Cont'd
Rules governing section 2254 cases, **HCR 8**
Executions, death penalty, stay of proceedings, **28 § 2262**
Exhaustion of remedies, state courts, **28 § 2254**
Extradition, **28 § 2253**
Fees, **28 § 1914**
Filing, **28 § 1914**
Rules governing section 2254 cases, **HCR 3**
Finality, orders, **28 § 2244**
Forma pauperis, **28 § 2250**
Attorneys, death penalty, **28 §§ 2261, 2265**
Death penalty, attorneys, **28 §§ 2261, 2265**
Transcripts, **28 § 753**
Witnesses, **28 § 1825**
Geneva Conventions of 1949, **28 § 2241 nt**
Hearings, **28 §§ 2243, 2244**
Rules governing section 2254 cases, **HCR 8**
Indigent persons. Forma pauperis, generally, ante
Issuance, **28 §§ 1446, 2243**
Limitation of actions,
Death penalty, **28 § 2266**
Pending actions, **28 § 2251 nt**
State courts, **28 § 2244**
Magistrate judges, rules governing section 2254 cases, **HCR 10**
Motions, death penalty, **28 § 2266**
New grounds, **28 § 2244**
Notice, **28 § 2252**
Orders of court, **28 § 2241**
Final orders, **28 § 2244**
Indigent persons, **28 § 2250**
Show cause orders, generally, post
Pending actions, limitation of actions, **28 § 2251 nt**
Petitions, **28 § 2244**
Rules governing section 2254 cases, **HCR 2 et seq.**
Plea or answer. Answer, generally, ante
Postponement, state courts, **28 § 2074 nt**
Preliminary review, rules governing section 2254 cases, **HCR 4**
Presumptions, **28 § 2254**
Priorities and preferences, **28 § 1657**
Records and recordation,
Rules governing section 2254 cases, **HCR 7**
State courts, **28 § 2254**
Removal of case, **28 § 1446**
Reports, Administrative Office of the United States Courts, death penalty, **28 § 2266**
Returns, **28 § 2248**
Certified copies, **28 § 2249**
Show cause orders, **28 § 2243**

HABEAS CORPUS—Cont'd
Rules governing section 2254 cases, **28 § 2254; HCR 1 et seq.**
Answer, **HCR 5**
Civil procedure rules, **HCR 11**
Discovery, **HCR 6**
Evidence, **HCR 8**
Filing, **HCR 3**
Forms, **foll. HCR 11**
Hearings, **HCR 8**
Magistrate judges, **HCR 10**
Petitions, **HCR 2 et seq.**
Preliminary review, **HCR 4**
Records and recordation, **HCR 7**
Second or successive petitions, **HCR 9**
Time, **28 § 2071 nt**
Rules of Appellate Procedure, this index
Rules of Civil Procedure, this index
Second or successive petitions, **28 § 2244**
Rules governing section 2254 cases, **HCR 9**
Show cause orders, **28 § 2243**
Answer, **28 §§ 2248, 2249**
State courts, **28 § 2241 et seq.**
Exhaustion of remedies, **28 § 2254**
Limitation of actions, **28 § 2244**
Postponement, **28 § 2074 nt**
Stay of proceedings, **28 § 2251**
Statutes, **28 § 2241**
Procedures, **28 § 2284**
States, **28 § 2254**
Stay of proceedings,
Executions, death penalty, **28 § 2262**
State courts, **28 § 2251**
Supreme Court, this index
Time,
Death penalty, applications, **28 § 2263**
Rules governing section 2254 cases, **28 § 2071 nt**
Show cause orders, **28 § 2243**
State courts, postponement, **28 § 2074 nt**
Transcripts, **28 § 753**
Transfers, applications, **28 § 2241**
Venue, **28 § 2241**
Death penalty, forma pauperis, **28 § 2265**
Witnesses, forma pauperis, **28 § 1825**

HABIT FORMING DRUGS
Controlled Substances, generally, this index

HALFWAY HOUSES
Correctional Institutions, generally, this index

HANDICAPPED PERSONS
Attorney General, vacancy in office, **28 § 508**
Bankruptcy, this index
Contracts, disputes, Contract Disputes Act of 1978, **28 § 2401**
Director of Administrative Office of U.S. Courts, retirement and pensions, **28 § 611**
District Judges, this index

HANDICAPPED PERSONS—Cont'd
Fair Housing, generally, this index
Housing. Fair Housing, generally, this index
Judges or Justices, this index
Judicial Center, **28 §§ 621, 627**
Legal disability,
Contract Disputes Act of 1978, **28 § 2401**
United States Court of Federal Claims, limitation of actions, **28 § 2501**
Limitation of actions, U.S. Court of Federal Claims, legal disability, **28 § 2501**
Parties,
Contract Disputes Act of 1978, **28 § 2401**
United States Court of Federal Claims, **28 § 2501**
Supreme Court, this index

HANDWRITING
Evidence, **28 § 1731**

HARASSMENT
Civil Rights, generally, this index

HARBORING
Aliens, this index

HARBORS AND PORTS
Entry, forfeitures, **28 § 1395**
Improvements, oysters,
Jurisdiction, **28 § 1497**
Limitation of actions, **28 § 2501**
Ships and Shipping, generally, this index
Vessels. Ships and Shipping, generally, this index

HARDSHIP
Jury, excuse, **28 §§ 1863, 1866**

HARMLESS ERROR
Judgment on hearing on appeal or certiorari, **28 § 2111**

HATE CRIMES
Generally, **28 § 534 nt**
Definitions, sentence and punishment, **28 § 994 nt**
Sentence and punishment, **28 § 994 nt**

HAWAII
Actions and proceedings, Statehood, **28 § 91 nt**
Admission to statehood,
Actions and proceedings, **28 § 91 nt**
Appeal and review, **28 § 91 nt**
Judges or justices, retirement and pensions, **28 § 373 nt**
Appeal and review, Statehood, **28 § 91 nt**
Bankruptcy, judges or justices, appointments, **28 § 152**
Circuit court judges, **28 § 371 nt**
Court of Appeals for Ninth Circuit, generally, this index
Courts. District courts, generally, post

HAWAII—Cont'd
District courts,
Judges or justices, **28 § 133**
Retirement and pensions, **28 § 371 nt**
Statehood, **28 § 373 nt**
Locations, **28 § 91**
Powers and duties, **28 § 91 nt**
Judges or justices. District courts, ante
Judicial Circuit of U.S., **28 § 41**
Judicial districts, **28 § 91**
Bankruptcy, **28 § 581 nt**
Judges or justices, **28 § 133**
Supreme Court justices, **28 §§ 371 nt, 373 nt**
United States, judicial district trustees, appointments, **28 § 581**

HAZARDOUS SUBSTANCES AND WASTE
Controlled substances, **28 § 524**
Methamphetamine, **28 § 524**

HEADS OF DEPARTMENTS
Federal Officers and Employees, this index

HEALTH AND HUMAN SERVICES DEPARTMENT
Community development, neighborhood revitalization plan, **28 § 509 nt**

HEALTH AND SANITATION
Controlled Substances, generally, this index

HEALTH CARE PROVIDERS
Long term care. Nursing Homes, generally, this index
Nursing Homes, generally, this index

HEALTH INSURANCE
Long term care. Nursing Homes, generally, this index
Nursing Homes, generally, this index

HEARINGS
Administrative Law and Procedure, this index
Arbitration, this index
Bankruptcy, this index
Courts of appeals, **28 § 46 et seq.**
Federal Agencies, this index
Federal Debt Collection, this index
Habeas Corpus, this index
International Trade Court, this index
Judicial Panel On Multidistrict Litigation, this index
Judicial sale of realty, **28 § 2001**
Lost or destroyed documents, courts, **28 § 1734**
Military Departments, this index
Multidistrict litigation, pretrial proceedings, **28 § 1407**
Rules of Appellate Procedure, this index
Rules of Civil Procedure, this index
Three judge court, **28 § 2284**

HEARSAY
Rules of Evidence, this index

HEAVY TRUCKS
Motor Carriers, generally, this index

HIGHER EDUCATION
Colleges and Universities, generally, this index

HISPANIC AMERICANS
Fair Housing, generally, this index
Housing. Fair Housing, generally, this index

HISTORY
Rules of Evidence, this index
Supreme Court, gifts, **28 § 1 nt**

HOBBS ADMINISTRATIVE ORDERS REVIEW ACT
Generally, **28 §§ 41 et seq., 2341 et seq.**

HOG (PCP)
Controlled Substances, generally, this index

HOLIDAYS
Rules of Appellate Procedure, this index
Rules of Civil Procedure, this index

HOME CARE
Confidential or privileged information, criminal background checks, labor and employment, **28 § 534 nt**
Criminal background checks, labor and employment, **28 § 534 nt**
Fees, criminal background checks, labor and employment, **28 § 534 nt**
Labor and employment, criminal background checks, **28 § 534 nt**

HOMELAND SECURITY
Security, generally, this index

HOMELAND SECURITY DEPARTMENT
Secret Service, generally, this index

HOMEOWNERSHIP
Fair Housing, generally, this index

HOMES
Nursing Homes, generally, this index

HOMICIDE
Murder, generally, this index

HOMOSEXUALS AND HOMOSEXUALITY
Hate Crimes, generally, this index

HONORABLE DISCHARGES
Army, this index
Navy, this index

HORSE RACES
Application of law, unlawful sports gambling, **28 § 3704**

HOSPITALS
Home Care, generally, this index
Justice Department, officers and employees, overseas, **28 § 530A**
Long term care. Nursing Homes, generally, this index
Nursing Homes, generally, this index

HOSTAGES
Damages, terrorists and terrorism, Foreign States, **28 § 1605A**
Terrorists and Terrorism, this index

HOURS OF LABOR
Court of Federal Claims, this index

HOUSE OF REPRESENTATIVES
Bills, referrals, U.S. Court of Federal Claims, Chief Judge, **28 § 1492**
Committees. Congressional Committees, generally, this index
Congressional Committees, generally, this index
Disclosure of Federal Campaign Funds, generally, this index
District courts, action to recover possession of office, **28 § 1344**
Elections, apportionment, three judge court, **28 § 2284**
Journals of Congress, evidence, **28 § 1736**
Judicial Center, directors, **28 § 627**
Judicial Survivors Annuity Fund, **28 § 376**
Officers and employees, removal of cases or causes, **28 § 1442**
Records and recordation, U.S. Court of Federal Claims, **28 § 2507**
Rulemaking, financial disclosure, **5 App. 4 § 101 nt**

HOUSING
Civil rights. Fair Housing, generally, this index
Discrimination. Fair Housing, generally, this index
Fair Housing, generally, this index
Hispanic Americans. Fair Housing, generally, this index

HOUSING AND URBAN DEVELOPMENT DEPARTMENT
Neighborhood revitalization plans, **28 § 509 nt**

HOWLAND ISLAND
Judicial district, **28 § 91**

HUMAN RIGHTS
Torture, generally, this index

HUMAN TRAFFICKING
Trafficking, this index

HUSBAND AND WIFE
Assault and battery. Domestic Violence, generally, this index

HUSBAND AND WIFE—Cont'd
Disqualification, judges or justices, **28 § 455**
Domestic Violence, generally, this index
Judges or justices, disqualification, **28 § 455**

HYDRIODIC ACID
Controlled Substances, generally, this index

HYDROMORPHINOL
Controlled Substances, generally, this index

HYDROXYPETHIDINE
Controlled Substances, generally, this index

IBOGAINE
Controlled Substances, generally, this index

IDAHO
Bankruptcy, judges or justices, appointments, **28 § 152**
Court of Appeals for Ninth Circuit, generally, this index
District courts,
Judges or justices, **28 § 133**
Location, **28 § 92**
Judicial circuit, **28 § 41**
Judicial districts,
Bankruptcy, **28 § 581 nt**
Judges or justices, **28 § 133**
United States trustees, judicial districts, **28 § 581**

IDENTITY AND IDENTIFICATION
Authentication, generally, this index
Crimes and offenses,
Acquisition, **28 § 534**
Criminal Background Checks, generally, this index
Criminal Background Checks, generally, this index
Interstate Identification Index, violence against women, **28 § 534**
Missing persons, **28 § 534**
Other institutions, definitions, **28 § 534**
Parents, missing persons, unemancipated persons, information, **28 § 534**
Reports, theft, task forces, **28 § 509 nt, EON 13402**
Rules of Evidence, this index
Sentence and punishment, fraud, **28 § 994 nt**
Task forces, theft, **28 § 509 nt, EON 13402**
Theft,
Reports, task forces, **28 § 509 nt, EON 13402**
Task forces, **28 § 509 nt, EON 13402**
Unemancipated persons, **28 § 534**

ILLINOIS
Bankruptcy, judges or justices, appointments, **28 § 152**

ILLINOIS—Cont'd
District courts,
Judges or justices, **28 §§ 93 nt, 133**
Location, **28 § 93**
Grand jury, designated courts, **28 § 93 nt**
Judicial circuit, **28 § 41**
Judicial districts, **28 § 93**
Bankruptcy, **28 § 581 nt**
Judges or justices, **28 §§ 93 nt, 133**
United States attorneys, **28 § 93 nt**
United States Marshals, **28 § 93 nt**
United States trustees, judicial districts, **28 § 581**

IMMIGRANT VISA
Visas, this index

IMMIGRATION
Aircraft, Immigration and Naturalization Service, funds, **28 § 530C**
Bringing in aliens, sentencing guidelines, **28 § 994 nt**
Detention, Military Justice Code, **28 § 2241**
Fences, funds, **28 § 530C**
Funds, fences, **28 § 530C**
Harboring aliens, sentencing guidelines, **28 § 994 nt**
Immigrant visa. Visas, this index
Immigration and Naturalization Service, generally, this index
Military Justice Code, detention, **28 § 2241**
Permanent residence, diversity of citizenship, **28 § 1332**
Smuggling, sentencing guidelines, **28 § 994 nt**

IMMIGRATION AND NATURALIZATION SERVICE
Aircraft, funds, **28 § 530C**
Ammunition, funds, **28 § 530C**
Boats and boating, funds, **28 § 530C**
Detention facilities, Assets Forfeiture Fund, **28 § 524 nt**
Real estate, fences, funds, **28 § 530C**
Uniforms, appropriations, **28 § 509 nt**
Weapons, funds, **28 § 530C**

IMMUNITIES
Privileges and Immunities, generally, this index

IMPACT STATEMENTS
Crime Victims, this index

IMPEACHMENT
Judges or justices, complaints, **28 § 355**

IMPORTS AND EXPORTS
Exports and Imports, generally, this index

IMPOSTS
Customs Duties, generally, this index
Taxation, generally, this index

IMPRISONMENT
Sentence and Punishment, generally, this index

IMPROVEMENTS
See specific index headings

IN FORMA PAUPERIS
Generally, **28 § 1915**
Forma Pauperis, generally, this index

IN REM
Admiralty, stay of proceedings, **28 § 2464**
Attachment, U.S. marshal, fees, **28 § 1921**
United States, change of venue, **28 § 1404**

INCARCERATION
Correctional Institutions, generally, this index

INCENTIVE PAY OR AWARDS
Administrative Office of United States Courts, **28 §§ 602 nt, 604**
Clerks of courts, **28 § 604**
Clerks of district courts, **28 § 604**
Courts, **28 § 604**
Courts of appeals, **28 § 604**
Law clerks, **28 § 604**

INCOME TAX
Actions and proceedings. Refunds, post
Aliens, this index
Assessments,
District courts, **28 § 1346**
Interest, **28 § 2411**
Judgments and decrees, interest, **28 § 2411**
Jury, **28 § 2402**
Tort Claim Act, **28 § 2680**
Venue, **28 § 1402**
Claims. Refunds, generally, post
Collection,
Errors, **28 § 2402**
Excessive collection, **28 § 1402**
Interest, **28 § 2411**
Jurisdiction, **28 § 1346**
Removal of cases or causes, **28 § 1442**
Tort Claims Act, **28 § 2680**
Venue, **28 § 1396**
Corporations, this index
Court of Federal Claims, this index
Federal Judicial Center Foundation, gifts, **28 § 629**
Inspection and inspectors. Returns, post
Internal Revenue Service, generally, this index
IRS. Internal Revenue Service, generally, this index
Jurisdiction, **28 §§ 1340, 1346**
Collection, ante
Removal of cases or causes, **28 § 1442**
Levy. Collection, generally, ante
Liens and incumbrances. Tax Liens, generally, this index
Limitation of actions, United States, **28 § 2415**

INCOME TAX—Cont'd
Nonresidents. Aliens, this index
Overpayment, interest, **28 § 2411**
Partnership, this index
Payment,
Collection, generally, ante
Executions, **28 § 2006**
Judgments and decrees, officers and employees, **28 § 2006**
Real estate, fines, penalties and forfeitures, **28 § 2402**
Refunds,
Actions and proceedings, aliens, **28 § 2502**
Aliens, **28 § 2502**
Corporations, this index
District courts, **28 § 1346**
Executions, **28 § 2006**
Judgments and decrees, **28 § 2006**
Venue, **28 § 1402**
Returns, inspection and inspectors, Independent Counsel, **28 § 594**
Tax Court. United States Tax Court, generally, this index
United States Tax Court, generally, this index
Venue, **28 § 1402**
Collection, **28 § 1396**
Wrongful levy,
Jurisdiction, **28 § 1346**
Venue, **28 § 1402**

INCOMPETENCY
Diversity of citizenship, jurisdiction, **28 § 1332**
Jurisdiction, diversity of citizenship, **28 § 1332**
Jury, **28 §§ 1865, 1869**
Limitation of actions, United States, **28 § 2416**
Rules of Civil Procedure, this index
United States, limitation of actions, **28 § 2416**

INCONVENIENCE
Jury service, excuse, **28 §§ 1863, 1866**

INCUMBRANCES
Liens and Incumbrances, generally, this index

INDEBTEDNESS
Bankruptcy, generally, this index
Collection. Federal Debt Collection, generally, this index
Federal Debt Collection, generally, this index
Garnishment, generally, this index
Municipal corporations, chapter 9 proceedings. Bankruptcy, this index
Receivers and Receivership, generally, this index
United States. Federal Debt Collection, generally, this index

INDEPENDENT COUNSEL
Generally, **28 § 591 et seq.**

INDEPENDENT COUNSEL—Cont'd
Access, records and recordation, exceptions, **28 § 594**
Administrative support, **28 § 594**
Amicus curiae, **28 § 597**
Briefs, disclosure, **28 § 593**
Appeal and review, **28 § 592**
Removal, **28 §§ 593, 596**
Appointment, **28 § 593**
Application, **28 § 592**
Appropriations, authorization, **28 § 591 nt**
Assistant Attorney General, appointment, investigations, **28 § 591**
Attorneys fees, **28 § 593**
Audits and auditors, **28 § 596**
Central Intelligence Agency, appointment, **28 § 591**
Certificates and certification, expenses and expenditures, compliance, **28 § 594**
Compensation and salaries, **28 § 594**
Conduct,
Investigations, **28 § 592**
Oversight, **28 § 595**
Conflicts of interest, investigations, **28 § 591**
Contents, appointment, applications, **28 § 592**
Contingency funds, **28 § 591 nt**
Costs, control, **28 § 594**
Custody, records of, **28 § 594**
Disclosure, **28 §§ 592, 593**
Dismissal and nonsuit, **28 § 594**
Ethics, **28 §§ 530B, 594**
Evidence, appeal and review, **28 § 594**
Examinations and examiners, investigations, **28 § 591**
Extension, time, investigations, **28 § 592**
Grounds, removal, **28 § 596**
Impeachment, information, **28 § 595**
Income tax, powers, limitations, **28 § 594**
Indictment and information, **28 § 594**
Information,
Impeachment, **28 § 595**
Investigations, **28 § 591**
Investigations, **28 § 591**
Jurisdiction, **28 § 593**
Investigations, revocation or suspension, **28 § 597**
Justice Department,
Assistance, **28 § 594**
Investigations, **28 § 591**
Officers and employees, **28 § 594**
Relationship, **28 § 597**
Maintenance, records and recordation, **28 § 594**
National campaign committee, Chairman, Treasurer, investigations, **28 § 591**
Notice, **28 § 593**
Investigations, **28 § 592**
Officers and employees, compensation and salaries, **28 § 594**
Offices, termination, **28 § 596**
Payment, **28 § 594**

INDEPENDENT COUNSEL—Cont'd
Post employment, restrictions, **28 § 594**
Powers and duties, **28 § 594**
Privileges and immunities, **28 § 594**
Prosecutions, **28 § 594**
Publication, reports, **28 § 594**
Qualifications, **28 § 593**
Reappointment, **28 § 596**
Records and recordation, maintenance, **28 § 594**
Recusal, **28 § 591**
Referrals, **28 § 594**
Removal, **28 § 596**
Reports, **28 § 592**
Audits and auditors, **28 § 596**
Disclosure, **28 § 594**
Expenses and expenditures, time, **28 § 594**
Financial statements and reports, **28 § 591 nt**
Oversight, **28 § 595**
Removal, **28 § 596**
Restrictions, labor and employment, **28 § 594**
Security,
Clearances, evidence, **28 § 594**
Evidence, clearances, **28 § 594**
Standards, conduct, **28 § 594**
Tax return, inspection and inspectors, **28 § 594**
Termination, **28 §§ 596, 599**
Time, investigations, **28 § 591**
Extension, **28 § 592**
Transfer, records and recordation, **28 § 594**
Traveling expenses, **28 § 594**
United States Attorney, powers and duties, **28 § 594**
Vacancies in office, **28 § 593**
Vice President, investigations, **28 § 591**
Warrants, subpoenas, **28 § 594**
Witnesses, privileges and immunities, **28 § 594**

INDEPENDENT PROSECUTOR
Independent Counsel, generally, this index

INDEXES
DNA (Deoxyribonucleic Acid), tests, **28 § 531 nt**
Interstate Identification Index, national crime information databases, **28 § 534**
Judgments and decrees, liens and incumbrances, **28 § 1962**
Liens and incumbrances, judgments and decrees, **28 § 1962**
National crime information databases, Interstate Identification Index, **28 § 534**
Pending actions, district courts, **28 § 1964**

INDIAN LANDS AND RESERVATIONS
Actions and proceedings,
Money damages, **28 § 2415**

INDIAN LANDS AND RESERVATIONS
—Cont'd
Actions and proceedings—Cont'd
Restricted lands, **28 § 2415**
States, **28 § 1360**
Allotments,
District courts, **28 § 1353**
Limitation of actions, trusts and trustees, **28 § 2415**
Estates. Trusts and trustees, generally, post
Fires and fire protection, damages, **28 §§ 2415, 2416**
Jurisdiction, States, civil actions, **28 § 1360**
Limitation of actions, **28 § 2415**
Allotments, trusts and trustees, **28 § 2415**
Proceedings. Actions and proceedings, generally, ante
Quieting title, **28 § 2409a**
States, jurisdiction, **28 § 1360**
Trespass, **28 §§ 2415, 2416**
Trusts and trustees,
Actions and proceedings, **28 §§ 2415, 2415 nt**
Taxation, **28 § 1360**

INDIAN TRIBES
Indians, generally, this index

INDIANA
Bankruptcy, judges or justices, appointments, **28 § 152**
District courts,
Judges or justices, **28 § 133**
Location, **28 § 94**
Judicial circuit, **28 § 41**
Judicial districts, **28 § 94**
Bankruptcy, **28 § 581 nt**
Judges or justices, **28 § 133**
United States trustees, judicial districts, appointments, **28 § 581**

INDIANS
Actions and proceedings,
States, jurisdiction, **28 § 1360**
United States, money damages, **28 §§ 2415, 2415 nt**
Alaska, this index
Allotments. Indian Lands and Reservations, this index
California, this index
Claims, Court of Federal Claims, **28 § 1505**
Court of Federal Claims, this index
Crimes and offenses,
Jurisdiction, district courts, **28 § 1362**
Registry, **28 § 534 nt**
Damages, limitation of actions, **28 § 2415**
District courts, **28 § 1362**
Allotments, **28 § 1353**
Federal Register, Indian Claims Limitation Act of 1982, **28 § 2415 nt**
Jurisdiction,
Crimes and offenses, ante
District courts, **28 § 1362**

INDIANS—Cont'd
Jurisdiction—Cont'd
States, civil actions, **28 § 1360**
Lands. Indian Lands and Reservations, generally, this index
Law enforcement, women, violent crimes, **28 § 534**
Limitation of actions, tribes, **28 § 2415**
Minnesota, this index
Nebraska, this index
Oregon, this index
Proceedings. Actions and proceedings, generally, ante
Quapaw Indian Agency, **28 § 1353**
Real estate. Indian Lands and Reservations, generally, this index
Registry, crimes and offenses, **28 § 534 nt**
Reservations. Indian Lands and Reservations, generally, this index
Secretary of the Interior, claims, **28 § 2415 nt**
Statutes, U.S. Court of Federal Claims, **28 § 1505**
Tracking, women, violent crimes, **28 § 534**
Treaties,
Allotments, **28 § 1353**
Jurisdiction, **28 § 1362**
Tribes,
Actions and proceedings, **28 § 1360**
Limitation of actions, **28 § 2415**
Wisconsin, this index
Women,
Law enforcement, violent crimes, **28 § 534**
Tracking, violent crimes, **28 § 534**

INDICTMENT AND INFORMATION
Dismissal and nonsuit, **28 § 1867**
Fines, penalties and forfeitures, notice, **28 § 2461**
Habeas corpus, **28 § 2249**
Independent Counsel, this index
Notice, fines, penalties and forfeitures, **28 § 2461**

INDICTMENT OR INFORMATION
Selection procedures, noncompliance, **28 § 1867**

INDIGENT PERSONS
Forma Pauperis, generally, this index
Rules of Appellate Procedure, this index

INDORSEMENT
Rules of Civil Procedure, this index

INFANTS
Children and Minors, generally, this index

INFORMATION
See specific index headings

INFORMATION SYSTEMS
Computers, generally, this index

INFORMERS
Appropriations, Justice Department, **28 § 524**
Justice Department, appropriations, **28 § 524**

INFRINGEMENT
See specific index headings

INJUNCTIONS
Appeal and review, **28 § 1292**
Athletics, gambling, **28 § 3703**
Attorney General, this index
Comptroller of the Currency, this index
Courts of Appeals, this index
District Courts, this index
Exports and Imports, this index
Foreign countries, **28 § 2467**
Interlocutory injunctions,
Orders, **28 § 2284**
State laws, **28 § 2284**
Three judge court, **28 § 1253**
Vacating or setting aside, **28 § 2284**
International Trade Court, this index
Interpleader, **28 § 2361**
National Banks, this index
Removal of cases, **28 § 1450**
Rules of Civil Procedure, this index
State agencies, rates and charges, **28 § 1342**
State laws, three judge court, **28 § 2284**
Stay of proceedings, **28 § 2283**
Surface Transportation Board, this index
Three judge court, **28 §§ 1253, 2284**

INJURIES
Personal Injuries, generally, this index

INMATES
Correctional Institutions, generally, this index

INSANE PERSONS
Incompetency, generally, this index

INSIGNIA
Emblems and Insignia, generally, this index

INSOLVENCY
Bankruptcy, generally, this index

INSPECTION AND INSPECTORS
District court records, **28 § 753**
Federal Legal Council, opinions, **28 § 509 nt, EON 12146**
International Trade Court, this index
Jury,
Commission or clerk of district court, records and papers, **28 § 1868**
Selection procedures, challenging compliance with, records or papers, **28 § 1867**
Rules of Civil Procedure, this index

INSPECTORS
Inspection and Inspectors, generally, this index

INSTALLMENTS
Bankruptcy, this index
Judges or justices, annuities, survivors, **28 § 376**

INSTITUTIONS OF HIGHER EDUCATION OR LEARNING
Colleges and Universities, generally, this index

INSTRUCTIONS
Jury, this index
Rules of Civil Procedure, this index
Rules of Evidence, this index
Supreme Court, certification of questions, **28 § 1254**

INSTRUMENTALITIES OF THE UNITED STATES
Federal Agencies, generally, this index

INSULAR POSSESSIONS AND DEPENDENCIES
Admiralty, **28 §§ 2071 nt, 2073**
Appeal and review. Federal agencies, post
Courts,
Admiralty, **28 §§ 2071 nt, 2073**
Full faith and credit, **28 § 1738**
Officers and employees, jury, exemptions, **28 § 1863**
Records and recordation, **28 § 1738**
Evidence, **28 §§ 1738, 1739**
Federal agencies,
Appeal and review,
Compensation and salaries, **28 § 373**
Official station, **28 § 456**
Compensation and salaries, **28 § 373**
Official station, **28 § 456**
Firefighters and fire departments, jury, exemptions, **28 § 1863**
Government publications, **28 § 414**
Legislature, jury, exemptions, **28 § 1863**
Limitation of actions, **28 § 2416**
Officers and employees, jury, exemptions, **28 § 1863**
Police, jury, exemptions, **28 § 1863**
Records and recordation, evidence, **28 § 1738**
Seal (official seals), **28 § 1739**

INSURANCE
Court of Federal Claims, judges and justices, retirement and pensions, **28 § 179**
Justice Department, motor vehicles, funds, **28 § 530C**
Long term care. Nursing Homes, generally, this index
Motor Vehicles, this index
Nursing Homes, generally, this index

INSURRECTION AND SEDITION
Proclamations, forfeitures, **28 § 1395**
Venue, **28 § 1395**

INTEGRATED CIRCUITS
Semiconductors, generally, this index

INTELLECTUAL PROPERTY
Copyrights, generally, this index
Patents, generally, this index

INTELLIGENCE
Federal Bureau of Investigation, this index
Gangs, national gang intelligence center, **28 § 534 nt**
National gang intelligence center, **28 § 534 nt**
Training, **28 § 509 nt**

INTENT
See specific index headings

INTERCEPTION OF WIRE, ORAL, OR ELECTRONIC COMMUNICATIONS
Attorney General, this index

INTERCOURSE
Sex, generally, this index

INTEREST
Bankruptcy, this index
Court of Federal Claims, this index
Fines, Penalties and Forfeitures, this index
Internal Revenue Service, **28 § 2411**
International Trade Court, this index
Judgments and decrees, **28 § 1961**
Internal Revenue Service, **28 § 1961**
T-bill rate table, **28 § 1961 nt**
United States, **28 § 2674**
United States Court of Appeals for the Federal Circuit, **28 § 1961**
United States Court of Federal Claims, **28 §§ 1961, 2516**
Jurisdiction, amount in controversy, exclusion, **28 § 1332**
Postal Service, this index
Searches and seizures, returns, **28 § 2465**
Supreme Court, this index
Taxation, this index
United States, this index
United States Court of International Trade, **28 § 2644**

INTERESTED PARTIES
See specific index headings

INTERFERENCE
Federal debt collection, prejudgment remedies, **28 § 3101**

INTERGOVERNMENTAL AGREEMENTS
Treaties, generally, this index

INTERGOVERNMENTAL COOPERATION
Judicial Center, **28 § 624**

INTERLOCUTORY INJUNCTIONS
Injunctions, this index

INTERLOCUTORY ORDERS
Bankruptcy, **28 § 158**

INTERLOCUTORY ORDERS—Cont'd
Courts of appeals, **28 § 1292**

INTERLOCUTORY PROCEEDINGS
Court of Appeals for the Federal Circuit, this index
Court of Federal Claims, this index
Rules of Civil Procedure, this index

INTERNAL REVENUE CODE
Income Tax, generally, this index
Internal Revenue Service, generally, this index

INTERNAL REVENUE SERVICE
Actions and proceedings, errors, **28 § 2402**
Boards and commissions. Commissioner, generally, post
Checks, judgments and decrees, **28 § 2411**
Commissioner,
Appointments, **28 § 591**
Checks, **28 § 2411**
Investigations, **28 § 591**
Damages, jurisdiction, **28 § 1357**
Errors, actions and proceedings, **28 § 2402**
Execution, **28 § 2006**
Financial institutions, fraud, **28 § 509 nt**
Fines, penalties and forfeitures,
District courts, **28 § 1346**
Interest, **28 § 2411**
United States attorneys, collection, **28 § 547**
Venue, **28 § 1402**
Forfeitures. Fines, penalties and forfeitures, generally, ante
Interest, **28 § 2411**
Judgments and decrees,
Interest, **28 § 2411**
Money judgments, **28 §§ 1961, 2411**
Officers and employees, **28 § 2006**
Jurisdiction, **28 § 1346**
Jury, **28 § 2402**
Liens and incumbrances. Tax Liens, generally, this index
Officers and employees,
Commissioner, generally, ante
Judgments and decrees, **28 § 2006**
Removal of cases or causes, **28 § 1442**
Penalties. Fines, penalties and forfeitures, generally, ante
Quieting title, **28 § 2409a**
Removal of cases or causes, **28 § 1442**
Sales. Tax Sales, generally, this index
Tax Sales, generally, this index
Third parties,
District courts, **28 § 1346**
Venue, **28 § 1402**
Tort Claims Act, **28 § 2680**
United States, attorneys, powers and duties, **28 § 547**

INTERNATIONAL CONVENTIONS
Conventions, generally, this index

INTERNATIONAL CRIMINAL POLICE ORGANIZATION
Criminal background checks, **28 § 509 nt**

INTERNATIONAL LAW
Aliens, torture victims, torts, **28 § 1350**
Torture, **28 § 1350 nt**

INTERNATIONAL TERRORISM
Terrorists and Terrorism, generally, this index

INTERNATIONAL TRADE
Exports and Imports, generally, this index

INTERNATIONAL TRADE COMMISSION
Actions and proceedings, disclosure, **28 § 2631**
Counterclaims, **28 § 1446**
Court of Appeals for the Federal Circuit, this index
Decisions, presumptions, **28 § 2639**
Presumptions, decisions, **28 § 2639**

INTERNATIONAL TRADE COURT
Generally, **28 § 2631 et seq.**
Abstracts, decisions, publication, **28 § 257**
Additional findings, **28 § 2645**
Administrative law and procedure, exhaustion of remedies, **28 §§ 1582, 2637**
Admiralty, searches and seizures, **28 § 1356**
Affidavits, evidence, **28 § 2639**
Affirmative statements, filing, **28 § 2635**
African Americans, judges, **28 § 133 nt**
Age,
Chief Judge, **28 § 258**
Judges or justices, **28 § 253**
Ambassadors and consuls, evidence, **28 § 2646**
Amendments,
Findings, **28 § 2645**
Judgments and decrees, **28 § 2645**
Pleading, **28 § 2633**
Summons, **28 § 2633**
American manufacturers, **28 §§ 1582, 2631**
Antidumping duties, **28 § 2635**
Appeal and review, **28 § 2640**
Contests, **28 § 2631**
Evidence, **28 § 2639**
Free trade areas, **28 § 2643**
Jurisdiction, **28 §§ 1581, 1584**
Protective orders, **28 § 1581**
Time, **28 § 2636**
Appeal and review, **28 § 2635**
Exclusive jurisdiction, **28 § 1581**
Final decisions, **28 § 2645**
Interlocutory appeals, **28 § 256**
Judges or justices, discipline, **28 § 372**
Standards, **28 § 2640**
Applications,
Disclosure, **28 § 2635 et seq.**
Three judge court, **28 § 255**

INTERNATIONAL TRADE COURT —Cont'd
Appointments, bailiffs and messengers, **28 § 872**
Appraisal and appraisers, jurisdiction, **28 § 1582**
Assistants, clerks of courts, **28 § 871**
Attorneys, evidence, **28 § 2641**
Bailiffs, **28 § 872**
Bonds (officers and fiduciaries),
Application of law, **28 § 1352**
Goods, wares and merchandise, **28 § 1582**
Recovery, **28 § 2643**
Setoff and counterclaim, **28 § 1583**
Books and papers,
Inspection and inspectors, **28 § 2641**
Mail and mailing, **28 § 2632**
Process, **28 § 2633**
Budget, **28 § 605**
Catalogs, evidence, **28 § 2639**
Certified copies, transcripts, **28 § 2632**
Chief deputy clerk of court, **28 § 871**
Chief Judge or Justice,
Age, mandatory retirement, **28 § 251 nt**
Clerks of courts, district courts, **28 § 751**
Designation, **28 § 253 et seq.**
Disability, **28 § 372**
Dockets and docketing, **28 § 253**
Financial statements and reports, **28 § 253**
Judicial Conference of the United States, **28 § 331**
Powers and duties, **28 § 253**
Qualifications, **28 § 258**
Reassignment, **28 § 253**
Vacancy in office, **28 § 253**
Claims, United States, payment, **28 § 2414**
Classification,
Jurisdiction, **28 § 1581**
Rates and charges, **28 § 1582**
Clerks of courts,
Appointments, **28 § 871**
Chief deputy clerk of court, **28 § 871**
Confidential or privileged information, **28 § 2635**
Customs officers, **28 § 2635**
District courts, **28 §§ 751, 1876**
Removal from office, **28 § 871**
Supervision, **28 § 253**
Commencement of action, **28 § 2631 et seq.**
Communities, adjustment assistance, **28 §§ 1581, 2631 et seq.**
Compensation and salaries,
Judges or justices, post
Jury, **28 § 1876**
Complaints, **28 § 2632**
Commencement of action, **28 § 2632**
Judges or justices, post
Compromise and settlement, United States, claims, payment, **28 § 2414**
Conclusions of law, **28 § 2645**

INTERNATIONAL TRADE COURT —Cont'd
Confidential or privileged information, **28 § 2635**
Jurisdiction, **28 § 1581**
Orders, **28 § 2631**
Trade secrets, **28 § 2641**
Consolidations and mergers, **28 § 2633**
Constitution of United States, **28 § 251**
Copies, decisions, **28 § 257**
Costs, dismissal or nonsuit, **28 § 1919**
Countervailing duties,
Actions and proceedings, **28 §§ 2635, 2643**
Appeal and review, **28 § 2640**
Evidence, **28 § 2639**
Exclusive jurisdiction, **28 §§ 1581, 1584**
Limitation of actions, **28 § 2636**
Protective orders, **28 § 1581**
Standing to sue, **28 § 2631**
Court of Appeals for the Federal Circuit, this index
Criers, powers and duties, **28 § 872**
Cross claims, **28 § 1583**
Money judgments, **28 § 2643**
Cross examination, witnesses, **28 § 2641**
Customs brokers,
Actions and proceedings, licenses and permits, **28 § 2636**
Appeal and review, licenses and permits, **28 § 2640**
Fines, penalties and forfeitures, **28 §§ 1582, 2643**
Jurisdiction, licenses and permits, **28 § 1581**
Licenses and permits,
Actions and proceedings, **28 § 2636**
Appeal and review, **28 § 2640**
Fines, penalties and forfeitures, **28 § 1582**
Jurisdiction, **28 § 1581**
Standing to sue, **28 § 2631**
Standing to sue, licenses and permits, **28 § 2631**
Customs Court, **28 § 251 nt**
Customs duties,
Interlocutory appeals, **28 § 2636**
Three judge court, **28 § 255**
Customs officers,
Actions and proceedings, **28 § 2635**
Decisions, **28 § 257**
Evidence, **28 § 2639**
Filing, **28 § 2635**
Death, judges or justices, **28 § 372**
Decisions. Opinions and decisions, generally, post
Declaratory judgments and decrees, **28 § 2643**
Interlocutory appeals, **28 § 256**
Decrees. Judgments and decrees, generally, post
Depositions, customs officers, **28 § 2639**
Deputy clerks of court, **28 § 871**
Disability. Judges or justices, post
Discipline, judges or justices, **28 § 372**

INTERNATIONAL TRADE COURT
—Cont'd
Disclosure,
Orders of court, **28 § 2643**
Trade secrets, **28 § 2641**
Discrimination, jury, **28 § 1862**
Dismissal and nonsuit, jurisdiction, **28 § 1919**
District courts,
Bonds (officers and fiduciaries), **28 § 1352**
Fines, penalties or forfeitures, **28 § 1355**
Judges or justices, **28 § 292 et seq.**
Jurisdiction, **28 §§ 1337, 1340**
Jury, **28 § 1876**
Powers and duties, **28 § 1585**
Dockets and docketing, **28 § 253**
Drawbacks, jurisdiction, **28 §§ 1581, 1582**
Embargoes, **28 § 1581**
Employees. Officers and employees, generally, post
Entry,
Judgments and decrees, post
Jurisdiction, **28 § 1581**
Equity, **28 § 1585**
Evidence, **28 §§ 2639, 2641**
Foreign countries, post
Retrials, **28 § 2643**
Exhaustion of remedies, **28 §§ 1582, 2637**
Federal Government. United States, generally, post
Federal Register, **28 § 2636**
Federal Rules of Evidence, **28 § 2641**
Fees, **28 § 2633**
Filing,
Jurisdiction, protest, **28 § 1582**
Official documents, **28 § 2635**
Summons, post
Financial statements and reports, **28 § 253**
Findings, **28 § 2645**
Fines, penalties and forfeitures, **28 §§ 1355, 1582**
Firms, adjustment assistance, **28 §§ 1581, 2631 et seq.**
Foreign countries,
Evidence,
Interlocutory appeals, **28 § 256**
Jurisdiction, **28 § 1292**
Manufacturers and manufacturing, **28 § 2631**
Forms. Summons, post
Grand jury, **28 § 1862**
Hearings,
Foreign countries, **28 § 256**
Harbors and ports, **28 § 256**
Three judge court, **28 § 255**
Time, **28 § 2634**
Witnesses, **28 § 2641**
Immoral articles, exports and imports, jurisdiction, **28 § 1581**
Injunctions,
Findings, **28 § 2645**

INTERNATIONAL TRADE COURT
—Cont'd
Injunctions—Cont'd
Labor and employment, adjustment assistance, **28 § 2643**
Orders of court, **28 § 2643**
Summons, **28 § 2633**
Inspection and inspectors,
Decisions, **28 § 257**
Samples, **28 § 2641**
Interest, money judgments, **28 § 2644**
Interlocutory orders, **28 § 1292**
Intervention, **28 § 2631**
Investigations, judges or justices, complaints, **28 § 351 et seq.**
Judges or justices, **28 § 251 et seq.**
Additional judges, **28 § 372**
Age, **28 § 253**
Annuities, survivors, **28 § 376**
Appointments, **28 § 251**
Chief Judge or Justice, generally, ante
Compensation and salaries,
Annual rates, **28 § 252**
Disability, **28 § 372**
Survivors annuities, deductions, **28 § 376**
Complaints, **28 § 351 et seq.**
Disability, **28 § 372**
District courts, **28 § 292**
Foreign countries, evidence, **28 § 256**
Judicial Conference, **28 § 335**
Law books, successors, **28 § 414**
Nominations, **28 § 133 nt**
Official duty station, **28 § 456**
Political affiliations, **28 § 251**
Precedence, **28 § 253**
Presiding judges, **28 § 253**
Reassignments, **28 § 253**
Seniority, **28 § 253**
Single judges, **28 § 254**
Tenure, **28 § 252**
Three judge court, **28 § 255**
Traveling expenses, **28 § 456**
Vacancies in office, **28 § 372**
Judgments and decrees, **28 § 1583**
Entry, money judgments, **28 § 2643**
Money judgments, **28 § 2643 et seq.**
United States, payment, **28 § 2414**
Judicial Conference of the United States, **28 §§ 331, 335**
Judicial review. Appeal and review, generally, ante
Jurisdiction, **28 §§ 1337, 1581 et seq.**
Countervailing duties, **28 § 1581**
Customs duties, **28 § 1583**
Dismissal and nonsuit, **28 § 1919**
District courts, **28 § 1340**
Immoral articles, exports and imports, **28 § 1581**
Transfer of cases or causes, **28 § 1631**
Jury,
Challenges, **28 § 1876**
Compensation and salaries, **28 § 1876**
Exemptions, **28 § 1862**
Qualifications, **28 § 1876**
Selection, **28 § 1876**

INTERNATIONAL TRADE COURT
—Cont'd
Labor organizations, **28 § 2631**
Laboratories,
Jurisdiction, **28 § 1581**
Reports, **28 § 2642**
Leave of court, intervention, **28 § 2631**
Licenses and permits. Customs brokers, ante
Limitation of actions, **28 § 1582**
Countervailing duties, **28 § 2636**
Liquidations,
Jurisdiction, **28 § 1582**
Sureties and suretyship, **28 § 2643**
Location, notice, **28 § 2634**
Mandamus, **28 § 2643**
Marking, exports and imports, jurisdiction, **28 § 1581**
Motions,
Amendments, **28 § 2645**
Retrials, **28 § 2646**
Time,
Findings, amendments, **28 § 2645**
Retrials, **28 § 2646**
New trial, **28 § 2645**
Orders of court, **28 § 2643**
New York City, NY, **28 § 251**
Judges or justices, official station, **28 § 456**
Nomination, judges or justices, **28 § 133 nt**
Notice, hearings, **28 § 2634**
Numbers and numbering, goods, wares and merchandise, **28 § 1582**
Officers and employees, **28 § 871**
Depositions, **28 § 2646**
Jurisdiction, **28 § 1581**
Summons, **28 § 2633**
Offices, **28 § 251**
Official station, judges or justices, **28 § 456**
Opinions and decisions, **28 § 2645**
Evidence, **28 § 2643**
Inspection and inspectors, **28 § 257**
Publication, **28 § 257**
Oral argument, **28 § 518**
Orders of court, **28 § 2643**
Confidential or privileged information, **28 § 2635**
Exports and imports, **28 § 2642**
Retrials, **28 § 2643**
Trade secrets, disclosure, **28 § 2641**
Papers. Books and papers, generally, ante
Parties,
Evidence, **28 § 2641**
Foreign countries, **28 § 256**
Three judge court, **28 § 255**
Party at interest, definitions, **28 § 2631**
Petitions,
Appeal and review, **28 § 2640**
Contest, **28 § 2637**
Denial, **28 § 2631**
Evidence, **28 § 2639**
Jurisdiction, **28 § 1581**
Official documents, filing, **28 § 2635**

INTERNATIONAL TRADE COURT
—Cont'd
Petitions—Cont'd
Time, **28 § 2636**
Pleading,
Amendments, **28 § 2633**
Injunctions, **28 § 2633**
Mail and mailing, filing, **28 § 2632**
Powers and duties, **28 § 1585**
Precedence, chief judge and judges, **28 §§ 253, 258**
Preservation, opinions and decisions, **28 § 257**
Presumption, opinions and decisions, correctness, **28 § 2639**
Price lists, evidence, **28 § 2639**
Privileged information. Confidential or privileged information, generally, ante
Process, **28 § 2633**
Pleadings, **28 § 2633**
Summons, generally, post
Prohibition, writ of, **28 § 2643**
Proof. Evidence, generally, ante
Protective orders, countervailing duties, **28 § 1581**
Protests, **28 § 2640**
Administrative law and procedure, **28 § 2637**
Evidence, **28 § 2639**
Filing, **28 § 2635**
Jurisdiction, **28 §§ 1581, 1582**
New grounds, **28 § 2638**
Standing to sue, **28 § 2631**
Time, **28 § 2636**
Publication, opinions and decisions, **28 § 257**
Race, jury, discrimination, **28 § 1862**
Rates and charges, **28 § 1581 et seq.**
Reassignments, **28 § 253**
Records and recordation, **28 §§ 251, 2640**
Official records, **28 § 2635**
Registered or certified mail, time, **28 § 2632**
Rehearing, application of law, **28 §§ 2643, 2645**
Remand, **28 § 2643**
Removal, criers, **28 § 872**
Removal of cases or causes, jurisdiction, **28 § 1631**
Reports,
Customs officers, merchandise, **28 § 2639**
Laboratories, **28 § 2642**
Resignation, judges or justices, **28 § 372**
Retirement and pensions, judges or justices, disability, **28 § 372**
Revenue, exports and imports, jurisdiction, **28 § 1581**
Review. Appeal and review, generally, ante
Revocation or suspension, **28 § 2633**
Samples, inspection and inspectors, **28 § 2641**
Schedule, fees, **28 § 2633 nt**

INTERNATIONAL TRADE COURT
—Cont'd
Sealing, books and papers, confidential or privileged information, **28 § 2635**
Searches and seizures, admiralty, **28 § 1356**
Seniority, Chief Judge, **28 § 258**
Sessions, **28 § 254**
Set-off and counterclaim,
Jurisdiction, **28 § 1583**
Money judgments, **28 § 2643**
Severance of cases, **28 § 2633**
Solicitor General, **28 § 518**
Standards, appeal and review, **28 § 2640**
Stay of proceedings, interlocutory appeals, **28 § 1292**
Stipulations,
Books and papers, **28 § 2635**
Interest, **28 § 2644**
Style, summons and complaint, **28 § 2632**
Summons,
Amendments, **28 § 2633**
Filing, **28 § 2632**
Pleadings, **28 § 2633**
Forms, **28 § 2632**
Injunctions, **28 § 2633**
Mail and mailing, **28 § 2632**
Tariffs, **28 § 1581**
Temporary restraining orders. Injunctions, generally, ante
Third parties,
Goods, wares and merchandise, jurisdiction, **28 § 1583**
Money judgments, **28 § 2643**
Three judge court, **28 § 255**
Time,
Commencement of action, **28 § 2636**
Findings, amendments, **28 § 2645**
Motions, ante
Retrials, **28 § 2646**
Trial, **28 § 2634**
Trade secrets, disclosure, **28 § 2641**
Traveling expenses, judges or justices, **28 § 456**
Trial,
Harbors and ports, **28 § 256**
Notice, time, **28 § 2634**
Single-judge trials, **28 § 254**
Three judge court, **28 § 255**
Time, notice, **28 § 2634**
United States,
Claims, payment, **28 § 2414**
Evidence, **28 § 2639**
Jurisdiction, exports and imports, **28 §§ 1581, 1582**
Money judgments, **28 § 2643**
Process, **28 § 2633**
Vacancy in office, Chief Judge, **28 § 253**
Valuation, goods, wares and merchandise,
Depositions, **28 § 2639**
Jurisdiction, **28 § 1581**
Vessels, repairs, jurisdiction, **28 § 1581**
Witnesses, **28 § 2641**
Women, judges or justices, selection, **28 § 133 nt**

INTERNATIONAL TRIBUNALS
Foreign Courts or Tribunals, generally, this index

INTERNET
Bankruptcy, reports, **28 § 589b**
Children and Minors, this index
Minors. Children and Minors, this index

INTERPLEADER
District Courts, this index
Process and procedure, **28 § 2361**
Rules of Civil Procedure, this index
Tax liens, **28 § 2410**
Venue, **28 § 1397**

INTERPRETERS
Generally, **28 § 1827 et seq.**
Administrative Office of United States Courts, **28 § 1827**
Special interpretation services, **28 § 1828**
Appropriations, **28 §§ 602 nt, 1827**
Bankruptcy, **28 § 1827**
Certificates and certification, **28 § 1827**
Clerks of courts, **28 § 1827**
Compensation and salaries, **28 § 1827**
Contracts, **28 § 1827 nt**
Costs, **28 § 1920**
Deaf persons, certificates and certification, **28 § 1827**
Definitions, **28 § 1827**
Electronic sound recordings, **28 § 1827**
Examinations and examiners, **28 § 1827**
Federal Bureau of Investigation,
Reports, **28 § 509 nt**
Terrorists and terrorism, **28 § 532 nt**
Fees, **28 § 1827**
Justice Department, **28 § 530C**
Lists, master list, **28 § 1827**
Master list, **28 § 1827**
Qualifications, **28 § 1827**
Reports, Federal Bureau of Investigation, **28 § 509 nt**
Simultaneous interpretation, **28 § 1827**
Special interpretation services, **28 §§ 1827, 1828**
Costs, **28 § 1920**

INTERROGATORIES
Rules of Civil Procedure, this index
Senate, **28 § 1365**

INTERVENTION
Act of Congress, constitutionality, **28 § 2403**
Court of Federal Claims, this index
District courts, multiparties, **28 § 1369**
Federal Agencies, this index
International Trade Court, this index
Judges or justices, complaints, **28 § 359**
Outsourcing, **28 § 1491**
Quieting title, **28 § 2409a**
Rules of Civil Procedure, this index
State laws, constitutionality, **28 § 2403**
Surface Transportation Board, this index
United States, this index

INTERVENTION—Cont'd
United States Court of International Trade, **28 § 2631**

INVEIGLE AND INVEIGLING
Kidnapping, generally, this index

INVENTIONS
Patents, generally, this index

INVESTIGATIONS
Attorney General, this index
Bureau of Alcohol, Tobacco, Firearms, and Explosives, undercover investigations, **28 § 533 nt**
Bureau of Investigation. Federal Bureau of Investigation, generally, this index
Civil Rights, this index
Court of Federal Claims, this index
Emergency Federal Law Enforcement Assistance, this index
Executive Agencies, this index
Executive Departments, this index
Federal Agencies, this index
Federal Bureau of Investigation, generally, this index
Independent Counsel, generally, this index
International Trade Court, this index
Judges or justices, complaints, **28 §§ 353, 354**
Justice Department, this index
Military Departments, this index
Rules of Civil Procedure, this index
Secret Service, this index
State Department, this index
Studies, generally, this index
United States Attorneys, this index

INVESTMENTS
Courts, deposits, pending actions, **28 § 2045**
Judicial Survivors Annuity Fund, **28 § 376**
Postal Service, this index
Securities, generally, this index

INVOLUNTARY SERVITUDE
Elections, jurisdiction, **28 § 1344**

IOWA
Bankruptcy, judges or justices, appointments, **28 § 152**
District courts,
Cities, **28 § 95**
Judges or justices, **28 § 133**
Judicial circuit, **28 § 41**
Judicial districts, **28 § 95**
Bankruptcy, **28 § 581 nt**
Judges or justices, **28 § 133**
United States trustees, judicial districts, appointments, **28 § 581**

IRAQ
Liability, terrorists and terrorism, **28 § 1605A nt**
Waiver, **28 § 1605A nt, PD 2008–9**

IRAQ—Cont'd
Terrorists and terrorism,
Liability, **28 § 1605A nt**
Waiver, **28 § 1605A nt, PD 2008–9**
Waiver, liability, **28 § 1605A nt, PD 2008–9**
Waiver, terrorists and terrorism, liability, **28 § 1605A nt, PD 2008–9**

IRS
Internal Revenue Service, generally, this index

ISLANDS
Insular Possessions and Dependencies, generally, this index
Northern Mariana Islands, generally, this index
Virgin Islands, generally, this index

ISOMETHADONE
Controlled Substances, generally, this index

ISONIPECAINE
Controlled Substances, generally, this index

ISRAEL
Conventions, evidence, Convention on the Taking of Evidence Abroad in Civil or Commercial Matters, **28 § 1781 nt**

ISSUANCE
See specific index headings

ISSUES
Rules of Civil Procedure, this index

ITALY
Convention on the Taking of Evidence Abroad in Civil or Commercial Matters, **28 § 1781 nt**
Evidence, Convention on the Taking of Evidence Abroad in Civil or Commercial Matters, **28 § 1781 nt**

ITC
International Trade Commission, generally, this index

JACKSON, MS
Court of Appeals for Fifth Circuit, generally, this index

JAI ALAI
Gambling, **28 § 3704**

JAILS
Correctional Institutions, generally, this index

JARVIS ISLAND
Judicial District of Hawaii, **28 § 91**

JET AIRCRAFT
Aircraft, generally, this index

JOBS
Labor and Employment, generally, this index

JOHNSTON ISLAND
Judicial District of Hawaii, **28 § 91**

JOINDER
Collusive joinder, **28 § 1359**
Rules of Civil Procedure, this index
United States, actions and proceedings, **28 § 1391**

JOINT COMMITTEE ON PRINTING
Reports, Supreme Court, **28 § 411**
Supreme Court, reports, **28 § 411**

JOINT COUNCILS ON SENTENCING
Generally, **28 § 334**

JOINT TENANTS
United States, partition, **28 §§ 1347, 1399, 2409**

JOURNALS
Clerk of House of Representatives, this index
Congress, this index
Patents, foreign patent offices, **28 § 1745**

JOURNALS OF CONGRESS
House of Representatives, this index
Senate, this index

JUDGES OR JUSTICES
Absence and absentees, **28 § 296**
Acknowledgments, **28 § 459**
Active duty or service, retired judges, **28 § 294**
Adjustments. Compensation and salaries, post
Administrative Office of United States Courts, generally, this index
Adverse or pecuniary interest, disqualification, **28 § 455**
Age,
Dependents, annuities, termination, **28 § 376**
Retirement and pensions, **28 § 371**
Agency, definitions, **28 § 451**
Alaska, this index
Alternative writs, powers and duties, **28 § 1651**
Amicus curiae, complaints, **28 § 359**
Annuities, **28 § 371 et seq.**
Definitions, **28 §§ 376, 377**
Increases, **28 § 376 nt**
Judicial Survivors Annuity Fund, generally, this index
Lump sum payments, **28 §§ 376, 377**
Remarriage, **28 § 376**
Territories, **28 § 373**
United States magistrates, **28 § 377**
United States possessions, **28 § 373**
Appeal and review,
Complaints, **28 §§ 352, 357**
Disqualification, **28 § 455**
Appearance, complaints, **28 § 358**

JUDGES OR JUSTICES—Cont'd
Application of law,
Annuities, remarriage, **28 § 376 nt**
Complaints, **28 §§ 362, 363**
Appointments,
Disability, **28 § 372**
Judge, Office of Federal Judicial Administration, **28 § 133**
Judicial branch agency director, **28 § 133**
Relatives, **28 § 458**
Armed Forces, this index
Assassination, **28 § 376**
Assault and battery, sentence and punishment, guidelines, **28 § 994 nt**
Assignments, **28 § 291 et seq.**
Absence and absentees, **28 § 296**
Annuities, survivors, **28 § 376**
Conditions, **28 § 295**
Judicial Conference of the United States, **28 § 331**
New assignments, **28 § 295**
Ninth Circuit, **28 § 297**
Retired judges, **28 §§ 294, 296**
Revocation, **28 § 295**
Time, **28 § 296**
Attorney General, appointments, challenges, **28 § 503 nt**
Attorneys, this index
Bankruptcy, this index
Black persons, selection, **28 § 133 nt**
Books and publications, succession, **28 § 414**
Censure, complaints, **28 § 354**
Certificates and certification,
Disability, retirement and pensions, **28 § 372**
Habeas corpus, evidence, **28 § 2245**
Territories, evidence, **28 § 1739**
United States possessions, evidence, **28 § 1739**
Certificates of public convenience and necessity, **28 § 291 et seq.**
Chief Judge or Justice, generally, this index
Child, definitions, **28 § 376**
Civil service. Retirement and pensions, generally, post
Commissions. Commissions of Officers, generally, this index
Committees, complaints, **28 § 353**
Compensation and salaries,
Adjustments, **28 § 461**
Increases, **28 § 461 nt**
Appropriations, **28 § 461 nt**
Deductions, **28 § 376**
Definitions, **28 § 377**
Increases, **28 §§ 376, 461 nt**
Life insurance, group premiums, **28 § 604**
Reduction, **28 § 461**
Resignation, **28 § 372**
Retired judges, **28 § 371**
Uniformed Services, former members, **28 § 371**

JUDGES OR JUSTICES—Cont'd
Complaints, **28 § 351 et seq.**
Amicus curiae, **28 § 359**
Appeal and review, **28 §§ 352, 357**
Appearance, **28 § 358**
Application of law, **28 §§ 362, 363**
Censure, **28 § 354**
Committees, **28 § 353**
Confidential or privileged information, **28 § 360**
Conviction, crimes and offenses, **28 § 364**
Copies, **28 § 351**
Crimes and offenses, conviction, **28 §§ 355, 364**
Definitions, **28 § 351**
Disclosure, confidential or privileged information, **28 § 360**
Dismissal and nonsuit, **28 §§ 352, 354**
Evidence, **28 § 358**
Expenses and expenditures, reimbursement, **28 § 361**
Frivolous actions, **28 § 352**
Impeachment, **28 § 355**
Intervention, **28 § 359**
Investigations, **28 §§ 353, 354**
Notice, **28 §§ 353, 354**
Orders of court, **28 § 352**
Records and recordation, confidential or privileged information, **28 § 360**
References, **28 §§ 352, 354**
Reimbursement, expenses and expenditures, **28 § 361**
Removal, **28 § 354**
Reprimand, **28 § 354**
Subpoenas, **28 § 356**
Witnesses, **28 § 358**
Confidential or privileged information, complaints, **28 § 360**
Conflict of interest, disqualification, **28 § 455**
Contributions, Judicial Survivors Annuity Fund, **28 § 376 nt**
Conviction, complaints, crimes and offenses, **28 §§ 355, 364**
Copies, complaints, **28 § 351**
Cost of living adjustments, retirement and pensions, **28 § 377**
Court of Appeals for First Circuit, this index
Court of Appeals for Second Circuit, this index
Court of Appeals for Third Circuit, this index
Court of Appeals for Fourth Circuit, this index
Court of Appeals for Fifth Circuit, this index
Court of Appeals for Sixth Circuit, this index
Court of Appeals for Seventh Circuit, this index
Court of Appeals for Eighth Circuit, this index

JUDGES OR JUSTICES—Cont'd
Court of Appeals for Ninth Circuit, this index
Court of Appeals for Tenth Circuit, this index
Court of Appeals for Eleventh Circuit, this index
Court of Appeals for the District of Columbia, this index
Court of Appeals for the Federal Circuit, this index
Court of Federal Claims, this index
Courts of Appeals, this index
Creditable service, survivors annuities, **28 § 376**
Crimes and offenses,
Complaints, **28 §§ 355, 364**
Practice of law, **28 § 454**
Death, survivors annuities, **28 § 376**
Defenses, costs, **28 § 463**
Definitions,
Annuities, **28 §§ 376, 377**
Complaints, **28 § 351**
Disqualification, **28 § 455**
Retirement and pensions, post
Degree of relationship, definitions, **28 § 455**
Department, definitions, **28 § 451**
Dependents. Annuities, generally, ante
Disability. Handicapped persons, generally, post
Discipline, complaints, **28 § 372**
Disclosure, complaints, confidential or privileged information, **28 § 360**
Dismissal and nonsuit, complaints, **28 §§ 352, 354**
Disqualification, **28 § 455**
District, definitions, **28 § 451**
Divorce, court decree of, **28 §§ 376, 376 nt**
Domicile and residence,
Changes, notice, **28 § 456**
Official duty stations, **28 § 456**
Retired judges, **28 § 374**
Duties. Powers and duties, generally, post
Elections,
Annuities, **28 §§ 376, 377**
Judicial Center Board, **28 § 621**
Nominations, generally, post
Employment. Labor and employment, generally, post
Evidence, complaints, **28 § 358**
Expenses and expenditures,
Complaints, reimbursement, **28 § 361**
Director of Administrative Office of U.S. Courts, **28 §§ 463, 604**
Judicial Center,
Boards and commissions, **28 § 621**
Director, **28 § 625**
Traveling expenses, generally, post
Fees, taxation of costs, **28 § 1920**
Fiduciary, definitions, **28 § 455**
Former spouse, survivors annuities, **28 § 376**
Frivolous actions, complaints, **28 § 352**

JUDGES OR JUSTICES—Cont'd
Funds,
Judicial Officers' Retirement, **28 § 377**
Judicial Survivors Annuity Fund, generally, this index
Habeas Corpus, generally, this index
Handicapped persons, **28 § 371 et seq.**
Appointments, **28 § 372**
Bankruptcy judges, **28 § 377**
Certificates and certification, **28 § 371**
Dependents, annuities, **28 § 376**
Retirement and pensions, **28 §§ 372, 377**
Survivors annuities, **28 § 376**
United States magistrates, **28 § 377**
Impeachment, complaints, **28 § 355**
Incumbents, retirement and pensions, **28 §§ 376 nt, 377 nt**
Insurance, group insurance, premiums, compensation and salaries, **28 § 604**
International Trade Court, this index
Intervention, complaints, **28 § 359**
Investigations, complaints, **28 §§ 353, 354**
Judge of the United States, definitions, **28 § 451**
Judicial Center, **28 §§ 620, 626**
Judicial Conference of the Circuit, **28 § 333**
Judicial Conference of the United States, **28 § 331**
Judicial Discipline and Removal National Commission, **28 § 372 nt**
Judicial Officers' Retirement Fund, **28 § 377**
Judicial official, definitions, **28 §§ 376, 377**
Judicial Panel on Multidistrict Litigation, assignments, **28 § 1407**
Judicial Survivors Annuity Fund, generally, this index
Labor and employment,
Receivers and receivership, **28 § 958**
Retired judges, **28 § 377**
Veterans, **28 § 601 nt**
Law. Practice of law, generally, post
Law books, successors, **28 § 414**
Life insurance, group insurance, premiums, compensation and salaries, **28 § 604**
Lump sum credit, definitions, **28 § 377**
Lump sum payment, retirement and pensions, **28 §§ 376, 377**
Magistrate judges. United States Magistrate Judges, generally, this index
Marriage, annuities, survivors, **28 § 376**
Newspapers, notice, **28 § 296**
Nominations, **28 § 133 nt**
Black persons, **28 § 133 nt**
President of the United States, time, **28 § 44 nt, EON 13300**
Time, President of the United States, **28 § 44 nt, EON 13300**
Women, **28 § 133 nt**
Notice,
Annuities, elections, **28 § 377 nt**
Complaints, **28 §§ 353, 354**

JUDGES OR JUSTICES—Cont'd
Oaths and affirmations, **28 § 453**
Administration, **28 § 459**
Offenses. Crimes and offenses, generally, ante
Office expenses, Director of Administrative Office of U.S. Courts, **28 § 604**
Official stations, retired judges, **28 § 374**
Orders of court, complaints, **28 § 352**
Payment, lump sum payment, retirement and pensions, **28 §§ 376, 377**
Pensions. Retirement and pensions, generally, post
Powers and duties,
Alternative writs, issuance, **28 § 1651**
Assignments, **28 § 296**
Rule nisi, issuance, **28 § 1651**
Practice of law,
Bankruptcy judges, retirees, **28 § 377**
High misdemeanor, **28 § 454**
Retired judges, **28 § 377**
President of the United States, **28 § 44 nt**
Disability, **28 § 372**
District courts, **28 § 133**
Judicial Center, **28 § 627**
Nominations, time, **28 § 44 nt, EON 13300**
Possessions, **28 § 373**
Territories, **28 § 373**
Time, nominations, **28 § 44 nt, EON 13300**
Proceeding, definitions, **28 § 455**
Puerto Rico, this index
Reappointments, retirement and pensions, **28 § 377**
Recall, **28 § 375**
Bankruptcy, **28 §§ 155, 375, 377**
Records and recordation,
Complaints, confidential or privileged information, **28 § 360**
Retirement and pensions, **28 § 377**
Recusal, **28 § 455**
Reduction, Judicial Survivors' Annuities Fund, **28 § 376**
References, complaints, **28 §§ 352, 354**
Rehearing,
Assignments, **28 § 296**
Courts of appeals, **28 § 46**
Reimbursement, complaints, **28 § 361**
Relatives, appointments, **28 § 458**
Remand, generally, this index
Remarriage, annuities, survivors, **28 § 376**
Removal,
Complaints, **28 § 354**
Territories, **28 § 373**
United States possessions, **28 § 373**
Reprimand, complaints, **28 § 354**
Residence. Domicile and residence, generally, ante
Retirement and pensions, **28 § 371 et seq.**
Active duty, retired judges, **28 § 294**
Annuities, generally, ante
Assignments, **28 §§ 294, 296**

JUDGES OR JUSTICES—Cont'd
Retirement and pensions—Cont'd
Bankruptcy, this index
Chief Judge, **28 § 294**
Cost of living adjustments, **28 § 377**
Deductions, **28 § 377**
Definitions,
Judicial Officers' Retirement Fund, **28 § 377**
Lump sum payment, **28 § 377**
Survivors annuities, **28 § 376**
Deposits, prior service, **28 § 377**
Domicile and residence, **28 § 374**
Handicapped persons, **28 §§ 372, 377**
Incumbents, **28 §§ 376 nt, 377 nt**
Judicial Officers' Retirement Fund, **28 § 377**
Judicial Survivors Annuity Fund, generally, this index
Lump sum payment, **28 §§ 376, 377**
Official duty station, **28 § 456**
Reappointments, **28 § 377**
Records and recordation, **28 § 377**
Roster of senior judges, special duties, **28 § 294**
Senior status, **28 § 371**
Subsistence, **28 § 456**
Substitutes, **28 § 372**
Tables, **28 § 371**
Traveling expenses, **28 § 456**
Review. Appeal and review, generally, ante
Revocation,
Assignments, **28 § 295**
Designations, **28 § 295**
Survivors annuities, **28 § 376 nt**
Roster of senior judges, special duties, **28 § 294**
Rule nisi, powers and duties, **28 § 1651**
Rules of Appellate Procedure, this index
Rules of Civil Procedure, this index
Salaries. Compensation and salaries, generally, ante
Secretaries,
Bankruptcy, **28 § 156**
Circuit judges, **28 § 712**
Compensation and salaries, **28 §§ 603 nt, 604**
Supreme Court, **28 § 675**
Sentence and punishment, assault and battery, threats, guidelines, **28 § 994 nt**
Special duties, retired judges, **28 § 294**
Spouses, survivors annuities, **28 § 376 nt**
Subpoenas, complaints, **28 § 356**
Subsistence, **28 §§ 456, 604**
Ninth Circuit, temporary assignments, **28 § 297**
Substitutes, retirement and pensions, **28 § 372**
Surviving spouses. Annuities, generally, ante
Survivor annuity, increases, **28 § 376 nt**
Tables, retirement and pensions, **28 § 371**
Territories, this index

JUDGES OR JUSTICES—Cont'd
Threats, sentence and punishment, guidelines, **28 § 994 nt**
Three Judge Court, generally, this index
Time, nominations, President of the United States, **28 § 44 nt, EON 13300**
Training, Judicial Center, **28 § 620 et seq.**
Traveling expenses, **28 §§ 456, 604**
Judicial Center, Director, **28 § 625**
Ninth Circuit, temporary assignments, **28 § 297**
Unfunded liability, definitions, **28 §§ 376, 377**
United States District Court for District of Columbia, this index
United States Magistrate Judges, generally, this index
United States Tax Court, this index
Vacancies in office,
Death, **28 § 372**
Disability, **28 § 372**
President of the United States, nominations, time, **28 § 44 nt, EON 13300**
Veterans, priorities and preferences, **28 § 601 nt**
Virgin Islands, this index
Waivers, disqualification, **28 § 455**
Widows and widowers. Annuities, generally, ante
Witnesses,
Complaints, **28 § 358**
Disqualification, **28 § 455**
Women, **28 § 133 nt**

JUDGMENT AS A MATTER OF LAW
Rules of Civil Procedure, this index

JUDGMENTS AND DECREES
Generally, **28 § 1961 et seq.**
Absent defendant, lien enforcement, **28 § 1655**
Affirmance, appellate courts, **28 § 2106**
Appeal and Review, generally, this index
Arbitration, this index
Bankruptcy, this index
Bill of costs included in, **28 § 1920**
Certified copies,
Habeas corpus, **28 § 2249**
Satisfaction, registration, **28 § 1963**
Computation, interest, **28 § 1961**
Court of Appeals for the Federal Circuit, this index
Court of Federal Claims, this index
Court record lost or destroyed, enforcement where U.S. is interested, **28 § 1735**
Declaratory Judgments and Decrees, generally, this index
Default Judgment, generally, this index
District Courts, this index
Docketing, lien, **28 § 1962**
Entry, appellate court directing entry, **28 § 2106**
Execution, generally, this index

JUDGMENTS AND DECREES—Cont'd
Federal Debt Collection, this index
Foreign Countries, this index
Foreign courts or tribunals, **28 § 2414**
Foreign judgments, registration of, **28 § 1963**
Forma pauperis, proceedings in, **28 § 1915**
Garnishment by U.S. against corporation, **28 § 2405**
Habeas Corpus, generally, this index
Index, lien, **28 § 1962**
Interest, this index
Internal Revenue Service, this index
International Trade Court, this index
Judicial Panel On Multidistrict Litigation, generally, this index
Judicial Sales, generally, this index
Liens and Incumbrances, this index
Motions, action by U.S. against delinquents for public money, **28 § 2407**
Payment,
IRS, certificates and certification, **28 § 2006**
Postal officers, **28 § 2717**
United States, **28 § 2414**
Postal Service, this index
Quieting title, **28 § 2409a**
Recognizances, docket fees, **28 § 1923**
Recording, lien, **28 § 1962**
Registration, this index
Removal of cases, **28 § 1450**
Revenue laws property taken under subject to, **28 § 2463**
Rules of Appellate Procedure, this index
Rules of Civil Procedure, this index
Rules of Evidence, this index
Sentence and Punishment, generally, this index
Setting aside, appellate courts, **28 § 2106**
States, this index
Subpoena of witness in foreign country, service, **28 § 1783**
Taxation, interest, **28 §§ 1961, 2411**
Three judge court, **28 § 2284**
Tort claims, against U.S., bar to action against employees, **28 § 2676**
United States, this index

JUDICIAL AGENCIES
Appointments, **28 § 133**
Definitions, **28 § 451**
Office of Federal Judicial Administration, **28 § 133**

JUDICIAL AMENDMENTS ACT OF 1994
Generally, **28 §§ 1 nt, 471 nt, 612**

JUDICIAL CENTER
Generally, **28 § 620**
Accommodations, **28 § 604**
Accounting and other fiscal services provided for, **28 § 628**
Administrative Office of U.S. Courts,
Accounting, auditing, and other fiscal services, providing, **28 § 628**

JUDICIAL CENTER—Cont'd
Administrative Office of U.S. Courts —Cont'd
Director,
Membership on Board of, **28 § 621**
Notice, election by Director of Center respecting retirement coverage, **28 §§ 376, 627**
Payment of retirement annuity to Director of Center, **28 §§ 376, 627**
Powers and duties, **28 § 604**
Retroactive effect, retirement and survivorship benefits, **28 § 611 nt**
Salary of Director of Center to be same as, **28 § 626**
Annuities, retirement, director of, **28 §§ 376, 627**
Appropriations, **28 § 628**
Audits and auditors, **28 § 604**
Boards and commissions,
Chairman,
Chief Justice of U.S. as, **28 § 621**
Request of Federal agencies, to furnish information, **28 § 624**
Special meeting held on call of, **28 § 622**
Composition, **28 § 621**
Conduct of business, **28 § 622**
Congressional committees, informing, **28 § 623**
Contracts, research projects and other services, **28 § 624**
Direction of activities, **28 § 623**
Director of Center, duties concerning, **28 § 624**
Duties, **28 § 623**
Expenses and expenditures, reimbursement, **28 § 621**
Meetings, **28 § 622**
Policies, establishment, **28 § 623**
Powers, **28 § 624**
Programs, development, **28 § 623**
Quorum, **28 § 622**
Recommendations, **28 § 623**
Reelection to, eligibility for, **28 § 621**
Report, **28 § 623**
Resignation of member, election for unexpired term caused by, **28 § 621**
Studies, automatic data processing and systems procedures, **28 § 623**
Supervision of activities, **28 §§ 621, 623**
Terms of office of members, **28 § 621**
Clerical and secretarial employees,
Appointment and compensation, **28 § 625**
Federal Employees' Life Insurance and Health Benefits Programs, applicability, **28 § 627**
Retirement and pensions, **28 § 627**
Compensation and salaries,
Board members, **28 § 621**
Deputy Director, **28 § 626**

JUDICIAL CENTER—Cont'd
Compensation and salaries—Cont'd
Director, **28 § 626**
Government and private agencies for research projects, **28 § 624**
Professional personnel, **28 § 625**
Deputy Director,
Appointment, duties, **28 § 624**
Compensation, **28 § 626**
Retirement and pensions, employee benefits, **28 § 627**
Director,
Administrative Office of U.S. Courts, ante
Annuities, retirement and pensions, **28 §§ 376, 627**
Cost of living adjustment, **28 § 627 nt**
Appointment and duties, **28 §§ 624, 625**
Assumption of duties by judge, appointment of additional judge by President, **28 § 133**
Compensation and salary, **28 § 626**
Deemed judicial official, for purposes of annuities to widows and dependent children of justices or judges, **28 § 376**
Delegation of Board's contract authority, **28 § 624**
Disability, retirement annuity, **28 § 627**
Election, coming within provisions for annuities to survivors of justices and judges, filing, **28 § 376**
Federal Employees' Life Insurance and Health Benefit Programs, applicability, **28 § 627**
Judge or justice as, service without additional compensation, **28 § 626**
Personal services, procurement, **28 § 625**
Professional personnel, appointment and fixing compensation, **28 § 625**
Request of Federal agencies, to furnish information, **28 § 624**
Retirement and pensions, **28 §§ 376, 627**
Secretarial and clerical personnel, appointment and compensation, **28 § 625**
Supervision of activities of employed persons, **28 § 625**
Traveling expenses, **28 § 625**
Federal Foundation, establishment, members, powers, duties, **28 § 629**
Judicial Conference of U.S.,
Assistance to, **28 § 620**
Election of members to Board of, **28 § 621**
Submission by Board of report to, **28 § 623**
Law books, **28 § 604**
Machinery and equipment, **28 § 604**

JUDICIAL CENTER—Cont'd
Nonprofit organizations or associations,
Boards and commissions, contracts for research projects and other services, **28 § 624**
Coordination, research and study, operation of courts, **28 § 620**
Operations of courts worthy of special study, recommendation, **28 § 623**
Office of Federal Judicial Administration,
Effect of appointment of judge as director of certain judicial branch agencies, **28 § 133**
Federal Courts Study Committee implementation, **28 § 133**
Officers and employees, traveling expenses, **28 § 604**
Policies, establishment by Board, **28 § 623**
Professional staff,
Employment, **28 § 625**
Federal Employees' Life Insurance and Health Benefits Programs, applicability, **28 § 627**
Retirement benefits, **28 § 627**
Programs, development by Board, **28 § 623**
Recommendations, **28 §§ 620, 623**
Research, conduct of, **28 § 620**
Retirement and pensions, civil service,
Director, professional staff, **28 § 627**
Reemployed annuitant, adjustment, **28 § 625**
Service, definitions, retirement, Director, professional staff, **28 § 627**
Staff, research and planning assistance provided by, **28 § 620**
Studies, functions respecting, **28 §§ 620, 623**
Subsistence, officers and employees, **28 § 604**
Supervision of, **28 § 621**
Supplies, **28 § 604**
Training, court personnel, recommendations by Board, **28 § 623**
Traveling expenses,
Director, **28 § 625**
Officers and employees, **28 § 604**
Wages. Compensation and salaries, generally, ante
Waiver, director of, coverage under civil service retirement, **28 §§ 376, 627**

JUDICIAL CIRCUITS
Assignments, **28 §§ 292, 294**
Civil justice expense and delay reduction plans, **28 § 471 et seq.**
Courts of appeals, **28 § 41 et seq.**
Judicial Council, generally, this index
Plans and specifications, civil justice expense and delay reduction plans, **28 § 471 et seq.**
Retired justices or judges, assignments, **28 § 294**

JUDICIAL CODE
Generally, **28 § 1 et seq.**

JUDICIAL CONFERENCE (CIRCUIT COURTS OF APPEALS)
Generally, **28 § 333**

JUDICIAL CONFERENCE OF THE UNITED STATES
Generally, **28 § 331**
Administrative Office of U.S. Courts, Personnel Management System, **28 § 602 nt**
Annuities, survivors, **28 § 376**
Bankruptcy, this index
Budget, **28 § 605**
Chief judges of judicial circuits, **28 § 331**
Committees, **28 § 2073**
Consultants, security, **28 § 331**
Court of Federal Claims, this index
Court of International Trade, representation, **28 § 331**
Courts of Appeals, this index
Director of Administrative Office of the U.S. Courts, **28 § 604**
Disability, annuities, **28 § 376**
Evidence, recommendations, rules of evidence, **28 § 2073**
Federal agencies, orders, appeal and review, **28 § 2352 nt**
Fees,
District courts, **28 § 1914**
Judicial Panel on Multidistrict Litigation, **28 § 1932**
International Trade Court, this index
Interpreters, **28 § 1827**
Judicial Panel on Multidistrict Litigation, fees, **28 § 1932**
Jury,
Commissioners, **28 § 1863**
Qualifications, forms, **28 § 1869**
Selection, **28 § 1878**
Law clerks, **28 §§ 603 nt, 604 nt, 794**
Obsolete papers, **28 § 457**
Powers and duties, **28 § 331**
Pretrial services, **28 § 604**
Priorities and preferences, civil actions, **28 § 1657**
Procedural rules, recommendations, **28 § 2073**
Proposed rules, reports, **28 § 2073**
Recommendations, rules of practice, **28 § 2073**
Records and recordation, district courts, **28 §§ 753, 753 nt**
Reporters, district courts, **28 § 753**
Reports,
District courts, **28 § 753**
Jury, selection, **28 § 1863**
Proposed rules, **28 § 2073**
Retired judges or justices, **28 § 371**
Secretaries, **28 §§ 603 nt, 604 nt, 794**
Security, consultants, **28 § 331**
Sentence and punishment, **28 §§ 334, 994**
Studies, procedures, **28 § 331**
Subsistence, allowances, **28 § 456**

JUDICIAL CONFERENCE OF THE UNITED STATES—Cont'd
Supervision, Director of Administrative Office of the U.S. Courts, **28 § 604**
Traveling expenses, **28 § 456**
United States Magistrate Judges, this index
United States Sentencing Commission, **28 §§ 991, 997**

JUDICIAL COUNCIL
Generally, **28 § 332**
Accommodations, **28 § 462**
Bankruptcy, this index
Circuit Executive, **28 § 332**
Consent,
Assignments, **28 § 295**
Sessions, **28 § 140**
Disability, retirement and pensions, **28 § 372**
Discipline, **28 § 372**
District courts,
Reporters, **28 § 753**
Sessions, **28 § 140**
Domicile and residence, **28 § 134**
Jury,
Exclusions, **28 § 1866**
Random selection, **28 § 1863**
Orders, **28 §§ 137, 332**
Records and recordation, **28 § 457**
Reports, **28 § 332**
Retired judges, assignments, **28 § 294**
United States Magistrate Judges, this index

JUDICIAL DISCLOSURE RESPONSIBILITY ACT
Generally, **5 App. 4 §§ 101 nt, 105**

JUDICIAL DISTRICTS
Alabama, this index
Alaska, this index
Arizona, this index
Arkansas, this index
Bankruptcy, this index
Connecticut, this index
District Courts, this index
Division,
Definitions, Jury Selection and Service Act, **28 § 1869**
Jury wheel, **28 § 1863 nt**
Georgia, this index
Hawaii, this index
Idaho, this index
Illinois, this index
Indiana, this index
Iowa, this index
Jury wheel, **28 § 1863 nt**
Kentucky, this index
Louisiana, this index
Maryland, this index
Massachusetts, this index
Michigan, this index
Mississippi, this index
Missouri, this index
Montana, this index
Multidistrict litigation, **28 § 1407**

JUDICIAL DISTRICTS—Cont'd
Nebraska, this index
Nevada, this index
New York, this index
North Carolina, this index
Ohio, this index
Oklahoma, this index
Oregon, this index
Pennsylvania, this index
Puerto Rico, this index
South Carolina, this index
South Dakota, this index
Tennessee, this index
Texas, this index
Utah, this index
Venue, generally, this index
Vermont, this index
Virginia, this index
Washington (State), this index
West Virginia, this index
Wisconsin, this index
Wyoming, this index

JUDICIAL NOTICE
Rules of Evidence, this index
Seals (official seals), Director of Administrative Office of U.S. Courts, **28 § 608**

JUDICIAL OFFICERS
See specific index headings

JUDICIAL PANEL ON MULTIDISTRICT LITIGATION
Generally, **28 § 1407; MDL 1.1 et seq.**
Accompaniments, notice, **MDL 25.2**
Admission to practice, attorneys, **MDL 1.4**
Adverse or pecuniary interest, corporate disclosure statements, **MDL 5.3**
Affidavits, **MDL 7.6**
Antitrust laws, definitions, **28 § 1407**
Appeal and review, **MDL 1.6**
Petitions, **28 § 1407**
Applications, extension of time, **MDL 6.2**
Attorneys, transferred actions, **MDL 1.4**
Averments, **MDL 7.1**
Briefs, **MDL 7.1**
Motions, **MDL 7.2**
Remand, **MDL 7.6**
Chairman, definitions, **MDL 1.1**
Clerks of courts,
Definitions, **MDL 1.1**
Motions, **MDL 7.2**
Notice, **MDL 25.1 et seq.**
Records and recordation, **MDL 5.1**
Refusal, filing, **MDL 1.3**
Service of process, **MDL 5.2**
Tag-along actions, **MDL 7.4**
Transfers, files, **MDL 1.6**
Composition, **28 § 1407**
Computer generated disks, filing, **MDL 5.13**
Conditional orders,
Remand, **MDL 7.6**
Tag-along actions, **MDL 5.2, 7.4, 7.5**
Copies, **MDL 5.12, 25.1 et seq.**

JUDICIAL PANEL ON MULTIDISTRICT LITIGATION—Cont'd
Corporate disclosure statements, **MDL 5.3**
Counterclaims, **MDL 1.6, 7.6**
Courts of appeals, **MDL 17.1**
Cross claims, **MDL 1.6, 7.6**
Definitions, **MDL 1.1**
Disclosure, corporate disclosure statements, **MDL 5.3**
Dismissal and nonsuit, **MDL 7.6**
Extension of time, **MDL 5.2, 5.12, 6.2**
Federal records center, **MDL 5.1**
Fees, **28 § 1932**
Copies, **MDL 5.1**
Filing, **MDL 5.11 et seq.**
Forms, **MDL 7.1**
Forms,
Filing, **MDL 7.1**
Notice, **MDL 25.4**
Government Services Administration, records and recordation, disposal, **MDL 5.1**
Hearings, **MDL 16.1**
Joinder of actions, **MDL 7.2**
Judges or justices, assignments, **28 § 1407**
Judicial Conference of the U.S., fees, **28 § 1932**
Mail and mailing, **MDL 5.11**
Monopolies and combinations, **28 § 1407**
Motions, **MDL 5.12 et seq.**
Corporate disclosure statements, **MDL 5.3**
Pretrial proceedings, transfer of cases, **28 § 1407**
Remand, **MDL 7.6**
Noncompliance, **MDL 1.3**
Notice,
Filing, **MDL 5.12**
Motions, **MDL 7.2**
Oral argument, **MDL 5.12, 16.1**
Pending actions, **28 § 1369**
Petitions, **MDL 25.1 et seq.**
Pretrial proceedings, transfer of cases, **28 § 1407**
Show cause orders, **MDL 7.3**
Tag-along actions, **MDL 7.4**
Transfers, files, **MDL 1.6**
Oral argument, **MDL 5.12, 16.1**
Orders of court,
Conditional orders, generally, ante
Pretrial proceedings, transfer of cases, **28 § 1407**
Show cause orders, generally, post
Pending actions, **MDL 1.5**
Notice, **28 § 1369**
Tag-along actions, **MDL 7.4**
Petitions,
Extraordinary writs, **28 § 1407**
Notice, **MDL 25.1 et seq.**
Place, records and recordation, **MDL 5.1, 5.11**
Pleading, **MDL 7.1**
Motions, **MDL 7.2**
Practice of panel, **MDL 1.2**

JUDICIAL PANEL ON MULTIDISTRICT LITIGATION—Cont'd
Process, **MDL 5.2, 5.12**
Notice, **MDL 25.3**
Panel, consolidation orders, **MDL 25.5**
Proof of service, **MDL 5.2, 25.3**
Tag-along actions, **MDL 7.5**
Questions of fact, **MDL 7.5**
Random selection, multi-circuit petition, **MDL 17.1**
Remand, **MDL 7.6, 16.1**
Tag-along actions, **MDL 7.5**
Transfers, **28 § 1407; MDL 1.6**
Responsive pleadings, **MDL 7.1, 7.2**
Show cause orders, **MDL 7.3, 7.6**
Corporations, disclosure, **MDL 5.3**
Stipulations, **MDL 7.6**
Summary judgment, **MDL 7.6**
Tag-along actions, **MDL 7.5, 16.1**
Conditional transfer orders, **MDL 7.4**
Definitions, **MDL 1.1**
Termination, **MDL 7.6**
Third parties, claims, **MDL 1.6, 7.6**
Time,
Extension of time, **MDL 5.2, 5.12, 6.2**
Filing, **MDL 5.12**
Motion practice, **MDL 7.2**
Service of process, **MDL 5.2**
Show cause orders, **MDL 7.3**
Tag-along actions, **MDL 7.4**
Transfers, **MDL 1.4, 5.2**
Coordination, **28 § 1407**
Records and recordation, **MDL 1.6, 5.1**
Vacating or setting aside, **MDL 7.4**
Waiver, oral argument, **MDL 5.12, 16.1**

JUDICIAL REVIEW
Appeal and Review, generally, this index

JUDICIAL SALES
Generally, **28 § 2001 et seq.**
Appraisals, **28 § 2005**
Bids and bidding, **28 § 2410**
Bona fide offers, **28 § 2001**
Federal debt collection, **28 § 3201 et seq.**
Fees, United States Marshal, **28 § 1921**
Goods, wares and merchandise, **28 § 2005**
Liens and incumbrances, United States, **28 § 2410**
Partition, United States, **28 § 2409**
Personalty, **28 § 2004**
Real estate, **28 § 2001 et seq.**
Receivers and receivership, **28 § 2001**
Separate parcels, **28 § 2001**
Tax liens, **28 § 2410**
United States, **28 § 2409 et seq.**
United States Marshal, **28 §§ 1921, 2003 et seq.**

JUDICIAL SURVIVORS ANNUITY FUND
Generally, **28 §§ 376, 376 nt**
Examinations and examiners, **28 § 605**

JUDICIARY COMMITTEE
Congressional Committees, this index

JURATS
United States magistrate judges, seals, **28 § 638**

JURISDICTION
Admiralty, this index
Alaska, this index
Ambassadors, Supreme Court, **28 § 1251**
Amendment of pleadings to show, **28 § 1653**
Antitrust, laws, preventing and restraining violations, regulations, district courts, **28 § 1337**
Bankruptcy, this index
Certificates, district courts jurisdiction, interpleader, **28 § 1335**
Civil action, removal, **28 § 1441**
Civil Rights, this index
Commerce regulations, district court, carrier cases, amount in controversy, **28 § 1337**
Constitution of the United States, this index
Copyrights, this index
Court of Appeals for First Circuit, this index
Court of Appeals for Third Circuit, this index
Court of Appeals for the District of Columbia, this index
Court of Appeals for the Federal Circuit, this index
Court of Federal Claims, this index
Courts of Appeals, this index
Customs Duties, this index
District Courts, this index
District of Columbia, this index
Exports and imports, monopolies and combinations, **28 § 1368**
Federal Maritime Commission, **28 § 2342**
Fines, Penalties and Forfeitures, this index
Foreign Countries, this index
Foreign Diplomatic and Consular Officers, this index
Foreign ministers, Supreme Court, **28 § 1251**
Guam, this index
Income Tax, this index
Indian Lands and Reservations, this index
Indians, this index
International Trade Court, this index
Interpleader proceedings, **28 § 1335**
Maritime cases, **28 § 1333**
Mask work cases, semiconductor chip products, **28 § 1338**
Monopolies and Combinations, this index
National Banks, this index
Nebraska, this index
Patents, **28 § 1338**
Plant Variety Protection, this index
Postal Service, this index
Prize (Vessels), this index
Public Contracts, this index

JURISDICTION—Cont'd
Removal, civil action, **28 § 1441**
Restraints of trade, **28 § 1337**
Rules of Civil Procedure, this index
Set-Off and Counterclaim, this index
States, this index
Statutes, **28 § 1346**
District courts, original jurisdiction, **28 § 1331**
Fines, penalties and forfeitures, recovery, **28 § 1355**
Indians, **28 § 1362**
Supplemental jurisdiction, district courts, **28 § 1367**
Supreme Court, this index
Taxation, States, **28 § 1341**
Territories, this index
Torture, **28 § 1350 nt**
Trademarks and Trade Names, this index
Unfair competition, **28 § 1338**
United States, this index
Virgin Islands, this index
Want of jurisdiction, transfer to cure, **28 § 1631**

JUROR QUALIFICATION FORM
Generally, **28 § 1864 et seq.**
Grand Jury, this index

JURY
Generally, **28 § 1861 et seq.**
Admiralty cases, **28 § 1873**
Adverse effect upon deliberations, exclusion, **28 § 1866**
Affidavits, summons, **28 § 1866**
Age, **28 § 1865**
Alphabetical lists, master jury wheels, **28 §§ 1864, 1865**
Appropriations,
Bailiffs, **28 § 524**
Refreshments, **28 § 1871 nt**
Assignments, **28 §§ 1863, 1866**
Attachment, Postal Service, **28 § 2713**
Attendance, fees, **28 § 1871**
Attorneys, fees, labor and employment, protection, **28 § 1875**
Bailiffs,
Appropriations, **28 § 524**
Labor and employment, **28 § 755**
Bankruptcy, this index
Bonds (officers and fiduciaries), **28 § 1874**
Books and papers, preservation, **28 § 1868**
Canal Zone, this index
Certificates and certification, fees, **28 § 1871**
Challenges, **28 § 1870**
Exclusion, good cause, **28 § 1866**
Peremptory challenges, **28 §§ 1866, 1870**
Selection procedures, **28 § 1867**
Chief judge of district court, **28 § 1863 et seq.**
Citizens and citizenship, **28 § 1865**
Civil Rights, this index

JURY—Cont'd
Clerks of district courts, **28 § 1863 et seq.**
Commission. Jury Commission, generally, this index
Compensation and salaries. Fees, generally, post
Composition, **28 § 1863 nt**
Conditions, eligibility, **28 § 1865**
Crimes and offenses,
Qualifications, **28 §§ 1865, 1869**
Service of process, **28 § 1865**
Definitions, **28 § 1869**
Deputy clerks of district courts, **28 § 1866**
Disclosure,
Master jury wheels, **28 § 1864**
Selection process, **28 § 1867**
Time, **28 § 1863**
Discrimination, **28 § 1862 et seq.**
Dismissal of indictment, **28 § 1867**
Disqualification, **28 §§ 1863, 1865, 1866**
Disruption of proceedings, **28 § 1866**
District courts,
Definitions, **28 § 1869**
Subsistence allowance, outside contiguous 48 States, **28 § 1871**
Domicile and residence, **28 § 1865**
Drawings, names, master jury wheels, **28 §§ 1864, 1866**
Evidence,
Qualifications, **28 § 1865**
Selection, **28 § 1867**
Examinations and examiners, random selection, **28 § 1863**
Exclusion, **28 § 1862 et seq.**
Excuse, **28 § 1863**
Exemptions, **28 § 1863 et seq.**
Extreme inconvenience, **28 § 1869**
Federal Officers and Employees, this index
Fees, **28 § 1871**
Attorneys, labor and employment, protection, **28 § 1875**
Forms, **28 § 1864**
Traveling expenses, generally, post
Ferries, toll charges, **28 § 1871**
Fines, penalties and forfeitures, **28 § 1864 et seq.**
First-class mail, summons, **28 § 1866**
Forms, juror qualification form, **28 § 1864 et seq.**
Grand Jury, generally, this index
Impartial service, exclusion, **28 § 1866**
Inconvenience, extreme inconvenience, **28 § 1869**
Inspection and inspectors, **28 § 1868**
Instructions,
Qualifications, **28 § 1864**
Rules of Civil Procedure, this index
Rules of Evidence, this index
Interim travel allowances, **28 § 1871**
Internal Revenue Service, erroneously paid taxes, recovery, **28 § 2402**
International Trade Court, this index

JURY—Cont'd
Judicial Conference of the United States, this index
Juror qualification form, **28 § 1864 et seq.**
Jury wheel,
Definitions, **28 § 1869**
Master jury wheel, **28 § 1863 et seq.**
Labor and employment,
Bailiffs, **28 § 755**
Protection, attorneys, fees, **28 § 1875**
Lists, **28 § 1863 et seq.**
Definitions, **28 § 1869**
Master jury wheels, **28 §§ 1864, 1865**
Voter registration lists, **28 §§ 1863, 1866, 1869**
Literacy, **28 § 1865**
Lodging, **28 § 1871**
Mail and mailing,
Qualification form, **28 § 1864**
Summons, **28 § 1866**
Maritime cases, **28 § 1873**
Master jury wheel, **28 § 1863 et seq.**
Meals, **28 § 1871**
Mental capacity, **28 § 1865**
Mileage. Traveling expenses, generally, post
Modification, random selection, **28 § 1863**
Motions, challenges, **28 § 1867**
Names, juror qualification form, **28 § 1869**
Notice, random selection, modification, **28 § 1863**
Numbers and numbering, exclusions, **28 § 1866**
Offenses. Crimes and offenses, generally, ante
One-step summoning and qualification procedure, **28 § 1878**
Orders of court, appearance, **28 §§ 1864, 1866**
Original jurisdiction, district courts, labor and employment, protection, **28 § 1363**
Overnight stays, **28 § 1871**
Panels, **28 §§ 1866, 1867**
Reviewing panels, random selection, **28 § 1863**
Parking, fees, **28 § 1871**
Peremptory challenges, **28 §§ 1866, 1870**
Physical capacity, **28 § 1865**
Postal Service, attachment, **28 § 2713**
Preservation, books and papers, **28 § 1868**
Protection, labor and employment, **28 § 1875**
Public policy, **28 § 1861**
Publicly draw, definitions, **28 § 1869**
Punishment, **28 § 1864 et seq.**
Qualification form, **28 § 1864 et seq.**
Race, color, and previous condition of servitude, **28 § 1862 et seq.**
Random selection, **28 § 1861 et seq.**
Receivers and receivership, **28 § 959**

JURY—Cont'd
Records and recordation, **28 §§ 1863, 1866 et seq.**
Inspection and inspectors, **28 § 1868**
Nondisclosure, **28 § 1867**
Preservation, **28 § 1868**
Voter registration, **28 §§ 1863, 1866, 1869**
Refreshments, appropriations, **28 § 1871 nt**
Registered mail, summons, **28 § 1866**
Reinstatement, labor and employment, **28 § 1875**
Religion,
Exclusion, **28 § 1862**
Qualification form, **28 § 1869**
Selection, **28 § 1867**
Reports, selection, **28 § 1863**
Residence, **28 § 1865**
Restoration, civil rights, qualifications, **28 § 1865**
Returns, qualification form, **28 § 1864**
Reviewing panels, random selection, **28 § 1863**
Rules of Civil Procedure, this index
Rules of Evidence, this index
Secrecy of proceedings, exclusion, **28 § 1866**
Selection, random selection, **28 § 1861 et seq.**
Sentence and punishment, **28 § 1864 et seq.**
Sequestration, subsistence, **28 § 1871**
Stay of proceedings, selection procedures, noncompliance, **28 § 1867**
Subsistence allowance, **28 § 1871**
Summons, **28 § 1864 et seq.**
Definitions, **28 § 1869**
One-step summoning and qualification procedure, **28 § 1878**
Panels, **28 § 1866**
Preservation, **28 § 1868**
Qualification form, **28 § 1864**
Supreme Court, original actions at law, **28 § 1872**
Time,
Random selection, **28 § 1863**
Selection procedures, challenges, **28 § 1867**
Service by jurors, **28 § 1866**
Tolls, highways and roads, **28 § 1871**
Traveling expenses, **28 §§ 1824, 1871**
Appearance, qualifications, **28 § 1864**
Jury commissioner, **28 § 1863**
Trusts and trustees, **28 § 959**
Undue hardship, **28 § 1869**
United States, **28 § 2402**
United States Marshals Service, this index
Virgin Islands, this index
Volunteer safety personnel, definitions, **28 § 1863**
Voter registration lists, **28 §§ 1863, 1866, 1869**
Waiver, Postal Service, attachment, **28 § 2713**

JURY—Cont'd
Wheels,
Definitions, **28 § 1869**
Master jury wheels, **28 § 1863 et seq.**

JURY COMMISSION
Generally, **28 § 1863 et seq.**
Appointments, **28 § 1863**
Compensation and salaries, **28 § 1863**
Deputies, **28 § 1866**
Disclosure, **28 § 1867**
Domicile and residence, **28 § 1863**
Expenses and expenditures, **28 § 1863**
Forms, **28 § 1864**
Jury wheel, **28 § 1866**
Lists, names, **28 § 1864**
Names, lists, **28 § 1864**
Panels, **28 § 1866**
Recommendations, **28 § 1865**
Records and recordation, **28 § 1868**
Reimbursement, **28 § 1863**

JURY SELECTION AND SERVICE ACT OF 1968
Generally, **28 § 1861 et seq.**

JUSTICE DEPARTMENT
Generally, **28 § 501 et seq.**
Accounts and accounting, transfers, **28 § 524 nt**
Actions and proceedings,
Civil justice reform, **28 § 519 nt, EON 12988**
Expenses less than certain amounts related to, availability of appropriations, **28 § 524**
Reimbursement, salaries and expenses, **28 § 509 nt**
Administrative expenses, appropriations, **28 § 524**
Administrative law and procedure, enforcement, reports, **28 § 530D**
Agents and agencies,
Delegation, Attorney General's authority, **28 § 510**
Functions vested in Attorney General, **28 § 509**
Aircraft, funds, **28 § 530C**
Ammunition, funds, **28 § 530C**
Appointments, investigations, **28 § 533**
Appropriations, **28 § 501 nt**
Administrative expenses, **28 § 524**
Drugs and medicine, civil enforcement enhancement, authorization, **28 § 509 nt**
Fact witness fees, incarcerated persons, payment, prohibition, **28 § 1821 nt**
Travel and health care expenses, personnel serving abroad, authorization, **28 § 530A**
Assets Forfeiture Fund, **28 § 524**
Appropriations, **28 § 524**
Definitions, **28 § 524**
Deposits in, **28 § 524**
Rewards, **28 § 524**
Attorney General, generally, this index

JUSTICE DEPARTMENT—Cont'd
Attorneys. United States Attorneys, generally, this index
Awards for information or assistance leading to forfeiture, **28 § 524**
Boats and boating, funds, **28 § 530C**
Buildings, construction, funds, **28 § 530C**
Bureau of Alcohol, Tobacco, Firearms, and Explosives, generally, this index
Chief Financial Officer, **28 § 507**
Civil debt collection, **28 § 527 nt**
Civil justice reform, **28 § 519 nt, EON 12988**
Compromise and settlement, enforcement, reports, **28 § 530D**
Conduct of litigation reserved to, **28 § 516**
Conferences, funds, **28 § 530C**
Confidential or privileged information, funds, **28 § 530C**
Conflict of interest, **28 § 528 et seq.**
Construction, buildings, funds, **28 § 530C**
Consultants, funds, **28 § 530C**
Contracts, personal services, funds, **28 § 530C**
Correctional, activities, Assets Forfeiture Fund, **28 § 524**
Counterterrorism Fund, **28 § 524 nt**
Credits, working capital funds, **28 § 527 nt**
Criminal division, United States Sentencing Commission, **28 § 994**
Definitions, attorneys, ethics, **28 § 530B**
Dependents, schools and school districts, funds, **28 § 530C**
Designation as Executive Department, **28 § 501**
Discipline, conflicts of interest, **28 § 528**
Drug Enforcement Administration, generally, this index
Drugs and medicine, civil enforcement enhancement, **28 § 509 nt**
Elections, reports, **28 § 529**
Emergencies, funds, **28 § 530C**
Employees. Officers and employees, generally, post
Enforcement,
Assets Forfeiture Fund, **28 § 524**
Statutes, reports, **28 § 530D**
Estates and trusts, United States trustees, oaths and affirmations, **28 § 583**
Ethics, attorneys, **28 § 530B**
Expenses and expenditures, conferences, reports, **28 § 530C nt**
Experts, funds, **28 § 530C**
Federal agencies,
Assets Forfeiture Fund, **28 § 524**
Reimbursement, funds, **28 § 530C**
Federal Bureau of Investigation, generally, this index
Federally insured financial institutions, fraud, **28 § 509 nt**
Foreign countries, reimbursements, funds, **28 § 530C**
Forfeited vessels, **28 § 524**

JUSTICE DEPARTMENT—Cont'd
Funds,
Assets Forfeiture Fund, generally, ante
Powers and duties, **28 § 530C**
Working capital funds, generally, post
Gifts, bequests and devises, **28 § 524**
Health care expenses, overseas personnel, **28 § 530A**
Independent Counsel, this index
Injunctions, enforcement, reports, **28 § 530D**
Institutes and joint councils on sentencing, **28 § 334**
Insurance, motor vehicles, funds, **28 § 530C**
Interpreters, funds, **28 § 530C**
Investigations, appointments, **28 § 533**
Lobbying, reports, **28 § 529**
Marshals. United States Marshals Service, generally, this index
Meals and lodging for bailiffs, appropriations, **28 § 524**
Meetings, funds, **28 § 530C**
Money, gifts, devises, and bequests, acceptance, use, **28 § 524**
Motor vehicles, funds, **28 § 530C**
National Crime Information Center, generally, this index
National security division, **28 § 509A**
Notarial fees, appropriations, **28 § 524**
Notice, rewards, payment, **28 § 530C**
Oaths and affirmations, United States trustees, **28 § 583**
Office of Justice for Victims of Overseas Terrorism, **28 § 501 nt**
Officers and employees,
Actions and proceedings, **28 § 515**
Conduct, **28 § 516**
Conflicts of interest, **28 § 528**
Delegation of authority, **28 § 510**
Overseas, **28 § 530A**
Pending actions, **28 § 517**
Privacy officer, **28 § 509 nt**
Public Integrity Section, **28 § 529**
Reimbursement, **28 § 509 nt**
Special agents, **28 § 530**
United States courts, **28 § 518**
Opinions and decisions, enforcement, reports, **28 § 530D**
Payment, special agents, **28 § 530**
Personal services, contracts, **28 § 530C**
Powers and duties, funds, **28 § 530C**
President, appointment, Solicitor General, **28 § 505**
Privacy officer, **28 § 509 nt**
Property taxes, Assets Forfeiture Fund, **28 § 524**
Public Integrity Section, reports, **28 § 529**
Public policy, statutes, enforcement, reports, **28 § 530D**
Receptions, funds, **28 § 530C**
Removal from office,
Conflict of interest, **28 § 519 nt**
Violation of conflict of interest rules, penalty, **28 § 528**

JUSTICE DEPARTMENT—Cont'd
Reports,
Banking law offenses, **28 § 522 nt**
Business and statistics, **28 § 522**
Conferences, expenses and expenditures, **28 § 530C nt**
Drugs and medicine, civil enforcement enhancement, **28 § 509 nt**
Money laundering, **28 § 994 nt**
Privacy officer, **28 § 509 nt**
Statutes, enforcement, **28 § 530D**
United States Sentencing Commission, **28 § 994 nt**
Requisitions, advance or payment of moneys, **28 § 523**
Rewards, **28 § 530C**
Rules and regulations, conflicts of interest, **28 § 528**
Schools and school districts, dependents, funds, **28 § 530C**
Seal, **28 § 502**
Seat of government, location, **28 § 501**
Security, national security division, **28 § 509A**
Solicitor General,
Appointment, **28 § 505**
Arguments, **28 § 518**
Pending suits, **28 § 517**
Succession, **28 § 508**
United States courts, powers and duties, **28 § 518**
Special agents, payment, **28 § 530**
Statutes, enforcement, reports, **28 § 530D**
Stenographic services, appropriations, **28 § 524**
Subdivisions, **28 § 501 nt**
Terrorists and terrorism, Office of Justice for Victims of Overseas Terrorism, **28 § 501 nt**
Training, funds, **28 § 530C**
Translators, funds, **28 § 530C**
Traveling expenses,
Funds, **28 § 530C**
Newly appointed special agents, **28 § 530**
Overseas employees, **28 § 530A**
Trusts and trustees, United States trustees, bankruptcy, **28 § 581 et seq.**
Undercover operations, reports, **28 § 533 nt**
Uniforms, funds, **28 § 530C**
United States Attorneys, generally, this index
United States Marshals Service, generally, this index
United States trustees, bankruptcy, **28 § 581 et seq.**
Violation of Controlled Substances Act or Controlled Substances Import and Export Act, **28 § 524**
Warranties, funds, **28 § 530C**
Weapons, funds, **28 § 530C**
Witnesses,
Appropriations, **28 § 524**
Fees, **28 § 1821 nt**

JUSTICE DEPARTMENT—Cont'd
Witnesses—Cont'd
Funds, **28 § 530C**
Procurement, **28 § 509 nt**
Working capital funds, **28 § 527**
Credits, **28 § 527 nt**
Retention, **28 § 527 nt**
Transfers, **28 § 527 nt**

JUSTICES
Judges or Justices, generally, this index

JUVENILE DELINQUENTS AND DEPENDENTS
Prosecutions, weapons, **28 § 509 nt**
Rules of Evidence, this index
United States Sentencing Commission, studies, **28 § 995**
Weapons, prosecutions, **28 § 509 nt**

KANSAS
Bankruptcy, judges or justices, appointments, **28 § 152**
District courts, **28 § 96**
Judges or justices, **28 § 133**
Vacancies in office, **28 § 133 nt**
Judicial circuit, **28 § 41**
Judicial district, **28 § 96**
Number of district judges, **28 § 133**
United States trustees, appointments, **28 § 581**

KEEPER OF THE GREAT SEAL
Generally, **28 § 1739**

KENTUCKY
Bankruptcy, judges or justices, appointments, **28 § 152**
District courts, **28 § 97**
Judges or justices, **28 § 133**
Places of holding, **28 § 97**
Judicial circuit, **28 § 41**
Judicial districts,
Bankruptcy, **28 § 581 nt**
Judges or justices, **28 § 133**
United States trustees, judicial districts, **28 § 581**

KETOBEMIDONE
Controlled Substances, generally, this index

KIDNAPPING
Children and Minors, this index
Domestic violence, parental kidnapping, reports, **28 § 1738A nt**
Morgan P. Hardiman Child Abduction and Serial Murder Investigative Resources Center, **28 § 531 nt**
Reports, parental kidnapping, domestic violence, **28 § 1738A nt**
United States-Mexico Border Violence Task Force, **28 § 509 nt**

KIN
Relatives, generally, this index

KINGMAN REEF
Judicial District of Hawaii, **28 § 91**

KNOWLEDGE
See specific index headings

LABOR AND EMPLOYMENT
Attorneys,
Fees, jury, discharge, **28 § 1875**
Jury, discharge, **28 § 1875**
Civil Service, generally, this index
Compensation and Salaries, generally, this index
Correctional Institutions, this index
Exports and Imports, this index
Guards, criminal background checks, **28 § 534 nt**
Judges or Justices, this index
Jury, this index
Wages. Compensation and Salaries, generally, this index

LABOR DEPARTMENT
Community development, neighborhood revitalization plan, **28 § 509 nt**

LABOR DISPUTES
Collective bargaining, motion pictures, copyrights, **28 § 4001**

LABORATORIES
Controlled Substances, this index
DNA (Deoxyribonucleic Acid), generally, this index
International Trade Court, this index
United States Court of International Trade, **28 § 2642**

LABORERS
Labor and Employment, generally, this index

LACHES
See specific index headings

LANDLORD AND TENANT
Joint Tenants, generally, this index

LANDS
Real Estate, generally, this index

LANGUAGE
Interpreters, generally, this index
Translators. Interpreters, generally, this index

LARCENY
Stores, organized retail theft task force, **28 § 509 nt**

LAW BOOKS
Attorney General, **28 § 413**
Procurement, **28 § 525**
Director of Administrative Office of U.S. Courts, **28 §§ 413, 604**
Successors in office, **28 § 414**
United States, **28 § 414**
United States magistrate judges, **28 § 604**

LAW CLERKS
Annual leave, **28 § 752**
Bankruptcy, **28 § 156**
Compensation and salaries, **28 § 603 nt**
District court judges, **28 § 752**
Incentive pay or awards, **28 § 604**
Supreme Court, **28 § 675**
Court of Federal Claims, this index
Courts of Appeals, this index
District Judges, this index
Incentive pay or awards, **28 § 604**
Sick leave, **28 § 752**

LAW ENFORCEMENT
Assets Forfeiture Fund, **28 § 524**
Indians, this index
Officers and employees. Law Enforcement Officers, generally, this index
Secretary of the Treasury, this index

LAW ENFORCEMENT AGENCIES OR INSTRUMENTALITIES
Bureau of Investigation. Federal Bureau of Investigation, generally, this index
Federal Bureau of Investigation, generally, this index
Grants, terrorists and terrorism, **28 § 509 nt**
National Crime Information Center Project 2000, **28 § 534 nt**
Officers and employees. Law Enforcement Officers, generally, this index
Terrorists and Terrorism, this index

LAW ENFORCEMENT OFFICERS
Automated legal research and information system, **28 § 509 nt, EON 12146**
Bailiffs, generally, this index
Crimes and offenses, violence, torts, scope of employment, **28 § 2671 nt**
Definitions, torts, acting within the scope of office or employment, **28 § 2671 nt**
Escape, torts, acting within the scope of office or employment, **28 § 2671 nt**
Felonious killings of, investigation by Attorney General and FBI, **28 § 540**
Force, torts, acting within the scope of office or employment, **28 § 2671 nt**
Torts, acting within the scope of office or employment, **28 § 2671 nt**
United States Marshals Service, generally, this index

LAW LIBRARIES
Librarians,
Courts, compensation and salaries, **28 §§ 603 nt, 604**
Courts of appeals, **28 § 713**
Supreme Court, **28 §§ 672, 674**

LAW REPORTS
Supreme Court reports, **28 § 412**

LAWS
Questions of Law or Fact, generally, this index
Statutes, generally, this index

LAWYERS
Attorneys, generally, this index

LEARNING DISABILITIES
Handicapped Persons, generally, this index

LEASES
Bankruptcy, this index

LEAVE OF ABSENCE
See specific index headings

LEAVE OF COURT
International Trade Court, this index
Rules of Civil Procedure, this index
Trusts and trustees, **28 § 959**

LEGAL DISABILITY
Handicapped Persons, this index

LEGAL REPRESENTATIVES
Attorneys, generally, this index

LEGAL RESEARCH
Federal law offices, automation, **28 § 509 nt, EON 12146**

LEGAL SERVICES
Attorneys, generally, this index

LEGAL TENDER
Money, generally, this index

LEGATIONS
Foreign Service, generally, this index

LEGISLATION
Civil justice, reform, **28 § 519 nt, EON 12988**

LEGISLATURE
Officers and employees, jury, exemptions, **28 § 1863**
States, this index

LETTERS AND OTHER CORRESPONDENCE
Tort Claims Act, **28 § 2680**

LETTERS PATENT
Patents, generally, this index

LETTERS ROGATORY
Convention on the Taking of Evidence Abroad in Civil or Commercial Matters, **28 § 1781 nt**
Foreign countries, **28 § 1696**
International tribunals, **28 § 1782**
Transmittal, **28 § 1781**

LEVOMETHORPHAN
Controlled Substances, generally, this index

LEVOMORAMIDE
Controlled Substances, generally, this index

LEVOPHENACYLMORPHAN
Controlled Substances, generally, this index

LEVORPHANOL
Controlled Substances, generally, this index

LEVY
Federal debt collection,
Postjudgment remedies, **28 § 3203**
Prejudgment remedies, **28 § 3102**
Justices and judges, annuities, exemptions, **28 § 376**

LIABILITY
See specific index headings

LIABILITY INSURANCE
Diversity of citizenship, jurisdiction, district courts, **28 § 1332**
Foreign diplomatic missions, **28 § 1364**

LIBEL AND SLANDER
Tort Claims Act, **28 § 2680**

LIBEL (PROCEEDINGS)
Admiralty, this index

LIBRARIANS
Law Libraries, this index

LIBRARIES
Compensation and salaries, Supreme Court, **28 § 674**
Courts of Appeals, this index
Law Libraries, generally, this index
Supreme Court, this index

LIBYA
Claims, terrorists and terrorism, United States nationals, **28 § 1605A nt**
Compromise and settlement, terrorists and terrorism, United States nationals, **28 § 1605A nt**
Privileges and immunities, terrorists and terrorism, United States nationals, claims, **28 § 1605A nt**
Terrorists and terrorism,
Claims, United States nationals, **28 § 1605A nt**
Compromise and settlement, United States nationals, **28 § 1605A nt**
Privileges and immunities, United States nationals, claims, **28 § 1605A nt**

LIBYAN CLAIMS RESOLUTION ACT
Generally, **28 § 1605A nt**

LICENSES AND PERMITS
Customs Duties, this index
Parimutuel betting, **28 § 534 nt**

LIENS AND INCUMBRANCES
Absent defendants, **28 § 1655**
Bankruptcy, this index
Creation of new judicial district or division, **28 § 1656**

LIENS AND INCUMBRANCES—Cont'd
District courts,
Absent defendants, **28 § 1655**
New districts, **28 § 1656**
United States, **28 § 2410**
Federal Debt Collection, this index
Income tax. Tax Liens, generally, this index
Internal Revenue Service. Tax Liens, generally, this index
Judgments and decrees, absent defendants, **28 §§ 1655, 1962, 1963**
Quieting title, **28 § 2409a**
Removal, district courts, **28 § 1655**
Sales, satisfaction, United States, **28 § 2410**
Ships and Shipping, this index
Tax Liens, generally, this index
Transfer of territory to another district or division, **28 § 1656**
United States, this index

LIFE INSURANCE
Judges or justices, group insurance, premiums, compensation and salaries, **28 § 604**

LIMITATION OF ACTIONS
Generally, **28 § 1658**
Acts of Congress, **28 § 1658**
Congressional reference cases, **28 § 2509**
Contract Disputes Act of 1978, **28 § 2401**
Copyrights, this index
Court of Federal Claims, this index
Customs Duties, this index
Drug patents, declaratory judgments, **28 § 2201**
Federal Agencies, this index
Federal Officers and Employees, this index
Fines, penalties and forfeitures, **28 § 2462**
Habeas Corpus, this index
Handicapped Persons, this index
Income Tax, this index
Incompetency, this index
Indian Lands and Reservations, this index
Indians, this index
Insular possessions and dependencies, **28 § 2416**
International Trade Court, this index
Oyster growers, dredges and dredging, **28 § 2501**
Public Contracts, this index
Puerto Rico, **28 § 2416**
Quieting title, States, **28 § 2409a**
Rules of Appellate Procedure, this index
Securities, this index
Terrorists and terrorism, Foreign States, **28 § 1605A**
Torture, **28 § 1350 nt**
United States, this index

LINER VESSELS
Ships and Shipping, generally, this index

LIQUIDATED DAMAGES
United States Court of Federal Claims, **28 §§ 1491, 1499**

LIQUIDATIONS
International Trade Court, this index

LIS PENDENS
Terrorists and terrorism, Foreign States, **28 § 1605A**

LISTS
Court of Federal Claims, this index
Federal agencies, appeal and review, **28 § 2112**
Interpreters, this index
Jury, this index

LITERACY
Jurors, **28 § 1865**

LITERARY ASSOCIATIONS AND ORGANIZATIONS
Attorneys, fees, prevailing parties, **28 § 2412**
Costs, prevailing parties, **28 § 2412**

LITERATURE
Copyrights, generally, this index

LOANS
Colleges and Universities, this index
Interpleader, district court, jurisdiction, **28 § 1335**
Security Interest, generally, this index

LOCAL GOVERNMENT
Political Subdivisions, generally, this index

LODGING
Aliens, funds, **28 § 530C**
Bailiffs, **28 § 524**

LONG TERM CARE
Nursing Homes, generally, this index

LOS ANGELES, CA
Court of Appeals for Ninth Circuit, generally, this index

LOSSES
See specific index headings

LOST OR DESTROYED DOCUMENTS
Evidence, **28 §§ 1734, 1735**

LOUISIANA
Bankruptcy, judges or justices, appointments, **28 § 152**
District courts,
Cities, **28 § 98**
Judges or justices, **28 §§ 98 nt, 133**
Judicial circuit, **28 § 41**
Judicial districts, **28 § 98**
Bankruptcy, **28 § 581 nt**
Judges or justices, **28 § 133**
United States attorneys, appointments, **28 § 98 nt**

LOUISIANA—Cont'd
United States Marshals, appointments, **28 § 98 nt**
United States trustees, judicial districts, appointments, **28 § 581**

LOW INCOME FAMILIES OR PERSONS
Community Development, generally, this index

LOWER INCOME HOUSING
Community Development, generally, this index

LUXEMBOURG
Evidence, conventions, **28 § 1781 nt**

LYSERGIC ACID
Controlled Substances, generally, this index

LYSERGIC ACID AMIDE
Controlled Substances, generally, this index

MAGAZINES
Periodicals, generally, this index

MAGISTRATES
United States Magistrate Judges, generally, this index

MAIL AND MAILING
Certified or Registered Mail, generally, this index
First-class mail, jury, summons, **28 § 1866**
Government Accountability Office, this index
Jury, this index
Orders of court, remand, **28 § 1447**
Registered mail. Certified or Registered Mail, generally, this index
Rules of Appellate Procedure, this index
Rules of Civil Procedure, this index
Tort Claims Act, **28 § 2680**

MAINE
Court of Appeals for First Circuit, generally, this index
District courts,
Cities, **28 § 99**
Judges or justices, **28 § 133**
Judicial circuit, **28 § 41**
Judicial districts, **28 §§ 99, 133**
United States trustees, judicial districts, appointments, **28 § 581**

MALES
Domestic Violence, generally, this index

MALICE
See specific index headings

MALICIOUS PROSECUTION
Tort Claims Act, exception, claim arising from, **28 § 2680**

MANAGERS AND MANAGEMENT
Bankruptcy, this index
Property, this index

MANDAMUS
Carriers, equal facilities, **28 § 2321 et seq.**
District Courts, this index
Rules of Appellate Procedure, this index

MANDATES
See specific index headings

MANUFACTURERS AND MANUFACTURING
Customs Duties, this index
Patents, generally, this index

MARIANA ISLANDS
Northern Mariana Islands, generally, this index

MARINE CORPS
Cemeteries and dead bodies. National Cemeteries, generally, this index
Justice code. Military Justice Code, generally, this index
National Cemeteries, generally, this index
Reserves,
National Cemeteries, generally, this index
Retirement and pensions, United States magistrate judges, appointment, eligibility, **28 § 631**
United States magistrate judges, appointment, eligibility, **28 § 631**
Retirement and pensions, enlisted members, United States magistrate judges, appointment, eligibility, **28 § 631**
Tort Claims Act, **28 § 2680**

MARINE CORPS EXCHANGES
Commissary stores. Armed Forces, this index

MARINE CORPS RESERVE
Reserves. Marine Corps, this index

MARINERS
Seamen, generally, this index

MARINES
Marine Corps, generally, this index

MARITIME ADMINISTRATION
Appeal and review, orders, **28 § 2341 et seq.**
Orders, **28 § 2341 et seq.**

MARITIME CLAIMS
Admiralty, generally, this index

MARITIME COMMISSION
Federal Maritime Commission, generally, this index

MARKETS AND MARKETING
Exports and Imports, generally, this index

MARKETS AND MARKETING—Cont'd
Telemarketing. Telecommunications, this index

MARRIAGE
Assault and battery. Domestic Violence, generally, this index
Domestic Violence, generally, this index
Judges or justices, annuities, survivors, **28 § 376**
Same sex marriages, **28 § 1738C**

MARSHALS
Rules of Civil Procedure, this index
Supreme Court Marshal, generally, this index
United States Marshals Service, generally, this index

MARYLAND
Bankruptcy, judges or justices, appointments, **28 § 152**
District courts,
Judges or justices, **28 § 133**
Location, **28 § 100**
District of Columbia, generally, this index
Judicial Circuit of U.S., **28 § 41**
Judicial districts, **28 § 100**
Bankruptcy, **28 § 581 nt**
Judges or justices, **28 § 133**
United States trustees, judicial districts, **28 § 581**

MASSACHUSETTS
Bankruptcy, judges or justices, appointments, **28 § 152**
Court of Appeals for First Circuit, generally, this index
District courts,
Cities, **28 § 101**
Judges or justices, **28 § 133**
Judicial circuit, **28 § 41**
Judicial districts, **28 § 101**
Judges or justices, **28 § 133**
Jury, Federal courts, **28 § 1863**
United States trustees of judicial districts, appointment, **28 § 581**

MASTER AND SERVANT
Rules of Civil Procedure, this index

MASTER JURY WHEEL
Generally, **28 § 1863 et seq.**
Grand Jury, this index

MASTER OF VESSEL
Customs Duties, generally, this index

MASTERS
Clerks of courts, appointment, **28 § 957**
Rules of Civil Procedure, this index
Three judge court, appointment, **28 § 2284**

MDMA
Controlled Substances, this index

MEALS
Jury, **28 § 524**

MEDIATION AND MEDIATORS
Alternative Dispute Resolution, generally, this index
Federal Judicial Center, training, of, **28 § 620**

MEDICAL CARE AND TREATMENT
Correctional Institutions, this index
Drugs and Medicine, generally, this index
Long term care. Nursing Homes, generally, this index
Nursing Homes, generally, this index
Rules of Evidence, this index

MEDICAL EXAMINATION
Judges or justices, annuities, survivors, **28 § 376**

MEDICARE
Physicians and surgeons, Judicial Center, **28 § 2073**

MEDICINE
Drugs and Medicine, generally, this index

MEETINGS
See specific index headings

MENTAL HEALTH
Annuities, dependents, judges or justices, **28 § 376**
Bankruptcy, this index
Rules of Civil Procedure, this index

MENTAL INCOMPETENTS
Incompetency, generally, this index

MENTALLY RETARDED PERSONS
Incompetency, generally, this index

MEPROBAMATE
Controlled Substances, generally, this index

MERCHANT VESSELS
Ships and Shipping, generally, this index

MERIT SYSTEMS PROTECTION BOARD
Administrative Office of U.S. Courts, appeal and review, **28 § 602 nt**
Appeal and review,
Administrative Office of U.S. Courts, **28 § 602 nt**
U.S. Court of Appeals for the Federal Circuit, **28 § 1295**
United States Marshals, reemployment rights, **28 § 569**
Discrimination, United States Court of Appeals for the Federal Circuit, **28 § 1295**
United States Court of Appeals for the Federal Circuit, **28 § 1295**
United States Marshals, reemployment rights, **28 § 569**

MESCALINE
Controlled Substances, generally, this index

MESSENGERS
Courts, compensation and salaries, **28 §§ 603 nt, 604**
Courts of appeals, **28 § 714**
District courts, criers, **28 § 755**
United States attorneys, **28 § 550**
United States Court of Federal Claims, **28 § 795**
United States Court of International Trade, criers, **28 § 872**

METAZOCINE
Controlled Substances, generally, this index

METHADONE
Controlled Substances, generally, this index

METHAMPHETAMINES
Controlled Substances, this index

METHOHEXITAL
Controlled Substances, generally, this index

METHYLDESORPHINE
Controlled Substances, generally, this index

METHYLHYDROMORPHINE
Controlled Substances, generally, this index

METHYLPHENIDATE
Controlled Substances, generally, this index

METHYLPHENOBARBITAL
Controlled Substances, generally, this index

METHYPRYLON
Controlled Substances, generally, this index

MEXICO
Boundaries, United States-Mexico Border Violence Task Force, **28 § 509 nt**
United States-Mexico Border Violence Task Force, **28 § 509 nt**

MICHIGAN
Bankruptcy, judges or justices, appointments, **28 § 152**
District courts,
Judges or justices, **28 § 133**
Location, **28 § 102**
Western district, **28 § 133 nt**
Judicial circuit, **28 § 41**
Judicial districts, **28 § 102**
Bankruptcy, **28 § 581 nt**
Judges or justices, **28 § 133**

MICHIGAN—Cont'd
United States trustees, judicial districts, appointments, **28 § 581**

MICROCHIPS
Semiconductors, generally, this index

MICROFILMS AND MICROPHOTOGRAPHS
Business records, evidence, **28 § 1732**
Records and recordation, business records, evidence, **28 § 1732**
Supreme Court, **28 § 674**

MICROPHOTOGRAPHS
Microfilms and Microphotographs, generally, this index

MIDDLE EAST
Iraq, generally, this index

MIDWAY ISLANDS
Judicial District of Hawaii, **28 § 91**

MILEAGE
Traveling Expenses, generally, this index

MILITARY APPEALS COURT
Court of Appeals for the Armed Forces, generally, this index

MILITARY COURTS
Court of Appeals for the Armed Forces, generally, this index
Military Justice Code, generally, this index

MILITARY DEPARTMENTS
Administrative law and procedure, enforcement, reports, **28 § 530D**
Attorney General, **28 § 513**
Attorneys,
Fees, prevailing parties, **28 § 2412**
Prevailing parties, fees, **28 § 2412**
Civil Service, generally, this index
Claims, torts, **28 § 2671 et seq.**
Compromise and settlement, reports, **28 § 530D**
Costs, prevailing parties, **28 § 2412**
Enforcement, statutes, reports, **28 § 530D**
Fees, attorneys, prevailing parties, **28 § 2412**
Foreign Service, generally, this index
Hearings, witnesses, **28 § 2412**
Injunctions, reports, **28 § 530D**
Investigations, **28 § 535**
Opinions and decisions, reports, **28 § 530D**
Public policy, statutes, enforcement, reports, **28 § 530D**
Reports,
Injunctions, **28 § 530D**
Opinions and decisions, **28 § 530D**
Statutes, enforcement, **28 § 530D**
Statutes, enforcement, reports, **28 § 530D**
Torts, claims, **28 § 2671 et seq.**

MILITARY DEPARTMENTS—Cont'd
United States Court of Appeals for the Federal Circuit, petitions, **28 § 520**
United States Court of Federal Claims, petitions, **28 § 520**
Witnesses, **28 § 2412**

MILITARY FORCES
Armed Forces, generally, this index

MILITARY JUSTICE CODE
Aliens, detention, **28 § 2241**
Appeal and review. Court of Appeals for the Armed Forces, generally, this index
Combatants, enemy combatants, **28 § 2241**
Detention,
Aliens, **28 § 2241**
Combatants, enemy combatants, **28 § 2241**
Enemies, combatants, enemy combatants, **28 § 2241**
Immigration, detention, **28 § 2241**
Terrorists and terrorism, aliens, **28 § 2241**

MILITARY REVIEW COURTS
Court of Appeals for the Armed Forces, generally, this index

MILITIA
Navy, this index

MINITRIALS
Administrative Law and Procedure, generally, this index
Alternative Dispute Resolution, generally, this index

MINNESOTA
Bankruptcy, judges or justices, appointments, **28 § 152**
District courts, **28 § 103**
Judges or justices, **28 § 133**
Location, **28 § 103**
Indians,
Actions and proceedings, **28 § 1360**
Proceedings, **28 § 1360**
Judicial circuit, **28 § 41**
Judicial districts, **28 §§ 103, 133**
United States trustees, judicial districts, appointments, **28 § 581**

MINOR OR PETTY OFFENSES
United States Magistrate Judges, this index
United States Sentencing Commission, reports, **28 § 994**

MINORITY GROUPS
Antidiscrimination in Federal employment. Discrimination, generally, this index
Discrimination, generally, this index
United States magistrate judges, merit selection panel, **28 § 631 nt**

MINORS
Children and Minors, generally, this index

MINUTES
See specific index headings

MISCONDUCT
See specific index headings

MISDEMEANORS
Crimes and Offenses, generally, this index

MISLEADING STATEMENTS
Fraud, generally, this index

MISREPRESENTATION
Fraud, generally, this index

MISSING CHILDREN
Information, collection, **28 § 534**
Unemancipated persons, **28 § 534**

MISSIONS
See specific index headings

MISSISSIPPI
Bankruptcy, judges or justices, appointments, **28 § 152**
District courts,
Cities, **28 § 104**
Judges, **28 § 133**
Places of holding, **28 § 104**
Judicial Circuit of U.S., **28 § 41**
Judicial districts, **28 § 104**
Bankruptcy, **28 § 581 nt**
Number of district judges, **28 § 133**
United States trustees of judicial districts, appointment, **28 § 581**

MISSOURI
Bankruptcy, judges or justices, appointments, **28 § 152**
District courts,
Cities, **28 § 105**
Judges, **28 § 133**
Judicial Circuit of U.S., **28 § 41**
Judicial districts, **28 § 105**
Bankruptcy, **28 § 581 nt**
Judges, **28 § 133**
United States trustees, judicial districts, **28 § 581**

MISTAKE
See specific index headings

MOBILE COMMUNICATIONS
Telecommunications, generally, this index

MOBILE TELEPHONES
Telecommunications, generally, this index

MODIFICATION
See specific index headings

MONEY
Actions and proceedings, **28 § 2407**
Appropriations, generally, this index
Bankruptcy, this index
Budget, generally, this index
Counterfeiting, generally, this index
Delinquencies, actions and proceedings, payment, **28 § 2407**
Disbursing Officials, Clerks, and Agents, generally, this index
Federal Aid, generally, this index
Funds, generally, this index
Government Accountability Office, generally, this index
Interpleader, jurisdiction, **28 § 1335**
Rules of Civil Procedure, this index
Tort Claims Act, exemptions, **28 § 2680**
Treasury of United States, generally, this index

MONEY LAUNDERING
Attorneys, Special Counsel, **28 § 509 nt**
Reports, Federal prosecutors, **28 § 994 nt**

MONOPOLIES AND COMBINATIONS
Actions and proceedings, Judicial Panel on Multidistrict Litigation, **28 § 1407**
District courts, **28 § 1337**
Jurisdiction, **28 § 1337**
Exports and Imports, this index
Jurisdiction, **28 §§ 1337, 1338**
Multidistrict litigation, exemptions, **28 § 1407**
Patents, generally, this index

MONTANA
Bankruptcy, judges or justices, appointments, **28 § 152**
Court of Appeals for Ninth Circuit, generally, this index
District courts,
Judges or justices, **28 § 133**
Location, **28 § 106**
Judicial circuit, **28 § 41**
Judicial districts, **28 § 106**
Bankruptcy, **28 § 581 nt**
Judges or justices, **28 § 133**
United States trustees, judicial districts, appointments, **28 § 581**

MORAMIDE
Controlled Substances, generally, this index

MORGAN P. HARDIMAN CHILD ABDUCTION AND SERIAL MURDER INVESTIGATIVE RESOURCES CENTER
Generally, **28 § 531 nt**

MORPHERIDINE
Controlled Substances, generally, this index

MORPHINE
Controlled Substances, generally, this index

MORTGAGES
Discharge, **28 § 2410**
Fair Housing, generally, this index
United States, actions and proceedings, **28 § 2410**

MOTHERS
Children and Minors, generally, this index

MOTION PICTURES
Collective bargaining agreements, copyrights, **28 § 4001**
Copyrights, collective bargaining agreements, **28 § 4001**

MOTIONS
Bankruptcy, this index
Dismissal and nonsuit, **28 § 2284**
International Trade Court, this index
Judicial Panel On Multidistrict Litigation, this index
Jury, challenges, **28 § 1867**
Multidistrict litigation, pretrial proceedings, **28 § 1407**
Open courts, **28 § 452**
Remand, **28 § 1448**
Rules of Appellate Procedure, this index
Rules of Civil Procedure, this index
Sentence and Punishment, this index
Supreme Court, this index
Surface Transportation Board, **28 § 2323**
United States, public money, delinquencies, **28 § 2407**

MOTOR BOATS
Boats and Boating, generally, this index

MOTOR CARRIERS
Actions and proceedings, connecting carriers, **28 § 1337**
Connecting carriers, actions and proceedings, **28 § 1337**
Receipts, **28 § 1337**
Surface Transportation Board, generally, this index

MOTOR VEHICLES
Common carriers. Motor Carriers, generally, this index
Federal Agencies, this index
Insurance, Justice Department, funds, **28 § 530C**
Justice Department, funds, **28 § 530C**

MOTORBOATS
Boats and Boating, generally, this index

MULTIDISTRICT LITIGATION
Judicial Panel On Multidistrict Litigation, generally, this index

MULTIPARTY AND MULTIFORUM
District Courts, this index

MUNICIPAL CORPORATIONS
Chapter 9 proceedings. Bankruptcy, this index
Criminal background checks, exchanges, **28 § 534**
Indebtedness, chapter 9 proceedings. Bankruptcy, this index

MURDER
Attorney General, serial killings, **28 § 540B**
Child Abduction and Serial Murder Investigative Resources Center, **28 § 531 nt**
FBI, serial killings, **28 § 540B**
Foreign officials, conspiracy, **28 § 956**
Morgan P. Hardiman Child Abduction and Serial Murder Investigative Resources Center, **28 § 531 nt**
Serial killings,
Child Abduction and Serial Murder Investigative Resources Center, **28 § 531 nt**
Investigations and investigators, **28 § 540B**

MUTUAL FUNDS
Disqualification, judges or justices, **28 § 455**
Judges or justices, disqualification, **28 § 455**

MUTUAL INSURANCE
Disqualification, judges or justices, **28 § 455**
Judges or justices, disqualification, **28 § 455**

MYROPHINE
Controlled Substances, generally, this index

N–A ACETYLANTHRANILIC ACID
Controlled Substances, generally, this index

N–PHENYL–N–[1–(2–PHENYLETHYL)–4–PIPERIDINYL] PROPANAMIDE
Controlled Substances, generally, this index

NAFTA
Customs Duties, this index

NALORPHINE
Controlled Substances, generally, this index

NAMES
Rules of Civil Procedure, this index
United States Bankruptcy Court, **28 § 151**

NARCOTICS
Controlled Substances, generally, this index

NATIONAL BANKS
Citizens and citizenship, **28 § 1348**
Conservators,
Jurisdiction, **28 § 1348**
Personal property, **28 § 2004**
Real estate, **28 § 2001 et seq.**
Injunctions,
Jurisdiction, **28 § 1348**
Venue, **28 § 1394**
Insolvency,
Conservators, generally, ante
Receivers and receivership, generally, post
Jurisdiction,
Conservators, **28 § 1348**
Injunctions, **28 § 1348**
Personal property, conservators, **28 § 2004**
Real estate, conservators, **28 § 2001 et seq.**
Receivers and receivership,
Injunctions, **28 § 1348**
Personal property, sales, **28 § 2004**
Real estate, sales, **28 §§ 2001, 2002**
Venue, **28 § 1394**
Winding up, jurisdiction, **28 § 1348**

NATIONAL CEMETERIES
Crimes and offenses, **28 § 994 nt**
Protection, property offenses, enhanced penalties, **28 § 994 nt**
Sentence and punishment, **28 § 994 nt**

NATIONAL COMMISSION ON JUDICIAL DISCIPLINE AND REMOVAL
Generally, **28 § 372 nt**

NATIONAL COUNTERINTELLIGENCE EXECUTIVE OFFICE
Espionage, **28 § 519 nt**

NATIONAL CRIME INFORMATION CENTER
Appropriations, **28 § 534 nt**
Definitions, **28 § 534**
Domestic violence, **28 § 534 nt**
Public policy, **28 § 534 nt**
Stalkers, **28 § 534 nt**

NATIONAL CURRENCY
Money, generally, this index

NATIONAL DEFENSE
Air Force, generally, this index
Army, generally, this index
Espionage, generally, this index
Intelligence, generally, this index
Marine Corps, generally, this index
National Guard, generally, this index
Navy, generally, this index
Secretary of Defense, generally, this index
Spies. Espionage, generally, this index

NATIONAL GANG INTELLIGENCE CENTER
Generally, **28 § 534 nt**

NATIONAL GUARD
Claims, torts, **28 § 2671 et seq.**
District of Columbia, United States magistrate judges, **28 § 631**
Officers and employees, torts, **28 § 2671 et seq.**
Torts, officers and employees, **28 § 2671 et seq.**
United States magistrate judges, **28 § 631**

NATIONAL INTELLIGENCE WORKFORCE
Federal Bureau of Investigation, **28 § 532 nt**

NATIONAL NARCOTICS ACT OF 1984
Controlled Substances, generally, this index

NATIONAL ORIGIN
Civil Rights, generally, this index
Civil service. Discrimination, generally, this index
Discrimination, generally, this index
Judges or justices, nominations, **28 §§ 44 nt, 133 nt**
Jury, **28 §§ 1862, 1867, 1869**

NATIONAL PARK SERVICE
United States magistrate judges, appointment and qualification in bi-State area under administration of, **28 § 631**

NATIONAL SECURITIES ACT
Securities, generally, this index

NATIONAL SECURITY
Armed Forces, generally, this index
Federal Bureau of Investigation, generally, this index
Intelligence, generally, this index
National Guard, generally, this index
Security, generally, this index

NATIVE AMERICANS
Indians, generally, this index

NATURAL RESOURCES
Attorney General, violations, **28 § 509 nt**

NATURALIZATION
Clerks of courts, payment, fees, **28 § 751**
Immigration and Naturalization Service, generally, this index

NAVY
Cemeteries and dead bodies. National Cemeteries, generally, this index
Commissary stores. Armed Forces, this index
District court crier or bailiff, appointments, preferences, **28 § 755**
Exchanges,
Contracts, claims, **28 § 1346**

NAVY—Cont'd
Exchanges—Cont'd
Express or implied contracts, United States Court of Federal Claims, jurisdiction, **28 § 1491**
Honorable discharges,
Bailiffs, **28 § 755**
Court criers, **28 § 755**
Justice code. Military Justice Code, generally, this index
Marine Corps, generally, this index
Military Justice Code, generally, this index
Militia, United States magistrate judges, eligibility, **28 § 631**
National Cemeteries, generally, this index
Reserves,
National Cemeteries, generally, this index
United States magistrate judges, appointments, eligibility, **28 § 631**
Retirement and pensions, United States magistrate judges, appointments, **28 § 631**
Stores and supplies, commissary stores. Armed Forces, this index
Tort Claims Act, **28 § 2680**
United States magistrate judges, retirees, eligibility, **28 § 631**

NAVY DEPARTMENT
Attorney General, advice, **28 § 513**

NCIC
National Crime Information Center, generally, this index

NEBRASKA
Bankruptcy, judges or justices, appointments, **28 § 152**
District courts,
Judges or justices, **28 § 133**
Location, **28 § 107**
Indians, jurisdiction, **28 § 1360**
Judicial circuit, **28 § 41**
Judicial districts, **28 § 107**
Bankruptcy, **28 § 581 nt**
Judges or justices, **28 § 133**
Jurisdiction, Indians, **28 § 1360**
United States trustees, judicial districts, appointments, **28 § 581**

NEGLIGENCE
Customs Duties, this index
Federal Officers and Employees, this index
Federal Tort Claims Act, **28 §§ 1346, 1402, 2401, 2402, 2411, 2412, 2671 et seq.**
Rules of Civil Procedure, this index

NEGOTIABLE INSTRUMENTS
Garnishment by U.S. in action commenced against corporation, **28 § 2405**
Interest, generally, this index

NEGOTIABLE INSTRUMENTS—Cont'd
Interpleader, district courts, jurisdiction, **28 § 1335**
Securities, generally, this index
Treasury Bills, generally, this index

NEGROES
Black Persons, generally, this index

NETHERLANDS
Convention on the Taking of Evidence Abroad in Civil or Commercial Matters, **28 § 1781 nt**
Evidence, Convention on the Taking of Evidence Abroad in Civil or Commercial Matters, **28 § 1781 nt**

NEUTRALITY
Alternative dispute resolution, **28 § 653**

NEVADA
Bankruptcy, judges or justices, appointments, **28 § 152**
Court of Appeals for Ninth Circuit, generally, this index
District courts, **28 § 108**
Judges or justices, **28 § 133**
Judicial districts, **28 § 108**
Bankruptcy, **28 § 581 nt**
Judges or justices, **28 § 133**
United States trustees of judicial districts, appointment, **28 § 581**

NEW DRUGS
Drugs and Medicine, this index

NEW HAMPSHIRE
Bankruptcy, judges or justices, appointments, **28 § 152**
Court of Appeals for First Circuit, generally, this index
District courts,
Judges or justices, **28 § 133**
Location, **28 § 109**
Judicial circuit, **28 § 41**
Judicial districts, **28 §§ 109, 133**
United States trustees, judicial districts, appointments, **28 § 581**

NEW JERSEY
Bankruptcy, judges or justices, appointments, **28 § 152**
District courts,
Judges or justices, **28 § 133**
Location, **28 § 110**
Judicial circuit, **28 § 41**
Judicial districts, **28 §§ 110, 133**
United States trustees, judicial districts, appointment, **28 § 581**

NEW MEXICO
Bankruptcy, judges or justices, appointments, **28 § 152**
District courts, **28 § 111**
Judges or justices, **28 § 133**
Judicial circuit, **28 § 41**
Judicial districts,
Bankruptcy, **28 § 581 nt**

NEW MEXICO—Cont'd
Judicial districts—Cont'd
Judges or justices, **28 § 133**
United States trustees, judicial districts, appointments, **28 § 581**

NEW ORLEANS, LA
Court of Appeals for Fifth Circuit, generally, this index

NEW TRIAL
Arbitration, **28 § 657**
Court of Federal Claims, this index
International Trade Court, this index
Rules of Civil Procedure, this index

NEW YORK
Bankruptcy, judges or justices, appointments, **28 § 152**
District courts,
Judges or justices, **28 §§ 133, 134**
Location, **28 § 112**
Eastern District, U.S. Attorneys, **28 § 545**
Judicial districts, **28 §§ 41, 112**
Bankruptcy, **28 § 581 nt**
Judges or justices, **28 § 133**
Southern District, clerks of court, **28 § 751**
United States trustees, appointments, **28 § 581**
Southern District,
United States attorneys, **28 § 545**
United States Marshals, **28 § 561**
United States attorneys, Southern District, **28 § 545**
United States Marshals, Southern District, **28 § 561**
United States trustees, judicial districts, appointments, **28 § 581**

NEW YORK CITY, NY
Court of Appeals for Second Circuit, generally, this index
International Trade Court, this index

NEWLY DISCOVERED EVIDENCE
Torts, United States, **28 § 2675**
United States, torts, **28 § 2675**

NEWS MEDIA
Copyrights, generally, this index

NEWSPAPERS
Attachment against delinquent postmasters and postal officers, employees, publication of executed warrant, **28 § 2715**
Legal notices, designation by assigned justices or judges, exception, **28 § 296**

NEXT OF KIN
Relatives, generally, this index

NICOCODEINE
Controlled Substances, generally, this index

NICOMORPHINE
Controlled Substances, generally, this index

NONCITIZENS
Aliens, generally, this index

NONCONTIGUOUS STATES
Alaska, generally, this index
Hawaii, generally, this index

NONPROFIT CORPORATIONS
Federal Judicial Center Foundation, establishment, **28 § 629**

NONPROFIT ORGANIZATIONS OR ASSOCIATIONS
Judicial Center, this index

NONRESIDENTS
Aliens, generally, this index
Courts, records and recordation, lost or destroyed property, **28 § 1734**
Income tax. Aliens, this index
Patents, service of process, **28 § 1694**
Postal Service, attachment, **28 §§ 2710, 2715**
Removal of cases or causes, Federal officers and employees, **28 § 1442**

NONSUIT
Dismissal and Nonsuit, generally, this index

NORACYMETHADOL
Controlled Substances, generally, this index

NORLEVEORPHANOL
Controlled Substances, generally, this index

NORLEVORPHANOL
Controlled Substances, generally, this index

NORMETHADONE
Controlled Substances, generally, this index

NORMORPHINE
Controlled Substances, generally, this index

NORPIPANONE
Controlled Substances, generally, this index

NORPSEUDOEPHEDRINE
Controlled Substances, generally, this index

NORTH CAROLINA
Bankruptcy, judges or justices, appointments, **28 § 152**
District courts, **28 § 133**
Cities, **28 § 113**
Judicial districts, **28 § 113**
Bankruptcy, **28 § 581 nt**

NORTH CAROLINA—Cont'd
Judicial districts—Cont'd
Judges or justices, **28 § 133**
United States trustees, judicial districts, appointments, **28 § 581**

NORTH DAKOTA
Bankruptcy, judges or justices, appointments, **28 § 152**
District courts,
Judges or justices, **28 § 133**
Location, **28 § 114**
Judicial circuit, **28 § 41**
Judicial districts, **28 §§ 114, 133**
United States trustees, judicial districts, appointments, **28 § 581**

NORTHERN MARIANA ISLANDS
District courts,
Judges or justices,
Annuities, survivors, **28 § 376**
Compensation and salaries, **28 § 373 nt**
U.S. Court of Appeals for the Federal Circuit, **28 § 1295**
Judicial districts, bankruptcy, **28 § 581 nt**
Tort Claims Act, **28 § 2680 nt**
United States Attorney, **28 § 545**
United States Court of Appeals for the Federal Circuit, **28 § 1295**
United States Marshal, **28 §§ 545, 561**
United States trustees of judicial districts, **28 § 581**

NORTHERN MARIANAS, COMMONWEALTH OF
Northern Mariana Islands, generally, this index

NORWAY
Evidence, Convention on the Taking of Evidence Abroad in Civil or Commercial Matters, **28 § 1781 nt**

NOTICE
Administrative Law and Procedure, this index
Administrative Office of United States Courts, this index
Appeal and Review, this index
Attachment, Post Office, officers and employees, **28 § 2716**
Attorney General, this index
Bankruptcy, this index
Class actions, fairness, **28 § 1715**
Clerks of District Courts, this index
Congress, this index
Copyrights, this index
Court of Federal Claims, this index
Courts of Appeals, this index
Depository Institutions, this index
Deposits in courts, claimant of fund, **28 § 2042**
District Courts, this index
Federal Agencies, this index
Federal Debt Collection, this index

NOTICE—Cont'd
Federal Officers and Employees, this index
Foreign Countries, this index
Foreign States, immunities, **28 § 1608**
Habeas corpus, **28 § 2252**
Indictment and information, fines, penalties and forfeitures, **28 § 2461**
Interlocutory injunctions, Federal agencies, **28 § 2349**
International Trade Court, this index
Judges or Justices, this index
Judicial Center, director of, election of retirement coverage, **28 §§ 376, 627**
Judicial Panel On Multidistrict Litigation, this index
Judicial sale of realty, **28 §§ 2001, 2002**
Jury, this index
Justices and judges, change of residence, **28 § 456**
Litigation notice system, **28 § 509 nt, EON 12146**
Lost or destroyed court records, **28 § 1734**
Maritime liens, **28 § 1605**
Multidistrict litigation, pretrial proceedings, **28 § 1407**
Postal Service, this index
Removal of case, **28 § 1446**
Rules of Appellate Procedure, this index
Rules of Civil Procedure, this index
Rules of Evidence, this index
Senate, this index
Special sessions,
Circuit courts, **28 § 48**
District courts, **28 § 141**
Supreme Court, this index
Terrorists and Terrorism, this index
Three judge court, hearing by, **28 § 2284**
United States Attorneys, this index
United States magistrate judges, appointment of, **28 § 631**
United States Marshal, fee for preparing public notice, **28 § 1921**
United States trustees, judicial districts, **28 § 581 nt**

NUMBERS AND NUMBERING
See specific index headings

NURSING HOMES
Confidential or privileged information, criminal background checks, labor and employment, **28 § 534 nt**
Criminal background checks, labor and employment, **28 § 534 nt**
Fees, criminal background checks, labor and employment, **28 § 534 nt**
Fines, penalties and forfeitures, criminal background checks, labor and employment, **28 § 534 nt**
Labor and employment, criminal background checks, **28 § 534 nt**

OATHS AND AFFIRMATIONS
Arbitration, referral from alternative dispute resolution, **28 § 655**

OATHS AND AFFIRMATIONS—Cont'd
Bankruptcy, this index
Clerks of Courts, this index
Congressional reference cases, **28 § 2509**
Convention on the Taking of Evidence Abroad in Civil or Commercial Matters, power of diplomatic officer, consular agent or commissioner to administer, **28 § 1781 nt**
Court of Federal Claims, this index
Courts of Appeals, this index
Delinquents for public money, continuance of action by U.S. against, **28 § 2407**
District court reporters, **28 § 753**
Evidence, this index
Habeas corpus, denial of facts set forth in return, **28 § 2243**
Judges or Justices, this index
Party, proof of amount in controversy for review by court of appeals, **28 § 2108**
Perjury, generally, this index
Reporters, district courts, **28 § 753**
Rules of Appellate Procedure, this index
Special Assistant to Attorney General or special attorney, **28 § 515**
United States attorneys, **28 § 544**
United States magistrate judges, **28 §§ 631, 636**
United States trustees, **28 § 583**
Unsworn declarations, perjury, **28 § 1746**

OBJECTIONS AND EXCEPTIONS
Rules of Civil Procedure, this index

OBSOLETE PAPERS
Courts, disposition, **28 § 457**

OCEAN LINERS
Ships and Shipping, generally, this index

OCEANS
Admiralty, generally, this index
Fines, penalties and forfeitures, **28 § 2461**
Ships and Shipping, generally, this index
Solid waste, United States Marshals, appointment, advice and consent, **28 § 561**
Vessels. Ships and Shipping, generally, this index

OFFENSES
Crimes and Offenses, generally, this index

OFFICE OF MANAGEMENT AND BUDGET
Courts, budget, **28 § 605**

OFFICERS AND EMPLOYEES
Administrative Office of United States Courts, this index
Bureau of Alcohol, Tobacco, Firearms, and Explosives, this index
Circuit executive (Courts of appeals), **28 § 332**

OFFICERS AND EMPLOYEES—Cont'd
Civil Service, generally, this index
Congress, this index
Court of Federal Claims, this index
Courts, this index
Courts of Appeals, this index
District Courts, this index
Districts, this index
Drug Enforcement Administration, this index
Executive Departments, this index
Federal Officers and Employees, generally, this index
Foreign Diplomatic and Consular Officers, generally, this index
Government Accountability Office, this index
Governor, generally, this index
Guards, generally, this index
House of Representatives, this index
Insular Possessions and Dependencies, this index
Internal Revenue Service, this index
International Trade Court, this index
Judges or Justices, generally, this index
Justice Department, this index
Law Enforcement Officers, generally, this index
Legislature, this index
National Guard, this index
Political Subdivisions, this index
Probation, this index
Rules of Appellate Procedure, this index
Rules of Civil Procedure, this index
Senate, this index
States, this index
Supreme Court, this index
Treasury Department, this index

OFFICES
Crime Victims, this index
Review, orders, certain Federal agencies, venue, **28 § 2343**
Terrorists and Terrorism, this index
United States Court of International Trade, location, **28 § 251**
United States Marshals, **28 § 561**

OFFICIAL DUTY STATION
Justices and judges, **28 § 456**

OFFICIAL NOTICE
Notice, generally, this index

OFFICIAL SEALS
Seals (Official Seals), generally, this index

OFFICIAL STATIONS
Bankruptcy, courts, judges or justices, **28 § 152**
Clerks of district court, **28 § 751**
United States attorneys, **28 § 545**
United States Marshals, **28 § 561**

OGDEN, UT
United States District Court, location, **28 § 125**

OHIO
Bankruptcy, judges or justices, appointments, **28 § 152**
District courts,
Cities, held at, **28 § 115**
Judges, **28 § 133**
Places of holding, **28 § 115**
Judicial Circuit of U.S., **28 § 41**
Judicial districts, **28 § 115**
Bankruptcy, **28 § 581 nt**
Number of district judges, **28 § 133**
United States trustees of judicial districts, appointment, **28 § 581**

OKLAHOMA
Bankruptcy, judges or justices, appointments, **28 § 152**
District courts,
Judges or justices, **28 § 133**
Location, **28 § 116**
Judicial circuit, **28 § 41**
Judicial districts,
Bankruptcy, **28 § 581 nt**
Judges or justices, **28 § 133**
United States trustees, judicial districts, appointments, **28 § 581**

OKLAHOMA CITY, OK
Counterterrorism Fund, **28 § 524 nt**
Court of Appeals for Tenth Circuit, generally, this index

OLD PERSONS
Aged Persons, generally, this index

OMAHA, NE
Court of Appeals for Eighth Circuit, generally, this index

OMISSIONS
See specific index headings

OPERATORS
See specific index headings

OPINIONS AND DECISIONS
Attorney General, this index
Court of Federal Claims, this index
International Trade Court, this index
Rules of Appellate Procedure, this index
Rules of Civil Procedure, this index
Supreme Court, this index

ORAL ARGUMENT
Court of Appeals for the Federal Circuit, this index
International Trade Court, this index
Rules of Appellate Procedure, this index
Supreme Court, this index

ORAL TESTIMONY
Evidence, generally, this index

ORDERS
See specific index headings

ORDERS OF COURT
Bankruptcy, this index
Change of venue, **28 § 1404**

ORDERS OF COURT—Cont'd
Court always open for making, **28 § 452**
Court of Appeals for Fifth Circuit, this index
Court of Appeals for the District of Columbia, this index
Court of Federal Claims, this index
District Courts, this index
Fines, Penalties and Forfeitures, this index
Grand Jury, this index
Habeas Corpus, this index
International Trade Court, this index
Judges or justices, complaints, **28 § 352**
Judicial Panel On Multidistrict Litigation, this index
Lost or destroyed record, verified application for order establishing record, **28 § 1734**
Mail and Mailing, this index
Moneys paid into court, criminal appearance bail bond, use to pay fine, assessment, **28 § 2044**
Property in different districts affected, **28 § 1692**
Protective orders,
International Trade Court, this index
Rules of Civil Procedure, this index
Removal of Cases or Causes, this index
Revenue laws, property taken under subject to, **28 § 2463**
Rules of Appellate Procedure, this index
Rules of Civil Procedure, this index
Show Cause Orders, generally, this index
Support, this index
Supreme Court, this index
Withdrawal of money deposited in court, **28 § 2042**
Witnesses, this index

OREGON
Bankruptcy, judges or justices, appointments, **28 § 152**
Court of Appeals for Ninth Circuit, generally, this index
District courts,
Judges or justices, **28 § 133**
Location, **28 § 117**
Indians, jurisdiction, **28 § 1360**
Judicial circuit, **28 § 41**
Judicial districts, **28 § 117**
Bankruptcy, **28 § 581 nt**
Judges or justices, **28 § 133**
United States trustees, judicial districts, appointments, **28 § 581**

ORIGIN
National Origin, generally, this index

ORIGINAL JURISDICTION
Generally, **28 § 1251**
District Courts, this index

ORTHOPEDICALLY IMPAIRED PERSONS
Handicapped Persons, generally, this index

OSAGE INDIANS
Allotments, real estate, **28 § 1353**
Real estate, allotments, **28 § 1353**

OUTLYING POSSESSIONS
Insular Possessions and Dependencies, generally, this index

OUTSOURCING
Intervention, **28 § 1491**

OVERPAYMENT
See specific index headings

OYSTERS
Dredges and dredging,
Actions and proceedings, **28 §§ 1497, 2501**
Damages, **28 § 1497**

PACKERS
Orders, **28 § 2351**

PALMYRA ISLAND
Judicial District of Hawaii, **28 § 91**

PAMPHLETS
Supreme Court, this index

PANAMA, REPUBLIC OF
Canal Zone, generally, this index

PANAMA CANAL COMPANY
Tort Claims Act, **28 § 2680**

PANAMA CANAL ZONE
Canal Zone, generally, this index

PANELS
Bankruptcy appellate panels. Bankruptcy, this index
Court of Appeals for the Federal Circuit, this index
Courts of appeals, senior circuit judge, in banc court, **28 § 46**
Judicial Panel On Multidistrict Litigation, generally, this index
Jury, this index

PAPER AND PAPER PRODUCTS
Books and Papers, generally, this index

PAPER MONEY
Money, generally, this index

PAPERBACK BOOKS
Books and Papers, generally, this index

PAPERS
Books and Papers, generally, this index

PARALDEHYDE
Controlled Substances, generally, this index

PARDON
Jurors, qualifications, **28 § 1869**

PARENT AND CHILD
Children and Minors, generally, this index

PARIMUTUEL BETTING
Definitions, **28 § 534 nt**
Licenses and permits, **28 § 534 nt**

PARIMUTUEL LICENSING SIMPLIFICATION ACT OF 1988
Generally, **28 § 534 nt**

PARKING
Jurors, fees, **28 § 1871**

PAROLE
Aliens, this index
Supervised release. Sentence and Punishment, this index

PARTIES
Absence and absentees, defendants, orders of court, **28 § 1655**
Administrative Law and Procedure, this index
Change of venue, **28 § 1404**
Collusive joinder, **28 § 1359**
Court of Federal Claims, this index
Depositions, generally, this index
Disability, time for commencing action against U.S., **28 § 2401**
Disqualification, judges or justices, **28 § 455**
Federal Agencies, this index
Handicapped Persons, this index
Improper joinder, lack of jurisdiction of district court, **28 § 1359**
International Trade Court, this index
Intervention, generally, this index
Judges or justices, disqualification, **28 § 455**
Jury, number of challenges permitted, **28 § 1870**
Multidistrict litigation, pretrial proceedings, **28 § 1407**
Peremptory challenges in civil cases, additional, multiple plaintiffs and defendants, **28 § 1870**
Personal conduct of case in court, **28 § 1654**
Review, orders, certain Federal agencies, **28 § 2348**
Rules of Appellate Procedure, this index
Rules of Civil Procedure, this index
Rules of Evidence, this index
Supreme Court, this index
Surface Transportation Board, proceedings to enforce orders of Board, **28 § 2323**
Tax liens, quieting title, **28 § 2410**
United States, this index
Venue, generally, this index

PARTITION
Liens and incumbrances, **28 § 2410**
United States, this index
United States Marshals, fees, **28 § 1921**

PARTNERSHIP
Attorneys, fees, prevailing parties, **28 § 2412**
Bankruptcy, this index
Income tax, final partnership administrative adjustments, **28 § 1346**
Rules of Civil Procedure, this index

PARTY
Parties, generally, this index

PASADENA, CA
Court of Appeals for Ninth Circuit, generally, this index

PASSENGERS
Customs Duties, generally, this index

PATENT AND TRADEMARK OFFICE
Disclaimer, infringement, **28 § 1928**
Records and recordation, evidence, **28 § 1744**
Seals (official seals), copies, documents, **28 § 1744**

PATENTS
Board of Patent Appeals and Interferences, United States Court of Appeals for the Federal Circuit, jurisdiction, **28 § 1295**
Claims, foreign countries, **28 § 1498**
Copies, letters patent, **28 § 1744**
Costs, infringement, **28 § 1928**
Court of Appeals for the Federal Circuit, this index
Court of Federal Claims, this index
Disclaimers, costs, **28 § 1928**
District Courts, this index
Drugs and Medicine, this index
Evidence, **28 § 1744**
Foreign Patents, generally, this index
Infringement,
Costs, **28 § 1928**
Nonresidents, service of process, **28 § 1694**
Patent and Trademark Office, generally, this index
Process, nonresidents, **28 § 1694**
Rules of Civil Procedure, this index
Summons,
Infringement, **28 § 1694**
Interference, **28 § 1694**
Venue, **28 § 1400**

PAY AND ALLOWANCES
Compensation and Salaries, generally, this index

PAY (REMUNERATION)
Compensation and Salaries, generally, this index

PAYMENT
See specific index headings

PENAL CODE
Crimes and Offenses, generally, this index

PENAL INSTITUTIONS
Correctional Institutions, generally, this index

PENAL LAWS
Crimes and Offenses, generally, this index

PENALTIES
Fines, Penalties and Forfeitures, generally, this index

PENDING ACTIONS
See specific index headings

PENITENTIARIES
Correctional Institutions, generally, this index

PENNSYLVANIA
Bankruptcy, judges or justices, appointments, **28 § 152**
District courts, **28 § 118**
Judges or justices, **28 § 133**
Judicial circuit, **28 § 41**
Judicial districts, **28 § 118**
Bankruptcy, **28 § 581 nt**
Judges or justices, **28 § 133**
United States trustees, appointments, **28 § 581**

PENOLOGISTS
Sentence and punishment, **28 § 334**

PENSIONS
Retirement and Pensions, generally, this index

PER DIEM
Courts of appeals, structural alternatives for the Federal Courts of Appeals Commission, **28 § 41 nt**
Ninth Circuit Court of Appeals, judges or justices, **28 § 297**
Structural alternatives for the Federal Courts of Appeals Commission, **28 § 41 nt**
Witnesses, **28 § 1821**

PEREMPTORY CHALLENGES
Jury, **28 §§ 1866, 1870**

PERFORMANCE BONDS
Bonds (Officers and Fiduciaries), generally, this index

PERIODICALS
Administrative Office of U.S. Courts, **28 § 413**
Attorney General, procurement, **28 §§ 413, 525**
Foreign patent offices, copies, evidence, **28 § 1745**
Rules of Evidence, this index
Supreme Court, **28 §§ 672, 674**

PERISHABLE GOODS
Federal debt collection, presumptions, **28 § 3007**

PERJURY
Actions and proceedings, unsworn declarations, **28 § 1746**
Evidence, unsworn declarations, **28 § 1746**
Unsworn declarations, **28 § 1746**

PERMANENT RESIDENCE
Immigration, this index

PERSONAL INJURIES
Bankruptcy, this index
Damages, generally, this index
Definitions, district courts, multiparty and multiforum, **28 § 1369**
District courts, jurisdiction,
Civil rights, interference with, **28 § 1343**
Damages in enforcing right of citizens to vote, **28 § 1357**
Foreign States, privileges and immunities, **28 § 1605**

PERSONAL PROPERTY
Damages, generally, this index
Federal Debt Collection, this index
Judicial sales, **28 § 2004**
National Banks, this index

PERSONAL REPRESENTATIVES
Executors and Administrators, generally, this index
Guardian and Ward, generally, this index

PETHIDINE
Controlled Substances, generally, this index

PETIT JURY
Jury, generally, this index

PETITIONS
Court of Appeals for the Federal Circuit, this index
Court of Federal Claims, this index
Customs Duties, this index
Habeas Corpus, this index
International Trade Court, this index
Judicial Center Board, special meetings, **28 § 622**
Judicial Panel On Multidistrict Litigation, this index
Petitioner, definitions, review, orders of Federal agencies, **28 § 2341**
Rules of Appellate Procedure, this index
Supreme Court, this index

PETRICHLORAL
Controlled Substances, generally, this index

PHENADOXONE
Controlled Substances, generally, this index

PHENAMPROMIDE
Controlled Substances, generally, this index

PHENAZOCINE
Controlled Substances, generally, this index

PHENMETRAZINE
Controlled Substances, generally, this index

PHENOBARBITAL
Controlled Substances, generally, this index

PHENOMORPHAN
Controlled Substances, generally, this index

PHENOPERIDINE
Controlled Substances, generally, this index

PHENYLACETIC ACID
Controlled Substances, generally, this index

PHILADELPHIA PA
Court of Appeals for Third Circuit, generally, this index

PHOLCODINE
Controlled Substances, generally, this index

PHONOGRAPHS AND PHONOGRAPH RECORDS
District courts, sessions, **28 § 753**

PHOTOGRAPHY AND PICTURES
Business records, evidence, **28 § 1732**
Copyrights, generally, this index
Microfilms and Microphotographs, generally, this index
Rules of Civil Procedure, this index
Rules of Evidence, this index

PHOTOSTATIC COPIES
See specific index headings

PHYSICAL EXAMINATIONS
Rules of Civil Procedure, this index

PHYSICAL INFIRMITIES
Jurors, qualification for service, **28 § 1865**
Form, contents concerning, **28 § 1869**

PHYSICAL INJURIES
Personal Injuries, generally, this index

PHYSICAL SECURITY
Security, generally, this index

PHYSICALLY HANDICAPPED PERSONS
Handicapped Persons, generally, this index

PHYSICIANS AND SURGEONS
Drugs and Medicine, generally, this index
Medicare, this index

PIMINODINE
Controlled Substances, generally, this index

PIPRADOL
Controlled Substances, generally, this index

PIRITRAMIDE
Controlled Substances, generally, this index

PISTOLS AND REVOLVERS
Weapons, generally, this index

PLACE OF TRIAL
Venue, generally, this index

PLANS AND SPECIFICATIONS
Community Development, this index
District courts, civil justice expense and delay reduction plans, **28 § 471 et seq.**
Judicial Conference of the United States, assignments, **28 § 331**
Jurors, random selection, **28 § 1863**
Rules of Civil Procedure, this index
Rules of Evidence, this index

PLANT VARIETY PROTECTION
Generally, **28 § 1498**
Appeal and review,
Refusal, application for protection of variety, jurisdiction, U.S. Court of Appeals for the Federal Circuit, **28 § 1295**
United States Court of Appeals for the Federal Circuit and other review, **28 § 1295**
Applications, protection of varieties, appeals from refusal, jurisdiction, U.S. Court of Appeals for the Federal Circuit, **28 § 1295**
Cease and desist, false marking, appeal and review, jurisdiction, U.S. Court of Appeals for the Federal Circuit, **28 § 1295**
Certificates and certification, reexamination, appeal and review, jurisdiction, **28 § 1295**
Damages, infringement cases, action against U.S. for infringement, **28 § 1498**
District courts, original jurisdiction of actions relating to, **28 § 1338**
False markings, cease and desist orders, appeal and review, jurisdiction, **28 § 1295**
Infringement, by U.S., or federally owned or controlled corporation, exclusive remedy by action in U.S. Court of Federal Claims for recovery of damages, **28 § 1498**
Jurisdiction, appeal and review, **28 § 1295**
Priorities and preferences, appeal and review, **28 § 1295**

PLANT VARIETY PROTECTION —Cont'd
Public interest in wide usage, appeals from decisions respecting, jurisdiction, U.S. Court of Appeals for the Federal Circuit, **28 § 1295**
Reexamination, appeal and review, **28 § 1295**
United States Court of Appeals for the Federal Circuit, jurisdiction, appeals from decisions, **28 § 1295**
United States Court of Federal Claims, exclusive remedy of owner of certificate by action against U.S. for damages for infringement, **28 § 1498**

PLANTS AND PLANT PRODUCTS
Protection. Plant Variety Protection, generally, this index
Variety protection. Plant Variety Protection, generally, this index

PLEA BARGAINING
Rules of Criminal Procedure, this index

PLEA IN ABATEMENT
Postal Service, attachment, **28 § 2713**

PLEA OF NOLO CONTENDERE
Rules of Evidence, this index

PLEA OR ANSWER
Rules of Appellate Procedure, this index
Rules of Civil Procedure, this index

PLEADING
Absent defendants, **28 § 1655**
Amendments, jurisdiction, **28 § 1653**
Bankruptcy, this index
Court of Federal Claims, this index
Declaratory judgments, **28 § 2201**
District courts, continuance, **28 § 143**
Espionage, **28 § 519 nt**
Federal Agencies, this index
Habeas corpus, **28 § 2244**
International Trade Court, this index
Interpleader, generally, this index
Judicial Panel On Multidistrict Litigation, this index
Removal of cases, **28 § 1446**
Rules of Civil Procedure, this index
Tax liens, **28 § 2410**
United States, this index

POISONS
Controlled Substances, generally, this index

POLICE
Federal Bureau of Investigation, **28 § 540C**
Jury service, exemption, **28 § 1863**
Railroads, this index
Secret Service, generally, this index

POLITICAL ACTIVITIES
Disclosure of Federal Campaign Funds, generally, this index

POLITICAL ACTIVITIES—Cont'd
Federal Officers and Employees, this index

POLITICAL CONTRIBUTIONS
Disclosure of Federal Campaign Funds, generally, this index

POLITICAL PARTIES
Disclosure of Federal Campaign Funds, generally, this index
Jury Commission, **28 § 1863**
United States Court of International Trade, judges, **28 § 251**

POLITICAL SUBDIVISIONS
Bankruptcy, this index
Bureau of Investigation, records and recordation, exchanges, **28 § 534 nt**
Community Development, generally, this index
Counterfeiting, officers and employees, emblems and insignia, **28 § 994 nt**
Crimes and offenses. Officers and employees, post
Districts, generally, this index
Emblems and insignia, officers and employees, counterfeiting, **28 § 994 nt**
Employees. Officers and employees, generally, post
Firefighters and firefighting, jury, exemptions, **28 § 1863**
Officers and employees,
  Crimes and offenses,
    Emblems and insignia, **28 § 994 nt**
    Reports, **28 § 529**
    Uniforms, **28 § 994 nt**
  Emblems and insignia, counterfeiting, **28 § 994 nt**
  Jury, exemptions, **28 § 1863**
  Reports, crimes and offenses, **28 § 529**
  Uniforms, crimes and offenses, **28 § 994 nt**
Police, exemption from jury service, **28 § 1863**
Rate orders, jurisdiction of district courts, **28 § 1342**
Taxation, court officers, liability, **28 § 960**
Uniforms, officers and employees, crimes and offenses, **28 § 994 nt**

PORTLAND, OR
Court of Appeals for Ninth Circuit, generally, this index

PORTS
Harbors and Ports, generally, this index

PORTUGAL
Convention on Taking Evidence Abroad in Civil or Commercial Matters, **28 § 1781 nt**

POSSESSION
See specific index headings

POSSESSION, WRIT OF
Marshals, fees, **28 § 1921**

POSSESSIONS OF UNITED STATES
Insular Possessions and Dependencies, generally, this index

POST OFFICE DEPARTMENT
Actions and proceedings, interest, **28 § 2718**
Interest, actions and proceedings, **28 § 2718**

POST OFFICES
Postal Service, generally, this index

POSTAL SERVICE
Actions and proceedings, district courts, **28 § 1339**
Affidavits, attachment, **28 § 2711**
Alias warrants, attachment, **28 § 2710**
Answer, attachment, **28 § 2716**
Attachment, **28 § 2710 et seq.**
  Affidavits, **28 § 2711**
  Alias warrants, **28 § 2710**
  Answer, **28 § 2716**
  Applications, **28 § 2711**
  Bonds (officers and fiduciaries), discharge, **28 § 2717**
  Damages, **28 § 2713**
  Discharge, **28 § 2717**
  Evidence, **28 § 2711**
  Fraudulent conveyances, **28 § 2710**
  Interest, **28 § 2718**
  Investments, **28 § 2714**
  Issuance, **28 § 2712**
  Judgments and decrees, discharge, **28 § 2717**
  Jurisdiction, **28 §§ 2710, 2711**
  Jury, **28 § 2713**
  Nonresidents, **28 §§ 2710, 2715**
  Notice, personal notice, **28 § 2716**
  Personal notice, **28 § 2716**
  Plea in abatement, **28 § 2713**
  Process, **28 § 2716**
  Publication, **28 § 2715**
  Returns, discharge, **28 § 2717**
  Rights, **28 § 2710**
  Service of process, **28 § 2716**
  Trespass, **28 § 2713**
  Trial, **28 § 2713**
  United States Marshals Service,
    Execution, **28 § 2712**
    Personal notice, **28 § 2716**
    Publication, **28 § 2715**
    Searches and seizures, **28 § 2710**
  Waiver, jury, **28 § 2713**
  Warrants, **28 § 2710 et seq.**
Bonds (officers and fiduciaries), attachment, discharge, **28 § 2717**
Certified or Registered Mail, generally, this index
Damages, attachment, **28 § 2713**
Discharge, attachment, **28 § 2717**
Evidence, attachment, **28 § 2711**
Fraudulent conveyances, attachment, **28 § 2710**

POSTAL SERVICE—Cont'd
Indebtedness. Attachment, generally, ante
Interest, attachment, **28 § 2718**
Investments, attachment, **28 § 2714**
Judgments and decrees, attachment, discharge, **28 § 2717**
Jurisdiction, **28 § 1339**
  Attachment, **28 §§ 2710, 2711**
Jury, attachment, **28 § 2713**
Nonresidents, attachment, **28 §§ 2710, 2715**
Notice, attachment, personal notice, **28 § 2716**
Plea in abatement, attachment, **28 § 2713**
Process, attachment, **28 § 2716**
Publication, attachment, **28 § 2715**
Registered mail. Certified or Registered Mail, generally, this index
Returns, attachment, discharge, **28 § 2717**
Torts, **28 § 2680**
Trespass, attachment, **28 § 2713**
United States Marshals Service. Attachment, ante
Waiver, attachment, jury, **28 § 2713**
Warrants, attachment, **28 § 2710 et seq.**

POSTMASTER GENERAL
Accounts and accounting, certificates and certification, **28 § 1743**
Certificates and certification, accounts and accounting, **28 § 1743**

POSTMASTERS
Certificates and certification, **28 § 1743**
Demands, evidence, **28 § 1743**

POSTPONEMENT
See specific index headings

POSTSECONDARY EDUCATION AND SCHOOLS
Colleges and Universities, generally, this index

POSTSENTENCE ADMINISTRATION
Sentence and Punishment, this index

POWERS AND DUTIES
See specific index headings

PRACTICE OF LAW
See specific index headings

PRECEDENCE
International Trade Court, this index

PREEMPTION
Federal debt collection, **28 § 3003**

PREFERENCES
Priorities and Preferences, generally, this index

PRELIMINARY EXAMINATION
Rules of Evidence, this index

PRESENTS
Gifts, generally, this index

PRESERVATION
Identity and identification, records and recordation, **28 § 534**
Jury Commission, records and recordation, **28 § 1868**
United States Court of International Trade, decisions, **28 § 257**

PRESERVING UNITED STATES ATTORNEY INDEPENDENCE ACT OF 2007
Generally, **28 §§ 1 nt, 456, 456 nt**

PRESIDENT OF SENATE PRO TEMPORE
Federal Judicial Center Foundation, appointments, **28 § 629**

PRESIDENT OF THE UNITED STATES
Accountability. Presidential and Executive Office Accountability, generally, this index
Administrative law and procedure, enforcement, reports, **28 § 530D**
Alaska, United States District Court for District of Alaska, **28 § 81A nt, EON 10867**
Attorney General, this index
Bankruptcy, this index
Closings, ports of entry, ships and shipping, **28 § 1395**
Compromise and settlement, reports, **28 § 530D**
Courts of appeals, judges or justices, **28 § 44**
Discrimination, nominees for appointment, **28 § 44 nt**
District Judges, this index
Enforcement, statutes, reports, **28 § 530D**
Executive Office, accountability. Presidential and Executive Office Accountability, generally, this index
Illinois, Southern District, judges or justices, appointments, **28 § 93 nt**
Independent Counsel, generally, this index
Injunctions, enforcement, reports, **28 § 530D**
Investigations, protection, **28 § 533**
Judges or Justices, this index
Justice Department, seals, **28 § 502**
Officers and employees, accountability. Presidential and Executive Office Accountability, generally, this index
Opinions and decisions, enforcement, reports, **28 § 530D**
Police. Secret Service, generally, this index
Protection, investigations, **28 § 533**
Public policy, statutes, enforcement, reports, **28 § 530D**
Reports,
Statutes, enforcement, **28 § 530D**

PRESIDENT OF THE UNITED STATES—Cont'd
Reports—Cont'd
United States Sentencing Commission, **28 § 997**
Seals (Official Seals), generally, this index
Secret Service, generally, this index
Solicitor General, appointment, **28 § 505**
Special prosecutors, **28 § 592 et seq.**
Statutes, enforcement, reports, **28 § 530D**
United States attorneys, powers and duties, **28 § 541**
United States Court of Appeals for Federal Circuit, appointments, **28 § 44 nt**
United States Court of Federal Claims, appointments, **28 § 171**
United States Court of International Trade, appointments, **28 § 251**
United States Marshals, appointments, **28 § 561**
United States Sentencing Commission, appointments, **28 § 991**
Virgin Islands, this index

PRESIDENTIAL AND EXECUTIVE OFFICE ACCOUNTABILITY
Appeal and review, **28 § 3901 et seq.**
Attorneys, fees, **28 § 3905**
Definitions, **28 § 3908**
Expedited appeals, **28 § 3904**
Jurisdiction, **28 § 3904**
Jury, **28 § 3901**
Payments, **28 § 3906**
Rules and regulations, **28 §§ 3902, 3903**
Supreme Court, **28 § 3904**
United States Court of Appeals for the Federal Circuit, **28 § 1296**
Attorneys, fees, appeal and review, **28 § 3905**
Awards, appeal and review, **28 § 3906**
Compromise settlements, appeal and review, **28 § 3906**
Covered employee, definitions, appeal and review, **28 § 3908**
Damages, punitive damages, **28 § 3905**
Employing office, definitions, **28 § 3908**
Judgments and decrees, **28 § 3906**
Jurisdiction, expedited review, **28 § 3904**
Jury, **28 § 3901**
Punitive damages, **28 § 3905**
Supreme Court, expedited review, **28 § 3904**
United States Court of Appeals for the Federal Circuit, **28 § 1296**
United States District Court for the District of Columbia, **28 § 1413**
Venue, **28 § 1413**

PRESIDENTIAL ELECTORS
Jurisdiction, **28 § 1344**

PRESUMPTIONS
Habeas corpus, **28 § 2254**

PRESUMPTIONS—Cont'd
Rules of Evidence, this index
United States Court of International Trade, **28 § 2639**

PRETRIAL CONFERENCES
Rules of Civil Procedure, this index

PRETRIAL SERVICES
Crimes and Offenses, this index

PREVIOUS CONDITION OF SERVITUDE
Race, Color, and Previous Condition of Servitude, generally, this index

PRICES
See specific index headings

PRIMA FACIE EVIDENCE
Evidence, generally, this index

PRINCIPAL AND SURETY
Bonds (Officers and Fiduciaries), generally, this index

PRINTING
Admiralty, appeal and review, briefs, **28 § 1923**
Costs, **28 § 1920**
Fees, **28 § 1920**
In forma pauperis proceedings, **28 § 1915**
Public Printing and Documents, generally, this index
Supreme Court, this index

PRINTS
Copyrights, generally, this index

PRIORITIES AND PREFERENCES
Civil actions, determination of priority by court, exception, **28 § 1657**
Courts, civil cases, **28 § 1657**
Criminal cases on appeal from State court, **28 § 2102**
Federal Debt Collection, this index
Lien of U.S. on property, **28 § 2410**
Plant Variety Protection, this index
Rules of Civil Procedure, this index

PRISONS AND PRISONERS
Correctional Institutions, generally, this index

PRIVACY PROTECTION
Justice Department, privacy officer, **28 § 509 nt**

PRIVATE CORPORATIONS
Corporations, generally, this index

PRIVATE SECURITY
Guards, generally, this index

PRIVATE SECURITY OFFICER EMPLOYMENT AUTHORIZATION ACT OF 2004
Generally, **28 § 534 nt**

PRIVILEGED INFORMATION
Confidential or Privileged Information, generally, this index

PRIVILEGES AND IMMUNITIES
Aircraft, this index
Arbitrators, **28 § 655**
Attachment, terrorists and terrorism, waiver, **28 § 1610 nt, PD 2001–03**
Certifying officer, courts, **28 § 613**
Civil rights, **28 § 1343**
Court of Federal Claims, this index
Diplomatic immunity, limitation of actions, **28 § 2416**
Disbursing officials, clerks, and agents, courts, **28 § 613**
Execution, terrorists and terrorism, waiver, **28 § 1610 nt, PD 2001–03**
Fines, penalties and forfeitures, **28 § 2465**
Foreign Countries, this index
Foreign Missions, this index
Foreign Service, this index
Libya, terrorists and terrorism, United States nationals, claims, **28 § 1605A nt**
Rules of Evidence, this index
Searches and seizures, **28 § 2465**
Terrorists and Terrorism, this index
United Nations, this index
Witnesses, this index

PRIZE (VESSELS)
Jurisdiction, **28 § 1333**

PRO HAC VICE
See specific index headings

PRO SE
See specific index headings

PROBATE PROCEEDINGS
Wrongful death, **28 § 2404**

PROBATION
Conditions,
Modifications, sentencing guidelines, **28 § 994**
Sentencing guidelines, duties of Commission, **28 § 994**
Officers and employees,
Accommodations, **28 § 462**
Investigations, official acts, by Attorney General, **28 § 526**
Judicial Center, conduct of programs of continuing education and training, **28 § 620**
Revocation or modification, sentencing guidelines, **28 § 994**
Supervised release. Sentence and Punishment, this index
United States Sentencing Commission, **28 § 994**

PROCEEDINGS
Actions and Proceedings, generally, this index

PROCEEDS
See specific index headings

PROCESS
Absence and absentees, liens and incumbrances, **28 § 1655**
Abuse of process, Tort Claims Act, **28 § 2680**
Admiralty, stay of proceedings, **28 § 2464**
Agent for service of process, patents, infringement, **28 § 1694**
Arbitration, this index
Attachment,
Post Office, officers and employees, **28 § 2716**
U.S. Marshals, fees, **28 § 1921**
Capias, U.S. marshal, fees, **28 § 1921**
Certified or registered mail,
Federal officers and employees, **28 § 1391**
Liens and incumbrances, United States, **28 § 2410**
Clerks of Courts, this index
Continuance, **28 § 143**
Corporations, derivative actions, **28 § 1695**
Evidence, Taking of Evidence Abroad in Civil or Commercial Matters Convention, **28 § 1781 nt**
Federal agencies, **28 § 2344**
Federal Debt Collection, this index
Federal officers and employees, **28 § 1391**
Fines, penalties and forfeitures, foreign countries, **28 § 2467**
Foreign Countries, this index
Foreign States, privileges and immunities, **28 § 1608**
Forma pauperis proceedings, **28 § 1915**
Habeas corpus, **28 §§ 1446, 2241**
ICC orders, **28 § 2321**
Indebtedness, **28 § 2007**
International Trade Court, this index
Interpleader, **28 § 2361**
Judicial Panel On Multidistrict Litigation, this index
Justices and judges, survivor annuities, exemptions, **28 § 376**
Multiparty and multiforum, **28 § 1697**
Multiple districts, property, **28 § 1692**
Patents, this index
Postal Service, this index
Process servers, **28 § 550**
Receivers and receivership, **28 § 1692**
Removal of Cases or Causes, this index
Rules of Appellate Procedure, this index
Rules of Civil Procedure, this index
Seal of court, **28 § 1691**
Stocks and stockholders, derivative actions, **28 § 1695**
Subpoenas, generally, this index
Summons, generally, this index
Supreme Court, this index
Surface Transportation Board, **28 § 2321**
Tax liens, **28 § 2410**
Time, **28 § 452**

PROCESS—Cont'd
Torts, United States, **28 § 2679**
United States, claims, **28 § 2408**
United States Attorney, liens and incumbrances, **28 § 2410**
United States Marshals Service, this index
Venue, **28 § 1693**

PROCLAMATIONS
Admiralty, United States Marshals, fees, **28 § 1921**
Insurrection and Sedition, this index

PROCTORS
Docket fees, **28 § 1923**

PROCUREMENT
Purchasers and Purchasing, generally, this index

PRODUCERS
See specific index headings

PRODUCTION OF BOOKS AND PAPERS
Arbitration, **28 § 656**
Assistance, foreign tribunals, **28 § 1782**
Contempt, foreign countries, **28 § 1784**
Rules of Civil Procedure, this index
Senate action to secure, District Court for District of Columbia, jurisdiction, **28 § 1365**

PROFESSIONAL SPORTS
Gambling, **28 § 3701 et seq.**

PROFESSIONS AND OCCUPATIONS
Guards, generally, this index
Juror qualification form, **28 § 1869**
Messengers, generally, this index
Receivers and Receivership, generally, this index
Stenographers, generally, this index

PROGRAMS
See specific index headings

PROHEPTAZINE
Controlled Substances, generally, this index

PROHIBITION, WRIT OF
Supreme Court, this index

PROOF
Evidence, generally, this index

PROPERIDINE
Controlled Substances, generally, this index

PROPERTY
Bankruptcy, generally, this index
Damages, Foreign States, privileges and immunities, **28 § 1605**
Exchange of Property, generally, this index

PROPERTY—Cont'd
Interpleader, district court, jurisdiction, **28 § 1335**
Liens and Incumbrances, generally, this index
Loss, tort claims against U.S., adjustment of claims, **28 § 2672**
Managers and management, actions and proceedings, **28 § 959**
Real Estate, generally, this index
Rules of Evidence, this index
Searches and Seizures, generally, this index
United States Marshals, commissions, sales, **28 § 1921**

PROSECUTIONS
See specific index headings

PROTECTION
See specific index headings

PROTESTS
Customs Duties, this index
Customs Officers, this index
International Trade Court, this index

PROTHONOTARIES
Books and papers, evidence, **28 § 1739**

PSILOCYBIN
Controlled Substances, generally, this index

PSILOCYN
Controlled Substances, generally, this index

PSYCHIATRY AND PSYCHIATRISTS
Sentence and punishment, **28 § 334**

PUBLIC BUILDINGS AND WORKS
General Services Administration, generally, this index

PUBLIC CONTRACTS
Aeronautics and Space Administration, Exchange Councils, **28 § 1491**
Appeal and review. Executive agencies, post
Attorney General,
Appeal and review, **28 § 1295**
Compromise and settlement, **28 § 2414**
Executive agencies, post
Civil Rights, generally, this index
Claims. Executive agencies, post
Contractors, generally, this index
Executive agencies,
Appeal and review,
Attorney General, certificates and certification, **28 § 2414**
Court of Appeals for the Federal Circuit, **28 § 1295**
Attorney General,
Decrees, **28 § 2414**
Judgments and decrees, **28 § 2414**

PUBLIC CONTRACTS—Cont'd
Executive agencies—Cont'd
Claims,
Contractors, Court of Federal Claims, **28 § 2517**
Court of Federal Claims, **28 § 2517**
Contractors, claims, Court of Federal Claims, **28 § 2517**
Court of Federal Claims, **28 §§ 1491, 2517**
Judgments and decrees, **28 § 2414**
Limitation of actions, **28 § 2401**
Payment, judgments and decrees, **28 § 2414**
Secretary of the Treasury, **28 § 2414**
State courts, judgments and decrees, **28 § 2414**
Torts, **28 § 2401**
United States Court of Federal Claims, **28 § 2517**
Jurisdiction, claims, **28 § 1346**
Limitation of actions, executive agencies, **28 § 2401**
Payment. Executive agencies, ante

PUBLIC DEFENDERS
Consultants, United States Sentencing Commission, **28 § 994**
Subpoenas, witnesses, **28 § 1825**
United States Sentencing Commission, consultants, **28 § 994**
Witnesses, subpoenas, **28 § 1825**

PUBLIC DOCUMENTS
Public Printing and Documents, generally, this index

PUBLIC EDUCATION
Colleges and Universities, generally, this index

PUBLIC FUNDS
Funds, generally, this index

PUBLIC LANDS
Fires and fire protection, damages, **28 §§ 2415, 2416**
Quieting title, **28 § 2409a**
Trespass, action by U.S. for damages, limitations, **28 §§ 2415, 2416**

PUBLIC MONEYS
Money, generally, this index

PUBLIC OFFICE
Offices, generally, this index

PUBLIC OFFICERS AND EMPLOYEES
Federal Officers and Employees, generally, this index
Political Subdivisions, this index
Rules of Civil Procedure, this index
States, this index

PUBLIC POLICY
See specific index headings

PUBLIC PRINTER
Supreme Court reports, **28 §§ 411, 412**

PUBLIC PRINTING AND DOCUMENTS
Attorney General, opinions, **28 § 521**
Courts of appeals, rules of practice, **28 § 2077**
Supreme Court, reports, **28 §§ 411, 412**

PUBLIC RECORDS
Records and Recordation, generally, this index

PUBLIC TELECOMMUNICATIONS SERVICE
Telecommunications, generally, this index

PUBLIC UTILITIES
Rate orders, State agencies, jurisdiction, **28 § 1342**
Telecommunications, generally, this index

PUBLIC UTILITIES REVIEW ACTS
Generally, **28 § 1342**

PUBLICATION
Attorney General's opinions, **28 § 521**
Courts of appeals, rules of practice, **28 § 2077**
Judicial sale of realty, **28 §§ 2001, 2002**
Periodicals, generally, this index
Postal Service, attachment, **28 § 2715**
Private sale under order of court, terms of, **28 § 2001**
United States Court of International Trade, decisions and abstracts thereof, **28 § 257**
United States trustees, judicial districts, **28 § 581 nt**

PUBLICLY HELD CORPORATIONS
Corporations, generally, this index

PUERTO RICO
Certiorari, Supreme Court of Puerto Rico, **28 § 1258**
Courts. District courts, generally, post
District courts,
Diversity of citizenship, jurisdiction, **28 § 1332**
Judges or justices, **28 §§ 133, 134 nt**
Jury, **28 § 1861 et seq.**
Location, **28 § 119**
Diversity of citizenship, district courts, jurisdiction, **28 § 1332**
Grand jury, **28 § 1861 et seq.**
Judges or justices,
Judicial districts, **28 § 133**
United States magistrate judges, **28 § 631**
Judicial circuit, **28 § 41**
Judicial districts, **28 § 119**
Bankruptcy, **28 § 581 nt**
Judges or justices, **28 § 133**

PUERTO RICO—Cont'd
Jurisdiction, diversity of citizenship, district courts, **28 § 1332**
Jury, **28 § 1861 et seq.**
Limitation of actions, **28 § 2416**
Supreme Court of Puerto Rico, **28 § 1258**
United States magistrate judges, **28 § 631**
United States trustees of judicial districts, **28 § 581**

PUNISHMENT
Sentence and Punishment, generally, this index

PUNITIVE DAMAGES
Foreign States, liabilities, **28 § 1606**
Presidential and Executive Office Accountability, **28 § 3905**
United States, torts, **28 § 2674**

PURCHASE MONEY SECURITY INTEREST
Security Interest, generally, this index

PURCHASERS AND PURCHASING
Attorney General, law books, **28 § 525**
Federal Agencies, this index
Judiciary Information Technology Fund, **28 § 612**
Law books, **28 § 413**
Supreme Court, books, pamphlets, **28 § 674**

QUALIFICATIONS
See specific index headings

QUAPAW INDIAN AGENCY
Real estate, allotments, **28 § 1353**

QUARANTINE
Torts, **28 § 2680**

QUESTIONS OF LAW OR FACT
Attorney General,
Executive departments, **28 § 512**
Military departments, **28 § 513**
President of the United States, **28 § 511**
Certified Questions, generally, this index
Constitution of the United States, this index
Multidistrict litigation, **28 § 1407**
Rules of Civil Procedure, this index

QUIETING TITLE
Jurisdiction, **28 § 1346**
Limitation of actions, **28 § 2409a**
States, **28 § 2409a**
Tax liens, **28 §§ 2409a, 2410**
United States, **28 §§ 2409a, 2410**

QUORUM
See specific index headings

RACE, COLOR, AND PREVIOUS CONDITION OF SERVITUDE
Crimes and offenses. Hate Crimes, generally, this index
Elections, **28 § 1344**
Hate Crimes, generally, this index
Judges or justices, nominations, **28 §§ 44 nt, 133 nt**
Jury, **28 § 1862 et seq.**

RACEMETHORPHAN
Controlled Substances, generally, this index

RACEMORAMIDE
Controlled Substances, generally, this index

RACEMORPHAN
Controlled Substances, generally, this index

RACKETEERING
Assets Forfeiture Fund. Justice Department, this index
Fines, penalties and forfeitures, Assets Forfeiture Fund. Justice Department, this index
Stores, organized retail theft task force, **28 § 509 nt**

RAIL CARRIERS
Railroads, generally, this index

RAILROADS
Police, training, funds, **28 § 530C**
Receivers and receivership, Federal Employers Liability Act, **28 § 1445**
Safety, appeal and review, **28 § 2342**
Training, police, funds, **28 § 530C**
Trusts and trustees, Federal Employers Liability Act, nonremovable actions, **28 § 1445**
Workers compensation,
Nonremovable actions, **28 § 1445**
Removal of cases or causes, **28 § 1445**

RAILWAYS
Railroads, generally, this index

RANDOM SELECTION
Grand Jury, this index
Jury, **28 § 1861 et seq.**

RATES AND CHARGES
Customs Duties, this index
International Trade Court, this index
State agencies, orders, district courts, **28 § 1342**
Surface Transportation Board, this index
Tolls, generally, this index

REAL ESTATE
Aliens, this index
Appraisal and appraisers, orders of court, **28 § 2001**
Condemnation. Eminent Domain, generally, this index

REAL ESTATE—Cont'd
Constructive notice, pending actions, **28 § 1964**
Correctional institutions, funds, **28 § 530C**
Eminent Domain, generally, this index
Exchange of Property, generally, this index
Income Tax, this index
Indian Lands and Reservations, generally, this index
Judicial sales, **28 § 2001 et seq.**
National Banks, this index
Public Lands, generally, this index
Quieting Title, generally, this index
Records and Recordation, generally, this index
Redemption, generally, this index
Sales, private sales, court orders, **28 § 2001**
States, registration, **28 § 1964**
Tenants In Common, generally, this index

REAL PROPERTY
Real Estate, generally, this index

REAPPORTIONMENT
Three judge court, **28 § 2284**

REASONABLE CAUSE CERTIFICATES
Searches and seizures, **28 § 2465**

RECALL
Bankruptcy, judges or justices, **28 §§ 155, 375, 377**
Judges or Justices, this index

RECEIPTS
Motor Carriers, this index
Treasury of United States, generally, this index

RECEIVERS AND RECEIVERSHIP
Generally, **28 § 958 et seq.**
Ancillary districts, **28 § 2001**
Appeal and review, interlocutory orders, **28 § 1292**
Bankruptcy, this index
Banks and Banking, this index
Carriers, nonremovable actions, **28 § 1445**
Clerks of courts, appointments, **28 § 957**
District courts,
Appeal and review, **28 § 1292**
Judicial sales, **28 § 2001**
Multiple properties, **28 §§ 754, 1692**
Orders or court, **28 § 754**
Federal Debt Collection, this index
Interlocutory orders, appeal and review, **28 § 1292**
Judicial sales, **28 § 2001**
Managers and management, **28 § 959**
Multiple districts, **28 § 754**
National Banks, this index
Rules of Civil Procedure, this index

RECIPROCITY
Bankruptcy, abstention, **28 § 1334**

RECOMMENDATIONS
See specific index headings

RECORDS AND RECORDATION
Authentication, generally, this index
Bankruptcy, this index
Carriers, this index
Classification, criminal identification records, **28 § 534**
Clerks of Courts, this index
Clerks of District Courts, this index
Consuls, evidence, **28 § 1740**
Court of Federal Claims, this index
Courts, this index
Courts of Appeals, this index
Criminal Background Checks, generally, this index
Customs Duties, this index
Disbursing officers, **28 § 1496**
District Courts, this index
Documentary Evidence, generally, this index
Evidence, this index
Exports and Imports, this index
Federal Agencies, this index
Federal Bureau of Investigation, this index
Federal debt collection, postjudgment remedies, **28 § 3203**
Federal records,
Admissibility of evidence, **28 § 1733**
Documentary evidence, **28 § 1733**
Standards, **28 § 1733**
Foreign countries, authentication, **28 § 1741**
Habeas Corpus, this index
House of Representatives, this index
International Trade Court, this index
Judges or Justices, this index
Jury, this index
Liens and incumbrances,
Certified copies, **28 § 1656**
Judgments and decrees, **28 § 1962**
Microfilms and Microphotographs, this index
Patent and Trademark Office, this index
Pending actions, real estate, constructive notice, **28 § 1964**
Possessions of U.S., evidence, **28 §§ 1738, 1739**
Production of Books and Papers, generally, this index
Rules of Appellate Procedure, this index
Rules of Civil Procedure, this index
Rules of Evidence, this index
Senate, this index
State Courts, this index
States, this index
Supreme Court, this index
Territories, this index
Transcripts, generally, this index
United States Magistrate Judges, this index
Vice Consuls, evidence, **28 § 1740**

RECOVERY
See specific index headings

RECREATION AND RECREATIONAL FACILITIES
Boats and Boating, generally, this index

RECREATIONAL VESSELS
Boats and Boating, generally, this index

RECUSAL
Judges or justices, **28 § 455**
United States magistrate judges, **28 § 455**

RECYCLING AND RESOURCE RECOVERY
Courts, **28 § 604**

REDEMPTION
Federal debt collection, postjudgment remedies, **28 § 3203**
Judicial sale, U.S., **28 § 2410**
Tax liens, **28 § 2410**

REDUCTION
See specific index headings

REEXAMINATION
See specific index headings

REFEREE
References, generally, this index

REFERENCE BOOKS
Attorney General, procurement, **28 § 525**

REFERENCES
Bankruptcy, this index
Clerks of court, appointments, **28 § 957**
Court of Federal Claims, this index
Federal agencies, orders, injunctions, **28 § 2349**
Judges or justices, complaints, **28 §§ 352, 354**
Real estate, pending actions, notice, **28 § 1964**
Rules of Civil Procedure, this index
Three judge court, **28 § 2284**

REFERRALS
References, generally, this index

REFORM
See specific index headings

REFORMATORIES
Correctional Institutions, generally, this index

REFUNDS
Income Tax, this index
Judicial Survivors Annuity Fund, **28 § 376**
Taxation, this index

REGISTERED MAIL
Certified or Registered Mail, generally, this index

REGISTRATION
Certified copy of satisfaction of judgment, **28 § 1963**
Child support, orders, full faith and credit, **28 § 1738B**
Elections, this index
Judgments and decrees,
Lien, **28 § 1962**
Other districts, **28 § 1963**
Pending actions, real estate, constructive notice, **28 § 1964**

REGISTRY
Indians, crimes and offenses, **28 § 534 nt**

REHEARING
Court of Appeals for the Federal Circuit, this index
International Trade Court, this index
Judges or Justices, this index
Rules of Appellate Procedure, this index
Supreme Court, this index

REIMBURSEMENT
See specific index headings

REINSTATEMENT
See specific index headings

RELATIVES
Annuities, justices and judges, survivors, **28 § 376**
Disqualification, judges or justices, **28 § 455**
Judges or justices, disqualification, **28 § 455**
Justice, judge or Magistrate Judge, ineligible to appointment to office or duty in any court, **28 § 458**
Missing persons, children and minors, **28 § 534**

RELEASE
Generally, **28 § 2465**
Bail, generally, this index
Federal debt collection, judgment liens, **28 § 3201**
Liens and incumbrances, United States, **28 § 2410**
Negligence, Federal officers and employees, claims, **28 § 2672**
Rules of Civil Procedure, this index
Ships and shipping, arrest, **28 § 2464**
Supervised release. Sentence and Punishment, this index
Tax Liens, this index
United States magistrate judges, **28 § 636**

RELEVANCY
See specific index headings

RELIGION
Associations and societies. Religious Organizations and Societies, generally, this index
Civil Rights, generally, this index

RELIGION—Cont'd
Corporations. Religious Organizations and Societies, generally, this index
Discrimination, generally, this index
Hate Crimes, generally, this index
Judges or justices, **28 §§ 44 nt, 133 nt**
Jury, this index
Religious Organizations and Societies, generally, this index

RELIGIOUS ORGANIZATIONS AND SOCIETIES
Attorneys, fees, awards, **28 § 2412**
Discrimination, generally, this index
Disqualification, judges or justices, **28 § 455**
Judges or justices, disqualification, **28 § 455**
Rules of Evidence, this index

REMAND
Bankruptcy, this index
Court of Federal Claims, this index
Courts of Appeals, this index
Federal officers and employees, motor vehicles, accidents, **28 § 2679**
Judicial Panel On Multidistrict Litigation, this index
Motor vehicles, Federal officers and employees, accidents, **28 § 2679**
State courts, **28 §§ 1447, 1448**

REMARRIAGE
Judges or justices, annuities, **28 § 376**

REMOVAL
See specific index headings

REMOVAL FROM OFFICE
See specific index headings

REMOVAL OF CASES OR CAUSES
Generally, **28 § 1441 et seq.**
Affidavits, **28 § 1449**
Aliens, **28 § 1442**
Appeal and review, **28 § 1447**
Armed Forces, **28 § 1442a**
Attachment of goods or estate of defendant, **28 § 1450**
Bankruptcy, this index
Bonds (officers and fiduciaries), **28 § 1450**
Carriers, **28 § 1445**
Civil rights, **28 §§ 1443, 1445**
Class actions, **28 § 1453**
Congress, **28 § 1442**
Constitutional questions, **28 § 1441**
Costs, **28 § 1447**
Court of Federal Claims, this index
Custody, defendants, **28 § 1446**
Discretion of court, **28 § 1441**
Evidence, **28 § 1446**
Exports and imports, monopolies and combinations, **28 § 1446**
Federal agencies, **28 §§ 1442, 2347**
Federal Employers Liability Act, **28 § 1445**

REMOVAL OF CASES OR CAUSES—Cont'd
Federal officers and employees, **28 § 1442**
Filing, **28 § 1446**
Foreclosure, United States, **28 § 1444**
Foreign States, **28 § 1441**
Goods, wares and merchandise, sequestration, **28 § 1450**
Hearings, **28 § 1446**
Improvident removals, **28 § 1447**
Injunctions, **28 § 1450**
Internal Revenue Service, **28 § 1442**
International Trade Commission, setoff and counterclaim, **28 § 1446**
International Trade Court, this index
Joinder, **28 § 1441**
Judicial officers and employees, **28 § 1442**
Jurisdiction, **28 §§ 1441, 1631**
Liens and incumbrances, foreclosure, United States, **28 § 1444**
Marshals, **28 § 1446**
Mortgages, foreclosure, United States, **28 § 1444**
Motions, **28 § 1448**
Multiparties, **28 § 1441**
Notice, **28 § 1446**
Orders of court,
Filing, **28 § 1446**
Issuance, **28 § 1447**
Preremoval orders, **28 § 1450**
Remand, **28 § 1447**
Original jurisdiction, **28 § 1441**
Pleadings, **28 § 1446**
Pretrial proceedings, multidistrict litigation, **28 § 1407**
Procedure, **28 § 1446 et seq.**
Process, **28 § 1446 et seq.**
Copies, **28 § 1446**
Defects, **28 § 1448**
Issuance, **28 § 1447**
Records and recordation, **28 § 1449**
Records and recordation, **28 § 1449**
Remand, **28 § 1447**
Sequestration, goods, wares and merchandise, **28 § 1450**
Service of process. Process, generally, ante
State, definitions, **28 § 1451**
State court, definitions, **28 § 1451**
Time, **28 § 1446**
Class actions, **28 § 1453**
United States, foreclosure, **28 § 1444**
United States Court of Claims (former court), **28 § 171 nt**
United States Court of Customs and Patent Appeals (former court), **28 § 171 nt**
Workers compensation, State laws, **28 § 1445**

RENEWAL
See specific index headings

REOPENING
See specific index headings

REORGANIZATION
See specific index headings

REPARATIONS
Restitution, generally, this index

REPEALS
Rules of court, **28 § 2072**

REPLEVIN
Federal debt collection, **28 § 3203**
Revenue laws, **28 § 2463**

REPLY
Rules of Civil Procedure, this index

REPORTERS
Compensation and salaries,
District courts, **28 § 753**
Supreme Court, **28 § 673**
Costs, **28 § 1920**
Court of Federal Claims, this index
District Courts, this index
Investigations, **28 § 526**
Oaths and affirmations, district courts, **28 § 753**
Supreme Court, this index
United States Magistrate Judges, this index

REPORTING SERVICES
United States Court of Federal Claims, **28 § 796**

REPORTS
Administrative Office of United States Courts, this index
Attorney General, this index
Bankruptcy, this index
Bureau of Alcohol, Tobacco, Firearms, and Explosives, undercover investigations, **28 § 533 nt**
Carriers, this index
Chief Justice of the Supreme Court, Judicial Conference of the United States, **28 § 331**
Comptroller General, this index
Congress, this index
Congressional Committees, this index
Court of Federal Claims, this index
Courts of Appeals, this index
Crimes and Offenses, this index
Customs Duties, this index
Disclosure of Federal Campaign Funds, this index
DNA (Deoxyribonucleic Acid), this index
Domestic Violence, this index
Executive Agencies, this index
Federal Bureau of Investigation, this index
Federal debt collection, receivers and receivership, **28 § 3103**
Federal Legal Council, **28 § 509 nt, EON 12146**
Federal Officers and Employees, this index
Fines, Penalties and Forfeitures, this index

REPORTS—Cont'd
Foreign Service, this index
Gangs, national gang intelligence center, **28 § 534 nt**
Government Accountability Office, this index
Grand Jury, this index
Identity theft task force, **28 § 509 nt, EON 13402**
Independent Counsel, this index
International Trade Court, this index
Interpreters, Federal Bureau of Investigation, **28 § 509 nt**
Joint Committee On Printing, this index
Judicial Center, **28 § 623**
Judicial Conference of the United States, this index
Justice Department, this index
Kidnapping, parental kidnapping, domestic violence, **28 § 1738A nt**
Military Departments, this index
Money Laundering, this index
National gang intelligence center, **28 § 534 nt**
President of the United States, this index
Rules of Civil Procedure, this index
Rules of Evidence, this index
Searches and Seizures, this index
Secretary of the Interior, this index
Sentence and Punishment, this index
Statistics, generally, this index
Supreme Court, this index
Surface Transportation Board, this index
Translators, Federal Bureau of Investigation, **28 § 509 nt**
United States Attorneys, this index
United States Sentencing Commission, evaluation of sentencing guidelines, time limitation, **28 § 994 nt**

REPRESENTATIVES AND REPRESENTATION
Bankruptcy, this index
Congress, generally, this index
House of Representatives, generally, this index
Rules of Civil Procedure, this index

REPRODUCTIONS
See specific index headings

REPUGNANCY
Statutes, this index

REQUESTS
See specific index headings

REQUISITIONS
Justice Department, **28 § 523**

RESEARCH
Judicial Center, **28 §§ 620, 624**

RESERVATIONS (LANDS)
Indian Lands and Reservations, generally, this index

RESERVES
Air Force, this index
Army, this index
Marine Corps, this index
Navy, this index

RESIDENCE
Domicile and Residence, generally, this index

RESIDENT ALIENS
Aliens, generally, this index

RESIDENT COMMISSIONER
Judges or justices, Judicial Survivors Annuity Fund, **28 § 376**

RESIDENTS
Domicile and Residence, generally, this index

RESIGNATION
See specific index headings

RESOLUTION TRUST CORPORATION
Attorney General, fraud, **28 § 509 nt**
Fraud,
Attorney General, **28 § 509 nt**
Justice Department, **28 § 509 nt**
Justice Department, fraud, **28 § 509 nt**

RESPONSES
See specific index headings

RESTITUTION
Generally, **28 § 994 nt**
Administrative Office of U.S. Courts, Director, powers and duties, **28 § 604**
Bail bonds, **28 § 2044**

RESTRAINING ORDERS
Injunctions, generally, this index

RESTRAINT OF TRADE
Monopolies and Combinations, generally, this index

RETAILERS
Stores, generally, this index

RETENTION
See specific index headings

RETIREMENT AND PENSIONS
Actions and proceedings, district courts, **28 § 1346**
Air Force, this index
Annuities, generally, this index
Army, this index
Bankruptcy, this index
Bills, exceptions, U.S. Court of Federal Claims, **28 §§ 1492, 2509**
Chief Justice of U.S., elections, coverage, **28 § 677**
Civil Service, this index
Coast Guard, this index
Coast Guard Reserve, this index
Court of Federal Claims, this index
Judges or Justices, this index

RETIREMENT AND PENSIONS—Cont'd
Jurisdiction, claims, **28 § 1346**
Marine Corps, this index
Navy, this index
Supreme Court, this index
United States Court of Federal Claims, **28 §§ 1492, 2509**
Jurisdiction, **28 § 1501**
United States Magistrate Judges, this index

RETURNS
Clerks of District Courts, this index
Court of Federal Claims, this index
Fines, penalties and forfeitures, **28 § 2465**
Habeas Corpus, this index
Income Tax, this index
Postal Service, this index
Rules of Civil Procedure, this index
Searches and seizures, **28 § 2465**

REVENUE
See specific index headings

REVERSAL
See specific index headings

REVIEW
Appeal and Review, generally, this index

REVIVAL OF ACTION
Abatement and Revival, generally, this index

REVOCATION OR SUSPENSION
See specific index headings

REVOLVERS
Weapons, generally, this index

REWARDS
Justice Department, **28 § 530C**
Terrorists and Terrorism, this index

RHODE ISLAND
Bankruptcy, judges or justices, appointments, **28 § 152**
Court of Appeals for First Circuit, generally, this index
District courts,
Judges,
Additional, **28 § 133 nt**
Number, **28 § 133**
Places of holding, **28 § 120**
Judicial Circuit of U.S., **28 § 41**
Judicial district, **28 § 120**
Number of district judges, **28 § 133**
United States trustees of judicial districts, appointment, **28 § 581**

RIFLES
Weapons, generally, this index

RTC
Resolution Trust Corporation, generally, this index

RULE NISI
Power to issue, **28 § 1651**

RULES AND REGULATIONS
See specific index headings

RULES GOVERNING SECTION 2254 CASES
Habeas Corpus, this index

RULES OF APPELLATE PROCEDURE
Generally, **28 § 2071 et seq.; FRAP 1 et seq.**
Abatement and revival, **FRAP 43**
Administrative law and procedure, **FRAP 15 et seq.**
Administrative Office of the United States Courts, powers and duties, **FRAP 45**
Admission to bar, **FRAP 46**
Advisory committees, **28 § 2077**
Affidavits,
Indigent persons, **FRAP 24; FRAP Form 4**
Injunctions, **FRAP 8**
Motions, **FRAP 27**
Stay of proceedings, **FRAP 8**
Agency, definitions, **FRAP 15**
Agreed statement, records and recordation, **FRAP 10**
Amendments,
Habeas corpus, **FRAP 23**
Judgments and decrees,
Interest, **FRAP 37**
Time, **FRAP 4**
Records and recordation, **FRAP 10, 16**
Amicus curiae,
Briefs, **FRAP 21, 29**
Oral argument, **FRAP 29**
Answer. Plea or answer, generally, post
Appeal as of right, **FRAP 3, 4**
Appeals by permission, **FRAP 5**
Appearances,
Arguments, **FRAP 34**
Mandamus, **FRAP 21**
Prohibition, **FRAP 21**
Appellants, definitions, **FRAP 20**
Appellees, definitions, **FRAP 20**
Appendices. Briefs, post
Application of rules, **FRAP 1, 2**
Applications,
Attorneys, admission to bar, **FRAP 46**
Extraordinary writs, **FRAP 21**
Habeas corpus, **FRAP 22**
Indigent persons, **FRAP 24**
Mandate, **FRAP 41**
Arguments. Oral argument, generally, post
Assignments, district court judges, **28 § 292**
Attorney General, constitutional questions, **FRAP 44**
Attorneys, **FRAP 46**
Admission to bar, **FRAP 46**
Books and papers, **FRAP 25**
Conferences, **FRAP 33**
Costs, **FRAP 30**

RULES OF APPELLATE PROCEDURE —Cont'd
Attorneys—Cont'd
Crimes and offenses, **FRAP 46**
Disbarment, **FRAP 46**
Discipline, **FRAP 46**
Fees, **FRAP 4**
Notice, **FRAP 3**
Statements, **FRAP 12**
Suspension, **FRAP 46**
Banc, court in banc, **FRAP 35**
Bankruptcy,
Corporate disclosure statements, **FRAP 26.1**
Judgments and decrees, **FRAP 6**
Panels, **FRAP 6; FRAP Form 5**
Bill of costs, **FRAP 39**
Binding, briefs, **FRAP 32**
Bonds (officers and fiduciaries),
Clerks of courts, **FRAP 45**
Costs, **FRAP 5 et seq.**
Indigent persons, **FRAP 24**
Mandate, **FRAP 41**
Permissive appeals, **FRAP 5**
Supersedeas or stay, **FRAP 7 et seq.**
Books and papers,
Briefs, generally, post
Clerks of courts, **FRAP 45**
Filing, generally, post
Forms, **FRAP 32**
Motions, **FRAP 27**
Signatures, **FRAP 32**
Briefs, **FRAP 28 et seq.**
Amicus curiae, **FRAP 29**
Appendices, **FRAP 30**
Costs, **FRAP 39**
Filing, **FRAP 25**
Forms, **FRAP 32**
Arguments, **FRAP 34**
Certificates of compliance, **FRAP 32; FRAP Form 6**
Copies, **FRAP 30 et seq.**
Corporate disclosure statement, **FRAP 26.1**
Costs, **FRAP 30, 39**
Cross appeals, **FRAP 28.1, 30**
Deferred appendix, **FRAP 30**
Dismissal and nonsuit, **FRAP 31**
Exhibits, **FRAP 30**
Extraordinary writs, **FRAP 21**
Filing, **FRAP 25**
Amicus curiae, **FRAP 29**
Appendices, **FRAP 30**
Time, **FRAP 31**
Forms, **FRAP 32; FRAP Form 6**
Jurisdiction, **FRAP 28**
Length, **FRAP 32**
Lists, appendices, **FRAP 30**
Mandamus, **FRAP 21**
National Labor Relations Board, **FRAP 15.1**
Omissions, appendices, **FRAP 30**
Parties, **FRAP 28**
Printing, **FRAP 39**
Prohibition, **FRAP 21**
References, **FRAP 28, 30**

RULES OF APPELLATE PROCEDURE —Cont'd
Briefs—Cont'd
Reply briefs, **FRAP 28 et seq.**
Amicus curiae, **FRAP 29**
Time, **FRAP 31**
Service of briefs, **FRAP 31**
Signatures, **FRAP 32**
Statutes, **FRAP 28**
Submission on briefs, **FRAP 34**
Time,
Amicus curiae, **FRAP 29**
Appendices, **FRAP 30**
Filing, **FRAP 31**
Typewriting, **FRAP 32**
Cross appeals, **FRAP 28.1**
Calendars, clerks of courts, **FRAP 45**
Certificates and certification,
Briefs, **FRAP 32; FRAP Form 6**
Habeas corpus, **FRAP 22**
Indigent persons, **FRAP 24**
Lists, filing, **FRAP 17**
Certiorari, **FRAP 41**
Class actions, notice, **FRAP 3**
Clerks of courts, **FRAP 45**
Attorneys, admission to bar, **FRAP 46**
Exhibits, **FRAP 34**
Notice, **FRAP 3**
Records and recordation, **FRAP 11**
Commercial carriers, process, **FRAP 25**
Compromise and settlement, **FRAP 19**
Conferences, **FRAP 33**
Voluntary dismissal, **FRAP 42**
Conferences, **FRAP 33**
Congressional Acts, constitutional questions, **FRAP 44**
Consolidated appeals, **FRAP 3**
Constitutional questions, **FRAP 44**
Contracts, voluntary dismissal, **FRAP 42**
Copies,
Briefs, **FRAP 30 et seq.**
Clerks of courts, **FRAP 45**
Corporate disclosure statements, **FRAP 26.1**
Costs, **FRAP 39**
Distribution, **28 § 2077**
District courts, **FRAP 3, 5**
Extraordinary writs, **FRAP 21**
Filing, **FRAP 25**
Indigent persons, **FRAP 24**
Judgments and decrees, **FRAP 36**
Mandamus, **FRAP 21, 41**
Motions, **FRAP 27**
Opinions and decisions, **FRAP 32.1, 36**
Prohibition, **FRAP 21**
Rehearings, **FRAP 40**
Tax Court, **FRAP 13**
Corporate disclosure statements, **FRAP 26.1**
Correctional institutions,
Filing, **FRAP 4, 25**
Habeas corpus, **FRAP 22, 23**
Release, **FRAP 9**
Corrections. Amendments, generally, ante

RULES OF APPELLATE PROCEDURE
—Cont'd
Costs, **FRAP 39**
Appendices, **FRAP 30, 39**
Attorneys, sanctions, **FRAP 30**
Bonds (officers and fiduciaries), **FRAP 5 et seq.**
Dismissal and nonsuit, **FRAP 42**
Frivolous appeals, **FRAP 38**
Mandate, **FRAP 39, 41**
Masters, **FRAP 48**
Permissive appeals, **FRAP 5**
United States, **FRAP 39**
Counsel. Attorneys, generally, ante
Crimes and offenses,
Attorneys, **FRAP 46**
Corporate disclosure statements, **FRAP 26.1**
Indigent persons, generally, post
Notice, **FRAP 3**
Release, **FRAP 9**
Supersedeas or stay, **FRAP 8**
Time, **FRAP 4**
Cross appeals,
Arguments, **FRAP 34**
Briefs, **FRAP 28.1, 30**
Oral arguments, **FRAP 34**
Cross-applications, **FRAP 5, 15**
Damages, frivolous appeals, **FRAP 38**
Death, parties, substitution, **FRAP 3, 43**
Decrees. Judgments and decrees, generally, post
Default, **FRAP 15**
Definitions,
Agency, **FRAP 15**
Appellant, **FRAP 20**
Appellee, **FRAP 20**
Legal holidays, **FRAP 26**
Record on appeal, **FRAP 10**
Destruction, exhibits, **FRAP 34**
Discipline, attorneys, **FRAP 46**
Disclosure, corporations, statements, **FRAP 26.1**
Dismissal and nonsuit, **FRAP 31, 42**
District courts, **FRAP 3 et seq.**
Dockets and docketing, **FRAP 12**
Clerks of courts, **FRAP 45**
Entry of judgment, **FRAP 36**
Tax Court, **FRAP 13**
Documents. Books and papers, generally, ante
Duplicates. Copies, generally, ante
Electronic filing, **FRAP 25**
Employees. Officers and employees, generally, post
En banc, **FRAP 35**
Entry of judgment, **FRAP 36**
Escape, habeas corpus, **FRAP 22, 23**
Evidence, statement of evidence, absence of report or transcript, **FRAP 10**
Excusable neglect, **FRAP 4**
Exhibits, **FRAP 34**
Briefs, **FRAP 30**
Extension of time, **FRAP 4, 11, 26**
Extraordinary writs, **FRAP 2, 21**
Facsimile transmissions, filing, **FRAP 25**

RULES OF APPELLATE PROCEDURE
—Cont'd
Federal agencies, **28 §§ 2072, 2073 nt, 2352 nt; FRAP 15 et seq.**
Fees,
Administrative law and procedure, **FRAP 15**
Attorneys, admission to bar, **FRAP 46**
Copies, **28 § 2077**
Dismissal and nonsuit, **FRAP 42**
Permissive appeals, **FRAP 5**
Filing, **FRAP 25**
Administrative law and procedure, **FRAP 17**
Amicus curiae, briefs, **FRAP 29**
Appendix to briefs, **FRAP 30**
Attorneys, admission to bar, **FRAP 46**
Briefs, ante
Clerks of courts, **FRAP 45**
Electronic filing, **FRAP 25**
Indigent persons, **FRAP 24**
Mail and mailing, **FRAP 25**
Notice, **FRAP 3**
Tax Court, **FRAP 13**
Tax Court, **FRAP 13**
Forma pauperis. Indigent persons, generally, post
Forms, **28 § 2072; FRAP 32**
Administrative law and procedure, **FRAP Form 3**
Attorneys, admission to bar, **FRAP 46**
Briefs, **FRAP 32; FRAP Form 6**
Indigent persons, **FRAP 24; FRAP Form 4**
Notice,
District courts, **FRAP Forms 1, 5**
Tax Court, **FRAP Form 2**
Friend of court. Amicus curiae, generally, ante
Frivolous appeals, **FRAP 38**
Habeas corpus, **FRAP 2, 22 et seq.**
Hearings,
En banc, **FRAP 35**
Oral argument, **FRAP 34**
Rehearing, generally, post
Holidays,
Clerks of courts, hours, **FRAP 45**
Time, **FRAP 26**
Hours, clerks of courts, **FRAP 45**
Indexes, clerks of courts, **FRAP 45**
Indigent persons, **FRAP 24**
Affidavits, **FRAP Form 4**
Forms, **FRAP Form 4**
Injunctions, **FRAP 8**
Interest, judgment and decrees, **FRAP 37**
Interlocutory injunctions, **FRAP 8**
Intervention, **FRAP 15**
Joint appeals, **FRAP 3, 15**
Judges or justices,
En banc, **FRAP 35**
Habeas corpus, **FRAP 22**
Judgments and decrees,
Amendments, **FRAP 4**
Bankruptcy, **FRAP 6**
Clerks of courts, **FRAP 45**
Copies, **FRAP 36**

RULES OF APPELLATE PROCEDURE
—Cont'd
Judgments and decrees—Cont'd
Crimes and offenses, **FRAP 9**
En banc, **FRAP 35**
Entry, **FRAP 4, 36**
Interest, **FRAP 37**
Magistrate judges, **FRAP 3**
Notice, **FRAP 4, 36**
Rehearings, **FRAP 40**
Release, **FRAP 9**
Renewal, **FRAP 4**
Judicial Conference of the Circuit, **28 § 333**
Jurisdiction, briefs, **FRAP 28**
Lawyers. Attorneys, generally, ante
Length, briefs, **FRAP 32**
Limitation of actions, **FRAP 4**
Lists,
Administrative law and procedure, **FRAP 17**
Briefs, appendices, **FRAP 30**
Local rules, **FRAP 47**
Magistrate judges, **FRAP 3, 5**
Mail and mailing,
Clerks of courts, **FRAP 45**
Filing, **FRAP 25**
Notice, **FRAP 3**
Opinions, **FRAP 36**
Time, **FRAP 26**
Mandamus, **FRAP 21, 41**
Mandates, **FRAP 1 et seq.**
Masters, **FRAP 48**
Misstatements, administrative law and procedure, **FRAP 16**
Modifications. Amendments, generally, ante
Motions, **FRAP 27**
Administrative law and procedure, **FRAP 18**
Admiralty, **28 § 2072**
Amicus curiae, **FRAP 29**
Appeal as of right, **FRAP 4**
Arguments, **FRAP 34**
Clerks of courts, **FRAP 45**
Corporate disclosure statements, **FRAP 26.1**
Death, parties, substitution, **FRAP 43**
Dismissal and nonsuit, **FRAP 42**
Filing, **FRAP 25**
Forms,
Briefs, **FRAP 32**
Indigent persons, **FRAP Form 4**
Indigent persons, **FRAP 24; FRAP Form 4**
Injunctions, **FRAP 8**
Oral arguments, **FRAP 34**
Replies, **FRAP 27**
Statements, **FRAP 27**
Stay of proceedings,
Administrative law and procedure, **FRAP 18**
Mandate, **FRAP 41**
Substitution, parties, death, **FRAP 43**
Time, **FRAP 26, 27**
Typewriting, **FRAP 27**

RULES OF APPELLATE PROCEDURE
—Cont'd
Multiple parties, **FRAP 28**
National Labor Relations Board, **FRAP 15.1**
New trial, **FRAP 4**
Nonappearance, **FRAP 34**
Notice,
Administrative law and procedure, **FRAP 17, 18**
Argument, oral arguments, **FRAP 34**
Attorneys, discipline, **FRAP 46**
Clerks of courts, hours, **FRAP 45**
Constitutional questions, **FRAP 44**
Death, parties, substitution, **FRAP 43**
Entry of judgment, **FRAP 36**
Exhibits, **FRAP 34**
Filing, **FRAP 3, 13, 17**
Forms, ante
Judgments and decrees, entry of judgment, **FRAP 36**
Oral arguments, **FRAP 34**
Partial transcripts, **FRAP 10**
Tax Court, **FRAP 13; FRAP Form 2**
Oaths and affirmations,
Attorneys, admission to bar, **FRAP 46**
Clerks of courts, **FRAP 45**
Offenses. Crimes and offenses, generally, ante
Officers and employees,
Attorneys, **FRAP 46**
Clerks of courts, **FRAP 45**
Constitutional questions, **FRAP 44**
Substitution, **FRAP 43**
Offices, clerks of courts, **FRAP 45**
Omissions,
Administrative law and procedure, **FRAP 16**
Briefs, appendices, **FRAP 30**
Opinions and decisions, **FRAP 36**
Copies, **FRAP 32.1**
Oral argument, **FRAP 34**
Amicus curiae, **FRAP 29**
Extraordinary writs, **FRAP 21**
Mandamus, **FRAP 21**
National Labor Relations Board, **FRAP 15.1**
Permissive appeals, **FRAP 5**
Prohibition, **FRAP 21**
Rehearings, **FRAP 40**
Orders of court, **FRAP 4**
Attorneys, discipline, **FRAP 46**
Bankruptcy, **FRAP 6**
Clerks of courts, **FRAP 45**
Conferences, **FRAP 33**
Dismissal and nonsuit, **FRAP 42**
En banc, **FRAP 35**
Extraordinary writs, **FRAP 21**
Mandamus, **FRAP 21**
Motions, **FRAP 27**
Prohibition, **FRAP 21**
Records and recordation, **FRAP 11**
Rehearings, **FRAP 35**
Substitution, parties, **FRAP 43**
Papers. Books and papers, generally, ante

RULES OF APPELLATE PROCEDURE
—Cont'd
Partial transcripts, **FRAP 10**
Parties,
Administrative law and procedure, **FRAP 15, 43 et seq.**
Arguments, **FRAP 34**
Briefs, **FRAP 28**
Conferences, **FRAP 33**
Constitutional questions, **FRAP 44**
Costs, **FRAP 39**
Judgments and decrees, **FRAP 36**
Opinions, **FRAP 36**
Representation, statements, **FRAP 12**
Substitution, **FRAP 43**
Paupers. Indigent persons, generally, ante
Permissive appeals, **FRAP 5**
Personal representatives, substitution, **FRAP 43**
Petitions,
Administrative law and procedure, **FRAP 15; FRAP Form 3**
Corporate disclosure statements, **FRAP 26.1**
Extraordinary writs, **FRAP 21**
Forms, **FRAP 32**
Mandamus, **FRAP 21**
Permissive appeals, **FRAP 5**
Prohibition, **FRAP 21**
Rehearings, **FRAP 40**
Writs, extraordinary writs, **FRAP 21**
Plea or answer, **28 § 2072**
Administrative law and procedure, **FRAP 15**
Corporate disclosure statements, **FRAP 26.1**
Extraordinary writs, **FRAP 21**
Permissive appeals, **FRAP 5**
Rehearings, **FRAP 40**
Preliminary hearings, **FRAP 11**
Printing, briefs, **FRAP 32, 39**
Prisons and prisoners. Correctional institutions, generally, ante
Privacy protection, **FRAP 25**
Pro se, **FRAP 3**
Process, **FRAP 25**
Acknowledgments, **FRAP 25**
Briefs, **FRAP 27, 31**
Carriers, **FRAP 25**
Copies, **FRAP 25**
Evidence, **FRAP 21, 25**
Extraordinary writs, **FRAP 21**
Mandamus, **FRAP 21**
Notice of appeal, **FRAP 3, 13**
Prohibition, **FRAP 21**
Tax Court, **FRAP 13**
Time, **FRAP 26**
Prohibition, **FRAP 2, 21**
Proposed judgments, administrative law and procedure, **FRAP 19**
Publication, **28 § 2077**
Records and recordation, **FRAP 10**
Administrative law and procedure, **FRAP 16, 17**
Bankruptcy, **FRAP 6**

RULES OF APPELLATE PROCEDURE
—Cont'd
Records and recordation—Cont'd
Briefs, **FRAP 28, 30**
Clerk of courts, **FRAP 45**
Copies, **FRAP 39**
Filing,
Administrative law and procedure, **FRAP 17**
Tax Court, **FRAP 13**
Printing,
Indigent persons, **28 § 1915**
Magistrate judges, **28 § 1915**
Supreme Court, **28 § 2101**
Tax Court, **FRAP 13**
Rehearing,
Bankruptcy, **FRAP 6**
En banc, **FRAP 35**
Mandate, **FRAP 41**
Release, habeas corpus, **FRAP 23**
Removal, exhibits, **FRAP 34**
Reply briefs. Briefs, ante
Reports, evidence, **FRAP 10**
Representation, statements, **FRAP 12**
Response,
Corporate disclosure statements, **FRAP 26.1**
Motions, **FRAP 27**
Retention, records and recordation, **FRAP 11, 17**
Reversal, judgments and decrees,
Costs, **FRAP 39**
Interest, **FRAP 37**
Right to appeal, **FRAP 3, 4**
Saturdays,
Clerks of courts, **FRAP 45**
Time, **FRAP 26**
Separate appeals, oral arguments, **FRAP 34**
Service of process. Process, generally, ante
Sessions, **28 § 48**
Signatures, **FRAP 32**
Single judges, motions, **FRAP 27**
Standard of review, briefs, **FRAP 28**
State courts, habeas corpus, **FRAP 22, 23**
State laws, constitutional questions, **FRAP 44**
Statements,
Agreed statement, records and recordation, **FRAP 10**
Attorneys, **FRAP 12**
Misconduct, **FRAP 46**
Evidence, **FRAP 10**
Extraordinary writs, **FRAP 21**
Statutes,
Briefs, **FRAP 28**
Constitutional questions, **FRAP 44**
Time, **FRAP 26**
Stay of proceedings,
Bonds (officers and fiduciaries), **FRAP 7 et seq.**
Mandate, **FRAP 41**
Pending appeals, **FRAP 8**

RULES OF APPELLATE PROCEDURE —Cont'd
Stipulations,
Administrative law and procedure, **FRAP 17**
Records and recordation, **FRAP 11**
Voluntary dismissal, **FRAP 42**
Substitution, parties, **FRAP 43**
Sundays,
Clerks of courts, **FRAP 45**
Time, **FRAP 26**
Suspension,
Attorneys, **FRAP 46**
Rules, **FRAP 2**
Tax Court. United States Tax Court, generally, post
Taxation of costs, **FRAP 39**
Temporary injunctions, **FRAP 8**
Time, **FRAP 26**
Administrative law and procedure, **28 § 2112; FRAP 17**
Arguments, **FRAP 34**
Briefs, ante
Certiorari, **FRAP 41**
Clerks of court, hours, **FRAP 45**
Computation, **FRAP 26**
En banc, **FRAP 35**
Legal holidays, **FRAP 26**
Mandate, **FRAP 41**
Motions, **FRAP 27**
Oral arguments, **FRAP 34**
Process, **FRAP 26**
Rehearings, **FRAP 35, 40**
Reply, motions, **FRAP 27**
Tax Court, notice, **FRAP 13**
Transcripts, **FRAP 10**
Administrative law and procedure, **FRAP 17**
Briefs, **FRAP 28**
Typewriting,
Briefs, **FRAP 32**
Cross appeals, **FRAP 28.1**
Motions, **FRAP 27**
United States,
Constitutional questions, **FRAP 44**
Costs, **FRAP 39**
Rehearings, **FRAP 40**
United States Tax Court, **FRAP 2, 14**
Decisions, **FRAP Form 2**
Notice, **FRAP 13; FRAP Form 2**
Vacating and setting aside, judgments and decrees, **FRAP 39**
Voluntary dismissals, **FRAP 42**
Weather, delays, **FRAP 26**
Writs, **28 § 2072**

RULES OF BANKRUPTCY
Bankruptcy, generally, this index

RULES OF CIVIL PROCEDURE
Generally, **FRCVP 1 et seq.**
Abatement of actions, public officers and employees, **FRCVP 25**
Absence, joinder of parties, **FRCVP 19**
Abstracts, business records, interrogatories, **FRCVP 33**

RULES OF CIVIL PROCEDURE —Cont'd
Accord and satisfaction, affirmative defenses, **FRCVP 8**
Accounts and accounting,
Default judgments, **FRCVP 55**
Masters, **FRCVP 53**
Stay of proceedings, **FRCVP 62**
Addresses,
Forms, **FRCVP Form 2**
Summons, **FRCVP 4**
Adjournment, masters, **FRCVP 53**
Administrative Office of the United States Courts, **FRCVP 79**
Administrators, **FRCVP 17**
Admiralty,
Application of rules, **FRCVP A**
Arrest, **FRCVP C**
Third parties, **FRCVP 14**
Warrants, **FRCVP D**
Attachment, **FRCVP A et seq.**
In personam actions, **FRCVP B**
In rem, **FRCVP E**
Quasi in rem, **FRCVP E**
Complaints, **FRCVP B et seq.**
Derivative actions, **FRCVP 23.1**
Injunctions, **FRCVP 65**
Condemnation, supplemental rules, **FRCVP A**
Costs,
In rem, **FRCVP E**
Quasi in rem, **FRCVP E**
Security, **FRCVP E, F**
Deposits,
Liability, **FRCVP F**
Searches and seizures, **FRCVP E**
Eminent domain, **FRCVP A**
Exoneration, **FRCVP A, F**
Expenses and expenditures, **FRCVP E**
Filing,
In rem, **FRCVP C**
Liability, **FRCVP F**
Fines, penalties and forfeitures, **FRCVP A, C, G**
Garnishment, **FRCVP A et seq.**
In personam actions, **FRCVP B**
In rem, **FRCVP E**
Quasi in rem, **FRCVP E**
In personam actions, **FRCVP B, C, E**
In rem, **FRCVP A**
Fines, penalties and forfeitures, **FRCVP G**
Process, **FRCVP C, E, G**
Quasi in rem, **FRCVP E**
Special matters, **FRCVP C**
Interrogatories, **FRCVP B, C, G**
Joinder, **FRCVP 18**
Judgments and decrees,
In rem, **FRCVP C**
Quasi in rem, **FRCVP C**
Release, **FRCVP E**
Jury, **FRCVP 38**
Liability, **FRCVP A, F**
Marshals,
Process, **FRCVP 4.1; FRCVP E**

RULES OF CIVIL PROCEDURE —Cont'd
Admiralty—Cont'd
Marshals—Cont'd
Property, powers and duties, **FRCVP C**
Masters, **FRCVP 53**
Motions,
Fines, penalties and forfeitures, **FRCVP G**
Liability, **FRCVP F**
Property, payment, **FRCVP C, E**
Supreme Court, **28 § 2072**
Notice,
Attachment, **FRCVP B**
Clearance, vessels, **FRCVP E**
Custody, **FRCVP E**
Fines, penalties and forfeitures, **FRCVP G**
Garnishment, **FRCVP B**
Liability, **FRCVP F**
Petitory actions, **FRCVP D**
Possessory actions, **FRCVP D**
Release, **FRCVP C, E**
Vessels, clearance, **FRCVP E**
Oaths and affirmations,
Depositions, **FRCVP 28**
Garnishment, **FRCVP B**
In lieu of oath, **FRCVP 43**
In rem, **FRCVP C**
Orders of court,
Liability, **FRCVP F**
Notice, **FRCVP C**
Sales, **FRCVP E**
Partition, **FRCVP A**
In rem, **FRCVP E**
Notice, **FRCVP D**
Process, **FRCVP D**
Quasi in rem, **FRCVP E**
Release, **FRCVP E**
Payment, **FRCVP C, E**
Permissive joinder, **FRCVP 20**
Plea or answer,
Garnishment, **FRCVP B**
In rem, **FRCVP C, E**
Liability, **FRCVP F**
Quasi in rem, **FRCVP C, E**
Pleading, **FRCVP 9**
Fines, penalties and forfeitures, **FRCVP G**
Supreme Court, **28 § 2072**
Prize proceedings, **FRCVP 81**
Process,
Attachment, **FRCVP B**
Garnishment, **FRCVP B**
In rem, **FRCVP C, E, G**
Liability, **FRCVP F**
Petitory actions, **FRCVP D**
Possessory actions, **FRCVP D**
Quasi in rem, **FRCVP C, E**
Supreme Court, **28 § 2072**
Quasi in rem, **FRCVP E**
Sales, **FRCVP C, E, G**
Searches and seizures, **FRCVP E**
United States vessels, **FRCVP C**
Security interest, **FRCVP D et seq.**

RULES OF CIVIL PROCEDURE
—Cont'd
Admiralty—Cont'd
Supreme Court, **28 §§ 2072, 2073 nt**
Third parties, **FRCVP 14**
Time,
In rem, **FRCVP C**
Liability, **FRCVP F**
Trial, fines, penalties and forfeitures, **FRCVP G**
Trusts and trustees, **FRCVP F**
Venue, **FRCVP 82**
Admissibility of evidence. Evidence, generally, post
Admissions,
Amendments, **FRCVP 36**
Answers, requests, **FRCVP 36**
Expenses and expenditures, requests, **FRCVP 36, 37**
Forms, requests, **FRCVP Form 51**
Pending actions, **FRCVP 36**
Pleading, **FRCVP 8**
Requests, **FRCVP 36, 37**
Forms, **FRCVP Form 51**
Stipulations, **FRCVP 29**
Supplementation, **FRCVP 26**
Stipulations, requests, **FRCVP 29**
Summary judgment, **FRCVP 56**
Supplementation, requests, **FRCVP 26**
Withdrawal, **FRCVP 36**
Adverse or pecuniary interest, depositions, **FRCVP 28**
Advisory juries, **FRCVP 39, 52**
Affidavits,
Admiralty, **FRCVP B**
Bad faith, **FRCVP 56**
Contempt, **FRCVP 56**
Default judgments, **FRCVP 55**
Hearings, **FRCVP 43**
New trial, **FRCVP 59**
Service, **FRCVP 6**
Proof, **FRCVP 4**
Summary judgment, **FRCVP 56**
Temporary restraining orders, **FRCVP 65**
Affirmative defenses,
Pleading, **FRCVP 8**
Service, **FRCVP 5**
Service, pleading, **FRCVP 5**
Age,
Depositions, **FRCVP 32**
Service of process, **FRCVP 4**
Agents and agencies,
Admiralty, **FRCVP E**
Federal agencies, generally, post
Alterations,
Class actions, **FRCVP 23**
Judgments and decrees,
Motions, **FRCVP 59**
Stay of proceedings, **FRCVP 62**
Amendments,
Admissions, **FRCVP 36**
Class actions, **FRCVP 23**
District courts, **FRCVP 83**
Findings, post
Judgments and decrees, post

RULES OF CIVIL PROCEDURE
—Cont'd
Amendments—Cont'd
Modifications, **28 § 2074 nt**
New trial, **FRCVP 59**
Pleading, post
Service, proof, **FRCVP 4**
Summons, **FRCVP 4**
Time, **FRCVP 86**
Ancillary process, admiralty, **FRCVP C**
Answer. Plea or answer, generally, post
Appeal and review,
Admiralty, **FRCVP E**
Supreme Court, **28 § 2072**
Application of rules, **FRCVP 81**
Bonds (officers and fiduciaries), **FRCVP 62**
Class actions, **FRCVP 23**
Clerical errors, **FRCVP 60**
Costs, **FRCVP 54**
Depositions, **FRCVP 27**
District of Columbia, **FRCVP 81**
Dockets and docketing, **FRCVP 6, 60**
Entry of judgment, **FRCVP 77**
Extension of time, **FRCVP 6**
Federal agencies, **28 § 2347; FRCVP 62**
Filing, **28 § 2072**
Final judgments, **FRCVP 79**
Findings, **FRCVP 52**
Habeas corpus, **FRCVP 81**
Injunctions, **FRCVP 62**
Longshoremen and harbor workers, workers compensation, **FRCVP 81**
Magistrate judges, **FRCVP 73**
Pending appeals, **FRCVP 62**
Records and recordation, **FRCVP 5**
Stay of proceedings, **FRCVP 62**
Time,
Costs, **FRCVP 54**
Entry of judgment, **FRCVP 77**
Extension of time, **FRCVP 6**
Stay of proceedings, **FRCVP 62**
Appearances,
Admiralty, **FRCVP E**
Dockets and docketing, **FRCVP 79**
Eminent domain, **FRCVP 71.1**
Service, **FRCVP 5**
Applications, **FRCVP 81**
Injunctions, **FRCVP 65**
Intervention, **FRCVP 24**
Appointment,
Class actions, attorneys, **FRCVP 23**
Interpreters, **FRCVP 43**
Masters, **FRCVP 53**
Process servers, **FRCVP 4**
Arbitration, **FRCVP 81**
Affirmative defenses, **FRCVP 8**
Arrest,
Admiralty, ante
Satisfaction of judgment, **FRCVP 64**
Assessments, masters, **FRCVP 53**
Assistance,
Foreign tribunals, testimony, **28 § 1782**
Writ of assistance, **FRCVP 70**

RULES OF CIVIL PROCEDURE
—Cont'd
Associations and societies,
Business associations, summons, **FRCVP 4**
Capacity, **FRCVP 9, 17**
Cross examination, **FRCVP 43**
Depositions, **FRCVP 32, 37**
Examinations and examiners, **FRCVP 43**
Interrogatories, **FRCVP 33**
Summons, **FRCVP 4**
Unincorporated associations, generally, post
Witnesses, **FRCVP 43**
Assumption of risk, affirmative defenses, **FRCVP 8**
Attachment, **FRCVP 64**
Admiralty, ante
Compulsory counterclaims, **FRCVP 13**
Disobeying judgments, **FRCVP 70**
Attestation, official records, **FRCVP 44**
Attorney General, parties, changes, **FRCVP 15**
Attorneys,
Admiralty, **FRCVP F**
Class actions, **FRCVP 23**
Compensation and salaries. Fees, generally, post
Depositions, **FRCVP 32**
Fees, **FRCVP 30, 37**
Disclosure, **FRCVP 37**
Discovery, **FRCVP 37**
Documents, genuineness, **FRCVP 37**
Entry upon land, **FRCVP 37**
Fees,
Class actions, **FRCVP 23**
Depositions, **FRCVP 30, 37**
Disclosure, **FRCVP 37**
Discovery, **FRCVP 37**
Documents, genuineness, **FRCVP 37**
Entry upon land, **FRCVP 37**
Interrogatories, **FRCVP 37**
Judgments and decrees, **FRCVP 58**
Motions, **FRCVP 54**
Orders, **FRCVP 37**
Pleading, **FRCVP 11**
Pretrial conferences, **FRCVP 16**
Pretrial orders, **FRCVP 16**
Production of documents or things, **FRCVP 37**
Sanctions, **FRCVP 11**
Summary judgment, **FRCVP 56**
Summons, **FRCVP 4**
Interrogatories,
Fees, **FRCVP 37**
Signatures, **FRCVP 33**
Judgments and decrees, **FRCVP 58**
Jury, instructions, **FRCVP 51**
Masters, **FRCVP 53**
Motions,
Fees, **FRCVP 54**
Signatures, **FRCVP 11**
Orders, fees, **FRCVP 37**
Pleading,
Fees, **FRCVP 11**

RULES OF CIVIL PROCEDURE —Cont'd
Attorneys—Cont'd
Pleading—Cont'd
Service, **FRCVP 5**
Signatures, **FRCVP 11**
Pretrial conferences, fees, **FRCVP 16**
Pretrial orders, fees, **FRCVP 16**
Production of documents or things, fees, **FRCVP 37**
Sanctions, fees, **FRCVP 11, 16**
Signatures,
Admissions, **FRCVP 36**
Discovery, **FRCVP 26**
Pleading, **FRCVP 11**
Summary judgment, fees, **FRCVP 56**
Summons, fees, **FRCVP 4**
Temporary restraining orders, **FRCVP 65**
Audiovisual media, depositions, **FRCVP 30**
Audita querela, abolition of writ, **FRCVP 60**
Audits and auditors,
Business records, **FRCVP 33**
Masters, **FRCVP 53**
Authentication, official records, **FRCVP 44**
Avoidance, pleading, **FRCVP 5, 8**
Bad faith, depositions, sanctions, **FRCVP 30**
Bailment, **FRCVP 17**
Bankruptcy,
Affirmative defenses, discharge, **FRCVP 8**
Discharge, affirmative defenses, **FRCVP 8**
Bills of review, abolition, **FRCVP 60**
Boards and commissions,
Eminent domain, **FRCVP 71.1**
Masters, **FRCVP 53**
Pleading, **FRCVP 9**
Bonds (officers and fiduciaries), **FRCVP 65.1**
Admiralty, **FRCVP E**
Appeal and review, **FRCVP 62**
Injunctions, **FRCVP 62**
Books and papers,
Delivery, **FRCVP 70**
Discovery, **FRCVP 26**
Masters, **FRCVP 53**
Pleading, **FRCVP 9**
Production of books and papers, generally, post
Retention, **FRCVP 79**
Subpoenas, **FRCVP 45**
Business associations, summons, **FRCVP 4**
Business records, interrogatories, **FRCVP 33**
Calendars,
Declaratory judgments, **FRCVP 57**
Preparation, **FRCVP 79**
Pretrial calendar, **FRCVP 16**
Trial, **FRCVP 40**
Capacity, **FRCVP 9, 17**

RULES OF CIVIL PROCEDURE —Cont'd
Captions,
Forms, **FRCVP Form 1**
Motions, **FRCVP 7**
Pleading, **FRCVP 10**
Certificates and certification,
Class actions, **FRCVP 23**
Constitutional challenges, statutes, **FRCVP 5.1**
Depositions, **FRCVP 30**
Discovery, attorneys, **FRCVP 26**
Habeas corpus, probable cause, **FRCVP 81**
Official records, authentication, **FRCVP 44**
Service of process, **FRCVP 5**
Temporary restraining orders, attorneys, **FRCVP 65**
Certified copies, summary judgment, **FRCVP 56**
Certified public accountants, masters, **FRCVP 53**
Challenges, jury, **FRCVP 47**
Chambers, **FRCVP 77**
Chief Justice of Supreme Court, reports, **28 § 2072**
Children and minors,
Default judgments, **FRCVP 55**
Depositions, **FRCVP 27**
Parties, **FRCVP 17**
Summons, **FRCVP 4**
Citations,
Federal Rules of Civil Procedure, **FRCVP 85**
Local district rules, **FRCVP 83**
Citizens and citizenship, admission to citizenship, **FRCVP 81**
Civil commitment, orders, **FRCVP 4.1**
Civil justice, reform, **28 § 519 nt, EON 12988**
Claims,
Admiralty, generally, ante
Cross claims, generally, post
Multiple claims or parties, generally, post
Set-off and counterclaim, generally, post
Third parties, generally, post
Class actions, **FRCVP 23**
Joinder, **FRCVP 19**
Shares and shareholders, derivative actions, **FRCVP 23.1**
Unincorporated associations, **FRCVP 23.2**
Clerical mistakes, corrections, **FRCVP 60**
Clerks of courts,
Admiralty, release, **FRCVP E**
Appeal and review, costs, **FRCVP 54**
Books and papers, **FRCVP 79**
Business hours, **FRCVP 77**
Calendars, **FRCVP 79**
Chambers, **FRCVP 77**
Copies, **FRCVP 79**
Costs, taxation, **FRCVP 54**
Default judgments, **FRCVP 55**

RULES OF CIVIL PROCEDURE —Cont'd
Clerks of courts—Cont'd
Entry of judgment, **FRCVP 58**
Executions, **FRCVP 70**
Masters, **FRCVP 53**
Notice, **FRCVP 77**
Office hours, **FRCVP 77**
Orders of court, **FRCVP 77, 79**
Pleading, **FRCVP 5**
Records and recordation, **FRCVP 79**
Service of process, **FRCVP 65.1**
Summons, **FRCVP 4**
Writ of assistance, **FRCVP 70**
Commissions and commissioners. Boards and commissions, generally, ante
Committees, incompetents, **FRCVP 17**
Commonwealth, official records, authentication, **FRCVP 44**
Compensation and salaries,
Eminent domain, **FRCVP 71.1**
Interpreters, **FRCVP 43**
Masters, **FRCVP 53**
Complaints,
Admiralty, ante
Conversion, **FRCVP Form 15**
Copyrights, infringement, **FRCVP Form 19**
Eminent domain, **FRCVP 71.1; FRCVP Form 61**
Federal officers and employees, **28 § 1391**
Filing, **FRCVP 3**
Fraudulent conveyances, **FRCVP Form 21**
Interpleader, **FRCVP Form 20**
Merchant Marine Act, **FRCVP Form 14**
Money, sum certain, **FRCVP Form 10**
Negligence, **FRCVP Form 11 et seq.**
Patents, infringement, **FRCVP Form 18**
Specific performance, **FRCVP Form 17**
Summons, **FRCVP 4**
Third parties, **FRCVP 7; FRCVP Form 16**
Title of action, **FRCVP 10**
Complicated issues, masters, **FRCVP 53**
Compromise and settlement,
Class actions, **FRCVP 23**
Derivative actions, **FRCVP 23.1**
Unincorporated associations, **FRCVP 23.2**
Compulsory counterclaims, pleading, **FRCVP 13**
Compulsory process, admiralty, **FRCVP B**
Computation, time, **FRCVP 6**
Conciseness, pleading, **FRCVP 8**
Conclusions of law, **FRCVP 52 et seq.**
Masters, **FRCVP 53**
New trial, **FRCVP 59**
Condemnation. Eminent domain, generally, post
Conditional rulings, motions, **FRCVP 50**

RULES OF CIVIL PROCEDURE
—Cont'd
Conditions, pleading, **FRCVP 9**
Conferences, pretrial conferences, **FRCVP 16**
Confidential or privileged information, discovery, **FRCVP 26**
Conflict of interest, depositions, **FRCVP 28**
Conflict of laws, capacity, **FRCVP 17**
Consent,
Admiralty, release, **FRCVP E**
Court trial, **FRCVP 39**
Jury trial, **FRCVP 39**
Withdrawal, **FRCVP 38**
Magistrate judges, jurisdiction, **FRCVP 73; FRCVP Form 81**
Conservators and conservatorship, **FRCVP 17**
Consideration, pleading, defenses, **FRCVP 8**
Consolidations and mergers. Merger and consolidation, generally, post
Constitutional challenges, statutes, **FRCVP 5.1**
Contempt,
Depositions, **FRCVP 37**
Discovery, **FRCVP 37**
Masters, **FRCVP 53**
Service of order, **FRCVP 4.1**
Subpoenas, **FRCVP 45**
Summary judgment, **FRCVP 56**
Continuances,
Pleading, **FRCVP 15**
Summary judgment, **FRCVP 56**
Contradicting testimony, depositions, **FRCVP 32**
Contribution, admiralty, third parties, **FRCVP 14**
Contributory negligence, affirmative defenses, **FRCVP 8**
Conversion, complaints, **FRCVP Form 15**
Copies,
Admiralty, **FRCVP E**
Admissions, documents, **FRCVP 36**
Business records, **FRCVP 33**
Eminent domain, **FRCVP 71.1**
Foreign official records, authentication, **FRCVP 44**
Masters, **FRCVP 53**
Orders of court, **FRCVP 27**
Written instruments, **FRCVP 10**
Copyrights,
Application of rules, **FRCVP 81**
Infringement, complaints, **FRCVP Form 19**
Coram nobis, writ abolished, **FRCVP 60**
Coram vobis, writ abolished, **FRCVP 60**
Corporations,
Admiralty, security, **FRCVP E**
Capacity, **FRCVP 17**
Depositions, **FRCVP 32, 37**
Disclosure, statements, **FRCVP 7.1**
Interrogatories, **FRCVP 33**
Shares and shareholders, derivative actions, **FRCVP 23.1**

RULES OF CIVIL PROCEDURE
—Cont'd
Corporations—Cont'd
Statements, disclosure, **FRCVP 7.1**
Summons, **FRCVP 4**
Correctional institutions,
Depositions, **FRCVP 30 et seq.**
Habeas corpus, **FRCVP 81**
Corrections, clerical errors, **FRCVP 60**
Costs,
Admiralty, ante
Default judgments, **FRCVP 55**
Depositions, **FRCVP 30**
Disclosure, parties, refusal, **FRCVP 37**
Discovery, **FRCVP 26**
Injunctions, **FRCVP 65**
Interpreters, **FRCVP 43**
Judgments and decrees, **FRCVP 58**
Offer of judgment, **FRCVP 68**
Pretrial conferences, sanctions, **FRCVP 16**
Pretrial orders, sanctions, **FRCVP 16**
Previously dismissed actions, **FRCVP 41**
Service of process, **FRCVP 4**
Signatures, sanctions, **FRCVP 11**
Summary judgment, **FRCVP 56**
Summons, **FRCVP 4**
Counterclaims. Set-off and counterclaim, generally, post
Court trials. Trial, post
Courts of appeals,
Extension of time, **FRCVP 6**
Time, extension of time, **FRCVP 6**
Cross claims, **FRCVP 8, 13**
Answers, **FRCVP 7, 12**
Dismissal and nonsuit, **FRCVP 41**
Entry of judgment, **FRCVP 54**
Joinder, **FRCVP 18**
Judgments and decrees, **FRCVP 54**
Separate trial, **FRCVP 42**
Service, **FRCVP 5**
Third parties, **FRCVP 14**
Time, answers, **FRCVP 12**
Cross examination, depositions, **FRCVP 30**
Cross questions, depositions, **FRCVP 31**
Custody, admiralty, **FRCVP E**
Customs, admiralty, vessels, clearance, **FRCVP E**
Damages,
Admiralty, **FRCVP E**
Default judgments, **FRCVP 55**
Discovery, **FRCVP 26**
Injunctions, **FRCVP 65**
Masters, **FRCVP 53**
Special damages, **FRCVP 9**
Summary judgment, **FRCVP 56**
Date, forms, **FRCVP Form 2**
Death,
Admiralty, **FRCVP F**
Parties,
Statements, **FRCVP Form 9**
Substitution, **FRCVP 25**
Public officers and employees, substitution, **FRCVP 25**

RULES OF CIVIL PROCEDURE
—Cont'd
Death—Cont'd
Witnesses, depositions, **FRCVP 32**
Decisions. Opinions and decisions, generally, post
Declaratory judgments and decrees, **FRCVP 57**
Class actions, **FRCVP 23**
Decrees. Judgments and decrees, generally, post
Default judgment, **FRCVP 54, 55**
Admiralty, **FRCVP B**
Demands, **FRCVP 54**
Discovery, **FRCVP 37**
Pleading, **FRCVP 54, 55**
Summons, **FRCVP 4**
Defenses. Pleading, post
Definitions, filing, **FRCVP 5**
Delays,
Depositions, **FRCVP 30**
Discovery, **FRCVP 26**
Delivery,
Admiralty, process, **FRCVP E**
Examinations and examiners, reports, **FRCVP 35**
Pleadings, copies, **FRCVP 5**
United States, process, **FRCVP 15**
Demand,
Judgments and decrees, **FRCVP 8, 54**
Jury, post
Process, post
Denials, **FRCVP 8**
Conditions precedent, **FRCVP 9**
Depositions, **FRCVP 26 et seq.**
Admissibility of evidence, **FRCVP 32**
Adverse or pecuniary interest, **FRCVP 28**
Age, attendance, **FRCVP 32**
Alterations, **FRCVP 26**
Associations and societies, **FRCVP 32, 37**
Attorneys, ante
Audiovisual media, **FRCVP 30**
Certificates and certification, **FRCVP 30**
Compelling answers, **FRCVP 37**
Competency, **FRCVP 32**
Completion, notice, **FRCVP 31**
Conflict of interest, **FRCVP 28**
Contradicting testimony, **FRCVP 32**
Corporations, **FRCVP 32, 37**
Correctional institutions, **FRCVP 30 et seq.**
Costs, **FRCVP 30**
Cross questions, **FRCVP 31**
Death, **FRCVP 32**
Delays, **FRCVP 30**
Disqualification, **FRCVP 28, 32**
Errors, **FRCVP 32**
Evasive answers, **FRCVP 37**
Exhibits, **FRCVP 30**
Expenses and expenditures, **FRCVP 37**
Expert witnesses, **FRCVP 26**
Federal agencies, **FRCVP 32, 37**
Foreign countries, **FRCVP 28**

RULES OF CIVIL PROCEDURE
—Cont'd
Depositions—Cont'd
Forms, **FRCVP 32**
Hearings, **FRCVP 32**
Illness, attendance, **FRCVP 32**
Incomplete answers, **FRCVP 37**
Interrogatories, **FRCVP 31, 33**
Irregularities, **FRCVP 32**
Letters of request, foreign countries, **FRCVP 28**
Mental examinations, **FRCVP 35**
Motions, compelling answers, **FRCVP 37**
Multiple depositions, leave of court, **FRCVP 30, 31**
Nonattendance, **FRCVP 37**
Notice, **FRCVP 28 et seq.**
Completion, **FRCVP 31**
Errors, **FRCVP 32**
Foreign countries, **FRCVP 28**
Irregularities, **FRCVP 32**
Oral examinations, **FRCVP 30**
Stipulations, **FRCVP 29**
Written questions, **FRCVP 31**
Oaths and affirmations, **FRCVP 28**
Oral examinations, **FRCVP 30**
Objections and exceptions, **FRCVP 26**
Depositions, **FRCVP 30**
Errors, **FRCVP 32**
Irregularities, **FRCVP 32**
Subpoenas, **FRCVP 45**
Officers and employees, **FRCVP 28, 30**
Oral examinations, **FRCVP 30 et seq.**
Orders of court, **FRCVP 27, 37**
Outside United States, **FRCVP 32**
Partnership, **FRCVP 32, 37**
Pending appeals, **FRCVP 27**
Petitions, **FRCVP 27**
Physical examinations, **FRCVP 35**
Place, **FRCVP 32**
Prior actions, **FRCVP 32**
Prisoners, **FRCVP 30 et seq.**
Protective orders, **FRCVP 32**
Records and recordation, **FRCVP 30**
Recross questions, **FRCVP 31**
Redirect questions, **FRCVP 31**
Returns, **FRCVP 32**
Sanctions, **FRCVP 30**
Service, **FRCVP 27**
Sound recordings, **FRCVP 30**
Stipulations, **FRCVP 29**
Subpoenas, **FRCVP 45**
Nonattendance, **FRCVP 32**
Written questions, **FRCVP 31**
Substitution, parties, **FRCVP 32**
Summary judgment, **FRCVP 56**
Supplementation, **FRCVP 26**
Termination, **FRCVP 30**
Time, **FRCVP 27**
Stipulations, **FRCVP 29**
Written questions, **FRCVP 31**
Trial, **FRCVP 32**
United States, post
Venue, **FRCVP 32, 37**
Written questions, **FRCVP 31 et seq.**

RULES OF CIVIL PROCEDURE
—Cont'd
Deposits,
Admiralty, ante
Court of appeals, **FRCVP 73**
Courts, **FRCVP 67**
Eminent domain, **FRCVP 71.1**
Derivative actions, shares and shareholders, **FRCVP 23.1**
Diagnoses, reports, **FRCVP 35**
Directed verdict. Judgment as a matter of law, generally, post
Disclosure,
Corporations, statements, **FRCVP 7.1**
Electronically stored information, **FRCVP 16, 26, 33 et seq.**
Motions, **FRCVP 37**
Discovery, **FRCVP 26 et seq.**
Attorneys, fees, **FRCVP 37**
Conferences, **FRCVP 26**
Executions, **FRCVP 69**
Expenses and expenditures, **FRCVP 37**
Foreign countries, **FRCVP 37**
Modification, **FRCVP 16**
Orders of court, **FRCVP 37**
Plans and specifications, **FRCVP 26**
Pretrial conferences, **FRCVP 16**
Pretrial disclosures, **FRCVP 26**
Protective orders, **FRCVP 26, 37**
Sanctions, **FRCVP 37**
Service, **FRCVP 5**
Signatures, **FRCVP 26**
Stipulations, **FRCVP 29**
Summary judgment, **FRCVP 56**
Supplementation, **FRCVP 26**
Time,
Modification, **FRCVP 16**
Pretrial disclosures, **FRCVP 26**
Stipulations, **FRCVP 29**
Trial preparation materials, exemptions, **FRCVP 26**
Witnesses, **FRCVP 26 et seq.**
Discretion of court,
Interpreters, **FRCVP 43**
Jury trial, **FRCVP 39**
Masters, **FRCVP 53**
Dismissal and nonsuit, **FRCVP 41**
Admiralty, **FRCVP F**
Class actions, **FRCVP 23**
Derivative actions, **FRCVP 23.1**
Discovery, **FRCVP 37**
Eminent domain, **FRCVP 71.1**
Forms, motions, **FRCVP Form 40**
Joinder, **FRCVP 19**
Jurisdiction, post
Motions,
Conclusions of law, **FRCVP 52**
Findings, **FRCVP 52**
Forms, **FRCVP Form 40**
Pleading, **FRCVP 12**
Real party in interest, **FRCVP 17**
Receivers and receivership, **FRCVP 66**
Substitution, parties, **FRCVP 25**
Summons, **FRCVP 4**
Third parties, **FRCVP 41**

RULES OF CIVIL PROCEDURE
—Cont'd
Dismissal and nonsuit—Cont'd
Unincorporated associations, **FRCVP 23.2**
Voluntary dismissal, **FRCVP 41**
Dispositions, admiralty, property, **FRCVP E**
Distributions,
Admiralty, funds, **FRCVP F**
Eminent domain, **FRCVP 71.1**
District courts,
Depositions, **FRCVP 37**
Hearings, **FRCVP 77**
Local rules, **FRCVP 83**
Time, **FRCVP 6**
Motion day, **FRCVP 78**
Official records, authentication, **FRCVP 44**
Time, local rules, **FRCVP 6**
District of Columbia, **FRCVP 81**
Dockets and docketing,
Appeal and review, **FRCVP 6, 60**
Entries, **FRCVP 79**
Jury trial, **FRCVP 39**
Notice, **FRCVP 77**
Domestic official records, authentication, **FRCVP 44**
Domicile and residence, parties, capacity, **FRCVP 17**
Duress, pleading, affirmative defenses, **FRCVP 8**
Dwellings,
Pleading, service, **FRCVP 5**
Summons, service, **FRCVP 4**
E-mail, forms, **FRCVP Form 2**
Electronic filing, **FRCVP 5**
Electronically stored information, disclosure, **FRCVP 16, 26, 33 et seq.**
Eminent domain, **FRCVP 71.1**
Admiralty, supplemental rules, **FRCVP A**
Complaints, **FRCVP 71.1; FRCVP Form 61**
Forms,
Complaints, **FRCVP Form 61**
Notice, **FRCVP Form 60**
Notice, **FRCVP 71.1; FRCVP Form 60**
Employees. Officers and employees, generally, post
Entry of judgment. Judgments and decrees, post
Entry upon land, **FRCVP 34**
Forms, requests, **FRCVP Form 50**
Requests, **FRCVP 34; FRCVP Form 50**
Sanctions, **FRCVP 37**
Stipulations, **FRCVP 29**
Equity,
Joinder, **FRCVP 18, 19**
Pleading, **FRCVP 8**
Error. Mistake, generally, post
Estoppel, pleading, affirmative defenses, **FRCVP 8**

RULES OF CIVIL PROCEDURE
—Cont'd
Evidence,
Admiralty, default judgments, **FRCVP B**
Affidavits, **FRCVP 43**
Compelling testimony, **FRCVP 81**
Costs, **FRCVP 68**
Eminent domain, **FRCVP 71.1**
Foreign laws, **FRCVP 44.1**
Forms, **FRCVP 43**
Harmless error, **FRCVP 61**
Injunctions, **FRCVP 65**
Interpreters, **FRCVP 43**
Letters of request, **FRCVP 28**
Masters, **FRCVP 53**
Motions, **FRCVP 43**
Oaths and affirmations, **FRCVP 43**
Objections and exceptions, **FRCVP 52**
Official records, **FRCVP 44**
Perpetuating testimony, **FRCVP 27**
Pleading, amendments, **FRCVP 15**
Pretrial procedure, **FRCVP 16**
Process, **FRCVP 4, 4.1**
Stenographers, **FRCVP 80**
Subpoenas, **FRCVP 45**
United States, **FRCVP 55**
Voluntary dismissal, **FRCVP 41**
Ex parte proceedings, masters, **FRCVP 53**
Examinations and examiners, **FRCVP 35, 37**
Business records, **FRCVP 33**
Depositions, generally, ante
Jury, **FRCVP 47**
Masters, **FRCVP 53**
Mental health, **FRCVP 35, 37**
Physical examinations, **FRCVP 35, 37**
Sanctions, **FRCVP 37**
Exceptions. Objections and exceptions, generally, post
Excusable neglect, **FRCVP 6, 60**
Execution,
Admiralty, **FRCVP E**
Discovery, **FRCVP 69**
Dockets and docketing, **FRCVP 79**
Masters, **FRCVP 53**
Possession, **FRCVP 70**
Stay of proceedings, **FRCVP 62**
Time, **FRCVP 62**
Executors and administrators, **FRCVP 17**
Exemptions,
Depositions, **FRCVP 32**
U.S. vessels, arrest, supplemental rules, **FRCVP C**
Exhibits,
Depositions, **FRCVP 30**
Discovery, **FRCVP 26**
Masters, **FRCVP 53**
Written instruments, **FRCVP 10**
Exoneration, admiralty, **FRCVP A, F**
Expenses and expenditures,
Admiralty, **FRCVP E**
Admissions, requests, **FRCVP 36**
Depositions, **FRCVP 37**
Discovery, **FRCVP 37**

RULES OF CIVIL PROCEDURE
—Cont'd
Expenses and expenditures—Cont'd
Documents, genuineness, **FRCVP 37**
Entry upon land, **FRCVP 37**
Interrogatories, **FRCVP 37**
Production of documents or things, **FRCVP 37**
Experts, **FRCVP 43**
Depositions, **FRCVP 26**
Discovery, **FRCVP 26**
Pretrial conferences, **FRCVP 16**
Facsimile transmissions, **FRCVP 5**
Facts. Questions of law or fact, generally, post
Fair conduct, class actions, **FRCVP 23**
Federal agencies,
Answers, **FRCVP 12**
Appeal and review, **28 § 2347; FRCVP 62**
Depositions, **FRCVP 32, 37**
Injunctions, **FRCVP 65**
Interrogatories, **FRCVP 33**
Process, **FRCVP 15**
Subpoenas, **FRCVP 45, 81**
Federal Employers Liability Act, negligence, complaints, **FRCVP Form 13**
Federal officers and employees,
Answer, **FRCVP 12**
Appeal and review, **FRCVP 62**
Compelling testimony, **FRCVP 81**
Definitions, **FRCVP 81**
Injunctions, **FRCVP 65**
Process, **FRCVP 15**
Subpoenas, **FRCVP 45**
Fees. Attorneys, ante
Fellow servant, pleading, affirmative defenses, **FRCVP 8**
Filing,
Admiralty, ante
Complaints, **FRCVP 3**
Definitions, **FRCVP 5**
Electronic filing, **FRCVP 5**
Eminent domain, **FRCVP 71.1**
Facsimile transmissions, **FRCVP 5**
Masters, **FRCVP 53**
Numbers and numbering, dockets and docketing, **FRCVP 79**
Pleading, **FRCVP 3 et seq.**
Privacy protection, **FRCVP 5.2**
Findings, **FRCVP 52, 53**
Admiralty, **FRCVP F**
Amendments,
Extension of time, **FRCVP 6**
New trial, motions, **FRCVP 59**
Stay of proceedings, **FRCVP 62**
Class actions, **FRCVP 23**
Jury, unanimity, **FRCVP 48**
New trial, **FRCVP 59**
Special verdict, **FRCVP 49**
Stay of proceedings, **FRCVP 62**
Fines, penalties and forfeitures,
Admiralty, **FRCVP A, C, G**
Conferences, **FRCVP 16**
Depositions, **FRCVP 30**
Disclosure, parties, **FRCVP 37**

RULES OF CIVIL PROCEDURE
—Cont'd
Fines, penalties and forfeitures—Cont'd
Discovery, **FRCVP 37**
Motions, **FRCVP 11**
Pleading, **FRCVP 11**
Pretrial conferences, **FRCVP 16**
Pretrial orders, **FRCVP 16**
Subpoenas, **FRCVP 45**
Witnesses, **FRCVP 53**
Foreign countries,
Authentication, **28 § 1741**
Depositions, **FRCVP 28**
Discovery, **FRCVP 37**
Judgments and decrees, **FRCVP 9**
Laws, **FRCVP 44.1**
Official records, authentication, **FRCVP 44**
Subpoenas, **FRCVP 45**
Summons, **FRCVP 4**
Foreign diplomatic and consular officers,
Authentication, **FRCVP 44**
Depositions, **FRCVP 28**
Forfeitures. Fines, penalties and forfeitures, generally, ante
Forms, **FRCVP Form 1 et seq.**
Addresses, **FRCVP Form 2**
Admissions, requests, **FRCVP Form 51**
Appendix forms, **FRCVP 84**
Captions, **FRCVP Form 1**
Conversion, complaints, **FRCVP Form 15**
Copyrights, infringement, complaints, **FRCVP Form 19**
Date, **FRCVP Form 2**
Defenses, plea or answer, **FRCVP Form 30**
Depositions, **FRCVP 32**
Dismissal and nonsuit, motions, **FRCVP Form 40**
E-mail, **FRCVP Form 2**
Eminent domain,
Complaints, **FRCVP Form 61**
Notice, **FRCVP Form 60**
Entry upon land, requests, **FRCVP Form 50**
Evidence, **FRCVP 43**
Fraudulent conveyances, complaints, **FRCVP Form 21**
Interpleader, complaints, **FRCVP Form 20**
Intervention, **FRCVP Form 42**
Judgments and decrees, **FRCVP Form 71**
Jurisdiction, statements, **FRCVP Form 7**
Magistrate judges, jurisdiction, **FRCVP Form 80 et seq.**
Masters, **FRCVP 53**
Merchant Marine Act, complaints, **FRCVP Form 14**
Money,
Had and received, plea or answer, **FRCVP Form 31**
Sum certain, complaints, **FRCVP Form 10**

RULES OF CIVIL PROCEDURE
—Cont'd
Forms—Cont'd
Motions, **FRCVP Form 40 et seq.**
Negligence, complaints, **FRCVP Form 11 et seq.**
Notice, **FRCVP Form 5 et seq.**
Parties, post
Patents, infringement, complaints, **FRCVP Form 18**
Pleading, **FRCVP 10; FRCVP Form 10 et seq.**
Process, **28 § 2072**
Production of books and papers, requests, **FRCVP Form 50**
Public policy, **FRCVP 84**
Sanctions, nonuse, **FRCVP 83**
Signatures, **FRCVP Form 2**
Specific performance, complaints, **FRCVP Form 17**
Subpoenas, **FRCVP 45**
Summons, post
Telephone numbers, **FRCVP Form 2**
Third parties, post
Verdict, **FRCVP Form 70**
Fraud,
Judgments and decrees, **FRCVP 60**
Pleading, **FRCVP 9**
Fraudulent conveyances,
Complaints, **FRCVP Form 21**
Joinder, **FRCVP 18**
Garnishment, **FRCVP 64**
Admiralty, ante
Good cause,
Electronically stored information, access, **FRCVP 26**
Examinations and examiners, **FRCVP 35**
Grounds, new trial, **FRCVP 59**
Guardian and ward, **FRCVP 17**
Habeas corpus, **FRCVP 81**
Harmless error, **FRCVP 61**
Hearings,
Admiralty, **FRCVP E, F**
Consolidation and merger, **FRCVP 42**
Depositions, motions, **FRCVP 32**
Discovery, **FRCVP 37**
Injunctions, **FRCVP 65**
Judges or justices, inability to proceed, **FRCVP 63**
New trial, **FRCVP 59**
Nonoral hearings, motions, **FRCVP 78**
Notice, **FRCVP 6**
Outside district, **FRCVP 77**
Preliminary hearings, **FRCVP 12**
Subpoenas, **FRCVP 45**
Successor judges, **FRCVP 63**
Temporary restraining orders, **FRCVP 65**
Voluntary dismissal, **FRCVP 41**
Holidays,
Clerks of courts, business hours, **FRCVP 77**
Definitions, **FRCVP 6**
Time, computation, **FRCVP 6**

RULES OF CIVIL PROCEDURE
—Cont'd
Houses,
Pleading, service, **FRCVP 5**
Summons, service, **FRCVP 4**
Illegality, pleading, affirmative defenses, **FRCVP 8**
Illness, depositions, **FRCVP 32**
Immigration, privacy protection, **FRCVP 5.2**
Impeachment, depositions, **FRCVP 32**
Imprisonment, depositions, **FRCVP 32**
In forma pauperis, process, **FRCVP 4**
In personam actions, admiralty, **FRCVP B, C, E**
In rem. Admiralty, ante
Inadvertence, judgments and decrees, **FRCVP 60**
Incompetency, **FRCVP 17**
Default judgments, **FRCVP 55**
Depositions, **FRCVP 27**
Substitution, **FRCVP 25**
Summons, **FRCVP 4**
Indexes, **FRCVP 79**
Indorsement,
Admiralty, **FRCVP E**
Temporary restraining orders, **FRCVP 65**
Infirmities, depositions, **FRCVP 32**
Infringement, stay of proceedings, accounts and accounting, **FRCVP 62**
Initial discovery, **FRCVP 26**
Injunctions, **FRCVP 65**
Admiralty, **FRCVP F**
Appeal and review, **FRCVP 62**
Class actions, **FRCVP 23**
Inspection and inspectors,
Business records, **FRCVP 33**
Entry upon land, generally, ante
Orders, **FRCVP 27**
Production of books and papers, generally, post
Instructions, jury, **FRCVP 49, 51**
Insular possessions, official record, authentication, **FRCVP 44**
Insurance, discovery, **FRCVP 26**
Intangible property, admiralty, **FRCVP C, E**
Intent, pleading, **FRCVP 9**
Interest, admiralty, **FRCVP F**
Interested parties,
Class actions, **FRCVP 23**
Depositions, **FRCVP 28**
Intervention, **FRCVP 24**
Joinder, **FRCVP 19**
Interlocutory proceedings,
Admiralty, **FRCVP E**
Injunctions, **FRCVP 52**
Internal Revenue Service, judgments and decrees, **FRCVP 69**
International agreements, summons, **FRCVP 4**
Interpleader, **FRCVP 22**
Complaints, **FRCVP Form 20**
Injunctions, **FRCVP 65**
Interpreters, **FRCVP 43**

RULES OF CIVIL PROCEDURE
—Cont'd
Interrogatories, **FRCVP 33**
Admiralty, **FRCVP B, C, G**
Alterations, **FRCVP 26**
Attorneys, ante
Business records, **FRCVP 33**
Compelling answers, **FRCVP 37**
Electronically stored information, **FRCVP 33**
Evasive answers, **FRCVP 37**
Experts, **FRCVP 26**
General verdicts, **FRCVP 49**
Incomplete answers, **FRCVP 37**
Jury, **FRCVP 49**
Masters, **FRCVP 53**
Motions, **FRCVP 33 et seq.**
Objections and exceptions, **FRCVP 33**
Orders of court, **FRCVP 33, 37**
Sanctions, **FRCVP 37**
Service, **FRCVP 33**
Stipulations, **FRCVP 29**
Summary judgment, **FRCVP 56**
Supplementation, **FRCVP 26**
Time, **FRCVP 33**
Trial, **FRCVP 33**
Written interrogatories, **FRCVP 49**
Intervention, **FRCVP 24**
Constitutional challenges, statutes, **FRCVP 5.1**
Forms, **FRCVP Form 42**
Motions, **FRCVP 24; FRCVP Form 42**
Investigations,
Admiralty, **FRCVP E**
Foreign official records, **FRCVP 44**
Involuntary plaintiffs, joinder, **FRCVP 19**
Issues,
Court trial, **FRCVP 39**
Jury trial, **FRCVP 38, 39**
Pretrial procedure, **FRCVP 16**
Separate trials, **FRCVP 42**
Joinder,
Claims, **FRCVP 18**
Eminent domain, **FRCVP 71.1**
Fraudulent conveyances, **FRCVP 18**
Parties, post
Remedies, **FRCVP 18**
Joint hearings, **FRCVP 42**
Judges or justices,
Filing, **FRCVP 5**
Inability to proceed, **FRCVP 63**
Magistrate judges, generally, post
Masters, **FRCVP 53**
Official records, authentication, **FRCVP 44**
Successor judges, **FRCVP 63**
Judgment as a matter of law, **FRCVP 50**
Extension of time, **FRCVP 6**
Stay of proceedings, **FRCVP 62**
Judgments and decrees,
Admiralty, ante
Amendments,
Findings, **FRCVP 52**
Stay of proceedings, **FRCVP 62**
Time, **FRCVP 59**
Attachment, **FRCVP 70**

RULES OF CIVIL PROCEDURE
—Cont'd
Judgments and decrees—Cont'd
Attorneys, fees, **FRCVP 58**
Audita querela, **FRCVP 60**
Bills of review, **FRCVP 60**
Class actions, **FRCVP 23**
Clerical mistakes, corrections, **FRCVP 60**
Compulsory counterclaims, **FRCVP 13**
Copies, **FRCVP 79**
Coram nobis, **FRCVP 60**
Costs, **FRCVP 58**
Cross claims, **FRCVP 13, 54**
Default judgment, generally, ante
Definitions, **FRCVP 54**
Demand, **FRCVP 8, 54**
Discovery, **FRCVP 69**
Dockets and docketing, entries, **FRCVP 79**
Entry of judgment, **FRCVP 58**
Advisory juries, **FRCVP 52**
General verdicts, **FRCVP 49**
Multiple claims, **FRCVP 54**
Multiple parties, **FRCVP 54**
New trial, **FRCVP 59**
Partial findings, **FRCVP 52**
Excusable neglect, **FRCVP 60**
Finality, **FRCVP 60**
Forms, **FRCVP Form 71**
Fraud, **FRCVP 60**
Inadvertence, **FRCVP 60**
Indexes, **FRCVP 79**
Joinder, **FRCVP 19**
Masters, reports, **FRCVP 54**
Misconduct, **FRCVP 60**
Mistake, **FRCVP 60**
Modifications, **FRCVP 61**
Motions,
Amendments, **FRCVP 6, 59**
Clerical mistakes, **FRCVP 60**
Conclusions of law, **FRCVP 52**
Excusable neglect, **FRCVP 60**
Findings, **FRCVP 52**
Matter of law, **FRCVP 50**
Mistake, **FRCVP 60**
Multiple claims, **FRCVP 54**
Multiple parties, **FRCVP 54**
Objections and exceptions, **FRCVP 52**
Pleading, judgment on the pleading, **FRCVP 12**
Stay of proceedings, **FRCVP 62**
New trial, **FRCVP 59, 62**
Newly discovered evidence, **FRCVP 60**
Notwithstanding the verdict, judgment as a matter of law, **FRCVP 50**
Offer of judgment, **FRCVP 5, 68**
Partial findings, **FRCVP 52**
Pleading, post
Possession, **FRCVP 70**
Prior proceedings, records and recordation, **FRCVP 54**
Recitals, **FRCVP 54**
Requests, entry of judgment, **FRCVP 58**

RULES OF CIVIL PROCEDURE
—Cont'd
Judgments and decrees—Cont'd
Reversals, **FRCVP 60**
Satisfaction, **FRCVP 60**
Admiralty, **FRCVP E**
Separate judgments, **FRCVP 54**
Sequestration, property, **FRCVP 70**
Set-off and counterclaim, **FRCVP 13**
Entry of judgment, **FRCVP 54**
Specific performance, **FRCVP 70**
State laws, enforcement, **FRCVP 62**
Stay of proceedings, **FRCVP 62**
Summary judgment, generally, post
Surprise, **FRCVP 60**
Suspension, **FRCVP 60**
Third parties, **FRCVP 54**
Admiralty, **FRCVP 14**
Time,
Enforcement, **FRCVP 62**
Entry of judgment, **FRCVP 58**
Excusable neglect, **FRCVP 60**
Extension of time, **FRCVP 6**
Mistake, **FRCVP 60**
Title to property, **FRCVP 70**
United States, **FRCVP 62**
Vacating or setting aside, **FRCVP 60, 61**
Void judgment, **FRCVP 60**
Written interrogatories, jury, verdicts, **FRCVP 49**
Judicial Conference, **28 § 2073**
Jurisdiction,
Application of rules, **FRCVP 82**
Defenses, **FRCVP 12**
Dismissal and nonsuit, **FRCVP 41**
Subject matter jurisdiction, **FRCVP 12**
Forms, statements, **FRCVP Form 7**
Magistrate judges, post
Objections and exceptions, **FRCVP 4**
Personal jurisdiction, **FRCVP 4, 12**
Pleading, **FRCVP 9**
Searches and seizures, **FRCVP 4**
Statements, **FRCVP Form 7**
Subject matter jurisdiction, dismissal and nonsuit, **FRCVP 12**
Summons, **FRCVP 4**
Sureties and suretyship, **FRCVP 65.1**
Jury, **28 § 2072; FRCVP 38 et seq.**
Admiralty, **FRCVP 38**
Advisory juries, **FRCVP 39, 52**
Calendars, **FRCVP 79**
Declaratory judgments, **FRCVP 57**
Default judgments, **FRCVP 55**
Demand, **FRCVP 38 et seq.**
Dockets and docketing, **FRCVP 79**
Removal of cases or causes, **FRCVP 81**
Disclosure, parties, **FRCVP 37**
Dockets and docketing, demand, **FRCVP 79**
Examinations and examiners, **FRCVP 47**
Excusing jurors, **FRCVP 47**
Findings, unanimity, **FRCVP 48**

RULES OF CIVIL PROCEDURE
—Cont'd
Jury—Cont'd
Injunctions, **FRCVP 65**
Instructions, **FRCVP 49, 51**
Issues, **FRCVP 38**
Judgment as a matter of law, **FRCVP 50**
Masters, **FRCVP 53**
Numbers and numbering, **FRCVP 48**
Peremptory challenges, **FRCVP 47**
Removal of cases or causes, **FRCVP 81**
Separate trials, **FRCVP 42**
Stipulations, **FRCVP 39**
Verdict, generally, post
Waiver, **FRCVP 38**
Instructions, omissions, **FRCVP 49**
Removal of cases or causes, **FRCVP 81**
Withdrawal of demand, **FRCVP 38**
Knowledge, pleading, **FRCVP 9**
Laches, pleading, affirmative defenses, **FRCVP 8**
Laws,
Judgment as a matter of law, generally, ante
Questions of law or fact, generally, post
Lawsuits, notice, **FRCVP Form 5**
Leave of court,
Admissions, requests, **FRCVP 36**
Depositions, **FRCVP 30**
Legal holidays. Holidays, generally, ante
Legal representatives, judgments and decrees, **FRCVP 60**
Letters of request, foreign countries, depositions, **FRCVP 28**
Liability, admiralty, **FRCVP A, F**
Licenses and permits, pleading, affirmative defenses, **FRCVP 8**
Liens and incumbrances, admiralty, **FRCVP C**
Limitation of actions, pleading, affirmative defenses, **FRCVP 8**
Longshoremen and harbor workers, workers compensation, **FRCVP 81**
Magistrate judges, **28 § 636; FRCVP 72 et seq.**
Appeal and review, **FRCVP 73**
Attorney, fees, **FRCVP 54**
Consent, jurisdiction, **FRCVP 73; FRCVP Form 81**
Forms, jurisdiction, **FRCVP Form 80 et seq.**
Jurisdiction, **FRCVP 72, 73**
Forms, **FRCVP Form 80 et seq.**
Masters, **FRCVP 53**
Notice, jurisdiction, **FRCVP 73; FRCVP Form 80**
Orders of court, assignments, **FRCVP Form 82**
Pretrial matters, **FRCVP 72**
Trial, **FRCVP 72, 73**
Forms, **FRCVP Form 80 et seq.**
Mail and mailing,
Admiralty, **FRCVP F**

RULES OF CIVIL PROCEDURE
—Cont'd
Mail and mailing—Cont'd
Business associations, summons, **FRCVP 4**
Corporations, summons, **FRCVP 4**
Masters, **FRCVP 53**
Notice,
Admiralty, **FRCVP F**
Judgments and decrees, entries, **FRCVP 77**
Orders of court, entries, **FRCVP 77**
Process, **FRCVP 4 et seq.**
Admiralty, **FRCVP B**
Foreign countries, **FRCVP 4**
Pleadings, **FRCVP 5**
Sureties and suretyship, **FRCVP 65.1**
Time, **FRCVP 6**
United States, **FRCVP 4**
United States, summons, **FRCVP 4**
Malice, pleading, **FRCVP 9**
Mandamus, writ abolished, **FRCVP 81**
Maritime claims. Admiralty, generally, ante
Marshals,
Admiralty, ante
Process, **FRCVP 4, 4.1**
Master and servant, injunctions, **FRCVP 65**
Masters, **FRCVP 52 et seq.**
Attorneys, fees, **FRCVP 54**
Compensation and salaries, **FRCVP 53**
Definitions, **FRCVP 53**
Findings, **FRCVP 52, 53**
Reports, **FRCVP 53, 54**
Mental health,
District of Columbia, **FRCVP 81**
Examinations and examiners, **FRCVP 35, 37**
Merchant Marine Act, complaints, **FRCVP Form 14**
Merger and consolidation,
Defenses, **FRCVP 12**
Hearings, **FRCVP 42**
Injunctions, **FRCVP 65**
Trial, **FRCVP 42**
Mileage, subpoenas, **FRCVP 45**
Minors. Children and minors, generally, ante
Misconduct, judgments and decrees, **FRCVP 60**
Misjoinder, parties, **FRCVP 21**
Misnomers, public officers and employees, substitution, **FRCVP 25**
Mistake,
Clerical mistakes, **FRCVP 60**
Depositions, **FRCVP 32**
Judgments and decrees, **FRCVP 60**
Jury, instructions, **FRCVP 51**
Pleading, post
Modification,
Discovery, **FRCVP 29**
Masters, **FRCVP 53**
Money,
Complaints, sum certain, **FRCVP Form 10**

RULES OF CIVIL PROCEDURE
—Cont'd
Money—Cont'd
Had and received, plea or answer, **FRCVP Form 31**
Motions,
Additional findings, **FRCVP 52**
Admiralty, ante
Admissions, **FRCVP 36**
Adoption by reference, **FRCVP 10**
Advisory juries, **FRCVP 39**
Amendments, findings, **FRCVP 52**
Applications, orders of court, **FRCVP 7**
Attorneys, ante
Clerical mistakes, corrections, **FRCVP 60**
Compelling discovery, **FRCVP 37**
Conclusions of law, **FRCVP 52**
Days, **FRCVP 78**
Defenses, consolidation and merger, **FRCVP 12**
Depositions, **FRCVP 32, 37**
Disclosure, parties, **FRCVP 37**
Dismissal and nonsuit, ante
Entry upon land, **FRCVP 37**
Examinations and examiners, reports, **FRCVP 35**
Extension of time, **FRCVP 6**
Findings, **FRCVP 52**
Forms, **FRCVP Form 40 et seq.**
Technical forms, **FRCVP 8**
Interrogatories, **FRCVP 33 et seq.**
Intervention, **FRCVP 24; FRCVP Form 42**
Judgments and decrees, ante
Jury trial, **FRCVP 39**
Masters, **FRCVP 53**
More definite statement, pleading, **FRCVP 12**
New trial, post
Notice,
Clerical mistakes, corrections, **FRCVP 60**
Discovery, **FRCVP 37**
Sureties and suretyship, **FRCVP 65.1**
Oral hearing, **FRCVP 78**
Particularity, **FRCVP 7**
Pleading, post
Process, **FRCVP 5 et seq.**
Intervention, **FRCVP 24**
Judgments and decrees,
Modification, **FRCVP 59**
Summary judgment, **FRCVP 56**
Substitution, parties, **FRCVP 25**
Summary judgment, **FRCVP 56**
Sanctions, **FRCVP 11**
Severance, third parties, **FRCVP 14**
Signatures, **FRCVP 7**
Sanctions, **FRCVP 11**
Striking,
Pleading, **FRCVP 12**
Third parties, **FRCVP 14**
Substitution, parties, **FRCVP 25**
Summary judgment, **FRCVP 12, 56**
Suppression, depositions, **FRCVP 32**

RULES OF CIVIL PROCEDURE
—Cont'd
Motions—Cont'd
Sureties and suretyship, **FRCVP 65.1**
Technical forms, **FRCVP 8**
Temporary restraining orders, **FRCVP 65**
Third parties,
Complaints, service, **FRCVP 14**
Forms, **FRCVP Form 41**
Time,
Excusable neglect, judgments and decrees, **FRCVP 60**
Inadvertence, judgments and decrees, **FRCVP 60**
Judgment on the pleadings, **FRCVP 12**
Mistake, judgments and decrees, **FRCVP 60**
New trial, **FRCVP 59**
Pleading, responsive pleadings, **FRCVP 12**
Service, **FRCVP 6**
Summary judgment, **FRCVP 56**
Surprise, judgments and decrees, **FRCVP 60**
Writings, **FRCVP 7**
Multiple claims or parties,
Judgments and decrees, **FRCVP 54, 62**
Stay of proceedings, **FRCVP 62**
Summons, **FRCVP 4**
Municipal corporations, Foreign States, summons, **FRCVP 4**
Names,
Depositions, **FRCVP 28**
Discovery, **FRCVP 26**
Nonjoinder, **FRCVP 19**
Pleading, **FRCVP 10, 19**
National Labor Relations Board, **FRCVP 81**
Naturalization, **FRCVP 81**
Negligence,
Complaints, **FRCVP Form 11 et seq.**
Federal Employers Liability Act, **FRCVP Form 13**
Unknown defendants, **FRCVP Form 12**
New trial, **FRCVP 59**
Affidavits, **FRCVP 59**
Alternative motion, judgment as a matter of law, **FRCVP 50**
Courts own initiative, **FRCVP 59**
Harmless error, **FRCVP 61**
Judgment as a matter of law, alternative motion, **FRCVP 50**
Judgments and decrees, **FRCVP 59, 62**
Motions, **FRCVP 59**
Additional findings, **FRCVP 52**
Alternative motion, judgment as a matter of law, **FRCVP 50**
Amended findings, **FRCVP 52**
Extension of time, **FRCVP 6**
Judgment as a matter of law, alternative motion, **FRCVP 50**
Time, **FRCVP 59**
Orders of court, **FRCVP 59**
Extension of time, **FRCVP 6**

RULES OF CIVIL PROCEDURE
—Cont'd
New trial—Cont'd
Stay of proceedings, **FRCVP 62**
Written interrogatories, answers, inconsistencies, **FRCVP 49**
Newly discovered evidence, judgments and decrees, **FRCVP 60**
Newspapers, admiralty, notice, **FRCVP C, F**
Next friend, claims, **FRCVP 17**
Nonjoinder, pleading, **FRCVP 19**
Nonresidents, depositions, **FRCVP 45**
Nonsuit. Dismissal and nonsuit, generally, ante
Notice,
Admiralty, ante
Amended rules, **FRCVP 83**
Class actions, **FRCVP 23**
Constitutional challenges, statutes, **FRCVP 5.1**
Costs, **FRCVP 54**
Default judgments,
Applications, **FRCVP 55**
Summons, **FRCVP 4**
Depositions, ante
Derivative actions, **FRCVP 23.1**
Dismissal and nonsuit, **FRCVP 41**
Dockets and docketing, **FRCVP 77**
Eminent domain, **FRCVP 71.1; FRCVP Form 60**
Examinations and examiners, **FRCVP 35**
Extension of time, **FRCVP 6**
Forms, **FRCVP Form 5 et seq.**
Injunctions, **FRCVP 65**
Lawsuits, **FRCVP Form 5**
Magistrate judges, jurisdiction, **FRCVP 73; FRCVP Form 80**
Mail and mailing, ante
Masters, **FRCVP 53**
Motions, ante
New trial, **FRCVP 59**
Offer of judgment, acceptance, **FRCVP 68**
Orders of court, **FRCVP 77**
Pleading, post
Process, **FRCVP 5 et seq.**
Default judgments, **FRCVP 55**
Depositions, **FRCVP 27**
Hearings, **FRCVP 6**
Orders of court, **FRCVP 77**
Third parties, **FRCVP 14**
Service, waiver, **FRCVP 4**
Temporary restraining orders, **FRCVP 65**
Time,
Admiralty, **FRCVP F**
Costs, **FRCVP 54**
Extension of time, **FRCVP 6**
Service, **FRCVP 6**
Writings, **FRCVP 7**
Numbers and numbering,
Claims, **FRCVP 42**
Cross claims, **FRCVP 42**

RULES OF CIVIL PROCEDURE
—Cont'd
Numbers and numbering—Cont'd
Experts, pretrial conferences, **FRCVP 16**
Jury, **FRCVP 48**
Separate trials, **FRCVP 42**
Oaths and affirmations,
Admiralty, ante
Depositions, ante
Objections and exceptions,
Admiralty, **FRCVP F**
Admissions, requests, **FRCVP 36**
Depositions, ante
Electronically stored information, **FRCVP 34**
Eminent domain, **FRCVP 71.1**
Entry upon land, **FRCVP 34**
Evidence, **FRCVP 52**
Findings, **FRCVP 52**
Formal exceptions, **FRCVP 46**
Interrogatories, **FRCVP 33**
Jury, instructions, **FRCVP 51**
Magistrates, **FRCVP 72**
Masters, **FRCVP 53**
Motions, **FRCVP 12**
Pleading, **FRCVP 12**
Production of documents and things, **FRCVP 34**
Service, **FRCVP 37**
Sufficiency, **FRCVP 36**
Offer of judgment, **FRCVP 5, 68**
Officers and employees,
Federal officers and employees, generally, ante
Parties, substitution, **FRCVP 25**
Pleading, **FRCVP 9**
Records and recordation, **FRCVP 44**
Official acts, pleading, **FRCVP 9**
One form of action, **FRCVP 2**
Open court, trial, **FRCVP 77**
Opinions and decisions,
Court trial, **FRCVP 52**
Formal exceptions, **FRCVP 46**
Pleading, **FRCVP 9**
Oral examinations, depositions, **FRCVP 30 et seq.**
Orders of court,
Admiralty, ante
Admissions, requests, **FRCVP 36, 37**
Class actions, **FRCVP 23**
Clerical mistakes, corrections, **FRCVP 60**
Clerks of courts, **FRCVP 77, 79**
Consolidations and mergers, **FRCVP 65**
Depositions, **FRCVP 27, 37**
Discovery, **FRCVP 37**
Dockets and docketing, **FRCVP 79**
Documents, genuineness, **FRCVP 37**
Entry upon land, **FRCVP 37**
Examinations and examiners, **FRCVP 35**
Fraud, **FRCVP 60**
Interrogatories, **FRCVP 33, 37**
Joinder, **FRCVP 19**

RULES OF CIVIL PROCEDURE
—Cont'd
Orders of court—Cont'd
Judgments and decrees, **FRCVP 54**
Magistrate judges, assignments, **FRCVP Form 82**
Masters, **FRCVP 53**
Mental examinations, **FRCVP 27**
Misconduct of party, relief from order, **FRCVP 60**
Multiple claims or parties, **FRCVP 54**
New trial, ante
Newly discovered evidence, **FRCVP 60**
Notice, **FRCVP 77**
Objections and exceptions, **FRCVP 46**
Parties, substitution, **FRCVP 25**
Physical examinations, **FRCVP 35**
Pretrial orders, **FRCVP 16**
Production of documents and things, **FRCVP 37**
Protective orders, generally, post
Receivers and receivership, **FRCVP 66**
Service, **FRCVP 5**
Time, computation, **FRCVP 6**
Unincorporated associations, **FRCVP 23.2**
Voluntary dismissal, **FRCVP 41**
Owners and ownership, admiralty, **FRCVP F**
Papers. Books and papers, generally, ante
Paragraphs, pleading, **FRCVP 10**
Partial findings, judgments and decrees, **FRCVP 52**
Parties,
Additional parties, **FRCVP 13**
Capacity, **FRCVP 17**
Children and minors, **FRCVP 17**
Class actions, **FRCVP 23**
Compelling discovery, **FRCVP 37**
Corporations, **FRCVP 17**
Cross claims, **FRCVP 13**
Death,
Statements, **FRCVP Form 9**
Substitution, **FRCVP 25**
Default judgments, **FRCVP 55**
Discovery, **FRCVP 26 et seq.**
Eminent domain, **FRCVP 71.1**
Forms,
Death, statements, **FRCVP Form 9**
Meetings, planning meetings, reports, **FRCVP Form 52**
Omissions, reasons, statements, **FRCVP Form 8**
Incompetency, **FRCVP 17, 25**
Indispensable parties, dismissal and nonsuit, **FRCVP 41**
Interested parties, generally, ante
Joinder, **FRCVP 19 et seq.**
Cross claims, **FRCVP 13**
Dismissal and nonsuit, **FRCVP 41**
Misjoinder, **FRCVP 12, 21**
Nonjoinder, **FRCVP 12, 21**
Set-off and counterclaim, **FRCVP 13**
Summons, **FRCVP 4**
Jurisdiction, **FRCVP 12**

RULES OF CIVIL PROCEDURE
—Cont'd
Parties—Cont'd
Jury trial, consent, **FRCVP 38**
Masters, **FRCVP 53**
Meetings, planning meetings, reports, **FRCVP Form 52**
Misjoinder, **FRCVP 12, 21**
Multiple claims or parties, generally, ante
Nonjoinder, **FRCVP 12, 21**
Partnerships, **FRCVP 17**
Planning meetings, reports, **FRCVP Form 52**
Pleading, post
Process, **FRCVP 71**
Public officers and employees, **FRCVP 17**
Substitution, **FRCVP 25**
Real party in interest, **FRCVP 17**
Receivers and receivership, **FRCVP 17**
Reports, planning meetings, **FRCVP Form 52**
Representatives, **FRCVP 17**
Service, **FRCVP 5**
Statements,
Death, **FRCVP Form 9**
Omissions, reasons, **FRCVP Form 8**
Substitution, **FRCVP 25**
Depositions, **FRCVP 32**
Eminent domain, **FRCVP 71.1**
Third parties, generally, post
United States, **FRCVP 17**
Voluntary dismissal, **FRCVP 41**
Partition. Admiralty, ante
Partnership,
Capacity, **FRCVP 17**
Depositions, **FRCVP 32, 37**
Interrogatories, **FRCVP 33**
Summons, **FRCVP 4**
Patents,
Infringement, complaints, **FRCVP Form 18**
Stay of proceedings, **FRCVP 62**
Payment, **FRCVP 67**
Admiralty, **FRCVP C, E**
Pleading, affirmative defenses, **FRCVP 8**
Penalties. Fines, penalties and forfeitures, generally, ante
Pending actions,
Discovery, **FRCVP 37**
Set-off and counterclaim, **FRCVP 13**
Peremptory challenges, jury, **FRCVP 47**
Permissive counterclaims, pleading, **FRCVP 13**
Permissive intervention, parties, **FRCVP 24**
Permissive joinder, parties, **FRCVP 20**
Perpetuation of testimony, **FRCVP 27**
Personal jurisdiction, **FRCVP 4, 12**
Personal representatives, **FRCVP 81**
Personal service, summons, **FRCVP 4**
Petroleum control boards, orders, appeal and review, **FRCVP 81**

RULES OF CIVIL PROCEDURE
—Cont'd
Photography and pictures,
Court orders, **FRCVP 27**
Orders of court, **FRCVP 27**
Physical examinations, **FRCVP 35, 37**
Place,
Depositions, **FRCVP 29**
Examinations and examiners, **FRCVP 35**
Pleading, averments, **FRCVP 9**
Venue, generally, post
Plans and specifications,
Discovery, **FRCVP 26**
Parties, planning meetings, reports, **FRCVP Form 52**
Plea or answer,
Admiralty, ante
Admissions, requests, **FRCVP 36**
Defenses, **FRCVP Form 30**
Depositions, **FRCVP 37**
Eminent domain, **FRCVP 71.1**
Evasive answers, **FRCVP 37**
General verdict, interrogatories, answers, **FRCVP 49**
Incomplete answers, **FRCVP 37**
Removed actions, **FRCVP 81**
Service, **FRCVP 12**
Pleading, **FRCVP 7 et seq.**
Additional claims, **FRCVP 5**
Admiralty, ante
Admissions, **FRCVP 8**
Adoption by reference, **FRCVP 10**
Affirmative defenses, **FRCVP 8**
Alternative statements, **FRCVP 8**
Ambiguity, **FRCVP 12**
Amendments, **FRCVP 15**
Eminent domain, **FRCVP 71.1**
Evidence, **FRCVP 15**
Omissions, **FRCVP 12**
Pretrial procedure, **FRCVP 16**
Relation back, **FRCVP 15**
Associations and societies, **FRCVP 9**
Attorneys, ante
Boards and commissions, **FRCVP 9**
Capacity, **FRCVP 9**
Captions, **FRCVP 7, 10**
Class actions, **FRCVP 23**
Compulsory counterclaims, **FRCVP 13**
Conciseness, **FRCVP 8**
Conditions precedent, **FRCVP 9**
Consistency, **FRCVP 8**
Consolidations and mergers, **FRCVP 12**
Damages, special damages, **FRCVP 9**
Default judgments, **FRCVP 54, 55**
Defects, supplemental pleading, **FRCVP 15**
Defenses, **FRCVP 8, 12**
Discovery, **FRCVP 37**
Eminent domain, **FRCVP 71.1**
Forms, **FRCVP Form 30**
Paragraphs, **FRCVP 10**
Removed actions, **FRCVP 81**
Summary judgment, **FRCVP 56**
Third parties, **FRCVP 14**

RULES OF CIVIL PROCEDURE
—Cont'd
Pleading—Cont'd
Denials, **FRCVP 8**
Conditions precedent, **FRCVP 9**
Directness, **FRCVP 8**
Dismissal and nonsuit, **FRCVP 41**
Eminent domain, **FRCVP 71.1**
Evidence, amendments, **FRCVP 15**
Exhibits, **FRCVP 10**
Filing, **FRCVP 3 et seq.**
Foreign judgments, **FRCVP 9**
Foreign laws, **FRCVP 44.1**
Forms, **FRCVP 10; FRCVP Form 10 et seq.**
Technical forms, **FRCVP 8**
Fraud, **FRCVP 8, 9**
Fraudulent conveyances, **FRCVP 18**
General denials, **FRCVP 8**
Hypothetical statements, **FRCVP 8**
Insufficiency, **FRCVP 7**
Intent, **FRCVP 9**
Interpleader, generally, ante
Joinder, **FRCVP 18**
Judgments and decrees, **FRCVP 9**
Demand, **FRCVP 8**
Recitals, **FRCVP 54**
Jurisdiction, **FRCVP 9**
Knowledge, **FRCVP 9**
Mail and mailing, service, **FRCVP 5**
Malice, **FRCVP 9**
Mental condition, **FRCVP 9**
Mistake, **FRCVP 9**
Amendments, relation back, **FRCVP 15**
Set-off and counterclaim, **FRCVP 8**
Motions,
Defenses, **FRCVP 12**
Judgment on the pleading, **FRCVP 12**
More definite statement, **FRCVP 12**
Responsive pleadings, **FRCVP 12**
Striking, **FRCVP 12**
Summary judgment, **FRCVP 12**
Supplemental pleadings, **FRCVP 15**
Names, **FRCVP 10, 19**
Negative averments, **FRCVP 9**
Negligence, **FRCVP Form 11 et seq.**
New claims, **FRCVP 5**
Nonjoinder, **FRCVP 12**
Notice,
Filing, **FRCVP 5**
Foreign laws, **FRCVP 44.1**
Parties, amendments, relation back, **FRCVP 15**
Numerous defendants, **FRCVP 5**
Objections and exceptions, **FRCVP 12**
Official documents, **FRCVP 9**
Outside matters, **FRCVP 12**
Paragraphs, numbers and numbering, **FRCVP 10**
Particularity, conditions precedent, **FRCVP 9**
Parties,
Amendments, relation back, **FRCVP 15**

RULES OF CIVIL PROCEDURE
—Cont'd
Pleading—Cont'd
Parties—Cont'd
Captions, names, **FRCVP 10**
Defects, **FRCVP 12**
Defenses, **FRCVP 12**
Title of action, **FRCVP 10**
Permissive counterclaims, **FRCVP 13**
Place, **FRCVP 9**
Preliminary hearings, **FRCVP 12**
Quasi-judicial tribunals, **FRCVP 9**
Removed cases, **FRCVP 81**
Set-off and counterclaim, **FRCVP 13**
Signatures,
Motions, **FRCVP 7**
Sanctions, **FRCVP 11**
Statements, **FRCVP 8**
Special matters, **FRCVP 9**
Striking of pleadings, generally, post
Summary judgment, **FRCVP 12, 56**
Supplemental pleadings, **FRCVP 12, 15**
Supreme Court, **28 § 2072**
Powers and duties, **28 § 2073 nt**
Third parties, **FRCVP 8**
Time, **FRCVP 9**
Amendment, **FRCVP 15**
Dismissal of action, **FRCVP 41**
Service, **FRCVP 12**
Summary judgment, **FRCVP 56**
Title of action, **FRCVP 10**
United States,
Reply, time, **FRCVP 12**
Set-off and counterclaim, **FRCVP 13**
Waiver, defenses, **FRCVP 8**
Political subdivisions, Foreign States, summons, **FRCVP 4**
Possession,
Admiralty, **FRCVP D**
Judgments and decrees, **FRCVP 70**
Preliminary hearings, pleading, **FRCVP 12**
Preliminary injunctions, **FRCVP 65**
Preservation of defenses, **FRCVP 12**
Pretrial conferences, **FRCVP 16**
Pretrial disclosures, **FRCVP 26**
Prevailing parties, costs, **FRCVP 54**
Priorities and preferences,
Admissions, requests, **FRCVP 36**
Declaratory judgments, **FRCVP 57**
Interrogatories, **FRCVP 33**
Trial, calendar, **FRCVP 40**
Privacy protection, **FRCVP 5.2**
Privileges and immunities, subpoenas, **FRCVP 45**
Prize proceedings, admiralty, **FRCVP 81**
Process, **FRCVP 4 et seq.**
Admiralty, ante
Admissions, **FRCVP 36**
Age, servers, **FRCVP 4**
Answer, **FRCVP 12, 36**
Appearance, **FRCVP 5**
Attorneys, **FRCVP 5**
Certificates and certification, **FRCVP 5**
Compulsory counterclaims, **FRCVP 13**
Contempt, **28 § 1783**

RULES OF CIVIL PROCEDURE
—Cont'd
Process—Cont'd
Defenses, **FRCVP 12**
Demand, **FRCVP 5**
Jury trial, **FRCVP 38**
Depositions, objections and exceptions, **FRCVP 32**
Discovery, **FRCVP 5**
Dockets and docketing, **FRCVP 79**
Eminent domain, **FRCVP 71.1**
Evidence, **FRCVP 4, 4.1**
Federal agencies, **FRCVP 15**
In forma pauperis, **FRCVP 4**
Interrogatories, **FRCVP 33, 37**
Joinder of parties, **FRCVP 19**
Mail and mailing, ante
Motions, ante
Multiple defendants, **FRCVP 5**
Nonparties, **FRCVP 71**
Notice, ante
Offer of judgment, **FRCVP 5, 68**
Orders of court, **FRCVP 5**
Parties, substitution, **FRCVP 25**
Pleadings, **FRCVP 5, 11 et seq.**
Process servers, **FRCVP 4**
Production of books and papers, **FRCVP 34**
Records and recordation, appeal and review, **FRCVP 5**
Searches and seizures, **FRCVP 5**
Substitution, parties, **FRCVP 25**
Summons, generally, post
Supreme Court, powers and duties, **28 § 2072**
Sureties and suretyship, **FRCVP 65.1**
Third parties, **FRCVP 14**
Time, **FRCVP 6 et seq.**
United States Marshals, **FRCVP 4**
Production of books and papers, **FRCVP 34**
Application of rules, **FRCVP 81**
Compelling production, **FRCVP 37, 45**
Depositions, **FRCVP 27**
Forms, requests, **FRCVP Form 50**
Nonparties, **FRCVP 34**
Objections and exceptions, **FRCVP 34**
Requests, **FRCVP 34; FRCVP Form 50**
Sanctions, **FRCVP 37**
Service, requests, **FRCVP 34**
Stipulations, **FRCVP 29**
Subpoenas, **FRCVP 45**
Supplementation, **FRCVP 26**
Proof. Evidence, generally, ante
Property, admiralty, disposition, **FRCVP E**
Protective orders,
Depositions, **FRCVP 32**
Discovery, **FRCVP 26, 37**
Privacy protection, **FRCVP 5.2**
Psychologists and psychology, examinations and examiners, **FRCVP 35**
Public officers and employees,
Parties, **FRCVP 17**
Substitution, **FRCVP 25**

RULES OF CIVIL PROCEDURE
—Cont'd
Public policy, **FRCVP 1**
Forms, **FRCVP 84**
Publication, official records, evidence, **FRCVP 44**
Quasi in rem, admiralty, **FRCVP E**
Quasi-judicial tribunals, pleading, **FRCVP 9**
Questions of law or fact,
Class actions, **FRCVP 23**
Foreign laws, **FRCVP 44.1**
Sanctions, **FRCVP 37**
Quo warranto, **FRCVP 81**
Railroads, labor disputes, **FRCVP 81**
Real party in interest, **FRCVP 17**
Receipts, service, **FRCVP 4**
Receivers and receivership, **FRCVP 66**
Capacity, **FRCVP 17**
Stay of proceedings, **FRCVP 62**
Recitals, judgments and decrees, **FRCVP 54**
Records and recordation,
Authentication, **FRCVP 44**
Business records, **FRCVP 33**
Clerical mistakes, corrections, **FRCVP 60**
Clerks of court, **FRCVP 79**
Depositions, **FRCVP 30**
Discovery, **FRCVP 26**
Evidence, **FRCVP 44**
Findings, **FRCVP 52**
Injunctions, **FRCVP 65**
Judgments and decrees, **FRCVP 54**
Magistrates, **FRCVP 72, 73**
Masters, **FRCVP 5, 53**
Recross questions, depositions, **FRCVP 31**
Redacted filings, **FRCVP 5.2**
Redirect questions, depositions, **FRCVP 31**
Redundancy, pleading, **FRCVP 12**
References,
Default judgments, **FRCVP 55**
Magistrates, **FRCVP 73**
Masters, **FRCVP 53**
Pleading, adoption by reference, **FRCVP 10**
Reform, civil justice, **28 § 519 nt, EON 12988**
Release,
Admiralty, **FRCVP E**
Notice, **FRCVP C**
Pleading, affirmative defenses, **FRCVP 8**
Removal of cases or causes, **FRCVP 81**
Repleading, removed cases, **FRCVP 81**
Replevin, **FRCVP 64**
Reply, **FRCVP 7 et seq.**
Admissions, **FRCVP 8**
Discovery, **FRCVP 29**
New trial, **FRCVP 59**
Omissions, **FRCVP 12**
Time, **FRCVP 12**
Reports,
Discovery, **FRCVP 26**

RULES OF CIVIL PROCEDURE
—Cont'd
Reports—Cont'd
Mental examinations, **FRCVP 35**
Parties, planning meetings, **FRCVP Form 52**
Physical examinations, **FRCVP 35**
Representatives and representation,
Capacity, **FRCVP 17**
Children and minors, **FRCVP 17**
Death, substitution, **FRCVP 25**
Incompetents, **FRCVP 17**
Requests,
Admissions, ante
Electronically stored information, **FRCVP 34**
Entry upon land, **FRCVP 34; FRCVP Form 50**
Examinations and examiners, **FRCVP 35**
Findings, **FRCVP 52**
Judgments and decrees, entries, **FRCVP 58**
Jury, instructions, **FRCVP 51**
Masters, **FRCVP 53**
Production of books and papers, **FRCVP 34; FRCVP Form 50**
Res judicata, pleading, **FRCVP 8**
Restraining orders, **FRCVP 65**
Returns,
Admiralty, marshals, **FRCVP E**
Habeas corpus, **FRCVP 81**
Reversals,
Judgments and decrees, **FRCVP 60**
New trial, **FRCVP 50**
Review. Appeal and review, generally, ante
Salaries. Compensation and salaries, generally, ante
Sales, admiralty, **FRCVP C, E, G**
Sanctions,
Attorneys, fees, **FRCVP 11, 16**
Depositions, **FRCVP 30**
Discovery, **FRCVP 37**
Electronically stored information, **FRCVP 37**
Entry upon land, **FRCVP 37**
Forms, nonuse, **FRCVP 83**
Interrogatories, **FRCVP 37**
Pretrial conferences, **FRCVP 16**
Pretrial orders, **FRCVP 16**
Production of books and papers, **FRCVP 37**
Signatures, **FRCVP 11**
Satisfaction, judgments and decrees, **FRCVP 60**
Admiralty, **FRCVP E**
Saturday,
Business hours, **FRCVP 77**
Time, computation, **FRCVP 6**
Scandalous matter, motion to strike, **FRCVP 12**
Scire facias, abolition of writ, **FRCVP 81**
Seals (official seals),
Records and recordation, authentication, **FRCVP 44**

RULES OF CIVIL PROCEDURE
—Cont'd
Seals (official seals)—Cont'd
Summons, **FRCVP 4**
Seamen, process, service, **FRCVP 4**
Searches and seizures, **FRCVP 64**
Admiralty, **FRCVP E**
United States vessels, **FRCVP C**
Service, **FRCVP 4, 5**
United States vessels, **FRCVP C**
Secretary of Agriculture, **FRCVP 81**
Secretary of embassy, official records, authentication, **FRCVP 44**
Secretary of the Interior, **FRCVP 81**
Security interest,
Admiralty, **FRCVP D et seq.**
Injunctions, **FRCVP 62, 65**
Masters, **FRCVP 53**
Stay of proceedings, **FRCVP 62**
Sureties and suretyship, **FRCVP 65.1**
Seizures. Searches and seizures, generally, ante
Separate trials. Trial, post
Sequestration, property, **FRCVP 70**
Service of process. Process, generally, ante
Set-off and counterclaim, **FRCVP 7 et seq.**
Admiralty, **FRCVP E**
Compulsory counterclaims, **FRCVP 13**
Dismissal and nonsuit, **FRCVP 41**
Entry of judgment, **FRCVP 54**
Joinder, **FRCVP 18**
Judgments and decrees, **FRCVP 13, 54**
Mistake, **FRCVP 8**
Money had and received, interpleader, **FRCVP Form 31**
Omissions, **FRCVP 13**
Permissive counterclaims, **FRCVP 13**
Reply, **FRCVP 7**
Time, service, **FRCVP 12**
Separate trials, **FRCVP 42**
Service, **FRCVP 5**
Third parties, **FRCVP 14**
United States, **28 § 2675; FRCVP 12, 13**
Voluntary dismissal, **FRCVP 41**
Setting aside. Vacating or setting aside, generally, post
Settlement. Compromise and settlement, generally, ante
Shares and shareholders, derivative actions, **FRCVP 23.1**
Ships and shipping, mortgages, foreclosure, **FRCVP C**
Show cause orders, admiralty, **FRCVP C**
Signatures,
Admiralty,
Affidavits, **FRCVP B**
Release, **FRCVP E**
Admissions, **FRCVP 36**
Attorneys, ante
Discovery, **FRCVP 26**
Electronic signatures, **FRCVP 5**
Foreign official records, authentication, **FRCVP 44**

RULES OF CIVIL PROCEDURE
—Cont'd
Signatures—Cont'd
Forms, **FRCVP Form 2**
Interrogatories, **FRCVP 33**
Motions, ante
Pleading, ante
Summons, **FRCVP 4**
Social security, privacy protection, **FRCVP 5.2**
Societies. Associations and societies, generally, ante
Sound recordings, depositions, **FRCVP 30**
Special pleadings, **FRCVP 9**
Special verdict, **FRCVP 49**
Specific performance,
Complaints, **FRCVP Form 17**
Execution, **FRCVP 70**
Statements,
Corporations, disclosure, **FRCVP 7.1**
Defenses, **FRCVP 12**
Jurisdiction, **FRCVP Form 7**
Official records, **FRCVP 44**
Parties,
Death, **FRCVP Form 9**
Omissions, reasons, **FRCVP Form 8**
States,
Admiralty, **FRCVP B**
Execution, **FRCVP 69**
Jury trial, **FRCVP 81**
Official records, authentication, **FRCVP 44**
Prior actions, **FRCVP 32**
Summons, **FRCVP 4**
Statute of frauds, pleading, **FRCVP 8**
Statute of limitations, pleading, **FRCVP 8**
Statutes,
Admiralty, **FRCVP C**
Capacity, **FRCVP 17**
Constitutional challenges, **FRCVP 5.1**
Intervention, **FRCVP 24**
Time, **FRCVP 6**
Stay of proceedings,
Admiralty, **FRCVP E**
Appellate courts, **FRCVP 62**
Bonds (officers and fiduciaries), **FRCVP 62**
Class actions, **FRCVP 23**
Discovery, **FRCVP 37**
Execution, **FRCVP 62**
Injunctions, **FRCVP 62**
Judgments and decrees, **FRCVP 62**
Patents, accounts and accounting, **FRCVP 62**
Previously dismissed actions, costs, **FRCVP 41**
Receivers and receivership, **FRCVP 62**
State laws, **FRCVP 62**
United States, **FRCVP 62**
Stenographers, evidence, **FRCVP 80**
Stipulations,
Admiralty, **FRCVP E**
Court trials, **FRCVP 39**
Depositions, **FRCVP 29, 30**
Discovery, **FRCVP 29**

RULES OF CIVIL PROCEDURE
—Cont'd
Stipulations—Cont'd
Dismissal and nonsuit, **FRCVP 41**
Jury verdict, **FRCVP 48**
Masters, **FRCVP 53**
New trial, **FRCVP 59**
Production of books and papers, **FRCVP 29**
Sureties and suretyship, **FRCVP 65.1**
Striking of pleadings, **FRCVP 12**
Discovery, **FRCVP 37**
Motions, more definite statement, **FRCVP 12**
Third parties, **FRCVP 14**
Subclasses, class actions, **FRCVP 23**
Subject matter, jurisdiction, defenses, **FRCVP 12**
Subpoena duces tecum, **FRCVP 30**
Subpoenas, **FRCVP 45**
Depositions, ante
Electronically stored information, **FRCVP 45**
Federal agencies, **FRCVP 45, 81**
Foreign countries, **FRCVP 37**
Forms, **FRCVP 45**
Masters, **FRCVP 53**
Objections and exceptions, **FRCVP 45**
Production of books and papers, **FRCVP 81**
United States, **FRCVP 45, 81**
Substantial rights, mistake, **FRCVP 61**
Substitution. Parties, ante
Successors, parties, **FRCVP 25**
Summaries,
Business records, **FRCVP 33**
Foreign official records, **FRCVP 44**
Summary judgment, **FRCVP 56**
Motions, **FRCVP 12, 52, 56**
Pretrial conferences, **FRCVP 16**
Time, **FRCVP 41**
Summons, **FRCVP 4 et seq.**
Admiralty, **FRCVP B, C**
Federal officers and employees, **28 § 1391**
Forms, **FRCVP 4; FRCVP Form 3 et seq.**
Third parties, **FRCVP Form 4**
Waiver, **FRCVP Forms 5, 6**
States, **FRCVP 4**
Third parties, **FRCVP 14; FRCVP Form 4**
Time, **FRCVP 4**
Waiver, **FRCVP 4; FRCVP Forms 5, 6**
Sundays,
Clerks of court, business hours, **FRCVP 77**
Time, computation, **FRCVP 6**
Supersedeas or stay. Stay of proceedings, generally, ante
Supplemental pleadings, **FRCVP 12, 15**
Supplemental process, admiralty, **FRCVP C**
Supplementary proceedings, execution, **FRCVP 69**
Supplementation, discovery, **FRCVP 26**

RULES OF CIVIL PROCEDURE
—Cont'd
Supreme Court, **28 § 2072 et seq.**
Sureties and surety bonds. Bonds (officers and fiduciaries), generally, ante
Surprise, judgments and decrees, **FRCVP 60**
Telecommunications,
Depositions, **FRCVP 30**
Telephone numbers, forms, **FRCVP Form 2**
Temporary restraining orders, **FRCVP 65**
Territories, official record, authentication, **FRCVP 44**
Third parties, **FRCVP 14**
Admiralty, **FRCVP 14**
Answers, **FRCVP 7**
Complaints, **FRCVP 7; FRCVP Form 16**
Dismissal and nonsuit, **FRCVP 41**
Entry of judgment, **FRCVP 54**
Forms,
Complaints, **FRCVP Form 16**
Motions, **FRCVP Form 41**
Summons, **FRCVP Form 4**
Joinder, **FRCVP 18**
Judgments and decrees, **FRCVP 54**
Admiralty, **FRCVP 14**
Motions,
Complaints, service, **FRCVP 14**
Forms, **FRCVP Form 41**
Pleading, **FRCVP 8**
Separate trials, **FRCVP 42**
Summons, **FRCVP Form 4**
Three judge court, **28 § 2284**
Injunctions, **FRCVP 62**
Time, **FRCVP 6**
Admiralty, ante
Admissions, **FRCVP 36**
Amendments, **FRCVP 86**
Appeal and review, ante
Appearance, **FRCVP 4**
Complaints, **FRCVP 3**
Computation, **FRCVP 6**
Depositions, ante
Discovery, ante
Dismissal and nonsuit, **FRCVP 17**
Electronically stored information, **FRCVP 34**
Entry upon land, **FRCVP 34**
Execution, **FRCVP 62**
Filing, **FRCVP 5**
Habeas corpus, **FRCVP 81**
Interrogatories, **FRCVP 33**
Involuntary dismissal, **FRCVP 41**
Judgments and decrees, ante
Masters, **FRCVP 53**
Mental health, examinations and examiners, **FRCVP 35**
Motions, ante
New trial, affidavits, **FRCVP 59**
Notice, ante
Offer of judgment, **FRCVP 68**
Original rules, **FRCVP 86**
Physical examinations, **FRCVP 35**
Pleading, ante

RULES OF CIVIL PROCEDURE
—Cont'd
Time—Cont'd
Production of documents or things, **FRCVP 34**
Summary judgment, **FRCVP 56**
Summons, **FRCVP 4**
Supersedeas bonds, **FRCVP 62**
Temporary restraining orders, **FRCVP 65**
Third parties, **FRCVP 14**
United States, **FRCVP 4**
Voluntary dismissal, **FRCVP 41**
Title, **FRCVP 85**
Pleading, **FRCVP 10**
Title to property, judgments and decrees, **FRCVP 70**
Trade secrets,
Protective orders, **FRCVP 26**
Subpoenas, **FRCVP 45**
Transcripts,
Depositions, **FRCVP 30**
Stenographers, evidence, **FRCVP 80**
Traveling expenses, subpoenas, **FRCVP 45**
Treaties, depositions, **FRCVP 28**
Trial,
Admiralty, fines, penalties and forfeitures, **FRCVP G**
Advisory juries, **FRCVP 52**
Assignments, **FRCVP 40**
Consolidations and mergers, **FRCVP 42, 65**
Court trials, **FRCVP 52**
Dismissal and nonsuit, motions, **FRCVP 41**
Issues, **FRCVP 39**
Judgment and decrees, forms, **FRCVP Form 71**
Magistrates, **FRCVP 72**
Motions, dismissal and nonsuit, **FRCVP 41**
Stipulations, **FRCVP 39**
Cross claims, separate trials, **FRCVP 13**
Depositions, **FRCVP 32**
Discovery, preparation material, **FRCVP 26**
Dismissal and nonsuit, court trials, motions, **FRCVP 41**
Eminent domain, **FRCVP 71.1**
Interrogatories, **FRCVP 33**
Issues, court trials, **FRCVP 39**
Joinder, separate trials, **FRCVP 20**
Judges or justices, inability to proceed, **FRCVP 63**
Jury, generally, ante
Magistrate judges, ante
Masters, **FRCVP 53**
Motions, court trials, dismissal and nonsuit, **FRCVP 41**
New trial, generally, ante
Open court, **FRCVP 77**
Orders of court, separate trials, **FRCVP 42**

RULES OF CIVIL PROCEDURE
—Cont'd
Trial—Cont'd
Pretrial conferences, separate trials, **FRCVP 16**
Pretrial procedure, **FRCVP 16**
Separate trials,
Cross claims, **FRCVP 13**
Joinder, **FRCVP 20**
Orders of court, **FRCVP 42**
Pretrial conferences, **FRCVP 16**
Set-off and counterclaims, **FRCVP 13**
Third parties, **FRCVP 14**
Set-off and counterclaims, separate trials, **FRCVP 13**
Stipulations, court trials, **FRCVP 39**
Subpoenas, **FRCVP 45**
Successor judges, **FRCVP 63**
Third parties, separate trials, **FRCVP 14**
Verdict, generally, post
Voluntary dismissal, **FRCVP 41**
Trusts and trustees, **FRCVP 17**
Admiralty, **FRCVP F**
Undertakings. Bonds (officers and fiduciaries), generally, ante
Uniform numbering system, local rules, **FRCVP 83**
Unincorporated associations, **FRCVP 23.2**
Derivative actions, shares and shareholders, **FRCVP 23.1**
Shares and shareholders, derivative actions, **FRCVP 23.1**
Summons, **FRCVP 4**
United States,
Admiralty, **FRCVP E**
Answers, **FRCVP 12**
Appeal and review, **FRCVP 62**
Bonds (officers and fiduciaries), **FRCVP 62**
Costs, **FRCVP 54**
Depositions, **FRCVP 28, 55**
Leave of court, **FRCVP 30**
Outside country, **FRCVP 32**
Discovery, **FRCVP 37**
Federal officers and employees, generally, ante
Names, **FRCVP 17**
Official records, authentication, **FRCVP 44**
Process, **FRCVP 15**
Set-off and counterclaim, **28 § 2675; FRCVP 12, 13**
Stay of proceedings, **FRCVP 62**
Subpoenas, **FRCVP 45, 81**
Summons, **FRCVP 4**
United States attorneys,
Pleading, amendments, parties, changes, **FRCVP 15**
Service, **FRCVP 4, 12**
United States laws, calendar, **FRCVP 40**
United States magistrate judges. Magistrate judges, generally, ante

RULES OF CIVIL PROCEDURE
—Cont'd
Unknown defendants, negligence, complaints, **FRCVP Form 12**
Vacating or setting aside,
Alternative new trial motion, judgment as a matter of law, **FRCVP 50**
Default judgments, **FRCVP 55**
Findings, **FRCVP 52**
Judgments and decrees, **FRCVP 60, 61**
Verdict, **FRCVP 61**
Venue,
Admiralty, **FRCVP 82; FRCVP F**
Defenses, **FRCVP 12**
Depositions, **FRCVP 32, 37**
Discovery, **FRCVP 37**
Dismissal and nonsuit, **FRCVP 41**
Joinder, **FRCVP 19**
Objections and exceptions, **FRCVP 4**
Verdict,
Dockets and docketing, **FRCVP 79**
Forms, **FRCVP Form 70**
General verdict, interrogatories, **FRCVP 49**
Harmless error, **FRCVP 61**
Judgment as a matter of law, generally, ante
Special verdicts, **FRCVP 49**
Unanimity of jurors, **FRCVP 48**
Verification,
Admiralty, **FRCVP C**
Electronic verification, **FRCVP 5**
Vice consul, official records, authentication, **FRCVP 44**
Void judgment, **FRCVP 60**
Voluntary dismissal, **FRCVP 41**
Waiver,
Affirmative defenses, **FRCVP 8**
Defenses, **FRCVP 12**
Depositions, **FRCVP 32**
Eminent domain, **FRCVP 71.1**
Examinations and examiners, **FRCVP 35**
Jury, ante
Privacy protection, **FRCVP 5.2**
Summons, **FRCVP 4; FRCVP Forms 5, 6**
Withdrawal,
Admissions, **FRCVP 36**
Deposits, **FRCVP 67**
Jury trial, **FRCVP 38**
Offer of judgment, **FRCVP 68**
Witnesses,
Compelling testimony, **FRCVP 81**
Depositions, generally, ante
Discovery, **FRCVP 26 et seq.**
Experts, generally, ante
Masters, **FRCVP 53**
Oaths and affirmations, **FRCVP 43**
Pretrial conferences, **FRCVP 16**
Successor judges, **FRCVP 63**
Writings,
Admissions, requests, **FRCVP 36**
Depositions, **FRCVP 32**
Discovery, stipulations, **FRCVP 29**

RULES OF CIVIL PROCEDURE
—Cont'd
Writings—Cont'd
Examinations and examiners, **FRCVP 35**
Motions, **FRCVP 7**
Subpoenas, **FRCVP 45**
Writs, **FRCVP 81**
Abolished writs, **FRCVP 60**
Admiralty, **28 § 2072**
Assistance, **FRCVP 70**
Supreme Court, powers and duties, **28 § 2072**
Written interrogatories, **FRCVP 49**
Written questions, depositions, **FRCVP 31 et seq.**

RULES OF COURT
Advisory committees, **28 § 2077**
Appearance, **28 § 1654**
Comment, **28 § 2071**
Copies, **28 § 2077**
Court of Appeals for First Circuit, generally, this index
Court of Appeals for Second Circuit, generally, this index
Court of Appeals for Third Circuit, generally, this index
Court of Appeals for Fourth Circuit, generally, this index
Court of Appeals for Fifth Circuit, generally, this index
Court of Appeals for Sixth Circuit, generally, this index
Court of Appeals for Seventh Circuit, generally, this index
Court of Appeals for Eighth Circuit, generally, this index
Court of Appeals for Ninth Circuit, generally, this index
Court of Appeals for Tenth Circuit, generally, this index
Court of Appeals for Eleventh Circuit, generally, this index
Court of Appeals for the District of Columbia, generally, this index
Court of Appeals for the Federal Circuit, generally, this index
Fees, copies, **28 § 2077**
Notice, **28 § 2071**
Publication, **28 § 2077**
Rules of Appellate Procedure, generally, this index
Rules of Civil Procedure, generally, this index
Rules of Criminal Procedure, generally, this index
Rules of Evidence, generally, this index

RULES OF CRIMINAL PROCEDURE
Plea bargaining, sentencing guidelines, **28 § 994**
United States magistrate judges, **28 § 631 et seq.**
Terms of office, **28 § 631**

RULES OF EVIDENCE
Generally, **FRE 101 et seq.**
Absence and absentees,
Accidents, evidence of other crimes or wrongs, **FRE 404**
Hearsay rule, exception, **FRE 804**
Mistakes, evidence of other crimes or wrongs, **FRE 404**
Accidents, absence and absentees, evidence of other crimes or wrongs, **FRE 404**
Actions and proceedings,
Child molestation, relevancy of similar cases, **FRE 415**
Sexual assault, relevancy of similar cases, **FRE 415**
Acts of Congress, self-authentication, **FRE 902**
Admiralty, **FRE 1101**
Amendments, **FRE 1102**
Ancient documents,
Authentication, **FRE 901**
Hearsay rule, exceptions, **FRE 803**
Annulment, conviction of crime, impeachment, **FRE 609**
Appeal and review, conviction of crime, impeachment, pending appeals, **FRE 609**
Application of rules, **FRE 101, 1101**
Arrest warrants, **FRE 1101**
Attorneys, privileges and immunities, **FRE 502**
Authentication, **FRE 901 et seq.**
Bail, **FRE 1101**
Baptismal certificates, hearsay rule, exception, **FRE 803**
Bases of opinions, opinion and expert testimony, **FRE 703**
Best evidence rule, **FRE 1001 et seq.**
Bias and prejudice, exclusion, prejudicial evidence, **FRE 403**
Books and papers,
Best evidence, **FRE 1001 et seq.**
Federal agencies, **28 § 1733**
Federal departments, **28 § 1733**
Boundaries,
Judgments and decrees, hearsay rule, exception, **FRE 803**
Reputation, hearsay rule, exception, **FRE 803**
Burden of proof, presumptions, **FRE 301**
Capital punishment, impeachment, conviction of crime, **FRE 609**
Character and reputation,
Conviction of crime, **FRE 609**
Hearsay rule, exception, **FRE 803**
Methods of proof, **FRE 405**
Relevancy, **FRE 404**
Witnesses, **FRE 404, 608**
Children and minors, molestation, relevancy of similar crimes, **FRE 414, 415**
Citation of rules, **FRE 1102**
Collateral matters, **FRE 1004**
Commercial paper, self-authentication, **FRE 902**

RULES OF EVIDENCE—Cont'd
Commercial publications, hearsay rule, exception, **FRE 803**
Compensation and salaries, court-appointed experts, **FRE 706**
Competency. Witnesses, post
Compromise and settlement, relevancy, **FRE 408**
Confessions, admissibility, **FRE 104**
Confusing evidence, exclusion, **FRE 403**
Congress, approval, **28 § 2074 nt**
Contempt, **FRE 1101**
Conviction of crime. Crimes and offenses, post
Copies,
Admissibility, **FRE 1003**
Federal agencies, **28 § 1733**
Federal departments, **28 § 1733**
Public records, self-authentication, **FRE 902**
Court of International Trade, **28 § 2641**
Credibility,
Conviction of crime, **FRE 609**
Preliminary determinations, **FRE 104**
Crimes and offenses,
Conviction of crime,
Judgments and decrees, hearsay rule, exception, **FRE 803**
Witnesses, credibility, **FRE 609**
Judgments and decrees, conviction of crime, hearsay rule, exceptions, **FRE 803**
Other crimes or wrongs, relevancy, **FRE 404**
Relevancy, other crimes or wrongs, **FRE 404**
Witnesses, conviction of crime, credibility, **FRE 609**
Cross examination, **FRE 611**
Impeachment, conviction of crime, **FRE 609**
Preliminary matters, **FRE 104**
Cumulative evidence, exclusion, **FRE 403**
Death penalty, impeachment, conviction of crime, **FRE 609**
Definitions,
Attorney-client privilege, **FRE 502**
Best evidence, **FRE 1001**
Courts, **FRE 1101**
Hearsay, **FRE 801, 804**
Judges or justices, **FRE 1101**
Relevant evidence, **FRE 401**
Work product protection, **FRE 502**
Disclosure, attorneys, privileges and immunities, **FRE 502**
Dishonesty, impeachment, conviction of crime, **FRE 609**
Domestic public documents, self-authentication, **FRE 902**
Duplicates. Copies, generally, ante
Emotional condition then existing, hearsay rule, exception, **FRE 803**
Exceptions. Hearsay, post
Excited utterances, hearsay rule, exception, **FRE 803**
Exclusion, witnesses, **FRE 615**

RULES OF EVIDENCE—Cont'd
Exemptions, impeachment, conviction of crime, **FRE 609**
Expert witnesses. Opinions and expert testimony, generally, post
Extradition, **FRE 1101**
False statements, impeachment, conviction of crime, **FRE 609**
Family history,
Judgments and decrees, hearsay rule, exception, **FRE 803**
Statements, hearsay rule, exception, **FRE 804**
Federal agencies, records and recordation, admissibility, **28 §§ 1732, 1733**
Foreign public documents, self-authentication, **FRE 902**
Forfeiture by wrongdoing, hearsay rule, **FRE 804**
Former testimony, hearsay rule, exception, **FRE 804**
General history,
Judgments and decrees, hearsay rule, exception, **FRE 803**
Reputation, hearsay rule, exceptions, **FRE 803**
Grand jury, application of rules, **FRE 1101**
Habits, relevancy, **FRE 406**
Handwriting, authentication, **FRE 901**
Hearsay, **FRE 801 et seq.**
Admissibility, **FRE 802**
Credibility of declarant, **FRE 806**
Definitions, **FRE 801**
Exceptions,
Declarant availability immaterial, **FRE 803**
Declarant unavailable, **FRE 804**
Hearsay within hearsay, **FRE 805**
Residual exception, **FRE 807**
History,
Judgments and decrees, hearsay rule, exception, **FRE 803**
Reputation, hearsay rule, exception, **FRE 803**
Identity and identification, **FRE 901 et seq.**
Other crimes or wrongs, **FRE 404**
Immunities. Privileges and immunities, generally, post
Impeachment. Witnesses, post
Impending death, statement made under belief, hearsay rule, exception, **FRE 804**
Indictment and information, validity, jurors as witnesses, **FRE 606**
Instructions,
Judicial notice, jury, **FRE 201**
Jury,
Judicial notice, **FRE 201**
Limited admissibility, **FRE 105**
Limited admissibility, jury, **FRE 105**
Insurance, liability insurance, relevancy, **FRE 411**
Intent, evidence of other crimes or wrongs, **FRE 404**

RULES OF EVIDENCE—Cont'd
Interpreters, witnesses, **FRE 603**
Judges or justices, competency as witnesses, **FRE 605**
Judgments and decrees, conviction of crime, hearsay rule, exception, **FRE 803**
Judicial Conference of the United States, recommendations, **28 § 2073**
Judicial notice, **FRE 201**
Jury,
Competency as witnesses, **FRE 606**
Instructions,
Judicial notice, **FRE 201**
Limited admissibility, **FRE 105**
Photographs, **FRE 1008**
Preliminary determinations, **FRE 104**
Recordings, **FRE 1008**
Rulings, **FRE 103**
Writings, **FRE 1008**
Juvenile delinquents and dependents, impeachment, conviction of crime, **FRE 609**
Knowledge, evidence of other crimes or wrongs, **FRE 404**
Leading questions, witnesses, **FRE 611**
Learned treatises, hearsay rule, exception, **FRE 803**
Liability insurance, relevancy, **FRE 411**
Limited admissibility, instructions to jury, **FRE 105**
Lost or destroyed originals, other proof, admissibility, **FRE 1004**
Maritime cases, **FRE 1101**
Market reports, hearsay rule, exception, **FRE 803**
Marriage certificates, hearsay rule, exception, **FRE 803**
Medical care and treatment,
Payment, relevancy, **FRE 409**
Statements, hearsay rule, exception, **FRE 803**
Mental condition then existing, hearsay rule, exception, **FRE 803**
Mistakes,
Absence and absentees, evidence of other crimes or wrongs, **FRE 404**
Rulings, **FRE 103**
Motive, evidence of other crimes or wrongs, **FRE 404**
Newspapers, self-authentication, **FRE 902**
Notice,
Crimes or wrongs, **FRE 404**
Impeachment, conviction of crime, **FRE 609**
Offenses. Crimes and offenses, generally, ante
Opinions and expert testimony, **FRE 701 et seq.**
Bases of opinion, **FRE 703**
Character evidence, **FRE 405**
Court-appointed experts, **FRE 706**
Facts or data underlying expert opinion, disclosure, **FRE 705**
Lay witnesses, **FRE 701**

RULES OF EVIDENCE—Cont'd
Opinions and expert testimony—Cont'd
Ultimate issues, **FRE 704**
Witnesses, **FRE 608**
Opportunity, evidence of other crimes or wrongs, **FRE 404**
Original writings, recordings, or photographs, **FRE 1002**
Other crimes or wrongs, relevancy, **FRE 404**
Papers. Books and papers, generally, ante
Pardons, impeachment, **FRE 609**
Parties, writings, recordings, or photographs, **FRE 1004, 1007**
Past sexual history or predisposition, sex offenses, victims, relevancy, **FRE 412**
Pending appeals, impeachment, conviction of crime, **FRE 609**
Periodicals, self-authentication, **FRE 902**
Personal history,
Judgments and decrees, hearsay rule, exception, **FRE 803**
Statements, hearsay rule, exception, **FRE 804**
Personal knowledge, witnesses, competency, **FRE 602**
Photography and pictures, best evidence, **FRE 1001 et seq.**
Physical condition then existing, hearsay rule, exception, **FRE 803**
Plain errors, **FRE 103**
Plans and specifications, evidence of other crimes or wrongs, **FRE 404**
Plea of nolo contendere, admissibility, **28 § 2074 nt**
Pleas, relevancy, **FRE 410**
Prejudice or bias, exclusion, prejudicial evidence, **FRE 403**
Preliminary examination, **FRE 104**
Facts, **FRE 1101**
Preparation, evidence of other crimes or wrongs, **FRE 404**
Present sense impressions, hearsay rule, exception, **FRE 803**
Presumptions, **FRE 301**
State laws, **FRE 302**
Previous conviction of crime, hearsay rule, exception, **FRE 803**
Prior conviction, impeachment, conviction of crime, **FRE 609**
Prior inconsistent statements of witnesses, **FRE 613**
Privileges and immunities, **FRE 501**
Application of rules, **FRE 1101**
Attorneys, **FRE 502**
Preliminary determinations, **FRE 104**
Probation, **FRE 1101**
Procurement, witnesses, hearsay rule, exception, **FRE 804**
Property, records and recordation, hearsay rule, exception, **FRE 803**
Public records. Records and recordation, generally, post
Purpose of rules, **FRE 102**

RULES OF EVIDENCE—Cont'd
Rape shield, victims of crime, past sexual history or predisposition, **FRE 412**
Recorded recollections, hearsay rule, exception, **FRE 803**
Records and recordation,
Absence of entry, hearsay rule, exception, **FRE 803**
Authentication, **FRE 901**
Best evidence, **FRE 1001 et seq.**
Copies, admissibility, **FRE 1005**
Extrinsic evidence of contents, **FRE 1005**
Federal agencies, **28 § 1733**
Hearsay rule, exception, **FRE 803**
Offers of evidence, **FRE 103**
Self-authentication, **FRE 902**
Refreshing memory, witnesses, writings, **FRE 612**
Regularly conducted activities, records and recordation,
Hearsay rule, exception, **FRE 803**
Self-authentication, **FRE 902**
Rehabilitation certificates, conviction of crime, impeachment, **FRE 609**
Related writings, **FRE 106**
Relevancy, **FRE 401 et seq.**
Admissibility, **FRE 402**
Character evidence, **FRE 404, 405**
Compromise and settlement, **FRE 408**
Conditioned on fact, preliminary determinations, **FRE 104**
Confusing evidence, **FRE 403**
Cumulative evidence, **FRE 403**
Definitions, **FRE 401**
Habit, **FRE 406**
Liability insurance, **FRE 411**
Medical care and treatment, payment, **FRE 409**
Pleas, **FRE 410**
Prejudicial evidence, **FRE 403**
Routine practices, **FRE 406**
Sex offenses, post
Subsequent remedial measures, **FRE 407**
Religion, impeachment, **FRE 610**
Religious organizations and societies, records and recordation, hearsay rule, exception, **FRE 803**
Remainder of writings, **FRE 106**
Rendition, **FRE 1101**
Reports,
Authentication, **FRE 901**
Public reports, hearsay rule, exception, **FRE 803**
Reputation. Character and reputation, generally, ante
Routine, relevancy, **FRE 406**
Rulings, **FRE 103**
Scope of rules, **FRE 101**
Searches and seizures, warrants, **FRE 1101**
Self-authentication, **FRE 902**
Sentence and punishment, application of rules, **FRE 1101**

RULES OF EVIDENCE—Cont'd
Settlement and compromise, relevancy, **FRE 408**
Sex offenses, **FRE 412 et seq.**
Child molestation, similar crimes, **FRE 414**
Civil cases, similar crimes, **FRE 415**
Relevancy, **FRE 412 et seq.**
Child molestation, similar crimes, **FRE 414**
Civil cases, similar crimes, **FRE 415**
Similar crimes, **FRE 413 et seq.**
Victims past sexual behavior or predisposition, **FRE 412**
Similar crimes, **FRE 413 et seq.**
Victims past sexual behavior or predisposition, **FRE 412**
Specific instances of conduct,
Character evidence, **FRE 405**
Witnesses, **FRE 608**
Statements against interest, hearsay rule, exception, **FRE 804**
Subsequent remedial measures, relevancy, **FRE 407**
Summaries, writings, recordings, or photographs, admissibility, **FRE 1006**
Summons, criminal cases, **FRE 1101**
Supreme Court, powers and duties, **28 § 2074**
Suspension, **28 § 2071 nt**
Telecommunications, authentication, **FRE 901**
Time,
Conviction of crime, impeachment, **FRE 609**
Judicial notice, **FRE 201**
Title of rules, **FRE 1102**
Trade inscriptions, self-authentication, **FRE 902**
Ultimate issues, opinion and expert testimony, **FRE 704**
Unobtainable originals, other proof, admissibility, **FRE 1004**
Verdicts, validity, jurors as witnesses, **FRE 606**
Victims of crime,
Character evidence, **FRE 404**
Sex offenses, past sexual behavior or predisposition, relevancy, **FRE 412**
Vital statistics, records and recordation, hearsay rule, exception, **FRE 803**
Voices, authentication, **FRE 901**
Waiver, attorneys, privileges and immunities, **FRE 502**
Weight of evidence, preliminary determinations, **FRE 104**
Witnesses,
Calling by court, **FRE 614**
Character and reputation, **FRE 404, 608**
Competency, **FRE 601 et seq.**
Judges and justices, **FRE 605**
Jurors, **FRE 606**
Personal knowledge, **FRE 602**
Conviction of crime, credibility, **FRE 609**

RULES OF EVIDENCE—Cont'd
Witnesses—Cont'd
Cross examination, **FRE 611**
Exclusion, **FRE 615**
Hearsay, generally, ante
Impeachment, **FRE 607 et seq.**
Character and reputation, **FRE 608**
Conviction of crime, **FRE 609**
Religious beliefs or opinions, **FRE 610**
Specific instances of conduct, **FRE 608**
Interpreters, **FRE 603**
Interrogation, **FRE 611, 614**
Leading questions, **FRE 611**
Opinions, **FRE 608**
Presentation, **FRE 611**
Prior statements, **FRE 613**
Qualifications, preliminary determinations, **FRE 104**
Refreshing memory, writings, **FRE 612**
Specific instances of conduct, **FRE 608**
Writings, refreshing memory, **FRE 612**
Work product, **FRE 502**
Writings,
Original writings, recordings, or photographs, **FRE 1002**
Refreshing memory, witnesses, **FRE 612**

RURAL AREAS
Federal debt collection, postjudgment remedies, **28 § 3203**

RUTLAND, VT
District court, **28 § 126**

SABOTAGE
Aircraft, this index

SACRAMENTO, CA
Court of Appeals for Ninth Circuit, generally, this index

SAFETY
Attorneys, fees, **28 § 2412**
Railroads, this index

SAILORS (MERCHANT MARINE)
Seamen, generally, this index

SAINT CROIX
Virgin Islands, generally, this index

SAINT JOHN
Virgin Islands, generally, this index

SAINT THOMAS
Virgin Islands, generally, this index

SALARIES
Compensation and Salaries, generally, this index

SALES
Attachment, Post Office, **28 § 2714**
Attorney General, law books, **28 § 525**
Bankruptcy, this index

SALES—Cont'd
Courts of appeals, rules of practice, **28 § 2077**
Customs Duties, generally, this index
Federal Debt Collection, this index
Internal Revenue Service. Tax Sales, generally, this index
Judicial Sales, generally, this index
Notice, U.S. marshal, fees, **28 § 1921**
Real Estate, this index
Rules of Civil Procedure, this index
Stores, generally, this index
Supreme Court, **28 §§ 412, 676**
Tax Sales, generally, this index
Unappraised goods, execution, **28 § 2005**
United States Marshals Service, this index

SALT LAKE CITY, UT
United States District Court, location, **28 § 125**

SAMPLES
United States Court of International Trade, inspection and inspectors, **28 § 2641**

SAN DIEGO, CA
Court of Appeals for Ninth Circuit, generally, this index

SANCTIONS
See specific index headings

SAND ISLAND
Judicial District of Hawaii, **28 § 91**

SATISFACTION
See specific index headings

SATURDAY
Rules of Civil Procedure, this index

SAULT SAINTE MARIE MI
District court held at, **28 § 102**

SCHEDULES
See specific index headings

SCHOLARSHIPS
Fraud, sentence and punishment, **28 § 994 nt**
Sentence and punishment, fraud, **28 § 994 nt**

SCHOOLS AND SCHOOL DISTRICTS
Justice Department, this index
Postsecondary education and schools. Colleges and Universities, generally, this index
Prosecutions, weapons, **28 § 509 nt**
Weapons, prosecutions, **28 § 509 nt**

SCIENTIFIC ASSOCIATIONS, INSTITUTIONS OR ORGANIZATIONS
Attorneys fees, prevailing parties, **28 § 2412**

SCRANTON, PA
District court held at, **28 § 118**

SCULPTURE
Copyrights, generally, this index

SEALING
International Trade Court, this index

SEALS (OFFICIAL SEALS)
Books of States, territories or possessions, evidence, **28 § 1739**
Continuance in action by U.S. against delinquents for public money, **28 § 2407**
Courts, records and recordation, **28 § 1738**
Director of Administrative Office of U.S. Court, **28 § 608**
Judicial Notice, this index
Justice Department, **28 § 502**
Patent and Trademark Office, this index
Possession of U.S.,
Authentication of acts of legislature for evidence, **28 § 1738**
Books or records of, evidence, **28 §§ 1738, 1739**
Process, **28 § 1691**
Record of States, territories or possessions, evidence, **28 §§ 1738, 1739**
Rules of Civil Procedure, this index
State,
Authentication of acts of legislature for evidence, **28 § 1738**
Books or records of, evidence, **28 §§ 1738, 1739**
Territories,
Authentication of acts of legislature for evidence, **28 § 1738**
Books or records of territories, evidence, **28 §§ 1738, 1739**
United States magistrate judges, **28 § 638**
Writs, **28 § 1691**

SEAMEN
Actions and proceedings, fees, **28 § 1916**
Appeal and review, fees, **28 § 1916**
Costs,
Appeal and review, **28 § 1916**
Courts, **28 § 1916**
Fees,
Actions and proceedings, **28 § 1916**
Appeal and review, **28 § 1916**
Courts, **28 § 1916**

SEAPORTS
Harbors and Ports, generally, this index

SEARCHES AND SEIZURES
Admiralty, this index
Attorneys, claims, **28 § 2465**
Certificates and certification,
Foreign countries, judgments and decrees, **28 § 2467**
Reasonable cause, **28 § 2465**
Costs, claims, **28 § 2465**
District courts, admiralty, **28 § 1356**

SEARCHES AND SEIZURES—Cont'd
Federal debt collection, **28 § 3009**
Fees, U.S. marshal, **28 § 1921**
Interest, returns, **28 § 2465**
International Trade Court, this index
Jurisdiction, **28 § 1356**
Privileges and immunities, **28 § 2465**
Reasonable cause certificates, **28 § 2465**
Release, generally, this index
Reports, Attorney General, **28 § 524**
Returns, **28 § 2465**
Rules of Civil Procedure, this index

SECRET SERVICE
Federally insured financial institutions, fraud, investigations, **28 § 509 nt**
Fraud, Federally insured financial institutions, **28 § 509 nt**
Investigations, Federally insured financial institutions, fraud, **28 § 509 nt**

SECRETARIES
Bankruptcy, judges or justices, **28 § 156**
District judges, **28 § 752**
Judges or Justices, this index

SECRETARY OF AGRICULTURE
Appeal and review, orders, **28 § 2341 et seq.**
Crimes and offenses, special prosecutor, **28 § 592 et seq.**
Orders, appeal and review, **28 § 2341 et seq.**
Special prosecutor, crimes and offenses, **28 § 592 et seq.**

SECRETARY OF AIR FORCE
Attorney General, advice, **28 § 513**

SECRETARY OF ARMY
Attorney General, advice, **28 § 513**

SECRETARY OF COMMERCE
Customs Duties, this index
Special prosecutor, appointment, **28 § 592 et seq.**

SECRETARY OF DEFENSE
Automated legal research and information system, **28 § 509 nt, EON 12146**
Consultants, ethics, Office of Government Ethics, **5 App. 4 § 101**
Special prosecutor, appointment, **28 § 592 et seq.**

SECRETARY OF EDUCATION
Special prosecutors, **28 § 592 et seq.**

SECRETARY OF ENERGY
Special prosecutor, appointment, crimes and offenses, **28 § 592 et seq.**

SECRETARY OF HOUSING AND URBAN DEVELOPMENT
Special prosecutor, crimes and offenses, **28 § 591**

SECRETARY OF LABOR
Crimes and offenses, special prosecutor, **28 § 591**
Special prosecutor, crimes and offenses, **28 § 591**

SECRETARY OF NAVY
Admiralty, this index
Attorney General, powers and duties, **28 § 513**

SECRETARY OF SENATE
Journals, evidence, **28 § 1736**

SECRETARY OF STATE
Certificates and certification, records and recordation, evidence, **28 § 1739**
Special prosecutor, **28 § 591 et seq.**

SECRETARY OF THE INTERIOR
Indians, this index
Reports, Indian Claims Limitation Act of 1982, **28 § 2415 nt**

SECRETARY OF THE TREASURY
Judgments and decrees, interest, **28 § 1961**
Law enforcement, training, overseas, **28 § 509 nt**
Overseas law enforcement, training, **28 § 509 nt**
Payment, judgments and decrees, **28 § 2414**

SECRETARY OF TRANSPORTATION
Orders, Maritime Act of 1981, **28 § 2341**

SECRETS AND SECRECY
Espionage, generally, this index
Intelligence, generally, this index

SECURITIES
Equity security holders. Bankruptcy, this index
Fraud, limitation of actions, **28 § 1658**
Limitation of actions,
Fraud, **28 § 1658**
Private actions, **28 § 1658**

SECURITIES ACT
Securities, generally, this index

SECURITIES EXCHANGE ACT
Securities, generally, this index

SECURITY
Actions and proceedings, **28 § 2408**
Contempt, witnesses, foreign countries, **28 § 1784**
Diplomatic Security, generally, this index
Federal Bureau of Investigation, this index
Guards, generally, this index
Independent Counsel, this index
Judicial Conference of the United States, consultants, **28 § 331**
Justice Department, national security division, **28 § 509A**
National Guard, generally, this index

SECURITY—Cont'd
Private security. Guards, generally, this index
Stay of proceedings,
Admiralty cases, **28 § 2464**
Certiorari, **28 § 2101**
Terrorists and Terrorism, generally, this index
United States Marshals Service, **28 § 604**
Consultants, **28 § 566**
Witnesses, compensation and salaries, **28 § 1821**

SECURITY INTEREST
Copyrights, motion pictures, transfer of ownership, collective bargaining agreements, **28 § 4001**
Garnishment, corporations, **28 § 2405**
Pending actions, costs, **28 § 2041**
Quieting title, **28 § 2409a**
Removal of cases, **28 § 1450**
Rules of Civil Procedure, this index

SEGREGATION
Discrimination, generally, this index

SEIZURES
Searches and Seizures, generally, this index

SELECTION
See specific index headings

SEMIAUTOMATICS
Weapons, generally, this index

SEMICONDUCTORS
Copyrights,
Actions and proceedings, mask works, **28 §§ 1338, 1400, 1498**
Jurisdiction, mask works, **28 §§ 1338, 1498**
Mask works,
Actions and proceedings, **28 §§ 1338, 1400, 1498**
Jurisdiction, **28 §§ 1338, 1498**

SEMINARS
United States magistrate judges, **28 § 637**

SENATE
Actions and proceedings, subpoenas, **28 § 1365**
Assistant Attorneys General, appointment, **28 § 506**
Attorney General, appointment, **28 § 503**
Committees, definitions, jurisdiction in Senate actions, **28 § 1365**
Congressional Committees, generally, this index
Courts of appeals, judges or justices, appointments, **28 § 44**
Deposition, District Court for District of Columbia, jurisdiction, Senate action to require, **28 § 1365**
Deputies, Attorney General, appointment, **28 § 504**

SENATE—Cont'd
Disclosure of Federal Campaign Funds, generally, this index
District court judges, appointments, **28 § 133**
District courts, recover possession of office, **28 § 1344**
Illinois, Southern District of Illinois, judges or justices, appointments, **28 § 93 nt**
Interrogatories, District Court for the District of Columbia, jurisdiction, **28 § 1365**
Journals of Congress, evidence, **28 § 1736**
Judges or justices,
Disability, appointments, **28 § 372**
Judicial Survivors Annuity Fund, **28 § 376**
Judicial Center, Director, **28 § 627**
Notice, district court judges, selection, **28 § 133 nt**
Officers and employees, removal of cases or causes, **28 § 1442**
Orders, District Court for District of Columbia, enforcement, **28 § 1365**
Production of books and papers, District Court for District of Columbia, jurisdiction, **28 § 1365**
Records and recordation, committees, U.S. Court of Federal Claims, **28 § 2507**
Rulemaking, financial disclosure, **5 App. 4 § 101 nt**
Solicitor General, appointment, advice, **28 § 505**
Subpoenas, District Court for District of Columbia, **28 § 1365**
United States attorneys, appointment, **28 §§ 541, 546**
United States Court of Federal Claims, appointments, **28 § 171**
United States Court of International Trade, appointments, **28 § 251**
United States Sentencing Commission, appointments, **28 § 991**
Virgin Islands, this index
Witnesses, District Court for District of Columbia, **28 § 1365**

SENATORS
Senate, generally, this index

SENIOR CITIZENS
Aged Persons, generally, this index

SENIORITY
Circuit judges, **28 § 45**
Courts of appeals, judges or justices, **28 § 2109**
District judges, **28 § 136**
Supreme Court, **28 § 4**
United States Court of International Trade, judges or justices, **28 §§ 253, 258**

SENTENCE AND PUNISHMENT
Generally, **MAS 1 et seq.**
Aged persons, **28 § 994 nt**
Aliens, this index
Attacking sentence, **28 § 2255; MAS 1 et seq.**
Answer, **MAS 5**
Appeal and review, **MAS 11**
Civil procedure rules, **MAS 12**
Criminal procedure rules, **MAS 12**
Discovery, **MAS 6**
Evidence, **MAS 8**
Filing, motions, **MAS 3**
Forms, **foll. MAS 12**
Hearings, **MAS 8**
Magistrate judges, **MAS 10**
Motions, **MAS 2 et seq.**
Preliminary review, **MAS 4**
Records and recordation, **MAS 7**
Second or successive motions, **MAS 9**
Time, **MAS 11**
Attorneys,
Appointment, **28 § 2255**
Tort claims against U.S., **28 § 2678**
Banks and Banking, this index
Boards and commissions. United States Sentencing Commission, generally, post
Cloning, wireless telephones, **28 § 994 nt**
Contempt, generally, this index
Controlled Substances, this index
Correctional Institutions, generally, this index
Counterfeiting, this index
Court of Federal Claims, this index
Crime of violence, definitions, **28 § 994 nt**
Crime Victims, this index
Criminal Background Checks, generally, this index
Debts, writ of execution, **28 § 2007**
Detention, generally, this index
District courts,
Attacking sentence, generally, ante
Transcripts, **28 § 753**
Ecstasy, trafficking, guidelines, **28 § 994 nt**
Emblems and insignia, **28 § 994 nt**
Enhancement, child victims, **28 § 994 nt**
Escape, this index
Explosives, this index
False imprisonment, **28 § 2680**
Federal Officers and Employees, this index
Forms, reports, **28 § 994**
Fraud, this index
Grand Jury, this index
Guidelines. United States Sentencing Commission, generally, post
Habeas Corpus, generally, this index
Identity and identification, fraud, **28 § 994 nt**
Institutes, **28 § 334**
Interstate stalking. Stalking, this index
Joint councils, **28 § 334**

SENTENCE AND PUNISHMENT
—Cont'd
Judges or justices, threats, guidelines, **28 § 994 nt**
Judicial Conference of the United States, **28 §§ 334, 994**
Jury, **28 § 1864 et seq.**
Limitation of action, vacation of sentence, **28 § 2255**
List I chemicals, controlled substances, guidelines, **28 § 994 nt**
Methamphetamine, guidelines, **28 § 994 nt**
Modification, term of imprisonment, **28 § 994**
Motions,
Attacking sentence, **MAS 2 et seq.**
Vacating and setting aside, **28 § 2255**
National cemeteries, **28 § 994 nt**
Postsentence administration, temporary release, **28 § 994**
Pre-release custody, **28 § 994**
Probation, generally, this index
Psychiatry and Psychiatrists, this index
Public policy. United States Sentencing Commission, post
Reductions, **28 § 994**
Release, generally, this index
Reports,
Forms, **28 § 994**
United States Sentencing Commission, post
Restitution, generally, this index
Revocation or suspension, earned release credits, **28 § 1932**
Rules of Evidence, this index
Second and subsequent offenses, enhancement, **28 § 994 nt**
Section 2255 proceedings (motion attacking sentence). Attacking sentence, generally, ante
Sentencing Commission. United States Sentencing Commission, generally, post
Sexual Abuse, this index
Solicitation, children and minors, **28 § 994 nt**
Spam, guidelines, **28 § 994 nt**
Staff Director, United States Sentencing Commission, **28 § 995**
Stalking, this index
Standards, **28 § 334**
Statutes,
Minimum sentences, **28 § 994 nt**
Vacating or setting aside, motions, **28 § 2255**
Studies, guidelines, **28 § 994 nt**
Successive applications, vacating and setting aside, **28 § 2255**
Supervised release, **28 § 994**
Telecommunications, this index
Terrorists and Terrorism, this index
Time, motions, **28 § 2255**

SENTENCE AND PUNISHMENT
—Cont'd
United States Sentencing Commission, **28 § 991 et seq.**
Administrative Office of U.S. Courts, **28 § 995**
Aged persons, **28 § 994 nt**
Aliens, smuggling, **28 § 994 nt**
Annual report, Judicial Conference of the United States, **28 § 997**
Attorney General, members and membership, **28 § 991**
Attorneys, **28 § 995**
Bureau of Prisons, powers and duties, **28 § 994**
Categories of offenses, **28 § 994**
Chairperson, **28 § 991 et seq.**
Children and minors, **28 § 994 nt**
Common carriers, **28 § 994 nt**
Compensation and salaries,
Members, **28 § 992**
Staff Director, **28 § 995**
Computers, sexual exploitation, children and minors, **28 § 994 nt**
Consecutive terms, **28 § 994**
Consultation, **28 § 994**
Contracts, **28 § 995**
Cooperative agreements, **28 § 995**
Crack (cocaine), **28 § 994 nt**
Criminal background checks, **28 § 534**
Defendants, petitions, **28 § 994**
Definitions, **28 § 998**
Disparities, **28 § 994**
Domicile and residence, **28 § 992**
Drug free truck stops and safety rest areas, **28 § 994 nt**
Emergency guidelines, **28 § 994 nt**
Explosives, **28 § 994 nt**
Federal agencies, information, **28 § 995**
Federal Judicial Center, **28 § 995**
Federally insured financial institutions, **28 § 994 nt**
Firearms, **28 § 994 nt**
Forms, reports, **28 § 994**
Fraud, telemarketing, **28 § 994 nt**
Hate crimes, **28 § 994 nt**
Hearings, **28 § 995**
Identity theft, **28 § 994 nt**
Imprisonment, **28 § 994**
Incremental penalties, **28 § 994**
Information, criminal background checks, **28 § 534**
Judicial Conference of the United States, **28 §§ 991, 997**
Justice Department, reports, **28 § 994 nt**
Juvenile delinquents, studies, **28 § 995**
Labor and employment, **28 § 995**
Leases, **28 § 995**
Maximum imprisonment, **28 § 994**
Methamphetamines, trafficking, **28 § 994 nt**
National Crime Information Center, access, **28 § 534**
Officers and employees, **28 § 996**

SENTENCE AND PUNISHMENT
—Cont'd
United States Sentencing Commission
—Cont'd
Petitions, defendants, **28 § 994**
Petty offenses, **28 § 994**
Powers and duties, **28 §§ 994, 995**
President of the United States,
Appointments, **28 § 991**
Reports, **28 § 997**
Probation, **28 § 995**
Public policy, **28 § 994**
Statutory minimum, **28 § 994 nt**
Publication, **28 § 995**
Quorum, **28 § 995**
Reductions, **28 § 994**
Removal from office, **28 § 991**
Reports, **28 § 994**
Annual report, **28 § 995**
Research and Development Program, **28 § 995**
Restitution, **28 § 994 nt**
Rules and regulations,
Definitions, **28 § 998**
Powers and duties, **28 §§ 994, 995**
Seminars, **28 § 995**
Sex offenses, **28 § 994 nt**
Smokeable crystal methamphetamine, **28 § 994 nt**
Solicitation, children and minors, **28 § 994 nt**
Spam, **28 § 994 nt**
Staff Director, **28 §§ 995, 996**
Statutory minimum, **28 § 994 nt**
Studies, **28 § 994 nt**
Telemarketing, fraud, **28 § 994 nt**
Terms of office, **28 § 992**
Terrorist crimes, **28 § 994 nt**
Veterans' cemeteries, property offenses, **28 § 994 nt**
Vice chairs, **28 §§ 991, 992**
Victim impact statements, **28 § 994**
Weapons, **28 § 994 nt**
Wireless telephones, cloning, **28 § 994 nt**
Witnesses, **28 § 995**
Unjust imprisonment, damages, **28 § 1495**
Veterans, this index
Weapons, this index
Wireless telephones, cloning, **28 § 994 nt**

SENTENCING GUIDELINES ACT OF 1986
Generally, **28 §§ 1 nt, 994**

SENTENCING REFORM ACTS AND AMENDMENTS
Generally, **28 § 994**

SEQUESTRATION
See specific index headings

SERIAL KILLINGS
Child Abduction and Serial Murder Investigative Resources Center, **28 § 531 nt**

SERIAL KILLINGS—Cont'd
Investigations, **28 § 540B**

SERVICE OF PROCESS
Process, generally, this index

SESSIONS
Court of Appeals for the Federal Circuit, this index
Courts of appeals, **28 §§ 46, 48**
District Courts, this index
International Trade Court, this index
Jurisdiction, **28 § 452**
Supreme Court, this index

SET-OFF AND COUNTERCLAIM
Bankruptcy, this index
Claims by U.S. against opposing or third parties, time barred, **28 § 2415**
Court of Federal Claims, this index
Foreign States, privileges and immunities, **28 § 1607**
International Trade Court, this index
Jurisdiction, United States, **28 § 1346**
Pleading, United States, jurisdiction, **28 § 1346**
Rules of Civil Procedure, this index
United States, this index

SETTLEMENT
Compromise and Settlement, generally, this index

SEX
Abuse. Sexual Abuse, generally, this index
Courts, nominees, **28 § 44 nt**
Federal judgeships, nominees, **28 § 133 nt**
Jury, discrimination, **28 §§ 1862, 1867**

SEX OFFENSES
Rules of Evidence, this index

SEXUAL ABUSE
Computers, **28 § 994 nt**
Repeat offenders, **28 § 994 nt**
Sentence and punishment,
Children and minors, **28 § 994 nt**
Repeat offenders, **28 § 994 nt**

SEXUAL ASSAULT
Sentence and punishment, **28 § 994 nt**

SEXUAL EXPLOITATION
Children and Minors, this index

SEXUAL ORIENTATION
Hate crimes, **28 § 534 nt**

SHAREHOLDERS COMMUNICATIONS ACT OF 1985
Securities, generally, this index

SHARES AND SHAREHOLDERS
Actions and proceedings. Derivative Actions, generally, this index
Bankruptcy, this index
Derivative Actions, generally, this index

SHARES AND SHAREHOLDERS—Cont'd
Securities, generally, this index
Service of process on corporation in stockholder's derivative action, **28 § 1695**
United States, corporations, **28 § 1349**
Venue, derivative actions, **28 § 1401**

SHIPS AND SHIPPING
Actions and proceedings. Admiralty, generally, this index
Boards and commissions. Federal Maritime Commission, generally, this index
Bonds (officers and fiduciaries), answer, **28 § 2464**
Coastwise voyages, jury, **28 § 1873**
Damages, jurisdiction, **28 § 1337**
Entry. Harbors and Ports, this index
Federal Maritime Commission, generally, this index
Fines, penalties and forfeitures, venue, **28 § 1395**
Harbors and Ports, generally, this index
Jury, **28 § 1873**
Liens and incumbrances, privileges and immunities, **28 § 1605**
Maritime Commission. Federal Maritime Commission, generally, this index
Officers and employees. Seamen, generally, this index
Ports. Harbors and Ports, generally, this index
Recreational vessels. Boats and Boating, generally, this index
Seamen, generally, this index
Stay of proceedings, process in rem, admiralty, **28 § 2464**
Stipulations, **28 § 2464**
United States Marshal, fees, **28 § 1921**
Venue, fines, penalties and forfeitures, **28 § 1395**

SHOPS
Stores, generally, this index

SHORTHAND RECORDING
District courts, sessions, **28 § 753**

SHOTGUNS
Weapons, generally, this index

SHOW CAUSE ORDERS
Foreign countries, subpoenas, **28 §§ 1783, 1784**
Habeas Corpus, this index
Judicial Panel On Multidistrict Litigation, this index
Magistrate judges, contempt, **28 § 636**

SIGNATURES
Attorney General, requisitions for advance or payment of moneys, **28 § 523**
Clerks of courts, writs and process issuing from court, **28 § 1691**

SIGNATURES—Cont'd
Convention on the Taking of Evidence Abroad in Civil or Commercial Matters, party to, **28 § 1781 nt**
Copyrights, generally, this index
Habeas corpus, application for writ, **28 § 2242**
Rules of Civil Procedure, this index

SISTERS AND BROTHERS
Relatives, generally, this index

SKILLED NURSING FACILITIES
Nursing Homes, generally, this index

SMALL BUSINESSES
Bankruptcy, this index

SMUGGLING
Aliens, this index
Immigration, this index

SOCIAL SECURITY
Attorneys, fees, **28 § 2412 nt**
Fees, attorneys, **28 § 2412 nt**

SOCIETIES
Associations and Societies, generally, this index

SOLICITATION
Children and minors, sentence and punishment, **28 § 994 nt**

SOLICITOR GENERAL
Justice Department, this index

SOLID WASTE
Oceans, this index

SOUTH CAROLINA
Bankruptcy, judges or justices, appointments, **28 § 152**
District courts,
Judges or justices, **28 § 133**
Location, **28 § 121**
Judicial circuit, **28 § 41**
Judicial districts, **28 § 121**
Bankruptcy, **28 § 581 nt**
Judges or justices, **28 § 133**
United States trustees, judicial districts, appointment, **28 § 581**

SOUTH DAKOTA
Bankruptcy, judges or justices, appointments, **28 § 152**
District courts,
Judges or justices, **28 § 133**
Location, **28 § 122**
Judicial circuit, **28 § 41**
Judicial districts, **28 § 122**
Judges or justices, **28 § 133**
United States trustees, **28 § 581**
United States trustees, judicial districts, **28 § 581**

SOVEREIGN IMMUNITY
Indians, generally, this index

SPAM
Guidelines, sentence and punishment, **28 § 994 nt**
Sentence and punishment, guidelines, **28 § 994 nt**

SPEAKER OF THE HOUSE OF REPRESENTATIVES
Federal Judicial Center Foundation, appointments, **28 § 629**

SPECIAL ATTORNEYS
United States attorneys, **28 § 543 et seq.**

SPECIAL COUNSEL
Senior interagency group Chairman, **28 § 509 nt**

SPECIAL MASTERS
Court of Federal Claims, this index
Terrorists and terrorism, Foreign States, damages, **28 § 1605A**

SPECIAL PROSECUTOR
Independent Counsel, generally, this index

SPECIAL TERMS
Supreme Court, **28 § 2**

SPECIFIC PERFORMANCE
See specific index headings

SPECIFICATIONS
Plans and Specifications, generally, this index

SPEECH IMPAIRMENT
Court Interpreters Act, **28 § 1827**

SPEEDY TRIAL
Trial, this index

SPIES
Espionage, generally, this index

SPOUSAL ABUSE
Domestic Violence, generally, this index

SPYING
Espionage, generally, this index

STALKING
Records and recordation, **28 § 534**
Sentence and punishment, **28 § 994 nt**

STANDARDS
See specific index headings

STANDING TO SUE
See specific index headings

STATE AGENCIES
Officers and employees. States, this index

STATE COURTS
Appeals to Supreme Court,
Criminal cases, **28 § 2101**
Priority of criminal cases, **28 § 2102**

STATE COURTS—Cont'd
Certified or registered mail, service of process on U.S. in proceedings in which it has lien on property, **28 § 2410**
Certiorari,
Records and proceedings on removal of case, **28 § 1447**
Review by Supreme Court, decision involving validity of State statute, **28 § 1257**
State courts, decision involving validity of State statute, **28 § 1257**
Time, **28 § 2101**
Clerks of courts,
Copy of order of remand mailed to clerk, **28 § 1447**
Removal of case,
Duties, **28 §§ 1446, 1447**
Failure of clerk to supply records and proceedings, **28 § 1449**
Procedure on, **28 § 1446**
Contract Disputes Act of 1978, judgments against U.S., payment, exception, **28 § 2414**
Definitions, Superior Court of the District of Columbia, removal of cases or causes, **28 § 1451**
Habeas Corpus, this index
Judgments, against U.S., payment, **28 § 2414**
Marshal, removal of case, custody of defendant, **28 § 1446**
Officers and employees, exemption from jury service, **28 § 1863**
Priority of criminal cases on appeal from, **28 § 2102**
Process, United States, liens and incumbrances, **28 § 2410**
Records and recordation,
Evidence, **28 § 1738**
Full faith and credit, **28 § 1738**
Removal of cases or causes, **28 § 1449**
Removal of Cases or Causes, generally, this index
Review by Supreme Court, **28 § 1257**
Manner of taking, **28 § 2104**
Stay of proceedings,
Habeas corpus, **28 § 2251**
Injunction, **28 § 2283**
Tax liens, U.S. as party, actions to quiet title, foreclose, service of process, **28 § 2410**
United States,
Interests in pending suits, attending to, **28 § 517**
Lien on property affected by action, **28 § 2410**

STATE DEPARTMENT
Appointments, investigations, **28 § 533**
Espionage, reports, **28 § 533 nt**
Investigations, **28 § 533**
Letters rogatory, **28 § 1781**

STATE JUSTICE INSTITUTE
Generally, **28 § 620**

STATE JUSTICE INSTITUTE—Cont'd
Judicial Center, **28 § 620**

STATE LAWS
Appeal and review, Supreme Court, **28 § 1257**
District courts, judgments, execution levied for interest on, **28 § 1961**
Evidence, **28 § 1738**
Forfeitures, Justice Department Assets Forfeiture Fund, **28 § 524**
Injunctions, three judge court, **28 § 2284**
Repugnant to treaty, constitution or U.S. laws, review of State decision by Supreme Court, **28 § 1257**
Review by Supreme Court of State decision involving validity, **28 § 1257**
Rules of Appellate Procedure, this index
Rules of decision, exception, **28 § 1652**
Senate subpoenas, **28 § 1365**
Trusts and trustees, United States courts, **28 § 959**

STATEMENTS
See specific index headings

STATES
Actions and proceedings,
Rate orders, **28 § 1342**
Rules of decision, **28 § 1652**
Supreme Court, **28 § 1251**
Taxation, **28 § 1341**
Alabama, generally, this index
Alaska, generally, this index
Aliens, Supreme Court, **28 § 1251**
Apportionment, constitutionality, **28 § 2284**
Arizona, generally, this index
Arkansas, generally, this index
Attorney General,
Habeas corpus, **28 § 2252**
State statutes, constitutionality, intervention, **28 § 2403**
Three judge court, notice, **28 § 2284**
Bankruptcy, this index
California, generally, this index
Citizens of another State, Supreme Court jurisdiction of actions or proceedings against, **28 § 1251**
Civil actions. Actions and proceedings, generally, ante
Claims, U.S. Court of Federal Claims, **28 § 1491**
Colorado, generally, this index
Community Development, generally, this index
Connecticut, generally, this index
Constitution of the United States, this index
Counterfeiting, officers and employees, emblems and insignia, **28 § 994 nt**
Courts. State Courts, generally, this index
Crimes and offenses,
Emblems and insignia, **28 § 994 nt**
Indian lands and reservations, jurisdiction, **28 § 1360 nt**

STATES—Cont'd
Crimes and offenses—Cont'd
Jurisdiction, Indian lands and reservations, **28 § 1360 nt**
Records and recordation, exchanges, **28 § 534**
Uniforms, **28 § 994 nt**
Delaware, generally, this index
District court jurisdiction, diversity of citizenship, **28 § 1332**
Elections, generally, this index
Emblems and insignia, officers and employees, counterfeiting, **28 § 994 nt**
Employees. Officers and employees, generally, post
Executions in favor of U.S., **28 § 2413**
Exemptions. Officers and employees, post
Federal Aid, generally, this index
Federal Bureau of Investigation, this index
Firefighters, jury, exemptions, **28 § 1863**
Florida, generally, this index
Full faith and credit,
Courts, **28 § 1738**
Records and recordation, **28 §§ 1738, 1739**
Gambling, this index
Georgia, generally, this index
Governor, generally, this index
Idaho, generally, this index
Illinois, generally, this index
Indian lands and reservations, jurisdiction, **28 § 1360**
Indiana, generally, this index
Intervention, constitutional questions, **28 § 2403**
Iowa, generally, this index
Judgments and decrees,
Contract Disputes Act of 1978, **28 § 2414**
United States, **28 § 2414**
Judicial proceedings, evidence, **28 § 1738**
Jurisdiction,
Crimes and offenses, ante
United States Supreme Court, **28 § 1251**
Kansas, generally, this index
Kentucky, generally, this index
Land grants, **28 § 1354**
Legislature,
Apportionment, three judge court, **28 § 2284**
Officers and employees, jury, exemptions, **28 § 1863**
Louisiana, generally, this index
Maine, generally, this index
Maryland, generally, this index
Massachusetts, generally, this index
Michigan, generally, this index
Minnesota, generally, this index
Mississippi, generally, this index
Missouri, generally, this index
Montana, generally, this index
National Guard, generally, this index
Nebraska, generally, this index

STATES—Cont'd
Nevada, generally, this index
New Hampshire, generally, this index
New Jersey, generally, this index
New Mexico, generally, this index
New York, generally, this index
Noncontiguous states,
Alaska, generally, this index
Hawaii, generally, this index
Nonjudicial records, evidence, **28 § 1739**
North Carolina, generally, this index
North Dakota, generally, this index
Offenses. Crimes and offenses, generally, ante
Officers and employees,
Emblems and insignia, counterfeiting, **28 § 994 nt**
Exemptions, jury, **28 § 1863**
Governor, generally, this index
Habeas corpus, notice, **28 § 2252**
Jury, exemptions, **28 § 1863**
Reports, crimes and offenses, **28 § 529**
Uniforms, crimes and offenses, **28 § 994 nt**
Ohio, generally, this index
Oklahoma, generally, this index
Oregon, generally, this index
Pending suits, attending to interests of U.S. in, **28 § 517**
Pennsylvania, generally, this index
Police, exemption from jury service, **28 § 1863**
Proceedings. Actions and proceedings, generally, ante
Quieting title, **28 § 2409a**
Rate orders of agencies, jurisdiction of district courts, **28 § 1342**
Records and recordation, evidence, **28 § 1739**
Reports. Officers and employees, ante
Rhode Island, generally, this index
Rules of Civil Procedure, this index
Seals (official seals), evidence, **28 § 1739**
South Carolina, generally, this index
South Dakota, generally, this index
Supreme Court, controversies between states, **28 § 1251**
Taxation,
Court officers, liability, **28 § 960**
Jurisdiction of district courts, **28 § 1341**
Tennessee, generally, this index
Texas, generally, this index
Unjust conviction and imprisonment, damages, **28 § 2513**
Utah, generally, this index
Vermont, generally, this index
Virginia, generally, this index
Washington (State), generally, this index
West Virginia, generally, this index
Wisconsin, generally, this index
Wyoming, generally, this index

STATIONS
Official Stations, generally, this index

STATISTICS
Attorney General, crimes and offenses, **28 § 522**
Bankruptcy, this index
Hate crimes, **28 § 534 nt**
Savings and loan associations, **28 § 604**

STATUTE OF LIMITATIONS
Limitation of Actions, generally, this index

STATUTES
Civil rights, jurisdiction, **28 § 1343**
Conflict with rules of court, civil procedure, **28 § 2072**
Court rules,
Civil procedure, conflicts, **28 § 2072**
Consistency, **28 § 2071**
Extraordinary expenses, ministerial officers, payment, **28 § 1929**
Fines, penalties and forfeitures, **28 § 1918**
Full Faith and Credit, generally, this index
Habeas Corpus, this index
Indians, this index
Judicial Panel on Multidistrict Litigation, conduct, **28 § 1407**
Jurisdiction, this index
Limitation of Actions, generally, this index
Puerto Rico, repugnancy, **28 § 1258**
Questions of Law or Fact, generally, this index
Removal of cases and causes, **28 § 1441**
Repugnancy,
Puerto Rico, **28 § 1258**
State laws, **28 § 1257**
Rules of Appellate Procedure, this index
Rules of Civil Procedure, this index
Sentence and Punishment, this index
State courts, validity, **28 § 1257**
State Laws, generally, this index
U.S. Court of Federal Claims, jurisdiction, **28 § 1491**
United States, this index

STATUTORY LIENS
Liens and Incumbrances, generally, this index

STAY OF PROCEEDINGS
Arrest or process in rem issued in admiralty case, **28 § 2464**
Bankruptcy, this index
Court of Appeals for the Federal Circuit, this index
Court of Federal Claims, this index
Execution,
Admiralty, **28 § 2464**
Certiorari, **28 § 2101**
Exports and Imports, this index
Federal agencies, **28 § 2350**
Federal Debt Collection, this index
Fines, Penalties and Forfeitures, this index
Habeas Corpus, this index

STAY OF PROCEEDINGS—Cont'd
International Trade Commission, **28 § 1659**
International Trade Court, this index
Jury selection procedures, noncompliance, grounds for, **28 § 1867**
Rules of Appellate Procedure, this index
Rules of Civil Procedure, this index
Security, this index
State Courts, this index
Supreme Court, this index

STENOGRAPHERS
Administrative Office of United States Courts, compensation and salaries, **28 § 604**
Compensation and salaries,
Administrative Office of United States Courts, **28 § 604**
Courts, **28 § 603 nt**
Courts, compensation and salaries, **28 § 603 nt**
Transcripts, generally, this index

STIPULATIONS
Admiralty, this index
International Trade Court, this index
Judicial Panel On Multidistrict Litigation, this index
Rules of Appellate Procedure, this index
Rules of Civil Procedure, this index
Ships and Shipping, this index
Venue, change of venue, **28 § 1404**

STOCK AND STOCKHOLDERS
Shares and Shareholders, generally, this index

STORES
Clearinghouses, organized retail theft task force, **28 § 509 nt**
Larceny, organized retail theft task force, **28 § 509 nt**
Racketeering, organized retail theft task force, **28 § 509 nt**
Task forces, organized retail theft task force, **28 § 509 nt**

STREET GANGS
Gangs, generally, this index

STRIKING OF PLEADINGS
Rules of Civil Procedure, this index

STRUCTURAL ALTERNATIVES FOR THE FEDERAL COURTS OF APPEALS COMMISSION
Generally, **28 § 41 nt**

STUDENTS
Colleges and Universities, generally, this index

STUDIES
Comptroller General, this index
Courts of appeals, structural alternatives for the Federal Courts of Appeals Commission, **28 § 41 nt**

STUDIES—Cont'd
Judicial Center, **28 §§ 620, 623**
Sentence and Punishment, this index
Structural alternatives for the Federal Courts of Appeals Commission, **28 § 41 nt**

SUBPOENAS
Arbitration, **28 § 656**
Clerks of courts, **28 § 1825**
Congressional reference cases, **28 § 2509**
Contempt, generally, this index
Court of Federal Claims, this index
Federal Agencies, this index
Fees, United States Marshals, **28 § 1921**
Foreign countries, **28 §§ 1783, 1784**
Judges or Justices, this index
Multiparty and multiforum, **28 § 1785**
Patents, infringement, **28 § 1694**
Rules of Civil Procedure, this index
Senate, this index
United States, this index
United States Marshal, fees for serving, **28 § 1921**

SUBSISTENCE
Administrative Office of U.S. Courts, **28 § 604**
Court officers and employees, **28 § 604**
District courts, special sessions, **28 § 141**
Grand jurors, **28 § 1871**
Judges or Justices, this index
Judicial Center, officers and employees, **28 § 604**
Jury, **28 § 1871**
Jury commissioners, **28 § 1863**
Witnesses, United States courts, **28 § 1821**

SUBSTANCE ABUSE
Controlled Substances, generally, this index

SUBSTITUTION
See specific index headings

SUCCESSORS
See specific index headings

SUFFRAGE
Elections, generally, this index

SUITS
Actions and Proceedings, generally, this index

SULFONDIETHYLMETHANE
Controlled Substances, generally, this index

SULFONETHYLMETHANE
Controlled Substances, generally, this index

SULFONETHYLMETHONE
Controlled Substances, generally, this index

SULFONMETHANE
Controlled Substances, generally, this index

SUMMARIES
See specific index headings

SUMMARY JUDGMENT
Rules of Civil Procedure, this index

SUMMONS
Appraisal and Appraisers, this index
Federal officers and employees, **28 § 1391**
Garnishment, United States, **28 § 2405**
Grand Jury, this index
International Trade Court, this index
Jury, this index
Patents, this index
Rules of Civil Procedure, this index
United States Marshals, fees, **28 § 1921**
Witnesses, this index

SUNDAYS
Rules of Civil Procedure, this index

SUPERINTENDENT OF DOCUMENTS
Supreme Court reports,
Copies, **28 § 411**
Sales, **28 § 412**

SUPERSEDEAS
Stay of Proceedings, generally, this index

SUPERVISED RELEASE
Sentence and Punishment, this index

SUPERVISION
See specific index headings

SUPPLEMENTAL JURISDICTION
District courts, **28 § 1367**

SUPPLIES
Courts, Administrative Office of United States Courts, **28 § 604**

SUPPORT
Bankruptcy, this index
Definitions, orders of court, full faith and credit, **28 § 1738B**
Full faith and credit, orders of court, **28 § 1738B nt**
Modification, definitions, **28 § 1738B**
Orders of court, full faith and credit, **28 § 1738B**
Registration, orders of court, **28 § 1738B**

SUPREME COURT
Generally, **SCR 1 et seq.**
Absence, quorum, **28 § 2109**
Acts of Congress, appeal and review,
State court decisions, certiorari, **28 § 1257**
Supreme Court of Puerto Rico, decisions, **28 § 1258**
Adjourned terms, **28 § 2**

SUPREME COURT—Cont'd
Administrative Assistant to Chief Justice, **28 § 677**
Annuities, **28 § 376**
Admission to bar, **SCR 5**
Adverse or pecuniary interest, practice of law, court officers and employees, **SCR 7**
Affidavits, indigent persons, attorneys, **SCR 39**
Affirmance, judgments, **28 §§ 1912, 2106, 2109**
Affirmations and oaths, admission to bar, **SCR 5**
Always open, **28 § 452**
Ambassadors, **28 § 1251**
Amicus curiae,
Briefs, **SCR 37**
Oral argument, **SCR 28**
Appeal and review,
Attorney General, **28 §§ 503 nt, 518**
Criminal cases, **28 § 2101 et seq.**
Determinations, **28 § 2106**
Direct appeals, generally, post
District courts, post
Jurisdiction, **28 § 2106**
Courts of appeals, **28 § 1291 et seq.**
District courts, **SCR 18**
Quorum, **28 § 2109**
State court cases, **28 §§ 1257, 2101 et seq.**
Supreme Court of Puerto Rico, **28 § 1258**
Time, **28 § 2101**
United States Court of Federal Claims, **28 § 2516**
United States magistrate judges, **28 § 636**
Appearance, **28 § 1654**
Attorneys, **SCR 9**
Applications, individual justices, **SCR 22**
Appointments,
Administrative Assistant to Chief Justice, **28 § 677**
Attorney General, **28 § 503 nt**
Assignments,
Chief Judge or Justice, post
District judges, **28 §§ 292, 297**
Assistant librarians, **28 § 674**
Assistants, reporters, **28 § 673**
Associate Justices. Justices, generally, post
Attorney General,
Appointments, **28 § 503 nt**
Conduct, **28 § 518**
Judicial Conference of the United States, reports, **28 § 331**
Surface Transportation Board, orders, **28 § 2323**
Attorneys, **SCR 5 et seq.**
Admission to bar, **SCR 5**
Appearance, **SCR 9**
Conflict of interest, **SCR 7**
Discipline, **SCR 8**
Forma pauperis proceedings, **28 § 672; SCR 39**

SUPREME COURT—Cont'd
Attorneys—Cont'd
Identification, **SCR 34**
Pro hac vice, **SCR 6**
Bankruptcy, **28 § 2075**
Bonds (officers and fiduciaries), supersedeas or stay, **SCR 23**
Booklets, **SCR 33**
Books and papers,
Decisions, **28 §§ 411, 676**
Librarian, **28 § 674**
Marshals, **28 §§ 672, 674**
Sales, **28 § 676**
Successors, **28 § 414**
Briefs, **SCR 24 et seq.**
Amicus curiae, **SCR 37**
Certified questions, **SCR 19**
Certiorari, **SCR 15**
Copies, **SCR 25**
District courts, **SCR 18**
Electronic briefs, **SCR 25**
Amicus curiae, **SCR 37**
Extraordinary writs, petitions, **SCR 20**
Forma pauperis proceedings, **28 § 672**
Joint appendix, **SCR 26**
Original actions, **SCR 17**
Printing, **SCR 33**
Reply briefs, generally, post
Time, **SCR 25**
Calendars, **SCR 27**
Certificates and certification,
Admission to bar, **SCR 5**
Briefs, **SCR 33**
Questions, **SCR 19**
Certiorari, **28 § 1254; SCR 10 et seq.**
Armed Forces, **28 § 1259**
Briefs, **SCR 15**
Considerations, **SCR 10**
Costs, **28 § 2101**
Criminal cases, **28 § 2101**
Damages, **28 § 2101**
Disposition, **SCR 16**
Federal agencies, **28 § 2350**
Federal claims, **28 § 2101**
Habeas corpus, **28 § 2244**
Method, **SCR 12**
Prejudgment, **SCR 11**
Puerto Rico Supreme Court, **28 § 1258**
State courts, **28 § 1257**
Criminal cases, **28 § 2101**
Time, **28 § 2101; SCR 13**
Chief Judge or Justice, **28 § 1**
Allotments, **28 § 42**
Assignments, **28 § 291 et seq.**
Multidistrict litigation, **28 § 1407**
New assignments, **28 § 295**
Retired justices, **28 § 294**
Revocation, **28 § 295**
Senior judges, **28 § 294**
Special prosecutors, **28 § 49**
Temporary assignments, **28 §§ 292, 297**
Attorney General, Judicial Conference of the United States, reports, **28 § 331**

SUPREME COURT—Cont'd
Chief Judge or Justice—Cont'd
Circuit judges, temporary assignments, **28 § 291**
Civil service, retirement and pensions, **28 §§ 376, 611**
Compensation and salaries, post
Costs, **28 § 463**
Court of appeals, Chief Judge, relief, **28 § 45**
Decisions, **28 §§ 673, 676**
Director of Administrative Office of U.S. Courts, **28 §§ 601, 602 nt**
Disability, **28 § 3**
Certificates and certification, **28 § 372**
District judges,
Relief, **28 § 136**
Temporary assignments, **28 § 292**
Federal Judicial Center Foundation, **28 § 629**
Judicial Conference of the United States, **28 § 331**
Judicial Panel on Multidistrict Litigation, **28 § 1407**
Law clerks, **28 § 675**
Official duty station, **28 § 456**
Personnel Management System, **28 § 602 nt**
Printers, **28 § 676**
Reports, Judicial Conference of the United States, **28 § 331**
Retirement and pensions, **28 §§ 294, 371**
Rosters, senior judges, **28 § 294**
Rules of civil procedure, **28 § 2072**
Senior judges, rosters, **28 § 294**
Special prosecutors, **28 § 49**
United States Court of International Trade, **28 §§ 292, 293**
Vacancy in office, **28 § 3**
Circuit justices, **28 § 42 et seq.**
Temporary assignments, **28 § 291**
Clerks of courts, **28 § 671; SCR 1**
Appropriations, **28 § 671 nt**
Assistants, **28 § 671**
Compensation and salaries, **28 § 671**
Copies, **28 § 6**
Costs, **28 § 671**
Court of appeals, records and recordation, **28 § 6**
Deputy clerks, **28 § 671**
Fees, **28 § 1911; SCR 38**
Taxation, **28 § 1911**
Treasury, **28 § 671**
Messengers, **28 § 671**
Removal, **28 § 671**
Returns, fees, **28 § 671**
Treasury, fees, **28 § 671**
Compensation and salaries,
Administrative Assistant to Chief Justice, **28 § 677**
Chief Judge or Justice, **28 §§ 371, 372, 672**
Annual rates, **28 § 5**
Disability retirement, **28 § 372**

SUPREME COURT—Cont'd
Compensation and salaries—Cont'd
Law clerks, **28 § 675**
Librarians, **28 § 674**
Marshals, **28 § 672**
Reporters, **28 § 673**
Secretaries, **28 § 675**
Conditional cross-appeals, district courts, **SCR 18**
Conditional cross-petitions, certiorari, **SCR 12**
Conflict of interest, practice of law, **SCR 7**
Consuls, **28 § 1251**
Copies,
Briefs, **SCR 25**
Court of appeals, **28 § 6**
Corporations, disclosure, statements, **SCR 29**
Correctional institutions, habeas corpus, **SCR 36**
Corrections, petitions, rehearings, **SCR 44**
Costs, **SCR 43**
Affirmance, **28 § 1912**
Frivolous cases, **SCR 42**
Military cases, **SCR 40**
Process, **28 § 1911**
Stay of proceedings, **28 § 2101**
Taxation, **28 § 1911**
Court of Appeals for the Armed Forces, this index
Cross appeals, district courts, **SCR 18**
Cross-petitions, certiorari, **SCR 12**
Damages, **SCR 42**
Affirmance, **28 § 1912**
Stay of proceedings, **28 § 2101**
Death, parties, **SCR 35**
Decisions. Opinions and decisions, generally, post
Definitions, **28 nt prec § 1251**
Highest court of a State, **28 § 1257**
State courts, **SCR 47**
State laws, **SCR 47**
Determinations, **28 § 2106**
Diagrams, evidence, **SCR 32**
Direct appeals,
Dockets and docketing, **28 § 2101**
Quorum, **28 § 2109**
Records and recordation, **28 § 2101**
Remission, **28 § 2109**
Time, **28 § 2101**
Director of Administrative Office of U.S. Courts, **28 § 602 nt et seq.**
Retirement and pensions, **28 § 677**
Disbarment, attorneys, **SCR 8**
Disbursements, **28 § 1911**
Marshal, **28 § 672**
Discipline, attorneys, **SCR 8**
Discretion, **28 § 1912**
Damages for delay, **28 § 1912**
Dismissal and nonsuit, **SCR 18, 46**
District courts,
Admiralty rules, **28 § 2072**
Appeal and review, **SCR 18**
Remission, **28 § 2109**

SUPREME COURT—Cont'd
District courts—Cont'd
Appeal and review—Cont'd
Three-Judge Courts, **28 § 1253**
Chief judges, **28 § 136**
Civil procedure, **28 § 2072**
Evidence, **28 § 2072**
District judges,
Assignments, **28 §§ 292, 297**
Chief Judge or Justice,
Relief, **28 § 136**
Temporary assignments, **28 § 292**
Dockets and docketing,
Criminal cases, state courts, **28 § 2102**
Direct appeals, **28 § 2101**
Duties. Powers and duties, generally, post
Effective date, **SCR 47**
Elections, retirement and pensions, **28 § 677**
Electronic briefs, **SCR 25**
Amicus curiae, **SCR 37**
Employees. Officers and employees, generally, post
Evidence, **28 § 1731 et seq.; SCR 32**
Exclusive jurisdiction, **28 § 1251**
Exhibits, **SCR 32**
Extension of time, **SCR 30**
Certiorari, **SCR 13**
Extraordinary writs, **SCR 20**
Fees,
Clerks of courts, ante
Military cases, **SCR 40**
Filing, **SCR 29**
Applications, individual justices, **SCR 22**
Briefs, **SCR 25**
Forms, **SCR 34**
Motions, **SCR 21**
Printing, **SCR 33**
Rejection, **SCR 1**
Withdrawal, **SCR 1**
Foreign languages, records and recordation, translations, **SCR 31**
Frivolous cases, **SCR 42**
Gifts, history, **28 § 1 nt**
Habeas corpus, **28 § 2241 et seq.; SCR 36**
Applications, **28 § 2242**
Judgments and decrees, conclusiveness, **28 § 2244**
Petitions, **SCR 20**
State courts, **28 § 2254**
Handicapped persons,
Chief Justice, **28 § 3**
Retirement and pensions, **28 § 372**
History, gifts, **28 § 1 nt**
In forma pauperis proceedings, **SCR 12, 39**
Individual justices, applications, **SCR 22**
Instructions, courts of appeals, certification of questions, **28 § 1254**
Interest, **SCR 42**
Joint appendices, briefs, **SCR 26**
Judges or justices,
Chief Judge or Justice, generally, ante

SUPREME COURT—Cont'd
Judges or justices—Cont'd
Justices, generally, post
Jurisdiction, **28 § 1251 et seq.**
Appeal and review, ante
Certified questions, **SCR 19**
Extraordinary writs, **SCR 20**
Original actions, **SCR 17**
Petitions, **SCR 20**
Jury trials, **28 § 1872**
Justices,
Acknowledgments, **28 § 459**
Allotments, **28 § 42**
Assignments,
Circuits, **28 § 42**
Retired justices, **28 § 294**
Books and papers, **28 § 414**
Chief Judge or Justice, generally, ante
Circuit justices, courts of appeals, **28 § 43**
Costs, **28 § 463**
Disability, **28 § 3**
Certificate of disability, **28 § 372**
Habeas corpus, **28 §§ 2241, 2254**
Oaths and affirmations, **28 § 453**
Official duty station, **28 § 456**
Practice of law, **28 § 454**
Precedence, **28 §§ 3, 4**
Quorum, **28 §§ 1, 2109**
Relatives, **28 § 458**
Retired justices, **28 § 294**
Secretaries, **28 § 675**
Seniority, **28 § 4**
Traveling expenses, **28 § 456**
Librarian, **28 §§ 672, 674**
Libraries, **SCR 2**
Lodgings, **SCR 32**
Mail and mailing, process, **SCR 29**
Mandamus, petitions, **SCR 20**
Mandates, **SCR 45**
Marshal. Supreme Court Marshal, generally, this index
Microfilm, **28 § 674**
Military court cases, costs, **SCR 40**
Ministers, foreign countries, **28 § 1251**
Models, evidence, **SCR 32**
Modification, judgments and decrees, **28 § 2106**
Motions, **SCR 21**
Amicus curiae, **SCR 37**
Certiorari, **SCR 12**
Dismissal and nonsuit, **SCR 46**
Notice,
Amicus curiae, **SCR 37**
Appearance, **SCR 9**
District courts, **SCR 18**
Oaths and affirmations, admission to bar, **SCR 5**
Objections and exceptions, dismissal and nonsuit, motions, **SCR 46**
Officers and employees,
Law clerks, **28 § 675**
Payment, **28 § 672**
Practice of law, **SCR 7**
Reporters, **28 § 673**
Secretaries, **28 § 675**

SUPREME COURT—Cont'd
Officers and employees—Cont'd
Substitution, **SCR 35**
Opinions and decisions, **SCR 41**
Pamphlets, **28 § 673**
Prices, **28 § 676**
Printing, **28 §§ 411, 676**
Publication, **28 § 673**
Reporter, **28 § 673**
Oral argument, **SCR 28**
Motions, **SCR 21**
Pro hac vice, **SCR 6**
Orders of court,
Allotments, justices, **28 § 42**
Marshals, **28 § 672**
Original jurisdiction, **28 § 1251; SCR 17**
Pamphlets,
Decisions, **28 § 673**
Disbursements, **28 § 672**
Librarian, **28 § 674**
Printing, **28 § 676**
Parties,
Certiorari, **SCR 12**
Death, **SCR 35**
District courts, **SCR 18**
Pensions. Retirement and pensions, generally, post
Periodicals, librarian, **28 § 674**
Petitions,
Certiorari, generally, ante
Extraordinary writs, **SCR 20**
Rehearings, **SCR 44**
Place of holding court, **28 § 2**
Powers and duties,
Admiralty rules, **28 § 2072**
Civil procedure rules, **28 §§ 2072, 2074**
Evidence rules, **28 § 2072**
Habeas corpus, **28 § 2241**
Maritime rules, **28 § 2072**
Writs, **28 § 1651**
Printing, **28 § 676**
Decisions, **28 § 411**
Filed documents, **SCR 33**
Reports, **28 §§ 411, 412**
Prisons and prisoners, habeas corpus, **SCR 36**
Pro hac vice, attorneys, **SCR 6**
Procedure, **28 § 1651 et seq.**
Process, **SCR 29, 45**
Costs, **28 § 1911**
Marshals, **28 § 672**
Proof of service, **SCR 21, 29**
Prohibition, writ of, **SCR 20**
Property, **28 § 672**
Public officers, substitution, **SCR 35**
Publications, **28 § 672**
Quorum, **28 §§ 1, 2109; SCR 4**
Records and recordation, **SCR 1**
Certified questions, **SCR 19**
Certiorari, **SCR 12**
Direct appeal, **28 § 2101**
District courts, **SCR 18**
Former court of appeals, **28 § 6**
Translations, **SCR 31**
Rehearing, petitions, **SCR 44**
Remand, cause, **28 § 2106**

SUPREME COURT—Cont'd
Remission, **28 § 2109**
Reply briefs, **SCR 24, 25**
Certiorari, **SCR 15**
Original actions, **SCR 17**
Reporters, **28 § 673**
Reports, **28 § 411 et seq.**
Bound volumes, **28 § 412**
Preliminary prints, **28 §§ 411, 412**
Printing, **28 §§ 411, 676**
Publication, **28 § 673**
Sales, **28 §§ 411 et seq., 676**
Responses, motions, **SCR 21**
Retirement and pensions,
Chief Judge or Justice, **28 §§ 294, 371**
Director of Administrative Office of U.S. Courts, **28 § 677**
Reversal, **28 §§ 2105, 2106**
Review. Appeal and review, generally, ante
Revivor, parties, death, **SCR 35**
Rules of civil procedure, **28 § 2072 et seq.**
Rules of Evidence, this index
Salaries. Compensation and salaries, generally, ante
Seamen, **SCR 40**
Secretaries, **28 § 675**
Service of process. Process, generally, ante
Sessions, **SCR 4**
Marshals, **28 § 672**
Powers and duties, **28 § 452**
Solicitor General, **28 § 518**
Special terms, **28 § 2**
State Courts, generally, this index
State law, definitions, **SCR 47**
Statutes, unconstitutionality, **SCR 29**
Stay of proceedings, **SCR 23**
Mandate pending rehearing petition, **SCR 45**
Substitution, parties, **SCR 35**
Supplemental briefs, certiorari, **SCR 15**
Terms, **28 § 2; SCR 3**
Time,
Appeal and review, **28 § 2101**
Briefs, **SCR 25**
Certiorari, **28 § 2101; SCR 13**
Clerks, office hours, **SCR 1**
Computation, **SCR 30**
Rehearings, petitions, **SCR 44**
Translations, foreign languages, **SCR 31**
Treaties, certiorari, **28 § 1257**
United States, service of process, **SCR 29**
United States judges. Justices, generally, ante
United States magistrate judges, appeal and review, **28 § 636**
United States Tax Court, **28 § 2072 et seq.**
Vacancies in office, Chief Justice, **28 § 3**
Vacating or setting aside, **28 §§ 42, 2106**
Veterans, **SCR 40**
Volunteers, **28 § 677**
Widows and widowers, justices, annuities, **28 § 376**

SUPREME COURT—Cont'd
Writs, **28 § 1651**
Extraordinary writs, **SCR 20**

SUPREME COURT BUILDINGS AND GROUNDS
Architect of the Capitol, disbursement, funds, **28 § 672**
Disbursement of funds by marshal, **28 § 672**

SUPREME COURT MARSHAL
Generally, **28 § 672**
Appropriations, **28 § 671 nt**
Compensation and salaries, **28 § 672**
Disbursements, **28 § 672**
Forma pauperis proceedings, **28 § 672**
Transportation, **28 § 456 nt**
Vouchers, **28 § 674**

SURETIES AND SURETY BONDS
Bonds (Officers and Fiduciaries), generally, this index

SURFACE CARRIERS
Motor Carriers, generally, this index

SURFACE TRANSPORTATION BOARD
Actions and proceedings,
District courts, **28 § 1398**
United States as party, **28 § 2322**
Appeal and review,
Courts of appeals, **28 § 2342**
Injunctions, **28 § 1336**
Orders, **28 § 2341 et seq.**
Attorney General, **28 § 2323**
Attorneys, orders, representation to enforce, **28 § 2323**
Court of Federal Claims, this index
District courts,
Enforcement, judicial review of orders and decisions, procedures, **28 § 2321 et seq.**
Jurisdiction,
Civil actions to, enforce, orders of Board, **28 § 1336**
Orders, **28 § 1398**
Orders, proceedings to enforce or set aside orders, **28 § 2321 et seq.**
Enforce, enjoin or set aside orders, **28 § 2321 et seq.**
Fines, penalties and forfeitures,
District courts, cases and proceedings other than collection of fines, procedures, **28 § 2321 et seq.**
Jurisdiction, district courts in civil actions to enjoin or suspend collection, **28 § 1336**
Injunctions,
Jurisdiction,
Courts of appeals, **28 § 2321 et seq.**
District courts, **28 § 1336**
Orders,
Court of Federal Claims, **28 § 1336**
District courts, **28 § 2321 et seq.**

SURFACE TRANSPORTATION BOARD—Cont'd
Intervention, actions to enforce orders, **28 § 2323**
Jurisdiction, **28 § 1336**
Orders,
Appeal and review, **28 § 2321 et seq.**
Jurisdiction, **28 §§ 1336, 1398**
Rates and charges, equity, **28 § 2321 et seq.**
Referrals, **28 § 1336**
Reports, liability for loss, judicial review, procedures, **28 § 2321 et seq.**
Review. Appeal and review, generally, ante
Tariffs, **28 § 2321 et seq.**
United States, parties, **28 § 2322**
Venue, **28 § 1398**
Writs, **28 § 2321 et seq.**

SURVEYS AND SURVEYORS
Judicial Conference of the United States, **28 § 331**

SURVIVAL OF ACTIONS AND PROCEEDINGS
Abatement and Revival, generally, this index

SUSPENSION
See specific index headings

SWEDEN
Convention on the Taking of Evidence Abroad in Civil or Commercial Matters, party to, **28 § 1781 nt**

SWINDLING
Fraud, generally, this index

SWORN
Oaths and Affirmations, generally, this index

SYNDICATES
Income tax. Partnership, this index

TABLES
See specific index headings

TAG-ALONG ACTIONS
Judicial Panel On Multidistrict Litigation, this index

TARIFFS
Customs Duties, generally, this index

TASK FORCES
Banks and banking, fraud, **28 § 509 nt**
Corporate Fraud Task Force, **28 § 509 nt, EON 13271**
Crimes and Offenses, this index
Drugs and medicine, civil enforcement, **28 § 509 nt**
Fugitives apprehension task forces, **28 § 566 nt**
Identity theft, **28 § 509 nt, EON 13402**
Stores, organized retail theft task force, **28 § 509 nt**

TASK FORCES—Cont'd
Trafficking, this index
United States-Mexico Border Violence Task Force, **28 § 509 nt**

TAX AND TRADE BUREAU
Treasury Department, this index

TAX COURT
United States Tax Court, generally, this index

TAX LIENS
Actions and proceedings, **28 § 1346**
Appearance, **28 § 2410**
Complaints, **28 § 2410**
Condemnation, **28 § 2410**
Foreclosure, **28 § 2410**
Interpleader, **28 § 2410**
Judicial sales, **28 § 2410**
Partition, **28 § 2410**
Pleading, **28 § 2410**
Quieting title, **28 §§ 2409a, 2410**
Redemption, **28 § 2410**
Release, **28 § 2410**
Venue, **28 § 1402**

TAX SALES
District courts, **28 § 1346**
Venue, wrongful tax sales, **28 § 1402**
Wrongful tax sales, venue, **28 § 1402**

TAXATION
Bankruptcy, this index
Costs, this index
Court of Federal Claims, this index
Courts, officers and employees, liability, **28 § 960**
Income Tax, generally, this index
Interest,
Judgments and decrees, **28 §§ 1961, 2411**
Overpayment, judgments and decrees, **28 § 2411**
Internal Revenue Service, generally, this index
Judgments and decrees, interest, **28 §§ 1961, 2411**
Liens and incumbrances. Tax Liens, generally, this index
Political Subdivisions, this index
Refunds,
Income Tax, this index
Venue, **28 § 1402**
Sales. Tax Sales, generally, this index
States, this index
United States Tax Court, generally, this index

TECHNOLOGY
Semiconductors, generally, this index

TELECOMMUNICATIONS
Appeal and review, Communications Commission, **28 § 2341 et seq.**
Cellular telephones, cloning, sentence and punishment, **28 § 994 nt**

TELECOMMUNICATIONS—Cont'd
Cloning, wireless telephones, sentence and punishment, **28 § 994 nt**
Copyrights, generally, this index
Crimes and offenses,
Cloning, wireless telephones, **28 § 994 nt**
Wireless telephones, cloning, **28 § 994 nt**
Fines, penalties and forfeitures, cloning, wireless telephones, **28 § 994 nt**
Fraud,
Records and recordation, sentence and punishment, **28 § 994 nt**
Sentence and punishment,
Records and recordation, **28 § 994 nt**
Telemarketing, **28 § 994 nt**
Orders, **28 § 2341 et seq.**
Rules of Civil Procedure, this index
Semiconductors, generally, this index
Sentence and punishment, wireless telephones, cloning, **28 § 994 nt**
Telemarketing, fraud, sentence and punishment, **28 § 994 nt**
Wireless telephones, cloning, **28 § 994 nt**

TELEGRAPHS
Telecommunications, generally, this index

TELEMARKETING
Telecommunications, this index

TELEPHONE RECORDS AND PRIVACY PROTECTION ACT OF 2006
Generally, **28 § 994 nt**

TELEPHONES
Telecommunications, generally, this index

TEMPORARY EMERGENCY COURT OF APPEALS OF UNITED STATES
Court of Appeals for the Federal Circuit, generally, this index

TEMPORARY RESTRAINING ORDERS
Injunctions, generally, this index

TENANTS
Joint Tenants, generally, this index

TENANTS IN COMMON
Generally, **28 § 2409**
United States, partition,
Jurisdiction, **28 § 1347**
Venue, **28 § 1399**

TENDER
Legal tender. Money, generally, this index

TENNESSEE
Bankruptcy, judges or justices, appointments, **28 § 152**

TENNESSEE—Cont'd
District courts,
Cities, **28 § 123**
Judges or justices, **28 § 133**
Judicial circuit, **28 § 41**
Judicial districts, **28 § 123**
Bankruptcy, **28 § 581 nt**
Judges or justices, **28 § 133**
United States trustees, judicial districts, appointment, **28 § 581**

TENNESSEE VALLEY AUTHORITY
Attorneys, **28 § 171 nt**
Tort Claims Act, exception of claim arising from activities of authority, **28 § 2680**

TENURE
See specific index headings

TERM OF OFFICE
See specific index headings

TERMINATION
See specific index headings

TERMS OF COURT
Courts of appeals, **28 § 48**
District Courts, this index

TERMS OF OFFICE
See specific index headings

TERRITORIES
Books and papers, evidence, **28 § 1739**
Costs, **28 § 1927**
Courts, **28 § 460**
Courts of appeals, **28 § 1294**
Full faith and credit, **28 § 1738**
District courts,
Admiralty, **28 § 2073 nt**
Diversity of citizenship, jurisdiction, **28 § 1332**
Diversity of citizenship, district courts, jurisdiction, **28 § 1332**
Documentary evidence, **28 §§ 1738, 1739**
Executions, **28 § 2413**
Federal officers and employees, jury, exemptions, **28 § 1863**
Government publications, courts, **28 § 414**
Judges or justices, **28 § 460**
Official duty station, location, **28 § 460**
Removal, **28 § 373**
Jurisdiction, diversity of citizenship, district courts, **28 § 1332**
Jury, exemptions, **28 § 1863**
National Guard, generally, this index
Nonjudicial records, evidence, **28 § 1739**
Records and recordation, evidence, **28 § 1739**
U.S. Court of Federal Claims, unjust imprisonment, damages, **28 § 2513**

TERRORISTS AND TERRORISM
Actions and proceedings, Foreign States, **28 § 1605A**
Aircraft, this index

TERRORISTS AND TERRORISM
—Cont'd
Aliens,
Detention, Military Justice Code, **28 § 2241**
Military Justice Code, **28 § 2241**
Appeal and review, Foreign States, damages, **28 § 1605A**
Attachment, waiver, **28 § 1610 nt, PD 2001–03**
Attorney General,
Deputy Attorney General for Combating Domestic Terrorism, **28 § 504**
Detention, reports, **28 § 509 nt**
Reports, detention, **28 § 509 nt**
Combatants, enemy combatants, **28 § 2241**
Counterterrorism Fund, **28 § 524 nt**
Crime Victims, this index
Damages,
Foreign States, **28 § 1605A**
State sponsors, **28 §§ 1605 nt, 1605A**
Death, Foreign States, damages, **28 § 1605A**
Definitions, Foreign States, actions and proceedings, **28 § 1605A**
Detention,
Aliens, ante
Attorney General, reports, **28 § 509 nt**
Military Justice Code, **28 § 2241**
Reports, Attorney General, **28 § 509 nt**
Diplomatic Security, generally, this index
Emergency medical services, grants, **28 § 509 nt**
Enemy combatants, **28 § 2241**
Execution, **28 §§ 1605A, 1610**
Exemptions, privileges and immunities, Foreign States, **28 § 1605A**
Federal Bureau of Investigation,
Funds, **28 § 531 nt**
Interpreters, **28 § 532 nt**
Translators, **28 § 532 nt**
Fines, penalties and forfeitures, property, transfers, **28 § 524 nt**
Firefighters and firefighting, training, **28 § 509 nt**
First responders, grants, **28 § 509 nt**
Fraud, older victims, sentencing guidelines, **28 § 994 nt**
Funds,
Bureau of Investigation, **28 § 531 nt**
Counterterrorism Fund, **28 § 524 nt**
Rewards, **28 § 530C**
Grants,
Emergency medical services, **28 § 509 nt**
First responders, **28 § 509 nt**
Law enforcement agencies or instrumentalities, **28 § 509 nt**
Hostages, Foreign States, damages, **28 § 1605A**
Immunities. Privileges and immunities, generally, post
Iraq, this index

TERRORISTS AND TERRORISM
—Cont'd
Justice Department, Office of Justice for Victims of Overseas Terrorism, **28 § 501 nt**
Law enforcement agencies or instrumentalities, grants, **28 § 509 nt**
Liability. Damages, generally, ante
Libya, this index
Limitation of actions, Foreign States, **28 § 1605A**
Lis pendens, Foreign States, **28 § 1605A**
Military Justice Code, aliens, **28 § 2241**
Notice, Foreign States, pending actions, **28 § 1605A**
Offices, Justice for Victims of Overseas Terrorism Office, **28 § 501 nt**
Pending actions, Foreign States, **28 § 1605A**
Private right of action, Foreign States, **28 § 1605A**
Privileges and immunities,
Attachment, execution, waiver, **28 § 1610 nt, PD 2001–03**
Exemptions, Foreign States, **28 § 1605A**
Foreign States, **28 § 1605A**
Reports. Detention, ante
Rewards, funds, **28 § 530C**
Sentence and punishment, guidelines, **28 § 994 nt**
Special masters, Foreign States, damages, **28 § 1605A**
State sponsors, damages, **28 §§ 1605 nt, 1605A**
Statute of limitations, Foreign States, **28 § 1605A**
Torture, Foreign States, damages, **28 § 1605A**
Transfers, property, fines, penalties and forfeitures, **28 § 524 nt**
Waiver,
Attachment, privileges and immunities, **28 § 1610 nt, PD 2001–03**
Iraq, liability, **28 § 1605A nt**

TESTIMONY
Evidence, generally, this index

TETRAHYDROCANNABINOLS
Controlled Substances, generally, this index

TEXAS
Bankruptcy, judges or justices, appointments, **28 § 152**
District courts, **28 § 124**
Judges or justices, **28 § 133**
Judicial circuit, **28 § 41**
Judicial districts, **28 § 124**
Bankruptcy, **28 § 581 nt**
Judges or justices, **28 § 133**
United States-Mexico Border Violence Task Force, **28 § 509 nt**
United States trustees, judicial districts, appointments, **28 § 581**

THEBACON
Controlled Substances, generally, this index

THIRD PARTIES
Claims, United States, **28 § 2415**
Internal Revenue Service, this index
International Trade Court, this index
Rules of Civil Procedure, this index
United States, claims, **28 § 2415**

THREATS
Federal Officers and Employees, this index
Judges or Justices, this index
Terrorists and Terrorism, generally, this index

THREE JUDGE COURT
Generally, **28 § 2284**
Appeal and review, Supreme Court, **28 § 1253**
Apportionment, legislative districts, **28 § 2284**
Injunctions, **28 § 2284**
International Trade Court, this index
Legislative districts, apportionment, **28 § 2284**
Orders of court, **28 § 2284**
Rules of Civil Procedure, this index

TIME
See specific index headings

TITLE
Rules of Civil Procedure, this index

TITLE TO PROPERTY
Claims, liens and incumbrances, **28 § 1655**
Federal officers and employees, **28 § 1442**
Quieting Title, generally, this index
United States, this index

TOBACCO
Bureau of Alcohol, Tobacco, Firearms, and Explosives, generally, this index

TOLL BRIDGES
Jurors, fees, **28 § 1871**

TOLL ROADS
Jurors, fees, **28 § 1871**

TOLLS
Courts, witnesses, pay and allowances, **28 § 1821**
Jurors, fees, **28 § 1871**
Tunnels, this index
Witnesses, courts, pay and allowances, **28 § 1821**

TOLUENE
Controlled Substances, generally, this index

TORTS
Generally, **28 §§ 1346, 1402, 2401 et seq., 2671 et seq.**
Acting within scope of his office or employment, definitions, **28 § 2671**
Administrative law and procedure, **28 §§ 2672, 2675**
Aliens, **28 § 1350**
Alternative dispute resolution, **28 § 2672**
Arbitration, **28 §§ 2672, 2677**
Attorney General, this index
Attorneys, fees, **28 § 2678**
Coast Guard, this index
Commencement of action, **28 § 2675**
Compromise and settlement, **28 § 2672 et seq.**
Definitions, **28 § 2671**
Employee of the Government, definitions, **28 § 2671**
Exclusivity, remedies, **28 § 2679**
Exemptions, **28 § 2680**
Federal agencies, **28 §§ 2671, 2672**
Limitation of actions, **28 § 2401**
Filing, **28 § 2675**
Funds, **28 § 2672**
Investigative or law enforcement officer, definitions, **28 § 2680**
Judicial immunity, **28 § 2674**
Jurisdiction, **28 § 1346**
Aliens, **28 § 1350**
Law enforcement officers, **28 § 2671 nt**
Legislative immunity, **28 § 2674**
Limitation of actions, **28 §§ 2401, 2675**
Military departments, **28 § 2671**
Negligence, generally, this index
Payment, **28 § 2672**
Public policy, **28 § 2671 nt**
Quarantine, **28 § 2680**
Release, **28 § 2672**
Statute of limitations, **28 §§ 2401, 2675**
Time, **28 §§ 2401, 2675**
Torture, **28 § 1350 nt**
Venue, **28 § 1402**

TORTURE
Actions and proceedings, **28 § 1350 nt**
Aliens, this index
Civil rights, **28 § 1350 nt**
Crime victims, **28 § 1350 nt**
Damages, terrorists and terrorism, Foreign States, **28 § 1605A**
District courts, **28 § 1350 nt**
International Law, **28 § 1350 nt**
Jurisdiction, **28 § 1350 nt**
Limitation of actions, **28 § 1350 nt**
Terrorists and terrorism, Foreign States, damages, **28 § 1605A**
Torts, **28 § 1350 nt**

TORTURE VICTIM PROTECTION ACT OF 1991
Generally, **28 § 1350 nt**

TRACKING
See specific index headings

TRADE REPRESENTATIVE
Exports and Imports, this index

TRADE SECRETS
International Trade Court, this index
Rules of Civil Procedure, this index
United States Court of International Trade, **28 § 2641**

TRADEMARK TRIAL AND APPEAL BOARD
United States Court of Appeals for the Federal Circuit, **28 § 1295**

TRADEMARKS AND TRADE NAMES
Court of Appeals for the Federal Circuit, this index
Jurisdiction, **28 § 1338**
Patent and Trademark Office, generally, this index

TRADING WITH THE ENEMY
Exemptions, Tort Claims Act, **28 § 2680**
Tort Claims Act, exemptions, **28 § 2680**

TRAFFICKING
Classification, human trafficking, **28 § 534 nt**
Controlled Substances, this index
Human trafficking, classification, **28 § 534 nt**
Task forces, United States-Mexico Border Violence Task Force, **28 § 509 nt**
United States-Mexico Border Violence Task Force, **28 § 509 nt**

TRAINING
Clerks of courts, Judicial Center, **28 § 620**
Firefighters and Fire Departments, this index
Intelligence, this index
Judges or Justices, this index
Railroads, this index
United States Magistrate Judges, this index

TRAINS
Railroads, generally, this index

TRANSCRIPTS
Costs, **28 § 1920**
Forma pauperis, **28 § 1915**
Court of Federal Claims, this index
Court reporters, certificates and certification, **28 § 753**
Federal Agencies, this index
Habeas corpus, **28 § 2247**
Magistrate judges, **28 § 1915**
Rules of Appellate Procedure, this index
Rules of Civil Procedure, this index

TRANSFER OF CASES OR CAUSES
Removal of Cases or Causes, generally, this index

TRANSFERS
See specific index headings

TRANSLATORS
Interpreters, generally, this index

TRANSPORTATION
Aircraft, generally, this index
Carriers, generally, this index
Court of Appeals for the Federal Circuit, this index
District courts, special sessions, **28 § 141**
Expenses and expenditures. Traveling Expenses, generally, this index
Harbors and Ports, generally, this index
Mass transportation. Motor Carriers, generally, this index
Railroads, generally, this index
Ships and Shipping, generally, this index
Surface Transportation Board, generally, this index

TRANSPORTATION DEPARTMENT
Community development, neighborhood revitalization plans, **28 § 509 nt**
Surface Transportation Board, generally, this index

TRAVELING EXPENSES
Administrative Office of United States Courts, this index
Arbitration, **28 § 658**
Court officers and employees, **28 § 604**
Courts of appeals, practice rules, advisory committees, **28 § 2077**
Disclosure of Federal Campaign Funds, this index
Grand Jury, this index
Independent Counsel, **28 § 594**
Judges or Justices, this index
Jury, this index
Justice Department, this index
Magistrates, **28 § 635**
Parental Kidnapping Prevention Act, **28 § 1738A nt**
Sentence and punishment, institutes, **28 § 334**
Supreme Court, forma pauperis proceedings, attorneys, **28 § 672**
United States Marshals Service, **28 § 1921**
Witnesses, this index

TREASON
Espionage, generally, this index

TREASURER OF UNITED STATES
Exemptions, Tort Claims Act, **28 § 2680**
Tort Claims Act, exemptions, **28 § 2680**

TREASURY BILLS
Interest, judgments and decrees, **28 §§ 1961, 2516**
Judgments and decrees, interest, **28 §§ 1961, 2516**

TREASURY DEPARTMENT
Internal Revenue Service, generally, this index
Officers and employees, Tax and Trade Bureau, personnel management demonstration project, **28 § 599B**
Secretary of the Treasury, generally, this index
Tax and Trade Bureau, personnel management demonstration project, **28 § 599B**

TREASURY OF UNITED STATES
Awards, fees, **28 § 1931**
Bankruptcy, this index
Bills. Treasury Bills, generally, this index
Checking accounts, **28 § 2043**
Court of Federal Claims Judges Retirement Fund, **28 § 178**
Courts of appeals, fees, **28 § 711**
Department of Justice Assets Forfeiture Fund, **28 § 524**
District courts, fees, **28 § 751**
Dockets and docketing, fees, **28 § 1923**
Fees, awards, **28 § 1931**
Information technology, Judiciary Information Technology Fund, **28 § 612**
Judicial Officers' Retirement Fund, investments, **28 § 377**
Judicial Survivors Annuity Fund, **28 § 376**
Justice Department, requisitions, **28 § 523**
Partition, payments, **28 § 2409**
Pending actions, Registry Administration Account, **28 §§ 2041, 2041 nt**
Registry Administration Account, courts, **28 § 2041 nt**
Supreme Court, fees, **28 § 671**
Unclaimed funds, **28 § 2042**
Witnesses, fees, **28 § 1821 nt**

TREASURY SECRETARY
Secretary of the Treasury, generally, this index

TREATIES
Aliens, torts, jurisdiction, **28 § 1350**
Court of Federal Claims, this index
District courts, original jurisdiction, **28 § 1331**
Habeas corpus, **28 § 2241**
States, **28 § 2254**
Indians, this index
Puerto Rico, Supreme Court of Puerto Rico, **28 § 1258**
Removal of cases or causes, **28 § 1441**
State court cases, certiorari, **28 § 1257**
State laws, rules of decision, **28 § 1652**
U.S. Court of Federal Claims, **28 § 1502**

TRESPASS
Indian lands and reservations, **28 §§ 2415, 2416**
Postal Service, attachment, **28 § 2713**
Postmasters, **28 § 2713**

TRESPASS—Cont'd
Public lands, **28 §§ 2415, 2416**

TRIAL
By court, actions against U.S., **28 § 2402**
Certified Questions, generally, this index
Certiorari, generally, this index
Dismissal and Nonsuit, generally, this index
Disqualification, judges or justices, **28 § 455**
Evidence, generally, this index
Habeas corpus, **28 § 2241**
International Trade Court, this index
Judges or justices, disqualification, **28 § 455**
Jury, generally, this index
Motions, generally, this index
Pleading, generally, this index
Questions of Law or Fact, generally, this index
Quieting title, **28 § 2409a**
Removal of Cases or Causes, generally, this index
Rules of Civil Procedure, this index
Speedy trial, **28 § 604**
Transcripts, generally, this index
United States Magistrate Judges, this index
Venue, generally, this index

TRIBES
Indians, this index

TRIBUNALS
Courts, generally, this index

TRIMEPERIDINE
Controlled Substances, generally, this index

TRUCKS
Motor Carriers, generally, this index

TRUST TERRITORY OF PACIFIC ISLANDS
Northern Mariana Islands, generally, this index

TRUSTS AND TRUSTEES
Bankruptcy, this index
Indian Lands and Reservations, this index
Justice Department, United States trustees, bankruptcy, **28 § 581 et seq.**
Railroads, this index
Resolution Trust Corporation, generally, this index
Rules of Civil Procedure, this index
United States trustees. Bankruptcy, this index

TUCSON, AZ
Court of Appeals for Ninth Circuit, generally, this index

TUNNELS
Jurors, tolls, **28 § 1871**

TUNNELS—Cont'd
Tolls, jurors, **28 § 1871**

TYPEWRITING
Rules of Appellate Procedure, this index

UNAVOIDABLE ACCIDENTS
United States, actions and proceedings, **28 § 2406**

UNCLAIMED FUNDS
Courts, deposits, **28 § 2042**

UNDERCOVER OPERATIONS
See specific index headings

UNDERTAKINGS
Bonds (Officers and Fiduciaries), generally, this index

UNEMPLOYMENT
Labor and Employment, generally, this index

UNFAIR COMPETITION
Monopolies and Combinations, generally, this index

UNFAIR DISCRIMINATION
Discrimination, generally, this index

UNFAIR TRADE PRACTICES
Monopolies and Combinations, generally, this index

UNIFORM CODE OF MILITARY JUSTICE
Military Justice Code, generally, this index

UNIFORM FEDERAL CRIME REPORTING ACT OF 1988
Generally, **28 § 534 nt**

UNIFORMED SERVICES
Cemeteries and dead bodies. National Cemeteries, generally, this index
Money erroneously paid to members, actions by U.S. for recovery, limitation, **28 §§ 2415, 2416**
National Cemeteries, generally, this index

UNIFORMS
Correctional Institutions, this index
Counterfeiting, public officers and employees, **28 § 994 nt**
Federal Bureau of Investigation, this index
Federal Officers and Employees, this index
Justice Department, funds, **28 § 530C**
Political subdivisions, officers and employees, crimes and offenses, **28 § 994 nt**

UNIONS
Customs Duties, this index

UNITED NATIONS
Privileges and immunities, insurance, **28 § 1364**

UNITED STATES
Actions and proceedings,
Award, fees, prevailing party, **28 § 2412**
Civil justice reform, guidelines, **28 § 519 nt, EON 12988**
Controversy with State, original jurisdiction with Supreme Court, **28 § 1251**
Costs, **28 § 2412**
Credits in actions by U.S., **28 § 2406**
Death of defendant in damage action, **28 § 2404**
Delinquents for public money, **28 § 2407**
District courts, **28 § 1346**
Executions, **28 § 2413**
Guidelines, civil justice reform, **28 § 519 nt, EON 12988**
Judgments and decrees, generally, post
Judicial Officers, costs, **28 § 2412 nt**
Jury trial, **28 § 2402**
Liens and incumbrances, **28 § 2410**
Partition, **28 § 2409**
Payment, judgments and compromise settlements, **28 § 2414**
Prevailing party, costs, judgment, **28 § 2412**
Recommencement after dismissal without prejudice, **28 § 2415**
Security not required of U.S., **28 § 2408**
Agents and agencies. Federal Agencies, generally, this index
Appeal and review, judgments, certification, **28 § 2414**
Appearance, lien actions, **28 § 2410**
Attorney General, this index
Attorneys,
Civil justice reform, **28 § 519 nt, EON 12988**
Fees, **28 § 2412 nt**
Bids, judicial sales, actions affecting property on which U.S. has lien, **28 § 2410**
Boundaries. Mexico, this index
Civil justice reform, **28 § 519 nt, EON 12988**
Claims,
Civil justice reform, **28 § 519 nt, EON 12988**
Court of Federal Claims, generally, this index
Judgments and decrees, appropriations, **28 § 2414**
Limitation of actions, generally, post
Collection. Federal Debt Collection, generally, this index
Compromise and settlement,
Appropriations, **28 § 2414**
Civil justice reform, **28 § 519 nt, EON 12988**

UNITED STATES—Cont'd
Condemnation, tax liens, **28 § 2410**
Constitution of the United States, generally, this index
Contracts,
District courts, **28 § 1346**
Interest, **28 § 2516**
Limitation of actions, **28 §§ 2415, 2416**
Venue, **28 § 1402**
Copyrights, jurisdiction, **28 § 1498**
Costs, **28 § 2412**
Payment, **28 § 2408**
Security, **28 § 2408**
Courts, generally, this index
Credits, **28 §§ 2406, 2407**
Damages, **28 §§ 2402, 2415, 2416**
Security, **28 § 2408**
Death of defendant in damage action, **28 § 2404**
Defendant or res outside of, limitation of actions, **28 § 2416**
Detention, enemy combatants, **28 § 2241**
District Courts, this index
Eminent domain,
Jurisdiction, **28 § 1358**
Venue, **28 § 1403**
Enemy combatants, detention, **28 § 2241**
Executions, **28 § 2413**
Exports and Imports, generally, this index
Federal Debt Collection, generally, this index
Fees, district court reporters, **28 § 753**
Foreclosure, mortgages, **28 § 2410**
Foreign Service, generally, this index
Forma pauperis, proceedings in, costs, payment, **28 § 1915**
Fraud, forfeitures, **28 § 2514**
Garnishment proceedings by, **28 § 2405**
Hawaii, this index
Imports. Exports and Imports, generally, this index
In rem proceedings, change of venue, consent, **28 § 1404**
Indebtedness. Federal Debt Collection, generally, this index
Insular Possessions and Dependencies, generally, this index
Interest,
Judgments and decrees, **28 § 2411**
Torts, prejudgment interest, **28 § 2674**
Internal Revenue Service, this index
International Trade Court, this index
Interpleader, property on which U.S. has lien, **28 § 2410**
Intervention, **28 § 2403**
Joint tenants, partition, **28 §§ 1347, 1399, 2409**
Judgments and decrees,
Claims, ante
Costs, **28 § 2412**
Liens and incumbrances, **28 § 1962**
Mortgages, **28 § 2410**
Payment, **28 §§ 2412 nt, 2414**
Registration, **28 § 1963**
Judicial sales, **28 § 2410**
Jurisdiction, **28 § 1345**

UNITED STATES—Cont'd
Jury trial, **28 § 2402**
Liens and incumbrances, **28 § 2410**
Application of law, **28 § 1962**
Tax Liens, generally, this index
Limitation of actions, **28 §§ 2401, 2415**
Claims against U.S., **28 § 2401**
Exemptions, **28 § 2416**
Torts, **28 §§ 2401, 2675**
Marshals. United States Marshals Service, generally, this index
Mortgages, **28 § 2410**
Officers and employees. Federal Officers and Employees, generally, this index
Parties, **28 § 2401 et seq.**
Appeal and review, **28 § 2107**
Awards, **28 § 2412**
Banking associations, **28 § 1348**
Concurrent jurisdiction, **28 § 1346**
Costs, **28 § 2412**
Credits, **28 §§ 2406, 2407**
Death, **28 § 2404**
District courts, original jurisdiction, **28 § 1345**
Execution, **28 § 2413**
Garnishment, **28 § 2405**
Jurisdiction, original jurisdiction, **28 § 1346**
Liens and incumbrances, **28 § 2410**
Limitation of actions, **28 § 2401**
Partition, **28 §§ 1399, 2409**
Public monies, delinquencies, **28 § 2407**
Security, **28 § 2408**
Supreme Court, original jurisdiction, **28 § 1251**
Venue, **28 § 1402**
Witnesses, fees, **28 § 1825**
Partition, **28 § 2409**
Liens and incumbrances, **28 § 2410**
Tenants in common, **28 § 1347**
Venue, **28 § 1399**
Payment, costs, **28 § 2408**
Pending suits, **28 § 517**
Pleading,
Liens and incumbrances, **28 § 2410**
Set-off and counterclaim, jurisdiction, **28 § 1346**
Torts, **28 § 2679**
President of the United States, generally, this index
Public Lands, generally, this index
Punitive damages, torts, **28 § 2674**
Quieting title, **28 §§ 2409a, 2410**
Real estate. Public Lands, generally, this index
Removal of cases or causes, foreclosure, **28 § 1444**
Rules of Appellate Procedure, this index
Rules of Civil Procedure, this index
Security, generally, this index
Set-off and counterclaim, jurisdiction, **28 § 1346**
Statute of limitations. Limitation of actions, generally, ante

UNITED STATES—Cont'd
Statutes,
Claims, interest, **28 § 2516**
Trial by court, **28 § 2402**
Venue, **28 § 1402**
Subpoenas, **28 § 1825**
Tax Liens, generally, this index
Tax refunds, corporations, actions and proceedings, **28 § 1402**
Tenant in common, partition, **28 §§ 1347, 1399, 2409**
Territories, generally, this index
Title to property,
Actions and proceedings, **28 § 2415**
Judicial sales, **28 § 2003**
Torts, generally, this index
Trade representative. Exports and Imports, this index
Transcripts requested by, fees of district court reporter, **28 § 753**
Treaties, generally, this index
Venue,
Claims, **28 § 1402**
Partition, **28 § 1399**
Witnesses,
Fees, **28 § 1825**
Payment, **28 § 1825**

UNITED STATES AIR FORCE
Air Force, generally, this index

UNITED STATES ARMED FORCES
Armed Forces, generally, this index

UNITED STATES ARMY
Army, generally, this index

UNITED STATES ATTORNEYS
Generally, **28 § 541 et seq.**
Aircraft, funds, **28 § 530C**
Alaska, **28 § 81A nt, EON 10867**
Alternative dispute resolution, **28 § 2672**
Ammunition, funds, **28 § 530C**
Appointments, **28 § 541 et seq.**
Assistants, **28 § 542**
Special attorneys, **28 § 543**
Vacancies, **28 § 546**
Arbitration, **28 § 2672**
Assistants, **28 § 542 et seq.**
Certificate for payment of witness fees, **28 § 1825**
Domicile and residence, **28 § 545**
Labor and employment, **28 § 509 nt**
Oath of office, **28 § 544**
Official stations, **28 § 545**
Salaries, **28 § 548**
Bail, **28 § 2044**
Boats and boating, funds, **28 § 530C**
California, **28 § 84 nt**
Certificate for payment of witness fees, **28 § 1825**
Certified copies, lost or destroyed court records, **28 § 1735**
Civil justice, reform, **28 § 519 nt, EON 12988**
Clerical assistants, **28 § 550**
Compensation and salaries, **28 § 548**

UNITED STATES ATTORNEYS—Cont'd
Conflict of interest, **28 § 528**
Court interpreters, **28 § 1827**
Crimes and offenses, **28 § 547**
Delinquents for public money, **28 § 2407**
Dispute resolution, alternative means, **28 § 2672**
District of Columbia, this index
Domicile and residence, **28 § 545**
Duties, **28 § 547**
Ethics, **28 § 530B**
Exemptions, domicile and residence, **28 § 545**
Expenses and expenditures, **28 § 549**
Florida, **28 § 89 nt**
Guidelines, litigation, **28 § 519 nt, EON 12988**
Illinois, **28 § 93 nt**
Investigations, **28 § 526**
Law books, **28 § 414**
Liens and incumbrances, **28 § 2410**
Litigation, guidelines, **28 § 519 nt, EON 12988**
Lost or destroyed court records, **28 § 1735**
Louisiana, **28 § 98 nt**
Messengers, **28 § 550**
Northern Mariana Islands, domicile and residence, **28 § 545**
Notice,
Money deposited in court, **28 § 2042**
Sentence and punishment, **28 § 2255**
Three-Judge Courts, **28 § 2284**
Oath of office, **28 § 544**
Official stations, **28 § 545**
President of the United States, appointments, **28 § 541**
Private process servers, **28 § 550**
Process servers, **28 § 550**
Removal, **28 § 541 et seq.**
Reports, **28 § 547**
Revenue laws, violations, **28 § 547**
Rules of Civil Procedure, this index
Senate, vacancies in office, **28 § 546**
Special attorneys, **28 § 543 et seq.**
Subsistence, **28 § 509**
Tax liens, **28 § 2410**
Term of office, **28 § 541**
Tort claims, **28 § 2679**
Vacancies, filling, **28 § 546**
Weapons, funds, **28 § 530C**
Witnesses, fees, **28 § 1922**

UNITED STATES CODE
Administrative Office of U.S. Courts, copies, United States magistrate judges, **28 § 638**
United States magistrate judges, copies, **28 § 638**

UNITED STATES COMMISSIONER
Generally, **28 § 631 nt**
Appointments, United States magistrate judges, **28 § 631 nt**
Rules and regulations, United States magistrate judges, **28 § 636**

UNITED STATES COMMISSIONER
—Cont'd
United States magistrate judges, **28 §§ 631 nt, 636**

UNITED STATES COURT OF APPEALS FOR THE ARMED FORCES
Court of Appeals for the Armed Forces, generally, this index

UNITED STATES COURT OF APPEALS FOR THE DISTRICT OF COLUMBIA
Court of Appeals for the District of Columbia, generally, this index

UNITED STATES COURT OF APPEALS FOR THE FEDERAL CIRCUIT
Court of Appeals for the Federal Circuit, generally, this index

UNITED STATES COURT OF APPEALS FOR VETERANS CLAIMS
Court of Appeals for Veterans Claims, generally, this index

UNITED STATES COURT OF FEDERAL CLAIMS
Court of Federal Claims, generally, this index

UNITED STATES COURT OF INTERNATIONAL TRADE
International Trade Court, generally, this index

UNITED STATES COURT OF MILITARY APPEALS
Court of Appeals for the Armed Forces, generally, this index

UNITED STATES COURTS OF APPEALS
Courts of Appeals, generally, this index

UNITED STATES DISTRICT COURT FOR DISTRICT OF COLUMBIA
Generally, **28 §§ 451 nt, 1651 et seq.**
Chief Judge, **28 § 451 nt**
Civil rights, **28 § 1343**
Clerks of district courts, **28 § 751**
Evidence, **28 § 1731 et seq.**
Fees, **28 § 1914**
Judges or justices,
Acknowledgments, **28 § 459**
Domicile and residence, **28 § 134**
Numbers and numbering, **28 § 133**
Oaths and affirmations, **28 § 459**
Official duty station, **28 § 456**
Relatives, appointments, **28 § 458**
Location, **28 § 88**
Obsolete papers, **28 § 457**
Official duty station, **28 § 456**
Rules and regulations, **28 § 2071**
Senate, subpoenas, **28 § 1365**

UNITED STATES DISTRICT COURT FOR DISTRICT OF COLUMBIA
—Cont'd
Supreme Court of District of Columbia known as, **28 § 451 nt**
Traveling expenses, **28 § 456**

UNITED STATES DISTRICT COURTS
District Courts, generally, this index

UNITED STATES GOVERNMENT
United States, generally, this index

UNITED STATES INSTRUMENTALITY
Federal Agencies, generally, this index

UNITED STATES INTERNATIONAL TRADE COMMISSION
International Trade Commission, generally, this index

UNITED STATES JUDGES OR JUSTICES
Judges or Justices, generally, this index

UNITED STATES MAGISTRATE JUDGES
Generally, **28 § 631 et seq.**
Adverse or pecuniary interest. Conflict of interest, generally, post
Age, **28 § 631**
Annual leave, **28 § 631**
Appeal and review, disqualification, **28 § 455**
Appointment, **28 § 631**
Arrest, discharge, **28 § 2007**
Assignments, **28 § 636**
Assistants, **28 §§ 634, 635**
Black persons, **28 §§ 133 nt, 631 nt**
Certificates and certification,
Official acts, **28 § 638**
Witnesses, fees, **28 § 1825**
Civil service. Retirement and pensions, post
Clerks of district courts,
Compensation and salaries, **28 § 751**
Notice, **28 §§ 631, 636**
Compensation and salaries, **28 § 633 et seq.**
Clerks of district courts, **28 § 751**
Conflict of interest, **28 §§ 455, 631, 632**
Consent, parties, **28 § 636**
Contempt, **28 § 636**
Continuing education, **28 § 620**
Courtrooms, **28 §§ 604, 635**
Crimes and offenses, contempt, **28 § 636**
Definitions, **28 § 639**
Disqualification, **28 § 455**
Discipline, **28 § 372**
Disqualification, **28 § 455**
Dockets and docketing, **28 § 639**
Dual office holding, **28 § 631**
Emergencies, assignments, **28 § 636**
Expenses and expenditures, **28 § 635 et seq.**
In forma pauperis proceedings, **28 § 1915**

UNITED STATES MAGISTRATE JUDGES—Cont'd
Fees, **28 § 1920**
Jurors, **28 § 1871**
Seals (official seals), **28 § 638**
Witnesses, **28 § 1922**
Fines, penalties and forfeitures, contempt, **28 § 636**
Forms, **28 § 638**
Hearings, **28 § 636**
Hispanics, **28 § 631 nt**
Infractions, **28 § 636**
Investigations, official acts, **28 § 526**
Judicial Conference of the Circuit, **28 § 333**
Judicial Conference of the United States,
Compensation and salaries, **28 § 634**
Definitions, **28 § 639**
Evaluations, **28 § 604**
Locations, **28 §§ 631, 633**
Rules and regulations, **28 §§ 604, 635**
Seals (official seals), **28 § 638**
Selection, **28 § 631**
Judicial Council,
Definitions, **28 § 639**
Removal, **28 § 631**
Reports, **28 § 633**
Jurisdiction, **28 § 636**
Jurors, fees, **28 § 1871**
Law books, **28 § 604**
Legal assistants, **28 § 635**
Manuals, **28 § 604**
Merit selection panels, **28 § 631**
Minor or petty offenses, **28 § 636**
Minorities, **28 § 631 nt**
Misdemeanors, **28 § 636**
Nominations, **28 § 133 nt**
Notice, appointment, **28 § 631**
Oaths and affirmations, **28 §§ 631, 636**
Offices, **28 § 635**
Part-time Magistrate Judges, **28 §§ 604, 631 et seq.**
Parties, consent, **28 § 636**
Post-trial relief, **28 § 636**
Powers and duties, **28 § 636**
Qualifications, **28 § 631**
Recall, retired magistrate judges, **28 § 636**
Records and recordation, **28 § 636**
Appeal and review, **28 § 1915**
Appointment, **28 § 631**
Preservation, **28 § 604**
Reinstatement, **28 § 631**
Removal, **28 § 631**
Reporters, **28 § 636**
Reports, **28 § 604**
Retirement and pensions, civil service, **28 § 636**
Rules of Criminal Procedure, this index
Seal, **28 § 638**
Security, courtrooms, **28 § 604**
Sick leave, **28 § 631**
Special masters, **28 § 636**
Special sessions, **28 § 636**
Statistics, **28 § 604**
Supervision, **28 § 604**

UNITED STATES MAGISTRATE JUDGES—Cont'd
Supplies, **28 § 604**
Surveys, **28 § 633**
Temporary assignments, **28 § 636**
Term of office, **28 § 631**
Training, **28 § 620 et seq.**
Transcripts, **28 § 1915**
Trial, **28 § 636**
Veterans, **28 § 601 nt**
Virgin Islands, **28 § 631**
Waiver, disqualification, **28 § 455**
Witnesses,
Fees, **28 § 1922**
Per diem, **28 § 1821**
Women, **28 §§ 133 nt, 631 nt**

UNITED STATES MARINE CORPS
Marine Corps, generally, this index

UNITED STATES MARITIME COMMISSION
Federal Maritime Commission, generally, this index

UNITED STATES MARSHALS SERVICE
Generally, **28 § 561 et seq.**
Accounts and accounting, **28 § 566**
Administrative Office of U.S. Courts, disbursements, **28 § 604**
Aircraft, this index
Ammunition, funds, **28 § 530C**
Appointments, **28 § 561 et seq.**
Appraisers and appraisals, sales, **28 § 2005**
Arrest,
Admiralty, **28 § 2464**
Without warrant, **28 § 566**
Attachment, **28 § 1921**
Attorney General,
Appointments, **28 § 562**
Fees, **28 § 1921**
Bailiffs, **28 § 755**
Boats and boating, funds, **28 § 530C**
California, **28 § 84 nt**
Certified copies, evidence, **28 § 1735**
Collections, fees, **28 § 567**
Compensation and salaries, **28 § 1921**
Director, **28 § 561**
Consultants, security, **28 § 566**
Crimes and offenses, fees, **28 § 1921**
Death, real estate, sales, **28 § 2003**
Deposits, **28 § 1921**
Deputies,
Designation, **28 § 564**
Oaths and affirmations, **28 § 563**
Powers and duties, **28 § 564**
Practice of law, **28 § 568**
Special services, **28 § 1921**
Detention, facilities, Assets Forfeiture Fund, **28 § 524 nt**
Director, **28 § 561 et seq.**
Fees, collections, **28 § 1921 nt**
Disbursements, Administrative Office of U.S. Courts, **28 § 604**
District of Columbia, this index

UNITED STATES MARSHALS SERVICE—Cont'd
Domicile and residence, **28 § 561**
Execution,
Fees, **28 § 1921**
Money judgments, interest, **28 § 1961**
Real estate, **28 § 2003**
Expenses and expenditures, **28 § 565**
Attachment, **28 § 1921**
Traveling expenses, **28 § 1921**
Federal Debt Collection, this index
Firearms, **28 § 566**
Florida, **28 § 89 nt**
Forwarding writs, **28 § 1921**
Grand jury, **28 § 1866**
Habeas corpus, **28 § 1825**
Illinois, **28 § 93 nt**
Interpleader, **28 § 2361**
Investigations, **28 § 526**
Jury,
Fees, **28 § 1871**
Summons, **28 § 1866**
Lodging, bailiffs, **28 § 524**
Louisiana, **28 § 98 nt**
Machinery and equipment, forfeitures, **28 § 524**
Meals, bailiffs, **28 § 524**
Mileage, **28 § 1921**
Northern Mariana Islands, domicile and residence, **28 § 545**
Notice, sales, **28 § 1921**
Oaths and affirmations, **28 §§ 561, 563**
Official stations, **28 § 561**
Payment, U.S. Attorneys, **28 § 566**
Powers and duties, **28 §§ 564, 566**
Practice of law, **28 § 568**
President of the United States, appointments, **28 § 561**
Process,
Admiralty, **28 § 2464**
Executions, **28 § 566**
Expenses and expenditures, **28 §§ 565, 1921**
Fees, **28 § 1921**
Interpleader, **28 § 2361**
Public monies, **28 § 566**
Qualifications, **28 § 561**
Reemployment, **28 § 569**
Removal, **28 § 561**
Real estate, sales, **28 § 2003**
Resignations, **28 § 566**
Retirement and pensions, **28 § 566**
Sales,
Appraisers and appraisals, **28 § 2005**
Fees, **28 § 1921**
Incapacity, **28 § 2003**
Security, **28 § 604**
Consultants, **28 § 566**
Service of process. Process, generally, ante
Stay of proceedings, admiralty, **28 § 2464**
Successors, real estate, sales, **28 § 2003**
Supreme Court Marshal, generally, this index
Term of office, **28 §§ 541, 561**
Traveling expenses, **28 § 1921**

UNITED STATES MARSHALS SERVICE—Cont'd
Uniforms, **28 § 509 nt**
United States Court of Federal Claims, **28 § 2521**
Vacancies, **28 § 562**
Weapons, funds, **28 § 530C**

UNITED STATES–MEXICO BORDER VIOLENCE TASK FORCE
Generally, **28 § 509 nt**

UNITED STATES NAVY
Navy, generally, this index

UNITED STATES OFFICERS AND EMPLOYEES
Federal Officers and Employees, generally, this index

UNITED STATES PAROLE COMMISSION EXTENSION AND SENTENCING COMMISSION AUTHORITY ACT OF 2005
Generally, **28 § 994 nt**

UNITED STATES POSSESSIONS
Insular Possessions and Dependencies, generally, this index

UNITED STATES POSTAL SERVICE
Postal Service, generally, this index

UNITED STATES SECRET SERVICE UNIFORMED DIVISION
Secret Service, generally, this index

UNITED STATES SENTENCING COMMISSION
Sentence and Punishment, this index

UNITED STATES TAX COURT
Appeal and review, **28 § 2072**
Courts of appeals, **28 § 2072**
Supreme Court, **28 §§ 2072, 2073 nt**
Appearances, **28 § 1654**
Attorneys, bankruptcy, **28 § 1452**
Bankruptcy,
Attorneys, **28 § 1452**
Removal of cases or causes, **28 § 1452**
Black persons, judges or justices, **28 § 133 nt**
Clerks of courts, transportation, **28 § 456 nt**
Courts of appeals, **28 § 2072**
Judges or justices, nominations, **28 § 133 nt**
Nominations, judges or justices, **28 § 133 nt**
Removal of cases or causes, bankruptcy, **28 § 1452**
Review. Appeal and review, generally, ante
Rules of Appellate Procedure, this index
Supreme Court, this index
Women, judges or justices, **28 § 133 nt**

UNITED STATES TREASURY
Treasury of United States, generally, this index

UNITED STATES TRUSTEES
Bankruptcy, this index

UNIVERSITIES
Colleges and Universities, generally, this index

UNLAWFUL COMBINATIONS
Monopolies and Combinations, generally, this index

UNLAWFUL RESTRAINT
Kidnapping, generally, this index

UNSWORN DECLARATIONS
Perjury, this index

USMC
Marine Corps, generally, this index

USPS
Postal Service, generally, this index

UTAH
Bankruptcy, judges or justices, appointments, **28 § 152**
District courts,
Judges, **28 § 133**
Location, **28 § 125**
Judicial circuit, **28 § 41**
Judicial districts, **28 § 125**
Bankruptcy, **28 § 581 nt**
Judges or justices, **28 § 133**
United States trustees, judicial districts, appointments, **28 § 581**

VACANCY IN OFFICE
See specific index headings

VACATING OR SETTING ASIDE
See specific index headings

VALIDATION
See specific index headings

VALUATION
See specific index headings

VENUE
Generally, **28 § 1391 et seq.**
Acts of Congress, claims, United States, **28 § 1402**
Admiralty, this index
Aliens, this index
Alterations, districts, **28 § 1405**
Arrest, **28 § 1693**
Banking associations, **28 § 1394**
Bankruptcy, this index
Cargo, forfeitures, **28 § 1395**
Change of venue, **28 § 1404**
Defects, **28 § 1406**
Districts, **28 §§ 1405, 1406**
Divisions, **28 §§ 1405, 1406**
Motions, **28 § 1404**

VENUE—Cont'd
Common questions of fact, multidistrict litigation, **28 § 1407**
Comptroller of the Currency, banking associations, **28 § 1394**
Contracts, United States, **28 § 1402**
Corporations, this index
Damages, United States, **28 § 1402**
Definitions, change of venue, **28 § 1404**
Dismissal and nonsuit, **28 § 1406**
Diversity of citizenship, **28 § 1391**
Eminent domain, United States, **28 § 1403**
Excessive taxes, United States, **28 § 1402**
Executive departments, rules and regulations, **28 § 1402**
Federal agencies, orders, **28 § 2343**
Federal officers and employees, **28 § 1391**
Fines, Penalties and Forfeitures, this index
Foreign States, **28 § 1391**
Habeas Corpus, this index
Income Tax, this index
Interpleader, **28 § 1397**
Joinder of additional parties, **28 § 1391**
Liens and incumbrances, **28 § 1655**
Mask works, **28 § 1400**
Motions. Change of venue, ante
Multiparty and multiforum, **28 § 1391**
National banks, **28 § 1394**
Objections and exceptions, waiver, **28 § 1406**
Orders of court, **28 § 1404**
Partition, United States, **28 § 1399**
Patents, **28 § 1400**
Presidential and Executive Office Accountability, **28 § 1413**
Pretrial proceedings, multidistrict litigation, **28 § 1407**
Quieting title, **28 § 1402**
Rules of Civil Procedure, this index
Shareholder derivative actions, **28 § 1401**
Ships and Shipping, this index
Surface Transportation Board, orders, **28 § 1398**
Tax refunds, United States, **28 § 1402**
United States, this index
Waiver, objections and exceptions, **28 § 1406**

VERDICT
Garnishment, **28 § 2405**
Rules of Civil Procedure, this index

VERIFICATION
See specific index headings

VERMONT
Bankruptcy, judges or justices, appointments, **28 § 152**
District courts, **28 §§ 126, 133**
Judicial Circuit of U.S., **28 § 41**
Judicial districts, **28 § 126**
Bankruptcy, **28 § 581 nt**
Judges or justices, **28 § 133**
Rutland, VT, district court, **28 § 126**

VESSELS
Ships and Shipping, generally, this index

VETERANS
Appeal and review. Court of Appeals for Veterans Claims, generally, this index
Claims. Court of Appeals for Veterans Claims, generally, this index
Courts. Court of Appeals for Veterans Claims, generally, this index
National Cemeteries, generally, this index
Sentence and punishment, cemeteries, **28 § 994 nt**

VETERANS AFFAIRS DEPARTMENT
National Cemeteries, generally, this index

VETERANS CEMETERY PROTECTION ACT OF 1997
Generally, **28 § 994 nt**

VICE CONSULS
Foreign Diplomatic and Consular Officers, this index

VICE PRESIDENT OF THE UNITED STATES
Seals (Official Seals), generally, this index
Secret Service, generally, this index

VICTIMS
Crime Victims, generally, this index

VIRGIN ISLANDS
Appeal and review, **28 § 1291 et seq.**
U.S. Court of Appeals for the Federal Circuit, **28 § 1295**
Claims, United States, jurisdiction, **28 § 1346**
Court of Appeals for Third Circuit, this index
District courts,
Clerks of court, investigations, **28 § 526**
Definitions, **28 § 1869**
Evidence, **28 § 1731 et seq.**
Interlocutory orders, **28 § 1292**
Obsolete papers, **28 § 457**
Records and recordation, **28 § 457**
Reporters, **28 § 753**
Rules and regulations, **28 § 2071**
Transfers, **28 § 1631**
United States magistrate judges, **28 § 631**
Evidence, district courts, **28 § 1731 et seq.**
Grand jury, **28 § 1861 et seq.**
Judges or justices, **28 § 458 et seq.**
Acknowledgments, **28 § 459**
Annuities, survivors, **28 § 376**
Compensation and salaries, **28 § 373**
Judicial Conference of the Circuit, **28 § 333**
Judicial Circuit of U.S., **28 § 41**
Judicial districts, bankruptcy, **28 § 581 nt**

VIRGIN ISLANDS—Cont'd
Jurisdiction, United States, claims, **28 § 1346**
Jury, **28 § 1861 et seq.**
President of the United States, judges or justices, appointments, **28 § 133 nt**
Rules and regulations, district courts, **28 § 2071**
Senate, district court judges, appointments, **28 § 133 nt**
United States magistrate judges, **28 § 631**
United States trustees of judicial districts, **28 § 581**

VIRGINIA
Bankruptcy, judges or justices, appointments, **28 § 152**
District courts, **28 § 127**
Judges or justices, **28 § 133**
Judicial Circuit of U.S., **28 § 41**
Judicial districts, **28 § 127**
Bankruptcy, **28 § 581 nt**
Judges or justices, **28 § 133**

VISAS
Fraud, sentencing guidelines, **28 § 994 nt**
Immigrant visa, fraud, sentencing guidelines, **28 § 994 nt**

VOLUNTARY PROCEEDINGS
Bankruptcy, this index

VOLUNTEERS
Supreme Court, Administrative Assistant to Chief Justice, **28 § 677**

VOTES AND VOTING
Elections, generally, this index

VOTING RIGHTS ACT OF 1965
Civil Rights, generally, this index

VOUCHERS
Comptroller General, **28 § 2510**
Court of Federal Claims, this index
U.S. Court of Federal Claims, **28 § 1496**
United States, actions and proceedings, **28 § 2406**

WAGERING
Gambling, generally, this index

WAGERS AND WAGERING
Gambling, generally, this index

WAGES
Compensation and Salaries, generally, this index

WAIVER
See specific index headings

WAKE ISLAND
Judicial District of Hawaii, **28 § 91**

WAR
Actions and proceedings, United States, **28 § 2416**

WAR—Cont'd
Tort Claims Act, **28 § 2680**

WARD
Guardian and Ward, generally, this index

WARRANTIES
Justice Department, funds, **28 § 530C**

WARRANTS
Alias warrants, Postal Service, attachment, **28 § 2710**
Fees, U.S. marshal for serving, **28 § 1921**
Independent Counsel, this index
Postal Service, this index

WASHINGTON DC
District of Columbia, generally, this index

WASHINGTON (STATE)
Bankruptcy, judges or justices, appointments, **28 § 152**
Court of Appeals for Ninth Circuit, generally, this index
District courts, **28 § 128**
Judges or justices, **28 § 133**
Judicial circuit, **28 § 41**
Judicial districts, **28 § 128**
Bankruptcy, **28 § 581 nt**
Judges or justices, **28 § 133**
United States trustees, judicial districts, appointments, **28 § 581**

WATER RIGHTS
Quieting title, **28 § 2409a**

WATERCRAFT
Boats and Boating, generally, this index

WATERS AND WATER COURSES
Forfeitures, **28 § 2461**
Harbors and Ports, generally, this index
Ships and Shipping, generally, this index
Vessels. Ships and Shipping, generally, this index

WEAPONS
Ammunition, generally, this index
Bureau of Alcohol, Tobacco, Firearms, and Explosives, generally, this index
Correctional institutions, funds, **28 § 530C**
Drug Enforcement Administration, funds, **28 § 530C**
Federal Bureau of Investigation, this index
Immigration and Naturalization Service, funds, **28 § 530C**
Juvenile Delinquents and Dependents, this index
Schools and School Districts, this index
Sentence and punishment, semiautomatic firearms, **28 § 994 nt**
United States attorneys, funds, **28 § 530C**
United States Marshals Service, funds, **28 § 530C**

WEST VIRGINIA
Bankruptcy, judges or justices, appointments, **28 § 152**
District courts, **28 § 129**
Judges or justices, **28 § 133**
Judicial Circuit of U.S., **28 § 41**
Judicial districts, **28 § 129**
Bankruptcy, **28 § 581 nt**
Judges and justices, **28 § 133**

WHEELS
Jury,
Definitions, **28 § 1869**
Master jury wheels, **28 § 1863 et seq.**

WHITE HOUSE
Accountability. Presidential and Executive Office Accountability, generally, this index
Police. Secret Service, generally, this index
Secret Service, generally, this index

WICHITA KS
Court of Appeals for Tenth Circuit, generally, this index

WIDOWS AND WIDOWERS
See specific index headings

WINDING UP
See specific index headings

WIRE COMMUNICATIONS
Telecommunications, generally, this index

WIRELESS TELEGRAPHY
Telecommunications, generally, this index

WIRELESS TELEPHONE PROTECTION ACT
Generally, **28 § 994 nt**

WISCONSIN
Bankruptcy, judges or justices, appointments, **28 § 152**
District courts,
Cities, **28 § 130**
Judges or justices, **28 § 133**
Green Bay, WI, district courts, **28 § 130 nt**
Indians, jurisdiction, **28 § 1360**
Judicial Circuit of U.S., **28 § 41**
Judicial districts, **28 § 130**
Bankruptcy, **28 § 581 nt**
Judges or justices, **28 § 133**
United States trustees of judicial districts, appointment, **28 § 581**

WITHDRAWAL
See specific index headings

WITNESSES
Administrative law and procedure, fees, **28 § 2412**
Allowances, incarcerated persons, **28 § 1821**

WITNESSES—Cont'd
Appearance, detention, **28 § 1821**
Bail, **28 § 1826**
Books and papers, orders of court, **28 § 1826**
Certificates and certification, fees, United States Attorney, **28 § 1825**
Change of venue, **28 § 1404**
Compensation and salaries. Fees, generally, post
Competency,
Interested persons, **28 § 1822**
United States Court of Federal Claims, **28 § 2506**
Confinement, **28 § 1826**
Contempt, generally, this index
Costs, **28 § 1920**
United States magistrate judges, **28 § 1922**
Court of Federal Claims, this index
Depositions, generally, this index
Detention, this index
District Courts, this index
Examinations and Examiners, generally, this index
Expenses and expenditures. Fees, generally, post
Federal Agencies, this index
Federal Officers and Employees, this index
Fees, **28 §§ 1821, 1920**
Federal agencies, **28 § 2412**
Foreign countries, subpoenas, **28 § 1783**
Habeas corpus, in forma pauperis, **28 § 1825**
Incarcerated persons, **28 § 1821**
Parental Kidnapping Prevention Act, **28 § 1738A nt**
Payment, **28 § 1825**
Tender on service of subpoena, **28 § 1825**
United States Magistrate Judge, **28 § 1922**
United States Marshal, **28 § 1921**
Foreign tribunals, voluntary testimony, **28 § 1782**
Forma pauperis, **28 § 1915**
Grand Jury, this index
Incarcerated persons, **28 § 1821**
Independent Counsel, this index
Interested persons,
Competency, **28 § 1822**
United States Court of Federal Claims, **28 § 2506**
International Trade Court, this index
International tribunals, **28 § 1782**
Judges or Justices, this index
Justice Department, this index
Letters rogatory, **28 § 1781**
Mileage. Traveling expenses, generally, post
Military Departments, this index
Multidistrict litigation, pretrial proceedings, **28 § 1407**

WITNESSES—Cont'd
Orders of court, recalcitrant witnesses, **28 § 1826**
Per diem, **28 § 1821**
Privileges and immunities, foreign tribunals, **28 § 1782**
Recalcitrant witnesses, **28 §§ 1657, 1826**
Rules of Civil Procedure, this index
Rules of Evidence, this index
Security for appearance, **28 § 1821**
Senate, this index
Subpoenas, generally, this index
Subsistence expenses, **28 § 1821**
Summons, U.S. marshal, fees, **28 § 1921**
Traveling expenses, **28 § 1821**
Foreign countries, subpoenas, **28 § 1783**
Forma pauperis, **28 § 1825**
Habeas corpus, in forma pauperis, **28 § 1825**
Summons, **28 § 1824**
Tender, subpoenas, **28 § 1825**
United States, this index
United States Attorneys, this index
United States Magistrate Judges, this index

WOMEN
Battered women and children. Domestic Violence, generally, this index
Crimes and offenses,
Dating violence. Domestic Violence, generally, this index
Domestic Violence, generally, this index
Indians, this index
Reports, Federal rape sentencing analysis, **28 § 994 nt**
Dating violence. Domestic Violence, generally, this index
Domestic Violence, generally, this index
Federal judgeships, **28 § 133 nt**
Indians, this index
United States magistrate judges, merit selection panel, **28 § 631 nt**

WORDS AND PHRASES
Accident, district courts, multiparty and multiforum, **28 § 1369**
Acting within the scope of his office or employment, tort claims against U.S., **28 § 2671**
Affiliates, Federal debt collection procedures, **28 § 3301**
Agency,
Attorney General, civil litigation reform, **28 § 519 nt, EON 12988**
Civil penalty, Federal agencies, inflation adjustment, **28 § 2461 nt**
Courts and judges, **28 § 451**
Review, orders of Federal agencies, **28 § 2341**
Agency or instrumentality of a foreign state, jurisdictional immunities of foreign states, **28 § 1603**

WORDS AND PHRASES—Cont'd
Aircraft sabotage, terrorists and terrorism, Foreign States, privileges and immunities, **28 § 1605A**
Alternative dispute resolution, district courts, **28 § 651**
Amateur sports organization, gambling, **28 § 3701**
Antitrust laws, Judicial Panel on Multidistrict Litigation, **28 § 1407**
Appropriate committees of Congress, Federal Bureau of Investigation, analysts, intelligence, **28 § 532 nt**
Appropriate Congressional committees, Libya, terrorists and terrorism, claims, United States nationals, **28 § 1605A nt**
Appropriate Federal official, class actions, fairness, **28 § 1715**
Appropriate state official, class actions, fairness, **28 § 1715**
Assassinated, judges or justices, annuities, survivors, **28 § 376**
Assassination, judges or justices, annuities, surviving spouses, **28 § 376**
Asset, Federal debt collection procedures, fraudulent transfers, **28 § 3301**
Associated, Independent Counsel, ban on representation by members of firms of, **28 § 594**
Attorney for the Government, ethics, **28 § 530B**
Authorized employer, guards, criminal background checks, **28 § 534 nt**
Bankruptcy judge, recall, **28 § 375**
Brokers, financial disclosure requirements of Federal personnel, **5 App. 4 § 102**
Chief Judge, jury selection and service, **28 § 1869**
Child,
Full faith and credit for child support orders, **28 § 1738B**
Judges or justices, annuities for survivors, **28 § 376**
Parental kidnapping prevention, **28 § 1738A**
Child support, full faith and credit for child support orders, **28 § 1738B**
Child support order, full faith and credit for child support orders, **28 § 1738B**
Child's home State, child support, full faith and credit, **28 § 1738B**
Child's State, full faith and credit for child support orders, **28 § 1738B**
Civil action brought by or against the United States, attorneys, fees, **28 § 2412**
Civil monetary penalty, civil penalty, Federal agencies, inflation adjustment, **28 § 2461 nt**
Claim, Federal debt collection procedures, fraudulent transfers involving debts, **28 § 3301**

WORDS AND PHRASES—Cont'd
Claims agreement, Libya, terrorists and terrorism, United States nationals, **28 § 1605A nt**
Class, class actions, **28 §§ 1332, 1711**
Class action, **28 §§ 1332, 1711**
Class certification order, **28 § 1332**
Class counsel, **28 § 1711**
Class members, **28 §§ 1332, 1711**
Clerk,
Jury selection and service, **28 § 1869**
Review, orders of Federal agencies, **28 § 2341**
Clerk of court, jury selection and service, **28 § 1869**
Closed, undercover operations, **28 § 533 nt**
Commercial activities, Foreign States, privileges and immunities, **28 § 1603**
Commission, United States Sentencing Commission, **28 § 998**
Commissioner, United States Sentencing Commission, **28 § 998**
Committee, Senate, **28 § 1365**
Compensation, retirement of bankruptcy judges and Magistrate Judges, acceptance of employment, **28 § 377**
Complainant, judges or justices, **28 § 351**
Conference, United States magistrate judges, **28 § 639**
Congressional ethics committees, financial disclosures, **5 App. 4 § 109**
Consumer Price Index, civil penalty, Federal agencies, inflation adjustment, **28 § 2461 nt**
Contestant, parental kidnapping prevention, **28 § 1738A**
Core proceedings, bankruptcy, **28 § 157**
Cost of living adjustment, Federal agencies, civil penalties, **28 § 2461 nt**
Council, United States magistrate judges, **28 § 639**
Counsel for the United States, Federal debt collection procedures, **28 § 3002**
Court,
Administrative Office of U.S. Courts, **28 § 610**
Administrative proceedings, award of attorneys' fees and other expenses, **28 § 2412**
Federal debt collection procedures, **28 § 3002**
Full faith and credit for child support orders, **28 § 1738B**
Judges or justices, retirement salary, payment pursuant to court decree of divorce, **28 § 376 nt**
Jury selection and service, **28 § 1869**
Officers and employees, **28 § 963**
Retirement of bankruptcy judges and Magistrate Judges, **28 § 377**
United States Court of Federal Claims, retirement of judges, **28 § 178**
Court of the United States, **28 § 451**

WORDS AND PHRASES—Cont'd
Covered employee, Presidential and Executive Office Accountability, appeal and review, **28 § 3908**
Creditor, Federal debt collection procedures, fraudulent transfers involving debts, **28 § 3301**
Crime of violence, sentence and punishment, aged persons, **28 § 994 nt**
Criminal civil rights statutes, civil rights, unsolved crimes, investigations, **28 § 509 nt**
Custody determination, parental kidnapping prevention, **28 § 1738A**
Debt, Federal debt collection procedures, **28 § 3002**
Debtor, Federal debt collection procedures, **28 § 3002**
Degree of relationship, judges or justices, disqualification, **28 § 455**
Demand, administrative law and procedure, fees, **28 § 2412**
Department, courts and judges, **28 § 451**
Dependent child, financial disclosure requirements of Federal personnel, **5 App. 4 § 109**
Designated agency ethics official, financial disclosures, **5 App. 4 § 109**
Director,
Federal Bureau of Investigation, police, **28 § 540C**
United States magistrate judges, **28 § 639**
Disposable earnings, Federal debt collection procedures, **28 § 3002**
District,
Change of venue, **28 § 1404**
Courts and judges, **28 § 451**
Venue or district of trial, cure or waiver of defects, **28 § 1406**
District courts, **28 § 451**
Jury Selection and Service Act, **28 § 1869**
Venue, **28 §§ 1404, 1406**
District courts of the United States, **28 § 451**
Jury Selection and Service Act, **28 § 1869**
Division, Jury Selection and Service Act, **28 § 1869**
Earnings, Federal debt collection procedures, **28 § 3002**
Employee,
Guards, criminal background checks, **28 § 534 nt**
Tort claim against U.S., officers and employees of government, **28 § 2671**
Undercover operations, **28 § 533 nt**
Employee of the Government, torts, **28 § 2671**
Employing office, Presidential and Executive Office Accountability, judicial review, **28 § 3908**

WORDS AND PHRASES—Cont'd
Enterprise architecture, Federal Bureau of Investigation, computers, **28 § 531 nt**
Excess unobligated balance, Justice Department Assets Forfeiture Fund, appropriations, **28 § 524**
Executive branch, financial disclosure requirements of Federal personnel, **5 App. 4 § 109**
Extrajudicial killing, **28 § 1350 nt**
FBI buildings and grounds, Federal Bureau of Investigation, police, **28 § 540C**
FBI police, Federal Bureau of Investigation, police, **28 § 540C**
Federal agencies, tort claims, **28 § 2671**
Fees and other expenses, administrative procedure, costs and fees of parties, **28 § 2412**
Felony crime of violence, FBI, investigations, **28 § 540A**
Fiduciary, judges or justices, disqualification, **28 § 455**
Final judgment, administrative proceedings, award of attorneys' fees and other expenses, **28 § 2412**
Financial interest, judges or justices, disqualification, **28 § 455**
Firm, Independent Counsel, ban on representation by members of firms of, **28 § 594**
Foreign nation, fines, penalties and forfeitures, **28 § 2467**
Foreign state, jurisdictional immunities of foreign states, **28 § 1603**
Forfeiture or confiscation judgment, foreign countries, **28 § 2467**
Former Fifth Circuit, Fifth Circuit Court of Appeals Reorganization Act of 1980, **28 § 41 nt**
Former spouse, judges or justices, annuities for survivors, **28 § 376**
Full time Magistrate Judge, **28 § 639**
Garnishee, Federal debt collection procedures, **28 § 3002**
Geneva Conventions, habeas corpus, **28 § 2241 nt**
Gift, financial disclosure requirements of Federal personnel, **5 App. 4 § 109**
Governmental entity, athletics, gambling, **28 § 3701**
Guidelines, United States Sentencing Commission, **28 § 998**
Hate crime, sentencing guidelines, **28 § 994 nt**
Highest court of a State,
Appeal and review, **28 § 2113**
Supreme Court, **28 § 1257**
Home health care agency, criminal background checks, labor and employment, **28 § 534 nt**
Home state, parental kidnapping prevention, **28 § 1738A**
Honoraria, Federal officers and employees, disclosure, **5 App. 4 § 109**

WORDS AND PHRASES—Cont'd
Hostage taking, terrorists and terrorism, Foreign States, privileges and immunities, **28 § 1605A**
Income, financial disclosure requirements of Federal personnel, **5 App. 4 § 109**
Injury, district courts, multiparty and multiforum, **28 § 1369**
Insider, Federal debt collection, fraudulent conveyances, **28 § 3301**
Interested party,
Financial disclosure requirements of Federal personnel, **5 App. 4 § 102**
Persons entitled to commence civil action in U.S. Court of International Trade, **28 § 2631**
Investigative or law enforcement officer, Tort Claims Act, **28 § 2680**
Investment adviser, financial disclosures, **5 App. 4 § 102**
Judge, complaints, **28 § 351**
Judge of the United States, **28 § 451**
Judge of the United States Court of Federal Claims, recall, **28 § 375**
Judgment, Federal debt collection procedures, **28 § 3002**
Judicial Conference, financial disclosure, **5 App. 4 § 109**
Judicial district, **28 § 451**
Judicial employee, financial disclosure, **5 App. 4 § 109**
Judicial Officer,
Expense and delay reduction plans, **28 § 481 et seq.**
Financial disclosure, **5 App. 4 § 109**
Veterans, preference, **28 § 601 nt**
Judicial official,
Annuities, survivors, **28 § 376**
Retirement and pensions, lump sum payments, **28 § 377**
Judicial proceedings instituted by the United States, court interpreters, **28 § 1827**
Juror qualification form, Jury Selection and Service Act, **28 § 1869**
Jury summons, Jury System Improvements Act, **28 § 1869**
Jury wheel, Jury Selection and Service Act, **28 § 1869**
Justice of the United States, **28 § 451**
Killing, serial killings, investigations and investigators, **28 § 540B**
Knows or has reason to know, copyrights, motion pictures, transfer of ownership, collective bargaining agreements, **28 § 4001**
Legislative branch, financial disclosures, **5 App. 4 § 109**
Lending or finance business, income tax, torts, **28 § 2671 nt**
Lien, Federal debt collection procedures, fraud, **28 § 3301**
Lists of actual voters, Jury Selection and Service Act, **28 § 1869**

WORDS AND PHRASES—Cont'd
Litigation counsel,
Attorney General, civil justice reform, **28 § 519 nt, EON 12988**
Definitions, civil litigation reform, **28 § 519 nt, EON 12988**
Lump sum credit, retirement of bankruptcy judges and Magistrate Judges, **28 § 377**
Mass action, district courts, **28 § 1332**
Member, judges, relatives, appointments, **28 § 458**
Members of Congress, financial disclosure, **5 App. 4 § 109**
Modification,
Child support orders, **28 § 1738B**
Parental Kidnapping Prevention Act, **28 § 1738A**
Modify, Parental Kidnapping Prevention Act, **28 § 1738A**
National Cemetery, veterans cemetery protection, **28 § 994 nt**
National crime information databases, women, **28 § 534**
National of the United States, Libya, terrorists and terrorism, claims, **28 § 1605A nt**
New Fifth Circuit, Fifth Circuit Court of Appeals Reorganization Act of 1980, **28 § 41 nt**
Nonexempt disposable earnings, Federal debt collection, **28 § 3002**
Notice of suit, jurisdictional immunities of foreign states, **28 § 1608**
Nursing facility, criminal background checks, labor and employment, **28 § 534 nt**
Office of Federal Judicial Administration, judges or justices, appointments, **28 § 133**
Officer or employee of the Congress, financial disclosure, **5 App. 4 § 109**
Organized retail theft, task forces, **28 § 509 nt**
Other institutions, crimes and offenses, records and recordation, **28 § 534**
Other judicial act, Convention on the Taking of Evidence Abroad in Civil or Commercial Matters, **28 § 1781 nt**
Part time employee, magistrates, **28 § 639**
Party,
Administrative law and procedure, costs, **28 § 2412**
Award of costs and fees of party prevailing in action against U.S., **28 § 2412**
Party at interest, persons entitled to commence civil action in U.S. Court of International Trade, **28 § 2631**
Person,
Athletics, gambling, **28 § 3701**
Federal debt collection procedures, **28 § 3002**

WORDS AND PHRASES—Cont'd
Person—Cont'd
Parental Kidnapping Prevention Act, **28 § 1738A**
Petitioner, review, orders of Federal agencies, **28 § 2341**
Physical custody, Parental Kidnapping Prevention Act, **28 § 1738A**
Plaintiff class action, **28 § 1711**
Position of the United States, administrative proceedings, fees, awards, **28 § 2412**
Prejudgment remedy, Federal debt collection procedures, general provisions, **28 § 3002**
Presiding judicial officer, court interpreters, **28 § 1827**
Prevailing party, administrative proceedings, attorneys fees, **28 § 2412**
Prisoner,
Civil actions by, against Government, screening and dismissal, **28 § 1915A**
Forma pauperis proceedings, **28 § 1915**
Private security officer, criminal background checks, labor and employment, **28 § 534 nt**
Proceeding, judges or justices, disqualification, **28 § 455**
Professional sports organization, gambling, **28 § 3701**
Property, Federal debt collection procedures, **28 § 3002**
Proposed settlement, class actions, **28 § 1711**
Protection order,
Domestic violence, **28 § 534**
Sex offenses, **28 § 534**
Stalkers, **28 § 534**
Public officer, Jury Selection and Service Act, **28 § 1869**
Publicly draw, Jury System Improvements Act, **28 § 1869**
Qualified blind trust, financial disclosure requirements of Federal personnel, **5 App. 4 § 102**
Qualified magistrate judge, retirement and pensions, annuities, **28 § 377 nt**
Qualified retirement arrangement, Federal debt collection, **28 § 3010**
Reasonable and entire compensation, copyright actions, independent inventors, **28 § 1498**
Reasonable period of time, judicial officers and employees, survivors annuities, **28 § 376**
Reimbursement, financial disclosure requirements of Federal personnel, **5 App. 4 § 109**
Relative,
Federal debt collection procedures, fraudulent transfers, **28 § 3301**
Federal officers and employees, financial disclosures, **5 App. 4 § 109**

WORDS AND PHRASES—Cont'd
Retirement salary, judges or justices, annuities for survivors, **28 § 376**
Retirement system for Federal military or civilian personnel, Federal debt collection, **28 § 3010**
Rules or regulations, United States Sentencing Commission, **28 § 998**
Same court, judges, relatives, appointments, **28 § 458**
Secretary, Libya, terrorists and terrorism, claims, United States nationals, **28 § 1605A nt**
Secretary concerned, financial disclosure requirements of Federal personnel, **5 App. 4 § 109**
Security agreement, Federal debt collection procedures, **28 § 3002**
Security services, criminal background checks, labor and employment, **28 § 534 nt**
Semiautomatic firearm, Sentencing Commission, amendment of guidelines for crimes involving use of, **28 § 994 nt**
Senior judge, Court of Federal Claims, **28 § 797**
Serial killings, investigations and investigators, **28 § 540B**
Service,
Administrative Office of United States Courts, Director, retirement, **28 § 611**
Judicial Center, Director, professional staff, retirement, **28 § 627**
Sexual orientation, hate crimes, **28 § 534 nt**
State,
Athletics, gambling, **28 § 3701**
Bureau of Investigation, counterterrorism, **28 § 531 nt**
District courts, **28 § 1332**
Multiparty and multiforum, **28 § 1369**
FBI, investigations, **28 § 540A**
Federal debt collection procedures, **28 § 3002**
Full faith and credit for child support orders, **28 § 1738B**
Parental Kidnapping Prevention Act, **28 § 1738A**
Parimutuel betting, licenses and permits, **28 § 534 nt**
Removal of cases from State courts to district courts, **28 § 1451**
Serial killings, investigations and investigators, **28 § 540B**
Supplemental jurisdiction, district courts, **28 § 1367**
State court,
District courts, removal of cases, **28 § 1451**
Review, miscellaneous provisions, **28 § 2113**
State identification bureau, guards, criminal background checks, **28 § 534 nt**

WORDS AND PHRASES—Cont'd
State sponsor of terrorism,
Damages, **28 § 1605A**
Libya, claims, United States nationals, **28 § 1605A nt**
Supervising ethics office, financial disclosure, **5 App. 4 § 109**
Tide or submerged lands, quieting title, **28 § 2409a**
Torture, **28 § 1350 nt**
Transfers, Federal debt collection, fraudulent transfers, **28 § 3301**
Travel, FBI, investigations, **28 § 540A**
Undercover investigative operation, reports, **28 § 533 nt**
Undercover operations, reports, **28 § 533 nt**
Undue hardship, Jury System Improvements Act, **28 § 1869**
Unfunded liability,
Judicial Survivors' Annuities Fund, **28 § 376**
United States Court of Federal Claims Judges Retirement Fund, **28 § 178**
Uniform Crime Reports, FBI, **28 § 534 nt**
United States,
Administrative proceedings, award of costs and fees, **28 § 2412**
Jurisdictional immunities of foreign states, **28 § 1603**
United States district courts, court interpreters services, use, **28 § 1827**
United States Marshal, Federal debt collection procedures, general provisions, **28 § 3002**
Valid lien, Federal debt collection procedures, fraudulent transfers, **28 § 3301**
Value, financial disclosure requirements of Federal personnel, **5 App. 4 § 109**
Visitation determination, parental kidnapping prevention, **28 § 1738A**
Volunteer safety personnel, exemption from jury duty, **28 § 1863**
Voter registration lists, Jury Selection and Service Act, **28 § 1869**
Widow or widower, judges or justices, annuities for survivors, **28 § 376**
Year, judges or justices, annuities, survivors, **28 § 376**

WORK FARMS
Correctional Institutions, generally, this index

WORK HOURS AND SAFETY ACT OF 1962
Generally, **28 § 1499**

WORKERS COMPENSATION
Federal Officers and Employees, this index
Railroads, this index
Removal of cases or causes, **28 § 1445**

WORKING CAPITAL FUNDS
Justice Department, this index

WORKMEN
Labor and Employment, generally, this index

WRITINGS
Business and commerce, regular course of business, evidence, **28 § 1732**
Depositions, generally, this index
Habeas corpus, **28 §§ 2242, 2246**
Handwriting, evidence, **28 § 1731**
Interrogatories, **28 § 2246**
Rules of Civil Procedure, this index
Rules of Evidence, this index

WRITS
Admiralty rules, **28 §§ 2072, 2073 nt**
Alternative writs, **28 § 1651**
Appeal and Review, generally, this index
Bankruptcy, this index
Certiorari, generally, this index
Habeas Corpus, generally, this index
Issuance, **28 § 1651**
Judicial Panel on Multidistrict Litigation, **28 § 1407**
Process, generally, this index
Rules of Appellate Procedure, this index
Rules of Civil Procedure, this index
Seals (official seals), **28 § 1691**
Supreme Court, this index
Surface Transportation Board, **28 § 2321**
United States Marshals, fees, **28 § 1921**

WRITS OF ERROR
Abolition, **28 nt prec § 1**
Appeal and Review, generally, this index
Definitions, **28 § 1651 nt**

WRONGFUL DEATH
Bankruptcy, this index

WRONGFUL LEVY
Income Tax, this index

WRONGFUL TAX SALES
Tax Sales, this index

WYOMING
Bankruptcy, judges or justices, appointments, **28 § 152**
District courts,
Judges or justices, **28 § 133**
Places of holding, **28 § 131**
Judicial circuit, **28 § 41**
Judicial districts, **28 § 131**
Bankruptcy, **28 § 581 nt**
Judges or justices, **28 § 133**
United States trustees, judicial districts, **28 § 581**

YEAR
See specific index headings

YOUTH
Children and Minors, generally, this index

YOUTHFUL OFFENDERS
Juvenile Delinquents and Dependents, generally, this index

†